Prentice-Hall
1978
FEDERAL TAX COURSE

STUDENTS EDITION

1978 Advisory Board

PHYLLIS A. BARKER, CPA, Professor, Department of Accounting, School of Business, Indiana State University

HOLLIS, A. DIXON, Ph. D., CPA, Professor, Department of Accounting, College of Business and Public Administration, The University of Arizona

CHARLES B. EDELSON, CPA, Associate Professor, College of Business and Management, The University of Maryland

DENNIS GORDON, CPA, Head of Accounting Department, Professor of Accounting, College of Business Administration, The University of Akron

WILLIAM ROSS HECK, Ph. D., CPA, Professor—Accounting, College of Business, The Florida State University

ALLAN S. ROSENBAUM, Ph. D., CPA

THOMAS E. SCANLON, CPA, Associate Professor, Taxation, Pace University—Westchester

© Copyright 1977 by
PRENTICE-HALL, INC • ENGLEWOOD CLIFFS, N.J. 07632

A STATEMENT TO THE STUDENT ABOUT THE PRENTICE-HALL FEDERAL TAX COURSE

THE Prentice-Hall Federal Tax Course is designed to provide a *comprehensive* explanation of the Federal tax structure and to provide training in the application of the tax principles to specific problems. While the subject matter is arranged in logical sequence based upon accepted academic teaching principles, *any* part of the explanation may be referred to separately as a self-constituted unit. See the Table of Contents on the next page.

Throughout the explanation, specific problems are worked out to insure a thorough understanding of the material. The applicable sections of the law and the regulations are *directly* referred to in the explanation. When the explanation is affected by rulings, Tax Court decisions or Federal court decisions, footnotes provide the necessary citations and related *P-H "Federal Taxes"* references for a *further study* of the material.

Unless otherwise noted, references in this volume which are preceded by "Sec." are to sections of the 1954 INTERNAL REVENUE CODE except where the references have a decimal symbol (.), in which case such references are to sections of the Federal tax regulations. See ¶ 1014.

This publication is designed to provide accurate and authoritative information in regard to the subject matter covered. It is sold with the understanding that the publisher is not engaged in rendering legal, accounting or other professional service. If legal advice or other expert assistance is required, the services of a competent professional person should be sought.
—*From a Declaration of Principles jointly adopted by a Committee of the American Bar Association and a Committee of Publishers and Associations.*

Library of Congress Catalog Card Number: 54-1027

PRINTED IN U.S.A.

TABLE OF CONTENTS

An Introduction to Federal Taxes .... Page 1001

Explanation

Chap.		Page
1.	Individuals—Returns, Filing Status, Personal Exemptions and Rates ..	1101

Gross Income—Gain or Loss—Capital Gains—Dividends

2.	Gross Income—Exclusions	1201
3.	Gross Income—Inclusions	1301
4.	Gain or Loss—Recognition	1401
5.	Gain or Loss—Basis	1501
6.	Capital Gains and Losses of Individuals	1601
7.	Dividends	1701

Maximizing Business and Personal Deductions

8.	Deductions—Expenses	1801
9.	Deductions—Interest, Taxes, Contributions and Medical Expenses	1901
10.	Deductions—Depreciation	2001
11.	Deductions—Depletion	2101
12.	Deductions—Losses	2201
13.	Deductions—Bad Debts	2301

Tax Computation—Withholding—Inventories—Accounting

14.	Alternate Tax Methods—Tax Credits	2401
15.	Withholding—Estimated Tax	2501
16.	Inventory	2601
17.	Accounting	2701
18.	Installment and Deferred Payment Sales	2801

Handling Taxes of Partnerships, Estates, Trusts

19.	Partnerships	2901
20.	Estates and Trusts	3001

Figuring the Corporation Tax—Tax-Exempt Organizations

21.	Corporations—Normal Tax and Surtax, Income, Deductions	3101
22.	Corporations—Capital Gains and Losses, Net Operating Loss, Etc.	3201
23.	Corporations—Reorganizations	3301
24.	Corporations—Personal Holding Companies, Etc.—Exempt Organizations	3401

Filing the New Returns—Paying Taxes—Getting Refunds

25.	Returns and Payment of Tax	3501
26.	Assessment, Collection, Refunds	3601
27.	Foreign Income, Foreign Taxpayers	3701

Social Security Taxes—Estate Tax—Gift Tax

28.	Social Security Taxes	3801
29.	Federal Estate Tax	3901
30.	Federal Gift Tax	4001

Table of Contents

How Tax Fundamentals are Applied

	Page
An Introduction to Tax Planning	4501
An Overview of Tax Shelters	4601
Tax Considerations in Estate Planning	4701
Problems for all Chapters	5001

Short Cuts to Tax Knowledge

Tax Charts and Tables	5501
"ABC" Round-up of Federal Tax Rules	5701
Internal Revenue Code Finding List	5801
Index	6001

AN INTRODUCTION TO FEDERAL TAXES*
TABLE OF CONTENTS

	¶		¶
The study of taxation	1001	Court decisions	1016
		Tax services	1017

HISTORICAL DEVELOPMENT

The early laws	1002	
The Excise Tax Act of 1909	1003	
The Sixteenth Amendment	1004	
History of the Revenue Acts—Internal Revenue Codes	1005	

TAX PRACTICE

Ethics	1018
Tax planning	1019
Return preparation and filing	1020
Examination	1021
Litigation	1022

OVERVIEW OF FEDERAL TAX STRUCTURE

The revenue objectives of taxation	1006
The social objectives of taxation	1007
The economic objectives of taxation	1008
The concepts of taxation	1009
How a tax bill becomes law	1010

OVERVIEW OF BASIC TAX CONCEPTS

The layers of income and their effect on deductions	1023
The concepts of recognition and realization	1024
The meaning of basis	1025
The special rules on capital gains and losses	1026
The method of reporting income and deductions	1027
The different types of taxpayers	1028

METHODS OF TAX RESEARCH

The importance of tax research	1011
The sources of tax literature	1012
The statute	1013
Treasury regulations	1014
Administrative rulings	1015

¶ **1001 The study of taxation.** The study of taxation can be a very exciting and meaningful experience. The practical consequences of its study are varied. But this fact stands out—taxes affect us all. Even if one does not plan to be a tax practitioner, there is a definite relevancy in the study of taxes. Various aspects of one's personal life are affected by tax rules. These rules can be significant in such personal transactions as: selling a residence, paying an obligation, investing in stocks or bonds, handling marital settlements, estate planning and keeping records. Business transactions are also influenced by the rules of taxation. Some of these are: buying and selling business property, handling of mortgages, liquidating or reorganizing a business and transactions between an employer and employee.

HISTORICAL DEVELOPMENT

¶ **1002 The early laws.** While a federal income tax was proposed as early as 1815 and such a tax was actually collected during the Civil War period,[a] the his-

---

* Acknowledgment is gratefully given to Allan S. Rosenbaum, Ph.D., CPA, a member of the Advisory Board, in the preparation of the introductory material.

Footnote ¶ 1002 (a) Income taxes were collected during the period 1863-1873. The first income tax law was the Revenue Act of 1861. Personal exemption was $800 and the rates were as follows: residents 3%, nonresident citizens 5%, interest on U.S. securities 1½%. No revenue was actually collected under the Revenue Act of 1861.

The Act of 1862 reduced the personal exemption to $600. The basic rate continued to be 3% but a 5% rate was applied in the case of those having an income of more than $10,000. The 5% rate for nonresident citizens and the 1½% rate for interest on government securities was the same as in the 1861 Act.

Under the 1864 Act, discrimination against nonresident citizens was removed and the rates were further graduated as follows: $600 to $5,000 at 5%; $5,000 to $10,000 at 7½%; over $10,000 at 10%.

tory of the present period properly begins with the Revenue Act of 1894. The Civil War Acts had been upheld in two unanimous Supreme Court decisions,[b] but notwithstanding the fact, the 1894 law was attacked at the first opportunity and nine months after its passage was declared invalid by Pollock v. The Farmers' Loan and Trust Company.[c]

The issue in this historic case which invalidated the 1894 Act was simple. The Constitution in Article I, Section 9(4) provides that "no capitation or other direct tax shall be laid, unless in proportion to the census or enumeration hereinbefore directed to be taken." Obviously, an income tax cannot be apportioned as required by the above provision. For example, no one can say that the amount of tax collected in one state whose population entitles it to 30 representatives will be three times as great as the amount of tax collected in another whose population entitles it to 10.

Assuming as the Court did, that a property tax is a direct tax and that excise taxes and duties are indirect taxes, the issue then was simply this: did the fact that the tax fell on the income from real and personal property make it a direct tax in the constitutional sense and hence invalid? The Court held that it did, saying:

> "The tax * * * so far as it falls on the income of real estate, and of personal property, being a direct tax, within the meaning of the constitution, and therefore unconstitutional and void, because not apportioned according to representation, all these sections constituting one entire scheme of taxation, are necessarily invalid."

¶ 1003 **The Excise Tax Act of 1909.** While the decision in the Pollock case was by a vote of 5 to 4, it was perfectly clear that no income tax could be imposed as part of the national policy of finance without a constitutional amendment. Before such an amendment was adopted, however, an ingenious scheme was worked out to impose a tax on the income of corporations. Under the decision in the Pollock case an excise tax was not required to be apportioned. Decisions of the Supreme Court indicated that an income tax on corporations would be upheld if it were denominated an excise tax for the privilege of carrying on or doing business as a corporation.[a] Accordingly, the Corporation Excise Tax Act of 1909 was adopted. The rate was 1% and an exemption of $5,000 was allowed. The tax was held constitutional in Flint v. Stone Tracy Company.[b]

¶ 1004 **The Sixteenth Amendment.** The Sixteenth Amendment was passed by Congress on July 12, 1909 and ratified by the required number of state legislatures early in 1913. The amendment reads as follows:

> "The Congress shall have power to lay and collect taxes on incomes, from whatever source derived, without apportionment among the several States, and without regard to any census or enumeration."

The amendment, of course, overcomes the objections raised in the Pollock case. It was ratified February 25, 1913, and the Revenue Act of 1913 taxed income beginning March 1, 1913. The latter date is important since the value of property when the law went into effect is sometimes used as a basis for computing gain or loss as well as for other purposes. It is significant to note that the Revenue Act,

---

Footnote ¶ 1002 continued
(b) Pacific Insurance Co. v. Soule, 74 US (7 Wall.) 433, 19 L. Ed. 95, 2 AFTR 2233; Springer v. U.S., 102 US 586, 26 L. Ed. 253, 2 AFTR 2410.
(c) 157 US 429, 15 S. Ct. 673, 39 L. Ed. 759, 3 AFTR 2557; 158 US 601, 15 S. Ct. 912, 39 L. Ed. 1108, 3 AFTR 2602.

Footnote ¶ 1003 (a) In the Provident Institution for Savings v. Massachusetts, 6 Wall. (73 U.S.) 611, the Supreme Court upheld the right of a state to include interest on U.S. obligations in the basis of a state franchise or excise tax. While the interest on such obligations could not be constitutionally taxed by the state, the court adopted the theory that the tax was not an income tax, but an excise tax, and that the income from all sources, including tax-exempt sources was a proper measure of the excise.
(b) 220 US 107, 31 S. Ct. 342, 55 L. Ed. 389, 3 AFTR 2834.

although enacted in October, 1913, was retroactive to March 1, 1913. The constitutionality of the 1913 Act was upheld in Brushaber v. Union Pacific Railroad Co.[a]

¶ 1005 History of the Revenue Acts—Internal Revenue Codes. Various revenue acts were passed between the years 1913 and 1939. Early in 1939, all of the revenue laws were codified into the Internal Revenue Code of 1939. The Internal Revenue Code of 1939 embodied all previous revenue acts as well as all revenue acts that were enacted during the period 1939-1953 as amendments to the Code.

One of the most important of these acts was the Current Tax Payment Act of 1943. Here for the first time, the "pay-as-you-go" system was adopted. The Congress recognized the difficulties of taxpayers meeting their tax obligations on the due date as well as the revenue loss to the government.

The Internal Revenue Code of 1954 completely overhauled the federal tax laws. It made revisions in the form and arrangement of the 1939 Code as well as effecting fundamental changes in the substantive rules of taxation.

The Revenue Acts of 1958 and 1962 made a great many substantive changes. Principal changes of the 1962 Act were provisions preventing diversion of U.S. source income to foreign sources, taxing foreign investment income as it is earned and granting a tax credit for investment in business equipment. It also introduced the important concept of depreciation recapture. Here the sale of business equipment could result in gain being "recaptured" as ordinary income to the extent of the depreciation taken.

The Revenue Act of 1964 was enacted mainly to reduce the impact of taxes on the economy of the country. It provided the largest individual and corporate tax rate reduction since the Act of 1913, among other substantive changes. Probably one of the most significant of these substantive changes was that the principle of "depreciation recapture" was extended to business realty.

The Tax Adjustment Act of 1966 put most taxpayers on a more realistic pay-as-you-go basis, but did not alter the rate of taxation. Flat-rate wage withholding was replaced by graduated withholding. Payment of corporate estimated taxes was accelerated. Finally, self-employed individuals were required to include self-employment tax in computing estimated tax payments. Late in 1966, the Foreign Investors Tax Act overhauled the basic provisions for taxing nonresident aliens and foreign corporations to induce greater foreign investment and business activities in the U.S.

The Revenue and Expenditure Control Act of 1968 increased taxes in 1968 and 1969 by imposing an additional surcharge on the tax in those years; it also further accelerated corporate estimated tax payments so that corporations would be on a pay-as-you-go basis after 10 years. The purpose of the Act was to increase government revenues and curb inflation.

The Tax Reform Act of 1969 represented a substantive and comprehensive reform of the income tax laws. It has had an impact on every taxpayer. The law's most significant effect is on the ways people have used their capital to get the greatest economic advantage from the tax laws. The Act imposed a minimum tax on tax preferences. It drastically cut back depreciation allowances on commercial and industrial buildings. It also altered the recapture rules on them. The new law raised the limit on charitable deductions, while eliminating many tax advantages of charitable giving permitted under prior law. Substantial changes were made to private foundations. The Act repealed the investment credit and extended the surcharge for 6 months (at a reduced rate). The alternative tax on capital gains was increased. At the same time the Act also provided some substantial tax breaks. It set a maximum tax on earned income. The standard deduction and personal ex-

---

Footnote ¶ 1004   (a)   240 US 1, 36 S. Ct. 236, 60 L. Ed. 493, 3 AFTR 2926.

emptions were increased. It also decreased tax rates for single individuals and heads of household. Many low-income taxpayers were removed from the tax rolls.

The Revenue Act of 1971 introduced a variety of tax incentives including restoring the investment credit as well as increasing personal exemptions.

In 1974, Congress enacted the Employee Retirement Income Security Act. This was a massive overhaul of the entire private pension system.

The Tax Reduction Act of 1975 reduced both individual and corporate taxes. It was enacted to stimulate the economy.

The Tax Reform Act of 1976 was the most comprehensive, complex and massive overhaul of the tax system that was ever attempted.

OVERVIEW OF FEDERAL TAX STRUCTURE

¶ **1006 The revenue objectives of taxation.** Most beginning students of taxation are often left with the thought that the primary objective of any tax policy is to raise revenue. This view is somewhat justified. It should be noted that dissatisfaction with the Articles of Confederation and the Confederation's inability to tap revenue sources provided the impetus for the Constitutional Convention. A limited authority to raise revenue for the federal function resulted from this convention. The ultimate objective of a tax policy in those early years was for the government to attain a certain revenue base so that it could become self-sufficient and self-sustaining.

On the state and local level, the primary objective of revenue raising through taxation has not changed. The state and local taxing authorities are more concerned with finding suitable tax bases and alternatives to finance their activities rather than the macro-economic goals which are within the province of the federal government.

Presently, local taxing jurisdictions are faced with the serious threat of losing one of their more productive taxes, the property tax. The enactment of Revenue Sharing was designed to help the states meet their obligations.

¶ **1007 The social objectives of taxation.** The revenue raising objective of tax policy was uppermost in the minds of federal policy makers all the way into the 1950's. It continues to be of primary importance. However, in recent years, a multitude of tax provisions has been introduced into law suggesting that taxation policies can be used for something other than the raising of revenue. A brief look at some of this legislation will show how tax policy is serving as an instrument for the attainment of socially desirable goals.

The Tax Reform Act of 1969 added Code Section 169 which allows for the amortization of certified pollution control facilities over a period of 60 months. This section was thought desirable to induce industries to install the facilities necessary to control air and water pollution.

It is an accepted accounting principle that if an asset has a life of one year or more, it is capitalized and its cost can be recovered through depreciating it over its estimated useful life. Contemporary thinking is that if a taxpayer is allowed cost recovery on a basis that is faster than estimated useful life, that taxpayer will, if his business dictates the need for that particular piece of equipment, purchase the equipment. Such was probably the thinking when Congress passed the faster amortization of certain coal mine safety equipment.

Certain expenditures for on-the-job training and child care facilities were allowed a quicker cost recovery, and new Code Section 40 developed a tax credit for certain expenses incurred in work incentive programs.

Other provisions of the Code, which would be classified as relief provisions rather than incentive provisions, might also be classified as socially desirable: life insurance proceeds received by reason of death are not subject to income taxes; taxpayers are allowed deductions for dependents.

tion. Sometimes the problems are simple enough and solutions are readily available. Other times, however, the simple problem uncovers complexities of such a nature that only competent research can produce an acceptable solution. It is this type of question as well as the complex question to which tax research addresses itself.

Tax research is not only important from the point of view of enabling the practitioner to reach acceptable solutions, but also because it serves as an educational tool for the practitioner. The gains from research are considerable—familiar material adds depth; new material adds dimension. The practitioner's efforts in research eventually yield a respectful expertise which can be productively applied in what is probably the most difficult, yet most challenging aspect of tax practice—that of tax planning. See ¶ 1019 and ¶ 4501 et seq.

¶ 1012 **The sources of tax literature.** A strong familiarity with the sources of tax literature and where to find them are essential to effective research. Additionally, one must know what degree of authority each of these sources holds.

These sources of tax literature can be ranked in order of their authority. Heading the list is the Code which is statutory law [¶ 1013]. Next come the Regulations which are interpretations of the law [¶ 1014]. These are followed by Rulings [¶ 1015]. Rulings are issued and deal with a specific case in point, except a Treasury Decision which either promulgates or modifies a regulation and has the binding effect of law. Revenue Rulings, other than Treasury Decisions, do not have this binding effect. Revenue Procedures basically affect the duties and rights of the taxpayer. The system of checks and balances is instituted through court hearings and decisions [¶ 1016]. Supreme Court decisions are binding throughout the land, but other court decisions have only a partial effect on the Commissioner of Internal Revenue.

The more familiar a practitioner becomes with these sources, the easier will be the task of his research. This is not to say that the burden of his drawing a conclusion will be less, but does imply that his conclusion will be backed by objectivity and fact.

¶ 1013 **The Statute. (a) Organization of the Code.**[a] The Code is subdivided into Subtitles, Chapters, Subchapters, Parts, Subparts, Sections, Subsections, Paragraphs, and Subparagraphs. Fortunately, reference to statutory tax law is most often made to a particular section and its subdivisions. Code Sections are in numerical order while Subsections are alphabetical, using small letters and placing them within parentheses. Paragraphs are numerals placed within parentheses and Subparagraphs are cited as capitalized letters within parentheses. A typical Code Section will be subdivided as follows:

Section 2
    Subsection (b)
        Paragraph (1)
            Subparagraph (A)

Reference to this particular section would be written as I.R.C. Sec. 2(b) (1)(A). (In this volume, Code sections are cited by number without the "I.R.C." preface.)

For an Internal Revenue Code Finding List see ¶ 5801.

(b) Legislative materials. Before the issuance of Regulations and rulings on a particular statutory provision, and sometimes when Regulations and rulings have been issued but their validity is in doubt, a taxpayer may wish guidance in

---

Footnote ¶ 1013 (a) The Internal Revenue Code is available in the P-H paperbound publication, Internal Revenue Code. The *complete* Internal Revenue Code, currently *supplemented* is found in the IRC volume of P-H "Federal Taxes."

the interpretation of a statutory provision. Such guidance may sometimes be found in:

1. The published reports of the House Ways and Means Committee, of the Senate Finance Committee, and of any Conference Committee, on the Revenue Act embodying the provision in question. These reports are often authoritative as indicating the intent behind the wording of the statute.[b]

Example: The Internal Revenue Code of 1954 allowed individual taxpayers to deduct the expenses of tax litigation. The report of the House Committee on Ways and Means explained the deduction as follows:
"Section 212. Expenses for production of income
" * * * Paragraph (3) is new and is designed to permit the deduction by an individual of legal and other expenses paid or incurred in connection with a contested tax liability, whether the contest be Federal, State, or municipal taxes, or whether the tax be income, estate, gift, property, and so forth. Any expenses incurred in contesting any liability collected as a tax or as a part of the tax will be deductible." [House Report No. 1337, PA 59, 83rd Cong., 2nd Sess.]

2. The published committee hearings on the Revenue Act.
3. Discussion of the Revenue Act in the House and Senate as published in The Congressional Record (the only valuable parts of such a floor discussion are the statements by the member in charge of the tax bill and by the members who propose amendments to the bill that are adopted.)

¶ 1014 **Treasury Regulations.** The complexities of economic life cannot always be described and accounted for as succinctly as a law must be, although every attempt is made to write Code Sections so that their meaning is clear. It is therefore necessary to have available official interpretations and explanations of Code Sections.

Except where such authority is expressly given by this title to any person other than an officer or employee of the Treasury Department, the Secretary or his delegate shall prescribe all needful rules and regulations for the enforcement of this title, including all rules and regulations as may be necessary by reason of any alteration of law in relation to internal revenue [Sec. 7805(a)].

An analysis of the above Code Section would lead one to believe that the Secretary of the Treasury, or a delegate of his, can prescribe rules and regulations necessary to enforce the provisions of the Internal Revenue Code, unless authority to perform this function is expressly given to another person. To fully appreciate the Regulations, contrast the construction of the Code Section above with the analysis presented in this paragraph, and then contrast both with the following Regulation:

The Commissioner, with the approval of the Secretary, shall prescribe all needful rules and regulations for the enforcement of the Code (except where this authority is expressly given by the Code to any person other than an officer or employee of the Treasury Department), including all rules and regulations as may be necessary by reason of any alteration of law in relation to internal revenue [Sec. 301.7805-1(a)].

The purpose of this discussion on Regulations has been two-fold: (1) to indicate that Regulations are authoritative pronouncements and do have the effect of being law unless they contradict the statute, and (2) to suggest that the combined reading of the Statute and its interpretive Regulations provide a greater understanding of the intent of the law. In addition to the expository nature of the Regulations, many factual examples are also presented which tend to add clarity to the revenue law.

¶ 1015 **Administrative rulings. (a) General.** Rulings are issued by the Treasury Department and the Internal Revenue Service. The purpose for which

---
Footnote ¶ 1013 continued
(b) Pertinent portions of current committee reports are reproduced in the P-H "Federal Taxes."

these rulings are issued is threefold: (1) to indicate the Treasury Department's interpretation of certain points of tax law and thus establish guidelines which the Treasury will follow; (2) to inform taxpayers how the Code and the Regulations have been applied to a particular set of facts; and (3) to outline those procedures which affect the taxpayer's rights or duties.

(b) Organization of the rulings. Those rulings which establish guidelines or general principles are in reality regulations or amend existing regulations and are published in the Internal Revenue Bulletin as Treasury Decisions (TD). Treasury Decisions must be approved by the Secretary of the Treasury.

Treasury Decisions set binding precedents whereas other types of rulings, which are called Revenue Rulings (Rev. Rul.), do not have the same authority unless the specific facts of a particular case are the same. Revenue Rulings are published in the Internal Revenue Bulletin along with the Treasury Decisions.

The term Revenue Ruling has replaced the terms for a variety of rulings which were identified and cited by the division or office issuing them. General Counsel's Memoranda (GCM), Solicitor's Memoranda (SM), Solicitor's Opinions (Sol. Op.) are only a few of the identifications which were used prior to replacing them with Revenue Rulings. Internally, new rulings with these identifications are still used.

Practice and procedure requirements which either affect the rights or duties of taxpayers or which should be public knowledge are published as Revenue Procedures (Rev.Proc.). Certain rulings and instructions issued in the form of Mimeograph Letters (IR-Mim.) or Circulars (IR-Circ.) contain instructions with reference to procedure within the Treasury Department. They are no longer released to the public. Revenue Procedures, like Revenue Rulings and Treasury Decisions, are published in the Internal Revenue Bulletin and later in the Cumulative Bulletin.

(c) Special rulings. In the interest of sound tax administration, the National Office of the Internal Revenue Service will respond to specific inquiries of individuals and organizations regarding the tax effects of their acts or transactions [Sec. 601.201(a)]. Rulings may be issued on prospective transactions and on completed transactions before the return is filed. "However, rulings will not ordinarily be issued if the identical issue is present in a return of the taxpayer for a prior year which is under active examination or audit by a district office, or is being considered by a branch office of the Appellate Division." [Sec. 601.201(b)].

Generally, requests on prospective transactions are handled by the National Office of the Internal Revenue Service while requests on completed transactions are administered by the taxpayer's District Director. The District Director will respond to the taxpayer's request only "if the answer to the question presented is covered specifically by statute, Treasury Decision or regulation, or specifically by a ruling, opinion, or court decision published in the Internal Revenue Bulletin" [Sec. 601.201(c)]. The District Director's response is called a determination letter. Procedural requirements for obtaining a ruling or determination letter require that the taxpayer issue a statement giving all relevant facts relating to the transaction including: (1) names, addresses, and identifying numbers of all interested parties; (2) the district office that has or will have jurisdiction over the return; (3) the business reasons for the transaction, and copies of documents involved in the transaction.

(d) Income tax information releases. To inform the public of its general position with respect to the proper treatment of certain gains, expenses, losses, etc., the Treasury issues press releases of a timely and nontechnical nature. Copies are distributed to District Directors of Internal Revenue, who may distribute additional copies to taxpayer. These releases are called "Tax Information Releases" and are numbered consecutively.

¶ 1015

Admittedly, circumstances will arise wherein the practitioner will not be able to find any concrete examples of a particular transaction or the manner in which tax law might treat it. Only sound professional judgment and knowledge of general principles of taxation can aid the decision maker.

Literature sources dealing with the ethical responsibilities of a tax practitioner can be found in the various publications of the American Institute of Certified Public Accountants, the American Bar Association, and other professional organizations. For all tax practitioners who are enrolled to represent clients before the Internal Revenue Service, the primary source of ethical guide stems from Treasury Department Circular No. 230.

Subpart B of Treasury Department Circular No. 230 addresses itself to such topics as: What is required of an enrolled practitioner if he has knowledge of a client's omission or error; the necessity of due diligence; fees; conflicting interest; solicitations, and the practice of law.

¶ **1019 Tax planning.** Planning, as applied to tax practice, does not differ drastically from planning situations which are encountered elsewhere. Objectives or goals are defined, information is gathered, alternatives are researched, and a decision on the basis of the information and available alternatives is made. For a complete discussion on how tax fundamentals are applied, see ¶ 4501 et seq.

(a) Tax shelter practices. Generally, tax savings require (1) a decision by the taxpayer on the strategy to be used; (2) compliance with legal forms and requirements to put the strategy into operation; and (3) reflection of the strategy in taxpayer's accounting methods.

Tax saving devices fall into several categories. But they all have one thing in common: the taxpayer has a choice of alternative courses of action. The art in achieving tax shelter lies in making the right choice at the right time. Of course, if the taxpayer makes the right choice, he must first recognize that there is a choice. These optional courses of action may be opened up to the taxpayer by the Code, by the regulations, or by cases and rulings that interpret the Code.

≫**OBSERVATION**→ Tax saving suggestions or tax shelter practices have been included in the succeeding chapters where a particular subject is covered.

In some cases, the Code specifically gives the taxpayer an option. For example, husbands and wives may file joint or separate returns, individual taxpayers may itemize their deductions or take a flat amount, depreciation may be based on one of several methods, certain corporations may elect to be taxed as partners. Selecting the proper alternatives will usually result in a tax saving for the taxpayer.

The Code may leave the taxpayer a choice as to what action to follow to achieve a tax saving. For example, under certain circumstances, assets may be exchanged without incurring any gain. There is no obligation on the taxpayer to exchange the asset. He is free to sell it and buy another if that will work out better, tax-wise, for him, as is often the case. Similarly, taxpayers may take a deduction for medical expenses paid during the year in excess of 3% of their adjusted gross income. If the expense comes near the end of the year, the taxpayer may save tax money by carefully choosing the year in which to pay the bill. The opportunity to take advantage of such implied options often gives tax significance to what may seem to be the most routine transactions.

(b) Tax sheltered investments. Generally, a business that offers relatively high security against loss, that permits substantial deductions on the original investment and that at the same time builds up capital values or future income, will be attractive taxwise.

Some of the tax sheltered investments involve oil, gas and mining operations, timber and citrus groves, cattle, farming and real estate. See ¶ 4601 et seq.

An Introduction to Federal Taxes

¶ 1020 Return preparation and filing. The complexity of the Internal Revenue Code may preclude the average taxpayer from being able to comply with its requirements without the assistance of an accomplished tax practitioner. The expertise of the tax practitioner is sought by many individuals, whether their problems are complex and intricate, or routine in nature. Return preparation requires the practitioner to apply skillfully his knowledge to the problems at hand. In the area of return preparation, the interpretive function performed by the practitioner is of immeasurable value.

Many taxpayers are not even aware of the informational sources from which the practitioner draws the basic information to prepare the return. The practitioner must be able to aid the taxpayer in gathering the necessary information so that it can be assembled into a proper return.

¶ 1021 Examination. After the return has been prepared and the taxpayer has filed it, the Internal Revenue Service may begin its audit process. Most returns are subject to a mathematical verification while others are, for a variety of reasons, subject to either an office audit or field audit.

At the examination stage, there are two parties to the issue, the taxpayer and his representative, and the government's appointed representative, either a revenue agent, district conferee, or appellate conferee.

Although the practitioner is dealing with the government, the practitioner owes complete fidelity to the client and to the client's cause, so long as there is reasonable justification for the client's position and that that position is within the boundaries of the law.

In fulfilling his obligation to his client, the practitioner must not only be justified in his position, but must deal in an atmosphere of candor and fairness with the government. The practitioner must advocate his client's cause without resorting to any misleading representations or statements. That the practitioner exercise due diligence when representing his client before the Internal Revenue Service is axiomatic.

¶ 1022 Litigation. Practice before the courts, other than the Tax Court, is limited to lawyers. This aspect of tax practice, litigation, can be succinctly characterized by reference to Canon 15:

> The lawyer owes 'entire devotion to the interest of the client, warm zeal in the maintenance and defense of his rights and the exertion of his utmost learning and ability', to the end that nothing be taken or be withheld from him, save by the rules of law, legally applied. . . . But it is steadfastly to be borne in mind that the great trust of the lawyer is to be performed within and not without the bounds of the law. The office of attorney does not permit, must less does it demand of him for any client, violation of law or any manner of fraud or chicane. He must obey his own conscience and not that of his client.[a]

OVERVIEW OF BASIC TAX CONCEPTS

An "overview" of certain basic tax rules will be helpful to the beginning student. This section is designed to present the interrelationships that exist among rules found in the Federal Tax Course. Six basic subjects are examined in this section:

- The layers of income and their effect on deductions [¶ 1023].
- The concepts of recognition and realization [¶ 1024].
- The meaning of basis [¶ 1025].
- The special rules on capital gains and losses [¶ 1026].
- The method of reporting income and deductions [¶ 1027].

Footnote ¶ 1022 (a) American Bar Association, *Canons of Professional and Judicial Ethics* (Chicago: American Bar Association), p. 4.

- The different types of taxpayers [¶ 1028].

¶ 1023 The layers of income and their effect on deductions. Four main terms apply when computing an individual's tax liability: gross receipts; gross income; adjusted gross income; and taxable income. The "layers" of income serve to fit the various types of deductions into suitable categories. This categorizing is necessary since different rules apply to these classes of deductions.

(a) Gross receipts and cost of goods sold. An individual's income from his business is included in gross income after deducting the cost of goods sold. Since this is tied in with the rules of inventory, these are covered in a later chapter [¶ 2601 et seq.]. In any case, gross receipts are a factor in determining gross income.

(b) Gross income. This includes all items of income from whatever source unless specifically excluded. Income is not a gain accruing to capital, not an increment of value but something of exchangeable value proceeding from the property. The receipt of income can be in different forms such as cash, property, services or even a forgiveness of an indebtedness.

Gain does not constitute income until it is *realized*. Thus, the appreciation in the value of property is not income until a transaction involving the investment in that property has been completed. The gain is then capable of being measured by receiving something of value.

Some items are excluded from gross income because they are a return of capital, for example, the part of sale proceeds that equal the basis of the property sold or the part of an annuity payment that may represent premiums previously paid. Thus, rules exist to separate the part that is tax free (return of capital) from the taxable portion (gain on the appreciation).

Certain items are not part of gross income since they are excluded by law, as in the case of gifts, inherited property or insurance proceeds received by reason of death. The exclusion for life insurance proceeds involves the view of achieving certain socially desirable goals. The original intent for excluding gifts and inheritances was that these would be subject to separate tax rates.

Income involving compensation. The Code requires that all compensation for services be included in gross income. However, a number of factors exist to keep this requirement from being absolute. One of these factors involves the distinguishing between compensation, on the one hand, which is taxable, and gifts, on the other, which are tax free. The Supreme Court has held that the two terms are "mutually exclusive; and a bestowal of money cannot, under the statute, be both a gift and a payment of compensation."[a] It does not necessarily follow that all voluntary payments are gifts or that their designation as such is controlling. The proper designation rests on facts and circumstances [¶ 1302].

Another factor in the compensation question is fringe benefits. Although certain so-called fringe benefits are excluded from gross income, some of these are entitled to the exclusion only if specific requirements are met. Thus, for example, meals furnished to employees are excludable only if the meals are provided by the employer for a "substantially noncompensatory business reason" [¶ 1308(a)].

A third factor involves so-called bargain purchases by employees. Generally, they are regarded as compensation. However, the Congress recognized that some employer-employee arrangements are used as incentive devices designed to attract employees. In such cases, special tax treatment is provided as long as very strict requirements are met. Some benefits are not considered compensation since these involve relatively little value, such as courtesy discounts [¶ 1310; 1326-1329].

Footnote ¶ 1023 (a) Bogardus v. Comm., 302 US 34, 58 SCt 61, 19 AFTR 1195.

Deductions related to compensation. Since the Congress has the power to tax all income except the part specifically exempted, the right to take deductions "depends upon legislative grace."[b] The taxpayer must be able to point to some specific provision of the statute which authorizes the deduction. The general deduction rule rests on the requirement that a deduction must be "an ordinary and necessary expense incurred in carrying on a trade or business."

The "carrying on of a trade or business" clause includes the salaried employee, and specific Code provisions allow the employee to take certain deductions from gross income.

There are four types of expenses allowed the employee as deductions from gross income: (1) travel expenses; (2) transportation expenses; (3) outside salesperson's expenses; and (4) reimbursed expenses [¶ 1805].

The employee must satisfy the specific requirements to qualify for the job-related deductions since the expenses involved resemble personal nondeductible outlays. Thus, for example, a transportation expense might be a nondeductible commuting cost. A reimbursement by the employer for some personal expense incurred by the employee does not make that expense deductible.

Compensation paid by the employer to employees is deductible if *reasonable*, and *paid for services actually* rendered [¶ 1815].

The question of reasonableness can exist when there is a relationship between the employer and the employee as for example, when a parent hires his child. It can also apply when an ostensible salary is used to distribute dividends to shareholders.

Income involving investments. Certain income items are related to investment property. These include interest, dividends, rents and royalties.

Generally, all interest income is taxable except interest on certain government obligations. The exclusion for interest from state and local obligations is based on the original view that it would be unconstitutional to tax this kind of interest.

Dividends are generally included in income above a $100 exclusion. However, certain distributions not out of corporate earnings and profits are not taxed as ordinary dividends but are considered a return of capital. In addition, stock dividends are usually tax free. Here, taxability occurs only when the stock is sold [¶ 1700 et seq.].

A question sometimes arises on whether a payment by a corporation is a dividend or interest. The distinction is important since interest payments are deductible by the corporation but dividend payments are not [¶ 1901(a)].

The payment for the use of property is rent and must be included in the income of the property's owner [¶ 1316].

Deductions related to investments. Since activities involving investment property are not considered a trade or business, the deductibility of expenses resulting from this "nonbusiness" property rests on specific Code sanction. Thus, a taxpayer could have a gainful activity without it being his trade or business. The expenses this activity generates are deductible from gross income [¶ 1806].

The expense item must first meet the specific requirements of its particular classification. Therefore, an interest expense must fit into the deductible category before being considered as a "nonbusiness" expense.

An expenditure to correct a defect in investment (or business) property may be a deductible repair or a capital improvement. Generally, a substitution of material indicates a capital expenditure [¶ 1825(a)]. This is recovered through an allowance each year over the property's useful life called depreciation. The deduction is permitted for property used in the production of income as well as business property [¶ 2000].

Footnote ¶ 1023 continued
   (b) New Colonial Ice Co., Inc. v. Helvering, 292 US 435, 54 SCt 788, 13 AFTR 1180.

¶ 1023

The subject of losses affects a number of different tax concepts such as those involving nonrecognition [¶ 1024], basis [¶ 1025] and capital gains [¶ 1026].

Losses are clearly deductible from gross income when they have been incurred in a true business enterprise. The problem arises in determining if a transaction has been entered into for profit. There is no deduction for an activity not carried on for profit except under certain specific circumstances [¶ 2225].

When a taxpayer rents out part of his residence, the portion of the expenses related to that part are deductible from gross income.

(c) Adjusted gross income. The concept of "adjusted gross income" was introduced by Congress as part of a simplification program. No new deductions were created by the introduction of the "adjusted gross income" concept.

The concept of "adjusted gross income" serves other purposes besides separating certain deductions. The adjusted gross income provides a basis for calculating the allowable medical expense deduction. In addition, it is a factor in limiting the deduction for charitable contributions. [¶ 1801(a); 1941; 1945].

Zero bracket amount. The standard deduction has been repealed ending the distinction between the minimum standard deduction and the maximum standard deduction based on a percentage of income. In its place, is the zero bracket amount. This is a fixed standard deduction that has been built into the tax tables to simplify computing tax liability. The zero bracket amount is $3,200 for married people filing joint returns, and $2,200 for single taxpayers as well as heads of households.

Itemized deductions. Taxpayers who itemize must reduce their itemized deductions by the applicable zero bracket amount since the tables already reflect that deduction. So itemizers can only deduct excess itemized deductions (amounts exceeding $2,200 for single taxpayers and heads of households and $3,200 for married taxpayers filing jointly).

Itemized deductions are certain expenses of a personal nature that may be deducted. Generally, these involve four main groups called "itemized deductions" and are intended to accomplish some economic or social objective: (1) Deductions for extraordinary expenses; (2) Deductions to "subsidize" certain taxpayers; (3) Deductions for state and local taxes; (4) Deductions for expenses of earning income.[c]

Extraordinary expense deductions. A prime example of this group is the medical expense deduction. The original intent of this deduction was directed at extraordinary medical expenses to maintain the level of public health. Thus, levels were established below which no medical deduction was permitted. However, a more recent change eliminated this limitation as it applied to part of the medical insurance premium. The purpose of this revision was to encourage taxpayers to protect themselves against future medical expenses [¶ 1945 et seq.].

Another extraordinary and unexpected expense involved losses due to fire, storms or other casualties. A $100 floor applies since Congress felt it appropriate to allow the deduction for only those losses considered nonrecurring, extraordinary or unusual [¶ 2204].

"Subsidy" deductions. Certain expenses permitted as deductions, such as property taxes and mortgage interest, are designed to encourage home ownership [¶ 1900; 1910].

The deduction for contributions to qualified charities is intended to encourage taxpayer-support of organizations accomplishing socially desirable goals [¶ 1941 et seq.].

Footnote ¶ 1023 continued
(c) Pechman, *Federal Tax Policy,* Washington, D.C.: The Brookings Institution, 1966, p. 76.

State and local tax deductions. The deductibility of state and local taxes is intended to help reduce the impact of the total taxes levied against the individual.

Earned income expense deductions. While certain expenses connected with job-related or gainful activities may be taken as deductions *for* adjusted gross income, other expenses related to the earning of income can be deducted only in computing taxable income. These include expenses for work clothes, rental of safe deposit box containing income-producing property and child care expenses. [¶ 1806; 1807].

The personal exemption. The exemption deduction is in lieu of personal or family expenses not normally allowed to be deducted on the return. The Code specifically precludes personal, living or family expenses from being taken [¶ 1807]. The exemption is intended to relate to the ordinary costs of the average family. Additional exemptions for dependents are permitted to provide flexibility for different family sizes. Blind and older taxpayers are allowed extra exemptions since special economic and physical problems apply to them [¶ 1111; 1115].

The personal exemption is a basic allowance that does not call for precise recordkeeping to support the deduction. However, proof may be required that someone qualifies as a dependent for the taxpayer to be allowed the deduction. In any case, specific requirements must be met, before the dependency deduction applies.

(d) Taxable income. This is adjusted gross income reduced by "excess itemized deductions" [(c) above] and by personal exemptions. In a few cases, taxable income is increased by an "unused zero bracket amount" (excess of the zero bracket amount over itemized deductions).

(e) Tax credits. Any tax credits are applied against taxable income. It is significant here to note the difference between a tax *credit* and tax *deduction*. A deduction reduces income to which the rates applied and indirectly lessens the tax liability. A tax credit directly reduces the tax liability.

A general tax credit [¶ 1111(e)] is included as part of the tax tables.

The other principal credits are (1) earned income credit [¶ 2405]; (2) credit for the elderly [¶ 2406]; (3) credit for investing in certain business property [¶ 2410]; (4) credit for child care expenses [¶ 2415]; (5) foreign tax credit [¶ 3701]; (6) credit for withheld taxes [¶ 2500]; (7) credit for excess social security taxes withheld [¶ 2511(a)]; (8) prepaid estimated taxes [¶ 2516]; (9) credit for work incentive program expenses [¶ 2411]; and (10) credit for political contributions [¶ 2416].

One justification for tax credits is to equalize the tax treatment applied to one group of taxpayers as opposed to another group. The foreign tax credit is provided to eliminate the double taxation of foreign income earned by U.S. taxpayers.

Another reason for the tax credit method is to facilitate a bookkeeping arrangement. Thus, taxes withheld from wages are considered a credit. Since the employer is directly liable to the government for collecting the taxes from wages, the employee gets a credit on his return for the amount collected from his wages. In addition, any excess social security collected is treated as a tax credit to facilitate the refund.

The credit approach has been used as an incentive device. Thus, the investment credit is provided to encourage the modernizing of machinery and equipment. A similar reason applies to the credit for work incentive program expenses. This is designed to encourage employers to hire welfare recipients.

¶ 1024 The concepts of recognition and realization. The recognition doctrine was introduced early in the tax law to modify the presumption that all exchanges resulted in a taxable transaction. Before, when property was exchanged for other property, the property received was treated as being equivalent to cash. Its fair market value was used as a basis for taxing the transaction. As noted ear-

¶ 1024

lier, gain does not constitute income until it is *realized* through a completed transaction. An exchange is a completed transaction since the taxpayer's investment in the relinquished property is over and a new investment begins. However, many dispositions do not really involve a change in the kind of investment held by the taxpayer. He has realized nothing tangible by the transfer. Instead, the taxpayer's investment carries over and is continued in the property acquired by the exchange. In short, the purpose of the nonrecognition provisions is to offset situations that would normally be a taxable event under the realization rule. It should be noted that the nonrecognition concept involves a *postponement of* rather than an exemption from taxation. The concept of basis furnishes the method by which taxation is eventually applied.

Since the nonrecognition concept relates to transactions in which a "continuity of interest" exists, dispositions involving exchanges, involuntary conversions and the sale of a residence fall within the concept.

(a) Exchanges. The situation in which the continuity of interest is least affected by a disposition involves an exchange as contrasted from a sale. In a *sale*, property is transferred for an agreed price expressed in money terms while an *exchange* involves a reciprocal transfer of property. Exchanges covered by the nonrecognition provisions involve the following types of property: (1) property held for productive use or investment [¶ 1406]; (2) stock or securities of the same corporation [¶ 1404]; (3) mortgaged property [¶ 1409]; (4) insurance policies [¶ 1407]; and (5) the transfer of property to a corporation controlled by the transferor [¶ 1405].

Property held for productive use or investment. The nonrecognition principle applies to the disposition of the property if the following conditions are met: (1) It must be held for productive use in trade or business, or be held for investment; (2) It must be exchanged; (3) It must be transferred solely for property; and (4) It must involve an exchange of "like kind" property [¶ 1406].

The transfer must involve property related to a gainful activity. The original provision excluded from the nonrecognition provision exchanges involving stock in trade and property held primarily for sale. A later revision added various types of stock or securities to this exclusion since these exchanges involved abusive practices. A taxpayer with a gain once could exchange the stock or securities with a brokerage house for other property and get the difference in money. The taxpayer would have realized a profit but under existing law paid no taxes. However, the exclusion of stock or securities from the nonrecognition provisions was subsequently modified to permit exchanges of stock or securities within the same corporation [¶ 1404].

The exchange must be *solely* for property. The nonrecognition provisions were modified from the original version for transactions involving a straight exchange along with cash or other property called "boot." As already indicated, prior law enabled stock speculators to effect a profit and then simply by an exchange plus "boot" realize a gain not subject to tax. Now, if "boot" is *received* in a transfer then the nonrecognition rule does not apply. The fact that "boot" is given by a taxpayer is not significant since he has made an exchange "solely for property." The other party to the transaction would not get the benefit of the nonrecognition provisions. However, while an exchange involving "boot" may disqualify property from the nonrecognition provision, taxability is limited [¶ 1408].

The exchange must involve "like-kind" property. Thus, the property received must be of the same *nature or character* of the property given up. Both properties must fit into the business or investment category.

The nonrecognition provision in an exchange involving productive use or investment property applies to a loss as well as a gain situation. Realized losses in a transaction involving "boot" are not recognized the same as in exchange of "like-kind" property.

Insurance policies. The exchange of an insurance policy for another policy, or an endowment or an annuity contract results in nonrecognition. The principle was extended to these exchanges since the transactions merely involve transfers of one policy for another better suited to the taxpayer's needs. But it does not apply to the reverse situation. This is to prevent avoiding the tax due on the maturity of endowment contracts by converting to life insurance contracts whose proceeds, payable at death, are tax free [¶ 1407].

Transfer of property to corporation controlled by transferor. The provision extending nonrecognition to this kind of transaction was consistent with the general view of permitting necessary business readjustments. Thus, a partnership or sole proprietorship could change to the corporate form without immediate tax cost. Here again was the notion of the continuity of interest applying to the transaction [¶ 1405].

(b) Involuntary conversions. The continuity of interest status can exist when property has been stolen, destroyed by accident or seized through condemnation. These involuntary conversion situations somewhat resemble exchanges. However, while an exchange is a reciprocal transfer of like property, an involuntary conversion may involve the additional step of reinvesting a condemnation award or insurance proceeds to acquire similar property. Therefore, the nonrecognition of gain rule applies only when a taxpayer makes the qualified replacement. His realized gain will only be recognized when the amount realized exceeds the replacement property's cost. In some cases, there can be a conversion directly into other property similar to the original property. The taxpayer has the option to elect the nonrecognition rule [¶ 1411].

The involuntary conversion provisions enacted into law what had been Treasury Department practice. When property was involuntarily converted with insurance proceeds or a condemnation award recovered, generally no gain or loss was considered to have resulted if the property was replaced.[a] The congressional view was that since the taxpayer's investment was not terminated by his own choice, he ought not to be penalized by the involuntary conversion.

It should be noted that prior law provided nonrecognition treatment for both a gain as well as loss. This was modified since Congress felt it was more equitable to allow the taxpayer to recognize his loss.[b]

In order to qualify as replacement property, it must be *similar or related in service or use* to the converted property.

(c) Sale of personal residence. The nonrecognition principle was applied to the sale of a residence to eliminate certain hardships that arose when the sale of a residence was required because of an increase in family size or when the taxpayer changed jobs. Under prior law, capital gain resulted from the sale of a residence even when the taxpayer bought another residence. A taxable transaction had occurred under the realization doctrine. Congress felt that the sale of a residence was entirely different from the sale of stocks but more like an involuntary conversion.[c]

The rule for nonrecognition of gain comes into play when the taxpayer sells his *principal residence* and buys a new residence within the prescribed period. A special exception applies to those taxpayers 65 or over. Here, all or part of the gain may be excluded [¶ 1416; 1423].

Footnote ¶ 1024   (a)   61 Cong. Rec. 5296 (1921) (remarks of Congressman Hawley).
(b)   H.R. Rep. No. 2333, 77th Cong., 2d Sess. 97 (1942).
(c)   H.R. Rep. No. 586, 82d Cong., 1st Sess. 27-29 (1951).

(d) Nonrecognition of losses. The nonrecognition principle can extend to losses as well as gains. There is no loss recognized when a "wash sale" is involved. In addition, losses from sales between related parties are also not recognized.

The "wash sale" provision was enacted to prevent tax avoidance. A taxpayer could show a "paper loss" by selling the securities and buying them back within a short time. There was no real break in the taxpayer's continuity of interest yet, he could create a loss for tax purposes. A "wash sale" occurs when substantially identical stock or securities are bought within 30 days before or after the sale [¶ 2221].

The disallowance of losses from sales between related parties was to stop the deduction of losses where no real economic loss had been sustained [¶ 2223].

¶ 1025 The meaning of basis. The starting point for determining gain or loss and the deductions for depreciation, bad debts or casualty losses is basis. Generally, basis fixes the amount of the original outlay that can be recovered tax free. Subsequent capital improvements to the property increase basis. Items that are considered a return of capital reduce basis. They include such things as depreciation and casualty losses. The result of these additions and reductions is the *adjusted basis*.

As noted earlier, gain is not included in income until it is *realized*. At this point, the gain is determined by reference to the adjusted basis of the property and the amount realized. However, the nonrecognition provisions may postpone the application of the tax until the time a taxable transaction occurs. The concept of basis is the method by which tax liability is ultimately applied. When no gain or loss is recognized on a disposition, the adjusted basis of the property given up becomes the basis of the new property.

Generally, basis is the property's cost or purchase price [¶ 1501]. But the property may have been acquired by gift [¶ 1515], by nontaxable exchange [¶ 1517; 1518], or through an involuntary conversion [¶ 1519]. In these cases, the basis is determined by reference to the property given up. A "substituted basis" is used [¶ 1514]. In other cases, fair market value is used [¶ 1502]. This involves property acquired in a taxable exchange [¶ 1503], property acquired from a decedent [¶ 1507] or property transferred in contemplation of death [¶ 1508].

The postponement concept in the sale and replacement of a new residence requires that the nonrecognized gain be taken into account in determining the basis of the new residence. In this way, the nonrecognized gain does not escape taxation but is merely postponed [¶ 1526].

¶ 1026 The special rules on capital gains and losses. Gain or the appreciation in value, as noted earlier, is included in income when it is realized. The amount of the gain is figured by reference to the property's adjusted basis and the amount realized. However, the recognition rule may limit taxability. Once taxability attaches in a particular transaction, the issue becomes one of determining whether the preferential capital gain treatment applies [¶ 1600 et seq.].

The realization concept bears directly on the preferred treatment given to capital gains. Since these are taxable only when a capital asset is sold or exchanged, the timing of the transaction and therefore realization is at the taxpayer's discretion.

Generally, a distinction is considered to exist between capital gains, as those gains stemming from increases in the value of investments, and profits that result from the sale of goods or services, being the product of the taxpayer's economic activity.

Early in the tax law, Congress accorded capital gains special treatment to limit the taxing in a single year appreciation that may have accumulated over a longer period. Prior law tended to curtail the sales and exchanges of capital assets thereby affecting business or investment activity.[a]

Footnote ¶ 1026 (a) H.R. Rep. No. 350; 67th Cong., 1st Sess. 10-11 (1921).

SPECIAL SUPPLEMENT TO THE
PRENTICE-HALL
1978 FEDERAL TAX COURSE
(Students Edition)

1977 TAX TABLES

	Page
Tax Table A—Single taxpayers	3
Tax Table B—Married taxpayers filing jointly and qualifying widows and widowers	5
Tax Table C—Married taxpayers filing separately	10
Tax Table D—Heads of household	12

Copyright 1977 by
PRENTICE-HALL, INC. • Englewood Cliffs, N.J. **07632**
(013-310367-6)

1977 TAX TABLES
Table A – Single Taxpayers

If Tax Table Income is— Over—	But not over—	1	2	3	If Tax Table Income is— Over—	But not over—	1	2	3	If Tax Table Income is— Over—	But not over—	1	2	3
If $3,200 or less your tax is 0					5,800	5,850	419	264	100	8,400	8,450	890	748	580
					5,850	5,900	427	273	108	8,450	8,500	900	757	590
3,200	3,250	4	0	0	5,900	5,950	436	283	116	8,500	8,550	909	767	601
3,250	3,300	11	0	0	5,950	6,000	444	292	124	8,550	8,600	919	776	611
3,300	3,350	18	0	0										
3,350	3,400	25	0	0	6,000	6,050	453	302	133	8,600	8,650	928	786	622
					6,050	6,100	461	311	141	8,650	8,700	938	795	632
3,400	3,450	32	0	0	6,100	6,150	470	321	150	8,700	8,750	947	805	643
3,450	3,500	39	0	0	6,150	6,200	478	330	158	8,750	8,800	957	814	653
3,500	3,550	46	0	0										
3,550	3,600	54	0	0	6,200	6,250	487	340	167	8,800	8,850	966	824	664
					6,250	6,300	495	349	175	8,850	8,900	976	833	674
3,600	3,650	61	0	0	6,300	6,350	504	359	184	8,900	8,950	985	843	685
3,650	3,700	69	0	0	6,350	6,400	512	368	192	8,950	9,000	996	852	695
3,700	3,750	76	0	0										
3,750	3,800	84	0	0	6,400	6,450	521	378	201	9,000	9,050	1,007	862	706
3,800	3,850	91	0	0	6,450	6,500	529	387	210	9,050	9,100	1,018	871	716
3,850	3,900	99	0	0	6,500	6,550	538	397	219	9,100	9,150	1,029	881	727
3,900	3,950	106	0	0	6,550	6,600	546	406	229	9,150	9,200	1,040	890	737
3,950	4,000	114	0	0										
					6,600	6,650	555	416	238	9,200	9,250	1,051	900	748
4,000	4,050	122	0	0	6,650	6,700	563	425	248	9,250	9,300	1,062	909	758
4,050	4,100	130	0	0	6,700	6,750	572	435	257	9,300	9,350	1,073	919	769
4,100	4,150	138	0	0	6,750	6,800	580	444	267	9,350	9,400	1,084	928	779
4,150	4,200	146	0	0										
4,200	4,250	154	4	0	6,800	6,850	589	454	276	9,400	9,450	1,095	938	790
4,250	4,300	162	11	0	6,850	6,900	597	463	286	9,450	9,500	1,106	947	800
4,300	4,350	170	19	0	6,900	6,950	606	473	295	9,500	9,550	1,117	957	811
4,350	4,400	178	26	0	6,950	7,000	615	482	305	9,550	9,600	1,128	966	821
4,400	4,450	186	34	0	7,000	7,050	624	492	314	9,600	9,650	1,139	976	832
4,450	4,500	194	41	0	7,050	7,100	634	501	324	9,650	9,700	1,150	985	842
4,500	4,550	203	49	0	7,100	7,150	643	511	333	9,700	9,750	1,161	996	852
4,550	4,600	211	56	0	7,150	7,200	653	520	343	9,750	9,800	1,172	1,007	862
4,600	4,650	220	64	0	7,200	7,250	662	529	352	9,800	9,850	1,183	1,018	871
4,650	4,700	228	71	0	7,250	7,300	672	538	362	9,850	9,900	1,194	1,029	881
4,700	4,750	236	79	0	7,300	7,350	681	546	371	9,900	9,950	1,205	1,040	890
4,750	4,800	244	87	0	7,350	7,400	691	555	381	9,950	10,000	1,216	1,051	900
4,800	4,850	251	95	0	7,400	7,450	700	563	390	10,000	10,050	1,227	1,062	909
4,850	4,900	259	103	0	7,450	7,500	710	572	400	10,050	10,100	1,238	1,073	919
4,900	4,950	266	111	0	7,500	7,550	719	580	409	10,100	10,150	1,249	1,084	928
4,950	5,000	274	119	0	7,550	7,600	729	589	419	10,150	10,200	1,260	1,095	938
5,000	5,050	283	127	0	7,600	7,650	738	597	428	10,200	10,250	1,271	1,106	947
5,050	5,100	291	135	0	7,650	7,700	748	606	438	10,250	10,300	1,282	1,117	957
5,100	5,150	300	143	0	7,700	7,750	757	615	447	10,300	10,350	1,293	1,128	966
5,150	5,200	308	151	0	7,750	7,800	767	624	457	10,350	10,400	1,304	1,139	976
5,200	5,250	317	159	6	7,800	7,850	776	634	466	10,400	10,450	1,315	1,150	985
5,250	5,300	325	168	14	7,850	7,900	786	643	476	10,450	10,500	1,326	1,161	996
5,300	5,350	334	176	21	7,900	7,950	795	653	485	10,500	10,550	1,337	1,172	1,007
5,350	5,400	342	185	29	7,950	8,000	805	662	495	10,550	10,600	1,348	1,183	1,018
5,400	5,450	351	193	36	8,000	8,050	814	672	504	10,600	10,650	1,359	1,194	1,029
5,450	5,500	359	202	44	8,050	8,100	824	681	514	10,650	10,700	1,370	1,205	1,040
5,500	5,550	368	210	52	8,100	8,150	833	691	523	10,700	10,750	1,381	1,216	1,051
5,550	5,600	376	219	60	8,150	8,200	843	700	533	10,750	10,800	1,392	1,227	1,062
5,600	5,650	385	227	68	8,200	8,250	852	710	542	10,800	10,850	1,403	1,238	1,073
5,650	5,700	393	236	76	8,250	8,300	862	719	552	10,850	10,900	1,414	1,249	1,084
5,700	5,750	402	245	84	8,300	8,350	871	729	561	10,900	10,950	1,425	1,260	1,095
5,750	5,800	410	254	92	8,350	8,400	881	738	571	10,950	11,000	1,436	1,271	1,106
Continued next column					Continued next column					Continued on next page				

1977 TAX TABLES
Table A – Single Taxpayers (Continued)

If Tax Table Income is— Over—	But not over—	And the number of exemptions is— 1	2	3	If Tax Table Income is— Over—	But not over—	And the number of exemptions is— 1	2	3	If Tax Table Income is— Over—	But not over—	And the number of exemptions is— 1	2	3
		Your tax is—					Your tax is—					Your tax is—		
11,000	11,050	1,447	1,282	1,117	14,000	14,050	2,200	1,998	1,804	17,000	17,050	3,053	2,834	2,617
11,050	11,100	1,459	1,293	1,128	14,050	14,100	2,214	2,011	1,816	17,050	17,100	3,069	2,849	2,631
11,100	11,150	1,470	1,304	1,139	14,100	14,150	2,227	2,025	1,829	17,100	17,150	3,084	2,863	2,646
11,150	11,200	1,482	1,315	1,150	14,150	14,200	2,241	2,038	1,841	17,150	17,200	3,100	2,878	2,660
11,200	11,250	1,493	1,326	1,161	14,200	14,250	2,254	2,052	1,854	17,200	17,250	3,115	2,892	2,675
11,250	11,300	1,505	1,337	1,172	14,250	14,300	2,268	2,065	1,866	17,250	17,300	3,131	2,907	2,689
11,300	11,350	1,516	1,348	1,183	14,300	14,350	2,281	2,079	1,879	17,300	17,350	3,146	2,921	2,704
11,350	11,400	1,528	1,359	1,194	14,350	14,400	2,295	2,092	1,891	17,350	17,400	3,162	2,936	2,718
11,400	11,450	1,539	1,370	1,205	14,400	14,450	2,308	2,106	1,904	17,400	17,450	3,177	2,950	2,733
11,450	11,500	1,551	1,381	1,216	14,450	14,500	2,322	2,119	1,917	17,450	17,500	3,193	2,965	2,747
11,500	11,550	1,562	1,392	1,227	14,500	14,550	2,335	2,133	1,930	17,500	17,550	3,208	2,979	2,762
11,550	11,600	1,574	1,403	1,238	14,550	14,600	2,349	2,146	1,944	17,550	17,600	3,224	2,994	2,776
11,600	11,650	1,585	1,414	1,249	14,600	14,650	2,362	2,160	1,957	17,600	17,650	3,239	3,008	2,791
11,650	11,700	1,597	1,425	1,260	14,650	14,700	2,376	2,173	1,971	17,650	17,700	3,255	3,023	2,805
11,700	11,750	1,608	1,436	1,271	14,700	14,750	2,389	2,187	1,984	17,700	17,750	3,270	3,038	2,820
11,750	11,800	1,620	1,447	1,282	14,750	14,800	2,403	2,200	1,998	17,750	17,800	3,286	3,053	2,834
11,800	11,850	1,631	1,459	1,293	14,800	14,850	2,416	2,214	2,011	17,800	17,850	3,301	3,069	2,849
11,850	11,900	1,643	1,470	1,304	14,850	14,900	2,430	2,227	2,025	17,850	17,900	3,317	3,084	2,863
11,900	11,950	1,654	1,482	1,315	14,900	14,950	2,443	2,241	2,038	17,900	17,950	3,332	3,100	2,878
11,950	12,000	1,666	1,493	1,326	14,950	15,000	2,457	2,254	2,052	17,950	18,000	3,348	3,115	2,892
12,000	12,050	1,679	1,505	1,337	15,000	15,050	2,472	2,268	2,065	18,000	18,050	3,363	3,131	2,907
12,050	12,100	1,691	1,516	1,348	15,050	15,100	2,486	2,281	2,079	18,050	18,100	3,379	3,146	2,921
12,100	12,150	1,704	1,528	1,359	15,100	15,150	2,501	2,295	2,092	18,100	18,150	3,394	3,162	2,936
12,150	12,200	1,716	1,539	1,370	15,150	15,200	2,515	2,308	2,106	18,150	18,200	3,410	3,177	2,950
12,200	12,250	1,729	1,551	1,381	15,200	15,250	2,530	2,322	2,119	18,200	18,250	3,425	3,193	2,965
12,250	12,300	1,741	1,562	1,392	15,250	15,300	2,544	2,335	2,133	18,250	18,300	3,441	3,208	2,979
12,300	12,350	1,754	1,574	1,403	15,300	15,350	2,559	2,349	2,146	18,300	18,350	3,456	3,224	2,994
12,350	12,400	1,766	1,585	1,414	15,350	15,400	2,573	2,362	2,160	18,350	18,400	3,472	3,239	3,008
12,400	12,450	1,779	1,597	1,425	15,400	15,450	2,588	2,376	2,173	18,400	18,450	3,487	3,255	3,023
12,450	12,500	1,791	1,608	1,436	15,450	15,500	2,602	2,389	2,187	18,450	18,500	3,503	3,270	3,038
12,500	12,550	1,804	1,620	1,447	15,500	15,550	2,617	2,403	2,200	18,500	18,550	3,518	3,286	3,053
12,550	12,600	1,816	1,631	1,459	15,550	15,600	2,631	2,416	2,214	18,550	18,600	3,534	3,301	3,069
12,600	12,650	1,829	1,643	1,470	15,600	15,650	2,646	2,430	2,227	18,600	18,650	3,549	3,317	3,084
12,650	12,700	1,841	1,654	1,482	15,650	15,700	2,660	2,443	2,241	18,650	18,700	3,565	3,332	3,100
12,700	12,750	1,854	1,666	1,493	15,700	15,750	2,675	2,457	2,254	18,700	18,750	3,580	3,348	3,115
12,750	12,800	1,866	1,679	1,505	15,750	15,800	2,689	2,472	2,268	18,750	18,800	3,596	3,363	3,131
12,800	12,850	1,879	1,691	1,516	15,800	15,850	2,704	2,486	2,281	18,800	18,850	3,611	3,379	3,146
12,850	12,900	1,891	1,704	1,528	15,850	15,900	2,718	2,501	2,295	18,850	18,900	3,627	3,394	3,162
12,900	12,950	1,904	1,716	1,539	15,900	15,950	2,733	2,515	2,308	18,900	18,950	3,642	3,410	3,177
12,950	13,000	1,917	1,729	1,551	15,950	16,000	2,747	2,530	2,322	18,950	19,000	3,659	3,425	3,193
13,000	13,050	1,930	1,741	1,562	16,000	16,050	2,762	2,544	2,335	19,000	19,050	3,676	3,441	3,208
13,050	13,100	1,944	1,754	1,574	16,050	16,100	2,776	2,559	2,349	19,050	19,100	3,693	3,456	3,224
13,100	13,150	1,957	1,766	1,585	16,100	16,150	2,791	2,573	2,362	19,100	19,150	3,710	3,472	3,239
13,150	13,200	1,971	1,779	1,597	16,150	16,200	2,805	2,588	2,376	19,150	19,200	3,727	3,487	3,255
13,200	13,250	1,984	1,791	1,608	16,200	16,250	2,820	2,602	2,389	19,200	19,250	3,744	3,503	3,270
13,250	13,300	1,998	1,804	1,620	16,250	16,300	2,834	2,617	2,403	19,250	19,300	3,761	3,518	3,286
13,300	13,350	2,011	1,816	1,631	16,300	16,350	2,849	2,631	2,416	19,300	19,350	3,778	3,534	3,301
13,350	13,400	2,025	1,829	1,643	16,350	16,400	2,863	2,646	2,430	19,350	19,400	3,795	3,549	3,317
13,400	13,450	2,038	1,841	1,654	16,400	16,450	2,878	2,660	2,443	19,400	19,450	3,812	3,565	3,332
13,450	13,500	2,052	1,854	1,666	16,450	16,500	2,892	2,675	2,457	19,450	19,500	3,829	3,580	3,348
13,500	13,550	2,065	1,866	1,679	16,500	16,550	2,907	2,689	2,472	19,500	19,550	3,846	3,596	3,363
13,550	13,600	2,079	1,879	1,691	16,550	16,600	2,921	2,704	2,486	19,550	19,600	3,863	3,611	3,379
13,600	13,650	2,092	1,891	1,704	16,600	16,650	2,936	2,718	2,501	19,600	19,650	3,880	3,627	3,394
13,650	13,700	2,106	1,904	1,716	16,650	16,700	2,950	2,733	2,515	19,650	19,700	3,897	3,642	3,410
13,700	13,750	2,119	1,917	1,729	16,700	16,750	2,965	2,747	2,530	19,700	19,750	3,914	3,659	3,425
13,750	13,800	2,133	1,930	1,741	16,750	16,800	2,979	2,762	2,544	19,750	19,800	3,931	3,676	3,441
13,800	13,850	2,146	1,944	1,754	16,800	16,850	2,994	2,776	2,559	19,800	19,850	3,948	3,693	3,456
13,850	13,900	2,160	1,957	1,766	16,850	16,900	3,008	2,791	2,573	19,850	19,900	3,965	3,710	3,472
13,900	13,950	2,173	1,971	1,779	16,900	16,950	3,023	2,805	2,588	19,900	19,950	3,982	3,727	3,487
13,950	14,000	2,187	1,984	1,791	16,950	17,000	3,038	2,820	2,602	19,950	20,000	3,999	3,744	3,503

Continued next column

Continued next column

1977 TAX TABLES
Table B — Married Taxpayers Filing Jointly and Qualifying Widows and Widowers

If Tax Table Income is— Over—	But not over—	2	3	4	5	6	7	8	9	If Tax Table Income is— Over—	But not over—	2	3	4	5	6	7	8	9
\$5,200 or less your tax is 0										8,400	8,450	499	341	186	36	0	0	0	0
5,200	5,250	4	0	0	0	0	0	0	0	8,450	8,500	506	349	194	44	0	0	0	0
5,250	5,300	11	0	0	0	0	0	0	0	8,500	8,550	514	358	202	51	0	0	0	0
5,300	5,350	18	0	0	0	0	0	0	0	8,550	8,600	521	366	210	59	0	0	0	0
5,350	5,400	25	0	0	0	0	0	0	0	8,600	8,650	529	375	218	66	0	0	0	0
5,400	5,450	32	0	0	0	0	0	0	0	8,650	8,700	536	383	226	74	0	0	0	0
5,450	5,500	39	0	0	0	0	0	0	0	8,700	8,750	544	392	234	81	0	0	0	0
5,500	5,550	46	0	0	0	0	0	0	0	8,750	8,800	553	400	242	89	0	0	0	0
5,550	5,600	53	0	0	0	0	0	0	0	8,800	8,850	561	409	250	96	0	0	0	0
5,600	5,650	60	0	0	0	0	0	0	0	8,850	8,900	570	417	258	104	0	0	0	0
5,650	5,700	67	0	0	0	0	0	0	0	8,900	8,950	578	426	266	111	0	0	0	0
5,700	5,750	74	0	0	0	0	0	0	0	8,950	9,000	587	434	274	119	0	0	0	0
5,750	5,800	81	0	0	0	0	0	0	0	9,000	9,050	595	443	282	127	0	0	0	0
5,800	5,850	89	0	0	0	0	0	0	0	9,050	9,100	604	451	290	135	0	0	0	0
5,850	5,900	96	0	0	0	0	0	0	0	9,100	9,150	612	460	298	143	0	0	0	0
5,900	5,950	104	0	0	0	0	0	0	0	9,150	9,200	621	468	306	151	1	0	0	0
5,950	6,000	111	0	0	0	0	0	0	0	9,200	9,250	629	477	314	159	9	0	0	0
6,000	6,050	119	0	0	0	0	0	0	0	9,250	9,300	638	485	323	167	16	0	0	0
6,050	6,100	126	0	0	0	0	0	0	0	9,300	9,350	646	494	331	175	24	0	0	0
6,100	6,150	134	0	0	0	0	0	0	0	9,350	9,400	655	502	340	183	31	0	0	0
6,150	6,200	141	0	0	0	0	0	0	0	9,400	9,450	663	511	348	191	39	0	0	0
6,200	6,250	149	4	0	0	0	0	0	0	9,450	9,500	672	520	357	199	46	0	0	0
6,250	6,300	156	11	0	0	0	0	0	0	9,500	9,550	680	529	365	207	54	0	0	0
6,300	6,350	164	18	0	0	0	0	0	0	9,550	9,600	689	539	374	215	61	0	0	0
6,350	6,400	171	25	0	0	0	0	0	0	9,600	9,650	697	548	382	223	69	0	0	0
6,400	6,450	179	32	0	0	0	0	0	0	9,650	9,700	706	558	391	231	76	0	0	0
6,450	6,500	186	39	0	0	0	0	0	0	9,700	9,750	714	567	399	239	84	0	0	0
6,500	6,550	194	46	0	0	0	0	0	0	9,750	9,800	723	577	408	247	92	0	0	0
6,550	6,600	201	54	0	0	0	0	0	0	9,800	9,850	731	586	416	255	100	0	0	0
6,600	6,650	209	61	0	0	0	0	0	0	9,850	9,900	740	596	425	263	108	0	0	0
6,650	6,700	216	69	0	0	0	0	0	0	9,900	9,950	748	605	433	271	116	0	0	0
6,700	6,750	224	76	0	0	0	0	0	0	9,950	10,000	757	615	442	279	124	0	0	0
6,750	6,800	232	84	0	0	0	0	0	0	10,000	10,050	765	624	450	288	132	0	0	0
6,800	6,850	240	91	0	0	0	0	0	0	10,050	10,100	774	634	459	296	140	0	0	0
6,850	6,900	248	99	0	0	0	0	0	0	10,100	10,150	782	643	467	305	148	0	0	0
6,900	6,950	256	106	0	0	0	0	0	0	10,150	10,200	791	653	476	313	156	4	0	0
6,950	7,000	264	114	0	0	0	0	0	0	10,200	10,250	799	662	485	322	164	11	0	0
7,000	7,050	272	121	0	0	0	0	0	0	10,250	10,300	808	672	494	330	172	19	0	0
7,050	7,100	280	129	0	0	0	0	0	0	10,300	10,350	816	681	504	339	180	26	0	0
7,100	7,150	288	136	0	0	0	0	0	0	10,350	10,400	825	691	513	347	188	34	0	0
7,150	7,200	296	144	0	0	0	0	0	0	10,400	10,450	833	700	523	356	196	41	0	0
7,200	7,250	304	151	4	0	0	0	0	0	10,450	10,500	842	710	532	364	204	49	0	0
7,250	7,300	312	159	11	0	0	0	0	0	10,500	10,550	850	719	542	373	212	57	0	0
7,300	7,350	320	166	19	0	0	0	0	0	10,550	10,600	859	729	551	381	220	65	0	0
7,350	7,400	328	174	26	0	0	0	0	0	10,600	10,650	867	738	561	390	228	73	0	0
7,400	7,450	336	181	34	0	0	0	0	0	10,650	10,700	876	748	570	398	236	81	0	0
7,450	7,500	344	189	41	0	0	0	0	0	10,700	10,750	884	757	580	407	244	89	0	0
7,500	7,550	352	197	49	0	0	0	0	0	10,750	10,800	893	765	589	415	253	97	0	0
7,550	7,600	360	205	56	0	0	0	0	0	10,800	10,850	901	774	599	424	261	105	0	0
7,600	7,650	368	213	64	0	0	0	0	0	10,850	10,900	910	782	608	432	270	113	0	0
7,650	7,700	376	221	71	0	0	0	0	0	10,900	10,950	918	791	618	441	278	121	0	0
7,700	7,750	384	229	79	0	0	0	0	0	10,950	11,000	927	799	627	450	287	129	0	0
7,750	7,800	393	237	86	0	0	0	0	0	11,000	11,050	935	808	637	459	295	137	0	0
7,800	7,850	401	245	94	0	0	0	0	0	11,050	11,100	944	816	646	469	304	145	0	0
7,850	7,900	410	253	101	0	0	0	0	0	11,100	11,150	952	825	656	478	312	153	0	0
7,900	7,950	418	261	109	0	0	0	0	0	11,150	11,200	961	833	665	488	321	161	6	0
7,950	8,000	427	269	116	0	0	0	0	0	11,200	11,250	969	842	675	497	329	169	14	0
8,000	8,050	435	277	124	0	0	0	0	0	11,250	11,300	978	850	684	507	338	177	22	0
8,050	8,100	444	285	131	0	0	0	0	0	11,300	11,350	986	859	694	516	346	185	30	0
8,100	8,150	452	293	139	0	0	0	0	0	11,350	11,400	995	867	703	526	355	193	38	0
8,150	8,200	461	301	146	0	0	0	0	0	11,400	11,450	1,003	876	713	535	363	201	46	0
8,200	8,250	469	309	154	6	0	0	0	0	11,450	11,500	1,012	884	722	545	372	209	54	0
8,250	8,300	476	317	162	14	0	0	0	0	11,500	11,550	1,020	893	732	554	380	218	62	0
8,300	8,350	484	325	170	21	0	0	0	0	11,550	11,600	1,029	901	741	564	389	226	70	0
8,350	8,400	491	333	178	29	0	0	0	0										

Continued next column Continued on next page

1977 TAX TABLES

Table B – Married Taxpayers Filing Jointly and Qualifying Widows and Widowers (Continued)

If Tax Table Income is— Over—	But not over—	\multicolumn{8}{c}{And the number of exemptions is—}								If Tax Table Income is— Over—	But not over—	\multicolumn{8}{c}{And the number of exemptions is—}							
		2	3	4	5	6	7	8	9			2	3	4	5	6	7	8	9
		\multicolumn{8}{c}{Your tax is—}									\multicolumn{8}{c}{Your tax is—}							
11,600	11,650	1,037	910	751	573	397	235	78	0	15,200	15,250	1,756	1,591	1,426	1,266	1,080	902	725	547
11,650	11,700	1,046	918	760	583	406	243	86	0	15,250	15,300	1,767	1,602	1,437	1,277	1,089	912	734	557
11,700	11,750	1,054	927	770	592	415	252	94	0	15,300	15,350	1,778	1,613	1,448	1,288	1,099	921	744	566
11,750	11,800	1,063	935	779	602	424	260	102	0	15,350	15,400	1,789	1,624	1,459	1,299	1,108	931	753	576
11,800	11,850	1,071	944	789	611	434	269	110	0	15,400	15,450	1,800	1,635	1,470	1,310	1,118	940	763	585
11,850	11,900	1,080	952	798	621	443	277	118	0	15,450	15,500	1,811	1,646	1,481	1,321	1,127	950	772	595
11,900	11,950	1,088	961	808	630	453	286	126	0	15,500	15,550	1,822	1,657	1,492	1,332	1,137	959	782	604
11,950	12,000	1,097	969	817	640	462	294	134	0	15,550	15,600	1,833	1,668	1,503	1,343	1,146	969	791	614
12,000	12,050	1,105	978	827	649	472	303	142	0	15,600	15,650	1,844	1,679	1,514	1,354	1,156	978	801	623
12,050	12,100	1,114	986	836	659	481	311	150	0	15,650	15,700	1,855	1,690	1,525	1,365	1,165	988	810	633
12,100	12,150	1,122	995	846	668	491	320	158	3	15,700	15,750	1,866	1,701	1,536	1,375	1,176	997	820	642
12,150	12,200	1,131	1,003	855	678	500	328	166	11	15,750	15,800	1,877	1,712	1,547	1,385	1,187	1,007	829	652
12,200	12,250	1,139	1,012	865	687	510	337	174	19	15,800	15,850	1,888	1,723	1,558	1,395	1,198	1,016	839	661
12,250	12,300	1,148	1,020	874	697	519	345	183	27	15,850	15,900	1,899	1,734	1,569	1,405	1,209	1,026	848	671
12,300	12,350	1,156	1,029	884	706	529	354	191	35	15,900	15,950	1,910	1,745	1,580	1,415	1,220	1,035	858	680
12,350	12,400	1,165	1,037	893	716	538	362	200	43	15,950	16,000	1,921	1,756	1,591	1,426	1,231	1,045	867	690
12,400	12,450	1,173	1,046	903	725	548	371	208	51	16,000	16,050	1,932	1,767	1,602	1,437	1,242	1,054	877	699
12,450	12,500	1,182	1,054	912	735	557	380	217	59	16,050	16,100	1,943	1,778	1,613	1,448	1,253	1,064	886	709
12,500	12,550	1,190	1,063	922	744	567	389	225	67	16,100	16,150	1,954	1,789	1,624	1,459	1,264	1,073	896	718
12,550	12,600	1,199	1,071	931	754	576	399	234	75	16,150	16,200	1,965	1,800	1,635	1,470	1,275	1,083	905	728
12,600	12,650	1,207	1,080	941	763	586	408	242	83	16,200	16,250	1,976	1,811	1,646	1,481	1,286	1,092	915	737
12,650	12,700	1,216	1,088	950	773	595	418	251	91	16,250	16,300	1,987	1,822	1,657	1,492	1,297	1,102	924	747
12,700	12,750	1,225	1,097	960	782	605	427	259	99	16,300	16,350	1,998	1,833	1,668	1,503	1,308	1,111	934	756
12,750	12,800	1,235	1,105	969	792	614	437	268	107	16,350	16,400	2,009	1,844	1,679	1,514	1,319	1,121	943	766
12,800	12,850	1,245	1,114	979	801	624	446	276	115	16,400	16,450	2,020	1,855	1,690	1,525	1,330	1,130	953	775
12,850	12,900	1,255	1,122	988	811	633	456	285	123	16,450	16,500	2,031	1,866	1,701	1,536	1,341	1,141	962	785
12,900	12,950	1,265	1,131	998	820	643	465	293	131	16,500	16,550	2,042	1,877	1,712	1,547	1,352	1,152	972	794
12,950	13,000	1,275	1,139	1,007	830	652	475	302	139	16,550	16,600	2,053	1,888	1,723	1,558	1,363	1,163	981	804
13,000	13,050	1,285	1,148	1,017	839	662	484	310	148	16,600	16,650	2,064	1,899	1,734	1,569	1,374	1,174	991	813
13,050	13,100	1,295	1,156	1,026	849	671	494	319	156	16,650	16,700	2,075	1,910	1,745	1,580	1,385	1,185	1,000	823
13,100	13,150	1,305	1,165	1,036	858	681	503	327	165	16,700	16,750	2,086	1,921	1,756	1,591	1,396	1,196	1,010	832
13,150	13,200	1,315	1,173	1,045	868	690	513	336	173	16,750	16,800	2,099	1,932	1,767	1,602	1,407	1,207	1,019	842
13,200	13,250	1,325	1,182	1,054	877	700	522	345	182	16,800	16,850	2,111	1,943	1,778	1,613	1,418	1,218	1,029	851
13,250	13,300	1,335	1,190	1,063	887	709	532	354	190	16,850	16,900	2,124	1,954	1,789	1,624	1,429	1,229	1,038	861
13,300	13,350	1,345	1,199	1,071	896	719	541	364	199	16,900	16,950	2,136	1,965	1,800	1,635	1,440	1,240	1,048	870
13,350	13,400	1,355	1,207	1,080	906	728	551	373	207	16,950	17,000	2,149	1,976	1,811	1,646	1,451	1,251	1,057	880
13,400	13,450	1,365	1,216	1,088	915	738	560	383	216	17,000	17,050	2,161	1,987	1,822	1,657	1,462	1,262	1,067	889
13,450	13,500	1,375	1,225	1,097	925	747	570	392	224	17,050	17,100	2,174	1,998	1,833	1,668	1,473	1,273	1,076	899
13,500	13,550	1,385	1,235	1,105	934	757	579	402	233	17,100	17,150	2,186	2,009	1,844	1,679	1,484	1,284	1,086	908
13,550	13,600	1,395	1,245	1,114	944	766	589	411	241	17,150	17,200	2,199	2,020	1,855	1,690	1,495	1,295	1,095	918
13,600	13,650	1,405	1,255	1,122	953	776	598	421	250	17,200	17,250	2,211	2,031	1,866	1,701	1,506	1,306	1,106	927
13,650	13,700	1,415	1,265	1,131	963	785	608	430	258	17,250	17,300	2,224	2,042	1,877	1,712	1,517	1,317	1,117	937
13,700	13,750	1,426	1,275	1,139	972	795	617	440	267	17,300	17,350	2,236	2,053	1,888	1,723	1,528	1,328	1,128	946
13,750	13,800	1,437	1,285	1,148	982	804	627	449	275	17,350	17,400	2,249	2,064	1,899	1,734	1,539	1,339	1,139	956
13,800	13,850	1,448	1,295	1,156	991	814	636	459	284	17,400	17,450	2,261	2,075	1,910	1,745	1,550	1,350	1,150	965
13,850	13,900	1,459	1,305	1,165	1,001	823	646	468	292	17,450	17,500	2,274	2,086	1,921	1,756	1,561	1,361	1,161	975
13,900	13,950	1,470	1,315	1,173	1,010	833	655	478	301	17,500	17,550	2,286	2,099	1,932	1,767	1,572	1,372	1,172	984
13,950	14,000	1,481	1,325	1,182	1,020	842	665	487	310	17,550	17,600	2,299	2,111	1,943	1,778	1,583	1,383	1,183	994
14,000	14,050	1,492	1,335	1,190	1,029	852	674	497	319	17,600	17,650	2,311	2,121	1,954	1,789	1,594	1,394	1,194	1,003
14,050	14,100	1,503	1,345	1,199	1,039	861	684	506	329	17,650	17,700	2,324	2,136	1,965	1,800	1,605	1,405	1,205	1,013
14,100	14,150	1,514	1,355	1,207	1,048	871	693	516	338	17,700	17,750	2,336	2,149	1,976	1,811	1,616	1,416	1,216	1,022
14,150	14,200	1,525	1,365	1,216	1,058	880	703	525	348	17,750	17,800	2,349	2,161	1,987	1,822	1,627	1,427	1,227	1,032
14,200	14,250	1,536	1,375	1,225	1,067	890	712	535	357	17,800	17,850	2,361	2,174	1,998	1,833	1,638	1,438	1,238	1,041
14,250	14,300	1,547	1,385	1,235	1,077	899	722	544	367	17,850	17,900	2,374	2,186	2,009	1,844	1,649	1,449	1,249	1,051
14,300	14,350	1,558	1,395	1,245	1,086	909	731	554	376	17,900	17,950	2,386	2,199	2,020	1,855	1,660	1,460	1,260	1,060
14,350	14,400	1,569	1,405	1,255	1,096	918	741	563	386	17,950	18,000	2,399	2,211	2,031	1,866	1,671	1,471	1,271	1,071
14,400	14,450	1,580	1,415	1,265	1,105	928	750	573	395	18,000	18,050	2,411	2,224	2,042	1,877	1,682	1,482	1,282	1,082
14,450	14,500	1,591	1,426	1,275	1,115	937	760	582	405	18,050	18,100	2,424	2,236	2,053	1,888	1,693	1,493	1,293	1,093
14,500	14,550	1,602	1,437	1,285	1,124	947	769	592	414	18,100	18,150	2,436	2,249	2,064	1,899	1,704	1,504	1,304	1,104
14,550	14,600	1,613	1,448	1,295	1,134	956	779	601	424	18,150	18,200	2,449	2,261	2,075	1,910	1,715	1,515	1,315	1,115
14,600	14,650	1,624	1,459	1,305	1,143	966	788	611	433	18,200	18,250	2,461	2,274	2,086	1,921	1,726	1,526	1,326	1,126
14,650	14,700	1,635	1,470	1,315	1,153	975	798	620	443	18,250	18,300	2,474	2,286	2,099	1,932	1,737	1,537	1,337	1,137
14,700	14,750	1,646	1,481	1,325	1,162	985	807	630	452	18,300	18,350	2,486	2,299	2,111	1,943	1,748	1,548	1,348	1,148
14,750	14,800	1,657	1,492	1,335	1,172	994	817	639	462	18,350	18,400	2,499	2,311	2,124	1,954	1,759	1,559	1,359	1,159
14,800	14,850	1,668	1,503	1,345	1,181	1,004	826	649	471	18,400	18,450	2,511	2,324	2,136	1,965	1,770	1,570	1,370	1,170
14,850	14,900	1,679	1,514	1,355	1,191	1,013	836	658	481	18,450	18,500	2,524	2,336	2,149	1,976	1,781	1,581	1,381	1,181
14,900	14,950	1,690	1,525	1,365	1,200	1,023	845	668	490	18,500	18,550	2,536	2,349	2,161	1,987	1,792	1,592	1,392	1,192
14,950	15,000	1,701	1,536	1,375	1,211	1,032	855	677	500	18,550	18,600	2,549	2,361	2,174	1,998	1,803	1,603	1,403	1,203
15,000	15,050	1,712	1,547	1,385	1,222	1,042	864	687	509	18,600	18,650	2,561	2,374	2,186	2,009	1,814	1,614	1,414	1,214
15,050	15,100	1,723	1,558	1,395	1,233	1,051	874	696	519	18,650	18,700	2,574	2,386	2,199	2,020	1,825	1,625	1,425	1,225
15,100	15,150	1,734	1,569	1,405	1,244	1,061	883	706	528	18,700	18,750	2,586	2,399	2,211	2,031	1,836	1,636	1,436	1,236
15,150	15,200	1,745	1,580	1,415	1,255	1,070	893	715	538	18,750	18,800	2,599	2,411	2,224	2,042	1,847	1,647	1,447	1,247

Continued next column

Continued on next page

1977 TAX TABLES
Table C — Married Taxpayers Filing Separately (Continued)

If Tax Table Income is— Over—	But not over—	1	2	3	If Tax Table Income is— Over—	But not over—	1	2	3	If Tax Table Income is— Over—	But not over—	1	2	3
		Your tax is—					Your tax is—					Your tax is—		
10,600	10,650	1,672	1,441	1,219	13,800	13,850	2,627	2,352	2,078	17,000	17,050	3,778	3,453	3,148
10,650	10,700	1,686	1,454	1,231	13,850	13,900	2,643	2,368	2,093	17,050	17,100	3,798	3,471	3,166
10,700	10,750	1,700	1,466	1,244	13,900	13,950	2,659	2,384	2,109	17,100	17,150	3,817	3,490	3,184
10,750	10,800	1,714	1,479	1,256	13,950	14,000	2,675	2,400	2,125	17,150	17,200	3,837	3,509	3,202
10,800	10,850	1,728	1,491	1,269	14,000	14,050	2,691	2,416	2,141	17,200	17,250	3,856	3,529	3,220
10,850	10,900	1,742	1,504	1,281	14,050	14,100	2,707	2,432	2,157	17,250	17,300	3,876	3,548	3,238
10,900	10,950	1,756	1,516	1,294	14,100	14,150	2,723	2,448	2,173	17,300	17,350	3,895	3,568	3,256
10,950	11,000	1,770	1,529	1,306	14,150	14,200	2,739	2,464	2,189	17,350	17,400	3,915	3,587	3,274
11,000	11,050	1,784	1,541	1,319	14,200	14,250	2,755	2,480	2,205	17,400	17,450	3,934	3,607	3,292
11,050	11,100	1,798	1,554	1,331	14,250	14,300	2,771	2,496	2,221	17,450	17,500	3,954	3,626	3,310
11,100	11,150	1,812	1,567	1,344	14,300	14,350	2,787	2,512	2,237	17,500	17,550	3,973	3,646	3,328
11,150	11,200	1,826	1,581	1,356	14,350	14,400	2,804	2,528	2,253	17,550	17,600	3,993	3,665	3,346
11,200	11,250	1,840	1,595	1,369	14,400	14,450	2,822	2,544	2,269	17,600	17,650	4,012	3,685	3,364
11,250	11,300	1,854	1,609	1,381	14,450	14,500	2,840	2,560	2,285	17,650	17,700	4,032	3,704	3,382
11,300	11,350	1,868	1,623	1,394	14,500	14,550	2,858	2,576	2,301	17,700	17,750	4,051	3,724	3,400
11,350	11,400	1,882	1,637	1,406	14,550	14,600	2,876	2,592	2,317	17,750	17,800	4,071	3,743	3,418
11,400	11,450	1,896	1,651	1,419	14,600	14,650	2,894	2,608	2,333	17,800	17,850	4,090	3,763	3,436
11,450	11,500	1,910	1,665	1,431	14,650	14,700	2,912	2,624	2,349	17,850	17,900	4,110	3,782	3,455
11,500	11,550	1,924	1,679	1,444	14,700	14,750	2,930	2,640	2,365	17,900	17,950	4,129	3,802	3,474
11,550	11,600	1,938	1,693	1,456	14,750	14,800	2,948	2,656	2,381	17,950	18,000	4,149	3,821	3,494
11,600	11,650	1,952	1,707	1,469	14,800	14,850	2,966	2,672	2,397	18,000	18,050	4,168	3,841	3,513
11,650	11,700	1,966	1,721	1,481	14,850	14,900	2,984	2,688	2,413	18,050	18,100	4,188	3,860	3,533
11,700	11,750	1,980	1,735	1,494	14,900	14,950	3,002	2,704	2,429	18,100	18,150	4,207	3,880	3,552
11,750	11,800	1,994	1,749	1,506	14,950	15,000	3,020	2,720	2,445	18,150	18,200	4,227	3,899	3,572
11,800	11,850	2,008	1,763	1,519	15,000	15,050	3,038	2,736	2,461	18,200	18,250	4,246	3,919	3,591
11,850	11,900	2,022	1,777	1,532	15,050	15,100	3,056	2,752	2,477	18,250	18,300	4,266	3,938	3,611
11,900	11,950	2,036	1,791	1,546	15,100	15,150	3,074	2,769	2,493	18,300	18,350	4,285	3,958	3,630
11,950	12,000	2,050	1,805	1,560	15,150	15,200	3,092	2,787	2,509	18,350	18,400	4,306	3,977	3,650
12,000	12,050	2,064	1,819	1,574	15,200	15,250	3,110	2,805	2,525	18,400	18,450	4,327	3,997	3,669
12,050	12,100	2,078	1,833	1,588	15,250	15,300	3,128	2,823	2,541	18,450	18,500	4,348	4,016	3,689
12,100	12,150	2,092	1,847	1,602	15,300	15,350	3,146	2,841	2,557	18,500	18,550	4,369	4,036	3,708
12,150	12,200	2,106	1,861	1,616	15,350	15,400	3,164	2,859	2,573	18,550	18,600	4,390	4,055	3,728
12,200	12,250	2,120	1,875	1,630	15,400	15,450	3,182	2,877	2,589	18,600	18,650	4,411	4,075	3,747
12,250	12,300	2,134	1,889	1,644	15,450	15,500	3,200	2,895	2,605	18,650	18,700	4,432	4,094	3,767
12,300	12,350	2,148	1,903	1,658	15,500	15,550	3,218	2,913	2,621	18,700	18,750	4,453	4,114	3,786
12,350	12,400	2,163	1,917	1,672	15,550	15,600	3,236	2,931	2,637	18,750	18,800	4,474	4,133	3,806
12,400	12,450	2,179	1,931	1,686	15,600	15,650	3,254	2,949	2,653	18,800	18,850	4,495	4,153	3,825
12,450	12,500	2,195	1,945	1,700	15,650	15,700	3,272	2,967	2,669	18,850	18,900	4,516	4,172	3,845
12,500	12,550	2,211	1,959	1,714	15,700	15,750	3,290	2,985	2,685	18,900	18,950	4,537	4,192	3,864
12,550	12,600	2,227	1,973	1,728	15,750	15,800	3,308	3,003	2,701	18,950	19,000	4,558	4,211	3,884
12,600	12,650	2,243	1,987	1,742	15,800	15,850	3,326	3,021	2,717	19,000	19,050	4,579	4,231	3,903
12,650	12,700	2,259	2,001	1,756	15,850	15,900	3,344	3,039	2,734	19,050	19,100	4,600	4,250	3,923
12,700	12,750	2,275	2,015	1,770	15,900	15,950	3,362	3,057	2,752	19,100	19,150	4,621	4,271	3,942
12,750	12,800	2,291	2,029	1,784	15,950	16,000	3,380	3,075	2,770	19,150	19,200	4,642	4,292	3,962
12,800	12,850	2,307	2,043	1,798	16,000	16,050	3,398	3,093	2,788	19,200	19,250	4,663	4,313	3,981
12,850	12,900	2,323	2,057	1,812	16,050	16,100	3,416	3,111	2,806	19,250	19,300	4,684	4,334	4,001
12,900	12,950	2,339	2,071	1,826	16,100	16,150	3,434	3,129	2,824	19,300	19,350	4,705	4,355	4,020
12,950	13,000	2,355	2,085	1,840	16,150	16,200	3,452	3,147	2,842	19,350	19,400	4,726	4,376	4,040
13,000	13,050	2,371	2,099	1,854	16,200	16,250	3,470	3,165	2,860	19,400	19,450	4,747	4,397	4,059
13,050	13,100	2,387	2,113	1,868	16,250	16,300	3,488	3,183	2,878	19,450	19,500	4,768	4,418	4,079
13,100	13,150	2,403	2,128	1,882	16,300	16,350	3,506	3,201	2,896	19,500	19,550	4,789	4,439	4,098
13,150	13,200	2,419	2,144	1,896	16,350	16,400	3,525	3,219	2,914	19,550	19,600	4,810	4,460	4,118
13,200	13,250	2,435	2,160	1,910	16,400	16,450	3,544	3,237	2,932	19,600	19,650	4,831	4,481	4,137
13,250	13,300	2,451	2,176	1,924	16,450	16,500	3,564	3,255	2,950	19,650	19,700	4,852	4,502	4,157
13,300	13,350	2,467	2,192	1,938	16,500	16,550	3,583	3,273	2,968	19,700	19,750	4,873	4,523	4,176
13,350	13,400	2,483	2,208	1,952	16,550	16,600	3,603	3,291	2,986	19,750	19,800	4,894	4,544	4,196
13,400	13,450	2,499	2,224	1,966	16,600	16,650	3,622	3,309	3,004	19,800	19,850	4,915	4,565	4,215
13,450	13,500	2,515	2,240	1,980	16,650	16,700	3,642	3,327	3,022	19,850	19,900	4,936	4,586	4,236
13,500	13,550	2,531	2,256	1,994	16,700	16,750	3,661	3,345	3,040	19,900	19,950	4,957	4,607	4,257
13,550	13,600	2,547	2,272	2,008	16,750	16,800	3,681	3,363	3,058	19,950	20,000	4,978	4,628	4,278
13,600	13,650	2,563	2,288	2,022	16,800	16,850	3,700	3,381	3,076					
13,650	13,700	2,579	2,304	2,036	16,850	16,900	3,720	3,399	3,094					
13,700	13,750	2,595	2,320	2,050	16,900	16,950	3,739	3,417	3,112					
13,750	13,800	2,611	2,336	2,064	16,950	17,000	3,759	3,435	3,130					

Continued next column   Continued next column

1977 TAX TABLES
Table D — Heads of Household

If Tax Table Income is— Over—	But not over—	1	2	3	4	5	6	7	8	If Tax Table Income is— Over—	But not over—	1	2	3	4	5	6	7	8
		\multicolumn{8}{c|}{Your tax is—}			\multicolumn{8}{c}{Your tax is—}

Over—	But not over—	1	2	3	4	5	6	7	8	Over—	But not over—	1	2	3	4	5	6	7	8
\multicolumn{10}{l|}{If $3,200 or less your tax is 0}	6,000	6,050	432	289	127	0	0	0	0	0
3,200	3,250	4	0	0	0	0	0	0	0	6,050	6,100	440	298	135	0	0	0	0	0
3,250	3,300	11	0	0	0	0	0	0	0	6,100	6,150	448	307	143	0	0	0	0	0
3,300	3,350	18	0	0	0	0	0	0	0	6,150	6,200	456	316	151	0	0	0	0	0
3,350	3,400	25	0	0	0	0	0	0	0	6,200	6,250	464	325	159	4	0	0	0	0
3,400	3,450	32	0	0	0	0	0	0	0	6,250	6,300	472	334	167	12	0	0	0	0
3,450	3,500	39	0	0	0	0	0	0	0	6,300	6,350	480	343	175	20	0	0	0	0
3,500	3,550	46	0	0	0	0	0	0	0	6,350	6,400	488	352	183	28	0	0	0	0
3,550	3,600	53	0	0	0	0	0	0	0	6,400	6,450	496	361	191	36	0	0	0	0
3,600	3,650	60	0	0	0	0	0	0	0	6,450	6,500	504	370	200	44	0	0	0	0
3,650	3,700	67	0	0	0	0	0	0	0	6,500	6,550	512	379	209	52	0	0	0	0
3,700	3,750	74	0	0	0	0	0	0	0	6,550	6,600	520	388	218	60	0	0	0	0
3,750	3,800	81	0	0	0	0	0	0	0	6,600	6,650	528	397	227	68	0	0	0	0
3,800	3,850	88	0	0	0	0	0	0	0	6,650	6,700	536	406	236	76	0	0	0	0
3,850	3,900	95	0	0	0	0	0	0	0	6,700	6,750	544	415	245	84	0	0	0	0
3,900	3,950	102	0	0	0	0	0	0	0	6,750	6,800	552	424	254	92	0	0	0	0
3,950	4,000	109	0	0	0	0	0	0	0	6,800	6,850	560	433	263	100	0	0	0	0
4,000	4,050	117	0	0	0	0	0	0	0	6,850	6,900	568	442	272	108	0	0	0	0
4,050	4,100	125	0	0	0	0	0	0	0	6,900	6,950	576	451	281	116	0	0	0	0
4,100	4,150	133	0	0	0	0	0	0	0	6,950	7,000	584	460	290	124	0	0	0	0
4,150	4,200	141	0	0	0	0	0	0	0	7,000	7,050	593	469	299	132	0	0	0	0
4,200	4,250	149	4	0	0	0	0	0	0	7,050	7,100	601	478	308	140	0	0	0	0
4,250	4,300	157	11	0	0	0	0	0	0	7,100	7,150	610	487	317	148	0	0	0	0
4,300	4,350	165	18	0	0	0	0	0	0	7,150	7,200	618	496	326	156	1	0	0	0
4,350	4,400	173	25	0	0	0	0	0	0	7,200	7,250	627	504	335	165	9	0	0	0
4,400	4,450	181	32	0	0	0	0	0	0	7,250	7,300	635	512	344	174	17	0	0	0
4,450	4,500	189	39	0	0	0	0	0	0	7,300	7,350	644	520	353	183	25	0	0	0
4,500	4,550	197	46	0	0	0	0	0	0	7,350	7,400	652	528	362	192	33	0	0	0
4,550	4,600	205	53	0	0	0	0	0	0	7,400	7,450	661	536	371	201	41	0	0	0
4,600	4,650	213	60	0	0	0	0	0	0	7,450	7,500	669	544	380	210	49	0	0	0
4,650	4,700	221	67	0	0	0	0	0	0	7,500	7,550	678	552	389	219	57	0	0	0
4,700	4,750	229	74	0	0	0	0	0	0	7,550	7,600	686	560	398	228	65	0	0	0
4,750	4,800	236	82	0	0	0	0	0	0	7,600	7,650	695	568	407	237	73	0	0	0
4,800	4,850	243	90	0	0	0	0	0	0	7,650	7,700	703	576	416	246	81	0	0	0
4,850	4,900	250	98	0	0	0	0	0	0	7,700	7,750	712	584	425	255	89	0	0	0
4,900	4,950	257	106	0	0	0	0	0	0	7,750	7,800	720	593	434	264	97	0	0	0
4,950	5,000	264	114	0	0	0	0	0	0	7,800	7,850	729	601	443	273	105	0	0	0
5,000	5,050	272	122	0	0	0	0	0	0	7,850	7,900	737	610	452	282	113	0	0	0
5,050	5,100	280	130	0	0	0	0	0	0	7,900	7,950	746	618	461	291	121	0	0	0
5,100	5,150	288	138	0	0	0	0	0	0	7,950	8,000	754	627	470	300	130	0	0	0
5,150	5,200	296	146	0	0	0	0	0	0	8,000	8,050	763	635	479	309	139	0	0	0
5,200	5,250	304	154	4	0	0	0	0	0	8,050	8,100	771	644	488	318	148	0	0	0
5,250	5,300	312	162	11	0	0	0	0	0	8,100	8,150	780	652	497	327	157	0	0	0
5,300	5,350	320	170	18	0	0	0	0	0	8,150	8,200	788	661	506	336	166	6	0	0
5,350	5,400	328	178	25	0	0	0	0	0	8,200	8,250	797	669	515	345	175	14	0	0
5,400	5,450	336	186	32	0	0	0	0	0	8,250	8,300	805	678	524	354	184	22	0	0
5,450	5,500	344	194	39	0	0	0	0	0	8,300	8,350	814	686	533	363	193	30	0	0
5,500	5,550	352	202	47	0	0	0	0	0	8,350	8,400	822	695	542	372	202	38	0	0
5,550	5,600	360	210	55	0	0	0	0	0	8,400	8,450	831	703	551	381	211	46	0	0
5,600	5,650	368	218	63	0	0	0	0	0	8,450	8,500	839	712	560	390	220	54	0	0
5,650	5,700	376	226	71	0	0	0	0	0	8,500	8,550	848	720	569	399	229	62	0	0
5,700	5,750	384	235	79	0	0	0	0	0	8,550	8,600	856	729	578	408	238	70	0	0
5,750	5,800	392	244	87	0	0	0	0	0	8,600	8,650	865	737	588	417	247	78	0	0
5,800	5,850	400	253	95	0	0	0	0	0	8,650	8,700	873	746	598	426	256	86	0	0
5,850	5,900	408	262	103	0	0	0	0	0	8,700	8,750	882	754	607	435	265	95	0	0
5,900	5,950	416	271	111	0	0	0	0	0	8,750	8,800	890	763	617	444	274	104	0	0
5,950	6,000	424	280	119	0	0	0	0	0										

Continued next column | Continued on next page

1977 TAX TABLES
Table D – Heads of Household (Continued)

If Tax Table Income— Over—	But not over—	1	2	3	4	5	6	7	8	If Tax Table Income— Over—	But not over—	1	2	3	4	5	6	7	8
		Your tax is—										Your tax is—							
8,800	8,850	899	771	626	453	283	113	0	0	11,600	11,650	1,462	1,305	1,155	994	803	626	448	277
8,850	8,900	907	780	636	462	292	122	0	0	11,650	11,700	1,472	1,315	1,165	1,005	813	635	458	286
8,900	8,950	916	788	645	471	301	131	0	0	11,700	11,750	1,483	1,325	1,175	1,016	822	645	467	295
8,950	9,000	925	797	655	480	310	140	0	0	11,750	11,800	1,493	1,336	1,185	1,027	832	654	477	304
9,000	9,050	935	805	664	489	319	149	0	0	11,800	11,850	1,504	1,346	1,195	1,038	841	664	486	313
9,050	9,100	945	814	674	498	328	158	0	0	11,850	11,900	1,514	1,357	1,205	1,049	851	673	496	322
9,100	9,150	955	822	683	507	337	167	3	0	11,900	11,950	1,525	1,367	1,215	1,060	860	683	505	331
9,150	9,200	965	831	693	516	346	176	11	0	11,950	12,000	1,536	1,378	1,225	1,071	871	692	515	340
9,200	9,250	975	839	702	525	355	185	19	0	12,000	12,050	1,547	1,388	1,235	1,082	882	702	524	349
9,250	9,300	985	848	712	534	364	194	27	0	12,050	12,100	1,559	1,399	1,245	1,093	893	711	534	358
9,300	9,350	995	856	721	544	373	203	35	0	12,100	12,150	1,570	1,409	1,255	1,104	904	721	543	367
9,350	9,400	1,005	865	731	553	382	212	43	0	12,150	12,200	1,582	1,420	1,265	1,115	915	730	553	376
9,400	9,450	1,015	873	740	563	391	221	51	0	12,200	12,250	1,593	1,430	1,275	1,125	926	740	562	385
9,450	9,500	1,025	882	750	572	400	230	60	0	12,250	12,300	1,605	1,441	1,285	1,135	937	749	572	394
9,500	9,550	1,035	890	759	582	409	239	69	0	12,300	12,350	1,616	1,451	1,295	1,145	948	759	581	404
9,550	9,600	1,045	899	769	591	418	248	78	0	12,350	12,400	1,628	1,462	1,305	1,155	959	768	591	413
9,600	9,650	1,055	907	778	601	427	257	87	0	12,400	12,450	1,639	1,472	1,315	1,165	970	778	600	423
9,650	9,700	1,065	916	788	610	436	266	96	0	12,450	12,500	1,651	1,483	1,325	1,175	981	787	610	432
9,700	9,750	1,075	925	797	620	445	275	105	0	12,500	12,550	1,662	1,493	1,336	1,185	992	797	619	442
9,750	9,800	1,085	935	805	629	454	284	114	0	12,550	12,600	1,674	1,504	1,346	1,195	1,003	806	629	451
9,800	9,850	1,095	945	814	639	463	293	123	0	12,600	12,650	1,685	1,514	1,357	1,205	1,014	816	638	461
9,850	9,900	1,105	955	822	648	472	302	132	0	12,650	12,700	1,697	1,525	1,367	1,215	1,025	825	648	470
9,900	9,950	1,115	965	831	658	481	311	141	0	12,700	12,750	1,708	1,536	1,378	1,225	1,036	836	657	480
9,950	10,000	1,125	975	839	667	490	320	150	0	12,750	12,800	1,720	1,547	1,388	1,237	1,047	847	667	489
10,000	10,050	1,135	985	848	677	499	329	159	0	12,800	12,850	1,731	1,559	1,399	1,245	1,058	858	676	499
10,050	10,100	1,145	995	856	686	509	338	168	0	12,850	12,900	1,743	1,570	1,409	1,255	1,069	869	686	508
10,100	10,150	1,155	1,005	865	696	518	347	177	8	12,900	12,950	1,754	1,582	1,420	1,265	1,080	880	695	518
10,150	10,200	1,165	1,015	873	705	528	356	186	16	12,950	13,000	1,766	1,593	1,430	1,275	1,091	891	705	527
10,200	10,250	1,175	1,025	882	715	537	365	195	25	13,000	13,050	1,779	1,605	1,441	1,285	1,102	902	714	537
10,250	10,300	1,185	1,035	890	724	547	374	204	34	13,050	13,100	1,791	1,616	1,451	1,295	1,113	913	724	546
10,300	10,350	1,195	1,045	899	734	556	383	213	43	13,100	13,150	1,804	1,628	1,462	1,305	1,124	924	733	556
10,350	10,400	1,205	1,055	907	743	566	392	222	52	13,150	13,200	1,816	1,639	1,472	1,315	1,135	935	743	565
10,400	10,450	1,215	1,065	916	753	575	401	231	61	13,200	13,250	1,829	1,651	1,483	1,325	1,146	946	752	575
10,450	10,500	1,225	1,075	925	762	585	410	240	70	13,250	13,300	1,841	1,662	1,493	1,336	1,157	957	762	584
10,500	10,550	1,235	1,085	935	772	594	419	249	79	13,300	13,350	1,854	1,674	1,504	1,346	1,168	968	771	594
10,550	10,600	1,245	1,095	945	781	604	428	258	88	13,350	13,400	1,866	1,685	1,514	1,357	1,179	979	781	603
10,600	10,650	1,255	1,105	955	791	613	437	267	97	13,400	13,450	1,879	1,697	1,525	1,367	1,190	990	790	613
10,650	10,700	1,265	1,115	965	800	623	446	276	106	13,450	13,500	1,891	1,708	1,536	1,378	1,201	1,001	801	622
10,700	10,750	1,275	1,125	975	810	632	455	285	115	13,500	13,550	1,904	1,720	1,547	1,388	1,212	1,012	812	632
10,750	10,800	1,285	1,135	985	819	642	464	294	124	13,550	13,600	1,916	1,731	1,559	1,399	1,223	1,023	823	641
10,800	10,850	1,295	1,145	995	829	651	474	303	133	13,600	13,650	1,929	1,743	1,570	1,409	1,234	1,034	834	651
10,850	10,900	1,305	1,155	1,005	838	661	483	312	142	13,650	13,700	1,941	1,754	1,582	1,420	1,245	1,045	845	660
10,900	10,950	1,315	1,165	1,015	848	670	493	321	151	13,700	13,750	1,954	1,766	1,593	1,430	1,256	1,056	856	670
10,950	11,000	1,325	1,175	1,025	857	680	502	330	160	13,750	13,800	1,966	1,779	1,605	1,441	1,267	1,067	867	679
11,000	11,050	1,336	1,185	1,035	867	689	512	339	169	13,800	13,850	1,979	1,791	1,616	1,451	1,278	1,078	878	689
11,050	11,100	1,346	1,195	1,045	876	699	521	348	178	13,850	13,900	1,991	1,804	1,628	1,462	1,289	1,089	889	698
11,100	11,150	1,357	1,205	1,055	886	708	531	357	187	13,900	13,950	2,004	1,816	1,639	1,472	1,300	1,100	900	708
11,150	11,200	1,367	1,215	1,065	895	718	540	366	196	13,950	14,000	2,016	1,829	1,651	1,483	1,311	1,111	911	717
11,200	11,250	1,378	1,225	1,075	906	727	550	375	205	14,000	14,050	2,029	1,841	1,662	1,493	1,322	1,122	922	727
11,250	11,300	1,388	1,235	1,085	917	737	559	384	214	14,050	14,100	2,041	1,854	1,674	1,504	1,334	1,133	933	736
11,300	11,350	1,399	1,245	1,095	928	746	569	393	223	14,100	14,150	2,054	1,866	1,685	1,514	1,345	1,144	944	746
11,350	11,400	1,409	1,255	1,105	939	756	578	402	232	14,150	14,200	2,066	1,879	1,697	1,525	1,357	1,155	955	755
11,400	11,450	1,420	1,265	1,115	950	765	588	411	241	14,200	14,250	2,079	1,891	1,708	1,536	1,368	1,166	966	766
11,450	11,500	1,430	1,275	1,125	961	775	597	420	250	14,250	14,300	2,091	1,904	1,720	1,547	1,380	1,177	977	777
11,500	11,550	1,441	1,285	1,135	972	784	607	429	259	14,300	14,350	2,104	1,916	1,731	1,559	1,391	1,188	988	788
11,550	11,600	1,451	1,295	1,145	983	794	616	439	268	14,350	14,400	2,116	1,929	1,743	1,570	1,403	1,199	999	799

Continued next column

Continued on next page

1977 TAX TABLES
Table D — Heads of Household (Continued)

If Tax Table Income is— Over—	But not over—	1	2	3	4	5	6	7	8	If Tax Table Income is— Over—	But not over—	1	2	3	4	5	6	7	8
14,400	14,450	2,129	1,941	1,754	1,582	1,414	1,210	1,010	810	17,200	17,250	2,877	2,672	2,469	2,267	2,079	1,861	1,643	1,436
14,450	14,500	2,141	1,954	1,766	1,593	1,426	1,221	1,021	821	17,250	17,300	2,891	2,685	2,483	2,280	2,091	1,874	1,655	1,447
14,500	14,550	2,154	1,966	1,779	1,605	1,437	1,232	1,032	832	17,300	17,350	2,905	2,699	2,496	2,294	2,104	1,886	1,666	1,459
14,550	14,600	2,166	1,979	1,791	1,616	1,449	1,243	1,043	843	17,350	17,400	2,919	2,712	2,510	2,307	2,116	1,899	1,678	1,470
14,600	14,650	2,179	1,991	1,804	1,628	1,460	1,254	1,054	854	17,400	17,450	2,933	2,726	2,523	2,321	2,129	1,911	1,689	1,482
14,650	14,700	2,191	2,004	1,816	1,639	1,472	1,265	1,065	865	17,450	17,500	2,947	2,739	2,537	2,334	2,141	1,924	1,701	1,493
14,700	14,750	2,204	2,016	1,829	1,651	1,483	1,276	1,076	876	17,500	17,550	2,961	2,753	2,550	2,348	2,154	1,936	1,714	1,505
14,750	14,800	2,216	2,029	1,841	1,662	1,493	1,287	1,087	887	17,550	17,600	2,975	2,766	2,564	2,361	2,166	1,949	1,726	1,516
14,800	14,850	2,229	2,041	1,854	1,674	1,504	1,299	1,098	898	17,600	17,650	2,989	2,780	2,577	2,375	2,179	1,961	1,739	1,528
14,850	14,900	2,241	2,054	1,866	1,685	1,514	1,310	1,109	909	17,650	17,700	3,003	2,793	2,591	2,388	2,191	1,974	1,751	1,539
14,900	14,950	2,254	2,066	1,879	1,697	1,525	1,322	1,120	920	17,700	17,750	3,017	2,807	2,604	2,402	2,204	1,986	1,764	1,551
14,950	15,000	2,267	2,079	1,891	1,708	1,536	1,333	1,131	931	17,750	17,800	3,031	2,821	2,618	2,415	2,216	1,999	1,776	1,562
15,000	15,050	2,280	2,091	1,904	1,720	1,547	1,345	1,142	942	17,800	17,850	3,045	2,835	2,631	2,429	2,229	2,011	1,789	1,574
15,050	15,100	2,294	2,104	1,916	1,731	1,559	1,356	1,153	953	17,850	17,900	3,059	2,849	2,645	2,442	2,241	2,024	1,801	1,585
15,100	15,150	2,307	2,116	1,929	1,743	1,570	1,368	1,164	964	17,900	17,950	3,073	2,863	2,658	2,456	2,254	2,036	1,814	1,597
15,150	15,200	2,321	2,129	1,941	1,754	1,582	1,379	1,175	975	17,950	18,000	3,087	2,877	2,672	2,469	2,267	2,049	1,826	1,608
15,200	15,250	2,334	2,141	1,954	1,766	1,593	1,391	1,186	986	18,000	18,050	3,101	2,891	2,685	2,483	2,280	2,061	1,839	1,620
15,250	15,300	2,348	2,154	1,966	1,779	1,605	1,402	1,197	997	18,050	18,100	3,115	2,905	2,699	2,496	2,294	2,074	1,851	1,631
15,300	15,350	2,361	2,166	1,979	1,791	1,616	1,414	1,208	1,008	18,100	18,150	3,129	2,919	2,712	2,510	2,307	2,086	1,864	1,643
15,350	15,400	2,375	2,179	1,991	1,804	1,628	1,425	1,219	1,019	18,150	18,200	3,143	2,933	2,726	2,523	2,321	2,099	1,876	1,654
15,400	15,450	2,388	2,191	2,004	1,816	1,639	1,437	1,230	1,030	18,200	18,250	3,157	2,947	2,739	2,537	2,334	2,111	1,889	1,666
15,450	15,500	2,402	2,204	2,016	1,829	1,651	1,448	1,241	1,041	18,250	18,300	3,171	2,961	2,753	2,550	2,348	2,124	1,901	1,679
15,500	15,550	2,415	2,216	2,029	1,841	1,662	1,460	1,252	1,052	18,300	18,350	3,185	2,975	2,766	2,564	2,361	2,136	1,914	1,691
15,550	15,600	2,429	2,229	2,041	1,854	1,674	1,471	1,264	1,063	18,350	18,400	3,199	2,989	2,780	2,577	2,375	2,149	1,926	1,704
15,600	15,650	2,442	2,241	2,054	1,866	1,685	1,483	1,275	1,074	18,400	18,450	3,213	3,003	2,793	2,591	2,388	2,161	1,939	1,716
15,650	15,700	2,456	2,254	2,066	1,879	1,697	1,494	1,287	1,085	18,450	18,500	3,227	3,017	2,807	2,604	2,402	2,174	1,951	1,729
15,700	15,750	2,469	2,267	2,079	1,891	1,708	1,506	1,298	1,096	18,500	18,550	3,241	3,031	2,821	2,618	2,415	2,186	1,964	1,741
15,750	15,800	2,483	2,280	2,091	1,904	1,720	1,517	1,310	1,107	18,550	18,600	3,255	3,045	2,835	2,631	2,429	2,199	1,976	1,754
15,800	15,850	2,496	2,294	2,104	1,916	1,731	1,529	1,321	1,118	18,600	18,650	3,269	3,059	2,849	2,645	2,442	2,211	1,989	1,766
15,850	15,900	2,510	2,307	2,116	1,929	1,743	1,540	1,333	1,129	18,650	18,700	3,283	3,073	2,863	2,658	2,456	2,224	2,001	1,779
15,900	15,950	2,523	2,321	2,129	1,941	1,754	1,552	1,344	1,140	18,700	18,750	3,297	3,087	2,877	2,672	2,469	2,237	2,014	1,791
15,950	16,000	2,537	2,334	2,141	1,954	1,766	1,563	1,356	1,151	18,750	18,800	3,311	3,101	2,891	2,685	2,483	2,250	2,026	1,804
16,000	16,050	2,550	2,348	2,154	1,966	1,779	1,575	1,367	1,162	18,800	18,850	3,325	3,115	2,905	2,699	2,496	2,264	2,039	1,816
16,050	16,100	2,564	2,361	2,166	1,979	1,791	1,586	1,379	1,173	18,850	18,900	3,339	3,129	2,919	2,712	2,510	2,277	2,051	1,829
16,100	16,150	2,577	2,375	2,179	1,991	1,804	1,598	1,390	1,184	18,900	18,950	3,353	3,143	2,933	2,726	2,523	2,291	2,064	1,841
16,150	16,200	2,591	2,388	2,191	2,004	1,816	1,609	1,402	1,195	18,950	19,000	3,368	3,157	2,947	2,739	2,537	2,304	2,076	1,854
16,200	16,250	2,604	2,402	2,204	2,016	1,829	1,621	1,413	1,206	19,000	19,050	3,383	3,171	2,961	2,753	2,550	2,318	2,089	1,866
16,250	16,300	2,618	2,415	2,216	2,029	1,841	1,632	1,425	1,217	19,050	19,100	3,399	3,185	2,975	2,766	2,564	2,331	2,101	1,879
16,300	16,350	2,631	2,429	2,229	2,041	1,854	1,644	1,436	1,229	19,100	19,150	3,414	3,199	2,989	2,780	2,577	2,345	2,114	1,891
16,350	16,400	2,645	2,442	2,241	2,054	1,866	1,655	1,448	1,240	19,150	19,200	3,430	3,213	3,003	2,793	2,591	2,358	2,126	1,904
16,400	16,450	2,658	2,456	2,254	2,066	1,879	1,667	1,459	1,252	19,200	19,250	3,445	3,227	3,017	2,807	2,604	2,372	2,139	1,916
16,450	16,500	2,672	2,469	2,267	2,079	1,891	1,678	1,471	1,263	19,250	19,300	3,461	3,241	3,031	2,821	2,618	2,385	2,151	1,929
16,500	16,550	2,685	2,483	2,280	2,091	1,904	1,690	1,482	1,275	19,300	19,350	3,476	3,255	3,045	2,835	2,631	2,399	2,164	1,941
16,550	16,600	2,699	2,496	2,294	2,104	1,916	1,701	1,494	1,286	19,350	19,400	3,492	3,269	3,059	2,849	2,645	2,412	2,176	1,954
16,600	16,650	2,712	2,510	2,307	2,116	1,929	1,713	1,505	1,298	19,400	19,450	3,507	3,283	3,073	2,863	2,658	2,426	2,189	1,966
16,650	16,700	2,726	2,523	2,321	2,129	1,941	1,724	1,517	1,309	19,450	19,500	3,523	3,297	3,087	2,877	2,672	2,439	2,202	1,979
16,700	16,750	2,739	2,537	2,334	2,141	1,954	1,736	1,528	1,321	19,500	19,550	3,538	3,311	3,101	2,891	2,685	2,453	2,215	1,991
16,750	16,800	2,753	2,550	2,348	2,154	1,966	1,749	1,540	1,332	19,550	19,600	3,554	3,325	3,115	2,905	2,699	2,466	2,229	2,004
16,800	16,850	2,766	2,564	2,361	2,166	1,979	1,761	1,551	1,344	19,600	19,650	3,569	3,339	3,129	2,919	2,712	2,480	2,242	2,016
16,850	16,900	2,780	2,577	2,375	2,179	1,991	1,774	1,563	1,355	19,650	19,700	3,585	3,353	3,143	2,933	2,726	2,493	2,256	2,029
16,900	16,950	2,793	2,591	2,388	2,191	2,004	1,786	1,574	1,367	19,700	19,750	3,600	3,368	3,157	2,947	2,739	2,507	2,269	2,041
16,950	17,000	2,807	2,604	2,402	2,204	2,016	1,799	1,586	1,378	19,750	19,800	3,616	3,383	3,171	2,961	2,753	2,520	2,283	2,054
17,000	17,050	2,821	2,618	2,415	2,216	2,029	1,811	1,597	1,390	19,800	19,850	3,631	3,399	3,185	2,975	2,766	2,534	2,296	2,066
17,050	17,100	2,835	2,631	2,429	2,229	2,041	1,824	1,609	1,401	19,850	19,900	3,647	3,414	3,199	2,989	2,780	2,547	2,310	2,079
17,100	17,150	2,849	2,645	2,442	2,241	2,054	1,836	1,620	1,413	19,900	19,950	3,662	3,430	3,213	3,003	2,793	2,561	2,323	2,091
17,150	17,200	2,863	2,658	2,456	2,254	2,066	1,849	1,632	1,424	19,950	20,000	3,678	3,445	3,227	3,017	2,807	2,574	2,337	2,104

Continued next column

In some cases, capital gains treatment has been allowed as a convenient way of giving relief to certain types of income considered to be unable to carry the burden of full taxation. In other cases, it is provided in place of an averaging technique. In still others, it is used as an incentive device.

Generally, the capital gain rules are similar for both individual and corporate taxpayers. However, the differences involve an alternative tax that is applied to net long-term capital gains, a deduction for capital losses and a carryover of net capital losses. Also, corporations get no long-term capital gain deduction. This is a deduction from gross income of half the excess of net long-term capital gains over net short-term capital losses.

The alternative tax was adopted to place a ceiling on the effective rate that applied to the net capital gain. The alternative tax rate differs between individual and corporate taxpayers [¶ 1614; 3202].

The key factor in producing a capital gain or loss is a *sale or exchange* of a capital asset. The way the capital gain or loss is classified depends upon the period the capital asset was held.

(a) Holding period. Congress divided capital gains and losses on the basis of the capital asset's holding period. This was to separate speculative and investment transactions. It was felt that the short-term category generally included the speculative gains. Congress considered that these should be taxed the same way as earned income and business profits.[b]

The original holding period rule involved varying lengths of time. This was modified to encourage the realization of capital gains. The six-month holding period was considered "sufficient deterrent to the speculator as contrasted with the legitimate investor."[c] The Tax Reform Act of 1976 increased the holding period to 9 months starting in 1977 and to 1 year starting in 1978.

The holding period measures the time the capital asset was held. When the taxpayer's investment carries over into replacement property, as in an involuntary conversion, nontaxable exchange or the sale of a residence, the holding period continues on with the new property [¶ 1605; 1606].

(b) Capital asset. Generally, a capital asset is property held for personal use or for investment. The definition excludes some property related to a taxpayer's trade or business such as stock in trade although it can include business property [¶ 1601]. However, a special exception allows capital gain treatment for certain business assets. Losses from transactions involving these assets can be ordinary and therefore fully deductible. This is important since capital losses get a limited deduction.

(c) Capital losses. While the nonrecognition rules may postpone the consideration of capital gains and losses, certain losses are never taken into account. The sale of a residence involves such a situation. Recognized gain from the sale is a capital gain but a loss is never deductible since the loss does not fit into one of the allowable categories: (1) incurred in a trade or business; (2) incurred in any transaction entered into for profit; or (3) casualty loss [¶ 2200].

Allowable capital losses serve to reduce their respective counterparts on the gain side. Capital losses also lower the amount of long-term capital gains that could qualify for preferential capital gain treatment [¶ 1611].

Once capital losses of individuals completely offset capital gains, a limited amount of capital losses can be deducted from ordinary income. These limitations are applied since taxpayers can time their sales of capital assets to take losses when they are most advantageous. Capital losses of a corporation can be deducted only

---

Footnote ¶ 1026 continued
    (b)   H.R. Rep. No. 1860, 75th Cong., 3d Sess. 7, 8, 36 (1938).
    (c)   S. Rep. No. 1631, 77th Cong., 2d Sess. 50 (1942).

¶ 1026

from capital gains. An individual's losses that cannot be applied against ordinary income can be carried over to succeeding years until used up. Corporations are limited to a 3-year carryback and a 5-year carryover of capital losses [¶ 1613; 3201].

(d) Dispositions of business property. One of the exceptions in the definition of a capital asset relates to depreciable and real property used in a trade or business. In addition, to produce a capital gain or loss, there must be a *sale or exchange* of a *capital asset.* Thus, capital gain treatment would not normally apply in situations relating to depreciable and real property used in business or an involuntary conversion of property. A special rule called "Sec. 1231" treatment allows handling certain gains as capital gains and certain losses as ordinary losses when qualified business property held for over nine months is disposed of [¶ 1618]. This special treatment also applies to an involuntary conversion of a capital asset.

Depreciable business property was originally eliminated from the capital asset definition to permit the full deduction of losses from ordinary income. Later, it was felt that gains from this property ought to get the benefit of capital gain treatment.

Before the special rule can apply, the gains and losses must be segregated and compared. If net gains exceed net losses, *all* the gains and losses are treated as long-term capital gains and losses. If net losses exceed net gains, *all* the gains and losses are treated as ordinary. Once this calculation determines if the "Sec. 1231" treatment applies, then the gains and losses are included with those from the sale or exchange of capital assets. However, two factors might have to be taken into account before the special calculation is made: (1) the depreciaton recapture rules and (2) the separate "netting" of casualty gains and losses.

(e) Recapture of depreciation. This concept was added to the tax law because a substantial tax advantage was afforded to those using depreciable property in the production of their income. This advantage arose from the fact that depreciation offset income taxed at ordinary rates while all the gains were taken into income as capital gain. These gains may have been nothing more than the result of accelerated reduction of the asset's basis through depreciation. Now, when depreciable property is disposed of, gain is ordinary income to the extent the recapture rules apply. Since the recapture rules involve property qualifying for "Sec. 1231" treatment, the ordinary gain must be separated from the portion treated as capital gain [¶ 1619].

The key element in the recapture concept as it applies to business equipment ("Sec. 1245 property") is depreciation since it is the yardstick for measuring the amount of ordinary gain. Therefore, any gain is treated as ordinary to the extent of depreciation taken since 1961. The gain in excess of that qualifies for "Sec. 1231" treatment [¶ 1619(a)]. Additional factors are involved in the recapture concept for depreciable real property ("Sec. 1250 property"). Generally, the treatment of gain on real property depends on how the property is used, when it was acquired and whether an accelerated method of depreciation was taken [¶ 1619(b)].

(f) Involuntary conversion. An involuntary conversion is one of the types of transactions that can qualify for "Sec. 1231" treatment. However, a separate "netting" must first be done for casualty (or theft) gains and losses to determine if these are to be included in the "Sec. 1231" computation. If casualty gains exceed casualty losses then there is a further netting with the Sec. 1231 gains and losses. If casualty losses exceed casualty gains, all the casualty gains and losses are ordinary [¶ 1620].

¶ 1027 The method of reporting income and deductions. The discussion up to this point has involved the way income and deductions are determined. The coverage now relates to figuring the *time* and *manner* of reporting these. As noted earlier, the taxability of gross income stems from the concept of realization [¶ 1024]. Also, the deductibility of an expense item is based on specific legislative sanction [¶ 1023]. The standard for determining when taxability or deductibility occurs depends on the method of accounting. Since tax liability is computed on an annual basis, the way income and deduction items are timed can be significant. The matter of timing involves accounting periods and methods. However, treating each year as a separate unit has significance beyond the question of timing. This is true because a single transaction can involve more than one year but taxation can be applied in the tax year the benefit occurs. Also, a taxpayer's situation can change from one year to the next. Special relief provisions have been provided to mitigate the effects of the year-by-year application of tax liability. Some of these include the installment method of reporting income, the net operating loss deduction and income averaging. See also ¶ 4520 et seq.

(a) **Accounting methods.** A method of accounting is a set of rules by which the taxpayer determines when and how to record income and expenses on his books. Generally, no specific method is required except when inventories are an income producing factor. Here the accrual method is required (see below). In any case, the method used must "clearly reflect income." This usually means that generally accepted accounting principles must be applied consistently [¶ 2700].

The two principal methods of accounting are: (1) the cash receipts and disbursements method (cash basis method); and (2) the accrual basis method. A combination of these methods (hybrid accounting method) is permitted if it clearly reflects income [¶ 2701]. An installment method can be used for installment sales.

Early law provided that income tax be levied on the accrual basis only. Since two systems of bookkeeping were being used (cash and accrual basis), the Congress considered it advisable to allow either method if income was clearly reflected.[a] See also ¶ 4510 et seq.

Cash receipts and disbursements method. This method requires the taxpayer to include in gross income all income items he actually or constructively receives during the tax year. Constructive receipt occurs when an amount is credited to the taxpayer's account or set apart for him so that the taxpayer can draw on it at any time. Generally expenses must be deducted in the tax year in which they are actually paid [¶ 2702; 2703; 2705].

Accrual method. All items of income are included in gross income when earned, even though payment may be received in another tax year. Business expenses are deductible when incurred, whether or not they are paid in the same tax year. All events fixing the liability or the right to receive the income must have occurred. The taxpayer must be able to determine the amount with reasonable accuracy [¶ 2706]. Thus, the basic idea under the accrual system is that the books reflect expenses definitely incurred and income definitely earned regardless of whether payment has been made or is due.

Installment method. Generally, the accrual method is used when a taxpayer is engaged in the purchase and sale of merchandise. There is a problem when an installment sale is involved. Although payments are spread over a number of years, the gain would be taxable in a single year. The same would apply to sales of real or personal property by someone not a dealer. In this case, the notes received would be considered a realized gain. Thus, early in the tax law, Congress enacted the relief provision permitting the installment method.

The installment method recognizes that each installment payment contains two elements: (1) a return of part of the cost; and (2) part of the profit on the sale. It

---

Footnote ¶ 1027 (a) H.R. Rep. No. 922, 64th Cong., 1st Sess. 4 (1916).

permits the taxpayer to apportion his collections for the year between these two elements and to include in his gross income only the part that represents profit. Expenses must be deducted in the year paid or incurred [¶ 2802; 2811(a)].

(b) Accounting periods. The tax system in practical terms must be based on some measurement of time. Every taxpayer must compute his taxable income and file a return on the basis of period of time called a tax year. This is usually 12 consecutive months and it may be a calendar or fiscal year. In some cases, the tax year may be less than 12 months, but it cannot be more than that unless a 52-53 week year is used. A *calendar year* is 12 consecutive months ending on December 31. A *fiscal year* is 12 consecutive months ending on the last day of any month other than December, or a 52-53 week year. A *short period* is a tax year of less than 12 months [¶ 2714].

A return for a short period is permitted when the taxpayer files his first or final return or when he changes his accounting period. The first or final return is considered to have been filed for a 12-month period. However, when a taxpayer changes his accounting period, his return must be annualized. This annualizing provision was added in the 1924 Revenue Act because taxpayers were changing their accounting periods to effect a tax reduction [¶ 2717].[b]

(c) Income averaging. Since a graduated rate structure applies, inequities in the tax burden could result to taxpayers with fluctuating incomes. These fluctuations are generally beyond the taxpayer's control. Business and personal matters are not usually arranged to fit within the calendar requirements. Recognition of this problem has given rise to certain provisions in the tax law designed to mitigate the situation. For example, the special rules on capital gains and losses furnish some measure of averaging. The specific income averaging provision deals with the problem of income fluctuations. The effect of this is to tax income in the high income year as though it were spread over a 5-year period [¶ 2401].

(d) Net operating loss. The net operating loss rule is another means of reducing the impact of the annual accounting set-up and the problem of fluctuating income. Under prior law, no recognition was given to net losses. The excess could not be carried to another year. The settlement had to be made on the basis of each year's business by itself. The change was designed to provide an additional stimulus to business investment.

The net operating loss deduction requires that the taxpayer's true economic loss be determined. Thus certain modifications must be made. The loss shown on the return has to be reduced by such items as the personal exemption and long-term capital gain deduction. This prevents the creation of artificial losses [¶ 2242].

The net operating loss provision allows taxpayers to average their profits and losses to some extent by letting them use the losses of one year to offset the profits of another year. This averaging device is known as the carryback and carryover of net operating losses [¶ 2241].

¶ 1028 The different types of taxpayers. Under the federal income tax law, the term "person" includes not only an individual, but an estate, trust, partnership, company, association, or corporation. For our purposes, the "persons" who may be taxpayers are classified as follows: citizens of the United States; aliens (resident or nonresident); partnerships; estates and trusts; domestic corporations; foreign corporations (resident or nonresident); personal holding companies; citizens of U.S. possessions, not U.S. citizens.

Some corporations can elect to be taxed as partnerships [¶ 3140].

Footnote ¶ 10 27 continued
 (b) H.R. Rep. No. 179, 68th Cong., 1st Sess. 23 (1924).

(a) **Citizens of the United States.** The term "United States" includes the states and the District of Columbia. With two minor exceptions, citizens of the United States are required to report their entire taxable income, whether it is derived from sources within the United States or from foreign sources. The two exceptions are: (1) Certain citizens with earned income from sources outside the U.S., and (2) Some U.S. citizens who get the greater part of their income from U.S. possessions [¶ 3727]. Special rules apply to residents of Puerto Rico.

(b) **Domestic (U.S.) corporations.** A domestic corporation is a corporation organized in the United States or any state or territory. The term "corporation" includes not only technical corporations, but also joint-stock companies, associations, insurance companies, and certain limited partnerships.

Domestic corporations (other than those exempt by statute) must report their entire taxable income from United States and foreign sources. But, like an individual, they can exclude some foreign income, if the greater part of their income is from U.S. possessions [¶ 3727]. Corporations can also be taxed for unreasonably accumulating surplus [¶ 3421]. Some corporations can elect to have their income taxed to the shareholders [¶ 3141]. Personal holding companies generally are "family corporations," a large part of whose income is derived from investments. They pay a special tax on undistributed income.

Some types of corporations get special treatment. These include banks and trust companies [¶ 3433], insurance corporations [¶ 3434], regulated investment companies [¶ 3428], cooperatives [¶ 3455], real estate investment trusts [¶ 3432] and Domestic International Sales Corporations (DISC) [¶ 3460].

It is important to understand that the principles and concepts covered before in the "Overview" generally apply to corporations. Thus, for example, the realization and recognition rules are relevant to the discussion on corporations. However, while many Code provisions are common to all types of taxpayers, some principles apply differently to the corporate entity. The variations in the capital gain rules were covered briefly earlier [¶ 1026]. In addition, there is no distinction between deductions for adjusted gross income and net income since the term adjusted gross income does not apply to the corporate taxpayer. Some other differences involve the ceilings applied to charitable contributions made by corporations and individuals. Finally, certain provisions of the Code relate solely to problems that are themselves common to corporations.

(c) **Partnerships.** A partnership, as such, does not pay income taxes. Instead, each partner must include in his individual return his share of partnership income. The partnership itself files an information return showing the amount and character of each partner's distributive share [¶ 2901 et seq.].

(d) **Estates and trusts.** Estates and trusts are taxable entities. A fiduciary files the return. This serves as an income tax return as well as an information return for distributions to the beneficiaries [¶ 3001 et seq.].

(e) **Resident aliens.** With minor exceptions, resident aliens are taxed exactly the same as citizens of the United States (on income from both within and without the United States). The exceptions relate to the credit for foreign taxes and to certain exemptions [¶ 3708].

(f) **Nonresident aliens.** Nonresident aliens are taxed on their income from United States sources and on limited business income from foreign sources. Income effectively connected with a U.S. business (including net capital gains) [¶ 3711] is taxed at U.S. rates after deductions. Other income and net capital gains from U.S. sources are taxed at 30% without any deductions but the net capital

¶ 1028

1026 An Introduction to Federal Taxes

gains may be exempt [¶ 3709]. U.S. wages and investment income are subject to withholding [¶ 2535]. See chart at ¶ 5505.

One exemption deduction is permitted each nonresident alien except that Canadians and Mexicans get the same number as U.S. citizens.

(g) Foreign corporations are those not organized in the United States. They are taxed on their U.S. business income as domestic corporations. Limited foreign source business income is also taxed at U.S. rates after deductions [¶ 3710].

Chapter 1

INDIVIDUALS—RETURNS, FILING STATUS, PERSONAL EXEMPTIONS AND RATES

TABLE OF CONTENTS

INDIVIDUAL INCOME TAX RETURNS

	¶
Who must file returns	1100
Return forms	1101

ELEMENTS IN FIGURING THE TAX

What is involved in the computation	1102
Steps in figuring the tax	1103

FILING STATUS

Married couples	1104
Who may file a joint return	
Married persons filing separate returns	
Abandoned spouse	
Surviving spouse	1105
Head of household	1106

ZERO BRACKET AMOUNT—STANDARD DEDUCTION

Zero bracket amount	1107
Standard deduction	1108
Marital status	1109

PERSONAL EXEMPTIONS

Your personal exemptions	1111
Exemptions of married persons	1112
Old-age exemptions	1113
Exemptions for the blind	1114

EXEMPTIONS FOR DEPENDENTS

Your exemptions for dependents	1115
Support	1116
What is support	
Students	
Multiple support agreements	
Relationship of dependent	1117
Taxpayer's relatives	
Member of taxpayer's household	
Dependent's gross income	1118
Children under 19 or students	
If the dependent files a return	
Married dependents	1119
Citizens of foreign countries as dependents	1120

METHODS OF FIGURING THE TAX

Tax rate schedules	1121
Using the tax tables	1122

• Highlights of Chapter 1 .... Page 1161

INDIVIDUAL INCOME TAX RETURNS

You must file a return if you meet the general rule or are self-employed. It makes no difference if you are a minor or an adult. The general filing requirement for a U.S. citizen or resident alien depends on income, age as well as marital status. If your gross income is too small to require a return but tax was withheld from your wages, you should file to get a refund of the tax withheld. All returns are filed on regular Form 1040 unless Short Form 1040A is used.

¶ 1100 Who must file returns. To determine if you must file an income tax return, you need to know your gross income [Sec. 6012(a)], unless you are self-employed (see (c) below). Gross income is all your income subject to tax [¶ 1201]. It includes salary, fees, profits from business, interests, rents, dividends and gains [Sec. 61].

Footnotes appear at end of this Chapter.

¶ 1100

Background and purpose. The income levels at which a return must be filed are designed to correspond to the tax-free income levels. These income levels are set up to determine who must file and do not necessarily establish that the return when filed will show a tax due. The 1977 Tax Reduction and Simplification Act increased the levels in the filing requirements.

(a) Income levels. The income level filing requirements for tax years starting after 12-31-76 are [Sec. 6012(a)(1)]:

Single	$2,950
Single—65 or over	3,700
Married—filing jointly	4,700
Married—filing jointly (one 65 or over)	5,450
Married—filing jointly (both 65 or over)	6,200
Married—filing separately	750
Surviving spouse	3,950
Surviving spouse—65 or over	4,700

NOTE: The $750 filing requirement also applies if: (1) you can be claimed as a dependent; or (2) you are married but you do not share the same household at the end of the year, or another taxpayer is entitled to an exemption for you or your spouse. You can file a joint return if you are married at the end of the tax year, even if only one of you has income or deductions [¶ 1104]. You and your spouse are considered to have the same household at the end of the tax year even though one of you may be away temporarily due to business, vacation, military service or other special circumstances [Sec. 1.6012-1(a)(2)(iv)].

Example 1: Peter and Laurette Lee, both 42 years old, lived together since they were married in 1977. Neither is the dependent of another taxpayer. During the year, Peter received $4,010 in salary, and Laurette $740 in savings bank interest. They had no other income. Since they are entitled to file jointly and their gross income is not less than $4,700, a 1977 return is required.

Example 2: Assume the same facts as in Example 1, except that the Lees decide to file separate returns. In that case, only Peter need file since Laurette's gross income is less than $750.

Example 3: Assume the same facts as in Example 1, except Peter became 65 in 1977. No joint return need be filed since their gross income is less than $5,450.

Gross income, to determine if a return must be filed, means statutory gross income (generally, all income less exclusions).

Example 4: James Fegan gets all his income from a store he owns. He had sales of $10,000 and cost of goods sold was $9,700. The gross income is not $10,000, but $300, and no return is required [Sec. 1.61-3].

Excluded income from sale of a residence [¶ 1416 et seq.] and excluded foreign earned income [¶ 3725] must be counted in the gross income amounts that require filing a return [Sec. 6012(c); 1.6012-1(a)(3)].

Adjusted gross income does not affect the liability for filing a return. See ¶ 1102(c).

Income of minors. The same filing requirements for adults apply to children. Amounts they receive are taxed to them and not to their parents. A child who has taxable earnings is entitled to the same deductions as other taxpayers, whether the payments are business or personal expenses, if they come out of the child's earnings. It is immaterial whether the expenditure is made by the child or by the parent for the child [Sec. 73(b); 1.73-1(b)]. See also ¶ 3509.

(b) If no tax is due. If your gross income equals or exceeds the limit, you must file even if no tax is due because of your deductions and credits. You still remain subject to the return requirements when filing a certificate of nontaxability exempting your wages from withholding [¶ 2506(c)].

(c) If you are self-employed and you have $400 or more net earnings in your own business or profession, you must file a return no matter how small your gross income is. For self-employment income, see ¶ 3823.

(d) Missing persons. When a person disappears, the legal guardian must file a return for the missing person for the current year and for any later years until the person is found, declared legally dead, or established facts justify the belief the person is dead.[1] When the spouse of a missing person is appointed guardian, a joint return can be filed, as individual and as guardian, if the other requirements for a joint return are met. Proof of the appointment should be filed with the return.[2] The return and payment of tax is postponed for civilian employees of the U.S. Government and for members of the Armed Forces who are in a missing or prisoner of war status, or who are involuntarily detained by a foreign government,[3] until the earlier of the 15th day of the third month after release, or the 15th day of the third month an executor is appointed [37 USC 558].

(e) Citizens of Puerto Rico who are also citizens of the U.S., and nonresident aliens who were residents of Puerto Rico during the entire tax year, must file returns if they meet the income test [Sec. 1.6012-1(a)]. See ¶ 3727.

¶ 1101 Return forms. Individual taxpayers file their income tax returns on Form 1040 or Short Form 1040A. If they are not eligible to use the short form, they must use the regular Form 1040 [Sec. 1.6012-1(a)(6), (7)]. Forms are mailed to most taxpayers by the Revenue Service. However, you are not excused from filing even if the return has not been sent to you. You must attach to your return all the withholding statements (Forms W-2 or W-2P) received from your employers for the year [¶ 2508]. The time and place of filing and other details about returns are discussed in Chapter 25.

(a) Filing Form 1040. If you file Form 1040, you may have to attach additional schedules, such as Schedule A if you itemize deductions, as necessary.

(b) Who may use Short Form 1040A. You may use the short form if all your income was from wages, tips, other employee compensation, you received not over $400 of dividends or interest, and you do not itemize deductions. Specifically, you may not use Form 1040A if you:[1]

- Are a nonresident alien (use Form 1040NR), or were "married" (for tax purposes)[2] to a nonresident alien at the end of the year, unless you elect to file a joint return [¶ 1104(a), (b)]; or
- Received more than $400 in dividends or $400 in interest (unless you are filing solely to get your earned income credit refund, ¶ 2405); or
- Had any income other than wages, tips, dividends or interest; or
- Received at least $20 in tips in any month and you did not fully report them to your employer; or
- Show on your W-2 [¶ 2508] uncollected social security tax on tips; or
- Received capital gain dividends or nontaxable distributions; or

Footnotes appear at end of this Chapter.

- Want to make certain adjustments to gross income like moving expenses, employee travel expenses or outside salesperson's expenses [¶ 1801(a); 1831]; or
- Claim a deduction for payment to an individual retirement account [¶ 1838(1)]; or
- Claim exemption for income earned abroad [¶ 3725]; or
- Itemize deductions; or
- Are married and either of you itemizes deductions on a separate return (does not apply if you are an abandoned spouse [¶ 1104(c)]; or
- Want to claim certain credits against your tax; or
- Are a railroad employee representative and claim a credit for excess hospital insurance benefits taxes paid; or
- Had an interest in or authority over a foreign bank account; or
- Are the grantor of a foreign trust that was in existence during the tax year; or
- Choose the income averaging benefits [¶ 2401]; or
- Must file Form 2210 since your balance due is more than 20% of your tax and you may owe a penalty for not paying enough tax during 1977; or
- Claim a deduction for interest forfeited on a premature withdrawal from a time savings account; or
- Claim an exclusion for disability pensions [¶ 1219(c)].

ELEMENTS IN FIGURING THE TAX

Starting in 1977, most taxpayers must figure their taxes by using the tax tables based on tax table income. Relatively few taxpayers will use the rate schedules based on taxable income. In either case, adjusted gross income is a key figure to find their tax liabilities. This is also an important factor in figuring limitations on certain itemized deductions.

¶ **1102 What is involved in the computation.** Before you figure your tax, you should know your (a) gross income, (b) deductions for adjusted gross income, (c) adjusted gross income, (d) itemized deductions, (e) zero bracket amount, (f) unused zero bracket amount (in certain cases), (g) personal exemptions and (h) tax table income (if you use the tax table) or taxable income (if you use the rate schedule).

(a) **Gross income** includes all types of income not expressly exempt from tax. See Chapters 2-7.

(b) **Deductions for adjusted gross income** include business deductions not incurred as an employee, and travel expense, including meals and lodging while away from home in connection with employment. See also (c) below.

(c) **Adjusted gross income** is gross income less the following (¶ 1801(a)) [Sec. 62]:

1. Your deductions for expenses directly incurred in carrying on your trade or business (not as an employee).
2. Reimbursed expenses in connection with your employment. (The reimbursement must be offset against the expenses.)
3. Your traveling expenses, including the cost of meals and lodging while away from home in connection with your employment.
4. Your deductions for transportation expenses in the performance of services as an employee even though incurred while not away from home and even though not reimbursed.
5. Your deductions for expenses incurred in connection with services performed in your employment as an "outside salesperson."

6. A deduction equal to 50% of the excess of your net long-term capital gain over your net short-term capital loss.
7. Your deduction for losses from sales or exchanges of property.
8. Your deductions related to property held for the production of rents and royalties.
9. Your deductions for depreciation and depletion, if you are a life tenant or income beneficiary of property held in trust, or an heir, legatee or devisee of an estate.
10. Moving expenses in connection with an employment.
11. Deductions for contributions to self-employment retirement plans.
12. Deductions under retirement plans for a Subchapter S shareholder-employee owning more than 5% of the outstanding stock.
13. Deductible contributions to individual retirement arrangements.
14. Deductible ordinary income portion of lump-sum distributions from retirement plans.
15. Your deduction for penalties forfeited because of a premature withdrawal from time savings accounts or deposits.
16. For tax years starting after 12-31-76, your deductions for alimony [¶ 1320].

➤**OBSERVATION**➤ It is important not merely to take all allowable deductions, but to properly allocate them. Certain employee expenses should not be reported as itemized deductions.

Background and purpose. Adjusted gross income is used to place limits on some itemized deductions. This concept is designed to segregate those deductions that can be taken in addition to the zero bracket amount (standard deduction before 1977) from those that would be forfeited by using the zero bracket amount.

(d) Itemized deductions are allowable deductions other than deductions allowable in arriving at adjusted gross income, and deductions for personal exemptions [Sec. 63(f)]. For example, itemized deductions include property taxes and mortgage interest on a residence owned and occupied by taxpayer; sales tax on personal articles bought at retail; charitable contributions; unreimbursed union dues; and expenses of tools and uniforms.

Unless taxpayer elects to itemize for the tax year, no itemized deductions will be allowed for the tax year [Sec. 63(g)]. In general, only individuals who have itemized deductions in excess of the zero bracket amount ((e), below) can make that election.

If a married taxpayer files separately and has itemized deductions in excess of the zero bracket amount of $1,600 [(e) below], he or she can elect to itemize. In that case, the other spouse must also itemize, and add back any unused zero bracket amount [(f) below].

(e) Zero bracket amount is $3,200 for married taxpayers filing jointly and surviving spouses, $2,200 for single taxpayers and heads of household, $1,600 for a married taxpayer filing separately, and zero in any other case [Sec. 63(d)].

(f) Unused zero bracket amount is the excess (if any) of the zero bracket amount [(e) above] over the itemized deductions [Sec. 63(e)]. For certain taxpayers, tax table income or taxable income must be increased by the unused zero bracket amount, if any. These include: married taxpayers filing separately where either spouse itemizes deductions; nonresident aliens; U.S. citizens with excludable income from U.S. possession; a taxpayer who can be claimed as a dependent of another.

Footnotes appear at end of this Chapter.

¶ 1102

(g) Personal exemptions include: (1) personal exemptions for the taxpayer and spouse; (2) old-age exemptions for the taxpayer and spouse; (3) exemptions for blindness for the taxpayer and spouse; (4) exemptions for dependents [Sec. 151].

(h) Tax table income or taxable income. Those who use the tax tables must find "tax table income." Those using the rate schedules must compute "taxable income."

Tax table income is adjusted gross income [(c) above] reduced by the excess itemized deductions [¶ 1103(a)] and increased in certain cases by the unused zero bracket amount ((f), above) [Sec. 3(a)(4)].

➤**OBSERVATION**➤ For most taxpayers who do not itemize, tax table income is simply adjusted gross income.

Taxable income is adjusted gross income [(c) above] *reduced* by the excess itemized deductions [¶ 1103(a)] and deductions for personal exemptions [(g) above] and *increased* in certain cases by any unused zero bracket amount ((f) above) [Sec. 63].

¶ 1103 Steps in figuring the tax. You take steps 1-7 below in figuring your tax, unless you leave the tax computation to the IRS [(b) below] or use the rate schedule [¶ 1121].

➤**OBSERVATION**➤ The income and deduction facts and figures needed for each step are entered on different lines and schedules on the form, and in a different order than that given here. The order of steps used is designed to make it easier for you to understand the tax computation structure.

(a) Step by step procedures. Here are the steps:

STEP 1. Start with your GROSS INCOME. This includes, for example: compensation for services [¶ 1301]; bonuses and prizes [¶ 1302]; pensions [¶ 1304]; interest [¶ 1314; 1315]; rent and royalties [¶ 1316]; dividends (first $100 excluded) [Ch. 7]; gains from sales and exchanges of property [Ch. 5; Ch. 6]; income from business [¶ 2601; 2906]. But it *excludes,* wholly or partially, such items as: interest on certain government obligations [¶ 1203-1204]; annuities [¶ 1230-1232]; insurance proceeds [¶ 1213-1218]; gifts and bequests [¶ 1225]; some payments to members of armed forces and veterans [¶ 1218(c); 1306]. You include the income of your spouse, if any, in a joint return.

STEP 2. Subtract your DEDUCTIONS FOR ADJUSTED GROSS INCOME from your gross income [Step 1] to get your adjusted gross income. These include, among others: Trade or business deductions of an employee or outside salesperson [¶ 1805(a)]; deductions due to rent and royalty property [¶ 1806]; losses from sale or exchange of business or investment property [¶ 1613; 1801; 2200]; long-term capital gains deduction [¶ 1612].

STEP 3. Determine your ITEMIZED DEDUCTIONS and your zero bracket amount to find if you have any "excess itemized deductions." The amount of your excess itemized deductions (if any) is the excess (if any) of your itemized deductions over your zero bracket amount [Sec. 63(c)].

STEP 4. Subtract your excess itemized deductions, if any, from your adjusted gross income. Then, add your unused zero bracket amount [¶ 1102(f)], if any, to the adjusted gross income, to arrive at your tax table income.

➤**NOTE**➤ The steps here should be followed by those who use the tax tables. If you use the rate schedules, compute your taxable income and follow the steps shown at ¶ 1121.

STEP 5. Determine your PERSONAL EXEMPTIONS. These include: one exemption for yourself [¶ 1111] and an additional exemption (a) if you are 65 or over [¶ 1113]; (b) if you are blind [¶ 1114]; (c) for each of your dependents [¶ 1115]; (d) for your spouse [¶ 1112]; (e) if spouse is 65 or over [¶ 1113]; (f) if spouse is blind [¶ 1114]. You get the exemption for your spouse on a separate return only if your spouse has no gross income and is not a dependent of another.

STEP 6. Go to your tax tables to find your tax [¶ 1122].

STEP 7. Subtract your CREDITS, if any, from the tax found in Step 6 to figure the net tax payable or overpayment refundable. These credits include: tax withheld on wages or prepaid estimated taxes [Ch. 15]; earned income credit [¶ 2405]; credit for the elderly [¶ 2406]; any social security tax overpayment [¶ 2511(a)]; investment credit [¶ 2410]; credit for political contributions [¶ 2416]; credits for work incentive program expenses [¶ 2411]; credit for foreign taxes and taxes of U.S. possessions [¶ 3701]; credit for nonhighway use of gasoline [¶ 2417]; credit for child care [¶ 2415]; and job credit [¶ 2414].

(b) Tax figured by Revenue Service. You may leave the computation of your tax to the Revenue Service if you follow the instructions for Forms 1040 or 1040A [Sec. 6014; 1.6014-2]. In general, you make the election by omitting certain lines and by not showing your tax on your return. You cannot make this election if you itemize your deductions [¶ 1102(d)], or someone could claim you as a dependent. Also, your return must be filed by its due date (without extention). If the Revenue Service figures your tax, you get a refund if you overpaid, or a bill for additional tax due, payable within 30 days from the mailing date [Sec. 6151(b); 1.6151-1(b)]. A balance of less than $1 need not be paid, and an overpayment of less than $1 is refunded only if application for it is made.[1]

Your right to claim head of household or surviving spouse status [¶ 1105; 1106] is not lost. Nor do you lose any credits for withholding, the elderly, investment in business equipment, gasoline and lubricating oil tax, political contributions, or tax overpayment [Sec. 1.6014-2(c)].

Husband and wife who file jointly may have the Revenue Service compute their tax. The tax is the lesser of the tax for a joint return, or if sufficient information is given, the tax figured as if the return was the spouses' separate returns [Sec. 1.6014-2(d)].

FILING STATUS

Your filing status may well be the single most important item on your return since it alone fixes the kind of tax rates you use. Married persons are taxed at the lowest rates if they file jointly, and the highest rates if they file separately. Single persons who are heads of household use a set of rates halfway between those of other single persons and those for married couples filing jointly. All unmarried taxpayers who do not qualify for another filing status must file "single."

¶ 1104 Married couples. Taxpayers who file a joint return get the "split-income benefit" reflected in the tax rates. The tax tables and tax rate schedules for married persons filing jointly split the income and reflect the tax at a lower rate.

Footnotes appear at end of this Chapter.

Example: The tax on $35,200 taxable income on a joint return is $8,660. If this income were split, twice the tax on $17,600 taxable income for married persons filing separately is $8,660 (2 × $4,330).

Background and purpose. Income-splitting was originally provided in the Revenue Act of 1948. Before 1948, a married couple filing separate returns in a non-community property state frequently paid a higher combined tax than the couple in a community property state where a married couple's income is treated as earned equally by the two. To equalize the tax treatment in community and non-community property states, Congress decided to let all married couples split their combined taxable income (see (a) below).

(a) **Who may file a joint return.** The rules for filing as a married couple apply regardless of how much gross income each spouse had during the tax year. Taxpayers may file jointly, if on the last day of the tax year any one of the following apply [Sec. 6013; 1.6013-1]:

- They are married and living as husband and wife (but see NOTE, below).
- They are living together in a common-law marriage recognized by the state in which it was entered.[1]
- They are married and living apart, but not legally separated under a decree of divorce or separate maintenance.
- They are separated under an interlocutory decree of divorce.[2]

NOTE: Taxpayers are not considered single unless the decree is final on or before the last day of the tax year. However, a couple who filed a joint return but whose marriage is later annulled, must file amended returns as singles.[3] A couple would still be considered married for tax purposes if divorced by the year-end to avoid tax and then remarried to each other early next year.[3]

If one spouse dies, the other generally may file a joint return for the year of death and claim an exemption for the deceased spouse. If husband and wife in a community property state file separate returns, each must report one-half the combined community income, and each may deduct one-half of the total deductions paid with community income.

U.S. citizens married to nonresident aliens. Generally, a taxpayer who is married to a nonresident alien at any time during the tax year cannot file a joint return [Sec. 6013(a)]. He or she must file as a married person filing separately.[4] However, a nonresident alien who is married to a U.S. citizen or resident, may file a joint return for tax years ending on or after 12-31-75, if husband and wife both elect to be taxed on their worldwide income. An election applies to the tax year for which made and to all subsequent years until terminated. If the election is terminated for any 2 individuals, neither of them is eligible to make a new election [Sec. 6013(g), (h)]. If the election is not made, certain community property laws are inapplicable for income tax purposes [Sec. 879]. A similar election is available to a married couple, one of which was a nonresident alien during the year but becomes a U.S. resident at the year-end [Sec. 6013(h)]. Election to file a joint return must be made on a timely filed return (including extensions) [Temp. Reg. Sec. 7.0]. The alien spouse not subject to withholding may postpone the filing of the estimated tax declaration until June 15 [Sec. 6073].

(b) **Married persons filing separate returns.** A husband and wife may file separate returns, whether or not both had income. If they file separately, they should each report only their own income, and claim only their own exemptions and deductions on their individual returns. See also ¶ 3506.

➤**OBSERVATION**➔ If both husband and wife have income, they should generally figure their tax both jointly and separately to make sure they are using the method that will result in less tax.

(c) Abandoned spouse. You are not considered married if you file a separate return and furnish more than half the cost of maintaining a household that is the principal home of a dependent child *for more than half the year*, and your husband (or wife) lived apart from you for the entire year [Sec. 2(c), 143(b)]. The requirements of maintaining a household for a dependent relative are substantially the same as described in ¶ 1106(b), (c) except the dependent needs to occupy the home of an abandoned spouse for more than 6 months only [Sec. 1.143-1]. If the abandoned spouse's child lived with the spouse for the *entire year*, such spouse may file as a head of household. If the taxpayer qualifies as an abandoned spouse but the child does not live with her during the entire year she may file as a *single* person.

¶ 1105 Surviving spouse. A widow or widower may file a joint return for the year his or her spouse dies [¶ 1104(a)]. Additional income-splitting benefits are available in later years. Certain widows or widowers get the same benefits as on a joint return for the first two years after the year in which his or her spouse died, if [Sec. 2(a); 1.2-2]:

- Taxpayer is eligible to file a joint return the year the spouse died; and
- Taxpayer lives with his or her child, stepchild or foster child for the entire tax year (except for temporary absences), and may claim a dependency exemption for such child; and
- Over half the household costs are paid by the taxpayer (here the same tests apply as found in ¶ 1106(c) for heads of household); and
- The taxpayer did not remarry by the end of the tax year.

Background and purpose. Congress adopted a 2-stage approach to save the income-splitting benefits for a surviving spouse. This was to insure that a surviving spouse's taxload might not be increased over that which the couple paid when both were alive. The first stage allows the surviving spouse to file a joint return [¶ 1104(a)] and the second involves filing as a head of household [¶ 1106].

NOTE: A Vietnam serviceman's widow can claim surviving spouse status for 2 years following the declaration of death, instead of actual death [Sec. 6013(f)].

¶ 1106 Head of household. A taxpayer who qualifies as a head of household can compute the tax by using the special rate in the tax tables or tax rate schedules. This special rate is available for a tax year only if *all* of the following conditions are met [Sec. 2(b); 1.2-2(b)]:

- You must be unmarried on the last day of your tax year [see (a) below].
- Your household must be the principal residence for at least one relative for the entire year [see (b) below and also an exception for parents].
- You must (1) maintain a household and (2) contribute over half the cost of maintaining the home [see (c) below].
- You must not be a nonresident alien at any time during the year.

NOTE: If you satisfy these conditions, you need not add the income of relatives living in the household to your own and you can take all your exemptions for dependents.

Background and purpose. An unmarried person required to maintain a home for another person's benefit, is likely to have income that is shared with that other person in much the same way a married couple share their income [¶ 1104]. This, it is believed, justifies the extension of some of the income-splitting benefits to a head of household, and is the reason for a special rate for a head of household.

(a) Marital status. You are considered unmarried for head of household purposes if:

- You have never been married; or
- You are a widow or widower whose spouse died before the tax year; or
- You are separated from your spouse under a final decree of divorce or separate maintenance; or
- Your spouse is a nonresident alien.

NOTE: Since you are considered married for the tax year in which your spouse dies, you cannot use the special head of household tax rate. However, you may qualify as a "surviving spouse" [¶ 1105].

An abandoned spouse [¶ 1104(c)] is considered *unmarried* and therefore may (though not necessarily) qualify as a head of household.

(b) Maintenance of household for relative. Generally, you must maintain as your home for the entire tax year a household in which your children (including adopted), their descendants, or your stepchildren (but not their descendants) live; or in which any other relative lives who qualifies as your dependent (¶ 1117(a)) [Sec. 1.2-2(b)(3)]. But see "parents" below.

NOTE: Although the household must actually be the principal abode of your relative (except your parent) during the year or up to the date of his or her death, the 9th Circuit has held occupancy need not be actual or physical, and a token or implied occupancy may be sufficient;[1] but the Revenue Service[2] and the 4th Circuit[3] disagree. Temporary absences for vacation, sickness or school are disregarded in determining if a related person actually lived in your household.

Parents. Your father or mother must live in a home you maintain for your entire tax year and qualify you for a dependency exemption. You need not live in the same household as your parent. A rest home or home for the aged qualifies as a household for this purpose.[4]

Children. An unmarried child living in the home maintained by taxpayer can qualify taxpayer as head of household even though not taxpayer's dependent,[5] but not a married or foster child.

Cousins or unrelated persons living in household do not qualify you as a head of household even if they are dependents.

Alien spouse. A U.S. citizen or resident alien married to and living with a nonresident alien can use head of household rates if a dependent child lives with taxpayer (but see ¶ 1104(a)).[6]

Multiple support agreements. If the relative must qualify as your dependent, that status may not arise from a multiple support agreement [¶ 1116(c)].

(c) Furnishing costs of maintaining home. You must contribute over half the cost of maintaining the home. These costs include rent, mortgage interest, taxes, property insurance, upkeep and repairs, utility charges, and food consumed in the home. You cannot include the cost of clothing, education, medical treatment, vacations, life insurance, transportation, the rental value of the home,[7] or the value of services rendered by you or by a member of the household [Sec. 1.2-2(d)].

ZERO BRACKET AMOUNT—STANDARD DEDUCTION

The 1977 Tax Reduction and Simplification Act repeals the standard deduction for tax years starting after 12-31-76. Instead of the minimum standard deduction and the maximum standard deduction based on a percentage of the adjusted gross income as under prior law, the 1977 law substitutes the new zero bracket amount. The zero bracket amount is, in effect, a fixed standard deduction that has been built into new tax tables to simplify the computation of tax liability. This amount, which is tax-free to all taxpayers according to their marital status, establishes a floor under itemized deductions to enable itemizers to also use the tables.

¶ **1107 Zero bracket amount.** The zero bracket amount is $3,200 for married individuals filing a joint return or a surviving spouse, $2,200 for single taxpayers and heads of household, $1,600 for married individuals filing separately, and zero in any other case [Sec. 63(d)].

¶ **1108 Standard deduction.** For tax years ending in 1976 and starting before 1-1-77, the maximum standard deduction was $2,800 for a surviving spouse or married persons filing jointly, $2,400 for single individuals, or $1,400 for married individuals filing separately. For tax years ending in 1975, the standard deduction could never exceed $2,600 for a surviving spouse or persons filing jointly, $2,300 for single individuals, or $1,300 for married individuals filing separately. However, within these limits, the standard deduction was the larger of the low income allowance or 16% for tax years ending in 1975 or 1976 of adjusted gross income.

The low income allowance for tax years ending in 1976 was $2,100 for a married couple filing jointly or a surviving spouse, $1,700 for single individuals, or $1,050 for a married person filing separately. The low income allowance for tax years ending in 1975 was $1,900 for a married couple filing jointly or a surviving spouse, $1,600 for single individuals, or $950 for a married person filing separately.

¶ **1109 Marital status.** A taxpayer's marital status determines the zero bracket amount [¶ 1107]. Marital status is determined at the end of the tax year or on the date of the spouse's death. Persons legally separated under a final decree of divorce or separate maintenance at either time are not considered married and must file separate returns. Although married, an abandoned parent may usually file as a head of household (¶ 1104(c)) [Sec. 143; 1.143-1(a)]. Persons separated by an interlocutory decree of divorce are married until it becomes final.[1] A taxpayer is considered married if his spouse died during the year and on the date of her death the parties were not separated under a decree of divorce or separate maintenance (¶ 1107) [Sec. 143(a); 1.143-1].

PERSONAL EXEMPTIONS

Personal exemptions are flat allowances of $750 each that are deducted from adjusted gross income. If you file jointly with your spouse, you may claim the same exemptions for your spouse. Special rules limit the exemptions for your spouse when separate returns are filed. Personal exemptions should not be confused with exclusions which are income items exempt from tax.

¶ **1111 Your personal exemptions.** Effective for tax years starting after 12-31-76, the personal exemptions are built into the new tax tables. In figuring your tax, you are allowed $750 for each personal exemption. The $750 exemption has applied since 1972. But for 1971, it was $675 per exemption; for 1970, it was $625; and for 1969 and earlier, $600. For 1975 through 1978, there is also a *credit* for personal exemptions [(e) below].

Footnotes appear at end of this Chapter.

(a) For yourself. Whether you are married or single, you get at least one exemption for yourself. You get 2 exemptions if you reached your 65th birthday on or before January 1, 1978 [¶ 1113(a)] *or* were blind at the end of 1977. If you were both 65 or over *and* blind, you get 3 exemptions for yourself.

(b) For your spouse. On a joint return, you get one exemption for your spouse, if she (or he) is neither blind nor has reached age 65; 2 exemptions if blind *or* age 65 or over; 3 exemptions if blind *and* 65 or over.

If you file a separate return, you get the same exemptions, if your spouse had *no* gross income and is not a dependent of another taxpayer. You get no exemptions for your spouse if she (or he) had any gross income.

(c) For dependents. You get a $750 exemption for each "dependent" who qualifies [¶ 1115-1120] but no extra exemptions for dependents who are blind or 65 or over.

Example 1: A single person with no dependents is entitled to the following deductions for exemptions:
   (a) $750 if under 65 and of good vision.
   (b) $1,500 if *either* 65 (or over) or blind.
   (c) $2,250 if *both* 65 (or over) and blind.

Example 2: A husband and wife, with one dependent son who meets the tests for exemption explained in ¶ 1115-1120, are entitled to the following deductions for exemptions on a joint return:
   (a) $2,250 if both husband and wife are under 65 and of good vision.
   (b) $3,000 if husband (or wife) is at least 65 *or* blind but wife (or husband) is under 65 and of good vision.
   (c) $3,750 if both husband and wife are at least 65 but neither is blind.
   (d) $4,500 if both husband and wife are at least 65 and only one is blind.
   (e) $5,250 if both husband and wife are at least 65 and both are blind.

(d) Short tax year. The amount of the above deductions is not affected ordinarily when the return covers less than 12 months. Thus, the deduction on the return for a taxpayer (single, under 65, of good vision, with no dependents) who died on June 30, 1977, would be $750 even though the return covered only half of 1977. The exemption deduction must be prorated, however, in returns for short periods made necessary by a change in accounting period [Sec. 443(c)]. See ¶ 2717.

(e) General tax credit. For 1976 through 1978, the individual resident taxpayer gets a credit equal to the greater of: (A) 2% of taxable income (reduced by the zero bracket amount for 1977 and 1978), up to $9,000, or (B) $35 for each allowable personal exemption. *For 1977 and 1978 only:* Credit is allowed for additional exemptions of old-age or blindness. Married individuals filing separately are limited to the $35-per-exemption credit [Sec. 42]. The credit is built into the 1977 and 1978 tax tables, so the table users need not compute the credit.

For tax years ending in 1975, the individual could take a $30 credit for each allowable personal exemption. There was no credit for the additional exemptions of old-age or blindness in 1975 or 1976 (¶ 1113; 1114) [Sec. 42; 1.42-1].

¶ 1112 Exemptions of married persons. Husband and wife need not live together for the rules below to apply. They must, however, be man and wife at the close of the tax year or, if one dies, on the date death occurs [Sec. 153(1); 1.153-1]. Persons legally divorced or separated under a decree are considered single, not married [Sec. 153(2); 1.153-1]. Those separated under an interlocutory decree of divorce are considered married until the decree becomes final.[1]

(a) If a joint return is filed. A husband and wife who file a joint return get two exemption deductions of $750 each, or a total of $1,500 [Sec. 151(b); 1.151-

1(b)]. But in that case, neither the husband nor the wife may be claimed as a dependent by any other person [Sec. 151(b); 1.151-1(b)]. Extra exemptions are allowed for old-age or blindness of either spouse. If one spouse dies, the other generally may file a joint return for the year of death [¶ 1104(a)] and claim an exemption deduction for the deceased spouse, unless the surviving spouse remarries during the year of the spouse's death.

(b) If only one spouse files a return. If no joint return is filed and one spouse, for example, the husband, files a separate return, he may claim 2 exemptions (one for himself and one for his wife), but only if his wife, for the calendar year in which his tax year began, has no gross income and was not a dependent of another [Sec. 151(b); 1.151-1(b)]. Extra exemptions are allowed for old-age or blindness of either spouse.

> **NOTE:** A spouse who receives rents has gross income even if the rented property is actually operating at a loss.[2]

(c) If husband and wife file separate returns. If a separate return is filed by each spouse, the husband is entitled to one exemption for himself on his return, and the wife may claim one exemption for herself on her return [Sec. 151(b); 1.151-1(b)]. Neither may use the other's deduction. Each may claim an extra exemption for his or her own old age or blindness on his or her own return.

Most married couples file joint returns to take advantage of the split-income benefits. If they file separate returns, they may change to a joint return even after the due date of the return, if they pay the tax in full when they file the joint return [¶ 3506]. Also, if they filed separate returns in one year, they may file a joint return the next year, provided that they are eligible to file jointly for the year in question [¶ 1104(a)].

If one spouse dies. If, for example, the wife dies during the tax year, the husband may claim a $750 exemption for himself and a $750 exemption for his wife on his separate return, if she had no gross income and was not a dependent of someone else. (If she had been 65 or more, or blind, he could also claim these additional exemptions.) But if the wife dies, and the husband remarries during the same year, he cannot claim an exemption for his deceased wife.[3] He can, however, claim an exemption for his present wife, if she has no gross income and is not a dependent of another person.

If, for example, the husband dies during the tax year, and the wife has no gross income and is not a dependent of another taxpayer for the year, a $750 exemption for each spouse may be claimed on the final separate return filed for the deceased husband. If, however, each spouse has gross income, neither the husband nor the wife is entitled to an exemption for the other spouse, unless a joint return is filed [¶ 3507].

> **Example 1:** Wife received $1 in interest before she died on 9-30-77. Husband gets one $750 exemption for himself, but no exemption for his deceased wife on a separate return. If the conditions for filing a joint return are met, one may be filed and the exemptions for both husband and wife may be taken. In this example, it is assumed husband and wife are under 65 and not blind.

Although a widow who remarries in the same calendar year her husband dies cannot claim both husbands on her separate return, she can be claimed twice: once on her deceased husband's separate return and again on her new husband's separate calendar year return, but only if she had no gross income and was not a dependent of another.[4]

Footnotes appear at end of this Chapter.

¶ 1112

Example 2: Laura Sand's husband Charles died on Jan. 31, 1977, and the following week she married Arthur Young. She had no income or deductions of her own. A $750 exemption for the wife is allowed on both the separate returns of Charles and Arthur.

¶ 1113 Old-age exemptions. Additional deductions for exemptions on account of old age are allowed as follows:
(1) $750 additional for a taxpayer who is 65 or over;
(2) $750 additional for a spouse who is 65 or over (a) if a joint return is filed, or (b) if a separate return is filed and the spouse had no gross income and is not a dependent of another person for the calendar year in which the taxpayer's tax year begins [Sec. 151(c)(2); 1.151-1(c)(1)].

Example 1: A single person, 65 (or over), with good vision and no dependents, is entitled to a total exemption deduction of $1,500 ($750 personal exemption plus $750 old-age exemption).

Example 2: A husband and wife, with good vision and no dependents, get the following exemption deductions on a *joint return*:
(a) $1,500 (2 exemptions) if both husband and wife are under 65.
(b) $2,250 (3 exemptions) if husband is at least 65 but wife is under 65.
(c) $2,250 (3 exemptions) if wife is at least 65 but husband is under 65.
(d) $3,000 (4 exemptions) if both husband and wife are at least 65.

Example 3: Assume same facts as in Example 2 except that the husband files a *separate return.* If his wife has no gross income and is not a dependent of another person, his exemption deductions will be the same as those in (a)-(d), Example 2. If she has gross income or is a dependent of another person, his exemption deductions will be those of a single person (Example 1).

➤OBSERVATION→ If the taxpayer or his spouse is to become 65 sometime during the succeeding year, they might consider shifting the receipt of income into that year to take advantage of the increased exemption.

Background and purpose. This additional exemption was created immediately after World War II, in the setting of an inflationary spiral, as Congress in the postwar period found there was a very heavy concentration of small incomes among persons 65 or over, and the need for a special relief for this age group was pressing.

(a) Who is "65 or over." The additional old-age deductions may be taken only if the individual reached age 65 on or before the last day of the tax year covered by the return. A person is 65, for this purpose, on the first moment of the day preceding the 65th birthday. There is no old-age deduction for a spouse who died before reaching age 65 [Sec. 151(c); 1.151-1(c)].

Example 4: A taxpayer whose 65th birthday falls on 1-1-78 reaches age 65 on 12-31-77. He may take an additional $750 deduction on his return for calendar year 1977. If he is single, has no dependents and has good vision, he gets a total exemption deduction of $1,500.

(b) Aged dependent. There is no *additional* deduction for a dependent who has reached age 65 [Sec. 1.151-2(b)]. Each dependency exemption is limited to $750.

¶ 1114 Exemptions for the blind. Additional deductions for exemptions on account of blindness are allowed as follows:
(1) $750 additional for a taxpayer who is blind;
(2) $750 additional for a spouse who is blind (a) if a joint return is filed, or (b) if a separate return is filed and the spouse had no gross income and was not a dependent of another person for the calendar year in which the taxpayer's tax year begins [Sec. 151(d); 1.151-1(d)(1)].

Chapter 1—Personal Exemptions

Example 1: A single person with no dependents gets an exemption deduction of:
  (a) $1,500 (2 exemptions) if blind and under 65.
  (b) $2,250 (3 exemptions) if blind and 65 or over.

Example 2: A husband and wife, who have no dependents, are entitled to the following deductions for exemptions on a *joint return:*
  (a) $2,250 (3 exemptions) if one spouse is blind *or* at least 65, but the other spouse is of good vision and under 65.
  (b) $3,000 (4 exemptions) if both husband and wife are blind, but neither has reached 65.
  (c) $3,750 (5 exemptions) if both husband and wife are blind, and one spouse is at least 65 but the other spouse is under 65.
  (d) $4,500 (6 exemptions) if both are blind, and 65 or over.

Example 3: Assume same facts as in Example 2, except that the married taxpayer files a *separate return.* If the spouse has no gross income and is not a dependent of another person, taxpayer's exemptions will be the same as those in (a)-(d), Example 2. If the spouse has gross income or is a dependent of another person, taxpayer's exemptions are limited to those of a single person (Example 1).

Background and purpose. Congress originally granted blind persons a fixed expense deduction. But this relief was later changed to an exemption deduction so that the blind need not forfeit the right to use the then optional standard deduction (which has since been converted into the zero bracket amount; ¶ 1107). Moreover, an exemption affects withholding and automatically increases the blind person's take-home pay, while a deduction does not.

(a) Determining blindness. A person's blindness is determined as of the last day of the tax year covered by the return. But the blindness of a spouse who dies during the year is determined as of the date of death [Sec. 151(d)(2); 1.151-1(d)(1)]. Proof of blindness should be attached to the return.

NOTE: If a person is totally blind, a statement to that effect is sufficient. If partially blind, the person should attach a certificate from a qualified physician or registered optometrist, stating that (a) central visual acuity does not exceed 20/200 in the better eye with correcting lenses, or (b) the fields of vision are so limited that the widest diameter of the visual field is no greater than 20 degrees. If the doctor certifies that the partial blindness is irreversible, a statement to that effect is sufficient with subsequent returns [Sec. 1.151-1(d)(3)].

(b) Blind dependent. There is no *additional* exemption deduction for a blind dependent [Sec. 1.151-2(b)]. Each exemption is limited to $750.

EXEMPTIONS FOR DEPENDENTS

A "dependent" is someone related to you or a member of your household for whom you provide more than half the support. You may claim a dependency exemption of $750 for each person who meets *all* 5 dependency tests, with certain exceptions. For example, the gross income test does not apply if your child is a full-time student or under 19. Also, special support rules apply to children of divorced parents and to those dependents being claimed under multiple support agreements.

¶ 1115 Your exemptions for dependents. The following 5 tests must be met for a person to qualify you for a dependency exemption:

- Support [¶ 1116].
- Relationship or member of household [¶ 1117].

Footnotes appear at end of this Chapter.

- Gross income [¶ 1118].
- Joint return [¶ 1119].
- Citizenship or residency [¶ 1120].

Birth or death during the year. If the 5 tests or conditions are satisfied, the fact that a person was not in existence throughout the year will not affect your right to claim the *full* $750 exemption. Thus, if your child, whom you support, is born or dies during the tax year, you may claim a full exemption deduction for him. No proration of the $750 is required. But no exemption is allowed for an unborn or stillborn child.[1]

¶ **1116 Support.** You must furnish over one-half the total support of the person for the calendar year in which your tax year begins [Sec. 152(a); 1.152-1]. There are, however, exceptions covering students [(b) below], and multiple support agreements [(c) below]. If a husband or wife filing separate returns both contribute to the support of a child, the exemption is taken by the one furnishing more than half the support unless the special provisions for separated or divorced parents below apply.

If taxpayer has not actually paid for the support, he still may qualify for the deduction if he (1) takes affirmative steps to provide the support, and (2) incurs an unconditional obligation to pay for the items of support. But a promise to pay for the support "if and when it is possible for him to do so" is not enough.[1]

➤**OBSERVATION**➤ Adequate records may be necessary to justify the support requirement for the dependency deduction.

(a) What is support. Support includes amounts spent for food, shelter, clothing, medical and dental care, education, church contributions,[2] child care expenses,[3] wedding apparel and receptions,[4] and the like, but not the value of services performed for a dependent,[5] nor federal, state and local income taxes paid by the dependent from his own income,[6] nor scholarships received by the dependent student [see (b) below]. Items furnished in the form of property or lodging[7] are measured by their fair market value [Sec. 1.152-1(a)(2)]. Thus, if the taxpayer owns the house in which the dependent lives, the fair rental value of the lodging furnished (which includes the cost of upkeep[8]) is counted. If the taxpayer lives rent free in the dependent's home, the fair rental value of the lodging furnished must be offset against the amounts he spent in support of the dependent.[9] If the dependent lives in his own home, its fair rental value is considered as being contributed by the dependent for his own support.[9] Premiums for medical care insurance count toward support but not: (1) the benefits themselves; (2) payments for civil damages; (3) services provided in government medical facilities.[10] Basic (but not supplementary) medicare benefits are dependent's contribution to his own support,[11] as are social security benefits paid to a disabled parent's child.[12] But the Tax Court says neither basic nor supplementary benefits are support items.[13]

If the dependent is alive the entire year, the fact that you do not support him for the entire year does not affect your right to the exemption.[14]

Example 1: Joe supports his father for 7 months of the year, at a cost of $2,900, and Joe's sister supports the father for the remaining 5 months at a cost of $2,700. Joe can claim the entire $750 exemption for his father's support. If Joe's sister supported her father for 5 months at a cost of $3,000, she, rather than Joe, would get the exemption.

VETERANS AND SERVICEMEN

A person in the Armed Forces a full year cannot be claimed as a dependent. But if he is in the Armed Forces for only part of a year, he may be claimed as a dependent, if all tests are met [¶ 1115].[9]

If a serviceman is supporting another person, the entire amount of support he furnishes, including any nontaxable allowances for dependents, is counted for this test.[15] A serviceman who furnishes more than half the support of his 2 minor sisters by a dependency allotment to the mother is entitled to exemptions for all three.[16]

Dependent's income. If a dependent has funds of his own from any source, only the amounts he actually spends on his support are matched against the support furnished by taxpayer to determine if taxpayer furnished over one-half the support. For example, social security benefits[17] and state benefit payments based solely on need[18] are treated as contributions to the dependent's own support to the extent the benefits are so used.

> **Example 2:** Gray's father gets social security of $2,200 a year. This year, he put $600 into a savings account and spent the remaining $1,600 on clothing, entertainment, and the like. Gray contributed $1,800 to the support of his father who had no other income. Gray meets the support test.

»OBSERVATION→ If the support test cannot be met because the taxpayer's dependent is using tax-exempt income for his own support, the dependent ought to consider putting away some of this income in a bank account instead of applying it toward support.

The total support of the taxpayer's parents is presumed to be spent on both evenly, unless taxpayer proves otherwise.[19]

> **Example 3:** During the year, Well's parents received $3,000 total support: $1,000 in father's social security benefits and $2,000 from Well. He is considered to have provided more than half the support of both parents. The parents are treated as a unit; the benefits are allocated evenly between the two.

Group support. If a person contributes a lump sum amount for the support of two or more dependents, the amount is allocated among the dependents on a pro rata basis. If a member of a household contributes more to the support of the household than his pro rata share, the difference counts toward the support of the other members of the household in equal amounts.[20]

Children of divorced or separated parents. The support test is based on rules that apply only if: (1) the parents together furnish more than half the child's support and (2) the child is in the parents' custody for more than half the year. These rules do not apply if they file a joint return or the child is the subject of a multiple support agreement [Sec. 152(e); 1.152-4]. If a divorced parent remarries, support furnished by the new spouse is treated as furnished by that divorced spouse.[21]

Parent with custody. Generally, the parent who has custody of the child for the greater part of the year is entitled to the exemption (custody parent).

> **Example 4:** Fred and Sally Jones were divorced in 1976. The divorce decree specified that Sally was to have custody of their 2 children for 8 months of each year and be entitled to the exemption deductions for the children. Neither child has income and the total annual cost of support for each child is $1,800 paid by both parents. Sally can claim the exemptions for the children.

> **Example 5:** Assume the same facts as in Example 4, except that neither parent is entitled to the exemption deductions under the terms of the decree and Sally can prove $2,000 and Fred $1,600 in contributed child support. Sally can claim the exemptions for the children because they are in her custody and she can prove she provided a greater share of support than Fred.

Parent without custody or having it for a lesser period (noncustodial parent) can get the exemption if: (1) he spends at least $600 for the child's support and the decree or agreement provides he is to get the exemption; or (2) he provides at least $1,200 for each child's support and the custody parent cannot prove that he or she provided the greater share of support. For tax years beginning before 10-5-76, the noncustodial parent in (2) merely had to provide at least $1,200 for *all* the children's support.

Example 6: Assume the same facts as in Example 4, except that the decree specified Fred is entitled to the exemption deductions and he contributed $600 for the support of each child and Sally contributed $3,000 in child support. Fred can claim the exemptions for the children.

Example 7: Assume the same facts as in Example 4, except that Sally signs a written agreement assigning the dependency claim to Fred and he contributed $600 for the support of each child and Sally contributed $3,000 in child support. Fred can claim the exemption for the children.

Child support payments received from the parent without custody are counted as his contribution to support, whether or not the amounts are actually spent [Sec. 152(e)(2); 1.152-4(d)(4)]. Alimony or trust payments taxable to a divorced or legally separated wife [¶ 1320] and deductible by the husband, are not considered payment by him for support of a dependent [Sec. 152(b)(4); 1.152-2(b)].

Itemized statement. To determine which parent provided the greater amount of support, either parent is entitled to receive an itemized statement concerning the child's income, support and the like, from the other parent, if he requests that information and notifies the other parent of his intention to claim the child. He must send the other parent a similar itemized statement [Sec. 152(e)(3); 1.152-4(d)(3), (e)(1)]. If a parent who intends to claim the exemption makes or receives such a request before he files his return, or before the due date for filing, whichever is later, he must attach his own itemized statements and that of the other parent, if available, to his return [Sec. 1.152-4(e)(2), (3)].

Community property states. If separate returns are filed in community property states, and husband and wife contribute *equally* to the support of the dependent, either husband or wife must take the entire exemption.[22] Note also the provisions for multiple support agreements in (c) below.

(b) Students. If a son, daughter, stepchild, adopted child or foster child is a student, a scholarship at an educational institution is not counted in determining if the taxpayer furnished more than half the support [Sec. 152(d); 1.152-1(c)] unless it results from a promise of future services.[23]

Example 8: Ben gets $3,000 support from his father and $4,000 in scholarship granted by his university which only requires him to be a third-year medical student in good standing to qualify for the grant. Ben has no other income. His father can claim Ben as a dependent.

Who is a student. A child is a "student" if, during each of any 5 calendar months of the calendar year in which the taxpayer's tax year begins, (1) he is in full-time attendance at an "educational institution," or (2) he is taking a full-time course of institutional on-farm training [Sec. 151(e)(4); 1.151-3(b)].

An educational institution is one that maintains a regular faculty and curriculum, and normally has a regularly organized body of students in attendance where the educational activities are carried out [Sec. 151(e)(4); 1.151-3(c)]. Thus, primary, secondary, preparatory and normal schools, colleges, universities, technical and mechanical schools are covered, but not correspondence schools and on-the-job training.

On-farm training, to qualify, must be supervised by an accredited agent of an educational institution or a state or a political subdivision of a state.

Night school attendance only is not considered full-time attendance. But full-time attendance may include some night attendance related to a full-time course of study [Sec. 1.151-3(b)].

Military academies. Appointment to any U.S. military academy is not a scholarship award.[24]

Naval ROTC payment for tuition and books is a scholarship award.[25]

Schools for handicapped or maladjusted. Amounts spent by state to educate children (including room and board) committed to state training school are counted as support,[26] but not amounts it spends, considered scholarships, to educate and train handicapped persons.[27]

(c) Multiple support agreements. When two or more persons furnish the support of a dependent, one of the contributing group is entitled to take the deduction for the dependent if [Sec. 152(c); 1.152-3]:

• No one person contributed more than half the dependent's support, *and*
• Each member of the group, were it not for the support test, would have been entitled to claim the individual as a dependent, *and*
• The one claiming the deduction gave more than 10% of the dependent's support, *and*
• Every other person who gave more than 10% of the dependent's support files a written statement on Form 2120 that he will not claim the exemption in the same calendar year (or any tax year starting in the calendar year).

➤**OBSERVATION**➤ All those contributing to the support should consider who has the best tax advantage in taking the exemption.

Background and purpose. The support test presented certain problems where several persons supported another individual, but no one could claim the exemption because no one supplied more than half the support. Sometimes contributors could vary their contributions from year to year to qualify one of them. But in most cases, such arrangements were difficult and frequently all lost the exemption. Thus, an exception was made to the one-half support requirement by way of multiple support agreements.

¶ **1117 Relationship of dependent.** The person supported must be (a) the taxpayer's relative, or (b) a member of the taxpayer's household.

(a) A taxpayer's relatives are the following:
• Son, daughter, grandchild, or great grandchild,
• Stepchild,
• Brother, sister, half brother, half sister, stepbrother or stepsister,
• Parent, grandparent, or great grandparent,
• Stepmother or stepfather,
• Brother's or sister's son or daughter,
• Father's or mother's brother or sister, and
• Son-in-law, daughter-in-law, father-in-law, mother-in-law, brother-in-law, or sister-in-law [Sec. 152(a)].

Adopted children. A legally adopted child or one placed with the taxpayer for adoption is considered a child by blood (A taxpayer claiming an exemption for a child placed with him for adoption must file a statement with the return giving the child's name, the agency's name and address, and the date the application was filed with the agency) [Sec. 152(b)(2); 1.152-2(c)].

Foster children qualify if they meet the tests in (b) below [Sec. 152(b)(2); 1.151-3, 1.152-2].

Cousins do not qualify unless they meet the tests in (b) below.

Spouse's in-laws. The wife of the taxpayer's wife's brother is not the taxpayer's sister-in-law.[1]

Taxpayer's spouse is never his dependent [Sec. 152(a)(9); 1.152-1(b)].[2]

Joint returns. On a joint return, this condition is satisfied if the qualifying relationship exists between the person claimed as dependent and *either* spouse [Sec. 1.152-2(d)].

Footnotes appear at end of this Chapter.

¶ **1117**

Example: Taxpayer supported his wife's niece (the daughter of his wife's sister). The niece had her own home. Neither taxpayer nor his wife had legally adopted the wife's niece. If taxpayer and his wife file a joint return, an exemption for support of the wife's niece will be allowed. But if taxpayer files a separate return he cannot claim an exemption for his support of his wife's niece.[3]

Relationships created by marriage do not end by divorce or the death of a spouse. So, you may continue to claim an exemption for a dependent mother-in-law after your spouse dies [Sec. 1.152-2(d)].

(b) Member of taxpayer's household is one who during the taxpayer's entire tax year (or the part of it during which the household member lived) used the taxpayer's home as his principal place of abode [Sec. 152(a)(9)].

Illegal relationships. A person is not a member of the taxpayer's household if the relationship with the taxpayer is against the law [Sec. 152(b)(5); 1.152-1(b)].

¶ 1118 **Dependent's gross income** for the calendar year in which taxpayer's tax year begins, must be less than $750 [Sec. 151(e)(1)(A)]. This does not apply to taxpayer's children who are students or under 19 [(a) below].

Excludable income. In figuring a dependent's gross income, you exclude any type of exempt income. Generally, the tax-exempt benefits are considered in determining whether the support test is met [¶ 1116], if the claimed dependent has used them for his support [Sec. 1.152-1(a)(2)]. Thus, state aid benefits based solely on the dependent's needs are considered in determining support to the extent that they are used for his support.[1]

Example 1: Taxpayer's father earned $610 in 1977 at odd jobs. He also received $960 during the year in social security benefits. He put $300 in the bank, but used the rest for his own support. Taxpayer during the year paid $1,500 towards his father's support and claims him as a dependent. Since the social security payments are not considered income, the $750 gross income test is met. And while the father received a total of $1,570, only $1,270 was used for his support. Therefore, the taxpayer furnished more than half the support.

Dependent's depreciation deduction. No depreciation deduction is allowed on the dependent's property in figuring his gross income.

If the dependent has rental income, the gross rents are included, without deduction for taxes, repairs, etc.[2]

Background and purpose. Children who are under 19 or students are not required to meet the gross income test. This exception was made so that the parent who provides most of the support of a child who helps to pay his way through school by working part-time, does not lose a dependency exemption. Moreover, the test should not induce the child to stop work just before he reaches the maximum earnings level. Here, Congress relaxed the rule against doubling up of exemptions. Thus, a child under 19 or a child-student of any age may claim an exemption for himself on his own return even though his parents claim an exemption for him as a dependent.

(a) Children under 19 or students. The $750 gross income limitation does not apply if the dependent is the taxpayer's child and is (1) a student or (2) under 19 years old [Sec. 151(e)(1)(B); 1.151-2(a)].

Taxpayer's children include a stepson, stepdaughter, adopted son or daughter, or a foster child who is a member of the taxpayer's household [Sec. 152(b)(2); 1.151-3, 1.152-2].

"Students" are defined the same as for

the support test in ¶ 1116(b).
"**Under 19**" means child has not reached age 19 by end of calendar year in which taxpayer's tax year begins.

(b) If the dependent files a return. You may claim an exemption for a dependent whose gross income is less than $750, even if he files a separate return to claim a refund of the tax withheld from his income. However, his gross income must be less than $750 (unless he is a student or under 19 as noted in (a) above) even if he received more than one-half of his support from you.

> **Example 2:** Joe's 20-year-old bachelor brother earned $3,000 in 1977. He received more than half his support from Joe. Joe is not entitled to a $750 exemption deduction for his brother. The brother must file his own return, and gets a $750 exemption deduction for himself.
>
> Assume Joe also contributed more than half the support of his bachelor son who attended Harvard during 8 full months in 1977 and that his son earned $3,000 during the summer. Joe gets the $750 exemption for his son, even though the son must file his own return and can claim a $750 exemption for himself.

¶ 1119 Married dependents. Generally, a taxpayer loses an exemption for a married dependent who files a joint return [Sec. 151(e)(2); 1.151-2(a)].

> **Example:** Suppose you supported your married daughter for the entire year, and your daughter and her husband filed a joint return. Even though you meet all the other tests, you may not claim your daughter as a dependent. If, however, your son-in-law files a separate return, he may not claim an exemption for your daughter, since she would be your dependent.

However, taxpayer is entitled to the exemption if neither the dependent nor his spouse is required to file a return, but they file a joint return solely as a claim for refund of tax withheld, assuming, of course, that all the other requirements for the dependency exemption are met.[1]

¶ 1120 Citizens of foreign countries as dependents. A dependent, to qualify taxpayer for an exemption, must be a U.S. citizen or a resident of the U.S., Canada, Mexico, the Canal Zone, or the Republic of Panama at some time during the calendar year in which the taxpayer's tax year begins [Sec. 152(b)(3)], except in the circumstances described in (a) and (b) below. Children are usually citizens or residents of the country of their parents.[1] A resident of Puerto Rico does not qualify unless he is a U.S. citizen.

(a) Adopted alien child living abroad. If you are a U.S. citizen living abroad and legally adopt a child who is not a U.S. citizen nor a resident of the places named above, you may claim the child as a dependent providing that during the entire tax year your home is his or her principal residence and he or she is a member of your household [Sec. 152(b)(3); 1.152-2(a)(2)].

(b) Child living in Philippines. Residents of the Philippines can qualify as dependents if, before 1-1-56, they were born to or adopted by the taxpayer while he was in the U.S. Armed Forces [Sec. 152(b)(3); 1.152-2(a)].

METHODS OF FIGURING THE TAX

Basically, an individual uses either of two methods in figuring the tax liability: the tax tables or the tax rate schedules. Within this framework, options exist that serve to limit the individual's tax liability: the alternative capital gains tax [¶ 1614]; income averaging [¶ 2401]; a special ten-year averaging method involving lump-sum distributions [¶ 3024]; and the maximum tax on earned income [¶ 2402].

Chapter 1—Methods of Figuring Tax

¶ 1121 Tax rate schedules. The tax rates vary from 14% to 70% as provided in the Code for various types of taxpayers, although the income brackets to which the rates apply are different in each schedule [Sec. 1].

Who must use the rate schedules. For tax years starting after 1976, most taxpayers must use the tax tables [¶ 1122]. The relatively few taxpayers who are not eligible for the tables, must compute their taxable income (below) and use the rate schedule [Sec. 1, 3]. Such taxpayers include those:

- Whose tax table income exceeds the ceiling amount [¶ 1122];
- With large number of exemptions;
- Using income averaging [¶ 2401];
- Using the alternative capital gains tax [¶ 1614];
- Using the maximum tax [¶ 2402];
- Filing a short return on account of a change in accounting period [¶ 2715];
- Claiming a foreign income exclusion [¶ 3725];
- Estates and trusts [Ch. 20].

How to compute taxable income. First, start with your adjusted gross income [¶ 1102(c)]. Next, reduce the amount by any excess itemized deductions (the excess of your itemized deductions over your zero bracket amount, ¶ 1103(a)) and the deductions for personal exemptions [¶ 1111-1120]. Finally, increase your adjusted gross income by the unused zero bracket amount, if any (¶ 1102(f)) [Sec. 63(b)].

➤**NOTE→** Information on the Tax Rate Schedules is found in the Tax Charts at ¶ 5516.

¶ 1122 Using the tax tables. The use of the tax tables is simply a short-cut method of figuring the tax. The 1977 Tax Reduction and Simplification Act authorizes the IRS to incorporate the zero bracket amount [¶ 1107], the personal exemption, [¶ 1115-1120] and the general tax credit [¶ 1111(e)], into new tax tables based on tax table income. By establishing a floor amount under itemized deductions equal to the zero bracket amount, taxpayers who itemize will also use these tables.

Who must use tax tables. Those who must use tax tables include: unmarried individuals with tax table income of $20,000 or less and 3 or fewer exemptions; married individuals filing joint returns with tax table income of $40,000 or less and 9 or fewer exemptions [Sec. 3]. For how to compute tax table income, see ¶ 1102(h).

Who cannot use tax tables. Relatively few taxpayers are not eligible to use the tables. Those are the taxpayers who must use the rate schedules; see ¶ 1121.

➤**NOTE→** Information on the Tax Tables is found in the Tax Charts at ¶ 5517.

Footnotes to Chapter 1

(P-H "FEDERAL TAXES" related paragraphs are cited in brackets [ ] at the end of each footnote below)

Footnote ¶ 1100 [¶ 35,031 et seq.].
(1) Rev. Rul. 66-286, 1966-2 CB 485 [¶ 35,059(60)].
(2) Rev. Rul. 55-387, 1955-1 CB 131 [¶ 35,059(60)].
(3) Rev. Rul. 69-246, 1969-1 CB 300 [¶ 35,360(12)].

Footnote ¶ 1101 [¶ 35,036 et seq.].

Footnote ¶ 1101 continued
(1) Treas. Dept. booklet "Your Federal Income Tax" (1977 Ed.), p. 5.
(2) Instructions for Form 1040A.

Footnote ¶ 1102 [¶ 7611 et seq.].

Footnote ¶ 1103 [¶ 3410 et seq.].

Footnote ¶ 1103 continued
(1) Treas. Dept. booklet "Your Federal Income Tax" (1977 Ed.), pages 10-11.

Footnote ¶ 1104 [¶ 3436 et seq.].
(1) Treas Dept. booklet "Your Federal Income Tax" (1977 Ed.), p. 12.
(2) Comm. v. Eccles, 208 F.2d 796, 45 AFTR 34; W. G. Oster, 237 F.2d 501, 50 AFTR 314; Rev. Rul. 57-368, 1957-2 CB 896 [¶ 35,071(25)].
(3) Adv. Rev. Rul. 76-255 (IR-1632), IRB 1976-28 [¶ 9271(5)].
(4) Hoyle, ¶ 70,172 P-H Memo TC; Schinasi, 53 TC 383; Rev. Rul. 74-370, 1974-2 CB 7 [¶ 3431(30); 8981(10); 35,069(35)].

Footnote ¶ 1105 [¶ 3436 et seq.].

Footnote ¶ 1106 [¶ 3431 et seq.].
(1) Smith v. Comm., 13 AFTR 2d 1633, 332 F.2d 671 [¶ 3431(20)].
(2) Rev. Rul. 72-43, 1972-2 CB 4 [¶ 3431(20)].
(3) Muse v. U. S., 26 AFTR 2d 70-5771, 434 F.2d 349 [¶ 3431(20)].
(4) Rev. Rul. 70-279, 1970-1 CB 1; Robinson, 25 AFTR 2d 70-807 [¶ 3431(15)].
(5) Rev. Rul. 55-329, 1955-1 CB 205 [¶ 3431(30)].
(6) Rev. Rul. 55-711, 1955-2 CB 13; Rev. Rul. 74-370, 1974-2 CB 7 [¶ 3431(30)].
(7) Treas. Dept. booklet "Your Federal Income Tax" (1977 Ed.), p. 14.

Footnote ¶ 1108 [¶ 8951].

Footnote ¶ 1109 [¶ 8985].
(1) Rev. Rul. 57-368, 1975-2 CB 896 [¶ 9271(10)].

Footnote ¶ 1111 [¶ 9201 et seq.].

Footnote ¶ 1112 [¶ 9225; 9261].
(1) Rev. Rul. 57-368, 1957-2 CB 896 [¶ 9271(10)].
(2) Lewis, ¶ 50,015 P-H Memo TC [¶ 9227(10)].
(3) Rev. Rul. 71-158, 1971-1 CB 50 [¶ 9227(20)].
(4) Rev. Rul. 71-159, 1971-1 CB 50 [¶ 9227(20)].

Footnote ¶ 1113 [¶ 9225].

Footnote ¶ 1114 [¶ 9225].

Footnote ¶ 1115 [¶ 9231 et seq.].
(1) Treas. Dept. booklet "Your Federal Income Tax" (1977 Ed.) p. 16.

Footnote ¶ 1116 [¶ 9243 et seq.].
(1) Rev. Rul. 58-404, 1958-2 CB 56; Rev. Rul. 67-61, 1967-1 CB 27 [¶ 9243(5)].
(2) Rev. Rul. 58-67, 1958-1 CB 62 [¶ 9249(25)].
(3) Lustig v. Comm., 5 AFTR 2d 657, 274 F.2d 448 [¶ 9249(30)].
(4) Rev. Rul. 76-184, 1976-1 CB 44 [¶ 9249(150)].
(5) Markarian v. Comm., 16 AFTR 2d 5785, 352 F.2d 870 [¶ 9249(73)].

Footnote ¶ 1116 continued
(6) Rev. Rul. 58-67, 1958-1 CB 62 [¶ 9249(50)].
(7) Rev. Rul. 58-302, 1958-1 CB 62 [¶ 9245(20)].
(8) Treas. Dept. booklet "Your Federal Income Tax" (1977 Ed.), p. 18.
(9) Treas. Dept. booklet "Your Federal Income Tax" (1977 Ed.), p. 19.
(10) Rev. Rul. 64-223, 1964-2 CB 50 [¶ 9249(55)].
(11) Rev. Rul. 70-341, 1970-2 CB 31 [¶ 9249(75)].
(12) Rev. Rul. 74-543, 1974-2 CB 39 [¶ 9249(75)].
(13) Alfred Turecamo, 64 TC 71 [¶ 9249(75)].
(14) Scott, ¶ 50,248 P-H Memo TC [¶ 9251(40)].
(15) Rev. Rul. 70-87, 1970-1 CB 29 [¶ 9251(15)].
(16) Rev. Rul. 63-14, 1963-1 CB 29 [¶ 9239(95)].
(17) Rev. Rul. 57-344, 1957-2 CB 112; Rev. Rul. 58-419, 1958-2 CB 57 [¶ 9249(75)].
(18) Rev. Rul. 71-468, 1971-2 CB 115 [¶ 9249(95)].
(19) Abel, ¶ 62,192 P-H Memo TC; Rev. Rul. 64-222, 1964-2 CB 47 [¶ 9251(55)].
(20) Rev. Rul. 64-222, 1964-2 CB 47 [¶ 9251(50)].
(21) Rev. Rul. 73-175, 1973-1 CB 58 [¶ 9253(45)].
(22) Treas. Dept. booklet "Community Property and the Federal Income Tax" (1974 Ed.), p. 5.
(23) Rev. Rul. 58-403, 1958-2 CB 49 [¶ 9247(10)].
(24) Rev. Rul. 55-347, 1955-1 CB 21 [¶ 9247(10)].
(25) Comm. v. Ide, 14 AFTR 2d 5190, 335 F.2d 852 [¶ 9247(10)].
(26) Rev. Rul. 71-491, 1971-2 CB 114 [¶ 9247(50)].
(27) Rev. Rul. 59-379, 1959-2 CB 51, as modified by Rev. Rul. 60-190, 1960-1 CB 51; Rev. Rul. 61-186, 1961-2 CB 30; Rev. Rul. 64-221, 1964-2 CB 46 [¶ 9247(50)].

Footnote ¶ 1117 [¶ 9239].
(1) Rev. Rul. 71-468, 1971-2 CB 115 [¶ 9249(95)].
(2) See also Dewsbury v. U.S., 146 F. Supp. 467, 50 AFTR 955 [¶ 9239(170)].
(3) McCann, 12 TC 239 [¶ 9239(70)].

Footnote ¶ 1118 [¶ 9235].
(1) Rev. Rul. 71-468, 1971-2 CB 115 [¶ 9249(95)].
(2) Treas. Dept. booklet "Your Federal Income Tax" (1977 Ed.), p. 17.

Footnote ¶ 1119 [¶ 9237].
(1) Rev. Rul. 54-567, 1954-2 CB 108; Rev. Rul. 65-34, 1965-1 CB 86; Eason, ¶ 67,047 P-H Memo TC [¶ 9237].

Footnote ¶ 1120 [¶ 9241].
(1) Treas. Dept. booklet "Your Federal Income Tax" (1977 Ed.), p. 18.

Footnote ¶ 1121 [¶ 3411 et seq.].

Footnote ¶ 1122 [¶ 3446].

Highlights of Chapter 1

Individuals—Returns, Filing Status, Personal Exemptions and Rates

I. **Individual Income Tax Returns**
   A. **Who must file 1977 returns.** A citizen or resident alien files if [¶ 1100]:

   1. Single, under 65 and gross income of $2,950 or more.
   2. Single, 65 or over and gross income of $3,700 or more.
   3. Married, both spouses under 65 and gross income of $4,700 or more.
   4. Married, one spouse 65 or over and gross income of $5,450 or more.
   5. Married, both spouses 65 or over and gross income of $6,200 or more.
   6. Married filing separately with gross income of $750 or more.
   7. Surviving spouse with gross income of $3,950 or more.
   8. Surviving spouse 65 or over with gross income of $4,700 or more.
   9. Net earnings from self-employment of $400 or more.

   B. **Return forms.** Form 1040 with schedules, unless taxpayer uses Short Form 1040A [¶ 1101].
      1. Who may use Short Form 1040A [¶ 1101(b)]:
         a. All income from wages; tips (regardless of amount); not over $400 in dividends or interest.
         b. Cannot itemize deductions.
      2. Who cannot use Short Form 1040A [¶ 1101(b)]:
         a. Required to use other schedules of Form 1040.
         b. Claiming deductions for disability pension, moving expenses, forfeited interest penalty for premature withdrawal from time savings account, employee travel expenses, or outside salesperson's business expenses.
         c. Claiming investment credit, credit for the elderly, foreign tax, or gas tax for nonhighway use and such.
         d. Choosing income averaging.

II. **Elements in Figuring Tax**
   A. **Factors in tax computation [¶ 1102]:**
      1. Gross income
      2. Deductions for adjusted gross income
      3. Adjusted gross income
      4. Itemized deductions
      5. Zero bracket amount
      6. Unused zero bracket amount (in some cases)
      7. Personal exemptions
      8. Tax table income or taxable income
   B. **Steps in figuring tax [¶ 1103(a)].**
   C. **Tax figured by IRS [¶ 1103(b)]:**
      1. IRS will figure your tax if you leave out certain lines on your tax return, and file it by due date.
      2. Must not itemize deductions.

III. **Filing Status**
   A. **Married couples [¶ 1104]:**

1. Married taxpayers get income-splitting benefits if filing jointly.
2. Married taxpayers taxed at highest rates if filing separately.
3. Abandoned spouse not considered married.

B. **Surviving spouses [¶ 1105]:**
   1. First two years after year of spouse's death.
   2. A joint return could have been filed in year of spouse's death.
   3. Dependent son, daughter, stepchild or foster child lives with taxpayer.

C. **Head of household [¶ 1106]:**
   1. Unmarried.
   2. Maintain household for relative.
   3. Furnish costs of maintaining home.
   4. Citizen or resident status.
   5. Abandoned spouse may be able to file as head of household.

D. **Single taxpayers:**
   1. Single, divorced, legally separated or married to a nonresident alien.
   2. Not a head of household or surviving spouse.

IV. **Zero bracket amount (formerly standard deduction).**
   A. **Fixed amounts [¶ 1107]:**
      1. $3,200 if married filing jointly or surviving spouse.
      2. $2,200 if single, or head of household.
      3. $1,600 if married, filing separately.
      4. Zero in any other case.
   B. **Marital status [¶ 1109]:**
      1. Taxpayer's zero bracket amount determined by his or her marital status.
      2. Status determined at the end of tax year or on date of spouse's death.
      3. Abandoned spouse not considered married.

V. **Personal Exemptions**
   A. **Individual's exemptions [¶ 1111]:**
      1. $750 if single under 65 and not blind.
      2. $1,500 if single over 65 and not blind.
      3. $1,500 if single under 65 and blind.
      4. $2,250 if single, 65 or older and blind.
   B. **Married persons [¶ 1112—1114]:**
      1. $1,500 if filing jointly, both under 65 and not blind.
      2. $2,250 if filing jointly, one is 65 or older and neither blind.
      3. $2,250 if filing jointly, one is blind and both under 65.
      4. $3,000 if filing jointly, both 65 or older and neither blind.
      5. $3,000 if filing jointly, both blind and under 65.
      6. $3,000 if filing jointly, one is 65 or older and blind.
      7. $3,750 if filing jointly, one is 65 or older and both blind.
      8. $3,750 if filing jointly, one is blind and both 65 or older.
      9. $4,500 if filing jointly, both 65 or older and blind.
      10. Filing separately, exemption (or exemptions) for spouse allowed if:
          a. Spouse had no gross income;
          b. Spouse not a dependent of another taxpayer.
   C. **General tax credit** is greater of [¶ 1111(e)]:
      1. 2% of taxable income reduced by zero bracket amount, up to $9,000 ($4,500 if married and filing separately), or
      2. $35 for each personal exemption.
      3. Credit allowed for old-age or blindness.
      4. Married taxpayers filing separately must take $35-per-exemption credit.

VI. **Exemptions for Dependents [¶ 1115—1120]**
   A. **Support [¶ 1116]:**
      1. More than ½ of dependent's support.
      2. Dependent's gross income a factor in support requirement.

3. Children of divorced parents.
4. Multiple support agreements.
B. **Relationship [¶ 1117]:**
 1. Relative.
 2. Member of household.
C. **Dependent's gross income [¶ 1118]:**
 1. Must be less than $750.
 2. Gross income test does not apply to child who is student or under 19.
D. **Married dependent [¶ 1119]:**
 1. Cannot file jointly with spouse.
 2. Exemption allowed if joint return filed merely for refund.
E. Citizenship test [¶ 1120].
VII. Methods of Figuring Tax
 A. Tax rate schedules [¶ 1121].
 B. Tax table method [¶ 1122].

GROSS INCOME—GAIN OR LOSS
CAPITAL GAINS—DIVIDENDS

Chapter 2—GROSS INCOME—EXCLUSIONS
(Detailed Table of Contents below)

Chapter 3—GROSS INCOME—INCLUSIONS
(Detailed Table of Contents at page 1301)

Chapter 4—GAIN OR LOSS—RECOGNITION
(Detailed Table of Contents at page 1401)

Chapter 5—GAIN OR LOSS—BASIS
(Detailed Table of Contents at page 1501)

Chapter 6—CAPITAL GAINS AND LOSSES OF INDIVIDUALS
(Detailed Table of Contents at page 1601)

Chapter 7—DIVIDENDS
(Detailed Table of Contents at page 1701)

Chapter 2

GROSS INCOME—EXCLUSIONS
TABLE OF CONTENTS

INCOME IN GENERAL

	¶
Income—gross income—taxable income	1201
What an exclusion is	1202

INTEREST ON GOVERNMENT OBLIGATIONS

	¶
Interest on obligations of U.S., its possessions and instrumentalities	1203
U.S. obligations	
Obligations of U.S. possessions	
Obligations of U.S. instrumentalities	
Federal tax refunds	
Interest on state and municipal obligations	1204

INSURANCE PROCEEDS

	¶
Life insurance—amounts paid by reason of death of insured	1213
Sale of policy	
Proceeds held under agreement to pay interest	
Interest element taxable	
Proceeds payable to shareholders	
Life insurance—surrender of policy before death	1214
Life insurance—endowment contracts	1215
Lump sum payment	
Proceeds payable in installments	
Option to receive annuity instead of lump sum	
Dividends on life insurance and endowment policies	1216
Social security, unemployment insurance benefits and public assistance payment	1217

DISABILITY BENEFITS

	¶
Compensation for injuries or sickness	1218

Footnotes appear at end of this Chapter.

¶

Workmen's compensation
  Accident or health insurance benefits
  Pension and disability payments to members of armed service
Employee accident and health plans .. 1219
  Excluded benefits
  What plans qualify
  Certain disability payments (sick pay)
Employer contributions to accident or health plans 1220
Taxable benefits under employer accident or health plans 1221
Medicare benefits 1222

GIFTS AND DAMAGES

Gifts and bequests 1225
  What is a gift
  Gifts to minors
Damages 1226

ANNUITIES

Annuities in general 1230
  What are annuity payments
  Exclusion ratio
  Annuity starting date

¶

  Investment in the contract
  Expected return under the contract
  Dividends received under annuity contract
  Surrender, redemption or maturity of annuity
  Variable payment annuities
  Two annuities for single consideration
  Private annuities
Joint and survivor annuities 1231
Employees' annuities 1232
  Is it a "qualified" annuity plan?
  How contributions are treated
  Lump sum proceeds
  Proceeds taxed as an annuity
  Nonqualified plan—certain exempt organizations or educational institutions
  Employer an insurance company
  Federal employees
  State and municipal employees
  Servicemen

• Highlights of Chapter 2 .... Page 1261

INCOME IN GENERAL

¶ **1201 Income—gross income—taxable income.** Income (in the broad sense) means all wealth which flows to the taxpayer other than as a mere return *of* capital. It includes gains and profits from any source, including gains from the sale or other disposition of capital assets. It is *not* a gain *accruing* to capital, not a *growth* or *increment* of value in an investment, but a gain or profit, something of exchangeable value, proceeding from the capital.[1]

Example 1: Walsh bought 100 shares of X stock on August 2 for $20 per share, or a total of $2,000. On December 31, the stock was listed at $25 per share on the stock exchange. This $500 increase in the value of the 100 shares of stock (from $2,000 to $2,500) is *not* income but a growth or increment in the value of the stock. This growth or increment will not be income until it is realized by a sale or exchange of the stock.

Example 2: On January 2, Thomas Stone borrowed $300 from the Fourth National Bank. He repaid the loan, plus 8% interest, by the end of the year. Of the $324 received by the bank during the year, $300 is a return of capital (not income) to the bank. The $24 interest is income, since it constitutes a realized gain.

Gross income means income (in the broad sense) less income exempt from tax [Sec. 61]. Items included in gross income are known as *inclusions* [Sec. 71 et seq.]. Exempt items are excluded from gross income and are commonly referred to as *exclusions* (¶ 1202) [Sec. 101 et seq.]. They should not be confused with the *deductions* allowed by law. Taxable income is gross income less deductions.

Example 3: Assume that during the year John Hart received $12,000 salary, $400 interest on a bank deposit, and $100 interest on a municipal bond that he owned. He paid a property tax of $2,000 and $475 interest on a mortgage on his residence. His deduction for personal exemptions was $750.

Hart's *income* (in the broad sense) is $12,500. Interest from the municipal bond, however, is exempt, and in filing his return, Hart *excludes* it from gross income. His statutory *gross income* is, therefore, $12,400. He is entitled to *deductions* for the property tax of $2,000, mortgage interest of $475 and deduction for personal exemption of $750. His *taxable income* (gross income less deductions) is $9,175, expressed mathematically—

Income (in the broad sense) — Exclusions = Gross income
$12,500   — $100   = $12,400
Gross income — Deductions = Taxable income
$12,400 — $3,225 ($2,000 + $475 + $750) = $9,175

NOTE: In this example we show no deductions for adjusted gross income. If there are both deductions for adjusted gross income and excess itemized deductions, taxable income is gross income less (1) deductions for adjusted gross income, (2) excess itemized deductions and (3) deductions for personal exemptions. See ¶ 1102.

While income does not include a return of capital, it does include gains from sales or exchanges.

Example 4: Assume the same facts as Example 3, except that during the year Hart bought some building lots for $8,800 and sold them immediately for $10,000. The $10,000 is not all income. Part of it ($8,800) is a return of capital. The profit on the sale ($1,200) is income and is not exempt. It must be included in Hart's return as gross income, increasing his taxable income to $10,375.

Income (in the broad sense) — Exclusions = Gross income
$13,700   — $100   = $13,600
Gross income — Deductions = Taxable income
$13,600 — $3,225 ($2,000 + $475 + $750) = $10,375

¶ **1202 What an exclusion is.** Exclusion of an item from gross income means, in a practical sense, that the item is not a part of the gross income that is the starting point in computing the income tax. An item may be excluded from gross income for any one of the following reasons: (1) it is not taxable under the U.S. Constitution; (2) it does not come within the definition of the term "income" (e.g., a return of capital) [¶ 1201]; (3) it is expressly excluded by statute.

Items in classes (1) and (2) are *wholly* exempt (excluded). Items in class (3) may be either *wholly* or *partially* exempt, depending upon the language of the statute, which Congress may change at will.

NOTE: In addition to the specific categories of exclusions found in this chapter (certain interest and insurance proceeds, annuities, disability benefits, gifts and damages), some other items of excludable income covered later in the text are: (1) Certain payments made by an employer to an employee's beneficiaries by reason of the employee's death [¶ 1304]; (2) Gain in whole, or in part, on the sale of a residence by a taxpayer 65 or over [¶ 1423]; (3) First $100 in dividends received from domestic corporations [¶ 1705 et seq.]; (4) Certain stock distributions and stock rights [¶ 1708; 1711]; (5) Recovery of bad debts, prior taxes, delinquency amounts and other deductions taken in prior years, if tax benefit rule applies [¶ 2316]; (6) Certain pay of foreign government employees [¶ 3708]; (7) Income exempt by treaty [¶ 3709, 3710]; (8) Income of certain foreign central banks [¶ 3712]; (9) Earned income of citizens from sources outside U.S. [¶ 3725]; (10) Certain allowances to U.S. employees in foreign service [¶ 3726]; (11) Income from sources within U.S. possessions [¶ 3727].

INTEREST ON GOVERNMENT OBLIGATIONS

Interest on state and municipal bonds are entirely tax exempt. But this does not apply to interest on obligations of the U.S., its agencies and instrumentalities. Special rules apply to interest on arbitrage and industrial development bonds.

¶ 1203 **Interest on obligations of the United States, its possessions and instrumentalities.** **(a) U.S. obligations.** Interest on U.S. obligations generally is included in gross income [Public Debt Act of 1941, Sec. 4(a)]. For the taxation of U.S. bonds issued at a discount, see ¶ 2723.

(b) Obligations of U.S. possessions. Interest on obligations of U.S. possessions is excluded from gross income [Sec. 103(a); 1.103-1].

(c) Obligations of U.S. instrumentalities. Interest on obligations of U.S. agencies as instrumentalities issued on or after 3-1-41 is included in gross income [Sec. 1.103-4(b)].

(d) Federal tax refunds. Interest on a refund of a federal tax must be included in gross income.[1]

¶ 1204 **Interest on state and municipal obligations.** Generally interest on obligations of a state, territory, or political subdivision is excludable from gross income except on certain industrial development bonds. The term "political subdivision" includes counties, cities and towns. It may or may not include special assessment districts,[1] such as road, water, school districts and the like [Sec. 103; 1.103-1]. An obligation can be issued *on behalf of* a state or local government. However, the issuing authority must be specifically authorized by state law to issue the obligation for a definite public purpose [Prop. Reg. Sec. 1.103-1(c)(1)].

INTEREST EXCLUDED

Bonds of Triborough Bridge (N.Y.)[2] and Port of N.Y. Authorities;[3] N.Y. State Housing Finance Agency obligations;[4] federally backed bonds of local housing authorities;[5] notes given by a state political subdivision in payment of purchase price of property;[6] profit on sale of certificate of indebtedness for past due municipal bond interest coupons (tax-free interest, not taxable gain).[7]

INTEREST NOT EXCLUDED

Industrial development bonds. Interest on bonds issued after 4-30-68 taxable with exceptions: (1) bond issues of $1 million or less exempt; (2) issues of $5 million or less exempt if local government elects small-issue exemption; (3) issues for certain designated types of facilities (sports, trade shows, conventions, etc.); (4) bonds committed for sale before 5-1-68 and issued before 1-1-69 [Sec. 103(c); 1.103-7—12].

Arbitrage bonds. These are state and local obligations whose proceeds are intended to be used to acquire obligations with "materially higher" yields. Interest on such bonds issued after 10-9-69 are taxable except when proceeds are: (1) temporarily invested until needed for purpose for which issued; (2) used to a limited extent to buy securities for required reserve or replacement fund such as retirement fund; or (3) ultimately to provide certain residential housing [Sec. 103(d); Prop. Reg. 1.103-13, 14; Temp. Reg. Sec. 13.4].

Condemnation awards. Interest paid by a state or political subdivision on an award.[8]

Certain municipal bonds. Brokers' Class B interest coupons detached from bonds;[9] "market discount" from par value, extended to investors by a broker on the purchase of bonds.[10]

INSURANCE PROCEEDS

Generally, life insurance proceeds paid by reason of the death of the insured can be excluded from gross income. This is not the case for proceeds determined to be alimony. Excludability of payments made for reasons other than the insured's death depends on their nature.

¶ **1213 Life insurance—amounts paid by reason of death of insured.** Such benefits generally are excluded from gross income [Sec. 101(a); 1.101-1].

Example 1: Taxpayer takes out a life insurance policy for $20,000, with his wife as beneficiary. If taxpayer dies, the $20,000 received by the widow is exempt.

(a) Sale of policy. If a life insurance contract, or an interest in one, is transferred for a valuable consideration, the exclusion of the death proceeds is limited to the consideration paid plus the premiums or other sums subsequently paid by the buyer. However, all of the proceeds are excludable if:

(1) the buyer's basis is determined by reference to the seller's basis in the contract [¶ 1514 et seq.]; or

(2) the transfer of the contract was to the insured, his partner, a partnership that includes the insured, or a corporation in which the insured is a shareholder or officer [Sec. 101(a); 1.101-1(b)].

(b) Proceeds held under agreement to pay interest. If the proceeds are held by the insurer under an agreement to pay interest, the interest payments must be included in gross income [Sec. 101(c); 1.101-3].

Example 2: A $100,000 life insurance policy calls for payments of $3,000 a year for 10 years, with the $100,000 payable after 10 years. The beneficiary has $3,000 interest income in each of the 10 years. The $100,000 is tax free.

(c) Interest element taxable. If the life insurance contract contains an agreement or option to pay the proceeds at a time later than death, the interest element of the proceeds held by the insurer is taxable to the beneficiary. This interest element is determined by prorating the present value of the life insurance proceeds as of the date of death over the period of the payments. The prorated amount is excluded from the beneficiary's income. Amounts over that are taxable as interest [Sec. 101(d); 1.101-4(c)].

Example 3: A life insurance policy is worth $100,000 at the insured's death but the beneficiary elects under the policy to take $12,000 a year for 10 years instead of the lump sum. He gets $10,000 a year tax free, but the remaining $2,000 a year is taxable as interest.

Surviving spouse's exclusion. The insured's spouse may exclude up to $1,000 of interest each year unless paid under an agreement to pay interest only [Sec. 101(d); 1.101-4].

Background and purpose. Surviving spouses are granted this exclusion to encourage them to take the life insurance proceeds in installments so as not to waste the principal.

Example 4: Mr. Gerber made his wife the beneficiary of a $50,000 (face amount) insurance policy on his life. The policy provided that the proceeds were to be paid to Gerber's widow in 10 annual installments. The portion of each installment that can be excluded from gross income is $5,000 ($50,000 ÷ 10). Any amount that Gerber's widow actually receives as an installment in excess of $5,000 must be included in her gross income as interest, except to the extent that her $1,000 annual interest exclusion applies. Thus, if she actually receives an installment of $6,200, she must include $200 in her gross income.

Example 5: If the contract in Example 4 called for payments to Gerber's widow for life, instead of 10 equal payments, the $50,000 lump sum would be divided by the present life expectancy of Gerber's widow determined from the mortality tables used by the insurer. With a life expectancy of 20 years, $2,500 would be excluded each year ($50,000 ÷ 20), plus her annual interest exclusion of $1,000, making a total exclusion of $3,500.

Footnotes appear at end of this Chapter.

A "family income rider" provides term insurance with a lump-sum payment after the term. If a single life insurance contract has a "family income rider" and the insured dies during the term period, only the interest paid on the term insurance amount comes within the $1,000 exclusion [Sec. 1.101-4(h)].

Only one exclusion. A surviving spouse gets only one exclusion for each insured regardless of the number of policies, but gets a separate exclusion for each insured deceased spouse.

Example 6: Assume the same facts as in Example 4, except that Gerber had two $50,000 (face amount) policies, *each* paying his widow an annual installment of $6,200 for 10 years. The annual amount included in gross income is $1,400 ($6,200 + $6,200 — $5,000 — $5,000 — $1,000).

Example 7: Assume that Mrs. Smith is the widow of both Mr. Jones (husband no. 1) and Mr. Smith (husband no. 2). She is the beneficiary of a policy on each husband's life of the type set forth in Example 4. The annual amount included in gross income is $400 ($6,200 + $6,200 — $5,000 — $5,000 — $1,000 — $1,000).

Option to take lump sum. If one of the options in the insurance contract is to take a specific amount in a lump sum, that is the amount that is prorated. But if there is no option, the amount that can be excluded is determined by finding the value of the agreement (with respect to each beneficiary) as of the date the insured died, discounted on the basis of the interest rate and mortality tables used in determining the payments.[1]

Example 8: If a surviving spouse would receive an annuity for a fixed period (or life) under one option, and under the remaining option she would receive a different sum (or the same sum for a different time), and her daughter would receive an annuity for a given period, the values to each would be determined after the wife's selection of an option, as of the date the insured died. For instance, assume that the wife, having a life expectancy of 20 years, selected an option under which she is to receive $5,000 a year for life, and the daughter $5,000 a year for 10 years. Assume also that the discounted value to the wife under the selected option is $60,000 and to the daughter $35,000. The wife would then exclude $3,000 of each installment ($60,000 ÷ 20) and an additional $1,000 because of her special exclusion, for a total of $4,000 of each installment. Her daughter can exclude $3,500 of each installment ($35,000 ÷ 10).

(d) Proceeds payable to shareholders. The Revenue Service says life insurance proceeds paid to shareholders of a corporation will be taxed as dividends when the corporation uses its earnings to pay the premiums and has all the incidents of ownership, including the right to name itself beneficiary. This applies even if the corporation is not the beneficiary and so does not receive the proceeds.[2] However, the Sixth Circuit holds that the proceeds are not taxable as dividends if they were neither a corporation's assets nor distributed by the corporation.[3]

¶ 1214 **Life insurance—surrender of policy before death.** If a life insurance policy is surrendered by the insured for a lump sum, he has taxable income to the extent the amount received exceeds the net premiums paid [Sec. 72(e)(2); 1.72-11(d)]. No loss is recognized when a life insurance policy is surrendered before maturity and premiums paid exceed cash surrender value.[1] For surrender of an insurance policy taken out before 3-1-13 see ¶ 1506.

¶ 1215 **Life insurance—endowment contracts.** The general rules are:

(a) **Lump sum payment.** If the proceeds are received in a lump sum, on maturity or surrender, only the excess of the amounts received over the premiums paid is included in gross income [Sec. 72(e)(2); 1.72-11(d)]. Income averaging may reduce the tax liability [¶ 2401].

(b) Proceeds payable in installments. Proceeds payable in installments for life are taxed the same as other annuities (see ¶ 1230) [Sec. 72(a)]. If they are payable for a fixed number of years, as in the case of an endowment contract, the amount that can be excluded each year is determined by dividing the cost of the contract by the number of annual payments [Sec. 72(c)(3)(B)].

(c) Option to receive annuity instead of lump sum. Amounts received under a paid-up endowment or similar contract will be taxed as an annuity [¶ 1230], if the policyholder elects to receive the payments in installments. Election must be made within 60 days after he has the right to receive a lump sum. This merely eliminates any question of constructive receipt of the proceeds. If the election is not made until after the 60-day period, the conversion is treated as if the beneficiary constructively received the lump-sum proceeds and reinvested them in an installment contract. Any gain (excess of lump-sum proceeds over cost) is taxable in the year of conversion, and is added to the cost of the annuity. The installment payments will be taxed like other annuity payments [Sec. 72(h); 1.72-12].

¶ 1216 Dividends on life insurance and endowment policies. Dividends on unmatured life or endowment insurance policies are a partial return of premiums paid and are not includible in income until they exceed the accumulated net premiums paid for the contract. However, interest paid or credited by the insurance company on dividends left with it is taxable.[1]

When proceeds are paid at maturity, the tax-free dividends are added to them, and the excess of this sum over cost of the insurance is included in income. [Sec. 72(e)(1); 1.72-11].

Government insurance. Veterans' insurance proceeds and dividends are not taxable either to the veteran or to his beneficiaries. The proceeds of a veteran's endowment policy paid before his death are also exempt, but interest on dividends left on deposit with the Veterans Administration is taxable.[1] The "Veterans' Benefit Act of 1957," currently in force, continues the tax exemption of benefits under previous veterans' laws.[2]

¶ 1217 Social security, unemployment insurance benefits and public assistance payments. (a) Social security benefits. Benefits received (including medicare payments) under the U.S. social security program[1] or lump-sum payments under the Railroad Retirement Act[2] may be excluded from tax. Benefits received under social security systems of foreign countries may not be excluded; benefit payments representing a return of cost may be excluded under the annuity rules [¶ 1230 et seq.].[3]

(b) Unemployment insurance benefits received from a state are not taxable.[4] Likewise, unemployment compensation payments made to federal employees by state or federal agencies[5] and unemployment insurance benefits received from the federal government by railroad workers covered by the Railroad Unemployment Insurance Act are not taxable.[6] However, supplemental unemployment benefit payments from a company financed fund or from a former employer generally are taxable. See ¶ 1307(d).

(c) Public assistance payments. Benefit payments from a general welfare fund in the interest of the general public, such as payments because of blindness, are not included in gross income.[7]

Footnotes appear at end of this Chapter.

DISABILITY BENEFITS

Disability benefits fall into two main classes of exclusions: (1) compensation for injuries and sickness, and (2) employee accident and health plans. A taxpayer may receive a number of benefits for one injury or sickness, some of which fall into one class of exclusion and some into another. The fact that the payments overlap does not affect the right to respective exclusions. The exclusions are apportioned if benefits received from one source have been financed partly by the taxpayer and partly by the employer.

¶ 1218 **Compensation for injuries or sickness.** (a) **Workmen's compensation.** Amounts received under workmen's compensation acts as compensation for personal injuries or sickness are excluded from gross income [Sec. 104(a)]. Nonoccupational disability benefits or occupational benefits received in excess of workmen's compensation cannot be excluded under this provision, but may qualify for exclusion as benefits under an accident or health plan (¶ 1219) [Sec. 1.104-1].

NOTE: Payments received by firemen and policemen on pension for total permanent disability caused by or arising out of their duties are in the nature of workmen's compensation and exempt.[1] When a state court ruled that occupational benefits in lieu of workmen's compensation actually were workmen's compensation, the Revenue Service allowed the entire amount to be excluded, even though the benefits exceeded the normal benefits payable under workmen's compensation.[2]

(b) **Accident or health insurance benefits.** You may exclude:

• Benefits from accident or health insurance you purchased yourself.
• Benefits from state sickness or disability funds [Sec. 104(a); 1.104-1(d)].

You may not exclude:

• Benefits attributable to deductible contributions on behalf of a self-employed person to a qualified retirement plan.
• Benefits attributable to medical deductions allowed for an earlier year [Sec. 104(a)].
• Insurance proceeds that reimburse you for business overhead expenses.[3]

(c) **Pension and disability payments to members of armed service.** Pensions, annuities, or similar allowances for personal injuries or sickness resulting from active service in the armed forces of any country or in the Coast and Geodetic Survey, or in the Public Health Service are exempt from tax [Sec. 104(a)(4); 1.104-1(e)]. The exclusion is not available, however, for persons receiving noncombat related disability pensions who joined the armed forces after 9-24-75 [Sec. 104(b)].

EXCLUDED

Retirement pay of officer retired for age, but eligible for disability retirement;[4] retirement pay of officer originally retired for age, recalled to active duty, and later ordered home for disability;[5] when retirement is for disability, but officer elects to have his retirement pay computed on the basis of length of service, portion that he would have received for his disability is exempt;[6] disability pay and pensions paid to veterans or their widows;[7] reduction in retirement pay to provide survivor annuities [¶ 1232(i)]; grants to seriously disabled veterans for homes designed for "wheelchair living" and for motor vehicles to those who lost their sight or the use of their limbs;[7] VA death benefits to families of deceased veterans;[7] subsistence, education or training allowances to veterans;[8] bonus payments to veterans paid by their states.[9]

¶ 1219 **Employee accident and health plans.** (a) **Excluded benefits.** An employee can exclude from his income all or part of three benefits attributable to the employer's contributions to accident and health plans. These are: (1) sick pay [(c) below]; (2) reimbursement for medical expenses of the employee, his wife or dependents that are not deducted as itemized medical expenses [Sec. 105(b);

1.105-2]; (3) benefits paid for loss of an arm, leg, or other bodily function[1] by the employee, his wife, or dependent, *if* the amounts payable are based on the nature of the injury and not on the time the employee is absent from work (the employee can also take the medical expense deduction) [Sec. 105; 1.105-3].

(b) What plans qualify. A *qualified* accident or health plan must be a *prior* arrangement or practice for paying employees in the event of personal injuries or sickness.[1]

- It may cover one or more employees;
- There may be different plans for different employees or classes of employees;
- It can discriminate in favor of highly paid or key employees, even if they also are officer-shareholders,[2] but it must benefit employees, not officer-shareholders only;[3]
- It may be insured or uninsured;
- It may be contributory or noncontributory;
- The plan's notice must be reasonably available to the employee;
- It does not matter who pays the benefits provided by the plan [Sec. 1.105-5].
- The plan must be in writing.

NOTE: The employee's rights to benefits need not be enforceable. But if this is the case, the employee must be covered by a plan providing for payments to the employee for personal injuries or sickness.

(c) Certain disability payments (sick pay). A taxpayer can exclude a limited amount of disability pay from gross income if all four conditions are met [Sec. 105(d); Temp. Reg. Sec. 7.105-1]:

- The taxpayer has not reached age 65 before the end of the tax year.
- The taxpayer has not reached mandatory retirement age at the start of the tax year.

NOTE: This is the age at which the taxpayer would have been required to retire under the employer's retirement program.

- The taxpayer was permanently and totally disabled at the time of retirement (or was permanently and totally disabled on 1-1-77 if retired before then on disability or under circumstances that allowed taxpayer to retire on disability).

NOTE: The taxpayer must be unable to be gainfully employed because of a physical or mental impairment that has lasted, or can be expected to last at least 12 months, or which can be expected to result in death. Proof from a qualified physician must be furnished to the Revenue Service.

- The taxpayer has not made the irrevocable election not to claim the disability income exclusion.

NOTE: The taxpayer can make an irrevocable election not to claim the exclusion if (1) retired on disability before 1-1-77 and (a) on 12-31-76 was entitled to exclude any disability income as sick pay; or (b) on 1-1-77 was permanently or totally disabled; or (2) retired after 1976 and was permanently and totally disabled at retirement. The election is made by attaching a statement to the return.

Background and purpose. The Tax Reform Act of 1976 repealed the sick pay rules for tax years starting after 1975. However, the Tax Reduction and Simplification Act of 1977 changed the effective date of the new rules to tax years beginning after 1976. *Pre-1977 rules:* (1) For the first 7 days, up to $75 of the sick pay was excludable from gross income if the taxpayer was hospitalized for at least one of those days and the sick pay wasn't in excess of 75% of regular pay. (2) For the 8th

Footnotes appear at end of this Chapter.

¶ 1219

to the 30th day, up to $75 per week was excludable if the sick pay wasn't in excess of 75% of regular pay. (3) For the 31st day and on, $100 per week was excludable. Taxpayers who made "irrevocable" elections under the new rules can revoke the elections and file amended returns or continue to be treated by the Tax Reform Act changes.

Limitation on exclusion. The maximum amount of disability payments that can be excluded from income is $100 a week ($5,200 annually). The maximum amount excludable is reduced dollar-for-dollar for adjusted gross income (including disability income) above $15,000 [Sec. 105(d)(2)].

> **Example:** Charles Howell collected $5,200 disability pay during the year. He also received other income and his adjusted gross income for the year was $21,000. He cannot exclude any disability income because his adjusted gross income exceeds the limitation of $20,200 ($15,000 + 5,200).

Special rules. In order to claim the exclusion, a married taxpayer must file a joint return, unless the spouses have lived apart for the entire year [Sec. 105(d)(4)]. Persons who retired before 1-1-77 on disability (or were entitled to retire on disability) and who on 1-1-77 were totally and permanently disabled are allowed to claim the exclusion if they otherwise qualify [Sec. 105(d)(5)]. The exclusion allowed on disability income in the form of an annuity is deferred until the taxpayer reaches 65 or until an earlier year when he or she makes an irrevocable election to forego further sick pay benefits [Sec. 105(d)(7)].

¶ **1220 Employer contributions to accident or health plans.** Contributions by an employer to compensate his employees for personal injuries or sickness are excluded from the employees' gross incomes. The exclusion applies whether the contribution is made by paying an insurance premium or by some other means. It also applies whether the plan covers one employee or a group. Therefore, the premium paid by an employer for an individual policy of accident and health insurance would not be taxable to the employee[1] [Sec. 1.106-1]. A plan can discriminate in favor of highly paid or key employees, even if they also are officer-shareholders,[2] but it must also benefit employees, not only officer-shareholders.[3]

¶ **1221 Taxable benefits under employer accident or health plans.** Benefits that are not among the excluded ones [¶ 1219] must be included in the employee's gross income. These are benefits (other than sick pay, reimbursement for medical expenses or payments for loss of limb) paid by the employer or attributable to employer contributions that are not taxed to the employee [Sec. 104(a)(3), 105(a); 1.104-1(d), 1.105-1]. Benefits provided in contributory pension or profit-sharing plans are considered to be from employer contributions, unless the plan expressly provides otherwise [Sec. 1.72-15]. Benefits received by an owner-employee [¶ 1839] under a self-employed retirement plan are taxable [Sec. 1.105-1(a), 1.105-5(b)].

Allocating taxable benefits based on employee and employer contributions. When contributions are made jointly by the employee and the employer, the benefits received must be allocated between the two. In the case of an individual policy under a contributory insured plan, the amount resulting from the employer's contribution is proportionate to the premiums he paid for the policy year [Sec. 1.105-1(d)].

> **Example 1:** Gorham maintains a plan whereby he pays $2/3$ of the annual premiums on accident and health insurance for his employees. The remainder of each employee's premium is paid by a payroll deduction from the employee's wages. The annual premium for employee Frost is $24, of which $16 is paid by Gorham. $16/24$ or $2/3$ of all amounts received by Frost under the insurance policy are includible in Frost's gross income. The remaining $1/3$ is excludable.

When there is a group policy, the amount resulting from the employer's contribution is proportionate to the net premiums contributed by the employer for the last 3 policy years. If the policy has not been in force for 3 years, then the period it has been in force is used [Sec. 1.105-1(d)].

Example 2: Mr. Barnard has a plan under which he pays part of the cost of a group accident and health insurance policy and his employees pay the balance of the cost through payroll deductions. The policy year starts Nov. 1 and ends Oct. 31. The net premium for the policy year ended 10-31-76 is not known on 1-1-77, because certain retroactive premium adjustments cannot be determined until after Jan. 1. Therefore, the last 3 policy years are the policy years ended Oct. 31, 1973, 1974, 1975. Assume that net premiums were paid as follows:

Policy year	Net premiums	Employer's Contribution
10-31-75	$ 8,000	$3,000
10-31-74	9,000	3,500
10-31-73	7,000	1,500
	$24,000	$8,000

$8,000/$24,000, or 1/3 of the amounts received by an employee at any time during 1977, must be included in gross income.

If an employee receives amounts under a contributory noninsured plan, the portion resulting from the employer's contribution is proportionate to the employer's contributions for the 3 calendar years (or the lesser period the plan was in effect) before the year of receipt [Sec. 1.105-1(d)].

¶ **1222 Medicare benefits.** Basic medicare benefits received under the Social Security Act are excluded from gross income since they are considered social security payments. Supplementary benefits (covering costs of doctors' services and other items not covered under basic Medicare) are also excluded since they are in the nature of medical insurance payments.[1] The employer-paid medicare premiums are not income to an employee since these are considered contributions to employer accident or health plans.[2]

GIFTS AND DAMAGES

While there is no tax when gifts, bequests, devises or inheritances are received, income from such property is usually taxable. Generally, damages awarded for personal injury or libel are not taxable except for punitive damages.

¶ **1225 Gifts and bequests.** The value of property received by gift, bequest, devise or inheritance can be excluded, but the income from the property is taxable. Thus, when payment under the terms of a gift or bequest is to be made at intervals, the payments are taxable to the donee or beneficiary to the extent they are made out of income [Sec. 102; 1.102-1].

Problem: Sy Stone received $10,000 in cash under a testamentary trust. Shortly thereafter, he invested this sum in corporate bonds and received $1,600 in interest during the year. What must he report as gross income for the year?

Solution: $1,600. Property received under a will is exempt from income tax, but not income derived from property due to investment.

There is no exclusion when income from property, rather than the property itself, is the subject of a bequest or gift [Sec. 102; 1.102-1(c)]. But a gift or bequest of a specific sum of money or specific property can be excluded, even though paid out of income, if it is required under the terms of the governing instrument to be

Footnotes appear at end of this Chapter.

paid or credited all at once or in not more than 3 installments. If under the terms of the governing instrument, it is required to be paid or credited in more than 3 installments or if it can be paid or credited only out of income, the bequest or gift is taxable [Sec. 663(a)(1); 1.663(a)-1].

EXCLUDED

Amount received by an heir in settlement of a will contest;[1] settlement made by a legatee under a prior will who contested probate of a later will;[2] political contributions used for campaign or similar purposes[3] (but not when diverted to personal use[3] or payoffs for political favors[4]).

NOT EXCLUDED

Interest on an undistributed legacy paid out of income of the estate;[5] amount received in compromise of a claim against estate of person who died without a will, based upon his promise to take care of taxpayer in his will in exchange for taxpayer's personal services (no tax-exempt bequest or inheritance, and not an amount received in settlement of a will contest);[6] amount received for an annuity in consideration for taxpayer's surrender of her right to contest her father's will held taxable to the extent it exceeds the fair market value of the annuity.[7]

Background and purpose. Gifts and bequests are exclusions since these are taxed at rather highly graduated rates (for example, gift taxes).

(a) What is a gift. The courts have defined a gift as a gratuitous transfer of property.[8] The essential elements of a gift are:

- A donor competent to make the gift.
- A clear intention on donor's part to make a gift.
- A donee capable of taking the gift.
- An irrevocable conveyance, assignment or transfer sufficient to vest legal title in the donee.
- Relinquishing dominion and control of the subject matter of the gift by delivery to the donee.

⇒**OBSERVATION→** Gifts of income property to relatives or persons in a confidential relationship are scrutinized carefully by the Revenue Service.[9] This is especially true of gifts and lease-backs to donor of property used in the donor's business. Under this arrangement, the donor can shift some of his business income to the donee by making lease payments that are based in whole or in part on the profits of the business.

(b) Gifts to minors. Under model acts adopted by all the states and the District of Columbia, title to securities can be transferred to minors without the formalities of special guardianship or trust. Although income from gift property ordinarily is taxable to the donee, income from "model act" gifts used to satisfy anybody's legal obligation to support a minor is taxable to the person whose support obligation is satisfied, no matter who made the gift.[10]

¶ **1226 Damages.** Damages are a form of reimbursement, whether received under a judgment or in compromise of a claim. To determine whether damages are income, the nature of the item for which the damages are a substitute generally must be considered.[1] Damages relating to personal or family rights can be excluded from gross income.[2] Damages for loss of or injury to capital also can be excluded, unless they exceed the basis of the capital.[1] However, damages for loss of profits[3] and punitive damages, such as treble damages under antitrust laws and exemplary damages for fraud, must be included in gross income [Sec. 1.61-14].

EXCLUDED

Personal or family rights: Damanges for slander and libel (but not exemplary damages);[4] award for loss of life.[5]

Return of capital: Damages for injury to goodwill of a business,[1] except to the extent they exceed its basis.[6]

Patent infringement or antitrust damages: Damages received for patent infringement, breach of contract or fiduciary duty and recoveries (except punitive damages) under the Clayton Act for antitrust violations are excluded from gross income to the extent that the losses to which the damages relate did not give rise to a tax benefit either in the recovery year or earlier tax years [Sec. 186; 1.186-1].

NOT EXCLUDED

Punitive damages: Treble damages recovered under the Clayton Act;[7] "insider profits" recovered under the Securities Exchange Act of 1934 or the Investment Company Act of 1940.[8] The insider also pays tax on the profits, but gets a loss deduction in the year of repayment. The loss may be ordinary or capital, according to whether the stock transactions produce ordinary income or capital gain.[9]

➤**OBSERVATION**➔ In the complaint for damages, each cause of action (good will and loss of profits) should be separately stated and the payment allocated.

ANNUITIES

An annuity ordinarily is insurance that provides for regular payments to the insured to begin at a fixed date and continue through his life or for a term of years. Each regular payment consists of interest plus enough principal (cost of contract) to complete the guaranteed payment. This liquidation of principal is calculated to extend over the annuitant's life expectancy or the term of the annuity. The part of each payment that represents a return of the annuity's cost can be excluded. The part representing interest must be included. Annuities under self-employed retirement plans are covered in Chapter 8.

¶ **1230 Annuities in general.** (a) **What are annuity payments.** Annuity payments are amounts received under a life insurance, endowment or annuity contract. It is immaterial, however, whether the contract is issued by an insurance company. The amounts must be payable in periodic installments at regular intervals over a period of at least one year from the annuity starting date [see (c) below]. Finally, it must be possible to determine the total of the amounts to be received from the terms of the contract or by use of mortality tables, compound interest computations, or both [Sec. 1.72-1(b); 1.72-2(b)].

If the contract provides for periodic payments that can vary in amount or value (for example, payments in foreign currency) from payment to payment, the investment in the contract [(d) below] must be divided by the number of payments expected. The result is the maximum amount of each payment that can qualify as an amount received under an annuity [Sec. 1.72-2(b)(3)(i)].

Background and purpose. The purpose of spreading the tax-free portion of the annuity ratably over the annuitant's lifetime is to protect him from having to adjust his standard of living.

(b) **Exclusion ratio.** The part of each payment that can be excluded is based on a ratio determined by dividing the amount invested in the contract [(d) below] on the annuity starting date [(c) below] by the expected return under the contract [(e) below]. Generally, it also can be determined by dividing the cost of the annuity by annuitant's life expectancy on the annuity starting date[1] [Sec. 72(b); 1.72-4].

Footnotes appear at end of this Chapter.

Example 1: Mr. Bruckner bought an annuity for $12,650 that would pay him $100 a month starting January 1, 1977. His expected return, under the contract, is $16,000. The exclusion ratio is:

$12,650/$16,000, or 79.1% (79.06 rounded to the nearest tenth)

Mr. Bruckner can exclude from gross income $79.10 (79.1% × $100) of each $100 monthly payment he receives. Thus, for the year 1977 he can exclude a total amount of $949.20 ($79.10 × 12) and must include $250.80 in gross income.

Excluded amount does not change. Once the amount to be excluded is determined for a particular contract, it generally remains the same, even if the annuitant outlives his life expectancy or the payments are increased.[2]

Partial year. If the payments received the first year are for only part of the year, the exclusion ratio is applied to the amount received for the partial year. The result is the amount that can be excluded for that year.

Example 2: Assume the same facts as *Example 1*, except that the first annuity payment is received July 1, 1977, so that Mr. Bruckner receives only $600 in 1977. For 1977 he can exclude $474.60 ($600 × 79.1%). For 1978 and later years, he can exclude $949.20 each year ($1,200 × 79.1%).

Interest. There is no exclusion for interest payments on any amounts held under an agreement to pay interest [Sec. 72(j); 1.72-14(a)].

Alimony. Alimony payments funded with an annuity contract are not treated as annuity payments, if they are includible in the wife's gross income. They are taxed under the alimony provisions [¶ 1320], unless the husband and wife file a joint return [Sec. 72(k); 1.72-14(b)].

Actuarial tables. Complete annuity tables for annuity computations may be found in regulation Sec. 1.72-9. Sample portions are reproduced in this paragraph. Copies of the tables may be obtained from a Revenue Service office.[3] Actuarial information for the computation generally can be obtained from the insurance company that issued the annuity contract or the annuitant's employer (in the case of an employee's annuity [¶ 1232]).

(c) Annuity starting date. The annuity starting date generally is the first day of the first period for which an amount is received as an annuity under the contract [Sec. 72(c)(4); 1.72-4(b)].

(d) Investment in the contract. Investment in the contract is the total premiums paid (including any amounts the annuitant's employer contributed, if the annuitant was required to include them in income), less:

(1) Any premiums refunded, rebates, or dividends received on or before the annuity starting date; and
(2) The value of any refund feature [Sec. 72(c); 1.72-6, 1.72-7].

Refund feature. Subtraction for the refund feature is required if the expected return depends on life expectancy, and the contract provides either for refunds of the consideration or payment of a guaranteed amount. The adjustment for a single life annuity is made as follows:

(1) Divide the guaranteed amount by the amount to be received each year (to the extent it reduces the guaranteed amount). State this number in terms of the nearest whole year (12½ counts as 13; 12¼ counts as 12).
(2) Consult actuarial Table III for the appropriate percentage under the whole number of years found in (1) and the annuitant's age and sex.
(3) Multiply the percentage found in (2) by the smaller of (a) investment in the contract or (b) the total amount guaranteed.

(4) Subtract the amount found in (3) from the investment in the contract.

NOTE: In making the adjustment, the guaranteed amount and the annuitant's age are figured as of the annuity starting date.

The result is the investment in the contract adjusted for the present value of the refund feature [Sec. 1.72-7(b)].

Example 3: Mr. White, age 65, bought for $21,053, an immediate installment refund annuity payable $100 per month for life. The contract provided that if Mr. White did not live long enough to recover the full $21,053, payments were to be made to his wife until a total of $21,053 had been paid.
The investment in the contract is determined as follows:

Cost of the annuity (investment in the contract)		$21,053
Amount to be received annually	$1,200	
Number of years for which payment is guaranteed ($21,053 ÷ $1,200)	17.5	
Rounded to nearest number of whole years	18	
Percentage provided by actuarial Table III for age 65 (annuitant's age) and 18 (number of whole years) [see page 1217]	30%	
Less value of refund feature to the nearest dollar (30% × $21,053)		6,316
Investment in the contract adjusted for the present value of the refund feature		$14,737
The exclusion is determined as follows:		
Annual payment ($100 × 12)		$ 1,200
Multiple shown in Table I, male, age 65		15
Expected return ($1,200 × 15)		$18,000

Annual exclusion ratio is 81.9% ($14,737/$18,000); annual exclusion is $982,80 ($1,200 × 81.9%).

Adjustment for the refund feature in the case of a joint and survivor annuity or where more than one annuity element is provided for a single consideration is described in the regulations [Sec. 1.72-7(c), (e)].

Transfer for consideration. If an annuity or endowment contract is transferred for value, investment in the contract generally is the consideration paid, plus the amount of premiums and any other consideration paid by the transferee after the transfer [Sec. 72(g); 1.72-10]. The basis for gain or loss on the sale of annuity contracts is at ¶ 1527. For private annuities, see (j) below.

(e) Expected return under the contract. To determine the expected return under a contract involving life expectancy, actuarial tables prescribed by the Internal Revenue Service are used [Sec. 72(c)(3)(A); 1.72-9]. They provide a multiple that takes life expectancy into account in terms of total annual payments. Multiplying the amount of the annual payment by the multiple gives the expected return under the contract [Sec. 1.72-5].

In some cases, the multiple found in the tables must be adjusted by adding or subtracting decimal figures as indicated in the table on page 1216. Also if payments are to be made at intervals other than yearly, they must be annualized before applying the multiple. Thus, if payments are monthly, they are multiplied by 12 before applying the multiple [Sec. 1.72-5].

[Text continues on page 1218]

TABLE I.—ORDINARY LIFE ANNUITIES—ONE LIFE—EXPECTED RETURN MULTIPLES

Ages Male	Ages Female	Multiples	Ages Male	Ages Female	Multiples	Ages Male	Ages Female	Multiples
*	*	*	*	*	*	*	*	*
56	61	21.0	61	66	17.5	66	71	14.4
57	62	20.3	62	67	16.9	67	72	13.8
58	63	19.6	63	68	16.2	68	73	13.2
59	64	18.9	64	69	15.6	69	74	12.6
60	65	18.2	65	70	15.0	70	75	12.1
*	*	*	*	*	*	*	*	*

TABLE II.—ORDINARY JOINT LIFE AND LAST SURVIVOR ANNUITIES—TWO LIVES—EXPECTED RETURN MULTIPLES

Ages Male	Ages Male	61	62	63	64	65	66	67	68	69	70	71	72	73
Male	Female	66	67	68	69	70	71	72	73	74	75	76	77	78
*	*	*	*	*	*	*	*	*	*	*	*	*	*	*
61	66	23.0	22.6	22.2	21.9	21.6	21.3	21.0	20.7	20.4	20.2	20.0	19.8	19.6
62	67	22.6	22.2	21.8	21.5	21.1	20.8	20.5	20.2	19.9	19.7	19.5	19.2	19.0
63	68	22.2	21.8	21.4	21.1	20.7	20.4	20.1	19.8	19.5	19.2	19.0	18.7	18.5
64	69	21.9	21.5	21.1	20.7	20.3	20.0	19.6	19.3	19.0	18.7	18.5	18.2	18.0
65	70	21.6	21.1	20.7	20.3	19.9	19.6	19.2	18.9	18.6	18.3	18.0	17.8	17.5
*	*	*	*	*	*	*	*	*	*	*	*	*	*	*

TABLE IIA.—ANNUITIES FOR JOINT LIFE ONLY—TWO LIVES—EXPECTED RETURN MULTIPLES

Ages Male	Ages Male	61	62	63	64	65	66	67	68	69	70	71	72	73
Male	Female	66	67	68	69	70	71	72	73	74	75	76	77	78
*	*	*	*	*	*	*	*	*	*	*	*	*	*	*
61	66	12.0	11.8	11.5	11.2	10.9	10.6	10.3	10.0	9.7	9.4	9.1	8.8	8.5
62	67	11.8	11.5	11.2	11.0	10.7	10.4	10.1	9.8	9.6	9.3	9.0	8.7	8.4
63	68	11.5	11.2	11.0	10.7	10.5	10.2	9.9	9.7	9.4	9.1	8.8	8.5	8.2
64	69	11.2	11.0	10.7	10.5	10.2	10.0	9.7	9.5	9.2	8.9	8.7	8.4	8.1
65	70	10.9	10.7	10.5	10.2	10.0	9.8	9.5	9.3	9.0	8.8	8.5	8.2	8.0
*	*	*	*	*	*	*	*	*	*	*	*	*	*	*

Adjustment of Multiple

If payments are made quarterly, semi-annually, or annually, or if the interval between the annuity starting date and date of the first payment is less than the interval between future payments, the multiple found in Tables I, II, and IIA must be adjusted as shown in the following table, unless the payments are to be made more often than quarterly:

If the number of whole months from the annuity starting date to the first payment date is	0-1	2	3	4	5	6	7	8	9	10	11	12
And payments under the contract are to be made:												
Annually	+0.5	+0.4	+0.3	+0.2	+0.1	0	0	-0.1	-0.2	-0.3	-0.4	-0.5
Semiannually	+.2	+.1	0	0	-.1	-.2						
Quarterly	+.1	0	-.1									

Thus, at age 70, male, the multiple in Table I above, adjusted for quarterly payments, first payment one full month after the annuity starting date is 12.2 (12.1 + .1); semi-annual payments, first made 6 full months from the annuity starting date, the adjusted multiple is 11.9 (12.1 − .2); annual payments, first made one full month from the annuity starting date, the adjusted multiple is 12.6 (12.1 + .5).

No adjustment is necessary for Tables III and IV.

TABLE III.—PERCENT VALUE OF REFUND FEATURE

Ages		Duration of guaranteed amount											
Male	Female	14 years	15 years	16 years	17 years	18 years	19 years	20 years	21 years	22 years	23 years	24 years	25 years	26 years
		Percent	Percent	Percent	Percent	Percent	Percent	Percent	Percent	Percent	Percent	Percent	Percent	Percent
*	*	*	*	*	*	*	*	*	*	*	*	*	*	*
61	66	17	19	20	22	23	25	27	28	30	32	33	35	37
62	67	18	20	22	23	25	27	28	30	32	33	35	37	38
63	68	20	21	23	25	26	28	30	32	33	35	37	39	40
64	69	21	23	24	26	28	30	32	33	35	37	39	41	42
65	70	22	24	26	28	30	32	33	35	37	39	41	42	44
*	*													

TABLE IV.—TEMPORARY LIFE ANNUITIES[1]—ONE LIFE—EXPECTED RETURN MULTIPLES

Ages		Temporary period—maximum duration of annuity Years									
Male	Female	1	2	3	4	5	6	7	8	9	10
*	*	*	*	*	*	*	*	*	*	*	*
56	61	1.0	2.0	2.9	3.9	4.8	5.7	6.6	7.5	8.4	9.2
57	62	1.0	2.0	2.9	3.9	4.8	5.7	6.6	7.5	8.3	9.1
58	63	1.0	2.0	2.9	3.9	4.8	5.7	6.6	7.4	8.3	9.1
59	64	1.0	2.0	2.9	3.9	4.8	5.7	6.5	7.4	8.2	9.0
60	65	1.0	2.0	2.9	3.8	4.8	5.6	6.5	7.3	8.1	8.9
*	*										

(1) The multiples in this table do not apply to annuities for a term certain; for such cases, see ¶1215(b).

[Text continued from page 1215]

Example 4: Hoskins, age 65 on the annuity starting date, bought an annuity for $12,000 that will pay him $80 a month for his lifetime. His expected return is determined as follows:

Annual payment ($80 × 12)	$ 960
Multiple shown in Table I, male, age 65 [see page 1216]	15
Expected return ($960 × 15)	$14,400

His annual exclusion ratio is $12,000/$14,400 or ⅚. Hoskins would exclude annually from gross income $800 ($960 × ⅚).

Temporary annuities. If the contract provides for fixed payments to be made to an annuitant until death or for a specified period, whichever is earlier, expected return is found by multiplying the total annual payment by the multiple from Table IV [Sec. 1.72-9]. No adjustment of multiple is required [Sec. 1.72-5(a)(3)].

Example 5: Mr. Armstrong, age 60 (at his nearest birthday), is to get $60 a month for 5 years or until he dies, whichever is earlier. His expected return is $3,456, figured as follows:

Annual payment ($60 × 12 months)	$ 720
Multiple from Table IV [page 1217]	4.8
Expected return ($720 × 4.8)	$3,456

Decreasing annuities. If the contract provides for payments for life but the payments decrease after a specified time, expected return is determined by considering the contract as a combination of a whole life annuity for the smaller amount, plus a temporary life annuity for the amount of the difference between the larger and smaller amounts [Sec. 1.72-5(a)(4)].

Example 6: White, age 60, is to get $150 per month for 5 years or until his earlier death. After 5 years, he is to get $90 a month for the rest of his life. The expected return is determined as if White's contract consisted of a whole life annuity for $90 a month, plus a 5 year temporary life annuity of $60 a month:

Annual payments ($90 × 12)	$ 1,080
Multiple from Table I [page 1216]	18.2
Expected return for whole life annuity ($1,080 × 18.2)	$19,656
Expected return for 5 year temporary life annuity of $720 a year (as found in Example 5 above)	3,456
Total expected return	$23,112

Increasing annuities. If annuity payments are to be increased for life after a specified time, expected return is determined as if the contract consists of a whole life annuity for the larger amount, less a temporary life annuity for the amount of the difference between the larger and smaller amounts [Sec. 1.72-5(a)(5)].

Joint annuity. If a contract provides for payments to two people as long as both of them live, and nothing is to be paid to the survivor, expected return is determined by multiplying the annual payment by the multiple in Table IIA for the age and sex of the annuitants [Sec. 1.72-5(b)(4)].

Fixed period annuity. If no life expectancy is involved, for instance, an endowment contract for a fixed number of years, expected return is the total amount to be received under the contract [Sec. 72(c)(3)(B); 1.72-5(c)].

(f) Dividends received under annuity contract. Dividends received under an annuity contract are taxable, if received on or after the annuity starting date. If received before the annuity starting date, they are taxable only to the extent that they exceed the portion of the cost of the contract that has not been recovered tax free [Sec. 72(e)(1); 1.72-1, 1.72-2, 1.72-11].

Example 7: Mr. Kemper bought an annuity policy for an annual premium of $400. Each year, Kemper received $100 from the insurance company as a "dividend" or return of premium. The $100 is not taxable (but it reduces the cost of the annuity for the purpose of figuring the annual annuity exclusion). This year, Kemper received a final dividend of $100 in addition to his first annuity payment. Kemper must include the $100 in his gross income.

(g) Surrender, redemption or maturity of annuity. Amounts received in full discharge, or on surrender, redemption or maturity of the contract, are taxable only so far as they exceed the cost of the contract less amounts received tax free under the contract [Sec. 72(e)(1), (2); 1.72-11(c)].

Example 8: Harris bought an annuity contract that would pay him $1,000 a year starting in 20 years. He paid a premium of $600 a year. Each year he received a $50 dividend. After 5 years he surrendered the contract. At that time, he had received tax-free dividends totalling $250. His cost, therefore, is $2,750 ($3,000 — $250). Anything received over that amount is taxable.

(h) Variable payment annuities. There are special rules if an annuity contract provides for variable payments [Sec. 1.72-4(d)].

(i) Two annuities for single consideration. When an annuity is payable to two or more persons for a single consideration, the exclusion ratio is determined for the whole contract. The expected return of each annuity element is found separately by applying the multiples in Table I. The investment in the contract is divided by the total of the expected return to find the exclusion ratio [Sec. 1.72-2(a)(2), 1.72-5(e), 1.72-6(b)].

(j) Private annuities. Generally a private annuity involves the transfer of securities or real property to a private person or organization in exchange for a promise to make periodic annuity payments. The present value of the annuity is determined by tables in the regulations (Sec. 20.2031-10) [Sec. 1.101-2(e)(1)(iii)(b)(3)]. Gain is determined by comparing the transferor's basis in the property with the annuity's present value. A gift tax may apply if that present value is less than the property's fair market value.

The taxation of the annuity payments generally follows the usual rules on annuities. The annuitant figures his annual exclusion by dividing his life expectancy into the investment in the contract. The investment is his basis in the property he transferred to receive the annuity. The gain is reported ratably over the period of years measured by the annuitant's life expectancy and the portion of each annual payment must be reported as capital gain. Thus, the remainder of the annuity payment (annual proceeds less the exclusion [(b) above] plus the capital gain) is the amount includible in income. After the capital gain has been fully reported, later amounts (after applying the exclusion ratio) are to be reported as ordinary income.[4]

The value of an annuity contract issued by an organization such as a corporation, trust, fund or foundation (not a commercial insurance company), is determined by tables from the Revenue Service.[5] Its value becomes the investment for computing the annuity exclusion.[6]

¶ **1231 Joint and survivor annuities.** Generally, in determining the annual exclusion for a uniform payment joint and survivor annuity the rules in ¶ 1230 apply, and the combined life expectancy of the annuitants (Actuarial Table II) is used in determining expected return [Sec. 72(c)(3)(A); 1.72-5(b)].

Example 1: Mr. Hartley bought a joint and survivorship annuity contract providing for payments of $100 a month for life and, after his death, for the same amount to his wife for her life. At the annuity starting date, he is age 70, his wife is 67. Expected return is computed as follows:

Annual annuity payments ($100 × 12)	$ 1,200
Multiple shown in Table II [page 1216]	19.7
Expected return ($1,200 × 19.7)	$23,640

If the payments to the second annuitant will be different from those to the first annuitant, the expected return is determined as illustrated below [Sec. 1.72-5(b)]:

Example 2: Mr. Gilroy bought a joint and survivorship annuity contract providing for payments of $100 a month for life and, after his death, payments to his wife of $50 a month for life. At the annuity starting date, his nearest birthday is 70 and that of his wife is 67.

Multiple from Table II [page 1216]	19.7
Subtract: multiple from Table I [page 1216]	12.1
Multiple applicable to second annuitant	7.6
Portion of expected return (first annuitant), 12.1 × $1,200	$14,520
Portion of expected return (second annuitant), 7.6 × $600	4,560
Expected return under the contract	$19,080

The total expected return is used to find the exclusion. If Gilroy's investment in the contract is $14,310, the exclusion ratio is $14,310/$19,080, or 75%. He can exclude $75 ($100 × 75%) of each $100 payment he receives. After his death, his wife can exclude $37.50 ($50 × 75%) of each $50 payment.

If the contract calls for payment of one amount to two annuitants during their joint lives, and a different amount to the survivor, expected return is determined:

(1) From Table II [Sec. 1.72-9], find the multiple under both the annuitants' ages (as of the annuity starting date) and their appropriate sexes;

(2) From Table IIA [Sec. 1.72-9], find the multiple that applies to both annuitants' ages (as of the annuity starting date) and their appropriate sexes;

(3) Multiply the multiple found in (1) by the total of the amounts to be received annually after the death of the first to die; and

(4) Multiply the multiple found in (2) by the difference between the total of the amounts to be received annually before and the total of the amounts to be received annually after the death of the first to die.

(5) If the original annual payment is more than the annual payment to be made after the death of the first to die, the expected return is the sum of the amounts determined under (3) and (4) above.

(6) If the original payment is less than the annual payment to be made after the death of the first to die, the expected return is the difference between the amounts determined under (3) and (4) above [Sec. 1.72-5(b)(5)].

Example 3: Mr. Standish buys a joint and survivor annuity that provides for payments of $100 a month for as long as both he and his wife live. After the death of either, payments of $75 a month will be made to the survivor for life. At the annuity starting date, his age at his nearest birthday is 70 and his wife is 67. Expected return is figured as follows:

Multiple from Table II [page 1216]	19.7
Multiple from Table IIA [page 1216]	9.3
Portion of expected return ($900 × 19.7—sum per year after first death)	$17,730
Portion of expected return ($300 × 9.3—amount of change in sum at first death)	2,790
Expected return under contract	$20,520

The investment in this contract is $17,887, so the exclusion ratio is 87.2 percent ($17,887/$20,520). The amount that can be excluded from each monthly payment made while both are alive is 87.2% of $100, or $87.20. The remaining $12.80 of each payment must be included in gross income. After the death of either, 87.2% of each monthly payment of $75, or $65.40, can be excluded. The remaining $9.60 of each payment must be included in gross income.

If a contract provides for payment of life annuities to two persons during their lives, and after the death of either, provides that the survivor will receive for life both his own annuity payment and payments made formerly to the deceased person, expected return is figured as if there are two joint and survivor annuities under the same contract: (1) find the multiple for the ages and sexes of the annuitants in Table II [Sec. 1.72-9]; multiply the sum of the annual payments to both annuitants by the multiple. The result is the expected return for the contract [Sec. 1.72-5(b)(6); 1.72-5(e)(4)]. See also ¶ 3008.

¶ **1232 Employees' annuities.** If an employer buys retirement annuities for his employees, or contributes to a pension plan that buys annuities for the employees, three questions are involved: (1) Can the employer deduct the amounts he contributes? (See ¶ 1838). (2) Is the amount contributed by the employer income to the employee when contributed? (3) How are the annuity proceeds taxed? For self-employed retirement plans, see ¶ 1839.

(a) Is it a "qualified" annuity plan? The first step in determining the taxable status of the employees is to find out if the annuity plan meets the requirements for a "qualified" plan. The essential requirements for a qualified plan are set out in detail at ¶ 3024. An annuity plan without a trust may qualify, if the plan meets the same requirements a trusteed plan must meet in order to qualify, and any refunds of premiums are applied in the current or following tax year to the purchase of retirement annuities [Sec. 404(a)(2); 1.404(a)-8].

If a group or individual retirement annuity contract is not owned by the trustee of an exempt employees' trust, the contract must be nontransferable [Sec. 401(g); 1.401-9(b)].

(b) How contributions are treated. Amounts resulting from the employer's contributions to the purchase of an annuity under a qualified plan are not taxable to the employee until they are distributed or made available to him [Sec. 403(a); 1.403(a)-1]. Employer contributions made and premiums paid after 8-1-69 to a nonqualified plan are taxed to the employee when his interest in the employer contributions is vested, either in the year of contribution or at a later date (¶ 1326) [Sec. 83, 403(c)].

NOTE: Under proposed amendments to Regulation Sec. 1.403(c)-1, the employee's interest vests when his interest in the contribution or premium is either transferable or not subject to a substantial risk of forfeiture.

Example 1: Garrett Corp. entered into a group annuity contract for the benefit of its employees. Under the contract, each year for 20 years, Garrett Corp. will deduct $120 from Charles Regan's salary of $4,800 ($2,400 in all). During the same period, Garrett Corp. will contribute $150 a year ($3,000 in all) on behalf of Regan. At the end of 20 years when Regan retires, he will receive an annuity of $700 per year. At the time he gets the first payment, his expected return under the contract is $7,000. The plan provides that refunds of contributions will be applied to reduce subsequent premiums. Assume the plan is a qualified plan, or that the employees' rights are subject to substantial risk of forfeiture, the employer's contribution is not included in the employee's income. However, because the plan has a refund provision, Regan must include in gross income his salary of $4,800, without any decrease for his contribution of $120. For annuity proceeds, see Example 4.

Example 2: Assume the same facts as in Example 1, except that the plan is not a qualified plan. Regan must include the contribution made by his employer in the year his interest is not subject to a substantial risk of forfeiture. For annuity proceeds, see Example 7.

Footnotes appear at end of this Chapter.

¶ **1232**

An employee's contributions to an annuity plan through payroll deductions are included in his gross income if the plan has a refund provision or the employee participates voluntarily.[1]

NOTE: Under proposed amendment to regulation Sec. 1.403(a)-1, a contribution to an exempt plan under an optional salary reduction agreement would be income to the employee for the year the contribution would have been payable as compensation.

Example 3: An employee is required to contribute to a pension plan. Under the terms of the plan, the employer withholds the amount of the contributions from the employee's salary. When the employee retires, or when his employment terminates for any other reason, he is entitled to an annuity based on both his and the employer's contributions. The employee is required to include the withheld amounts in his gross income.

(c) Lump sum proceeds of an employee annuity contract that represent accumulations attributable to years of participation before 1974 are taxed as capital gain. Those that represent accumulations attributable to years of participation after 1973 are ordinary income [Sec. 403]. There is an *elective* 10-year forward averaging rule, as well as a $10,000 minimum distribution allowance, for taxing the ordinary income portion of the distribution. See ¶ 3024.

(d) Proceeds taxed as an annuity. If they are not paid in a lump sum, the proceeds (whether paid under qualified or nonqualified plans) generally are taxed the same as other annuity payments (¶ 1230) [Sec. 403(a), (c)]. However, if the amounts payable in the first 3 years equal or exceed the cost of the annuity to the employee (without reduction for any refund feature[2]), the life expectancy method does not apply. In that case the employee (or his beneficiary) excludes all amounts received until the cost is recovered. After that, all of the annuity payments are taxable [Sec. 72(d); 1.72-13].

Example 4: Assume the same facts as in Example 1. The cost of the annuity to Regan is $2,400, and each year he receives an annuity payment of $700, he will exclude $240 ($700 × 2,400/7,000) and include $460 ($700-$240).

Example 5: Assume the same facts as in Example 1, except that the entire annual contribution ($270) is made by Garrett Corp., and Regan contributes nothing. The cost of the annuity to Regan is zero, and all annuity payments received by him are taxable.

Example 6: Assume the same facts as in Example 1, except that the annuity payments to Regan will be $1,000 per year. The life expectancy method does not apply to the annuity payments, since the payments Regan will get in the first 3 years ($3,000) are more than his contributions ($2,400). Regan will not report any part of the annuity payments the first 2 years. The third year, he will exclude $400 and report $600. After that, he will report $1,000 each year.

Some trusts or plans make one payment for several programs or contracts. When the first payment is made, the amount for each program must be treated as a separate annuity.[3]

Employer's contributions. In figuring the consideration paid by the employee for an annuity, certain contributions by the employer may be treated as the employee's contributions. These are: (1) amounts contributed by the employer includible in the gross income of the employee; and (2) amounts contributed by the employer which, if paid directly to the employee at that time, would not have been includible in the employee's gross income. (This does not apply to employer contributions after 1962 that can be excluded as employee's foreign earned income [¶ 3725].) [Sec. 72(f), 403; 1.72-8].

Example 7: Assume the same facts as in Example 2. The cost of the annuity to Regan is $5,400, and each year he receives an annuity payment of $700, he will exclude $540 ($700 × 5,400/7,000) and include $160 ($700-$540).

Example 8: Assume the same facts as in Example 1, except that during the 20 years (1-1-58 to 12-31-77) Regan works and lives in Brazil, and his salary is not taxable. If Garrett paid its contributions directly to Regan they would not be taxable either. Regan's cost for figuring the tax-free amount of the annuity is $3,150. This includes 20 payments of $120 made by Regan, and 5 payments of $150 made by Garrett before 1963 that would not have been included in Regan's gross income if paid directly to him. Garrett's $150 contributions in 1963 through 1977 are not counted as employee contributions, even though they are excluded from Regan's gross income. Each year Regan receives his $700 annuity he will exclude $315 ($3,150/7,000 × $700) and include $385.

Death benefits. In the case of an employee's beneficiary, death benefits (except amounts paid as an annuity) that can be excluded from gross income [¶ 1304] are added to the amount of the employee's contributions to determine the whole consideration paid by the employee [Sec. 1.72-8(b)].

(e) Nonqualified plan—certain exempt organizations or educational institutions. An employee of an exempt organization or educational institution also includes his employer's contributions to an annuity contract under a nonqualified plan when his rights under the contract vest. Rights to the contributions vest when they are either transferable or not subject to a substantial risk of forfeiture (¶ 1326) [Sec. 83, 403(c); 1.403(c)-1(a)]. However, some contributions are tax free to the extent of an exclusion allowance. This applies if the contract is purchased by an employer that is a religious, scientific, literary or educational organization exempt under Sec. 501(c)(3), or an educational institution of a state, political subdivision of a state or their agencies or instrumentalities. The employee's rights must be nonforfeitable, except for failure to pay future premiums. The employee includes the contribution in gross income to the extent it exceeds an "exclusion allowance" for the year.[4] The exclusion allowance is 20% of the employee's pay for the last 12-month period, multiplied by the number of years of the employee's past service, reduced by any amounts contributed by the employer that were excluded in prior tax years [Sec. 403(b); 1.403(b)-1(b), (d)].

NOTE: For tax years starting after 1975, an election is available to have the exclusion computed under Sec. 415 rules. The amount that could be excluded is the amount that can be contributed to an annuity contract purchased by educational institutions, hospitals or home health service agencies as if it is part of a defined contribution plan maintained by such employers [Sec. 403(b)(2)(B); Temp. Reg. 11.415(c)(4)].

In determining service, full time employment for a full year is one year of service. Part time employees are credited with fractional years [Sec. 1.403(b)-1(f)]. Annuity payments by a school or hospital that is an integral part of local government do not qualify for the exclusion.[5] The cost of the annuity is the amount contributed by the employee (Examples 1, 4 and 5 above apply).

Example 9: O.S. University pays premiums of $2,000 in 1977 and $2,500 in 1978, for the purchase of an annuity for Jesse Aron, who became a full-time professor on January 1, 1977. Aron draws a salary of $8,000 for 1977 and $8,800 for 1978 reporting his income on a calendar year basis. Assume that the plan is not a qualified plan, and Aron's rights are nonforfeitable, except for the failure to pay premiums. For 1977, Aron will exclude $1,600 [20% × $8,000 (includible compensation for 1977)] and include $400 [$2,000 (contribution for 1977) less $1,600 (amount of 20% exclusion)]. For 1978 Aron will exclude $1,920 [20% × $8,800 (includible compensation for 1978, × 2 (number of years of service), less $1,600 (amount contributed by employer that was excluded in 1977)]. He will include $580 [$2,500 (contribution for 1978) less $1,920 (amount of exclusion)].

If the annuity contract is not under a qualified plan and the employee's rights change from forfeitable to nonforfeitable rights, the employer's contributions that exceed the 20% exclusion allowance are taxable to the employee when his rights vest [Sec. 403(b)(6); 1,403(b)-1(b)(2)]. An employee of an exempt employer who is not allowed an exclusion and is not under a qualified plan must include in gross income the value of the contract on the date his rights change from nonvested to vested during a tax year [Sec. 403(c); 1.403(c)-1(b)].

Example 10: Assume the facts in Example 9, except Aron's rights initially under the contract are forfeitable and Hale University changes Aron's rights to nonforfeitable on December 31, 1978. For 1977, Aron will exclude the $2,000 contribution because his rights are forfeitable. For 1977, Aron will exclude $1,760 [20% × $8,800 (includible compensation for most recent period when rights vested)] and include $740 [$2,500 (contribution for 1978) less $1,760 (amount of the 20% exclusion)].

Example 11: Assume the facts as in Example 10, except that the employer is the Horton Chamber of Commerce (exempt under Sec. 501(c)(6)), and the value of the contract on December 31, 1978, is $4,500. For 1978, the date the change occurred, Aron will include $4,500 as additional gross income.

(f) If the employer is an insurance company, the rules in (a), (b) and (c) apply, even if the employer does not actually deduct its contributions.

(g) Federal employees. Civil Service employees must include in gross income amounts withheld under the Civil Service Retirement Act. Amounts paid to retired employees are taxable as annuities.[6] The computation is made as illustrated in Examples 1 and 4. The amount that may be excluded remains the same, even if the annuity payment has been increased. Thus, increases in U.S. Civil Service annuity payments are taxable in full. Amounts received from an "additional annuity" bought with voluntary employee contributions should be treated as a separate annuity in figuring amounts to be included in gross income. Annuity payments to beneficiaries of deceased Civil Service employees are taxable the same as if paid to the employees.[3]

(h) State and municipal employees. Rules in (a), (b) and (c) above apply. If the plan is qualified, the employee is not required to include the employer's contributions in gross income. The cost of the annuity is the amount, if any, contributed by the employee, and the computation is made as shown in Example 1, 4 or 5. Thus, if the employee contributed nothing, all amounts received by him are taxable income. Amounts contributed by the state or local government before 1939 are treated as the employee's contribution.[7]

NOTE: Benefits received from a retirement fund established by an exempt policemen's benevolent and protective association for its members and their beneficiaries are taxable.[8]

(i) Servicemen. Servicemen (or former servicemen), except those electing not to participate in the Survivor Benefit Plan, receiving reduced retirement pay exclude the amount of the reduction from gross income [Sec. 122(a)]. If such reductions have been included in gross income in the past, retirement pay may be excluded until it equals the excess amounts previously included in income [Sec. 122(b); 1.122-1(b)]. If the retired serviceman dies before the already-taxed reductions in retirement pay have been offset against future retirement income, the surviving annuitant may exclude annuity payments until the already-taxed reductions are fully recovered [Sec. 72(n)]. Otherwise, the survivor-annuitant ordinarily will be taxed on the full annuity payments.

Footnotes to Chapter 2

(P-H "FEDERAL TAXES" related references are cited in brackets [ ] at the end of each footnote below.)

Footnote ¶ 1201 [¶ 7000 et seq.].
(1) Comm. v. Glenshaw Glass Co., 348 US 426, 75 SCt 473, 47 AFTR 162; Eisner v. Macomber, 252 US 189, 40 SCt 189, 3 AFTR 3020 [¶ 7016(5)].

Footnote ¶ 1202 [¶ 8101 et seq.]

Footnote ¶ 1203 [¶ 8271 et seq.].
(1) Treas. Dept. booklet "Your Federal Income Tax" (1977 Ed.), p. 36.

Footnote ¶ 1204 [¶ 8236 et seq.].
(1) 30 Op. A. G. 252; 38 Op. A. G. 563, 1937-1 CB 328 [¶ 8240(5)].
(2) White, 3 TC 156, affd. 144 F.2d 1019, 32 AFTR 1316, cert. den. [¶ 8240(10)].
(3) Shamberg, 3 TC 131 affd. 144 F.2d 998, 32 AFTR 1295, cert. den. [¶ 8240(10)].
(4) Rev. Rul. 60-248, 1960-2 CB 35 [¶ 8240(20)].
(5) Sec. 5(d), U.S. Housing Act of 1937, as amended.
(6) Comm. v. Meyer, 104 F.2d 155, 23 AFTR 31 [¶ 8244(30)].
(7) Palm Beach Tr. Co., 9 TC 1060, affd. 37 AFTR 1478 [¶ 8252(10)].
(8) Holley v. U.S. 124 F.2d 909, 28 AFTR 863 [¶ 8244(15)].
(9) Rev. Rul. 55-73, 1955-1 CB 236 [¶ 7072(40); 8252(15)].
(10) Rev. Rul. 57-49, 1957-1 CB 62; Rev. Rul. 60-210, 1960-1 CB 38 [¶ 8253(10)].

Footnote ¶ 1213 [¶ 8111].
(1) Senate Report No. 1622, p. 181-182, 83rd Cong., 2nd Sess.
(2) Rev. Rul. 61-134, 1961-2 CB 250 [¶ 8123(15), 17,042(40)].
(3) Ducros v. Comm., 4 AFTR 2d 5856, 272 F.2d 49 [¶ 8123(15)].

Footnote ¶ 1214 [¶ 7771 et seq.; 7775; 8116].
(1) London Shoe Co. v. Comm., 80 F.2d 230, 16 AFTR 1398, cert. den. [¶ 14,029(10)].

Footnote ¶ 1215 [¶ 7731 et seq.; 7777 et seq.].

Footnote ¶ 1216 [¶ 7098; 7771 et seq.].
(1) Treas. Dept. booklet "Your Federal Income Tax" (1977 Ed.), p. 36.
(2) PL 85-56, 71 Stat. 122 [¶ 7098].

Footnote ¶ 1217 [¶ 7032].
(1) Rev. Rul. 70-217, 1970-1 CB 12 [¶ 7032(35)].
(2) Rev. Rul. 74-561, 1974-2 CB 24 [¶ 7797(50)].
(3) Rev. Rul. 66-34, 1966-1 CB 22 [¶ 7300.20(5)].
(4) Rev. Rul. 70-280, 1970-1 CB 13 [¶ 7032(5)].
(5) Rev. Rul. 55-652, 1955-2 CB 21 [¶ 7032(5)].
(6) Sec. 2(e), Railroad Unemployment Insurance Act.
(7) Rev. Rul. 71-425, 1971-2 CB 76; Treas. Dept. booklet "Your Federal Income Tax" (1977 Ed.), p. 51. [¶ 7032(45)].

Footnote ¶ 1218 [¶ 8341; 8349].
(1) Rev. Rul. 72-45, 1972-1 CB 34 [¶ 8349(5)].
(2) Rev. Rul. 68-10, 1968-1 CB 50 [¶ 8349(20)].
(3) Rev. Rul. 55-264, 1955-1 CB 11 [¶ 7407(10)].
(4) Prince v. U.S., 127 Ct Cl 612, 119 F. Supp. 421, 45 AFTR 730 [¶ 8354(15)].
(5) McNair v. Comm., 250 F.2d 147, 52 AFTR 1028 [¶ 8354(15)].
(6) IT 4017, 1950-2 CB 12; Rev. Rul. 55-88, 1955-1 CB 241 [¶ 8354(25)].
(7) Veteran's Administration Release, 2-14-57 [¶ 7098(5)].
(8) Treas. Dept. booklet "Your Federal Income Tax" (1977 Ed.), p. 31.
(9) Rev. Rul. 68-158, 1968-1 CB 47 [¶ 7098(10)].

Footnote ¶ 1219 [¶ 8364 et seq.].
(1) Leo P. Kaufman, 35 TC 663; John C. Lang, 41 TC 352 [¶ 8388(9)].
(2) Bogene, Inc., ¶ 68,147 P-H Memo TC; Smith, ¶ 70,243 P-H Memo TC [¶ 8409(10)].
(3) Larkin, 21 AFTR 2d 1307, 394 F 2d 494 [¶ 8409(10)].

Footnote ¶ 1220 [¶ 8364 et seq.; 8411].
(1) Rev. Rul. 58-90, 1958-1 CB 88 [¶ 8388(25)].
(2) Bogene, Inc., ¶ 68,147 P-H Memo TC [¶ 8409(10)].
(3) Larkin, 21 AFTR 2d 1307, 394 F.2d 494 [¶ 8409(10)].

Footnote ¶ 1221 [¶ 8404 et seq.].

Footnote ¶ 1222 [¶ 8416].
(1) Rev. Rul. 70-341, 1970-2 CB 31 [¶ 7032(35)].
(2) Rev. Rul. 67-360, 1967-2 CB 71 [¶ 8416(30)].

Footnote ¶ 1225 [¶ 7046 et seq.; 8181 et seq.].
(1) Lyeth v. Hoey, 305 US 188, 59 SCt 155, 21 AFTR 986 [¶ 8191(5)].
(2) C. Keller, 41 BTA 478 [¶ 8191(5)].
(3) Rev. Rul. 71-449, 1971-2 CB 77 [¶ 8223(5)].
(4) Reichert, 19 TC 1027 [¶ 8223(5)].
(5) Wolf v. Comm., 84 F.2d 390, 17 AFTR 1306 [¶ 7210(5)].
(6) J. Davies, 23 TC 524 [¶ 7415(35)].
(7) Quigley v. Comm., 143 F.2d 27, 32 AFTR 908 [¶ 8191(15)].
(8) W. H. Cooper, ¶ 51,267 P-H Memo TC, affd. 197 F.2d 951, 42 AFTR 261 [¶ 8223(10)].
(9) Wodehouse v. Comm., 178 F.2d 987, 38 AFTR 1248 [¶ 7479; 8219(20)].
(10) Rev. Rul. 56-484, 1956-2 CB 23 [¶ 8216(15)].

Footnote ¶ 1226 [¶ 8350].
(1) Farmers's & Merchants Bk. v. Comm., 59 F.2d 912, 11 AFTR 619 [¶ 7412(5)].
(2) Rev. Rul. 74-77, 1974-1 CB 33 [¶ 7417(15)].
(3) Sternberg, 32 BTA 1039 [¶ 7414(65)].
(4) Hawkins, 6 BTA 1023; Rev. Rul. 58-418, 1958-2 CB 18 [¶ 7417(5); 7418(5)].

Footnote ¶ 1226 continued
(5) Rev. Rul. 54-19, 1954-1 CB 179 [¶ 8350(5)].
(6) Raytheon Prod. Corp. v. Comm., 144 F.2d 110, 32 AFTR 1155 [¶ 7412(15)].
(7) Comm. v. Glenshaw Glass Co., 348 US 426, 75 SCt 473, 47 AFTR 162 [¶ 7418(5)].
(8) General American Investors Co. v. Comm., 348 US 434, 75 SCt 478, 47 AFTR 167 [¶ 7418(15)].
(9) Marks, 27 TC 464; Rev. Rul. 61-115, 1961-1 CB 46 [¶ 12,116; 32,148(25)].

Footnote ¶ 1230 [¶ 7731 et seq.].
(1) Senate Report No. 1622, p. 11, 83rd Cong., 2nd Sess.
(2) Rev. Rul. 71-435, 1971-2 CB 84 [¶ 7768(5)].
(3) Treas. Dept. Publication 575, "Tax Information on Pensions and Annuities" (1974 Ed.), p. 13.
(4) Rev. Rul. 69-74, 1969-1 CB 43 [¶ 7755(5); 31,040(5)].
(5) Rev. Rul. 67-39, 1967-1 CB 18; Rev. Rul. 62-216, 1962-2 CB 30; Rev. Rul. 72-438, 1972-2 CB 38 [¶ 7776(10); 31,040(5)].

Footnote ¶ 1230 continued
(6) Rev. Rul. 62-137, 1962-2 CB 28; Rev. Rul. 62-216, 1962-2 CB 30; Rev. Rul. 72-438, 1972-2 CB 38 [¶ 7776(10)].

Footnote ¶ 1231 [¶ 7760 et seq.].

Footnote ¶ 1232 [¶ 19,076 et seq.].
(1) Treas. Dept. booklet "Your Federal Income Tax" (1977 Ed.), p. 30.
(2) Clifford H. Searl, 35 TC 1217 [¶ 7769(5)].
(3) Treas. Dept. booklet "Your Federal Income Tax" (1977 Ed.), p. 45.
(4) Letter Ruling dated 4-26-63, ¶ 54,636, P-H Fed. 1964 [¶ 19,088(15)].
(5) Rev. Rul. 68-294, 1968-1 CB 46 [¶ 8160(5)].
(6) Isaiah Megibow, 218 F.2d 687, 46 AFTR 1553 [¶ 7092(25)].
(7) Treas. Dept. Publication 575, "Tax Information on Pensions and Annuities" (1974 Ed.), p. 3.
(8) Rev. Rul. 68-161, 1968-1 CB 173 [¶ 19,063(55)].

Highlights of Chapter 2
Gross Income—Exclusions

I. **Income in General**
   A. Income defined [¶ 1201]:
      1. Gains and profits.
      2. Gains from sale of capital assets.
      3. Does not include return of capital.
      4. Gross income—income less exempt income (exclusions).
      5. Taxable income is gross income less deductions.
   B. Exclusions [¶ 1202]:
      1. Not taxable under U.S. Constitution.
      2. Not included in definition of income.
      3. Excluded by statute.

II. **Interest on Government Obligations**
   A. Interest on U.S. obligations, possessions and instrumentalities [¶ 1203]:
      1. U.S. obligations—wholly taxable.
      2. U.S. possessions—exempt.
      3. U.S. instrumentalities—wholly taxable.
      4. Federal tax refunds—taxable.
   B. Interest on state and municipal obligations generally exempt [¶ 1204].

III. **Insurance Proceeds**
   A. Life insurance benefits:
      1. Wholly exempt lump-sum proceeds [¶ 1213].
      2. Partially taxable:
         a. Surrender or sale of policy before death [¶ 1214].
         b. Endowments contracts payable in lump sum or installments [¶ 1215].
         c. Interest element taxable:
            (1) Proceeds held under agreement to pay interest [¶ 1213(b)].
            (2) Surviving spouse's exclusion up to $1,000 [¶ 1213(c)].
         d. Single premium insurance-annuity combinations—taxable in excess of net premiums [¶ 1213(e)].
         e. Dividends received—not taxable on unmatured life insurance or endowment policies [¶ 1216].
   B. Government insurance—generally exempt [¶ 1216].
   C. Government benefits—generally excluded [¶ 1217].

IV. **Disability Benefits**
   A. Excluded benefits:
      1. Workmen's compensation [¶ 1218(a)].
      2. Accident and health plans [¶ 1218(b)].
      3. Pension and disability payments to members of armed service [¶ 1218(c)].
   B. Partially or wholly excluded benefits:
      1. Employee's health or accident benefits [¶ 1219(a), (b); 1220].
      2. Disability benefits [¶ 1219(c)]:
         a. $100 a week maximum (annual exclusion $5,200) for taxpayers under age 65 who have retired on disability and who are permanently and totally disabled.
         b. Excludable amounts reduced as adjusted gross income exceeds $15,000.
         c. Married taxpayers must file jointly to claim exclusion.

V. **Gifts and Damages**
   A. Gifts and bequests [¶ 1225]:

1. Nontaxable gratuitous transfer of property.
2. Value excluded but not income from gift.
3. Gifts to minors—taxable if used for support.
B. Damages [¶ 1226]:
1. Personal, family rights, loss or injury to capital excluded.
2. Loss of profits, punitive or exemplary damages included.

VI. Annuities
A. Payments defined [¶ 1230(a)]:
1. Amounts received under:
a. Life insurance contract.
b. Endowment; or
c. Annuity contract.
2. Must be payable in periodic installments at regular intervals over period of at least one year from annuity starting date.
B. Exclusion for each payment [¶ 1230(b)]:
1. Based on ratio of cost to expected return.
2. Cost divided by annuitant's life expectancy.
C. Annuity starting date—generally, 1st day of 1st period of payment [¶ 1230(c)].
D. Cost of contract [¶ 1230(d)]:
1. Total premiums paid less any premiums refunded, rebates, dividends received before starting date; and
2. Value of refund feature.
E. Dividends [¶ 1230(f)]:
1. Wholly taxable if received after annuity starting date.
2. Partially taxable if received before annuity starting date.
F. Surrender, redemption or maturity of annuity—partially taxable [¶ 1230(g)].
G. Special rules apply for:
1. Variable payment annuities [¶ 1230(h)].
2. Two annuities for single consideration [¶ 1230(i)].
3. Private annuities [¶ 1230(j)].
4. Joint and survivor annuities [¶ 1231].
H. Employees annuities [¶ 1232]:
1. Treatment of employer contributions to qualified plans—not taxable to employee until distributed.
2. Lump sum proceeds of employee annuity contract [¶ 1232(c)]:
a. Pre-1974 as capital gain.
b. Post-1973 as ordinary income.
3. Special averaging rule [¶ 1232(c)].
4. Proceeds taxed as an annuity if not paid in lump sum [¶ 1232(d)].
5. Treatment of employer contributions to nonqualified plans [¶ 1232(e)]:
a. Forfeitable rights—not taxable at contribution.
b. Change to nonforfeitable rights—taxable when rights vest.
6. Exempt organizations or educational institutions—20% exclusion allowance.
7. Federal employees—taxed on amount withheld with amounts paid at retirement taxed as annuity at distribution [¶ 1232(g)].
8. State and municipal employees—qualified plan rules apply [¶ 1232(h)].
9. Servicemen—amount of reduced retirement pay for annuities excludable [¶ 1232(i)].

Chapter 3

GROSS INCOME—INCLUSIONS
TABLE OF CONTENTS

GROSS INCOME

	¶
What is gross income	1300
In general	
Amounts received by mistake	
To whom income is taxable	
Tenancy by the entirety	
Joint tenants and tenants in common	
Community property income	
Income from illegal activities	

COMPENSATION FOR SERVICES

	¶
Taxability of compensation	1301
Compensation distinguished from gift	1302
Payments held to be compensation	
Payments held to be gifts	
Awards and prizes	
Scholarships and fellowships	1303
Pensions and employee death payments	1304
Employee death benefits	
Nontaxable pensions	
Compensation of government employees	1305
Compensation of members of armed forces	1306
Compensation other than cash	1307
Insurance premiums	
Books and tuition	
Government bonds	
Guaranteed annual wage plans	
Compensation paid in stock	
Board and lodging as compensation	1308
Meals	
Lodging	
Property occupied rent free by stockholder	
Quarters allowance for government employees	
Clergymen	
Compensation paid in notes	1309
Bargain purchases by employees	1310
Compensation of children	1312

INTEREST, RENT, MISCELLANEOUS INCOME

	¶
Interest	1314
Interest accrued on bonds sold between interest dates	1315
Rents and royalties	1316
Improvements by lessee	1317
Forgiveness of debt	1318
Cancellation for consideration	
Cancellation as a gift	
Adjustment of purchase price	
Capital transaction	
Dividend	
Cancellation under Bankruptcy Act	
Insolvency	
Settlement of debt by delivery of property	
Settlement of mortgage for less than face value	
Election to exclude income from discharge of debt	
Alimony	1320
Source of payments	
Payments must be periodic	
Support payments	
Life insurance premiums	
Mortgage and other payments on residence	
Medical expenses	
Gambling income	1321

SPECIAL PROBLEMS

	¶
Restricted property as compensation	1326
General rule	
Election	
Restrictions that never lapse	
Holding period	
Tax-free exchanges	
Excluded transactions	
Transition rules	
Employee stock options	1327
Qualified stock options	
Stock purchase plan options	
Restricted stock options	

Footnotes appear at end of this Chapter.

¶	¶
Special rules	for less than fair market value ... 1329
Other stock options 1328	Profit on state and municipal contracts 1330
Option without readily ascertainable value	Business insurance proceeds 1331
Option with readily ascertainable value	
Property purchased by stockholders	• Highlights of Chapter 3 .... Page 1361

GROSS INCOME

Gross income is the starting point for determining the amount of income tax you owe. It includes all types of income not expressly exempt from tax. This chapter covers some major categories of income: compensation for services, interest, rents and royalties and certain miscellaneous income.

¶ **1300 What is gross income. (a) In general.** "Gross income" is all items of income not among the exclusions covered in the previous chapter. It includes compensation for personal and professional services, business income, profits from sales of and dealings in property, interest, rent, dividends, and gains, profits and income derived from any source whatever unless exempt from tax by law [Sec. 61(a); 1.61-1]. Questions as to the year income should be reported are treated in Chapter 17.

(b) Amounts received by mistake. When there is an obligation to return funds but it is impossible to discover the owner, the overpayment is income.[1] If the overpayment is kept in a separate fund from which reimbursement is made whenever possible, the overpayment is not income until there is very little chance that a refund will be made.[2]

(c) To whom income is taxable. Salaries and other forms of compensation for services generally are income to the person who performs the services. Income from property and gain from the sale of property generally are income to the owner of the property. However, as to a husband and wife, the income splitting benefits on a joint return have the effect of taxing the income as if one-half belonged to each. There are other important exceptions that are subject to special rules, such as income from partnerships and from estates and trusts.

If a person merely receives physical possession of income that belongs to another, he is not taxed on it.[3] If he receives it as an agent, it is taxable to his principal.[4] If he really owns the income, however, he cannot escape taxation on it by having it paid to another party.[5] See also ¶ 2704.

(d) Tenancy by the entirety. If a husband and wife file a joint return, the problem of who is entitled to the income from property held by them as tenants by the entirety (a form of joint ownership by a husband and wife) is of little importance, because of the split-income benefits available on such returns. However, when separate returns are filed, applicable state law controls as to who is taxable on the income. In most states, the husband can no longer claim an exclusive right to the income from property owned under a tenancy by the entirety.

(e) Joint tenants and tenants in common. When persons hold property as joint tenants or as tenants in common, state law determines who is taxed on the income from the property. In most cases, the income is divided equally among the tenants. If the property is sold, the sale price is allocated in equal amounts to the tenants.[6]

(f) Community property income. A husband and wife domiciled in a state that has the community property system of ownership of marital property (Arizona, California, Idaho, Louisiana, Nevada, New Mexico, Texas and Washington) may each report one-half the community income in separate returns. Each state has its own rules for determining whether income is community income or separate income. Generally, however, income earned by the spouses through their efforts or investments after their marriage is community income. Likewise, income from property acquired after marriage by either the husband, the wife or both (except property acquired by gift, bequest, devise or inheritance) is generally community income. Property acquired by either spouse before marriage is separate property.

For income tax purposes, the rules for community income are only important when *separate* returns are filed by a husband and wife in a community property state. If they file a joint return they get the benefit of income splitting.

(g) Income from illegal activities. Income from an illegal business,[7] swindling operations[8] or extortions[9] is taxable. Proceeds of embezzlement are taxable.[10]

COMPENSATION FOR SERVICES

Compensation includes wages, fees for services, commissions, bonuses, tips, and fringe benefits. Certain payments are noncompensatory and not includible in gross income. Gifts are not income. Generally, you may exclude scholarships and fellowships although limitations apply. Also, a limited exclusion is allowed for employee death benefits and group life insurance premiums paid by an employer.

¶ **1301 Taxability of compensation.** All compensation for personal services must be included in gross income [Sec. 61(a); 1.61-2]. For an employee, the amount of compensation included in gross income is the total amount *before payroll deductions* by the employer for such items as withheld taxes, bond purchases, employee's contributions to annuities, and union dues.

If compensation is received under a claim of right and there is no unconditional obligation to pay it back, it is taxable (unless it is returned before the close of the year). As to tax treatment when an item of income is required to be repaid in a later year, see ¶ 2729.

What the compensation is called, how it is figured, and the form of payment are immaterial. The fact that the services are merely part-time, casual, seasonal or temporary is also immaterial.

TAXABLE

Wages, salaries, commissions on sales or on insurance premiums (including commissions on life insurance on the agent's own life[1] and on the lives of his children[2]); commissions on real estate bought for salesman's own account;[3] back pay received by employees under the Fair Labor Standards Act or Walsh-Healey Public Contracts Act, which represents unpaid minimum wages or overtime pay (back pay representing liquidated damages is also taxable, though not "wages");[4] compensation received in the form of property, such as stocks, bonds, or notes; pay whether received in a lump sum on an hourly, daily, weekly, monthly or annual basis, or on the basis of piecework or a percentage of profits; amounts paid and received as compensation, even though they are disallowed as deductions by the employer as unreasonable [Sec. 1.162-8].

Substitute for wages: Amounts received under a claim as reimbursement for wages lost during a period of suspension from employment.[5]

Tips: If income from tips is not reported, the Revenue Service will estimate the amount. Estimates ranging from 10% to

18% of total fares have been approved as to taxicab operators; 10% of total sales, as to waiters.[6] For withholding on tips, see Ch. 15.

Fees, such as marriage fees, baptismal offerings, sums received for saying masses for the dead, and other contributions received by a clergyman, evangelist, or religious worker for services rendered [Sec. 1.61-2], directors' fees, fees for serving on a jury (but not mileage reimbursement payments[7]).

Executor's commissions, unless waived.[8]

Strike benefits based on need, paid by labor unions out of union dues to members or nonmembers, may be gifts or taxable income, depending on the facts of each case.[9] If the benefits are paid out of a special or private fund, as distinguished from a union established fund,[10] only the benefits received in excess of contributions can be taxed.[11]

Covenant not to compete: Proceeds are ordinary income, not gift or capital gain.[12]

Financial counseling fees paid by a corporation for the benefit of its executives.[13]

NONTAXABLE

Car pool receipts for transporting car pool members to and from work to the extent they do not exceed the expenses (repairs, gasoline, etc. are nondeductible personal expenses).[14]

Donated services: Value of services donated to an exempt charitable organization is not taxable to the person performing them. However, if by agreement, Moore renders services for Gold and Gold pays the compensation to an exempt charity instead of Moore, the amount paid is taxable to Moore.[15]

Job training benefits: Payments for attending classes or retraining under federal or state law are exempt, but not state payments to unemployed persons for short-term employment in disaster relief activities.[16]

Moving expense reimbursement. All reimbursements and other payments to both old and new employees as well as self-employed persons for the expenses of moving from one residence to another are included in gross income [Sec. 82; 1.82-1]. These reimbursements may be received directly or indirectly and in the form of money, property or services [Sec. 1.82-1(a)(2), (3)]. However, an employee or self-employed person may deduct moving expenses. For tax years starting after 1975, armed forces' members can exclude from income reimbursements or allowances to the extent of moving expenses actually paid or incurred. See ¶ 1831.

Employer's reimbursement for loss on sale of employee's residence must be included in the employee's gross income as "incentive compensation." [17]

¶ 1302 Compensation distinguished from gift. Frequently the question arises whether a payment is taxable compensation or a nontaxable gift. The intent of the parties and surrounding facts are examined to reach a determination.[1]

(a) Payments held to be compensation. The doctrine that bonus payments and gratuitous "additional compensation" may be income subject to tax has often been recognized.[2] For tax purposes, a voluntary transfer without compensation is not necessarily a gift. It is not a gift if there is a legal or moral obligation for it, or if the donor expects benefit from the transfer. But mere absence of a legal or moral obligation does not necessarily make it a gift. A transfer is a gift, if it is made from detached or disinterested generosity. What counts most in deciding the question is the donor's dominant reason for making the transfer.[3]

Factors establishing intent. If an employer takes a deduction for the payment, it is a strong indication that he considers it compensation.[4] If he does not, it is evidence, although not conclusive, that the payment is not compensation but a gift. The length and value of the employee's services, the manner in which the "additional compensation" or bonus was determined, the treatment of the payment on the books of the employer and all other pertinent factors are to be considered in determining the intent of the parties.

TAXABLE COMPENSATION

Bonuses: Payment received under a resolution of the directors, but not confirmed by the stockholders (directors have no authority to give away the corporate assets);[5] payment received by corporation president in consideration of his previous years of service or in appreciation of his loyalty and devotion;[6] payments made annually to reimburse officers for income taxes, even though called gifts in the corporate resolution and not deducted by the company;[7] stockholder's transfer of stock to corporate officer to induce him to remain in the corporation's employ;[8] Christmas bonuses,[9] but the value of a turkey, ham or similar item distributed to employees at Christmas or a comparable holiday is not taxable to the employee and is deductible by the employer.[10]

Voluntary payments: Severance pay, even though there was no legal obligation to make the payment (compensation for past services);[11] honorarium paid to lawyer as partial compensation for professional services, even though inadequate for services rendered and no legal obligation to make the payment;[12] amount received by lawyer in excess of fee allowed by law.[13]

Salary guaranty: Lump sum paid for an annuity or to an irrevocable trust to relieve guarantors of their personal obligation to pay an employee's salary.[14]

(b) Payments held to be gifts. If a taxpayer claims an amount paid to him by his employer is exempt from tax as a gift, the intention to make a gift must be established. The fact that the payment was made without legal obligation is not in itself evidence of a gift, since additional compensation for past services may be taxable.[15]

NONTAXABLE GIFTS

Substitute for compensation: Bequest to executor as a substitute for commissions or other pay, unless conditioned upon his performance of his duties.[16]

Honorarium to former president of corporation after he resigned when new owners took over the company.[17]

Bonuses paid to employees of Y Corporation by X Corporation upon acquiring certain assets of Y Corporation (X had no obligation to pay any additional compensation to employees of Y, and the payments were not made for services rendered or to be rendered).[17]

Option to buy stock at less than market acquired from a client when it came as a surprise and was conceived and suggested by the donor.[18]

Employee relief contributions: Tornado relief contributions made by an employer to his employees.[19]

Relocation payments to cover moving expenses and direct losses of property resulting from taxpayer's displacement by an urban renewal project are not includible in gross income to the extent spent for these purposes.[20]

(c) Awards and prizes. Contest awards or prizes are generally taxable [Sec. 74; 1.74-1]. However, amounts received as prizes and awards made primarily in recognition of religious, charitable, scientific, educational, artistic, literary, or civic achievement are not taxable, provided: (1) the winner was selected without action on his part to enter the contest or to submit his works in the proceeding; and (2) he is not required to render substantial future services as a condition to receiving the prize or award [Sec. 74; 1.74-1(b)].

Background and purpose. The basic thrust of this exclusion is to exclude only those prizes or awards given for past achievement of a particular type, the selection having been made without any action being taken by the recipient to enter the contest.

TAXABLE

Award for special services, such as an award for suggestions to employer, a reward for outstanding work;[21] or an award to army nurse for outstanding performance from fund contributed to Dept. of Army.[22]

Footnotes appear at end of this Chapter.

¶ 1302

Prizes won in competitive contest[23] (payment for services rendered);[24] fair market value of merchandise received as a prize in a radio quiz contest [Sec. 1.74-1], but the value is its value to the taxpayer, rather than its retail cost.[25]

Scholarships awarded as prizes if there is no requirement that the amounts be used for educational purposes.[26] See also ¶ 1303.

How treated on the return. Although prizes are taxable as compensation, they are reported on the return as "other income." [27]

≫**OBSERVATION**→ If an arrangement is made before an award or prize is given, it may be possible to split the proceeds among members of a family to reduce taxes.

¶ **1303 Scholarships and fellowships.** Amounts received as scholarships at educational institutions or fellowships can be excluded from gross income, subject to limitations noted below. Also excluded are: (1) the value of services and accommodations supplied (such as room, board and laundry); and (2) amounts received and used for travel, research, clerical help, or equipment incident to the grant [Sec. 117; 1.117-1]. College students in Naval ROTC may exclude amounts paid by Navy for tuition and books.[1] Armed forces scholarships received during 1973 through 1975 are also excludable when tied to future service commitment [P.L. 93-483].

Candidate for degree. If the student or fellow is a candidate for a degree at an educational institution, and the grant requires him to perform teaching, research or other services, the amount that represents salary for those services is taxable. But if the services are required of all candidates for a particular degree, the grant is excluded[2] [Sec. 117; 1.117-2]. The Supreme Court has held that an employer-paid scholarship was compensation when the recipient had to hold his position during the educational leave and return to work after finishing the doctoral program [Sec. 1.117-4(c)].[3]

Not a candidate for a degree. A limited exclusion is allowed when the student or fellow is not a candidate for a degree [Sec. 117; 1.117-2]. The grant must be made by: a tax-exempt organization; the U.S. or its instrumentalities; a state, territory, U.S. possession, or their political subdivision; District of Columbia; a foreign government; an international organization; an educational or cultural foundation or a commission set up by two or more nations under the 1961 Mutual Educational and Cultural Exchange Act.

The exclusion is limited to $300 times the number of months for which the recipient received grants during the tax year. This exclusion is only for a 36-month period (whether or not consecutive). The excess received over the exclusion is gross income, but is not wages for withholding tax or self-employment income.[4]

Example 1: In March 1977, Stark, a calendar year basis taxpayer, was awarded a postdoctorate fellowship grant to start 9-1-77 and end on 5-31-78. The grant is for $4,500, and he receives this amount in monthly installments of $500 on the first day of each month. During 1977, Stark gets a total of $2,000 for the four months of September through December. He can exclude $1,200 ($300 × 4) and must include the remaining $800.

Example 2: Assume the facts are the same as in Example 1 except that the grant was for a 24-month period and was paid in full on 9-1-77. Stark can exclude the full amount of $4,500 since the grant does not exceed an amount equal to $300 times the number of months (24) for which he receives the grant during the tax year.

Amounts designated for expenses incidental to the scholarship or fellowship grant are not subject to the $300 limitation, but the 36-month limitation applies.[5]

Medical trainees. The exclusion does not apply to pay received by interns and resident physicians performing services at a hospital to complete or receive specialized training[6] (unless the grant does not represent compensation[7]), nor to amounts received by an "administrative resident" who is a candidate for a degree in hospital administration.[8] However, the Tax Court holds that payments received by a trainee to enable him to pursue studies or research may be excluded, if the primary purpose of the payments is to further his education rather than to serve his grantor's interest.[9] The Revenue Service does not follow this position with respect to payments received after 6-30-70.[10]

Vocational trainees. Cost of vocational training and amounts received for room, board, transportation and tuition in state-run experimental training project are not income to participants.[11]

Student Loans. No amount is included in gross income from the discharge of a student loan when the discharge is made under a loan agreement providing for discharge if a student works for a certain period at a particular job or location. This rule applies only to loans made by the federal, state, or local governments, either directly or indirectly through educational organizations. It applies to loans that are discharged before 1-1-79 [Sec. 2117, P.L. 94-455].

¶ **1304 Pensions and employee death payments.** Pensions and retirement allowances generally are taxable. Usually, if the employee did not contribute to the cost of the pension, and was not taxable on his employer's contributions, the full amount of the pension must be included in his gross income [Sec. 1.61-11]. For exceptions in the case of amounts received under employee annuity, pension or profit-sharing plans, see ¶ 1232; 3024.

Payments to widow. Amounts paid by the employer to the widow of a deceased employee are taxable as compensation for past services of the deceased employee if the employer was required to make the payments.[1] Voluntary payments for past services are taxable unless a gift was intended.[2]

(a) Employee death benefits. Payments up to $5,000 made by or for an employer to a deceased employee's beneficiaries or estate on account of the employee's death can be excluded. It makes no difference whether the payments represent compensation or a gift, or whether the employer is legally obligated to make the payments [Sec. 101(b)(1); 1.101-2]. Benefits paid under a self-employed retirement plan for an owner-employee [¶ 1839] are not excludable. [Sec. 1.101-2(f)].

If excludable death benefits are held by an insurer or the employer under an agreement to pay interest, the interest payments are taxable [Sec. 101(c); 1.101-3].

A surviving annuitant under a joint and survivor's annuity contract gets no exclusion, if the employee received, or was entitled to receive, any annuity before his death [Sec. 101(b)(2)(C); 1.101-2(e)].

More than one beneficiary. If the payments exceed $5,000, and are made to more than one beneficiary of the employee, the nontaxable amount is allocated among the beneficiaries [Sec. 1.101-2(c)].

Example 1: One beneficiary who receives $8,000 excludes $5,000 from his gross income and is taxed on $3,000. If there are four beneficiaries and each receives $2,000, $1,250 will be excluded from the return of each and $750 taxed to each.

More than one employer. The total exclusion cannot exceed $5,000, even if payments are made by more than one employer [Sec. 101(b)(2)(A); 1.101-2(a)]. There is a separate exclusion, however, for each employee.

Footnotes appear at end of this Chapter.

Example 2: Assume a mother, as beneficiary of her two sons, received $4,000 under a death benefit contract for each son from one employer. She can exclude the entire $8,000 received.

Vested rights. There is no exclusion for amounts to which the employee had a vested right before his death, except when a lump sum distribution is paid to the beneficiary within one of his tax years by an exempt pension, profit-sharing or stock bonus trust, or under an annuity contract under a qualified annuity plan [Sec. 101(b)(2)(B)].

Example 3: Under the profit-sharing plan of the company where Martin worked, 50% of the total allocation for each employee could be withdrawn (that is, was vested) during the period of his employment. The rest was payable only when he retired or died. At the time of Martin's death before reaching retirement age, he had withdrawn $1,000. His remaining credits in the plan amounted to $7,000. Of this amount, $3,000 was vested, and $4,000 had not vested. The $7,000 was paid to Martin's widow over a period of 3 years. Only the $4,000 that had not vested qualifies for the exclusion. However, if the plan were exempt from tax and the $7,000 had been paid to Martin's widow during one of her tax years, $5,000 could be excluded.

The death benefit exclusion also may apply to total distributions payable under annuity contracts purchased by certain tax-exempt employers, even though the employee had vested rights in the contract. The benefit is restricted to annuities purchased by schools and colleges, publicly supported charities and religious organizations. However, there is no exclusion if the public school, college or hospital is an integral part of a local government.[3] The exclusion applies to the portion of the distribution represented by the employer's contributions which come within the 20% rule; see ¶ 1232(e). The following formula may be used:

$$\frac{\text{Amount excluded under 20\% rule}}{\text{Employer's total contributions}} \times \text{Total distribution} = \text{Exclusion}$$

The total distribution is the death benefit provided by the employer, less amounts contributed by the employee, and less employer's contributions taxable to the employee. The exclusion cannot exceed $5,000 [Sec. 101(b)(2)(B)].

Death benefits received as an annuity. If a death benefit is received in the form of an annuity, the amount that can be excluded is the value of the annuity at the time the employee died, less the larger of (1) the employee's contribution, or (2) the amount of his vested rights in the contract. However, the exclusion cannot be more than $5,000. The excludable amount is treated as consideration paid by the employee for the annuity, and is added to the employee's contributions for the purpose of computing the tax on the annuity payments [Sec. 101(b)(2)(D); 1.101-2(e)]. If the beneficiary will receive $5,000 or more during the first 3 years, he can exclude the first $5,000 received and pay tax on the remaining installments.[4]

The exclusion applies to an annuity paid under a retired serviceman's family protection plan only if the serviceman retired before normal retirement age and dies before reaching that age [Sec. 101(b)(2)(D)].

(b) Nontaxable pensions. A retired clergyman is not taxable on payments from his congregation when they were not made under an enforceable agreement, established plan or past practice, but were based on his financial needs and the financial capacity of his congregation.[5]

¶ **1305 Compensation of government employees.** Compensation of all federal, state and municipal officers and employees is taxable [Sec. 61].

¶ **1306 Compensation of members of armed forces.** Generally, the pay for service in the armed forces of the United States is fully taxable to officers as well as enlisted personnel, including students at Service Academies,[1] except pay for service in a combat zone. Monthly allotments chargeable to the serviceman's pay must be included in gross income but not monthly basic allowances for quarters to dependents.[2]

> **NOTE:** Pay while serving in a combat zone (Vietnam), or while hospitalized because of disease or injuries incurred during combat, can be fully excluded by enlisted personnel and warrant officers. Officers and personnel serving as temporary officers can exclude only $500 a month. The exclusion for hospitalized Vietnam veterans does not apply to any month beginning after Jan. 78 [Sec. 112].

TAXABLE

Re-enlistment bonus[3] (except for service in combat zone); payments received from former employers;[4] per diem allowance instead of subsistence and mileage allowance received while in a travel status or on temporary duty away from a permanent station (deductible travel expenses incurred for such travel may be deducted without offsetting the basic subsistence and quarters allowances received);[5] lump-sum payments received by officers on termination of service (but may be averaged, see ¶ 2401);[6] pay for accrued leave on separation (terminal leave pay);[7] combined sick pay, combat pay exclusions not to exceed active service pay.[8]

¶ **1307 Compensation other than cash.** If compensation is paid in a form other than money, the fair market vlaue of the property on the date received is the amount included as income [Sec. 1.61-2(d); Prop. Reg. 1.83-1]. If the property received has no fair market value, no income is reported. In that case, the entire amount received when the property is sold would be taxable.[1] If it is a capital asset, the capital gain or loss rules apply [¶ 1600 et seq.].

(a) Insurance premiums paid by an employer under policies that protect the employee, his family or estate are treated as follows:

Ordinary life insurance. Premiums paid by an employer on the life of an employee generally are taxable to the employee if the proceeds are payable to the employee's beneficiaries [Sec. 1.61-2(d)]. However, when a corporation is the beneficiary and owner of an insurance policy on the life of an employee or stockholder, premiums paid by the corporation are not income to the insured individual.[2]

Group life insurance. Premiums paid by an employer on group *permanent* life insurance, providing paid-up continued insurance are taxable to the employee, unless his rights are forfeited when he stops working for the employer.[3] However, if the group permanent life insurance reserves are accumulated for pension purposes, only the part of the premium paid for current life insurance protection is taxable. For tax years starting after 6-30-73, for a policy that includes permanent insurance, a paid up value, a cash surrender value, or an equivalent benefit, if an employer pays any premium that is not allocated by the policy to the group-term life insurance (below), then the entire payment is taxable to the employee. But if the payment is not greater than the amount allocated by the policy but is above the portion properly allocable to the group-term life insurance, then only the excess amount is taxable [Sec. 1.79-1(b)(1)].

Group-term life insurance. Premiums paid by an employer for coverage up to $50,000 are not taxed to the employee. The cost of coverage over $50,000 provided by one or more employers is taxable to the employee in his tax year in which the premiums are paid, even though his rights under the policy are assigned.[4] The cost is figured from uniform premium rates for 5-year age brackets (see table below).

Footnotes appear at end of this Chapter.

Employee contributions to the cost of the insurance reduce the taxable amount [Sec. 79(a), (c); 1.79-1, 3].

Uniform 1-month Group-Term Premiums for $1,000 of Life Insurance Protection [Sec. 1.79-3].

AGE	COST per $1,000	AGE	COST per $1,000
Under 30	8 cents	45-49	40 cents
30-34	10 cents	50-54	68 cents
35-39	14 cents	55-59	$1.10
40-44	23 cents	60-64	$1.63

Example 1: Martin, age 62, works for Fair Corporation. During the year, he is insured for $100,000 group-term life insurance. He pays $2 of the cost of each $1,000 of coverage, and Fair Corporation pays the balance. Cost of insurance over $50,000 in Martin's age bracket is $978 (50 × $19.56). Martin is taxed on $778 [$978—employee's payment (100 × $2)].

Employer paid premiums for coverage over $50,000 are not income to the employee if the employer is the beneficiary of the policy, or if the sole beneficiary is an organization for which a charitable contribution deduction may be taken [Sec. 79(b); 1.79-1,2].

NOTE: An employer must report group-term life insurance provided for employees [¶ 3535]. See ¶ 3530.

Health and hospitalization insurance. Premiums paid by an employer on group hospitalization insurance policies are not taxable to employees.[5] Premiums (including reimbursements to the employee[6]) paid by an employer under an accident or health plan to compensate employees for personal injuries or sickness are not taxed to the employee [¶ 1219; 1220].

Annuity. Premiums paid by an employer on qualified employee's retirement annuity generally are not taxable to the employee [¶ 1232].

Pension trust. Premiums paid for term life insurance protection out of the employer's contributions under a pension trust plan are taxable to the insured employees [Sec. 1.402(a)-1].

Split-dollar life insurance. Under split-dollar life insurance, an employer pays the premiums on an employee's life insurance policy to the extent of the annual increase in the cash surrender value of the policy. The employee pays the balance. When the employee dies, the employer receives the cash surrender value. The balance is paid to the employee's beneficiary.

For policies purchased after 11-13-64, the employee is taxed on the total value of all the benefits received under the arrangement during the year, including cash dividends or additional life insurance, less any part of the premiums he paid. Neither the employer, nor the employee's beneficiaries are taxed on their share of the proceeds of the policy.[7]

Example 2: Employer buys $100,000 accelerated 10-payment life policy for employee Brown, age 45. The premium is $7,899.50 a year. Employer pays $7,291.00 (cash value) and Mr. Brown pays $608.50. The cost of 1-year term protection on $92,709 of insurance ($100,000 less $7,291.00) is $584.07 (based on 1-year term premiums per $1,000 includible in employee income under qualified plans). Since Mr. Brown paid more than this, he has no income this year.

Example 3: Assume the same facts as above. In the 3rd year, the employer pays $7,690 (additional cash value for that year); Mr. Brown pays $209.50 for $77,535 of insurance protection ($567.56 value for 1 year). $358.06 ($567.56 less $209.50) is included in Mr. Brown's gross income.

(b) Books and tuition. The value of books and tuition paid by the employer for an employee who must attend school and maintain a certain average to retain the position is taxable to the employee.[8] The same applies for non-job related or non-degree courses.[9] However, the employee can exclude tuition payments for job-related courses that are not required to be taken.[10] For deductibility of payments, see ¶ 1833.

(c) Government bonds. Salary received in tax-exempt state or local bonds is not exempt.[11] The tax is not on the medium of payment, but on wages or salary received.

(d) Guaranteed annual wage plans. Taxability of benefits under guaranteed annual wage plans depends on how the plan is set up and on the nature of the employee's interest in it. It makes no difference whether the plan is union negotiated or is set up by the employer alone.[12] In general, supplemental unemployment benefit (SUB) payments made by an employer directly to former employees are includible in gross income.[13]

> **Example 4:** When the employee had exclusive right of ownership of the account, and also had a nonforfeitable beneficial interest in the cash benefits payable under the plan (glass industry), the employer's contributions to the plan were taxable to the employee.[14]

> **Example 5:** When the employee's eligibility for benefits depended upon meeting prescribed conditions after termination of the employment relationship (auto industry), the employee was taxed on the benefits actually received, rather than the employer's contributions.[15]

(e) Compensation paid in stock. If an employee[16] or independent contractor receives the employer's corporate stock as compensation, he must include the stock's fair market value in income at the time of the transfer.[17] Special rules apply to restricted property received as compensation as well as to restricted stock options and plans (¶ 1326-1328) [Sec. 1.61-2(d)(4), (5)].

¶ 1308 Board and lodging as compensation. The value of meals or lodging furnished to an employee for the convenience of his employer generally is not taxable. The exclusion does not apply if an employee can take cash instead. Nor does it apply to meals and lodging furnished to wives and children of employees.

(a) Meals. The exclusion is limited to meals furnished by the employer for a *substantial noncompensatory* business reason (generally, when employee must be on duty during the meal period). Meals furnished to food service employees are excludable. If the nature of the job requires that the employee reside on the premises, the value of all meals taken there qualifies for exclusion, even if not taken on a working day, and even if taking meals on the job is not a condition of employment [Sec. 1.119-1].

A cash allowance for meals or lodging must be included in gross income to the extent it is compensation [Sec. 1.119-1(c)]. But some courts have allowed state highway patrol officers to exclude a cash allowance for meals taken in restaurants during a tour of duty[1] although the Revenue Service and the Tax Court disagree.[2] Supper money could be treated as a cash allowance, but the Revenue Service has not indicated if it considers supper money taxable.

(b) Lodging. The exclusion is allowed only if the employee must accept the lodging on the employer's business premises to perform his duties properly. Lodging includes the value of utilities, unless the employee buys them directly from suppliers.³ The fact that a state statute or employment contract fixing the terms of the employment indicates the meals or lodging are intended as compensation does not necessarily mean that they were furnished for the convenience of the employer [Sec. 119; 1.119-1].

Example 1: A state civil-service employee is employed at an institution. He is required by his employer, for the convenience of the employer, to live and eat at the institution in order to be available for duty at any time. Under the state law, his meals and lodging are regarded as part of his pay. For tax purposes he can exclude the value of the meals and lodging from gross income.

Example 2: An employee of an institution, who is required to be on duty from 8 a.m. until 4 p.m., is given the choice of residing at the institution free of charge, or of residing elsewhere and receiving an allowance of $30 per month in addition to his regular salary. If he elects to reside at the institution, the value of the meals and lodging to the employee is taxable, because residence there is not a condition of employment necessary to the proper performance of his duties.

(c) Property occupied rent free by stockholder. The rental value of a corporation's property occupied rent free by a stockholder has been held taxable to the stockholder.⁴ But when there was no evidence that the rental value was compensation, the Fifth Circuit held that it was a nontaxable gift from the corporation to its stockholders.⁵

(d) Quarters allowance for government employees. The value of quarters furnished to officers and enlisted personnel of the Armed Forces, Coast and Geodetic Survey, and Public Health Service, or amounts received by them instead of quarters are not taxable [Sec. 1.61-2]. The value of quarters furnished to civilian employees of the federal government, including the Public Health Service and Veterans Administration, generally will be exempt as furnished for convenience of the government.

For exclusion of cost-of-living and post allowances paid to government employees, officers and representatives in the Foreign Service, see ¶ 3726.

(e) Clergymen. Rental value of a dwelling furnished to an active or retired,⁶ ordained,⁷ licensed, or commissioned clergyman, and cash allowances paid to such a clergyman to the extent used by him to rent or provide a home, are exempt if designated a rental allowance in advance by official action of the employer [Sec. 107; 1.107-1]. "Rental allowance" includes amounts spent for rent, utilities and for buying a home and furnishings. It can also include payments for a home (mortgage payments, interest, taxes, repairs) the clergymen own.⁸ Clergymen are still entitled to allowable deductions such as interest and taxes on their residences.⁹ Clergymen employed only to teach or as administrators by an organization not under authority of a church or church denomination do not get the exclusion.¹⁰ But it is allowed if they teach at a college operated as an integral agency of the church.¹¹ A cantor of the Jewish faith qualifies for the exclusion, since he performs ministerial services as defined in Reg. Sec. 1.1402(c)-5(b)(2); but the Revenue Service disagrees with the Tax Court.¹²

¶ 1309 Compensation paid in notes. Notes received in payment for services are income to the extent of their fair market value when received.¹ But a note received as additional security or to cover overdue interest, rather than in payment of a debt, does not result in income.² A taxpayer paid with a note regarded as good for its face value at maturity, but not bearing interest, reports as income the fair discounted value of the note. As payments are received on the note, taxpayer must include in income the portion of each payment that represents the proportionate part of the discount originally taken on the entire note [Sec. 1.61-2(d)(4), Prop. Reg. 1.83-4(c)].

¶ 1310 Bargain purchases by employees. When an employee or independent contractor buys property for less than its fair market value from a person for whom services are performed, the difference between the price and its fair market value is included in the buyer's gross income. Basis of the property is increased by the amount so included [Sec. 1.61(2)(d)(2), Prop. Reg. Sec. 1.83-1].

Example: R-Company sold to Conroy, an employee, shares of its stock with a fair market value of $2,000. He paid $1,700. Conroy reports $300 income, and the stock's cost to him is $2,000.

Employees' discounts. Facilities or privileges, such as "courtesy" discounts granted by an employer to his employee, are not taxable if they are of relatively small value, noncompensatory and furnished to promote employee welfare, or efficiency.[1]

¶ 1312 Compensation of children. Pay for a child's services and other income the child gets is included in the child's gross income and not in the parent's gross income [Sec. 73; 1.73-1]. Even if a contract of employment is made directly by the parent and the parent receives the pay, it is taxable to the child. See also ¶ 1100(a); 3509.

Payments for board and lodging received by a parent from an employed child are income to the parent only to the extent they exceed the cost of household expenses attributable to the child.[1]

INTEREST, RENT, MISCELLANEOUS INCOME

Generally, interest income like bank account and savings bond interest must be included in taxable income. Exceptions apply to certain state and local bonds. Other miscellaneous items that may be subject to tax and covered in this section relate to rent and royalty payments, lessee improvements, debt forgiveness, alimony and gambling income.

¶ 1314 Interest. All interest is taxable except excluded interest on government obligations [¶ 1204]. This includes interest on corporate bonds, mortgage bonds, notes and bank deposits, and interest received from tax-exempt organizations, such as charitable, religious or educational institutions [Sec. 61; 1.61-7]. Interest is defined as compensation for the use, forbearance or detention of money.[1] On deferred payment sales, interest may be imputed, even though not stated in the sales contract [¶ 2840].

Bonds bought "flat." If a taxpayer buys bonds "flat" (price covers unpaid interest as well as principal), the entire amount is a capital investment. Any accrued interest that is in arrears at the time of purchase is not income and is not taxable when paid later. These payments are returns of capital that reduce the remaining cost basis [Sec. 1.61-7(c)].

Example: On June 15, Brown bought for $800 "flat" a bond of Apex Corp. with a face value of $1,000. The bond bore interest at 8%, payable each Nov. 1. At the time of the purchase, $160 accrued interest was in default. On Nov. 1, Apex Corp. paid Brown $240 interest on the bond. The $160 accrued interest that was in arrears is considered to be a return of capital, and only $80 is reported as interest. The basis of the bond is $640 ($800−$160).

When payments of the accrued interest exceed the basis of the bonds, any further interest payments are entitled to capital gains treatment [¶ 1629].[2] Capital gains treatment applies, even if it appears certain that the bonds ultimately will be

Footnotes appear at end of this Chapter.

paid in full.³ However, capital gains treatment does not apply to interest that accrues after the bonds are purchased.⁴

Bonds redeemed before maturity. When bonds are redeemed before the maturity date, future interest paid for the period between the date of redemption and the maturity date is treated not as interest, but as part of the redemption proceeds.⁵

Taxable interest includes: interest on award paid for loss of life (but award itself is not income)⁶ [¶ 1226]; interest on refund of federal tax; interest on legacies (not property received by gift, but income from such property⁷) [¶ 1225]; interest on life insurance policies paid by reason of the death of the insured [¶ 1213]; usurious interest,⁸ unless under state law it is a payment of principal [Sec. 1.61-7].

Series E bonds: Cash basis taxpayer may defer tax on the interest increment until the certificates are redeemed, or he may elect to report the annual increase as taxable income [¶ 2723]. Interest increment on U.S. Series E bond issued to 2 persons as co-owners is taxable to them in proportion to the amount of purchase price contributed by each. If a third person is substituted for one of the co-owners, he is taxable on any increment earned after he becomes a co-owner in the same proportion as the co-owner whom he succeeds.⁹

Long-term savings accounts: Depositor must include in income the entire amount of interest credited on premature withdrawal subject to forfeiture penalty. For deduction of penalty loss, see ¶ 2203.

¶ 1315 Interest accrued on bonds sold between interest dates. When taxable bonds are sold between interest dates, the accrued interest *to* the date of sale is taxable to the seller; the accrued interest *from* the date of sale is taxable to the buyer. Both seller and buyer disregard the accrued interest in determining selling price and cost.¹

Example 1: Some years ago, Harold Wells purchased at face value a $1,000 bond of the Stanford Co. Interest at 6% is due Jan. 1 and July 1 (each interest payment, therefore, is $30). On June 1, Wells sold the bond to Edward Frey for $1,025 (of which $25 represented accrued interest to be collected July 1).

Wells reports $25 interest; Frey reports $5 interest. Since the accrued interest is disregarded in determining both selling price and cost, Wells has no gain or loss (cost $1,000; selling price $1,000). The basis of the bond to Frey is $1,000.

Example 2: Assume the same facts as in Example 1, except that the bond was an exempt municipal bond. Neither Wells nor Frey will report any interest; Wells has no gain or loss (cost $1,000; selling price $1,000), and the basis of the bond to Frey is $1,000.

The taxpayer must show how much of the money received or paid by him on the sale or purchase between interest dates is allocated to capital investment and how much to accrued interest. Otherwise, the construction most favorable to the government will be adopted.¹

¶ 1316 Rents and royalties—(a) Rents must be included in gross income [Sec. 61; 1.61-8]. The owner of property from which rents are received is entitled to deductions for depreciation, mortgage interest, taxes and other ordinary and necessary expenses of operating the property. These deductions are discussed in later chapters.

Payment to third parties. If, instead of rent, the tenant pays the interest on the landlord's bonds¹ or dividends on its stock,² the payments are rental income to the landlord and rental payments by the tenant. Amounts received by the stockholders and bondholders are dividends and interest to them.

Taxes paid by a tenant to or for a landlord for business property generally are additional rent taxable to the landlord [Sec. 1.162-11].

If the tenant's obligation to pay the landlord's federal income tax is not limited, the landlord's income includes not only the original tax, but also the tax on that amount, and so on until the added tax is less than 1¢.[3] There is an exception when a corporate tenant pays the tax for a corporate landlord under a pre-1954 lease or renewal option. The tax is not income to the landlord, and the tenant cannot deduct it [Sec. 110; 1.110-1].

Cancellation of lease. Payment to a landlord by a tenant to cancel, amend or modify a lease is taxable as ordinary income.[4] But an amount paid to a tenant to cancel a lease is treated as proceeds from sale or exchange of the lease [Sec. 1241; 1.1241-1]. If the lease is of nondepreciable property, it is a capital asset [Sec. 1221; 1.1221-1], and the payment results in capital gain [¶ 1601; 1602].

Example 1: Jones rents an apartment to Keltner. If Jones gives Keltner $1,000 to cancel the lease, Keltner has a capital gain of $1,000.

If a depreciable leasehold is used in trade or business, and it has been held for more than 9 months, payment received by the tenant to cancel the lease may be a long-term capital gain under certain conditions [¶ 1618].

Example 2: Parker rents Knight's store for a term of 5 years. At the end of the first year, Parker assigns the lease to Quayle for $1,000. Quayle has a depreciable leasehold. If, after holding the store for more than 9 months, Quayle cancels the lease for a consideration, he will have a long-term capital gain, if he meets the other conditions set out in ¶ 1618.

Cancellation of a lease, held for disposition to customers in the ordinary course of business by a tenant who is in the business of entering into and marketing leases, results in ordinary gain.

(b) Royalties are taxable.[5] Examples of royalties are payments made to the owner of a mine for permitting another to extract minerals from it, payments to an owner of a patent or private formula[6] for the use of it or the right to act under it, and payments to an author of a book. For treatment of coal and iron ore royalties, see ¶ 1623. For depletion deduction of mine owners who receive royalties, see Chapter 11.

¶ 1317 Improvements by lessee. Improvements made by a tenant that increase the value of the leased property are not income to the landlord [Sec. 109; 1.109-1]. Gain or loss is recognized only when the property is disposed of [Sec. 1019; 1.1019-1].

Example 1: On 7-1-67, Evans leased a parcel of land to Dugal for a 10-year term, with an annual rental of $800. The land had cost Evans $5,000 in 1964. Dugal in 1975 erected a building at a cost of $20,000. The lease expired and Evans repossessed the property on 6-30-77. On the next day Evans sold the land and building for $30,000. The annual rent was income. But Evans realized no income from the improvement when it was made in 1975. Nor did he realize income from the improvement when the lease expired on 6-30-77 and he repossessed the land and improvement. But when he sold the land and building for $30,000, his gain on the sale was $25,000 ($30,000 − $5,000).

(a) Adjustments to basis. No adjustment to the basis of the landlord's property is made for an improvement by the lessee for tax years starting after 1941. For 1941 and earlier years, a landlord realized income from an improvement by the lessee when the lease ended. Any amount included in gross income under this rule before 1942 can be added to the basis of the property [Sec. 1019].

Footnotes appear at end of this Chapter.

(b) Exception—Improvement instead of rent. The fair market value of an improvement that a tenant makes instead of paying rent is income to the landlord when it is placed on the property [Sec. 109; 1.109-1].

Example 2: In January, 1973, Evans leased another piece of land to Dugal for a period of 5 years. Under the lease terms, Dugal was not required to pay rent, but in lieu of rent he was to install an irrigation system before the end of the 5th year. Dugal installed the system in the fall of 1977, at which time it had a fair market value of $5,000. Evans realized $5,000 income in 1977.

¶ 1318 Forgiveness of debt. The cancellation of debt may result in the realization of income [Sec. 1.61-12].

(a) Cancellation for consideration. If the debt of a solvent taxpayer is cancelled or forgiven (in whole or in part) for consideration, the taxpayer realizes income in the amount of the debt cancelled [Sec. 1.61-12].

Example 1: Allen owes Bacon $300. Allen does certain work for Bacon in consideration of which Bacon cancels the debt. Allen must report income amounting to $300. The situation is exactly the same as if Bacon had paid Allen $300 in cash for his work, and Allen had used the amount received to pay his debt.

(b) Cancellation as a gift. When a creditor "gratuitously" forgives a debt, the amount forgiven is not income, whether debtor is solvent or insolvent.[1] Debtor must establish that there was no consideration for the cancellation. It cannot be inferred that the cancellation or reduction was done gratuitously, since creditors, as a rule, do not gratuitously forgive the obligations of their debtors.[2]

Example 2: Suppose that in Example 1 above, Bacon had cancelled the debt without receiving any consideration, but with the desire to benefit Allen. The situation is then the same as if Bacon had made a gift to Allen of $300. Since gifts are expressly exempt from tax, Allen receives no taxable income.

Business debts. The same rule could apply to the forgiveness of business debts by creditors. Suppose the taxpayer owed rent and interest which it had set up on its books as debts and had deducted in previous years. If the creditors gratuitously agreed to cancel the interest and the rent, the transaction would be a gift and no income would be realized. The creditors' motives are immaterial. The fact that there was no consideration for the forgiveness makes the transaction tax-exempt.[1]

Intent. If a creditor accepts less than full payment, intent to gratuitously forgive the unpaid amount depends on whether the transaction is simply a transfer of an obligation for the best price available or is a release of part of the debt for cash and the unpaid balance "for nothing."[3]

(c) Adjustment of purchase price. If the cancellation of debt is an adjustment of the purchase price, no income results.[4]

Example 3: Johnson bought stock, partly on credit. Later the stock went down in value. After trying to get a reduction on the purchase price, Johnson gave a note for the unpaid balance. Several years later, he settled the balance on the note for $6,200 less than the note called for. The settlement was an adjustment of the purchase price, and no income resulted.

(d) Capital transaction. A corporation owed one of its stockholders $10,000 and the latter cancelled the debt. This is considered a contribution to the capital of the corporation [Sec. 1.61-12]. The situation is the same as if the stockholder had paid $10,000 additional for his stock.[5] The contribution is not income to the corporation [Sec. 1.118-1; ¶ 3106]. This rule applies only to cancellation of principal.[6]

(e) Dividend. The release by a corporation of a debt owning to it by a stockholder is a taxable dividend [Sec. 1.301-1(m)].

> **Example 4:** Ames and Beach each own 50% of the stock of the X Corporation. Ames owes the corporation $5,000 and Beach, $3,000. If the corporation releases the debts, Ames gets a dividend of $5,000 and Beach a dividend of $3,000.

(f) Cancellation under Bankruptcy Act. No income is realized if a debt is discharged, cancelled or reduced as a result of:

- An adjudication in bankruptcy under Sec. 14 of the Bankruptcy Act;
- A corporate reorganization plan confirmed under Sec. 77B or Chapter X of the Bankruptcy Act; or
- A composition agreement, arrangement, or settlement confirmed under Chapters X, XI, XII, or XIII of the Bankruptcy Act [Sec. 1.61-12].

The basis of the debtor's property is reduced by the amount cancelled, but not below the fair market value of the property at the time of confirmation of the plan or agreement [Sec. 1.1016-7]. Basis is not reduced in an insolvency reorganization. See ¶ 3331(c).

(g) Insolvency. If the cancellation or reduction of debt does not result from an adjudication in bankruptcy or a plan or agreement confirmed under the Bankruptcy Act, and if it is not a "gift", these rules apply:

1. If the debtor in insolvent both before and after the forgiveness, no part of the amount forgiven is taxable income.[7]

> **Example 5:** Assume that the taxpayer has assets of $75,000 and liabilities of $100,000. If the taxpayer enters into an agreement with his creditors, under which all the assets are distributed to the creditors, no taxable income is received.

2. If the debtor is insolvent before, but solvent after, the forgiveness, he has income to the extent of his net worth *after* the forgiveness.[8]

> **Example 6:** Taxpayer has assets of $75,000 and liabilities of $100,000. If he enters into an agreement with his creditors under which all the assets are retained, but the indebtedness is reduced to $60,000 ($40,000 being forgiven), he receives income of $15,000 (his net worth after the forgiveness).

(h) Settlement of debt by delivery of property. If a debtor settles a debt by delivering to the creditor property having a basis less than the amount of the debt, the difference between the basis of the property and the amount of the debt is income to the debtor.[9] But no income results if the debtor is insolvent before and after the transaction.[10]

> **Example 7:** Carson owes Dark $5,000. He transfers property that cost $5,000, in full settlement of the debt. If $1,000 had been allowed to Carson as a depreciation deduction, the property's adjusted basis would be $4,000 ($5,000 cost, less depreciation) [¶ 1500(b)]. $1,000 is income to Carson (the difference between $4,000, the property's adjusted basis, and $5,000, the amount of the debt).

(i) Settlement of mortgage for less than face value. If settlement of a mortgage for less than its face value is gratuitous, no income results to the mortgagor.[1] If the settlement is not gratuitous, the following rules apply when the mortgagor is personally liable under the mortgage:

1. If the value of the property at the time of the settlement is at least equal to the face value of the mortgage, the mortgagor realizes income.[11] The basis remains the same.

Footnotes appear at end of this Chapter.

¶ 1318

Example 8: Taxpayer purchased real estate for $100,000 on terms of $30,000 cash and $70,000 first mortgage on which he was personally liable. He settled the mortgage for $60,000 at which time the value of the property was $70,000. He realized income of $10,000. The basis of the property is $100,000.

2. If the value of the property at the time of the settlement is equal to or less than the settlement price, the mortgagor realizes no income.[12] The basis, however, must be decreased by the amount saved.

Example 9: If the value of the property in Example 8 was $60,000 at the time of the settlement, the mortgagor realizes no income but the basis of the property to him becomes $90,000.

3. If the mortgage debt was not incurred at the time of or in connection with the acquisition of the property, settlement for less than face value results in income regardless of the value of the property at the time of the settlement.[13] The basis remains the same.

Example 10: If the taxpayer in Example 8 had purchased the real estate for $100,000 cash and then had placed a mortgage of $70,000 on the property, the mortgagor would realize income upon the settlement for $60,000 regardless of the value of the property. The basis would be $100,000.

If the mortgagor was *not* personally liable on the mortgage, no income would result in any case and the basis of the property would be reduced by the amount saved.[14]

(j) Election to exclude income from discharge of debt. If the debt was incurred by a corporation, or by an individual in connection with property used in his trade or business, taxpayer may exclude all or part of the income arising from discharge of the debt, if he applies the amount so excluded to reduce the basis of his property. To get the exclusion, taxpayer must file with his return a consent to the adjustment in basis. The consent is filed in duplicate on Form 982. The adjustment is made against particular properties in the order prescribed by regulations [¶ 3125(f)]. [Sec. 108(a), 1017; 1.108(a)-1, 1.108(a)-2, 1.1017-1, 1.1017-2].

¶ 1320 Alimony. Certain payments, generally called alimony, that a husband must pay to his wife because of their marital relationship may be taxable to the wife and deductible by the husband if all four of the following conditions exist [Sec. 71; 1.71-1]:

• Payments must be required under a (1) civil decree of divorce or separate maintenance, or written instrument incident to that decree;[1] (2) written separation agreement, or (3) a civil decree for support or maintenance (including an interlocutory decree of divorce or a decree of alimony pendente lite).

NOTE: The husband and wife must be separated and not file a joint return when payments are made under a separation agreement or support decree.

• There must be a legal obligation to support based on the marital relationship.
• The payments must be periodic [(b) below].
• The payments are not specifically made as child support [(c) below].

Periodic alimony or payments in place of alimony can be deducted in the year of payment by the spouse who pays it, or his estate,[2] if it is taxable to the spouse who gets it [Sec. 215; 1.215-1]. It is a deduction for adjusted gross income [Sec. 62(13)].

Background and purpose. By taxing alimony and separate maintenance payments to the wife receiving them, and allowing a corresponding deduction to the husband, the husband is relieved of a real hardship. Otherwise, after paying alimony he might not have enough cash to pay his income tax. The 1976 Tax Reform Act changed alimony to a deduction for adjusted gross income for tax years starting after 1976.

> **NOTE:** A husband has taxable gain if he transfers appreciated property (property worth more than its basis) to his wife for release of her rights to support and maintenance.[3] For the basis of property acquired in divorce or marital settlement, see ¶ 1505.

(a) Source of payments. The source of the payments is immaterial. The payment may be from property held in trust, life insurance, endowment or annuity contracts, any other interest in property or from income or capital of the husband whether paid directly or indirectly by him. Thus, payments are taxable although made by an estate or trust after the death of the husband [Sec. 71(a); 1.71-1(c)].[4] Payments made by father to son's former wife were held taxable to the wife as alimony when the payments were made under a guaranty to pay the son's alimony obligation under a separation agreement.[5]

> **Example 1:** If the husband buys or assigns an annuity contract to meet his alimony obligation, the full amount received by the wife is taxable to her. None of it is includible in the husband's income, or deductible by him. The annuity exclusion [¶ 1230] does not apply in such a case.

(b) Payments must be periodic. To qualify for alimony treatment, the payments must be periodic. "Periodic" means "payable over a period of indefinite duration." Thus, generally, a lump sum payment is not periodic, and is not includible in the wife's income.

Generally, installment payments of a fixed amount of alimony are not taxable to the wife, because they are not considered periodic payments. But they are considered periodic payments (a) if the principal sum is to be paid over a period of more than ten years, and (b) to the extent that the payments for the tax year do not exceed 10% of the principal sum [Sec. 1.71-1(d)].

> **Example 2:** If the decree provides for a lump sum settlement of $60,000 (cash or property), no part of the $60,000 is includible in the wife's income. If the $60,000 is to be paid over 15 years at the rate of $4,000 a year, $4,000 is includible each year in the wife's income. If the $60,000 is to be paid, $15,000 in 1977 and the balance ($45,000) over 15 years, the amount the wife would include as income in 1977 is limited to $6,000 (10% of $60,000). In the remaining years, the full $3,000 is includible each year.

Even if payments are to be paid for a period of 10 years or less, the payments are "periodic" (includible in wife's income) if certain contingencies, such as remarriage, death or reduced earnings, could vary the total amount payable [Sec. 1.71-1(d)].

No principal sum in decree. The Ninth Circuit held that payments for only 6 years were "periodic," even though they were to continue if the wife remarried, because the *decree* specified no principal sum.[6]

Rental value of house. Actual rent payments made by a husband under a decree are periodic and includible in wife's income,[7] but not the monthly rental value of a house furnished to the wife by a husband under a decree.[8]

(c) Support payments. The portion of the alimony that is specifically payable for the support of minor children of the husband is *not* includible in the wife's gross income. If the husband pays less than the amount the decree specifies, the amount paid is considered a payment for children's support up to the amount specified for the support [Sec. 71(b); 1.71-1(e)].

Footnotes appear at end of this Chapter.

Problem: Tom Jax's divorce decree requires him to pay $500 a month to his wife to defray the increase in her household expenses incurred in housing his 2 minor children. How much can he deduct as alimony?

Solution: Zero. These payments are for the support of the children and are not deductible as alimony.

If no specified amount is allocated to the minor children, the entire amount payable is taxable to the wife and deductible by the husband[9] [Sec. 1.71-1(e)]. But payments to a divorced wife after her remarriage are treated as child support and not taxed to her as alimony if state law ends the husband's obligations on her remarriage.[10]

Support of wife's relatives. If a husband makes payments for support of his stepchild, they are taxable to the wife, if it can be shown that she has a legal obligation to support her child.[11] The same rule applies, if payments are made for support of the wife's mother.[12]

(d) Life insurance premiums. Premiums paid by the husband under a decree on his life insurance policy naming the wife as beneficiary are additional alimony payments. They are included in the wife's gross income if she gets immediate benefits from the insurance arrangement.[13] But if she does not get an immediate benefit, the premiums are not considered alimony payments, and they are not included in her gross income.[14]

Example 4: Wife is irrevocable beneficiary of policy and policy is assigned to her absolutely under a property settlement agreement approved by the court decree. In this case, wife obtains immediate irrevocable benefit. Premiums paid by husband under this policy are considered alimony payments.

(e) Mortgage and other payments on residence. Periodic payments attributable to property transferred to the wife under the decree are alimony to be included in her gross income and deductible by the husband [Sec. 1.71-1(c)]. If the decree earmarks alimony to be used to reduce the mortgage on a residence owned jointly by husband and wife, and on which both are principal obligors, or if they hold the property as *tenants in common,* one half of the payments are taxable to the wife and deductible by the husband.[15] Regardless of the title to the property, payments for utilities are taxable to the wife and deductible by the husband.[16]

(f) Medical expenses, paid under a decree or separation agreement by the husband, are alimony payments taxable to the wife if they qualify as periodic payments, but she can deduct them to the extent they are allowable deductions as medical expenses [¶ 1945-1947].[17]

¶ **1321 Gambling income.** Total gambling winnings must be included in income. This can include the proceeds from lotteries, raffles, sweepstakes and the like. Gambling income may qualify for income averaging [¶ 2401]. Gambling losses are deductible to the extent of winnings, if deductions are itemized [¶ 2224].

SPECIAL PROBLEMS

The special problems covered in this section relate to restricted property as compensation, certain types of stock options, bargain purchases of corporate property by stockholders, profits on state and local contracts and business insurance proceeds.

¶ **1326 Restricted property as compensation.** Restricted stock or other property received by an employee or independent contractor after 6-30-69 as compensation is generally taxable in the year his rights in the property are transferable or are not subject to substantial risk of forfeiture. However, this general rule is limited by various exceptions and transition rules discussed below. For similar treatment of transfers under nonqualified employee annuity or trust plans, see ¶ 1232(e); 3024(f).

Background and purpose. Prior tax treatment allowed taxpayers to defer the tax on restricted property until the restrictions lapsed; at that time, if the property had appreciated, only the value at the time of the transfer to the employee was taxed as compensation. If the property had decreased in value, its value at the time of the lapse was taxed as compensation. As a result, the tax treatment of restricted stock plans was significantly more generous than the treatment given for similar types of deferred compensation arrangements.

(a) General rule. An employee (or independent contractor) who receives restricted property as compensation is taxed on the excess of the property's fair market value over any cost to him in the first tax year the stock is either transferable (other than by gift) or is not subject to a substantial risk of forfeiture. The fair market value of the property is determined without regard to any restriction except one which by its terms will never lapse [see (c) below].

Appreciation of the property between the time of receipt and time of inclusion in income is ordinary income. Appreciation after inclusion in income is treated as capital gain.

There is a substantial risk of forfeiture if the employee's rights to the full enjoyment of the property are conditioned on his performance of future substantial service. In other cases, whether forfeiture conditions are substantial is a question of fact. An interest in property is considered transferable only if the transferee would not be subject to the forfeiture conditions. If the employee gives forfeitable property to another person, he (and not the donee) is taxed at the time the donee's rights become nonforfeitable. However, if the employee sells the property in an arm's length transaction, he realizes income at that time [Sec. 83(a), (c); Prop. Reg. 1.83-1, 1.83-3].

Example 1: On Dec. 1, 1977, Ace Corp. transfers to Eaton, an employee, 100 shares of its stock valued at $90 a share. Under the terms of the transfer Eaton must sell the stock back to Ace Corp. for $90 a share if he leaves its employ before Dec. 1, 1987. Eaton's rights in the stock are subject to a substantial risk of forfeiture.

Example 2: Last year, Acme Co. contributed funds to an educational benefit trust to pay post-high school educational expenses for its key employees' children. No benefits were to be received if the employee terminated the employment for reasons other than death or permanent disability. This year, funds of $4,000 from the trust were given to Miller, an Acme employee, to send his daughter to college. Miller must include that amount in this year's income since his daughter has a vested right to receive the benefit.[1]

(b) Election. An employee may elect to treat restricted property subject to a substantial risk of forfeiture or nontransferable as compensation at the time he receives the property. His income is the amount equal to the excess of fair market value (ignoring restrictions except those that will never lapse; see (c) below) over any amount he paid for the property. Any later appreciation of the property would be available for capital gain treatment. However, if the election is made and the property is later forfeited, he gets neither a refund nor a deduction. The employee must make this election not later than 30 days after the date of transfer; he may not revoke it without the Commissioner's consent [Sec. 83(b); Temp. Reg. Sec. 13.1; Prop. Reg. 1.83-2].

Footnotes appear at end of this Chapter.

¶ 1326

NOTE: If the taxpayer makes this election, proposed regulation Sec. 1.83-2(a) would allow a loss deduction for any excess of the taxpayer's cost for the property over any amount realized at the time of forfeiture or premature sale.

(c) Restrictions that never lapse. Special rules apply to those restrictions that will never lapse (for example, a requirement that the employee sell his stock back to his employer when the employment relationship ends). They are the only ones considered in determining the property's fair market value in the year of its inclusion in the employee's gross income [see (a) and (b) above]. If, under such a restriction, the restricted property can only be sold at a formula price, then the formula price is treated as the property's fair market value unless the Revenue Service proves a higher value. If the restriction is later cancelled, the employee has compensation income when the cancellation occurs on the excess of the full value over the sum of the restricted value at that time and any consideration paid for cancellation. However, this does not apply if the employee can show that the cancellation was not compensatory and not treated as such by his employer [Sec. 83(d); Prop. Reg. 1.83-5].

(d) Holding period begins when the restricted property is included in income [Sec. 83(f); Prop. Reg. 1.83-4].

(e) Tax-free exchanges. The restricted property rules apply to securities with substantially similar restrictions received in certain tax-free exchanges [¶ 1404; 3309(a); 3317] or by exercising a conversion privilege, unless the securities received had been transferred before 7-1-69, or were transferred under a transition rule ((g) below). The exchange itself is disregarded [Sec. 83(g), (i); Prop. Reg. 1.83-8(b)(6)].

(f) Excluded transactions. The restricted property rules do not apply to: (1) the transfer of a qualified or restricted option or under an employee stock purchase plan [¶ 1327-1328]; (2) the transfer to or from a qualified employee trust [¶ 3024] or a transfer under a qualified annuity [¶ 1232(a)]; (3) the transfer of an option without a readily ascertainable market value; or (4) the transfer of property by exercising an option with a readily ascertainable market value at the time of the grant (¶ 1328) [Sec. 83(e); Prop. Reg. 1.83-8(a)].

(g) Transition rules. The restricted property rules do not apply to (1) transfers made under a pre-4-22-69 contract or option, or (2) certain transfers before 1-1-73 or transfers before 5-1-70 under a pre-7-1-69 plan [Sec. 83(i); Prop. Reg. 1.83-8(b)].

¶ 1327 Employee stock options. An employee stock option is essentially an offer by a corporation to sell stock to its employees at a bargain price. The employee does not become obligated to pay the purchase price until he elects to exercise the option.

Special treatment is permitted for 3 types of options [Sec. 421-425]:

• Qualified stock options [(a) below].
• Options granted under an employee stock purchase plan [(b) below].
• Restricted stock options *granted before 1964* (with minor exceptions) [(c) below].

Generally, when all requirements are met, the employee realizes no income when he receives an option or when he exercises it (but see (a) below). An employee may be subject to the minimum tax rules when an option is exercised (¶ 2403) [Sec. 57(a)(6)]. An option can meet the requirements even if the employee must first offer the stock to the corporation before selling it.[1] Gain on the disposition of the stock acquired usually is taxed as long-term capital gain. However, when the fair market value of the stock is more than the option price at the time the option is granted, ordinary income may be realized when a qualified stock option is exercised or when stock acquired under a restricted option or an employee purchase plan option is disposed of [Sec. 421(a)].

If stock acquired under an option is not held the required length of time, the employee realizes ordinary income. See ¶ 1328. Generally, the income is reported when the stock is disposed of, and the corporation can then deduct the same amount as compensation paid to the employee. No deduction is allowed to the corporation when it transfers the stock on exercise of an option [Sec. 421]. Payments received for cancellation of an option are taxed as ordinary income.[2]

A corporation must file an information return about options that are exercised. See ¶ 3534.

Background and purpose. Employee stock options are frequently used as incentive devices by corporations who wish to attract new management, to convert their officers into "partners" by giving them a stake in the business, to retain the services of executives who might otherwise leave, or to give their employees generally a more direct interest in the success of the corporation.

(a) Qualified stock options. These are individual options granted after 1963, but do not include restricted options granted after 1963 under an earlier binding written contract [see (c) below]. If the options meet the requirements listed below, they receive favored tax treatment.

Requirements. An option is a qualified stock option only if it meets all the following conditions [Sec. 422(b); 1.422-1(b)]:

1. Stockholder approval of plan. The option must be granted under a plan approved by shareholders who own a majority of the outstanding voting stock of the corporation within 12 months before or after the plan is adopted [Sec. 422(b)(1); 1.422-2(b)(2)].[3]

2. Plan requirements. The plan must not run for more than 10 years, and must state the total shares to be optioned and the employees or classes of employees entitled to receive options [Sec. 422(b)(2); 1.422-2(b)(4)].

3. Employment. The employee receiving the option must be an employee of the granting corporation, its parent or subsidiary *continuously* from the grant to 3 months before the exercise date [Sec. 422(a)(2); 1.422-1(a)].

4. Option provisions. The option must provide: (i) that it must be exercised within 5 years after it is granted; (ii) that only the employee can exercise it while he lives, and it can be transferred only at death by will or operation of law; (iii) that it cannot be exercised while the employee has a prior outstanding qualified stock option or restricted stock option (Failure to include this provision is immaterial if the employee has no prior option[4]) [Sec. 422(b); 1.422-2(d)]. This last requirement is designed to prevent downward readjustment of the price. There are these exceptions to the requirement: (a) a new option may be exercised until a prior restricted one first becomes exercisable; (b) the terms of a prior option may be modified to accelerate the exercise date; and (c) a new option may be exercised if it relates to the same stock and the option price is not lower than the price under all old options [Sec. 422(c)(6); 1.422-2(f)].

5. Option price. The option price must be at least equal to the fair market value of the stock at the time it is granted [Sec. 422(b)(4); 1.422-2(e)(1)]. If a real effort is made to meet this condition and the price turns out to be less than fair

Footnotes appear at end of this Chapter.

¶ 1327

market value, the option can qualify, but 1½ times the spread at grant becomes ordinary income when the option is exercised [Sec. 422(c)(1); 1.422-2(e)(2)(i)].

≫**WATCH THIS**→ For options granted after 7-1-66, if the price falls below fair market value because of imputed interest [¶ 2840], the regulations say there has not been a good faith attempt to meet the condition, and the whole qualification fails [Sec. 1.422-2(e)(2)(ii)].

6. *Stock ownership.* At the time the option is granted, the employee cannot own more than 5% of the stock (in voting power or value) of the employer or its parent or subsidiary corporations. Shares he holds options for are counted in the 5%. If an option puts the holdings over the 5% limit, it can qualify up to the limit. Shares first bought under the option within the 5% limit qualify for the special tax treatment as qualified option shares. Shares owned by related persons are also counted for the 5% limit (see (d) below).

The 5% stock ownership limit is increased to 10%, if the equity capital of the corporation or corporations is $1,000,000 or less when the option is granted. If the equity capital is between $1,000,000 and $2,000,000, the 5% limit is increased proportionately to a maximum of 10% [Sec. 422(b)(7); 1.422-2(h)(3)(i)]. Equity capital is specially defined [Sec. 422(c)(3)(A); 1.422-2(h)(3)(ii)].

Example 1: Ken Corporation has equity capital of $1,500,000. Options can be granted to employees who own 7½% or less of the stock. This is 5% plus (5% × 500,000/1,000,000).

NOTE: No qualified stock options can be granted in "tandem" with nonstatutory options after 1-2-73 but both may be separately granted at the same time without the "tandem" feature. Generally, a "tandem" option is one in which both qualified and nonqualified stock options exist at the same time with alternative purchase terms.[5] The exercise of either reduces the number of shares of stock available under the other.

Tax treatment. The Tax Reform Act of 1976 generally has repealed the rules giving favorable tax treatment to certain qualified plans. Under the new rules, options (whether or not they satisfy the requirements of Sec. 422) granted after 5-20-76 will be treated as nonqualified options [See ¶ 1328]. If an option has a readily ascertainable fair market value, the difference between the value of the option and lesser amount paid for it is ordinary income when the option is received. Where the option has no readily ascertainable fair market value, its receipt does not constitute taxable income. However, if the option is exercised and the market value of the stock exceeds the option price the excess is ordinary income [Sec. 422].

Options granted after 5-20-76 will be treated as qualified stock options if they are granted under a written qualified plan adopted before such date. Also, options granted after 5-20-76 as part of a corporate reorganization or liquidation that are substitutes for qualified options granted before 5-21-76 will be treated as qualified options. In either case the options will only retain their qualified status if they are exercised before 5-21-81 [Sec. 422(c)].

An employee ordinarily does not realize income when he receives or exercises a qualified stock option. However, he realizes ordinary income if he exercises an option that meets all the other requirements listed above except that the option price is inadvertently set at less than the fair market value of the stock at the time the option is granted. He must include in gross income the lesser of: (1) 150% of the spread between the option price and the fair market value of the stock when the option was granted; or (2) the spread when the option is exercised. The basis of the stock is increased by the amount of income reported [Sec. 422(c)(1); 1.422-1].

Example 2: Option granted for $100 in good-faith belief that stock value was $100. In fact, it was $110. On exercise:

(a) If stock is then worth $118, employee has $15 ordinary income (150% × $110 − $100), and basis of stock becomes $115.

(b) If stock is then worth $112, employee has $12 ordinary income ($112 − $100), and stock basis is $112.

If stock acquired by exercise of a qualified stock option is held at least 3 years, gain realized on sale or exchange of the shares is long-term capital gain [Sec. 422; 1.422-1].

If the stock is sold within 3 years, ordinary income is realized. If the sale or exchange is one for which a loss, if sustained, would be recognized [¶ 1400 et seq.], the amount reported as ordinary income is limited to the gain on the sale or exchange [Sec. 422(c)(4); 1.422-1(b)]. So, ordinary income generally will be the lesser of: (1) the difference between the option price and the value of the stock when the option is exercised [¶ 1328]; or (2) the amount of the gain. If the gain is more than the spread between option price and value, the excess is capital gain—short-term or long-term, depending on the holding period [¶ 1605].

Example 3: Employee Jones exercises a qualified stock option at the option price of $100 a share when the value is $120. One year later, he sells at $115 a share. Jones has $15 a share ordinary income. This is the gain on the sale. It is less than $20, the difference between the option price and the value of the shares when the option was exercised.

Example 4: Assume the same facts as Example 3, but the sale price is $125. The gain is $25 a share. Ordinary income is $20 (the difference between option price and stock value when the option was exercised). The excess gain ($5) is capital gain.

After 2-20-73, an employee realizes ordinary income on a short sale within the 3-year period if, at the time of the sale, the option stock is the only employer's stock he owns.[6] But an insolvent individual can transfer the shares for the benefit of creditors before he has held them 3 years without realizing ordinary income [Sec. 422(c)].

Minimum tax. The difference between purchase price and the value of the stock in the tax year the option is exercised is a tax preference item subject to the minimum tax [¶ 2403].

(b) Stock purchase plan options. These are options granted after 1963 to employees across-the-board. They receive separate tax treatment from qualified stock options ((a) above), which generally are granted only to key employees. The rules for restricted stock options apply, with modifications.

Requirements. Only employees owning less than 5% of the stock can participate. Stockholder approval of the plan is required. The plan must not discriminate in favor of officers or highly compensated personnel, but the amount of optioned stock may be proportionate to salary. All employees must be included under the plan, except officers, highly compensated personnel, certain part-time workers, and those employed less than 2 years. The price must be at least 85% of the value of the stock at the time of grant or exercise. If the price under the plan is 85% at time of exercise, the option may run for 5 years; otherwise 27 months. Finally, no more than $25,000 (valued at time of grant) of stock may accrue for purchase in any one year [Sec. 423(b); 1.423-2].

The employee receiving the option must be an employee of the granting corporation, its parent or subsidiary continuously from the grant to 3 months before the option is exercised [Sec. 423(a)(2)].

Example 5: I. M. Cool's employer granted him an option under a qualified stock purchase plan to buy 100 shares of company stock at $20 a share when the stock's value was $22 a share. Eighteen months later, he exercised the option when the value of the stock was $23 a share. Seven months after that he sold the stock for $30 a share. In the year of sale, Cool must report $200 as ordinary income and $800 as long-term capital gain, figured as follows:

Footnotes appear at end of this Chapter.

¶ 1327

Chapter 3—Gross Income—Inclusions

Selling price ($30 × 100 shares)	$3,000
Purchase price (option price) ($20 × 100 shares)	2,000
Gain realized	$1,000
Amount realized as ordinary income ($2,200 − $2,000)	200
Capital gain ($1,000 − $200)	$ 800

≫SUGGESTION→ If the employee is given a long time to pay for the stock, fix the price high enough so that any amount treated as imputed interest (¶ 2840) will not cause the purchase price to fall below 85%.

Tax treatment. An employee realizes no income when he receives or exercises an option granted under a stock purchase plan. When stock acquired by exercise of the option is held for a least 9 months after it was acquired *and* at least 2 years after the option is granted, gain on sale or exchange of the shares is long-term capital gain, if the option price was at least equal to the fair market value of the stock when the option was granted. However, the employee realizes ordinary income if the option price is less than 100% (but not less than 85%) when the option is granted or when it is exercised and the employee sells it after the required holding period, or dies while he still owns it. The amount of ordinary income is the lesser of the excess of: (1) fair market value of the stock when the option was granted, or (2) the fair market value at disposition, *over* the option price. If the option price is not fixed or determinable when granted, it is determined as if the option was exercised when granted [Sec. 423(c); 1.423-2].

NOTE: The Tax Reform Act of 1976 increased the holding period for long-term capital gains to over 9 months for tax years beginning in 1977 and to over one year for tax years beginning in 1978 (it was over 6 months for tax years begun before 1977)[¶ 1605].

If the holding requirements are not met (both 9 months and 2 years), when the taxpayer sells the stock he must report as ordinary income the difference between the fair market value of the stock when option is exercised and the option price. The basis of the stock is increased by the amount of the ordinary income. The difference between the increased basis and the selling price is capital gain or loss.

Example 6: Assume the same facts as in Example 5 except that Cool sold the stock 5 months after he bought it. In the year of sale, he must report $300 as ordinary income and $700 as short-term capital gain:

Selling price ($30 × 100 shares)	$3,000
Purchase price (option price) ($20 × 100 shares)	2,000
Gain realized	$1,000
Amount reported as ordinary income ($2,300 − $2,000)	300
Capital gain ($1,000 − $300)	$ 700

≫OBSERVATION→ Unlike qualified and restricted stock options, a stock purchase plan option is not a tax preference item when the option is exercised. However, when the stock is sold, one-half of any net long-term capital gain realized on sale of stock is a tax preference item at the time of the sale [Sec. 57(a)(9); Prop. Reg. 1.57-1(i)].

(c) **Restricted stock options.** These are individual options *granted* before 1964 (or later under a binding written contract made before 1964).

Requirements. The conditions a restricted stock option must meet are more liberal than those for qualified and stock purchase options. *Options* can be exercised up to 10 years after they are granted. They cannot be transferred except at the death of the employee by will or operation of law. *Price* of the option must be at least 85% of the fair market value of the stock when the option is granted. Variable price options[7] (price depends on market value of the stock) are allowed. *Stock ownership* can be as high as 10% of the voting stock when the option is granted, and greater than 10%, if the option price is at least 110% of the value of the stock when it is granted and a 5-year limit is set for exercise of the option. Stock held by related persons is counted for the 10% [Sec. 424(b); 1.424-1].

Tax treatment. An employee realizes income only when he disposes of stock acquired under a restricted stock option. When the stock is held at least 9 months after it was acquired *and* 2 years after the option was granted, the gain on a sale or exchange is long-term capital gain if the option price is at least 95% of the fair market value of the stock when the option is granted. If the option price is between 85% and 95% of the value, the employee realizes some ordinary income when he disposes of the stock. The amount included in gross income is the *lesser* of the excess of: (1) fair market value of the stock when the option was granted; or (2) the fair market value at disposition, *over* the option price. The employment must continue from the time the option is granted to 3 months before it is exercised [Sec. 424; 1.424-1].

NOTE: The Tax Reform Act of 1976 has increased the holdng period for long-term capital gains from over 6 months to over 9 months for tax years beginning in 1977 and over one year for tax years beginning in 1978 [¶ 1605].

Ordinary income is realized when the option is disposed of before it has been held the required length of time. See ¶ 1328. The 2nd and 7th Circuits have held that the bargain element of restricted stock options is an expense reducing a corporate employer's earnings and profits.[8]

Minimum tax. Restricted stock options are treated the same way as qualified options for minimum tax purposes (¶ 2403) [Sec. 57(a)(6); Prop. Reg. 1.57-1(f)].

(d) Special rules. *Stock owned by an employee* to determine whether he is within the percentage limit allowed for receipt of tax-favored options includes stock owned by his brothers and sisters of the whole or half blood, spouse, ancestors, lineal descendants and a proportionate share of stock owned by a corporation, partnership, estate or trust in which he is a shareholder, partner or beneficiary [Sec. 425(d); 1.425-1(d)].

Modification, extension or renewal of an option generally is treated as a new option grant [Sec. 425(h); 1.425-1(e)]. A substitution of options may be allowed because of the corporate merger, reorganization, liquidation, etc. [Sec. 425(a); 1.425-1(a)].

Options exercised by an estate or a person acquiring them by reason of the death of the employee, qualify the shares received for special tax treatment. The holding period and employment requirements do not apply, but a transfer by an estate of stock acquired under a stock purchase or restricted option is a transfer in which ordinary income is realized, if it would have been realized by the employee on a disposition of the stock. If ordinary income must be included in the gross income of an estate of the deceased employee for any option because the option price is less than fair market value, a deduction is allowed for the estate tax on the option value. There is a special basis adjustment for the shares acquired [Sec. 421(c); 1.421-8(c)].

¶ 1328 Other stock options. When an employee or other person receives a stock option as compensation, and it does not qualify as an employee stock option (¶ 1327), the tax treatment of the option depends on whether it has a readily ascer-

Footnotes appear at end of this Chapter.

¶ **1328**

tainable fair market value. A detailed statement must be filed with the return for the year the option is received [Sec. 1.61-15(c)].

NOTE: The following rules apply to all stock options, qualified or not, granted after 5-20-76 [See ¶ 1327(a)].

(a) Option without readily ascertainable value. There is no tax when the option is granted but the person has taxable compensation on its exercise. This is measured by the difference between the stock's fair market value and the lesser amount paid for it. However, the restricted property rules apply if the stock received under the option that has been granted after 6-30-69 is subject to a restriction which substantially affects it value [¶ 1326]. Otherwise as to options granted before 7-1-69, there is compensation when the restrictions lapse or when the stock is sold, whichever happens first. This is the lesser of the difference between: (1) the amount paid for the stock and its value when acquired (disregarding restriction), or (2) the amount paid for the stock and either its value when the restriction lapses or consideration received on the sale [Sec. 1.421-6(d)].

(b) Option with readily ascertainable value. If an option has a readily ascertainable fair market value, the difference between the value of the option and any lesser amount paid for it is taxable compensation when the option is received [Sec. 1.61-15, 1.421-6]. Any later appreciation can qualify for capital gains treatment.

A stock option has a readily ascertainable fair market value when it is actively traded on an established market. If there is no market value, a value may be ascertained by showing that certain conditions specified in the regulations exist [Sec. 1.421-6(c)(3)].

¶ 1329 Property purchased by stockholders for less than fair market value.-
If property is transferred in a sale or exchange by a corporation to a shareholder for an amount less than its fair market value, the shareholder is treated as having received a distribution from the corporation.[1] The distribution is taxable as a dividend to the extent it is dividend income as determined under rules explained in ¶ 1700 et seq. If the shareholder is an individual, the amount of the distribution is the difference between the amount paid for the property and its fair market value. If the shareholder is a corporation, a special rule applies, as explained in ¶ 3126. In determining gain or loss from a later sale of the property, its basis is the amount paid for the property, increased by the amount of the distribution [Sec. 1.301-1(j)].

¶ 1330 Profit on state and municipal contracts. The profit from a contract with a state, municipality or other political subdivision, such as a school district, must be included in gross income. If payment is in warrants, their fair market value should be reported as income. If the amount received when they are cashed is more than the amount previously reported, the excess is income; if less, the difference is deductible [Sec. 1.61-3].

Mileage allowance received by a parent from a school board for transporting his children to and from school in his personal automobile is not includible in gross income. The automobile expenses of such transportation are not deductible.[1]

¶ 1331 Business insurance proceeds. In the case of insurance received for the destruction of property, the income, if any, is not the gross insurance proceeds, but only the excess, if any, over the basis of the property destroyed. Even this excess may be relieved from recognition of gain if taxpayer complies with the requirements outlined at ¶ 1411. If the proceeds are less than the basis of the property, they reduce the amount of loss that may be deducted; see ¶ 2204 et seq.

Proceeds of insurance against loss of profits because of a fire or other casualty ordinarily are income. Use and occupancy insurance and business interruption insurance proceeds, are examples.[1]

Footnotes to Chapter 3

(P-H "FEDERAL TAXES" related references are cited in brackets [ ] at the end of each footnote below.)

Footnote ¶ 1300   [¶ 7011 et seq.].
(1) Chicago, R.I. & P. Ry. Co., 47 F.2d 990, 9 AFTR 1040 [¶ 7391(15)].
(2) Natl. Ry. Times Service Co., 88 F.2d 904, 19 AFTR 212 [¶ 7391(25)].
(3) Comm. v. Turney, 82 F.2d 661, 17 AFTR 679 [¶ 7542(35)].
(4) Strauss, 2 BTA 598 [¶ 20,170(40)].
(5) Comm. v. Sunnen, 333 US 591, 68 SCt 715, 92 L. Ed. 898, 36 AFTR 611 [¶ 7479(5)].
(6) Treas. Dept. booklet "Your Federal Income Tax" (1977 Ed.), p. 38.
(7) U.S. v. Sullivan, 274 US 259, 47 SCt 607, 6 AFTR 6753 [¶ 7438(5)].
(8) Akers v. Scofield, 167 F.2d 718, 36 AFTR 981 [¶ 7435(5)].
(9) Rutkin v. U.S., 343 US 130, 72 SCt 571, 41 AFTR 96 [¶ 7434(5)].
(10) James v. U.S., 7 AFTR 2d 1361, 81 SCt 1052, 366 US 313 [¶ 7432(5)].

Footnote ¶ 1301   [¶ 7026 et seq.].
(1) Comm. v. Minzer, 5 AFTR 2d 1572, 279 F.2d 338 [¶ 7035(5)].
(2) Ostheimer v. U.S., 3 AFTR 2d 886, 264 F.2d 789 [¶ 7035(5)].
(3) Comm. v. Daehler, 6 AFTR 2d 5082, 281 F.2d 823 [¶ 7035(8)].
(4) Rev. Rul. 72-268, 1972-1 CB 313 [¶ 7034(20)].
(5) Rev. Rul. 58-140, 1958-1 CB 15 [¶ 7414(30)].
(6) Roberts, 10 TC 581, aff'd 176 F.2d 221; Foster, ¶ 48,024 P-H Memo TC; Cesanelli, 8 TC 776; Wexler, ¶ 60,266 P-H Memo TC [¶ 7051(40); 33,979(45), (50)].
(7) Jernigan, ¶ 68,018 P-H Memo TC [¶ 7397(40)].
(8) Rev. Rul. 66-167, 1966-1 CB 20 [¶ 20,167(5)].
(9) U.S. v. Kaiser, 5 AFTR 2d 1611, 363 US 299; Rev. Rul. 61-136, 1961-2 CB 20 [¶ 7032(30)].
(10) Rev. Rul. 59-5, 1959-1 CB 12 [¶ 7032(15)].
(11) Rev. Rul. 57-383, 1957-2 CB 44 [¶ 7032(15)].
(12) Rogers v. U.S. 7 AFTR 2d 1318, 290 F.2d 501 [¶ 7427(5)].
(13) Rev. Rul. 73-13, 1973-1 CB 42 [¶ 7072(22)].
(14) Rev. Rul. 55-555, 1955-2 CB 20 [¶ 7397(40)].
(15) Rev. Rul. 71, 1953-1 CB 18 [¶ 7039(5)].
(16) Rev. Rul. 63-136, 1963-2 CB 19, distinguished by Rev. Rul. 74-413, 1974-2 CB 333; Rev. Rul. 68-133, 1968-1 CB 36 [¶ 7032(55)].
(17) Bradley v. Comm., 12 AFTR 2d 5967, 324 F.2d 610, affg. 39 TC 652; Lull v. Comm., 26 AFTR 2d 70-5788 [¶ 7031.1(5); 16,496(100)].

Footnote ¶ 1302   [¶ 7046 et seq.].

Footnote ¶ 1302 continued
(1) Bogardus v. Comm., 302 US 34, 58 SCt 61, 19 AFTR 1195; Comm. v. Duberstein, 5 AFTR 2d 1626, 363 US 278 [¶ 7048(5); 7051(10)].
(2) Fisher v. Comm., 59 F.2d 192, 111 AFTR 413 [¶ 7300.15(5)].
(3) Comm. v. Duberstein, 363 US 278, 5 AFTR 2d 1626 [¶ 7051(10)].
(4) Umstead, ¶ 55,157 P-H Memo TC [¶ 7300.15(10)].
(5) Wilcox, 27 BTA 580 [¶ 7415(15)].
(6) Nickelsburg v. Comm., 154 F.2d 70, 34 AFTR 1087; Wallace v. Comm., 219 F.2d 855, 47 AFTR 210 [¶ 7047(5); 7055(10)].
(7) Levey 26 BTA 889, aff'd 68 F.2d 401, 13 AFTR 517 [¶ 7377(15)].
(8) Batterman v. Comm., ¶ 43,098 P-H Memo TC, aff'd 142 F.2d 448, 32 AFTR 671 [¶ 7047(5)].
(9) Van Sicklen, 33 BTA 544 [¶ 7055(5)].
(10) Rev. Rul. 59-58, 1959-1 CB 17 [¶ 7055(8)].
(11) Hart, ¶ 53,361 P-H Memo TC [¶ 7300.15(5)].
(12) Hubert v. Comm., 212 F.2d 516, 45 AFTR 1465 [¶ 7052(10)].
(13) Silliman v. Comm. 220 F.2d 282, 47 AFTR 300 [¶ 7051(35)].
(14) Rev. Rul. 55-691, 1955-2 CB 21 [¶ 19,089(30)].
(15) Weagant, 57 F.2d 679, 11 AFTR 30, rev'g 49 F.2d 934, 9 AFTR 1527 [¶ 7047(15)].
(16) U.S. v. Merriam, 263 US 179, 4 AFTR 3673 [¶ 8187(5)].
(17) Cunningham v. Comm., 67 F.2d 205, 12 AFTR 1385 [¶ 7048(20)].
(18) Siegel, 39 BTA 60 [¶ 7051(35)].
(19) Rev. Rul. 131, 1953-2 CB 112 [¶ 7032(50)].
(20) Rev. Rul. 60-279, 1960-2 CB 11 [¶ 7397(45)].
(21) Griggs v. U.S., 11 AFTR 2d 965, 314 F.2d 515; Treas. Dept. booklet "Your Federal Income Tax" (1977 Ed.), p. 29 [¶ 7875(25)].
(22) Rev. Rul. 67-89, 1967-1 CB 20 [¶ 7875(25)].
(23) Robertson v. U.S., 343 US 711, 72 SCt 994, 41 AFTR 1053; Rev. Rul. 68-20, 1968-1 CB 55 [¶ 7877(5)].
(24) Stein, 14 TC 494; Robertson v. U.S., 343 US 711, 41 AFTR 1053 [¶ 7877(5)].
(25) R. Turner, ¶ 54,142 P-H Memo TC [¶ 7876(10); 7877(5)].
(26) Rev. Rul. 65-58, 1965-1 CB 37; Treas. Dept. booklet "Your Federal Income Tax" (1977 Ed.), p. 51 [¶ 7879(10)].
(27) Treas. Dept. booklet "Your Federal Income Tax" (1977 Ed.), p. 47; Instructions for Form 1040.

Chapter 3—Footnotes

Footnote 1303 [¶ 8621 et seq.].
(1) Charles P. Ide, 40 TC 721, aff'd 14 AFTR 2d 5190, 335 F.2d 852 [¶ 8634(25)].
(2) William Wells, 40 TC 40; Rev. Rul. 75-280, 1975-2 CB 47 [¶ 8630(45), (60)].
(3) Bingler v. Johnson, 23 AFTR 2d 69-1212, 394 US 741 [¶ 8629(30)].
(4) Peiss, 40 TC 78; Rev. Rul. 60-378, 1960-2 CB 38 [¶ 8630(65); 34,080(17); 34,528].
(5) Rev. Rul. 59-81, 1959-1 CB 37 [¶ 8638(20)].
(6) Rev. Rul. 57-386, 1957-2 CB 107; Parr v. U.S., 31 AFTR 2d 73-392 [¶ 8629(30); 8630(5)].
(7) Leathers v. U.S., 31 AFTR 2d 73-442; Rev. Rul. 73-255, 1973-1 CB 54 [¶ 8630(5), (15)].
(8) Rev. Rul. 57-385, 1957-2 CB 109; Rev. Rul. 73-255, 1973-1 CB 54 [¶ 8630(15); 34,528].
(9) Evans, 34 TC 720; Shuff, 28 AFTR 2d 71-5625 [¶ 8630(15), (30)].
(10) Rev. Rul. 70-283, 1970-1 CB 26 [¶ 8629(30)].
(11) Rev. Rul. 66-208, 1966-2 CB 38 [¶ 8630(85)].

Footnote ¶ 1304 [¶ 7026; 7054].
(1) Flarsheim v. U.S., 156 F.2d 105, 34 AFTR 1515 [¶ 7054(5)].
(2) Rev. Rul. 62-102, 1962-2 CB 37 [¶ 7054(10)].
(3) Rev. Rul. 68-294, 1968-1 CB 46 [¶ 8160(5)].
(4) Rev. Rul. 58-153, 1958-1 CB 43 [¶ 8164(5)].
(5) Schall v. Comm., 174 F.2d 893, 37 AFTR 1536; Mutch v. Comm., 209 F.2d 390, 45 AFTR 144; Hershman v. Kavanagh, 120 F. Supp. 956, affd. 210 F.2d 654, 45 AFTR 381; Abernethy v. Comm., 211 F.2d 651, 45 AFTR 1325; MacMillan v. Crenshaw (DC-Va., ED), 48 AFTR 1288 [¶ 7300.15(50)].

Footnote ¶ 1305 [¶ 7091 et seq.].

Footnote ¶ 1306 [¶ 7096 et seq.; 8567 et seq.; 8581 et seq.].
(1) Treas. Dept. booklet "Your Federal Income Tax" (1977 Ed.), p. 31.
(2) Rev. Rul. 70-87, 1970-1 CB 29 [¶ 7097(30)].
(3) IT 3473, 1941-1 CB 192 [¶ 7097(45)].
(4) Treas. Dept. Press Release 140, 11/19/40; Rev. Rul. 69-104, 1969-1 CB 33 [¶ 7047(30)].
(5) Rev. Rul. 55-572, 1955-2 CB 45 [¶ 7097(15)].
(6) Rev. Rul. 67-350, 1967-2 CB 58 [¶ 8586(5)].
(7) Rev. Rul. 55-249, 1955-1 CB 218 [¶ 8586(10)].
(8) Rev. Rul. 76-174, 1976-1 CB 36 [¶ 8391(20)].

Footnote ¶ 1307 [¶ 7071 et seq.].
(1) Jacques, 5 BTA 56; Davidson, 94 F.2d 1011, 20 AFTR 1033 [¶ 7081(5)].
(2) Casale v. Comm., 247 F.2d 440, 52 AFTR 122; Prunier v. Comm., 248 F.2d 818, 52 AFTR 693 [¶ 7076(70); 17,087(5)].
(3) Treas. Dept. booklet "Your Federal Income Tax" (1977 Ed.), p. 30.
(4) Rev. Rul. 73-174, 1973-1 CB 43 [¶ 7910.15(15)].
(5) Treas. Dept. booklet "Your Federal Income Tax" (1977 Ed.), p. 29.
(6) Rev. Rul. 61-146, 1961-2 CB 25, distinguished by Rev. Rul. 75-241, 1975-1 CB 316 [¶ 8416(10); 34,552].
(7) Rev. Rul. 64-328, 1964-2 CB 11; Rev. Rul. 66-110, 1966-1 CB 12 [¶ 7076(75)].
(8) IT 1304, I-1 CB 72 [¶ 7072(15)].
(9) Rev. Rul. 76-352, IRB 1976-38 [¶ 54,814].
(10) Rev. Rul. 76-71, 1976-1 CB 308 [¶ 8629(3)].

Footnote ¶ 1307 continued
(11) Hitner v. Lederer, 63 F.2d 877, 12 AFTR 329 [¶ 7072(30)].
(12) Rev. Rul. 58-128, 1958-1 CB 89 [¶ 7032(10)].
(13) Rev. Rul. 60-330, 1960-2 CB 46 [¶ 7032(10)].
(14) Letter Ruling, 3-22-56, in full at ¶ 76,448, P-H Fed. 1956 [¶ 7032(20)].
(15) Rev. Rul. 56-249, 1956-1 CB 488 [¶ 7032(10)].
(16) Rev. Rul. 67-402, 1967-2 CB 135 [¶ 7077(3)].
(17) Comm. v. Fender Sales, 14 AFTR 2d 6076, 338 F.2d 924 [¶ 7077(3)].

Footnote ¶ 1308 [¶ 8681 et seq.].
(1) U.S. v. Barrett, 12 AFTR 2d 5630, 321 F.2d 911; U.S. v. Morelan, 17 AFTR 2d 286, 356 F.2d 199; U.S. v. Keeton, 20 AFTR 2d 5688, 383 F.2d 429 [¶ 8687(5)].
(2) Kowalski, 65 TC 44, revd. 38 AFTR 2d 76-6125; TIR-741, ¶ 54,920 P-H Fed. 1965 [¶ 8687(5)].
(3) Rev. Rul. 68-579, 1968-2 CB 61 [¶ 8686(30)].
(4) Chandler v. Comm., 119 F.2d 623, 27 AFTR 172; Frueaff, 30 BTA 449 [¶ 7379(5), (8)].
(5) Richards v. Comm., 111 F.2d 376, 24 AFTR 931; Peacock v. Comm., 256 F.2d 160, 1 AFTR 2d 1931 [¶ 7379(15)].
(6) Rev. Rul. 63-156, 1963-2 CB 79 [¶ 8430(10)].
(7) Rev. Rul. 65-124, 1965-1 CB 60 [¶ 34,083(13)].
(8) Rev. Rul. 59-350, 1959-2 CB 45 [¶ 8427(20)].
(9) Rev. Rul. 62-212, 1962-2 CB 41 [¶ 13,048(55)].
(10) Rev. Rul. 63-90, 1963-1 CB 27 [¶ 8426(15)].
(11) Rev. Rul. 70-549, 1970-2 CB 16 [¶ 8426(15)].
(12) Salkov, 46 TC 190 (NA, 1969-2 CB XXVI) [¶ 8426(10)].

Footnote ¶ 1309 [¶ 7080 et seq.].
(1) Treas. Dept. booklet "Your Federal Income Tax" (1977 Ed.), p. 48.
(2) Schlemmer v. U.S., 94 F.2d 77, 20 AFTR 645 [¶ 7080(5)].

Footnote ¶ 1310 [¶ 7075].
(1) Treas. Dept. booklet "Your Federal Income Tax" (1977 Ed.), p. 29.

Footnote ¶ 1312 [¶ 7861 et seq.].
(1) Marinaccio, ¶ 49,081 P-H Memo TC [¶ 33,973(70)].

Footnote ¶ 1314 [¶ 7201 et seq.].
(1) Fall River Electric Light Co., 23 BTA 168 [¶ 7206(5)].
(2) W. Noll, 43 BTA 496; Campbell v. Sailer, 224 F.2d 641, 47 AFTR 1490 [¶ 7225(10); 7895(5)].
(3) Est. of Rickaby, 27 TC 886; Rev. Rul. 60-284, 1960-2 CB 464 [¶ 32,329(5)].
(4) Jaglom, 9 AFTR 2d 1686, 303 F.2d 847 [¶ 7225(20)].
(5) Treas. Dept. letter, 2/7/49 [¶ 7223(20)].
(6) Kieselbach v. Comm., 317 U.S. 399, 30 AFTR 371 [¶ 7226(5)].
(7) Rev. Rul. 73-322, 1973-2 CB 44 [¶ 7210(5)].
(8) Terrel, 7 BTA 773 [¶ 7209(5)].
(9) Rev. Rul. 54-143, 1954-1 CB 12 [¶ 20,509(15)].

Footnote ¶ 1315 [¶ 7223].
(1) Rev. Rul. 72-224, 1972-1 CB 30 [¶ 8252(5)].

Footnote ¶ 1316 [¶ 7241 et seq.].
(1) Wentz v. Gentsch (DC Ohio) 27 AFTR 1128 [¶ 7267(20)].
(2) U.S. v. Joliet & Chicago R.R. Co., 315 US 44, 28 AFTR 215 [¶ 7267(5)].

Chapter 3—Footnotes

Footnote ¶ 1316 continued
(3) Conn. Ry. & Lighting Co. v. U.S., 135 Ct Cl 650, 142 F. Supp. 907, 49 AFTR 1902 [¶ 7263(10)].
(4) Hort v. Comm., 313 US 28, 61 SCt 757, 25 AFTR 1207 [¶ 32,605(5)].
(5) Bankers Pocahontas Coal Co., 287 US 308, 53 SCt 150, 11 AFTR 1089 [¶ 7250(5)].
(6) Hopkins v. U.S., 82 F. Supp. 1015, 37 AFTR 1108 [¶ 7249(5)].

Footnote ¶ 1317 [¶ 8461 et seq.].

Footnote ¶ 1318 [¶ 7301 et seq.].
(1) Helvering v. American Dental Co., 318 US 322, 63 SCt 577, 30 AFTR 397 [¶ 7308(5)].
(2) Elizabeth Operating Corp., ¶ 43,434, P-H Memo TC [¶ 7308(15)].
(3) Comm. v. Jacobson, 336 US 28, 69 SCt 358, 37 AFTR 516 [¶ 7308(5)].
(4) Helvering v. Killian, 128 F.2d 433, 29 AFTR 528; Gehring Publishing Co., Inc. v. Comm., 1 TC 345 [¶ 7312(20)].
(5) U.S. v. Ore.-Wash. R.R. & Nav. Co., 251 Fed. 211, 1 AFTR 989, DeRoy & Bros., ¶ 44,154 P-H Memo TC [¶ 7314(5), (15)].
(6) Helvering v. Jane Holding Corp., 109 F.2d 933, 24 AFTR 426, rev. 38 BTA 960 [¶ 7320(15)].
(7) Burnet v. Campbell Co., 50 F.2d 487, 10 AFTR 33; Rev. Rul. 58-600, 1958-2 CB 29 [¶ 7307(5); 7329(25)].
(8) Lakeland Grocery Co., 36 BTA 289; Haden Co., Memo BTA, 10-20-39, affd. 118 F.2d 285, 26 AFTR 679 [¶ 7307(10)].
(9) Carlisle Packing Co., 29 BTA 514; Huberman, ¶ 43,323 P-H Memo TC; O'Dell & Sons Co., Inc. v. Comm., 169 F.2d 247, 37 AFTR 173 [¶ 31,107(5), (10)].
(10) Springfield Industrial Bldg. Co., 38 BTA 1445 [¶ 7307(30)].
(11) Coddon & Bros., Inc., 37 BTA 393 [¶ 7312(5)].
(12) Hirsch v. Comm., 115 F.2d 656, 25 AFTR 1038; Helvering v. Killian Co., 128 F.2d 433, 29 AFTR 528, affg. 44 BTA 169 [¶ 7312(20)].
(13) Frank v. U.S., 131 F.2d 864, 30 AFTR 497, affg. 29 AFTR 398 [¶ 7311(35)].
(14) Hiatt, 35 BTA 292, citing Fulton Gold Corp., 31 BTA 519 [¶ 7323(5)].

Footnote ¶ 1320 [¶ 7701 et seq.].
(1) Clark, 40 TC 57 [¶ 7717(20)].
(2) Rev. Rul. 65-283, 1965-2 CB 25 [¶ 7706(15)].
(3) U.S. v. Davis, 370 US 65, 9 AFTR 2d 1625 [¶ 31,111(5)].
(4) Est. of Laughlin, 167 F.2d 828, 36 AFTR 985 [¶ 7706(15)].
(5) Luckenbach v. Pedrick, 214 F.2d 914, 45 AFTR 1849 [¶ 7707(30)].

Footnote ¶ 1320 continued
(6) Myers v. Comm., 212 F.2d 448, 45 AFTR 1436 [¶ 7710(15)].
(7) Marinello, 54 TC 577 [¶ 7706(10)].
(8) Pappenheimer v. Allen, 164 F.2d 428, 36 AFTR 406 [¶ 7706(10)].
(9) Comm. v. Lester, 7 AFTR 2d 1445, 366 US 299; Rev. Rul. 70-557, 1970-2 CB 10 [¶ 7714(20)].
(10) Brown, 50 TC 865, affd. 24 AFTR 2d 69-5509, 415 F.2d 310; Hoffman, 54 TC 1607 [¶ 7722(10)].
(11) Faber v. Comm., 3 AFTR 2d 838, 264 F.2d 127 [¶ 7707(35)].
(12) Lehman, 17 TC 652 [¶ 7714(15)].
(13) Hart, 11 TC 16; Rev. Rul. 70-218, 1970-1 CB 19 [¶ 7712(5)].
(14) Blumenthal v. Comm., 183 F.2d 15, 39 AFTR 628; Gardner, 14 TC 1445; Carr, ¶ 54,050 P-H Memo TC; Smith, 21 TC 353; Rev. Rul. 70-218, 1970-1 CB 19 [¶ 7712(5)].
(15) Rev. Rul. 67-420, 1967-2 CB 63 [¶ 7706(13)].
(16) Rev. Rul. 62-39, 1962-1 CB 17 [¶ 7706(13)].
(17) Rev. Rul. 62-106, 1962-2 CB 21 [¶ 7707(20)].

Footnote ¶ 1321 [¶ 7011 et seq.].

Footnote ¶ 1326 [¶ 7921 et seq.].
(1) Rev. Rul. 75-448, 1975-2 CB 55 [¶ 7926(10)].

Footnote ¶ 1327 [¶ 19,311 et seq.].
(1) Rev. Rul. 64-312, 1964-2 CB 117 [¶ 19,414(10)].
(2) Dugan v. U.S., 14 AFTR 2d 5788, 234 F. Supp. 7 [¶ 32,381(55)].
(3) Rev. Rul. 75-256, 1975-2 CB 194 [¶ 19,376(7)].
(4) Rev. Rul. 67-166, 1967-1 CB 97 [¶ 19,376(5)].
(5) Rev. Rul. 73-26, 1973-1 CB 204 as modified by Rev. Rul. 73-330, 1973-2 CB 426; Rev. Rul. 74-128, 1974-1 CB 104 [¶ 19,376(5), (20)].
(6) Rev. Rul. 73-92, 1973-1 CB 208 [¶ 19,458(20)].
(7) Rev. Rul. 63-47, 1963-1 CB 97 [¶ 19,412(5)].
(8) Luckman v. Comm., 418 F.2d 381, 24 AFTR 2d 69-5901; Divine v. Comm., 34 AFTR 2d 74-5331, 500 F.2d 1041 [¶ 19,351(10)].

Footnote ¶ 1328 [¶ 19,331].

Footnote ¶ 1329 [¶ 17,086(15)].
(1) Timberlake v. Comm., 132 F.2d 259, 30 AFTR 583, affg. 46 BTA 1082; Comm. v. Gordon, 391 US 83, 21 AFTR 2d 1329 [¶ 17,042(5); 17,086(15)].

Footnote ¶ 1330 [¶ 7156].
(1) Rev. Rul. 57-60, 1957-1 CB 25 [¶ 7397(40)].

Footnote ¶ 1331 [¶ 7407].
(1) Oppenheim's, Inc. v. Cavanagh, 90 F. Supp. 107, 39 AFTR 468; Rev. Rul. 55-264, 1955-1 CB 11 [¶ 7407(10)].

Highlights of Chapter 3
Gross income—Inclusions

I. **Gross Income**
   A. **What is gross income.** Income from any source unless exempt by law [¶ 1300(a)]:
      1. Compensation for services.
      2. Business income.
      3. Profit from property sales and dealings.
      4. Interest.
      5. Rent.
      6. Dividends.
   B. **Amounts received by mistake taxable when [¶ 1300(b)]:**
      1. Owner cannot be found.
      2. Little chance refund will be made.
   C. **To whom taxable [¶ 1300(c), (d), (e), (f)]:**
      1. Salaries and wages—to performers of services.
      2. Property income—to owners of property.
      3. Tenants by the entirety:
         a. Joint return—no consequence, income splitting available.
         b. Separate return—state law controls, generally taxable to husband in common law state.
      4. Joint tenants and tenants in common—state law controls.
      5. Community property income:
         a. Joint return—no consequence, income splitting available.
         b. Separate return—state law controls, generally taxable to both.
II. **Compensation for Services**
   A. **All compensation for personal services taxable [¶ 1301].**
   B. **Distinguished from gift [¶ 1302]:**
      1. Intention of parties and facts controls.
      2. Awards and prizes taxable [¶ 1302(c)]:
         a. Reported as "other income" on return.
         b. Not taxable if primarily in recognition of religious, charitable, scientific, educational, artistic, literary or civil achievement and if:
            1) Winner selected without action on own part to enter contest; and
            2) Substantial future services not required as condition to receive prize.
   C. **Scholarships and fellowships [¶ 1303]:**
      1. Candidate for degree—taxed on amount representing salary when services required, unless all candidates required to work.
      2. Not candidate for degree—taxed on amount, excluding $300 times number of months grant received (limited to 36 months—consecutive or not).
      3. Medical trainees—taxed on amount received, unless grant not deemed compensation.
      4. Vocational trainees—training, room, board, transportation and tuition costs in state-run projects not income.
   D. **Pensions and employee death benefits [1304]:**
      1. Pensions and retirement allowances generally taxable.
      2. Payments to widows of deceased employees either taxable compensation for past services or nontaxable gift.
      3. Employee death benefits up to $5,000 excludable.
      4. Death benefits received as annuity excludable (subject to $5,000 limit) to value of annuity less larger of:

a. Employee's contribution; or
b. Amount of vested rights.
    5. Certain pensions awarded as gifts nontaxable.
E. **Compensation of government employees taxable [¶ 1305].**
F. **Compensation of members of armed forces generally taxable [¶ 1306].**
G. **Compensation other than cash [¶ 1307]:**
    1. Taxable at fair market value on date received.
    2. Employer paid insurance premiums generally taxable to insured employee [¶ 1307(a)], except:
        a. Ordinary life insurance—when employer is beneficiary.
        b. Group permanent life insurance—if employee's rights end when he stops working for employer.
        c. Group-term life insurance—premiums up to $50,000 coverage, and premiums over $50,000 when employer or recognized charity is beneficiary.
        d. Health and hospital insurance premiums.
    3. Employer paid qualified retirement annuity premiums not taxable.
    4. Employer paid pension trust premiums taxable.
    5. Split-dollar life insurance:
        a. Employee taxed on total yearly benefits received less premiums he paid.
        b. No tax on policy proceeds at death.
    6. Books and tuition for required schooling paid by employer taxable to employee [¶ 1307(b)].
    7. Government bonds received as salary taxable [¶ 1307(c)].
    8. Guaranteed annual wage plans generally taxable [¶ 1307(d)].
    9. Stock taxable on fair market value when received [¶ 1307(e)].
H. **Board and lodging generally not taxable [¶ 1308], except:**
    1. When cash is available instead.
    2. Meals and lodging furnished employee's family.
    3. Meals furnished without substantial noncompensatory business reason [¶ 1308(a)].
    4. Lodging not necessary for proper performance of duties [¶ 1308(b)].
    5. Property occupied rent-free by stockholder [¶ 1308(c)].
    6. Rental allowances for clergymen employed only to teach by organization not under church authority [¶ 1308(e)].
I. **Compensation paid in notes [¶ 1309]:**
    1. Payment for services—taxable to extent of fair market value when received.
    2. Additional security or cover for overdue interest—not taxable.
    3. Good for face value at maturity, but not bearing interest—taxable at fair discounted value.
    4. Portions of payments representing proportionate parts of original discount taxable when received.
J. **Employee's bargain purchases [¶ 1310]:**
    1. Difference between price and fair market value taxable.
    2. "Courtesy" discounts not taxable if relatively small value, noncompensatory and furnished to promote efficiency.
K. **Children's compensation taxable to child [¶ 1312].**
III. **Interest, Rent and Miscellaneous Income**
A. **Interest [¶ 1314]—all taxable, except:**
    1. Excluded interest on government obligations—not taxable.
    2. Accrued interest in arrears on bonds bought "flat"—treated as return of capital.
    3. Future interest on bonds redeemed before maturity—treated as redemption proceeds.
B. **Accrued interest on bonds sold between interest dates [¶ 1315]:**
    1. Accrued interest *to* date of sale—taxable to seller.
    2. Accrued interest *from* date of sale—taxable to buyer.
C. **Rents [¶ 1316(a)]—taxable, including:**

1. Payments by tenant to third party—rent income to landlord.
2. Taxes paid by tenant to or for landlord—rent income to landlord.
3. Cancellation of lease:
    a. Tenant pays landlord—ordinary income to landlord.
    b. Landlord pays tenant—proceeds from sale or exchange of lease.
D. Royalties [¶ 1316(b)]—taxable.
E. Improvements by lessee [¶ 1317].
    1. In addition to rent—not income to landlord (gain or loss recognized at property's disposal).
    2. In lieu of rent—fair market value taxable to landlord [¶ 1317(b)].
F. Debt forgiveness [¶ 1318].
    1. Cancellation for consideration—income in amount of debt cancelled [¶ 1318(a)].
    2. Cancellation as gift—no income [¶ 1318(b)].
    3. Cancellation as adjustment of purchase price—no income [¶ 1318(c)].
    4. Cancellation of corporate debts:
        a. Debt owed stockholder—no income, capital contribution [¶ 1318(d)].
        b. Debt owed corporation—taxable dividend [¶ 1318(e)].
    5. Cancellation under Bankruptcy Act [¶ 1318(f)]—no income if:
        a. Bankruptcy adjudication.
        b. Corporate reorganization plan.
        c. Composition agreement, arrangement or settlement.
    6. Insolvency [¶ 1318(g)]:
        a. Debtor insolvent before and after—no income.
        b. Debtor insolvent before and solvent after—income to extent of net worth after forgiveness.
    7. Delivery of property [¶ 1318(h)]—income if property basis less than debt.
    8. Mortgage settlement for less than face value [¶ 1318(i)]:
        a. Gratuitous—no income.
        b. Not gratuitous and personal liability:
            1) Property value at least equal to mortgage value—income.
            2) Property value equal to or less than settlement price—no income.
            3) Mortgage debt incurred after property acquired—income regardless of property value at settlement.
        c. Not gratuitous and no personal liability—no income.
    9. Election to exclude income and apply to reduce basis [¶ 1318(j)].
G. Alimony [¶ 1320]—taxable if:
    1. Periodic payments [¶ 1320(b)].
    2. In discharge of obligation to support under:
        a. Civil decree of divorce or separate maintenance or written instrument incident to divorce or separate maintenance.
        b. Written separation agreement, if spouses living apart and filing separately.
        c. Civil decree requiring payments for support and maintenance, provided spouses separated and filing separately.
    3. Not specifically for support of minor children [¶ 1320(c)].
    4. Other taxable alimony includes:
        a. Life insurance premiums (if immediate benefits) [¶ 1320(d)].
        b. Mortgage and other residence payments [¶ 1320(e)].
        c. Medical expenses [¶ 1320(f)].
H. Gambling income taxable [¶ 1321].
IV. Restricted Property As Compensation [¶ 1326]
    A. Generally [¶ 1326]:
        1. Transferred to employee after 6-30-69 generally taxable.
        2. Taxed on excess of fair market value over any cost in first year stock is transferable (other than by gift) or not subject to substantial risk of forfeiture [¶ 1326(a)].
        3. Appreciation between receipt and inclusion in income is ordinary income [¶ 1326(d)].

B. Election [¶ 1326(b)(c)]:
1. To treat restricted property subject to substantial risk of forfeiture or nontransferable as compensation when received [¶ 1326(b)]:
   a. Income in excess of fair market value over any amount paid for property.
   b. No deduction or refund if property later forfeited.
2. Special rules for restrictions that never lapse [¶ 1326(c)].

C. **Restricted property rules not applicable to [¶ 1326(f), (g)]:**
1. Transfers under employee stock purchase plan.
2. Transfers to or from qualified employee trust.
3. Transfers under qualified annuity.
4. Transfers of options without readily ascertainable market value.
5. Transfers of property by exercising options with readily ascertainable market value at time of grant.
6. Transfers made:
   a. Under pre-4-22-69 contracts or options, or
   b. Before 5-1-70 under pre-7-1-69 plans or under similar transition rules.

V. **Employee Stock Options [¶ 1327]**
A. **Qualified stock options—individual options granted after 1963 [¶ 1327(a)].**
1. Requirements (*all* must be met):
   a. Stockholder approval within 1 year before or after adoption.
   b. Must not run more than 10 years and must state total shares optioned and employees or classes to receive options.
   c. Available only to those employed by granting corporation continuously from grant to 3 months before exercise.
   d. Option must provide:
      1) For exercise within 5 years after grant.
      2) Only employee can exercise while alive, and transferable at death only by will or operation of law.
      3) Not exercisable while employee has prior outstanding qualified or restricted option.
   e. Price must at least equal fair market value of stock when granted.
   f. Employee cannot hold more than 5% of stock when option granted.
   g. Must be granted under a plan adopted prior to 5-20-76.
2. Tax treatment:
   a. No income when received or exercised.
   b. Ordinary income when exercise option meeting all requirements *but* price is less than fair market value when granted.
   c. Long-term capital gain or loss if stock held at least 3 years.
   d. Ordinary income if sold within 3 years.
3. Minimum tax on difference between purchase price and stock value in tax year option exercised.
4. Rules allowing favorable tax treatment of qualified plans repealed for options granted after 5-20-76 (except those granted under plan adopted prior to this date).
5. Tax treatment of option when received depends on whether it has readily ascertainable fair market value.

B. **Stock purchase plan options—across-the-board options granted after 1963 [¶ 1327(b)].**
1. Requirements:
   a. Participation limited to employees owning less than 5% stock.
   b. Stockholder approval.
   c. Non-discriminatory.
   d. All employees must be included (except officers, part-time workers and those employed less than 2 years).
   e. Price must be at least 85% of stock value when granted or exercised.
   f. Plan may run 5 years if price is 85% when exercised; otherwise 27 months.

g. No more than $25,000 of stock (valued at grant) may accrue for purchase in one year.
h. Available only to those employed by granting corporation continuously from grant to 3 months before exercise.
2. Tax treatment:
   a. No income when received or exercised.
   b. Long-term capital gain or loss if stock held at least 9 months after acquired, at least 2 years after option granted and price at least equal to fair market value when granted.
   c. Ordinary income if held as in b. above and price between 85% and 100% when granted or exercised.
   d. Ordinary income if disposed before required holding period ends.
3. No minimum tax when exercised, but one-half of long-term gain on sale is tax preference item.

C. **Restricted stock options—individual options granted before 1964 (or later under a binding written contract made before 1964) [¶ 1327(c)].**
1. Requirements:
   a. Exercisable for 10 years after grant.
   b. Not transferable except at death by will or operation of law.
   c. Price must be at least 85% of stock fair market value when granted.
   d. Variable price options allowed.
   e. Employee cannot hold more than 10% of stock when option granted, but more than 10% if price is at least 110% of stock value when granted and 5-year limit to exercise.
   f. Available only to those employed by granting corporation continuously from grant to 3 months before exercise.
2. Tax treatment:
   a. No income when received or exercised.
   b. Long-term capital gain or loss when held at least 9 months after acquired, at least 2 years after option granted, and price at least 95% when granted.
   c. Ordinary income when held as in b. above and price between 85% and 95% when granted.
   d. Ordinary income if disposed before required holding period ends.
3. Minimum tax on difference between purchase price and stock value in tax year option exercised.

D. **Special rules [¶ 1327(d)]:**
1. Employee owned stock in determining percentage limit includes stock of brothers, sisters, spouse, ancestors, lineal decendants and proportionate shares owned by corporations in which he is shareholder.
2. Modification, extension or renewal of option treated as new option grant.
3. Options exercised by reason of employee's death receive special treatment.

VI. **Other Stock Options [¶ 1328]**
A. **Applies to all options granted after 5-20-76.**
B. **Tax treatment:**
1. Readily ascertainable market value:
   a. Ordinary income when option received.
   b. Capital gains treatment when option sold.
2. No readily ascertainable market value:
   a. Unconditional right to receive stock—ordinary income when option exercised.
   b. Subject to substantial restriction—ordinary income when restriction lapses or stock transferred.
   c. Employee is officer or insider—ordinary income when option exercised.

VII. **Stockholder Purchases For Less Than Fair Market Value [¶ 1329]**
A. **Treated as corporate distribution.**
B. **Taxed as dividend.**

VIII. **Profit on State and Municipal Contracts [¶ 1330]**

A. Included in gross income (if warrants—fair market value taxed).
B. School board mileage allowance—not income.
IX. Business Insurance Proceeds Generally Taxable [¶ 1331]

Chapter 4

GAIN OR LOSS—RECOGNITION

TABLE OF CONTENTS

¶

GAIN OR LOSS IN GENERAL

	¶
Factors in figuring gain or loss	1400
Recognition of gain or loss	1401
Amount received for easement	
Gain recognized while loss not deductible	
Sale and exchange distinguished	1402

NONTAXABLE EXCHANGES

Common nontaxable exchanges	1403
Securities for securities of same corporation	1404
Transfer of property to corporation controlled by transferor	1405
Liability of transferor assumed by transferee	
When corporation assumes liabilities in excess of basis of property transferred	
Exchanges with an investment company	
Property held for productive use or investment	1406
Exchange of insurance policies	1407
Effect of giving or receiving "boot"	1408
Giving boot	
Receiving boot	
Exchange of mortgaged property	1409

INVOLUNTARY CONVERSION

What is involuntary conversion	1410
Condemnation	
Livestock—disease and drought	
Sales under federal reclamation laws	
Broadcasting property sales certified by FCC	
Gain or loss on involuntary conversion—general rules	1411
Conversion directly into other property	
Who must make the replacement	
How to make the election	
Information on the return	
Notice required	
Time limit on replacement in involuntary conversions	1412
Advance payment to contractor	

¶

	¶
Conversion directly into other property	
Making replacements in involuntary conversions	1413
What qualifies as replacement property	
Property similar or related in service or use	
Condemnation of real property	
How to figure recognized gain or loss in involuntary conversions	1414
If amount realized exceeds cost of replacement	
If basis of asset exceeds amount received	
If cost of replacement exceeds amount received	
Severance damages and special assessments in condemnations	1415

SALE OF RESIDENCE

Gain from sale or exchange of residence	1416
Sales price of old residence	
Adjusted sales price	
Fixing-up expenses	
Cost of new residence	
How to figure recognized gain	
Official worksheet	
Exchange	
Installment sale	
What is a residence	1417
Business or investment property	
Property used both for residence and business or investment	
More than one residence	
How special rules apply to husband and wife	1418
When benefits of special rule not available	1419
Special treatment for members of Armed Forces	1420
Condemnation of a residence	1421
How to report sale of residence	1422
Sales by persons 65 or over	1423
Sales of low-income housing projects	1426

• Highlights of Chapter 4 .... Page 1461

Footnotes appear at end of this Chapter.

GAIN OR LOSS IN GENERAL

A gain is not includible in income nor a loss deductible until realized. But even if a gain or loss is realized, it will not be reported until it is *recognized.* Usually, gain or loss realized on a sale or exchange is recognized. However, in certain exchanges the gain or loss is not recognized in the year of the exchange, but will be recognized when the property received is sold or otherwise disposed of in a taxable transaction. This chapter answers the question: "When is a gain or loss recognized?"

¶ 1400 **Factors in figuring gain or loss.** Even if there is a taxable gain or a deductible loss, a number of rules must be applied to find the amount of the gain or loss. To understand the factors and apply these rules, the following must be considered:

- *Basis* ordinarily is the tax cost at which the taxpayer got the property. Sometimes the value of the property or a substituted basis (someone else's basis) is used. See Chapter 5.

- *Adjustments to basis* (additions and reductions) involve capital expenditures and recoveries during the time the property was held. Basis is increased if capital is spent to add or permanently improve the value of property. Deductible losses and capital recoveries, such as capital investment returned or depreciation allowable, decrease basis. See ¶ 1500(b).

- *Amount realized* is both the money and fair market value of any property received for the property transferred. The type of consideration received for the property must be taken into account. Consideration includes: (a) cash; (b) property; (c) property and cash; or (d) fair market value of buyer's obligations. See (b) below.

- *The nature of the property* determines if capital gain or loss provisions apply. Types of property include: (a) securities; (b) real estate; (c) business property; (d) investment property; (e) inventory property and (f) intangible property. Also consider whether the property was held for more than nine months. See Chapter 6.

Steps in figuring gain or loss to be reported. When the above factors are known, the following formula is applied to arrive at the amount to be reported:

BASIS + ADDITIONS − REDUCTIONS = ADJUSTED BASIS
GAIN = AMOUNT REALIZED − ADJUSTED BASIS
LOSS = ADJUSTED BASIS − AMOUNT REALIZED

Amount realized. The excess of the amount realized over the adjusted basis is gain; the excess of the adjusted basis over the amount realized is loss [Sec. 1.1001-1]. The amount realized includes the seller's personal obligations assumed by the buyer, as well as encumbrances outstanding against the property that the buyer assumes or satisfies, or which remain a charge against the property. For example, a taxpayer who sells mortgaged property realizes an amount equal to the cash received plus the mortgage debt he is relieved from paying.[1] The seller also includes real estate taxes assumed by the buyer in the amount realized. Selling expenses, however, are deducted from the amount realized.[2] See also ¶ 1501; 1920. The amount realized in a taxable exchange of property [¶ 1503] generally is the fair market of the property received. Any money received with the property is included in the amount realized. Any money given with the property reduces the amount realized.[3] An employer transferring securities to his employee for services realizes taxable income measured by the excess of the fair market value of the securities over their adjusted basis in his hands on the date of the transfer[4] [¶ 3124].

Capital gain or loss. If the property is a capital asset held for more than nine months, a sale or exchange results in a long-term capital gain or loss. If it was held for nine months or less, the sale or exchange results in a short-term capital gain or loss. 50% of any excess net long-term capital gain over net short-term capital loss is deductible in figuring adjusted gross income of an individual. See Chapter 6. (For rules applying to corporations, see Chapter 22.)

NOTE: The holding period will be increased for long-term capital gain or loss to over one year for tax years starting in 1978.

¶ **1401 Recognition of gain or loss.** Generally, gain or loss is recognized for income tax purposes when property is sold or exchanged [Sec. 1001]. But gain or loss may not be recognized at the time of some exchanges [¶ 1403-1409; Chapter 23], involuntary conversions [¶ 1410-1415], the sale of a residence [¶ 1416-1423; 1426], sales between related persons [¶ 2223], repossessions of property [¶ 2821; 2823] and sales or exchanges by a corporation of its own stock [¶ 3124].

(a) **Amount received for easement.** If a taxpayer grants an easement on his property and is deprived of the beneficial interest of the entire property, it is treated as a sale of the entire property. But if he retains a beneficial interest, the amount received reduces the entire property's basis.[1] Any amount in excess of the basis is taxable gain.[2]

(b) **Gain recognized while loss not deductible.** In some cases, a gain on the sale of property may be recognized, while a loss on the sale of the *same* property is not deductible. Thus, gain on the sale of a pleasure car or residence is recognized, while a loss is not [¶ 2202; 2203]. Also, *loss* is not recognized on "wash sales" and sales between related taxpayers [¶ 2221; 2223].

¶ **1402 Sale and exchange distinguished.** An exchange is a reciprocal transfer of property, as distinguished from a property transfer for money only. The fact that the taxpayer pays cash in addition to giving up property does not prevent the transaction from being an exchange.[1] The distinction between a sale accompanied by a purchase, and an exchange is important. Generally, only exchanges qualify for nonrecognition of gain.

NONTAXABLE EXCHANGES

Gain or loss is generally recognized on an exchange. However, in certain instances the recognition of gain or loss is postponed. These are referred to as "nontaxable exchanges."

¶ **1403 Common nontaxable exchanges.** They include the following:

• Securities for securities of the same corporation. See ¶ 1404.
• Under certain conditions, the transfer of property to a corporation controlled by the transferor. See ¶ 1405.
• Property held for productive use or investment for property of a like kind. See ¶ 1406.
• Exchanges of certain insurance policies. See ¶ 1407.

Footnotes appear at end of this Chapter.

- Exchanges of certain government bonds. The Treasury can allow bonds issued under the Second Liberty Bond Act to be surrendered in exchange solely for other bonds issued under the act without gain or loss being recognized [Sec. 1037(a); 1.1037-1(a)]. State or municipal bonds may be exchanged for substantially identical bonds of the same obligor with no gain or loss being recognized.[1]
- Exchanges of stock and property in corporate reorganizations. Chapter 23.

Gain or loss may be recognized when "boot" is given or received in exchanges that are ordinarily nontaxable. See ¶ 1408. Assuming liabilities in certain otherwise nontaxable exchanges may also result in recognition of gain.

¶ **1404 Securities for securities of same corporation.** No gain or loss is recognized on an exchange of stock in the same corporation (common for common, preferred for preferred, or voting for nonvoting). The exchange is nontaxable whether it is between a stockholder and the corporation, or between two individual stockholders [Sec. 1036; 1.1036-1]. Exchanging bonds for similar bonds of the same corporation also is a nontaxable exchange.

NONTAXABLE EXCHANGES

Restricted stock for unrestricted stock in the same corporation.[1]

Exercising right found in debenture to convert it into obligor corporation's stock[2] (but exercising right to convert into stock of another corporation is a taxable exchange).[3]

Voting trust certificates turned in for common stock.[4]

Converting joint tenancy in corporate stock to tenancy in common; severing joint tenancy in corporate stock under partition action.[5]

TAXABLE EXCHANGES

Stock exchanged for bonds.

Preferred stock exchanged for common (but preferred exchanged for common in the same corporation *under a conversion privilege in the preferred stock certificate* is nontaxable).[6]

Common stock of one corporation exchanged for common stock in another.

(However, the above exchanges may be tax free when a corporate reorganization is involved. See ¶ 3300 et seq.)

¶ **1405 Transfer of property to corporation controlled by transferor.** No gain or loss is recognized if one or more persons transfer property to a corporation solely in exchange for its stock or securities, and immediately after the exchange such person or persons are in control of the corporation. Services are not considered property; but if services performed in a property transfer are not substantial, no gain or loss is recognized.[1] Gain or loss may be recognized in certain cases if stock or securities are issued for property of relatively small value compared to the value of the stock and securities already owned by the transferor. The transferred property is not considered of small value if its fair market value equals or exceeds 10% of the value of the stock or securities to be received[2] [Sec. 351(a); 1.351-1, 1.351-2]. Requests for rulings on the nonrecognition of gain must give complete details of the transaction.[3] When a transfer involves a foreign corporation, an otherwise tax-free exchange will be recognized unless a clearance request is filed with the IRS within 183 days after the transfer showing that it was not for tax avoidance purposes.[4] Certain transactions may be exempted from the request requirement [Sec. 367].

Control means owning at least 80% of the voting stock and at least 80% of all other classes of stock of the corporation [Sec. 368(c)]. In determining control, it is immaterial that a corporate transferor distributes to its shareholders the stock it gets for property [Sec. 351(c); 1.351-1(a)(1)].

Example 1: Carle owns 6,000 of 10,000 shares of the voting common stock of the Low Corp. and 4,000 of its 5,000 nonvoting preferred shares. Carle transfers property to Low Corp. in exchange for 2,000 of the remaining 4,000 common shares. No gain is recognized because

Carle was in control of the corporation immediately after the exchange. He owned at least 80% of the total voting power (8,000 out of the 10,000 common) and at least 80% of all other classes of stock (4,000 out of the 5,000 preferred).

Stock in proportion to interests before exchange. When more than one person transfers property, the stock and securities they receive need not be in the same proportion as their interest in the property. However, any stockholder who received stock and securities whose value was less than the property transferred may have made a gift or paid compensation to stockholders who received stock and securities of greater value than the property they transferred [Sec. 1.351-1(b)(1)].

Example 2: A and B, father and son, organize a corporation with 1,000 shares of common stock. A transfers property worth $800 in exchange for 200 shares of stock, while B transfers property worth $2,000 to the corporation in exchange for 800 shares of stock. No gain or loss is recognized. But, if in fact A has made a gift to B, it may be subject to gift tax. Similarly, if in fact B had rendered services to A and the disproportion in the amount of stock received was, in effect, the payment of compensation by A to B, the compensation would be taxed.

Information filed with return—records kept. Transferor and corporation must file information about the transfer with their income tax returns for the year the exchange is made. Permanent records must be kept so gain or loss on a later sale of the stock or securities and other property received in the exchange can be determined [Sec. 1.351-3].

(a) Liability of transferor assumed by transferee. If the corporation acquires the property subject to a liability or assumes transferor's liability, the assumption or acquisition does not prevent the exchange from being tax free [Sec. 357(a); 1.357-1(a)(b)]. See ¶ 1518. But if the purpose is to avoid taxes, or if the transaction is not for a real business purpose, the total liability assumed or acquired is considered as money received by the transferor [Sec. 357(b); 1.357-1(c)]. It is taxed as "boot" [¶ 1408].

(b) When corporation assumes liabilities in excess of basis of property transferred the excess is taxable gain to the transferor [Sec. 351, 357(c); 1.357-2].

(c) Exchanges with an investment company. Gain or loss is recognized when property is transferred to an investment company after 6-30-67, if the transfer results in diversification of transferor's interests. An investment company is: (1) a regulated investment company [¶ 3428-3431], (2) a real estate investment trust [¶ 3432], or (3) any corporation, if more than 80% of the value of its assets are: (a) held for investment, and (b) readily marketable stocks or securities, or interests in regulated investment companies or real estate investment trusts [Sec. 351(d); 1.351-1(c)].

¶ **1406 Property held for productive use or investment.** No gain or loss is recognized if property is exchanged for "like kind" property held for either purpose. This does not apply to property held only for personal purposes;[1] but if it is used for both business and personal purposes, it applies to the business part [¶ 1517(g)]. Property held for productive use in trade or business may be exchanged for property held for investment. The reverse is also true. "Like kind" means the nature or character of the property, not its grade or quality. Thus, a farm for a farm, an apartment house for building lots, city real estate for a ranch, a leasehold for 30 or more years for real estate, and improved for unimproved real estate qualify as "like kind" exchanges [Sec. 1031(a); 1.1031(a)-1], but not the exchange of livestock of different sexes [Sec. 1031(e); 1.1031(e)-1]. While the ex-

Footnotes appear at end of this Chapter.

change of realty for realty may generally qualify as a "like kind" exchange, exchange of realty for personalty will not. Stock in trade or property held for sale, shares of stock, bonds, notes or other securities are not considered properties held for productive use or investment. Converting U.S. currency into foreign currency and reconverting to U.S. currency are taxable transactions.[2]

Example 1: An exchange by an automobile dealer of a new car in his stock for an old one is a taxable exchange.

Example 2: An exchange of an automobile used entirely for pleasure purposes for a new car is a taxable exchange.

Example 3: An exchange of an automobile used by a salesman partly for business purposes for a new car results in a nontaxable exchange of the business part and a taxable exchange of the personal part.

¶ 1407 **Exchange of insurance policies.** No gain or loss is recognized on the exchange of—

• a life insurance contract for another life insurance contract or for an endowment or annuity contract;

• an endowment insurance contract for another endowment insurance contract providing for regular payments starting at a date not later than the starting date under the old contract, or for an annuity contract;

• one annuity contract for another, whether or not the issuer of the contract received in exchange is the same as the issuer of the original contract[1] [Sec. 1035(a); 1.1035-1].

Gain or loss is recognized on an exchange of an endowment or annuity contract for a life insurance contract, or an annuity contract for endowment contract. The recognized gain is the excess of property and cash received over the basis of the policy exchanged [Sec. 1.1035-1].

These definitions govern:

(1) An *endowment insurance contract* is a contract with a life insurance company that depends partly on the insured's life expectancy, but may be payable in full in a single payment during his life.

(2) An *annuity contract* is a contract to which definition (1) applies but which may be payable during the life of the annuitant only in installments.

(3) A *life insurance contract* is one to which definition (1) applies but which is not ordinarily payable in full during life of insured [Sec. 1035(b)].

Background and purpose. These rules allow taxpayers to exchange one insurance policy for another better suited to their needs.

¶ 1408 **Effect of giving or receiving "boot."** Boot is money or other property given or received in addition to the property on which no gain or loss is recognized.

(a) Giving boot. Gain or loss ordinarily is not recognized when boot is given in a nontaxable exchange. However, if the boot is property, gain or loss is recognized to the extent of the difference between the basis and fair market value of the boot [Sec. 1.1031(d)-1(e)].

Example 1: Hardy exchanged a machine with an adjusted basis of $3,000 for a new one. He also gave $100 cash and a $500 note. The following illustrates the tax treatment if he has (1) a gain, and (2) a loss on the transaction.

Chapter 4—Gain or Loss—Recognition

	Gain transaction	Loss transaction
Gave		
Old machine	$3,000	$3,000
Cash	100	100
Note	500	500
	$3,600	$3,600
Received		
New machine	$3,800	$3,400
Realized gain (loss)	$ 200	($ 200)
Recognized gain (loss)	None	None

The basis of the property acquired is the total basis of the properties transferred (adjusted to the date of exchange) increased by the amount of gain and decreased by the amount of loss recognized when the boot is property [Sec. 1.1031(d)-1(e)].

Example 2: Hardy exchanged real estate with an adjusted basis of $10,000 for similar real estate. He also gave stock with an adjusted basis of $4,000 and a fair market value of $3,000. Hardy is considered to have received a $3,000 portion of the acquired real estate in exchange for the stock, as well as recognizing a $1,000 loss. However, no gain or loss is recognized on the exchange of the real estate. The basis of the acquired real estate is determined as follows:

Adjusted basis of real estate transferred	$10,000
Adjusted basis of stock transferred	4,000
Total	$14,000
Less: loss recognized on stock transfer	$ 1,000
Basis of real estate acquired in exchange	$13,000

(b) Receiving boot. Gain is recognized, but only up to the amount of the boot received [Sec. 351(b), 1031(b); 1.351-2, 1.1031(b)-1].

Example 3: Hardy exchanges a machine with an adjusted basis of $5,000 for one similar having a fair market value of $5,500. The following illustrates the effect on gain if: (1) no boot received; (2) receipt of boot equals realized gain from the machines exchanged; and (3) receipt of boot is less than gain.

	Boot Received		Realized	Recognized
	Cash	Notes (FMV)	gain	gain
(1)	None	None	$ 500	None
(2)	$100	$400	$1,000	$500
(3)	None	$400	$ 900	$400

A fourth situation: receipt of boot exceeding realized gain would occur if Hardy received a machine with a fair market value of $4,800 plus $500 in cash and/or notes. The $500 would be boot, making the entire gain of $300 recognized.

No gain is recognized when the only cash received is allocated and used to liquidate a mortgage on the property given in exchange.[1]

Losses are not recognized [Sec. 351(b)(2), 1031(c); 1.351-2, 1.1031(c)-1].

Problem: Grade exchanged machinery having an adjusted basis of $10,000 for similar machinery valued at $7,000. He also received $1,100 as "boot." What, if any, was the recognized loss?

Solution: The realized loss was $1,900, but that loss would not be recognized.

When several assets are transferred to a corporation for stock and boot, a part of each kind of consideration received is allocated to each asset in the ratio that each asset's fair market value bears to their total fair market value.[2]

Footnotes appear at end of this Chapter.

¶ 1408

The gain recognized because of boot received can be reported on the installment plan if the transaction otherwise qualifies for installment reporting.[3] See ¶ 2801 et seq.

¶ 1409 Exchange of mortgaged property. When a taxpayer exchanges mortgaged property in a tax-free transaction, the mortgage debt he is relieved from paying will be treated as cash received in figuring his recognized gain. This is true whether the transferee takes the property subject to a mortgage or assumes personal liability for it. The amount of boot given by the taxpayer on the exchange, whether in the form of money, property, or a receipt by him of property subject to liabilities or mortgages, reduces the amount of liabilities or mortgages which are treated as boot received by him on the exchange. However, if a taxpayer assumes or takes subject to a mortgage which exceeds that which the other party assumes or takes subject to, the excess does not reduce any other boot received by the taxpayer [Sec. 1031(d); 1.1031(d)-2].

Example 1: Roe owns a ranch with an adjusted basis of $50,000 and subject to a $10,000 mortgage. He exchanges it for a farm worth $65,000, the transferee assuming the mortgage. Roe realizes a gain of $25,000, but only $10,000 of the gain is recognized (the mortgage is treated as cash):

Value of property received	$65,000
Mortgage on property exchanged	10,000
Total consideration received	$75,000
Less: Adjusted basis of property transferred	50,000
Gain realized	$25,000

Example 2: The facts are the same as in Example 1 except that the farm Roe received is subject to a mortgage of $6,000 which he assumed. Roe realized a gain of $19,000 on the exchange figured as follows:

Value of property received		$65,000
Mortgage on property exchanged, assumed by transferee		10,000
Total consideration received		$75,000
Less: Adjusted basis of property transferred	$50,000	
Mortgage on property received, assumed by transferor (Roe)	6,000	56,000
Gain realized		$19,000

The gain is recognized to the extent of $4,000 ($10,000 mortgage assumed by transferee less $6,000 mortgage assumed by transferor Roe).

If the transfer is to a controlled corporation, the mortgage is not considered "boot" received by the transferor in determining his recognized gain, unless the purpose is to avoid tax or there is no real business purpose [Sec. 357; 1.357-1]. See also ¶ 1405(a).

INVOLUNTARY CONVERSION

¶ 1410 What is involuntary conversion. Involuntary conversion occurs when property is stolen, destroyed by accident or seized by condemnation proceedings, and the taxpayer receives insurance or a condemnation award. If the amount received is more than the basis of the converted property, taxpayer has a gain. However, if the taxpayer buys new property to replace the old property within a certain period of time, the gain (or part of it) may not be recognized. See ¶ 1411.

Amounts received under use and occupancy (business interruption) insurance are proceeds of an involuntary conversion, if the policy measures recovery by a fixed periodic amount and not by lost profits.[1] See also ¶ 1331.

CONVERSIONS

Some borderline cases are: sale of property adjacent to that involuntarily converted when continued operation of business on adjacent property was impractical because of the conversion;[2] granting perpetual overflow easement[3] of sale of leasehold to railroad under condemnation threat.[4]

NOT CONVERSIONS

Sale of fertilizer plant because offensive to residents;[5] sale of stock because it could be held only by an officer;[6] sale of property to avoid meeting the requirements of a housing ordinance.[7]

(a) Condemnation. A property transfer under threat or imminence of condemnation qualifies as an involuntary conversion as well as an actual condemnation. Information from news media that a condemnation is being *considered,* even if confirmed by officials, is not a "threat or imminence." This exists only when officials or the news media indicate a *decision* has been reached by the condemning authority. Information obtained from news media must be confirmed by the condemning authority.[8] When there is a "threat or imminence," a sale to a private party can qualify as a conversion.[9]

(b) Livestock—disease and drought. The destruction of livestock by disease, or their sale or exchange because of disease, is treated as an involuntary conversion [Sec. 1033(d); 1.1033(e)-1].

Sale or exchange of livestock (except poultry) held for draft, breeding, or dairy purposes in excess of the number taxpayer would sell following his usual business practices is treated as an involuntary conversion, if they are sold or exchanged solely on account of drought [Sec. 1033(e); 1.1033(f)-1].

(c) Sales under federal reclamation laws. Sale or other disposition of property in an irrigation project to conform to the acreage limitations of federal reclamation laws is treated as an involuntary conversion [Sec. 1033(c); 1.1033(d)-1].

(d) Broadcasting property sales certified by F.C.C. The sale or exchange of broadcasting property or the stock of a corporation operating a broadcasting station is an involuntary conversion if required by the Federal Communications Commission. However, it must certify that the transaction is essential to fulfilling a change of its present or future policy. Gain is not recognized if the proceeds are used to buy other property similar or related in service or use. Moreover, any gain normally recognized under involuntary conversion rules can be deferred if the taxpayer elects to apply this gain in reducing the basis of his other business property [Sec. 1071; 1.1071-1—1.1071-4]. See also ¶ 1619(f). Buying stock of a corporation that does not operate broadcasting stations, but which owns all the stock of a subsidiary corporation operating stations, does not qualify as replacement property.[10]

¶ 1411   Gain or loss on involuntary conversion—general rules. If a taxpayer receives payment for property condemned or destroyed by casualty and he replaces it with property similar to related in service or use, the following rules apply [Sec. 1033; 1.1033(a)-1(a)]:

1. If the amount realized equals or is less than the cost of the replacement property, no gain is recognized.
2. If the amount realized exceeds the cost of replacement, gain is recognized to the extent of the excess.
3. A loss on an involuntary conversion is generally recognized [¶ 1414].

Rules 1 and 2 do not apply unless: (a) the replacement is made within a certain period of time [¶ 1412]; (b) the replacement is in kind [¶ 1413]; and (c) the taxpayer elects to have them apply [Sec. 1033(a)(3)(A); 1.1033(a)-2(c)].

(a) **Conversion directly into other property.** If property is converted *directly* into other property similar or related in service or use to the original property, no gain is recognized [Sec. 1033 (a)(1); 1.1033(a)-2(b)]. But if the property is converted into money (insurance or condemnation proceeds) or property not similar or related in service or use, the replacement property of a similar or related service or use is acquired, the rules above apply.

(b) **Who must make the replacement.** Generally, the property must be replaced by the taxpayer or one acting in his behalf. Leased property can be replaced by the tenant when required to return it in the same condition as received.[1] A purchase of property by taxpayer's controlled corporation does not qualify as a replacement.[2] Nor does replacement by a partner. It must be made by the partnership.[3] A decedent's executor has been allowed to make replacement,[4] but the Revenue Service disagrees.[5]

(c) **How to make the election.** Election is made on the return by including gain in gross income only to the extent it is recognized under the above rules. If the converted property is not replaced within the time limit, or replacement is made at a cost lower than anticipated, or a decision is made not to replace, the tax liability for the year the election was made must be recomputed, and an amended return filed. If no election was made when the return was filed, an election may be made later, within the time limit, by filing an amended return[6] or claim for refund [Sec. 1.1033(a)-2(c)(2)]. Generally, the election is made by the taxpayer. The grantor of a reversionary trust must make the election not to recognize gain on the sale of condemned trust property, if he is taxable on the income of the trust.[7] Partnerships must make the election, not the individual partners.[3]

(d) **Information on the return.** When there is a gain on an involuntary conversion the details must be reported on the return for the year the gain was realized. These details relate to the replacement of the converted property, decision not to replace, or end of the replacement period. If replacement is made in a year when no gain is realized, details of the replacement are reported on the return for that year [Sec. 1.1033(a)-2(c)(2)].

(e) **Notice required.** The Revenue Service must be notified of a replacement, or of an intention not to replace, or of a failure to replace within the required period. The notice limits the time for assessment of a deficiency [Sec. 1.1033(a)-2(c)(5)]. For details, see ¶ 3611.

¶ **1412 Time limit on replacement in involuntary conversions.** If the property is converted into money, or into property not similar or related in service or use, replacement with qualified property [¶ 1413] must be made during a period:

Beginning with the earlier of these dates: (1) date of destruction, seizure, etc., of the converted property; (2) earliest date of the threat or imminence of requisition or condemnation.

Ending (1) two years after the close of the first tax year in which any part of the gain is realized [Sec. 1033(a)(2)(B)], or (2) a later date set by the Revenue Service on taxpayer's application before the end of the above period. (Late application may be considered if there was reasonable cause for delay.)[1]

NOTE: A three-year replacement period applies to the condemnation of certain real property [¶ 1413(c)] disposed of after 12-31-74 (unless the proceedings began before 10-4-76) [Sec. 1033(f)(4)].

(a) **Advance payment to a contractor** to construct replacement property is not a timely replacement, if construction is not completed before the replacement period ends.[2]

(b) Conversion directly into other property. If property is converted *directly* into other property similar or related in service or use to the original property, there is no time limit [Sec. 1033(b); 1.1033(a)-1(a), 1.1033(a)-2(b)].

¶ **1413 Making replacements in involuntary conversions.** Replacement can be made by buying property, by building it, by acquiring it directly or by getting control of a corporation owning similar property. Control means owning 80% or more of the voting stock and 80% or more of the nonvoting stock [Sec. 1033(a); 1.1033(a)-2(c)].

Example 1: Riley's land was condemned by the state, which gave him similar land to replace the condemned property. This is direct replacement.

Example 2: Reese's warehouse was destroyed by fire. Soon afterwards, he bought another one. This is replacement by purchase. He also could have replaced by getting control of a corporation that owns a warehouse.

(a) What qualifies as replacement property. Replacement property must meet these qualifications [Sec. 1033(a)(2)(A); 1.1033(a)-2(c)(4)]:

- It must be similar or related in service or use to the converted property [(b) below], unless condemnation of real property used in business or held for investment is involved [(c) below].
- It must be held on the date the old property was converted if it was acquired before that date.
- It must be purchased to replace the old property.
- It must not be acquired by gift.

(b) Property similar or related in service or use, for an owner-user, means that it must be *functionally* the same as the property converted. The nature of the replacement property's service or use must be the same as that of the converted property.[1] Thus, a business vehicle must be replaced with another, and it must perform the same function. For a lessor, attention is directed primarily to the relationship of the services or uses that the original and replacement properties have to him.[2] New rental property can qualify to replace old, even though the tenant's functional uses differ.[3] However, the replacement of property rented as a parking lot with property rented as a warehouse did not qualify.[4] Also, the replacement of a rented residence by a personal residence does not qualify.[5]

(c) Condemnation of real property. Real property (except stock in trade or other property held for sale) held for productive use in trade or business or for investment that is involuntarily converted by *requisition, seizure, condemnation or threat of this action* may be replaced with "like kind" property [Sec. 1033(f)(1); 1.1033(g)-1(a)]. "Like kind" property has the same meaning, for this purpose, as it has in the rule for nontaxable exchanges of property held for productive use or investment [¶ 1406].[6] Thus unimproved realty would be similar to improved.

The nonrecognition of gain rule does not apply when: (1) replacement property is acquired by buying control of a corporation [Sec. 1033(f); 1.1033(g)-1]; (2) money received from the condemnation of one business property is used to reduce the mortgage of another business property;[7] and (3) a sole stockholder, who in complete liquidation of his corporation following condemnation of its property, received the condemnation proceeds awarded the corporation and reinvested them in similar property.[8] However, it does apply to real property sold, under threat of condemnation, for a lump sum as part of a going business.[9]

Footnotes appear at end of this Chapter.

¶ **1413**

¶ 1414 How to figure recognized gain or loss in involuntary conversions. - The following discussion shows how to apply the rules outlined in ¶ 1411 governing recognition of gain or loss on involuntary conversion [Sec. 1033(a)(2)(A); 1.1033(a)-2(c)]:

(a) If amount realized exceeds the cost of replacement, gain is recognized, but only to the extent of the excess, if the taxpayer so elects.

(b) If the basis of the asset exceeds the amount received, a loss is recognized.

≫**OBSERVATION**→ Only casualty or theft losses and those incurred in a trade, business or transaction entered into for profit are deductible [¶ 2200 et seq.]. Thus, an involuntary conversion loss from fire of a residence or business building is deductible (but only in excess of $100 for the residence). An involuntary conversion loss from condemnation is deductible only for the business building. See also ¶ 1421; 2204 and 2207.

(c) If cost of replacement exceeds amount received. If the amount received exceeds the adjusted basis of the old property and the cost of replacement exceeds the amount received, no gain is recognized, if the taxpayer so elects. The excess of the cost of replacement over the amount received cannot be taken as a loss. It is treated as a capital expenditure [¶ 1808]. Interest added to a condemnation award is taxable as ordinary income.[1]

Example: A manufacturing plant with an adjusted basis of $45,000 is destroyed by fire. The building is replaced at a cost of $55,000. The following table illustrates taxpayer's choices under the rules in (a), (b) and (c) above, depending on the amount of insurance proceeds he receives. In all three cases, the amounts realized include any liabilities assumed.[2]

	Adjusted basis	Amount received	Replacement cost	Gain or loss
(a)	$45,000	$60,000	$55,000	$5,000
(b)	$45,000	$40,000	$55,000	($5,000)
(c)	$45,000	$50,000	$55,000	none

NOTE: Under the first alternative, the realized gain is $15,000, but taxpayer can elect to limit the recognized gain to $5,000 (the difference between the amount received and the replacement cost). Under the third alternative, gain is not recognized if taxpayer so elects. However, if no replacement is made, his gain of $5,000 ($50,000 − $45,000) is taxable.

¶ 1415 Severance damages and special assessments in condemnations. Severance damages are amounts paid in addition to a condemnation award. Special benefit assessments are amounts levied against the retained property if that property is benefited by the improvement for which the land was condemned. Examples would be widening a street or installing a sewer.

(a) Severance damages are paid to a taxpayer when part of his property is condemned and the value of the retained part is decreased by the condemnation. They are not treated as income, but offset expenses in the following order: (1) expenses incurred in securing the damages; (2) any special benefit assessment [(b) below]; (3) expenses incurred in restoring the retained property to its former use; and (4) the basis of the retained property. Any excess is treated as recognized gain.[1] The IRS holds that the tax deferral benefits in involuntary conversions do not apply to severance damages,[2] but some courts disagree.[3] Also, the IRS and some courts maintain that severance damages must be separately stated, or the entire amount received is treated as the condemnation award.[4] However, the Tax Court has disagreed.[5]

(b) Special benefit assessments levied against the retained property are not deductible. They first reduce the severance damages. Any excess reduces the condemnation award.[6] Any unused amount is added to the retained property's basis.

SALE OF RESIDENCE

If the taxpayer sells his principal residence at a gain, the tax will be postponed to the extent the proceeds of the sale are used to buy a new principal residence within certain time limits. If the taxpayer is 65 or over when he sells his principal residence all or part of the gain is tax-free even though he does not buy a new residence.

¶ **1416 Gain from sale or exchange of residence.** Generally, gain is recognized on the sale or exchange of a residence. But a special rule applies if taxpayer sells his principal residence, and—

(1) he buys a new residence and uses it as his principal residence within 18 months (one year for sales before 1975) before or after he sells his old residence, or

(2) he starts to build a new residence before or within 18 months (one year for sales before 1975) after he sells the old residence, and uses the new property as his principal residence within two years (18 months for sales before 1975) after he sells his old residence.

If taxpayer meets either test, gain is recognized only to the extent the adjusted sales price of the old residence exceeds the cost of the new residence. This rule is mandatory [Sec. 1034(a), 1034(c)(5); 1.1034-1(a), (c)].

Example 1: Green sold his old residence for an adjusted sales price of $45,000 and realized a gain of $5,000 on the sale. Two months later in the year, he bought a new residence. The following table illustrates how the cost of the new residence affects the gain that will be recognized on the transaction.

Sales price	Realized gain	Cost of new residence	Recognized gain
$45,000	$5,000	$46,000	None
$45,000	$5,000	$44,000	$1,000
$45,000	$5,000	$45,000	None

Special provisions for members of the Armed Forces are at ¶ 1420. For taxpayers 65 or over, see ¶ 1423. For a residence that is repossessed, see ¶ 2823. To figure the adjusted basis of the old residence, see ¶ 1526.

≫**OBSERVATION**→ Any *recognized* gain on the sale of a residence, held for more than nine months is a long-term capital gain. See ¶ 1601; 1605; 1611. A *loss* on the sale of a residence, is not deductible [Sec. 1.165-3]. However, if the residence is converted to income-producing purposes, loss is deductible. See ¶ 2207 for complete discussion.

Background and purpose. The nonrecognition provision was added because of a similarity Congress saw between the exchange of residences and an involuntary conversion. With increasing frequency, taxpayers are moving for reasons that are not entirely voluntary, such as a change in business position. The thought was that they should be entitled to the same benefits as those who lose property in an involuntary conversion.

(a) Sales price of old residence includes the amount of any mortgage or other debt to which the property is subject in the buyer's hands, whether or not he assumes the debt and the face amount of any liabilities of the buyer which are part of the consideration for the sale [Sec. 1.1034-1(b)(4)].

>>OBSERVATION→ The deferred payment sale is one in which all or part of the payment is made at a later date [Chap. 18]. In figuring the recognized gain on such a sale, the sale price includes the *face* amount of the buyer's liabilities that are part of the consideration, but in figuring the realized gain, the buyer's liabilities are taken at *market value* [¶ 2816]. Therefore, if liabilities have a market value less than the face value, two computations must be made to find realized and recognized gain.[1]

(b) **Adjusted sales price** is the amount realized reduced by fixing-up expenses. The amount realized is the sales price less items properly offset against sales price to determine gain [Sec. 1034(b); 1.1034-1(b)]. Thus, both selling and fixing-up expenses are subtracted from the sales price to arrive at the adjusted sales price. Those items that offset the sales price include such selling expenses as commissions, expenses of advertising the property for sale, preparing the deed, other legal services related to the sale and "points" paid by the seller to obtain an FHA mortgage for the buyer (See also (d) below).[2] But when selling expenses are taken as a moving expense deduction, they cannot be used to reduce the sales price (¶ 1831) [Sec. 217(e), 1001(f); 1.217-2].

Example 2: Selling price of White's old residence was $46,500. Selling expense (broker's commission) was $1,000. Fixing-up expenses were $500. Adjusted sales price is $45,000 ($46,500 less $1,000 selling expense and $500 fixing-up expense).

(c) **Fixing-up expenses** are expenses for work performed on the old residence to assist in its sale. These are considered only to find the amount of gain not recognized. They must: (1) be for work performed during a 90-day period before the sale contract was made that results in a completed sale,[3] (2) be paid within 30 days after the sale date, (3) be otherwise nondeductible in figuring taxable income, and (4) not be capital expenditures or improvements [Sec. 1034(b); 1.1034-1(b)]. Papering and painting are examples of fixing-up expenses.

(d) **Cost of new residence** includes only so much of the costs of acquiring, building, rebuilding and improving that are properly chargeable to capital account within the 42-month period (30-month period for sales before 1975) starting 18 months before and ending 24 months after the sale of the old residence. This period also includes any time the period was suspended for persons in the Armed Forces.[4]

"Cost" also includes: debts the property is subject to at the time of purchase whether or not assumed by the buyer (including purchase money mortgages); the face amount of the liabilities of the taxpayer that are part of the consideration for purchase; and commissions or other buying expenses unless deducted as moving expenses [¶ 1831]. A loan processing fee ("points") paid by a mortgagor-borrower as a bonus or premium to get a conventional mortgage loan is deductible as interest.[5] However, loan origination fees ("points") paid in place of specified service charges in connection with a mortgage loan, such as a VA loan, are neither a cost of acquiring the property nor deductible as interest.[6] See also ¶ 1900. The cost of a tenant-stockholder's stock in a cooperative apartment house includes his share of the cooperative's mortgage.[7]

If any part of the new residence is acquired other than by purchase (such as by gift or inheritance), value of that part is not included in its cost [Sec. 1034(c)(2); 1.1034-1(b)(7), 1.1034-1(c)(4)].

Example 3: Sims inherited a residence, and spent $5,000 in rebuilding it. Only $5,000 is treated as cost.

NOTE: A taxpayer buying a new principal residence could get a 5% credit (up to $2,000) on the home's purchase or construction price. Since this is the adjusted basis on the date acquired, the credit is affected by any gain not recognized on the sale of the old residence [¶ 1526]. The taxpayer must be the new home's original user. A new home acquired and occupied between 3-13-75 and 12-31-76, and under construction before 3-26-75 qualifies. The credit is recaptured for the home's disposition within 3 years of purchase unless due to an involuntary conversion, the owner's death or from a divorce proceeding. Replacement can avoid or reduce the recapture. Form 5405 must be attached to the return along with the seller's certification that the price is the lowest at which the residence has been offered for sale after 2-28-75 [Sec. 44; 1.44-1—1.44-5].

(e) How to figure recognized gain is illustrated as follows:

Example 4: White sold his residence, which had an adjusted basis of $20,500. The selling price was $46,500. Selling expense (broker's commission) was $1,000. Cost of fixing up the old residence (papering and painting) to assist in its sale was $500. Two months later he bought a new residence for $44,000. Here is how White figures his realized gain, and his recognized gain.

Realized Gain
1.	Selling price of old residence	$46,500
2.	Less: Selling expenses	1,000
3.	Amount realized on sale	$45,500
4.	Less: Adjusted basis of old residence	20,500
5.	Realized gain	$25,000

Adjusted Sales Price
6.	Amount realized on sale (Line 3 above)	$45,500
7.	Less: Fixing-up expenses	500
8.	Adjusted sales price	$45,000

Recognized Gain
9.	Adjusted sales price (Line 8 above)	$45,000
10.	Less: Cost of new residence	44,000
11.	Recognized gain	$ 1,000

(f) Official worksheet. The optional Form 2119, for figuring recognized gain on sale of a residence, can be obtained at District Directors' offices.

(g) Exchange. The special rule explained and illustrated above also applies if the old residence is *exchanged* for a new one within the allotted periods [Sec. 1034(c)(1); 1.1034-1(b)(8)].

(h) Installment sale. The special rule applies even if taxpayer sells his residence on the installment plan [¶ 2811]. The recognized gain may be apportioned over the period of the installment transactions. The amount of recognized gain included in income each year is that portion of the installment payments received during the year which the total recognized gain bears to the total contract price.[8]

¶ 1417 What is a residence. The special rule for nonrecognition of gain on sale of a residence applies only to property used as taxpayer's *principal* residence. This can be a houseboat or trailer. Stock held by a tenant-stockholder in a cooperative apartment corporation qualifies if he lives in the apartment [Sec. 216(b); 1034(f); 1.1034-1(c)(3)]. A condominium would also qualify.[1]

(a) Business or investment property. Property used in a trade or business or held for investment is not a residence. But property may still be considered a personal residence even if taxpayer temporarily rents it out.

Footnotes appear at end of this Chapter.

Example 1: Bryant buys a new residence before he sells the old one. He rents out the new residence until he sells and vacates the old. Property is still considered his new residence for this special rule.

(b) Property used both for residence and business or investment. If a person uses his property partly for a residence and partly for business or for the production of income (for example, a storekeeper, doctor or owner of a two-family house), allocation must be made and the special rule applies only to the part allocated for residential purposes [Sec. 1.1034-1(c)(3)].

Example 2: Cole owns a 4-unit apartment building that cost him $42,000. He occupied one unit as his personal residence and rented out the other three. Depreciation on the rented portion totaled $6,000. Cole sold the entire property this year for $50,000 incurring selling expenses of $2,800 but with no fixing-up expenses. He bought a new residence for $20,000. Since 1/4 of the apartment building was Cole's residence, he figures his recognized gain as follows:

		Residence portion (1/4)	Rental portion (3/4)
1.	Selling price	$12,500	$37,500
2.	Less: Selling expenses	700	2,100
3.	Amount realized	$11,800	$35,400
4.	Basis (cost)	10,500	31,500
5.	Depreciation		6,000
6.	Adjusted basis	10,500	25,500
7.	Realized gain (Line 3 less line 6)	1,300	9,900
8.	Adjusted sales price	11,800	
9.	Cost of new residence	20,000	
10.	Gain not recognized	1,300	
11.	Gain recognized		$9,900

(c) More than one residence. If you have more than one residence you may apply the special rule only to the sale of the principal residence. If you rent your principal and own a secondary residence, the special rule does not apply to the secondary residence.[2]

¶ **1418 How special rules apply to husband and wife.** If husband and wife both use the old and new residences as their principal residence, and if they consent, the special rule for nonrecognition of gain on the sale or exchange of an old residence is applied to both as follows:

- Adjusted sales price of the old residence is the taxpayer's or the taxpayer and his spouse's adjusted sales price of the old residence.
- Cost of purchasing the new residence is the cost to the taxpayer, or to his spouse, or to both of them, of purchasing the new residence, whether such new residence is held by the taxpayer, or his spouse, or both.
- The gain on sale of the old residence that is not recognized, and the adjustment to the basis of the new residence, are allocated between taxpayer and his spouse.

Example 1: Smith individually owned a home which served as his and his wife's principal residence. It cost him $10,000 (adjusted basis to him in this example). He sold it at an adjusted sales price of $20,000. Within a year after the sale he and his wife contributed $10,000 each from their separate funds to buy their new principal residence, which they held as tenants in common. If they consent, the gain of $10,000 on sale of the old residence will not be recognized to him, and the adjusted basis of his interest in the new residence will be $5,000, and the adjusted basis of his wife's interest also will be $5,000.

Example 2: Brown and his wife own their principal residence as joint tenants. It has an adjusted basis of $5,000 to each of them ($10,000 together). They sold the house at an adjusted sales price of $20,000. Within a year after the sale, Mrs. Brown spent $20,000 of her own funds to buy a new principal residence for herself and her husband. She took title in her name only. If Mr. Brown and his wife consent, the adjusted basis to the wife of the new residence will be $10,000, and Mr. Brown's gain of $5,000 on the sale of the old residence will not be recognized. As a taxpayer herself, Mrs. Brown's $5,000 gain on the sale of the old residence will not be recognized.

≫**OBSERVATION**→ This means the husband and his wife acting singly or jointly benefit by the special rule, even if the spouse who sold the old residence is not the same as the one who bought the new one, or the rights of both in the new residence are not the same as their rights in the old residence.

Consent necessary. Consent must be filed with the Revenue Service for the year the gain from sale of the old residence is realized [Sec. 1034(g); 1.1034-1(f)]. Form 2119 can be used.

¶ 1419 **When benefits of special rule not available.** Rule limiting recognition of gain on sale or residence does not apply to the following:

New residence sold before old. If another residence is bought and sold before the old residence is sold, the purchased residence is not a new residence, and the special rule does not apply [Sec. 1034(c)(3); 1.1034-1(d)].

More than one new residence. If more than one residence is bought within the time allowed and is used by the taxpayer as his principal residence at some time within 18 months (one year for sales before 1975) after the old residence is sold, only the last of such residences so used is considered a new residence in applying the special rule. Furthermore, the special rule applies only to one sale or exchange within 18 months [Sec. 1034(c), (d)].

Example: Donovan sold his old residence on 1-15-77 and bought a new residence on 2-16-77. On 3-15-77, he sold the new residence and bought a second new residence on 4-16-77. The gain on the sale of the old residence on 1-15-77 is not recognized, except to the extent that Donovan's adjusted sal price of the old residence exceeded his cost of buying the second new residence bought on 4-16-77. Gain on the sale of the first new residence on 3-15-77 is recognized.

Sale of residence by a trust. A trust does not get the benefit of the special rule. It is not a person using property as a principal residence.[1]

Title in new residence held by another. The special rule does not apply if the proceeds from the sale of the old residence are reinvested in a new residence to which another party, for instance a daughter, holds title.[2]

Purchase of partially constructed new residence. If the taxpayer buys a partially built new residence from a builder who completes construction, the taxpayer did not start the construction of a new residence; the construction is by the builder and the taxpayer is considered a purchaser.[3]

¶ 1420 **Special treatment for members of Armed Forces.** The replacement period [¶ 1416] is suspended while taxpayer or spouse is on extended duty (active duty for more than 90 days or indefinitely) with the U.S. Armed Forces. The suspension cannot extend for more than 4 years from the date the old residence is sold. The suspension applies only when service begins before the end of the replacement period and only if the old and new residences are each used by the taxpayer and his spouse as their principal residence [Sec. 1034(h); 1.1034-1(g)].

Footnotes appear at end of this Chapter.

¶ **1421 Condemnation of a residence.** A transfer of taxpayer's residence as a result of condemnation or its threat or imminence is treated as a sale if the taxpayer so elects. This election to defer gain is made by attaching a statement to the return showing the basis, adjusted sales price, and the sale date of the old residence. If a new residence was acquired before the election was made, the statement must show its price, and occupancy and purchase dates [Sec. 1034(i); 1.1034-1(h)]. If no election is made, the general rules on involuntary conversions apply [¶ 1411].

¶ **1422 How to report sale of residence.** If you sold or exchanged your residence during the tax year, and the special rules for nonrecognition of gain apply, report the details on your return as follows [Sec. 1034(j)]:

If replacement is made, report only the amount of taxable gain, if any, on Schedule D and attach a statement showing the purchase price and occupancy and purchase dates of the new home. You may use Form 2119.

If replacement is intended but not made by filing date and the replacement period has not expired, no gain is reported. However, attach a statement to the return showing how the gain was figured and that replacement has not been made. If you do replace within the required period, advise the district director in writing, giving full details. If you decide not to replace, or if the period has passed without replacement, report the taxable gain in the regular way. Since any additional tax bears interest from the due date of the original return until paid, take final action as soon as possible.

Unreported gain. If there has been an unreported taxable gain on the sale of a residence, either because a new one was not bought or because some of the requirements were not met, the Revenue Service should be notified. This notice limits the time for assessment of a deficiency. See ¶ 3611(a).

¶ **1423 Sales by persons 65 or over.** If a person 65 or over at the time of sale sells his residence, all or part of the gain is tax-free. The property must have been used as his residence for a period totaling at least 5 out of the 8 years before the sale. This 5-year rule is met by using the residence for 60 full months or 1,825 days (365 × 5). Short temporary absences are counted as periods of use [Sec. 121(a); 1.121-1].

The entire gain is tax-free if the *adjusted sales price* [¶ 1416(b)] is $35,000 or less. If more, the gain is tax-free in the ratio that $35,000 is to the adjusted sales price ($35,000/adjusted sales price × realized gain = tax-free gain) [Sec. 121(b)(1); 1.121-2].

> **Example 1:** Brand, who is 66 years old, sold his home for $47,000. He had bought it 10 years ago. His adjusted basis is $10,000. Selling and fixing-up expenses were $1,000 each. His adjusted sales price is, therefore, $45,000. Since his realized gain is $36,000 ($46,000, amount realized less $10,000, adjusted basis), his tax-free gain is $28,000 ($35,000/$45,000 × $36,000).

The relief applies to gain on an involuntary conversion. Thus, gain from fire insurance proceeds or from a condemnation can qualify. If taxpayer buys a replacement residence, the rules for nonrecognition of gain on the sale and replacement of a residence [¶ 1416] apply to any part of the gain that is not exempt. The amount realized from the sale (sales price less selling expenses) is reduced by the tax-free gain. This decreases the amount the taxpayer must reinvest for nonrecognition of gain. His taxable gain is the amount remaining after deducting any fixing-up expenses and the cost of the new residence [Sec. 121(d)(7); 1.121-5].

Example 2: Assume the same facts as in Example 1, except that Brand bought a new residence for $15,000. His taxable gain is $2,000 figured as follows:

Sales price		$47,000
Less: Selling expenses		1,000
Amount realized		$46,000
Less:		
Tax-free gain	$28,000	
Fixing-up expenses	1,000	29,000
Amount required to be reinvested		$17,000
Cost of new residence		15,000
Taxable gain		$ 2,000

When only part of the property was used as a residence during 5 of the 8 years, only the gain on the residence part qualifies for relief. If the taxpayer's residence was a two-family house, the gain on the rented unit does not qualify. If part of the residence was used in a trade or business, a doctor's office for example, gain on that part would not qualify [Sec. 121(d)(5); 1.121-5(e)].

The election to exclude the gain can be made only once by the taxpayer. It can be made or revoked at any time before the time a refund claim can be made (generally 3 years) for the sales year. If taxpayer is married, an election or revocation must be made by both spouses [Sec. 121(c); 1.121-4].

Property may qualify under special rules when it is disposed of by a surviving spouse or only one spouse meets the requirements and the property is jointly owned [Sec. 121(d); 1.121-5]. The executor of taxpayer's estate cannot elect if the taxpayer died after signing an executory contract but before title to the property had passed.[1] For repossessed residence, see ¶ 2823.

Background and purpose. The provisions that allow the deferral of gain from the sale of a residence are adequate for younger taxpayers who sell one house and buy another but do nothing to ease the burden of the elderly taxpayer who no longer has the need for a house and sells it without purchasing another. Recognizing the fact that many elderly persons sell their houses and move to apartments or other rental property, Congress added the exclusion of gain provisions of Sec. 121. The 1976 Tax Reform Act increased the adjusted sales price limit from $20,000 to $35,000 for tax years beginning after 12-31-76.

Joint ownership. An unmarried individual, 65 or over, who sells his residence, which he holds as joint tenant or tenant in common, can get the exclusion in proportion to his undivided interest.[2]

¶ 1426 Sales of low-income housing projects. The nonrecognition of gain rules on the sale and replacement of a residence generally apply to the sale of a low-income housing project. However, the sale must be to tenants of the project or to a condominium or cooperative for their benefit. In addition, the gain is not recognized only if the property is replaced with similar low-income housing property within a year of the sale or any other period approved by the Revenue Service. These rules apply only to housing projects constructed under FHA Sec. 221(d)(3) and Sec. 236 and certain state assisted programs. For treatment of basis, see ¶ 1526; for depreciation recapture, see ¶ 1619 [Sec. 1039; 1.1039-1].

Footnotes to Chapter 4

(P-H "FEDERAL TAXES" related references are cited in brackets [ ] at the end of each footnote below.)

Footnote ¶ 1400   [¶ 31,005 et seq.]
(1) Crane v. Comm., 331 US 1, 67 SCt 1047, 35 AFTR 776 [¶ 31,162(25)].
(2) Treas. Dept. booklet "Tax Guide for Small Business" (1977 Ed.), p. 86.
(3) Rev. Rul. 57-535, 1957-2 CB 513 [¶ 31,037(10)].
(4) Rev. Rul. 69-181, 1969-1 CB 196 [¶ 31,110(5)].

Footnote ¶ 1401   [¶ 31,005 et seq.]
(1) H.L. Scales, 10 BTA 1024 [¶ 31,098(15)].
(2) Rev. Rul. 70-510, 1970-2 CB 159 [¶ 31,098(15)].

Footnote ¶ 1402   [¶ 31,097; 31,666].
(1) G. E. Hamilton, 30 BTA 160; W. H. Hartman Co., 20 BTA 302; G. L. DeBlois. et al. Exs., 12 BTA 1138, aff'd. 36 F.2d 11, 8 AFTR 9821 [¶ 18,106(30); 31,666(35)(40)].

Footnote ¶ 1403   [¶ 31,651 et seq.]
(1) Motor Products Corp., 47 BTA 983, aff'd. 142 F.2d 449, 32 AFTR 672; City Bank Farmers Trust Co., Trustee (Astor) v. Hoey, 52 F. Supp. 665, aff'd. 138 F.2d 1023, 31 AFTR 974 [¶ 31,068(5)].

Footnote ¶ 1404   [¶ 31,771 et seq.]
(1) Clark v. Comm., 77 F.2d 89, 15 AFTR 1343 [¶ 31,775(5)].
(2) Rev. Rul. 72-265, 1972-1 CB 222 [¶ 31,071(10)].
(3) Rev. Rul. 69-135, 1969-1 CB 198 [¶ 31,071(15)].
(4) Rev. Rul. 72-319, 1972-1 CB 224 [¶ 31,070].
(5) Rev. Rul. 56-437, 1956-2 CB 507 [¶ 31,092(10)].
(6) Rev. Rul. 69-20, 1969-1 CB 202 [¶ 31,776(15)].

Footnote ¶ 1405   [¶ 18,006 et seq.]
(1) Rev. Rul. 64-56, 1964-1 CB 133 [¶ 18,023(5)].
(2) Rev. Proc. 76-22, 1976-1 CB 562 [¶ 18,027(5)].
(3) Rev. Proc. 73-10, 1973-1 CB 466 [¶ 18,021; 39,777(5)].
(4) Rev. Proc. 77-5, IRB 1977-5 [¶ 55,173].

Footnote ¶ 1406   [¶ 31,655 et seq.]
(1) Treas. Dept. booklet "Tax Guide for Small Business" (1977 Ed.), p. 87.
(2) Rev. Rul. 74-7, 1974-1 CB 198 [¶ 31,667(20)].

Footnote ¶ 1407   [¶ 31,761].
(1) Rev. Rul. 73-124, 1973-1 CB 200 [¶ 31,767(5)].

Footnote ¶ 1408   [¶ 18,006; 31,655; 31,666; 31,671].
(1) Comm. v. North Shore Bus Co., 143 F.2d 114, 32 AFTR 931 [¶ 31,672(25)].
(2) Rev. Rul. 68-55, 1968-1 CB 140 [¶ 18,043(5)].
(3) Rev. Rul. 65-155, 1965-1 CB 356 [¶ 20,421(30)].

Footnote ¶ 1409   [¶ 18,186 et seq.; 31,672].

Footnote ¶ 1410   [¶ 31,695 et seq.; 31,851].
(1) Piedmont-Mt. Airy Guano Co., 3 BTA 1009; Miller v. Hocking Glass Co., 80 F.2d 436, 16 AFTR 1448; Treas. Dept. booklet "Tax Guide for Small Business" (1977 Ed.), p. 116. [¶ 31,721(5), (15)].
(2) Masser, 30 TC 741 [¶ 31,712(50)].
(3) Rev. Rul. 72-433, 1972-1 CB 470 [¶ 31,098(15)].
(4) Davis Regulator Co., 36 BTA 437 [¶ 31,712(65); 31,715(10)].

Footnote ¶ 1410 continued
(5) Piedmont-Mt. Airy Guano Co., 8 BTA 72 [¶ 31,712(65)].
(6) Rev. Rul. 69-550, 1969-2 CB 161 [¶ 31,712(10)].
(7) Rev. Rul. 57-314, 1957-2 CB 523 [¶ 31,712(25)].
(8) Rev. Rul. 63-221, 1963-2 CB 332 [¶ 31,712(65)].
(9) Creative Solutions, Inc. v. U.S., 12 AFTR 2d 5229, 320 F.2d 809 [¶ 31,712(70)].
(10) Rev. Rul. 66-33, 1966-1 CB 183 [¶ 31,860(5)].

Footnote ¶ 1411   [¶ 31,695 et seq.].
(1) Adams, 16 BTA 497 [¶ 31,734(15)].
(2) Feinberg, 19 AFTR 2d 1366, 377 F.2d 21 [¶ 31,734(40)].
(3) Rev. Rul. 66-191, 1962-2 CB 300 [¶ 31,734(45)].
(4) Goodman v. Comm., 199 F.2d 895, 42 AFTR 877 [¶ 31,734(5)].
(5) Rev. Rul. 64-161, 1964-1 CB 298 [¶ 31,734(5)].
(6) Rev. Rul. 63-127, 1963-2 CB 333 [¶ 31,735(5)].
(7) Rev. Rul. 70-376, 1970-2 CB 164 [¶ 31,735(8)].

Footnote ¶ 1412   [¶ 31,735].
(1) Rev. Rul. 56-300, 1956-1 CB 624 [¶ 31,735(10)].
(2) Rev. Rul. 56-543, 1956-2 CB 521 [¶ 31,735(20)].

Footnote ¶ 1413   [¶ 31,731; 31,732].
(1) Rev. Rul. 64-237, 1964-2 CB 319, [¶ 31,731(25)].
(2) Treas. Dept. booklet "Tax Guide for Small Business" (1977 Ed.), p. 117.
(3) Liant Records Inc. v. Comm., 9 AFTR 2d 1557, 303 F.2d 326 [¶ 31,731(40)].
(4) McCaffrey v. Comm., 5 AFTR 2d 777, 275 F. 2d 27 [¶ 31,731(40)].
(5) Rev. Rul. 70-466, 1970-2 CB 165 [¶ 31,731(47)].
(6) Senate Report No. 1983, p. 202, 85th Cong., 2d Sess.
(7) Rev. Rul. 70-98, 1970-1 CB 169 [¶ 31,731(60)].
(8) Rev. Rul. 73-72, 1973-1 CB 368 [¶ 31,734(35)].
(9) Rev. Rul. 70-465, 1970-2 CB 162 [¶ 31,725(35)].

Footnote ¶ 1414   [¶ 31,742].
(1) Kieselbach, 317 US 399, 30 AFTR 371 [¶ 7226(5)].
(2) Comm. v. Fortee, 211 F.2d 915, 45 AFTR 1347; but see Comm. v. Babcock, 2 AFTR 2d 5819, 259 F.2d 689 [¶ 31,722(10)].

Footnote ¶ 1415   [¶ 31,724].
(1) Rev. Rul. 68-37, 1968-1 CB 359; Treas. Dept. booklet "Your Federal Income Tax" (1977 Ed.), p. 131. [¶ 31,724(5)].
(2) Rev. Rul. 69-240, 1969-1 CB 199 [¶ 31,731(50)].
(3) McKitrick, 33 AFTR 2d 74-811; Conran, 27 AFTR 2d 71-745 [¶ 31,724(5); 31,731(50)].
(4) Rev. Rul. 59-173, 1959-1 CB 201; Lapham v. U.S., 178 F.2d 994, 38 AFTR 1255; Allaben, 35 BTA 327; Greene v. U.S., 3 AFTR 2d 1461, 173 F. Supp. 868 [¶ 31,725(30)].
(5) L. A. Beeghly, 36 TC 154 [¶ 31,725(30)].
(6) Treas. Dept. booklet "Your Federal Income Tax" (1977 Ed.), p. 131.

Footnote ¶ 1416   [¶ 5918; 31,748 et seq.].
(1) Rev. Rul. 54-380, 1954-2 CB 155 [¶ 31,755(5)].
(2) Rev. Rul. 68-650, 1968-2 CB 78 [¶ 13,008(10)].

Footnote ¶ 1416 continued
(3) Rev. Rul. 72-118, 1972-1 CB 227, [¶ 31,755(20)].
(4) Rev. Rul. 55-90, 1955-1 CB 348 [¶ 31,755(10)].
(5) Rev. Rul. 69-188, 1969-1 CB 54 [¶ 13,008(10)].
(6) Rev. Rul. 67-297, 1967-2 CB 87; Treas. Dept. booklet "Your Federal Income Tax" (1977 Ed.), p. 87. [¶ 31,177(95)].
(7) Rev. Rul. 60-76, 1960-1 CB 296 [¶ 31,755(10)].
(8) Rev. Rul. 75, 1953-1 CB 83 [¶ 20,420(10)].

Footnote ¶ 1417   [¶ 31,753].
(1) Rev. Rul. 64-31, 1964-1 CB 300 [¶ 31,753(47)].
(2) Treas. Dept. booklet "Your Federal Income Tax" (1977 Ed.), p. 107.

Footnote ¶ 1418   [¶ 31,755].

Footnote ¶ 1419   [¶ 31,753].
(1) Rev. Rul. 54-583, 1954-2 CB 158 [¶ 31,753(25)].
(2) Rev. Rul. 55-37, 1955-1 CB 347 [¶ 31,753(30)].
(3) Rev. Rul. 57-234, 1957-1 CB 263 [¶ 31,753(40)].

Footnote ¶ 1420   [¶ 31,754].

Footnote ¶ 1421   [¶ 31,748].

Footnote ¶ 1422   [¶ 31,756].

Footnote ¶ 1423   [¶ 8705].
(1) Rev. Rul. 70-469, 1970-2 CB 179 [¶ 34,455(5)].
(2) Rev. Rul. 67-234, 1967-2 CB 78; Rev. Rul. 67-235, 1967-2 CB 79 [¶ 8713(5)].

Footnote ¶ 1426   [¶ 31,799].

Highlights of Chapter 4

Gain or Loss—Recognition

I. **Recognition of Gain or Loss**
   A. **In general [¶ 1400]:**
      1. Must be realized *and* recognized.
      2. Factors in figuring [¶ 1400]:
         a. Basis.
         b. Adjustments to basis.
         c. Amount realized and type of consideration.
         d. Nature of property determines treatment.
      3. Steps in figuring:
         a. Following formulas used:
         BASIS + ADDITIONS − REDUCTIONS = ADJUSTED BASIS
         GAIN = AMOUNT REALIZED − ADJUSTED BASIS
         LOSS = ADJUSTED BASIS − AMOUNT REALIZED
         b. Amount realized increased by:
            1) Seller's personal obligations assumed by buyer.
            2) Outstanding encumbrances assumed or satisfied by buyer, or which remain.
            3) Real estate taxes assumed by buyer.
            4) Any money received in taxable exchange of property.
         c. Amount realized reduced by:
            1) Selling expenses.
            2) Money given in taxable exchange of property.
   B. **Recognition generally when property sold or exchanged [¶ 1401]:**
      1. Amount received for easement [¶ 1401(a)]:
         a. Deprived of whole beneficial interest—sale of entire property.
         b. Beneficial interest remains—amount received reduces property's basis.
      2. Gain recognized while loss not deductible [¶ 1401(b)].
   C. **Sale and exchange distinguished [¶ 1402]:**
      1. Exchange—reciprocal transfer of property.
      2. Sale—property transferred for money only.

II. **Nontaxable Exchanges**
   A. **Common nontaxable exchanges [¶ 1403]:**
      1. Gain or loss postponed until property disposed of.
      2. Includes:
         a. Securities for securities of same corporation.
         b. Some transfers of property to corporation controlled by transferor.
         c. Exchanges of certain government bonds.
         d. Property held for productive use or investment property of like kind.
         e. Exchange of stock and property in corporate reorganizations.
         f. Exchange of certain insurance policies.
   B. **Securities for similar securities of same corporation [¶ 1404]**
   C. **Transfer of property to corporation controlled by transferor [¶ 1405]:**
      1. Control—owning 80% of voting stock and 80% of all other classes of stock.
      2. Stock received need not be in proportion to interests before exchange.
      3. Information on exchange filed with tax return.
      4. Liability of transferor assumed by transferee [¶ 1405(a)].
      5. Assumed liabilities in excess of transferred property's basis taxable gain to transferor [¶ 1405(b)].

1462 Highlights of Chapter 4

6. Gain or loss may be recognized on transfers to investment company [¶ 1405(c)].
D. **Property held for productive use or investment [¶ 1406]:**
   1. Must be "like-kind" exchange.
   2. Not personal property exchange.
E. **Exchange of insurance policies [¶ 1407]:**
   1. One life insurance contract for another, or for endowment or annuity contract.
   2. Endowment insurance contract for certain others, or annuity contract.
   3. One annuity contract for another.
   4. Gain or loss recognized on:
      a. Endowment or annuity for life insurance contract.
      b. Annuity for endowment contract.
F. **Boot [¶ 1408]:**
   1. Defined—money or other property in addition to property not taxed.
   2. Giving boot—gain or loss generally not recognized, unless property [¶ 1408(a)].
   3. Receiving boot [¶ 1408(b)]:
      a. Gain recognized up to amount of boot received (no gain if cash boot used to liquidate mortgage).
      b. No loss recognized.
      c. Boot gain reportable on installment plan if otherwise qualified.
G. **Exchange of mortgaged property [¶ 1409]:**
   1. Relieved mortgage debts treated as boot (cash received) to figure gain.
   2. Boot given reduces amount of liabilities treated as boot received.
   3. Transfer to controlled corporation—mortgage generally not considered boot received.

III. **Involuntary Conversions**
   A. **Defined [¶ 1410]:**
      1. Occurs when money received for property stolen, accidentally destroyed or condemned.
      2. Condemnation [¶ 1410(a)]:
         a. Transfer under threat or imminence of condemnation—involuntary conversion.
         b. Condemnation considered—not threat or imminence.
         c. Condemnation decided—threat or imminence.
      3. Livestock [¶ 1410(b)]:
         a. Destruction by, or sale because of, disease—involuntary conversion.
         b. Sale of draft, breeding or dairy livestock because of drought—involuntary conversion.
      4. Disposition under federal reclamation laws [¶ 1410(c)].
      5. Broadcasting property sales required by FCC [¶ 1410(d)].
   B. **Gain or loss [¶ 1411]:**
      1. Payment received and replaced with similar or related use property:
         a. Amount realized equals or less than replacement cost—no gain.
         b. Amount realized exceeds replacement cost—gain.
         c. Loss recognized.
      2. Property converted directly into other similar property [¶ 1411(a)]—no gain.
      3. Generally must be replaced by taxpayer or one acting in his behalf [¶ 1411(b)].
      4. Election made on return, or amended return, by taxpayer [¶ 1411(c)].
      5. Gain must be reported in year realized [¶ 1411(d)].
      6. Notice of replacement, intention not to replace or failure to replace to IRS [¶ 1411(e)].
   C. **Time limit on replacement [¶ 1412]:**
      1. If conversion to money or nonsimilar property, qualified replacement required during period:
         a. Beginning with earlier of (1) converted property's date of destruction, seizure, etc., or (2) earliest date of threat or imminence of requisition or condemnation.

b. Ending (1) 2 years after first tax year gain realized, or (2) at later date set by IRS after taxpayer application (3-year limit applies to certain condemned realty).
 2. If converted directly into other property—no time limit.
D. **Making replacements [¶ 1413]:**
 1. Replacement property can be:
    a. Bought.
    b. Built.
    c. Acquired directly.
    d. Acquired by getting control of corporation owning similar property.
 2. Qualifications—replacement must be [¶ 1413(a)]:
    a. Similar or related in service or use to converted property (unless condemnation of real business or investment property).
    b. Held on date old property converted if acquired before conversion.
    c. Purchased to replace old property.
    d. Non-gift acquisition.
 3. Similar or related in service or use—means functionally same as converted property [¶ 1413(b)].
 4. Real business or investment property replacable by "like kind" property [see ¶ 1406].
E. **Figuring recognized gain or loss [¶ 1414]:**
 1. If amount realized exceeds replacement cost—gain recognized to extent of excess, if so elected [¶ 1414(a)].
 2. If basis exceeds amount received—loss recognized [¶ 1414(b)].
 3. If replacement cost exceeds amount received which exceeds basis—no gain, if so elected, but no loss either [¶ 1414(c)].
F. **Severance damages and special assessments [¶ 1415]:**
 1. Severance damages received when property condemned [¶ 1415(a)]:
    a. Not treated as income.
    b. Offset expenses in following order:
       1) Expenses incurred in securing damages.
       2) Any special benefit assessments.
       3) Expenses incurred in restoring retained property.
       4) Basis of retained property.
    c. Excess treated as gain—no postponement election.
 2. Special benefit assessments levied against retained property [¶ 1415(b)]:
    a. Not deductible.
    b. Used in following order:
       1) Reduce severance damages.
       2) Excess reduces condemnation award.
       3) Unused amount added to retained property's basis.
IV. **Sale of Residence**
 A. **Gain from sale or exchange [¶ 1416]:**
  1. Generally, gain recognized.
  2. Special rule if principal residence sold and:
     a. New principal residence bought and used within 18 months (one year for sales before 1975) before or after old residences sold, or
     b. Construction of new residence begun before or within 18 months (one year before 1975) after old residence sold *and* used as principal residence within 24 months (18 months for sales before 1975), after old residence sold.
  3. Gain recognized under special rule only to extent adjusted sales price of old exceeds cost of new residence.
  4. Sales price of old residence—includes [¶ 1416]:
     a. Mortgage to which property subject in buyer's hands, whether assumed or not.
     b. Face amount of buyer's liabilities that are partial consideration for sale.
  5. Adjusted sales price—amount realized less fixing-up expenses [¶ 1416(b)].

6. Amount realized—sales price less offsets to determine gain (selling and fixing-up expenses).
7. Selling expenses include commissions, sale advertising expenses, deed preparation, legal services and FHA mortgage "points."
8. Fixing-up expenses—must be [¶ 1416(c)]:
   a. For work on old residence to help sale during 90-day period before contract of completed sale.
   b. Paid within 30 days after sale.
   c. Otherwise nondeductible in figuring taxable income.
   d. Noncapital expenditures or improvements.
9. Cost of new residence—includes [¶ 1416(d)]:
   a. Costs of acquiring, building, rebuilding and improving chargeable to capital account within 42-month period (30-month period for sales before 1975) from 18 months before to 24 months after old residence sold.
   b. Assumed or unassumed debts property subject at purchase.
   c. Face amount of taxpayer's liabilities part of purchase consideration.
   d. Commissions and other buying expenses not deducted as moving expenses.
10. Exchange of residences—special rule applies [¶ 1416(g)].
11. Installment sale—special rule applies [¶ 1416(h)].

B. **What is a residence**—only property used as principal residence [¶ 1417]:
   1. Business or investment property not residence [¶ 1417(a)].
   2. Property used for residence *and* business or investment—allocation required [¶ 1417(b)].
   3. More than one house—special rule applies only to principal residence [¶ 1417(c)].

C. **Special rule for husband and wife**—nonrecognition of gain rule applies if elected, whether acting jointly or singly [¶ 1418].

D. **When special rule benefits not available [¶ 1419]:**
   1. New residence sold before old.
   2. More than one new residence—only last qualifies.
   3. Sale of residence by a trust.
   4. Title in new residence held by another.
   5. Purchase of partially constructed new residence.

E. **Special treatment for Armed Forces members [¶ 1420]:**
   1. Special nonrecognition rule replacement period suspended 4 years while on extended duty.
   2. 4-year limit deferred for service in combat zone and resultant hospitalization, and additional 180 days.

F. **Condemnation of residence**—treated as sale, if elected [¶ 1421].

G. **How sale reported [¶ 1422]:**
   1. If replacement made—only taxable gain reported (Form 2119).
   2. If replacement intended—no gain reported.
   3. If no replacement, or replacement period expired—taxable gain reported in usual way.

H. **Sale by persons 65 or over [¶ 1423]:**
   1. Election for all tax-free gain if:
      a. Old home was principal residence for 5 of 8 years before sale, *and*
      b. Adjusted sales price $35,000 or less.
   2. If adjusted sales price over $35,000—tax-free gain in ratio $35,000 is to adjusted sales price.
   3. Only one election per taxpayer.
   4. Spouses must both elect.
   5. Allocation of election when sale of part residence/part business or by joint tenant or tenant in common.

I. **Low-income housing project sales**—nonrecognition of gain rule applies if [¶ 1426]:
   1. Constructed under FHA or certain state assisted programs.
   2. Sale to tenants or co-op for their benefit.
   3. Property replaced within year with similar low-income housing.

Chapter 5

GAIN OR LOSS—BASIS

TABLE OF CONTENTS

¶

BASIS IN GENERAL
Basis—the key factor in figuring gain or loss 1500
  Basis
  Adjusted basis

COST AS BASIS
Cost basis—property acquired by purchase 1501

FAIR MARKET VALUE CONSIDERED IN BASIS DETERMINATION
Fair market value as basis 1502
  What is fair market value
  Evidence of value
Property acquired in a taxable exchange 1503
  Property received for other property
  Property acquired in trade-in
Property received as compensation for services 1504
Property acquired in divorce or separation settlement 1505
Property acquired before 3-1-13 1506
  Basis for determining gain
  Basis for determining loss
Property acquired from a decedent 1507
  What is carryover basis property
  The adjustments to carryover basis
  Special adjustment to basis
  Generation-skipping transfers
Property transferred within three years of decedent's death 1508
Joint ownership 1509
  Joint ownership in general
  Husband and wife
Life estates and remainders 1510

SUBSTITUTED BASIS
Using substituted basis 1514
Property acquired by gift 1515
  Determining the basis
  Adjustment for gift tax
Property acquired in nontaxable exchange 1517

¶

  When no "boot" is given or received
  When "boot" is given
  When cash "boot" is received and taxpayer has a gain
  When cash "boot" is received and taxpayer has a loss
  When taxpayer has a gain and not only money, but other property is received
  When transferee acquires property encumbered by a mortgage
  Exchange of property used partly for business
Property acquired in nontaxable transfer to controlled corporation 1518
  Basis of stock received in exchange for property
  Basis of property acquired by issuance of stock of controlled corporation or as paid-in surplus
Property acquired upon involuntary conversion 1519
  When no gain is recognized because of direct conversion
  When loss is recognized
  When gain is recognized because amount received exceeds cost of replacement
  When no gain is recognized because cost of replacement exceeds amount received

IDENTIFICATION OF BASIS
Allocation of basis 1521
  Corporate securities bought as a unit
  Basis of property partly condemned
  Sports franchises
  Other situations requiring allocation of basis
First-in, first-out rule 1522

SPECIAL RULES
Basis of patents and copyrights 1523
Sale of good will 1524

Footnotes appear at end of this Chapter.

Replacement for old residence	1526
Basis of annuity contract	1527
Additions to basis for circulation expenses, taxes and carrying charges	1528
• Highlights of Chapter 5	Page 1561

BASIS IN GENERAL

Basis of property is generally its cost if acquired by purchase. A basis other than cost may be required when property was acquired in some other manner. Once basis is known, adjustments are generally additions to basis for investment of capital and reductions of basis for recovery of capital. The gain from a sale or other disposition of property is the excess of the amount realized over the adjusted basis of the property. If the adjusted basis exceeds the amount realized there is a loss.

¶ **1500 Basis—the key factor in figuring gain or loss.** Basis and adjusted basis are the key factors in the formula for figuring gain or loss when property is disposed of. As explained in Chapter 4, the formula is:

BASIS + ADDITIONS − REDUCTIONS = ADJUSTED BASIS
GAIN = AMOUNT REALIZED − ADJUSTED BASIS
LOSS = ADJUSTED BASIS − AMOUNT REALIZED

Basis and adjusted basis also are important in determining the amount of certain deductions, such as depreciation, bad debts and casualty losses [Sec. 1001, 1012; 1.1001-1].

(a) **Basis** is determined by the way the taxpayer acquired the property. In most cases, basis is the property's cost or purchase price [¶ 1501]. However, the property may have been acquired by gift, inheritance or some other way that requires using a basis other than cost [¶ 1502 et seq.]. When special basis rules apply to a particular transaction, they are explained where the transaction is covered.

(b) **Adjusted basis.** While the taxpayer holds property, he may spend money on improvements, or he may take deductions for depreciation. Before he can figure his gain or loss when he disposes of the property, these items must be added to or subtracted from the basis. The basis after these adjustments are made is called the adjusted basis.

The taxpayer *increases* his basis for all items or expenditures chargeable to capital account. These include improvements, purchase commissions, legal costs for defending or perfecting title (including title insurance), surveying expenses, and recording fees. Expenditures that are currently deductible generally cannot be added to basis. But see ¶ 1528.

The taxpayer *reduces* the basis for any items that are a return of capital: depreciation, depletion, obsolescence, tax-free dividends, recognized losses on involuntary conversions and *deductible* casualty losses [Sec. 1011, 1016; 1.1011-1, 1.1016-1].[1] The basis cannot be reduced below zero.[2]

Example: In 1973, Sommers bought real property for $80,000 to be used as a factory. In addition to the purchase price he paid commissions of $2,000 with title search and legal fees of $600. Of the total cost of $82,600, $10,325 was allocated to the land and $72,275 to the building. Sommers spent $20,000 in remodeling the building and was allowed depreciation of $9,600 for the years 1973, 1974, 1975 and 1976. In 1976, he sustained an uninsured casualty loss to the building of $5,000 as a result of a fire. This loss was claimed as a deduction. The property's adjusted basis as of 1-1-77 is as follows:

	Land	Building
Original cost, including fees and commissions	$10,325	$72,275
Adjustments to basis:		
Add: Improvements		20,000
		$92,275
Subtract: Depreciation $9,600		
Casualty loss 5,000		14,600
Adjusted basis 1-1-77	$10,325	$77,675

COST AS BASIS

¶ 1501 **Cost basis—property acquired by purchase.** The original basis of property the taxpayer buys is the purchase price or cost to him. The cost of property is the amount paid for it either in cash or other property plus commissions and other expenses connected with the purchase. If mortgaged property is acquired the basis is the amount paid for the property plus the unpaid amount of the mortgage. This eliminates the need for making adjustments as the mortgage is paid. When the property is disposed of, any remaining portion of the mortgage is treated as part of the amount realized [¶ 1400].

Example: Smith paid $20,000 cash for a house worth $30,000 that was subject to a $10,000 mortgage. His basis for the house is $30,000 whether or not he assumes the mortgage. If Smith does assume the mortgage and pays off $2,000 of it, and then sells the house for $25,000 cash, subject to the remaining mortgage, his gain is $3,000, computed as follows:

Selling price:		
Cash	$25,000	
Mortgage	8,000	$33,000
Less: Basis		30,000
Gain		$ 3,000

The basis of property bought through exercising an option to purchase includes the option price and the option's cost or other basis (if purchased at a bona fide sale).

Capitalized expenditures in buying, building or developing an asset having a useful life of over 1 year [¶ 1808] form the cost basis of the asset. Real estate taxes are figured in as part of the property's cost if the buyer assumes the seller's obligation to pay them. See ¶ 1920 [Sec. 1012; 1.1012-1]. When the "price" paid for property includes payments made for reasons other than acquisition, such as family reasons, as a capital contribution, or to shift deductions, the amount in excess of fair market value is not part of the buyer's cost.[1]

NOTE: If property is bought under a deferred payment contract with interest not stated or at a low rate, a part of the price may be treated as interest. This "imputed" interest is not included in the property's basis [¶ 2840]. Special rules allow taxpayers to elect an average basis for mutual fund shares held in a custodial account and with different bases [Sec. 1.1012-1(e)].

FAIR MARKET VALUE CONSIDERED IN BASIS DETERMINATION

Generally, in a taxable exchange, the basis of property received is its fair market value when the exchange is made. Fair market value is also used in determining the basis of property received as compensation for services, acquired in divorce or separation settlement, acquired before 3-1-13 and acquired from a decedent.

¶ 1502 **Fair market value as basis.** The value of property on a specific date frequently is a factor in determining its basis. See ¶ 1503 et seq.

Footnotes appear at end of this Chapter.

(a) What is fair market value. Fair market value is the price a willing buyer and a willing seller would probably reach after negotiation, when neither is acting under compulsion.[1] Property may have a fair market value although no buyers exist.[2] However, there must be some assurance the value is what a market would establish.[3] It may not be based on assumptions[4] or the price in a forced sale.[5]

(b) Evidence of value. Actual sales of similar property on the open market are reliable evidence of value.

Example: Stock exchange quotations are good evidence of the fair market value of stock, but might not be conclusive as to a large block of stock that could not be sold on the market without affecting the market prices.[6] In one case, the court declined to use stock market prices at the peak of inflation.[7]

For real estate, leaseholds and patents, the testimony of experts is usally given great weight. Negotiable promissory notes of a responsible and solvent maker are regarded as the equivalent of cash.[8]

¶ 1503 Property acquired in a taxable exchange. If the taxpayer acquires property for other property in a taxable exchange (where gain or loss is recognized), the basis of the property received is generally its fair market value at the time of the exchange.

(a) Property received for other property. Some cases and rulings measure the cost of the property received in the exchange by its fair market value at receipt.[1] In other decisions, the new property's basis is measured by the fair market value of the property exchanged for it, increased or decreased by payments made or received by the taxpayer when the properties are of unequal value.[2] In most cases, the result will be the same under both methods. However, if the value of the property received is not equal to the value of the property given up, and no payment is made to compensate for the difference, the result may differ.

When it is impractical to determine a property's fair market value by the basis of the property received, their values are presumed to be equal.[3]

(b) Property acquired in trade-in. A dealer who sells new property and accepts used property in part payment, usually includes the traded-in property in inventory at a value equal to its bona fide selling price less direct selling costs (¶ 2607) [Sec. 1.471-2(c)]. If not put into inventory, its basis is equal to the amount included for it in the amount realized on the new property's sale.[4]

Automobile dealers may value used cars received as trade-ins at valuations equal to those listed in an official used car guide as the average wholesale prices for comparable cars.[5]

Generally, there is a nontaxable exchange [¶ 1517] when a buyer gives used business or investment property in part payment for new like property. However, in a taxable exchange, the trade-in is treated as part of the consideration given by the buyer for the new property.[6]

The basis of property used partly for business exchanged for similar property is discussed in ¶ 1517(g).

¶ 1504 Property received as compensation for services. If the taxpayer received property for services, its original basis to him is the property's fair market value, which he included in income [Sec. 1.61-2(d)(2)]. The basis of restricted property received after 6-30-69 as compensation for services is the sum of any amount paid for the property and any amount the taxpayer includes in gross income when the property is no longer subject to a substantial risk of forfeiture [Prop. Reg. Sec. 1.83-4]. See also ¶ 1326.

¶ **1505 Property acquired in divorce or separation settlement.** If a husband transfers property, such as a lump sum alimony payment, to his wife in settlement of his obligation to support her or for her release of her rights to his estate, it is a taxable exchange (unless the wife has a co-ownership interest in the property, as in community property states or in states where the wife's inchoate rights in her husband's property constitute co-ownership). The value of the marital rights surrendered is the fair market value of the transferred property. Therefore, the husband has gain to the extent that the fair market value of the property he gives up exceeds his basis for it. The wife's basis for the property she receives is its fair market value when she receives it.[1] She has no gain or loss on the transfer.[2]

¶ **1506 Property acquired before 3-1-13.** The basis for determining gain or loss on the sale or exchange of property acquired before 3-1-13, depends on whether it is disposed of at a gain or loss. The reason for this is that the increase in value before 3-1-13 is not taxed [Sec. 1053; 1.1053-1].

(a) **Basis for determining gain** is the greater of cost or fair market value on 3-1-13.

(b) **Basis for determining loss** is the cost of the property.

When selling price is greater than cost, but less than 3-1-13 value, there is neither a taxable gain nor a deductible loss.

For improved real estate and other depreciable property, the above rules apply, but the cost must be adjusted to 3-1-13, and the basis must also be adjusted for the period after 2-28-13 [Sec. 1053; 1.1053-1].

> **Example:** Todd owns property that cost $6,000 on which $1,000 of depreciation was sustained before 3-1-13. The fair market value on 3-1-13, was $5,500. The basis for gain is the fair market value of $5,500, since this is greater than the adjusted basis of $5,000 ($6,000 less $1,000 depreciation). The basis for loss is the adjusted basis of $5,000.

¶ **1507 Property acquired from a decedent.** The basis of *carryover basis property* inherited from a decedent dying after 12-31-76 is generally the same as the decedent's basis immediately before death, with adjustments. However there is an important exception—appreciated "carryover basis property" acquired before 1977 will get a stepped-up basis for its pre-1977 appreciation [Sec. 1023].

Background and purpose. Before the 1976 Tax Reform Act, the cost or other basis of property acquired from a decedent was its fair market value at the date of death (or the alternate valuation date, if elected). Therefore, if the property's fair market value had appreciated since the decedent acquired it, the resulting gain would never be taxed. On the other hand, if the property depreciated in value after the decedent acquired it, the loss could never be deducted. The basis of property acquired from a decedent was often referred to as a "stepped-up basis." Generally now, the beneficiary will receive no step-up in basis and that appreciation will not escape taxation. An exception remains for carryover basis property with pre-1977 appreciation.

(a) **What is carryover basis property.** Carryover basis property is property acquired from the decedent except for: (1) income in respect of a decedent [¶ 3008(b)]; (2) life insurance proceeds [¶ 3914]; (3) taxable joint and survivor annuities and deferred compensation plans [¶ 1231; 1232; 1838; 1839; 3024]; (4) property includible in decedent's gross estate disposed of in a taxable transaction before death [¶ 3907-3909; 3912]; (5) taxable stock options [¶ 1327]; (6) foreign

Footnotes appear at end of this Chapter.

personal holding company stock [Sec. 1023(b)(2)]. Noncarryover basis property continues to be governed by the existing basis rules.[1]

Personal and household effects can be excluded from carryover basis property to the extent of $10,000 of fair market value on election by the executor. This election must be made no later than the due date for the estate tax return [¶ 3943]. When the executor makes the election, the personal and household effects to which the election applies will receive a stepped-up basis.[1] [Sec. 1023(b)(3)].

(b) The adjustments to carryover basis. There are three adjustments that must be made to the adjusted basis carried over from the decedent in the following order: (1) the adjustment for federal and state estate taxes; and (2) the minimum carryover basis; and (3) the adjustment in basis attributable to state succession taxes [Sec. 1023(c), (d), (e)].

NOTE: These increases in basis are only used to determine gain. The basis for loss is the decedent's adjusted basis immediately before death.

All these adjustments cannot increase basis above fair market value. To determine the appreciation of carryover basis property and the limit on adjustments in the carryover basis of the property, the fair market value of property is considered to be its value for federal estate tax purposes [Sec. 1023(f), (g)].

Adjustments for federal and state estate taxes. This adjustment is to prevent part of the appreciation from being subject to both the estate tax and the income tax. Part of each individual carryover basis asset is found by multiplying the net federal and state estate tax after all credits by a fraction: the numerator is the appreciation in the individual carryover basis asset; the denominator is the total value of all decedent's property subject to the estate tax. The appreciation is determined on an asset by asset basis. There is no "netting" to determine unrealized appreciation for the estate as a whole. [Sec. 1023(c)].

Minimum carryover basis. The aggregate bases of all carryover basis property can be increased to a minimum of $60,000. Here, the finding of whether the aggregate bases exceed $60,000 is made after the increase in the basis for federal and state estate taxes, but before the increase in the basis for state succession taxes. If the aggregate bases of the carryover properties is under $60,000, the basis of each *appreciated* carryover basis property will increase by allocating the excess up to $60,000 in the ratio of net appreciation of the property to total net appreciation [Sec. 1023(d)].

State succession taxes. After the other adjustments are made, the carryover basis can be increased for the part of any state succession taxes paid by the recipient of the property that is attributable to the net appreciation on that property. The portion of the state succession taxes attributable to the net appreciation in the property received is figured by mutiplying total succession taxes paid by the recipient by a fraction: the numerator is the net appreciation in that particular property; the denominator is the fair market value of all property acquired by that person subject to the succession taxes [Sec. 1023(e)].

(c) Special adjustment to basis. The basis for computing gain (but not loss) of property which the decedent is treated as holding on 12-31-76 is increased by the excess of the fair market value of the property on 12-31-76 over its adjusted basis on that date. The basis cannot be increased above its estate tax value [Sec. 1023(h)].

Marketable bonds and securities. The fair market value of marketable bonds on 12-31-76 is determined from daily quotation prices on that day. The basis for gain will be the fair market value if it exceeded the adjusted basis [Sec. 1023(h)(1)].

Other carryover basis property. Carryover basis property other than marketable bonds and securities has its fair market value on 12-31-76 determined by formula. The property is assumed to have appreciated ratably over the years and the basis is increased by the appreciation attributable to the pre-1977 period. The basis increase formula is as follows: (1) Subtract the adjusted basis from the fair market value on the date of death; (2) Reduce that excess by the depreciation, depletion, and amortization taken while held by the decedent; (3) Multiply that figure by the ratio of the number of days the property was held before 1977 to the total number of days held; (4) Add the adjustments to basis for depreciation, depletion and amortization attributable to pre-1977 [Sec. 1023(h)(2)].

Substantial improvements are considered as separate properties for the purpose of these calculations [Sec. 1023(h)(2)(D)].

(d) Generation-skipping transfers. A generation-skipping trust is a trust with two or more generations of beneficiaries who belong to generations that are younger than the generation of the trust's grantor. Special basis rules apply to generation-skipping transfers. See ¶ 3912 [Sec. 2614].

¶ 1508 Property transferred within three years of decedent's death. Property transferred by the decedent without adequate consideration (a gift) within three years of his death is includible in the decedent's gross estate. The amount includible is the fair market value of the property on the date of death. There is no inclusion for bona fide sales or gifts excludable under the $3,000 annual exclusion. The sale or gift would be subject to the usual basis rules. If the decedent paid gift tax on a gift made after 12-31-76 and the value of that gift is included in the decedent's estate, the estate is increased by the amount of gift tax paid. This would not apply to the half of the gift attributable to a spouse under a joint gift [¶ 4009] [Sec. 2035].

NOTE: Before 12-31-76, transfers without consideration were includible in the decedent's estate only if they were made within three years of death *and* were in contemplation of death.

Example: Thurman gave Moore a gift with a fair market value of $100,000 on 1-31-77. When Thurman died on 10-1-77, the $100,000 gift (assuming the fair market value remained constant) would be added to his gross estate. Also, the gift tax of $22,960 would be added into the gross estate. Moore's basis in the gift remains at $100,000, its fair market value on the date of death.

¶ 1509 Joint ownership. The death of a joint tenant or tenant by the entirety may pose a basis problem for the survivor. However, a special rule applies to joint tenancies created after 1976 when a husband and wife are involved.

(a) Joint ownership in general. The part of the property included in the decedent's estate [¶ 3904] is considered acquired from the decedent by the survivor. Its basis is the value at which it was included in the estate (market value on date of decedent's death or on alternate date). The basis of the part not included in the decedent's estate is cost or other basis.

The basis of the property is reduced by depreciation on the property taken by the survivor before the other died. If the property was owned by husband and wife, and joint returns were filed, a part of the depreciation taken on these returns must be allocated to the surviving spouse for this purpose. The part allocated to the surviving spouse is determined under the following formula:

Survivor's income from property/Total income × depreciation = part allocated

(b) Husband and wife. For qualified joint interests created after 12-31-76, only one-half of the value of the interest is included in the the gross estate regardless of who furnished the consideration. An interest is a qualified joint interest only if: (1) created by the decedent, his spouse, or both; (2) for personal property, it was a completed gift for gift tax purposes; (3) for real property, the election was made to treat the creation of the joint tenancy as a taxable event; (4) only the decedent and spouse were joint tenants. [Sec. 2040].

NOTE: A joint tenancy created before 12-31-76, but severed and recreated after 12-31-76 will qualify if it meets the four requirements.

Background and purpose. Formerly, property owned jointly or by the entirety by husband and wife was includible in full in decedent's estate unless the survivor proved contribution. If contribution was shown, the portion contributed by the survivor was excluded. The excluded portion retained its original cost basis. For property acquired by gift or inheritance, only the deceased co-owner's fractional interest was includible. These rules still apply to joint interests of spouses that are unqualified or are qualified but were created before 12-31-76.

¶ **1510 Life estates and remainders.** The basis of a term interest (term of years, life interest or income interest in a trust) acquired by gift or from a decedent is zero. Thus, the entire amount realized from a sale is gain. However, this does not apply to a remainder interest, a resale by a purchaser of the term interest or to a joint sale of the term and remainder interests in a single transaction [Sec. 1001(e); 1.1001-1]. The basis for the remainder interest is found by multiplying the uniform basis of the entire property (adjusted to the time of sale) by a percentage. This percentage called a "factor" comes from mortality tables ("Tables of Factors" in Estate Tax Regulation Sec. 20.2031-7(f)) [Sec. 1.1014-5]. Mortality tables include a 6% discount factor.[1]

SUBSTITUTED BASIS

A substituted basis is one derived by reference to the basis of a transferor, donor or grantor. Either the basis for the taxpayer's old property is carried over to the new property, or the transferor's basis for the property is carried over to the property in the hands of the transferee. Transactions involving a substituted basis are gifts received after 1920, nontaxable exchanges and replacement property acquired as a result of an involuntary conversion.

¶ **1514 Using substituted basis.** A substituted basis is one derived from a transferor's or a donor's basis, or other property held by the person for whom the basis is to be determined [Sec. 1016(b); 1.1016-10]. The basis must be adjusted, as described in ¶ 1500, not only for the period that it was held by the present owner, but also for the period it was held by the transferor or donor.

Example: On 1-2-75, Alston bought an apartment building having an estimated useful life of 30 years. The purchase price was $30,000. On 1-2-77, Alston gave the building to his daughter. (Assume no gift tax was paid on the transfer.) On 1-2-78, the daughter sold the building for $35,000. The recognized gain on the sale (assuming no figures other than those mentioned) is $8,000. The basis is adjusted for depreciation while in the hands of both the donor (2 years) and the donee (1 year). Since the rate of depreciation is $1,000 a year (straight line depreciation), the adjusted basis is $27,000, and the recognized gain on the sale $8,000. The daughter recovers the same capital investment that Alston would have recovered, had he continued to own the property.

¶ 1515 Property acquired by gift. The basis of property acquired by gift after 12-31-20, depends on whether a sale of the property results in a gain or loss, as indicated below. These rules also apply to property acquired by a transfer in trust made by gift.

(a) Determining the basis. If a transfer of the property results in a gain, its basis is the same as in the hands of the donor or the last preceding owner by whom it was not acquired by gift. The basis for depreciation, amortization, or depletion is the donor's adjusted basis regardless of whether the fair market value of the property is greater or less than the donor's adjusted basis at the time of the gift.[1]

If the transfer results in a loss, the basis is (1) the same as in the hands of the donor or the last preceding owner by whom it was not acquired by gift, or (2) the fair market value of the property at the time of the gift, whichever is lower [Sec. 1015(a); 1.1015-1]. If the taxpayer uses the basis for determining a gain and computes a loss, and then uses the basis for determining a loss and computes a gain, he has neither a gain nor a loss.[1]

Example: On 4-11-69, Mason bought bonds for $1,000. On 6-11-77, Mason gave the bonds to Doran when their fair market value was $800. No gift tax was payable on this gift. The basis of the bonds to Doran is as follows:

For determining gain $1,000
  (same as in hands of donor)
For determining loss .... $ 800
  (fair market value on date of gift, since that is less than basis in hands of donor)

If Doran sold the bonds for $1,200, his gain would be $200 ($1,200 − $1,000).
If Doran sold the bonds for $700, his loss would be $100 ($800 − $700).
If Doran sold the bonds for any amount between $800 and $1,000 (for example, $925), there would be neither gain nor loss.

Exception. The above rules do not apply to gifts included in the donor's estate as property transferred within three years of donor's death, and disposed of by the donee after the donor's death. Such gifts are considered property acquired from a decedent, and the basis is governed by the rules in ¶ 1507-1510. For the basis of a term or life interest when disposed of, see ¶ 1510.

(b) Adjustment for gift tax. For gifts made after 12-31-76, the basis is increased by the portion of the gift tax attributable to the net appreciation on the gift [Sec. 1015(d)(6)].

Background and purpose. For gifts made between 9-2-58 and 12-31-76, the basis was increased by the total gift tax paid. But the basis could not be increased to more than the fair market value of the property at the time of the gift. For gifts made before 9-2-58 and not disposed of before that date, the basis of the property was increased by the amount of the gift tax. But the increase could not be more than the excess of the property's fair market value at the time of the gift over its basis at that time.

¶ 1517 Property acquired in nontaxable exchange. The basis of property acquired in a nontaxable exchange is generally the adjusted basis of the property traded, plus any "boot" given, additional costs incurred, and gain recognized. The basis is reduced by any cash or unlike property (boot) received, and loss recognized on the exchange [Sec. 1031(d); 1.1031(d)-1]. See also ¶ 1403 et seq. If two or more properties are received, the basis is allocated among the properties according to their fair market values (in proportion to the total value) on the date of exchange.

(a) When no "boot" is given or received the basis of the property acquired is the same as the basis of the property transferred (adjusted to the date of exchange).

Example 1: Chambers exchanges an apartment house with an adjusted basis of $30,000 for a dairy farm. The basis of the farm becomes $30,000, regardless of its fair market value.

The total of the bases of two or more properties acquired in an exchange will be the same as the basis of the property given up. This basis is allocated among the properties according to their respective fair market values (in proportion to the total value) on the date of exchange.[1]

(b) When "boot" is given, the basis of the property acquired is the same as the basis of the property transferred (adjusted to the date of exchange), plus the amount of the boot.

Example 2: Tilson in acquiring a new truck listed at $1,500 was allowed $1,000 on his old truck. He paid the additional $500 in cash. The adjusted basis of the old truck was $900 (cost less depreciation). The basis of the new truck is $1,400 ($900 plus $500), regardless of its actual or fair market value.

When gain or loss is recognized. The basis of the property received is the same as that of the property transferred (adjusted to the exchange date) *increased* by the recognized gain or *decreased* by the recognized loss.

Example 3: Lewis exchanges an apartment building with an adjusted basis of $100,000 and a fair market value of $150,000, plus shares of stock with a basis of $60,000 and a value of $50,000, for an apartment building worth $200,000. Since the exchange of the stock in part consideration for the apartment is not within the nontaxable exchange provisions, Lewis has a recognized loss of $10,000 ($60,000 less $50,000). The basis of the property received is $150,000:

Adjusted basis of old apartment building	$100,000
Basis of stock surrendered	60,000
	$160,000
Less: Loss recognized on the exchange	10,000
Basis of new apartment building	$150,000

(c) When cash "boot" is received and taxpayer has a gain, the basis of the property acquired is the basis of the property transferred (adjusted to the date of exchange) *decreased by* the cash received and *increased by* the amount of gain recognized on the exchange.

Example 4: If Doe exchanges a machine having an adjusted basis of $1,000 for a similar one with a fair market value of $900, and also receives $300, his gain is $200, all of which is recognized (since it does not exceed the cash received). Basis of the new machine is $900:

Adjusted basis of old machine	$1,000
Less: Amount of money received	300
	$ 700
Plus: Gain recognized on exchange	200
Basis of new machine	$ 900

The reason for this computation becomes clear if it is assumed that the new machine is sold immediately for $900 (its basis). Gordon originally had a machine with an adjusted basis of

$1,000. He now has $1,200 cash ($300 received on the exchange and $900 on the sale). His profit is $200.

(d) When cash "boot" is received and taxpayer has a loss, the basis of the property received is the basis of the property transferred (adjusted to the date of exchange), *decreased by* the amount of money received.

Example 5: If Wright exchanges a machine with an adjusted basis of $1,000 for a similar machine having a fair market value of $700, and also receives $100 in cash, his loss is $200, but that loss is not recognized. The basis of the new machine becomes $900 ($1,000 − $100). The reason for this is readily seen. If the new machine were destroyed in an accident, Wright's actual loss would be $900—basis of the old machine less $100 in cash he had received.

(e) When taxpayer has a gain and not only money, but other property is received. When a taxpayer not only receives money, but other property not permitted to be received without the recognition of gain, the basis must be apportioned, an amount equal to the fair market value of the other property being assigned to it.

Example 6: Assume that Simon exchanges a machine with an adjusted basis of $8,000 for a similar machine having a fair market value of $8,500, and also receives $1,500 in cash and the note of the purchaser having a fair market value of $1,000. Simon's gain is $3,000 of which $2,500 is recognized (the cash plus the fair market value of the note). The bases of the new machine and the note are figured as follows:

Adjusted basis of old machine	$8,000
Less: Amount of money received	1,500
	$6,500
Plus: Gain recognized on exchange	2,500
Combined bases of new machine and note	$9,000
Basis of note (its fair market value)	1,000
Basis of new machine	$8,000

The reason for this computation is clear, if it is assumed that the note and new machine are sold immediately for $9,000 (their bases). Simon originally had a machine with an adjusted basis of $8,000. He now has $10,500 cash ($1,500 received on the exchange and $9,000 on the sale). His profit is $2,500.

(f) When transferee acquires property encumbered by a mortgage. Generally, if property encumbered by a mortgage is transferred in a tax-free exchange, and the transferee assumes or takes the property subject to the mortgage, the mortgage is considered the equivalent of cash in figuring the *basis* of the property received [Sec. 1031(d); 1.1031(d)-2]. This is true whether or not it is treated as "boot" in determining the amount of *recognized gain* [¶ 1409]. Thus, identical figures may result in different bases. This can occur in determining *recognized gain* when the assumption of liability is treated as money in one case, but not in another.

Example 7: *When mortgage is considered "boot."* Kent bought a farm for $25,000 and immediately put a $5,000 mortgage on it. He exchanged the farm for an office building worth $32,500 and owned by Clark who assumed the mortgage. Kent has a recognized gain of $5,000 (the indebtedness assumed by Clark is considered the same as cash), and the office building's basis is $25,000:

Adjusted basis of farm	$25,000
Less: Amount of money received (assumption of indebtedness)	5,000
	$20,000
Plus: Gain recognized on exchange (mortgage assumed treated as money)	5,000

Footnotes appear at end of this Chapter.

¶ 1517

Basis of office building $25,000

Example 8: *When mortgage is not considered "boot," because of transfer to controlled corporation.* White bought property for $25,000 and immediately put a $5,000 mortgage on it. He transferred the property to a controlled corporation for its stock worth $32,500, the corporation assuming the mortgage. His gain is $12,500, but none of it is recognized (the indebtedness assumed by the corporation is not considered "boot"), and the basis of the shares is $20,000, figured as follows:

Adjusted basis of old property	$25,000
Less: Amount of money received (assumption of indebtedness)	5,000
	$20,000
Plus: Gain recognized on exchange (mortgage assumed not treated as money)	0
Basis of shares of stock	$20,000

(g) Exchange of property used partly for business. When property used partly for business is exchanged for similar property, the part of the acquired property's basis allocated to business use is decreased by any gain not recognized, or increased by any loss not recognized on the exchange.[2] A gain realized on the personal part is taxable, but a loss on that part is not deductible.

Example 9: Clark owned a car driven two-thirds for business use. It had cost him $3,600, and prior years' depreciation totaled $1,350. He traded it in on a new car also costing $3,600 and was given a $1,200 trade-in allowance. The new car was also to be used two-thirds for business. Assume there is no salvage value. The basis is figured as follows:

Cost of old car allocable to business use (⅔ of $3,600)		$2,400
Less: Trade-in allowance for business portion (⅔ of $1,200)	$800	
Total depreciation allowed on old car	1,350	2,150
Unrecognized loss on business portion		($ 250)
Cost of new car		$3,600
Portion of new car's cost for business use (⅔ of $3,600)		$2,400
Plus: Unrecognized loss on trade-in		250
Basis of new car (business portion)		$2,650

(Note that if salvage value is a factor [¶ 2005] it is subtracted from the cost of the new car and reduces its basis for computing depreciation.)

¶ 1518 Property acquired in nontaxable transfer to controlled corporation. When property is transferred in a nontaxable exchange to a corporation controlled by the transferor [¶ 1405], the basis must be found for (a) the stock received in exchange for the transferred property, and (b) the property transferred to the corporation in return for its stock.

(a) Basis of stock received in exchange for property. The basis of stock received in a nontaxable transfer of property to a corporation is the same as that of the property exchanged, *less* the money and fair market value of other property received, and *increased* by any gain recognized on the exchange [Sec. 358(a)(1); 1.358-1]. The basis of any other property (except money) received is its fair market value [Sec. 358(a)(2); 1.358-1].

Example 1: Stanley transfers property to Sterling Corporation in exchange for its controlling stock. He had bought the property for $10,000. No gain is recognized on the transaction. His basis for the stock is $10,000.

Example 2: Assume that in Example 1, the stock received was worth $9,800 and Stanley also received $750 cash. He has a recognized gain of $550 ($9,800 plus $750, minus $10,000). The basis of the stock is $9,800 ($10,000 minus $750, plus $550).

When liability is assumed. If the property received is taken subject to a liability, or if the corporation receiving it assumes a liability of the transferor, gain is not recognized, but the liability is treated as money received by the person who transferred the property and is subtracted in figuring his basis [Sec. 358(d); 1.358-3].

Example 3: Harper transfers property with an adjusted basis of $100,000, and subject to a mortgage of $25,000, in a nontaxable exchange to a controlled corporation. He receives in exchange stock of the corporation worth $150,000. No gain or loss is recognized on the exchange [¶ 1405(a)]. The basis of the stock to Harper is $75,000; basis of the property transferred ($100,000) less the amount of money received (amount of liability, $25,000).

A mortgage assumed by a corporation in a nontaxable transfer has the same effect on stock received by a transferor [¶ 1517(f)].

(b) Basis of property acquired by issuance of stock of controlled corporation or as paid-in surplus. If property was acquired by a corporation on or after 6-22-54, in a tax-free transfer to a corporation controlled by the transferor, or as paid-in capital or as a contribution to capital, the basis of the property acquired is the transferor's basis increased by any gain recognized to the transferor [Sec. 362(a); 1.362-1].

Example 4: Frank Harris owns land with an adjusted basis of $25,000, but which now has a fair market value of $75,000. He organizes the Frank Corp. to which all the property is transferred in exchange for all of its stock. Frank is in control of the corporation immediately after the exchange which, therefore, is tax free. Obviously, if the basis of the property to Frank Corp. is its cost ($75,000), the basis of the property will have been stepped up from $25,000 to $75,000, and no one will have paid any tax on the increment. This provision prevents the increase. Accordingly the basis of the property to the Frank Corp. is $25,000. The basis of the stock to Frank is also $25,000.

¶ 1519 Property acquired upon involuntary conversion. Rules follow for determining the basis of property that replaces similar property that has been involuntarily converted [Sec. 1033(b); 1.1033(c)-1].

(a) When no gain is recognized because of direct conversion of property into other property similar or related in service or use, the basis of the new asset is the same as that of the old (adjusted to the time of conversion).

Example 1: Land owned by Byrd and having an adjusted basis of $8,000 was condemned by the county, and Byrd received similar land from the county to replace his condemned land. The basis of the new land is $8,000.

(b) When loss is recognized, the basis of the new property is its replacement cost. A loss from an involuntary conversion is recognized. See ¶ 1414(b).

Example 2: Lee's factory with an adjusted basis of $30,000 was destroyed by fire. The insurance proceeds were $25,000. He bought a new plant for $33,000. A loss of $5,000 is recognized and the new factory's basis is $33,000.

(c) When gain is recognized because amount received exceeds cost of replacement, the basis of replacement property is its cost less gain not recognized. If more than one property is bought, the basis is allocated to these properties in proportion to their respective costs.[1] See ¶ 1411; 1414(a).

Example 3: Woods owned a garage with an adjusted basis of $14,000 which the State condemned. He received a $20,000 award and bought a new garage for $18,000. His realized gain is $6,000 but only $2,000 of it is recognized (excess of condemnation proceeds over cost of new property). The new garage's basis is $14,000, figured as follows:

Realized gain	$ 6,000
Recognized gain	2,000

Footnotes appear at end of this Chapter.

Gain not recognized	$ 4,000
Cost of new garage	$18,000
Less: Gain not recognized	4,000
Basis of new garage	$14,000

Example 4: Jones owned a farm with an adjusted basis of $14,000 which the State condemned. He received a $20,000 award and bought 2 adjoining farms totaling about the same acreage as the condemned land. He paid $10,800 for farm #1 and $7,200 for farm #2. His realized gain is $6,000 but only $2,000 of it is recognized (excess of condemnation proceeds over new properties' total cost). The basis of each of the new properties is figured as follows:

Realized gain	$ 6,000
Recognized gain	2,000
Gain not recognized	$ 4,000
Cost of new property (both farms)	$18,000
Less gain not recognized	4,000
Basis of new property (both farms)	$14,000

Basis of farm #1 10,800/18,000 × $14,000 = $8,400.
Basis of farm #2 7,200/18,000 × $14,000 = $5,600.

(d) When no gain is recognized because cost of replacement exceeds amount received, the basis of replacement property is its cost less gain not recognized. If more than one property is bought, the basis is allocated to these properties in proportion to their respective costs. See ¶ 1411; 1414(c).

Example 5: Miller's plant with a $30,000 adjusted basis was destroyed by fire. The insurance proceeds were $37,000. Miller bought a new plant for $40,000. No gain is recognized and the basis of the new plant is figured as follows:

Realized gain	$ 7,000
Recognized gain	0
Gain not recognized	$ 7,000
Cost of new plant	$40,000
Less: Gain not recognized	7,000
Basis of new plant	$33,000

Example 6: Assume the same facts as in Example 5 above, except that Miller bought two new plants: (1) at cost of $10,000; (2) at cost of $30,000. Basis of each new plant is figured as follows:
Basis of plant #1: 10,000/40,000 × $33,000 = $8,250
Basis of plant #2: 30,000/40,000 × $33,000 = $24,750

NOTE: A special allocation must be made when there is unrecognized Sec. 1250 gain. See ¶ 1619(d).

IDENTIFICATION OF BASIS

Generally, when various kinds of property are purchased for a lump sum, an allocation of their cost or other basis is required if gain, loss or depreciation is to be figured for a part of that property. The first-in, first-out rule is a different kind of basis identification involving the sale of stocks or bonds. It is applied when various lots are bought at different prices or their identity cannot be determined when sold.

¶ **1521 Allocation of basis.** In the situation in which an allocation of basis is required, it is usually determined on the relative value of each unit to the value of the whole.[1] If allocation is impractical, no gain or loss is realized until the entire cost is recovered [Sec. 1.61-6].[2]

(a) Corporate securities bought as a unit. If an allocation is practicable, the cost is apportioned among the securities to provide their respective bases for gain or loss on resale or worthlessness. In the case of a block of the same securities, the allocation is pro rata.[3]

If no reasonably accurate method of allocation exists, the purchased securities are treated as a unit for computing gain or loss. Problems of practicability of allocation usually involve securities whose market value is difficult or impossible to determine, and particularly securities that are required to be resold as a unit.[4]

(b) Basis of property partly condemned. If part of the taxpayer's property was condemned, he must determine the basis of the condemned and retained portions. There is no problem for unimproved land acquired at a certain amount per acre, or when land and improvement costs were separately shown in a purchase contract. He merely allocates the total cost between the two portions. For lump-sum purchases of improved realty, separate local tax assessments for land and buildings may serve as a measure for allocation.[5] See also ¶ 1415(a) on severance damages.

(c) Sports franchises. The amount the buyer allocates to player contracts on a sale or exchange of a franchise cannot exceed what the seller allocates to the contracts. However, this is limited to no more than 50% unless the taxpayer can prove a greater allocation is proper. This applies to sales or exchanges after 12-31-75 in tax years ending after that date [Sec. 1056].

(d) Other situations requiring allocation of basis. These include:

- Business bought as a unit [¶ 1601(d)].
- Property sold with separate elements [¶ 1619(b)].
- Nontaxable stock dividend in stock of a class different from that on which the dividend was declared [¶ 1708].
- Bargain sales to charity [¶ 1942(b)].
- Land and buildings acquired together [¶ 2003(d)].
- Aggregating operating oil and gas interests [¶ 2107].
- Subdivided real estate [¶ 2841].
- Partnership distributions or transfers [¶ 2937; 2938].
- Several kinds of securities received in a nontaxable exchange [¶ 3313].

¶ **1522 First-in, first-out rule.** When shares of stock are sold from lots bought at different dates or prices, and the identity of the lots cannot be determined, the stock sold must be charged against the earliest purchase. The first-in, first-out rule also applies to bonds sold or exchanged after 7-13-65 [Sec. 1.1012-1(c)]. Use of average cost generally is not allowed.[1] However, special rules allow taxpayers to elect an average basis for mutual fund shares held in a custodial account and with different bases [Sec. 1.1012-1(e)].

> **Example:** Simms bought 100 shares of Phillips Co. stock on 4-30-64 and another 100 shares of Phillips Co. stock on 3-1-77. On 8-1-77, he sold 100 shares of Phillips Co. stock. Unless Simms can show that the stock sold was that bought in 1977, it will be assumed that the sale was from the earlier purchase in 1964.

Usually, difficulty can be avoided by keeping records that identify the stock sold. If the stock is registered in the taxpayer's name, he can identify it by keeping a record of dates and prices by certificate numbers. If the stock certificate is in a broker's custody, or if the taxpayer holds a single certificate representing stock from different lots, identification may be made by giving the broker instructions (confirmed by him in writing) as to which particular stock to sell [Sec. 1.1012-

Footnotes appear at end of this Chapter.

1(c)]. Stock identified in this manner is the stock sold even though the broker delivers stock certificates from a different lot.[2] When the broker is authorized to sell stock without an owner's prior approval, the owner may identify the particular shares sold before the settlement date (usually 4 business days after trade date).[3] Special rules apply to identify sold Treasury bonds and notes[4] [Sec. 1.1012-1(c)(7)].

Stock received in reorganization. The first-in, first-out rule does not apply to shares of stock received in a tax-free reorganization. Here the "average cost" rule is used.[5] The basis of each new share of stock received in exchange is determined by dividing the total cost of the old stock by the number of new shares received. But if the new shares received in a reorganization can be traced to specific old shares, the "average cost" rule does not apply and the cost of the new shares is the adjusted cost of the old shares with which they are identified.[6] If taxpayer receives new stock in a split-up, the first-in, first-out rule applies, unless taxpayer identifies the new shares with purchases made before the split-up.[7] A split-up is defined in ¶ 3316(a).

SPECIAL RULES

The paragraphs that follow cover basis rules pertaining to certain special situations. These involve: Patents and copyrights; good will; replacement of old residence; annuity contracts; and deductible circulation expenses, taxes and carrying charges.

¶ **1523 Basis of patents and copyrights** include cost if purchased, governmental fees, cost of drawings, experimental models, attorney's fees, and development or experimental expenses [Sec. 1.167(a)-6(a)]. (But if research and experimental expenditures have been deducted [¶ 1842], they are not included in the basis.) The inventor's own time is not an element of cost.[1]

¶ **1524 Sale of good will.** When all or a large part of the assets of a business are sold, it must be determined whether the sale included good will. Good will may be included in the basis if it was purchased, or was in existence on 3-1-13. Good will developed by the seller since 3-1-13 may not be included in the basis regardless of the value; it is subject to tax as capital gain [¶ 1601].

To determine whether or not the good will has been sold, the courts consider: (a) what part of the business was sold,[1] (b) whether the buyer had the right to use the seller's name,[2] and (c) whether the contract of sale required the seller to cease doing business.[3]

¶ **1526 Replacement for old residence.** The basis of a new residence is its purchase price reduced by the nontaxable gain after the old residence is sold or exchanged. The adjusted basis of the *old* residence is its original cost, including commissions and other expenses at the time of its purchase, plus subsequent improvements [¶ 1825(a)] less allowable depreciation, if any, deductible casualty losses and the nontaxable gain on the sale of the previous residence. Expenses of buying the new residence are not added to basis if deducted as moving expenses [¶ 1416 et seq.].

Taxpayers 65 and over do not reduce the basis of the new residence for the gain they can exclude from income (¶ 1423) [Sec. 121, 1016(a)(7), 1034(e); 1.121-5(g), 1.1016-5(d), 1.1034-1(e)]. However, they do reduce basis for any remaining nonrecognized gain.

Example 1: Foster sold the house he had used as his residence for 10 years. Its adjusted basis was $10,000, and the selling price was $32,000. Selling expenses (broker's commissions) and "fixing-up" expenses were $1,000 each. Two months later, he bought a new residence for $14,000. Basis of his new residence is $9,000.

Realized Gain

1.	Selling price of old residence	$32,000
2.	Less: Selling expenses	1,000
3.	Amount realized on sale	$31,000
4.	Less: Adjusted basis of old residence	10,000
5.	Realized gain	$21,000

Adjusted Sales Price

6.	Amount realized on sale (Line 3 above)	$31,000
7.	Less: Fixing-up expenses	1,000
8.	Adjusted sales price	$30,000

Recognized Gain

9.	Adjusted sales price (Line 8 above)	$30,000
10.	Less: Cost of new residence	14,000
11.	Recognized gain	$16,000

Gain Not Recognized

12.	Gain realized (Line 5 above)	$21,000
13.	Gain recognized (Line 11 above)	16,000
14.	Gain not recognized	$ 5,000

Basis of New Residence

15.	Cost of new residence	$14,000
16.	Less: Gain not recognized (Line 14 above)	5,000
17.	Basis of new residence	$ 9,000

NOTE: If Foster was 65 or over, the basis of the new residence would be the same. However, the amount of the recognized gain ($16,000) would be reduced to zero by electing the tax-free exclusion [¶ 1423].

Example 2: On 1-1-77, Strong bought a new residence for $10,000. His old residence had cost him $5,000 (adjusted basis of old residence to him in this example). He sold the old residence on 3-1-77, at an adjusted sales price of $15,000. In May, 1977, he had a garage built on the new premises for $2,000. During March and April, 1977, only $5,000 of the $10,000 gain on the sale of the old residence is recognized. After completion of the garage in May, 1977, the cost of the new residence is $12,000 ($10,000 + $2,000 for garage addition) and then only $3,000 of the $10,000 gain on the old residence is recognized.

The adjusted basis of the new residence during January and February, 1977, is $10,000 (cost) because the rule above does not apply—no reduction is made in determining adjusted basis of the new residence *before* the old one is sold.

The adjusted basis of the new residence during March and April, 1977, is $5,000—the rule above applies—the basis (cost) of $10,000 is reduced by $5,000, the amount of gain not recognized on the sale of the old residence.

The adjusted basis of the new residence following the completion of the garage in May, 1977, is $5,000—the rule above applies—the basis (cost) of $12,000 is *reduced* by $7,000, the gain not recognized on the sale of the old residence.

Residence acquired by gift or inheritance. If any part of the new residence was acquired by gift or inheritance, the value of that part is not treated as a cost in determining the recognized gain on the sale of the old residence, but it is included in the basis of the inherited or donated residence in figuring the gain on a later sale.[1]

Example 3: Bruckner inherited a residence having a fair market value of $12,000. He made improvements totaling $14,000. He then sold his old residence, acquired at a cost of $10,000, for $15,000. There were $200 fixing-up expenses on the old residence. Gain recognized on the sale of the old residence is $800, figured as follows: Adjusted sales price of

Footnotes appear at end of this Chapter.

¶ 1526

$14,800 ($15,000 less $200) less $14,000 improvements. The adjusted basis of the new residence to be used in figuring gain or loss on a later sale of the new residence is $21,800 (the $12,000 fair market value of the new residence plus the $14,000 improvements less the $4,200 gain not recognized on the sale of the old residence).

Sale of low-income housing projects. When certain low-income housing projects are sold, the basis of the qualified replacement property is its cost less any gain not recognized (¶ 1426) [Sec. 1039].

Residence acquired by repossession. See ¶ 2823.

¶ **1527 Basis of annuity contract.** If an annuity contract is sold, the amounts recovered tax free as a return of investment [¶ 1230 et seq.] are subtracted from the cost basis of the annuity contract. A long-lived annuitant may receive excludable payments exceeding his cost. Nevertheless, the basis of the contract may not be reduced below zero [Sec. 1021; 1.1021-1]. On the transfer of appreciated property for a private annuity, the investment in the contract is the transferor's basis in the property transferred; the gain (excess of the value of the annuity over the basis of the property transferred) is reported ratably over the annuitant's life expectancy.[1] In the case of a secured private annuity, the Tax Court has held that the excess of the annuity's value, as determined under the actuarial tables, over the transferor's basis in the property exchanged is includible in income in the year of exchange.[2]

¶ **1528 Additions to basis for circulation expenses, taxes and carrying charges.** A taxpayer can elect to capitalize (add to property basis) deductible circulation expenditures, taxes and other carrying charges *instead* of deducting them, if sound accounting principles allow them to be charged to capital account [Sec. 173, 266, 1016(a)(1); 1.173-1, 1.266-1, 1.1016-2(c)]. In general, these expenses are carrying charges, interest and certain taxes during the construction period of property or on unimproved and unproductive real property. An example of a circulation expenditure that is properly chargeable to capital account is the cost of hiring extra employees for a limited time to get new subscribers through telephone calls.

≫**OBSERVATION**→ Whether to capitalize or deduct these items depends on what the taxpayer's tax bracket is for the tax year in which the charges were paid or incurred.

Example: Rhodes paid $5,000 for an unimproved and unproductive lot with the idea of building a store at some future date. From 1967 to 1977 he paid taxes of $1,500 on the property, but instead of deducting the taxes he elected to capitalize them. The basis of the property to Rhodes is $6,500 ($5,000 + $1,500).

MAY BE CAPITALIZED

Deductible expenditures by publishers of newspapers, magazines and other periodicals, to establish or increase circulation [Sec. 1.173-1].

Deductible expenditures incurred in developing or building improvements to real property; also taxes and interest incurred in installing machinery and other fixed assets. For example: interest on loans to pay for improvements or machinery; social security taxes on wages paid for services in developing and building improvements, or in transporting or installing machinery; taxes paid on the purchase, storage or consumption of material, such as sales or use taxes.

Delay rentals paid or accrued on non-producing oil and gas leases [¶ 2101(b)];[1] insurance premiums paid on a construction loan for business improvements.[2]

MAY NOT BE CAPITALIZED

The following are not "carrying charges:" advertising expenses on the property; cost of maintenance and upkeep (for example, salaries of manager, etc., wages of laborers for minor repairs, supervising properties); rent of office to do business, and bookkeepers' salaries to maintain records;[3] real estate taxes and mortgage interest paid while property is being used as own residence.[4]

(a) Making the election. The election to capitalize is made by filing a statement with the return showing what charges have been capitalized. Taxes, mortgage interest and other carrying charges on unimproved and unproductive real property for a tax year may either be capitalized or deducted as the taxpayer chooses without reference to what he has done in other tax years. However, once taxpayer elects to capitalize charges for improvements or installation of machinery, he must continue to capitalize charges of the same type on the same project in all future years [Sec. 1.266-1]. A subdivided plat is unimproved and unproductive land until it is recorded.[5]

The election to capitalize circulation expenses is binding for all later years unless the Revenue Service permits revocation [Sec. 173; 1.173-1; ¶ 1808].

(b) Charges on improvements may be capitalized only until the development or construction work is completed, and for machinery, until it is installed or put into use, whichever is later.

Allocation of charges is permitted. For example, when an employee spends 1/3 of his time on a new factory's construction, and 2/3 on the company's general business, 1/3 of his social security tax may be capitalized.

The construction work does not have to be for a productive asset, such as a factory, but may be for personal residences. Of course, the charges cannot be capitalized unless they are otherwise deductible. The charges may be for additions to an improvement, such as building another floor in a factory, or installing insulation in a building.

When several charges of the same type are incurred on a project, if one charge is capitalized, all others of the same type also must be capitalized. If the charges are not of the same type, however, one or more may be capitalized without the others being capitalized. If the same type of charges are incurred on different projects, they may be capitalized on one project and not the other [Sec. 1.266-1].

Footnotes to Chapter 5

(P-H "FEDERAL TAXES" related references are cited in brackets [ ] at the end of each footnote below)

Footnote ¶ 1500 [¶ 31,141 et seq.; 31,446 et seq.].
(1) Other adjustments are in Sec. 1011-1022 and in the regulations.
(2) Rev. Rul. 75-451, 1975-2 CB 330 [¶ 31,484(5)].

Footnote ¶ 1501 [¶ 31,151 et seq.].
(1) McDonald, 28 BTA 64; Mountain Wholesale Co., 17 TC 870 [¶ 31,175(5), (10)].

Footnote ¶ 1502 [¶ 31,257].
(1) Williams Est. v. Comm., 1 AFTR 2d 834, 256 F.2d 217 [¶ 31,257(5)].
(2) Alvary v. U.S., 9 AFTR 2d 1633, 302 F.2d 790 [¶ 31,257(10)].
(3) Helvering v. Walbridge, 70 F.2d 683, 13 AFTR 1062, cert. den. [¶ 31,257(10)].
(4) Roe, ¶ 65,100 P-H Memo TC [¶ 31,257(15)].
(5) Acme Mills, Inc., 6 BTA 1065; Harris, 14 BTA 1259 [¶ 31,257(20)].
(6) General Securities Co., 38 BTA 330 [¶ 31,300(50)].

Footnote ¶ 1502 continued
(7) Rogers v. Strong, 72 F.2d 455, 14 AFTR 468, cert. den. [¶ 31,300(45)].
(8) Corbett v. Burnet, 50 F.2d 492, 10 AFTR 38, cert. den. [¶ 20,469(15)].

Footnote ¶ 1503 [¶ 31,196 et seq.].
(1) Phila. Pk. Amusement Co. v. U.S., 126 F. Supp. 184, 46 AFTR 1293; Williams, 37 TC 1099; Rev. Rul. 57-535, 1957-2 CB 513; Rev. Rul. 55-27, 1955-1 CB 350 [¶ 31,197(5)].
(2) Countway v. Comm., 127 F.2d 69, 29 AFTR 80; Myers, 1 TC 100 [¶ 31,197(15)].
(3) Phila. Pk. Amusement Co. v. U.S., 126 F. Supp. 184, 46 AFTR 1293; Countway v. Comm., 127 F.2d 69, 29 AFTR 80 [¶ 31,197(10), (20)].
(4) A & A Tool & Supply Co. v. Comm., 182 F.2d 300, 39 AFTR 517 [¶ 31,201(5)].
(5) Rev. Rul 67-107, 1967-1 CB 115 [¶ 31,201(5)].
(6) Ives Ice Cream Co., 15 BTA 376 [¶ 31,201(10)].

Footnote ¶ 1504 [¶ 7081].

¶ 1528

Chapter 5—Footnotes

Footnote ¶ 1505 [¶ 31,111].
(1) U.S. v. Davis, 370 US 65, 9 AFTR 2d 1625 [¶ 31,111(5)].
(2) Rev. Rul. 67-221, 1967-2 CB 63 [¶ 7706(20)].

Footnote ¶ 1506 [¶ 31,824 et seq.].

Footnote ¶ 1507 [¶ 31,361 et seq.; ¶ 31,556 et seq.].
(1) P.L. 94-455, Sec. 2005 [¶ 31,558].

Footnote ¶ 1508 [¶ 31,389].

Footnote ¶ 1509 [¶ 31,386; 120,400].

Footnote ¶ 1510 [¶ 31,373 et seq.].
(1) Valuation Tables [¶ 31,375].

Footnote ¶ 1514 [¶ 31,492].

Footnote ¶ 1515 [¶ 31,401 et seq.].
(1) Treas. Dept. booklet "Your Federal Income Tax" (1977 Ed.), p. 103.

Footnote ¶ 1517 [¶ 31,651 et seq.].
(1) Rev. Rul. 68-36, 1968-1 CB 357 [¶ 31,675(30)].
(2) Treas. Dept. booklet "Tax Guide for Small Business" (1977 Ed.), p. 20.

Footnote ¶ 1518 [¶ 18,206; 18,251].

Footnote ¶ 1519 [¶ 31,741 et seq.].
(1) Rev. Rul. 73-18, 1973-1 CB 368 [¶ 31,743(15)].

Footnote ¶ 1521 [¶ 31,206 et seq.].
(1) C. D. Johnson Lumber Corp., 12 TC 348 [¶ 31,214(10)].
(2) Atwell, 17 TC 1374 [¶ 31,218(15)].
(3) Bancitaly Corp., 34 BTA 494 [¶ 31,216(5)].
(4) Collin v. Comm., 32 F.2d 753, 7 AFTR 8733 [¶ 31,216(25)].
(5) Treas. Dept. booklet "Your Federal Income Tax" (1977 Ed.), p. 131.

Footnote ¶ 1522 [¶ 31,231 et seq.].
(1) Skinner v. Eaton, 45 F.2d 568, 9 AFTR 663 [¶ 31,237(15)].
(2) Rev. Rul. 61-97, 1961-1 CB 394 [¶ 31,233(5)].
(3) Rev. Rul. 67-436, 1967-2 CB 266 [¶ 31,233(5)].
(4) Rev. Rul. 71-21, 1971-1 CB 221; Rev. Rul. 73-37, 1973-1 CB 374 [¶ 31,232(3)].
(5) Rev. Rul. 55-355, 1955-1 CB 418 [¶ 31,237(5)].
(6) Letter Ruling, 9-1-55 [¶ 31,237(5)].
(7) Bloch v. Comm., 148 F.2d 452, 33 AFTR 955 [¶ 31,237(5)].

Footnote ¶ 1523 [¶ 31,331 et seq.].
(1) Treas. Dept. booklet "Your Federal Income Tax" (1977 Ed.), p. 103.

Footnote ¶ 1524 [¶ 31,321 et seq.].
(1) Stratton Grocery Co., 8 BTA 317 [¶ 31,049(35)].
(2) Acme, Palmers & De Mooy Foundry Co., 3 BTA 1126 [¶ 31,049(20)].
(3) Devoy & Kuhn Coal & Coke Co., 66 F.2d 1012, 12 AFTR 1388 [¶ 31,049(35)].

Footnote ¶ 1526 [¶ 31,755].
(1) Treas. Dept. booklet "Your Federal Income Tax" (1977 Ed.), p. 109.

Footnote ¶ 1527 [¶ 31,545 et seq.].
(1) Rev. Rul. 69-74, 1969-1 CB 43 [¶ 31,040(5)].
(2) Estate of Bell, 60 TC 469 [¶ 31,040(5)].

Footnote ¶ 1528 [¶ 31,461; 31,465].
(1) Rev. Rul. 55-118, 1955-1 CB 320 [¶ 16,810(15)].
(2) Rev. Rul. 56-264, 1956-1 CB 153 [¶ 16,810(5)].
(3) Rev. Rul. 71-475, 1971-2 CB 304 [¶ 31,465(20)].
(4) Megibow v. Comm., 218 F.2d 687, 46 AFTR 1553 [¶ 16,813(5)].
(5) Rev. Rul. 69-105, 1969-1 CB 88 [¶ 16,813(15)].

Highlights of Chapter 5

Gain or Loss—Basis

I. **Basis In General**
   A. Determined by way property acquired [¶ 1500(a)].
   B. Increased by items or expenditures chargeable to capital account, such as [¶ 1500(b)]:
      1. Improvements.
      2. Purchase commissions.
      3. Legal costs for defending or perfecting title.
      4. Surveying expenses.
      5. Recording fees.
   C. Decreased for items that are return of capital, such as [¶ 1500(b)]:
      1. Depreciation.
      2. Depletion.
      3. Obsolescence.
      4. Tax-free dividends.
      5. Recognized losses on involuntary conversions.
      6. Deductible casualty losses.

II. **Cost as Basis**
   A. Cost equals amount paid plus commissions and purchase expenses [¶ 1501].
   B. Property subject to mortgage—basis is amount paid plus unpaid amount of assumed mortgage [¶ 1501].

III. **Fair Market Value Considered In Basis Determination**
   A. Fair market value as basis—price willing buyer and seller would reach after noncompulsory negotiation [¶ 1502].
   B. Property acquired in taxable exchange—basis generally fair market value at time of exchange [¶ 1503].
      1. Property received for other property—basis either [¶ 1503(a)]:
         a. Fair market value of new property at receipt, or
         b. Fair market value of exchanged property, plus or minus payments made when properties unequal in value.
      2. Property acquired in trade-in—dealers value traded-in property in inventory at bona fide selling price less direct selling costs [¶ 1503(b)].
   C. Property received as compensation for service [¶ 1504]:
      1. Original basis is fair market value.
      2. Restricted property after 6-30-69—basis is value when no longer subject to substantial risk of forfeiture.
   D. Property received in divorce or separation—basis is fair market value when transferred [¶ 1505].
   E. Property acquired before 3-1-13 [¶ 1506]:
      1. Basis for determining gain—greater of cost or fair market value [¶ 1506(a)].
      2. Basis for determining loss—cost of property [¶ 1506(b)].
      3. No gain or loss when selling price exceeds cost but less than 3-1-13 value.
   F. Property acquired from decedent [¶ 1507]
      1. Carryover basis is generally same as decedent's basis immediately before death.
      2. Carryover basis is property acquired from decedent except [¶ 1507(a)]:
         a. Income in respect of a decedent.
         b. Life insurance proceeds.
         c. Taxable joint and survivor annuities and deferred compensation plans.

d. Property includible in decedent's gross estate disposed of in taxable transaction before death.
e. Taxable stock options.
f. Foreign personal holding company stock.
3. Adjustments to carryover basis [¶ 1507(b)]:
   a. Federal and state estate taxes.
   b. Minimum carryover basis.
   c. State succession taxes.
4. Basis of carryover basis property is increased by appreciation attributable to period held before 1977 [¶ 1507(c)]:
   a. Stocks and bonds get increase in basis up to market price on 12-31-76.
   b. Other carryover basis property gets increase in basis for ratable portion of pre-1977 appreciation.
5. Generation-skipping transfers [¶ 1507(d)].

G. **Property transferred within three years of decedent's death [¶ 1508]:**
1. Includible in decedent's gross estate.
2. Basis is fair market value on date of death.
3. Does not apply to sales, or gifts within $3,000 annual exclusion.
4. Estate is increased by gift tax paid.
5. Includible regardless of transferor's intent.

H. **Joint ownership [¶ 1509]:**
1. Part included in decedent's estate—basis is market value on date of death or alternate date.
2. Part not included in decedent's estate—basis is cost or other basis.
3. Reduced by depreciation taken by survivor before other died.
4. For qualified joint tenancies created by spouses after 12-31-76, only one-half of the value of the property owned in joint tenancy is includible in the decedent's gross estate regardless of the contribution made by each joint tenant.

I. **Life estates and remainders**—generally, basis is zero [¶ 1510].

IV. **Substituted Basis**

A. **In general [¶ 1514]:**
1. Used for post-1920 gifts, nontaxable exchanges and involuntary conversion replacement property.
2. Derived from transferor's or donor's basis, or other property held by taxpayer.
3. Must be adjusted for periods held by present and prior owners.

B. **Property acquired by gift [¶ 1515]:**
1. Gift after 12-31-20—basis is [¶ 1515(a)]:
   a. For determining gain—same as donor's or last preceding owner by whom not acquired by gift.
   b. For determining loss—lower of (a) above or fair market value.
2. Gift before 1-1-21—basis is fair market value at time of gift for determining both gain and loss.
3. Basis increased by amount of gift tax paid, but is limited to gift tax attributable to net appreciation of gift (for gifts made after 12-31-76). [¶ 1515(b)].

C. **Property acquired in nontaxable exchange**—following table summarizes rules for figuring new basis [¶ 1517]:

Condition of exchange	Basis of property acquired
No boot given or received.	Same as old property (adjusted to date of exchange).
Boot given.	Same as old property (adjusted to date of exchange) plus amount of "boot."
Taxpayer has gain and boot received.	Same as old property (adjusted to date of exchange) minus cash received and plus recognized gain.

Taxpayer has loss and boot received.	Same as old property (adjusted to date of exchange) minus cash received.
Taxpayer has gain and money and other property is received.	Basis apportioned (using fair market of other property).
Property used partly for business.	Business part decreased by gain not recognized or increased by loss not recognized.
Mortgage assumed by transferee or property acquired by transferee subject to mortgage.	Mortgage considered equivalent of cash in determining basis.

    D. **Property acquired in nontaxable transfer to controlled corporation [¶ 1518]:**
        1. Stock received in exchange for property—basis is same as property exchanged, *less* money and value of other property received, *plus* any gain recognized on exchange [¶ 1518(a)].
        2. Property transferred to corporation—basis is transferor's basis *plus* any gain recognized to transferor [¶ 1518(b)].
    E. **Property acquired upon involuntary conversion:**
        1. When no gain recognized because:
            a. Direct conversion into similar property—basis of new asset same as old (adjusted to time of conversion) [¶ 1519(a)].
            b. Replacement cost exceeds amount received—basis of new is cost less gain not recognized [¶ 1519(d)].
        2. When loss recognized—basis of new is replacement cost [¶ 1519(b)].
        3. When gain recognized—basis of new is cost less gain not recognized [¶ 1519(c)].

V. Identification of Basis
    A. **Allocation of basis**—usually when part of property subject to gain, loss or depreciation [¶ 1521]:
        1. Lump sum purchase of various properties.
        2. Corporate securities purchased as unit [¶ 1521(a)]:
            a. Block of same securities—pro rata allocation.
            b. No reasonable allocation possible—treated as unit.
        3. Property partly condemned [¶ 1521(b)].
    B. **First-in, first-out rule**—stock sold from unidentified lots bought at different times or prices charged against earliest purchase [¶ 1522].

VI. Special Rules
    A. **Basis of patents and copyrights**—basis is cost, if bought [¶ 1523].
    B. **Sale of good will [¶ 1524]:**
        1. Included in basis if:
            a. Purchased, or
            b. Owned by the seller on 3-1-13.
        2. Good will developed since 3-1-13 not includible in basis.
        3. Factors determining whether good will sold:
            a. What part of business sold.
            b. Whether buyer has right to use seller's name.
            c. Whether contract required seller to cease doing business.
    C. **Replacement for old residence [¶ 1526]:**
        1. Basis of new residence—purchase price less nontaxable gain on sale of old residence.
        2. Adjusted basis of old residence—cost, plus commissions, purchase expenses and subsequent improvements, minus depreciation, deductible casualty losses and nontaxable gain on sale of previous residence.
        3. Taxpayers 65 and over—new residence basis not reduced by nontaxable gain on sale of old residence.
        4. Residence acquired by gift or inheritance—value of donated or inherited part:
            a. Not treated as cost to determine gain on sale of old residence, but
            b. Included in basis of gift or inherited residence to figure gain on later sale.
    D. **Basis of annuity contract [¶ 1527]:**

1. If sold—cost basis reduced by tax-free investment return (but not below zero).
2. If transferred for appreciated property—investment in contract is transferor's basis in transferred property.

E. **Additions to basis for circulation expenses, taxes and carrying charges**—election to capitalize or deduct [¶ 1528]:
   1. Election made by filing statement with return [¶ 1528(a)]:
      a. Taxes, mortgage interest, etc.—non-binding election each year.
      b. Improvements, machinery installation and circulation expenses—election to capitalize binding on future years.
   2. Charges on improvements [¶ 1528(b)]—can capitalize only till development or construction completed, or machinery installed or used.

SUMMARY OF BASIS RULES

Types: Cost; Fair Market Value; Substituted Basis

Type of Acquisition	Basis for Gain or Loss
Annuity contract	Generally cost less tax-free recoveries but not below zero [¶ 1527]
Bargain purchases by employees	Cost [¶ 1310]
Cash purchase	Cost [¶ 1501]
Mortgage also assumed or property taken subject to mortgage	Full price, included mortgage [¶ 1501]
Gift property	*Gain:* Donor's basis plus portion of gift tax attributable to net appreciation [¶ 1515] *Loss:* Limited to lesser of donor's basis or FMV at time of gift [¶ 1515]
Joint tenancy	Estate tax value for portion included in estate [¶ 1509]
Life estate	Zero [¶ 1510]
Property acquired from decedent	Estate tax value with adjustments for appreciation in value if acquired after 12-31-76. [¶ 1507; 3920]
Property acquired under stock options	FMV when issued [¶ 1327]
Residence after sale of old residence without recognition of gain	Cost less gain not recognized on old residence [¶ 1526]
Taxpayer 65 or over	Basis not reduced for excluded gain [¶ 1526]
Tenancy by the entirety	For qualified joint interests created after 12-31-76, only ½ of value of the interest is included in gross estate regardless of who furnished consideration [¶ 1509]

Chapter 6

CAPITAL GAINS AND LOSSES OF INDIVIDUALS*
TABLE OF CONTENTS

¶		¶

Capital gains and losses in general 1600
   What produces capital gain or loss
   Holding period
   Figuring capital gains and losses
   Capital gain as tax preference item
What is a capital asset 1601
Necessity for a sale or exchange 1602

HOLDING PERIOD

Effect of holding period 1605
Determining the holding period 1606
   Gift after 12-31-20
   Property acquired by bequest, devise or inheritance
   Tax-free exchanges
   Partnership interest
   New residence replacing old residence
First-in, first-out rule 1607
Short sales 1608
   Special rules for short sales
   "When issued" transaction
   Commodity futures and hedging transactions
"Put" and "call" options 1609
   When option is sold
   When option is exercised
   When options lapse

FIGURING CAPITAL GAIN OR LOSS

How to report gain or loss 1611
   Short-term and long-term transactions
   Determine net short-term capital gain or loss
   Determine net long-term capital gain or loss
   Determine net gain or loss from capital asset transactions
   Net gain or loss on return
Long-term capital gain deduction 1612
   How treated on return
   Capital gain as tax preference item
Capital loss deduction 1613
   Amount of loss deductible
   Husband and wife
   Capital loss carryover

Alternative tax for net long-term capital gain 1614

DISPOSING OF BUSINESS PROPERTY

Sale or exchange of property receiving capital gain treatment 1618
   What property is involved
   How to figure the computation
Recapture of depreciation 1619
   Gain from disposing of certain depreciable property
   Gain from disposing of certain depreciable real property
   Exceptions
   Like kind exchanges
   Involuntary conversions
   Sale or exchange by order of FCC or SEC
   Player contracts
Involuntary conversion 1620
Timber 1621
Farmers' Sec. 1231 transactions 1622
Coal and domestic iron ore 1623
How to figure net gain or loss on Sec. 1231 assets 1624
Sale of depreciable property between related parties 1625

SPECIAL RULES

Collapsible corporations 1627
   What is a collapsible corporation
   When gains will be ordinary income
   Exceptions to rule
Dealers in securities 1628
Original issue discount bonds 1629
Sale of tax-exempt securities 1630
Subdividing realty for sale 1631
Loss on small business stock 1632
   Qualification requirements
   What is a small business corporation

● Highlights of Chapter 6 .... Page 1661

---

* For special rules on domestic corporations see ¶ 3201. See Chapter 27 for rules for nonresident aliens and foreign corporations.

Footnotes appear at end of this Chapter.

Chapter 6—Capital Gains and Losses of Individuals

¶ 1600 **Capital gains and losses in general.** An individual's taxable gain or deductible loss often depends on the nature of the asset sold or exchanged to produce the gain or loss and the length of time it was held. Ordinary business gains and losses are usually includible in, or deductible from, income in full. *Capital gains* and *capital losses* are subject to special rules and limitations. The gain limitations benefit the taxpayer since they limit his tax liability. But the loss rules limit his deduction [Sec. 1201 et seq.].

> NOTE: Generally, the capital gain rules for individuals apply to corporations as well, except: (1) no long-term capital gain deduction is allowed; (2) capital losses may be deducted only from capital gains; (3) a capital loss may be carried over as a short-term capital loss for 5 years and offset against net capital gains in those years and carried back for 3 years; and (4) the maximum alternative tax is 30%.

Background and purpose. The special treatment for capital gains was originally enacted to limit the taxing of property in a single year that may have appreciated in value over a longer period. It gave relief to those taxpayers with fluctuating or bunched income. It also provided an incentive to businesses and private investors.

(a) **What produces capital gain or loss.** A capital gain or loss results from a *sale or exchange* [¶ 1602] of a *capital asset* [¶ 1601].

(b) **Holding period.** When the property sold or exchanged is a capital asset, or treated like one, the next step is to determine how long it was held [¶ 1605-1609]. For tax years starting in 1977, if the property was held for *more than 9 months*, a sale or exchange results in a long-term capital gain or loss.

> NOTE: For tax years starting after 12-31-77, the asset must be held for more than 1 year to have a long-term capital gain or loss [Sec. 1222]. The 6-month holding period applied to tax years starting before 1977.

(c) **Figuring capital gains and losses.** These steps are taken:

- Long-term capital losses offset long-term capital gains to find net long-term capital gains or losses.
- Short-term capital losses offset short-term capital gains to find net short-term capital gains or losses.
- The net long-term figure and the net short-term figure are offset to find the net gain or net loss from the sale or exchange of capital assets.
- *Net gain* is included in taxable income.
- *Net loss* offsets ordinary income but is limited to the lesser of: (a) taxable income reduced (but not below zero) by the zero bracket amount [¶ 1107] for tax years starting after 1976, figured without regard to either capital gains and losses or personal exemptions; (b) $2,000 for tax years starting in 1977; or (c) the actual net capital loss [¶ 1613]. Four other provisions may require additional figuring:

> NOTE: For tax years starting after 1977 the capital loss deduction limit will be increased to $3,000. For tax years starting before 1977, the deduction limit was $1,000.

(1) **Long-term capital gain deduction** is 50% of the excess of the net long-term capital gain over the net short-term capital loss [¶ 1612].

(2) **Alternative tax** limits the tax on long-term capital gain to 25% of the first $50,000 of this gain ($25,000 for spouses filing separately) [¶ 1614]. A special computation is required for long-term capital gain above that amount. The alternative tax does not apply if income averaging is elected [¶ 2401].

(3) Capital loss carryovers allow the nondeductible part of a capital loss to offset income of later years, except for the disallowed half of a long-term capital loss [¶ 1613].

(4) Some business property can get special treatment if held for a required length of time and disposed of in a tax year [¶ 1618 et seq.].

(d) Capital gain as tax preference item. An amount equal to one-half of net long-term capital gains over net short-term capital losses is a tax preference item subject to the minimum tax [¶ 1612; 2403].

¶ 1601 What is a capital asset. The principal capital assets are investment property (stocks and bonds held by investor) and property held for personal use (jewelry, residence or automobile). Gain or loss from the sale or exchange of the investment property is a capital gain or loss. Gain from a transaction on the property held for personal use is a capital gain but losses are never deductible unless an involuntary conversion is involved [¶ 1620]. A capital asset is any property (whether or not connected with a trade or business), *except:*

• Stock in trade or other inventory property.
• Property held *primarily* for sale to customers in the ordinary course of the taxpayer's trade or business. "Primarily" means "of first importance" or "principally."[1]
• Depreciable property used in a trade or business [but see ¶ 1618 et seq.].
• Real property used in a trade or business [but see ¶ 1618; 1619(b); 1631].
• Copyrights; literary, musical or artistic compositions; a letter or memorandum; or similar property; held by (1) a taxpayer whose personal efforts created the property; or (2) a taxpayer for whom a letter, memorandum or similar property was prepared or produced; or (3) one receiving the property as a gift from the person who created it.
• Accounts or notes receivable acquired in the ordinary course of trade or business (a) for services rendered, or (b) from the sale of stock in trade, inventory or property held for sale to customers.
• Certain short-term government obligations issued on a discount basis such as the U. S. treasury bills [¶ 2723(c)].
• Certain U.S. Government publications received without charge or at a reduced price [Sec. 1221; 1.1221-1].

Background and purpose. The exceptions were included since the original intent for the preferred treatment of capital assets was to provide incentives to investment and to reduce the tax impact on long-term appreciation. Thus, for example, inventories and stock in trade were excluded since these assets were involved in a rapid sales turnover.

(a) Stocks, bonds, notes, debentures, and similar securities are capital assets, unless they fall under one of the above exceptions. Special rules apply to collapsible corporation stock [¶ 1627] and dealers in securities [¶ 1628]. Small business stock and stock in a small business investment company are not considered capital assets if sold at a loss under certain conditions [see ¶ 1632; 3459]. Securities bought to get inventory or guarantee performance of a contract are not capital assets if the purpose for which they are acquired is accomplished and the securities are disposed of within a relatively short time after acquisition.[2] Gain on transfers of stock in controlled foreign corporations may be ordinary income [¶ 3728].

Footnotes appear at end of this Chapter.

¶ 1601

(b) **Real property** not used in a trade or business is a capital asset, for example, taxpayer's private residence. If property is used in trade or business it is not a capital asset. There is a conflict as to whether a taxpayer who rents a single piece of real property is engaged in a trade or business. The Tax Court says he is.[3] But the Second Circuit Court of Appeals and the Court of Claims disagree.[4] See also ¶ 1618; 1631.

(c) **Property held for the production of income,** but not used in the trade or business of the taxpayer, is included in the term "capital assets" [Sec. 1.1221-1]. This rule is not in conflict with the decisions on income-producing rental property mentioned in (b) above, since the property there was "used in the trade or business of the taxpayer."[3]

(d) **An unincorporated business.** The sale of a sole proprietorship is not a sale of a single asset. It is the sale of the individual business assets, such as inventory, fixtures and other items.[5] Some of the assets may be capital assets and others may not. For example, inventory is not a capital asset. But records maintained for the business, as well as intangible assets such as good will, are capital assets (not including records that are in fact inventory or stock in trade).[6] A professional can make a partial transfer of good will when admitting partners to his practice.[7]

(e) **Partnership interest.** The portion of an individual partner's partnership interest that is attributable to certain partnership noncapital assets (primarily acccounts receivable and appreciated inventory) is an ordinary asset, while the remainder of his interest is a single capital asset.[8] Transfer of a partnership interest is discussed in ¶ 2935; 2945.

(f) **Copyrights, literary, musical or artistic compositions, letters or memorandums, and similar property** are not capital assets. "Similar property" includes a radio program created by taxpayer's personal efforts, a theatrical production, a newspaper cartoon strip, or other property eligible for copyright protection. It does not include a patent, invention, or a design protected only under the patent law and not under the copyright law [Sec. 1.1221-1]. Letters and memorandums include manuscripts and any other writings or recordings of a business or personal nature. A letter or memorandum addressed to a person is considered as prepared or produced for him [Sec. 1.1221-1(c)(2)].

(g) **Lease.** Amounts received by a *tenant* for cancelling a lease are considered as received in exchange for the lease [Sec. 1241; 1.1241-1]. This also applies to giving up a restriction on the landlord.[9] The type of gain or loss depends on the lease's character. A nondepreciable leasehold is a capital asset. A depreciable lease used in a trade or business and held for the required period is a Sec. 1231 asset [Sec. 1221, 1231; 1.1221-1]. Part of a gain from the sale or exchange of the depreciable leasehold may be ordinary income to the extent the recapture rules apply [¶ 1618 et. seq.]. An amount received by the *landlord* for cancelling[10] or amending[11] a lease is ordinary income.

(h) **Options.** Gain or loss from sale or exchange of options to buy or sell property (or loss on failure to exercise the option) is treated the same as gain or loss from the sale or exchange of the property underlying the option would be treated. If the loss results from failure to exercise the option, the option is considered to have been sold or exchanged on the day it expired [Sec. 1234; 1.1234-1]. The rule does not apply to the following:

- An option that is part of taxpayer's inventory or stock in trade.
- Gain from the sale of an option if income derived from the option would be treated as ordinary income without regard to the rule. For example, if

gain on sale of an employee stock option is in the nature of compensation, the gain is not treated as a capital gain merely because the stock, if acquired, would be a capital asset in the employee's hands.
• Loss from failure to exercise a "put" bought on the same day as the stock used to fulfill the contract [¶ 1609].

For options granted on or before 9-1-76 the rule *also* does not apply to gain from the sale or exchange of options acquired before 3-1-54 if the option is a capital asset in the taxpayer's hands [Sec. 1234; 1.1234-1].

(i) Distributor's agreement. Amounts received by a distributor of goods for cancelling a distributor's agreement (if the distributor has made a substantial capital investment) are considered received in exchange for the agreement (usually, capital gain treatment applies) [Sec. 1241; 1.1241-1].

(j) Patents. A patent held for investment is a capital asset. Long-term capital gain treatment is granted to amateur or professional inventors or certain other holders who transfer *all substantial rights* in the patent under certain conditions and regardless of the length of time the patent right was held. There is no such transfer when the patent is sold limited as to use or all rights of value to the patent are not released. But there can be a transfer of substantial rights even though there is a restriction as to geographical use.[12] Payments for the inventor's interest can be made periodically during transferee's use of the patent or be contingent on production, profits, sales, etc. However, the transfer must not be made to certain related persons, including a trust in which the inventor is a grantor or beneficiary and a controlled corporation, but not including a brother or sister. An individual backer of an inventor who got his interest by putting up money before the invention was completed also may be entitled to long-term capital gains. Patent transfers not qualifying for long-term capital gains treatment under Sec. 1235 may still qualify under other Code provisions.[13] Long-term capital gains treatment also applies to a sale of rights under patent applications, even if no patent has been obtained[14] [Sec. 1235; 1.1235-1, 1.1235-2(b)].

(k) Other items. The following have been held capital assets: life estate;[15] bank account;[16] cotton acreage allotment.[17] The following have been held *not* to be capital assets: right to receive a dividend sold by stockholder;[18] employment contract sold by employee;[19] trade acceptance received as incident to sale of merchandise;[20] an exclusive or perpetual right to exploit and use one's name;[21] covenant not to compete;[22] a franchise, trademark or trade name, if the transferor retains any signficant power, right or continuing interest [Sec. 1253; Prop. Reg. 1.1253-1–1.1253-3].

¶ **1602 Necessity for a sale or exchange.** There is no capital gain or loss unless the asset disposed of was *sold or exchanged*. Some transactions that are not actually sales or exchanges will be treated as such, since their effect is similar. These include:

• Retirement of bonds. Bonds issued before 1-1-55 must have had interest coupons or been in registered form on 3-1-54 to qualify. For tax-exempt securities and other bonds issued at a discount, see ¶ 1629; 1630 [Sec. 1232(a)(1); 1.1232-2].
• Involuntary conversion [¶ 1620].
• Cutting of timber [¶ 1621].
• Liquidating dividends [¶ 1717].
• Securities becoming worthless during the tax year [¶ 2208; 2312].
• Nonbusiness debts becoming worthless in the tax year [¶ 2307].

Footnotes appear at end of this Chapter.

- Pension, profit-sharing and stock bonus distributions [¶ 3024].

HOLDING PERIOD

Whether gains or losses from the sale or exchange of capital assets are short-term or long-term capital gains or losses depends on the period the capital asset was held. Those held *not* more than 9 months are short-term. Those held more than 9 months are long-term.

¶ **1605 Effect of holding period.** Although 100% of long-term and short-term capital gains and losses are taken into account, it is important to distinguish between them, because net long-term capital gains are given special treatment when (1) they exceed net short-term capital losses or (2) there are no net short-term capital losses. In these cases, there is a deduction from gross income of 50% of the excess of net long-term capital gain over net short-term capital loss [¶ 1612], and there may be a lower alternative tax [¶ 1614].

¶ **1606 Determining the holding period.** It is essential to determine the exact length of time property was held. An error of one day can change the type of capital gain or loss the taxpayer has. His records should show the exact date property was acquired and disposed of.

In figuring the period held, the date the property was acquired is *excluded;* the day it was disposed of is *included*.[1] The reverse is true when figuring a prescribed period *before* a designated event (as in timber and coal transactions, ¶ 1621; 1623).[2] The holding period is figured by calendar months and fractions of months, not by days.[3] In other words, the day after the property was acquired is the start of the holding period and this same date in each succeeding calendar month is the start of a new month regardless of the number of days in the preceding month.[4] Thus, for tax years starting in 1977, property acquired on the last day of the month must be held on or after the first day of the tenth succeeding month to be held for more than 9 months.

> NOTE: For tax years starting after 1977, you must hold the asset for more than 1 year to qualify for the long-term treatment. For tax years starting before 1977, you must have held it for more than 6 months to qualify for this treatment. But see commodity futures below.

Commodity futures. The 6-month holding period applies to all futures transactions in any commodity subject to the rules of a board of trade or commodity exchange[5] [Sec. 1222(11)]. This is the only exception to the general increases in the holding period made by the 1976 Tax Reform Act (see NOTE, above). If a taxpayer accepts delivery of a commodity in satisfaction of a commodity futures contract, the holding period of the commodity includes the period for which the taxpayer held the futures contract [Sec. 1223(8); 1.1223-1(h)]. For short sale rules, see ¶ 1608(c).

FIGURING HOLDING PERIOD

Securities bought and sold through stock exchange transactions use trade dates, rather than settlement dates as the dates of acquisition or disposition.[6] For other purchases and sales, see ¶ 2725(a), (b) on what is a closed transaction.

For over-the-counter purchases, the date acquired is the date broker notifies customer purchase was made, not the date title passed.[7]

Real Property. The holding period begins on the day after title passes, or on the day after delivery of possession is made and the buyer assumes ownership privileges, whichever occurs first. A delivery of possession under a mere option agreement is without significance until a contract of sale comes into being through exercise of the option.[8]

Newly erected building. Parts of a new building may be considered as having been completed before the entire building. Their holding period starts at their completion.[9]

Patents. The special rule under Sec. 1235 [¶ 1601(j)] for long-term capital gain treatment on transfer of a patent applies regardless of the period held. When capital gain is sought under general capital gains rules, a patent's holding period runs from the earlier of the date the invention is reduced to actual practice or the patent is issued.[10]

Community property. The holding period of a surviving spouse's share generally runs from the date the property was acquired by the spouses. However, the share inherited from a deceased spouse gets the long-term capital gain or loss treatment [Sec. 1223(11)].

Optioned property. The period during which a taxpayer holds an option cannot be added to the period he owns property acquired under the option.[11]

The holding period of stock dividends and stock rights is given in ¶ 1707 et seq. and 1710 et seq.; wash sales in ¶ 2221. For holding period of worthless securities, see ¶ 2208; 2312. See below for other special cases.

(a) Gift after 12-31-20. The holding period begins with the date the property was acquired by the donor. However, if the property had a value at the date of the gift lower than cost, and the sale results in a loss, the holding period begins on the date of the gift [Sec. 1223(2); 1.1223-1(b)].

For property acquired at death, see (b) below.

(b) Property acquired by bequest, devise or inheritance. Generally, the holding period runs from the date of the decedent's death.

Property acquired from a decedent and disposed of within 9 months after decedent's death will be considered as being held for over 9 months. This rule applies to decedents dying after 1970 [Sec. 1223(11)].

> **NOTE:** The holding period was 6 months for tax years starting after 1977. It is 1 year for tax years starting after 1977.

For property acquired from a decedent *dying after 12-31-76*, the basis is generally determined by the carryover basis rules [¶ 1507]. Thus, if the recipient later disposes of the property, the holding period on that property for determining the gain or loss, includes the decedent's holding period [Sec. 1223(2)].

(c) Tax-free exchanges. The holding period of property received in a nontaxable exchange after 3-1-54 includes the holding period of the property given in exchange, if the property exchanged was a capital asset or depreciable property used in taxpayer's trade or business [Sec. 1223(1); 1.1223-1(a)].

> **Example:** On 6-1-77, Frank, a calendar year taxpayer, exchanged shares of Class A stock, bought 2-10-77 for $1,200, for shares of Class B stock in a tax-free exchange. The holding period of the Class B shares began on 2-11-77. If the Class B shares were sold on 12-1-77 for $1,000, Frank held them over 9 months. His loss of $200 is a long-term loss.

(d) Partnership interest. The holding period runs from the date the interest is acquired. A partner's death does not interrupt the holding period of the other partners' interest, as long as the business continues.[12]

(e) New residence replacing old residence. The holding period of a new residence that replaces one transferred without gain being recognized [¶ 1416], includes the old residence's holding period [Sec. 1223(7); 1.1223-1(g)].

¶ 1607   First in, first-out rule. Stock sold must be charged against the earliest purchase when shares of stock are sold from lots bought at different dates or prices, and the identity of the lots cannot be determined [¶ 1552]. This is important in determining the period held as well as fixing gain or loss.

¶ 1608 **Short sales.** Selling what you do not own, but expect to buy and deliver, is called selling short. Short sales involve two kinds of property: (1) stocks and securities, and (2) commodity futures.

A short sale of stock occurs when a speculator who believes that the price of a certain stock will fall, sells the stock short anticipating that he will be able to buy it for less than he got for it on the short sale. A short seller must deliver the certificates to the buyer like any other seller. Since he does not have them, a broker borrows the stock for him. The seller *closes* the short sale when he returns the borrowed stock. If the stock sold short declines in price, the short seller makes a profit; if the price goes up, he has a loss. Gains or losses from short sales of property are considered gains or losses from sales or exchanges of capital assets to the extent the property used to close the short sale is a capital asset [Sec. 1233(a); 1.1233-1(a)]. For a short sale that is also a wash sale, see ¶ 2221. For "put" and "call" options, see ¶ 1609.

(a) Special rules for short sales. The following rules apply to short sales of stock, securities, or commodity futures [Sec. 1233; 1.1233-1(c)].

Rule 1. Short-term capital gain. Gain on closing a short sale is short-term capital gain if [Sec. 1233(b)(1); 1.1233-1(c)]:

- Taxpayer on the date of the short sale has held substantially identical property for not more than 9 months (6 months for tax years before 1977; 1 year for tax years starting after 1977); or
- After the short sale, but on or before the closing date, he acquired property substantially identical to that sold short.

Example 1: On 4-3-76, Dalton ordered his broker to sell short 100 shares of West stock at 63. At that time Dalton owned no West Co. stock and had no other dealings in that stock until 6-4-77, when he ordered a covering purchase made at 55. Dalton's gain is a short-term capital gain of $800 ($6,300 − $5,500).

Example 2: On 2-11-77, Roland, a calendar year taxpayer, buys 100 shares of Rose Co. stock at $10 per share. On 5-17-77, he sells short 100 shares at $16 per share. On 12-1-77, he closes the short sale by delivering the 100 shares bought on 2-11-77 to the lender of the stock used to effect the short sale. Since 100 shares of Rose Co. stock had been held by Roland on the date of the short sale for not more than 9 months, the gain of $600 on the transaction is a short-term capital gain.

This rule does not apply to property sold short that exceeds the substantially identical property [Sec. 1233(e)(1)].

Rule 2. Holding period of substantially identical property. If the substantially identical property has not been held over 9 months (6 months for tax years starting before 1977; 1 year for tax years starting after 1977) before the date of the short sale, or if it was acquired between the date of the sale and the date of the closing, the holding period begins on the earlier of:

(1) The date of the closing of the short sale; or
(2) The date of a sale, gift or other disposition of the property.

If several quantities of property substantially identical to that sold short are acquired at different times, this rule applies to such property in the order of the dates of its acquisition [Sec. 1233(b)(2); 1.1233-1(c)].

Example 3: On 1-11-77, Wein, a calendar year taxpayer, buys 100 shares of Cooper Co. stock at $10 a share. On 6-26-77, he sells short 100 shares at $16 a share. On 10-20-77, he buys 100 shares at $18 a share with which to close the short sale. On 10-21-77, he sells at $18 a share the 100 shares bought 1-11-77.

The $200 loss on closing the short sale is short-term capital loss. The holding period of the stock bought on 1-11-77 is considered to begin 10-20-77 (short sale closing date). The $800 gain on the sale of the stock is short-term capital gain.

This rule does not apply to substantially identical property that exceeds in quantity the property sold short [Sec. 1233(b)(2)].

Example 4: On 1-11-77, Joe, a calendar year taxpayer, sells short 100 shares of Gemstone stock at $16 a share. On 6-26-77, he buys 250 shares of the same stock at $10 a share. He holds the latter stock until 10-20-77, when he delivers 100 shares to close the short sale made 1-11-77.

Since substantially identical property was acquired after the short sale and before it was closed, the $600 is short-term capital gain (Rule 1). The holding period of the remaining 150 shares is not affected since to that extent the substantially identical property exceeds the quantity of the property sold short.

Exception. An exception applies to substantially identical property held for investment, if the short sale is part of an arbitrage operation. An arbitrage operation involves the purchase and sale of substantially identical assets, including securities, to profit from a current difference between the price of the asset purchased and the price of that sold. If a short sale is entered into as part of an arbitrage operation, the rule applies first to the substantially identical assets acquired for arbitrage operations held on the day the short sale is made. The rule applies to other substantially identical assets only to the extent that the quantity sold short exceeds the substantially identical assets held for arbitrage operations. However, the rule becomes applicable if assets acquired for arbitrage are disposed of in such a way as to create a net short position in assets acquired for arbitrage. To the extent of the net short position the open short sale in the arbitrage operations is a short sale made on the date that the net short position is created [Sec. 1233(f); 1.1233-1(f)].

A special provision prevents security dealers from avoiding the rule by closing the sale with securities held in inventory (non-capital assets). Normally the rule only applies if the short sale is closed with a capital asset. But the rule applies to short sales of stock by security dealers, regardless of how they close the sale, if (a) the substantially identical property is a capital asset in the dealer's hands and on the date of the short sale has been held for not more than 9 months (6 months for tax years starting before 1977; 1 year for tax years starting after 1977), and (b) the short sale is closed more than 20 days after it was made. Stock includes bonds convertible into stock and rights to stock or convertible bonds [Sec. 1233(e)(4); 1.1233-1(e)].

Rule 3. Long-term losses. If property substantially identical to that sold short has been held over 9 months (6 months for tax years starting before 1977; 1 year for tax years starting after 1977) on the date of the short sale, loss on closing the short sale is a long-term capital loss [Sec. 1233(d); 1.1233-1(c)].

Example 5: On 1-11-77, Lee, a calendar year taxpayer, buys 100 shares of Silver Co. stock at $10 a share. On 11-1-77, he sells short 100 shares at $16 a share. On 12-1-77, he sells the 100 shares of stock (bought 1-11-77) at $18 a share. On 12-1-77, he also buys 100 shares at $18 a share and closes the short sale by delivering these shares.

The $800 gain on sale of the stock Lee bought on 1-11-77, is, of course, long-term capital gain. Since Lee had held 100 shares of Silver Co. stock for more than 9 months on the date of the short sale, the $200 loss on closing the short sale is long-term capital loss.

This rule does not apply to property sold short that exceeds the substantially identical property [Sec. 1233(e)(1); 1.1233-1(c)].

¶ 1608

What is substantially identical property depends on the circumstances. Generally, preferred stocks or bonds are not identical with common stock of the same corporation. Securities of one corporation are not substantially identical with securities of another (except in special situations as, for example, the securities of corporations in a reorganization).

When preferred stock or bonds are convertible into common stock of the same corporation, the relative values and price changes may be so similar as to make them substantially identical to the common stock [Sec. 1.1233-1(d)].

The term "taxpayer" means the "taxpayer or his spouse." Consequently, if taxpayer's spouse (not legally separated or divorced) holds stock substantially identical to that sold short by the taxpayer, the three rules apply as if the taxpayer himself owned the property [Sec. 1233(e)(2)(C); 1.1233-1(d)(3)].

Short sale of small business investment company stock. If taxpayer acquired the stock merely to close a short sale, he does not get the ordinary loss deduction allowed for this stock.[1] See ¶ 3459.

(b) "When issued" transaction. Securities to be issued as a stock dividend, or in a reorganization or recapitalization may be bought and sold on a "when issued" basis. A contract to sell stock or other securities on a "when issued" basis is a short sale, and the performance or assignment for value of the contract is a closing of the short sale [Sec. 1233(e)(2)(A); 1.1233-1(c)(1)].

(c) Commodity futures and hedging transactions. The short sale rules in (a) above apply to transactions in commodity futures that are capital assets [Sec. 1233(b)]. A commodity future is a standard form contract to deliver a fixed quantity of a commodity (wheat, cotton, hides etc.) in a future month for a fixed price. Their purchase and sale results in capital gain or loss, unless the transaction is a hedge [Sec. 1233(a), (g); 1.1233-1(b)]. A hedge is a form of price insurance to avoid the risk of change in the market price of commodities used in a business.[2] The purchase and sale of futures acquired as hedges result in ordinary gain or loss.[3] However, the Revenue Service does not apply this to a short sale of currency to hedge against devaluation.[4]

In applying the short sale rules to capital transactions, futures that cover different commodities (corn and wheat), or that call for different delivery months (May wheat and July wheat) are not substantially identical. Futures obtained in different markets may be treated as substantially identical in particular cases. When a taxpayer engages in two futures transactions, one to deliver and the other to receive a substantially identical commodity in two different markets, only the excess quantity in either market is considered a short sale if both transactions are made the same day and closed the same day [Sec. 1233(e); 1.1233-1(d)(2)].

¶ 1609 **"Put" and "call" options.** A "put" is an option that gives an investor (holder of the option) the right to sell stock to the maker of the option at a stated price within a limited time. A "call" is an option that gives the holder the right to buy stock from the maker of the option at a stated price within a limited time. The option's maker is paid a premium for his obligation to buy or sell the stock.

A "straddle" is a simultaneous granting of a combination of an option to buy and an option to sell the same quantity of a security at the same price during the same period. The maker of the straddle allocates the premium to each option on the basis of their respective fair market values at the time of the issuance of the straddle.

Background and purpose. Investors buy puts when they expect the value of the stock to fall. They then can sell the stock at the higher option price. If the market price goes up they can sell the stock at the higher market price rather than ex-

4. Tax on taxable income (line 3)		$21,319.50
5. Add: 50% of line 2 (25% of the $20,000 excess of net long-term capital gain over net short-term capital loss		5,000.00
Alternative tax		$26,319.50

Alternative computation is used, since it gives the lower tax.

Excess net long-term capital gain more than $50,000. If the net capital gain exceeds $50,000 ($25,000 if married filing separately), the alternative tax is the total of three tax computations [Sec. 1201(b)(3), (c)(1); 1.1201-1(e)(1)]:

- Determine the regular tax on your ordinary income.
- Add $12,500 (25% of first $50,000 of net long-term capital gains).
- Add the difference between: (1) the tax on taxable income (with half the net long-term capital gain included); and (2) the tax on the sum of taxable income (*excluding* capital gain and loss) plus $25,000 of net long-term capital gain.

Example 2: Assume the same facts as in Example 1, except that Burton has a net capital gain of $80,000 (instead of $20,000). His tax under the regular and alternative methods should be figured as follows:

Tax Using Regular Computation

Salary			$ 60,000.00
Taxable interest			6,000.00
Capital gain or loss:			
Net capital gain		$80,000	
Less: Long-term capital gain deduction (50% of $80,000)		40,000	
Net capital gain (included in income)			40,000.00
Adjusted gross income			$106,000.00
Less: Excess itemized deductions ($6,350 — $3,200)		$3,150	
Deduction for exemptions		1,500	4,650.00
Taxable income			$101,350.00
Tax			$ 44,070.00

Tax Using Alternative Method

1. Regular tax on ordinary income [$61,350 ($101,350 — $40,000]			$21,319.50
2. Tax on first $50,000 of net capital gain (25% × $50,000)			12,500.00
3. Tax on net capital gain greater than $50,000:			
Tax on taxable income ($101,350)		$44,070	
Less: Tax on $86,350 ($61,350 + ½ of $50,000 excess net long-term gain)		35,167	8,903.00
Alternative tax			$42,722.50

The tax figured by the alternative method is used since it is less than the tax computed under the regular method.

DISPOSING OF BUSINESS PROPERTY

Certain assets qualify for an annual deduction related to their becoming worn out, exhausted or obsolete (depreciation). The idea is to spread their cost over the period of expected usefulness. These assets, called depreciable property, are specifically excluded from the capital asset category. Thus, their disposal would not normally result in capital gain or capital loss. However, a special rule, called "Sec. 1231 treatment," allows the taxpayer to treat certain gains as capital gains and certain losses as ordinary losses when disposing of this kind of property. But before any gain gets this treatment, some of it may be "recaptured" as ordinary income. This occurs since all or part of the gain might have resulted from the depreciation previously taken. In addition to the recapture computation, certain involuntary conversions are netted separately to determine if the Sec. 1231 treatment applies.

ercise their option. Conversely, investors buy calls when they expect the value of the stock to rise. They can buy the stock at the lesser option price. If the market goes down they can buy the stock at the market price rather than use the option. It is not unusual for one person to write, or to acquire, at the same time, a "straddle."

>>**OBSERVATION**→ Puts and calls can be used for four different purposes: (1) to speculate on price changes—up or down; (2) to establish paper gains; (3) to delay the tax impact of a security transaction to a later time; and (4) to prevent or limit capital loss. The use of a put is generally preferred to the use of a call. Using a call requires the sale of stock and entails a current tax. However, if you use a put, you may not have to sell the stock.

(a) When option is sold. Generally, capital gain or loss results from the sale or exchange of the option unless taxpayer is a dealer (¶ 1601(h)) [Sec. 1.1234-1]. A dealer is one who trades in puts and calls written by others, but not someone who writes puts and calls for a premium.[1] The maker or writer of the put or call is not affected by the sale or exchange.

(b) When option is exercised. The maker of a call option includes the premium received for the option with the option price to find the amount he realized on the exercise. The holder of the call adds the premium he paid to the property's cost in determining his basis for the stock.[1] When the holder sells a 30-day call option and reacquires it before the exercise period expires, the excess cost to reacquire over the option's selling price is added to the stock's basis.[2]

When a put option is exercised, the maker subtracts the premium he received for the option from the price paid for the stock to find his basis for the acquired stock.[1] The holder subtracts the premium he paid from the stock's price to determine the amount he realized on the sale.[3]

Gain or loss on the option's exercise is determined when the sale is closed. It is a capital gain or loss if the stock is a capital asset. The holding period runs from the time the option is exercised.

Short sales. Since a put is an option to sell, the holder generally is making a short sale when he acquires the put and has a short-term capital gain under Rules 1 and 2 of ¶ 1608 when he exercises the option. Rule 3 of ¶ 1608 does not apply. The acquisition of a put is not a short sale if the holder owns substantially identical stock for more than 9 months (6 months for tax years starting before 1977; 1 year for tax years starting after 1977) before he buys the put. Accordingly, the holder can cover the put with this stock for a long-term capital gain or loss or cover it by other stock held less than 9 months (6 months for tax years starting before 1977; 1 year for tax years starting after 1977) for a short-term gain or loss. Also, the short sale rules do not apply when the put and the stock to be used to cover it are bought on the same day. A call is not substantially identical to the stock subject to the call [Sec. 1233(c); 1.1233-1(c)].[4]

(c) When options lapse. For stock or commodity options granted after 9-1-76, the option grantor realizes short-term capital gain or loss on a "closing transaction" or lapse of the option without exercise. A "closing transaction" means any end to the grantor's obligation other than by exercise or lapse of the option. This rule does not apply to dealers [Sec. 1234(b)]. Prior to this rule grantors of options have realized ordinary income when they received a premium for the option. They would report as ordinary gain or loss the difference between the amount paid in the closing transaction and the premium received.

Footnotes appear at end of this Chapter.

Chapter 6—Capital Gains and Losses of Individuals

Puts. The holder of a put has a loss for the amount he paid for the option, unless the put was bought on the same day as the stock to be used to cover it. A capital loss is a long-term loss if the put was held more than 9 months (6 months for tax years starting before 1977; 1 year for tax years starting after 1977). There is no loss when the put and the stock to cover it are bought at the same time. Instead, the amount paid for the put is added to the cost of the stock [Sec. 1233(c)].

FIGURING CAPITAL GAIN OR LOSS

The mechanics of computing gains and losses, including the long-term capital gain deduction, the capital loss limitation and the alternative tax on long-term capital gains, are handled on Schedule D of Form 1040.

¶ **1611 How to report gain or loss.** These steps are taken to figure the capital gain or loss to be entered on Schedule D of the individual's return:

(a) **Short-term and long-term transactions.** Separate short-term capital assets transactions from long-term capital assets transactions.

(b) **Determine net short-term capital gain or loss.** This is the difference between the gain and the loss on all short-term transactions [Sec. 1222(1)(2)(5)(6); 1.1222-1].

Example 1: On 7-6-77, Frank, a calendar year taxpayer, sold for $4,800 stock bought on 3-5-77 for $3,600. The short-term capital gain was $1,200, since the shares had been held not more than 9 months.
On 8-5-77, Frank sold for $2,800 bonds bought 3-2-77 for $3,000. The short-term capital loss was $200, since the bonds were held not over 9 months. His *net* short-term capital gain for 1977 was $1,000 ($1,200 — $200).

Example 2: On 3-3-77, Yvonne, a calendar year taxpayer, sold for $7,500 stock bought on 10-3-76 for $7,200. The short-term capital gain was $300, since the stock had not been held for more than 9 months. On 5-20-77, she sold for $6,000 stock bought on 12-12-76 for $8,000. The short-term capital loss was $2,000, since the stock had not been held more than 9 months. Yvonne's *net* short-term capital loss for 1977 was $1,700 ($2,000 — $300).

(c) **Determine net long-term capital gain or loss.** This is the difference between the gain (in excess of any ordinary gain resulting from recapture [¶ 1619]) and the loss on all long-term transactions [Sec. 1222(3)(4)(7)(8); 1.1222-1]. For dividends treated as long-term capital gains, see ¶ 3431(a).

Example 3: On 2-17-77, Frank in Example 1 sold for $15,700 stock bought on 2-2-74 for $16,400. The loss is a long-term capital loss of $700, since the stock had been held for more than 9 months. On 7-20-77, Frank sold for $10,000 stock bought on 11-8-74 for $9,900. The gain is a long-term capital gain of $100, since the stock had been held for more than 9 months. His *net* long-term capital loss for 1977 was $600 ($700 — $100).

Example 4: On 8-10-77, Yvonne in Example 2 sold for $11,000 bonds bought on 3-4-75 for $10,500. The gain is a long-term capital gain of $500, since the bonds had been held for more than 9 months. On 12-7-77, Yvonne sold for $5,000 stock bought on 5-2-74 for $5,300. The loss is a long-term capital loss of $300, since the stock had been held for more than 9 months. Her *net* long-term capital gain for 1977 was $200 ($500 — $300).

(d) **Determining net gain or loss from capital asset transactions.** This is the total of the net figures arrived at in steps (b) and (c) above.

Chapter 6—Capital Gains and Losses of Individuals

Example 5: In 1977, Frank had a net short-term capital gain of $1,000 and a net long-term capital loss of $600 (Examples 1 and 3 above). Frank's *net gain* in that year from the sale or exchange of capital assets was $400 ($1,000 − $600).

Example 6: In 1977, Yvonne had a net short-term capital loss of $1,700 and a net long-term capital gain of $200 (Examples 2 and 4 above). Her *net loss* from the sale or exchange of capital assets was $1,500 ($1,700 − $200).

(e) Net gain or loss on return. Net gain from capital asset transactions is added to other income in figuring adjusted gross income. If the net long-term capital gain is more than the net short-term capital loss, the net gain is reduced by 50% of the excess before it is added to other income on the return [see ¶ 1612]. But if there is a net loss from capital asset transactions, generally all or part of it is deductible from ordinary income [¶ 1613]. However, losses from transactions of personal-use property are deductible only if an involuntary conversion is involved [¶ 1620].

¶ 1612 Long-term capital gain deduction. If net long-term capital gains exceed net short-term capital losses, one-half the excess may be deducted.

Example 1: Net long-term capital gain; no net short-term capital gain or loss.

1. Net long-term capital gain or loss .... $2,000 G
2. Net short-term capital gain or loss .... NONE
3. Excess of net long-term capital gain over net short-term capital loss $2,000
4. Deduction (50% of line 3) $1,000

Example 2: Net long-term capital gain; net short-term capital loss.

1. Net long-term capital gain or loss .... $2,000 G
2. Net short-term capital gain or loss .... $1,500 L
3. Excess of net long-term capital gain over net short-term capital loss .... $ 500
4. Deduction (50% of line 3) .... $ 250

Example 3: Net long-term capital gain; net short-term capital gain.

1. Net long-term capital gain or loss .... $2,000 G
2. Net short-term capital gain or los .... $1,500 G
3. Excess of net long-term capital gain over net short-term capital loss $2,000
4. Deduction (50% of line 3) $1,000

Example 4: Net long-term capital *loss;* net short-term capital gain.

1. Net long-term capital gain or loss .... $ 500 L
2. Net short-term capital gain or loss .... $1,500 G
3. Excess of net long-term capital gain over net short-term capital loss .... NONE
4. Deduction (50% of line 3) .... NONE

Note: There is no deduction for a *short*-term gain.

(a) How treated on return. The long-term capital gain deduction is a deduction from gross income to arrive at adjusted gross income [Sec. 62(3)]. On the return the deduction is taken in figuring the net gain from sales or exchanges of capital assets, instead of being deducted directly from gross income. The net gain from sale of capital assets included in income is the net gain after being reduced by the long-term capital gain deduction.

Example 5: Net long-term capital gain; no net short-term capital gain or loss.
White had the following income: Salary, $10,000; net long-term capital gain, $2,000; net short-term capital loss, none. His adjusted gross income is $11,000, figured as follows:

Salary $10,000
Capital gain or loss:

Footnotes appear at end of this Chapter.

¶ 1612

1614 Chapter 6—Capital Gains and Losses of Individuals 1978

Net long-term capital gain or loss	$2,000 G	
Net short-term capital gain or loss	0	
Net gain or loss from sale of capital assets (before long-term capital gain deduction)	$2,000 G	
Less: Long-term capital gain deduction (Ex. 1)	1,000	
Net gain from sale of capital assets (included in income)		1,000
Adjusted gross income		$11,000

Example 6: Net long-term capital gain; net short-term capital *loss*.

Black had the following income: Salary, $10,000; net long-term capital gain, $2,000; net short-term capital loss, $1,500. His adjusted gross income is $10,250, figured as follows:

Salary		$10,000
Capital gain or loss:		
Net long-term capital gain or loss	$2,000 G	
Net short-term capital gain or loss	1,500 L	
Net gain or loss from sale of capital assets (before long-term capital gain deduction)	$ 500 G	
Less: Long-term capital gain deduction (Ex. 2)	250	
Net gain from sale of capital assets (included in income)		250
Adjusted gross income		$10,250

Example 7: Net long-term capital gain; net short-term capital gain.

Brown had the following income: Salary, $10,000; net long-term capital gain, $2,000; net short-term capital gain, $1,500; His adjusted gross income is $12,500, figured as follows:

Salary		$10,000
Capital gain or loss:		
Net long-term capital gain or loss	$2,000 G	
Net short-term capital gain or loss	1,500 G	
Net gain or loss from sale of capital assets (before long-term capital gain deduction)	$3,500 G	
Less: Long-term capital gain deduction (Ex. 3)	1,000	
Net gain from sale of capital assets (included in income)		2,500
Adjusted gross income		$12,500

Example 8: Net long-term capital *loss*; net short-term capital gain.

Green had the following income: Salary, $10,000; net long-term capital loss, $500; net short-term capital gain, $1,500; His adjusted gross income is $11,000, figured as follows:

Salary		$10,000
Capital gain or loss:		
Net long-term capital gain or loss	$ 500 L	
Net short-term capital gain or loss	$1,500 G	
Net gain or loss from sale of capital assets (before long-term capital gain deduction)	$1,000 G	
Less: Long-term capital gain deduction (Ex. 4)	0	
Net gain from sale of capital assets (included in income)		1,000
Adjusted gross income		$11,000

(b) Capital gain as tax preference item. An amount equal to one-half of the net long-term capital gain over the net short-term capital loss is a tax preference item for the minimum tax [¶ 2403]. This is true even if the long-term capital gain deduction is not taken, as when the alternative tax is used [Sec. 57(a)(9)].

¶ **1613 Capital loss deduction.** Generally, a net loss from capital asset transactions is partially or fully deductible from other income in computing adjusted gross income [Sec. 1211(b)]. However, losses from transactions of personal-use property are never deductible unless an involuntary conversion is involved [¶ 1620].

(a) Amount of loss deductible. A net short-term loss from capital asset transactions is deductible up to the lesser of taxable income (reduced, but not below zero, by the zero bracket amount; ¶ 1107) from noncapital asset sources (without personal exemption deductions) or $2,000 ($1,000 for tax years starting before 1977; $3,000 for tax years starting after 1977); the balance is not deductible in the year the loss is sustained, but may be carried over to later tax years. A net long-term loss from capital asset transactions is deducted in the same way, but only one-half the net long-term capital loss can be taken into account in computing the deduction. Thus, $4,000 of net long-term capital loss is needed to produce a $2,000 deduction.

The $2,000 limit also applies to the deduction for net long-term capital losses. The two-for-one ratio of net long-term capital loss to allowable deduction only applies to the net amount deducted from adjusted gross income from noncapital asset sources; long-term losses are taken into account fully as an offset against long-term capital gains. If taxpayer has both net long-term and net short-term capital losses, the net short-term loss is deducted first from adjusted gross income. As with net short-term capital losses, a carryover is also available for net long-term capital losses except for disallowed half. See (c) below.

Background and purpose. The present 2-for-1 rule on the capital loss deduction was enacted because the prior treatment was inconsistent with the way long-term capital gains were treated. Although half of net long-term capital gain is ordinary income, net capital losses were once fully deductible up to the limit.

Example 1: When both net short-term loss and taxable income reduced (but not below zero) by the zero bracket amount (without capital asset transactions) exceed $2,000, $2,000 of the loss is deductible in the tax year sustained. The balance is carried over to later years. (NOTE: In this and following examples, it is assumed that taxpayer does not itemize.)

Adjusted gross income (without capital asset transactions)		$10,000
Net short-term loss	$3,000	
Limited deduction for tax year loss sustained		2,000
Adjusted gross income		$ 8,000

The part of the net short-term loss not deductible ($1,000) is carried over to later tax years.

Example 2: If the net long-term loss is $4,000 or less and is not greater than adjusted gross income (without capital asset transactions), half is deductible in the tax year sustained. The disallowed half cannot be carried over.

Adjusted gross income (without capital asset transactions)		$10,000
Net long-term loss	$4,000	
Amount deductible ($4,000 × 50%)		$ 2,000
Adjusted gross income		$ 8,000

Example 3: Assume capital asset transactions produce a net short-term loss of $600 and a net long-term loss of $500. The short-term loss is fully deductible from ordinary income within the limit but only half of the long-term loss can be used.

Adjusted gross income (without capital asset transactions)		$10,000
Net short-term loss	$600	
Net long-term loss ($500 × 50%)	250	850
Adjusted gross income		$ 9,150

(b) Husband and wife. A husband or wife filing separately is only allowed to offset the excess of capital losses against $1,000 ($500 for tax years starting before 1977; $1,500 for tax years starting after 1977) of ordinary income. Neither spouse may use the other's loss in this case [Sec. 1211(b)(2)]. On a joint return,

Footnotes appear at end of this Chapter.

they combine their capital gains and losses [Sec. 1.1201-1(d), 1.1211-1(d), 1.1212-1(c)].

NOTE: Instead of the $500 limit, carryovers from years starting before 1-1-70 are subject to a special transitional rule [Sec. 1.1211-1(b)(1)].

(c) Capital loss carryover. If your capital losses in the current year exceed the limits in (a), above, you may carry over the excess until completely exhausted [Sec. 1212(b)]. In determining the amount of the carryover, short-term losses are applied first even if incurred after a long-term loss. Then, if the capital loss limitation has not been reached, long-term losses are applied up to the limit. Form 4798 can be used to compute the carryover.

Example 4: In 1977, White's capital loss limitation is $2,000. He has short-term losses of $1,300 and long-term losses of $1,800. His carryover to 1978 and later years is $400, computed as follows:

1.	Maximum capital loss deduction	$2,000
2.	Less: Short-term capital loss	1,300
3.	Remaining capital loss deduction allowable	$ 700
4.	Long-term capital loss	$1,800
5.	Amount of long-term loss needed to reach $2,000 limitation in Line 1 (50% of $1,400 = $700)	$1,400
6.	Long-term capital loss carryover to 1978 (and later years)	$ 400

Long-term capital loss carryovers from previous years offset long-term capital gains of the current year before offsetting short-term gains for the current year, and short-term loss carryovers offset short-term gains before offsetting long-term gains. Long-term capital losses are carried over in full. The capital loss carryovers are applied dollar for dollar against gains. However, long-term loss carryovers from post-1969 years are deducted from ordinary income at the 50% rate up to the limit. Long-term capital losses from years beginning before 1970 need not be reduced by 50% before being deducted.[1]

Example 5: In 1976, Mr Kemp's only capital asset transaction is a long-term capital loss of $3,600. He deducted $1,000. Only $1,600 is available for carryover [$3,600 − $2,000 ($1,000 × 2)]. In 1977, Kemp's only capital transaction is a $600 gain. $600 of the $1,600 carryover is offset against the gain in full. The 50% rule is applied to the remaining $1,000 resulting in a $500 deduction against his ordinary income. There is no carryover to a future year.

Example 6: Mr. Beasley had a long-term capital loss carryover from 1969 of $10,000. He had ordinary income of $12,000 in each year from 1970 to 1976. On each return for these years he deducted a $1,000 long-term capital loss. $3,000 remains as a carryover to future years.

When carrying over capital losses from more than one year, deduct the earliest loss first. This rule applies even though the loss is carried over from years before 1970.

NOTE: Since the 50% limitation does not apply to carryovers from years starting before 1970, transitional rules apply to pre-1970 loss carryovers. Regulations set forth the following order of applying capital losses to the transitional additional allowance: (1) Apply any excess of net short-term capital loss over net long-term capital gain; (2) apply any excess of net long-term capital loss over net short-term capital gain to the extent of the transitional net long-term capital loss component for the tax year, (3) apply one-half of any balance of the excess net long-term capital loss not applied under (2) above [Sec. 1.1211-1].

Capital loss carryovers from separate returns must be combined if a joint return is filed for the current year. However, a capital loss carryover from any joint return can be deducted only on the separte return of the person who actually sustained the loss.[2]

¶ 1614 Alternative tax for net long-term capital gain. If an individual's net long-term capital gain exceeds his net short-term capital loss, the tax may be figured in two ways (regular and alternative computations) and the one that produces the *smaller* tax is used.

Background and purpose. The present rule on the alternative tax was enacted because the prior treatment differed with the intent of the progressive rate structure to tax individuals on their ability to pay. High-bracket taxpayers were revising their investment strategies to convert as much as possible of their income into capital gain. The effect of the alternative method is to tax the first $50,000 of net long-term capital gain at 25% and the balance of the gain at a higher rate.

(a) Regular way. The tax is figured in the usual way on the taxable income, which includes net gain from the sale or exchange of capital assets.

(b) Alternative way. The alternative tax computation depends on whether the excess of net long-term capital gain over any net short-term capital loss is above or below $50,000 ($25,000 if married filing separately). This excess is known as net capital gain [Sec. 1222(11); 1.1222-1(h)]. Regardless of the amount of net capital gain, the taxpayer first computes the tax on his taxable income less 50% of the net capital gain at the regular tax rate [Sec. 1201(b)(1); 1.1201-1(b)(2)]. In effect, taxable income used in this computation does not include any net capital gain since the other 50% has already been eliminated by the long-term capital gain deduction in arriving at taxable income [¶ 1612].

Excess net long-term capital gain of $50,000 or less. If the net capital gain is $50,000 or less ($25,000 if married filing separately), the total tax under the alternative method is figured by adding 25% of the gain to the tax on taxable income (computed exclusive of capital gains and losses) [Sec. 1201(b)(2); 1.1201-1(b)(2)].

Example 1: During 1977, Burton's salary was $60,000, his taxable interest was $6,000, and the excess of net long-term capital gain over net short-term capital loss was $20,000 (net capital gain). Burton was married and had no children. His wife had no income or deductions. His itemized deductions were $6,350. His tax on a joint return should be figured by the regular and alternative computations as shown below.

Tax Using Regular Computation

Salary		$60,000.00
Taxable interest		6,000.00
Capital gain or loss:		
Net capital gain	$20,000	
Less: Long-term capital gain deduction (50% of $20,000)	10,000	
Net capital gain (included in income)		10,000.00
Adjusted gross income		$76,000.00
Less: Excess itemized deductions ($6,350 — $3,200)	$3,150	
Deduction for exemptions	1,500	4,650.00
Taxable income		$71,350.00
Tax		$26,702.50

Tax Using Alternative Computation

1.	Taxable income	$71,350.00
2.	Less: 50% of net capital gain	10,000.00
3.	Taxable income exclusive of capital gains and losses	$61,350.00

¶ 1614

¶ **1618 Sale or exchange of property receiving capital gain treatment.** If certain property is disposed of by sale, exchange or involuntary conversion, the net result of the gains and losses determines how the transaction will be treated.

Background and purpose. As originally enacted during a depression period, the Revenue Act of 1938 excluded depreciable property used in taxpayer's trade or business as a capital asset to remove the limitation on the amount of loss that could be deducted when such property was disposed of at a loss. Before this, taxpayers tended to retain in use, or abandon, their old obsolete properties rather than sell them, since a loss on the sale was a capital loss and not fully deductible as ordinary losses. However, this made any gains from these properties ordinary. So an additional change permitted capital gain treatment under certain circumstances.

(a) **What property is involved.** The special tax treatment applies to the following property known as "Sec. 1231 assets:"

• Depreciable personal property used in a trade or business and held for more than 9 months.
• Real property used in a trade or business and held for more than 9 months.
• Property held for the production of income (including rented real property) and held for more than 9 months.
• Leaseholds used in a trade or business and held for more than 9 months [¶ 1601(g)].
• Timber under certain conditions [¶ 1621].
• Certain unharvested crops [¶ 1622(b)].
• Coal or domestic iron ore under certain conditions [¶ 1623].
• Cattle and horses acquired for draft, breeding, dairy or sporting purposes and held for 24 months or more [¶ 1622(a)].
• Livestock (except cattle, horses and poultry) acquired for draft, breeding, dairy or sporting purposes and held 12 months or more [¶ 1622(a)].
• Capital assets held for more than 9 months that have been involuntarily converted [¶ 1620].
• Business property held for more than 9 months that has been involuntarily converted [¶ 1620].

Inventory; property held for sale to customers; certain copyrights; artistic, musical, or literary compositions; letters or memorandums or similar property are not "Sec. 1231 assets."

NOTE: The 9-month holding period rule increases to 1 year for tax years starting in 1978 and later. It was 6 months for tax years starting before 1977.

(b) **How to figure the computation.** Since the net result of the sales or exchanges of "Sec. 1231 assets" determines the tax treatment of *each* individual sale, a special computation must be made. But before this can be completed, the following steps must be taken into account:

• First, the portion of the gain that is "recaptured" as ordinary income is handled separately [¶ 1619].
• Casualty or theft gains and losses must be netted to determine if they are to be included in the Sec. 1231 computation for further netting [¶ 1620].
• Sec. 1231 assets are segregated and netted:

1. If net gains exceed net losses, *all* the gains and losses are treated as long-term capital gains and losses:

Footnotes appear at end of this Chapter.

¶ 1618

2. If net losses exceed net gains, *all* the gains and losses are treated as ordinary.

Form 4797 (Supplemental Schedule of Gains and Losses) is used to report gains and losses on Sec. 1231 transactions, including gain that is recaptured and casualty or theft gains and losses.

NOTE: Form 4684 can be used instead of Form 4797 if taxpayer has only personal casualty or theft losses. [¶ 2206].

¶ **1619 Recapture of depreciation.** Depreciation once offset income taxed at ordinary income rates. Now, however, gain from disposing of depreciable assets is ordinary income to the extent the recapture rules apply.

NOTE: The cost or other basis of depreciable property is written off over the property's life. It can be done evenly as in the straight line method [¶ 2011], or in an accelerated way as in the declining balance or sum of the years-digits methods [¶ 2012 et seq.]. In all these methods, a useful life or rate is applied to the property's cost or other basis which remains constant under the straight line or sum of the years-digits methods but is always reducing under the declining balance methods. A comparison of the methods can be seen in the following table. Assume the property cost $4,000, has a 10-year useful life and no salvage value:

	Straight line method		Declining balance method			Sum of the years-digits		
Year	Annual deduction 10%	Cumulative amount recovered	Balance (unrecovered cost)	Annual deduction (20% of balance)	Cumulative amount recovered	Rate (fraction of cost)	Annual deduction	Cumulative amount recovered
1st...	$400	$ 400	$4,000.00	$800.00	$ 800.00	10/55	$727.27	$ 727.27
2nd..	400	800	3,200.00	640.00	1,440.00	9/55	654.55	1,381.82
3rd...	400	1,200	2,560.00	512.00	1,952.00	8/55	581.82	1,963.64
4th..	400	1,600	2,048.00	409.60	2,361.60	7/55	509.09	2,472.73
5th..	400	2,000	1,638.40	327.68	2,689.28	6/55	436.36	2,909.09

NOTE: The excess of accelerated over straight line depreciation on real property or leased personal property, is a tax preference subject to the minimum tax [¶ 2403].

(a) Gain from disposing of certain depreciable property. If depreciable personal or similar property ("Section 1245 property") is disposed of, any gain is treated as ordinary income to the extent of depreciation taken, generally, after 1961. If a sale or exchange is not involved, gain is the excess of the property's fair market value over its adjusted basis at the time of disposition [Sec. 1245(a); 1.1245-1].

"Section 1245 property" includes [Sec. 1245(a)(3); 1.1245-3]:

• Personal property (both tangible and intangible).
• Elevators and escalators.
• Other tangible property (except a building or its structural components) such as research, or storage or structure facilities used as integral parts of specified business activities.
• Amortized pollution control facilities; certain railroad equipment; and on-job training and child care facilities [¶ 2040; 2041; 2043].

Special recapture rules apply to player contracts [(g) below].

Recomputed basis is the key factor. This is adjusted basis plus depreciation taken after 1961 (after 6-30-63 for elevators or escalators and after 1969 for livestock). The depreciation added back must include any taken by another person if the taxpayer has a carryover basis (such as gift property). Any gain up to the recomputed basis is Section 1245 ordinary income. Gain above recomputed basis is included in Sec. 1231 computations [¶ 1624]. Ordinary income is limited to actual gain on a sale or exchange for less than the full recomputed basis. If the taxpayer can prove depreciation taken was lower than the maximum allowable, the lower figure is used. Permanent records must be kept to determine the recomputed basis [Sec. 1245(a)(2); 1.1245-2].

Example 1: Ramsey sold a business machine for $3,000 on 1-2-77 that he had bought on 12-31-75. The machine had an adjusted basis of $2,500 and the depreciation deduction for 1976 was $300. Thus the recomputed basis is $2,800. Ramsey's Section 1245 income is $300 figured as follows:

Amount realized	$3,000
Adjusted basis	2,500
Gain	$ 500
Recomputed basis ($2,500 + $300)	$2,800
Adjusted basis	$2,500
Section 1245 ordinary income	$ 300
Section 1231 capital gain	$ 200

Depreciation or amortization includes farmers' land clearing depreciation expenses [¶ 1845(d)], certain costs of acquiring a leasehold and lessee's improvement costs [¶ 2002], the additional first-year depreciation, the depreciation of improvements under the depletion allowance and amortization of pollution control facilities, certain railroad equipment, and expenditures for on-the-job training and child care facilities (¶ 2040; 2041; 2043) [Sec. 1245(a)(2)(D); 1.1245-2(a)(3)(i)].

(b) Gain from disposing of certain depreciable real property. The treatment of gain from a sale or exchange of depreciable real property ("Section 1250 property") depends on how the property is used, when it was acquired, and whether an accelerated method of depreciation was taken. Generally, the taxpayer has ordinary income to the extent of a percentage of (1) gain or (2) excess depreciation (the amount that exceeds what would have been taken by straight line depreciation), whichever is less; any gain not recaptured as ordinary income gets Sec. 1231 treatment.

"Section 1250 property" is depreciable real property, which includes all real property that is subject to depreciation allowance and is not depreciable personal property at any time [(a), above]. It also includes intangible real property such as a leasehold of land [Sec. 1.1250-1(e)(3)].

If Sec. 1250 property is acquired in certain tax-free transactions (other than like-kind exchanges or involuntary conversions), information, including depreciation deductions by prior owners, should be filed with the return for the year the property is acquired [Sec. 1.1250-2(f)].

General rule. The taxpayer has ordinary income to the extent of all depreciation taken since 1963 if he disposes of property held for one year or less. If the property has been held over a year, the amount of the ordinary income is the applicable percentage of (1) the recognized gain, or (2) the excess depreciation, whichever is less [Sec. 1250(a); 1.1250-1]. To determine what part of the gain is to be treated as ordinary income, the following steps must be taken:

STEP 1. Figure the amount of the gain.

NOTE: If the disposition is not a sale, exchange or involuntary conversion, the gain is the fair market value less adjusted basis.

Footnotes appear at end of this Chapter.

¶ 1619

STEP 2. Determine excess depreciation for periods after 1975.
STEP 3. Multiply the gain or excess depreciation, whichever is less, by the applicable percentage.

NOTE: The applicable percentage on new or used real property is 100% for periods after 1975, except for certain low income residential rental property [See (c) below].

STEP 4. Determine excess depreciation for periods after 1969 and before 1976.
STEP 5. Multiply the unabsorbed gain (amount remaining above the post '75 depreciation) or excess depreciation for periods after 1969 and before 1976, whichever is less, by the applicable percentage [see below].

Commercial or industrial property. The applicable percentage on new or used property is 100%. This applies even though the property was acquired before 1970. There is no applicable percentage for used property acquired after 1969 since the depreciation deduction for this property must be computed under the straight line method [¶ 2017].

Residential rental property. The applicable percentage for this property (at least 80% of gross rents from dwelling units) is 100% until the property is held 100 full months; then it declines 1% for each full month of ownership.

STEP 6. If there is any unabsorbed gain, determine excess depreciation for periods after 1963 and before 1970.
STEP 7. Multiply the unabsorbed gain (amount remaining above depreciation for periods after 1969 and before 1976) or excess depreciation, whichever is less, by the applicable percentage (100% until the property is held for 20 full months; then the percentage declines 1% for each full month).
STEP 8. Add STEPS 3, 5 and 7 to arrive at the gain to be treated as ordinary income.

Excess depreciation is the difference between the amount actually deducted after 12-31-63 by an accelerated depreciation method [¶ 2012 et seq.] and the amount that would have been deducted under the straight line method [¶ 2011], using the same salvage value [¶ 2005] and useful life (¶ 2031). Proper salvage value must be used in the as-if straight line computation even if it is not used in the accelerated method. If taxpayer can prove depreciation taken was lower than the maximum allowable, the lower figure is used [Sec. 1250(b); 1.1250-2]. The special 5-year writeoff of rehabilitation expenses [¶ 2018] is recaptured under the general rule if the property is sold within a year after the improvement is placed in service; otherwise, excess depreciation is the amount that exceeds what the straight line depreciation would have been if the improvement's actual useful life had been used [Sec. 1250(b)(4)].

Special rules on applicable percentage. Depreciable real property acquired under a contract binding on and after 7-24-69 and qualified low-income housing acquired before 1976 [¶ 1426] use the more liberal percentage in effect before 1970: 100% until the property is held 20 full months, declining at 1% a month thereafter. The applicable percentage for the recapture of depreciation taken under the special 5-year writeoff of rehabilitation expenditures [¶ 2018] is the same as for new residential rental property acquired after 1969 [Sec. 1250(a)(1), (b)(4); 1.1250-2(a)(2)]. A special rule applies to foreclosures. Once proceedings start, reduction of the recapture potential will cease [Sec. 1250(d)(10)].

The holding period used to find the "applicable percentage" begins the day after Sec. 1250 property is acquired. For property built or rebuilt by the taxpayer, it starts the first day of the month the property is placed in service. If Sec. 1250 property has a transferred basis (gifts, tax-free transactions, transfers at death, etc.) the holding period includes that of the transferor [Sec. 1250(e); 1.1250-4].

When qualified low-income housing is disposed of [¶ 1426], the Sec. 1250 property acquired includes the holding period of the same disposed element [Sec. 1250(e)(4)].

Leased property. If the taxpayer erects a building or makes improvements on property he has leased, he includes all renewal periods in his lease term to figure depreciation recapture [Sec. 1250(b)(2); 1.1250-2(c)].

Property sold with separate elements. If real property disposed of has more than one separate element, the amount of ordinary gain is the total of the ordinary income figured for each element. A separate element can be: (1) a separate improvement; (2) units placed in service before the depreciable real property was completed; (3) depreciable real property plus improvements not considered as a separate improvement [Sec. 1250(f); 1.1250-5].

To figure ordinary income for each element: (1) determine the ratio that excess depreciation taken after 1975 for the element bears to the total excess depreciation taken after 1975 for all the elements; (2) next, multiply this ratio by the lesser of the entire property's excess depreciation taken after 1975, or the gain from disposing of the entire property; and (3) then multiply this result by the applicable percentage for the element. If there is any unabsorbed gain, the following additional steps must be taken: (4) determine the ratio that the excess depreciation taken after 1969 for the element bears to the total excess depreciation taken after 1969 for all the elements; (5) next, multiply this ratio by the lesser of the excess depreciation taken after 1969 and before 1976 for the entire property or the unabsorbed gain from disposing of the entire property; and (6) multiply this result by the applicable percentage for the element. If there is still any unabsorbed gain, take the following additional steps: (7) determine the ratio that the excess depreciation taken before 1970 for the element bears to the total excess depreciation taken before 1970 for all the elements; (8) next, multiply this ratio by the lesser of the excess depreciation taken before 1970 for the entire property or the unabsorbed gain from disposing of the entire property; and (9) multiply this result by the applicable percentage for the element [Sec. 1250(f)(2); 1.1250-5(b)].

A *separate improvement* is each improvement added to the property's capital account if the cost during a 3-year period ending on the last day of any one tax year exceeds the greater of: (a) $5,000; (b) 25% of adjusted basis; or (c) 10% of unadjusted basis. The basis for (b) and (c) is determined as of the first day of the 36-month period, or the first day of the property's holding period, whichever is later. In applying the 3-year period test, improvements in any of the 3 years are omitted entirely if for such year their total does not amount to the greater of: (a) $2,000, or (b) 1% of the property's unadjusted basis figured as of the start of the year or the property's holding period, whichever is later [Sec. 1250(f)(4); 1.1250-5].

(c) Exceptions. The recapture rule applies to most dispositions of depreciable personal or real property used in trade or business, even if they would otherwise be without immediate tax consequences. Exceptions to this include [Sec. 1245(b), 1250(d); 1.1245-4, 1.1245-6(b), 1.1250-1(a)(4), 1.1250-3]:

Gifts. The taxpayer can give depreciable property without realizing income. His Sec. 1245 or 1250 potential is passed on to the person receiving the property. Thus when the donee sells the property he must take into account the donor's depreciation deductions that are subject to the recapture rules.

Charitable contributions. If the taxpayer gives depreciable business property to a charity, he realizes no income. However, his charitable contribution is reduced by Sec. 1245 or 1250 income that would have resulted had he sold the property for fair market value (¶ 1942) [Sec. 170(e); 1.170A-4(b)(4)].

Transfers at death. Both the decedent and his successor are completely free from the recapture rules once the property is transferred at death, except that the successor is subject to the rules for those amounts that would have been taxed to the decedent if he had remained alive and received them. Generally, this applies only to installment obligations (¶ 3008(b)) [Sec. 691, 1245(b)(2), 1250(d)(2); 1.1245-4(b), 1.1250-3(b)]. For basis of inherited property, see ¶ 1507.

Personal residence. The depreciation recapture rules apply to gain on the part used in trade or business, except to the extent a taxpayer 65 or over can exclude the gain from income (¶ 1423) [Sec. 1250(d)(7)(B); 1.1250-3(g)(1)(ii)].

Certain qualified low-income housing projects. Special rules apply to any ordinary income recaptured from the partial or total nonrecognition of gain from the sale of a housing project [¶ 1426]. In general, the recapture amount cannot exceed the greater of recognized gain or that part of the proceeds not reinvested in Sec. 1250 property [Sec. 1250(d)(8); 1.1250-3(h)]. For tax years ending after 1975, there is full recapture on certain low-income residential rental housing, if the owner sells the property during the first 100 months. After that, there will be 1% reduction in recapture for each month the property is held, so that there will be no recapture at all after 200 months [Sec. 1250(a)].

Contributions and distributions. Special rules apply to depreciation deductions taken before a new partner's admission to a partnership [¶ 2925]; partnership distributions [¶ 2945]; and to corporate distributions [¶ 3204].

(d) Like kind exchanges. A like kind exchange [¶ 1403] does not result in ordinary income when Sec. 1245 or 1250 property is disposed of unless "boot" is received. The *Sec. 1245 gain* is limited to the lesser of: (1) gain to the extent of depreciation taken since 1961, or (2) the gain recognized in a like kind exchange, plus the fair market value of the qualified property received that is not Sec. 1245 property. *Sec. 1250 gain* cannot exceed the greater of two limitations: (1) the total amount of the "boot," or (2) the amount of Sec. 1250 gain that would be recognized if the exchange was fully taxable, less the fair market value of the Sec. 1250 property received [Sec. 1245(b)(4), 1250(d)(4); 1.1245-4(d), 1.1250-3(d)].

The basis of property received in exchange. The rules are similar to those for involuntary conversions. See (e) below.

Sale or exchange of Sec. 1250 property received in exchange. The unrecognized Sec. 1250 gain of property disposed of in a like kind exchange is carried over to the Sec. 1250 property received in the trade-in. This carryover is added to the "excess" depreciation taken after the exchange when the property is later disposed of. The holding period begins when the Sec. 1250 like kind property is acquired. To find the recognized gain on the resale, the carryover gain and the "excess" depreciation are multiplied by the applicable percentage [Sec. 1250(d)(4)(E); 1.1250-3(d)].

(e) Involuntary conversions. Gain that is generally not recognized in an involuntary conversion [¶ 1411] may be affected by the depreciation recapture rules when Sec. 1245 or 1250 property is disposed of. However, the amount taxed as ordinary income is limited to the unreinvested conversion proceeds [Sec. 1245(b)(4), 1250; 1.1245-4(d), 1.1250-3(d)].

Sec. 1245 gain cannot exceed the gain recognized in an involuntary conversion, plus the fair market value of qualified replacement property that is not Sec. 1245 property [Sec. 1245(b)(4); 1.1245-4(d)]. Sec. 1250 gain cannot exceed the greater of two limitations: (1) the total amount of the unreinvested conversion proceeds increased by the value of controlling shares acquired in a corporation to get replacement property [¶ 1413(a)]; or (2) the amount of Sec. 1250 gain that would be recognized if the proceeds were fully taxable less the cost of Sec. 1250 property acquired [Sec. 1250(d)(4); 1.1250-3(d)].

The basis of replacement property acquired is cost reduced by the Sec. 1245 or 1250 gain not recognized on the conversion. If more than one piece of Sec. 1245 or 1250 replacement property is bought, the basis allocated to the properties is in proportion to their respective costs (see also ¶ 1519). If other replacement property also is bought, all the bases are combined to find the total cost of the replacement property. This amount is reduced by the gain not recognized under replacement rules [¶ 1414] and the Sec. 1245 or 1250 gain not taken into account. The total is then allotted in proportion to their respective costs [Sec. 1245(b)(4); 1250(d)(4)(D); 1.1245-5(a); 1.1250-3(d)(2)].

Example 2: Bailey's warehouse was condemned and he received an award of $90,000. He spent $10,500 to buy a storage shed and $31,500 for a garage. The land for the storage shed cost $12,000, and for the garage, $36,000. The unrecognized gain on the condemnation was $60,000 of which $10,000 is Sec. 1250 gain. The tentative total basis of the shed and the garage is $32,000 ($42,000 property cost less $10,000 nonrecognized Sec. 1250 gain). The tentative basis of the shed is $8,000 ($32,000 × $10,500/$42,000), and the tentative garage basis is $24,000 ($32,000 × $31,500/$42,000). The basis of all the properties replaced is $30,000 figured as follows:

Cost (tentative basis) of shed		$ 8,000
Cost (tentative basis) of garage		24,000
Cost of land for shed		12,000
Cost of land for garage		36,000
Cost of properties bought		$80,000
Less: gain not recognized under replacement rules	$60,000	
Minus Sec. 1250 unrecognized gain	10,000	
		$50,000
Total basis of properties bought		$30,000

The total basis of $30,000 is allocated to each property:

Shed: $30,000 × ($8,000/$80,000)	$ 3,000
Garage: $30,000 × ($24,000/$80,000)	9,000
Land for shed: $30,000 × ($12,000/$80,000)	4,500
Land for garage: $30,000 × ($36,000/$80,000)	13,500
Total	$30,000

Sale or exchange of Sec. 1250 replacement property. These rules are similar to the sale or exchange of property received in a like kind exchange. See (d) above.

(f) Sale or exchange by order of F.C.C. or S.E.C. When property is disposed of by order of the Federal Communications Commission [¶ 1410(d)] or Securities and Exchange Commission [¶ 3330(a)], the recapture rules that apply are similar to those of other tax-free dispositions. See above.

(g) Player contracts. Special recapture rules apply to player contracts transferred in a franchise sale after 12-31-75. They apply only to the sale of the entire sports franchise or substantial portion of the assets. The sale of an individual player contract is governed by the general recapture rules [(a) above]. Under the special rules, the amount recaptured is the greater of: (1) the sum of depreciation taken and not previously recaptured plus any loss deductions (i.e., abandonment

Chapter 6—Capital Gains and Losses of Individuals

losses) on these contracts that are initially acquired as a part of the original acquisition of the franchise, or (2) depreciation taken on the contracts that are owned by the seller at the time of the franchise sale [Sec. 1245(a)(4)]. The transferee's basis is discussed at ¶ 1521(c).

¶ 1620 Involuntary conversion. A recognized gain or deductible loss from the condemnation or other involuntary conversion [¶ 1410] of both business property and capital assets, held over 9 months may enter into the Sec. 1231 computation [¶ 1618]. Recognized gains and deductible losses from fire, storm, shipwreck or other casualty or theft of this property are treated separately. This separate "netting computation" is made to determine how *all* the casualty or theft gains and losses will be treated on the return. If the casualty or theft gains exceed the casualty or theft losses, there is a further netting with the Sec. 1231 gains and losses. As indicated earlier [¶ 1618], if the result of this netting is a gain, *all* the gains and losses are capital; if a net loss, *all* the gains and losses are ordinary. If the separate netting of the casualty or theft losses is a net loss, all the casualty or theft gains and losses are separately treated as ordinary income or deductible losses. This separate treatment applies whether or not the property is insured. Thus, the treatment of gains and losses from involuntary conversions of business property, personal property and capital assets held over 9 months depends on the amount of gain and loss from the sale or exchange of other Sec. 1231 assets, but the treatment of gains and losses from casualties and thefts depends on the amount of other gains and losses from casualties and thefts as well. In addition, unreinvested conversion proceeds for Sec. 1245 or 1250 property are ordinary income to the extent the recapture rules apply (¶ 1619(e)) [Sec. 1231, 1245, 1250; 1.1231-1(e), 1.1245-4, 1.1250-3]. These recapture rules apply first to the assets, before the separate netting of the casualty and theft gains and losses. Form 4797 is filed with Form 1040 to show the netting computation.

NOTE: For tax years starting in 1978, the holding period will be increased to 1 year. For tax years starting before 1977, a 6-month holding period applied.

Background and purpose. The Congress concluded that it was not appropriate to allow a business taxpayer to deduct an uninsured casualty loss on business property in full from ordinary income when he also had a larger casualty gain on insured business property that was treated as a capital gain.

NOTE: These rules apply to capital assets held for personal purposes, such as a residence or automobile but not a condemnation loss on a personal residence. A personal casualty or theft loss in excess of the $100 floor [¶ 2204] and deductible as an ordinary loss is an itemized deduction.

Example 1: Mr. Smith sold at a gain of $30,000, a warehouse that he used in his business and had bought in 1975. During the year, his personal car was badly damaged in an accident to the extent of $1,500. It was not insured. The car casualty is treated separately and deductible in full. Mr. Smith, therefore, has a fully deductible ordinary loss of $1,400 ($1,500 less the $100 floor) and a Section 1231 capital gain of $30,000 from the sale of the business property.

Example 2: In 1977, Mr. Green sold several depreciable business assets held more than 9 months. The first sale resulted in a gain of $3,400 ($400 of this amount recaptured as Sec. 1245 ordinary income), the second sale in a loss of $2,000, and the third sale in a loss of $4,000. He had a $10,000 fire loss to one of his business garages built in 1973. Insurance proceeds were $13,500. Sec. 1250 recapture applied to $1,000 of these proceeds. He also had a $600 theft loss on an uninsured ring that he had bought in January 1973. The $1,400 subject to recapture is separated first before the netting computation is made. Then Green nets his casualty gains and losses; next, he further nets his casualty gain with his Sec. 1231 gains and losses as follows:

1st netting: Casualty gains and losses:
Gain from fire damage	$2,500
Loss from ring theft ($600 less $100 floor)	(500)

Chapter 6—Capital Gains and Losses of Individuals

Net casualty gain		$2,000
2nd netting: Casualty gains with Sec. 1231 gains and losses:		
Net casualty gain		$2,000
Section 1231 gains and losses:		
Gain from 1st sale		$3,000
Total gains		$5,000
Less: Loss on sales:		
Loss on 2d sale	$2,000	
Loss on 3d sale	$4,000	
Total loss from sales of Sec. 1231 assets		($6,000)
Difference		($1,000)
Ordinary loss		($1,000)

Since the netting produces a net loss, all the gains and losses are treated as ordinary [¶ 1618]. The $500 theft loss becomes an itemized deduction.

Example 3: Mr. White has a loss from Section 1231 sales of $3,000. He has a net gain from casualties of $4,500. The net overall gain of $1,500 ($4,500 − $3,000) is capital.

¶ 1621 **Timber.** The cutting of standing[1] timber, or disposal under certain contracts, if taxpayer retains an economic interest, may be treated as a sale of the timber. Gains or losses from these fictional sales come under Sec. 1231. Timber includes evergreen trees over 6 years old when cut down, and sold for ornamental purposes (for example, Christmas trees).

Cutting timber is treated as a sale if: (1) the taxpayer owned the timber or contract right to cut it for more than 9 months (1 year for tax years starting after 1977) before he cuts it; (2) it was cut for sale, or use in taxpayer's trade or business; and (3) taxpayer so elects on his return. For holding period see ¶ 1606. For tax years starting before 1977, taxpayer must have owned the timber or had a contract right to cut it more than 6 months before the start of the tax year when it was cut, to qualify for capital gain treatment.

In figuring gain or loss on this assumed sale, the basis is the adjusted basis for depletion. The fictional selling price is the fair market value of the timber as of the first day of the tax year. This market value also becomes the cost of the cut timber for future transactions.

Background and purpose. The present rule was enacted since gain from the sale of timber was regarded as having accrued over the period during which the trees matured. It also gave similar treatment to the taxpayer selling timber under a cutting contract as to those who sold the standing timber.

≫**OBSERVATION**→ Congressional action has encouraged investments in timber and has provided two instruments to enable the investor to get a favorable return: capital gain and depletion. See also ¶ 2110.

(a) How to elect. The election is made by reporting the gain or loss on the return and attaching a copy of the figures. It applies to all timber owned by the taxpayer, or that he has a contract right to cut, and is binding for later years. It can be revoked with the Revenue Service's permission on showing undue hardship. Any new election would then require the Revenue Service's consent [Sec. 631(a); 1.631-1].

(b) Disposal of timber under contract by a taxpayer who retains an economic interest in the timber, may be considered a sale. Taxpayer must have owned the timber for more than 9 months (6 months for tax years starting before 1977; 1 year for tax years starting after 1977) before the disposal. The disposal date is when the timber is cut, but if the owner receives payment before then, he may treat the pay-

Footnotes appear at end of this Chapter.

¶ 1621

ment date as the disposal date. Owner means any person who owns an interest in the timber, including a sublessor and a holder of a contract to cut timber. No election is needed. The difference between the amounts received for the timber in any tax year and the adjusted basis for depletion of the timber sold is considered gain or loss [Sec. 631(b); 1.631-2].

¶ **1622 Farmers' Sec. 1231 transactions.** Gain or loss from the sale of livestock or unharvested crops may get Sec. 1231 treatment.

(a) **Livestock.** The provisions of Sec. 1231 apply to livestock held for draft, breeding, dairy, or sporting purposes; but the animals must be held for at least 12 months, except cattle and horses which must be held for 24 months or more. The holding period starts from the date of acquisition, not the date the animal was put to draft, breeding, dairy or sporting purposes. Livestock includes hogs, mules, donkeys, sheep, goats, fur-bearing animals, and other mammals, as well as cattle and horses. It does not include chickens, turkeys, pigeons, geese, other birds, fish, frogs, reptiles, etc. The holding period for all other livestock held for draft, breeding or dairy purposes and acquired before 1970 is 12 months [Sec. 1231(b)(3); 1.1231-2].

HELD FOR DRAFT, BREEDING OR DAIRY PURPOSE

An animal to be used for breeding is found to be sterile, and is sold "a reasonable time" afterwards.

A farmer retires from the breeding or dairy business and sells his whole herd, including young animals never used for such purpose.

A farmer raises hogs for slaughter; he customarily breeds sows once to get a litter which he raises for sale, and he sells the brood sows after obtaining the litter. The sows are held for breeding purposes, even though intended for ultimate sale to customers in the ordinary course of the farmer's business.

NOT HELD FOR DRAFT, BREEDING OR DAIRY PURPOSE

A person raises horses for sale to others, to be used by them for draft purposes. He uses the horses as draft animals on his own farm to train them. Since this use is incidental to his purpose of selling the horses, they are not held by him for draft purposes.

A taxpayer is in the business of raising registered cattle for sale to be used by the buyers for breeding. Business practice calls for such cattle to be bred before the sale to show their fitness for breeding. The test breeding does not, of itself, establish that the animal was held for breeding. (But any animal bred to add the calves to the taxpayer's herd would be held for breeding).

The taxpayer's business is buying cattle and fattening them for slaughter. He buys cows with calf, and the calves are born while owned by him. These cows are not held for breeding.

(b) **Unharvested crops** get Sec. 1231 treatment if (1) raised on land used in the trade or business and held for more than 9 months (6 months for tax years starting before 1977; 1 year for tax years starting after 1977); (2) the crop and land are sold (or exchanged or involuntarily converted) to the same person at the same time; and (3) no right or option is kept by the taxpayer, at the time of the sale, exchange, or conversion to acquire the land, directly or indirectly. (This does not bar rights under a mortgage or other security transaction.) The time the crop, as distinguished from the land, has been held does not matter. A leasehold or estate for years is not considered land [Sec. 1231(b)(4); 1.1231-1(f)].

If an unharvested crop is sold or exchanged and the gain is treated as capital gain under Sec. 1231, no deductions for production of the crop are allowed. This applies whether the deduction is for expenses, depreciation or otherwise, and whether or not it is for the tax year of the sale or exchange. If the deduction is not for the tax year, refigure the tax for the year to which the deduction applies [Sec. 268; 1.268-1].

The disallowed deductions are added to the basis of the crop. For example, if the deductions are for $100 wages and $50 depreciation on a tractor used only to cultivate the particular crop, the basis of the crop is increased by $150. The basis of the tractor is reduced by the $50 depreciation even though this depreciation was disallowed as a deduction [Sec. 1016(a)(11); 1.1016-5(g)].

(c) Ordinary income recapture when farm property disposed of. The sale or exchange of farm property can result in the recapture of certain deductions as ordinary income. Farm losses in excess of $25,000 may cause part of the gain on the sale or exchange of farm property to be treated as ordinary income (¶ 2226) [Sec. 1251]. Deducted soil and water conservation expenditures and land clearing costs may also be recaptured (¶ 1845) [Sec. 1252].

¶ 1623 Coal and domestic iron ore. An owner (or sublessor) of a coal mine who disposes of coal (or lignite) under a royalty contract may get Sec. 1231 treatment for a gain or loss (except when recapture of exploration expenditures is involved, see ¶ 1843). This can also apply to iron ore royalties. The coal or iron ore must be owned for more than 9 months (6 months for tax years starting before 1977; 1 year for tax years starting after 1977) before disposal (date of extraction). To figure the holding period, see ¶ 1606. In addition, an economic interest must be retained in the mineral. The difference between the amount realized and the adjusted depletion basis [¶ 2103(b)] (plus certain disallowed deductions) is the gain or loss. The taxpayer is not entitled to percentage depletion. Nor is he entitled to Sec. 1231 treatment if involved in the mining operation [Sec. 272, 631(c); 1.272-1, 1.631-3].

¶ 1624 How to figure net gain or loss on Sec. 1231 assets. The following example illustrates how to figure the gain or loss:

Example: David West is a calendar-year accountant. In 1977, he received $20,000 in professional fees. On May 4, he had a $2,000 gain from the sale of stock held 10 months. On Jan. 15, he sold a year-old car used only in his practice for $2,700. The car had an adjusted basis of $2,200, and he had taken $400 depreciation last year. On July 1, he received royalties of $3,000 (in excess of his depletion basis) from coal lands he owned for 6 years. On July 15, fire damage to his home, owned for 5 years, resulted in a loss of $700. On Aug. 12, he sold, at a gain of $1,000, a vacant lot held for 4 months as an investment. On Sept. 15, he sold other depreciable investment property he owned for 3 years at a $500 loss. Sale of an office machine on Oct. 7 (3 months after purchase) resulted in a $200 loss.

Net professional fees	$20,000
Other business income (recapture of depreciation on car)	400
Less: Loss on office machine	(200)

Sec. 1231 transactions:

	Gain	Loss
Sale of car used in business	$ 100	
Coal royalties	3,000	
Sale of investment property		$500
Total gains	$3,100	
Total losses		$500
Excess of gains over losses	$2,600	

Capital gain or loss:

1.	Net long-term capital gain ($2,600 + $2,000)	$4,600	
2.	Net short-term capital gain	1,000	
3.	Total	$5,600	
4.	Less: Long-term capital gain deduction (50% of line 1)	2,300	3,300

Adjusted gross income	$23,500

The net professional fees and $400 of the gain on the car sale are ordinary income. The gain on the stock sale is a long-term capital gain. The rest of the gain on the sale of the car, the coal royalties and the loss from the depreciable investment property are all Sec. 1231 gains and losses, resulting in a net Sec. 1231 gain of $2,600 (if the result were a net loss, the gains and losses would be ordinary gains and losses). The gain on sale of the lot is a short-term capital gain. The loss on the office machine is an ordinary loss deductible in full from ordinary income. Since West has a casualty loss from the fire, it is treated as an ordinary loss, deductible above the $100 floor if he itemizes his deductions.

¶ **1625 Sale of depreciable property between related parties.** Gain from sales or exchanges, directly or indirectly, of depreciable property is ordinary income, if made between (a) husband and wife, (b) an individual and his controlled corporation, or (c) 2 or more corporations controlled by the same individual. The rule in (c) applies to sales made after 10-4-76, unless made under a contract entered into before such date. A corporation is "controlled corporation" if the individual, his spouse, his children, his grandchildren, his parents and any trust, estate or partnership of which he is a beneficiary or partner, own (together) 80% or more in value of its outstanding stock [Sec. 1239].

SPECIAL RULES

A special rule prevents the use of a temporary (collapsible) corporation to convert what would be ordinary income to the corporation into capital gains for the stockholders. The remainder of the chapter deals with gain or loss on sales or exchanges of: Securities owned by dealers, tax-exempt securities, original issue discount bonds, subdivided realty and small business stock.

¶ **1627 Collapsible corporations.** Generally, the stockholder's gain can be taxed as ordinary income, even though the gain would otherwise qualify as capital gain, if he sells or exchanges collapsible corporation stock, or receives a distribution in payment for this stock in a partial or complete liquidation [Sec. 341(a); 1.341-1].

(a) What is a collapsible corporation. A collapsible corporation is one formed or used principally to (1) manufacture, construct, or produce property, or (2) buy "Sec. 341 assets" or (3) hold stock in such a corporation. The corporation must be formed or used with a view to (1) having the shareholders realize gain through a sale of stock or distribution to them before the corporation realizes a *substantial part* of the taxable income from the property, and (2) having the shareholders realize gain from the property. Sec. 341 assets are property held primarily for sale, Sec. 1231 property held less than 3 years, or unrealized receivables or fees [Sec. 341(b); 1.341-2].

A corporation is presumed to be collapsible if the fair market value of its Sec. 341 assets is (1) 50% or more of the fair market value of its total assets (exclusive of cash, obligations that are capital assets, and stock in any other corporation) *and* (2) 120% or more of the adjusted basis of its Sec. 341 assets [Sec. 341(c); 1.341-3].

"**A substantial part of income**" is an indefinite term determined by the facts of each case.[1] It refers to the part of the total income remaining to be realized at the time of the stock sale or dissolution of the corporation.[2] However, the Fifth Circuit considered 33⅓% of the anticipated total income from the property as substantial,[1] while 17% was not.[3]

(b) When gains will be ordinary income. Gains will be ordinary income only if [Sec. 341(d); 1.341-4]: (1) The shareholder owns directly or indirectly, over 5% of the corporation's shares. This ownership must exist anytime after manufacturing, construction or production was started, or at the time the property was bought or any time after that. (Stock ownership rules are the same as those found in ¶ 3402 but also include the spouses of taxpayer's brothers and sisters and of his lineal descendants); (2) 70% or more of the gain is related to the property manufactured, built, produced or bought; and (3) the gain was realized within 3 years after completion of the manufacture, construction, or purchase of the property (but gain realized from property after 3 years is counted for the 70% limit above[4]). Land and buildings are considered one unit in applying the 70% rule.[5] If stock is sold on the installment method within the 3-year period, gain is considered realized within that period, even if a payment is received after the 3-year period.[6]

(c) Exceptions to rule. A corporation is not a collapsible corporation if the unrealized appreciation in "ordinary income assets" does not exceed 15% of the corporation's net worth. Thus, if the only unrealized appreciation was in the corporation's inventory, and that equals only 10% of its net worth, a stockholder's gain on the sale of his stock normally will be capital gain. However, the exception does not apply to stock sales to the corporation or by a more-than-20% stockholder to a "related" person [Sec. 341(e); 1.341-6].

Ordinary income assets include inventory, copyrights, letters, memorandums and the like, and in certain cases, assets that would have such character if held by a shareholder. Sec. 1231 assets [¶ 1618 et seq.] generally are not ordinary income assets; but they can be when they would be inventory if held by a stockholder. Net unrealized depreciation in Section 1231 assets is subtracted to determine the net unrealized appreciation of all ordinary income assets. The exception applies in a similar way if the corporation is completely liquidated, but with certain additional restrictions [Sec. 341(e)(2), (5); 1.341-6]. The Supreme Court holds that collapsible corporation rules can apply to capital asset property.[7]

An asset does not become an "ordinary income asset" merely because its sale would result in ordinary income by applying the rules on depreciation recapture [¶ 1619], farm property recapture [¶ 2226], recapture related to certain farm land expenses [¶ 1845(e)], recapture applying when certain mining property is disposed of [¶ 1843], or, for tax years ending after 1975, the recapture of intangible drilling costs (¶ 2103(c)) [Sec. 341(e)(12)].

The exception removes a corporation from the collapsible corporation status for purposes of liquidation under Sec. 337 [¶ 3128], and limited tax-free liquidations under Sec. 333 [¶ 3335] if certain generally similar conditions are met [Sec. 341(e)(3), (4); 1.341-6].

Collapsible subsidiary. If a corporation holding stock in a collapsible subsidiary sells such stock and the gain is taxable as ordinary income under the collapsible corporation rule, the rule will not be applied again to tax as ordinary income the gain realized later by the stockholders of the holding corporation upon its liquidation.[8]

Corporation consenting to recognize gain. Collapsible corporation treatment does not apply to a sale of stock in a corporation which consents to recognize gain when it later disposes of assets owned or under option on the sale date (except certain capital assets), as if the assets had been sold for fair market value at the time of the stock sale. The consent applies to each stock sale made within 6 months after the consent is filed. If a consenting corporation owns 5% or more of another corporation, that corporation must file a consent within the 6 month period ending on the sale date to make the owning corporation's consent valid. The consenting corporation is taxed on any gain that otherwise would not be recognized [¶ 3128]. When assets are transferred to another consenting corporation in one of the various tax-free transactions [¶ 1405; 3309; 3311; 3331(a); 3334] the first corporation is not taxed on the transfer. However, the rule applies to the second corporation. A stockholder can use this rule only once in 5 years. A consenting cor-

Footnotes appear at end of this Chapter.

¶ 1627

poration loses its right to claim it was not collapsible [Sec. 341(f)]. Rules for filing agreements from transferee corporations have been issued.[9]

¶ 1628 **Dealers in securities** usually report ordinary gain or loss on the sale or exchange of securities they own. They can hold securities as an investment for capital gain or loss, if identified in their records as such within 30 days after acquired, and they are not later offered for sale to customers in their trade or business. A "security" is a stock, certificate of stock or interest in any corporation, note, bond, debenture, or evidence of indebtedness, or of an interest in or right to subscribe to or buy any of these [Sec. 1236; 1.1236-1].

¶ 1629 **Original issue discount bonds.** If the taxpayer sells, exchanges or retires bonds or other evidences of indebtedness issued at a discount and held more than 9 months (6 months for tax years starting before 1977; 1 year for tax years starting after 1977), the treatment of the gain due to the original issue discount (OID) depends on the type of bond, when it was issued and the intention of the issuer of the bond at the time it was issued (see below). Original issue discount means the difference between the issue price and the stated redemption price at maturity. The discount is zero if this original issue discount is less than ¼ of 1% of the redemption price at maturity multiplied by the number of years to maturity. Issue price generally is the initial offering price to the public. Special rules apply to define the issue price for bonds that are privately placed, bonds issued with options that are investment units, bonds issued for stock or other property, and to face-amount certificates [Sec. 1232; 1.1232-1(c), 1.1232-3(b), 1.1232-3A(f)].

If an obligation is exchanged for another in a tax-free reorganization, the obligation received carries over the same original issue discount as the one surrendered. This OID carryover is reduced by any ordinary gain recognized and the original issue discount on the surrendered obligation already reported as interest [Sec. 1.1232-3(b)(1)(iv), 1.1232-3A(a), (d)].

> **Example 1:** On 1-1-69, Dale bought Plymouth Corp.'s 20-year 6% bond for $8,000. The redemption price was $10,000 with its OID being $2,000. Since the bond was issued before 5-28-69, the ratable inclusion rules do not apply. On 1-2-77, Dale exchanged his bond, under Plymouth's tax-free reorganization plan, for a 10-year 6% bond that also has a $10,000 redemption price. The $2,000 OID carried over to the new bond. Since it was issued after 5-27-69, Dale must begin ratable inclusion of the $2,000 of OID as interest in income for 1977. The ratable monthly part of OID taxable to Dale is $16.67 ($2,000 ÷ 120 months).

The rules for taxing bond discount do not apply to state and local government bonds whose interest is fully exempt [¶ 1630], nor to discount bonds bought at a premium [Sec. 1232(a)(2)(D)(i)].

(a) Corporate bonds issued before 5-28-69 and government bonds. The tax treatment of corporate bonds issued before 5-28-69 (or under a contract binding before that date) and certain govenment bonds continues to apply as before the changes made by the 1969 Tax Reform Act. If at the time of original issue, there was no intention to call the bond or other evidence of indebtedness before maturity, the discount is apportioned over the entire period to the maturity of the bond. If the bond is sold before maturity, only a pro rata portion of the discount is treated as ordinary income. Any gain in excess of that amount is long-term capital gain (if the bond is a capital asset (¶ 1601)) [Sec. 1232(a)(2)(B); 1.1232-3].

> **Example 2:** Gregory, on 2-1-69, paid $900 to an investment bank for a 10-year bond. The redemption price was $1,000. The bank had no intention of calling the bond before maturity. Gregory sells the bond on 2-20-77 for $940. In this case, he has held the bond for 96 months of its life of 120 months. The part of his gain that would be ordinary income is determined as follows:
>
> 96/120 × $100 (amount of the discount) = $80 (ordinary income).
>
> Thus, the entire gain of $40 is ordinary income. If Gregory sells the bond for $990, only $80 of

his $90 gain is ordinary income. The balance of $10 is long-term capital gain. If he sells the bond for $800, he will have a $100 capital loss.

The discount is not apportioned if, at the time of original issue, there was an intention to call it before maturity. The entire gain due to the discount is ordinary income when realized [Sec. 1232(a)(2)(B)].

(b) Corporate bonds issued after 5-27-69. If the taxpayer sells or exchanges an original issue discount bond issued after 5-27-69 before maturity or if it is redeemed, the taxpayer treats any amount in excess of his adjusted basis as capital gain. However, as with bonds issued before 5-28-69 and certain government bonds, if the issuing corporation intended at the time of original issue to call the bond before maturity, any realized gain is ordinary income to the extent of the original issue discount less any amounts previously included in income [Sec. 1232(a)(2)(A)].

The owner of an original issue discount bond issued after 5-27-69 is required to include the discount in his gross income on a ratable basis over the life of the bond [Sec. 1232(a)(3)(A); 1.1232-3A(a)]. This parallels the treatment of the discount to the issuing corporation [¶ 3125(c)]. The bondholder includes a ratable monthly portion of original issue discount multiplied by the number of full months the bond was held during the tax year. If a bond is sold during a month, the monthly portion of discount is allocated on a daily basis between the seller and the buyer. The taxpayer increases the basis of the bond by the discount that has been included in his gross income [Sec. 1232(a)(3)(E); 1.1232-3A(c)]. A purchaser of the bond continues to include the ratable monthly portion of the discount in his gross income, but he can reduce the inclusion by the ratable amount of any excess he paid over the seller's adjusted basis for the bond [Sec. 1232(a)(3)(B); 1.1232-3A(a)].

> **Example 3:** On January 1, 1977 Mr. Amory bought a 10-year 7% bond for $76, with a stated redemption price of $100. The ratable monthly portion of original issue discount that he includes in gross income for each month he holds the bond is $0.20 [(1/120 months) × $24 ($100 stated redemption price less $76 issue price)]. Amory's basis is the original purchase price, $76, plus $0.20 multiplied by the number of complete months he holds the bond until maturity.
>
> On January 1, 1985, he sells the bond to Mr. Fletcher for $97.60. Fletcher includes in gross income the ratable monthly portion of original issue discount. However, Fletcher can reduce the $0.20 ratable monthly portion by $0.10 [1/24 × ($97.60 (cost of bond) − $76 (issue price) − $19.20 (original issue discount previously includible in Amory's gross income))]. Thus Fletcher includes $1.20 (12 months × $0.10 ratable monthly portion of original issue discount) in his 1985 and 1986 income respectively, and increases his basis by the same amount.

The treatment of original issue discount bonds issued after 5-27-69 is among those provisions designed to discourage the use of the debt in corporate acquisitions [¶ 1901(a); 2811; 3125; 3300]. An information return must be filed by corporations that issue original issue discount bonds after 5-27-69 [¶ 3532].

Interest on bank certificates of deposits and similar deferred interest bank accounts. Taxpayers with certificates of deposit, time deposits, bonus plans and other deposit arrangements made after 1970 that have a term of more than one year and are issued by banks, savings and loan associations and similar financial intitutions, must report interest ratably over the term of the instrument in the same manner as original issue discount bonds (¶ 2722) [Sec. 1.1232-3A(e)].

> **Example 4:** Mr. Smith bought a certificate of deposit from the Bloomton Bank on 1-1-77 for $10,000. Interest was not expressly stated in the obligation. The bond was not redeemable until 12-31-81. The stated redemption price at maturity was $13,382.26. Smith includes $676.45 in his gross income for 1977. This is 12/60 months multiplied by $3,382.26, the excess of the

Footnotes appear at end of this Chapter.

¶ 1629

stated redemption price ($13,382.26) over the issue price ($10,000). The amount included in gross income for 1977 is the same as if the certificate provides for "an amount equal to $10,000 plus 6% compound interest from 1-1-77 to 12-31-81."

Example 5: On 1-1-77, Brown bought a 4-year savings certificate from Jones Building and Loan Corporation. The certificate cost $4,000 and was redeemable for $5,000 on 12-31-80. Brown redeems the certificate on 12-31-79 for $4,660. Brown had included $250 of original issue discount in his gross income for 1977, $250 for 1978 and $250 in his 1979 gross income for a total of $750. Since the excess of the redemption amount over the issue price ($660) is lower than the discount included in gross income ($750) by $90, the $90 is treated as an ordinary loss deductible in computing adjusted gross income, and thus decreases the basis of the certificate by that amount. He has no gain or loss from the redemption, computed as follows:

Adjusted basis on 1-1-79	$4,500
Increase in basis in 1979	250
Subtotal	$4,750
Decrease in basis for loss	90
Basis at redemption	$4,660
Amount realized at redemption	$4,660
Gain or loss	-0-

If a bond is sold with a number of coupons detached, an artificial discount is created. This rule applies regardless of when the bond was issued. A buyer of such a bond must report as ordinary income any gain on the later sale or redemption of the bond up to the amount of the artificial discount created by detaching coupons. If the bond was bought after 1957 the rule applies if any unmatured coupons are detached. If the bond was bought before 1958 the rule only applies if coupons payable more than 12 months after the date of purchase are detached [Sec. 1232(c); 1.1232-4].

A time deposit open account is an arrangement with a fixed maturity date where deposits may be made from time to time. Generally, no interest is paid or constructively received until that fixed date. If part of the account is redeemed before maturity and under withdrawal terms the amount received is based on the principal amount of a specific deposit and interest earned from the deposit date, then the terms control on which deposit was withdrawn. If there are no terms, the withdrawal is considered to be of specific deposits with interest earned from the deposit date on a first-in, first-out basis [Sec. 1.1232-3A(e)].

¶ **1630 Sale of tax-exempt securities.** An original buyer of tax-exempt securities holding them until maturity generally realizes neither gain nor loss on their redemption. The amount realized equals the holder's cost plus the tax-free interest and discount factor [Sec. 1232(a); 1.1232-1]. If redeemed before maturity at a premium, the taxpayer will have a capital gain to the extent of any premium paid.[1] If the bonds are sold before maturity for more or less than their basis, the taxpayer (not a dealer) will have a capital gain or loss. However, short-term bonds are considered noncapital assets, and their sale will result in ordinary gain or loss [¶ 1601]. Similar rules on the sale of tax-exempts apply to a subsequent buyer. However, he must figure his basis by reducing his cost for amount paid to acquire any accrued interest. When such bonds are bought on the open market at a discount over the original issue discount, the bargain element of the sale is not considered tax-exempt interest. The amount of the discount treated as tax-exempt interest is limited to the amount of the discount at which the bonds were originally issued.[2]

¶ **1631 Subdividing realty for sale** can result in capital gain treatment if an individual: (1) is not a real estate dealer in the year the lots are sold; (2) did not make substantial improvements on the tract that increased the value of the particular lots sold; (3) held the lots for at least 5 years (unless he inherited the property); and (4) did not previously hold the tract or any lot in it as a dealer (but even if he did, he can still qualify if conditions (2) and (3) were met in the year he was a dealer).

If these conditions are met, and taxpayer has not sold more than 5 lots or parcels from a single tract through the end of the tax year, the entire proceeds get capital gain treatment. In computing the number of lots or parcels sold, two or more adjoining lots sold to a single buyer in a single sale are counted as one parcel.[1] All sales made during or after the year the 6th lot or parcel from a single tract is sold come under a special rule: gain up to 5% of the selling price is ordinary income; the balance is long-term capital gain. Selling expenses first offset the gain taxable as ordinary income, and any excess offsets the capital gain. If, after selling any lot or tract, no other sales are made from the same tract until at least 5 years later, the seller can start counting the sales of the first 5 lots again before the 5% rule goes into operation. Corporate taxpayers selling subdivided realty receive capital gain treatment in limited cases only [Sec. 1237; 1.1237-1].

¶ 1632 **Loss on small business stock.** Loss on the sale, exchange or worthlessness of certain small business stock (called "Section 1244 stock") is fully deductible as an ordinary loss [Sec. 1244]. Any amount not absorbed in the year sustained becomes part of the stockholder's net operating loss carryback and carryover [¶ 2242].

The rule applies only to an individual, and he must be the original buyer, either directly or through a partnership [Sec. 1244(a); 1.1244(a)-1]. The maximum allowable as an ordinary loss in one tax year is $25,000; on a joint return, it is $50,000 whether the stock is owned by one or both spouses. Any excess loss is subject to capital-loss limitations [Sec. 1244(b); 1.1244(b)-1].

> **Example 1:** Yardley buys Sec. 1244 stock for $200,000 cash. In 1977, he sells half of it for $80,000. His $20,000 loss is deductible as an ordinary loss on a separate or joint return. In 1978, he sells the rest of the stock for $30,000. On a separate return, he deducts $25,000 as ordinary loss and $45,000 as capital loss. On a joint return, he deducts $50,000 as ordinary loss, and $20,000 as capital loss.

> **Example 2:** The Ames-Byrd partnership, of which Ames is an equal member, has a loss of $80,000 on Sec. 1244 stock purchased by it. Assume Ames files a joint return, and also has individually a $20,000 loss on Sec. 1244 stock. His total loss is $60,000 ($40,000 partnership and $20,000 individual); on his return, he treats $50,000 as ordinary loss and $10,000 as capital loss.

(a) Qualification requirements. Only common stock (voting or non-voting) of a domestic corporation qualifies as Sec. 1244 stock. Also:

- The stock must be issued under a *written* plan to issue the stock within 2 years (no other stock offering may be outstanding at time of issue);
- The corporation must be a "small business corporation" when the plan is adopted (its status at the time of issue or of loss is immaterial);
- The stock must be issued for money or property (other than stock, securities or services) [Sec. 1244(c)(1); 1.1244(c)-1].

(b) What is a small business corporation. A "small business corporation" is one which, when the plan is adopted, (a) has not more than $1,000,000 equity capital (assets, taken at basis for gain, less liabilities, except debt to stockholders); and (b) whose capital paid-in after 6-30-58 does not exceed $500,000. In both cases, the amount of stock that can be offered under the plan is taken into account [Sec. 1244(c)(2); 1.1244(c)-2].

The rule applies only if, for the 5 tax years of the corporation ended before the loss, less than 50% of its gross receipts was from investment sources, such as interest, dividends, rents, and stock and security gains; but this limitation does not ap-

Footnotes appear at end of this Chapter.

ply if deductions (excluding those for operating loss, partially tax-free interest, and dividends received) exceed gross income [Sec. 1244(c)(1); 1.1244(c)-1]. However, the corporation must be largely an operating company [Sec. 1.1244(c)-1(g)(2).

In general, stock received in a reorganization does not qualify. However, a stock dividend or stock received in a recapitalization or change of name, identity, etc., reorganization may qualify [Sec. 1244(d)(2); 1.1244(d)-3].

If property with value less than basis is transferred tax-free to a corporation for Sec. 1244 stock, ordinary loss (but not total loss) is that value minus whatever is realized on disposition [Sec. 1244(d)(1)(A); 1.1244(d)-1].

Example 3: Property valued at $1,000 and with a $3,000 basis is transferred tax-free to a small business corporation for all its stock. The stock becomes worthless. There is an ordinary loss to the extent of $1,000 and a capital loss of $2,000.

If after acquiring Sec. 1244 stock, a stockholder's basis for his stock is increased (for example, by additional capital contribution), a loss on the stock is allocated [Sec. 1244(d)(1)(B); 1.1244(d)-2].

Example 4: Stock cost $10,000 and the stockholder made a capital contribution of $2,000, thus increasing the basis to $12,000. He sold the stock for $9,000. Of the $3,000 loss, only 10/12, or $2,500, is an ordinary loss.

The plan to issue Sec. 1244 stock must appear on the corporation's records. Records also should be kept showing (1) to whom stock was issued, stock certificates, dates of issue, amount and type of consideration received from each shareholder, including shareholder's basis and value of property; (2) amount of money and corporation's basis of property received for its stock after 6-30-58 and before adoption of the plan, as a contribution to capital, and as paid-in surplus; (3) equity capital on date of adoption of plan; and (4) stock dividends and reorganizations. Minutes of a corporation's board meeting can qualify as a "plan" if they contain all of these required elements.[1] Taxpayer claiming deduction must file a statement with his return showing the corporation's address, how the stock was acquired, and the nature and amount of the consideration paid, including the type, value and basis of property given in a nontaxable exchange. Taxpayer should also keep records to distinguish Sec. 1244 stock from other stock owned in the same corporation [Sec. 1.1244(e)-1].

Footnotes to Chapter 6

(P-H "FEDERAL TAXES" related references are cited in brackets [ ] at the end of each footnote below.)

Footnote ¶ 1600 [¶ 32,001 et seq.].

Footnote ¶ 1601 [32,065 et seq.].

(1) Malat v. Riddell, 17 AFTR 2d 604, 383 US 569 [¶ 32,076(2)].
(2) Rev. Rul. 58-40, 1958-1 CB 275 [¶ 32,461(5)].
(3) Hazard, 7 TC 372 [¶ 32,491(30); 32,493(5)].
(4) Grier v. U.S., 120 F. Supp. 395, 45 AFTR 1975, affd. 218 F.2d 603, 46 AFTR 1536; Bauer v. U.S., 2 AFTR 2d 6191, 168 F. Supp. 539 [¶ 32,493(10)].
(5) Williams v. McGowan, 152 F.2d 570, 34 AFTR 615 [¶ 32,097(5)].
(6) Michaels, 12 TC 17; Rev. Rul. 55-79, 1955-1 CB 370 [¶ 32,091(5); 32,097(15)].

Footnote ¶ 1601 continued
(7) Rev. Rul. 70-45, 1970-1 CB 17 [¶ 32,091(10)].
(8) Comm. v. Shapiro, 125 F.2d 532, 28 AFTR 1079 [¶ 28,774(5)].
(9) Comm. v. Ray, 210 F.2d 390, 45 AFTR 334 [¶ 32,607(5)].
(10) Hort v. Comm., 313 US 28, 25 AFTR 1207 [¶ 32,605(5)].
(11) Thorpe, 42 BTA 654 [¶ 32,605(10)].
(12) Rodgers, 51 TC 927 [¶ 32,408(15)].
(13) Rev. Rul. 69-482, 1969-2 CB 164 [¶ 32,407(1)].
(14) Lan Jen Chu, 58 TC 598 [¶ 32,582(12)].
(15) Bell's Estate v. Comm., 137 F.2d 454, 31 AFTR 411 [¶ 32,102].
(16) Perkins, 41 BTA 1225 [¶ 32,101(5)].

Chapter 6—Footnotes

Footnote ¶ 1601 continued
(17) Rev. Rul. 66-58, 1966-1 CB 186 [¶ 32,116(40)].
(18) Rhodes' Est. v. Comm., 131 F.2d 50, 30 AFTR 220 [¶ 32,144(5)].
(19) Finch, ¶ 42,641 P-H Memo TC [¶ 32,099.15].
(20) Hercules Motor Corp., 40 BTA 999 [¶ 32,076(10)].
(21) Rev. Rul. 65-261, 1965-2 CB 281 [¶ 32,116(10), (145)].
(22) Beals' Est. v. Comm., 82 F.2d 268, 17 AFTR 621 [¶ 32,093].

Footnote ¶ 1602 [¶ 32,131].

Footnote ¶ 1605 [¶ 32,176].

Footnote ¶ 1606 [¶ 32,176 et seq.].
(1) Rev. Rul. 66-5, 1966-1 CB 91; Rev. Rul. 70-598, 1970-2 CB 168 [¶ 32,179(5), (10)].
(2) Rev. Rul. 66-6, 1966-1 CB 160 [¶ 32,179(5)].
(3) Rev. Rul. 66-5, 1966-1 CB 91 [¶ 32,179(15)].
(4) Rev. Rul. 66-7, 1966-1 CB 188 [¶ 32,179(15)].
(5) IR-1787, 3-30-77 [¶ 55,373].
(6) Rev. Rul. 66-97, 1966-1 CB 190; Rev. Rul. 70-344, 1970-2 CB 50 [¶ 20,251(15); 32,463(5)].
(7) Otto v. Comm., 101 F.2d 1017, 22 AFTR 620 [¶ 32,463(5)].
(8) Rev. Rul. 54-607, 1954-2 CB 177 [¶ 32,198].
(9) Paul v. Comm., 206 F.2d 763, 44 AFTR 319; Rev. Rul. 75-524, 1975-2 CB 342 [¶ 32,198(10)].
(10) Kronner v. U.S., 43 AFTR 574, 110 F.Supp. 730 [¶ 32,410].
(11) Comm. v. San Joaquin Fruit and Investment Co., 297 US 496, 17 AFTR 470 [¶ 31,169(5); 32,203(10)].
(12) Humphrey, 32 BTA 280; Lehman, 7 TC 1088, affd. 165 F.2d 383, 36 AFTR 545 [¶ 32,205].

Footnote ¶ 1607 [¶ 31,231].

Footnote ¶ 1608 [¶ 32,345].
(1) Rev. Rul. 63-65, 1963-1 CB 142 [¶ 32,349(5)].
(2) Fulton Bag & Cotton Mills, 22 TC 1044 [¶ 32,361(5)].
(3) Corn Products Refining Co. v. Comm., 350 US 46, 47 AFTR 1789 [¶ 32,363].
(4) International Flavors & Fragrances, Inc., 62 TC 232; rev'd 36 AFTR 2d 75-6054 [¶ 32,361(60); 56,615].

Footnote ¶ 1609 [¶ 32,383].
(1) Rev. Rul. 58-234, 1958-1 CB 279 [¶ 20,255; 32,383(5), (10)].
(2) Rev. Rul. 70-205, 1970-1 CB 174 [¶ 32,383(17)].
(3) Rev. Rul. 71-521, 1971-2 CB 313 [¶ 32,383(5)].

Footnote ¶ 1609 continued
(4) Rev. Rul. 58-384, 1958-2 CB 410 [¶ 32,351(5)].

Footnote ¶ 1611 [¶ 32,011].

Footnote ¶ 1612 [¶ 32,035 et seq.].

Footnote ¶ 1613 [¶ 32,045; 32,051 et seq.].
(1) Rev. Rul. 71-195, 1971-1 CB 225 [¶ 32,051].
(2) Treas. Dept. booklet, "Your Federal Income Tax" (1977 Ed.), p. 120.

Footnote ¶ 1614 [¶ 32,021 et seq.].

Footnote ¶ 1618 [¶ 32,231 et seq.].

Footnote ¶ 1619 [¶ 32,695; 32,761].

Footnote ¶ 1620 [¶ 32,231 et seq.; 32,695; 32,761].

Footnote ¶ 1621 [¶ 22,431 et seq.].
(1) Rev. Rul. 56-434, 1956-2 CB 334 [¶ 22,443(10)].

Footnote ¶ 1622 [¶ 32,259 et seq.; 32,275].

Footnote ¶ 1623 [¶ 22,431].

Footnote ¶ 1624 [¶ 32,231 et seq.].

Footnote ¶ 1625 [¶ 32,576 et seq.].

Footnote ¶ 1627 [¶ 17,771 et seq.].
(1) Comm. v. Kelley, 8 AFTR 2d 5232, 293 F.2d 904; Rev. Rul. 72-48, 1972-1 CB 102. [¶ 17,787(5)].
(2) Abbot v. Comm., 2 AFTR 2d 5479, 258 F.2d 537 [¶ 17,787(5)].
(3) Heft v. Comm., 8 AFTR 2d 5465, 294 F.2d 795 [¶ 17,787(5)].
(4) Rev. Rul. 65-184, 1965-2 CB 91; Rev. Rul. 70-93, 1970-1 CB 71 [¶ 17,793(10), (15)].
(5) Rev. Rul. 68-476, 1968-2 CB 139 [¶ 17,793(15)].
(6) Rev. Rul. 60-68, 1960-1 CB 151 [¶ 17,793(10)].
(7) Braunstein, et al. v. Comm., 11 AFTR 2d 1606, 83 SCt. 1663 [¶ 17,791(10)].
(8) Rev. Rul. 56-50, 1956-1 CB 174 [¶ 17,792(5)].
(9) Rev. Rul. 69-32, 69-33, 1969-1 CB 100 [¶ 17,793(20); 17,795(25)].

Footnote ¶ 1628 [¶ 32,446 et seq.].

Footnote ¶ 1629 [¶ 32,315; 32,337].

Footnote ¶ 1630 [¶ 8252; 8253].
(1) Rev. Rul. 72-587, 1972-2 CB 74 [¶ 32,329(10)].
(2) Rev. Rul. 73-112, 1973-1 CB 47 [¶ 8253(5)].

Footnote ¶ 1631 [¶ 32,476 et seq.].
(1) Treas. Dept. booklet, "Your Federal Income Tax" (1977 Ed.), p. 101.

Footnote ¶ 1632 [¶ 32,655 et seq.].
(1) Rev. Rul. 66-67, 1966-1 CB 191 [¶ 32,685].

Highlights of Chapter 6
Capital Gains and Losses of Individuals

I. **What Produces Capital Gain or Loss**
   A. Sale or exchange of capital asset [¶ 1602].
   B. Capital asset is any property *except* [¶ 1601]:
      1. Inventory.
      2. Property held primarily for sale in ordinary course of business.
      3. Depreciable or real property used in business.
      4. Accounts or notes receivable in ordinary course of business.
      5. Copyrights, literary and musical composition or similar property held by the creator or his donee.
      6. Certain short-term government bonds issued at discount.
      7. Certain U. S. government publications received without charge or at reduced price.

II. **Holding Period**
   A. Short- or long-term [¶ 1605]:
      1. Short-term, if asset held not over 9 months.
      2. Long-term, if held over 9 months.
      3. Exception: 6-month holding period applies to commodity futures.
   B. Start of holding period [¶ 1606–1607]:
      1. Ordinary sales: day after property acquired.
      2. Gift after 1920: date property acquired by donor, or date of gift if sold at a loss.
      3. Sale of inherited property gets long-term gain or loss treatment generally.
      4. Tax-free exchange: same date as property given.
      5. New residence replacing old: same date as old residence.
      6. Stock sold from lots: subject to FIFO rule unless identified.
   C. Short sales [¶ 1608]:
      1. Gain is short-term if holding substantially identical property not over 9 months on date of sale, or acquiring such property after sale but before closing.
      2. Substantially identical property's holding period starts on earlier of closing date or date of sale.
      3. Loss is long-term if substantially identical property held over 9 months on date of sale.
   D. "Puts" & "calls" [¶ 1609]:
      1. Option price enters into basis of stock received.
      2. On lapse, option maker has short-term capital gain or loss; holder has capital loss.
      3. Gain or loss on option sale is capital, generally.

III. **Figuring Capital Gain or Loss**
   A. How to report gain and loss [¶ 1611–1612]:
      1. Determine net short-term capital gain or loss.
      2. Determine net long-term capital gain or loss.
      3. Determine net gain or loss (difference between 1 & 2).
      4. Deduct 50% of excess net LTCG (2) over net STCL (1).
      5. Amount in 4 subject to minimum tax on preferences.
   B. Limits on capital loss deduction [¶ 1613]:
      1. Net loss deductible against ordinary income up to lesser of other income or $2,000.
      2. 2-for-1 ratio applies to net long-term loss after 1969.
      3. Balance not deductible carried over indefinitely.

Highlights of Chapter 6

C. **Alternative tax [¶ 1614]:**
 1. Net LTCG up to $50,000: tax on gain not over 25%.
 2. Over $50,000: use 3-step computation and add total.

IV. **Disposing of Business Property**
 A. **Special treatment of Sec. 1231 gains and losses [¶ 1618]:**
  1. If net gains exceed net losses, all gains and losses treated as long-term capital gains and losses.
  2. If net losses exceed net gains, all gains and losses treated as ordinary.
 B. **Sec. 1231 assets [¶ 1618(a)].**
 C. **Gain is ordinary to extent of recaptured depreciation [¶ 1619; 1624]:**
  1. Depreciable property except building: recapture applies to depreciation allowable since 1961.
  2. Depreciable realty: recapture hinges on use, acquisition date, depreciation methods; figured generally on lesser of percentage of gain or excess depreciation.
 D. **Exceptions to recapture rule.** Gifts; charitable contributions; transfers at death; sale of senior citizen's home; low-income housing; like kind exchanges; involuntary conversions; sales under government order; sale of player contracts [¶ 1619].
 E. **Involuntary conversions [¶ 1620]:**
  1. Separate netting of casualty gains and losses of personal and business property (insured or not) held over 9 months.
  2. If 1st netting is net loss, all casualty gains and losses are ordinary.
  3. If 1st netting is net gain, further netting with Sec. 1231 gains and losses.
 F. **Sec. 1231 treatment also applies to [¶ 1621–1623]:**
  1. Cutting or disposal of timber.
  2. Farmers' sale of livestock held for draft, breeding or sporting, and unharvested crops.
  3. Sale of coal or domestic iron ore.
 G. **Gain on sale of depreciable property is ordinary, if between [¶ 1625]:**
  1. Husband and wife.
  2. Individual and his 80%-controlled corporation.
  3. Two corporations controlled by one individual.

V. **Special Rules**
 A. **Collapsible corporations [¶ 1627]:**
  1. Corporation "collapsible" if formed principally to manufacture, construct, or produce property (or hold stock in such corporation) with view to let shareholders realize gain before corporation realizes substantial part of taxable income.
  2. Shareholders denied capital gains treatment.
 B. **Security brokers** usually get ordinary gain or loss on sale of securities they own unless identified [¶ 1628].
 C. **Original issue discount bonds [¶ 1629]:**
  1. Issued before 5-28-69: No tax until bond is sold; portion of gain due to original issue discount is ordinary income; balance long-term capital gain.
  2. Issued after 5-27-69: holder currently reports ratable portion of original issue discount; inclusion increases bond basis.
 D. **Sale of tax-exempt bonds [¶ 1630].**
 E. **Subdividing realty for sale** can result in capital gain treatment [¶ 1631].
 F. **Loss on small business stock [¶ 1632]:**
  1. Loss on "Sec. 1244 stock" is ordinary if stock is issued under written plan and meets other requirements.
  2. Ordinary loss limited to $25,000 ($50,000 on joint return) yearly.
  3. Any excess loss subject to capital loss limitation.

Chapter 7

DIVIDENDS

TABLE OF CONTENTS

ORDINARY DIVIDENDS

	¶
What is a dividend	1700
Source of distribution	1701
Presumption as to source	
What are available earnings and profits	
Matching cash dividends and distribution source	
Reporting dividends when earnings are unknown	
How distributions are taxed	1702
Distributions in kind	
Capital gain dividends	
Consent dividends	
Tax-exempt and specially treated dividends	
Constructive dividends	1703
Tax-exempt and specially treated distributions	1704
Dividends from federal agencies	
Dividends from tax-exempt earnings	
Other common examples of tax-exempt or specially treated distributions	

THE DIVIDEND EXCLUSION

Dividends excluded from income	1705
Joint returns	
Jointly owned stock	
When exclusion is not allowed	1706
Dividends that do not qualify	
Short sales of stock	

STOCK DIVIDENDS

What is a stock dividend	1707
Other definitions	
How stock dividends are taxed	
Transactions treated as distributions	
Effect of nontaxable stock distributions	1708
Basis of old and new stock	
Holding period of new stock	
Effect of taxable stock distributions	1709
Amount distributed	
Basis of stock	
Holding period of new stock	

STOCK AND BOND RIGHTS

	¶
Rights in general	1710
Effect of nontaxable stock rights	1711
Basis of stock and rights	
The election to allocate	
Holding period of stock and rights	
Taxable stock rights	1712
Rights to bonds	1714

LIQUIDATING DIVIDENDS

What is a liquidating dividend	1715
What is a partial liquidation	1716
How liquidating dividends are treated	1717
Amount and character of gain or loss	
Reporting gain or loss	

STOCK REDEMPTIONS

Stock redemptions in general	1718
Sale and dividend distinguished	
Is redemption essentially equivalent to a dividend?	
Is redemption substantially disproportionate?	
Was all the shareholder's stock redeemed?	
Stock ownership	
Other rules	
Complete redemption of taxpayer's stock	1719
When constructive ownershp rules do not apply	
Prior stock transfers to avoid tax	
Redemption through use of a related corporation	1720
Sale to related corporation (other than a subsidiary)	
Sale to subsidiary	
What is control	
Constructive ownership	
Stock redeemed to pay death taxes	1721
Special relief	
What stock qualifies	
The "preferred stock bail-out"	1722
Constructive ownership of stock	1727
Family members	
Partnerships and estates	
Trusts	

Footnotes appear at end of this Chapter.

Corporations
Options
Constructive ownership as actual ownership

• Highlights of Chapter 7 .... Page 1761

ORDINARY DIVIDENDS

Most corporations pay their dividends in cash. Dividends paid by taxable domestic corporations to individuals usually qualify for an *exclusion* of up to $100 per person. The balance of the dividend, after the exclusion, is generally ordinary income, but there are exceptions. One of these applies if the total distribution exceeds the corporation's earnings and profits. The excess is first a nontaxable reduction of the shareholders' stock basis. The excess over basis is usually a capital gain. No exclusion is allowed for dividends paid to corporations; they get relief by a dividends-received *deduction*.

¶ **1700 What is a dividend.** The term "dividend" is used in a broad sense to mean any corporate distribution. For tax purposes, a distribution is a "dividend" only to the extent made from current earnings and profits or from those accumulated after 2-28-13 [Sec. 316(a); 1.316-1]. For determinations after 10-4-76, dividends include deficiency dividends paid by real estate investment trusts (¶ 3432) [Sec. 316(b)(3)].

Example: Acme Corporation has no accumulated earnings and profits. In 1977, it has earnings and profits of $16,000. During the year, it distributed $20,000 in cash to its sole stockholder. The amount of the dividend is $16,000.

The corporation must make the distribution to a shareholder *as a shareholder*. A distribution to him as a creditor in payment of a debt is not a dividend. However, the label given to a distribution is not controlling. A distribution could, in fact, give rise to a dividend even though it was made to look like a debt payment or some other type of payment [¶ 1703].

Earnings and profits. There is no comprehensive definition of "earnings and profits" in the statute or regulations. There are only rules for determining the effect of particular transactions and certain nonstatutory rules on the computation of earnings and profits [Sec. 312; 1.312-1—1.312-12].

NOTE: In some cases, the tax concepts and terminology in this area will correspond with the accounting concepts and terminology; in other cases, they will differ.

The amount of the corporation's accumulated earnings and profits available for dividend payments is the excess of its earnings and profits (profit years) over its deficits (loss years). There can be no accumulated earnings or profits until an operating deficit is made good.[1]

How distributions are taxed. The general rules are summarized in ¶ 1702. Some distributions are tax-exempt in whole or in part; others (those paid in property, for example) are subject to special rules [¶ 1702; 1704].[2]

¶ **1701 Source of distribution. (a) In general.** Determination of source is important because a distribution is a "dividend" only to the extent it comes from current or accumulated earnings and profits. However, the corporation may not pick the source at random.

Chapter 7—Dividends

Presumption as to source. It is conclusively presumed that every distribution comes from earnings and profits to the extent there are any; and from current earnings and profits first [Sec. 316(a); 1.316-2(a)].

> **Example 1:** At the beginning of the year Bellar Corp. had $12,000 earnings and profits accumulated since 2-28-13. Its earnings for the year amounted to $30,000. Assume it paid a single annual dividend as follows:
> a. Dividend of $20,000. The entire dividend would be taxable, since it did not exceed the $30,000 earnings of the tax year.
> b. Dividend of $40,000. The entire dividend would be taxable since it did not exceed the $30,000 earnings of the tax year, plus the $12,000 earnings and profits accumulated since 2-28-13 ($30,000 plus $12,000, or a total of $42,000).
> c. Dividend of $60,000. The dividend would be taxable to the extent of $42,000 ($30,000 plus $12,000). The remaining $18,000 is not taxable.

Current earnings and profits are computed at the end of the tax year, without reduction for distributions during the year. Thus, a distribution made when the corporation had no earnings and profits could turn out to be a dividend if the corporation ended the year with a profit.

(b) What are available earnings and profits. In determining the amount of accumulated earnings and profits still available for dividend payments, an adjustment is made for payments that come from, and therefore reduce, the earnings and profits. The adjustment is made for the tax year as a whole, if the dividend is paid from current earnings and profits; and on the payment date, if payment comes from accumulated earnings and profits [¶ 3129]. See examples (2) and (3) in (c) below.

For definition of "accumulated earnings and profits" see ¶ 1700.

Effect of depreciation on earnings and profits. In figuring earnings and profits for tax years starting after 6-30-72, a corporation can deduct depreciation or amortization only on the straight line method, or on a similar method that provides for ratable depreciation reductions over an asset's useful life [Sec. 312(k)].

> **NOTE:** The corporation may still use accelerated depreciation in figuring its taxable income, since the above restrictions apply only to the computation of earnings and profits. However, as to a particular asset, the corporation must use the same remaining useful life for both income tax and earnings and profits purposes.[1]

Foreign corporation with less than 20% U.S. source income during the year may use the accelerated methods in figuring their earnings and profits. See also ¶ 2024.

Carryover earnings in reorganizations. Earnings and profits (or a deficit) of a predecessor corporation in a reorganization may be carried over to the successor under certain conditions [¶ 3336-3338].

(c) Matching cash dividends and distribution source. Allocation of earnings and profits to cash dividends paid during the year is sometimes necessary to determine the taxable amount of each payment. Usually, the allocation is necessary only where stock changes hands during the year or total distributions exceed the current earnings and profits. In these cases, the current and accumulated earnings and profits are allocated to each distribution under the rules below [Sec. 1.316-2(b), (c)].

Current earnings. First allocate the earnings of the tax year to each individual dividend. The proportion of each dividend which the total of the earnings or prof-

Footnotes appear at end of this Chapter.

¶ 1701

its of the year bears to the total dividends paid during the year is regarded as out of the earnings of that year.

Example 2: Current earnings and profits are $30,000. Four dividends of $15,000 were paid, or a total of $60,000. The proportion which the current earnings and profits ($30,000) bears to the total dividends ($60,000) is 30,000/60,000 or 50%. Thus 50%, or $7,500, of each dividend is regarded as out of current earnings and profits and taxable to that extent.

If current earnings and profits exceed the current year's distributions, the excess either reduces prior deficits, if any, or is added to accumulated earnings and profits at the beginning of the following year.

Accumulated earnings and profits. Allocate the earnings and profits accumulated since 2-28-13 in sequence to the portion of each individual dividend not out of current earnings and profits. The allocation is made to the extent of such earnings and profits available on the date of each distribution.

Example 3: Assume the same facts in Example 2, except that earnings and profits accumulated since 2-28-13 amount to $12,000. Four dividends of $15,000 each were paid on March 15, June 15, Sept. 15, and Dec. 15. On Mar. 15 the entire $12,000 earnings and profits accumulated since 2-28-13 were available. Thus, $7,500, the portion of the Mar. 15 dividend not regarded as out of earnings or profits of the tax year, is entirely taxable, since it does not exceed $12,000. As of June 15, date of the second dividend, only $4,500 of the $12,000 is available ($12,000 less $7,500 allocated to the Mar. 15 dividend). Thus, only $4,500 of the $7,500 portion of the second dividend not regarded as out of earnings of the year is taxable. After the second dividend is paid, there are no more earnings or profits accumulated since 2-28-13 available, since the entire $12,000 was allocated to the first two dividends. The portions of the third and fourth dividends not out of the earnings of the year ($7,500 each) are nontaxable.

Date	Dividends Amount	Portion out of earnings or profits of the tax year	Portion out of earnings accumulated since 2-28-13	Taxable amount of each dividend	Nontaxable amount of each dividend
Mar. 15	$15,000	$ 7,500	$ 7,500	$15,000	$ ....
June 15	15,000	7,500	4,500	12,000	3,000
Sept. 15	15,000	7,500	....	7,500	7,500
Dec. 15	15,000	7,500	....	7,500	7,500
Total	$60,000	$30,000	$12,000	$42,000	$18,000

Each shareholder should report as taxable income:
(a) 100% of his Mar. 15 dividend.
(b) 80% of his June 15 dividend.
(c) 50% of his Sept. 15 dividend.
(d) 50% of his Dec. 15 dividend.

➤**OBSERVATION**➤ Tables showing the tax status of dividends paid during the year appear in the P-H Capital Adjustments Service.

(d) Reporting dividends when earnings are unknown. If the corporation's current earnings and profits are unknown when the shareholder files his return, he should tentatively report the entire distribution as taxable. A situation of this kind might occur, for example, if the corporation had a fiscal year ending June 30 and the shareholder used the calendar year.[2] If necessary, the shareholder may file a refund claim later.

➤**OBSERVATION**➤ Corporations must send their shareholders a copy of Form 1099-DIV showing the payments made to them. If the information needed is not received, or if there is any doubt as to the status of a particular payment, the shareholder may get full details from the dividend tables in the P-H Capital Adjustments Service.

¶ 1702 **How distributions are taxed.** The rules are summarized below.

(a) In general. The distribution is a "dividend" to the extent covered by earnings and profits of the tax year, or still-available earnings and profits accumulated after 2-28-13. Except for the partial exclusion allowed individuals (or the deduction allowed corporations), the dividend portion is taxed as ordinary income to the shareholder in the year he or his agent actually or constructively receives the dividend. In figuring his tax, the shareholder may assume the distribution is from earnings and profits unless the corporation indicates otherwise [¶ 1701(a); 1705; 1706; 3114].

To the extent the distribution exceeds earnings and profits, it is not a dividend. The excess is treated first as a nontaxable reduction of the shareholders' basis (in effect, the shareholders are recovering their investment).[1] Any excess over basis is usually a capital gain, but is exempt if it comes from an increase in value before 3-1-13. Any capital gain is long-term or short-term, depending on how long the stock was held [Sec. 301(c); 1.301-1, 1.316-2].

(b) Distributions in kind. Special problems arise when corporations distribute property (including stock in other corporations) to their shareholders. The dividend portion cannot exceed the corporation's earnings and profits [Sec. 1.316-1(a)(2)].

> **Example:** Adelphi Corporation has earnings and profits of $10,000. It distributes to the shareholders property with a basis of $6,000 and a fair market value of $16,000. The amount taxable to the shareholders is $10,000.

The distribution could also result in a gain to the distributing corporation [¶ 3127–3129].

Amount of distribution. The amount distributed to an individual is the fair market value of the property on the distribution date, reduced (but not below zero) by any liability assumed by the shareholder or to which the property remains subject [Sec. 301(b); 1.301-1, 1.305-2(c)].

Basis of property. The individual shareholder's basis for the property is its fair market value on the distribution date [Sec. 301(d)(1); 1.301-1(h)].

Special rules for corporate shareholders. The amount distributed and the shareholder's basis are determined under special rules when the shareholder is a corporation [¶ 3107; 3309 et seq.].

(c) Capital gain dividends. Mutual funds, regulated investment companies and real estate investment trusts may designate part of a distribution as a capital gain dividend. The shareholder treats this part as long-term gain regardless of how long he held the stock [¶ 1706(a); 3431(a); 3432].

(d) Consent dividends. In the case of personal holding companies and the accumulated earnings tax, a "consent dividend" has the effect of a taxable cash dividend paid by the corporation and reinvested by the shareholder. Thus, the basis of the original stock is increased by the amount of the "consent dividend" [¶ 3132(b); 3404(b)].

Footnotes appear at end of this Chapter.

¶ 1702

Chapter 7—Dividends

(e) Tax-exempt and specially treated dividends. Some dividends are tax-exempt in whole or in part; others are specially treated [see (a)–(d) above; also ¶ 1704].

When a corporation makes partially or wholly tax-free distributions to its shareholders, it must file Form 5452 by February 28 of the following year. These distributions are considered wholly or partially nontaxable only because the paying corporation's earnings and profits are less than the distributions.[2]

NOTE: If you do not furnish the required information, the Revenue Service may assume you have redetermined your distributions to be fully taxable as dividends.

¶ 1703 Constructive dividends. Some transactions not in the form of dividends are taxed as such because their effect is the same. They are taxed even though a dividend was not formally declared[1] and payment was not made to all the shareholders in proportion to stock ownership.

The contested cases usually involve distributions of profits in a form that would give the corporation a deduction (dividends are not deductible) or would avoid a tax on the shareholder.

Payments to shareholders taxed as dividends include excessive salaries paid to them as employees [¶ 1817], excessive royalties[2] and rents,[3] and "interest" on notes held to be an equity investment (stock)[4] rather than evidence of a corporate debt.

Shareholder withdrawals that were called loans have been taxed as dividends when the facts showed they were really distributions of profits. Some of the factors considered were:

LOAN

Withdrawal (1) charged to account of shareholder and carried on books of corporation as accounts receivable; (2) secured by shareholder's note or otherwise and interest paid on it; (3) greater than any dividends shareholder may be entitled to on shares he holds; (4) regarded as an indebtedness by shareholder and reduced by cash payments from time to time.

TAXABLE DIVIDEND

Withdrawal (1) made by sole stockholder or by principal shareholders; (2) not secured and no interest paid by shareholder or charged by corporation; (3) when corporation has a substantial surplus; (4) without any evidence of intention of shareholder to repay.

The Tax Court has held a corporation's interest-free loan to shareholders to be a real loan, not constructive dividends.[5] But the Revenue Service disagrees.[5]

Business deals with shareholders. A taxable dividend resulted from these transactions:

- Bargain sales of securities and other property to shareholders [¶ 1329];
- Release of shareholder's debt to corporation [¶ 1318];
- Corporation's purchase of shareholder's property for more than its value;[6]
- Bargain sales of inventory items to shareholders.[7]

Life insurance proceeds paid to shareholders might give rise to dividends if corporation paid the premiums and held incidents of ownership. See ¶ 1213(d).

¶ 1704 Tax-exempt and specially treated distributions. Some distributions are fully or partly tax-exempt; others are specially treated. Dividends paid to policyholders by mutual life insurance companies and certain other insurance companies are exempt, unless paid after an annuity starting date. Dividends paid to the shareholders of these insurance companies are taxable (¶ 1216) [Sec. 316(b); 1.34-3, 1.316-1].

NOTE: For tax years starting after 6-30-72, corporations can no longer make tax-free distributions by using accelerated depreciation in figuring earnings and profits [¶ 1701(b)]. For restrictions on the use of depreciation methods allowable to public utilities, see ¶ 2019.

(a) Dividends from federal agencies on obligations issued after 3-27-42 are fully taxable [Sec. 1.103-2]. Prior dividends are treated as follows:

Wholly exempt. Dividends on obligations issued before 3-28-42 by federal land banks, national farm loan associations and federal reserve banks (but dividends of member banks are treated the same as dividends of ordinary corporations).

Partially exempt. Dividends on share accounts of federal savings and loan associations issued before 3-28-42.

(b) Dividends from tax-exempt earnings. The fact that the earnings of a corporation are exempt from tax does not make a dividend exempt to the shareholders. For example, a dividend received from a corporation is not exempt merely because part or all of the corporate earnings consisted of interest on municipal bonds.

NOTE: Generally, income that is tax-exempt to a trust or partnership *does* retain its exemption when distributed to the beneficiary or partner.

(c) Other common examples of tax-exempt or specially treated distributions include the following: some stock dividends and rights [¶ 1708; 1710; 1714]; dividends paid in corporate liquidations and reorganizations [¶ 1715; 3300; 3316]; dividends paid by Subchapter S corporations [¶ 3140 et seq.] and dividends paid by certain personal holding companies [Sec. 316(b)].

THE DIVIDEND EXCLUSION

Taxable dividends from domestic corporations, if paid to individuals, can usually qualify for an exclusion of up to $100 per person. The principal exceptions deny an exclusion for dividends from certain types of corporations and grant it to nonresident aliens only in certain cases. In lieu of an exclusion, corporate shareholders get their relief from double taxation in the form of a dividends-received deduction.

¶ 1705 Dividends excluded from income. An individual may exclude from gross income the first $100 of most taxable dividends received from domestic corporations during the tax year. The exclusion applies to eligible dividends whether they are paid in stock, other property or cash. However, some distributions and corporations do not qualify for the exclusion (¶ 1706) [Sec. 116(a); 1.116-1].

Example 1: In 1977, Smith, a calendar-year taxpayer, received dividends of $200 each on March 1, June 1, September 1 and December 1. He may exclude $100 of the dividend received on March 1. The $700 balance of the dividends is included in gross income.

Background and purpose. The main purpose of the dividend exclusion is to eliminate the double taxation of corporate earnings that are the source of the taxpayer's first $100 of dividend income. Otherwise, all corporate earnings are taxed once as corporate income and again as dividend income when received by shareholders. Another purpose is to encourage investment in corporations by individuals with relatively low incomes.

Nonresident aliens get the exclusion only for dividends effectively connected with a U.S. trade or business. However, if they are taxed as expatriates, they may exclude qualified dividends from their other taxable U.S. source income (¶ 3709(c); 3711) [Sec. 116(d)].

(a) Joint returns. The husband and wife are treated as separate individuals and compute their exclusions separately. Thus, if each receives $100 or more of eligible dividends, each may exclude the first $100 received if they file separate returns, or a total of $200 on a joint return. However, neither may use any part of the other's exclusion.

Example 2: Assume Smith in Example 1 files a joint return with his wife who also received $70 of dividends in 1977. The exclusion on the joint return is $170. Although Smith and his wife, together, received more than $200 in dividends, the wife received only $70, and her exclusion may not exceed this amount. She may not take an exclusion for any part of her husband's dividends.

➤**OBSERVATION**➤ Smith should consider a gift of some stock to his wife to take full advantage of each exclusion. But see ¶ 4001 et seq. for possible gift tax consequences. Smith should take the tax into account in deciding what to do.

(b) Jointly owned stock. If stock is owned jointly, in common, or by the entirety, each co-owner must first determine his share of any dividends on the stock before he can compute his exclusion. For this purpose, his interest in the dividend is determined under local law. If the stock is community property, the dividend is treated as received one-half by each spouse.

Example 3: Frank and his sister, Marie, are equal joint owners of Dektar Corp. stock. The stock pays an annual dividend of $220. For the tax year 1977, each can exclude $100 because, as joint owners, each one is entitled to $110 (one-half) of the annual dividend. If dividend were $100, each would exclude $50.

Example 4: Frank Bolder and his wife are equal joint owners of stock that pays an annual dividend of $130. Frank also gets a $70 annual dividend from stock he owns individually. For the tax year 1977, Frank can exclude $100 and his wife can exclude $65. On a joint return, the total exclusion is $165.

¶ 1706 When exclusion is not allowed. The exclusion does not apply to dividends from certain types of corporations, or to certain distributions.

(a) Dividends that do not qualify. Dividends from the following do not qualify for the exclusion [Sec. 116(a), (b); 1.116-1]:

- Foreign corporations.
- Exempt corporations (religious, charitable, educational, etc.).
- Exempt farmers' cooperative associations.
- Corporations deriving 80% or more of their income from U.S. possessions and 50% or more from business activity there.
- Real estate investment trusts.
- China Trade Act corporations (however, for tax years starting after 1977, such corporations will no longer exist).

Banks and savings and loan associations. Dividends (commonly referred to as interest) from mutual savings banks, cooperative banks, domestic building and loan associations, domestic savings and loan associations, and Federal savings and loan associations, on deposits or withdrawable accounts do not qualify. These dividends are reported as interest. Dividends on the permanent nonwithdrawable stock of savings and loan associations do qualify for the exclusion [Sec. 1.116-1].

Patronage dividends. Patronage dividends paid by farm cooperatives do not qualify for the exclusion (¶ 3458) [Sec. 1.116-1].

Mutual funds dividends. Dividends from regulated investment companies are subject to a special rule. The part that is a capital gain dividend does not qualify for the exclusion; the part representing dividends from income qualifies, with certain limits. The company usually notifies shareholders of the qualified and nonqualified portions [Sec. 1.116-1]. See also ¶ 3431(c).

Corporate distributions. Certain liquidating distributions and certain stock redemptions do not qualify [¶ 1715 et seq.; 1718 et seq.]. Distributions from corporations electing to be treated as partnerships (Subchapter S corporations) do not get the exclusion, unless paid out of earnings and profits of prior years on which the corporation was taxed [¶ 3140 et seq.].

(b) Short sales of stock. The borrower of stock used to cover a short sale has to pay the lender an amount equal to any cash dividends paid while the stock is on loan. The lender may not exclude any part of this amount; it is not a dividend.[1]

STOCK DIVIDENDS

Under the general rule, as stated in the Code, stock dividends are nontaxable unless they come within a specific exception. The exceptions are so broad that shareholders should closely examine any distribution beyond a common stock dividend on common stock to determine its tax status under the exceptions.

¶ 1707 What is a stock dividend. A stock dividend is a distribution by a corporation to its shareholders in its *own* stock. A corporation might decide to issue stock dividends, for example, if it needed its cash for other purposes.

(a) Other definitions. "Stock," as used in this area, includes stock rights. "Shareholder," for purposes of (b) and (c) below, includes a holder of rights or convertible securities.

(b) How stock dividends are taxed. Stock dividends are nontaxable unless they come within a specific exception.

Stock dividends can be used either to split a shareholder's interest into more parts or to alter that interest. Ordinarily, a dividend of the first type is nontaxable. There would be no tax, for example, if a corporation with only common stock outstanding issued additional common as a dividend. But the shareholder should closely examine any other dividend to determine its status under the exceptions below [Sec. 305; 1.305-1—1.305-7].

Background and purpose. Stock dividends are generally nontaxable so that equity interests in a corporation may be distributed to the greatest extent possible. The reasoning behind the provision is that as long as a shareholder's rights in the corporation remain subject to the same risks, the investment is not separate but is a continuing one, presenting no occasion for the imposition of tax. To understand the exceptions listed below, it is necessary to understand their purpose. Each of

Footnotes appear at end of this Chapter.

the exceptions is aimed at a sophisticated technique developed under prior law. Under these techniques, a shareholder who did not want cash could receive an increased stock interest with much the same effect as if he had received cash and reinvested it in the corporation.

Exceptions. The 1969 Tax Reform Act broadened the prior exceptions to outlaw these techniques. The general rule of nontaxability does not apply, and the stock dividend is considered taxable, if:

(1) *Any* shareholder can *elect* to take cash or other property, in lieu of the stock [Sec. 1.305-2].

(2) The result of the distribution (or a series of distributions) is disproportionate (some shareholders get cash or other property; the others have an increase in their proportionate interests). However, the distribution is nontaxable in certain cases where the cash or other property is received more than 36 months before or after the stock distribution. In determining whether a distribution is disproportionate, convertible bonds and stock rights are treated as stock [Sec. 1.305-3(b)].

Example 1: Corporation has 2 classes of common, A and B, having equal rights, except that A pays only cash dividends and B only equivalent stock dividends. Since the stock dividend increases the B shareholders' proportionate interest, it is taxable.

Example 2: X Corporation has outstanding class A common and class B nonconvertible preferred. If dividends are declared, payable in additional shares of class A on the common and cash on the preferred, the distribution of stock is nontaxable because there is no increase in the class A shareholders' proportionate interest. However, taxability results if the dividend on class A is payable in class B stock.

Example 3: P. Y. Corporation has outstanding common stock and convertible debentures. It pays cash interest on the debentures and distributes a stock dividend on the common stock. The stock dividend and interest payment are taxable since the shareholders' equity increases and the corporation is considered to have 2 classes of outstanding stock, the debentures here being treated as stock.

NOTE: The distribution of cash for fractional shares in connection with a stock dividend would not make the stock distribution taxable as a dividend. Cash of 5% or less of the stock's fair market value is considered in lieu of fractional shares. In Example 3, above, the stock dividend, as well as the interest payment, is treated as a distribution of property (¶ 1709) [Sec. 1.305-3].

(3) The result of the distribution (or a series of distributions) is the receipt of preferred stock by some common shareholders, and of common stock by other common shareholders [Sec. 1.305-4].

(4) The distribution is *on* preferred stock, except in the case of an increase in conversion ratio solely to reflect a stock dividend or split (otherwise, the conversion privilege might be diluted). "Conversion ratio" is defined in (c) below [Sec. 1.305-5].

(5) There is a distribution of convertible preferred, except where its effect is not disproportionate under (2) above [Sec. 1.305-6].

Example 4: N. T. Corporation distributes convertible preferred on common, the only prior outstanding issue. The conversion period is 4 months only. Since those who wish to increase investment will convert and those who wish cash will sell, it is likely that the result will be a disproportionate distribution. So the distribution is taxable. But suppose the conversion period is long, say 20 years. It is likely that by the end of the conversion period substantially all the preferred would be converted. So the distribution would not be disproportionate and is not taxable.

NOTE: The rules under the 1969 Tax Reform Act generally apply to distributions after 1-10-69 with exceptions. Subject to transitional rules, the rule in (2) may not apply until 1991 as to distributions on stock outstanding on 1-10-69 or issued later under a contract binding on that date. In addition, the rule in (4) does not apply until 1991 if the stock is issued under terms in effect on 1-10-69 [Sec. 1.305-8].

(c) Transactions treated as distributions. Transactions which increase the shareholders' proportionate interest through a redemption, change in conversion ratio, recapitalization, change in redemption price and the like, are treated as taxable distributions. An actual distribution of stock is not required [Sec. 305(c); 1.305-7].

> **NOTE:** "Conversion ratio" is best defined by an example. Suppose that each share of a corporation's Class B stock is convertible into 1.05 shares of its Class A stock. The conversion ratio is 1.05 to 1. Any change in this ratio could result in a taxable distribution as to any shareholder whose proportionate interest in the corporation was increased by such change.

¶ 1708 Effect of nontaxable stock distributions. The distribution has no effect on the shareholder's income in the year received, unless the stock is sold or exchanged. But the distribution does raise two problems: the basis of the old and new stock, and the holding period of the new.

(a) Basis of old and new stock. The basis of the stock depends on whether the old and new stock is identical.

When old and new stock identical. Examples include stock splits[1] and dividends of common on common. To find the basis of each share (old and new), divide the basis of the old stock by the total number of old and new shares [Sec. 307(a); 1.307-1].

> **Example 1:** Harrison owned 100 shares of Haron Corporation common stock bought in 1975 for $12,000 ($120 a share). In 1977, Haron Corporation declared a 50% stock dividend and Harrison received 50 new common shares. After the stock dividend, the basis of each share is $80 ($12,000 ÷ 150).

If the old stock is bought at different times and prices, basis is found by allocating to each lot of the old stock the proportionate amount of dividend stock attributable to it.[2] This could raise an identification problem [¶ 1521 et seq.].

Old and new stock not identical. An example would be preferred on common. The basis of the old stock is allocated to the old and new stock in proportion to their relative market values on the distribution date.

> **Example 2:** Jackson bought 100 shares of Redy Corp. common stock for $12,000. He received a nontaxable stock dividend of 50 shares of Redy preferred stock having a fair market value of $5,000. The value of the old stock when the dividend was received was $15,000. After the stock dividend, the bases of the old and new stock are determined as follows:
>
> | | |
> |---|---:|
> | Basis of 100 shares of old stock | $12,000 |
> | Fair market value of old stock | $15,000 |
> | Fair market value of new stock | 5,000 |
> | Total | $20,000 |
>
> Basis of 100 shares of old stock after dividend: $12,000 × 15,000/20,000 = $9,000
> Basis of 50 shares of new stock after dividend: $12,000 × 5,000/20,000 = $3,000

➤**OBSERVATION**➔ Tables showing the required allocation between old and new stock appear in the P-H Capital Adjustments Service.

(b) Holding period of new stock. The holding period of the new shares starts on the same date as the holding period of the old [Sec. 1223(5); 1.1223-1].

Footnotes appear at end of this Chapter.

Example 3: Assume the same facts as in Example 1, except that 4 months after receipt of the stock dividend, Harrison sold the 50 new shares for $4,800. Since the date basis of the new shares is 1975, his holding period is more than 9 months. He realizes a long-term capital gain of $800, figured as follows:

Selling price	$4,800
Basis (50 × $80)	4,000
Long-term capital gain	$ 800

¶ 1709 Effect of taxable stock distributions. (a) Amount distributed. A taxable stock distribution is considered a property distribution treated as explained at ¶ 1702. The amount distributed is the fair market value of the stock on the distribution date, except in the case of certain regulated investment company distributions where the shareholder may take cash or stock of equal value (¶ 3431) [Sec. 305(b); 1.305-1(b)].

Example 1: Mutual Growth, Inc., a regulated investment company, declared a dividend of $1 a share on common stock on 1-9-77, payable 2-9-77, in cash or in Mutual Growth stock of equal value determined as of 1-23-77. The election to take stock or cash had to be made by 1-23-77. George Gaines owns 100 shares and elected to take the dividend in stock. He received a taxable dividend of $100. The result is the same if he elected to take cash. (In this case, the result would also be the same if the shareholder was a corporation.)

(b) Basis of stock. The basis of the new stock is its fair market value at the time of receipt. The basis of old stock remains the same [Sec. 301(d)(1); 1.301-1(h)(1)].

(c) Holding period of new stock. The holding eriod begins on the date the stock dividend is received.

Example 2: In 1967, Ken, a calendar year taxpayer, bought 100 shares of Joyce Co. stock for $12,000. Joyce paid a taxable stock dividend on 3-22-77, and Ken received 50 shares having a fair market value of $5,000. He must include the $5,000 in income as a dividend in 1977. On 10-20-77, Ken sold the 100 old shares for $11,000 and the 50 new shares for $5,300. In his return, he will show a long-term capital loss of $1,000 and a short-term capital gain of $300.

Basis of 100 old shares	$12,000
Selling price of 100 old shares	11,000
Long-term capital loss (since the old shares had been held for more than 9 months)	$ 1,000
Selling price of 50 new shares	$ 5,300
Basis of new shares (fair market value when received)	5,000
Short-term capital gain (since the new shares had been held for not more than 9 months—March 22 to Oct. 20)	$ 300

STOCK AND BOND RIGHTS

¶ 1710 Rights in general. (a) Stock rights. A corporation may issue to its shareholders *rights* to subscribe to a new issue of its stock—usually at less than the quoted price. For that reason, the rights have a market value. A shareholder may sell his rights, exercise them, or let them expire.

The rules for determining whether a stockright is taxed to its recipient are the same as those for stock dividends (¶ 1707(b)) [Sec. 305(d); 1.305-1].

(b) Bond rights. These are discussed at ¶ 1714.

¶ 1711 Effect of nontaxable stock rights. The rights have no effect on the shareholder's income in the year received. It is necessary, however, to determine the basis of the stock and rights and the holding period of the rights.

(a) Basis of stock and rights. The basis of the rights is zero if their market value when distributed is less than 15% of the stock's value at that time, unless the shareholder elects to allocate part of his stock basis to the rights. If the value is 15% or more, a basis *must* be allocated to the rights, but only if the rights are exercised or sold [Sec. 307(b)(1), (2); 1.307-1, 1.307-2].

How to allocate basis. The taxpayer's stock basis is allocated between the stock and rights in proportion to their relative market values on the *distribution* date [Sec. 1.307-1].

Example 1: On 6-1-77, Hanson bought 100 shares of Carr Corp. stock at $100 per share. On 7-1-77, he received 100 rights entitling him to subscribe to an additional 100 shares at $95 per share. On the day the rights were issued, the fair market value of the stock was $110 a share and that of the rights at $15 each. The basis of the rights and the common stock to determine the gain or loss on a later sale is computed as follows, if the election is made:

Original cost of stock (100 × $100)	$10,000
Value of old stock when rights issued (100 × $110)	$11,000
Value of rights when issued (100 × $15)	1,500
Value of both old stock and rights when rights issued	$12,500
Basis of old stock after rights issued ($11,000/$12,500 × $10,000)	$ 8,800
Basis of rights ($1,500/$12,500 × $10,000)	$ 1,200
Basis of one share of old stock after rights issued ($8,800 ÷ 100)	$ 88
Basis of one right ($1,200 ÷ 100)	$ 12

If the rights are *sold,* the basis for determining gain or loss will be $12 per right. If the rights are *exercised,* the basis of the new stock acquired will be the subscription price paid for it ($95) plus the basis of the rights exercised ($12). In both cases, the basis of the old stock will be set at $88 per share.

➤OBSERVATION➤ If an allocation is not required and the taxpayer is eligible to elect, such an election provides no tax benefit unless a sale of the rights is being considered.

NOTE: In Example 1, Hanson could either assign a zero basis to the rights or allocate the cost of the original stock between that stock and the new right. Assume Hanson sold his rights for $15 each. If his other capital transactions for the year result in a net long-term capital *gain,* he would probably want to keep his gain on the sale of the rights to a minimum by electing to allocate basis. Thus, his gain would be $3 per right instead of $15 and the basis of his old stock would change from $100 to $88 per share. This is also an effective way to convert a short-term gain that would arise on the sale of the rights, into a long-term gain on the sale of the old stock. If his other capital transactions for the year result in a net *loss,* he would probably want to elect a zero basis to offset as much of the loss as possible. Thus his gain would be $15 per right instead of $3, and the basis of his old stock would remain at $100 per share.

(b) The election to allocate. The election in (a) above applies to all rights received in any one distribution on the same class of stock owned when the rights were distributed. The election is made in a statement attached to the return for the year the rights were received and is irrevocable. Shareholders should keep a copy of the election and tax return to support the allocated basis when they sell the new stock [Sec. 1.307-2].

(c) Holding period of stock and rights. If the rights are sold, their holding period runs from the date the stock was acquired. If the rights are exercised, the holding period of the new stock starts on the date of exercise [Sec. 1223(5), (6); 1.1223-1].

Footnotes appear at end of this Chapter.

Example 2: On 6-5-67, Arnold Rice bought 100 shares of Delphi Corporation stock. On 7-1-77, he received 100 nontaxable rights entitling him to subscribe to 25 additional shares at $120 a share. Assume the basis of each right is $4. He sold 60 of the rights on 7-12-77 for $6 each. Rice has a long-term capital gain of $120 ($360 sales price less $240 basis), since the rights were held for more than 9 months—6-5-67 to 7-12-77.

Example 3: Assume that Arnold Rice of Example 2 exercised the remaining 40 rights on 7-12-77. He turned in the 40 rights with $1,200 for 10 new shares. On 11-3-77, he sold the new shares for $1,500. He has a short-term capital gain of $140, figured as follows:

Selling price	$1,500
Basis of 10 new shares ($160 + $1,200)	1,360
Short-term capital gain (since date basis is 7-12-77)	$ 140

¶ **1712 Taxable stock rights.** A distribution of taxable stock rights is considered a property distribution treated as explained at ¶ 1702. The amount distributed, or the basis of the rights, is generally the fair market value of the rights on the distribution date, whether the shareholder is an individual or a corporation. If the rights are exercised, the basis of the new shares is the basis of the rights plus the subscription price. The basis of the old stock remains the same [Sec. 305(b), (d)(1); 1.305-1(b)].

NOTE: There is no clear express rule in the Code or Regulations as to when you must report a taxable stock right. The taxable event under current rules seems to take place when you receive the rights.[1]

Holding period of stock and rights. If taxable rights are exercised, the date basis of the new shares is the date the rights were exercised. The date basis of the old shares remains unchanged [Sec. 1223(6); 1.1223-1].

Example: Charles Kane bought 100 shares of Derby Corp. common stock on 5-1-67. On 6-1-77, he received 100 taxable rights to subscribe to 50 new shares. He exercised the rights on 6-8-77. The date basis of the new shares is 6-8-77. The date basis of the old shares is 5-1-67.

¶ **1714 Rights to bonds. (a) Nontaxable bond rights.** Rights to subscribe to bonds are treated in a manner similar to nontaxable stock rights if (1) the bonds are convertible into stock that, if distributed, would not result in a taxable dividend, and (2) the value of the rights arises from the conversion privilege. The basis of the original stock is allocated between the stock and the rights in proportion to their relative market values. The computation is similar to that used in ¶ 1711, Example 1. The basis of the bonds is the basis of the rights plus the subscription price. If the bonds are converted into stock, the basis of such stock is the basis of the bonds plus any consideration paid at the time of the conversion.[1]

(b) Taxable bond rights. If the bonds are not convertible into stock, the rights are property dividends.[2] The basis of the shares remains unchanged, and the basis of the bonds is determined as if they were new stock [¶ 1702; 1712].

LIQUIDATING DIVIDENDS

A corporation generally liquidates by redeeming its stock for cash, property, or both. A distribution of this kind is known as a "liquidating dividend." The material below relates to the tax effect of either a complete or partial liquidation at the shareholder level. If certain requirements are met, the transaction is treated as though the shareholder had sold his stock to the corporation (he usually gets capital gain or loss). The tax effect of the liquidation at the corporate level is discussed at ¶ 3128.

¶ **1715 What is a liquidating dividend.** A corporation may liquidate by redeeming its stock for cash, or by exchanging its assets for the stock. We call this a liquidating dividend. In some cases, the liquidation is only partial, rather than complete.

¶ **1716 What is a partial liquidation.** There are three types, each of which can qualify for favorable tax treatment [Sec. 346; 1.346-1]:

(1) A distribution that is one of a series in a planned redemption of all the corporation's stock.

(2) A distribution in a planned redemption of part of the stock, if it is not essentially equivalent to a dividend and if it is made in the year the plan is adopted, or the year after.

> **Example 1:** In 1977, Tara Corp. adopted a plan to redeem all its preferred stock, leaving only the common outstanding. In 1978, the taxpayer, who had bought 100 shares of Tara preferred in 1969, received a final liquidating dividend. The distribution qualifies as a partial liquidation.

A genuine contraction of the corporation's business is usually involved in this type of partial liquidation.

(3) A distribution that terminates one of the businesses of the distributing corporation, if:

(a) The terminated business was actively conducted (whether or not by the present corporation) during the 5 years before the distribution, and was not acquired in a gain or loss transaction, *and*

(b) The distributing corporation continues the active conduct of its other business or businesses immediately after the distribution.

> **Example 2:** In 1969, Audio Corp. was organized and began the manufacture of electronic equipment and household appliances in separate plants. It actively conducted both businesses until late 1977, when it sold the household appliance business and distributed the proceeds. The recipient shareholders can treat the distributions as received in a partial liquidation.

Working capital attributable to the discontinued business can be added to the proceeds from the sale of assets and included in the distribution.[1]

¶ **1717 How liquidating dividends are treated.** The amount received in a partial or complete liquidation is treated as the proceeds from the sale of the redeemed stock by the shareholder. In computing the amount received, any property received is taken into account at its fair market value [Sec. 331(a); 1.331-1].

(a) **Amount and character of gain or loss.** The amount of gain or loss is the difference between the cost or other basis of the redeemed stock and the amount received in liquidation.

> **Example 1:** In 1969, Barnett bought 100 shares of Rocket Corp. stock for $10,000. In 1977, the Corp. dissolved and Barnett received a final liquidating dividend of $4,000. His recognized loss is $6,000.

> **Example 2:** In 1969, Dickens bought 100 shares of Storm Corp. stock for $10,000. In 1977, the Corp. dissolved and Dickens received a final liquidating dividend of $12,000. His recognized gain is $2,000.

> **Example 3:** John Karen bought 100 shares of Wire Reel Corp. preferred stock in 1975 for $15,000. In 1977, Wire Reel Corp. adopted a plan to redeem all its preferred stock, but none of its common stock. In 1978, Karen received a final liquidating dividend of $12,000. His recognized loss is $3,000.

Footnotes appear at end of this Chapter.

Since the stock is usually a capital asset, the shareholder will have capital gain or loss, unless the special rule below applies. The gain or loss will be short-term or long-term, depending on how long the stock was held. If the shares were acquired at different times and prices, the gain or loss is computed separately on each block for a single distribution.[1] The distribution is allocated among the various blocks in the same proportion that the number of shares in each block bears to the total number of shares outstanding[2] [Sec. 1.331-1(e)].

Example 4: In 1973, Able bought 40% of the 200 shares outstanding of the Black Corporation for $800. He acquired the remaining 60% of Black stock in 1974 for $3,600. In 1977, Able receives a final liquidating dividend of $10,000 from the Black Corporation. Able has $3,200 in long-term capital gain on the stock bought in 1973 [(40% × $10,000) − $800] and $2,400 in long-term gain on the stock acquired in 1974 [(60% × $10,000) − $3,600].

Example 5: Assume the same facts as in Example 4 except that $5,000 in liquidating dividends are distributed in December, 1976, and $5,000 in January, 1977. In 1976, Able has $1,200 in long-term capital gain on the stock bought in 1973 [$2,000 ($5,000 × 40%) less $800 basis] but has no gain recognized on the second block because he has not recovered his adjusted basis [$3,000 ($5,000 × 60%) and $3,600 basis]. In 1977, Able has $2,000 in long-term capital gain on the first block since the entire basis of that stock has been recovered. Long-term gain of $2,400 is recognized on the second block since $600 of the $3,000 prorated distribution represents recovery of basis.

Shareholders who report capital gain on a liquidating dividend are sometimes called on as transferees to pay the corporation's tax deficiencies. These payments are treated as capital losses.[3]

Special rule for certain distributions. A liquidating dividend may give rise to ordinary income if paid by a collapsible corporation, or if the dividend includes undistributed personal holding company income [¶ 1627; 3404].

A corporation may have ordinary income if it distributes property subject to recapture under Secs. 1245, 1250, 1251, 1252 or 1254 [¶ 1619; 1845(c); 2103(c); 2226].

If a liquidation is followed or preceded by a transfer to another corporation of all or part of the liquidating corporation's assets, the liquidating distribution may give rise to an ordinary dividend (taxable as ordinary income), or as a transaction in which no loss is recognized and gain is recognized only to the extent of other property received (see ¶ 3319) [Sec. 1.331-1(c)].

(b) Reporting gain or loss. When liquidating dividends are distributed in installments, gain need not be reported until the cost or other basis of the stock is recovered[4] (see Example 5). Ordinarily, loss through liquidation is deductible in the year the final distribution is made. However, when a corporation distributes all of its assets, except a small amount of cash reserved for expenses of dissolution, there is in practical effect a final distribution. Loss to a shareholder may be taken in that year, instead of being postponed until a later year when the remaining cash is distributed.[5]

Information filed with return. A shareholder who transfers stock to the issuing corporation in exchange for property should report all the facts and circumstances on his return, unless the dividend is paid under a corporate resolution reciting that it is made in liquidation of the corporation, and the corporation is completely liquidated and dissolved within one year after the distribution. The distributing corporation must file Form 966 within 30 days after adopting the plan of liquidation, but liquidating distributions will be treated as such whether or not the corporation filed Form 966[6] (¶ 3128(b)) [Sec. 1.331-1(d)].

STOCK REDEMPTIONS

Chapter 7—Dividends

A redemption occurs when a corporation acquires its stock from a shareholder for money or other property, whether or not the stock is cancelled, retired, or held as treasury stock. The principal problem here is how to distinguish between a true redemption (capital gain), and a disguised dividend (ordinary income). Some redemptions are subject to special rules aimed, for the most part, at preventing tax avoidance.

¶ **1718 Stock redemptions in general.** Usually, when stock is redeemed, the transaction is treated as if the shareholder sold his stock to the corporation. The shareholder pays only a capital gains tax on any gain. However, what looks like a redemption is sometimes a disguised dividend (taxable as ordinary income). It is therefore necessary to distinguish between them. This is done by applying the rules below.

(a) Sale and dividend distinguished. A redemption is treated as a sale if it meets *any* of the following conditions:

- It is *not* essentially equivalent to a dividend under the rules in (b) below [Sec. 302(b)(1)], or

NOTE: In determining whether a redemption is not equivalent to a dividend, the fact that it fails to meet the other conditions is not considered.

- It meets the "substantially disproportionate" (or 80%) test in (c) below *and* leaves the shareholder with less then 50% of the total voting power after redemption, or
- The corporation redeems all the shareholder's stock in the corporation [Sec. 302(b)(3); 1.302-4]. See ¶ 1719.
- A fourth condition relates to stock of certain railroads and affects few taxpayers [Sec. 302(b)(4)].

(b) Is redemption essentially equivalent to a dividend? It is (and is taxed as a dividend) if it meets a "net effects" test. It meets the test if all the circumstances show that, as a practical matter, the shareholder's relationship to the corporation did not really change.[1] If the test is met, the mere presence of a business purpose for the redemption will not change the result.[2]

Ordinarily, a dividend results if there is a prorata redemption of the only class of stock outstanding, or a redemption of one class of stock (except Sec. 306 stock) when all the other classes are held in the same proportion.

(c) Is redemption substantially disproportionate? It is if it meets an 80% test. First, figure what percentage of the corporation's *voting stock* the shareholder owned before and after the redemption. Then figure what percentage of the corporation's *common stock* (voting and nonvoting) he owned before and after (if there is more than one class of common, the percentage is determined by using market values). Under the 80% test (which applies to the *voting stock*, as well as the *common stock*[3]), the percentage after the redemption must be less than 80% of the percentage before. An option to acquire treasury or unissued stock must be included in applying the 80% test (¶ 1727(e)) [Proposed reg. Sec. 1.302-3(a)]. If the 80% test and the 50% test in (a) above are met, the redemption qualifies as a sale, with one exception. If the redemption is one of a series in total redemption, the total redemption must also meet the 80% test [Sec. 302(b); 1.302-3].

Example: Arko, Inc. has 400 shares of common stock outstanding. Arlen, Branch, Cole and Darby each own 100 shares, or 25%. Arko redeems 55 shares from Arlen, 25 shares from Branch, and 20 shares from Cole. The redemption will be disproportionate as to any shareholder

Footnotes appear at end of this Chapter.

owning less than 20% after the redemption (80% of 25%). After the redemptions, Arlen owns 45 shares (15%), Branch owns 75 shares (25%), and Cole owns 80 shares (26⅔%). Only the redemption of Arlen's shares is disproportionate.

(d) Was all the shareholder's stock redeemed? This looks like an easy question to answer, but the rules are complex and, for that reason, are discussed separately [¶ 1719].

(e) Stock ownership. In applying the above tests, the shareholder must take into account stock attributed to him although it actually belongs to others. The attribution rules are explained at ¶ 1727. They apply here except as otherwise noted in ¶ 1719.

(f) Other rules. A formal retirement of the redeemed stock is not required. The corporation may continue to hold it as treasury stock.

Special rules apply to redemptions from a controlled corporation; redemptions to pay death taxes; redemption of Sec. 306 stock, and liquidating dividends [¶ 1715-1717; 1720-1722].

≫OBSERVATION→ If a redemption is treated as a dividend, taxpayer should adjust the basis of his remaining shares. Suppose, for example, that taxpayer owns 100 shares of stock with a basis of $5,000 and redeems 20 of the shares. If the redemption is treated as a dividend, taxpayer should add the basis of the 20 redeemed shares to the 80 remaining shares, giving these 80 shares a basis of $5,000. Otherwise, the basis of the 20 redeemed shares would just disappear.

¶ 1719 Complete redemption of taxpayer's stock. A complete redemption of taxpayer's stock qualifies for capital gains treatment if, after the redemption, he owns no stock in the corporation, either actually or constructively. In determining his constructive ownership, the constructive ownership rules in ¶ 1727 apply, with one exception. The exception prevents application of the family attribution rules, if the conditions in (a) below apply and if there are no prior transfers of the kind described in (b).

(a) When constructive ownership rules do not apply. The rules for attribution between family members do not apply if [Sec. 302(c)(2); 1.302-4]:

• Immediately after the redemption, taxpayer had no interest in the corporation other than as a creditor (he cannot even be an officer,[1] director or employee);

• Taxpayer does not re-acquire an interest (other than by bequest or inheritance) within 10 years from the redemption date. If he acquires such interest, an additional tax, at dividend rates, is assessed for the redemption year (the statute of limitations is automatically extended);

NOTE: The 10-year ban on re-acquisition of an interest in the corporation does not apply if complete redemption of shareholder's stock was not essentially equivalent to a dividend, was substantially disproportionate, or the stock was issued in a railroad Bankruptcy Act reorganization.

• Taxpayer files an agreement: (1) to notify IRS within 30 days if he acquires such interest and (2) to keep copies of his return and other records showing the tax that would have been payable if the redemption had been a dividend. The agreement is filed with his return.

Example 1: Husband and wife each own 50% of the stock of a corporation. All the husband's stock is redeemed, and husband meets the above conditions. The husband is entitled to treat this as a sale of his stock, because the family constructive ownership rules do not apply. If they did apply, he would still constructively own his wife's shares, and the redemption would not be complete.

(b) Prior stock transfers to avoid tax. The family attribution rules *do* apply under either of the following two conditions, but only if tax avoidance was a principal purpose [Sec. 302(c)(2)(B)].

• If taxpayer acquired any part of the redeemed stock, directly or indirectly, within the previous 10 years from a person whose stock would have been attributed to taxpayer at the time of redemption.

Example 2: Solely to reduce taxes, the only shareholder of a corporation gives half of the stock to his son. Five years later, there is a complete redemption of all of his son's shares. The rules relating to constructive ownership between members of a family apply.

• If, at the time of redemption, any person owned stock that would be attributed to taxpayer, and he acquired *any* stock in the corporation from the taxpayer, directly or indirectly, within the previous 10 years (unless this stock is also redeemed).

Example 3: If, in Example 2, the father's shares were redeemed and the father otherwise terminated his interest in the corporation, rules relating to constructive ownership between members of family would apply.

NOTE: These rules do not apply to distributions in liquidation [Sec. 1.302-1].

¶ **1720 Redemption through use of a related corporation.** Under prior law, taxpayers sometimes sold their stock in one corporation to another "related" corporation. This gave them the benefits of a redemption in certain cases where they could not otherwise qualify for those benefits [¶ 1718]. This is no longer possible because of the special rules below.

(a) Sale to related corporation (other than a subsidiary). If one or more persons control two corporations (the so-called brother-sister situation) and sell the stock of one to the other, the transaction is treated as a redemption of the *purchasing* corporation's stock. If a direct redemption by the *issuing* corporation would result in a dividend [¶ 1718], the dividend portion (the amount covered by the *purchasing* corporation's earnings and profits) is taxed as such and reduces the corporation's earnings and profits [Sec. 304(b)(2)(A), 312(e); 1.312-5].

Effect on basis. The purchasing corporation's basis for the stock is the same as the shareholder's basis, plus any recognized gain [Sec. 304(a)(1); 1.304-2].

If the amount received is a dividend, the basis of the shareholder's stock in the purchasing corporation is increased by his basis for the redeemed stock. If the amount received is from a sale, the basis of his stock in the purchasing corporation remains the same [Sec. 1.304-2].

(b) Sale to subsidiary. If a shareholder sells stock in one corporation to another corporation controlled by the first (the so-called parent-sub situation), the transaction is treated as though the sub distributed the purchase price to the parent, which then redeemed its own stock from the shareholder [Sec. 304(a)(2); 1.304-3]. Assuming dividend treatment under the rules in ¶ 1718, the dividend portion is the amount covered by the *parent's* earnings and profits.

(c) What is control. Control means ownership of 50% or more of the voting power or 50% or more of the total value of all classes of stock. In one case where a transaction was covered by both Sec. 304 and 351, the Sixth Circuit held that Sec. 351 took precedence[1] [¶ 1405].

Example: Arnold Baker owns control of Arba Corp. Arba Corp. owns 52% of the voting power of Baar Corp. Baker is considered to control Baar Corp.

(d) Constructive ownership. The rules in ¶ 1727 apply in determining control, except that the corporate attribution rules are applied without the 50% limitation [Sec. 304(c)(2); 1.304-2].

¶ 1721 Stock redeemed to pay death taxes. (a) Special relief. When a shareholder dies, it may be necessary to redeem some of his stock to pay death taxes. This is a disadvantage if the redemption would result in a dividend. However, relief is granted and the proceeds will qualify for capital gain or loss treatment, if all these 4 conditions are met [Sec. 303; 1.303-1—1.303-3]:

- The value of the stock is included in decedent's gross estate for estate tax purposes [see (b) below].
- The stock is redeemed after death and within 3 years and 90 days after the filing of the estate tax return; or, if a petition was filed with the Tax Court, within 60 days after its decision becomes final; or, if death occurs after 1976 and deferred payment of estate taxes is elected, within the time permitted for the estate tax installments in a closely held business interest [3944(a)].
- The stock is redeemed for an amount not more than the estate and inheritance taxes (including interest), plus the funeral and administration expenses allowable as deductions to the estate; there is no requirement that the proceeds be needed to pay these items or that they be used to pay them. However, any excess over the allowable amount is a dividend. For decedents dying after 1976, the 1976 Tax Reform Act limits qualifying redemptions to those from shareholders whose interest in the estate is reduced (directly or through a binding obligation to contribute) by the payment of death taxes and funeral and administrative expenses and only to the extent of this reduction. Special rules also limit the amount of qualifying redemption distributions made over 4 years after the death.
- The value of the stock, for decedents dying after 1976, must exceed 50% of the value of the adjusted gross estate (gross estate less deductions for administration expenses, debts, taxes and losses) and, for decedents dying before 1977, must exceed 35% of decedent's gross estate, or more than 50% of the decedent's taxable estate. For this purpose, the stock of 2 or more corporations may be treated as stock of a single corporation if more than 75% of the stock of each *directly*[1] owned by the decedent is included in his estate. For purposes of the 75% rule, stock is treated as part of the decedent's estate, if it represents the community property interest of his surviving spouse [Sec. 303(b)].

Example 1: The gross estate of decedent who died in 1976, is valued at $1,000,000; taxable estate is $700,000; sum of death taxes and funeral and administration expenses is $275,000. Included in gross estate is stock, valued as follows:

Corporation A	$200,000
Corporation B	400,000
Corporation C	200,000

The stock of Corporations A and C included in the estate is all of their outstanding stock. If treated as the stock of a single corporation, it has a value of over $350,000 (35% of gross estate or 50% of taxable estate). Likewise, Corporation B's stock has a value of over $350,000. A distribution in redemption by one or more of these corporations of amounts not totaling more than $275,000 would be considered a stock redemption qualifying for capital gain treatment.

Example 2: Adjusted gross estate of decedent who died 1-1-77, is $700,000. Sum of death taxes and funeral and administration expenses is $275,000. Included in gross estate is stock, valued as follows:

Corporation X	$200,000
Corporation Y	400,000
Corporation Z	200,000

Stock of corporations X and Z included in estate is all of their outstanding stock. If treated as stock of a single corporation, it has value of over $350,000 (50% of adjusted gross estate). Likewise, Corporations Y's stock has value of over $350,000. Distribution in redemption of stock X and Z, or stock Y, in amounts not totaling more than $275,000 can be considered distribution in payment for stock.

(b) **What stock qualifies.** The stock need not be owned by decedent at death, nor does it have to be redeemed from his estate, *as long as its value is includible in the estate.* Examples of this could include stock the estate distributed before the redemption. However, stock redeemed from a purchaser for value does not qualify even though it was part of the decedent's estate.

Stock received after death can qualify if its basis is determined by reference to qualified stock included in the estate. An example would be a nontaxable stock dividend paid to the estate after decedent's death.

¶ **1722 The "preferred stock bail-out." (a) Sale of stock.** The amount realized is ordinary income up to the stock's ratable share of the earnings at the time of issuance. If the amount realized exceeds the stock's ratable share of the corporation's earnings and profits, the excess, to the extent of gain, is treated as capital gain. However, no loss is recognized [Sec. 306(a)(1); 1.306-1].

Background and purpose. It was once possible to withdraw earnings from a corporation without paying a dividend tax. The corporation would pay a nontaxable dividend in preferred stock. The shareholder could then redeem the stock or sell it. In either case, the shareholder got capital gain treatment,[1] although the effect was the same as a taxable dividend. This is no longer possible because of the rules that now apply. The term "Sec. 306 stock" is used for this stock, and it can include rights, and common stock that is reclassified in a recapitalization proceeding.[2]

(b) **Redemption of stock.** The general dividend rules apply in determining the tax status of the proceeds [¶ 1700]. The portion that is covered by corporate earnings and profits at the time of the redemption is a dividend and is taxed as ordinary income [Sec. 306(a)(2); 1.306-1].

(c) **Exceptions.** The bail-out rules do not apply if [Sec. 306(b); 1.306-2]:

• The shareholder completely terminates his actual and constructive interest in the corporation.
• The redemption is in complete or partial liquidation.
• The taxpayer proves a principal purpose was not tax avoidance.
• The transaction is one in which gain or loss is not recognized.

¶ **1727 Constructive ownership of stock.** The tax consequences of some transactions depend on how much stock taxpayer owns in a particular corporation. In these cases, taxpayer is deemed to own not only his own stock, but also stock belonging to others that is treated as his under the "attribution" rules below. In applying these rules, a person is considered the owner of stock whether he owns

Footnotes appear at end of this Chapter.

it directly or indirectly, and whether it is owned by or for him [Sec. 318; 1.318-1—1.318-4].

The general attribution rules below apply to stock redemptions [¶ 1718-1720]; preferred stock bail-outs [¶ 1722]; liquidation of subsidiaries [¶ 3334] and net operating loss carryovers [¶ 3221; 3338]. Special rules apply to sales between corporations and shareholders [¶ 2223(d)]; personal holding companies [¶ 3402] and in determining whether a corporation comes within a controlled group [¶ 3222].

(a) **Family members.** An individual is considered as owning the stock of his spouse (unless legally separated or divorced), his children and adopted children, his grandchildren, and parents.

Example 1: An individual, H, owns 20 of the 100 outstanding shares of stock of a corporation. His wife, W, owns 20 shares of such stock. His son, S, owns 20 shares. His grandson, G, owns 20 shares. H is considered to own 80 shares. W and S also are each considered to own 80 shares. But the grandson is considered to own only 40 shares, that is, his own and his father's.

Example 2: Hicks owns no stock of the Ecks Corp. His wife, however, owns 25% and his son owns 26% of the stock. Hicks is constructive owner of 51% of the Ecks Corp. stock.

(b) **Partnerships and estates.** A partnership or estate owns the stock of its partners or beneficiaries. Partners or beneficiaries own proportionately the stock of the partnership or estate [Sec. 318(a)(2), (3); 1.318-2, 1.318-3].

Example 3: John Heeney has a 50% interest in a partnership. The partnership owns 50 of the 100 outstanding shares of stock of a corporation, the remaining 50 shares being owned by Heeney. The partnership is considered as owning 100 shares. Heeney is considered as owning 75 shares.

(c) **Trusts.** A trust owns the stock of its beneficiary, unless the beneficiary has only a remote, contingent interest (it is remote if its value cannot exceed 5% of the value of the trust property). Trust beneficiaries own the trust's stock in proportion to their interests in the trust. These trust rules do not apply to exempt employee trusts.

Example 4: A testamentary trust owns 25 of the outstanding 100 shares of stock of a corporation. James Drake, who holds a vested remainder in the trust having a value, determined actuarially equal to 4% of the value of the trust property, owns the remaining 75 shares. Since Drake's interest in the trust is vested rather than contingent (whether or not remote), the trust is considered as owning 100 shares. Drake is considered as owning 76 shares. (75 + 4% of 25).

Grantor-owned trust [¶ 3022]. There is mutual attribution between the trust and any grantor or other person treated as its owner [Sec. 318(a)(2), (3)].

(d) **Corporations.** If any person owns or is deemed to own 50% or more in value of a corporation's stock, he is considered as owning any stock the corporation owns, in the ratio of the value of his stock to the value of all the corporation's stock. The corporation in turn owns his stock in other corporations [Sec. 318(a)(2), (3); 1.318-1, 1.318-2].

Example 5: A and B, unrelated individuals, own 70% and 30% in value of the stock of M Corp. M owns 50 of the 100 outstanding shares of stock of O Corp., the remaining 50 shares being owned by A. M Corp. is considered as owning 100 shares of O Corp., and A is considered as owning 85 shares. (50 + 70% of 50).

(e) **Options.** If a person has an option to acquire stock (or an option to acquire the option), the stock is considered his [Sec. 318(a); 1.318-3]. A warrant or convertible debenture is considered an option if its holder can obtain the stock at his election.[1]

Chapter 7—Dividends

Example 6: A and B, unrelated individuals, own all of the 100 outstanding shares of stock of a corporation, each owning 50 shares. A has an option to acquire 25 of B's shares, and has an option to acquire a further option to acquire the remaining 25 of B's shares. A is considered as owning the entire 100 shares of stock of the corporation.

(f) Constructive ownership as actual ownership. Stock constructively owned by a taxpayer under the above rules is treated as actually owned (it can be reattributed from taxpayer to others).

Example 7: Assume the facts of Example 1. The rules provide that H, W, and S are each considered as owning 80 shares. If the remaining 20 shares are owned by another corporation wholly owned by H, then H, W, and S are all considered to own the stock in fact owned by that corporation.

Exceptions. There are two exceptions to the above rules:
(1) Stock attributed to a partnership, estate, trust or corporation under the rules in (b), (c) or (d) above cannot be reattributed under those rules [Sec. 318(a)(5)(C); 1.318-4];
(2) Stock attributed to an individual under the rules in (a) above cannot be reattributed under those rules [Sec. 1.318-4].

Example 8: Assume the facts of Example 1. Grandson G owns 20 of the outstanding 100 shares. His father, S, owns in fact 20 of such shares, but is considered to own in addition to the stock owned by his parents H and W and his son. But G is not considered to own the stock of H and W.

Overlapping rules. If stock can be attributed to an individual under either the family or option rule, it is attributed under the option rule, and exception (2) above does not apply [Sec. 318(a)(5)(D)].

Footnotes to Chapter 7

(P-H "FEDERAL TAXES" related references are cited in brackets [ ] at the end of each footnote below.)

Footnote ¶ 1700   [¶ 17,011].
(1) Shorb, 22 BTA 644; Foley Securities Corp. v Comm., 106 F.2d 731, 23 AFTR 404 [¶ 17,398(40), (50)].
(2) Detailed treatment of the taxable status of each distribution by individual companies is given in the P-H Capital Adjustments Service.

Footnote ¶ 1701   [¶ 17,031; 17,343].
(1) Rev. Rul. 76-12, 1976-1 CB 91 [¶ 17,371(25)].
(2) Young, 6 TC 357 [¶ 17,398(15)]. P-H Capital Adjustment Service has a cumulative record of the total nontaxable amounts of prior dividends.

Footnote ¶ 1702   [¶ 17,011].
(1) Treas. Dept. booklet "Your Federal Income Tax" (1977 Ed.), p. 39.
(2) Treas. Dept. Publication No. 542 "Corporations and the Federal Income Tax" (1975 Ed.), p. 13.

Footnote ¶ 1703   [17,081—17,093].
(1) Hadley v. Comm., 8 AFTR 9877, 36 F.2d 543 [¶ 17,090(5)].

Footnote ¶ 1703 continued
(2) Peterson & Pegau Baking Co., 2 BTA 637 [¶ 17,085(25)].
(3) Limericks, Inc. v. Comm., 165 F.2d 483, 36 AFTR 649 [¶ 17,085(10)].
(4) Peco Company, ¶ 67,041 P-H Memo TC [¶ 13,096].
(5) Dean, 35 TC 1083; Announcement of Nonacquiescence, 1973-2 CB 4 [¶ 7378(5)].
(6) Comm. v. Pope, 50 AFTR 1240, 239 F.2d 881 [¶ 17,086(10)].
(7) Dellinger, 32 TC 1178 [¶ 17,086(17)].

Footnote ¶ 1704   [¶ 8284].

Footnote ¶ 1705   [¶ 8615].

Footnote ¶ 1706   [¶ 8619; 8620].
(1) Rev. Rul. 60-177, 1960-1 CB 9 [¶ 8620.20(25)].

Footnote ¶ 1707   [¶ 17,201 et seq.].

Footnote ¶ 1708   [¶ 17,216].
(1) Treas. Dept. booklet "Your Federal Income Tax" (1977 Ed.), p. 106.
(2) Rev. Rul. 71-350, 1971-2 CB 176 [¶ 17,315(50)].

¶ 1727

Chapter 7—Footnotes

Footnote ¶ 1709 [¶ 17,216].
Footnote ¶ 1710 [¶ 17,261 et seq.].
Footnote ¶ 1711 [¶ 17,261].
Footnote ¶ 1712 [¶ 17,261 et seq.].
(1) Treas. Dept. booklet "Your Federal Income Tax" (1977 Ed.), p. 106.

Footnote ¶ 1714 [¶ 17,327(5)].
(1) GCM 13275, XIII-2 CB 121 [¶ 17,327(5)].
(2) GCM 13414, XIII-2 CB 124 [¶ 17,272(10)].

Footnote ¶ 1715 [¶ 17,571 et seq.].

Footnote ¶ 1716 [¶ 17,831 et seq.].
(1) Rev. Rul. 60-232, 1960-2 CB 115 [¶ 17,849(25)].

Footnote ¶ 1717 [¶ 17,571 et seq.].
(1) Cooledge, 40 BTA 110 [¶ 17,587(15)].
(2) Rev. Rul. 68-348, 1968-2 CB 141 [¶ 17,587(15)].
(3) Arrowsmith v. Comm., 344 US 6, 73 SCt 71, 42 AFTR 649 [¶ 32,149].
(4) Ludorff, 40 BTA 32 [¶ 17,587(35)].
(5) Comm. v. Winthrop, 98 F.2d 74, 21 AFTR 657 [¶ 17,587(30)].
(6) Rev. Rul. 65-80, 1965-1 CB 154 [¶ 17,583(5)].

Footnote ¶ 1718 [¶ 17,102 et seq.].
(1) Seabrook Sr. v. U.S., 17 AFTR 2d 1041, 253 F. Supp. 652 [¶ 17,118(30)].
(2) U.S. v. Davis, 25 AFTR 2d 70-827, 397 US 301, 91 SCt 1041 [¶ 17,118(25)].
(3) Treas. Dept. booklet "Tax Guide for Small Business" (1977 Ed.), p. 136.

Footnote ¶ 1719 [¶ 17,131].
(1) Rev. Rul. 75-2, 1975-1 CB 99 [¶ 17,133(25)].

Footnote ¶ 1720 [¶ 17,149].
(1) Comm. v. Stickney, 22 AFTR 2d 5502, 399 F.2d 828 [¶ 17,155(20)].

Footnote ¶ 1721 [¶ 17,138].
(1) Byrd v. Comm., 21 AFTR 2d 313, 388 F.2d 223 [¶ 17,145(25)].

Footnote ¶ 1722 [¶ 17,281 et seq.].
(1) Chamberlin v. Comm., 207 F.2d 462, 44 AFTR 494 [¶ 17,299(5)].
(2) Rev. Rul. 66-332, 1966-2 CB 108 [¶ 17,293(15)].

Footnote ¶ 1727 [¶ 17,441 et seq.].
(1) Rev. Rul. 68-601, 1968-2 CB 124 [¶ 17,451(50)].

Highlights of Chapter 7
Dividends

I. **Ordinary Dividends**
   A. **What is dividend [¶ 1700]:**
      1. Tax definition—a corporate distribution is a "dividend" only to the extent made from current earnings and profits or from those accumulated after 2-28-13.
      2. Earnings and profits—no statutory definition; tax concepts may differ from accounting concepts.
      3. Accumulated earnings and profits—excess of earnings and profits over deficits.
   B. **Source of distribution [¶ 1701]:**
      1. Every distribution presumed to come from earnings and profits, and from current earnings first.
      2. To figure available earnings and profits:
         a. If dividend paid from current earnings—available earnings are reduced by payments for whole year.
         b. If from accumulated earnings—available earnings are reduced by payment on payment date.
         c. Use straight line, not accelerated depreciation.
         d. Carryovers from predecessor corporation in reorganization allowed.
      3. Matching cash dividends and distribution source:
         a. Current earnings are considered first source, and accumulated earnings and profits second.
         b. If dividends are paid more than once a year, allocation of current and accumulated earnings is required to determine amount taxable.
      4. Shareholders tentatively report distribution as dividends if earnings unknown.
   C. **How dividends are taxed [¶ 1702]:**
      1. Ordinary dividends are includible in gross income in full, subject to dividends-received exclusion (see II, below).
      2. Return-of-capital distributions reduce shareholder's basis in stock; excess below zero basis is taxable as capital gain.
      3. If dividend is paid in property:
         a. To an individual—property basis is its value on distribution date, and amount distributed is that value less liability assumed by him.
         b. To a corporation—special rules apply (covered in chapters 21, 23).
      4. Treat capital gain dividends of mutual funds as long-term capital gain.
   D. **Constructive dividends**—taxable as ordinary dividends, though not so declared by corporation; for example [¶ 1703]:
      1. Payments to shareholders in the form of excessive salaries, royalties, rents, interest.
      2. Loan to majority shareholder without intention to repay.
      3. Bargain sales to shareholders, release of their debts, sale of property to corporation for more than worth.
   E. **Tax-exempt dividends [¶ 1704]:**
      1. Paid by insurance companies on policies.
      2. Paid on obligation issued before 3-28-42 by various federal agencies.
      3. Dividends paid from tax-exempt earnings at corporate level are not exempt to shareholders.
II. **Dividend Exclusion**
   A. **Allowance of exclusion [¶ 1705]:**
      1. Amount of exclusion:

a. Individuals exclude first $100 of most dividends paid by domestic corporations.
b. Up to $200 total on joint return but neither spouse can use any part of other's exclusion.
2. Dividends paid on stock commonly or jointly owned are considered to be received by individual to the extent he shares them; dividends paid on community property stock are shared equally.

B. **Exclusion is not allowed for [¶ 1706]:**
1. Dividends paid by foreign corporations.
2. Dividends paid by tax-exempt corporations.
3. Patronage dividends.
4. Capital gains portions of mutual funds dividends.
5. Dividends paid on withdrawable savings accounts.
6. Liquidating distributions and stock redemptions.
7. Subchapter S corp. distributions, unless paid out of earnings and profits on which corp. was previously taxed.
8. Amount equal to dividends paid in short sale.

III. Stock Dividends
A. **General rules [¶ 1707]:**
1. Stock dividends—distribution of corporation's own stock to its shareholders—are generally not taxable.
2. Stock dividend is taxable if:
   a. Any shareholder can elect to take cash or property.
   b. Distribution (or series of distributions) is disproportionate, in that some shareholders receive cash or property and others increase their equity interests.
   c. Distribution results in receipt of preferred stock by some common shareholders and receipt of common by others.
   d. Declared on preferred stock, unless increase in conversion ratio solely to reflect stock dividend or stock split.
   e. Distribution of convertible preferred unless its effect is not disproportionate under (b), above.
3. Redemptions and recapitalizations may be treated as disproportionate distributions.

B. **Nontaxable stock dividends [¶ 1708]:**
1. To find basis of old and new stock:
   a. If old and new shares are identical—divide basis of old stock by total number of shares.
   b. If in a, above, old shares were bought at different times and prices, allocate proportionate amount of dividend stock to each lot.
   c. If old and new shares are not identical—allocate basis by values on distribution date.
2. Holding period of new stock is same as that of the old.

C. **Taxable stock dividends [¶ 1709]:**
1. Amount of distribution is generally fair market value of stock on date of distribution.
2. Basis of new stock is its fair market value when received. Basis of old stock remains unchanged.
3. Holding period of new stock begins when received.

IV. Stock and Bond Rights
A. **Stock rights [¶ 1710—1712]:**
1. Rules to determine whether taxed are same as those for stock dividends.
2. Nontaxable stock rights:
   a. Basis of rights is zero if its market value when distributed is less than 15% of stock value, unless shareholder elects to allocate part of stock's basis to right.
   b. If value of right is 15% or more, allocate basis to right according to market values of stock and right on distribution date.

c. If right is sold, holding period begins on date old stock acquired.
3. Taxable stock rights:
   a. Amount distributed or basis of rights is generally fair market value of rights on distribution date.
   b. Holder of rights taxed on receipt of rights.
   c. Basis of new stock is basis of rights plus subscription price.
   d. Holding period of new shares begins on date of exercise.

B. **Rights to bonds [¶ 1714]:**
   1. Bond rights are nontaxable if:
      a. Bonds are convertible into stock that, if distributed, would be nontaxable dividend, and
      b. Value of rights arises from conversion privilege.
   2. Taxable bond rights are treated as property dividends if bonds are not convertible into stock.

V. Liquidating Dividends

A. **Liquidating dividend**—distribution of cash or assets in exchange for corporation's outstanding stock [¶ 1715].

B. **Partial liquidations that qualify for capital gains treatment [¶ 1716]:**
   1. A distribution as one in a series toward redeeming all stock, or
   2. Distribution under plan to redeem part of stock if made in year plan of liquidation adopted or following year, or
   3. Distribution on closing out of branch business if:
      a. Terminated business was actively conducted for 5 years and was not acquired in gain or loss transaction, and
      b. Distributing business is actively conducted immediately after distribution.

C. **How liquidating dividends are treated [¶ 1717]:**
   1. Difference between amount received (fair market value, if property) and basis of stock is usually capital gain or loss.
   2. Gain or loss must be computed separately on each block.
   3. Gain is not reportable until cost recovered.
   4. Ordinarily, loss is not deductible until year final distribution made.
   5. Ordinary income may result from asset distribution if:
      a. The corporation is collapsible, or
      b. Distribution is of undistributed personal holding company income, or
      c. Property distributed is subject to recapture.

VI. Stock Redemptions

A. **Redemptions qualify for capital gains treatment if [¶ 1718]:**
   1. Not essentially equivalent to a dividend ("net effect" test), or
   2. Redemption is substantially disproportionate, i.e., shareholder owns less than 50% of total voting power after redemption, *and* shareholder's ownership of all voting and common stock is decreased by more than 20% as result of redemption, or
   3. There is complete redemption of shareholder's stock.

B. **Complete redemption and constructive ownership rules [¶ 1719]:**
   1. Constructive ownership rules do not apply to complete redemption if:
      a. Immediately after redemption, shareholder has no interest (except as creditor) in corporation, and
      b. Shareholder does not reacquire interest in corporation within 10 years, and
      c. He files an agreement to notify IRS on reacquisition.
   2. Constructive ownership rules apply if tax avoidance was principal aim and:
      a. Stock redeemed was acquired from related person within 10 years before redemption, or
      b. Stock was transferred to related person within 10 years before redemption.

C. **Redemption through use of controlled corporations [¶ 1720]:**
   1. Sales between "brother-sister" corporations:

a. Treated as if purchasing corp. redeemed own stock. If direct redemption would result in dividend, dividend portion is taxed as such.
b. Purchasing corp.'s basis for redeemed stock is same as shareholder's, plus any recognized gain.
c. If dividend, shareholder increases basis of his purchasing corp. stock by redeemed stock basis.
2. Sale of parent stock to sub is treated as if parent redeemed own stock.
3. Control is at least 50% of total voting power, or value of all shares.

D. **Stock redeemed to pay death taxes is subject to capital gain and loss treatment if [¶ 1721]:**
1. Value of stock is included in decedent's gross estate, and
2. Stock is timely redeemed after decedent's death, and
3. Stock is redeemed for not more than sum of estate and inheritance taxes, plus funeral and administration expenses; if dying after 1976, redemption qualifies only if made from shareholder whose estate interest is reduced by payment of death taxes and funeral expenses and only to that extent, and
4. Value of stock, for decedents dying after 1976, exceeds 50% of value of adjusted gross estate.

E. **"Preferred stock bail-out" [¶ 1722]:**
1. Nontaxable dividend in preferred stock creates "Section 306 stock" if corporation has earnings and profits.
2. If Section 306 stock is sold:
   a. Amount realized is ordinary income up to stock's ratable share of earnings at time of issuance—excess is capital gain.
   b. No loss is recognized.
3. If Section 306 stock is redeemed, amount realized is treated as distribution of property; ordinary income is measured by earnings at time of redemption.
4. "Bail-out" rules do not apply in case of:
   a. Complete termination of shareholder interest.
   b. Liquidation.
   c. No tax avoidance purpose.
   d. No gain or loss recognized on the transaction.

F. **Constructive ownership of stock [¶ 1727]:**
1. An individual is deemed to own stock of his spouse, children, grandchildren, and parents.
2. Partnership or estate owns stock of its partners or beneficiaries. Partners or beneficiaries own proportionately stock of partnership, estate or trust.
3. Trust owns beneficiary's stock unless beneficiary has only a remote, contingent interest. Each beneficiary owns a portion of trust's stock.
4. A 50%-or-more owner of a corporation is attributed an amount of corporate-owned stock in proportion to his holdings in the corporation. All his outside stock is attributed to the corporation.
5. Options are same as stock for constructive ownership rule.

MAXIMIZING BUSINESS AND PERSONAL DEDUCTIONS

Chapter 8—DEDUCTIONS—EXPENSES
(Detailed Table of Contents below)

Chapter 9—DEDUCTIONS—INTEREST, TAXES, CONTRIBUTIONS AND MEDICAL EXPENSES
(Detailed Table of Contents at page 1901)

Chapter 10—DEDUCTIONS—DEPRECIATION
(Detailed Table of Contents at page 2001)

Chapter 11—DEDUCTIONS—DEPLETION
(Detailed Table of Contents at page 2101)

Chapter 12—DEDUCTIONS—LOSSES
(Detailed Table of Contents at page 2201)

Chapter 13—DEDUCTIONS—BAD DEBTS
(Detailed Table of Contents at page 2301)

Chapter 8

DEDUCTIONS—EXPENSES

TABLE OF CONTENTS

¶

DEDUCTIONS IN GENERAL

The deductible items in general 1800
Two basic deduction groups for individuals 1801
    Deductions for adjusted gross income
    Deductions from adjusted gross income
Deductions disallowed 1802

EXPENSES IN GENERAL

What is a deductible expense 1803
    Ordinary and necessary
    Expenses related to business or nonbusiness activities
Expenses incurred in trade, business or profession 1804

Expenses incurred in trade or business by employee 1805
    Expenses of outside salespersons
    Reimbursed expenses
    Reporting requirements
Nonbusiness expenses 1806
    Expenses of rental or royalty property
    Expenses of investors
    Property not currently productive
    How treated on return
Personal expenses distinguished from business or nonbusiness expenses 1807
Expenses distinguished from capital expenditures 1808
Expenses for tax-exempt income 1809
Expenses for donated property 1810

Footnotes appear at end of this Chapter.

Chapter 8—Deductions—Expenses

	¶		¶
Expenses for political purpose	1811		
Illegal business or payment	1812		

COMPENSATION FOR SERVICES

Deduction for compensation 1815
Reasonableness of compensation 1816
Payment for services 1817
Commissions 1818
   Advances to salespersons
   Buying and selling commissions
Bonuses and other additional compensation 1819
   Wages during military reserve leaves
   Employee benefits
   Employer's deduction for restricted property
Compensation for services performed in prior years 1821
Pensions—payments to former employees or their dependents 1822
   Pensions
   Payments to employees in armed forces or their dependents
Fees to attorneys, accountants and other professional people 1823
   Capital expenditures
   How treated on return

REPAIRS, RENT, ADVERTISING, INSURANCE

Repairs 1825
   Distinction between capital expenditures and repairs
   Simultaneous repairs and improvements
   How treated on return
Rent 1826
   Personal expenses
   Residence used partly for business
   Advance rental
   Lease cancellation payments
   Payments under lease
   How treated on return
Advertising expenses 1827
   "Nonbusiness" expense
   How treated on return
Insurance premiums 1828
   Life insurance premiums
   Premiums on insurance other than life—fire, burglary, etc.
   How treated on return

TRAVELING, ENTERTAINMENT AND MOVING EXPENSES

Travel and transportation expenses 1829
   Business traveling expenses
   Transportation expenses
   Necessity of proof
   How treated on return

Entertainment expenses 1830
   General rules
   Exceptions
   Business gifts
   Employer's deduction
   Employee's deduction
   Family expenses
   Necessity for records
   How treated on return
Moving expenses 1831
   Dollar limits on indirect expenses
   Deductible sale, purchase and lease expenses
   Qualification tests
   Deduction for self-employed persons
   How treated on return

MISCELLANEOUS TRADE OR BUSINESS EXPENSES

Expenses of professional people 1832
   Home and office combined
   How treated on return
Education expenses 1833
   What expenses are deductible
   Teachers
   How treated on return
Expenses of persons in the armed forces 1834
   Uniform—equipment
   Overseas duty; travel

BENEFIT AND RETIREMENT PLANS

Contributions under pension, stock bonus and profit-sharing plans 1838
   Reasonableness and time of contributions
   Special deduction provisions for qualified plan
   Requirements for qualified plan
   Deduction for qualified pension trust
   Deduction for qualified stock bonus or profit-sharing trust
   Overall limitations on contributions to qualified plans
   Contributions toward purchase of retirement annuities
   Contributions to combination of plans
   Contributions to plans that do not qualify
   Contributions when there is no plan
   Information required
   Individual retirement arrangements
Self-employed retirement plans 1839
   Who can get coverage

Chapter 8—Deductions—Expenses

Ceiling on contributions
Ceiling on deductions
Qualifying the plan
Retirement fund
Treatment of excess contributions
Treatment of distributions

SPECIAL PROBLEMS

Leaseholds 1840
Research and experimental expenditures 1842
  Deductible in year paid or incurred
  Deferred expenses
  Exceptions
  Adjustment of basis
Mining expenditures 1843
  Exploration expenditures
  Development expenditures
  Expenditures not included
  Deduction for adjusted gross income
  Adjusted basis of mine or deposit
Expenses of farmers 1844
  Business expenses
  Capital expenditures
  Farming for pleasure
  Farming syndicates
  How treated on return
Soil and water conservation expenditures 1845
  Limitation
  Adoption of method
  Assessments
  Expenses of clearing land for farming
  Recapture of deductions
Amortizable bond premium 1846
  Tax-exempt obligations
  Taxable obligations
  Adjustment for period before election
  Bond premiums due to conversion privilege
  Determination of amount amortizable
  Called bonds
  How treated on return

• **Highlights of Chapter 8** 1861

DEMDUCTIONS IN GENERAL

Deductions are important because every deduction allowed under the law reduces the income subject to tax. The basic principles covering deductions from gross income apply to all taxpayers. The taxpayer must be able to point to some specific provision of the statute which authorizes the deduction.

¶ **1800 The deductible items in general.** There are three categories of allowed deductions:

(1) Expenses or costs. This class includes expenses of carrying on any trade, business or profession [¶ 1804; 1831]; expenses for production of income ("nonbusiness" expenses) [¶ 1806]; interest [¶ 1900 et seq.]; taxes [¶ 1910 et seq.]; contributions [¶ 1941 et seq.]; and medical expenses [¶ 1945 et seq.].

(2) Realized losses. The principal deductions in this class are losses incurred in a trade, profession or business [¶ 2202]; losses incurred in transactions entered into for profit though not connected with trade, profession or business [¶ 2203]; casualty losses [¶ 2204]; and bad debts [¶ 2300 et seq.].

(3) Reductions in value of property or interest in property. This class includes the deduction for depreciation of business property or property held for the production of income [Ch. 10], depletion [Ch. 11], amortization of bond premiums [¶ 1846], pollution control facilities [¶ 2040] and railroad rolling stock [¶ 2041].

Notice that some of the deductible items are allowed only if they are related to a trade, profession or business or to a "nonbusiness activity." A taxpayer who uses a truck for business or an automobile to look after his income-producing property may deduct expenses of operation and depreciation of the vehicle, but no such deductions are permitted if an automobile is used solely for pleasure.

Footnotes appear at end of this Chapter.

¶ 1800

Some items are deductible whether or not they relate to a trade, profession or business, or to a nonbusiness activity. These include interest, taxes, contributions and medical expenses [Ch. 9]; certain losses [Ch. 12]; and bad debts [Ch. 13]. For example, real property taxes are deductible whether paid on a residence occupied by the taxpayer or on property used in businss. The same is true of interest; it is deductible whether it is paid on a residence mortgage or on a business loan.

¶ 1801 **Two basic deduction groups for individuals.** For individuals, there are two groups of deductible items: (1) those deductible from gross income to arrive at adjusted gross income, called "deductions *for* adjusted gross income," and (2) those deductible from adjusted gross income to arrive at taxable income, called "deductions *from* adjusted gross income."

NOTE: The deduction for personal exemptions [¶ 1111 et seq.] is disregarded for purposes of this discussion.

(a) **Deductions for adjusted gross income.** These deductions include:

- Expenses of carrying on a trade, business or profession [¶ 1804];
- Reimbursed expenses of employee [¶ 1805(b)];
- Expenses of travel, meals and lodging while away from home in connection with employment [¶ 1805; 1829];
- Transportation expenses incurred while not away from home in the performance of services as an employee [¶ 1805; 1829];
- Expenses incurred in connection with services performed in employment as an "outside salesperson" [¶ 1805(a)];
- A deduction for long-term capital gain [¶ 1612];
- Deduction for losses allowed on sales or exchanges of property [¶ 1613; 1620; 1806; 2200; 2307; 2312];
- Deductions due to rent and royalty property [¶ 1806];
- Certain deductions of life tenant and income beneficiaries of property [¶ 2002(c); 2101(c); 3014];
- Moving expenses [¶ 1831];
- Deductions for contributions to self-employed retirement plans [¶ 1839(b)];
- Excess contributions by Subchapter S corporations to retirement plans for benefit of shareholder-employees [¶ 3146(a)];
- Deductible contributions to individual retirement arrangements [¶ 1838(l)];
- Deductible ordinary income portion of lump-sum distributions for retirement plans [¶ 1839(g)];
- Alimony payments [¶ 1320];
- Deduction for premature time deposit withdrawal penalties [¶ 2203].

Importance of deductions for adjusted gross income. The difference between deductions for and from adjusted gross income for individuals is important because it determines the amount of adjusted gross income. The amount of the adjusted gross income is important since it controls (1) the limit on charitable contribution deduction [¶ 1943]; and (2) the medical expense deduction [¶ 1945].

(b) **Deductions from adjusted gross income.** These deductions include: deductible medical expenses, charitable contributions, personal interest, personal taxes, personal casualty losses, and some other less common deductions. They are sometimes referred to as "itemized deductions." Schedule A of Form 1040 must be used to take the "itemized deductions." "Adjusted" itemized deductions may be a tax preference item subject to the minimum tax. See ¶ 2403.

Zero bracket amount. All taxpayers get a tax-free amount according to their marital status called the zero bracket amount [¶ 1107]. If an election is not made to take "excess itemized deductions", then the taxpayer can file the Short Form 1040A.

¶ 1802 Deductions disallowed. Deductions may be disallowed either because they do not come within the statutory requirements, or because they are of a type expressly disallowed by the statute. The law expressly prohibits deduction of the items mentioned below.

- Personal, living or family expenses [¶ 1807].
- Capital expenditues [¶ 1808].
- Amounts allocable to exempt income [¶ 1809].
- Certain accrued, but unpaid, expenses and interest [¶ 2748].
- Certain payments for insurance [¶ 1828].
- Certain charges to capital account [¶ 1528].
- Deductions related to production of unharvested crop [¶ 1622(b)].

A deduction may also be disallowed or only partially allowed if it results from the acquisition of property or stock and if the principal purposes of such acquisition is evasion or avoidance of tax [¶ 3226].

➢**OBSERVATION**➤ When expenses are incurred that are partly personal, it is advisable to get an itemized statement allocating the charges between the personal and business portions.

EXPENSES IN GENERAL

An expense is deductible if ordinary and necessary. It must be business related or incurred in the production of income. Personal and family expenses generally are not deductible.

¶ 1803 What is a deductible expense. An expense, to be deductible, must be [Sec. 162; 1.162-1]:

- Ordinary and necessary; and
- Paid or incurred during the tax year; and
- Related to carrying on a trade or business.

(a) Ordinary and necessary. An *ordinary* expense is one that is commonly incurred in the taxpayer's trade or business. It may vary, depending on the time, place and circumstances under which it is incurred.[1] A *necessary* expense need not be "essential." It may be necessary if it is "appropriate and helpful" to the taxpayer's business or occupation.[2]

(b) Expenses related to business or nonbusiness activities. Generally, a trade or business involves a line of work or an occupation carried on for a livelihood or profit. However, many types of expenses that do not qualify as being paid or incurred in "carrying on any trade or business" may be deductible as "nonbusiness" expenses. These are expenses for (1) producing or collecting income; (2) managing, conserving, or maintaining property held for the production of income, or (3) in determining, collecting, or refunding any tax (¶ 1806) [Sec. 212; 1.212-1].

Footnotes appear at end of this Chapter.

¶ **1804 Expenses incurred in trade, business or profession.** Expenses paid or incurred in a trade, business or profession carried on by the individual taxpayer, not consisting of services as an employee, are deductions for adjusted gross income [Sec. 62(l); 1.62-1]. They are not limited to "expenses," but may include losses, bad debts, depreciation, etc. Two requirements must be met for the deduction of ordinary and necessary expenses of a trade, business or profession:

- The expense must be *directly* connected with the taxpayer's trade, business or profession [Sec. 162(a); 1.162-1]; and
- The expense must be *reasonable* in amount.[1]

State income taxes on gross income from a trade or business are deductible in computing adjusted gross income. These taxes on *net income* from business profits are *not* deductible in computing adjusted gross income.[2] Both the Tax Court and Revenue Service hold that state income taxes are business expenses for purposes of the net operating loss deduction.[3]

Business use of home. For tax years starting after 12-31-75, the taxpayer must show that a specific part of the residence is set aside and used exclusively on a regular basis as (1) a principal place of business, or (2) a place where the taxpayer meets with patients, clients or customers. A deduction is also allowed when the taxpayer maintains a structure separate from the residence used exclusively and regularly in a trade or business. A taxpayer who carries on a business from the residence can take deductions for space in the home that is used regularly for storing inventory. In this case, the home must be the sole fixed location for the business. The deduction for the business use of the home is limited to the amount of gross income from that use less the deductions allocable to the home-office [Sec. 280A].

NOTE: For tax years after 1975, a home-office deduction is allowed for licensed day-care services regularly provided in the home for compensation. If not used exclusively for business purposes, expenses for the facility are only allowed to the extent attributable to business use [Sec. 280A(c)(4)].

¶ **1805 Expenses incurred in trade or business by employee.** Any expense incurred by an employee is not deductible unless it was required by the employment agreement,[1] or is incident to performing his or her duties.[2] The only deductions *for* adjusted gross income available to an employee are for expenses of travel and transportation [¶ 1829], moving expenses [¶ 1831], expenses incurred by an outside salesperson and reimbursed expenses. All other deductible employee business expenses are "itemized deductions."

DEDUCTIBLE

Employment agency fees and other expenses in seeking employment in the same trade or business even if employment is not secured, but not if employment is sought in new trade or business.[3]

Cost of telephone installed to receive calls from employer,[4] but not when telephone is only incidentally used in business.[5]

Cost of medical examination required as condition of employment.[6]

If office is maintained in employee's home. An employee is allowed a home-office deduction only if the exclusive use is for the convenience of the employer. See ¶ 1804 [Sec. 280A].

(a) **Expenses of outside salespersons.** An individual's expenses connected with services as an "outside salesperson" are deductions for adjusted gross income [Sec. 62(2)(D); 1.62-1(h)].

Who is an outside salesperson. An "outside salesperson" is one who solicits business away from employer's place of business as a full time salesperson. A salesperson whose principal activity is service and delivery is not an "outside salesperson," nor is an inside salesperson who makes incidental outside calls and sales. If an individual must perform inside activities as part of the employment for a specified period each week, he or she is not considered an outside salesperson.[7] However, outside salespersons who have incidental activities at the employer's place of business, such as writing up and transmitting orders, can take the deduction.[8]

DEDUCTIBLE ITEMS

Cost of telephone and telegraph, secretarial help, entertainment, split commissions paid on subcontracts,[8] transportation expenses while not away from home, travel, meals and lodging expenses while away from home [¶ 1829].

(b) Reimbursed expenses. Employee business expenses are deductions for adjusted gross income to the extent they are reimbursed under a reimbursement for other expense allowance arrangement. This is a wash transaction since reimbursements are offset against deductible expenses. If the reimbursements exceed the expenses, the excess must be included in gross income. If traveling, transportation or outside salesperson's expenses exceed the reimbursements, the excess is deducted from gross income. If other expenses exceed the reimbursements, the excess is deductible *from* adjusted gross income, as an itemized deduction. A reimbursement that covers both kinds of expenses must be allocated between them [See below]. For reimbursed moving expenses, see ¶ 1831(e).

> **Example 1:** A police officer received a $100 cash allowance (reimbursement) for his uniform. It cost him $125. Of this, $100 (offset by the $100 reimbursement) is a deduction for adjusted gross income. The $25 balance is deductible *from* adjusted gross income.[9]

Reimbursement must be claimed. Employees get no deduction for amounts they would have been reimbursed by their employers if they had made a claim.[10]

(c) Reporting requirements. The employee's method of reporting business expenses on the return depends on whether or not an accounting is made to the employer. Form 2106 can be used to report business deductions on the return. No accounting, reporting or record-keeping is required for incidental expenses [Sec. 1.162-17, 1.274-5].

Employees who account to the employer. They generally need not report their expenses or reimbursements on the return. But see ¶ 1831(e). If reimbursements equal expenses, the employee reports neither the business expenses nor the reimbursements on the return. If reimbursements exceed expenses, the employee reports the excess reimbursement on the return as miscellaneous income unless the employer has reported the excess as wages.[11] If expenses exceed reimbursements, and the employee claims a deduction for the excess, an explanatory statement must be submitted showing [Sec. 1.162-17, 1.274-5]:

- The total of any charges paid or borne by the employer and any other amounts received from the employer for expenses;
- Occupation;
- Number of days away from home on business;
- Total expenses paid or incurred by employee (including those charged to employer) under headings like transportation, meals and lodging while away from home overnight, entertainment expenses, and other business expenses.

Employees who do not account to employer. These employees must report their business expenses and reimbursements on the return. Therefore, they must

Footnotes appear at end of this Chapter.

¶ 1805

submit an explanatory statement described above, whether or not they are reimbursed.

Proving expenses. Employees ordinarily will not be called on to prove their expenses unless [Sec. 1.162-17(d)(1), 1.274-5]:

- They do not account to their employer; or
- They claim a deduction for an excess of expenses over reimbursements; or
- They are related to the employer [¶ 2223]; or
- It is determined that the employer's accounting procedures for reporting and substantiating employees' expenses were not adequate.

Allocation of expenses. In preparing the explanatory statement and claiming expenses, employees must separate the deductions *for* adjusted gross income from the "itemized deductions." For example, if the total expenses exceed a reimbursement intended to cover all expenses, only part of the expenses other than for travel and transportation is deductible for adjusted gross income (unless the employee is an outside salesperson). That part is figured as follows [Sec. 1.62-1(f)]:

$$\frac{\text{Expenses (other than travel or transportation)}}{\text{Total expenses}} \times \text{Reimbursement}$$

Example 2: Bacon (not an outside salesperson) received an expense allowance of $1,200. He had $800 meals and lodging expenses while away from home, $500 transportation expenses, and $300 entertainment expenses. Of the $300 entertainment expenses, $225 ($300/$1,600 × $1,200) is the amount of entertainment expense covered by the allowance and deductible for adjusted gross income as a reimbursed employee expense. The $75 balance is an "other itemized deduction." The expenses would be reported in the statement as follows:

Expense allowance		$1,200
Deductions for adjusted gross income:		
Meals and lodging (away from home)	$800	
Transportation expenses	500	
Entertainment expense ($300/$1,600 × $1,200)	225	1,525
Deductible from gross income ($1,525 − $1,200)		$ 325
Deductible from adjusted gross income:		
Entertainment expense		$ 75

What an "accounting" is. To "adequately account" to an employer, the employee must submit a record describing each element (amount, date, place, business purpose and business relationship) of the expenditure that has been recorded at or near the time of the expenditure. There also must be supporting documentary evidence. Only this kind of proof will qualify as "adequate accounting," except when records were destroyed or when it was impossible to get the evidence [Sec. 1.162-17(b)(4); 1.274-5]. See also ¶ 1830(g).

Reasonable per diem allowance. Reimbursement arrangements, per diem and mileage allowances when conforming to reasonable business practices may be treated as adequate accounting and substantiation of employee expenses. Generally, employer-paid reimbursements or per diem allowances up to $44 per day for employee travel expenses while away from home (but not transportation expenses to and from destination) satisfy the adequate accounting and substantiation requirements. These requirements can also be met by using a higher per diem allowance set by the U.S. for its employees in the particular travel areas. An employee can also receive a mileage allowance up to 15¢ per mile for travel expenses away from home or for local transportation expenses without actually accounting to the employer.[12] Reimbursement arrangements or per diem allowances are not allowed when employer and employee are related [¶ 2223(b)]. Here, a "10% stock ownership" rule applies. In any case, the 15¢ fixed mileage allowance can be used.[13]

¶ **1806 "Nonbusiness" expenses.** Many types of expenses that do not qualify as business expenses are deductible as "nonbusiness expenses." Nonbusiness expenses are the ordinary and necessary expenses paid or incurred by an individual in [Sec. 212; 1.212-1]:

- producing or collecting income, or
- managing, conserving or maintaining property held for the production of income, or
- the determination, collection or refund of any tax.

Two requirements must be met for a nonbusiness expense to be deductible: (1) it must be reasonable in amount, and (2) it must bear a reasonable and close relation to the above activities [Sec. 1.212-1(d)].

Example 1: The cost of this Tax Course generally would be deductible as an expense of determining the purchaser's income tax.

(a) Expenses of rental or royalty property. Expenses incurred in the rental of property or in the production of royalty income are deductible as nonbusiness expenses. Property held for the production of royalties includes both tangible and intangible property (such as patents and copyrights). Thus, expenses for repairs, maintenance and upkeep of rental property are included with other deductions (interest, taxes and depreciation) in calculating the net profit or loss from renting property.

Vacation home. For tax years starting after 1975, there is a limit on the amounts deductible on the rental of a dwelling when it is used for personal purposes for more than 14 days or 10% of the rental, whichever is greater. If these limitations are exceeded, deductions attributable to the rental of the property are limited to the amount by which gross rental income exceeds the deductions otherwise available (e.g., interest, taxes, casualty losses). Deductions attributable to rental activity are those type of expenses normally allowable when incurred in connection with a trade or business or the production of income (e.g., maintenance and depreciation). If the vacation home is rented for less than 15 days during the year, no deductions attributable to the rental are allowable and any revenue from the rental is excluded from gross income.

Example 2: Joe Morgan rented out his vacation home for four months during the year at a gross rental of $4,000. He used the home himself for two months. Joe paid $1,000 in taxes and $1,400 in mortgage interest on the property for the year. His expenses allocable to the rental of the home were: maintenance, $500; utilities, $400; depreciation, $800.

The limit on rental expenses that can be deducted by Joe is $1,600 (gross rental less interest and taxes). He can therefore deduct the utility and maintenance expenses (total of $900), but his depreciation deduction is limited to $700.

The "personal use" of a vacation home includes days it is used by other family members, by someone who owns an interest in the home, or by anyone for less than a fair rental [Sec. 280A(d)(2)]. A vacation home can be a house, apartment, condominium, mobile home, boat, or similar property [Sec. 280A(f)(1)].

In allocating expenses between personal use and rental use, the expenses allocable to the rental use are limited to an amount that bears the same ratio to such expenses as the number of days the home is actually rented out for the year bears to the total number of days the home is actually used for all purposes during the year.

Footnotes appear at end of this Chapter.

(b) Expenses of investors. Expenses incurred related to investment activities are deductible as nonbusiness expenses. Deductible items include custodian fees, cost of investment advice, wages paid to clerical help and safe deposit rentals (but not if used for personal effects).

DEDUCTIBLE

State transfer taxes on security sales [¶ 1912(d)]; travel expenses incurred in looking after income-producing property;[1] insurance and storage charges on merchandise purchased and held by taxpayer as a speculative investment;[2] amounts, equal to dividends, paid by an investor for stock borrowed to cover short sales and premiums paid in acquiring such stock[3] (but amounts paid to repay lender for stock dividends or liquidating dividends on such stock are capital expenditures and not deductible).[4]

NOT DEDUCTIBLE

Expense of attending stockholders' meetings for information on *future* investments.[5]

(c) Property not currently productive. Deduction of nonbusiness expenses is allowed even if the property involved is not currently productive and it is unlikely that it will be sold at a profit or produce income [Sec. 1.212-1(b)].

DEDUCTIBLE

Maintenance expenses of a residence from the time it is abandoned as a residence and offered for sale or rent, but not if the residence was held for sale only.[6]

Legal and other fees: Attorneys' and accountants' fees for services in getting adjustment of property taxes;[7] attorney's fees for services to get increased alimony,[8] reasonable administrative expenses of estate and trust, including fiduciaries' fees and litigation expenses (except expenses allocated to tax-exempt income or deducted for estate tax purposes) [Sec. 1.212-1(i)].

Legal fees for advice on distribution of trust property[9] or terminating a trust;[10] accountants' fees for keeping books of income-producing properties;[11] appraisal fees to establish personal casualty loss or charitable contribution (considered expense to determine tax liability);[12] legal fees for advice on tax consequences of divorce action;[13] trustee's fees to maintain self-employed retirement plan.[14]

Expense paid in recovering income-producing property deductible (1) to extent allocable to recovery of interest on principal amount involved[15] or (2) in full, if the action is brought to recover *specific* income-producing property;[16] expenses of conserving and managing income-producing property of infant, such as guardians' commissions, legal fees, accounting and court fees.[17]

NOT DEDUCTIBLE

Legal and other fees: Expense of defending title to income-producing property;[18] legal fees of public officer in successful defense of contested election.[19]

Hobby expenses: See ¶ 2225.

Miscellaneous: Campaign expenses of candidate for re-election,[20] even if elected.[21] But see ¶ 2416.

(d) How treated on return. Deductible nonbusiness expenses are *not* deductions for adjusted gross income, unless they are related to property held for the production of rents and royalties.

¶ 1807 **Personal expenses distinguished from business or "nonbusiness" expenses.** Personal and family expenses generally are not deductible [Sec. 262; 1.262-1]. The tests that take an expense item out of this category have already been mentioned: is the expense ordinary and necessary *and* has it been incurred in connection with the taxpayer's trade, business or profession or in a "nonbusiness" activity? In each case, the question is whether the expenditure arose independently of the taxpayer's business or nonbusiness activities, or primarily because of them. If it arose independently of such activity, it is a personal expenditure and is not deductible, unless there is a specific provision in the law for some deduction, as for medical expenses [¶ 1945 et seq.].

DEDUCTIBLE

Uniforms and work clothes: The cost and maintenance of uniforms and work clothes are deductible if they are required as a condition of employment and are not suitable for regular wearing apparel off duty or away from work.[1] Special accessories, such as gloves, boots or shoes are also deductible.[2] The deduction for the cost of special clothes is reduced for any salvage value they have.[3] (Cost of armed forces uniforms generally is not deductible. See ¶ 1834.)

Fees and dues: Labor union initiation fees, dues (including fines[4]) or non-union employee's monthly service charge paid as condition of employment under employer-union contract, and pension fund assessments that must be paid to stay employed[5] (assessment for sickness, accident and death benefit funds are not deductible[6]); dues paid employer's association to protect against labor union;[7] dues to trade association [Sec. 1.162-15(c)]; social club dues if club is used more than half the time for business (see ¶ 1830) [Sec. 274(a)].[8]

NOT DEDUCTIBLE

Family expenses: Allowance by husband to wife for household expenses and by father to children for living expenses; child adoption expenses.[9] Amounts paid to real estate company for maintenance charges assessed on residential lot (deductible if property converted to rental property);[10] insurance premiums paid by individual on his life, home, pleasure car or craft, jewelry [Sec. 1.262-1]; funeral expenses [but see ¶ 3926]; employees' contributions to voluntary plan for disability benefits under state unemployment insurance laws;[11] the extra cost of personal benefits derived from business purchases.[12]

Career expenses: Expenses of training for a career, securing a license, seeking public office, or improving personal appearance [Sec. 1.212-1(f)].

¶ 1808 Expenses distinguished from capital expenditures. A charge against income is an expenditure incurred in earning income and is deductible. A capital expenditure is an outlay that results in the acquisition of property or in a permanent improvement that extends beyond the tax year. Such an expenditure, generally, is not deductible as an expense [Sec. 263(a); 1.263(a)-1]. However, the taxpayer can still get a deduction through depreciation. This is spread over the useful life of the property. The more important capital expenditures are listed in Sec. 1.263(a)-2.[1]

> **NOTE:** The Class Life ADR system concedes a portion of the taxpayer's outlays for repair, maintenance, rehabilitation and improvement (except "excluded additions" which are clearly capital expenditures) to be currently deductible expenses; only the remaining portion is treated as capital expenditure [Sec. 263(e)]. This system provides a simplified procedure for handling those expenditures that have the characteristics of both deductible expenses and capital expenditures [¶ 2033(f)].

DEDUCTIBLE AS EXPENSES

Expenses of installing accounting and cost system;[2] moving machinery;[3] cost of automobile worn out and junked by company in six months.[4]

NOT DEDUCTIBLE (CAPITAL EXPENDITURE)

Cost of legal fees for acquiring and disposing of assets;[5] conversion of equipment for use of different fuel;[6] cost of paying stock dividends;[7] cost of producing films, books, records and similar property must be deducted over the life of the income stream generated by the property (effective for amounts paid or incurred after 12-31-75 for property begun after 12-31-75) [Sec. 280].

SPECIAL RULES

Trademark expense. Expenses paid or incurred for protection, expansion, registration or defense of a trademark or trade name that are properly chargeable to capital account may be amortized ratably over 60 months or more at taxpayer's election. This does not apply to the cost of buying an existing trademark, trade name or business, but other acquisition expenses may be included [Sec. 177; 1.177-1]. The election is made the year the expenses are paid or incurred; otherwise they must be capitalized.

Transfer of franchise, trademark or trade name. Amounts paid or incurred in the tax year because of a sale or transfer of a franchise, trademark or trade name contingent on its productivity, use or disposition are deductible by the transferee as business expense [Sec. 1253; Proposed Reg. 1.1253-1(c)(1)]. Taxpayer may elect to treat contingent payments made after 1969 on account of transfers before 1970 under this rule [Proposed Reg. Sec. 1.1253-3]. Lump-sum initial payments can be amortized, and installments may be deducted when made [Proposed Reg. Sec. 1.1253-1(c)(3)]. If transferor retains no significant rights, the payments are subject to amortization [Proposed Reg. Sec. 1.1253-1(c)(2)]. See also ¶ 1601.

Costs of investigating a new business are capital expenditures generally recoverable only on sale or final disposition of the business. If the taxpayer actually enters into a project for profit and the project is later abandoned, the expenses are deductible as a loss in the year of abandonment.[8]

Payments to eliminate competition: If the restraint is for a definite term, the cost may be exhausted over such term, but if the restriction is permanent or indefinite, no deduction is allowed. If agreement not to compete is part of indivisible contract for sale of all assets of a business, no deduction is allowed.[9]

Cost of catalogs held deductible as a current business expense even if their use extends beyond one year, if the benefits in future years are not reasonably certain.[10] But Revenue Service says cost must be capitalized.[11]

Circulation expenditures of periodicals may be deducted as ordinary business expenses. This does not include expenditures for buying land, depreciable property or part of the business of another publisher. The deduction may be taken only in the year paid or incurred [Sec. 173; 1.173-1(a)(3)]; publishers may elect to capitalize expenses to establish or increase circulation [¶ 1528].

Stock exchange dues and fees: Deduction allowed if used by exchange to defray current expenses rather than for capital purchases;[12] initiation fee[13] and cost of listing stock not deductible;[14] assessment for operating expenses deductible.[15]

Dissolution and liquidation expenses of a corporation are deductible as ordinary and necessary business expenses in year dissolution occurs.[16]

Research, experimental and development expenditures are covered in ¶ 1842.

Organizational expenditures of corporation are covered in ¶ 3116.

Construction equipment. Depreciation of equipment used in constructing capital assets must be capitalized and deducted over the assets' lives.[17]

Expenses for handicapped. Costs up to $25,000 to make any facility or vehicle used in a trade or business more accessible and usable to the handicapped or elderly are currently deductible. This applies for tax years starting after 1976 and ending before 1980 [Sec. 190; Temp. Reg. 7.190-1—3].

¶ 1809 Expenses for tax-exempt income. Business expenses due to tax-exempt income, except interest, are not deductible. "Nonbusiness" expenses due to wholly tax-exempt income, including interest, are not deductible [Sec. 265(1); 1.265-1]. An unrecognized involuntary conversion gain [¶ 1411 et seq.] is not tax-exempt income for this purpose.[1] In addition, no deduction is allowed for interest on a loan to buy or carry tax-exempt securities [¶ 1905(a)].

Example: Lee paid a nonbusiness expense (investment service fee) of $4,000. Of $16,000 income derived from the property serviced, $2,000 was tax-exempt interest. One-eighth of the fee ($500) is disallowed ($2,000/$16,000 × $4,000).[2]

¶ 1810 Expenses for donated property. A taxpayer need not include in income the fair market value of agricultural or manufactured products or property held for sale that is donated to charity or is given to any other donee, including individuals [¶ 1942; 2601; 2614]. But costs and expenses incurred in the year of contribution in acquiring or producing the donated property are deductible and are part of the cost of goods sold if the property was acquired in the year of contribution. If such related costs and expenses of prior years are reflected in the cost of goods sold in the year of contribution, the cost of goods sold must be reduced to eliminate these amounts [Sec. 1.170A-1(c)(4)].

¶ 1811 **Expenses for political purpose.** Generally no business deduction is allowed for direct or indirect payments for political purposes. Indirect contributions include: (1) admission to a dinner or program where the proceeds of the affair would benefit a political party or candidate; (2) admission to an inaugural ball, parade, concert, or similar event which is identified with a candidate or party; and (3) advertising in a publication (including a convention program) where the proceeds benefit a party or candidate [Sec. 276].

Individuals are allowed a deduction or credit for political contributions. See ¶ 2416.

¶ 1812 **Illegal business or payment.** Operating expenses of an illegal or questionable business are deductible,[1] but not expenses of an inherently illegal nature, such as bribery and protection payments[2] [Sec. 162(c), (f), (g); 1.162-18, 1.162-21].

COMPENSATION FOR SERVICES

Compensation paid for personal services are deductible business expenses if:

- Ordinary and necessary;
- Reasonable;
- For personal services actually rendered in connection with a trade or business, or related to "nonbusiness" activities;
- Actually paid or incurred during the tax year.

The name by which the compensation is designated, the basis on which it is determined and the form in which it is paid are immaterial.

¶ 1815 **Deduction for compensation.** Taxpayers may deduct what they pay for personal services actually rendered for them in connection with their trade, business or profession or in connection with their "nonbusiness" activities (¶ 1806) [Sec. 162(a); 1.162-7; 1.212-1]. Wages paid *solely* for services that are personal to the employer (for example, to domestics) are not deductible [Sec. 262]. For time of the deduction, see ¶ 2735.

Child employed by parent. Wages (except the cost of meals and lodging) paid by a parent to an unemancipated minor child for services actually rendered as a bona fide employee in the parent's business, or for the production of income, are deductible even if the child uses the wages for part of his or her own support.[1]

¶ 1816 **Reasonableness of compensation.** The question of reasonableness of compensation generally arises only if there is some relationship between the parties in addition to that of employer and employee; for example, if the employee is also a stockholder of a corporate employer or if he is a child or parent of an individual proprietor.

There is no precise rule to determine the exact amount of compensation that is considered reasonable. This is an amount that would ordinarily be paid for like services by like enterprises under like circumstances [Sec. 1.162-7]. The facts in each case control.

Footnotes appear at end of this Chapter.

¶ 1816

Factors of reasonableness are: the character and amount of responsibility, difficulty of the work itself, time required, working conditions, future prospects, living conditions of the locality, individual ability, technical training, profitableness to the employer of the services rendered and the number of available persons capable of performing the duties of the position.

≫**OBSERVATION**→ The Revenue Service may examine a situation in which an officer-stockholder with a controlling interest in a corporation receives a large payment of compensation, especially when the corporation has a history of paying small dividends.

¶ **1817 Payment for services.** In addition to being reasonable, the compensation must be paid purely for services to be deductible. If the purported compensation is actually a payment for the transfer of property by the employee, then such payment is a nondeductible capital expenditure. A payment may be a dividend if purported compensation is excessive and bears a close relationship to the employee's stockholdings [Sec. 1.162-7, 1.162-8].

¶ **1818 Commissions** paid for services are deductible the same as ordinary salaries [Sec. 1.162-1; 1.162-7; 1.212-1].

(a) Advances to salespersons, originally intended as loans, but later considered paid by the employer, are compensation to the salespersons and deductible by the employer in the year charged-off.[1]

(b) Buying and selling commissions. Commissions paid in *buying* property, such as securities and real estate, are not deductible by the investor, trader or dealer, but are added to the cost of the property used in determining the gain or loss on its later sale.[2] Commissions paid in *selling* property are not deductible but are offset against the selling price used to figure gain or loss on the sale, except for a dealer[3] who may deduct commissions as an expense [Sec. 1.263(a)-2]. Selling commissions deducted for estate tax purposes may also be offset against the selling price.[4] Commissions paid for the purchase or sale of a residence can be deductible if they are the moving expenses of an employee or self-employed person [¶ 1831(b)].

¶ **1819 Bonuses and other additional compensation.** Compensation paid to employees in addition to their regular salary or wage, is deductible by the employer only if the additional compensation plus the basic salary or wage is reasonable. Any excess amount is not deductible [Sec. 1.162-9].

Cash or property: Bonuses, including Christmas payments, to employees are deductible if made in good faith and for services rendered, whether paid in cash, property, or both[1] [Sec. 1.162-9]. The deduction for a bonus paid in the employer corporation's stock is its fair market value. The deduction for a bonus payable in stock of another corporation also is the fair market value;[2] but if the bonus is payable in a stated dollar amount, the deduction is limited to the cost of the other corporation's stock, plus any cash distributed, when using market value would exceed the authorized dollar amount.[3] For treatment of stock received under a stock option plan, see ¶ 1327.

Contingent compensation, such as a percentage of profits or sales, is deductible if a free bargain was made in advance between the employee and the employer for the pay [Sec. 1.162-7].

Reconditioning or health restoring expenses paid by employer for executives at a hotel are deductible if payments can be considered compensation.[4]

Life insurance premiums. See ¶ 1828.

(a) Wages during military reserve leaves. Amounts paid by employers to employees while they are on leave to attend National Guard or Army and Navy Reserve training are additional compensation and are deductible.[5]

(b) Employee benefits. Amounts paid for dismissal wages, unemployment benefits and guaranteed annual wages are deductible.

Payments to an employee because of injuries, even when paid in a lump sum, are deductible to the extent not compensated for by insurance or otherwise [Sec. 1.162-10].

Amounts paid under sickness, accident, hospitalization (including reimbursement of medicare premiums to active or retired employees and contributions to welfare fund for these premiums[6]), recreational, welfare or similar benefit plans are also deductible. If, however, these amounts may be used to provide benefits under a deferred compensation pension, or profit-sharing plan as described in ¶ 1838, they are deductible under the rules covering such plans [Sec. 1.162-10].

(c) Employer's deduction for restricted property. An employer who gives restricted property as compensation to his employee may deduct an amount equal to the amount included in the employee's gross income. It is allowed in the employer's accounting period that includes the close of the tax year in which the employee treats the restricted property as income [Sec. 83(h); Proposed Reg. 1.83-6]. See also ¶ 1326.

¶ 1821 Compensation for services performed in prior years. Reasonable payments for services peformed in prior years are deductible.[1] However, payment must be authorized in the year that the deduction is claimed.[2]

¶ 1822 Pensions—payments to former employees or their dependents— (a) Pensions. Pensions paid by an employer directly to retired employees or to their beneficiaries and death benefits paid to beneficiaries are generally considered proper deductions. Contributions by an employer to an employees' trust or plan, under which annuities or pensions are paid to former employees, are deductible up to certain limits. [¶ 1838].

(b) Payments to employees in armed forces or their dependents. Salary payments to employees who are absent in the military or naval service or who are serving the government in other ways at a nominal salary are deductible.[1] Payments (under a plan adopted by an employer) made to dependents of former employees serving in the armed forces of the United States also are deductible.[2]

¶ 1823 Fees to attorneys, accountants and other professional people. Fees to attorneys and other professional people are deductible if incurred (1) in a transaction directly connected with, or proximately resulting from, the taxpayer's trade, business or profession, or (2) in the production or collection of income or the management, conservation or maintenance of property held for the production of income, or (3) in connection with determination, collection or refund of any tax [Sec. 212(3); 1.162-1; 1.212-1]. Fees that are reasonable administration expenses of an estate or trust also are deductible [¶ 1806]. Fees paid for legal advice concerning investments, loans to protect stockholdings, and the rearrangement of an estate are deductible.[1] Fees paid for general personal services are not deductible, but fees paid for medical and dental treatment are deductible to a certain extent [¶ 1945 et seq.].

The Supreme Court has held that legal fees paid in defending a criminal action are deductible if they are an ordinary and necessary business expense, even if the defense is unsuccessful.[2] The same rule would seem to apply to fees related to a "nonbusiness" activity [¶ 1806]. Previously, some courts had disallowed deductions for fees paid in an unsuccessful criminal defense on the grounds that the deduction would frustrate public policy.[3] Under the Supreme Court rule, the disal-

Footnotes appear at end of this Chapter.

¶ 1823

lowance must be supported by some governmental statement of a national or state public policy considered to be frustrated.[2]

DEDUCTIBLE

Fees for defense of malpractice suit, disbarment proceedings, mail fraud proceedings,[4] suit against a director of a corporation,[5] expense of defending a court martial;[6] attorney's fees in connection with additional income tax on taxpayer's (or transferor's) business,[7] or in suit to recover income tax deficiencies assessed on property held for production of income,[8] or in will contest resulting in increase of taxpayer's share of trust income;[9] legal and accounting fees in contesting income tax deficiency and fraud penalties and effecting compromise settlement;[10] tax or investment counseling fees paid by a corporation for the benefit of its executives;[11] legal fees in suit for negligent destruction of rental property.[12]

NON DEDUCTIBLE

Fees in suing for slander[13] or libel[14] (unless livelihood threatened);[15] fees to recover nontaxable damages for personal injuries suffered on business trip;[16] defense of contested election by public officer;[17] defense of title to property;[18] legal advice as to selection of securities for gift; preparation of a will;[19] obtaining or defending a suit for divorce or separate maintenance,[20] even if expenses are to conserve income-producing property;[21] (But fees are deductible if incurred for the production or collection of alimony includible in gross income [Sec. 1.262-1]); defense of assault or bribery charges (neither business connected).[22]

(a) Capital expenditures. Occasionally, an attorney's fees may be a capital expenditure, for example, fees paid to secure a long-term lease of real estate,[23] fee for reducing an assessment for a local benefit;[24] and fee for tax advice on changing corporate capital structure (merger, stock split and proposed redemption).[25]

NOTE: Fee relating to redemption above would be deductible if and when the proposal is abandoned.

(b) How treated on return. Fees paid to attorneys and others that are business expenses of an individual are deductions for adjusted gross income. Expenses related to property held for the production of rent or royalties are deductible for adjusted gross income. [¶ 1806(a)]. Employees can deduct for adjusted gross income fees that are reimbursed employee expenses [¶ 1801; 1805].

REPAIRS, RENT, ADVERTISING, INSURANCE

This section deals with some of the expenses that could be used to offset income from business or income-producing property—repairs, rent, advertising and insurance. In the case of an outlay to "fix-up" property, the question often arises of whether it is a deductible expense or a nondeductible capital expenditure.

¶ **1825 Repairs.** The cost of repairs to property used in a trade, business or profession and of repairs to property held for the production of income is deductible as an ordinary and necessary expense [Sec. 162(a); 1.162-4; 1.212-1]. The cost of repairs to the taxpayer's residence is not deductible. If the property is held by the taxpayer as rental property, the cost of repairs is deductible even though it was formerly his residence [Sec. 1.212-1(h)]. This rule applies even though the property is not actually rented, if it has been abandoned as a residence and is listed for rent or sale or for sale only [¶ 1806].

(a) Distinction between capital expenditures and repairs. For business property and property held for production of income, the question is whether the expenditure is an expense (deductible in the year paid or incurred) or a capital expenditure (recoverable usually through annual depreciation deductions spread over the life of the property) [Sec. 162(a); 1.162-4]. The distinction between improvements (capital expenditures) and repairs (expense) is not always clear. But here is a useful general guide: "A repair is an expenditure for the purpose of keeping the property in an ordinarily efficient operating condition. It does not add to the value of property, nor does it appreciably prolong its life. It merely keeps the property in an operating condition over its probable useful life for the uses for which it was acquired. Expenditures for that purpose are distinguishable from those for replacements, alterations, improvements or additions which prolong the life of the property, increase its value, or make it adaptable to a different use. The one is a maintenance charge, while the others are additions to capital investment which should not be applied against current earnings." [1]

Examples relating to business property: Cost of a new roof is a capital expenditure, but cost of repairing roof is an expense;[2] cost of new concrete floor and new foundation for machinery is capital expenditure;[3] however, cost of concrete lining added to basement floor and walls is expense;[4] cost of small parts of large machine to keep it in operating condition is expense.[5] Also deductible as expenses are cost of repairing leaks,[6] tuck pointing,[7] and painting and redecorating;[8] but cost of rearranging lighting system,[3] and bricking up walls[9] are capital expenditures.

> **NOTE:** The Class Life ADR system contains an elective rule which simplifies handling expenditures that have characteristics of both repair expenses and capital expenditures [¶ 2033(f)]. Generally, ADR allows expenses related to a particular depreciable asset account to be deducted currently and provides a specific percentage repair allowance. The allowance applies to expenditures on assets placed in service before 1971 as well as after 1970 [Sec. 263(e)].

(b) Simultaneous repairs and improvements. Repairs and improvements are often made at the same time. If the repair items are merely part of the general plan of improvements, cases hold that the *entire* amount spent for both repairs and improvements must be treated as a capital expenditure.[10] Even if the repairs and improvements are not part of a general plan of improvement, the repairs are not a deductible expense unless they are segregated from the nondeductible improvements.[11] When the exact cost of repairs is not shown, some deduction may be allowed depending on the evidence submitted, though not necessarily the amount claimed by the taxpayer.[12]

(c) How treated on return. An individual's deductible expense for repairs to business property, or property held for production of rents or royalties, is a deduction for adjusted gross income [¶ 1801; 1804; 1806(a)].

¶ 1826 Rent. A tenant may deduct rent for the use of property to the extent it is used in his trade, business or profession [Sec. 162(a)(3), 212; 1.162-11]. Rent also may be deductible as a nonbusiness expense [¶ 1806]. Payments for leasing machinery and equipment also can be deducted.

(a) Personal expenses. Rent is not deductible if it is a personal expense as distinguished from a business expense. For that reason rent for a home used entirely for residential purposes is not deductible.

(b) Residence used partly for business. If property is rented primarily for use as a residence, but part of it is used for business, an apportionment may be made, based generally on the number of rooms used for each purpose.[1] If the property is rented primarily for business purposes, the rental value of the living quarters should be estimated and the difference between such rental value and the total rent paid should be deducted as a business expense.[2] So if an individual pays $400

Footnotes appear at end of this Chapter.

a month for a store and five rooms, and the rental value of similar rooms is $150 he should deduct $250 as business rent.

If the owner of a building occupies it for business purposes or for both business and residential purposes, he cannot deduct any rent. However, if the owner, reserving no interest to himself, makes an irrevocable gift of business property to a valid trust for his family, and then leases the property back from the independent trustee, the amount he pays as rent is deductible.[3]

(c) Advance rental payments are not deductible when paid. The deduction is allowed only for the portion allocable to the particular tax year.[4]

Example: Ed Dolan paid $5,000 rent in 1977 for use of a store under a lease covering the years 1977-1981 inclusive. $5,000 is not deductible in full in 1977, but $1,000 is deductible in each of the five years.

(d) Lease cancellation payments. Amounts paid by a landlord for the cancellation of a lease are capital expenditures.[5] If the sum is paid by the tenant for cancellation of his lease, the total cost of cancelling the lease and any unamortized improvements to the leasehold is deductible in the year of cancellation.[6] If the tenant's payment is considered as a personal expense, it can only be deductible if it is a moving expense [¶ 1831(b)]. A forfeited lease deposit on property used in trade or business is deductible as a business loss.[7]

(e) Payments under lease. Payments for the use of machinery and equipment under lease agreements are deductible as rent if there is compelling evidence of a true rental and not a sale. Otherwise, the payments (except for interest and other charges) are part of the purchase price and are not deductible; but the payor will be allowed depreciation on the property.

NOTE: Special rules apply to equipment leasing unless there was a binding contract entered into before 1976. See ¶ 2736.

Lease agreement treated as purchase or sale. No general rule can be given, and each case must be decided on its own facts. However, generally, *in the absence of evidence of a true rental,* agreements for the lease of property will be treated as purchases and sales if one or more of the following conditions are present:

- Portions of periodic payments apply specifically to an equity to be acquired by the lessee.
- Lessee will acquire title on payment of a stated amount of "rent" which must be paid in any event.
- Total amount that lessee must pay for a relatively short period of use is very large compared with the amount needed to get transfer of title.
- Periodic payments materially exceed current fair rental value.
- Property may be bought under an option at a price that is (a) nominal in relation to value of property at time option may be exercised, or (b) relatively small compared with total required payments.
- Part of the "rent" is specifically designated interest, or is easily recognizable as the equivalent of interest.
- Total rental payments plus option price approximate price at which property could have been bought plus interest and carrying charges.

Transfer of title not essential. The fact that the agreement does not provide for the transfer of title or specifically precludes transfer of title does not prevent the contract from being a sale of an equitable interest in the property. Thus, the agreement is a sale if (1) total rents over a relatively short period approximate the price at which the property could have been bought plus interest and carrying charges, and (2) the lessee may continue to use the property over its entire useful life for relatively nominal or token payments, even if there is no provision for the passage of title.[8]

(f) How treated on return. Rent paid by an individual for property used in his trade, business or profession is a deduction for adjusted gross income. But if he is an employee, rent paid in connection with his employment is a deduction for adjusted gross income only if it can be considered a travel expense [¶ 1829] or reimbursed employment expense, or if the employee is an outside salesperson [¶ 1805].

¶ 1827 Advertising expenses. Advertising expenditures (except indirect political contributions [¶ 1811]) are deductible as business expenses if they are ordinary and necessary and bear a reasonable relation to the business activities of the taxpayer. Cost of goodwill advertising that keeps the advertiser's name before the public is deductible, but not advertising intended to promote or defeat legislation. Advertising that encourages charitable contributions or the buying of U.S. savings bonds qualifies [Sec. 1.162-20].

(a) "Nonbusiness" expense. Advertising costs of an individual may be deducted as a "nonbusiness" expense if they are reasonable in amount and bear a reasonable and proximate relation to the production or collection of income or to the management, conservation or maintenance of property held for the production of income [¶ 1806].

(b) How treated on return. Deductible advertising expenses incurred by an individual in carrying on a trade, business or profession are deductions for adjusted gross income, except for employees [¶ 1801; 1804]. Employees who incur advertising expenses in connection with their employment can deduct them for adjusted gross income only if they can be considered expenses of travel or a reimbursed employment expense, or if employee is an outside salesperson [¶ 1805]. Deductible nonbusiness advertising expenses are deductible for adjusted gross income only if they are related to property held for the production of rents and royalties [¶ 1806(a)].

¶ 1828 Insurance premiums. The following rules prevail:

(a) Life insurance premiums. 1. Not deductible if paid by the person insured [Sec. 262; 1.262-1]. Such premiums are personal rather than business or "nonbusiness" expenses; for example, premiums paid on an ordinary life policy taken out by the taxpayer and naming his wife or other dependents as beneficiaries are not deductible.

2. Not deductible if paid by the taxpayer on the life of an officer, employee, or other person financially interested in the taxpayer's business, when the taxpayer is directly or indirectly a beneficiary under the policy [Sec. 264(a)(1); 1.264-1]. Thus, premiums paid by an employer on the life of any employee are not deductible while the employer is a beneficiary, even if only to the extent of the cash surrender value.[1]

3. Deductible if paid by the taxpayer on the life of an officer or employee, if the taxpayer is neither directly nor indirectly a beneficiary *and* the premium is an ordinary and necessary business expense.[2]

Example: The Blaine Corp. insured the life of John Watson, its treasurer, for $50,000. The premiums were $2,000 a year. Watson, who earns $25,000 annually, named his wife as beneficiary. The $2,000 is considered additional compensation. If the total compensation ($25,000 plus $2,000 insurance premium) is reasonable in amount it is deductible in full.

Footnotes appear at end of this Chapter.

Group insurance premiums. Premiums paid by an employer on group life insurance are deductible.[2] For taxability of the employee, see ¶ 1307.

Loan insurance. An individual insuring his own life to get a loan for business purposes (policy in favor of lender) may not deduct the premiums. The proceeds would be used to liquidate the debt so the borrower is indirectly a beneficiary.[3]

Certain partnership insurance. A partner cannot deduct premiums on insurance on his own life, irrevocably naming his copartners as sole beneficiaries to induce them to stay in the business. (In accomplishing his purpose, jeopardy to taxpayer's interest in the partnership is removed and his interest in the business favorably affected[4]) [Sec. 1.264-1(b)].

(b) Premiums on insurance other than life—fire, burglary, etc. Premiums on fire,[5] burglary, storm, theft and accident insurnce covering property used in a trade, business or profession, or in connection with the production of income or the management, conservation or maintenance of property held for the production of income, are deductible [Sec. 162(a); 212; 1.162-1; 1.212-1]. The Tax Court has held that premiums paid after a business use ends and the property is offered for sale must be capitalized.[6] Insurance on property used for personal purposes, for example, fire insurance on a taxpayer's dwelling is a nondeductible personal expense [Sec. 262; 1.262-1]. For deductibility of hospitalization insurance premiums, see ¶ 1946.

Employers' liability, etc. Premiums on other insurance such as public liability, workmen's compensation, credit, fidelity, indemnity bonds, use and occupancy and the like are deductible, if incurred in carrying on a trade, business or profession or in the production or collection of income or in the management, conservation or maintenance of property held for the production of income [¶ 1804; 1806]. Some premiums may have to be capitalized [¶ 1808].

Premiums on overhead insurance that reimburses taxpayer for business overhead expenses incurred during prolonged periods of disability are deductible, if the policy expressly states that it is overhead insurance.[7]

Health, accident, and disability. If an employer buys group hospitalization and surgical insurance for employees and their families, the premiums paid are deductible as ordinary and necessary business expenses. The purchase must be in consideration of services rendered. The employees need not include the premiums in taxable income.[8] Employers who are beneficiaries of employee accident and health policies cannot deduct premiums they pay.[9]

Premiums a person pays for his own medical insurance are included in the deduction for medical expenses [¶ 1945 et seq.].

(c) How treated on return. Insurance premiums paid by an individual, if deductible as a business expense, are deductions for adjusted gross income, except in the case of an enployee [¶ 1801; 1804]. Employees, in figuring, adjusted gross income, may deduct only premiums that are a reimbursed employment expense unless the employee is an outside salesperson [¶ 1805]. Deductible "nonbusiness" insurance premiums are not deductions for adjusted gross income unless they are related to property held for the production of rents and royalties [¶ 1806(a)].

TRAVELING, ENTERTAINMENT AND MOVING EXPENSES

This section deals with the deductibility of costs incurred in entertaining and in going from one place to another (traveling, transportation and moving expenses) in connection with your trade, business or "nonbusiness" activities.

Chapter 8—Deductions—Expenses

¶ 1829 Travel and transportation expenses. Traveling expenses are deductible if they are ordinary and necessary business or "nonbusiness" expenses as distinguished from personal expenses [¶ 1804-1807]. The only exception is those personal traveling expenses that are considered moving expenses [¶ 1831].

(a) Business traveling expenses. To be deductible by an employer or employee, the expense must be:

- *Reasonable and necessary* as the term is generally understood. This includes transportation fares and traveling expenses for food and lodging that are not lavish or extravagant under the circumstances [Sec. 162(a)(2)].
- Incurred while *"away from home"* except for certain transportation expenses (see below).
- Incurred in *pursuing a trade, business or profession* (expenditure must be directly connected with trade, business or profession of the taxpayer or his employer).
- *Necessary or appropriate* to the development of the trade, business or profession.[1]

NOTE: The Revenue Service has issued guidelines for the traveling expense deduction. These enable employers to meet the substantiation requirements as to the mileage and per diem requirements.[2] See ¶ 1805(c).

Personal and business activities combined.—*trip within U.S.:* When a taxpayer engages in both personal and business activities at his destination, travel expenses there and back are deductible only if the trip is related primarily to business. If the trip is primarily personal, travel expenses to and from the destination are not deductible, even if he engages in business activities while there. Expenses at the destination that are properly allocable to business are deductible whether the trip is primarily business or personal. Travel within the U.S. means travel from one point in the U.S. to another point in the U.S. [Sec. 274(c)(3)]. When one or more family members accompany the taxpayer on a business trip, the additional amount spent for the family members is not deductible unless their presence has a bona fide business purpose. The performance of incidental services by a family member is not a "business purpose"[3] [Sec. 1.162-2].

Trip outside U.S.: For conventions beginning after 12-31-76, a taxpayer can only deduct costs for two foreign conventions per year. Foreign conventions include meetings held outside the U.S., its possessions or the Trust Territory of the Pacific. To deduct transportation costs, at least half of the total trip days must be spent on business related activities, and the deduction is limited to the lowest coach or economy rate. Deductions for meals, lodging and other subsistence costs are allowed if 2/3 of the scheduled business activities are attended. 6 hours constitutes a full day's business schedule; 3 hours is a half-day. These subsistence costs are limited to the per diem rates applicable to U.S. civil servants in that area of the world. If transportation and subsistence costs are not separately stated, all costs are assumed to be for subsistence. A detailed expense statement must be submitted by the attending individual and by the organization sponsoring the convention [Sec. 274(h)].

DEDUCTIBLE

Convention expenses directly related to taxpayer's trade or business [Sec. 1.162-2] or incurred by an employee if attendance is connected with services as an employee (but for conventions outside U.S., see above).[4]

Trips for business or investment interests. Traveling expenses (including passport fee[5]) in making trips to look after business and investment interests or to inspect business or investment properties.[6]

Entertainment expenses incurred on a business trip are not part of traveling expenses. But they may be deductible under the rules applying to entertainment expenses [¶ 1830].

Footnotes appear at end of this Chapter.

Sale of automobile. A loss on the sale of an employee's automobile that he uses in business is a deduction for adjusted gross income [¶ 1613].

Laundry and cleaning expenses are deductible in reasonable amounts while away from home.[7]

NOT DEDUCTIBLE

Investigating business locations. Expense of seeking location for contemplated business (capital expenditure added to cost of new property).[8]

Away from home overnight. The cost of meals and lodgings may be deducted as a travel expense only when the taxpayer is away from home "overnight." "Overnight" is a time period substantially longer than an ordinary day's work that requires relief from duty to obtain sleep or rest away from home.[9] It need not be 24 hours or from dusk to dawn. If the taxpayer neither sleeps nor rests while away from home (for example, one-day travelers or intra-city travelers), the cost of meals is a nondeductible personal expense and not a travel expense.[10]

"Home" is the location of the taxpayer's business, employment, station, or post of duty (even if for an indefinite period[11]) regardless of where the family residence is maintained (but see also "work in widely scattered locations" below). It is not confined to a particular building or property, but includes the entire city or general area where taxpayer's business or place of employement is located.[12] The Second Circuit disagrees with this, holding that "home" means the taxpayer's permanent residence.[13]

If the taxpayer must work away from home for a *strictly temporary period,* and cannot return home each day, he is *away from home* for the entire period. *Temporary period* means that its termination can be foreseen within a reasonably short period. The Revenue Service considers this to be less than a year,[14] but the Tax Court has allowed the deduction when the temporary employment was much longer than a year.[15]

NOTE: For tax years beginning before 1-1-77, a state legislator could elect to treat his legislative district residence as his tax home [Sec. 307, P.L. 95-30].

Work in widely scattered locations. - The IRS uses the following to determine if taxpayer has a "home" for the travel expense deduction: (1) If taxpayer does part of the business near claimed "home" while living there; (2) If living expenses incurred at claimed "home" are duplicated when business requires him or her to be away; and (3) If taxpayer (a) has not left the vicinity in which his or her historical place of abode and claimed "home" are both located, (b) has family residing at the claimed "home," or (c) uses the claimed "home" often for lodging.[16]

Employment abroad: If taxpayer is employed abroad indefinitely,[17] home for tax purposes is the place of employment abroad. Thus, taxpayer is *not* away from home while employed there, even if not permitted to take the family.[18] A ship with living facilities is a naval officer's tax home when permanently assigned to it.[19]

Two places of business or employment. If the taxpayer regularly works in two or more separate areas, the general area where principal business or employment is located is considered "home." Taxpayer is away from "home" when away from that general area, even while working at the minor place of business or employment.[18] This applies even if taxpayer's minor place of business is in the same location as the family residence; he is "traveling away from home" when business requires his presence at the location of his residence.[20]

Factors in determining the *principal place of business* are time spent at each place, "degree of business activity," and financial reward of each business.[21]

(b) Transportation expenses. A deduction is allowed for transportation expenses incurred by an individual in a trade, business or profession. However, expenses in going to and from one's personal residence and a place of business or employment are generally nondeductible personal expenses. Transportation expenses while away from home are deducted as travel expenses. An individual's transportation expenses are deductions for adjusted gross income [Sec. 62(2)(c), 162(a); 1.62-1(g), 1.162-2(e)].

These expenses include transportation fares of all kinds, including taxis, buses and also the cost of operating and maintaining an auto. See (c) below. It does not include "travel items" such as meals and lodging.

Commuting expenses distinguished from certain transportation expenses. After 7-1-77, transportation expenses between taxpayer's residence and place of work, even though temporary, are nondeductible commuting expenses regardless of the work's nature, distance traveled, mode of transport, or degree of necessity.[22] A deduction is allowed for transportation costs above normal commuting expenses, incurred for transporting work implements used in taxpayer's trade or business to and from work.[23]

Commuting between jobs for more than one employer. If an employee works for two (or more) separate employers, each position is considered part of the employee's over-all trade or business. Therefore, local transportation expenses in getting from one job to another are deductible. If the employee goes home between jobs, the amount of the deduction is the lesser of (1) the cost of transportation between jobs, or (2) the amount actually spent.[24]

Example: Assume employee has two jobs. Transportation cost to and from home to Job 1 is $.75 each way; between Job 1 and 2, $1.00; and between home and Job 2, $.50. If he goes home between Job 1 and 2, the deduction is $1.00 (cost of going from Job 1 to 2), although he actually spent $1.25 ($.75 from Job 1 to home plus $.50 from home to Job 2).

"Nonbusiness" transportation expenses. Ordinary and necessary transportation expenses are deductible if incurred in connection with the production or collection of income or the management, conservation or maintenance of property held for the production of income, or in connection with the determination, collection or refund of any tax. Of these expenses, those related to property held for the production of rents and royalties are deductions for adjusted gross income [¶ 1807(a)]; the remainder are itemized deductions [¶ 1801].

Transportation for medical treatment. Transportation expenses paid to get medical treatment are included in computing the medical expense deduction [¶ 1946].

(c) Necessity of proof. Traveling expenses are disallowed if the taxpayer does not keep adequate records or other proof of the amount, time, place and business purpose of the expense[25] [Sec. 274(d); 1.274-5(b)(1)].

Mileage rate. A self-employed individual or an employee, instead of figuring the exact cost of operating his own passenger automobile (or pickup or panel truck) for business use, may deduct 15¢ a mile for the first 15,000 miles of business use and 10¢ for each additional business mile.[26] If he alternates vehicles, the total business mileage determines the amount of the deduction. If 2 or more vehicles are in use at the same time he cannot use the mileage rate reduction. A taxpayer who uses the mileage rate cannot deduct operating or fixed costs related to business use of the vehicle. These include oil, repair, license fee, gasoline (including state or local tax), insurance and depreciation; but not parking fees or tolls. However, the basis of the vehicle must be reduced by the amount of straight line depreciation otherwise allowable.

You cannot use the mileage rate for a vehicle if accelerated or additional first-year depreciation [¶ 2013—2016] has been deducted, or if it is used for hire, for example, as a taxicab. Also, if an auto used for business has been, or is considered fully depreciated under the straight line method, a mileage rate of 10¢ a mile must be used if the taxpayer does not use the "actual cost" method.[27] Employees who are reimbursed for these expenses must report the reimbursement on the return if they use the mileage rate deduction. Use of the standard mileage rate does not affect the taxpayer's itemized deductions for interest and state and local taxes (but taxes included in the cost of gasoline that is an operating cost related to business use are not itemized deductions).[28] An employee who is partially reimbursed for his car expenses must keep adequate records or other proof in order to claim a deduction for the difference between his reimbursement and the standard mileage rate.[29]

(d) **How treated on return.** Traveling expenses incurred by an individual in carrying on a trade, business or profession as an employer or employee, or for moving, are deductions for adjusted gross income. See ¶ 1801; 1804. Those deductible from adjusted gross income are deductible on Schedule A of Form 1040 as itemized deductions. For employee's reimbursed expenses see ¶ 1805(b), (c).

¶ **1830 Entertainment expenses.** Deductible entertainment expenses must be ordinary and necessary expenses of carrying on a business or "nonbusiness" activity. They must also be "directly related to" or "associated with" the active conduct of a trade or business (see (a) below) or come within the exceptions stated in (b) below [Sec. 274].

Entertainment includes activities involving entertainment, amusement, or recreation. These activities include entertaining guests at night clubs, country clubs, theaters, sporting events and on vacation trips. They also include the furnishing of food, beverages, hotel rooms, vacation cottages or automobiles to a business customer or his family. Lavish or extravagant expenses are not deductible [Sec. 1.274-1]. However, entertainment expenses will not be disallowed merely because they exceed a fixed dollar amount or are incurred at a "high priced" hotel, restaurant, etc.[1]

(a) **General rules.** *Directly related entertainment rule.* The entertainment expenses must be *directly related* to the active conduct of taxpayer's trade or business or "nonbusiness activity." Thus the taxpayer must show a closer relation between the outlay and his business than is required for an ordinary business expenses. Unless proven otherwise, outlays will not be treated as "directly related" if the taxpayer is not present or if the distractions are substantial [Sec. 1.274-2(c)].

Associated with entertainment rule. Outlays not "directly related" to the taxpayer's trade or business are deductible if they are "associated with" that business and precede or follow a substantial and bona-fide business discussion. Usually the business discussions should be on the same day as the entertainment. However, under certain circumstances a deduction will be allowed for entertainment on the evening before the day of discussion or on the evening of the day following [Sec. 1.274-2(d)(1)—(4)].

Entertainment facilities. If you own or rent a facility for entertaining, your expenditures, as to the facility, are deductible providing you use the facility more than 50% of the time for business purposes. Only the portion of the expenditures directly related to the active conduct or your trade or business is deductible as an entertainment expense. Items that are deductible under the facility rules include depreciation, rent and social club dues. Out-of-pocket expenses, however, such as for food and beverages, do not come under these rules [Sec. 1.274-2(e)].

Directly related means the expense has to meet one of the following conditions: (1) taxpayer expected to derive a specific business benefit, other than goodwill at some time because of the entertainment, and business was actually conducted; (2) expense was incurred in a clear business setting; (3) entertainment was compensation for services or was for prizes for nonemployees; or (4) expense was for club dues to the extent that club was used to furnish business meals, and similar expenses, described below [Sec. 1.274-2(c)].

Associated with business. There must be a business purpose for incurring the expense. For example, obtaining new business, or continuing existing business (goodwill).

The cost of entertaining a person not at the business discussion, or not closely connected with a person at the discussion, (see above) is not deductible. The cost of entertaining the spouses of the participants is deductible [Sec. 1.274-2(d)(2)].

Entertainment facilities. In determining whether the facility was used more than 50% of the time for business, the time spent for entertainment that is "directly related" or "associated with" business counts, as well as time spent for other business connected entertainment, such as business meals. The deduction for the facility's upkeep is the amount allocable to "directly related" entertainment. For this purpose, time spent for business meals, and so forth, counts as "directly related" entertainment [Sec. 274; 1.274-2(a), (e)].

Example: Hollis is a member of a club that he uses 30% of the time for pleasure, 25% of the time for entertainment "directly related" to his business, 35% of the time for entertainment "associated with" his business, and 10% of the time for business meals, as explained below. Club dues are $1,000. Since the club is used for business purposes more than half of the time (70%), Hollis may take a deduction for part of the dues. His deduction is $350 ($1,000 × [25% + 10%] the time that the club was used for entertainment directly related to his business, including business meals).

(b) Exceptions. An entertainment expense (including the cost of related facilities) will not have to meet the "directly related" and "associated with" rules in (a) above if it meets one of the following tests [Sec. 274(e)]:

Quiet business meal exception. If a taxpayer provides a meal or refreshment for a business associate in a place conducive to a business discussion, the expense of such entertainment does not have to meet the "directly related to" or the "associated with" business tests if taxpayer, or his agent, is present. No business discussion need have occurred for this exception to apply; but reciprocal exchanges of "treats" do not qualify.[1] A place is conducive to a business discussion if there are no substantial distractions, such as a floor show. For example, entertainment at a restaurant, or at a cocktail lounge will usually qualify. Expenses for a dinner that is part of a business program or banquet also is covered by this exception, even if the taxpayer is not present [Sec. 1.274-2(f)(2)(i)].

Other exceptions. There are eight other exceptions to the application of the "directly related to" and "associated with" business tests: (1) Food and beverages furnished to employees; (2) items treated as compensation (such as an employer-paid vacation); (3) some reimbursed expenses; (4) general employee recreation expenses; (5) business meetings of employees, stockholders, etc.; (6) business league meetings; (7) items made available to the general public; (8) expenses of an entertainment business [Sec. 1.274-2(f)(2)].

(c) Business gifts. A deduction for business gifts is limited to $25 a person each year. This does not include advertising gifts each costing $4 or less distributed generally by the taxpayer with his name on them, or any promotional material used in the recipient's place of business. Also not included is an employee's gift for length of service, or safety award, that costs $100 or less [Sec. 274(b); 1.274-3].

Gifts made indirectly to an individual (to his wife, other family member, or to a corporation on his behalf) are considered made to him. The $25 limit applies to the partnership, as well as the partners [Sec. 1.274-3].

(d) Employer's deduction. If the entertainment expense is deductible, the employer who spends the money directly, or who reimburses an employee who spends the money, gets the deduction. See also ¶ 1804.

(e) Employee's deduction. A salaried employee may only deduct entertainment expenses if he can show that his employer expected him to incur the expenses

Footnotes appear at end of this Chapter.

¶ 1830

in connection with his work. He must have proper records (see (g) below) to support the deduction.[2] For reimbursed employee expenses, see ¶ 1805(b), (c). Outside salespersons may deduct entertainment expenses even if not reimbursed [¶ 1805(a)].

(f) Family expenses. The portion of entertainment costs for the expenses of the taxpayer and his family is not deductible, unless taxpayer can prove in each instance that they exceed or are different from the amounts he would have spent for his personal purposes.[3]

(g) Necessity for records. Entertainment expenses can be deducted only when supported by adequate records of the amount, time, place, business purpose, and business relation of persons entertained[4] [Sec. 274(d); 1.274-5(b)(2)]. This means that the taxpayer must maintain an account book or diary in which each element of an expenditure is contemporaneously recorded. Documentary evidence is required to support all expenditures for lodging while traveling away from home and for any other expenditures of $25 or more. However, it will not be required for transportation charges if the evidence is not readily available. If a taxpayer fails to keep adequate records, each element of expense must be established by a written or oral statement giving the exact details of the expense and by other corroborating evidence [Sec. 1.274-5(c)].

(h) How treated on return. Deductible entertainment expenses incurred by an individual in carrying on a trade, business or profession are deductions for adjusted gross income [¶ 1801; 1804]. Employee's reimbursed entertainment expenses and expenses of an outside salesperson are also deductions for adjusted gross income [¶ 1805]. "Nonbusiness" entertainment expenses are deductible for adjusted gross income only if they are related to property held for the production of rents or royalties [¶ 1806(a)].

¶ 1831 Moving expenses. Moving expenses related to starting work by an employee at a new job location can be deducted whether the employment is new or is a transfer in an existing job. The expenses are deductible in the year paid or incurred, but a taxpayer may also elect to deduct them in the year reimbursed. These expenses can also be deducted by self-employed persons, including partners. The following reasonable expenses are deductible [Sec. 217(a), (b); 1.217-2]:

• Moving household goods and personal effects from the old to the new residence.[1]

NOTE: The standard mileage rate of 7¢ a mile is allowed for moving an automobile[2] but depreciation on it cannot be deducted.[3]

• Traveling (including meals and lodging) to the new residence.
• Traveling (including meals and lodging) after obtaining employment, from the old residence to the general area of the new job and return to search for a new residence.
• Meals and lodging in temporary quarters in the new job site's general area for up to 30 days while waiting to move into the new residence after obtaining employment.
• Certain expenses of selling the old residence and buying the new one by the taxpayer or his spouse, as well as the expenses of settling an old lease and acquiring a new one [(b) below].

The moving expenses of a member of the taxpayer's household can also be deducted if that person resided with the taxpayer before and after the move. However, the taxpayer's spouse is the only member of his household for the sale, purchase and lease expense deduction. In addition, none of the moving expenses of a tenant in the taxpayer's residence, or an individual such as a servant, governess, chauffeur, nurse, valet, or personal attendant are deductible [Sec. 217(b); 1.217-2(b)(10)].

(a) Dollar limits on indirect moving expenses. Direct moving expenses are fully deductible. However, the aggregate deduction for each job move for the indirect expenses of househunting trips, temporary quarters and acquiring or disposing of a residence is limited to $3,000. Furthermore, the deduction for househunting trips and temporary quarters cannot exceed $1,500 [Sec. 219(b)(3)].

> NOTE: For tax years starting before 1977, the dollar limits were $2,500 and $1,000 respectively.

Other indirect expenses, such as the expenses of refitting rugs and draperies,[4] cannot be deducted at all. The taxpayer may deduct any combination of deductible indirect expenses within the dollar limits. Note that those costs of acquiring and disposing of residences not treated as moving expenses may be used to offset the amount realized from a sale or increase the basis of a purchased residence [(b) below; ¶ 1416(b), (d)].

> NOTE: The dollar limits are halved if spouses file separately. The limits remain at the $1,500—$3,000 level when spouses filing jointly both start work in the same general location [Sec. 217(b)(3)(B)]. However, the dollar limits are not split for separate filers if: (1) only one spouse makes the job change; or (2) both spouses make job changes—but they live apart and work at sites at least 35 miles apart. Also, spouses filing jointly who meet the conditions of (2) above get the benefit of a $3,000—$6,000 limitation.

(b) Deductible sale, purchase and lease expenses. Deductible sale-related expenses are those that would be offset against the amount realized on the sale [¶ 1416(b)]. These include the real estate agent's commission, escrow fees, expenses of advertising the property for sale, the cost of preparing the deed and other legal expenses related to the sale, "points" paid to obtain an FHA mortgage for the buyer, and state transfer taxes paid or incurred in the sale or exchange; but not fixing-up expenses on the residence, or any loss sustained on the sale. Deductible purchase-related expenses are the cost of a loan (but not payments or prepayments of interest or "points" paid to obtain a conventional mortgage [¶ 1900]) and those expenses that would be added to the basis of the new residence, such as legal fees, title costs and appraisal fees [¶ 1416(d)]. A taxpayer may also treat as deductible moving expenses, the expenses of settling a lease and acquiring a new one. However, payments or prepayments of rent on a lease for the new residence cannot be deducted [Sec. 217(b)(2); 1.217-2(b)(7)].

> NOTE: To prevent a double benefit, selling expenses taken as a moving expense deduction cannot be used to reduce the amount realized on the sale of the old residence nor can deducted purchase expenses be added to the cost basis of the new [Sec. 217(e); 1.217-2(e)].

(c) Qualification tests. Moving expenses are deductible only if certain time and distance requirements are met [Sec. 217(c), (d); 1.217-2]:

• *Distance.* The new principal place of work must be at least 35 miles farther from the taxpayer's old residence than his old residence was from his old place of work. If taxpayer had no old place of work, the new place must be at least 35 miles from his old residence.

> NOTE: For tax years starting before 1977, the distance requirement was 50 miles.

• *Time.* During the 12 months following the move, the taxpayer must be employed full-time by any employer in the general vicinity of the new job location for

Footnotes appear at end of this Chapter.

¶ 1831

39 weeks. This is waived if the taxpayer cannot meet this requirement because of discharge (other than willful misconduct) or transfer by his employer if it was otherwise reasonable to expect that the taxpayer would have fulfilled the condition, or because of the taxpayer's death or disability.

> NOTE: The taxpayer can elect to take the deduction in the year the moving expenses were paid or incurred even if he has not met the 39-week test by filing date (including extensions) of the return for that year. If he later fails to meet the test, he must include an amount equal to the deduction in his gross income for the first tax year the 39-week test cannot be met [Sec. 217(d)(2), (3); 1.217-2(d)(2), (3)]. If the taxpayer does not claim the moving expense deduction until he has met the 39-week test in the year after the expenses were paid or incurred, he files for a refund for the year of the expenses. For tax years starting after 1975, military personnel are exempted from the time and distance requirements [Sec. 217(g)].

(d) Deduction for self-employed persons. A person who performs personal services as the owner of an unincorporated trade or business or as a partner may deduct moving expenses in the same way as employees [Sec. 217(a), (f); 1.217-2(f)]. The only two differences are: (1) the self-employed taxpayer must work full time either as an employee or self-employed person in the general vicinity of the new job for 78 weeks during the 24 months after the move (39 of these weeks must be during the first 12-month period) [Sec. 217(c)(2); 1.217-2(c)(4)(i)(b)]; and (2) for purposes of the deductions for househunting and temporary quarters, the self-employed taxpayer does not "obtain employment" at the new location until he has made substantial arrangements to commence his work [Sec. 217(c)(2), (f); 1.217-2(f)].

(e) How treated on return. Reimbursements and other payments for moving expenses are included in gross income [¶ 1301]. These payments must be reported to the employee on Form 4782 and included in total wages on the employee's Form W-2. Moving expenses are deductions for adjusted gross income and Form 3903 should be attached to the return.

MISCELLANEOUS TRADE OR BUSINESS EXPENSES

The following will cover some of the miscellaneous expenses, such as educational expenses, that may be deductible by individuals in their trade, business or profession.

¶ 1832 Expenses of professional people. A physician, attorney or other professional person may deduct automobile expenses [¶ 1829], depreciation on office furniture and equipment [Ch. 10], insurance premiums [¶ 1828], travel and entertainment expenses [¶ 1829; 1830], office rent [¶ 1826] and other expenses ordinarily and necessarily incurred in the practice of his profession [Sec. 162(a); 1.162-6]. Professionals and other self-employed individuals, including partners, can also deduct the cost of moving their households as well as their offices [¶ 1831(d)].

Membership dues in medical, technical, or professional societies, chambers of commerce, etc., may be deducted.

Magazines and books: The cost of magazines and newspapers is usually a personal expense. Physicians and dentists can deduct the cost of magazines and newspapers kept in their waiting rooms. The cost of technical magazines, newspapers and looseleaf services is deductible. The original cost of technical books is not a deduction; but the professional person may deduct a proportionate amount for each year's depreciation of technical books. See also ¶ 1806.

Fees for right to practice: The following items are *not* deductible: bar examination fees and other expenses incurred in securing admission to the bar; similar fees and expenses incurred by physicians, dentists, accountants and others for securing the right to practice their professions [Sec.

1.212-1(f)]; fees paid to hospital to practice as staff member (capital expenditure).[1]

Teachers: Dues paid to professional societies, subscription price of educational journals connected with profession, and traveling expenses, costs of meals and lodging incurred in attending teachers' conventions are deductible.

(a) Home and office combined. Specific rules apply to using part of the residence as an office. See ¶ 1804.

The professional may deduct as a business expense the rental value of rooms occupied as an office if rent is actually paid; also the cost of light and heat furnished these rooms. So too, the wages of a domestic who takes care of office is deductible to the extent the domestic's time is involved in that care.

>>**OBSERVATION**> The taxpayer should not forget to add to the cash wages of domestics the value of their food and lodging, light, and special privileges furnished to them.

(b) How treated on return. Allowable professional expense deductions are deductions for adjusted gross income, unless the professional services are performed by the individual as an employee [¶ 1801; 1804]. Employees, in figuring adjusted gross income, may deduct expenses of travel, meals and lodging while away from home in connection with their professional employment; transportation expenses while not away from home in connection with services as professional employees; and all of their other professional expenses which are reimbursed by the employer [¶ 1805]. If the employee's expenditures do not fall within such limitation, but are otherwise deductible, they are deductible as itemized deductions in figuring taxable income.

¶ 1833 Education expenses. The taxpayer can deduct education expenses as ordinary and necessary business expenses if the education either:

- *Maintains or improves* skills required in his job; or
- *Meets new requirements* of his employer or the law, to *keep* his job or rate of pay [Sec. 1.162-5(a)].

However, even if any of the above requirements are met, expenses are not deductible if the education either:

- *Meets minimum educational requirements* for qualifying taxpayer in his present job; or
- *Qualifies taxpayer for a new trade or business* [Sec. 1.162-5(b)].

Problem: Steele, who is an attorney licensed to practice in Ohio, incurs state bar examination fees in order to take the Kentucky bar exam. Are these expenditures deductible?

Solution: No. Passing the bar is the minimum educational requirement for the practice of law in each individual state.

Maintaining or improving skills. Deductible educational costs to maintain or improve skills include refresher courses or courses dealing with current developments as well as academic and vocational courses [Sec. 1.162-5(c)].

Requirements of employer. If, having met the minimum educational requirements for the job, the taxpayer must obtain additional education to keep the present job status or pay rate, those expenses for the least education that will meet the minimum requirements are deductible. Education that also allows advancement in the employer-firm will not necessarily be disallowed under the "requirements of employer" criterion. The deduction is allowed if education resulting in advancement is required for the taxpayer to be kept as an employee at the present level [Sec. 1.162-5(c)].

Footnotes appear at end of this Chapter.

(a) **What expenses are deductible.** Deductible education expenses include amounts spent for tuition, books, supplies, typing,[1] lab fees, and similar items as well as certain travel and transportation costs.

Travel and transportation expenses. The cost of commuting from work to classes is at least partially deductible; if the classes are located within the city or general area of the taxpayer's work, he may deduct the cost of the one-way trip from work to class; however, if the classes are outside the city or general area of the work, the entire round trip is a fully deductible transportation expense.[2] The costs of travel (including sabbatical leaves) as a form of education are deductible only to the extent the expenditures are attributable to a period of travel directly related to the taxpayer's duties in his employment, trade or business, and only if the major portion of the activities during the period directly maintain or improve the taxpayer's skills. The cost of travel for personal reasons is not deductible [Sec. 1.162-5(d)].

(b) **Teachers.** The education expenses of teachers are often deductible. The minimum educational requirements for a position in an educational institution is the minimum level of education (in college hours or degree) normally required when the person is first employed. If there are none, he meets the minimum educational requirements (with reference to the deductibility of expenses) when he becomes a faculty member. All teaching and related duties are considered to be the same general type of work. Thus, education expenses incurred by a classroom teacher for a change from elementary to secondary school or from one subject to another or from teacher to principal would be deductible, as would expenses incurred to qualify for a permanent certificate to teach in another state[3] [Sec. 1.162-5(b), (2), (3)]. Teacher was allowed education expense deduction for full-time graduate study, even though not actively employed at the time.[4] The Revenue Service limits this to a suspension of a year or less to qualify for the deduction.[5]

> **Example:** Joe Frank, who holds a bachelor's degree, is employed by UPI University as an instructor in economics. He undertakes graduate courses as a candidate for a graduate degree. Joe may become a faculty member only if he obtains a graduate degree. He may continue as an instructor only so long as he shows satisfactory progress toward obtaining his degree. The costs of the graduate courses are not deductible, since they constitute education required to meet the minimum educational requirements for qualification in Joe's trade or business.

(c) **How treated on return.** Employees deduct unreimbursed education expenses as an "itemized deducton" [¶ 1801(b)], but related travel and transportation expenses are deductions for adjusted gross income. Both types of expense are deductions for adjusted gross income for outside salespersons, whether or not reimbursed.[2] A professional or self-employed person includes allowable education and related expenses with other expenses of the business as deductions for adjusted gross income.

¶ 1834 **Expenses of persons in the armed forces.** Generally, a person in the armed forces of the U.S. gets the same deductions as a civilian.

(a) **Uniform-equipment.** Officers can deduct the cost of equipment that is especially required by their profession [Sec. 1.262-1]. If the item merely takes the place of an article required in civilian life, it is not deductible. Generally, the cost of the uniform and its maintenance (cleaning, repairs, etc.) is a nondeductible personal expense when it can replace civilian clothing; but reserve personnel on inactive duty can deduct the excess of these costs over a uniform gratuity received for uniforms required for training and drills.[1]

(b) Overseas duty; travel. Members of the armed forces on *permanent* duty overseas may not deduct expenses for meals and lodging at such locations although they are required to maintain homes in the United States for their families.[2] Expenses incurred by servicemen while in a travel status or on temporary assignments *away from their permanent posts,* are deductible in full, and need not be offset by the nontaxable, basic subsistence allowance.[3]

A reservist may deduct the transportation costs of going from his regular job to his meetings. If he goes home first, he cannot deduct more than it would cost to go directly from the job to the meeting.[4]

BENEFIT AND RETIREMENT PLANS

¶ **1838 Contributions under pension, stock bonus and profit-sharing plans.** The employer can take a limited deduction for contributions made to pension, annuity, stock bonus and profit-sharing plans. To get the deduction, it must be shown that the contribution is an ordinary and necessary expense paid or incurred in carrying on a trade or business [Sec. 162; 1.162-1], or is an expense for the production of income [Sec. 212]. Also, see (i) below.

(a) Reasonableness and time of contributions. The contributions plus regular salaries must not exceed reasonable compensation for past and present services rendered. Any contribution for an employee pension over the amount necessary to provide a reasonable pension is not deductible. The deduction is generally allowed in the tax year the contribution is made. However, an employer, whether on cash or accrual basis, may treat its contribution made after the end of its tax year but before the return due date (including extensions) as payment for the preceding year, if the employer so designates in writing to the plan administrator or trustee, or claims the deduction on the return for the preceding year.[1]

(b) Special deduction provisions for qualified plan. Contributions to a qualified plan or trust may be deductible under special provisions. These provisions do not apply to a plan that does not defer compensation. Nor do they apply to a plan that is *solely* a dismissal wage, hospitalization, medical expense, recreational, welfare or similar benefit plan (these contributions are deductible as a business expense [¶ 1819(c)]). But if contributions to a *qualified plan* can be used to provide these benefits, they are deductible under these provisions, not as a business expense [Sec. 1.404(a)-1(a)].

(c) Requirements for qualified plan. See ¶ 3024(a).

(d) Deduction for qualified pension trust. For plan years beginning after 9-2-74 (after 12-31-75 for plans existing on 1-1-74), an employer can deduct the amount necessary: (a) to satisfy the minimum funding standard, or (b) to provide all employees with their remaining unfunded cost of past and current service credits, distributed as a level amount or a level percentage of compensation, over the remaining life of each employee (at least 5 years if 3 individuals account for over 50% of the remaining unfunded cost), or (c) to amortize past service liabilities and other supplementary pension or annuity credits over 10 years, plus the normal cost of the plan. The maximum deduction cannot exceed the amount of the full funding limitation for the year [Sec. 404(a)(1)]. For plan years beginning on or before 9-2-74 (before 12-31-75 for plans existing on 1-1-74), the deduction is generally limited to 5% of the tax year's compensation paid or accrued to all participating employees.

Footnotes appear at end of this Chapter.

¶ **1838**

Any amount paid in one tax year over the limits can be deducted in a succeeding tax year to the extent that year's contribution is less than the maximum allowable deduction [Sec. 404(a)(1)(D); 1.404(a)-7].

(e) Deduction for qualified stock bonus or profit-sharing trust. The deduction is limited to 15% of the compensation otherwise paid or accrued during the tax year to all beneficiaries of the plan. Any amount paid in one tax year *over* the limit is deductible in the succeeding tax years in the order of time, if the deduction in the succeeding year does not exceed the 15% limits for the current year's deduction. This contribution carryover deduction may be taken even in the year following the year the plan is terminated.

If the amount contributed during any tax year is *less* than the 15% maximum, the difference between the amount contributed and the 15% maximum may be carried over as a potential credit and deducted when contributed in a later tax year. The amount that can be carried over and deducted is in addition to the 15% maximum current year's deduction. Up to 25% of the compensation may be deducted in a year the credit is used (for tax years beginning before 1976, a carryover of up to 15% of compensation was allowed, so that up to 30% of compensation was deductible). Two or more stock bonus or profit-sharing trusts are considered a single trust for the purpose of the above limit [Sec. 404(a)(3)(A); 1.404(a)-9]. However, a special rule applies after 1970 to credit carryovers of corporations electing to be taxed as partnerships [¶ 3146(c)].

Affiliated corporations. Affiliated corporations that can file a consolidated tax return may establish and maintain a joint profit-sharing plan. If one corporation fails to make any profits, the participating corporations may share the total contributions in any proportions they choose. However, if the affiliated group does not file a consolidated return, the members of the group must divide the contribution made on behalf of the loss corporation so that each contributes in the proportion that its profits bear to the total profits of the members that make profits. A contribution is deductible by the corporation making it, but the corporation for whose employees the contribution was made does not get a carryover for succeeding tax years because of its failure to contribute the full deductible amount. Affiliated corporations may also maintain a common stock bonus plan *if* the contributions are measured by a percentage of profits [Sec. 404(a)(3)(B); 1.404(a)-10].

(f) Overall limitations on contributions to qualified plans. Annual additions to an employee's account under a qualified plan can not exceed the lesser of $28,175 or 25% of the individual's compensation from the employer during the tax year.

NOTE: The dollar limitation is subject to cost-of-living adjustments [Sec. 415(d)(1)(B)].

The term "annual addition" includes (1) the employer's contribution, (2) the lesser of the employee's contributions in excess of 6% of compensation or half the employee's total contribution, and (3) forfeitures added to the employee's account. When contributions are made above the 25%, they may be carried forward and deducted in subsequent years. However, the limitation for these years remains at 25% [Sec. 415].

NOTE: For tax years starting after 1975, the Tax Reform Act of 1976 allows a self-employed individual to set aside up to $750 in a defined contribution plan without regard to the 25% limitation, provided the individual's adjusted gross income for the tax year is not over $15,000 [Sec. 415(c)(5)].

Background and purpose. At one time, there was no limit on the amount that could be contributed to an employee's retirement account, although the employer could not, in a single year, deduct contributions above 15% of total compensation paid to employees covered by a qualified plan. ERISA retained the 15% limit [(e) above], but imposed the limitations on the annual additions that could be made to an individual employee's account under a defined contribution plan. This was done to achieve some measure of comparability with limitations imposed on the benefits which could be paid under a defined benefit plan. The limitations apply to contributions and benefits accrued in years starting after 12-31-75.

(g) Contributions toward purchase of retirement annuities. Employer's contributions paid to buy retirement annuities under a qualified plan that is not part of a trust, are subject to the rules governing pension trusts. See (d) above. Any refunds of premiums, however, must be applied in the current or next succeeding tax year toward the purchase of retirement annuities [Sec. 404(a)(2); 1.404(a)-8].

(h) Contributions to combination of plans. If contributions are made either to (1) a pension trust and a profit-sharing or stock bonus trust, or (2) a profit-sharing or stock bonus trust and under an annuity plan, or (3) both pension and profit-sharing or stock bonus trusts and under an annuity plan, and the plans meet the requirements of Sec. 401(a), the amount deductible for contributions may not exceed the greater of (a) 25% of the compensation otherwise paid or accrued during the tax year to the employee beneficiaries, or (b) the contributions made to the extent they do not exceed the contributions needed to satisfy the minimum funding standard. This rule applies to plan years starting after 9-2-74. If the contributions in the tax year exceed the limit, the excess may be deducted in succeeding years, but the deduction in any one succeeding year may not exceed 25% (30% for plan years started on or before 9-2-74) of the compensation otherwise paid or accrued during such tax year to the employees covered by the plan [Sec. 404(a)(7)].

(i) Contributions to plans that do not qualify. For contributions made after 8-1-69, the employer is allowed a deduction equal to the amount included in the employee's income when the employee's rights become nonforfeitable and he reports the income. However, if the plan is one in which more than one employee participates, the deduction is permitted only if separate accounts are kept for each employee [Sec. 404(a)(5)]. For contributions made before 8-2-69, a deduction was allowed only if the employees' rights arising from the contribution were nonforfeitable when the contribution was made [Sec. 1.404(a)-(12)].

If a trust qualifies except for the fact that it was organized outside the United States, an employer may deduct his contribution as if it were made to a qualified trust [Sec. 404(a)(4); 1.404(a)-11]. Contributions are deductible as a business expense if made to plans established before 1-1-54 as a result of an agreement between employees and the U.S. Government during a period of Government operation of the industry [Sec. 404(c); 1.162-10, 1.404(c)-1].

(j) Contributions when there is no plan. If there is no plan, but a method of employer contributions or compensation has the effect of a stock bonus, pension, profit-sharing, or annuity plan, or similar plan deferring compensation, the contribution or compensation is also subject to the provisions discussed in this paragraph. This method would exist where (1) a corporation pays pensions to retired employees or their beneficiaries in amounts determined from time to time by the board of directors or officers, or (2) a corporation is obligated to pay a pension or deferred compensation to an employee or his beneficiaries. An accrual basis taxpayer who defers compensation under such an arrangement can take the deduction only in the year paid [Sec. 404(b); 1.404(b)-1].

Footnotes appear at end of this Chapter.

¶ 1838

(k) Information required. See ¶ 3521; 3537(d).

(l) Individual retirement arrangements. An individual who is not covered by an employer plan, self-employed retirement plan or charitable annuity, can set up his or her own plan to which he or she can contribute and deduct 15% of compensation up to $1,500 from gross income annually for tax years starting after 1974 [Sec. 219, 408, 409, 4973, 4974; Prop. Reg. 1.219-1(b)]. This deduction is disallowed if one is taken on retirement savings for certain married individuals [see below]. The maximum deduction is figured separately for each individual. Thus, a husband and wife must account for his or her own compensation, whether or not they file a joint return or live in a community property state. There is no deduction for contributions made in or after the tax year an individual reaches age 70½ [Prop. Reg. Sec. 1.219-1(b), (c)]. The contribution may be made to an individual retirement account or for an individual retirement annuity or bond. An employer can also set up and contribute to an employee's plan. The employer gets the deduction even if it exceeds the maximum limit, provided the deduction meets reasonable compensation standards (¶ 1815-1817) [Prop. Reg. Sec. 1.219-1(c)(3)]. The employer's contribution is taxable income to the employee. See ¶ 3027.

NOTE: For tax years stating after 1976, contributions can be made at any time within 45 days after the close of the tax year. For tax years starting after 1975, reservists, national guard members and volunteer firefighters can participate in individual retirement arrangements under certain conditions [Sec. 219(c)].

Retirement savings for certain married individuals. For tax years starting after 1976, an employee has the option of setting up retirement savings with a subaccount for the benefit of a nonworking spouse. The maximum deduction is $1,750 to a single account that has a subaccount for the spouse. The taxpayer may also deduct up to $875 to his or her own account and up to $875 to a separate account for the spouse. In either case, the total deduction is limited to 15% of compensation, including earned income. This deduction is disallowed if one has been taken under a regular IRA [Sec. 220].

NOTE: For tax years starting after 1977, contributions can be made at any time within 45 days after the close of the tax year [Sec. 220(c)(4)].

Excess contributions. Contributions to an individual retirement account or annuity in excess of permissible limits are subject to a 6% excise tax [Sec. 4973; Prop. Reg. 54.4973-1]. The tax is nondeductible, cumulative, and payable by the participant. For tax years beginning after 1976, the tax is not applied if excess contributions, plus any income earned on them, are withdrawn before the due date of the return for the contribution year. Excess contributions made after 3-3-76 and before 1-1-77 are subject to the excise tax even if withdrawn by the due date for filing the tax return.[2] The tax can be avoided for a subsequent year by contributing less than the maximum limit for that year.

Premature distributions. Distributions from retirement accounts or annuity plans which occur before an individual reaches age 59½ are subject to a 10% nondeductible excise tax unless the individual is disabled [Sec. 408(f)(1); Proposed Reg. 1.408-1]. The penalty cannot be offset by investment, retirement, or WIN credits [Proposed Reg. Sec. 1.408-1(c)(1)]. The tax applies to actual, as well as "deemed" distributions. Thus, if an individual benefits from a prohibited transaction, the tax can apply to the amount of the benefit.

Late distributions. Distributions from individual retirement plans must begin by the end of the year in which the participant reaches age 70½ [Proposed Reg. Sec. 1.408-2(b)(6)]. If not, a nondeductible 50% excise tax is imposed on the difference between what was paid out and what should have been paid out [Sec. 4974; Proposed Reg. 54.4974-1].

Rollover contributions. An individual can withdraw his entire interest in a retirement plan without penalty or tax if that interest is recontributed to an individual retirement arrangement within 60 days of receipt. A rollover contribution to an arrangement is an allowable contribution not deductible on the taxpayer's return. There are two types [Sec. 402(a), 403(a), 408(d)(3), 409(b)(3)]:

• A lump-sum distribution from a qualified pension, profit-sharing or stock bonus plan within the taxpayer's tax year.

NOTE: A lump-sum distribution is the receipt of the taxpayer's entire interest in one tax year which must occur at least when a taxpayer reaches age 59½ unless: (1) he becomes disabled before then; (2) leaves the company when employment is ended provided he has been a plan participant for at least 5 years before tax year in which the distribution is made; or (3) receives a "termination distribution" after 7-3-74 because the employer either ended the plan or discontinued contributions to it. In this case, the distribution can be rolled over at any time before 12-31-76, regardless of the 60-day rollover period [Sec. 805(d)(1)].

• An entire distribution is made from one arrangement (not an endowment contract) to another.

NOTE: This transfer will be taxable if there was a prior tax-free rollover of an amount received from another arrangement within 3 years of the current distribution's receipt date.

Information required. Persons who have an individual retirement arrangement must file Form 5329, with Form 5498 attached, with their tax return whether or not any contributions were made during the tax year. This form must also be filed by a surviving spouse or other surviving beneficiary as long as there is a balance remaining in the account. Form 5498 is provided by the trustee, custodian or insurance company responsible for the arrangement. Persons not required to file a tax return should file on a completed Form 5329. See also ¶ 3537(d).

¶ **1839 Self-employed retirement plans.** Self-employed individuals can take tax deductions for contributions they make to formal pension or profit-sharing plans for themselves and their employees. Income earned on their contributions is not taxed until it is withdrawn from the retirement fund.

(a) Who can get coverage. Self-employed individuals who have earnings from self-employment for the tax year can participate in qualified pension and profit-sharing plans. An inactive owner or partner who gets income entirely from his investment cannot participate.

Self-employed who are "owner-employees" cannot get coverage for themselves unless they provide coverage for all full-time employees (including those whose services and wage cost are shared by others[1]) with 3 or more years service [Sec. 401(d)(3); 1.401-12(e)]. An owner-employee is an individual who owns all of an unincorporated business or is a partner owning a more-than-10% capital or profits interest [Sec. 401(c)(3); 1.401-10(d)].

Two or more businesses. Any owner-employee (or group of owner-employees) who controls more than one business must cover all the qualifying employees in all the businesses that are controlled. An owner-employee (whether or not he controls the business) who also is an owner-employee of another business which he controls cannot be covered under the plan of the first business unless he has set up a plan for the employees of the business he controls. The plan for the controlled business must provide contributions and benefits that are at least as favorable as those provided for owner-employees under the plan of the first business [Sec. 401(d); 1.401-12(1)].

(b) **Ceiling on contributions.** An owner-employee can contribute for himself each year the lesser of $7,500 or 15% of his earned income for that year. A minimum of $750 is deductible without regard to the percentage limitation (but see (c) below). After 1975, in applying the percentage limit, generally no more than $100,000 of each owner-employee's earned income is taken into account. In general, earned income is net earnings from self-employment in a trade, business, or profession in which the taxpayer performs personal services. However, persons who create property, such as authors, inventors and artists may count net earnings derived from the property and ordinary gain on its sale as earned income [Sec. 401; Prop. Reg. 1.401(e)-5]. Ordinarily, interest is not included as earned income, but if it is generated by personal services, such as by a real estate broker arranging sales, it may be counted as part of the net business profits.[2]

NOTE: The contribution limit may exceed $7,500 after 1975 by using the defined-benefit plan formula [Sec. 401(j)]. However, the limit on nondeductible voluntary contributions of owner-employees remains unchanged—10% of earnings or $2,500, whichever is less.

Generally, only money may be contributed to a plan [1.401-12(k)]. A partner who is not an owner-employee apparently can make a contribution for himself (out of earned income) in excess of the percentage or amount limitations outlined above.

NOTE: Effective for 1975, and subsequent years, an employer may elect to have a contribution to a plan treated as having been made for a given year even though it was not in fact made until after the end of that year. However, the contribution must have in fact been made by the time for filing the tax return for that year (including extensions for filing) [Temp. Reg. Sec. 11.404(a)(6)-1].

(c) **Ceiling on deductions.** A self-employed person (including an owner-employee) can deduct his entire contribution on his own behalf up to $7,500 or 15% of his earned income, whichever is less (see the limit in (b), above). However, the minimum deduction is not less than the lesser of $750, or 100% of his earned income (for tax years starting after 1975, the $750 minimum applies unless the person's adjusted gross income exceeds $15,000 without taking the plan contribution into account) [Sec. 404(e)(4)]. A self-employed person cannot deduct his own voluntary "employee" contributions [Sec. 404(a)(8); 1.404(e)-1(b)(1)].

The self-employed individual can deduct contributions for his employees in full if they are within the general deduction limits applying to all qualified plans. However, the amount the self-employed individual can deduct for himself is determined on a year-to-year basis, without any carryover. But he can take advantage of the various carryover provisions for contributions made for his employees.

NOTE: An individual proprietor who sets up a plan cannot deduct for his contributions made after the business operates as a partnership, unless the partnership adopts the plan[3] or he is covered by a partnership plan [Sec. 401(d)(4)(A); 1.401-10(e)(1), 1.401-12(b)].

How treated on return. The self-employed person calculates what he is allowed to deduct for contributions on his own behalf for the year. Then he subtracts it from gross income in arriving at "adjusted gross income." He treats the contribution for his employees like any other business expense.

(d) Qualifying the plan. In addition to meeting the nondiscrimination requirements for qualified employee plans generally [¶ 3024], a plan also must [Sec. 401(d); 1.401-11, 1.401-12]:

- Provide for immediate vested benefits for all covered employees.
- If it is a profit-sharing plan, have a definite formula for determining contributions to be made for employees (other than owner-employees).
- Require that benefits to an employee start not later than age 70½ or the year he retires, or to an owner-employee, not later than age 70½.
- Require that benefits cannot be paid to an owner-employee before he reaches age 59½ unless he becomes disabled, even if the plan is ended before then.[4] For tax years ending after 9-2-74, this rule applies to benefits in excess of contributions made by an owner-employee as an employee. A premature payout to him does not adversely affect the qualification of a plan in regard to his employees covered under the plan;[5] however, for tax years after 1974, a penalty tax is payable on the premature payout. But a plan can allow an owner-employee to withdraw his voluntary contributions without penalty [Sec. 408(f)].
- After 1975, provide that contributions made and benefits payable will not exceed the overall limits on benefits and contributions [Sec. 415].

Medical benefits may be paid as part of a qualified plan [Sec. 401(h); 1.401-14].

Revenue Service approval of the initial qualification or amendment of an individually designed plan can be obtained by filing a request on Form 4574 for a Revenue Service determination letter.

Master or prototype plans may be submitted for approval by trade or professional associations, banks, and insurance or regulated investment companies by filing Form 3672.[6]

Information required on return. See ¶ 3537(d).

(e) Retirement fund. The retirement fund set up by a self-employed person may be lodged with a bank as trustee [Sec. 401(d)(1); 1.401-12(c)] or as custodian. Persons other than banks may serve as trustees or custodians providing they can show the Revenue Service that they can properly perform the service [Temp. Reg. Sec. 11.401(d)(1)-1; Prop. Reg. 1.401-12]. Custodial account assets must be invested in open-end mutual funds or annuity, endowment, or life insurance contracts. Annuity contracts, meeting the same requirements of custodial accounts, can also be treated as qualified trusts [Sec. 401(f)]. The retirement fund can be invested in nontransferable annuities or face amount certificates [Sec. 401(g); 1.401-9], or it can be invested in a special series of U.S. bonds authorized for this purpose. These bonds are nontransferable, nonredeemable before age 59½ (except in case of disability or death), and are issued only in the names of individuals [Sec. 405; 1.405-1].

> NOTE: For tax years starting after 1975, a qualified pension plan can invest in an insurance contract with a segregated asset account even though the contract does not provide for the payment of annuities. Assets of a qualified plan can be held in annuity contracts or certain nonannuity contracts instead of trusts if the investment is otherwise allowable under law [Sec. 401(f)].

(f) Treatment of excess contributions. Contributions over the maximum allowed must be returned to the owner-employee for whom it was made. If a contribution is not repaid within 6 months after notice by the Revenue Service that it

¶ 1839

was excessive, the plan is disqualified (until the excess is returned) as to the person for whom the excess contribution was made. In that case, he will be taxed on his share of the annual income earned by the fund. If the excess contribution was made wilfully his entire interest in all plans in which he is an owner-employee must be distributed to him and he is disqualified from participating in any pension plan as an owner-employee for 5 years. An exception to these rules allows an owner-employee to buy annuity, life insurance or endowment policies at level premiums without fear of making excess contributions [Sec. 401(e)(3); 1.401-13(b)].

NOTE: Excess contributions to qualified plans of Subchapter S corporations are included in the gross income of shareholder-employees [¶ 3146(a)].

(g) Treatment of distributions. Lump-sum distributions representing employer contributions in 1973 and earlier years receive capital gain treatment. Distributions from accumulations after 1973 are ordinary income. However, the tax on the ordinary income portion can be computed under a special 10-year forward-averaging device. There is a penalty for premature distributions made after 12-31-75 [Sec. 72(m), 402(e)]. For more details on taxing lump-sum distributions, see ¶ 3024(d).

SPECIAL PROBLEMS

The special problems covered in this section relate to leaseholds, research and experimental expenditures, mining expenditures, farmer's expenses, soil and water conservation expenditures and amortizable bond premiums.

¶ 1840 Leaseholds. The cost of property having a useful life longer than the tax year is not deductible as *a business expense*, but is spread over the useful life of the property and recovered by way of depreciation. This basic principle is applied to (a) improvements by tenant [¶ 2002], and (b) purchase of a lease.

Purchase of lease. A lease is sometimes bought from a tenant. The buyer pays a fixed sum and undertakes the rent obligations of the seller for the remaining period of the lease. The buyer may deduct each year a proportionate part of the cost of acquiring the lease, based on the number of years the lease has to run [Sec. 1.162-11].[1]

Renewable lease. The renewable period must be considered in writing off the acquisition cost if less than ¾ of the cost is for the initial (unexpired) lease period, unless the tenant establishes that, as of the close of the tax year, the probabilities favor the termination, rather than renewal, of the lease [Secs. 178(a); 1.178-1(b)]. The renewal period must be considered in any event if the lease is renewed or it is reasonably certain that it will be renewed [Secs. 178(c); 1.178-1(c); 1.178-3].

Example: Taxpayer buys a lease for $10,000. The unexpired term of the lease is 10 years, but there is a renewal option for 5 years. If less than $7,500 (¾ × $10,000) is paid for the 10 remaining years of the lease, the cost must be written off over 15 years, unless the tenant shows that, as of the end of the tax year, the odds favor the termination of the lease. But, if $7,500 or more is paid for the 10 remaining years of the lease, the cost is written off over 10 years, unless it is certain that the lease will be renewed.

¶ 1842 Research and experimental expenditures. Research and experimental expenditures of an existing[1] trade or business may be deducted in the year paid or incurred, or over a period of 60 months or more. A new venture is allowed a deduction for the costs of a new product even though the product is not finished or marketable the year the expenses are incurred.[2] It is not necessary that the expenses be related to the current product lines or manufacturing processes of the trade or business; they may be for new products or processes.[3] This rule applies whether the research and experiments were made by the taxpayer, or by another for him (such as an institute or foundation). If neither method is used, the expenditures must be capitalized [Sec. 174; 1.174-1, 1.174-2].

(a) Deductible in year paid or incurred. If this method is elected, the expenses are not chargeable to capital account. However, they may be deducted currently regardless of how they are recorded on the books.[4]

Election of method. This method can be adopted without consent if the deduction is claimed on the return in the first tax year the expenditures are paid or incurred. Consent is required for adoption at any other time. The request should be in writing, signed by the taxpayer (or representative), and addressed to the Commissioner, Att: T: R, Wash., D.C. It should state: (1) taxpayer's name and address, (2) first tax year for which the request is made; and (3) description of the projects for which the request is made. It must be filed by the end of the first tax year for which the request is made [Sec. 1.174-3(b)(2)].

Once adopted, this method applies to *all* research and experimental expenditures regularly incurred by the taxpayer starting with the election year [Sec. 1.174-3(a), (b)(2)], and must be followed unless the Commissioner consents to a change for all or a part of the expenditures [Sec. 174(a); 1.174-3(a)]. The taxpayer may request authorization to capitalize research and experimental expenditures for a special project [Sec. 1.174-3(a)].

Change of method. The application for change must be in writing, signed by taxpayer (or representative) and filed by the end of the first tax year to which the change applies. It must include: (1) reason for the change; (2) all necessary information relating to the change; and (3) a note that proper accounting records will be maintained for the expenditures involved. A copy of the letter of permission must be attached to the return for the first tax year to which the change applies [Sec. 1.174-3(b)(3)].

(b) Deferred expenses. If the taxpayer defers his research and experimental expenditures and charges them to capital account, he must deduct them ratably over a period of 60 months or more. He starts with the month he first benefits from the expenditures. If there are two or more projects, different periods may be selected for each. If, however, the property resulting from such expenditures has a determinable useful life, such capitalized expenditures are recoverable by way of depreciation or depletion. Also, if the expenditures which the taxpayer elected to defer result in the *development* of depreciable property, the unrecovered costs, from the time the asset first becomes depreciable, must be recovered by way of depreciation.

Election of method. Election must be made no later than the time for filing the return for the tax year (including extensions) the expenditures are paid or incurred. The election is made by a signed statement attached to the return. It should include: (1) taxpayer's name and address; (2) all necessary information relating to the expenditures; and (3) a note stating proper accounting records will be kept for the expenditures [Sec. 1.174-4(b)(1)]. However, the election to defer expenses can be made by claiming an appropriate deduction on the return.[5] The election does not apply to an expenditure paid or incurred before the year of election [Sec. 174(b); 1.174-4].

Change of method. Once adopted this method must be followed unless Commissioner consents to a change. The application must be in writing, signed by taxpayer (or representative) and filed by the end of the first tax year for which the change applies. It should contain: (1) taxpayer's name and address; and (2) all necessary information relating to the change. A copy of the permission must be attached to the return for the first tax year to which the change applies [Sec. 1.174-4(b)(2)].

(c) **Exceptions.** Generally, the options to defer the expenses or deduct them in the year paid or incurred do not apply to (1) expenditures for land or depreciable or depletable property even if it is to be used in research or experimentation (but depreciation and depletion on such property are considered research and experimental expenditures); or (2) exploration expenditures incurred for minerals, oil or gas [Sec. 174(c)(d); 1.174-2(b), (c)]. However, research and experimental expenditures, themselves, are deductible (under (a) above) even if they result (as a product of the research and experimentation) in depreciable property to be used in taxpayer's trade or business. If the expenditures are for the construction or manufacture of depreciable property by another, they are so deductible only if incurred at taxpayer's order or risk.

(d) **Adjustment of basis.** Expenses deferred (under (b) above) are included in figuring the adjusted basis of the property for which they are paid or incurred. The adjusted basis, however, must be reduced by the deferred expenses allowed as deductions to the extent there is a tax benefit (but not less than the amount allowable for the tax year and prior years) [Sec. 1016(a)(1), (14); 1.1016-5(j)].

¶ **1843 Mining expenditures.** The rules for deducting exploration and development expenditures in connection with mines follow:

(a) **Exploration expenditures.** These are expenditures made to ascertain the existence, location, extent or quality of any deposit of ore or other mineral (except oil or gas) before the development stage begins [Sec. 617(a); 1.617-1]. Instead of capitalizing these expenses, a taxpayer may elect to deduct those paid or incurred after 12-31-69. Before 1970, a taxpayer could elect a limited as well as an unlimited deduction for the same type of expenses [Sec. 617(i); 1.615-1—1.615-8]. A taxpayer who elected the pre-1970 limited deduction (not subject to recapture) is deemed to have elected the unlimited deduction (subject to recapture) for expenditures after 12-31-69, unless he notifies the Revenue Service to the contrary. Notification must be made with the return for the first tax year that includes post-1969 expenditures [Sec. 1.615-9].

The general or unlimited deduction applies only to ores or minerals located in the U.S. (or the Outer Continental Shelf). This election allows the taxpayer to deduct the expenditures currently as they are paid or incurred; but none can be capitalized. The election may be made for a tax year as long as a refund claim can be filed for that year (generally 3 years). It is made by taking the deduction on the return or an amended return for the first tax year it is to apply. The election applies to all later years and cannot be revoked without Revenue Service consent (except during the period ending before 10-1-72) [Sec. 617(a), (h); 1.617-1(c)].

The deduction eventually is recaptured as ordinary income either when the property reaches the production stage or when it is disposed of at a gain [Sec. 617(b); 1.617-3]. When a mine goes into production, the taxpayer may elect either to include in income the adjusted exploration expenditures deducted for all mines that reach the production stage that year and capitalize them as an expenditure for the year, or to forego the depletion allowance until the amount that could have been deducted as depletion equals the adjusted expenditure. The adjusted expenditure is the total exploration expenses for a mine or property, reduced by the excess of what the percentage depletion would have been (if the expense deduction were not elected) over the amount of allowable cost depletion [See Ch. 11]. This amount is reduced by any amounts reported as income when the property goes into production or as ordinary gain on a disposition of the property [Sec. 617(f)]. Ordinary gain is the lesser of (1) adjusted exploration expense or, (2) the gain, measured by the difference between adjusted basis and amount realized (for sale, exchange or involuntary conversion) or fair market value (for other dispositions). The entire expense for a property is attributed to a portion of the property that is disposed of, but is allocated when an undivided interest is transferred. This does not apply to mines in production or expenses not related to the portion disposed of [Sec. 617(d); 1.617-4].

The exceptions and limitations that apply to receipt of ordinary income on dispostions of Sec. 1245 property [¶ 1619(c)] also apply to mining property transferred by gift, inheritance and tax-free transfers in which the transferee's basis is determined from the transferor's basis [Sec. 617(d)]. Bonus and royalty payments generally are subject to the same recapture rules for the depletion deduction, and gain on the disposition of coal or iron ore that usually is treated as capital gain [¶ 1617] may be ordinary income [Sec. 617(c); (f)]Special rules apply to partnership distributions [Sec. 617(g)].

A limited deduction is allowed for ores or minerals from foreign (and oceanographic) deposit. If the taxpayer makes the election, he may deduct up to $400,000. A taxpayer generally may deduct expenditures for foreign explorations within the $400,000 limit, reduced by the aggregate of any amounts previously deducted or deferred under the pre-1970 limited deduction and any post-1969 deductions (whether for foreign or domestic exploration); any expenses in excess of this limit are capitalized. The general recapture rules (above) apply to the amounts deducted for expenditures made after 12-31-69 [Sec. 617(h); 1.617-2]. Before 1970, there was no recapture of deducted foreign expenditures.

Mineral property transfers with a substituted basis. When the transferee's basis for the transferred property is determined from the transferor's basis and the transferor has made no election to deduct or defer exploration expenses, the transferor cannot make an election for expenses related to the property for the period between 9-12-66 and the date of transfer. An election made before the transfer and revoked after it, is disregarded. If transferor elected the pre-1970 limited deduction and the transferee elects or applies the unlimited deduction, transferor's deductions are counted as recapturable deductions and his deferred expenses are capitalized [Sec. 617(i); 1.615-7].

(b) Development expenditures. Expenses for the development of a mine or natural deposit (other than oil or gas well) that contains commercially marketable quantities of the ore or mineral, are deductible as follows:

(1) They can be deducted in the year paid or incurred [Sec. 616(a); 1.616-1]; *or*

(2) The taxpayer may elect to deduct them proportionately as the ore or mineral benefited by them is sold (deferred expense). While the mine or deposit is in the development stage, this election is limited to the development expenses in excess of the net receipts from production within the tax year. (Expenditures not in excess of such receipts are deductible in full.) This election is not binding on future years. It may be made either on the return or by a statement filed with the Director with whom the return was filed not later than the time for filing the return (including extensions) for the tax year to which the election applies [Sec. 616(b); 1.616-2].

Example 1: Mine A was in the development stage throughout the year 1977. If the development expenses incurred during the year are $5,000, the whole amount is either deductible in 1977, or, at the election of the taxpayer, deferred to be deducted ratably as the ore or mineral is sold.

Example 2: Mine C was in the development stage from January to August 1977: From August to December 1977, it was in the productive stage. Development expenses from January

¶ 1843

to August amounted to $5,000 and from August to December, $1,000. If the net receipts from the sale of minerals produced in 1977 is $3,000, the taxpayer has an option to—

(1) deduct $6,000 in 1977, or

(2) deduct $3,000 in 1977 and defer $3,000 to be deducted ratably as the ore or mineral is sold. (The $3,000 to be deducted in 1977 represents his $5,000 preproduction development expenses not in excess of the $3,000 net receipts. The $3,000 to be deferred, represents the $1,000 development expenses incurred in the productive stage plus the $2,000 which is the excess of his $5,000 of preproduction development expenses over the $3,000 of net receipts.)

(c) **Expenditures not included.** The options in (a) and (b) above do not apply to expenditures (1) to acquire or improve depreciable property (but depreciation on such property is an exploration or development expenditure); (2) deductible without regard to these provisions; or (3) that are part of the cost of acquiring the property [Sec. 616, 617; 1.616-1(b)].

(d) **Deduction for adjusted gross income.** An individual's deductible business exploration or development expenses are deductions for adjusted gross income [¶ 1804].

(e) **Adjusted basis of mine or deposit.** Development or pre-1970 exploration expenses that are deferred are included in figuring the adjusted basis of the mine or deposit when the mine is sold. However, the adjusted basis must be reduced by the deferred expenses allowed as deductions to the extent that they reduced tax liability (but not less than the amount allowable for the tax year and prior years). These expenses are not considered in figuring the adjusted basis of the mine or deposit for purposes of depletion [Sec. 616(c); 617(i); 1.1016-5(f)]. Depletion disallowed when the unlimited exploration expenditure is elected does not reduce the property basis [Sec. 617(e)].

¶ **1844 Expenses of farmers.** A farmer's expenses of preparing, developing and operating his farm are either ordinary and necessary current business expenses or capital expenditures. Special rules limit the deductions available to farm syndicates. See (d) below. Losses of farmers are discussed in ¶ 2211.

(a) **Business expenses.** During the productive period of the farm, the ordinary and necessary current expenses of farming are deductible. They cannot be capitalized [Sec. 1.162-12].

EXAMPLES OF DEDUCTIBLE EXPENSES[1]

Rations purchased and furnished sharecroppers

Feed purchased (grain, hay, silage, mill feeds, concentrates and other roughages, and cost of grinding, mixing, and processing feed) [but see (d) below]

Machine hire (payments for use of threshing, combining, silo filling, baling, ginning, and other machines)

Seeds and plants purchased (but see (d) below)

Supplies purchased (spray material, poisons, disinfectants, cans, barrels, baskets, egg cases, bags, etc.)

Repairs and maintenance of farm machines and equipment

Breeding fees

Fertilizers and lime (cost of commercial fertilizers, lime, and manure purchased during the year, the benefit of which is of short duration) [see also election]

Veterinary and medicine for livestock

Storage and warehousing expense

Insurance on farm property, except farmer's dwelling (buildings, improvements, equipment, crops and livestock)

Water rent (farm share of expense)

Blacksmith and harness repair

Subscription to farm journals

EXAMPLES OF NONDEDUCTIBLE EXPENSES[1]

Value of products raised by farmer and used for board of hired help

Expense of raising products consumed by farmer and his family

Cost of producing or acquiring donated products[2] [see ¶ 1810]
Value of labor of farmer, his wife, or minor children (but reasonable wages paid to child for his service on farm are deductible)
Cotton acreage allotments[3]
Expenses of planting and developing citrus groves (see below)

During the development of the farm, a farmer may elect to capitalize ordinary and necessary expenses incidental to current operation instead of deducting them[4] [Sec. 1.162-12].

Citrus and almond grove expenses. The costs of planting, cultivating, maintaining and developing citrus and almond groves must be capitalized rather than deducted currently through the end of the fourth tax year after planting. The rule does not apply to the cost of replanting a grove lost by disease, freeze or other casualty [Sec. 278].

NOTE: The farm syndicate rules discussed in (d) below do not apply to any groves planted or replanted before 1976.

Election to deduct fertilizer and lime expenditures. A farmer may elect to treat as a deductible expense expenditures for fetilizer, lime, ground limestone, marl, or other materials used to enrich, neutralize, or condition his farmland, or for the application of these materials. The election is made by taking the deduction on a timely filed return for the year. It may not be revoked without consent of the Revenue Service [Sec. 180; 1.180-1, 1.180-2].

(b) Capital expenditures. Expenditures during the preparatory period, when the property is made ready for development, are not deductible as business expenses. They are capital expenditures[4] [Sec. 1.162-12; ¶ 1808; 2001], except for fertilizer and lime expenditures (above) the farmer elects to deduct.

The cost of farm machinery, equipment, and buildings (other than dwelling) whether incurred in the preparatory period or another period, is not deductible as an expense, but is a capital expenditure, and deduction is allowed for depreciation [Sec. 1.162-12; ¶ 1804; 2001]. Likewise, amounts spent to buy work, breeding or dairy animals are regarded as investments of capital, and a depreciation deduction is allowed, unless the animals are included in inventory [Sec. 1.162-12; see ¶ 2614 et seq.].

(c) Farming for pleasure. If a farm is operated for recreation or pleasure and not on a commercial basis, and the farm expenses exceed the receipts from operation of the farm, the receipts from the sale of farm products need not be included in income. The expenses will be treated as personal expenses, that is, not deductible [Sec. 1.162-12]. Farm expenses in excess of receipts are deductible only if the farming is engaged in for profit [¶ 2225]. Deductible farm losses can also be recaptured as ordinary income when farm property is sold by taxpayers who farm but have large amounts of income from other sources [¶ 2226].

NOTE: No additions can be made to an excess deductions account for tax years starting after 1975. See ¶ 2226.

(d) Farming syndicates. Farm syndicates can only deduct during the tax year; feed, seed, seed fertilizer and other similar farm supplies when actually used or consumed. Poultry production costs and certain grove expenses must be capitalized [Sec. 464(a)].

NOTE: The farm syndicate rules are effective for tax years starting after 12-31-75. However, the rules are effective for tax years starting after 1976 for a farm syndicate in existence on 12-31-75 and that has had no change of membership throughout its tax year starting in 1976.

What are farming syndicates. A farm syndicate is a partnership or any other enterprise (other than a corporation not having made a Subchapter S election [¶ 3140]) that engages in farming and has registered securities for sale with a federal or state agency. It also includes a partnership or any other enterprise (other than a corporation not electing Subchapter S) that allocates more than 35% of its losses to a limited entrepreneur (someone who does not actively participate in the enterprise's management) or limited partner. However, an individual can avoid being treated as a limited partner or entrepreneur by actively participating in the management for at least 5 years or by living on the farm [Sec. 464(c)].

(e) How treated on return. Deductions by an individual farmer under (a) or (b) above are deductions for adjusted gross income [¶ 1804]. For a credit on the federal excise tax on nonhighway-use gasoline and lubricating oils, see ¶ 2417.

¶ 1845 Soil and water conservation expenditures. A farmer can deduct in the tax year paid or incurred, expenses for soil and water conservation and the prevention of erosion of land used in farming [Sec. 175; 1.175-1]. The deduction cannot be more than 25% of his gross income from farming during the tax year (see (a) below). The expenditure must be made to further the business of farming and if not deducted, must be capitalized [Sec. 1.175-1, 1.175-2]. A portion of any deduction taken after 1969 may be recaptured as ordinary income if farm land is held less than ten years when it is sold or exchanged (see (e)).

The deduction applies to land used by the taxpayer or his tenant for the production of crops, fruits or other agricultural products or for the sustenance of livestock [Sec. 175(c)(2)]. It does not apply when the taxpayer rents farm land at a fixed rental (unless he materially helps manage or operate the farm), engages in forestry or timber growing, or runs a farm as a hobby [Sec. 1.175-3]. If the expenditures are made for newly-acquired farm land, the deduction applies if the land is put to the same type of farming use as that immediately preceding its acquisition. However, if land will be put to a different use (i.e., pasture or timber land cultivated for crops) the expenditures are preparatory expenses and must be capitalized [Sec. 1.175-4].

DEDUCTIBLE

Expenditures for treatment and moving of earth (including—but not limited to—leveling, conditioning, grading, terracing, contour furrowing, and restoration of soil fertility); eradication of brush; planting of windbreaks; construction, control and protection of diversion channels, drainage ditches, irrigation ditches, earthen dams, watercourses, outlets and ponds.

NOT DEDUCTIBLE

Expenditures to buy, construct, install, or improve depreciable structures, appliances, or facilities, or any amount deductible under other provisions. Expenditures for depreciable property include cost of materials, supplies, wages, fuel, hauling and dirt moving for structures such as tanks, reservoirs, pipes, conduits, canals, dams, wells or pumps made of masonry concrete, tile, metal or wood [Sec. 175(c); 1.175-2]. For deductibility of assessments for depreciable property, see (c) below.

(a) Limitation. (1) the amount deductible for the tax year cannot exceed 25% of gross income from farming during the tax year. "Gross income from farming" means gross income from *all* of the taxpayer's farms. It does not, however, include gains from sale of assets such as farm machinery or gains from the disposition of land [Sec. 1.175-5].

(2) Expenditures over the amount allowable for any tax year can be carried over to the following tax year, and considered the first expenditure in that year.

However, the total deduction for each succeeding year (carryover plus actual expenditures made during the tax year) is still limited to 25% of gross income from farming during the tax year.

> **Example 1:** Taxpayer had $12,000 gross income from farming in 1976. His soil and water conservation expenditures were $3,500. Taxpayer can deduct $3,000 (.25 × $12,000) for 1976. The balance, $500, can be carried over to 1977 and considered the first such expenditure in that year.
>
> **Example 2:** Assume same taxpayer had $10,000 gross income from farming in 1977, and that his soil and water conservation expenditures were $2,100. Taxpayer can deduct $2,500 for 1977, and his carryover to 1978 would be $100, figured as shown below:
>
> | | |
> |---|---:|
> | Carryover from 1976 | $ 500 |
> | Expenditures in 1977 | 2,100 |
> | Total | $2,600 |
> | Deduction (limited to .25 × $10,000) | 2,500 |
> | Carryover to 1978 | $ 100 |

Amounts deducted either in the year paid or incurred or a carryover year are considered in figuring a net operating loss (¶ 2241 et seq.) [Sec. 1.175-5].

(b) Adoption of method. The method (deduction or capitalization) can be adopted without consent for the first tax year the expenditures are paid or incurred. For adoption at any other time, the consent of the Renvenue Service is required. Once adopted, the method applies to all soil and water conservation expenditures for the tax year and later tax years, and must be followed consistently, unless the Revenue Service consents to a change. However, taxpayer may request authorization to capitalize (or, if the election to deduct is not made, to deduct) soil and water conservation expenditures for a special project or a single farm.

The request for adoption (or a change) must be in writing, signed by the taxpayer (or representative), and must be filed not later than the time required for filing the return. The request should state: (1) taxpayer's name and address; (2) first tax year to which the method or change applies; (3) whether it applies to all expenditures or only a special project or farm (if so, identify it); (4) amount of soil and water conservation expenditures for the first tax year to which the method or change applies; and (5) that an accounting segregation will be made of the expenditures [Sec. 175(d); 1.175-6].

➤ **OBSERVATION**➤ The taxpayer should distinguish between (1) soil and water conservation *expenditures* and (2) expenses for *maintenance and repair* of structures built for soil and water conservation purposes or to prevent erosion. Expenses for maintenance and repair are deductible when paid or incurred without limit. They cannot be carried over and deducted in a succeeding year.[1]

(c) Assessments. Amounts paid to a soil or water conservation or drainage district are deductible to the extent they are (1) not otherwise allowable as a deduction and (2) they defray expenses by such a district, which, if made by the taxpayer, would be deductible as soil or water conservation expenditures [Sec. 175(c); 1.175-2(c)]. Also, for tax years ending after 10-22-68, a limited deduction is allowed for assessments levied by a district to acquire depreciable property used in the district's conservation or drainage activities. The deduction for any one member of a district is limited to 10% of the depreciable cost of the property to the district (any balance is capitalized as land cost). Payment in any year is deductible currently only to the extent of 10% of a member's assessment for equipment cost to the district; the balance is spread over 9 succeeding years if it exceeds 10% of the assessment plus $500 [Sec. 175(c), (f)]. If a member sells his land before he has

Footnotes appear at end of this Chapter.

taken the full allowable deduction, the unwritten amounts enters into his gain or loss. If he dies, the unwritten-off amount is deductible on his last return but subject to the 25% limit in (a) above [Sec. 175(f); 1.175-5].

(d) **Expenses of clearing land for farming.** Farmers can deduct costs incurred to clear land for farm use. The deduction applies to outlays that otherwise would be treated as capital expenditures. The deduction cannot exceed the lesser of: $5,000 or 25% of that year's taxable income from farming [Sec. 182; 1.182-1—1.182-6].

(e) **Recapture of deductions.** Both soil and water conservation expenditures and land clearing costs previously deducted in a tax year starting after 1969 may be partially or fully recaptured as ordinary income when farm land held less than ten years is sold or exchanged. The amount of the recapture is the gain up to the applicable percentage of such deductions allowed to the taxpayer in the year of disposition and nine preceding years. There is complete recapture of the deductions if the land is held less than six years, 80% recapture if the land is disposed of within the sixth year after it was acquired, 60% recapture if disposed of in the seventh year, 40% in the eighth year and 20% in the ninth year after the date it was acquired [Sec. 1252; Prop. Reg. 1.1252-1].

NOTE: If ordinary income could be recaptured from the sale or exchange of farm land for previously deducted farm losses [¶ 2226] as well as deducted soil and water conservation expenditures and land clearing costs, the ordinary income recaptured first is the amount attributable to the deducted farm losses [Sec. 1252(a)(1); Prop. Reg. 1.1252-1(a)].

¶ **1846 Amortizable bond premium.** The amount you pay above the face value of bonds you buy is called the premium. Amortization of this premium means the writing off of the premium's amount. It is required for tax exempts but is optional for bonds that are taxable. In every case, however, the amortized premium for the year reduces the bond's basis. The rules are summarized below:

AMORTIZABLE BOND PREMIUMS

Type of Bond	Mandatory or Elective Amortization - Corporations	Mandatory or Elective Amortization - Others	Basis of Bond Reduced by Amortizable Premiums	Amortization Deducted from Adjusted Gross Income
Tax exempt	Manadatory	Mandatory	Yes	No
Taxable	Elective	Elective	Yes	Yes

Notes

1. Callable bonds—The premium on any wholly taxable bond acquired after 1957 (regardless of the date of issue) must be amortized to maturity date. However, the premium must be amortized to an earlier call date if that results in a smaller deduction.
On wholly taxable bonds issued after Jan 22, 1951 and acquired after Jan. 22, 1954 but before 1958, the premium must be amortized to maturity if the call date is 3 years or less after the date of issue (but see (e) below).
There is a special rule for deducting the remaining unamortized bond premium if the bond is called during the tax year ((f) below).
2. Convertible bonds—amortization is not allowed for premium attributable to the conversion feature of the bond ((d) below).
3. Capitalized expenditures in connection with acquisition may be amortized.
4. Amortization will not be required if no interest is received during taxable year by cash basis taxpayer.

5. Provisions as to amortization of premium do not apply to dealers in securities, except in the case of *certain* short-term municipal bonds ((a) below).

Background and purpose. Before enactment, a bond premium was a capital loss when the bond matured or was disposed of. Thus, while periodical payments on taxable bonds were included in income as interest, no current deduction was allowed on the premium. This resulted in an inequity in favor of tax-exempts whose current payments were tax-free but which received a capital loss deduction at maturity.

(a) Tax-exempt obligations. Every taxpayer (corporate, individual, or other) must amortize the premium paid for tax-exempt obligations. Because the interest is exempt, the amortization is not deductible; but it reduces the basis of the obligations [Sec. 171, 1016(a)(5); 1.171-1(b), 1.1016-5(b)].

> **Example 1:** On 1-4-77, Baxter bought five $1,000 bonds of the State of Y for $5,100, maturing on 1-1-97. In 1977, he got interest of $150 which would be excluded from gross income. However, he must reduce the basis by the amount of amortization ($5). If the bonds are held until maturity, taxpayer's basis will be $5,000 ($5,100 — $100).

Dealer in securities. Dealers must amortize the premium on all tax-exempt obligations of a government or political subdivision acquired after 1957,[1] unless the bonds are disposed of at a gain and are either (1) held 30 days or less by the dealer or (2) have a maturity or call date more than 5 years from the date of acquisition. [Sec. 75; 171; 1016(a)(6); 1.171-4]. When amortization is required, the dealer must reduce the cost basis by the amortizable bond premium.

If the dealer figures his gross income by the use of inventories, and values the inventories on any basis other than cost, he must reduce the cost of securities sold during the year by the amortizable bond premium that would be disallowed as a deduction, if the dealer were an ordinary investor. But no reduction is made for bonds maturing more than 5 years after acquisition and still held by the dealer at the close of the year. If these bonds are later disposed of at a loss, the cost of the securities sold is reduced by the total amortizable premium in the year the bond is disposed of. [Sec. 75].

"Cost of securities sold" is the sum of opening inventory, plus cost of securities bought during the year, less closing inventory.

If the dealer figures his gross income without the use of inventories, or values his inventories at cost, he must reduce the cost of the municipal bonds sold during the year by the amortization that would be disallowed as a deduction if the dealer were an investor. [Sec. 75; 171; 1016(a)(6); 1.75-1].

(b) Taxable obligations. Amortization of bond premium of a taxable bond is optional, at taxpayer's election, whether taxpayer is a corporation, individual or other taxpayer [Sec. 171; 1.171-1(a)]. The amortizable bond premium is deductible from adjusted gross income, if the election is made. Basis must be reduced by the amortization. [Sec. 1016(a)(5); 1.1016-5(b)].

Election. If election is made for any particular bond issue, it applies to all bonds owned at the date of election and all bonds later acquired. The election must be made in the return and is binding for all future years, unless it is revoked on application to the Revenue Service. Elections made in a refund claim after the return is filed are not recognized.[2]

> **Example 2:** On 1-4-77, taxpayer bought five X Corporation $1,000 4% bonds for $5,100, maturing on 1-1-97. The interest ($200) would be included in gross income. If the taxpayer elects to amortize the premium, he can deduct $5 for 1977 and for each later year he owns the bonds.

Footnotes appear at end of this Chapter.

¶ 1846

(c) **Adjustment for period before election.** Adjustment must be made to reflect the unamortized bond premium for the period before the year of election [Sec. 1.171-2].

> **Example 3:** On 1-1-77, taxpayer owned five $1,000 bonds bought on 1-1-67 for $5,100, maturing on 1-1-87. Taxpayer elects to take a deduction for the premium. In determining the premium to be amortized over the remaining ten years of the life the original premium must be reduced by the amount of amortization due to the previous years. He would treat $50 of the premium as having been amortized over the previous ten years and would amortize the balance ($50) over the remaining ten years to maturity or $5 in 1977 and later tax years. At maturity in 1987, the taxpayer will have a recognized loss of $50, since the basis at maturity will be $5,050 ($5,100 less the amortization *since* the election year).

(d) **Bond premiums due to conversion privilege.** Amortization is not allowed for any part of the premium due to the conversion features of the bond [Sec. 171(b)(1); 1.171-2(c)]. The amount of the premium that represents the conversion feature may be found by getting the yield on similar bonds without conversion features selling on the open market, and adjusting the price of the convertible bond to this yield. This adjustment may be made by using standard bond tables.[3]

> **Example 4:** Suppose you want to appraise the 5% convertible bonds of Loe Company. Assume these bonds have 5 years to run to maturity. A study of similar bonds without conversion features on which quotations are available shows that they sell at an average yield of 5.75. To reduce these bonds to a price which will give an equivalent yield, turn to a standard bond table for 5% bonds with a 5-year maturity, and read across from 5.75. The corresponding price is 96.78. Subtracting this value from the amount paid for the bond gives the amount attributable to the conversion feature.

(e) **Determination of amount amortizable.** The premium on any bond is determined by finding the excess of the basis that is used for determining loss on the sale or exchange of the bond, over the amount payable at maturity or on an earlier call date [except as noted in (1) and (2) below].

The part of the bond premium that is due to the current year is amortizable (but see special rule for called bonds in (f) below) [Sec. 171(b)(2); 1.171-2].

> **Example 5:** On 1-1-77, taxpayer received a gift of five $1,000 wholly taxable bonds, maturing on 1-1-87. Assume no gift tax was payable on the gift. The donor had bought the bonds on 1-1-66 for $5,100, and the fair market value at the time of the gift was $5,200. Taxpayer elects to amortize the premium, beginning in 1977. The basis for figuring loss in case of a gift after 12-31-20 is the lower of the donor's cost ($5,100) or the fair market value at the time of the gift ($5,200). The amount of premium to be amortized, adjusted for the period before acquisition is $50. Thus, he may deduct $5 amortization in 1977, reducing the basis by that amount. In 1987, upon redemption, taxpayer will have a recognized loss of $50 ($5,100 less $50 amortization deduction).

(1) *Taxable bonds issued after 1-22-51 and acquired after 1-22-54 but before 1-1-58.* The premium must be amortized to maturity if the call date is 3 years or less after the date of issue.

NOTE: This provision has been repealed. However, the bond premium for a tax year starting after 1975 is determined by the amount payable on maturity. If the bond is called before then, the premium is determined under (e) above.

(2) *Taxable bonds acquired after 12-31-57.* The premium must be amortized to maturity. However, it is amortized to an earlier call date, if that results in a smaller deduction.[4]

> **Example 6:** On 1-3-77, you pay $1,200 for a $1,000 taxable bond which matures 12-31-96. The bond is callable on 1-1-82, at $1,165. The premium to maturity date is $200, but it is $35 if figured to call date. Although the premium amortized ratably to maturity would yield a deduction of $10 for each year ($200 ÷ 20 years), under the law the deduction for each tax

year for the period before 1-1-81 will be $7 ($35 ÷ 5 years). If the bond is not called, the deduction for each tax year in the period from 1982 through 1996 will be $11 ($165 ÷ 15 years). If the earliest call date had been 1-1-80, the premium amortized ratably to maturity would be used to get a deduction of $10 per year since this would be less than the premium amortized ratably to earlier call date of $11.67 ($35 ÷ 3, the number of years to the earliest call date).

(f) Called bonds. If a bond described in either (e)(1) or (2) above is called in the tax year, taxpayer may deduct the unamortized premium remaining as of the start of the tax year. The deduction cannot exceed the adjusted basis of the bond as of the start of the tax year less the greater of: (1) amount received on redemption or (2) amount payable at maturity [Sec. 171(b)(2)]. This provision applies if the bonds were acquired after 1957.

(g) How treated on return. The amortization deduction is deductible on Schedule A of Form 1040 as an "other itemized deduction."

Footnotes to Chapter 8

(P-H "FEDERAL TAXES" related references are cited in brackets [ ] at the end of each footnote below.)

Footnote ¶ 1801 [¶ 11,002 et seq.].

Footnote ¶ 1803 [¶ 11,005; 16,310].
(1) Welch v. Helvering, 290 US 111, 54 SCt. 8, 12 AFTR 1456, affg. 63 F.2d 976, 12 AFTR 348; Dunn & McCarthy, Inc. v. Comm., 139 F.2d 242, 31 AFTR 1043; Cf. Kentucky Util. Co. v. Glenn, 21 AFTR 2d 1263, 394 F.2d 631 [¶ 11,031; 11,045(5); 11,102(15)].
(2) Comm. v. Heininger, 320 US 467, 64 SCt. 249, 31 AFTR 783 [¶ 11,033].

Footnote ¶ 1804 [¶ 7611; 7627].
(1) Comm. v. Lincoln Elec. Co., 176 F.2d 815, 38 AFTR 411 [¶ 11,043].
(2) Rev. Rul. 70-40, 1970-1 CB 50 [¶ 7628(10)].
(3) Rev. Rul. 70-40, 1970-1 CB 50; Reise, 9 AFTR 2d 887, 299 F.2d 380 [¶ 7628(10); 16,192(70)].

Footnote ¶ 1805 [¶ 7631; 7632; 11,362 et seq.; 12,067].
(1) Magill, 4 BTA 272 [¶ 11,191].
(2) Tyler, 13 TC 186 [¶ 11,335(10)].
(3) Cremona, 58 TC 219; Rev. Rul. 75-120, 1975-1 CB 55; Rev. Rul. 77-16, IRB 1977-3 [¶ 11,220(5); 16,371(85); 55,160].
(4) Roth, 17 TC 1450 [¶ 11,230(20)].
(5) Lanier, ¶ 52,125 P-H Memo TC [¶ 11,230(20)].
(6) Rev. Rul. 58-382, 1958-1 CB 59 [¶ 11,230(8)].
(7) Rev. Rul. 62-85, 1962-1 CB 13 [¶ 7637(15)].
(8) Senate Report No. 1622, 83 Cong., 2nd Sess., p. 10, 170.
(9) Rev. Rul. 72-110, 1972-1 CB 24 [¶ 7399(5); 7632(5)].
(10) Podems, 24 TC 21; Kennelly, 56 TC 936, aff'd., 29 AFTR 2d 72-855 [¶ 11,411(20)].
(11) Treas. Dept. booklet, "Your Federal Income Tax" (1977 Ed.), p. 65.
(12) Rev. Rul. 74-433, 1974-2 CB 92 [¶ 12,067(10)].

Footnote ¶ 1805 continued
(13) Rev. Rul. 74-433, 1974-2 CB 92; Treas. Dept. booklet "Your Federal Income Tax" (1977 Ed.), p. 66 [¶ 12,067(10)].

Footnote ¶ 1806 [¶ 7648; 16,310 et seq.]
(1) Coffey, 1 TC 579; Kanelos, ¶ 43,429 P-H Memo TC [¶ 16,366(5), (15)].
(2) Higgins, 72 F.Supp. 252, 36 AFTR 1198 [¶ 16,371(5)].
(3) Rev. Rul. 62-42, 1962-1 CB 133; Rev. Rul. 72-521, 1972-2 CB 178 [¶ 16,328(25)].
(4) Rev. Rul. 72-521, 1972-2 CB 178 [¶ 16,328(25)].
(5) Rev. Rul. 56-511, 1956-2 CB 170 [¶ 16,328(5)].
(6) Robinson, 2 TC 305; F. A. Newcombe, 54 TC 1298. But see Smith, ¶ 67,028 P-H Memo TC, affd. 22 AFTR 2d 5096, 397 F.2d 804 [¶ 16,337(5), (10)].
(7) Coffey, 1 TC 579 [¶ 16,357(50)].
(8) Gale, 13 TC 661, affd. 191 F.2d 79, 40 AFTR 1192 [¶ 16,351(10)].
(9) Bingham Trust v. Comm., 325 US 365, 65 SCt. 1232, 33 AFTR 842 [¶ 16,342(5)].
(10) Herbst, ¶ 43,309 P-H Memo TC [¶ 16,328(30)].
(11) Frost, ¶ 43,155 P-H Memo TC [¶ 16,357(40)].
(12) Rev. Rul. 58-180, 1958-1 CB 153; Rev. Rul. 67-461, 1967-2 CB 125 [¶ 16,357(75), (77)].
(13) Carpenter v. U.S., 14 AFTR 2d 5897, 338 F.2d 366 [¶ 16,357(37)].
(14) Rev. Rul. 68-533, 1968-2 CB 190 [¶ 19,287(10)].
(15) Stormfeltz, 142 F.2d 982, 32 AFTR 770 [¶ 16,704(10)].
(16) Megargel, 3 TC 238 [¶ 16,704(10)].
(17) Spear v. Gagne, 49 F.Supp. 263, 30 AFTR 1241 [¶ 16,342(10)].
(18) Bowers v. Lumpkin, 140 F.2d 927, 32 AFTR 201; Martin v. U.S., 17 AFTR 2d 330, 249 F.Supp. 204 [¶ 16,702(50); 16,704(8)]. See also ¶ 1808.

Footnote ¶ 1806 continued
(19) Rev. Rul. 1, 1953-1 CB 36 [¶ 16,975(15)].
(20) McDonald v. Comm., 323 US 57, 65 SCt. 96, 32 AFTR 1404 [¶ 16,975(5)].
(21) Mays v. Bowers, 201 F.2d 401, 43 AFTR 170 [¶ 16,975(5)].

Footnote ¶ 1807 [¶ 11,421; 16,655].
(1) Rev. Rul. 70-474, 1970-2 CB 34 [¶ 11,214; 11,215].
(2) Rev. Rul. 55-235, 1955-1 CB 274; Russell, ¶ 52,098 P-H Memo TC [¶ 11,217(15)].
(3) Leacock, ¶ 47,328 P-H Memo TC [¶ 11,215(20)].
(4) Treas. Dept. booklet "Your Federal Income Tax" (1977 Ed.), p. 92; Rev. Rul. 69-214; 1969-1 CB 52 [¶ 11,226(5)].
(5) Rev. Rul. 54-190, 1954-1 CB 46; Rev. Rul. 68-82, 1968-1 CB 68 [¶ 11,226(5)].
(6) Rev. Rul. 72-463, 1972-2 CB 93 [¶ 11,226(5), (10)].
(7) Campen, 16 BTA 543 [¶ 12,023(5)].
(8) Senate Report No. 1881, p. 170, 87th Cong., 2d Sess.
(9) Rev. Rul. 56-401, 1956-2 CB 169, modified by Rev. Rul. 60-255, 1960-2 CB 105 [¶ 16,393; 16,667(5)].
(10) Rev. Rul. 55-154, 1955-1 CB 216 [¶ 16,662(5)].
(11) Rev. Rul. 75-48 1975-1 CB 62 [¶ 11,115(5)].
(12) Rev. Rul. 66-289, 1966-2 CB 43 [¶ 11,239(30)].

Footnote ¶ 1808 [¶ 16,681].
(1) Rev. Rul. 66-18, 1966-1 CB 59, classifies expenses of growing and selling Christmas trees; modified by Rev. Rul. 71-228, 1971-1 CB 53 [¶ 11,923(15)].
(2) Schlosser Bros., 2 BTA 137 [¶ 11,074(5)].
(3) MacAdam & Foster, Inc., 8 BTA 967 [¶ 11,152(10)].
(4) Harbeson Lumber Co., 24 BTA 542 [¶ 16,736(5)].
(5) Spangler v. Comm., 323 F.2d 913, 12 AFTR 2d 5831; U.S. v. St. Joe Paper Co., 284 F.2d 430, 432, 6 AFTR 2d 6058 [¶ 11,106(40); 16,353(10)].
(6) Bonwit Teller & Co., 17 BTA 1019, rev'd in part without discussion of this point, 53 F.2d 381, 10 AFTR 656; Beaven, ¶ 47,339 P-H Memo TC [¶ 11,482(5)].
(7) Rev. Rul. 60-254, 1960-1 CB 42 [¶ 11,018(10)].
(8) Rev. Rul. 57-418, 1957-2 CB 143; Finch v. U.S. (DC Minn. 6-30-66), 18 AFTR 2d 5259 [¶ 14,078(20); 14,249(15)].
(9) Babbitt, 32 BTA 693; The Toledo Blade Co., 11 TC 1079 [¶ 15,342(10), (25)].
(10) E. H. Sheldon & Co. v. Comm., 214 F.2d 655, 45 AFTR 1791 [¶ 11,960(5)].
(11) Rev. Rul. 68-360, 1968-2 CB 197 [¶ 11,964(10)].
(12) Whitney v. Comm., 73 F.2d 589, 14 AFTR 744 [¶ 11,204(5)].
(13) GCM 4015, VII-1 CB 120; Bradley, 41 BTA 153 [¶ 11,204(10)].
(14) Motion Pictures Capital Corp., 32 BTA 339, affd., 80 F.2d 872, 17 AFTR 138 [¶ 16,597(20)].
(15) Lowell, 30 BTA 1297 [¶ 11,204(5)].
(16) Liquidating Co., 33 BTA 1173; Meurer Steel Barrel Co., Inc., ¶ 43,113 P-H TC Memo, affd. 144 F.2d 282, 32 AFTR 1189 [¶ 16,602(5); 16,604(5)].
(17) Idaho Power Co. v. Comm., 34 AFTR 2d 74-5244, 94 SCt 2757 [¶ 16,740(30)].

Footnote ¶ 1809 [¶ 16,785].
(1) Cotton States Fertilizer Co., 28 TC 1169 [¶ 16,796(5)].
(2) Herbst, ¶ 43,309 P-H Memo TC [¶ 16,798(5)].

Footnote ¶ 1810 [¶ 7488; 16,011; 16,075].

Footnote ¶ 1811 [¶ 11,958].

Footnote ¶ 1812 [¶ 11,269].
(1) Comm. v. Sullivan, 1 AFTR 2d 1158, 356 US 27, 78 SCt. 512 [¶ 11,269(5)].
(2) Comeaux, G.A., 10 TC 201; Excelsior Baking Co. v. U.S., 82 F. Supp. 423, 37 AFTR 1066 [¶ 11,268(5), (10)].

Footnote ¶ 1815 [¶ 11,541].
(1) Rev. Rul. 72-23, 1972-1 CB 43; Rev. Rul. 73-393, 1973-2 CB 33 [¶ 11,562(5)].

Footnote ¶ 1816 [¶ 11,611].

Footnote ¶ 1817 [¶ 11,741 et seq.].

Footnote ¶ 1818 [¶ 11,746 et seq.].
(1) Rev. Rul. 69-465, 1969-2 CB 27 [¶ 11,748(5)].
(2) Helvering v. Winmill, 305 US 79, 59 SCt. 45, 21 AFTR 962 [¶ 16,722(10)].
(3) Spreckles v. Helvering, 315 US 626, 62 SCt. 777, 28 AFTR 1010; Davis, 34 AFTR 335, 151 F.2d 441 [¶ 16,712(10)].
(4) Rev. Rul. 71-173, 1971-1 CB 204; Bray, Viola E. Est., 46 TC 577, affd. 21 AFTR 2d 1517, 396 F.2d 452 [¶ 28,070.15(45)].

Footnote ¶ 1819 [¶ 11,541 et seq.].
(1) Brandenburg, 4 BTA 108 [¶ 11,556(5)].
(2) Int'l Freighting Corp., 135 F.2d 310, 30 AFTR 1433 [¶ 11,757(35)].
(3) The Liquid Carbonic Corp., 34 BTA 1191; Edgecomb Steel Corp., ¶ 45,101 P-H Memo TC [¶ 11,757(10)].
(4) Rev. Rul. 57-130, 1957-1 CB 108 [¶ 11,163-A(10)].
(5) Treas. Dept. Press Release, 6-2-47, [¶ 11,772(5)].
(6) Rev. Rul. 67-315, 1967-2 CB 85 [¶ 11,774(35)].

Footnote ¶ 1821 [¶ 11,651].
(1) Lucas v. Ox Fibre Brush Co., 281 US 115, 50 SCt. 273, 8 AFTR 10901; Associated Theatres Corp., 14 TC 313 [¶ 11,580(30)].
(2) Reub Isaacs & Co., Inc., 1 BTA 45 [¶ 11,577(5)].

Footnote ¶ 1822 [¶ 11,766 et seq.].
(1) Rev. Rul. 71-260, 1971-1 CB 57 [¶ 11,772(5)].
(2) Rev. Rul. 69-104, 1969-1 CB 33 [¶ 35,219(20)].

Footnote ¶ 1823 [¶ 11,071; 11,131 et seq.].
(1) Bagley, 8 TC 130 [¶ 16,322(10); 16,330(5)].
(2) Comm. v. Tellier, 17 AFTR 2d 633, 86 SCt 118, 383 U.S. 687 [¶ 11,262(3)].
(3) Burroughs Bldg. Mat. Co. v. Comm., 47 F.2d 178, 9 AFTR 892; Sanitary Earthenware Specialty Co., 19 BTA 641 [¶ 11,261(15)].
(4) Comm. v. Heininger, 320 US 467, 64 SCt. 249, 31 AFTR 783. See ¶ 1808 [¶ 11,260].
(5) Hurt, 30 BTA 653; Hochschild, 161 F.2d 817, 36 AFTR 1373 [¶ 11,135(15)].
(6) Howard v. Comm., 202 F.2d 28, 43 AFTR 249 [¶ 11,229(5)].
(7) O'Neal, 18 BTA 1036; Kelley, 38 BTA 1292 [¶ 11,139(5)].
(8) Commack, 5 TC 467 [¶ 16,357(15)].
(9) Tyler, 6 TC 135 [¶ 16,344(5)].

Footnote ¶ 1823 continued
(10) Greene Motor Co., 5 TC 314 [¶ 11,261(10)].
(11) Rev. Rul. 73-13, 1973-1 CB 42 [¶ 16,322(5)].
(12) U.S. v. Pate, 254 F.2d 480, 1 AFTR 1530 [¶ 16,717(13)].
(13) Lloyd, 22 BTA 674, affd. 55 F.2d 842, 10 AFTR 1195 [¶ 11,017(10)].
(14) Kleinschmidt, 12 TC 921 [¶ 11,516(15)].
(15) Draper, 26 TC 201 [¶ 11,516(15)].
(16) Murphy, 48 TC 569 [¶ 16,353(5)].
(17) Rev. Rul. 1, 1953-1 CB 36 [¶ 16,975(15)].
(18) Bowers v. Lumpkin, 140 F.2d 927, 32 AFTR 201; Coughlin, 3 TC 420 [¶ 16,702(10), (50)].
(19) Treas. Dept. booklet "Your Federal Income Tax" (1977 Ed.), p. 94.
(20) Robins, 8 BTA 523 [¶ 16,667(40)].
(21) Gilmore, 372 US 39, 11 AFTR 2d 758; Patrick, 372 US 53, 11 AFTR 2d 764 [¶ 16,351(5)].
(22) Nadiak v. Comm., 17 AFTR 2d 396, 356 F.2d 911; Margoles, ¶ 68,058 P-H Memo TC [¶ 16,353(50)].
(23) Davidson, 27 BTA 158 [¶ 11,295(5)].
(24) Rev. Rul. 70-62, 1970-1 CB 30 [¶ 31,462(15)].
(25) Rev. Rul. 67-125, 1967-1 CB 31 [¶ 11,132(17)].

Footnote ¶ 1825 [¶ 11,471 et seq.].
(1) Illinois Merchants Trust Co., Ex., 4 BTA 103 [¶ 11,471].
(2) Munroe Land Company, ¶ 66,002 P-H Memo TC [¶ 11,477(15)].
(3) Parkersburg Iron & Steel Co. v. Burnet, 48 F.2d 163, 9 AFTR 1078 [¶ 11,482(45)].
(4) Midland Empire Packing Co., 14 TC 635 [¶ 11,479(25)].
(5) Libby & Blouin, Ltd., 4 BTA 910 [¶ 11,478(5)].
(6) Buckland v. U.S., 66 F. Supp. 681, 35 AFTR 161 [¶ 11,480(10)].
(7) City National Bank, ¶ 52,112 P-H Memo TC [¶ 11,477(10)].
(8) Treas. Dept. booklet "Tax Guide for Small Business" (1977 Ed.), p. 44.
(9) Marble & Shattuck Chair Co., 13 BTA 657 [¶ 11,486(20)].
(10) Cowell, 18 BTA 997; University Nat'l Bk., 21 BTA 71 [¶ 11,485(5), (20)].
(11) Modesto Lumber Co., 5 BTA 598 [¶ 11,486(5)].
(12) Markovits, ¶ 52,245 P-H Memo TC [¶ 11,486(40)].

Footnote ¶ 1826 [¶ 11,811 et seq.].
(1) Harder, R.J., ¶ 58,097 P-H Memo TC [¶ 11,817(5)].
(2) McCaulley, R., ¶ 64,004 P-H Memo TC [¶ 11,817(5)].
(3) Skemp v. Comm., 168 F.2d 598, 36 AFTR 1089 [¶ 11,835(5)].
(4) Baton Coal Co., 19 BTA 169, affd. 51 F.2d 469, 10 AFTR 270 [¶ 11,320(5)].
(5) Miller, 10 BTA 383 [¶ 11,304(5)].
(6) Cassatt v. Comm., 137 F.2d 745, 31 AFTR 576 [¶ 11,877(10)].
(7) Treas. Dept. booklet "Tax Guide for Small Business" (1977 Ed.), p. 43.
(8) Rev. Rul. 55-540, 1955-2 CB 39 [¶ 11,840(15)].

Footnote ¶ 1827 [¶ 11,951].

Footnote ¶ 1828 [¶ 11,111 et seq.].
(1) Rev. Rul. 66-203, 1966-2 CB 104 [¶ 16,765(10)].
(2) Treas. Dept. booklet "Tax Guide for Small Business" (1977 Ed.), p. 66.

Footnote ¶ 1828 continued
(3) Rev. Rul. 68-5, 1968-1 CB 99 [¶ 16,762].
(4) Rev. Rul. 73, 1953-1 CB 63 [¶ 16,770(5)].
(5) Bell, 13 TC 344 [¶ 11,113(10)].
(6) Lenington, ¶ 66,264 P-H Memo TC [¶ 11,120].
(7) Rev. Rul. 55-264, 1955-1 CB 11 [¶ 11,112(5)].
(8) Rev. Rul. 56-632, 1956-2 CB 101 [¶ 16,767].
(9) Rev. Rul. 66-262, 1966-2 CB 105 [¶ 16,765(10)].

Footnote ¶ 1829 [¶ 11,219; 11,351 et seq.].
(1) Flowers v. Comm., 326 US 465, 66 SCt. 250, 34 AFTR 301 [¶ 11,368(5)].
(2) Rev. Rul. 72-508, 1972-2 CB 200, modifying Rev. Rul. 71-412, 1971-2 CB 170 [¶ 12,067(10)].
(3) Rev. Rul. 56-168, 156-1 CB 93 [¶ 11,368(15)].
(4) Rev. Rul. 60-16, 1960-1 CB 58 [¶ 7634(15)].
(5) Rev. Rul. 72-608, 1972-2 CB 100 [¶ 13,251(30)].
(6) Coffey, 1 TC 579 [¶ 16,366(5)].
(7) Rev. Rul. 63-145, 1963-2 CB 86 [¶ 11,362(10)].
(8) Frank, 20 TC 511 [¶ 11,237(10)].
(9) Williams v. Paterson, 7 AFTR 2d 462, 286 F.2d 333; Rev. Rul. 75-168, IRB 1975-19; Comm. v. Bagley, 19 AFTR 2d 924, 374 F.2d 204 [¶ 11,367(3); 11,381(15), (20); 16,959(20)].
(10) U.S. v. Correll, 20 AFTR 2d 5845, 389 US 299, 88 SCt. 445 [¶ 11,367(3)].
(11) Smith, ¶ 66,247 P-H Memo TC; English, ¶ 66,256 P-H Memo TC [¶ 11,378(20); 11,378-A(5)].
(12) Rev. Rul. 71-247, 1971-1 CB 54 [¶ 11,366(5)].
(13) Rosenspan v. U.S. 27 AFTR 2d 71-707, 438 F.2d 905; Six v. U.S. 28 AFTR 2d 71-5839, 450 F.2d 66 [¶ 11,366(5); 11,368(5)].
(14) Rev. Rul. 60-189, 1960-1 CB 60; Treas. Dept. booklet "Your Federal Income Tax" (1977 Ed.), p. 61 [¶ 11,379(15)].
(15) Cowger, ¶ 66,095 P-H Memo TC [¶ 11,378(5)].
(16) Rev. Rul. 73-529, 1973-2 CB 37 [¶ 11,366(5)].
(17) Dowd, 37 TC 399 [¶ 11,378(5)].
(18) Rev. Rul. 54-147, 1954-1 CB 51; Joseph H. Sherman et al., 16 TC 332 [¶ 11,372].
(19) Rev. Rul. 67-438, 1967-2 CB 82 [¶ 11,368(15)].
(20) Rev. Rul. 75-432, 1975-2 CB 60; Rev. Rul. 75-169, 1975-1 CB 59; Rev. Rul. 54-497, 1954-2 CB 75; Rev. Rul. 55-604, 1955-2 CB 49 [¶ 11,373].
(21) Rev. Rul. 54-147, 1954-1 CB 51; Treas. Dept. booklet "Your Federal Income Tax" (1977 Ed.), p. 61. [¶ 11,372].
(22) Rev. Rul. 76-453, IRB 1976-47; Announc. 77-23, IRB 1977-7 [¶ 54,980; 55,214].
(23) Fausner v. Comm., 413 US 838, 32 AFTR 2d 73-5202; Rev. Rul. 75-380, 1975-2 CB 59 [¶ 11,407(10)].
(24) Rev. Rul. 55-109, 1955-1 CB 261 [¶ 11,408(5)].
(25) Poletti, ¶ 66,047 P-H Memo TC [¶ 11,052(15)].
(26) Rev. Proc. 74-23, 1974-2 CB 476 [¶ 11,426(3)].
(27) Rev. Proc. 74-23, 1974-2 CB 476, amplified by Rev. Proc. 75-3, 1975-1 CB 643 [¶ 11,426(3)].
(28) Rev. Proc. 70-25, 1970-2 CB 506 [¶ 11,426(3)].
(29) Rev. Rul. 73-191, 1973-1 CB 151 [¶ 12,067(10)].

Footnote ¶ 1830 [¶ 16,945].
(1) Treas. Dept. booklet "Tax Guide for Small Business" (1977 Ed.), p. 61.
(2) Treas. Dept. booklet "Your Federal Income Tax" (1977 Ed.), p. 67.
(3) Rev. Rul. 67-421, 1967-2 CB 84 [¶ 11,504(15)].
(4) Poletti, ¶ 66,047 P-H Memo TC [¶ 11,052(15)].

Chapter 8—Footnotes

Footnote ¶ 1831 [¶ 16,493].
(1) Rev. Rul. 70-625, 1970-2 CB 67 [¶ 16,496(5)].
(2) Rev. Proc. 74-25, 1974-1 CB 284 [¶ 16,496(3)].
(3) Rev. Rul. 70-656, 1970-2 CB 67 [¶ 16,496(35)].
(4) Comm. v. Starr, 22 AFTR 2d 5567, 399 F.2d 675; Lull, 26 AFTR 2d 70-5789, 434 F.2d 615 [¶ 16,496(90), (100)].

Footnote ¶ 1832 [¶ 11,511 et seq.].
(1) Heigerick, 45 TC 475 [¶ 12,035(5)].

Footnote ¶ 1833 [¶ 11,501 et seq.].
(1) Rev. Rul. 67-421, 1967-2 CB 84 [¶ 11,504(15)].
(2) Treas. Dept. booklet "Your Federal Income Tax" (1977 Ed.), p. 71.
(3) Rev. Rul. 71-58, 1971-1 CB 55 [¶ 11,504(5)].
(4) Furner, 21 AFTR 2d 794, 393 F.2d 292 [¶ 11,504(5)].
(5) Rev. Rul. 68-591, 1968-2 CB 73 [¶ 11,504(5)].

Footnote ¶ 1834 [¶ 11,215].
(1) Treas. Dept. booklet "Your Federal Income Tax" (1977 Ed.), p. 92.
(2) Comm. v. Stidger, 19 AFTR 2d 959, 386 US 287, 87 SCt. 1065 [¶ 11,382].
(3) Rev. Rul. 55-572, 1955-2 CB 45 [¶ 11,382].
(4) Rev. Rul. 55-109, 1955-1 CB 261 [¶ 11,383].

Footnote ¶ 1838 [¶ 16,498; 19,000 et seq.].
(1) Rev. Rul. 76-28, 1976-1 CB 106 [¶ 54,899].
(2) TIR-1446 [¶ 19,201(90)].

Footnote ¶ 1839 [¶ 19,251 et seq.].
(1) Rev. Rul. 68-391, 1968-2 CB 180 amplifying Rev. Rul. 67-101, 1967-1 CB 82 [¶ 19,266(10)].
(2) Rev. Rul. 66-56, 1966-1 CB 87 [¶ 19,266(25)].
(3) Rev. Rul. 67-3, 1967-1 CB 94 [¶ 19,266(30)].
(4) Rev. Rul. 65-21, 1965-1 CB 174 [¶ 19,266(15)].
(5) Rev. Rul. 69-380, 1969-2 CB 97 [¶ 19,266(45)].

Footnote ¶ 1839 continued
(6) Rev. Proc. 72-7, 1972-1 CB 715; Rev. Proc. 75-38, 1975-2 CB 567 [¶ 39,780(15)].

Footnote ¶ 1840 [¶ 11,866].
(1) Miller, 10 BTA 383 [¶ 16,707(25)].

Footnote ¶ 1842 [¶ 16,209 et seq.].
(1) Koons, 35 TC 1092; Mayrath v. Comm., 17 AFTR 2d 375, 357 F.2d 209 [¶ 16,209(17)].
(2) Snow v. Comm., 33 AFTR 2d 74-1251, 416 US 500 [¶ 16,209(17)].
(3) Rev. Rev. 71-162, 1971-1 CB 97 [¶ 16,209(38)].
(4) Rev. Rul. 58-78, 1958-1 CB 148 [¶ 16,209(20)].
(5) Rev. Rul. 71-136, 1971-1 CB 97 [¶ 16,209(37)].

Footnote ¶ 1843 [¶ 22,356 et seq.; 22,378 et seq.].

Footnote ¶ 1844 [¶ 11,911 et seq.].
(1) Treas. Dept. booklet "Farmers' Tax Guide" (1977 Ed.), pp. 24-29.
(2) Rev. Rul. 55-531, 1955-2 CB 520 [¶ 7488(5)].
(3) Rev. Rul. 66-58, 1966-1 CB 186 [¶ 15,351(40)].
(4) Treas. Dept. booklet "Farmers' Tax Guide" (1977 Ed.), p. 28.

Footnote ¶ 1845 [¶ 11,911 et seq.; 16,211 et seq.; 32,801].
(1) Treas. Dept. booklet "Farmers' Tax Guide" (1977 Ed.), p. 52.

Footnote ¶ 1846 [¶ 16,110 et seq.].
(1) Sec. 2(c), Technical Amendments Act of 1958.
(2) Barnhill, 241 F.2d 496, 50 AFTR 1675 [¶ 16,132(5)].
(3) The P-H Capital Adjustments Service contains a table listing convertible bonds of individual corporations indicating the amortizable and nonamortizable portions of the premium on each bond.
(4) Sec. 13(b) Technical Amendments Act of 1958.

Highlights of Chapter 8
Deductions—Expenses

I. **Deductions in General**
   A. **Deductible items [¶ 1800]:**
      1. Expenses or costs.
      2. Realized losses.
      3. Reductions in value of property or interest in property.
   B. **Deductions for adjusted gross income [¶ 1801(a)]:**
      1. Trade, business, or professional expenses.
      2. Employee reimbursed expenses.
      3. Travel expenses.
      4. Transportation expenses.
      5. Outside salesperson's expenses.
      6. Long-term capital gain deduction.
      7. Losses on sales and exchanges of property.
      8. Deductions attributable to rents and royalties.
      9. Certain deductions of life tenants and income beneficiaries of property.
      10. Moving expenses.
      11. Contributions to self-employed retirement plans.
      12. Excess contributions by Subchapter S corporations to shareholder-employee retirement plans.
      13. Deductible contributions to individual retirement arrangements.
      14. Deductible ordinary income portion of lump-sum distributions for retirement plans.
      15. Alimony payments.
      16. Deduction for premature time deposit withdrawal penalties.
   C. **Disallowed deductions [¶ 1802]:**
      1. Do not satisfy statutory requirements.
      2. Disallowed by statute.
II. **Expenses in General**
   A. **General requirements for deduction [¶ 1803]:**
      1. Ordinary and necessary.
      2. Paid or incurred during year.
      3. Business or "nonbusines" expense.
   B. **Requirements for deduction of business expenses [¶ 1804]:**
      1. Directly connected to taxpayer's trade, business or profession.
      2. Reasonable in amount.
   C. **Expenses incurred in trade or business by employee [¶ 1805]:**
      1. Not deductible unless required by employment agreement or is incident to performance of duties.
      2. Expenses of outside salespersons [¶ 1805(a)]:
         a. Expenses connected with services are deductions for adjusted gross income.
         b. Outside salesperson is one who solicits business away from employer's place of business.
      3. Reimbursed expenses [¶ 1805(b)]:
         a. Generally reimbursements offset deductible expenses.
         b. Excess reimbursements over expenses are included in gross income.
         c. When traveling, transportation or outside salesperson's expenses exceed reimbursements, excess is deductible from gross income.

d. When other employee business deductions exceed reimbursements, excess is deductible from adjusted gross income.
   e. No deduction is allowed for amounts employees would have been reimbursed had they filed a claim.
4. Method of reporting depends on whether the employee accounts to his employer for expenses.
5. Employee moving expenses are deductions for adjusted gross income.
6. Employees who account to employer [¶ 1805(c)]:
   a. If reimbursements equal expenses—No reporting required.
   b. Excess reimbursements reported as miscellaneous income unless employer reports excess as wages.
   c. Excess expenses are deductible only if proper statement is filed.
      1) Allocation may be necessary if reimbursement covers all types of expenses.
      2) Allocation separates itemized deductions from deductions for adjusted gross income.
7. Employees who do not account to employer must report business expenses and reimbursements on return.
8. Expenses do not generally have to be proved except under certain circumstances.

D. **Nonbusiness expenses [¶ 1806]:**
   1. Paid or incurred in:
      (a) Producing or collecting income.
      (b) Managing, conserving or maintaining property held for the production of income, or
      (c) Determining, collecting, or refunding of any tax.
   2. Requirements for deduction:
      (a) Reasonable in amount.
      (b) Closely related to nonbusiness activities.

E. **Deductions relating to rents and royalties [¶ 1806]:**
   1. They are deductions for adjusted gross income if directly incurred in connection with rental of property or production of royalties.
   2. Employee's rental payments are deductible for adjusted gross income if travel expense, reimbursed employment expense, or if an outside salesperson.
   3. Expenses must be prorated where property rented for part of the year, or property only used partly for rental purposes.
   4. Special rules apply for vacation homes.
   5. Investor's expenses not deductions for adjusted gross income unless investor in trade or business or expenses related to rents and royalties.

F. **Personal expenses [¶ 1807]:**
   1. Arise independently of business or nonbusiness activities.
   2. Not deductible.

G. **Expense and capital expenditure distinguished [¶ 1808]:**
   1. Expense:
      (a) Incurred in earning income.
      (b) Deductible.
   2. Capital expenditure:
      (a) Outlay of capital resulting in acquisition of property or permanently improving it.
      (b) Not deductible.

H. **Expenses in earning tax-exempt income [¶ 1809]:**
   1. Generally not deductible.
   2. Business expense attributable to tax-exempt interest may be deductible.

I. **Payments for political purposes**—generally not deductible [¶ 1811].

J. **Expenses of illegal business [¶ 1812]:**
   1. Generally deductible.
   2. Not deductible if business inherently illegal.

III. **Compensation for Services**

A. **Deduction in general [¶ 1815]:**
   1. Deduction allowed for compensation paid in connection with business and "nonbusiness" activities.
   2. Wages for personal services to employer aren't deductible.
   3. Wages (except meals and lodging) paid by parent to unemancipated minor child are deductible.
B. **Reasonable compensation [¶ 1816]:**
   1. Defined as amount ordinarily paid for like services by like enterprises under like circumstances.
   2. Responsibility, work difficulty, ability, and training are some factors to be considered.
   3. As to officers, special considerations apply.
C. **Payment for services**—must be reasonable, and paid purely for services [¶ 1817].
D. **Commissions [¶ 1818]:**
   1. Deductible as ordinary salaries.
   2. Loans to salespersons, but later considered paid by employer, are deductible compensation [¶ 1818(a)].
   3. Buyer's commissions are added to the cost of the property [¶ 1818(b)].
   4. Seller's commissions (except dealer's) are offset against the selling price.
   5. Selling commissions of a dealer are deductible as an expense.
E. **Bonuses and additional compensation [¶ 1819]:**
   1. Deductible if additional compensation plus salary are reasonable.
   2. Amounts paid to employees while performing reservist training are deductible.
   3. Amounts paid for employee benefits are deductible.
F. **Compensation for service in prior years is deductible if authorized in the year claimed [¶ 1821].**
G. **Pensions, death benefits, and salary payments to employees in military service are generally deductible [¶ 1822].**
H. **Legal, accounting, appraisal, and other professional fees [¶ 1823].**
   1. Generally deductible.
   2. Legal fees in unsuccessful defense of criminal action are generally deductible if connected with a "business" or "nonbusiness activity."
   3. Attorneys' fees may in some instances be capital expenditures and therefore not deductible.
IV. **Repairs, Rent, Advertising, Insurance**
   A. **Repairs [¶ 1825]:**
      1. Repairs to business property or property held for production of income are deductible.
      2. Expenditures resulting in improvements are capital expenditures.
      3. If repairs are part of general plan of improvement, amounts spent for both repairs and improvements are capitalized.
   B. **Rent [¶ 1826]:**
      1. Deductible to extent property used in trade, business, or profession.
      2. If residence is used partly for business purposes, portion of rental payment allocable to business use is deductible.
      3. Advance rentals are deductible in year paid and only for portion allocable to the particular tax year.
      4. Landlord's lease cancellation payment is a capital expenditure, but tenant's is a deductible expense, if not personal.
      5. Payments under lease:
         (a) Deductible.
         (b) In absence of evidence of true rental, leases are treated as purchases if one or more or certain conditions are present.
   C. **Advertising expenses [¶ 1827]:**
      1. Deductible when ordinary and necessary and bear a reasonable relationship to business.

2. Cost of goodwill advertising is generally deductible.
3. Deductible as "nonbusiness expense" when reasonable and proximately relate to the "nonbusiness activity."

D. **Insurance premiums [¶ 1828]:**
1. Life insurance premiums:
   (a) Generally not deductible.
   (b) Deductible if paid on the life of officer or employee where taxpayer is not directly or indirectly a beneficiary and the premium is an ordinary and necessary expense.
   (c) Individual's payment of premiums on own life insurance to get business loan isn't deductible.
   (d) No deduction is allowed where partner insures own life and names co-partners as beneficiaries to induce them to stay in business.
   (e) Employer's payment of group life insurance premiums is deductible.
2. Premiums on fire, burglary, storm, theft and accident insurance are generally deductible if paid in connection with business or "nonbusiness property".
3. Premiums on employer's liability insurance covering employees, public liability insurance, workmen's compensation, etc. are deductible if paid in connection with a business or "nonbusiness activity."
4. Premiums paid by the employer on group health and accident insurance for employees are deductible providing the insurance is purchased in consideration for the services rendered.

V. **Traveling, Entertainment, and Moving Expenses**
   A. **Traveling expenses**—except for moving expenses are deductible only if ordinary and necessary business or "nonbusiness" expenses [¶ 1829].
   1. Business traveling expenses:
      (a) Deductible by employer or employee if following conditions are met:
         1) Expenses are reasonable and necessary.
         2) Except for certain transportation expenses, expenses must be incurred while away from home overnight.
         3) Expenses must be incurred in trade, business, or profession and must be necessary and appropriate to the development of the trade, business, or profession.
      (b) "Home" means principal place of business, employment, or post of duty.
      (c) Trips must involve sleep or rest to be considered "overnight".
   2. Ordinary and necessary transportation expenses incurred in connection with "nonbusiness activity" are deductible.
   3. Proof:
      (a) Adequate records required.
      (b) Self-employed persons or employees may use standard mileage rate in determining cost of operating motor vehicles.
   B. **Entertainment expenses [¶ 1830]:**
   1. Ordinarily deductible if directly related to active conduct of trade or business or production of income.
   2. Where expense relates to entertainment facility there is the additional requirement that the facility be used more than 50% of time to further business.
   3. Costs are deductible though not directly related to taxpayer's business if they are "associated with" the business and precede or follow substantial business discussion.
   4. Quiet business meal is one of nine exceptions to the "directly related" and "associated with" tests.
   5. Deduction for business gifts is limited to $25 a person each year.
   6. Adequate records must show amount, time, place, business purpose, and business relation of persons entertained.
   C. **Moving expenses [¶ 1831]:**
   1. Deductible by employees or self-employed persons (including partners) where incurred in moving to new job location.

2. Deductible are reasonable expenses of:
   (a) Moving household goods and personal effects to new residence.
   (b) Traveling to new residence.
   (c) Traveling after obtaining employment from old residence to general area of new job and return in search for new residence.
   (d) Meals and lodging in temporary quarters up to 30 days while waiting for new residence at new job location.
   (e) Expenses of sale of old residence and purchase of new one.
   (f) Expenses of settling old lease and acquiring new one.
3. Deduction on indirect moving expenses:
   (a) $3,000 limit on expenses of househunting trips, temporary quarters and acquiring and disposing of residence.
   (b) $1,500 limit on househunting trips and temporary quarters.
4. Expenses relating to the purchase and sale of a residence, and those relating to the settling or acquisition of a lease are deductible.
5. Taxpayer's move must be somewhat permanent and new work area must be 35 miles from old job site.
6. A self-employed person or partner who performs personal services may deduct moving expenses the same as an employee.

VI. Miscellaneous Expenses

A. **Physicians, attorneys, and other professionals**—may deduct the ordinary and necessary expenses incurred in the practice of their profession [¶ 1832].

B. **Educational expenses [¶ 1833]:**
   1. Expenses incurred to meet minimum educational requirements of employment or trade or business aren't deductible.
   2. Expenses incurred to maintain or improve skills required in employment, trade or business are deductible.
   3. Also deductible are expenses incurred to meet express requirements of employer, or requirements of law, imposed as a condition for retaining salary status or employment.
   4. Directly related research, travel, transportation, and typing expenses are deductible.
   5. Expenses incurred by teachers are deductible even though the education may qualify the teacher for a higher position in the profession.

C. **Armed forces personnel [¶ 1834]:**
   1. Generally have same deductions as civilian.
   2. Cost of equipment required by profession is deductible, but cost of uniforms and their maintenance is generally not deductible.
   3. Traveling expenses incurred while on permanent duty overseas aren't deductible, but such expenses incurred while assigned away from permanent posts are deductible.

VII. Benefit and Retirement Plans

A. **Contributions under pension, stock bonus and profit-sharing plans [¶ 1838]:**
   1. Limited deduction allowed employers.
   2. Contributions plus regular salaries may not exceed reasonable compensation [¶ 1838(a)].
   3. Special provisions allow deductions to certain qualified plans [¶ 1838(b)].
   4. Employer deductions for qualified pension trust for plan years beginning after 9-2-74 (after 12-31-75 for plans existing on 1-1-74) [¶ 1838(d)]:
      (a) Amount necessary to satisfy minimum funding standard; or
      (b) Amount necessary to provide all employees with their remaining unfunded cost of past and current service credits distributed as a level amount or a level percentage of compensation, over remaining life of employee; or
      (c) Normal cost of plan plus amount necessary to amortize past service liabilities and other supplementary pension or annuity credits over 10 years.
      (d) Maximum deduction can't exceed amount of full funding limitation for year.

(e) For plan years beginning on or before 9-2-74 (before 1-1-76 for plans existing on 1-1-74), deduction limited to 5% of tax year's compensation paid or accrued to all participating employees.

(f) Amounts paid in one tax year over limits can be deducted in succeeding tax year to extent that year's contribution is less than maximum allowable deduction.

5. Deduction for qualified stock bonus or profit-sharing trust [¶ 1838(e)]:
    (a) Deduction limited to 15% of compensation otherwise paid or accrued during tax year to all beneficiaries of plan.
    (b) Amounts paid in one tax year over limit is deductible in succeeding tax years in order of time, if deduction in succeeding year doesn't exceed 15% limit for current year's deduction.
    (c) If amount contributed during tax year is less than 15% maximum, difference between amount contributed and 15% maximum may be carried over as credit and deducted when contributed.
6. Rules on pension trusts apply to contributions to buy employee retirement annuities under a qualified plan not part of a trust [¶ 1838(g)].
7. Deductions for contributions to certain combinations of qualified plans may not exceed the greater of [¶ 1838(h)]:
    (a) 25% of compensation otherwise paid or accrued during tax year to employee beneficiaries; or
    (b) Contributions made to extent they don't exceed contributions needed to satisfy minimum funding standard.
8. Contributions to nonqualified plans are deductible if [¶ 1838(i)]:
    (a) Participating employees include the contribution in income, and the employer maintains separate accounts for each employee; or
    (b) The method of paying contributions has the effect of a plan.
9. Individual not covered by plan can set up individual retirement arrangement [¶ 1838(1)]:
    (a) Can contribute and deduct 15% of compensation up to $1,500 each year.
    (b) Income earned by plan is tax-free until paid out.
    (c) Excess contributions, premature distributions and late distributions are subject to nondeductible penalty taxes.
    (d) Retirement plan benefits can be "rolled-over" tax-free into IRA if made within 60 days of receipt.

B. **Self-employed retirement plans [¶ 1839]:**
1. Self-employed persons with "earned income" may set up retirement plans for themselves [¶ 1839(a)].
2. For tax years starting after 1973, an owner-employee can contribute for himself each year the lesser of $7,500 or 15% of his "earned income" for that year [¶ 1839(b)].
3. Earned income means net earnings from self-employment [¶ 1839(b)].
4. Deduction for contributions [¶ 1839(c)]:
    (a) Self-employed person can deduct his entire contribution on his own behalf up to $7,500 or 15% of earned income, whichever is less.
    (b) Voluntary "employee" contributions aren't deductible.
    (c) Contributions for employees are deductible to the extent they are within the general deduction limits applying to all plans.
5. To qualify, the plan must meet [¶ 1839(d)]:
    (a) Special requirements, and
    (b) Requirements for plans for employees, except to the extent the special rules for the self-employed are inconsistent with those for employees.
6. A plan may be disqualified if excess contributions are made and not returned to owner-employee within specified time [¶ 1839(f)].
7. Treatment of distributions [¶ 1839(g)]:
    (a) Lump-sum distributions representing employer contributions in 1973 and earlier years receive capital gain treatment.

Highlights of Chapter 8

    (b) Distributions from accumulations after 1973 are ordinary income.
    (c) Tax on ordinary income portion can be computed under special 10-year forward averaging device.

C. Leaseholds [¶ 1840]:
1. Cost of improvements by lessee which extend beyond tax year are not currently deductible, but recoverable by depreciation over useful life of property.
2. Purchaser of lease may deduct each year the proportionate part of cost of acquiring lease. Special rule applies to renewal period in writing off acquisition cost.

D. Research and experimental expenses [¶ 1842]:
1. Deductible.
2. Election as to when to deduct:
    (a) In year incurred.
    (b) Ratably over period of 60 months or more.
3. Election does not apply where:
    (a) Expenditures for land or depreciable or depletable property.
    (b) Exploration expenditures for minerals, gas or oil.

E. Mining expenses [¶ 1843]:
1. Exploration expenses [¶ 1843(a)]:
    (a) Defined as expenses incurred to determine existence, location, extent, or quality of mineral deposits (except oil and gas) before development begins.
    (b) Deductible if incurred after 1969.
    (c) Limited and unlimited deduction available for expenses incurred before 1970.
    (d) Deduction is recaptured as orginary income when production stage reached or when property disposed of at gain.
    (e) Limited deduction allowed on foreign deposits.
2. Development expenses (other than for oil and gas) [¶ 1843(b)]:
    (a) Deduction may be taken:
        1) In year paid or incurred, or
        2) Proportionately, as the ore or mineral benefited is sold.
    (b) Following expenses do not qualify for this election [¶ 1843(c)]:
        1) Expenses to acquire or improve depreciable property.
        2) Expenses not deductible as development expenses.
        3) Expenses of acquiring property.

F. Farmer's expenses [¶ 1844]:
1. Ordinary and necessary expenses incurred during productive period of farm are deductible.
2. Farmers may elect to deduct fertilizer and lime expenses currently.
3. Capital expenditures:
    (a) Except where farmer elects to deduct fertilizer and lime expenses, expenses during preparatory period are capital expenditures.
    (b) Cost of farm machinery, equipment and buildings (other than dwellings) are capital expenditures.
    (c) Cost of planting, cultivating, maintaining and developing citrus and almond groves must be capitalized through end of fourth tax year after planting.
4. No business deduction is allowed for pleasure farm expenses.

G. Soil and water conservation expenses [¶ 1845]:
1. Farmers cannot take a deduction for more than 25% of their farm gross income for the year for soil and water conservation expenses.
2. Assessments by soil or water conservation or drainage districts under certain conditions.
3. Expenses of clearing farm land:
    (a) Deductible.
    (b) Deduction cannot exceed lesser of: $5,000 or 25% of taxable income from farming.
4. Soil and water conservation expenses and land clearing costs may be partially or fully recaptured where farm land held for less than 10 years is sold or exchanged.

H. Amortizable bond premium [¶ 1846]:

1. Amortization of premium of wholly tax-exempt bonds:
   (a) Mandatory.
   (b) No deduction allowed and basis of obligations is reduced.
   (c) Special rules apply to dealers in securities.
2. Amortization of premium of wholly taxable bonds:
   (a) Optional.
   (b) Deduction allowed, but basis of obligations is reduced.
3. Bond premiums due to conversion privilege are not amortized.

Chapter 9

DEDUCTIONS—INTEREST, TAXES, CONTRIBUTIONS AND MEDICAL EXPENSES
TABLE OF CONTENTS

¶

DEDUCTIONS—INTEREST

	¶
What interest is deductible	1900
Indebtedness must exist	1901
Interest and dividends distinguished	
Indebtedness must be that of the taxpayer	1902
Discount	1903
Installment payments	1904
Interest charge stated	
Finance charges on installment purchases	
Interest charge not stated	
Disallowed interest	1905
Interest for tax-exempt securities	
Interest for single premium insurance contract	
Life insurance loans	
Accrued but unpaid interest	
Disallowed interest deduction in corporate mergers	
Special treatment of investment interest	1906

DEDUCTIONS—TAXES

The deductibility of taxes	1910
Federal taxes	1911
Deductible as expense	
State and local taxes	1912
Social security taxes	1913
Federal social security tax	
Federal unemployment insurance tax	
State unemployment insurance contributions	
State disability tax	
Foreign taxes and taxes of U.S. possessions	1914
Who may deduct taxes	1915
Who may deduct federal taxes	1916
Who may deduct state and local taxes	1917
State capital stock taxes	1918

	¶
Taxes must be imposed on taxpayer	1919
Buyer and seller apportion real property tax deduction	1920
Apportionment	
Adjustment of amount realized by seller and basis to buyer	
Time for deduction	
Adjustment for deduction in prior year	

DEDUCTIONS—CONTRIBUTIONS

Deduction for charitable contributions	1941
Qualified organizations	
Benefits received for contributions	
Time for deduction	
How treated on return	
Contributions other than money	1942
Valuation	
Appreciated property	
Contributions of services	
Right to use property	
Partial interests	
Student living in taxpayer's home	
Reduction for certain interest	
Limitations on contribution deduction	1943
Carryover of excess charitable contributions	1944

DEDUCTIONS—MEDICAL EXPENSES

Deduction for medical expenses	1945
Amount of deduction	
Amount paid for decedents	
Taxpayer-spouse-dependent	
What are medical expenses	1946
Medical expense reimbursed in later years	1947

• Highlights of Chapter 9 .... Page 1961

The law allows certain deductions from adjusted gross income in computing taxable income. This chapter deals with the main categories of itemized deductions (interest, taxes, charitable contributions and medical deductions).

Footnotes appear at end of this Chapter.

DEDUCTIONS—INTEREST

Interest is deductible if paid on a debt for which the taxpayer is legally liable. Special rules may limit the deduction or disallow it entirely.

¶ **1900 What interest is deductible.** "Interest" is compensation for the use or forbearance of money.[1] A loan processing fee (points) paid by a mortgagor-borrower as a bonus or premium to get a conventional mortgage loan is deductible as interest.[2] However, a loan origination fee (points) paid in place of specified service charges in connection with a loan (such as a VA loan) is a charge for services rendered and is not deductible as interest. Nor is a loan placement fee paid by seller to get a loan for the buyer (such as FHA loan).[3] But see ¶ 1416(b). There may be an unstated interest element in deferred payment sales [¶ 2840]. The interest must be paid on a real debt to be deductible. Interest is deductible whether the debt is a business, "nonbusiness" or personal debt. Exceptions to the general rule are discussed in ¶ 1905.

> **Example:** Interest paid by a taxpayer on a mortgage on his property is deductible whether the property is a business building or his private residence. Also, a taxpayer who borrows money to repair his home, or to build a garage for his pleasure auto can deduct the interest on the loan.

A taxpayer may not charge his business with interest on the money he has invested [Sec. 1.163-1(a)].

How treated on return. Deductible interest of an individual is a deduction for adjusted gross income only if (1) it is directly incurred in carrying on trade, business or profession or (2) it is incurred in connection with property held for the production of rents or royalties [¶ 1804; 1806]. In all other cases, interest is deductible on Form 1040, Schedule A, as an "other itemized deduction." Certain excess itemized deductions (including interest) may be a tax preference item subject to the minimum tax. See ¶ 2403. For time for deducting interest see ¶ 2739.

¶ **1901 Indebtedness must exist.** If no indebtedness exists, no deduction is allowed[1] [Sec. 163(a); 1.163-1(a)]. A deduction has been denied when the debt did exist, but was incurred solely for tax savings purposes.[2]

Gifts. Generally, interest paid on a note executed as a gift is not deductible because no debt exists when the note cannot be enforced;[3] but if the note can be collected, for example, a note under seal, the interest is deductible.[4]

Mortgage prepayment penalty is deductible as interest.[5] But amounts designated "interest on mortgage" paid for occupying a home *before settlement of mortgage* are not deductible.[6]

Redeemable ground rents are deductible as interest [Sec. 163(c); 1.163-1].

Delinquent taxes. Interest paid on delinquent taxes[7] is deductible. But if the interest is a part of a lump-sum payment in compromise of proposed tax deficiency plus penalty and interest, the interest cannot be deducted.[8]

Judgments. Interest paid on a judgment is deductible (judgment is a debt).[9]

Bank deposits. The relation of a bank to depositors is that of debtor and creditor, so a bank may deduct interest paid on its deposits [Sec. 1.163-1(c)]. But there is a special rule for mutual bank withdrawable accounts [¶ 3433(b)].

Insurance policy conversion. Payments called "interest" that in fact are a part of the property's cost are not deductible. For example, when a life policy is converted into a higher premium policy by paying the difference in premium plus interest to conversion date, the amount designated as interest is part of the cost of the new policy.[10]

Credit cards. Finance charges on credit card holders for purchases can be deducted as interest.[11] See also ¶ 1904(b).

Interest and dividends distinguished. Payments by a corporation on its stock are dividends (not deductible). But payments made on its evidences of indebtedness are interest (deductible). Classification of the instrument under which the payments are made is sometimes difficult. The intent of the parties as determined from the facts and circumstances controls.[12]

Stocks and evidences of indebtedness are distinguished from each other by their respective features. The *characteristics of stock of a corporation* are: evidence of the right to participate in the net profits of the corporation proportionate to the stockholding; the right to participate in the management of the corporation through voting power; the right to share proportionately in the distribution of net assets on the liquidation of the corporation. Stock may have any or all of the foregoing features, and may and usually does have other features. The *characteristics of an evidence of indebtedness* are: a definite obligor: a definite obligee (either by name or designation); a definite ascertainable obligation; a time of maturity, either definite or that will become definite. It may, of course, have other features.[13]

NOTE: In a "thin corporation," where the debt greatly exceeds the stock, part of the debt may be treated as stock for tax purposes.

Factors given more weight under the general debt-equity guidelines are: (1) whether the instrument is an unconditional promise to pay a sum certain either on demand or on a specific date, with fixed interest; (2) whether there is subordination to or preference over any indebtedness of the corporation; (3) corporation's ratio of debt to equity; (4) whether the interest is convertible into stock of the corporation; and (5) the relationship between stock holdings and interest in question [Sec. 385].

¶ 1902 Indebtedness must be that of the taxpayer. Interest is not deductible unless it is paid on a debt owed by the taxpayer.[1]

Corporation and stockholder. A corporation may not deduct interest paid for a stockholder[2] and a stockholder may not deduct interest paid for the corporation.[3]

Estate and heirs. An estate may not deduct interest paid on state inheritance taxes owed by the heirs.[4]

Joint obligors can deduct interest paid on the indebtedness; for example, an obligor on a mortgage bond[5] or the comaker on a note.[6]

Husband and wife. A husband may not deduct interest paid by him on a mortgage on his wife's property[7] (not his debt). But if a husband and wife own real estate as tenants by entireties, either spouse may deduct the interest he or she pays on the mortgage[8] (essentially a joint obligation). Of course, if they file a joint return, the interest may be deducted whether it is paid by the husband or wife.

Condominiums. Taxayer may deduct interest on the mortgage of his condominium apartment even if it is a part of a master mortgage.[9]

When direct liability not essential. The rule that interest is not deductible unless paid on a debt owed by the taxpayer is relaxed in some instances to allow a deduction even if taxpayer was not *directly* liable.

Real estate owners. A deduction is allowed for interest paid on a mortgage on real estate the taxpayer owns, even though he is not liable directly on the bond or note [Sec. 1.163-1(b)].

Cooperative apartments and housing. Tenant-stockholders of cooperative apartment or housing corporations may take a deduction for amounts paid to the corporation that represent interest on the mortgage[10] [Sec. 216; 1.216-1].

Interest on taxes paid by transferee. A transferee or a beneficiary may deduct interest on income, estate or gift taxes determined against him, that accrues after the transfer of property to which the tax relates.[11]

G.I. loan. The veteran can deduct payments made by the U.S. government and applied to interest owed by the veteran if the government did not assume that liability; but not if the government insured the interest payment.[12]

Loan for taxpayer's benefit. There is some authority to the effect that a taxpayer may deduct interest that he pays on a loan made for his benefit, although he is not directly liable.[13]

Footnotes appear at end of this Chapter.

¶ **1903 Discount.** When money is borrowed from a bank, the interest may be adjusted in advance; that is, taxpayer's note may be discounted. The discount can be deducted as interest. For time of deduction, see ¶ 2739.

> **Example:** Kent borrows money from a local bank. He signs a note for $1,000. The note is discounted. Kent receives only $940. The $60 difference is deductible interest.[1]

¶ **1904 Installment payments.** When a purchase of property is made on an installment plan or a purchase is repaid in installments, a part of each payment may be deductible interest (for example, monthly payments made on the purchase of household appliances or on a mortgage on one's home may cover both interest charges and principal). The rules for deducting the interest are in (a) and (c) below. The rules for personal property in (c) below, also apply to payments to an educational institution for educational services (including lodging) on behalf of a student [Sec. 163(b)(1)]. For payments treated as interest, see ¶ 2840.

Background and purpose. Formerly, it was the practice to deny any deduction for carrying charges on installment purchases unless the interest element was stated separately. This denial was based on the belief that part of the carrying charge represented charges other than that for the use of money.

(a) Interest charge stated. If the interest charge is separately stated or can be ascertained by the taxpayer and proven, the interest part of each installment payment is deductible[1] [Sec. 163(a)]. This rule applies whether the property involved is real property or personal property.

> **NOTE:** A creditor-lender subject to the federal "Truth in Lending Act" and its "Regulation Z" must furnish the borrower with a detailed statement for the interest to be charged on the installment loan.

(b) Finance charges on installment purchases. Finance charges on installment accounts or paid on a retail or an educational institution installment contract, including prepayment charges, are deductible as interest.[2]

(c) Interest charge not stated. The interest deduction depends on whether the property bought is real or personal.

Real property. When the interest charge is hidden in the carrying charges or purchase price of real property paid for in installments and the rules for unstated interest [¶ 2840] do not apply, interest may be deducted only if the taxpayer can prove what is the interest element.[3]

Personal property. If an installment purchase of personal property (or educational services) is made on a charge account and a flat fee or service charge is separately stated, but the interest charge is not, an interest deduction is allowed. The portion of the flat fee or service charge that may be deducted as interest is the lesser of: (1) the amount equal to 6% of the average unpaid balance under the contract during the year; or (2) the portion of the total fee or service charge properly allocable to the tax year.[4] The average unpaid balance is the sum of the unpaid balances outstanding on the first day of each month beginning in the tax year divided by 12 [Sec. 163(b); 1.163-2].

¶ **1905 Disallowed interest.** Certain interest that would otherwise qualify as a deduction is disallowed to prevent abuses in the use of the interest deduction.

Background and purpose. Disallowing the interest deduction in certain cases eliminates the tax advantage of a taxpayer incurring a debt to secure income that is not currently taxed, for example, tax-exempt securities.

(a) Interest for tax-exempt securities. No deduction is allowed for interest paid on a debt incurred or continued to buy or carry wholly tax-exempt obligations or securities [Sec. 265(2); 1.265-2]. A deduction has been allowed for interest on money borrowed for working capital needs and *temporarily* invested in tax-exempt securities,[1] or when there is no direct relationship between the borrowing and the tax-exempt transactions.[2] When part of the total interest is disallowed, the proportionate share of disallowance is determined by multiplying the total interest by the average amount of tax-exempt obligations (valued at their adjusted basis) over the average amount of total assets (valued at their adjusted basis) minus the indebtedness the interest on which is not subject to disallowance.[3]

(b) Interest to buy or carry a single premium insurance contract. No deduction is allowed for interest paid or accrued on a debt incurred or continued to buy or carry a single premium life insurance or endowment contract; or a single premium annuity contract. This includes a contract on which (a) substantially all the premiums are paid within four years from the date of purchase or (b) an amount is deposited with the insurer for payment of a substantial number of future premiums [Sec. 264].

(c) Life insurance loans. No deduction is allowed for interest on a debt to buy or carry life insurance, endowment, or annuity contracts bought after 8/6/63, under a systematic plan to borrow the cash surrender value of the contract. This does not apply if the annual interest is $100 or less, the loan is incurred due to unforeseen circumstances, the loan is for business purposes, or no part of 4 of the first 7 annual premiums are paid with funds borrowed under the plan [Sec. 264]. Interest deductions will be allowed until 4 of the first 7 premiums are paid by debt. The deductions will then be disallowed for the earlier years, if open [Sec. 1.264-4(b)].

> **NOTE:** A borrowing in one of the seven years in excess of the annual premium can be attributed to the payment of premiums paid for years before or after the borrowing occurred [Sec. 1.264-4(d)].

(d) Accrued but unpaid interest is not deductible if the parties are related and certain other conditions are present. See ¶ 2748.

(e) Disallowed interest deduction in corporate mergers. A corporation gets no deduction for interest that exceeds $5,000,000 paid or incurred during a tax year on *corporate acquisition indebtedness* incurred after 10-9-69. To be considered corporate acquisition indebtedness, four tests must be met: (1) the use test; (2) the subordination test; (3) the convertibility test; (4) and either debt-equity or projected earnings-annual interest test. The $5,000,000 allowable limit is reduced by any interest paid or incurred in a tax year on corporate acquisition indebtedness after 1967 that does not meet one of the 4 tests [Sec. 279; 1.279-1—7].

¶ **1906 Special treatment of investment interest.** Interest on funds borrowed to buy or carry investment property is deductible up to an allowable limit for all taxpayers except corporations. To determine an allowable limit, pre-1970, pre-1976, and post-1975 interest deduction rules apply. For tax years starting after 1975 the investment interest deduction limit is an amount equal to the sum of the following [Sec. 163(a), (d)]:

Footnotes appear at end of this Chapter.

¶ **1906**

- $10,000 ($5,000 for married persons filing separately). Trusts have no dollar exemption. A special rule applies when the taxpayer owns 50% or more of a corporation or partnership. See below.
- Net investment income. A proportionate share of current year net investment income must be allocated to current and prior tax years where the investment interest is attributable to more than one period (pre-1970, pre-1976 and post-1975). See (b) below.
- Excess deductions for business (or investment) expenses, interest, and property taxes on net lease property over rental income from such property.

NOTE: Similar rules apply to net lease property [(b), below]. Form 4952 is used to compute the deduction and must be attached to the return. Pre-1976 limitations apply to investment indebtedness attributable to a specific property for a specified term that was incurred before 9-11-75, or under a contract binding on and after 9-11-75.

Example 1: In 1977, Bob Brown, a married taxpayer filing a joint return, had an investment interest expense of $200,000 for a loan he was granted in January 1977. His investment income from dividends, interest and net short-term capital gains from sales of investment property totaled $25,000 and his investment expenses were $5,000. Thus, his net investment income was $20,000 ($25,000 less $5,000). Brown also had $20,000 in net long-term capital gain from sale of investment property. This gain does not enter into the computation. Brown's disallowed investment interest deduction for 1977 is thus $170,000, and deductible investment interest is $30,000 computed as follows:

1.	Investment interest expense		$200,000
2.	Exemption	$10,000	
3.	Net investment income	20,000	
4.	Total deduction allowed (total exemptions)		30,000
5.	Disallowed investment interest		$170,000

50%-owned corporations or partnerships. For tax years starting after 1975, the $10,000 limitation (see above) is increased by the lesser of $15,000 ($7,500 for married taxpayers filing separately) or the amount of interest on the indebtedness incurred or continued which is used to acquire any 50%-owned corporation or partnership. To qualify, the taxpayer, his spouse, and children must own at least 50% of the stock or capital interest in the enterprise [Sec. 163(d)(7)].

Pre-1976 rules. For tax years starting in 1972 through 1975, the investment interest that can be deducted is an amount equal to the sum of the following:[1] (1) $25,000 ($12,500 for married taxpayers filing separately; trusts have no dollar exemption); (2) net investment income (see (b) below); (3) excess deductions for business (or investment) expenses, interest and property taxes on net lease property over rental income from this property; (4) excess net long-term capital gains over net short-term capital losses on investment property (see below); (5) one-half of the investment interest that exceeds the total of these four items. The remaining half, if any, is disallowed.

NOTE: Similar rules apply to net lease property [(b), below]. These pre-1976 limitations do not apply to investment indebtedness attributable to a specific item of property for a specified term that was incurred before 12-17-69 or under a contract binding on and after 12-16-69.

Example 2: In 1974, Bill Jones, a married taxpayer filing a joint return, had an investment interest expense of $20,000. His investment income from dividends, interest and net short-term capital gains from sales of investment property totaled $25,000 and his investment expenses were $5,000. Thus, his net investment income was $20,000 ($25,000 less $5,000). Jones also had $20,000 in net long-term capital gains from sales of investment property. Jones' disallowed investment interest deduction for 1974 is $67,500, and deductible investment interest is $132,500, computed as follows:

1. Investment interest expense $200,000

2.	Exemption	$25,000	
3.	Net investment income	20,000	
4.	Net long-term capital gain	20,000	
5.	Total of lines 2—4	$65,000	
6.	½ the difference between amounts on lines 1 and 5: $135,000 ($200,000 less $65,000)	$67,500	
7.	Deduction allowed (total exemptions)		132,500
8.	Disallowed investment interest		$ 67,500

Special pre-1976 rule for net long-term capital gains. For tax years starting in 1972 through 1975, any excess net long-term capital gains from investments that offset investment interest (and therefore allowed the interest to be deducted) are treated as ordinary income; the alternative tax and net long-term capital gain deduction cannot be used for these gains.

Background and purpose. At one time, taxpayers could incur a substantial interest expense on funds borrowed to buy growth stocks (or other investments initially producing low income) and then use the interest deduction to shelter other income from tax. The effect of allowing a current deduction for interest on funds used to make the investment was to allow the interest deduction to offset other ordinary income even though the gains might result in capital gains. The Tax Reform Act of 1976 reduced the deduction.

(a) Carryover of disallowed deduction. Investment interest that can not be deducted in the year paid or accrued can be carried over to succeeding tax years. The carryovers retain their character. Carryovers of pre-1976 interest will be subject to the pre-1976 limitations. Carryover of post-1975 interest is treated as investment interest paid or accrued in the succeeding taxable year [Sec. 163(d)(2)].

Pre-1976 carryover rules. For tax years starting in 1972 through 1975 the amount of the pre-1976 carryover deductible in the carryover year is limited to one-half the excess of (1) the sum of $25,000 plus any net investment income in the carryover year over (2) the greater of $25,000 or any investment interest actually paid in the carryover year. Any carryover that is not deductible can be carried over to the next succeeding year. This carryover is first reduced by the amount of any net long-term capital gain deduction to which the taxpayer is entitled in the carryover year. The carryover must be reduced by 50% of any excess net long-term capital gains whether or not the taxpayer claimed the deduction.[2]

Example 3: In addition to the same facts as in Example 2, Bill Jones had net investment income of $100,000, investment interest expense of $80,000 and net long-term capital gain of $20,000 in 1975. $22,500 of the $67,500 in disallowed interest carried over from 1974 is deductible in 1975, and $35,000 of the same carryover is carried over to 1976, computed as follows:

1.	Net investment income ($100,000) + $25,000	$125,000
2.	Greater of investment interest ($80,000) or $25,000	80,000
3.	Investment interest deduction [½ the difference between amounts on lines 1 and 2: $45,000 ($125,000 less $80,000)]	22,500
4.	Nondeductible carryover ($67,500 less $22,500)	45,000
5.	50% of net long-term capital gain	10,000
6.	Disallowed interest which can be carried to 1976 from 1975 ($45,000 less $10,000)	$ 35,000

The actual investment interest expense in 1975 of $80,000 is fully deductible in that year. The $25,000 exemption plus the $100,000 in net investment income permits full deduction in that year.

Footnotes appear at end of this Chapter.

¶ 1906

(b) Net investment income defined. Net investment income is the excess of the taxpayer's investment income over investment expenses. If a taxpayer has investment interest attributable to a pre-1976 tax year, a proportionate share of the current net investment income must be allocated between the pre-1976 and post-1975 tax years [see below]. A taxpayer's investment income is the gross income from interest, dividends, rents and royalties, the net short-term capital gain from disposing of investment property, and the recapture of depreciation and intangible drilling costs [¶ 1619; 2103(c)]. However, investment income may not be attributable to a trade or business. The investment expenses are expenses deductible as trade or business [¶ 1804], property taxes [¶ 1910], bad debts [¶ 2300], straight line depreciation [¶ 2011], amortizable bond premium [¶ 1846], cost depletion [¶ 2103], and other deductible investment expenses [Sec. 163(d)(3)].

Allocation of net investment income. For tax years starting after 12-31-75, a proportionate share of current net investment income must be allocated to pre-1976 and to post-1975 tax years for investment interest attributable to pre-1976 years. These proportionate allocations are computed as follows: (1) The proportionate share of pre-1976 net investment income is determined by multiplying the current net investment income by the interest attributable to the pre-1976 tax year over the total investment interest; (2) The proportionate share of the post-1975 net investment income is determined by multiplying the current net investment income by the interest attributable to the post-1975 year over the total investment interest. The interest deduction for each tax period is limited to an amount equal to the sum of the allocated investment income plus the limitations that apply to each period (post-75, pre-76, pre-70). [Sec. 163(d)(3)(A)].

Example 4: In 1976, Sam Smith, a married taxpayer filing a joint return, had investment income of $45,000. He had $90,000 in investment interest: $30,000 attributable to 1975 and $60,000 attributable to 1976. The current investment income of $45,000 is allocated as follows: (1) one-third, $15,000 [$30,000/$90,000 × $45,000] to 1975; (2) two-thirds, $30,000 [$60,000/$90,000 × $45,000] to 1976. The 1976 total interest deduction is limited to $70,000 [$30,000 for 1975 and $40,000 for 1976] because pre-1976 interest is deductible under pre-1976 limitations and post-1975 interest under post-1975 limitations. The interest attributed to 1975 is fully deductible since the pre-1976 limitation of $25,000 plus $15,000 of allocated investment income exceeds the $30,000 of pre-1976 interest. But only $40,000 of investment interest attributable to 1976 is deductible in 1976 because the post-1975 limitation of $10,000 plus $30,000 of allocated investment income equals $40,000. The remaining $20,000 [$60,000 less $40,000] is carried to 1977.

Net lease property. Property subject to a net lease entered into after 10-9-69 is investment property. Property is subject to a net lease if: (1) the lessor-taxpayer is guaranteed a specific return or against loss of income; or (2) expenses (excluding rent paid and reimbursed expenses) deductible solely as trade or business expenses are less than 15% of rental income from the property. The *return test* analyzes the entire leasing arrangement to find if the guarantee applies for any period covered by the lease. However, the *15% expense ratio test* is made annually and applies to each lease. There are 2 elections related to this test: (1) multiple leases on single (or adjacent) parcels may be combined to determine if they are net leases; or (2) property in commercial use more than 5 years can be eliminated from the 15% test. Either election must be made each year by the return due date (including extensions). No election can be made later than the time for filing a refund or credit claim for the election year. It is made by attaching a statement to the return for each election year [Sec. 57(c); Proposed Reg. 1.57-3; Temp. Reg. Sec. 12.8].

DEDUCTIONS—TAXES

There is a distinction between a tax and a fee. A tax is imposed to raise revenue, but a fee is a charge for a particular act or service. Certain state, local and foreign levies are deductible as taxes. Federal taxes are not deducted as such. However, some levies not deductible as taxes may be deducted as business expenses or expenses of "nonbusiness" activities.

¶ **1910 The deductibility of taxes.** A tax must meet three conditions to be deductible during the tax year: (1) it must be a deductible tax [¶ 1912]; (2) it must be imposed on the taxpayer [¶ 1915-1920]; and (3) generally it must be paid during the tax year [¶ 1920(c); 2740]. A tax may fall under one of the following headings:

(1) Taxes not deductible at all. Certain taxes are not deductible under any circumstances, for example, an inheritance tax [Sec. 275].

(2) Taxes deductible as a tax. Sec. 164 provides a deduction for specified state, local and foreign taxes. A tax deductible under this section is said to be deductible as such since the only requirement for the deduction is that the tax be of a certain character. For example, state property taxes and state income taxes are always deductible *as taxes,* even if they are personal expenses (as distinguished from business or "nonbusiness" expenses).

(3) Taxes deductible as an expense. Sec. 164 permits a deduction for state, local and foreign taxes incurred in carrying on a trade or business, or in a "nonbusiness" activity (¶ 1806). In addition, Sec. 162 provides a deduction for ordinary and necessary expenses of carrying on a trade or business. Sec. 212 provides a deduction for expenses incurred for "nonbusiness" activities. A tax not deductible as such, may nevertheless be deductible as a business or "nonbusiness" expense. For example, the federal excise tax on telephone messages is deductible only when related to business or "nonbusiness" activity.

Treatment on the return. Deductible taxes of an individual are deductions for adjusted gross income only if (1) they are directly incurred in carrying on a trade or business or (2) they are incurred in connection with property held for the production of rents or royalties [¶ 1804; 1806]. In all other cases they are deductible on Schedule A Form 1040 itemized deductions. Certain excess itemized deductions (including taxes) may be a tax preference item subject to the minimum tax. See ¶ 2403.

¶ **1911 Federal taxes.** Federal taxes fall under one of two headings:

(a) Not deductible. The following federal taxes are not deductible [Sec. 275]: income taxes; estate tax (but see ¶ 3008(b); gift tax.

(b) Deductible as expense. Federal import (customs) duties, excise taxes and social security taxes [¶ 1913] are deductible if they are incurred in a trade or business [¶ 1804] or in a "nonbusiness" activity (¶ 1806) [Sec. 162; 212]. All or part of the interest equalization tax (tax imposed on the acquisition of foreign stock or debt obligations) is deductible as a business or "nonbusiness" expense in the year equivalent reimbursement is reported as income [Sec. 263(d)].

¶ **1912 State and local taxes.** Some of these taxes are not deductible at all while others may be deducted in certain cases. Local taxes include those imposed by counties, cities, municipalities, villages, towns, school districts, and other political subdivisions of the state. For a state and local tax to be deductible as a personal property tax, it must be imposed on an annual basis and be based on the value of the personal property (for example, auto registration fees in some states). The rules on who may deduct state and local taxes are in ¶ 1915 and 1917.

(a) Not deductible. State and local death taxes (estate, inheritance, legacy and succession taxes) and gift taxes are not deductible at all [Sec. 164].

(b) Special assessments. Assessments for local benefits (special assessments) are not deductible *unless* made (1) for maintenance or repair; (2) to meet interest charges; or (3) levied by a special taxing district to retire debt existing on 12-31-63 if (i) the district covers at least one county, (ii) tax covers at least 1,000 persons, and (iii) the assessment is levied annually at a uniform rate on the same assessed property value used for real estate tax purposes[1] [Sec. 1.164-4]. When an assessment is made for several purposes, the part deductible must be ascertained from local officials.

(c) Deductible as taxes. State and local taxes, deductible as such, are limited to the following: property taxes; general sales and compensating use taxes; gasoline taxes; and state and city income taxes. This includes taxes on interest income that is exempt from federal tax but not taxes on other exempt income[2] [Sec. 164(a); 1.164-1]. Some fees may be deductible as taxes (for example, Indiana, fee for capital stock increase[3] and Pennsylvania, payment for corporate franchise[4]).

(d) Deductible as business expenses. Any state and local tax not deductible as such (for example, stamp and stock transfer taxes or a cigarette tax), or any charges collected primarily for regulatory purposes (such as fishing license) may be deductible if they are incurred in the taxpayer's business or "nonbusiness" activities [Sec. 164(a); 1.164-1(a)]. See also ¶ 1913(c), (d).

> NOTE: In personal transactions, such as buying a residence, a transfer tax paid by the buyer is capitalized. Tax paid by the seller is an expense of sale.[5] For treatment of the taxes as deductible moving expenses, see ¶ 1831(b).

¶ 1913 Social security taxes. (a) Federal social security tax paid by an employer generally is deductible, but not the tax paid by an employee or self-employed person.

Tax on employers. The federal tax on employers is an excise tax [¶ 3800]. So it is deductible if it is a business expense [¶ 1804] or related to a "nonbusiness" activity [¶ 1806], but not if it is a personal expense.

Tax on employees. The federal tax on employees is an income tax and is not deductible by the employee [¶ 1911(a)]. If an employer does not withhold the tax from the employee's wages, but pays it for the employee, it is additional compensation to the employee.[1] As such, the employer can deduct the amount paid if it is an ordinary and necessary business or "nonbusiness" expense [¶ 1815].

Tax on self-employed persons. The federal tax on self-employed persons is not deductible since it is an income tax.

(b) Federal unemployment insurance tax. The federal tax on *employers* is an excise tax. It is deductible to the same extent as the federal social security tax on employers [see (a) above]. There is no federal unemployment insurance tax on employees.

(c) State unemployment insurance contributions by employers are deductible, if paid in connection with a business or "nonbusiness" activity.

Voluntary contributions. Employer voluntary contributions over the amounts required by state law are deductible as business expense so long as they effect a reduction in the rate of required contribution.[2]

Employee contributions. At present, *employees* are required to contribute to state unemployment funds in Alabama, Alaska, Rhode Island and New Jersey. Contributions to the New Jersey fund have been ruled deductible as taxes.[3] Contributions to the Alabama, Alaska and Rhode Island funds also would seem to be deductible.

(d) State disability tax. Employers may deduct as business expenses, contributions that provide nonoccupational disability benefits to employees.

Employees can deduct as state income taxes their contributions to state disability funds in Rhode Island,[4] but not in California, New Jersey, and New York.[5]

¶ **1914 Foreign taxes and taxes of U.S. possessions.** Generally, the rules for deducting taxes imposed by a U.S. possession are the same as those for state and local taxes [¶ 1912]. However, a taxpayer who elects to take the credit against his tax [¶ 3701-3706] allowed for an income, war profits or excess profits tax of a possession cannot deduct that tax [Sec. 275].

Foreign taxes. Real property taxes and income, war profits or excess profits taxes imposed by a foreign country are deductible as taxes. Estate, legacy, inheritance, succession and gift taxes are not deductible in any event. Other foreign taxes are deductible only if they are paid or incurred as a trade or business expense [¶ 1804] or are related to a "nonbusiness" activity (¶ 1806) [Sec. 164, 275]. If the taxpayer elects to take a credit against his tax for foreign income, war profits or excess profits tax [¶ 3701-3706], he cannot deduct that tax [Sec. 275].

¶ **1915 Who may deduct taxes.** A tax that is deductible *as such* is deductible by the person on whom it is imposed. A tax that is deductible *as an expense* is deductible by the person incurring the expense.

(a) Tax not imposed on payor. Liability for a tax depends on the law imposing it. For example, a state retail sales tax may be imposed on the consumer, although payment is made by the retailer. In that case, the retailer is, in effect, a collection agency for the state. If the retailer includes the collections in gross income, he gets a corresponding deduction. If the retailer does not include the collections in gross income, but simply transmits them to the state, he gets no deduction [¶ 1917(b)]. Also, on certain sales of real property, the property tax deduction is divided between buyer and seller regardless of who pays it [¶ 1920].

(b) Deduction of same tax by two taxpayers. In effect, the same tax may be deducted by two taxpayers. For example, a retailer may sometimes deduct a state gasoline tax as a tax and the consumer of the fuel may deduct it as a tax [¶ 1917(a)].

(c) Consumers. The right of a consumer to deduct a tax as a personal expense usually depends on the wording of the statute imposing the tax. For example, if a consumer buys gasoline for his personal use and the state gasoline tax is imposed on the dealer, the consumer may not deduct it unless separately stated; if imposed on the consumer, he may deduct it.

Footnotes appear at end of this Chapter.

(d) **Excise taxes included in inventory.** The buyer of goods included in his inventory may not take a deduction for excise taxes paid by the seller, whether the tax is included in the price or billed to him separately. The tax is part of the cost of goods sold.

¶ **1916 Who may deduct federal taxes.** All deductible federal taxes now are either import duties or excise taxes. They are, therefore, deductible only by persons to whom they are an expense of a trade or business or a "nonbusiness" activity (¶ 1806). See also ¶ 1911(b).

¶ **1917 Who may deduct state and local taxes.** Generally, state and local taxes are deductible as such only by the person on whom they are imposed. There are exceptions to this rule. See (a) and (b) below and ¶ 1920.

(a) **Gasoline taxes.** Different rules apply depending on whether the tax is imposed on the retailer or consumer.

Tax imposed on retailer. In the states listed below, the tax is imposed on the wholesaler or retailer and deductible by him as a tax [Sec. 164]. Under a special provision, a consumer who pays the tax can deduct it as a personal expense if the amount is separately stated [Sec. 164(c); 1.164-5]. If the consumer pays the tax in connection with his trade or business, it is deductible as an expense even if not separately stated [¶ 1910].

California, Georgia, Hawaii, Louisiana, Montana, Nebraska, New Jersey, New Mexico and Wyoming.

Tax imposed on consumer. Gasoline taxes in all the other states and the District of Columbia, are imposed on consumers and are deductible by them (even if a personal expense and if not separately stated). If taxpayer deducted part of his car's expenses for business [¶ 1829], his deductible gasoline taxes can include only the part allocated to the car's personal use.[1]

State gasoline tax rates per gallon.

Ala., 7¢; Alaska, 8¢; Ariz., 8¢; Ark., 8.5¢; Calif., 7¢; Colo., 7¢; Conn., 11¢; Del., 9¢; D.C., 10¢; Fla., 8¢; Ga., 7.5¢; Hawaii: *Hawaii Cty.*—11$\frac{1}{2}$¢ (8¢ after 6-30-77); *Honolulu Cty.*—12¢ (8$\frac{1}{2}$¢ before 6-30-77); *Kauai Cty.*—12$\frac{1}{2}$¢ (9¢ before 6-30-77); *Maui Cty.*—13$\frac{1}{2}$¢ (10¢ before 6-30-77); Idaho, 9$\frac{1}{2}$¢; Ill., 7.5¢; Ind., 8¢; Iowa, 7¢; Kan., 8¢; Ky., 9¢; La., 8¢; Maine, 9¢; Md., 9¢; Mass., 8$\frac{1}{2}$¢; Mich., 9¢; Minn., 9¢; Miss., 9¢; Mo., 7¢; Mont., 8¢; Neb., 8.5¢; Nev., 6¢; N.H., 9¢; N.J., 8¢; N.M., 7¢; N.Y., 8¢; N.C., 9¢; N.D., 8¢ (7¢ before 7-1-77); Ohio, 7¢; Okla., 6.58¢; Ore., 7¢; Pa., 9¢; R.I., 10¢; S.C., 8¢; S.D., 8¢; Tenn., 7¢; Tex., 5¢; Utah, 7¢; Vt., 9¢; Va., 9¢; Wash., 9¢; W.Va., 8.5¢; Wis. 7¢; Wyo., 8¢.

NOTE: These are the rates at press time. Check for any later changes.

(b) **General retail sales taxes.** To qualify for deduction, the tax must be imposed at one rate on a broad range of classes of items. Retail services may be included. A use tax that complements the sales tax is treated the same as the sales tax [Sec. 1.164-3]. Different rules apply depending on whether the tax is imposed on the retailer or consumer. Specialized rates on food, liquor, machinery, farm equipment, rentals, vehicles, etc., may be in effect in some states.

Tax imposed on retailer. In the states listed below, the tax is imposed on the retailer and is deductible by him as a tax [Sec. 164; 1.164-5]. It is also deductible by the consumer as a tax if the amount is separately stated and is paid by the consumer otherwise than in connection with his trade or business [Sec. 164(b)(5); 1.164-5]. If the tax is paid by the consumer in connection with his trade or business and the item bought is not a capital item the tax is deductible as an expense, even if not separately stated. On capital items for a trade or business the tax is capitalized.[2]

Ariz., 4%; Calif., 6%; D.C., 5%; Hawaii, 4%; Ill., 4%; Ky., 5%; Me., 5%; Mich., 4%; Miss., 5%; Mo., 3⅛% (3% before 7-1-77); N.Mex., 4%; N.C., 3%; S.C., 4%; S.Dak., 4%; Tenn., 4½% ; Va., 3%; Wis., 4%.

Tax imposed on consumer. In the following states, the tax is imposed on the consumer and is deductible by him as a tax (even if in the nature of a personal expense and even if not separately stated). It is deductible by the retailer as an expense if he includes the collections in gross income.

Ala., 4%; Ark., 3%; Colo., 3%; Conn., 7%; Fla., 4%; Ga., 3%; Ida., 3%; Ind., 4%; Iowa, 3%; Kans., 3%; La., 3%; Md., 4%; Mass., 5%; Minn., 4%; Neb., 3%; Nev., 3%; N.J., 5%; N.Y., 4%; N.D., 3%; Ohio, 4%; Okla., 2%; Pa., 6%; R.I., 6%; Tex., 4%; Utah, 4¾%; Vt., 3%; Wash., 4.5% (4.6% before 7-1-77); W.Va., 3%; Wyo., 3%.

NOTE: Whether a state or local tax is a general retail sales tax and, if so, whether it is imposed on the retailer or consumer depends on the local law. The rates listed are the state rates as we go to press. They should be checked for any later change. Statewide local taxes are included in the rates for Calif., Nev., Utah and Va. Additional local taxes may be levied in Ala., Alaska, Ariz., Ark., Calif., Colo., Ga., Ill., Kan., La., Minn., Mo., Neb., Nev., N.M., N.Y., N.C., Ohio, Okla., S.D., Tenn., Tex., Utah, Wash., W.Va., Wis. and Wyo.

¶ **1918 State capital stock taxes.** In several states a tax imposed on the owners of shares of stock of banks and other corporations is collected directly from the corporation. A corporation that absorbs such a tax is entitled to a deduction for it. The amount so paid need not be included in the income of the shareholder [Sec. 164(e); 1.164-7].

NOTE: A state dividends tax that must be deducted and withheld from dividends by the payor corporation is not deductible by the corporation.[1]

¶ **1919 Taxes must be imposed on taxpayer.** To be deductible, as such, taxes generally must be paid by the person on whom they are imposed [¶ 1915].

Corporations and stockholders. A corporation may not deduct taxes paid for another corporation[1]; a stockholder may not deduct taxes paid for a corporation[2] and a corporation may not deduct taxes paid for a stockholder.[3] Stockholder allowed deduction when residential property was placed in the hands of the corporation solely for convenience in transferring title (corporate entity disregarded).[4]

Husband and wife. A husband may not deduct taxes paid on his wife's property.[5] But if husband and wife own property as tenants by entireties, the taxes are deductible by the spouse who pays them[6] (essentially a joint obligation). If husband and wife file a joint state income tax return and are jointly and severally liable for the state tax, either spouse paying the tax may deduct it.[7] Of course, if husband and wife file a joint return, the taxes paid may be deducted whether paid by husband or wife. Husband was allowed deduction when he had all the incidents of ownership except bare legal title and taxes were imposed on the property itself.[8]

Tenant and landlord. The situations outlined above should be sharply distinguished from one in which taxes are paid by a tenant to or for his landlord. In that case, the tenant generally gets a deduction; not because he is paying the taxes of another, but because he is, in effect, paying additional rent. The deduction generally is allowed only when the taxes are paid by a tenant on business property. If paid on property used for residential purposes, the "additional rent" is a personal expense [Sec. 1.162-11]. However, if under state law the tax is directly assessed against the tenant, it is deductible as a tax.[9] In the case of certain leases entered into before 1-1-54 (or renewals) between corporations, requiring the tenant to pay rent to the landlord free of federal income tax, the tenant cannot deduct for the tax payment [¶ 1316].

Footnotes appear at end of this Chapter.

¶ 1919

Condominiums. Taxpayer can deduct taxes imposed on his condominium apartment.[10]

Cooperative apartments and housing. Tenant-stockholders of cooperative apartment or housing corporations may take a deduction for amounts paid to the corporation that represent taxes[11] on property owned and maintained by the corporation.[12] The deduction is allowed even though a government or governmental unit owns some shares. To qualify as a cooperative housing corporation, at least 80% of the co-op's gross income for the tax year must come from the individual tenant stockholders (not including gross income attributable to governmental ownership) [Sec. 216; 1.216-1].

Reserved interests. The owner of a reserved term of years may deduct tax on real property even though another holds title.[13]

¶ **1920 Buyer and seller apportion real property tax deduction.**

(a) **Apportionment.** If real property is sold during the real property tax year, the property tax deduction is divided between buyer and seller as follows [Sec. 164(d); 1.164-6]:
1. The part of the tax allocable to that part of the property tax year *preceding* date of sale is considered imposed on the seller.
2. The part of the tax allocable to that part of the property tax year *beginning* on date of sale is considered imposed on the buyer.

This applies whether the parties are on the cash or accrual basis, and whether or not they actually apportion the tax between them.

> **Example 1:** Assume the real property tax year is the calendar year. The date of sale is April 1, 1977. The seller can deduct the part of the tax for the period from Jan. 1, 1977 through March 31, 1977 (90/365). The buyer can deduct the part of the tax for the period from April 1, 1977 through Dec. 31, 1977 (275/365).

(b) **Adjustment of amount realized by seller, and basis to buyer.** Since the tax deduction is divided between buyer and seller regardless of who pays the tax, adjustments may have to be made to the amount realized by the seller and the cost basis to the buyer.

When buyer pays the tax. The tax treated as imposed on the buyer is not considered part of cost [Sec. 1012; 1.1012-1(b)]. However, the part of the tax *paid by the buyer and treated as imposed on the seller* is considered part of the amount realized and is an additional cost of the property to the buyer [Sec. 1001(b)(2); 1.1001-1(b)].

> **Example 2:** On April 1, 1977, John Sellers sold Edward Beyers real property. The price was $100,000. On January 1, 1977, annual state property taxes of $3,650 became a lien on the property for the calendar year 1977. The tax, however, was not due until December 31, 1977. Beyers paid the entire tax when due. Sellers could deduct $900 (90/365 × $3,650) and Beyers, $2,750 (275/365 × $3,650) for taxes; the amount realized by Sellers and the cost to Beyers is $100,900.

When seller pays the tax. The tax treated as imposed on the seller is not considered part of the amount realized. However, the part of the tax *paid by the seller and treated as imposed on the buyer* reduces both the amount realized by the seller and the basis of the property to the buyer.

> **Example 3:** Assume the same facts as in Example 2 except that the tax was due on January 15, 1977 and that Sellers paid the tax when due. The tax deduction for Sellers is still $900 and for Beyers, $2,750; the amount realized by Sellers and the cost to Beyers is $97,250.

However, *if the buyer reimburses the seller* for the taxes paid by the seller but deductible by the buyer, neither the amount realized by the seller nor the cost to the buyer need be adjusted [Sec. 1001(b)(1); 1.1001-1(b)].

Example 4: Assume that in Example 3 Beyers reimburses Sellers for $2,750, representing the portion of the tax paid by Sellers and deductible by Beyers. Sellers still deducts $900 and Beyers, $2,750 for taxes. However, the amount realized by Sellers and the cost to Beyers is $100,000.

There is one exception to this rule. If the seller paid the tax *before* the year of the sale *and elected to capitalize it* [¶ 1528], then he must increase the amount realized by the reimbursement [Sec. 1.1001-1(b)].

(c) Time for deduction. Generally, the cash basis taxpayer deducts his share of taxes in the year paid; the accrual taxpayer, in the year accrued. There are, however, some important exceptions. These are covered below.

Cash basis seller. The cash basis seller deducts his share of the tax as if he had paid it on the date of the sale if: (1) the buyer is liable;† or (2) the seller, himself, is liable† but the tax is payable after the date of sale. In either of these cases if the tax (or an amount representing the tax) is paid in a *tax year* occurring *after* the year of sale, the seller may take the deduction either in the year of payment or the year of sale [Sec. 1.164-6(d)(1), (2)].

Cash basis buyer. The cash basis buyer deducts his share of the tax as if he had paid it on the date of the sale if the seller is liable.† In that case, if the tax (or an amount representing the tax) is paid in a *tax year* occurring *after* the year of sale, the buyer may take the deduction either in the year of payment or the year of sale.

Accrual basis taxpayers. The following applies to accrual basis taxpayers who have not elected to deduct property taxes ratably as they accrue [¶ 2740]: The part of the property tax which is treated as imposed on the taxpayer and which he could not deduct for any tax year is treated as having accrued on the date of the sale [Sec. 1.164-6(d)(4)].

(d) Adjustment for deduction in prior year. If in any tax year before the sale the taxpayer deducted more than his share of the tax, the excess is includible in gross income in the year of the sale subject to the rules governing bad debt recoveries (¶ 2316) [Sec. 1.164-6(d)(3)].

DEDUCTIONS—CONTRIBUTIONS

Cash or property contributions made to a "qualified organization" before the end of the tax year are deductible, but not the contribution of services. Special rules apply to the valuing of property contributions and to the limits on deductible contributions.

¶ 1941 Deduction for charitable contributions. Individuals may deduct contributions they make to or for the use of qualified organizations. Contributions to individuals are generally not deductible. A qualified organization may be public or private, or a governmental unit. There is a limit on the deduction allowed [¶ 1943]. Contributions to public charities that cannot be deducted in the year they are paid may be carried over and deducted in a following year [¶ 1944]. Corporations and estates and trusts may also deduct charitable contributions [¶ 3013; 3118]. Partnership contributions are passed through and deducted by the partners [¶ 2915].

(a) Qualified organizations. A contribution to an organization may be deducted only when the organization meets the following qualifications and when, in some cases, the gift is used for a stated purpose [Sec. 170(c)]:

---

† Either personally liable or holds property when tax becomes a lien (if no one liable).

Footnotes appear at end of this Chapter.

Corporations, trusts, community chests, funds or foundations. These organizations must be created under federal or state laws or laws of U.S. possessions and operated exclusively for religious, charitable, scientific, literary or educational purposes, or after 10-4-76, to foster national or international amateur sports competition if no part of its activities is to provide athletic facilities or equipment, or for the prevention of cruelty to children or animals. An organization is not disqualified for the exemption under Sec. 501(c)(3) by attempting to influence legislation or by participating in or intervening in a political campaign for any candidate [Sec. 170(a), (c); 1.170A-1(h)(5), (6)]. No individuals may benefit from net earnings. Contributions to a U.S. organization earmarked for use by a foreign organization are not deductible;[1] but a distribution to a foreign organization by a U.S. organization that has full discretion as to the use of contributions received in aid of its purposes does not bar the deduction.[2]

NOTE: For tax years starting in 1977, a taxpayer may not deduct actual out-of-pocket expenses incurred to lobby for a public charity that is not a church, integrated auxiliary of a church, or convention, or association of churches or its affiliated groups [Sec. 170(f)(6)].

Veterans' organizations. A post, group, or a trust or foundation for war veteran's organizations must be organized in the U.S. or its possessions and no individual may benefit from the net earnings.

Fraternal organizations. Only contributions used for the same religious, charitable, etc., purposes as community chests or funds (above) qualify as deductible contributions. The society, order or association must be a domestic organization operating under the lodge system.

Cemetery organizations. This must be company owned and operated solely for the benefit of its members or a non-profit corporation chartered solely for burial purposes and no other business. Also, no individual may benefit from the net earnings. The funds must be irrevocably dedicated to the cemetery as a whole, and not for a particular lot or crypt.[3]

Governmental units. Only contributions made exclusively for a public purpose may be deducted. They may be made to a state, U.S. possession, or any political subdivision, or the U.S. or the District of Columbia.

Disallowed deductions. Contributions cannot be deducted if they are [Sec. 170(f)(1); 1.170A-1(h)(2)]: (1) gifts to certain private foundations and nonexempt trusts that must pay tax on termination of their exempt status (¶ 3437; 3453) [Sec. 508(d)(1), (3); 1.508-2(a)]; (2) gifts to certain taxable private foundations and nonexempt trusts organized after 1969 whose charter does not include prohibitions against conduct that would subject them to excise taxes [¶ 3437; 3453]; foundations and trusts organized before 1970 had until 1972 to modify their charters (¶ 3437; 3453) [Sec. 508(d)(2)(A); 1.508-2(b)]; and (3) gifts to charitable organizations organized after 10-9-69 that do not notify the Revenue Service they are claiming exempt status (¶ 3437) [Sec. 508(d)(2)(B); 1.508-2(b)]. Contributions to foreign private foundations are similarly disallowed [Sec. 4948(c)(4); 53.4948-1(d)].

Gifts to individuals. Gifts or donations to needy persons are not deductible.[4] They must be made to qualified organizations. But actual out-of-pocket expenses incurred to care for hurricane evacuees referred to the taxpayer by qualified organizations are counted as charitable contributions.[5] See also ¶ 1942(f).

EXAMPLES OF QUALIFIED ORGANIZATIONS

Contributions to the following are deductible[3]—nonprofit schools; nonprofit hospitals; churches; synagogues; Salvation Army; United Funds; Community Chests; YMCA—YMHA; YWCA—YWHA; Red Cross; Family Service Association; Boy Scouts; American Legion; Multiple Sclerosis Society; CARE; Tuberculosis Society; Cancer Association; Heart Association; Cerebral Palsy.

EXAMPLES OF ORGANIZATIONS THAT DO NOT QUALIFY

Contributions to the following held not deductible—American Institute of Certified Public Accountants; Anti-Cigarette League; communist-action and communist-front organizations; fund to attract industry to a city; college fraternity, if purpose is primarily social.[6]

Government's list of qualified organizations. The Treasury Department publishes a booklet (with supplements) of organizations to which contributions are deductible (Pub. 78). It may be obtained from the Superintendent of Documents, Government Printing Office, Washington, D.C. 20402.

(b)   Benefits received for contributions. Dues paid to a qualified organization are deductible to the extent they exceed the value of the benefits and privileges received.[7] Tuition paid to parochial and other church-sponsored schools is not deductible.[8] Payments to qualified organizations for benefit performances are deductible only to the extent of the actual gift. Thus, if a patron of a charitable function receives anything of value, such as a ticket for a play or concert, he may not deduct the entire price of the ticket, rather only the excess over the fair market value of the ticket. Whether the ticket or other privilege is used has no bearing on the deduction. The taxpayer must be able to prove the amount of the contribution; he cannot rely solely on the indicated amount of the contribution on the ticket or in an advertisement. The Revenue Service will scrutinize deductions when publicity for charities misinforms contributors as to the amount deductible. Usually the cost of chances for raffles, drawings, etc., is not deductible.[9]

(c)   Time for deduction. The deduction is allowable only for the tax year in which the contribution is actually paid (or in a carryover year [¶ 1944]), whether the taxpayer is on the cash or the accrual basis [Sec. 170(a); 1.170A-1(a)(1)]. Thus, a mere pledge of a contribution[10] even if enforceable, does not give rise to a deduction. Ordinarily, a contribution is made at the time delivery is effected. Contributions made by check delivered unconditionally and cleared in due course are effective contributions when mailed or delivered. If the check is postdated, it is a contribution for the year the check is dated.[11] As with checks, gifts of stock certificates are treated the same way except certificates delivered to the donor's agent are an effective gift as of the date the stock is transferred on the books of the corporation [Sec. 1.170A-1(b)]. A contribution made by a bank credit card charge is deductible in the tax year the taxpayer pays the bank for the amount contributed [¶ 2742].[12]

(d)   How treated on return. Deductible contributions are entered on Schedule A of Form 1040 as an itemized deduction. Certain excess itemized deductions (including contributions) may be a tax preference item subject to the minimum tax. See ¶ 2403.

¶ 1942   Contributions other than money. Deductible contributions may be made in property as well as in money. Under specified conditions a gift of a partial interest in property or a transfer in trust can also be deducted. No deduction is allowed for the donation of services or for the use of property. Generally, the deductible amount is the property's fair market value, but special rules apply to appreciated property.

(a)   Valuation. The deduction for contributed property is usually measured by the property's fair market value at the time of the contribution. However, the deductible amount may be less than the value if the gift involves appreciated property [(b) below] or deductible interest [(g) below]. The fair market value of a do-

Footnotes appear at end of this Chapter.

nor's stock in trade is the price he could have sold it for in his lowest usual market (without reduction for any cash discounts)[1] where he contributed it [Sec. 1.170A-1(c)]. The donor must attach to his return a description of the property given and a statement of how the property was valued. For appreciated property, the statement must show the cost of the property and the manner in which the reduction ((b) below) was determined. Contributed property worth more than $200 must be fully described [Sec. 1.170A-1(a)(2)]. The Revenue Service has issued guidelines for appraising contributed property.[2] An appraisal fee is a separate miscellaneous deduction.[3]

(b) Appreciated property. Appreciated property (value greater than basis) is generally deductible at its full fair market value. However, the total deductions for appreciated capital assets are usually limited to a lower percentage of adjusted gross income than other contributions to public charities [¶ 1943(b)]. In addition, the individual deduction of certain contributions of appreciated property must be reduced depending on the type of appreciated property or the identity of the donee [Sec. 170(e); 1.170A-4].

Background and purpose. The combined effect of not taxing appreciation in value and allowing a contribution deduction for the fair market value of the property given produced tax benefits above those available for cash contributions. In addition, these rules were designed to prevent a greater advantage in the giving of appreciated property than would have been realized if the property were sold. Also, a sale of appreciated property to a charity at cost would result in no taxable gain to the taxpayer and a deduction equal to the appreciation.

Contribution of ordinary income property. The deduction for contributions of property is limited to the property's basis if it would give rise solely to ordinary income when sold at its fair market value [Sec. 170(e)(1)(A); 1.170A-4(a)(1)]. This rule applies regardless of the identity of the donee. Examples of the types of property giving rise to ordinary income are inventory [¶ 2601], capital assets held nine months or less, letters and memorandums (only those given after 7-25-69 if prepared for donor), and works of art created by the donor [Sec. 1.170A-4(b)(1)].

> **NOTE:** The Tax Reform Act of 1976, has increased the holding period for capital assets giving rise to ordinary income from 6 to 9 months or less for tax years starting in 1977, and to 1-year or less for tax years starting in 1978 and later years [¶ 1606].

> **Example 1:** On 12-1-77, Jones gave Black Corp. stock that he had bought on 9-1-77 for $800. The stock's value on 12-1-77 was $1,000. Jones' deduction is limited to the stock's basis of $800 since Jones would have had a short-term capital gain (ordinary income) if the stock had been sold.

Other examples of property giving rise to ordinary income when sold is property that had a portion of gain recaptured as ordinary income because of previously deducted depreciation [¶ 1619], mining expenses [¶ 1843], farm losses [¶ 2226], soil and water conservation expenditures [¶ 1845(e)], and intangible drilling expenses paid or incurred for tax years ending after 12-31-75 [¶ 2103(c)]. The deduction for contributions of this type of appreciated property is the property's fair market value less the amount of ordinary income that would have been recaptured if the property had been sold. Any appreciation in excess of the recapture potential is treated as a contribution of capital gain property [Sec. 170(e)(1)(B); 1.170A-4(b)(4)].

Contribution of capital gain property. Capital gain property is appreciated property that would be long-term capital gain if sold at its fair market value. If capital gain property is given to a private foundation (other than one qualifying for the 50% limitation [¶ 1943(a); 3441]), the taxpayer must reduce the deduction by one-half the amount that would have been long-term capital gain if the property had been sold [Sec. 170(e)(1)(B)(ii); 1.170A-4(b)(2)].

Example 2: On 12-1-77, Bill Jones contributed a painting worth $12,000 to the Black Foundation, a private foundation. He had bought the painting on 2-1-77 for $9,000. Jones' deduction is $10,500 ($12,000 less ½ of $3,000).

The deduction for contributed capital gain property that is tangible personal property is reduced in the same way if the use of the contributed property by the donee is unrelated to the donee's exempt purpose or function. A taxpayer can treat the property as being related to the donee's exempt purpose or function if: (1) the property is actually not used in an unrelated way, or (2) the taxpayer reasonably anticipated that the property would not be put to an unrelated use [Sec. 170(e)(1)(B)(i); 1.170A-4(b)(3)]. This rule applies regardless of the identity of the donee.

Example 3: Jones contributed a painting to Morgen University for its library. It was used for display and study by art students. If Morgen sold the painting and the proceeds were used for educational purposes, the painting would be put to an unrelated use.

A taxpayer can elect to reduce *all* his contributions of capital gain property for the tax year by one-half the appreciation in exchange for a more liberal limitation (50% instead of 30% of his adjusted gross income) on his charitable contribution deduction for his capital gain property contributions during the tax year (¶ 1943(b)) [Sec. 170(b)(1)(D)(iii); 1.170A-8(d)(2)].

NOTE: The taxpayer who contributes less than his entire interest in appreciated property must allocate the property's basis between the donated interest in the property and the retained interest [Sec. 170(e)(2); 1.170A-4(c)(1)].

Bargain sales to charity. A special rule applies if property is sold to a charity for less than the property's fair market value. Such a transfer may be partly a sale or exchange and partly a contribution of appreciated property. When the transfer is treated as two separate transactions, the taxpayer can get a charitable deduction for the contributed element, but must report any gain on the sale or exchange element. If the sale or exchange results in an *allowable* charitable deduction, the property's basis has to be allocated between the part sold and the part contributed. If *no* charitable deduction is allowable, all the property's basis is allocated to the sale or exchange [Sec. 170(e)(1), 1011(b); 1.170A-4(c)(2), (3), (4), 1.1011-2]. The following test is made to determine if a charitable deduction is allowable:

1. Figure the gift element (difference between property's fair market value and amount realized).
2. Figure the gain that would result if the *entire* property were sold at its fair market value.
3. Reduce the gift element by either (a) the ordinary gain, or (b) half the long-term capital gain if the transaction is to a private foundation (20% limitation) or is to a public charity and consists of tangible personal property that will not be used in line with the charity's exempt function.

When the property's basis must be allocated between the part sold and the part contributed, the allocation is made as follows:

• To the part sold, allocate the property's basis in the same proportion as the amount realized bears to the property's fair market value.
• To the contributed part, allocate the property's basis in the same proportion as the conributed element's fair market value (difference between the property's

Footnotes appear at end of this Chapter.

¶ 1942

fair market value and the amount realized) bears to the property's fair market value.

Example 4: Fall sold ordinary income property having a fair market value of $10,000 to a church for $6,000. The property's basis was $4,000. Fall made no other contribution during the year. Although Fall's gift element was $4,000 ($10,000 fair market value less $6,000 amount realized), this amount is reduced to zero in the allowability test [$4,000 — ($10,000 — $4,000 adjusted basis)]. Thus, all the property's basis is allocated to the sale and no basis allocation is required. Fall has a recognized gain on the bargain sale of $2,000 ($6,000 — $4,000 adjusted basis).

Example 5: Hall sells short-term stock to his church, having a fair market value of $10,000 and a $4,000 basis, for $2,000. He made no other contributions during the year. Hall's gift element is $8,000 ($10,000 value — $2,000 amount realized). The allowability test produces a $2,000 amount [$8,000 gift element—($10,000 fair market value — $4,000 basis)]. An allocation of basis must be made between the part sold and the part contributed. Hall's allocated for determining gain on the bargain sale is $800 ($4,000 basis × $2,000 amount realized/ $10,000 fair market value of stock). He has short-term capital gain on the bargain sale of $1,200 ($2,000 amount realized — $800 allocated basis) and a charitable deduction of $3,200: $8,000 gift element—[$8,000 — ($4,000 basis × $8,000 gift element/ $10,000 value)].

(c) Contributions of services. The value of services donated to an organization described in ¶ 1941(a) is not deductible; but unreimbursed expenses related to the services rendered may be deducted [Sec. 1.170A-1(g)].

Deductible items include traveling expenses (even board and lodging when away from home overnight) [¶ 1829], automobile expenses for gasoline and oil (but not depreciation),[3] cost and maintenance of uniforms, cost of stamps, secretarial and telephone, and other expenses directly connected with and due solely[4] to the donated services [Sec. 1.170A-1(g)]. Excess reimbursement must be reported as income.[5] A taxpayer may deduct 7¢ for each mile he uses his automobile in the work he contributes to a charitable organization, instead of itemizing the actual expenses. Parking fees and tolls are deductible in any case.[6] There is no deduction for blood donations,[7] or baby sitting expenses incurred specially to render donated services.[8]

(d) Right to use property. No deduction is allowed for the contribution (not made by a transfer in trust) after 7-31-69 of the right to use property for a period of time [Sec. 170(f)(3)(A); 1.170A-7(a)(1)]. However, the taxpayer can exclude from his income the value of the right to use the property contributed to charity.[9]

(e) Partial interests. With certain major exceptions, a taxpayer cannot deduct a contribution to a qualified organization after 7-31-69 of less than an entire interest in property [Sec. 170(f)(3)(A); 1.170A-7(a)(1)]. However, in no case can he deduct gifts of future interests in tangible personal property as long as he, or a related person [¶ 2223], has any interest in, or right to actual possession or enjoyment of the property; the deduction may be taken when these rights or interests are cut off [Sec. 170(a)(3); 1.170A-5(a)(1)].

Example 6: On 12-31-77, Jones gave Center City Museum title to a $90,000 painting, but reserved the right to the use, possession, and enjoyment of the painting during his lifetime. The contribution is a gift of a future interest because Jones has retained an intervening interest. When Jones gives up that right and delivers the painting to the museum he will be entitled to his deduction.

The major exceptions to the general rule are an undivided portion of an entire interest (for example, one-half the taxpayer's interest in a plot of land), a remainder interest in the taxpayer's personal residence or farm, or in other property contributed exclusively for "conservation purposes" (see below). The term "personal residence" need not be taxpayer's principal residence, and may include stock in a cooperative housing corporation [Sec. 170(f)(3)(B); 1.170A-7(b)]. The value of the deduction of a remainder interest in real property must be reduced by straight line depreciation and by depletion. The Revenue Service has prescribed tables to figure the deduction for the remainder interest taking into account actuarial and other factors [Sec. 1.170A-12]. This reduced value must be discounted at an annual rate of 6% (except that the Revenue Service may prescribe a different rate) [Sec. 170(f)(4); 1.170A-7(c)]. The remaining exception is transfers in trust after 7-31-69 of charitable remainders with noncharitable income interests and of charitable income interests with noncharitable remainders [Sec. 170(f)(2); 1.170A-6].

Transfers for conservation purposes. A taxpayer can deduct the following transfers to a qualified organization made exclusively for conservation purposes after 6-13-76 and before 6-14-81: (1) a lease on, option to buy, or easement for real property (for contributions made before 6-14-77 the interest must be for 30 years' duration, from 6-14-77 to 6-13-81 such interest must be in perpetuity) or (2) a remainder interest in real property [Sec. 170(f)(3)(B), (C)].

Transfer in trust of remainder interest. No income tax deduction is allowed for the transfer in trust of a charitable remainder unless the trust is an annuity trust, a unitrust or a pooled income fund [Sec. 170(f)(2)(A); 1.170A-6(b)].

NOTE: A remainder interest is a future interest to take effect at the end of the preceding estate, as when property is conveyed to Jones for life and then to Smith and his heirs.

Transfer in trust of charitable income interest. The only transfers in trust of charitable income interests that can be deducted are those after 7-31-69 that are guaranteed annuities or gifts of a fixed percentage distributed yearly of the trust's fair market value determined annually and where the grantor is taxed on the trust's income [¶ 3022]. No further deduction is allowed for the charitable contribution by the trust. If the grantor-donor of the interest ceases to be taxed on the trust income, he must include in his income at that time an amount equal to his previous deduction for the charitable income interest reduced by the trust income taxed to him to that point and discounted to the date of the contribution [Sec. 170(f)(2); 1.170A-6(c), (d)]. This recapture of the previously deducted charitable contribution deduction prevents the double tax benefit of receiving a deduction for contribution from future trust income not taxed to the taxpayer.[10]

(f) **Student living in taxpayer's home.** Up to $50 a month paid to maintain a student as a member of the taxpayer's household is counted as a charitable contribution if: (1) the student lives with the taxpayer under a written agreement with an organization in the first 3 of the 5 groups described in ¶ 1941(a) that provides educational opportunities for children; (2) the student is neither the taxpayer's dependent [¶ 1115] nor his relative [¶ 1117(a)]; and (3) he is a full-time student in the 12th or lower grade of a U.S. educational institution [¶ 1116(b)]. The amount deductible is limited to $50 a month for each full month of residence during which the student is attending school. Fifteen or more days in a month count as a full month. There is no deduction if taxpayer received any reimbursement for the student's ordinary maintenance costs. Property received and services rendered by the student for the taxpayer, count as reimbursements [Sec. 170(h); 1.170A-2].

(g) **Reduction for certain interest.** The contribution deduction is reduced by any interest paid by the donor on a loan secured by the donated property

Footnotes appear at end of this Chapter.

¶ 1942

where such interest is attributable to the post-contribution period. This rule prevents the taxpayer from getting both the deduction for the prepared interest and the increase in the charitable deduction resulting from an increase in the value of the donated property. If the property is a bond or other debt instrument, the value is further reduced by any interest paid that is attributable to the pre-contribution period [Sec. 170(f)(5); 1.170A-3].

¶ **1943 Limitations on contribution deduction.** The individual taxpayer's deduction for the tax year for contributions to qualified organizations is limited to various percentages of his adjusted gross income [¶ 1122(a)] (computed before any net operating loss carryback [¶ 2241] and termed the contribution base). In general, the deduction for contributions to public charities is limited to 50% of the taxpayer's adjusted gross income, the deduction for appreciated capital gain property contributions is limited to 30%, and the deduction for donations to most private foundations is 20% (or a lesser amount) [Sec. 170(b); 1.170A-8]. Contributions over the 30% and 50% limits may be carried over 5 years [¶ 1944].

Background and purpose. The Tax Reform Act of 1969 increased the deduction limitation on contributions to public charities from 30% to 50% for tax years starting after 1969 to strengthen the incentive effect of the contribution deduction especially since the unlimited deduction was eliminated. It also introduced the 30% limit on appreciated capital gain property.

(a) 50% limit. The deduction in a tax year for the total contributions *directly to* (not merely for the use of) the following public charities is limited to 50% of the taxpayer's adjusted gross income [Sec. 170(b)(1)(A); 1.170A-8(b), 1.170A-9]:

• A church, or a convention or association of churches.
• An educational organization that normally maintains a regular faculty and curriculum, and has a regularly enrolled student body in attendance where its educational activities are carried on.
• An organization, the principal purposes or function of which are providing of medical or hospital care.
• A medical research organization directly engaged in the continuous active conduct of medical research in conjunction with a hospital, if certain conditions are met.
• A governmental unit described in ¶ 1941(a).
• A state university fund.
• A corporation, trust, fund, community chest or foundation [¶ 1941] that gets a substantial part of its support, directly or indirectly, from a governmental unit or from the general public. Support is not limited to contributions. It includes any investment income or unrelated business income. An organization is publicly supported for the current tax year and the next tax year if at least $1/3$ of its total support for the 4 years before the current year is from donations by the general public and government units.

NOTE: Even if the organization does not qualify as "publicly supported" under the $1/3$ public support test, it qualifies as "publicly supported," if at least 10% of the 4-year total support is from public or governmental sources. Under the 10% test other factors are considered: the sources of support, investment income from endowment funds, solicitation of funds, methods of operation and the organization's character and purpose. Contributions by one individual, trust, or corporation (counting those of related persons in ¶ 2223) that exceed 2% of the 4-year total support are not counted as general public support for computing the $1/3$ of 10% test. However, unusual grants in excess of 2% are counted. New organizations can be treated as publicly supported for their first two years (or first 3 tax years if the first tax year is less than 8 full months[1]) by obtaining a ruling to that effect [Sec. 1.170A-9(e)].

- Certain private foundations [¶ 3437]. These include: (1) private operating foundations (¶ 3441) [Sec. 4942(j); 53.4942(b)-1]; (2) private nonoperating foundations that distribute contributions within 2½ months after the year of receipt provided the distribution is treated as a distribution of corpus [Sec. 1.170A-9(g)]; and (3) a pooled income fund [Sec. 170(b)(1)(E)].
- Exempt charitable organizations that normally receive more than ⅓ their support from the general public and ⅓ or less from gross investment income. Other charitable organizations set up for and controlled by "⅓ charitable organizations" are also allowed the 50% limitation [Sec. 509(a)(2), (3); 1.509(c)-2].
- Certain community trusts if they meet the tests specified in the regulations [Sec. 1.170A-9(e)(10)].

On a joint return, the percentage limits apply to the total adjusted gross income of husband and wife [Sec. 1.170-2(a); 1.170A-8(a)].

(b) 30% limit. The deduction for contributions to qualified organizations of appreciated capital gain property that are not reduced by any amount of the appreciation [¶ 1942(b)] is subject to a separate limitation of 30% of the taxpayer's adjusted gross income. For this purpose, appreciated capital gain property is any capital asset or Sec. 1231 asset [¶ 1618] that would be long-term capital gain if sold at its fair market value [Sec. 170(b)(1)(D); 1.170A-8(d)].

> **Example 1:** Adams' adjusted gross income is $50,000. On 12-1-77, Adams contributed to a public art museum a painting worth $12,000 and appreciated stock held over 9 months worth $10,000. The painting was to be exhibited. Adams had bought the painting on 2-1-77 for $9,000. The deduction for these two contributions ($22,000) is limited to 30% of Adams' adjusted gross income for the tax year ($15,000). If Adams had donated the painting to the Red Cross to hang in an office, the limitation would be 50% instead of 30% of adjusted gross income since the deduction would be reduced from $12,000 to $10,500 ($12,000 less ½ of $3,000) as a contribution of appreciated tangible personal property used in a way unrelated to the donee's exempt function; the limitation on the stock contribution would remain at 30%.

When applying the limitations, contributions to which the 30% limit applies are the last taken into account [Sec. 170(b)(1)(D)(i); 1.170A-8(d)].

> **Example 2:** Sam Jones's adjusted gross income is $10,000. He contributed $2,800 in cash to Blue University and stock held over 9 months to the Red Cross that is worth $4,000. The appreciated stock valued at $4,000 is first limited to $3,000 (30% of $10,000). That contribution plus the cash contribution totals $5,800, but the actual deduction is limited to $5,000 (50% of $10,000). This is made up of $2,800 in cash and $2,200 in stock. The excess of capital gain property over both percentage limitations can be carried over [¶ 1944(a), Example 4].

Election. The taxpayer may elect to reduce the deductible amount of *all* his contributions of appreciated capital gain property during the tax year (or carried over to the tax year from a tax year starting after 1969) by one-half the property's appreciation in value. The reduction would apply to those contributions to which it does not otherwise apply [¶ 1942(b)]. If the taxpayer makes the election, the deduction for contributions of this type of property is not subject to the 30% limitation for the tax year [Sec. 170(b)(1)(D)(iii); 1.170A-8(d)(2)]. In effect, the taxpayer can elect to exchange a reduced deduction for each separate contribution of appreciated capital gain property for the more liberal 50% limitation.

> **NOTE:** The election is made by a statement filed with the return for the election year. The statement must show the basis of recomputation for any carryovers and indicate the District Director or Service Center where the previous returns were filed for any earlier years. Special rules apply to married couples who file separate returns in some years and joint returns in others [Sec. 1.170A-8(d)(2)].

Footnotes appear at end of this Chapter.

¶ 1943

Example 3: Smith's adjusted gross income is $10,000. He contributed to the Boy Scouts stock held over 9 months that cost $2,900 and was worth $3,500. His only other contribution during the tax year was another block of stock held over 9 months to the Community Chest that cost $1,400 and was worth $1,800. Without the election, the contributions totaled $5,300 but the deduction was limited to $3,000 (30% of $10,000). If Smith made the election, his deduction would be $4,800 [$5,300 less ½ of $1,000 appreciation ($600 and $400)]. The deduction would not exceed the 50% limit ($5,000).

(c) **20% limit.** The deduction for contributions to qualified organizations [¶ 1941(a)] that are not among the public charities listed at ¶ 1943(a) is limited to a lower percentage of the taxpayer's adjusted gross income. These organizations are primarily private nonoperating foundations. These contributions also include ones made for the use of, rather than directly to, public charities. The deduction for the total of these contributions is the lesser of: (1) 20% of the taxpayer's adjusted gross income; or (2) the excess of 50% of the taxpayer's adjusted gross income over the amount of his contributions to public charities without regard to the 30% limitation [Sec. 170(b)(1)(B); 1.170A-8(c)]. The excess of the total of these contributions over the limitation cannot be carried over [¶ 1944].

Example 4: Green's adjusted gross income is $10,000. He contributed $2,000 to his church and $3,000 to the Blue Foundation, a private foundation. His contribution deduction is $4,000, the sum of the $2,000 contribution to the church and $2,000 of $3,000 given to the Foundation which is limited to 20% of Green's adjusted gross income.

Example 5: Assume the same facts as in Example 4 except that Green contributed $3,500 to his church. His contribution deduction is $5,000, the sum of the $3,500 contribution to the church and $1,500 to the Foundation. The deduction for the contribution to the Foundation is limited to the excess of 50% of Green's adjusted gross income ($5,000) over the amount of the contribution to his church ($3,500).

Example 6: Assume the same facts as in Example 4 except that Green contributed to the Girl Scouts $3,500 worth of appreciated stock held over 9 months, $2,500 to the Blue Foundation and $1,000 to the Community Chest. His contribution deduction is $4,500, the sum of the $1,000 contribution to the Community Chest, $3,000 to the Girl Scouts and $500 to the Foundation. The deduction for the contribution of appreciated stock is limited to 30% of Green's adjusted gross income ($3,000). The deduction for the contribution to the Foundation is limited to the excess of 50% of his adjusted gross income ($5,000) over the sum of his contributions to the Community Chest ($1,000) and to the Girl Scouts without applying the 30% limit ($3,500 worth of stock).

(d) **Contributions as business expenses.** Payments to recipients generally described in ¶ 1941(a) that are in fact business expenses and not contributions are deductible without limit[2] [Sec. 162(b); 1.162-15, 1.170A-1(C)].

(e) **Unlimited deduction repeal.** The unlimited deduction is repealed for tax years starting after 1974. Rules that phase out the deduction apply to tax years starting after 1969 and before 1975 [Sec. 170(b)(1)(C), (g)].

¶ **1944 Carryover of excess charitable contributions.** Contributions to public charities [¶ 1943(a)] that are over the limit for a tax year starting after 1969 may be carried over to the next succeeding 5 years. In figuring the carryover, contributions subject to the 20% limitation [¶ 1943(c)] are disregarded. Contributions that are carried over, plus the actual contributions in the tax year must fall within the 50% limit. However, any excess contributions of appreciated capital gain property are subject to the 30% limit in the carryover year [See (a) below]. The carryover does not apply to an estate or trust charitable deduction (¶ 3013) [Sec. 170(d)(1); 1.170A-10(a)].

NOTE: Carryovers to 1970 and later years are limited to the excess over 30% of adjusted gross income in the pre-1970 contribution year [Sec. 170(d)(1)(A)]. A supporting statement must be filed with the return showing the deduction for the amounts carried over and treated as paid in the tax year [Sec. 1.170A-10(e)].

Example 1: Joe Brown's adjusted gross income is $20,000. In 1977, he contributes $2,000 to his private nonoperating foundation and $9,000 to the Red Cross. He can deduct $10,000 in 1977, but there is no carryover. The only contribution that qualifies for a carryover (Red Cross) does not exceed 50% of his adjusted gross income.

Example 2: Assume the same facts as in Example 1, except that Brown's contribution to the Red Cross is $11,000. He can deduct $10,000 in 1977. In addition he may carry over $1,000 ($11,000 less $10,000 (50% of $20,000)) of his contribution to the Red Cross until 1982 unless it is used up earlier.

The amount of the carryover from any contribution year deducted in a carryover year is the lesser of: (1) the excess of 50% of adjusted gross income over the sum of any actual contributions to public charities in that year and any deducted carryovers (except carryovers of appreciated capital gain property) from a year before the contribution year of this carryover, or (2) the total carryovers available in that year [Sec. 170(d)(1)(A); 1.170A-10(b)].

Example 3: Joe Brown had the following adjusted gross incomes and contributions to public charities in the years 1977-1981:

	1977	1978	1979	1980	1981
Adjusted gross income	$20,000	$14,000	$30,000	$20,000	$18,000
Contributions to public charities (no other contributions)	12,000	8,000	16,500	6,500	3,000
Contribution deductions (without regard to carryover)	10,000	7,000	15,000	6,500	3,000
Excess contributions carried over	$ 2,000	$ 1,000	$ 1,500	$ 0	$ 0

Since Brown's contributions in 1980 and 1981 are less than 50% of his adjusted gross income, the excess contributions for 1977, 1978 and 1979 are treated as having been paid in 1980 and 1981 as follows:

1980

Contribution year	Total excess	Less: Amount treated as paid in year prior to 1980	Available charitable contribution carryovers
1977	$2,000	-0-	$2,000
1978	1,000	-0-	1,000
1979	1,500	-0-	1,500
			$4,500

50% of Brown's gross income for 1980	$10,000
Less: Charitable contributions made in 1980	6,500
	$ 3,500

Carryovers treated as paid in 1980—the lesser of $4,500 (available carryovers to 1980) or $3,500 [excess of 50% limit ($10,000) over contributions actually made in 1980 ($6,500)] $3,500

1981

Contribution year	Total-excess	Less: Amount treated as paid in 1980	Available charitable contribution carryovers
1977	$2,000	$2,000	-0-
1978	1,000	1,000	-0-

¶1944

1979	1,500	500	$1,000
1980	0	0	-0-
			$1,000

50% limit for 1981	$9,000
Less: Charitable contributions made in 1981	3,000
	$6,000

Carryovers treated as paid in 1981—the lesser of $1,000 (available carryovers to 1981) or $6,000 [50% limit ($9,000) over contributions actually made in 1981 ($3,000)] $1,000

(a) Special carryover of contributions of appreciated capital gain property. Contributions of appreciated capital gain property that are over the 30% limit [¶ 1943(b)] for tax years starting after 1969 may be carried over the same as other contributions, whether or not the taxpayer's total contributions exceed 50% of his adjusted gross income. However, the excess carried over is added to actual contributions of capital gain property in future years to determine the 30% limit for such year and any further carryover. Contributions of capital gain property are subject to both the 50% as well as the 30% limitation in the contribution year and the carryover years. In other words, the excess of contributions of capital gain property over both percentage limitations can be carried over [Sec. 170(b)(1)(D)(ii); 1.170A-10(c)].

Example 4: In 1977, Joe Brown's adjusted gross income is $10,000. He contributed $2,800 in cash to Blue University and stock held over 9 months to the Red Cross that is worth $4,000. His deduction for the appreciated stock is first limited to $3,000 (30% of $10,000). The total contribution deduction in 1977 is limited to $5,000 (50% of $10,000) [¶ 1943(b), Example 2]. His contribution carryover is made up solely of appreciated property contribution and totals $1,800 (the sum of the $1,000 in excess of the 30% limit and the $800 in excess of the 50% limit).

The capital gain property carryover is deducted only to the extent of the difference between the 30% limit and the actual contributions of capital gain property made in the carryover year the same way as other contribution carryovers [Sec. 170(b)(1)(D)(ii); 1.170A-10(c)(1)].

Example 5: Assume the same facts as in Example 4. In 1978, Brown's adjusted gross income is $7,000. He contributes $500 in cash to Blue University and $400 in long-term stock to the Red Cross. His deduction in 1978 for appreciated property contributions is limited to $2,100 (30% of $7,000). This is made up of $400 actually contributed in 1978 and $1,700 carried over from 1977. Brown's carryover of appreciated capital gain property to 1979 is $100 ($1,800 carryover from 1977 less $1,700 deducted in 1978). His total deduction in 1977 is $2,600 ($500 in cash and $2,100 in appreciated capital gain property).

The amount of any carryover of appreciated capital gain property from a contribution year deducted in a carryover year that has available both appreciated capital gain contribution carryovers and other contribution carryovers is the least of: (1) the excess of 30% of the adjusted gross income in the carryover year over the sum of the actual contributions of appreciated capital gain property to public charities in that year (subject to the 30% limit) and any deducted carryovers of appreciated capital gain property from a year before the contribution year of this carryover; or (2) the excess of 50% of adjusted gross income in the carryover year over the sum of all actual contributions to public charities in that year and any deducted carryovers of public charity contributions from a year before the contribution year; or (3) the total appreciated capital gain carryovers available to that year [Sec. 1.170A-10(c)(2)].

A taxpayer who elects to reduce his deduction for all his contributions of capital gain property in a tax year and apply the 50% instead of the 30% limitation [¶ 1943(b)] continues to apply the 50% limit to any excess in carryover years. A carryover of contributions of appreciated capital gain property from a year the election was not in effect to carryover years under the election must be reduced by

½ the appreciation in value in the contribution year [Sec. 170(b)(1)(D)(iii); 1.170A-8(d)(2)(b)].

Example 6: In 1978, Brown's adjusted gross income is $50,000; he contributed capital gain property to his church that cost $10,000 and worth $60,000. Brown did not make an election in 1978. His 1978 contribution deduction is $15,000 (30% of $50,000), and he is allowed a carryover to 1978 of $45,000 ($60,000 less $15,000). In 1979, Brown's adjusted gross income is $60,000; he contributed capital gain property to his church that cost $10,000 and worth $11,000, and he made no other contributions. In 1979, Brown elects to reduce by ½ the appreciation in value his contributions of capital gain property made in 1978 and 1979. Accordingly, Brown must recompute his carryover from 1978 as if the ½ reduction had been made in 1978. Brown's 1978 contribution would have been reduced from $60,000 to $35,000 ($60,000 less ½ of $50,000 appreciation). Brown's recomputed carryover to 1979 is $20,000 ($35,000 less $15,000 deduction allowed in 1978. The 1979 capital gain property contribution is $10,500 ($11,000 less ½ of $1,000 appreciation). Thus, in 1979 Brown is allowed a deduction of $30,000 ($30,500 total contributions [$20,000 carryover from 1977 plus $10,500 contribution for 1979] but not to exceed 50% of $60,000 adjusted gross income for 1979). The $500 carryover is treated as a carryover from 1978 since current year contributions are deducted before carryover contributions.

(b) Special rules. Once an excess contribution is made, a net operating loss carryback [¶ 2241] from later years does not change the contribution carryover amount; but a net operating loss carryover to the contribution year reduces the contribution carryover to the extent it increases the net operating loss carryover to later years [Sec. 1.170-2(g); 1.170A-10(d)(2), (3)].

Change to joint returns in carryover year. When individuals with contribution carryovers change to joint returns (or spouses change from joint to individual returns) in later years, the carryover deduction must be specially computed. An unused carryover of a deceased spouse can be applied only on a return (separate or joint) for the year the spouse dies [Sec. 1.170A-10(d)(4)]. After that, the carryover is lost.

DEDUCTIONS—MEDICAL EXPENSES

Deductible medical expenses include the cost of care, insurance and travel related to medical purposes. Generally, these are deductible above certain limits although half (up to $150) the insurance premiums are fully deductible.

¶ 1945 Deduction for medical expenses. An individual taxpayer who itemizes personal deductions [¶ 1801(b)] may deduct medical expenses he pays for himself, his spouse and his dependents [Sec. 213]. The expenses may include the cost of items not commonly considered as medical costs, as well as the usual medical or dental services and medicines [¶ 1946]. Any medical expense that is reimbursed during the year is reduced by the amount of the reimbursement before the percentage limitations are applied.

Only amounts actually paid during the tax year for expenses incurred in the tax year or prior tax years may be included in computing the deduction ((a) below), even when the taxpayer uses the accrual basis of accounting. Prepayment of expenses to be incurred in later years generally is not deductible in the current year.[1] However, a lump-sum prepayment fee is deductible if it is paid to a retirement home or other private institution for a life-care medical plan.[2] See also ¶ 1946 on prepaid premiums. Any expense compensated for by insurance or otherwise during the same tax year is disregarded. Payments for permanent injury are not considered compensation for medical expenses [Sec. 1.213-1]. Special rules apply to reimbursements received after the close of the tax year [¶ 1947].

(a) Amount of deduction. Medical expenses are deductible only to the extent they exceed 3% of adjusted gross income. However, a taxpayer can deduct ½ of his medical insurance costs up to $150 without regard to this limit. The balance is included in with his other medical expenses subject to the 3% limit. In addition, his other medical expenses include the cost of drugs and medicines that exceed 1% of adjusted gross income and is disregarded when it is 1% or less of adjusted gross income.

Example 1: Assume Tom, John and Frank all have adjusted gross incomes of $8,000. Tom pays $75 for medicines and John and Frank each pay $100. Tom pays $380 for hospitalization insurance premiums and John and Frank each pay $150. Each also pays medical or dental bills in varying amounts. Their deductions are computed as follows:

	Tom		John		Frank	
Medical insurance deduction		$150		$ 75		$75
Medicine (excess over 1% of $8,000)	$-0-		$20		$20	
Balance of medical insurance	230		75		75	
Doctor or dentist bills	500		250		100	
Total	730		345		195	
Reimbursement received during the same year	175		50		-0-	
Net expense	555		295		195	
Less: 3% of adjusted gross income	240	315	240	55	240	-0-
Total deduction		$465		$130		$75

»OBSERVATION→ Timing the payment of medical expenses may reduce taxes. For example, if Frank in the above example will have the same expenses and adjusted gross income next year and defers paying current expenses (except medical insurance) to next year, his medical deduction for the 2 years would be $305 instead of $150 ($75 for each year).

Joint returns. On a joint return the 1% and 3% limits apply to the aggregate adjusted gross income of husband and wife. In most cases, the joint return results in a lower tax. However separate returns may occasionally yield a larger total medical deduction than joint returns. Whenever both husband and wife have medical expenses and adjusted gross income, the tax should be figured both for separate returns and a joint return.

Example 2: John and Mary Ayle are married and each has an adjusted gross income of $6,000. They have no dependents. Each pays $200 a year for hospitalization insurance. Mary paid $500 in doctor bills and $125 for medicine. John paid $100 in dental bills and $25 for medicine. Their total medical deduction on separate returns is $35 more than the deduction on a joint return.

	Individual returns				Joint return	
	Husband		Wife			
Medical insurance deduction		$100		$100		$150
Medicines (Excess over 1% of adjusted income)	$-0-		$65		$30	
Balance of medical insurance	100		100		250	
Other medical bills	100		500		600	
Total	200		665		880	
Less: 3% of adjusted gross income	180	20	180	485	360	520
Total deduction		$120		$585		$670

≫**OBSERVATION**→ Factors other than medical deduction must be considered in determining whether to file joint or separate returns.

(b) Amounts paid for decedents. Medical expenses of a decedent, paid out of his estate within one year from the date of his death, are considered paid by a decedent at the time the expenses were incurred.

This rule does not apply where these expenses are also deductible for estate tax purposes, unless the taxpayer files (1) a statement that the deduction has not been allowed for estate tax purposes and (2) a waiver of the right to the deduction for estate tax purposes [Sec. 213(d); 1.213-1(d)].

(c) Taxpayer—spouse—dependent. Expense paid must be for medical care of the taxpayer, his spouse or dependent. The status as spouse or a dependent must exist either when (1) the expenses were incurred, or (2) they were paid [Sec. 213; 1.213-1(e)(3)].

Expenses for spouse. A husband may deduct medical expenses of his wife if paid by him even though incurred before their marriage. But in determining whether two persons are married at any time during the tax year, the status at the close of the tax year or at the date of the death of one of them governs, and an individual legally separated from his spouse under a decree of divorce or separate maintenance is not considered married [Sec. 6013(d)]. As to husband paying medical expenses of divorced wife as part of alimony, see ¶ 1320.

Community property states. In community property states, medical expenses paid out of community funds are deductible in equal amounts on separate returns. However, those paid out of the separate funds of either are deductible only by the spouse paying them.[3]

Joint checking accounts—non-community property states. Expenses paid from joint checking accounts in non-community property states are considered paid equally by both spouses when filing separate returns, unless there is competent evidence to the contrary.[3]

Who is a "dependent." A person is a taxpayer's "dependent" for the medical expense deduction if he meets only the support, relationship and citizenship or residency tests [¶ 1115]. The other conditions required for a dependency exemption need not be met[4] [Sec. 213(a); 1.213-1(a)(3)].

Medical expenses taxpayer actually paid for a dependent may be deducted under a multiple support agreement [Sec. 1.213-1] (even though an exemption deduction cannot be claimed because the dependent had a gross income of $750 or more).[5]

Transplant expenses are deductible whether paid by donor, or prospective donor.[6]

¶ 1946 What are medical expenses. "Medical expenses" include any payment for diagnosis, cure, treatment, mitigation or prevention of disease, or for purpose of affecting any bodily function or structure; cost of insurance to cover medical care; and transportation expenses primarily for and essential to medical care [Sec. 213(e); 1.213-1].

(a) Fees and services. The deductibility of fees and services depends on the nature of the services rendered and not on the experience, qualifications or title of the person performing them.[1]

DEDUCTIBLE FEES AND SERVICES

Fees for doctors, dentists and other services. These include fees of surgeons, eye doctors, authorized Christian Science practitioners, chiropodists, chiropractors, osteopaths, qualified psychologists,[2] practical or registered nurses (including cost of nurses' board and social security taxes[3] where paid by taxpayer); cost of clerk in family business to let wife perform nursing services;[4] fees for healing services, laboratory, X-Rays, fees to health institutes if prescribed by physician as necessary to health;[5] membership fees in association furnishing medical services, hospitalization and clinical care; part of lump-sum tuition or retirement hotel (or home) fees allocated to medical care if breakdown is provided or is readily obtainable;[6] a portion of housekeeper's salary where duties

Footnotes appear at end of this Chapter.

include medical care;[7] obstetrical expenses; therapy treatment; cost of operation, including legal abortion or vasectomy;[8] legal fees paid in guardianship proceeding to commit an incompetent;[9] cost of acupuncture;[10] and cosmetic surgery even for purely nonmedical reasons.[11]

Hospitalization and institutional costs. These include hospital fees; cost of renting and equipping an apartment in lieu of hospitalization;[4] cost of special schools or institutions for mentally or physically handicapped (including board, lodging and ordinary education incidental to special services) if medical resources of institution are primary reasons for being there[12] [Sec. 1.213-1(e)]; and also the cost of keeping mentally retarded in a specially selected home to aid in his adjusting to community life after institutional care.[13] The Tax Court has held tuition for special training may be deductible, although not the cost of board and lodging.[14]

NOT DEDUCTIBLE

Cost of illegal operation; cost of personal analysis required by students in psychoanalytic training schools;[15] fees for practical nurses hired to care for motherless but healthy child;[16] (but see below); cost of dancing lessons even though recommended by doctors;[17] funeral and burial expenses.[18]

Child care expenses as medical expense. If an expense (such as a nurse's fee) qualifies both as a child care expense [¶ 2415] and as a medical expense, the following rules apply: (1) that part allowed as a child care expense cannot also be treated as a medical expense; and (2) the amount treated as a medical expense for determining the medical expense deduction cannot also be allowed as a child care expense [Sec. 213(f)].

(b) Cost of medicines or drugs. Amounts paid for medicines or drugs (legally obtained with or without prescription) are deductible as a medical expense within limits (¶ 1945(a)) [Sec. 213(b); 1.213-1(e)(2)]. The cost of special foods and beverages prescribed by doctors for medicinal purposes *in addition to* the normal diet is counted as a medicine and drug expense.[5] Vitamins are deductible only if prescribed or recommended by a doctor.[19] But the cost of toilet articles are not includible.[20]

(c) Medical care insurance. Only the cost of insurance providing reimbursement[21] (including for prescription drugs only[22]) or indemnity[23] for medical care is included as a medical cost. If a policy covers other items, such as accidental loss of life, no part of the premium may be deducted, unless the policy or separate insurance company statement specifies the amount attributable to medical care. Also, no deduction is allowed if the charge for medical care is unreasonably large in relation to the total cost of all items [Sec. 213(e); 1.213-1(e)(4)].

Prepaid premiums. A taxpayer under 65 may deduct current payments for medical care insurance to cover the expenses for a spouse, dependent or himself after the taxpayer reaches 65. To qualify, the premiums must be payable on a level payment basis for at least 10 years or until the taxpayer reaches 65. If the taxpayer will reach 65 before 10 years lapse, the premiums must be payable for at least 5 years [Sec. 213(e)(3)].

Social security program. The monthly premiums paid under the voluntary medicare program are deductible, but not the hospital insurance paid as part of the social security tax.[24]

(d) Special aids and supplies. Facilities and supplies purchased to alleviate a physical defect or provide relief for an ailment can be included with other medical expenses.

DEDUCTIBLE EXPENSES

These include artificial limbs and teeth; braces and crutches; dental supplies (but not toothpaste or toothbrushes[20]); eyeglasses (or contact lens), including examination fees; hearing aids;[18] oxygen and oxygen equipment;[5] iron lung and operating expenses;[5] special mattress and plywood boards for arthritic condition;[5] air conditioning units (less resale or salvage value) and operating expenses, if primarily for illness and they do not become a permanent part of dwelling (but see (f) below);[5] cost of "seeing-eye" dog and its maintenance;[18] wheel chair [Sec. 1.213-1(e)] or "autoette" and its costs to operate and maintain[25] if used primarily to alleviate sickness or disability and not merely as transportation to work;[26] cost of special equipment for physically handicapped to enter and operate automobile;[27] excess cost of auto specially designed to accommodate wheelchair passengers;[28] special aids (special typewriter, tape recorder, etc.) to assist in educating child becoming progressively blind;[29] clarinet and lessons recommended by orthodontist to help correct teeth;[30] fees for notetaker for deaf child at college;[14] cost and repair of special equipment for deaf person to communicate effectively over a regular telephone.[31]

NOT DEDUCTIBLE

Personal expenses. Maternity clothing, diaper service, and similar personal expenses. Generally wigs, unless ordered by doctor as essential to health.[32]

(e) Medical transportation and travel. Amounts paid for travel and transportation primarily for and essential to medical care are deductible as expenses for medical care. You may deduct 7¢ for each mile your car is used for transportation related to medical treatment instead of itemizing your car expenses. Parking fees and tolls can be deducted separately.[33]

DEDUCTIBLE EXPENSES

Transportation expenses. These include ambulance hire; transportation expenses primarily to get medical services, such as railroad fare to hospital or recuperation home, cab fare in obstetrical cases and cases of "occupational therapy";[34] any other transportation expense primarily for and essential to medical care.[35] If you travel to a favorable climate on advice of your physician to alleviate a specific chronic ailment, you can deduct the transportation expenses to get there[36] [Sec. 1.213-1(e)].

NOT DEDUCTIBLE

Meals and lodging (unless included in hospital bill[37] or while en route between home and distant hospital[38]) at a location away from home prescribed by physician,[36] or as an outpatient.[37] However, the Seventh Circuit allowed the cost of meals and lodgings at a hotel used as an interim place of convalescence while away from home after discharge from a hospital.[39]

Travel expenses not connected with medical treatment even though prescribed by doctor[40] (unless part of occupational therapy[34]).

Vacation costs for rehabilitation.[41]

(f) Home improvement costs. The full cost of installing an elevator or making similar permanent improvements to property is deductible if the improvement does not increase the value of the property and otherwise qualifies as a medical expense. If the improvement increases the property's value, only the part of the cost that exceeds the increase in value is deductible. But a taxpayer can deduct the full cost of operating and maintaining medically necessary permanent home improvements even if none of the original costs were deductible [Sec. 1.213-1(e)(1)(iii)]. The District Court of Hawaii allowed the cost of constructing a specially-designed swimming pool that qualified as a medical expense, even though it had increased the value of the property.[42] A tenant's cost of medically necessary home improvements is deductible.[43]

(g) Records. Complete records of all "medical expenses" should be kept. Taxpayers must furnish the name of each person to whom such expenses were paid, the amount and the approximate date paid.

Footnotes appear at end of this Chapter.

¶ 1946

(h) Medical reimbursement plans. An employer may deduct, as a business expense, medical expenses paid for an employee under a medical reimbursement plan, even if the plan covers only a few selected [¶ 1838], high salaried or key employees and even if they are also officer-stockholders. But the plan must benefit employees as well.[44] The employer's contribution to the plan is not income to the employee [¶ 1219]; nor is reimbursement under the plan, unless the employee has deducted it. But the exclusion does not apply if payments under a plan could be made to an employee regardless of whether he had medical expenses.[45]

¶ 1947 Medical expense reimbursed in later years. In general, compensation for personal injuries or sickness under workmen's compensation acts or health, accident or hospitalization policies, or damages received in such cases through suit or agreement are not taxable income (¶ 1218) [Sec. 104(a)(2); 1.104-1]. However, if the receipt represents reimbursement for medical expenses[1] deducted in a previous year, it is income to the extent attributable to, but not in excess of the deduction [Sec. 1.213-1(g)]. The amount taxable is the *lesser* of: (1) the reimbursement; or (2) the deduction allowed. But if the zero bracket amount (standard deduction before 1977) was taken for the medical expense deduction, any reimbursement for these expenses is not taxable.[2]

NOTE: Reimbursement for medical expenses does not include disability benefits received as indemnification for loss of earnings.[1]

Footnotes to Chapter 9

(P-H "FEDERAL TAXES" related references are cited in brackets [ ] at the end of each footnote below.)

Footnote ¶ 1900   [¶ 13,000 et seq.].
(1) Old Colony R.R. Co. v. Comm., 284 US 552, 52 SCt 211, 10 AFTR 786; Deputy v. DuPont, 308 US 488, 60 SCt 363, 23 AFTR 808 [¶ 13,003].
(2) Rev. Rul. 69-188, 1969-1 CB 54, amplified by Rev. Rul. 69-582, 1969-1 CB 54 [¶ 13,008(10)].
(3) Rev. Rul. 67-297, 1967-2 CB 87; Rev. Rul. 68-650, 1968-2 CB 78; Rev. Rul. 69-188, 1969-1 CB 54, amplified by Rev. Rul. 69-582, 1969-1 CB 54 [¶ 13,008(10)].

Footnote ¶ 1901   [¶ 13,019 et seq.].
(1) Knetsch v. U.S., 6 AFTR 2d 581, 364 US 361 [¶ 13,006(5)].
(2) Goldstein v. Comm., 18 AFTR 2d 5328, 364 F.2d 734 [¶ 13,006(8)].
(3) Benson, 9 BTA 279; Day, 42 BTA 109 [¶ 13,021(5), (20)].
(4) Comm. v. Park, 113 F.2d 352, 25 AFTR 367, affd. 38 BTA 1118; Preston v. Comm., 132 F.2d 763, 30 AFTR 680 [¶ 13,021(20)].
(5) Rev. Rul. 57-198, 1957-1 CB 94 [¶ 13,012].
(6) Rev. Rul. 58-129, 1958-1 CB 93 [¶ 13,048(25)].
(7) Scripps v. Comm., 96 F.2d 492, 21 AFTR 130, cert. den.; Rev. Rul. 70-284, 1970-1 CB 1 [¶ 13,023(3), (5)].
(8) Rev. Rul. 73-304, 1973-2 CB 42 [¶ 13,023(10)].
(9) Bettendorf, 3 BTA 378 [¶ 13,029].

Footnote ¶ 1901 continued
(10) S. J. Johnson, ¶ 43,275 P-H Memo TC [¶ 13,015(5)].
(11) Rev. Rul. 73-136, 1973-1 CB 68; Rev. Rul. 72-315, 1972-1 CB 49, modifying Rev. Rul. 71-98, 1971-1 CB 57 [¶ 13,008(20); 13,088(12)].
(12) Hemenway-Johnson Furniture Co., Inc., ¶ 48,113 P-H Memo TC affd. 174 F.2d 793, 37 AFTR 1515 [¶ 13,096].
(13) See Northern Fire Apparatus Co., 11 BTA 355; Comm. v. Hood, 141 F.2d 467, 32 AFTR 423; Rev. Rul. 68-54, 1968-1 CB 69 [¶ 13,096].

Footnote ¶ 1902   [¶ 13,037 et seq.].
(1) Chester A. Sheppard, Trustee, 37 BTA 279 [¶ 13,049(5)].
(2) Morris Plan Co. of Binghamton, 26 BTA 772 [¶ 13,038].
(3) Griffin, 7 BTA 1094 [¶ 13,039].
(4) Est. of McClatchy, 12 TC 370, affd. 179 F.2d 678, 38 AFTR 1287 [¶ 13,023(5)].
(5) Williams, 3 TC 200 [¶ 13,041].
(6) Larson, 44 BTA 1094; Neracher, 32 BTA 236 [¶ 13,021(35); 13,042].
(7) Colston, 21 BTA 396, affd. 59 F.2d 867, 11 AFTR 606, cert. denied [¶ 13,042].
(8) Rev. Rul. 71-268, 1971-1 CB 58; Nicodemus, 26 BTA 125 [¶ 13,042].
(9) Rev. Rul. 64-31, 1964-1 CB 300 [¶ 13,048(27)].

Chapter 9—Footnotes

Footnote ¶ 1902 continued
(10) Evans, L. M. v. U.S., 17 AFTR 2d 574, 251 F. Supp. 296 [¶ 16,490(30)].
(11) Koppers Co., 3 TC 62; Comm. v. Breyer, 151 F.2d 267, 34 AFTR 151; W. D. Haden Co. v. Comm., 165 F.2d 588, 36 AFTR 670 [¶ 13,043].
(12) Letter ruling dated 2-3-47 reported in full at ¶ 76,114 P-H Fed. 1947.
(13) U.S. Fidelity & Guaranty Co., 40 BTA 1010. See Watson, 42 BTA 52 [¶ 13,046(15), (20)].

Footnote ¶ 1903   [¶ 13,091].
(1) U.S. v. Collier, 104 F.2d 420, 23 AFTR 60 [¶ 13,091].

Footnote ¶ 1904   [¶ 13,086].
(1) House Report No. 1337, p. A44, 83rd Cong. 2nd Sess.
(2) Rev. Proc. 74-8, 1974-1 CB 419 [¶ 16,801(3)].
(3) Hudson-Duncan & Co., 36 BTA 554 [¶ 13,088].
(4) Treas. Dept. booklet "Your Federal Income Tax" (1977 Ed.), p. 88.

Footnote ¶ 1905   [¶ 13,001 et seq.; 16,751; 16,785; 16,978].
(1) Rev. Rul. 55-389, 1955-1 CB 276 [¶ 16,785].
(2) Wisconsin Cheeseman v. U.S., 21 AFTR 2d 383, 388 F.2d 420; but see Leslie v. Comm., 24 AFTR 2d 69-5219, revg. 50 TC 11 [¶ 16,801(20)].
(3) Rev. Proc. 72-18, 1972-1 CB 740 [¶ 16,801(3)].

Footnote ¶ 1906   [¶ 6125; 13,001].
(1) P.L. 91-172, Sec. 221(a); P.L. 92-178, Sec. 304(b).
(2) P.L. 91-172, Sec. 221(a).

Footnote ¶ 1910   [¶ 13,145 et seq.; 13,171 et seq.; 13,255 et seq.].

Footnote ¶ 1911   [¶ 13,100].

Footnote ¶ 1912   [¶ 13,100].
(1) Sec. 207(c)(1), P.L. 88-272.
(2) Rev. Rul. 61-86, 1961-1 CB 41 [¶ 13,211].
(3) Rev. Rul. 66-184, 1966-2 CB 50 [¶ 13,108(60)].
(4) Rev. Rul. 66-185, 1966-2 CB 51 [¶ 13,217].
(5) Rev. Rul. 65-313, 1965-2 CB 47 [¶ 13,262(5)].

Footnote ¶ 1913   [¶ 12,039; 13,255 et seq.].
(1) Rev. Rul. 74-75, 1974-1 CB 19 [¶ 13,255(25)].
(2) Rev. Rul. 71-59, 1971-1 CB 56; Grossman v. Glenn, 91 F. Supp. 1005, 39 AFTR 885, aff'd USCA-6 [¶ 11,966(5); 12,039(5)].
(3) Letter signed by Lester W. Utter, Chief, Individual Tax Branch, I.R.S., 4/1/65, in full at ¶ 54,818 P-H Fed. 1965; Rev. Rul. 75-48, 1975-1 CB 62 [¶ 11,227(10)].
(4) James R. McGowan, 67 TC No. 43; IR 1742, 1-28-77 [¶ 57,454; 55,195].
(5) Rev. Rul. 71-73, 1971-1 CB 52; Rev. Rul. 75-48, 1975-1 CB 62, Rev. Rul. 75-149, 1975-1 CB 64 [¶ 11,227(10); 13,260].

Footnote ¶ 1914   [¶ 13,229].

Footnote ¶ 1915   [¶ 13,100; 13,113 et seq.].

Footnote ¶ 1916   [¶ 13,247 et seq.; 13,261 et seq.].

Footnote ¶ 1917   [¶ 13,100(b); 13,181; 13,275].
(1) Rev. Proc. 70-25, 1970-2 CB 506 [¶ 11,426(3)].
(2) Rev. Rul. 58-292, 1958-2 CB 106 [¶ 13,279(30)].

Footnote ¶ 1918   [¶ 13,291 et seq.].
(1) Wis. Gas and Elec. Co. v. U.S. 322 US 526, 64 SCt 1106, 32 AFTR 368 [¶ 13,295(25)].

Footnote ¶ 1919   [¶ 13,149; 13,291].

Footnote ¶ 1919 continued
(1) Falk Corp., 23 BTA 883, aff'd 60 F.2d 204, 11 AFTR 733 [¶ 13,111(5)].
(2) Railey, 36 BTA 543 [¶ 13,149(10)].
(3) Eastern Gas & Fuel Assoc., 44 BTA 1225, aff'd 128 F.2d 369, 29 AFTR 511 [¶ 13,295(20)].
(4) Watson, 42 BTA 52, affd. 124 F.2d 437, 28 AFTR 788 [¶ 13,149(10)].
(5) Colston, 21 BTA 396, aff'd 59 F.2d 867, 11 AFTR 606 [¶ 13,149(5)].
(6) Rev. Rul. 71-268, 1971-1 CB 58; Nicodemus, 26 BTA 125 [¶ 13,149(5)(6)].
(7) Rev. Rul. 72-79, 1972-1 CB 51 [¶ 13,203(5)].
(8) Bernstein, ¶ 40,270 P-H Memo TC [¶ 13,149(5)].
(9) Rev. Rul. 68-84, 1968-1 CB 71 [¶ 13,149(42)].
(10) Rev. Rul. 64-31, 1964-1 CB 300 [¶ 13,149(45)].
(11) Evans v. U.S., 17 AFTR 2d 574, 251 F. Supp. 296 [¶ 16,490(30)].
(12) Rev. Rul. 69-76, 1969-1 CB 56 [¶ 16,490(30)].
(13) Rev. Rul. 67-21, 1967-1 CB 45 [¶ 13,149(55)].

Footnote ¶ 1920   [¶ 13,283].

Footnote ¶ 1941   [¶ 16,011; 16,021 et seq.].
(1) Rev. Rul. 63-252, 1963-2 CB 101 [¶ 16,035(25)].
(2) Rev. Rul. 66-79, 1966-1 CB 48 [¶ 16,035(25)].
(3) Treas. Dept. booklet "Your Federal Income Tax" (1977 Ed.), p. 83.
(4) Libby, ¶ 42,252 P-H Memo TC, aff'd 133 F.2d 203, 30 AFTR 751 [¶ 16,027].
(5) Rev. Rul. 66-10, 1966-1 CB 47 [¶ 16,078(35)].
(6) Rev. Rul. 69-573, 1969-2 CB 125 [¶ 16,029(20)].
(7) Rev. Rul. 68-432, 1968-2 CB 104 modifying Rev. Rul. 54-565, 1954-2 CB 95 [¶ 16,081(10)].
(8) Rev. Rul. 54-580, 1954-2 CB 97 [¶ 16,083(45)].
(9) Rev. Rul. 67-246, 1967-2 CB 104; Rev. Rul. 74-348, 1974-2 CB 80; Goldman v. U.S., 21 AFTR 2d 301, 388 F.2d 476 [¶ 16,079(5); 16,081(5)].
(10) Johnson v. U.S., 20 AFTR 2d 5873, 280 F. Supp. 412 [¶ 16,048].
(11) Griffin, 49 TC 253 [¶ 13,052-A].
(12) Rev. Rul. 71-216, 1971-1 CB 96 [¶ 16,083(120)].

Footnote ¶ 1942   [¶ 16,011; 16,075 et seq.].
(1) Rev. Rul. 69-514, 1969-2 CB 36 [¶ 16,079(15)].
(2) Rev. Proc. 66-49, 1966-2 CB 1257 [¶ 16,079(5)].
(3) Treas. Dept. booklet "Your Federal Income Tax" (1977 Ed.), p. 85.
(4) Rev. Rul. 56-509, 1956-2 CB 129 [¶ 16,078(5)].
(5) Rev. Rul. 67-30, 1967-1 CB 9 [¶ 16,078(5)].
(6) Rev. Proc. 74-24, 1974-1 CB 244 [¶ 16,078(5)].
(7) Rev. Rul. 162, 1953-2 CB 127 [¶ 16,076(15)].
(8) Rev. Rul. 73-597, 1973-2 CB 69 [¶ 16,078(45)].
(9) Senate Report No. 91-552, p. 84, 91st Cong. 1st Sess.
(10) House Report No. 91-413 (Part 1), p. 61, 91st Cong. 1st Sess.

Footnote ¶ 1943   [¶ 16,011; 16,057 et seq.].
(1) Rev. Rul. 74-487, 1974-2 CB 82 [¶ 16,057(35)].
(2) U.S. v. Jefferson Mills, 18 AFTR 2d 5757, 367 F.2d 392 [¶ 12,057(5)].

Footnote ¶ 1944   [¶ 16,011; 16,055 et seq.].

Footnote ¶ 1945   [¶ 16,380 et seq.].
(1) Bassett, 26 TC 619 [¶ 16,396(5)].
(2) Rev. Rul. 75-302, 1975-2 CB 86; Rev. Rul. 75-303, 1975-2 CB 87 [¶ 16,429(5)].

Chapter 9—Footnotes

Footnote ¶ 1945 continued
(3) Rev. Rul. 55-479, 1955-2 CB 57 [¶ 16,403].
(4) Rev. Rul. 59-66, 1959-1 CB 60 [¶ 16,402].
(5) Treas. Dept. booklet "Your Federal Income Tax" (1977 Ed.), p. 79.
(6) Rev. Rul. 68-452, 1968-2 CB 111; Rev. Rul. 73-189, 1973-1 CB 139 [¶ 16,413(55)].

Footnote ¶ 1946 [¶ 16,411 et seq.].
(1) Dodge Est., ¶ 61,346 P-H Memo TC [¶ 16,413(5)].
(2) Rev. Rul. 143, 1953-2 CB 129 [¶ 16,413(20)].
(3) Rev. Rul. 57-489, 1957-2 CB 207 [¶ 16,413(5)].
(4) Ungar, ¶ 63,159 P-H Memo TC [¶ 16,413(5); 16,431(5)].
(5) Rev. Rul. 55-261, 1955-1 CB 307 [¶ 16,411; 16,416; 16,419; 16,431(5)].
(6) Rev. Rul. 54-457, 1954-2 CB 100; Rev. Rul. 67-185, 1967-1 CB 70 [¶ 16,417; 16,429(5)].
(7) Hentz, ¶ 53,110 P-H Memo TC [¶ 16,413(5)].
(8) Rev. Rul. 73-201, 1973-1 CB 140 [¶ 16,413(5)].
(9) Rev. Rul. 71-281, 1971-2 CB 165 [¶ 16,413(5)].
(10) Rev. Rul. 72-593, 1972-2 CB 180 [¶ 16,413(5)].
(11) Rev. Rul. 76-332, IRB 1976-36 [¶ 54,783].
(12) Rev. Rul. 58-280, 1958-1 CB 157 [¶ 16,427(5)].
(13) Rev. Rul. 69-499, 1969-2 CB 39 [¶ 16,429(5)].
(14) Baer, ¶ 67,034 P-H Memo TC [¶ 16,424(10)].
(15) Rev. Rul. 56-263, 1956-1 CB 135 [¶ 16,427(5)].
(16) Wendell, 12 TC 161 [¶ 16,437].
(17) Thoene, 31 TC 62 [¶ 16,427(5)].
(18) Treas. Dept. booklet "Your Federal Income Tax" (1977 Ed.), p. 77.
(19) Treas. Dept. booklet "Your Federal Income Tax" (1977 Ed.), p. 76.
(20) O. G. and Thelma L. Russell, ¶ 53,357 P-H Memo TC [¶ 16,418].
(21) Rev. Rul. 19, 1953-1 CB 59 [¶ 16,421].
(22) Rev. Rul. 68-433, 1968-2 CB 110 [¶ 16,421].

Footnote ¶ 1946 continued
(23) Rev. Rul. 58-602, 1958-2 CB 109 [¶ 16,421].
(24) Rev. Rul. 66-216, 1966-2 CB 100 [¶ 16,421].
(25) Rev. Rul. 67-76, 1967-1 CB 70 [¶ 16,432(5)].
(26) Rev. Rul. 58-8, 1958-1 CB 154 [¶ 16,424(10); 16,431(5)].
(27) Rev. Rul. 66-80, 1966-1 CB 57 [¶ 16,431(5)].
(28) Rev. Rul. 70-606, 1970-2 CB 66 [¶ 16,431(5)].
(29) Rev. Rul. 58-223, 1958-1 CB 156 [¶ 16,431(5)].
(30) Rev. Rul. 62-210, 1962-2 CB 89 [¶ 16,431(5)].
(31) Rev. Rul. 71-48, 1971-1 CB 99 [¶ 16,431(5)].
(32) Rev. Rul. 62-189, 1962-2 CB 88 [¶ 16,431(5)].
(33) Rev. Rul. 74-24, 1974-2 CB 477 [¶ 16,424(25)].
(34) Misfeldt v. Kelm (DC, Minn., 1952) 44 AFTR 1033 [¶ 16,425(5)].
(35) Rev. Rul. 58-533, 1958-2 CB 108; Rodgers, 25 TC 254 [¶ 16,424(15)].
(36) Comm. v. Bilder, 369 US 499, 9 AFTR 2d 1355, 82 SCt 881 [¶ 16,424(5), (10)].
(37) O'Hare, 54 TC 874 [¶ 16,413(19)].
(38) Montgomery, 26 AFTR 2d 70-5001, 428 F.2d 243 [¶ 16,424(10)].
(39) Kelly v. Comm., 27 AFTR 2d 71-912, 440 F.2d 307 [¶ 16,424(10)].
(40) Havey, 12 TC 409 [¶ 16,424(5)].
(41) Rev. Rul. 57-130, 1957-1 CB 108 [¶ 16,660(45)].
(42) Mason v. U.S. (DC, Hawaii, 1957) 52 AFTR 1593 [¶ 16,432(5)].
(43) Rev. Rul. 70-395, 1970-2 CB 65 [¶ 16,432(5)].
(44) Bogene, ¶ 68,147 P-H Memo TC; Larkin, 21 AFTR 2d 1307, 394 F.2d 494 [¶ 11,774(35)].
(45) Rev. Rul. 69-141, 1969-1 CB 48 [¶ 19,062(10)].

Footnote ¶ 1947 [¶ 16,461 et seq.].
(1) Deming, 9 TC 383 [¶ 16,464].
(2) Treas. Dept. booklet "Your Federal Income Tax" (1977 Ed.), p. 80.

Highlights of Chapter 9

Deductions—Interest, Taxes, Contributions and Medical Expenses

I. **Deductions—Interest**
   A. **Generally all interest deductible [¶ 1900]:**
      1. It is compensation for use or forbearance of money.
      2. Itemized deduction unless business or "nonbusiness" expense.
   B. **Deductible interest:**
      1. Debt can be business, nonbusiness, or personal debt [¶ 1900].
      2. Must be real debt of taxpayer [¶ 1901].
      3. Interest vs. dividends—dividends not deductible [¶ 1901].
      4. Must be taxpayer's indebtedness—direct liability not essential [¶ 1902].
      5. Discount on note—generally deductible as interest [¶ 1903].
   C. **Installment payments:**
      1. Interest and finance charges—separately stated; deductible [¶ 1904(a), (b)].
      2. Interest charge not stated [¶ 1904(c)]:
         a. Real property—not deductible unless proven.
         b. Personal property—unstated interest rules apply [¶ 1904(c)].
   D. **Disallowed interest:**
      1. Interest for tax-exempt securities [¶ 1905(a)].
      2. Interest to buy or carry single premium insurance [¶ 1905(b)].
      3. Certain life insurance loans [¶ 1905(c)].
      4. Interest paid between certain related parties [¶ 1905(d)].
      5. Interest paid in certain corporate mergers [¶ 1905(e)].
   E. **Investment interest [¶ 1906]:**
      1. Post-1975 rules:
         a. Deduction limited to sum of the following:
            1) $10,000 ($5,000 for married persons filing separately).
            2) Net investment income, but allocable if any investment interest attributable to pre-1970, pre-1976 and post-1975 period.
         b. 50%-owned corporations and partnerships: Limitation is increased by the lesser of $15,000 ($7,500 for married taxpayers filing separately) or interest on debt used to buy the 50% firm. A 50% interest includes taxpayer, his spouse and children's interests.
         c. Investment income defined:
            1) Certain depreciation recapture.
            2) Short-term gains from sale of investment property.
            3) Other investment income such as interest, dividends, etc.
            4) Income allocated to pre-1976 and post-1975 tax years if investment interest attributable to pre-1976 year.
         d. Investment expense defined:
            1) Trade or business expenses.
            2) Property taxes.
            3) Bad debts.
            4) Straight line depreciation.
            5) Amortizable bond premium.
            6) Cost depletion.
            7) Deductible investment expenses.
         e. Carryovers retain their character:
            1) Carryover of pre-1976 interest subject to pre-1976 limitations.
            2) Carryover of post-1975 interest subject to post-1975 limitations.

f. Net lease property—subject to same rules as investment property.
  2. Pre-1976 rules:
   a. Deduction limited to sum of the following:
    1) $25,000 ($12,500 for married persons filing separately).
    2) Net investment interest plus excess of out-of-pocket expenses over gross rents from net lease.
    3) Excess of net long-term capital gains over net short-term capital losses from disposition of investment property.
    4) One-half of investment interest that exceeds (a) (b) and (c).
   b. Investment income defined same as rules in item 1(c).
   c. Investment expense defined same as rules in 1(d).
   d. Net lease property—subject to same rules as investment property.
   e. Net long-term capital gains:
    1) Any excess that offsets investment interest treated as ordinary income.
    2) Alternative tax does not apply.
    3) Net long-term capital gain deduction cannot be used.
   f. Disallowed investment interest deduction can be carried over indefinitely but limited.

II. Deductions—Taxes
  A. **The deductibility of taxes [¶ 1910]:**
   1. Must meet three conditions:
    a. It must be a deductible tax.
    b. It must be imposed on taxpayer.
    c. It must be paid during tax year.
   2. May fall under three headings:
    a. Not deductible.
    b. Deductible as tax.
    c. Deductible as expense.
  B. **Federal taxes [¶ 1911]:**
   1. Not deductible as a tax (income, estate & gift taxes).
   2. Deductible as business or "nonbusiness" expense [¶ 1911(b)]: import, excise and social security taxes.
  C. **State and local taxes [¶ 1912]:**
   1. Not deductible at all—death and gift taxes.
   2. Deductible as taxes—state & city income, sales & use, gasoline and property.
   3. Deductible as business or "nonbusiness" expense—not deductible as a tax.
  D. **Federal social security [¶ 1913]:**
   1. Employer tax:
    a. Deductible only if business or "nonbusiness" expense.
    b. Not deductible if it is personal expense (e.g., tax on domestics).
   2. Employee tax—not deductible (income tax).
   3. Self-employed tax—not deductible (income tax).
  E. **Federal Unemployment tax:**
   1. Employer only—deductible only if business or "nonbusiness" expense.
  F. **State unemployment insurance [¶ 1913(c)]:**
   1. Employer contribution—deductible as business expense.
   2. Employee contribution—deductible as a tax (some states).
  G. **State disability benefits [¶ 1913(d)]:**
   1. Employer contribution—deductible as business expense.
   2. Employee contribution—not deductible as a tax or medical expense.
  H. **Taxes of foreign countries and U.S. possessions:**
   1. Not deductible [¶ 1914].
   2. Deductible if not taken as credit [¶ 1914].
   3. Deductible as special assessment [¶ 1912(b); 1914].
   4. Deductible as taxes [¶ 1914].
   5. Deductible as business or "nonbusiness" expense [¶ 1914].

I. **Who may deduct taxes:**
   1. Federal—person incurring the business or "nonbusiness" expenses [¶ 1916].
   2. State and local—the payor except gasoline taxes and retail sales taxes that are separately stated [¶ 1917(b)].
J. **State capital stock taxes [¶ 1918].**
K. **Tax must be imposed on taxpayer to be deductible [¶ 1919].**
L. **Buyer and seller apportion real property deduction [¶ 1920]:**
   1. Apportionment tax is divided between buyer and seller.
   2. Adjustment of selling price and cost when buyer or seller pays tax imposed on the other.
   3. Time for deduction—special rules apply to accrual basis taxpayers not election to deduct taxes ratably; and cash basis taxpayers.

III. **Deductions—Contributions**
   A. **Deduction in general [¶ 1941]:**
      1. When made to qualified tax-exempt organization.
      2. Qualified organizations.
      3. Benefits received for contributions—no deduction if donor receives personal benefits.
      4. Time for deduction—generally in tax year contribution actually paid.
   B. **Contributions other than money [¶ 1942].**
      1. Valuation—generally measured by property's fair market value.
      2. Appreciated property:
         a. Ordinary income property—deduction is basis.
         b. Property, if sold, would result in portion recaptured as ordinary income—deduction fair market value less amount recaptured.
         c. Long-term capital gain property to private foundation—deduction fair market value less ½ appreciation.
         d. Tangible personal property put to unrelated use by donee and if sold would result in long-term capital gain—deduction fair market value less ½ appreciation.
         e. Long-term capital gain property and 50% limit elected by qualified organization except private foundation—deduction fair market value less ½ appreciation.
         f. Other property, if sold, would result in long-term capital gain and not described above—deduction is fair market value.
      3. Bargain sales to charity—allocate property's basis between part sold and part contributed.
      4. Contributions of services—not deductible but unreimbursed related expenses are.
      5. Right to use property—generally not deductible.
      6. Partial interests:
         a. Generally not deductible except remainder interest in personal residence or farm and undivided portion of entire interest.
         b. Transfer in trust of remainder interest—deduction allowed if trust is annuity trust, unitrust or pooled income fund.
         c. Transfer in trust of remainder interest—generally no deduction for value of income interest except if: grantor is taxed on income and charity gets fixed dollar amount or fixed percentage of trust each year.
      7. Student living in taxpayer's home—deduction up to $50 per month applies:
         a. Written agreement with qualified charity.
         b. Not taxpayer's dependent or relative.
         c. Full-time student in 12th or lower grade.
      8. Deduction reduced for prepaid interest.
   C. **Limitations on contribution deduction [¶ 1943]:**
      1. Public charities—cash and property (including appreciated capital gain property)—50% of adjusted gross income with 5-year carryover of excess.
      2. Public and private organizations—appreciated capital gain property—30% of adjusted gross income with 5-year carryover of excess.

3. To or for use of other qualified organizations (generally private in nature) or for use of public charities:
   a. Cash and property including appreciated capital gain property.
   b. Lesser of 20% of adjusted gross income or difference between 50% of adjusted gross income and contributions to public charities—no carryover.

IV. Deductions—Medical expenses
   A. Deduction for medical expenses [¶ 1945]:
      1. Itemized deduction.
      2. Deductible in year paid.
      3. Amount deductible:
         a. Generally must exceed 3% of adjusted gross income.
         b. One-half (up to $150) of medical insurance deductible without regard to 3% limit.
         c. Drugs and medicine costs must exceed 1% limit.
      4. Amounts paid for decedents—generally deductible.
      5. Taxpayer-spouse-dependent—deductible if status exists when expenses incurred or expenses paid.
   B. What are medical expenses [¶ 1946]:
      1. Medical expenses include:
         a. Fees and services.
         b. Medicines or drugs.
         c. Medical care insurance.
         d. Special aids and supplies.
         e. Transportation and travel.
         f. Home improvement costs.
      2. Medical reimbursement plans—generally deductible by employer.
   C. Medical expense reimbursed in later years [¶ 1947]:
      1. Not taxable if standard deduction taken.
      2. Otherwise taxable up to deduction taken in earlier year.
      3. Excluded—pay received under workmen's compensation, accident and hospitalization policies or damages through suit or agreement.

Chapter 10

DEDUCTIONS—DEPRECIATION

TABLE OF CONTENTS

DEPRECIATION IN GENERAL

	¶
Depreciation	2000
What property may be depreciated	2001
Business and investment property	
When to deduct depreciation	
Who is entitled to deduct depreciation	2002
Buyer and seller	
Landlord and tenant	
Life tenant and remainderman	
Basis for depreciation	2003
Property acquired from a decedent	
Taxpayer losing tax-exempt status	
Change in use of property	
Allocation of lump-sum purchase price between land and building	
Adjusting basis	2004
Salvage value	2005

FIGURING THE DEPRECIATION DEDUCTION

	¶
Methods of figuring depreciation	2010
Election of method	
Change of method	
Agreements on depreciation	
Straight line depreciation	2011
Declining balance depreciation	2012
Property subject to declining balance	
Use of limited declining balance	
Sum of the years-digits method	2013
General rule	
Remaining life plan	
Comparison of straight line, declining balance and sum of the years-digits methods	2014
Other methods of depreciation	2015
Unit of production method	
Operating day method	
Income forecast method	
Additional first-year depreciation allowance	2016
Qualifying property	
Election	
Controlled group of corporations	
Partnerships	
Methods usable for depreciable real property	2017

	¶
New depreciable real property	
Used depreciable real property	
Exceptions	
Change of method	
Depreciation on qualified low-income housing	2018
Depreciation on public utility property	2019

ACCOUNTING FOR DEPRECIATION

	¶
Reserve for depreciation	2021
Depreciation property accounts	2022
Item accounts	
Multiple asset accounts	
Depreciation records	2023
Effect of depreciation on earnings and profits	2024

USEFUL LIFE AND OBSOLESCENCE

	¶
Useful life of depreciable property	2032
Class Life Asset Depreciation Range system	2033
Asset depreciation ranges	
Vintage account	
Property eligible for Class Life ADR treatment	
When asset is placed in service	
Salvage value	
Repairs	
Class Life ADR table	
Obsolescence	2034

RETIREMENT

	¶
Gain or loss on retirement of assets	2036
Sale or exchange	
Abandonment	
Other disposition	
Basis of retired assets	2037
Retirement from vintage accounts	2038
Recognition of gain	
Recognition of loss	
Salvage value	

SPECIAL AMORTIZATION

	¶
Amortization of pollution control facilities	2040
Basis for amortization	

Footnotes appear at end of this Chapter.

How to make the election Amortization of railroad grading and tunnel bores and railroad rolling stock ¶ 2041	the-job training and child care centers ¶ 2043
Amortization of real property construction period interest and taxes ¶ 2042	Amortization of rehabilitation expenses for historic structures ¶ 2044
Amortization of expenditures for on-	• Highlights of Chapter 10 .... Page 2061

DEPRECIATION IN GENERAL

A reasonable allowance, called depreciation, may be deducted each year to compensate the taxpayer for exhaustion, wear and tear, and normal obsolescence of property used in a trade or business or held for the production of income. Such property must have a determinable useful life of more than one year.

¶ 2000 Depreciation. Depreciation enables a taxpayer to recover the cost or other basis of qualifying property during its estimated useful life. But no asset may be depreciated below a reasonable salvage value (¶ 2005) [Sec. 167; 1.167(a)-1].

Depreciation may be figured in any way consistent with recognized trade practices, but methods of depreciation usable for certain depreciable real property may be limited [¶ 2017]. Moreover, special rules may apply to low-income housing and to public utilities [¶ 2018; 2019]. Instead of a depreciation deduction, special amortization may be available for pollution control facilities, railroad rolling stock and right-of-way investments, real property construction period interest and taxes, expenditures for on-the-job training and child care centers, and rehabilitation expenses for historic structures [¶ 2040-2044].

Three methods of depreciation are listed specifically in the 1954 Code: straight line, declining balance, and sum of the years-digits. These are described and compared in ¶ 2011-2014. Other methods are discussed in ¶ 2015.

Regardless of the method of depreciation used, an additional first-year depreciation deduction is allowed for certain tangible personal property as explained in ¶ 2016. Also, provisions are made for extraordinary obsolescence of property [see ¶ 2034], and for retirement of assets [see ¶ 2036 et seq.].

The tests for determining what property may be depreciated are given in ¶ 2001; the rules explaining who may take the deduction are in ¶ 2002.

In the following example we use the straight line method to illustrate (1) the basic principles applied in figuring the depreciation deduction and (2) the effect of the deduction on the basis of the property.

Example: New property was acquired 1-1-77 at a cost of $5,000. It has a useful life of 5 years, during which there were no capital additions. The depreciation deduction and its effect on the basis of the property is as follows:

	1977	1978	1979	1980	1981
Cost Jan. 1	$5,000	$5,000	$5,000	$5,000	$5,000
Useful Life from Jan. 1	5 yrs.	4 yrs.	3 yrs.	2 yrs.	1 yr.
Depreciation Allowable Dec. 31	$1,000	$1,000	$1,000	$1,000	$1,000
Accumulated Depreciation Dec. 31	$1,000	$2,000	$3,000	$4,000	$5,000
Adjusted Basis Dec. 31	$4,000	$3,000	$2,000	$1,000	0

(1) On 1-1-80, the adjusted basis is $2,000, and if the property were sold at that time for $3,000, the recognized gain would be $1,000. The basis of the property in the hands of the new owner would be $3,000.

(2) Failure to deduct the full amount of depreciation allowable each year does not prevent that amount from reducing the adjusted basis, nor does it entitle the taxpayer to a greater deduction in a later year. So, if the allowable $1,000 had not been deducted in 1978, the adjusted basis at the end of that year would still be $3,000 and the deductions for 1979, 1980 and 1981 would still be limited to $1,000 each year. See ¶ 2004 for more details.

(3) After 1981, no further depreciation may be deducted, even though the property remains in use.

Background and purpose. The depreciation deduction would be questionable without specific permission in the Code. A deduction is allowed for expenses paid or incurred in a trade or business. On the other hand, a capital expenditure is not deductible. Since the original investment for property is a capital expenditure and its yearly wear and tear is not an expense paid or incurred, the deduction had to be specifically provided by Code Section 167.

⇒ OBSERVATION→ Since depreciation is a deduction from otherwise taxable income, but does not require a cash outlay as most expense deductions do, the result is "tax-free cash."

Accelerated depreciation and the minimum tax. Accelerated depreciation above the straight line method on real property [¶ 2017; 2018] and on leased personal property are tax preference items subject to the minimum tax. See ¶ 2403.

Property owned only part of year. If the property is not owned for the entire year, depreciation may be taken only for the part of the year it was owned (but see ¶ 2016; 2022(b); 2033(d)).

How treated on return. For individuals, the deduction for depreciation on property used in his trade or business is a deduction for adjusted gross income purposes. If the depreciation is on property held for the production of income, it is a deduction for adjusted gross income purposes only if the property is held for the production of rents or royalties or is held by a life tenant or by a trustee for an income beneficiary [¶ 1801(a); 1804; 1806].

¶ 2001 What property may be depreciated. A depreciation allowance is necessary because certain property gradually approaches a point when its usefulness is exhausted. Property with a definite useful life [¶ 2032; 2033] of more than one year may be depreciated. This property includes buildings, machinery, equipment and vehicles. Land is generally not depreciable, but depreciation may be allowed for pasture land (see (a) below). The cost of excavating, grading and removal directly associated with constructing buildings and roadways is part of their cost and therefore depreciable.[1]

(a) **Business and investment property.** The depreciation deduction is allowable *only* on [Sec. 167(a); 1.167(a)-1(a)]:
• Property used in trade or business.
• Property held for the production of income (whether or not used in the taxpayer's trade or business).

These tests relate to the use to which the property is put in the tax year. A change in use may affect the right to deduct depreciation.

No allowance is made for taxpayer's residence or automobile [Sec. 1.167(a)-2]. But if the residence is abandoned as such and is rented or is listed for rent or sale, a deduction is allowed.[2] It is also allowed for an auto used for both business and personal purposes. A proportionate part of depreciation sustained may be deducted.[3] If the percentage of business use changes each year, the basis for depreciation must be recomputed. See also ¶ 1517(g).

Footnotes appear at end of this Chapter.

Inventories and stock in trade are not depreciable property [Sec. 1.167(a)(2)]. See ¶ 2600 et seq. for inventory valuations.

Returnable, durable containers having a useful life over 1 year may be depreciated if they qualify as property used in business. Some factors to be considered are: whether taxpayer retains title in the sales contract, invoice or order acknowledgement; treatment as separate items on the invoice; and proper recording of basis in taxpayer's records.[4]

Intangible property can be depreciated, if its use in business or in the production of income is definitely limited in duration [Sec. 1.167(a)-3]. Thus, depreciation is allowed for a patent, copyright or leasehold [Sec. 1.162-11; 1.167(a)-3]; also for a license, franchise,[5] contract,[6] patent license contract,[7] or baseball contract.[8] A covenant not to compete when separately stated in the sales agreement is also depreciable.[9] These items may not be depreciated under the declining balance or sum of the years-digits methods. See ¶ 2012(a); 2013. Goodwill,[10] trade names, trademarks (but see ¶ 1808) and trade brands are not depreciable because of the indefinite duration of their usefulness.

Property of farmers. Depreciation may be claimed on farm buildings (other than a dwelling occupied by the owner), farm machinery, and other physical property, whether or not a crop was planted. Pasture land is depreciable when the grass is planted and would lose its economic usefulness over a period of time.[11] Livestock acquired for work, breeding or dairy purposes also may be depreciated unless they are included in an inventory used to determine profits (see ¶ 2615) [Sec. 1.167(a)-6(b)].

Depreciation is also allowed for fruit trees with a definite useful life (such as lemon or peach groves), but not for fruit trees with an indeterminate age and productivity that increases with age (such as avocado, mango and some citrus groves).[12]

Professional libraries with a diminishable value can be depreciated if used exclusively for business purposes.[13]

(b) When to deduct depreciation. The period for depreciation starts when the asset is placed in service. A new building is placed in service when it is completed and capable of being used.[14] Depreciation is claimed only for the year it is allowable [¶ 2004] regardless of the way income is figured. The Supreme Court has held that it may be taken the year the asset is sold although sales price exceeds the adjusted basis.[15] But the Revenue Service has ruled that depreciation for any open tax year (including year of sale) can be adjusted if the estimate of salvage value or useful life is unreasonable.[16] If property acquired for personal use is converted to business or investment use, depreciation is allowable from time of conversion.[2]

¶ 2002 Who is entitled to deduct depreciation. The person who sustains an economic loss from the decrease in property value due to depreciation gets the deduction.[1] Ordinarily, this is the person who owns and has a capital investment in the property.[2]

> **Example 1:** Ames leases a building to Bates, with Bates required merely to maintain the property in good and safe condition and to make necessary repairs and replacements. Ames may claim the depreciation allowance; Bates may not.[3] But see (a) below.

Tenant-stockholders of cooperative housing corporations may take depreciation for the part of the property they use for business or investment purposes, determined by their share of the depreciation allowable to the corporation [Sec. 216(c); 1.216-2(b)(1)].

(a) Buyer and seller. When property is sold, transferring title, delivering possession and paying the full purchase price, do not necessarily occur at the same time. Thus, there may be a period of time when it is a question whether the buyer or seller is entitled to deduct depreciation on the property. A buyer under an executory contract of sale may claim depreciation on the property from the time he gets possession and ownership privileges, though transfer of title may occur later.[4]

(b) Landlord and tenant. When a property owner leases his property to another for a period shorter than its useful life, under a lease that merely requires the tenant to maintain the property and make necessary repairs, the owner is entitled to depreciation.[5] The tenant can take depreciation for permanent improvements he makes if their useful life is less than the remaining lease term.[6] If their useful life is longer, he can write off (deduct) the cost evenly over the remaining life of the lease [Sec. 1.167(a)-(4)]. Neither the lessor nor his heir is entitled to depreciation on improvements made by the lessee without cost to the lessor, under a lease extending beyond the improvement's useful life.[7] In one case, an heir was denied depreciation even though the improvement's life outlasted the lease term.[8]

> **Example 2:** Tenant erected a building with an estimated life of 20 years at a cost of $20,000. At that time, the lease had 25 years left to run. Assuming straight line depreciation [¶ 2011] is used, tenant will take an annual deduction for depreciation of $1,000 ($20,000 ÷ 20) rather than a deduction based on the total cost of the improvements ($20,000) divided by the number of years remaining of the term of the lease (25), or $800.

> ≫**OBSERVATION 1**→ Writing off the unrecovered cost of the improvements is not the same as taking a depreciation allowance, because the law permits a choice of depreciation methods.

> ≫**OBSERVATION 2**→ A lessee, obligated under a lease to replace worn-out or discarded machinery, equipment, and furniture, may be allowed to deduct the cost as a business expense.[9] See also Ch. 8.

Renewable lease. If the initial (unexpired) term of the lease is shorter than ⅗ of the estimated life of the improvements, the renewal period is considered in determining the period for writing off the cost of improvements, unless the tenant establishes that it is unlikely the lease will be renewed at the close of the tax year [Sec. 178(a); 1.178-1(b)]. The renewal period is considered in any event if the lease is renewed or it is reasonably certain that it will be renewed [Sec. 178(c); 1.178-1(c); 1.178-3].

> **Example 3:** The estimated life of a building constructed by tenant on leased property is 35 years. The unexpired term of the lease is 20 years; there is a renewal option for 10 years. ⅗ of the useful life is 21 years. Since the remaining term of the lease (20 years) is shorter than 21 years, building cost must be written off over 30 years (unexpired term plus renewal term), unless the tenant can show that at the close of the tax year the lease will not be renewed.

If the tenant and landlord are "related," the depreciation period must be at least as long as the remaining useful life of the improvements [Sec. 178(b)(1); 1.178-1(d)].

"Related" person includes the relationships outlined in ¶ 2223(a)-(d) except that "at least 80%" is substituted for "more than 50%." It also includes a landlord and tenant who are members of an affiliated group. In determining stock ownership, the constructive ownership rules of ¶ 2223(d) apply, but brother and sister are excluded from the family rule [Sec. 178(b)(2); 1.178-2].

Footnotes appear at end of this Chapter.

¶ 2002

(c) Life tenant and remainderman. A life tenant deducts depreciation over the useful life of the property and not on his life expectancy[10] [Sec. 167(h); 1.167(h)-1]. After the death of the life tenant, the remainderman gets the deduction. Anyone who buys a life estate, whether or not he is the remainderman, can recover the amount of his investment through annual deductions spread over the life expectancy of the life tenant.[11]

¶ 2003 Basis for depreciation is the adjusted basis for determining *gain* from a sale [Sec. 167(g); 1.167(g)-1]. See ¶ 1500 et seq.

> **Example 1:** On 1-1-77, Hart bought for $12,000 a machine having an estimated useful life of 8 years. The basis for figuring depreciation is $12,000, and the amount allowable for 1977 using the straight line method [¶ 2011], is $1,500 ($12,000 ÷ 8). Ordinarily the deduction for each of the 7 succeeding years, will be the same. Technically, however, the basis for figuring 1978 depreciation is $10,500, and the allowance, $10,500 ÷ 7, or $1,500.
>
> **Example 2:** Assume the same facts as in Example 1, and also that at the close of 1978 it developed that the machine would be used for 10 more years. The adjusted basis of the machine at the close of 1978 was $9,000 (cost of $12,000 less two years depreciation amounting to $3,000). Using the straight line method, the deduction for each of the succeeding years will be $900 ($9,000 ÷ 10).

(a) Property acquired from a decedent. The basis for depreciation of property acquired from a decedent dying *before* 1977 is the fair market value at decedent's death unless the executor elected the alternate valuation date (¶ 1507) [Sec. 1014]. In that case, the basis is the value on the alternate valuation date reduced for depreciation since the date of death.[1] The basis is not reduced for a mortgage on the property whether or not it is assumed by the person acquiring the property.[2] If the mortgage is settled for less than face value, the basis for depreciation for the current and future years must be reduced by the amount saved.[3]

The basis of property acquired from a decedent dying *after* 1976 is generally the decedent's basis in the property immediately before his death, with certain adjustments (¶ 1507) [Sec. 1023].

(b) Taxpayer losing tax-exempt status. A taxpayer losing tax-exempt status must reduce the basis for depreciation of property he holds by depreciation that would have been sustained (using the straight line method) during the period held by the taxpayer while exempt [Sec. 1016(a)(3); 1.1016-4]. See also ¶ 2004.

(c) Change in use of property. If property originally acquired for personal use is converted to income-producing use, the basis for depreciation is the adjusted basis on the date of conversion or the fair market value on the date of conversion, whichever is lower [Sec. 1.167(g)-1].

(d) Allocation of lump sum purchase price between land and building. If a parcel of improved real estate is bought for a lump sum, the purchase price must be allocated between the land (nondepreciable property) and the building (depreciable property) in the same proportion that their values bear to the total value. Only the price allocable to the building may be recovered through depreciation [Sec. 1.167(a)-5].

To apply this rule, the taxpayer must determine: (1) the value of the entire property—in the ordinary arm's-length transaction this may be the same as the lump-purchase price; and (2) the value of the building.

> **Example 3:** Assume value of entire property is the same as the purchase price ($45,000); and the value of building is $30,000. Lump price would be split, ⅔ or $30,000 to building, and $15,000 to land.

Example 4: Assume value of entire property is $50,000 and the purchase price is $45,000, with the value of building, $25,000. Lump price would be split, ½ or $22,500 to building, and $22,500 to land.

(e) If basis cannot be proven, depreciation will be disallowed.[4]

¶ 2004 Adjusting basis. A taxpayer must deduct his full depreciation in the year it is allowable. He cannot deduct in later years any amount he fails to deduct currently [Sec. 1.167(a)-10]. The property's basis must be reduced by the full amount allowable, even if he does not take the full deduction or the amount allowable does not reduce his tax [Sec. 1.1016-3(b)].

Tax benefit rule for excessive depreciation. A taxpayer who deducts more than the allowable depreciation must reduce the property's basis by the amount allowed that reduced the tax (but not less than the full amount allowable) [Sec. 1.1016-3(b)]. This is the tax benefit amount allowed.

In figuring the "tax-benefit amount allowed," the income tax enters into the computation but not the self-employment tax. Net operating loss carrybacks and carryovers affecting taxes of years other than the year when depreciation was taken must be considered. If a partnership or trust holds property, the partners' or beneficiaries' tax benefit must be accounted for in figuring the "tax-benefit amount allowed." If several properties are involved, an allocation is made. The taxpayer may use the tax-benefit rule only for years that he can prove the tax-benefit amount [Sec. 1.1016-3(e)].

Example: On 1-1-74, Cook purchased a truck for $8,000. Since the life of the truck was 8 years, and it had no salvage value, allowable depreciation, using the straight line method, was $1,000 a year. However, depreciation was actually taken and allowed as follows:

1974	$1,000
1975	NONE
1976	NONE
1977	$3,000

Of the $3,000 depreciation allowed for 1977, assume only $2,000 resulted in a tax benefit. The basis of the truck should be reduced as follows:

	Year	Allowed	Tax benefit amount allowed (amount allowed which reduced taxpayer's tax)	Allowable	Reduction of basis
(1)	1974	$1,000	......	$1,000	$1,000
(2)	1975	0	......	1,000	1,000
(3)	1976	0	......	1,000	1,000
(4)	1977	3,000	$2,000	1,000	2,000
			Total reduction		$5,000

The basis is reduced to $3,000 ($8,000 less $5,000), and the remaining basis should be written off at the rate of $750 per year ($3,000 divided by 4).

Technically, Cook should not be allowed a $3,000 deduction for 1977. Failure to deduct $1,000 allowable depreciation in each of the years 1975 and 1976 does not entitle him to a greater deduction in a later year. However, when the excessive depreciation was allowed, basis must be adjusted as shown.

The basis must also be reduced by the amount of depreciation allowable in 1975 and 1976, even though Cook took no deduction in those years.

¶ 2005 Salvage value. Salvage value, determined when property is acquired, is the amount that can be realized when property is no longer useful to the taxpayer. It may be no more than junk value or a large proportion of the original ba-

Footnotes appear at end of this Chapter.

sis. This depends on how long before the end of the asset's inherent useful life [¶ 2032] the taxpayer plans to dispose of it. The salvage value of personal property (except livestock) with at least a 3-year useful life may be reduced by up to 10% of its cost or other basis [Sec. 167(f); 1.167(f)-1]. No asset may be depreciated below a reasonable salvage value (less the 10% reduction, if applicable) [Sec. 1.167(a)-1(a)].

The salvage value as determined above must be subtracted from the basis for depreciation in figuring straight line [¶ 2011] and sum of the years-digits [¶ 2013] depreciation. It is not subtracted in figuring declining balance depreciation [¶ 2012] or the additional first-year allowance [¶ 2016], but must be accounted for when the assets are retired. Instead of salvage value, taxpayer may use net salvage value. Net salvage value is salvage value reduced by cost of removal. Either value must be used consistently. When an asset is retired or disposed of [¶ 2036 et seq.], adjustments must be made in the asset and depreciation reserve account (¶ 2021) [Sec. 1.167(a)-1(c)].

Once salvage value is determined, it cannot be changed merely because of change in price levels. If there is a redetermination of useful life [¶ 2032], salvage value may be redetermined. Taxpayer may enter into an agreement with Revenue Service on salvage value [¶ 2010(c)].

A taxpayer who elects the Class Life ADR system [¶ 2033] must specify the salvage value of each vintage account and the 10% reduction, if applicable [Sec. 1.167(a)-11(d)]. He can disregard salvage completely even though it exceeds 10% of the cost. The salvage value is not changed by the Revenue Service in this case, unless the final salvage is substantially higher than the estimate.

FIGURING THE DEPRECIATION DEDUCTION

The taxpayer can use any reasonable and consistently applied method for computing depreciation. Accelerated methods will give greater depreciation deductions in the earlier years. In addition to regular depreciation, taxpayers may elect an additional first-year depreciation allowance for certain tangible personal property.

¶ **2010 Methods of figuring depreciation.** Annual depreciation may be figured in any way consistent with recognized trade practice. Listed below are the methods specifically mentioned in the 1954 Code. Others may be used. Any method adopted must be reasonable [Sec. 167; 1.167(b)-0].
1. Straight line method [¶ 2011].
2. Declining balance method [¶ 2012].
3. Sum of the years-digits method [¶ 2013].
4. Any other consistent method [¶ 2015].

For comparison of methods (1), (2) and (3), see ¶ 2014.

NOTE: The depreciation of certain depreciable real property is limited [¶ 2017]. Also, there are special rules for rehabilitating low-income housing [¶ 2018] and public utilities [¶ 2019].

(a) **Election of method.** A taxpayer who has not previously filed a return may adopt the appropriate method in his first return. If the taxpayer qualifies for, and wants to use, the liberalized methods, no formal election of method is necessary. He just uses the appropriate method for the first tax year in which he acquires the property [Sec. 1.167(c)-1(c)]. Form 4562, an optional form for depreciation, may be used as an attachment to the return.

NOTE: By "liberalized methods" we mean declining balance at *twice* the straight line rate [¶ 2012], the sum of the years-digits method [¶ 2013], and the methods mentioned in ¶ 2015.

A taxpayer need not use the same method for all his depreciable property. But once he chooses a method for any particular property he must continue it for that property (but see (b) below). He may choose a different depreciation method for similar property acquired later, if the new property is set up in a separate account [Sec. 1.167(b)-(0)(c)]. See also ¶ 2022(b).

(b) Change of method. Any change in an adopted method of depreciation is a change in the accounting method [¶ 2708(b)], and generally requires Revenue Service approval. But consent for most changes can be assumed when the taxpayer has properly filed Form 3115 and complied with certain conditions. Form 3115 must be filed with the Service Center during the first 180 days of the year of change. Thus, a taxpayer who wants to change his method for the calendar year 1978 must apply by 6-29-78. The application must include specific information indicated in the form and refer to Rev. Proc. 74-11.[1]

No Revenue Service permission is needed generally to change from the declining balance (including limited declining balance[2]) to the straight line method unless there is an agreement prohibiting the change (see (c) below) [Sec. 167(e); 1.167(e)-1(b)]. The change must be applied to all the assets in a particular account and may only be made on the original return for the tax year in which the change is made.[3] A statement must be attached to the return showing date asset was acquired, basis, amounts recovered through depreciation and other allowances, salvage value, character of the property, remaining useful life, and any other information that may be required. The change must be adhered to until the Revenue Service consents to a later change [Sec. 1.167(e)-1(b)]. See ¶ 2012 for depreciation under the straight line method after the change. A taxpayer electing the Class Life system [¶ 2033] may change from the declining balance to the sum of the years-digits and from the declining balance or the sum of the years-digits to the straight line without Revenue Service consent [Sec. 1.167(a)-11(c)(1)(iii)].

> NOTE: A change in depreciation method resulting from property qualifying or not qualifying as residential rental property does not need Revenue Service consent (¶ 2017(d)) [Sec. 1.167(j)-3(c)].

(c) Agreements on depreciation. The taxpayer and Revenue Service may enter into a binding written agreement on Form 2271 as to useful life, depreciation rate and method, and salvage value of any property. The agreement generally will not be changed until facts and circumstances not taken into account in making it are proven by the one initiating the change. A change is effective starting with the tax year a written notice is served by registered or certified mail by the one proposing the change [Sec. 167(d); 1.167(d)-1]. If the taxpayer elects to apply the ADR system to any eligible property, he can withdraw any agreement made before 1971 as to that property (¶ 2033) [Sec. 1.167(a)-11(g)(2)].

> NOTE: Before making the agreement the Revenue Service may examine the taxpayer's return (or returns) for the tax year (or years) immediately preceding the first tax year to be covered by the agreement. There also may be a physical examination of the property involved.[4]

¶ 2011 Straight line depreciation. The cost or other basis of the property, less the estimated salvage value, is deducted in equal amounts each year over the period of its remaining estimated useful life [¶ 2003; 2032]. Salvage value up to 10% of the cost or other basis may be ignored for personal property with at least a 3 year useful life (¶ 2005) [Sec. 167; 1.167(b)-1]. The salvage in excess of 10% is also ignored if the Class Life ADR system is elected [¶ 2033].

Footnotes appear at end of this Chapter.

¶ 2011

Example: If Nelson bought a machine with a useful life of 10 years, for $5,000, and the salvage value at the end of that period is $500 (10% of cost), the annual deduction would be $5,000 divided by 10, or $500 since the salvage value up to 10% of cost can be disregarded.

For convenience, the depreciation allowance may be expressed as a percentage. In the above example the rate (unadjusted for salvage) is 10% (100% divided by the number of years of useful life). If this rate is used, it is applied to the cost (or other basis). The rate would be 10% (100% ÷ 10).

The straight line method may be used for any depreciable property [¶ 2001]. For change from declining balance method, see ¶ 2012. For an additional first-year allowance for certain tangible personal property, see ¶ 2016.

¶ 2012 Declining balance depreciation. The depreciation that can be taken each year under this method is generally twice the straight line rate (unadjusted for salvage) [Sec. 167(b)(2); 1.167(b)-(2)]. See (a) below. However, it may be limited to 1½ times [(b) below] or even 1¼ times [¶ 2017(b)] the straight line rate.

NOTE: The useful life under the Class Life ADR system, if elected, determines the asset's depreciation rate and whether it qualifies for the depreciation method (¶ 2033) [Sec. 1.167(a)-11(g)(1)].

A uniform rate is applied to the unrecovered basis of the property. Since the basis is always reduced by prior depreciation, the rate is applied to a constantly declining basis. Although salvage value [¶ 2005] is not deducted from the basis, it must be considered when assets are retired. For estimated useful life, see ¶ 2032. This method gives the greatest amount of depreciation in the first year of use, with continually decreasing amounts in later years [¶ 2014]. For additional first-year allowance, see ¶ 2016.

NOTE: When the term "declining balance" is used in this text, the method at twice the straight line rate is meant. The term "limited declining balance" refers to the method at 1½ times the straight line rate.

Example 1: On Jan. 1, Marcus bought a new machine with a useful life of 5 years. It cost him $5,000 and its salvage value was $700. Under the declining balance method, he may use a 40% rate (twice the 20% straight line rate [unadjusted for salvage] for this asset). Depreciation for the first year is $2,000, reducing the basis to $3,000. For the second, it will be $1,200, and so on.

Change in useful life. When a change in the estimated useful life is justified, subsequent computations are made as if the revised useful life had been originally estimated [Sec. 1.167(b)-2(c)].

Example 2: A machine has an estimated useful life of 10 years and a declining balance rate of 20%. After 6 years, it is determined that the remaining life of the machine is 6 years. Depreciation is then figured as if the original life had been estimated as 12 years, and the new rate, 16⅔%, is then applied to the unrecovered cost or other basis.

Change to straight line method. A taxpayer may switch to the straight line method from declining balance, basing future allowances on the asset's unrecovered cost (less salvage, if taken) and its remaining life. Both salvage value and useful life must be redetermined from circumstances existing at the time of change [Sec. 1.167(e)-1(b)].[1]

(a) Property subject to declining balance. The declining balance method may be used only for property [Sec. 167(c); 1.167(c)-1]:

- With a useful life of at least 3 years;
- Built or rebuilt by or for the taxpayer after 1953, or
- Acquired by taxpayer after 1953 if the original user.

NOTE: Used or reconditioned property does not qualify for the declining balance method. But see (b) below. Special rules apply to depreciable real property acquired after 7-24-69 [¶ 2017].

Example 3: Lee bought a machine from Roe in 1977. The machine was made in 1971. Roe had leased the machine to another in 1971 before selling it to Lee in 1977. Lee cannot use the declining balance method since he is not the original user of the machine acquired in 1977.

Nonqualifying property. The declining balance method cannot be used for intangible property, such as patents, copyrights and leases [Sec. 167(c)]. Nor can it be used on property in the hands of a distributee, vendee, transferee, donee, or grantee, unless he is the original user and the property otherwise qualifies [Sec. 1.167(c)-1(a)(6)].

New or used depreciable real property acquired after 7-24-69, except *new* residential rental housing acquired after that date, does not qualify for the declining balance method [¶ 2017]. In addition, this method generally is not allowed for real property, if construction was begun or ordered during the suspension period (10-10-66 through 3-9-67) and actual construction was started before 5-24-67. However, this only applies to the part of the construction completed before 5-24-67. The rest of the construction's cost on or after 5-24-67 qualifies for declining balance [Sec. 167(i)].

Property that does not qualify for declining balance may qualify for straight line, limited declining balance ((b) below) or any reasonable method, except the other liberalized methods explained in ¶ 2013; 2015(a).

(b) Use of limited declining balance. There is a maximum rate of 1½ times the straight line rate that can be used under the declining balance method for certain property. This maximum rate applies to:

• Used tangible personal property (or new tangible personal property acquired before 1954)[2] having a useful life of 3 or more years.

• Used depreciable real property acquired before July 25, 1969.

• New real property (other than residential rental property) acquired after July 24, 1969.[3]

There is a maximum rate of 1¼ times the straight line rate for certain used residential rental property acquired after July 24, 1969. [¶ 2017(b)].

Used property with a useful life of less than 3 years generally can only use the straight line method.[4] Limited declining balance for new or used property was not affected by the suspension rules. Salvage value is not considered in figuring the deduction,[5] but the depreciation taken must be reasonable.

¶ 2013 Sum of the years-digits method. This method may be used for the same kind of property that qualifies for the declining balance method, as described in ¶ 2012(a) [Sec. 167(b)(3), (c); 1.167(b)-3]. It is generally not allowed for new or used depreciable real property acquired after 7-24-69, except *new* residential rental housing acquired after that date [¶ 2017]. In addition, real property does not qualify if construction was begun or ordered during the suspension period (10-10-66 through 3-9-67) and actual construction was started before 5-24-67 with exceptions same as those applicable to declining balance depreciation [¶ 2012(a)].

For change of method, see ¶ 2010(b). For additional first-year depreciation, see ¶ 2016.

(a) General rule. The annual depreciation deduction is figured by applying a changing fraction to the taxpayer's cost of the property less any salvage value taken [¶ 2005]. The numerator of the fraction is the number of remaining years of the property's estimated useful life [¶ 2032]. The denominator is the sum of the

Footnotes appear at end of this Chapter.

¶ 2013

numbers representing the years of life of the property. Salvage value [¶ 2005] is disregarded if the Class Life system is elected [¶ 2033].

Example 1: An asset has a 5-year life. The fraction used in figuring the depreciation for the first year would be $5/15$, 5 being the number of remaining years of life, and 15 being the sum of $1 + 2 + 3 + 4 + 5$. For the second year, the fraction would be $4/15$, and so on.

NOTE: You can get the sum of years-digits for the denominators of the fraction by using the following formula:

$$S = N \left(\frac{N + 1}{2} \right) \quad \text{when:} \quad \begin{array}{l} S = \text{sum of the digits} \\ N = \text{number of years of estimated useful life.} \end{array}$$

Thus, substituting in the formula, for an asset with 5 years of estimated useful life, you get $S = 5 \left(\frac{5 + 1}{2} \right) = 5 \times 3 = 15.$

Example 2: Blue acquires a new machine on 1-1-77 at a cost of $150. It had an estimated useful life of 5 years. Its estimated salvage value is $15 (which can be ignored).

Year	Fraction of cost	Cost or other basis	Depreciation
1	$5/15$	$150	$ 50
2	$4/15$	150	40
3	$3/15$	150	30
4	$2/15$	150	20
5	$1/15$	150	10
	Total cost		$150

Assets acquired during year. Depreciation is figured in the usual manner for each 12-month period of service. Allocation is then made to the respective tax years according to the proportion of the service year that falls within the respective tax years [Sec. 1.167(b)(3)(a)].

Example 3: On 4-1-75 Jones bought a new machine for $30,000 having an estimated useful life of 5 years. Assume no salvage value. Annual depreciation using the sum of the years-digits method would be figured as follows:

Asset Year	Deductions for 12-month periods	1975	1976	1977	1978	1979	1980
1	$5/15$ $10,000	$(9/12)$7,500	$(3/12)$2,500				
2	$4/15$ 8,000		$(9/12)$6,000	$(3/12)$2,000			
3	$3/15$ 6,000			$(9/12)$4,500	$(3/12)$1,500		
4	$2/15$ 4,000				$(9/12)$3,000	$(3/12)$1,000	
5	$1/15$ 2,000					$(9/12)$1,500	$(3/12)$500
15	$15/15$ $30,000	$7,500	$8,500	$6,500	$4,500	$2,500	$500

Change in useful life. When a change in useful life is justified for a single asset account [¶ 2022], subsequent computations are made as if the remaining useful life at the start of the tax year of change were the useful life of a new asset acquired at that time. The basis is the unrecovered cost or other basis of the asset at that time [Sec. 1.167(b)-3(a)(1)(ii)].

Example 4: On 1-1-77, Tyson bought a new asset with a 10-year estimated life. When making his return in 1982, he finds that the asset has a remaining useful life of 7 years from 1-1-82. Depreciation for 1982 is figured as if 1982 were the first tax year of life. The asset has a 7-year useful life, and the allowance for 1982 is $7/28$ of the unrecovered basis adjusted for any salvage.

(b) Remaining life plan. Under the sum of the years-digits method, depreciation may also be figured by applying changing fractions to the *unrecovered cost* less any salvage value taken [¶ 2005]. The numerator of the fraction changes each year to correspond with remaining useful life of the asset (including the year for which the allowance is figured), and the denominator changes each year to correspond with the sum of the numbers representing the remaining useful life [Sec. 1.167(b)-3(a)2].

Example 5: Assume the same facts as in Example 1. Under remaining life the fraction for the first year would be 5/15, 5 being the remaining years of life, and 15, the sum of 5 + 4 + 3 + 2 + 1. For the second year the fraction would change to 4/10, 4 being the remaining years of life and 10 being the sum of 4 + 3 + 2 + 1. For the third year the fraction would change to 3/6, and so on. These fractions are then applied to the *unrecovered cost.*

Official table. The Revenue Service has prepared a table showing decimal equivalents of the sum of the years-digits fractions corresponding to remaining lives from 1 to 100 years. Instead of figuring the fractions, the taxpayer merely checks the table for remaining life, finds the decimal equivalent, and then multiplies the *unrecovered cost* (less salvage, if applicable) by this decimal. Exhibit 1 shows decimal equivalents of such fractions for remaining lives from 1 to 20 years. The complete table is in P-H Federal Taxes at ¶ 15,473, and in the regulations at Sec. 1.167(b)-3. Copies can be obtained from the Revenue Service.[1]

[Table appears on page 2014]

NOTE: For determination of decimal equivalents of remaining lives falling between those shown in the table, the taxpayer may use the next longest life shown in the table, interpolate from the table, or use the following formula:

D = 2R / (W + 2F) (W + 1). D = Decimal equivalent; R = Remaining life; W = Whole number of years in remaining life and F = Fractional part of year in remaining life. If the taxpayer wants to carry his calculations of decimal equivalents to more decimal places than found in the table, he may use the formula. The procedure adopted must be consistently followed. This formula may also be used if the remaining life is longer than 20 years. Thus substituting in the formula, for an asset with 30.1 years of estimated useful life we get:

$$D = \frac{2 \times 30.1}{(30 + .2)(30 + 1)} = \frac{60.2}{30.2 \times 31} = \frac{60.2}{936.2} = .0643$$

Multiple asset accounts. The sum of the years-digits method may be applied to composite, classified, or group accounts [¶ 2022] using the remaining life plan. Revenue Service consent is required when using any other plan with the sum of the years-digits [Sec. 1.167(b)-3(b)].

When remaining life plan is used for a multiple asset account, the remaining useful life of the account must be redetermined each year. This annual redetermination may be made (1) by analysis (determine the remaining lives for each of the components in the account, and average them); or (2) by use of the following formula [Sec. 1.167(b)-3(b)(2)]:

$$\frac{\text{Unrecovered cost (or other basis) of account using straight line method}}{\text{Gross cost (or other basis) of account}} \times \text{Average life of assets in account}$$

Use of the formula may be illustrated by the following example:

Footnotes appear at end of this Chapter.

¶ 2013

Example 6: A group account has an average life of 10 years. On Jan. 1, it has a gross asset balance of $12,600 and a depreciation reserve (figured on the straight line basis) of $9,450. The remaining useful life of the account as of Jan. 1 is 2.5 years figured as follows:

$$\frac{\$12,600 - \$9,450\dagger}{12,600} \times 10 = 2.5$$

†The gross asset balance ($12,600) minus the depreciation reserve by the straight line method ($9,450) equals the unrecovered cost figured by the straight line method.

EXHIBIT 1

Decimal Equivalents for Use of the Sum of the Years-Digits Method, Based on Remaining Life (1-20 years)

Remaining life (years)	Decimal equivalent	Remaining life (years)	Decimal equivalent	Remaining life (years)	Decimal equivalent	Remaining life (years)	Decimal equivalent	Remaining life (years)	Decimal equivalent
20.0	0.0952	16.1	0.1169	12.2	0.1514	8.4	0.2121	4.6	0.3538
19.9	.0957	16.0	.1176	12.1	.1526	8.3	.2145	4.5	.3600
19.8	.0961	15.9	.1183	12.0	.1538	8.2	.2169	4.4	.3667
19.7	.0966	15.8	.1190	11.9	.1549	8.1	.2195	4.3	.3739
19.6	.0970	15.7	.1197	11.8	.1561	8.0	.2222	4.2	.3818
19.5	.0975	15.6	.1204	11.7	.1573	7.9	.2244	4.1	.3905
19.4	.0980	15.5	.1211	11.6	.1585	7.8	.2267	4.0	.4000
19.3	.0985	15.4	.1218	11.5	.1597	7.7	.2292	3.9	.4063
19.2	.0990	15.3	.1226	11.4	.1610	7.6	.2317	3.8	.4130
19.1	.0995	15.2	.1234	11.3	.1624	7.5	.2344	3.7	.4205
19.0	.1000	15.1	.1242	11.2	.1637	7.4	.2372	3.6	.4286
18.9	.1005	15.0	.1250	11.1	.1652	7.3	.2401	3.5	.4375
18.8	.1010	14.9	.1257	11.0	.1667	7.2	.2432	3.4	.4474
18.7	.1015	14.8	.1265	10.9	.1680	7.1	.2465	3.3	.4583
18.6	.1020	14.7	.1273	10.8	.1693	7.0	.2500	3.2	.4706
18.5	.1025	14.6	.1281	10.7	.1707	6.9	.2527	3.1	.4844
18.4	.1030	14.5	.1289	10.6	.1721	6.8	.2556	3.0	.5000
18.3	.1036	14.4	.1297	10.5	.1736	6.7	.2587	2.9	.5088
18.2	.1041	14.3	.1306	10.4	.1751	6.6	.2619	2.8	.5185
18.1	.1047	14.2	.1315	10.3	.1767	6.5	.2653	2.7	.5294
18.0	.1053	14.1	.1324	10.2	.1783	6.4	.2689	2.6	.5417
17.9	.1058	14.0	.1333	10.1	.1800	6.3	.2727	2.5	.5556
17.8	.1063	13.9	.1342	10.0	.1818	6.2	.2768	2.4	.5714
17.7	.1069	13.8	.1350	9.9	.1833	6.1	.2811	2.3	.5897
17.6	.1074	13.7	.1359	9.8	.1849	6.0	.2857	2.2	.6111
17.5	.1080	13.6	.1368	9.7	.1865	5.9	.2892	2.1	.6364
17.4	.1086	13.5	.1378	9.6	.1882	5.8	.2929	2.0	.6667
17.3	.1092	13.4	.1387	9.5	.1900	5.7	.2969	1.9	.6786
17.2	.1098	13.3	.1397	9.4	.1918	5.6	.3011	1.8	.6923
17.1	.1105	13.2	.1407	9.3	.1938	5.5	.3056	1.7	.7083
17.0	.1111	13.1	.1418	9.2	.1957	5.4	.3103	1.6	.7273
16.9	.1117	13.0	.1429	9.1	.1978	5.3	.3155	1.5	.7500
16.8	.1123	12.9	.1438	9.0	.2000	5.2	.3210	1.4	.7778
16.7	.1129	12.8	.1448	8.9	.2018	5.1	.3269	1.3	.8125
16.6	.1135	12.7	.1458	8.8	.2037	5.0	.3333	1.2	.8571
16.5	.1142	12.6	.1469	8.7	.2057	4.9	.3379	1.1	.9167
16.4	.1148	12.5	.1479	8.6	.2077	4.8	.3429	1.0	1.0000
16.3	.1155	12.4	.1490	8.5	.2099	4.7	.3481		
16.2	.1162	12.3	.1502						

¶ 2014 **Comparison of straight line, declining balance and sum of the years-digits methods.** The chief advantage of the declining balance and the sum of the years-digits methods over the straight line method is that they increase available working capital during the early years of the life of the assets. The stepped-up tax-free recovery of costs also assists the manufacturer and other users of machinery to replace obsolete machinery and equipment with up-to-date facilities. However, the straight line method gives full recovery of cost, and charges an equal amount each year. Deductions under both the other methods are unequal, and the declining balance method does not permit full recovery of cost unless taxpayer elects to switch to the straight line method at some point. But full recovery can be made by deducting the unrecovered cost as a loss by sale or abandonment if the asset is a single item. For group assets, the entire remaining unrecovered cost of a given year's acquisition can be deducted when the last unit is retired if records show when the assets were acquired. The unrecovered balance can also be depreciated gradually over later years if the asset is used beyond its normal life [¶ 2036]. In any case, the tax advantages of the liberalized methods have been reduced by the recapture of depreciation rules [¶ 1619].

The following provides a comparison between the straight line and declining balance methods:

Life	Straight Line Rate	1¼ DB	1½ DB	DB
10	10 %	12.5 %	15 %	20 %
15	6.66	8.33	10	13.33
20	5	6.25	7.5	10
25	4	5	6	8
30	3.33	4.17	5	6.67
40	2.5	3.125	3.75	5

¶ **2015 Other methods of depreciation.** Any other consistent method may be used to determine the annual depreciation allowance for property like that for which the declining balance method may be used (¶ 2012(a)) [Sec. 167(b)(4), (c); 1.167(b)-4, 1.167(c)-1]. These methods may be used only if the total allowances for the property, at the end of each year do not exceed, during the first two-thirds of the useful life of the property, the total allowances that would result if the declining balance method were used [Sec. 167(b)(4); 1.167(b)-4].

Some other methods than can be used are the unit of production method [Sec. 1.167(b)-0(b)], the operating day method, and the income forecast method. For an additional first-year allowance for certain property, see ¶ 2016.

(a) **Unit of production method** provides equal depreciation per unit of work done during the useful life of the asset under normal conditions of use, irrespective of the lapse of time.

Example: The difference between cost and salvage value of a machine is $4,800; it is estimated that during its useful life the machine will produce 20,000 units, and during the tax year 2,500 units were produced. The deduction would be $600 ($4,800 × 2,500/20,000).

(b) **Operating day method** may be used when the major depreciation factor on equipment (such as rotary oil drilling rigs) is wear and tear from use rather than obsolescence [¶ 2034]. Useful life is estimated in terms of number of days the equipment can be operated, and the depreciable basis is prorated on the actual number of days used. Estimated life and salvage are subject to revision according to actual experience.[1]

(c) **Income forecast method** may be used to depreciate the cost of rented television film, taped shows and motion picture films.[2] A fraction is applied using the film's income for the year as the numerator and the estimated income to be received over the film's useful life as the denominator. This fraction is mutiplied by the adjusted cost of films that produced income during the year. Adjustments can be made for substantial overestimates or underestimates.[3]

¶ **2016 Additional first-year depreciation allowance.** In addition to regular depreciation deducted in the first year, taxpayers, except trusts, can elect an initial deduction equal to 20% of the cost of tangible personal property ((a) below) [Sec. 179]. This extra 20%, however, applies only to $10,000 of investment. The full cost or a fractional part of the cost of an item may be selected for the extra write-off, but only up to a total cost of $10,000 [Sec. 1.179-1(c)]. The limit applies to each

Footnotes appear at end of this Chapter.

taxpayer, not to each business in which he has an interest [Sec. 1.179-2(a)(2)]. No proration is required regardless of when the property is placed in service [Sec. 1.179-1(b)].

Salvage value is not considered in applying the 20%. But in figuring normal depreciation, the basis must be reduced by both the additional allowance and salvage value (if salvage value is a factor) [Sec. 1.179-1(d)]. See also ¶ 2033(b).

Example 1: On 1-1-77, Rogers, who uses straight line depreciation, bought for $10,000 a machine having a useful life of 10 years. Salvage value is $1,500. The initial first-year allowance is $2,000 (20% of $10,000). This reduces the basis for normal depreciation to $8,000. Normal depreciation for the first year is $750 (10% × $7,500 [$8,000 − $500 salvage value in excess of 10% of cost]). The total first-year depreciation is $2,750.

Example 2: Assume the same facts as in Example 1 except that Rogers bought the machine on 7-1-77. The first-year allowance is still $2,000, but the normal depreciation for 1977 is only half of $750 or $375.

Joint return. On a joint return, the 20% is applied to $20,000 of cost [Sec. 179(b)]. For a joint return filed after the due date [¶ 3506], the deduction is limited to the total amount taken on the separate returns [Sec. 1.179-2(e)].

Trade-ins. If property is acquired by a trade-in of like property, the adjusted basis of the property traded in is not considered in determining the cost of the newly acquired property [Sec. 179(d)(3)].

(a) Qualifying property is new or used tangible personal property (such as machinery) with a useful life of at least six years when acquired. If the taxpayer elects the Class Life ADR system, the useful life requirement for this purpose reflects the asset depreciation range (¶ 2033) [Sec. 1.167(a)-11(g)].

The additional allowance does not apply if the property: (1) was acquired from a "related" person; (2) was acquired by a component member of a controlled group from another component member of the same group; or (3) has its basis determined (a) with reference to the adjusted basis in the hands of the person from whom it is acquired (as in the case of gifts); or (b) under the rules for the basis of property acquired from a decedent [Sec. 179(d); 1.179-3].

Related person includes the relationships outlined in ¶ 2223(a)—(d) and ¶ 2924 (under disallowed losses) except that brother and sister are excluded from the family rule [Sec. 179(d)].

Controlled group of corporations is defined in ¶ 3223(a) except "more than 50%" is substituted for "at least 80%."

(b) Election. Election is made by showing the *total* additional first-year depreciation for the year as a separate item on the taxpayer's timely filed return. The taxpayer must keep records that identify each piece of property for which the allowance is claimed and show how it was acquired. Additional first-year depreciation cannot be taken until the first year the taxpayer's depreciation method lets him take regular depreciation.[1] The election cannot be revoked unless the Revenue Service consents. A separate election must be made for each year the additional first-year election is claimed [Sec. 1.179-4(a)].

A request to revoke, or change the selection of property, must be filed no later than 6 months after the time for filing (disregarding extensions) for the year the allowance was claimed. The request should state the reason. Ordinarily, it will not be allowed just to get a tax advantage [Sec. 1.179-4(b)].

(c) A controlled group of corporations (see (a) above) is treated as one taxpayer. The allowance may be taken by any one member or allocated among the members in any way they agree. However, the allowance allocated to any member cannot exceed 20% of the cost of the qualifying property actually purchased by that member during the year [Sec. 179(d); 1.179-2(c)].

(d) Partnerships. In figuring the allowance, each partner is considered to have bought his share in the qualifying asset. Thus, a partnership is allowed up to 20% of the total cost of qualifying property. However, for partnership tax years starting after 1975, the cost of the property on which additional first-year depreciation is calculated for the partnership as a whole can not exceed $10,000 [Sec. 179(d)].

Each partner's share of additional first-year depreciation is entered in Schedule K-1 on Form 1065. In addition, the amounts must also be included in column (e) of Schedule M of Form 1065.[2] See ¶ 2918.

¶ 2017 Methods usable for depreciable real property. Generally, the methods available for new or used depreciable real property acquired after 7-24-69 are limited. Property that is not depreciable when its use starts (first used as a personal residence) but becomes depreciable after 7-24-69, is not treated as original-use property.

NOTE: Excess depreciation on real property may be a tax preference item subject to the minimum tax. See ¶ 2403. Accelerated depreciation methods are not allowed for real property constructed on a site that had been occupied by a certified historic structure demolished or substantially altered (other than by certified rehabilitation) after 6-30-76 and before 1-1-81 [Sec. 167(n)].

Components of a new building (elevators, wiring, heating, etc.) can be depreciated separately from each other and from the building.[1] This can also apply to used buildings if the cost is properly allocated to the various components based on their value, and useful lives are assigned to the components based on their condition when acquired.[2]

Background and purpose. Certain high-income individuals used the prior tax treatment of real estate as a tax shelter device. The rapid depreciation methods allowed made it possible for taxpayers to deduct amounts above those required to service the mortgage during the property's early life. In addition, since accelerated depreciation produced a deduction in excess of the actual decline in the property's usefulness, profitable real estate was normally converted into a tax loss. This sheltered economic profits from income tax, permitting tax avoidance on other ordinary income.

(a) New depreciable real property. New construction other than residential rental housing is limited to the straight line method, limited declining balance method, or certain other consistent methods (¶ 2015) [Sec. 167(j)(1); 1.167(j)-1, 1.167(j)-2].

New residential rental property is eligible for all appropriate methods of depreciation, including the accelerated methods [¶ 2010 et seq.]. "Residential rental property" generally is a building or structure with 80% or more of its gross rentals for the tax year from dwelling units. The rental value of the part of the building occupied by the taxpayer counts into gross rental income. The 80% test is applied on a year-by-year basis. Foreign residential rental housing can qualify for accelerated methods if the foreign country allows the depreciation for similar housing [Sec. 167(j)(2); 1.167(j)-3].

Any of the accelerated methods can be used for construction or reconstruction started before 7-25-69, or if a binding contract for any part of the construction or a substantial portion of the permanent financing was entered into before 7-25-69 [Sec. 167(j)(3)].

Footnotes appear at end of this Chapter.

(b) Used depreciable real property. Generally, used depreciable real property acquired after 7-24-69 is limited to the straight line or a comparable ratable method of depreciation. This limitation does not apply to property acquired under a binding contract or when a substantial portion of the financing was entered into before 7-25-69 [Sec. 167(j)(4); 1.167(j)-1, 1.167(j)-5].

Used residential rental property acquired after 7-24-69 is limited to the straight line method, a declining balance method not exceeding 1¼ times the straight line rate, or certain other consistent methods [¶ 2015]. This property must have a useful life of 20 years or more [Sec. 167(j)(5); 1.167(j)-6].

NOTE: Historic property that is substantially rehabilitated after 6-30-76 and before 7-1-81 is allowed a 150% (200% in case of residential rental property) declining balance method of depreciation [Sec. 167(o)].

(c) Exceptions. Rules similar to certain exceptions applying when the investment credit was suspended [¶ 2410] (plant facility rule, certain transfers, property acquired from affiliated corporation, and certain property replacing casualty loss property) may apply to property built before 7-24-69 or used depreciable real property [Sec. 167(j)(6); 1.167(j)-1, 1.167(j)-4, 1.167(j)-7].

(d) Change of method. A change in computing depreciation resulting from property qualifying or not qualifying as residential rental property can be made without Revenue Service consent [¶ 2010(b)]. If a change is made, future allowances are based on the asset's unrecovered cost (less salvage, if applicable) and its remaining life. The taxpayer should attach a statement to his return in the year of change [Sec. 1.167(j)-3(c)].

¶ 2018 Depreciation on qualified low-income housing. A taxpayer can elect to depreciate rehabilitation expenditures incurred after 7-24-69 and before 1978 (after 12-31-77 if made under binding contracts entered into before 1-1-78) under the straight line method using a 60-month useful life with no salvage value. Capital expenditures qualify if they are for additions or improvements to property having at least a 5-year useful life and are related to rehabilitating an existing building for low income rental housing. Although the limit on expenditures is $20,000 ($15,000 before 1976) per dwelling unit, total expenditures must exceed $3,000 for each unit over 2 consecutive tax years including the tax year. The rule does not apply to hotels, motels or similar places if over half of the units are rented on a transient basis. The election is made by a statement with the return filed for the first year the special depreciation is used, and with a statement for the returns for such later years [Sec. 167(k); 1.167(k)-1—1.167(k)-4].

NOTE: Excess depreciation on qualified low-income housing may be a tax preference item subject to the minimum tax [¶ 2403]. If the taxpayer elects amortization, he forfeits any investment credit otherwise allowable (¶ 2410) [Sec. 48(a)(8)].

¶ 2019 Depreciation on public utility property. Certain regulated public utilities may be limited to the use of the straight line method. The rules, in effect, "freeze" the utilities' existing depreciation practices to those used on the last return filed before 8-1-69 [Sec. 167(l); 1.167(l)-1]. An election made by 6-29-70 on the method of depreciation for property acquired after 1969 to increase production capacity continues to apply to all future acquisitions of the same type of property [Sec. 1.167(l)-2].

Background and purpose. Certain regulated utilities were shifting to accelerated depreciation methods. In addition, some regulatory agencies required them to reduce their rates ("flow-through") from the resulting tax saving. Other agencies required utilities to set rates as if they had used accelerated method. The combination of accelerated depreciation and flow-through was causing substantial revenue losses to the government.

Normalization method. An alternative to flow-through is the normalization method of accounting. Under this method, the tax savings from accelerated depreciation are set up in a reserve to offset future tax expense when accelerated depreciation runs out. Utilities using a normalization method of accounting can continue to use accelerated depreciation under certain conditions. A Class Life ADR election is also permitted (¶ 2033) [Sec. 1.167(a)-11(b)(6), 1.167(1)-1].

ACCOUNTING FOR DEPRECIATION

Generally, depreciation is accounted for on the books by crediting a depreciation reserve account. The cost or other basis of every depreciable asset is recorded in either a single item or multiple asset account.

¶ **2021 Reserve for depreciation.** Depreciation may be taken care of on the books by reducing the property account, but the usual method and the method preferred by the Revenue Service [Sec. 1.167(a)-7(c)] is to credit a depreciation reserve account.

Example: Oakes owned two storage sheds (Nos. 1 and 2) used in connection with his business, the estimated useful life of which was 10 years. The sheds (exclusive of land) were bought for $20,000 on 1-1-73. No additions or improvements have been made since they were acquired. During 1977, Oakes erected two new sheds for use in his business. No. 3 was completed on 7-1-77 at a cost of $12,000, and No. 4 was completed on 10-1-77 at a cost of $9,000. The new sheds also have an estimated useful life of 10 years. Oakes maintains an account entitled "Storage Sheds—Depreciation Reserve Account." The depreciation for 1977, using the straight line method, would be figured as follows:

$20,000	1 year	$2,000
12,000	6 mos.	600
9,000	3 mos.	225
		$2,825

The entries on the books would indicate the following:

STORAGE SHEDS

Jan. 1	Balance	$20,000
July 1	Shed No. 3 erected	12,000
Oct. 1	Shed No. 4 erected	9,000

STORAGE SHEDS—DEPRECIATION RESERVE

Jan. 1	Balance	$8,000
Dec. 31	Depreciation	2,825

Replacements and repairs. In the above example, the additions were carried directly into the asset account. Improvements are capitalized the same way.

Incidental repairs [¶ 1825] that neither materially add to the value of the property nor appreciably prolong its life, but keep it in an ordinary efficient operating condition, may be deducted as a business or investor's expense. For example, if Oakes spent $25 to repair the roof of Shed No. 1, he could deduct it as a business expense, and it would not appear in the above accounts. Suppose, however, that he spent $500 replacing the foundations of Shed No. 1. That would not be deductible

Footnotes appear at end of this Chapter.

¶ **2021**

as an expense. Instead, the $500 can be either capitalized and depreciated, or charged against the depreciation reserve [Sec. 1.162-4]. The method of handling additions, improvements, alterations and repairs depends to some extent on the type of business and its accounting practices. See also ¶ 2033(f).

¶ 2022 Depreciation property accounts. Depreciable property may be accounted for by treating individual items as an account, or by combining two or more assets in a single account [Sec. 1.167(a)-7].

(a) Item accounts. The cost of each asset is kept separately with the useful life, salvage value and depreciation rate determined individually.

Method and rate. Any reasonable method may be selected for each item of property, but it must be applied consistently until the asset is disposed of or the basis, less salvage, is completely recovered [Sec. 1.167(b)-0(c)]. For retirement of assets, see ¶ 2036(c). The depreciation rate for each asset may be based on the asset's maximum expected useful life or the average useful life of all the assets [Sec. 1.167(a)-8].

(b) Multiple asset accounts. A number of assets with the same or different useful lives may be combined into one account, and a single rate of depreciation used for the entire account. Multiple asset accounts are generally broken down into group, classified, and composite accounts. However, they may be further broken down on the basis of location, acquisition dates, cost, character and use [Sec. 1.167(a)-7(a)]. Any of the assets in an account disposed of at a gain may be treated as a unit to find the Sec. 1245 gain (¶ 1619) [Sec. 1.1245-1(a)(4)]. An "open-end" multiple asset account is one containing the cost of assets acquired in the current year and in prior years.

Group accounts contain assets similar in kind with approximately the same average useful lives.

Composite accounts include assets without regard to their character or useful lives.

Classified accounts consist of assets classified as to use without regard to useful life, such as machinery and equipment, furniture and fixtures, or transportation equipment [Sec. 1.167(a)-7(a)].

Methods and rates. Any reasonable method may be selected for each account, but it must be applied to that account consistently, although it need not be applied to similar property acquired later if these are set up in separate accounts [Sec. 1.167(b)-0(c)]. Under the straight line method, the rate may be based on the maximum expected useful life of the longest-lived asset in the account or on the average expected useful life of the assets in the account. In group accounts, the rate is found from the average of the useful lives of the assets. In classified or composite accounts, the average rate is generally figured by getting one year's depreciation for each item (or each group of similar items) and dividing the total depreciation thus obtained by the assets' cost or other basis [Sec. 1.167(b)-1(b)]. Special rules apply in using the sum of the years-digits method. See ¶ 2013(b). For retirement of assets, see ¶ 2036(c).

Example:

Cost or other basis	Estimated useful life	Annual depreciation
$10,000	5 years	$2,000
10,000	15 years	667
$20,000		$2,667

Based on these facts, the average straight line rate would be
13.33% ($2,667 ÷ $20,000).

Average useful life and rate must be redetermined whenever additions, retirements, or replacements substantially alter the relative proportion of types of assets in the classified or composite account [Sec. 1.167(a)-7(d)].

When a liberalized depreciation method [¶ 2012; 2013; 2015] is used, assets having an estimated useful life of less than 3 years cannot be included in a multiple asset account [Sec. 1.167(c)-1(a)(3)].

Averaging convention methods. The annual allowance may be determined under either one of the averaging convention methods explained below:

Method I: It is assumed all additions and retirements occur uniformly throughout the year. The depreciation rate is applied to the average of the beginning and ending balances in the asset account for the tax year.

Method II: It is assumed (1) all additions and retirements during the first half of the year were made on the first day of the year and (2) all those during the second half of the year were made on the first day of the following year. So, a full year's depreciation is taken on (1) additions in the first half of the year and (2) retirements in the second half of the year. On the other hand, no depreciation is taken on (1) additions in the second half of the year and (2) on retirements in the first half of the year.

An averaging convention method, once chosen, must be consistently followed. A change in an averaging convention method can be made the same way as changing a depreciation method [¶ 2010(b)].[1] But an averaging convention method may not be used in any year in which it substantially distorts the depreciation allowance [Sec. 1.167(a)-10].

¶ 2023   Depreciation records. Depreciation deductions must be recorded on taxpayer's books so that they can be verified. He must be able to justify the deduction [Sec. 1.167(b)-0(a)]. The amount measuring a reasonable depreciation allowance may be deducted directly from an asset's book value. But the preferred method is to credit the amount to a depreciation reserve account. A separate reserve account should be kept for each asset account. Regular books or auxiliary records should show for each account the basis of the property, including adjustments to basis, and depreciation allowances for tax purposes. If the reserves for book purposes do not correspond with reserves for tax purposes, permanent auxiliary records should be kept with the regular books reconciling the differences in depreciation methods, bases, rates, salvage value, etc. Depreciation schedules filed with the return should show the accumulated reserves figured for tax purposes [Sec. 1.167(a)-7(c)]. Generally, these supporting schedules should show cost or other basis, later additions, credits to accounts for retirements and sales, annual depreciation accrual, estimated useful life in years and the rate.

A taxpayer must set up separate depreciation records for assets described in ¶ 2012(a), if he wants to use the liberalized depreciation methods for them.

> **Example:** Alcorn bought 2 identical new machines, one in 1955 and the other in 1977. Separate records for each are required if he wants to use the declining balance method for the 1977 purchase.

For depreciation property accounts, see ¶ 2022. For depreciation reserve under the Class Life ADR system, see ¶ 2033(b).

Footnotes appear at end of this Chapter.

¶ 2023

¶ 2024   Effect of depreciation on earnings and profits. A corporation is considered to use straight line depreciation to figure its earnings and profits for tax years starting after 6-30-72. A similar method that provides for ratable depreciation reductions over the asset's useful life may also be permitted [Sec. 312(k); 1.312-15(a)]. See also ¶ 1701(b). This rule is not intended to affect any available accelerated depreciation methods in figuring taxable income.[1]

USEFUL LIFE AND OBSOLESCENCE

An asset is depreciated over the period of its useful life. This may be determined on the basis of the taxpayer's own operating conditions and experience or general experience in the industry. Alternatively the taxpayer may elect the Class Life ADR system which permits the taxpayer to select a useful life from a designated range of years.

¶ 2032   Useful life of depreciable property. Useful life is the period over which the asset is expected to be of service to the taxpayer. Some of the factors to be considered in determining useful life are: (1) wear and tear and decay or decline from natural causes; (2) normal progress of the arts, economic changes, inventions and current developments; (3) climatic and other local conditions; (4) taxpayer's policy on repairs, renewals and replacements. Salvage value is not a factor. Estimated useful life can be redetermined only when the change in the useful life is significant and there is a clear and convincing basis for redetermination [Sec. 1.167(a)-1(b)]. For agreement on useful life with the Revenue Service, see ¶ 2010(c).

Patents and copyrights. A patent term in the U.S. is 17 years. Copyrights run 28 years from first publication date. They may be renewed, under certain conditions, for another 28 years.[1] If a patent or copyright becomes obsolete in any year before its expiration, the unrecovered cost or other basis may be deducted in that year [Sec. 1.167(a)-6(a)].

Stepped-up use of property. Changing conditions may warrant changes in the amount deducted for depreciation. For instance, accelerated property use may warrant a greater deduction than in a year of normal use.[2] Changes in the amount deducted from year to year, however, must be based on the facts of the property use and should not be made merely because, for another reason, the taxpayer has more or less than normal income.

Taxpayers claiming abnormal depreciation must give detailed information about the assets. Mere proof of accelerated use is not enough. Taxpayer must prove that the useful life of the property was shortened.[3]

If there is a decrease in the estimated useful life of the property due to conditions *other than wear and tear,* the annual depreciation deduction may be increased by an allowance for obsolescence. See ¶ 2034.

¶ 2033   Class Life Asset Depreciation Range system. The Class Life Asset Depreciation Range (ADR) system allows taxpayers to take as a reasonable allowance for depreciation an amount based on any period of years selected by them within a range specified for designated classes of assets [Sec. 167(m)(1)]. Once the period is selected, the taxpayer determines his depreciation allowance under one of the methods permitted [¶ 2010 et seq.].

Background and purpose. The key to the Class Life ADR system is the lower useful life. It is designed to minimize disputes between the taxpayer and the Revenue Service as to the useful life of property, salvage value, repairs and the like. The Class Life system was established by the 1971 Revenue Act. It combined the ADR

(Asset Depreciation Range) system initially set up by Regulations in 1971 and the 1962 Guideline system. This system applies to assets placed in service after 1970.

(a) Asset depreciation ranges. The Class Life ADR system allows taxpayers to choose from a range of depreciation lives that are not more than 20% shorter nor 20% longer than the prior guideline lives. The lower and upper limits of each range are rounded to the nearest half year. The taxpayer must specify in the election the asset depreciation period chosen for the assets in each account. If the Revenue Service lengthens an asset depreciation range during a year, a taxpayer may choose a depreciation period from the old range for asset acquisitions in that year [Sec. 1.167(a)-11(b)(4)].

>   NOTE: Rev. Proc. 77-10 includes a table that sets forth the asset guideline classes, asset guideline periods and asset depreciation ranges, as well as the asset guideline class repair allowance percentages [(g) below].[1]

Guideline class. An asset is classified according to its primary use. The classification is not changed because of a change in primary use after the tax year. An incorrect classification does not void the election. However, all necessary adjustments must be made to correct the unadjusted and adjusted basis, the salvage value and depreciation reserve of vintage accounts and the allowable depreciation for all tax years involved [Sec. 1.167(a)-11(b)(4)(iii)].

Annual election. The taxpayer must elect the Class Life ADR system. It is made on Form 4832 and filed with the return for the year the assets are placed in service. If the taxpayer does not file a timely return, the election must be filed when the first return for the tax year is filed. The election may be made on an amended return only if it is filed no later than the due date of the return. While the election is a method of accounting, Revenue Service consent is considered granted (¶ 2708) [Sec. 167(m)(3); 1.167(a)-11].

Once the election is made for a year, the taxpayer must write off all depreciable assets falling within a particular Guideline Class and placed in service during the year under the Class Life ADR system only. The taxpayer must use the straight line, sum of the years-digits or declining balance methods within the ADR system. However, the taxpayer can use another method [¶ 2015] excluding certain property from the election if this property has an unadjusted basis of 75% or more of the unadjusted basis of all eligible property first placed in service in the tax year in the same class. Unless those methods under the ADR election are used, a change of method usually requires Revenue Service consent. See ¶ 2010(b).

(b) Vintage account. A vintage account contains assets to which the taxpayer elects to apply Class Life ADR system, first placed in service during the year of the election [Sec. 1.167(a)-11(b)(3)]. In other words, the vintage of an account is the tax year during which assets in the account are first placed in service by the taxpayer. The account includes an asset or a group of assets within a single guideline class. The taxpayer must use the same depreciation method for all assets in a single vintage account [Sec. 1.167(a)-11(c)(1)(iv)]. But different depreciation methods can be used for each separate vintage account for the same year [¶ 2010]. A taxpayer can set up any number of vintage accounts for a particular year. More than one account for the same vintage may be set up for different assets of the same guideline class. Separate vintage accounts must be set up in some cases [Sec. 1.167(a)-11(b)(3)(ii)]. For example, used property cannot be in the same account with new property. In the same way, property that qualifies for additional first-year depreciation [¶ 2016] or 10% reduction in salvage value [¶ 2005] cannot be in the same vintage account with property that does not qualify. If additional first-

Footnotes appear at end of this Chapter.

¶ 2033

year depreciation is deducted, the amount of the deduction is subtracted from the asset cost before computing depreciation.[2]

Example 1: In 1977, Daniel Corporation, a furniture manufacturer, bought and placed in service the following equipment:

	Cost
Machine A	$10,000
Machine B	10,000
Machine C	20,000
Special Machine D	36,000

Daniel Corporation elects the Class Life ADR system, so there is an 8-to-12 year depreciation range (Asset Guideline Class 24.4; see (g) below). Some of the choices available to the corporation are: (1) to put all the machines in one vintage account for 1977 and give an 8-year life to the account; (2) to put Machines A, B and C in one vintage account and Special Machine D in a separate account; (3) to put Machines A and B in one account, Machine C in another, and Machine D in a third; or (4) to set up separate accounts for each of the machines. In (2), (3) and (4), the taxpayer can assign different lives (within the ADR range) for the different accounts.

Example 2: Assume that in Example 1 above, Daniel Corporation makes choice (3) and chooses a different depreciation method for each account. Assuming an 8-year life under Class Life ADR, the depreciation for 1977 is as follows:

	Cost	Depreciation Method	Depreciation
Machines A & B	$20,000	Straight line	$2,500
Machine C	20,000	Declining bal.	5,000
Machine D	36,000	Sum of years-digits	8,000

Note that salvage value is disregarded for the straight line and the sum of the years-digits methods as well as the declining balance method [see (e) below].

Depreciation reserve. The taxpayer must set up a depreciation reserve for each vintage account. The amount of reserve must be stated on the return on which depreciation for the amount is determined. The depreciation deduction for a tax year cannot exceed the amount by which the unadjusted basis of the account (the total cost or other basis of the assets in the account) exceeds the depreciation reserve plus the salvage value of the account. The reserve for an account is the accumulated depreciation adjusted for retirements, reduction of the salvage value, transfers to supplies and scrap, and property amortized under special provisions and removed from the account. In any case, the reserve cannot be reduced below zero [Sec. 1.167(a)-11(c)(1)].

(c) Property eligible for Class Life ADR treatment. The Class Life ADR system generally applies to all types of tangible property if: (1) an asset guideline class and asset guideline period is in effect for the property for the election year; (2) the property is placed in service by the taxpayer after 1970; and (3) it is Sec. 1245 or Sec. 1250 property. However, the taxpayer who elects the ADR system may exclude from the election the following types of property: (1) certain used property (see below); (2) certain property subject to the investment credit; (3) certain property subject to special methods of depreciation or amortization; and (4) certain subsidiary assets (such as jigs, dies, returnable containers, etc.) placed in service before 1974 [Sec. 1.167(a)-11(b)].

NOTE: The Class Life System was to apply to real estate after 1973. However, depreciable realty has been exempted from the ADR system until new class lives have been set for this property. Taxpayers electing ADR may continue to use shorter lives for their real estate acquisitions if justified under the old Guideline rules as in effect on 12-31-70, or on the basis of facts and circumstances.[3]

Used property. The Class Life ADR system applies to both new and used equipment placed in service in the year. However, if the cost of the used property is more than 10% of the total cost of the new and used eligible property placed in service during the year, the taxpayer can exclude all (but not less than all) used property from ADR treatment [Sec. 1.167(a)-11(b)(5)(iii)].

(d) When asset is placed in service. The taxpayer who elects the Class Life ADR system determines when the asset is placed in service by using either the *half-year convention* or the *modified half-year convention.* Under the half-year convention, the taxpayer treats all assets placed in service during the year as placed in service at the midpoint of the year. Under the modified half-year convention, the taxpayer treats each asset put in service during the first half of a tax year as placed in service on the first day of that tax year, and each asset placed in service in the last half of the tax year as placed in service on the first day of the *following* tax year. The same convention must be elected for all vintage accounts established during the year. However, a different convention may be elected for the accounts in later years [Sec. 167(m)(2); 1.167(a)-11(c)(2)].

> **Example 3:** Kurth Corp. keeps its books on a calendar year basis. During the year, it buys two machines, placing Machine A in service on 3-15-77 and Machine B in service on 10-15-77. Under the half-year convention, both machines are treated as placed in service on 7-1-77. Under the modified half-year convention, Machine A is treated as placed in service on 1-1-77 and Machine B as placed in service on 1-1-78.

> **Example 4:** Assume the same facts as in Example 3, except that the corporation keeps its books on a fiscal year basis beginning September 1. Under the half-year convention, Machine A would be treated as placed in service on 3-1-77 and Machine B as placed in service on 3-1-78 (the midpoints of the corporation's respective fiscal years). Under the modified half-year convention, both machines would be treated as placed in service on 9-1-77 (Machine A was placed in service in the last half of the '76-'77 tax year, and Machine B was placed in service in the first half of the '77-'78 tax year).

(e) Salvage value. Under the Class Life ADR system, the taxpayer can disregard salvage value completely even though it exceeds 10% of the cost [¶ 2005]. But in no case can a vintage account be depreciated below a reasonable salvage value. The taxpayer must keep sufficient records of the facts relevant to his estimate. The Revenue Service will not change the taxpayer's estimate unless (1) the estimate turns out to exceed the true salvage value by more than 10% of the unadjusted basis of the account at the end of the tax year in which the account is set up, or (2) the taxpayer follows the practice of understating his estimates to take advantage of this provision [Sec. 1.167(a)-11].

> **Example 5:** Kane elects ADR and places assets A and B with a total unadjusted basis of $80,000 in a multiple asset vintage account. He estimates the gross salvage value to be $55,000 and sets up a salvage value of $47,000 for the account (the assets qualify for the 10% salvage reduction). Kane has not followed a practice of understating his estimates, but true salvage value is $52,000 (after 10% reduction). Since the $47,000 value is within the 10% range ($8,000), it will not be redetermined.

> **Example 6:** Assume the same facts as in Example 4, except that Kane sets up a salvage value of $42,000 for the account. Since the $42,000 value is not within the 10% range ($52,000 is more than $8,000 greater than $42,000), the salvage value will be adjusted.

(f) Repairs. The taxpayer can elect a simplified procedure to determine if an outlay with respect to property eligible for Class Life ADR treatment is a currently deductible repair or is a capital improvement subject to depreciation [Sec. 263(f); 1.263(f)-1]. When the expenditures have characteristics of both deductible expenses and capital expenditures, a repair allowance can be currently deducted for the taxpayer's expenses with respect to his assets in any of the guideline classes listed in Rev. Proc. 77-10.[1] However, a taxpayer cannot deduct a repair allowance

¶ 2033

for capital expenditures, such as those for an additional unit or those that substantially increase production or change the property's use. The increase must be more than 25% to be considered substantial. Property acquired before 1971 is eligible for repair allowance treatment, but the allowance can be elected only if the taxpayer elects Class Life ADR in a tax year after 1970 [Sec. 1.167(a)-11(d)(2)].

The repair allowance for a tax year is the result of multiplying the appropriate repair allowance percentage by the average of the unadjusted basis of the taxpayer's property in any guideline class (less retirements) at the beginning and at the end of the tax year. The repair allowances percentage for each guideline class is listed in Rev. Proc. 77-10[1] (see (g) below) [Sec. 1.167(a)-11(d)(2)(iii)]. Thus, if a taxpayer has repair, maintenance, rehabilitation or improvement expenses for property eligible for the repair allowance, he can (1) elect the allowance for one or more of the guideline classes and treat the amount of his expenses that does not exceed the repair allowance as deductible repairs (any excess is included in a special basis vintage account [Sec. 1.167(a)-11(d)(2)(viii)]) or (2) take a deduction for those expenses he can prove are entitled to a current deduction.

Example 7: Daniel Corporation elects repair allowance treatment for tax year 1977. The corporation has machinery and equipment used in the sugar business in asset guideline class 20.2 under Rev. Proc. 77-10 [(g) below] with an average unadjusted basis of $100,000, and machinery used in the manufacture of furniture in asset guideline class 24.4 with an average unadjusted basis of $300,000. The repair allowance percentage for asset guideline class 20.2 is 4.5% and for asset guideline class 24.4 is 6.5%. The two asset guideline class repair allowances for 1977 are $4,500 and $19,500, respectively, determined as follows:

Asset Guideline Class 20.2
$100,000 average unadjusted basis multiplied by 4.5% .... $ 4,500
Asset Guideline Class 24.4
$300,000 average unadjusted basis multiplied by 6.5% $19,500

The election of the repair allowance is an annual election. A taxpayer can make the election for one guideline class and not for another, and the election can be changed from year to year in the same guideline class. The taxpayer must keep books and records sufficient to identify the amount and nature of the expenses as to the property in the various guideline classes [Sec. 1.167(a)-11(d)(2)].

(g) Class Life ADR table. The table on the following pages sets forth the asset guideline classes, asset guideline periods, asset depreciation ranges [(a) above], and asset guideline class repair allowance percentages [(f) above].

[Table appears on page 2027-2030]

Chapter 10—Deductions—Depreciation

Asset Guideline Class	Description of Assets	Asset Depreciation Range (in years) Lower limit	Asset Guideline Period	Upper limit	Annual Asset Guideline Repair Allowance Percentage
Specific Depreciable Assets Used in All Business Activities, Except as Noted:					
00.11	Office Furniture, Fixtures, and Equipment	8	10	12	2
00.12	Information Systems (computers and their peripheral equipment)	5	6	7	7.5
00.13	Data Handling Equipment, except Computers	5	6	7	15
00.21	Airplanes (except commercial or charter) and helicopters	5	6	7	14
00.22	Automobiles, Taxis	2.5	3	3.5	16.5
00.23	Buses	7	9	11	11.5
00.241	Light General Purpose Trucks	3	4	5	16.5
00.242	Heavy General Purpose Trucks	5	6	7	10
00.25	Railroad Cars and Locomotives	12	15	18	8
00.26	Tractor Units For Use Over-The-Road	3	4	5	16.5
00.27	Trailers and Trailer-Mounted Containers	5	6	7	10
00.28	Vessels, Barges, Tugs	14.5	18	21.5	6
00.3	Land Improvements	—	20	—	—
00.4	Industrial Steam and Electric Generation and/or Distribution Systems	22.5	28	33.5	2.5
Depreciable Assets Used in the Following Activities:					
01.1	Agriculture (includes machinery and equipment, grain bins, and fences)	8	10	12	11
01.11	Cotton Ginning Assets	9.5	12	14.5	5.5
01.21	Cattle, Breeding or Dairy	5.5	7	8.5	—
01.22	Horses, Breeding or Work	8	10	12	—
01.23	Hogs, Breeding	2.5	3	3.5	—
01.24	Sheep and Goats, Breeding	4	5	6	—
01.3	Farm Buildings	20	25	30	5
10.0	Mining	8	10	12	6.5
13.1	Drilling of Oil and Gas Wells	5	6	7	10
13.2	Exploration for and Production of Petroleum and Natural Gas Deposits	11	14	17	4.5
13.3	Petroleum Refining	13	16	19	7
13.4	Marketing of Petroleum and Petroleum Products	13	16	19	4
15.1	Contract Construction Other than Marine	4	5	6	12.5
15.2	Marine Contract Construction	9.5	12	14.5	5
20.1	Manufacture of Grain and Grain Mill Products	13.5	17	20.5	6
20.2	Manufacture of Sugar and Sugar Products	14.5	18	21.5	4.5
20.3	Manufacture of Vegetable Oils and Related Products	14.5	18	21.5	3.5
20.4	Manufacture of Other Food and Kindred Products	9.5	12	14.5	5.5
20.5	Manufacture of Food and Beverages-Special Handling Devices	3	4	5	20
21.0	Manufacture of Tobacco and Tobacco Products	12	15	18	5
22.1	Manufacture of Knitted Goods	6	7.5	9	7
22.2	Manufacture of Yarn, Thread, and Woven Fabric	9	11	13	16

Footnotes appear at end of this Chapter.

¶ 2033

Asset Guideline Class	Description of Assets	Asset Depreciation Range (in years) Lower limit	Asset Guideline Period	Upper limit	Annual Asset Guideline Repair Allowance Percentage
22.3	Manufacture of Carpets, and Dyeing, Finishing, and Packaging of Textile Products	7	9	11	15
22.4	Manufacture of Textured Yarns	6.5	8	9.5	7
22.5	Manufacture of Nonwoven Fabrics	8	10	12	15
23.0	Manufacture of Apparel and Other Finished Products	7	9	11	7
24.1	Cutting of Timber	5	6	7	10
24.2	Sawing of Dimensional Stock from Logs (permanent sawmills)	8	10	12	6.5
24.3	Sawing of Dimensional Stock from Logs (temporary facilities)	5	6	7	10
24.4	Manufacture of Wood Products, and Furniture	8	10	12	6.5
26.1	Manufacture of Pulp and Paper	10.5	13	15.5	10
26.2	Manufacture of Converted Paper, Paperboard, and Pulp Products	8	10	12	15
27.0	Printing, Publishing, and Allied Industries	9	11	13	5.5
28.0	Manufacture of Chemicals and Allied Products	9	11	13	5.5
30.1	Manufacture of Rubber Products	11	14	17	5
30.11	Manufacture of Rubber Products—Special Tools and Devices	3	4	5	—
30.2	Manufacture of Finished Plastic Products	9	11	13	5.5
30.21	Manufacture of Finished Plastic Products—Special Tools	3	3.5	4	5.5
31.0	Manufacture of Leather and Leather Products	9	11	13	5.5
32.1	Manufacture of Glass Products	11	14	17	12
32.11	Manufacture of Glass Products—Special Tools	2	2.5	3	10
32.2	Manufacture of Cement	16	20	24	3
32.3	Manufacture of Other Stone and Clay Products	12	15	18	4.5
33.1	Manufacture of Primary Ferrous Metals	14.5	18	21.5	8
33.11	Manufacture of Primary Ferrous Metals—Special Tools	5	6.5	8	4
33.2	Manufacture of Primary Nonferrous Metals	11	14	17	4.5
33.21	Manufacture of Primary Nonferrous Metals—Special Tools	5	6.5	8	4
34.0	Manufacture of Fabricated Metal Products	9.5	12	14.5	6
34.01	Manufacture of Fabricated Metal Products—Special Tools	2.5	3	3.5	3.5
35.1	Manufacture of Metalworking Machinery	9.5	12	14.5	5.5
35.11	Manufacture of Metalworking Machinery—Special Tools	5	6	7	12.5
35.2	Manufacture of Other Machines	9.5	12	14.5	5.5
35.21	Manufacture of Other Machines—Special Tools	5	6.5	8	12.5
36.1	Manufacture of Electrical Equipment	9.5	12	14.5	5.5
36.11	Manufacture of Electrical Equipment—Special Tools	4	5	6	—
36.2	Manufacture of Electronic Products	6.5	8	9.5	7.5
37.11	Manufacture of Motor Vehicles	9.5	12	14.5	9.5

Chapter 10—Deductions—Depreciation

Asset Guideline Class	Description of Assets	Asset Depreciation Range (in years) Lower limit	Asset Guideline Period	Upper limit	Annual Asset Guideline Repair Allowance Percentage
37.12	Manufacture of Motor Vehicles—Special Tools	2.5	3	3.5	12.5
37.2	Manufacture of Aerospace Products	8	10	12	7.5
37.31	Ship and Boat Building Machinery and Equipment	9.5	12	14.5	8.5
37.32	Ship and Boat Building Dry Docks and Land Improvements	13	16	19	2.5
37.33	Ship and Boat Building—Special Tools	5	6.5	8	0.5
37.41	Manufacture of Locomotives	9	11.5	14	7.5
37.42	Manufacture of Railroad Cars	9.5	12	14.5	5.5
38.0	Manufacture of Professional, Scientific, and Controlling Instruments; Photographic and Optical Goods; Watches and Clocks	9.5	12	14.5	5.5
39.0	Manufacture of Athletic, Jewelry and Other Goods	9.5	12	14.5	5.5
	Railroad Transportation:				
40.1	Railroad Machinery and Equipment	11	14	17	10.5
40.2	Railroad Structures and Similar Improvements	24	30	36	5
40.3	Railroad Wharves and Docks	16	20	24	5.5
40.51	Railroad Hydraulic Electric Generating Equipment	40	50	60	1.5
40.52	Railroad Nuclear Electric Generating Equipment	16	20	24	3
40.53	Railroad Steam Electric Generating Equipment	22.5	28	33.5	2.5
40.54	Railroad Steam, Compressed Air, and Other Power Plant Equipment	22.5	28	33.5	7.5
41.0	Motor Transport-Passengers	6.5	8	9.5	11.5
42.0	Motor Transport-Freight	6.5	8	9.5	11
44.0	Water Transportation	16	20	24	8
45.0	Air Transport	9.5	12	14.5	15
45.1	Air Transport (restricted)	5	6	7	15
46.0	Pipeline Transportation	17.5	22	26.5	3
	Telephone Communications:				
48.11	Telephone Central Office Buildings	36	45	54	1.5
48.12	Telephone Central Office Equipment	16	20	24	6
48.13	Telephone Station Equipment	8	10	12	10
48.14	Telephone Distribution Plant	28	35	42	2
48.2	Radio and Television Broadcastings	5	6	7	10
	Telegraph, Ocean Cable, and Satellite Communications (TOCSC):				
48.31	TOCSC-Electric Power Generating and Distribution Systems	15	19	23	—
48.32	TOCSC-High Frequency Radio and Microwave Systems	10.5	13	15.5	—
48.33	TOCSC-Cable and Long-line Systems	21	26.5	32	—
48.34	TOCSC-Central Office Control Equipment	13	16.5	20	—
48.35	TOCSC-Computerized Switching, Channeling, and Associated Control Equipment	8.5	10.5	12.5	—

Footnotes appear at end of this Chapter.

Chapter 10—Deductions—Depreciation

Asset Guideline Class	Description of Assets	Lower limit	Asset Guideline Period	Upper limit	Annual Asset Guideline Repair Allowance Percentage
48.36	TOCSC-Satellite Ground Segment Property	8	10	12	—
48.37	TOCSC-Satellite Space Segment Property	6.5	8	9.5	—
48.38	TOCSC-Equipment Installed on Customer's Premises	8	10	12	—
48.39	TOCSC-Support and Service Equipment	11	13.5	16	—
	Cable Television (CATV):				
48.41	CATV-Headend	9	11	13	5
48.42	CATV-Subscriber Connection and Distribution Systems	8	10	12	5
48.43	CATV-Program Origination	7	9	11	9
48.44	CATV-Service and Test	7	8.5	10	2.5
48.45	CATV-Microwave Systems	7.5	9.5	11.5	2
	Electric, Gas, Water and Steam, Utility Services:				
49.11	Electric Utility Hydraulic Production Plant	40	50	60	1.5
49.12	Electric Utility Nuclear Production Plant	16	20	24	3
49.121	Electric Utility Nuclear Fuel Assemblies	4	5	6	—
49.13	Electric Utility Steam Production Plant	22.5	28	33.5	5
49.14	Electric Utility Transmission and Distribution Plant	24	30	36	4.5
49.15	Electric Utility Combustion Turbine Production Plant	16	20	24	4
49.21	Gas Utility Distribution Facilities	28	35	42	2
49.221	Gas Utility Manufactured Gas Production Plants	24	30	36	2
49.222	Gas Utility Substitute Natural Gas Production Plant	11	14	17	4.5
49.223	Substitute Natural Gas—Coal Gasification	14.5	18	21.5	15
49.23	Natural Gas Production Plant	11	14	17	4.5
49.24	Gas Utility Trunk Pipelines and Related Storage Facilities	17.5	22	26.5	3
49.25	Liquefied Natural Gas Plant	17.5	22	26.5	4.5
49.3	Water Utilities	40	50	60	1.5
49.4	Central Steam Utility Production and Distribution	22.5	28	33.5	2.5
50.0	Wholesale and Retail Trade	8	10	12	6.5
50.1	Wholesale and Retail Trade Service Assets	2	2.5	3	—
70.2	Personal and Professional Services	8	10	12	6.5
70.21	Personal and Professional Services Service Assets	2	2.5	3	—
79.0	Recreation	8	10	12	6.5
80.0	Theme and Amusement Parks	10	12.5	15	12.5

¶ **2034 Obsolescence.** Obsolescence may make an asset economically useless to the taxpayer regardless of its physical condition. It is caused by many conditons, including technological improvements and reasonably foreseeable economic changes. Among these causes are normal progress of the arts and sciences, supersession or inadequacy caused by developments in the industry, products, methods, markets, sources of supply, and like changes, and legislative and regulatory actions.

Ordinarily, the depreciation deduction includes an allowance for normal obsolescence. However, if the taxpayer shows that the estimated useful life will be shortened by obsolescence greater than that originally considered in determining useful life, a change to a shorter life will be allowed with depreciation computed over the shorter life [Sec. 1.167(a)-9].

Generally, obsolescence is limited to relatively few years. A taxpayer's opinion that his property will be obsolete in, say, 10 years, will not warrant the deduction.[1] He might have to wait for another 7 years for events to justify his opinion and enable him to prove an obsolescence claim with reasonable certainty. The property's remaining cost would then be recoverable over the three years left, through a deduction for depreciation including obsolescence. For obsolescence of nondepreciable property, see ¶ 2210. For treatment of demolition of buildings, see ¶ 2209.

RETIREMENT

Retirement of an asset means that it is permanently withdrawn from use in a trade or business or in the production of income. This may happen by sale or exchange, by abandonment, or by placing the depreciable asset in a supplies or scrap account. The tax results of a retirement depend on the form of the transaction, the reason for it, the timing of the retirement, the estimated useful life used in figuring depreciation, and whether multiple or item accounts are used. Special rules apply to retirements from a vintage account.

¶ 2036 Gain or loss on retirement of assets. Here are the rules [Sec. 1.167(a)-8]:

(a) Sale or exchange. If the asset is sold or exchanged the ordinary rules for recognition of gains or losses apply [¶ 1400 et seq.].

(b) Abandonment. Here, recognized loss is the difference between the adjusted basis of the asset when it is abandoned and its salvage value.

(c) Other disposition. If the asset is not disposed of by sale or exchange or abandoned (for example, if it is transferred to a supplies or scrap account), no gain is recognized. Loss may or may not be recognized, depending on whether the retirement is normal or abnormal.

Difference between abnormal and normal retirement. Generally, a retirement is considered normal unless the withdrawal is due to a cause not contemplated in setting the depreciation rate. For example, a retirement is normal if it is made within the range of years used in fixing the rate, and the asset has reached a condition at which the taxpayer customarily retires assets. It may be abnormal, if it is withdrawn at an earlier time, or under other conditions, for example, when damaged by casualty or when suddenly made useless by extraordinary obsolescence [Sec. 1.167(a)-8(b)].

Recognition of loss on abnormal retirement. Loss is recognized equal to the excess of the adjusted basis at the time of retirement over the greater of (a) salvage value or (b) fair market value at the time of retirement.

Recognition of loss on normal retirement. Different rules apply to multiple asset accounts and to item accounts [¶ 2022].

Multiple asset accounts. If the depreciation rate is based on the maximum expected life of the longest-lived asset in the account, the loss as figured for abnormal retirement (above) is recognized. If the rate is based on average life, no loss is recognized since the use of this rate assumes that some assets will be retired before and others after the expiration of the average life [Sec. 1.167(a)-8(a); 1.167(a)-8(e)]. In that case, the full cost of the asset, reduced by salvage is charged to the depreciation reserve [Sec. 1.167(a)-8(e)]. A change in the treatment of salvage proceeds from the retirement of assets can be made the same way as changing a depreciation method [¶ 2010(b)]. But such a change must be made for all the items in the account.[1]

Item accounts. If the rate is based on average useful life, and taxpayer has a large number of assets, no loss is recognized. If there are a few assets, the loss as figured for abnormal retirement above will be recognized only if the use of average life does not substantially disort income. Generally this would apply when the assets cover a relatively narrow range of lives [Sec. 1.167(a)-8(d)].

When no loss is recognized, the taxpayer may (from the time of retirement) take an annual deduction equal to the unrecovered cost (less salvage, if applicable) divided by the average expected life. For example, if an asset that was depreciated at an average rate of 10 years is retired after 6 years, the unrecovered cost less salvage (if applicable) would be amortized over 10 years from the time of retirement [Sec. 1.167(a)-8(e)].

For basis of retired assets, see ¶ 2037. For retirement from a vintage account, see ¶ 2038.

¶ 2037   Basis of retired assets. The basis for figuring gain or loss on retirement of assets [¶ 2036] is the adjusted basis for determining gain or loss on a sale [¶ 1500 et seq.] with the following modifications for multiple asset accounts (¶ 2022(b)) [Sec. 1.167(a)-8(c)]:

(1) If an asset is *normally* retired and the rate is based on average life, the "adjusted basis" of the retired asset is the salvage value.

(2) If an asset is *normally* retired and the rate was based on the maximum expected life of the longest lived asset in the account, the depreciation adjustment [¶ 1500] for the retired asset is figured as if the asset were depreciated in a single asset account using the maximum expected useful life of the asset.

(3) If an asset is *abnormally* retired, the depreciation adjustment for the retired asset is figured as if the asset were depreciated in a single item account using a rate based on either (a) average expected useful life or (b) maximum expected useful life of the asset, itself, depending on the method used in determining the rate for the multiple asset account.

¶ 2038   Retirement from vintage accounts. Under the Class Life ADR system, the recognition of gain or loss when an asset is retired from a vintage account depends on whether the retirement is ordinary or extraordinary.

Difference between extraordinary and ordinary retirement. A retirement is extraordinary if the asset is Sec. 1245 property that is retired as a direct result of: (1) casualty (for example, fire, storm, shipwreck), and the taxpayer consistently treats these retirements as extraordinary; or (2) termination, curtailment or sale of a business, manufacturing, or income-producing operation or unit if the unadjusted basis of the assets retired from the account in the tax year exceeds 20% of the account's unadjusted basis immediately before the event. Here all accounts are treated as a single vintage account if they contain property with the same vintage and asset guideline class. A retirement is also extraordinary if it is Sec. 1250 property. All other retirements (such as a sale or physical abandonment) are ordinary [Sec. 1.167(a)-11(d)(3)(ii)].

Note: The taxpayer would adopt the same convention for the extraordinary retirements from a vintage account as he does the depreciation allowances from that account (¶ 2033(d)) [Sec. 1.167(a)-11(c)(2)].

(a) Recognition of gain. Gain is recognized on an extraordinary retirement in the tax year the asset is retired (unless it is a tax-free transaction). Unlike an ordinary retirement, the asset's unadjusted basis is removed from the account's unadjusted basis, and the depreciation reserve is reduced by the depreciation allowable for the retired asset [Sec. 1.167(a)-11(d)(3)(iv)].

Gain may or may not be recognized on an ordinary retirement. In any case, all proceeds from ordinary retirements are added to the account's depreciation reserve and reduce total depreciation. Gain is recognized to the extent the reserve at the end of the year exceeds the account's unadjusted basis [Sec. 1.167(a)-11(d)(3)(iii)].

> **Example:** Wein's vintage account shows an unadjusted basis of $1,000 and a depreciation reserve of $700. During the tax year, he received $500 from the sale of the assets in the account. Wein must add $500 to the reserve, thus increasing it to $1,200. Gain is recognized to the extent of $200 (difference between $1,200 and the $1,000 basis).

The gain is recaptured and treated as ordinary income to the extent of the total depreciation allowances in the reserve that were not previously recaptured [¶ 1618-1619]. The depreciation reserve is reduced by the amount of the gain so that after the reduction, the reserve is equal to the account's unadjusted basis, and there is no depreciation allowable for the tax year [Sec. 1.167(a)-11(d)(3)(ix)].

(b) Recognition of loss. No loss is recognized on an ordinary retirement. However, loss is recognized in the tax year an extraordinary retirement occurs (except in a tax-free transaction) [Sec. 1.167(a)-11(d)(3)(iii), (iv)].

(c) Salvage value. A taxpayer may reduce the salvage value for the account by the amount of salvage value attributable to the retired asset, or he may elect the Class Life ADR system without reducing the salvage value for a vintage account. If the depreciation reserve unadjusted for retirements during the year exceeds the account's unadjusted basis minus salvage value, the salvage value for the account is reduced (but not below zero) as of the start of the tax year [Sec. 1.167(a)-11(d)(3)].

SPECIAL AMORTIZATION

Certain facilities and other properties having an important national interest may be amortized over a 60-month period, regardless of useful life. The amortization taken in place of depreciation usually results in faster write-offs.

¶ 2040 Amortization of pollution control facilities. A taxpayer can elect to amortize (in place of depreciation) a *certified pollution control facility* over a 60-month period. The amortization may begin the month after the facility is completed or acquired, or in the following tax year. It applies only to new facilities placed in service in plants (or other properties) in existence before 1-1-76 [Sec. 169].

> **NOTE:** An investment credit of 50% is allowed on the amortizable basis (see (a) below) of qualified pollution control facilities acquired or built in tax years starting after 1976 that have a useful life not less than 5 years [Sec. 46(c)(5)].

(a) Basis for amortization. The 60-month amortization is allowed only for the proportion of the facility's cost attributable to the first 15 years of its normal useful life. If a facility's useful life exceeds 15 years, it is treated as two separate facilities. One facility (representing the cost attributable to the first 15 years of useful life) gets the amortization. Regular depreciation is allowed for the other facility (the remaining cost) based on the facility's entire useful life [Sec. 169(f); 1.169-3].

NOTE: Any gain on the sale or other disposition is subject to the recapture rules [¶ 1619(a)]. Gain is recaptured to the extent of the total amortization deductions [Sec. 1245(a)]. The amortization deduction for the entire year above accelerated depreciation methods that would otherwise be allowable is a tax preference item subject to the minimum tax (¶ 2403) [Sec. 57(a)(4)].

(b) How to make the election. The election is available for any tax year ending after 12-31-68 in which the facility is completed or acquired, or the next tax year. It is made by attaching a statement to the return giving the necessary information [Sec. 1.169-4].

¶ 2041 Amortization of railroad grading and tunnel bores and railroad rolling stock. Railroads can elect to amortize qualified railroad grading and tunnel bores over a 50-year period. The amortization is in lieu of other amortization and depreciation deductions for that property. Election is made by filing a statement attached to the return [Sec. 185; 1.185-1—1.185-3; Temp. Reg. 13.0].[1]

Railroads can also elect to amortize qualified rolling stock placed in service after 1969 and before 1976. Stock is generally written off over a 60-month period, but if placed in service during 1969, it may be amortized over a 48-month period to the extent of costs unrecovered as of 1-1-70. The deduction is in place of regular depreciation [Sec. 184; Temp. Reg. Sec. 13.0].[1]

NOTE: If amortization is elected, no investment credit is allowed (¶ 2410) [Sec. 48(a), 185(h)]. Amortization above the depreciation that would otherwise be allowable is a tax preference item (¶ 2403) [Sec. 57(a)(5)].

¶ 2042 Amortization of real property construction period interest and taxes. Construction period interest and taxes (excluding carrying charges [¶ 1528]) incurred by individuals and Subchapter S corporations on property held for business or investment purposes must be capitalized in the year in which paid or incurred and amortized over a 10-year period. Part of the amount capitalized may be deducted for the tax year in which paid or incurred. The balance must be amortized over the remaining years in the amortization period starting with the year in which the property is ready to be placed in service or is ready to be held for sale [Sec. 189].

(a) Amortization period. Separate rules apply to nonresidential real estate (amortization applies only to property when construction begins after 12-31-75) (see NOTE below), residential real estate (amortization applies only to interest and taxes paid or accrued after 12-31-77) and government subsidized low-income housing (amortization applies only to interest and taxes paid or accrued after 12-31-81). The length of the amortization periods for the three types of property are to be phased in over three separate 7-year periods. It will be 4 years (25% per year; but see Note below) for interest and taxes paid or accrued in the first year to which these rules apply, and increases by one year for each succeeding year after initial effective dates until the amortization period becomes 10 years (10% per year).

NOTE: For nonresidential real property for 1976 only, the amount that could be deducted currently was 50% (instead of 25%) and the remaining 50% was to be amortized over a 3-year period beginning in the year the property is ready to be placed in service or is ready for sale.

(b) Sales or exchanges. For a sale or exchange, the unamortized balance of the construction period interest and taxes is to be added to the property's basis to determine gain or loss. For a nontaxable transfer or exchange, the *transferor* is to continue to deduct the amortization allowable over the amortization period remaining after the transfer.

¶ **2043 Amortization of expenditures for on-the-job training and child care centers.** A taxpayer can elect to amortize (in place of depreciation) on-the-job training or child care facilities over a 60-month period. The property must be depreciable and located within the U.S. The amortization begins with the month the facility is placed in service. It applies to expenditures made after 1971 and before 1977 for on-the-job training centers and to expenditures made after 1971 and before 1982 for child care facilities [Sec. 188]. No investment credit is allowed if the taxpayer elects the amortization (¶ 2410) [Sec. 48(a)(8)].

NOTE: Amortization deduction above depreciation (including accelerated depreciation) that would otherwise be allowable is a tax preference item subject to the minimum tax (¶ 2403) [Sec. 57(a)(10)].

Recapture. Gain on the sale or other disposition of amortized property is recaptured to the extent of the amortization deductions (¶ 1619) [Sec. 1245(a), 1250].

¶ **2044 Amortization of rehabilitation expenses for historic structures.** Taxpayers can elect to amortize over a 60-month period (in place of depreciation) the capital expenditures incurred in the rehabilitation of a certified historic structure. The amortization begins with the month (or year) following the month (or year) the property is acquired. It applies only to expenditures made after 6-14-76 and before 6-15-81 [Sec. 191]. Amortization in excess of depreciation otherwise allowable is recaptured as ordinary income on sale of the property (¶ 1619(a)) [Sec. 1245(a); Temp. Reg. 7.191-1].

Footnotes to Chapter 10

(P-H "FEDERAL TAXES" related references are cited in brackets [ ] at the end of each footnote below.)

Footnote ¶ 2000 [¶ 15,011 et seq.].

Footnote ¶ 2001 [¶ 15,326 et seq.].
(1) Rev. Rul. 65-265, 1965-2 CB 52; Rev. Rul. 68-193, 1968-1 CB 79 [¶ 15,332(10)].
(2) Robinson, 2 TC 305; Newberry, 1945 P-H TC Memo ¶ 45,077; Smith, 1967 P-H TC Memo ¶ 67,028; 22 AFTR 2d 5096, 397 F.2d 804 [¶ 15,335(15)].
(3) Carey, 6 BTA 539; Harroun, 1945 P-H TC Memo ¶ 45,252 [¶ 15,336(5)].
(4) Treas. Dept. booklet, "Tax Guide for Small Business" (1977 Ed.), p. 45.
(5) Automatic Heating and Cooling Co., 1942 P-H BTA Memo ¶ 42,561 [¶ 15,346(15)].
(6) Hill, 3 BTA 761 [¶ 15,341(30)].
(7) Int'l. Curtis Marine Turbine Co. v. U.S., 63 Ct Cl 597, 6 AFTR 6789 [¶ 15,341(5)].
(8) Rev. Rul. 67-379, 1967-2 CB 727 [¶ 15,341(95)].
(9) Johnson, 1966 P-H TC Memo ¶ 66,031 [¶ 15,342(5)].
(10) Red Wing Malting Co., 15 F.2d 626, 6 AFTR 6360 [¶ 15,343(10)].

Footnote ¶ 2001 continued
(11) Johnson v. Westover (DC, Calif. 3/21/55), 48 AFTR 1671 [¶ 15,389(40)].
(12) Kaweah Lemon Co., 5 BTA 992; Krome, 1950 P-H TC Memo ¶ 50,064 [¶ 15,333(30)].
(13) Arthur Beaudry, 1943 P-H TC Memo ¶ 43,156, aff'd. 150 F.2d 20, 33 AFTR 1495; Treas. Dept. booklet, "Tax Guide for Small Business" (1977 Ed.), p. 45 [¶ 15,336(70)].
(14) Batman, 1950 P-H TC Memo ¶ 50,070, aff'd. 189 F.2d 107, 40 AFTR 656 [¶ 15,462(10)].
(15) Fribourg Navigation Co., Inc. v. Comm., 17 AFTR 2d 470, 86 SCt. 862 [¶ 15,311(5)].
(16) Rev. Rul. 67-272, 1967-2 CB 99 [¶ 15,311(5)].

Footnote ¶ 2002 [¶ 15,021].
(1) Weiss V. Weiner, 279 US 333, 7 AFTR 8865 [¶ 15,023(5)].
(2) Frank Holton & Co., 10 BTA 1317; Railey, 36 BTA 543 [¶ 15,023(5)].
(3) Gulf, Mobile & Northern R.R. Co. v. Comm., 83 F2d 788, 17 AFTR 1187 cert. denied; Brevoort Hotel Co. v. Rienecke, 36 F.2d 51, 8 AFTR 9826 [¶ 11,849; 15,357(10)].

Chapter 10 Footnotes

Footnote ¶ 2002 continued
(4) Rev. Rul. 69-89, 1969-1 CB 59 [¶ 15,024(10)].
(5) Terminal Realty Corp., 32 BTA 623 [¶ 15,357(10)].
(6) First Nat. Bank of Kansas City v. Nee, 85 F. Supp. 840, 38 AFTR 473 [¶ 15,357(25)].
(7) Comm. v. Moore, 207 F.2d 265, 44 AFTR 470; Rowan, 22 TC 865; Rev. Rul. 55-89, 1955-1 CB 284 [¶ 15,357(40)].
(8) Schubert v. Comm., 286 F.2d 573, 7 AFTR 2d 550 [¶ 15,357(40)].
(9) Journal-Trib. Pub. Co. v. Comm., 216 F.2d 138, 46 AFTR 660 [¶ 11,820(5)].
(10) Penn v. Comm. 199 F.2d 210, 42 AFTR 682 [¶ 15,549(10)].
(11) Keitel, 15 BTA 903; Bell v. Harrison, 108 F. Supp. 300, 42 AFTR 1045 [¶ 15,350(5)].

Footnote ¶ 2003 [¶ 15,537 et seq.].
(1) Rev. Rul. 63-223, 1963-2 CB 100 [¶ 31,373(20)].
(2) Crane v. Comm., 331 US 1, 35 AFTR 776 [¶ 31,162(25)].
(3) Blackstone Theatre, 12 TC 801 [¶ 31,463(20)].
(4) Pittsburgh & West Virginia Ry., 30 BTA 843; Camp Wolters Land Co., 160 F.2d 84, 35 AFTR 873 [¶ 15,416(5)].

Footnote ¶ 2004 [¶ 31,483 et seq.].

Footnote ¶ 2005 [¶ 15,301 et seq.].

Footnote ¶ 2010 [¶ 15,467 et seq.].
(1) Rev. Proc. 74-11, 1974-1 CB 420 [¶ 15,526(10)].
(2) Rev. Rul. 74-324, 1974-2 CB 66 [¶ 15,526(25)].
(3) Rev. Rul. 73-467, 1973-2 CB 66 [¶ 15,526(25)].
(4) Rev. Proc. 57-10, 1957-1 CB 735 [¶ 15,514(5)].

Footnote ¶ 2011 [¶ 15,468].

Footnote ¶ 2012 [¶ 15,468; 15,482; 15,501 et seq.].
(1) Rev. Rul. 58-420, 1958-2 CB 83 [¶ 15,306(20)].
(2) Rev. Rul. 57-352, 1957-2 CB 150 [¶ 15,482(5)].
(3) Treas. Dept. booklet "Tax Guide for Small Business," (1977 Ed.), p. 48.
(4) Rev. Rul. 67-248, 1967-2 CB 98 [¶ 15,482(5)].
(5) Rev. Rul. 60-8, 1960-1 CB 113 [¶ 15,482(20)].

Footnote ¶ 2013 [¶ 15,468, 15,501 et seq.].
(1) Treas. Dept. booklet "Tax Guide for Small Business," (1977 Ed.), p. 49.

Footnote ¶ 2014 [¶ 15,468].

Footnote ¶ 2015 [¶ 15,468; 15,486; 15,487].
(1) Rev. Rul. 56-652, 1956-2 CB 125 [¶ 15,487(25)].
(2) Rev. Proc. 71-29, 1971-2 CB 568 [¶ 15,487(5)].
(3) Rev. Rul. 60-358, 1960-2 CB 68, amplified by Rev. Rul. 64-273, 1964-2 CB 62 [¶ 15,487(5)].

Footnote ¶ 2016 [¶ 16,238 et seq.].
(1) Rev. Rul. 63-30, 1963-1 CB 50 [¶ 16,243(5)].

Footnote ¶ 2016 continued
(2) Treas. Dept. booklet "Tax Guide for Small Business," (1977 Ed.), p. 163.

Footnote ¶ 2017 [¶ 15,556].
(1) Shainberg, 33 TC 241 [¶ 15,395(5)].
(2) Rev. Rul. 75-55, 1975-1 CB 74, clarifying Rev. Rul. 73-410, 1973-2 CB 53 [¶ 15,395(7)].

Footnote ¶ 2018 [¶ 15,566].

Footnote ¶ 2019 [¶ 15,576].

Footnote ¶ 2021 [¶ 15,391].

Footnote ¶ 2022 [¶ 15,391; 15,393].
(1) Rev. Proc. 74-11, 1974-1 CB 420 [¶ 15,526(10)].

Footnote ¶ 2023 [¶ 15,391 et seq.].

Footnote ¶ 2024 [¶ 17,343].
(1) Senate Report No. 91-552, p. 177, 91st Cong., 1st Sess.

Footnote ¶ 2032 [¶ 15,191 et seq.].
(1) Treas. Dept. booklet "Tax Guide for Small Business" (1977 Ed.), p. 45.
(2) Lewis, 1941 P-H TC Memo ¶ 41,228; Ellis, 1943 P-H TC Memo ¶ 43,199 [¶ 15,318(20)].
(3) Copifyer Lithograph, 12 TC 728 [¶ 15,318(10), (25)].

Footnote ¶ 2033 [¶ 15,466].
(1) Rev. Proc. 77-10, IRB 1977-12 (superseding Rev. Proc. 72-10, 1972-1 CB 721, as supplemented, clarified and modified), modified and supplemented by Rev. Proc. 77-14, IRB 1977-21. However, the taxpayer may elect to apply Rev. Proc. 72-10 without regard to Rev. Proc. 77-10 for property placed in service in a tax year beginning before 3-21-77 and ending on or after that date [¶ 55,328; 55,481].
(2) TIR-1097 [¶ 15,466].
(3) P.L. 93-625, 1-3-75 [¶ 15,466.2].

Footnote ¶ 2034 [¶ 15,431 et seq.].
(1) Wooten v. Comm., 181 F.2d 502, 39 AFTR 405 [¶ 15,437(40)].

Footnote ¶ 2036 [¶ 14,224; 15,421].
(1) Rev. Proc. 74-11, 1974-1 CB 420 [¶ 15,526(10)].

Footnote ¶ 2037 [¶ 14,224; 15,421].

Footnote ¶ 2038 [¶ 15,466.4-C].

Footnote ¶ 2040 [¶ 15,665].

Footnote ¶ 2041 [¶ 16,266; 16,273].
(1) TD 7032, 3-10-70 [¶ 15,017].

Footnote ¶ 2042 [¶ 16,293].

Footnote ¶ 2043 [¶ 16,290].

Footnote ¶ 2044 [¶ 16,297].

Highlights of Chapter 10
Deductions—Depreciation

I. **Depreciation in General [¶ 2000—2005]**
   A. **What is depreciation.** Reasonable allowance deducted each year for exhaustion, wear and tear and normal obsolescence of business or investment property [¶ 2000].
   B. **Depreciable property [¶ 2001(a)]:**
      1. Used in a trade or business, or
      2. Held for production of income.
   C. **When to deduct.** Depreciation period starts when asset is placed in service [¶ 2001(b)].
   D. **Who can deduct [¶ 2002]:**
      1. One sustaining economic loss—usually owner.
      2. Buyer under executory contract may get deduction.
      3. Tenant may write off permanent improvements.
      4. Life tenant deducts depreciation over property's useful life; after he dies, remainderman gets deduction.
   E. **Basis for depreciation [¶ 2003]:**
      1. Adjusted basis for determining gain from sale, generally.
      2. Inherited property:
         a. Decedent dying before 1977: market value at death unless executor elects alternate valuation date.
         b. Decedent dying after 1976: decedent's basis in property immediately before death, with certain adjustments [¶ 1507].
      3. Taxpayer denied exempt status: basis reduced by "as-if" straight line depreciation during exemption period.
      4. Property converted to income-producing use: lower of adjusted basis or market value on conversion date.
      5. Lump-sum purchase price: allocate between land and building.
   F. **Adjusted basis [¶ 2004]:**
      1. Each year property basis must be reduced by full depreciation allowable; amount not currently deducted cannot be deducted later.
      2. Taxpayer deducting more than allowable must reduce basis by amount allowed that reduced tax, but not less than full amount allowable. ("Tax benefit rule.").
   G. **Salvage value [¶ 2005].**
      1. Salvage value of personal property with at least 3-year useful life can be reduced by up to 10% of cost.
      2. To figure straight line or sum of years-digits depreciation—subtract salvage value from basis for depreciation. Not subtracted in figuring declining balance depreciation, additional first-year allowance or investment credit.

II. **How To Figure Depreciation [¶ 2010—2020]:**
   A. **Straight line method.** Cost, less salvage, deducted in equal amounts each year over remaining useful life [¶ 2011].
   B. **Declining balance [¶ 2012]:**
      1. Generally twice straight line rate, unadjusted for salvage (but rate can be limited).
      2. Apply uniform rate to unrecovered basis.
   C. **Sum of years-digits [¶ 2013]:**
      1. Apply changing fraction to cost less salvage.

2. Numerator is number of remaining years of useful life: denominator is sum of numbers representing years of asset's life.
D. **Other methods [¶ 2015]:**
1. Unit of production.
2. Operating day.
3. Income forecast.
E. **Additional first-year depreciation [¶ 2016]:**
1. Each taxpayer allowed 20% of cost; deduction limit, $2,000 a year.
2. Only tangible personalty with at least 6-year useful life qualifies.
F. **How to elect.** Just use appropriate method for first tax year property is acquired [¶ 2010(a)].
G. **How to change method.** File Form 3115 for IRS approval, same as change in accounting method [¶ 2010(b)].
H. **Agreement on depreciation.** Made with IRS on Form 2271 as to useful life, depreciation rate and method, and salvage [¶ 2010(c)].
I. **Most liberal method available for depreciable realty [¶ 2010; 2012; 2013; 2017]:**
1. Used residential rental or commercial property acquired before 7-25-69 with useful life under 20 years: limited declining balance.
2. Used residential rental property acquired after 7-24-69 with useful life of 20 years or more: declining balance at 1¼ times straight line rate.
3. Used commercial property acquired after 7-24-69 with useful life of 3 years or more: straight line.
4. New residential rental or commercial property acquired before 7-25-69 with useful life of at least 3 years: declining balance or sum of years-digits.
5. New residential rental property acquired after 7-24-69 with useful life of at least 3 years: declining balance or sum of years-digits.
6. New commercial property acquired after 7-24-69 with useful life of at least 3 years: limited declining balance.
J. **Low-income housing.** Taxpayer can elect to deduct pre-1978 expenditures under straight line using 60-month useful life without salvage. Limit: $20,000 per dwelling unit [¶ 2018].
K. **Public utilities.** Normalization method provided [¶ 2019].

III. **Accounting For Depreciation**
A. **Depreciation reserve.** Usual method of accounting for depreciation is to credit a depreciation reserve account [¶ 2021].
B. **Depreciation property accounts [¶ 2022]:**
1. Item accounts: Cost of each asset kept separately with useful life, salvage and depreciation rate determined individually.
2. Multiple asset accounts: Generally broken down into group, classified and composite accounts. Single depreciation rate used for one account combining number of assets.
C. **Depreciation records.** Taxpayer must set up depreciation records so that deductions can be verified [¶ 2023].
D. **Effect of depreciation on earnings and profits.** Corporation must use straight line to figure earnings and profits (but this does not restrict available accelerated depreciation methods in figuring taxable income) [¶ 2024].

IV. **Useful Life and Obsolescence [¶ 2032—2034]**
A. **Useful life determined by [¶ 2032]:**
1. Operating conditions, experience and informed judgment, or
2. Election of Class Life ADR system.
B. **Class Life ADR system of depreciation [¶ 2033]:**
1. Choose from official table range of depreciation lives not over 20% shorter nor 20% longer than guideline lives. Elect annually.
2. Set up vintage accounts for assets first placed in service.
3. Generally all types of tangible property eligible if:
   a. Asset guideline class and period in effect for election year,

b. Placed in service after 1970, and
c. Sec. 1245 or Sec. 1250 property.
4. When asset acquired:
   a. Half-year convention: treat all assets placed in service during year as acquired at mid-year.
   b. Modified half-year convention: treat assets placed in service in first ½ of year as acquired on first day of that year, and assets placed in service in last ½ of year as acquired on first day of following year.
5. Salvage value can be disregarded, but vintage account cannot be depreciated below reasonable salvage value.
6. Repair allowance is result of multiplying appropriate repair allowance percentage (in official table) by average of unadjusted basis of property in guideline class at start and end of tax year.

C. **Obsolescence.** If taxpayer shows estimated useful life shortened by obsolescence greater than originally considered in determining useful life, change of shorter life allowed [¶ 2034].

V. **Retirement of Assets [¶ 2036—2038]**
   A. **Gain or loss [¶ 2036]:**
      1. Sale or exchange: Apply ordinary rules for recognition of gains or losses.
      2. Abandonment: Recognized loss is difference between adjusted basis and salvage.
      3. Other disposition: No gain recognized. On *abnormal* retirement, loss is excess of adjusted basis over greater of salvage or market value on retirement. On *normal* retirement, different rules apply to multiple asset and item accounts.
   B. **Basis of retired assets.** Use adjusted basis for gain or loss on a sale, with following modifications for multiple asset accounts [¶ 2037]:
      1. If asset *normally* retired and rate based on average life, adjusted basis is salvage value.
      2. If asset *abnormally* retired and rate based on maximum expected life of longest lived asset, depreciation adjustment figured as if asset were depreciated in single asset account using maximum expected useful life of asset.
      3. If *abnormally* retired, depreciation adjustment figured as if asset were depreciated in single item account using rate based on average or maximum expected useful life, depending on method used to determine rate for the account.
   C. **Retirement from vintage accounts [¶ 2038]:**
      1. Gain recognized on extraordinary retirement generally. On ordinary retirement, gain recognized to extent reserve at end of year exceeds account's unadjusted basis.
      2. On ordinary retirement, no loss recognized. Loss recognized in year extraordinary retirement occurs.
      3. If depreciation reserve unadjusted for retirements during the year exceeds account's unadjusted basis minus salvage, account's salvage value is reduced (but not below zero) as of start of tax year.

VI. **Special Amortization**
   A. **Pollution control.** Taxpayer can elect to amortize certified pre-1976 pollution control facilities over 60-month period [¶ 2040].
   B. **Railroad grading and tunnel bores and railroad rolling stock [¶ 2041].**
   C. **Coal mine safety equipment [¶ 2042].**
   D. **Expenditures for on-job training and child care centers.** Taxpayer can elect to amortize qualified expenditures over 60-month period [¶ 2043].
   E. **Rehabilitation expenses for historic structures [¶ 2044].**

Chapter 11

DEDUCTIONS—DEPLETION

TABLE OF CONTENTS

DEPLETION IN GENERAL

What is depletion 2100
Who is entitled to the deduction for depletion 2101
   Owner of an economic interest
   Lessor and lessee
   Life tenant and remainderman
   Sale of entire economic interest
   Mineral production payments

FIGURING THE DEPLETION DEDUCTION

Two methods of figuring depletion 2102
   Cost method
   Percentage method
Cost depletion 2103
   How to figure cost depletion
   Determining adjusted basis
   Charges to capital account
   Incorrect estimate of remaining units
Percentage depletion 2104
   Oil and gas wells
   Other depletable mineral interests
   Percentage depletion allowed though no cost basis*

Treatment of bonuses and royalties 2105

AGGREGATING DEPLETABLE INTERESTS

Treating separate interests as one property 2106
Aggregating operating oil and gas interests 2107
Aggregating operating mineral interests other than oil and gas 2108
   Aggregation rules
   Breakup of single interest into more than one property
   Making the election
Aggregating nonoperating mineral interests 2109

SPECIAL PROBLEMS

Depletion of timber 2110
Depreciation 2111
Books of account 2112
Distributions from depreciation or depletion reserves 2113

• Highlights of Chapter 11 2161

DEPLETION IN GENERAL

The law allows an annual depletion deduction in figuring taxable income. You must have the requisite "economic interest" in the depletable property to get the deduction. It may have to be apportioned between interested parties.

¶ **2100 What is depletion.** Minerals, oil and gas, other natural deposits (including soil in place[1]), and timber are known as wasting assets. The gradual reduction of the original amount by removal for use is known as "depletion." The theory is that the annual deduction for depletion and depreciation, in the aggregate, will return the cost or other basis of the property plus later allowable capital additions [Sec. 1.611-1, 1.611-5].

Property means each separate interest owned by a taxpayer in each mineral deposit in each separate tract or parcel of land. It includes working or operating interests, royalties, overriding royalties, production payments and net profits interests. Contiguous areas acquired at the same time from the same owner constitute a single separate tract or parcel of land. Areas included in separate conveyances or grants from separate owners are separate tracts or parcels, even if the areas are contiguous [Sec. 614(a); 1.614-1].

Footnotes appear at end of this Chapter.

¶ 2100

¶ 2101 **Who is entitled to the deduction for depletion. (a) Owner of an economic interest.** An individual or a corporation that is the sole owner and operator of a property is the only one entitled to deduct depletion on it. But a deduction may be allowed to more than one taxpayer if the owner is a trust or partnership, or has transferred a part of his economic interest in mineral deposits or standing timber to another. The deduction must be apportioned between lessor and lessee and between trustee and beneficiary [Sec. 611(b); 1.611-1(b)]. A deduction for depletion will be allowed only if the taxpayer has an "economic interest" in the mineral deposit or standing timber which gives rise to the income. A taxpayer has an economic interest when he has both: (1) acquired an interest in minerals in place or standing timber, and (2) receives income from mineral extraction or timber cutting to which he must look for recovery of his investment [Sec. 1.611-1(b)].[1]

The Supreme Court has ruled that contract coal miners have no economic interest in the coal they mine.[2] For estates and trusts, see ¶ 3014.

> **Example 1:** An adjacent upland owner who provides the only available drilling site for oil from submerged coastal lands, is entitled to depletion on the share of net profits received from the producer for use of the lands.[3]
>
> **Example 2:** A processor under contracts with oil producers to extract casinghead gasoline from natural gas they deliver to it is not entitled to depletion, since it has no capital investment in the mineral deposit being depleted.[4]

In the case of an individual the deduction is subtracted from gross income to arrive at adjusted gross income [¶ 1801(a); 1806].

(b) Lessor and lessee. No specific rule can be laid down for making the apportionment, and each case must be decided on its own merits.

If the value of any leased mineral property must be ascertained to determine the basis for depletion, the value of the interests of the lessor and lessee may be determined separately. If they are determined as of the same date, they may not exceed the value of the property on that date [Sec. 1.611-1(c)].

Minimum royalties. If a lessee agrees that he will pay a minimum royalty to be applied against the price or royalty per unit, even if the minerals covered by that royalty are not extracted, the lessor takes depletion to the same extent as if the minerals had been removed. No further deduction is allowed, of course, when actual removal takes place [Sec. 1.612-3(b)(1)]. If all the minerals are not extracted, and the lease is ended, the lessor must adjust his capital account by restoring the depletion deductions taken in prior years for the minerals paid for in advance, *but not extracted*. The same amount must be reported as income [Sec. 1.612-3(b)(2)].[5]

Overriding royalties. A lessee who transfers his interest in the property, but retains his royalty interests, shares an equitable portion of the depletion allowance with the lessor. It is immaterial whether the transfer is by assignment or by a sublease, since an economic interest in the property has been retained.[6]

Delay rentals. Amounts paid for the privilege of deferring development are ordinary income to the lessor and not subject to depletion [Sec. 1.612-3(c)(1)].

Shut-in royalties are treated the same as delay rentals.[7]

(c) Life tenant and remainderman. The life tenant gets depletion until his death. Then the remainderman gets it [Sec. 1.611-1(c)(3)].

(d) Sale of entire economic interest. If the taxpayer leases or transfers property subject to depletion, but retains an economic interest in that property, he is entitled to the deduction. The income from such a transfer is not a capital gain.[8]

If the taxpayer *sells* the property or his entire economic interest (for example, an interest in an oil and gas lease, or a mineral deposit), any gain ordinarily is capital gain (but see ¶ 2103(c)),[9] and no depletion deduction is allowed against the gain.[10]

(e) Mineral production payments. A production payment is a right to a share of the production from a mineral property (or a sum of money in place of the production) when that production occurs.

1. Carved-out payments are created when the owner of a mineral property sells—or carves out—a portion of his future production. They are treated as mortgage loans rather than economic interests in the mineral property [Sec. 636(a); 1.636-1(a), 1.636-3]. Income will be taxable to the property owner, subject to depletion, as income is derived from the property.

2. Retained payments are created when the owner of a mineral interest sells the working interest, but retains production payments for himself. Retained payments are treated as purchase money mortgage loans rather than economic interests in the mineral property [Sec. 636(b); 1.636-1(c)]. The production payment is part of the sales proceeds entering into the seller's gain or loss. The income from the property used to satisfy the payment is taxable to the buyer and is subject to depletion; he can deduct operating costs.

3. Payments retained by lessors on leases of mineral interests are treated by the lessee as a bonus payable by him in installments; the lessee capitalizes the payments and recovers them through depletion. The lessor treats the production payments as depletable income [Sec. 636(c); 1.636-2(b)].

FIGURING THE DEPLETION DEDUCTION

The cost method is the general way to calculate depletion. However, some property qualifies for the percentage method which can produce a larger allowance.

¶ 2102 Two methods of figuring depletion. (a) **Cost method** applies to all types of property subject to depletion. Under it the basis is the same as that for determining a gain on the sale of the property, and may be more or less than cost. The basis is divided by the number of units (tons of ore, barrels of oil, thousands of cubic feet of natural gas, feet of timber) to arrive at the depletion unit. Deduction for a tax year is the depletion unit multiplied by the number of units sold within the year. See ¶ 2103.

(b) **Percentage method.** The tax year's percentage depletion allowance is a specified percentage of the "gross income from the property" subject to the limitation that it generally may not exceed 50% of the "taxable income from the property" (figured without depletion allowance). But see ¶ 2104(a) [Sec. 613]. It applies to oil and gas wells, coal mines, metal mines, and certain other deposits, but not to timber. For those properties to which the percentage method applies, the deduction should be figured under both the cost method and the percentage method, and the larger deduction taken [Sec. 613(a); 1.613-1]. Also, the basis of the property must be reduced by the larger allowance [Sec. 1.1016-3(b)]. See ¶ 2104.

Footnotes appear at end of this Chapter.

¶ 2102

NOTE: The excess of the depletion deduction over the property's adjusted basis is a tax preference item subject to the minimum tax (¶ 2403) [Sec. 57(a)(8); Proposed Reg. 1.57-1(h)].

¶ 2103 Cost depletion is the general rule for figuring the depletion deduction, and can be applied to all types of depletable property. The deduction by this method is often called valuation depletion.

(a) How to figure cost depletion. The basis for depletion under the cost method is the adjusted basis for determining gain on a sale [Sec. 612; 1.612-1]. Even when the cost method is not used, it is often necessary to figure depletion under that method to insure the maximum deduction.

Depletion under the cost method is figured as follows [Sec. 1.611-2]:

Adjusted basis/total remaining mineral units × number of units sold

≫**OBSERVATION**→ It is the number of units sold (not the number produced) that determines the allowance.

Example 1: On Jan. 1, the Russell Co. owned property subject to depletion, with a basis in its hands of $1,000,000. The recoverable reserves (the total remaining mineral units) were estimated at 100,000 units. The unit cost was $10, and if 5,000 units were sold during the year, the depletion deduction would be $50,000 (assuming no capital additions).

Important exceptions to the cost method are considered in ¶ 2104; 2105; 2110. As to aggregating interests for depletion purposes, see ¶ 2106 et seq.

(b) Determining adjusted basis. In determining the basis of property under the cost method, either cost or the value on a particular date may be used [¶ 1500 et seq.]. Value on a particular date is used, for example, when the property was acquired before 3-1-13, or was transmitted at death. Rules for determining that value are given in the regulations [Sec. 1.611-2(d)]. Usually the following factors are determinative (the order indicates the preferential weight to be given to each): (1) actual bona fide sale price, (2) a bona fide offer to buy, (3) a bona fide offer of sale, (4) the sale price of similar properties, similarly situated, (5) market value of stocks that fairly and clearly represents the property's value, (6) royalties or rentals, paid or received, (7) analytical appraisals by the present worth method, (8) valuation for purposes of state and local taxation and appraisals for court proceedings. The regulation also provides for the use of the "present value method."[1]

When a valuation as of a specific date has been fixed, no revaluation is allowed the same owner, except in the case of a later discovery or because of misrepresentation, fraud, or gross error [Sec. 1.611-2(f)].

(c) Charges to capital account. In figuring the adjusted basis, certain additions must be made to capital account. In the case of mines and oil and gas properties, capital expenditures allocable to the mine or well itself are recoverable through depletion; capital expenditures allocable to plant or equipment are recoverable through depreciation.

Capital additions to mines. Expenditures for plant and equipment (except maintenance and repairs) are ordinarily recoverable through depreciation but in certain cases, expenditures for equipment necessary to maintain normal output are chargeable to expense (deductible) [Sec. 1.612-2]. For a discussion of when certain exploration expenditures may be deducted see ¶ 1843.

Election to expense or capitalize. An operator can either charge intangible drilling and development costs to capital, recovering them through depletion or depreciation (depending on the nature of the expenditure), or can deduct the costs as expenses. A binding election must be made on the return for the first tax year

tion is claimed. Deductions not directly related to the property are fairly allocated [Sec. 1.613-5]. The charitable contribution deduction is not subtracted.[4] This applies to qualifying gas well production.

(b) Other depletable mineral interests. The allowance is the following percentage of the gross income from the property [Sec. 613(b); 1.613-2].

(1) Sulfur and uranium; and, if from deposits in the United States, anorthosite, clay, laterite, and nephelite syenite (to the extent that alumina and aluminum compounds are extracted from it), asbestos, bauxite, celestite, chromite, corundum, fluorspar, graphite, ilmenite, kyanite, mica, olivine, quartz crystals (radio grade), rutile, block steatite talc, zircon, and ores of the following metals: antimony, beryllium, bismuth, cadmium, cobalt, columbium, lead, lithium, manganese, mercury, molybdenum nickel, platinum and platinum group metals, tantalum, thorium, tin, titanium, tungsten, vanadium and zinc 22%

(2) Domestic gold, silver, oil shale, (except shale to which (5) applies), copper and iron ore 15%

(3)(a) Ball clay, bentonite, china clay, sagger clay, metal mines (if not allowed in the 22% group above), rock asphalt, vermiculite; and

(b) All other minerals [including, but not limited to, aplite, barite, borax, calcium carbonates, clay (refractory and fire), diatomaceous earth, dolomite, feldspar, fullers earth, garnet, gilsonite, granite, limestone, magnesite, magnesium carbonates, marble, mollusk shells (including clam and oyster shells), phosphate rock, potash, quartzite, slate, soapstone, stone (used or sold for use by the mine owner or operator as dimension stone or ornamental stone) thenardite, tripoli, trona and (if not allowed in the 22% group above) bauxite, flake graphite, fluorspar, lepidolite, mica, spodumene, and talc, including pyrophyllite] except as specified in (A) and (B) below 14%

(A) When minerals in group 3(b) are used or sold for use by the mine owner or operator as rip rap, ballast, road material, rubble, concrete aggregates, or for similar purposes the percentage is 5% (unless sold on bid in direct competition with a bona fide bid to sell a mineral listed in 3(a)).

(B) Group 3(b) does not include soil, sod, dirt, turf, water or mosses; or minerals from sea water, the air or similar inexhaustible sources, or oil and gas wells.

(4) Asbestos (if from deposits outside U.S.), brucite, coal,[5] lignite, perlite, sodium chloride, and wollastonite 10%

(5) Clay and shale used or sold for use in the manufacture of sewer pipe or brick, and clay, shale, and slate used or sold for use as sintered or burned lightweight aggregates 7½%

(6) Gravel, peat, peat moss,[6] pumice, sand, scoria, shale (except shale to which 15% or 7½% rate applies), and stone, except stone described in the 14% group above; and, if from brine wells—bromine, calcium chloride, and magnesium chloride 5%

An amount equal to any rents and royalties paid or incurred for the property must be excluded in determining gross income [Sec. 613(a); 1.613-2(c)(5)].

Gross income from property in connection with percentage depletion for mines means gross income *from mining*. Mining includes not merely the extraction of ores or minerals from the ground but also (1) the treatment processes considered as mining to the extent they are applied by the mine owner or operator to the mineral or the ore, and (2) the transportation of ores or minerals from the point of extraction from the ground to the plants or mills where the ordinary treatment processes are applied, but not in excess of 50 miles (unless the Revenue Service rules otewise) [Sec. 613(c); 1.613-4(h)]. Any process that is not necessary to bring the minerals to shipping form is not part of the treatment process.[7] The Supreme Court holds that a lessee of mining property must deduct ad valorem and royalty

Footnotes appear at end of this Chapter.

¶ 2104

taxes it paid before figuring gross income from property for percentage depletion purposes.[8]

> **NOTE:** Percentage depletion is to be based on the constructive income from the raw product if marketable in that form (whether or not marketable at a profit) and not on the value of the finished product.[9]

The percentage depletion on oil shale is figured on its value after the extraction and retorting of the shale oil, but before hydrogenating and refining [Sec. 613(c)].

Cash or trade discounts actually allowed by a taxpayer must be subtracted from his sales price in determining "gross income from the property" [Sec. 1.613-4(e)].

> **NOTE:** The "extraction of ores or minerals from the ground" includes the extraction by *mine owners or operators* of ores or minerals from the waste or residue of their prior mining such as a tailing dump, or a culm bank. This does not apply to a buyer of the waste or residue or a buyer of the rights to extract ores or minerals from the waste or residue [Sec. 613(c); 1.613-4(i)].

The depletion deduction may be figured (without regard to any election) either on the percentage basis, or on the general rule basis, whichever gives the greater deduction [Sec. 613(a); 1.613-1].

Business interruption insurance. Proceeds from a policy insuring against loss of mining profits are not taken into account in figuring percentage depletion, since they are not considered gross income from mining.[10]

Taxable income from the property generally has the same meaning as in (a), above. However, the deduction for mining expenses is reduced by gain on sale of depreciable property [¶ 1619(a)] that is taxed as ordinary income, and which is allocable to the property. Records must be kept in determining the gain on the property [Sec. 613(a); 1.613-5(b)(5)].

(c) Percentage depletion allowed though no cost basis. It is possible and not unusual for a taxpayer to recover tax free, through percentage depletion, an amount greater than the cost of the property. It follows that a taxpayer may recover a larger amount tax free through depletion than he could through a sale or other disposition of the property. The statute ignores such inequalities and allows the deduction although the cost has been recovered.[11] However, any depletion in excess of cost basis is a tax preference item subject to the minimum tax [¶ 2102(b); 2403].

¶ 2105 Treatment of bonuses and royalties. If a lessor receives a bonus in addition to royalties, the depletion deduction is figured as follows [Sec. 1.612-3(a)]:

Basis for depletion × Bonus/Bonus + expected royalties = Depletion deduction

Example 1: Assume that the lessor's basis for depletion is $2,000,000, that he receives a bonus of $1,000,000 and that he is to receive a royalty of one-fourth of the minerals produced by the lessee, it being estimated that the royalty payments will amount to $3,000,000. The depletion deduction on account of the receipt of the bonus would be $500,000, figured as follows:

$2,000,000 × $1,000,000 / $1,000,000 + $3,000,000 = $500,000

If percentage depletion may be used, the lessor is entitled to apply the applicable rate to the bonus [Sec. 1.612-3(d)]. Since percentage depletion in the above case would amount only to $220,000 ($1,000,000 × 22%), it would not be used.

Obviously, if the basis equals or exceeds the bonus and expected royalties, the entire bonus is a return of capital.

Even if there is no well on the property, the bonus is subject to percentage depletion, since it is a payment in advance for oil and gas to be extracted.[1] Any such depletion deduction must be added to income in the tax year the lease expires if there has been no income from the extraction of the mineral [Sec. 1.612-3(a)(2)]. This is so even if no tax benefit resulted.[2] However, if the entire mineral interest is transferred by any means, before the end of the lease, the bonus depletion does not have to be added to income.[3]

The above rule, however, does not apply to delay rentals [¶ 2101(b)].[4]

⇒**OBSERVATION**→ It is the income from the property, and not production, that determines the depletion deduction on the bonus. The production factor, however, is used to figure the depletion on royalties.

Example 2: After the $500,000 depletion deduction is taken in Example 1 the basis is $1,500,000. Assume that in a succeeding year one-tenth of the minerals are extracted and sold, and the lessor receives $400,000. His depletion deduction is $150,000 (1/10 of $1,500,000). If he had received $750,000, his depletion deduction would have been $165,000 ($750,000 × 22%).

AGGREGATING DEPLETABLE INTERESTS

If you own more than one depletable interest, you may, under certain conditions, elect to form one aggregation of two or more of them and treat the aggregation as one property. You are not permitted to aggregate a nonoperating interest with an operating interest.

¶ 2106 Treating separate interests as one property. If an election to aggregate two or more interests is made, depreciation for each interest may be taken separately [¶ 2111]. However, the total depreciation taken on the aggregated property must be used in figuring the depletion limitation.[1]

Operating interests are those for which the costs of production are required (or would be required if the property were in production) to be taken into account in figuring the percent of taxable income limit for percentage depletion (¶ 2104(a)) [Sec. 614(d); 1.614-2(b)]. So royalties and similar interests are *not* operating interests. But aggregation of these may be allowed under the rules for nonoperating interests [¶ 2109].

NOTE: An operating *interest* is different from an operating *unit.* An operating unit generaly consists of a number of operating interests which may be conveniently and economically operated as a single unit [Sec. 1.614-2(c)].

¶ 2107 Aggregating operating oil and gas interests. A taxpayer's operating mineral interests in oil and gas in a separate tract or parcel of land (lease) are combined and treated as one property. However, the taxpayer may elect to combine some of his interests into *one* combination and to treat all his other interests in the tract separately [Sec. 614(b)(2); 1.614- 8(a)(1)]. A new interest found or acquired in the property is combined with any existing combination of interests unless the taxpayer elects to treat it separately. If there is no existing combination, it is treated separately unless the taxpayer elects to combine it with *one* other interest [Sec. 1.614-8(a)(2)].

Example: Cox owns under one lease operating interests A, B, C, and D. Cox elects to combine A and B, and to treat C and D as separate properties. When Cox acquires E, a new operating interest in the same property, he can elect to treat E separately; otherwise, he must treat it as part of the AB combination. If Cox had elected to treat the interests separately, E would also be treated separately unless he elected to combine it with *one* other interest.

Footnotes appear at end of this Chapter.

Election to treat part or all operating interests in each separate tract or parcel of land as separate properties must be made when filing the return for the first tax year in which a development or operation expenditure is made by the taxpayer after acquisition [Sec. 614(b)(4); 1.614-8(a)(3)].

Unitization and pools. When these are compelled by state law, the taxpayer's interest in the unit or pool is considered one property. When the unit or pool is voluntary, the same rule applies, but the interests must be in the same deposit, or if in more than one, must be logical and either contiguous or in close proximity [Sec. 614(b)(3); 1.614-8(b)].

Unitizations made before 1964 may continue, if previous treatment was then legally proper [Sec. 614(b)(3)(C); 1.614-8(b)].

Basis unscrambled. When made necessary because of new arrangements, any basis may be divided among the separate properties in accordance with the fair market value of each property, or taxpayers may take the adjusted basis of each property when first aggregated and adjust it down reasonably so that the total adjusted base equals the adjusted basis of the former aggregation [Sec. 614; 1.614-6].

¶ **2108 Aggregating operating mineral interests other than oil and gas. (a) Aggregation rules.** A taxpayer may elect to aggregate and treat as one property all the interest in a mine, or all the interests in 2 or more mines within an operating unit. It does not matter whether the interests are in the same or contiguous tracts, or if taxpayer makes more than one aggregation in an operating unit. But any aggregation must include all the interests in the mine. Nonaggregated interests are treated as separate properties [Sec. 614(c)(1); 1.614-3(a)].

> **Example:** North Co. owns 25 operating interests comprising 5 mines of 5 interests each. All are in one operating unit. North may elect to aggregate, for example, all 15 interests in mines 1, 3 and 4 and treat them as one property; to aggregate its 5 interests in mine 2 and treat them as one property; and to treat each of the 5 interests in mine 5 as separate properties.

> **NOTE:** For pre-1977 elections, if exploration expenditures were deducted before the interests were aggregated, the depletion deduction and the tax had to be recomputed for the prior years to recover the tax benefit. In the recomputation, it was assumed that the interests were aggregated for the prior years. The basis of the aggregated property was adjusted as if the tax for the prior years was determined in accordance with the recomputation [P.L. 94-455, Sec. 1901(a)(87)(A)(i)].

Invalid aggregations. If a taxpayer acquires an interest in a mine whose other interests were validly aggregated, it becomes part of that aggregation, even if he invalidly adds it to a different aggregation [Sec. 1.614-3(f)(8)].

(b) Breakup of single interest into more than one property. A taxpayer may elect to break up a single interest or tract containing one deposit into 2 or more properties if there is a mine (for which development or operation expenditures have been made) in each segment. The separate property on which the mine is located then can be aggregated with other properties as explained above. However, once an interest has been included in an aggregation, it cannot be broken off and treated as a separate property without the consent of the Revenue Service [Sec. 614(c)(2); 1.614-3(b)].

(c) Making the election. The election under either (a) or (b) is binding for all later years unless the Revenue Service consents to a different treatment for any interest to which the election applies [Sec. 614(c)(3); 1.614-3(f)(7)].

Election under (a) must be made by the time for filing returns (including extensions) for the first tax year in which development or operation expenditure for the separate operating mineral interest is made by the taxpayer after acquiring the property [Sec. 614(c)(3); 1.614-3(f)].

Election under (b) must be made by the time for filing returns (including extensions) for the first tax year in which development or operation expenditures for more than one mine are made by the taxpayer after acquiring the property [Sec. 614(c)(3); 1.614-3(f)].

¶ 2109 **Aggregating nonoperating mineral interests.** If the taxpayer owns more than one separate nonoperating mineral interest in a single tract or parcel of land or in 2 or more adjacent tracts or parcels of land, he may treat all the interests in each separate kind of mineral deposit as one property. He must, however, secure the permission of the Revenue Service and must show that the principal purpose is not tax avoidance. Permission must be requested by the later of the following: (1) within 90 days after the start of the first tax year for which aggregation is desired; or (2) within 90 days after acquiring an interest includible in the aggregation [Sec. 1.614-5(e)]. If permission is granted, he must continue to treat such interests as one property unless the Revenue Service consents to a different treament[Sec. 614(e); 1.614-5(d), (e)(5)].

SPECIAL PROBLEMS

¶ 2110 **Depletion of timber** is based on the adjusted basis for determining gain on a sale. It does not include any part of the land's cost. Depletion occurs when the timber is cut and is figured by the cost method only. The deduction each year is the number of timber units cut multiplied by the depletion unit. The unit is figured as follows [Sec. 1.611-3]:

$$\frac{C + P + A}{U + (or-) X + (or-) Y} = \text{depletion unit}$$

when
C equals the capital sum remaining at the beginning of the year.
P equals the cost of any purchases during the year.
A equals capital additions during the year other than purchases.
U equals total units of timber at the beginning of the year.
X equals the units to be added or deducted in order to adjust the total remaining units (U) to conform to the actual quantity of units remaining.
Y equals the units added through purchase or deducted on account of sale en bloc.

The loss to be deducted in case of forest fire is found the same way. If timber contains turpentine, that portion of the total cost or other basis reasonably allocable to turpentine may be amortized or recovered through depletion deductions on any reasonable basis over the period of actual turpentining.[1]

NOTE: A map and statement (Form T) giving the data required by the regulations must be attached to the return if depletion of timber is claimed [Sec. 1.611-3(h)].

¶ 2111 **Depreciation.** In the case of mines, oil and gas wells, and timber, depreciation of improvements may be taken under any reasonable method of depreciation [¶ 2000 et seq.]. A reasonable allowance for depreciation may also be taken due to obsolescence or decay during periods when the improvement is not used or is producing at a rate below normal capacity. For operating oil and gas properties, depreciation is allowed on machinery, tools, equipment, pipes and similar items, and installation costs not deducted as intangible drilling and development expenses (¶ 2103(c)) [Sec. 1.611-5].

¶ 2112 **Books of account.** Separate accounts should be kept in which there should be recorded the basis of the property on the basic date, any allowable capital additions, and all other adjustments. The annual depletion deduction should be

Footnotes appear at end of this Chapter.

credited to the mineral property accounts or to the depletion reserve accounts [Sec. 1.611-2(b)]. It is not necessary to adopt any particular method of bookkeeping. But records must be accurate.

As to timber, there are special requirements for the books of account [Sec. 1.611-3(c)], and, as a general rule, separate accounts must be kept for each "block" of timber [Sec. 1.611-3(d)].

¶ 2113 **Distributions from depreciation or depletion reserves.** This can be illustrated best by an example.

> **Example:** The Nile Co. bought a building on 1-2-69 for $100,000. No capital additions have been made since that date, but depreciation has been taken at the rate of 2½% a year. On 1-2-77, the depreciation reserve showed a credit of $20,000. The Nile Co.'s capital investment, however, is still $100,000. The situation is the same as if the Nile Co. had taken $2,500 each year and put it in a separate fund, so that at the end of 40 years, it would have $100,000 in that fund to buy or erect a new building. After 8 years, the building (as it then stands) plus $20,000 credit in the depreciation reserve will be the exact equivalent of the building when bought. Each represents the Nile Co.'s capital investment. Suppose now that the Nile Co. decides to distribute the $20,000 attributable to the depreciation reserve. What the stockholders get is not a taxable dividend, but a return of capital.

The following points should be noted [Sec. 1.316-2(e)]:

1. No distribution can be made from such a reserve until all earnings or profits of the corporation accumulated after 2-28-13 have been first distributed.

2. The distribution reduces the basis of the stock on which declared. Therefore, if the Nile Co. in the above example distributed $20,000, the stockholders' capital investment is reduced by that amount.

3. When percentage depletion is used, the annual deduction may exceed the allowance under the general rule. The difference is earnings and profits, and, on distribution, is a taxable dividend.

4. A distribution made from that part of a depletion reserve based on a valuation as of 3-1-13, that is in excess of the depletion reserve based on cost, will not be considered as having been paid out of earnings or profits, but the distribution reduces the basis of the stock. In short, if 3-1-13 value exceeds cost, the taxpayer is entitled to a return of 3-1-13 value. To hold otherwise would mean taxing the increase in value accrued before 3-1-13.

Footnotes to Chapter 11

(P-H "FEDERAL TAXES" related references are cited in brackets [ ] at the end of each footnote below.)

Footnote ¶ 2100 [¶ 22,011 et seq.].
(1) Rev. Rul. 78, 1953-1 CB 18 [¶ 22,050(15)].

Footnote ¶ 2101 [¶ 22,016; 22,475].
(1) Palmer v. Bender, 287 US 551, 53 SCt 225, 77 L Ed 489, 11 AFTR 1106. See GCM 22730, 1941-1 CB 214 [¶ 22,037(60); 22,038(5)].
(2) Paragon Jewel Coal Co., Inc. v. Comm., 380 US 624, 15 AFTR 2d 812 [¶ 22,037(5); 22,073(5)].
(3) Comm. v. Southwest Exploration Co., 350 US 308, 48 AFTR 683 [¶ 22,046(10)].
(4) Helvering v. Bankline Oil Co., 303 US 362, 20 AFTR 782 [¶ 22,076(5)].
(5) Douglas v. Comm., 322 US 275, 32 AFTR 358 [¶ 22,140(5)].
(6) Palmer v. Bender, 287 US 551, 11 AFTR 1106 [¶ 22,044(5)].

Footnote ¶ 2101 continued
(7) Johnson v. Phinney, 7 AFTR 2d 860, 287 F.2d 544 [¶ 22,146(15)].
(8) Badger Oil Co. v. Comm., 118 F.2d 791, 26 AFTR 910 [¶ 22,061(35)].
(9) Johnson, ¶ 63,321 P-H Memo TC [¶ 32,545(5)].
(10) Helvering v. Elbe Oil Land Development Co., 303 US 372, 20 AFTR 787 [¶ 22,037(40); 22,061(5)].

Footnote ¶ 2102 [¶ 22,081; 22,186 et seq.].

Footnote ¶ 2103 [¶ 22,084 et seq.].
(1) A full explanation of the "present value method" appears in P-H "Federal Taxes" [¶ 22,106].
(2) Hardesty v. Comm., 127 F.2d 843, 29 AFTR 420; Comm. v. Rowan Drilling Co., 130 F.2d 62,

Footnote ¶ 2103 continued
29 AFTR 1050; Hunt v. Comm., 135 F.2d 697, 31 AFTR 49 [¶ 22,171(20); 22,181(5)].
(3) Rev. Rul. 71-579, 1971-2 CB 225 [¶ 20,567(25)].

Footnote ¶ 2104 [¶ 22,186 et seq.; 22,271 et seq.].
(1) Canadian River Gas Co. v. Higgins, 151 F.2d 954, 34 AFTR 411 [¶ 22,142(5)].
(2) Kirby Petroleum Co. v. Comm., 326 US 599, 66 SCt 409, 34 AFTR 526 [¶ 22,046(5)].
(3) Handelman v. U.S., 17 AFTR 2d 609, 357 F.2d 694 [¶ 22,267(20)].
(4) Rev. Rul. 60-74, 1960-1 CB 253 [¶ 22,272(20)].
(5) However, no percentage depletion on coal is allowed to a lessor receiving royalties which are given capital gain treatment under Sec. 631(b). See ¶ 1623.
(6) Rev. Rul. 57-336, 1957-2 CB 325 [¶ 22,209(40)].
(7) Rev. Rul. 62-5, 1962-1 CB 88 and Rev. Rul. 64-49, 1964-1 CB 218 [¶ 22,227(20)].
(8) U.S. Steel Corp. v. U.S., 19 AFTR 2d 1493, 270 F. Supp. 253, affd. 28 AFTR 2d 71-5053, 445 F.2d 520 [¶ 22,267(20)].
(9) U.S. v. Cannelton Sewer Pipe Co., 364 US 76, 5 AFTR 2d 1773, 80 SCt 1581 [¶ 22,247(15)].
(10) Guthrie v. U.S., 12 AFTR 2d 5666, 323 F.2d 142 [¶ 22,267(15)].

Footnote ¶ 2104 continued
(11) Comm. v. Elliott Petroleum Corp., 82 F.2d 193, 17 AFTR 595; Louisiana Iron & Supply Co., Inc., 44 BTA 1244 [¶ 22,200(5)].

Footnote ¶ 2105 [¶ 22,138 et seq.].
(1) Herring v. Comm., 293 US 322, 55 SCt 179, 14 AFTR 717 [¶ 22,139(5), (20)].
(2) Douglas v. Comm., 322 US 275, 32 AFTR 358 [¶ 22,140(5)].
(3) Rev. Rul. 60-336, 1960-2 CB 195 [¶ 22,140(25)].
(4) Sneed, 33 BTA 478 [¶ 22,146(10)].

Footnote ¶ 2106 [¶ 22,291 et seq.].
(1) Rev. Rul. 59-415, 1959-2 CB 158 [¶ 22,306(100); 22,330(100)].

Footnote ¶ 2107 [¶ 22,291].

Footnote ¶ 2108 [¶ 22,291 et seq.].

Footnote ¶ 2109 [¶ 22,291 et seq.].

Footnote ¶ 2110 [¶ 22,093 et seq.].
(1) Income Tax Information Release No. 1, 12/28/49 [¶ 22,094(20)].

Footnote ¶ 2111 [¶ 22,326 et seq.].

Footnote ¶ 2112 [¶ 22,316].

Footnote ¶ 2113 [¶ 17,391].

Highlights of Chapter 11
Deductions—Depletion

I. **Depletion in General**
   A. **What is depletion**—gradual reduction of original amount of wasting asset by removal for use [¶ 2100].
   B. **Who is entitled to depletion deduction [¶ 2101]:**
      1. Owner of economic interest.
      2. Lessor and lessee.
      3. Life tenant and remainderman.
      4. Sale of entire economic interest—capital gain results (no depletion allowed) [¶ 2101(d)].
      5. Mineral production payments—right to share of production when production occurs [¶ 2101(e)]:
         a. Carved-out payments (created when *property* owner sells portion of future production):
            1) Treated as mortgage loans not taxable to owner.
            2) Seller taxed on amounts used for production payments, subject to depletion.
         b. Retained payments (created when interest owner sells working interest, but retains production payments):
            1) Treated as purchase money mortgage loans.
            2) Property income used to satisfy payment taxable to buyer and subject to depletion.
            3) Operating costs deductible by buyer.
         c. Payments retained by lessors:
            1) Treated by lessee as bonus payable in installments (capitalized and recovered through depletion).
            2) Treated by lessor as depletable income.
II. **Figuring the Depletion Deduction**
   A. **Two methods [¶ 2102]:**
      1. Cost method—applies to all types of depletable property [¶ 2102(a)].
      2. Percentage method [¶ 2102(b)]:
         a. Applies to oil and gas wells, coal and metal mines and certain other deposits, but not to timber.
         b. Depletion deduction in excess of property's adjusted basis allowed, but subject to minimum tax on tax preferences.
   B. **Cost depletion**—often called valuation depletion.
      1. How figured [¶ 2103(a)]:
         a. Basis for depletion—adjusted basis for determining gain on sale.
         b. Following formula used:

            $$\frac{\text{Adjusted basis}}{\text{Total remaining mineral units}} \times \text{Number of units } sold$$

      2. Determining adjusted basis—either cost or value on particular date used [¶ 2103(b)].
      3. Revaluation not allowed same owner unless later discovery, misrepresentation, fraud or gross error.
      4. Charges to capital account—capital expenditures for mines and oil and gas properties [¶ 2103(c)]:
         a. Allocable to mine or well itself—recoverable through depletion.

b. Allocable to plant or equipment—recoverable through depreciation.
c. Intangible drilling and development costs—binding election to expense or capitalize required in first year costs sustained.
5. Incorrect estimate of remaining units—depletion allowance based on revised estimate after discovery [¶ 2103(d)].

C. **Percentage depletion**—depletion allowance is percentage of gross income from property [¶ 2104]:
1. Oil and gas wells—generally repealed but 22% rate applies for certain gas well production and small independent producers (subject to phase-down) [¶ 2104(a)].
    a. Small producer's exemption subject to certain limitations:
        1) Transferred property—transferees generally not entitled to percentage depletion.
        2) Income limitations—depletion allowance cannot exceed 65% of taxpayer's net income from all sources (figured without depletion allowance, net operating loss and capital loss carrybacks). Also, the 50% limitation (II A 2 b above) limits percentage depletion to 50% of taxable income from property.
        3) Retailers and refiners—percentage depletion not available to them.
    b. Gross income from property—generally amount oil or gas sold for in immediate vicinity of well.
    c. Taxable income from property—gross income from qualifying gas well production property less allowable deductions directly related to property on which depletion claimed.
2. Other depletable mineral interests—depletion allowance varies from 5% to 22% depending on type of mineral [¶ 2104(b)].
    a. Gross income from property—gross income from *mining*.
    b. Taxable income from property—gross income from property less allowable deductions directly related to property on which depletion claimed.
    c. *Mining* includes:
        1) Extraction from ground (includes owner's extraction from prior mining waste or residue).
        2) Treatment processes considered mining and necessary to bring minerals to shipping form (to extent applied by mine owner).
        3) Transportation from point of extraction to plants where ordinary treatment process applied (50 mile limit without Revenue Service consent).
    d. Cash or trade discount subtracted from sales price in determining gross income from property.
    e. Business interruption insurance proceeds—not considered gross income from mining.

D. **Bonuses and royalties** [¶ 2105]:
1. Lessor receives bonus *plus* royalties—depletion deduction from following formula:

$$\text{Basis for depletion} \times \frac{\text{Bonus}}{\text{Bonus plus expected royalties}}$$

2. Bonus subject to percentage depletion even if no well or production.

III. **Aggregating Depletable Interests**
A. **Separate interests treated as one property** [¶ 2106]:
1. May aggregate two or more depletable interests.
2. May not aggregate operating with non-operating interests.
3. Operating interests—those for which production costs are considered in figuring % of taxable income limit for percentage depletion.

B. **Operating oil and gas interests**—election to treat part or all operating interests in each tract as separate properties [¶ 2107].
1. New interests combined with existing interests unless elect to separate.

2. Election required with return for first year after acquisition in which development or operation expenditures made.
3. Unitization and pools—taxpayer's interest considered one property.
4. Basis may be divided among separate properties when necessary.
C. **Operating mineral interests other than oil and gas [¶ 2108].**
1. Aggregation rules [¶ 2108(a)]:
   a. May aggregate all interests in one mine, or in two or more mines (each aggregation must include all interests in mine).
   b. Interests need not be in same or continguous tracts.
   c. Nonaggregated interests treated as separate properties.
2. Breakup of single interest [¶ 2108(b)]:
   a. May be broken into two or more properties if mine in each segment.
   b. Consent required to break up already aggregated interest.
   c. Exploration expenditures before aggregation—recomputation of preaggregation depletion deductions required for tax years before 1977.
3. Making the election [¶ 2108(c)]:
   a. Binding for later years unless consent received to change.
   b. Required by return due date for first year after acquisition in which development or operation expenditures made.
D. **Nonoperating mineral interests [¶ 2109]:**
1. Permission to aggregate required—must be requested by later of:
   a. Within 90 days after start of first year for which aggregation desired, *or*
   b. Within 90 days after acquiring interest includible in aggregation.
2. Permission binding for later years unless consent to change received.

IV. **Special Problems**
A. **Depletion of timber [¶ 2110]:**
1. Based on adjusted basis for determining gain on sale (does not include land's cost).
2. Occurs when timber cut.
3. Figured by cost method only:
   a. Yearly deduction equals number of timber units cut multiplied by depletion unit.
   b. Forest fire loss deduction figured same way.
4. Cost allocable to turpentining recoverable through depletion.
B. **Depreciation**—any reasonable method allowed on improvements and obsolescence or decay of improvement from nonuse or below normal capacity use [¶ 2111].
C. **Account books**—no special requirements, except for timber [¶ 2112].
D. **Distributions from depreciation or depletion reserves [¶ 2113].**
1. No distribution allowed till all earnings or profits accumulated after 2-28-13 first distributed.
2. Distribution reduces basis of stock on which declared.
3. When percentage depletion used:
   a. Annual deduction may exceed allowance under cost depletion.
   b. Difference is taxable dividend on distribution.
4. Distribution from part of depletion reserve where valuation using 3-1-13 basis exceeds valuation using cost basis not taxable, but reduces basis of stock.

Chapter 12

DEDUCTIONS—LOSSES
TABLE OF CONTENTS

LOSSES IN GENERAL
Deductible losses 2200
Amount deductible 2201

LOSSES IN BUSINESS OR PROFIT TRANSACTIONS
Losses incurred in trade or business .. 2202
   Anticipated profits or wages
   Legal damages
   How treated on return
Transaction entered into for profit 2203
   Sale of gift property
   Sale of stock
   How treated on return

CASUALTY AND THEFT LOSSES
Casualty losses 2204
   Deduction limited to property losses
   Deductible whether business or personal
   Amount deductible as personal casualty loss
   Figuring business casualty loss
   When to deduct a casualty loss
   Carrybacks and carryovers
   How treated on return
Theft 2205
   Amount deductible
   When to deduct theft loss
   Carrybacks and carryovers
   How treated on return
Handling casualties and thefts on return 2206

SPECIAL RULES
Property converted to business use 2207
Worthless stock 2208
   Loss as a capital loss
   How treated on return
Demolition of buildings 2209
   Intent to demolish formed at time of purchase
   Intent to demolish formed after acquisition
   Buildings demolished to get lease
Abandonment losses 2210
Losses of farmers 2211
   Deterioration of crops in storage
   Destruction of prospective crops
   Destruction of livestock
   Loss reflected in inventory
   Operating a farm and another business
   How treated on return
Loss distinguished from capital expenditure 2212
   Contributions to corporation or partnership
   Surrender of stock to corporation

DISALLOWED LOSSES
Wash sales 2221
   Date basis—period held
   Substantially identical stock or securities
   Dealers and traders
   Partners and partnerships
Sham sales 2222
Sales to related taxpayers 2223
   Family losses
   Sales between corporation and shareholders
   Sales between taxpayer and exempt organization
   Constructive ownership of stock
   Recognized gain on resale
Gambling losses 2224
Hobby losses and expenses 2225
Recapture of farm losses as ordinary income 2226
   Farm recapture property
   Excess deductions account
   Transfer of excess deductions account
   Special rules

NET OPERATING LOSS DEDUCTION
Special treatment of net operating losses 2241
   Years to which a net operating loss may be carried
   Who is entitled to net operating loss relief
Determining net operating loss 2242
   Adjustments in figuring net operating loss

Footnotes appear at end of this Chapter.

Capital loss carryover	How treated on return
Carryover of unused portion of net operating loss 2243	Carryovers or carrybacks from more than one year 2244
Determining the carryover	
Recomputing taxable income	
Refund claim	• Highlights of Chapter 12 .... Page 2261

LOSSES IN GENERAL

A loss actually sustained by an individual during the tax year not compensated for by insurance qualifies as a deduction *only* if incurred: (1) in a trade or business; (2) in a transaction entered into for profit; and (3) in a casualty or theft.

¶ **2200 Deductible losses.** An individual may deduct only the following types of losses [Sec. 165(c); 1.165-1(e)]:

- losses incurred in trade or business;
- losses incurred in any transaction entered into for profit, though not connected with trade or business;
- losses from fires, storms, shipwreck, or other casualty, or from theft.

Losses from involuntary conversions need not be connected with a trade or business, or be incurred in a transaction entered into for profit.

Example: Corwin used his auto solely for pleasure and sold it at a loss. The loss is not deductible because it is not in the above classes. If the auto had been used in business, to the extent that it was so used, the loss on the sale would be deductible as a loss incurred in business. If the auto was destroyed by fire, the loss would be deductible as a casualty loss.

All losses of a corporation generally are deductible [Sec. 165(a); 1.165-1(a)].

Voluntary s well as involuntary losses are deductible. For example, losses from the voluntary sale of business property are deductible. Also, an involuntary loss, such as from theft or a casualty, is deductible.

Deductible losses must be evidenced by closed and completed transactions, fixed by identifiable events. They must be real losses actually sustained during the tax period for which claimed [Sec. 1.165-1(b)]. The amount of the loss must be reduced by salvage value and insurance or other compensation received [Sec. 1.165-1(c)(4)].

Special rules apply to certain losses, such as loss on sale of income-producing property that was formerly used as a residence, loss from worthless stock, loss from voluntary removal of buildings, loss due to obsolescence of nondepreciable property, and losses of farmers [¶ 2207 et seq.]. Farm losses that are deducted may be recaptured as ordinary income by taxpayers with over $50,000 from other sources [¶ 2226].

Some losses are specifically disallowed, such as loss on "wash sales," loss on sham sales, loss on sale to certain related taxpayers, gambling losses in excess of winnings, and hobby losses [¶ 2221 et seq.].

Taxpayers may be able to offset business, casualty and theft losses of the current year against income from past and future years. This is the "net operating loss" deduction [¶ 2241 et seq.]. A net operating loss also affects a taxpayer's liability for the minimum tax on tax preferences [¶ 2403].

The distinction between a loss and a bad debt is explained in ¶ 2315. Deduction of a reserve for losses is discussed at ¶ 2744. Time for deducting losses is covered in ¶ 2743(b).

¶ **2201 Amount deductible.** In general, the amount of the loss deduction is figured the same way as a loss on a sale [Sec. 165(b)]. It is the difference between the amount realized and the adjusted basis of the property [See ¶ 1500 for rules on adjusted basis]. In any event, the amount of the loss cannot be more than the adjusted basis of the property [Sec. 1.165-1(c)]. Insurance, salvage value and other recoveries reduce the deductible loss [Sec. 165(a); 1.165-1(c)].

There are special rules that apply to personal casualty and theft losses and losses of business property by casualty and theft [¶ 2206].

LOSSES IN BUSINESS OR PROFIT TRANSACTIONS

Deductible losses from taxpayer's trade or business involve those arising from taxpayer's regular occupation or calling. On the other hand, a qualified loss from a transaction entered into for profit results from an activity entered into primarily to make a profit outside the individual's regular trade or business.

¶ **2202 Loss incurred in trade or business.** A trade or business is a regular occupation or calling engaged in by the taxpayer for a living or for profit. The loss does not have to be incurred in his principal trade or business[1] if he is engaged in several occupations. An isolated activity or transaction generally is not a trade or business. The distinction is very similar to the difference between business and personal expenses discussed in Chapter 8. For loss from farm operation, see ¶ 2211.

> **Example 1:** Smith bought a new ice-box for his summer home and sold it at a loss after learning that he could not get any ice. He is not entitled to a deduction. Jones is a butcher who bought a refrigerator and sold it at a loss because it did not fit his requirements. He has a deductible loss.

A loss deduction on the sale of an entertainment facility is not allowed as to any part used for personal purposes [Sec. 274]. See also ¶ 1830; 2207.

> **Example 2:** Brown bought a yacht that he used three-fourths of the time for business and one-fourth of the time for pleasure and then sold at a loss. The transaction in its business aspect should be treated as if he had bought a yacht for business use only at three-fourths of purchase price, taken depreciation on that reduced price and sold it for three-fourths of selling price.[2]

(a) Anticipated profits or wages. No deduction is allowed for loss of anticipated profits or wages.

> **Example 3:** As a result of personal injuries, taxpayer had to cancel his contract of employment. Difference between amount received on cancellation, and amount receivable if the contract is not cancelled, is not deductible.[3]

(b) Legal damages. Damages paid under a judgment to settle a suit or claim arising out of trade or business, or transaction entered into for profit are deductible. But see ¶ 1804. Damages for personal losses are not deductible.[4]

> **Example 4:** Payment by president and director to settle suit for mismanagement is deductible;[5] payment to settle a suit for malicious prosecution not related to taxpayer's business is not deductible.[6] Damages paid for fraudulent claim of fire loss are not deductible when it frustrates public policy.[7]

(c) How treated on return. An individual's losses in a trade or business are deducted from gross income to arrive at adjusted gross income [¶ 1804]. This type of deduction (called deductions *for* adjusted gross income, as explained in Chapter

8) should be distinguished from "itemized deductions" such as *personal* casualty losses [¶ 2204(g); 2206].

¶ 2203 Transaction entered into for profit. A loss incurred in any transaction entered into for profit is deductible, though not connected with trade or business [Sec. 165(c)(2); 1.165-1(e)]. Profit is used in its ordinary and usual sense. It has been defined as the gain on invested capital or the receipt of money in excess of the amount spent.[1] It must be of a tangible or pecuniary nature and capable of measurement.

>   **Examples:** Payment made on a promise to a relative to repay him for any loss sustained on securities he bought is not deductible.[1] This is not a profit transaction. Loss on sale of a residence converted to rental use is a transaction entered into for profit and is deductible.[2] An individual depositor of a bank time savings account can take a loss deduction by forfeiting part of the interest previously paid on the account for a premature withdrawal of the principal. See ¶ 1801.

(a) Sale of gift property. A sale of property acquired by gift, bequest, or inheritance may be a transaction for profit. This property is treated as bought when acquired. The important question is—what was the property used for after it was acquired? Ordinary investment property is acquired for profit unless recipient's conduct shows contrary intent.[3]

>   **Examples:** Loss allowed where devisee of a private residence planned to rent or sell it from time of acquisition. A joint owner was also allowed to deduct loss on the sale of personal residence when there was an intention to sell it after it was inherited from the co-owner.[4] Loss on sale of inherited necklace deductible when taxpayer had no intention of using the necklace, but always intended to dispose of it at the best possible price; loss allowed on sale of inherited yacht never used for personal purposes when there was no intent to use it for such purposes.

(b) Sale of stock. Under ordinary conditions, the purchase of stock shows an intention to receive profits, and a loss on its sale would be allowed. But the decisions are conflicting as to deductibility of loss on sale of stock when purchaser has both a profit and nonprofit motive.[5]

>   **Examples:** Loss on sale of apartment house stock is deductible, even if one motive in acquiring it was to have a voice in management; loss on sale of stock in country club is not deductible when bought to become a member. Loss on sale of stock known to be worthless when bought is not deductible [¶ 2208].

(c) How treated on return. An individual's deductible losses in any transaction entered into for profit, even though not for a trade or business, are deductions *for* adjusted gross income if (1) the property involved was held for the production of rents or royalties, or (2) the loss is from the sale or exchange of capital assets (deduction is subject to capital loss limitation), or (3) the loss is due to securities becoming worthless (subject to capital loss limitation) [¶¶ 1613; 1806; 2307; 2312].

CASUALTY AND THEFT LOSSES

This section defines what is a casualty or theft and covers how losses arising from these events are handled on the return. An uncompensated casualty or theft loss is deductible even though not incurred in a trade or business or in a transaction entered into for profit.

¶ 2204 Casualty losses. Losses from fire, storm, shipwreck or other casualty are deductible [Sec. 165(c)(3); 1.165-7]. A "casualty" is an event due to some sudden, unexpected or unusual cause.[1] Generally, this means an accident or some sudden invasion by a hostile agency. It need not be due to natural causes.[2] The progressive deterioration of property through a steadily operating cause is not a casualty;[3] nor is it a casualty when an individual loses an article through his own negligence or carelessness.[4]

(a) Deduction limited to property losses. The deduction is limited to *property* losses, and the loss must be of *taxpayer's* property.[5]

> **Example 1:** Damages paid by Brown for injuries to White's property are not deductible by Brown unless the damages arose out of Brown's business.

The Revenue Service and some courts[6] hold that a loss is allowed only for the actual physical damage to the property resulting from the casualty.

> **Example 2:** Smith's cottage on the shore escaped damage when a hurricane demolished neighboring cottages. But the value was reduced because the area might suffer again from hurricanes. No loss is allowed for the reduction in value.

But a district court[7] allowed a deduction for loss in value of property resulting from a casualty even though there was no physical damage to the property.

> **Example 3:** Muller's home built on a bluff was partially isolated when the bluff suddenly slid and the home's value declined because of poor access to it. Loss in value was allowed even though the home itself was not physically damaged.

Expenses of taking care of personal injuries and the cost of temporary lights, fuels, moving, or rental of temporary quarters are not a part of the casualty loss deduction.[8] But the cost of cleaning up can be (see (c) below).

(b) Deductible whether business or personal. Casualty losses are deductible whether business, investment or personal property is involved. However, the type of property determines the amount of the deduction [(c) below; Sec. 165(c); 1.165-7].

> **Example 4:** King shipped goods manufactured in his business, and also some personal belongings. Both the business and personal articles were lost in a shipwreck. The entire loss on the business property is deductible, but the loss on personal articles is deductible only to the extent it exceeds $100.

➤**OBSERVATION**➤ Loss from destruction of personal property must qualify as a casualty to be deductible; loss from destruction of business or investment property may be deductible even though it fails to qualify as a casualty [¶ 2202; 2203]. For example, a condemnation loss of business or investment property is deductible; a condemnation loss of personal property, such as a residence, is not.

DEDUCTIBLE

Automobile damages to the taxpayer's pleasure car caused by faulty driving (but not taxpayer's wilful act or wilful negligence); damages to taxpayer's auto from faulty driving by operator of another auto [Sec. 1.165-7(a)(3)].

Drought damages if unusual in area (not from normal dry spell);[9] foundation of residence weakened by subsoil shrinkage due to unusually severe drought.[10]

Mine cave-in damage to residence.[8]

Sonic boom damage caused by airplane breaking the sound barrier.[11]

Vandalism damage.[12]

Damage to exterior house paint from sudden and severe smog containing high chemical fume concentration.[13]

Attorney's fees and court costs paid from amount awarded in suit to recover casualty losses, if court finds a deductible casualty.[14]

Footnotes appear at end of this Chapter.

¶ 2204

NOT DEDUCTIBLE

Damages paid to another to cover personal injury by the taxpayer's car[15] (unless used for business purposes).[16]

Moth damage to fur coat.[17]

Loss of livestock from disease (does not meet the suddenness test).[18]

Foundation damage caused by steady effect of wind and weather (but sudden damage by storm is deductible).[3]

Tree and shrub damage on residential property caused by disease or insects[19] (but damage by freeze and mass attack by southern pine beetles are deductible).[20]

Loss of purse, package or other article left on a bus or train; loss of valuable ring that slipped from finger.[4]

Termite damage (unless it meets suddenness test).[21]

Loss on sale of residence due to condemnation of property as part of a site for flood prevention construction.[22]

(c) Amount deductible as personal casualty loss is the lesser of (1) the sustained loss—that is, the value of the property just before the casualty less its value immediately afterward, or (2) the adjusted basis of the property for determining loss on a sale (¶ 1500(b)) [Sec. 1.165-7(b)]. This amount must be reduced by: (1) insurance; (2) amounts received from an employer or disaster relief agencies to restore the property; (3) other compensation for lost property; and (4) $100. But there is no reduction for food, medical supplies, other forms of subsistance received that are not replacements of lost property,[8] or unrestricted cash gifts.[23] Proceeds received after the year the casualty loss was deducted are income in the year received [¶ 2204(e)]. When insurance proceeds exceed the loss and the property is replaced, gain is recognized only to the extent that the amount realized exceeds replacement cost.

If the taxpayer sustains more than one loss from a single event, only one $100 reduction is made. Husband and wife filing jointly are treated as one taxpayer. Separate losses sustained, therefore, by the same act bring only one reduction [Sec. 1.165-7(b)(4)].

Background and purpose. Since casualty and theft losses are generally nonrecurring, extraordinary losses which go beyond the normal losses of everyday living, it was considered appropriate to limit the deduction to those personal out-of-pocket casualty or theft losses above a minimum amount.

Example 5: Johnson's personal summer residence was damaged by hurricane. The home, bought for $18,000, was worth $8,000 just before the storm, but only $1,000 afterward. It was not insured against loss by hurricane.

(1)	Value before casualty	$ 8,000
(2)	Value after casualty	1,000
(3)	Difference	$ 7,000
(4)	The property's cost (adjusted basis)	$18,000
(5)	Lesser of (3) or (4)	$ 7,000
(6)	Casualty loss	$ 7,000
(7)	Less $100 reduction	100
(8)	Deductible loss	$ 6,900

Example 6: Residential property that cost $10,000 and had a value before casualty of $18,000 was completely destroyed. The owner received a $7,000 insurance payment.

(1)	Value before casualty	$18,000
(2)	Value after casualty	0
(3)	Difference	$18,000
(4)	The property's cost (adjusted basis)	10,000
(5)	Lesser of (3) or (4)	10,000
(6)	Less: Insurance recovery	7,000
(7)	Casualty loss	$ 3,000
(8)	Less $100 reduction	100
(9)	Deductible loss	$ 2,900

Exclusion of reimbursed living expenses. A taxpayer who cannot use his principal residence because of a fire, storm or other casualty may exclude part of any insurance proceeds that reimburse him for living expenses. He may exclude an amount that equals the extraordinary (the actual less the normal) expenses for him and the members of his household to live somewhere other than their residence. This exclusion also applies to living expense reimbursements received when a governmental authority forces the evacuation of a residence because of the threat of a fire, storm or other casualty. The exclusion does not apply to recoveries for loss of rental income or damage to the property. If the property is used only partly as a principal residence, the exclusion does not apply to that part of the proceeds that compensates for the nonresidential use of temporary replacement property. Formulas are provided for lump-sum settlements that do not identify the amount allocated to the excludable living costs [Sec. 123; 1.123-1].

How to prove loss in value. The difference between the value of the property immediately before and immediately after the casualty should be proved by competent appraisals. The reasonable cost of repairs necessary to restore the damaged property to its condition immediately before the casualty may be acceptable evidence of the loss of value. However, the loss is measured by the difference in value, not the repair bill.[24] Repairs must be limited to damage sustained [Sec. 1.165-7(a)(2)].

A personal loss involving both realty and improvements (buildings, ornamental trees and shrubbery) is treated as a single loss measured by the actual decrease in the entire property's value[25] [Sec. 1.165-7(b)]. However, when more than one item of *personal* property is involved, the decrease in fair market value of adjusted basis is figured separately for each item and then combined to find the deduction.[26] The cost of clearing property of debris is part of the loss deduction.[27]

Sentimental values are not considered in determining loss on the destruction, damage or theft of family portraits, heirlooms or keepsakes.[28]

(d) Figuring business casualty loss. The amount of a business casualty loss depends on whether the property was *completely* destroyed or only *partially* destroyed. If the entire property is destroyed, the loss is the adjusted basis for determining loss on a sale [¶ 1500(b)] less any insurance, salvage value, or other recovery [Sec. 165(b); 1.165-1(c)(4), 1.165-7(b)(1)].

> **Example 7:** Flynn's shop was demolished by hurricane. The shop was bought for $18,000. It was worth $8,000 just before the storm, but salvage value was only $1,000 thereafter. It was not insured against loss by hurricane. Its adjusted basis immediately before the hurricane was $12,000. The deduction is $11,000 ($12,000 − $1,000), the difference between the adjusted basis and the salvage value after the casualty.

If only part of the property is destroyed, the loss is the lesser of the sustained loss or adjusted basis.

Allocation of loss. The loss for each part of the business property destroyed must be figured separately [Sec. 1.165-7(b)(2)(i)]. See also ¶ 2207.

(e) When to deduct a casualty loss. The time to deduct a casualty loss is the tax year in which the loss was *actually sustained.*

If the extent of the damage is not determined until a later year, deduction is taken in the later year.[29]

If insurance or other reimbursement is not collected in the loss year, but there is a reasonable prospect of recovery by insurance or other reimbursement, the loss is

Footnotes appear at end of this Chapter.

¶ 2204

not sustained until it can be determined with reasonable certainty whether the reimbursement will be received. If a portion of the loss is not covered by insurance or other claim for reimbursement, the loss on that portion is sustained in the year the casualty occurs.

Example 8: Property with a $10,000 basis, insured for $8,000, is destroyed in 1977. Taxpayer expects the $8,000 insurance claim to be paid in full in 1978. Taxpayer has a $2,000 loss in 1977. If he recovers only $7,500 in 1978 with no chance of getting the full $8,000, he has a $500 loss in 1978.

If taxpayer deducts a loss in one year and in a later year is paid for the loss, he does not change the tax for the earlier year. Instead, he includes the payment in income for the year he gets it but only to the extent his taxable income was reduced by the loss deduction [Sec. 1.165-1(d)(2)].

Special rule for some disaster losses. The taxpayer can elect to deduct losses from certain disasters on his return for the tax year immediately preceding the tax year in which the disaster occurred. This applies only to losses in an area the President declares a disaster area entitled to federal assistance. The loss is measured as of the date of the disaster. If the election is not made, the loss is deducted in the year sustained [Sec. 165(h)].

Example 9: A calendar-year taxpayer's property was damaged by hurricane in February 1977, but repairs were not made until 1978. The deductible loss is taken for tax year 1977 and is not taken for 1978, even though taxpayer is on a cash basis and pays the repair bill in 1978. If the President declared the area to be a disaster area after the hurricane, the taxpayer could deduct the loss on his return for tax year 1976.

(f) Carrybacks and carryovers. When casualty losses exceed income for the tax year, the excess is considered a net operating loss and may be carried back to offset income of prior years and carried over to offset income of future years under the net operating loss provisions [Sec. 172]. All casualty losses qualify even though the propety involved is personal, and the taxpayer is not in business [Sec. 1.172-3]. See ¶ 2241 et seq.

(g) How treated on return. Casualty losses on business property or property held for the production of rents or royalties are deductible for adjusted gross income [¶ 1801; 1806(a)]. In general, personal casualty losses are not deductible for adjusted gross income, but are "other itemized deductions" [¶ 2206]. The casualty loss of inventory is reflected in inventory [¶ 2601]. Insurance proceeds for loss of inventory are included in income.

¶ 2205 Theft. Losses from theft or embezzlement are deductible if proven[1] [Sec. 165; 1.165-8]. The cost of recovering stolen property is deductible as a theft loss.[2]

(a) Amount deductible. The amount to deduct is determined the same as a casualty loss [¶ 2204(c) and (d)]. Personal theft losses are deductible only to the extent each theft exceeds $100. In applying these rules, the fair market value of the property immediately after a theft is considered to be zero [Sec. 1.165-8(c)]. The loss must be reduced by (a) amounts received from an insurance company, or value of taxpayer's claim against the company, and (b) surety or fidelity bond proceeds, or amount of claim against the bonding company.[3] A taxpayer cannot take a theft deduction for unreported income that has been embezzled,[4] but may deduct, as a theft loss, amounts loaned to a corporation as a result of fraudulent financial reports issued by the corporation before it became bankrupt.[5]

(b) When to deduct theft loss. Losses from theft or embezzlement generally are considered sustained and deductible in the year the taxpayer discovers the loss

[Sec. 165(e); 1.165-8(a)]. However, if there is a reasonable prospect of recovery on a claim for reimbursement, the deduction is postponed until the year when it can be determined with reasonable certainty whether or not there will be reimbursement [Sec. 1.165-1(d)(3), 1.165-8(a)]. If taxpayer deducts a loss in one year and in a later year is paid for the loss, he includes this amount in income for the tax year it is received. The amount included in income is limited to the amount the taxable income was reduced by the loss deduction [Sec. 1.165-1(d)(2)].

Background and purpose. Losses are generally deducted in the year they are sustained. However, in the case of embezzlements and other thefts, the taxpayer may not find out about the loss until the statute of limitations has run for the year in which the loss was sustained. So that the deduction is not lost, the special rule provides that theft losses are deducted only in the year they are discovered.

(c) Carrybacks and carryovers. The excess of theft losses over income is treated the same as casualty losses [¶ 2204]. It is considered a net operating loss and carried to other years, possibly resulting in a refund for prior years as well as a reduction of income in future years. See ¶ 2241 et seq.

(d) How treated on return. Theft losses are treated on the return the same way as casualty losses. As with casualty losses, theft losses on business property or property held for the production of rents or royalties are deductible for adjusted gross income [¶ 1801; 1806(a)]. In general, personal theft losses are not deductible for adjusted gross income, but are "other itemized deductions" [¶ 2206]. Theft of inventory is reflected in inventory [¶ 2601]. Insurance proceeds for theft of inventory are included in income.

¶ 2206 Handling casualties and thefts on return. Generally, the way casualties and thefts are reported depends on whether there is a net gain or loss from casualties and thefts and if the property is held for personal purposes or for business or investment. A special computation is required to figure the casualty or theft loss (or gain) if there is a mixture of casualty or theft losses and gains.

(a) Personal casualty or theft losses. Personal casualty and theft losses are deductible above the $100 floor on Schedule A of Form 1040. A statement must be attached to the return. The taxpayer can use a special worksheet, Form 4684, for this purpose.

Example: Brown's home was burglarized on 3-15-77 and the following items were stolen: a diamond ring costing $900 bought 2 years ago; negotiable stock certificate costing $1,200 held for 5 months; and a television set costing $550 bought over 1 year ago. He figures his deductible loss and includes the information on his attachment as follows:

		Item Ring	Item Stock	Item TV set
1.	Description	Ring	Stock	TV set
2.	Cost or other basis	$ 900	$1,200	$ 550
3.	Decrease in fair market value:			
	a. Value before theft	$1,400	$1,500	$ 250
	b. Value after theft	0	0	0
	c. Excess	$1,400	$1,500	$ 250
4.	Lesser of lines 2 or 3c	$ 900	$1,200	$ 250
5.	Insurance recovery	720	960	200
6.	Excess	$ 180	$ 240	$ 50
7.	Total of line 6			$ 470
8.	Amount of income-producing property			240

9. Line 7 less line 8	$ 230
10. $100 limit	100
11. Excess	$ 130
12. Deductible theft loss (lines 8 & 11)	$ 370

Allocation of loss. Losses on property used for *both* business and pleasure must be allocated to the respective uses before deducting. This is because business losses are wholly deductible for adjusted gross income, but personal losses are deductible only above the $100 floor as an itemized deduction.

Problem: Sym's car, which he used 75% of the time for business and 25% for pleasure, was totally destroyed in an accident. The car was worth $6,000 when destroyed, but Sym received only $4,800 insurance. What amount is deductible on his return?

Solution: $1,100. A $900 business casualty loss (75% × $1,200) plus a $200 personal casualty loss [$300 (25% × $1,200) minus $100 floor].

(b) Gains and losses from casualties or thefts. A taxpayer may have gains from casualties and thefts as well as losses. This occurs when an insurance recovery or other reimbursement exceeds the loss. When the taxpayer has both gains and losses from casualties or thefts, a special computation is made on Form 4797, Supplemental Schedule of Gains and Losses, and then entered in the applicable place on the return. Generally, if a casualty or theft gain is attributable to Sec. 1231 assets subject to depreciation recapture [¶ 1619], the gain is first computed on Form 4797 to determine the amount recaptured; the gain recaptured as Sec. 1245 or 1250 ordinary income is not included in the special computation. All other casualty or theft gains and losses (not including any condemnation gains or losses) of property held over 9 months are netted separately from any other gains and losses from Sec. 1231 assets [Sec. 1231(a)(2)]. If the result is a net gain (gains exceed losses), this gain is netted again with the gains and losses from other Sec. 1231 assets. If this also results in a net gain, the casualty or theft gains and losses are treated as capital gains and losses (except to the extent the recapture rules apply [¶ 1619]); if it results in a net loss, the casualty gains and losses are treated as ordinary gains and losses [¶ 1620]. However, if the result of the separate netting of the casualty or theft gains and losses is a net loss, the casualty or theft gains and losses are kept separate from any gains and losses from other Sec. 1231 assets; the losses are treated as fully deductible ordinary losses, and the gains are treated as ordinary gains. This special rule determines the treatment of casualty and theft gains and losses from both insured and uninsured property (either as ordinary or as capital gains and losses). It therefore determines whether these gains and losses are fully taxable and fully deductible (ordinary gain and loss treatment) or taxed at a lower effective rate and subject to limitations on the loss deduction (capital gain and loss treatment) [¶ 1612-1614].

NOTE: For tax years starting in 1978, an asset must be held for more than 1-year to get long-term capital gain treatment. See ¶ 1606.

Because the special "netting" rule applies to casualty and theft gains and losses from capital assets held over 9 months (6 months for tax years starting before 1977), as well as assets used in trade or business held over 9 months (6 months for tax years starting before 1977), the special rule also applies to capital assets held for personal purposes, such as a residence or automobile. However, only the deductible amount of casualty or theft loss from personal property in excess of insurance or other reimbursement and $100 is netted with other casualty and theft gains and losses, and if the loss is treated as an ordinary loss, it is an itemized deduction.

SPECIAL RULES

Special rules relate to how losses are figured for: property converted to business use, worthless stock, the abandonment of business or investment property and for farm operations.

¶ 2207 Property converted to business use. Generally, a loss on the sale of property used for personal purposes is not deductible. This is usually the case when a taxpayer sells his personal residence at a loss, although a recognized gain would be taxable [¶ 1416].

When the taxpayer converts personal-use property to business or income-producing property, the basis for loss when sold is the lesser of the fair market value or the adjusted basis of the property on the conversion date.[1] This is the unadjusted basis for loss on the sale. The basis is adjusted for improvements and additions, depreciation and casualty loss deductions for the period since the property was converted to business use [Sec. 1.165-9]. The loss is the excess of the adjusted basis on the sale date over the amount realized.

Example 1: Property bought by Allen on 7-1-73, for $28,000 ($7,000 allocable to the land and $21,000 to the building) was used as a residence until 1-1-76, when it was used by Allen solely as an office for his real estate business. On 1-1-76 the fair market value of the property was $25,000 ($5,000 allocable to the land and $20,000 to the building, which at that time had an estimated useful life of 20 years). The property was sold on 10-1-77, and the amount realized was $22,400 ($4,400 allocable to the land and $18,000 to the building). Allen put an addition on his house in 1974 at a cost of $4,000. There were no casualty losses. Since property was converted to business use before sale there is an adjustment for depreciation from date of conversion.

Basis of land on conversion date (cost)		$ 7,000
Basis of building on conversion date:		
Cost	$21,000	
Plus: Improvements (1974)	4,000	
Less: Casualty loss before conversion	0	
Depreciation before conversion (no depreciation on a personal residence)	0	$25,000
Basis of land and building on conversion date		$32,000
Fair market value of land and building on conversion date		$25,000

(The fair market value of the property on conversion date ($25,000) is less than the adjusted basis on that date ($32,000). This is the unadjusted basis for loss on the sale.)

Basis of land on date of sale (fair market value on conversion date)		$ 5,000
Basis of building on date of sale:		
Value on conversion date	$20,000	
Plus: Improvements after conversion	0	
Less: Casualty loss after conversion	0	
Depreciation after conversion (allowed on business property)	1,750	18,250
Adjusted basis of land and building on date of sale		$23,250
Amount realized from sale of land and building		22,400
Recognized loss on sale		$ 850

If property was acquired and used by taxpayer for rental purposes, but was later occupied as his personal residence and was so used at the time of sale, *no part of loss on sale is deductible*.[2]

Footnotes appear at end of this Chapter.

¶ 2207

Taxable gain. The basis for figuring gain on the sale of property converted from personal use, such as a converted residence, is cost or other basis adjusted to the conversion date. Fair market value on the conversion date is disregarded. However, the fair market value on conversion date is considered for computing depreciation if it is lower than the adjusted basis on conversion date [¶ 2003(c)]. This basis is again adjusted from the date of conversion to the date of sale. The difference between this adjusted basis and the amount realized on the sale is the recognized gain.

Example 2: Assume the same facts as in Example 1, except that the property was sold for $32,000.

Basis of land on conversion date (cost)		$ 7,000
Basis of building on conversion date:		
Cost	$21,000	
Plus: Improvements (1974)	4,000	
Less: Casualty loss before conversion	0	
Depreciation before conversion (no depreciation on a personal residence)	0	25,000
Basis for sale (fair market value is not considered)		$32,000
Plus: Improvements after conversion		0
Less: Casualty loss after conversion		0
Depreciation after conversion (allowed on business property)†		1,750
Adjusted basis of property on date of sale		$30,250
Amount realized from sale of land and building		32,000
Recognized gain on sale		$ 1,750

---

† Even though basis for computing gain is cost, generally the basis for computing depreciation is adjusted basis on conversion date or value of the property on coversion date, whichever is lower. See ¶ 2003(c).

Neither gain nor loss will result on sale of the converted personal residence, if the amount realized is between the basis for gain and the basis for loss.[3]

Example 3: Assume the same facts as in Example 1, except that the property was sold for $25,000. There would be neither gain nor loss on the sale of the property. Since the basis for gain is $30,250, there is no gain on a sale at $25,000. Since the basis for loss is $23,250, there is no loss on a sale at $25,000.

¶ 2208 Worthless stock entitles the owner to a deduction for the year it becomes worthless [Sec. 1.165-5]. The basis for figuring the deduction is the same as for a loss on a sale. No deduction is allowed until the stock is completely worthless[1] [Sec. 1.165-4, 1.165-5(f)]. If taxpayer owes money on the purchase price, he cannot take a deduction until the money owed is paid.[2] A loss may be established by a *bona fide* sale before stock becomes entirely worthless.

Example 1: Stock bought for $20,000 became worthless in 1975. Stockholder auctions it for $10 in 1977 at an expense of $80. Deduction must be taken for 1975.

Losses on worthless bonds are also deductible. See ¶ 2312.

»OBSERVATION» A complete list of worthless securities, indicating the time for deduction, is given in the P-H Capital Adjustments Service.

(a) Loss as a capital loss. Generally, loss on worthless stock is a capital loss on the last day of the tax year it becomes worthless [Sec. 165(g); 1.165-5(c)]. Whether it is a long-term or a short-term capital loss depends on the period it was held.[3]

Example 2: Evans kept his books on a fiscal year ending Sept. 30. On 5-1-77, stock he had bought on 12-1-76 for $5,000 became worthless. It is considered as having been held from

12-1-76 to 9-30-77 ("for more than 9 months"), and Evans has a long-term capital loss [¶ 1613]. The rule also applies to corporations [¶ 3201 et seq.].

Stock of corporate subsidiary. The loss is not a capital loss if the taxpayer is a domestic corporation and sustains the loss on stock of an affiliated corporation. A corporation is affiliated with the taxpayer only if all these conditions are satisfied: (1) the taxpayer owns directly at least 80% of each class of the voting stock and at least 80% of each class of the nonvoting stock of this corporation (nonvoting stock which is limited and preferred as to dividends is not considered); (2) none of the stock was acquired solely to convert a capital loss into an ordinary loss under this rule; (3) more than 90% of the gross receipts for all tax years of this corporation is from sources other than royalties, rents (except rents from rental of properties to employees of the company in the ordinary course of its operating business), dividends, interest (except interest received on the deferred purchase price of operating assets sold), annuities, or gains from sales or exchanges of stocks and securities. Gross receipts from the sale or exchange of stock and securities are taken into account only to the extent of the gains [Sec. 165(g)(3); 1.165-5(d)].

Bank stock owned by another bank. If a bank owns directly at least 80% of each class of stock of another bank, loss sustained on the stock of the other bank is not a capital loss [Sec. 582(b); 1.582-1].

Small business stock. Loss on small business stock or small business investment company stock is not a capital loss [¶ 1632; 3459]. This does not apply to loss on closing of short sale of small business investment company stock.[4]

(b) How treated on return. The capital loss from worthless stock is a deduction for adjusted gross income; see ¶ 1801.

¶ 2209 Demolition of buildings. Generally, a loss from the voluntary demolition of old business buildings and the scrapping of old equipment is deductible, unless taxpayer intended to demolish the building when he acquired it [Sec. 165(a); 1.165-3].

NOTE: Any loss sustained from a demolition starting after 6-30-76 and before 1981 on a certified historic structure is not deductible. The expenses must be charged to the basis of the land [Sec. 280B].

(a) Intent to demolish formed at time of purchase. A taxpayer who intends to demolish the building when he acquires property for business or investment use, cannot take a loss deduction for the demolition, even if he defers the demolition or the replacement of the demolished building[1] [Sec. 1.165-3].

Allocation of basis. Generally, the entire basis of the property is allocated to the land only. The basis is increased by the net cost of demolition, or decreased by the net proceeds from demolition. However, if the building is not immediately demolished, part of the property's basis may be allocated to the building and depreciated over the period the building is used. The part allocated may not exceed the present value of the right to receive rentals from the building over the period of its intended use. The present value of this right is determined at the time the building is first used in trade or business or first held for production of income. Any part of this value not depreciated before demolition can be taken as a loss in the year demolition occurs [Sec. 1.165-3].

(b) Intent to demolish formed after acquisition. A loss from demolition is allowed when the plan to demolish is formed after the buildings are acquired. The

Footnotes appear at end of this Chapter.

amount of the loss is the adjusted basis of the buildings demolished, increased by the net cost of demolition, or decreased by the net proceeds from demolition [Sec. 1.165-3(b)]. It cannot be a capital loss, since there is no sale or exchange [¶ 1602].

(c) Buildings demolished to get lease. If a landlord or tenant must demolish, or if a tenant is merely permitted to demolish buildings on the property by the lease terms or an agreement resulting in a lease, the landlord gets no deduction. The adjusted basis of the demolished buildings, increased by the net cost of demolition, or decreased by the net proceeds from demolition, is considered part of the cost of the lease, and may be amortized over the lease term [Sec. 1.165-3(b)].

¶ 2210 Abandonment losses. A loss arising from the *sudden* end of usefulness of nondepreciable business or investment property is deductible if the abandonment is permanent. If it is not permanent, there may still be a deduction for obsolescence [¶ 2034 et seq.]. Losses from sales or exchanges, or from casualties, are not included. The deduction is not allowed for stock in trade or property held in inventory. The deduction is taken in the year the loss is actually sustained. This is not necessarily the tax year when the act of abandonment or the loss of title to the property occurs [Sec. 1.165-2].

Example: Amounts spent in drilling test holes to find water for a business are capital expenditures. However, if sufficient water is not found and the project is abandoned, the entire cost is deductible as a loss.[1]

A loss deduction is available for good will allocable to the abandoned part of a business.[2]

¶ 2211 Losses of farmers. Generally, losses incurred in the operation of farms as business enterprises are deductible from gross income [Sec. 1.165-6].

(a) Deterioration of crops in storage. If farm products are held for favorable markets, no deduction is allowed for deterioration or shrinkage in weight or decline in value, except as shrinkage is reflected in inventory [Sec. 1.165-6(b)].

(b) Destruction of prospective crops by frost, storm, flood or fire is not a deductible loss. This is a loss of anticipated profits [Sec. 1.165-6(c)]. See ¶ 2202(a).

(c) Destruction of livestock. A farmer raising and selling livestock cannot take a loss for the value of animals that were raised on the farm and die, except as the loss is reflected in an inventory. A loss not reflected in inventory that results from the death of any *purchased* livestock may be deducted if the loss is not compensated for by insurance or otherwise. This applies when death is the result of disease, exposure, injury, or an order of state or federal authorities. The amount deductible is the actual purchase price less any depreciation allowable. The cost of any feed, pasture or care that has been deducted as an expense of operation cannot be included as part of the cost of the stock to determine the amount of the loss [Sec. 1.165-6].

NOTE: If a state or the Federal Government pays for a stock killed or other property destroyed for which a loss was claimed in a prior year, the amount received is income in the year the payment is made.

(d) Loss reflected in inventory. If gross income is determined by the use of inventories, no deduction can be taken separately for livestock or products lost during the year, whether bought for resale or produced on the farm. These losses will be reflected in the inventory by reducing the livestock, or products on hand at the close of the year. This reduces gross income from business by the amount of the loss [Sec. 1.165-6(f)(2)].

(e) Operating a farm and another business. If an individual owns and operates a farm and also has another trade, business or calling, farm operation losses may be deducted from gross income received from other sources only if the farming is engaged in for profit [¶ 2225]. Even if the farming is engaged in for profit, farm losses that are deducted may be recaptured as ordinary income when farm property is sold [¶ 2226].

(f) How treated on return. Losses of a farmer are deductions for adjusted gross income if the farm is operated as a business or the property is held for the production of rents or royalties [¶ 1801; 1806(a)].

¶ 2212 Loss distinguished from capital expenditure. There is no loss deduction if an item is a capital expenditure [¶ 1808]. Generally, the capital expenditure issue arises when taxpayer is considered to have received something of value in return for what he paid out, or the expenditure is related to property he owns. This issue usually will not exist when the ground claimed for the loss is worthlessness, abandonment, or theft. See also loss distinguished from bad debts, ¶ 2311.

(a) Contributions to corporation or partnership. A stockholder gets no loss deduction for voluntary capital contributions to a corporation. These are treated as capital expenditures and increase his stock's basis. However, he has a loss, if forced to make advances to the corporation from which he can expect no return.[1] Advances by partners to partnerships are generally treated the same as advances by stockholders to corporations.[2] See also ¶ 3106 on assessments against stockholders.

(b) Surrender of stock to corporation. A stockholder makes a capital contribution by surrendering part of his stock to a corporation. The cost of the surrendered stock increases the retained stock's basis.[3] However, if surrendered to the corporation's bankers to be used to pay new management and the remaining stock's value is not increased, a loss may be recognized.[4]

DISALLOWED LOSSES

This section deals with special rules that limit or disallow losses arising from certain transactions: wash sales, sham sales, sales among related taxpayers, gambling losses, hobby losses and farm loss recapture.

¶ 2221 Wash sales. A wash sale occurs when substantially identical stock or securities are bought within 30 days before or after the sale. Losses on wash sales (including wash sales on margin[1]) are not deductible. The disallowed loss is added to the basis of the newly acquired stock or security [Sec. 1091; 1.1091-1, 1.1091-2].

Background and purpose. The rule denying a loss deduction on a wash sale was enacted to prevent a tax avoidance scheme. Taxpayers used to sell securities on which they could show a loss, and immediately buy back substantially identical securities. They incurred no real loss, but had paper losses they used to wipe out or minimize their taxable income. The indicated loss added to the price of the new securities gives taxpayer the basis for gain or loss when they are sold. Thus, while the taxpayer cannot prematurely claim losses, he receives the return of his entire investment tax free.[2]

Footnotes appear at end of this Chapter.

Example:

	Item	Date of Purchase	Cost	Date of Sale	Selling Price	Indicated Loss
(A)	100 shares of X stock	1-5-74	$10,000	2-10-77	$8,500	$1,500
(B)	100 shares of X stock	2-2-77	$9,000			

The indicated loss of $1,500 on the sale of the 100 shares in a lot A is disallowed because within 30 days before the sale, identical stock (lot B) was bought. The basis of stock in lot B becomes $10,500 ($9,000 + $1,500). The result would be the same if identical securities were bought within 30 days *after* the sale.

The wash sales provisions apply if the taxpayer contracts or gets an option to acquire substantially identical securities within 30 days before or after the sale [Sec. 1091; 1.1091-1]. They also apply when the taxpayer sells and his wife or a controlled corporation buys substantially identical stocks or securities.[3] The provisions may apply if taxpayer enters into a contract to sell stock. The date of sale is the date the contract is entered into, not when the stock is delivered to the buyer.[4]

If a wash sale also is a short sale [¶ 1608], the rules for closing a short sale apply, except that the date of entering into the short sale is treated as the date of sale to determine the 61-day wash sale period [Sec. 1.1091-1(g), 1.1233-1(a)(5)].

The wash sales provisions do not apply to sales of stock or securities that result in a profit.[5] Nor do they apply to commodity futures contracts since these are not considered stock or securities.[6]

Shares acquired within the 61-day period need not be in the same quantity as the shares sold for the wash sale provisions to apply.[7]

(a) Date basis—period held. The holding period for securities bought in connection with a wash sale includes the period for which the original securities were held [Sec. 1223(4); 1.1223-1].

Example:

	Item	Date of Purchase	Cost	Date of Sale	Selling Price	Indicated Loss
(C)	100 shares of X stock	8-2-75	$5,000	8-31-77	$4,500	$ 500
(D)	100 shares of X stock	9-15-77	$4,600	3-1-78	$4,200	$ 400

The indicated loss of $500 on the sale of 100 shares in lot C is disallowed because within 30 days after the sale identical stock or securities (lot D) were bought. The basis of the securities in lot D becomes $5,100 ($4,600 + $500). The recognized loss on the sale of lot D is $900 ($5,100 − $4,200). The period held is counted as follows: From 8-2-75 to 8-31-77 and 9-15-77 to 3-1-78. Thus the securities in lot D were held more than 9 months. Note: The original securities (lot C) were not held from 9-1-77 to 9-15-77, so that period cannot be included in the holding period.

The holding period is not one consecutive period. It may be fractional parts of months. This holding period may be found by a Revenue Service formula.[8] It is only necessary when the holding period is so close to nine months that one day more or less would make the difference between a long- or short-term capital gain or loss.

NOTE: For tax years starting before 1977, an asset must have been held only for more than 6 months to get long-term capital gain treatment. See ¶ 1606.

(b) Substantially identical stock or securities. The wash sales provisions apply only when the security purchased is substantially identical to that sold. "Substantially identical" means the same in all important particulars. Thus, common stock and voting trust certificates representing common stock are substantially identical.[9] But the following would not be substantially identical: highway authority bonds with same maturity date but different interest rates and bonds of same corporation differing with respect to interest rates, and dates of maturity;[10] stock in a different corporation.[11]

(c) Dealers and traders. The wash sales provisions do not apply to any individual who is a *trader*, that is, one who buys and sells securities on his own account to a degree sufficient to be in a "trade or business." The wash sales provisions do not apply to individuals or corporations who are *dealers*. They buy and sell securities to customers.[12] A corporation that trades in securities but is not a dealer, is subject to the wash sales provisions.

(d) Partners and partnership. The wash sales provisions apply to losses of a partnership when a partner buys substantially identical stock or securities, with his own funds, within 30 days before or after the sale by the partnership.[13]

¶ 2222 Sham sales. When a taxpayer transfers assets for the sole purpose of realizing a loss, the loss is deductible only if the sale is bona-fide. A sham transaction made only for the record will not do. Generally, if there is a repurchase agreement in connection with the purported sale, the sale will be termed a sham and the loss deduction disallowed. The Revenue Service will consider the following circumstances in showing that there has been a repurchase agreement: (a) the relationship, business association or friendship between taxpayer and purchaser, or (b) actual repurchase of the property.[1] A loss on a real sale to a related taxpayer may be disallowed [¶ 2223].

¶ 2223 Sales to related taxpayers. No loss deduction is allowed, even in a real sale or exchange, between certain related taxpayers. If the buyer later sells the property, any gain he realizes is reduced by the amount of the disallowed loss. The following rules apply to losses from sales or exchanges of property other than those resulting from distributions in corporate liquidations [Sec. 267].

(a) Family losses. No deduction is allowed if the sale or exchange was made, directly or indirectly, between:

- Husband and wife;
- Brothers and/or sisters (whole or half blood);
- Ancestors and lineal descendants [Sec. 267(b), 267(c); 1.267(b)-1].

The loss is disallowed even if the sale is made indirectly. The sale of stock on a stock exchange by one member of a family followed the same day by purchase on the stock exchange of the same number of shares of the same stock at similar prices by another family member is considered an indirect sale between members of the family.[1]

A forced sale is treated the same as a voluntary sale. For example, a loss sustained by a mortgagor on foreclosure sale to a family member as mortgagee is not deductible.[2]

(b) Sales between corporation and shareholders. No deduction is allowed if a sale is made, directly or indirectly, between a corporation and an individual who owns more than 50% in value of the outstanding stock, directly or indirectly [Sec. 267(b)(2); 1.267(c)-1].

(c) Sales between taxpayer and exempt organization. No deduction is allowed if the sale is made between a taxpayer and an exempt organization controlled by it, or, if the taxpayer is an individual, controlled by him or his family [Sec. 267(b)(9); 1.267(b)-1].

(d) **Constructive ownership of stock.** In applying the above rules, an individual is considered to own not only the stock he actually owns, but stock he constructively owns under the so-called "stock ownership, family, and partnership rules" explained below [Sec. 267(c); 1.267(c)-1].

1. **Stock ownership rule.** Stock owned, directly or indirectly, by or for a corporation, partnership, estate or trust, is considered as being owned proportionately by or for its shareholders, partners, or beneficiaries.

Example 1: A owns 60% of Corp. P's stock, and Corp. P owns all the stock of Corp. Q. A is the constructive owner of 60% of Corp. Q's stock. Since A is the owner of more than 50% in value of the outstanding stock of Corp. Q, if A sold property to the corporation at a loss, the loss would be disallowed. Furthermore, if the corporation sold property to A at a loss, that loss would also be disallowed.

Example 2: B is the beneficiary of the R Trust that owns 600 of the 1,000 shares of Corp. T's stock. Assume that B's proportionate interest in the trust is 75% and B owns personally 100 shares of Corp. T's stock. B is the constructive owner of 450 shares of T stock (75% of 600) and the actual owner of 100 shares (550 shares or 55% in all). Since B is the owner of more than 50% in value of the outstanding stock of corporation T, if B sold property to the corporation at a loss, the loss would be disallowed. A loss in a sale by the corporation to B also would be disallowed.

Example 3: C and D are members of the partnership of C & D that owns 4,000 of the 5,000 shares of corporation U. C's proportionate interest in the partnership is 60%. C owns personally 500 shares of stock of corporation U. D does not own personally any shares of corporation U. C is the constructive owner of 2,400 shares of U stock (60% of 4,000) and the actual owner of 500 shares. Since C is the owner of more than 50% in value of the outstanding stock of corporation U, a loss would be disallowed on any sale of property between them.

NOTE: Under the partnership rule ((3) below), C also would be the constructive owner of the 1,600 shares constructively owned by D (40% of 4,000). By applying the partnership rule and the stock ownership rule, C would constructively own a total of 4,000 shares, so that he would own over 50% of the stock even without considering the 500 shares he owned personally. Similarly, D would be the constructive owner of over 50% of the stock.

2. **Family rule.** An individual is considered as owning the stock owned, directly or indirectly, by or for his family (husband or wife; brothers and sisters, whether by the whole or half blood; ancestors and lineal descendants).

Example 4: E owns 30%, his wife 10%, and his wife's brother (E's brother-in-law) 20% of the stock of corporation V. Under the statute, E is the constructive owner of 10% of V stock and the actual owner of 30% (40% in all). Since E is the owner of less than 50% in value of the outstanding stock of corporation V, a loss would be allowed on a sale of property between them.

Under the statute, Mrs. E is the constructive owner of 50% of V stock (the 30% owned by E plus the 20% owned by her brother) and the actual owner of 10% (60% in all). Since Mrs. E is the owner of more than 50% in value of the outstanding stock of corporation V, a loss would be disallowed on a sale of property between them.

3. **Partnership rule.** An individual actually owning stock of a corporation and an individual constructively owning stock of a corporation under the rule (1) above, is considered as owning the stock owned, directly or indirectly, by or for his partner.

Example 5. F owns 40% and his partner G owns 20% of the stock of corporation W. Under the statute, F is the constructive owner of 20% of W stock and the actual owner of 40%

(60% in all). Since F is the owner of more than 50% in value of the outstanding stock of corporation W, a loss on a sale of property between them would be disallowed.

Under the statute, G is the constructive owner of 40% of W stock and the actual owner of 20% (60% in all). Since G is the owner of more than 50% in value of the outstanding stock of corporation W, a loss on a sale of property between them would be disallowed.

NOTE: Stock constructively owned by an individual under the stock ownership rule, (1) above, is considered to be actually owned by the constructive owner so as to make another the constructive owner of the stock. Stock constructively owned by an individual under the family and partnership rules, (2) and (3) above, is not considered to be actually owned by the constructive owner so as to make another the constructive owner of stock [Sec. 267(c)(5); 1.267-1(a)(3)].

Example 6: H and J (not related) are members of the partnership of H & J which owns 4,000 of the 10,000 shares of corporation X. H's proportionate interest in the partnership is 60% and J's 40%. H owns personally 500 shares of stock of corporation X, Mrs. H owns personally 600 shares of corporation X, and J owns personally 700 shares. Mrs. H also owns 100% of the stock of corporation Y which owns 1,000 shares of corporation X.

Under the statute, H is the constructive owner of 2,400 shares actually owned by the partnership (60% of 4,000). He is also the constructive owner of the 600 shares actually owned by Mrs. H, the 1,000 shares constructively owned by Mrs. H, the 700 shares actually owned by J, and the 1,600 shares constructively owned by J. Under the statute, therefore, H is the constructive owner of 6,300 shares and the actual owner of 500 shares (6,800 shares or 68% in all). Since H is the owner of more than 50% in value of the outstanding stock of corporation X, a loss on a sale of property between them would be disallowed.

Under the statute, Mrs. H is the constructive owner of the 500 shares actually owned by H and the 2,400 shares constructively owned by H through his interest in the partnership. She is not the constructive owner of the 700 shares constructively owned by H, because of actual ownership by J, his partner, nor is she the constructive owner of the 1,600 shares constructively owned by H because of J's constructive ownership of 1,600 shares by virtue of his 40% share of the partnership. Mrs. H is also the constructive owner of the 1,000 shares owned by corporation Y. Altogether, Mrs. H is the constructive owner of 3,900 shares and the actual owner of 600 shares of corporation X (4,500 shares or 45% in all). Since Mrs. H is the owner of less than 50% in value of the outstanding stock of corporation X, either could deduct a loss on a sale of property between them.

(e) Recognized gain on resale. When a loss on a sale to a related taxpayer is disallowed and the buyer later sells the property at a gain, a special rule limits the gain. Gain on the sale of the property is recognized only to the extent that it exceeds the disallowed loss [Sec. 267(d); 1.267(d)-1].

Example 7: Clark bought stock for $7,500 and sold the stock to his wife for $5,000. The $2,500 loss is disallowed. The wife sells the stock for $8,000. The wife's recognized gain is $500 figured as follows:

Selling price by wife	$8,000
Basis to wife	5,000
Realized gain	$3,000
Disallowed loss	2,500
Excess of realized gain over disallowed loss (gain recognized)	$ 500

This special rule does not apply if the loss was disallowed under the wash sales provisions [¶ 2221].

Divisible property. Suppose the property sold at a loss to a related purchaser is sold as a whole, but is divisible into parts, and the buyer sells a part. The buyer's basis for that part may be found by allocating a portion of the basis of the whole property in the proportion that the fair market value of the part bears to the fair market value of the whole when the buyer acquired the property. The amount realized by the seller for that part is figured by a similar allocation.

¶ 2223

Example 8: H sold class A stock which had cost him $1,100, and common stock which had cost him $2,000, to his wife W for a lump sum of $1,500. The loss of $1,600 ($3,100 less $1,500) was disallowed. When W bought the stocks, the value of class A stock was $900 and the value of the common stock was $600. W sold the class A stock for $2,500. Her recognized gain is $1,400 determined as follows:

Selling price by W of class A stock	$2,500
Less: Basis allocated to class A stock ($900/$1,500 × $1,500)	900
Realized gain	$1,600
Less: Disallowed loss sustained by H on class A stock sale:	
Basis to H of class A stock $1,100	
Amount realized by H on class A stock	
($900/$1,500 × $1,500) 900	
Disallowed loss to H on class A stock sale	200
Recognized gain on sale of class A stock by W	$1,400

If the seller's basis for figuring loss on the part is not known, the loss may be figured by allocating to the part a portion of the loss on the whole property in the proportion that the fair market value of the part bears to the fair market value of the whole property on the date the buyer acquired it.

Example 9: Assume the same facts as in Example 8 except that H originally bought both classes of stock for a lump sum of $3,100. The disallowed loss to H on the sale of all the stock to W is $1,600 ($3,100 less $1,500). An exact determination of the disallowed loss sustained by H on sale to W of class A stock cannot be made because H's basis for class A stock cannot be determined. A determination of the disallowed loss is made by allocating to class A stock a portion of H's loss on the entire property sold to W in the porportion that the fair market value of class A stock at the time acquired by W ($900) bears to the fair market value of both classes of stock at the time ($1,500). The allocated portion if $900/$1,500 × $1,600, or $960. W's recognized gain is $640 (W's realized gain of $1,600 less $960).

Exchange or gift of property by buyer. Suppose the buyer exchanges the property for other property in a *nontaxable* exchange, and then sells the other property. The gain on the sale of the other property is limited by this rule, just as though the property sold were the original property bought. But only the person who bought the original property gets the benefit of the rule. Thus, if the buyer gave the property to another person, the other person would have to pay the full tax if he sold the property at a gain.

Losses may also be disallowed in transactions between parties to a trust [¶ 3018], a partner and his partnership [¶ 2923] and controlled corporations when one is a personal holding company [¶ 3408].

¶ 2224 Gambling losses. Losses from wagering transactions are allowed only to the extent of gains from such transactions [Sec. 165(d); 1.15-10].

Example: Carson whose gambling transactions result in losses of $500 and gains of $400 must report the $400 gain to obtain a deduction for $400 of the loss. The $100 excess of the loss over the gains is not deductible. If the gains are $500 and the losses $400, the $100 excess of gains over losses is taxable.

How treated on return. When gambling is a person's trade or business, he gets a loss deduction for adjusted gross income up to the amount of his gambling gains. If it is not a trade or business, he can take the losses, up to the gains, as "other itemized deductions."[1]

¶ 2225 Hobby losses and expenses. An individual or Subchapter S corporation [¶ 3140 et seq.] engaged in an activity not carried on for profit cannot take a deduction attributable to that activity except: (1) deductions that would be allowed whether or not the activity was carried on for profit (for example, interest, state and local property taxes and capital gains deduction); and (2) deductions that would be allowed if the activity was carried on for profit but only to the extent the gross income from the activity for the tax year exceeds the allowable deductions in (1) [Sec. 183; 1.183-1(b)(1)]. An activity is presumed to be "engaged in for profit" if it produces a profit in any 2 or more tax years out of 5 consecutive years ending with the current year [Sec. 1.183-1(a)]. For the breeding, training, showing or racing of horses, there must be a profit in 2 out of 7 consecutive years [Sec. 1.183-1(c)(1)]. The taxpayer can elect to suspend the presumption until 5 (or 7) tax years, starting after 1969, from the time the activity is started. Generally, this is made by filing a statement with the Revenue Service no later than 3 years after the due date of the return for the year the activity is started [Sec. 183(e); Temp. Reg. Sec. 12.9]. By making the election, the taxpayer automatically extends the statute of limitations for any deficiency during any year in the suspension period to at least two years after the return's due date (not including extensions of time to file) for the last year in the 5 (or 7) year period [Sec. 183(e)(4)]. But this does not apply to any deficiency in a tax year ending before 10-4-76, the assessment of which is barred by the statute of limitations.[1]

Background and purpose. The taxpayer has the burden of proving he was engaged in an activity for profit; this burden shifts to the Revenue Service if the taxpayer made a profit in any 2 years of the period of 5 consecutive years ending with the current tax year. A literal application of these rules would preclude a taxpayer from taking advantage of the presumption if he showed a loss at the end of the first tax year after starting an activity. There would be no profit years in the consecutive 5-year (or 7-year) period ending with the current year. The Revenue Act of 1971 corrected this situation by allowing the taxpayer to elect to temporarily suspend the presumption.

¶ 2226 **Recapture of farm losses as ordinary income.** Farm losses after 1969 may be recaptured as ordinary income when farm recapture property is sold or exchanged in a tax year starting after 1969 [Sec. 1251]. This rule applies to all taxpayers who do not report farm income on the accrual method, but applies only to the individual taxpayer who in any year has nonfarm adjusted gross income that exceeds $50,000 and then only to the extent the farm loss exceeds $25,000. In tax years starting before 1976, each year's net farm losses had to be added to an excess deductions account. For tax years starting after that date, no additions can be made (see (b) below). When farm recapture property is sold, the portion of any gains that are treated as ordinary income is limited to the taxpayer's balance in his excess deductions account.

NOTE: This rule does not disallow the deduction of farm losses, but the hobby loss provisions may [¶ 2225].

Background and purpose. The farm accounting rules were adopted to relieve farmers of bookkeeping burdens. However, they were also used by some high-income taxpayers who were not primarily engaged in farming to obtain a tax, but not an economic, loss which was then deducted from their high-bracket, nonfarm income. In addition, these high-income taxpayers often received capital gains treatment when they sold farm assets. The excess deductions account concept provided for the recapture of farm losses previously used to offset nonfarm income. However, the Tax Reform Act of 1976, terminated additions to the account for tax years beginning after 12-31-75.

(a) **Farm recapture property.** Farm recapture property is: (1) farm land held over nine months (six months for tax years starting before 1977), (2) depreciable personal property held over nine months (six months for tax years starting before 1977), (3) livestock and (4) unharvested crops (¶ 1622) [Sec. 1251(c)(1), (e)(1)].

NOTE: For tax years starting in 1978 and later, the "over 9 months" rule is increased to "over 1-year."

The amount of the ordinary income recapture is the lesser of: (1) the total of the differences between the amount realized (or fair market value if the property is not sold, exchanged or in an involuntary conversion) and the adjusted basis of each farm recapture property disposed of during the year, and (2) the amount in the taxpayer's excess deductions account (see (b) below) at the end of the year [Sec. 1251(c)]. However, the ordinary income recapture from farm land is limited to an amount equal to the deductions in the current and four preceding years for soil and water conservation expenditures [¶ 1845] and land clearing costs (¶ 1845(d)) [Sec. 1251(c)(2)(C), (e)(5); 1.1251-1(b)(2)]. In addition, the recapture rule does not apply to depreciable real property nor is any ordinary income recognized when farm property is given (but see (c) below) or transferred at death [Sec. 1251(d)(1), (2); 1.1251-2(e)(2), 1.1251-4(b)].

NOTE: When Sec. 1245 [¶ 1619(a)] and Sec. 1251 both apply to a sale or exchange of farm depreciable personal property, ordinary income is first recaptured to the extent of the depreciation [Sec. 1.1251-1(b)(5)]. The recapture provisions are applied first to Sec. 1245 assets, then to Sec. 1251 assets. In addition, if ordinary income may be recaptured for previously deducted soil and water conservation expenditures and land clearing costs [¶ 1845(e)] as well as for deducted losses under Sec. 1251, Sec. 1251 applies first [Sec. 1252(a)(1); 1.1252-1(a)]. Although farm buildings are not subject to the recapture rule under Sec. 1251, there may be recapture under Sec. 1250 [¶ 1619(b)].

(b) Excess deductions account. The aggregate of ordinary income recaptured in any tax year after 1969 is limited by the balance in the taxpayer's excess deductions account at the end of the year [Sec. 1251(c)(2)]. Every taxpayer in the business of farming that sustains a farm net loss in a tax year starting after 1969 must establish an excess deductions account, unless the taxpayer reports farm income on the accrual basis (see below), using inventories and capitalizing all costs which may be either capitalized or deducted as expenses [¶ 1845]. However, for tax years starting after 1975, there will be no additions made although the rules still apply to existing accounts. For tax years starting before 1976, the taxpayer must add any farm net loss in a tax year to the account and maintain the account as long as there is a balance. But an individual taxpayer only adds a net loss to his account for a year he has over $50,000 in nonfarm adjusted gross income and then only to the extent his loss exceeds $25,000. If both spouses have nonfarm adjusted gross income and they file separately, a $25,000—$12,500 exemption applies rather than $50,000—$25,000. The $50,000—$25,000 exemption also applies to a small business corporation [¶ 3140 et seq.] for taxable years ending before 12-10-71, unless any of its shareholders has a farm net loss. For tax years ending after 12-10-71, there are two exceptions: (1) to determine whether nonfarm adjusted gross income exceeds $50,000, the corporation's nonfarm income is combined with the nonfarm income of that shareholder with the largest nonfarm income, and (2) the $25,000 net farm loss exclusion is disallowed if any shareholder also is a shareholder of another small business corporation with a farm net loss [Sec. 1251(b)].

If a taxpayer has farm net income rather than loss in a tax year starting after 1969, he subtracts the income from the excess deductions account in any year he has a balance in the account [Sec. 1.1251-1(a), 1.1251-2(a)(1)]. A taxpayer also subtracts any adjustments for deductions that did not result in a tax reduction. Gains and losses from the disposition of farm recapture property are not included in the computation of farm net income or loss. However, the ordinary income recapture of previously deducted losses is subtracted from the excess deductions account after the adjustment of the account for the year's farm net income or loss

[Sec. 1251(b)(3), (e)]. At the end of a year, the taxpayer adjusts his account for any farm net income or loss and then compares the account balance with the total of any gains from the sales or exchanges of farm recapture property; if the balance exceeds the gain, all the gain is treated as ordinary income, but if the gain exceeds the balance, the gain is treated as ordinary income only to the extent of the balance [Sec. 1251(c); 1.1251-1(b)]. The recaptured ordinary income is then subtracted from the account and the resulting balance is the opening balance in the following year [Sec. 1251(b)(3); 1.1251-2(c)].

Example: Farmer Brown has a farm net income of $5,000 and $20,000 in his excess deductions account in 1977. He subtracts the income from the account and compares this amount ($15,000) with his total gains from sales of farm recapture property in 1977. This total is $3,500. Because the account balance exceeds the gains, Brown treats all the gains from the sales of farm recapture property as ordinary income. The balance in his excess deductions account at the end of 1977 is $11,500 ($15,000 less $3,500).

Election of accrual accounting. A taxpayer can avoid an excess deductions account and therefore the recapture of deducted losses as ordinary income by using accrual basis accounting. The taxpayer may elect the accrual method for this purpose without Revenue Service consent and certain income and deduction adjustments [¶ 2709(b)]. The election for a tax year must be filed by the return filing date (including extensions) for that year and is binding for later years [Sec. 1251(b)(4); 1.1251-2(c)(4)].

(c) Transfer of excess deductions account. When farm recapture property (see (a) above) is given, some or all of the excess deductions account may also be transferred and maintained by the recipient of the property. The account is transferred only if in any one-year period, the donor makes gifts of farm recapture property that have a potential gain (difference between fair market value and adjusted basis, but for land, limited to the deductions for soil and water conservation expenditures and land clearing costs [¶ 1845]) that is more than 25% of his total potential gain on farm recapture property at the time of the first such gift [Sec. 1.1251-2(e)(2)]. If a transfer is necessary, each recipient of recapture property succeeds to the same proportion of the donor's excess deductions account as the potential gain of the property received by him bears to the aggregate of potential gain for all farm recapture property held by the donor at the beginning of the one-year period. The recipient of the property succeeds to the account at the time of the gift, but the amount of the account balance is computed at the end of the donor's tax year after any adjustments for the donor's farm net income or loss [Sec. 1251(b)(5)(B); 1.1251-2(e)(2)]. In addition, the excess deductions account is also carried over to the successor corporation in the liquidation of a subsidiary corporation and in most tax-free reorganizations (¶ 3331; 3332; 3336(a)). For transfers in 1976 and later years, the entire account is applied to both the transferor and transferee corporations in a Type "D" reorganization (¶ 3306) [Sec. 1251(b)(5)(A); 1.1251-2(e)(1)]. The recapture potential is not carried over in the case of a transfer to a controlled corporation [¶ 1405]; the transferor of the farm recapture property recaptures ordinary income on the sale or other disposition of the stock received on the transfer [Sec. 1251(d)(6)].

(d) Special rules. The amount of ordinary income recaptured in otherwise tax-free corporate transactions involving farm recapture property is limited to the gain recognized because of boot received. This rule applies to the tax-free liquidation of a subsidiary [¶ 3334], the transfer of property to a controlled corporation [¶ 1405; 1406(b)] and corporate transfers in reorganizations (¶ 3309(b)) [Sec. 1251(d)(3); 1.1251-4(c)]. Note that any recapture potential that is not recognized is carried over. In certain situations, otherwise nontaxable gains become taxable [Sec.

¶ 2226

1.1251-1(e)(2)]. This occurs in a 12-month corporate liquidation [¶ 3128] and the distribution of farm recapture assets to shareholders [¶ 3204]. Contributions of farm recapture property to partnerships are generally exempt from recapture. However, the partners must account for the recapture income on disposition of the property by the partnership. The partnership agreement can allocate the income to the contributing partner [Sec. 1251(d)(5)]. Ordinary income recapture is also limited in otherwise tax-free property transfers [¶ 1406(b)] and involuntary conversions [¶ 1411] to any recognized gain plus the fair market value of property received that is not farm recapture property [Sec. 1251(d)(4); 1.1251-4(d)].

NET OPERATING LOSS DEDUCTION

This section covers the method of computing the net operating loss deduction. This was created to cushion the impact of the year-by-year principle as to net losses. This device allows the taxpayer to carry the losses of one year and offset them against the income of another year.

¶ 2241 **Special treatment of net operating losses.** A taxpayer's income and deductions for a particular year ordinarily are the only items considered in computing his taxable income or loss for the year [¶ 2719; 2735]. If this were always the case, a taxpayer who had a bad year followed by a good year would be taxed on the income of the good year without any offsetting benefit for the loss of the bad year. However, the Code gives some relief in this situation. It allows taxpayers to average their profits and losses to some extent by letting them use the losses of one year to offset the profits of another year. This averaging device is known as the carryback and carryover of net operating losses [Sec. 172; 1.172-1—1.172-8]. In addition, a carryforward election may be made, instead of the regular carryback and carryover, for any loss year that ends after 12-31-75. The election must be made by due date of the return (including extensions of time to file). Once it is made and applies to any loss year, it is irrevocable. However, a taxpayer may terminate the election after the period of irrevocability has expired. The taxpayer may make a new carryforward election at any time [Sec. 172(b)(3)].

> **Example 1:** Hays owns a store. In the tax year he had sales receipts of $104,000. However, his operating expenses were $108,000, so he has a loss of $4,000. He has no other income or expenses. In a prior year, he had a net profit of $6,000. He can use the $4,000 loss (after certain adjustments) as an offset against the profit of the prior year if he makes a timely election. Since he has already paid the tax for the prior year, he can file a refund claim based on his reduced income for that year. He can also elect not to carry back the loss, but instead carry it forward.

The loss must be from the operation of a trade, business or profession, or from casualty or theft. A loss due to confiscation of a business by a foreign government can also qualify for the net operating loss.[1]

(a) Years to which a net operating loss may be carried. If the carryforward election (discussed above) is not made, the net operating loss can be used to offset profits of the 3 years before the year of the loss under the regular carryback-carryforward rules. This is the "carryback" of net operating loss mentioned above. If any of the loss remains after this carryback, taxpayer can use it to offset profits of the 7 years following the year the loss was sustained. The carryover is five years for tax years ending before 1976. This is the carryover provision [Sec. 172(b)(1); 1.172-4]. The loss must be carried first to the earliest year and then to the next earliest year, and so on. For example, if taxpayer has a net operating loss for 1977, he can apply it to offset profits of these years: 1974, 1975, 1976, 1978, 1979, 1980, 1981, 1982, 1983, 1984. Taxpayer must follow this sequence. Thus, he cannot use any of the 1977 loss to offset 1975 income until 1974 income has been entirely absorbed.

> **NOTE:** The Tax Reform Act of 1976, has provided for two additional carryover years on losses incurred in tax years ending after 12-31-75, for business taxpayers in general, insurance companies (making a 7-year carryover) as well as for regulated transportation corporations (making a 9-year carryover). In addition, these taxpayers who are eligible to carry their losses back 3 years may elect to forego the entire carryback period and carry forward the loss for the 7 or 9 year period. [Sec. 172(b)(1)(B), (C)].

Regulated transportation companies are allowed a carryover of 9 years for tax years ending after 1975. This is in addition to the 3-year carryback. This carryover was seven years for tax years ending before 1976. Special rules apply to firms with losses caused by the Trade Expansion Act of 1962 [Sec. 172(b)(1); 1.172-4].

A foreign expropriation loss gives rise to a carryover or carryback if the loss cannot be fully offset against income of the loss year. However, at taxpayer's option, a foreign expropriation loss sustained after 1958 can be carried over for 10 years (but not carried back) if it is at least 50% of the net operating loss. The loss is treated separately from any remaining operating loss. In the carryover years, the remaining loss is applied first. This treatment of expropriation losses must be elected on the return for the expropriation year and cannot be revoked after the return's due date [Sec. 172(b); 1.172-11]. For treatment of recoveries of expropriation losses, see ¶ 2316(d).

(b) Who is entitled to net operating loss relief. All taxpayers are entitled to the net operating loss deduction. It can be taken even if the individual is not in business during the deduction year [Sec. 172; 1.172-1]. When the taxpayer's marital status has changed, the net operating loss can be carried back only to his vested part of joint return income.[2] Special rules apply to partnerships [¶ 2914], estates and trusts [¶ 3015], corporations [¶ 3215 et seq.], real estate investment trusts [¶ 3432], and when partnership-type taxation is elected [¶ 3143(c)].

¶ 2242 Determining net operating loss. The starting point for computing the net operating loss is the loss shown on the tax return for the year. Unless the return shows a loss, there can never be a net operating loss.

Assume that deductions exceed income, so the return shows a loss for the year. Because of the special treatment of long-term capital gains and the deduction for personal exemptions, the loss shown on the return may not be an economic loss. To limit the net operating loss carryback and carryover to economic loss, certain adjustments have to be made in the loss figure shown on the return. The resulting amount is the net operating loss.

> **NOTE:** The net operating loss may affect the minimum tax on tax preference items. The part of a net operating loss that remains to be carried forward from the current year may result in a deferral of all or part of any minimum tax liability until later years when the loss is absorbed. See ¶ 2403.

(a) Adjustments in figuring net operating loss. In order to convert a tax loss into economic loss, the following items reduce the amount of the loss shown on the return [Sec. 172(d); 1.172-3]:

- Net operating loss from any other year.
- Long-term capital gain deduction.
- Deduction for personal exemptions.
- Any excess of capital losses over capital gains. Also nonbusiness capital losses may be offset only against nonbusiness capital gains. If nonbusiness

Footnotes appear at end of this Chapter.

¶ 2242

capital losses exceed nonbusiness capital gains, the excess cannot be deducted, even if there are enough business capital gains.
- Any excess of nonbusiness deductions over nonbusiness income.
- Contributions for a self-employed person to a self-employment retirement plan (¶ 1839) [Sec. 172(d)(4)(D); 1.172-3(a)].

Nonbusiness income and deductions. Nonbusiness income is income from sources other than taxpayer's trade, business or profession. Dividend income is not business income, so the income of a small business corporation that must be included in a stockholder's income as a dividend [¶ 3142(b)] is not business income to the stockholder.[1] Salaries and rent, however, are considered business income [Sec. 1.172-3(a)(3)].[2] Nonbusiness deductions for net operating loss purposes generally are taxpayer's itemized deductions, except casualty or theft losses. Gains or losses from disposing of depreciable business property (Sec. 1231 property, see ¶ 1618) are treated as business income or expense [Sec. 172(d)(4); 1.172-3(a)(3)].

BUSINESS DEDUCTIONS

Accounts receivable. Loss from sale of accounts receivable on disposing of a business, if they arose under the accrual method of accounting in ordinary course of taxpayer's trade or business.[3]

Small business stock. Loss from disposition or worthlessness of small business stock or stock in small business investment companies [Sec. 1244(d)(3); 1.1244(d)-4].

State income taxes on income from taxpayer's business, interest on state and federal income taxes on his business income, and litigaton expenses in connection with these taxes.[4]

Moving expenses paid by an employee for the start of work at a new principal place of employment.[5]

Nonbusiness deductions may be offset only against nonbusiness income. You cannot deduct them from business income to increase or create a net operating loss.

Example: The following illustrates how net operating loss is computed. Miller owns a hardware store. In 1977, he had sales receipts of $242,000. His expenses were $248,000. His tax return for 1977 (joint return) shows the following figures:

Loss from business operations		$(6,000)
Dividend income after $100 exclusion		325
Capital gains—long and short term		2,000
Capital losses—long and short-term		(2,900)
Itemized deductions, including an allowable casualty loss of $500		1,050
Personal exemptions		1,500

His taxable income is computed as follows:

Business loss		$(6,000)
Dividend income after $100 exclusion		325
Capital loss—subject to capital loss limitations		0
Adjusted gross income		$(5,675)
Less: Itemized deductions	$1,050	
Personal exemptions	1,500	2,500
Taxable income (loss)		$(8,225)

To find Miller's net operating loss, you must make the following adjustments to this taxable income figure:

Taxable income (loss)	$(8,225)
Remove:	
1. Net operating loss from another year	0
2. Long-term capital gain deduction	0
3. Excess of capital losses over capital gains (this was already left out in computing taxable income)	0
4. Excess of nonbusiness deductions over nonbusiness income. Nonbusiness deductions:	

Total itemized	$1,050	
Allowable casualty loss	500	
	$ 550	
Nonbusiness income:		
Dividends	$ 325	$ 225
5. Personal exemptions		1,500 1,725
Net operating loss		$ 6,500

NOTE: Allowable casualty losses, whether business or nonbusiness, increase the net operating loss.

(b) Capital loss carryover. Because of the distinction between business and nonbusiness capital gains and losses, a taxpayer who has a capital loss carryover must determine how much of the capital loss carryover is a business capital loss and how much is a nonbusiness capital loss [Sec. 1.172-3(b)].

¶ 2243 Carryover and unused portion of net operating loss. A net operating loss is used first to reduce the income of the third preceding year. If any loss remains, it is carried to the second preceding year, then to the first preceding year, as described in ¶ 2241(a). However, taxpayer must make adjustments to the taxable income for each year to which the loss is applied [Sec. 172(b)(2); 1.172-4(b)]. Here is what you do:

(a) Determining the carryover. First determine the amount that can be carried to the following year. To do this, apply the net operating loss directly to taxable income of the year to which it is being carried back. If any loss remains, reduce it by the following deductions in that year [Sec. 1.172-5]:

- Personal exemptions.
- Long-term capital gain deduction.
- Net capital loss.
- An expense adjustment, if any, recomputed because of a percentage limitation for taxable income (for example, a charitable deduction) or adjusted gross income (medical deduction).

Any loss that remains after making these adjustments is the amount that can be carried over to the next applicable year.

In determining the amount of net operating loss to be carried to the second preceding tax year, the taxable income of the third preceding tax year is reduced by the amount of any unclaimed deduction.[1] This is true even though the deduction is barred by the statute of limitations.

(b) Recomputing taxable income. Taxpayer also must recompute the taxable income of the year to which the loss has been applied. This is done to find the new tax liability for the year and the amount of the refund. This computation also gives the amount of income for that year that will be available to absorb further losses. In recomputing the tax liability, a charitable contributions deduction is determined without regard to carryovers carryback. Any other deductions claimed, however, that are based on or limited to a percentage of adjusted gross income or taxable income (such as the medical expenses) must be recomputed as to adjusted gross or taxable income, determined after applying the carryback. Also, any credits based on or limited by the tax must be recomputed on the tax liability after applying the carryback.

Footnotes appear at end of this Chapter.

Chapter 12—Deductions—Losses

Example: Referring to the example at ¶ 2242 where Miller had a net operating loss of $6,500, assume that Miller's return for the third preceding year (1974) showed the following facts:

Return for 1974

Profit from business			$3,125
Dividends after $100 exclusion			250
Net long-term capital gain		$550	
Less: long-term capital gain deduction		275	275
Adjusted gross income			3,650
Less: itemized deductions:			
Interest		150	
Taxes		175	
Contributions		250	
Medical expenses paid	$450		
Less: 3% adjusted gross income	110	340	915
			$2,735
Personal exemption			$1,500
Taxable income			$1,235
Tax payable			$ 176

The amount of net operating loss remaining to be carried to 1975 is computed as follows:

Net operating loss carried to 1974		$6,500
Taxable income for 1974		1,235
Excess of loss		$5,265
Adjustments:		
Personal exemptions	$1,500	
Long-term capital gain deduction	275	
Medical expense†	8	1,783
Loss remaining to be carried to 1975		$3,482

---

†For purposes of recomputing the medical deduction, a revised adjusted gross income is figured. This is the original adjusted gross income for 1974 ($3,650) plus the capital gain deduction ($275). The 3% floor is then applied to the revised adjusted gross income ($3,925). The recomputed medical deduction then would be $332 [$450 − 118 (3% × $3,925, rounded off)]. This is subtracted from the original medical expense deduction ($340) giving the $8 medical expense adjustment.

The recomputed tax liability and refund for 1974 are figured as follows:

Adjusted gross income on return			$3,650
Less: net operating loss			6,500
Revised adjusted gross income			$(2,850)
Itemized deductions:			
Interest		$150	
Taxes		175	
Contributions		250	
Medical expenses paid	$450		
Less: 3% of adjusted gross income	0	450	1,025
			$(3,875)
Personal exemptions			$ 1,500
Revised taxable income			$(5,375)
Revised net tax liability			0
Tax paid			$ 176
Refund claimed for 1974			$ 176

Assume further that Miller's return for 1975 showed the following facts:

Return for 1975

Profit from business	$ 4,800
Dividends after $100 exclusion	970

Net long-term capital gain		$700	
Less: long-term capital gain deduction		350	350
Adjusted gross income			$ 6,120
Itemized deductions:			
Interest		$130	
Taxes		200	
Contributions		325	
Medical expenses paid	$550		
Less: 3% adjusted gross income	184	366	1,021
			$ 5,099
Personal exemptions			$ 1,500
Taxable income			$ 3,599
Tax liability			$ 548

Since taxable income 1975 ($3,599) is greater than the loss carried to 1975 ($3,482), no loss remains to be carried to 1976.

The recomputed tax liability and refund for 1975 are determined as follows:

Adjusted gross income on return			$ 6,120
Less: net operating loss carried to 1975			3,482
Revised adjusted gross income			$ 2,638
Itemized deductions:			
Interest		$130	
Taxes		200	
Contributions		325	
Medical expenses paid	$550		
Less: 3% of adjusted gross income	79	471	1,126
			$ 1,512
Personal exemptions			1,500
Revised taxable income			$ 12
Tax liability			$ 2
Revised tax liability			$ 2
Tax paid			548
Refund claimed for 1975			$ 546

(c) Refund claim. Refunds can be claimed by filing an amended return on Form 1040X with the appropriate supporting evidence [¶ 3622; 3626]. The refund can be speeded up, however, by filing Form 1045, Application for Tentative Carryback Adjustment [¶ 3630]. For special refund period, see ¶ 3624.

(d) How treated on return. A prior year's net operating loss carried to the current year is entered on the return as a "minus" figure in miscellaneous income. A separate statement must be attached to the return showing how it was computed.[2]

¶ 2244 Carryovers or carrybacks from more than one year. Since a net operating loss generally can be carried back 3 years and then forward 7 years the net operating loss deduction for a particular year may involve carryovers or carrybacks from more than one year. When this happens, the available carryovers and carrybacks are added, and the total is the net operating loss deduction [Sec. 172(a); 1.172-1(a)].

Example: Assume the following facts:

1974 taxable income (adjusted)	$ 3,018
1975 taxable income (adjusted)	$ 3,899

Footnotes appear at end of this Chapter.

¶ 2244

1976 taxable income (adjusted)	$ 5,600
1977 net operating loss	$ (6,500)
1978 net operating loss	$ (3,400)

The 1977 net operating loss of $6,500 is carried back to 1974. The unused $3,482 ($6,500 minus $3,018) is carried over to 1975. The 1978 net operating loss of $3,400 is carried back to 1975. Thus, the net operating deduction for 1975 is $6,882 ($3,482 plus $3,400).

Footnotes to Chapter 12

(P-H "FEDERAL TAXES" related references are cited in brackets [ ] at the end of each footnote below)

Footnote ¶ 2200 [¶ 14,011 et seq.].

Footnote ¶ 2201 [¶ 14,011].

Footnote ¶ 2202 [¶ 14,011 et seq.].
(1) Schwinn, 9 BTA 1304 [¶ 11,011].
(2) Rev. Rul. 72-111, 1972-1 CB 56 [¶ 14,494(5)].
(3) Jones, ¶ 42,324 P-H Memo BTA [¶ 14,112(5)].
(4) Tallman, 37 BTA 1060 [¶ 14,066(40)].
(5) The Great Island Holding Corp., 5 TC 150 [¶ 14,068(5)].
(6) Dickey, 14 BTA 1295, aff. 56 F.2d 917, 10 AFTR 1449 [¶ 14,424(20)].
(7) O'Brien, 12 AFTR 2d 5411, 321 F.2d 227 [¶ 14,108(70)].

Footnote ¶ 2203 [¶ 14,061 et seq.].
(1) Goldsborough v. Burnet, 46 F.2d 432, 9 AFTR 765 [¶ 14,038(15); 14,074(5)].
(2) Heiner v. Tindle, 276 US 582, 6 AFTR 7366 [¶ 14,095(5)].
(3) Campbell, 5 TC 272 [¶ 14,093(5)].
(4) Miller, ¶ 67,044 P-H Memo TC [¶ 14,093(10)].
(5) Weir, 109 F.2d 996, 24 AFTR 453; Riker, 6 BTA 890; Dresser, 55 F.2d 499, 10 AFTR 1096 [¶ 14,069(20); 14,074(5); 14,083(5)].

Footnote ¶ 2204 [¶ 14,361 et seq.].
(1) Matheson & Wood, Exs. v. Comm., 54 F.2d 537, 10 AFTR 945 [¶ 14,367(5)].
(2) Shearer v. Anderson, 16 F.2d 995, 6 AFTR 6483 [¶ 14,367(10)].
(3) Fay v. Comm., 120 F.2d 253, 27 AFTR 432 [¶ 14,367(5)].
(4) Stevens, ¶ 47,191 P-H Memo TC [¶ 14,367(10)].
(5) Stoll, ¶ 46,202 P-H Memo TC [¶ 14,151(10)].
(6) Treas. Dept. Publication 547, "Tax Information on Disasters, Casualty Losses and Thefts" (1977 Ed.), p. 1; Treas. Dept. booklet "Your Federal Income Tax" (1977 Ed.), p. 135; West, 2 AFTR 2d 6003, 259 F.2d 704; Peterson, 30 TC 660; Rev. Rul. 70-16, 1970-1 CB 441 [¶ 14,148(85); 14,368(120); 14,377(60)].
(7) Stowers v. U.S., 3 AFTR 505, 169 F. Supp. 246 [¶ 14,368(140)].
(8) Treas. Dept. Publication 547 "Tax Information on Disasters, Casualty Losses and Thefts" (1977 Ed.), p. 1; Treas. Dept. booklet "Your Federal Income Tax" (1977 Ed.), p. 135.
(9) Letter ruling [¶ 14,368(40)].
(10) Rev. Rul. 54-85, 1954-1 CB 58 [¶ 14,368(140)].
(11) Rev. Rul. 60-329, 1960-2 CB 67 [¶ 14,368(145)].

Footnote ¶ 2204 continued
(12) Davis, 34 TC 586 [¶ 14,368(160)].
(13) Rev. Rul. 71-560, 1971-2 CB 126 [¶ 14,368].
(14) Hayutin, ¶ 72,127 P-H Memo TC [¶ 14,368(120)].
(15) Dickason, 20 BTA 496 [¶ 14,368(15)].
(16) Anderson v. Comm., 81 F.2d 457, 17 AFTR 369 [¶ 14,378(5)].
(17) Rev. Rul. 55-327, 1955-1 CB 25 [¶ 14,368(90)].
(18) Rev. Rul. 61-216, 1961-2 CB 134 [¶ 14,368(30)].
(19) Rev. Rul. 57-599, 1957-2 CB 142 [¶ 14,368(30)].
(20) Lloyd v. U.S., (DC, Wash.; 8-22-61) 8 AFTR 2d 5586; Nelson, ¶ 68,035 P-H Memo TC [¶ 14,368(80), (90)].
(21) Rev. Rul. 63-232, 1963-2 CB 97 [¶ 14,368(155)].
(22) Rev. Rul. 70-16, 1970-1 CB 441 [¶ 14,368(120)].
(23) Rev. Rul. 64-329, 1964-2 CB 58 [¶ 14,377(15)].
(24) Conner, 439 F.2d 974, 27 AFTR 2d 71-858 [¶ 14,377(15)].
(25) Rev. Rul. 68-29, 1968-1 CB 74 [¶ 14,377(10)].
(26) Rev. Rul. 66-50, 1966-1 CB 40 [¶ 14,377(100)].
(27) Walton, ¶ 61,130 P-H Memo TC [¶ 14,377(25)].
(28) Treas. Dept. Publication 547, "Tax Information on Disasters, Casualty Losses and Thefts" (1977 Ed.), p. 2; Treas. Dept. booklet "Your Federal Income Tax" (1977 Ed.), p. 139.
(29) Barret v. U.S., 202 F.2d 804, 43 AFTR 443 [¶ 14,385(10)].

Footnote ¶ 2205 [¶ 14,400 et seq.].
(1) Felton, 5 TC 256; Gilpin, ¶ 47,085 P-H Memo TC [¶ 14,453(15)].
(2) Earle v. Comm., 72 F.2d 366, 14 AFTR 453; Vincent v. Comm., 219 F.2d 228, 49 AFTR 1698 [¶ 14,443(5)].
(3) Treas. Dept. Publication 547, "Tax Information on Disasters, Casualty Losses and Thefts" (1977 Ed.), p. 5.
(4) Alsop v. Comm., 7 AFTR 2d 1438, 290 F.2d 726 [¶ 14,114(5)].
(5) Rev. Rul. 71-381, 1971-2 CB 126 [¶ 14,418(27)].

Footnote ¶ 2206 [¶ 14,361 et seq.].

Footnote ¶ 2207 [¶ 14,061 et seq.].
(1) Heiner v. Tindle, 276 US 582, 48 SCt. 326, 6 AFTR 7366 [¶ 14,095(5)].
(2) Blalock, ¶ 41,434 P-H Memo BTA [¶ 14,092(50)].
(3) Treas. Dept. booklet "Your Federal Income Tax" (1977 Ed.), p. 129.

Footnote ¶ 2208 [¶ 14,290 et seq.].
(1) Davis, 6 BTA 1267 [¶ 14,300(5)].

Chapter 12—Footnotes

Footnote ¶ 2208 continued
(2) Rev. Rul. 74-80, 1974-1 CB 117 [¶ 54,641].
(3) Seeligson, ¶ 53,300 P-H Memo TC [¶ 14,295(5)].
(4) Rev. Rul. 63-65, 1963-1 CB 142 [¶ 32,349(5)].

Footnote ¶ 2209 [¶ 14,257 et seq.].
(1) Liberty Baking Co. v. Heiner, 34 F.2d 513, 7 AFTR 9381 [¶ 14,262(5)].

Footnote ¶ 2210 [¶ 14,224 et seq.].
(1) Rev. Rul. 61-206, 1961-2 CB 57 [¶ 14,251(5)].
(2) Strauss v. U.S., 8 AFTR 2d 5952, 199 F. 2d 845 [¶ 14,250(10)].

Footnote ¶ 2211 [¶ 14,350 et seq.].

Footnote ¶ 2212 [¶ 14,016 et seq.].
(1) Kohler, 37 BTA 1019 [¶ 14,327(35)].
(2) Hambuechen, 43 TC 90 [¶ 14,715(20)].
(3) Comm. v. Burdick, Exec., 59 F.2d 395, 11 AFTR 513 [¶ 14,024(20)].
(4) Wright, 18 BTA 471, affd. 47 F.2d 871, 9 AFTR 1031 [¶ 14,024(5)].

Footnote ¶ 2221 [¶ 31,917 et seq.].
(1) Rev. Rul. 71-316, 1971-2 CB 311 [¶ 31,921.15(5)].
(2) Richard Coulter, 32 BTA 617 [¶ 31,921.35(5)].
(3) Brochon, 30 BTA 404; Security First Nat'l Bank, 28 BTA 289 [¶ 31,921.40(20), (40)].
(4) Rev. Rul. 59-418, 1958-2 CB 184 [¶ 31,921.35(15)].
(5) Treas. Dept. booklet "Your Federal Income Tax" (1977 Ed.), p. 100.
(6) Rev. Rul. 71-568, 1971-2 CB 312 [¶ 31,921.20(5)].
(7) Rev. Rul. 70-231, 1970-1 CB 171 [¶ 31,921.35(25)].
(8) Rev. Rul. 66-5, 1966-1 CB 91 [¶ 32,192].
(9) Kidder, 30 BTA 59 [¶ 31,921.30(15)].
(10) Rev. Rul. 58-210, 1958-1 CB 523 [¶ 31,921.30(40)].

Footnote ¶ 2221 continued
(11) Knox, 33 BTA 972 [¶ 31,921.30(25)].
(12) Donander Co., 29 BTA 312 [¶ 312 [¶ 31,921.10(10)].
(13) Letter Ruling dtd. 10/11/46 [¶ 31,921.40(30)].

Footnote ¶ 2222 [¶ 14,463 et seq.].
(1) Shoenberg v. Comm., 77 F.2d 446, 16 AFTR 95 [¶ 14,477(30)].

Footnote ¶ 2223 [¶ 16,825(a), (c)].
(1) McWilliams v. Comm., 331 US 694, 67 SCt. 1477, 35 AFTR 1184 [¶ 16,862(5)].
(2) Zacek, 8 TC 1056 [¶ 16,862.5(5)].

Footnote ¶ 2224 [¶ 14,548 et seq.].
(1) Rev. Rul. 54-339, 1954-2 CB 89 [¶ 14,551(10)].

Footnote ¶ 2225 [¶ 16,259 et seq.].
(1) P.L. 94-455, Tax Reform Act of 1976, Sec. 214(c).

Footnote ¶ 2226 [¶ 32,791].

Footnote ¶ 2241 [¶ 16,141 et seq.].
(1) Alvary v. U.S., 9 AFTR 2d 1633, 302 F.2d 790 [¶ 16,192(155)].
(2) Rev. Rul. 65-140, 165-1 CB 127 [¶ 16,149(25)].

Footnote ¶ 2242 [¶ 16,141 et seq.].
(1) Rev. Rul. 66-327, 1966-2 CB 357 [¶ 16,192(55)].
(2) Lagriede, 23 TC 508 [¶ 16,192(45), (95)].
(3) Rev. Rul. 57-563, 1957-2 CB 175 [¶ 16,192(165)].
(4) Rev. Rul. 70-40, 1970-1 CB 50 [¶ 16,192(70), (75)].
(5) Rev. Rul. 72-195, 1972-1 CB 95 [¶ 16,192(25)].

Footnote ¶ 2243 [¶ 16,141 et seq.].
(1) Rev. Rul. 65-96, 1965-1 CB 126 [¶ 16,179(20)].
(2) Instructions to Form 1040.

Footnote ¶ 2244 [¶ 16,141 et seq.].

Highlights of Chapter 12
Deductions—Losses

I. **Losses in General**
   A. **Deductible losses for individuals [¶ 2200]:**
      1. Incurred in trade or business.
      2. Incurred in transaction entered into for profit.
      3. From casualties and thefts.
   B. **Amount deductible [¶ 2201]:**
      1. Generally, difference between amount realized and adjusted basis.
      2. Cannot exceed adjusted basis.
      3. Reduced by salvage value, insurance and other recoveries.

II. **Losses in Business or Profit Transactions**
   A. **Business losses [¶ 2202]:**
      1. Need not be principal business.
      2. Anticipated profits or wages—not deductible [¶ 2202(a)].
      3. Legal damages (not for personal losses)—deductible [¶ 2202(b)].
      4. Deductions *for* adjusted gross income [¶ 2202(c)].
   B. **Losses from transactions entered into for profit [¶ 2203]:**
      1. Deductible, whether connected with business or not.
      2. Sale of gift property—use after being acquired determines treatment [¶ 2203(a)].
      3. Sale of stock—usually deductible [¶ 2203(b)].
      4. Deductions *for* adjusted gross income if [¶ 2203(c)]:
         a. Property involved held for production of rents or royalties.
         b. From sale or exchange of capital assets.
         c. Due to securities becoming worthless.

III. **Casualty and Theft Losses**
   A. **Casualty losses [¶ 2204]:**
      1. Defined:
         a. From fire, storm, shipwreck or other casualty.
         b. Due to sudden unexpected or unusual cause.
         c. Generally, accident or sudden invasion by hostile agency.
         d. Need not be natural causes.
      2. Negligent or careless loss not casualty.
      3. Progressive deterioration not casualty.
      4. Limited to property losses [¶ 2204(a)].
      5. Deductible whether business or personal [¶ 2204(b)].
      6. Amount deductible—personal casualty loss [¶ 2204(c)]:
         a. Lesser of sustained loss or adjusted basis for determining loss on sale, reduced by:
            1) Insurance.
            2) Amount from employer or disaster relief agencies to restore property.
            3) Other compensation.
            4) $100.
         b. Living expense reimbursements do not reduce loss.
         c. Proof of loss through competent appraisals.
      7. Amount deductible—business casualty loss [¶ 2204(d)]:
         a. Completely destroyed—adjusted basis for determining loss on sale, less salvage, insurance, etc.
         b. Partially destroyed—lesser of sustained loss or adjusted basis, less salvage, insurance, etc.

8. When deductible [¶ 2204(e)]:
    a. Tax year when loss sustained.
    b. Special rule for Presidentially declared disaster areas.
9. Carryback and carryover-casualty losses in excess of income [¶ 2204(f)].
10. How treated on return [¶ 2204(g)]:
    a. Losses on business property or property held for production of rents and royalties—deductible *for* adjusted gross income.
    b. Personal losses—generally, "other itemized deduction."
    c. Inventory losses reflected in inventory.

B. **Theft losses [¶ 2205]:**
 1. Defined—from theft or embezzlement.
 2. Amount deductible [¶ 2205(a)]:
    a. Same as casualty losses.
    b. Fair market value of property after theft is zero.
    c. Must be reduced by insurance proceeds or claim and surety bond proceeds or claim.
 3. When deductible [¶ 2205(b)]:
    a. Tax year when loss discovered.
    b. Postponed if reasonable prospect of recovery.
 4. Carryback and carryover—theft losses in excess of income [¶ 2205(c)].
 5. How treated on return—same as casualty losses [¶ 2205(d)].

C. **Special "netting" rule when gains and losses from casualties or thefts [¶ 2206(b)].**

IV. **Special Rules**

A. **Property converted to business use—loss on sale deductible [¶ 2207]:**
 1. Personal-use property—loss on sale not deductible.
 2. Basis for loss—lesser of fair market value or adjusted basis on conversion date.
 3. Basis adjusted for improvements, depreciation, casualty deductions since conversion.
 4. Loss equals excess of adjusted basis when sold over amount realized from sale.
 5. Gain equals excess of amount realized from sale over adjusted basis when sold.
 6. No gain or loss on converted personal residence sale if amount realized between gain basis and loss basis.

B. **Worthless stock [¶ 2208]:**
 1. Deductible in year completely worthless.
 2. Capital loss on last day of tax year worthless [¶ 2208(a)].
 3. Not capital if:
    a. Stock of corporate subsidiary.
    b. Bank stock owned by another bank.
    c. Small business or small business investment company stock.
 4. Deduction *for* adjusted gross income.

C. **Demolition of buildings [¶ 2209]:**
 1. Intent to demolish when purchased—no loss deduction (basis allocated to land) [¶ 2209(a)].
 2. Intent to demolish after purchase—loss deduction equal to building's adjusted basis plus demolition cost and minus demolition proceeds [¶ 2209(b)].
 3. Demolished to get lease—no loss deduction (basis amortized over lease term) [¶ 2209(c)].

D. **Abandonment losses**—deductible if end of usefulness sudden and permanent [¶ 2210].

E. **Farm losses [¶ 2211]:**
 1. Incurred in operation as business—generally, deductible *for* adjusted gross income.
 2. Deterioration of crops in storage—no loss deduction [¶ 2211(a)].
 3. Prospective crop destruction—no loss deduction [¶ 2211(b)].
 4. Destruction of livestock [¶ 2211(c)]:
    a. Raised on farm—no loss deduction.

b. Purchased for farm—deductible.
5. Reflected in inventory—no separate deductions allowed [¶ 2211(d)].
F. **Loss distinguished from capital expenditure [¶ 2212]:**
 1. Capital contributions [¶ 2212(a)]:
    a. Voluntary—no loss deduction.
    b. Involuntary and no return expected—deductible.
 2. Stock surrender [¶ 2212(b)]:
    a. To corporation with increase in retained stock basis—no loss deduction.
    b. To corporation's bankers with no basis increase—deductible.

V. **Disallowed Losses**
 A. **Wash sales [¶ 2221]:**
  1. Occur when substantially identical stock or securities bought within 30 days before or after sale.
  2. Loss on sale not deductible (added to basis of new stock).
  3. Gain on sale recognized.
  4. Holding period of new securities includes period original securities held [¶ 2221(a)].
  5. Dealers and traders not subject to wash sales provisions [¶ 2221(c)].
 B. **Sham sales**—losses not deductible [¶ 2222].
 C. **Sales to related taxpayers**—no loss deduction if [¶ 2223]:
  1. Family loss—sale between [¶ 2223(a)]:
     a. Husband and wife,
     b. Brothers and/or sisters (whole or half blood),
     c. Ancestors and lineal descendants, or
  2. Sale between corporation and shareholder owning over 50% stock [¶ 2223(b)], or
  3. Sale between taxpayer and taxpayer's controlled exempt organization [¶ 2223(c)].
  4. Constructively owned stock included to determine percentage stock owned [¶ 2223(d)]:
     a. Stock ownership rule.
     b. Family rule.
     c. Partnership rule.
  5. Disallowed loss limits recognized gain on resale [¶ 2223(e)].
 D. **Gambling losses deductible only to extent of gains [¶ 2224].**
 E. **Hobby losses [¶ 2225]:**
  1. No deduction for individual or small business corporation engaged in activity not carried on for profit, except:
     a. Deductions allowed whether or not activity carried on for profit, and
     b. Deductions allowed if activity carried on for profit, but only to extent activity's gross income exceeds deductions allowed in (a).
  2. "Engaged in for profit" presumed if profit in 2 of 5 consecutive years (2 of 7 for horses).
 F. **Farm loss recaptured as ordinary income [¶ 2226]:**
  1. When farm recapture property sold or exchanged after 1969.
  2. Applies to all taxpayers not reporting farm income on accrual method.
  3. Applies to individual taxpayer only if nonfarm adjusted gross income over $50,000 (but only to extent farm loss exceeds $25,000).
  4. Excess deductions account must be kept [¶ 2226(b)], to which:
     a. Yearly net farm loss is added.
     b. Yearly net farm income is subtracted.
  5. Ordinary income gain on sale limited to excess deductions account balance.
  6. Farm recapture property is [¶ 2226(a)]:
     a. Farm land held over 6 months.
     b. Depreciable personal property held over 6 months.
     c. Livestock.
     d. Unharvested crops.
  7. Excess deductions account transferable with farm recapture property [¶ 2226(c)].

8. Special rules for otherwise tax-free corporate transactions [¶ 2226(d)].
VI. **Net Operating Loss Deduction**
   A. **Special treatment [¶ 2241]:**
      1. Loss from operation of trade, business or profession, or from casualty or theft.
      2. 3-year carryback and 7-year (5-years before 1976) carryover; 9-years (7-years before 1976) for regulated transportation companies) [¶ 2241(a)].
      3. Special election: All taxpayers may elect not to carryback.
      4. Foreign expropriation loss—special option for 10 - year carryover.
      5. Available to all taxpayers.
   B. **Determination [¶ 2242]:**
      1. Net operating loss equals loss shown on return, less [¶ 2242(a)]:
         a. Net operating loss from another year.
         b. Long-term capital gain deduction.
         c. Personal exemption deduction.
         d. Capital loss excess over capital gains.
         e. Nonbusiness deductions excess over nonbusiness income.
         f. Self-employment retirement plan contributions.
      2. Casualty losses increase net operating loss.
   C. **Carryover of unused portion [¶ 2243]:**
      1. Applied directly to taxable income of 3rd prior year.
      2. Remaining loss reduced by 3rd prior year deductions for [¶ 2243(a)]:
         a. Personal exemptions.
         b. Long-term capital gain deduction.
         c. Net capital loss.
      3. Remaining loss applied and reduced till used up.
      4. Taxable income of year to which loss applied must be recomputed [¶ 2243(b)].
      5. Refunds claimed by filing amended return on Form 1040X [¶ 2243(c)].
   D. **Losses from more than one year added for total net operating loss deduction [¶ 2244].**

Chapter 13

DEDUCTIONS—BAD DEBTS

TABLE OF CONTENTS

BAD DEBT DEDUCTION IN GENERAL

	¶
The deduction for bad debts	2300
Existence of debt	2301
Amount deductible	2302

WHAT BAD DEBTS ARE DEDUCTIBLE

	¶
Business bad debts	2305
Partially worthless business debts	2306
Charge-off not mandatory	
Collateral need not be liquidated	
Debt must be specific	
Nonbusiness bad debts	2307
Advances to relatives	2308
Advances to corporations by stockholders	2309
Deposits in closed banks	2310
Method of deducting bad debts	2311
Specific charge-off method	
Reasonable addition to reserve	
Election	
Sale of receivables	

	¶
Worthless bonds	2312
Taxpayers other than banks and trust companies	
Banks and trust companies	

SPECIAL PROBLEMS

	¶
Bad debt and loss distinguished	2315
Voluntary cancellation or forgiveness	
Endorsers and guarantors	
Recovery of bad debts	2316
Specific charge-off method	
Reserve method	
Tax benefit rule—recovery exclusion	
Prior taxes, delinquency amounts and other deductions recovered	
Loss on sale of pledged property	2317

• Highlights of Chapter 13 .... Page 2361

BAD DEBT DEDUCTION IN GENERAL

The treatment of bad debts depends on whether the debt is a business or a nonbusiness bad debt.

¶ 2300 The deduction for bad debts affects taxpayers who loan money to others or who have included in gross income debts due from others for property sold or services rendered. The loss resulting from the worthlessness or uncollectibility of these debts is deductible, provided the debts had a value when acquired or created.[1] If a worthless debt arises from unpaid wages, salaries, rents, etc. the loss is not deductible unless the unpaid amount has been included in income [Sec. 166; 1.166-1].

When and how deductible. Bad debts are deductible in the year they become worthless. A corporation generally may claim the full amount of the loss as an ordinary deduction, but a special rule applies to worthless securities [¶ 2312]. Other taxpayers also may claim the full amount of the loss as an ordinary deduction, except that special rules apply to (1) nonbusiness bad debts [¶ 2307] and (2) worthless securities [¶ 2312].

Deductions for partial worthlessness are allowed, except for (1) partially worthless securities and (2) partially worthless nonbusiness bad debts of taxpayers other than corporations.

Footnotes appear at end of this Chapter.

¶ 2300

Business bad debts are deductible in full. Nonbusiness bad debts are treated as short-term capital losses subject to the capital loss limitation.

¶ 2301 **Existence of debt.** The debt must really exist to be deductible. There must be a debtor-creditor relationship. This exists when one person, by contract or law, is obliged to pay another an amount of money, certain or uncertain, either presently or at some future date.[1] There is no debt however, when the obligation to repay is subject to a contingency and that contingency has not occurred.[2] Only banks can deduct for a worthless debt owed by a political party (see ¶ 1811); but the debt must be created under its usual commerical practice [Sec. 271; 1.271-1]. For example, a debt motivated only by a bank officer's political interest would not qualify.

¶ 2302 **Amount deductible.** The amount deductible is the debt's adjusted basis for determining loss from a sale or exchange [Sec. 166(b); 1.166-1(d)]. This may or may not be the same as the face amount of the debt. See ¶ 1500 et seq. No deduction is allowed when the basis cannot be proved.[1]

Example: If Ames buys a $1,000 note for $700, its basis to him is $700, and that is the amount deductible if the debt becomes worthless.

WHAT BAD DEBTS ARE DEDUCTIBLE

It is not always easy to determine if a debt is business or nonbusiness. The difference is important: no deduction is allowed for the partial worthlessness of a nonbusiness bad debt, and noncorporate taxpayers must treat nonbusiness bad debts as short-term capital losses.

¶ 2305 **Business bad debts.** An individual's business bad debt is a debt incurred in *his* trade or business that became worthless during the year. A proximate relationship must exist between the creation of that debt and his trade or business [Sec. 1.166-5(b)(2)]. The Supreme Court holds that the relationship is proximate only if the taxpayer's motivation for making the debt is primary and dominant to his trade or business; significant motivation is not sufficient.[1] A business bad debt is a deduction for adjusted gross income (¶ 1804) [Sec. 166(d)(2); 1.166-1].

FACTORS INDICATING DEBT WORTHLESS

Bankruptcy generally indicates that at least part of an unsecured and unpreferred debt is worthless [Sec. 1.166-2(c)]. The deduction is limited to the difference between the claim and the amount received on distribution of the bankrupt's assets [Sec. 1.166-1(d)(2)].

Statute of limitations having run on the debt is strong, but not conclusive, evidence of worthlessness.[2]

Other factors: Collateral worthlessness,[3] debtor's disappearance,[4] insolvency,[5] ill health,[6] or receivership,[7] debtor without assets,[8] or out of business[9] (but when a loan to business was guaranteed by life insurance proceeds, the deduction was allowed in the year the policy was found to be worthless, even though the business failed in an earlier year[10]); foreign expropriation [Sec. 1351(b)].

FACTORS INDICATING DEBT NOT WORTHLESS

No serious effect to collect[11] (but legal action against debtor is not necessary if it would be futile[12]); debtor still in business,[13] or earning substantial income.[14]

¶ 2306 **Partially worthless business debts.** If a business debt is partially worthless, the taxpayer can deduct the part he elects to charge off within the tax year [Sec. 166(a)(2); 1.166-3(a)]. See also ¶ 2311.

(a) **Charge-off not mandatory.** The charge-off does not have to be made in the tax year the debt became partially worthless [Sec. 1.166-3]. For instance, if a debt became partially worthless in 1977, the charge-off may be made in 1978, and a deduction taken in the 1978 return.

You do not have to claim partial worthlessness as a deduction, and failure to do so does not preclude a deduction for partial worthlessness in a greater amount, or for total worthlessness, in a later year.[1]

≫OBSERVATION→ Partial charge-offs allow you to take the deduction in the year it will do the most good.

(b) **Collateral need not be liquidated.** Generally, collateral securing a debt need not be liquidated to establish the worthless part of the debt.[2]

(c) **Debt must be specific.** Partial deductions are allowed for specific debts only. For example, the taxpayer may not deduct a percentage of the total of certain accounts.

(d) **Partially worthless bonds.** Only banks or trust companies are allowed a deduction for partially worthless bonds [¶ 2312].

¶ **2307 Nonbusiness bad debts** are debts not related to your trade or business when they are created, acquired or become worthless. Thus, even if a debt arose in a trade or business, it is a nonbusiness debt in the hands of a donee, executor or transferee who was not, and never had been, in the trade or business in which the debt arose. No deduction is allowed for a partially worthless nonbusiness bad debt [Sec. 166(d); 1.166-5].

(a) **Loans by an officer or employee** to a corporation usually are not closely related to his business, since the business of the corporation is not the business of its employees or officers. These loans, if uncollectible, are nonbusiness bad debts.[1] But a loan may be a business debt if required as a condition of employment,[2] not just to protect an investment in the company. The Second Circuit, in denying a business bad debt deduction to the majority shareholder-president of a corporation, discussed the taxpayer's motives in guaranteeing a loan made to the corporation.[3] In another case, the Tax Court allowed a business bad debt deduction to a corporate president for a loss on a business-related guarantee of the corporation's debt when his primary motive was to protect his job.[4]

(b) **Loans by a stockholder.** The Supreme Court holds that a stockholder who lends money to his corporation is not in business when his only return is that of an investor, even though his return on the loan is substantially due to his services. A loss would be a nonbusiness bad debt.[5] Similarly, loans by a stockholder-employee do not receive business bad debt treatment unless the dominant motivation for making the loan was business oriented.[6]

(c) **Nonbusiness bad debt as short-term capital loss.** A nonbusiness bad debt is treated as a short-term capital loss in the year of worthlessness. Corporations are excepted from the nonbusiness bad debt provision.

Example: Zale had a nonbusiness bad debt of $2,200 which became worthless in 1977. The debt of $2,200 is considered a short-term capital loss. If Zale had no other capital gains and losses in 1977, the debt is deductible only to the extent of $2,000 and the balance ($200) is carried over to 1978. See ¶ 1613.

Footnotes appear at end of this Chapter.

Background and purpose. Congress provided that nonbusiness bad debts be treated differently from business bad debts to eliminate abuses that arose from loans made by taxpayers who did not expect to be repaid.

¶ **2308 Advances to relatives** raise these questions: (1) Was the advance a gift? If so, there is no bad debt deduction, since no debtor-creditor relationship exists;[1] (2) Was it a real loan? If the advance was a loan, it ordinarily results in a nonbusiness debt. However, the way the recipient uses the funds does not determine the debt's character. It depends, rather on whether the debt was created in taxpayer's trade or business, or the loss from the worthless debt is related to taxpayer's trade or business.

¶ **2309 Advances to corporations by stockholders** may be loans or capital contributions (additional investment). If the advance is in fact a loan, it is subject to the rules governing bad debts.[1]

≫**OBSERVATION→** It is important that the nature of the advance be established at the time it is made. If the purpose is to make a loan to the corporation, later complications may be avoided if the stockholder takes the corporation's note to cover the advance.[2]

¶ **2310 Deposits in closed banks** usually give rise to a bad debt deduction for a depositor. The problem is finding the right year to take the deduction. Although depositors usually do not receive 100 cents on the dollar, some lesser sum is paid. If the debt is a nonbusiness debt, any loss from complete worthlessness is treated as a short-term capital loss [Sec. 166(d)(1); 1.166-5].

¶ **2311 Method of deducting bad debts.** Bad debts may be deducted either by the *specific charge-off method* or by the *reserve method* [Sec. 166; 1.166-1, 1.166-4]. Bad debt recoveries reduce the deduction. See ¶ 2316.

(a) Specific charge-off method allows the taxpayer to deduct the bad debts that have become worthless during the tax year [Sec. 1.166-1].

(b) Reasonable addition to reserve. Business debts that have become worthless during the year are not deducted directly from income but rather are charged against a reserve. Although there is no specific formula for figuring the reserve, the addition to the reserve must be reasonable. What is a "reasonable addition to a reserve" depends on the collection history of the business or other facts. It is based primarily on the total amount of debts outstanding at the end of the year and the total amount of the existing reserve [Sec. 1.166-4(b)].

Example: Jones uses the reserve method to arrive at his deduction for bad debts. At the end of 1977, the reserve had a balance of $500 and Jones wanted to add $2,000 to the reserve account. His books disclose the following facts:

	Accounts receivable at end of year	Bad debt Losses	Recoveries
1972	$ 18,000	$ 795	$ 75
1973	17,500	875	80
1974	18,500	740	50
1975	17,000	765	75
1976	18,000	995	90
1977	19,000	570	50
Six-year total	$108,000	$4,740	$420
Average	18,000	790	70

He figures the reasonable addition to his reserve for bad debts as follows:[1]

1. Average net bad debt losses ($790 less $70 average recoveries) is $720.
2. $720 ÷ average receivables of $18,000 = 4%.
3. 4% of $19,000, receivables at end of year, is $760.
4. $760 is the balance that should be in reserve at end of year.
5. Books show $500 balance in the reserve account at end of year.
6. To bring this up to a credit balance of $760, Jones may add $260 to his bad debt reserve account and claim a bad debt deduction for that amount.

NOTE: A taxpayer cannot take an addition to a reserve and a separate bad debt deduction except in the year of change to the reserve method or in the first year of starting a new business. A special technique applies to those in business changing to the reserve method. See (c) below.

If the reserve method is used, a statement must be attached to the return showing: (1) the volume of charge sales for the year; (2) the percentage of the reserve to that amount; (3) the total amount of notes and accounts receivable at the start and end of the year; and (4) the amount of the debts that have become worthless and have been charged against the reserve account during the year [Sec. 1.166-4].

(c) **Election.** A taxpayer filing his first return may select either of the two methods subject to approval of the Revenue Service on examining the return. But a taxpayer can make an initial election of the reserve method without Revenue Service consent if made for the first tax year in which there is a bad debt claim.[2] The method selected must be followed in returns for later years, unless permission to change is granted. The change must be applied for within 180 days after the start of the tax year for which the change is desired. See ¶ 2708.

Changing method of treating bad debts. In changing from the specific charge-off to the reserve method, the initial reserve for the year of change is found by (1) dividing the total of accounts receivable at the close of each of 5 preceding years into the total bad debt losses for those years, and then (2) multiplying the outstanding accounts receivable at the end of the year of change by the percentage found in (1).

The initial reserve is deducted ratably over a 10-year period starting with the year of change. The bad debt deduction for the year of change will be those bad debts charged off during the year plus 1/10 of the initial reserve. If the business is ended during the 10-year period, Form 3115 must be attached to the return for the termination year. A statement with the form must show the adjustment balance not previously considered in computing taxable income.[3]

(d) **Sale of receivables.** A dealer in property can deduct a reasonable addition to a reserve for bad debts arising from his contingent liability as guarantor, endorser or indemnitor of debt obligations, which arose originally from his sale of real or tangible personal property in the course of business. This is the only way he can deduct additions to a reserve for bad debts for obligations of this type. The customer's debt can include service charges related to the sale [Sec. 166(f)]. But a deduction for an addition to a reserve is not allowed to a dealer for lost finance charges when a customer prepays his discounted notes.[4]

The yearly addition to the bad debt reserve is figured in the usual way [(b) above]. However, for the first year, an opening reserve is figured as if taxpayer had been on the reserve method all along. This initial reserve must be set up in a suspense account that is not currently deductible. This prevents a double deduction for both the reserve and current charge-offs in the initial year. In any year in which the reserve (after year-end adjustment) is less than the suspense account, the suspense account is written down accordingly, and the write-down is allowed as an additional current deduction. But when the year-end reserve is more than the suspense account as written down, the excess is added to the suspense account. This

Footnotes appear at end of this Chapter.

¶ 2311

addition is not increased above the original amount. The add-back must be reported as income for the tax year in which the increase is required [Sec. 81, 166(f)].

(e) Installment basis. Taxpayers reporting on the installment basis may use the reserve method. The installment sales reserve must be kept separate from the reserve for other accounts receivable. A reserve may be maintained for either type of account, or both.[5]

(f) Transfer of a bad debt reserve to a controlled corporation is not income to the transferor in the year of transfer. Transferor received a tax benefit in the year the reserve was originally taken as a deduction.[6]

(g) Banks and trust companies. Special rules apply to banks and trust companies using a reserve for bad debts [¶ 3433(a)].

¶ 2312 Worthless bonds—(a) Taxpayers other than banks and trust companies. The following rules apply to both noncorporate and corporate taxpayers (¶ 3201 et seq.) [Sec. 165(g); 1.165-5]:

1. If a corporate bond becomes completely worthless during the tax year, the loss is a capital loss on the last day of that year.

Example: On 2-1-77, Henderson bought a bond of the Bigley Co. for $600. On 4-3-77, the bond became completely worthless. The bond is considered as having been held from 2-1-77 to 12-31-77 ("for more than 9 months"), and the loss is a long-term capital loss for Henderson as explained in ¶ 1605.

2. No deduction is allowed if a corporate bond becomes partially worthless during the tax year.

Exception—Affiliated corporations. In certain cases a corporation may claim the full deduction (rather than the limited deduction as a capital loss) for worthless securities of an affiliated corporation [Sec. 165(g)(3); 1.165-5(d)].

What is a bond. The term "bond" as used in the law, means bonds, debentures, notes or certificates, or other evidences of indebtedness, issued by any corporation (including issues of a government or political subdivision) with interest coupons or in registered form [Sec. 165(g)(2); 1.165-5(a)(3)].

(b) Banks and trust companies. The following rules apply [Sec. 582; 1.582-1, 1.166-2(d)]:

1. A conclusive presumption of complete or partial worthlessness is established when a bank or trust company [Sec. 581] must charge off a debt in whole or in part in obedience to specific orders of the banking authorities.
2. The loss is an ordinary loss even if secured by a corporate bond.
3. A deduction for partial worthlessness is allowed. The bank or trust company, however, does not have to claim partial worthlessness as a deduction, and failure to do so does not bar a deduction for partial worthlessness in a greater amount, or for total worthlessness, in a later year.

SPECIAL PROBLEMS

The remainder of this Chapter points out the differences between a bad debt and a loss, and explains how the recovery of a bad debt is treated.

¶ 2315 Bad debt and loss distinguished. The difference between a bad debt and loss may be important for at least two reasons: (1) Partial losses are not deductible, but business bad debts partially worthless may be; and (2) ordinarily, the statute of limitations on filing a refund claim for a loss deduction is 3 years after filing of return. It is 7 years for a bad debt.

(a) Voluntary cancellation or forgiveness of a debt does not give rise to a deductible loss.[1] However, if the debt is actually worthless, there may be a bad debt deduction. That deduction would be allowed because the debt was worthless, not because it was forgiven.[2] For example, the difference between a note's face value and the amount received in compromise is deductible as a bad debt, *if* the debtor has no assets out of which the entire amount can be collected by suit.[3] In some cases, even though the debt when forgiven was *not* worthless, a loss deduction was allowed when there was consideration for the forgiveness.

DEDUCTIBLE AS A LOSS

Consideration: The cancellation is a loss when made in consideration of the giving of security for other debts previously unsecured.[4]

Compromised accounts: A loss resulting from a dispute over the correctness of book charges and credits in connection with business transactions is deductible in the year in which settled by compromise or otherwise.[5]

Composition agreement: Loss under composition agreement is deductible in year agreement was made.[6]

NOT DEDUCTIBLE

Capital transaction: If a shareholder gratuitously forgives a debt owing to him by the corporation, the transaction amounts to a contribution to the capital of the corporation [Sec. 1.61-12]. No loss deduction is allowed.

(b) Endorsers and guarantors. Individuals having a loss from a loan guaranty receive the same treatment as if they had made the loan directly. Thus, the loss is ordinary if the guaranty is connected with the guarantor's trade or business. A loss on a guaranty that was entered into for profit is a short-term capital loss. These rules apply to tax years starting after 1975 [Sec. 166(f)]. A cash basis taxpayer paying his principal's debt with a note gets no bad debt deduction until he pays the note.[7]

Example 1: F endorses J's note. J defaults and F has to pay. Ordinarily J owes F the amount paid. If this debt is worthless, F may take a deduction.[8]

The deduction may be disallowed if the endorser cannot prove he intended to collect the debt.[9]

Example 2: Father endorsed his son's note, without investigating the son's financial prospects. Father made no effort to collect from the son when he had to pay the son's debt. Bad debt deduction was denied on the ground that the transaction was in effect a gift to the son.[9]

¶ **2316 Recovery of bad debts—(a) Specific charge-off method.** Bad debts taken as a deduction, but later recovered, must be included in gross income for the year received.

Example 1: In 1976, Stone's return showed a taxable income of $3,000 [gross income $6,200—deduction $3,200 (including $1,500 exemption deduction in effect)]. Included in the deductions for that year was a bad debt of $500. In 1977, the debtor paid Stone the $500. Stone would include the $500 in gross income for 1977. He would *not* make the adjustment by filing an amended return for 1976.

(b) Reserve method. If the reserve method is used, the recoveries are not included in gross income, but are credited to the reserve [Sec. 1.111-1]. The credit, in effect, decreases the deduction of the reasonable addition to the reserve for the year. See also ¶ 2311(b).

Footnotes appear at end of this Chapter.

¶ **2316**

Chapter 13—Deductions—Bad Debts

(c) Tax benefit rule—recovery exclusion. Under the specific charge-off method [(a), above] all of the recovery is included in gross income in the year received. However, the recovery is excluded to the extent that the bad debt deduction did *not* result in a reduction of tax. The balance of the recovery, if any, is taxable in the year received [Sec. 111; 1.111-1]. In determining if there was a tax benefit, consideration must be given to the net operating loss carrybacks and carryovers or capital loss carryover resulting from the bad debt deductions [Sec. 1.111-1]. Gain on sale of property taken to satisfy a debt cannot be excluded under the tax benefit rule.[1]

Example 2: In 1976, Smith, single with no dependents, had a net operating loss of $375, figured as follows:

Nonbusiness income			$4,600
Income (or loss) from business:			
Gross profit from business		$3,700	
Less: Business deductions:			
Business deductions other than bad debts	$3,000		
Bad debt	1,700	4,700	
Net loss from business			1,000 Loss
Adjusted gross income			$3,600
Less: Other itemized deductions		$3,975	
Deduction for exemption		750	4,725
Income tax net loss shown on return for 1976			$1,125
Less: Adjustment for deduction for exemption			750
Net operating loss for 1976 (see ¶ 2243)			$ 375

It is assumed there were no other Sec. 172 net operating loss adjustments required and the $375 net operating loss for 1976 was carried back, reducing the 1973 taxable income to the full extent of the $375 carryback.

In 1977, Smith recovered the $1,700 bad debt. If all of the bad debt deduction had resulted in a tax reduction, all of the recovery would have been taxable. However, $750 of the deduction did not effect a reduction as shown below. Therefore, $750 of the recovery is excluded and only $950 is taxable in 1977.

1976 nonbusiness income		$4,600
Income (or loss) from business:		
Gross profit from business	$3,700	
Less: Business deductions (excluding $1,700 bad debt)	3,000	
Net income from business		700
Adjusted gross income		$5,300
Less: Other itemized deductions	$3,975	
Deduction for exemption	750	4,725
1976 taxable income (excluding bad debt deduction)		$ 575
1976 bad debt deduction		$1,700
Less: Portion that offset 1976 taxable income		575
Balance of no benefit for 1976		$1,125
Less: Amount carried back to reduce 1973 tax		375
Net amount that did not reduce the tax (recovery exclusion)		$ 750
Balance of recovery that is taxable ($1,700 − $750)		$ 950

If a recovery exclusion is claimed, the taxpayer must submit with his return a statement showing the computation of the amount excluded.[2] If the original year is closed, the recovery exclusion is figured from the return as filed. The return is not reopened to include deductions not previously taken but allowable.[3] The "tax benefit" rule applies to all business and nonbusiness bad debts, including worthless bonds. It does not apply if the reserve method is used [Sec. 1.111-1].

(d) Prior taxes, delinquency amounts and other deductions recovered.
The tax benefit rule ((c) above) is not limited to the recovery of bad debts but also includes the recovery of taxes paid and interest on delinquent taxes, as well as the recovery of other losses, expenditures and accruals made the bases for deductions [Sec. 111; 1.111-1]. So if a tax paid in 1974 is later declared invalid, any recovery is subject to the above rules. Since federal income taxes are not deductible, refunds of these taxes, except for interest, are not income.[4]

Recoveries on or after 1-1-65 of foreign expropriation losses by a domestic corporation are included in income to the extent a deduction was taken in the loss year. The tax on the recovery is limited to the tax benefit, except that current tax rates apply. The types of income offset by the loss, carrybacks or carryovers and the effect of tax credits are taken into account [Sec. 1351]. See also ¶ 2241.

The tax benefit rule does not apply to items affected by prior deductions for depreciation, depletion, amortization or amortizable bond premiums. As to tax benefit resulting from excess depreciation allowed, see ¶ 2004.

¶ 2317 Loss on sale of pledged property other than on purchase money mortgage. If a mortgagor makes a voluntary conveyance of the property to the mortgagee, the property's fair market value is considered as payment of the unpaid balance of the obligation. If the fair market value of the property is less than the basis of the obligation, the difference, if worthless, is a bad debt deductible by the mortgagee. If there is a foreclosure and someone other than the mortgagee bids in the property for less than the obligation, the mortgagee has a bad debt deduction for the difference between the obligation and the amount received. If the mortgagee bids in the property, his deduction is the difference between the obligation and the bid price [Sec. 1.166-6]. For repossessions of installment sale property, see Chapter 18.

Footnotes to Chapter 13

(P-H "FEDERAL TAXES" related references are cited in brackets [ ] at the end of each footnote below)

Footnote ¶ 2300   [¶ 14,701 et seq.].
(1) Eckert v. Burnet, 283 US 140, 51 SCt. 373, 9 AFTR 1413 [¶ 14,753(5)].

Footnote ¶ 2301   [¶ 14,711 et seq.].
(1) Birdsboro Steel F & M Co. v U.S., 3 F. Supp. 640, 12 AFTR 1048 [¶ 14,712(10)].
(2) Clark, 205 F.2d 353, 44 AFTR 70 [¶ 14,712(15)].

Footnote ¶ 2302   [¶ 14,766].
(1) Skinner v. Eaton, 34 F.2d 576, 7 AFTR 9394, affd. 44 F.2d 1020, 9 AFTR 491 [¶ 14,767(20)].

Footnote ¶ 2305   [¶ 14,701 et seq.].
(1) U.S. v. Generes, 405 U.S. 93, 29 AFTR 2d 72-609 [¶ 14,904(5); 14,914(5)].
(2) Nichols, 17 BTA 580 [¶ 14,796(25)].
(3) Lyon, Inc., 127 F.2d 210, 29 AFTR 205 [¶ 14,804(10)].
(4) Brickell, 17 BTA 711 [¶ 14,786(5)].
(5) City National Bank of Commerce, 17 BTA 637 [¶ 14,782(10)].
(6) Smyth v. Motter, 77 F.2d 77, 15 AFTR 1339 [¶ 14,787(5)].

Footnote ¶ 2305 continued
(7) Richards & Hirschfield, Inc., 24 BTA 1289 [¶ 14,811(15)].
(8) Perine Machinery Co., 22 BTA 450 [¶ 14,783(5)].
(9) Burdine Realty Co., 20 BTA 54 [¶ 14,784(5)].
(10) Propp. ¶ 55,322 P-H Memo TC[¶ 14,804(20)].
(11) C.S. Webb, Inc., 1 BTA 269 [¶ 14,796(25)].
(12) Amer. Natl. Bank, 31 F.2d 47, 7AFTR 8537 [¶ 14,796(45)].
(13) Lutz, 9 BTA 23 [¶ 14,782(5)].
(14) Nathan H. Gordon Corp., 2 TC 571 [¶ 14,782(10)].

Footnote ¶ 2306   [¶ 14,829].
(1) Moock Electric Supply Co., 41 BTA 1209 [¶ 14,830(5)].
(2) Ross v. Comm., 72 F.2d 122, 14 AFTR 400 [¶ 14,837(5)].

Footnote ¶ 2307   [¶ 14,701 et seq.; 14,901].
(1) Treas. Dept. booklet "Your Federal Income Tax" (1977 Ed.), p. 118.
(2) Trent v. Comm., 7 AFTR 2d 1599, 291 F.2d 669 [¶ 14,914(5)].

Chapter 13—Footnotes

Footnote ¶ 2307 continued
(3) Weddle, 12 AFTR 2d 6103, 325 F.2d 849 [¶ 14,914(10)].
(4) Rosati, ¶ 70,343 P-H Memo TC [¶ 14,914(10)].
(5) Whipple v. Comm., 373 US 193; 11 AFTR 2d 1454 [¶ 14,904(5); 14,914(5)].
(6) U.S. v. Generes, 405 U.S. 93, 29 AFTR 2d 72-609 [¶ 14,904(5); 14,914(5)].

Footnote ¶ 2308 [¶ 14,720].
(1) Price, 7 BTA 1237; Sooy, 10 BTA 493, affd. 40 F.2d 634, 8 AFTR 10788; Griffiths, 70 F.2d 946, 14 AFTR 225 [¶ 14,720(10), (25)].

Footnote ¶ 2309 [¶ 14,731].
(1) Nicolai, 42 BTA 899, affd. 126 F.2d 927, 29 AFTR 36; Amer. Cigar Co. v. Comm., 66 F.2d 425, 12 AFTR 1268; Estate of Kent Avery, ¶ 69,064 P-H Memo TC [¶ 14,735(5), (45); 14,737(10)].
(2) Gimbel, 36 BTA 539 [¶ 14,735(60)].

Footnote ¶ 2310 [¶ 14,810].

Footnote ¶ 2311 [¶ 14,701 et seq.].
(1) Treas. Dept. booklet "Tax Guide for Small Business" (1977 Ed.), p. 53.
(2) Rev. Rul. 69-548, 1969-2 CB 32 [¶ 14,868(3)].
(3) Rev. Proc. 64-51, 1964-2 CB 1003, amplified by Rev. Proc. 70-15, 1970-1 CB 20 [¶ 14,871(5); 21,913(10)].
(4) Quality Chevrolet Co., 24 AFTR 2d 69-5532, 415 F.2d 116 [¶ 14,848(15); 14,965(40)].
(5) Rev. Rul. 70-139, 1970-1 CB 39 [¶ 14,849(10); 20,403(10)].

Footnote ¶ 2311 continued
(6) Nash v. U.S., 398 US 1, 25 AFTR 2d 70-1177 [¶ 8538(15)].

Footnote ¶ 2312 [¶ 14,290 et seq.; 21,829].

Footnote ¶ 2315 [¶ 14,045 et seq.].
(1) Johnson, Drake & Piper, Inc., 69 F.2d 151, 13 AFTR 657 [¶ 14,034(5)].
(2) MacRae, 9 BTA 428 [¶ 14,794(40)].
(3) Feltex Corp., ¶ 53,119 P-H Memo TC [¶ 14,794(5)].
(4) First National Bank of Durant, Okla., 6 BTA 545 [¶ 14,034(10)].
(5) Kansas City Pump Co., 6 BTA 938 [¶ 14,183(10)].
(6) Pacific Novelty Co., 5 BTA 1017 [¶ 14,046(40)].
(7) Eckert v. Burnet, 283 US 140, 9 AFTR 1413; Perry, 49 TC 508 [¶ 14,954(5)].
(8) Howell v. Comm., 69 F.2d 447, 13 AFTR 716 [¶ 14,950(5)].
(9) Ellisberg, 9 TC 463 [¶ 14,720(15)].

Footnote ¶ 2316 [¶ 8481 et seq.].
(1) Rev. Rul. 66-320, 1966-2 CB 37 [¶ 8487(50)].
(2) Treas. Dept. booklet "Tax Guide for Small Business" (1977 Ed.) p. 54.
(3) First National Bank, 221 F.2d 959; 47 AFTR 797 [¶ 8499(5)].
(4) Treas. Dept. Booklet "Your Federal Income Tax" (1977 Ed.), p. 47.

Footnote ¶ 2317 [¶ 14,921 et seq.].

Highlights of Chapter 13
Deductions—Bad Debts

I. **Bad Debt Deduction in General**
   A. **Defined [¶ 2300]:**
      1. From loans of money.
      2. From inclusion in gross income of debts due from others.
      3. Loss resulting from worthlessness deductible in year becomes worthless.
      4. Partial worthlessness deductible except for securities and nonbusiness bad debts of noncorporate taxpayers.
   B. **Existence of debt [¶ 2301]:**
      1. Must be real debtor-creditor relationship.
      2. No debt when repayment subject to contingency that has not yet occurred.
      3. Debt owed by political party—deductible only by banks.
   C. **Amount deductible [¶ 2302]:**
      1. Adjusted basis for determining loss from sale or exchange.
      2. No deduction if basis unprovable.
II. **What Bad Debts Are Deductible**
   A. **Business bad debts [¶ 2305]:**
      1. Incurred in taxpayer's business.
      2. Proximate relationship between debt creation and business.
      3. Deduction *for* adjusted gross income.
      4. Factors indicating worthless include bankruptcy, expired statute of limitations, etc.
      5. Factors indicating not worthless include no serious collection effort, debtor still in business, etc.
   B. **Partially worthless business debts [¶ 2306]:**
      1. Part charged-off in tax year deductible.
      2. Charge-off not mandatory [¶ 2306(a)].
      3. Collateral need not be liquidated [¶ 2306(b)].
      4. Must be specific debt [¶ 2306(c)].
      5. Partially worthless bonds—deductible only by banks [¶ 2306(d)].
   C. **Nonbusiness bad debts [¶ 2307]:**
      1. Not related to taxpayer's trade or business when created, acquired or become worthless.
      2. Partially worthless—not deductible.
      3. Loans by officer or employee to corporations—usually nonbusiness debt [¶ 2307(a)].
      4. Loans by stockholders to corporation—nonbusiness debt [¶ 2307(b)].
      5. Treated as short-term capital loss [¶ 2307(c)].
   D. **Advances:**
      1. To relatives [¶ 2308]:
         a. As gift—no bad debt deduction.
         b. As real loan—usually nonbusiness debt.
      2. To corporations by stockholders [¶ 2309]:
         a. Either loan (debt created) or capital contribution (no debt).
         b. Important to establish nature of advance when made.
   E. **Deposits in closed banks**—usually bad debt deduction for depositor [¶ 2310].
   F. **How deducted [¶ 2311]:**
      1. Specific charge-off method—deducted as become worthless during tax year [¶ 2311(a)].
      2. Reserve method [¶ 2311(b)]:
         a. Not directly deducted from income during year.
         b. Reasonable addition charged against a reserve.
         c. Must attach statement to return.

3. Election of methods subject to IRS approval [¶ 2311(c)].
4. Change of methods allowed subject to IRS approval.
5. Sale of receivables—slightly different reserve method deductions allowed [¶ 2311(d)].
6. Installment basis sales—reserve method allowed [¶ 2311(e)].
7. Transfer of bad debt reserve to controlled corporation [¶ 2311(f)].
8. Banks and trust companies—special rules [¶ 2311(g)].

G. **Worthless bonds [¶ 2312]:**
 1. Taxpayers other than banks and trust companies [¶ 2312(a)]:
    a. Completely worthless corporate bond—capital loss on last day of tax year.
    b. Partially worthless corporate bond—no deduction allowed.
    c. Exception—certain affiliated corporation securities.
 2. Banks and trust companies [¶ 2312(b)]:
    a. Conclusive presumption of worthlessness when debt charged-off under banking authority orders.
    b. Fully deductible loss (not capital).
    c. Partial worthlessness deduction allowed.

III. **Special Problems**
 A. **Bad debt and loss distinguished [¶ 2315]:**
  1. Refund claim statute of limitations:
     a. Loss deduction—3 years.
     b. Bad debt deduction—7 years.
  2. Voluntary cancellation or forgiveness of debt [¶ 2315(a)]:
     a. Loss deduction—not allowed.
     b. Bad debt deduction—allowed, if actually worthless.
  3. Endorsers and guarantors [¶ 2315(b)]:
     a. Pay principal's debt and claim against principal worthless—bad debt deduction.
     b. No proof of intent to collect—no bad debt deductions.
     c. Noncorporate guarantors paying principal's debt—business bad debt deduction if:
        1) Debt noncorporate.
        2) Loan proceeds used in debtor's business.
        3) Right to collect from principal worthless at time of payment.

 B. **Recovery of bad debts [¶ 2316]:**
  1. Specific charge-off method [¶ 2316(a)]—include in gross income in year received.
  2. Reserve method [¶ 2316(b)]—credit to reserve.
  3. Tax benefit rule [¶ 2316(c)]:
     a. Recovery excluded under specific charge-off method—income to extent that bad debt deduction did not result in tax reduction.
     b. Not applicable to reserve method deductions
     c. Applies to all business and nonbusiness bad debts, including worthless bonds.
     d. Also applies to recovery of prior taxes, delinquency amounts and other deductions [¶ 2316(d)].
     e. Not applicable to items affected by prior deductions for depreciation, depletion, amortization or amortizable bond premiums.

 C. **Loss on sale of pledged property other than on purchase money mortgage [¶ 2317]:**
  1. Voluntary conveyance to mortgagee:
     a. Property's fair market value is unpaid balance of debt.
     b. If fair market value is less than debt's basis, difference, if worthless, is bad debt deduction for mortgagee.
  2. Foreclosure and property bid in by third party for less than debt—bad debt deductible by mortgagee for difference between debt and amount received.
  3. If mortgagee bids in property—bad debt deduction for difference between debt and bid price.

TAX COMPUTATION—WITHHOLDING—INVENTORIES—ACCOUNTING

Chapter 14—ALTERNATE TAX METHODS—TAX CREDITS
(Detailed Table of Contents below)

Chapter 15—WITHHOLDING—ESTIMATED TAX
(Detailed Table of Contents at page 2501)

Chapter 16—INVENTORY
(Detailed Table of Contents at page 2601)

Chapter 17—ACCOUNTING
(Detailed Table of Contents at page 2701)

Chapter 18—INSTALLMENT AND DEFERRED PAYMENT SALES
(Detailed Table of Contents at page 2801)

Chapter 14

ALTERNATE TAX METHODS—TAX CREDITS
TABLE OF CONTENTS

	¶
Tax computation in general	2400

METHODS OF FIGURING THE TAX

Income averaging 2401
   What income is eligible
   What benefits are not available
   Who is eligible for income averaging
   How income averaging is figured
   Married couples
How to compute the maximum tax on personal service income 2402
   What is personal service income
   What is personal service taxable income
   How to figure the maximum tax
How to compute the minimum tax 2403
   What are the tax preferences
   Effect of net operating loss on minimum tax
   Estates, trusts and certain corporations

What forms to use

CREDITS FOR EARNED INCOME AND THE ELDERLY

Earned income credit 2405
   Who can get the credit
   What earned income qualifies
Credit for the elderly 2406
   Figuring the credit
   Husband and wife
   Public retirees

INVESTMENT, WORK INCENTIVE AND JOBS CREDITS

Figuring the investment credit 2410
   Qualified property
   Property that does not qualify
   Useful life
   Credit carryback and carryover
   Credit recapture
   Leased property

Footnotes appear at end of this Chapter.

Chapter 14—Alternate Tax Methods—Tax Credits

¶
- Special rules
- Credit for employee stock ownership plan (ESOP)
- **Credit for work incentive program expenses** 2411
  - Amount of credit
  - Limitations on credit
  - Credit carryback and carryover
  - Credit recapture
  - Special rules
  - Employment of federal welfare recipients
- **Jobs credit** 2412

OTHER TAX CREDITS

Expenses of child care and care of

¶
- disabled dependent of spouse 2415
- Who may take the credit
- What expenses qualify
- Limitation on credit
- Payments to relatives
- Special rules
- **Political campaign contributions** 2416
  - Eligible contributions
  - Donation of appreciated property
  - "Tax check-off" system
- **Credit for certain uses of gasoline, special fuels and lubricating oil** 2417

• **Highlights of Chapter 14** .... Page 2461

¶ **2400 Tax computation in general.** There are basically two methods of computing an individual's tax liability which were covered earlier in Chapter 1: the tax rate schedules and the tax tables. However, certain optional methods serve to reduce the tax impact. This chapter deals with some of the principal methods that can minimize an individual's tax liability: income averaging and the maximum tax on personal service income. Other alternate methods exist that have a similar effect. These methods are covered in the chapters dealing with the general subject to which they relate: the alternative capital gains tax [¶ 1614], the net operating loss [¶ 2241 et seq.] and the ten-year averaging method involving lump-sum distributions [¶ 3024(d)].

The minimum tax on tax preference items is also covered in this chapter. It is an additional tax which is added to the taxpayer's tax liability.

One of the final steps on the tax return involves applying any tax credits to which the taxpayer may be entitled. There is a basic difference between a credit and a deduction. A deduction only indirectly reduces tax liability since it is subtracted from gross or adjusted gross income. However, a credit is deducted directly from the tax due. The principal credits are for earned income, child care expenses, political campaign contributions, investment in qualified property, hiring individuals under a work incentive program, hiring new employees and credit for the elderly. Some other credits, such as the general tax credit [¶ 1111(e)], the foreign tax credit [¶ 3701 et seq.] and the credits for withholding and estimated taxes [¶ 2501 et seq.] are discussed in the chapters to which they closely relate.

METHODS OF FIGURING THE TAX

This section deals with certain methods that serve to reduce an individual's tax liability (income averaging and the maximum tax on personal service income) and a method that is an additional tax. The minimum tax is an additional levy designed to tax certain preference items that would normally escape taxation.

¶ **2401 Income averaging.** Income averaging permits a part of an unusually large amount of taxable income to be taxed in lower brackets. This method is not an alternative to computing your tax under the tax rate schedules. But rather it serves to place a ceiling on your tax liability and results in a reduction of the overall amount of tax due. Briefly, the income averaging method operates to tax a part (the averageable income) of the unusually large amount of income in the peak year at the same lower effective tax rate that applies to the first $1/5$ of this averageable income. This method has the effect of taxing income of a high income year *as if* it were spread over a 5-year period.

Background and purpose. Before income averaging was enacted, those whose incomes varied widely (for example, authors, actors, artists and athletes) paid substantially more in taxes than others with comparable amounts of income spread more evenly over the same years. This was caused by the progressive nature of the individual tax rates. By spreading income over a 5-year period, income averaging treats those with fluctuating income as near equal as possible to those with stable incomes.

≫**OBSERVATION**→ Every year, a taxpayer should check carefully to see if the benefits of income averaging are available no matter what is the taxpayer's economic status.

(a) What income is eligible. Generally, all types of income can be averaged, including long-term capital gains, wagering income and income from gifts and inherited property. The only exceptions are premature payouts from self-employed retirement plans [¶ 1839(g)] and accumulation distributions from trusts (¶ 3023) [Sec. 1302(a)(2); 1.1302-1(b), 1.1302-2(c)(2)].

(b) What benefits are not available: If the taxpayer chooses the benefits of income averaging, the following provisions are not available in the same computation year: (1) the alternative tax on net long-term capital gains [¶ 1614]; (2) the maximum tax [¶ 2402]; (3) the exclusion of foreign source earned income [¶ 3725]; and (4) the exclusion of the income from sources within the U.S. possessions (¶ 3727) [Sec. 1304(b)].

(c) Who is eligible for income averaging. You are eligible for income averaging if you meet two tests: (1) citizenship or residence test; and (2) support test [Sec. 1303; 1.1303-1].

Citizenship or residence test. You must have been either a citizen or a resident of the U.S. throughout your computation year and your base period years. Thus, if you were married to a nonresident alien during any part of the averaging period, you cannot use income averaging if you file a joint return [Sec. 1303; 1.1303-1(b)].

Support test. You must have furnished at least ½ of your own support in all of the 4 base period years. Support, for this purpose, is defined in ¶ 1116. If you file a joint return, both you and your spouse must meet the support test. However, there are three exceptions [Sec. 1303(c)(2); 1.1303-1(c)]:

• You are at least 25 in the current tax year and you were not a full time student (5 months or more a year) for at least 4 tax years after age 21;
• You received more than half of your current year's taxable income for work done in 2 or more base period years; or
• Your income is not more than 25% of the aggregate adjusted gross income reported on a joint return.

(d) How income averaging is figured. A qualified individual can elect income averaging when *averageable income* for a current tax year is more than $3,000 and taxable income for the same tax year is more than ⅕ higher than average income for a base period of the 4 preceding years [Sec. 1301; 1.1301-1]. For this purpose, taxable income is reduced by accumulations distributed to the taxpayer by a trust during the tax year [¶ 3023] and premature payouts from self-

Footnotes appear at end of this Chapter.

employed retirement plans (¶ 1839(g)) [Sec. 1302(a)(2); 1.1302-1(b)]. The election can be made or revoked as long as the high income tax year is open. If the taxpayer elects this method, he computes his tax on Schedule G, Form 1040, and attaches it to his return. The tax is computed using the rate schedule method (¶ 1121) [Sec. 1301, 1304; 1.1304-1].

NOTE: For tax years beginning before 1-1-77, add the zero bracket amount [¶ 1107] to the base period income. Next, apply the following test on Schedule G merely to determine whether you can use income averaging: Adjusted taxable income must be *more than* $3,000 higher than 120% of your average taxable income for the last 4 years.

Example 1: A single taxpayer wants to use income averaging in 1977. His taxable income for the four prior years was $7,000, $9,000, $11,000 and $13,000 for an average of $12,200 (the $2,200 zero bracket amount is added to each year). 120% of $12,200 is $14,460, so the taxpayer can average if his 1977 taxable income is over $17,460.

➤**OBSERVATION**➤ A base period year may be a short year due to a change in the accounting period [Sec. 1.1304-6(a)(1)].

A tax is computed for $1/5$ of the averageable income and multiplied by 5 to find the tax on this income. The tax on the nonaverageable income is added to this amount, and the total is the tax liability for the year. There is no adjustment of prior year's returns.

When the current year's income does not include nonaverageable items, the tax can be computed in 7 steps:

STEP 1. Find the average base period income. This is the average of the 4 years immediately before the year for which averaging is elected. Add the zero bracket amount to base period income for tax years beginning before 1-1-77.

NOTE: The taxable income in the base period years is decreased by accumulation trust payouts [¶ 3023] and is increased by otherwise excludable income from foreign sources and U.S. possessions, less deductible related expenses (¶ 3725; 3727) [Sec. 1302(b)(2); 1.1302-2(c)]. Base period income for any tax year may never be less than zero[1] [Sec. 1.1302-2(b)]. If there is a discrepancy between taxable income reported and the correct taxable income for a base period year, the latter figure is applied even if the base year is closed.[2]

STEP 2. Multiply the average base period income by $1\frac{1}{5}$ (120%). This is the *nonaverageable income*.

NOTE: Return Schedule G streamlines Steps 1 and 2. All you need do to determine the nonaverageable income is multiply the sum of the taxable incomes for the 4 base period years by 30%.

STEP 3. Subtract nonaverageable income from the current year's taxable income. If the remainder exceeds $3,000, all of it is *averageable income*.

STEP 4. Add $1/5$ of averageable income to nonaverageable income and compute the tax on the total.

STEP 5. Find the tax on nonaverageable income only.

STEP 6. Subtract the tax in Step 5 from the tax in Step 4 and multiply by 5.

STEP 7. Add the amounts in Step 5 and Step 6. The sum of the two taxes is the total tax.

Example 2: Wilhelm Jones, single, has taxable income of $45,000 in 1977. Taxable income for the base period 1973-1976, consisting of both ordinary income and capital gain, was $5,000, $6,000, $4,000 and $9,000, respectively. Jones must add the $2,200 zero bracket amount to each year.

Step 1:	Average base period income ($32,800 ÷ 4)	$ 8,200
Step 2:	Nonaverageable income ($8,200 × 120%)	9,840
Step 3:	Averageable income ($45,000 − $9,840)	35,160
Step 4:	Nonaverageable income	9,840

	⅕ of averageable income ($35,160 ÷ 5)	7,032
	Total	16,872
	Tax on above (Tax Rate Schedule)	3,418
Step 5:	Tax on nonaverageable income ($9,840)	1,504
Step 6:	Increase in tax	1,914
	Increase multiplied by 5	9,570
Step 7:	Plus tax on nonaverageable income	1,504
	Tax for 1977	11,074

(e) Married couples. When a married couple files a joint return for the current year, the computations are made on their joint income and the combined incomes for the base year. If either was married to another spouse in a base period year, his or her base period income is considered to be not less than 50% of what it would have been if a joint return had been filed [Sec. 1304(c); 1.1304-3]. If separate returns are filed for the current year and joint returns had been filed for any year in the base period, the separate income and deductions of the spouses must be determined for the year a joint return was filed [Sec. 1.1304-3]. Taxpayer's separate deductions are determined as follows:

$$\text{Separate deductions} = \text{Total deductions} \times \frac{\text{Taxpayer's adjusted gross income}}{\text{Combined adjusted gross income}}$$

However, if 85% or more of the combined adjusted gross income is attributable to only one spouse, that spouse is allowed all the deductions.

Example 3: George Young, a calendar year taxpayer, is married to Nora and files a separate return for 1977, electing the income averaging method. In 1976 George and Nora filed a joint return in which their combined adjusted gross income was $10,000, consisting entirely of salaries. Of this amount, $8,000 was attributable to George. Their deductions in 1976 totaled $3,000. The amount of George's separate deductions in 1976 is $2,400 ($8,000/$10,000 × $3,000). His separate income in 1976 is $5,600 ($8,000 minus $2,400).

Example 4: Assume the same facts as in Example 3, except that $9,000 of their combined adjusted gross income was attributable to George. George would be entitled to all of the deductions ($3,000) as his separate deductions, since his portion of the combined income was more than 85% of the total ($9,000/$10,000 = 90%). His separate income would be $6,000 ($9,000 minus $3,000).

¶ 2402 How to compute the maximum tax on personal service income. The top marginal tax rate applicable to an individual's personal service taxable income is limited to 50%. The limit does not apply to the separate return of a married person, or if the taxpayer elects income averaging (¶ 2401) [Sec. 1348; 1.1348-1].

Background and purpose. The Congress concluded that extremely high rates of tax, particularly for earned income, are unrealistic and tend to create distortions in our tax system. It was decided that a 50% maximum marginal rate on earned income would be an effective method of reducing the disincentive effect of high rates for earned income. The Tax Reform Act made changes effective for tax years starting after 1976. The term "earned income" was replaced by "personal service income" and now includes pensions, annuities and deferred compensation. The 5-year averaging of tax preferences and the $30,000 exemption for tax preferences were eliminated.

(a) What is personal service income. Personal service income includes: (1) wages, salaries, professional fees and other compensation as defined in Sec. 911(b) [¶ 3725(a)]; (2) ordinary gains and net earnings from the disposition or licensing of property (other than good will) owned by an author or inventor; (3) pensions, annuities and deferred compensation [Sec. 1348(b)(1)(A)]. If both services and capital are material income-producing factors, a reasonable amount (up to 30%) can be treated as earned income. Personal service income does *not* include: (1) payments made by a corporation that represent a distribution of earnings and profits rather than a reasonable allowance for personal services rendered; (2) lump-sum and penalty distributions from qualified plans [¶ 1838]; (3) distributions from self-employed retirement plans [¶ 1839]; (4) early redemption of retirement bonds (¶ 1838) [Sec. 1348(b)(1)(B)].

A nonresident alien's personal service income does not include wages, compensation and other fixed or determinable annual or periodical gains, profits and income subject to the 30% tax (or lower treaty rate) [¶ 3709(b); 3711(a)].

(b) What is personal service taxable income. Personal service taxable income is determined as follows (see ¶ 1614 for computation of alternative tax):

(1) Determine personal service net income, which is personal service income less allocable deductions for adjusted gross income.
(2) Find your adjusted gross income [¶ 1102(c)].
(3) Divide personal service net income (1) by the amount in (2) (but this amount cannot be in excess of 100%).
(4) Multiply the percentage in (3) by taxable income [¶ 1102(g)].
(5) Reduce the figure determined in (4) by the items of tax preference [¶ 2403(a)] for the tax year.

NOTE: The maximum tax does not apply if you are single or a head of household and your personal service taxable income is $40,200 or less; $55,200 or less if you are married filing jointly or a surviving spouse.

Example 1: In 1977, J. P. Snodgrass has wages of $150,000, other taxable income of $25,000, and no deductions for adjusted gross income or excess net long-term capital gains. His excess itemized deductions and personal exemptions total $20,000. He has no tax preferences in 1977. His personal service taxable income (PSTI) is $132,857.14, figured as follows:

$$\$155{,}000 \text{ (taxable income)} \times \frac{\$150{,}000 \text{ (personal service net income)}}{\$175{,}000 \text{ (adjusted gross income)}} = \$132{,}857.14 \text{ (PSTI)}$$

(c) How to figure the maximum tax. The maximum tax is the sum of three separate tax computations: (1) regular tax on taxable income through the 50% rate bracket; (2) 50% of the excess of personal service taxable income over the amount of taxable income in (1); (3) the excess of the tax on taxable income (determined without regard to the maximum tax) over the tax on personal service taxable income.

Example 2: J. P. Snodgrass in Example 1 files a joint return for 1977. His tax (before credits) without the benefit of the maximum tax is $78,168. With the maximum tax, it is $71,296.00, figured as follows:

(1) Regular tax on income through 50% bracket ($55,200) $18,060.00
(2) 50% × ($132,857.14 − $55,200) 38,828.57
(3) Tax on $155,000 .... $78,168.00
    Tax on $132,857.14 .... 63,760.57   14,407.43

Tax payable $71,296.00

¶ 2403 How to compute the minimum tax. Individuals, trusts, estates and corporations that have substantial tax preferences are liable for a minimum tax in addition to all other taxes [Sec. 56]. For tax years starting after 1975, individuals pay a minimum tax that is a flat 15% (10% in earlier years) of the tax preferences reduced by the greater of:

- $10,000 ($5,000 if married filing separately) [Sec. 58(a)], or
- One-half of the regular income tax imposed for the tax year (see NOTE below), less the general tax credit [¶ 1111(e)], the credits for foreign taxes [¶ 3701], elderly persons [¶ 2406], investment in qualified property [¶ 2410], work incentive program expenses [¶ 2411], jobs credit [¶ 2412], political contributions [¶ 2416], purchase of a new home [¶ 1416(d)], and child care expenses [¶ 2415].

> NOTE: The tax imposed that is applied to reduce the minimum tax does not include the tax on lump-sum distributions or on premature distributions from certain retirement plans, or the accumulated earnings and personal holding company taxes [¶ 1838(1); 1839; 3024(d); 3131; 3405]. The regular tax can be the tax determined by using the maximum tax, the alternative tax or under income averaging [¶ 1614; 2401; 2402]. However, income averaging may not be used when determining the minimum tax itself.[1] Special rules apply to corporations. See ¶ 3102. The carryover of unused regular taxes to offset preference income has been repealed effective for tax years after 1975.

(a) What are the tax preferences. The following are tax preference items subject to the minimum tax [Sec. 57]:

- Capital gains.
- Accelerated depreciation on real property.
- Accelerated depreciation on leased personal property.
- Adjusted itemized deductions.
- Intangible drilling costs.
- Depletion.
- Amortization of certified pollution control facilities [¶ 2040], railroad rolling stock [¶ 2041], and child care facilities [¶ 2043].
- Stock options.
- Bad debt deductions of financial institutions.

Capital gains. The tax preference for individuals, estates and trusts involves an amount equal to one-half of the excess of net long-term capital gain over net short-term capital loss. This is true even if the long-term capital gain deduction is not taken, as when the alternative tax is used [¶ 1612; 3009]. For corporations, see ¶ 3201.

> NOTE: Any excess net long-term capital gain used to offset disallowed investment interest is not a tax preference item. This also applies for an amount equal to a long-term capital gain deduction that reduces a disallowed investment interest carryover (¶ 1906(a)) [Proposed Reg. Sec. 1.57-1(i)(1)].

Accelerated depreciation. The "excess" depreciation on leased personal property and real property is considered a tax preference item [Sec. 57(a)(2), (3)].

Real property. The "excess" depreciation is the depreciation deduction above the "as-if" straight line method allowable for each of the tax years the taxpayer held the property. Grouping of assets with similar useful lives and depreciation methods is permitted. Depreciation recaptured as ordinary income is not considered allowable depreciation for tax preference (¶ 1619; 1942(b)) [Proposed Reg. Sec. 1.57-1(b)].

Personal property. The "excess" depreciation on a lease is the depreciation above the straight line method. This is not a preference item for corporations except Subchapter S corporations [¶ 3140] and personal holding companies (¶ 3400) [Proposed Reg. Sec. 1.57-0; 1.57-3].

Adjusted itemized deductions. If total itemized deductions (including the zero bracket amount) exceed 60% of adjusted gross income, then the excess, up to

Footnotes appear at end of this Chapter.

¶ 2403

100% of adjusted gross income, is a tax preference item. Deductions for adjusted gross income, medical expenses and casualty losses are not included. The rule is for tax years starting after 1975 and does not apply to corporations. Deductions taken by estates or trusts for (1) certain contributions passed on to beneficiaries [¶ 3006; 3013]; (2) net operating losses [¶ 3015]; (3) depreciation or depletion [¶ 3014]; (4) distributions to beneficiaries [¶ 3017]; or (5) administration expenses [¶ 3016] are considered deductions for adjusted gross income and are not included [Sec. 56(a), (b)].

Intangible drilling costs. Intangible drilling costs in excess of the amount deductible if such costs were capitalized and either deducted as cost depletion or written off over 10 years are tax preferences [¶ 2103(c)]. This rule is for tax years starting after 1975, and does not apply to nonproductive wells or to corporations [Sec. 56(a)(11)].

NOTE: For tax years beginning after 12-31-76 and before 1-1-78, the tax preference base for intangible drilling costs is reduced by: (1) the amount that could have been deducted if the costs had been amortized and capitalized; (2) the net income from all oil and gas properties [¶ 2104].

Depletion. This is the excess, if any, of the depletion deduction for the year over the property's cost reduced for depletion taken in prior years [Proposed Reg. Sec. 1.57-1(h)]. Each property is separately determined. So, once the taxpayer has taken depletion deductions in an amount equal to the cost of the property, any further depletion deductions are tax preferences.

Stock options. The tax preference involves the difference between the purchase price and the value of the stock in the tax year the option is exercised. However, the minimum tax does not apply if in the same tax year the option is exercised, the stock transferred is disposed of or the stock plan under which the option is exercised is modified so as to result in the income being taxed as ordinary income. Also, the tax does not apply if the employment requirements are not met when the option is exercised. No adjustment is made to the basis of the stock for any minimum tax liability [Sec. 57(a)(6), (9); Proposed Reg. 1.57-1(f)]. The rule applies to both qualified and restricted stock options [¶ 1327]. It does not apply to corporations.

Financial institutions' bad debt deduction. This is the excess of the additions to the bad debt reserve over the reserve which would have been allowable if it had been based on the institution's actual experience (¶ 3433) [Proposed Reg. Sec. 1.57-1(g)].

(b) Effect of net operating loss on minimum tax. In a year the taxpayer has tax preferences in excess of $10,000 ($30,000 for tax years starting before 1-1-76) and also sustains a net operating loss large enough to carry over to a succeeding year, he defers all or part of his minimum tax liability to the tax year his taxable income is reduced by the net operating loss attributable to the excess tax preferences. No minimum tax is imposed if the taxpayer does not benefit from this portion of the loss during the carryover period. The tax deferred is the lesser of the minimum tax or 15% of either the net operating loss for the year or unused net operating loss carried over from the year the loss was sustained (10% in tax years starting before 1-1-76). He pays the tax in any of the years that carried over loss attributable to the tax preferences in excess of $10,000 reduces taxable income. The net operating loss not attributable to the tax preferences is applied first [Sec. 56(b)].

Example 3: In 1976, Guido sustained a net operating loss and had an unused carryover from this loss of $100,000 of which $75,000 was from tax preferences. Guido carried over his net operating loss to 1977 when he had a taxable income of $80,000 (no tax preferences). He would pay no minimum tax in 1976 and in 1977 would pay the deferred tax of $9,750 plus the 1977 minimum tax of $6,750, computed as follows:

1976

Minimum tax [15% × $65,000 ($75,000 − $10,000)]	$ 9,750
15% × Net operating loss carryover ($100,000)	15,000
Deferred minimum tax (lesser of above)	9,750

1977

Taxable income	$80,000
NOL carryover not attributable to excess tax preferences ($25,000 + $10,000 minimum tax exclusion)	35,000
NOL carryover attributable to excess tax preferences	45,000
Minimum tax in 1977 (15% × $45,000)	$ 6,750
Remaining NOL to be carried forward and attributable to excess tax preference ($100,000 NOL less $80,000 taxable income)	$20,000

Limit on tax preferences. Because of the adjustments on figuring net operating loss [¶ 2242], a taxpayer's net operating loss does not usually equal the excess of his deductions over his gross income. A taxpayer in that situation in a year he has tax preference items does not fully benefit from the preferences and can therefore limit the preferences subject to minimum tax to the amount that does benefit him. If the taxpayer has no taxable income in a year (without regard to the net operating loss deduction), his tax preferences equal his "recomputed income" if he has no net operating loss or, if he does have a net operating loss, the net operating loss (expressed as a positive amount) increased by his "recomputed income" or decreased by his "recomputed loss." In either case, stock option preferences are added to the limitation. Recomputed income or loss means the taxable income or net operating loss computed without regard to any tax preferences (except corporate capital gains [¶ 3201(b)]), or the net operating loss deduction. When the sum of the tax preference items is reduced, the capital gains preference and any other item related to a deduction disallowed in computing the net operating loss are reduced first and pro rata. The balance of the reduction is from the remaining tax preferences, pro rata [Sec. 56(b); Proposed Reg. 1.57-4].

(c) Estates, trusts and certain corporations. There are special rules for applying the minimum tax to estates and trusts [¶ 3020(d)], Subchapter S corporations [¶ 3140], related corporations [¶ 3223(a)], personal holding companies [¶ 3400] and regulated investment companies [¶ 3431].

(d) What forms to use. Individuals with preference items in excess of $10,000 ($5,000 if married filing separately) must file Form 4625, even if there is no minimum tax due. Form 4626 is used by corporations having tax preferences in excess of $10,000. See also ¶ 3541.

CREDITS FOR EARNED INCOME AND THE ELDERLY

This section deals with the earned income credit for certain low income taxpayers and the new credit for the elderly. This new credit was enacted as part of the Tax Reform Act of 1976 replacing the old retirement income credit. It offers individuals over age 65 a credit based on all types of income and is available regardless of prior work experience.

The *earned income credit* is 10% up to a maximum $400 on earned income for certain taxpayers with dependent children. There is a phase-out as income levels exceed $4,000. This credit has been extended through 1978.

Footnotes appear at end of this Chapter.

¶ **2405 Earned income credit.** Certain individuals can get a refundable tax credit of 10% of earned income up to a maximum of $400. The credit is phased out as adjusted gross income, or earnings if higher, exceeds $4,000 [Sec. 43(a), (b); Prop. Reg. 1.43-1(b)(1)].

Background and purpose. The earned income credit was enacted to provide some tax relief from the social security and self-employment taxes for low income individuals.

(a) Who can get the credit. An individual must maintain a household in the U.S. for himself and for at least one child either under age 19 or a student, or a disabled child for whom a dependency exemption may be claimed. A single taxpayer qualifies by providing over half the cost of maintaining a household for himself or herself and a dependent child. A married individual is considered to be maintaining a household if both spouses together furnish over half the cost of supporting it. Married taxpayers must file a joint return to be eligible. However an abandoned spouse can qualify for the credit (¶ 1104(c)) [Sec. 43(c)(1), (d); Prop. Reg. 1.43-1(c), (i)].

(b) What earned income qualifies. Earned income includes wages, salaries, tips and other employee compensation along with any net earnings from self-employment. Pension and annuity payments cannot be included [Sec. 43(c)(2); Prop. Reg. 1.43-1(c)(2)].

¶ **2406 Credit for the elderly.** Individuals age 65 or over can receive a 15% credit against their tax on all types of income, including earned income. No prior work experience is necessary. The credit is available for tax years starting after 1975. Nonresident aliens do not qualify [Sec. 37].

Background and purpose. The Tax Reform Act of 1976 liberalized the elderly credit (formerly the retirement credit) by making it available for earned as well as retirement income. The major changes occurred in the following four areas: (1) the credit base was 15% of the first $1,524 of retirement income; (2) earned income was not eligible; (3) the credit was not based on joint income; (4) the individual had to have received earned income in the prior four years. The Tax Reduction and Simplification Act allowed taxpayers to elect to be treated under the old rules for the first tax year beginning in 1976.

(a) Figuring the credit. The maximum amount of income against which the 15% credit can be claimed is $2,500 for single persons age 65 or over and married persons filing jointly when only one is 65 or over. The maximum is $3,750 when both spouses, filing joint returns, are age 65 or over ($1,875 on separate returns). The maximum credit base must be reduced by social security, railroad retirement benefits or other exempt pension benefits. It is also reduced by one-half of the amount of adjusted gross income above certain income levels ($7,500 for single persons; $10,000 for married persons filing jointly; or $5,000 for married persons filing separately) [Sec. 37(b)(2), (3)].

(b) Husband and wife. Generally, the credit is available to married couples only if they file a joint return. The credit is figured on their combined income and the credit base is reduced by the total exempt pension income above the permitted level. An abandoned spouse can qualify for the credit (¶ 1104(c)) [Sec. 37(d)(1)].

(c) Public retirees. Persons under age 65 and retired under a public retirement system have similar rules as to maximum credit base as those retirees age 65 or over. Retirement income for those under 65 generally includes pension or annuity income under a public retirement system. For those 65 or over, retirement income includes the taxable portion of income from annuities [¶ 1230; 1231]; pensions [¶ 1304]; qualified U.S. bonds received under a retirement plan and distribution under self-employed retirement plans [¶ 1839]; interest [¶ 1314]; rents [¶ 1316]; dividends [¶ 1705]; and certain individual retirement arrangements [¶ 1838(1)].

A special rule applies when one spouse is under age 65 and the other is 65 or over. They must elect for the year either the elderly credit or to use essentially the old retirement income credit rules. If the prior rules are elected, they must allocate the $3,750 ($1,875 on separate returns) maximum credit base between themselves as they decide. However, no more than $2,500 ($1,875 on separate returns) can go to any one spouse. Then this credit base is reduced by (1) social security, railroad retirement benefits or other exempt pension benefits; (2) earned income over $900 if an individual is under age 62; or (3) one-half of earned income between $1,200 and $1,700 plus all earned income over $1,700 if the individual is 62 or over, but not 72 years old [Sec. 37(e)].

INVESTMENT, WORK INCENTIVE AND JOBS CREDITS

An investment credit is allowed when certain qualified business property is placed in service. It can also apply to amounts paid in the building or acquiring of qualified property ("progress payments"). The credit has no effect on regular depreciation. A special credit is available to those who employ persons in training under a Work Incentive Program. Employers can also get a credit for hiring new or handicapped employees.

¶ **2410 Figuring the investment credit.** Taxpayers can take a 10% credit for investments in certain qualified business property (including utility property) acquired and placed in service after 1-21-75 and before 1-1-81. The credit can also apply to expenditures made during this period in the building of certain property ("progress payments"). For property built or rebuilt by the taxpayer, the 10% credit applies to the extent of the property's basis attributable to construction after 1-21-75 and before 1-1-81. A corporate taxpayer may elect an 11% credit for qualified investment during the 1-22-75 through 12-31-80 period if an amount equal to 1% of this investment is contributed to an employee stock ownership plan ("ESOP," see (h) below). Starting in 1977, an extra ½% may be claimed (in addition to the 11%) if an additional ½% employer contribution is matched by employee contributions to the ESOP. The credit cannot be more than the first $25,000 of the tax liability ($12,500 for a married person filing separately, unless his spouse is not entitled to any credit), plus ½ of the excess [Sec. 46(a), (c)].

Example 1: Wilson's tax before the credit is $100,000. The maximum credit allowable, is $62,500 ($25,000 + ½ of $75,000). If he bought and placed into service qualified property on 5-1-77 costing $200,000, his credit would be $20,000, and his net tax payable would be $80,000. Depreciation on the property is computed on the basis of $200,000.

NOTE: Certain public utilities can use the investment credit to offset 100% of their tax liabilities for years ending in 1976. After 1976 this percentage is phased down 10% annually until 1981, when it reaches 50% [Sec. 46(a)(7)]. Certain railroads and airlines can also use the investment credit to offset 100% of their tax liability for tax years ending in 1977 and 1978 (50% for 1976). After 1978 this percentage is phased down 10% annually until 1983 when it is again 50% [Sec. 46(a)(8), (9)].

The amount of the "qualified investment" depends on the useful life of the property ((c) below). It is determined from the cost of used property that qualifies or the basis of new property. Items like installation and freight costs added to basis for depreciation are included. The basis of new property acquired in a nontaxable exchange is the same as the property transferred plus any boot given [¶ 1517]. The cost of used property is equal to its basis except for any part of the basis that is determined from the basis of other property that was held by the taxpayer. The basis is not reduced for the credit taken [Sec. 46(a); 1.46-1(b); 1.46-3(c); 1.48-3(b)].

Example 2: Cole traded in an old business machine with an adjusted basis of $8,000 for a new similar machine and paid $1,000 in cash. The trade-in is tax free and the basis of the new machine is $9,000 (basis of old plus boot).

Example 3: On 2-1-77, James Clinton traded in a used business machine bought in 1974 with an adjusted basis of $1,600 for a used machine which has an estimated life of 8 years. He paid $4,000 cash on the deal. The basis of the machine just acquired is $5,600 ($1,600 adjusted basis of the traded-in machine plus $4,000 cash). But the *cost* of the machine which is used to compute the investment credit is $4,000 ($5,600 basis minus $1,600 adjusted basis of the traded-in machine). The credit, therefore, is $400 (10% of $4,000).

Example 4: On 9-18-77, Ian Krassner sold his truck which he bought in September, 1976, and which has an adjusted basis of $5,200. On 10-10-77, he bought a used truck for $6,000 to replace the old one. The cost of the replacement truck which is used to compute the credit is $800 ($6,000 − $5,200).

Tax liability is the tax less all credits except for withholding and investment credit. However, it does not include accumulated earnings tax [¶ 3130], personal holding company tax [¶ 3400], tax on capital gains of small business corporations [¶ 3143(b)], tax added for investment credit recapture [(e) below], tax on lump-sum distributions [¶ 3024(d)], additional tax on income from certain retirement accounts [¶ 1839(d)], or the minimum tax for tax preferences (¶ 2403) [Sec. 46(a)].

NOTE: A taxpayer whose financial reports are subject to the jurisdiction of a federal agency must use the "flow-through" or deferred method of accounting for the investment credit, and specify the method used in the report. The entire investment credit is not available to a utility if a public service commission requires the utility to flow through any part of additional credit to customers [Sec. 46(f)(4)].

Background and purpose. The investment credit was intended as a device for stimulating increased business investment in machinery and equipment. As originally enacted in the Revenue Act of 1962, the credit was equal to 7% of qualified investment. The Tax Reduction Act of 1975 raised it to 10% to increase investment activities in a recessionary period. It allowed a credit on so-called "progress payments" for property being built. This was permitted to avoid delaying its application on property with a long construction lead time. It also allowed corporations a credit for setting up an employee stock ownership plan (ESOP). This was to encourage employee ownership in the companies for which they work. The Tax Reform Act of 1976 has extended the investment credit, making it available for tax years ending before 1-1-81.

Progress payments. Generally, the investment credit is available only for property acquired and placed in service during the year. However, you can also take a credit for expenditures, called progress payments, made in the building or acquiring qualified investment property [(a) below]. The property must have a normal construction period of at least two years and have an estimated useful life in the taxpayer's hands of at least seven years. When the property is put into service, the credit is on the property's basis reduced by the basis on which credits were previously taken [Sec. 46(d)].

The normal construction period generally begins when physical work on the property commences and ends when the property can reasonably be expected to be placed into service. In determining the two year period, no construction before 1-22-75 is taken into account. If your election year begins after 1-21-75, the construction period is computed from the first day of the election tax year if construction began before the tax year.

Qualified progress payments generally equal amounts properly chargeable to your capital account for self-constructed property. When you acquire property, these payments are amounts paid to the manufacturer to the extent of actual progress made in the construction. It is presumed that progress will occur ratably over the construction period. This may be rebutted by clear and convincing evidence [Sec. 46(d)(4)].

The election to take a credit for progress payments cannot be revoked without permission from the Revenue Service [Sec. 46(d)(6)].

(a) **Qualified property.** The credit applies to depreciable tangible personal property, including livestock (but not horses). However, if the taxpayer disposes of substantially identical livestock during a 1-year period starting 6 months before the date he acquires other livestock, the cost of the acquired livestock is reduced by the amount of the sale. (But this rule does not apply if the sale is due to an involuntary conversion or results in a credit recapture). [Sec. 1.48-1(1)]. The credit also applies to depreciable real property, except buildings and their structural components, such as central air conditioning and heating systems (unless essential in the manufacturing process), plumbing, wiring and lighting fixtures [Sec. 1.48-1(e)(2)]. However, to qualify, the real property must (a) be used in manufacturing, production, extraction or the furnishing of utility-like services, or (b) constitute a research facility or a facility for the bulk storage of fungible commodities (including those in a liquid or gaseous state) of an activity under (a). Property is an integral part of manufacturing, etc., or the furnishing of utility-like services when used directly to produce the product or service [Sec. 48(a)(1); 1.48-1(a)-(e)].

Examples of depreciable tangible property include: outside gasoline pumps, hydraulic car lift, counters, printing press, office equipment, neon signs, and motion picture and TV film (qualified investment is the cost of production capitalized by the taxpayer). Examples of other tangible, real-property-like assets are: blast furnaces, oil derricks, oil and gas pipelines, fractionating towers, broadcasting towers, tracks, certain farm improvements,[1] elevators and escalators acquired or completed after 6-30-63 (do not qualify for additional first-year allowance [2]) [Sec. 1.48-1], and citrus trees (qualify as new property if bought before income-producing stage, otherwise, they qualify as used property).[3]

When to claim the credit. The credit is allowed for the year the property is placed in service. This is the earlier of (1) the first tax year depreciation can be taken, or (2) the tax year it becomes ready to be used for its intended purpose [Sec. 46(c); 1.46-3(d)]. Form 3468 is used to report the credit.

The credit on "qualified progress payments" may be taken on payments made after 1-21-75. The progress payment rule is phased in over a 5-year period by treating a percentage of progress payments as qualified investments for each year, as follows: 20% for 1975, 40% for 1976, 60% for 1977, 80% for 1978 and 100% for 1979. The excess over the percentage is taken into account ratably over the transition period [Sec. 46(d)(7)].

Rental property is placed in service in the earlier of the year possession is transferred to the lessee, or the year it first can be depreciated [Sec. 1.46-3(d)(3)].

Used property. The credit is available to qualified investment in either new or used property. However, only $100,000 of the cost of used property is eligible for the credit. For a married peson filing separately, the limit is $50,000, unless one spouse acquired no qualified used property. The $100,000 limit applies to a partnership as a whole, and to each partner [Sec. 48(c)(2); 1.48-3(c)].

NOTE: The dollar limitations above apply to tax years beginning after 1974 and before 1981. Before and after those years, the dollar limitations are $50,000 and $25,000 respectively.

Footnotes appear at end of this Chapter.

¶ 2410

In a nontaxable exchange, the cost of used property is limited to boot given. If the property replaces similar property in a 60-day period before or after the disposition, and the exchange is taxable, "cost" is the basis of the replacement property reduced by the adjusted basis of the property replaced. If the property disposed of results in a recapture of credit (see (e) below), the full cost of the purchased property is used to figure the credit [Sec. 48(c); 1.48-3(b)].

Example 5: Wilkins exchanges a machine with an adjusted basis and fair market value of $8,000 for a similar used machine, paying $1,000 "boot." The exchange is nontaxable. The "cost," for applying the credit, is $1,000.

Example 6: Assume the same facts as in Ex. 5, except that Wilkins had to add back part of the credit previously taken on the old machine. The "cost" taken into account is $9,000.

Example 7: Assume the same facts as in Ex. 6, except that Wilkins sold the old machine for $8,000 on 4-1-77, and bought a used machine as replacement on 5-1-77 for $10,000. The "cost" for applying the credit is $2,000 ($10,000 less $8,000 adjusted basis of the old machine).

(b) Property that does not qualify. No credit is allowed for property with a useful life of less than 3 years. Nor is it allowed for property used by a government agency or an exempt organization (except property used in a business subject to the unrelated business income tax) [¶ 3445], or property amortized under special provisions (¶ 2018; 2041; 2043) [Sec. 48(a)(4), (5), (8); 1.48-1]. Used property will not qualify if, after acquisition by taxpayer, it is used by the person from whom acquired (such as in a sale and leaseback arrangement[4]). Property the taxpayer used before will not qualify for the investment credit (such as repossessed property). Nor will property qualify if acquired from a "related" party [Sec. 48(c); 1.48-3]. (Related party is the same as defined in ¶ 3223) except that "more than 50%" is substituted for "at least 80%," and the excepted corporations listed are not excepted for this purpose).

Property converted from personal use does not qualify for the credit [Sec. 1.46-3(d)(4)]. Property disposed of in the year acquired does not qualify, unless taxpayer dies, property is involuntarily converted (and replaced), or disposition is due to certain changes in business [Sec. 1.46-3(a)(2)].

Lodging facilities. No credit is allowed for property used mainly to furnish lodging or in connection with providing lodging, unless used by transients more than half of the time. Nonlodging commercial facilities open to the public, such as a restaurant in a hotel, or coin-operated laundry machines in an apartment house, qualify for the credit [Sec. 48(a)(3); 1.48-1(h)].

(c) Useful life. The useful life that can be used for an asset in determining the amount of credit is the same as that used for computing its depreciation [Sec. 46(c)(2); 1.46-3(b)]. But the amount of credit does not reduce the property basis for depreciation[5] [¶ 2003].

If the property has a useful life of at least 3 but less than 5 years, only one-third of the investment will qualify for the credit. If the useful life is at least 5 but less than 7 years, two-thirds will qualify. The entire investment will qualify for property with longer lives [Sec. 46(c); 1.46-3(b)]. This is illustrated as follows:

Asset	Useful life	Cost	Applicable percentage	Taken in acc't
Truck	3	$12,000	33⅓%	$ 4,000
Office machine	6	18,000	66⅔%	12,000
Plant equipment	7	20,000	100 %	20,000
				$36,000
Credit ($36,000 × .10)			$3,600	

NOTE: Movie and television films created primarily for entertainment or educational purposes and placed in service after 1974 generally qualify for a 66⅔% credit regardless of useful life [Sec. 48(k)].

(d) Credit carryback and carryover. If the credit is not used up because it exceeds the amount allowed for the year under the tax limitations, it may be carried back to the 3 prior years and forward 7. In figuring the limitation, credits carried over are used first and then credits earned currently; after that, any carryback credits may be applied. If there are unused credits from 2 or more years, they are used up in the order that they occur. The credit for investment in the current year, plus any carryover credits cannot exceed the general limitations [Sec. 46(b)].

Special rules for pre-1971 carryovers. Unused credits from 1970 and earlier can be carried over for 10 years. The limitation for a year after 1971 is first absorbed by pre-1971 carryovers, then by the credits arising in the current year, and finally by any carryover from 1971 and later years [Sec. 46(b); 1.46-2].

(e) Credit recapture. If qualified property is disposed of, ceases to be qualified, or becomes public utility property before its useful life ends, part or all of the credit may be recaptured. The difference between the credit taken (including carrybacks and carryforwards) and the credit allowed for actual use is added back to the tax due in the year of disposition [Sec. 47(a); 1.47-1(a)].

> **Example 8:** In July 1975, the Butler Corp. bought a machine with a useful life of 8 years for $6,000 that qualified for the investment credit. On its return for 1975, it claimed a $420 credit (7% of $6,000) against its $2,400 tax due. In May, 1978, the uninsured machine was destroyed in a fire. This involuntary conversion is considered a disposition for recapture purposes and the Butler Corp. must recapture the appropriate amount of investment credit taken in 1975. Since the machine's actual use was less than 3 years (7-75 to 5-78), no investment credit would be allowed and the total $420 credit must be added back to the tax due in 1978. If the machine had been destroyed two months later, it would have had an actual use of 3 years and the Butler Corp. would be entitled to a 7% investment credit on ⅓ of the cost. In this case, the Butler Corp. would have to add back only $280 to its 1978 tax due, the difference between the credit taken, $420, and the credit allowed for actual use, $140 [7% of $2,000 (⅓ of $6,000)].

NOTE: The shortening of the useful life brackets by the 1971 Revenue Act [(c) above] applies equally for recapture purposes.[6]

A corporation that changes its status to exempt organization must recapture investment credit claimed on property that has remaining useful life when the status change occurs.[7]

Disposition for recapture purposes includes sales, exchanges, gifts, trade-ins and involuntary conversions. It also includes a sale in a sale-leaseback transaction and a transfer on the foreclosure of a security interest. It does not include: a transfer of title to a credit or on the creation of a security interest; transfers at death; corporate tax-free transfers [¶ 3336]; and changes in the form of doing business [Sec. 1.47-1—1.47-3]. Property may be treated as disposed of if the taxpayer fails to keep adequate records showing: (1) cost or other basis (2) estimated useful life; (3) the date property was placed in service; and (4) the date of disposition.

Amounts which were treated as "progress payments" are subject to recapture: (1) if you dispose of property before it is placed in service; (2) if it becomes apparent that the property will not be qualified investment property when placed in service; (3) if the property in your hands may actually have a shorter useful life than originally estimated; (4) if there is a sale-leaseback transaction and the seller-lessee makes progress payments, but the property is sold to a lessor before the property is placed into service. If the recapture rate for the recapture year differs from the

Footnotes appear at end of this Chapter.

¶ 2410

date in effect for the year you took progress payment treatment, the rate in effect when progress payment treatment was allowed applies [Sec. 47(a)].

(f) Leased property. For leases entered into after 9-22-71, an individual or other noncorporate lessor (including a Subchapter S corporation) can claim the credit only if he manufactured or produced the leased property, or is in the business of making short-term leases. A short-term lease is one where (1) the lease period (including renewal options) is less than 50% of the leased property's useful life, and (2) the lessor's allowable business deductions on the property exceeds 15% of the rental income during the first 12 months of the lease. The above limitation as to noncorporate lessors does not prevent a corporate partner from getting its share of the lessor-partnership's credit [Sec. 46(e)(3); 1.46-4(d)].

A lessor—corporate or noncorporate—may waive the credit for new property and let the lessee claim it. In figuring the credit, the useful life of the property is the useful life to the lessor, not the term of the lease. However, if the lease is ended, an adjustment of the credit may be required [Sec. 48(d); 1.48-4]. See recapture of credit ((e) above).

The lessee uses the fair market value of the property as his basis for figuring the credit; but the lessor's basis for the property is used for leases between controlled corporations [Sec. 48(d); 1.48-4(k)(2)].

To prevent the pass-through of a disproportionately large credit, for leases entered into after 11-8-71, a lessor can pass through the *full* credit only if the lease is for a period of at least 80% of the class life of the property. However, this rule does not apply if the class life is 14 years or less or the lease is a net lease. For a short-term lease not qualifying for the full credit, the lessor is still allowed to pass through to the first lessee part of the credit which the lease period bears to the class life of the property [Sec. 48(d); 1.48-4(a)].

Election is made by filing a statement with lessee by the return due date (including extension) for the lessee's return of the year the property is transferred to the lessee [Sec. 1.48-4(f)].

(g) Special rules apply to the following:

• *Thrift savings institutions,* such as mutual savings banks, are limited to 50% of otherwise qualified property [Sec. 46(e); 1.46-4(a)].

• *Regulated investment companies* [¶ 3429], real estate investment trusts [¶ 3432], and cooperatives [¶ 3455] are limited to the amount that is in proportion to the income not passed through [Sec. 46(e); 1.46-4(b)].

• *Corporations electing partnership taxation.* Stockholders on the last day of the tax year are considered to have made the proportionate part of the investment of the corporation. Each shareholder takes the credit limit into account separately. The $100,000 limit ($50,000 for tax years beginning before 1975 and after 1980) as to used property applies at both the corporate and shareholder levels [Sec. 48(e); 1.48-5(a)].

➢OBSERVATION➜ The end of the interest of a beneficiary in an estate or trust, or a stockholder in an electing small business corporation, is a disposition that may require a credit adjustment. See (e) above.

• *Controlled groups* apportion the $25,000 among the component members as specified in regulations to be issued. Controlled group is the same as defined in ¶ 3223(a) [Sec. 46(a)]. The group is limited to one $100,000 amount ($50,000 for tax years beginning before 1975 and after 1980) as to used property [Sec. 48(c)].

• *Estates and trusts,* see ¶ 3019.
• *Partnerships,* see ¶ 2913(c).

(h) Credit for employee stock ownership plan (ESOP). Corporations (except Subchapter S) can elect, through 1980, an 11% investment credit for setting up an employee stock ownership plan that is funded by 1% of its qualified investment. For tax years beginning after 1976 an extra ½% credit may be claimed (in addition to the 11%) if an additional ½% is matched by employee contributions to the ESOP. An ESOP is a written, defined contribution plan designed primarily for investing in employer securities. It cannot be used as a replacement for any existing employee benefits. Thus, if an employer already has a pension, profit-sharing or other plan, the contribution for investment credit purposes must be in addition to existing benefits. However, if an existing plan meets the requirements of an ESOP or if it is amended to meet those requirements, the benefits under the existing plan may be increased and a new plan need not be established. The plan must allocate the securities to plan participants as of the end of each plan year. The stock allocation is made on the basis of the relative compensation of each employee to the total compensation. Compensation to any employee over $100,000 is disregarded. There must be immediate vesting in the employee of stock allocated and the employee must have the right to direct how his allocable stock is voted. Specific limits apply on the amount of stock that can be allocated to the employee. Even nonqualified plans must meet the minimum participation rules and limits on benefits and contributions (¶ 1838; 1839).[8]

The stock or securities transferred or bought must have at least the same voting power and dividend rights as other common or convertible securities of the corporation or parent.

An employee cannot withdraw his allocated stock (no distributions are allowed) until at least 84 months after the month the stock is allocated to his account, except if the employee is separated from service, is disabled or dies.

The stock allocated to the employee and the dividends are not currently taxable if the plan fails to meet the limitations for qualified plans. The employer is subject to a civil penalty for the amount involved in the failure if it violates ESOP rules. The penalty cannot exceed an amount in excess of 1% of the qualified investment of the corporation for the tax year. However, there is no penalty if corrected within 90 days of Revenue Service notice of noncompliance.

¶ 2411 Credit for work incentive program expenses. Taxpayers can take a tax credit equal to 20% of the wages of employees undergoing training under a Work Incentive Program (Sec. 432(b)(1) of the Social Security Act) certified by the Secretary of Labor [Sec. 40, 50A, 50B]. The allowable credit is for tax years starting after 12-31-71 and is subject to various limitations explained below. Unused credits may be carried back or carried forward. The credit may be recaptured because of premature job termination or other causes.

NOTE: The limitations on credit and carrybacks and carryovers [(b) and (c) below] are similar to those for the investment credit [¶ 2410].

Background and purpose. The 1971 Revenue Act established a work incentive credit to incude employers in the private sector to hire individuals placed in on-the-job training or employment through the Work Incentive Program. It is designed to open up job opportunities for welfare recipients, and to strengthen the administrative framework of the Program so as to make participants ready for the jobs when the jobs are ready for them.

(a) Amount of credit. The amount of credit is 20% of cash wages paid or accrued to employees during first 12 months of employment under a Work Incentive Program. The 12 months of employment need not be consecutive; but no credit is allowed for wages incurred more than 24 months after the initial starting date [Sec. 50A(a), (b), (c); 1.50A-1, 1.50B-1]. Form 4874 (or 4874-FY) must be

Footnotes appear at end of this Chapter.

¶ 2411

attached to the taxpayer's income tax return to claim the credit for salaries paid or incurred during the year.

Credit is not allowed for wages of an employee who displaces another or is closely related to the taxpayer as described in ¶ 1117; 2223(d). Nor is it allowed for reimbursed expenses or for employment outside the U.S., or for expenses not qualifying as business deductions [Sec. 50B(a)(2), (b); 1.50B-1].

(b) Limitations on credit. The credit cannot exceed the first $50,000 of the tax liability for the year ($25,000 on a married person's separate return unless his spouse is not entitled to the credit) plus ½ of the excess [Sec. 50A(a)].

Tax liability is the income tax less investment credit [¶ 2410] and credits for foreign taxes [¶ 3701(a)], the elderly [¶ 2406] and political contributions [¶ 2416]. The credit may *not* be offset against the minimum tax for tax preferences [¶ 2403], tax on lump-sum distributions [¶ 3024(d)], additional tax on income from certain retirement accounts [¶ 1839(d)], accumulated earnings tax [¶ 3130], personal holding company tax [¶ 3400], tax on capital gains of Subchapter S corporations [¶ 3143(b)], tax added for recapture of work incentive credit [(d) below], and tax on foreign expropriation loss recoveries (¶ 2316(d)) [Sec. 50A(a)(3), (c)(3), (d)(2)].

(c) Credit carryback and carryover. If the credit is not used up because it exceeds the limit [(b) above], the unused credit can be carried back to the 3 prior years and forward 7. The credit is first carried back to the third preceding year and then to the following years in consecutive order. However, carryback is allowed only for tax years starting after 12-31-71. The credit earned in the current year, plus any carryover and carryback credits, cannot exceed the general limitations [Sec. 50A(b); 1.50A-2].

(d) Credit recapture. The credit is recaptured if: (a) wages paid to an employee for which credit was claimed are less than wages of other employees performing comparable services, or (b) employment is terminated either before the employee is employed 90 days (whether or not consecutive) or during the next 90 days after the 90-day employment is completed [Sec. 50A(c), (d); 1.50A-3]. There is no recapture, however, if the employee is fired for misconduct, quits voluntarily, or is disabled (unless the taxpayer fails to offer reemployment after receiving notice of the removal of the disability). Employment is not considered terminated if the employee is hired by a successor in a reorganization described in ¶ 3336, if there is a mere change in the form of the business and the taxpayer retains a substantial interest in the business, or if the employee is laid off due to lack of business. Temporary lay-offs due to a valid reason and lasting no more than 60 days do not cause recapture [Sec. 50A(c)]. Recapture does apply to corporations electing Subchapter S treatment after having claimed the credit, unless all Subchapter S shareholders and the electing corporation agree to be jointly and severally liable to pay any recapture tax resulting from termination of employment or non-comparable wages [Sec. 1.50A-5(b)].

(e) Special rules. Controlled corporations apportion the $50,000 [(b) above] among the component members in any manner the members select, provided each member consents [Sec. 1.50A-1(f)]. Stockholders of a Subchapter S corporation on the last day of the tax year are considered to have made the proportionate part of the investment of the corporation [Sec. 50B(d); 1.50B-2]. Estates and trusts apportion the wages entitled to the WIN credit between the estate or trust and its beneficiaries on the basis of income allocable to each [Sec. 50B(e); 1.50A-6, 1.50B-3]. In the case of partnerships, each partner takes his own share of the WIN expenses separately, with WIN expenses for each employee allocated separately [Sec. 1.50A-7, 1.50B-4]. Mutual savings banks, cooperatives [¶ 3455], regulated investment companies [¶ 3429] and real estate investment trust [¶ 3432] are subject to special limitations similar to rules for the investment credit [¶ 2410(g)) [Sec. 1.50B-5].

(f) Employment of federal welfare recipients. If you hire federal welfare recipients who have been on welfare for at least 90 days before being hired you are entitled to an incentive tax credit equal to 20% of the gross wages paid to them (or incurred) after 3-29-75. Once a qualified employee has been on the payroll for more than 30 days you get the credit for salary from the first day of employment, and subsequently, until 6-30-76. This credit is available to both business and nonbusiness employers. There is, however, a $1,000 annual limitation on credits for nonbusiness salaries. Child day care centers also get a 20% credit ($1,000 per year per employee) for wages paid for services rendered through 9-30-77 to welfare recipients hired after 9-6-76 [Sec. 50A, 50B].

¶ **2412 Jobs credit.** Employers can get a 50% credit on the first $4,200 of each new employee's wages, with an overall annual ceiling of $100,000 per employer. The credit is refundable and can be carried back three years and carried forward for seven years [Sec. 44B, 51(d), 53]. This applies to tax years starting after 12-31-76.

Eligibility. The employment must be in the U.S. and over one-half of the wages must be paid for services performed in a trade or business in the United States [Sec. 51(g)(1)].

Payroll deductions. The amount allowed for payroll deductions is decreased by the amount of the jobs credit [Sec. 280C].

(a) Amount of credit. For tax years beginning in 1977, the credit is equal to 50% of the excess of Federal Unemployment Tax wages paid during 1977 over 102% of such wages paid in 1976. This figure may not exceed 50% of the excess of total 1977 payroll over 105% of FUTA wages paid in 1976. Furthermore the figure arrived at for 1976 in multiplying by the 102% may not be less than 50% of the wages paid in 1977 [Sec. 51(a)-(c)].

> NOTE: To determine the 1978 base amount, use 1977 as the first base year. Although FUTA increases to $6,000 in 1978, it remains at $4,200 for the purposes of jobs credit determination [Sec. 51(f)(1)].

(b) Credit for handicapped employees. An additional credit, not subject to the $100,000 ceiling is allowed for hiring new employees who are handicapped. To qualify the employer must also qualify for the regular jobs credit. The amount of the credit is 10% of the FUTA wages paid to the handicapped employees during the year. For tax years beginning in 1978, the credit is 10% of the excess of the 1978 FUTA wages over the 1977 FUTA wages. The credit is limited to 20% of the jobs credit [Sec. 51(e)].

(c) Special situations:

(1) *Controlled groups,* defined as 50%-owned corporations or partnerships, are only allowed one job credit for the entire control group [Sec. 52(a), (b), (c)].

(2) *Agricultural employees* are not eligible for the credit until 1978, and will count social security tax paid up to $4,200 as the FUTA base [Sec. 51(f)(2)].

(3) *Railroad employees* will use 87.5% of Railroad Unemployment Insurance as the FUTA base [Sec. 51(f)(3)].

(4) *Self-employed individuals* who become employees can use the first $4,200 of net earnings as the FUTA base [Sec. 52(e)].

(5) *Tax-exempt organizations* are not eligible for the credit [Sec. 52(d)].

(6) *Estates and trusts, Subchapter S corporations, mutual savings banks, regulated investment companies, real estate investment trusts and certain cooperatives*

2420 Chapter 14—Alternate Tax Methods—Tax Credits 1978

will apportion the credit, e.g., trust and beneficiary, among the shareholders [Sec. 52(f)—(h)].

(7) *Short tax years*—Employers should use the last taxable year beginning in 1977 or 1978, as the case may be [Sec. 52(j)].

OTHER TAX CREDITS

In addition to the main credits covered earlier in the chapter, there are other credits such as the general tax credit [¶ 1111(e)], the credit for withheld taxes and excess social security [¶ 2511; 2535], and the foreign tax credit [¶ 3701 et seq.]. These are explained in the chapters where the general subject to which they relate is covered. This section covers the credit for expenses of child care and care of disabled dependents or spouse as well as the handling on the return of political campaign contributions. It also covers the credit for federal taxes on certain uses of gasoline, special fuels and lubricating oils.

¶ **2415 Expenses of child care and care of disabled dependent or spouse.** A taxpayer can claim a credit against tax for household and dependent care expenses when paying these expenses allows the taxpayer to be gainfully employed [Sec. 44A(a)].

Background and purpose. Effective for tax years starting after 1975, the Tax Reform Act of 1976 did away with the child care deduction that could not exceed $4,800 a year and phasing out when taxpayer's adjusted gross income exceeded $35,000. It converted the deduction to a nonrefundable credit but generally retained the old rules for determining what expenses qualify. The credit can now be taken when one spouse works part-time or is a student. Also, child care payments to certain relatives now qualify.

(a) Who may take the credit. The credit is allowed a taxpayer who maintains a household (pays more than half the expense) for any of the following individuals: a person under the age of 15 for whom the taxpayer can claim a dependency exemption; a dependent of the taxpayer (regardless of age) who is incapable of self-care; and a spouse who is incapable of self-care [Sec. 44A(c)(1), (f)(1)].

(b) What expenses qualify. The expenses must be employment-related, that is, they must be incurred to enable the taxpayer to be gainfully employed. No credit is allowed as to out-of-home costs in caring for a spouse or a dependent over 15 [Sec. 44A(c)(2)].

Expenses for services outside the taxpayer's home qualify, but only if incurred for the care of dependent under 15 years old.

(c) Limitation on credit. A $2,000 limit applies when the taxpayer has one qualifying dependent and a $4,000 limit for two or more qualifying dependents. Thus, the maximum credit would be $400 for one dependent or $800 for two more more [Sec. 44A(d)]. In addition, employment-related expenses may not exceed an individual's earned income for the year. If the person is married the expenses may not exceed the lesser of the individual's earnings for the year or the earnings of the taxpayer's spouse. If one spouse is a student or is incapable of self-care and so has no earned income, he or she is treated as having earnings of $166 a month if there is one dependent or $333 a month for two or more dependents. This earned income limit also applies to unmarried taxpayers [Sec. 44a(e)].

(d) Payments to relatives. The credit is available for child care payments made to a relative providing the relative is not one for whom the taxpayer may claim a dependency exemption and the payments received by the relative for child care are subject to social security taxes [Sec. 44A(f)(6)].

(e) Special rules. Married couples will be allowed the credit only if they file a joint return. A divorced or legally separated parent of a child under 15 or physically or mentally disabled may be allowed the credit if the parent has custody of the child for a longer period than the other parent. The child must receive more than one-half the support from the parents during the calendar year. An abandoned spouse is also eligible for the credit when the deserting spouse is not a member of the household for the last six months of the tax year [Sec. 44(f)].

¶ **2416 Political campaign contributions.** Individuals may either elect a limited credit or deduction for political contributions [Sec. 41, 218]. Only payments made during the tax year qualify for the credit or deduction, regardless of the contributor's accounting method [Proposed Reg. Sec. 1.41-1(a), 1.218-1(a)]. A credit or deduction may be claimed for the tax year prior to the year the candidacy is formally announced [Sec. 41(c)(2)(A)].

≫**OBSERVATION**→ It is important to determine whether the credit or deduction produces the greatest tax saving. Generally, for taxpayers who itemize, the deduction is preferable in the higher tax brackets while the credit is better in the lower and middle brackets.

(a) Tax credit. The credit is one-half of the amount of the political contributions made during the year. The maximum credit is $50 on a joint return and $25 for single persons or married persons filing separately (for contributions after 1974 in tax years starting after that date). The credit cannot exceed an individual's tax liability for the year reduced by credits for foreign taxes, the elderly, partially tax-exempt interest, and investment in business equipment [Sec. 41].

The credit is allowed on a joint return regardless of which spouse makes the contribution. Thus, a political contribution of $200 or more by the husband alone will enable the couple to take a $50 credit on their joint return.

(b) Deduction. An individual may elect to take a deduction for his political contributions instead of the credit. The maximum deduction is $200 on a joint return with $100 for single persons and married couples filing separately (for contributions after 1974 in tax years starting after that date) [Sec. 218].

(c) Eligible contributions. Contributions to the following persons and organizations will qualify for the credit or deduction: (1) to any candidate for nomination or election to any federal, state, or local office in a general, primary or special election, (2) to any committee sponsoring such candidate, and (3) to a national, state or local committee of a national political party [Sec. 41(c)].

A credit or deduction can be taken for the cost of a ticket to a political dinner only if the dinner is devoted primarily to speeches and fund raising, and not to entertainment. Otherwise, the credit or deduction is reduced by the value of the benefits received by the contributor. No credit or deduction is allowed for the cost of raffle tickets [Prop. Reg. Sec. 1.41-1(b)].

(d) Donation of appreciated property. If a donor contributes appreciated property to a political organization, he is taxed on the difference between the fair market value of the property and its adjusted basis. The transfer is treated as a sale; so if the property is a capital asset, he will receive capital gain treatment. The political organization acquires the donor's basis plus any gain recognized to the donor. No loss will be recognized on the transfer [Sec. 84].

Footnotes appear at end of this Chapter.

(e) "Tax Check-Off" System. Individuals (other than nonresident aliens) may designate on their returns that $1 of their tax liability ($2 if each spouse makes the designation on a joint return) be paid into the Presidential Election Campaign Fund. If no designation is made on the return, the taxpayer has 20 and one-half months after the due date of the original return to designate to the fund [Sec. 301.6096-1, 301.6096-2].

¶ 2417 Credit for certain uses of gasoline, special fuels and lubricating oil. Generally, the taxpayer can claim a credit on the tax return for the federal excise taxes on the nonhighway use of gasoline, special fuels and lubricating oil. These include gasoline or special fuels used in farming and special fuels used in local transit systems and for aviation purposes. Quarterly refund payments are allowed for claims of at least $1,000 [Sec. 39, 6420, 6421, 6424, 6427].

NOTE: Examples of nonhighway use include operating a motor boat, power lawn mower, stationary engines or for use in construction, mining, or timbering projects.

Any individual, estate, trust or corporation claiming the credit must file and attach Form 4136 to the tax return.

Footnotes to Chapter 14

(P-H "FEDERAL TAXES" related references are cited in brackets [ ] at the end of each footnote below.)

Footnote ¶ 2400 [¶ 3428 et seq.; 5801; 6125 et seq.; 33,005 et seq.].

Footnote ¶ 2401 [¶ 33,005 et seq.].
(1) Fabian Tebon, Jr., 55 TC 410 [¶ 33,035(10)].
(2) Rev. Rul. 74-61, 1974-1 CB 239 [¶ 33,006(5)].

Footnote ¶ 2402 [¶ 33,295].

Footnote ¶ 2403 [¶ 6125].
(1) Riley, 66 TC 141 [¶ 6171(5)].

Footnote ¶ 2405 [¶ 5917].

Footnote ¶ 2406 [¶ 5881].

Footnote ¶ 2410 [¶ 5921 et seq.].
(1) Rev. Rul. 66-89, 1966-1 CB 7; Rev. Rul. 72-222, 1972-1 CB 17 [¶ 5987(45)].
(2) Rev. Rul. 65-230, 1965-2 CB 75 [¶ 16,242(10)].
(3) Rev. Rul. 65-104, 1965-1 CB 28 [¶ 5988(10)].

Footnote ¶ 2410 continued
(4) Thompson, 49 TC 230, affd. 23 AFTR 2d 69-1495, 410 F.2d 1195 [¶ 5988(5)].
(5) Senate Report No. 92-437, p. 45, 92d Cong., 1st Sess.
(6) House Report No. 92-533, p. 28, 92d Cong., 1st Sess.; Senate Report No. 92-437, p. 43.
(7) Rev. Rul. 73-76, 1973-1 CB 31 [¶ 55,024].
(8) P.L. 94-12, 3-29-75, Sec. 301(d); TIR-1413, 11-4-75 [¶ 19,245; 34,990.75(5)].

Footnote ¶ 2411 [¶ 6015].

Footnote ¶ 2412 [¶ 6031].

Footnote ¶ 2415 [¶ 5920].

Footnote ¶ 2416 [¶ 5914; 16,497].

Footnote ¶ 2417 [¶ 5905].

Highlights of Chapter 14
Alternate Tax Methods—Tax Credits

I. Tax Computation in General [¶ 2400]
II. Methods of Figuring the Tax
   A. **Income averaging [¶ 2401]:**
      1. Who can qualify:
         a. Must be a U.S. citizen or resident during 5-year averaging period.
         b. Must furnish at least ½ own support during 4 base period years.
         c. Adjusted taxable income must be more than $3,000 higher than 120% of average taxable income for last 4 years.
      2. Nonaverageable income—premature payouts from self-employed retirement plans and accumulation distributions from trusts.
      3. Benefits unavailable if averaging elected:
         a. Optional tax tables.
         b. Maximum tax on personal service income.
         c. Alternative tax on capital gains.
         d. Exclusion of foreign source earned income or income from U.S. possessions.
      4. Special computations for married couples [¶ 2401(e)].
   B. **Maximum tax [¶ 2402]:**
      1. Limits top tax rate on earned taxable income to 50%.
      2. Personal service income generally means wages, professional fees, pensions and annuities.
   C. **Minimum tax on tax preferences [¶ 2403]:**
      1. Flat 15% tax on tax preferences reduced by greater of $10,000 or one-half the regular income tax.
      2. The tax preferences [¶ 2403(a)] are: capital gains; accelerated depreciation; adjusted itemized deductions; intangible drilling costs; depletion; fast amortization; stock options; financial institutions' bad debt deductions.
   D. **Effect of net operating loss on minimum tax [¶ 2403(b)]:**
      1. Deferral of minimum tax liability to year taxpayer actually benefits from tax preferences.
      2. Limit on tax preferences to amount actually benefiting taxpayer.
III. Credits for earned income and the elderly.
   A. **Earned income credit [¶ 2405].**
      1. 10% of earned income—maximum of $400.
      2. Available to individuals maintaining household for child under 19, student, or disabled child.
      3. Earned income does not include pensions and annuities.
   B. **Credit for the elderly [¶ 2406].**
      1. 15% credit against income for individuals over 65.
      2. Maximum amount of income against which credit can be claimed is:
         a. single—$2,500;
         b. married (and both over 65)—$3,750.
      3. Credit reduced by one-half of excess over adjusted gross income of:
         a. $7,500 for singles;
         b. $10,000 for marrieds.
IV. Investment and Work Incentive Credits
   A. **Figuring investment credit [¶ 2410]:**

1. Credit is 10% of investment, not to exceed $25,000 of tax ($12,500 if married, filing separately) plus ½ of excess. Property must be acquired and placed in service after 1-21-75 and before 1-1-81.
    a. 11% credit if 1% of investment is put into an employee stock ownership plan (ESOP).
    b. After 1976, 11½% credit if additional ½% employer contribution is matched by employee contribution.
2. Qualified property: Depreciable tangible personal property and some depreciable realty (except buildings). Only $100,000 of cost of used property eligible.
3. Property not qualified: Property's useful life under 3 years; lodging facilities.
4. Asset with useful life of 3-4 years: ⅓ of investment qualifies; 5-6 years: ⅔ qualifies; 7 or more years: all qualify.
5. Unused credit can be carried back 3 years and forward 7.
6. Credit recaptured on disposing asset prematurely.
7. Individual lessor can claim credit only if he manufactured or produced leased property or is in short-term leasing business. Any lessor can waive credit for new property and let lessee claim it.
8. Special rules apply to thrift savings institutions, regulated investment companies, Subchapter S corporations, controlled groups, estates and trusts, partnerships.

B. **Work incentive tax credit [¶ 2411]:**
1. Credit is 20% of cash wages paid employees in first 12 months of employment (not necessarily consecutive) under Work Incentive Program. No credit allowed for wages incurred over 24 months after starting date.
2. Credit limited to $25,000 of tax plus ½ of excess.
3. Unused credit can be carried back 3 years and forward 7.
4. Credit recaptured in case of substandard wages and premature dismissal.
5. Special rules apply to estates and trusts, controlled corporations, Subchapter S corporations, financial institutions.
6. A similar credit, the federal welfare recipient employment incentive credit applies for a limited period starting after 3-29-75.

C. **Jobs credit [¶ 2412]:**
1. Must be trade or business in the U.S.
2. Limited to $100,000 per employer.
3. Amount of credit. Lesser of 50% of excess of: (1) 1977 FUTA wages over 102% of 1976 FUTA wages; or 1977 payroll over 105% of 1976 FUTA wages.
4. Additional credit for hiring handicapped if employer qualifies for regular jobs credit.
5. Other special rules apply in reference to determining FUTA base, eligibility, and apportionment.

V. **Other Tax Credits**
   A. **Expenses for child care and care of disabled dependent or spouse [¶ 2415].**
   1. Credit equals 20% of expenses, limited to $400 for one dependent and $800 for two or more dependents.
   2. Taxpayer must maintain household for:
      a. Dependent under 15; or
      b. Dependent incapable of self-care; or
      c. Spouse incapable of self-care.
   3. Expenses must be incurred to enable taxpayer to be gainfully employed.
   4. Expenses can't exceed earned income.
   5. Married couples must file jointly to claim credit.
   B. **Political campaign contributions made after 1971 [¶ 2416]:**
   1. Individuals allowed limited credit—$50 for couple filing joint return, $25 on returns of single persons or married persons filing separately, or
   2. Deduction—not in excess of $200 for married persons filing joint returns, and $100 for single persons and married persons filing separately.
   C. **Credit for nonhighway use of gasoline, special fuels and lubricating oil [¶ 2417].**

Chapter 15

WITHHOLDING—ESTIMATED TAX

TABLE OF CONTENTS

WITHHOLDING TAX ON WAGES

Who must withhold 2501
  Employers
  Persons who control wage payments
Who is subject to withholding 2502
  Who are employees
  Self-employed persons
Wages subject to withholding 2503
  What are wages
  No withholding on pay for excluded employment
  Combined wages and nonwages
How to figure withholding 2504
  Percentage method
  Wage-bracket withholding method
  Alternative methods
  Payments made without regard to specified payroll periods
  Supplemental wage payments
  Vacation pay
  Wage disability payments
  Wages paid for two or more employers
  Withholding on average estimated wages
  Voluntary withholding
  Withholding on pension and annuity payments
  Part-time employment method of withholding
Withholding exemptions 2505
  Standard deduction allowance
  Additional withholding allowances
  Penalties
Withholding exemption certificates 2506
  New employees
  Filing an amended certificate on change in status
  Certification of nontaxability
Records 2507
  Employers
  Employees
Statements to employees, Form W-2 .. 2508
  What to include
  When employment ends
  Extension of time
  Filing requirements

RETURNS AND PAYMENT OF TAXES WITHHELD

How the employer reports and pays the tax 2509
  When deposits are made
  When to file quarterly return
  Where return is filed
  Employers who fail to collect or pay tax
  Extension of time
Withholding adjustments 2510
  Errors found before quarterly return filed
  Errors found after quarterly return filed
  Adjusting tax reported on tips
Refunds and credits 2511
  Employee refunds and credits
  Nonresident aliens
Penalties 2512
  Employer penalties
  Employee penalties
  Taxpayer identifying numbers

DECLARATION AND PAYMENT OF ESTIMATED TAX BY INDIVIDUALS

The declaration 2515
  What is estimated tax
  Changes during year
Who must file a declaration 2516
  Married couples
  Declaration by agent
  Declaration not required
Filing declaration and payment of estimated tax 2517
  Declaration and payment for 1978
  Amended declarations
  Farmers and fishermen
  Fiscal year taxpayers
  Extension of time
  Nonresident aliens
How to figure estimated tax 2518
Penalties for underpaying estimated taxes 2519
  How to avoid the underpayment penalty
  How the penalty is applied

Footnotes appear at end of this Chapter.

SPECIAL PROBLEMS

Payments to nonresident aliens 2535
Who must withhold
Payments subject to withholding

Who is subject to withholding
Returns and payment of tax withheld 2536
Tax treaties on withholding rates 2537

• Highlights of Chapter 15 .... Page 2561

WITHHOLDING TAX ON WAGES

The withholding provisions were enacted to enable taxpayers to meet their tax obligations while also permitting current payment of taxes as wages were earned. In addition, the estimated tax requirements were adopted to reach those wages falling into higher brackets and other types of income on which there was no withholding. Thus, individual income taxes are collected on a current basis, in the year the income is earned, instead of the following year. Employers must withhold the tax from wages paid to their employees. Some individuals must estimate their tax, file a declaration of estimated tax and pay a lump-sum or installments. For income tax purposes, withholding is not an allowable deduction either to the employer or the employee.

¶ 2501 **Who must withhold.** Every employer who pays wages [¶ 2503] to an employee [¶ 2502] must withhold from the wages paid, an amount determined according to the formula or tables at ¶ 2504. The number of employees and the length of time they are employed do not matter.

(a) **Employers** required to withhold include individuals, partnerships, estates, trusts, trustees in bankruptcy,[1] corporations, and unincorporated organizations. Churches, colleges and organizations exempt from income tax must withhold; also, the governments of the United States, Puerto Rico, the District of Columbia, states, cities, school districts and other political subdivisions, instrumentalities, and agencies [Sec. 3401(d); 31.3401(d)-1].

Mechanical details of the withholding process may be handled by representatives of the employer. When a corporate employer has branch offices, the branch manager or other representative may actually perform the duties of the employer. Nevertheless, the legal responsibility rests with the corporate employer [Sec. 31.3403-1].

(b) **Persons who control wage payments.** Persons other than the actual employer may be required or permitted to withhold tax.

• If the person for whom an individual performs services does not have control of the wage payments, then the person having control must withhold [Sec. 3401(d)(1); 31.3401(d)-1]. As a general rule, bonding companies or sureties are not liable for the withholding taxes of the insured contractor.[2]

• One who pays wages on behalf of a nonresident alien individual, foreign partnership, or foreign corporation, not engaged in trade or business within the U.S., is considered as an employer even though the services are not performed for him [Sec. 3401(d)(2); 31.3401(d)-1]. See also ¶ 2535(a).

• Fiduciaries, agents, and others who have control or pay wages of employees may perform the employer's duties when authorized by the Revenue Service [Sec. 3504; 31.3504-1].

• Lenders, sureties or other persons who pay wages directly to employees of another are liable to the U.S. for withholding taxes related to these wages plus interest. In addition, any creditor who lends money knowing that the loan will be used to meet payrolls is subject to a limited liability [Sec. 3505]. Form 4219 must be submitted with the payment.[3]

¶ **2502 Who is subject to withholding.** An employer is required to withhold the individual's tax only if the legal relationship of employer-employee exists with respect to the services for which the compensation is paid. It is not necessary that the services be continuing at the time the wages are paid [Sec. 31.3401(d)-1]. Thus, for example, a person who pays wages to a former employee on January 28, 1978, for services the latter performed during the week of January 2-6, 1978, when the employer-employee relationship existed, must withhold the tax when the wages are paid.

(a) **Who are employees.** Generally, there is an employer-employee relationship when the person for whom services are performed has the right to control and direct the individual who performs the services, not only as to the result to be accomplished by the work, but also as to the details and means by which that result is accomplished. The employer does not have to actually direct or control the way the services are performed; it is enough if he has the right to do so. The following factors are also important in determining whether a person is an "employer:" right to discharge; furnishing of tools; furnishing a place to work [Sec. 31.3401(c)-1].

So-called partners. If the employer-employee relation in fact exists, it does not matter that the employee is called a partner or an independent contractor.

Managers, officers, directors. No distinction is made between classes or grades of employees. Generally, a corporate officer is an employee, but a director as such is not. Withholding, therefore, is required on officers' salaries, but not on directors' fees.

Minors—students. Minors are treated the same as other employees. For example, tax is withheld from wages of a student working during vacation, even if he will not earn enough to pay an income tax (unless he files a proper withholding exemption certificate of nontaxability [¶ 2506(c)]). As to refund of tax withheld, see ¶ 3509; see also ¶ 2503(b) for newsboys under 18.

Substitutes who are properly working in place of regular employees are considered employees for purposes of withholding. However, if a person is engaged without the company's knowledge or consent, he is not an employee for withholding purposes.[1]

Unlawful business. An individual performing services in an illegal activity for wages may be an employee.[2]

Contract landmen who obtain oil and gas leases for a corporation are its employees for purposes of withholding.[3]

(b) **Self-employed persons.** Individuals who are in fact partners, independent contractors, or sole proprietors of a business are not subject to withholding on their drawings or earnings [Sec. 31.3401(c)-1].

Examples: Auctioneers, contractors and subcontractors, dentists, doctors, freelance professional models,[4] lawyers, public stenographers, veterinarians, and others who follow an independent trade, business or profession, in which they offer their services to the public, are not employees.

¶ **2503 Wages subject to withholding.** Only those payments that are "wages" are subject to withholding [Sec. 3401].

(a) **What are wages.** "Wages" means pay to employees for services [Sec. 3401(a)]. A payment can be wages whether it is called a salary, fee, bonus, commission, vacation pay, or even retirement pay. Wages can be paid in property, such as stocks, bonds or other property transferred in exchange for the employee's services. The value of the property when it is transferred is the amount of the wages [Sec. 3401(a); 31.3401(a)-1].

The same kind of payment may be wages subject to withholding under some conditions but not under other conditions, or only a portion of a payment may be subject to withholding as wages. Also, some payments for employment may be excluded from wages [Sec. 3401(a)].

Footnotes appear at end of this Chapter.

ITEMS THAT ARE WAGES SUBJECT TO WITHHOLDING

Suggestion awards;[1] vacation, dismissal and overtime pay [Sec. 31.3401(a)-1(b), 31.3402(g)-1]; old age benefit or state unemployment tax, paid without deduction from employee's pay [Sec. 31.3401(a)-1(b)(6)]; payments equivalent to difference between employees' normal wages and amounts received from the state while serving in the National Guard;[2] reimbursed employment agency fees[3] (unless paid directly to the agency by the employer);[4] guaranteed annual wage payments;[5] financial counseling fees paid by a corporation for the benefit of its executives.[6]

ITEMS THAT ARE NOT SUBJECT TO WITHHOLDING

Compensation paid to former employees in the Armed Forces or National Guard;[7] facilities or privileges of small value furnished to employees generally, to promote health, good will or efficiency, such as entertainment, medical service and courtesy discounts on purchases [Sec. 31.3401(a)-1(b)(10)]; merchandise of nominal value;[8] scholarship and fellowship grants;[9] union strike benefits;[10] reimbursement for uniforms;[11] supper money; direct payment or reimbursement for employee's tuition for job-related courses [¶ 1833].[12]

SPECIAL RULES

Back pay and overtime paid under the Fair Labor Standards Act are subject to withholding whether paid as a result of a settlement or court judgment, but not liquidated damages paid under the Act.[13] The employer should withhold tax when back wages are paid over to the administrator of the Wage and Hour Div., Dept. of Labor and report it on his current return.[14]

Moving expenses are not subject to withholding if, when paid, it is reasonable to believe that an employee can deduct them. Reimbursements or allowances in excess of moving expenses are subject to withholding (¶ 1831) [Sec. 3401(a)(15); Proposed Reg. 31.3401(a)(15)-1(a)].[15]

Board and lodging. The employer must withhold tax for meals or lodging that is taxable income to the employee [¶ 1308]; but not for the excludable amounts [Sec. 31.3401(a)-1(b)(9)].

Commissions generally are wages subject to withholding. But if a retail commission salesperson, usually paid in cash, receives a noncash payment (such as a sales prize), it is not subject to withholding if the prize's fair market value is included as "other compensation" reported on his Form W-2 (¶ 2508) [Sec. 3402(j); 31.3402(j)-1].[16] An insurance salesperson is not a retail commission salesperson for this purpose.[17]

Insurance and annuity premiums. Payments to employees to buy individual hospitalization coverage that are includible in employees' income, are subject to withholding,[18] but not group-term life insurance premiums [Sec. 3401(a)(14)]. Nor are premiums paid by an organization exempt under Sec. 501(c)(3) [¶ 3436] to buy an employee annuity.[19]

Wages to nonresident aliens. See ¶ 2535.

Payments after employee's death representing unpaid compensation for services rendered by deceased employee are not subject to withholding.[20]

Pensions and retirement pay are generally subject to withholding unless taxable as an annuity or not includible in gross income. Thus, no withholding is required on pensions received for personal injuries or sickness due to active service in the Armed Forces, Coast and Geodetic Survey, or the Public Health Service; retirement payments from the U.S. Civil Service Retirement Fund or similar funds [Sec. 31.3401(a)-1]; or pensions based on services in excluded employment (see (b) below), such as agricultural labor.[21] The credit for elderly [¶ 2406] does not affect withholding on such income.[22] For withholding on annuities, see ¶ 2504(k).

Gambling winnings. Withholding applies to proceeds from (1) state-connected lotteries on winnings over $5,000 and (2) sweepstakes, lotteries (not state-connected), wagering pools on winnings over $1,000. But for certain parimutuel pools and jai alai (for payments made after 4-30-77) payments are not subject to withholding unless odds are at least 300 to 1. Winnings from slot machines, keno, and bingo are exempt. Also, each person who receives a payment must furnish a statement that contains his name, address and identification number as well as each person entitled to part of payment (¶ 3521) [Sec. 3402(q)].

Retirement savings. Amounts paid for an individual to a retirement arrangement are not wages subject to withholding as long as it is reasonable to believe that the employee will be entitled to a deduction for such payment (¶ 1838(1)) [Sec. 219(a), 220, 3401(a)(12)(D)].

Tax-exempt employee trust or plan. Payments to or from a trust or annuity plan, made to, or for, an employee or his beneficiary, are not subject to withholding, unless payment is compensation for services [Sec. 31.3401(a)(12)-1].

Tips (cash or charge[23]) of $20 or more a month received by an employee during one employment and reported to the employer are wages subject to withholding. The employer withholds only if he can collect the tax from the employee's wages after social security taxes have been deducted. The employee can voluntarily furnish funds if his regular pay cannot cover withholding. Tips are considered paid when the employee reports them to his employer. He must report them in writing by the 10th of the month after the month they were received. Form 4070 can be used for this purpose. Unreported tips are considered paid when received [Sec. 3401(a)(16), 3401(f), 3402(k), 6053(a); 31.3401(f)-1, 31.3402(k)-1, 31.6053-1]. "Service charges" added to patron's bill and distributed to employees are wages for withholding.[24] Also, tips which charge customers add to their checks must be reported to employers with other tips. The employer must report such tips on Form W-2.[23]

Traveling expenses and other necessary expenses incurred, or reasonably expected to be incurred in employer's business, and specifically advanced or reimbursed to employees are not wages [Sec. 31.3401(a)-1(b)(2)]. However, after 7-1-77, reimbursements for expenses incurred in traveling from home to the place of work are subject to withholding regardless of work's nature, distance traveled, mode of transport or degree of necessity.[25] Wages and expense money need not be paid separately, but if one payment includes both items, each should be shown separately [Sec. 31.3401(a)(1)].

State unemployment benefits are not taxable income.[26]

Supplemental unemployment benefits (SUB) are subject to withholding to the extent that the benefits are taxable. Withholding is required on benefits paid under a plan to which the employer is a party due to employee's involuntary separation from employment (whether or not temporary), resulting directly from a reduction in force, discontinuing operation or similar conditions [Sec. 3402(o); 31.3401(a)-1(b)(14), 31.3402(o)-1]. "Involuntary separation" is a factual question. The fact that the employees' collective bargaining agreed to job termination due to automation does not make the subsequent unemployment voluntary [Sec. 1.501(c)(17)-1(b)].

Wages as community property. Total wages paid to the husband are wages subject to withholding. The wife's share of the tax withheld may be credited against her tax if she files separately.[27]

Fishing wages. Crewmen are not subject to withholding on pay for services rendered after 12-31-71, consisting of a share of the boat's or fleet's catch if the operating crew is less than ten[28] [Sec. 3121(b)(20), 3401(a)(17)]. For recordkeeping requirements, see ¶ 3521.

Employee stock options. When an employee exercises his rights in nonqualified stock options, the excess of the stock's fair market value over the option price is wages and may be treated as a supplemental wage [¶ 2504(e)].[29]

(b) No withholding on pay for excluded employment. Pay for services in certain excluded employment is not "wages" [Sec. 3401(a)].

Agricultural labor. Pay for services in agricultural labor is not subject to withholding [Sec. 31.3401(a)(2)-1]. But hatching poultry off the farm or processing maple sap is not considered agricultural labor.[30] For voluntary withholding on nonwage payments, see ¶ 2504(j).

Armed forces. Pay that can be excluded from income because of service in a combat area is not wages subject to withholding [Sec. 31.3401(a)(1)-1].

Church ministers. Payments to a duly ordained, commissioned or licensed minister of a church when performing his duties, or to a member of a religious order performing duties required by the order are not wages subject to withholding [Sec. 31.3401(a)(9)-1]. Pay for secular services by a minister in a headquarters office of a national organization qualifies, but withholding is required on pay for routine clerical work.[31]

Domestics. Pay for services in a private home, local college club, or local chapter of a college fraternity or sorority is not wages for withholding [Sec. 31.3401(a)(3)-1]. But see ¶ 2504(j).

Pay for employment NOT in the course of employer's trade or business is not subject to withholding if it is a noncash payment [Sec. 31.3401(a)(11)-1], or if the cash payment is less than $50 for a calendar quarter. Withholding is required when the

Footnotes appear at end of this Chapter.

¶ 2503

employee receives $50 or more in cash for any calendar quarter in which he does such work for the employer on each of 24 days during the quarter [Sec. 31.3401(a)(4)-1].

Foreign country, U.S. possessions, international organization. Pay for services *for* a foreign country or an international organization is not wages [Sec. 31.3401(a)(5)-1]. Pay for services by a U.S. citizen *in* a foreign country or U.S. possession (except compensation paid by the U.S. or its agencies) is not wages if (1) the employer is required to withhold tax for the foreign country or possession, or (2) it is reasonable to believe payments will be excluded from gross income (such as income earned abroad, ¶ 3725) or (3) it is reasonable to believe payments for services in a U.S. possession (Puerto Rico excepted) will be at least 80% of the compensation the employer pays to the employee during the calendar year [Sec. 31.3401 (a) (8) (A) -1, 31.3401 (a)(8)(B)-1]. Although Puerto Rico is not included in proviso (3), no withholding is required if it is reasonable to believe the employee will be a bona fide resident there for the entire year [Sec. 31.3401(a)(8)(C)-1]. The employer may rely on the employee's filed statement that he qualifies for proviso (2). A duplicate copy of the statement should be filed with the quarterly return [¶ 2509], Form 941 [Sec. 31.3401(a)(8)(A)-1].

Newsboys and news vendors. Pay of newboys under 18 is not wages. But withholding is required on pay for delivery or distribution to a point from which further delivery or distribution is made. Pay of news vendors who sell papers and magazines for a fixed price is not wages when that pay is the excess of what they receive for the papers and magazines over what they pay for them. This applies even though they are guaranteed a minimum amount or credited with unsold papers or magazines [Sec. 31.3401(a)(10)-1].

Peace Corps allowances for services performed by volunteers are not subject to withholding; but readjustment allowances (termination payments) will be treated for withholding purposes as if received at the rate of $75 a month [Sec. 3401(a)(13)].

Public service. Fees paid for performing a public duty (such as a notary, clerk or sheriff), amounts paid to jurors and witnesses, or to precinct workers at election booths in state, county or municipal elections are not wages subject to withholding. But salaries paid to officials by the government or government agencies are subject to withholding [Sec. 31.3401(a)-2(b)].

(c) Combined wages and nonwages. The amount of time spent in each kind of work determines whether or not withholding is required when an employment for one employer for a payroll period of not over 31 days combines work for "wages" and work for pay in excluded employment.

• Withholding is required on the entire payment if one-half or more of the time is spent in work for "wages."

• Withholding is not required if more than one-half of the time is spent for pay in excluded employment [Sec. 3402(e); 31.3402(e)-1].

¶ 2504 How to figure withholding. Withholding from gross wages may be figured ordinarily by either the *wage-bracket withholding tables* (illustrated in Exhibit at (b) below) or the *percentage method*. Graduated rates apply in figuring withholding. Each method is arranged by payroll periods and divided into two separate schedules for married (including surviving spouse) and single (including head of household) taxpayers. The percentage method may be used for some employees and the wage-bracket tables for others. An employer can change from one method to the other without Revenue Service approval.[1] The percentage method must be used for quarterly, semiannual, or annual payroll periods, unless an authorized alternative method (see (c) below) is used.

Graduated withholding results in an amount withheld that closely approximates final tax liability.

The amount of withholding under either method depends on the schedule used (as to the payroll period and the employee's marital status), the number of withholding exemptions and allowances claimed by the employee on the withholding exemption certificate [¶ 2505; 2506] and on the amount of the employee's earnings.

Employers may use alternative methods of withholding that result in substantially the same amount as the percentage or wage-bracket method. See (c) below.

An employer cannot withhold less tax than is required, even though the amount withheld exceeds employee's tax liability for the year.[2]

NOTE: The income tax withholding tables reflect the current withholding rates for wages paid after 5-31-77 through 12-31-78. They reflect the zero bracket amount [¶ 1107], the general tax credit [¶ 1111(e)] and the earned income credit [¶ 2405].

(a) Percentage method. The amount to be withheld using the percentage method is determined as follows [Sec. 3402(a); 31.3402(b)-1]:

(1) Multiply the amount of one withholding exemption shown in the table below by the number of exemptions and allowances allowed [¶ 2505]:

EXEMPTION TABLE

Payroll period	Amount of one withholding exemption
Weekly	$ 14.40
Biweekly	28.80
Semimonthly	31.30
Monthly	62.50
Quarterly	187.50
Semiannual	375.00
Annual	750.00
Daily or miscellaneous (per day of such period)	2.10

(2) Next, subtract the amount arrived at in (1) from the periodical wage to find the "net wages" used to figure withholding.

(3) Apply the proper rate found in the tables to the "net wages":

[Percentage withholding tables appear on pages 2508-2509.]

Footnotes appear at end of this Chapter.

¶ 2504

PERCENTAGE WITHHOLDING TABLES
(Effective 6-1-77 to 12-31-78)

TABLE 1. WEEKLY Payroll Period

(a) SINGLE person—including head of household:

If the amount of wages is:		The amount of income tax to be withheld shall be:	
Not over $33		0	
Over—	But not over—		of excess over—
$33	—$76	16%	—$33
$76	—$143	$6.88 plus 18%	—$76
$143	—$182	$18.94 plus 22%	—$143
$182	—$220	$27.52 plus 24%	—$182
$220	—$297	$36.64 plus 28%	—$220
$297	—$355	$58.20 plus 32%	—$297
$355		$76.76 plus 36%	—$355

(b) MARRIED person—

If the amount of wages is:		The amount of income tax to be withheld shall be:	
Not over $61		0	
Over—	But not over—		of excess over—
$61	—$105	15%	—$61
$105	—$223	$6.60 plus 18%	—$105
$223	—$278	$27.84 plus 22%	—$223
$278	—$355	$39.94 plus 25%	—$278
$355	—$432	$59.19 plus 28%	—$355
$432	—$509	$80.75 plus 32%	—$432
$509		$105.39 plus 36%	—$509

TABLE 2. BIWEEKLY Payroll Period

(a) SINGLE person—including head of household:

If the amount of wages is:		The amount of income tax to be withheld shall be:	
Not over $65		0	
Over—	But not over—		of excess over—
$65	—$152	16%	—$65
$152	—$287	$13.92 plus 18%	—$152
$287	—$363	$38.22 plus 22%	—$287
$363	—$440	$54.94 plus 24%	—$363
$440	—$594	$73.42 plus 28%	—$440
$594	—$710	$116.54 plus 32%	—$594
$710		$153.66 plus 36%	—$710

(b) MARRIED person—

If the amount of wages is:		The amount of income tax to be withheld shall be:	
Not over $121		0	
Over—	But not over—		of excess over—
$121	—$210	15%	—$121
$210	—$445	$13.35 plus 18%	—$210
$445	—$556	$55.65 plus 22%	—$445
$556	—$710	$80.07 plus 25%	—$556
$710	—$863	$118.57 plus 28%	—$710
$863	—$1,017	$161.41 plus 32%	—$863
$1,017		$210.69 plus 36%	—$1,017

TABLE 3. SEMIMONTHLY Payroll Period

(a) SINGLE person—including head of household:

If the amount of wages is:		The amount of income tax to be withheld shall be:	
Not over $71		0	
Over—	But not over—		of excess over—
$71	—$165	16%	—$71
$165	—$310	$15.04 plus 18%	—$165
$310	—$394	$41.14 plus 22%	—$310
$394	—$477	$59.62 plus 24%	—$394
$477	—$644	$79.54 plus 28%	—$477
$644	—$769	$126.30 plus 32%	—$644
$769		$166.30 plus 36%	—$769

(b) MARRIED person—

If the amount of wages is:		The amount of income tax to be withheld shall be:	
Not over $131		0	
Over—	But not over—		of excess over—
$131	—$227	15%	—$131
$227	—$482	$14.40 plus 18%	—$227
$482	—$602	$60.30 plus 22%	—$482
$602	—$769	$86.70 plus 25%	—$602
$769	—$935	$128.45 plus 28%	—$769
$935	—$1,102	$174.93 plus 32%	—$935
$1,102		$228.37 plus 36%	—$1,102

TABLE 4. MONTHLY Payroll Period

(a) SINGLE person—including head of household:

If the amount of wages is:		The amount of income tax to be withheld shall be:	
Not over $142		0	
Over—	But not over—		of excess over—
$142	—$329	16%	—$142
$329	—$621	$29.92 plus 18%	—$329
$621	—$788	$82.48 plus 22%	—$621
$788	—$954	$119.22 plus 24%	—$788
$954	—$1,288	$159.06 plus 28%	—$954
$1,288	—$1,538	$252.58 plus 32%	—$1,288
$1,538		$332.58 plus 36%	—$1,538

(b) MARRIED person—

If the amount of wages is:		The amount of income tax to be withheld shall be:	
Not over $263		0	
Over—	But not over—		of excess over—
$263	—$454	15%	—$263
$454	—$965	$28.65 plus 18%	—$454
$965	—$1,204	$120.63 plus 22%	—$965
$1,204	—$1,538	$173.21 plus 25%	—$1,204
$1,538	—$1,871	$256.71 plus 28%	—$1,538
$1,871	—$2,204	$349.95 plus 32%	—$1,871
$2,204		$456.51 plus 36%	—$2,204

Chapter 15—Withholding

TABLE 5. QUARTERLY Payroll Period

(a) SINGLE person—including head of household:

If the amount of wages is:	The amount of income tax to be withheld shall be:
Not over $425	0

Over—	But not over—		of excess over—
$425	—$988	16%	—$425
$988	—$1,863	$90.08 plus 18%	—$988
$1,863	—$2,363	$247.58 plus 22%	—$1,863
$2,363	—$2,863	$357.58 plus 24%	—$2,363
$2,863	—$3,863	$477.58 plus 28%	—$2,863
$3,863	—$4,613	$757.58 plus 32%	—$3,863
$4,613		$997.58 plus 36%	—$4,613

(b) MARRIED person—

If the amount of wages is:	The amount of income tax to be withheld shall be:
Not over $788	0

Over—	But not over—		of excess over—
$788	—$1,363	15%	—$788
$1,363	—$2,894	$86.25 plus 18%	—$1,363
$2,894	—$3,613	$361.83 plus 22%	—$2,894
$3,613	—$4,613	$520.01 plus 25%	—$3,613
$4,613	—$5,613	$770.01 plus 28%	—$4,613
$5,613	—$6,613	$1,050.01 plus 32%	—$5,613
$6,613		$1,370.01 plus 36%	—$6,613

TABLE 6. SEMIANNUAL Payroll Period

(a) SINGLE person—including head of household:

If the amount of wages is:	The amount of income tax to be withheld shall be:
Not over $850	0

Over—	But not over—		of excess over—
$850	—$1,975	16%	—$850
$1,975	—$3,725	$180.00 plus 18%	—$1,975
$3,725	—$4,725	$495.00 plus 22%	—$3,725
$4,725	—$5,725	$715.00 plus 24%	—$4,725
$5,725	—$7,725	$955.00 plus 28%	—$5,725
$7,725	—$9,225	$1,515.00 plus 32%	—$7,725
$9,225		$1,995.00 plus 36%	—$9,225

(b) MARRIED person—

If the amount of wages is:	The amount of income tax to be withheld shall be:
Not over $1,575	0

Over—	But not over—		of excess over—
$1,575	—$2,725	15%	—$1,575
$2,725	—$5,788	$172.50 plus 18%	—$2,725
$5,788	—$7,225	$723.84 plus 22%	—$5,788
$7,225	—$9,225	$1,039.98 plus 25%	—$7,225
$9,225	—$11,225	$1,539.98 plus 28%	—$9,225
$11,225	—$13,225	$2,099.98 plus 32%	—$11,225
$13,225		$2,739.98 plus 36%	—$13,225

TABLE 7. ANNUAL Payroll Period

(a) SINGLE person—including head of household:

If the amount of wages is:	The amount of income tax to be withheld shall be:
Not over $1,700	0

Over—	But not over—		of excess over—
$1,700	—$3,950	16%	—$1,700
$3,950	—$7,450	$360.00 plus 18%	—$3,950
$7,450	—$9,450	$990.00 plus 22%	—$7,450
$9,450	—$11,450	$1,430.00 plus 24%	—$9,450
$11,450	—$15,450	$1,910.00 plus 28%	—$11,450
$15,450	—$18,450	$3,030.00 plus 32%	—$15,450
$18,450		$3,990.00 plus 36%	—$18,450

(b) MARRIED person—

If the amount of wages is:	The amount of income tax to be withheld shall be:
Not over $3,150	0

Over—	But not over—		of excess over—
$3,150	—$5,450	15%	—$3,150
$5,450	—$11,575	$345.00 plus 18%	—$5,450
$11,575	—$14,450	$1,447.50 plus 22%	—$11,575
$14,450	—$18,450	$2,080.00 plus 25%	—$14,450
$18,450	—$22,450	$3,080.00 plus 28%	—$18,450
$22,450	—$26,450	$4,200.00 plus 32%	—$22,450
$26,450		$5,480.00 plus 36%	—$26,450

TABLE 8. DAILY or MISCELLANEOUS Payroll Period

(a) SINGLE person—including head of household:

If the wages divided by the number of days in such period are:	The amount of income tax to be withheld shall be the following amount multiplied by the number of days in such period:
Not over $4.70	0

Over—	But not over—		of excess over—
$4.70	—$10.80	16%	—$4.70
$10.80	—$20.40	$.98 plus 18%	—$10.80
$20.40	—$25.90	$2.71 plus 22%	—$20.40
$25.90	—$31.40	$3.92 plus 24%	—$25.90
$31.40	—$42.30	$5.24 plus 28%	—$31.40
$42.30	—$50.50	$8.29 plus 32%	—$42.30
$50.50		$10.91 plus 36%	—$50.50

(b) MARRIED person—

If the wages divided by the number of days in such period are:	The amount of income tax to be withheld shall be the following amount multiplied by the number of days in such period:
Not over $8.60	0

Over—	But not over—		of excess over—
$8.60	—$14.90	15%	—$8.60
$14.90	—$31.70	$.95 plus 18%	—$14.90
$31.70	—$39.60	$3.97 plus 22%	—$31.70
$39.60	—$50.50	$5.71 plus 25%	—$39.60
$50.50	—$61.50	$8.44 plus 28%	—$50.50
$61.50	—$72.50	$11.52 plus 32%	—$61.50
$72.50		$15.04 plus 36%	—$72.50

Example 1: Davis is on a weekly payroll receiving $109.95. His withholding exemption certificate shows he is married and claiming a total of 3 withholding exemptions. Total income tax to be withheld each week is $1.50, figured as follows:

Step 1
Amount of one withholding exemption for weekly payroll period .... $ 14.40
Multiplied by number of withholding exemptions claimed by employee ...... × 3
Total withholding exemptions .... $ 43.20

Step 2
Total wage payment .... $110.00†
Less amount determined in Step 1 .... 43.20
Net wages .... $ 66.80

¶ 2504

Chapter 15—Withholding

Step 3

The employer uses the weekly table for a married person to determine the amount to withhold from Davis' wages. Since the $66.80 "net wages" is "over $61 but not over $105," the amount withheld is $0.87, or 15% of $5.80 (the excess over $61).

† In this formula employers may round out the wage to the nearest dollar [Sec. 3402(b)(5)], or reduce the last digit of the wage amount to zero [Sec. 31.3402(b)-1]. Thus, if the wage is $109.95, the employer may round out to $110, or determine the tax on the basis of $109.90.

Miscellaneous payroll period. If withholding is figured for a "miscellaneous" payroll period, the wages and the amounts shown in the percentage method withholding table must be placed on a comparable basis. This may be done by either of the following methods [Sec. 31.3402(b)-1]:

1. Adjust the percentage method withholding table to accord with the number of days in the period by multiplying the amounts shown in the table for the daily or miscellaneous period by the number of days in the miscellaneous period.
2. Reduce the wages paid for the period to a daily basis by dividing the total wages by the number of days in the period.

(b) Wage-bracket withholding method. The amount to be withheld is determined directly from the wage-bracket tables (illustrated below). They are set up by payroll period (weekly, biweekly, semimonthly, monthly and daily or miscellaneous), with separate tables for married and single taxpayers. The employer uses the bracket in which the wage payment fits and withholds the amount found in the column for the number of withholding exemptions claimed (¶ 2506) [Sec. 3402(c); 31.3402(c)-1].

SEMIMONTHLY PAYROLL PERIOD – continued   MARRIED PERSONS

WAGES: $940–$2,040 and over

And the wages are—		And the number of withholding allowances claimed is—									
At least	But less than	0	1	2	3	4	5	6	7	8	9	10 or more

The amount of income tax to be withheld shall be—

At least	But less than	0	1	2	3	4	5	6	7	8	9	10 or more
$940	$960	$179.70	$170.30	$161.60	$152.80	$144.10	$135.30	$126.80	$119.00	$111.10	$103.30	$95.50
960	980	186.10	176.10	167.20	158.40	149.70	140.90	132.20	124.00	116.10	108.30	100.50
980	1,000	192.50	182.50	172.80	164.00	155.30	146.50	137.80	129.00	121.10	113.30	105.50
1,000	1,020	198.90	188.90	178.90	169.60	160.90	152.10	143.40	134.60	126.10	118.30	110.50
1,020	1,040	205.30	195.30	185.30	175.30	166.50	157.70	149.00	140.20	131.50	123.30	115.50
1,040	1,060	211.70	201.70	191.70	181.70	172.10	163.30	154.60	145.80	137.10	128.30	120.50
1,060	1,080	218.10	208.10	198.10	188.10	178.10	168.90	160.20	151.40	142.70	133.90	125.50
1,080	1,100	224.50	214.50	204.50	194.50	184.50	174.50	165.80	157.00	148.30	139.50	130.80
1,100	1,120	231.20	220.90	210.90	200.90	190.90	180.90	171.40	162.60	153.90	145.10	136.40
1,120	1,140	238.40	227.30	217.30	207.30	197.30	187.30	177.30	168.20	159.50	150.70	142.00
1,140	1,160	245.60	234.30	223.70	213.70	203.70	193.70	183.70	173.80	165.10	156.30	147.60
1,160	1,180	252.80	241.50	230.30	220.10	210.10	200.10	190.10	180.10	170.70	161.90	153.20
1,180	1,200	260.00	248.70	237.50	226.50	216.50	206.50	196.50	186.50	176.50	167.50	158.80
1,200	1,220	267.20	255.90	244.70	233.40	222.90	212.90	202.90	192.90	182.90	173.10	164.40
1,220	1,240	274.40	263.10	251.90	240.60	229.40	219.30	209.30	199.30	189.30	179.30	170.00
1,240	1,260	281.60	270.30	259.10	247.80	236.60	225.70	215.70	205.70	195.70	185.70	175.70
1,260	1,280	288.80	277.50	266.30	255.00	243.80	232.50	222.10	212.10	202.10	192.10	182.10
1,280	1,300	296.00	284.70	273.50	262.20	251.00	239.70	228.50	218.50	208.50	198.50	188.50
1,300	1,320	303.20	291.90	280.70	269.40	258.20	246.90	235.70	224.90	214.90	204.90	194.90
1,320	1,340	310.40	299.10	287.90	276.60	265.40	254.10	242.90	231.60	221.30	211.30	201.30
1,940	1,960	533.60	522.30	511.10	499.80	488.60	477.30	466.10	454.80	443.60	432.30	421.10
1,960	1,980	540.80	529.50	518.30	507.00	495.80	484.50	473.30	462.00	450.80	439.50	428.30
1,980	2,000	548.00	536.70	525.50	514.20	503.00	491.70	480.50	469.20	458.00	446.70	435.50
2,000	2,020	555.20	543.90	532.70	521.40	510.20	498.90	487.70	476.40	465.20	453.90	442.70
2,020	2,040	562.40	551.10	539.90	528.60	517.40	506.10	494.90	483.60	472.40	461.10	449.90

36 percent of the excess over $2,040 plus—

| $2,040 and over | | 566.00 | 554.70 | 543.50 | 532.20 | 521.00 | 509.70 | 498.50 | 487.20 | 476.00 | 464.70 | 453.50 |

EXHIBIT. Wage-Bracket Table

Example 2: Jones is married and properly claims 2 withholding exemptions. He receives a salary of $965 semimonthly. In using the wage-bracket table as shown in the Exhibit above, Jones' employer would withhold $167.20 each pay period. This amount appears in the column for two exemptions across from the $960-980 bracket into which Jones' $965 salary fits.

A weekly table combining the income tax and social security tax can be obtained from the Revenue Service.

If wages exceed the highest bracket, the excess subject to the 36% rate may be rounded off to the nearest dollar [Sec. 3402(c)(5)]. Thus, if a married employee claiming 2 exemptions has a semimonthly salary of $2,170.33, the employer may withhold $543.50, plus 36% of either $130.33 or $130 (see Exhibit above).

(c) Alternative methods. In addition to the percentage and wage-bracket methods (see (a) and (b) above), several alternative methods of computing withholding are available.

An employer can use his own method of figuring withholding without Revenue Service approval if it gives the same result as the percentage or wage-bracket methods.[3]

In addition, rules have been prescribed for employers to withhold on the basis of (1) annualized wages, (2) cumulative wages (at the employee's request), (3) wages for part-time employment (at the employee's request), or (4) any other method of computing withholding that comes within the maximum permissible deviation amounts set forth in the regulations [Sec. 3402(h); 31.3402(h)(2)-1, 31.3402(h)(3)-1, 31.3402(h)(4)-1].

Employers may also withhold quarterly on the basis of the employee's average estimated wages [see (i) below].

(d) Payments made without regard to specified payroll periods. If wages are paid without regard to any payroll period, or if they are paid for a period not otherwise provided for by the percentage method schedule or wage-bracket tables, the employer determines the amount withheld by using the table for a "daily or miscellaneous payroll period," or if the percentage method is used, by applying the exemption for such period [Sec. 3402(b)(2), (3); 3402(c)(2), (3); 31.3402(b)-1, 31.3402(c)-1].

Short period. The employer may use the weekly payroll period table or exemption to determine the amount to be withheld *when the period covered by the payments is less than one week.* This method can be used only if the employer gets a written statement from the employee that (1) he works for no other employer during the calendar week and (2) he will notify the employer within 10 days after he starts any other employment. This statement must be certified under penalty of perjury [Sec. 3402(b)(4), 3402(c)(4); 31.3402(b)(1), 31.3402(c)-1].

Figuring withholding by annualizing wages. Withholding can be figured by annualizing wages and finding the amount as follows: (1) multiply wages for the payroll period by the number of these periods in the calendar year; (2) determine the amount to be withheld from step (1) on an annual basis; (3) divide the result by the number of payroll periods [Sec. 31.3402(h)(2)-1].[3]

Example 3: Smith, who is single and claims 1 withholding exemption, earns $105 weekly. His employer can multiply his weekly wage by 52 to find his annual wage. The employer would then subtract $750 and arrive at a net wage of $4,710. The percentage table for the annual payroll period shows that the tax to be withheld for $4,710 is $360 plus 18% of the excess over $3,950, or a total of $496.80. The annual withholding of $496.80, when divided by 52 to arrive at the weekly share, equals $9.55.

(e) Supplemental wage payments. If an employee, in addition to regular wages, receives supplemental wages, such as bonuses, commissions or overtime pay, the tax to be withheld may be determined in several ways.

Footnotes appear at end of this Chapter.

¶ 2504

Paid with regular wages. A supplemental payment and the regular wage for the regular payroll period paid at the same time are treated as a *single* wage payment for the *regular* payroll period [Sec. 31.3402(g)-1].

Example 4: A salesman, married and properly claiming 3 withholding exemptions is employed at a semimonthly salary of $500 plus commissions on sales made during the payroll period. Between November 15 and the end of the month, he earns $675 and is paid this amount plus his regular $500 salary on November 30. The wage-bracket table is used to figure the income tax to be withheld. $1,175 ($675 commissions + $500 salary) is considered a single wage payment for the semimonthly period. $1,175 falls in the $1,160-$1,180 bracket; withholding for that bracket for a married taxpayer claiming 3 withholding exemptions is $220.10.

Not paid with regular wages. If a supplemental wage is paid at a different time than the regular wage payment, it may be added to regular wages for the current payroll period *or* to regular wages for the last preceding payroll period within the same calendar year, and the total treated as a single wage payment for the regular payroll period [Sec. 31.3402(g)-1].

Example 5: Roberts is married and employed at a salary of $23,400 a year paid semimonthly on the 15th and last days of each month, plus a bonus determined at the end of each 3-month period. Three withholding exemptions are properly claimed. The bonus for August 1 to October 31, amounted to $180, which was paid on November 10. Employer uses the wage-bracket table to figure the income tax to be withheld. Under the above rule, the amount withheld on the aggregate of the $180 bonus and the last preceding semimonthly wage payment of $975, or $1,155 is $213.70. Since income tax in the amount of $158.40 was withheld on the semimonthly wage payment of $975, the income tax to be withheld on November 10 is $55.30.

Tax previously withheld on regular wages. When the tax has been withheld on regular wages, an employer can figure the tax to be withheld from supplemental wage payments by using a flat rate of 20% without allowance for exemptions and without reference to any regular wage payment [Sec. 31.3402(g)-1].

Example 6: If his employer used this method, the income tax withheld from Roberts' semimonthly salary (Example 5) would remain the same ($158.40). But the employer would deduct $36 from the bonus payment of Nov. 10 (20% of $180), making the total income tax withheld $194.40.

When exemptions exceed regular wages. When the amount of regular wages paid to an employee for two or more consecutive payroll periods of one week or more is less than the amount of his withholding exemptions, the employer may elect to use a special method to find the tax to be withheld on supplemental wages received for those payroll periods. First the employer averages the total of regular and supplemental wages over the payroll periods. Then he figures the tax to be withheld on the average amount for each payroll period. Finally he subtracts the tax withheld on the regular wages from the tax to be withheld on the averaged wages. The remainder is the tax to be withheld on the supplemental wages [Sec. 31.3402(g)-1(b)].

Example 7: Smith, who is married and claims 2 exemptions, receives $74 a week salary, plus a production bonus of $125, for 5 weeks' work. The employer used the percentage method table. The amount to be withheld is figured as follows:

Wages for 5 weeks ($74 × 5)	$370.00
Production bonus	125.00
Total wage payments	$495.00
Average wages per payroll period ($495 ÷ 5)	$ 99.00
Less: withholding exemptions ($14.40 × 2)	28.80
Remainder subject to tax	$ 70.20
Tax on average wages for 1 week [$9.20 ($70.20 − $61.00) × 15%]	$ 1.38

Tax on average wages for 5 weeks ($1.38 × 5)	$ 6.90
Less: Tax previously withheld on weekly wage of $74	NONE
Tax to be withheld on supplemental wages	$ 6.90

Tips. Employers may treat reported tips as supplemental payments in determining the proper amount of withholding. These may be treated as if part of the current or preceding wage payment, or if the tax has been previously withheld from the regular wage payment, figure the tax using the flat 20% rate.[4]

(f) Vacation pay. Withholding on vacation allowances is the same as regular wage payments made for the vacation period [Sec. 31.3402(g)-1].

Example 8: Smith who is married and claims 1 withholding exemption earns $100 a week. On April 30, he will receive his pay for the week just closed and for his vacation, the first two weeks in May. His employer uses the percentage method to figure withholding. The income tax withheld should be 3 times that shown for Smith's weekly wage, or $11.07 (3 × $3.69).

If the employee gets *extra pay* for working during his vacation, it is treated as a supplemental payment [Sec. 31.3402(g)-1]. See (e) above.

(g) Wage disability payments. There is no withholding on payments made by a person for whom the employee does not work such as payments by a trust or an insurance company under an accident or health plan, or by a state under a disability fund [Sec. 31.3401(a)-1(b)(8)].

NOTE: Qualifying disability income payments would not be subject to withholding [¶ 1219(c)]. Thus, payments under a wage continuation plan that were generally described as "sick pay" for tax years before 1977, would be subject to withholding unless they qualify as exempt disability income.

(h) Wages paid for two or more employers. If an agent, fiduciary, or other person pays the wages of an employee of two or more employers, withholding is figured on the total amount [Sec. 31.3402(g)-3].

Example 9: Alma Co. and Ball Co. maintain a joint agency; Alma pays 60% of the expense and Ball 40%. James works in the agency. He receives $56.50 weekly, paid in one sum by the agency manager with funds supplied by Alma and Ball. James is single and claims 1 withholding exemption. The agency manager uses the percentage method to figure withholding. It is figured on the aggregate salary of $56.50, not on the respective amounts contributed by Alma and Ball. The tax withheld on $56.50 weekly wage of a single person claiming 1 withholding exemption is $1.46, using the percentage method. The tax is apportioned between Alma and Ball in proportion to their contributions to James' salary. Thus, Alma must report and pay $0.88 (60% of $1.46) and Ball $0.58 (40% of $1.46). They may authorize (with Revenue Service permission) the agency manager to file the return of taxes withheld and to pay the aggregate tax, but they remain responsible if he fails to pay.

(i) Withholding on average estimated wages other than tips can be made, with necessary adjustments for any quarter, without Revenue Service approval. An estimate can also be used in figuring tips an employee will report in a given quarter. The employer can determine the amount to be withheld and then deduct it from each regular wage payment. Adjustments can be made during the quarter and within 30 days thereafter to reflect tips actually reported by the employee [Sec. 3402(h)(1); 31.3402(h)(1)-1].

(j) Voluntary withholding. When an employee finds that withholding will not cover the tax liability, fewer exemptions can be claimed on the withholding exemption certificate than allowed [¶ 2506]. For this purpose, a married person can indicate single status. In addition, the employee can increase withholding by

Footnotes appear at end of this Chapter.

¶ 2504

entering into a written agreement with the employer. It can be effective for any period and any amount agreed on. If the agreement does not state an earlier termination date, either party may end it by giving written notice at least 30 days before any "status determination date." Termination is effective for the first wage payment on or after that date. Amounts withheld under the agreement are treated the same as other withheld taxes [Sec. 3402(i); 31.3402(i)-1]. Additional withholding may relieve an employee from penalties for underpaying estimated taxes [¶ 2519(a)].

Withholding on nonwage payments. A voluntary agreement between an employer and an employee can cover payments for an employee's service not within the usual definition of "wages" [¶ 2503(a)] (for example, domestic and farm workers' wages, ¶ 2503(b)). But certain payments such as noncash pay for services not in the course of employer's business, certain moving expense reimbursements and employer-paid group-term life insurance premiums, may *not* be covered by a voluntary agreement [Sec. 3402(p)-1; 31.3401(a)-3]. The agreement is effective for such period as the employer and employee mutually agree on, but either one can terminate it by giving notice to the other. No special form is prescribed for the employee's request, but Form W-4 [¶ 2505] must be attached to the request [Sec. 31.3402(p)-1].

For withholding on pension and annuity payments, see (k) below; for withholding on supplemental unemployment compensation, see ¶ 2503(a).

(k) Withholding on pension and annuity payments. Those receiving pension or annuity payments can request withholding on these payments by filing a Form W-4P with the one making the payments. A whole-dollar amount of at least $5 a month that does not reduce the net payment below $10 must be specified [Sec. 3402(o); Temp. Reg. Sec. 32.1]. The request takes effect no later than 3 months after filing if no previous request is in effect. In other cases, it is the first status determination date occurring at least 30 days after the request. The request may be terminated by a written notice. Form W-2P is used instead of Form W-2 as the statement of the amount withheld [¶ 2508].

(l) Part-time employment method of withholding. Withholding can be figured by the part-time employment method at the employee's request. This request must state under penalty of perjury: (1) the last day of employment (if any) by any employer before the current term of continuous employment during the year when the term began, (2) that employee will work no more than 245 days during the year or during the current term of continuous employment during the current and following years, and (3) that no more than $30,000 gross wages from all employers is expected. Withholding is figured by the following steps [Sec. 31.3402(h)(4)-1(c)]:

1. Add the wages for the current payroll period to the total wages paid to the employee for all prior periods included in the current term of continuous employment;
2. Divide total wages computed in (1) above by the total payroll periods to which that amount relates plus an equal number of payroll periods in the employee's continuous unemployment just before the current term of continuous employment. Omit from the term of continuous unemployment any days before the start of the employee's current tax years;
3. Determine the total tax that would have been withheld if average wages (computed in (2) above) had been paid for the number of payroll periods determined in (2) above (including equivalent number of payroll periods);
4. Determine the excess, if any, of the tax computed in (3) above over the total tax already withheld for all payroll periods during the current term of continuous employment.

Example 10: Ecks was unemployed from May 23 to Oct. 26. He began part-time work with Ace Corp. for 8 weeks from Oct. 27 to Dec. 21. Ecks gave Ace his Form W-4 properly claiming 3 exemptions and married status. He also requested the part-year employment method of withholding. Ecks works for a period starting Oct. 27 and ending Nov. 9 earning $2,700. Wages are paid on a biweekly basis. Using the part-year method, Ace determines that $28.20 is to be withheld from Ecks' wages paid Oct. 27 to Nov. 9 as follows:

Wages to be paid for biweekly payroll period		$2,700.00
Number of payroll periods 10-27 to 11-9		1
Equivalent number of payroll periods for period of unemployment, disregarding fractional payroll period	11	12
Average wages per payroll period including equivalent number of payroll periods ($2,700 ÷ 12)		$ 225.00
Amount to be withheld from $225.00 for biweekly period to married person with 3 exemptions (percentage methods)		2.64
Total to be withheld under percentage method for all payroll periods (including equivalent number of payroll periods) ($2.64 × 12)		$ 31.68
Amounts already withheld by employer		0
Amount to be withheld under part-year employment method ($31.68 — 0)		$ 31.68

¶ **2505 Withholding exemptions.** Generally, an employee can list on his Form W-4 [¶ 2506] as many exemptions as he is allowed on his return [¶ 1111; 1115]. In addition, he can also claim a "zero bracket allowance" or an additional withholding allowance for large itemized deductions. The employer treats each of these allowances as a withholding exemption. A husband and wife who are employed must allocate these exemptions and allowances on their exemption certificates. An allocation also must be made if the taxpayer holds more than one job at the same time [Sec. 3402(f), 3402(m)].

A nonresident alien who is not a resident of Canada or Mexico and who is not a resident of Puerto Rico during the entire tax year is allowed only one exemption [Sec. 3402(f)(6); 31.3402(f)(6)-1].

(a) Zero bracket allowance. An employee can take a special withholding allowance on the Form W-4. This allowance cannot be claimed by a married taxpayer whose spouse is employed or by any employee who has more than one job. [Sec. 3402(f)(1)(G)].

(b) Additional withholding allowances. An employee with substantial itemized deductions can prevent overwithholding by taking additional withholding allowances. To take an allowance for the current year, the estimated deductions cannot exceed the itemized deductions (or zero bracket amount) taken in the prior year's return, plus additional determinable deductions for the estimation year. The estimate can be based on the second prior year if a claim is made before prior year's return is filed. The allowances remain in effect until the employee files a new Form W-4. Determinable additional deductions mean certain identifiable itemized deductions that the taxpayer estimates will cause his total estimated deductions to be larger in the current year than those claimed in the prior year. An example of this would be an increase in property taxes due to the purchase of real estate [Sec. 3402(m)].

> NOTE: Although alimony is considered a deduction for adjusted gross income in tax years starting in 1977 and later, it is treated as an itemized deduction for these "withholding allowances" purposes [Sec. 3402(m)(2)].

A husband and wife figure their withholding allowances on the basis of their combined wages and deductions, unless they filed separate returns for the prior year and expect to file separately for the current year. An employee with two employers can claim withholding allowances only with one employer [Sec. 3402(m); 31.3402(m)-1]. A fiscal year taxpayer should see his District Director.

The allowances are figured from the table below.

WITHHOLDING ALLOWANCE TABLE
(Effective 6-1-77)

Table for Determining Number of Withholding Allowances Based on Tax Credits

Number of additional withholding allowances for the amount of tax credits for child care expenses, earned income, or credit for the elderly from the appropriate column

Estimated salaries and wages	0	1		2		3		4		5		6	
	Under	At least	But less than	At least	But less than	At least	But less than	At least	But less than	At least	But less than	At least	But less than

Part I — Single Employees

Under $5,000	NO ADDITIONAL ALLOWANCES												
5,000– 7,000		$75	75	200	200								
7,001–10,000		125	125	260	260	300	300 or more						
10,001–15,000		175	175	370	370	400	400	530	530	650	650	770	770 or more
15,001–20,000		200	200	450	450	550	550	700	700 or more				
20,001–25,000		250	250	525	525	670	670 or more						
25,001–30,000		400	400	700	700 or more	800	800 or more						
30,001–35,000		800	800 or more										

Part II — Head of Household Employees

Under $5,000	NO ADDITIONAL ALLOWANCES												
5,000– 10,000		$90	90	210	210	340	340	475	475	600	600	710	710 or more
10,001–15,000		50	50	210	210	400	400	560	560	725	725 or more		
15,001–20,000		1	1	190	190	400	400	610	610	800	800 or more		
20,001–25,000		1	1	120	120	350	350	630	630 or more				
25,001–30,000		1	1	75	75	375	375	640	640 or more				
30,001–35,000		75	75	350	350	620	620 or more						
35,001–45,000		475	475	750	750 or more								

Part III — Married Employees (When Spouse Is Not Employed)

Under $7,000	NO ADDITIONAL ALLOWANCES												
7,000–15,000		$125	125	250	250	390	390	525	525	660	660	800	800 or more
15,001–20,000		180	180	375	375	540	540	700	700 or more				
20,001–25,000		210	210	420	420	630	630	800	800 or more				
25,001–30,000		240	240	480	480	720	720 or more						
30,001–35,000		270	270	550	550	800	800 or more						
35,001–45,000		425	425	750	750 or more								

Part IV — Married Employees (When Both Spouses Are Employed)

Under $8,000	NO ADDITIONAL ALLOWANCES												
8,000–10,000		$150	150 or more										
10,001–12,000		220	220 or more										
12,001–14,000		300	300 or more										
14,001–16,000		450	450	590	590	670	670 or more						
16,001–18,000		560	560	710	710 or more								
18,001–20,000		650	650 or more										
20,001–25,000		800	800 or more										

Determining Withholding Allowances for Itemized Deductions and Payments of Alimony

The worksheet below will be helpful to you in determining whether your expected itemized deductions and adjustment to gross income for alimony payments entitle you to claim one or more additional withholding allowances

(a) Total estimated annual salary or wages (from all sources) . . . . $
(b) Total estimated itemized deductions . . . . $
(c) Enter $3,200 for joint return or $2,200 for all others . . . .
(d) Line (b) or line (c), whichever is larger . . . .
(e) Total estimated deduction for alimony payments . . . .
(f) Add lines (d) and (e) . . . .
(g) Appropriate amount from column (A), (B), or (C) in the table below . . . .
(h) Balance (subtract line (g) from line (f)). If less than $1, you are not entitled to additional withholding allowances and may be having too little tax withheld. You can generally avoid this by claiming 1 less allowance than the total number to which you are entitled for each $750 by which line (g) exceeds line (f) . . . . .
(i) You are entitled to 1 allowance for each $750 or fraction thereof that line (h) exceeds $1. Enter number here . . . .
(j) Withholding allowances from Part I, II, III, or IV . . . .
(k) Total of lines (i) and (j) . . . .

Table for Determining Number of Withholding Allowances Based on Deductions

Estimated salaries and wages	(A) Single Employees (With One Job) and Head of Household Employees	(B) Married Employees (Wife or Husband is Not Working)	(C) Married Employees (Both Husband and Wife Working) and Employees Working in More Than One Job
Under $10,000	$2,500	$3,500	$4,300
10,000–15,000	2,500	3,500	5,100
15,001–20,000	2,500	3,600	6,000
20,001–25,000	2,600	3,600	6,600
25,001–30,000	2,800	3,600	7,300
30,001–35,000	3,600	3,600	8,000
35,001–40,000	4,700	3,900	8,900
40,001–45,000	6,000	4,600	9,800
45,001–50,000	7,600	5,600	10,900
Over $50,000	21% of estimated salaries and wages	15% of estimated salaries and wages	24% of estimated salaries and wages

(c) **Penalties.** Civil and criminal penalties are imposed on the employee for giving the employer false or fraudulent information as to exemptions and allowances [Sec. 31.6682-1]. See ¶ 2512(b).

¶ 2506 **Withholding exemption certificates.** Each employee must file a withholding exemption certificate (Form W-4) with the employer listing his withholding exemptions and allowances (unless he files Form W-4E explained in (c) below). Without Form W-4, he gets no exemptions or allowances [Sec. 31.3402(f)(2)-1]. Furthermore, he is treated as a single person unless he files and his Form W-4 indicates that he is married [Sec. 3402(1)]. Penalties are imposed for false or fraudulent statements, for failing to supply a certificate or for misstating withholding allowances [¶ 2512(b)].

An employee can claim a special withholding allowance or additional withholding allowances on Form W-4 [¶ 2505]. Claims for withholding allowances remain in effect until the employee files a new certificate because of a change in circumstances [see (b) and (c) below]. A new certificate is not required even when these allowances were claimed by using itemized deductions from the second prior year and the deductions on the prior year's return are lower.

(a)   New employees must furnish a Form W-4 with their identifying numbers [¶ 3500] to their employers before employment starts. The form must be given immediate effect by the employer [Sec. 3402(f); 31.3402(f)].

> **Example 1:**   Kane starts work on Feb. 3 giving his employer a Form W-4 that lists 3 exemptions. The next payroll period ends on Feb. 15. In figuring the withholding from Kane's salary on that date and thereafter, these 3 exemptions will be used.

(b)   Filing an amended certificate on change in status.   An employee's withholding exemption certificate (Form W-4) on file with the employer remains in effect until a new one is furnished.[1]

> **NOTE:**   Since the employer will not request an amended certificate, an employee who claimed additional allowances but whose circumstances have been changed later, should file a new certificate.[2]

Change in status.   An amended withholding certificate may be required or permitted when an employee's withholding exemptions change. Here are the rules [Sec. 3402(f)(2)(B); 31.3402(f)(2)-1]:

Exemptions reduced.   An employee *must* file an amended certificate within 10 days after exemptions decrease, if entitled to less than the exemptions originally claimed on the withholding exemption certificate.

> **Example 2:**   Green is married, with one dependent daughter, and has on file a Form W-4 properly claiming 4 withholding exemptions [¶ 2505]. On May 3, the daughter was married, and since then she has been supported by her husband. Within 10 days after the wedding, Green must file a new Form W-4 with his employer, claiming 3 exemptions instead of 4.

Exemptions increased.   An employee *may* (but is not required to) file an amended certificate increasing the number of exemptions if he becomes entitled to more exemptions than those originally claimed.

> **Example 3:**   Barnes, a married employee, with one dependent, has on file a Form W-4 properly claiming three withholding exemptions. On June 15, a second child is born. Barnes may (but is not required to) furnish his employer with a new Form W-4 claiming four exemptions instead of three. The law prescribes no specific time for filing the new certificate.

When employer gives effect to amended certificate.   The employer *may* give effect to a new certificate filed by the employee for any wages *paid after* it is furnished. He *must* give effect to it by the "status determination date" (Jan. 1, May 1, July 1 and Oct. 1 of each year) if the new certificate is filed at least 30 days before that date [Sec. 3402(f)(3)(B); 31.3402(f)(3)-1].

> **Example 4:**   In Example 2, the employer must give effect to the new certificate for the first wages paid on or after July 1, but he may give effect to it for any wages paid on or after the date he gets the new certificate.

Footnotes appear at end of this Chapter.

¶ 2506

Marital status. An employee can give his employer a Form W-4 showing he is married only if that is his status on that date. A person who is married to a nonresident alien, or is legally separated or divorced under a final decree is single for withholding purposes. A person is considered married if a "surviving spouse", or if his spouse died during the tax year [Sec. 3402(1); 31.3402(f)(1)-1(c)].

(c) Certification of nontaxability. An employee who had no tax liability last year and anticipates none this year may complete an exemption certificate on Forms W-4 or W-4E, claiming exemption from withholding. An employer cannot withhold income tax from an employee who has filed a properly executed form [Sec. 3402(n); 31.3402(n)-1].

NOTE: The exemption does not affect the liability for social security taxes.

¶ **2507 Records.** All required records must be retained until the later of four years after the tax is paid or after the due date of the tax. Records relating to a claim for refund, credit or abatement should be held until four years after the claim is filed [Sec. 31.6001-1].

(a) Employers. Employer records must show the persons employed during the year, their account numbers, addresses, wages and reported tips subject to withholding, periods of employment, and amounts and dates of payments and deductions [Sec. 31.6001-5]. Withholding exemption certificates and employees' notices of changes in status should also be kept.

(b) Employees generally are not required to keep records (except for claims) but they should retain the duplicate copy of the Form W-2 furnished by their employer [Sec. 31.6001-1(d)].

¶ **2508 Statements to employees, Form W-2.** An employer must give each employee two copies of the Wage and Tax Statement, Form W-2, or Form W-2P for those requesting withholding of annuity or pension payments, ¶ 2504(k), by January 31 of each calendar year. They must be given (even though no social security or income tax is withheld) if wages equal or exceed one withholding exemption. This applies if an employee is covered by certain deferred compensation plans [¶ 1838].[1] Form W-2 must also be given even if an employer withholds no tax from an employee who files a proper certificate of nontaxability (¶ 2506(c)) [Sec. 6051; 31.6051-1]. Penalties are imposed for fraudulent statements and failure to furnish statements [¶ 2512].

(a) What to include. Form W-2 must show the wages paid (including tips reported) and the taxes deducted during the preceding year for income and social security taxes. It must include the name and address of employer and employee, employer's identification number and the employee's account number (¶ 3500) [Sec. 6051(a); 31.6051-1(a), 31.6109-1].

Other compensation must be reported on Form W-2 even though not subject to withholding. This includes traveling and other expense allowances, moving expense reimbursements unless included as wages, group-term life insurance premiums to the extent includible in the employee's gross income, certain noncash prizes or awards to retail commission salespersons and employer contributions to individual retirement accounts whether or not deductible by employee [¶ 2503(a)].[1]

Wage continuation payments made directly by the employer under a "plan" must be included in the wages shown, regardless of whether tax was withheld on such payments [Sec. 31.6051-1(a)(1)(iii)]. Wage continuation payments made by persons who control wage payments [¶ 2501] (not including payments made for nonresident aliens or foreign partnerships, and corporations not doing business in the U.S.) need not be reported on Form W-2 [Sec. 31.6051-1(a)(1)(iv)].

Social security tax. Wages subject to social security tax should be shown separately, unless the wages subject to income tax were also subject to social security tax up to the maximum amount [¶ 3818(a)].

Tips. The amount required to be shown on Form W-2 includes only the tips (cash or charge) reported to the employer [Sec. 6051; 31.6051-1(a)(1)(vi)]. However, the Form must show the uncollected social security tax. For tips required to be reported to the employer, see ¶ 2503(a).

Adjustments made during the year for incorrect W-2 Forms of prior years should be indicated on the current form. Forms marked "corrected by employer" should be given to the employee for those years involved. Corrected forms not delivered to employees must be filed with the Revenue Service ((d) below) [Sec. 31.6051-1].

Armed Forces. A statement must be furnished covering pay for service in the Armed Forces if any tax is withheld or if any taxable compensation was paid. It must show (1) the total taxable compensation paid and (2) the tax withheld [Sec. 6051(b); 31.6051-1(a)(2)].

Employer going out of business. An employer who goes out of business ordinarily must furnish a Form W-2 to each employee by the 30th day after the day final payment is made [Sec. 31.6051-1(d)]. However, if another employer acquires the business, and the employees' services are continued, the predecessor employer may be relieved from furnishing the W-2 forms, if the successor employer agrees. In that case, all wages paid by both employers (including "other compensation" paid or the uncollected employee tax on tips) are included in the W-2 form given to the employees by the successor employer.[2] No Revenue Service consent is required. See also ¶ 2509(c).

(b) When employment ends. If an employee's services are ended or the expectation of further work ceases, the duplicate Form W-2 generally must be given to the employee within 30 days after the last payment of wages [Sec. 6051(a); 31.6051-1(d)(1)], unless the employment is only interrupted and both the employer and employee expect further employment.[3]

(c) Extension of time. The Revenue Service may extend for a reasonable time the due date for furnishing the employee's Form W-2. It cannot be more than 6 months except for taxpayers abroad [Sec. 6081(a)]. The application must be filed when the Form W-2 would be given to the employee. It must be in writing, signed by the employer or his agent, and must state detailed reasons for the request [Sec. 31.6051-1(d)(2)].

(d) Filing requirements. *Employees* must attach the tax return copy of each statement they receive to their final income tax return for the year. If the employee gets an additional Form W-2 after filing his return, he must file an amended return with the Form W-2 attached. An employer may replace lost or destroyed copies, marked "Reissued by Employer."[1]

Employers must make a reasonable effort to deliver the Form W-2 to an employee. Mailing it to the last known address is enough. If it cannot be delivered, it should be kept as part of the employer's records for four years.[4]

Footnotes appear at end of this Chapter.

¶ 2508

RETURNS AND PAYMENT OF TAXES WITHHELD

An employer required to withhold income taxes from wages or liable for social security taxes must make a quarterly return on Form 941. When to deposit the withheld taxes depends on the total amount withheld. The time for filing the quarterly return depends on whether the tax is paid by timely deposit. There are civil and criminal penalties for failing to file returns or pay the tax.

¶ **2509 How the employer reports and pays the tax. (a) When deposits are made.** Combined withheld taxes and employer-employee social security taxes are paid into an authorized bank with a preinscribed Federal Tax Deposit Form designating Form 501 (Form 511 for agricultural workers). The date of receipt by the authorized bank determines the timeliness of the deposit (¶ 3523) [Sec. 31.6302(c)-1(a)(3)]. A deposit mailed two or more days before the due date is timely even though received after the due date [Sec. 7502(e)]. The amount of tax withheld determines the frequency of deposits. Large employers must make 4 deposits each month.

NOTE: Proposed rules would require employers with employment taxes of less than $25,000 in a prior calendar quarter to make a deposit within 7 calendar days after any day during the current calendar quarter withheld taxes were $2,000 or more. The proposal would also eliminate the 90% exception [Proposed Reg. Sec. 31.6302(c)-1].

Weekly undeposited taxes of $2,000 or more. A deposit is required within 3 banking days after the end of a quarter-monthly period if combined withheld taxes and employee-employer social security taxes for the period are $2,000 or more. This includes the tax for periods since the start of the calendar quarter, excluding quarter-monthly periods for which deposits were already made. A quarter-monthly period ends on the 7th, 15th, 22d and last day of the month [Sec. 31.6302(c)-1(a)(1)].

Example 1: During April, Smith's taxes for each quarter-monthly period were $3,000. He had to deposit the $3,000 within 3 banking days after April 7, 15, 22 and 30.

Example 2: During January and February, Jones collected withheld taxes and social security, making required deposits as follows:

Period	Liability	Deposit amount and due date
Jan. 1-7	$1,500	Add to next period
Jan. 8-15	1,700	$3,200 by Jan. 18
Jan. 16-22	2,100	$2,100 by Jan. 25
Jan. 23-31	1,800	Add to next period
Feb. 1-7	1,700	$3,500 by Feb. 10
Feb. 8-15	1,200	Add to next period
Feb. 16-22	1,600	$2,800 by Feb. 25
Feb. 23-28	2,000	$2,000 by Mar. 3

Local banking holidays, Saturdays, Sundays and legal holidays in the District of Columbia are excluded in counting the 3 banking days.[1] The deposit requirements are considered met if: (1) at least 90% of the actual tax liability for the period is deposited, and (2) resulting underpayments for the first and second month of each calendar are added to the first required deposit made after the 15th of the following month [Sec. 31.6302(c)-1(a)]. Any underpayment for a quarter-monthly period occurring during the third month of the quarter that is $200 or more must be deposited by the end of the next month. An overdeposit of employment taxes because of incorrect estimate of tax liability may be applied to reduce the amount of tax required to be deposited for a later period.[2]

Undeposited taxes for first two months of calendar quarter of $200 or more. A deposit is required within 15 days after the end of the month if at the end of the first or second month of a quarter the total amount of undeposited taxes for the quarter is $200 or more and less than $2,000. This does not apply if a deposit was made for a quarter-monthly period that occurred during the month under the $2,000 rule [Sec. 31.6302(c)-1(a)]. For deposits involving the last month of the calendar quarter, see below.

Example 3: During the second quarter, Brown's taxes for April and May totaled $300 each. He must deposit $300 within 15 days after both April 30 and May 31.

Undeposited taxes for calendar quarter of $200 or more. A deposit is required on or before the last day of the next month if the total amount of undeposited taxes is $200 or more at the end of the quarter. If $2,000 or more, see above [Sec. 31.6302(c)-1(a)].

This rule would also apply to taxpayers who have made deposits for either of the first two months of a calendar quarter (see above).

Example 4: During the second quarter of the year, Green's taxes for each month were $75. He must deposit $225 on or before July 31.

Example 5: During February and March, Carr collected withheld taxes and social security, making required deposits as follows:

Period	Liability	Deposit amount and due date
Feb. 1-7	$50	Add to next period
Feb. 8-15	55	Add to next period
Feb. 16-22	50	Add to next period
Feb. 23-28	60	$215 by Mar. 15
Mar. 1-7	50	Add to next period
Mar. 8-15	55	Add to next period
Mar. 16-22	55	Add to next period
Mar. 23-31	60	$220 by April 30

Undeposited taxes for quarter of less than $200. An early deposit is not required. It can be either included with the quarterly return submitted to the Revenue Service [(b) below] or deposited.

(b) When to file quarterly return. The quarterly return, Form 941 (with exceptions), and payment are due by the last day of the month following the period covered by the return. However, if timely deposits in full payment are made for all 3 months of a quarter, the employer is allowed 10 additional days for filing [Sec. 31.6071(a)-1]. Form 942 is used for withholding on wages of domestics (unless the employer has elected to use Form 941), and Form 943 is used for farm workers' pay (¶ 2503(b); 2504(j)) [Sec. 31.6011(a)-4(a)]. State and local government employers and tax-exempt organizations that do not report social security taxes to the Revenue Service should use Form 941E to report income taxes withheld. Those paying pensions and annuities with no employees covered by social security should also use Form 941E [¶ 2504(k)].

Quarters	Quarter ending	Due date	Due date if timely deposits have been made
Jan.-Feb.-Mar.	March 31	April 30	May 10
Apr.-May-June	June 30	July 31	Aug. 10
July-Aug.-Sept.	Sept. 30	Oct. 31	Nov. 10
Oct.-Nov.-Dec.	Dec. 31	Jan. 31	Feb. 10

Footnotes appear at end of this Chapter.

¶ 2509

Amounts deposited with banks are credited against the taxes shown on the quarterly return [Sec. 6302(c); 31.6302(c)-1].

(c) **Where return is filed.** The return is filed with the Regional Service Center where the employer's principal place of business or legal residence in the U.S. is located. If there is no address in the U.S., return is filed with the Regional Service Center at Philadelphia, Pa. Employers located outside the U.S. file with the Director of International Operations, Washington, D.C. 20225 or, if located in the Virgin Islands or Puerto Rico, with the Director of Internal Operations, United States Internal Revenue Service, Hato Rey, Puerto Rico 00917. Permission to file in other districts may be granted [Sec. 31.6091-1].

Withholding tax statements. The employer must file the Revenue Service's copy of each withholding statement on Form W-2 (or W-2P) for wages paid during the calendar year (as well as any corrected statements for prior years), together with Form W-3, Reconciliation of Income Tax Withheld from Wages, by the end of February following the calendar year for which the return is made [Sec. 31.6071(a)-1]. Form W-3 must be accompanied by a list of the amounts of income tax withheld. The Revenue Service prefers an adding machine tape. The Revenue Service's copies of corrected Forms W-2 for a prior year must be kept separate from the forms for the current year and must be accompanied by a statement explaining the corrections [Sec. 31.6011(a)-4(b)].

Final return. The final return of an employer who goes out of business or ceases to pay wages must be marked "final return." The return must be accompanied by a statement indicating where required records will be kept, the name and address of the person who will keep them. If the business has been sold, the name and address of the purchaser and the date of sale must be stated [Sec. 31.6011(a)-6]. Copies of Form W-2 (or W-2P) and Form W-3, also must be filed as for a fourth quarter return. However, if both employers agree, the successor must furnish the W-2 Forms to employees working for both employers. When filing Forms 941 and W-3, the successor must include the predecessor's name, address, identification number and refer to Rev. Proc. 69-9. The prior employer does the same as to the successor employer when filing his Forms 941 and W-3. He also must file W-2 Forms for those employees who worked only for him.[3] See also ¶ 2508(a).

Seasonal employers and those who only temporarily stop paying wages continue filing returns even though no tax is reported [Sec. 31.6011(a)-6(a)].

(d) **Employers who fail to collect or pay tax.** Any employer failing to pay over employee tax or income tax withheld from wages, or who fails to make deposits, payments or tax returns may be required to deposit the taxes in a special trust account for the U.S. Government [Sec. 7512; 301.7512-1]. In addition, monthly returns, Form 941-M, and monthly payments of tax may be required. In this case, the employer's quarterly returns are filed on Schedule A of Form 941-M. Severe penalties are provided for failing to make deposits and payments (¶ 2512) [Sec. 31.6011(a)-5(a), 31.6071(a)-1, 31.6151-1(a), 31.6302(c)-1].

December return. If a return for December, or a final return, is filed, the employer must also file an information statement (Form W-3M) and the Revenue Service copies of Form W-2 for the year, by the last day of the following month [Sec. 31.6011(a)-5(b)(2)].

(e) **Extension of time.** Generally, there is no extension of time to file any return or document. However, the Revenue Service, on application made by the due date, may extend the time up to 30 days for filing Form W-3 and its copies of Form W-2 [Sec. 31.6081(a)-1(a)(1), (3)]. No extension will be granted for payment of the tax [Sec. 31.6161(a)(1)-1]. When the due date falls on a Saturday, Sunday, or legal holiday, the next business day is the due date [Sec. 7503; 301.7503-1].

¶ **2510 Withholding adjustments.** Errors made by employers in withholding or paying the tax for any quarter may be adjusted without interest, in a later quarter of the same year [Sec. 6205(a)(1), 6413(a)(1)]. The method of making the adjustment depends on when the error was discovered.

(a) Errors found before quarterly return filed. If too little was withheld, the correct amount should be shown on the return and the undercollection deducted from the employee's next wage payment. If too much was withheld, a receipt should be taken from the employee showing date and amount of repayment to him. If repayment to the employee is not made before Form 941 is filed, the amount collected must be included in the return and the adjustment is made in the return for a following quarter [Sec. 31.6205-1(c), 31.6413(a)-1].

(b) Errors found after quarterly return filed. If the employer collects and pays more than the correct amount of the employee's tax, unless the employee has so agreed [¶ 2504(j)], the employer may adjust the overcollection by repaying or reimbursing the employee for the amount of the overcollection in any quarter of the same calendar year. The employer may also reimburse the employee by applying the overcollection against taxes to be withheld in any later quarter of the same calendar year [Sec. 31.6413(a)-1(b)(2)(ii)]. If the overcollection is repaid, a written receipt with the amount and date should be obtained and kept as part of the employer's records. The necessary adjustment is made by a deduction on the return for any later quarter of the same calendar year [Sec. 31.6413(a)-2(b)].

The employer may report an underpayment on the return for any later quarter of the same calendar year or file a supplemental return for the period when the wages were paid. An underpayment reported by the due date of the return for the period in which the error was found is considered an adjustment. If the error is not reported as an adjustment, the underpayment should be reported on the return for the next period in the calendar year or immediately on a supplemental return [Sec. 31.6205-1(c)(2)]. This is a correction and interest can be charged.

The employer may reimburse himself for an undercollection of tax by deductions from the employee's pay (whether or not it is wages) on or before the last day of the calendar year. The employer and employee can settle the item between themselves within the year, if the deduction is not made [Sec. 31.6205-1(c)(4)].

(c) Adjusting tax reported on tips. If the employer does not have enough wages or funds available to collect the correct amount of social security employee tax on tips, he should deduct the amount of uncollected tax as an adjustment on Form 941.[1]

¶ **2511 Refunds and credits.** When the employer pays the Revenue Service more than the amount withheld from his employees, he can get a refund or credit [Sec. 6402(a), 6414; 301.6402-1]; see ¶ 3621 et seq. The credit for an overpayment that was not withheld from the employee may be taken as a deduction, on a return of tax withheld, on Form 941. A statement explaining the deduction must be attached to the return [Sec. 31.6414-1].

(a) Employee refunds and credits. The amount withheld during the year from any employee is credited against his tax liability for the year. If the amount withheld exceeds the tax due, the excess will be refunded on timely application [Sec. 6401(b), 6402(a); 301.6402-2]. Fiscal year taxpayers must claim credit for the entire tax withheld during the calendar year that ends in the fiscal year for which the return is filed.[1]

Footnotes appear at end of this Chapter.

Special refund of social security tax. If more than $962.25 of social security tax (F.I.C.A.) is withheld from salary or wages in 1977, because the taxpayer worked for more than one employer, taxpayer gets a special refund. If he has to file an income tax return, the excess must be claimed as a credit against the income tax on the return form [Sec. 1.31-2]. Otherwise, a refund claim is filed [¶ 3626; 3627]. (See ¶ 2509(c) if employee has no U.S. residence.) [Sec. 31.6413(c)-1]. A refund also is allowed for excess hospital insurance tax when withheld under both the Railroad Retirement Act and F.I.C.A. [Sec. 6413(c)(3)]. See ¶ 3800; 3818.

(b) Nonresident aliens. Any withholding agent [¶ 2535(a)] who pays more than the correct amount withheld from nonresident aliens may file a claim for credit or refund of the overpayment on the appropriate Form [¶ 3626], or may claim a credit for the overpayment on Form 1042. The withholding agent cannot claim credit for the overpayment on Form 1042, if he files a claim for credit or refund on the appropriate Form or a claim for refund on Form 1042 [Sec. 301.6402-2, 1.6414-1].

NOTE: Before 7-1-76, Form 843 also was used for filing claims for income tax refund or credit.

¶ 2512 Penalties. An employer may be liable for penalties and interest for not collecting tax, not filing a return, not depositing taxes, nonpayment of tax, fraud in connection with withholding statements or for failing to supply taxpayer identifying numbers. He may also be subject to criminal penalties. An employee may be subject to criminal penalties for fraud on withholding exemption certificates.

(a) Employer penalties. The employer penalties are:

Failure to withhold. Employers are liable for payment of the tax that must be withheld [Sec. 3403; 31.3403-1], unless the employee later pays the tax. However, employer is liable for interest, or other penalties for failure to withhold, file the return and pay the amount withheld to the Revenue Service.[1] (See below) [Sec. 3402(d); 31.3402(d)-1]. He can be *penalized* an amount equal to the total amount of tax not collected or paid over if the failure is willful [Sec. 6672; 301.6672-1]. Interest runs from the date the tax was due to the earlier of, the next April 15, or the date the employee pays the tax.[2] A corporate officer may be held personally liable if he willfully fails to pay the tax.[3]

Employers are not liable for withholding on tips not reported to them by their employees on written statements [Sec. 3402(k); 31.3402(k)-1].

Failure to file return. Unless due to reasonable cause and not to willful neglect, penalty is 5% of the net amount due for delay up to 30 days, with an added 5% for each additional month or fraction (25% maximum penalty) [Sec. 6651(a); 301.6651-1]. If this penalty is assessed for an employer's failure to file Form 941 [¶ 2509], it runs from the return's due date to the date the Form is filed.[4] It is considered filed by the employer when prepared and executed by the Revenue Service. This stops the delinquency period.[5] Additional penalty of $1 must be paid for each copy of Form W-2 that taxpayer, without reasonable cause, fails to file on time [¶ 2509]; maximum penalty is $1,000 for any one year [Sec. 6652; 301.6652-1].

Failure to pay tax. Unless adjustment is made [¶ 2510], interest is charged at 7% (9% between 7-1-75 and 1-31-76; 6% before 7-1-75)[6] per annum from the date the tax became due until paid [Sec. 6601(a)]. An additional penalty is imposed for failure to pay the amount shown as tax on any return to which the penalty for failure to file applies, and for failure to pay a deficiency after notice; the penalty is 1/2% of the unpaid tax (less credits) for each month or fractional month of delinquency, with a maximum of 25%, unless failure is due to reasonable cause and not willful neglect [Sec. 6651(a), (b)]. If the amount demanded is paid within 10 days after notice and demand, interest will not be imposed for the period after the date of the notice [Sec. 6601(e)(4); 301.6601-1(f)(4)]. If the deficiency is due to fraud, the penalty is 50% of the unpaid tax. [Sec. 6653(b); 301.6653-1(b)]. The 50% penalty does not apply if the penalty for failure to withhold applies (see above) [Sec. 301.6672-1].

A $10,000 fine, or 5 years imprisonment, or both, can be imposed for a willful failure to collect or pay over taxes which should be withheld [Sec. 7202] or for any willful attempt to evade or defeat the tax [Sec. 7201]. It is a misdemeanor, punishable by a $10,000 fine, or one year imprisonment, or both, willfully to fail to make a required return or to pay a tax [Sec. 7203].

Fraudulent withholding statement or failure to furnish withholding statement. - The employer will, for each such failure, be subject to (1) a civil penalty of $50 *and* (2) a fine not more than $1,000, and/or imprisonment for not more than one year [Sec. 6674, 7204; 31.6674-1, 301.6674-1]. These penalties are instead of any other penalties that might otherwise be imposed. Ordinarily, a willfully fraudulent return is a felony carrying up to 3 years jail sentence, $5,000 fine, or both [Sec. 7206].

Failure to deposit taxes. For failure without reasonable cause to deposit tax in a government depositary, a penalty of 5% is imposed. The penalty does not continue beyond the due date of the return or the date the tax was paid, whichever is earlier [Sec. 6656].

If an employer fails to comply with a notice to collect and deposit the tax within two banking days thereafter [¶ 2509], it is a misdemeanor punishable by a $5,000 fine, a year in prison, or both. Compliance may be excused if there is reasonable doubt that a tax should be collected, who should collect it, or for circumstances beyond employer's control (not including lack of funds) [Sec. 7215].

(b) Employee penalties. Both civil and criminal penalties are imposed for supplying the employer with false or fraudulent information on the withholding exemption certificate [¶ 2506].

A civil penalty of $50 is imposed for claiming excess deductions or showing too little wages in claiming withholding allowances [¶ 2505(a)]. Only one $50 penalty is imposed even if the employee misstates both the amount of his itemized deductions and wages. However, the penalty does not apply if withholding is not reduced or the tax liability is paid by withholding and estimated taxes [Sec. 6682(a)].

A criminal penalty is imposed if false or fraudulent information is willfully given on the withholding exemption certificate or if there is an intentional failure to give information requiring increased withholding. The employee is subject to a fine up to $500, imprisonment for not over one year, or both [Sec. 7205].

(c) Taxpayer identifying numbers. There is a $5 penalty for each failure to include a required identifying number in a return or other tax document. See ¶ 3500.

DECLARATION AND PAYMENT OF ESTIMATED TAX BY INDIVIDUALS

The income tax of many individuals is not satisfied by withholding. They must file a declaration and pay an estimated tax in a lump sum or installments to keep on a current basis. A penalty may apply for underpaying estimated taxes.

¶ **2515 The declaration.** The declaration of estimated tax (Form 1040-ES) is a statement of what the taxpayer expects his tax to be for the year based on what he expects his income to be. (Corporations do not file declarations, but must make estimated tax payments [¶ 3523(a)].)

(a) What is estimated tax. The estimated tax is the amount of income tax a person figures he will pay, plus any self-employment tax [¶ 3821 et seq.], less any credits against his tax [¶ 2518].

Footnotes appear at end of this Chapter.

NOTE: The minimum tax on tax preferences (see ¶ 2403) is not part of the estimated tax [Sec. 6015(c)(1); Proposed Reg. 1.6015(c)-1].

(b) Changes during year. Changes in income or deductions may make the original estimate wrong. The estimate may be corrected by filing an amended declaration when the next installment of estimated tax is due. The later installments are ratably increased or decreased to reflect the change [¶ 2517]. If the error is due to a "substantial" underestimate, an amended declaration may be necessary to avoid penalties [¶ 2519].

If the final return for a tax year shows that the tax for the year was overestimated by the taxpayer, he will be entitled to a refund of the excess if there is no other tax due (for example, the first installment of the estimated tax for the succeeding tax year).

¶ 2516 Who must file a declaration. Individuals must file a declaration of estimated tax for a tax year, if the estimated tax is $100 or more and they expect to meet either the *gross income* requirement or expect to exceed *certain income levels* [Sec. 6015(a)(1), (2); 1.6015(a)-1(a)(1)].

Gross income. The gross income requirement is met if an individual estimates that there will be more than $500 of gross income not subject to withholding [Sec. 6015(a)(2); 1.6015(a)-1(a)(1)].

Income levels. The following are the gross income levels that are expected to be exceeded [Sec. 6015(a)(1); 1.6015(a)-1(a)(1)]:
1. $20,000 for a single person, including a head of household [¶ 1106], and a surviving spouse [¶ 1105].
2. $20,000 for a married person entitled to file a joint declaration with spouse, but only if the spouse did not receive wages during the tax year.
3. $10,000 for a married person entitled to file a joint declaration with spouse, but only if both received wages during the tax year.
4. $5,000 for a married person not entitled to file a joint declaration with spouse.

> **Problem:** Healy is married and is the sole support of his wife and 2 daughters. His wife has no gross income. Healy estimated 1978 wages of $19,000 subject to withholding and dividends of $275. Is he required to file a declaration for 1978?
>
> **Solution:** No. He is not required to file a declaration because (1) his gross income is not expected to exceed $20,000 and (2) his estimated income from sources other than wages subject to withholding is not in excess of $500.

NOTE: Expected income includes employees' transportation and per diem allowances in excess of expenses, when no tax is withheld.[1]

(a) Married couples. Husband and wife may file a joint declaration, but this does not require them to file a joint tax return. On a joint declaration, liability is both joint and several [Sec. 6015(b); 1.6015(b)-1]. This declaration may be filed even if one spouse has no gross income, but not if either spouse is a nonresident alien or has died, or if the couple have different tax years or are divorced or separated under a final decree.

A surviving spouse may figure the estimated tax as if a joint declaration had been filed for the tax year death occurred [Sec. 1.6015(b)-1(c)].

Credit for estimated tax paid. If a husband and wife make a joint declaration but do not file a joint return, payments of estimated tax may be applied against the tax liability of either, or divided between them as they see fit. If they do not agree on the division, the payments are allocated in proportion to the tax paid on separate returns [Sec. 6015(b); 1.6015(b)-1].

(b) Declaration by agent. The declaration should be made by an authorized agent, guardian, or other person charged with the care of his person or property, when a taxpayer is unable to do it himself. A power of attorney must be filed with a declaration made by an agent [Sec. 6012(b)(2); 1.6015(a)-1(f)]. See also ¶ 3510.

(c) Declaration not required.

• *Corporations* do not file declarations, but must pay estimated taxes; see Ch. 25.

• *Estates and trusts* do not file declarations [Sec. 6015; 1.6015(h)-1], and no declaration need be filed after a decedent dies [Sec. 1.6015(g)-1(a)(4)].

• *Nonresident aliens* do not file declarations unless withholding applies to their wages, they have effectively connected income, or they have resided in Puerto Rico during the entire tax year [Sec. 1.6015(a)-1(d)].

• *Partnerships* do not file declarations, but *partners* must include in their declarations an estimate of their distributive share of the profits.

¶ 2517 Filing declaration and payment of estimated tax. A taxpayer required to file a declaration must file it on Form 1040-ES with an Internal Revenue Service Center. Installment payments are sent with an Estimated Tax Declaration-Voucher included in the Form 1040-ES. The Revenue Service does not send out periodic statements of taxes due [Sec. 1.6073-1(c)].

(a) Declaration and payment for 1978. The declaration for the *calendar year* 1978 is due by April 17, 1978 [Sec. 6073(a); 1.6073-1]. See special rule for farmers, fishermen and for fiscal year taxpayers ((c) and (d) below). When the due date falls on Saturday, Sunday or legal holiday, the next business day is the due date [¶ 3517].

If the requirements are first met after April 1, 1978, the original declaration is to be filed according to the following schedule [Sec. 6073(a); 1.6073-1]:

Requirement first met after	and	before	Declaration is to be filed on or before
April 1		June 2	June 15
June 1		Sept. 2	Sept. 15
Sept. 1			Jan. 15, 1979

Early income tax return as declaration. A calendar year taxpayer who first meets the requirement for filing a declaration after September 1, 1978, may file the annual income tax return on or before January 31, 1979, pay the tax due, and it will be treated as the declaration on amended declaration, that otherwise would have been due [Sec. 6015(f); 1.6015(f)-1]. For farmers and fishermen, see (c) below; for fiscal year returns, see (d) below.

When payments are due. The payment for a declaration filed 4-17-78 is due in 4 equal installments on 4-17-78, 6-15-78, 9-15-78 and 1-15-79. For declarations filed 6-15-78, the payment is due in 3 equal installments on 6-15-78, 9-15-78 and 1-15-79. For a declaration filed 9-15-78, the payment is due in 2 equal installments on 9-15-78 and 1-15-79. For a declaration filed on 1-15-79, payment in full is due with the declaration (but the taxpayer may instead file an early return, with payment, by 1-31-79 as explained above) [Sec. 6153; 1.6153-1].

NOTE: If a declaration is not made on time, all of the past due installments are payable immediately and the balances are due and payable as described above.

A credit for overpayment of the previous year's income tax may be applied against the first installment or equally divided among all the installments.[1]

Footnotes appear at end of this Chapter.

(b) Amended declarations. If a taxpayer has to amend an original declaration, the amendment should be filed where the original declaration was filed, by the fifteenth day of the last month of any quarter following the quarter in which a declaration was filed. However, an amendment after September 15 of the tax year may be filed by January 15 of the next year [Sec. 6015(e); 1.6015(e)-1].

Filing a final return and paying the tax in full by January 31 takes the place of a declaration or amendment due January 15. This will not avoid penalties incurred for the earlier declaration dates, but it stops the accrual of additional penalties as of January 15 [Sec. 6015(f); 1.6015(f)-1]. For farmers and fishermen, see (c) below; for fiscal year taxpayers, see (d) below.

Successive amendments may be made during the year, but not more than one may be made in each quarter [Sec. 1.6015(e)-1].

Example 1: Ade files his declaration on April 17, 1978. One amendment may be made during each of the following periods:

April 17 to June 15, 1978
June 16 to Sept. 15, 1978
Sept. 16, 1978 to Jan. 15, 1979

Example 2 (decrease): Taxpayer filed a 1978 declaration on April 17, 1978, showing an estimated tax of $800. An amended declaration was later filed reducing the estimated tax by $150. The amount payable on each installment date will depend on the time of filing the amendment:

(a) Amendment filed June 15, 1978:
Original estimated tax		$800
Reduction by amended declaration		150
Revised estimated tax		$650
Paid on April 17, 1978		200
Unpaid balance		$450
Remaining payments due:		
June 15, 1978	$150	
September 15, 1978	150	
January 15, 1979	150	
	$450	

(b) Amendment filed September 15, 1978:
Revised estimated tax		$650
Payments April 17 and June 15 at $200 each		400
Unpaid balance		$250
Remaining payments due:		
September 15, 1978	$125	
January 15, 1979	125	
	$250	

(c) Amendments filed after September 15, 1978:
Revised estimated tax	$650
Payments April 17, June 15 and September 15, at $200 each	600
Balance payable January 15, 1979	$ 50

Example 3 (increase): Taxpayer filed a 1978 declaration on April 17, 1978, showing an estimated tax of $600. An amended declaration was later filed increasing the estimated tax by $300. Installments will be payable on the dates and in the amounts illustrated below, depending upon the time of filing the amendment.

(a) Amendments filed June 15, 1978:
Original estimated tax	$600
Increase by amended declaration	300
Revised estimated tax	$900
Paid on April 17, 1978	150
Unpaid balance	$750
Remaining payments due:	

June 15, 1978	$250	
September 15, 1978	250	
January 15, 1979	250	
	$750	

(b) Amendment filed September 15, 1978:

Revised estimated tax		$900
Payments April 17 and June 15 at $150 each		300
Unpaid balance		$600

Remaining payments due:

September 15, 1978	$300	
January 15, 1979	300	
	$600	

(c) Amendment filed after September 15, 1978:

Revised estimated tax		$900
Payments April 17, June 15 and September 15, at $150 each		450
Unpaid balance		$450

Since the amendment was made after September 15, the $450 unpaid balance of estimated tax is payable immediately upon filing the amended declaration on or before January 15, 1979.

Amended declarations may be made on page 1 (Amended Computation schedule) of Form 1040-ES. The amended estimated tax must be shown in Block A of the next declaration-voucher filed.[1]

(c) Farmers and fishermen are allowed to file a declaration and pay their estimated tax (for a calendar year) by January 15th of the next year when at least two-thirds of their estimated gross income comes from farming or fishing. They can also file an income tax return [¶ 3517] and pay the tax by March 1 of the next year instead of filing a declaration [Sec. 6015(f), 6073(b); 1.6015(f)-1, 1.6073-1(b)]. Wages paid to a farm employee are not gross income from farming, so the special filing dates for farmers do not apply to his declaration of estimated taxes.[2]

(d) Fiscal year taxpayers substitute corresponding months in their fiscal year instead of those indicated for filing the original declaration and amendments and for paying the installments by calendar year taxpayers [Sec. 6073(e); 1.6073-2, 1.6153-2]. Thus, for a fiscal year starting July 1, the month corresponding to April would be October (fourth month of fiscal year).

Example 4: Holt's fiscal year begins Oct. 1, 1978. His declaration for the fiscal year is due Jan. 15, 1979, together with a quarterly installment of his estimated tax. The other 3 installments are due Mar. 15, June 15 and Oct. 17, 1979.

(e) Extension of time. The District Director may extend the due date for filing and payment. It is limited to six months, except when the taxpayer is abroad [Sec. 6081(a); 1.6073-4, 1.6081-(a), 1.6153-4]. No interest is charged [Sec. 6601(f); 301.6601-1(f)(5)].

(f) Nonresident aliens required to file a declaration of estimated tax use Form 1040-ES (OIO) and file it with the Internal Revenue Service Center, Philadelphia, Pa. 19155.

NOTE: Nonresident aliens who do not have wages subject to withholding can file estimated returns by June 15, the due date of the return (¶ 3522(b)) [Sec. 6073(a)]. Before 1977, the estimated returns were due first by April 15.

¶ **2518 How to figure estimated tax.** In his declaration, the taxpayer must estimate his tax for the year and reduce it by estimated withholding and other

Footnotes appear at end of this Chapter.

¶ **2518**

credits against his tax [Sec. 6015(c); 1.6015(c)-1, 1.6015(d)-1]. He should consider all available facts that will affect his income, deductions, and credits during the year.[1] In estimating his tax before reducing it for estimated withholding and other credits he may use:

- Last year's income tax and any self-employment tax.
- Last year's income using current rates and exemptions.
- Annualizing income.
- Actual estimate.

For the lowest amount of estimated taxes that must be paid to avoid penalties, see ¶ 2519.

Example 1: Carl Sanders, age 66, is single and is employed at a salary of $520 a week. On April 17, 1978, he files his 1977 income tax return, and also a joint declaration of estimated tax for 1978, estimating that his salary in 1978 will total $27,500 and that he will receive other income (taxable interest on bonds) of $3,100. He estimates that his excess itemized deductions will amount to $1,000. He also estimates that $6,635 will be withheld from his salary from January 1, to December 31, 1978. The declaration of estimated tax filed by Sanders for 1978 will show an estimated tax of $915 as follows:

Estimated salary	$27,500
Estimated other income	3,100
Estimated gross income	$30,600
Less: Excess itemized deductions ($1,000) plus deductions for exemptions ($1,500)	2,500
Estimated taxable income	$28,100
Tax on $28,100 before credits	$ 7,550
Less estimated withholding on salary	6,635
Estimated tax payable	$ 915

The $915 will be payable in 4 equal installments of $228.75 each on April 17, June 15, September 15, 1978 and January 15, 1979.

Example 2: Assume that Sanders in Example 1, discovers in May 1978 that his actual income is running above the estimated income in the declaration of April 17, and that the estimated tax will be $90 higher ($1,005 instead of $915). He will file an amended declaration on June 15, 1978, and pay $228.75 plus a prorated part of the $90 increase, or $30. Thus, the June 15th installment will total $258.75. If the actual income is running under the estimate made in the declaration in April, the remaining installments would be proportionately reduced. See ¶ 2517(b).

¶ 2519 Penalties for underpaying estimated taxes. There is no penalty for failing to *file* a declaration of estimated tax [Sec. 6651(d)]. However, there is a charge of 7% (9% between 7-1-75 and 1-31-76; 6% before 7-1-75)[1] a year for underpaying the estimated tax. This cannot be deducted as interest.[2] The penalty can be avoided for a given installment, if the installment qualifies under any one of four exceptions. A different test may be applied to each installment to avoid the penalty.

NOTE: For individuals, until 4-15-77, there is relief from additions to tax, interest and penalties (but not liability for tax) for Tax Reform Act changes applying to 1976.

(a) How to avoid the underpayment penalty. The taxpayer adds all estimated payments and withholdings for the current year that are made on or before the installment due date. There is no penalty for underpayment if they equal or exceed the smallest amount that would be due by the installment due date if the estimated tax (including self-employment tax) were any of the following [Sec. 6654(d); 1.6654-2]:

1. Last year's tax. This is the regular tax shown on last year's return (if one was filed and it covered 12 months) plus any self-employment tax. The payment on the due date for the current year's first installment must equal or exceed 25% of

last year's tax. Payments on the due dates of the current year's succeeding installments must be at least 50%, 75% and 100% respectively [¶ 2517(a)].

Example 1: Brown's return for last year showed a tax of $2,760 (unreduced by withholdings and estimated tax payments). By June 15 of the current year, he paid 2 installments of $250 each and had $900 withheld. The second installment is penalty-free since the estimated tax plus withholding ($500 + $900) exceeds 50% of last year's tax ($1,380).

2. A tax based on last year's income, but at current rates and exemptions. This exception applies even if there was no taxable income because of a net operating loss carryover.[3] Since facts shown on the prior year's return apply, except for rates and exemptions, income averaging used in that return would be a factor.[4] The payments on the due date for the current year's installment are the same as (1) above.

Example 2: Assume the same facts as in Example 1, except that (a) withholding up to June 15 was $1,000 and (b) last year's recomputed tax was $2,970 because Brown has one less exemption for the current year. The second installment is penalty-free since estimated tax plus withholdings ($500 + $1,000) exceeds 50% of the recomputed tax ($1,485).

3. 80% (66⅔% for farmers and fishermen) of the total tax (including any self-employment tax) figured by annualizing the income received during the year up to the month in which the installment is due [Prop. Reg. Sec. 1.6654-1]. The payment on the due date for the current year's first installment must equal or exceed 20% of the tax figured on the annualized income. For succeeding installments, payments must be at least 40%, 60% and 80% of the annualized tax.

4. 90% of the tax (including any self-employment tax) figured at current rates on taxable income for the period ending before the month in which the installment is due [Sec. 6015(c)(1); Prop. Reg. 1.6015(c)-1].

➤**OBSERVATION**➤ The first two exceptions are most advantageous when the current year's income is greater than that of the prior year. Taxpayer may not adjust the amount figured under these exceptions by eliminating the tax from capital gains or other nonrecurring items received during the prior year. The last two exceptions are most useful if the greater part of income is received in the latter part of the year. They require an accurate determination of income and deductions for the computation period under taxpayer's method of accounting. For instance, if amount of a year-end bonus is determined in last month of the year, it should be deducted only for the final installment period. Also, cost of goods sold generally is allocated to the period in the ratio of gross receipts from sales for the year to gross receipts for the period.

The year's withholdings are equally divided between the installment periods, unless taxpayer proves a different allocation, or unless more than one tax year begins in a calendar year [Sec. 6654(e)(2); 1.6654-1(a)(3)]. This allows a taxpayer to adjust his withholding to avoid a penalty. See also ¶ 2504(j).

Partnerships. Partners must include an estimate of income from the partnership, along with other estimated income. When applying tests 3 or 4, a partner includes the following in his income for the period: (1) his distributive share of partnership items under Sec. 702; (2) guaranteed payments from the partnership; and (3) gains and losses on partnership distributions treated as gains and losses on sales of property [Sec. 1.6654-2(d)(2)].

Beneficiary of estate or trust who applies tests 3 or 4 includes in income his share of currently distributable estate or trust income for the period (whether or not distributed) and actual distributions of income not currently distributable [Sec. 1.6654-2(d)(2)].

Footnotes appear at end of this Chapter.

¶ 2519

Form 2210. Computations relating to the penalty and the exceptions may be made on Form 2210. It should be attached to the return in case of any underpayment and a reliance on the exceptions [Sec. 1.6654-1].

(b) How the penalty is applied. The 7% (9% between 7-1-75 and 1-31-76; 6% before 7-1-75)[1] penalty for underpaying estimated taxes is figured separately for each installment, on the difference between the amount actually paid and the amount that should have been paid if the estimated tax were 80% (66⅔% for farmers and fishermen) of the amount shown on the final return. The charge runs until the amount is paid or until the filing date of the tax return, whichever is earlier. Any overpayment is first a payment of prior underpayments, and the excess is credited to later installments [Sec. 1.6654-1]. The penalty may be assessed and collected without a deficiency notice [¶ 3618(a)], except when no income tax return has been filed. [Sec. 6659(b)]. Even if the underestimate is due to reasonable cause, the penalty will be imposed.[5]

Example 3: A store owner with a net tax payable (without regard to prepaid taxes) of $40,000 on his final return, pays four equal installments of estimated tax of $6,000 during the year. (He has no withholding.) Since what he pays in each quarter is less than $8,000 ($40,000 × 80% × ¼), the penalty charge applies to each quarter and would be figured as follows:

1.	Net tax payable (without regard to prepaid taxes)	$40,000.00
2.	80% of item 1	$32,000.00
3.	¼ of item 2	$ 8,000.00
4.	Less quarterly prepayment	$ 6,000.00
5.	Balance on which charge is figured	$ 2,000.00
6.	Additional charge:	
	(a) 1st quarter ($2,000 at 7% for 365 days)	$ 140.00
	(b) 2nd quarter ($2,000 at 7% for 304 days)	$ 116.60
	(c) 3rd quarter ($2,000 at 7% for 212 days)	$ 81.32
	(d) 4th quarter ($2,000 at 7% for 90 days)	$ 34.52
	Total	$ 372.44

If the storekeeper had paid $1,000 on the first installment, $9,000 on the second installment, and $8,000 each on the third and fourth installments, the 7% penalty would first be applied on the $7,000 which was underpaid on the first installment for a period of 2 months, and then on the remaining $6,000 until the date it is paid or until the filing date of the income tax return, April 15 of the following year, whichever is earlier.

In addition to the 7% (9% between 7-1-75 and 1-31-76; 6% before 7-1-75)[1] charge, willful failure to *pay* estimated taxes is a misdemeanor punishable by a fine of $10,000, or jail for not more than one year, or both [Sec. 7203].

SPECIAL PROBLEMS

Withholding may also be required for payments to nonresident aliens.

¶ 2535 Payments to nonresident aliens. Payments (except wages) to nonresident aliens may be exempt from withholding, if the income is effectively connected with a trade or business in the U.S. (see (b) below). Wages paid to a nonresident alien for services in the U.S. are subject to withholding [¶ 2503 et seq.]. In addition, withholding may be required for certain periodic payments from U.S. sources. Generally, withholding on these periodic payments is at least at a 30% rate [Sec. 1441, 1442; 1.1441-1—1.1441-4, 1.1442-1]. See also ¶ 3711.

(a) Who must withhold. Those responsible for withholding are called "withholding agents." This means any U.S. citizens, resident alien or resident fiduciary making the income payments. It also includes resident partnerships, U.S. and resident foreign corporations [Sec. 1465; 1.1465-1].

A corporation that pays dividends may assume that a shareholder is a resident or citizen of the U.S. when his address is in the U.S., if it does not know his status. If the address is a foreign one, or changed from a foreign one to one in the U.S., tax must be withheld, unless a written statement is obtained [Sec. 1.1441-3(b)(3)].

(b) Payments subject to withholding. Withholding may be required on fixed or determinable periodical income. This includes dividends, interest, rents, royalties, premiums, annuities, remuneration, emoluments and other income of this type. In addition, withholding may be required on the gross amount of certain items considered to be gains from the sale or exchange of capital assets. These generally include lump-sum distributions from exempt employees' trust and annuity plans [¶ 1232(c); 3024(d)]; royalties on the sale of timber, coal or domestic iron ore [¶ 1621; 1623]; and contingent income from the sale of patents and other intangibles. Income from original discount on bonds issued after 9-28-65 [¶ 1630] may also be subject to withholding [Sec. 1441].

Income effectively connected with U.S. trade or business. Withholding on payments (except wages, ¶ 2503) to nonresident aliens is *not* required, if: (a) the income is effectively connected with the nonresident alien's U.S. trade or business and is includable in his gross income, and (b) he files a withholding exemption statement with the withholding agent (¶ 3711) [Sec. 1441(c); 1.1441-4].

Withholding rates. When withholding is required, the rate is generally 30% of the income items, unless a lower treaty rate applies [¶ 2537]. The withholding rates on wages paid to nonresident aliens for services in the U.S. are the same as for U.S. citizens. Special rules apply to original issue discount bonds [¶ 1630] held by foreign taxpayers. Foreign students and exchange visitors are subject to a 14% withholding rate on the taxable portion of their scholarships or grants [Sec. 1441, 1442; 1.1441-1, 1.1441-2, 1.1441-4(b)(1)].

(c) Who is subject to withholding. Withholding on *noneffectively connected* income applies to nonresident alien individuals (including alien residents of Puerto Rico), foreign partnerships and foreign corporations. Foreign students and exchange visitors are subject to the same withholding rates as other nonresident aliens except for the taxable portion of their scholarships or grants (¶ 1303) [Sec. 1441; 1.1441-1, 1.1441-2].

¶ 2536 Returns and payment of tax withheld. Tax withheld on payments to nonresident alien individuals, foreign partnerships or foreign corporations must be reported by the withholding agent on Form 1042. In addition, there is also an information return (Form 1042S) to be submitted. These are filed with the Director, Internal Revenue Service Center, Philadelphia, Pennsylvania [Sec. 1461; 1.1461-3].

The withholding agent deposits withheld taxes into an authorized bank using a Federal Tax Deposit Form designating Form 512 under rules similar to the rules for deposits of withheld income and employment taxes at ¶ 2509(a) [Sec. 1.1461-3, 1.1461-4, 1.6302-2].

A nonresident alien, foreign partnership or corporation must file a Form 4224 to get an exemption from withholding on effectively connected income.

¶ 2537 Tax treaties on withholding rates. Lower withholding rates are provided in a number of tax conventions with foreign countries. To obtain the lesser treaty rate or exemption, the receipt must file Form 1001 with the withholding agent [¶ 2535(a)]. The reduced rate for dividends applies when the payor's records show the stockholder's address is in the foreign country concerned.[1]

Footnotes to Chapter 15

(P-H "FEDERAL TAXES" related references are cited in brackets [ ] at the end of each footnote below.)

Footnote ¶ 2501   [¶ 34,505 et seq.].
(1) Otte v. U.S., 419 US 43, 34 AFTR 2d 74-6194 [¶ 34,718].
(2) Firemen's Fund Indemnity Co. v. U.S., 210 F.2d 472, 45 AFTR 342 [¶ 34,717].
(3) Rev. Proc. 67-41, 1967-2 CB 677 [¶ 34,957].

Footnote ¶ 2502   [¶ 34,655 et seq.].
(1) Rev. Rul. 70-471, 1970-2 CB 199 [¶ 34,555].
(2) Rev. Rul. 60-77, 1960-1 CB 386 [¶ 34,697].
(3) Rev. Rul. 65-277, 1965-2 CB 393 [¶ 34,699].
(4) Rev. Rul. 71-144, 1971-1 CB 285 [¶ 34,666].

Footnote ¶ 2503   [¶ 34,520 et seq.].
(1) Rev. Rul. 70-471, 1970-2 CB 199 [¶ 34,555].
(2) Rev. Rul. 68-238, 1968-1 CB 420 [¶ 34,542].
(3) Rev. Rul. 66-41, 1966-1 CB 233 [¶ 34,582(c)].
(4) Rev. Rul. 73-351, 1973-2 CB 323 [¶ 34,582(c)].
(5) Rev. Rul. 61-68, 1961-1 CB 429 [¶ 34,813].
(6) Rev. Rul. 73-13, 1973-1 CB 42 [¶ 34,588].
(7) Rev. Rul. 69-136, 1969-1 CB 252 [¶ 34,542].
(8) Rev. Rul. 59-58, 1959-1 CB 17 [¶ 34,568].
(9) Rev. Rul. 60-378, 1960-2 CB 38 [¶ 34,528].
(10) U.S. v. Kaiser, 5 AFTR 2d 1608, 80 SCt. 1204; Rev. Rul. 61-136, 1961-2 CB 20; Rev. Rul. 68-424, 1968-2 CB 419 [¶ 7032(30); 34,576].
(11) Rev. Rul. 72-110, 1972-1 CB 24 [¶ 34,582(b)].
(12) Rev. Rul. 76-71, 1976-1 CB 308 [¶ 34,564].
(13) Rev. Rul. 72-268, 1972-1 CB 313 [¶ 34,554].
(14) Rev. Rul. 55-203, 1955-1 CB 114 [¶ 34,554].
(15) Rev. Rul. 65-158, 1965-1 CB 34; Allstate Ins. Co. v. US (US Ct. Claims, 2-18-76) 37 AFTR 2d 76-844 [¶ 7031(5); 76-463].
(16) Rev. Rul. 57-18, 1957-1 CB 354; Rev. Rul. 68-216, 1968-1 CB 413 [¶ 34,833; 34,836].
(17) Rev. Rul. 57-551, 1957-2 CB 707 [¶ 34,837].
(18) Rev. Rul. 57-33, 1957-1 CB 303; Rev. Rul. 61-146, 1961-2 CB 25 [¶ 34,552].
(19) Rev. Rul. 181, 1953-2 CB 111 [¶ 34,539].
(20) Rev. Rul. 71-279, 1971-2 CB 81; Rev. Rul. 71-456, 1971-2 CB 354 [¶ 7628(10); 34,540].
(21) Rev. Rul. 54-122, 1954-1 CB 223 [¶ 34,538].
(22) Rev. Rul. 55-484, 1955-2 CB 454 [¶ 34,538].
(23) Rev. Rul. 75-400, 1975-2 CB 464; Ann. 76-20 (TIR-1436), IRB 1976-8 [¶ 54,513; 54,606].
(24) Rev. Rul. 57-397, 1957-2 CB 628; Rev. Rul. 59-252, 1959-2 CB 215 [¶ 34,572].
(25) Rev. Rul. 76-453, IRB 1976-47; Announc. 77-23, IRB 1977-7 [¶ 54,980; 55,214].
(26) Rev. Rul. 70-280, 1970-1 CB 13 [¶ 7032(5)].
(27) D. W. Smith, ¶ 50,249 P-H MemoTC [¶ 5815(10)].
(28) Rev. Rul. 77-102, IRB 1977-15 [¶ 55,333].
(29) Rev. Rul. 67-257, 1967-2 CB 359 [¶ 34,580; 34,812(5)].
(30) Treas. Dept. booklet "Agricultural Employer's Tax Guide" (1976 Ed.), p. 7.

Footnote ¶ 2503 continued
(31) Rev. Rul. 57-129, 1957-1 CB 313 [¶ 34,083(5); 34,632].

Footnote ¶ 2504   [¶ 34,741 et seq., 34,825 et seq.].
(1) Ltr. ruling 7/27/43 [¶ 34,756].
(2) Rev. Proc. 75-7, 1975-1 CB 648 [¶ 34,550(e)].
(3) Rev. Rul. 66-328, 1966-2 CB 454 [¶ 34,775; 34,777].
(4) Rev. Rul. 66-190, 1966-2 CB 457 [¶ 34,572].

Footnote ¶ 2505   [¶ 34,783 et seq.].

Footnote ¶ 2506   [¶ 34,783].
(1) Treas. Dept. booklet "Employer's Tax Guide" (1976 Ed.), p. 6.
(2) Senate Report No. 92-437, p. 58, 92d Cong., 1st Sess.

Footnote ¶ 2507   [¶ 34,550; 34,913].

Footnote ¶ 2508   [¶ 34,852; 34,857].
(1) Treas. Dept. booklet "Employer's Tax Guide" (1976 Ed.), p. 10.
(2) Rev. Proc. 69-9, 1969-1 CB 400 [¶ 34,857; 34,919].
(3) Rev. Rul. 55-145, 1955-1 CB 503 [¶ 34,857].
(4) Treas. Dept. booklet "Employer's Tax Guide" (1976 Ed.), p. 12.

Footnote ¶ 2509   [¶ 34,912 et seq.].
(1) Rev. Rul. 66-230, 1966-2 CB 494 [¶ 34,912].
(2) Rev. Rul. 68-544, 1968-2 CB 581 [¶ 34,915].
(3) Rev. Proc. 69-9, 1969-1 CB 400 [¶ 34,857; 34,919].

Footnote ¶ 2510   [¶ 34,926 et seq.].
(1) Treas. Dept. booklet "Employer's Tax Guide" (1977 Ed.), p. 7.

Footnote ¶ 2511   [¶ 34,926(b)].
(1) Treas. Dept. booklet "Your Federal Income Tax" (1977 Ed.), p. 40.

Footnote ¶ 2512   [¶ 34,792; 34,912; 37,366; 38,536; 38,541].
(1) Kellems v. U.S. (DC Conn. 1951), 97 F. Supp. 681, 40 AFTR 872 [¶ 37,367.35(75)].
(2) Rev. Rul. 58-577, 1958-2 CB 744 [¶ 34,875].
(3) Paddock v. Siemoneit, (Texas SCt), 218 S.W.2d 428; 38 AFTR 1173 [¶ 37,367.35(10)].
(4) Rev. Rul. 66-113, 1966-1 CB 244 [¶ 34,875].
(5) Rev. Rul. 69-397, 1969-2 CB 263 [¶ 37,213(35)].
(6) Rev. Rul. 75-487, 1975-2 CB 488 [¶ 54,533].

Footnote ¶ 2515   [¶ 35,081 et seq.].

Footnote ¶ 2516   [¶ 35,081 et seq.].
(1) IRS Doc. No. 5125 (11-58).

Footnote ¶ 2517   [¶ 35,361 et seq.; 35,362.45].
(1) Treas. Dept. booklet "Your Federal Income Tax" (1977 Ed.), p. 24.
(2) Rev. Rul. 65-280, 1965-2 CB 433 [¶ 35,362.45(15)].

Chapter 15—Footnotes

Footnote ¶ 2518 [¶ 35,081.70].
(1) Treas. Dept. booklet "Your Federal Income Tax" (1977 Ed.), p. 22.

Footnote ¶ 2519 [¶ 37,317].
(1) Rev. Rul. 75-487, 1975-2 CB 488 [¶ 54,533].
(2) Senate Report No. 1622, p. 593, 83rd Cong., 2nd Sess.
(3) Rev. Rul. 58-369, 1958-2 CB 894 [¶ 37,317.45(15)].
(4) Rev. Rul. 69-307, 1969-1 CB 304

Footnote ¶ 2519 continued
  [¶ 37,317.45(15)].
(5) Ruben, 33 TC 1071 [¶ 37,317.45(5)].

Footnote ¶ 2535 [¶ 34,105 et seq.].

Footnote ¶ 2536 [¶ 34,241 et seq.; 35,706 et seq.].

Footnote ¶ 2537 [¶ 3151 et seq.; 34,106(c); 34,122; 42,001 et seq.].
(1) Rev. Rul. 60-288, 1960-2 CB 265 [¶ 3153; 34,122].

Highlights of Chapter 15
Withholding—Estimated Tax

I. **Withholding Tax on Wages**
   A. **Who must withhold [¶ 2501]:**
      1. Every employer who pays employee wages.
      2. Persons who control wage payments (not necessarily employer) may be required or permitted to withhold.
   B. **Who subject to withholding [¶ 2502]:**
      1. Tax withheld from "employees" only.
      2. Self-employed not subject to withholding.
   C. **What is subject to withholding [¶ 2503]:**
      1. Only wages are subject to withholding.
      2. No withholding on pay for excluded employment such as farm labor, church ministers, domestics, public services.
   D. **How to figure withholding [¶ 2504]:**
      1. Using official tables under percentage method [¶ 2504(a)].
      2. Using official tables under wage bracket method [¶ 2504(b)].
      3. Alternative methods available [¶ 2504(c)].
      4. Figuring tax without regard to payroll periods by annualizing or using table for daily or miscellaneous payroll period [¶ 2504(d)].
      5. Supplemental wages added to regular pay or subject to 20% withholding [¶ 2504(e)].
      6. Treat vacation pay as regular pay [¶ 2504(f)].
      7. Sick pay subject to withholding unless payments qualify as exempt disability income [¶ 2504(g)].
      8. To increase withholding, claim fewer exemptions or sign agreement with employer. Nonwages can be covered by voluntary withholding [¶ 2504(j)].
      9. Requesting withholding on pension and annuity payments [¶ 2504(k)].
   E. **Withholding exemptions [¶ 2505]:**
      1. Everyone entitled to personal exemptions plus 1 zero bracket allowance, except no extra allowance for employee with more than 1 job or married employee whose spouse works.
      2. Claim additional withholding allowances to avoid overwithholding if you have big deductions.
   F. **Exemption certificates (W-4) [¶ 2506]:**
      1. New employee files W-4 before work.
      2. Amended certificate *required* if exemption decreases; *permitted* if exemption increased.
      3. Certificate of nontaxability, W-4 or W-4E, exempts employee from withholding.
   G. **Records to be kept 4 years generally [¶ 2507].**
   H. **Statement to employee (W-2) [¶ 2508]:**
      1. Employer gives employee W-2 by Jan. 31, showing wages paid and taxes withheld in preceding year.
      2. Employee attaches W-2 to his return.
II. **Withholding Returns and Payments**
   A. **When to deposit tax [¶ 2509(a)]:**
      1. Within 3 banking days after quarter-monthly period for weekly undeposited taxes of $2,000 or more.
      2. Within 15 days after end of month for undeposited taxes of $200 or more at end of 1st or 2d month of quarter.

3. By end of next month for undeposited taxes of $200 or more at end of quarter.
B. **When to file employer's return [¶ 2509(b)]:**
   1. Quarterly returns due by end of month following period of return.
   2. Timely depositors get 10 extra days to file.
C. **Where to file.** With Regional Service Center where employer's principal place of business is [¶ 2509(c)].
D. **Withholding adjustments.** Employers can correct withholding errors interest-free in a later quarter of same year [¶ 2510].
E. **Refund or credit [¶ 2511]:**
   1. Employers allowed refund or credit for overpayment.
   2. Withholding tax credited against employee's income tax.
   3. Employee gets refund on excess over $962.25 of social security tax withheld.
F. **Penalties [¶ 2512]:**
   1. Employer punishable for failure to collect or deposit taxes or file returns.
   2. Employees punishable for false information.

III. **Estimated Tax of Individuals**
  A. **Who must file declaration [¶ 2516]:**
   1. No declaration if estimated tax under $100.
   2. Declaration required if gross income from nonwages exceeds $500.
   3. Declaration required if gross income exceeds:
      a. $20,000 for single person, head of household, surviving spouse, or married couple entitled to file jointly.
      b. $10,000 for working couple.
      c. $5,000 for married couple not entitled to file jointly.
  B. **When to file [¶ 2517]:**
   1. April 15 for most taxpayers except farmers, fishermen and those using fiscal year or meeting requirements later.
   2. Early return (by Jan. 31) in place of declaration.
   3. Amended declaration required or permitted due to changing circumstances.
  C. **When to pay.** April 15 filers pay ¼ by 15th of April, June, Sept. (current year), and Jan. (following year). Fewer installments or full payment for those filing later [¶ 2517].
  D. **How to figure estimated tax and avoid penalty [¶ 2518-2519]:**
   1. Estimate based on last year's tax. Pay 25% of last year's tax on 1st installment; then 50%, 75%, 100%.
   2. Estimate based on last year's income using current rates and exemptions.
   3. Estimate based on annualized income. Pay 20% of annualized tax on 1st installment; then 40%, 60%, 80%.
   4. Pay 90% of tax figured at current rates on taxable income for period ending before month in which installment due.

IV. **Withholding From Nonresident Aliens**
  A. Alien's withholding tax on wages same as citizen's [¶ 2535].
  B. **Periodical income.** Nonresident alien's dividends, interest, and certain income items are subject to withholding, generally at 30% or lower treaty rates. But effectively connected income is exempt [¶ 2535(b), (c); 2537].
  C. Withholding agent's special filing and payment requirements [¶ 2535(a); 2536].

Chapter 16

INVENTORY

TABLE OF CONTENTS

INVENTORIES IN GENERAL

Need for inventory 2600
Income from business 2601
   Gross profit
   Net profit
   Segregation of items on return
Goods included in inventory 2602

PRICING INVENTORIES

Valuation of inventories 2604
   Inventories at cost
   Inventories at lower of cost or market
First-in first-out method 2605
Last-in first-out method 2606
   Difference between last-in first-out ("lifo"), and first-in first-out ("fifo")
   Costing inventory under "lifo"
   Application for, and use of, "lifo"
Goods unsalable at normal prices 2607
Book inventories 2608
Methods of valuation in special classes of businesses 2609

Dealers in securities
Farmers and livestock raisers
Manufacturers
Miners and like producers—allocation of costs
Retail merchants
Methods disapproved 2610
Basis 2611

FARM INVENTORY AND ACCOUNTING

Income from farming 2614
   Accounting methods of farmers
   Items included in income
   Items not included in income
Inventories of farmers and livestock raisers 2615
   Farm-price method
   Unit-livestock-price method
   Livestock included in inventory

• Highlights of Chapter 16 .... Page 2661

INVENTORIES IN GENERAL

¶ **2600 Need for inventory.** An inventory is a list of goods on hand held for sale. In every business in which the production, purchase, or sale of merchandise is an income-producing factor, the inventory of unsold goods on hand at the beginning and end of each year is required to clearly reflect the income of the taxpayer [Sec. 471; 1.446-1, 1.471-1]. This is necessary because (1) all the merchandise produced or bought during the year may not be sold during the year, or (2) the merchandise sold during the year may include all that was produced or bought during the year, plus some that was produced or bought in a prior year. In addition, those who use inventory must use accrual accounting for purchases and sales [¶ 2706]. In some businesses the use of inventories is not a practical method of figuring income and is not permitted. For example, flower growers, oyster and fish hatcheries, and real estate dealers may not use an inventory method.

There are four main issues related to the subject of inventory: (1) the extent to which inventory must be used in figuring gross profit [¶ 2601]; (2) the determining of what goods must be included [¶ 2602]; (3) the identifying of goods sold from those remaining in inventory [¶ 2605; 2606]; and (4) the determining of inventory value [¶ 2604; 2607-2611; 2614; 2615].

¶ **2601 Income from business.** Determining the net profit from a business involves (a) finding the gross profit and (b) deducting from it the operating expenses.

Footnotes appear at end of this Chapter.

¶ 2601

In the individual taxpayer's return, the net profit (or loss) is determined from a separate schedule, and the net amount is then entered in gross income (as a minus quantity if a loss) [Sec. 1.61-3]. Examples 1 and 2 below illustrate the method used in making the computation.

(a) Gross profit. Gross profit from a business means the total receipts (less returns and allowances) minus the cost of goods sold. The cost of goods sold is figured by adding to the inventory at the start of the tax year the cost of merchandise and materials bought or produced during the year, plus all other costs related to obtaining or producing the merchandise. Inventory at the close of the tax year is subtracted from this total to get the net cost of goods sold. The usual items included in the cost of goods sold are direct and indirect labor, materials and supplies consumed, freight-in and a proportion of overhead expenses. Generally, unreimbursed casualty and theft losses during the year of inventory are reflected in closing inventory,[1] except for such losses sustained by manufacturers and producers using the full absorption method, which are excluded (¶ 2609(c)) [Sec. 1.471-11(c)(2)(g)].

Example 1: A business shows receipts of $30,000 ($31,500 gross sales less $1,500 returns and allowances); inventory of goods at start of the year, $3,700; inventory of goods at the end of the year, $3,000; merchandise bought during the year for sale, $15,000; costs during year in purchase and production of goods for sale: labor, $7,500; material and supplies, $600; other costs, $200. The gross profit is not $6,700 (the excess of receipts [$30,000] over disbursements [$23,300]), but $6,000:

1. Total receipts from business, $31,500, less returns and allowances $1,500 .... $30,000

COST OF GOODS SOLD

2. Inventory at beginning of year	$ 3,700
3. Merchandise bought for sale	15,000
4. Labor	7,500
5. Material and supplies	600
6. Other costs	200
7. Total (lines 2 to 6)	$27,000
8. Less inventory at end of year	3,000
9. Net cost of goods sold (line 7 minus line 8)	$24,000
10. Gross profit from business	$ 6,000

Donated items. The fair market value of agricultural or manufactured products or property held for sale that taxpayer gives away is not includible in income. The opening inventory must be adjusted in the year of the gift to remove the cost or other basis of the donated asset.[2] In case of contributions to charity, this adjustment is necessary to avoid a double deduction for the gift. However, because only property in opening inventory is taken into account for the charitable deduction, there is no deduction for property donated in the same year it is acquired; the cost or other basis of this property is treated as part of the costs of the goods sold in the contribution year (¶ 1810; 1942(b)) [Sec. 1.170A-1(c)(4)].

Goods withdrawn for personal use. The cost of goods withdrawn for personal use is excluded from the total amount of merchandise bought for sale, unless the proprietor pays for the withdrawn goods with his own private funds. If he does not pay for the withdrawn goods, he must adjust his account of the merchandise bought for sale. This is necessary to avoid an understatement of the net profit from business. Without the adjustment, the cost of goods used by the taxpayer would be charged against the total sales. The adjustment may consist of crediting the purchases account with the merchandise withdrawn for personal use, and charging the proprietor's drawing account with the cost of the withdrawn merchandise. A separate account of all goods withdrawn for personal or family use should be kept.[3]

(b) Net profit. In figuring net profit from a business, the expenses of operating the business (except those that apply to cost of goods sold) are deducted from gross profit determined as in (a) above.

Example 2: Taxpayer in Example 1 has the following business deductions other than those that apply to the cost of goods sold:

OTHER BUSINESS DEDUCTIONS

11. Salaries (not included in line 4 above)	$1,200
12. Interest on business indebtedness	150
13. Taxes on business and business property	150
14. Bad debts arising from sales	200
15. Depreciation, obsolescence, and depletion	250
16. Rent, repairs, and other expenses	750
17. Total (lines 11 to 16)	$2,700

The net profit from business is $3,300 figured as follows:

18. Gross profit from business (from line 10, Example 1)	$6,000
19. Total of "other business deductions" line 17	2,700
20. Net profit (or loss) from business	$3,300

NOTE: Depreciation and cost depletion may be considered in determining gross profit of a mining, manufacturing or merchandising business. When depreciation and cost depletion are included in the cost of goods produced under the full absorption method [¶ 2609(c)], these items should be reported in the same amounts as in the taxpayer's financial report [Sec. 1.471-11(c)(3)].

(c) Segregation of items on return. For individual taxpayers, all business expenses and deductions should be properly segregated on the return to figure the taxpayer's adjusted gross income accurately. For example, interest paid on a business debt should be entered as a business deduction on Schedule C (Form 1040), but interest paid on a personal loan should be included in the "other itemized deductions" on separate Schedule A.

¶ 2602 Goods included in inventory. The inventory includes all finished or partly finished goods. Raw materials and supplies (including containers) are included only if they have been acquired for sale, or will physically become a part of merchandise intended for sale. Merchandise is included only if the taxpayer has title. Goods (including containers) in transit are included in the buyer's inventory if he has title, although he does not have physical possession yet. Goods (including containers) out on consignment are not inventoried by the buyer-consignee but by the seller [Sec. 1.471-1]. The inventory at the start of the tax year should be identical with that of the close of the preceding year. Depreciation is not allowed on inventories and stock in trade.

➤**OBSERVATION**→ Including goods in inventory only to which taxpayer has title can be significant if the taxpayer values his inventory at the lower of cost or market. His failure to get title to goods that have declined in price will prevent him from getting the tax benefit of the reduced market price.

Excluded from inventory. Among the items *not* included in inventory are cash, notes, accounts, capital assets, investments, equipment, and similar assets.

PRICING INVENTORIES

¶ 2604 Valuation of inventories. There are two popular ways to value inventories:

Footnotes appear at end of this Chapter.

- Cost.
- Cost or market, whichever is lower.

A new concern may adopt either method. Once a method is adopted, it may not be changed without permission of the Revenue Service [Sec. 1.471-2]. The method adopted must be used for the entire inventory. But there are exceptions for (1) goods inventoried by the last-in, first-out method [¶ 2606] and (2) animals inventoried by the unit livestock-price method [¶ 2615(c)]. Generally consistency in valuing inventory from year to year is important.[1]

Background and purpose. The criteria for the correct valuation of inventories is that the method must conform to the best accounting practice in the trade or business and must clearly reflect income.

More than one trade or business. If the taxpayer has more than one trade or business, the Revenue Service may require that the method used for goods in one trade or business also be used for similar goods of the others if necessary to clearly reflect income [Sec. 1.471-2(d), 1.472-2(i)].

Change of method. Application to change the method of valuation must be filed on Form 3115 within 180 days after the start of the year for which the change is desired [Sec. 1.446-1(e)].

> **Example 1:** A taxpayer who has been reporting on the cost basis and wants to change to cost or market for the calendar year 1978 must file an application with the Revenue Service by 6-29-78.

Permission will not be granted if tax reduction is the principal reason.

In recent years, many businesses, with the approval of the Revenue Service, have elected to figure inventories under the so-called "last-in, first-out" method described in ¶ 2606. In addition, special rules have been adopted governing the value of inventories in certain classes of businesses [¶ 2609].

(a) Inventories at cost. The cost of merchandise *bought* during the year is the invoice price minus trade or other discounts. Freight and other charges paid to get the goods are added to the net invoice price [Sec. 1.471-3].

Cash discounts may be treated in either of two ways, but the taxpayer must be consistent. He may:

1. Deduct the cash discounts from purchases. This reduces the cost of goods sold. The invoices show the net price after the cash discount, and this is the price at which the goods in the inventory are valued.
2. Credit the cash discount to a discount account. The credit balance in this account at the end of the tax year is included in income. The cost of goods sold is not reduced by the cash discounts taken.

The Revenue Service holds that if the second method is used, the taxpayer, in valuing the closing inventory, may not deduct from the invoice price of the merchandise on hand at the close of the tax year, the average amount of cash discount received on the merchandise.[2] However, the Tax Court has allowed the use of this practice if it was followed consistently.[3]

Merchandise manufactured by taxpayer. The cost of merchandise manufactured by the taxpayer is the total of (1) the cost of the raw materials and supplies consumed in the process (2) the expenditures for direct labor including overtime costs[4] and (3) indirect production costs including a reasonable proportion of management expenses, but excluding all selling expenses [Sec. 1.471-3]. When straight line depreciation is used for book purposes and an accelerated method is used for taxes, the straight line depreciation is treated as an indirect cost; the excess is a business deduction in the year incurred.[5]

NOTE: Loss on sale of supplier's stock bought to get merchandise for use in taxpayer's business, is part of cost, not a capital loss.[6] But taxpayer *must prove* that he bought the stock to get merchandise.[7]

(b) Inventories at lower of cost or market. "Market" ordinarily means the bid price prevailing at the date of the inventory. This applies to goods bought and on hand, and to the basic elements of cost (materials, labor, and overhead) in goods in process of manufacture and finished goods on hand. It does not apply to goods on hand or in process for delivery on a contract at fixed prices, if the contract legally cannot be cancelled by either party. These goods must be inventoried at cost.

On the date the inventory is being valued, the market value of each article is compared with its cost and the lower figure is taken as the inventory value of the article [Sec. 1.471-4]. For this comparison, the cost of goods in the closing inventory that were also on hand at the beginning of the year is their opening inventory price.[8]

Example 2: At the close of the year, a taxpayer had on hand:

	Cost	Market
Bricks	$2,000	$2,400
Coal	2,000	1,700

The bricks would be inventoried at $2,000; the coal at $1,700.

Example 3: 100 tons of sugar were bought at 7¢ a pound on August 15 and on October 1 another 50 tons were bought at 6¢ a pound. The entire 150 tons were on hand at the close of the year. The market value of the sugar at the close of the year was 6½¢ a pound. If "cost or market whichever is lower" is used, the 100 tons of sugar would be inventoried at market or 6½¢ a pound; the 50 tons would be inventoried at cost, or 6¢ a pound.

¶ 2605 **First-in, first-out method.** The first-in, first-out method is a way to identify and not value goods in closing inventory. This can be used with value at cost or value at lower of cost or market. Generally, it is used if the same type of merchandise is bought at different prices during the year and is so intermingled that it cannot be identified with specific invoices. Under this method, the goods first bought are considered those first sold. The "cost" of the amount on hand at the end of the year is the cost of the goods last bought. But if the quantity is greater than the amount bought at the last price, the excess is inventoried at the next to the last price, and so on [Sec. 1.471-2].

Example: Assume that the inventory at the end of the year shows 275,000 units of a certain article on hand and the last three invoices for that article are June 29, 100,000 at $1.00; September 30, 80,000 at $1.10; December 10, 125,000 at 95¢. If the goods cannot be identified with specific invoices, the inventory would show 125,000 at 95¢, 80,000 at $1.10, and the remainder (70,000) at $1.00.

¶ 2606 **Last-in, first-out method.** With Revenue Service approval, any taxpayer who must take inventory can use the "last-in, first-out" method [Sec. 472; 1.472-1; 1.472-3]. The inventory must be valued at cost. The goods most recently bought or produced are treated as the first goods sold so that the goods on hand at the close of the year are treated as those bought or produced earliest. In determining income for the tax year preceding the tax year for which the "lifo" method is first used, the closing inventory of the preceding year must be at cost. This adjustment includes any writedown from actual cost for "subnormal goods" as well as normal goods that have been written down to market value.[1] The "last-in, first-

Footnotes appear at end of this Chapter.

out" method may be applied to the entire inventory or to specified items. However, its use may be required by the Commissioner for other items in the inventory or for similar goods in another business of the taxpayer if necessary to clearly reflect income [Sec. 1.472-2].

(a) Differences between last-in, first-out ("lifo") and first-in, first-out ("fifo"). Under "lifo," the inventory at the end of the year is treated as being derived from the *earliest* acquired goods. Under "fifo" inventory at the end of the year is treated as derived from the *latest* acquired goods. See ¶ 2605.

Example 1: Assuming the same facts in each case, taxpayer figures closing inventory under (1) "fifo" and (2) "lifo" as follows:

	(1) First-in first-out	(2) Last-in first-out
Sales 5000 units @ $4.00	$20,000	$20,000
Cost of sales:		
Opening inventory (2000 units @ $1.00)	$ 2,000	$ 2,000
Purchases (5000 units @ $3.00)	15,000	15,000
Total	$17,000	$17,000
Less: Closing inventory:		
(Fifo) 2000 units @ $3.00	$ 6,000 $11,000	
(Lifo) 2000 units @ $1.00		$ 2,000 $15,000
Gross profit on sales	$ 9,000	$ 5,000

Inventory value will be different under the "lifo" and "fifo" methods when goods are bought or manufactured at various costs during the year. Example 2 (with the opening inventory omitted for simplicity) illustrates the difference under general accounting theory.[2]

Example 2: Assume there are 150 units in inventory and purchases during the period are:

1st purchase 100 units @	$1.00	$100.00
2nd purchase 200 units @	1.10	220.00
3rd purchase 250 units @	1.20	300.00
4th purchase 100 units @	1.25	125.00

First-in first-out method. The goods on hand are considered to have been acquired by the most recent purchases; therefore the inventory is composed of:

From 4th purchase:	100 units @	$1.25	$125.00
From 3rd purchase:	50 units @	1.20	60.00
Cost of inventory			$185.00

Last-in first-out method. The sales are assumed to consist of the last goods purchased, and the inventory at the end of the period is assumed to consist of any opening inventory and the earliest purchases. Therefore the inventory is composed of:

From the 1st purchase:	100 units @	$1.00	$100.00
From the 2nd purchase:	50 units @	1.10	55.00
Cost of inventory			$155.00

Advantages of last-in, first-out method over first-in, first-out. The chief advantage of "lifo" is that it reduces taxable income during an inflationary period such as the one since World War II. The spread between costs and selling prices is reduced under "lifo" as both are affected by the same market conditions. Businesses most likely to benefit by the "lifo" method are those in which: (1) the value of the inventory is large compared with other assets and sales; (2) production covers a long period; and (3) the price of goods included in inventory is subject to wide fluctuations.

(b) Costing inventory under "lifo." The opening inventory for the first tax year that "lifo" is used must be valued at the actual cost of the goods on hand. The unit cost for an item is the average of the cost of all items, as if they were all bought at the same time at the same price [Sec. 1.472-2]. If this unit cost is $5 and the inventory remained constant at 1,000 units, the inventory value would always be $5,000 because these first units would always be considered to remain in stock.

When the closing inventory is larger than the opening inventory, the cost of the increase, or "increment," generally is determined from purchases or manufacturing costs during the year in one of three ways. The Revenue Service may accept another method that correctly reflects income [Sec. 1.472-2(d)]. The cost of the increase in inventory can be determined from the cost of the earliest units bought or produced during the year, the latest units, or from the average cost of all units. The method first used must be followed in later years and the method for increases also must be used when the closing inventory is less than the opening inventory. These methods are used only if closing is larger than opening inventory. If the closing is less than opening inventory, the standard LIFO approach is used (See Ex. 4, below).

Example 3: Bell Co. adopted the "lifo" method for the tax year 1976. The opening inventory was 10 units at 10¢ a unit. During the year Bell Co. bought 10 units: 1 in January at 11¢, 2 in April at 12¢, 3 in July at 13¢ and 4 in October at 14¢. On 12-31-76, the closing inventory had 15 units. Depending on the method used for *inventory increases,* the closing inventory will be:

(a) Most recent purchases		(b) In order of acquisition		(c) At an annual average	
10 @ 10	100	10 @ 10	100	10 @ 10	100
4 @ 14 (October)	56	1 @ 11 (January)	11	5 @ 13 (130/10)	65
1 @ 13 (July)	13	2 @ 12 (April)	24		
		2 @ 13 (July)	26		
Totals:					
15	169	15	161	15	165

Example 4: Bell Co.'s closing inventory for 1977 is 13 units. This is a decrease of 2 units from the opening inventory from Example 3. The value of the reduced inventory must be determined from the 15 units in opening inventory in the order of acquisition and by the method used to value inventory increases. The 1977 closing inventory value depends on the method used to value the increases. If the increase for the preceding tax year was taken:

(a) By reference to most recent purchases		(b) In order of acquisition		(c) On basis an average	
10 @ 10 (from 1975)	100	10 @ 10 (from 1975)	100	10 @ 10 (from 1975)	100
1 @ 13 (July 1976)	13	1 @ 11 (Jan. 1976)	11	3 @ 13 (from 1976)	39
2 @ 14 (Oct. 1976)	28	2 @ 12 (April 1976)	24		
13	141	13	135	13	139

Merchandisers and first producers. Unless the Commissioner approves another proper method (such as FIFO or weighted average) that clearly reflects income, retailers, wholesalers and other enterprises that buy and sell goods must use one of the LIFO methods to value inventory. So, too, must those that *initially* produce and sell materials without processing, like raw mined ore [Sec. 1.472-2(d)(1)]. See ¶ 2609 for retailers who use the "lifo" method with the retail inventory method.

Manufacturers can limit their use of the "lifo" method to raw materials only. The cost of finished goods and goods in process can be figured any way that clearly reflects income; but adjustment may be required for raw material integrated in the goods [Sec. 1.472-1(c)].

Footnotes appear at end of this Chapter.

¶ 2606

Example 5: Opening inventory consists only of 20 units of raw material at 6¢ a unit. Raw material bought during the year cost 10¢ a unit. Closing inventory has 12 units or raw material and 12 units of finished goods. Processing cost is 4¢ a unit, overhead 1¢ a unit. The closing inventory value is figured:

Raw materials	Raw material	Finished goods
12 at 6¢	72	
8 at 6¢		48
4 at 10¢		40
Processing cost		48
Overhead		12
	72¢	$1.48

Dollar-value costing. This method uses dollar values rather than physical quantities. The inventory is viewed as a pool not as individual items. The pool may be classified by broad product categories, by departments or by any other logical grouping. The "dollar-value lifo" method requires the matching of dollar values in the closing and opening inventories at base year (first lifo year) prices and then adjusted to dollar variations to reflect the increase or decrease in current prices. The "base year cost" is established for the entire inventory in the "pool" at the beginning of the tax year the method is first adopted. This pool remains the same for all later years unless the Revenue Service approves a change as a change of accounting method [¶ 2708]. The base-year cost is the total cost of all items in the pool. The closing inventory value for the pool must be established by the double extension method unless the District Director accepts an index method or link chain method because the double extension is impractical. A detailed explanation of the index or link chain method used must be attached to the first return when dollar value is adopted [Sec. 1.472-8].

The double extension method basically is a way to state the value of the increase or decrease in current closing inventory in dollar amounts in relation to the base year cost. The base year unit cost of a new item entering the pool in later years is its price or production cost; but the Revenue Service may accept a reconstructed base year unit cost. To apply the method you find the cost of the closing inventory at the unit cost for the base year and the unit cost for the current year; then divide the total current cost by the total cost at base year unit cost to get a ratio that is applied to increases in inventory for the year. The current year cost may be consistently determined by one of the methods described above for valuing inventory increase or decrease. There is an inventory increase for the year when the total dollar value of the closing inventory at base year unit costs exceeds the base year cost. The inventory increase is converted to current dollar value by applying the ratio, or percentage, derived from the comparative base year and current year costs. This figure is the "lifo" value of the increase.

Each year's increase must be recorded and accounted for as a separate unit, and decreases or liquidations of inventory must be absorbed first by the latest previous increase and then successively by the next earlier increases until the decrease is fully absorbed. The ratio established for each year's increase is also used when that increase is liquidated. Base year inventory is reduced only when the total of all decreases is more than the total of all increases. There is an inventory decrease when the closing inventory for a year is less than the opening inventory with both computed at base year unit costs.

Example 6: Electing the dollar value "lifo" method for 1977, Bay Co. properly establishes a pool for items A, B, and C. The inventory on January 1 is: A-1,000 units at a cost of $5 a unit; B-2,000 units at $4; C-500 units at $2; for a total base year cost of $14,000. The total current year cost of the December 31st closing inventory, determined from items last bought during the year, is $24,250. This includes: A-3,000 units at a unit cost of $6; B-1,000 units at $5; C-500 units at $2.50. At the base year unit costs (A-$5, B-$4, C-$2) the closing inventory cost is $20,000. The closing inventory value is $21,275 computed as follows:

(1) Closing inventory at base year cost $20,000
    Base year inventory cost 14,000

    Increase in inventory* $6,000
(2) $24,250 (inventory at current year unit cost)/$20,000 (inventory at base year unit cost)
    = 121.25% (ratio of current cost to base year cost)

---

* If cost of the closing inventory at base year unit costs were equal to or less than base year inventory cost, that would be the closing inventory value.

Closing inventory base year cost		Ratio of current year cost to base year cost	Closing inventory value
Base cost	$14,000	100%	$14,000
Increase	6,000	121.25%	7,275
Total	$20,000		$21,275

Example 7: On 12-31-78, Bay Co. of Example 6 has a current year cost of $27,000 and a cost of $18,000 at base year unit costs for its closing inventory. The base year cost of the opening inventory was $20,000 so the $2,000 reduction in inventory reduces the $6,000 increase of 1977. In 1978 closing inventory value is $18,850 computed as follows:

Closing inventory base year cost		Ratio of current year cost to base year cost	Closing inventory value
Base cost	$14,000	100%	$14,000
1977 increase	4,000	121.25%	4,850
Total	$18,000		$18,850

Manufacturers and processors pools include the entire inventory of a natural business unit. This may be an entire business or a separate division of a business. The circumstances surrounding the operation of an organization determine whether it has one or more natural business units. You can establish separate pools for substantially similar inventory items that are not part of a natural business pool. Goods bought from others for wholesaling or retailing must be pooled as for merchandisers.

Merchandisers pools must be established by major lines, types or classes of goods, according to customary business classification. One example is a department of a department store. The Revenue Service may allow a natural business pool for wholesalers, retailers, jobbers or distributors.

(c) **Application for, and use of, lifo.** Application is made on Form 970, or by a statement acceptable to the Commissioner, with the return for the tax year the method is first to be used [Sec. 1.472-3]. So, if a taxpayer uses this method for the first time in valuing closing inventories for calendar year 1977, Form 970 (or attachment) must be filed with the 1977 return. Once adopted, this method must be continued unless the Revenue Service requires a change to another method, or authorizes a change [Sec. 1.472-5, 1.472-6].

The Revenue Service will invalidate a "lifo" election if during the election year a taxpayer uses "fifo", or any other valuation method, for its financial reports.[3] But an election remains valid, after a "lifo" switch, if later financial reports merely comply with income disclosure rules set by the SEC[4] [Sec. 1.472-2(g)].

You cannot change to "dollar-value lifo" from another "lifo" method without Revenue Service consent. Special adjustments are required when a change is allowed or when a change in the content of pools is allowed or required.

In the application, the taxpayer must specify the part of his inventory to which the election of the "lifo" method is to apply.

Footnotes appear at end of this Chapter.

¶ 2606

A taxpayer who adopts this method for a specified part of his inventory may continue to take the rest of his inventory for tax purposes, on a cost or market basis, or any other basis that was properly adopted and approved for prior years. The Revenue Service, however, can require use of the "lifo" method for other items in the taxpayer's inventory if necessary for a clear reflection of income. It may also require its use for similar goods of any other trade or business of the taxpayer [Sec. 1.472-2(i)].

If a new taxable entity is created, approval to use "lifo" is required even if the new business is formed from companies that had permission to use "lifo" and the transaction was tax-free.[5]

¶ 2607 **Goods unsalable at normal prices.** Goods in inventory that cannot be sold at normal prices or used in the normal way should be valued at "bona fide selling prices" less the direct cost of disposition. This applies whether the inventory is taken at cost or at cost or market. "Bona fide selling price" is the actual offering price of the goods during a period ending not later than 30 days after the inventory date. Goods may be unsalable at normal prices because of imperfection, shop wear, change of style, odd lots, or other causes, including second hand goods taken in exchange [Sec. 1.471-2].

¶ 2608 **Book inventories.** The use of book or perpetual inventories is allowed [Sec. 1.471-2]. The purpose of a book inventory is to show the goods on hand as of any given date. It must show proper credit for goods sold or used during the year, as well as charges for goods bought or produced. The additions and subtractions to the book inventory are on the basis of actual cost of the goods bought or produced. The balances shown by the book inventories must be verified by physical inventories at reasonable intervals and adjusted to conform with them. If the taxpayer uses the "lower of cost or market" method, inventory at the close of each tax year should be adjusted for each article, as shown in ¶ 2604(b).

¶ 2609 **Methods of valuation in special classes of businesses.** (a) **Dealers in securities.** A dealer in securities is one who regularly buys securities for resale to customers. Three methods of inventory valuation are open to these dealers (1) cost; (2) cost or market, whichever is lower; (3) market value [Sec. 1.471-5]. (The cost of securities sold must be reduced by the amortized premium on certain short term municipal bonds. See ¶ 1846(a).)

(b) **Farmers and livestock raisers.** See ¶ 2615.

(c) **Manufacturers.** Taxpayers involved in the manufacturing operations must use the full absorption method of inventory costing. All direct production costs must be included as inventoriable costs. Certain indirect production costs that are necessary for production must also be included regardless of their financial report treatment; for example, expenses for repair and maintenance, utilities, rent, indirect labor, supervisory wages, indirect materials, tools and equipment (if not capitalized) and quality control costs. Some indirect production costs are specially excluded; for example, expenses for marketing, advertising, selling, distribution, interest, research and development, losses, percentage depletion in excess of cost depletion, depreciation and amortization reported but in excess of that reported in financial reports. Other indirect costs such as state and local property taxes are treated for tax purposes the same as in the taxpayer's financial reports. The indirect costs to be included must be allocated to goods in ending inventory by using an allocation method that fairly apportions these costs among the various items produced. Those manufacturers who did not switch to the full absorption method immediately could have elected a 2-year transition provision by filing Form 3115 [Sec. 1.471-11]. In addition, the Revenue Service has issued guidelines that set forth procedures for switching to the full absorption method.[1]

(d) Miners and like producers—allocation of costs. This method may be used when two or more products of a different selling value are produced by a uniform process [Sec. 1.471-7].

> **Example 1:** When coal is used to produce gas, a by-product (coke) may result. The cost of production may be allocated to the gas and to the coke in proportion to their respective selling values.

(e) Retail merchants. The most common methods for retailers to value their inventory are the conventional "retail method" and the "lifo" retail method.[2] Under the conventional "retail method," goods in inventory are valued at the retail selling price. This is then reduced to approximate cost. A separate ratio must be determined for each department or class of goods [Sec. 1.471-8].

> **Example 2:**
>
> | | | |
> |---|---:|---:|
> | Opening inventory (retail selling price) | $100,000 | |
> | Goods purchased during year (retail selling price) | 900,000 | $1,000,000 |
> | Opening inventory (cost of goods) | 75,000 | |
> | Goods purchased during year (cost) | 725,000 | 800,000 |
> | | | $ 200,000 |
>
> $200,000 \div $1,000,000 = 20\%$

> To determine its correct inventory under the conventional "retail method," the taxpayer ascertains the retail selling price of the goods in inventory at the end of the year and applies the percentage. For example, assume sales were $850,000, then the closing inventory (retail selling price) is $150,000. $150,000 × 20% is $30,000. The closing inventory is $120,000 ($150,000 − $30,000). Multiplying the closing inventory (retail selling price) of $150,000 by 80% ($800,000/$1,000,000) produces the same result. In this method, the cost-to-retail ratio is computed by adding the markups to retail purchases. Markdowns are excluded from the computation and added to retail sales to get net sales.

Under the "lifo" retail method, the cost of starting inventory is usually the bottom (first) layer in the closing inventory. The next layer is the increment purchased for the year. As this is a "lifo" cost layer, it is based on the cost-to-retail ratio which recognizes mark-ups and mark-downs. Thus, in our example the closing inventory under the "lifo" retail method would be $115,500 consisting of the first layer (opening inventory) $75,000 plus the second layer $40,500 [81%, rounded ($725,000/$900,000) × $50,000 ($150,000 − $100,000) retail purchase increment].[2]

Subject to approval of the Revenue Service, selling prices can be adjusted for mark-ups only; but mark-ups that cancel mark-downs or are canceled by mark-downs are not counted. Retailers who use the "lifo" method with retail inventory must use both mark-ups and mark-downs in valuing inventory. However, mark-downs that are not actual sales price reductions, such as mark-downs for depreciation or obsolescence, are never counted [Sec. 1.471-8(d)-(g)]. Unsalable obsolete or damaged merchandise [¶ 2607] should not only be excluded from inventory but a loss should be taken in the period when the loss developed.[3]

Conversion to "lifo" cost. Since the "lifo" method requires inventory to be valued at cost price changes during the year must be eliminated from the apparent cost of the closing inventory by using a price index [Sec. 1.472-1(k)].

> **Example 3:** John Jones uses "lifo" to value his hardware store inventory with the retail method. His closing inventory in 1976 (his base year) was retail selling price, $40,000, and cost, $24,000. The retail price of his 1977 closing inventory is $52,000. His retail ratio for 1977 is 40% so he used 60% of retail price for retail cost. There was a general price increase for hard-

Footnotes appear at end of this Chapter.

¶ **2609**

ware in 1977 in relation to the base year 1976 and his price index is 104%. The value of his 1977 closing inventory is $30,240 computed as follows:

(1)	$52,000 (selling prices) ÷ 1.04% = closing inventory at base year prices	$50,000
	Less base year inventory (retail selling prices)	40,000
	Inventory increase at base year prices	$10,000
(2)	$10,000 × 1.04 = inventory increase at current prices	$10,400
(3)	$10,400 × 60% = cost of increase	6,240
(4)	Cost of base year inventory	24,000
	"Lifo" value of closing inventory	$30,240

¶ 2610 **Methods disapproved.** The following methods are specifically disapproved [Sec. 1.471-2]:

• Deducting from the inventory a reserve for price changes, or an estimated depreciation in its value.
• Taking work in process, or other parts of the inventory, at a nominal price or at less than its proper value.
• Omitting portions of the stock on hand.
• Using a constant price or nominal value for so-called normal quantity of materials or goods in stock.
• Including stock in transit, either shipped to or from the taxpayer, when the title is not vested in the taxpayer.
• Using the "direct cost" method by allocating only the variable indirect production costs to the costs of goods produced while treating fixed costs as currently deductible period costs.
• Using the "prime cost" method by treating all indirect production costs as currently deductible period costs.

¶ 2611 **Basis.** If property should have been included in inventory, its basis is the last inventory value [Sec. 1013; 1.1013-1].

FARM INVENTORY AND ACCOUNTING

¶ 2614 **Income from farming. (a) Accounting methods of farmers.** Farmers may keep their records and file their returns of income either on the cash basis or on the accrual basis of accounting [see ¶ 2701-2706]. A consistent method, however, must be used. Schedule F (Form 1040) must be filed with the tax return, whether the farmer is on the cash or accrual basis.

A farmer who wants to change from the cash to the accrual method must get Revenue Service permission [Sec. 1.471-6]. Application must be filed within 180 days after the start of the tax year to be covered by the return. See ¶ 2708.

Cash basis. A farmer who reports income on the cash receipts and disbursements basis (in which no inventories to determine profits are used) must include in gross income for the tax year (1) the cash or the value of merchandise or other property received during the tax year from the sale of livestock or produce that was raised; (2) profits from the sale of any livestock or other items that were bought; (3) all miscellaneous income during the year; (4) all subsidy and conservation payments that must be considered as income; and (5) gross income from all other sources [Sec. 1.61-4(a)]. However a farmer on the cash basis can elect to include crop insurance proceeds in gross income for the tax year following the damage or destruction if he normally would have reported the income from the crop in that following year. If insurance is received as a result of damage to two or more specific crops and an election is made to include part of the proceeds in the following tax year, the farmer must include all the proceeds then unless the portion is attributable to a crop that represents a separate trade or business. The election is made by a statement with the return for the tax year of the recovery [Sec. 451(d); 1.451-6]. Some cash basis farmers also recapture farm losses when farm property is sold [¶ 2226]. In tax years starting after 12-31-75, a farmer on a cash basis can elect to include in gross income the gain from livestock sales due to drought conditions for the tax year following the sale or exchange. The drought conditions must be in areas designated for federal disaster assistance. In addition, this election applies only if the number of sales exceed the usual business practice and if the sales would not have been made but for the drought [Sec. 451(e)].

NOTE: Certain Federal crop disaster payments can be treated for the election as any other crop insurance proceeds [Sec. 451(d)].

Accrual basis. If the farmer is on the accrual basis, and inventories are used to determine the profits, his gross profits are found by first adding together: (1) sales price of all livestock and produce sold during the year; (2) inventory value of livestock and produce on hand and not sold at the end of the year; (3) all miscellaneous items of income; (4) any subsidy or conservation payment that must be considered as income; and (5) gross income from all other sources. From this sum, he subtracts: (1) the inventory value of livestock and produce on hand not sold at the beginning of the year, and (2) the cost of livestock and produce bought during the year [Sec. 1.61-4(b)]. For inventories of farmers and livestock raisers, see ¶ 2615.

NOTE: A farmer may elect the accrual basis without Revenue Service consent if the election is made to avoid the recapture of deducted farm losses as ordinary income (¶ 2226) [Sec. 1251(b)(4)].

Crop basis. The income from crops that take more than a year to grow and sell, may be figured on the crop basis. This is a special variation of the accrual basis, and the entire cost of producing the crop is deducted in the year the gross income from the crop is realized [Sec. 1.61-4(c)]. Application to use this method must be filed within 180 days after the start of the tax year to be covered by the return. See ¶ 2708.

(b) Items included in income. The rules are summarized below.

Products exchanged for groceries, etc. If farm produce is exchanged for merchandise, groceries, or the like, the market value of the articles received in exchange is included in gross income.

Crop shares (whether or not considered rent under state law) are reported as income the year they are reduced to money or its equivalent [Sec. 1.61-4(a)(5), (b)(7)].

Insurance proceeds, such as hail and fire insurance on growing crops, are included in gross income [Sec. 1.61-4(c)]. But see the election for cash basis farmer in (a) above.

Government subsidies. All Government payments, such as those for approved conservation practices, Soil Bank payments, Wheat Stabilization and Feed Grain Programs payments, must be included in income, whether received in cash or in materials. If fertilizer or lime is received, its value is included in income, but its receipt is offset by an expense deduction plus any cash handling charges. If payments are based on improvements such as a pollution control facility, the full cost is capitalized without reduction for payments received, since they have been included in income. Its cost should be depreciated or amortized starting on the date the facility is placed into service. If certified and placed into service before 1976, amortization is allowed over a 60-month period.[1] Farmers receiving feed grain payments for 2 crop years in one year can report the second crop year payments in 10 annual installments.[2]

Patrons' income from cooperative includes patronage dividends, nonpatronage payments and per-unit retains [¶ 3458].

(c) Items not included in income. The following need not be added to the farmer's income:

Footnotes appear at end of this Chapter.

¶ 2614

Products used by family. The value of farm products produced by a farmer and consumed by his family.[3]

Donated products. The fair market value of farm products that the farmer gives away[4] (but see ¶ 1810).

¶ 2615 Inventories of farmers and livestock raisers. As in the case of other taxpayers, a farmer who makes his return on an inventory basis may value his inventory on the basis of cost, or cost or market whichever is lower. However, a simpler method for farmers is the "farm-price method." In addition, farmers raising livestock may value their inventories of animals according to either the "farm-price method" or the unit-livestock-price method."

(a) Farm-price method. The "farm-price method" provides for valuation of inventories at market price less cost of disposition. When used, it must be applied to the entire inventory except to livestock inventory that the farmer elects to value under the "unit-livestock-price method." If the use of the "farm-price method" involves a change in valuing inventories from that used in prior years, permission to change must be secured from the Revenue Service [Sec. 1.446-1(e), 1.471-6].

(b) Unit-livestock-price method. The "unit-livestock-price method" provides for valuation of classes of animals raised at a standard unit price within a class. The classification, made by the taxpayer, is subject to approval of the Revenue Service.[1] In determining the unit cost for each classification, effect must be given to the age and kind of animals included within each class, so as to reflect normal cost incurred in producing the animals.

> **Example:** If it cost $15 to produce a calf and $7.50 each year to raise a calf to maturity, the classification and unit prices would be as follows: calves, $15; yearlings, $22.50; two-year olds, $30; mature animals, $37.50.

If a taxpayer using the "farm-price method" wants to adopt the "unit-livestock-price method" he must get the approval of the Revenue Service[1] for the change. However, a taxpayer who has filed returns on the basis of inventories at cost, or cost or market, whichever is lower, may adopt the "unit-livestock-price method" without formal application [Sec. 1.471-6].[2]

(c) Livestock included in inventory. The rules are summarized below:

All livestock raised or purchased *for sale* must be included in the inventory of the accrual basis farmer. But livestock acquired for draft, breeding, or dairy purposes may be treated as capital assets and depreciated, or it may be included in inventory. Either method can be used, but it must be consistent from year to year.[1]

If the unit-livestock method is used, it applies to all livestock *raised*, whether for sale or for breeding, draft or dairy purposes, but livestock *purchased* must be included in inventory at *cost*. However, the farmer still has the option to either inventory or capitalize livestock *purchased* for breeding, draft or dairy purposes [Sec. 1.471-6]. The election can be changed only with the consent of the Revenue Service [¶ 2708].[3]

In figuring gain or loss from livestock in inventory, the inventory value takes the place of the original cost, if any.[3]

Footnotes to Chapter 16

(P-H "FEDERAL TAXES" related references are cited in brackets [ ] at the end of each footnote below)

Footnote ¶ 2600 [¶ 20,650 et seq.].
Footnote ¶ 2601 [¶ 11,444; 20,650].

Footnote ¶ 2601 continued
(1) Treas. Dept. booklet "Tax Guide for Small Business" (1977 Ed.), p. 113.

Footnote ¶ 2601 continued
(2) Rev. Rul. 55-138, 1955-1 CB 223; Rev. Rul. 55-531, 1955-2 CB 520. (But see ¶ 1515) [¶ 7488(5), (10)].
(3) Rev. Rul. 28, 1953-1 CB 20 [¶ 7149(10)].

Footnote ¶ 2602 [¶ 20,650 et seq.].

Footnote ¶ 2604 [¶ 20,675 et seq.].
(1) The Buss Co., 2 BTA 266 [¶ 20,667(5)].
(2) Rev. Rul. 69-619, 1969-2 CB 111 [¶ 20,710(25)].
(3) Higgenbotham-Bailey-Logan Co., 8 BTA 566 [¶ 20,710(30)].
(4) Rev. Rul. 69-373, 1969-2 CB 110 [¶ 20,707(70)].
(5) Rev. Rul. 70-346, 1970-2 CB 106 [¶ 20,690(25)].
(6) Western Wine and Liquor Co., 18 TC 1090; Clark, 19 TC 48 [¶ 11,462].
(7) McGhee Upholstery Co., ¶ 54,014 P-H Memo TC [¶ 32,461(5)].
(8) Rev. Rul. 70-19, 1970-1 CB 123 [¶ 20,722(30)].

Footnote ¶ 2605 [¶ 20,709; 20,775].

Footnote ¶ 2606 [¶ 20,775 et seq.].
(1) Rev Proc. 76-6 (TIR-1433), 1976-1 CB 545; Rev. Rul. 76-282, IRB 1976-30, Rev. Proc. 76-28 (IR-1630), IRB 1976-28 [¶ 20,787(17)].
(2) Johnson and Gentry, Finney and Miller's Principles of Accounting, (7th Ed.), Prentice-Hall, Inc., p. 206 et seq.
(3) Rev. Rul. 75-49, 1975-1 CB 151 [¶ 20,789(10)].
(4) Rev. Proc. 75-10, 1975-1 CB 651 [¶ 20,789(10)].
(5) Textile Apron Co., Inc., 21 TC 147 [¶ 20,789(5)].

Footnote ¶ 2607 [¶ 20,695].

Footnote ¶ 2608 [¶ 20,675].

Footnote ¶ 2609 [¶ 20,727; 20,755; 20,761; 20,764].
(1) Rev. Proc. 74-21, 1974-2 CB 475; Rev. Proc. 75-22, 1975-1 CB 717; Rev. Proc. 75-34, 1975-2 CB 560; Rev. Proc. 75-40, 1975-2 CB 571 [¶ 20,773(10)].
(2) Horngren and Lear, CPA Problems and Approaches to Solutions (Vol. 1, 4th Ed.), Prentice-Hall, Inc., p. 70 et seq.
(3) Johnson and Gentry, Finney and Miller's Principles of Accounting, (7th Ed.), Prentice-Hall, Inc., p. 217.

Footnote ¶ 2610 [¶ 20,675].

Footnote ¶ 2611 [¶ 31,351].

Footnote ¶ 2614 [¶ 7161 et seq.].
(1) Treas. Dept. booklet "Farmer's Tax Guide" (1977 Ed.), p. 33.
(2) Rev. Proc. 64-16, 1964-1 CB 677; Rev. Rul. 65-97, 1965-1 CB 211; Rev. Rul. 65-98, 1965-1 CB 213 [¶ 20,083(7); 20,166(5)].
(3) Morris, 9 BTA 1273 [¶ 7174(10)].
(4) Rev. Rul. 55-138, 1955-1 CB 223; Rev. Rul. 55-531, 1955-2 CB 250 [¶ 7488(5), (10)].

Footnote ¶ 2615 [¶ 20,736 et seq.].
(1) Treas. Dept. booklet "Farmer's Tax Guide" (1977 Ed.), p. 29.
(2) U.S. v. Catto, 86 US 1311, 17 AFTR 2d 881 [¶ 20,747(20)].
(3) Rev. Rul. 60-60, 1960-1 CB 190 [¶ 20,747(5)].

Highlights of Chapter 16
Inventory

I. **Inventories in General**
   A. **Need for inventory [¶ 2600]:**
      1. To clearly reflect income.
      2. Method to identify and value items intended for sale.
   B. **Four problems related to inventory:**
      1. Extent to which it is used to figure gross profit.
      2. Determination of what goods are included.
      3. Identification.
      4. Valuation.
   C. **Income from Business [¶ 2601]:**
      1. Gross profit—total receipts (less returns and allowances) less cost of goods sold [¶ 2601(a)].
         a. Cost of goods sold:
            1) Inventory at start of year.
            2) Goods and materials bought or produced during year.
            3) Direct and indirect labor.
            4) Closing inventory excluded.
         b. Net cost of goods sold is total cost less closing inventory.
      2. Net profit is direct expenses deducted from gross profit [¶ 2601(b)].
   D. **Goods Included in Inventory [¶ 2602]:**
      1. Finished products.
      2. Raw materials.
      3. Merchandise or stock in trade.
      4. Work in process.
II. **Pricing Inventories**
   A. **Valuation:**
      1. Cost [¶ 2604(a)].
      2. Lower of cost or market [¶ 2604(b)].
   B. **First-in, First-out Method [¶ 2605]:**
      1. Value at lower of cost or market can be used.
      2. Goods first bought are considered first sold.
   C. **Last-in, First-out Method [¶ 2606]:**
      1. Inventory must be valued at cost.
      2. Goods most recently bought or produced treated as first sold.
      3. Advantages of LIFO over FIFO [¶ 2606(a)]:
         a. Spread between cost and selling price reduced.
         b. Reduces taxable income during inflationary period.
      4. Costing inventory under LIFO [¶ 2606(b)]:
         a. Opening inventory for first tax year—valued at cost.
         b. When closing inventory larger than opening—cost of increase found by reference to:
            1) earliest units bought or produced; or
            2) latest units, or
            3) average cost.
         c. Dollar-value costing—requires matching of dollar values in closing and opening inventories.
   D. **Goods Unsalable at Normal Prices.** Valued at selling prices less direct cost of disposition [¶ 2607].

E. **Book Inventories [¶ 2608]:**
 1. to show goods on hand as of any given date.
 2. Proper credit for goods sold, or used, as well as charges must be shown.
 3. Actual cost of goods bought or produced.
 4. Balances must be verified by physical count.
 5. Adjustment required if lower of cost or market is used.
F. **Methods of Valuation in Special Classes of Businesses:**
 1. Dealers in securities can be valued by [¶ 2609(a)]:
    a. Cost.
    b. Lower of cost or market.
    c. Market.
 2. Manufacturers and other producers [¶ 2609(c)]:
    a. Must use "full absorption" method of costing for allocating direct and indirect costs used in determining cost of goods sold.
    b. Treatment in financial reports of certain indirect costs can determine their status as inventoriable costs.
 3. Miners and like producers [¶ 2609(d)]:
    a. May allocate costs.
    b. Cost allocated to each kind and size or grade of product.
 4. Retail merchants [¶ 2609(e)]:
    a. Use of retail methods.
    b. Markup and markdown adjustments.
    c. Special rules allow use with LIFO and FIFO methods.
G. **Methods Disapproved [¶ 2610]:**
 1. Deducting reserve for price changes.
 2. Taking work in process or other parts of inventory at nominal prices.
 3. Omitting part of stock.
 4. Using a constant price or nominal value for normal quantity of materials or stock.
 5. Including stock in transit when title is not vested.
 6. Using "direct cost" method.
 7. Using "prime cost" method to currently deduct all indirect costs.
H. **Basis.** Last inventory value [¶ 2611].

III. **Farm Inventory and Accounting**
 A. **Income from farming:**
  1. Accounting methods of farmers [¶ 2614(a)]:
     a. Cash basis.
     b. Accrual basis.
     c. Crop basis.
  2. Items included in income [¶ 2614(b)]:
     a. Products exchanged for groceries.
     b. Crop shares.
     c. Insurance proceeds.
     d. Government subsidies.
     e. Patrons' income from cooperatives.
  3. Items excluded from income [¶ 2614(c)]:
     a. Products used by family.
     b. Donated products.
 B. **Inventories of farmers and livestock raisers [¶ 2615]:**
  1. Farm-price method.
  2. Unit-livestock-price method.
  3. Certain livestock included in inventory.

Chapter 17

ACCOUNTING

TABLE OF CONTENTS

ACCOUNTING METHODS

	¶
Methods of accounting	2701
Cash receipts and disbursements method	2702
Constructive receipt—cash basis	2703
Income paid to third parties—assignments	2704
Constructive payment—cash basis	2705
Accrual basis	2706
Accounting methods must clearly reflect income	2707
Change in accounting method	2708
Revenue Service consent required	
Consent may be assumed	
Alternative method for changing accounting method	
Adjustments required by change in accounting method	2709
If adjustments are substantial	
Change initiated by Revenue Service	
Change initiated by taxpayer	
Records	2710
Reconstruction of income	2711
Net worth method	
Percentage method	
Bank deposit method	
Excess cash expenditure method	

ACCOUNTING PERIODS

Accounting periods	2714
52-53 week fiscal year	
Change in accounting period	2715
Application to change accounting period	2716
Returns for periods of less than 12 months	2717
First or final returns	
Change of accounting period	
Alternative method	

WHEN TO REPORT INCOME

Period in which items of gross income reported	2719
Cash basis	
Accrual basis	
Compensation for services	2720
Dividends	2721
Loans, interest, discounts, and commissions	2722

	¶
Discount and interest on federal, state and local obligations	2723
Rent	2724
Income from sale of property or stock	2725
Prepaid income	2726
Prepaid subscriptions	
Prepaid membership dues	
Advance payments	
Dealers' reserves	2727
Disputed income	2728
Repaid Income	2729
Other types of income	2730
Blocked foreign income	
Merit credit under state unemployment compensation law	

WHEN TO TAKE DEDUCTIONS

Period when deductions may be taken	2735
Cash basis	
Accrual basis	
Contested items	
Overlapping items	
Payment by check	
When deductions are limited to amounts at risk	2736
Vacation pay and incentive bonuses	2737
Advertising expenses	2738
Interest	2739
Taxes	2740
Cash basis	
Accrual basis	
Medical expenses	2741
Contributions	2742
Bad debts and losses	2743
Reserves for expenses and losses	2744
Farming syndicate expenses	2745
Elections available for certain expenses	2746

SPECIAL PROBLEMS

Accounting for trading stamps and coupons	2747
Disallowance of unpaid expenses and interest	2748
Circulation expenses	2749

• Highlights of Chapter 17 .... Page 2761

Footnotes appear at end of this Chapter.

ACCOUNTING METHODS

The regular method of accounting you use in keeping your books is generally used in computing your income for tax purposes. The method used must clearly reflect taxable income.

¶ **2701 Methods of accounting.** The law recognizes that no uniform method of accounting can be prescribed for taxpayers. It expects each taxpayer to adopt the forms and methods of accounting suitable for his purpose [Sec. 1.446-1]. The two principal methods of accounting are:
  (1) The cash receipts and disbursements, or "cash basis," method [¶ 2702];
  (2) The accrual basis method [¶ 2706].

Generally, the cash basis taxpayer takes income into account when received and deducts expenses when paid. The accrual basis taxpayer takes income into account when earned and deducts expenses when incurred. Other methods used include the installment sales [¶ 2801 et seq.], long-term contracts [¶ 2842], and farmers' crop basis [¶ 2614]. See (d) below for farm corporations.

(a) Hybrid accounting method. A combination of accounting methods is permitted if it clearly reflects income and is consistently used. If the accrual basis is used for purchase and sales, the cash basis may be used for all other income and expense items. But a cash basis for income cannot be combined with accruals of expenses [Sec. 446(c); 1.446-1(c)(1)(iv)].

(b) More than one trade or business. A taxpayer engaged in two or more separate and distinct businesses may use a different method for each. Separate books and records must be kept [Sec. 446(d); 1.446-1(d)].

(c) Income solely from wages. A taxpayer whose income is solely from wages need not keep formal books. His accounting method may be established from his tax returns, copies of them, or other records [Sec. 1.446-1(b)(2)].

(d) Farm corporations. For tax years starting after 1976, corporations with annual gross receipts over one million dollars (except Subchapter S [¶ 3140] and family corporations), and certain partnerships, engaged in farming (except nurseries and timber farmers) must use the accrual method of accounting *and* must capitalize preproductive period expenses. A family corporation is one at least 50% owned by members of the same family. Only partnerships with a corporate partner that by itself would be subject to these rules must use the accrual method and must capitalize expenses. The change to accrual accounting is treated as a change of accounting not initiated by the taxpayer [¶ 2708] and any adjustments can be spread over the 10 tax years beginning with the year of change. A corporation that has used the accrual method for at least 10 years, and raises crops that are harvested at least one year after planting, can continue to use that method and need not capitalize its preproductive expenses [Sec. 447]. See also ¶ 1844.

> NOTE: The mandatory use of accrual basis accounting and capitalization of preproductive expenses has been postponed until tax years starting after 1977 for farming corporations if: (1) at least 65% of total combined voting power of stock and at least 65% of all stock is owned by members of two farming families, or (2) at least 50% of voting power and total shares is owned by members of three farming families and substantially all the balance of stock is owned by corporate employees or a trust for their benefit [P.L. 95-30].

¶ **2702 Cash receipts and disbursements method.** A taxpayer on the cash basis includes in gross income all income subject to tax that he received during the year in cash or its equivalent [¶ 2719]. He deducts all disbursements made during the year in cash or its equivalent, if deduction for the expenditures is authorized [¶ 2735]. Items of income and expenditures that are elements in figuring taxable income do not have to be in cash. It is enough that the items can be valued in terms of money.

¶ **2703 Constructive receipt—cash basis.** A cash basis taxpayer may be required to add to the income actually received, the amount of income constructively received. This is income that the taxpayer does not actually possess, but which is so much within his control and disposition as to amount to actual receipt [Sec. 1.451-2].

EXAMPLES OF CONSTRUCTIVE RECEIPT

Interest on savings bank deposits is fully taxable to the depositor when credited, without reduction for any forfeiture on a premature withdrawal.[1] For deductibility of the forfeiture, see ¶ 1801(a) for reporting requirements, see ¶ 3532(a).

Interest coupons. If matured and payable, but not cashed, the interest is reported for the year the coupons matured, unless there are no funds available for payment [Sec. 1.451-2(b)].

Brokerage accounts. Profits from a brokerage account not withdrawn by a taxpayer are taxable in the year earned, even if the account may be wiped out by losses in later years.[2]

Check. Check issued in one year and received in another, is constructively received in the year of issuance, if it was available in the earlier year[3] or the taxpayer agreed to accept payment in that year.[4] Also constructively received in the year of issuance is a salary check mailed for deposit in taxpayer's bank according to practice.[5]

Agent's receipt of income is the same as receipt by the principal.[6]

SPECIAL RULES

Acceptance. The taxpayer need not legally accept income to be taxed under the constructive receipt doctrine. If the money is subject to his command, it is constructively received whether he actually accepts it or not. Taxpayer cannot shift income to another year by refusing to accept what has been properly tendered under a prior agreement.[7]

Examples: A taxpayer verbally refused to accept a pension, and kept uncashed checks received under the pension plan. The checks were income constructively received.[8] but there was no constructive receipt when taxpayer refused to accept salary voted but not credited to him, and corporation used money for charitable purposes suggested by taxpayer.[9]

Pay. An employee may constructively receive pay if the money is credited to him, and he may withdraw it at any time.[10] There does not have to be a book entry setting the money apart, if it is otherwise made available[11] However, whether or not there is constructive receipt depends on the facts in each case. If there are no funds to make the payment for example, when the employer is insolvent, there is no constructive receipt.[12] Merely because an employer on the accrual basis deducted the pay does not necessarily result in constructive receipt by the employee.

Amounts taken out of wages by employer to pay insurance, buy savings bonds, pay union dues, or pay income taxes, are constructively received by the employee and must be included in gross income for that year.[13]

If a taxpayer's employer uses the taxpayer's wages to pay the latter's debts, or if the taxpayer's wages are attached, the full amounts are constructively received by the employee.[13]

Agreement to execute promissory notes in a later year is not the equivalent of cash.[14]

Dividends. For constructive receipt of dividends, see ¶ 2721.

Endowment and life insurance proceeds. See ¶ 1215(c).

Footnotes appear at end of this Chapter.

¶ 2704 Income paid to third parties—assignments.

Taxpayers may agree that income they are entitled to receive is to be paid to a third party. This raises the question of who pays the tax on the income—the one making the agreement or the person to whom it is paid.

(a) Assignment of income from property. A person owning an interest in property agrees that the income from the property will be paid to a third party. If the interest of the third party is merely in *income,* and there is no transfer of title to the property producing the income, it is not taxable to the third party, but to the owner of the property. It does not matter whether the income is to be earned in the future or has already been earned.[1] But if there is a legal transfer of a *property interest* to a third party, he is taxable on the income arising under the agreement.[2]

(b) Assignment of earnings. Income received for personal services is taxable to the person who earns it, even if he assigns it to another. The result is the same whether the assignment is for income to be earned,[3] or income already earned for past services.[1]

EXAMPLES OF ASSIGNED INCOME

Taxable to assignor. Assignment of earned commissions to third party by insurance agent[4]; assignment of cash dividends on stock (ownership of stock itself retained by assignor)[5]; assignment of rent[6] or lease[7] (real property owned by assignor); assignment by a beneficiary of trust income for a short period (one year)[8]; assignment of dividends after declaration date and before payment date by a life income beneficiary of a trust[9]; share of partnership income assigned[10]; assignment by husband to wife of patent license contracts between husband and a corporation, when husband, as majority stockholder in the corporation, had power to cancel the contract[11]; Medicare fees assigned by physicians to exempt organizations, but can be deducted as charitable contributions.[12]

Taxable to assignee. Transfer of stock and subsequent dividends on the stock[13]; assignment by life beneficiary of trust of part of the trust income for rest of his life.[14]

¶ 2705 Constructive payment—cash basis.

Generally, a cash basis taxpayer cannot deduct expenses before actual payment. However, when a payment due from, or made on behalf of, a cash method taxpayer is offset against amounts due him, he may deduct it for the year of the offset.[1] In such cases, his obligation with respect to the deducted expense is fully discharged by the offset. For example, interest charged by a broker on debt owed by a customer on the usual type of margin account is constructively paid when the broker makes collections for the account of the customer.[2]

¶ 2706 Accrual basis.

If income is reported when earned, even though not actually received, and expenses are reported when incurred, whether paid or not, taxpayer is using the accrual method of accounting. For prepaid income, see ¶ 2726. These are the basic rules:

1. The *right* to receive income (as distinguished from actual receipt) determines its inclusion in gross income under the accrual method [¶ 2719].
2. A deduction is accrued when an actual *liability is incurred* [¶ 2735].[1]

Example 1: On 9-1-77, a paving contractor laid a sidewalk for Mason City. Payment was not received until 1978. If the taxpayer reports on the accrual basis, the income is included in his 1977 return (when earned). If he reports on the cash basis, the payment is included in his 1978 return (when received).

Example 2: On 11-1-77, Walker bought a machine and gave his one-year 9% note for $500. On 11-1-78, he paid the note and interest ($545). If he reports on the accrual basis, $7.50 interst is deductible in 1977, and $37.50 is deductible in 1978, (over the period the liability is *actually incurred*). If he reports on the cash basis, the $45 is deductible in 1978 (when paid).

Accrual basis mandatory when inventories used. When it is necessary to use an inventory [¶ 2600], the accrual method must be used for purchases and sales, unless the Revenue Service authorizes another method [Sec. 1.446-1(c)(2)].

¶ 2707 Accounting methods must clearly reflect income. The statute does not sanction any method of accounting unless it clearly reflects income [Sec. 446(b); 1.446-1(a)(2)]. So, even if the taxpayer's accounts are kept and the return made on a cash basis, unusual cases may arise when a payment made during the year is not deductible.

Commissions, fees, and printing costs paid in one year by a taxpayer in securing a loan for 10 or 15 years covered by a mortgage on property to be leased are not deductible in full in the year of payment, but should be spread over the period of the loan, even if taxpayer's return is made on the "cash basis." [1]

Insurance premiums that are business or investor's expenses paid in advance for more than one year by cash basis taxpayer are deductible ratably over the period to which they relate (Revenue Service and 1st Circuit).[2] But the 8th Circuit holds that these premiums may be deducted in the year paid.[3]

Taxpayers may round-off amounts on internal transactions to the nearest dollar, if a penny elimination account is maintained, and the procedure is followed with reasonable consistency.[4]

¶ 2708 Change in accounting method. A taxpayer who changes his method of accounting must get the consent of the Commissioner before computing his income under the new method even if the new method is proper and permitted by the Code and the regulations [Sec. 1.446-1(e)(2)]. Exceptions to this general rule are noted below. Application to change the accounting method used is made on Form 3115. It ordinarily must be filed with the Commissioner of Internal Revenue, Washington, D.C. 20224, within 180 days after the start of the year for which the change is desired [Sec. 1.446-1(e)(3)(i)].

Example: A taxpayer who wants to change his method of accounting for calendar year 1978 must file Form 3115 by 6-29-78.

(a) Revenue Service consent required. A change in the method of accounting includes a change in the over-all method of accounting for items of gross income or deduction, as well as a change in the treatment of a material item. A material item is any item that involves the proper time for the inclusion of an item in income or the taking of a deduction [Sec. 1.446-1(e)(2)(ii)(a)]. Specifically a change includes: change from the cash to an accrual method, or vice versa;[1] a change from the cash or accrual method to a long-term contract method, or vice versa [¶ 2842]; a change in the method or basis used in valuing inventories [¶ 2604]; a change involving any other specialized method of figuring taxable income, such as the crop method [¶ 2614]; a change in the treatment of any other material items of income or expense, or a change that specifically requires Revenue Service consent [Sec. 1.446-1(e)(2)(ii)(a)]. A change in the method of accounting does not include: (1) the correction of mathematical or posting errors; (2) errors involving the computation of tax liability; (3) the adjustment of income or deduction items that do not involve the proper timing for inclusion of the items (for example, the correction of items deducted as interest or salary when they are in fact dividend payments); (4) the adjustment of an addition to a bad debt reserve or the useful life of a depreciable asset; or (5) changes in the treatment of any item that results from a change of underlying facts [Sec. 1.446-1(e)(2)(ii)(b)]. Permission to change will not be granted, unless the taxpayer and the Revenue Service agree to the terms and con-

Footnotes appear at end of this Chapter.

ditions under which the change will be made [Sec. 1.446-1(e)]. Consent to a changed method may be implied from Revenue Service acceptance of its use.[2] When the accounting method is changed, certain adjustments in income and deductions are required [¶ 2709].

REVENUE SERVICE CONSENT NOT REQUIRED

When installment method is adopted, changed to, or discontinued, but consent is required if a new election is made within 5 years of discontinuance [¶ 2804]; when a subsidiary corporation must change its method to conform to that of the consolidated group of which it is a member[3]; when changing from the declining balance to the straight line depreciation method (¶ 2012) [Sec. 1.167(e)-1(b)]; when changing to accrual method to avoid recapture of deducted farm losses as ordinary income (¶ 2226) [Sec. 1251(b)(4)(C); Temporary Reg. Sec. 13.0]; when changing to straight line depreciation despite contrary agreement to avoid depreciation recapture (¶ 2010(c)) [Sec. 1.167(e)-1(c)(2); Temporary Reg. Sec. 13.0]; when changing depreciation methods under ADR system (¶ 2033) [Sec. 1.167(a)-11(c)(1)(iii)].

(b) Consent may be assumed. A procedure to expedite getting consent has been instituted for: (1) a change in the method of accounting for bad debts from the specific charge-off to the reserve method, unless taxpayer uses the installment method [¶ 2311],[4] and (2) a change in depreciation method [¶ 2010].[5] In these instances, the taxpayer within the first 180 days of the tax year may file Form 3115 with the Service Center where the taxpayer normally files his return. Unless the Revenue Service notifies taxpayer that the Form 3115 is not timely filed, taxpayer is deemed to have obtained the Commissioner's consent. A copy of Form 3115 must be attached to the return for the year in which the change is made. If the taxpayer is changing his method of accounting for bad debts, he must attach a copy of Form 3115 to this return for the succeeding 9 years, together with a statement showing the computation used in arriving at the adjustments required by the change [¶ 2709]. The adjustments must be spread over the 10-year period.

(c) Alternative method for changing accounting method. An administrative procedure has also been instituted under which a taxpayer's request to change his accounting practice with respect to a material item or to change any other accounting method will receive favorable consideration, if he agrees to take the resulting adjustment into account ratably over an appropriate period, generally 10 tax years. Application is made by filing Form 3115 with the Commissioner of Internal Revenue, with a request for the change within 180 days after the start of the tax year for which the change is requested. A request may be considered timely filed if it is filed after the 180-day period but within 9 months of the tax year for which the change is requested if the taxpayer can show good cause for the delay.[6]

NOTE: The approval of the deferral of prepayments for services depends on the principles set forth in this procedure [¶ 2720]. A taxpayer who wants to change his method of accounting for prepayments for services may file Form 3115 under this procedure for the last tax year for which a return has been filed.[7]

¶ 2709 Adjustments required by change in accounting method. When the accounting method is changed (except a change from the accrual to the installment method [¶ 2804]), an adjustment is required to avoid duplication or omission of items of income or deductions [Sec. 481(a); 1.481-1]. So the income of the transition year may consist of two elements: (1) taxable income figured under the new method; and (2) adjustments to take up the slack between the old and the new method.

Example 1: A taxpayer changing from the cash to the accrual basis in 1977 has taxable income of $20,000 figured on the accrual basis. His books at the start of 1977 showed the following: Accounts receivable, $30,000; accounts payable $14,000; inventory, $5,000.

The taxable income after adjustments for the transition period is $41,000:

(1)	Taxable income figured on accrual basis		$20,000
(2)	Adjustments:		
	(a) Add: (1) Items not previously reported as income:		
	Accounts receivable 1-1-77	$30,000	
	(2) Items previously deducted:		
	Inventory 1-1-77	5,000	
	Total to be added		35,000
	Total		$55,000
	(b) Subtract items not previously deducted:		
	Accounts payable 1-1-77		14,000
(3)	Taxable income after adjustments		$41,000

If a taxpayer is required to change his accounting method and use inventories, and his closing inventory on 12-31-53 exceeds his opening inventory for the year of change, no adjustment is needed as to the inventory.[1]

(a) Limitations on tax if adjustments are substantial. If the net amount of the adjustments attributable to the 1954 Code years is an increase in taxable income of not more than $3,000, or is any decrease, the entire amount of the adjustment is made in the year of change [Sec. 481]. But if the increase in income attributable to 1954 Code year exceeds $3,000, the adjustment may be made by (1) a three-year allocation method, (2) an allocation under the new method of accounting, or (3) any other method agreed upon by the taxpayer and the Commissioner [Sec. 481(c); 1.481-5].

NOTE: Election of a relief method generally is made in a written statement filed with the Revenue Service at the time permission to change the accounting method is requested [¶ 2708].

Three-year allocation method. If the taxpayer used the old method of accounting for the 2 years preceding the change-over year, the tax is reduced to the amount that would have been paid if one third of the increase in income had been received in the year of the change and one third in each of the 2 preceding years [Sec. 481(b)(1); 1.481-2(a), (d)].

Example 2: Assume the same facts as in Example 1, and that taxpayer used the cash method in 1975 and 1976, and that the adjustments are all post-1954. Since the adjustments increase taxable income by $21,000 ($41,000 adjusted taxable income less $20,000 taxable income before adjustments), taxpayer may reduce the tax on the increase by allocating $7,000 to 1975, $7,000 to 1976, and $7,000 to 1977.

Allocation under new method of accounting. If the taxpayer can establish his taxable income (under the new method) for one or more years *consecutively* preceding the year of the change, he may reduce his tax to the amount that would have been paid if the new method had been used during those years, except that any remaining adjustments would be allocated to the year of the change [Sec. 481(b)(2); 1.481-2(b), (d)].

Example 3: Assume the same facts as in Example 1, and that the taxpayer recomputed the tax for 1975 and 1976 on the accrual basis. On this basis, the taxable income for 1975 was increased by $6,000 and for 1976 by $7,000. Thus, $13,000 of the $21,000 adjustments were allocated to 1975 and 1976. The balance, $8,000, is taken into account in figuring the tax for 1977 (the change-over year).

Effect of net operating loss and capital loss carryover or carryback. In the recomputation under either relief method, net operating losses and capital loss carryovers or carrybacks (only carrybacks of losses sustained in tax years starting after 1969) are

Footnotes appear at end of this Chapter.

¶ 2709

taken into account for years to which no adjustment is allocated [Sec. 481(b)(3)(A); 1.481-2(c)(2)]. Any net operating loss incurred in a later year is carried back to the year involved before either of the above spread-backs are computed.[2]

Closed years. If any tax year involved is a closed year, the adjustments are made in accordance with Sec. 1314(a) (mitigation of statute of limitations, ¶ 3631) [Sec. 481(b)(3)(B)].

(b) Change initiated by Revenue Service. If the Revenue Service initiates the change, no adjustment is required for items of income and deductions applicable to a tax year starting before 1-1-54 [Sec. 481(a)(2); 1.481-3].

Example 4: Assume the same facts as in Example 1 and that the Revenue Service initiated the change and $1,000 of the inventory adjustment resulted from pre-1954 Code years. The net adjustments taken into account would be only $20,000 and the taxable income after adjustments. $40,000.

(c) Change initiated by taxpayer. If the change in method is initiated by the taxpayer in tax years starting after 1963, all pre-1954 adjustments must be treated the same way as an adjustment for 1954 Code years [Sec. 481(b)(4)(D); 1.481-4(a)]. However, if taxpayer initiates certain changes in the method of accounting [¶ 2708(b), (c)], a 10-year spread forward remains available. In addition, taxpayers requesting discontinuance of the LIFO method of inventory [¶ 2606] may also request permission to allocate any adjustment over a period of 10 years;[3] if they have used the LIFO method for 6 or more years up to the year of the change, they may allocate the adjustment over a period of twice the number of years the LIFO method was used, but not more than 20 years.[4]

NOTE: A change made by a taxpayer on his own initiative to conform to a federal income tax regulation or ruling, or one required by another governmental regulatory agency is considered initiated by the taxpayer.

Change in tax years starting before 1-1-64. Special rules applied to a taxpayer-initiated change made in tax years starting before 1-1-64. If he elected to spread forward pre-1954 adjustments, he could allocate them ratably over 10 years starting with the change-over year [Sec. 481(c); 1.481-4]. The election thus affects tax years after 1963.

Change of status. If the taxpayer's status changes before the full amount of the pre-1954 adjustments have been reported, the balance is reported (i) by an individual, in the year he dies or goes out of business; (ii) by a partner, in the year the partnership terminates or his interest is transferred or liquidated; (iii) by a corporation, in the year it ceases business (except for "acquired" corporations (¶ 3337)) [Sec. 481(b)(4)(C); 1.481-4(c)].

¶ 2710 Records. The taxpayer must keep accounting records that will enable him to make a return of his true income. Among the essentials are the following [Sec. 1.446-1(a)(4)]:

- If the production, purchase, or sale of merchandise is an income producing factor, inventories must be taken into account at the beginning and end of the year [See Chapter 16].
- Expenditures during the year must be properly classified as between capital and expense [See Chapter 8].
- If the cost of assets is being recovered through depreciation, amortization or depletion, any expenditure (other than ordinary repairs) made to restore the property or prolong its useful life must be added to the property account or charged against the appropriate reserve and not to current expense [See Chapter 8; 10; 11].

¶ 2711 Reconstruction of income. If the taxpayer has no regular method of accounting, or if his records are incomplete, inaccurate, lost, or destroyed, the

Revenue Service may reconstruct his income by whatever method seems appropriate [Sec. 446(b)].

(a) **Net worth method.** The Revenue Service first establishes the "net worth" (difference between the assets and the liabilities) at the start of the tax year. Any increase in net worth during the tax year is added to the nondeductible expenses. This amount is compared with the amount reported on the return. If the reported amount is smaller than the income as reconstructed, and the additional funds did not come from a nontaxable source (such as gift or inheritance[1]), they are unreported income on which an additional tax is due. The Courts have approved the use of the net worth method in reconstructing income from gambling, tavern-restaurant, slot machines, general store, used car business, black market operations, and income of a doctor, among others. The net worth method has also been upheld by the Supreme Court as a basis for conviction for tax evasion.[2]

(b) **Percentage method.** The Revenue Service reconstructs income by determining the total sales or receipts and applying to this amount an average percentage of gross profit to the total sales or receipts.[3] It can also reconstruct taxable income by applying to gross income an average percentage of taxable income to gross income.[4] The percentage used is either taken from returns filed in previous years or from figures reflecting percentages of taxpayers in similar trades or businesses.[5] However, the experience of other taxpayers cannot be used if the taxpayer's business conditions are unlike those of the businesses used for comparison.[6]

(c) **Bank deposit method.** The Revenue Service includes in income the total amounts deposited in the tax year, after eliminating (1) duplications (such as transfers of funds between banks); (2) amounts identified as not being income receipts; and (3) total receipts reported as income by the taxpayer. Unexplained bank deposits are presumed to be income, and the burden of proving otherwise is on the taxpayer.[7]

(d) **Excess cash expenditure method.** The Revenue Service usually reconstructs income by comparing the amount spent by the taxpayer with the amount the return shows is available to him as income. Income has been reconstructed from amounts spent for machinery, equipment, real estate and living expenses, and from amounts spent for medical and entertainment expenses.

ACCOUNTING PERIODS

Accounting periods are ordinarily for 12 months—either for a calendar or fiscal year. A 52-53 week year can be elected if books are kept accordingly. A change of accounting period can only be made for valid business reasons.

¶ 2714 **Accounting periods.** (a) **General rules.** Taxable income is figured on the basis of the taxpayer's annual accounting period, which may be either the calendar year or a fiscal year [Sec. 441(b)(1); 1.441-1(b)]. A fiscal year means (1) an accounting period of twelve months ending on the last day of any month other than December or (2) an annual accounting period varying from 52 to 53 weeks, subject to the rules in (b) below [Sec. 1.441-1(e)].

No books kept. If the taxpayer does not keep books, a calendar year must be used [Sec. 441(b)(2); 1.441-1(b)].

Footnotes appear at end of this Chapter.

New taxpayers. A taxpayer who adopts an accounting period ending on a date other than the last day of a calendar month has failed to establish an annual accounting period within the meaning of the Code. He must compute his net income on a calendar year basis.[1] Electing a 52-53 week period [(b) below] is an exception to this rule.

A newly-organized corporation may file its return on a fiscal year basis without applying to the Revenue Service for permission, provided the fiscal year basis is definitely established and the books are kept in accordance with it before close of the first fiscal year.[2]

Sole proprietor—one tax year. A sole proprietor must report business and personal income on the basis of the same tax year. For example, he may not operate his business on a fiscal year basis, and file his individual return on a calendar year basis.[3]

(b) 52-53 week fiscal year. A taxpayer who regularly keeps his books on the basis of a period varying from 52 to 53 weeks always ending on the same day of the week which either (1) occurs for the last time in a calendar month or (2) falls nearest to the end of the calendar month, may elect to figure his taxable income on the basis of that period [Sec. 441(f)(1); 1.441-2(a)].

Under (1) above, the year may end as many as 6 days before the end of the month, but must end within that month. Under (2) above, the year may end as many as 3 days before or after the end of the month. [Sec. 1.441-2(a)].

If the taxpayer does not regularly keep books on the basis of a 52-53 week year, he may elect this period if at the time of election he conforms his books to this basis, and after that continues to keep his books and report income on this basis [Sec. 1.441-2(c)].

Effective dates. To determine the due dates of returns or the effective dates of other law provisions that are expressed in terms of tax years beginning or ending with reference to the first or last day of a specified calendar month, a 52-53 week year is considered to begin on the first day of the calendar month nearest to the first day of the 52-53 week year. It is considered to end or close on the last day of the calendar month ending nearest to the last day of the 52-53 week year [Sec. 441(f)(2)(A); 1.441-2(b)].

Example 1: Assume a new tax rate applies to years beginning after Dec. 31, 1976. A 52-53 week year starting on Dec. 26 is treated as starting on Jan. 1.

Example 2: Assume a return is due by the 15th of the 3rd month following the close of the fiscal year. A 52-53 week year ending on June 1 is considered as ending on May 31.

Exception—rate change. These rules do not apply when a tax rate changes *during* the 52-53 week tax period [Sec. 1.441-2(b)].

Example 3: Assume a rate of tax is reduced from 30% to 25% for tax years starting after 12-31-76, and that taxpayer is on a 52-53 week fiscal year ending 8-26-77. The new rate is not effective as of 9-1-77, but as of 1-1-77. The tax for the fiscal year ending 8-26-77 must be figured on the basis of the number of days in the tax year before 1-1-77 and the number of days in the tax year after 12-31-76.

Figuring taxable income. Generally, income and deduction items are determined on the basis of a 52-53 week year. They may, however, be determined as if the year contained 12 calendar months, if the practice is consistent and clearly reflects income. Depreciation and amortization deductions are taken as if the year contained 12 calendar months, unless (in the case of depreciation) some other practice is consistently followed [Sec. 1.441-2(d)].

Election is made by a statement with the return for the first period for which the election is made. It should show: (1) the calendar month with reference to which the new 52-53 week year ends: (2) the day of the week on which the tax year will always end; and (3) whether it will end on (a) the date the day occurs for the last time in the calendar month or (b) the date it occurs nearest to the end of the calendar month [Sec. 1.441-2(c)].

¶ 2715 **Change in accounting period.** The change may be from a calendar year to a fiscal year, from a fiscal year to a calendar year, or from one fiscal year to another fiscal year. A fractional year return is required for the part of the year between the close of the old period and the start of the new. This period is called the short tax year [Sec. 7701(a)(23)].

Special rules apply to short tax periods resulting from a change to or from a 52-53 week accounting period. In the year the 52-53 week period is adopted, periods of more than 358 days and periods of less than 7 days are not considered short periods. The former are treated as full years; the latter are added to the following tax year [Sec. 441(f)(2)(B); 1.441-2(c)].

Example 1: Assume a corporation is on the calendar year basis for 1976. It elects to report income for 1977 on the basis of a 52-53 week period ending on the Monday nearest to the end of December. The first tax period will consist of the period from 1-4-77 through 1-2-78, plus the short period of 3 days, 1-1-77 through 1-3-77. No fractional return is required for the short period.

Example 2: Assume the same facts as in Example 1, except that taxpayer was on a fiscal year ending Nov. 30. The first full tax year will consist of the period from 1-4-77 through 1-2-78. A fractional year return will be required for the short tax year beginning 12-1-76 and ending 1-3-77, since this period consists of more than 6 days, but less than 359 days.

¶ 2716 **Application to change accounting period.** Generally, an application on Form 1128 to make the change must be sent to the Commissioner of Internal Revenue, Washington, D.C. 20224, on or before the 15th day of the second calendar month following the close of the short tax year. Usually a change will be approved if there is a substantial business reason for it (for example, to change to a natural business year[1]) and the taxpayer and the Revenue Service agree to the terms, conditions, and adjustments required. The change ordinarily will not be approved if it substantially reduces a taxpayer's tax liability by shifting a taxpayer's income or deductions to another year or to another taxpayer. If the short tax year has a substantial net operating loss or if a substantial part of the income of an electing small business [¶ 3140 et seq.] for the short period is long-term capital gain, the change will not be approved [Sec. 1.442-1(b)]. There are special rules for partners and partnerships [¶ 2920 et seq.], bank or trust company fiduciaries[2] and tax-exempt organizations.[3]

(a) **Special rule for corporations.** No prior approval is needed if (1) corporation has not changed its accounting period within the 10 calendar years ending with the year the short tax year begins; (2) the short tax year has no net operating loss; (3) the taxable income for the short tax year when annualized [¶ 2717] is at least 80% of the taxable income for the preceding full tax year; and (4) the corporation has the same special status (if any) for the short period and for the tax year immediately preceding the short period. (Special status includes: personal holding company [foreign or domestic], exempt organization, foreign corporation not engaged in trade or business within U.S., Western Hemisphere trade corporation, China Trade Act corporation.) [Sec. 1.442-1(c)].

A statement must be filed with the District Director by the time (including extensions) for filing the return for the short tax year. Statement should show that above conditions have been met, and that the change is authorized by Sec. 1.442-

1(c). If, because of later adjustments in establishing tax liability, the Revenue Service finds that the corporation did not meet all the requirements, this statement will be considered a timely application for change of accounting period [Sec. 1.442-1(c)].

NOTE: The special rule explained above does not apply to corporations that are subject to partnership-type taxation [¶ 3140 et seq.] during the short period. These must get prior approval to change the accounting period [Sec. 1.442-1(c)]. Another special rule would require, in addition to (1) through (4) above, that the corporation not attempt a Subchapter S election for a tax year (a) immediately following the short tax year, and (b) beginning after 8-23-72 [Sec. 1.442-1(c)(2)(v)]. The special rules also do not apply to DISCs (¶ 3460) [Sec. 1.442-1(c)(4)].

(b) 52-53 week year. Prior approval is *not* required if the change is made to a 52-53 week year that ends on a day that refers to the same month in which taxpayer's prior tax year ended. The necessity for approval for other changes is governed by the general rules outlined above, or the special rules for partners and partnerships in Chapter 19.

Example: Compton currently reports on a fiscal year ending June 30. If he changes to a 52-53 week year ending on the last Saturday in June or on the Saturday nearest to the last day of June, approval is not required. If he changes to a 52-53 week period ending on a particular day with reference to any other month, approval will be required.

When permission is not required, election to change to a 52-53 week year should be indicated by a statement attached to the return for the first tax year to which the election applies [¶ 2714(b)].

(c) Husband and wife cannot file a joint return and take advantage of the split-income benefits unless each has the same accounting period, that is, the same tax year [¶ 1104; 3504-3507]. If a change in the period of one spouse is desired in order to file a joint return, permission may be granted, even though there is no business reason for the change [Sec. 1.442-1(b)].

Newly married couples. A newly married person may change his accounting period to conform to that of the other spouse so that a joint return may be filed for the first or second year of such spouse ending after the marriage date. The spouse making the change must file a return for the short tax year by the 15th of the 4th month following the close of the short tax year, with a statement that it is authorized by Sec. 1.442-1(e). If the couple marries after the due date of the short tax year return, the first tax year of the nonchanging spouse that ends after the marriage date cannot be adopted [Sec. 1.442-1(e)].

(d) A subsidiary corporation required to change its accounting period because it has elected to file consolidated returns [¶ 3222] need not file Form 1128 when the consolidated return is filed [Sec. 1.442-1(d)]. However, the Revenue Service recommends that this form be filed.[4]

(e) If book and tax periods differ. If the taxpayer regularly keeps books on the calendar or fiscal year, but erroneously files returns on a different basis, permission is not required to file returns for later years based on the way the books are kept.[5]

¶ 2717 Returns for periods of less than 12 months. Most income tax returns cover an accounting period of 12 months. On two occasions, however, a taxpayer's accounting period is less than 12 months: (1) when he files a first or final return; and (2) when he changes his accounting period.

(a) First or final returns. Short period returns are required of new taxpayers filing their first returns and of taxpayers ending their existence. This applies to all kinds of taxpayers, such as corporations, partnerships, estates and trusts, decedents, departing aliens and taxpayers whose tax years are terminated for jeopardy. These returns are prepared and filed, and the taxes paid, as if they were returns for a 12-month period ending on the last day of the short period. The income of the short period is not annualized, nor are personal exemptions or other credits prorated. A decedent's return, however, may be filed and the tax paid as if he had lived throughout his last tax year [Sec. 443; 1.443-1].

(b) Change of accounting period. A taxpayer who changes his accounting period may have to file a return for a period of less than 12 months. Such a return must be placed on an annual basis [Sec. 443(b)]. This is done as follows [Sec. 443; 1.443-1(b)(1)]:

1. Multiply the short period gross income (minus deductions allowed for the short period and the proportionate amount of any personal exemptions for the short period) by 12.
2. Divide the result by the number of months in the short period.
3. Add the appropriate zero bracket amount to the result.
4. Compute the tax on the result on an annual basis using the tax rate schedules.
5. Divide the result by 12.
6. Multiply the result by the number of months in the short period.

Exemption deduction. The deduction for exemptions for the short tax year is apportioned in the ratio that the number of months in the short tax year bears to 12 [Sec. 443(c); 1.443-1(b)(1)].

Net operating loss. In computing taxable income for a short year, a net operating loss deduction is applied against the actual income for the short period before placing the income on an annual basis.[1]

Minimum tax. The $10,000 exclusion ($5,000 for married persons filing separately) from the tax on preference items [¶ 2403] is prorated in the ratio that the number of days in the short tax year bears to 365 [Sec. 443(d)].

Credits. If any credit against the tax depends upon the amount of any item of income or deduction, the credit must be annualized, and then applied against the tax figured on an annual basis. If credit limitation is based on taxable income, the income must be annualized [Sec. 1.443-1(b)(1)].

52-53 week year. In annualizing income for short tax years resulting from a change to or from a 52-53 week accounting period [¶ 2715], the computation is made on a daily basis [Sec. 441(f)(2)(B); 1.441-2(c)].

When to annualize. The rule for annualizing income applies only to a change in accounting periods. It does *not* apply to the first or last *income* tax return of a taxpayer for a short period [Sec. 443(b); 1.443-1(a)(2)], such as the return of a newly organized corporation; the final return of a dissolving corporation; the return for a decedent; the first or final returns of an estate; or to a new member of an affiliated group filing a consolidated return.[2]

(c) Alternative method. To prevent hardship, taxpayer can apply for a refund, if the tax figured under the annualized method is greater than the tax figured on actual income for the 12-month period starting with the first day of the short period. This is determined by establishing the actual taxable income for the 12 months *beginning* with the first day of the short period. The tax figured on the actual taxable income for the 12-month period is then multiplied by a fraction, the numerator of which is the *actual* taxable income for the short period and the denominator of which is the taxable income for the 12-month period. But, the tax for the short period cannot be less than if the income for the short period were not annualized [Sec. 443(b); 1.443-1(b)(2)].

Footnotes appear at end of this Chapter.

¶ 2717

A taxpayer, other than a corporation, that was not in existence at the end of the 12-month period may figure its tax based on the 12 months *ending* with the last day of the short period. The same rule applies to a corporation that has disposed of substantially all of its assets before the end of the 12-month period. Application to use this method must be attached to the return. The computation is the same as that explained above [Sec. 443(b)(2)(B); 1.443-1(b)(2)].

WHEN TO REPORT INCOME

The question often is not whether an item should be included in income but when it should be included. The rules generally have evolved from Revenue Service rulings and court decisions.

¶ **2719 Period in which items of gross income reported.** (a) **Cash basis** taxpayer reports all income subject to tax actually or constructively received during the year in cash or its equivalent [Sec. 451; 1.451-1].

Checks are income in the year received, although cashed in a later year by taxpayer on cash basis.[1] This is so even if the check is received too late to be cashed in the year of receipt.[2] However, if the check is not cashed until the next year at the request of the drawer, it is income in the year cashed.[3] As to dividend checks, see ¶ 2721; for constructive receipt, see ¶ 2703.

(b) **Accrual basis.** A taxpayer on the accrual basis includes in gross income all income subject to tax that accrues during the year. Income accrues when all the events have occurred that fix the right to receive it, and the amount can be reasonably estimated. When a reasonable estimate is made, any difference in the estimated and exact amount is taken into account in the year the exact amount is determined [Sec. 1.451-1]. A taxpayer is not required to accrue an amount that probably will never be received. If the obligation is not collectible when the right to receive arises, nothing accrues.[4]

Prepaid income is reported in the year received. It cannot be prorated over the period that the services are to be performed.[5] See ¶ 2726.

¶ **2720 Compensation for services.** (a) **Cash basis.** If the taxpayer is on the cash basis, compensation is included in income for the year it is actually or constructively received.[1] This includes income deferred by an employment contract.[2] Generally, it is immaterial that the employer, using the accrual basis, deducted the compensation in the previous year. However, an employer making deferred compensation payments can deduct only those amounts in the year they are actually made.[2] Special rules apply to a salaried partner [¶ 2920]. Money placed in an educational benefit trust set up by a corporation for the education of employees' children is deferred compensation taxable to the employees and deductible by the corporation when paid out of the trust.[3]

Advances to salespersons. If, under the employment contract, advances are a debt due the employer, they are not taxable when received by a cash basis salesperson. However, if advances to commission salespersons were orginally intended as loans but are later charged off, they are additional compensation to the salespersons and deductible by the employer in the year charged-off.[4] If the contract guarantees the salesperson a certain monthly sum, advances up to the guarantee are income when received.[5]

(b) Accrual basis. For an accrual basis taxpayer, pay is usually income in the year earned. But if it is not determined until the services are completed, it is income for the year of determination [Sec. 1.451-1]. An accrual basis taxpayer may defer reporting of an advance payment received for services to be performed until the year next succeeding the year of payment if, under an agreement, the services are to be performed before the end of the year succeeding the year of payment. If any part of the services are not performed by this time, the taxpayer must include the amount allocable to that portion of the services not so performed, in his gross income in that succeeding year, regardless of when the services are performed.[6]

¶ **2721 Dividends** are subject to tax when unqualifiedly made subject to the demand of the shareholder [Sec. 1.301-1]. This applies to both cash and accrual basis taxpayers.

> **Example 1:** A dividend is fully and unqualifiedly available to Turner in 1977. It can be reduced to actual possession and realization in 1977, merely for the asking. Turner does not receive the dividend until 1978. It is taxable in 1977.

> **Example 2:** Benton, a stockholder, buys stock for Mason in Benton's name. Benton receives a dividend for Mason on 12-14-77 but transmits it to Mason by check on 1-2-78. It is taxable to Mason on 12-14-77.

Dividend checks mailed on last day of tax year. If a dividend is declared payable on December 31, but the corporation follows the practice of mailing the dividend checks so that they will not be received until January, there is no constructive receipt in December, and the dividend is January income [Sec. 1.451-2(b)], even if taxpayer is on the accrual basis.[1] For other checks received on the cash basis, see ¶ 2719(a).

(a) Income from building and loan associations. An amount credited to the shareholders of a building and loan association is constructively received in the year of credit, if it passes without restriction to the shareholder. However, if the amount accumulated does not become available to the shareholder until maturity, the total amount credited is income to the shareholder in the year of maturity [Sec. 1.451-2(b)].

(b) Patronage dividends and per-unit retains are generally taxable in the year received, whether taxpayer is on the cash or accrual basis [Sec. 1385(a); 1.1385-1(a)]. See ¶ 3458 for patrons' income from cooperatives.

¶ **2722 Loans, interest, discounts and commissions. (a) Interest.** If the taxpayer is on the cash basis, interest is taxable when actually or constructively [¶ 2703] received. Accrual method taxpayers report interest for the year in which it accrues, unless received earlier. Property given a depositor by a bank is taxable as interest income when paid or made available to the taxpayer.[1]

Discount on a note. When installment payments of a loan made at discount are first applied to reduce principal under a bona fide agreement, a lender on the cash basis does not receive interest until after the principal has been recovered.[2]

A special rule applies to interest on capital received by partners [¶ 2923(d)].

(b) Loans and mortgages bought at discount. The time for reporting the income depends on whether the loan bears interest.

If the loan is interest-bearing, no income from the discount is reportable until all or a part of the loan is paid, or until it is resold, whether the taxpayer is on the

Footnotes appear at end of this Chapter.

cash or accrual basis.[3] If the debt is payable in full at maturity, the discount is income when the payment is made.[3]

If the loan is payable in installments, the following rules apply: (1) a part of each payment, representing interest, is reported as paid or earned (depending on accounting method); a proportionate part of the balance is treated as repayment of the principal, and a proportionate part (figured on the basis of the entire discount) is treated as income; (2) upon final payment, the discount not reported in prior years, is income in the year of payment; (3) if the note is resold, the gain or loss is the difference between the selling price and the purchase price, adjusted for any prior recovery of cost.

If the loan is non-interest bearing, the rules governing bank discount on money loaned apply. On the cash basis, the discount is reported as the loan is paid; on the accrual basis, as the discount is earned.[4]

(c) Commissions on bank loans. When a bank arranges for or makes a loan, the commission or service charge is deducted from the face amount of the loan before payment to the borrower. If the bank is on the cash basis, the commission is income to the bank only when it is actually received or realized on payment, sale or other disposition of the loan.[5] If the bank is on the accrual basis, the commission is income when the loan is made.[6]

(d) Commodity Credit loans. The taxpayer may elect to treat as income loans from the Commodity Credit Corporation [Sec. 77; 1.77-1]. If the election is made, he reports the amounts authorized by interest certificates in the year actually disbursed to him or as directed by him.[7] The election is made by attaching a statement to the return,[8] and is binding unless the Revenue Service authorizes a change to a different method. When the loan is treated as income, it increases the basis of the property pledged as security [Sec. 1016(a)(8); 1.1016-5(e)]. The Fifth Circuit held that a loan redeemed the same year received and elected to be treated as income then, was not income until the crops were sold later.[9] The Ninth Circuit disagreed, holding the redeemed loan income in the year received and repaid.[10] If no election is made, and the loan is not repaid, the loan is income in the year the redemption period ends. Any additional amount the taxpayer realizes from CCC's sale of the security for more than the amount owed is also income.[11]

(e) Savings certificates. Increment in growth savings certificates and non-negotiable savings certificates issued by banks is included in a cash basis taxpayer's gross income in the year the increase occurs, since certificate holders can redeem the certificate in that year.[12]

(f) Original issue discount. The discount on certificates of deposit, time deposits, bonus plans and other deposit arrangements issued after 1970 with a term of more than one year and issued by banks, savings and loan associations, and similar financial institutions, as well as face-amount certificates issued after 12-31-74 is reported ratably over the term of the instrument in the same manner as original issue discount bonds (¶ 1629) [Sec. 1232; 1.1232-3A(e), (f)]. The amount reported is the original issue discount divided by the total number of months of the instrument's term, times the number of months it was held during the tax year [Sec. 1.1232-3A(a)]. Basis is increased by the amount of included interest [Sec. 1.1232-3A(c)]. A taxpayer who redeems before maturity for less than the stated redemption price gets a deduction for discount reported but not received [Sec. 1.1232-3A(e)(2)]. See ¶ 3532 for information returns required for such interest.

¶ 2723 **Discount and interest on federal, state and local obligations.**

(a) U.S. savings bonds issued on a discount basis on or after 3-1-41. Series E bonds are the only U.S. Savings bonds issued at a discount and currently outstanding. These bonds increase in value depending on how long they are held. The entire increase is taxable. The amount that accrues in any tax year is measured by the actual increases in the redemption price occurring in that year.[1]

Cash basis. If the taxpayer is on the cash basis, he may treat the taxable increment as income received in the year of redemption or maturity, or he may elect in his return to report the taxable increment for each year as income for that year. The election applies to all bonds owned by him at the start of the year for which he made the election and to bonds he acquires later. It is binding for all future years, unless, on application by the taxpayer [¶ 2708], the Revenue Service permits a change. The increment for all prior years must be included in income for the year the election is made [Sec. 454(a); 1.454-1]. If the taxpayer dies, the increment is reported as income in respect of a decedent [¶ 3008(b)], unless the decedent's personal representative makes the election and reports it in the decedent's final return.[2] An election cannot be made in an amended return filed after the due date of the original return or in an original return not timely filed.[3]

> **Example 1:** Taxpayer on the cash basis bought a Series E bond for $75 (maturity value $100) in January 1976. According to the Table of Redemption Values, the first increase in value occurs ½ year after issue ($76.20). If the taxpayer elects to report the increment annually, he reports $1.20 in 1976. Any increases in 1977 and later years are reported in the same way.

Accrual basis. If the taxpayer is on the accrual basis, he must report the taxable increment for each year as income for that year.[4]

Series E bonds held beyond maturity. Cash basis taxpayers holding Series E bonds after maturity who have elected to report the taxable increment on the accrual basis must continue to do so, unless permission to change is granted. Those who have elected to report on redemption or maturity, report the entire increment in the year of *final* redemption or *extended* maturity.[5]

(b) U.S. savings bonds issued on a current income basis after 3-1-41. Unlike the bonds issued on a discount basis [see above], these current income bonds are issued at par with interest payable semiannually by Treasury check. The interest is taxable when received or accrued. The interest accrues when it becomes payable.[6] The only current income U.S. Savings Bonds currently outstanding are Series H bonds. Owners of matured Series H bonds may continue to hold the bonds at interest after maturity.[7] Interest for the extended period should be reported when received or accrued.

(c) Discount on federal, state and local short-term obligations. U.S. treasury bills and other U.S. obligations, or obligations of any U.S. possession, state or any political subdivision, or the District of Columbia issued on or after March 1, 1941 on a discount basis and payable without interest at a fixed maturity date not exceeding one year from the date of issue are affected by a special rule [Sec. 454(b); 1.454-1(b)]. These obligations are treated as noncapital assets [Sec. 1221].

The effect of these provisions is twofold: (1) the discount does not accrue until the obligation is paid at maturity, sold or otherwise disposed of; (2) they eliminate the necessity for making an allocation between interest and capital gain or loss, for federal obligations (Example 2) [Sec. 1.1221-1]. But for obligations of a U.S. possession, a state or any political subdivision or the District of Columbia, it is necessary to separate the interest from the selling price, because the interest is exempt [Example 3].[8]

Footnotes appear at end of this Chapter.

¶ 2723

Example 2 (federal obligation): Assume that a U.S. Treasury bill issued for $994 has a maturity value of $1,000 at the end of 90 days. At the end of 60 days, the obligation is sold by the original buyer for $997.

Selling price	$997
Cost	994
Ordinary income	$ 3

Example 3 (Other obligations): Assume that a state obligation issued for $994 has a maturity value of $1,000 at the end of 90 days. At the end of 60 days, the obligation is sold by the original buyer for $997.

Cost		$994
Selling price	$997	
Less: Tax-exempt discount for the period from date of acquisition to date of disposition (60/90 of $6)	4	993
Ordinary loss		$ 1

Assume the buyer held the security until its maturity, his tax results would be as follows:

Amount realized		$1,000
Less: Tax-exempt discount for the period from date of acquisition until maturity (30/90 of $6)	2	$998
Cost		997
Ordinary gain		$ 1

¶ 2724 Rent. If the taxpayer is on the cash basis, rent is taxable when received. Rent accrues ratably over the period of the lease, unless paid in advance, in which case, it accrues when received. [Sec. 1.61-8].

Example: Davis owns an apartment house. Rent for December 1977 and for January 1978 is paid in January 1978. If Davis reports on the cash basis, the rent is 1978 income. If he reports on the accrual basis, the rent paid for December is 1977 income and that paid for January is 1978 income. But if Davis rented an apartment for 5 years in December 1977, and the rent for the whole period was paid to him in advance at that time, it would be 1977 income whether he reports on the cash or accrual basis. The same rule would apply to other types of prepaid income (but see ¶ 2726 for exceptions).

Lease cancellation. Amount received from a tenant for cancellation of a lease is income in the year received, even if landlord is on the accrual basis.[1]

¶ 2725 Income from sale of property or stock. (a) **Sale of property.** In determining the year gain from the sale of property should be reported, the question is when was there a *closed transaction?* For a *cash basis* taxpayer, that is usually when the purchase price is received. *Accrual basis* taxpayers realize gain when a sale is completed (see below), and they have an unqualified right to receive payment. This usually is when the buyer becomes unconditionally liable to pay the purchase price.

When sale completed. A sale of real property generally occurs at the time (1) title is conveyed by a deed, or (2) possession and the burdens and benefits of ownership, are, from a practical standpoint, transferred to the buyer, whichever occurs first. The transfer of possession and of the burdens and benefits of ownership need not be complete. When the "bundle of rights" or attributes of ownership acquired by the buyer outweigh those retained by the seller, the sale is completed.[1] Sales of personal property are governed by the same rules. But most sales of personal property will occur when title passes. For tax purposes, the local law of sales will prevail in determining when title passes.

Contingent payments. If all or part of the consideration for the sale of property is an agreement to make future payments of *a contingent character*, the transaction is not closed for tax purposes. No part of the contingent payments is income until taxpayer has recovered his capital. After that the payments are taxed as a gain (subject to capital gain limitations if the asset was a capital asset).[2]

Example: Taxpayer sold property to a corporation for a percentage of its profits for 5 years. Since the payments were contingent on earnings, they were not income until received, and then only to the extent that they represented gain over the basis of the property.[3] See also ¶ 2816.

(b) Sale of stock through broker. The question when a sale of stock becomes a closed transaction arises when a sale is made at the end of one tax year but delivery of the certificates is not made until the next year. An accrual basis taxpayer realizes gain or loss on sale of securities on the day a broker completes the transaction on a stock exchange. A cash basis taxpayer realizes a loss when the broker completes the transaction,[4] but does not realize gain until the settlement date of the contract.[5] The foregoing does not apply to short sales of stock or to sales of stock on a "when issued" basis [¶ 1608(b)].

(c) Payments or property in escrow. If part or all of the purchase price of property is placed in escrow by the buyer, the seller should not include the amount placed in escrow in his gross sales until it is actually or constructively received, whether he is on the cash or accrual basis. However, on performance of the terms of the contract and escrow agreement, the seller realizes taxable income, even though he may not accept the money until the following year.[6]

If property is sold and placed in escrow to secure notes accepted in payment, the proceeds of the sale (cash and fair market value of notes received) are includible in income on the date received.[6]

¶ 2726 Prepaid income. Generally, prepaid income is taxable in the year received whether the taxpayer is on the cash or accrual basis.[1] However, there are exceptions for *accrual* basis taxpayers receiving prepaid subscription income, certain prepaid membership dues and advance payments.

(a) Prepaid subscriptions. Publishers on the accrual basis may elect to report prepaid subscriptions over the subscription period instead of reporting it all in the year received. But if the taxpayer's liability ends or taxpayer dies or goes out of existence, any unreported amount must be reported in that year [Sec. 455(a)(b); 1.455-4].

The election generally applies to all prepaid subscriptions of the trade or business for which it is made. However, income that will be earned within 12 months of receipt may either be included in the election or reported in the year received [Sec. 455(c); 1.455-6(c)].

How to elect. The election can be made without consent for the first tax year in which subscription income is received [Sec. 455(c); 1.455-6(a)]. It is made by a statement attached to the return. Statement should show the following for each trade or business to which the election applies: (1) name and type of business; (2) method of accounting used; (3) total amount of prepaid subscription income for the tax year; (4) period or periods over which the liability of the taxpayer extends; (5) amount of prepaid subscription income for each period; and (6) method of allocation [Sec. 1.455-6(a)]. Consent is required at any other time. The application must be filed with the Commissioner in Washington, within 90 days after the start of the first year to which the election is to apply [Sec. 1.455-6(b)].

The election is effective for the year of election and all later years. It can be revoked only with the consent of the Revenue Service [Sec. 455(c); 1.455-2(c)].

Footnotes appear at end of this Chapter.

¶ 2726

If the election is not made, taxpayers may continue to report subscription income by the method used in the past [Sec. 455(e); 1.455-5(a)].

(b) Prepaid membership dues. Certain membership organizations without capital stock, operating on the accrual basis, may elect to spread dues covering 36 months or less over the membership period. This would apply to automobile clubs like the A.A.A., for example [Sec. 456; 1.456-1—1.456-7].

(c) Advance payments. Taxpayers on the accrual basis or using the long-term contract method [¶ 2842] who receive advance payments for goods to be delivered in some future year or for building, installing, constructing or manufacturing under an agreement not completed in the tax year can include the advance payments in income in either (a) the tax year the payments are received or (b) the tax year they are properly accruable under the taxpayer's method of accounting (either the method used for tax purposes or the method used for financial reports that includes the advance payments earlier in gross receipts). The financial reporting requirement is ignored for payments under a long-term contract method of accounting [Sec. 1.451-5(b)]. For example, if the taxpayer would normally account for his sales when goods are shipped, advance payments for the goods could be included in income in the year of shipment. However, an exception to this exclusion rule applies if the taxpayer receives an advance payment under an agreement to sell goods that are includible in inventory and, on the last day of the tax year, he (1) has received "substantial advance payments" and (2) has on hand (or has readily available to him) enough goods that are substantially similar in kind to satisfy the agreement in that year [Sec. 1.451-5(c)]. If this exception applies, all advance payments received by the last day of the second tax year after the tax year of the "substantial advance payments" (and not previously included in income) must be included in income in that second year [Sec. 1.451-5(c)(1)]. Any payments received after the second tax year must be included in the tax year of receipt [Sec. 1.451-5(c)(2)]. Advance payments are "substantial" if the payments received during the tax year plus advance payments received prior to that year equal or exceed total costs and expenditures reasonably estimated as includible in inventory [Sec. 1.451-5(c)(3)]. If the taxpayer elects this special method of reporting advance payments, he must attach an information schedule to his income tax return each year that shows the amount of advance payments received in the year and those received in prior years that have and those that have not been included in income [Sec. 1.451-5(d)].

¶ 2727 Dealers' reserves. Amounts credited by a finance company to an accrual basis dealer's reserve on discount of customers' notes are taxable in the year credited.[1] A cash basis taxpayer reports the amount credited to him when he gets a fixed right to the money.

Required increase in a suspense account set up by a dealer deducting a reasonable reserve for bad debts arising from his liability as a guarantor of debt obligations he sells, is income to the dealer in the tax year for which the increase is required [Sec. 81]. See also ¶ 2311(d).

¶ 2728 Disputed income. A dispute as to the taxpayer's right to receive an amount he claims is due, postpones the time for taxability of his claim. Amounts recovered as a result of the dispute usually are taxable: (1) under the accrual method when the dispute is finally terminated by a settlement, a final judgment by the highest court, or a final judgment of a lower court when no appeal is taken and the time for appeal expires;[1] and (2) under the cash method when the amounts are received by taxpayer.[2] However, taxability is not postponed beyond the time when the taxpayer receives disputed amounts under a claim of right and without restriction as to their disposition, even when the receipt takes place during a dispute.[3]

Income impounded, withheld or escrowed during a dispute as to the taxpayer's right to receive it, is not taxable until the funds are released to him or the dispute is terminated.[3]

An offer to compromise a claim for a lesser amount does not create taxable income,[4] but an unconditional concession as to part of the claim fixes the time for accrual of the conceded amount.[5]

¶ **2729 Repaid income.** When taxpayer receives income under a claim of right and without restriction as to its disposition, it is income in the year received. The taxpayer must include the income even though his right to retain it is disputed and all or part of it may have to be repaid in a later year because the right to its use proves not to have been unrestricted. The repayment, however, is deductible in the later year,[1] even if the government received no tax benefit the year the income was reported, because taxpayer had a net loss.[2] The Supreme Court has held that the deduction of repayment must be reduced by any depletion taken on the income received under a claim of right.[3]

(a) Special relief. A number of factors may prevent taxpayer from receiving enough benefit from the deduction to offset the tax paid when the income was received. For instance, taxpayer may be in a lower tax bracket or the tax rates may be lower. If the repayment exceeds $3,000, a relief provision applies. The inequity is corrected by reducing the tax for the year of repayment. In essence, the tax reduction is equal to the amount taxpayer would have saved if he had never received the income and never made the repayment. If the reduction exceeds the tax for the current year, the excess is refunded or credited as an overpayment [Sec. 1341; 1.1341-1(i)].

In making the computations, the following must be considered:

- If the prior year is not open for adjustments, it is not opened by this provision. Computations are made to determine the tax for the year in which the repayment is made.
- If the prior year is still open, other adjustments by way of carrybacks, carryovers, credits and allowances are made before any computations are made for the purpose of this section.
- In either event, deductions that depend on the amount of adjusted gross income, taxable income, or net income (such as contributions and medical expense), are recomputed under this section [Sec. 1.1341-1(d)(4)].

Exceptions to relief provisions. The above provisions do not apply to: (1) bad debts [¶ 2301 et seq.], (2) legal expenses incurred in contesting repayment of the income previously included, or (3) sales of inventory or stock in trade, except as indicated below [Sec. 1341(b)(2); 1.1341-1(f), (g), (h)].

The relief provisions apply to: (1) refunds or repayments involving rate adjustments made by a regulated public utility when the refunds or repayments are required by a regulatory body, a court order, or in settlement of litigation; and (2) refunds or repayments made under price redetermination provision of subcontracts involving the U.S. under the following conditions: (a) the subcontract was entered into before 1-1-58, (b) the subcontract is between "unrelated" taxpayers, (c) the subcontract is subject to statutory renegotiation, and (d) the refund or repayment is made to a contractor (not the U.S.) [Sec. 1341(b)(2); 1.1341-1]. Taxpayers are "unrelated" when they are not related as described in ¶ 2223, as parties to a trust [¶ 3018] or as controlled corporations when one is a personal holding corporation [¶ 3409].

Footnotes appear at end of this Chapter.

¶ **2729**

Subcontracts made after 1957. For repayments resulting from contracts similar to those in (2) entered into after 1957, a different provision applies. Both the payor-subcontractor and the payee recompute the tax for the year of original payment as if the original payment of the repaid amount was not made. Any resulting overpayment to the payor, or deficiency for the payee, is taken into account in the year of repayment. The provision applies whether or not payor and payee are "related" [Sec. 1482; 1.1341-1(f)(3)].

(b) Accounting methods. The foregoing explanation has been made in terms of a cash basis taxpayer. An accrual basis taxpayer is entitled to the relief in the year the repayment accrues as a charge. The year in which the income first accrued is considered the year of receipt of the income.

Cash basis taxpayers who reported the income on the constructive receipt basis, but who have never actually received the income, are considered to have made the repayment in the year they were required to relinquish their right to receive the income.

¶ **2730 Other types of income. (a) Blocked foreign income.** Some foreign countries impose monetary or exchange restrictions that prevent conversion of foreign currency into U.S. dollars. Taxpayers with income from these sources can elect to defer the taxation of the nonconvertible income until: (1) conversion can be made, (2) conversion is actually made, despite the existence of restrictions, (3) the income is used for nondeductible personal expenses, (4) the income is disposed of as a gift, bequest, devise, inheritance, dividend or other distribution, or (5) in the case of a resident alien, the taxpayer terminates his residence in the U.S.

Election is made by filing with the regular return a special return for each country (using same type of form) reporting the deferable income. Return is headed "Report of Deferable Foreign Income, pursuant to Rev. Rul. 74-351."[1] Once made, the election may not be changed without the Commissioner's consent. The election must be made by the due date for filing the return for the first year the election will apply.[1]

For payment of tax in nonconvertible funds, see ¶ 3527(b).

Business expenses paid in the foreign currency are deductible only when and to the extent the deferred income is reported. Costs and direct expenses in U.S. dollars incurred in earning deferable income also are deferred. Their treatment, however, is not identical. Costs are a first charge, to their full extent, against such income when it ceases to be deferred. Direct expenses are deductible, however, only in the proportion that the net recovery after deducting costs, bears to the gross profit on the transaction.[1]

> **NOTE:** When blocked foreign income is received, it is included in income on the basis of first-in, first-out.[2]

(b) Merit credit under state unemployment compensation law. If the taxpayer is on the cash basis, the credit is income when it becomes available to him in satisfaction of liability for contributions. On the accrual basis, it is reported as income in the year taxpayer becomes liable for contributions against which the credit may be applied.

WHEN TO TAKE DEDUCTIONS

Generally cash basis taxpayers deduct expenses in the year paid while accrual basis taxpayers deduct them in the year of accrual. However, certain expenses must be ratably deducted over the future periods they benefit regardless of the accounting method used.

¶ **2735 Period when deductions may be taken.** **(a) Cash basis.** Deductions must be taken by a cash basis taxpayer in the year payment is made in cash or its equivalent [Sec. 461, 7701(a)(25); 1.461-1(a)(1)]. But a taxpayer's note is not the equivalent of cash. So, if a cash basis taxpayer gives his note in payment, he cannot take the deduction until he pays the note, even if it is secured by collateral.[1] However, a payment with borrowed money is deductible when paid; not later, when the loan is repaid.[2]

(b) Accrual basis. An accrual basis taxpayer takes all deductions when they accrue [Sec. 461, 7701(a)(25); 1.461-1(a)(2)]. There must be an actual liability before any amount may be accrued. If a liability has actually been incurred, and is uncertain only as to the exact amount and date it must be discharged, a reasonable estimate may be set up as an accrual. Any difference in the estimate and the exact amount is taken into account in the year of exact determination [Sec. 1.461-1(a)(2)]. But if an actual liability is not incurred until the happening of some contingency, no amount can be accrued until the contingency happens.[3]

(c) Contested items. When an accrual method taxpayer disputes his liability to pay a claimed amount, deduction of the resulting settlement, judgment or award is postponed until the dispute is settled by the parties or it is finally adjudicated by the courts [Sec. 1.461-1(a)(3)(ii)]. However, when taxpayer pays an expense, the liability for which he then contests, payment accrues the item, so as to permit and require immediate deduction, even though the contest is continued [Sec. 461(f); 1.461-2]. Putting the money in escrow qualifies. If taxpayer later settles the liability for less than the amount transferred, the excess must be included in income to the extent a tax benefit results [¶ 2316]. The deduction was denied for amounts deposited with the Revenue Service while taxpayer was contesting a proposed tax, since the Service had not made an assessment of the tax to create a liability.[4] These rules apply to all contested items, except foreign taxes and taxes of U.S. possessions. Cash method taxpayers deduct disputed liabilities for the year in which they actually pay them[5] or make an escrow deposit [Sec. 461(f); 1.461-2].

(d) Overlapping items. While the expenses, liabilities, or deficit of one year cannot be used to reduce the income of a later year, regulations recognize that in a business of any magnitude there are certain overlapping items. The important thing is that the taxpayer follow a consistent policy, making sure the income of any year is not distorted [Sec. 1.461-1(a)(3)].

(e) Payment by check by a cash basis taxpayer can be deducted when it is delivered, if paid on presentation.[6] Checks postdated to another tax year cannot be deducted before the date shown.[7]

> **Example:** Taxpayer contributes to a college fund. He sends the college a check late in December 1977. The check is dated 12-31-77. The college does not deposit or cash the check until January 1978. The contribution is considered made in 1977. Deduction is taken in the 1977 return [Sec. 1.170A-1(b)].

In the case of accrual basis taxpayers, the method of payment usually does not affect the time for deducting the expenses.

¶ **2736 When deductions are limited to amounts at risk.** Investors can deduct losses only to the extent of investments in the following tax shelter activities: (1) holding, producing or distributing movies or video tapes; (2) certain kinds of farming [¶ 1844(d); 2745]; (3) leasing any personal property subject to depreciation recaputre [¶ 1619(a)]; and (4) exploring for, or exploiting, oil and gas re-

Footnotes appear at end of this Chapter.

sources. These provisions do not apply to corporations (except Subchapter S) [Sec. 465].

NOTE: These rules generally apply to tax years starting after 1975. For equipment leasing, the rules do not apply to net leases under a binding contract on or before 4-30-76. For movie arrangements, the rules do not apply to a film purchase if the photography began before 9-11-75, there was a binding written contract for the film's purchase on that date and the taxpayer held his interest in the film on that date. For movie production costs, the same rules apply except there is no need for a written binding contract. For a film produced in the U.S., the at risk rule does not apply if photography began before 1-1-76 and by 9-10-75 either there was an agreement with the principal star or the director, or the lower of 10% of estimated costs or $100,000 had been spent or committed to the production.

Any allowable loss from these activities can be deducted only to the extent of the amount an investor has at risk for each activity at the end of each tax year. Any loss exceeding the at risk investment is treated as a deduction allocable to the activity in the first succeeding tax year and is also subject to the at risk limits. A deductible loss reduces the amount at risk in subsequent tax years [Sec. 465(a)]. However, it does not have any effect on the bases of assets or a partner's interest in the partnership.

Amount considered at risk. An investor is at risk to the extent of money or the adjusted basis of other property contributed to the activity, as well as loans on which the investor is personally liable or for which property has been pledged (other than property used in the activity). Despite personal liability, an investor is not at risk for loans if the creditor is a related taxpayer [¶ 2223] or has an interest in the activity other than as a creditor. Also, an investor is not at risk for amounts protected against loss by insurance, nonrecourse financing, guarantees, stop loss agreements or other similar arrangements [Sec. 465(b)].

¶ **2737 Vacation pay and incentive bonuses.** Special rules govern the time for deducting (a) vacation pay on the accrual basis and (b) incentive bonuses payable by accrual taxpayers.

(a) **Accrual of vacation pay.** An accrual basis employer may elect to accrue and deduct vacation pay when earned by his employees, even though they do not actually take vacations or receive vacation pay until a subsequent year. If the employer elects this treatment, he must set up a vacation pay accrual account. Reasonable additions are made to this account, representing the employer's liability for vacation pay earned by employees before the close of the tax year and payable within that year or 12 months thereafter. In addition, the employer must set up a suspense account to prevent the permanent loss of vacation pay deductions contained in the opening balance of the vacation pay accrual account [Sec. 463].

The suspense account is set up with an initial amount equal to the opening balance of the vacation accrual account. This amount is reduced by accruals allowed as deductions for prior years, but not yet paid at the beginning of the election year. At the end of each year, the suspense account is reduced by the amount, if any, by which the beginning balance in the suspense account exceeds the ending balance in the vacation pay accrual account. The amount of this reduction, plus the reasonable additions (above), constitute the annual deduction for vacation pay.

Vacation pay includes amounts paid or to be paid to an employee while he is on vacation or in lieu of a vacation (so long as the choice is solely the employee's). It does not include sick pay or holiday pay.[1]

The employer first electing this method of deducting accrued vacation pay may do so for tax years beginning after 1973 without the Commissioner's consent. The election must be made by the later of 7-21-75, or the due date for filing the return (without regard to extensions) for the first tax year for which the election may be made. The Commissioner's consent is required to revoke the election and is a change of accounting method [Temp. Reg. 10.2].

(b) Accrual of bonuses under incentive compensation plan. When the exact amount of a bonus cannot be determined and paid until the year following the year of accrual, such amounts may be deducted by the accrual basis taxpayer in the year of accrual if: (1) the total bonuses are determinable through a formula in effect before the end of the year; (2) the employer before the end of the year obligates itself to make payment by notifying each employee (individually, or in a group) either orally or in writing of the percentage of the total bonus payment to be awarded to him; and (3) payment is made as soon after the close of the year as is administratively feasible.[2] For time for deducting contributions to employees' trust, see ¶ 1838.

¶ 2738 Advertising expenses are deductible by a cash basis taxpayer in the year paid; by an accrual basis taxpayer in the year they accrue. Although the benefits of advertising may continue for several years, the cost may not be capitalized and written off over the later years.[1]

¶ 2739 Interest. A taxpayer on the cash basis ordinarily deducts interest when it is actually paid,[1] unless it is prepaid [below]. An accrual basis taxpayer deducts interest as it accrues; interest accrues ratably over the period.[2]

> **Example 1:** On April 1, 1977, Barnes bought a machine, giving his one-year note for $1,000. The note bore interest at 9%. On April 1, 1978, he paid the note and interest ($1,090). If he reports on the cash basis, the $90 interest is deductible for 1978 (when paid). If he reports on the accrual basis, $67.50 interest is deductible for 1977 and $22.50 for 1978.

Prepaid interest. If interest is paid in advance (after 12-31-75), a cash basis taxpayer must allocate the interest deduction over the period of the loan. However, this rule does not apply to interest prepaid before 1-1-77 under a binding contract or written loan commitment that existed on 9-16-75 and required prepayment. Also, deductible mortgage "points" paid in connection with the purchase or improvement of, and secured by, the taxpayer's principal residence can be fully deducted in the year of payment if the payment of "points" is an established business practice in the area and does not exceed amounts generally charged for such home loans (¶ 1416(d); 1900) [Sec. 461(g)].

Insurance policy loan. Interest on a life insurance policy loan, which by the terms of the contract is added to the principal of the loan if not paid when due, cannot be deducted as "interest paid" by a cash basis taxpayer.[3]

Discount on a note (other than an installment note) is deductible by a cash basis taxpayer when paid, and by an accrual basis taxpayer as it accrues.[4]

In the case of discount on an installment note payable in equal monthly installments, part of each payment made by the cash basis borrower represents interest and is deductible in the year paid,[5] unless there is an agreement to apply all of the payments to principal until it is fully recovered.[6]

> **Example 2:** If Coe, on the cash basis, receives $100 cash for a $114.98 note payable in 36 equal monthly installments, $1/36$ of $14.98 is the deductible part of each payment. If 12 monthly payments are made in the year, $12/36$ of $14.98 is deductible in that year.[5]

¶ 2740 Taxes. (a) Cash basis. A taxpayer on the cash basis may deduct as taxes only the amount actually paid during the year.[1]

(b) Accrual basis. A taxpayer on the accrual basis deducts taxes as they accrue. A tax accrues when all the events have occurred that fix the amount of the tax and determine the taxpayer's liability to pay it.[2] A tax that is imposed retroactively cannot accrue before enactment of the law imposing it.[3] For contested taxes see ¶ 2735(c).

Foreign tax credit. A foreign tax taken as a credit accrues for the year to which it relates even if contested and not paid until a later year. But the accrual cannot be made until the contested liability is finally determined.[4]

State income taxes. State income taxes generally accrue in the year the income (on which the state tax is paid) is earned.[5] But an increase in state taxes accrues when the amount is finally determined by litigation or default, or taxpayer acknowledges liability.

Corporate franchise taxes. Several states impose corporate franchise taxes based on income. These taxes accrue when all the events have occurred that fix the liability. A list of states imposing franchise taxes and the accrual dates is given in the P-H "Federal Taxes" at ¶ 13,217.

Property taxes. Generally, property taxes accrue on the date liability for the tax becomes fixed. This is usually the lien date or the date the owner becomes personally liable. If the state changes the accrual date, there may be 2 accrual dates in one year. In that case, unless the deduction would be lost for good, only one accrual for state taxes is available in any one tax year and the date of accrual before the state change determines the time of deduction. Thus, all taxpayers continue to use the original accrual date.

> **Example:** A state changes its lien (accrual) date from 1-1-77 to 12-31-77. Taxpayer cannot deduct 2 years' taxes in 1977 (those accruing on 1-1-77 and those accruing on the new lien date, 12-31-77). Instead, he deducts 12 months' taxes for 1977 and 12 months for 1978.

Election to ratably accrue real property taxes. Instead of taking the deduction based on the accrual date as explained above, taxpayers may elect to accrue and deduct them ratably over the period imposed. The election may be made for each separate trade or business (or for "nonbusiness" activities if accounted for separately). It can be adopted *without consent* for the first year the taxpayer incurs real property taxes, if the election is made by the return due date for the tax year (including extensions). For adoption at any other time, written request to the Revenue Service must be made not later than 90 days after the start of the tax year to which the election applies. With the election or request, taxpayer should submit a computation of the deduction for the first year of election and any other information necessary to explain the deduction. Election is binding unless on application by taxpayer [¶ 2708], the Revenue Service permits a change [Sec. 1.461-1(c)].

¶ 2741 Medical expenses. The deduction allowed individuals for expenses for medical care [¶ 1945] is for amounts actually paid during the tax year. No deduction is allowed for accruals or prepaid expenses.

¶ 2742 Contributions. Generally, charitable contributions are deductible in the year paid. Pledge or accrual is not enough[1] [¶ 1942]. Thus, a charitable contribution made through a bank credit card is only deductible in the year the charge amount is paid to the bank.[2] A special rule, however, allows accrual basis corporations to deduct contributions before they are actually paid [¶ 3118]. Contributions in property are deductible in the year the gift is completed.

Contribution of stock certificate. A contribution of a properly endorsed stock certificate is made when the certificate is unconditionally delivered to donee or donee's agent. If delivered to donor's agent or to issuing corporation for transfer, the contribution is made when stock is transferred on the corporate books [Sec. 1.170-1(b)]. See also payment by check [¶ 2735(e)].

¶ 2743 Bad debts and losses. (a) **Bad debts** are deductible in the year they become worthless [¶ 2300]. But see ¶ 2311, if a reserve is used.

(b) **Losses** generally are deductible in the year sustained. They must be evidenced by closed and completed transactions fixed by identifiable events.

Sales of property and stock. Losses from sales of property or stock generally are deductible in the year there is a "closed transaction" [¶ 2725].

Mortgage foreclosure. Generally, loss to the mortgagor resulting from a foreclosure is sustained when the period of redemption expires.[1] However, circumstances may warrant deduction in year of foreclosure sale as where the taxpayer, though financially able, refused to pay the taxes because of the low value of the property.[2] In effect, he has abandoned the property. If he litigates the validity of the foreclosure sale, no loss occurs until the litigation is finally settled.[3] Also, if he makes a bona fide claim that the sale is invalid, time for deduction may be postponed until that claim is settled, although there is no formal court action.[4]

¶ 2744 Reserves for expenses and losses. A reserve is an amount set aside out of current income for meeting expenditures to be made in a later tax year. As to reserve for bad debts, see ¶ 2311.

(a) **Cash basis.** Under the cash basis, deduction may be taken only in the year of payment. So there can be no deduction for a reserve.

(b) **Accrual basis.** If the books are kept on the accrual basis, a deduction may be taken if there is a present liability to support the deduction. The cases are in conflict as to whether reasonably accurate estimates of expenses are deductible before the year in which the services actually are rendered and taxpayer's liability to make actual payments arises. Some Circuit Courts have allowed the deduction for the year in which the income for the services was taxable, or in which the obligation to perform them arose.[1] The Tax Court disagrees.[2] See ¶ 2735(b) for the rule when an actual liability has been incurred, but the amount is uncertain.

EXAMPLES OF RESERVES HELD NOT DEDUCTIBLE

Anticipated loss on contract to buy merchandise.[3]

Reserve for self-insurance.[4]

Reserve representing estimate of cash discounts that taxpayer may have to allow customers in later years.[5]

¶ 2745 Farming syndicate expenses. Generally, for tax years starting after 1975, farming syndicates must (1) deduct expenses for feed, seed and similar farm supplies only when used (not when paid), and (2) capitalize poultry production costs and preproductive orchard, vineyard or citrus grove expenses (except for trees and vines planted or bought on or before 12-31-75, or under a binding contract to purchase in effect on 12-31-75) [Sec. 464]. A preproductive cost is one incurred in the year before the year the property becomes productive. See ¶ 1844(d).

¶ 2746 Elections available for certain expenses. Both the cash and accrual basis taxpayer have a choice as to the time for, and the method of, deducting certain expenses. Among these are:

Footnotes appear at end of this Chapter.

¶ 2746

- Research and experimental expenses [¶ 1842];
- Exploration and development expenses of mines [¶ 1843];
- Farm development expenses [¶ 1844];
- Soil and water conservation expenses [¶ 1845];
- Intangible drilling and development costs of mines [¶ 2103(c)];
- Corporate organizational expenses [¶ 3116].

SPECIAL PROBLEMS

¶ 2747 Accounting for trading stamps and coupons. If a taxpayer issues trading stamps or coupons with sales or is engaged in the business of selling such stamps and coupons redeemable in merchandise, cash, or other property, he is allowed to deduct from gross receipts an amount equal to the cost of redemptions plus the net addition to (or minus the net subtraction from) the provision for future redemptions during the tax year [Sec. 1.451-4(a)(1)]. The provision for future redemptions is computed by multiplying "estimated future redemptions" by the estimated average redemption cost of each stamp or coupon [Sec. 1.451-4(b)(1)(i)]. "Estimated future redemptions" are the number of stamps or coupons outstanding at the end of the year that can be reasonably expected to be presented for redemption [Sec. 1.451-4(b)(1)(ii)]. Any method that is reasonably accurate and consistently used (for example, a determination based on taxpayer's past redemption experience or the experience of similar businesses) may be used to determine estimated future redemptions [Sec. 1.451-4(c)(1)—(6)].

¶ 2748 Disallowance of unpaid expenses and interest. No deduction will be allowed to a debtor:

1. If the debtor reports on the accrual basis, and the creditor reports on the cash basis;
2. If within 2½ months after the close of the debtor's tax year (a) payment is not made and (b) the amount is not includible (either actually or constructively) in the gross income of the creditor; *and*
3. If, at the close of the debtor's tax year or at any time within 2½ months after that, both the debtor and creditor are so related that losses between them would be disallowed under Sec. 267(b); see ¶ 2223.

Disallowance occurs only when *all three* conditions are present. Payment in notes meets the payment condition.[1]

Example 1: A corporation is on the accrual basis, and Smith, its president, is on the cash basis. The corporation pays its employees on the first business day of each month, and Smith received his December, 1977 salary of $2,000 on January 2, 1978. Since Smith is on the cash basis, he will report this payment as 1978 income. The corporation, however, will take a deduction in its 1977 return (the year liability to make payment was incurred).

Ordinarily, no objection can be offered to this plan. Suppose, however, Smith owns all the stock of the corporation, and instead of paying his salary monthly, the corporation merely accrues his annual salary of $24,000 and never pays Smith anything, except possibly in a year he has a loss to offset the payment. Obviously, Smith's salary, for which the corporation is taking a deduction, may never be taxed to him. The law prevents this by providing that the corporation does not get a deduction unless within 2½ months after the close of the corporation's tax year (a) the corporation actually pays Smith's salary or (b) makes the pay available to Smith in such a manner that it is includible in his income as constructively received [¶ 2703].

Example 2: Assume the tax year ends 12-31-77. The 2½-month period ends at the close of 3-15-78. Payment on 3-16-78 would be too late.[2]

¶ 2749 Circulation expenses attributable to prepaid subscriptions [¶ 2726(a)] formerly were required to be spread over the life of the subscriptions, if the publisher as a consistent practice so spread the subscription income. The Regulations provide for the current deduction of such expenditures in the year paid or incurred, and this rule apparently applies even if the prepaid subscription income is spread over the life of the subscriptions, and regardless of the method of accounting used by the taxpayer [Sec. 1.173-1(a)].

Footnotes to Chapter 17

(P-H "FEDERAL TAXES" related references are cited in brackets [ ] at the end of each footnote below.)

Footnote ¶ 2701 [¶ 20,060 et seq.].
Footnote ¶ 2702 [¶ 20,065 et seq.].
Footnote ¶ 2703 [¶ 20,161 et seq.].
(1) Rev. Rul. 73-511, 1973-2 CB 402; Rev. Rul. 75-21, 1975-1 CB 367 [¶ 20,137(7)].
(2) Webb v. Comm., 67 F.2d 859, 13 AFTR 408 [¶ 20,166(95)].
(3) McEuen v. Comm., 196 F.2d 127, 41 AFTR 1169 [¶ 20,171(5)].
(4) Rev. Rul. 68-126, 1968-1 CB 194 [¶ 20,171(25)].
(5) Kuhn v. U.S., 1 AFTR 2d 825, 157 F. Supp. 331 [¶ 20,171(10)].
(6) Strauss, 2 BTA 598 [¶ 20,170(40)].
(7) Hurd, 12 BTA 368 [¶ 20,167(10)].
(8) Hedrick, 154 F.2d 90, 34 AFTR 1090 [¶ 20,167(20)].
(9) Comm. v. A.P. Giannini, 129 F.2d 638, 29 AFTR 952 [¶ 20,167(25)].
(10) Burns v. Comm., 31 F.2d 399, 7 AFTR 8567 [¶ 20,166(80)].
(11) Cooney, 18 TC 883 [¶ 20,166(10)].
(12) Northern Trust Co., 8 BTA 685 [¶ 20,169(5)].
(13) Treas. Dept. booklet "Your Federal Income Tax" (1977 Ed.), p. 7.
(14) Evans, 5 BTA 806 [¶ 20,469(10)].

Footnote ¶ 2704 [¶ 7463; 7476].
(1) Helvering v. Eubank, 311 US 122, 61 SCt 149, 24 AFTR 1063; Helvering v. Horst, 311 US 112, 61 SCt 144, 24 AFTR 1058 [¶ 7466(5); 7483(10)].
(2) Holmes, 1 TC 508; Austin v. Comm., 161 F.2d 666, 35 AFTR 1350 [¶ 7483(5), (15)].
(3) Lucas v. Earl, 281 US 111, 8 AFTR 10287 [¶ 7464(5)].
(4) Helvering v. Eubank, 311 US 122, 61 SCt 149, 24 AFTR 1063 [¶ 7466(5)].
(5) Van Brunt, 11 BTA 406 [¶ 7482(5)].
(6) Bing v. Bowers, 22 F.2d 450, 6 AFTR 7045 [¶ 7477(5)].
(7) U.S. v. Shafto, 52 AFTR 1748 [¶ 7477(15)].
(8) Harrison v. Schaffner, 312 US 579, 61 SCt 759, 25 AFTR 1209 [¶ 7485(15)].
(9) Rev. Rul. 74-562, 1974-2 CB 28 [¶ 7482(15)].
(10) Mitchell v. Bowers, 15 F.2d 287, 6 AFTR 6329 [¶ 7470(5)].
(11) Comm. v. Sunnen, 333 US 591, 68 SCt 715, 36 AFTR 611 [¶ 7479(5)].
(12) Rev. Rul. 70-161, 1970-1 CB 15 [¶ 7464(30)].
(13) Capel, 7 BTA 1076 [¶ 8215(15)].
(14) Blair v. Comm., 300 US 5, 57 SCt 330, 18 AFTR 1132 [¶ 7485(10)].

Footnote ¶ 2705 [¶ 20,565].
(1) Rollin C. Reynolds, 44 BTA 342 [¶ 20,565(15)].

Footnote ¶ 2705 continued
(2) Rev. Rul. 70-221, 1970-1 CB 33 [¶ 13,060].

Footnote ¶ 2706 [¶ 20,065; 20,068].
(1) U.S. v. Anderson, 269 US 422, 46 SCt 131, 5 AFTR 5674 [¶ 20,571(5)].

Footnote ¶ 2707 [¶ 20,065].
(1) Lovejoy, 18 BTA 1179 [¶ 11,312(5)].
(2) Rev. Rul. 70-413, 1970-2 CB 103; Comm. v. Boylston Market Ass'n, 131 F.2d 966, 30 AFTR 512 [¶ 11,286; 11,323(5), (10)].
(3) Waldheim Realty & Investment Co. v. Comm., 245 F.2d 823, 51 AFTR 801 [¶ 11,323(10)].
(4) Rev. Rul. 54-4, 1954-1 CB 75 [¶ 20,074(5)].

Footnote ¶ 2708 [¶ 20,081].
(1) Rev. Proc. 72-52, 1972-2 CB 833 [¶ 20,082(5)].
(2) Fowler Bros. & Cox, Inc. v. Comm., 138 F.2d 774, 31 AFTR 830 [¶ 20,085(20)].
(3) Rev. Rul. 55-732, 1955-2 CB 379 [¶ 34,459(10)].
(4) Rev. Proc. 64-51, 1964-2 CB 1003, amplified by Rev. Proc. 70-15, 1970-1 CB 441 [¶ 14,871(5)].
(5) Rev. Proc. 74-11, 1974-1 CB 420 [¶ 15,526(10)].
(6) Rev. Proc. 70-27, 1970-2 CB 509 as modified by Rev. Proc. 74-51, 1974-2 CB 507 [¶ 20,083(7)].
(7) Rev. Proc. 71-21, 1971-2 CB 549 [¶ 20,307(3)].

Footnote ¶ 2709 [¶ 20,801].
(1) Rev. Rul. 64-191, 1964-2 CB 132 [¶ 20,810(10)].
(2) Rev. Rul. 64-245, 1964-2 CB 130 [¶ 20,810(10)].
(3) Rev. Proc. 72-24, 1972-1 CB 102 [¶ 17,792(10)].
(4) Rev. Proc. 71-16, 1971-1 CB 682 [¶ 20,083; 20,775].

Footnote ¶ 2710 [¶ 35,016 et seq.].

Footnote ¶ 2711 [¶ 33,956 et seq.].
(1) Goodman, ¶ 61,201 P-H Memo TC [¶ 33,964(5)].
(2) Holland v. U.S., 348 US 121, 75 SCt 127, 46 AFTR 943; Freidberg v. U.S. 348 US 142, 75 SCt 138, 46 AFTR 954; Smith v. U.S., 348 US 147, 75 SCt 194, 46 AFTR 968; U.S. v. Calderon, 348 US 160, 75 SCt 186, 46 AFTR 962 [¶ 33,958(5); 38,443(5), (15), (40)].
(3) B. Fairman, et al., ¶ 49,006 P-H Memo TC [¶ 33,978(5)].
(4) M. & B. Rubin, Inc., 10 BTA 866 [¶ 33,978(20)].
(5) F. G. Bishoff, 27 F.2d 91, 6 AFTR 7870 [¶ 33,978(20)].
(6) Stratman, ¶ 49,143 P-H Memo TC [¶ 33,977(55)].
(7) Hague, 132 F.2d 775, 30 AFTR 686 [¶ 33,972(5)].

Footnote ¶ 2714 [¶ 20,012 et seq.].
(1) Rev. Rul. 54,273, 1954-2 CB 110 [¶ 20,020(5)].
(2) Rev. Rul. 66-68, 1966-1 CB 197 [¶ 20,023(5)].
(3) Rev. Rul. 57-389, 1957-2 CB 298 [¶ 20,026(5)].

Footnote ¶ 2715 [¶ 20,031 et seq.].

¶ 2749

Footnote ¶ 2716 [¶ 20,031 et seq.].
(1) Rev. Proc. 74-33, 1974-2 CB 489 [¶ 20,039].
(2) Rev. Proc. 68-41, 1968-2 CB 943 [¶ 20,031].
(3) Rev. Proc. 76-9, 1976-1 CB 547 [¶ 20,035(10)].
(4) Instructions to Form 1128 (Rev. 7-76).
(5) Rev. Rul. 58-256, 1958-1 CB 215 [¶ 20,022(20)].

Footnote ¶ 2717 [¶ 20,045 et seq.].
(1) Rev. Rul. 65-163, 1965-1 CB 205 [¶ 20,050(10)].
(2) Rev. Rul. 67-189, 1967-1 CB 255 [¶ 34,459(5)].

Footnote ¶ 2719 [¶ 20,125 et seq.].
(1) Butler, 19 BTA 718; Lavery v. Comm., 158 F.2d 859, 35 AFTR 616 [¶ 20,134(5), (20)].
(2) Kahler, 18 TC 31 [¶ 20,134(10)].
(3) Fischer, 14 TC 792 [¶ 20,134(20)].
(4) American Central Utilities Co., 36 BTA 688; Cuba RR Co., 9 TC 211 [¶ 7217(10); 20,149(5)].
(5) Amer. Auto. Ass'n. v. U.S., 367 US 687, 7 AFTR 2d 1618 [¶ 20,307(10)].

Footnote ¶ 2720 [¶ 7061 et seq.].
(1) Zittel, 12 BTA 675; Massey v. Comm., 143 F.2d 429, 32 AFTR 986 [¶ 7062(25); 7073(25)].
(2) Rev. Rul. 69-650, 1969-2 CB 106 [¶ 19,157(5)].
(3) Rev. Rul. 75-448, 1975-2 CB 55 [¶ 7926(10)].
(4) Shockey, ¶ 47,274 P-H Memo TC; Rev. Rul. 69-465, 1969-2 CB 27 [¶ 7063(30)].
(5) Drummond, 43 BTA 529 [¶ 7063(30)].
(6) Rev. Proc. 71-21, 1971-2 CB 549 [¶ 20,307(3)].

Footnote ¶ 2721 [¶ 17,031(g); 17,066].
(1) Tar Prods. Corp., 130 F.2d 866, 29 AFTR 1190; Comm. v. American Light & Traction Co., 156 F.2d 398, 34 AFTR 1544 [¶ 17,067(5)].

Footnote ¶ 2722 [¶ 7215 et seq.; 7896 et seq.].
(1) TIR-1032, 4-14-70 [¶ 7214(5)].
(2) Rev. Rul. 63-57, 1963-1 CB 103 [¶ 7215(10)].
(3) SM 3820, 1925-2 CB 32 [¶ 7215(35)].
(4) Vancoh Realty Co., 33 BTA 918 [¶ 7215(40)].
(5) GCM 14839, 1935-1 CB 73, modifying SM 3820, 1925-2 CB 35 [¶ 7215(5)].
(6) Bonded Mtg. Co. v. Comm., 70 F.2d 341, 13 AFTR 979 [¶ 7215(15)].
(7) Rev. Rul. 60-211, 1960-1 CB 35 [¶ 7904(25)].
(8) Rev. Rul. 56-358, 1956-2 CB 99 [¶ 7901(5)].
(9) Thompson v. Comm., 12 AFTR 2d 5451, 322 F.2d 122 [¶ 7904(7)].
(10) U.S. v. Isaak, 22 AFTR 2d 5632, 400 F.2d 869 [¶ 7904(7)].
(11) Rev. Rul. 75-57, 1975-1 CB 141 [¶ 7904(10)].
(12) Rev. Rul. 66-44, 66-45, 1966-1 CB 94 [¶ 20,166(125); 20,169(20)].

Footnote ¶ 2723 [¶ 8231 et seq.].
(1) Table of Redemption Values and Investment Yields for U.S. Savings Bonds, Series E [¶ 3205; 20,507; 20,510].
(2) Treas. Dept. booklet "Your Federal Income Tax" (1977 Ed.), p. 37; Rev. Rul. 68-145, 1968-1 CB 203 [¶ 20,509(10)].
(3) Rev. Rul. 55-655, 1955-2 CB 253 [¶ 20,509(10)].
(4) Treas. Dept. booklet "Your Federal Income Tax" (1977 Ed.), p. 37.
(5) Treas. Dept. booklet "Your Federal Income Tax" (1977 Ed.), p. 36.
(6) Treas. Dept. Circular 905, 5th Rev. Amendment 1 [¶ 3205; 8281(15)].

Footnote ¶ 2723 continued
(7) Sec. 22(b) of 2nd Liberty Act as amended by P.L. 86-346, 9-22-59; Treas. Dept. Release, 7-24-61 [¶ 8281(15)].
(8) Letter ruling, 10/14/49 [¶ 8253(5)].

Footnote ¶ 2724 [¶ 20,309; 20,310].
(1) Farrelly-Walsh, Inc., 13 BTA 923 [¶ 20,147(10)].

Footnote ¶ 2725 [¶ 20,215 et seq.].
(1) 2 Lexington Avenue Corp., 26 TC 816 [¶ 20,240; 20,244(10)].
(2) Burnet v. Logan, 283 US 404, 9 AFTR 1453 [¶ 20,468(10)].
(3) U.S. v. Yerger, 55 F. Supp. 521, 32 AFTR 855 [¶ 20,468(20)].
(4) Rev. Rul. 70-344, 1970-2 CB 50; Mott v. Comm. 103 F.2d 1109, 22 AFTR 1169; Comm. v. Dashiell, 100 F.2d 625, 22 AFTR 163 [¶ 20,251(10)].
(5) Rev. Rul. 72-381, 1972-2 CB 581; Taylor, 43 BTA 563 [¶ 20,217(5); 20,251(5)].
(6) Treas. Dept. booklet "Tax Guide for Small Business" (1977 Ed.), p. 27.

Footnote ¶ 2726 [¶ 20,300; 20,305; 20,520; 20,535].
(1) Schlude v. Comm., 372 US 128, 11 AFTR 2d 751 [¶ 20,307(20)].

Footnote ¶ 2727 [¶ 20,144; 20,145].
(1) Comm. v. Hansen, 360 US 446, 79 SCt 1270, 3 AFTR 2d 1690 [¶ 20,144(5)].

Footnote ¶ 2728 [¶ 20,181 et seq.].
(1) Burnet v. Sanford & Brooks Co., 282 US 359, 9 AFTR 603; H. Liebes & Co. v. Comm., 90 F.2d 932, 19 AFTR 965 [¶ 20,182(5), (40)].
(2) Koelle, 7 BTA 917 [¶ 20,182(55)].
(3) North American Oil Consolidated v. Burnet, 286 US 417, 11 AFTR 16 [¶ 20,202(5)].
(4) Triboro Coach Corp., 29 TC 1274 [¶ 20,185(5)].
(5) Johnson, ¶ 47,057 P-H Memo TC [¶ 20,185(20)].

Footnote ¶ 2729 [¶ 20,201; 33,261].
(1) Universal Oil Products Co. v. Campbell, 181 F.2d 451, 39 AFTR 377 [¶ 20,210(5)].
(2) O'Meara, 8 TC 622 [¶ 20,210(10)].
(3) U.S. v. Skelly Oil Co., 23 AFTR 2d 69-1186; 394 US 678 [¶ 33,265(70)].

Footnote ¶ 2730 [¶ 8542; 20,293 et seq.].
(1) Rev. Rul. 74-351, 1974-2 CB 144 [¶ 20,293(5)].
(2) Rev. Rul. 57-379, 1957-2 CB 299 [¶ 20,293(15)].

Footnote ¶ 2735 [¶ 20,551 et seq.].
(1) Quinn v. Comm., 111 F.2d 372, 24 AFTR 927 [¶ 20,564(10)].
(2) Crain v. Comm., 75 F.2d 962, 15 AFTR 343 [¶ 20,562(10)].
(3) Blaine, Mackay, Lee Co. v. Comm., 141 F.2d 201, 32 AFTR 273, revg ¶ 42,032 P-H Memo BTA [¶ 20,591(5)].
(4) Charles Leich v. U.S., 13 AFTR2d 869, 329 F.2d 649 [¶ 20,607(42)].
(5) Sidney-Hill System of Health Building Co., 12 BTA 548 [¶ 20,614].
(6) Est. of Spiegel, 12 TC 524 [¶ 20,561(5)].
(7) Griffin, 49 TC 253 [¶ 13,052-A].

Footnote ¶ 2736 [¶ 20,645 et seq.].

Footnote ¶ 2737 [¶ 11,590; 20,631].
(1) Senate Report No. 93-625, 93rd Cong. 2d Sess. [¶ 20,633].

Footnote ¶ 2737 continued
(2) Rev. Rul. 55-446, 1955-2 CB 531; as modified by Rev. Rul. 61-127, 1961-2 CB 36 [¶ 11,590].

Footnote ¶ 2738 [¶ 11,960].
(1) Sheldon & Co. v. Comm., 214 F.2d 655, 45 AFTR 1791 [¶ 11,960(5)].

Footnote ¶ 2739 [¶ 13,051 et seq.].
(1) Massachusetts Mutual Life Ins. Co. v. U.S., 288 US 269, 53 SCt 337, 11 AFTR 1389, XII-1 CB 286 [¶ 13,052].
(2) Higgenbotham-Bailey-Logan Co., 8 BTA 566 [¶ 13,068].
(3) Prime, 39 BTA 487; Keith v. Comm., 139 F.2d 596, 31 AFTR 1100 [¶ 13,055].
(4) Rev. Rul. 75-12, 1975-1 CB 62 [¶ 13,061(5)].
(5) Hopkins, 15 TC 160; Rev. Rul. 72-100, 1972-1 CB 122, as clarified by Rev. Rul. 72-562, 1972-2 CB 231 and Rev. Rul. 74-607, 1974-2 CB 149 [¶ 13,061(10)].
(6) Rev. Rul. 63-57, 1963-1 CB 103 [¶ 13,061(10)].

Footnote ¶ 2740 [¶ 13,117 et seq.].
(1) Powell, 26 BTA 509 [¶ 13,118].
(2) U.S. v. Anderson, 269 US 422, 46 SCt 131, 5 AFTR 5674 [¶ 13,121].
(3) Union Bleachery v. U.S., 97 F.2d 226, 21 AFTR 336 [¶ 13,131(5)].
(4) Rev. Rul. 58-55, 1958-1 CB 266 [¶ 30,564(25)].
(5) Rev. Rul. 72-490, 1972-2 CB 100 [¶ 13,205(10)].

Footnote ¶ 2741 [¶ 16,396].

Footnote ¶ 2742 [¶ 16,048].
(1) Rev. Rul. 68-174, 1968-1 CB 81 [¶ 16,079(53)].
(2) Rev. Rul. 71-216, 1971-1 CB 96 [¶ 16,083(120)].

Footnote ¶ 2743 [¶ 14,176 et seq.; 14,701 et seq.].
(1) Derby Realty Corporation, 35 BTA 335. Pet. for review dis. 92 F.2d 999, 20 AFTR 370 [¶ 14,517(5)].
(2) Comm. v. Peterman, 118 F.2d 973, 26 AFTR 930; Abelson, 44 BTA 98 (NA 1944 CB 32) [¶ 14,517(20); 14,518(25)].
(3) Morton v. Comm., 104 F.2d 534, 23 AFTR 85 [¶ 14,517(30)].
(4) Burke, Ltd., 3 TC 1031 [¶ 14,518(40)].

Footnote ¶ 2744 [¶ 20,575 et seq.].
(1) Harrold v. Comm., 192 F.2d 1002, 41 AFTR 442; Schuessler v. Comm., 230 F.2d 722, 49 AFTR 322 [¶ 20,577 (5), (55)].
(2) Natl. Bread Wrapping Machine Co., 30 TC 550 [¶ 20,577(25)].
(3) Adams-Roth Baking Co., 8 BTA 458 [¶ 20,587(5)].
(4) Rev. Rul. 69-512, 1969-2 CB 24 [¶ 20,584(5)].
(5) Farmville Oil & Fertilizer Co., 78 F.2d 83, 16 AFTR 305; Brown v. Helvering, 291 US 193, 54 SCt 356, 13 AFTR 851 [¶ 20,580(5); 20,583(5)].

Footnote ¶ 2745 [¶ 16,977.5; 20,640 et seq.].

Footnote ¶ 2747 [¶ 20,296 et seq.].

Footnote ¶ 2748 [¶ 16,825 et seq.].
(1) Musselman-Hub-Brake Co. v. Comm., 139 F.2d 65, 31 AFTR 1001; Miller, Inc. v Comm., 164 F.2d 268, 36 AFTR 250; Rev. Rul. 55-608, 1955-2 CB 546 [¶ 16,853(5)].
(2) Mansuss Realty, 143 F.2d 286, 32 AFTR 962, modifying 1 TC 932 [¶ 16,848].

Footnote ¶ 2749 [¶ 16,199 et seq.].

Highlights of Chapter 17

Accounting

I. **Accounting Methods**
   A. **No uniform method [¶ 2701]**, but two principal—cash and accrual:
      1. Hybrid accounting method—Combination allowed if consistent and clear [¶ 2701(a)].
      2. More than one trade or business—Different methods for same taxpayer allowed [¶ 2701(b)].
      3. Income solely from wages—Formal records not required [¶ 2701(c)].
      4. Farm corporations—Generally, accrual method [¶ 2701(d)].
   B. **Cash basis method [¶ 2702]:**
      1. Include income only when actually received.
      2. Deduct expenses only when actually paid.
      3. Constructive receipt—income actually not possessed, but within control and disposition [¶ 2703].
      4. Assignment of income [¶ 2704]:
         a. From property—taxable to owner of property [¶ 2704(a)].
         b. Earnings—taxable to wage earner [¶ 2704(b)].
      5. Constructive payment—deductible if offset against income due [¶ 2705].
   C. **Accrual basis method [¶ 2706]:**
      1. Include income when earned.
      2. Deduct expenses when liability is incurred.
   D. **Change of accounting method [¶ 2708]:**
      1. Generally, Revenue Service consent required [¶ 2708(a)].
      2. Application within 180 days after start of year change desired.
      3. Consent assumed in specific changes [¶ 2708(b)].
      4. Change with ratable adjustment over 10-year period [¶ 2708(c)].
   E. **Adjustments required by change [¶ 2709]:**
      1. Change initiated by Revenue Service—pre-1954 adjustments not considered [¶ 2709(b)].
      2. Change initiated by taxpayer—pre-1954 and post-1954 adjustments considered [¶ 2709(c)].
      3. Tax limitation if adjustments substantial [¶ 2709(a)]:
         a. Increase taxable income by more than $3,000.
         b. Election to allocate increase over period of years.
   F. **Reconstruction of income**—Revenue Service reconstructs income when no regular accounting method [¶ 2711]:
      1. Net worth method [¶ 2711(a)].
      2. Percentage method [¶ 2711(b)].
      3. Bank deposit method [¶ 2711(c)].
      4. Excess cash expenditure method [¶ 2711(d)].

II. **Accounting Periods**
   A. **Annual basis [¶ 2714]:**
      1. Calendar year (required when no books kept).
      2. Fiscal year:
         a. Twelve months ending last day of any month not December.
         b. 52-53 week fiscal year [¶ 2714(b)].
   B. **Change in accounting period [¶ 2715—2716]:**
      1. From calendar to fiscal, or fiscal to calendar.

2. Application to change—filed by last day of month following close of short tax year, except:
   a. Special rule for corporations [¶ 2716(a)].
   b. Certain 52-53 week years [¶ 2716(b)].
   c. Husband-wife tax year changes [¶ 2716(c)].
   d. Subsidiary corporation [¶ 2716(d)].
C. **Fractional (short) year returns [¶ 2717]:**
   1. When first or final return—filed as if 12-month return [¶ 2717(a)]:
      a. Income not annualized.
      b. Personal exemption etc. not prorated.
   2. Resulting from change of accounting period [¶ 2717(b)]:
      a. Income annualized.
      b. Exemption deduction prorated.
      c. Net operating loss applied before annualization.
      d. $10,000 minimum tax exclusion prorated.
      e. Credits annualized before application to annualized basis.
   3. Alternative method—when annualized tax greater than actual 12-month period tax [¶ 2717(c)].

III. **When To Report Income**
   A. **Cash basis**—when actually or constructively received in cash or its equivalent [¶ 2719(a)].
   B. **Accrual basis**—when accrued (i.e., when enforceable right to collect arises) [¶ 2719(b)].
   C. **General examples of when to report** (subject to numerous exceptions):

Item	Cash Basis	Accrual Basis
Compensation for Services [¶ 2720].	Year actually or constructively received. (Special relief in case of "lump sum" payments covering more than one year).	Year earned (but when amount not determined, income in year determined).
Interest [¶ 2722(a)].	Year actually or constructively received.	Accrues ratably over period involved.
Dividends [¶ 2721].	Year actually or constructively received.	Year actually or constructively received.
Rent [¶ 2724].	Year actually or constructively received.	Accrues ratably over period involved (except rent paid in advance, then total advance rent taxable in year received).
Sale of property (Question—when closed transaction?) [¶ 2725(a)].	Usually when cash is received.	Year binding agreement to sell is entered into.
Sale of stock (Question—when closed transaction?) [¶ 2725(b)].	Gain on sale: year cash or equivalent actually or constructively received. Loss on sale: year sale is executed regardless of settlement date.	Gain or loss on sale: year sale is executed regardless of settlement date.
Disputed income [¶ 2728].	Year income is realized in money or property.	When judgment becomes final.

Item	Cash Basis	Accrual Basis
Discount on U. S. Sav. Bonds [¶ 2723].	Optional—May either include in year of maturity or each year based on the increment earned.	Year income (increment) is accruable.

IV. **When To Take Deductions**
   A. **Cash basis**—when payment actually made in cash or its equivalent [¶ 2735(a)].
   B. **Accrual basis**—when accrued (i.e., when actual liability exists); but when liability certain and amount indefinite—reasonable amount deductible [¶ 2735(b)].
   C. **General examples of when to deduct** (subject to numerous exceptions) [¶ 2735–2746]:

Deductible Item	Cash Basis	Accrual Basis
Business and investor's expenses.	Year payment is made in cash or equivalent.	Year liability arose.
Interest [¶ 2739].	Year paid (except prepaid interest deductible ratably over loan period).	Accrues ratably over period involved.
Taxes [¶ 2740].	Year payment actually made.	Year when all events have occurred that fix amount of tax and determine liability of taxpayer to pay. (a) Property taxes—date liability becomes fixed or, in the case of *real* property taxes, if election is made, accrue ratably over period for which imposed. (b) State income taxes—year that income (on which tax is paid) is earned (but increase accrues on final determination or when liability acknowledged).
Bad debts [¶ 2743(a)].	Year debt becomes worthless.	Year debt becomes worthless.
Losses [¶ 2743(b)].	When a closed transaction fixed by identifiable events and actually sustained during year.	When a closed transaction fixed by identifiable events and actually sustained during year.
Reserves for expenses and losses [¶ 2744].	Not allowed (since deductions allowable only in year of payment).	Year actual liability exists to support deduction.
Judgments, claims, damages [¶ 2735(c)].	Year paid or payment put in escrow.	Year liability becomes fixed by final judgment, or when paid or payment put in escrow, if that is earlier.
Medical expenses [¶ 2741].	Year paid.	Year paid.

V. **Special Problems**
  A. **Trading stamps and coupons**—subtractable from sales income [¶ 2747].
  B. **Debtor's unpaid expenses and interest**—not deductible if (all three conditions necessary) [¶ 2748]:
    1. Debtor on accrual basis and creditor on cash basis.
    2. Within 2½ months of close of debtor's tax year:
       a. Payment is not made, and
       b. Amount not includible in creditor's gross income.
    3. At close of debtor's tax year, or within 2½ months later, debtor and creditor are persons between whom losses are disallowed.
  C. **Circulation expenses from prepaid subscriptions**—currently deductible [¶ 2749].

Chapter 18

INSTALLMENT AND DEFERRED PAYMENT SALES
TABLE OF CONTENTS

Special methods of deferring income .. 2800

INSTALLMENT SALES BY DEALERS IN PERSONAL PROPERTY

How dealers report income from installment sales 2801
  Who is a dealer
  Accounting procedure
  Information required on the return
Figuring the profit 2802
Repossession by dealer 2803
Change of accounting method 2804
  Adjustments on change from accrual basis
  Information required on return

OTHER INSTALLMENT SALES

Sales of real property on the installment plan 2811
  Figuring the profit
  Information required
Casual sales of personal property on the installment plan 2812
Capital gain on installment sales 2813
Expenses and losses 2814

DEFERRED PAYMENT SALES

Deferred payment sales not on the installment plan 2816

  Gain or loss in year of sale
  Collections on discounted notes
  Indeterminate market value

REPOSSESSIONS

Repossession of personal property 2821
Real property repossessed by seller .. 2823

DISPOSITION OF INSTALLMENT OBLIGATIONS

Gain or loss on disposition of installment obligations 2831
  Acquisition from decedent
  Distributions in liquidation
  Tax-free transfers of installment obligations

SPECIAL PROBLEMS

Imputed interest 2840
Sale of real property in lots 2841
Long-term contracts 2842
  Percentage of completion
  Completed contract
  Comparison of percentage of completion method with completed contract method

• Highlights of Chapter 18 .... Page 2861

¶ **2800 Special methods of deferring income.** A taxpayer who gets a large part of his gross income from selling merchandise on the installment plan may find it difficult to pay the tax on the income. The problem becomes particularly acute under the accrual method of accounting where all of the profit from the sales is recognized at the time of the sale.

To alleviate this situation, special provisions allow taxpayer to spread his profit from installment sales over the years in which he receives payments. To accomplish this, he first segregates the part of each payment that represents profit from the part that represents recovery of his cost. Then he includes in gross income each year only the part of each payment that is profit. This relief applies to:

- Installment sales by dealers in personal property [¶ 2801–2804].
- Certain sales of real property [¶ 2811].
- Casual sales of personal property [¶ 2812].

The installment method generally must be elected on a timely filed original return for the year of sale [Sec. 1.453-8]. However, as to real property sales and casual sales of personal property, if the taxpayer in good faith failed to make the

Footnotes appear at end of this Chapter.

¶ 2800

election that way, he may make it on an amended or delinquent return for the year of sale under certain conditions, provided assessment or collection of the tax will not be barred.[1]

For treatment of deferred payment sales that do not qualify for the installment sales method, see ¶ 2816.

INSTALLMENT SALES BY DEALERS IN PERSONAL PROPERTY

Dealers in personal property, including those using revolving credit plans, may report income from installment sales on the installment method. There is great flexibility in using this method. For example, you may use it in one department and not in another.

¶ 2801 How dealers report income from installment sales. Dealers using the installment method report income proportionately as collections are made [Sec. 453(a); 1.453-2].

> **Example:** During 1977, the Lee Co., which uses the installment basis, sold for $100 an article that had cost $60, receiving $20 down, the balance being payable in monthly installments of $5 each. During the year, the total payments (including the down payment) amounted to $55. The profit on the sale was $40, which must be accounted for as the $100 due on the contract is received. Accordingly, *40% of each payment is reported as profit.* Since $55 was received in 1977, the profit reported for that year was $22. *The same percentage is applied each year on later collections made on the 1977 sale* [see ¶ 2802].
>
> If property is sold for a down payment and the balance in deferred payment notes, and the notes are immediately discounted to a finance company, the entire profit is reportable in the year of sale.[1]

(a) Who is a dealer. Persons who "regularly sell" personal property on the installment plan qualify as dealers. Neither the law nor the regulations indicate what part of the year's total sales must be on the installment plan. However, they do define the term "installment sale"; this is generally any sale in which payment is made in two or more installments [Sec. 1.453-2(b)]. The amount of the down payment, and whether title to the goods passes to the buyer, is immaterial. Sales on the revolving credit plan also may qualify, but special rules apply[2] [Sec. 1.453-2(d)].

(b) Accounting procedure. Accounting records must permit allocation of all collections to the year the sales were made and yield enough information to set up adequate gross profit percentages for each year [Sec. 1.453-2(c)].

Hybrid accounting system permitted. A regular dealer in personal property, starting installment selling, may elect to report income from installment sales on the installment basis and continue to report sales on open account on the accrual basis.[3]

(c) Information required on the return. The dealer should attach a statement showing the method of figuring the profits reported for each year.

¶ 2802 Figuring the profit. If the property is to be paid for over a period of more than one year, the dealer must allocate his profit as he receives the payments, using his percentage of profit *for the year of sale.*

> **Example 1:** In 1976, Wilson, a dealer, sold for $100,000 goods which cost $60,000. During 1976, he received total cash payment of $55,000. His profit to be reported for 1976 is $22,000 (40% of $55,000). If only $30,000 of the remaining $45,000 was collected in 1977, 40% of that sum or $12,000 will be reported as profit for 1977. If Wilson in 1977 had also collected $16,000 from sales made in 1975, he would have to refer to his profit percentage for

1975 to determine how much to report as profit in 1977. The percentage applicable to 1975 sales may be quite different from that on 1976 sales. See also Example 2.

Example 2: The balance sheet of the Lorring Co., as of 12-31-77 disclosed the following accounts receivable and unrealized profits:

Year of sale	Installment accounts receivable	Per cent of gross profit	Unrealized profit
1975	$ 9,000	38%	$ 3,420
1976	15,000	40%	6,000
1977	52,000	42%	21,840

Collections for the year 1977 totaled $126,000, divided as follows:

Year of sale	Payments
1975	$16,000
1976	30,000
1977	80,000

The amount to be reported as income from 1977 collections is $51,680:

1975 sales, collections from	$16,000 × 38% or	$ 6,080
1976 sales, collections from	30,000 × 40% or	12,000
1977 sales, collections from	80,000 × 42% or	33,600
		$51,680

Items included in sales price. Finance or carrying charges generally are included in the selling price [Sec. 453(a)]. An accrual basis taxpayer accrues these charges ratably over the contract period or until the installment notes are sold, if the charges are subject to abatement in case the contract price is prepaid.[1] But part of the charges must be allocated to the down payment and reported as gross profit.[2] Also, any retailer's excise tax and any state sales tax on the dealer are included in the sales price when figuring profit. These taxes do not reduce installment payments received.[3]

Business expenses not included in cost of goods sold may not be spread over the term of the installment payments. They must be deducted in the year paid or incurred.[4]

¶ 2803 Repossession by dealer. When a dealer repossesses personal property he sold, he has gain or loss equal to the difference between the fair market value of the repossessed goods and the unpaid amount of the outstanding obligations, less the amount that would be returnable as income if the notes were paid in full. The repossessed goods are then included in inventory at their fair market value.[1] The following examples show how to figure gain or loss when a dealer repossesses personal property he sold.

Example 1: On 6-15-76, Ross, a dealer who reports on the installment basis, sold for $100 an article that had cost $60, receiving $20 down, the balance payable in 16 monthly installments of $5 each. After paying 9 installments (6 in 1976 and 3 in 1977), the buyer defaulted. Under the agreement Ross repossessed the article when it was worth $25. His gain on the repossession is $4, and his 1977 income from this sale is $10, figured as follows:

Value of property at time of repossession		$25.00
Basis of obligations surrendered (7 unpaid installments):		
Face value (7 × $5)	$35.00	
Less: Unrealized profit (40% of $35)	14.00	21.00
Taxable gain on repossession in 1977		$ 4.00

Footnotes appear at end of this Chapter.

Chapter 18—Installment and Deferred Payment Sales

Profit to be reported on 3 installments in 1977 (40% of $15)	$ 6.00
Income in 1977	$10.00

The repossessed article must be put back in inventory at $25 (its value when repossessed).

The same principles apply when the repossessions are numerous.

Example 2: Assume that in Example 2 of ¶ 2802 goods were repossessed as follows:

	Unpaid balance of accounts	Value of property at time of repossession		
1975 accounts	$ 4,000	$ 2,000		
1976 accounts	6,000	4,000		
1977 accounts	12,000	9,000		
Value of property at time of repossessions				$15,000
Basis of obligations, 1975 accounts				
Face value		$ 4,000		
Less: Unrealized profit (38%)		1,520	$ 2,480	
Basis of obligations, 1976 accounts				
Face value		$ 6,000		
Less: Unrealized profit (40%)		2,400	$ 3,600	
Basis of obligations, 1977 accounts				
Face value		$12,000		
Less: Unrealized profit (42%)		5,040	$ 6,960	$13,040
Taxable gain on repossessions in 1977				$ 1,960
Amount to be reported as income from 1977 collections				51,680
Total profit to be shown in 1977 return				$53,640

Bad debts. If the seller does not repossess the goods, or if they are valueless when recovered, seller is entitled to a bad debt deduction equal to the unrecovered cost of the goods.[1]

Example 3: Assume the same facts as in Example 1, except that the article was valueless when repossessed. Then, the taxpayer would have a bad debt deduction of $15 on the repossession instead of a gain of $4.

Value of property at time of repossession		0
Basis of obligations surrendered (7 unpaid installments):		
Face value (7 × $5)	$35	
Less: Unrealized profit (40%)	14	$21
Loss on repossession in 1977		$21
Profit to be reported on 3 installments paid in 1977 (40% of $15)		6
Deduction for 1977		$15

¶ 2804 Change of accounting method. A dealer in personal property may adopt, or change to, the installment method without prior approval of the Revenue Service [Sec. 453(c)(1); 1.453-8]. The dealer may also retroactively revoke his election to use the installment method without Revenue Service consent. This is done by filing a notice of revocation within 3 years after the filing date of the return for the year of the change to installment reporting. The statute of limitations for assessment of deficiencies is extended 2 years from the date the notice is filed. Any resulting refunds and credits are allowed for at least 1 year from the date the notice is filed. No interest is allowed for any period prior to filing of the notice. A dealer who revokes the election cannot make a new election before the fifth tax year following the year of revocation without Revenue Service consent [Sec. 453(c)(4), (5); 1.453-8]. A dealer who does not use the 3-year retroactive revocation must get Revenue Service permission to change from the installment to another method of accounting [Sec. 1.453-8(c)]. Application for permission must be filed within 180 days after the start of the year for which the change is desired [¶ 2708].

(a) Adjustments on change from accrual basis. If an accrual basis dealer changes to the installment basis or revolving credit plan, receipts from prior installment sales are included in income when collected. In determining which receipts from sales under a revolving credit plan must be included when collected, the percentage of charges for the year of sale may be used instead of the percentage determined under Sec. 1.453-2(d)(2) [Sec. 453(c); 1.453-7]. The result is that in many cases the profits are taxed twice. To remedy this, the tax for the year in which the amounts are included a second time may be reduced. To compute the reduction, you determine the following for each amount that was included a second time [Sec. 453(c)]:

(1) The tax that resulted from including the amount in the first year.
(2) The tax that resulted from including the amount in the second year.

The tax that results from including an amount is determined by the following formula:

$$\text{Total tax} \times \frac{\text{Amount included}}{\text{Gross income}}$$

The lesser of (1) or (2) is the reduction for each amount. Add them up to get the total reduction. The total tax in the above formula does not include the minimum tax on tax preferences (¶ 2403) [Sec. 453(c)(3)].

Example: Assume the following facts for a noncorporate taxpayer changing from the accrual to the installment basis in 1977:

	1975	1976	1977	
Gross profit from installment sales (receivable in periodic payments over 5 years)	$100,000.00	$ 50,000.00	$ 20,000.00	(1975 sales)
			10,000.00	(1976 sales)
			20,000.00	(1977 sales)
Other income	80,000.00	200,000.00	150,000.00	
Gross income	$180,000.00	$250,000.00	$200,000.00	
Deductions	60,000.00	50,000.00	50,000.00	
Taxable income	$120,000.00	$200,000.00	$150,000.00	
Tax liability	67,090.00	123,090.00	86,550.00	

The adjustment would be figured as follows:

Adjustment for 1975 Amount

Tax attributable to 1975 inclusion:
   $20,000/180,000 × $67,090.00 = $7,454.44
Tax attributable to 1977 inclusion:
   $20,000/200,000 × $86,550.00 = $8,655.00
Lower of these amounts .... $ 7,454.44

Adjustment for 1976 Amount

Tax attributable to 1976 inclusion:
   $10,000/250,000 × $123,090.00 = $4,923.60
Tax attributable to 1977 inclusion:
   $10,000/200,000 × $86,550.00 = $4,327.50
Lower of these amounts 4,327.50
1977 tax is reduced by $11,781.94

Footnotes appear at end of this Chapter.

¶ 2804

(b) Information required on return. A taxpayer changing to the installment method should attach a statement to the return showing (1) the accounting method used before the change; (2) the span of years over which the adjustments must be figured; and (3) a schedule similar to the above showing computation of the adjustments. A dealer who adopts the method in the first year he makes installment sales, must indicate in his return for that year that he is adopting the installment method [Sec. 1.453-8, 1.453-10(b)].

OTHER INSTALLMENT SALES

You may use the installment method to report your profit from sales of real property involving deferred payments and certain casual sales of personal property.

¶ **2811 Sales of real property on the installment plan.** The gain (but not loss) from a sale of real property involving deferred payments may be reported on the installment method, whether or not the seller is a dealer in real estate, if (1) there is no payment in the year of sale *or* (2) payments in the year of sale do not exceed 30% of the selling price [Sec. 453(b)(2)(A); 1.453-4]. Payment must be made in 2 or more installments.[1]

Example 1: In 1977 White sold real property having an adjusted basis of $30,000 for $40,000 (exclusive of 6% interest on installments), payable as follows: $10,000 in 1978, and the balance in annual installments of $5,000 starting on 7-1-79. Since there is no payment in the year of sale, the income can be reported on the installment basis. Therefore, the profit will be accounted for as the $40,000 due on the contract is paid.

Example 2: Assume same facts as in Example 1, except there was cash payment of $10,000 in 1977. Since payments in the year of sale ($10,000) are less than $12,000 (30% of selling price), the income can be reported on installment plan.

(a) Figuring the profit. Total profit is the difference between the *selling price* and adjusted basis. This total profit is divided by the *contract price* to find the proportion of each year's payment to be returned as profit.

Example 3: In 1976, Smith sold real property having an adjusted basis of $60,000 for $100,000 (exclusive of 6% interest on installments), payable as follows: cash $30,000; mortgage for $70,000, payable by the buyer in semi-annual installments of $10,000 each, the first to be paid on 4-1-77. The profit was $40,000 ($100,000 selling price less $60,000 basis), which will be accounted for as the $100,000 due on the contract is paid. Accordingly, 40% ($40,000 profit divided by $100,000 contract price) of each payment is recognized gain.

1976 payments	$ 30,000	of which	$12,000 is recognized gain
1977 payments	20,000	of which	8,000 is recognized gain
1978 payments	20,000	of which	8,000 is recognized gain
1979 payments	20,000	of which	8,000 is recognized gain
1980 payments	10,000	of which	4,000 is recognized gain
Total payments	$100,000	of which	$40,000 is recognized gain

Payments in the year of sale include all cash or property received in the year of sale, reported separately for each transaction, except generally the buyer's evidences of indebtedness. There is included, however, the buyer's bonds and other evidences of indebtedness that are payable on demand or readily marketable and received in a sale or other disposition after 5-27-69 [Sec. 453; 1.453-3, 1.453-4(c)]. There is not included the assumption or payment of the seller's liabilities incurred in the ordinary course of the seller's business and not to avoid the 30% limit.[2]

A mortgage on the property, which the buyer assumes or takes subject to, is included to the extent that it exceeds seller's adjusted basis of the property sold

[Sec. 1.453-4(c)]. Any property received outright in payment is included, but not property received by seller merely as collateral for buyer's note. The proceeds of any mortgage obtained from a financial institution by the buyer or for him by the seller, and paid at the closing of title, are included, but not the proceeds of any disposition of the buyer's notes to a third person [Sec. 1.453-4]. Payments received in prior years for options or as down payments on signing a contract are included.[3]

Selling price is the total amount involved in the sale. It includes cash, the fair market value of any other property received by the seller,[4] and the amount of any notes or other evidences of indebtedness of the buyer [Sec. 1.453-4]. If there is an existing mortgage on the property, it is also included as part of the selling price, whether it is assumed by the buyer or the property is merely sold subject to the mortgage [Sec. 1.453-4(c)].

Contract price is the total amount to be received by the seller; in other words, it is the seller's equity in the property.

>**Example 4:** Jones sells for $100,000 real property (with a $25,000 basis encumbered by a mortgage of $20,000. The buyer takes title subject to the mortgage. The selling price is $100,000, but the contract price is $80,000.

As shown in Example 4, if the buyer assumes or takes title subject to an existing mortgage, the mortgage is generally not included in determining the contract price. However, if the mortgage exceeds the basis, the difference is treated as part of the "payments in the year of sale" and part of the "total contract price," [Sec. 1.453-4(c)].

>**Example 5:** Property having a basis of $10,000 was sold for $80,000 (cash, $10,000; assumption of existing mortgage, $15,000; and a new mortgage of $55,000). These payments were in addition to installment payments at 6% interest. The contract price is $70,000 ($10,000 + $55,000 + $5,000). The "payments in the year of sale" are $15,000 ($10,000 + $5,000). The excess of the assumed mortgage over the basis is treated as cash. The result would be the same if the buyer took the property subject to the mortgage.

Imputed interest. The amount of imputed interest [¶ 2840] is used to reduce the stated sales price or the total contract price [Sec. 1.453-1(b)].

>**Example 6:** John Silver sold a house for $8,500, payable $2,500 down and the balance $2,000 annually. His total imputed interest is $763.10 [see ¶ 2840]. His selling price is $7,736.90 ($8,500 contract price less $763.10 total imputed interest). Since the $2,500 down payment is more than $2,321.07 (30% of the $7,736.90 selling price), the sale does not qualify as an installment sale.

Commissions and selling expenses do not reduce selling price, payments made in the year of sale, or contract price [Sec. 1.453-4(c)]. Except for dealers, such expenses are an offset against selling price, not reducing selling price itself, but reducing the profit from the transaction.[5] Dealers in real estate can deduct the commissions as a business expense.[6]

>**Example 7:** The taxpayer (not a dealer) owned real property encumbered by a mortgage of $25,000. In 1977, he sold this property, which had an adjusted basis of $65,000, for $100,000 payable as follows: cash, $30,000; first mortgage assumed, $25,000; second mortgage for $45,000, payable in semi-annual installments of $5,000 each, the first to be paid in 1978. In addition, the contract called for 6% interest on the installment payments. Commissions on the sale were $5,000, the abstract of title, $75, and the recording fees, $25.

Selling price	$100,000
Less: Adjusted basis	65,000
Gross profit	$ 35,000

Footnotes appear at end of this Chapter.

¶ 2811

Chapter 18—Installment and Deferred Payment Sales

Less: Selling expenses			
Commissions paid		$5,000	
Abstract of title		75	
Recording fees		25	5,100
Gross profit to be realized			$29,900
Selling price			$100,000
Less: First mortgage assumed by buyer			25,000
Total contract price			$ 75,000
Payments in the year of sale			$ 30,000

The $29,900 profit will be accounted for as the $75,000 on the contract is paid, and 299/750 of each payment will be reported as profit.

(b) Information required. Computation of the gross profit from sales on the installment plan is shown in the return (or an attached statement) for the year of sale. The taxpayer should also show in his return computation of the reportable income for any year in which payments are received on account of such sales. Separate computations must be made for each sale, but they may be shown in a single statement [Sec. 1.453-8(b), 1.453-10].

¶ **2812 Casual sales of personal property on the installment plan.** The rules in ¶ 2811 also apply to casual sales of personal property, except stock in trade, if the selling price exceeds $1,000 [Sec. 453(b)]. Thus, a taxpayer selling shares of stock, even if he is not qualified as a dealer, may return the gain on the transaction on the installment basis if (1) there is no payment in the year of sale or (2) the payments in the year of sale do not exceed 30% of the selling price.[1] If the seller repossesses the property, he computes his gain or loss as a dealer does [¶ 2803]. The gain or loss has the same character as the gain or loss on the original sale.[2] Thus, if the sale initially resulted in a capital gain, any repossession gain also will be a capital gain [Sec. 1.453-1(d)].

¶ **2813 Capital gain on installment sales.** When the gain on a sale of real property or on a casual sale of personal property is reported on the installment plan, and the property is a capital asset [¶ 1601] the gain reported each year is a short-term or long-term capital gain depending on how long the property was held [Sec. 1223; 1.1223-1]. If the property is a Sec. 1231 asset, special benefits apply [¶ 1618]. The amount if any, of imputed interest [¶ 2840] is ordinary income. On a sale of Sec. 1245 or 1250 property [¶ 1619], all the gain on each installment, other than interest, will be taxed as ordinary income until all Sec. 1245 or 1250 income is recaptured [Sec. 1.1245-6(d), 1.1250-1(b)(6)].

Example: On 9-1-77, Brown sold for $40,000, shares of stock that he had bought on 2-1-75 for $30,000. Brown received $10,000 in cash and two notes of the buyer, each of which had a face value of $15,000 at 6% simple interest annually. The first note was due on 9-1-78, the second on 9-1-79. Since the payments in the year of sale ($10,000) do not exceed 30% of the selling price ($40,000), the sale may be reported on the installment basis. The profit is $10,000 which will be accounted for as the $40,000 on the contract is paid. Accordingly, 25% of each payment, exclusive of interest, will be reported as profit, and will be treated as a long-term capital gain [see ¶ 1605; 1612; 3201 et seq.], since the stock had been held for the required period. Brown will report a long-term capital gain of $2,500 in 1977. In 1978, he will report a long-term capital gain of $3,750 and an ordinary income of $900. In 1979, he will report a long-term capital gain or $3,750 and an ordinary income of $1,800. His taxable and nontaxable amounts are shown as follows:

	Payment	Return of capital	Recognized capital gain	Interest (Ordinary income)
1977 payment	$10,000	$ 7,500	$2,500	
1978 payment	15,900	11,250	3,750	$ 900
1979 payment	16,800	11,250	3,750	1,800

¶ **2814 Expenses and losses.** Business expenses not included in cost of goods sold and loss on sale of realty [¶ 2811] or casual sale of personal property [¶ 2812] cannot be spread over the term of the installment payments.[1]

DEFERRED PAYMENT SALES

A taxpayer who sells property for obligations of the buyer and does not qualify or elect the installment method of reporting income may be subject to the deferred payment rules.

¶ **2816 Deferred payment sales not on the installment plan.** If a deferred payment sale does not qualify for the installment method of reporting, or if the seller does not make the election, gain or loss must be reported in the year of sale, even if the sale is covered by obligations of the buyer that are payable to the seller over a period of years. However, in the case of a sale of real property, the buyer's obligations are treated as cash to the extent of their fair market value [Sec. 1.453-6]. Any gain reflected in the difference between the fair market value of the obligations and their face value is reported only when and if collected. This so-called deferred payment sales method applies also to casual sales of personal property by a cash basis taxpayer;[1] but an accrual basis seller must take the whole purchase price into income in the year of sale.[2]

(a) Gain or loss in year of sale. When a taxpayer sells realty for deferred payments not on the installment plan, treatment depends on whether the obligations received were worth their face amount or less than face or had no immediate determinable value. If worth face, the obligations are treated as cash received and included in income in the year of sale [Sec. 1.453-6]. If the property sold is a capital asset [¶ 1601], gain or loss on the sale is a capital gain or loss. If the property is a Sec. 1231 asset [¶ 1618 et seq.], the Sec. 1231 rules apply.

Example 1:
Sale price:

Cash	$20,000	
Notes (worth face value)	$30,000	$50,000
Adjusted basis of property		$35,000
Taxable gain		$15,000

If a fair market value of less than face was reported at the time of sale, however, the amount reported becomes taxpayer's basis in the obligation; and a proportionate part of each payment collected later represents income [see (b) below]. If the obligation has an indeterminable fair market value, subsequent payments are exempt until taxpayer's basis in the obligation is recovered [see (c) below]. The distinction between collections on obligations with a discounted value and those with no determinate value is important, because the former results in ordinary income, while the latter may qualify for capital gain treatment. Only in rare and extraordinary circumstances will obligations be considered to have no fair market value [Sec. 1.453-6].

(b) Collections on discounted notes. When the fair market value of an obligation is less than face value, the fair market value (1) is included in the amount realized to compute gain or loss at the time of sale; and (2) determines the creditor's basis in the obligation for purpose of computing future gain. In later years, part of each payment received is regarded as return of capital, and the remainder is taxable income. The portion that is exempt as a return of capital bears the same ratio to each payment received as the fair market value of the obligation at time of sale bore to its face value.[3] If the issuer of the obligation was an individual, the taxable portion of each payment is ordinary income. If the issuer of the obligation was a corporation, the gain is capital gain only if the collection qualifies as a bond retirement; see ¶ 1602.

Example 2: In 1976 Brown sold realty, which had an adjusted basis of $60,000, for $100,000, payable as follows: cash $35,000; first mortgage assumed, $20,000; second mortgage for $45,000 payable by the buyer in 5 annual installments of $9,000 each (exclusive of 6% stated interest), the first to be paid in 1977. The fair market value of the second mortgage note was 66⅔% of face value, or $30,000. The $40,000 realized gain is reported as follows:

Proceeds realized:		
Cash		$35,000
First mortgage (assumed by purchaser; therefore valued at par)		20,000
Second mortgage	$45,000	
Discount on second mortgage (33⅓%)	15,000	30,000
		$85,000
Adjusted basis		60,000
Realized gain reported in 1976		$25,000

The balance of the realized gain ($15,000) will be reported as the 5 annual installments are paid:

	1977	1978	1979	1980	1981
Collected	$9,000	$9,000	$9,000	$9,000	$9,000
Less 66⅔% already reported	6,000	6,000	6,000	6,000	6,000
Realized (ordinary) gain to be reported	$3,000	$3,000	$3,000	$3,000	$3,000

(c) **Indeterminate market value.** If the fair market value of an obligation cannot be determined, taxpayer is entitled to a return of capital before reporting any profits [Sec. 1.453-6(a)(2)]. The basis of the property sold, reduced by any cash or other property having a fair market value that he receives on the sale, becomes his basis in the obligation with an indeterminate market value for computing gain or loss on collection. If the property sold was a capital asset, collection may result in capital gain [Sec. 1.453-6]. Contingent rights to future payments have been held to be without fair market value.[4]

Example 3: Assume the same facts as in Example 2, except that the second mortgage notes had an indeterminate fair market value. The order of the payment is:

Cash	$ 35,000
First mortgage (assumed by purchaser and therefore valued at par)	20,000
First annual installment	9,000
Second annual installment	9,000
Third annual installment	9,000
Fourth annual installment	9,000
Fifth annual installlment	9,000
Total	$100,000

The adjusted basis is $60,000. The cash ($35,000), first mortgage ($20,000) and $5,000 of the first annual installment (total $60,000) are a return of capital. $4,000 of the first annual installment and all of the subsequent installments are recognized gain *when received*. If all the installments are paid when due, the taxpayer will report recognized gain as follows: return for 1977, $4,000; 1978, $9,000; 1979, $9,000; 1980, $9,000; 1981, $9,000 (total $40,000).

REPOSSESSIONS

If the seller repossesses personal property sold in a deferred payment transaction not reported on the installment basis, the rules for determining gain or loss or a bad debt on the defaulted installment obligation are basically the same as for sales on the installment basis discussed at ¶ 2803. If real property is repossessed, no loss is recognized and no bad debt deduction allowed.

¶ **2821 Repossession of personal property.** The gain or loss on the repossession of personal property in a deferred payment sale *not* on the installment plan [¶ 2816], is the difference between the fair market value of the property on the date of repossession and the basis of the defaulted obligation adjusted for other amounts realized or costs incurred in the repossession. However, the entire taxable gain or deductible loss is reported in the year of sale. Therefore, the basis of the obligation to be used is its face value or fair market value, whichever was used in computing gain or loss for the year of sale. Nature of the gain or loss depends on the obligation, rather than the original sale. If the obligation is discharged by repossession of the property, any gain will be ordinary income. If the repossession results in a loss that is a nonbusiness bad debt, it will be reported as a short-term capital loss. If the loss is a business bad debt, it will be so reported.[1]

Special rules apply to foreclosures by mutual banks and certain other mutual savings institutions [¶ 3433(b)].

¶ **2823 Real property repossessed by seller.** No loss is recognized and no bad debt deduction is allowed when real property is repossessed by the seller to satisfy a purchase obligation. Gain will be recognized to the seller on repossession only to the extent of the cash (or other property) received, less the gain on the original sale already included in income. The amount of the gain that is taxable, however, is limited to the gain on the original sale less repossession costs and gain previously reported as income [Sec.1.1038-1]. The nonrecognition of gain rules do not apply when real property is reconveyed to the estate of a deceased seller.[1]

If the original sale was reported on the installment basis, the repossession gain retains the same character as the gain on the original sale. If the sale was by a dealer, the gain is ordinary income; otherwise, it is either capital gain or Sec. 1231 gain [Sec. 1038; 1.1038-1]. Seller's holding period includes the period he held the property before its original sale, but excludes the period starting with the day after date of the original sale and ending with date property is reacquired [Sec. 1.1038-1(g)]. If the original sale was not an installment sale, and the title passed to the buyer, repossession gain from a voluntary reconveyance generally is ordinary income. However, if the obligations satisfied are bonds as defined in ¶ 2312(a), any gain from the reacquistion is capital gain [Sec. 1.1038-1(d)].

Example 1: Brown sold a building in 1973 for $60,000, $10,000 cash and a $50,000 mortgage, payable $10,000 annually starting 6-3-74. His adjusted basis was $48,000. Brown elected to report income from the sale on the installment basis. His gain was $12,000, or 20% of selling price, and he reported $2,000 gain in 1973, 1974, 1975 and 1976. The buyer defaulted in 1977, and Brown repossessed the property at a cost of $500. Brown's gain on repossession is $32,000 ($40,000 cash received minus $8,000 already reported as income), but his recognized gain is limited to $3,500 ($12,000 gain on the original sale minus $500 repossession costs and $8,000 already reported as income).

If any part of the debt obligation remains unsatisfied, its basis becomes zero. Hence, any later recovery is income. The basis of the repossessed property is the adjusted basis of the obligations (including the basis of unsatisfied obligations) plus any repossession gain and plus repossession costs. Adjusted basis of the obligations is the excess of the face amount of the obligations over the gain that would be reported if the obligations were satisfied in full [Sec. 1038; 1.1038-1(g)].

Footnotes appear at end of this Chapter.

Example 2: The basis of the repossessed property in Example 1 is $20,000, determined as follows:

Obligations (face amount)	$20,000
Less 20% unreported profits	4,000
Adjusted basis of obligations	$16,000
Repossession gain	3,500
Repossession costs	500
Basis of repossessed property	$20,000

If, before the repossession, the seller took a bad debt deduction for the partial or complete worthlessness of the obligations, repossession satisfies the debt and the deduction must be added back to income if a tax benefit resulted from it. Basis is increased accordingly [Sec. 1038(d); 1.1038-1(f)].

Repossession of seller's residence. When the repossessed property was the seller's principal residence and gain was either excluded or not recognized on the original sale, special rules apply. If the property is not resold within a year after repossession, the rules above apply. If it is resold within a year, in effect the repossession is disregarded and the resale is considered a sale of the property occurring on the original sales date; the price deemed received is the resale price, including mortgages plus the cash or other property retained from the original sale. Using this selling price, the amount of the gain exempt under Sec. 121 or not recognized under Sec. 1034 is recomputed [¶ 1416; 1423]. If the recomputation shows the taxable gain is more or less than that reported in the year of the original sale, an adjustment is made by taking the difference into account in the return for the year of resale [Sec. 1.1038-2].

DISPOSITION OF INSTALLMENT OBLIGATIONS

Disposing of an installment obligation usually results in a gain or loss from the sale or exchange of the property for which the obligation was received.

¶ 2831 Gain or loss on disposition of installment obligations. A person who disposes of the installment obligations after he makes an installment sale must report the gain or loss. The basis is the excess of the face value of the obligation over an amount equal to the income that would be returnable if the obligation were fully satisfied [Sec. 453(d)]. Since this is always equal to the unrecovered cost, *the basis is the unrecovered cost.* Gain or loss is the difference between the basis and (i) the amount realized when the obligation is sold or exchanged, or satisfied at other than face value, or (ii) the fair market value when the obligation is disposed of other than by sale or exchange. The gain or loss is treated as a gain or loss from the property for which the installment obligation was received [Sec. 453(d); 1.453-9].

Example: In 1976, Hobson sold for $100,000 (exclusive of 6% interest) real property which he had purchased in 1962 and which had an adjusted basis of $60,000. Payment was to be made as follows: cash $30,000; mortgage for $70,000, payable by the buyer in semi-annual installments of $10,000 each, the first to be paid on 4-1-77. The profit was $40,000 which will be accounted for as the $100,000 due on the contract is paid. Accordingly, 40% of each payment is profit.

	Face value	Recognized gain (40%)	Return of capital or basis (60%)
1976 payments	$ 30,000	$12,000	$18,000
1977 payments	20,000	8,000	12,000
1978 payments	20,000	8,000	12,000
1979 payments	20,000	8,000	12,000
1980 payments	10,000	4,000	6,000
Total	$100,000	$40,000	$60,000

Assume that before any payment is made in 1978, Hobson assigns the 1978, 1979 and 1980 notes that he still has (face value $50,000) for $35,000. The basis of the notes is the unrecovered cost of $30,000 ($12,000 + 12,000 + 6,000). The recognized gain is $5,000 ($35,000 − 30,000).

There are conflicting authorities as to whether a gift of the obligation is a taxable disposition.[1]

(a) Acquisition from decedent. Installment obligations which the decedent would have reported on the installment basis had he lived, are taxed to the successor as "income in respect of a decedent" to the extent the obligation's face value exceeds its basis in decedent's hands. The successor must report as income the same proportion of payments in satisfaction of the obligation as would be returnable by the decedent if he had lived [Sec. 691(a)(4); 1.691(a)(5)].

(b) Distributions in liquidation. No gain or loss is recognized to a corporation on the distribution of installment obligations if:

• An installment obligation is distributed by one corporation to another in liquidation, and, under the rules for complete liquidations of subsidiaries, [¶ 3334] no gain or loss is recognized to the recipient.

• An installment obligation is distributed by a corporation in liquidation and, under the nonrecognition rules stated in ¶ 3128, no gain or loss would have been recognized to the corporation if the corporation had sold or exchanged the installment obligations on the day of distribution [Sec. 453(d)(4); 1.453-9(c)].

≫**OBSERVATION→** The liquidating corporation may have ordinary income if the installment obligations represent Sec. 1245 or 1250 property [¶ 1619], or Sec. 1251 or 1252 farm property [¶ 1845(e); 2226], or mining property (¶ 1843), or stock of a consenting collapsible corporation (¶ 1627(c)), or interest in oil or gas property (¶ 2103(c)) [Sec. 453(d)(4)].

(c) Tax-free transfers of installment obligations. In some cases installment obligations may be transferred without tax being imposed on disposition. These include: transfers to a controlled corporation in exchange for stock or securities [¶ 1405]; contributions to a partnership in exchange for partnership interest; distributions in liquidations ((b), above); distributions by a partnership to a partner; certain exchanges of property for stock or securities involving corporate reorganizations [¶ 3306; 3309].

SPECIAL PROBLEMS

The special problems covered in this section relate to imputed interest, sale of real property in lots, and long-term contracts.

¶ 2840 Imputed interest. Taxpayers entitled to capital gain treatment on deferred payment sales formerly could save taxes by either specifying no interest, or an unreasonably low interest rate, on the sales contract. This increased the capital

Footnotes appear at end of this Chapter.

2814　Chapter 18—Installment and Deferred Payment Sales

gain and reduced or wiped out interest taxable as ordinary income. To prevent this, part of the deferred payments is now treated as interest, both to seller and buyer for all tax purposes. Thus basis of property in buyer's hands does not include the part of his payments treated as interest, and he gets a deduction for the interest element [Sec. 483].

(a) Figuring imputed interest. Interest is not imputed if the stated simple interest rate is at least 6% (4% for contracts entered into before 7-24-75). If interest is specified, but the amount is not stated as a percent, the unstated interest must be detemined:

Step 1: Determine the sum of the sale price payments (excluding any stated interest) deferred for more than 6 months.

Step 2: Find the present value of all payments (including any stated interest) deferred for more than 6 months, using the 6% columns in the Table on page 2815. If the amount in Step 2 is less than the amount in Step 1, there is unstated interest and you must take Step 3.

Step 3: Find the present value of the payments in Step 2, using the 7% columns in the Table. Subtract this amount from the amount in Step 1. The difference is the amount that will be treated as interest [Sec. 483; 1.483-1].

Example 1: A capital asset, adjusted basis $10,000, is sold for $16,000, payable $4,000 within 3 months, and the balance in 4 annual installments of $3,000 starting a year after sale. The contract does not provide for interest.

There's no interest element in the $4,000 payment—it's within 6 months of sale. The interest element imputed in the remaining $12,000 is $1,866.42:

Sum of payments deferred more than 6 months		$12,000.00
Less: present values of $3,000 due every 12 mos. for 4 yrs. figured from Table:		
$3,000 deferred 12 mos. ($3,000 × .93351)	$2,800.53	
$3,000 deferred 24 mos. ($3,000 × .87144)	2,614.32	
$3,000 deferred 36 mos. ($3,000 × .81350)	2,440.50	
$3,000 deferred 48 mos. ($3,000 × .75941)	2,278.23	10,133.58
Unstated interest		$ 1,866.42

Seller's capital gain (reportable at once or on installment basis) is $4,133.58 ($16,000 − $1,866.42 − $10,000). On cash basis, he has interest income of $466.61 ($1,866.42/4) as each $3,000 installment is received. Buyer's unadjusted basis is $14,133.58. Assuming he is on the cash basis, he deducts $466.61 interest as each installment is paid.

Late payments. Total unstated interest must be recomputed if any payment is made more than 90 days after its due date [Sec. 483; 1.483-1(f)(1), (2)]. If imputed interest must be recomputed, the recomputed amount does not disqualify use of the installment method[1] [¶ 2811(a)].

(b) Sale at loss. The rules for imputing interest apply even if the property is sold at a loss, or would be sold at a loss when the interest element is separated from the contract amount.

Example 2: Assume that seller's basis in Example 1 were $16,000. Seller has the same interest income. He also has a capital loss of $1,866.42.

Chapter 18—Installment and Deferred Payment Sales

TABLE—PRESENT VALUE OF DEFERRED PAYMENT
Applies to Contracts Entered into after 7-23-75

[Col. (a) 6 percent simple interest; col. (b) 7 percent interest, compounded semiannually]

Number of months deferred More than	But not more than	Col. (a) Present value of $1 at 6 percent simple interest	Col. (b) Present value of $1 at 7 percent compounded semi-annually	Number of months deferred More than	But not more than	Col. (a) Present value of $1 at 6 percent simple interest	Col. (b) Present value of $1 at 7 percent compounded semi-annually	Number of months deferred More than	But not more than	Col. (a) Present value of $1 at 6 percent simple interest	Col. (b) Present value of $1 at 7 percent compounded semi-annually
0	6	1.00000	1.00000	243	249	.44843	.24403	489	495	.28902	.05955
6	9	.97087	.96618	249	255	.44248	.23578	495	501	.28653	.05754
9	15	.94340	.93351	255	261	.43668	.22781	501	507	.28409	.05559
15	21	.91743	.90194	261	267	.43103	.22010	507	513	.28169	.05371
21	27	.89286	.87144	267	273	.42553	.21266	513	519	.27933	.05190
27	33	.86957	.84197	273	279	.42017	.20547	519	525	.27701	.05014
33	39	.84746	.81350	279	285	.41494	.19852	525	531	.27473	.04845
39	45	.82645	.78599	285	291	.40984	.19181	531	537	.27248	.04681
45	51	.80645	.75941	291	297	.40486	.18532	537	543	.27027	.04522
51	57	.78740	.73373	297	303	.40000	.17905	543	549	.26810	.04369
57	63	.76923	.70892	303	309	.39526	.17300	549	555	.26596	.04222
63	69	.75188	.68495	309	315	.39062	.16715	555	561	.26385	.04079
69	75	.73529	.66178	315	321	.38610	.16150	561	567	.26178	.03941
75	81	.71942	.63940	321	327	.38168	.15603	567	573	.25974	.03808
81	87	.70423	.61778	327	333	.37736	.15076	573	579	.25773	.03679
87	93	.68966	.59689	333	339	.37313	.14566	579	585	.25575	.03555
93	99	.67568	.57671	339	345	.36900	.14073	585	591	.25381	.03434
99	105	.66225	.55720	345	351	.36496	.13598	591	597	.25189	.03318
105	111	.64935	.53836	351	357	.36101	.13138	597	603	.25000	.03206
111	117	.63694	.52016	357	363	.35714	.12693	603	609	.24814	.03098
117	123	.62500	.50257	363	369	.35336	.12264	609	615	.24631	.02993
123	129	.61350	.48557	369	375	.34965	.11849	615	621	.24450	.02892
129	135	.60241	.46915	375	381	.34602	.11449	621	627	.24272	.02794
135	141	.59172	.45329	381	387	.34247	.11062	627	633	.24096	.02699
141	147	.58140	.43796	387	393	.33898	.10688	633	639	.23923	.02608
147	153	.57143	.42315	393	399	.33557	.10326	639	645	.23753	.02520
153	159	.56180	.40884	399	405	.33223	.09977	645	651	.23585	.02435
159	165	.55249	.39501	405	411	.32895	.09640	651	657	.23419	.02352
165	171	.54348	.38165	411	417	.32573	.09314	657	663	.23256	.02273
171	177	.53476	.36875	417	423	.32258	.08999	663	669	.23095	.02196
177	183	.52632	.35623	423	429	.31949	.08694	669	675	.22936	.02122
183	189	.51813	.34423	429	435	.31646	.08400	675	681	.22779	.02050
189	195	.51020	.33259	435	441	.31348	.08116	681	687	.22624	.01981
195	201	.50251	.32134	441	447	.31056	.07842	687	693	.22472	.01914
201	207	.49505	.31048	447	453	.30769	.07577	693	699	.22321	.01849
207	213	.48780	.29998	453	459	.30488	.07320	699	705	.22173	.01786
213	219	.48077	.28983	459	465	.30211	.07073	705	711	.22026	.01726
219	225	.47393	.28003	465	471	.29940	.06834	711	717	.21882	.01668
225	231	.46729	.27056	471	477	.29674	.06603	717	723	.21739	.01611
231	237	.46083	.26141	477	483	.29412	.06379				
237	243	.45455	.25257	483	489	.29155	.06164				

(c) **Contract revised.** If the contract is revised, the interest element in future payments must be recalculated [Sec. 483(e); 1.483-1(f)].

(d) **Contingent payments.** If deferred payments are contingent as to time, amount or liability, the interest element is determined separately from the interest element in the noncontingent payments [Sec. 483(d); 1.483-1(e)].

> **Example 3:** Assume same facts as Example 1, except the buyer is also to pay 5% of profits over a stated period. The $16,000 fixed price is treated as explained in Example 1. Any payment of profits is to be discounted back to the contract date. The excess of the payment over the discounted amount is interest.

(e) **Exceptions to imputed interest rule.** As stated above, interest is not imputed if the stated interest is at least 6% (4% before 7-24-75). In addition, the rule will not apply in any of these cases: (1) Sales price is $3,000 or less; (2) No payment is deferred by the contract for more than a year; (3) Patents are being sold under conditions described in ¶ 1601(j); (4) Property is neither a capital nor a Sec. 1231 asset (only affects seller); (5) Property is exchanged for annuity payments

Footnotes appear at end of this Chapter.

¶ 2840

based on life expectancy; or (6) Buyer can take a deduction for carrying charges [¶ 1904] (only affects buyer) [Sec. 483(f); 1.483-2].

(f) Accounting for imputed interest. If taxpayer is on the cash basis, the imputed interest is income when received or deductible when paid.

NOTE: This results in different treatment than if reasonable interest had been stated. Imputed interest is prorated ratably to the deferred payments. Stated interest normally would be payable on declining balances.

An accrual basis taxpayer reports imputed interest or deducts it for the tax year the payment is due [Sec. 1.483-2(a)(1)].

¶ 2841 Sale of real property in lots. A real estate development company will often acquire a tract of land and divide it into parcels or lots for easier sales. Ordinarily this requires an outlay for development such as surveying, installation of sewerage, paving, and the like. These costs must be recorded on company books and equitably apportioned to the separate lots.

The sale of each lot is treated as a separate transaction. This means that there will be a separate gain or loss on every lot sold, and not deferred until the entire tract is disposed of before determining taxable gain or deductible loss [Sec. 1.61-6(a)].

The allocation of costs is a big problem in making the computation. Foot frontage, release prices, tentative sales prices and assessed valuation have all been used. The tentative sales price method is illustrated below.

Example: The cost of the land, including the improvements, was $25,000 and the development company expects to sell the lots for $100,000. The cost of any one lot is 25% of the sale price at which it was offered for sale to the public on the day the tract was first opened.

Lot No.	No. of lots	Tentative sales price Each	Total	Estimated cost price Each	Total
1-10	10	$5,500	$55,000	$1,375	$13,750
11-20	10	3,000	30,000	750	7,500
21-25	5	2,000	10,000	500	2,500
26-30	5	1,000	5,000	250	1,250

¶ 2842 Long-term contracts. Generally, the long-term contract method may be used to report income from a building, installation, construction, or manufacturing contract which is not completed within the tax year in which it is entered into. A manufacturing contract is a long-term contract only if it involves the manufacture of (a) unique items of a type not normally carried in the taxpayer's finished goods inventory, or (b) items that normally require over 12 months to complete (regardless of the actual contract duration) [Sec. 1.451-3]. A statement that this method is being used should be attached to the return. Permission to change to or from this method must be obtained the same way permission is obtained to change from the cash to the accrual basis, or vice versa [¶ 2708]. Special rules apply to advance payments [¶ 2726(c)]. The income from long-term contracts may be reported under either of the following methods:

(a) Percentage of completion. If this method is used, there should be available for inspection, certificates of architects or engineers showing the percentage of completion during the tax year. That percentage determines the gross income to be reported for that year, regardless of when payment is made. Expenditures made on the contract during the year are deductible. No deduction is allowed for materials and supplies on hand at the end of the year but not yet in process. Sec. 1.451-3(c)(3).

Example 1: If the amount to be received under the contract is $100,000 and the certificate shows that 40% was completed during the year, the gross income for that year is $40,000 (regardless of the time payment is actually made).

(b) Completed contract. Under this method, the gross income from the contract is reported in the year the contract is completed, a deduction being permitted at that time for all expenditures properly allocable to the contract over its life. Thus, loss from the abandonment of a hole by an oil-well driller using a modified long-term contract method, was deductible in the year the contract was completed, not the year the loss was sustained.[1] Indirect costs and overhead expenses *not directly attributable* to the contract are deductible only in the year paid or incurred.[2] Those that cannot be accurately allocated may be similarly deducted.[3] Franchise and capital stock taxes may be apportioned between the long-term contract and other business activities.[4]

(c) Comparison of percentage of completion method with completed contract method. When a change to either of these methods is contemplated, the probable result should be checked against the method in present use by the taxpayer. A comparison of the percentage of completion method and the completed contract method is given in the example below.

Example 2: Harmon, a contractor, entered into three contracts in 1977 for various construction jobs. Contract No. 1 was for $100,000 and was to be completed by December 1, 1979. Contract No. 2 was for $200,000 and was to be completed by November 15, 1979. Contract No. 3 was for $300,000 and was to be completed by December 15, 1980.

Harmon's estimated expenditures on account of the contract are as follows:
Contract No. 1, 1978, $60,000; 1979, $20,000.
Contract No. 2, 1978, $125,000; 1979, $50,000.
Contract No. 3, 1978, $115,000; 1979, $110,000; 1980, $35,000.

The percentage of completion at the end of each year for each contract is estimated to be as follows:
Contract No. 1, Dec. 31, 1978, 60%; Dec. 31, 1979, 100%.
Contract No. 2, Dec. 31, 1978, 75%; Dec. 31, 1979, 100%.
Contract No. 3, Dec. 31, 1978, 40%; Dec. 31, 1979, 80%; Dec. 31, 1980, 100%.

PERCENTAGE OF COMPLETION METHOD

Contract No. 1	1978	1979	1980
Gross income	$ 60,000	$ 40,000	
Expenses	60,000	20,000	
Net	0	$ 20,000	
Contract No. 2			
Gross income	$150,000	$ 50,000	
Expenses	125,000	50,000	
Net	$ 25,000	0	
Contract No. 3			
Gross income	$120,000	$120,000	$60,000
Expenses	115,000	110,000	35,000
Net	$ 5,000	$ 10,000	$25,000
Contract No. 1	0	$ 20,000	
Contract No. 2	$ 25,000	0	
Contract No. 3	5,000	10,000	25,000
Total	$ 30,000	$ 30,000	$25,000

Footnotes appear at end of this Chapter.

¶ 2842

Chapter 18—Installment and Deferred Payment Sales

COMPLETED CONTRACT METHOD

	Receipts	Expenses	Net Income
Year 1978	0	0	0
Year 1979			
Contract No. 1	$100,000	$80,000	$20,000
Contract No. 2	200,000	175,000	25,000
Total	$300,000	$255,000	$45,000
Year 1980			
Contract No. 3	$300,000	$260,000	$40,000

Footnotes to Chapter 18

(P-H "FEDERAL TAXES" related references are cited in brackets [ ] at the end of each footnote below.)

Footnote ¶ 2800 [¶ 20,375 et seq.].
(1) Rev. Rul. 65-297, 1965-2 CB 152; Rev. Rul. 76-44, 1976-1 CB 27 [¶ 20,421(5)].

Footnote ¶ 2801 [¶ 20,395].
(1) Alworth-Washburn Co., 67 F.2d 694, 13 AFTR 381 [¶ 20,451(5)].
(2) Rev. Proc. 65-5, 1965-1 CB 720 [¶ 20,409].
(3) Rev. Rul. 54-111, 1954-1 CB 76 [¶ 20,396(15)].

Footnote ¶ 2802 [¶ 20,397].
(1) Rev. Rul. 67-316, 1967-2 CB 171; Federated Department Stores, Inc., 25 AFTR 2d 70-1269, 426 F.2d 417 [¶ 20,141(75); 20,144(30); 20,311(10); 20,401(20)].
(2) Rev. Rul. 74-156, 1974-1 CB 114 [¶ 20,397(25)].
(3) Rev. Rul. 60-53, 1960-1 CB 185; Rev. Rul. 68-163, 1968-1 CB 201 [¶ 20,397(20); 20,425(25)].
(4) Blum's Inc., 7 BTA 737 [¶ 20,401(5)].

Footnote ¶ 2803 [¶ 20,403].
(1) Blum's Inc., 7 BTA 737 [¶ 20,403(5)].

Footnote ¶ 2804 [¶ 20,405 et seq.].

Footnote ¶ 2311 [¶ 20,415 et seq.].
(1) Rev. Rul. 69-462, 1969-2 CB 107; Rev. Rul. 71-595, 1971-2 CB 223 [¶ 20,416(5)].
(2) Rev. Rul. 73-555, 1973-2 CB 159; U.S. v. Marshall, 17 AFTR 2d 596, 357 F.2d 294; Irwin V. Comm., 21 AFTR 2d 779, 390 F.2d 91 [¶ 20,427(40)].
(3) Newaygo Portland Cement Co., 27 BTA 1097; Treas. Dept. booklet "Tax Guide for Small Business" (1977 Ed.), p. 99 [¶ 20,429(5)].
(4) Tombari, 9 AFTR 2d 672, 299 F.2d 889 [¶ 20,424(18)].
(5) Rev. Rul. 74-384, 1974-2 CB 153 [¶ 20,435(5)].
(6) Solly K. Frankenstein, 31 TC 431, 4 AFTR 2d 5809, 272 F.2d 135; Highland, E.-L. Subdivision, etc., 32 BTA 760, 19 AFTR 131, 88 F.2d 355 [¶ 16,712(30), (35)].

Footnote ¶ 2812 [¶ 20,415 et seq.].
(1) 50 East 75th St. Corp. v. Comm., 78 F.2d 158,

Footnote ¶ 2812 continued
16 AFTR 332; Greenwood, 34 BTA 1209 [¶ 20,419(5); 20,435(5)].
(2) Treas. Dept. booklet "Your Federal Income Tax" (1977 Ed.), p. 116.

Footnote ¶ 2813 [¶ 20,415].

Footnote ¶ 2814 [¶ 20,401; 20,416].
(1) Martin V. Comm., 61 F.2d 942, 11 AFTR 1019; Rev. Rul. 70-430, 1970-2 CB 51 [¶ 20,416(10)].

Footnote ¶ 2816 [¶ 20,461].
(1) Powell, ¶ 62,195 P-H Memo TC [¶ 20,466(7)].
(2) George L. Castner Co., Inc., 30 TC 1061 [¶ 20,467(15)].
(3) Culbertson, 14 TC 1421 [¶ 20,465(5)].
(4) Burnet v. Logan, 283 US 404, 51 SCt 550, 9 AFTR 1453 [¶ 20,468(10)].

Footnote ¶ 2821 [¶ 20,403].
(1) Treas. Dept. booklet "Your Federal Income Tax" (1977 Ed.), p. 116.

Footnote ¶ 2823 [¶ 31,791].
(1) Rev. Rul. 69-83, 1969-1 CB 202 [¶ 31,796(10)].

Footnote ¶ 2831 [¶ 20,445 et seq.].
(1) Rev. Rul. 55-157, 1955-1 CB 293; Miller v. Usry, 1 AFTR 2d 1295, 160 F. Supp. 368; Treas. Dept. booklet "Tax Guide for Small Business" (1977 Ed.), p. 104 [¶ 20,453(10)].

Footnote ¶ 2840 [¶ 20,921].
(1) Rev. Rul. 68-247, 1968-1 CB 199 [¶ 20,427(65)].

Footnote ¶ 2841 [¶ 31,210].

Footnote ¶ 2842 [¶ 20,260 et seq.].
(1) Smith v. Jones, 193 F.2d 381, 41 AFTR 488 [¶ 20,272(10)].
(2) Treas. Dept. booklet "Tax Guide for Small Business" (1977 Ed.), p. 13.
(3) Brown & Root, Inc. v. Scofield, 44 AFTR 1325 [¶ 20,272(15)].
(4) Patrick McGovern, Inc., 40 BTA 706 [¶ 20,272(25)].

Highlights of Chapter 18
Installment and Deferred Payment Sales

I. **Installment Sales by Dealers in Personal Property**
   A. **How income reported [¶ 2801]:**
      1. Proportionately as collections made.
      2. Who is dealer [¶ 2801(a)]:
         a. No definition of dealer.
         b. Installment sale—payment made in 2 or more installments.
      3. Accounting [¶ 2801(b)]:
         a. Must permit allocation of collections to year sale made.
         b. Hybrid accounting allowed.
      4. Statement with tax return required [¶ 2801(c)].
   B. **Figuring the profit [¶ 2802]:**
      1. Payment period over one year—profit allocation required:
         a. Figured as payments received.
         b. Percentage of profit for year of sale used.
      2. Finance or carrying charges—generally included in sales price.
      3. Retailer's excise and state sales taxes—included in sales price.
      4. Business expenses not in cost of goods sold—must be deducted in year paid or incurred.
   C. **Repossession by dealer [¶ 2803]:**
      1. Gain or loss—difference between:
         a. Fair market value of repossessed goods, and
         b. Unpaid outstanding obligations less unrealized profit.
      2. Repossessed goods included in inventory at fair market value.
      3. No repossession, or valueless when recovered—bad debt deduction equal to unrecovered cost of goods.
   D. **Change of accounting method [¶ 2804]:**
      1. Installment method adoptable without prior IRS approval.
      2. Installment method retroactively revocable without prior IRS approval.
      3. Adjustments required on change from accrual to installment [¶ 2804(a)]:
         a. Receipts from prior installment sales income when collected.
         b. Reduction allowed to prevent double taxation of profits—lesser of taxes from inclusion in first and second years.
      4. Information required on return [¶ 2804(b)]:
         a. Accounting method used before change.
         b. Span of years over which adjustments required.
         c. Schedule showing adjustment computations.
II. **Other Installment Sales**
   A. **Sales of real property**—reportable on installment method if [¶ 2811]:
      1. Two or more payments, and
      2. Payments in year of sale not over 30% of selling price.
      3. Figuring profit [¶ 2811(a)]:
         a. Difference between selling price and adjusted basis—gross profit.
         b. Gross profit divided by contract price—each payment's proportionate return of profit.
         c. Payments in year of sale include:
            1) All cash or property received in year of sale (except buyer's evidences of indebtedness, generally).

2) Bonds, etc. payable on demand or readily marketable (received after 5-27-69) of buyer, corporation or government.
3) Excess of mortgage (which buyer assumes or takes property subject to) over property's adjusted basis.
4) Payments received in prior years as options or down payments.
   d. Selling price—total amount involved in sale.
   e. Contract price—total amount received by seller (seller's equity).
   f. Amount of imputed interest reduces selling or contract price.
   g. Commissions and selling expenses:
1) Do not reduce selling or contract prices or payments in year of sale.
2) Offset selling price by reducing profit from sale.
3) Business expense deduction for real estate dealers.
4. Gross profit computations required on tax return [¶ 2811(b)].
B. **Casual sales of personal property**—if sales price over $1,000 and not stock in trade [¶ 2812]:
1. Same rules as installment sales of real property.
2. Repossession—same rules as for repossession by dealer.
C. **Capital gain on installment sales [¶ 2813]:**
1. Long or short-term capital gain depending on how long property held.
2. Imputed interest is ordinary income.
3. Sec. 1231 assets—special benefits.
4. Sec. 1245 or 1250 property—ordinary income until all Sec. 1245 or 1250 income recaptured.

III. **Deferred Payment Sales**
A. **Defined [¶ 2816]:**
1. Not qualified or elected for installment method treatment.
2. Gain or loss reported in year of sale, except buyer's obligations treated as cash only to extent of fair market value for:
   a. Sales of real property.
   b. Casual sales of personal property by cash basis taxpayers.
B. **Gain or loss in year of sale [¶ 2816(a)]:**
1. Obligations worth face value—report everything in year of sale.
2. Obligations worth less than face—report proportionate part of each payment collected later as income:
   a. Discounted value—ordinary income.
   b. Indeterminate value—qualify for capital gain treatment.
C. **Collections on discounted notes [¶ 2816(b)]**
1. Fair market value:
   a. Included in amount realized to compute gain or loss at sale.
   b. Determines creditor's basis for future gain computations.
2. Future payments treated proportionately as:
   a. Return of capital.
   b. Taxable income.
3. Obligation issued by individual—ordinary income.
4. Obligation issued by corporation—capital gain if bond retirement.
D. **Indeterminate market value [¶ 2816(c)]:**
1. Taxpayer entitled to return of capital before reporting profits.
2. Basis of property sold less cash or property received in sale becomes basis for computing gain or loss.

IV. **Repossessions**
A. **Personal property [¶ 2803; 2821]:**
1. Installment sales—rules summarized at I, C, above.
2. Other deferred-payment sales:
   a. Gain or loss or bad debt determined generally as in I, C, above.
   b. Nature of gain or loss depends on obligation, not on original sale.
B. **Real property [¶ 2823]:**

1. Amount of gain or loss:
   a. No loss recognized.
   b. No bad debt deduction allowed.
   c. Recognized gain—to extent of cash (or other property) received, less original sale gain already included in income.
   d. Limit on taxable gain—original sale gain less repossession costs and gain previously reported as income.
2. Character of gain or loss:
   a. Original sale on installment basis—same as original sale.
   b. Original sale by dealer—ordinary income.
   c. Other original sale—capital or Sec. 1231 gain.
3. Seller's holding period:
   a. Includes period held before original sale.
   b. Excludes period from day after original sale to day of repossession.
4. Basis of repossessed property:
   a. Adjusted basis of obligations (excess of face amount over reportable gain if fully satisfied), plus
   b. Repossession costs and gain.
5. On repossession, report prior bad debt deduction as income.
6. Seller's residence—special rules.

V. **Disposition of Installment Obligations**
   A. **Gain or loss [¶ 2831]**—difference between:
      1. Basis (unrecovered cost), and
      2. Amount realized when sold, exchanged or satisfied at other than face, or fair market value, when disposed other than by sale or exchange.
      3. Gift of obligation—taxability subject to conflicting views.
   B. **Acquisition from decedent [¶ 2831(a)]:**
      1. Payment to successor is "income in respect of decedent."
      2. Successor reports same portion of payments as decedent would have.
   C. **Distribution in liquidation [¶ 2831(b)]:**
      1. No gain or loss to liquidating corporation generally.
      2. Corp. realizes ordinary income on disposing notes representing sale of depreciable, farm, or mining property and the like.
   D. **Tax-free transfers**—no tax when exchange involving certain [¶ 2831(c)]:
      1. Transfers to controlled corporations for stock.
      2. Contributions to partnerships for interest.
      3. Corporate liquidation distributions.
      4. Distributions by partnerships to partners.
      5. Corporate reorganizations.

VI. **Imputed Interest**
   A. **When and how to impute interest [¶ 2840(a)]:**
      1. Interest is imputed if:
         a. No interest specified, or
         b. Post-7-23-75 contract sets lower than 6% interest.
      2. Use official table to impute.
   B. **Sale at loss**—rules still apply [¶ 2840(b)].
   C. **Contract revised**—recalculation required [¶ 2840(c)].
   D. **Contingent payments**—interest element figured separately from noncontingent payments [¶ 2840(d)].
   E. **Exceptions**—interest not imputed when [¶ 2840(e)]:
      1. Stated interest at least 6% (4% before 7-24-75).
      2. Sales price is $3,000 or less.
      3. No payment deferred more than one year.
      4. Patents are sold under certain conditions.
      5. Property neither capital nor Sec. 1231 asset (seller only).
      6. Property exchange for life expectancy annuity payments.

7. Buyer can deduct carrying charges (buyer only).
F. Accounting [¶ 2840(f)]:
1. Cash basis—income (or deduction) when installment received (or paid).
2. Accrual basis—income (or deduction) for year payment due.
VII. Sale of Real Property in Lots
A. Development cost allocated to separate lots.
B. Taxable gain or loss when each lot sold.
VIII. Long-term Contract Method
A. For income from building, installation, construction, or manufacturing contracts.
B. Income reportable two ways:
1. Percentage of completion—income reported yearly as work completed [¶ 2842(a)].
2. Completed contract—income reported in year contract completed [¶ 2842(b)].
C. Change to or from requires permission.

HANDLING TAXES OF PARTNERSHIPS, ESTATES, TRUSTS

Chapter 19—PARTNERSHIPS
(Detailed Table of Contents below)

Chapter 20—ESTATES AND TRUSTS
(Detailed Table of Contents at page 3001)

Chapter 19

PARTNERSHIPS

TABLE OF CONTENTS

¶

WHAT IS A PARTNERSHIP

Tax definition	2900
How group enterprises are classified	2903
Family partnerships	2904
Recognition of family member as partner	
Service partnerships	
Allocation of income to family members	2905

PARTNERSHIP INCOME, DEDUCTIONS, CREDITS

How partnerships report their income, deduction and credit items	2906
Segregation of partnership income, deduction and credit items	
Partnership's taxable income or loss	
Elections affecting computation of income	
Book profit and taxable income reconciled	2907

DETERMINATION OF PARTNER'S TAX LIABILITY

Partner's income, deductions and credits	2908
Loss is limited	
Gross income	
Partnership tax preferences	
Partnership earned income	
How partner's distributive share is determined	2909
Distributive share of items due to contributed property	2910

¶

Allocation by agreement	
Allocation for undivided interests	
Capital gains and losses	2911
Capital assets	
Sales and exchanges of business property—involuntary conversions	
Partnership items specially reported	2913
Limited deductions or exclusions	
Change to installment accounting	
Investment tax credit	
Work incentive program credit	
Partner's net operating loss deduction	2914
Charitable contributions	2915
Dividends received	2916
Credit or deduction for foreign taxes paid	2917
Distribution and reconciliation schedules	2918
Purpose of distribution schedule	
Purpose of reconciliation schedule	

TAX YEAR OF PARTNER AND PARTNERSHIP

When partner reports partnership income	2920
When partner disposes of his interest	
Gain or loss on distribution or transfer	
Choice of tax year	2921
Partnership tax year	
Partner's tax year	
Application to adopt or change a tax year	
When partnership's tax year closes	2922
Change of partners	

Footnotes appear at end of this Chapter.

When partnership ends
When partnerships combine
Split-up of partnership

TRANSACTIONS BETWEEN PARTNERSHIP AND PARTNER OR PERSON RELATED TO PARTNER

Partner not acting in capacity as partner 2923
   When loss is disallowed
   When gain is ordinary income
   Ownership of an interest
   Salaries and interest paid to partner
Transactions between partnership and person related to partner 2924

CONTRIBUTIONS TO PARTNERSHIP

Tax effect of contribution 2925
   Nonrecognition of gain or loss
   Partnership's basis for contributed property
   Basis of contributing partner's interest

PARTNER'S BASIS FOR PARTNERSHIP INTEREST

Partner's original basis and how to adjust it 2926
   General rule
   Alternative rule
   Effect of liabilities

DISTRIBUTIONS OTHER THAN TO A RETIRED PARTNER OR A DECEASED PARTNER'S SUCCESSOR

Gain or loss on distribution 2927
   Recognition of gain or loss
   Specially treated transactions
   Constructive distributions
Partner's basis and holding period for distributed property other than money 2928
   Distributions not in complete liquidation of partner's interest
   Distributions in complete liquidation of partner's interest
   Specially treated transactions
   Partner's holding period for distributed property
How to allocate partner's basis for distributed property 2929
   Allocation to receivables and inventory
   Allocation to other property
   Loss for unallocated basis
   Special rules

Special elective partnership basis for transferee 2930
   Excluded property
   When partner must use special basis
Distribution of property with special basis 2931
   Basis allocated to distributed property
   Reallocating special basis adjustment
   Unused special basis adjustment
Partnership's elective adjustment to basis of undistributed property 2932
   Method of adjustment
   Allocation of basis

TRANSFER OF PARTNERSHIP INTEREST

Gain or loss on transfer 2935
   How current earnings are treated
   Transfers involving receivables or inventory
   Statement must be filed
Basis of transferee partner 2936
Partnership's elective adjustment to basis of partnership property 2937
   Method of adjustment
   How partnership agreement affects special basis adjustment
   Effect on depletion allowance

ALLOCATION OF ELECTIVE PARTNERSHIP ADJUSTMENTS TO BASIS

How to allocate adjustments to basis 2938
   Allocation under general and special rule
   Optional allocation
   Who is affected by adjustment

SPECIAL PROBLEMS RETIREMENT OR DEATH OF A PARTNER

Payments to retiring partner or deceased partner's successor in interest 2941
   Payments for interest in partnership assets
   Other liquidating payments
   Reporting gain or loss on installment payments for interest in assets
How installment payments are allocated 2942
   Fixed payments
   When amount varies
   Allocation by agreement

DISTRIBUTIONS OF UNREALIZED RECEIVABLES OR SUBSTANTIALLY APPRECIATED INVENTORY

Distributions treated as sales or exchanges 2944
Excluded transactions
When is distribution a sale or exchange
Tax consequences of distribution
Definitions
Transfer of distributed property 2945
Recapture property
Unrealized receivables
Inventory items

• **Highlights of Chapter 19** .... Page 2961

WHAT IS A PARTNERSHIP

¶ **2900 Tax definition.** For tax purposes, a partnership usually exists when 2 or more persons join together to carry on a trade or business and share its profits and losses, with each person contributing cash, property, labor or skill.[1] This definition is broad enough to include several groups that are not commonly called partnerships. Examples include syndicates, groups, pools, joint ventures and similar busines or financial organizations that are not corporations, trusts or estates [Sec. 761(a); 1.761-1(a)(1)].

Exclusion from partnership treatment. Certain groups formed only for investment or for the joint production, extraction, or use of property, may avoid partnership treatment in whole or in part, if all the members so elect.[2] The election applies only if the group *as such* does not actively conduct a business and if the members can determine their income without reference to a partnership taxable income for the group. The procedure for making the election is set forth in the regulation [Sec. 761(a); 1.761-2].

¶ **2903 How group enterprises are classified.** Classifying an enterprise depends on whether its characteristics more closely resemble those of a partnership [¶ 2900], a corporation [¶ 3101], or a trust [¶ 3000]. For instance, the Revenue Service might classify an investment club as either a corporation or partnership, depending on how it was organized and operated. Federal law sets the classification standards. These standards control, no matter what the organization is called under state law[1] [Sec. 301.7701-1—301.7701-4].

Tenants in common. Mere co-ownership of property does not, of itself, constitute a partnership. Thus, tenants in common who own real estate, rent it out and divide the profits, are not considered partners. But a partnership may exist if they carry on a trade, business or venture, and divide the profits [Sec. 1.761-1(a)].

> **Example 1:** John and Harry own a farm as tenants in common, and rent it to farmer Brown. John and Harry are not treated as partners.
>
> **Example 2:** John and Harry own a fully rented apartment house as tenants in common. They furnish maid service, meals and other services to the tenants. They are carrying on a business as joint venturers [Sec. 1.761-1(a)].

¶ **2904 Family partnerships.** A family partnership is one whose members are closely related by blood or marriage. The Revenue Service recognizes these partnerships but looks closely to see whether each partner actually owns his alleged interest. This depends on the intent of the parties, determined from all the facts—the agreement, the relationship of the parties, their conduct, statements, individual abilities and capital contributions, who controls the income and how it is used, and any other facts showing their true intent.[1]

Footnotes appear at end of this Chapter.

Background and purpose. Family partnerships are sometimes created to shift income from the organizer of a business to members of his family. This reduces the family taxes if the family members are in lower tax brackets. Although tax saving is sometimes the only motive, the Revenue Service will recognize the arrangement if the family members actually own their partnership interests.

(a) Recognition of family member as partner. An example of a partnership where capital is a material income producing factor is the firm that requires large inventories or investments in plant and equipment. The Revenue Service will recognize the family member if he actually owns a *capital interest* (even if he got it from another family member), provided the transaction vested him with dominion and control [Sec. 704(e)(1); 1.704-1(e)(1)].

NOTE: The donor may retain substantial powers as managing partner if other facts show that he really gave up part of his interest and made the donee its true owner.

(b) Service partnerships. An example is the firm whose business income is primarily from fees, commissions, or other pay for personal services. The Revenue Service generally will *not* recognize the family member unless he contributes substantial or necessary services.

¶ **2905 Allocation of income to family members.** Ordinarily, each partner is taxed on his distributive share of the firm's income, as fixed by the partnership agreement [¶ 2909]. But the Revenue Service will disregard the agreement when a partnership interest is created by gift *and* (1) the donor is paid less for his services than they are worth, or (2) the donee gets more than his share of the partnership's income. Here the Revenue Service allows a reasonable amount for each partner's services and allocates the rest as to the capital interest of each partner. But it will not reduce a partner's share if in military service [Sec. 704(e)(2); 1.704-1(e)(3)(i)].

NOTE: For purposes of this provision, a partnership interest bought by one member of a "family" from another is treated as a gift from the seller. "Family," here, is limited to a husband or wife, ancestors (for example, father, grandfather) and lineal descendants (for example, son or grandson) and any trusts for their primary benefit [Sec. 704(e)(3); 1.704-1(e)(3)(i)(a)].

Example: Father gave his son a half interest in a partnership having net profits for the year of $50,000. The son performs no duties, while the father contributes services worth $10,000. $30,000 is allocated to the father ($10,000 salary plus 50% of the remaining $40,000). $20,000 is allocated to the son. If father and son performed equal services, $25,000 would be allocated to each.

The Revenue Service may also disregard the agreement and make an allocation when a gift interest in the partnership is created indirectly [Sec. 1.704-1(e)(3)(ii)]. Thus, the father giving property to a son who then transfers it to a partnership of father and son, is considered the donor of the son's interest.

PARTNERSHIP INCOME, DEDUCTIONS, CREDITS

A partnership is not a taxable entity. It is a mere conduit for passing through its income, deduction and credit items to the partners. The rules in this area are designed to pass through each item in a way that preserves its tax characteristics. Briefly, the partnership return segregates any item that has special tax significance for any partner, and lists it separately along with each partner's distributive share. Each partner then picks up his share, combines it with his own items of the same nature, and gives tax effect to the total on his individual return.

Items with no special tax significance to the partners are used to figure the partnership's taxable income or loss. Each partner picks up his share and reports it as ordinary income or loss.

¶ 2906 How partnerships report their income, deduction and credit items. A partnership is not a tax-paying entity, but it must file a return (Form 1065) signed by one of the partners [¶ 3539]. The partnership's income, deductions and credits are passed through to the partners and are given tax effect on their individual returns. The pass-through is accomplished as follows:

(1) The partnership segregates certain income, deduction and credit items, lists them separately on its return, and allocates to each partner his distributive share of each item. See (a) below.

(2) The partnership then computes its "taxable income or loss" as explained in (b) below. In doing so, it disregards the items that were separately listed, since these are picked up directly by the partners. The partnership must also allocate to each partner his distributive share of its taxable income or loss.

(3) Each partner then picks up his distributive share of each separately listed item and his distributive share of the partnership's taxable income or loss, as explained in ¶ 2908.

Partnership tax preferences are treated the same as partnership income: the partnership does not pay any minimum tax but passes through its preference items to the partners who include them in their minimum tax returns (¶ 2403) [Sec. 56, 57; Proposed Reg. 1.58-2(b)].

(a) Segregation of partnership income, deduction and credit items. The segregated items are those that require separate consideration by the partners. Each partner must combine these items with his own items of the same nature before he can determine their tax effect.

The partnership must separately list its long-term and short-term capital gains and losses and its Sec. 1231 gains and losses [¶ 2911]; its charitable contributions [¶ 2915]; dividends from most domestic corporations [¶ 2916] and foreign taxes paid or accrued [¶ 2917]. The partnership must also separately list any deduction that is disallowed in computing the partnership's taxable income or loss (see (b) below) and any other item required by the regulations (these items are listed in ¶ 2913) [Sec. 703(a); 1.703-1(a)].

(b) Partnership's taxable income or loss. The partnership's taxable income or loss is figured like that of an individual except that separately listed items (see (a) above) are not taken into account and the following deductions are not allowed: the deduction for personal exemptions; the deduction for foreign taxes and for charitable contributions; the net operating loss deduction [¶ 2914]; the long-term capital gain deduction; the deduction for capital-loss carryovers; the other deductions listed in ¶ 2913; and as to tax years ending after 12-31-74, the depletion allowance for oil and gas wells (¶ 2104(a)) [Sec. 703(a)(2)].

The partnership is also denied the benefit of the exclusion for dividends received and the foreign tax credit.

For deductibility of salary and interest paid to partners, see ¶ 2923.

NOTE: A partnership can deduct a state tax based on the firm's income.[1]

Organization and syndication fees. For partnership tax years starting after 1975, no deduction is allowed to a partnership or partner for amounts paid or incurred to organize a partnership or promote the sale of a partnership interest.

Footnotes appear at end of this Chapter.

However, for amounts paid or incurred in tax years starting after 1976, a partnership may elect to deduct its organizational expenses ratably over a period of not less than 60 months. The expenses eligible for the 60-month amortization must be (a) incident to the partnership's creation, and (b) chargeable to the capital account, and (c) of a character which, if expended for the creation of the partnership with an ascertainable life, would be amortized over that life [Sec. 709]. The special amortization does not apply to capitalized syndication fees. These fees include commissions, professional fees and printing costs for issuing and marketing partnership interests.

(c) Elections affecting computation of income. Most elections affecting the computation of partnership income are made by the partnership and bind all the partners [Sec. 703(b); 1.703-1(b)]. The only exceptions are:

(1) The election as to foreign taxes [¶ 2917; 3701];
(2) The election as to deduction and recapture of certain mining exploration expenditures [¶ 1843];
(3) The election as to investment interest deduction relating to net leases of property [¶ 1906];
(4) A nonresident alien's or foreign corporation's election to treat income from U.S. real property as "effectively connected" income [¶ 3711].

The excepted elections are made by each partner separately. For example, each partner can use his distributive share of foreign taxes either as a credit or as a deduction, as he chooses.

Examples of elections made by partnership include the election as to method of accounting, method of figuring depreciation, use of installment sales provisions, option to expense intangible drilling and development costs, etc., and nonrecognition of gain from condemnation of partnership property.[2]

¶ 2907 Book profit and taxable income reconciled. Book profit of a partnership should be distinguished from its taxable income. Many items enter into the determination of book profit that are not considered in figuring taxable income. For example, the items listed in ¶ 2906(b), or items exempt from tax such as interest on municipal and state obligations, do not affect partnership taxable income; yet under ordinary methods of accounting, they are taken into account in figuring book profit. Thus, when a partnership return is prepared directly from the books, it is easy for errors to occur by neglecting to exclude or include certain items.

It is best first to determine the partnership's taxable income as it will appear in the partnership return by taking the regular profit and loss statement and either decreasing or increasing the book profit or loss, as required.

Example: The profit and loss statement of the Smith & Brown partnership for the tax year is as follows:

Gross receipts from sales		$316,418.00
Less cost of goods sold		173,618.00
Gross profit		$142,800.00
Dividends received		1,000.00
Interest (tax-exempt)		3,200.00
Short-term capital gain		1,600.00
Long-term capital gain		4,400.00
Gross profit and misc. income items		$153,000.00
Deduct:		
Charitable contributions	$ 3,000	
Partners' salaries ($12,500 for each partner)	25,000	
Other operating expenses	15,000	$ 43,000.00
Net profit from operations and capital transactions		$110,000.00
Deduct interest on capital		10,000.00
Net profit for the year		$100,000.00

From this profit and loss statement, the taxable income of the Smith & Brown partnership is figured as follows:

Book profit (from profit and loss statement)		$100,000.00
Capital gains and losses segregated:		
Book gains on short-term transactions	$1,600	
Book gains on long-term transactions	4,400	
Subtract net book gain (add back net book loss) on capital asset transactions		6,000.00
		$ 94,000.00
Segregated income items:		
Tax-exempt interest	$3,200	
Dividends received from domestic corporations	1,000	
Subtract total segregated income items		4,200.00
		$ 89,800.00
Deductions not allowed:		
Charitable contributions	$3,000	
Add back total deductions not allowed		3,000.00
Partnership's taxable income		$ 92,800.00

The taxable income and the segregated items of the partnership would appear on the partnership return as follows:

Ordinary income	$ 92,800.00
Net gain from short-term capital asset transactions	1,600.00
Net gain from long-term capital asset transactions	4,400.00
Dividends received from domestic corporations	1,000.00
Charitable contributions	3,000.00

DETERMINATION OF PARTNER'S TAX LIABILITY

The partnership return lists the various items the partners must pick up, together with the distributive share of each partner. Each partner determines his tax liability by combining his share of each item he picks up with his own items of the same nature and by taking each combined total into account in figuring his own income or loss.

Special rules may apply in computing the deductible amount of the partner's share of partnership losses, and in computing his distributive share of certain items.

¶ **2908 Partner's income, deductions and credits.** Each partner must pick up his distributive share of each income, deduction or credit item that is separately listed on the partnership return. He must also pick up his distributive share of the partnership's taxable income or loss. See ¶ 2906. He must pick up his share whether or not he received it, even if he is on a cash basis and the partnership is on an accrual basis.[1] In addition, he must report his salaries and other guaranteed payments received from the partnership [¶ 2920; 2923(d)].

    Example 1: A partnership equally owned by R and S has taxable income of $34,000 for the current year. It had no transactions involving the items at ¶ 2906(a). During the year the partners each withdrew $2,000 of the profits. The partnership files Form 1065 showing partnership taxable income of $34,000 and the partners' distributive shares of taxable income as $17,000 each. Both R and S must report his $17,000 share on his own Form 1040. This is true even if it is not all distributed to them, and even if the partnership agreement prohibited distribution during the current year.

A partner's share of each separately listed item takes, in his hands, the same character it would have if the partner had realized it directly [Sec. 702; 1.702-1].

His share of the partnership's taxable income or loss is treated as ordinary income or loss.

>Example 2:< The WXYZ partnership sold depreciable property used in the business at a gain. Each partner reports his share of the gain as though he received it directly from the sale of depreciable property.

➤**OBSERVATION**➜ Ordinary gain realized by the partnership from recapture of depreciation is not included in the partners' distributive shares of gain from the property [¶ 1619; 2911]. The ordinary income generally is reported as part of the partnership taxable income, but a special allocation rule may apply [¶ 2910].

The partner combines his share of each item he picks up with his own items of the same nature and takes each combined total into account in figuring his own income or loss [Sec. 702; 1.702-1]. The combined total is, of course, subject to any limitation or special rules that apply to the particular item [¶ 2913].

(a) **Loss is limited.** A partner may deduct his share of partnership losses (including capital losses) only up to the amount of his adjusted basis for his partnership interest at the end of the partnership year.[2] His adjusted basis is computed without deducting the current year's loss [¶ 2926(a)]. For purposes of deducting partnership losses, the adjusted basis does not include any portion of a partnership liability incurred after 1976 for which the partner has no personal liability, except to the extent the "at risk" rules apply [¶ 2736], or unless the partnership's principal activity is investing in real (non-mineral) property [Sec. 704(d); Temp. Reg. Sec. 7.704-1]. The partner may deduct any excess loss at the end of later partnership years to the extent his adjusted basis for his partnership interest exceeds zero [Sec. 704(d)].

>Example 3:< A and B form a partnership. A contributes $5,000. B contributes property worth $5,000, but with a basis to him of $1,000. The first year's operations result in a loss of $3,000. A has a loss of $1,500, but B, whose loss is limited to his basis, can take only $1,000. A has a basis for his partnership interest of $3,500 ($5,000 less $1,500 loss); B's basis is zero. If B contributes $500 to the partnership, then he can take the remaining $500 loss at the end of the year in which the contribution was made.

If the partnership has more than one type of loss, and the partner's basis is too small to cover his share of each type, the limitation applies proportionately to each type. The partner's basis is allocated among the types as illustrated in the example below [Sec. 1.704-1(d)(2)].

>Example 4:< A partner's distributive share of partnership losses is $6,000, consisting of a long-term capital loss of $4,000, and a short-term capital loss of $2,000. If his basis for his interest at the end of the partnership's tax year and before deducting the losses is $5,000, he is allowed only $5,000/$6,000 of each loss, that is, $3,333 of his long-term loss, and $1,667 of his short-term loss. He may carry forward to later years $667 as a long-term loss and $333 as a short-term loss.

(b) **Gross income.** Whenever a partner must determine the amount or character of his gross income for tax purposes, he includes his distributive share of partnership gross income [Sec. 702(c); 1.702-1(c)].

>Example 5:< In figuring his gross income to determine if he must file a return, a partner must include his distributive share of partnership gross income.

(c) **Partnership tax preferences.** Partnership tax preference items are passed through to the partners and treated as if realized directly by each partner. Because the partnership does not pay the minimum tax, it does not have the minimum tax exclusion for itself or to allocate among the partners (¶ 2403). A partner must take into account separately his distributive share of tax preference items subject to minimum tax [Sec. 56, 57; Prop. Reg. 1.58-2(b)].

(d) Partnership earned income. Each partner must include his distributive share of partnership earned income for maximum tax purposes (¶ 2402) [Sec. 702; 1.702-1]. Such income includes fees for consulting services performed by engineers, draftsmen, architects and administrative personnel under partners' supervision.[3]

¶ 2909 How partner's distributive share is determined. The partner's share of each item is generally fixed by the partnership agreement. For partnership tax years starting after 12-31-75, a partner's distributive share of income, gain, loss, deduction or credit (or item thereof) is determined by his interest in the partnership, if (a) the partnership agreement is silent on the allocation, or (b) the allocation under the agreement lacks substantial economic effect [Sec. 704(a), (b)]. Special allocations may be used for bona fide business purposes only. The partner's interest in the partnership is determined by taking into account all the facts and circumstances, including interests of the respective partners in profits and losses (if different from that of taxable income or loss), cash flow, and their rights to distributions of capital on liquidation.

> **Example:** The provisions of a partnership agreement for a year the partnership has losses on the sale of depreciable property used in the business are amended to allocate the losses to one partner who has no such gains individually. An equivalent amount of partnership loss or deduction of a different character is allocated to other partners who individually have gains from the sale of depreciable property used in the trade or business. Since the purpose and effect of this allocation is solely to reduce the taxes of certain partners without actually affecting their shares of partnership income, it will not be recognized. The items will be allocated among the partners according to their share of partnership income or loss generally.

Changes in agreement. The agreement includes any change agreed to by all the partners or made under the terms of the agreement. Changes as to a particular taxable year are possible up to the original due date of the partnership return for that year [Sec. 761(c); 1.761-1(c)].

Depreciation recapture. The above rules apply in allocating depreciation recapture to the partners [¶ 1619]. But if the partner is a transferee with a special basis adjustment [¶ 2937], his share of the ordinary gain is specially computed.

Sec. 1245 income. In general, the partner finds his share of Sec. 1245 gain by first adding his special basis adjustment to (or subtracting it from) his share of partnership basis. This is his adjusted basis.

The partner then adds depreciation deducted by the partnership that is allocable to him (depreciation deducted before he became a partner is not included). This is his recomputed basis.

The partner's Sec. 1245 gain is the difference between his adjusted basis and recomputed basis, but it may not exceed the difference between his adjusted basis and his share of the amount realized [Sec. 1.1245-1(e)].

Sec. 1250 income. Sec. 1250 gain is allocated to the partner in the same way as for Sec. 1245 income, above [Sec. 1.1250-1(f)].

¶ 2910 Distributive share of items due to contributed property. The partnership takes the contributor's basis for contributed property. It uses this basis in figuring depreciation, depletion, gain and loss on the property. The partners share these items in the general profit and loss ratio, without taking into account any

Footnotes appear at end of this Chapter.

difference between the contributor's basis and the property's value at contribution, unless the partnership agreement provides otherwise [Sec. 704(c)(1); 1.704-1(c)(1)].

Example 1: A and B form an equal partnership. A contributes building worth $1,000 with an adjusted basis of $400. B contributes $1,000 in cash. The basis of A's interest in the partnership is $400, B's is $1,000. There is no provision in the partnership agreement relating to contributed property. The property has an annual straight line depreciation rate of 10%. The partnership has an annual depreciation deduction of $40. This results in a deduction of $20 in figuring each partner's distributive share of partnership income.

If the property is sold after one year for $900, the partnership gain will be $540 ($900 the amount realized less $360 the adjusted basis of the property). Each partner's share is $270. If we assume that the partnership had no other transactions that year, each partner will have capital gain of $270 from the partnership to report on his individual return.

(a) Allocation by agreement. If the agreement so provides, the partnership may allocate depreciation, depletion, gain and loss in a way that attributes all or part of the pre-contribution appreciation or depreciation in value to the contributor. Thus, the agreement may provide for allocating gain or loss on sale of the property to the contributor to the extent it represents the difference between value and basis at contribution. The agreement may also allocate any depreciation or depletion on contributed property in a way that offsets the smaller deduction a partner gets because of the low basis of property contributed by another partner. However, the total depreciation, depletion, gain or loss may not exceed the gain or loss realized by the partnership or the depreciation or depletion allowable to it [Sec. 704(c)(2); 1.704-1(c)(2)(i)]. The agreement may also allocate the gain from disposition of farm recapture property to the contributing partner (¶ 2226) [Sec. 1251(d)(5)].

Example 2: C and D form an equal partnership. C contributes a building worth $10,000 with an adjusted basis to him of $4,000. D contributes $10,000 cash. The partners agree to attribute to C, the potential gain of $6,000 represented by the difference between its adjusted basis and its fair market value. With the contribution of $10,000 cash, D has, in effect, bought an undivided half interest in the property for $5,000. If the property depreciates at an annual rate of 10%, D should have been entitled to a depreciation deduction of $500 per year. However, since there is a ceiling on D's deduction (the partnership deduction of 10% of $4,000 (or $400)), no more than $400 may be allocated between the partners. Therefore, the $400 deduction for depreciation is allocated entirely to D and none to C, the contributor. At the end of the first year, the adjusted basis of the contributed property will be $3,600. Since the $400 deduction was allocated entirely to D, if the partnership had no other taxable income or loss, C will have no income or loss, and D will have a deduction of $400. C's basis for his interest will remain $4,000. D's adjusted basis for his interest will be $9,600 ($10,000, the original basis of his interest, reduced by the deduction of $400).

Example 3: Suppose that in Example 2, above, the building is sold after one year for $9,000. The partners have agreed that the portion of the proceeds attributable to the excess of its original fair market value (less accumulated depreciation on the value) over its basis upon contribution (as depreciated) will result in gain to the contributing partner. The sale results in a partnership gain of $5,400 ($9,000 realized, less $3,600, the adjusted basis of the property). The original fair market value of the property (as depreciated) is $9,000 ($10,000 original value, less $1,000 accumulated depreciation). Under the partnership agreement the difference between the $9,000 and the basis of the property, $3,600 (or $5,400), is allocated to C. None of the gain is allocated to D.

If the property had been sold for more than $9,000, the gain in excess of $5,400 would be divided between the partners in accordance with their agreement for sharing gains (equally, in this case). If the property were sold for less than $9,000, the entire gain would be allocated to C and nothing to D.

(b) Allocation for undivided interests. A special rule applies to undivided interests in property contributed by *all* the partners, if their relative undivided interests before contribution were in the same ratio as their interest in partnership capital and profits after the contribution. Unless the partnership agreement provides otherwise, the depreciation, depletion, gain or loss on such undivided interests is determined as though they were still held by the partners outside the partnership. This avoids the shifting of rules for computing depreciation, depletion, and gain or loss when a joint tenancy or similar undivided interest is unintentionally handled in a way that results in partnership classification [Sec. 704(c)(3); 1.704-1(c)(3)].

Example 4: X and Y own undivided half interests in a factory and the land on which the factory is situated. They each contribute their interests in the real estate to a partnership in which the profits and the assets on dissolution are to be divided equally. X's basis for his undivided half interest is $4,000, of which $1,000 is allocable to the land and $3,000 to the factory. Y's basis for his undivided half interest is $10,000, of which $3,000 is allocable to the land and $7,000 to the factory. The partnership agreement is silent as to the allocation of depreciation or gain or loss on disposition of property. The factory depreciates on a straight line basis at a rate of 5% per year. The annual allowance to he partnership is $500 (5% of $10,000). It will be allocated between the partners by allowing X a deduction of $150 (5% of $3,000, his basis for the factory), and by allowing Y a deduction of $350 (5% of $7,000, his basis for the factory).

If the partnership, after one year's operation, sells the factory and land for $12,000, each partner's share of the gain is determined as follows: X's share of the proceeds is $6,000, and his basis for the contributed property is $3,850 ($1,000 for the land and $2,850 for the factory); therefore his capital gain from the sale is $2,150. Y's share of the proceeds is also $6,000, and his basis in the contributed property is $9,650 ($3,000 for the land and $6,650 for the factory); his loss, therefore, is $3,650.

The result is the same whether the contribution by the partners is expressly made in exchange for interest in a partnership, or whether a partnership is held to exist because X and Y conduct their business jointly.

¶ **2911 Capital gains and losses. (a) Capital assets.** Long-term and short-term capital gains and losses are not taken into account in figuring partnership taxable income [Sec. 702(a)(1), (2); 1.702-1(a)(1), (2)]. They are reported on the capital gain and loss schedule of the partnership return. The short-term capital asset transactions are segregated from the long-term capital asset transactions. The net recognized gain or loss from the short-term transactions and the net recognized gain or loss from the long-term transactions are figured separately and *100%* of each is shown on the schedule. Each partner must pick up his share of these gains and losses from the distribution schedule [¶ 2918] and include them in his individual return *whether distributed to him or not* [Sec. 702(a)(1), (2); 1.702-1(a)(1), (2)]. Short-term or long-term treatment depends on the partnership's holding period, not the length of time a partner held his partnership interest.[1]

Partner's long-term capital gain deduction. The partnership does not take a long-term capital gain deduction [¶ 1612] on the partnership return. Each partner takes the deduction on his individual return after he combines his personal net capital gain or loss, if any, with his share of capital gain or loss of the partnership.

Capital loss limited. A partner's share of partnership capital loss is limited to the adjusted basis (before reduction by the current year's losses) of his partnership interest at the end of the partnership year in which the loss occurred. Because a partner's shares of all types of partnership losses are subject to the same limit [¶ 2908(a)], he must allocate his adjusted basis among his share of partnership short-term and long-term capital losses, Sec. 1231 losses and ordinary losses, if their total exceeds the adjusted basis of his interest. Any excess can be deducted in later partnership years to the extent of the adjusted basis of his interest at the end of the year. [Sec. 704(d)]. See also ¶ 2908(a).

Example 1: N is a partner in the MNO partnership. Without regard to any losses during the year, he has an adjusted basis for his partnership interest at the end of the tax year of $5,000. His current year's distributive share of MNO losses is $2,000 of short-term capital losses

Footnotes appear at end of this Chapter.

and $4,000 of ordinary losses. N is allowed only $5,000/$6,000 of each loss or $1,667 of short-term capital loss and $3,333 of ordniary loss. N can carry forward $333 as a short-term capital loss and $667 as an ordinary loss.

Wash sales. A loss by the partnership is not allowed when a partner buys securities in a wash sale [¶ 2221].

(b) Sales and exchanges of business property—involuntary conversions (Sec. 1231 assets). Gains and losses from the sale, exchange or involuntary conversion of Sec. 1231 assets [¶ 1618] are excluded in figuring partnership taxable income. Each partner must segregate his distributive share of such gains and losses and set them off against his individual gains and losses of the same type [Sec. 702(a)(3); 1.702-1(a)(3)]. Sec. 1231 losses are limited by the partner's adjusted basis, as discussed above.

Example 2: A partnership equally owned by M and N has a taxable income of $40,000 and a loss of $9,000 from the sale of trucks used in the business. Partner M also has a Sec. 1231 gain of $5,000 from the sale of a depreciable asset used in another business he operates as a proprietor. He has no other income from this other business. M has $20,000 as his distributable share of partnership taxable income (50% of $40,000) and a capital gain of $500 ($5,000 from the depreciable assets less $4,500, his share of the partnership Sec. 1231 loss).

When property subject to the recapture of depreciation [¶ 1619] is sold at a gain, only the gain in excess of the recaptured gain is picked up by the partners as Sec. 1231 gain. The recaptured gain is included in partnership taxable income. Gains and losses from partnership casualties and thefts are passed through separately to the partners. Each partner includes his partnership gains and losses from casualties and thefts with the same type of personal gains and losses when determining how they should be treated [¶ 1620].

¶ 2913 Partnership items specially reported. Any partnership items of income, gain, loss, deduction or credit that would affect the determination of *any* partner's income tax when combined with his own items of the same class are disregarded in computing the partnership's taxable income or loss. Such items are separately stated and allocated to the partners on separate distribution schedules [¶ 2918]. These items include [Sec. 1.702-1(a)(8)(i)]:

- Recovery of bad debts, prior taxes and delinquency amounts [¶ 2316(d)];
- Additional first-year depreciation [¶ 2016];
- Medical expenses [¶ 1945];
- Contributions and deductions for partners under self-employed retirement plans [¶ 1839];
- Nonbusiness expenses [¶ 1803(b); 1806];
- Exploration, soil and water conservation expenditures [¶ 1843; 1845];
- Gains and losses from wagering [¶ 1331; 2224];
- Alimony [¶ 1320];
- Income, gain or loss to partnership in a disproportionate distribution [¶ 2944];
- Taxes and interest paid to cooperative housing corporations [¶ 1902; 1919];
- Intangible drilling and development costs [¶ 2103(c)];
- Any items subject to a special allocation under partnership agreement that differs from the allocation of partnership taxable income or loss generally [¶ 2909; 2910].

Partners must also take into account their distributive share of any partnership farm net losses, gains from dispositions of farm recapture property or other items (¶ 2226) [Sec. 1251(d)(5)].

Each partner also must report his distributive share of any item which, if separately taken into account by *any* partner, would change that partner's tax liability.

Thus, if one partner could get a credit for the elderly [¶ 2406] if partnership pensions, annuities, etc. were separately stated, such items must be separately stated for all partners. The same rule applies to earned income for all partners when a partner residing in a foreign country can exclude a portion of his income earned in that country[1] (¶ 3725(a)) [Sec. 1.702-1(a)(8)(ii)].

(a) Limited deductions or exclusions. Each partner must total his individual deductions or exclusions and his distributive share of partnership deductions and exclusions of the same item in figuring the deductions or exclusions allowable to him when the deduction or exclusion is subject to a limitation [Sec. 1.702-1(a)(8)(iii)]. For example, a partnership's investment interest is passed through and added to the partner's investment interest in figuring whether the limitation on the investment interest deduction applies (¶ 1906) [Sec. 163(d)(4)(B)].

(b) Change to installment accounting. If a partnership changes from the accrual basis to the installment method of accounting [¶ 2804], each partner's distributive share of the profits from installment sales included in the partnership taxable income for the year of sale and for each "adjustment year" is separately stated [Sec. 1.453-7].

(c) Investment tax credit. Each partner gets his share of any tax credit allowed for certain business property [¶ 2410]. The allocation is made according to each partner's interest in the partnership general profits, unless the partnership agreement requires a special allocation of items related to the property [¶ 2909]. The agreement may also include a provision that allows a partner with a minor interest to avoid recapture when he retires [Sec. 1.46-3(f)]. Special rules apply to used property that qualifies for the credit [Sec. 48(c)(2)(D); 1.48-3(c)(3), (4)].

Credit recaptured. When the partnership distributes or sells the property prematurely, the actual credit allowable, if any, is recomputed for each partner's qualified investment and the excess credit originally taken is added to the partner's tax [¶ 2410(e)]. When a partner's interest in partnership profits or a particular item of qualified property is reduced (for example, by admission of a new partner) by more than ⅓ before qualified property is held for the useful life on which the partner's credit was based, his qualified investment is reduced proportionately [Sec. 1.47-6].

> **Example 1:** Partner A sells half of his 60% interest in Partnership ABC 2 years after he had a tax credit of $1,000 on his share of qualified investment of $10,000. His qualified investment is now $5,000 for a tax credit of $500. Since his partnership interest is reduced by more than ⅓, $500 of the original credit is recaptured in the year of the sale.

Once credit is recaptured for an item of property, there is no further recapture for that item until the partner's profit interest is reduced to less than ⅓ of what it was when the property was acquired.

> **Example 2:** Assume the same facts as in Example 1, except that A sells another 10% interest in ABC in the next tax year. There is no further recapture because the sale reduces A's interest to only 20% or ⅓ of what it was when the propety was acquired.

(d) Work incentive program credit. Each partner gets his share of any credit under a Work Incentive Program for expenses of training employees during the partnership's tax year [Sec. 1.50B-4]. If employment is terminated prematurely, the recapture rules [¶ 2411(d)] apply to each partner [Sec. 1.50A-7].

NOTE: Each partner also gets his or her share of the new jobs credit [¶ 2414].

Footnotes appear at end of this Chapter.

¶ 2913

¶ **2914 Partner's net operating loss deduction.** In figuring his net operating loss deduction [¶ 2241], a partner takes into account his distributive share of items of gain, loss, deduction or credit of the partnership. The character of such items is determined as if they were realized directly from the same source, or in the same manner, as by the partnership [Sec. 1.702-2].

To determine his allowable nonbusiness deductions, a partner must combine his individual nonbusiness deductions with his distributive share of the partnership nonbusiness deductions. He must also separately take into account and add to his nonbusiness income, his distributive share of the partnership's gross income not derived from a trade or business [Sec. 1.702-2].

¶ **2915 Charitable contributions** are not deductible in figuring partnership taxable income. Each partner deducts his proportionate share of the contributions on his individual return, within the limitations (¶ 1943) [Sec. 702(a)(4); 1.702-1(a)(4)].[1]

> **Example:** Under a partnership agreement, Archer's share of the income or loss is $2/3$. During the year, the partnership made charitable contributions of $12,000. Those contributions are not deductible by the partnership. In his personal income tax return, Archer will assume that he made contributions of $8,000 (regardless of the income of the partnership).
>
> If Archer also made a personal contribution of $2,000 to his chruch, his deduction for contributions on his individual return is $10,000, if that amount does not exceed the limitations [¶ 1943].

¶ **2916 Dividends received.** The dividends of domestic corporations for which individual taxpayers are entitled to an exclusion [¶ 1705; 1706] are disregarded in figuring taxable income of the partnership. They must be allocated among the partners on the distribution schedule [Sec. 702(a)(5); 1.702-1(a)(5)]. The partners include their shares of these dividends in their individual returns (whether distributed to them or not) together with dividends they receive personally. The proper exclusion may then be taken. Corporations that are members of a partnership do the same thing for the dividends received deduction (¶ 3114) [Sec. 702(a)(5); 1.702-1(a)(5)].

¶ **2917 Credit or deduction for foreign taxes paid.** Individuals who are partners are entitled to a credit or a deduction for taxes paid by the partnership to foreign countries and possessions of the United States [Sec. 702(a)(6); 1.702-1(a)(6)]. These taxes are not deductible by the partnership in figuring its taxable income. They are allocated among the partners. The election to take the foreign taxes paid by partnership as either a credit or a deduction is made by the partners individually [¶ 2906(c)].

¶ **2918 Distribution and reconciliation schedules. (a) Purpose of distribution schedule.** Schedule K, Form 1065, shows the partners' total shares of income, deductions, credits, etc. Schedule K-1, Form 1065, shows each partner's distributive share of these items allocated to him, as well as reconciliation of his capital account [see (b) below]. A sample distribution schedule appears in Example 1 below.

(b) Purpose of reconciliation schedule. Schedule M, Form 1065, reconciles the capital accounts of the partners at the beginning and end of the tax year. This schedule shows the relationship between the partnership's income and its capital transactions for the year. The items needed for the schedule are found in the partnership's balance sheet and distribution schedule. Each partner's capital account is reconciled on Schedule K-1, Form 1065. A sample reconciliation schedule appears in Example 2 below.

Example 1: The partnership agreement for the Smith and Brown partnership (See Example, ¶ 2907), provides that all partnership items other than fixed salaries and 5% interest on investment are distributed 80% to Smith and 20% to Brown. Since the taxable income of a parntership is figured without taking into account any of the items that must be separately stated [¶ 2906], it is apportioned directly. So also are the other partnership items.

SAMPLE DISTRIBUTION SCHEDULE

1. Name, address and social security number of each partner	2. Percentage of time devoted to business	3. Ordinary income	4. Additional first-year depreciation
(a) J. Smith 049-11-2822	50%	$74,240 (80%)	......
(b) B. Brown 125-15-1118	50%	18,560 (20%)	......
Totals		$92,800	......

5. Payments to partner*	6. Qualifying dividends	7. Net short-term gain or loss from capital assets	8. Net long-term gain or loss from capital assets
(a)... $21,000	$ 800 (80%)	$1,280 (80%)	$3,520 (80%)
(b)... 14,000	200 (20%)	320 (20%)	880 (20%)
Totals $35,000	$1,000	$1,600	$4,400

9. Net gain or loss under Sec. 1231	10. Net gain or loss from involuntary conversions under Sec. 1231	11. Net earnings from self-employment†	12. Contributions
(a)...	....	$95,240	(a)... $2,400 (80%)
(b)...	....	32,560	(b)... 600 (20%)
Totals	....	$127,800	Totals $3,000

13. Expense account allowance	14. Property qualified for investment credit	15. Tax preferences††		
		Short-term gains	Long-term gains	Other
None	....	(a)... $1,280(80%)	(a)... $3,520(80%)	......
None	....	(b)... 320(20%)	(b)... 880(20%)	......
		Totals $1,600	Totals $4,400	

*Payments are figured on partner's salary plus his interest on investment.

†Figuring these amounts requires special steps: (a) Determine total net earnings from self-employment; (b) Subtract total payments to partners; (c) Apportion remainder on 80%, 20% basis; (d) Add back appropriate payments.

††The partnership in this example, had only net short-term and long-term gains to pass through as tax preferences.

Example 2: On the facts of Example 1 above, the reconciliation schedule will be as follows:

SAMPLE RECONCILIATION SCHEDULE

	1. Capital account at beginning of year	2. Capital contributed during year	3. Ordinary income	4. Income not included in column 3 plus nontaxable income	5. Losses not included in column 3 plus unallowable deductions	6. Withdrawals and distributions	7. Capital account at end of year
(a) Smith	$170,000	......	$74,240	$ 8,160	$2,400	......	$250,000
(b) Brown	30,000	......	18,560	2,040	600	......	50,000
Totals	$200,000	......	$92,800	$10,200	$3,000	......	$300,000

Explanation of reconciliatiion figures:

Column 1. Capital account at the beginning of the year. The figures $170,000 and $30,000 are taken from the balance sheet of the partnership as of the beginning of the tax year. Since Example 1 does not include a balance sheet, we are assuming these figures for the purposes of the reconciliation schedule.

Footnotes appear at end of this Chapter.

¶ 2918

Column 2. *Additional capital contributed during year.* Additional capital includes property as well as cash. It would be entered here at its fair market value. No additional capital was contributed by either partner.

Column 3. *Ordinary income.* The partner's shares of ordinary income may be found in the Distribution Schedule in Example 1.

Column 4. *Income not included in column 3 plus nontaxable income.* Smith's share of income not included in column 3 and nontaxable income is $8,160, figured as follows: Capital gain $4,800 ($1,280 short-term and $3,520 long-term); dividends $800 and tax-exempt interest $2,560.

Brown's share of income not included in column 3 and nontaxable income is $2,040, figured as follows: Capital gain $1,200 ($320 short-term and $880 long-term); dividends $200 and tax-exempt interest $640.

Column 5. *Losses not included in column 3 plus unallowable deductions.* There were no capital losses. Charitable contributions constitute the unallowable deductions. Smith's share of the contributions was $2,400; Brown's $600. If the partnership took additional first-year depreciation during the year, that too would be entered here in proportion to the partners' shares.[1]

Column 6. *Withdrawals.* There are no withdrawals by either partner. We assume the partners left the net profit in the business. Partnership contributions for the partners to a self-employed retirement plan would be entered here.

Column 7. *Capital account at end of year.* This figure is the sum of columns 1, 2, 3, and 4 less the sum of columns 5 and 6. It must agree with the capital account on the balance sheet of the partnership as of the end of the tax year.

TAX YEAR OF PARTNER AND PARTNERSHIP

As a general rule, the partner includes in his return his share of partnership items for any partnership tax year that ends with or within his own tax year. Under prior law, this rule resulted in a postponement of tax on partnership income where the partnership used a fiscal year and the partners reported on a calendar year basis. See the observation and Examples 1 and 2 below. Current law prevents this by limiting the partnership's right to use a fiscal year and the partner's right to change his own tax year.

Ordinarily, a partnership's tax year does not close before the last day of such year. A premature closing could result in a bunching of more than one year's income into a single return. Current law prevents a premature closing when a partner dies or makes a gift of his interest.

¶ 2920 When partner reports partnership income. Each partner includes in his return his share of partnership items and his "guaranteed payments" for any partnership tax year that ends with or within his tax year (¶ 2923(d)) [Sec. 706(a); 1.706-1(a)].

➤**OBSERVATION**➤ If a partner reports on a calendar year basis, and the partnership uses a fiscal year ending June 30, the partner will be 6 months behind in reporting and paying tax on his partnership income.

Example 1: The E-H partnership uses a fiscal year ending September 30. Partner Edge uses a calendar year. For the year ending September 30, 1977, the partnership has a taxable income of $30,000. Edge includes his distributive share of this $30,000 in his individual return for the year 1977, his tax year within which the partnership's year ends.

Example 2: Partner Ames is on a calendar year while his partnership is on a fiscal year ending June 30. Ames receives payments regularly during the partnership year ending June 30, 1977, representing a guaranteed salary and guaranteed payments for the use of capital. During this partnership fiscal year, half of the total amount paid to him is received between July 1 and December 31, 1976. The other half is received between January 1 and June 30, 1977. The entire amount received is includable in Ames' return for the calendar year ending December 31, 1977, along with his distributive share of partnership taxable income for the partnership year ending June 30, 1977.

(a) When partner disposes of his interest. A partner whose entire interest is sold, exchanged or liquidated includes his share of partnership items, and his guaranteed payments, up to the date of disposition, as though the partnership year had ended on that date [Sec. 1.706-1(c)(2)(ii)].

NOTE: To avoid closing the partnership books, the partners may agree that the retiring partner may estimate his share of partnership items by prorating the amount of the items he would have included had he remained a partner until the end of the partnership year. A partner to whom the interest is transferred must then include in his taxable income the pro rata part of the items he would have included had he been a partner from the beginning of the tax year of the partnership [Sec. 1.706-1(c)(2)(ii)].

(b) Gain or loss on distribution or transfer. A partner receiving partnership distributions, or selling or exchanging all or part of his partnership interest, must include any gain or loss in his tax year in which the payment is made. This is not partnership gain or loss [Sec. 1.706-1(a)(2)].

¶ 2921 **Choice of tax year.** (a) **Partnership tax year.** A partnership may adopt a calendar or fiscal year under the rules below [Sec. 706(b); 1.442-1(b)(2), 1.706-1(b)].

Newly formed partnership. A newly formed partnership may, without prior Revenue Service approval, adopt either (1) a tax year which is the same as the tax year of all its principal partners (or the same as the tax year to which all its principal partners with different tax years are concurrently changing), or (2) a calendar year if all its principal partners are not on the same taxable year. In all other cases, prior approval is needed. Thus, prior approval is needed for adoption of a fiscal year different from that of all its principal partners. A principal partner is one who has an interest of 5% or more in the partnership's profits or capital.

Existing partnership. An existing partnership may, without prior approval, change to a tax year which is the same as the tax year of all its principal partners (or the same as the tax year to which all its principal partners are concurrently changing). In all other cases, it must satisfy the Commissioner that a good business reason exists for the change.[1]

(b) Partners tax year. A partner cannot change his tax year, unless he can show that there is a good business reason for the change [Sec. 706(b)(2); 1.442-1(b)(2), 1.706-1(b)(2)].

Partners who change their tax year to the partnership tax year must file a return for the short period ending on the last day of the first tax year of the partnership.[2]

Example: A and B are calendar year taxpayers. On September 1, 1976, they form a partnership with a fiscal year ending August 31. On approval of the change of their tax year to that of the partnership, A and B must file returns for the short period from January 1 to August 31, 1977.

(c) Application to adopt or change a tax year. The application is made on Form 1128. The applicant must file it with the Revenue Service by the 15th of the second month after the end of the short period for which a return is required because of the change [Sec. 1.706-1(b)].

¶ 2922 **When partnership's tax year closes.** A partnership's tax year normally closes on the last day of such year. In some cases, however, it may close prematurely for all the partners, or only for a particular partner.

Footnotes appear at end of this Chapter.

The partnership's tax year closes prematurely for all the partners only when the partnership terminates under the rules in (b). It does not close prematurely for all partners on the death, withdrawal, substitution or addition of a partner, or on a shift of interest among existing partners.

A partnership's tax year is not prematurely closed when a partner sells less than his entire interest in the partnership or reduces his interest. However, his distributive share of the partnership items must be determined by his "varying interest" in his partnership during the tax year [Sec. 706(c)(2)(B)].

NOTE: Partnership income and losses are allocated to a partner only for the part of the year he is a partnership member. Furthermore, for partnership tax years starting after 1975, the varying interests rule must apply to any partner whose interest in a partnership is reduced, whether by a new partner's entry who purchased his interest directly from the partnership, partial liquidation of a partner's interest, gift, or otherwise. This rule must also apply to the incoming partner so as to take into account his varying interests during the year.

The rules on a premature closing for a particular partner, assuming the partnership did not terminate, are summarized below [Sec. 706(c); 1.706-1(c)].

(a) Change of partners. The partnership's tax year does not close as to a partner who dies during the year. It continues until the normal end of the partnership's year, or until the decedent's entire interest is sold, exchanged, or liquidated by the decedent's successor, if that occurs earlier. The decedent's final return includes his share of partnership income for the partnership's tax year ending on or before his death. His share of income not reported on his final return must be reported by his estate or other successor in interest.

Example 1: A, B, C, and D own equal shares in the ABCD partnership. For the fiscal year ending June 30, 1977, the partnership has a taxable income of $124,000. Partner A, who reports on a calendar year basis, dies July 15, 1977. The last return for this deceased partner must report $31,000 (¼ of $124,000), his share of the partnership earnings for the year ending with or before his death.

Example 2: Assume the same partnership as in Example 1. Partner A, however, dies on June 15, 1977. His return for the shortened period ending with his death will not include his share of the $124,000. This amount will be picked up and reported by his estate.

The partnership's tax year does not close for a donor who transfers his interest by gift. Income attributable to his interest up to the date of the gift is allocated to him.

The partnership's tax year closes as to a partner who sells, exchanges or liquidates his entire interest, but not for a partner who sells, exchanges or liquidates less than his entire interest.

Example 3: Again assume the same partnership as in Example 1, but with A living. On November 30, 1977, partner A sells his entire interest to E. The partnership's tax year ends on November 30, 1977 *as to A*. On his return for 1977 (due April 15, 1978), A must include his share of partnership income for the partnership year ending June 30, 1977, *and* his share of partnership income for the short year, July 1, 1977 to November 30, 1977. Partners B, C, and D are not affected by the sale, and the partnership tax year does not close before its normal end as to them.

(b) When partnership ends. A partnership's tax year closes as to all partners when the partnership terminates. The partnership terminates only if (1) its operations cease, or (2) within a 12-month period 50% or more of the total interest in both capital and profits is *sold* or *exchanged*. There may be a "winding up period" after the partners agree to dissolve the firm [Sec. 708(b)(1); 1.708-1(b)].

Example 4: The ABCD partnership is owned, 50% by A, 20% by B, 15% by C and 15% by D. On March 31, 1977, A sells his interest to F. Since there is a transfer of a 50% or more interest within a 12-month period, the partnership is ended and its tax year closes as to all the partners.

Disposition of a partnership interest by gift, bequest, inheritance, or liquidation is not a sale or exchange for termination purposes [Sec. 1.708-1(b)]. Thus, 50% or more of the partnership's assets may be distributed in liquidation of a partner's interest without terminating the partnership. But a contribution of property to a partnership, followed shortly by a distribution, may constitute a sale or exchange [Sec. 1.731-1(c)(3)].

> **NOTE:** The partnership business is not considered to end on the death of one member of a 2-man partnership, if the deceased partner's estate or successor continues to share in the profits and losses of the partnership [Sec. 1.708-1(b)].

Termination by the sale or exchange of an interest is deemed to involve a distribution of assets and their contribution immediately to a new firm to continue business or wind it up [Sec. 1.708-1(b)(1)(iv)].

(c) **When partnerships combine.** On a merger or consolidation of partnerships, the tax year of the new partnership is considered a continuation of the tax year of the merging partnership whose members own an interest of more than 50% in the capital and profits of the new partnership. The tax years of partnerships whose members own 50% or less interest in the new partnership are closed. If none of the members of the merging partnerships have an interest of more than 50% in the resulting partnership, the partnership starts with a new tax year [Sec. 708(b)(2); 1.708-1(b)(2)(i)].

> **Example 5:** Partnerships AB and CD merge and form partnership ABCD. Partners A and B each own 30% and partners C and D each own 20% interest in the new partnership. Since partners A and B together own an interest of more than 50% in the new partnership, partnership ABCD is considered a continuation of and will have the same tax year as partnership AB. Partnership CD's tax year is closed on the merger.

(d) **Split-up of partnership.** When a partnership divides into two or more partnerships, any new partnership is considered a continuation of, and will have the same tax year as, the first partnership if the members of the new partnership owned a more than 50% interest in the capital and profits of the first partnership. All other new partnerships whose members owned an interest of 50% or less in the first partnership start with a new tax year. If however, the members of none of the new partnerships owned a more than 50% interest in the first partnership, the tax year of the first partnership is closed [Sec. 708(b)(2)(B); 1.708-1(b)(2)(ii)].

> **Example 6:** A owns a 40%, B, C and D each own a 20% interest in the capital and profits of partnership ABCD. When partnership ABCD is split into partnership AB and partnership CD, the tax year of partnership AB is considered a continuation of the tax year of partnership ABCD since A and B together own more than a 50% interest in partnership ABCD. Partnership CD is considered a new partnership and starts with a new tax year.

TRANSACTIONS BETWEEN PARTNERSHIP AND PARTNER OR PERSON RELATED TO PARTNER

¶ 2923 **Partner not acting in capacity as partner.** A partner sometimes does business with his partnership just as an outsider would. In such cases the transaction is generally treated as one between the partnership and a nonpartner [Sec. 707(a); 1.707-1(a)(1)]. Exceptions to this rule are found in (a) to (c), below.

Footnotes appear at end of this Chapter.

¶ 2923

Example 1: Perkins, an equal member of the OPQ partnership, has a basis of $1,000 for a particular asset. If he sells it to the partnership for $1,500, its fair market value, he will report a gain of $500.

Example 2: Assume, now that Perkins pays $2,000 for partnership property, that has a basis to it of $1,100. The partnership reports a gain of $900. Since the partners share equally, $300 of this gain ($1/3$ of $900) must be reported by P on his individual return as part of his distributive share of partnership gain.

(a) When loss is disallowed. No deduction is allowed for losses from the sale or exchange of property (except an interest in the partnership) between (1) the partnership and a partner who owns more than a 50% interest in its capital or profits, or (2) the partnership and another partnership, when the same persons own more than a 50% interest in the capital or profits of each [Sec. 267(d), 707(b)(1)(A), (B); 1.707-1(b)(1)(i)].

Example 3: The AFG partnership in which partner Frank owns a 60% interest in capital and profits transfers property at a loss of $500 to the DFH partnership, in which Frank owns a 55% interest in capital and profits. The AFG partnership is not allowed a deduction for the loss.

Any recognized gain on a later sale or exchange of the property by the purchaser is taxable only to the extent it exceeds that part of the disallowed loss allocable to the property sold [Sec. 267(d), 707(b)(1); 1.707-1(b)(1)(ii)].

Example 4: The DFH partnership in Example 3, sells the property it got from the AFG partnership at a gain of $600. Only $100 of the gain is taxable.

Example 5: The DFH partnership sells only half the property received from the AFG partnership at a gain of $300. Only $50 of the gain is taxable.

(b) When gain is ordinary income. Any recognized gain from the sale or exchange of property that is not a capital asset [¶ 1601] *in the hands of the person getting it* is ordinary income, if the transaction is between (1) a partnership and a partner who owns over 80% of the capital or profits interest in the partnership, or (2) two partnerships in which the same persons own more than 80% of the capital or profits interest [Sec. 707(b)(2); 1.707-1(b)(2)].

Example 6: Corby, who owns an 82% interest in the capital and profits of the CDE partnership which sells paintings, transfers a painting from his personal collection to the partnership at a gain of $100. This amount is ordinary income to Corby.

(c) Ownership of an interest. In determining the extent of the ownership of a capital or profits interest when there is a sale or exchange between a partner and partnership, the rules for constructive ownership of stock apply [¶ 2223(d)]. In applying these rules, however, the partnership rule (Rule 3), is not used [Sec. 707(b)(3); 1.707-1(b)(3)].

Example 7: If in Example 3 above Frank owned only a 30% interest in the DFH partnership, the loss would be allowed. If, however, H, who also owns a 30% interest, were Frank's brother, the loss would not be allowed.

(d) Salaries and interest paid to partner. Payments to a partner for services or for the use of capital are "guaranteed payments" to the extent determined without regard to partnership income. [Sec. 707(c)]. They are treated as payments to a nonpartner, but only for purposes of determining their taxability to the partner and their deductibility by the partnership. The payments are not wages or interest for any other purpose but are considered self-employment income (¶ 3823) [Sec. 1.1402(a)-1(b)].

The partner includes these guaranteed payments as ordinary income [¶ 2920] and the partnership may deduct them as business expenses in computing taxable income or loss if they meet the business expense deduction tests [¶ 1803]. In determining their deductibility, for partnership tax years starting after 1975, the partnership must also take into account the capital expenditure rules (¶ 1808) [Sec. 707(c)]. The payments are not subject to wage withholding and are not part of an employee's deferred compensation plan [Sec. 1.707-1(c)].

NOTE: The Fifth Circuit treats a partner as an employee for the purpose of the meals and lodging exclusion [¶ 1308].[1]

A partnership may set up a self-employed retirement plan [¶ 1839], but it gets no deduction for contributions for the partners [¶ 2913]. When the employer of a medical partnership contributes directly to its retirement plan, the Supreme Court held that each doctor-partner must report as income his share of the contribution.[2]

¶ 2924 Transactions between partnership and person related to partner. - The rule disallowing losses [¶ 2223] and deductions for expenses and interest paid later than 2½ months after the payor's tax year [¶ 2748], in transactions between related parties, does not apply in transactions between partners and partnerships. However, the rule does apply in transactions between a partnership and a person related to a partner in any of the ways listed in ¶ 2223. The regulations treat a transaction of this kind as one between the other person and the members of the partnership separately. Such treatment disallows the loss or deduction otherwise allowable [Sec. 1.267(b)-1(b)]:

- To the partner to the extent his distributive share of any such partnership loss or deduction is treated as occurring in a transaction he had with the other (related) person;
- To the other person to the extent that any such loss or deduction of his is treated as occurring in a transaction with the related partner.

Example 1: A, an equal partner in the ABC partnership, personally owns all of M Corporation's stock. B and C are not related to A. The partnership and all the partners are on the accrual basis and calendar year. M Corp. is on the cash basis and calendar year. During 1976, the partnership borrowed money from M Corp. and also sold property to M Corp. at a loss. On December 31, 1976, the partnership accrued its interest liability to M Corp., and on April 1, 1977 (more than 2½ months after the close of its tax year) it paid M Corp. the interest. B and C may deduct their shares of the partnership deductions for the loss and interest. But no deduction is allowed to A for his distributive share of these partnership deductions

Example 2: Assume that the partnership and all the partners in Example 1 are on the cash basis and M Corporation is on the accrual basis. During 1976, M Corp. borrowed money from the partnership and sold property to it at a loss. On December 31, 1976, M Corp. accrued its interest liability on the borrowed money, and on April 1, 1977, it paid the interest to the partnership. The corporation's interest deduction is disallowed to the extent of A's distributive share (one-third) of such interest income. M Corporation's deduction for the loss on the sale is disallowed to the extent of A's one-third interest in the purchased property.

CONTRIBUTIONS TO PARTNERSHIPS

The contribution rules are best summarized on the basis of a simplified statement of facts such as the following:

A, B and C form an equal partnership. A contributes $100 in cash. B contributes property X (basis $40, value $100). C contributes property Y (basis $100, value $90).

Tax rules. As a general rule, no gain or loss is recognized to any partner or the partnership.

The partnership's basis for each property is the same as the contributor's basis.

A's original basis for his partnership interest is $100. B's basis is $40. C's basis is $100.

Footnotes appear at end of this Chapter.

¶ 2924

Special rules may apply if the partner acquires his interest for sevices, or if the contribution is considered a sale by the partners.

¶ 2925 **Tax effect of contribution.** When a partnership is formed, each partner contributes money, other property, or services in return for his interest. A new partner may also acquire an interest by making a contribution after the partnership is formed and operating.

> NOTE: Amounts received by a partnership as beneficiary of life insurance policies transferred to the partnership as part of the partners' capital contribution are exempt from income tax.[1]

(a) **Nonrecognition of gain or loss.** Except as otherwise noted below, no gain or loss is recognized on a contribution of money, installment obligations or other property to a partnership in return for a partnership interest. This rule applies whether the partnership was just formed or is already formed and operating [Sec. 721; 1.721-1(a)].

Capital interest acquired for services. The value of a partnership interest in *capital* acquired for services is ordinary income to the partner. The interest is valued (1) when received, if received for past services, or (2) when the services are rendered if the interest depends on future services [Sec. 1.721-1(b)].

Contribution of property with recapture potential. On a contribution of depreciable property, any ordinary income potential carries over to the partnership (¶ 1619) [Sec. 1245, 1250; 1.1245-4(c), 1.1250-3(c)].

If farm recapture property is contributed, ordinary gain is recognized to the extent of the difference between the fair market value of the property and the fair market value of the partnership interest attributable to such property (¶ 2226) [Sec. 1251(d)(5)].

A contribution of investment credit property will not cause recapture of the credit if there is merely a change in the form of conducting business and the partner has a substantial interest (¶ 2410(e)) [Sec. 47(b); 1.47-3(f)].

Partner acting as outsider. The above rules do not apply if the transaction is actually a sale, rather than a contribution [¶ 2923].

Exchange funds. Any gain (but not loss) realized by a partner on property transferred to a partnership in exchange for a partnership interest will be recognized if the partnership is an investment company. A partnership is an investment company if, after the exchange, more than 80% of its assets' value are held for investment and consist of readily marketable stocks or securities. This rule generally applies to transfers after 2-17-76 in tax years ending after that date although special transitional rules may apply [Sec. 721(b)].

(b) **Partnership's basis for contributed property.** The partnership takes the contributor's basis for any contributed property. It may also add the contributor's holding period to its own [Sec. 723, 1223(2); 1.723-1].

(c) **Basis of contributing partner's interest.** The partner's *original* basis for an interest acquired by a *contribution* is the amount of money contributed plus his adjusted basis for any property contributed. Effective for transfers after 2-17-76 in tax years ending after that date generally, the property's adjusted basis is increased by the amount of any gain recognized to the partner at the time of contribution [Sec. 722]. Additional contributions increase his basis [Sec. 1.705-1(a)].

Example 1: A and B form a partnership. A contributes $1,000 in cash, and B contributes property worth $1,000 but with an adjusted basis of $600. The basis of the property to the partnership is $600. This is also B's basis for his partnership interest.

The basis of an interest acquired by gift, purchase or inheritance is determined under the rules in ¶ 2926.

Any taxable income received on a contribution of services for an interest (see above) is included in the contributor's basis [Sec. 1.722-1].

Adjustment of partner's original basis for his interest. The partner's original basis is adjusted from time to time to prevent the unintended benefit or detriment that would otherwise result [¶ 2926].

An increase in the partner's share of partnership liabilities, in any of the ways mentioned in ¶ 2926(c), is considered a contribution of money to the partnership.

Example 2: A and B form a partnership. A contributes $5,000 in cash. B contributes property worth $5,000, but subject to a chattel mortgage of $1,000. This property has a basis to B of $3,000. A's basis for his partnership interest will be $5,500 (the $5,000 cash plus $500, his share of the encumbrance). B will have $2,500 as a basis for his partnership interest ($3,000 his basis for the property less $500, the amount of his liability assumed by A).

PARTNER'S BASIS FOR PARTNERSHIP INTEREST

¶ 2926 Partner's original basis and how to adjust it. A partner's original basis for an interest acquired by a contribution is the amount of money contributed, plus his adjusted basis for any property contributed and plus any taxable income realized on acquisition of the interest [¶ 2925(c)]. His basis for an interest acquired in some other way is determined by applying the general rules for property basis [Chapter 5].

The partner's original basis must be adjusted from time to time to prevent the unintended benefit or detriment that would otherwise result. Suppose, for example, that the value of a partner's interest increased because the partnership retained its current income. The partner is taxed on his share of this income even though the partnership retains it. If his basis for his interest remained the same, a later sale of the interest would result in a second tax to the extent of any gain due to such increased value.

The partner's adjusted basis for his interest is determined under the general rule ((a) below) or under an alternative rule ((b) below).

(a) General rule. Adjustments to original basis are required under this rule. These adjustments may increase or decrease the partner's basis for his interest.

Basis increased. A partner's original basis is increased by any further contributions to the partnership and by his distributive share of:

- Partnership taxable income, capital gains and other income items separately allocated to the partners [¶ 2906(a)];
- Partnership tax-exempt income;
- The excess of the depletion deduction over the basis of the depletable property [Sec. 705(a)(1); 1.705-1(a)(2)].

Example 1: A's share of taxable income of the AB partnership is $2,000. He also is entitled to a $100 share in tax-exempt interest received by the partnership. The basis of A's partnership interest must be increased by $2,100.

An increase in the partner's share of partnership liabilities, in any of the ways mentioned in (c) below, is considered a contribution of money to the partnership.

Footnotes appear at end of this Chapter.

Basis reduced. A partner's original basis for his interest is reduced (but not below zero) by cash distributions, his basis for other property distributed to him, and by his distributive share of:

- Partnership losses (including capital losses), and
- Nondeductible partnership expenditures that are not capital expenditures [Sec. 705(a)(2), 733; 1.705-1(a)(3), 1.733-1].

Example 2: At the end of the year, the AB partnership distributes $2,100 to partner A in Example 1. A must decrease the basis of his partnership interest by that amount. Thus the transactions in Examples 1 and 2 cancel each other out. This leaves A with his basis unchanged.

For tax year starting after 12-31-74, the partner's basis is reduced (but not below zero) by the amount of the partner's depletion deduction for oil and gas wells (¶ 2104) [Sec. 705(a)(3)].

A decrease in the partner's share of partnership liabilities, in any of the ways mentioned in (c) below, is considered a distribution of money to him.

(b) Alternative rule. In certain cases, the partner may take as the adjusted basis of his interest an amount equal to his share of the partnership's adjusted basis for the property it would distribute if the partnership terminated. The partner may use this method only where adjustment under the general rule is not practicable, or where IRS concludes that the result will not vary substantially from the result under the general rule. If this method is used, certain adjustments are required in figuring the partner's adjusted basis for his interest. Examples include adjustments to reflect any significant differences due to contributions or distributions of property or transfers of partnership interests [Sec. 705(b); 1.705-1(b)].

Example 3: The ABC partnership, in which A, B, and C are equal partners, owns various properties with a total adjusted basis of $1,500, and has earned and retained an additional $1,500. The total adjusted basis of partnership property is thus $3,000. Each partner's share in the adjusted basis of partnership property is one-third of this amount, or $1,000. Under the alternative rule, this amount represents each partner's adjusted basis for his partnership interest.

Example 4: Assume that partner A in Example 3 sells his partnership interest to D for $1,250 when the partnership property (with an adjusted basis of $1,500) had appreciated in value to $3,000, and when the partnership also had $750 in cash. The total adjusted basis of all partnership property is $2,250, and the value of the property is $3,750. D's basis for his partnership interest is his cost, $1,250. However, his one-third share of the adjusted basis of partnership property is only $750. Therefore, for purposes of the alternative rule, D has an adjustment of $500 in determining the basis of his interest. This amount represents the difference between the cost of his partnership interest and his share of partnership basis at the time of his purchase. If the partnership later earns and retains an additional $1,500, its property will have an adjusted basis of $3,750. D's adjusted basis for his interest under the alternative rule is $1,750, determined by adding $500, his basis adjustment, to $1,250 (his 1/3 share of the $3,750 adjusted basis of partnership property). If the partnership distributes $250 to each partner in a current distribution, D's adjusted basis for his interest will be $1,500 ($1,000, his 1/3 share of the remaining basis of partnership property ($3,000) plus his $500 basis adjustment). D's adjusted basis for his partnership interest, after the $500 adjustment, may be shown as follows:

		D bought interest for $1,250	ABC later earns and retains additional $1,500	ABC then distributes $250 to each partner
1.	Total adjusted basis of all ABC's property	$2,250 ($1,500 + $750)	$3,750 ($2,250 + $1,500)	$3,000 ($3,750 − $750)
2.	D's share of adjusted basis of ABC property (1/3 of 1.)	$ 750	$1,250	$1,000
3.	Plus basis adjustment	$ 500	$ 500	$ 500
4.	D's adjusted basis for his interest (2 + 3)	$1,250	$1,750	$1,500

(c) Effect of liabilities. The rules are as follows [Sec. 752; 1.752-1]:

A partner's assumption of partnership liabilities, or an increase in his share of such liabilities, is considered a contribution of money to the partnership. The contribution increases his basis for his interest.

A decrease in the partner's share of partnership liabilities, or an assumption of his liabilities by the partnership, is considered a distribution of money to the partner. The distribution reduces his basis for his interest and may result in gain [¶ 2927; 2944].

Liability to which property is subject is considered the owner's liability to the extent of the property's fair market value. Thus, if property subject to a liability is contributed to a partnership, or is distributed to a partner, the transferee is deemed to have assumed the liability.

DISTRIBUTIONS OTHER THAN TO A RETIRED PARTNER OR A DECEASED PARTNER'S SUCCESSOR

Gain or loss on most distributions is recognized only to a limited extent, if at all.

On a nonliquidating distribution, the partner takes the partnership's basis for the distributed property. But such "carryover" basis may not exceed the partner's basis for his interest, less any money received. On a liquidating distribution, he uses his basis for his interest, less any money received.

A nonliquidating distribution reduces the partner's basis for his interest (but not below zero).

The partnership's basis for its assets is subject to an *elective* adjustment to reflect the effect of distributions and transfers of partnership assets. An *elective* adjustment is also available to a transferee as to certain distributions after he acquires his interest.

Specific rules are provided for allocating the partner's basis for distributed property among the properties received. Specific rules also govern the nature of the gain or loss on a disposition of distributed property, and on the sale of a partnership interest [¶ 2935; 2945].

¶ 2927 Gain or loss on distribution. This paragraph discusses distributions by a partnership to its partners of money or property other than their distributive share of earnings. The distribution may reduce or liquidate the partner's interest.

The issue here is not whether a gain or loss was realized, but whether the amount realized is "recognized" (given tax effect) at the time of distribution.

(a) Recognition of gain or loss. Gain or loss is recognized only to a limited extent, if at all [Sec. 731; 1.731-1]. The general rules are summarized below. Specially treated transactions are in (b).

Partner's gain or loss. When a partner receives money, gain is recognized only to the extent the money exceeds his basis for his partnership interest.[1] The gain is usually a capital gain, but it may be taxed as ordinary income to the extent of his share in the partnership's unrealized receivables[2] [¶ 2944]. When he receives property other than money, gain or loss is generally not recognized until the partner disposes of the property. Disposition usually results in capital gain or loss, but an exception may apply if the property is unrealized receivables or substantially appreciated inventory [¶ 2945].

Footnotes appear at end of this Chapter.

¶ 2927

Example 1: Brady has $10,000 as the basis of his partnership interest. He receives a distribution of $8,000 in cash and property with a value of $3,000. No gain is recognized. If Brady received a distribution of $11,000 in cash, a capital gain of $1,000 would be recognized.

A partner's loss is recognized only on distributions in liquidation of his entire interest and only if he receives no property other than money, unrealized receivables and/or inventory. The potential ordinary income from Sec. 1245 or Sec. 1250 property [¶ 1619]; farm recapture property [¶ 2226]; farm land [¶ 1845(e)]; mining property [¶ 1843]; certain oil and gas property, for tax years ending after 1975 [¶ 2103(c)]; stock in certain foreign corporations, for exchanges starting after 10-9-75 and to exchanges and distributions taking place after that date [¶ 3728]; and stock in a DISC, as to dispositions after 12-31-75 in tax years ending after that date [¶ 3460] is treated as a receivable. Foreign investment company stock is treated as inventory [¶ 2944(d)]. The basis of Sec. 1245 and 1250 potential ordinary income is zero [Sec. 1.751-1(c)(5)].

The loss is the excess of (1) the partner's basis for his interest over (2) the money he receives plus his basis for the other property [¶ 2928]. The loss is a capital loss.

Example 2: Frey has $10,000 as the basis of his interest in the FGH partnership. He retires from the partnership receiving $5,000 in cash and inventory items with a basis to the partnership of $3,000. Frey realizes a capital loss of $2,000. The basis of his interest is first reduced by the $5,000 cash. $3,000 of the remaining $5,000 basis for his interest is allocated to the inventory. The remaining $2,000 is capital loss.

Partnership's gain or loss. A partnership has no gain or loss on its usual distributions. But it may elect to adjust the basis of its assets to reflect the effect of the distribution on its asset basis [¶ 2932].

(b) Specially treated transactions. (1) A retiring partner or a deceased partner's successor may have recognized gain or loss, or other income, on receipt of payments from the partnership [¶ 2941].

(2) Both partnership and partners may have recognized gain or loss on distributions treated as sales or exchanges. These include unequal distributions of receivables or inventory [¶ 2944] and distributions shortly before or after a contribution to the partnership [Sec. 1.731-1(c)(3)].

Recapture potential. When depreciable property is distributed, the partnership's ordinary income potential carries over to the partner but is reduced for gain recognized in a disproportionate distribution (¶ 2944; 2945) [Sec. 1245(b)(6), 1250(d)(6); 1.1245-4(f), 1.1250-3(f)].

A distribution before the end of the useful life used for investment credit purposes may result in recapture of the credit from the partners (¶ 2410(e); 2913(c)) [Sec. 47; 1.47-6].

(c) Constructive distributions. A decrease in a partner's share of partnership liabilities, or an assumption of his liabilities by the partnership, is considered a distribution of money to the partner [Sec. 722, 752(b); 1.722-1, 1.752-1(b)].

Distributions are loans if the partner is obligated to return them. Cancellation of the obligation is considered a distribution [Sec. 731(c); 1.731-1(c)].

A partnership contribution to a self-employed retirement plan for a partner is treated as a distribution to him.

¶ 2928 Partner's basis and holding period for distributed property other than money. The general rules are summarized in (a) and (b) [Sec. 732; 1.732-1]. Specially treated situations are in (c).

(a) Distributions not in complete liquidation of partner's interest. The partner takes the partnership's basis for the distributed properties. But such "carryover" basis may not exceed the partner's basis for his interests, less any money he received. If the limitation applies, the reduced basis is allocated among the distributed properties [¶ 2929]. The distribution reduces the partner's basis for his partnership interest (but not below zero); see examples below [Sec. 733].

A transferee partner taking a "carryover" basis may have a special basis adjustment for distributed property [¶ 2930].

Example 1: Armstrong, whose basis for his interest is $2,500, receives a distribution of partnership property. If the partnership's basis for the property is $1,500, he takes that as his basis. The $1,500 reduces the basis of his partnership *interest* to $1,000.

Example 2: Armstrong has a basis of $10,000 for his partnership interest. He receives a distribution, other than in liquidation of his interest, of $4,000 in cash, and properties with a basis to the partnership of $8,000. Armstrong's basis in the distributed properties is $6,000—his basis of $10,000 reduced by the cash distribution of $4,000. (If the partnership had made the election to adjust basis [¶ 2932], it could add the $2,000 difference to the basis of its retained properties.) Armstrong's basis for his partnership *interest* becomes zero ($10,000 less the cash of $4,000 and his $6,000 basis for the distributed property.)

(b) Distributions in complete liquidation of partner's interest. The partner's basis for the distributed properties is the same as his adjusted basis for his partnership interest, less any money he received [Sec. 732(b); 1.732-1(b)]. This reduced basis is allocated among the distributed properties. Unallocated basis may give rise to a capital loss. See ¶ 2929.

Example 3: The adjusted basis of Brown's interest in the partnership is $12,000. When he retires from the partnership, he receives in a liquidating distribution $2,000 cash and $14,000 worth of real estate with an adjusted basis of $6,000 to the partnership. Brown will take $10,000 as his basis for the distributed real estate (his basis for his partnership interest, $12,000, less $2,000 cash received).

(c) Specially treated transactions. Certain disproportionate distributions are treated as sales or exchanges between the partner and the partnership. In effect, the partner gives up his interest in certain partnership property in exchange for a distribution of other property [¶ 2944].

The basis of the property the partner *received* is his cost. The basis of the property he *gave up* (by giving up his interest in it) is the basis it would have in his hands if distributed to him just before he transferred it to the partnership.

A partner's basis for distributed receivables or inventory may not exceed the basis they had in the partnership. However, this rule does not apply if the distribution is treated as a sale or exchange or if the partner has a special basis adjustment for the property (¶ 2930) [Sec. 732(c); 1.732-1(c)(1)].

The basis of Sec. 1245 potential ordinary income and of potential Sec. 1250 income is zero [Sec. 1.751-1(c)(5)].

(d) Partner's holding period for distributed property. The partner includes the partnership's holding period in figuring his own, with a possible exception for distributed inventory [¶ 2945]. If he contributed the property to the partnership, he may also include his own original holding period [Sec. 735(b); 1.735-1(b)].

¶ 2929 How to allocate partner's basis for distributed property. A distributee partner who must allocate the basis of his partnership interest among the properties he received [¶ 2928(a), (b)] must first allocate the basis to receivables and inventory and then to other property under the rules below [Sec. 732(c); 1.732(c)].

Footnotes appear at end of this Chapter.

¶ 2929

(a) **Allocation to receivables and inventory.** The partner's basis (less distributed cash) is first allocated to any unrealized receivables and inventory in an amount equal to the partnership's basis for such property, taking into account the transferee's special basis adjustment, if any [¶ 2928(c)]. If the allocable basis is less than the partnership's basis for such property, an allocation in proportion to the partnership's bases for the items is required.

(b) **Allocation to other property.** Any basis remaining after the first allocation is given to the other properties in proportion to their bases to the partnership [Sec. 732(c)(2); 1.732-1(c)(1)].

Example 1: Harper has a basis of $17,000 for his partnership interest. He receives a distribution from the partnership in liquidation of his interest of $2,000 cash, inventory with a basis to the partnership of $3,000, real estate (capital asset) with a basis of $2,000 and a depreciable asset with a basis of $4,000. The basis to be allocated to the property is $15,000 (the basis of his interest, $17,000, less the cash distributed, $2,000). This amount is first allocated to the inventory in an amount equal to its basis to the partnership. His basis in the inventory is therefore $3,000. The remaining $12,000 of the basis of his partnership interest is allocated to the capital and depreciable assets in proportion to their bases to the partnership. Since the basis of the capital asset is $2,000 and the basis of the depreciable asset is $4,000, the $12,000 is allocated $4,000 to the capital assets and $8,000 to the depreciable asset.

(c) **Loss for unallocated basis.** If the basis of the partner's interest to be allocated on a distribution *in liquidation of his entire interest*, is greater than the amount allocable under the rules in (a) above, and there is no other property to absorb the excess, the unallocated amount is a capital loss [Sec. 731(a)(2); 1.732-1(c)(2)].

Example 2: Frost's interest in partnership FGH has an adjusted basis to him of $9,000. He receives, as a distribution in liquidation, cash of $1,000 and inventory items having a basis to the partnership of $6,000. The cash payment reduces Frost's basis to $8,000, which can be allocated only to the extent of $6,000 to the inventory items. The remaining $2,000 basis, not allocable to distributed property, is a capital loss to Frost.

(d) **Special rules.** Special rules apply to certain distributions to a partner who acquired his interest from another partner [¶ 2931(a), (b)], and to distributions treated as sales or exchanges. See ¶ 2930; 2944; 2945.

¶ 2930 Special elective partnership basis for transferee. A transferee partner is one who acquired his interest by purchase or on a partner's death.

If the partnership had elected to adjust the bases of its assets on transfers of partnership interests, its adjusted bases for such assets would reflect the transferee's acquisition cost for his interest in the assets. See ¶ 2936; 2937.

A transferee who did not get the benefit of an adjustment by the partnership, may get a similar benefit by electing a special method to fix and allocate his basis for distributed property other than money [Sec. 732(d); 1.732-1(d)]. He starts with the basis the property would have if the partnership had made the adjustment when he acquired his interest [¶ 2937]. In effect, he treats as the partnership's special basis for the distributed property the amount he paid for his interest in such property. See ¶ 2931. The partnership's basis is not changed as to all the partners. Instead, the transferee gets a special basis adjustment. The adjustment is a specific amount that increases or decreases the partnership's basis for the distributed property when it is distributed to the transferee.

The transferee may make his election only if he receives a distribution within 2 years after he acquired his interest. In some cases, the Revenue Service may require the adjustment whether or not the distribution occurred within the 2-year period.

Example 1: The basis to transferee partner K of his one-fourth interest in partnership WJKS is $17,000. At the time he acquired such interest by purchase, the election under section 754 was not in effect and the partnership inventory had a basis to the partnership of $14,000 and a value of $16,000. K's purchase price reflected $500 of this difference. Thus, $4,000 of the $17,000 paid by K for his one-fourth interest was attributable to his share of partnership inventory with a basis of $3,500. Within 2 years after acquiring his interest K retired from the partnership and received in liquidation of his entire interest cash of $1,500, inventory with a basis to the partnership of $3,500, property X (a capital asset), with an adjusted basis to the partnership of $2,000, and property Y (a depreciable asset), with an adjusted basis to the partnership of $4,000. The value of the inventory received by K was one-fourth of the value of all partnership inventory and was his share of such property. It is immaterial whether the inventory K received was on hand when K acquired his interest. In accordance with K's election under section 732(d), the amount of his share of partnership basis which is attributable to partnership inventory is increased by $500 (one-fourth of the $2,000 difference between the value of such property, $16,000 and its $14,000 basis to the partnership at the time K acquired his interest). This adjustment under section 732(d) applies only for purposes of distributions to partner K, and not for purposes of partnership depreciation, depletion, or gain or loss on disposition. Thus, the amount to be allocated among the properties received by K in the liquidating distribution is $15,500 ($17,000, K's basis for his interest, reduced by the amount of cash received, $1,500). This amount is allocated as follows: The basis of the inventory items received is $4,000, consisting of the $3,500 common partnership basis for such items, plus the special basis adjustment of $500 which K would have had under Sec. 743(b). The remaining basis of $11,500 ($15,500 — $4,000) is to be allocated to the remaining property distributed to K in proportion to their adjusted bases to the partnership. Since the adjusted basis to the partnership of property X is $2,000, and that of property Y is $4,000, the $11,500 is allocated $3,833 (2,000/6,000 × $11,500) to X, and $7,667 (4,000/6,000 × $11,500) to Y.

(a) Excluded property. The optional method cannot be used to determine the basis for the portion of a distribution to a partner that is treated as received by him in a sale or exchange under Sec. 751. It does apply to the portion treated as exchanged by him, since such property is treated as currently distributed before the exchange [¶ 2944]. His basis for the property he received is cost [Sec. 1.732-1(e)].

(b) When partner must use special basis. The transferee must determine his basis under the special method whether or not the distribution was made within 2 years after he acquired his interest, if at the time he acquired the interest [Sec. 732(d); 1.732-1(d)(4)]:

(1) The fair market value of all partnership property (except money) exceeds 110% of its adjusted basis to the partnership,

(2) An allocation [¶ 2929] on a liquidation of his interest immediately after its transfer, would have resulted in a shift of basis from property not subject to an allowance for depreciation, depletion or amortization, to property subject to such an allowance, *and*

(3) A special partnership basis adjustment on a transfer [¶ 2937(a)] would change the basis, to the transferee partner, of the property actually distributed [Sec. 732(d); 1.732-1(d)(4)].

Example 2: Partnership ABC owns 3 parcels of land, each of which has a basis to the partnership of $5,000 and each of which is worth $55,000. It also has depreciable property with a basis and value of $150,000. D purchases A's partnership interest for $105,000 when the election under Sec. 754 is not in effect. At this time, the value of all the partnership property is $315,000 which exceeds 110% of $165,000, its basis to the partnership. Four years later the partnership dissolves and D receives 1 of the 3 parcels of land which had a basis to the partnership of $5,000 and one-third of the depreciable property which had a basis to the partnership at that time of $45,000, one-third of $135,000 ($150,000 original basis less $15,000 depreciation). If D's basis for his interest at the time of distribution was $100,000, and it was allocated to the properties received by him in proportion to their respective basis to the partnership, the basis to him for the distributed land would be $10,000 (5,000/50,000 × $100,000), and the basis of the depreciable property would be $90,000 (45,000/50,000 × $100,000). As a result, D would, in effect, apply as the basis of depreciable property a portion of the amount which he had paid for nondepreciable property. If the partnership adjustment for transfers [¶ 2937(a)] had been applied to the transfer of the interest, D would have had a different basis for the distributed property. Therefore D *must* increase the basis of the land by a special adjustment of $50,000 ($55,000 value less $5,000 partnership basis). Hence his basis for the land will be $55,000 and for the depreciable property, $45,000.

¶ 2931 **Distribution of property with special basis.** A partnership may elect to make certain optional adjustments to the bases of its remaining assets after distributions or transfers of partnership interest [¶ 2932; 2937].

Adjustments after a distribution affect only the partnership's undistributed assets. They apply to all the partners and the partnership must reflect them in its basis for any affected property included in a later distribution. The method of adjustment is covered at ¶ 2932(a).

Adjustments after transfers of partnership interests. These adjustments are for the transferee only. The partnership's basis remains the same for all the other partners. The transferee gets a special basis adjustment. When he receives a distribution of any affected property, he must increase or decrease the partnership's basis for such property by the amount of his special adjustment [¶ 2937]. A similar rule applies to the special adjustment the transferee acquires through his own election (¶ 2930) [Sec. 1.734-2(a)].

> **Example 1:** Partner D acquired his interest in the ABD partnership from a previous partner. Since the partnership had made an election to adjust basis [¶ 2937], D acquired a special basis with respect to partnership property X. The adjusted basis to the partnership for this property is $1,000. D's special adjustment is $500. Upon the distribution of property X to D in a current distribution, the adjusted basis of such property to the partnership before the distribution is $1,500. D, under the rules for determining basis [¶ 2928(a)], takes $1,500 as his basis for X. If property X had been distributed to partner A, a nontransferee partner, its adjusted basis to the partnership would only have been $1,000 and A would have acquired only $1,000 as his carryover basis for X.

(a) Basis allocated to distributed property. If a partner receives more than one property, he must allocate his basis among them. Such basis is allocated first to any unrealized receivables or appreciated inventory included in the distribution. Ordinarily, the amount allocated to such property is an amount equal to its basis to the partnership. But a special rule applies to a transferee who has a special basis adjustment for receivables or inventory. He gets the full benefit of his special adjustment only if he receives his share or more of the fair market value of the receivables or inventory. If he gets less than his full share, the partnership'basis for the distributed receivables or inventory is increased or decreased by only a proportionate part of the special adjustment. The proportionate part is determined by the ratio between (1) the value of receivables or inventory distributed to the transferee and (2) his entire share of the total value of all such partnership items [Sec. 1.732-2(c)].

> **Example 2:** Partner F acquired a one-third interest in the EFG partnership from a previous partner. Since the partnership had elected to adjust the basis of partnership property for transfers [¶ 2937], F has a special basis of $800 for partnership inventory items and $200 for unrealized receivables. F retires from the partnership when the adjusted basis of his partnership interest is $3,000. He receives in liquidation of his interest $1,000 cash, certain depreciable assets, inventory, and unrealized receivables. The common partnership bases for the inventory he received is $500 and for the unrealized receivables, zero.
>
> If the value of inventory items and unrealized receivables distributed to F is his share or more (33⅓% or more) of the total value of all partnership inventory items and unrealized receivables, then his adjusted basis will be $1,300 for the inventory items ($500 plus $800 adjustment) and $200 for the unrealized receivables (zero plus $200). His basis for the depreciable property is

$500, figured as follows: $3,000 (the basis of F's partnership interest) less $1,000 (cash distributed) or $2,000 (the amount to be allocated to the basis of all distributed property). This $2,000 is then reduced by the amount allocated to the inventory and receivables ($2,000 less $1,500).

If the value of the inventory items and unrealized receivables distributed to F consisted of only $1/6$ of the total fair market value of such property (i.e., only $1/2$ of F's share), then only $1/2$ of F's special basis adjustment of $800 for partnership inventory items and $200 for unrealized receivables will be taken into account. Thus, the basis of the inventory items in F's hands is $650 ($250, the common partnership basis for inventory items distributed to him, plus $400, $1/2$ of F's special basis adjustment for inventory items). The basis of the unrealized receivables in F's hands would be $100 (zero plus $100, $1/2$ of F's special basis adjustment for unrealized receivables).

(b) Reallocating special basis adjustment. If property for which a transferee has a special basis adjustment is distributed to another partner, the other partner may not take the adjustment into account. However, the transferee does not lose his adjustment. He reallocates it to like kind property retained by the partnership or, if he receives a distribution of like kind property, to such distributed property [Sec. 1.743-1(b)(2)(ii)].

A transferee may also reallocate his special basis adjustment if he receives a distribution of property (whether or not he has a special adjustment for it) at the same time he gives up his interest in other like kind property for which he has a special adjustment. He reallocates his adjustment to the property he received [Sec. 1.743-1(b)(2)(ii)].

Like kind property. Like kind property means property of the same class (stock in trade, property used in the trade or business, capital assets, and so forth) [Sec. 1.743-1(b)(2)(ii)].

>**Example 3:** X is a transferee partner in the XY partnership. The partnership owns, among other assets, A, a depreciable asset with a common basis to the partnership of $1,000 and a special basis adjustment to X of $200, and B, another depreciable asset with a common basis of $800 and a special basis adjustment to X of $300. X and Y agree that X will receive a distribution of A, and Y will receive a distribution of B, with all other property to remain in the partnership. As to Y, the partnership basis of property B is $800, the common partnership basis. Property B will, therefore, have a basis of $800 in Y's hands. As to X, however, the partnership basis of property A is $1,500, the common partnership basis of $1,000 plus X's special basis adjustment of $200 for property A, plus X's additional special basis adjustment of $300 for property B in which he hs relinquished his interest.

(c) Unused special basis adjustment. A transferee partner, in liquidation of his entire partnership interest, sometimes get property for which he has *no* special basis adjustment, in exchange for his interest in property for which he has a special basis ajdustment. If he does not use his entire adjustment in determining his basis for the distributed property under the rules above, the unused amount is used by the partnership to adjust its basis for its retained property [Sec. 1.734-2(b)(1)].

>**Example 4:** On the death of his father, partner B acquired by inheritance a $1/2$ interest in partnership ABC. Partners A and C each have a $1/4$ interest. The assets of the partnership consist of $100,000 in cash, and real estate worth $100,000 with a basis to the partnership of $10,000. Since the partnership elected, at the time of transfer, to adjust the basis of its property, partner B has a special basis adjustment of $45,000 for his undivided half interest in the real estate. The basis of B's partnership interest is $100,000, the basis his father had. B retires from the partnership and receives $100,000 in cash in exchange for his entire interest. Since B received no part of the real estate, his special basis adjustment of $45,000 will be allocated to the real estate, the remaining partnership property, and will increase its basis to the partnership to $55,000.

¶ 2932 Partnership's elective adjustment to basis of undistributed property. A distribution by a partnership to a partner may cause a basis problem if the partnership's basis for the distributed property differs from the partner's basis. Suppose, for example, that the partnership distributes property with a basis of $1,000 to a partner who must take the property at a basis of $600. In effect, there was an overall loss of $400 in basis. The optional adjustment discussed below prevents the loss.

The optional adjustment also reflects the distributee's gain or loss in the partnership's basis for its retained assets. Example 1, below, illustrates the reason for this. Because of the appreciation in value of its property, the partnership had a potential gain of $3,000 ($22,000 minus $19,000). After the distribution, the potential gain was really only $2,000, since the distributee had realized his share of the appreciation in the form of his $1,000 gain. The upward adjustment of partnership basis reflects this. After the adjustment, the spread between basis and value is only $2,000 ($22,000 minus $20,000).

(a) **Method of adjustment.** The adjustment is made only if the partnership election described in ¶ 2937 is in effect. The adjustment may increase or decrease the partnership's basis.

Increase in basis. The partnership increases its basis for the retained assets by (1) gain recognized to the distributee [¶ 2927], or (2) the excess of the partnership's basis for the distributed property immediately before the distribution over the distributee's basis for it [Sec. 734(b)(1); 1.734-1(b)(1)].

> **Example 1:** Ander's basis for his one-third partnership interest is $10,000. The partnership has assets consisting of cash $11,000 and property with a basis of $19,000 and a value of $22,000. Ander realizes a gain of $1,000 when he receives, in a liquidating distribution, a payment of $11,000 cash. If the partnership elects to adjust the basis of undistributed partnership property, the partnership basis for the property becomes $20,000 ($19,000 plus $1,000).

> **Example 2:** Boyle's basis for his one-third partnership interest is $10,000. The partnership has assets consisting of cash $4,000 and properties X and Y with bases of $11,000 and $15,000 and values of $11,000 and $18,000 respectively. Boyle receives property X in liquidation of his entire interest in the partnership. His basis for property X is $10,000 [¶ 2928(b)]. The excess of the partnership basis for X over Boyle's basis for X after the distribution is $1,000 ($11,000 − $10,000). If the partnership elects to adjust the basis of undistributed partnership property, the basis of property Y to the partnership becomes $16,000 ($15,000 plus $1,000).

Decrease in basis. In a liquidation of the partner's complete interest, the partnership decreases its basis for the retained assets by (1) loss recognized to the distributee [¶ 2927], or (2) the excess of the distributee's basis for the distributed property over the partnership's basis for it [Sec. 734(b)(2); 1.734-1(b)(2)].

> **Example 3:** Engle's basis for his one-third partnership interest is $11,000. The partnership has assets consisting of $10,000 cash and property with a basis of $23,000 and a value of $20,000. Engle receives $10,000 in cash in liquidation of his entire interest in the partnership. He sustains a loss of $1,000. If the partnership elects to adjust the basis of undistributed partnership property, the partnership basis for the property becomes $22,000 ($23,000 less $1,000).

> **Example 4:** Forest's basis for his one-third partnership interest is $11,000. The partnership has assets consisting of $5,000 cash, properties X and Y with bases of $10,000 and $18,000 and values of $10,000 and $15,000 respectively. In liquidation of his entire interest in the partnership, Forest receives property X with a basis of $10,000 to the partnership (but a basis of $11,000 to him [¶ 2928(b)]). If the partnership elects to adjust the basis of undistributed partnership property, the basis of Y becomes $17,000 ($18,000 less $1,000).

(b) **Allocation of basis.** The partnership must allocate any increase or decrease in basis among its property. Specific rules are provided for making the allocation [¶ 2938].

TRANSFER OF PARTNERSHIP INTEREST

The sale or exchange of a partnership interest usually results in capital gain or loss. But a special rule applies if the interest includes unrealized receivables or substantially appreciated inventory (defined in ¶ 2944(d)). Any gain or loss due to such property is ordinary gain or loss.

The price a transferee pays for his interest will, of course, reflect any increase or decrease in the value of partnership assets. The transferee thus gets a basis for his interest that differs from the transferor's. The partnership may, if it so elects, adjust (for the transferee's benefit only) the basis of its assets to reflect the transferee's acquisition cost. If it does, it must thereafter adjust its basis for all distributions and transfers unless the election is revoked.

¶ **2935 Gain or loss on transfer.** A partner who sells or exchanges his partnership interest has a recognized gain or loss measured by the difference between the amount realized and the adjusted basis of his partnership interest [Sec. 741; 1.741-1(a)].

The amount of any partnership liabilities allocable to the interest and transferred to the purchaser is considered part of the amount realized (¶ 2926(c)) [Sec. 1.752-1(d)].

Example 1: If Abbot sells his interest in the AB partnership for $750 cash and, at the same time, the buyer assumes his $250 share of partnership liabilities, the amount realized on the transaction is $1,000. This amount is then applied against the basis of his partnership interest to determine gain or loss.

The partnership may elect to adjust the basis of its property after the transfer to reflect the transferee's acquisition cost [¶ 2937].

Character of gain or loss. As a general rule, the partner has capital gain or loss, except to the extent the rules in (a) or (b) apply.

(a) How current earnings are treated. The partner's distributive share of current earnings is taxed to him whether or not he receives it[1] [¶ 2920]. The amount so taxed increases the basis of his partnership interest [¶ 2926], so the net gain on the sale of his interest does not include the current earnings. It is only this net gain that is taxed as capital gain.

Example 2: A partner sold his interest (basis $5,000) on June 30. His share of partnership income to date of sale was $15,000. The sale price was $20,000. The $15,000 is taxed to the partner and increases his basis for the interest to $20,000. No gain was realized on the sale since the selling price and his basis were the same.

(b) Transfers involving receivable or inventory. Any recognized gain or loss due to unrealized receivables or substantially appreciated inventory[2] is ordinary gain or loss (¶ 2944) [Sec. 751(a); 1.751-1].

The ordinary gain or loss is found by allocating a portion of the sales proceeds and a portion of the transferee's basis to the receivables and inventory [Sec. 1.741-1(a)].

The definitions of "unrealized receivables" and "inventory" are very broad. They include amounts received for foreign investment company stock; Sec. 1245 or 1250 property, farm recapture property [¶ 2226]; farm land [¶ 1845(e)]; mining property [¶ 1843]; certain oil and gas property, for tax years ending after 12-31-75 [¶ 2103(c)]; stock in certain foreign corporations, for exchanges starting after 10-9-75 and to exchanges and distributions taking place after that date [¶ 3728]; and stock in a DISC, as to dispositions after 12-31-75 in tax years ending after

Footnotes appear at end of this Chapter.

that date [¶ 3460] to the extent ordinary gain would result if the partnership sold the property at the time of transfer. The investment credit recapture rules also may apply (¶ 2410(e)) [Sec. 47(a); 1.47-6].

Background and purpose. A partnership interest is considered a capital asset, the sale or exchange of which gives rise to capital gain or loss. However, an exception for receivables and inventory was deemed necessary to prevent the conversion of ordinary income into capital gain. Since a sale or exchange by the partnership gives rise to ordinary income, a sale or exchange by the partner should have the same effect.

Example 3: C buys B's 50% interest in the AB partnership which keeps its books on a cash basis. At the time, the balance sheet of the firm shows:

Assets	Basis	Market value	Liabilities & Capital	Basis	Market value
Cash	$ 3,000	$ 3,000	Notes payable	$ 2,000	$ 2,000
Advances for clients	10,000	10,000	Capital:		
Other assets	7,000	7,000	A	9,000	15,000
Accounts receivable	0	12,000	B	9,000	15,000
	$20,000	$32,000		$20,000	$32,000

The cash price C paid for his partnership interest is $15,000, representing C's share in the net assets shown above, including $6,000 for B's interest in accounts receivable. B realizes $6,000 in ordinary income, attributable to his partnership interest in unrealized receivables.

➤OBSERVATION→ When a partner decides to withdraw from a partnership he may dispose of his entire interest by alternative methods, having different tax consequences to the partners. If the value of his interest exceeds its adjusted basis, he will probably want to follow the Sec. 741 transfer route to get capital gain treatment. On the other hand, the taxable distributive shares of the continuing partners may be reduced, or the firm may get a deduction, by liquidating the interest under Sec. 736 [¶ 2941]. Thus, the tax consequences become dollars and cents factors in negotiating the amount to be paid by the continuing partners or by the partnership. By clearly stating their intent in the agreements, the partners can increase their control over the tax consequences of the transaction and reduce the chance of later litigation over such consequences.

(c) Statement must be filed. A partner who sells or exchanges all or part of his interest when the partnership has any unrealized receivables or substantially appreciated inventory, must submit a prescribed statement with his income tax return for the year of sale or exchange [Sec. 1.751-1(a)(3)].

¶ 2936 Basis of transferee partner. The transferee finds his *original* basis for his interest by applying the basis rules for property in general (¶ 1500 et seq.) [Sec. 742; 1.742-1].

The transferee's *original* basis must be adjusted from time to time to prevent the unintended benefit or detriment that would otherwise result [¶ 2926].

¶ 2937 Partnership's elective adjustment to basis of partnership property. A partnership may elect to adjust the basis of its property for distributions and for transfers of partnership interests. If it makes the election, it must adjust its basis for all distributions *and* all transfers during the affected tax year and all later years, unless the election is revoked [Sec. 754; 1.754-1]. The adjustment for transfers affects only the transferee partner, but the adjustment after a distribution applies to all the partners [¶ 2931].

Adjustments for transfers. A transferee partner is one who acquired his interest by purchase or on the death of a partner. The optional adjustment discussed below reflects the transferee's acquisition cost [¶ 2936] in the partnership's basis for its assets. The adjustment benefits the transferee, especially if he paid more for his interest in appreciated assets than the partnership's basis for the assets. The transferee benefits from the higher basis used in computing his gain on partnership sales of the appreciated assets, or his deduction for depreciation or depletion. See Examples 2 and 3, below.

(a) Method of adjustment. This adjustment is made only if the partnership election described above is in force. The election must be filed with the partnership return for the tax year during which the transfer or distribution occurs. It has almost the same effect as the election the transferee may make under the rules in ¶ 2930. The adjustment may increase or decrease the partnership's basis for its assets, but the change is solely for the benefit of the transferee. The partnership's basis is not changed as to all the partners. Instead, the transferee gets a special basis adjustment. Thereafter, the transferee's special basis for any affected property is the partnership's basis for the property, plus or minus his own special basis adjustment [Sec. 1.743-1(b)]. See Example 1 below.

Increase in basis. The partnership increases the basis of its assets to the transferee by the excess of the transferee's basis for his interest over his proportionate share of adjusted basis of all partnership property.

Decrease in basis. The partnership decreases the basis of its assets to the transferee by the excess of his proportionate share of the basis of partnership property over the basis of his interest. The transferee's proportionate share is determined by his interest in partnership capital (plus his share of partnership liabilities), taking into account any partnership agreement on contributed capital [Sec. 743(b); 1.743-1(b)(2)]. See also (b) below.

Example 1: Partner A of the ABC partnership sells his interest to M for $22,000 when the firm's balance sheet is as follows:

Assets	Adjusted basis	Market value	Liabilities & Capital	Adjusted basis	Market value
Cash	$ 5,000	$ 5,000	Liabilities	$10,000	$10,000
Accounts receivable	10,000	10,000	Capital:		
Property X (inventory)	20,000	21,000	A	15,000	22,000
Property Y (capital asset)	20,000	40,000	B	15,000	22,000
			C	15,000	22,000
Total	$55,000	$76,000	Total	$55,000	$76,000

All partners share equally in profits, and the partnership has made the election to adjust the basis of partnership assets on the transfer of a partnership interest.

The amount of the adjustment is determined by comparing the transferee's basis for his interest in the partnership with his proportionate share of the adjusted basis of partnership properties. The basis of M's interest is $25,333, the cash paid for A's interest, $22,000, plus his proportionate share of partnership liabilities $3,333 ($10,000, the total partnership liabilities, divided by 3). M's proportionate share of the adjusted basis of the partnership property is $18,333, i.e., ⅓ of $45,000 ($55,000 less $10,000 liabilities) plus $3,333 (M's share of the liabilities). Thus, the amount to be added to the bases of the partnership properties, is $7,000 ($25,333 − $18,333). See also Ex. 1 of ¶ 2938 for basis allocation.

Footnotes appear at end of this Chapter.

¶ 2937

Allocation of basis. The allocation of basis among partnership properties is made by applying the rules in ¶ 2938.

(b) How partnership agreement affects special basis adjustments. In some cases, the partnership agreement may provide for a special allocation of depreciation, depletion, gain or loss on contributed property whose basis differed from its value at contribution [¶ 2910]. The agreement must be taken into account in determining the transferee's proportionate share of the partnership's basis for special basis adjustment ((a) above) [Sec. 743(b); 1.743-1(b)(2)(i)].

Example 2: (a) A and B form partnership AB to which A contributes property X, worth $1,000, with an adjusted basis to him of $400. B contributes $1,000 in cash. During the partnership's first tax year property X appreciates in value to $1,200, and A sells his half interest in the partnership to C for $1,100.

If there is no agreement for special allocation and the partnership has elected to adjust the basis, the adjusted basis of the partnership property to C will be increased by the excess of the transferee partner's basis for his partnership interest, $1,100, over his proportionate share of the adjusted basis of the partnership property, $700 ($400, the basis of property X, plus $1,000, the money, or a total partnership basis of $1,400, divided by 2). The amount of the adjustment is $400, applied as an increase in the basis of partnership property X as to C only. If X is sold for $1,400, the gain to the partnership is $1,000 ($1,400, less partnership basis of $400 for X). Each partner has gain of $500 on the sale. C has a special basis adjustment of $400 for X, thus reducing his gain to $100.

If C bought his interest from B (the partner contributing cash), C's adjustment would also be $400, figured the same way as for a purchase from A.

(b) If, in this example, the original partnership AB had a special agreement about property X, stating that on the sale of that property, any gain, to the extent of the precontribution appreciation, was to be allocated entirely to the contributing partner, A, then C's special basis would be different. Under the partnership agreement, A had, in effect, a basis of only $400 in the partnership assets (his basis for property X before its contribution to the partnership), and B had a basis of $1,000 (the full basis of his investment). C, who is A's successor, has a proportionate share in the adjusted basis of partnership property of only $400 (A's share of partnership basis). The amount of the increase to C in the adjusted basis of partnership property is $700 (the excess of $1,100, C's basis for his interest, over $400, C's share of partnership basis). This amount is an adjustment to the basis of partnership property as to C only. If X is sold by the partnership for $1,400, the gain is $1,000 ($1,400 received less the partnership basis of $400). Under the partnership agreement, $600 of this gain which is attributable to precontribution appreciation, is allocable to C as A's successor. The remaining $400 gain is not subject to the agreement, and is allocable to B and C equally, i.e., $200 each. However, C's recognized gain is only $100 (his $800 distributive share of the gain, reduced by $700, his special basis adjustment for X). B has a gain of $200, and is unaffected by the transfer of A's interest.

(c) Effect on depletion allowance. If an adjustment is made to the basis of depletable property, any depletion allowance is figured separately for each partner, including the transferee partner [Sec. 743(b); 1.743-1(b)(2)(iii)].

Example 3: A and B each contribute $5,000 to partnership AB, which buys property for $10,000. Shortly after that certain depletable minerals are discovered, and B sells his interest in the partnership to C for $100,000. The difference between B's and C's bases, $95,000, is allocated to the mineral property. A's share of basis with respect to the property remains $5,000. C's basis is $100,000: $5,000, his half of the common partnership basis, plus $95,000, his additional transferee basis. At the end of the partnership year, cost depletion as to A's ½ interest which has a basis of $5,000 is $500, and cost depletion as to C's ½ interest with a basis of $100,000 is $10,000. Under the percentage depletion method [¶ 2104], however A and B would each be entitled to $7,000 allowance. Percentage depletion is greater for A. He will therefore be allowed a deduction of $7,000. Cost depletion is greater for C, and he is allowed a deduction of $10,000.

ALLOCATION OF ELECTIVE PARTNERSHIP ADJUSTMENTS TO BASIS

¶ 2938 How to allocate adjustments to basis. Adjustments to the basis of partnership properties for distributions and transfers must be allocated among the partnership assets. The partnership may make the allocation under a general and special rule, or apply for permission to use some other method.

(a) **Allocation under general and special rule.** The allocation involves these steps [Sec. 755; 1.755-1(a)(1), (b)]:

(1) **Classification of assets.** The basis adjustment must be allocated to the kind of property involved in the distribution or transfer. For this purpose, there are 2 kinds of property: (a) capital assets or Sec. 1231 assets, and (b) other property. Thus, an adjustment for a distribution of capital assets or Sec. 1231 assets or for a transfer of an interest in such assets, is allocated only to capital assets or Sec. 1231 assets.

Where an adjustment is required because of the recognition of gain or loss on a distribution [¶ 2927] the adjustment is made only to capital assets or Sec. 1231 assets [Sec. 1.755-1(b)(1)(ii)].

If, on a distribution, the partnership owns no undistributed property of the kind it has to adjust, the adjustment is made when the partnership acquires such property.

(2) **Allocation within the class.** The idea is to reduce the difference between the value and basis of the assets within the class. Thus, a plus adjustment (one that increases basis) is allocated only to assets whose values exceed their bases in proportion to the difference between the value and basis for each. A minus adjustment is allocated only to assets whose bases exceed their values, again in proportion to the difference between the basis and value of each.

> **NOTE:** If good will is involved in the transaction, some of the basis adjustment also must be allocated to the good will [Sec. 1.755-1(a)(1)(iv)].

> **Example 1:** In Example 1 of ¶ 2937, the total appreciation is $21,000 ($1,000 on property X and $20,000 on property Y). The basis adjustment of $7,000 is, therefore, one third of the $21,000 appreciation. When the allocation rules are applied, $333 ($1/3$ of $1,000, the excess of the market value over the basis of property X) is allocated to property X and $6,666 ($1/3$ of $20,000, the excess of the market value over the basis of property Y) is allocated to property Y.

If, on a distribution, a decrease in basis of undistributed property is required, and the amount of the decrease is more than the basis of the required kind of property, the basis of such property is reduced to zero, and the balance of the decrease is applied when the right kind of property is acquired.

(b) **Optional allocation.** A partnership (or a partner who has made his own election, ¶ 2930) may apply for permission to use another method of allocation. The increase or decrease under the method used must also reduce the difference between the value and basis of the asset [Sec. 1.755-1(a)(2)].

(c) **Who is affected by adjustment.** The basis ajustment affects only the transferee. It takes the form of a special basis adjustment that only he can use. The basis of the partnership's property remains the same for the other partners [¶ 2937].

Example 2: Assume that the partnership in Example 1, ¶ 2937, sells the inventory, property X, for $24,000, after M buys his interest. Since the basis to the partnership is $20,000, there is $4,000 ordinary income to be allocated to each of the partners, $1,333 to each. The tax positions of B and C remain unchanged as a result of the transfer to M. Each therefore has $1,333 of income to report. M, on the other hand, has an additional basis of $333 for the inventory (see Example 1 above). This reduces his gain to $1,000.

SPECIAL PROBLEMS
RETIREMENT OR DEATH OF A PARTNER

Payments to a retiring partner or a deceased partner's successor, in liquidation of his entire interest, are allocated between (1) payments for the interest in partnership assets, and (2) other payments. The intent is to separate the payments into those that result in capital gain or loss, and those that result in ordinary income. However, the division is not precise and payments for certain assets are specially treated to prevent tax avoidance.

Payments for the interest in assets are treated as distributions and generally result in capital gain or loss. Other payments are taxed as ordinary income. If mixed payments are made in installments, each annual amount is allocated between payments for the interest in assets and other payments. Specific rules are provided for making the allocation.

If a fixed sum is payable in installments, the recipient may elect to report the gain or loss on each annual amount proportionately over the years of receipt.

¶ 2941 Payments to retiring partner or deceased partner's successor in interest. Payments to a withdrawing partner (that is, a retiring partner or a deceased partner's successor), in liquidation of his entire interest in the partnership, are allocated [¶ 2942] between (1) payments for his interest in partnership assets, and (2) other payments [Sec. 736(b); 1.736-1(a)(2)]. The term "payments" includes any assumption of the partner's liabilities that is treated as a distribution of money to the partner [¶ 2926(c)].

The rules below apply only to payments by the partnership. They do not apply to payments by the remaining partners or outsiders.

(a) Payments for interest in partnership assets. As a general rule, such payments are treated as distributions in exchange for the partner's interest in assets [Sec. 736(b)(1); 1.736-1(b)(1)]. But such assets do not include unrealized receivables, good will, or substantially appreciated inventory, *to the extent indicated* under "specially-treated assets" below. See Example 2 below.

The remaining partners get no deduction for payments treated as distributions. The payments reduce the withdrawing partner's basis for his interest and result in gain to the extent they exceed any remaining basis, or loss to the extent of any remaining basis after all payments are received. Assuming that only cash is received, the gain or loss is recognized immediately under the rules in ¶ 2927 [Sec. 731(a); 1.731-1(a)].

Special rules for reporting gain or loss on installment payments are in (c) below.

Example 1: The ABC partnership pays retired partner C $15,000 per year for 10 years for his interest in the partnership. The basis of C's interest is $90,000. Of the $150,000 which C will receive over the 10 years, $90,000 will go in reduction of his basis and the remaining $60,000 will be capital gain.

When payments are made for unrealized receivables [¶ 2944(d)], the value of the partner's interest in that property is reduced by the amount of the ordinary income potential in the property [Sec. 1.736-1].

Specially treated assets. Payments for certain assets are not subject to the above general rule and are not treated as distributions [Sec. 736(b); 1.736-1(b)].

Amounts paid for unrealized receivables *in excess of their partnership basis* are not payments for the withdrawing partner's interest in partnership assets. They are "other payments" subject to the rules in (b).

Amounts paid for good will in excess of its partnership basis are not treated as distributions unless the partnership agreement expressly[1] provides for *reasonable* payments for good will. If the agreement does *not* so provide, such amounts are "other payments" subject to the rules in (b).

Amounts paid for the partner's interest in *substantially appreciated inventory* are treated as proceeds from the sale or exchange of a noncapital asset under the rules in ¶ 2944.

Example 2: Assume that in Example 1 above, C's interest in partnership property included an interest worth $50,000 in substantially appreciated inventory. Assume also that $15,000 of C's basis of $90,000 is attributable to this inventory. Then of the $150,000 C will receive $90,000 goes in reduction of his basis, $35,000 ($50,000 − $15,000) is ordinary income, and $25,000 ($100,000 − $75,000) is capital gain.

(b) Other liquidating payments. Payments for unrealized receivables and good will, to the extent indicated in (a) above, and all other payments that are not made for the interest in partnership assets, are either distributive shares of income or guaranteed payments, depending on whether or not they are based on income.

Payments based on income. Payments measured by partnership income are distributive shares of partnership income regardless of the period over which they are paid [Sec. 736(a)(1); 1.736-1(a)(3)(i)]. They are taxable to the recipient as though he continued to be a partner and thus reduce the amount of the remaining partner's distributive shares [Sec. 1.736-1(a)(4), (6)].

Example 3: Each year AB partnership pays retired partner C 10% of partnership net income. Payments are taxed to C as if he still had a 10% distributive share of the partnership income, loss, deductions and credits.

Payments not based on income. If the payments are determined without regard to the partnership income and are not payments for an interest in partnership property [(a) above], they are guaranteed payments (salary) made to one not a partner. They are ordinary income to the recipient, and a deductible partnership expense [Sec. 736(a)(2); 1.736-1(a)(3)(ii), 1.736-1(a)(4)].

Example 4: If in Example 3 above, the payments were $100 per week rather than 10% of partnership net income, the payments received by C are ordinary income to him, and are deductible by the partnership as salary.

Amounts includable as "other payments" in the gross income of the successor in interest of a deceased partner are taxed to the successor the same way they would have been taxed to the decedent [Sec. 753; 1.753-1(a), (d)]. Payments to the successor determined without regard to partnership income are taxed to him as if he were a partner and the payments were salary or interest on capital, that is, as ordinary income. Payments determined with reference to partnership income, are taxed to the successor as if he were a partner receiving his distributive share of partnership income. The successor is allowed a deduction for any amounts that may have been included in the gross estate of the decedent [¶ 3008], but is not allowed an optional adjustment [¶ 2937] to the basis of a deceased partner's share of receivables existing at the partner's death.[2]

(c) Reporting gain or loss on installment payments for interest in assets.- Gain on such installments is not recognized until capital is recovered, unless the election below applies.

Footnotes appear at end of this Chapter.

¶ 2941

Partner's election. If the amount paid for the interest is a fixed sum payable in installments, the withdrawing partner may elect to report any gain or loss proportionately over the years of receipt. The gain or loss for each year is the difference between (1) the amount treated as a distribution in that year, and (2) the portion of the partner's basis for his partnership interest attributable to such distribution [Sec. 1.736-1(b)(6)].

Example 5: ABC is a personal service partnership. When partner A retires, the partnership's balance sheet is as follows:

Assets	Basis	Value	Liabilities & Capital	Basis	Value
Cash	$13,000	$13,000	Liabilities	$ 3,000	$ 3,000
Capital assets	$20,000	$23,000	Capital:		
	$33,000	$36,000	A	$10,000	$11,000
			B	$10,000	$11,000
			C	$10,000	$11,000
				$33,000	$36,000

It is agreed that A's capital interest is valued at $12,000 (⅓ of $36,000) and that A will receive $5,000 a year for 3 years after his retirement. The first $5,000, however, will include A's share of the liabilities ($1,000) assumed by B and C.

Tax treatment of A: The basis of A's interest is $11,000 ($10,000 investment plus $1,000, his share of liabilities). Of the $15,000 A is to receive, only $12,000 is in payment of his interest in partnership property. The remainder is ordinary income. Thus A will have $1,000 capital gain ($12,000 minus $11,000), and $3,000 ordinary income. A may report the $1,000 gain at the time he receives his last payment, or he may elect to allocate the gain over the 3 years. If he elects to allocate, he may report $333 capital gain and $1,000 ordinary income each year (⅓ of the total amounts of capital gain and ordinary income, respectively). The remainder of the payment is a return of capital.

Tax treatment of remaining partners: The partnership cannot deduct A's $1,000 capital gain since the amount represents a purchase of A's capital interest by the partnership. The partnership may deduct A's $3,000 ordinary income.

Example 6: Assume the same facts as in Example 5 except that the agreement provides for payments to A for three years of a percentage of annual income instead of a fixed amount. In this case, all payments received by A up to $12,000 are treated as payments for A's interest in partnership property. His gain of $1,000 is taxed only after he has received his full basis. Any payment in excess of $12,000 is treated as a distributive share of partnership income to A.

¶ **2942 How installment payments are allocated.** Amounts paid in liquidation of the partner's interest are often paid in installments over several years. The methods of dividing these payments between those made for the partner's interest in assets and "other payments" are as follows:

(a) Fixed payments. If a fixed amount is payable over a fixed number of years (whether or not supplemented by additional amounts), a proportionate part of each year's fixed agreed payments is treated as a payment for the partner's interests in assets. The proportionate part is in the ratio of the total fixed agreed payments for the interest in assets to the total fixed agreed payments for the partner's interest in assets and for other items (guaranteed payments and distributive share of income). The balance of the annual payments is treated as "other payments." If the amount the partner receives in a given year is less than the amount treated as payable for his interest in assets in that year, the deficiency is carried over and is added to the amount paid for his interest in the following year or years [Sec. 1.736-1(b)(5)(i)].

Example: Retiring partner Marks who is entitled, for 10 years, to an annual payment of $6,000 for his interest in partnership property, receives only $3,500 in 1976. In 1977, he receives $10,000. Of this amount, $8,500 ($6,000 plus $2,500 from 1976) is treated as a distribution [¶ 2941(a)], $1,500 as a payment governed by the rules in ¶ 2941(b).

(b) When amount varies. If the payments are not fixed in amount, they are treated as payments for the partner's interest in assets until he receives the full value of that interest. After that, all payments are treated as "other payments" [Sec. 1.736-1(b)(5)(ii)].

(c) Allocation by agreement. The withdrawing partner and all the remaining partners may agree on any other method that does not allocate to the partner's interest in assets an amount in excess of its value at death or retirement [Sec. 1.736-1(b)(5)(iii)].

DISTRIBUTIONS OF UNREALIZED RECEIVABLES OR SUBSTANTIALLY APPRECIATED INVENTORY

Distributions have been used in the past to avoid tax by shifting assets among the partners. Suppose, for example, that a partnership distributes ordinary income assets to a partner whose losses will offset his gain on a later sale. The partnership also distributes capital assets to another partner. To the extent a transaction of this kind is really an exchange of assets between the partners, it is now taxed as such under the rules below, if it involves unrealized receivables or substantially appreciated inventory. If the distribution is not a sale or exchange, a later disposition of such distributed property will result in ordinary gain or loss.

¶ **2944 Distributions treated as sales or exchanges.** When a partner receives a distribution from a partnership that owns Sec. 751 assets, he must determine whether the distribution is, in effect, a sale or exchange. If it is, it may result in ordinary income to the partner or the partnership.

As used here, "Sec. 751 assets" means unrealized receivables or substantially appreciated inventory (defined in (d) below). "Other property" means all partnership property, including money, except "Sec. 751 assets."

(a) Excluded transactions. There are two exceptions to the general rule that treats certain distributions as sales or exchanges.

• A distribution to a partner of property he contributed is either a reduction or liquidation of his interest [¶ 2927] or a payment to a retiring partner or deceased partner's successor [¶ 2941].

• A payment for unrealized receivables to a retiring partner or deceased partner's successor *in excess of his partnership basis*, is either a distributive share of partnership income or a guaranteed payment (¶ 2941) [Sec. 751(b)(2)(A), (B); 1.751-1(b)(4)(i), (ii)]. However, payments to such a partner which are considered as made in exchange for an interest in partnership property as explained in ¶ 2941(a), are subject to the general rule.

(b) When is distribution a sale or exchange. Briefly, a distribution is a sale or exchange to the extent that (1) the distributee partner receives more than his share of property other than Sec. 751 assets in exchange for some or all of his interest in Sec. 751 assets, or (2) he receives more than his share of Sec. 751 assets in exchange for some or all of his interest in property other than Sec. 751 assets [Sec. 751(b); 1.751-1(b)].

Before a partner can tell whether he comes under the above rule, he must know (1) whether the distribution exceeded his proportionate share of the distributed property, and (2) if there was an excess, what property he gave up in return.

Assuming there was a sale or exchange, the partner must then determine its tax consequences. See (c) below.

(1) Was there an excess distribution? The rules in this area do not apply to the extent that the partner receives only his share of Sec. 751 assets or his share of other property. But in figuring his share for this purpose, the regulations require that he take into account any interest he still has in the partnership after the distribution. The regulations give as an example a partnership whose Sec. 751 assets are valued at $100,000. A partner with a 30% interest (worth $30,000) receives a distribution of $20,000 of these assets, and continues to have a 30% interest in the $80,000 of such assets remaining in the partnership after the distribution. Only $6,000 ($30,000 less 30% of $80,000) represents his share of the Sec. 751 assets. The balance ($14,000) is an excess distribution [Sec. 1.751-1(b)(1)(ii)].

Distributions are sometimes made in partial liquidation of a partner's capital and profits interest. In these cases, the distribution of a particular asset is not an excess distribution as to that asset to the extent it merely reflects the reduction of the partner's interest in it [Sec. 1.751-1(g), Example 5].

A partner who received a distribution in complete liquidation of his interest would, of course, have no interest left after the distribution. Here, the distribution of each type of asset is an excess distribution only to the extent its value exceeds the partner's proportionate share. See Examples 1 and 2 below.

(2) What property did the partner give up? The partner must determine what property he gave up for the excess distribution. The rules in this area do not apply unless he receives a distribution of Sec. 751 assets in exchange for an interest in other property, or a distribution of other property in exchange for an interest in Sec. 751 assets.

The partners may identify the property for which the excess distribution is made. See Example 3 below. Otherwise, the partner is presumed to have sold or exchanged a proportionate amount of each property in which he relinquished an interest [Sec. 1.751-1(g), Example 5].

(c) Tax consequences of distribution. The rules for the portion of the distribution treated as a sale or exchange are summarized in (1) and (2) below. The balance of the distribution is subject to the rules for distributions in general [¶ 2927 et seq.; 2941; 2945]. The exchange and distribution elements are treated separately [Sec. 1.751-1(b)]. See Example 2 below.

(1) Other property distributed in exchange for Sec. 751 assets. Such distributions, to the extent treated as sales or exchanges under the rules in (a) and (b) above, are considered sales or exchanges between the partner and the partnership (as constituted after the distribution) [Sec. 751(b); 1.751-1(b)].

Tax consequences to partner. The partner has ordinary gain or loss on the sale or exchange of the Sec. 751 assets he gave up in the exchange. His gain or loss is the difference between (1) his basis for the Sec. 751 assets treated as sold or exchanged, and (2) the fair market value of the other property he received in exchange [Sec. 1.751-1(b)(3)].

The partner's basis for the Sec. 751 assets treated as sold or exchanged is the basis they would have if distributed to him just before the actual distribution [Sec. 1.751-1(b)(3)].

Tax consequences to partnership. The partnership has gain or loss on the sale or exchange of the distributed property other than Sec. 751 assets. Its gain or loss is the difference between (1) its basis for the distributed property treated as sold or exchanged, and (2) the fair market value of the partner's interest in the Sec. 751 assets he gave up in exchange. The character of the partnership's gain or loss depends on the kind of property it sold or exchanged [Sec. 1.751-(b)(3)].

Example 1: The balance sheet of the DEF partnership is as follows:

Assets	Basis	Market Value	Capital	Per books	Market Value
Cash	$ 60,000	$ 60,000	Dayton	$ 35,000	$ 60,000
Unrealized receivables	0	60,000	Edwards	35,000	60,000
Land & building	45,000	60,000	Fitter	35,000	60,000
	$105,000	$180,000		$105,000	$180,000

The partnership distributed to Dayton the land and building it had owned for 15 years in complete liquidation of his partnership interest. Dayton is treated as if he sold his share of the unrealized receivables for $20,000. He is taxed on $20,000 ordinary income as follows:

Fair market value of the assets (land & building) received in exchange for Sec. 751 property (unrealized receivables)	$20,000
Basis allocable to partner's relinquished interest in Sec. 751 property	0
Difference (treated as ordinary income)	$20,000

The following schedule may be set up to analyze the transaction:

	Dayton's interest (market value)	Value of assets received	Dayton's interest (basis)
Sec. 751 property:			
Unrealized receivables	$20,000	0	0
Other property:			
Cash	20,000	0	$20,000
Land & building	20,000	$60,000	15,000
	$60,000	$60,000	$35,000

Dayton's interest (at market value) in the unrealized receivables, cash, and land & building amounted to $20,000 each, or a total of $60,000. Instead of receiving his interest in each of these assets in the form of the assets themselves, at $20,000 each (total $60,000), he received his total $60,000 in land & building. Thus, $20,000 of the land & building was in exchange for his $20,000 interest in the land & building to which he was entitled; another $20,000 share of the land & building was in exchange for his $20,000 interest in the cash; the other $20,000 was in exchange for his interest in the unrealized receivables.

Example 2: The 3-man wholesale sales partnership, ABC, which keeps its books on the accrual basis, agreed to liquidate the interest of C by a distribution to him. At that time the firm's balance sheet was as follows:

Assets	Basis	Market Value	Liabilities & Capital	Per books	Market Value
Cash	$15,000	$ 15,000	Current liabilities	$15,000	$ 15,000
Accounts receivable	9,000	9,000	Mortgage	21,000	21,000
Inventory	21,000	30,000	Capital, A	20,000	25,000
Buildings	42,000	48,000	Capital, B	20,000	25,000
Land	9,000	9,000	Capital, C	20,000	25,000
	$96,000	$111,000		$96,000	$111,000

Footnotes appear at end of this Chapter.

¶ 2944

The partnership distributed to C $10,000 cash and a 20 year-old building worth $15,000 with a basis to the partnership of $15,000. C will rent the land. C is treated as if he sold his share of Sec. 751 assets (with a $10,000 basis) for $13,000. Thus, on the sale, he is taxed on the $3,000 ordinary income. The transaction is analyzed in the following schedules:

	C's interest (market value)		Value of assets received		C's interest (basis)
Sec. 751 property					
Accounts receivable	$ 3,000		0	$ 3,000	
Inventory	10,000		0	7,000	
		$13,000			$10,000
Other property					
Cash	$ 5,000		$22,000*	$ 5,000	
Buildings	16,000		15,000	14,000	
Land	3,000	24,000	0	3,000	22,000
Total		$37,000	$37,000		$32,000

Value of assets received in exchange for Sec. 751 property $13,000**
Basis of relinquished interest in Sec. 751 property 10,000
Difference (ordinary income) .... $ 3,000

---

* $10,000 cash plus $12,000 liabilities assumed.
** The $13,000 value of assets received in exchange for Sec. 751 property is arrived at as follows: The market value of C's interest in "other property" was $24,000. But he received $37,000 worth of "other property," which is $13,000 more than his share ($37,000 less $24,000, or $13,000). This additional $13,000 was in exchange for the $13,000 market value of the Sec. 751 property which he relinquished.

Sec. 751 property (see definitions in (d) below) is figured as follows:

Accounts receivable. Since the partnership is on the accrual basis, the receivables are not unrealized receivables. However, receivables are considered inventory items for the purpose of Sec. 751. As the inventory items are substantially appreciated (as shown below), the receivables are included in Sec. 751 property as part of the substantially appreciated inventory items.

Substantially appreciated inventory items.

	Adjusted basis	Market value
Accounts receivable	$ 9,000	$ 9,000
Inventory	21,000	30,000
Total inventory items	$30,000	$39,000

The fair market value of the inventory items ($39,000) exceeds 120% of the basis ($30,000). (120% of $30,000 is $36,000.)
The value also exceeds 10% of the fair market value of all the partnership property other than money (10% of $96,000 is $9,600).
The aggregate of inventory items meets the 120% and 10% tests. They are substantially appreciated, and are considered Sec. 751 property.

Sec. 751 sale. Since the entire payment was made in liquidation of C's interest in partnership property, no part of it is considered as a guaranteed payment or a distributive share. In the distribution, C received his share of cash ($5,000) and a $15,000 building ($1,000 less than his $16,000 share). In addition, he received other partnership property ($5,000 cash and $12,000 in liabilities assumed by the partners) in exchange for his interest in accounts receivable ($3,000), inventory ($10,000), land ($3,000), and the balance of his interest in buildings ($1,000). Only the accounts receivable and inventory are Section 751 property. Hence $13,000 of the amount C received is considered as received for Sec. 751 property. Since his basis for Sec. 751 property is $10,000 ($7,000 for inventory and $3,000 for accounts receivable), C realizes $3,000 of ordinary income on the sale of his share of Sec. 751 property.

The part of the distribution not under Sec. 751. Before the distribution, C's basis for his partnership interest was $32,000 ($20,000 plus $12,000, his share of partnership liabilities). Taking away the $10,000 allocable to Sec. 751 property items (see above), he has a basis of $22,000 for the rest of his interest. The total distribution to C was $37,000 ($22,000 in cash and liabilities assumed by the partnership, and a $15,000 building). Since C received no more than his share of buildings, none of that property constitutes the proceeds of a sale. He did, however, receive more than his share of money. Hence, the sales proceeds must consist of money and must be deducted from the money distribution. Consequently, in liquidating the balance of his interest, C receives the building and $9,000 in money ($22,000 less $13,000). Therefore C had no gain or loss on this part of the distribution. His basis for the building is $13,000 (the remaining basis of his partnership interest, $22,000, less $9,000 of money received).

(2) Sec. 751 assets distributed in exchange for other property. Such distributions, to the extent treated as sales or exchanges under the rules in (a) and (b) above, are considered sales or exchanges between the partner and the partnership (as constituted after the distribution) [Sec. 751(b)(1); 1.751-1(b)(2)].

Tax consequences to partner. The partner has gain or loss on the sale or exchange of the other property he gave up in the exchange. His gain or loss is the difference between (1) his basis for the other property treated as sold or exchanged, and (2) the fair market value of the Sec. 751 assets he received in exchange [Sec. 1.751-1(b)(2)].

The partner's basis for the other property treated as sold or exchanged, is the basis it would have if distributed to him just before the actual distribution [Sec. 1.751-1(b)(2)].

The character of the partner's gain or loss depends on the kind of property he gave up [Sec. 1.751-1(b)(2)].

Tax consequences to partnership. The partnership has ordinary gain or loss on the sale or exchange of the distributed Sec. 751 assets. Its gain or loss is the difference between (1) its basis for the Sec. 751 assets treated as sold or exchanged, and (2) the fair market value of the partner's interest in the other property he gave up in exchange [Sec. 1.751-1(b)(2)].

Example 3: Partner C, who has no special basis adjustment, receives a depreciated machine in liquidation of his $1/3$ interest in the ABC partnership. The machine has a recomputed basis [¶ 1619] of $18,000 and the partnership books show at the time:

Assets	Adjusted basis	Market value	Liabilities and Capital	Per books	Market value
Cash	$ 3,000	$ 3,000	Liabilities	$ 0	$ 0
Machine (Sec. 1245 prop.)	9,000	15,000	Capital: A	10,000	15,000
			B	10,000	15,000
Land	18,000	27,000	C	10,000	15,000
Total	$30,000	$45,000		$30,000	$45,000

The partnership has Sec. 751 property of $6,000 [see (d) below], since the Sec. 1245 ordinary income potential for the machine is $6,000 ($15,000 fair market value less $9,000 adjusted basis). In the distribution, C got his share of Sec. 751 property ($1/3 \times $6,000) of $2,000 and Sec. 1231 property with a fair market value of $3,000 [$1/3 \times ($15,000 - $6,000)] and adjusted basis of $3,000 ($1/3 \times $9,000). He also received $4,000 of Sec. 1245 ordinary income property ($6,000 potential less $2,000 share above) and Sec. 1231 property with a fair market value and adjusted basis of $6,000 ($9,000 - $3,000 above). C gave up his $1,000 interest in cash and $9,000 interest in land.

Footnotes appear at end of this Chapter.

¶ **2944**

The partners agree the $4,000 of Sec. 751 property (Sec. 1245 potential) in excess of C's share, was in exchange for $4,000 of his land interest. C is treated as receiving 4/9 of his interest in land in a current distribution with a basis of $2,667 (18,000/27,000 × $4,000) and selling it to the partnership for $4,000 at a $1,333 gain. The basis of his remaining partnership interest is then $7,333 ($10,000 less $2,667 land distribution). Of the $15,000 total distribution to C, $11,000 ($2,000 ordinary income potential plus $9,000 Sec. 1231 property) is *not* subject to the special rules of Sec. 751 (above), but is treated as a distribution explained in ¶ 2928. C's basis for his share of Sec. 1245 potential is zero. His basis for the remaining property is $7,333 ($7,333, remaining basis for his partnership interest, reduced by zero, his Sec. 1245 potential). Thus, C's basis for the machine received from the partnership is $11,333 ($7,333 + $4,000) and his recomputed basis $13,333 ($11,333 plus $2,000 share of Sec. 1245 potential).

The partnership of A and B has an ordinary gain of $4,000 on the exchange of C's 4/9 interest in land for $4,000 of Sec. 1245 income potential (basis zero). The partnership basis for the land becomes $19,333 ($18,000, less $2,667 treated as distributed to C, plus $4,000 paid for that share).

(d) Definitions. Pertinent terms used in this area are defined below [Sec. 751(c), (d); 1.751-1(c), (d)].

Unrealized receivables. Unrealized receivables include the following amounts to the extent not previously includable in income under the partnership's method of accounting [Sec. 751(c); 1.751-1(c)]:

• Amount due for goods delivered or to be delivered, to the extent they are payments for noncapital assets.

• Amounts due under existing contracts for past or future services. Uncompleted service contracts are included.[1]

Unrealized receivables also include the potential ordinary gain in the following types of property: Sec. 1245 or 1250 property [¶ 1619]; farm recapture property [¶ 2226]; farm land [¶ 1845(e)]; mining property [¶ 1843]; certain oil and gas property, for tax years ending after 12-31-75 [¶ 2103(c)]; stock in certain foreign corporations, as to exchanges starting after 10-9-75 and to exchanges and distributions taking place after that date [¶ 3728]; and stock in a DISC, as to dispositions after 12-31-75 in tax years ending after such date [¶ 3460]. For transactions after 1976 in tax years ending after 1976, unrealized receivables also include the ordinary income potential from a franchise, trademark or trade name. The gain is measured as if the partnership sold the property at fair market value at distributions [Sec. 751(c)(2)].

A partner's Sec. 1245 or 1250 income is specially computed if he has a special basis adjustment (¶ 2909; 2937) [Sec. 1.751-1(c)(6)].

What is inventory? The term "inventory" is not limited to stock in trade, goods held for sale, or other items generally considered inventory. The term includes all assets of the partnership except capital assets and Sec. 1231 assets. The term also includes any other partnership property that would qualify under the above rules if held by the selling or distributee partner.

Some examples of inventory items are: accounts receivable or any unrealized receivable acquired for services or stock in trade, copyrights, literary, musical or artistic compositions [Sec. 751(d)(2); 1.751-1], and foreign investment company stock (or stock substituted for it) if gain on its sale would constitute ordinary gain.

What is substantial appreciation? Inventory items are substantially appreciated if their value is more than (1) 120% of their basis to the partnership *and* (2) 10% of the value of all partnership property other than money [Sec. 751(d)(1); 1.751-1(d)(1)]. See Example 2 above.

"Substantially appreciated inventory items" refers to the aggregate of all partnership inventory and not to specific items or groups of items. If the whole inventory has substantially appreciated in value, Sec. 751 will apply even if specific items distributed have not appreciated in value [Sec. 1.761-1(d)(1)]. See Example 2 above.

¶ 2945　Transfer of distributed property. As a general rule, no gain or loss is recognized on a distribution of property other than money until the property is disposed of. The character of the gain or loss as capital or ordinary depends on the character of the property to the partner when he disposes of it. Exceptions to the general rule are discussed in (a)-(c), below.

Holding period. The partner includes the partnership's holding period in figuring his own, except as noted in (c). If he contributed the property, his original holding period is also included [Sec. 735(b); 1.735-1(b)].

> **Example 1:** On 7-15-77, the partnership distributed to Archer his proportionate share of vacant land it had acquired on 6-1-75. When Archer sold this on 7-20-77, he realized a long-term capital gain.

The above rule does not apply to a surviving partner in a 2-man partnership who buys the decedent's interest. The survivor's holding period runs from the date of purchase.[1]

(a)　Recapture property. When a partner disposes of depreciable property distributed to him, all or part of the depreciation deducted by the partnership may be recaptured as ordinary income to the distributee partner.

Sec. 1245 property. For Sec. 1245 property [¶ 1619] the amount is determined as usual, except that the recomputed basis for the property is the partner's adjusted basis for the property plus (1) depreciation he deducted after distribution, and (2) the Sec. 1245 ordinary gain the partnership would have had if it had sold the property at fair market value when it was distributed. If the partner got the property in a disproportionate distribution involving Sec. 751 property [¶ 2944], the recomputed basis above is reduced by the amount of Sec. 1245 ordinary gain taxed in that distribution [Sec. 1245(b)(6); 1.1245-4(f)].

> **Example 2:** All the assets of ABC partnership are Sec. 1245 properties. A's basis for his partnership interest is $75,000. In complete liquidation of his interest, A receives one asset worth $100,000. The partnership's adjusted basis for the property is $85,000 and the recomputed basis is $110,000. A's basis for the property is $75,000 (basis of partnership interest allocated to the property). He does not depreciate the property, and later sells it for $103,000. A has a Sec. 1245 ordinary gain of $15,000 on the sale. The partnership Sec. 1245 gain on a sale before distribution would have been $15,000 ($100,000 FMV less $85,000 partnership adjusted basis). A's recomputed basis is $90,000 ($75,000 adjusted basis plus $15,000 partnership "as-if" ordinary gain).

Sec. 1250 property. For Sec. 1250 property [¶ 1619], the distributee partner's additional depreciation when he disposes of the property includes (1) additional depreciation he deducted and (2) additional depreciation for the partnership deductions. The partnership amount is the ordinary gain the partnership would have had to report if, at the time of distribution, it had sold the property at fair market value and the applicable percentage was 100%. This is reduced by any Sec. 1250 ordinary gain (again using 100%) recognized in a disproportionate distribution [¶ 2944]. The distributee partner includes the partnership holding period to determine the percentage he applies to find his ordinary gain [Sec. 1250(d), (e); 1.1250-3(f)].

> **NOTE:** Exploration expenses related to the distributed property also may be recaptured as ordinary gain on a sale by the partner [¶ 1843]. Ordinary gain realized in a dis-

proportionate distribution [¶ 2944] reduces the recapturable amount for both the partner and the partnership [Sec. 617(g)].

Losses recaptured for farm property [¶ 2226] and certain farm expenses recaptured for farm land [¶ 1845(e)] may also result in ordinary income when the partner disposes of such property.

(b) Unrealized receivables. A partner has odinary gain or loss when he disposes of unrealized receivables distributed *to him* by the partnership [Sec. 735(a)(1); 1.735-1(a)(1)].

NOTE: The distribution itself may give rise to ordinary gain or loss if treated as a sale or exchange under the rules in ¶ 2944.

Example 3: On 3-10-77, the partnership distributes to Bowen his proportionate share of unrealized receivables. The partnership's basis in this property, which Bowen acquired as his basis, was $1,000. If, on 11-10-77, Bowen sells these receivables for $1,500, he will realize $500 ordinary income.

For purposes of the above rule, "unrealized receivables" does not include the potential ordinary gains in the type of property listed in ¶ 2944(d) such as Sec. 1245 or 1250 property. Such potential gains are taxed as indicated in (a) above.

(c) Inventory items. A partner has ordinary gain or loss if he disposes of *any* inventory items within 5 years from the distribution date. Otherwise, the character of the gain or loss depends on the character of the items to the partner when sold or exchanged [Sec. 735(a)(2); 1.735-1(a)(2)]. In computing the 5-year period, the partnership's holding period is not included.

NOTE: The distribution itself may give rise to ordinary gain or loss if treated as a sale or exchange under the rules in ¶ 2944.

Example 4: On 2-10-75, the partnership distributed to Corwin his proportionate share of partnership inventory items. The partnership's basis in this property, which Corwin acquired as his basis, is $3,000. If Corwin sells the inventory items on 4-10-77 for $4,000, he will realize ordinary income of $1,000.

Example 5: If Corwin, in Example 4 above, disposes of the distributed inventory on 4-10-80, he will realize capital gain if the property is a capital asset in his hands.

Footnotes to Chapter 19

(P-H "FEDERAL TAXES" related references are cited in brackets [ ]at the end of each footnote below.)

Footnote ¶ 2900 [¶ 28,871; 33,325; 41,702 et seq.].
(1) Comm. v. Tower, 327 US 280, 34 AFTR 799 [¶ 28,576].
(2) Rev. Rul. 65-118, 1965-1 CB 30; Rev. Rul. 68-344, 1968-1 569 [¶ 28,878(17); 41,722(10)].

Footnote ¶ 2903 [¶ 28,871].
(1) Alexander Trust Property, 12 BTA 1226 [¶ 41,620].

Footnote ¶ 2904 [¶ 28,571 et seq.; 28,593].
(1) Comm. v. Tower, 327 US 280, 34 AFTR 799; Lusthaus v. Comm., 327 US 293, 34 AFTR 806; Comm. v. Culbertson, 337 US 733, 37 AFTR 1391 [¶ 28,576; 28,593].

Footnote ¶ 2905 [¶ 28,588].

Footnote ¶ 2906 [¶ 28,526].
(1) Rev. Rul. 71-278, 1971-2 CB 75 [¶ 28,535(15)].

Footnote ¶ 2906 continued
(2) Mihran Demirjian, 29 AFTR 2d 72-741, 457 F.2d [¶ 72-460].

Footnote ¶ 2907 [¶ 28,526].

Footnote ¶ 2908 [¶ 6125; 28,551].
(1) Truman v. U.S., 4 F. Supp. 447, 12 AFTR 1415 [¶ 28,556(20)].
(2) Rev. Rul. 66-93, Rev. Rul. 66-94, 1966-1 CB 165, 166 [¶ 28,560(5); 28,606(20)].
(3) Rev. Rul. 74-231, 1974-1 CB 240 [¶ 28,517(5)].

Footnote ¶ 2909 [¶ 28,556 et seq.].

Footnote ¶ 2910 [¶ 28,557].

Footnote ¶ 2911 [¶ 28,511].
(1) Rev. Rul. 68-79, 1968-1 CB 310 [¶ 28,517(15)].

Footnote ¶ 2913 [¶ 28,511; 28,514].
(1) Rev. Rul. 67-158, 1967-1 CB 294 [¶ 30,639(10)].

Footnote ¶ 2914 [¶ 28,511; 28,526].

Footnote ¶ 2915 [¶ 28,511].
(1) The Revenue Service booklet, "Cumulative List of Organizations—Contributions to Which are Deductible," may be obtained from the Superintendent of Documents, Government Printing Office, Washington D.C. 20402.

Footnote ¶ 2916 [¶ 28,511; 28,517(15)].

Footnote ¶ 2917 [¶ 28,511; 30,487(40)].

Footnote ¶ 2918 [¶ 28,551 et seq.].
(1) Treas. Dept. booklet "Tax Guide for Small Business" (1977 Ed.), p. 163.

Footnote ¶ 2920 [¶ 28,616 et seq.].

Footnote ¶ 2921 [¶ 28,616 et seq.].
(1) Rev. Rul. 60-182, 1960-1 CB 264 [¶ 28,621(15)].
(2) Rev. Rul. 60-268, 1960-2 CB 206 [¶ 28,621(20)].

Footnote ¶ 2922 [¶ 28,616 et seq.; 28,646 et seq.].

Footnote ¶ 2923 [¶ 28,631 et seq.].
(1) Armstrong v. Phinney, 21 AFTR 2d 1260, 394 F.2d 661 [¶ 28,636(55)].
(2) U. S. v. Basye, 31 AFTR 2d 73-802 [¶ 28,517(10)].

Footnote ¶ 2924 [¶ 16,825 et seq.; 28,631].

Footnote ¶ 2925 [¶ 28,661 et seq.; 28,816 et seq.].
(1) Rev. Rul. 72, 1953-1 CB 23 [¶ 28,676(5)].

Footnote ¶ 2926 [¶ 28,601 et seq.; 28,816 et seq.].

Footnote ¶ 2927 [¶ 28,724; 28,816].

Footnote ¶ 2927 continued
(1) Rev. Rul. 66-94, 1966-1 CB 166 [¶ 28,606(20)].
(2) Rev. Rul. 73-300, 1973-2 CB 215 [¶ 28,807(10)].

Footnote ¶ 2928 [¶ 28,726].

Footnote ¶ 2929 [¶ 28,726].

Footnote ¶ 2930 [¶ 28,601; 28,726].

Footnote ¶ 2931 [¶ 28,696 et seq.; 28,726; 28,730].

Footnote ¶ 2932 [¶ 28,696 et seq.; 28,730; 28,761].

Footnote ¶ 2935 [¶ 28,761].
(1) Sherlock v. Commissioner, 8 AFTR 2d 5530, 294 F.2d 863 [¶ 28,774(45)].
(2) C. F. Phillips, 40 TC 157 [¶ 28,774(5)].

Footnote ¶ 2936 [¶ 28,761].

Footnote ¶ 2937 [¶ 28,696 et seq.; 28,730; 28,761 et seq.].

Footnote ¶ 2938 [¶ 28,696 et seq.; 28,730; 28,761].

Footnote ¶ 2941 [¶ 28,746].
(1) Comm. v. Jackson Investment Co., 15 AFTR 2d 1125, 346 F.2d 187; V. Zay Smith, 37 TC 1033 [¶ 28,750(20)].
(2) Rev. Rul. 66-325, 1966-2 CB 249 [¶ 28,750(25)].

Footnote ¶ 2942 [¶ 28,746].

Footnote ¶ 2944 [¶ 28,724; 28,801].
(1) John W. Wolcott, 39 TC 538; U.S. v. Woolsey, 13 AFTR 2d 311, 326 F.2d 287 [¶ 28,807(15)].

Footnote ¶ 2945 [¶ 28,696 et seq.].
(1) Rev. Rul. 67-65, 1967-1 CB 168 [¶ 28,732(10)].

Highlights of Chapter 19
Partnerships

I. **What Is Partnership**
   A. **Tax definition [¶ 2900]:**
      1. Association of 2 or more persons to carry on business.
      2. Share profits and losses, with each contributing cash, property, labor or skill.
      3. Certain groups such as investment clubs may elect to avoid partnership treatment [¶ 2900].
   B. **How group enterprises are classified [¶ 2903]:**
      1. Federal, not state, law sets classification standards; classification depends on enterprise's characteristics.
      2. How tenants in common are treated:
         a. Partnership—if carrying on business and sharing profit.
         b. Not partnership—if merely co-owning property.
   C. **Family partnership.** Family members recognized as partners only if facts show true intent to form partnership [¶ 2904]:
      1. Firms that need capital investment—Partners must actually own a capital interest.
      2. Service partnerships—Partners must contribute substantial services.
   D. **How family partnership's income is allocated.** IRS will allocate reasonable shares regardless of partnership agreement if [¶ 2905]:
      1. Partnership interest is directly or indirectly created by gift, and
      2. Donor's service is underpaid or donee's share overpaid.

II. **Partnership Income, Deductions, Credits**
   A. **How partnership handles its income, deductions and credits [¶ 2906]:**
      1. Partnership is not taxable entity, but must file return showing each partner's share of its income, deductions and credit.
      2. Partnership return shows each partner's share of:
         a. Separately listed income, deduction and credit items that have special tax significance for any partner (e.g., capital gains and losses).
         b. Partnership taxable income or loss (figured as individual's with exceptions).
         c. Partnership tax preferences.
      3. Partnership must make elections that affect income computation (e.g., accounting method), with exceptions [¶ 2906(c)].
   B. **Book profit vs. taxable income.** Book profit or loss may have to be decreased or increased to arrive at partnership taxable income [¶ 2907].

III. **Determination of Partner's Tax Liability**
   A. **Partner's income, deductions and credits [¶ 2908]:**
      1. Each partner, in figuring his income, picks up his distributive share of:
         a. Separately listed items on partnership return, and combine his share of each item with his own items of same nature.
         b. Partnership taxable income or loss (treated as ordinary income or loss).
         c. Partnership tax preferences.
         d. Partnership earned income for maximum tax purposes.
      2. Loss is limited to adjusted basis of partner's partnership interest.
         a. Adjusted basis excludes partnership liabilities for which partner has no personal liability.
         b. Limitation in a. doesn't apply to partnerships in realty investment or activities limited by "at risk" rules.

3. To figure whether partner must file and the like, include his share of partnership's *gross* income.
B. **How to determine partner's distributive share [¶ 2909]:**
   1. Generally fixed by partnership agreement.
   2. Determined by his partnership interest if:
      a. Agreement silent on allocation, or
      b. Allocation lacks substantial economic effect.
C. **Figuring distributive share when partner contributes property [¶ 2910]:**
   1. Partnership uses contributor's basis to figure depreciation, depletion, gain or loss on contributed property; partners share these items in general profit-and-loss ratio, unless agreed on otherwise.
   2. Partnership agreement may allocate [¶ 2910(a)]:
      a. Depreciation, depletion, gain or loss to attribute precontribution appreciation or depreciation to contributor.
      b. Gain from sale of farm recapture property, to contributor.
   3. Depreciation, depletion, gain or loss on undivided interests in property contributed by all partners may be allocated as if interests were held by partners outside partnership [¶ 2910(b)].
D. **Capital gains and losses [¶ 2911]:**
   1. Capital assets [¶ 2911(a)]:
      a. Gains and losses excluded from partnership taxable income.
      b. Each partner picks up his share of partnership gain or loss whether distributed or not.
      c. Short-term or long-term treatment depends on partnership's holding period.
      d. Only partner can take long-term capital gain deduction after netting all his capital gains and losses.
      e. Partner's share of capital, Sec. 1231, and ordinary losses limited to adjusted basis for his partnership interest.
      f. Wash sale losses not allowed.
   2. Sale of business property—involuntary conversion (Sec. 1231 assets) [¶ 2911(b)]:
      a. Gain or loss excluded in figuring partnership taxable income except recaptured gain.
      b. Each partner picks up his share of separately listed partnership gains and losses and combines with his items of same type.
E. **Partnership items specially reported [¶ 2913]:**
   1. Disregarded in figuring partnership taxable income, but allocated to partners.
   2. In applying certain limitations to deduction or exclusion, partner combines distributive share with same item of his own [¶ 2913(a)].
   3. On changing to installment accounting, partnership must separately state each partner's profit share each year [¶ 2913(b)].
   4. Each partner gets allocated share of investment, work incentive program, and new jobs credits [¶ 2913(c), (d)].
F. **Net operating loss deduction [¶ 2914]:**
   1. No such deduction for partnership [¶ 2906(b)].
   2. To figure partner's NOL deduction:
      a. Partnership's gain, loss, deduction and credit items are passed through without changing their tax characteristics.
      b. Combine distributive share of partnership nonbusiness income with his. Do the same with such deductions.
G. **Charitable contributions [¶ 2915]:**
   1. Not deductible by partnership.
   2. Partner combines share of partnership contribution with his own.
H. **Dividends received [¶ 2916]:**
   1. Not included in partnership taxable income.
   2. Partner includes his share with dividends he receives personally.
I. **Foreign taxes paid [¶ 2917]:**

1. Not deductible by partnership.
2. Each partner gets allocated share of taxes paid, and elects to treat them as credit or deduction.

J. **Distribution and reconciliation schedules:**
1. Distribution schedule (Schedule K-1) shows each partner's share of various partnership items he must pick up [¶ 2918(a)].
2. Reconciliation schedule (Schedule M) shows relation between partnership income and its capital transactions for the year. Schedule K-1 reconciles each partner's capital account at start and end of the year [¶ 2918(b)].

IV. **Tax Year of Partner and Partnership**

A. **When partner reports partnership income [¶ 2920]:**
1. Partner generally includes his share of partnership items (including guaranteed payments) for any partnership year ending with or within his tax year.
2. Partner whose entire interest is sold or liquidated reports his share as if partnership year ended on disposition date.
3. Partner receiving partnership distribution or selling partnership interest, reports gain or loss in payment year.

B. **Choice of tax year [¶ 2921]:**
1. New partnership can adopt:
   a. Tax year of all its principal partners (without IRS approval), or
   b. Calendar year if all its principal partners are not on same tax year (without IRS approval), or
   c. Any other tax year (with prior IRS approval).
2. Existing partnership can change to any tax year:
   a. Which is same as tax year of all its principal partners (without IRS approval), or
   b. In all other cases (with prior IRS approval).
3. Partner who changes his tax year to partnership tax year must:
   a. Show good business reason, and
   b. File return for short period ending on last day of partnership's first tax year.

C. **When partnership tax year ends:**
1. Partnership's tax year ends prematurely for all partners only if [¶ 2922(b)]:
   a. It stops to operate, or
   b. 50% or more interest is sold or exchanged within 12 months.
2. Change of partners [¶ 2922(a)]:
   a. Partnership's tax year ends prematurely as to particular partner who sells or liquidates his entire interest.
   b. Partnership's tax year does not end prematurely for:
      1) Partner who dies during the year, or
      2) Donor who gives away his partnership interest.
3. When partnerships combine [¶ 2922(c)]:
   a. New partnership tax year same as merging partnership's if merging partnership's members own more than 50% interest in new partnership.
   b. New partnership starts with new tax year and the merging partnership tax year is closed if merging partnership's members do not own more than 50% interest in new partnership.
4. Split-up of partnership [¶ 2922(d)]:
   a. Tax year of new partnership same as first partnership if members of new partnership owned more than 50% interest in first partnership.
   b. Any other new partnership starts with new tax year if its members owned not over 50% interest in first partnership.

V. **Transactions Between Partnership and Partner or Person Related to Partner**

A. **Sales between partnership and partner or 2 partnerships**—Gain or loss treated usual way, with exceptions [¶ 2923]:
1. Loss disallowed on exchange between [¶ 2923(a)]:
   a. Partnership and partner who owns more than 50% interest.
   b. Two partnerships if same persons own more than 50% interest in each.

2. Gain is ordinary income if noncapital asset in hands of person getting it, is transferred between [¶ 2923(b)]:
   a. Partnership and partner who owns over 80% of partnership interest, or
   b. Two partnerships in which same persons own over 80% interest.
3. To determine extent of ownership, constructive ownership rules apply [¶ 2923(c)].
4. "Guaranteed payments" are ordinary income to partner and deductible by partnership; not subject to withholding [¶ 2923(d)].

B. The 2½-month rule disallowing loss and interest deduction (see ¶ 2223) applies to transactions between partnership and person related to partner [¶ 2924].

VI. Contributions to Partnership
1. Generally no gain or loss recognized to partnership or partner on contributions to partnership in return for partnership interest, except [¶ 2925(a)]:
   a. Value of capital interest acquired for services is ordinary income to partner.
   b. Contributions of property with recapture potential.
   c. Gain (not loss) on transfer of property to partnership that would be treated as investment company.
2. Partnership takes contributor's basis and holding period for contributed property [¶ 2925(b)].
3. Contributor's basis for interest is [¶ 2925(c)]:
   a. Money contributed plus his adjusted basis for contributed property plus any gain recognized to him.
   b. Increased by additional contributions.
   c. Adjusted sometimes to prevent unintended consequences.

VII. Partner's Basis for Partnership Interest
A. How to figure original basis [¶ 2926]:
   a. Interest acquired by contribution—see VI, 3, above.
   b. Apply general rules for property basis if acquired by some other way.

B. Adjusted basis [¶ 2926(a), (b)]:
   1. General rule—Basis is:
      a. Increased by further contributions and by distributive share of:
         1) Partnership taxable income, capital gain, separately listed income.
         2) Partnership tax-exempt income.
         3) Excess depletion deduction.
      b. Reduced by cash and property distributions and by distributive share of:
         1) Partnership losses.
         2) Nondeductible, noncapital partnership expenses.
   2. Alternative rule:
      a. Adjusted basis equals partner's share of adjusted basis of partnership property distributable on partnership termination.
      b. Adjustments needed to reflect significant differences due to contributions or distributions of property or transfers of interest.

C. Effect of liabilities. Basis for partnership interest is [¶ 2926(c)]:
   1. Increased by partner's assumption of partnership liabilities.
   2. Reduced by partnership's assumption of partner's liabilities.

VIII. Distributions Other Than to Withdrawing Partners
A. Recognition of gain or loss on distribution other than earnings distributions [¶ 2927]:
   1. Partnership has no gain or loss, but may elect to adjust asset basis.
   2. Partner's gain or loss [¶ 2927(a)]:
      a. Gain recognized only in cash distribution; capital gain if it exceeds his basis for partnership interest.
      b. Loss recognized only if he gets money, unrealized receivables or inventory on liquidating partnership interest; capital loss if basis exceeds such distribution.
   3. Gain or loss recognized on [¶ 2927(b)]:
      a. Payments to retiring partner or deceased partner's successor.

     b. Distributions treated as sales (e.g., unequal distributions of receivables or inventory).
4. Carryover of recapture potential [¶ 2927(b)].
5. Constructive distributions include decrease in partner's share of partnership liabilities or partnership's assumption of his liabilities [¶ 2927(c)].

B. **Partner's basis for distributed property [¶ 2928]:**
1. Nonliquidating distribution [¶ 2928(a)]:
   a. Partner takes partnership's basis.
   b. "Carryover" basis not to exceed partner's basis for his interest less money received; if limitation applies, allocate basis.
2. In complete liquidation—partner's basis for property same as his basis for partnership interest, less money received [¶ 2928(b)].
3. Special rules apply on disproportionate distributions treated as sales between partner and partnership [¶ 2928(c)].

C. **Partner includes partnership's holding period for distributed property in his [¶ 2928(d)].**

D. **How to allocate partner's basis for distributed property [¶ 2929]:**
1. First, allocate basis of his partnership interest to unrealized receivables and inventories.
2. Then, allocate remaining basis to other properties in proportion to their bases to partnership.
3. On liquidation, loss for unallocated basis is capital [¶ 2929(c)].

E. **Adjustment to basis of property distributed to transferee partner [¶ 2930]:**
1. Transferee gets special basis adjustment through own election as if partnership made such adjustment on transfer.
2. Generally, he can elect only if distribution occurs within 2 years after he acquires interest.
3. Optional method not allowed for disproportionate Sec. 751 distribution [¶ 2930(a)].
4. Special basis must be used if at time transferee acquires interest [¶ 2930(b)]:
   a. Value of all partnership property exceeds 110% of its adjusted basis;
   b. Allocation (see D, above) would result in shift of basis from property not subject to depreciation allowance to depreciable property; and
   c. Partnership adjustment would change transferee's basis.

F. **Distribution of property with special basis [¶ 2931]:**
1. Partnership can elect to adjust:
   a. For all partners—basis of remaining undistributed property, after distribution.
   b. For transferee only—basis of transferred property after transfer; transferee increases or decreases partnership's basis for property by amount of special adjustment.
2. Partner who gets several properties allocates basis first to unrealized receivables or appreciated inventory received [¶ 2931(a)].
   a. If he gets at least his full share of receivables or inventory—apply special adjustment in full.
   b. If less than his share—apportion special adjustment between values received.
3. Transferee can reallocate his special basis adjustment [¶ 2931(b)]:
   a. To like kind property partnership retains or distributes to him, or
   b. Because he is giving up interest in other like kind property for which he has special adjustment.
4. In liquidating distribution, partnership may use transferee's unused special basis adjustment for remaining property [¶ 2931(c)].

G. **Partnership's elective adjustment to basis of undistributed property [¶ 2932]:**
1. Partnership's basis for retained property is [¶ 2932(a)]:
   a. Increased by distributee's gain, or excess of partnership's basis for distributed property over distributee's.
   b. Decreased by distributee's loss, or excess of his basis for distributed property over partnership's.

2. Partnership must allocate basis increase or decrease among its assets [¶ 2932(b)].
IX. **Transfer of Partnership Interest**
   A. **Gain or loss on transfer [¶ 2935]:**
      1. Sale of partnership interest usually results in capital gain or loss.
      2. Only net gain after excluding distributive share of current earnings is taxed as capital gain [¶ 2935(a)].
      3. Portion of sales proceeds and transferee's basis allocable to unrealized receivables and substantially appreciated inventory is ordinary gain or loss [¶ 2935(b)].
      4. Statement to be filed with returns of selling partners [¶ 2935(c)].
   B. **Transferee partner applies general rules for property basis (see ch. 5) to find his original basis [¶ 2936].**
   C. **If partnership elects to adjust its property basis [¶ 2937]:**
      1. Basis for all later distributions and transfers must be adjusted unless election revoked.
      2. Transferee gets special basis adjustment; other partners not affected.
      3. Basis of partnership assets to transferee is [¶ 2937(a)]:
         a. Increased by excess of basis of transferee's interest over his share of total partnership property basis.
         b. Decreased by excess of transferee's share of partnership property basis over basis of his interest.
      4. Partnership must figure transferee's proportionate share of partnership property basis, taking agreement into account [¶ 2937(b)].
      5. Each partner's depletion allowance figured separately if depletable property basis was adjusted [¶ 2937(c)].
X. **Allocation of Elective Partnership Adjustments to Basis**
   A. **How to allocate partnership adjustments to basis [¶ 2938]:**
      1. Step 1—Basis adjustment allocated only to same kind of assets involved in distribution or transfer; assets classified as:
         a. Capital or Sec. 1231 assets.
         b. Other property.
      2. Step 2—Allocate within class to reduce gap between value and basis of assets within same class.
         a. Plus adjustment is allocated only to assets whose values exceed bases.
         b. Minus adjustment is allocated only to assets whose bases exceed values.
      3. If partnership has no property to adjust, make adjustment as in 1-2 above when proper kind of property acquired.
      4. Other allocation methods may be allowed.
XI. **Payments to Retiring Partner or Deceased Partner's Successor**
   A. **Payments for withdrawing partner's interest in partnership assets generally result in capital gain or loss [¶ 2941(a)].**
   B. **Payments for "specially treated assets" and all other liquidating payments not made for interest in partnership assets are taxed as ordinary income [¶ 2941(b)].**
   C. **How to allocate installment payments [¶ 2941(c); 2942]:**
      1. Recipient may apportion each year's fixed amount between payments in A and B above [¶ 2942(a)].
      2. If amount varies, treat installments as payments for interest in assets until full value recovered; after that all payments treated as "other payments" [¶ 2942(b)].
      3. Partners may agree to allocate some other way [¶ 2942(c)].
XII. **Distributions of Unrealized Receivables or Substantially Appreciated Property**
   A. **Distributions treated as sales or exchanges [¶ 2944]:**
      1. Distribution is "sale or exchange" to the extent distributee gets more than his share of [¶ 2944(b)]:
         a. Property other than Sec. 751 assets (unrealized receivables or substantially appreciated inventory; see [¶ 2944(d)]) in exchange for his interest in Sec. 751 assets, or

b. Sec. 751 assets in exchange for his interest in property other than Sec. 751 assets.
2. Other property distributed in exchange for Sec. 751 assets [¶ 2944(c)(1)]:
   a. Partner has ordinary gain or loss on difference between his basis for Sec. 751 assets sold and value of other property distributed.
   b. Partnership has gain or loss on difference between basis for distributed property and value of partner's interest in Sec. 751 assets exchanged.
3. Sec. 751 assets distributed in exchange for other property [¶ 2944(c)(2)]:
   a. Partner has gain or loss on difference between his basis for other property and value of Sec. 751 asset received.
   b. Partnership has ordinary gain or loss on difference between its basis for Sec. 751 asset and value of partner's interest in other property exchanged.
4. Excluded transactions [¶ 2944(a)]:
   a. Distribution of contributed property.
   b. Payment for unrealized receivables to withdrawing partner in excess of his partnership basis is ordinary income treated as under XI, B, above.

B. **Transfer of distributed property [¶ 2945]:**
1. Distributee may get ordinary income on disposing recapture property distributed to him [¶ 2945(a)].
2. He has ordinary gain or loss on disposing [¶ 2945(b), (c)]:
   a. Unrealized receivables distributed to him.
   b. Any inventory item within 5 years of distribution.

Chapter 20

ESTATES AND TRUSTS

TABLE OF CONTENTS

¶

ESTATES AND TRUSTS IN GENERAL

How estates and trusts are taxed 3000
   Allocation of income
   Returns
   Exempt trusts
Who is a fiduciary 3001
   Fiduciary, receiver and agent distinguished
   Liability for tax
   Terminable interests
Nature of estates and trusts 3002
   Estates
   Multiple trusts

WHO IS TAXABLE ON ESTATE AND TRUST INCOME

To whom estate or trust income is taxable 3003
   General rules
   Different tax years
   Income when trust terminates
Distributable net income 3004
Distributions by simple trusts 3005
   Income taxable to beneficiaries
   Distributions of corpus
Distributions by estates and complex trusts 3006
   Allocation by tiers—distributions of current income
   Allocation by tiers—other distributions
   Allocation by separate shares
   Special distributions
   Throwback rule
   Sixty-five day rule
   Charitable remainder trust distributions
Beneficiary's share of each item of distributable net income 3007
   Method of apportionment
   Apportionment formulas
   Allocation of deductions

INCOME—CAPITAL GAINS AND LOSSES

Gross income 3008
   Estates and trusts
   Decedents

¶

Capital gains and losses 3009
   Capital loss
   Long-term capital gain deduction
   Asset distributions in lieu of cash
   Distributable net income
   Deduction for state tax
Basis of property to estate or trust 3010
   Transfer in trust after 12-31-20
   Transfer in trust before 1-1-21
   Property acquired from decedent

DEDUCTIONS AND CREDITS

Deductions in general 3011
   Losses
   Termination of estate or trust
   Dividend exclusion
Deduction for personal exemption 3012
Contributions 3013
   Contributions from gross income
   Contributions permanently set aside
Depreciation or depletion 3014
   Life tenant
   Trusts
   Estates
Net operating loss deduction 3015
Expenses 3016
   Waiver of estate tax deduction
   Statement required
Deduction for distributions to beneficiaries 3017
   Simple trusts
   Estates and complex trusts
Disallowed expenses and losses 3018
Credits against tax 3019

RATES AND RETURNS FOR DECEDENTS, ESTATES AND TRUSTS

Rates and returns 3020
   Decedents
   Estates
   Trusts
   Minimum tax on estates and trusts
Distribution computations 3021

SPECIAL PROBLEMS

Trust income taxable to grantor or others 3022

Footnotes appear at end of this Chapter.

¶	¶
Reversionary interest	Exemption of trust income
Power to control beneficial enjoyment	Trust must prove exemption
Administrative powers	Deduction for employer's contributions
Power to revoke	Taxability of amounts received by employee
Income for benefit of grantor, his spouse or dependent	Curtailment or termination of a plan
Income taxable to others	Treatment of a nonqualified plan
Taxing transfer of appreciated property to trust	How treated on return
Foreign trust with U.S. beneficiary	U.S. bond purchase plan
Throwback of excess distributions by complex trusts 3023	**Common trust funds** 3025
Undistributed net income	Withdrawal of participating interest
Accumulation distribution	Different tax years
How to handle the throwback rule	**Business trusts** 3026
Tax added to distribution	Business purpose test
Tax paid by beneficiaries on excess distributions	Agent in a real estate trust
Refunds or credits	Depositor in a fixed investment trust
Determining the new undistributed net income	Liquidating trusts
Capital gain distributions	**Individual retirement arrangements** .. 3027
Foreign trusts	
Employees' trusts 3024	• **Highlights of Chapter 20** .... **Page 3061**

ESTATES AND TRUSTS IN GENERAL

An estate of a decedent, or a trust, is a separate taxable entity for which a return must be filed and taxes paid. The fiduciary (an executor or administrator for an estate, a trustee for a trust) must file the return and pay the tax. *Generally* estates and trusts are taxed in the same manner as individuals.

¶ **3000 How estates and trusts are taxed.** For tax years starting after 1976, estates and trusts must compute their taxes by using the rate schedule specially provided for them [¶ 3020]. Special rules affecting computation of their taxable income, deductions and credits are discussed in this chapter. If the entity is a business trust, it is considered an "association" and is taxed as a corporation [¶ 3026].

Some trusts, however, are not taxable entities. For example, a revocable trust is a separate entity for trust law purposes, but is not a separate taxable entity for federal income tax purposes. The grantor of such a trust must report the income and deductions of the trust on his individual return as if there were no trust. Trusts that do not become separate taxable entities are discussed at ¶ 3022. The balance of this chapter explains the income tax on (1) trusts that are taxable entities, and (2) decedents' estates. In certain cases, the trust is taxed as the grantor or transferor; see ¶ 3022(g).

For the *estate tax* on the estate of a decedent, see Chapter 29.

(a) Allocation of income. Generally, the income of an estate or trust is taxed either to the estate or trust (through its fiduciary [¶ 3001]), or to the beneficiaries, or in part to each, depending upon the disposition of the income determined under the terms of the will or trust and state law. In this way the entire taxable income of the estate or trust is taxed. In its simplest form, the rule may be illustrated as follows:

	Estate or Trust		Allocation of Income		
			Fiduciary	Beneficiaries	
				A	B
Gross income		$10,000			
Deduction for expenses, etc.		1,500			
Difference		$ 8,500			
Distributions:				$1,000	$3,500
Beneficiary A	$1,000				
Beneficiary B	3,500	4,500			
Balance		$ 4,000	$4,000		

In figuring taxable income of the estate or trust, a deduction is allowed for amounts paid, credited, or required to be distributed to the beneficiaries [¶ 3017]. The amounts generally are taxed to the beneficiaries [¶ 3003-3007].

(b) Returns. The fiduciary who acts for an estate or trust must file a return (Form 1041) and pay its tax. The rquirements for filing are listed in ¶ 3020. Separate Schedule K-1 that the fiduciary files for each beneficiary is explained in ¶ 3021. The fiduciary generally files the final return for the decedent [¶ 3020; 3517]. Those fiduciaries who do not act for an estate or trust, such as guardians and receivers, must file income tax returns otherwise required to be filed by the taxpayers whom they represent [¶ 3511].

(c) Exempt trusts (charitable, educational, etc.) are subject to tax on unrelated business income, see ¶ 3450 et seq.

¶ 3001 Who is a fiduciary. A fiduciary is a person who (a) holds in trust an estate for another who has beneficial title or has a beneficial interest, or (b) receives and controls income of another [Sec. 7701(a)(6); 301.7701-6]. He files a return and pays a tax for the individual, estate or trust for which he acts.

Example 1: When John Jones died, Edward Smith was appointed his executor. Smith must file a return and pay a tax for Jones, for the period before his death [¶ 3020(a)]. A new taxable entity came into being, namely, Jones' estate, and the executor must file returns and pay taxes for that entity [¶ 3020(b)].

(a) Fiduciary, receiver and agent distinguished. The term "fiduciary" applies to persons who occupy positions of peculiar confidence toward others, such as trustees, guardians, executors, administrators, receivers for individuals and conservators. Receivers for corporations are not fiduciaries [Sec. 6012(b)(3); 1.6012-3(b)(4)]. Similarly, if one acts as a mere agent without legal title to the property in question, no fiduciary relationship is established. The principal and not the agent must file the return and pay the tax.

Example 2: An agent who is given complete control over the management of property by a power of attorney and who must turn over the net profits from the property to his principal is not a fiduciary [Sec. 301.7701-7].

Example 3: When a taxpayer who buys stock on margin and furnishes all the collateral directs his broker to pay all of the profits to certain individuals, the broker is an agent and not a trustee.[1]

In some situations even though the agent is given legal title, he is not considered a fiduciary.

Footnotes appear at end of this Chapter.

Example 4: An agency may result when a trustee has no active duties to perform but merely holds title to the property subject to the directions of the beneficiaries[2] or when the trustee is given legal title and power to sell and lease property for a limited time jointly with the transferor of the property.[3]

(b) Liability for tax. Although a fiduciary assumes the rights and duties of the taxpayer with respect to the income tax, he ordinarily is not personally liable for the tax. Usually it is paid from the assets of the estate or trust [Sec. 6903; 301.6903-1]. However, if the fiduciary uses these assets to pay the taxpayer's debts without first satisfying the tax claim of the federal government, he will be personally liable for the tax deficiency up to the amounts paid[4] if: (1) the estate is too small to pay all the debts of the deceased;[5] (2) the government's claim has priority over the claims of creditors who were paid;[6] or (3) the fiduciary has notice of the debt.[7] Similarly, this personal liability also applies to the fiduciary of an estate or trust who knew or should have known about government tax claims before making distributions to beneficiaries and legatees [Sec. 1.641(b)-2].

Discharge from personal liability. An executor or administrator can obtain a discharge from personal liability for a decedent's income taxes by applying to the Commissioner. This application may be made anytime after the return is filed. The Commissioner may notify him of the amount of the tax due. On payment of this amount, or if he is not notified of any payment due, within 9 months after the Commissioner receives the application, the executor or administrator is discharged from personal liability for any deficiency in the decedent's tax found later [Sec. 6905(a), (b); 301.6905-1].

(c) Terminable interests. A life tenant ordinarily is not taxable on any gain from the sale or exchange of property, because he is not a fiduciary, is not an owner, and is only entitled to the income from the property. However, if he also has a right to sell the property, he is a trustee for the remainderman. If he then sells or exchanges it, he reports and pays the tax on any recognized gain as a fiduciary.[8]

¶ **3002 Nature of estates and trusts.** In legal terms, a trust is an advisory relationship in which one person—the trustee—is the owner of the title to property, subject to an obligation to keep or use the property for the benefit of another—the beneficiary. A trust created by an instrument other than a will is an inter vivos or living trust. A trust created by will is a testamentary trust. The subject matter of the trust is often referred to as the trust res, trust principal, trust property or trust corpus. The most common types of property held in trust are bonds, stocks, mortgages, titles to land and bank accounts. A trust generally is a taxable entity for which returns must be filed and taxes paid on the income produced by the trust corpus and retained by the trust [Sec. 641; 1.641(a)-1].

Example 1: John Doe, while living, transfers to Richard Roe certain shares of stock and bonds, in trust, to pay the income to Henry Doe every month, or, perhaps, to accumulate the income for Henry's benefit until he becomes 21 years of age. Under this instrument, a *new taxable entity has been created*, for which returns must be filed and taxes paid. The trust is a "person" separate and distinct from the individuals with whom it is related.

John Doe may be called the grantor, creator, donor, founder, trustor or settlor of the trust. Some of these terms are synonymous; some depend upon how the trust was created. Richard Roe is the trustee, and Henry Doe, the beneficiary or cestui que trust. The stocks or bonds (or other items constituting the trust property) transferred to the trustee are the corpus of the trust.

Example 2: The trust in Example 1 is a living trust. If the same trust had been created by the will of John Doe, who left the stocks and bonds to Richard Roe in trust for Henry Doe, it would have been a testamentary trust.

(a) Estates. Suppose, however, that the will does not create a trust, but, after naming an executor, merely leaves certain stocks and bonds to the decedent's son. During the period of administration, the executor (or the administrator if there was no will) must file a return and pay a tax for the estate. So an estate, during the period of administration, also is a taxable entity.

(b) Multiple trusts. A person can create several (multiple) trusts in one instrument and have the same trustee administer all of them. The income of each trust is taxable as income of a separate entity.[1] Whether only one trust or more than one trust has been created depends upon the intention of the grantor as determined from the trust agreement.[2] The Supreme Court has held that separate trusts were created, even if there was only one trust instrument and the trust assets were not segregated, when each beneficiary had a separate account and was granted a fixed share in the trust property.[3]

WHO IS TAXABLE ON ESTATE AND TRUST INCOME

An estate's or trust's "distributable net income" (taxable income with modifications) is the yardstick for determining the amount the estate or trust may deduct and the amount the beneficiaries must include in income. For trusts, the use of this yardstick will depend on whether the trust is simple or complex.

¶ **3003 To whom estate or trust income is taxable. (a) General rules.** A beneficiary generally is taxed on distributions he gets or is entitled to get from the estate or trust, but only to the extent of his share of its "distributable net income" [¶ 3004-3006].

A fiduciary is taxed on the taxable income of the estate or trust. Taxable income is gross income [¶ 3008] less the deductions discussed in ¶ 3011 et seq.

Under certain conditions, the income of a trust is not taxed to either the beneficiaries or the fiduciary. Instead, it is taxed to the grantor or other persons having control of the trust property or income [¶ 3022].

(b) Different tax years. If the tax year of a beneficiary is not the same as that of the estate or trust, he is taxed on the distributions for the tax year or years of the estate or trust that end within or with his tax year [Sec. 652(c), 662(c); 1.652(c)-1, 1.662(c)-1].

> **Example:** A beneficiary filing a return for the calendar year 1977 would include in the return distributions received from an estate or trust having a fiscal year beginning in 1976 and ending in 1977.

(c) Income when trust terminates. When a trust terminates, its separate status ceases. After that, its income, deductions and credits are attributed to the termination beneficiaries. However, a trust does not terminate automatically. A reasonable period is allowed for the trustee to wind up its affairs. During this period, the status of the trust income is determined under the terms of the trust instrument and state law [Sec. 1.641(b)-3].

¶ **3004 Distributable net income.** The law sets up a yardstick called "distributable net income" to limit (1) the amounts the beneficiaries must include in their gross income, and (2) the deductions the fiduciary may take for distributions. A beneficiary never reports more than his share of distributable net income. The fiduciary's deduction for distributions cannot be more than the trust's distributable net income [Sec. 643, 652, 662; 1.643-1, 1.652(a)-2, 1.662(a)-2].

Footnotes appear at end of this Chapter.

¶ **3004**

(a) **How to figure distributable net income.** Distributable net income is computed by making the following modifications to taxable income (gross income [¶ 3008] less deductions [¶ 3011 et seq.]) [Sec. 1.643(a)(1)—(7)]:

(1) Add back: (a) the personal exemption [¶ 3012]; (b) the distributions deduction [¶ 3017]; (c) the dividend exclusion [¶ 3011(c)]; (d) any net capital losses deducted by the trust or estate [¶ 3009]; and (e) the long-term capital gains deduction [¶ 3009(b)].

(2) Add net tax-exempt interest to taxable income as modified in (1). Tax-exempt interest is reduced by any portion of the interest that is paid or set aside for charitable purposes and by related nondeductible expenses (such as commissions and general expenses) [¶ 1809]. The reductions for charitable contributions from unspecified sources and for expenses not directly attributable to other items of income are in the same proportion as total tax-exempt interest bears to total gross income (including tax-exempt interest).

(3) Subtract the net capital gains taxable to the trust or estate [¶ 3009]. In other words, net capital gains paid, credited or required to be distributed to beneficiaries or paid or set aside for charitable purposes are included in distributable net income, but the gains allocated to corpus are excluded.

Example: A trust has $40,000 gross income for the year, including $9,000 long-term capital gain, which under the trust instrument is to be distributed one-third to the beneficiary and two-thirds to the corpus of the trust. Gross income also includes $5,000 dividends of domestic corporations. The trust is entitled to deductions for interest, taxes, depreciation and charitable contributions amounting to $8,000. In addition to the $40,000 gross income, the trust also receives $7,000 tax-exempt interest. Distributable net income is $33,000:

Gross income	$40,000
Less: deductions	8,000
Taxable income as modified	$32,000
Plus: tax-exempt interest	7,000
	$39,000
Less: long-term capital gain to be added to trust corpus (⅔)	6,000
Distributable net income	$33,000

(b) **Special rules apply to simple and foreign trusts.** In the case of simple trusts [¶ 3005], extraordinary dividends and taxable stock dividends allocated to corpus by a trustee are not included in distributable net income. A foreign trust's gross income from foreign sources reduced by nondeductible expenses [¶ 1809] is included. See also ¶ 2023(i).

¶ **3005 Distribution by simple trusts.** A simple trust is one which, under the trust terms, distributes current income only (that is, distributes no corpus), has to distribute all its income, and has no charitable beneficiaries [Sec. 651; 1.651(a)-1]. A simple trust is primarily a conduit of income in that the trust takes a deduction for the income which is required to be distributed currently and the beneficiaries include that amount in their gross income. The terms of the trust instrument and state law determine what is income for this purpose. However, if the trust instrument departs fundamentally from state law concepts in defining income, the trust instrument may be disregarded [Sec. 1.643(b)-1]. For example, if the trust instrument directs that all of the trust income shall be paid to the beneficiary, but defines ordinary dividends and interest as corpus, the trust will not be considered one that has to distribute all its income and will not qualify as a simple trust. Because income for this purpose may be less than the trust's taxable income, a simple trust can be a conduit and yet have a taxable income.

(a) **Income taxable to beneficiaries.** Generally, the beneficiaries must include in their gross income all trust income required to be distributed to them to the extent of the trust's distributable net income [¶ 3004]. For asset distributions in lieu of cash, see ¶ 3009.

Example 1: Covington placed certain securities in trust for the sole benefit of his wife. The trust instrument provided that all the income be distributed to her at least annually, that the securities themselves not be distributed to her, and that no distributions be made to anyone else. This is a simple trust. The wife will include the trust income in her gross income each year whether or not the fiduciary actually makes the payment to her during the tax year.[1]

If the income required to be distributed exceeds the distributable net income, each beneficiary is taxed only on his proportionate share of the distributable net income [Sec. 652(a); 1.652(a)-2].

Example 2: A simple trust provides that Barnes is to receive 60% of the trust income and Cox is to receive 40%. The trust has the following income and disbursements during the year: $9,000 interest on corporate bonds; $4,000 net short-term capital gains allocable to corpus; $1,500 commissions, legal fees and other deductible expenses allocable to corpus; and $400 expenses allocable to income. The trust income required to be distributed is $9,000 less $400, or $8,600. The trust's distributable net income is $9,000 (capital gains are excluded), less $1,900 (all deductible expenses), or $7,100. Although Barnes receives $5,160 ($8,600 × 60%), he will include only $4,260 ($7,100 × 60%) in income. Cox will receive $3,440 ($8,600 × 40%), but will include only $2,840 ($7,100 × 40%).

(b) Distributions of corpus. A trust may be a simple trust one year and a complex trust another year. For example, a trust is required to distribute all of its income currently. The trustee also has a discretionary power to distribute corpus to the income beneficiary. In years when only income is distributed, the trust is a simple trust, but when corpus is distributed, the trust becomes a complex trust for that year. When a trust ends, it is treated as a complex trust because corpus is distributed that year [Sec. 1.651(a)-3].

¶ 3006 Distributions by estates and complex trusts. Complex trusts are those that are not simple trusts. They include discretionary trusts, trusts with charitable beneficiaries, and trusts that accumulate income or distribute corpus. In determining the inclusions of beneficiaries and the deductions for distributions by the fiduciary, complex trusts and estates are treated similarly [Sec. 661-663; 1.661(a)-1].

The distributions of estates and complex trusts consist of (1) current income required to be distributed to the beneficiaries, and (2) all other amounts properly paid, credited, or required to be distributed to the beneficiaries. The beneficiaries include the sum of these amounts in their gross income, with certain restrictions indicated below. For asset distributions in lieu of cash, see ¶ 3009.

(a) Allocation by tiers—distributions of current income. Each beneficiary must inlude in gross income the income of the estate or trust that must be distributed to him currently. This includes an amount required to be paid out of either income or corpus to the extent it is paid out of trust income [Sec. 662(a)(1); 1.662(a)-1, 1.662(a)-2]. These are called first tier distributions.

Example 1: A trust provides that Anson is to receive $5,000 annually, even if the corpus has to be invaded to make the payment. The trust has income of $7,000 and distributes $5,000 to Anson. He will include $5,000 in his gross income.

Distributions that exceed distributable net income. If the first tier distributions to all beneficiaries exceed the distributable net income (figured without any deduction for charitable contributions), the amount to be included in the beneficiary's gross income is figured as follows [Sec. 1.662(a)-2].

Footnotes appear at end of this Chapter.

$$\frac{\text{First tier distributions to the beneficiary}}{\text{First tier distributions to all beneficiaries}} \times \begin{pmatrix} \text{Distributable net income} \\ \text{(without deduction for} \\ \text{charitable contributions)} \end{pmatrix} = \begin{pmatrix} \text{Amount beneficiary in-} \\ \text{cludes in gross income} \end{pmatrix}$$

Example 2: A trust is required to distribute one-half of its current income for the tax year to A, the grantor's son, one-quarter to B, the grantor's daughter, and one-quarter to C, a charity. The trust income is $10,000. The charitable contribution is $2,500 ($\frac{1}{4} \times$ $10,000). The amount required to be distributed to A is $5,000 and the amount required to be distributed to B is $2,500. Hence, the amount required to be distributed to all beneficiaries is $7,500, since the charity is not considered a beneficiary [Sec. 663(a)]. Assume the distributable net income of the trust is $7,000 before the charitable deduction is taken. A will include $4,666.67 ($5,000/$7,500 × $7,000) in his gross income. B will include $2,333.33 ($2,500/$7,500 × $7,000) in her gross income.

(b) Allocation by tiers—Other distributions. Each beneficiary also must include in his gross income, all other amounts properly paid, credited, or required to be distributed to him (so-called "second tier" distributions) [Sec. 662(a)(2); 1.662(a)-3]. An amount is not treated as credited to a beneficiary, unless it is so definitely allocated to him as to be beyond recall. Thus "credit" for practical purposes is the equivalent of "payment." A mere entry on the books of the fiduciary will not serve, unless it cannot be changed.[1]

Example 3: A trust provides that each year the fiduciary must distribute $3,000 of the corpus to beneficiary B. B will include $3,000 in his gross income to the extent of the trust's distributable net income.

Distributions exceeding distributable net income. When the sum of the first and second tier distributions exceeds the distributable net income, the beneficiary must include in his gross income only a proportionate share of the distributable net income (less first tier distributions). His share is determined as follows [Sec. 662(a)(2); 1.662(a)-3]:

$$\begin{pmatrix} \text{Distributable net in-} \\ \text{come less first tier dis-} \\ \text{tributions} \end{pmatrix} \times \frac{\text{Second tier distributions to the beneficiary}}{\text{Second tier distributions to all beneficiaries}} = \begin{pmatrix} \text{The beneficiary's share} \\ \text{of distributable net income} \end{pmatrix}$$

Thus, beneficiaries are taxed on second tier distributions only if the first tier distributions fail to exhaust the distributable net income of the estate or trust. This is so, even if the distributions are made from income.

Example 4: A trust requires the distribution annually of $8,000 of income to A. Any remaining income may be accumulated or distributed to B, C, and D in the trustee's discretion. He may also invade corpus for the benefit of A, B, C, or D. During the year, the trust has $20,000 income after deducting expenses. Distributable net income is $20,000. The trustee distributes $8,000 of income to A. He also distributes $4,000 each to B and C, $2,000 to D, and an additional $6,000 to A. The amounts taxable to A, B, C, and D are determined as follows:

Distributable net income	$20,000
Less: first tier distribution to A	8,000
Available for second tier distributions	$12,000
Second tier distributions:	
A—6,000/16,000 × $12,000	$ 4,500
B—4,000/16,000 × $12,000	$ 3,000
C—4,000/16,000 × $12,000	$ 3,000
D—2,000/16,000 × $12,000	$ 1,500

A includes $12,500 in income ($8,000 first tier distribution plus $4,500 second tier distribution). B and C each include $3,000 in income. D includes $1,500.

(c) **Allocation by separate shares.** In determining the amount taxable to the beneficiaries, allocation by tiers may work an injustice when a trust is administered in substantially separate shares.

Example 5: A trust with two beneficiaries has distributable net income of $20,000. The trustee makes a mandatory distribution of one-half of this amount, or $10,000, to beneficiary A. He accumulates the other $10,000 for future distribution to beneficiary B. He also makes a discretionary distribution of $10,000 out of corpus to A. Under the tier system, the entire distributable net income would be allocated to A, and A would be taxed on the $20,000 received. His tax is being measured, in part, by $10,000 of current income that can only go to B.

But suppose that the above trust is divided into two separate trusts, one for each beneficiary. Each trust then will have distributable net income of $10,000. The trustee of the trust for A distributes all the income of that trust and $10,000 of the corpus to A. The trustee of the trust for B makes no distribution. Under these facts, A would be taxed on $10,000. He actually received $20,000, but his taxable share may not exceed the distributable net income of his trust. The B trust makes no distributions, so its income of $10,000 is taxable to the trustee.

The separate share device achieves the two-trust result in a one-trust case. The two-trust result in the above example seems more equitable, since it exempts the corpus distribution and limits the tax on the beneficiaries to current income. To accomplish this, if a single trust has more than one beneficiary, and they have substantially separate and independent shares, their shares are treated as separate trusts for the sole purpose of determining the amount taxable to the beneficiaries. This treatment cannot be used to get more than one deduction for the personal exemption [¶ 3012] or to split the undistributed income of the trust into several shares for being taxed at lower-bracket rates [Sec. 663(c); 1.663(c)-1].

(d) **Special distributions.** The following items are not deductible as distributions by a trust or estate, nor are they included in a beneficiary's gross income for the current tax year [Sec. 663(a)]:

(1) Any gift or bequest of a specific sum of money or of specific property which, under the terms of the governing instrument, is paid in a lump sum or in not more than 3 installments. If, however, the governing instrument provides that the gift or bequest is payable *only* from the income of the estate or trust (whether from the income for the payment year or accumulated from a prior year), it will not be treated as a gift. Instead, it will be deductible by the trust and taxable to the beneficiary [Sec. 663(a)(1); 1.663(a)-1]. For property used to satisfy a cash legacy, see ¶ 3009.

Example 6: Under the trust instrument, A received a lump-sum distribution of $10,000 on reaching age 25. Since, under the terms of the trust instrument, it was payable out of income only, it is not regarded as a lump-sum gift.

Example 7: Assume the same facts as in Example 6 except that the amount is payable out of income or corpus. The amount is treated as a lump-sum gift, even if the trustee charges the amount paid to income.

Example 8: Under the terms of the trust instrument, A received the accumulated income of the trust on reaching the age of 25. This distribution is not considered a lump-sum gift, even if the amount is payable only out of accumulated income or is payable either out of income or corpus [Sec. 1.663(a)-1(b)].

(2) Charitable distributions [Sec. 1.663(a)-2]; but see ¶ 3013.
(3) Any distribution in the current tax year that was deducted by the estate or trust in a preceding tax year [Sec. 1.663(a)-3].

Footnotes appear at end of this Chapter.

¶ 3006

(e) **Throwback rule.** If a trust distributes less than its distributable net income, the undistributed excess may have to be reported by the beneficiaries in later years [¶ 3023].

(f) **Sixty-five day rule.** To avoid accumulations and the application of the throwback rule [¶ 3023], this rule allows amounts paid or credited in the first 65 days of a trust tax year to be attributed to the preceding tax year [Sec. 663(b)(1); 1.663(b)-1]. The 65-day rule applies only if the trustee elects it [Sec. 663(b)(2); 1.663(b)-1, 2]. Distributions eligible for the election cannot exceed the greater of the trust income for the year of election, or distributable net income for such year. The limitation is further reduced by distributions in the election year except those amounts for which the election was claimed in a preceding tax year [Sec. 1.663(b)-1]. The election is made on the return for the tax year in which the distribution is considered made. If no return is due, a statement of election must be filed with IRS where the return would normally be filed. In either case, it must be made within the tine for filing the return for that year (including extensions) and cannot be revoked after the return due date [Sec. 1.663(b)-2].

(g) **Beneficiary's share of charitable remainder trust distributions.** Unlike other trust distributions, distributions to income beneficiaries of charitable annuity trusts or unitrusts [¶ 3927(b)] are separated into four categories for tax purposes: (1) ordinary income and loss; (2) short-term capital gain and loss; (3) long-term capital gain and loss; and (4) other income, including tax-exempt income and related loss. Any distribution in excess of these four categories is treated as a nontaxable distribution of corpus. The beneficiaries are taxed on the amounts in each category to the extent of the trust's current income and undistributed prior years' income in that category. Undistributed capital gains (long and short-term) for the current and prior years are computed without regard to any capital loss limitation, that is, on a cumulative net basis. In addition, the amount of current and prior years' income is computed without regard to a net operating loss deduction. A loss in one of these categories may not be used to offset a gain in another. However, within a category, losses may be carried over indefinitely to future years to reduce later income in the same category [Sec. 664(b); 1.664-1(d)(1)]. Income items are distributed proportionately among the income recipients [Sec. 1.664-1(d)(3)]. Generally, income is taxed to the recipient in the year it is paid to him. However, if additional income is payable for a particular year because of an incorrect valuation of trust assets, it is taxed in the year paid, not the earlier year to which it relates [Sec. 1.664-1(d)(4)]. Expenses are also allocated among the beneficiaries. However, any expense that is not deductible in determining the trust's taxable income or related to a specific category is allocable to corpus [Sec. 1.664-1(d)(2)].

¶ **3007 Beneficiary's share of each item of distributable net income.** If distributable net income includes items with a special tax status, such as exempt interest, you must determine how much of the item is included in the distribution to the beneficiary. The reason for this is that such items retain their status in the hands of the beneficiary [Sec. 652(b), 662(b); 1.652(b)-1, 1.662(b)-1]. Thus, to the extent that a distribution includes exempt interest, the beneficiary can exclude it from his return.

(a) **Method of apportionment.** To determine how much of each item is included in a given distribution, the net amount of each item (the gross amount of the item, less the deductions allocable to it (see (c) below)) is apportioned among the beneficiaries on a simple proportion basis, unless the governing instrument or state law requires a different allocation. [Sec. 652(b), 662(b); 1.652(b)-1, 1.662(b)-1]. An allocation in the trust instrument will be recognized only to the extent that it has an economic effect independent of the income tax consequences of the allocation. Thus, when the trustee can allocate different classes of income to different beneficiaries, it is not a specific allocation by terms of the trust instrument [Sec. 1.652(b)-2].

(b) Apportionment formulas. To determine a beneficiary's share of a particular item of distributable net income, the following formulas are used [Sec. 652(b), 662(b); 1.652(b)-2, 1.662(b)-1]:

Formula I

$$\frac{\text{Beneficiary's total share of distributable net income}}{\text{Total distributable net income of trust}} \times \text{Total of particular item of distributable net income} = \text{Beneficiary's share of the particular item of distributable net income}$$

When an estate or trust distributes only a part of its distributable net income, the total amount of a particular item of distributable net income that is being distributed must be determined before the beneficiary's share of the item can be determined. This total amount is determined as follows:

Formula II

$$\frac{\text{Total distribution}}{\text{Total distributable net income}} \times \text{Total of particular item of distributable net income} = \text{Total of particular item of distributable net income being distributed}$$

When the total of each item of distributable net income distributed is known, Formula I determines the beneficiary's share of the particular item.

(c) Allocation of deductions. As noted above in (a), in determining the total of a particular item of distributable net income, the gross amount of each income item must be reduced by the deduction allocable to it. In the absence of specific instructions in the governing instrument, the deductions are allocated in the following manner [Sec. 1.652(b)-3]:

(1) Any deduction directly allocable to a particular class of gross income (except excluded dividends) is allocated to that class.

(2) If the deduction exceeds the income, the excess may be applied against any other income class the trustee chooses, with these limitations: (a) the income chosen must be included in figuring distributable net income, (b) a proportionate share of nonbusiness deductions must be allocated to nontaxable income (except excluded dividends); and (c) excess deductions attributable to tax-exempt income (except excluded dividends) may not be offset against any other class of income.

(3) Deductions that are not directly allocable to any particular class of income (trustee's commissions, safe deposit rentals, state income and personal property taxes, for example) are treated the same as the excess deductions; see (2) above.

Example 1: A trust has rents, taxable interest, dividends, and tax-exempt interest. Deductions directly attributable to the rents exceed the rental income. The excess may be allocated to the taxable interest and dividends in whatever proportions the trustee elects. However, if the excess deductions are attributable to the tax-exempt interest, they may not be allocated to the other income items.

Charitable contributions adjustment. In determining the tax status of currently distributable income items in the hands of the beneficiary, distributable net income is figured without regard to any part of a charitable deduction that is not attributable to income of the tax year. This prevents a charitable contribution from reducing the amount of current income otherwise taxable to a beneficiary, except

¶ 3007

to the extent that the contribution is itself paid out of current income [Sec. 662(b); 1.662(b)-2].

Example 2: A trust provides that one-half of its income must be distributed to A and the other half may either be (1) accumulated for B, (2) distributed to Charity X, or (3) accumulated for Charity X. During the year, the trust had $40,000 taxable income and $10,000 tax-exempt income. It distributed $25,000 to A and $50,000 (consisting of both current and accumulated income) to Charity X. The distributable net income is $25,000 (the charitable deduction is taken into account only to the extent of $25,000. A will include in his gross income only $20,000 ($25,000 received less $5,000 which is his share of the tax-exempt income).

The regulations indicate that the charitable contributions deduction does not reduce the amount taxable to beneficiaries who receive currently distributable income, but it can reduce the amount taxable to beneficiaries who receive other amounts [Sec. 1.662(b)-2].

INCOME—CAPITAL GAINS AND LOSSES

The gross income of an estate or trust is determined the same as for an individual. All the gross income realized by a decedent under his method of accounting must be reported on his final return. Amounts excluded from the final return are income with respect to a decedent, taxable to the recipient (the estate or beneficiary). Capital gains or losses of an estate or trust are, with exceptions, subject to the same rules as for an individual.

¶ **3008 Gross income. (a) Estates and trusts.** The gross income of an estate or trust includes: income accumulated in trust for the benefit of unborn, unascertained or contingent beneficiaries; income accumulated or held for future distribution; income to be distributed currently to beneficiaries; income collected by a guardian of an infant; income received by an estate during its administration or settlement; and income to be distributed or accumulated in the fiduciary's discretion [Sec. 641; 1.641(a)-1, 1.641(a)-2].

In the case of an estate, title to personal property usually passes to the executor or administrator, but title to real property often passes to the heirs or persons named in a will at the decedent's death. Therefore, in most cases, the person who gets the real property reports the income from the property or the gain or loss from its sale [¶ 3009]. The only complication is the proper treatment of income accrued to a decedent at the time of his death.

(b) Decedents. When a person dies, his executor or administrator may be required to file returns for two separate and distinct taxable entities: (1) the decedent, for the period before his death; and (2) the decedent's estate.

Final return for decedent. If the decedent was on the cash basis, the final return filed for him will include only income he actually or constructively received while he was alive. A bonus received after a cash basis taxpayer's death will not be reported on his final return, unless it was constructively received during his life.[1] If he used the accrual method of accounting, his final return will include only income that accrued before his death. Income that accrues only because of his death is not included in his final return [Sec. 451(b); 1.451-1(b)]. Deductions get similar treatment. See ¶ 3011.

Income in respect of a decedent. Amounts that are excluded from the decedent's final return under the above rule are taxed to the persons who receive them as a result of the decedent's death. This would include his estate, heirs, devisees and legatees. The amounts are treated as income of the same nature and to the same extent as they would have been income to the decedent if he had remained alive and received them [Sec. 691(a)]. A person who transfers the right to receive such amounts must include in income either what he gets for the right, or its fair market value, whichever is greater, See also ¶ 1304(a).

Example 1: Decedent kept his books on the cash basis. Shortly before his death in November, he was voted a salary payment of $10,000, to be paid in 5 equal annual installments beginning the following January. He could not draw any of these payments before the actual payment date. His estate collected 2 installments, and distributed the right to the remaining 3 installments to the residuary legatee. The $4,000 must be included in the gross income of the estate; the residuary legatee must include $6,000 in its income when received. However, if the estate had sold the right to the 3 reamining installments to a person not entitled to them as a legatee, devisee or heir, or by reason of the death of the decedent, the estate would be required to include in the gross income the amount received or the fair market value of the right, whichever was greater.

Successive decedents. This treatment extends to a successive decedent if the right to an item of gross income in respect of a prior decedent was acquired by reason of the death of the prior decedent or by bequest, devise, or inheritance [Sec. 691(a)(1); 1.691(a)-1].

Example 2: The widow of a life insurance agent acquires by reason of the death of her husband the right to receive renewal commissions on life insurance sold by him in his lifetime and payable over a period of years. However, she dies before getting the commissions, leaving the right to receive them to her son. The son includes the renewal commissions in his gross income as he gets them.

Installment obligations. Decedent's uncollected installment obligations transmitted at his death directly to his estate or beneficiaries are treated as income in respect of a decedent. The recipient will report the installment gain the same way the decedent would have reported it [Sec. 691(a)(4); 1.691(a)-5]. Income in respect of a deceased partner is discussed in Chapter 19.

Deductions and credits accruing after death. Just as income in respect of a decedent is reported by his successor, so the deductions and credits (for example, the foreign tax credit) denied to the decedent on his final return will be allowed to his successor for obligations outstanding against property of the decedent that the successor receives. Business and nonbusiness expenses of the decedent, and deductions for interest and taxes, ordinarily can be deducted by the estate, if it pays them or is liable for them. If it is not liable for their payment, and they are paid by an heir or other beneficiary who got property subject to them, he gets the deduction.

A deduction for depletion also can be taken, but it is allowed to the person who gets the income to which the depletion relates, whether or not he gets the property from which the income is derived [Sec. 691(b); 1.691(b)-1].

Deduction for estate taxes. Income in respect of a decedent is included in his gross estate for estate tax purposes, so it is subject to a double tax. As a relief measure, the person who reports the income can deduct the estate tax attributable to the right he received. For decedents dying after 1976, the income recipient can deduct all federal and state estate taxes that are attributable to income in respect of a decedent. The amount of deduction is computed by multiplying the amount of these taxes by a fraction, the numerator of which is the net amount of the income in respect of a decedent and the denominator of which is the gross estate value. For any generation-skipping transfers made after 4-30-76 [¶ 3912], if any amount distributed out of a generation-skipping trust is included in the transferee's gross income, the transferee is allowed an income tax deduction to the extent of any generation-skipping tax that is attributable to the transferred property (reduced by any credit attributable to that tax) [Sec. 691(c)].

Footnotes appear at end of this Chapter.

¶ **3008**

NOTE: For decedents dying before 1977, a deduction was allowed only as to federal estate taxes. Also, there was a different method of computing the tax deduction.

Any estate tax resulting from inclusion of an employee stock option in the decedent's estate is deductible in the year the estate or beneficiary has increased income resulting from disposition of the stock acquired under the option (¶ 1327) Sec. 421(c)(2)].

The surviving annuitant of a joint and survivor annuity gets a deduction each year during his life expectancy, if the deceased annuitant died after December 31, 1953, and after the annuity starting date. This annual deduction approximately equals the estate tax that results from the net value of the annuity included in the estate of the deceased annuitant divided by the life expectancy of the survivors [Sec. 691(d); 1.691(d)-1].

¶ 3009   Capital gains and losses. The gain on the sale or exchange of a capital asset by an estate or trust must be included in its gross income. The gain is either a short-term or long-term capital gain, and the rules prescribed for individuals apply [¶ 1601 et seq.; 1605; 1612; 1614]. However, a special rule accords long-term treatment to the trust or estate even if it sells the property right after the decedent's death (¶ 1606(b)) [Sec. 1223(1)]. Any part of the gain that is properly paid, credited or required to be distributed during the year to the beneficiary is deductible by the fiduciary. It is taxable to the beneficiary (to the extent of the distributable net income) even if allocated to corpus.

(a)   Capital loss. A capital loss usually is deductible only by the estate or trust, and not by the beneficiary.[1] The loss is either a short-term or long-term capital loss, and the rules for individuals apply. However, a special rule requires trusts and estates to treat losses as long-term even if the assets were sold soon after the decedent's death [¶ 1606(b)]. In most states, title to real property passes directly from the decedent to his heirs (not to the executor). In such states, gain or loss on the sale of the property is reported directly by the heir. For treatment of an unused capital loss in the trust's or estate's year of termination, see ¶ 3011.

(b)   Long-term capital gain deduction. In determining the taxable income of an estate or trust, a deduction is allowed equal to 50% of the excess of the net long-term capital gain over the net short-term capital loss. In determining the amount of the deduction, capital gain allocable to the income beneficiaries must be excluded [Sec. 1202; 1.1202-1]. In computing the alternative tax, the trustee may exclude that portion of long-term capital gain set aside for charities.[2] [¶ 3013], and an estate may deduct the estate tax paid on income in respect of a decedent.[3]

NOTE: An amount equal to one-half the net long-term capital gain is a tax preference item subject to the minimum tax (¶ 2403; 3020(d)) [Sec. 57(a)(9); Prop. Reg. 1.57-1(i)].

(c)   Asset distributions in lieu of cash. When a fiduciary pays a *cash* legacy by transferring an asset to the legatee, it is treated as if a sale or exchange took place between them. Gain or loss to the fiduciary is recognized equal to the difference between the fair market value of the property at its transfer and its adjusted basis in the hands of the fiduciary.[4]

Example: The fiduciary is required to pay $50,000 to the testator's child when he becomes 25. The fiduciary is authorized to pay this amount in either cash or property worth $50,000. He elects to transfer securities worth $50,000 to satisfy the legacy. Assuming the basis of the securities in the fiduciary's hands was $40,000, a capital gain of $10,000 is recognized. If the property transferred was not a capital asset, the $10,000 gain would be taxable as ordinary income.

The legatee is treated as a purchaser of the property. He has a basis equal to the fair market value of the property at the time of the distribution.[5]

If a trustee distributes a capital asset with the same value as a required distribution of income, it is also treated as a sale or exchange. The value is deductible by the trustee and taxable to the beneficiary to the extent of the trust's distributable net income.[6]

(d) Distributable net income. In determining the distributable net income [¶ 3004], the fiduciary excludes capital gains allocated to corpus and not paid or credited to any beneficiary or used for charitable purposes. Capital gains allocated to income are included in distributable net income. Capital losses are excluded, except to the extent they enter into the determination of any capital gains that are paid, credited, or required to be distributed to any beneficiary during the tax year [Sec. 643(a)(3); 1.643(a)-3]. Special rules apply to foreign trusts [Sec. 643(a)(6)].

(e) Deduction for state tax. A simple trust can deduct state income tax on capital gain properly retained by the trust, in arriving at its taxable income and distributable net income.[7]

¶ 3010 Basis of property to estate or trust. (a) Transfer in trust after December 31, 1920. The following rules apply to transfers other than by bequest or devise discussed in (c) below.

- If the transfer is for a valuable consideration, the basis of the property to the trust is the basis in the hands of the grantor, increased by the gain or decreased by the loss recognized to the grantor on the transfer [Sec. 1.1015-2].

    Example: In 1963, A bought certain bonds for $10,000. In 1977, in consideration of $15,000, he transferred the bonds in trust. A's gain is $5,000, and the basis of the bonds to the trust is $15,000 (the basis of the bonds in the hands of A ($10,000) plus the gain recognized to A on the transfer ($5,000)).

- If the transfer is by gift, the basis for gain or loss is the same as for other gifts (¶ 1515) [Sec. 1015(a); 1.1015-1].

(b) Transfer in trust before January 1, 1921. The basis of property acquired by gift or transfer in trust before 1921 is its fair market value on the date of the gift or transfer [Sec. 1015(c); 1.1015-3].

(c) Property acquired from decedent. The basis of property acquired from a decedent depends on when the decedent died. For property acquired in respect of a decedent dying after 12-31-76, the decedent's basis immediately before death is generally carried over, with certain adjustments explained in ¶ 1507. The stepped-up basis rule (using the fair market value on date of death or an alternate valuation date) applies if the decedent died before 1977 [Sec. 1014(a), (d); 1.1014-1].

DEDUCTIONS AND CREDITS

Estates and trusts ordinarily get the same deductions and credits as individuals, but special rules apply to certain deductions such as contributions and depreciation. There is a special deduction for distributions to beneficiaries.

¶ **3011 Deductions in general.** Estates and trusts ordinarily get the same deductions as individuals [Sec. 1.641(b)-1]. Exceptions for contributions, the special rule for depreciation, and disallowance of losses are explained below. Unlike the individual taxpayers, there is no zero bracket amount for estates or trusts [Sec. 63(d)(4)]. For distributions to beneficiaries, see ¶ 3017.

The deductions allowed to a decedent depend on his accounting method. If he reported on the cash basis, the deductions would be those actually paid. If he used the accrual basis, deduction is allowed for amounts that accrue up to the date of death. Deduction cannot be taken, however, for amounts that accrued only because of his death [Sec. 1.461-1(b)]. As to deductions that accrue after his death, see ¶ 3008.

> **NOTE:** Funeral, medical and dental expenses are never deductible in determining the income tax of an estate.[1] No credits or deductions are allowed estates and trusts for political contributions (¶ 2416) [Sec. 642(a)(3), (i)].

(a) Losses. If a trust sustains a loss, the loss usually is not deductible by a beneficiary. The trust and the beneficiary are separate taxable entities, and one taxpayer cannot deduct another's losses.[2]

(b) Termination of estate or trust. When an estate or trust terminates, any unused capital loss or net operating loss carryovers or any deductions (except for personal exemption or charity) in excess of gross income for the last tax year can be deducted by the beneficiaries getting the estate or trust property. This is limited to: (a) the remaindermen of a trust; (b) the heirs and next of kin of a person who dies without a will; and (c) the residuary legatees (including a residuary trust) of a person leaving a will. A person entitled to a dollar legacy qualifies only to the extent the deductions reduced his share. An income beneficiary does not qualify [Sec. 642(h); 1.642(h)-1].

(c) Dividend exclusion. Noncorporate taxpayers can exclude from gross income the first $100 of dividends received from domestic corporations during the tax year [¶ 1705]. The fiduciary is entitled to this exclusion for dividends *not* allocated to beneficiaries. However, on the return, the exclusion is treated as a deduction. That is, the fiduciary reports all dividends received and later deducts a proportionate part of $100, depending on the proportion of dividends retained by the estate or trust.

> **Example:** If an estate received dividends of $4,000, and distributed $3,000 to beneficiaries, accumulating the remaining $1,000, it would report $4,000 dividend income. It then could deduct $25 ($100 $\times$ 1/4) for the exclusion.

Each beneficiary also gets an exclusion on his individual return. If dividends allocated to him by the estate or trust (plus dividends from other sources) amount to $100 or more, his exclusion is $100. But he cannot count dividends allocated to him from the trust if the trust in its last tax year has deductions that exceed its gross income.[3]

¶ **3012 Deduction for personal exemption.** The following deductions are allowed [Sec. 642(b); 1.642(b)-1]:

- An estate gets a deduction of $600.
- A trust that is required to distribute all income currently gets a deduction of $300, even though it is not a "simple"trust that year [¶ 3005]. A trust for the payment of an annuity also gets a deduction of $300 in any tax year the annuity equals or exceeds current income.
- All other trusts get a deduction of $100.

The benefit of the exemption is lost if the estate or trust does not have retained income for the taxable period at least equal to the amount of the exemption.[1]

On a decedent's final return, full deduction is allowed for personal exemptions *for which he qualified* [¶ 1111-1120]. No proration is required [¶ 2717(a)].

> **Example:** Before his death on 11-1-77, Edward Grant, 68 years of age, was the sole support of his wife, Joan, age 63 and his daughter, Ruth, age 18 and single. All have good vision. Neither his wife nor daughter has income of her own. In a separate return filed for the decedent for the period from 1-1-77 to 11-1-77, the following personal exemptions may be claimed *in full:* (1) one exemption for the decedent; (2) another exemption for his old age since he became 65 before he died; (3) another for his spouse if she was not another taxpayer's dependent; (4) another for dependent daughter, if decedent provided more than half her support for 1977.

¶ 3013 Contributions. An estate or a complex trust gets a deduction for gross income which, under the terms of the will or trust deed, is *paid* for charitable purposes[1] [Sec. 642(c)]. Unlike the charitable deduction allowed individuals, no limitation is placed on the amount that can be deducted by a trust or estate. To enable a trustee or administrator to act after he knows the exact income for the year, he can elect to treat a current contribution as paid during the preceding tax year [Sec. 642(c)(1); 1.642(c)-1]. The election must be made not later than the due date (including extensions) of the income tax return for the year after the year for which the election is made. [Temporary Reg. Sec. 13.0(b)(2)]. Estates and certain inter vivos and testamentary trusts in existence on 10-9-69 also get a deduction for gross income which, under the terms of the will or trust deed, *is permanently set aside* for charitable purposes. Pre-10-10-69 inter vivos trusts qualify if the set-aside is required and is for an irrevocable remainder interest or the grantor at all times after 10-9-69 was under a mental disability to change the trust. Testamentary trusts executed before 10-10-69 qualify if: (1) the testator died before 10-9-72 without having republished the will; (2) the will was not republished by 10-9-72 because the testator was under a mental disability; or (3) the testator at no time after 10-9-69 had the right to change the trust provisions in the will. In these trusts, however, the deduction is limited to income earned on property transferred to the trust before 10-0-69, or property transferred under the will [Sec. 642(c)(2)]. The set-aside deduction also is available to pooled income funds [¶ 3927] but only for long-term gain from sale of capital assets [Sec. 642(c)(3),(5); 1.642(c)-1—1.642(c)-5]. A trust claiming the deduction must file an information return [¶ 3538]. Charitable trusts and split interest trusts may be liable for the same excise taxes as private foundations [¶ 3453].

(a) Contributions from gross income. Generally, the charitable contribution must be from the gross income of the trust or estate.[2] Thus, no deduction will be allowed for a contribution out of the estate or trust corpus. However, a contribution from *income* allocable to corpus, such as capital gains, will qualify for the deduction, since such income is included in the gross income of the estate or trust. But no deduction is allowed to a trust for contributions allocable to its unrelated business income for the tax year [¶ 3452].

> **Example 1:** A trustee, under the terms of a will, is directed to pay to X charity one-half of the accretion to corpus each year for the duration of the trust. The only addition to the corpus for the tax year consisted of $12,000 of capital gains and the trustee distributed $6,000 to X charity. Capital gains allocated to corpus under the terms of the will are included in trust gross income, so a charitable contribution deduction will be allowed.

Adjustment for exempt income. When a trust or estate has both taxable and tax-exempt income, the charitable contribution deduction is allowed only for contributions considered as coming from gross income. Unless the governing instrument makes a different allocation, the contribution considered as coming from

Footnotes appear at end of this Chapter.

¶ 3013

gross income bears the same proportion to the total contribution as the total gross income bears to the total income (including tax-exempt items) [Sec. 1.642(c)-2].

Example 2: A trust had income of $8,000 consisting of $5,000 rent and $3,000 tax-exempt interest on municipal bonds. The trustee was directed to pay 25% of the income to charity. He made a charitable contribution of $2,000 (25% of $8,000). The amount considered as coming from the gross income of the trust is $1,250 ($5,000/$8,000 × $2,000). Hence, the trust can deduct $1,250.

Adjustment for long-term capital gain. An adjustment also must be made when an amount is paid or permanently set aside from long-term capital gains and the long-term capital gain deduction is allowed. First you determine the amount of the contribution coming from the long-term capital gains. This bears the same proportion to the total contribution made as the total of the long-term capital gains allocated to income bears to the total income. Then 50% of this amount is subtracted from the contribution. The remainder can be deducted [Sec. 642; 1.642(c)-3].

Example 3: A trust has ordinary income of $20,000 and long-term capital gains of $30,000. Under the trust instrument, a charitable contribution of $15,000 from the trust income is to be made. The amount of the contribution made from the long-term capital gains is $9,000 ($30,000/$50,000 × $15,000). The charitable deduction allowed is $10,500 ($15,000 less 50% of $9,000).

(b) Contributions permanently set aside. To determine whether an amount has been *permanently* set aside by those pre-10-10-69 trusts that can claim a deduction for these amounts, attention is given to capital gains allocated to a charitable remainder trust corpus that can be invaded for the benefit of others. A charitable remainder trust is one in which the trustee is directed to distribute the trust corpus for a charitable purpose when the trust terminates. When the extent to which the corpus can be invaded cannot be measured with certainty, the capital gains allocated to corpus are not considered to have been permanently set aside.[3] Consequently, no charitable contribution deduction can be taken. The instrument creating the trust or estate must establish the extent to which the corpus will be invaded in order for the deduction to be allowed.[4]

NOTE: The problem of invading corpus is unlikely to apply to transfers to inter vivos trusts after 7-31-69 or testamentary trusts created after 1969. Neither the income, estate, nor gift tax charitable deduction is allowed for transfers of remainder interests after these dates if the trust is not a charitable remainder annuity trust or unitrust or a pooled income fund [¶ 1942(e); 3927; 4022].

¶ **3014 Depreciation or depletion.** The depreciation deduction allowed to a life tenant, income beneficiary of a trust, or distributee of an estate is a deduction *for* adjusted gross income; see ¶ 1801(a). Who gets the depreciation deduction is discussed in the following paragraphs; similar rules apply to the deduction for depletion. See also Ch. 10; 11.

(a) Life tenant. The holder of property for life (life tenant) is entitled to the deduction for depreciation during his lifetime. After his death, the remainderman gets the deduction [Sec. 1.167(h)-1(a)].

(b) Trusts. The Code provides that the deduction for depreciation of trust property is to be divided between the income beneficiaries and the trustee as directed in the trust instrument. If the trust instrument makes no allocation, the deduction is apportioned on the basis of the trust income (determined under the trust instrument and state law) allocable to each [Sec. 167(h)].

The regulations limit the allocation in the trust instrument. They provide that the share of the deduction allocated to either the trustee or a beneficiary ordinarily cannot be more than his pro rata share of the trust income. One exception is recognized: if the trust instrument or state law requires or allows the trustee to maintain a reserve for depreciation, the deduction is first allocated to the trustee for income set aside for a depreciation reserve. Any part of the deduction not used up is then divided between the beneficiaries and the trustee on the basis of the trust income (in excess of the amount set aside as a reserve) allocable to each [Sec. 1.167(h)-1(b); 1.642(e)-1].

Example: Mr. Hyde establishes a trust for the benefit of his son, John, and his daughter, Mary. The trust property includes an apartment house on which a depreciation allowance could be claimed. Under the terms of the trust instrument, the income of the trust is to be distributed to John and Mary in equal shares. The trust instrument also authorizes the trustee, in his discretion, to set aside income for a depreciation reserve. During the year, the trustee sets aside $2,000 income as a depreciation reserve. Depreciation on the trust property amounts to $2,500. The trustee gets a depreciation deduction of $2,000. John and Mary each get a depreciation deduction of $250.

When the income beneficiary is entitled to the entire income, and the governing instrument is silent on depreciation, he gets the deduction. Even when the trust has no income during the year, the sole beneficiary is still entitled to take the depreciation deduction.[1]

(c) Estates. For an estate, the depreciation deduction is divided between the estate and the heirs, legatees and devisees on the basis of the income of the estate that is allocable to each [Sec. 1.167(h)-1(c)].

Any additional first-year allowance [¶ 2016] allocated to an heir, legatee or devisee under this provision is not considered in applying the $10,000 (or $20,000 on a joint return) limitation to qualifying property of the heir, legatee, or devisee not held by the estate [Sec. 179(d)(5); 1.179-2(b)].

→**OBSERVATION**→ An estate or trust that shares in depreciation or depletion of another trust or a partnership (or takes the deduction into account separately), divides the deduction among its own distributees on the same basis as it allocates its income.[2]

¶ 3015 Net operating loss deduction. Generally, estates and trusts are entitled to the net operating loss deduction. This may reduce distributable net income for the year to which the operating loss is carried back, so that beneficiaries may recompute their share of the estate or trust income for the prior year.[1] However, in computing the net operating loss, the estate or trust cannot take deductions for charitable contributions or for distributions to beneficiaries. A trust also must exclude income and deductions that are attributable to the grantor [Sec. 642(d); 1.642(d)-1]. If a trust's income is allocable entirely among income beneficiaries, and the governing instrument makes no provision for depreciation, the trustee cannot take a depreciation deduction in computing the net operating loss.[2]

On termination of an estate or trust any unused net operating loss carryovers are deductible by the beneficiaries succeeding to the estate or trust property [Sec. 642(h); 1.642(h)-1].

The net operating loss deduction of a common trust fund [¶ 3025] is allowed to the participants in the fund and not to the trust [Sec. 584(g); 1.584-6].

¶ 3016 Expenses. Ordinary and necessary expenses paid or incurred by an estate or trust are deductible if they are: (1) trade or business expenses; (2) expenses for the production or collection of income or for the management, conservation or maintenance of property held for the production of income; (3) reasonable administration expenses, including fiduciaries' fees and litigation expenses in connection with the duties of administration (except expenses allocable to the pro-

Footnotes appear at end of this Chapter.

¶ 3016

duction or collection of tax-exempt income[1]); (4) expenses for the determination, collection or refund of any tax [Sec. 162, 212; 1.212-1]. Deductible expenses chargeable only to the corpus of a trust reduce distributable net income and thus the amount taxable to the beneficiary. However, these expenses do not reduce the amount of income available for the income beneficiary.[2] The fiduciary must file Forms 1096 and 1099 if he makes certain payments of $600 or more related to a trade or business [¶ 3531].

DEDUCTIBLE

Legal fees: Counsel fees and expenses paid in contesting unsuccessfully an income tax deficiency; legal fees and other expenses paid in connection with tax and other problems arising after the expiration of the trust connection with the final distribution to the legatees.[3]

Interest: Interest on overdue estate tax;[4] interest on legacies.[5]

NOT DEDUCTIBLE

Interest paid by an estate on deficiencies in state inheritance taxes when the taxes are not an obligation of the estate under state law.[6]

(a) Waiver of estate tax deduction. Administration expenses and casualty and theft losses that can be deducted from the gross estate of a decedent [¶ 3926(a), (d)] cannot for income tax purposes be deducted or, for tax years ending after 10-4-76, offset a property's selling price, unless a waiver of the estate tax deduction is filed. A portion of expenses and losses can be allocated to the estate income and a waiver filed for only that part. This rule does not bar deductions related to income in respect of a decedent or for claims against the estate [¶ 3926(c)], such as periodic payments under a divorce decree[7] [Sec. 642(g)].

(b) Statement required. To deduct administration expenses and casualty and theft losses, a statement that they have not been deducted on decedent's estate tax return must be filed in duplicate with the income tax return. This statement is required even if the gross estate is not large enough to require an estate tax return.[8] Waiver of right to deduction under estate tax also is required, and it forfeits the right to deduct the items at any time under the estate tax. However, a claim of deduction on the estate tax return may be withdrawn, if it has not yet been allowed, and a claim for an income tax deduction substituted [Sec. 1.642(g)-1]. If the estate files the statement and waiver and deducts administrative expenses on its income tax return [Sec. 212], it does not forfeit its deduction for *administrative expenses paid in another year* in determining the taxable estate for estate tax purposes [Sec. 2053].[9]

¶ 3017 Deduction for distributions to beneficiaries. (a) Simple trusts. A simple trust gets a deduction for trust income required to be distributed currently, whether or not distributed [Sec. 651; 1.651(a)-2, 1.651(b)-1]. For asset distributions in lieu of cash, see ¶ 3009.

Example 1: The trust instrument requires all the income to be distributed currently. The trust has $10,000 income for 1977, of which $2,500 is collected in December. The trustee pays the usual quarterly payment of $2,500 to its sole beneficiary A in January, 1978. The trust can deduct $10,000 for 1977.

The deduction is limited to the distributable net income [¶ 3004]. For this purpose, distributable net income does not include income items (adjusted for related deductions) not included in gross income [Sec. 651; 1.651(b)-1].

Example 2: Distributable net income is $99,000. This includes tax-exempt interest totaling $9,000. The deduction for distributions to beneficiaries cannot be more than $90,000.

(b) Estates and complex trusts. An estate or complex trust gets a deduction for amounts paid, credited, or required to be distributed to beneficiaries. The deduction consists of the sum of (1) income required to be distributed currently (including an amount payable out of income or corpus to the extent that it is paid out of income), and (2) any other amounts paid, credited, or required to be distributed for the tax year. However, the deduction may not exceed the distributable net income, excluding items not included in the gross income of the estate or trust [Sec. 661(a), 661(c); 1.661(a)-2, 1.661(c)-1]. For asset distributions in lieu of cash, see ¶ 3009.

The amount deductible is treated as consisting of the same proportion of each class of items entering into the computation of distributable net income as the total of each class bears to the total distributable net income, unless the governing instruments or state law allocates different classes of income to different beneficiaries [Sec. 661(b); 1.661(b)-1].

> **Example 3:** A trust has gross income of $100,000, consisting of $50,000 taxable income and $50,000 tax-exempt income. Its distributable net income is $98,000. It has deductions of $2,000, one-half of which is attributable to tax-exempt income. The deduction to the trust is limited to $49,000, since the rest of the distributable net income ($49,000) is deemed to be tax-exempt income.

¶ 3018 Disallowed expenses and losses. A fiduciary of a trust who reports on the accrual basis cannot deduct accrued but unpaid interest, business or "production of income" expenses due a cash basis creditor who is "related" to the trust at the close of the trust's tax year or within 2½ months thereafter. To deduct such amounts, they must be paid or constructively received within 2½ months after the close of the trust's tax year. Issuance of a promissory note during the prescribed period is considered payment to the extent of its fair market value [Sec. 267(a)(2); 1.267(a)-1(b)].

The deduction for these accruals may be disallowed if the related creditor is the grantor of the trust, another trust with the same grantor, a beneficiary of the trust, a beneficiary of another trust with same grantor, or a corporation in which the trust or its grantor actually or constructively owns more than 50% of the stock [Sec. 267(b)]. See also ¶ 2748.

Similarly, no loss deduction is allowed either party to a sale or exchange if they are related when the transaction occurs [Sec. 267; 1.267(a)-1(a)].

¶ 3019 Credits against tax. An estate or trust gets a credit against tax for the following [Sec. 642(a)]:

- *Foreign taxes* not allocable to the beneficiaries [Sec. 1.642(a)(2)-1].
- *Investment credit* not allocated to the beneficiaries [Sec. 48(f)]. Any investment in qualified property is divided between the estate or trust and the beneficiaries according to the income allocable to each. The recapture rules apply to the estate or trust and to each beneficiary if the property is disposed of prematurely or ceases to qualify (¶ 2410(e)) [Sec. 1.47-5].
- *Work incentive program expenses* not allocated to the beneficiaries. The expenses are divided between the estate or trust and the beneficiaries according to the income allocable to each. The recapture rules apply to the estate or trust and to each beneficiary if employment is terminated prematurely (¶ 2411) [Sec. 50B(e); 1.50A-6; 1.50B-3].
- New jobs credit allocated to the estate or trust (¶ 2414) [Sec. 52(g)].

RATES AND RETURNS FOR DECEDENTS, ESTATES AND TRUSTS

An estate or trust uses its special rate schedule to figure its tax. It can't use the tax tables.

Footnotes appear at end of this Chapter.

A fiduciary for an estate or trust which meets certain income requirements, or which has at least one nonresident alien beneficiary, must file Form 1041. An executor or administrator must also file a Form 1040 or 1040A for a decedent who would have been required to file. The fiduciary must file Schedule K-1 with Form 1041 showing each beneficiary's share of income, deductions and credits. A copy is given to each beneficiary.

¶ 3020 **Rates and returns.** (a) **Decedents.** If a decedent would have been required to file a return, his executor, administrator, legal representative, or survivor must file a final return for him.[1] The return is made on Form 1040 or 1040A.[1] An executor or administrator may disaffirm a joint return filed by the surviving spouse [¶ 3507].

The return for the decedent covers the period from the beginning of his tax year up to and including the date of his death (¶ 2717(a)) [Sec. 443; 1.443-1]. For rates, see ¶ 1121; 1122.

(b) **Estates.** The fiduciary must file Form 1041 for every estate for which he acts, if (a) a gross income is $600 or over, or (b) any beneficiary is a nonresident alien [Sec. 6012(a); 1.6012-3(a)]. An ancillary executor or administrator must file an information return on Form 1041 for the part of the estate he controls [Sec. 1.6012-3(a)(3)].

In his first return, the fiduciary chooses the accounting period for the estate. This may be either a calendar year or any fiscal year he selects. Estate gross income is figured from the day following the decedent's death [Sec. 1.443-1]. Thus, a return may have to be filed for the short period from that date to the start of the estate's regular tax year. The tax rate schedule appears below.

TAXABLE INCOME	TAX
Not over $500	14% of the taxable income.
Over $500 but not over $1,000	$70, plus 15% of excess over $500.
Over $1,000 but not over $1,500	$145, plus 16% of excess over $1,000.
Over $1,500 but not over $2,000	$225, plus 17% of excess over $1,500.
Over $2,000 but not over $4,000	$310, plus 19% of excess over $2,000.
Over $4,000 but not over $6,000	$690, plus 22% of excess over $4,000.
Over $6,000 but not over $8,000	$1,130, plus 25% of excess over $6,000.
Over $8,000 but not over $10,000	$1,630, plus 28% of excess over $8,000.
Over $10,000 but not over $12,000	$2,190, plus 32% of excess over $10,000.
Over $12,000 but not over $14,000	$2,830, plus 36% of excess over $12,000.
Over $14,000 but not over $16,000	$3,550, plus 39% of excess over $14,000.
Over $16,000 but not over $18,000	$4,330, plus 42% of excess over $16,000.
Over $18,000 but not over $20,000	$5,170, plus 45% of excess over $18,000.
Over $20,000 but not over $22,000	$6,070, plus 48% of excess over $20,000.
Over $22,000 but not over $26,000	$7,030, plus 50% of excess over $22,000.
Over $26,000 but not over $32,000	$9,030, plus 53% of excess over $26,000.
Over $32,000 but not over $38,000	$12,210, plus 55% of excess over $32,000.
Over $38,000 but not over $44,000	$15,510, plus 58% of excess over $38,000.
Over $44,000 but not over $50,000	$18,990, plus 60% of excess over $44,000.
Over $50,000 but not over $60,000	$22,590, plus 62% of excess over $50,000.
Over $60,000 but not over $70,000	$28,790, plus 64% of excess over $60,000.
Over $70,000 but not over $80,000	$35,190, plus 66% of excess over $70,000.
Over $80,000 but not over $90,000	$41,790, plus 68% of excess over $80,000.
Over $90,000 but not over $100,000	$48,590, plus 69% of excess over $90,000.
Over $100,000	$55,490, plus 70% of excess over $100,000.

(c) **Trusts.** The fiduciary must file Form 1041 if (a) the trust has any taxable income for the tax year, or (b) the gross income is $600 or over, or (c) any beneficiary is a nonresident alien [Sec. 6012; 1.6012-3(a)]. The fiduciary also must file Form 1041-A if the trust claims charitable or other deductions under Sec. 642(c) [Sec. 6034(a); 1.6034-1(a)]. But this return is not required if the trust must distribute all of its net income to its beneficiaries [Sec. 6034(b); 1.6034-1(b)]. Exempt employees' trusts do not file Form 1041, but instead file information returns explained in ¶ 3537.

The trustee chooses the accounting period to be used by the trust. He may select either the calendar year or a fiscal year. The first period for which a return is required starts on the day the trust is created. It covers the period up to the beginning of the trust's regular tax year.

The tax rates applicable to estates also apply to trusts; see (b) above.

Short-form return for simple trust. The fiduciary of a simple trust can use a short-form method to file Form 1041. He need fill in only the appropriate entries on page 1 of the return. He can disregard the schedule for charitable deduction (Sch. B) and the schedule for distributable net income and distributions deduction (Sch. C). The capital gain or loss schedule (Sch. D) is used only if the estate or trust has gains or losses from sales or exchanges of capital assets. However, he must attach separate Schedules K-1 (Beneficiary's share of income, deductions and credits) or an appropriate substitute [¶ 3021].[2]

Will or trust deed. First return of an estate or trust, when gross income is $5,000 or over, must be accompanied by a copy of the will or trust instrument. It also must contain a statement by the fiduciary indicating the provision that determines the taxability of the income to the estate or trust, beneficiaries, or the grantor. Once a copy of the will or trust instrument, and statement, have been filed, they need not again be filed if the fiduciary return contains a statement showing when and where they were filed. If the trust instrument is amended in a later year, a copy of the amendment and a statement of its effect on the taxability of the trust income, must be attached to the return for that year. [Sec.1.6012-(a)(2)].

(d) Minimum tax on estates and trusts. Estates and trusts must pay the minimum tax on the same tax preference items as individuals (¶ 2403) [Sec. 56(a); Prop. Reg. 1.56-1(a)]. The tax itself is also computed the same way. However, the preference items are apportioned between the estate or trust and the beneficiaries on the basis of the estate or trust income allocable to each. Income for this purpose is income received or accrued by the trust or estate which is not subject to current taxation by reason of the tax preference. Preference items allocated to each beneficiary are reported on the tax preference part of Schedule K-1. The exclusion is shared by the estate or trust and the beneficiaries in the same proportion [Sec. 58(c); Prop. Reg. 1.58-1(d)]. Form 4626 is used for filing the minimum tax return of an estate or trust. An estate or trust with tax preference items of $10,000 or less allocated to it needn't file, unless the preference items exceed the amount of the exclusion allocated to it.[3]

NOTE: Proposed amendment to Reg. Sec. 1.6012-3(a) would require a fiduciary to file a minimum tax return if the estate or trust has *any* tax preference, whether or not the minimum tax applies.

¶ 3021 Distribution computations. (a) Simple trust. In the following example, under the terms of a trust, all of the income is to be distributed equally to the grantor's widow and son. Capital gains are to be allocated to corpus. The trust and both beneficiaries file returns on the calendar year basis. No provision for depreciation is made in the trust instrument. During the tax year 1977, the trust had the following items of income and expense:

Rents	$25,000
Dividends of domestic corporations	50,000
Tax-exempt interest on municipal bonds	25,000

Footnotes appear at end of this Chapter.

Long-term capital gains	15,000
Taxes and expenses attributable to rent	5,000
Trustee's commissions allocable to income	2,600
Trustee's commissions allocable to corpus	1,300
Depreciation	5,000

The tax on a simple trust is figured on Form 1041 and amounts to be included in each beneficiary's return are reported on separate Schedule K-1 (Copy A). Form 1041 and its separate schedules are in a different order than given below. The order used here is designed for simplicity.

Income required to be distributed currently (income for trust accounting purposes) is figured as follows:

Rents		$ 25,000
Dividends		50,000
Tax-exempt interest		25,000
Total		$100,000
Deductions: Expenses attributable to rent	$5,000	
Trustee's commissions allocable to income account†	2,600	7,600
Income required to be distributed currently		$ 92,400

† In determining income for trust accounting purposes, expenses allocable to corpus are ignored.

Distributable net income of the trust is figured as follows:

Rents		$25,000
Dividends		50,000
Tax-exempt interest	$25,000	
Less: expenses allocable to tax-exempt interest (25,000/100,000 × $3,900)‡	975	24,025
Total		$99,025
Deductions: Expenses attributable to rent	$5,000	
Trustee's commissions ($3,900 less $975 allocable to tax-exempt interest)‡	2,925	7,925
Distributable net income		$91,100

‡ In determining distributable net income, expenses allocable to corpus are taken into account.

Deduction allowable for distributions is determined as follows:

Distributable net income	$91,100
Less: Tax-exempt interest as adjusted for expenses allocable thereto	24,025
Deduction allowable for distributions	$67,075

The trust's taxable income upon which its tax is based, is computed as follows:

Rents		$25,000
Dividends		50,000
Long-term capital gains		15,000
Gross income		$90,000
Deductions: Rental expenses	$5,000	
Trustee's commission	2,925	
Capital gain deduction	7,500	
Distributions to beneficiaries	67,075	
Personal exemption	300	82,800
Taxable income		$7,200

Amounts allocable to beneficiaries (in determining the character of the amounts includable in, or deductible from gross income of the beneficiaries, it is assumed the trustee elects to allocate to rents the expenses not directly attributable to a specific item of income other than the portion ($975) of such expenses allocated to tax-exempt interest):

	Rents	Dividends	Tax-exempt interest	Total
Income for trust accounting purposes	$25,000	$50,000	$25,000	$100,000
Less: Rental expenses	5,000	......	......	5,000
Trustee's commissions	2,925	......	975	3,900
Total deductions	7,925	0	975	8,900
Beneficiaries' share of income items	$17,075	$50,000	$24,025	$91,100

Since the trust income is to be distributed equally to the widow and son, each is deemed to have received one-half of each form of income; that is, rents of $8,537.50, dividends of $25,000, and tax-exempt interest of $12,012.50. The dividends of $25,000 allocated to each beneficiary are to be added to his or her other dividends (if any) for purposes of the dividend exclusion. Also each beneficiary is allowed a deduction of $2,500 for depreciation of rental property.

(b) Complex trust. In the following example, under the terms of a testamentary trust created in 1973, one-half of the trust income is to be distributed currently to the decedent's widow for her life. The remaining trust income, in the trustee's discretion, may be paid to the decedent's daughter or to designated charities, or it may be accumulated. The trust is to terminate on death of the widow, and the principal will then be payable to the daughter. No provision is made in the trust instrument for depreciation of rental property. Capital gains are allocable to the principal account under state law. The trust and beneficiaries file returns on the calendar year basis. The records of the fiduciary show the following income and deductions for 1977:

Rents	$ 60,000
Dividends of domestic corporations	50,000
Tax-exempt interest	20,000
Capital gains (long-term)	20,000
Depreciation of rental property	10,000
Expenses attributable to rental income	15,400
Trustee's commissions allocable to income account	2,800
Trustee's commissions allocable to principal account	1,100

Income for trust accounting purposes is figured as follows:

Rents		$ 60,000
Dividends		50,000
Tax-exempt interest		20,000
Total		$130,000
Less: Rental expenses	$15,400	
Trustee's commissions allocable to income account	2,800	18,200
Income for trust accounting purposes		$111,800

The trustee, after distributing one-half the income ($55,900) to the widow, made a contribution of one-quarter ($27,950) to charity X and distributed the remaining one-quarter ($27,950) to the daughter.

The items of income, deductions and credits of a complex trust to be included in each beneficiary's return, are computed as illustrated in the schedules below. However, these do not follow the same order or design as in Form 1041. For ex-

Footnotes appear at end of this Chapter.

¶ 3021

ample, the distribution schedule shown below does not follow the design of separate Schedule K-1. The schedules used here are designed to make it easier to understand the computations involved.

Distributable net income of the trust is figured as follows:

Rents			$60,000
Dividends			50,000
Tax-exempt interest		$20,000	
Less: Trustee's commissions allocable thereto (20,000/130,000 × $3,900)	$600		
Charitable contributions allocable thereto (20,000/130,000 × $27,950)	4,300	4,900	15,100
Total			$125,100
Deductions:			
Rental expenses		$15,400	
Trustee's commissions ($3,900 less $600 allocated to tax-exempt interest)		3,300	
Charitable deduction ($27,950 less $4,300 attributable to tax-exempt interest)		23,650	42,350
Distributable net income			$ 82,750

Deduction allowable for distributions is determined as follows:

Distributable net income	$82,750
Less: Tax-exempt interest (as adjusted for expenses and the charitable contributions)	15,100
Deduction allowable for distributions	$67,650

The trust's taxable income upon which its tax is based, is determined as follows:

Rents		$60,000.00
Dividends		50,000.00
Capital gains		20,000.00
Gross income		$130,000.00
Deductions:		
Rental expenses	$15,400	
Trustee's commissions	3,300	
Charitable contributions	23,650	
Capital gain deduction	10,000	
Distributions to beneficiaries	67,650	
Personal exemption	100	120,100.00
Taxable income		$9,900.00

Amounts distributable to beneficiaries and contributed to charity. (In determining the character of the amounts distributable to beneficiaries, the trustee elected to offset the trustee's commissions (other than the portion required to be allocated to tax-exempt interest) against the rental income):

	Rents	Dividends	Tax-exempt interest	Total
Trust income	$60,000	$50,000	$20,000	$130,000
Less:				
Charitable contributions	12,900	10,750	4,300	27,950
Rental expenses	15,400	.....	.....	15,400
Trustee's commissions	3,300	.....	600	3,900
Total deductions	31,600	10,750	4,900	47,250
Amounts distributable to beneficiaries	$28,400	$39,250	$15,100	$ 82,750

The character of the charitable contribution is determined by multiplying the total charitable contribution ($27,950) by a fraction consisting of each item of trust income respectively, over the total trust income. For example, the charitable contribution is deemed to consist of rents of $12,900 (60,000/130,000 × $27,950).

Amounts includible in widow's gross income: The $55,900 distribution to the widow ($111,800 × ½) is deemed to be composed of the following proportions of the items of income deemed to have been distributed to her:

Rents (28,400/82,750 × $55,900)	$19,185
Dividends (39,250/82,750 × $55,900)	26,515
Tax-exempt interest (15,100/82,750 × $55,900)	10,200
Total	$55,900

Thus, the widow will exclude $10,200 of tax-exempt interest from gross income. She will get the exclusion for dividends received with respect to the dividends ($26,515) deemed to have been distributed to her. Her share of the dividends will be added to any other dividends she gets for purposes of the exclusion. In addition, she can deduct a share of the depreciation deduction proportionate to the trust income allocable to her; that is, one-half the total depreciation deduction, or $5,000.

Amounts includible in daughter's gross income: Since the sum of the amount of income required to be distributed currently to the widow ($55,900) and the other amounts properly paid, credited or required to be distributed to the daughter ($27,950) exceeds the distributable net income ($82,750), the daughter is deemed to have received $26,850 ($82,750 less $55,900) for income tax purposes. The character of the amounts deemed distributed to her is determined as follows:

Rents (28,400/82,750 × $26,850)	$ 9,215
Dividends (39,250/82,750 × $26,850)	12,735
Tax-exempt interest (15,100/82,750 × $26,850)	4,900
Total	$26,850

The daughter can exclude $4,900 of tax-exempt interest. She will get the exclusion for dividends received ($12,735) deemed to have been distributed to her. Her share of the dividends will be added to any other dividends she gets for purposes of the exclusion. In addition, she can deduct a share of the depreciation deduction proportionate to the trust income allocable to her: that is, one-fourth of the total depreciation deduction, or $2,500. The remaining $2,500 of the depreciation deduction is allocable to the amount distributed to the charity X, and hence is not deductible by the trust, the widow or the daughter.

SPECIAL PROBLEMS

The paragraphs that follow cover "Clifford" trusts, the throwback rule, employees' trusts, and individual retirement accounts.

¶ 3022 Trust income taxable to grantor or others. Under certain conditions, the income of a trust is not taxed to the trust or beneficiaries. It may be taxed instead to the grantor or other persons who have substantial dominion and control over the trust property or income. When the grantor is taxed on the income of the trust, he is allowed the deductions and credits related to the income [Sec. 671; 1.671-3]. The tax year and the method of accounting used by the trust are disregarded. The gross income from the trust properties is determined by the grantor as if the trust had not been created.[1] The trustee still must file a return on Form 1041, but the income, deductions and credits of the trust are shown on a separate statement attached to the return, instead of on the return itself [Sec. 1.671-4].

A special rule applies when a grantor places property in trust, having unrealized appreciation, to shift the payment of tax to the trust at its lower progressive rates. See (g) below.

Footnotes appear at end of this Chapter.

¶ 3022

(a) **Reversionary interest.** The grantor is taxable on the trust income from property in which he retains a reversionary interest (in the corpus or income) that may take effect within 10 years after the last transfer to the trust. If he has an interest in the corpus that will revert to his estate at death, the trust income is taxable to him if his life expectancy is less than 10 years[2] [Sec. 673(a); 1.673(a)-1].

Example 1: Harvey sets up a trust with income payable to his son for 8 years. Then the corpus is to return to Harvey. Harvey is taxable on the entire income from the trust during the 8 year period.

Example 2: Harvey sets up a trust with income payable to his son for 11 years (a so-called "short-term" or "Clifford" trust). Then the corpus is to return to Harvey. Five years later, Harvey transfers more property to the trust, but does not extend the period of the trust. Harvey is taxable on the income from the property involved in the second transfer. He is not taxable on the income from the property originally transferred until the end of the trust.

However, if trust income is payable to a beneficiary for life, with a reversion in the grantor, the grantor is not taxable on the income even if the life expectancy of the beneficiary is less than 10 years [Sec. 673(c); 1.673(a)-1(b)].

Although ordinary income of a trust is taxable to the beneficiaries when the trust principal cannot revert to the grantor until after 10 years, capital gains that must be added to the trust corpus under state law are taxable to the grantor as income accumulated for future distribution[3] (see (e) below).

(b) **Power to control beneficial enjoyment.** The grantor is taxable on the trust income if he or a nonadverse party, or both, have the power to dispose of the corpus or income without the consent of any adverse party [Sec. 674; 1.674(a)-1]. An adverse party is any person having a substantial beneficial interest in the trust that would be adversely affected by the exercise or nonexercise of the power (such as a general power of appointment over the trust property) he possesses respecting the trust. A nonadverse party is any other person [Sec. 672(a)(b); 1.672(a)-1].

Exceptions: The following powers *in anyone* will not cause the income to be taxed to the grantor [Sec. 674(b); 1.674(b)-1]:

(1) To apply trust income to support grantor's dependents, except to the extent so applied (see also (e) below);
(2) To change the distribution of income, but only 10 years after the creation of the trust;
(3) To affect income distribution by will (except accumulated income);
(4) To shift corpus or income from one charity to another;
(5) To invade corpus for the benefit of any designated beneficiary;
(6) To postpone payment of income to a beneficiary temporarily;
(7) To postpone payment of income to a beneficiary during his minority or disability;
(8) To apportion receipts and disbursements between corpus and income.

The grantor is not taxed on the trust income when a power to allocate income or corpus among a class of beneficiaries is held by any person other than the grantor or a person who is both related to the grantor and subservient to his wishes [Sec. 1.674(c)-1]. Nor will he be taxed when a trustee (other than the grantor or his wife) holds a power to apportion income among a class of beneficiaries according to a reasonably definite external standard spelled out in the trust instrument [Sec. 1.674(d)-1] (see note below).

NOTE: The exceptions noted in the preceding paragraph and in paragraphs (5), (6) and (7) above do not apply if any person has a power to add to the designated beneficiaries, except to provide for children born or adopted after the grantor dies [Sec. 1.674(d)-2(b)].

(c) **Administrative powers.** The grantor is taxable on the trust income when administrative control of the trust may be exercised primarily for his benefit instead of the beneficiaries [Sec. 675; 1.675-1]. The following situations illustrate this type of administrative control:

- Power in the grantor or a nonadverse party, or both, without the approval of any adverse party, to deal with the trust property or income for less than an adequate consideration;
- Power in the grantor or a nonadverse party, or both, that enables the grantor to borrow the corpus or income without adequate interest or security, except when a trustee (other than the grantor) is authorized to make loans to *any* persons without regard to interest or security;
- When the grantor has borrowed the corpus or income and has not repaid the loan before the start of the tax year, unless the loan was made for adequate interest and security by a trustee (other than the grantor or a trustee subservient to the grantor);
- General powers of administration exercisable by anyone in a nonfiduciary capacity so as to benefit the grantor individually rather than the beneficiaries.

(d) **Power to revoke.** The grantor generally is taxable on the income of a trust if he reserves the power to revoke the trust. However, he is not taxable if he can revoke it only with the consent of an adverse party. If he cannot exercise the power to revoke until 10 years after inception of the trust, he is not taxed on the income during that time. He will be taxed after that time, unless he gives up the power [Sec. 676; 1.676(a)-1, 1.676(b)-1].

(e) **Income for benefit of grantor, his spouse or dependent.** The grantor is taxable on the income of a trust when, without the consent of an adverse party, it *is,* or *may be,* paid or accumulated for the grantor's benefit, or used to pay his life insurance premiums (except policies irrevocably payable to charity). In addition, the grantor is taxable on the income from property transferred in trust after 10-9-69 for the benefit of his spouse. In transfers for the benefit of himself or his spouse, the grantor is treated as the owner of the property transferred [Sec. 1.677(a)-1]. Trust income used to support a child or other beneficiary the grantor is legally obligated to support generally is taxable to the grantor, for example, when it is used to pay his son's college tuition[4] [Sec. 677; 1.677(a)-1, 1.677(b)-1]. But in the case of an alimony or support trust, the wife is taxed on the payments (including any tax preference items) except to the extent the payments are for the support of minor children [Sec. 682; 1.682(a)-1, 1.682(b)-1, 1.682(c)-1]. Some courts hold that tax-exempt income received by an alimony trust is not taxed when it is distributed to the wife,[5] but the Revenue Service disagrees.[6]

(f) **Income taxable to others.** A person other than the grantor may be taxed on the trust income if he has a power to acquire the corpus or income of the trust. Thus, a person who has exclusive power to vest the corpus or income of a trust in himself, or who has released such power but retained controls similar to those outlined in (a) to (e) above is taxed on the trust income [Sec. 678; 1.678(a)-1], subject to these modifications:

(1) If the grantor of the trust, or the transferor in (h), below, is taxed as the owner, the other person will not be taxed under the above rule;

(2) If the other person can merely use trust income to support a dependent, he will be taxed only to the extent it is so used [Sec. 1.678(c)-1];

(3) If the other person renounces the power within a reasonable time after learning of it, he will not be taxed on the trust income [Sec. 1.678(d)-1].

Footnotes appear at end of this Chapter.

¶ 3022

(g) Taxing transfer of appreciated property to trust. For transfers in trust made after 5-21-76, if property with unrealized appreciation is transferred to a trust and the trust sells it within 2 years of the transfer, the trust is taxed, at the grantor's tax rates, on the "includible gain" (below). The tax is equal to the additional tax the transferor would have paid (including any minimum tax) had the gain been included in his income for his tax year in which the sale occurred. For a short sale, the 2-year period is extended to the closing date [¶ 1608]. Whether the property is a capital asset, is determined by looking at its character in the transferor's hands [Sec. 644].

"Includible gain" is the lesser of (1) the gain realized by the trust on the sale or exchange, or (2) the excess of the property's fair market value at the time of the initial transfer over the trust's basis in the property immediately after the transfer [Sec. 644(b)]. The trust's basis will include any increase in basis for gift tax paid. Any additional gain on the property occurring after the transfer is subject to the normal rules for gains realized by the trust. The "includible gain" is excluded from trust's taxable income and distributable net income (¶ 3004(a)).

When to report "includible gain". In general, the additional tax is reported by the trust for its tax year that begins with or within the transferor's tax year in which the sale or exchange occurred [Sec. 644(a)(3)].

Exceptions. The above rules do not apply to property acquired by a trust from a decedent, or by a pooled income fund or a charitable remainder annuity trust or unitrust [¶ 1942(e)]. Nor does it apply if the property is sold or exchanged after the transferor's death [Sec. 644(e)].

(h) Foreign trust with U.S. beneficiary. For tax years ending after 12-31-75, a U.S. person (grantor) who directly or indirectly transfers property after 5-21-74 to a foreign trust created after 5-21-74, is taxed as the owner of the portion of the trust attributable to such property if the trust has a U.S. beneficiary for such tax year [Sec. 679(a)(1)].

A grantor will not be treated as owner of a foreign trust if the transfers are made to the foreign trust because of the grantor's death, or if the transferor has recognized gain on the transfer [Sec. 679(a)(2)].

A trust having a foreign corporation as a beneficiary is treated under the attribution rules as "having a U.S. beneficiary" if over 50% of the total combined voting power of all classes of stock is owned by U.S. shareholders. The attribution rules apply if a foreign trust has a foreign partnership as a beneficiary and a U.S. person is a partner. Similarly, if the foreign trust has a foreign trust or estate as a beneficiary, the attribution rules apply if the second trust or estate has a U.S. person as beneficiary [Sec. 679(c)(2)].

¶ 3023 "Throwback" of excess distributions by complex trusts. The throwback rule ordinarily applies only to complex trusts [Sec. 1.665(a)-OA]. But a simple trust that makes an accumulation distribution allocable to an earlier year is treated as a complex trust for that year [Sec. 1.665-1A(b)].

Background and purpose. The throwback rule prevents the tax avoidance that occurs when a trust in a lower tax bracket accumulates and pays the tax on its income rather than distribute the income to a beneficiary in a higher tax bracket. When the income is distributed at a future date, little or no additional tax is paid by the beneficiary because distributions in excess of the distributable net income in the year of distribution are tax-exempt to the beneficiary [¶ 3004]. Thus, trust income can be split between the trust and the beneficiary in a way that avoids the high tax to the beneficiary in a year his other income puts him in a substantially higher tax bracket than the trust. This tax avoidance device is compounded when multiple accumulation trusts—each in a low tax bracket—are used. To forestall this, *the throwback rule taxes the beneficiaries as if the amounts had been distributed each year instead of accumulated.* In other words, the rule "throws back" the accumulated income to the years it was accumulated. The 1969 Tax Reform Act changed the mechanics of applying the throwback rule, provided for the throwback of capital gains distributions, eliminated certain exceptions, and did away with the 5-year limitation on the rule's application. The 1976 Tax Reform Act repeals the capital gain throwback, simplifies the method of computation and exempts minors and unborn children from the throwback rule.

Two throwback concepts are basic to understanding the rule: (a) "undistributed net income" and (b) "accumulation distribution" [Sec. 665(a), 665(b); 1.665(a)-1A, 1.665(b)-1A]. There can only be a throwback from a year with an accumulation distribution to a year with undistributed net income.

(a) Undistributed net income. A trust has undistributed net income for a tax year when the amounts distributed are less than the distributable net income for the year [Sec. 665(a)(2), 665(d); 1.665(a)-1A]. Undistributed net income is computed as follows:

1. Find the distributable net income of the trust [¶ 3004].
2. Subtract the following from amount in (1):

(a) the amount of *income* required to be distributed currently including any amount that may be paid out of income or corpus to the extent it was paid out of trust income for the year; and

(b) any other amounts paid, credited or required to be distributed; and

(c) the income tax on the undistributed portion of the trust's distributable net income. This is the same amount as the total tax paid by the trust (not including any minimum tax) except when the trust has capital gains not included in distributable net income (for example, capital gains to corpus) [Sec. 1.665(d)-1A].

Example 1: Under the terms of a trust, the trustee is required to distribute $10,000 of income currently to Bill Brown. He also has discretion to make additional distributions to Brown. In 1977, the trust's distributable net income of $30,100 was derived from royalties, and the trustee distributed $20,000 to Brown. The trust's taxable income is $10,000 on which a tax of $2,190 is paid. The undistributed net income of the trust for 1977 is $7,910, computed as follows:

Distributable net income		$30,100
Less:		
Income currently distributable to Brown	$10,000	
Other amounts distributed to Brown	10,000	
Tax attributable to undistributed net income	2,190	22,190
Undistributed net income		$7,910

(b) Accumulation distribution. A trust has an accumulation distribution when it distributes more than the distributable net income for the year. To determine the accumulation distribution, find the total distribution for the tax year reduced by the amount of income required to be distributed currently (including any amount that may be paid out of income or corpus to the extent it was paid out of trust income for the year) and subtract the distributable net income reduced (but not below zero) by the income required to be distributed currently. This difference is the accumulation distribution for the tax year. For distributions in tax years starting after 1975, a distribution made or required to be distributed by a trust in a year that does not exceed the trust income for the year is not treated as an accumulation distribution for that year [Sec. 665(b); 1.665(b)-1A].

Example 2: During the tax year 1977, a trustee properly distributes $20,000 to a beneficiary, of which $7,000 is income required to be distributed currently to him. The distributable net

Footnotes appear at end of this Chapter.

¶ 3023

income of the trust is $15,000. There is an accumulation distribution of $5,000, computed as follows:

Total distribution		$20,000
Less: Income required to be distributed currently		7,000
Other amounts distributed		13,000
Distributable net income	$15,000	
Less: Income required to be distributed currently	7,000	
Balance of distributable net income		8,000
Accumulation distribution		$5,000

(c) **How to handle the throwback rule.** When a trust makes an accumulation distribution for any tax year, the distribution is thrown back to the earliest year the trust has undistributed net income, and so on, up to the year of the distribution. The accumulation being thrown back is deemed to have been distributed on the last day of the year to which it is thrown back, but only to the extent of the undistributed net income of that year. The rest of the accumulation distribution is then thrown back to the next succeeding year that had undistributed net income, and so on through the tax years until the accumulation distribution is used up [Sec. 666(a); 1.666(a)-1A]. The trustee must file Schedule J (attached to Form 1041), showing allocation of accumulation distribution to each beneficiary.

Sixty-five day rule. A trustee can avoid the throwback rule by electing to treat any distribution during the first 65 days of a trust year as an amount paid during the preceding year (¶ 3006(f)) [Sec. 663(b); 1.663(b)-1, 2].

Extent of throwback. The 1969 Tax Reform Act applied the unlimited throwback rule to accumulations earned in tax years starting after 1968. This means that accumulations in tax years starting before 1969 are not included in accumulation distributions in tax years starting after 1973 but are added to the trust corpus [Sec. 1.666(a)-1A(b)(1)]. In the same way, accumulation distributions in tax years starting before 1974 would not include any accumulations earned more than 5 years before the date of distribution [Sec. 665(e); 1.665(e)-1A; 1.666(a)-1A(b)(2)]. The net effect of these transition rules is that no distributions would be thrown back more than 5 years until 1975. Also, any distributions after 1968 from accumulations from tax years starting before 1969 are not thrown back (and thus are tax-free in the year of distribution) if they are within any of the following exceptions [Sec. 1.665(b)-2A]:

1. Amounts paid, credited, or required to be distributed to a beneficiary as income accumulated before his birth or before he reaches 21;

NOTE: This exception has been restored for tax years beginning after 12-31-75. See (e) below.

2. Amounts paid or credited to a beneficiary for emergency needs;
3. Amounts paid or credited to a beneficiary upon his reaching a specified age, provided (a) the total distributions cannot exceed four, (b) the distributions are at least 4 years apart, and (c) the distributions were required by the trust instrument as of January 1, 1954;
4. Amounts paid or credited to a beneficiary as a final distribution of the trust if made more than 9 years after the last transfer to the trust.

Example 3: In 1977, a trust reporting on the calendar year basis makes an accumulation distribution of $33,000. Therefore, years before 1969 are ignored. In 1969, the trust had $6,000 of undistributed net income; in 1970, $4,000; in 1971, none; in 1972, $7,000; in 1973, $5,000; in 1974, $8,000; in 1975, $6,000; and in 1976, $4,000. The accumulation distribution is deemed distributed $6,000 in 1969, $4,000 in 1970, none in 1971, $7,000 in 1972, $5,000 in 1973, $8,000 in 1974, $3,000 in 1975.

Lack of records. If records are not available to determine the undistributed net income of any tax year of the trust, the accumulation distribution is deemed to have been determined on 12-31-69 or the earliest subsequent date the trust was in existence. If the trustee establishes that the loss of records for some tax years was due to circumstances beyond his control, the accumulation distribution is first allocated to tax years for which he has adequate records [Sec. 666(d); 1.666(d)-1A].

Example 4: In 1977, a trust makes a distribution of $100,000. The trustee has adequate records for 1975, 1976 and 1977. These records show that the trust is on a calendar year basis, had $20,000 distributable net income in 1977 and $15,000 undistributed net income in 1976 and $16,000 in 1975. The trustee has no other records except a copy of the instrument showing that the trust was created on 1-1-67. He establishes that the loss of records was due to circumstances beyond his control. Since the distribution is made in 1977, the earliest tax year of the trust to which a throwback is made is 1969. Since $80,000 of the distribution is an accumulation distribution, and $31,000 of it is allocated to 1975 and 1976, $49,000 is deemed to have been distributed on the last day of 1969.

(d) Tax added to distribution. When an accumulation distribution is thrown back to a particular year, all or part of the tax imposed on the trust for that year (other than any tax on capital gains) is also deemed distributed. This is done because the accumulation deemed distributed in the year to which the accumulation is thrown back would have increased the trust's distribution deduction in that year [¶ 3017], and thereby reduced or eliminated the trust's tax. If the accumulation distribution thrown back to a particular year is at least as much as the undistributed net income for that year, the tax paid by the trust for that year is eliminated and is therefore added to the distribution [Sec. 666(b); 1.666(b)-1A]. If the accumulation distribution thrown back is less than the undistributed net income, the portion of the tax added to the accumulation distribution is determined as follows [Sec. 666(c); 1.666(c)-1A]:

$$\text{Tax on the trust for the year to which the throwback is made} \times \frac{\text{Accumulation distribution thrown back to the particular year}}{\text{Undistributed net income for that particular year}} = \text{The amount of the tax deemed to have been distributed on the last day of that particular year}$$

(e) Tax paid by beneficiaries on excess distribution. The beneficiary must pay an additional tax in the year in which the accumulation distribution is actually paid, credited, or required to be distributed on the amount deemed to have been distributed to him by the trust in any year to which the throwback is made. He is taxed on the accumulation distribution thrown back to a particular year and also an amount equal to the tax paid by the trust on the accumulation distribution so thrown back. The tax on the beneficiary in the year the accumulation is actually distributed is the sum of (1) the partial tax on the beneficiary's taxable income computed without regard to the accumulation distribution and (2) the partial tax on the accumulation distribution [Sec. 667]. The partial tax is computed on a 3-year average basis, as follows:

First, the beneficiary takes his taxable income for the 5 years immediately preceding the distribution year, and disregards the lowest and highest years. If he has a loss year in any of the 5 preceding years, that year's taxable income is deemed to be not less than the zero bracket amount, for a beneficiary who is an individual [¶ 1107], or zero, for a corporate beneficiary. Using the averaging device, he then adds an amount equal to the trust income accumulation distribution, divided by the number of years the trust earned it, to the taxable income for the remaining 3 years and figures a tax for each year. Finally, he multiplies the average increase in tax for the 3-year period by the number of years the trust earned the income. The

Footnotes appear at end of this Chapter.

¶ 3023

result is his tax on the accumulation [Sec. 667(b)]. The tax so computed may be offset by a credit for any taxes previously paid by the trust with respect to this income, and the remaining tax liability is then payable by the beneficiary in the distribution year. But no refund or credit is allowed as a result of accumulation distribution; see (f) below. Special rules apply to multiple trusts [Sec. 667(c)].

For distributions in tax years starting after 12-31-75, accumulations for beneficiaries before they are born or for children up to age 21 are exempt from the throwback rules. However, a beneficiary of a multiple trust gets the exemption only for the first 2 trusts. A beneficiary of a foreign trust is not entitled to this exemption [Sec. 665(b)(2), 667].

(f) Refunds on credits. For distributions in tax years starting after 12-31-75, the 1976 Tax Reform Act does not allow any refunds or credits to be made to any beneficiary or trust as a result of any accumulation distributions [Sec. 666(e)].

(g) Determining the new undistributed net income. After the taxes paid by the beneficiaries under the throwback rule have been determined, it is necessary to determine what the remaining undistributed net income for the trust will be for the prior year involved. This is determined as explained in ¶ 3023(a) with this exception: The amount distributed by the trust includes not only the amounts actually paid or credited for the prior year involved but also amounts *deemed* distributed under the throwback rule [Sec. 1.665(a)-1A(c); 1.666(a)-1A(d)]. In other words, it must be assumed that the trust distributed all the amounts attributable to the prior year involved. In addition, when a throwback results in taxes paid by the trust being deemed distributed to the beneficiaries, the taxes imposed on the trust attributable to any remaining undistributed net income are reduced by the taxes deemed distributed [Sec. 1.665(d)-1A(b)(2)].

(h) Capital gain distribution. The 1976 Tax Reform Act repeals the capital gain throwback rule for distributions in tax years starting after 12-31-75. However, the Act provides a special rule for taxing the trust on the gain on its sale of the transferred property (within 2 years of transfer) when there was a bargain element on the initial transfer. See ¶ 3022(g).

(i) Foreign trusts. The general accumulation rules explained earlier also apply to foreign trusts. However, for tax years starting after 12-31-75, foreign trusts are not allowed an exclusion from the throwback rule for accumulation distributions covering years before the beneficiary reached 21 or was born. Beneficiaries cannot gross up taxes paid by the trust for the covered years; they cannot get any kind of credit for taxes paid by the trust [Sec. 643, 665(b), (c), 666(e), 667]. Special rules apply to foreign trusts not created by U. S. persons [Sec. 665(c); 1.665(c)-1A]. For taxation of foreign trusts with a U. S. beneficiary, see ¶ 3022(h).

NOTE: A beneficiary who receives accumulation distribution from a foreign trust may be liable for an interest charge [Sec. 668].

¶ 3024 Employees' trusts. Employers setting up a stock bonus, pension, or profit-sharing plan for the benefit of their employees frequently create a trust to hold, invest, and distribute the fund. For self-employed retirement plans, see ¶ 1839; for individual retirement accounts, see ¶ 3027.

Background and purpose. The growth of these plans reflects a number of influences, including employer realization that they improve the attitudes and performance of employees, and a general concern for economic security. This growth has also been encouraged by tax provisions which allow tax deferral on contributions made on behalf of covered employees. The Employee Retirement Income Security Act sets new standards for participation, vesting and funding. It changes limits on deductible contributions and taxation of lump-sum payouts. It also provides for individual retirement savings plans, more tax benefits for the self-employed, and comprehensive rules on reports and prohibited transactions. The 1976 Tax Reform Act eases the limitations on contributions to Keogh plans and individual accounts [¶ 1838; 1839]. It also permits recipients of lump-sum payouts to elect ordinary income treatment subject to the 10-year averaging.

(a) Exemption of trust income. Income of these trusts ordinarily is exempt (except for tax on unrelated business income, ¶ 3446) if the trust is created or organized in the United States and all of the following requirements are met [Sec. 401(a), 501(a); 1.401-1; Temp. Reg. Sec. 11.401(a)-14; Prop. Reg. 1.401(a)-14]:

(1) The plan is for the employees' and their beneficiaries' exclusive benefit.

(2) The sole purpose of the plan is to offer the employees or their beneficiaries either (a) a share of the profits of the business, or (b) an income after retirement.

(3) The contributions or benefits provided under the plan do not discriminate in favor of employees who are officers, shareholders, or highly paid employees.

(4) The employer intends the plan to be permanent (but an irrevocable lump sum contribution to be distributed in 10 years, with no provision for future contributions, was held to qualify).[1]

(5) The plan is in writing and is communicated to the employees.

(6) A *pension* plan must prohibit forfeitures that increase employee benefits.

(7) It must be impossible, under the trust instrument, for any of the trust corpus or income at anytime to be used other than for the exclusive benefit of the employees or their beneficiaries [Sec. 1401-2].

(8) The plan must meet the standards of minimum participation, vesting, commencement of benefits and the like [Temp. Reg. Sec. 11.411(a)-2; Prop. Reg. 1.411(a)-2].

Minimum participation standards. A plan, whether or not trusteed, does not qualify for exemption if it requires, as a condition of plan participation, that an employee complete a period of service with the employer extending beyond (a) 1 year of service, or (b) the date the employee reaches age 25, whichever is later [Sec. 410; Temp. Reg. Sec. 11.410(a)-1—11.410(a)-6; Prop. Reg. 1.410(a)-1—1.410(a)-6]. However, a plan that provides for 100% vesting after 3 years of service can defer participation until an employee has put in 3 years of service. A defined or target benefit plan can exclude employees who are hired at an age within 5 years of the plan's normal retirement age. A "year of service" is any 12-month period during which the employee puts in at least 1,000 "hours of service." These standards do not apply to government, church and certain other plans. However, certain church plans may elect to have the minimum participation, vesting, etc. provisions apply to the plan [Temp. Reg. Sec. 11.410(d)-1; Prop. Reg. 1.410(d)-1].

Minimum vesting standards. A qualified plan must provide an employee with complete vesting of all accrued benefits from his own contributions, and complete vesting of his normal retirement benefits on attaining normal retirement age [Sec. 411]. In addition, the employer's contributions must be 100% vested under: (a) the 10 years of service rule, (b) the graduated 15-year rule, or (c) the "rule of 45." Under the 10-year rule there is complete vesting after 10 years. Under the 15-year rule, the employee's right to his accrued benefit is 25% vested after 5 years of service, plus 5% for each of the next 5 years, and 10% for each of the following 5 years. Under the "rule of 45," an employee with at least 5 years of service has at least 50% of his rights vested, if the sum of his age and years of service adds up to

Footnotes appear at end of this Chapter.

¶ 3024

45. 10% is added for each succeeding year of service, so the employee has 100% vested after an additional 5 years of service [Temp. Reg. Sec. 11.411(a)-1—11.411(a)-9; Prop. Reg. 1.411(a)-1—1.411(a)-9].

A plan that meets these requirements is referred to as a "qualified" plan. When a trust for a pension plan negotiated by a union and at least one or more employers substantially complied with the requirements, the Revenue Service can qualify it from the date contributions were first made, rather than from the date it actually qualified [Sec. 401(i)].

A domestic corporation can cover under its own qualified plan U.S. citizens employed by the corporation's foreign subsidiaries for whom it has elected social security coverage. The parent corporation's contribution is deductible only by the foreign subsidiary, and unreimbursed contributions become part of the subsidiary's capital. A similar rule applies to U.S. citizens employed abroad by an 80% owned subsidiary doing substantially all its business abroad [Sec. 406, 407].

> NOTE: A pension or annuity plan may provide for sickness, hospitalization and accident expenses of retired employees and their families. These benefits must be subordinate to the plan's retirement benefits. A separate account must be kept for the benefit funds, and they cannot be used for other purposes. Contributions under the plan for medical benefits and for life insurance are limited to not more than 25% of the total contribution for all benefits that the plan provides [Sec. 1.401-14(c)(1)]. Unused funds must be returned to the employer [Sec. 401(h)].

A plan is not discriminatory if (a) 70% or more of all employees participate in the plan, or (b) 70% or more of all employees are eligible and 80% of those eligible are in the plan, or (c) the plan benefits employees qualifying under a classification set up by the employer, which the IRS does not find discriminatory in favor of employees who are officers, shareholders, or highly paid employees [Sec. 401(a), 410(b); 1.401-3; Temp. Reg. Sec. 11.410(b)-1; Prop. Reg. 1.410(b)-1].

Limitations on benefits. Benefits under employee pension, profit-sharing or stock bonus plans are subject to overall limitations[2] [Sec. 415]. Generally, for a defined benefit plan, the maximum annual benefit allowed for an employee with at least 10 years of service cannot, at anytime within the limitation year, exceed the lesser of $75,000 or 100% of his average compensation for his high 3 consecutive years of service. For a defined contribution plan, the annual addition to a participant's account in a limitation year cannot exceed the lesser of $25,000 or 25% of his compensation for the year. The $75,000 and $25,000 limits are, effective 1-1-77, increased to $84,525 and $28,175, respectively, for cost-of-living adjustments.[3] See also ¶ 1838.

As long as the plan meets the above requirements, it may cover the employer's only employee, even if the employer deals exclusively in the services of its employee who is also its principal or sole shareholder,[4] or give a new employee credit in a qualified pension plan for the employee's past service for another employer.[5] The former employer must be a member in a group plan with the new employer or be specified in the new employer's plan. Other special conditions must also be fulfilled. Also, the trust may make loans to, or invest in the securities of the employer contributing to the plan if full disclosure is made[6] and make adequately secured loans at reasonable interest to employee-participants in excess of their vested interests[7] [Sec. 1.401-1(b)(5)]. A determination letter on the effect of investing in employer's stock can be obtained from the District Director by filing Form 4575.[8] An electing small business corporation [¶ 3140 et seq.] can adopt a plan that includes shareholder-employees.[9]

(b) Trust must prove exemption. The employer who establishes or amends a pension, profit-sharing or stock bonus plan or trust will want to know in advance if the proposed plan or trust qualifies for exemption from tax. For the convenience of taxpayers, the Service will issue a determination letter. Requests for determination letters as to defined contribution plans are filed with the district director generally on Form 5301. Form 4577 permits the administrators or trustees of an industry wide plan to file for employer-members of the plan.[8] Advance approval can be obtained for master and prototype employee plans. Application is made on Form 4461 by a sponsoring employer group and on Form 4462 by an employer.[10]

Information return. An information return must be filed by the trustee each year to prove the trust's right to continued exemption [¶ 3537]. A qualified employees' trust may be excused from reporting information reported in returns of the employer establishing the trust [Sec. 6033(a); 1.6033-2(a)].

Prohibited transactions. The Employee Retirement Income Security Act specifies certain prohibited transactions involving an employee benefit plan, and defines fiduciary responsibilities. An excise tax is imposed on disqualified persons who participate in prohibited transactions [Sec. 4975; 54.4975-9]. This tax is similar to the penalty tax on those of a private foundation engaged in self-dealings [¶ 3440].

(c) Deduction for employer's contributions. An employer can take a limited deduction for contributions to a pension, annuity, stock bonus or profit-sharing plan [¶ 1838].

Information required. Deductions for contributions made on behalf of employees or self-employed are shown on Form 5500, or Form 5500-C, or Form 5500-K (depending on the type and size of the plan) filed by the employer each year during which he maintains a plan (whether or not qualified) [Sec. 1.404(a)-2A]. For other filing requirements of an employee's pension and profit-sharing trust, see ¶ 3537(d).

(d) Taxability of amounts received by employee. The employee generally treats the amounts received or made available to him under a qualified plan as an annuity. His consideration is the amounts he contributed [Sec. 402(a)(1); Prop. Reg. 1.402(a)-1]. Lump-sum distributions, however, are taxed under special rules discussed below. If an employee under the terms of the plan elects within 60 days to take an annuity instead of a lump sum, no part of the lump sum is includible in his gross income. He pays taxes on the annuity receipts under the usual annuity rules;[11] see ¶ 1232. If the lump-sum distribution includes the employer's appreciated stock or securities, the net unrealized appreciation is not taxable at the time of distribution [Sec. 402(e)(4)(J)]. Subsequent sale will result in long-term capital gain to the extent of the appreciation. The balance of any gain will be long or short term, depending on the holding period [Prop. Reg. Sec. 1.402(a)-1(b)].

Tax on lump-sum distributions. All lump-sum distributions attributable to post-1973 plan participation are taxed at ordinary income rates, subject to an *elective* 10-year forward averaging rule. However, lump-sum distributions attributable to plan participating years starting before 1974 are long-term capital gains [Sec. 402(a)(2)]. This tax treatment applies to all qualified plans, including self-employment retirement plans [¶ 1838; 1839]. A death payout to more than one person cannot qualify as a lump-sum distribution unless all the beneficiaries are trusts [Prop. Reg. Sec. 1.402(e)-2(d)(1)]. For payouts made after 1975 in tax years starting after 1975, the taxpayer may elect to treat all of a lump-sum distribution as if it were earned after 1973 so that it is taxed as ordinary income subject to the 10-year averaging discussed below. This election, once made, is irrevocable and

Footnotes appear at end of this Chapter.

¶ 3024

applies generally to all lump-sum distributions from plans in which he participated [Sec. 402(e)(4)(L)].

NOTE: Under prior law, Keogh distributions were 100% ordinary income [¶ 1839]. But now Keogh distributions attributable to pre-1974 participation may be converted from ordinary income to capital gain. However, to permit recipients to avoid the minimum tax on the capital gain portion of the payouts [¶ 2403], the 1976 Tax Reform Act provides the above election.

10-year averaging. Individuals, as well as estates and trusts, can elect a 10-year forward averaging rule for lump-sum distributions in tax years starting after 1973 [Sec. 402(e); Temp. Reg. Sec. 11.402(e)(4)(B)-1; Prop. Reg. 1.402(e)-3]. To elect this rule, an employee must have been a plan participant for at least 5 years before the year of distribution. Moreover, the entire balance of his account must have been paid to him within one of his tax years after he attains age 59½, or by reason of his death or separation from service. An owner-employee under a Keogh plan [¶ 1839] cannot qualify for the election unless the distribution was made after he has reached age 59½ or on account of death or disability. Also, an owner-employee can make the election only once in a lifetime. However, a regular employee may elect as many times as he can qualify up to age 59½, plus once more after that. Moreover, a common-law employee at least 59½ years old, can continue to work for the employer and still make the election. To determine lump-sum distributions, all trusts which are part of a plan are treated as a single trust, and all pension plans maintained by an employer are treated as a single plan. The same rules apply to profit-sharing or stock bonus plans. But a nonqualified plan does not count.

If a taxpayer elects the 10-year averaging, his tax is the tax on the ordinary income portion plus the tax on the other income, explained below. A single beneficiary makes the election by filing Form 4972 as part of his income tax return or amended return for the tax year [Temp. Reg. Sec. 11.402(e)(4)(B)-1]. Where there are two or more beneficiaries of a lump-sum distribution, Form 5544 is used by each to elect the 10-year averaging.

Tax on ordinary income portion of distribution is computed separately from all other income, as follows: (1) Find the total taxable distribution less the minimum distribution allowance (below), and divide the amount by 10. (2) Find the tax on the result in (1) plus $2,200, using the rates for single individuals, and multiply this tax by 10. (3) Multiply the result in (2) by the percentage of the taxpayer's plan participation after 1973 [Sec. 402(e); Proposed Reg. 1.402(e)-2]. This tax is computed without regard to the community property laws of any state. If the 10-year averaging is elected, the general 5-year averaging provisions cannot be used on the ordinary income portion, though it can be used on the "other" income (below). Multiple distributions and distributions of annuity contracts are subject to special rules (below).

Minimum distribution allowance. The minimum distribution allowance for the tax year is an amount equal to: (a) 50% of the first $20,000 of the taxable distribution, up to $10,000, less (b) 20% of the amount by which the distribution exceeds $20,000 [Sec. 402(e)(1)(D); Proposed Reg. 1.402(e)-2(b)(3)].

Tax on other income. A taxpayer electing the 10-year averaging must compute his tax on his other income, including the capital gain portion of the distribution. The capital gain portion is the total distribution (unreduced by any minimum allowance) multiplied by the percentage of the taxpayer's plan participation before 1-1-74 [Sec. 402(a)(2); Proposed Reg. 1.402(a)-1(a)(9)]. This tax is computed either in the regular way, or using the alternative capital gain tax method or regular income averaging [¶ 1102; 1614; 2401], whichever produces the least tax.

5-year "lookback" rule. If a taxpayer receives more than one distribution during the 5 years preceding the year of current distribution, all the lump-sum distributions after 12-31-73 are included for purposes of computing his tax under the 10-year averaging rule. The tax on the prior distribution is then subtracted from the tax so computed to find the tax on the current distribution [Sec. 402(e); Prop. Reg. 1.402(e)-2(c)(2)]. The tax on the other income, including the capital gain portion of the distribution is not affected by this rule.

Distribution of annuity contracts. If a taxpayer who elects the 10-year averaging, takes an annuity in addition to a lump-sum distribution, the annuity payments themselves are not taxed until received. However, a separate tax must be computed on the cash value of the annuity less its portion of the minimum distribution allowance. Subtracting this tax from the tax computed under the 10-year rule on all of the ordinary income, including the annuity, produces the tax on the ordinary income portion of the cash distributed under the 10-year averaging rule [Sec. 402(e); Prop. Reg. 1.402(e)-2(c)(1)]. For this purpose, the value of an annuity is its cash surrender value if it has one; if not, the present value of the total payments which the annuitant will receive over his life expectancy.

Separation from service. Following distributions were held not to have been made by reason of "separation from service": An employee had election to receive a lump-sum distribution on account of a reorganization under a plan continued by a successor corporation and he continued to work for the successor;[12] a subsidiary separated from the parent and continued as a separate entity, the employee continued employment with the subsidiary;[13] a lump sum was paid to an employee on a plan's termination not directly caused by the employer corporation's dissolution;[14] no real separation from service occurred as new ownership ended a plan and the employees continued to work.[15]

When employee's interest not taxable. An employee's interest in a trust is not taxable to him if: (1) there are substantial conditions on his right to withdraw his share, such as a requirement that the employee discontinue his participation in the trust or forfeit a portion of his interest in the trust, or a requirement that the employee may elect irrevocably to have distribution of his interest deferred to a definite future time;[16] or (2) he can withdraw only after getting approval of an administrative committee in a case of proven financial necessity.[17] However, the plan itself may become disqualified if actual withdrawals by lower-paid employees result in the plan becoming discriminatory in favor of higher-paid employees.[18]

Retirement insurance contracts. If the trust buys retirement insurance contracts, contributions by the employer for the "current insurance protection" in excess of the reserve accumulation needed to secure retirement benefits constitute income taxable to the employees. If an employee dies before retirement, amounts paid to a beneficiary on account of such "current insurance protection" are exempt from tax [Sec. 1.72-16]. See ¶ 1213.

Accident or health benefits. The annuity rules do not apply to pension or profit-sharing payments received as accident or health benefits [Sec. 1.72-15(a)]. Such benefits resulting from employee contributions are tax-free. However, amounts treated as employee contributions for this purpose are not counted as employee contributions in figuring the annuity exclusion for pension or profit-sharing benefits [Sec. 1.72-15(c)]. Thus, the employee cannot get a double exclusion for the same amount. Benefits resulting from employer contributions can be excluded to the extent discussed in ¶ 1219-1221 [Sec. 1.72-15(d)]. Employer contributions for

¶ 3024

these benefits are limited to 25% of the total contributed for all benefits [Sec. 1.401-14(c)(1)].

(e) Curtailment or termination of a plan. Curtailment or termination of a qualified plan may result in retroactive disqualification of the plan. This, in turn, may void the employer's deductions for contributions to the plan in prior years still open under the statute of limitations (generally three years) as well as for any contributions in the year of termination or curtailment. To prevent such disallowance, the employer must show:

(1) The plan was intended to be permanent and curtailment or termination was due to business necessity that could not be foreseen when the plan was adopted; and

(2) The curtailment or termination did not result in discrimination in favor of officers, shareholders, supervisory and highly-paid employees; and

(3) The plan was qualified during actual operation.[19]

The employer may obtain a determination letter on the effect of the proposed curtailment or termination by filing Form 5310.[8]

(f) Treatment of a nonqualified plan. Contributions made by an employer after 8-1-69 to a nonqualified plan are included in the employee's gross income according to the restricted property rules [¶ 1326]. Thus, when an employee's forfeitable interest becomes nonforfeitable, he must include in income the value of his interest in the plan at that time. Later employer contributions are income to the employee if he has a nonforfeitable interest. A beneficiary is not considered the owner of any portion of the trust; undistributed income is not taxed to the employee before its distribution. However, any distribution of income from nonqualified pension and profit-sharing plans before the annuity starting date is included in the employee's income without regard to the employee contribution to the trust (¶ 1230(f)) [Sec. 402(b); Prop. Reg. 1.402(b)-1].

When payments are made to the employee, they are taxed as annuity payments [¶ 1232], and the employee's cost basis (investment in the contract) is increased by the amount of the employer's contributions taxed to the employee. The employee does not get the long-term capital gain privilege [Sec. 402(b); Proposed Reg. 1.402(b)-1(b)].

(g) How treated on return. Taxpayers who elect the 10-year averaging method generally should use Form 4972 [see (d) above]. Payouts that qualify for long-term capital gain treatment are reported on Schedule D, Form 1040. Those treated as annuities are reported on Schedule E, Form 1040. Those that do not qualify for annuity or long-term capital gain treatment are reported on Form 1040 as fully taxable pensions and annuities.

(h) U.S. bond purchase plan. A qualified trust or employer plan can invest in special U.S. bonds bought in the name of the employee (¶ 1839(e)) [Sec. 405; 1.405-1—1.405-3]. The face of the bond shows whether it is issued for an employee or self-employed individual. The employer's contributions are deductible the same as if made to a qualified trust [see (c) above]. The annual contribution for an employee must be rounded to a multiple of $50. The employee or beneficiary is taxed when the bond is redeemed, not when it is distributed. The taxable redemption proceeds are ordinary income, whether the bond is received from a trust or a bond purchase plan. An employee's basis is the amount of his own contributions. A self-employed individual's basis must be specially computed [Sec. 1.405-3(b)]. The application for approval of a bond purchase plan is made on Form 4578.[8] See also purchase of individual retirement bonds at ¶ 3027.

¶ 3025 Common trust funds. Common trust funds maintained by banks are exempt from tax [Sec. 584(b); 1.584-1]. Each participant in the fund, however, is taxed on his share of the fund's income, whether distributed or not [Sec. 1.584-2]. Consequently, the bank must file an information return for the fund [Sec. 6032; 1.6032-1]. The fund computes its taxable income in the same manner as an individual, except that capital gains and losses are segregated, and the fund is not allowed the charitable contributions deduction or a net operating loss deduction [Sec. 584(d); 1.584-3, 1.584-6]. The partnership return Form 1065 may be used [Sec. 1.6032-1].

A participant in a common trust fund in computing his taxable income takes into account his proportionate share of the capital gains or losses, and the taxable income or net loss of the fund. Dividends are allocated to the participants, as is the fund's net operating loss [Sec. 584(c); 1.584-2]. A participant must also account for his pro rata share of the fund's items of tax preference subject to minimum tax (¶ 2403) [Sec. 58(e)].

(a) Withdrawal of participating interest. No gain or loss is realized by the fund on the admission or withdrawal of a participant. But the withdrawal of a participating interest by a participant is treated as a sale or exchange of his interest resulting in a recognized gain or loss to him [Sec. 584(e)]. A transfer into a new trust is not a withdrawal of a participating interest.[1]

(b) Different tax years. If the tax years of the fund and the participant are not the same, the participant will include in his gross income his share of the taxable income of the fund for the tax year of the fund ending within or with his tax year [Sec. 584; 1.584-2].

¶ 3026 Business trusts. Ordinary trusts are taxed at the same rates as married individuals filing separate returns [¶ 3020]. But if the trust resembles a corporation in form and has as its purpose the conduct of a business, it is considered an association, taxed at corporate rates [¶ 3101], regardless of its classification under state law[1] [Sec. 7701(a)(3)].

A trust has the structural features of a corporation when:[2]
- the trustee exerts centralized management over the property,
- the trustee is authorized to issue transferable certificates,
- the enterprise continues even though a beneficiary may die or transfer his interest, and
- limited liability exists.

This is not an all-inclusive rule,[3] but it does show that it is not necessary for the trust to adhere to the strict corporate form to be considered an association. While the beneficiaries do not have to have the powers of stockholders,[4] if they do, it is evidence of an association [Sec. 301.7701-2(a), 301.7701-4(b)].

(a) Business purpose test. A trust must have been created for a business purpose for it to be treated as an association. There is no definite rule as to when such a purpose exists. However, when the trustee has extensive control over the acquisition, disposal, and operation of the corpus similar to the powers of a director of a corporation, a business purpose may be present.[2]

> **Example 1:** Real estate is the corpus of a trust. The trustees are authorized to acquire new land, sell, encumber, and manage the realty as if they were its owners. They are also authorized to build and operate golf courses and club houses. A business purpose for developing the land exists.[2]

> **Example 2:** A trust is created to drill a single oil well. The trustees are authorized to manage the property, pay off any debts incurred, supervise the production, and sell the oil produced. A business purpose exists even though only one oil well is involved. The size and extent of the activity engaged in under the trust instrument is not a determining factor.[5]

Footnotes appear at end of this Chapter.

Sometimes, however, even when the trustee has extensive managerial control, no business purpose exists. This occurs when the primary purpose for establishing the trust is to conserve the corpus and distribute income. The trustee's managerial powers are regarded as incidental to this main purpose.[6]

The courts may examine not only the extent of the managerial powers of the trustee but also the type of business activity conductd by the creators of the trust before its formation. When the creators formerly were engaged in a business closely related to the type of activity carried on by the trustee, a business purpose was found to exist.[7]

(b) Agent in a real estate trust. The powers of the agent and trustee in a real estate trust are considered separately. When the agent is the exclusive selling agent and manager of the property and the trustee has only the ministerial powers to collect and distribute income and convey title only upon the agent's directions, no business purpose exists.[8]

(c) Depositor in a fixed investment trust. The powers of the trustee and depositor (who serves in a capacity similar to that of an agent or manager) must be considered together in a fixed investment trust. When the trustee's powers are to conserve the property and distribute the income, and the depositor is authorized to sell the securities forming the corpus of the trust to eliminate unsound investments, the trust is not taxable as a corporation. In effect, the depositor's powers are considered necessary to conserve the trust corpus.[9] When, however, the trust depositor has the power to vary the investment of the certificate holders, the trust may be taxed as a corporation.[10]

(d) Liquidating trusts. Although a liquidating trust may have the qualities of a business trust it is taxed as a trust if it was created primarily to liquidate a business. If operation of the business is only incidental to this purpose and is continued to conserve the property, the trust is still considered a liquidating trust.[11] If, however, the trust is used to disguise the establishment of a new business or to continue the operation of the old enterprise for profit only, it will be taxed as a corporation.[12]

¶ **3027 Individual retirement arrangements.** A taxpayer who is not covered by an employer or Keogh plan [¶ 1838; 1839] can set up his own plan and deduct limited contributions [¶ 1838(1)]. Income from the plan is exempt from income tax (except the unrelated business income tax, ¶ 3445), until paid out [Sec. 408(d), (e), 409(b); Proposed Reg. 1.408-1]. Under certain conditions, an employer or union can also set up and contribute to an individual retirement arrangement (IRA) for the benefit of the employee or member [Sec. 408(c)]. A participant who has been in a retirement plan at least 5 years, under tax-free rollover provisions, can withdraw his entire interest in the plan without tax or penalty, if he recontributes it to another such plan within 60 days of receipt [Sec. 408(d)(3), 409(b)(3)]. Also, one may set up an IRA as a conduit to make tax-free rollovers from one qualified plan to another.

(a) Plan requirements. An individual may set up either an individual retirement account, an individual retirement annuity plan, or an individual retirement bond plan. In any case, the interest is not transferable. Use form 5305 to adopt an officially prescribed model individual retirement trust account; Form 5306 to apply for approval of a prototype individual retirement account; Form 5304 to apply for determination of individual retirement account established by an employer or employee association. See also ¶ 1838(1).

Individual retirement accounts are domestic trusts organized for the exclusive benefit of an individual or his beneficiaries [Sec. 408(a); Proposed Reg. 1.408-2].

Normally the trustee must be a bank. The plan must include these written terms: (1) No contribution (which must be in cash) will exceed $1,500 a year except for a tax-free rollover; (2) The trust assets must be kept separately from other property except a common or trust investment fund; (3) A participant's entire interest must be paid out by the end of the year he reaches 70½, or distribution over the life of the participant (or participant and spouse) must start by that time; (4) If the participant dies before a complete payout, any balance must be paid out within 5 years or used to buy an annuity for beneficiaries; (5) The account must be nonforfeitable.

Individual retirement annuities are annuity or endowment contracts issued by an insurance company to the individual participants [Sec. 408(b); Proposed Reg. 1.408-3]. The contract must be nonforfeitable and must contain no life insurance element. The annual premium cannot exceed $1,500. Also, similar payout provisions as in (3) and (4) above, apply here.

Individual retirement bonds. Instead of setting up an IRA or buying an annuity, the taxpayer can invest in U.S. bonds issued under the Second Liberty Bond Act, in his name or his beneficiary's [Sec. 409; Proposed Reg. 1.409-1]. The bonds cannot bear interest or provide investment income after the day he reaches age 70½ or 5 years after the date of death (but no later than the day he would have been 70½ had he lived). He must pay a tax on 10% of the proceeds on early redemption, unless (a) it occurs within 12 months after issuance, or (b) he reached age 59½, or (c) he is disabled.

(b) Deductions for contributions to IRA. The maximum annual deduction is 15% of compensation up to $1,500 [Sec. 408, 409]. See ¶ 1838(1).

(c) Tax on distributions. Generally, payouts from IRA are taxed as ordinary income in the year the taxpayer actually receives the cash payments [Sec. 408(d), 409(b); Proposed Reg. 1.408-1]. Since he was entitled to a deduction for the contribution [(b) above], his basis in an account, or annuity, or bond is zero, so the full amount of the distribution is taxable. A transfer of interest under a divorce settlement is tax free.

A distribution of a qualified retirement annuity is taxed under the annuity rules [¶ 1230 et seq.]. Since the participant has a zero basis, the annuity payments are taxable when and as received [Sec. 408(d)].

A distribution of a retirement bond is not immediately taxable. If the bond is later redeemed, the entire proceeds are taxable as ordinary income [Sec. 409(b)]. If the owner of a bond had not redeemed it by the end of the year he reaches the age of 70½, he must include the value in his income for that year, unless the tax-free rollover provisions apply.

NOTE: IRA distributions are not eligible for capital gains treatment, or the special 10-year averaging rule available to retirement plan participants [¶ 3024(d)]. However, an IRA participant can use the general 5-year averaging [¶ 2401]. Furthermore, an IRA distribution is income eligible for the credit for the elderly [¶ 2406].

¶ 3027

Footnotes to Chapter 20

(P-H "FEDERAL TAXES" related references are cited in brackets [ ] at the end of each footnote below.)

Footnote ¶ 3000 [¶ 28,001 et seq.]

Footnote ¶ 3001 [¶ 41,755 et seq.]
(1) Hellman v. Glenn, 36 F. Supp. 423, 26 AFTR 500 [¶ 7547(15)].
(2) Meeker v. Durey, 92 F.2d 697, 20 AFTR 285 [¶ 28,017(10)].
(3) T. Munger, 16 BTA 168 [¶ 28,282(50)].
(4) Rev. Stats. Sec. 3467, 31 USC 192 [¶ 37,706].
(5) Rev. Stats. Sec. 3466, 31 USC 191 [¶ 37,703].
(6) U.S. v. Weisburn, 48 F. Supp. 393, 30 AFTR 856 [¶ 37,706(15)].
(7) Est. of L. E. McNight, 8 TC 871; Livingston v. Becker, 40 F.2d 673, 8 AFTR 10790; M. Viles, ¶ 55,142 P-H memo TC [¶ 37,706(60), (75)].
(8) De Bonchamps v. U.S., 5 AFTR 2d 1323, 278 F.2d 127, rev. U.S. v. Cooke, 228 F.2d 667, 48 AFTR 789, Rev. Rul. 61-102, 1961-1, CB 245 [¶ 28,282(65)].

Footnote ¶ 3002 [¶ 28,001; 28,283].
(1) Fred W. Smith, 25 TC 143 [¶ 28,283(90)].
(2) Fiduciary Trust Co. v. U.S., 36 F. Supp. 653, 26 AFTR 545, Boyce v. U.S., 8 AFTR 2d 6001, 296 F.2d 731 [¶ 28,283(25), (95)].
(3) United States Tr. Co. v. Comm., 296 US 481, 16 AFTR 1306 [¶ 28,283(75)].

Footnote ¶ 3003 [¶ 28,000 et seq.; 28,172].

Footnote ¶ 3004 [¶ 28,099].

Footnote ¶ 3005 [¶ 28,100; 28,111; 28,131; 28,153].
(1) Rev. Rul. 62-147, 1962-2 CB 151 [¶ 28,125(15)].

Footnote ¶ 3006 [¶ 28,111; 28,131; 28,153; 28,194; 28,201].
(1) Comm. v. Stearns, 65 F.2d 371, 12 AFTR 786 [¶ 28,101(20)].

Footnote ¶ 3007 [¶ 28,131; 28,153].

Footnote ¶ 3008 28,006; 28,016; 28,493; 28,494.26].
(1) Basch, 9 TC 627; O'Daniel, 10 TC 631, affd. 173 F.2d 966, 37 AFTR 1249; Rev. Rul. 65-217, 1965-2 CB 214 [¶ 28,494.17(20)].

Footnote ¶ 3009 [¶ 28,102; 28,138.10; 31,106].
(1) Beatty, 28 BTA 1286 [¶ 28,102(20)].
(2) Statler v. Comm., 17 AFTR 2d 1012, 361 F.2d 128 [¶ 32,029].
(3) Meissner v. U.S., 18 AFTR 2d 5126, 364 F.2d 409 [¶ 28,494.26(5)].
(4) Suisman v. Eaton, 15 F. Supp. 113, 18 AFTR 24; Kenan v. Comm., 114 F.2d 217, 25 AFTR 607; Rev. Rul. 66-207, 1966-2 CB 243 [¶ 28,195(20); 31,107(25)].
(5) Sherman Ewing, 40 BTA 912 [¶ 31,165(15)].
(6) Rev. Rul. 67-74, 1967-1 CB 194 [¶ 28,125(10)].
(7) Rev. Rul. 74-257, 1974-1 CB 153 [¶ 28,138(55)].

Footnote ¶ 3010 [¶ 31,361; 31,401].

Footnote ¶ 3011 [¶ 28,031 et seq.].
(1) Instructions for Form 1041 (1976), p. 5.
(2) Beatty, 28 BTA 1286 [¶ 28,102(20)].
(3) Treas. Dept. booklet "Your Federal Income Tax" (1977 Ed.), p. 39.

Footnote ¶ 3012 [¶ 28,031; 28,033; 28,067]
(1) Instructions for Form 1041 (1976), p. 6.

Footnote ¶ 3013 [¶ 28,064; 28,473].
(1) A list of qualifying organizations (Pub. 78) may be purchased from the Superintendent of Documents, Govt. Printing Office, Washington, D.C. 20402.
(2) Wellman v. Welch, 99 F.2d 75, 21 AFTR 847; Marion C. Tyler Trust, 5 TC 729 [¶ 28,066(5), (70)].
(3) Bank of America Nat'l. Tr. & Savings Ass'n. v. Comm., 126 F.2d 48, 28 AFTR 1276 [¶ 28,066(55)].
(4) Ithaca Trust Co. v. U.S., 279 US 151, 7 AFTR 8856; Merchants' Nat'l. Bank of Boston v. Comm., 320 US 256, 31 AFTR 753 [¶ 28,066(55)].

Footnote ¶ 3014 [¶ 28,067].
(1) Sue Carol, 30 BTA 443 [¶ 15,551(10)].
(2) Rev. Rul. 61-211, 1961-2 CB 124; Rev. Rul. 74-71, 1974-1 CB 158 [¶ 15,551(10)].

Footnote ¶ 3015 [¶ 28,067].
(1) Rev. Rul. 61-20, 1961-1 CB 248 [¶ 28,070(25)].
(2) Kearney v. U.S., 116 F. Supp. 922, 45 AFTR 523 [¶ 15,551(15)].

Footnote ¶ 3016 [¶ 28,031; 28,033; 28,067 et seq.].
(1) Rev. Rul. 63-27, 1963-1 CB 57 [¶ 28,138.5; 28,168(15)].
(2) Erdman v. Comm., 11 AFTR 2d 1209, 315 F.2d 762 [¶ 28,167(60)].
(3) Bingham v. Comm., 325 US 365, 33 AFTR 842 [¶ 28,070.20(50)].
(4) Penrose v. U.S., 18 AFTR 1289, 23 AFTR 1166, 18 F.Supp. 413 [¶ 13,023(5)].
(5) Rev. Rul. 73-322, 1973-2 CB 44 [¶ 28,150(48)].
(6) Est. of McClatchy, 12 TC 370, affd. 179 F.2d 678, 38 AFTR 1287 [¶ 13,203(10)].
(7) Rev. Rul. 67-304, 1967-2 CB 224 [¶ 28,070.15(45)].
(8) Letter Ruling (2-11-47) in full at ¶ 76,136 P-H Fed. 147 [¶ 28,070.15(45)].
(9) Rev. Rul. 70-361, 1970-2 CB 133 [¶ 28,070.15(45)].

Footnote ¶ 3017 [¶ 28,001; 28,111; 28,131; 28,153].

Footnote ¶ 3018 [¶ 16,825 et seq.].

Footnote ¶ 3019 [¶ 28,033 et seq.].

Footnote ¶ 3020 [¶ 35,059].
(1) Treas. Dept. booklet "Your Federal Income Tax" (1977 Ed.), pp. 14-15.
(2) Instructions for Form 1041 (1976), p. 3.
(3) Instructions for Form 4626 (1975).

Footnote ¶ 3021 [¶ 28,099].

Footnote ¶ 3022 [¶ 28,104; 28,351 et seq.; 28,446 et seq.; 28,458].
(1) Rev. Rul. 57-390, 1957-2 CB 326 [¶ 28,363(5)].
(2) Rev. Rul. 55-34, 1955-1 CB 226; Rev. Rul. 56-601, 1956-2 CB 458, modified by Rev. Rul. 73-251, 1973-1 CB 324. [¶ 28,393(5), (15)].

Chapter 20—Footnotes

Footnote ¶ 3022 continued
(3) Rev. Rul. 58-242, 1958-1 CB 251 [¶ 28,452(25)].
(4) Morrill, Jr. v. U.S., 13 AFTR 2d 1334, 228 F. Supp. 734 [¶ 28,455(5)].
(5) Ellis v. U.S., 24 AFTR 2d 69-5671, 416 F.2d 894; A.Q. Stewart, 9 TC 195 [¶ 28,482(5)].
(6) Rev. Rul. 65-283, 1965-2 CB 25 [¶ 28,482(25)].

Footnote ¶ 3023 [¶ 28,211 et seq.].

Footnote ¶ 3024 [¶ 19,001 et seq.].
(1) Lincoln Elec. Co. Tr. v. Comm., 190 F.2d 326, 40 AFTR 1018 [¶ 19,039(15)].
(2) Announcement 76-13, IRB 1976-5 [¶ 19,025(20)].
(3) News Release, IR-1782, 3-25-77 [¶ 55,369].
(4) Rev. Rul. 55-81, 1955-1 CB 392, amplified by Rev. Rul. 72-4, 1972-1 CB 105; but see Rev. Rul. 63-108, 1963-1 CB 87 [¶ 19,029(10); 19,031(15)].
(5) Rev. Rul. 62-139, 1962-2 CB 517 [¶ 19,034(73)].
(6) Rev. Rul. 71-311, 1971-2 CB 184 [¶ 19,038(50)].
(7) Rev. Rul. 67-288, 1967-2 CB 151 [¶ 21,153(10)].
(8) Rev. Proc. 72-6, 1972-1 CB 710; Rev. Proc. 72-8, 1972-1 CB 716; Rev. Proc. 75-47, 1975-2 CB 581; Rev. Proc. 76-15 (TIR-1447), 1976-1 CB 553 [¶ 19,025.1].
(9) Rev. Rul. 66-218, 1966-2 CB 120 [¶ 19,031(50)].
(10) Rev. Proc. 72-8, 1972-1 CB 716; Rev. Proc. 76-15 (TIR-1447) 1976-1 CB 553; Rev. Proc. 76-31, IRB 1976-38 [¶ 19,025(20); 19,025.1(5)].
(11) Rev. Rul. 59-94, 1959-1 CB 25 [¶ 19,062(20)].
(12) Gitten, 49 TC 419; but see Houg, 54 TC 792; Nonacquiescence in Houg, Announcement, 1973-1 CB 2 [¶ 19,061(10), (30)].
(13) Rev. Rul. 58-99, 1958-1 CB 202; modified by Rev. Rul. 72-440, 1972-2 CB 225 [¶ 19,061(10)].
(14) Beecher v. U.S., 13 AFTR 2d 889, 226 F. Supp. 547; U.S. v. Haggart, 410 F.2d 449, 23 AFTR 2d 69-1326 [¶ 19,061(10)].
(15) U.S. v. Johnson, 13 AFTR 2d 1371, 331 F.2d 943; U.S. v. Peebles, 13 AFTR 2d 1382, 331 F. 2d 955; Robert E. Beaulieu, ¶ 65,303 P-H Memo TC [¶ 19,061(10)].
(16) Rev. Rul. 55-423, 1955-1 CB 41; Rev. Rul. 55-425, 1955-1 CB 43; Rev. Rul. 60-292, 1960-2

Footnote ¶ 3024 continued
CB 153 [¶ 19,062(15)].
(17) Rev. Rul. 55-424, 1955-1 CB 42 [¶ 19,062(15)].
(18) Rev. Rul. 57-587, 1957-2 CB 260 [¶ 19,039(30)].
(19) Rev. Rul. 55-60, 1955-1 CB 37; Rev. Rul. 69-24, 1969-1 CB 110 [¶ 19,030(10)].

Footnote ¶ 3025 [¶ 21,832].
(1) Wiggin v. U.S., (DC Mass.) 3 AFTR 2d 998; Rev. Rul. 60-256; 1960-2 CB 193 [¶ 21,832(15)].

Footnote ¶ 3026 [¶ 41,631 et seq.].
(1) Swanson v. Comm., 296 US 362, 16 AFTR 1268; Helvering v. Coleman-Gilbert Assoc., 296 US 369, 16 AFTR 1270; Helvering v. Combs, 296 US 365, 16 AFTR 1272; Morrissey v. Comm., 296 US 344, 16 AFTR 1274 [¶ 41,616(5)].
(2) Morrissey v. Comm., 296 US 344, 16 AFTR 1274; Mid-Ridge Investment Co. v. U.S., 12 AFTR 2d 945, 324 F.2d 945 [¶ 41,616; 41,620; 41,633(10)].
(3) Davidson v. U.S., 115 F.2d 799, 25 AFTR 1073 [¶ 41,636(5)].
(4) Hecht v. Malley, 265 US 144, 16 AFTR 3976 [¶ 41,633(10)].
(5) Helvering v. Combs, 296 US 365, 16 AFTR 1272 [¶ 41,635(5)].
(6) Cleveland Trust Co. v. Comm., 115 F.2d 481, 25 AFTR 137 [¶ 41,634(10)].
(7) Main-Hammond Ld. Tr. v. Comm., 200 F.2d 308, 42 AFTR 958 [¶ 41,634(15)].
(8) Lewis & Co. v. Comm., 301 US 385, 19 AFTR 486 [¶ 41,617(25)].
(9) Comm. v. Chase Nat. Bank, 122 F.2d 540, 27 AFTR 887 [¶ 41,637(5), (15)].
(10) Comm. v. No. Amer. Bond Tr., 122 F.2d 545, 27 AFTR 892 [¶ 41,637(15)].
(11) Helvering v. Washburn, 99 F.2d 478, 21 AFTR 1140 [¶ 41,636(15)].
(12) U.S. v. Hill, 142 F.2d 622, 32 AFTR 699; Anderson, et al. v. U.S., 120 F. Supp. 99, 45 AFTR 1947, affd. 222 F.2d 176, 47 AFTR 840 [¶ 41,636(5), (15)].

Footnote ¶ 3027 [¶ 19,197].

Highlights of Chapter 20
Estates and Trusts

I. **Estates and Trusts in General**
   A. **Estates and trusts are taxed as separate taxable entities.**
      1. Allocation of income. Income taxed to estate or trust or beneficiaries or in part to each, depending on will or trust deed [¶ 3000(a)].
      2. Returns. Form 1041 is used with separate schedules [¶ 3000(b)].
      3. Exempt trusts are taxed on unrelated business income [¶ 3000(c)].
   B. **Who is a fiduciary [¶ 3001]:**
      1. Person who holds in trust for another with beneficial interest; or
      2. Person who receives or controls income of another.
      3. Fiduciary is not a receiver or an agent [¶ 3001(a)].
      4. Generally fiduciary is not personally liable for tax; he also can obtain discharge from personal liability [¶ 3001(b)].
      5. Terminable interests. Life tenant ordinarily not considered a fiduciary unless he has right to sell property [¶ 3001(c)].
   C. **Nature of estates and trusts [¶ 3002]:**
      1. Administrator, executor and trustee must file returns and pay tax on trust's or estate's taxable income.
      2. Single instrument can create multiple trusts [¶ 3002(b)].
II. **Who Is Taxable on Estate and Trust Income**
   A. **To whom estate or trust income is taxable [¶ 3003]:**
      1. If all income is distributable, taxed to beneficiary.
      2. If all income is not distributable (e.g., accumulated), taxed to fiduciary.
      3. If income is partly distributable, taxed partly to fiduciary and partly to beneficiaries.
      4. Different tax years—Beneficiary taxed on distributions for estate's or trust's tax year ending within or with his tax year [¶ 3003(b)].
      5. Income when trust ends—Separate status ceases and income, deductions and credits are attributed to beneficiaries [¶ 3003(c)].
   B. **Distributable net income**—Generally computed by making certain modifications to taxable income [¶ 3004(a)].
   C. **Distribution by simple trust [¶ 3005]:**
      1. A simple trust must:
         a. Distribute current income only.
         b. Distribute all its income.
         c. Have no charitable beneficiaries.
      2. Beneficiary includes in income all income required to be distributed to him, not to exceed his share of distributable net income.
      3. Simple trust turns complex in any year it distributes corpus.
   D. **Distributions by estates and complex trusts**—Consists of [¶ 3006]:
      1. Current income required to be distributed to beneficiaries, and
      2. All other amounts properly paid, credited, or required to be distributed to the beneficiaries.
   E. **Allocation by tiers—distributions of current income [¶ 3006(a)]:**
      1. Generally called first tier distributions.
      2. If distribution exceeds distributable net income, only a portion of that income included in beneficiary's income.
   F. **Allocation by tiers—other distributions [¶ 3006(b)]:**
      1. Generally called "second tier" distributions.

2. If 1st and 2d tier distributions exceed distributable net income (DNI), beneficiary includes in income a portion of DNI.
G. **Allocation by separate shares**—This rule limits the amount taxable to beneficiaries to current income excluding corpus distribution [¶ 3006(c)].
H. **Special distributions**—Not included in beneficiary's gross income nor deductible by estate or trust [¶ 3006(d)]:
   1. Gift or bequest of specific sum of money or specific property which, under governing instrument, is paid in lump sum or in not more than 3 installments.
   2. Charitable distributions; but see IV, C, below.
   3. Current distribution deducted by estate or trust in prior year.
I. **Throwback rule**—If trust distributes less than its distributable net income, undistributed excess may have to be reported in distribution year. See VI, B, below.
J. **65-day rule**—Trustee can elect to attribute distributions within first 65 days of year to preceding year, to avoid throwback (I, above) [¶ 3006(f)].
K. **Beneficiary's share of charitable remainder trusts** [¶ 3006(g)]:
   1. Distributions separated into 4 categories:
      a. Ordinary income and loss.
      b. Short-term capital gain and loss.
      c. Long-term capital gain and loss.
      d. Other income, including tax-exempt income and related loss.
   2. Any distribution in excess of 4 categories treated as nontaxable distribution of corpus.
   3. Beneficiaries taxed on amount in each category to extent of trust's current income and undistributed prior year's income in that category.
   4. Undistributed capital gains (long- and short-term) for current and prior years computed without regard to any capital loss limitation.
   5. Amount of current and prior year's income is computed without regard to net operating loss deduction.
   6. Loss in one category may not be used to offset gain in another.
   7. Within a category, losses may be carried over indefinitely to future years to reduce later income in same category.
   8. Income items distributed proportionately among income recipients.
   9. Generally, income taxed to recipient in year it is paid.
   10. Allocate deductible and income-related expenses to beneficiaries, and other expenses to corpus.
L. **Beneficiary's share of each item of distributable net income:**
   1. Find each beneficiary's share of any item with special tax status (e.g., exempt interest) included in distributable net income [¶ 3007].
   2. Method of apportionment [¶ 3007(a)]:
      a. Net amount of each item apportioned among beneficiaries on simple proportion basis unless instrument or state law requires otherwise.
      b. Allocation in trust instrument recognized only to extent that it has an economic effect independent of tax consequences of allocation.
   3. Apportionment formulas [¶ 3007(b)].
   4. Allocation of deductions—Each income item includible in distributable net income must be reduced by deductions allocable to it [¶ 3007(c)].
   5. Charitable contributions adjustment [¶ 3007(c)].

III. **Income—Capital Gains and Losses**
   A. **Gross income of estates and trusts**—Determined the same as for individuals and includes [¶ 3008(a)]:
      1. Income accumulated in trust for benefit of unborn, unascertained or contingent beneficiaries.
      2. Income accumulated or held for future distribution.
      3. Income to be distributed currently to beneficiaries.
      4. Income collected by guardian of infant.
      5. Income received by an estate during its administration or settlement.

6. Income to be distributed or accumulated in fiduciary's discretion.
B. **Decedent's gross income**—When a person dies, two separate and distinct taxable entities arise [¶ 3008(b)]:
1. Final return of decedent—includes only income actually or constructively received before death.
2. Income in respect of decedent—If excluded on decedent's final return, amounts are taxed and reported on return of his estate or other person who receives them [¶ 3008(b)]:
    a. Successive decedents—Income taxed to person receiving income.
    b. Installment obligations reported the same way decedent would have reported them.
    c. Deductions and credits accruing after death—Generally allowed to successor.
    d. Federal and state estate taxes attributable to income in respect of decedent are deductible by recipient.
C. **Capital gains and losses of estate or trust [¶ 3009]:**
1. Gain included in estate's or trust's income, except that part of gain paid, credited or distributable to beneficiary is taxed to beneficiary and deductible by fiduciary.
2. Capital loss usually deductible only by estate or trust [¶ 3009(a)].
3. Long-term capital gain deduction allowed estate or trust [¶ 3009(b)].
4. Fiduciary has gain or loss on distribution of asset to pay cash legacy [¶ 3009(c)].
5. In figuring distributable net income, fiduciary [¶ 3009(d)]:
    a. Includes capital gain allocated to income.
    b. Excludes capital gain allocated to corpus and not paid to beneficiary or used for charity.
    c. Excludes capital loss unless used to determine capital gains paid or credited to beneficiary during the year.
6. Simple trust can deduct state income tax on retained capital gain [¶ 3009(e)].
D. **Basis of property to estate or trust [¶ 3010]:**
1. Transfers after 1920:
    a. For value—Same as grantor's basis, increased by gain or decreased by loss recognized to grantor on transfer.
    b. By gift—Same as donor's, unless transfer results in loss.
    c. By bequest or devise—Use carryover basis for decedents dying after 1976.
2. Transfers before 1921—Fair market value when acquired.

IV. **Deductions and Credits**
A. **Estate's or trust's deductions in general [¶ 3011]:**
1. Same as for individuals except:
    a. No zero bracket amount.
    b. Beneficiary usually cannot deduct trust's loss [¶ 3011(a)].
    c. Special rules for contributions and depreciation (see C and D below).
2. Termination of estate or trust—Certain beneficiaries are allowed unused capital loss or net operating loss carryovers and other deductions [¶ 3011(b)].
3. Dividend exclusion—Fiduciary gets exclusion based on proportion of dividend retained by estate or trust; beneficiary gets exclusion for dividends allocated to him [¶ 3011(c)].
B. **Deduction for personal exemption [¶ 3012]:**
1. Estate—$600.
2. Trusts which must distribute all income currently—$300.
3. All other trusts—$100.
C. **Contributions [¶ 3013]:**
1. Estates and complex trusts get unlimited deduction for donations *paid*.
2. Estates also get unlimited deduction for amounts *permanently set aside* for charity.
3. Set-aside deduction generally not available to trusts after 10-9-69 except under transition rules [¶ 3013(b)].
4. What contributions are deductible [¶ 3013(a)]:
    a. Generally contributions must come from estate's or trust's gross income.

b. Deduction generally denied if contribution is out of corpus, but income allocable to corpus may qualify.
c. No deduction for contributions allocable to unrelated business income.
d. Adjustments necessary if contribution comes from tax exempt income or long-term capital gain.

D. **Depreciation or depletion [¶ 3014]:**
1. Generally apportioned to beneficiary on basis of trust or estate income but if trustee sets aside depreciation reserve, deduction is first allocated to trustee for income so set aside.
2. Deduction allowed to a life tenant, income beneficiary of trust or distributee of estate is deduction for adjusted gross income.

E. **Net operating loss**—Generally deductible by estates and trusts [¶ 3015].

F. **Expenses deductible by estate or trust [¶ 3016]:**
1. Must be ordinary and necessary for:
   a. Trade or business.
   b. Production or collection of income or management, conservation or maintenance of property for producing income.
   c. Administration expenses.
   d. Collection, determination or refund of tax.
2. On filing waiver of estate tax deduction and statement, estate can deduct [¶ 3016(a), (b)]:
   a. Administration expenses.
   b. Casualty and theft losses.

G. **Deductions for distributions to beneficiaries [¶ 3017]:**
1. Simple trusts—deductible by fiduciary up to distributable net income (excluding items not included in gross income) [¶ 3017(a)].
2. Estate and complex trusts [¶ 3017(b)]:
   a. Deduction consists of:
      1) Income required to be distributed currently.
      2) Any other amounts paid, credited, or required to be distributed.
   b. Limitation: Amount up to distributable net income (excluding items not included in gross income).

H. **Fiduciary-debtor loses interest, expense or loss deduction, if [¶ 3018]:**
1. He is on accrual basis but "related" creditor is on cash basis; and
2. Debt not paid within 2½ months after end of trust's tax year.

I. **Credits against tax [¶ 3019]:**
1. Foreign taxes.
2. Investment credit.
3. Work incentive program expenses.
4. New jobs credit.

V. **Rates and Returns for Decedents, Estates and Trusts**

A. **Rates and returns [¶ 3020]:**
1. Decedents—Generally filed by administrator, executor or surviving spouse and covers period from start of decedent's tax year to his death [¶ 3020(a)].
2. Estates [¶ 3020(b)]:
   a. Form 1041 with separate schedules is used.
   b. Return required if gross income is $600 or over or any beneficiary is a nonresident alien [¶ 3020(b)].
   c. Use special rate schedule provided for estates and trusts.
3. Trusts [¶ 3020(c)]:
   a. Form 1041 with separate schedules is used.
   b. Return required if: trust has any taxable income; or gross income is $600 or more; or any beneficiary is nonresident alien.
   c. See A(2c) above.
   d. Short-form return for simple trust; fiduciary disregards Schedules B & C (charitable deductions, distributable net income and distributions deduction).

e. Attach copy of will or trust deed to first return if gross income is $5,000 or more.
4. Minimum tax on estates and trusts [¶ 3020(d)]:
   a. Must pay tax on same preference items as individuals.
   b. Preference items apportioned between estate or trust and beneficiaries on basis of estate or trust income allocable to each; exclusion is shared the same way.

B. **Distribution computations:**
   1. Simple trusts [¶ 3021(a)].
   2. Complex trusts [¶ 3021(b)].

VI. Special Problems

A. **Trust income taxable to grantor or others** [¶ 3022]:
   1. Grantor taxed on trust income if he retains:
      a. Reversionary interest that may take effect in 10 years after transfer [¶ 3022(a)], or
      b. Power to control beneficial enjoyment (but retaining certain powers not necessarily fatal) [¶ 3022(b)], or
      c. Administrative control of trust primarily for his benefit [¶ 3022(c)], or
      d. Power to revoke trust [¶ 3022(d)].
   2. Trust income also taxed to grantor if [¶ 3022(e)]:
      a. It is or may be paid for his benefit or life insurance premiums, or
      b. Property transferred for spouse's benefit, or
      c. Income used for someone whom he is legally obligated to support.
   3. If a person other than grantor can acquire trust corpus or income, then trust income may be taxed to that person [¶ 3022(f)].
   4. Trust must pay tax on "includible gain" [¶ 3022(g)], if:
      a. Property with unrealized appreciation is transferred to trust, and
      b. Trust sells it within 2 years of transfer.
   5. Grantor transferring property to foreign trust with U.S. beneficiary is taxed as owner [¶ 3022(h)].

B. **Throwback of excess distributions by complex trusts.** Generally does not apply to simple trusts [¶ 3023]:
   1. Undistributed net income—amounts distributed are less than distributable net income [¶ 3023(a)].
   2. Accumulation distribution—amounts distributed are more than distributable net income for tax year [¶ 3023(b)].
   3. How to handle throwback rule—Excess over current distributable net income is taxed to beneficiary as if distributed and includable in his income first, from the earliest accumulation year, then from the next succeeding year and following years in regular order [¶ 3023(c)]:
      a. Transition rules—No distribution is thrown back to tax years before 1969 [¶ 3023(c)].
      b. Lack of records—Accumulation distribution is deemed distributed on last day of 1969 or earliest later date trust was in existence [¶ 3023(c)].
   4. Tax added to distribution—Distribution is increased by tax of trust in accumulation year attributable to undistributed net income [¶ 3023(d)].
   5. Beneficiary's tax in year of excess distribution is sum of:
      a. Partial tax on his taxable income, excluding accumulation distribution.
      b. Partial tax on accumulation distribution figured by short-cut method [¶ 3023(e)].
   6. No refund or credit allowed as result of accumulation distribution [¶ 3023(f)].
   7. Undistributed net income affected by partial tax paid by beneficiary [¶ 3023(g)].
   8. Capital gain throwback repealed [¶ 3023(h)].
   9. Foreign trusts—General accumulation rules apply, with exceptions [¶ 3023(i)].

C. **Employees' trusts** [¶ 3024]:
   1. Income of qualified stock bonus, pension or profit-sharing plan is tax-exempt if certain requirements are met [¶ 3024(a)].

2. Trust knows its exemption status in advance through determination letter, and proves continued exemption by filing annual information return [¶ 3024(b)].
3. Employer can deduct contributions to qualified plans within limits [¶ 3024(e)].
4. How is employee taxed on *qualified* plan distribution and similar benefits [¶ 3024(d)]:
   a. Distributions normally treated as ordinary income under annuity rules, unless (b) below applies.
   b. Lump-sum distribution paid on job termination in employee's tax year is treated as:
      1) long-term capital gain as to accumulations attributable to pre-1974 participation, unless taxpayer elects to treat all payouts as post-1973 accumulations.
      2) ordinary income as to post-1973 accumulations, subject to elective 10-year forward averaging rule.
   c. Employee's interest in trust not taxed to him if conditions are attached to withdrawal.
   d. Employer contribution to retirement insurance may be taxed to employee.
   e. Pension or profit-sharing payouts received as accident or health benefits are tax-free.
5. Plan can be disqualified *retroactively* on its curtailment or termination [¶ 3024(e)].
6. How is employee of *nonqualified* plan taxed [¶ 3024(f)]:
   a. He is taxed on employer contribution when made, if his rights are nonforfeitable.
   b. Distributions are taxed as annuities.
   c. No capital gain treatment.
7. U.S. bond purchase plan [¶ 3024(h)]:
   a. Taxed to employee or his beneficiary when bond is redeemed.
   b. Employer can deduct contributions.

D. **Common trust funds [¶ 3025]:**
   1. Fund not taxable, but bank that maintains it must file information return.
   2. Each participant in fund taxed on his share of fund's income, whether or not distributed.

E. **Business trusts [¶ 3026]:**
   1. Taxed at corporate rates.
   2. Business purpose test must be met [¶ 3026(a)].
   3. Agent, trustee in real estate trust are considered separately [¶ 3026(b)].
   4. Depositor in a fixed investment trust—May be taxed as corporation or trust depending on depositor's powers [¶ 3026(c)].
   5. Liquidating trusts—Taxed as trust if created primarily to liquidate a business [¶ 3026(d)].

F. **Individual retirement accounts [¶ 3027]:**
   1. Employees not covered by other qualified employee benefit plan can set up own individual retirement accounts or annuities.
   2. Plan income is generally tax-free.
   3. Maximum annual deduction for contributions is 15% of compensation up to $1,500.
   4. Cash payouts generally taxed as ordinary income.

FIGURING CORPORATION TAX
SPECIAL CORPORATION PROBLEMS

Chapter 21—CORPORATIONS—NORMAL TAX AND SURTAX, INCOME, DEDUCTIONS
(Detailed Table of Contents below)

Chapter 22—CORPORATIONS—CAPITAL GAINS AND LOSSES, NET OPERATING LOSS, ETC.
(Detailed Table of Contents at page 3201)

Chapter 23—CORPORATIONS—REORGANIZATIONS
(Detailed Table of Contents at page 3301)

Chapter 24—CORPORATIONS—PERSONAL HOLDING COMPANIES, ETC.—EXEMPT ORGANIZATIONS
(Detailed Table of Contents at page 3401)

Chapter 21

CORPORATIONS
NORMAL TAX AND SURTAX, INCOME, DEDUCTIONS
TABLE OF CONTENTS

	¶
TAXING THE CORPORATION	
Corporation taxes	3100
What is a "corporation"	3101
FIGURING THE TAX	
Normal tax and surtax	3102
Minimum tax	3103
CORPORATE INCOME	
Income of corporations	3105
Capital contributions	3106
Voluntary payments and assessments	
Contributions made by non-shareholders	
Property distributions received by corporations	3107
Corporate rental income paid directly to shareholders	3108
Income from a sinking fund	3109

	¶
Reconciliation of taxable income with book income	3110
CORPORATE DEDUCTIONS	
Deductions of corporations in general	3112
Special deductions for corporations	3113
Deduction for certain dividends received	3114
Dividends from domestic corporations	
Dividends from affiliated corporations	
Dividends from foreign corporations	
Dividends on certain public utility preferred stock	
Limitation	
Deduction for dividends paid on pre-10-1-42 preferred stock of public utility	3115

Footnotes appear at end of this Chapter.

¶	¶
Organizational expenditures 3116	Figuring the tax—illustration 3134
Special deductions based on income .. 3117	
Western Hemisphere Trade Corporations	**SUBCHAPTER S CORPORATIONS**
China Trade Act Corporations	Subchapter S corporations 3140
Charitable contributions 3118	Electing Subchapter S taxation 3141
Time for deduction	Who may elect
Amount deductible	How to elect
Carryover	Return by electing corporation
Contribution as business expense	Terminating the election
	How shareholders are taxed on the corporation's income 3142
PURCHASES, SALES, AND DISTRIBUTIONS OF CORPORATE SECURITIES AND PROPERTIES	Actual distributions
	Undistributed taxable income
	Distribution of previously taxed income
Corporation dealing in its own stock .. 3124	Allocation of current earnings and profits
Corporation dealing in its own obligations 3125	Treatment of capital gains and net operating losses 3143
Property bought by stockholder for less than market value 3126	Adjustments to basis of shareholder's stock 3144
Gain or loss to corporation on property distributions 3127	Adjustments to earnings and profits .. 3145
Gain or loss to liquidating corporation 3128	Special rules for retirement plans of electing corporations 3146
12-month liquidation	
Filing requirements	
Effects of distributions on corporation's earnings and profits 3129	**CHOOSING THE BEST FORM OF BUSINESS (CORPORATION, PARTNERSHIP, SOLE PROPRIETORSHIP)**
Appreciated inventory	
Adjustments for liabilities and gains	
Distribution not taxed to distributee	The different forms of business organizations 3152
Partial liquidations and certain redemptions	Tax advantages of corporation over unincorporated business 3153
Allocation of earnings	Splitting income
Distribution of proceeds of loan insured by U.S.	Disposition of business interest
	Fringe benefits for shareholder-employees
ACCUMULATED EARNINGS TAX	Additional tax advantages to corporations electing Subchapter S tax treatment 3154
The accumulated earnings tax 3130	Avoiding the double tax
Corporations liable for tax 3131	Fringe benefits retained
Burden of proof	Pass-through of corporate net operating loss
Guides in determining whether accumulations are reasonable or unreasonable	Pass-through of corporate capital gain
Income subject to the tax 3132	Elimination of penalty for unreasonable accumulation
Adjusted taxable income	
Dividends paid deduction	
Accumulated earnings credit	
Accumulated taxable income	
Rate of accumulated earnings tax 3133	• Highlights of Chapter 21 .... Page 3161

TAXING THE CORPORATION

¶ **3100 Corporation taxes.** The ordinary business corporation is subject to two taxes: a normal tax and a surtax. An additional penalty surtax, the accumulated earnings tax, may be imposed when a corporation retains earnings beyond the reasonable needs of the business [¶ 3130 et seq.]. Corporations must also pay a minimum tax in much the same way as individuals [¶ 3103].

In general, a corporation's taxable income is determined on the same principles as an individual's. Several items that are peculiar to corporations are discussed in this Chapter and in Chapter 22.

Returns. The ordinary business corporation files a return on Form 1120. A corporation electing Subchapter S taxation [¶ 3140 et seq.] uses Form 1120S. Corporations with tax preferences over $10,000 must file a minimum tax form [¶ 3103]. Consolidated returns are discussed in ¶ 3222.

Special treatment corporations. Certain corporations are taxed in different ways, at different rates or with additional deductions. For example, banks and trust companies are taxed as ordinary business corporations, but are allowed additional deductions [¶ 3433].

Earnings of exempt farmers' cooperatives are taxed as corporate income [¶ 3455]. Certain corporations are allowed a tax exemption on income related to their exempt purposes. Exempt private foundations are subject to an investment tax and also may pay some penalty excise taxes [¶ 3435 et seq.]. Other corporations receiving special treatment include:

Corporations electing Subchapter S taxation [¶ 3140 et seq.].
Personal holding companies [¶ 3400 et seq.; 3411 et seq.].
Regulated investment companies [¶ 3428 et seq.].
Real estate investment trusts [¶ 3432].
Insurance companies [¶ 3434].

Exempt organizations with unrelated business income [¶ 3454 et seq.].
Small business investment companies [¶ 3459].
Domestic International Sales Corporations (DISCs) [¶ 3460].
Foreign corporations [¶ 3710 et seq.].

¶ 3101　What is a "corporation." The term "corporation," as used in the income tax law, is not limited to those organizations actually incorporated under a charter or certificate of incorporation [Sec. 7701(a)(3)]. An organization is treated as a corporation if its characteristics are such that it more nearly resembles a corporation than a partnership or trust [Sec. 301.7701-2]. For example, some trusts are taxed as corporations [¶ 3026]. For insurance companies, see ¶ 3434.

(a) Corporate characteristics. The major corporate characteristics are: (1) associates; (2) purpose to conduct a business and distribute its profits; (3) continuity of life on the death or withdrawal of a member; (4) centralized management; (5) limited liability; and (6) free transferability of interests in the organization. The combination of these characteristics in a particular fact situation will determine if an organization is taxable as a corporation. Other factors also may affect the determination [Sec. 301.7701-2(a)]. Associations of doctors, lawyers and other professional people organized under state professional association acts are considered corporations for tax purposes and the criteria set forth above need not be applied.[1]

(b) Limited partnerships. A limited partnership may be classified as an ordinary partnership or as an association taxable as a corporation. Partnerships may be taxed as corporations if they more closely resemble a corporation than any other type of business entity [Sec. 301.7701-3(b)].

FIGURING THE TAX

¶ 3102　Normal tax and surtax. The normal tax and surtax are imposed on a corporation's taxable income (with some adjustments for the surtax) [Sec. 11; 1.11-1]. The corporate tax rate schedule is as follows:

Footnotes appear at end of this Chapter.

(1) Tax years ending after 1974 and before 1979.—The normal tax rates are 20% on the first $25,000 of taxable income, plus 22% on the excess. The surtax rate is 26% on taxable income over the $50,000 surtax exemption. A corporation with a 1974-1975 fiscal year must prorate its tax (see ¶ 3546) [Sec. 21; 1.21-1].

(2) Tax years ending after 1978.—The normal tax rate is 22% on total taxable income and the surtax rate is 26% on taxable income over the $25,000 surtax exemption. This rate also applies to tax years beginning after 1964 and ending before 1975.

The total tax may be reduced by any allowable investment credit [¶ 2410] and foreign tax credit [¶ 3701]. The tax is computed as follows:

Computation of Tax—Calendar Year 1977

Example: Armstrong Corporation had gross income of $101,000, and itemized deductions of $11,000. The gross income included cash dividends of $4,000 from taxable domestic industrial corporations (for which there is a special 85% deduction [¶ 3114(a)]).

Gross income		$101,000
Less:	Itemized deductions	11,000
Difference		$ 90,000
Less:	Special deductions [Dividends received (85% of $4,000)]	3,400
Taxable income		$ 86,600

1.	Taxable income		$ 86,600
2.	Normal tax:		
	a. 20% of first $25,000	$ 5,000	
	b. 22% of $61,600 ($86,600 less $25,000)	13,552	
	c. Total normal tax		$ 18,552
3.	Taxable income		$ 86,600
4.	Less: $50,000 surtax exemption		50,000
5.	Balance subject to surtax		$ 36,600
6.	Surtax (26% of line 5)		$ 9,516
7.	Normal tax (line 2c)		$ 18,552
8.	Surtax (line 6)		9,516
9.	Tax before credits		$ 28,068

The same result may be achieved by the following method:

1.	Taxable income	$ 86,600
2.	48% of line 1	$ 41,568
3.	Subtract $13,500*	13,500
4.	Tax before credits	$ 28,068

---

* $50,000 × 27% [26% surtax + 1% (48% minus 26% surtax minus 21% average normal tax)] = $13,500.

¶ 3103 Minimum tax. For tax years starting after 1975, the minimum tax on corporations is 15% of the tax preference items reduced by the greater of (a) $10,000, or (b) the regular income tax imposed for the tax year, less credits for foreign taxes (¶ 3701), investment in qualified property (¶ 2410), and work incentive program expenses (¶ 2411), and the adjustment for timber income [Sec. 56(a), (c), (d), (e)]. The regular income tax for the purpose of the reductions does not include the accumulated earnings or personal holding company taxes [¶ 3130; 3406]. Form 4626 is used by corporations to compute the minimum tax if the corporation's tax preferences exceed $10,000.

There are special rules for applying the minimum tax to Subchapter S corporations (¶ 3140), related corporations (¶ 3222) and regulated investment companies (¶ 3428) [Sec. 58(b), (d), (e); Prop. Reg. 1.58-1(c); 1.58-4].

Chapter 21—Corporations—Normal Tax, Surtax

NOTE: Before the 1976 Tax Reform Act, the corporate minimum tax was 10% of tax preference items reduced by: (1) $30,000, (2) regular income tax for the year less credits, and (3) tax carryover after 1969 (excess of regular tax computed without minimum tax, less credits, over sum of tax preferences less $30,000 exclusion). The tax preferences for corporations before the 1976 Tax Reform Act were the same as under current law. Except for income from timber, the carryover of taxes to offset preference income was repealed for tax years starting after 6-30-75.

Tax preference items.—The following are tax preference items for corporations (see ¶ 2403 for definitions):

- Capital gain. To figure excess net long-term capital gains as a tax preference, corporations use a different percentage (37.5%) than that of other taxpayers. Special rules apply to timber income, see Note below. [Sec. 56(d), (e); 57(a)(9), (e); Prop. Reg. 1.57-1(i)].
- Accelerated depreciation on real property [Sec. 57(a)(2); Prop. Reg. 1.57-1(b)].
- Depletion [Sec. 57(a)(8); Prop. Reg. 1.57-1(h)].
- Fast amortization [Sec. 57(a)(4), (5), (10); Prop. Reg. 1.57-1(d), (e)].
- Bad debt deduction of financial institutions [Sec. 57(a)(7); Prop. Reg. 1.57-1(g)].
- Accelerated depreciation on leased personal property only for Subchapter S corporations (¶ 3140) and personal holding companies (¶ 3400) [Sec. 57(a)(3); Prop. Reg. 1.57-1(c)(8); 1.57-2(a)].

NOTE: Banks and other financial institutions (¶ 3433) are not affected by the changes made by the 1976 Tax Reform Act until tax years starting after 1977. Timber companies may still continue to carry over taxes against preference income. In addition, special rules under the 1976 Tax Reform Act have the effect of exempting timber income from the increase in minimum tax. Under these rules the item of tax preference for timber gains is reduced by one-third and further reduced by $20,000. Also the deduction for regular taxes is reduced by the lesser of (1) one-third, or (2) the preference reduction, described in preceding sentence.

CORPORATE INCOME

¶ 3105 Income of corporations. Gross income of a domestic corporation generally includes the same items and is figured the same as gross income of an individual. A "domestic" corporation is one created or organized in the United States or under the laws of the United States or of any State or Territory [Sec. 7701(a)(4)]. A foreign corporation is one that is not domestic.

Taxable income is gross income less the deductions allowed to corporations [¶ 3112]. There is no provision for adjusted gross income as in the case of an individual.

The following are the major sources of corporate income:
- Gross profit from sales [¶ 2601].
- Dividends [¶ 1700 et seq.].
- Interest [¶ 1315].
- Rents and royalties [¶ 1316].
- Gains and losses [¶ 3201 et seq.].

The following are additional factors that must be considered in determining corporate income:
- Receipts that are contributions to capital [¶ 3106].
- Property distributions received by corporations [¶ 3107].
- Rentals paid to shareholders of a lessor corporation [¶ 3108].
- Income from a sinking fund [¶ 3109].

Footnotes appear at end of this Chapter.

¶ 3105

¶ **3106 Capital contributions.** Contributions to capital of the corporation are not income [Sec. 118; 1.118-1]. This includes contributions in aid of construction made after 1-31-76 (basically, money or other property contributed by a person whether or not a shareholder) to a regulated public utility providing water or sewage disposal services. For this rule to apply, the contributions must be used to acquire or construct qualified tangible property, and may not be included in the rate base for rate making purposes [Sec. 118(b)].

(a) Voluntary payments and assessments. Voluntary pro rata payments by shareholders are neither income to the corporation, nor deductible by the shareholder. They are capital contributions similar to the original investment and are added to the cost of the stock. This also applies to assessments against the stockholders by the corporation.[1] If the stock becomes worthless, the assessment increases the loss [Sec. 1.118-1]. For the basis of property acquired as a contribution to capital, see ¶ 1518(b).

(b) Contributions made by nonshareholders. Contributions to capital of the corporation by persons not shareholders are not income to the corporation. However, special rules govern the basis of contributions by non-shareholders.

Property other than money. When property other than money is contributed to capital by someone not a stockholder, the basis of the property is zero [Sec. 362(c)(1)].

Property acquired with money contributions. If a capital contribution of money is made by someone not a stockholder, the basis of any property bought with the money during the 12-month period beginning on the day the contribution is received is reduced by the contribution. Any money not used during that period reduces the basis of other property held by the corporation at the end of the 12-month period in the following order: (1) depreciable property; (2) property subject to amortization; (3) property subject to depletion (except percentage depletion); (4) other property. The basis of property in each category is reduced in proportion to the relative bases of the properties. But the bases of the various units of property within a category may be adjusted differently of the Revenue Service consents. Request for the change should be filed with the return for the tax year the property was transferred to the corporation [Sec. 362(c)(2); 1.362-2].

These rules on contributions made by nonshareholders do not apply where there is a contribution in aid of construction to a public utility under Sec. 118(b) [Sec. 362(c)(3)].

¶ **3107 Property distributions received by corporations.** When a corporation receives distributions in property, the amount of the distribution is the lesser of: (1) fair market value of the property on date of distribution; or (2) adjusted basis of the property (in distributing corporation's hands immediately before the distribution), increased by any gain recognized to the distributing corporation in distributions of LIFO inventory, property subject to a liability in excess of its basis [¶ 3127], appreciated property in redemption of its own stock, or recapture income under Sec. 1245, 1250, 1251, 1252 or 1254 (¶ 1619; 1622(c); 1845(e); 2103(c); 2226) [Sec. 301(b)(1)(B)]. See also ¶ 3127 for gain or loss to the distributing corporation on property distributions. For property bought by a corporate shareholder below its value, see ¶ 3126.

NOTE: Fair market value *must* be used for distributions by a foreign corporation unless the shareholder gets a dividends received deduction [¶ 3114(c)] for the distribution. Then a special rule applies [Sec. 301(b)(1)(C)]. Fair market value also must be used by foreign corporate shareholders receiving property distributions unless the distribution is effectively connected income (¶ 3710) [Sec. 301(b)(1)(D)].

The amount of the distribution is reduced (but not below zero) by any liability of the distributing corporation assumed by the recipient shareholder in connection with the distribution, and any liability to which the property is subject immediately before and after the distribution [Sec. 301(b)(2); 1.301-1(g)].

Basis. The basis of the property received in the distribution is the same as the amount of the distribution, as determined above, without reduction for liabilities [Sec. 301(d)(2), (3); 1.301-1(h)].

¶ **3108 Corporate rental income paid directly to shareholders.** If a corporation leases its property, the rent is taxable to it, although paid directly to its shareholders and bondholders.[1] This applies even if the lease is in perpetuity and without a condition defeating its force or operation.[2]

> **Example:** X Railroad leased property to Y Railroad, the annual rental being $500,000. Instead of paying $500,000 to X, Y paid $200,000 to X's shareholders and $300,000 to its bondholders. The transaction is treated as if Y had paid the $500,000 rent to X (which must include it in gross income), and X had then paid a dividend of $200,000 to its shareholders (who would include it in gross income as dividends), and $300,000 to its bondholders (who would include it in gross income as interest).

The rent is deemed constructively received by the lessor corporation. Its shareholders may be held liable as transferees for the corporation's tax on the income[3] [¶ 3614].

¶ **3109 Income from a sinking fund.** A corporation that issues bonds may establish a sinking fund to pay the debt. Usually, a trustee is appointed to whom the corporation has to make payments at stated intervals. Property in the fund is a corporate asset and any income or gain from it must be reported (for example, interest on bonds the trustee holds) [Sec. 1.61-13(b)].

¶ **3110 Reconciliation of taxable income with book income.** The net income on the books of a corporation may differ from the taxable income on its return. This is because certain book income items are excluded from income on the return, and some expenses on the books are not deductible.

The corporation return (Form 1120) has two schedules in this area: Sched. M-1 reconciles book income with taxable income, and Sched. M-2 is an analysis of surplus.

Schedule M-1 has two columns. In the left hand column, entries are made for book income, federal income tax, excess of capital losses over capital gains, income items in the return not included in the books (such as prepaid rent) and expenses deducted on the books but not on the return (such as gifts costing over $25). In the right hand column, entries are made for income reported on the books and not included in the return (such as tax-exempt interest) and expenses deducted on the return but not on the books (for example, if the corporation used accelerated depreciation for tax purposes and straight line depreciation on its books). The difference between the right hand column and left hand column should equal the corporation's taxable income before the net operating loss deduction [¶ 3215 et seq.] and special deductions [¶ 3113 et seq.].

Schedule M-2 also has 2 columns. The left hand column is for opening surplus, book income for year and any increases in surplus. The right hand column is for distributions and other items that decrease surplus. For example, adjustment of prior year's earnings would affect one of these columns, depending on adjustment. The difference between these two columns is the ending surplus. This figure should equal the corporation's unappropriated retained earnings at the end of the tax year entered in the Schedule L balance sheets.

Footnotes appear at end of this Chapter.

¶ 3110

Chapter 21—Corporations—Income, Deductions

Form 1120S, filed by a corporation electing partnership-type taxation also has Schedules M-1 and M-2. They are substantially the same as those in Form 1120. The major difference is the Schedule M-2 entry on Form 1120S for undistributed taxable income or net operating loss [¶ 3142(b); 3143(c)].

NOTE: 1976 return schedules M-1 and M-2, discussed here, may be different on the 1977 return.

Example 1: In the first column of the following worksheet are items taken from the books of a corporation. The net income on the books is $137,450, but taxable income on the return is $237,100. Columns 2 and 3 are for items to be entered in Schedule M-1. The fourth column is for items to be entered on the return. The worksheet and Schedule M-1 (Form 1120) are filled out as follows:

Schedule M-1 Worksheet

Income	(1) Profit & Loss Account	(2) Schedule M-1 Left-hand Column	(3) Schedule M-1 Right-hand Column	(4) Taxable Income
Sales (net)	$1,900,000			$1,900,000
Interest:				
From bank & income tax refund $10,000				
On State bond 1,000	11,000		$ 1,000(a)	10,000
Proceeds from life insurance (death of corporate officer)	15,000		15,000(b)	
Total	$1,926,000			$1,910,000
Cost of goods sold	$1,550,000			$1,550,000
Insurance premiums on life of corporate officer (corporation is beneficiary of policy)	3,000	$ 3,000(c)		
Compensation of officers	35,000			35,000
Salaries and wages	32,000			32,000
Repairs	1,000			1,000
Taxes (property)	9,000			9,000
Contributions:				
Charities .... $ 5,000				
Political party 500	5,500	500(d)		5,000
Interest paid on loan to purchase New York State bonds	400	400(e)		
Depreciation	20,400			20,400
Depletion	20,500			20,500
Capital loss on sale of securities	200	200(f)		
Federal income tax	111,550	111,550(g)		
Total	$1,788,550			$1,672,900
Net income:				
Per books	137,450			
Taxable income				237,100

Notes to Schedule M-1 worksheet:
  (a) Nontaxable interest on State bonds. ¶ 1204.
  (b) Proceeds of life insurance not taxable. ¶ 1213.
  (c) Insurance premium not deductible where paid by corporation on life of officer and corporation is beneficiary. ¶ 1828(a).
  (d) Contribution made by a corporation to a political party is not deductible. ¶ 3112.
  (e) Interest paid to purchase tax-exempt bonds is not deductible. ¶ 1905.
  (f) A net capital loss is not deductible in year sustained. ¶ 3201.
  (g) Federal income taxes are not deductible. ¶ 1911.

Schedule M-1

Left-hand column
1. Net income per books $137,450
2. Federal income tax 111,550
3. Excess of capital losses over capital gains 200
4. Taxable income not recorded on books 0
5. Expenses recorded on books, not deducted on return:
   - Insurance premiums .... $ 3,000
   - Political contribution 500
   - Interest to purchase tax-exempt securities 400   3,900
6. Total of lines 1-5 .... $253,100

Right-hand column
7. Income recorded on books, not included in return:
   - Interest on state bond .... $ 1,000
   - Insurance proceeds .... 15,000 $ 16,000
8. Deductions on return, not made on books 0
9. Total of lines 7 and 8 .... $ 16,000
10. Taxable income (line 6 minus line 9) $237,100

Example 2: The corporation mentioned in Example 1 had an opening balance of $300,000. During the year, it paid cash dividends of $75,000. It received a federal tax refund of $13,000 due to an adjustment of its 1975 return. The worksheet and Schedule M-2 would appear as follows:

Schedule M-2 Worksheet

	Retained Earnings Account	Schedule M-2 (Left-hand Column) Credits	Schedule M-2 (Right-hand Column) Debits
Balance at start of year	$ 300,000	$300,000	
Net book income	137,450	137,450	
	437,450		
Dividends	75,000		$ 75,000
	362,450		
Federal income tax refund	13,000	13,000	
Balance at end of year	$ 375,450		375,450
		$450,450	$450,450

Schedule M-2

Left-hand column
1. Balance at beginning of year $300,000
2. Net income per books 137,450
3. Other increases:
   - 1975 tax refund 13,000
4. Total of lines 1, 2 and 3 .... $450,450

Right-hand column
5. Distributions: (a) Cash .... $ 75,000
   - (b) Stock 0
   - (c) Property 0
6. Other decreases 0
7. Total of lines 5 and 6 .... $ 75,000
8. Balance at end of year (line 4 minus line 7) $375,450

Footnotes appear at end of this Chapter.

¶ 3112

CORPORATE DEDUCTIONS

¶ **3112 Deductions of corporations in general.** Corporations generally get the same itemized deductions as individuals [Sec. 161-175]. However, they cannot take purely personal deductions, such as the statutory deductions for medical expenses or alimony payments [Sec. 211-217]. Nor can the corporation claim a deduction or tax credit for political contributions [¶ 2416]. Similarly, they cannot take the zero bracket amount and the deductions for personal exemptions. The following are the more common deductions:

Salaries and wages [¶ 1815 et seq.].
Rent [¶ 1826].
Repairs [¶ 1825].
Bad debts [¶ 2300 et seq.].
Interest [¶ 1900 et seq.].
Taxes [¶ 1910 et seq.].
Charitable contributions [¶ 3118].

Casualty losses [¶ 2204; 2207].
Depreciation and amortization [¶ 2000].
Amortizable bond premium [¶ 1846].
Depletion [¶ 2100 et seq.].
Advertising [¶ 1827; 2738].
Contributions to pension and profit-sharing plans [¶ 1838].
Net operating loss deduction [¶ 3215].

≫**OBSERVATION**→ Since there is no provision for adjusted gross income for a corporation, there is no division of deductions between those for adjusted gross income and other itemized deductions.

¶ **3113 Special deductions for corporations.** In addition to itemized deductions, corporations get special deductions for [Sec. 241; 1.241-1]:
- Dividends received from domestic corporations [¶ 3114(a)];
- Dividends received from foreign corporations [¶ 3114(c)];
- Organizational expenditures [¶ 3116].

There are also other special deductions for Western Hemisphere Trade Corporations and China Trade Act Corporations [¶ 3117].

≫**OBSERVATION**→ Except for a deduction for dividends paid on certain preferred stock of public utilities [¶ 3115], and the deduction for organizational expenditures, the special deductions differ from itemized deductions in that the former are for amounts *received* rather than *paid*.

¶ **3114 Deduction for certain dividends received** is allowed to corporations.

Background and purpose. If Corporation A owns stock in Corporation B, receives a dividend from B and then distributes the dividend income to its own individual stockholders, B's earnings would be taxed twice at the corporate level and once at the individual stockholders' level. The dividends-received relief provisions were designed to cushion this triple tax impact by taxing only a small portion of dividend income received by corporations.

(a) Dividends received from domestic corporations. Corporations generally can deduct an amount equal to 85% of the dividends received from taxable domestic corporations. See (e) below for limitation on the amount deductible. There is a special limitation for dividends received from a regulated investment company [¶ 3431] or a DISC [¶ 3460(c)].

Dividends not included in figuring the deduction [Sec. 246(a); 1.246-1]: (1) dividends from corporations exempt from tax in year of distribution or preceding year; (2) dividends, usually referred to as interest, from mutual savings banks, cooperative banks and domestic building and loan associations [¶ 3433]; (3) dividends from real estate investment trusts [¶ 3432]; (4) dividends from public utilities on preferred stock issued before 10-1-42 ((d) below).

100% dividend deduction. Small business investment companies [¶ 3459] may deduct 100% of dividends received, and members of an affiliated group may elect to deduct 100% of dividends received from another member ((b) below). The 85% of taxable income limitation ((e) below) does not apply to this deduction [Sec. 246(b); 1.246-2].

Dividends from certain foreign corporations. Generally, dividends from foreign corporations are treated as shown in (c) below. However, a dividend from a foreign corporation paid out of earnings and profits accumulated by a domestic corporation when it was subject to the U.S. income tax is treated as a dividend from a taxable domestic corporation [Sec. 243(d); 1.243-3, 1.245-1(a)(2)].

Deduction not allowed. To get the deduction, the corporation must own the stock (1) on the dividend record date[1] (the day that a stock must be held if the stockholder is to receive a dividend), and (2) for a period of at least 16 days (a preferred stock whose dividend covers a period of more than 366 days must be owned for 91 days). Only 15 (or 90) days after the ex-dividend date (day after dividend record date) may be counted in the 16 (or 91) day period. Also, the corporation cannot count the days the original stock in a wash sale was held or any time that a short sale of substantially identical securities is pending. This includes an option to sell, a contract to sell or an actual short sale that has not been closed by the corporation [Sec. 1.246-3].

The deduction is disallowed to the extent the corporation has to make payments for substantially identical securities corresponding to the dividends received. This usually covers payments by the corporation equivalent to dividends declared on stock "borrowed" to cover a short sale; but it is not restricted to that situation. Payments equivalent to dividends are deductible as expenses[2] [Sec. 246(c); 1.246-3].

(b) Dividends received from another corporation in the same affiliated group. Corporations may elect to deduct the entire dividend received from another corporation in the same affiliated group [¶ 3222(a)]. For this purpose, affiliated groups may include insurance companies. This election applies only to dividends either (a) paid out of post-1963 earnings and profits or (b) for tax years beginning after 1975 paid by a corporation electing the Puerto Rico and possession tax credit (¶ 3727) [Sec. 243(a)(3); 1.243-4].

If the election is made, the group is limited to one surtax exemption, one $150,000 credit for accumulated earnings tax ($100,000 for tax years starting before 1975) and one exemption for estimated tax. The group also is treated as one corporation in figuring the limited exploration expense deduction [¶ 1843], and each member of the group must treat foreign taxes [¶ 3701-3703] in the same manner [Sec. 243(b); 1.243-5].

Election is made by the parent. Every corporation that is a subsidiary on the last day of the parent's tax year must consent to the election. The election terminates automatically if a new corporation joins the group and does not file a consent. Otherwise, it will continue until all the members of the group agree to its revocation [Sec. 243(b)(2); 1.243-4(c)-(e)].

(c) Dividends received from foreign corporations. A deduction for dividends received from a foreign corporation (other than a foreign personal holding company) is allowed, if: (1) the foreign corporation is subject to federal income tax; and (2) for an uninterrupted period of at least 36 months by the end of the tax year the dividends were paid (or the corporation's entire existence, if less), it was engaged in trade or business in the U.S.; and (3) at least 50% of its gross income during the period was effectively connected with a U.S. trade or business (¶ 3711) [Sec. 245(a)]. See (e) below for limitation on the amount deductible.

Figuring the deduction. The deduction is the sum of:

Footnotes appear at end of this Chapter.

¶ 3114

(1) 85% of dividends out of earnings and profits of tax year × $\dfrac{\text{foreign corp. gross income effectively connected with U.S. trade or business in tax year}}{\text{total gross income of foreign corp. for tax year}}$

plus

(2) 85% of dividends out of earnings and profits of uninterrupted period × $\dfrac{\text{foreign corp. gross income effectively connected with U.S. trade or business (excluding tax year)}}{\text{total gross income of foreign corp. for uninterrupted period (excluding tax year)}}$

Wholly owned foreign corporations. A foreign corporation that only has income effectively connected with a U.S. business [¶ 3711] for a tax year is taxed at U.S. rates. A domestic corporation that owns all the stock of such a foreign corporation for the entire year may deduct 100% of the dividends paid out of these earnings and profits, if it also owns all of the stock for its entire tax year when the dividends are received. This does not apply if a multiple surtax exemption is elected for the respective tax year of either corporation [Sec. 245(b)].

(d) Dividends on certain public utility preferred stock. Corporate taxpayers also deduct a percentage of the dividends received on public utility preferred stock issued before 10-1-42 for which the utilities were allowed a dividends paid deduction[3] [¶ 3115]; dividends on public utility preferred stock issued after 9-30-42 are treated the same as those from other domestic corporations ((a) above). The percentage, based on the tax rate, is 60.208% on pre-10-1-42 preferred stock [Sec. 244; 1.244-1, 1.244-2]. If the public utility is a member of an affiliated group that makes the election in (b) above, the percentage is 70.833%. See (e) below for limitation on amount deductible.

(e) Limitation. The total amount deductible for domestic dividends received ((a) above), dividends received from certain public utilities ((d) above), and dividends received from foreign corporations ((c) above) is limited to 85% of the corporation's taxable income computed without regard to these deductions: (1) the net operating loss, (2) dividends received from domestic corporations, (3) dividends paid or received on certain public utility preferred stock, (4) dividends received from certain foreign corporations, and (5) capital loss carryback to the tax year [Sec. 246(b)(1)]. Taxable income for this purpose includes the excess of net long-term capital gain over net short-term capital loss, even if the alternative method is used (¶ 3202) [Sec. 1.1201-1(a)]. This limitation does not apply if the corporation has a net operating loss for the year [¶ 2242], computed without regard to the 85% taxable income limitation [Sec. 246(b)(2); 1.246-2].

Example: Assume the Rex Corporation has dividend income from domestic corporations of $100,000 and business income of $85,000. Its deductions for the current tax year are $100,000 in business deductions and a $10,000 net operating loss deduction. The dividends received deduction is computed as follows:

1.	Gross income		$185,000
2.	Business deductions		100,000
3.	Taxable income before net operating loss deduction and dividends received deduction		$ 85,000
4.	Div. rec. ded. (85% × $85,000 instead of 85% × $100,000)	$72,250	
5.	Net operating loss deduction	10,000	82,250
6.	Taxable income		$ 2,750

If the corporation's business deductions totaled $100,001 so that item 3 is $84,999, the taxable income limitation would not apply. In this case, after deducting the 85% of dividends received ($85,000), item 6 would be a net operating loss of $1; so the dividend received deduction would not be limited to 85% of taxable income.

¶ 3115 Deduction for dividends paid on pre-10-1-42 preferred stock of public utility. Public utilities get a deduction for dividends paid on preferred stock issued before 10-1-42. The deduction is a percentage of the lesser of (a) dividends paid during the tax year on this preferred stock, or (b) taxable income for the tax year (figured without this deduction). For this deduction, taxable income includes the excess of net long-term capital gain over the net short-term capital loss, even if the corporation uses the alternative method[1] [¶ 3202]. The percentage is 29.167% [Sec. 247; 1.247-1].

¶ 3116 Organization expenditures. Ordinarily, these are deductible only in the year of dissolution. But if certain conditions are met, the corporation can elect to amortize them ratably over a period of 60 months or more, beginning with the month the corporation starts business. When the corporate charter or certificate is issued for a limited time only, the expenses can be amortized over that period. The election applies only to expenditures incurred before the end of the tax year the corporation begins business, regardless of whether the corporation files its returns on the cash or accural basis, or whether the expenditures are paid in the tax year they were incurred [Sec. 248; 1.248-1].

To be deductible, the expenditure must be (1) incident to the creation of the corporation; (2) chargeable to capital account; and (3) of a character that would be amortizable over the life of the corporation [Sec. 248(b); 1.248-1]. These expenditures include fees paid for legal services in drafting the corporate charter, by-laws, minutes of organizational meetings, and terms of original stock certificates; fees paid for accounting services; expenses of temporary directors, and of organizational meetings of directors or stockholders; and fees paid to the state of incorporation.

Election to amortize does not apply to expenditures for (1) issuing or selling shares of stock or other securities, such as commissions, professional fees, and printing costs, (2) transfer of assets to a corporation, (3) reorganization of a corporation, unless directly incident to the creation of a corporation.

Election must be made by the time for filing the return (including extensions) for the tax year the corporation begins business. It is made in a statement attached to the return showing (1) amount and description of the organizational expenditures, (2) date the expenditures were incurred, (3) month the corporation began business, and (4) number of months over which the expenditures are to be deducted. The period elected must be adhered to in figuring the taxable income of the corporation [Sec. 248(c); 1.248-1(c)].

¶ 3117 Special deductions based on income. Some specially treated corporations are allowed a deduction based on income.

(a) Western Hemisphere Trade Corporations can deduct a percentage of their taxable income as a special deduction. For this purpose, taxable income is figured without regard to the deduction, and it includes the excess of net long-term capital gain over net short-term capital loss, even if the corporation uses the alternative method[1] [¶ 3202]. The percentage was 29.167% for tax years starting before 1976 [Sec. 992; 1.992-1].

NOTE: The Western Hemisphere Trade Corporation deduction is repealed for tax years starting after 1979. During the transitional period from 1976 through 1979, the

Footnotes appear at end of this Chapter.

¶ 3117

special tax deduction percentage is phased out as follows: 1976, 22.917%; 1977, 16.667%; 1978, 10.417% and 1979, 4.617% [Sec. 922(b)].

A Western Hemisphere Trade Corporation is a domestic corporation all of whose business (other than incidental purchases) is done in North, Central, or South America, or the West Indies, and: (1) at least 95% of gross income for the 3-year period before the close of the tax year (or the corporation's entire existence, if less) was from sources outside the U.S., and (2) at least 90% of gross income for the period was from the active conduct of a trade or business [Sec. 921; 1.921-1]. The source of income from sales depends on where title passes.[2] This tax reduction does not apply to a Virgin Islands' or U.S. corporation in computing the Virgin Island tax.[3]

(b) China Trade Act Corporations are allowed a special deduction for income from sources within Formosa and Hong Kong [Sec. 941; 1.941-1].

NOTE: The China Trade Act Corporation deduction is repealed for tax years starting after 1977. The special deduction is reduced by (a) one-third for tax years starting in 1976 and (b) two-thirds for tax years starting in 1977 [Sec. 941(d).]

¶ **3118 Charitable contributions.** A corporation may deduct charitable contributions. Gifts or donations that are deductible by individuals [¶ 1941] qualify for the corporate deduction, except those made to fraternal societies and those made to trusts, community chests, funds or foundations for use outside the U.S. or its possessions [Sec. 170(c); 1.170A-11(a)]. Deduction was denied for a contribution to a tax-exempt parent corporation [¶ 3436].[1] The same special rules apply to contributions of income and remainder interests in trust and the contribution of the right to use property [¶ 1942(d), (e)].

For contributions made after 10-4-76, corporations (other than a Subchapter S corporation) contributing certain types of ordinary income property (basically, inventory items) to a public charity or private operating foundation are allowed a deduction equal to the sum of: (a) the corporation's basis in the property plus (b) up to one-half of the unrealized appreciation. However, no deduction exceeding twice the basis of the property is allowed. No deduction is allowed for any part of the unrealized appreciation which would be ordinary income resulting from recapture of certain items if the property were sold. To qualify, the following conditions must be met: (1) the donee's use of the property must be related to its exempt purpose and solely for the care of the ill, the needy or infants; (2) the donee must not exchange the property for money, other property, or services; and (3) the donee must give the donor a statement representing compliance with conditions (1) and (2) above [Sec. 170(e)(3)].

(a) Time for deduction. The deduction ordinarily is allowed only for the tax year the contribution is actually paid [Sec. 1.170A-1]. However, an accrual basis corporation can elect to deduct contributions authorized by its board of directors during the tax year, if they are paid by the 15th day of the third month after the tax year ends [Sec. 1.170A-11(b)]. See also ¶ 2735(e); 2742.

The election is made by reporting the contribution on the return, and attaching a declaration that the resolution authorizing the contribution was adopted by the board of directors during the tax year. This must be verified by a statement signed by an officer authorized to sign the return that it is made under the penalties of perjury. A copy of the resolution authorizing the contribution also must be attached to the return [Sec. 1.170A-11(b)].

(b) Amount deductible. The corporation's deduction cannot exceed 5% of its taxable income, figured without regard to the contributions deduction, special deductions [¶ 3113] (other than organizational expenditures), any net operating loss carryback to the tax year [¶ 3215 et seq.], any capital loss carryback to the tax year [¶ 3201(a)], and the special deduction for Western Hemisphere Trade Corporations [Sec. 170(b)(2); 1.170A-11(a)]. The same general rules apply to corporate contributions of appreciated property [¶ 1942(b)]. However, when it is required, a corporate donor of appreciated capital gain property reduces its contribution deduction by 62.5% of the appreciation rather than 50%. As with individual donors, the corporation reduces its deduction only for contributions to or for the use of private foundations (other than an operating foundation [¶ 3441]) or for a contribution of tangible personal property that is used by the donee in a way that is not related to the donee's exempt purpose [Sec. 170(e)(1)(B); 1.170A-4(a)(3)].

Example 1: In 1977, Sims Co. (not a Western Hemisphere Trade Corporation) gave $2,500 to a domestic community chest. Its taxable income before deducting contributions was $30,000, and it had special deductions (other than organizational expenditures) of $15,000. It had no capital loss during the tax year. The deduction is figured as follows:

Taxable income (without benefit of contributions deduction)	$30,000
Plus: Special deductions	15,000
Taxable income figured without regard to contributions, special deductions, net operating loss carryback and capital loss carryback	$45,000
Contributions deduction (5% × $45,000)	$ 2,250

(c) Carryover. Contributions over the 5% limit are carried over 5 succeeding tax years. However, contributions actually made during the later year plus the carryover must fall within the 5% limit [Sec. 170(d)(2); 1.170A-11(c)].

Example 2: Assume that in 1978, Sims Co. in Example 1 had a taxable income (figured without contributions, special deductions, net operating loss carryback and capital loss carryback) of $50,000, and that it gave $2,300 to the American Red Cross. The deduction would be figured as follows:

Contributions actually made in 1978	$ 2,300
Carryover from 1977 (1977 excess)	250
Total	$ 2,550
Amount deductible (5% × $50,000)	2,500
Excess (available for carryover to 1979)	$ 50

If a charitable contribution for a tax year results in a carryover to later years because a net operating loss carryover to that year reduces or eliminates taxable income, the charitable contribution carryover must be reduced. This prevents a double deduction. Since the net operating loss carryover to later years is computed after the charitable deduction, it is increased to the extent that the charitable deduction has reduced taxable income for this purpose. Therefore, the charitable contribution carryover is reduced to the extent the net operating loss carryover is increased [Sec. 170(d)(2); 1.170A-11(c)].

(d) Contribution as business expense. If the payments do not qualify as contributions, but are in fact business expenses, the amount is deductible without limitation [Sec. 1.162-15]. Contributions in excess of the 5% limit cannot be deducted as business expenses [Sec. 1.162-1].

PURCHASES, SALES, AND DISTRIBUTIONS OF CORPORATE SECURITIES AND PROPERTIES

¶ 3124 Corporation dealing in its own stock. No gain or loss is recognized to a corporation that receives money or other property in exchange for its own stock, including treasury stock. Nor is gain or loss recognized if a corporation transfers its stock as payment for services [Sec. 1032; 1.1032-1(a)]. However, gain or loss is recognized in the case of restricted property transferred to an employee to the extent of the amount allowed as a deduction to the employer (¶ 1819(c)) [Prop. Reg. Sec. 1.83-6(b)]. For the recognition of gain to a corporation that distributes the stock of another corporation as payment for services, see ¶ 1400.

Gain or loss may be recognized if the corporation receives its own stock in the exchange, unless it receives it in exchange for its own stock (including treasury stock) [Sec. 1.1032-1(b)].

Example: Yale Co. owns real estate worth $3,000, but having an adjusted basis of $2,500, which it exchanges for shares of its own stock having a fair market value of $3,000. The $500 gain is taxable.

¶ 3125 Corporation dealing in its own obligations. Bonds, debentures, notes or other obligations bearing interest may be issued (1) at face value (price equal to amount printed on the bonds); (2) at a premium (price in excess of face value); or (3) at a discount (price less than face value). Obligations that are part of investment units that include options are subject to special rules [Sec. 1.61-12(c)(4), 1.163-3(a)(2), 1.1232-3(b)]. For special rules on repurchases of convertible bonds at a premium after 4-22-69, see (b) below.

(a) Obligations issued at face value. No gain or loss is realized when the obligations are issued [Sec. 1.61-12(c)(1)]. If they are bought later by the issuing corporation for a price over the issuing price, the excess is a deductible expense [Sec. 1.163-3(c)]. If they are bought for less than the issuing price, the difference is income[1] [Sec. 1.61-12(c)(3)]. (The purchase constitutes the closed transaction. The fact that they are not retired does not prevent application of the rule.[2]).

Example 1: In 1960, Burke Co. issued 500 bonds of the face value of $1,000 each, receiving $500,000 for them. If, in 1977, it repurchased 100 bonds for $95,000, it has income of $5,000 ($100,000 − $95,000); if it repurchased the 100 bonds for $103,000, it can deduct $3,000 ($103,000 − $100,000).

NOTE: Railroad corporations, as defined in Sec. 77(m) of the Bankruptcy Act, are not taxed on income from discharge of indebtedness for less than face value, if made on court order in a receivership or Sec. 77 Bankruptcy Act proceeding that began before 1-1-60.[3]

(b) Obligations issued at a premium. A premium received on obligations issued after 2-28-13 is income and should be amortized over the life of the obligations [Sec. 1.61-12(c)(2)]. If they are repurchased by the corporation before maturity, the premium that has been reported as income is subtracted from the issuing price. If the result is less than the purchase price, the difference is a deduction in the year of purchase [Sec. 1.163-3(c)]. If the result is greater than the purchase price, the difference is income in the year of purchase [Sec. 1.61-12(c)(3)].

Example 2: If Hale Co. issues $100,000 of its 20-year bonds for $110,000, 1/20 of the premium (1/20 of $10,000 or $500) will be reported as income each year. Assume that after 5 years (after Hale has reported $2,500 as income), the bonds are repurchased for $115,000.

Purchase price		$115,000
Issuing price	$110,000	
Premium already returned as income	2,500	107,500
Deductible expense in year of purchase		$ 7,500

Example 3: Assume the same facts as in Example 2, except that the bonds were repurchased for $95,000.

Issuing price	$110,000	
Premium already returned as income	2,500	$107,500
Purchase price		95,000
Income in year of purchase		$ 12,500

Obligations issued before 3-1-13 at a premium are treated the same as obligations issued at face value ((a) above) when they are repurchased [Sec. 1.61-12(c)(3), 1.163-3(c)].

Deduction of convertible bond premium on repurchase. The deduction for any premium paid by a corporation on the repurchase of its indebtedness convertible into its own stock (or that of a controlling or controlled corporation) is limited to the amount by which the repurchase price exceeds the issue price increased by discounts previously deducted ((c) below) and decreased by premiums previously included in gross income ((b) above) plus a normal call premium for nonconvertible obligations. Any premium paid in excess of this deductible amount is attributable to the conversion feature unless the Revenue Service is shown that it is actually interest and thus deductible [Sec. 249; 1.249-1(a), (b), (e)]. A normal call premium is an amount stated in dollars equal to a call premium on a nonconvertible obligation that is comparable to the convertible obligation [Sec. 1.249-1(d)(1)]. This term also includes a specified call premium on a convertible obligation, if the premium at the time of the repurchase does not exceed one year's interest payable on the obligation, increased by the deductible discount or reduced by issue premium includible in income [Sec. 1.249-1(d)(2)]. This provision is among those designed to discourage the use of debt in corporate acquisitions [¶ 1630; 1905(e); 2811(a); 3300]. In the case of repurchases under a binding commitment existing on 4-23-69, the above rule does not apply, and the proper deduction is left to court decisions [Sec. 1.249-1(f)].

(c) **Obligations issued at a discount.** If obligations are issued by a corporation at a discount, the net amount of the discount is deductible, and should be prorated or amortized over the life of the obligations [Sec. 1.163-3(a)]. If they are bought by the corporation before maturity, add the discount already deducted to the issuing price. If the result is less than the purchase price, the difference is a deduction in the year of purchase; but if the result is greater than the purchase price, the difference is income in the year of purchase [Sec. 1.61-12(c)(3), 1.163-3(c)].

NOTE: Amortizable premium and discount are reflected in earnings and profits in the same amount and in the same tax year that they are included in taxable income.[4]

Example 4: If Judd Co. issues $100,000 of its 20-year bonds for $90,000, 1/20 of the discount (1/20 of $10,000, or $500) will be deducted each year as interest.

Assume that after five years (after Judd has deducted $2,500 as interest), the bonds are repurchased for $95,000.

Purchase price		$95,000
Issuing price	$90,000	
Discount already deducted	2,500	92,500
Deductible expense in year of purchase		$ 2,500

Example 5: Assume the same facts as in Example 4, except that the bonds were repurchased for $85,000.

Issuing price	$90,000	
Discount already deducted	2,500	$92,500
Purchase price		85,000
Income in year of purchase		$ 7,500

(d) **Issuance of new bonds at time corporation buys old bonds.** If old bonds are bought with proceeds from the sale of new bonds, the unamortized discount or premium on the old bonds is treated as explained in (b) and (c) above. But if there is an exchange of new for old bonds, before the old bonds mature, the unamortized premium or discount on the old bonds is amortized over the life of the new bonds.[5]

(e) **Carryover of bond discount or premium to successor corporation.** A successor corporation may continue to amortize bond discount or premium on bonds taken over from its predecessor in certain liquidations and reorganizations. See ¶ 3337.

(f) **Election to exclude income from discharge of indebtedness.** A corporation may elect to have excluded from gross income the gain realized when it discharges its indebtedness for less than the amount due [Sec. 108(a); 1.108(a)-1]. However, if it so elects, the basis of the property against which the obligations were issued is reduced by the amount of the gain [Sec. 1017; 1.1017-1]. This may more than offset the advantage of not reporting the gain realized, since it lowers the basis used to figure depreciation and gain or loss on a sale.

Example 6: If Shelby Co. bought for $70,000, outstanding bonds it had issued for $100,000, the $30,000 gain may be excluded from gross income. However, the basis of the property then would be reduced by $30,000.

When the income exclusion is elected, the taxpayer must file a consent to have the basis of his property reduced. Ordinarily, it is filed in duplicate on Form 982 with the return for the tax year. However, it may be filed with an amended return or claim for credit or refund, if taxpayer establishes reasonable cause for failure to file with the original return [Sec. 1.108(a)-2].

The reduction in basis is made to the property used in a trade or business in this order [Sec. 1.1017-1]: (1) the property for which the debt is incurred, except inventories and receivables; (2) property against which there is a lien, except inventories and receivables; (3) any other property, except inventories and receivables; (4) inventories and receivables. In the case of an individual taxpayer, the reduction is further made to: (5) his property held for the production of income and (6) his other property.

Taxpayer also may request that the basis of his property be adjusted in a particular way. For instance, he can ask that the basis of only part of his property be reduced. Or he can request that the basis of all his property be reduced according to a fixed allocation. Agreement between taxpayer and the Commissioner as to any variations in the adjustment must be made by a closing agreement (see ¶ 3608(b)) [Sec. 1.1017-2].

¶ **3126 Property bought by stockholder for less than fair market value.** If a corporation transfers property to a corporate shareholder in a sale or exchange for less than its fair market value and also less than its adjusted basis, the amount of distribution is determined under the rules summarized below [Sec. 1.301-1(j)]. The distribution is taxable as a dividend to the extent it qualifies as such under the rules in ¶ 1701; 1702. Property distributions received by corporations, generally, are explained at ¶ 3107; those received by noncorporate shareholders are at ¶ 1702(b).

(a) **Amount distributed.** If property is transferred for less than its fair market value and adjusted basis, the amount of distribution is determined as follows [Sec. 1.301-1(j)]:

Value equal to or greater than basis. If the fair market value of the property equals or exceeds its adjusted basis in the hands of the distributing corporation, the amount of the distribution is the excess of the adjusted basis over the amount paid for the property.

Example 1: Y Corp. sold property to X Corp., one of its shareholders, for $20. The property's fair market value was $100, and its basis to Y was $25. The amount of the distribution is $5 ($25 — $20).

Value less than basis. If the fair market value of the property is less than its adjusted basis to the distributing corporation, the distribution is the excess of the fair market value over the amount paid for the property.

Example 2: If, in Example 1, the basis of the property to Y had been $120, the amount of the distribution would have been $80 ($100 — $20).

(b) Basis to recipient. In figuring gain or loss from the later sale of the property, its basis is the amount paid for it, plus the distribution.

(c) Adjustment to earnings and profits. The distributing corporation must decrease its earnings and profits by the excess of the basis for the property in its hands over the amount received for it [Sec. 1.301-1(j)(2)]. For effect of distributions on earnings and profits in general, see ¶ 3129.

¶ 3127 Gain or loss to corporation on property distributions. (a) General rule. A corporation ordinarily realizes no gain or loss when it distributes its stock, stock rights or property to its stockholders [Sec. 311(a); 1.311-1].

Example: A corporation owned securities that cost it $100,000. When the market value of the securities rose to $150,000, the corporation distributed the securities to its shareholders. The corporation realized no gain even though the securities had appreciated in value.

NOTE 1: Distributions to which this rule applies are limited to those made by reason of the corporation-stockholder relationship. The rule does not apply to transactions between a corporation and a shareholder in his capacity as debtor, creditor, employee, or vendee, where the fact he is a shareholder is incidental to the transaction. Thus, if the corporation gets its own stock on the sale of property, or in satisfaction of indebtedness, gain or loss is figured as if the payment had been made in any other property [Sec. 1.311-1(e)].

NOTE 2: If inventory is distributed, the corporation must adjust its accounts to eliminate any deduction for the cost of the inventory.[1]

A corporation can distribute a part interest in a corporate asset without incurring tax liability—unless the distribution is solely to avoid corporate tax on a later sale of the property. Retirement of a shareholder's interest in the corporation is a good reason to distribute a part interest. When the property is later sold, the corporation and retired shareholder each transfer their own part interest.[2]

(b) Exceptions. A corporation may realize taxable gain when it distributes LIFO inventory, a property subject to a liability, property subject to recapture under Sec. 1245, 1250, 1251 or 1252 [¶ 1619; 1845(e); 2226], mining property [¶ 1843], appreciated property used to redeem stock, or installment obligations. Installment obligations are discussed at ¶ 2831.

LIFO inventory. If a corporation using the LIFO method [¶ 2606] distributes inventory, gain is recognized equal to (1) the inventory value under a method other than LIFO, less (2) the inventory value under LIFO. If the corporation uses the retail method of valuing its LIFO inventory, the retail method must be used in (1). Otherwise, the lower of cost or market is used [Sec. 311(b); 1.311-1(b), (c)].

Footnotes appear at end of this Chapter.

Property subject to a liability. Suppose (1) a corporation distributes property that is subject to a liability, or the shareholder assumes a liability of the corporation in connection with the distribution, and (2) the liability exceeds the adjusted basis in the hands of the corporation. Then, gain is recognized to the corporation equal to the amount of the liability *less* the adjusted basis of the distributed property. If the liability is not assumed by the shareholder, the gain may not exceed the fair market value of the property less the adjusted basis [Sec. 311(c); 1.311-1(d)].

Depreciable property. If a corporation distributes, as a dividend, property subject to recapture under Sec. 1245, 1250, 1251, 1252 or 1254 [¶ 1619; 1622(c); 2104(c)], any ordinary income on the disposition will be measured as if it sold the property for its fair market value [Sec. 312(c)(3), 1245(a), (d), 1250(a), (i); 1.312-3, 1.1245-1 et seq., 1.1250-1 et seq.]. See ¶ 3204.

Appreciated property used to redeem stock. If a corporation distributes property (other than an obligation of the corporation) with a value in excess of the adjusted basis in the corporation's hands, to a shareholder in redemption of part or all of the shareholder's stock, gain is recognized to the corporation for the excess as if the property had been sold [Sec. 311(d)(1)]. This rule does not apply to: complete termination of the interest of an at-least-10% shareholder within a 12-month period; certain distributions of stocks of 50%-owned subsidiaries; distributions under an antitrust decree; distributions to pay death taxes [¶ 1721]; certain redemptions from private foundations [¶ 3442]; a redemption by a regulated investment company on stockholders' demand; and exceptions under transitional rules [Sec. 311(d)(2); 1.311-2].

¶ 3128 **Gain or loss to liquidating corporation.** A corporation generally has no gain or loss when it distributes property in exchange for stock in a partial or complete liquidation [Sec. 336; 1.336-1]. The shareholders treat the transaction as a sale of the stock to the corporation. They have a recognized gain or loss depending on whether the value of the property received is more or less than the basis of their stock [¶ 1717].

(a) **12-month liquidation.** Under prior law, when a corporation sold its assets and distributed the proceeds, a tax was imposed on both the corporate and shareholder level. This double tax led to serious conflicts of fact as to whether the corporation or the shareholders actually sold the property.[1] Also, the corporation could avoid any tax in a liquidation by simply distributing the assets to the shareholders.

To remedy this situation, the law provides that no gain or loss is recognized to a corporation when it sells or exchanges its property within a 12-month period beginning with the adoption of a plan, if, within the 12-month period, all the assets of the corporation (less assets retained to meet claims) are distributed in complete liquidation [Sec. 337(a); 1.337-1, 1.337-2]. (Ordinary income will be recognized to the extent that the sale proceeds represent a recovery of amounts previously deducted for those items,[2] or a recapture of depreciation [¶ 1619], or previously deducted farm losses [¶ 2226] or other farm expenses (¶ 1845(e)) [Sec. 1251(c), 1252(a); 1.1245-6(b), 1.1250-1(b)(2)].) For purposes of the nonrecognition treatment, "property" generally does not include stock in trade, inventory, property held primarily for sale to customers, unused bad debt reserve,[3] and certain installment obligations, such as accounts receivable[4] [Sec. 337(b); 1.337-3]. However, inventories are included as "property" if substantially all the inventory is sold or exchanged to one person in one transaction, and there is no replacement. In that case, installment obligations received on the sale or exchange also are included as "property" [Sec. 337(b)(2); 1.337-3]. Involuntary conversion of property involved in a corporate liquidation is considered a sale or exchange. However, the Supreme Court has held that the nonrecognition treatment of the 12-month liquidation does not extend to insurance proceeds received from involuntary conversions that predate the adoption of a liquidation plan.[5]

Example 1: A corporation owns a grocery store at one location and a hardware store at another. The stores do not handle similar items. Both are served by a common warehouse. Under a liquidation plan, the grocery store and all its inventory, including the part held in the warehouse, are sold to one person in one transaction. Later, and within 12 months of adoption of the plan, all the corporation's assets are distributed to the shareholders. No gain or loss is recognized on the sale of the grocery store's assets, including the inventory.

Example 2: A corporation owns 2 department stores. One is downtown, the other in a suburban shopping center. Both handle the same items, which come from a common warehouse, the inventory items being intermingled. Under a liquidation plan, the suburban store's assets, including the store's inventory, but not any part of the warehouse inventory, are sold to one person in one transaction. Later, and within 12 months of adoption of the liquidation plan, all the corporation's assets are distributed to the shareholders. No gain or loss is recognized on the sale of property other than the inventory, but gain or loss is recognized on the sale of the inventory.

Example 3: Assume the same facts as in Example 2, except that the part of the warehouse inventory for the suburban store can be clearly determined, and that this part of the warehouse inventory and the suburban store's inventory are both sold. No gain or loss is recognized on the sale of the inventory.

When gain or loss is recognized in a 12-month liquidation. The rule for the nonrecognition of gain or loss on the sale or exchange of assets by a corporation in a 12-month liquidation does not apply to a sale or exchange made by [Sec. 337(c); 1.337-4]:

- a collapsible corporation, unless certain conditions are met[6] [¶ 1627];
- a corporation that adopted a plan of complete liquidation with a one-month distribution of assets [¶ 3335].

Liquidating subsidiary. The rule that gain or loss is not recognized when a corporation sells or exchanges its assets in a 12-month liquidation generally does not apply, or is limited, in the case of nontaxable liquidation of a controlled subsidiary [¶ 3334]. However, the nonrecognition rule may apply where there is a simultaneous liquidation of the parent and subsidiary. See below.

The nonrecognition rule does not apply if the parent's basis for the property received is the same as the basis in the hands of the subsidiary. However, a special provision gives relief to minority shareholders in this situation. It puts the minority shareholder in the same position after taxes as he would have been if the nonrecognition rule has applied. The amount realized by a minority shareholder during the first tax year he receives a distribution in complete liquidation is increased by his proportionate share of the amount by which the tax imposed on the subsidiary would have been reduced if the nonrecognition rule had applied, and the shareholder is deemed to have paid a tax equal to the increase. This may give rise to an overpayment of tax, for which credit or refund may be granted [Sec. 337(d); 1.337-5].[7]

If the parent's basis for the property is the cost of the subsidiary's stock, gain will not be recognized on the sale or exchange of the subsidiary's assets only to the extent that the parent's basis for the stock allocable to those assets exceeds their adjusted basis to the subsidiary [Sec. 337(c)(2); 1.337-4].

After 1975, the nonrecognition rule *does* apply to a controlled subsidiary that sells property and makes a liquidating distribution within 12 months after adopting a plan of complete liquidation *if* the parent corporation also liquidates completely within the same 12-month period (the parent may retain assets to meet claims). Furthermore, if the liquidating subsidiary is a member of an affiliated group with a common parent, then all other subsidiaries in the direct line of stock

Footnotes appear at end of this Chapter.

¶ 3128

ownership above the liquidating subsidiary must also liquidate completely within the same 12-month period [Sec. 337(c)(2)].

(b) Filing requirements. The liquidating corporation must attach the following information to its return for a 12-month liquidation: A copy of the minutes of the stockholder's meeting that adopted the plan of liquidation with a copy of the plan; a statement of the assets sold after the adoption of the plan and the dates of the sales; information as to date of the final liquidating distribution; and a statement of the assets retained to pay liabilities and the nature of the liabilities [Sec. 1.337-6]. Failure to give the information will not disqualify the liquidation for tax-free treatment, but the corporation may be subject to criminal penalties under Sec. 7203 for not supplying required information[8] [¶ 3620].

Within 30 days after a corporation adopts a resolution or plan of dissolution or liquidation, it must file Form 966 and a certified copy of the resolution or plan with the District Director for the district where the corporation files its income tax return[9] [Sec. 6043; 1.6043-1]. Any change or addition to the original plan requires the filing of another Form 966, showing the changes.

Every liquidating corporation must file Form 1099L (accompanied by Form 1096) for each shareholder who gets a liquidating distribution of $600 or more during any calendar year [Sec. 6043; 1.6043-2]. See also ¶ 3536.

¶ 3129 Effects of distributions on corporation's earnings and profits. As explained in ¶ 1702(a), a distribution by a corporation to its shareholders is an ordinary dividend only to the extent the corporation has earnings and profits. What effect the distribution has on the corporation's earnings and profits is discussed below.

(a) General rules. Generally, the earnings and profits of a corporation must be adjusted when it distributes property to its shareholders. The earnings and profits are decreased by the amount of cash, the principal amount of the corporation's own obligations, and the adjusted basis of other property that are distributed [Sec. 312(a); 1.312-1]. There are special adjustments for foreign investment companies [Sec. 312(j)].

> **Example 1:** Maple Co. distributes property with an adjusted basis of $50 and a fair market value of $100. Before the distribution, Maple's earnings and profits are $75. The distribution decreases earnings by $50, leaving a balance of $25 in the earnings and profits account.

The adjustment is made on the payment date for dividends paid out of accumulated earnings and profits. Earnings and profits at the end of the tax year reflect dividends paid out of current earnings and profits.[1]

(b) Appreciated inventory. When a corporation distributes inventory whose fair market value exceeds its adjusted basis, the earnings and profits of the corporation are:
1. Increased by value of inventory less adjusted basis, *and*
2. Decreased by the lesser of (a) fair market value of inventory, or (b) corporation's earnings and profits as increased in (1) [Sec. 312(b)(1); 1.312-2].

> **Example 2:** Akers Co. has earnings and profits of $20,000. It distributes inventory with a fair market value of $10,000 and an adjusted basis of $7,000. To figure the effect of the distribution on earnings and profits do the following:
>
> | | |
> |---|---|
> | $ 20,000 | Earnings and profits before the distribution |
> | + 3,000 | Value less basis |
> | $ 23,000 | (Step 1 above) |
> | − 10,000 | Value of inventory (2(a) above) |
> | $ 13,000 | Earnings and profits after the distribution |

Example 3: Assume the same facts as in Example 2, except that Akers has earnings and profits of $2,000 before the distribution.

$ 2,000		Earnings and profits before the distribution
+ 3,000		Value less basis
$ 5,000		(Step 1 above)
− 5,000		2(b) above)
$ 0		Earnings and profits after the distribution

For purposes of this rule, "inventory" includes items normally included in inventory, property held primarily for sale to customers, and unrealized receivables or fees from sales or exchanges of such inventory items. Unrealized receivables or fees include rights to payment (1) for goods (other than capital assets) delivered, or to be delivered, and (2) for services rendered or to be rendered, but only to the extent the rights to payment were not previously includible in income [Sec. 312(b)(2); 1.312-2].

(c) **Adjustments for liabilities and gains.** The amount of any reductions in earnings and profits described in (a) and (b) above must be reduced by any liability on the distributed property assumed by a shareholder in connection with the distribution. Also, the earnings and profits are increased by any gain recognized to the corporation on distribution of LIFO inventory, Sec. 1245, 1250, 1251, 1252 or 1254 property, appreciated property used to redeem stock, mining property [¶ 1843], or property subject to a liability greater than its adjusted basis [Sec. 312(c); 1.312-3, 1.312-4].

Example 4: On 12-1-77, Engel Co. distributed to its sole shareholder, John Kane, as a dividend in kind, a vacant lot that was not an inventory asset. On that date, the lot had a fair market value of $5,000 and was subject to a mortgage of $2,000. The adjusted basis of the lot was $3,100. The earnings and profits were $10,000. The dividend received by Kane is $3,000 ($5,000, the fair market value, less $2,000 mortgage). The reduction in the earnings and profits of Engel is $1,100 ($3,100, the basis, less $2,000 mortgage).

Example 5: The facts are the same as in Example 4 above except that the amount of the mortgage on the property was $4,000. The dividend received by Kane is $1,000, and there is no reduction in the earnings and profits of the corporation (disregarding any tax on Engel Co.) as a result of the distribution. There is, however, a gain of $900 recognized to Engel, the difference between the basis of the property ($3,100) and the mortgage ($4,000), and an increase in earnings and profits of $900 [¶ 3127].

Example 6: Trent Co. distributed in kind to its shareholders, not in liquidation, inventory assets which had a basis on the "Lifo" method of $46,000, and on the basis of cost or market ("Fifo") of $50,000. The inventory had a fair market value of $55,000, and was subject to a liability of $35,000. The distribution results in a net decrease of $11,000 in earnings and profits of Trent (without regard to any tax on Trent), figured as follows:

"Fifo" (cost or market) basis of inventory	$50,000	
Less: "Lifo" basis of inventory	46,000	
Gain recognized—addition to earnings and profits (¶ 3127)		$ 4,000
Adjustment to earnings and profits:		
Fair market value of inventory	$55,000	
Less: "Lifo" basis plus adjustment (¶ 3127)	50,000	5,000
Total increase in earnings and profits		$ 9,000
Decrease in earnings and profits	$55,000	
Less: Liability assumed	35,000	
Net amount of distribution (decrease in earnings)		20,000
Net decrease in earnings and profits		$11,000

Footnotes appear at end of this Chapter.

¶ 3129

(d) Distribution not taxed to distributee. A distribution by a corporation does not decrease earnings and profits if (1) no gain was recognized to the distributee, or (2) the distribution was a nontaxable stock dividend or right [Sec. 312(d); 1.312-1]. But the corporation must file a statement with Form 1096 proving that the distribution was not from current or accumulated earnings and profits[2] [¶ 1702(e)].

(e) Partial liquidations and certain redemptions. The part of distributions in partial liquidation or in redemption, properly chargeable to capital, does not decrease corporate earnings and profits[3] [Sec. 312(e); 1.312-5].

(f) Allocation of earnings. When a corporation distributes the stock of a corporation it controls [¶ 3318 et seq.], part of the earnings and profits of the distributing corporation must be allocated to the controlled corporation [Sec. 312(h); 1.312-10]. This allocation of earnings and profits between distributing and controlled corporations must be made in most tax-free distributions, exchanges, or transfers of property [Sec. 1.312-11].

(g) Distribution of proceeds of loan insured by the U.S. If a corporation distributes property when it has an outstanding loan made, guaranteed, or insured by the U.S. or its agency or instrumentality, and the loan exceeds the adjusted basis of the property securing it, a special rule applies [Sec. 312; (i); 1.312-12]. The earnings and profits are (1) at the time of distribution, increased by the amount of the excess, and (2) immediately after the distribution, decreased by the amount of the excess. This creates earnings and profits taxable as dividends to the shareholders receiving the distribution. For this purpose, the adjusted basis of the property does not reflect adjustment for depreciation. Further, a commitment to make, guarantee, or insure a loan is treated as the making, guaranteeing, or insuring of the loan.

ACCUMULATED EARNINGS TAX

¶ 3130 The accumulated earnings tax is aimed at corporations that retain earnings to avoid having the earnings taxed to the shareholders as dividends.

Background and purpose. Corporate earnings are subject to a "double tax" [¶ 3152–3154]—one on the corporate level as the income is earned, and another on the shareholder level when these earnings are distributed as dividends. Shareholders may be tempted to avoid the second tax by accumulating the earnings. If there are no dividends, there is no immediate tax at the shareholder level. The shareholders could wait until their retirement (when they would be in lower tax brackets), or until they have offsetting losses, before taking dividends. They could also divide the stock (and the tax brackets) among their families, and then declare dividends. Since stock prices reflect accumulations, they could liquidate, or sell the stock at an appreciated price, and pay a tax on the increment at favorable capital gains rates. To prevent arrangements of this kind, a penalty surtax is imposed on the income of a corporation for any year it accumulates earnings *to avoid tax on its shareholders.* This is in addition to the regular corporate normal tax and surtax. There is no penalty when sound business management requires earnings to be plowed back in the business or retained for future use.

It is the responsibility of the directors to determine the amount of dividends that must be paid to avoid liability for accumulated earnings tax. Under certain conditions, the directors may be personally liable to the corporation for allowing the corporation to become subject to that tax and if there is evidence of negligence in permitting the accumulation and consequent underpayment of tax, an additional penalty tax can be imposed.[1]

¶ **3131 Corporations liable for tax.** A manufacturing, mercantile,[1] or any other type of corporation (other than a domestic or foreign personal holding company) may be subject to the accumulated earnings tax when it is formed or used to avoid the income tax that would otherwise be paid by its shareholders [Sec. 532(a), (b); 1.532-1]. However, if the shareholders elect to be taxed as partners, the corporation avoids the penalty tax on accumulated earnings.

NOTE: Proposed regulation 1.533-1(a)(3) would extend accumulated earnings tax liability to subsidiary corporations whose parent makes a nondividend distribution to its shareholders from funds borrowed against the subsidiary's stock or assets while the parent has no current or accumulated earnings and profits. The subsidiary will have been used to avoid tax on the parent's shareholders and therefore be liable for the tax. The rule would not apply before 1976 to affiliated corporations that elected to pay any accumulated earnings tax on a consolidated basis.

Liability for the accumulated earnings tax is incurred whenever one of the purposes for an accumulation beyond the reasonable needs of the business is to prevent the imposition of income tax on the shareholders.[2] If the accumulation is reasonable, the finding of a tax avoidance purpose and a liability for the penalty surtax is unlikely.

Reasonable needs of the business. The most important question is whether or not the surplus is beyond the reasonable needs of the business. These needs include those that are reasonably anticipated. In other words, accumulated earnings and profits do not have to be invested immediately, so long as there is an indication that future needs of the business require the accumulation. If there is a definite plan for investment of earnings and profits, it is not necessary to complete the plan immediately after the close of the tax year; but when future use of the funds is uncertain or vague, the accumulated earnings tax applies [Sec. 1.537-1]. Corporations are also allowed to accumulate earnings in a tax year ending after 5-26-69 for either of two types of redemptions: (1) redemption of a shareholder's stock to pay death taxes [¶ 1721] (but the corporation cannot accumulate earnings in a year before the year of the shareholder's death); and (2) redemption of any stock held by a private foundation on 5-26-69 that are excess business holdings (¶ 3442) [Sec. 537; 1.537-1(c), (d)].

NOTE: The Supreme Court has held that a corporation's appreciated and readily marketable securities, bought with earnings and profits, are valued at net liquidation value rather than cost in deciding if earnings have been unreasonably accumulated.[3]

Evidence of purpose to avoid income tax on shareholders. Whether a tax avoidance purpose existed depends on the circumstances in each case. Among other things, the following are considered: (1) dealings between corporation and shareholders, such as withdrawals by shareholders as personal loans, or expenditure of corporate funds for the shareholders' personal benefit; (2) investment by the corporation of undistributed earnings in assets having no reasonable connections with the business; and (3) the extent of corporate distributions of earnings and profits [Sec. 1.533-1(a)(1)].

(a) Burden of proof. The burden of proving whether the accumulated surplus is beyond the reasonable needs of the business depends on what takes place before proceedings in the Tax Court [Sec. 534; 1.534-1—1.534-4].

Burden of proof on government. The burden falls on the government if:
1. The taxpayer, on receipt of notice of a proposed deficiency for accumulated earnings tax, files a statement of the grounds, supported by facts, on which it relies to establish to reasonableness of the accumulation. The statement

Footnotes appear at end of this Chapter.

must be filed within 60 days after the notice. But an additional 30 days may be granted upon request.

2. The taxpayer is not notified of a proposed deficiency before a deficiency notice is issued.

Burden of proof on taxpayer. The burden falls on the taxpayer if:
1. It fails to file the statement within the proper time after it receives a notice of proposed deficiency.
2. It presents grounds in its statement not supported by the facts.

Generally, the taxpayer must prove that an accumulation is reasonable *or* that there was no tax avoidance purpose. Filing the statement makes the government prove that the accumulation was unreasonable. Since a valid reason for accumulation is strong evidence that the accumulation was not made to avoid taxes, when the government fails to prove unreasonableness, it may have to prove a tax avoidance purpose.[4] The 7th Circuit, however, has held that the taxpayer always has the burden of proving there was no tax-avoidance purpose, even when a statement is filed.[5]

(b) Guides in determining whether accumulations are reasonable or unreasonable. Whether a particular ground for accumulating earnings and profits indicates that the accumulation is for the reasonable needs of the business or is beyond such needs depends on the circumstances in each case.[6] However, the following may be used as guides [Sec. 1.537-2].

Reasonable accumulation. The following grounds may indicate that the earnings and profits are being accumulated for reasonable needs:

- To provide for expansion of business or replacement of plant;
- To acquire a business enterprise through buying stock or assets;
- To provide for the retirement of bona fide indebtedness created in connection with the trade or business, such as the establishment of a sinking fund to retire bonds issued by the corporation in accordance with contract obligations incurred on issue;
- To provide necessary working capital for the business, such as, to procure inventories; or
- To provide for investments or loans to suppliers or customers if necessary to maintain the business of the corporation.

Unreasonable accumulation. Accumulation to meet the following objectives may be considered as accumulations beyond reasonable needs:

- Loans to shareholders, or the expenditure of funds of the corporation for the personal benefit of shareholders;
- Loans having no reasonable relation to the conduct of the business made to relatives or friends of shareholders, or to other persons;
- Loans to another corporation, the business of which is not that of the taxpayer corporation, if the capital stock of the other corporation is owned, directly or indirectly, by the shareholder or shareholders of the taxpayer corporation, and the shareholder or shareholders are in control of both corporations;
- Investments in properties, or securities that are unrelated to the business activities of the corporation; or
- Retention of earnings and profits to provide against generalized or unrealistic hazards.

¶ **3132 Income subject to the tax.** The accumulated earnings tax is imposed on "accumulated taxable income," not on surplus [Sec. 531]. Accumulated taxable income is adjusted taxable income ((a) below), minus the sum of the dividends paid deduction ((b) below) and the accumulated earnings credit ((c) below) [Sec. 535(a); 1.535-2].

(a) **Adjusted taxable income** is taxable income with the following adjustments [Sec. 535(b); 1.535-2]:
 (1) Add back the net operating loss deduction;
 (2) Add back the capital loss carryback or carryover;
 (3) Add back the deduction for dividends received;
 (4) Add the excess of the charitable deduction allowed on the return over the amount actually paid during the year;
 (5) Subtract the excess of charitable contributions actually paid during the tax year over the charitable contributions allowed;
 (6) Subtract federal income tax;

The deduction for federal income taxes includes the alternative capital gains tax, but does not include the accumulated earnings tax or the personal holding company tax. A cash basis corporation may subtract the taxes accrued during the tax year even though not actually paid in that year.

 (7) Subtract income, war-profits and excess-profits taxes of a foreign country or U.S. possession included in foreign tax credit;
 (8) Subtract disallowed net capital loss;
 (9) Subtract the excess of net long-term capital gains over net short-term capital losses (figured without regard to the carryover or carryback) reduced by the taxes attributable to the excess;

The tax attributable to the excess is the difference between (1) the tax figured on total taxable income and (2) the tax figured on taxable income excluding the excess of the long-term capital gain over the short-term capital loss (determined without the capital loss carryover or carryback).

 (10) Bank affiliates are allowed the special deduction for earnings and profits invested in readily marketable assets.

(b) **Dividends paid deduction.** From adjusted taxable income, subtract: dividends paid during the tax year; dividends paid with 2½ months after close of tax year; and consent dividends.
The rules for the dividends paid deduction of personal holding companies [¶ 3404(b)] also apply here, except that no dividend carryover is allowed, and the deduction for dividends paid after the close of the tax year is mandatory and unlimited.

(c) **Accumulated earnings credit.** From adjusted taxable income, also subtract the accumulated earnings credit. This credit is so designed that the accumulated earnings tax applies *only* to the amount unreasonably accumulated. The tax is not imposed on any corporation that does not accumulate earnings over $150,000 ($100,000 for years before 1975). [Sec. 535(c); 1.535-3].

Amount allowed. The accumulated earnings credit is the *greater* of:

A. Earnings and profits of the tax year retained for the reasonable needs of the business, *less* [(the excess of the net long-term capital gain over the net short-term capital loss computed without any capital loss carryover) minus (the capital gains tax)]; or

B. $150,000, *less* (accumulated earnings and profits at the end of preceding tax year reduced by dividends paid during the first 2½ months of the tax year).[1] Holding and investment companies can only use this formula.

Example: Assume that at the end of 1976, calendar-year corporation XYZ had accumulated earnings and profits of $120,000. On 3-1-77, it distributed $50,000 as a taxable dividend.

Footnotes appear at end of this Chapter.

In 1977, XYZ's long-term capital gain, minus the tax attributable to such gain, was $10,000. It had no short-term capital loss. The corporation retained $30,000 for the reasonable needs of the business. Applying formula A, the credit would be $20,000 ($30,000 less $10,000). Applying formula B, the credit would be $80,000 ($150,000 less ($120,000 less $50,000)). The XYZ Corporation would get an accumulated earnings credit of $80,000 under formula B.

(d) Accumulated taxable income. The balance that remains after subtracting dividends paid and the accumulated earnings credit from adjusted taxable income is the accumulated taxable income. The tax rates are applied to this balance to determine the tax.

¶ 3133 **Rate of accumulated earnings tax.**

Accumulated taxable income	Tax
Up to $100,000	27½%
Over $100,000	$27,500 plus 38½% of the amount over $100,000 [Sec. 531].

NOTE: The Tax Reduction act of 1975 altered *only* the amount of the accumulated earnings credit under Sec. 535. It did not affect the rate or income levels of the accumulated earnings tax under Sec. 531.

¶ 3134 **Figuring the tax—illustration.** Assume the following facts for a business corporation subject to the accumulated earnings tax for 1977. The corporation uses the calendar year and accrual basis.

Taxable income	$971,000.00
Dividends received from taxable domestic corporations and included in gross income	$ 20,000.00
Federal normal tax and surtax (alternative method)	$455,180.00
Federal normal tax and surtax (on taxable income excluding excess of long-term capital gain over short-term capital loss)	$453,680.00
Foreign taxes	$ 0
Contributions allowed—5% limitation applicable	$ 52,000.00
Contributions actually made of the character deductible by an individual	$ 70,000.00
Long-term capital gain $10,000; short-term capital loss $5,000 (no carryover); net capital gain	$ 5,000.00
Dividends paid during 1977	$260,000.00
Consent dividends	$ 30,820.00
Dividends paid on 3-1-78	$ 40,000.00
Accumulated earnings credit	$ 21,600.00

The accumulated earnings tax is figured as follows [Sec. 535]:

Taxable income		$971,000.00
Add: Deduction for dividends received (85% of $20,000)		17,000.00
Taxable income (without regard to special deductions)		$988,000.00
Less: Federal income tax	$455,180	
Foreign tax credit	0	
Excess of actual contributions ($70,000) over contributions allowed ($52,000)	18,000	
Disallowed net capital loss	0	
Excess of long-term capital gains over short-term capital losses $5,000		
Tax on such amount 1,500		
Difference	3,500	476,680.00
Adjusted taxable income		$511,320.00
Less: Dividends-paid deduction ($260,000 during 1977 and $40,000 paid on 3-1-78)	$300,000	
Consent dividends	30,820	
Accumulated earnings credit	21,600	352,420.00
Accumulated taxable income		$158,900.00
Tax on portion of accumulated taxable income not in excess of $100,000 ($100,000 at 27½%)		$ 27,500.00

Tax on portion of accumulated taxable income in excess of $100,000 ($58,900 at 38½%)	$ 22,676.50
Total accumulated earnings tax	$ 50,176.50

Avoiding the accumulated earnings tax. There is no penalty surtax, if accumulations are for the reasonable needs of the business. If there is no reasonable need for further accumulations, the penalty tax can be avoided by paying or crediting sufficient dividends. If the dividends paid deduction plus the accumulated earnings credit is at least equal to the adjusted taxable income, there is no accumulated taxable income, and the tax is zero.

SUBCHAPTER S CORPORATIONS

¶ **3140 Subchapter S corporations.** The Code allows shareholders in certain corporations with 10 or less shareholders to elect partnership-type taxation [Sec. 1371, 1372; 1.1371-1, 1.1372-1]. See ¶ 3141(a) as to an increase to 15 shareholders. Here, income generally is taxed directly to the shareholders whether distributed or not. They report the income without benefit of the dividend exclusion, but benefit by the corporation's long-term capital gain, and net operating loss, which are passed through as such to them. The shareholders do not get the foreign tax credit[1] [¶ 3701]. But those who are shareholders on the last day of the corporation's tax year are considered to have made ratably the corporation's investments in qualified property and can thus claim the investment credit (¶ 2410) [Sec. 48(e); 1.48-5]. The election affects the corporation's earnings and profits and the shareholder's basis for stock, and may cause an investment credit recapture [¶ 3141(b)].

The electing corporation is treated as a corporation for all purposes except as specifically provided in Sec. 1371-1377 [Sec. 1.1372-1(c)]. No corporate tax is imposed, but the corporation may have to pay a tax on capital gains for the first 3 years under the election [¶ 3143].

Corporation tax preferences. The items of tax preference of an electing corporation are the same as those for an individual taxpayer [¶ 2403], except that stock options do not apply to corporations and are therefore not a tax preference item for them [¶ 1327]. Unlike regular corporations, electing corporations treat accelerated depreciation on leased personal property as a tax preference (¶ 2403(a)) [Sec. 57(a); Prop. Reg. 1.57-1(c)(8), 1.57-2(a)]. The electing corporation's tax preference items are passed through to and apportioned among the shareholders in a similar manner as net operating losses are apportioned (¶ 3143(c)) [Sec. 58(d)(1); Prop. Reg. 1.58-4(a), (b)]. Corporate capital gains may be tax preferences at both the corporate and shareholder levels and therefore taxed at both levels [¶ 3143(b)].

¶ **3141 Electing Subchapter S taxation.** The special treatment is available only to certain qualified corporations [(a) below] whose shareholders elect it [(b) below]. The electing corporation must file a return [(c) below], even if it pays no tax. Termination of the election [(d) below] may be voluntary or involuntary.

(a) Who may elect. Only a "small business corporation" may elect the special tax treatment. Generally, a small business corporation is one that meets the following requirements [Sec. 1371; 1.1371-1]:

1. It must be a domestic corporation. It cannot be a member of an affiliated group eligible to file a consolidated return with any other corporation; but owning stock in another corporation that has not begun business during the tax year and has no taxable income for the year does not make it a member of the group [Sec. 1371(a), (d)].

2. It must not have more than 10 shareholders. However, for tax years starting after 1976, it can have up to 15 shareholders if: (1) it has been a Subchapter S corporation for at least 5 consecutive years, or (2) during the 5-year period, above, additional shareholders are added solely by reason of persons acquiring stock through inheritance (but at no time can the number exceed 15) [Sec. 1371(a), (e)].

In counting shareholders these rules apply: Each co-owner tenant by the entirety, tenant in common or joint tenant is counted as a shareholder. But a husband and wife count as one shareholder, if they hold the stock as joint tenants, tenants by the entirety, or tenants in common, or if the stock is community property. However, husband and wife who each own shares separately as well as jointly are counted as two shareholders.[1] Also, where either husband or wife, or both, die, the estate of the deceased will be treated as one shareholder with the surviving spouse (or spouse's estate) if the husband and wife were treated as one shareholder while both were living and the stock continues to be held in the same proportions as before death. Persons for whom stock in a corporation is held by a nominee agent, guardian or custodian generally will be considered shareholders. Stock owned by a trust, voting trust or partnership is considered held by the trust or partnership [Sec. 1371(c); 1.1371-1(d)].

3. All shareholders must be individuals, decedents' estates (but not a bankrupt individual's estate)[2] or, for tax years starting after 1976, the following trusts: (1) grantor trusts, (2) voting trusts (each beneficiary is considered a shareholder), and (3) any trust that receives stock under a will (but only for 60 days after being transferred to the trust) [Sec. 1371(a), (f)].

A corporation cannot elect if it has another corporation, a partnership or a trust as a shareholder [Sec. 1.1371-1(e)]. However, district courts have held this regulation invalid to the extent it prohibits an election by a corporation that has a voting trust as a shareholder.[3]

4. No nonresident alien may be a shareholder.

5. The corporation may not have more than one class of stock.

Only issued and outstanding stock is counted. The issued stock must be identical as to rights, interest and preferences. But different groups of stock can qualify as one class if they are identical, except for the right of each group to elect a proportionate number of directors[4] [Sec. 1.1371-1(g)]. This regulation says debt obligations not held in the same proportion as stock ownership may be treated as a second class of stock, but the 5th and 7th Circuits and the Tax Court hold that an election is valid even though the debt is not proportionate.[5]

6. The corporation may not get more than 80% of its gross receipts from sources outside the U.S. [Sec. 1372(e)(4); 1.1372-4(b)(4)].

7. The corporation may not get more than 20% of its gross receipts from interest, dividends, rents, royalties, annuities, and gains from sales or exchanges of securities. Gross receipts from sales or exchange of stock or securities do not include amounts received as payments in exchange for stock in the liquidation of a corporation more than 50% owned (each class of stock) by the electing corporation [Sec. 1372(e)(5); 1.1372-4(b)(5)]. Gain from the sale of investment real estate is not subject to the 20% limit.[6]

➤ **OBSERVATION** ➤ The first five requirements must be met *before* the corporation can make a valid election. Failure to meet *any* of the requirements will automatically terminate an otherwise valid election for the tax year the condition is not met (see (d) below).

(b) How to elect. A valid election can be made only if all shareholders consent. For this purpose, the shareholders are those of record as of the first day of the tax year in question, or, if the election is made after that, shareholders of record when it is made. However, a stockholder of record who does not own a beneficial interest in a share of the company's stock, need not consent.[7] Husband and wife *each* must consent, even if the stock is held jointly, in common, as tenants by the entirety, or is community property.[8] If the shareholder is a minor, the guardian must consent for him.[9] For an estate, the executor or administrator gives consent. The election is made by filing Form 2553 with the internal revenue officer designated in the instructions to the form. For a bankrupt corporation, only the trustee or receiver can sign the election.[10]

The election must be made in the first month before the start of the tax year for which it will apply, or in the first month of that year. For new corporations, the first month of the tax year begins when the earliest of the following occurs: (1) the corporation has shareholders; or (2) it acquires assets; or (3) it begins doing business. Once the election is made, it is effective for all later years, unless it is terminated [(d) below].

> **Example:** Perry Martin subscribed to all the shares of stock in a new electing small business corporation on 3-15-77. The corporation filed its articles of incorporation on the same date but did not acquire assets or start business until 6-26-77. Under the state law, the subscribers become shareholders on the day a new corporation files its articles. Therefore, the last day for the corporation to file its election under Subchapter S for its first tax year is 4-14-77.[11]

New shareholders. For tax years starting after 1976, consent of a new shareholder is not required. A Subchapter S election continues unless a new shareholder affirmatively acts to terminate it (see (d) below) [Sec. 1372(e)(1)].

Investment credit recapture. If the corporation has property at the time of the election that is subject to the investment credit recapture [¶ 2410], the credit is recaptured at time of the election, unless the shareholders and the corporation file an agreement stating that the shareholders will be liable for any recapture during the period of the election. The agreement must be filed with the Revenue Service by the due date of the corporation's last return before the election [Sec. 1.47-4(b)].

> **NOTE:** Although the shareholders assume the recapture of credits for investments before the election, they cannot share any investment credit carried over or back from nonelection years. The corporation counts the election years to determine the years to which the unused credit may be carried [Sec. 1.46-2(h)].

The termination of the election does not cause a recapture of the credit [Sec. 1.47-4(d)]. The premature sale or disposition of qualified property by the corporation or the reduction of the shareholder's stock interest causes a recapture of the investment credit for a shareholder the same way it does for a partner (¶ 2913(c)) [Sec. 1.47(a)].

(c) Return by the electing corporation. Every electing corporation must file a return on Form 1120S each tax year, even though it may not be subject to tax. It reports gross income and allowable deductions, as well as information concerning the shareholders, including their stock holdings and distributions made to them [Sec. 6037; 1.6037-1].

(d) Terminating the election. The election will be terminated in *any one* of the following circumstances [Sec. 1372(e); 1.1372-4]:

1. A new shareholder affirmatively refuses to consent to the election within 60 days after becoming a shareholder. If the new shareholder is a decedent's estate, the affirmative refusal to consent must be made within 60 days after the earlier of (a) the date the executor or administrator qualifies, or (b) the last day of the corporation's tax year in which the decedent died. Such termination is effective for the corporate tax year in which the person becomes a shareholder and for all later years.

2. All the shareholders consent to its revocation.

Footnotes appear at end of this Chapter.

¶ 3141

The shareholders who must consent are those who were shareholders at the beginning of the day of revocation. A statement of revocation must be filed with the internal revenue officer with whom the election was filed. It should show the first year for which the revocation is effective. A statement of the consent to the revocation signed by each person who is a shareholder on the day the statement of revocation is filed should be attached [Sec. 1.1372-4(b)(2)].

➤ **OBSERVATION**➔ A revocation is effective only for later years, unless it is made in the first month of the tax year. All other terminations including filing a voluntary petition in bankruptcy by a shareholder,[12] are effective in the year the disqualifying event occurs [Sec. 1.1372-4(c)].

3. The corporation ceases to qualify as a small business corporation.

The corporation should notify the internal revenue officer, stating cause and date. If stock transfer is the cause, the notice should show number of shares transferred and names of transferor and transferee. If issuance of new stock is the cause, notice should describe the stock and state number of shares issued [Sec. 1.1372-4(b)(3)]. Unreasonably long administration of decedent shareholder's estate disqualifies estate as shareholder, disqualifying the corporation [Sec. 1.641(b)-3(a)]. Merger of electing corporation into new qualifying corporation organized by same stockholders in another state does not terminate election.[13] Likewise, the election is not terminated by the acquisition of a non-electing corporation in a statutory merger.[14]

4. The corporation gets more than 80% of its gross receipts from sources outside the United States.

Gross receipts are total amounts received or accrued before deducting returns and allowances, cost of goods sold, or other expenses. Notes are included at face value. The following are not included: unrecognized gains (except those under sec. 337 referring to property sales in liquidation [¶ 3128]), loans or repayment of loans, contributions to capital, and amounts received on issuance of the corporation's own stock [Sec. 1.1372-4(b)(5)(iv)]. A district court held Reg. Sec. 1.1372-4(b)(5) invalid to the extent it excludes the repayment of loans from the gross receipts of a loan or finance company,[15] but the Tax Court disagrees.[16]

5. More than 20% of the corporation's gross receipts are from interest, dividends, rents, royalties, annuities, and sales or exchanges of stock or securities (with only gains being taken into account). This does not apply when the income from these sources is less than $3,000 for the first or second tax year ending on or after 4-15-66 in which the corporation first actively engages in a trade or business.

Gross receipts has the same meaning here as above. Rents generally do not include payments for the use or occupancy of space if you render significant services to the occupant. Examples of this are payments for parking, if attendant parks auto in any available space, and for handling and storage of goods in refrigerated warehouse, or of grain when warehouse supplies services to prevent spoilage and is responsible for maintenance.[17] Payments for leasing autos on a daily basis are not rents if corporation provides all maintenance;[18] nor are payments for use of silverware, glassware, chairs and tables rent, if services include pickup and delivery, washing, polishing, repairing and storing before their lease to a customer.[19] Payments for quarters in hotels, boarding houses, tourist homes and motels[20] [Sec. 1.1372-4(b)(5)(vi)] and payments received under a share-farming arrangement[21] are not rents.

When an election has been terminated or revoked, a new election cannot be made for 5 years, unless the Revenue Service consents to an earlier election [Sec. 1372(f); 1.1372-5].

¶ 3142 How shareholders are taxed on the corporation's income. A shareholder of an electing corporation is taxed on his pro rata share of corporate income. See chart on p. 3133). He is taxed not only on actual dividend distributions, but also on his share of the corporation's undistributed income for the year as a constructive dividend. The amount previously taxed, however, may be distributed tax free in later years [(c) below].

Chapter 21—Subchapter S Corporations

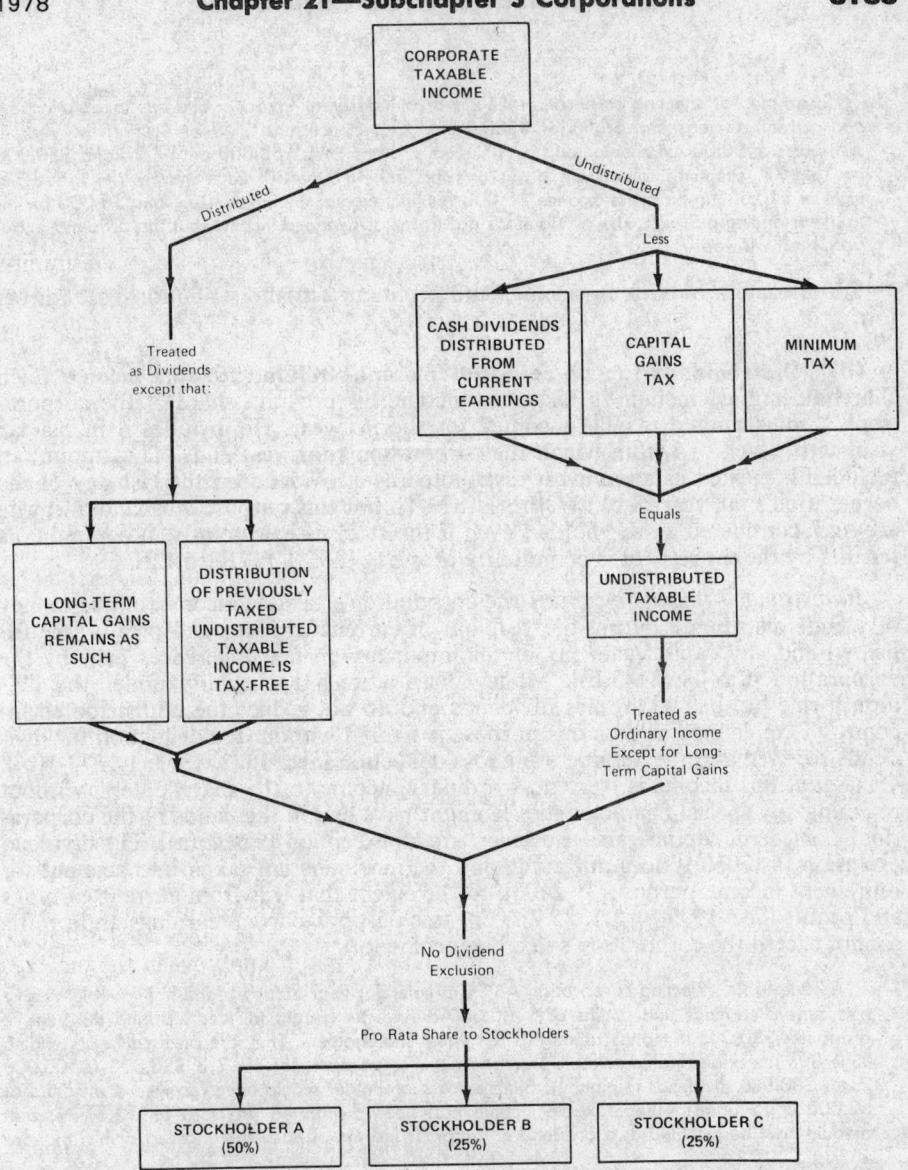

[Flowchart: CORPORATE TAXABLE INCOME branches into Distributed and Undistributed paths.

- Distributed → Treated as Dividends except that:
  - LONG-TERM CAPITAL GAINS REMAINS AS SUCH
  - DISTRIBUTION OF PREVIOUSLY TAXED UNDISTRIBUTED TAXABLE INCOME IS TAX-FREE

- Undistributed Less:
  - CASH DIVIDENDS DISTRIBUTED FROM CURRENT EARNINGS
  - CAPITAL GAINS TAX
  - MINIMUM TAX
  Equals UNDISTRIBUTED TAXABLE INCOME → Treated as Ordinary Income Except for Long-Term Capital Gains

No Dividend Exclusion

Pro Rata Share to Stockholders:
- STOCKHOLDER A (50%)
- STOCKHOLDER B (25%)
- STOCKHOLDER C (25%)]

NOTE: In family corporations the Revenue Service may allocate any distribution (actual or otherwise) received by a shareholder among the members of a shareholder's family, if this is necessary to reflect the value of services rendered to the corporation[1] [Sec. 1375(c); 1.1375-3].

(a) Shareholders' tax on actual distributions. Actual distributions are taxed to shareholders as dividends in the year received, except that (1) long-term capital gains are treated as such by the shareholders [¶ 3143(a)]; (2) distributions of previously taxed undistributed taxable income are tax-free [(c) below]; and (3) the shareholders get no dividends received exclusion [¶ 1706(a)] nor retirement income credit [¶ 2406] for the distribution to the extent made out of current earnings and profits. (For this purpose current earnings and profits cannot exceed the corporation's taxable income.)

Footnotes appear at end of this Chapter.

¶ 3142

Example 1: Electing corporation ABC is a calendar year taxpayer and has taxable income and current earnings and profits of $100,000 during the current tax year. During the year, it distributes $100,000 in cash among its 10 equal shareholders, $50,000 on 4-1-77 and $50,000 on 10-1-77. The shareholders are on fiscal years ending June 30. Each shareholder includes a total of $10,000 in his gross income: $5,000 for his tax year ending 6-30-77 and $5,000 for his tax year ending 6-30-78. The distributions are taxed as dividend income, but the dividend exclusion is not allowed.

For allocation of current earnings and profits to actual distributions, see (d) below.

(b) Shareholder's tax on corporation's undistributed taxable income Each shareholder must include in his gross income his pro rata share of the corporation's "undistributed taxable income" for the tax year. He includes it in his tax year with which or within which the corporation's tax year ends. The amount so included is treated as an amount distributed as a dividend on the last day of the corporation's tax year [Sec. 1373(b); 1.1373-1]. For this purpose, husband and wife are *each* considered a shareholder, even if the stock is held jointly in common, as tenants by the entirety, or is community property [Sec. 1.1371-1(d)(2)].

Undistributed taxable income is the corporation's taxable income, minus money dividends distributed during the year out of current earnings and profits [see (d) below] and any capital gain tax or minimum tax on tax preferences paid by the corporation [¶ 2403; 3143(b)]. Money distributions that qualify under the 2½-month rule [(c) below] are not dividends and do not reduce the undistributed income. "Taxable income" for this purpose is figured without the deduction for dividends received and the net operating loss deduction [Sec. 1372, 1373; 1.1373-1(b)]. Generally, this income is treated as ordinary income to the shareholders, without retaining any special characteristics it might have had in the hands of the corporation. Long-term capital gains, however, are an exception [¶ 3143(a)]. The dividend exclusion [¶ 1706(a)] does not apply and the income is not taken into account for retirement income purposes [¶ 2406], to the extent that it is from current earnings and profits [Sec. 1375(b); 1.1375-2]. (For this purpose, current earnings and profits cannot exceed the corporation's taxable income.)

Example 2: Electing corporation ABC is a calendar year taxpayer and has taxable income and current earnings and profits of $100,000 during the current tax year. During the year, it distributes $80,000 in money among its ten equal shareholders. They are on fiscal years ending June 30. The undistributed taxable income of the corporation for 1977 is $20,000 ($100,000 minus $80,000 dividends in money). Since each shareholder would have received a dividend of $2,000 if the undistributed taxable income had been distributed pro rata on 12-31-77, that amount must be included as a dividend in the gross income of each shareholder for his tax year ending 6-30-78.

(c) Distribution of previously taxed income. Since a shareholder is taxed on the undistributed taxable income [(b) above], he may receive a later distribution of the previously taxed income (PTI) tax-free. Two separate rules are provided, setting forth different conditions for the tax-free payouts. Under either rule, however, a distribution of previously taxed income does not reduce the corporation's earnings and profits [Sec. 1375(d), (f)].

The 2½-month rule. Cash distributions made within 2½ months after the close of a tax year are treated as previously taxed earnings of that year to the extent that the recipient shareholder was required to include such income in his gross income. The distribution is not a dividend, is tax-free to the shareholder, and does not reduce the current year's undistributed income taxed to the shareholders at the end of the current year. It would reduce the stock's basis if the basis has been increased by the prior year's constructive dividend. This rule applies even though the corporation may have lost its Subchapter S status in the distribution year [Sec. 1375(f); 1.1375-6(a)].

Example 3: Electing corporation ABC, a calendar year taxpayer, had undistributed taxable income of $20,000 in 1976 and has taxable income and current earnings and profits of $100,000 during the current tax year. During the year, it makes two distributions in money among its ten equal shareholders who are also on the calendar year: the first distribution is $10,000 on 3-1-77 and the second is $80,000 on 10-1-77. Since the first distribution is within 2½ months after 12-31-76, it is counted as previously taxed earnings and is not taxed to the shareholders. The second distribution of $8,000 to each shareholder is included in gross income as a dividend from current earnings and profits (but no exclusion is allowed). A pro rata share of the corporation's undistributed taxable income for 1977 ($100,000 minus $80,000 dividend in money) is included in the gross income of each shareholder for 1977.

The general PTI rule. Unlike the 2½-month rule, the second rule permits tax-free distribution of the undistributed income of all prior years. First, however, all earnings and profits of the distribution year must be paid out in cash. Any money distributions in excess of that amount are tax-free only to the extent of the shareholder's *net share* of previously taxed income. Any such money distributions in excess of the net share are treated as dividend income if covered by accumulated earnings and profits; if not, the excess is treated as a return of capital, tax free up to the stock's basis, and gain (usually capital gain) to the extent it exceeds the stock's basis [Sec. 1375(d); 1.1375-4].

A shareholder's net share of previously taxed income at distribution is undistributed taxable income included in his income in prior years less (1) amounts *allowable* (whether or not claimed or resulting in a tax benefit) as his share of the corporation's net operating losses in prior years, and (2) all his tax-free distributions of previously taxed income [Sec. 1375; 1.1375-4]. To the extent of his net share of previously taxed income, money distributions that ordinarily would be distributions of accumulated earnings and profits are treated as tax-free distributions [Sec. 1.1375-4(b)]. However, if all shareholders consent, the corporation may elect to treat them as distributions of accumulated earnings and profits. The election applies to all distributions in excess of earnings and profits in the year of the election and may be renewed annually [Sec. 1.1375-4(c)].

If a corporation loses its Subchapter S status, any distribution during that or later years is not a distribution of previously taxed income accruing before the loss of status (except to the extent the 2½-month rule applies) [Sec. 1.1375-4(a)]. Thus, the distribution is taxable if covered by earnings and profits.

The corporation must keep a record of each shareholder's net share of previously taxed income. Each shareholder, too, should keep a record of his share and make it available to the corporation [Sec. 1.1375-4].

A shareholder's right to these tax-free distributions is personal and cannot be transferred to another. For example, a surviving joint owner of stock does not receive decedent's right to his share of earnings previously taxed.[2] The shareholder loses his right only when he transfers *all* his stock [Sec. 1.1375-4(e), 1.1375-6(a)(4)]. The right can be regained only if he again becomes a shareholder under the same election.

(d) Allocation of current earnings and profits. The amount of money distributed as dividends during the year out of current earnings and profits must be determined in figuring the shareholder's dividend income [(a) and (b) above]. This amount is determined by allocating current earnings and profits to distributions during the year in this order [Sec. 1.1373-1(d), (e)]:

(1) Distributions of money that are not (1) in exchange for stock or (2) distributions in the first 2½ months of undistributed taxable income for the immediately preceding year.

Footnotes appear at end of this Chapter.

¶ 3142

NOTE: If money distributions exceed current earnings and profits, the latter are allocated ratably to each money distribution [Sec. 1.1373-1(d)].

(2) Ratably to undistributed taxable income and distributions of property (other than money) not in exchange for stock.

(3) Distributions in exchange for stock.

¶ **3143 Treatment of capital gains and net operating losses.** The corporation's capital gains and net operating losses retain their character in the hands of the shareholders.

(a) **Long-term capital gains of the corporation** keep that status in the hands of the shareholders, whether or not actually distributed. The amount passed through to the shareholders is the excess of the net long-term capital gain over the net short-term capital loss. However, this cannot exceed the corporation's taxable income,[1] or its current earnings and profits. For any year the corporation pays a capital gains tax ((b) below), the gain passed through to the shareholders is reduced by the amount of the tax [Sec. 1.1375-1(a)]. The gain is also reduced by any minimum tax on tax preferences paid by the corporation (¶ 2403; 3134(b)) [Sec. 1375(a)(3); Prop. Reg. 1.1375-1]. If there is more than one dividend distribution (including amounts treated as dividends [¶ 3142(b)]) made during the corporation's tax year, the capital gains must be allocated ratably among them [Sec. 1.1375-1(c)]. If corporate net gains from Sec. 1231 transactions exceed corporate net losses from the same type transactions, they are treated as long-term capital gains and losses. Capital gain from installment sale payments is included in this treatment;[2] but see ¶ 2813 when Sec. 1245 or Sec. 1250 assets are sold. A shareholder's share of any gain from pre-10-9-69 contracts (subject to the 25% maximum alternative tax [¶ 1614(b)]) is the same proportion of his long-term capital gain (not over 100% of such gain) as the corporate gain from pre-10-9-69 contracts bears to its total excess net gain [Sec. 1.1375-1(e)]. Net capital losses are not passed through to the shareholders but are carried forward 5 years and applied against the corporation's capital gains, if any, and then unused amounts would expire [¶ 3201]. Also, net capital losses incurred by a Subchapter S corporation are not allowed as a carryback, and net capital losses incurred by a non-Subchapter S corporation cannot be carried back to a year in which the corporation operated under the Subchapter S election [Sec. 1212(a)(3)].

> **Example 1:** Electing corporation ABC, a calendar year taxpayer, has taxable income and current earnings and profits of $100,000 (including $20,000 net long-term capital gains) during the current tax year. During the year, it distributes $80,000 in money among its ten equal shareholders who are also on the calendar year. The corporation's undistributed taxable income for 1977 is $20,000 ($100,000 minus $80,000 dividend in money). One-fifth ($20,000/$100,000) of both the actual distribution to each shareholder ($8,000) and each shareholder's pro rata share of undistributed taxable income ($2,000) is treated as long-term capital gain ($1,600 and $400 respectively); the remainder of each share ($6,400 and $1,600) is taxed as dividend income but the dividend exclusion is not allowed.

(b) **Corporate capital gains tax.** Existing corporations that make the election to be taxed as a partnership may have to pay a capital gains tax for the first 3 years they operate under the election [Sec. 1378; 1.1378-1]. They are liable for tax only if the taxable income of the corporation for the year is more than $25,000, and the excess of net long-term capital gain over net short-term capital loss is both more than $25,000 and more than 50% of taxable income [Sec. 1378(a); 1.1378-2]. The tax is not imposed after 3 years under the same election, and it does not apply to new corporations with less than 4 tax years that operate under a continuing election for each of their tax years. However, electing corporations may be subject to a tax in any event when they dispose of property acquired from a nonelecting corporation in a tax-free transfer (see below).

The tax is the lesser of (1) the tax under the alternative method [¶ 3202] (generally, a tax rate of 30%) on the excess net long-term capital gains less $25,000, or (2) the regular corporate tax on taxable income (computed without the net operating loss deduction and the special corporation deductions [¶ 3113] (except organization expenses)) [Sec. 1378(b); 1.1378-3]. No credit is allowed against the tax except credit for nonhighway use of oil and gasoline.

Example 2: ABC Corporation was organized in 1963 and elected partnership-type taxation in 1975. In 1977, it has an excess of net long-term capital gain over net short-term capital loss of $73,000 and taxable income of $100,000. ABC is liable for the tax on capital gains because, during one of the first three years of operation under the election, its taxable income is more than $25,000 and its excess of net long-term capital gains is both more than $25,000 and 50% of its taxable income. The amount of the tax is $14,400 [30% × ($73,000 minus $25,000)]. This is less than the total tax under the regular method ($34,500).

Gain on property acquired tax free. If a corporation need not pay a capital gain tax only because it is a new corporation or has operated under an election for more than 3 years, it still may have to pay tax on the gain from property acquired from a nonelecting corporation. The tax is figured as above, but not to exceed the alternative tax on the excess of net long-term capital gains over net short-term capital losses from such transactions. The tax is payable with respect to property acquired any time during a 4-year period ending on the last day of the tax year the property is disposed of, if its basis is derived from property in the hands of a corporation that was a nonelecting corporation during the entire period, or the shorter term it existed [Sec. 1378(c)(3); 1.1378-2(b)].

Capital gains as a tax preference. If an electing corporation pays a capital gains tax, 37.5% of the excess net long-term capital gains subject to the tax is a tax preference [Sec. 58(d)(2)]. This is the only instance of an electing corporation paying the minimum tax (assuming the corporation has net long-term capital gains in excess of the tax exclusions [¶ 2403]). However, the shareholder's capital gains tax preference item is reduced by the capital gains tax and any minimum tax paid by the corporation [Sec. 58(d)(1); Prop. Reg. 1.58-4(c)].

(c) Net operating losses of the corporation are passed through to the shareholders. But a shareholder's pro-rata share may not exceed the adjusted basis of his stock, plus the adjusted basis of any indebtedness owed him by the corporation.[1] An operating loss passed through to a shareholder is deductible on his return as a business deduction, and is not subject to the limitations relating to nonbusiness deductions [¶ 2242(a)]. He takes the deduction for his tax year with which or within which the corporation's tax year ends. (He gets the deduction for his final tax year if he dies before the end of the corporation's tax year). If it is not currently absorbed, it gives rise to an operating loss carryback or carryover. The shareholder's proportionate share of the loss is computed on a daily basis. For example, a shareholder who disposes of his shares in the middle of the year would be entitled to his share of about one-half the corporation's operating loss for the year, assuming continued qualification of the corporation [Sec. 1374; 1.1374-1, 1.1374-2, 1.1374-3]. The corporation cannot carry back or forward a net operating loss arising during an electing year. And the corporation or its shareholders may not apply a loss carryback or carryover from a non-electing year against the income of an electing year. The carryback or carryover is not terminated by the election, but every year in which the election applies is counted in figuring the years of the carryback or carryover [Sec. 172(h); 1.172-1(g), 1.1374-1(a)].

Footnotes appear at end of this Chapter.

¶ 3143

Example 3: Electing corporation ABC, a calendar year taxpayer, has a net operating loss of $73,000 during the current tax year. Blaine, one of the 10 equal shareholders, has an adjusted basis of $6,000 for his shares of ABC stock. He sells the shares on 6-22-77. Blaine's pro rata share of the corporation's net operating loss to be deducted on his return is $3,460 (173 days/365 days × $7,300). Note that the stock is considered held by the buyer on the day of the sale. If the corporation had undistributed taxable income instead of a net operating loss in 1977, none of it would have been taxed to Blaine; only those who own shares at the close of the corporation's tax year include undistributed taxable income in their gross income.

¶ **3144 Adjustments to basis of shareholder's stock.** When partnership-type taxation has been elected, the basis of a shareholder's stock is increased for any of the corporate earnings taxed to him but not distributed. The basis is later reduced if the previously taxed income is distributed.

The basis of the shareholder's stock is reduced for any corporate net operating losses which are passed through to him [¶ 3143(c)]. However, the basis of the stock cannot be reduced below zero. The basis of any indebtedness of the corporation to its shareholders also is reduced (but not below zero) by such amount, but only to the extent that the amount exceeds the basis of the shareholder's stock [Sec. 1376; 1.1376-1, 1.1376-2]. Any debt repayment in excess of the shareholder's reduced basis for the note or bond is capital gain. Payments are allocated between capital gain and tax-free return of basis.[1]

Only the stock owned at the end of the corporation's tax year is adjusted. However, the net operating loss decrease in the basis of stock disposed of before the end of the corporation's tax year is made the day before disposition [Sec. 1.1376-1, 1.1376-2].

¶ **3145 Adjustments to earnings and profits.** To avoid double taxation of the income of an electing corporation that does not distribute all of its income currently, the accumulated earnings and profits must be reduced as of the close of the corporation's tax year by the amount of the undistributed taxable income for that year taxed to the shareholders [Sec. 1377(a); 1.1377-1].

The current year's earnings and profits of an electing corporation cannot be reduced by any amount that is not allowable as a deduction in figuring the taxable income of the corporation for the year [Sec. 1377(b); 1.1377-2].

Neither the current nor the accumulated earnings and profits of an electing corporation are affected by any item of gross income or any deduction taken into account in determining the amount of any net operating loss of the corporation deductible by the shareholders (¶ 3143(c)) [Sec. 1377(c)].

For tax years starting after 1975, previously taxed income can be distributed to shareholders, even though the corporation's current earnings and profits exceed its taxable income, if the excess is due to deductions for accelerated depreciation that did not reduce earnings and profits [Sec. 1377(d)].

¶ **3146 Special rules for retirement plans of electing corporations.** Qualified retirement plans of electing corporations are subject to the following special rules. The usual rules apply to these qualified plans in all other respects [¶ 1232; 1838; 3024].

(a) Excess contributions as gross income. Excess contributions to a qualified retirement plan made for the benefit of a shareholder-employee are included in the shareholder-employee's gross income. For this purpose, a shareholder-employee is any officer or employee who owns more than 5% of the corporation's stock [Prop. Reg. Sec. 1.1379-4]. The family attribution rules apply in determining percentage of stock ownership [¶ 2223(d)]. After 1973, any shareholder-employee for whom a contribution is made in excess of the lesser of $7,500 or 15% of his compensation must include the excess in his income. The excess is treated as a contribution made by him and thus is not taxed when paid out [Sec. 1379(b); Prop. Reg. 1.1379-2]. If the total payouts to the shareholder-employee (or his beneficiary) are less than the amount included in income in all years, then he (or his beneficiary) may deduct the excess in figuring his adjusted gross income when his rights to the payouts end (¶ 1801(a)) [Sec. 62(9); 1379(b)(3)]. An excess deduction does not necessarily disqualify the plan and is fully deductible by the corporation within the plan limits.

(b) Added qualification requirement. An electing corporation's profit-sharing or stock bonus plan is not qualified [¶ 3024] unless it provides that forfeitures cannot benefit an employee who is also a more-than-5% shareholder. This rule applies to tax years starting after 1970 and to forfeitures attributable to contributions deductible in tax years starting after 1970. This requirement is satisfied if it is made effective for the full tax year within 2½ months after the close of the tax year [Sec. 1379(a); Prop. Reg. 1.1379-1(b), (f)].

(c) Carryover of contribution deduction. Unlike a nonelecting corporation, an electing corporation cannot carry over any unused portion of the limitation [¶ 1838(e)] and apply that portion to a succeeding tax year after 1970 that is not under the election [Sec. 1379(c); Prop. Reg. 1.1379-3].

CHOOSING THE BEST FORM OF BUSINESS (CORPORATION, PARTNERSHIP, SOLE PROPRIETORSHIP)

¶ 3152 The different forms of business organization. The problem of determining the "best" form in which to run a business is one that has long plagued businessmen and their advisors. Basically, there are three primary forms available:
- Sole proprietorship.
- Partnership.
- Corporation.

For tax purposes only, there is the corporation that elects Subchapter S tax treatment [¶ 3140]. The tax advantages are discussed in ¶ 3154.

Tax considerations, as well as common-sense business considerations, help determine which form is "best." Some of the important tax advantages of operating a business as a corporation are outlined here. See also ¶ 4505-4509.

(a) General tax considerations. For federal income tax purposes, a partnership is treated as a conduit. No tax is imposed at the partnership level, but each partner is taxed on his distributive share of the partnership income as it is earned. In the case of a business operated as a proprietorship, income is taxed directly to the proprietor as it is earned. A corporation, unlike a partnership or proprietorship, is a separate taxable entity. Thus, income tax is imposed at the corporate level, and another tax is imposed on the earnings as they are distributed to the stockholders.

➤**OBSERVATION**➤ This "double tax" is slightly minimized by the individuals' $100 dividend exclusion [¶ 1705], and can be substantially eliminated if the corporation elects Subchapter S tax treatment [¶ 3154].

Character of income. In the case of a proprietorship or partnership, income and deductions retain their character in the hands of the recipient. In the case of a corporation, the same items usually change their character. For example, a partner picks up in his tax return his share of tax-exempt interest, dividends, capital gains and losses. In the case of a corporation, such items lose their character on distribution to the stockholder. Thus, a current distribution may be taxed as an ordinary dividend, even if it includes tax-exempt interest and capital gains. On the other hand, a stockholder through the sale of his stock may realize at capital gain rates ordinary income retained by the corporation.

Double taxation in the case of a corporation (i.e., a tax at both the corporate and individual level) does not mean that the tax rates in the aggregate will necessarily be higher than if the same business were carried on as a partnership or proprietorship. The ultimate tax cost of doing business as a corporation compared with the cost of doing business as a partnership or proprietorship depends on many factors, including the character of the income, present and future tax rates on corporations and individuals, salaries paid to the owners of the business, capital structure, dividend policy, financial needs of the company, deferred compensation plans, fringe benefits, and outside sources of income of the owners of the business.

(b) Comparing the tax rates. Corporation income tax rates depend on the type of income. Interest from obligations of states and their subdivisions is exempt from tax. Since, with limited exceptions, a corporation is entitled to deduct at least 85 percent of dividends received from domestic corporations, the effective tax rate on dividends is 3.0 percent when the corporations's earnings are $25,000 or less, approximately 3.3 percent when the earnings are between $25,000 and $50,000, and approximately 7.2 percent when the corporation's income exceeds $50,000. The alternative tax serves to limit the tax on capital gain [¶ 3201] and by setting up multiple corporations it might be possible to reduce the corporate tax even further [¶ 3223].

Source of income. In the case of a proprietorship and a partnership, the tax payable is, with one exception, the same, whether the income is paid out in the form of salary, interest or net profit. The exception relates to the case of a partnership having losses [¶ 2927]. Under the corporate form, since guaranteed drawings are income, the ultimate tax burden will vary considerably, depending on the character of the distributions made to the owners of the business, i.e., whether the distribution is in the form of dividends, interest, or salaries. Interest and salaries are deductible by a corporation for income tax purposes, but no deduction is allowed for dividends. In other words, interest and salaries are subject to a single tax at the individual level, but income distributed via the dividend route is subject to the double tax—on the corporation when it is earned, on the individual when distributed to him.

> **Example:** A corporation owned by Adams and Baker has earnings of $70,000 before any payments to the owners for salaries and interest. If Adams and Baker are each paid $25,000 as salary and interest, only $20,000 is subject to tax at the corporate level.

Dividend policy. When the entire profits are distributed currently, and a portion consists of dividends, the corporate form results in a higher tax than a partnership or proprietorship. If income can be deferred, if it can be leveled out, or if it can be pulled out at the capital-gain rate, the corporate form may save taxes. If the earnings are distributed currently, they are then taxed at the ordinary rates for individuals (less a dividend exclusion). If the earnings can be taken out of the business via the capital-gain route, i.e., by sale or redemption of stock, they are subject to the lower capital-gain rate.

Nature of distributions. Ideally, the best arrangement from a tax standpoint is to have all current distributions in the form of salary and interest, which are deductible. This may not be possible, since salaries must be reasonable to be deductible [¶ 1816]. In closely held corporations, salaries paid to principal stockholders are closely scrutinized. When they are found to be excessive, the excessive portion is deemed to be a dividend, and to that extent the salary deduction is disallowed. A problem also exists in the case of interest. If a small portion of the total capital of the business is in the form of capital and retained earnings, the Revenue Service may take the position that the entire indebtedness owed to stockholders is equity rather than debt, and not allow the interest on it as a deduction [¶ 1901].

Unreasonable accumulations. Another factor to be kept in mind in determining the amount of dividends to be paid currently is the surtax on unreasonable accumulations [¶ 3130]. A surtax is imposed on the retained earnings of a given year that are beyond the reasonable needs of the business. The rate is 27½% on the first $100,000 of unreasonably retained earnings and 38½% of the excess. For individuals in the top tax brackets, it may be cheaper to retain the earnings and pay the surtax than to distribute the profits as dividends. The first $150,000 of accumulated earnings is exempt.

➤**WARNING**➤ Directors of publicly held and semi-publicly held corporations should think twice before running a risk of subjecting the corporation to the accumulated earnings tax. *Reason:* Minority stockholders may be able to hold them liable for the accumulated earnings tax the corporation has to pay.

➤**REMEMBER**➤ Shareholders in closely held corporations can elect Subchapter S tax treatment [¶ 3140 et seq.]. If the election is made, the corporate tax is avoided. Proper timing in making the election will enable them to eliminate the accumulated earnings tax as well [¶ 3154].

Personal holding company tax. The ability to use the corporation as a tax shelter, i.e., to pay the corporate rate, and postpone the higher rates that apply to individuals, is not available to holding or investment companies [¶ 3401]. These companies are generally those with the bulk of their income from dividends, interest, gains from the sales of securities, rents and royalties. Personal holding companies pay a tax on their undistributed personal holding company income at the rate of 70%. In brief, these companies pay the ordinary income tax on their entire income and a surtax on retained earnings. See ¶ 3400 et seq.

(c) Leveling taxes. In determining the tax cost of the corporate form of doing business, consider the fact that, under the corporate form, it is possible to minimize taxes to some extent by evening off income at the individual level, thereby transferring income from higher to lower tax brackets. For example, a business operated as a partnership or proprietorship with income subject to high variations will throw such income into higher tax rates of the owner in profitable years. The same peak profits earned by a corporation can be leveled out for the individual stockholders by dividends, executive bonus plans and accounting methods. Profits of an extremely good year may be distributed as dividends over a number of years, taking such income out of top brackets. Under executive profit-sharing plans, profits earned in peak years can be paid pro rata over a number of years. When the corporation is on the accrual basis, and the executive is on the cash basis, year-end bonuses paid shortly after the end of the year may be deducted by the corporation in the year earned, and reported as income in the year received by the owner-executive. Dividends covering the profits for the current year may be declared at year-end, and paid to the individuals in the following year. Interest may be deducted by the corporation in the year incurred, and paid out in the early part of the following year. The corporation deducts the interest in the current year, and the recipient includes the income in the following year. On the other hand, income averaging may be more advantageous to the partners or to the sole owner of a business [¶ 2401].

Accumulation of capital. When funds are needed in the business, the corporate form permits the accumulation of additional working capital. Thus, if members of a partnership, or a sole proprietor, are in the 60% tax bracket, only 40% of

¶ **3152**

their share of the earnings would be available for reinvestment. Under the corporate form, approximately 78 percent of the first $50,000 of income and 52 percent of the remaining income would be available for reinvestment. Also, the income derived from the reinvested earnings would be subject to a ceiling rate of approximately 48 percent under the corporate form. In the case of a partnership or proprietorship, the income would be subject to rates up to 70 percent.

¶ **3153 Tax advantages of corporation over unincorporated business.** Corporations have certain tax advantages over unincorporated businesses. The most important of these advantages relate to splitting income, disposition of business interests, and availability of fringe benefits for shareholder-employees. Certain closely held corporations can keep these benefits, and also be taxed as partnerships, if they so elect.

(a) Splitting income. An advantage of doing business as a corporation lies in the fact that it is normally easier to split income among members of the family through a gift of corporate stock than through the creation of a family partnership. Splitting the income of a proprietorship with family members is impossible, unless they work for the business.

(b) Disposition of business interest. An advantage to incorporating is that when you are ready to liquidate or sell out, you can do so at capital gain rates, as long as the corporation is not "collapsible." And this is true whether you sell the stock or the assets under Section 337 (assuming, of course, any inventory is sold to one person in one transaction).

The sale of a proprietorship, however, is a sale of the individual assets comprising the business. Hence, any gain attributable to inventory would be ordinary income. The sale of a partnership interest suffers from a similar inhibition, in that gain due to substantially appreciated inventory and receivables is taxed as ordinary income.

(c) Fringe benefits for shareholder-employees. Some important advantages arise out of the fact that the officers of a corporation are also considered employees, entitled to all of the tax privileges specifically reserved to employees. Here are some of the important fringe benefits:

Stock options. One of the most important employees' privileges is the stock option. Substantial interest in an expanding business may be acquired with minimum tax cost through the use of stock options. See ¶ 1327.

Deferred pay plans. Deferred pay plans are available to executive owners of a corporation, but not to the sole owner of a business or partners of a business, since they must pay a tax on the income of the business as it is earned.

These plans take income out of high tax brackets and defer its realization until some future time, when it will be taxed at lower rates. Such payments are not subject to the discrimination rules, i.e., they may apply only to key executives. Under such plans, the corporation does not get a deduction for the payment until it is actually made. The executive, on the other hand, defers the tax until he gets the amount.

These plans usually take the form of a contract with the executive, which requires the company to pay him for active service and, after retirement, say, a reduced amount for life or a specified period of years.

Insurance. Premiums on group-term life insurance policies, the beneficiaries of which are designated by employees, are not income to the stockholder-executive when paid if the policy is for $50,000 or less. Proceeds of a group policy are exempt from income tax as amounts received under a life insurance contract. The proceeds also may be exempt from estate tax, if the executive has no right to designate the beneficiary. There are no requirements with respect to discrimination between employees or dollar amount limits. Partners and proprietors are not eligible for the benefits of group insurance. See also ¶ 1307; 1819; 1828(a).

Death benefit payments. Certain death benefit payments are available to the family of an executive-stockholder but are not available to the families of partners or sole proprietors. See ¶ 1304(a); 1822(a).

Medical payments and wage continuation plans. Under the corporate form, the executive-stockholders can have their entire medical expenses and medical insurance paid for by the corporation. These payments can be deducted by the corporation, even though the benefits are extended only to a limited number of individuals or to a single individual. The executive-stockholders receive no income as a result of the payments. See ¶ 1219; 1220.

Meals and lodging. The value of meals and lodging furnished the employee for the convenience of the employer is not taxable to the employees but their cost is deductible by the employer, if: (1) the meals are furnished on the business premises of the employer; and (2) the employee is required to accept lodging on the business premises of the employer as a condition of his employment. Corporate executives get this privilege. A sole proprietor cannot, and generally neither can partners. See ¶ 1308; 1815.

Other fringe benefits. Other fringe benefits are: executive dining rooms; company automobiles; home financing plans; co-operative purchases of merchandise; recreational facilities; country club membership; and expense accounts. Most of these can be limited to one or few employees. However, the Revenue Service is more likely to question luxury-type fringe benefits available only to a few, especially in a closely held corporation.

¶ 3154 Additional tax advantages to corporations electing Subchapter S tax treatment.[1] Certain closely held corporations have an additional advantage over unincorporated businesses. They can elect special tax treatment [¶ 3140 et seq.].

≫**OBSERVATION**→ Every closely held business—whether now operating as a sole proprietorship, partnership, or corporation—should re-examine its setup in light of this election. A partnership or sole proprietor can obtain the advantages of incorporating—limited liability, ease in transferring interests, continuity of business after death, and stockholder-employee fringe benefits—while avoiding the corporation income tax. A corporation can retain the advantages of the corporate form and at the same time substantially cut its stockholders' tax burden.

Here are some of the advantages of electing Subchapter S tax treatment:

(a) **Avoiding the double tax.** A corporation that elects Subchapter S taxation escapes paying tax on its earnings (except on certain capital gains [¶ 3143(a)]. Then, the stockholders pay individual taxes on their shares of the corporation's earnings. In effect, they pay taxes on the business earnings much as though they were partners.

(b) **Fringe benefits retained.** Fringe benefits to shareholder-employees available under the corporate form (profit-sharing to a limited extent [¶ 3146], deferred payments plans, stock options, etc., discussed at ¶ 3153(c)) may be retained.

Footnotes appear at end of this Chapter.

(c) Pass-through of corporate net operating losses. If a corporation has a net operating loss, it does not pass to any of the stockholders. But when the election is made, stockholders can offset any income they get from other sources against their shares of the loss [¶ 3143(c)]. An operating loss of a corporation that does not make the election cannot be deducted by its stockholders. It is wasted, except as reflected in a carryback or carryforward, or in its stockholders' capital loss on disposing of their stock. But the stockholders of a corporation that makes the election, can deduct the corporation's net operating losses, not only for the year the corporation suffers a loss and they have outside income, but also in prior or later years.

(d) Pass-through of corporate capital gain. Normally, if an existing corporation makes a capital gain, it pays 22% or 30% tax on the gain; then when and if it distributes the rest, the stockholder pays a regular income tax of 14% to 70% on it. When a corporation makes the election, the long-term capital gains generally are passed through to the stockholders. Thus, if the corporation has 10 stockholders and has a $10,000 capital gain, each stockholder pays a maximum capital gain tax of 25% on the $1,000 (assuming his entire capital gain from all sources is under $50,000) instead of the corporation paying 22% or 30% and the stockholders each paying 14% to 70% on $700. See ¶ 3143(a) for some limitations.

(e) Elimination of penalty for unreasonable accumulation. If the corporation accumulates income until it reaches the point over $150,000 where it is unreasonable, further accumulations are penalized [¶ 3130 et seq.]. However, if the corporation then makes the election, it avoids the penalty, since shareholders are taxed at individual rates, and there is no corporate tax.

Footnotes to Chapter 21

(P-H "FEDERAL TAXES" related references are cited in brackets [ ] at the end of each footnote below.)

Footnote ¶ 3100 [¶ 3910 et seq.].

Footnote ¶ 3101 [¶ 41,602; 41,605; 41,608].
(1) Rev. Rul. 70-101, 1970-1 CB 278; Rev. Rul. 72-468, 1972-2 CB 647; Rev. Rul. 73-596, 1973-2 CB 424 [¶ 41,608(5)].

Footnote ¶ 3102 [¶ 3916 et seq.].

Footnote ¶ 3103 [¶ 6125].

Footnote ¶ 3105 [¶ 7011].

Footnote ¶ 3106 [¶ 8661; 18,251].
(1) Paxton, 7 BTA 92 [¶ 14,018(10)].

Footnote ¶ 3107 [¶ 17,011 et seq.; 17,332].

Footnote ¶ 3108 [¶ 7261].
(1) Rensselaer & Saratoga R.R. Co. v. Irwin, 249 Fed. 726, 1 AFTR 754 [¶ 7267(15)].
(2) U.S. v. Joliet R.R. Co., 315 US 44, 28 AFTR 215 [¶ 7267(5)].
(3) Comm. v. Western Union Tel. Co., 141 F.2d 774, 32 AFTR 492 [¶ 38,025(45)].

Footnote ¶ 3109 [¶ 7361].

Footnote ¶ 3112 [¶ 11,002 et seq.].

Footnote ¶ 3113 [¶ 16,555 et seq.].

Footnote ¶ 3114 [¶ 16,559].
(1) O'Brien Co. v. Comm., 9 AFTR 2d 1217, 301 F.2d 813 [¶ 16,567(70)].

Footnote ¶ 3114 continued
(2) Rev. Rul. 62-42, 1962-1 CB 133 [¶ 16,328(25)].
(3) A list of public utility preferred stocks subject to this deduction appears in the P-H Capital Adjustment Service.

Footnote ¶ 3115 [¶ 16,569].
(1) Rev. Rul. 56-151, 1956-1 CB 382 [¶ 32,027(5)].

Footnote ¶ 3116 [¶ 16,575].

Footnote ¶ 3117 [¶ 30,666; 30,719].
(1) Rev. Rul. 56-161, 1956-1 CB 382 [¶ 32,027(5)].
(2) Comm. v. Pfaudler Inter-American Corp., 13 AFTR 2d 1216, 330 F.2d 471; Rev. Rul. 64-198, 1964-2 CB 189 [¶ 30,677(25)].
(3) Senate Report No. 92-437, p. 70, 92d Cong., 1st Sess.

Footnote ¶ 3118 [¶ 16,011 et seq.].
(1) Crosby Valve & Gage Co., 19 AFTR 2d 1731, 380 F.2d 146 [¶ 16,021].

Footnote ¶ 3124 [¶ 17,338(35); 31,681].

Footnote ¶ 3125 [¶ 7346].
(1) U.S. v. Kirby Lumber Co., 284 US 1, 52 SCt 4, 10 AFTR 458 [¶ 7306(5)].
(2) Garland Coal & Mining Co. v. Helvering, 75 F.2d 663, 15 AFTR 275 [¶ 7311(25)].
(3) P.L. 94-455, 10-4-76 [¶ 8441].
(4) Rev. Rul. 66-35, 1966-1 CB 63 [¶ 17,373(48)].

Footnote ¶ 3125 continued
(5) TD 4603, XIV CB 58; Virginia Electric & Power Co. v. Early, 52 F. Supp. 835, 31 AFTR 1186 [¶ 7356(10)].

Footnote ¶ 3126 [¶ 17,011 et seq.].

Footnote ¶ 3127 [¶ 17,331].
(1) Rev. Rul. 57-490, 1957-2 CB 231 [¶ 7573(30)].
(2) U.S. v. McNair Realty Co., 9 AFTR 2d 332, 298 F.2d 35 [¶ 17,727(40)].

Footnote ¶ 3128 [¶ 17,691 et seq.].
(1) Compare U.S. v. Cumberland Public Service Co., 338 US 451, 38 AFTR 978 with Comm. v. Court Holding Co., 324 US 331, 65 SCt 707, 33 AFTR 593. Also see, Hines, Jr. v. U.S., 31 AFTR 2d 73-1215 [¶ 17,727(5), (10)].
(2) Rev. Rul. 61-214, 1961-2 CB 60; Comm. v. Anders, 24 AFTR 2d 69-5133, 414 F.2d 1283; Spitalny v. U. S., 26 AFTR 2d 70-5351, 430 F.2d 195 [¶ 17,718(25)].
(3) Rev. Rul. 57-482, 1957-2 CB 49; Bird Management, 48 TC 586; but see West Seattle Nat. Bk. of Seattle v. Comm., 7 AFTR 2d 790, 288 F.2d 47; see also Nash v. U.S. (U.S. Sup.Ct., 5-18-70), 25 AFTR 2d 70-1177 [¶ 8538(15), (20); 18,031(5)].
(4) Family Record Plan, 36 TC 305, aff'd. at 10 AFTR 2d 5794, 309 F.2d 208; Coast Coil Co., 50 TC 528; aff'd. 25 AFTR 2d 70-787, 422 F.2d 402 [¶ 17,721(10)].
(5) Rev. Rul. 64-100, 1964-1 (Pt. 1) CB 130; Central Tablet Manufacturing Co. v. U.S., 34 AFTR 2d 74-5200 [¶ 17,718(10)].
(6) Rev. Rul. 63-125, 1963-2 CB 146 [¶ 17,788(10)].
(7) Senate Report No. 1983, pp. 30, 141, 85th Cong., 2d Sess.
(8) Rev. Rul. 65-30, 1965-1 CB 155 [¶ 17,737(15)].
(9) Instructions, Form 966.

Footnote ¶ 3129 [¶ 17,343 et seq.].
(1) Rev. Rul. 62-131, 1962-2 CB 94 [¶ 17,365(5)].
(2) Rev. Proc. 75-17, 1975-1 CB 677 [¶ 17,398(10)].
(3) Rev. Rul. 70-531, 1970-2 CB 76, as modified by Rev. Rul. 73-550, 1973-2 CB 108 [¶ 17,369(5); 21,614(15)].

Footnote ¶ 3130 [¶ 21,301 et seq.; 21,331].
(1) Rev. Rul. 75-330, 1975-2 CB 496 [¶ 37,262(5)].

Footnote ¶ 3131 [¶ 21,331; 21,334].
(1) Helvering v. Nat'l Grocery Co., 304 US 282, 58 SCt 932, 20 AFTR 1269, rehearing denied, 305 US 669, 59 SCt 56, 21 AFTR 969 [¶ 21,331(5); 21,334].
(2) U.S. v. The Donruss Co., 393 US 297, 23 AFTR 2d 69-418 [¶ 21,334].
(3) Ivan Allen Co. v. U.S., 36 AFTR 2d 75-5200 [¶ 21,334].
(4) Gsell & Co., Inc. v. Comm., 8 AFTR 2d 5507, 292 F.2d 321; Young Motor Co., Inc. v. Comm., 6 AFTR 2d 5350, 281 F.2d 488; same case on remand, TC Memo 1962-135 [¶ 21,334].
(5) Pelton Steel Casting Co. v. Comm., 1 AFTR 2d 542, 251 F.2d 278; [¶ 21,334].
(6) Factors the courts consider are covered in the Prentice-Hall "Federal Taxes" [¶ 21,334].

Footnote ¶ 3132 [¶ 21,332].

Footnote ¶ 3132 continued
(1) Rev. Rul. 73-139, 1973-1 CB 295 [¶ 21,332(5)].

Footnote ¶ 3133 [¶ 21,331].

Footnote ¶ 3134 [¶ 21,332].

Footnote ¶ 3140 [¶ 33,361 et seq.].
(1) Rev. Rul. 68-128, 1968-1 CB 381 [¶ 33,420(25)].

Footnote ¶ 3141 [¶ 33,361 et seq.].
(1) Hicks Nurseries, Inc. v. Comm., 517 F.2d 437, 35 AFTR 2d 75-1478 [¶ 33,367.5(25)].
(2) Rev. Rul. 66-266, 1966-2 CB 356 [¶ 33,367.5(20)].
(3) A & N Furniture & Appliance Co. v. U.S., 19 AFTR 2d 1487, 271 F. Supp. 40; Lafayette Distributors, Inc. v. U.S., 36 AFTR 2d 75-5479, 397 F. Supp. 719 [¶ 33,367.5(10)].
(4) Pollack, 47 TC 92, affirmed at 21 AFTR 2d 1056; 392 F.2d 409 [¶ 33,367(15)].
(5) Amory Cotton Oil Co. v. U.S., 30 AFTR 2d 72-5665; Shores Realty Co., Inc. v. U.S., 30 AFTR 2d 72-5672; Portage Plastics Co. v. U.S., 31 AFTR 2d 73-864; Stinnet, 54 TC 221; Allison, 57 TC 174 [¶ 33,367(25)].
(6) Rev. Rul. 75-188, 1975-1 CB 276 [¶ 33,377.10].
(7) Rev. Rul. 70-615, 1970-2 CB 169, clarified by Rev. Rul. 75-261, 1975-2 CB 350 [¶ 33,377.10].
(8) Clemens, ¶ 69,235 P-H Memo TC, aff'd. at 20 AFTR 2d 72-390, 453 F.2d 869 [¶ 33,377.10].
(9) Rev. Rul. 66-116, 1966-1 CB 198; Rev. Rul. 68-227, 1968-1 CB 381 [¶ 33,367.5(15)].
(10) Levy, 46 TC 527 [¶ 33,377.10].
(11) Rev. Rul. 72-257, 1972-1 CB 270 [¶ 33,377(10)].
(12) Rev. Rul. 74-9, 1974-1 CB 241 [¶ 33,367.5(55)].
(13) Rev. Rul. 64-250, 1964-2 CB 333 [¶ 33,377.35(15)].
(14) Rev. Rul. 69-566, 1969-2 CB 165 [¶ 33,377.35(5)].
(15) Valley Loan Association v. U.S., 18 AFTR 2d 5793, 258 F. Supp. 673 [¶ 33,377.20].
(16) I. J. Marshall, 60 TC 242 [¶ 33,377.20].
(17) Rev. Rul. 65-91, 1965-1 CB 431 [¶ 33,377.15].
(18) Rev. Rul. 65-40, 1965-1 CB 429 [¶ 33,377.15].
(19) Rev. Rul. 64-232, 1964-2 CB 334 [¶ 33,377.15].
(20) Feingold, 49 TC 461 [¶ 33,377.15].
(21) Rev. Rul. 61-112, 1961-1 CB 399 [¶ 33,377.15].

Footnote ¶ 3142 [¶ 33,361 et seq.].
(1) Krahenbuhl, ¶ 68,034 P-H Memo TC [¶ 33,407(15)].
(2) Rev. Rul. 66-172, 1966-1 CB 198 [¶ 33,407(10)].

Footnote ¶ 3143 [¶ 33,361 et seq.].
(1) Byrne v. Comm., 17 AFTR 2d 1272, 361 F.2d 939 [¶ 33,397(5); 33,407(5)].
(2) Rev. Rul. 65-292, 1965-2 CB 319 [¶ 33,407(5)].

Footnote ¶ 3144 [¶ 33,361 et seq.].
(1) Rev. Rul. 64-162, 1964-1 (Pt. 1) CB 304 [¶ 33,417(5)].

Footnote ¶ 3145 [¶ 33,361 et seq.].

Footnote ¶ 3146 [¶ 33,443].

Footnote ¶ 3152 [¶ 33,443].

Footnote ¶ 3154
(1) For a more detailed discussion of the tax advantages, see Prentice-Hall's "Tax Ideas," ¶ 15,013.

Highlights of Chapter 21
Corporations—Normal Tax and Surtax, Income, Deductions

I. **Taxing the Corporation**
   A. **Kinds of tax.** Normal tax and surtax, accumulated earnings tax, minimum tax [¶ 3100].
   B. **What is corporation [¶ 3101]:**
      1. Characteristics: associates, purpose to conduct business and distribute profits, continuity of life, centralized management, limited liability, free transferability of interest [¶ 3101(a)].
      2. Partnerships can be taxed as corporations [¶ 3101(b)].
II. **Figuring Income Tax**
   A. **Normal tax and surtax for tax years ending after 1974 and before 1979.** Normal tax is 20% of first $25,000, plus 22% of excess. Surtax is 26% of income over $50,000 [¶ 3102].
   B. **Minimum tax.** 15% tax on preferences [¶ 3103].
III. **Corporate Income**
   A. **Taxable income [¶ 3105]:**
      1. Gross income less deductions.
      2. Major sources of income: gross profit from sales, dividends, interest, rents and royalties, gains and losses.
   B. **Capital contributions.** Not income to corporation, whether made by shareholders or non-shareholders [¶ 3106].
   C. **Property distributions.** Measured by lesser of property's fair market value on distribution, or distributor's adjusted basis increased by gain recognized on distributing LIFO inventory, recapture income and such [¶ 3107].
   D. **Rental paid directly to shareholders.** Taxed to lessor corporation, but shareholders may be liable for tax [¶ 3108].
   E. **Sinking fund.** Income or gain from it taxed to corporation [¶ 3109].
   F. **Taxable income vs. book income.** Taxable income reconciled with book income in return schedules [¶ 3110].
IV. **Corporate Deductions**
   A. **Deductions generally.** Corporations get same itemized deductions as individuals except purely personal deductions [¶ 3112].
   B. **Dividends-received deduction [¶ 3113-3114]:**
      1. 85% of dividends received from taxable domestic corporations and certain foreign corporations [¶ 3114(a)].
      2. 85% of dividends received from foreign corporations out of effectively connected U.S. business [¶ 3114(c)].
      3. 60.208% of dividends on public utility preferred stock issued before 10-1-42 [¶ 3114(d)].
      4. Deductions in 1-3 limited to 85% of corporate taxable income figured without net operating loss, dividends received, capital loss carryback; limitation not applied if corporation has net operating loss [¶ 3114(e)].
      5. 100% of dividends received from affiliated corporation if parent so elects. Entire group then limited to one surtax exemption, one $100,000 accumulated earnings tax credit, one estimated tax exemption [¶ 3114(b)].
   C. **Deduction for dividends paid on public utilities' pre-10-1-42 preferred stock** [¶ 3115].
   D. **Organizational expenses amortized over 60-month period** [¶ 3116].

E. Western Hemisphere Trade Corporation's special deduction [¶ 3117(a)].
F. China Trade Act Corporation's special deduction [¶ 3117(b)].
G. Charitable contributions [¶ 3118]:
  1. Gifts deductible by individuals qualify for corporate deduction, except gifts to fraternity or for use abroad.
  2. Accrual basis corporation can deduct board-approved contributions if paid by 15th of 3d month after tax year.
  3. Deduction limited to 5% of taxable income. Deduction for appreciated capital gain property reduced by 62.5% of appreciation.
  4. 5-year carryover of unused contributions allowed.

V. Purchase, Sale or Distribution of Corporate Property or Securities
  A. Dealing in own stock. No gain or loss recognized on receiving money or property for company's own stock. Gain or loss recognized if receiving own stock on selling property or to settle debt [¶ 3124].
  B. Dealing in own obligations [¶ 3125]:
    1. No gain or loss if issued at face value.
    2. Premium is income amortizable over life of obligation.
    3. Deduction allowed for discount amortized over life of obligation.
    4. On exchange of new for old bonds before maturity, unamortized premium or discount on old bonds is amortized over new bonds' life.
    5. Successor can continue to amortize bond discount or premium.
    6. Gain on discharge of debt for less than amount due excluded, provided basis of property (against which obligations issued) is reduced by gain.
  C. Property bought by stockholder below market value [¶ 3126]:
    1. If market value equals or exceeds distributor's adjusted basis, distribution is excess of adjusted basis over amount paid.
    2. If market value is less than adjusted basis, distribution is excess of market value over amount paid.
    3. Basis to recipient is amount paid plus distribution figured in 1 or 2.
    4. Distributing corporation's earnings and profits decreased by excess of property basis over amount received.
  D. Distributing property to shareholders [¶ 3127]:
    1. Ordinarily, no gain or loss to corporation distributing stock, stock rights or property to shareholders.
    2. Corporation realizes taxable gain if it distributes LIFO inventory, property subject to liability or recapture, mining property, appreciated property used to redeem stock, or installment obligation.
  E. Liquidation. No gain or loss recognized, generally, on distributing assets in 12-month liquidation [¶ 3128].
  F. Effect of distributions on earnings and profits [¶ 3129]:
    1. Earnings and profits decreased by cash, principal amount of corporate bonds, and adjusted basis of other property distributed.
    2. If corporation distributes inventory whose value exceeds adjusted basis, earnings and profits (a) increased by inventory value less adjusted basis and (b) decreased by lesser of inventory's market value or earnings and profits as increased in (a).
    3. Earnings and profits adjusted by liability on distributed property, gain on distributing LIFO inventory and such.

VI. Accumulated Earnings Tax
  A. Corporations liable [¶ 3131]:
    1. Any corporation accumulating surplus beyond reasonable needs can be liable except personal holding companies and electing small business corporations.
    2. Burden of proof on government if taxpayer files statement after receiving notice or is not notified; otherwise burden on taxpayer.
    3. Guides: providing for business expansion, for example, "reasonable"; providing against generalized hazards, not.
  B. Figuring the tax [¶ 3132-3134]:

1. 27.5% of accumulated taxable income up to $100,000 plus 38.5% of amount over $100,000.
2. Accumulated taxable income is adjusted taxable income (3 below) minus dividends-paid deduction and accumulated earnings credit (4 below).
3. Adjusted taxable income is taxable income *increased* by net operating loss deduction, capital loss carryback or carryover, dividends-received deduction, and excess of allowed charitable deduction over actual donation; *decreased* by excess of actual donation over allowed deduction, federal income tax, foreign income taxes included in foreign tax credit, disallowed net capital loss, and excess of NLTCG over NSTCL reduced by tax on excess.
4. Accumulated earnings credit is greater of (a) earnings and profits of year less excess of NLTCG over NSTCL minus gains tax, or (b) $150,000 less prior year-end accumulated earnings and profits reduced by dividends paid in first 2½ months of tax year.

VII. **Subchapter S Corporations**
   A. **Tax advantages [¶ 3140; 3143(b)]:**
      1. Electing corporation pays no tax except capital gains tax and minimum tax for first 3 years of operation.
      2. Shareholders pay tax on their share of earnings, whether or not distributed.
   B. **Who can elect—Corporation meeting following requirements [¶ 3141]:**
      1. Domestic corporation.
      2. 10 or less shareholders (exceptions allow up to 15).
      3. Shareholders are individuals, decedents' estates or certain specific trusts.
      4. No nonresident alien shareholders.
      5. Only one class of stock.
      6. Not over 80% of gross receipts from abroad.
      7. Not over 20% of gross receipts from passive income (interest, dividends, etc.).
   C. **Shareholders' tax [¶ 3142]:**
      1. Actual distributions taxed as dividends (but generally no dividends-received exclusion).
      2. Undistributed taxable income also taxed to shareholders.
      3. Distribution of previously taxed earnings tax-free.
      4. Cash distributed in 2½ months after year-end treated as previously taxed earnings [¶ 3142].
   D. **Long-term capital gain passed through as such [¶ 3143(a)].**
   E. **Net operating loss treated as shareholder's business deduction [¶ 3143(c)].**
   F. **Adjustments to shareholder's stock basis [¶ 3144].**
   G. **Adjustments to earnings and profits [¶ 3145].**
   H. **Special rules for electing corporation's retirement plans [¶ 3146].**

VIII. **Choosing Best Form of Business**
   A. **Primary forms [¶ 3152]:**
      1. Partnership—no tax at partnership level; each partner taxed on distributive share.
      2. Proprietorship—income taxed directly to proprietor.
      3. Corporation—income taxed to corporation; distributed earnings taxed to shareholders (double tax).
   B. **Factors affecting ultimate cost of doing business [¶ 3152-3153]:**
      1. Income character.
      2. Tax rates.
      3. Owner's salary.
      4. Capital structure.
      5. Dividend policy.
      6. Company's financial needs.
      7. Deferred compensation plans.
      8. Fringe benefits.
   C. **Tax advantages of doing business in corporate form [¶ 3152-3153]:**

1. Leveling taxes.
2. Stock options.
3. Deferred pay.
4. Insurance.
5. Death benefit payments.
6. Medical payments.
7. Meals and lodging.
8. Disposition of business.
9. Splitting income.

D. **Tax advantages to corporations electing Subchapter S tax treatment [¶ 3154]:**
1. Double tax (corporation on earnings, stockholder on share of earnings) avoided.
2. Corporate fringe benefits retained.
3. Pass-through of corporate net operating loss.
4. Pass-through of corporate capital gain.
5. Elimination of accumulated earnings tax.

CHAPTER 22

CORPORATIONS
CAPITAL GAINS AND LOSSES, NET OPERATING LOSS, ETC.

TABLE OF CONTENTS

CAPITAL GAINS AND LOSSES OF CORPORATIONS

	¶
Capital gains and losses in general	3201
Carrybacks and carryovers of net capital losses	
Minimum tax	
Figuring alternative tax for net long-term capital gain	3202
Worthless stocks and bonds	3203
Gain on disposition of depreciable property	3204

NET OPERATING LOSSES OF CORPORATIONS

	¶
Net operating losses in general	3215
Years to which a net operating loss may be carried	3216
Figuring the net operating loss	3217
Figuring the net operating loss deduction	3218
Carryover of unused portion of net operating loss	3219
Table illustrating net operating loss carrybacks and carryovers	3220
Net operating loss carryover disallowed for substantial change of ownership	3221
50% change of ownership	
Changing trade or business	

AFFILIATED AND RELATED CORPORATIONS

	¶
Affiliated corporations—consolidated returns	3222
What is an affiliated group	
Changing the election	
Advantages and disadvantages of filing a consolidated return	
Controlled corporations—surtax exemption	3223
Splitting corporations—disallowance of surtax exemption and accumulated earnings credit	3224
Related corporations—allocation of income, deductions, credits and allowances	3225
Related corporations—acquisitions to avoid tax	3226

• Highlights of Chapter 22 .... Page 3261

CAPITAL GAINS AND LOSSES OF CORPORATIONS

¶ 3201 Capital gains and losses in general. Generally, the capital gains and losses of a corporation are the same as for an individual. They result from the sale or exchange of a capital asset. Gain from dispositions of Sec. 1245 and 1250 property may be ordinary income [¶ 1619]. Gain on a sale or exchange of depreciable property between an individual and his controlled corporation is also treated as ordinary income [¶ 1625]. For details on what is a capital asset and what is treated as a capital asset, see ¶ 1601 and ¶ 1618.

Just as for individuals, net long-term capital gain or loss and net short-term gain or loss are balanced off to get the net capital gain or loss for the year [¶ 1605; 1606; 1611]. However, unlike an individual, a corporation cannot take the long-term capital gain deduction [Sec. 1202; 1.1202-2], nor deduct any part of a net capital loss in the year it is sustained [Sec. 1211(a); 1.1211-1]. Corporate capital gains and losses are reported on Schedule D of Form 1120, or Form 1120S if the corporation has elected Subchapter S tax treatment [¶ 3140 et seq.].

(a) Carrybacks and carryovers of net capital losses. Generally, corporations are allowed to carry back and carry over their net capital losses. The net cap-

Footnotes appear at end of this Chapter.

¶ 3201

ital losses from tax years starting after 1969 can be carried back to each of the 3 tax years before the loss year. These are deductible in the earlier years only if they do not increase or create a net operating loss [¶ 3217] for the tax year in which the carryback is applied. A corporation with a net capital loss is also allowed a capital loss carryover to each of the 5 tax years after the loss year. The carrybacks and carryovers are treated as short-term capital losses. The net capital loss is first carried back to the earliest tax year to which it is allowed. The excess of the net capital loss over the net capital gains of this earliest year is then carried to the succeeding tax year. In figuring the net capital gains of a carryback year, the capital loss of the loss year and of any tax year thereafter is disregarded. If the net capital loss cannot be carried back in full because it would increase or create a net operating loss, the net capital gain for such prior year cannot be treated as greater than the loss which is allowed to be carried back. Foreign expropriation capital losses cannot be included in the capital loss carryback. Instead, a special 10-year carryforward is allowed. Also, regulated investment companies are allowed an 8-year carryover, but no carryback, for years ending after 1969 [Sec. 1212(a)(1)]. A tentative carryback adjustment [¶ 3630] is available.

Example 1: In 1977, Dart Corp. has a net capital loss of $40,000. Its net capital gains in 1974, 1975 and 1976 were $23,000, $12,000 and $6,000 respectively. The first year to which Dart can carry back its 1977 net capital loss is 1974. The $23,000 net capital gain for that year is completely used up by the $40,000. The excess ($17,000) is carried to 1975 where it entirely offsets the $12,000 net capital gain for that year. The $5,000 remaining of the 1977 net capital loss is deducted in 1976 from the $6,000 net capital gain for that year, reducing it to $1,000. The 1977 net capital loss has been completely used up, so there is no capital loss carryover for tax years 1978-1982.

Example 2: Baker Corp. has a net capital loss of $32,000 in 1977. Its net capital gains in 1974, 1975 and 1976 were $15,000, $102,000 and $10,000 respectively. It also had a net operating loss of $100,000 in 1975. Baker can carry back its net capital loss to 1974 and wipe out that year's $15,000 net capital gain. Since taxable income for 1975 is only $2,000, Baker can only deduct the 1977 net capital loss in 1975 to the extent of $2,000 of taxable income. If a greater amount were deducted, it would create an operating loss. For 1976, Baker can carry back $10,000 of the 1977 net capital loss to offset the $10,000 net capital gain of 1976. The balance of the 1977 net capital loss ($5,000) will be available as a short-term loss carryover for tax years 1978-1982.

Net capital losses cannot be carried back to or from a tax year the corporation operates under the Subchapter S election (¶ 3143(a)) [Sec. 1212(a)(3)].

For a denial of capital loss carryovers on a substantial change of ownership, see ¶ 3339.

Special rules on carrybacks. Net capital losses cannot be carried back to any tax year in which the corporation is:

- a foreign personal holding company [¶ 3412]; or
- a regulated investment company [¶ 3429]; or
- a real estate investment trust [¶ 3432]; or
- a foreign investment company in a year in which it elects to distribute income currently [Sec. 1212(a)(4)].

(b) Minimum tax. An amount equal to a portion of the corporation's net capital gain is a tax preference item subject to the minimum tax [¶ 2403]. It is figured by applying a fraction of 37.5% to the net long-term capital gain over net short-term capital loss [Sec. 57(a)(9); Prop. Reg. 1.57-1(i)(2)]. This fraction is the sum of the normal tax and surtax rates [¶ 3102] less the alternative tax rate [¶ 3202] over the normal tax and surtax.

¶ **3202 Figuring alternative tax for net long-term capital gain.** If the net long-term capital gain exceeds the net short-term capital loss, the tax is figured two ways: the regular and the alternative methods. The method is used that produces the smaller tax [Sec. 1201(a); 1.1201-1(a)].

1. In the regular method, the tax is figured on taxable income, which includes net capital gain.
2. In the alternative method, two steps are taken:

(a) a tax is figured on taxable income less the excess of net long-term capital gain over the net short-term capital loss, if any. This excess is known as the net capital gain [Sec. 1222(11)].

(b) 30% of the net capital gain is added to the tax figured on the taxable income without regard to the net capital gain.

Example: The Logan Corporation in 1977 had gross income (other than capital gains) of $190,000 and itemized deductions of $110,000. Its gross income included $2,000 dividends from unrelated taxable domestic corporations. Its capital gains and losses were as follows:

Short-term capital gain	$ 2,000	
Short-term capital loss	7,000	
Net short-term capital loss		$ 5,000.00
Long-term capital gain	$11,000	
Long-term capital loss	3,000	
Net long-term capital gain		$ 8,000.00
Excess of net long-term capital gain over net short-term capital loss (net capital gain)		$ 3,000.00

Tax Under Regular Method of Computation

Gross income (including capital gains)		$193,000
Itemized deductions		110,000
Difference		$ 83,000
Less: Special deductions Dividends received (85% of $2,000)	1,700	1,700
Taxable income		$ 81,300

1. Taxable income		$ 81,300
2. Normal tax:		
a. 20% of first $25,000	$ 5,000	
b. 22% of $56,300 (taxable income over $25,000)	12,386	
c. Total normal tax		$ 17,386
3. Surtax: 26% of $31,300 (taxable income over $50,000)		8,138
4. Total tax (line 2c plus line 3)		$ 25,524

Tax Under Alternative Method

1. Taxable income		$ 81,300
2. Less: Excess of net long-term capital gain over net short-term capital loss (net capital gain)		3,000
3. Taxable income without regard to net capital gain		$ 78,300
4. Normal tax:		
a. 20% of first $25,000	$ 5,000	
b. 22% of $53,300 (taxable income over $25,000)	11,726	
c. Total normal tax		$ 16,726
5. Surtax: 26% of $28,300 (taxable income over $50,000)		7,358
6. Tax on taxable income without regard to net capital gain (line 4c plus line 5)		$ 24,084
7. Add: 30% of net capital gain ($3,000)		900
8. Alternative tax		$ 24,984

Footnotes appear at end of this Chapter.

The alternative method is used since it produces the *smaller* tax ($24,984).

No net short-term capital loss. If the corporation had a net short-term capital gain instead of a net short-term capital loss or if the corporation had no net short-term capital gain or loss, but did have a net long-term capital gain, the alternative tax would be the tax, figured on taxable income less the net long-term capital gain, plus 30% of the net long-term capital gain.

¶ **3203 Worthless stocks and bonds.** If securities owned by a corporation become worthless, the corporation has a capital loss. However, the loss is an ordinary loss if the securities are those of an affiliated corporation [Sec. 165; 1.165-5(d)]. Rules governing this loss are set forth at ¶ 2208; 2312. Special rules apply to banks [¶ 2312] and small business investment companies [¶ 3459].

¶ **3204 Gain on disposition of depreciable property.** All or part of the gain from the sale, exchange, or other disposition of Sec. 1245 property or Sec. 1250 property may be ordinary income [¶ 1619]. The deduction for mining exploration expenses [¶ 1843], certain farm expenses [¶ 1845(e)] and farm losses [¶ 2226] may be recaptured under similar rules.

A corporation that distributes Sec. 1245 property or Sec. 1250 property to a shareholder measures its ordinary income from the distribution as if the property had been sold at its fair market value at the time of distribution [Sec. 1245(a), 1250(a); 1.1245-1(c), 1.1250-1(a)(4)]. This applies to dividend distributions, liquidations and stock redemptions that otherwise would be tax-free [Sec. 1245(d), 1250(h); 1.1245-6(b), 1.1250-1(b)(2)]. However, the amount of ordinary gain from the disposition is limited to the corporation's recognized gain when the distributee or transferee takes the corporation's basis for the property as its own basis in:

- liquidation of a controlled subsidiary [¶ 3334]
- transfer to a controlled subsidiary [¶ 1405]
- exchange for stock or securities in a reorganization [¶ 3309(a)]
- insolvency reorganizations [¶ 3331(a)].

This limitation applies to exempt farmer's cooperatives [¶ 3455] but not to other tax-exempt organizations [Sec. 1245(b)(3), 1250(d)(3); 1.1245-4(c), 1.1250-3(c)].

NET OPERATING LOSSES OF CORPORATIONS

¶ **3215 Net operating losses in general.** All corporations are entitled to the net operating loss deduction in computing their tax, except: (1) mutual insurance companies other than life or marine, (2) regulated investment companies, (3) corporations electing to be taxed substantially as partnerships. The general rules governing a net operating loss are similar to those for individuals [¶ 2241-2244]; but the adjustments for figuring net operating losses and net operating loss carryovers are different. However, a net operating loss limits and defers a corporation's minimum tax liability in much the same way it does an individual's [¶ 2403].

NOTE: Special loss carryover rules allow an insurance company that changes its tax status to carry over losses from the period under one status to the period under the other [Sec. 844].

Corporations and individuals—adjustments compared. Corporations need not make the adjustments required of individuals to eliminate the long-term capital gain deduction and excess of capital losses over capital gains, because corporations are not allowed the long-term capital gain deduction, and are not permitted to deduct any excess of capital losses over capital gains on their returns. Corporations have no personal exemption deductions and no nonbusiness deductions to adjust. But corporations must make adjustments for "special deductions" (see ¶ 3217) which do not apply to individuals.

¶ 3216 Years to which a net operating loss may be carried. A net operating loss may be carried back to each of the 3 preceding years, and carried forward to each of the 7 following years (to each of 5 following years for losses in tax years ending before 1976). The loss is first carried to the earliest year, and then to the next earliest year, etc. For example, a net operating loss for 1977 may be used until exhausted in the following years: 1974, 1975, 1976, 1978, 1979, 1980, 1981, 1982, 1983, 1984. This sequence must be followed. Thus, no part of the 1977 loss may be used to offset 1975 income until 1974 income has been absorbed. However, a corporation can elect to give up the 3-year carryback for losses in tax years ending after 1975 if the election is made by the due date for filing the return for the year of the loss [Sec. 172(b)(1), (3)(E)].

There are several exceptions to the general rule: business firms seriously hurt by increased imports due to U.S. trade agreement concessions are allowed a 5-year carryback; certain regulated transportation companies get a 9-year carryover (7-year carryover for losses for tax years starting before 1976); foreign expropriation losses cannot be carried back, but a 10-year carryover can be elected (20-year carryover for Cuban expropriation losses); certain financial institutions for tax years starting after 1975 are allowed a 10-year carryback; a Bank for Cooperatives with a net operating loss for any tax year starting after 1969, has a 10-year carryback. See also ¶ 3433(a) [Sec. 172(b); 1.172-4, 1.172-11].

Special rules apply to mutual savings banks, building and loan associations and cooperative banks [Sec. 1.581-2(c)], farm cooperatives [Sec. 1.522-2], and new life insurance companies [Sec. 812].

NOTE: A corporation that is in fact dissolved cannot carry back a net operating loss, even though it is not legally dissolved.[1]

¶ 3217 Figuring the net operating loss. Net operating loss is the amount by which the corporation's deductions, adjusted as follows, exceed its gross income [Sec. 172(c), (d); 1.172-2]:

1. Net operating loss deduction is *not allowed.*
2. The following special deductions are *not allowed:*
   a. Deduction for partially tax-exempt interest.
   b. Deduction applicable to Western Hemisphere Trade Corporations.
3. The following special deductions *are allowed without limitation:*
   a. Deduction for 85% of dividends received from domestic corporations.
   b. Deduction for dividends received on certain public utility preferred stock.
   c. Deduction for dividends received from certain foreign corporations.
   d. Deduction for dividends paid on certain preferred stock of public utilities.

➤**OBSERVATION**➤ The adjustment allowing certain special deductions without limitation is a relief measure. The effect of the adjustment is to give the corporation the benefit of the deductions in figuring net operating loss. For example, in a year when the corporation has a net operating loss there would be no taxable income, and the deduction for dividends received would be completely eliminated if the 85% taxable income limitation were applied [¶ 3114].

Example: In 1977, Coen Trading Corporation had a gross profit of $250,000 and deductions of $375,000, excluding any net operating loss deduction and any dividend received deduction. Coen also received taxable dividends of $100,000 from Malcolm Corp., a domestic corporation, and $50,000 from Acapulco Corp., a foreign corporation not doing business in U.S. Coen's net operating loss is $60,000:

Footnotes appear at end of this Chapter.

Chapter 22—Net Operating Losses of Corporations

Gross income:		
Gross business profit	$250,000	
Dividends, domestic corporation	100,000	
Dividends, foreign corporation	50,000	$400,000
Deductions	$375,000	
Add: Dividends received deduction	85,000	$460,000
Net operating loss		($ 60,000)

¶ 3218 **Figuring the net operating loss deduction.** When a net operating loss occurs in only one year and is absorbed by income of the first carryback year, determining the net operating loss deduction is simple. A problem arises, however, when some years show losses and others show income. The net operating loss deduction that can be taken in any given year is arrived at by figuring the total net operating loss carryovers and carrybacks to that tax year [Sec. 172(a); 1.172-1]. See ¶ 3220.

¶ 3219 **Carryover of unused portion of net operating loss.** When a net operating loss deduction is taken in a tax year, the amount of the loss remaining to be carried forward to the following year is determined only after making adjustments to the corporation taxable income for the year the deduction is taken. For this purpose, the taxable income is computed without the special deduction for partially tax-exempt interest and the Western Hemisphere Trade Corporation deduction. Also, the net operating loss deduction is determined without regard to (1) the net operating loss being carried forward, or (2) a loss for any year after that in which the net operating loss was incurred. The taxable income may not be less than zero. The balance of the net operating loss that remains after offsetting the adjusted taxable income is the amount carried forward to the following year [Sec. 172(d); 1.172-5(a)(3)].

NOTE: A net operating loss carried back to a year in which a corporation used the alternative method of computing tax [¶ 3202] is "absorbed" by capital gains as well as ordinary income, so that it survives as a carryover to a succeeding year only to the extent that it exceeds the earlier year's *taxable income* (both ordinary income *and* capital gains).[1]

Example: Assume the corporation in the example at ¶ 3217 had taxable income of $3,500 on its 1974 return. The return showed a $1,000 WHTC deduction.

The carryover to 1975 would be $55,500, figured as follows:	
Taxable income for 1974	$3,500
Plus adjustments:	
Deduction for Western Hemisphere Trade Corporation	$1,000
1974 taxable income adjusted	$4,500
Net operating loss carried back from 1977 to 1974	
(from Example in ¶ 3217)	$60,000
Less: Taxable income adjusted	4,500
Carryover to 1975	$55,500

NOTE: Net operating loss carryovers may be disallowed when ownership of the corporation changes substantially, see ¶ 3221. For net operating loss carryover by a successor corporation in a tax-free reorganization, see ¶ 3336 and 3337.

¶ 3220 **Table illustrating net operating loss carrybacks and carryovers.** The following table illustrates the net operating loss carrybacks and carryovers. The minus sign indicates a net operating loss and the plus sign taxable income. It is assumed that (1) no adjustments apply and (2) there was no net operating loss for any year other than those shown.

	After 1977 return	After 1978 return	After 1979 return	After 1980 return	After 1981 return
1974 + 5,000	0	0	0	0	0
1975 + 15,000	0	0	0	0	0
1976 + 35,000	+30,000	0	0	0	0
1977 − 25,000	0	0	0	0	0
1978 − 50,000		−20,000	−20,000	0	0
1979 − 40,000			−40,000	−30,000	0
1980 + 30,000				0	0
1981 + 85,000					+55,000

After 1977 return is filed. The 1977 net operating loss of $25,000 cancels the 1974 taxable income of $5,000 and the 1975 taxable income of $15,000. It reduces the 1976 taxable income by $5,000 (to $30,000). After the 1977 return is filed, the taxpayer should claim a refund for 1974, 1975, and 1976.

After 1978 return is filed. The 1978 net operating loss of $50,000 cancels the remainder of the 1976 taxable income of $30,000, leaving $20,000 that may be carried forward. After the 1978 return is filed, the taxpayer should file another claim for refund for 1976.

After 1979 return is filed. The 1979 return shows a net operating loss of $40,000, but since there is now no taxable income for 1976, 1977, or 1978, no carryback is made.

After 1980 return is filed. The 1980 return shows a taxable income of $30,000 before deduction of net operating loss. The remainder of the 1978 net operating loss ($20,000) reduces 1980 taxable income to $10,000. The 1979 net operating loss of $40,000 eliminates this $10,000 and leaves $30,000 to be carried over.

After 1981 return is filed. The 1981 return shows a taxable income of $85,000 before deduction of net operating loss. The remainder of the 1979 net operating loss ($30,000) reduces this to $55,000.

¶ 3221 Net operating loss carryover disallowed for substantial change of ownership. The net operating loss carryover will not be allowed when the ownership of the corporation changes substantially under these conditions: (1) 50% or more of the corporation's stock changes hands (2) during a two-year period, (3) as a result of purchase or redemption of stock (except redemption to pay death taxes), and (4) the corporation changes its trade or business. If all the conditions exist, the carryover is disallowed [Sec. 382(a); 1.382(a)-1].

NOTE: For tax years starting after 6-30-78, the NOL carryover is only reduced, not disallowed, for a substantial change of ownership.

(a) 50% change of ownership condition. This condition applies only to the 10 stockholders owning the largest percentage of stock at the end of the tax year. The condition is met if one or more of them owns a percentage of the total fair market value of the stock that is at least 50 percentage points more than the percentage they owned at the beginning of the year, or at the beginning of the prior year, whichever percentage was lower. If another stockholder owns as much stock as one of the 10, the other stockholder is also considered. If there are less than 10 stockholders, all are considered.

NOTE: An increase of 50% does not necessarily mean an increase of 50 percentage points. A stockholder who owns 6% of the stock and increases his holdings to 9% has a 50% increase in ownership, but only a 3 percentage point increase.

Constructive ownership rules. Constructive ownership rules apply (but the corporate ownership rule is applied without the 50% requirement). See ¶ 1727. However, in selecting the 10 largest stockholders, persons related to each other so that the stock of one is constructively owned by the other are considered together as one person [Sec. 1.382(a)-1(c)].

Increase in percentage ownership. The increase in percentage ownership must be the result of (1) purchase of stock in the corporation, or an interest in another corporation, partnership or trust owning stock in the corporation; *or* (2) a decrease in the outstanding stock, or stock of another corporation owning stock in the corporation (except a decrease resulting from redemption to pay death taxes) [Sec. 1.382(a)-1(f), (g)].

In applying these rules, stock is considered to be purchased only if the transferee's basis is his cost and he would not have been a constructive owner of the stock before the transfer. Thus, an acquisition through a tax-free reorganization, gift or devise is not counted [Sec. 1.382(a)-1(e)]. Nonvoting stock limited and preferred as to dividends is not considered [Sec. 1.382(c)-1].

(b) Changing trade or business. If the loss corporation continues to carry on a trade or business substantially the same as that conducted before the change in ownership, the net operating loss carryover will be allowed. But if there is a change of ownership (see (a) above), and the loss corporation shifts from one type of business to another, discontinues any except a minor portion of its business, substantially changes its location, or otherwise fails to carry on substantially the same trade or business that was conducted before the change in ownership, the carryover is disallowed [Sec. 1.382(a)-1(h)].

AFFILIATED AND RELATED CORPORATIONS

¶ 3222 Affiliated corporations—consolidated returns. An affiliated group of corporations may choose to be taxed as a single unit and thus eliminate intercompany gains and losses. This is achieved by granting the affiliated group the privilege of filing a consolidated return rather than separate returns. This is allowed only if all the corporations that have been members of the affiliated group *at any time* during the tax year consent to it before the last day for filing the return. Each member must signify its consent by filing Form 1122 for the first consolidated year only. However, the filing of a consolidated return by all of the affiliated corporations may be considered such consent [Sec. 1501, 1502; 1.1502-75(b)].

Affiliated corporations can also establish joint profit-sharing or stock bonus plans [¶ 1838].

(a) What is an affiliated group. An affiliated group is formed when (1) at least 80% of all classes of voting stock and at least 80% of each class of nonvoting stock of each includible corporation (except the common parent) is owned directly by one or more of the other includible corporations, and (2) the common parent corporation owns directly 80% of all classes of the voting stock and at least 80% of each class of nonvoting stock of at least one of the other includible corporations. The term "stock" does not include nonvoting preferred stock or, for tax years starting after 1974, employer securities held under a qualified employee stock ownership plan [Sec. 1504(a)]. Any corporation is an includible corporation except [Sec. 1504-(b), (c), (e)]:

1. Corporations exempt from tax, other than a title-holding company described in Sec. 501(c)(2) and the exempt organizations deriving income from it (¶ 3436) [Sec. 1504(e)],
2. Life insurance or mutual insurance companies [¶ 3434] (but insurance companies taxable under the same code section may file consolidated returns),
3. Foreign corporations,
4. Corporations electing the possession tax credit [¶ 3727],
5. China Trade Act corporations,
6. Regulated investment companies [¶ 3428],
7. Real estate investment trusts [¶ 3432],
8. Domestic International Sales Corporations (DISCs) [¶ 3460].

(b) Changing the election. Once a group files a consolidated return, it must continue to do so as long as it exists, unless the Revenue Service consents to a discontinuance. A group continues to exist as long as the common parent and at least one subsidiary remain. In some situations, the group may continue even without the common parent. Permission to discontinue consolidated returns may be granted on application by the common parent filed with the Commissioner in Washington, D.C. not later than 90 days before the due date for filing the consolidated return. Changes in the tax law, or other facts and circumstances that substantially reduce the advantage of a consolidated return for the group are considered as grounds for discontinuance. Blanket permission also may be announced for all groups or certain classes of groups without application [Sec. 1.1502-75].

(c) Advantages and disadvantages of filing a consolidated return. - Whether a consolidated return will be advantageous depends on the facts in each particular case. For example, a consolidated return may result in a tax advantage if one corporation in the group has a capital loss and another corporation has a capital gain. The net capital loss of one offsets the net capital gain of the other. Unless a consolidated return is filed, the loss could not be used in the tax year, since a corporation may not deduct a net capital loss in the year sustained (though it is entitled to a capital loss carryback and carryover against its own gain, if any) [¶ 3201]. The losses of one corporation from business operations will offset the profits of another in a group if a consolidated return is filed. And, for affiliated corporations that filed separate returns in previous tax years, a loss corporation's net operating loss carryover may be applied against the consolidated income of the group on consolidated returns. The loss corporation must have been affiliated with the group in the loss year; but if multiple surtax exemptions had been elected [¶ 3223] for a loss year after 1962, the loss cannot offset consolidated income [Sec. 1.1502-21]. However, if no consolidated return is filed, the loss could be used to reduce the loss corporation's taxes of other years under the net operating loss carryback and carryover provisions [¶ 3215].

In prior years, many related corporations filed separately in order to get multiple surtax exemptions. In fact, it was not uncommon for a single corporation to be split up into a number of corporations for this purpose, in addition to a nontax business reason [¶ 3224]. However, this advantage has been eliminated first by imposing an additional 6% tax on multiple surtax exemptions of related corporations, and later by the phasing out of the multiple exemptions under the 1969 Tax Reform Act [¶ 3223].

¶ 3223 Controlled corporations—surtax exemption. For tax year starting after 1974, members of a controlled group of corporations are limited to one surtax exemption which can be divided equally among them or shared as they elect (see (b) below) [Sec. 1561(a); Proposed Reg. 1.1561-3].

> **NOTE:** The surtax exemption is $50,000 for tax years ending after 1974 and before 1979 ($25,000 for years ending after 1978). See ¶ 3102. The first $25,000 of taxable income and the second $25,000 of taxable income are allocated among the members of a controlled group of corporations in the same manner as the surtax exemptions [Sec. 1561(a)].

Background and purpose. Before the Tax Reform Act of 1969, related corporations in a controlled group either had to divide one $25,000 exemption among them or, if they elected to retain separate exemptions, each had to pay an additional 6% tax on the first $25,000 income. Under the Act, the election to retain multiple exemptions was gradually phased out from 1970 to 1974 by reducing each exemption above one by one sixth (or $4,167) each successive year. During the transition period, the group chose which member was to receive the full $25,000 and which were to be limited to the reduced exemptions. If the exemptions were elected the extra 6% tax was imposed, but only on the income equal to the amount of the exemption [Sec. 1564; 1.1564-1].

Accumulated earnings credit. For tax years starting after 1974, members of a controlled group of corporations are limited to one accumulated earnings credit totalling $150,000 which must be divided equally among the component members [Sec. 1561(a)]. Before 1970, each corporation received an accumulated earnings credit of $100,000. However, the Tax Reform Act of 1969 limited related corporations to one credit starting in 1975 and the Tax Reduction Act of 1975 increased the amount of the credit from $100,000 to $150,000 for tax years starting after 1974. For 1970 to 1974, the credits in excess of one were each reduced by $16,667 for each successive year. The special relief for small life insurance companies was similarly phased out (¶ 3434(a)) [Sec. 1564; 1.1564-1].

Minimum tax. The $10,000 ($30,000 for tax years beginning before 1976) tax preference exclusion is divided equally among the members of a controlled group unless all members agree to share the $10,000 according to an adopted plan [Sec. 58(b)]. The consent of an apportionment plan must be filed with the District Director or the Service Center where the component member files its return [Prop. Reg. Sec. 1.58-1(c)].

(a) Controlled groups are defined as [Sec. 1563(a); 1.1563-1(a)(3)]:

(1) Parent corporations and their 80% subsidiaries (basically the same as the parent-subsidiary group that is eligible to file a consolidated return [¶ 3222]);

(2) Brother-sister corporations. These are defined as 2 or more corporations at least 80% owned by 5 or fewer individuals, estates or trusts, who must also own more than 50% of the stock, taking into account as stock owned by each only his least percent of ownership in each corporation. In determining the 80% control test, the 5 or fewer shareholders do not have to own stock in each corporation.[1]

Special attribution rules apply to determine stock ownership [Sec. 1563(d), (e); 1.1563-2, 1.1563-3].

Excluded corporations. Some corporations are not counted as members of a group, even if they are controlled. They are (1) tax-exempt corporations that have no unrelated business income; (2) corporations that were members of the group for less than half the days in the tax year before the designated December 31 ((c) below); (3) foreign corporations that do not have income effectively connected with a U.S. business [¶ 3711]; (4) certain insurance companies (but there can be a controlled group of these companies); and (5) franchised corporations (the stock is sold to the corporate employees, and the corporation sells or distributes products of another group member) [Sec. 1563(b)(2); 1.1563-1(b)].

(b) Election. The election to apportion the surtax exemption is made with reference to a designated December 31st. All corporations that were members of the group on that day must consent by filing an original statement of consent with the service center where they file their tax returns. Each member should also attach a copy of the consent to its income tax return for the year including such December 31st. Component members of a controlled group filing a consolidated return are treated as a single member so that only one consent to an apportionment plan need be filed by the common parent. The election is effective for the year that includes the designated day and continues until terminated or amended. The election can be amended or terminated, also with reference to a designated December 31st, by the consent of the corporations who were members then. The election is also terminated if a new member fails to file a consent or a member leaves and no amendment of the election is made or the group goes out of existence [Sec. 1561(a); Proposed Reg. 1.1561-3].

¶ **3224 Splitting corporations—disallowance of surtax exemption and accumulated earnings credit.** If a corporation, or five or fewer individuals, in control of a corporation, transfer property (other than money), directly or indirectly, to a newly created, or formerly inactive controlled corporation, the transferee corporation loses its surtax exemption and $150,000 accumulated earnings credit [¶ 3132], unless it is proven that getting an extra exemption and credit was not the main purpose of the transfer. However, the Revenue Service can allow the exemption and credit in part or allocate it among the corporations [Sec. 1551(a); 1.1551-1(a)-(d)].

Control of a corporation means ownership of at least 80% of the voting power or value of all classes of stock [Sec. 1551(b); 1.1551-1(e)].

A group of five or less individuals controls both corporations if they own at least 80% of the voting power or value of the stock of each corporation and they own more than 50% taking into account only each one's least percentage of ownership in each corporation [Sec. 1551(b)(2)].

In either case, the constructive ownership rules at ¶ 2223(d) apply.

¶ **3225 Related corporations—allocation of income, deductions, credits and allowances.** The Revenue Service can distribute, apportion, or allocate gross income, deductions, credits or allowances among organizations, trades or businesses owned or controlled by the same interests if it determines that it is necessary to prevent tax evasion or to clearly reflect the income of the taxpayer [Sec. 482; 1.482-1].

> **Example:** A subsidiary corporation rented a building that it owned, to the parent corporation. The parties arbitrarily adjusted the rental each year so as to result in the lowest possible combined tax. In such case, an adjustment of the accounts to show the fair rental value is in order.[1]

The Revenue Service will also impute interest on interest-free or low-interest intercompany loans or advances; impute payment for certain services rendered by one related corporation for another and for the use or occupation of tangible or intangible property of one related corporation by another; and impute profit to the seller of tangible property to a related party [Sec. 1.482-1(d), 1.482-2]. Income or deductions so allocated may later actually be transferred between the involved corporations without further tax consequences.[2]

> **NOTE:** The Tax Court has held that without an enabling statute, the Revenue Service cannot create income where in fact none exists.[3]

¶ **3226 Related corporations—acquisitions to avoid tax.** Deductions, credits and other allowances may be disallowed if the main purpose for organizing a corporation[1] or acquiring control or property of a corporation is to get tax benefits. The disallowance will apply if:

- a person or persons get control of a corporation, or
- a corporation get property (with a carried over or transferred basis) from another corporation not then controlled by the former or its stockholders; *and*
- the *principal purpose* for the acquisition is *evasion* or *avoidance* of taxes through the benefits of a deduction, credit or allowance that would not otherwise be available [Sec. 269; 1.269-1—1.269-6].

Footnotes appear at end of this Chapter.

Chapter 22—Affiliated Corporations

Control means ownership of stock with at least 50% of the total combined voting power of all classes of stock entitled to vote; or at least 50% of total value of shares of all classes of stock.

Person includes an individual, trust, estate, partnership, association, company, or corporation [Sec. 269(a)(2); 1.269-1].

The Revenue Service may (1) allow any deductions or credits that will not result in the tax evasion or avoidance for which the acquisition was made; or (2) allocate gross income and the deductions, credits or allowances, between or among the corporations or properties [Sec. 269(b); 1.269-4].

See also ¶ 3221 for limitation of net operating loss carryover when one corporation acquires another; and ¶ 3337 for treatment of various carryovers when corporation acquires another in a reorganization.

Footnotes to Chapter 22

(P-H "FEDERAL TAXES" related references are cited in brackets [ ] at the end of each footnote below.)

Footnote ¶ 3201 [¶ 32,001 et seq.].
Footnote ¶ 3202 [¶ 32,001].
Footnote ¶ 3203 [¶ 14,290].
Footnote ¶ 3204 [¶ 32,695; 32,761].
Footnote ¶ 3215 [¶ 16,141 et seq.; 16,150].
Footnote ¶ 3216 [¶ 16,141 et seq.; 16,163].
(1) Rev. Rul. 61-191, 1961-2 CB 251; Rev. Rul 74-462, 1974-2 CB 82 [¶ 16,150(5)].
Footnote ¶ 3217 [¶ 16,168].
Footnote ¶ 3218 [¶ 16,156 et seq.; 16,179].
Footnote ¶ 3219 [¶ 16,173].
(1) U.S. v. Foster Lumber Co., 38 AFTR 2d 76-6024 [¶ 56,999.93].
Footnote ¶ 3220 ¶ 16,164].
Footnote ¶ 3221 [¶ 18,501(c)].

Footnote ¶ 3222 [¶ 34,345 et seq.].
Footnote ¶ 3223 [¶ 34,475].
(1) Fairfax Auto Parts of Northern Virginia, Inc., v. Comm., 39 AFTR 2d 77-670 [¶ 77-400].
Footnote ¶ 3224 ¶ 34,463].
Footnote ¶ 3225 [¶ 20,901 et seq.].
(1) Senate Report No. 1622, p. 224, 83rd Cong., 2d Sess.
(2) Rev. Proc. 65-17, 1965-1 CB 833 as amplified by Rev. Proc. 65-31, 1965-2 CB 1024 [¶ 20,906(10)].
(3) Smith-Bridgman & Co., 16 TC 287 [¶ 20,909(10)].
Footnote ¶ 3226 [¶ 16,886 et seq.].
(1) Joe Dillier, 41 TC 762, affd. Made Rite Investment Co. v. Comm., 17 AFTR 2d 466, 357 F.2d 647 [¶ 16,897(10)].

Highlights of Chapter 22
Corporations—Capital Gains and Losses, Net Operating Loss, Etc.

I. **Capital Gains and Losses of Corporations**
   A. **How to figure corporation's capital gains and losses [¶ 3201]:**
      1. Net long-term gain or loss and net short-term gain or loss balanced off to get net capital gain or loss.
      2. Corporations get no long-term capital gain deduction or deduction for net capital loss in year sustained.
   B. **Net capital loss carryback and carryover [¶ 3201(a)]:**
      1. Losses are carried back 3 years and forward 5. Carrybacks and carryovers treated as short-term capital losses.
      2. Special rules apply to pre-1970 losses; foreign expropriation losses; foreign personal holding companies; regulated, real estate, or foreign investment companies.
   C. **Minimum tax.** 37.5% of net long-term capital gain is preference item subject to 10% tax [¶ 3201(b)].
   D. **Alternative tax for net long-term capital gain [¶ 3202]:**
      1. Alternative method—add 30% of excess net long-term capital gain over net short-term capital loss to tax on taxable income minus the excess.
      2. Use above method if you get smaller tax than under regular method, which figures tax on taxable income (including capital gains).
   E. **Worthless securities.** Usually capital loss, but loss in affiliates' securities is ordinary [¶ 3203].
   F. **Disposing depreciable assets [¶ 3204]:**
      1. All or part of gain from sale of Sec. 1245 or 1250 property may get ordinary gain treatment.
      2. If property distributed to shareholders, ordinary gain realized as if property sold at open market, with certain limitations.

II. **Corporation's Net Operating Loss**
   A. **Who can deduct.** Every corporation except Subchapter S, mutual insurance (not life or marine) and regulated investment companies [¶ 3215].
   B. **Figuring net operating loss [¶ 3215; 3217; 3218]:**
      1. Net operating loss is excess of deductions over gross income.
      2. Deductions are adjusted as follows:
         a. No net operating loss deduction allowed.
         b. No deduction for partially tax-exempt interest or for WHTC.
         c. Dividends-received deductions allowed without limitation.
   C. **Loss carrybacks and carryovers [¶ 3216; 3219; 3220]:**
      1. Loss carried back 3 years and forward 7, generally.
      2. Unused portion of net operating loss carried over after proper adjustments as in B above [¶ 3216; 3219; 3220].
   D. **Carryover disallowed for substantial change of ownership**—Conditions of substantial change [¶ 3221]:
      1. After purchase or stock redemption (except redemption to pay death tax) 10 largest stockholders own 50 percentage points more at year-end than start of current or prior year.
      2. Corporation's business substantially changed.

III. **Affiliated Corporations**
   A. **Affiliates can elect consolidated return [¶ 3222]:**

1. Elimination of intercompany gains and losses is major advantage of consolidated return.
2. Discontinuance of consolidated return needs IRS approval.

B. **What is affiliated group [¶ 3222(a)]:**
   1. At least 80% of all classes of voting stock and 80% of each class of nonvoting stock of each includible corporation owned directly by one or more of other includible corporations, and
   2. Parent owns directly 80% of all classes of voting stock and 80% of each class of nonvoting stock of at least one of the other includible corporations.
   3. Any corporation is includible corporation except exempt and foreign corporations, life and mutual insurance companies, and other special-type organizations.

C. **Controlled corporations—surtax exemption [¶ 3223]:**
   1. After 1974, group shares equally or apportions one surtax exemption.
   2. $150,000 accumulated earnings credit shared equally.
   3. Controlled groups may be affiliates (B above) or brother-sister corporations.

D. **Loss of surtax exemption and accumulated earnings credit**—Exemption and credit denied transferee, if main purpose to transfer property is to avoid tax [¶ 3224].

E. **Allocation of income, deductions, credits and allowances by IRS among related corporations [¶ 3225].**

F. **Denial of deductions, credits and allowances on acquisition to avoid tax [¶ 3226].**

Chapter 23

CORPORATIONS—REORGANIZATIONS
TABLE OF CONTENTS

REORGANIZATIONS

Corporate reorganizations 3300
Who is party to a reorganization 3301
Basic requirements for tax-free reorganization 3302

TYPES OF REORGANIZATIONS

Statutory merger or consolidation (Type A) 3303
Acquiring another corporation's stock (Type B) 3304
Acquiring another corporation's property (Type C) 3305
   Giving other property
   Amount of property acquired
   Transfer of acquired assets to controlled subsidiary
Transfer of assets to another corporation (Type D) 3306
   Control
   Distributions of stock
   If no distribution is made
Change in capital structure or form of corporation 3307
   Recapitalization (Type E)
   Change in identity, form, etc. (Type F)
Reorganization chart 3308

GAIN OR LOSS ON EXCHANGES

Recognition of gain or loss 3309
   Holders of stocks and securities
   Corporation exchanging property for stock or securities
   Corporation exchanging its own stock or securities for property
Tabular synopsis 3310
Treatment of boot 3311
Gain taxed as dividend 3312

BASIS

Basis to distributee-stockholder 3313
Basis to corporation 3314
Liabilities assumed 3315
   In general
   In excess of basis (transfers to controlled corporation)

DIVISIVE REORGANIZATIONS

Divisive reorganizations generally 3316
   Types of divisive reorganizations
   Information to be filed
Stock or securities received tax-free .. 3317
   What is required
   Qualifying distributions
   Limitation
Requirements as to active business 3318
When boot is received 3319
Basis to distributee-stockholder 3320
   When no stock is surrendered
   When stock is surrendered

SPECIAL TYPES OF REORGANIZATIONS

Transactions under orders of federal agencies 3330
   Securities and Exchange Commission
   Federal Reserve Board
Reorganization of insolvent corporation 3331
   Transfers by corporations
   Exchanges by security holders
   Basis to corporation
Railroad reorganizations 3332

LIQUIDATIONS

Nontaxable liquidation of subsidiary 3334
   Transfer to pay debt
   Basis of property received
Tax-free one-month liquidations 3335
   When liquidation qualifies
   What gain is taxed
   Basis of property received

CARRYOVERS

Carryovers to successor corporation .. 3336
   When carryover is allowed
   Dates are important for carryover benefits
Checklist of carryover items 3337
Special limit on net operating loss carryover 3338

Footnotes appear at end of this Chapter.

20% continuity of ownership requirement
How to figure continued ownership
How to figure the limit

Limits on carryovers of unused credits and capital losses 3339

• Highlights of Chap. 23 .... Page 3361

REORGANIZATIONS

¶ 3300 Corporate reorganizations. A reorganization is a readjustment of corporate structure or ownership. It may occur when one corporation (new or existing) acquires stock or property of one or more corporations, or when an existing corporation changes its capital structure, name or form, or place of organization.[1]

Reorganizations generally involve exchanges between corporations or between a corporation and its shareholders. Ordinarily, gain or loss on an exchange is fully recognized for tax purposes if the property given up differs in nature or amount from the property received [¶ 1401]. However, in many cases a reorganization merely modifies the corporate form without changing in substance the continuing interest [Sec. 368; 1.368-1, 1.368-2]. The reorganization provisions defer or limit recognition of gain or loss on exchanges made in connection with reorganizations, until the stock, securities or property received is disposed of. To benefit from a tax-free reorganization [¶ 3309], the taxpayer must be either a party to a reorganization or a holder of stock or securities in a party to a reorganization [Sec. 354, 361; 1.354-1, 1.361-1].

> NOTE: The reorganization provisions of the Code apply only to private corporations. They do not apply to municipal corporations.[2]

Background and purpose. Gains arising out of corporate reorganizations are treated under special provisions intended to minimize tax barriers to normal business adjustments which involve transactions that do not basically alter the continuity of an economic interest. A business purpose germane to the conduct of the corporate enterprise must form the basis for the transaction.

In general, the tax-free reorganizations discussed in this chapter involve the use of stock. In recent years, there has been a growing trend to use debt rather than stock in corporate mergers. In addition to certain nontax advantages, debt was preferred to stock because the corporation was allowed interest deductions and the shareholders could defer their gain with the same effect as in a tax-free reorganization. To reduce the tax inducements to this type of corporate merger, the Tax Reform Act of 1969 included the following changes: (1) the partial or total disallowance of deductions for interest payments on bonds and debentures used in corporate acquisitions [¶ 1905(e)]; (2) the treatment of marketable obligations as cash when the installment method is used [¶ 2811]; (3) a speed-up in the reporting of income from bonds issued at a discount [¶ 1629]; and (4) a limit on the deduction of the premium for the repurchase of a corporation's own convertible bonds and debentures [¶ 3125(b)].

¶ 3301 Who is party to a reorganization. A party to a reorganization includes:

• A corporation resulting from a reorganization.
• Both corporations, in a reorganization resulting from the acquisition by one corporation of the stock, securities or properties of the other.

A corporation that controls an acquiring corporation is a party to a reorganization if the controlling corporation's stock or securities were used to acquire stock or assets of a third corporation [Sec. 368(b)(2); 1.368-2(f)]. An acquiring corporation remains a party to a reorganization, even if it transfers all or part of the stock or assets acquired to a controlled subsidiary [Sec. 368(a)(2)(c); 1.368-2(f)].

A corporation that issues new stock certificates after a change of name (Type F reorganization), in exchange for its shareholder's stock, is a party to a reorganization. The same is true for the corporation that issues preferred stock in exchange for its shareholders' common, as part of a recapitalization (Type E).[1]

Definition of securities. The term "securities" includes bonds and debenture notes. It does not include short-term purchase money notes;[2] but long-term notes may be considered securities[3] [Sec. 1.368-1].

¶ 3302 Basic requirements for tax-free reorganization. Reorganizations must meet the following tests:

1. The reorganization (unless a divisive reorganization [¶ 3316]) must be pursuant to a plan adopted in advance by each of the corporations concerned. A copy of the plan must be filed as part of its return by each party to the reorganization [Sec. 1.368-3]. Unless an exchange comes within the scope of the plan, it is not tax-free. Obviously, if a long period intervenes between the adoption of the plan and the exchange, it will be difficult to show that the exchange was made pursuant to the plan.

2. The reorganization must have a business purpose. While an intention to avoid tax liability will not of itself make a transaction ineffective, a plan that complies literally with the statute will not accomplish the nonrecognition of gain, if it has no other business or corporate purpose.[1]

3. Except for a Type D reorganization [¶ 3306], there must be a continuity of interest in the business on the part of the owners of the enterprise before the reorganization [Sec. 1.368-1(b)].

4. The business enterprise must be continued under a modified corporate form [Sec. 1.368-1(b)]. However, the surviving corporation need not pursue the identical activities of its predecessors. For example, a corporation engaged in one type of manufacturing may succeed a corporation that was engaged in a different manufacturing activity.[2]

A statutory merger or other exchange of assets or stock involving two or more investment companies and made after 2-17-76 under Sec. 368(a)(1)(A), (B), (C), (D) or (F) [¶ 3303—3307] is *not* a tax-free reorganization if the result is to achieve significantly more diversity for shareholders than existed before the exchange. However, if the companies have diversified portfolios before the exchange, or if the stock of the companies is owned substantially by the same persons in the same proportions, the reorganization is still tax-free. For purposes of this rule, an investment company is (1) a regulated investment company, (2) a real estate investment trust, or (3) a corporation with over 50% of total asset value consisting of stocks or securities and over 80% of total asset value being held for investment [Sec. 368(a)(2)(F)].

TYPES OF REORGANIZATIONS

¶ 3303 Statutory merger or consolidation (Type A). A statutory merger or consolidation is generally a reorganization. In a merger, one corporation acquires another corporation. The acquired company is dissolved and its assets and liabilities are taken over by the acquiring company. In a consolidation, two or more corporations combine to form a new corporation. The original corporations are dissolved.

> **NOTE:** The Code does not specify the type of consideration that may be given in a merger or consolidation. But securities or other property (as opposed to stock) cannot be all or even too high a proportion of the consideration given to the stockholders. Receipt

of too much consideration other than stock has been held to break the continuity of interest [¶ 3302] with the result that the reorganization was denied tax-free treatment.[1] For transfer of acquired assets to controlled subsidiary, see ¶ 3305(c).

A controlled corporation can use its parent's stock to acquire substantially all the properties of another corporation which merges into the subsidiary after 10-22-68 if no subsidiary stock is used and the exchange would have been a Type A reorganization had the merger been into the parent (¶ 3306(b)) [Sec. 368(a)(2)(D)]. A merger of a subsidiary using parent stock, into another corporation after 1970, is also a Type A reorganization if: (1) the surviving corporation holds substantially all of the properties of the merged corporation (except voting stock of the controlled corporation distributed in the transaction); and (2) the former shareholders of the surviving corporation receive voting stock of the controlling corporation in exchange for control of the surviving corporation [Sec. 368(a)(2)(E); 1.368-2].

> **Example:** Co. T, an unrelated corporation may be absorbed (merged) into Co. J, a controlled subsidiary of Co. L, or vice versa, in exchange for the voting stock of Co. L. In either case, all 3 corporations are parties to the reorganization.

¶ 3304 Acquiring another corporation's stock (Type B). If a corporation exchanges any of its voting stock, or any of the voting stock of a corporation that controls it, for stock of another corporation, there is generally a reorganization, provided the first corporation has control of the second right after the exchange. It does not matter how much voting stock of either its own or its parent's the first corporation gives, but it must not give anything else [Sec. 368(a)(1)(B); 1.368-2(c)].[1] However, a small amount of cash merely to round off fractional shares[2] or a nonassignable contingent contract right to receive additional voting stock[3] does not disqualify the reorganization. Nor does the exchange of debentures, in a separate taxable transaction, if the debentures are not additional consideration for the acquired stock.[4] But convertible rights to purchase additional shares of stock does disqualify the reorganization.[5]

Control means owning at least 80% of the voting stock and at least 80% of all other classes of stock [Sec. 368(c); 1.368-2].

> **Example 1:** If Co. F exchanges 15% of its voting stock for at least 80% of the voting stock and at least 80% of the shares of all other classes of stock of Co. G, there is a reorganization with F and G as parties. If, however, F also gave nonvoting stock or bonds besides voting stock, no reorganization occurs.

It does not matter whether the acquiring corporation had control before the acquisition [Sec. 368(a)(1)(B); 1.368-2(c)]. Thus, the stock acquired need not represent 80% control, if there is control after the transaction.

> **Example 2:** Co. A bought 30% of the common stock of Co. W (with only one class of stock outstanding) for cash in 1960. In 1977, Co. A offers to exchange its own voting stock for all of the stock of Co. W within 6 months from the date of the offer. Within the 6-month period, Co. A acquires an additional 60% of Co. W stock for its own voting stock. Co. A now owns 90% of the stock of Co. W and reorganization has occurred. If Corporation A had acquired 80% of Corporation W's stock for cash in 1960, it could likewise acquire some or all of the remainder of such stock solely in exchange for its own voting stock and still have a reorganization.

¶ 3305 Acquiring another corporation's property (Type C). If a corporation exchanges any of its voting stock for substantially all the property of a second corporation, there is generally a reorganization. The acquiring corporation ordinarily must give only its voting stock [Sec. 368(a)(1)(C); 1.368-2(d)]. It may add a small amount of cash merely to round off fractional shares.[1] See also (a) below.

Example 1: If H Co. exchanges 15% of its voting stock for substantially all the properties of I Co., there is a reorganization, with H Co. and I Co. as parties. If, however, H Co. also gives nonvoting stock or bonds besides the voting stock, it usually is not a reorganization.

There also is a reorganization if a subsidiary acquires substantially all the properties of another corporation solely in exchange for the voting stock of the subsidiary's parent corporation [Sec. 368(a)(1)(C); 1.368-2(d)].

Example 2: P Co. owns all the stock of S Co. All the assets of W Co. are transferred to S Co. in exchange for voting stock of P Co. This transaction is a reorganization, with S, P and W as parties [Sec. 1.368-2(f)].

(a) Giving other property. The rule that the acquiring corporation must give only voting stock is relaxed to this extent: if the acquiring corporation gets at least 80% of the fair market value of all the second corporation's property for voting stock, it can add cash and other types of consideration without disqualifying the tax-free reorganization [Sec. 368(a)(2)(B); 1.368-2(d)].

Example 3: Co. Y acquires Co. A's assets worth $100,000 for $92,000 of Y's voting stock plus $8,000 cash. This is a reorganization, even though part of the assets of Co. A are acquired for cash.

Assumed liabilities. An exchange is still considered solely for voting stock if, besides giving voting stock, the acquiring corporation assumes a liability of the other corporation, or acquires property subject to a liability [Sec. 368(a)(1)(C); 1.368-2(d)].

Example 4: If Co. H acquires substantially all of the properties of Co. I solely for voting stock and the assumption of a mortgage on the property, the transaction will ordinarily qualify as a reorganization (but see Note 1 below).

If, however, the acquiring corporation gives cash or other property, the total of their value and the value of the assumed liabilities cannot exceed 20% of the fair market value of the property acquired. Otherwise there is no reorganization [Sec. 368(a)(2)(B); 1.368-2(d)].

Example 5: Co. Y is to acquire the assets of Co. A, worth $100,000. Co. A has liabilities of $50,000, which Co. Y is to assume. Co. Y can give only voting stock as consideration because the liabilities alone are over 20% of the fair market value of the property.

NOTE 1: If the assumed liabilities are too high a proportion of the consideration given for the property, the reorganization may be denied tax-free treatment because of lack of continuity of interest[2] (¶ 3302) [Sec. 1.368-2(d)].

NOTE 2: Even when insufficient to disqualify the tax-free reorganization, other consideration received usually is treated as boot [¶ 3309(b)]. In a Type C reorganization, however, other consideration in the form of non-voting stocks and securities of a party to the reorganization comprising 20% or less of the value of the acquired property is not regarded as boot [Sec. 1.361-1].

(b) Amount of property acquired. The term *"substantially all"* of the properties is a relative term. However, as an operating rule for issuing ruling letters, the Revenue Service considers "substantially all" to be at least 90% of the fair market value of the net assets and at least 70% of the fair market value of the gross assets of the transferring corporation.[3] Ultimately, it depends on the facts of any given situation.[4] Seventy percent of the assets was held to be substantially all, when the value of the retained assets approximately equaled the liabilities and consisted of cash, accounts receivable and 3% of the inventory.[5] But 81% of the assets was held not to be substantially all when most of the retained assets were operating assets,

Footnotes appear at end of this Chapter.

not retained to liquidate liabilities.[6] Eighty-six and 90% have been held substantially all.[7]

In determining the percentage of property transferred, value rather than cost is used.[8] The term "properties" does not include retained surplus cash which might have been paid out as a dividend before the transfer.[9]

(c) Transfer of acquired assets to controlled subsidiary. The acquiring corporation may transfer the acquired assets to a controlled subsidiary in exchange for its (acquiring corporation's) voting stock held by the subsidiary. This exchange is normally tax-free to both and will not disqualify the tax-free status of the reorganization [Sec. 368(a)(2)(C)]. This is true even if the then acquiring corporation transfers assets to its sub-subsidiary.[10]

NOTE 3: A transaction that qualifies as both a Type C and a Type D reorganization [¶ 3306] is treated as Type D [Sec. 368(a)(2)(A)].

¶ 3306 Transfer of assets to another corporation (Type D). A transfer by a corporation of some or all of its assets to a second corporation is generally a reorganization if:

1. Immediately after the transfer the corporation that transferred the assets (transferor), its shareholders (including persons who were shareholders immediately before the transfer), or any combination of these, are in control of the second corporation (transferee); and
2. Stock or securities of the transferee are distributed by the transferor under the conditions listed in (b) below.

(a) Control means owning at least 80% of the voting stock and at least 80% of the shares of all other classes of stock [Sec. 368(c); 1.368-2].

> **Example:** The J Co. transferred part of its assets to K Co., and immediately after the transfer J Co. and its stockholders together owned stock having 80% of the total voting power and 80% of all other classes of K Co. stock.

The stock owned by the shareholders need not be in the same proportion as it was before the transfer. However, disproportionate stock ownership may create taxable compensation or gifts from one shareholder to another [¶ 1405].

(b) Distributions of stock. The stock and securities received from the transferee corporation generally must be distributed to the transferor's shareholders in one of the following ways [Sec. 368(a)(1)(D)]:

- In pursuance of the plan of reorganization and together with substantially all of the transferor's remaining properties [Sec. 354(b); 1.354-1(a)].

➢OBSERVATION➔ The above distribution generally results in complete liquidation of the transferor.

- In a divisive reorganization [¶ 3316-3320]. Distributions may be made if the transferor transferred only part of its assets.

(c) If no distribution is made. Although there will be no reorganization, the transaction may nevertheless result in nonrecognition of gain or loss to the transferor corporation as an exchange of property for stock or securities in a corporation controlled by the transferor [Sec. 351]. See ¶ 1405.

¶ 3307 Change in capital structure or form of corporation. (a) Recapitalization (Type E). A recapitalization is a reorganization. A recapitalization is an arrangement by which the stock and bonds of the corporation are readjusted as to amount, income, or priority, or an agreement of all stockholders and creditors to increase or decrease the capitalization or debts of the corporation, or both [Sec. 368(a)(1)(E); 1.368-2(e)]. Cash payments received to round off fractional shares resulting from the recapitalization do not disqualify the reorganization.[1] The following illustrate recapitalization:

- A corporation has $200,000 par value of bonds outstanding. Instead of paying them off in cash, it discharges the obligation by issuing preferred shares, or new bonds,[2] to the bondholders.
- There is surrendered to a corporation for cancellation 25% of its preferred stock in exchange for no par value common stock.
- A corporation issues preferred stock, previously authorized but unissued for outstanding common stock.
- An exchange is made of a corporation's outstanding preferred stock, having certain priorities with reference to the amount and time of payment of dividends and the distribution of the corporate assets upon liquidation, for a new issue of the corporation's common stock having no such rights.
- A corporation's outstanding preferred stock with dividends in arrears is exchanged for a similar amount of a corporation's preferred stock plus stock (preferred or common) for the dividends in arrears.

NOTE: One of the effects of the 1969 Tax Reform Act's generally toughened stock dividend rules is that such an exchange is taxable to the extent of the dividend arrears (¶ 1707(b)) [Sec. 305(b)(4); 1.305-5].

(b) Change in identity, form, etc. (Type F). A mere change in identity, form, or place or organization is generally a reorganization [Sec. 368(a)(1)(F)]. For example, X Co. changes its name to Y Co. This type is not necessarily limited to the reorganization of a single business enterprise; it can, under certain conditions, also apply to the combination of 2 or more commonly owned operating corporations, or a merger of a wholly owned subsidiary into its parent.[3]

¶ 3308 Reorganization chart. The following chart summarizes the effects of the 6 types of reorganizations on the parties to the reorganizations.

[Chart appears on page 3308]

GAIN OR LOSS ON EXCHANGES

¶ 3309 Recognition of gain or loss. Subject to certain conditions, gain or loss on exchanges in reorganizations is not recognized either to those who participate only as shareholders or to parties to the reorganization. The only exception is gain from a reorganization involving a foreign corporation; this gain is recognized unless, within 183 days after the beginning of the exchange, a request is filed with the Revenue Service for a ruling that tax avoidance is not one of the principal purposes of the exchange.[1] This exception applies to exchanges made after 10-9-75 [Sec. 367(a)].

(a) Holders of stocks and securities. Corporate as well as noncorporate holders of stocks and securities in a corporation that is a party to a reorganization [¶ 3301] can exchange them without recognition of gain or loss if the exchange is solely for stock or securities in the same corporation or in another corporation that is a party to the same reorganization [Sec. 354; 1.354-1].

NOTE: This type of exchange is not made in divisive reorganizations (¶ 3316) [Sec. 354(b)(1)(A)]. If the reorganization qualifies as divisive, nontaxable exchanges may still be made under Sec. 355 [¶ 3317]. See also ¶ 3306(b).

Limit on tax-free exchange of securities. If the securities received are greater in principal amount than the principal amount of the securities given up, the fair

Footnotes appear at end of this Chapter.

¶ 3309

Chapter 23—Corporations—Reorganizations

REORGANIZATION CHART

Type of Reorg.	Parties Before Reorganization	Parties after reorganization
A	Y — merger (Y into X) — X	X
	X — consolidation (X + Y) — Y	W (new corp.)
B	X gives only its voting stock (all or part) for 80% control of stock of Y	X (parent) Y (subsidiary)
	W owns 80% control of X, which gives only W's voting stock (all or part) for 80% control of stock of Y	W owns 80% control of X which owns 80% control of stock of Y
C	X gives only its voting stock (all or part) for substantially all the property of Y	X owns former assets of Y; X's voting stock is only asset of Y
	W owns 80% control of X, which gives only W's voting stock (all or part) for substantially all the property of Y	W owns 80% control of X which owns the former assets of Y; W's voting stock is only asset of Y
D	(1) X transfers all or a part of its assets to Y in exchange for 80% stock control of Y	
	(2) X distributes all of its Y stock to its (X's) stockholders	X, Y controlled by X's stockholders
E	X has a capital and debt structure before recapitalization of:	X has a capital and debt structure after recapitalization of:
	common stock only [issues preferred stock in exchange for 50% of the common]	common and preferred stock
	common stock and bonds [issues preferred stock to pay off bonds]	common and preferred stock
	Class A common and preferred stock [50% of preferred is surrendered in exchange for class B common]	class A common, class B common, and preferred stock
	class A common and class B common stock [all of class B may be exchanged for class A or for (new) preferred]	class A common and preferred stock
F	Y [changes its name to X and substitutes stock for stock]	X
	X [N.Y. Corp.] reincorporates in New Jersey	X N.J. Corp.
	X [charter revoked or expired] (reincorporates)	X

NOTE: In types E and F only a few of the possible examples are given.

market value of the excess is treated as boot [¶ 3311]. If no securities are surrendered, the fair market value of the securities received is boot [Sec. 354(a)(2), 356(d)(2)(B); 1.354-1(b), 1.356-3].

Example: In a tax-free recapitalization [¶ 3307], Ames surrenders a bond in the principal amount of $1,000 in exchange for bonds in the principal amount of $1,500 with fair market value of $1,575. The fair market value of the excess principal amount is $525 ($1,575 × 500/1,500). It is treated as "boot" to Ames.

NOTE: If an exchange consists of the surrender of stock for securities, no securities are given up and no stock received, the transaction resembles a redemption of the stock. In such case the fair market value of the securities (boot) may be taxed at capital gain rates if the redemption is found to be disproportionate (¶ 1718).

Giving or receiving other consideration. If the security holder gives other property in the exchange besides stock or securities in a party to the reorganization, gain or loss on the property is recognized when the value he receives for it is more or less than its adjusted basis (¶ 1408(a)) [Sec. 1.358-1(a)]. If the security holder receives consideration other than the stock or securities in a party to the reorganization, it may be treated as boot (¶ 3311) [Sec. 356(a)(1); 1.356-1(a)].

NOTE: Stock rights and stock warrants are not counted as "stock or securities" [Sec. 1.354-1(e)].

(b) Corporation exchanging property for stock or securities. No gain or loss is recognized to a corporation that is a party to a reorganization when it exchanges property solely for stock or securities in another party to the same reorganization [Sec. 361; 1.361-1].

Receipt of other consideration. If the corporation receives anything besides stock or securities in a party to the reorganization, the value of this other consideration may be taxable as boot (but see ¶ 3305(a), note 2). It will not, however, be taxable to the corporation to the extent that it is redistributed to its shareholders pursuant to the plan of reorganization [Sec. 361(b)(1)(A); 1.361-1]. The assumption of liabilities is also a form of consideration to the corporation whose liabilities are assumed. These assumed liabilities may be taxable as boot if undertaken to avoid taxes, or are without a real business purpose [Sec. 357(b)(1); 1.357-1(c)].

(c) Corporation exchanging its own stock or securities for property will not have any recognized gain or loss [¶ 3124]. If other property is also given, gain or loss on the other property is recognized [¶ 1408(a)].

➤**OBSERVATION**➤ If the rules for recapture of depreciation [¶ 1619; 3204], mining exploration expenses [¶ 1843], certain farm expenses [¶ 1845(e)], or farm losses apply [¶ 2226], all or part of the gain may be ordinary income. Recapture of investment credit [¶ 2410(e)] also must be considered.

¶ 3310 Tabular synopsis. The following table shows under what Code Section participants in exchanges made under a plan of reorganization as defined in ¶ 3303-3307 derive their nonrecognition of gain or loss.

Exchanger	Section
1. Corporation, a party to a reorganization, giving stock and securities of its own issue.	§ 1032
2. Corporation, a party to a reorganization, giving property.	§ 361
3. A holder, giving stock or securities in a party to a reorganization [but see ¶ 3309(a)].	§ 354

➤**OBSERVATION**➤ A corporation giving stock or securities as a party to a reorganization may be a party giving property under Sec. 361 or a holder under Sec. 354.

Footnotes appear at end of this Chapter.

Chapter 23—Corporations—Reorganizations

¶ **3311 Treatment of boot.** When boot [¶ 1408] is received in exchanges connected with reorganizations, as well as the stocks or securities that can be received without gain or loss being recognized:

- No loss is recognized [Sec. 356(c), 361(b)(2); 1.356-1, 1.361-1].
- The corporation has recognized gain up to the value of boot received, unless boot is distributed under the plan of reorganization [¶ 3309(b)].

Example 1: Corporation J transferred part of its assets to Corporation K for 80% of the voting stock and 80% of all other classes of stock of Corporation K, plus $50,000 in cash. This cash is boot to J, unless distributed to its shareholders.

- Gain to the shareholders is recognized, but not in excess of the boot received [Sec. 356(a)(1); 1.356-1].

Example 2: Pursuant to a plan of reorganization, A exchanged 100 shares of stock of Co. X (cost to him, $5,000) for 200 shares of Co. Y into which Co. X is merging. In addition, A received $200 in cash. The Y Co. shares had a fair market value of $5,500. The gain to A is $700, but that gain is recognized only to the extent of $200. The basis of the Y shares becomes $5,000 [¶ 3313]. If the Y stock had a fair market value of only $4,000, the loss of $800 would not be recognized and the basis of the Y shares would be $4,800. If all of A's X stock did not have the same basis, the realized gain or loss would be computed separately for each basis.[1]

NOTE: For recognition of gain or loss to the giver of boot, see ¶ 3309(a), (c).

Exchange for Sec. 306 stock. To the extent that it is received in exchange for Sec. 306 stock [¶ 1722], the fair market value of boot is treated as a dividend to the shareholder [Sec. 356(e); 1.356-4]. This is true whether he realizes a gain or loss.

For treatment of bonds as boot, see ¶ 3309(a).

¶ **3312 Gain taxed as dividend.** If money or other property received from a corporation by its stockholders in connection with an exchange of stock or securities [¶ 3311] has the effect of a dividend, the gain recognized may be taxed as a dividend. The stockholder treats his proportionate share of the earnings and profits accumulated after 2-28-13 as a dividend [¶ 1701]. Any remainder is a capital gain[1] [Sec. 356(a)(2); 1.356-1].

Example: The X Co. has a capital of $100,000 and earnings and profits of $50,000 accumulated since February 28, 1913. In the current year the X Co. transferred all of its assets to the Y Co. in exchange for all of the stock of the Y Co. and the payment of $50,000 in cash to the stockholders of the X Co. This is a reorganization, and X and Y are parties to the reorganization. A, who owns 100 of the 1,000 shares of stock in the X Co. for which he paid $10,000, receives 100 shares of Y stock worth $10,000 and $5,000 in cash. The $5,000 is a dividend.

Suppose that instead of receiving $5,000 in cash, A received $7,500 in cash. $5,000 of that $7,500 would be taxable as a dividend, the remainder ($2,500) as capital gain.

BASIS

¶ **3313 Basis to distributee-stockholder.** The basis of the stock or securities received in a nontaxable exchange in a reorganization is the same as the basis of the stock or securities exchanged. This basis must be *decreased by* (1) any money received, (2) the fair market value of any other property received, and (3) any loss that was recognized [¶ 3309(a)]. It must be *increased by* any gain recognized on the exchange [Sec. 358(a)(1); 1.358-1]. The basis of any other property received is its fair market value on the date of exchange [Sec. 358(a)(2); 1.358-1].

NOTE: Basis may also be increased by amounts received as a dividend because Sec. 306 stock is received in the exchange (¶ 1722) [Sec. 358(a)(1)(B); 1.358-1(a)].

Example 1: Pursuant to a plan of reorganization, A exchanged 100 shares of stock of the X Co. he had bought for $10,000 on 7-1-73 for 200 shares of the Y Co. having a fair market value of $11,000. No gain is recognized on the exchange. The cost basis of the Y shares to A is $10,000; the date basis, 7-1-73.

Example 2: John Vickers surrenders stock that has a basis of $1,000 in his hands in a tax-free recapitalization. He receives in exchange stock that has a value of $500 and a bond with a value of $750. The bond is "boot" [¶ 3309]. Actual gain on the deal is $250. Any part treated as a dividend is taxed as such; the remainder, if any, is taxed as a capital gain. The basis of the new stock is $500 determined as follows: $1,000 (basis of old stock) minus $750 (value of the other property), plus $250 (gain taxed), or $500. The basis of the bond is $750.

Allocation of basis. If a distributee receives several kinds of stock or securities, the basis must be allocated among the properties received in proportion to their relative fair market values [Sec. 358(b)(1); 1.358-2].

Example 3: In a tax-free reorganization, A exchanged 100 shares of X Co. stock for 50 shares of Y Co. common stock (value $15,000) and 50 shares of Y Co. preferred stock (value $10,000). A's 100 shares of X Co. stock had a cost basis to him of $10,000. The total value of the Y Co. stock received is $25,000, of which $15,000 or three-fifths is represented by the common stock and $10,000 or two-fifths is represented by the preferred stock. The combined bases of the two classes of Y Co. stock ($10,000) are apportioned according to their respective values. The basis of the Y common stock is $3/5$ of $10,000, or $6,000. The basis of the Y preferred stock is $2/5$ of $10,000 or $4,000.

For basis in divisive reorganizations, see ¶ 3320.

¶ 3314 Basis to corporation. If property is acquired by a corporation in connection with a tax-free reorganization, the basis of the property ordinarily is the same as it would be in the hands of the transferor, increased by any gain recognized to the transferor on the transfer [Sec. 362(b); 1.362-1].

Example: X Corporation owns property with a basis of $10,000 and a fair market value of $20,000. X Corporation transfers the property to Y Corporation for all of Y's stock, and distributes the Y stock to the X Corp. shareholders. This is a reorganization, and the exchange is nontaxable. Y Corporation's basis in the property received from X Corporation is $10,000.

If stocks or securities in a party to the reorganization are acquired, the basis of the stock or securities is the same as the basis of the property exchanged, with the same basis adjustments discussed in ¶ 3313 [Sec. 358(a)(1); 1.358-1]. However, the acquired stock or securities retain the basis they had in the hands of the transferor if the transferee exchanges its stock, or securities (or its parent's stock or securities) as all or part of the consideration for the transfer [Sec. 362(b); 1.362-1].

¶ 3315 Liabilities assumed. A corporation may assume liabilities on property received, as part of the consideration for the exchange [¶ 1405(a)].

(a) In general. If the transferee acquires property subject to a liability of the transferor, or assumes a liability against property, the assumption or acquisition is not considered money or other property in that it does not prevent the exchange from being tax-free, unless the purpose was to avoid taxes or assumption had no business purpose [Sec. 357(a); 1.357-1]. However, assumption of liability decreases the basis to the transferor of the property he receives in the exchange [Sec. 358(d); 1.358-3].

Example: Corporation X transfers its property with a basis of $100,000 to Corporation Y in return for voting stock of Y and the assumption of a $25,000 mortgage on the property. No gain or loss is recognized to either corporation. X's basis for the stock received is $75,000.

Footnotes appear at end of this Chapter.

(b) In excess of basis (transfers to controlled corporation). In an exchange under a Type D reorganization [¶ 3306], if the liabilities assumed plus the liabilities to which the property is subject exceed the adjusted basis of the property transferred, the excess is treated either as a capital gain or an ordinary gain, as the case may be[1] [Sec. 357(c)(1); 1.357-2]. This does not apply to an exchange in which the assumption or acquisition of liability is treated as money received because of a tax avoidance or non bona fide business purpose (see (a) above) [Sec. 357(c)(2); 1.357-2].

DIVISIVE REORGANIZATIONS

¶ 3316 Divisive reorganizations generally. For various reasons, a corporation may want to dispose of a substantial part of its assets. If it sells them and distributes the proceeds, it may have to pay tax on the gain. Furthermore, the shareholders may have to pay tax on the distribution. It is possible to avoid this result through use of a "divisive reorganization." There are three types of divisive reorganizations, commonly called "split-ups," "split-offs," and "spin-offs." Each type is divisive because each divides what previously was held in one corporation into two corporations, with the shares of both in the hands of the original shareholders.

Background and purpose. The law permits the division of an existing corporation by divesting its subsidiaries or businesses for bona fide corporate reasons. To accomplish this tax-free separation, a number of complex statutory requirements must be met. The purpose for these rules is to prevent the divisions from being used as a device for distributing earnings and profits.

(a) Types of divisive reorganizations. There are three types of divisive reorganizations [Sec. 355]:

• *Split-up.* A corporation is split up into two or more separate corporations. The stock of the new corrporations is distributed to the shareholders of the old corporation, who surrender the stock of the old corporation.

• *Split-off.* A corporation transfers part of its assets to a new corporation in exchange for the stock of the new corporation. It then immediately distributes the stock to its shareholders, who *surrender* part of their stock in the original corporation. A split-off also may occur through a distribution by a parent of an existing controlled subsidiary company's stock.

• *Spin-off.* This is the same as a split-off, except that the shares of the new corporation or existing controlled subsidiary are distributed to shareholders *without* surrender of their stock in the original corporation.

(b) Information to be filed. A corporation distributing stock or securities of a controlled corporation must attach to its return for the year of the distribution a statement of facts showing compliance with the rules governing such distributions [¶ 3317 et seq.]. A taxpayer receiving such a distribution must attach to his return a statement of facts that includes a description of the stock and securities surrendered (if any) and received, and the names and addresses of all the corporations involved [Sec. 1.355-5].

¶ 3317 Stock or securities received tax-free. Generally, no gain or loss is recognized to a shareholder who receives only stock or securities on account of stock he owns, and no gain or loss is recognized to a security holder who receives only stock or securities in exchange for his securities. The tax-free amount is limited [(c) below]. Gain is recognized to the extent that the taxpayer receives "boot" [¶ 3319]. Gain is also recognized if a foreign corporation is involved in the divisive reorganization unless, within 183 days after the beginning of the exchange, a request is filed with the Revenue Service for a ruling that tax avoidance is not one of the principal purposes of the exchange.[1] Exchanges made after 10-9-75 are covered by this rule [Sec. 367(a)]. If a transfer is made to a controlled foreign corporation, the transferor is treated as having received stock equal in value to appreciated property transferred, even if no stock was in fact exchanged [Sec. 367(c)(2)].

(a) What is required. If the following requirements are met, stock and securities of a controlled corporation can be distributed without gain or loss being recognized to the shareholders or security holders:

(1) The distribution to a shareholder must be with respect to the distributing corporation's stock, while a distribution to a security holder must be in exchange for the distributing corporation's securities [Sec. 355(a)(1)].

(2) The distribution must be solely stock or securities of a controlled corporation. If anything else is distributed, the "boot" may be taxable [¶ 3319].

(3) The distribution must not be used principally as a device[2] for distributing earnings and profits of the distributing corporation, the controlled corporation, or both [Sec. 355(a)(1)(B); Prop. Reg. 1.355-2].

(4) Both corporations ordinarily must be engaged in a trade or business that has been actively conducted for at least 5 years [¶ 3318].

(5) The distributing corporation must distribute all the stock or securities of the controlled corporation that it held immediately before the distribution, or an amount of stock that constitutes control [Sec. 355(a)(1)(D); 1.355-2]. If more than one distribution is necessary to meet this requirement, the distributing corporation must commit itself at the time of the first distribution to enough later distributions to divest control.[3]

Sale of the stock. After the distribution, the shareholders or security holders who get the distribution may sell or exchange stock or securities of the corporations involved. This will not be construed as a device to distribute earnings or profits, unless it is negotiated or agreed upon before the distribution [Sec. 355(a)(1)(B); 1.355-2].

What is control. The test for control is the same as for other types of reorganizations. It means the ownership of stock with at least 80% of the total voting power and at least 80% of the total number of shares of all other classes of stock of the corporation [Sec. 368(c); 1.368-2].

(b) Qualifying distributions. If the requirements in (a) are met, gain or loss will not be recognized. It makes no difference whether the distribution is pro rata, there is a surrender of stock, or there is a plan of reorganization [Sec. 355(a)(2); 1.355-3].

Non pro rata distribution. Gain or loss is not recognized whether or not the distribution is proportionate to the shareholdings of the distributing corporation, provided all the requirements in (a) above are met [Sec. 355(a)(2)(A); 1.355-3].

Example 1: A Co. transfers all of its assets to B Co. and C Co. pursuant to an anti-trust decree. In distributing the stock of B Co. and C Co. to A Co. stockholders, it is not essential that the A Co. stockholders all get proportionate amounts of the B Co. and C Co. stock. This reorganization is a *split-up*.

Example 2: X and Y are sole proprietors. X transferred his jewelry business and Y transferred his optical business to A Corp. A Corp. then transferred the jewelry business to D Corp. for all of D's stock, and transferred the optical business to H Corp. for all of H's stock. Immediately after that, A Corp. transferred all the D stock to X and all the H stock to Y in return for their stock in A Corp. The transfer by A Corp. is a "split-up" type of reorganization. No gain is recognized even if the D and H stock received by X and Y isn't proportionate to the stockhold-

¶ 3317

ings they had in A Corp. However, there may be a gift or compensation to the stockholder (¶ 3306).

Stock surrender. The distribution is tax-free whether or not the shareholder surrenders stock in the distributing corporation [Sec. 355(a)(2)(B); 1.355-3].

Example 3: For business reasons, A Co. has transferred certain of its properties to B Co. in exchange for all of B Co.'s stock. B Co. will manufacture certain long-established products of the A Co.'s business. X, a stockholder of the A Co., is no longer interested in having stock in the A Co. He does want to continue as a stockholder of B Co. X surrenders his stock in the A Co. and gets B Co. stock in exchange. No gain or loss is recognized to X, if all of the requirements are met. This transaction is a *split-off*.

Example 4: A Co. transfers part of its assets to a newly formed B Co. in exchange for the stock of B Co. A Co. distributes the B Co. stock to its shareholders. This transaction is a typical *spin-off*. If all of the requirements are met, the reorganization is tax-free. In this example there is no surrender of stock in the distributing corporation.

≫**OBSERVATION**→ In the four preceding examples, preferred stock and bonds could be distributed along with common stock of the controlled corporation. However, if preferred stock is distributed, it might be "Section 306 stock" [¶ 1722].

No plan of reorganization. The distribution does not have to be pursuant to a plan of reorganization [Sec. 355(a)(2)(C); 1.355-3(c)]. Not all of the stock and securities of a controlled subsidiary must be distributed, if stock representing "control" is distributed, and the stock and securities are not retained to avoid tax [Sec. 355(a)(1)(D)(ii); 1.355-2(d)].

Example 5: A Co. owns a controlling interest in subsidiary B Co. which has been in existence for a long time. For business reasons A Co. distributes the controlling interest in B Co. to its stockholders. If all of the requirements are met, the transaction is a tax-free reorganization.

(c) Limitation. Only the principal amount of the securities surrendered for the securities received in the controlled corporation can be tax free [Sec. 355(a)(3)(A); 1.355-2(e)]. If securities in any greater amount are received, the fair market value of the excess is treated as boot [Sec. 356(b); 1.356-3]. If no securities are surrendered, the fair market value of the securities received is treated as boot or "other property" (¶ 3319) [Sec. 355(a)(3)(B); 1.355-2(e)].

Stock held 5 years or less. Stock in a controlled corporation acquired within 5 years of its distribution in a transaction in which gain or loss was recognized is treated as boot [¶ 3319].

Example 6: X Co. held an 80% stock interest in Y Co. for 5 years or more before the distribution. Within those 5 years X Co. purchased the remaining 20% of the Y Co. stock. Only the 20% stock purchased will be considered "other property" if Y Co. stock is distributed in a transaction that is otherwise tax free.

However, the acquired stock is included to determine whether the stock distributed constitutes control [Sec. 355(a)(3); 1.355-2(f)].

¶ 3318 Requirements as to active business. Right after the distribution, both the distributing corporation and the controlled corporation (or corporations) must be engaged in a trade or business that meets both of the following requirements:

(1) The trade or business must have been actively conducted throughout the five-year period ending on the date of the distribution [Sec. 355(b)(1)(A), 355(b)(2); 1.355-1, 1.355-4]. What is the "active conduct of a trade or business" depends on the circumstances.[1]

Example 1: Co. A has been in active business more than 5 years. It distributes to its stockholders stock of controlled Co. B, organized 2 years before the distribution to carry on a new business. The spin-off is not tax free because, immediately after the distribution, the controlled corporation was not actively engaged in business for the 5 years before the distribution date.

Example 2: Corporation X transfers its investment portfolio to a newly-formed subsidiary, Corporation S. The stock of the subsidiary is then spun off to the shareholders of Corporation X. The spin-off would not be tax free, because Corporation S is not engaged in the active conduct of a business.

However, if the distributing corporation was a holding company (had no assets other than stock of the controlled corporations) before the distribution, the 5-year requirement applies only to the controlled corporation [Sec. 355(b)(1)(B), 355(b)(2); 1.355-1, 1.355-4].

(2) The trade or business must have been acquired either (a) more than 5 years before the date of the distribution, or (b) in a transaction in which no gain or loss was recognized [Sec. 355(b)(2)(C),(D); 1.355-1, 1.355-4]. These provisions extend the scope of the 5-year rule to include acquisition as well as creation of controlled corporations.

NOTE: A corporation cannot escape recognition of gain or loss on a distribution by purchasing the stock of a second corporation, merging into it and then having the second corporation (without waiting 5 years) spin off the acquired assets to the shareholders of the absorbed corporation. The merger may be tax-free, but the prior purchase was made within the five-year period. It doesn't matter that both corporations were in business for over 5 years at the time of the spin-off.

Earnings of one business used for second business. The 5-year rule is not met if a large part of the earnings of a "spun-off" business is used to finance purchases of the retained business during the 5-year period. Such use of earnings is contrary to the purpose of the 5-year rule, which is intended to prevent earnings (that would otherwise be distributed and taxed as dividends) from being used to create a new enterprise that can be sold by stockholders for capital gains.[2]

Division of one business. Each corporation must be engaged immediately after the distribution in a separate trade or business [Sec. 1.355-1(a)]. The distributing corporation can meet this requirement by dividing a single business it operates, and transferring part to the controlled corporation [Prop. Reg. 1.355-3].[3]

¶ **3319 When "boot" is received.** If the holders exchange stock or securities in a divisive reorganization and *receive* not only stock or securities that can be received tax-free, but also "boot" (money or other property), the following rules apply [Sec. 356; 1.356-1]:

- Gain is recognized up to the value of the boot received.
- No loss is recognized.
- Part of the gain may be taxable as a dividend [¶ 3312].

If no stock or securities are surrendered (a spin-off), boot is treated as a dividend or return of capital (¶ 1702) [Sec. 356; 1.356-1, 1.356-2].

Example: Corporation D owned 80% of the stock of subsidiary Corporation E and distributed that stock to the shareholders of Corporation D, along with cash. Assuming that all of the requirements are met, the distribution of the stock is tax-free. However, the boot (cash) is taxed as a dividend to the extent that it is covered by Corporation D's earnings and profits.

Securities (bonds) may be treated as boot [Sec. 356(d)(1); 1.356-3]. The securities so treated are limited to the fair market value of any excess of the principal

Footnotes appear at end of this Chapter.

¶ **3319**

amount of securities received in the controlled corporation over the principal amount of securities surrendered. If no securities are surrendered, the boot is the fair market value of the entire principal amount of the securities received [Sec. 356(d)(2)(C); 1.356-3].

If any of the boot is received in exchange for Sec. 306 stock [¶ 1722], the value of the boot is treated as a dividend [Sec. 356(e); 1.356-4].

¶ **3320 Basis to distributee-stockholder.** For basis to distributee-stockholders generally, see ¶ 3313. Note however, the following provisions applicable to divisive reorganizations:

(a) **When no stock is surrendered.** In a tax-free divisive reorganization when no stock is surrendered, but stock of a controlled corporation is received, the basis of the old and the new stock is determined by allocating the basis of the original stock [Sec. 358(c); 1.358-2].

Example 1: A owns 100 shares of X Co. stock, which has a basis to him of $10,000 and a market value of $15,000. In a tax-free spin-off, he surrenders no X Co. stock, but receives 100 shares of Y Co. stock having a value of $5,000. The basis of X stock and Y stock after the spin-off is determined as follows:

Market value 100 shares X stock		$15,000
Market value 100 shares Y stock		5,000
Total		$20,000
Basis of X Co. stock after spin-off	15,000/20,000 × $10,000 =	$ 7,500
Basis of Y Co. stock after spin-off	5,000/20,000 × 10,000 =	2,500
	Total	$10,000

(b) **When stock is surrendered.** If some stock is surrendered in a tax-free divisive reorganization, for which the stockholder receives more than one class of stock of the controlled corporation, the basis must be allocated among the different classes of stock he holds [Sec. 358(b)(2); 1.358-2].

Example 2: A owns 200 shares of X Co. stock that cost him $14,000 and has a market value of $40,000. In a tax-free split-off, he gives up 100 shares of X Co. stock and receives 50 shares of preferred (value $10,000) and 50 shares of common (value $5,000) in the newly-formed Y Co. The basis of the stock of X Co. held before the transaction ($14,000) is allocated among the three kinds of stock he holds after the transaction [(1) X Co. stock retained; (2) Y Co. common; (3) Y Co. preferred] as follows:

Market value 100 shs. X Co. retained		$20,000
Market value 50 shs. Y Co. preferred		10,000
Market value 50 shs. Y Co. common		5,000
Total value		$35,000
Basis of X Co. stock retained	20,000/35,000 × $14,000 =	$ 8,000
Basis of Y Co. preferred	10,000/35,000 × 14,000 =	4,000
Basis of Y Co. common	5,000/35,000 × 14,000 =	2,000
	Total basis	$14,000

SPECIAL TYPES OF REORGANIZATIONS

¶ **3330 Transactions under orders of federal agencies.** Special tax relief is provided to postpone the recognition of gain or loss when certain holding companies are required by federal agencies to distribute or exchange a portion of their holdings. This is done by not recognizing gain or loss on the exchange or distribution, but requiring adjustments to basis of the property retained by the distributor or substitution of basis on an exchange. This relief is provided in the following cases:

(a) Securities and Exchange Commission. Exchanges and distributions ordered by the Securities and Exchange Commission under Sec. 11 of the Public Utility Holding Company Act of 1935. This Act provides for the simplification and geographical integration of public utility holding company systems [Sec. 1081-1083; 1.1081-1—1.1083-1].

(b) Federal Reserve Board. Distributions and exchanges certified by the Federal Reserve Board as necessary under the Bank Holding Company Act of 1956 and the Bank Holding Company Tax Act of 1976 [Sec. 1101-1103; 1.1101-1—1.1102-3].

See also: Sales or exchanges of radio broadcasting properties certified by the Federal Communications Commission [¶ 1410]; Railroad reorganizations approved by the Interstate Commerce Commission [¶ 3332].

¶ 3331 Reorganization of insolvent corporation. No gain or loss is recognized in certain insolvency reorganizations (a) on transfers of property by corporations; and (b) on exchanges by security holders.

(a) Transfers by corporations. No gain or loss is recognized on a transfer of property by a corporation, if the transfer is made under these conditions: (1) under a court order, (2) in a receivership, foreclosure, or similar proceeding, or in a proceeding under chapter X of the Bankruptcy Act, (3) to another corporation putting into effect a court-approved plan of reorganization, (4) in exchange solely for stock or securities in the other corporation [Sec. 371(a)(1); 1.371-1]. If other property or money is received, no gain is recognized if the corporation distributes the property or money pursuant to the plan of reorganization. Gain is recognized to the extent of the property or money not distributed [Sec. 371(a)(2); 1.371-1]. Similar and special provisions apply to railroad corporations [Sec. 354(d), 374]. See also ¶ 3332.

(b) Exchanges by security holders. No gain or loss is recognized on exchanges of stocks or securities of an insolvent corporation for stocks or securities of another corporation to which the property was transferred [Sec. 371(b)(1); 1.371-2]. Gain from "boot" is taxed, but not as a dividend.

(c) Basis to corporation. The basis of property acquired in an insolvency reorganization is the same as the transferor's basis, increased by any gain recognized to the transferor. It is not reduced by any exclusion of income from discharge of indebtedness. Special adjustments may be necessary if the property was acquired from a corporation that used the retirement method of depreciation and the acquiring corporation adopts a different method [Sec. 372; 1.372-1].

NOTE: The statutory definition of a reorganization [¶ 3303-3307] does not apply to insolvency reorganizations [Sec. 371, 372; 1.371-1].

¶ 3332 Railroad reorganizations. No gain or loss is recognized to a shareholder or security holder on an exchange of stock and securities under a reorganization approved by the Interstate Commerce Commission as being in the public interest [Sec. 354(c); 1.354-1]. See also ¶ 3331(a).

LIQUIDATIONS

¶ 3334 Nontaxable liquidation of subsidiary. No gain or loss is recognized to a parent corporation that receives property (including money[1]) in a complete liquidation of a subsidiary if [Sec. 332(b); 1.332-2—4]:

- The parent owns at least 80% of the voting stock, and at least 80% of all other classes of stock (except non-voting stock that is limited and preferred as to dividends). Such ownership must exist on the date the liquidation plan is adopted and continue until property is received in liquidation; and
- The subsidiary's distribution is in complete cancellation or redemption of all of the subsidiary's stock; and
- The distribution of all of the subsidiary's property is made to the parent in the same tax year,[2] unless there is a series of distributions. In that case, the transfer must be made within 3 years from the close of the tax year in which the first distribution is made [Sec. 332(b)(2)(3); 1.332-3, 1.332-4].

NOTE: The taxpayer may apply for an advance ruling on the proposed transaction by furnishing all pertinent information to the Revenue Service.[3] Gain may be recognized if the liquidation of a subsidiary involves a foreign corporation. If it does, the usual non-recognition rule applies only if, within 183 days after the beginning of the liquidation, a request is filed with the Revenue Service for a ruling that tax avoidance is not one of the principal purposes of the liquidation. This rule applies to exchanges made after 10-9-75 [Sec. 367(a)].[4]

(a) Transfer to pay debt. If on the date the plan of liquidation is adopted, the subsidiary was indebted to the parent corporation, no gain or loss is recognized to the subsidiary because of the transfer of property to satisfy the debt [Sec. 332(c); 1.332-7]. However, gain or loss is recognized to the parent if the property transferred is worth more or less than the debt.[5]

(b) Basis of property received. Generally, the parent's basis for the property received is the same as the subsidiary's basis [Sec. 334(b)(1); 1.334-1]. This rule applies where the parent receives property in satisfaction of the subsidiary's indebtedness.[6] However, if the parent (1) purchased, in a taxable exchange, at least 80% control (voting power and value) of the subsidiary within a 12-month period, and (2) adopts a plan of liquidation within 2 years after the stock acquisition, the parent's basis for the property received is the basis of its stock in the subsidiary [Sec. 334(b)(2), (3); 1.334-1]. Stock acquired from a related person is not counted for 80% control, if the stock would have been constructively owned [¶ 1727]. Parent corporations that do not qualify under Sec. 334(b)(2) may nevertheless use the cost of its stock in the subsidiary for the property received in the liquidation if the subsidiary's stock was purchased with the intent to liquidate.[7]

¶ **3335 Tax-free one-month liquidations.** A relief provision permits a corporation (except a collapsible corporation [¶ 1627]) to be liquidated without the shareholders being taxed on the increase in value of the property they get [Sec. 333; 1.333-1]. However, the tax is only postponed. This is accomplished by making the basis of property received in the liquidation the same as the basis (with certain adjustments) of shareholder's stock surrendered in the liquidation [Sec. 334(c); 1.334-2]. If the property is sold, this basis is used in figuring gain or loss on the sale. The provision is useful if a corporation has little or no earnings and profits and its assets consist largely of property that has appreciated in value and is distributed in kind.

Example: Dodd, a shareholder, surrendered at liquidation one share of stock with a basis of $40 and received property worth $100. Assume that under this relief provision, he was not taxed on the $60 gain at the time of liquidation. The basis of the property received is $40 (basis of the stock). If he later sells the property for $100, he is taxed on the $60 gain at the time of the sale.

These are the broad principles of the provision. Many technical requirements have to be met to get this tax relief.

(a) When liquidation qualifies. The relief is available only to qualified electing shareholders [Sec. 333(c); 1.333-2], and only if the following conditions are met [Sec. 333(a), (d); 1.333-1, 1.333-3]:

- Liquidation is made pursuant to a plan adopted on or after 6-22-54;
- Distribution is in complete cancellation or redemption of all the stock of a domestic corporation, other than a collapsible corporation;
- Transfer of all the property under the liquidation occurs within some *one* calendar month;
- Within 30 days after the adoption of the plan, the shareholder files his written election (on Form 964) to accept the benefits of the plan and the corporation files an information return on Form 966 [¶ 3536].

Who are qualified shareholders. Corporations holding 50% or more of the stock entitled to vote on adoption of the liquidation plan cannot qualify for this relief [Sec. 333(b); 1.333-2]. Other shareholders are divided into two groups to determine if they are qualified electing shareholders: (1) noncorporate shareholders, and (2) corporate shareholders. Any shareholder of either group, whether or not his stock can be voted on the issue of the adoption of the liquidation plan, is a qualified electing shareholder if:

- His written election has been properly filed; and
- Like elections have been made and filed by owners of stock possessing at least 80% of the voting power of all classes of stock owned by shareholders of the same group and entitled to vote on the adoption of the plan of liquidation. Such ownership must exist when the plan is adopted [Sec. 333(c); 1.333-2].

(b) What gain is taxed. The gain at the time of liquidation is not always completely nontaxable. The nontaxable portion is figured by imposing certain limitations on the amount of taxable gain. The recognized gain on each share of stock surrendered in the liquidation is limited to the greater of: (1) shareholder's ratable share of earnings and profits accumulated after February 28, 1913; or (2) money and market value of stock or securities received that were acquired by the corporation after 1953. Corporate shareholders report the entire recognized gain as capital gain. Noncorporate shareholders report the recognized gain representing earnings and profits accumulated after February 28, 1913 as a dividend, and the rest as capital gain.

NOTE: If depreciable business property is transferred, gain is recognized as ordinary income to the extent the depreciation recapture rules apply [¶ 1619]. Recapture of investment credit [¶ 2410(e)], mining expenses [¶ 1843], certain farm expenses [¶ 1845(e)] and farm losses [¶ 2226] also must be considered.

(c) Basis of property received. The basis to shareholders of the property received in the liquidation is the same as the basis of the stock cancelled or redeemed, decreased by the amount of money he receives, and increased by the amount of gain recognized to him [Sec. 334(c); 1.334-2].

CARRYOVERS

¶ 3336 Carryovers to successor corporation. When the assets of a corporation are acquired by another corporation in a tax-free liquidation or reorganization, the successor corporation may, under conditions described below, carry over certain tax benefits, privileges, elective rights, and obligations [¶ 3337] of the predecessor corporation [Sec. 381(a)(c); 1.381(a)-1].

Footnotes appear at end of this Chapter.

(a) **When carryover is allowed.** The carryover provisions apply to:

- *Liquidation of subsidiary.* When a controlling parent corporation takes over the property of a subsidiary in a complete liquidation of the subsidiary and takes the subsidiary's basis for the property acquired (see ¶ 3334) [Sec. 381(a)(1); 1.381(a)-1(b)(1)].

- *Reorganizations.* When assets of another corporation have been acquired in the following types of reorganization: a statutory merger or consolidation [¶ 3303]; an acquisition by one corporation of properties of another corporation for stock [¶ 3305]; a transfer of assets for controlling stock, if there is a single transferee corporation and the transferor distributes all of the stock, securities and properties it receives as well as its other properties under a plan of reorganization [¶ 3306]; a mere change in identity, form, or place of organization (¶ 3307(b)) [Sec. 381(a)(2); 1.381(a)-1(b)(1)].

NOTE: The carryover provisions do not apply to partial liquidations, divisive reorganizations or reorganizations not listed above [Sec. 1.381(a)-1(b)(3)].

(b) **Dates are important for carryover benefits.** The successor takes over the carryovers as of the close of the day of distribution (in the case of a liquidated subsidiary) or the day of transfer (in the case of a reorganization) [Sec. 381(a)]. When transfer of assets is referred to in the following explanation, it also includes a distribution of assets.

The following operating rules apply to liquidations and reorganizations entitled to carryover benefits; but they do not apply to a reorganization that is a mere change in identity, form, or place of organization[1] [Sec. 381(b); 1.381(b)-1, 1.381(c)(1)-1].

End of tax year. The tax year of the predecessor corporation ends on the date the assets are transferred from the predecessor to the successor corporation. Amounts retained to pay taxes, director fees and dissolution expenses do not affect this date.[2] The predecessor should file a return for the tax year ending with that date. If the predecessor remains in existence, it should also file a return for the tax year beginning on the day following date of transfer and ending with the date its year would have ended had there been no transfer.

Date of transfer. Generally, the date of transfer is the day the transfer is completed. However, it may be the day when substantially all the property has been transferred and the predecessor has ceased all operations except liquidating activities. The latter date applies if completion of the transfer is unreasonably postponed, or predecessor and successor corporations file statements specifying (1) the day considered to be the date of transfer, (2) nature and amount of assets transferred as of that date and dates of transfer, (3) nature and amount of assets not transferred and purpose for which retained, (4) date on which predecessor ceased all operations except liquidating activities. A predecessor files the statement with its return for the tax year ending with the date of transfer. Successor files it with return for first year ending after transfer date [Sec. 1.381(b)-1(b)].

Net operating loss or net capital loss after transfer. The successor corporation is not entitled to carry back to a tax year of a predecessor, a net capital loss sustained in a tax year starting after 1969, or a net operating loss, incurred in a tax year ending after the date of transfer [Sec. 381(b)]. However, in an "F" reorganization [¶ 3307(b)], the successor's loss can be carried back against the predecessor's pre-merger profits. The 2d Circuit held that a triangular merger of a 62% controlled subsidiary into a 100% controlled shell was an "F" reorganization, even though the subsidiary's minority shareholders had to exchange their stock for the controlled shell's parent's stock.[3]

Example 1: Corporations X and Y transfer on 12-31-77, all their property to Z in a consolidation. If Z has a net operating loss or net capital loss in 1978, it cannot be carried back to a tax year of X or Y.

Example 2: Corporation X merges into Corporation Y on 12-31-77, in a statutory merger, with Y's charter continuing after the merger. If Y has a net operating loss or a net capital loss in 1978, the loss cannot be carried back to a tax year of X, but is a carryback to a tax year of Y.

Example 3: X reorganizes by changing its name to Y. Y may carry back a net operating or net capital loss to a tax year of X before the reorganization.

¶ **3337 Checklist of carryover items.** The following items may be carried over subject to the conditions described:

Net operating loss. The successor corporation may carry over net operating losses of the predecessor, subject to the special limitations shown at ¶ 3338; but the carryover to the first tax year ending after the date of transfer is limited to an amount that bears the same ratio to the taxable income (determined without regard to a net operating loss deduction) of the successor in such tax year as the number of days in the tax year after the date of transfer bears to the total number of days in the tax year [Sec. 381(c)(1)(B); 1.381(c)(1)-1(d)]. Any deferred minimum tax liability attributable to the carryover is also acquired (¶ 2245) [Prop. Reg. Sec. 1.381(c)(1)-1(a)(3)].

Earnings and profits of the predecessor become the successor's. But an earnings and profits deficit of either corporation may only be applied against the successor's earnings and profits accumulated after the assets' date of transfer. The earnings and profits of the successor's first tax year that may be reduced by the predecessor's deficit is in the same ratio to the total undistributed successor's earnings for the year as the number of days of the year after the transfer bears to the total days in the year [Sec. 381(c)(2); 1.381(c)(2)-1(a)].

Capital loss carryover. The successor is entitled to use the unexhausted portion of the predecessor's capital loss carryover. The first year in which the loss may be deducted is the first tax year of the successor ending after the date of transfer of assets. The amount that can be used in the first year, however, is limited to a fraction of the successor corporation's capital gain net income for that year. The fraction is the number of days in the tax year after the transfer over the total number of days in the tax year [Sec. 381(c)(3); 1.381(c)(3)-1].

Method of accounting. If both successor and predecessor used the same method of accounting on the date of the transfer of assets, the successor continues to use that method. But if different methods were used by several predecessors, or by predecessor and successor, the successor uses a method prescribed by the Commissioner [Sec. 381(c)(4); 1.381(c)(4)-1].

Inventories. The successor values inventories received from the predecessor on the same basis as the predecessor. However, if the carryover of the method of taking inventory results in the successor having more than one method of taking inventory, the successor may adopt a particular method or combination of methods of taking inventory [Sec. 381(c)(5); 1.381(c)(5)-1].

Depreciation. The successor figures dpreciation on acquired assets the same way the predecessor did. But his total depreciaion on a particular asset may not exceed the predecessor's adjusted basis. A change of method may be made with Commissioner's consent. (¶ 2010(b)) [Sec. 381(c)(6); 1.381(c)(6)-1].

A successor corporation can use the ADR system on property acquired from a predecessor only if the predecessor elected it for the property (¶ 2033) [Sec. 1.167(a)-11(e)(3)].

Installment sales method. If the successor acquires installment obligations which the predecessor reported on the installment basis, the successor also reports the income

Footnotes appear at end of this Chapter.

on the installment basis [Sec. 381(c)(8); 1.381(c)(8)-1].

Amortization of bond discount or premium. If the successor assumes liability for bonds of the predecessor issued at a discount or premium, the successor is treated as the predecessor in determining the amortization deductible or includible in income [Sec. 381(c)(9); 1.381(c)(9)-1].

Exploration and development expenditures. The successor can deduct certain development expenditures [¶ 1843] when the predecessor has previously so elected [Sec. 381(c)(10); 1.381(c)(10)-1].

Contributions to pension trusts, employees' annuity plans, stock bonus and profit-sharing trusts. The successor is considered to be the predecessor in determining deductions for contributions of an employer under pension trusts, employees' annuity plans, stock bonus and profit-sharing plans [Sec. 381(c)(11); 1.381(c)(11)-1]. See ¶ 1838.

Recovery of bad debts, prior taxes or delinquent amounts. If successor is entitled to the recovery of bad debts, prior taxes or delinquency amounts previously deducted or credited by the predecessor, the successor must include in its income the amounts that would have been includible by the predecessor on the recovery [Sec. 381(c)(12); 1.381(c)(12)-1].

Involuntary conversions. The successor is treated as the predecessor when there is an involuntary conversion [Sec. 381(c)(13); 1.381(c)(13)-1].

Dividend carryover to personal holding company. A successor that is a personal holding company may include a dividend carryover of its predecessor in figuring the dividends paid deduction to the same extent as the predecessor [Sec. 381(c)(14); 1.381(c)(14)-1].

Indebtedness of certain personal holding companies. In figuring its undistributed personal holding company income for tax years ending after the date of the transfer, a successor that is a personal holding company, may deduct, to the same extent as its predecessor could have, amounts set aside to pay certain indebtedness (¶ 3404(a)) [Sec. 381(c)(15); 1.381(c)(15)-1].

Obligations of predecessor. The successor may deduct amounts that arise out of an obligation of the predecessor paid or accrued by the successor after the date of transfer, if: (1) the obligation is assumed by the successor; (2) the obligation gives rise to a liability after the date of transfer; (3) the liability, if paid or accrued by the predecessor after that date, would have been deductible by it; (4) the obligation was not reflected in the consideration transferred by the successor for the property [Sec. 381(c)(16); 1.381(c)(16)-1].

Deficiency dividend of personal holding company. If the successor pays a personal holding company deficiency dividend of its predecessor, it is entitled to the deficiency dividend deduction [Sec. 381(c)(17); 1.381(c)(17)]. See ¶ 3404(b).

Percentage depletion on ore extraction from prior mining residue. The successor can claim percentage depletion on prior mining residue acquired from the predecessor [Sec. 381(c)(18); 1.381(c)(18)-1].

Charitable contributions over prior years' limitation. If the predecessor corporation has a charitable contribution carryover on the date of the transfer, the successor corporation can use the carryover (within the 5% limit [¶ 3118]) only in tax years beginning after that date that are not more than 5 tax years after the year the excess contribution was made [Sec. 381(c)(19); 1.381(c)(19)-1].

Life insurance companies. A successor life insurance company may take into account, under special regulations, certain items of a predecessor life insurance company [Sec. 381(c)(22); 1.381(c)(22)-1, 1.381(d)-1].

Investment credit. The successor corporation stands in the shoes of the predecessor corporation as to carryovers of unused credits and adjustments because of early dispostions [Sec. 381(c)(23); 1.381(c)(23)-1].

Work incentive program credit. The successor can carry over unused WIN credits under rules similar to those of investment credit (above) [Sec. 381(c)(24); 1.381(c)(24)-1].

Deficiency dividend of real estate investment trust. If the successor pays a real estate investment trust deficiency dividend of its predecessor, such predecessor is entitled to the deficiency dividend deduction [Sec. 381(c)(25)]. See ¶ 3432.

Foreign tax credit. The successor may carry over any unused foreign taxes of the predecessor, but the credit is subject to a limitation that includes only post-merger foreign taxable income attributable to the same business that caused the predecessor's foreign tax liability[1] [¶ 3703(b)].

Excess deductions account for farm recapture property. The successor takes into account the precessor's excess deductions account as of the close of the day of distribution or transfer (¶ 2226) [Sec. 1251(b)(5)(A)].

Certain aircraft and vessels. An election to treat rentals from U.S.-built ships and aircraft as U.S. source income [¶ 3712] is binding on the successor corporation [Sec. 861(e)(4)].

¶ **3338 Special limit on net operating loss carryover.** Under certain conditions, a limit is placed on the net operating loss carryover that is available to the acquiring corporation in tax-free reorganizations described in Sec. 381(a) [¶ 3336(a)]. The net operating loss carryover after a substantial change of ownership may be disallowed [¶ 3221].

NOTE: The 1976 Tax Reform Act changed the limitations on net operating loss carryovers, effective for plans of reorganization adopted after 1-1-78. The minimum ownership requirement has been increased to 40%. If the loss company's shareholders get less than 40% and more than 20%, the carryover is reduced by 3½% for each 1% under 40%. The carryover is reduced by 1½% for each 1% below 20%. §382(b) will now apply to stock-for-stock (type B) exchanges and "triangular" reorganizations. "Stock" was redefined to exclude a wider range of preferred stock.[1]

(a) 20% continuity of ownership requirement. The full carryover is allowed only if the stockholders of the loss corporation own at least 20% of the fair market value of the outstanding common stock of the acquiring corporation immediately after the reorganization. The stockholders of the loss corporation must have been stockholders in the loss corporation immediately before the reorganization, and their ownership in the acquiring corporation must result solely from this prior interest [Sec. 382(b); 1.382(b)-1(a)]. The Eighth Circuit has held, however, that the 20% test can be met by a mere transfer of the acquiring corporation's stock to the loss corporation without its actually being distributed to the loss corporation shareholders after the reorganization.[2] If the 20% requirement is not met, the net operating loss carryover is reduced proportionately [see (c) below].

Example 1: Assume XYZ Corp. has a net operating loss carryover to 1977 of $100,000 and assets valued at approximately 4% of the fair market value of ABC Corp.'s outstanding stock. ABC merges into XYZ in a statutory merger on 12-31-75. ABC's stockholders own, as a result of the reorganization, 96% of the fair market value of YXZ's outstanding stock. XYZ's stockholders now own only 4% of the fair market value. The limit would apply to the net operating loss carryover to 1977 because the stockholders of the loss corporation own only a 4% interest in the successor. See also Example 5 following.

Example 2: Assume the same facts as in Example 1 and the additional fact that on 12-30-76 XYZ's stockholders bought one-third of ABC's stock from its stockholders. After the reorganization, XYZ's stockholders would own 4% of XYZ's stock as a result of owning stock of the loss corporation and 32% (⅓ of 96%) as a result of owning stock in ABC Corp. The limit would still apply. The 32% ownership is not the result of owning stock in the loss corporation.

What is stock. "Stock" is defined as "all shares except nonvoting stock that is limited and preferred as to dividends" [Sec. 382(c); 1.382(c)-1]. The expression "common stock" is used instead in this explanation.

The 20% requirement cannot be spread among several corporations. The continuity of ownership requirement applies to the corporation that includes the net operating loss carryover in its net operating loss deduction. Thus, the 20% requirement cannot be watered down by inserting one or more corporate entities between the corporation with the loss and the corporation deducting the loss [Sec. 382(b)].

Example 3: Assume Corporation X with a net worth of $2,000,000 wants to acquire the assets of Corporation Y, a loss corporation, which has a net worth of $100,000. Corporation X also wants the assets of Corporation Z. Trying to avoid the 20% continuity requirement, Corporation X arranges to have Z acquire the assets of Y in a reorganization to which Sec. 381 applies. Immediately after the reorganization, the former stockholders of Y own 20% of the fair

Footnotes appear at end of this Chapter.

¶ **3338**

market value of the outstanding common stock of Z. Shortly thereafter, X acquires the assets of Z in a reorganization under Sec. 381(a). Immediately after the reorganization the former stockholders of Y own 4% of the fair market value of the outstanding common stock of X and the limit applies.

Holdings of parties count towards the 20% requirement. If a corporate stockholder of the loss corporation is also a party to the tax-free reorganization, it will be considered to own a percentage of the common stock in the acquiring corporation in determining the percentage of continuous ownership [Sec. 382(b)(5); 1.382(b)-1(f)]. The corporate ownership counts even if the corporate stockholder disappears in the reorganization or becomes the acquiring corporation, thereby not owning common stock in the acquiring corporation immediately after the reorganization.

When limit does not apply. The limit on loss carryover does not apply if the transferor and acquiring corporations are owned substantially by the same persons in the same proportion[3] [Sec. 382(b)(3); 1.382(b)-1(d)].

(b) How to figure continued ownership. The percentage owned by the corporate stockholder in the acquiring corporation bears the same ratio to the percentage of common stock of the loss corporation owned immediately before reorganization as the value of the total outstanding common stock of the loss corporation immediately before the reorganization bears to the total value of outstanding common stock of the acquiring corporation immediately after the reorganization [Sec. 382(b)(5); 1.382(b)-1(f)].

> **Example 4:** X Corp. owns 6% of stock of Y Corp., a loss corporation. Fair market value of Y's outstanding stock is $3,000,000. X acquires Y in a tax-free reorganization. Immediately after reorganization, the fair market vaue of the outstanding stock of X Corp. is $8,000,000.
>
> x equals percentage of X corp. owned by itself after the reorganization
> $x: 6\% :: \$3,000,000 : \$8,000,000$
> $8x$ equals 18%
> x equals $2\frac{1}{4}\%$

Stockholders of a loss corporation who own common stock of a corporation controlling the acquiring corporation may treat the stock as if it were an equivalent amount (measured by value) of stock of the acquiring corporation in figuring the 20% continuity of ownership [Sec. 382(b)(6); 1.382(b)-1(g)].

(c) How to figure the limit. The reduction in the net operating loss carryover to the first tax year ending after the date of transfer of assets is figured as follows:

1. Multiply by 5 the percent of the fair market value of the outstanding common stock of the acquiring corporation that is owned by the stockholders of the loss corporation immediately after reorganization.
2. Subtract the percentage obtained in 1. from 100%.
3. The result is the percentage of reduction that must be applied to the net operating loss carryover [Sec. 382(b)(2); 1.382(b)-1(b)].

> **Example 5:** Assume the same facts as in Example 1. The carryover would be limited to $20,000, figured this way: $5 \times 4\% = 20\%$; $100\% - 20\% = 80\%$; 80% of $100,000 = $80,000, the reduction.

If the net operating loss carryover is not completely absorbed in the year the limit applies, the reduction is applied against the oldest net operating loss first, and then, against later net operating losses in order[4] [Sec. 382(b)(4); 1.382(b)-1(e); 1.383-1—1.383-3]. Any deferred minimum tax liability due to a net operating loss carryover reduces the net operating loss proportionately [Prop. Reg. Sec. 1.382(b)-1(h)].

¶ 3339 **Limits on carryovers of unused credits and capital losses.** Similar rules for disallowance or reduction of net operating loss carryovers for changes in ownership [¶ 3221; 3338] also apply to carryovers of capital losses and foreign tax credits, unused investment credits and unused work incentive program credits. The limitations apply to acquisitions occurring after 12-10-71 under contracts entered into after 9-28-71 [Sec. 383; 1.381(a)-1(a), 1.383-1—1.383-3]. In addition, to carry over unused foreign tax credit, the overall limitation [¶ 3703] must also be applied [Sec. 1.383-3(b)].

Footnotes to Chapter 23

(P-H "FEDERAL TAXES" related references are cited in brackets [ ] at the end of each footnote below.)

Footnote ¶ 3300 [¶ 18,321].
(1) A record of reorganizations of individual companies, with treatment for tax purposes of the exchanges of securities in the hands of the security holders under such reorganizations, will be found in the P-H Capital Adjustments Service.
(2) Girard Trust Co. (Moore) v. U.S., 166 F.2d 773, 36 AFTR 852 [¶ 18,348(5)].

Footnote ¶ 3301 [¶ 18,321].
(1) Rev. Rul. 72-206, 1972-1 CB 104 [¶ 18,348(15), (70)].
(2) Pinellas Ice and Cold Storage Co. v. Comm., 287 US 462, 11 AFTR 1112 [¶ 18,022(15)].
(3) Burnham, 86 F.2d 776, 18 AFTR 669, cert. den. [¶ 18,022(15)].

Footnote ¶ 3302 [¶ 18,321 et seq.].
(1) Gregory v. Helvering, 293 US 465, 55 SCt 266, 14 AFTR 1191; Wilson v. Comm., 16 AFTR 2d 6030, 353 F.2d 184 [¶ 18,133(25); 41,015].
(2) Rev. Rul. 63-29, 1963-1 CB 77 [¶ 18,352(5)].

Footnote ¶ 3303 [¶ 18,321 et seq.].
(1) Southwest Natural Gas Co. v. Comm., 189 F.2d 332, 40 AFTR 686 [¶ 18,350(5)].

Footnote ¶ 3304 [¶ 18,321 et seq.].
(1) Turnbow v. Comm., 8 AFTR 2d 5967, aff'g 286 F.2d 669; Rev. Rul. 70-65, 1970-1 CB 77 [¶ 18,335(5), (52)].
(2) Mills v. Comm., 13 AFTR 2d 1386, 331 F.2d 321; Rev. Rul. 66-365, 1966-2 CB 116 [¶ 18,335(10)].
(3) Rev. Rul. 66-112, 1966-1 CB 68 [¶ 18,335(12)].
(4) Rev. Rul. 69-142, 1969-1 CB 107; Rev. Rul. 70-41, 1970-1 CB 77 [¶ 18,335(42), (53)].
(5) Rev. Rul. 70-108, 1970-1 CB 78 [¶ 18,335(7)].

Footnote ¶ 3305 [¶ 18,321 et seq.].
(1) Rev. Rul. 66-365, 1966-2 CB 116 [¶ 18,335(10)].
(2) Civic Center Finance Co. v. Kuhl, 177 F.2d 706, 38 AFTR 835 [¶ 18,350(35)].

Footnote ¶ 3305 continued
(3) Rev. Proc. 74-26, 1974-2 CB 478; Rev. Proc. 76-26, IRB 1976-28 [¶ 18,336(50)].
(4) Daily Telegram Co., 34 BTA 101 [¶ 18,336(50)].
(5) Rev. Rul. 57-518, 1957-2 CB 253 [¶ 18,336(50)].
(6) Nat. Bk. of Commerce of Norfolk v. U.S., 1 AFTR 2d 894, 158 F. Supp. 87 [¶ 18,336(50)].
(7) Schuh Trading Co., 95 F.2d 404, 20 AFTR 1114 [¶ 18,336(50)].
(8) American Foundation Co., 120 F.2d 807, 27 AFTR 524 [¶ 18,336(50)].
(9) Gross v. Comm., 88 F.2d 567, 19 AFTR 158 [¶ 18,336(50)].
(10) Rev. Rul. 64-73, 1964-1 CB 142 [¶ 18,348(25)].

Footnote ¶ 3306 [¶ 18,321 et seq.].

Footnote ¶ 3307 [¶ 18,321 et seq.].
(1) Rev. Rul. 69-34, 1969-1 CB 105 [¶ 18,339(100)].
(2) Neustadt, 43 BTA 848, aff'd. 131 F.2d 528, 30 AFTR 320 [¶ 18,339(10)].
(3) Stauffer v. Comm., 22 AFTR 2d 5571, 403 F.2d 611; Associated Machine v. Comm., 22 AFTR 2d 5780, 403 F.2d 622; Davant v. Comm., 18 AFTR 2d 5523, 366 F.2d 874; Home Construction Corp. v. U.S., 27 AFTR 2d 71-837; Performance Systems, Inc. v. U.S., 34 AFTR 2d 74-5582; Rev. Rul. 75-561, 1975-2 CB 129 [¶ 18,340(40), (45)].

Footnote ¶ 3309 [¶ 18,100 et seq.; 18,231 et seq.].
(1) Rev. Proc. 77-5, (IR 1734), IRB 1977-5 [¶ 55,173].

Footnote ¶ 3311 [¶ 18,156 et seq.; 18,242].
(1) Rev. Rul. 68-23, 1968-1 CB 144 [¶ 18,167(30)].

Footnote ¶ 3312 [¶ 18,156 et seq.; 18,179(10), (15)].
(1) Comm. v. Bedford's Est., 325 US 283, 33 AFTR 832 [¶ 18,179(5)].

Footnote ¶ 3313 [¶ 18,206 et seq.].

Footnote ¶ 3314 [¶ 18,251 et seq.].

Footnote ¶ 3315 [¶ 18,186; 18,206].
(1) Rev. Rul. 68-629, 1968-2 CB 154 [¶ 18,200(20)].

Chapter 23—Footnotes

Footnote ¶ 3316 [¶ 18,121 et seq.].

Footnote ¶ 3317 [¶ 18,121].
(1) Rev. Proc. 77-5, (IR 1734), IRB 1977-5 [¶ 55,173].
(2) Rev. Rul. 64-102, 1964-1 CB (Pt. 1) 136 [¶ 18,133(20)].
(3) Comm. v. Gordon, 21 AFTR 2d 1329, 391 US 83 [¶ 18,130(15)].

Footnote ¶ 3318 [¶ 18,136].
(1) Comm. v. Morris, 18 AFTR 2d 5843, 367 F.2d 794; Curtis v. U.S., 14 AFTR 2d 5685, 336 F.2d 714 [¶ 18,136(30)].
(2) Rev. Rul. 59-400, 1959-2 CB 114 [¶ 18,133(10)].
(3) U.S. v. W. W. Marett, 12 AFTR 2d 5900, 325 F.2d 28; Comm. v. Coady, 7 AFTR 2d 1322, 289 F.2d 490; Rev. Rul. 64-147, 1964-1 (Pt. 1) CB 136; Rev. Rul. 75-160, 1975-1 CB 112 [¶ 18,136(5)].

Footnote ¶ 3319 [¶ 18,156].

Footnote ¶ 3320 [¶ 18,206 et seq.].

Footnote ¶ 3330 [¶ 31,851; 31,881; 31,925].

Footnote ¶ 3331 [¶ 18,401 et seq.].

Footnote ¶ 3332 [¶ 18,401 et seq.].

Footnote ¶ 3334 [¶ 17,611—17,630].
(1) Rev. Rul. 69-379, 1969-2 CB 48 [¶ 17,627(15)].
(2) Rev. Rul. 71-326, 1971-2 CB 177 [¶ 17,627(22)].

Footnote ¶ 3334 continued
(3) Rev. Proc. 73-17, 1973-2 CB 465 [¶ 17,627(50)].
(4) Rev. Proc. 77-5, (IR 1734), IRB 1977-5 [¶ 55,173].
(5) Rev. Rul. 259, 1953-2 CB 55; Rev. Rul. 59-296, 1959-2 CB 87; Rev. Rul. 70-489, 1970-2 CB 53 [¶ 17,630(5)].
(6) Rev. Rul. 69-426, 1969-2 CB 48 [¶ 17,685.15(5)].
(7) American Potash & Chemical Corp. v. U.S., 22 AFTR 2d 5161, 399 F.2d 194 [¶ 17,685.5(10)].

Footnote ¶ 3335 [¶ 17,646 et seq.].

Footnote ¶ 3336 [¶ 18,501 et seq.].
(1) Dunlap and Associates, Inc., 47 TC 542 [¶ 18,340(20)].
(2) Rev. Rul. 70-27, 1970-1 CB 83 [¶ 18,612(10)].
(3) The Aetna Cas. & Surety Co., 39 AFTR 2d 77-400 [¶ 77,328].

Footnote ¶ 3337 [¶ 18,502].
(1) Rev. Rul. 68-350, 1968-2 CB 159 [¶ 30551(5)].

Footnote ¶ 3338 [¶ 18,501 et seq.].
(1) P.L. 94-455, Sec. 806.
(2) World Service Life Ins. Co. v. U.S., 31 AFTR 2d 73-594, 471 F.2d 247 [¶ 18,593(5)].
(3) Commonwealth Container Corp., 48 TC 483 [¶ 18,593(5)].
(4) Senate Report No. 1635, p. 286, 83rd Cong., 2nd Sess.

Footnote ¶ 3339 [¶ 18,501 et seq.].

Highlights of Chapter 23
Corporations—Reorganizations

I. **Reorganizations**
   A. **Corporate reorganizations in general [¶ 3300]:**
      1. A reorganization is a readjustment of structure or ownership, which occurs when:
         a. Two or more corporations combine (Type A).
         b. Corporation acquires stock of another corporation in exchange for voting stock (Type B).
         c. Corporation acquires substantially all property of another corporation in exchange for voting stock (Type C).
         d. Corporation transfers assets to another corporation in exchange for control (Type D).
         e. Corporation is recapitalized (Type E).
         f. Corporation changes identity, form or place of organization (Type F).
      2. Generally in a reorganization, gain or loss on exchanges is deferred or limited until stock, securities, or property received in exchange is disposed of.
   B. **A party to a reorganization includes [¶ 3301]:**
      1. A corporation resulting from reorganization.
      2. Both corporations in reorganization resulting from acquisition by one corp. of stock, securities or property of the other:
         a. "Securities" are bonds and debentures, not short-term notes.
         b. Controlling parent corp. whose stock is used by subsidiary is party to reorganization.
         c. Parent corp. is still party to reorganization even if it immediately transfers acquired assets to subsidiary.
   C. **Basic requirements for reorganizations [¶ 3302]:**
      1. Must be pursuant to plan.
      2. Must have business purpose other than tax avoidance.
      3. Except for Type D reorganization, shareholder must maintain continuity of interest in new or successor corporation.
      4. Business enterprise must be continued, but different activities can be carried on.
II. **Types of Reorganizations**
   A. **Statutory merger or consolidation (Type A) [¶ 3303]:**
      1. A merger is absorption of one corp. into another.
      2. A consolidation occurs when 2 or more corporations transfer their properties to a third and then dissolve; shareholders receive stock of new corp.
      3. Under certain circumstances, a Type A reorganization results where subsidiary uses parent's stock to acquire substantially all properties of corporation which merges with subsidiary.
   B. **Acquiring another corporation's stock (Type B) [¶ 3304]:**
      1. Type B reorganization results where:
         a. Corporation exchanges its voting stock or its parent's for stock of another, and
         b. Acquiring corporation has control of acquired corporation after the exchange (control may be obtained in series of transactions over short period).
      2. To have control, acquiring corporation must obtain 80% of voting power and at least 80% of all other classes of stock.
      3. In 1. a. (above) acquiring corp. cannot give anything else except its own or parent's stock.

C. **Acquiring another corporation's property (Type C) [¶ 3305]:**
1. A Type C reorganization results where corporation exchanges any of its voting stock for substantially all the property (90% of fair market value of net assets and 70% of fair market value of gross assets) of the second corporation.
2. If acquiring corporation gets 80% of value of property for voting stock, it can add cash and other consideration.
3. Acquiring corporation may assume acquired corporation's liabilities or take property subject to liability.

D. **Transfer of assets to another corporation (Type D) [¶ 3306]:**
1. A transfer by a corporation of some or all of its assets to a second corporation is a reorganization if [¶ 3306]:
   a. Immediately after transfer, transferor corporation and/or any of its shareholders have 80% control of transferee corporation, and
   b. Stocks and securities received from transferee corporation are distributed to the transferor's shareholders together with its remaining properties.
2. To have control, 80% of voting stock and 80% of all other classes of stock must be owned.

E. **Recapitalization (Type E) [¶ 3307(a)].** This occurs where:
1. There is a change in capital structure under an arrangement by which stocks and bonds of a single corporation are readjusted as to amount, income or priority, or
2. An agreement is reached between the stockholders and creditors to increase or decrease the capitalization or debts of the corporation.

F. **Change in identity, form, etc. (Type F) [¶ 3307(b)].** This occurs where:
1. A corporation changes its name and issues new stock certificates.
2. A corporation reincorporates in a different state.
3. A corporation changes its charter.

III. **Gain or Loss on Exchanges**
   A. **Recognition of gain or loss [¶ 3309-3310]:**
   1. Generally, no gain or loss is recognized on exchanges by shareholders, corporate as well as individuals, of stocks and securities held in corporation that is a party to reorganization.
   2. If securities received are greater in principal amount than principal amount of securities given up, the fair market value of the excess is taxable as boot.
   3. If property is given in exchange (other than stock or securities), gain or loss on such property is recognized when value received for it is more or less than its adjusted basis.

   B. **Corporation exchanging property for stock or securities [¶ 3309(b)]:**
   1. The transferor corporation that exchanges property solely for stock or securities in another party to the reorganization does not recognize gain or loss.
   2. Property received (boot), other than stock or securities, may be taxable to the transferor corporation, unless it is distributed to its shareholders pursuant to the reorganization plan.
   3. Assumption of corporation's liabilities will not be taxable to it as boot unless there is tax avoidance, or no real business purpose.

   C. **Corporation exchanging its own stock or securities [¶ 3309(c)]** for property generally has no recognized gain or loss.

   D. **Treatment of boot [¶ 3311-3312]:**
   1. No loss is recognized.
   2. Transferor corp. has recognized gain up to value of undistributed boot.
   3. Gain to shareholders is recognized only to extent of boot received.
   4. If boot received has effect of dividend, stockholder treats recognized gain as dividend to extent of his share of corporation's earnings and profits; remainder gain is capital.
   5. If shareholder exchanges Sec. 306 stock for boot, value of boot is taxed as dividend.

IV. **Basis**

A. **Basis to distributee-stockholder** of stock or securities received in tax-free reorganization is same as basis of stock or securities given up, with adjustments [¶ 3313]:
   1. This basis is decreased by:
      a. Any money received.
      b. The fair market value of any other property received.
      c. Any loss that was recognized.
   2. Basis is increased by any gain recognized on the exchange.
   3. Basis of other property received (boot) is its fair market value.
   4. When several kinds of stock or securities are received, the basis must be allocated among them in proportion to relative fair market values.
B. **Basis to corporation** [¶ 3314]:
   1. Basis of property acquired in reorganization is same as it was in transferor corp.'s hands, increased by gain recognized to transferor on transfer.
   2. The carryover basis also applies to stocks or securities received, if the transferee exchanged its (or its parent's) stocks or securities as all or part of the consideration. Otherwise, the same substituted basis that applied to stock or securities in the hands of distributee-shareholders (see A, above), applies to corporations.
C. **Liabilities assumed.** If the transferor's liabilities are assumed as part of the consideration [¶ 3315]:
   1. The assumption is generally not considered boot, unless there was tax avoidance motivation or the assumption had no business purpose.
   2. The basis of property received by the transferor in the exchange is decreased by the amount of liability assumed.
   3. In a Type D reorganization, if liabilities exceed the adjusted basis of property transferred, excess is taxable as capital or ordinary gain depending on nature of property.

V. **Divisive Reorganizations**
   A. Through "divisive reorganizations" corporations may dispose of a substantial part of assets without paying tax on distribution of the sales proceeds, and shareholders may receive distributions without paying any tax [¶ 3316].
   B. **Types of divisive reorganizations** [¶ 3316(a)]:
      1. A *split-up* occurs where business of old corporation is split-up into two or more new corporations. New corporations' stock is distributed to shareholders of the old corporation who surrender their old corporation stock back to old corporation. Old corporation then dissolves.
      2. A *split-off* occurs where a corporation transfers part of assets to new corporation for new corporation's stock. The corporation distributes the new stock to its shareholders who surrender part of their stock in the corporation.
      3. A *spin-off* is the same as a split-off except that there is no surrender of the shares in the corporation.
   C. **Stock or securities received tax-free** [¶ 3317]:
      1. Within certain limitations shareholders have no recognized gain or loss where they receive only stock or securities:
         a. On account of stock they own.
         b. In exchange for their securities.
      2. Gain is recognized to the extent of boot received.
      3. The shareholders or security holders have no recognized gain or loss where following requirements are met:
         a. Distribution to shareholder must be for his stock, while distribution to security holder must be in exchange for his securities.
         b. Only stock or securities of a controlled corporation is distributed (any boot is taxable).
         c. Distribution must not be used as device for distributing earnings and profits of corporations involved.
         d. Both corporations must have actively conducted business for five years.
         e. All stock or securities of controlled corporation held immediately before distribution or an amount of stock constituting control, must be distributed.

4. Gain or loss not recognized if requirements in (3) above are met, even if distribution is not in proportion to shareholdings, shareholder does not surrender stock in distribution corp., and distribution is not made pursuant to plan of reorganization.
5. Only principal amount of securities surrendered for securities received is tax free; excess of securities received over securities surrendered is taxable.
6. Distribution of controlled corp. stock acquired within 5 years, is taxable.

F. **Active business requirements [¶ 3318]:**
1. Right after distribution, distributing corporation and the controlled corporation(s) must be engaged in a trade or business that meets both of the following requirements [¶ 3318]:
   a. Trade or business must have been actively conducted throughout 5-year period ending on date of distribution.
   b. Trade or business must have been acquired either:
      1) More than 5 years before the distribution date, or
      2) In a transaction in which no gain or loss was recognized.
2. The 5-year rule is not met if large part of earnings of "spun-off" business is used to finance purchases of retained business during 5-year period.

G. **If distributee-shareholder receives boot [¶ 3319]:**
1. Gain is recognized up to the value of the boot received.
2. No loss is recognized.
3. Part of the gain may be taxable as a dividend.
4. In a spin-off, boot is treated as a dividend or return of capital.
5. Value of boot received in exchange for Sec. 306 stock is dividend.

H. **Basis to distributee-shareholder [¶ 3320]:**
1. Apply the basis rules in IV, A (above) generally.
2. When no stock is surrendered, basis of old and new stock is determined by allocating basis of original stock according to relative values.
3. If stock is surrendered for more than one class of stock of controlled corp., basis is allocated among different classes of stock received.

VI. **Special Types of Reorganizations**
A. **Transactions under orders of Federal agencies.** Recognition of gain or loss is postponed when certain holding companies are ordered to distribute or exchange a part of their holdings [¶ 3330].
B. **Reorganization of insolvent corporation.** No gain or loss is recognized in certain insolvency reorganizations on transfers of property by corporations and on exchanges by security holders [¶ 3331].
C. **Railroad reorganizations** result in nonrecognition of gain or loss under special rules [¶ 3331(a); 3332].

VII. **Liquidations**
A. **Nontaxable liquidation of subsidiary [¶ 3334]:**
1. No gain or loss is recognized to a parent corporation that receives property (including money) in complete liquidation of a subsidiary if:
   a. Parent owns at least 80% of the voting stock, and at least 80% of all other classes of stock, except non-voting limited preferred, and
   b. Distribution is in complete cancellation or redemption of the subsidiary's stock, and
   c. Transfer of subsidiary's property takes place within the tax year liquidation plan is adopted, or in the case of a series of distributions, within 3 years from the close of the tax year in which first distribution made.
2. Subsidiary's transfer to pay debt will not result in recognition of gain or loss to subsidiary, but gain or loss may be recognized to parent.
3. Parent's basis of property received:
   a. Generally same as subsidiary's basis.
   b. Same as basis of its subsidiary stock, if liquidation plan is adopted within 2 years parent bought control of subsidiary.

B. **One month liquidations [¶ 3335]:**
  1. Relief provision permits qualified electing shareholders to receive property in a liquidation without being taxed on the increase in the property's value:
     a. Basis of property received is same as basis in shareholder's stock cancelled or redeemed.
        1) Decreased by money received, and
        2) Increased by gain recognized.
     b. When shareholder sells the property this basis is used in determining gain or loss.
  2. Liquidation qualifies for tax-free treatment only if:
     a. Liquidation plan is adopted.
     b. All the stock is cancelled or redeemed by distribution.
     c. Transfer of all property takes place in 1 month.
     d. Within 30 days after adoption, shareholders file election accepting plan; corp. must file information return.
  3. Qualified shareholders:
     a. Corporations holding 50% or more of stock entitled to vote on adoption of liquidation plan do not qualify for relief.
     b. Corporate or noncorporate shareholders (whether or not their stock is entitled to vote on the issue of the adoption of liquidation plan) qualify if:
        1) Written election has been properly filed, and
        2) Like elections have been made and filed by owners of stock possessing at least 80% of the total combined voting power of all classes of stock entitled to vote upon adoption of plan owned by shareholders of same group.
  4. Limited gain may be recognized: gain on each share of stock surrendered is limited to the greater of:
     a. Shareholder's ratable share of earnings and profits accumulated after February 28, 1913, or
     b. Money or market value of stock or securities received that were acquired by corporation after 1953.

VIII. **Carryovers.**
  A. **Carryovers to successor corporations [¶ 3336]:**
    1. Under following conditions, a corporation which acquires assets of predecessor corporation inherits various tax benefits, elective rights and obligations:
       a. When a controlling parent liquidates its subsidiary in a transaction in which the parent takes the subsidiary's basis in the property acquired.
       b. Following a Type A, Typce C, Type F or a non-divisive Type D reorganization.
    2. Except in the case of a Type F reorganization, the tax year of the predecessor corporation ends, and the tax attributes are carried over, on the date the assets are transferred to the successor corporation.
    3. Except for Type F reorganization, a successor may not carry back:
       a. A net capital loss sustained in a tax year starting after 1969.
       b. Net operating loss incurred in a tax year ending after date of transfer.
  B. **Checklist of carryover items.** Among the more important carryover items are [¶ 3337]:
    1. Net operating loss, subject to special limitations.
    2. Earnings and profits.
    3. Capital loss carryover.
  C. **Limit on net operating loss carryover to acquiring corporation in tax-free reorganization [¶ 3338]:**
    1. Full carryover is allowed if stockholders of loss corporation own at least 20% of fair market value of outstanding common stock of acquiring corporation immediately after reorganization.
    2. If 20% limit isn's met, the carryover is reduced proportionately.
    3. 20% requirement cannot be spread among several corporations.

4. 20% limit doesn't apply if transferor and acquiring corporation are owned substantially by same persons in same proportion.
5. Percentage of reduction is determined by multiplying percent of outstanding stock of acquiring corporation owned by stockholders of loss corporation by 5, and subtracting the product from 100.

D. **Limits on carryovers of unused credits and capital losses [¶ 3339]:**
1. Rules similar to those on NOL's apply to carryovers of capital losses and foreign tax credits, unused investment credits and unused WIN credits.

Chapter 24

CORPORATIONS—PERSONAL HOLDING COMPANIES, ETC.—EXEMPT ORGANIZATONS

TABLE OF CONTENTS

PERSONAL HOLDING COMPANIES

	¶
The personal holding company tax	3400
The personal holding company income requirement	3401
The stock ownership requirement	3402
Corporations exempt from the tax	3403
Income subject to the tax	3404
Undistributed personal holding company income	
Dividends paid deduction	
Foreign corporations	
Rate of tax, returns and payment	3405
Figuring the tax—illustration	3406
Deficiency dividend	3407
Disallowed losses	3408
Consolidated returns	3409

SHAREHOLDERS IN FOREIGN PERSONAL HOLDING COMPANIES

	¶
Tax on undistributed foreign personal holding company income	3411
What is a foreign personal holding company	3412
What is undistributed personal holding company income	3413
Corporation income taxed to United States shareholders	3414
Exempt corporations	3415
Returns	3416

REGULATED INVESTMENT COMPANIES

	¶
Tax on regulated investment companies	3428
Requirements for being taxed as a regulated investment company	3429
"Venture capital" companies	3430
Figuring the tax	3431
Capital gain dividends	
Exempt-interest dividend	
Foreign tax credit allowed to shareholders	
Shareholders' dividends received exclusion or deduction	
Dividends declared after close of tax year	
Tax preference items for minimum tax	

	¶
Real estate investment trusts	3432
General requirements	
Gross income requirement	
Diversification of income	
Distribution of income	
Net operating loss carryover	
Records and information required	
Tax preference items for minimum tax	

BANKS AND TRUST COMPANIES

	¶
Tax on banks and trust companies	3433
Special rules for all banks and trust companies	
Special rules for mutual banks and loan associations	

INSURANCE COMPANIES

	¶
Tax on insurance companies	3434
Life insurance companies	
Insurance companies other than life or mutual	
Mutual insurance companies other than life, marine or fire	
Foreign insurance companies	

EXEMPT ORGANIZATIONS

	¶
Exempt organizations in general	3435
Types of exempt organizations	3436
Feeder organizations	
Application for exemption	
Disallowed losses	
Loss of exemption	
Private foundations defined	3437
Notification of status	
Tax on termination of private foundation status	
Tax on investment income	3438
Prohibited acts of private foundations	3439
Tax on self-dealing	3440
Tax on undistributed income	3441
Tax on excess business holdings	3442
Tax on speculative investments	3443
Tax on improper expenditures	3444
Unrelated business income tax in general	3445

Footnotes appear at end of this Chapter.

Chapter 24—Personal Holding Companies

Exempt organizations subject to tax on unrelated business income .. 3446	Taxable organizations Returns
What is an unrelated trade or business 3447	Cooperative distributions 3456
Income from unrelated business 3448	Deduction for distributions 3457
Gross income	Farmers' cooperatives
Exclusions from gross income	Tax reduction for redemption of unqualified scrip or certificates
Deductions from gross income	
Special rules	Patrons' income from cooperative 3458
Unrelated debt-financed income 3449	Ordinary income
General rule	Excluded patronage dividends
Debt-financed property	
Acquisition indebtedness	
Exempt trusts 3450	**SMALL BUSINESS INVESTMENT COMPANIES**
Business income tax of exempt trusts 3451	
Trusts claiming charitable deductions 3452	Special treatment for small business investment companies 3459
Nonexempt trusts with charitable interests treated as private foundations 3453	
	DOMESTIC INTERNATIONAL SALES CORPORATIONS (DISC)
Unrelated business income tax rates, returns and payments 3454	Tax deferral for export sales profits .. 3460
COOPERATIVE ORGANIZATIONS	
Taxing cooperatives 3455	• Highlights of Chapter 24 .... Page 3461

PERSONAL HOLDING COMPANIES

¶ 3400   The personal holding company tax is aimed at closely-held corporations with income mainly from investments.

Example: Giles, in the 68% bracket, transfers his income-producing property to Argo Co. in return for all of Argo's stock. The income is taxed at corporate rates (up to 48% maximum), and is accumulated for several years. Giles then liquidates Argo, and receives the accumulated income at capital gains rates. If Argo is liquidated by his heirs after Giles dies the accumulation would escape the individual income tax.

To prevent this, a high surtax [¶ 3405] is imposed on undistributed earnings [¶ 3404] of personal holding companies in addition to the normal tax and surtax on corporate taxable income [Chapter 21].

Background and purpose. The purpose of the personal holding company tax is to prevent tax avoidance because of the difference between rates of tax on corporations and individuals.

Minimum tax. Like other corporations, personal holding companies pay a minimum tax on their tax preferences [¶ 3103]. However, unlike other corporations (except Subchapter S corporations [¶ 3140]), personal holding companies treat accelerated depreciation on leased personal property [¶ 2403(a)] as a tax preference [Sec. 57(a); Prop. Regs. 1.57-0, 1.57-1(c)(8), 1.57-2(a)].

What is a personal holding company. A corporation is a personal holding company only if: (1) its income is mainly "personal holding company income" [¶ 3401]; *and* (2) five, or less, individuals own more than 50% of its stock [¶ 3402]. The tests are applied each year to the situation as it exists that year. Thus, the classification may change from year to year.

¶ 3401   The personal holding company income requirement. A corporation becomes a personal holding company only when 60% or more of its adjusted ordinary gross income for the tax year is personal holding company income [Sec.

542(a)(1)]. To find adjusted ordinary gross income, first reduce gross income by capital gains and Sec. 1231 gains. This is ordinary gross income. Then reduce ordinary gross income by the amount of: *leasing income* (rents, etc.) received for the use of tangible personal property manufactured by the corporation as a substantial activity during the tax year; *interest* on judgments, tax refunds, condemnation awards and U.S. obligations held for sale by a dealer; *rents* to the extent of related deductions for property taxes, interest, rent incurred and depreciation (except depreciation on tangible personal property not customarily leased to any one lessee for more than 3 years); *mineral, oil, and gas royalties* and income from working interests to the extent of related deductions for depletion, property and severance taxes, interest and rent incurred [Sec. 543(b); Prop. Reg. 1.543-12(b),(c)]. Rents and royalties not eliminated are the adjusted amounts included in personal holding company income.

Personal holding company income is income from the items below. Any income disregarded to find adjusted ordinary gross income also is excluded from personal holding company income [Sec. 543(a); Prop. Reg. 1.543-3—1.543-11]:

(a) Dividends, interest, royalties, and annuities. Royalties are those other than mineral, oil, gas, and copyright royalties.

(b) Rent adjusted for the use of, or the right to use, corporate property. Adjusted rents are not personal holding company income if they are at least 50% of adjusted ordinary gross income, and any other personal holding company income that exceeds 10% of ordinary gross income is paid out in dividends.

(c) Adjusted mineral, oil and gas royalties. They are not personal holding company income if: (1) they are at least 50% of adjusted ordinary gross income; (2) trade or business deductions (except for compensation paid to shareholders) are at least 15% of adjusted ordinary gross income; and (3) other personal holding company income is 10% or less of ordinary gross income.

(d) Copyright royalties. Copyright royalties include film rents (except produced film rents). Produced film rents (payments received because the corporation held an interest in the film before it was substantially completed) are not counted if they are at least 50% of ordinary gross income.

(e) Payments for the use of tangible corporate property by a shareholder who owns, directly or indirectly, 25% or more in value of the outstanding stock at any time during the tax year. However, it applies only when the corporation has other personal holding company income for the tax year in excess of 10% of its ordinary gross income. Rules for determining stock ownership are at ¶ 3402.

(f) Payments under personal service contracts, if the individual who is to perform the services is named in the contract or can be designated by someone other than the corporation, and directly or indirectly, owns 25% or more in value of the outstanding corporate stock at any time during the tax year.[1] Rules for determining stock ownership are at ¶ 3402.

(g) Taxable income from estates and trusts [¶ 3003 et seq.] is personal holding company income.

¶ 3402 The stock ownership requirement. Even if the corporation meets the income test [¶ 3401], it is not classed as a personal holding company unless more than 50% in value of its outstanding stock is owned, directly or indirectly, by 5 or

Footnotes appear at end of this Chapter.

¶ 3402

less individuals any time during the last half of the tax year. In applying this rule, certain charitable foundations and trusts are considered to be individuals [Sec. 542(a)(2); 1.542-3].

The following rules determine whether a corporation meets the stock ownership requirement and whether amounts received under personal service contracts, compensation for use of property, and copyright royalties are personal holding company income (¶ 3401) [Sec. 544; 1.544-1—1.544-7]:

(1) Stock not owned by individual. Stock owned, directly or indirectly, by or for a corporation, partnership, estate, or trust is considered owned proportionately by its shareholders, partners, or beneficiaries.

(2) Family and partnership ownership. An individual is considered as owning the stock owned, directly or indirectly, by or for his family or his partner. His family includes only brothers and sisters (whole or half-blood), spouse, ancestors, and lineal descendants.

(3) Options. If a person has an option to acquire stock, he is considered the owner of it. This applies to an option to acquire an option, and each one of a series of options. The option rule takes precedence over the family and partnership rules.

(4) Constructive ownership as actual ownership. Stock constructively owned by a person through applying rule (1) or (3) above is treated as actually owned by that person in again applying rule (1) or in applying rule (2) so as to make another the stock's constructive owner. But stock constructively owned by an individual through applying rule (2) is not treated as owned by him in again applying rule (2) to make another the constructive owner of the stock.

(5) Convertible securities. Outstanding securities convertible into stock (whether or not convertible during the tax year) are considered as outstanding stock, but only if including all such securities will make the corporation a personal holding company.

¶ 3403 Corporations exempt from the tax. The following corporations are exempt from personal company tax [Sec. 542(c)]:
- Corporations exempt from the income tax [¶ 3436].
- Banks, domestic building and loan associations, life insurance companies, and surety companies.
- Certain finance and lending companies [Sec. 542(c)(6), (d); Prop. Reg. 1.542-5].
- Foreign personal holding companies [¶ 3411 et seq.], and other foreign corporations with no personal service contract income [¶ 3401] and wholly owned by nonresident alien individuals directly or indirectly (through foreign estates, trusts, partnerships or corporations) during the last half of the tax year [Sec. 542(c)(5), (7)].
- A small business investment company [¶ 3459], unless a shareholder owns a 5% or more proprietary interest in a concern receiving funds from the investment company [Sec. 542(c)(11)].

¶ 3404 Income subject to the tax. The personal holding company tax is a tax on the *undistributed* personal holding company income.

(a) Undistributed personal holding company income is taxable income with certain adjustments minus the dividends paid deduction ((b) below) [Sec. 545(b); 1.545-1]. Here are the rules for the adjustments:
- *Taxes.* The taxpayer can deduct federal income taxes, foreign income and profits taxes not deducted in figuring taxable income, and certain foreign taxes attributable to dividends received by domestic corporations from their foreign subsidiaries which are deemed to have been paid by the domestic corporations

[¶ 3706(b); 3728]. The accumulated earnings tax and the personal holding company tax are *not* deductible [Sec. 545(b)(1); 1.545-2(a)].

• *Charitable contributions.* A deduction for charitable contributions is allowed with the same taxable income limitation as for an individual [¶ 1943], but without any carryover. Taxable income for purposes of the contribution limitation is figured without the charitable contribution deduction [¶ 3118(b)], certain expense and depreciation deductions, special deductions (other than organizational expenditures), any net operating loss or capital loss carryback to the tax year, and the special deduction for Western Hemisphere Trade Corporations [Sec. 545(b)(2); 1.545-2(b)].

• *Expenses and depreciation* allocable to the operation and maintenance of property may not exceed rent received for the use of the property unless: (a) the rent was the highest obtainable, or if none was received, none was obtainable; (b) the property was held in the course of a business carried on in good faith for profit; and (c) it was reasonable to expect that operation of the property would result in a profit, or the property was necessary to the conduct of the business [Sec. 545(b)(6); 1.545-2(h)].

• *Net gains.* A deduction is allowed for the net capital gain, but reduced by the taxes on such net capital gain [Sec. 545(b)(5); 1.545-2(e)]. The reduction is the difference between (1) the tax on the total taxable income and (2) the tax on the taxable income excluding the net capital gain.

• *Net operating loss* deduction is not allowed; but a deduction is allowed for the net operating loss of the preceding year figured without the special deductions (except organizational expenditures) [Sec. 545(b)(4); 1.545-2(d)].

• *Retirement of other debt.* Reasonable amounts used, or irrevocably set aside, to pay or retire a debt incurred between 1-1-34 and 1-1-64, or indebtedness incurred after 1963 to retire such debt may be subtracted under certain conditions [Sec. 545(c)(2), (4); 1.545-3(c), (e)].

• *Dividends received* deduction is not allowed [Sec. 545(b)(3); 1.545-2(c)].

• *Income for a short period* [¶ 2713] does not have to be annualized [Sec. 546].

After these additions and subtractions are made, the dividends paid deduction then is subtracted to find undistributed personal holding company income [Sec. 545(a); 1.545-1].

(b) Dividends paid deduction. The corporation can subtract (1) dividends paid during the year, (2) consent dividends, (3) the dividend carryover, and (4) certain dividends paid after the close of the tax year. The figure arrived at is the "undistributed personal holding company income," which is the basis of the tax [Sec. 561; 1.561-1, 1.561-2].

Dividends paid during the tax year. Only taxable dividends can be subtracted. Thus, cash dividends must be paid out of earnings or profits of the tax year, or accumulated after 2-28-13 [Sec. 562; 1.562-1(a)]. However, any distribution to the extent of the undistributed personal holding company income is considered a taxable dividend, even if it is not paid out of earnings. Such dividends also are taxable to the stockholders [Sec. 316(b)(2); 1.316-1, 1.563-3]. The reason for this exception is to prevent an inequity when undistributed personal holding company income exceeds earnings, as it could when certain deductions are disallowed.

> NOTE: For a property distribution, the 6th Circuit held Reg. Sec. 1.562-1(a) invalid to the extent it limits the dividends-paid deduction to adjusted basis rather than fair market value.[1]

> **Example 1:** Assume a personal holding company with no accumulated earnings has $5,000 earnings for the tax year. However, its adjusted taxable income is $15,000, due to the

disallowance of $10,000 deductions. To avoid the personal holding company tax, the personal holding company must subtract $15,000 dividends. However, if it could only subtract dividends paid from earnings, the maximum subtracted would be $5,000, leaving an undistributed personal holding company income of $10,000 subject to personal holding company tax. The exception above ("NOTE") permits the subtraction of $15,000 in this case.

Generally, only the part of a liquidating dividend chargeable to earnings and profits accumulated after 2-28-13 may be subtracted. However, distributions of undistributed personal holding company income in a complete liquidation concluded within a 24-month period may be treated as dividends [Sec. 316(b)(2), 562(b)]. The dividend amount cannot be more than the undistributed personal holding company income for the year of distribution. The distributions must be allocated between corporate and noncorporate shareholders, and amounts paid to noncorporate shareholders may not be subtracted unless they are designated as dividend distributions [Sec. 1.316-1(b)(2), 1.562-1(b)(2)].

When a personal holding company files a consolidated return with other members of an affiliated group, and must also file a separate personal holding company schedule, a distribution of a dividend by the company to another member of the group can be subtracted, if it would be a taxable dividend to a recipient not a member of an affiliated group [Sec. 562(d); 1.562-3].

Dividends paid after the close of the tax year (see below) but subtracted in the tax year, may not be again subtracted in the year actually distributed [Sec. 563(b)]. This prevents a duplication of deductions.

The following dividends cannot be subtracted: Any nontaxable dividend, including nontaxable stock dividends and nontaxable stock rights [Sec. 312]; preferential dividends, including a distribution that is not made to all shareholders within the same class of stock in proportion to their shareholdings, or one that violates the dividend preference of any class of stock [Sec. 562(c); 1.562-2].

Consent dividends. The taxpayer can get the dividends paid deduction without impairing its cash position by paying cash dividends that are immediately returned to the corporation in the form of a loan or capital contribution [Sec. 565; 1.565-1—1.565-6]. However, if the consent of the shareholders is obtained it will be presumed that a dividend was paid, and that it was then invested by the shareholders in the corporation without an actual distribution.

> **NOTE:** On the part of the corporation, the consent dividend is considered as paid-in surplus or as a contribution to capital, with a corresponding reduction in its earnings and profits.
>
> On the part of the shareholders, the consent dividend is taxable the same as a cash dividend. Since it is theoretically reinvested by the shareholder, the basis of his stock is correspondingly increased [Sec. 1016(a)(12); 1.1016-5(h)].

Dividend carryover. If dividends exceeded adjusted taxable income in the two years before the tax year, the sum of the excess dividends for each of the two years may be carried over to the tax year. If there is an excess only in the first preceding year, only that amount is carried over. If the excess is in the second preceding year, it is reduced by the excess of taxable income over the dividends paid in the first year. Any balance is then carried over to the tax year [Sec. 564(b); 1.564-1].

Example 2:

	Taxable income adjusted	Dividends paid excluding carryover	Difference
1976	$25,000	$35,000	($10,000)
1975	$40,000	$55,000	($15,000)

The carryover to 1977 is $25,000 ($10,000 plus $15,000).

Example 3:

1976	$25,000	$15,000	$10,000
1975	$35,000	$62,000	($27,000)

The carryover to 1977 is $17,000 ($27,000 less $10,000).

NOTE: "Dividends" referred to above include (a) dividends paid during the tax year, (b) dividends paid before the 15th day of the third month following the close of the tax year and (c) consent dividends. They do not include the dividend carryover to the year [Sec. 564(b)(1)].

Dividends paid after the close of the tax year. A deduction for dividends paid after the close of the tax year and by the 15th of the third month following the close of the tax year can be elected. However, the amount deducted can not exceed (1) the undistributed personal holding company income figured without the deduction for dividends paid after the close of the tax year; or (2) 20% of the dividends paid during the tax year, not including consent dividends or the deduction for dividends paid after the close of the preceding tax year [Sec. 563(b); 1.563-2].

In figuring accumulated earnings tax [¶ 3130 et seq.], dividends paid after the close of the tax year and by the 15th of the third month following the close of the tax year are deductible without election or restriction on the amount [Sec. 563(a); 1.563-1].

(c) Foreign corporations. When 10% or less of the value of the outstanding stock of a foreign corporation subject to the tax is owned by U.S. citizens or residents, domestic corporations, partnerships, estates or trusts during the last half of the tax year, only the same percentage of the corporation's undistributed personal holding company income is taxed [Sec. 545(a)]. The greatest percentage of ownership during the period is used. For wholly foreign-owned foreign corporations, see ¶ 3403.

¶ 3405 Rate of tax, returns and payment. The tax is 70% of undistributed personal holding company income [Sec. 541]. A single return is made for both the income tax and the personal holding company tax. A separate schedule (P-H) is provided for the personal holding company tax. The tax is paid at the same time as the income tax [¶ 3517].

A foreign corporation that fails to file a return for its personal holding company tax must pay a penalty of 10% of the taxes (except employment taxes) payable by the corporation for the tax year, including the personal holding company tax [Sec. 6683].

¶ 3406 Figuring the tax—illustration. Assume the following facts on a personal holding company's 1977 calendar-year return on the accrual basis:

Taxable income	$126,900.00
Contributions allowed—5% limitation applicable	8,205.26
Contributions actually made of the character specified in Sec. 170 (all to hospitals)	82,100.00
Dividends received from taxable domestic corporations and included in gross income	34,117.65
Federal normal tax and surtax (alternative method)	46,512.00
Federal normal tax and surtax (on taxable income excluding excess of long-term capital gain over short-term capital loss)	45,012.00
Taxable dividends paid during current year	5,000.00
Consent dividends	3,200.00
Amount set aside during current year to apply toward retirement of indebtedness of $50,000 incurred before 1-1-34	7,500.00
Long-term capital gain $10,000.00; short-term capital loss $5,000.00; net capital gain	5,000.00
Dividends paid between Jan. 1 and Mar. 15 of following calendar year	900.00

Footnotes appear at end of this Chapter.

Under the above facts, the personal holding company tax for the current year would be figured as follows [Sec. 541, 545; 1.541-1]:

Undistributed Personal Holding Company Income Computation

1.	Taxable income		$126,900.00
2.	Add: Contributions allowed (5% limitation)	$ 8,205.26	
3.	Dividends received deduction	29,000.00	
4.	Net operating loss deduction	0	
5.	Disallowed expenses and depreciation under Sec. 545(b)(8)	0	37,205.26
6.	Total of items 1 to 5, inclusive		$164,105.26
7.	Less: Federal income tax	46,512.00	
8.	Income and profits taxes paid to a foreign country or U.S. possession not deducted in figuring taxable income	0	
9.	Contributions not exceeding 50% of taxable income adjusted as provided in Sec. 170(b)(2)	82,052.63†	
10.	Net operating loss for preceding tax year	0	
11.	Excess of long-term capital gains over short-term capital losses. $5,000.00 Tax on such amount 1,500.00		
	Difference	3,500.00	
12.	Amounts used or irrevocably set aside to pay or retire indebtedness of any kind accrued before 1-1-34	7,500.00	
13.	Lien in favor of the U.S.	0	139,564.63
14.	Adjusted taxable income		$ 24,540.63
15.	Less: Dividends paid deduction:		
	Taxable dividends paid	$ 5,000.00	
	Consent dividends	3,200.00	
	Dividends paid between Jan. 1, and Mar. 15, 1978 (Note limitation in Sec. 563(b))	900.00	
	Dividend carryover under Sec. 564	0	9,100.00
16.	Undistributed Personal Holding Company Income		$ 15,440.63

Computation of Tax

17.	70% of item 16		$ 10,808.44

---

† 50% of taxable income without regard to contributions, special deductions and net operating loss carryback. Here item 6.

NOTE: There is no penalty surtax if sufficient dividends are paid or credited. If the dividends paid deduction (item 15 above) is at least equal to the adjusted taxable income (item 14 above), there is no undistributed personal holding company income, and the tax is zero. Thus, in the above computation, no tax would have been payable, if the dividends paid plus the consent dividends credit had been increased by $15,440.63. The payment of additional dividends between January 1 and March 15, 1978. would also have helped to reduce the tax, but in that connection, care should be taken not to exceed the limitation in Sec. 563(b).

When a deficiency in the tax has been established for a prior year, a corporation may pay additional taxable dividends, subject to certain provisions, that will reduce or eliminate the deficiency. See ¶ 3407.

¶ **3407 Deficiency dividend.** If there is a deficiency in the personal holding company tax for a prior tax year, the company can pay a deficiency dividend in the current tax year. This will relieve it from paying the deficiency, or entitle it to a refund or credit if any part of the deficiency has been paid. The deficiency dividend is deducted in redetermining the undistributed personal holding company income, and so reduces or eliminates the tax. This remedy does not extend to interest and penalties, and it is not available at all if any part of the deficiency was due to fraud or wilful failure to file a timely return. In most cases, the first step toward paying a deficiency dividend is to sign an agreement with the Revenue Service relating to the liability of the taxpayer for the personal holding company tax. This is known as a determination. The determination date ordinarily is the date the agreement is mailed to the taxpayer, but it is the date the agreement is signed if a dividend is paid before the mailing date but on or after the date of signing. The term "determination" also means a decision by the Tax Court, a judgment, decree, or other Court order that has become final, or a closing agreement under Sec. 7121. The deficiency dividend must be paid within 90 days after the determination date. Claim for deduction must be filed within 120 days after the determination date. Refund claim can be filed within 2 years from the determination date [Sec. 547; 1.547-1—1.547-7].

¶ 3408 **Disallowed losses.** No deduction is allowed for a loss incurred on a sale made between two corporations, if (1) over 50% in value of the outstanding stock of each is owned, directly or indirectly by or for the same individual, and (2) either corporation was a personal holding company during the preceding tax year. This does not apply to distributions in liquidation [Sec. 267(b)(3); 1.267(b)-1]. In determining if over 50% in value of the stock is owned by an individual, the stock ownership, family and partnership rules explained in ¶ 2223 apply.

¶ 3409 **Consolidated returns.** The personal holding company tax does not apply to affiliated corporations filing a consolidated return, unless 60% or more of the adjusted ordinary gross income of the group is personal holding company income. This does not apply (except to affiliated railroad corporations) if any member of the group (including the common parent) (1) is exempt from the personal holding company tax, or (2) got 10% or more of its adjusted ordinary gross income from sources outside the affiliated group, and 80% or more of the income from outside sources was personal holding company income [Sec. 542(b); 1.542-4].

SHAREHOLDERS IN FOREIGN PERSONAL HOLDING COMPANIES

¶ 3411 **Tax on undistributed foreign personal holding company income.** The U.S. shareholders (including U.S. corporations, estates and trusts) of foreign personal holding companies must include undistributed foreign personal holding company income (determined by disregarding any liquidating distributions) in their gross income. Foreign corporations are classified as foreign personal holding companies depending upon the nature of their gross income and the ownership of their outstanding stock [Sec. 551]. Certain foreign corporations are exempt from this treatment [¶ 3415].

¶ 3412 **What is a foreign personal holding company.** A foreign corporation is a foreign personal holding company if [Sec. 552(a); 1.552-1]:
1. 60% or more of its gross income for the tax year is foreign personal holding company income (or 50%, if it was a foreign personal holding company in the prior year) [Sec. 552(a)(1); 1.552-2]; and
2. more than 50% in value of its outstanding stock is owned, directly or indirectly, by or for not over 5 individuals who are citizens or residents of the U.S. [Sec. 552(a)(2), 554; 1.552-3, Prop. Regs. 1.554-1—7].

NOTE: Foreign corporations that are not foreign personal holding companies may be subject to personal holding company tax [¶ 3403].

Foreign personal holding company income, in general, includes: (1) dividends, interest, royalties and annuities; (2) net gains from the sale of stocks and securities;

Footnotes appear at end of this Chapter.

¶ 3412

(3) net gains from commodity futures transactions (but bona fide business hedging transactions are disregarded); (4) income from estates and trusts, or from a disposition of an interest in an estate or trust; (5) income from personal service contracts [¶ 3401]; (6) payments for use of corporate property by a 25% or more shareholder; (7) rents (unless they are 50% or more of gross income) [Sec. 553; 1.553-1].

¶ 3413 **What is undistributed foreign personal holding company income.** Undistributed foreign personal holding company income is the taxable income of a foreign personal holding company (adjusted as shown below), minus the dividends paid deduction [Sec. 556; 1.556-1; 1.556-3]. The rules for dividends paid that apply to domestic holding companies [¶ 3404(b)], also apply to foreign holding companies with certain exceptions.

The adjustments made to taxable income to determine undistributed foreign personal holding company income are basically the same adjustments personal holding companies make for taxes, charitable contributions, special deductions, net operating losses and expenses and depreciation related to corporate property [¶ 3404(a)]. In addition, the taxes of a shareholder in a foreign personal holding company paid by the corporation and any deduction relating to pension trusts are disallowed [Sec. 556(b); 1.556-2].

¶ 3414 **Corporation income taxed to United States shareholders.** The undistributed foreign personal holding company income is included in the gross income of its U.S. shareholders.

Example: A owns 25% of the stock of X, a foreign personal holding company, and X's undistributed foreign personal holding company income is $100,000. A must include $25,000 in gross income for his tax year in which the end of the corporation's tax year falls [Sec. 551; 1.551-1, 1.551-2].

The undistributed foreign personal holding company income is treated as a contribution to capital, increasing the stockholders' basis for the stock [Sec. 551(d), (f); 1.551-5].

¶ 3415 **Exempt corporations.** Corporations exempt under Sec. 501 are not classed as foreign personal holding companies. Certain exempt corporations and corporations organized and doing business under foreign banking and credit laws also are excluded [Sec. 552(b); 1.552-4, 1.552-5].

¶ 3416 **Returns.** The following returns are required:
1. Information returns by shareholders owning over 5% in value of the stock are filed with the shareholder's annual tax return [Sec. 551(c); 1.551-4].
2. Annual returns on Form 957 by officers, directors and U.S. shareholders owning 50% or more in value of the outstanding stock, stating ownership of stock and convertible securities. Form 957 is due within 15 days after the tax year ends [Sec. 6035(a)(1), 6035(b)(1); 1.6035-1(a)(1), 1.6035-2].
3. Annual returns by officers and directors on Form 958 giving information on gross income, deductions, credits, taxable income and undistributed earnings, and on ownership of stock and convertible securities. Form 958 is due within 60 days after the tax year ends [Sec. 6035(a)(2); 1.6035-1(a)(2)].
4. Information returns must be filed for foreign corporations [¶ 3540(b)].

REGULATED INVESTMENT COMPANIES

¶ 3428 **The tax on regulated investment companies.** A regulated investment company is taxed only on undistributed income, since it can deduct most dividends paid. Corporations taking advantage of this provision are usually those known as "investment trusts" or "mutual funds." Personal holding companies are

Chapter 24—Regulated Investment Companies

specifically excluded. A periodic payment plan (an investment trust that sells shares in a mutual fund in installments) is generally not subject to tax; the investors are treated as owning the fund shares directly and are taxed on the shares only if sold [Sec. 851(f); 1.851-7].

¶ 3429 Requirements for being taxed as a regulated investment company. A corporation must meet the following requirements:

(1) The corporation must be registered under the Investment Company Act of 1940, or a certain type of common trust fund [Sec. 851(a); 1.851-1(b)].

(2) Election. The corporation must file with its return for the tax year an election to be taxed as a regulated investment company. The election is binding for future years [Sec. 851(b)(1); 1.851-2(a)].

(3) Gross income. At least 90% of the corporation's gross income must be from dividends, interest and gains from the sale or other disposition of stock or securities. Income from disposition of stock or securities held under 3 months must be less than 30% of gross income [Sec. 851(b)(2)(3); 1.851-2(b)].

(4) Diversification of income. At the close of each quarter of the tax year, at least 50% of the value of the corporation's total assets must be cash and cash items (including receivables), government securities and securities of other regulated investment companies. Other securities may also be included in this figure, but the amount that the taxpayer owns in any one corporation cannot be (1) greater in value than 5% of the value of the taxpayer's total assets and (2) over 10% of the outstanding voting securities of the issuing corporation. Also, at the close of each quarter, the taxpayer must not have more than 25% of the value of its total assets invested in the securities (other than government securities or the securities of other regulated investment companies) of any one corporation, or of two or more corporations, which the taxpayer controls, and which are engaged in the same or similar trades or businesses or related trades or businesses [Sec. 851(b)(4); 1.851-2(c)]. But exceptions are made in the case of "venture capital" companies [¶ 3430].

(5) Distribution of income. The company must distribute dividends (not counting capital gain dividends) at least equal to the sum of (a) 90% of its investment company taxable income, plus (b) 90% of the excess of its tax-exempt interest over its disallowed tax-exempt interest deductions [Sec. 852(a); 1.852-1]. The dividends may be paid during the tax year, or after the close of the tax year [¶ 3431(d)].

¶ 3430 "Venture capital" companies. An investment company that furnishes capital for corporations chiefly engaged in developing new products is a "venture capital" company. An exception to the requirements for diversification of income is made for "venture capital" companies. Under certain conditions, they may exceed the 10% voting stock limitation. To qualify as a "venture capital" company, the investment company must have the Securities and Exchange Commission certify, not earlier than 60 days before the close of the tax year, that it is principally engaged in the furnishing of capital to other corporations, which are principally engaged in the development or exploitation of inventions, technological improvements, new processes, or products not previously generally available [Sec. 851(e)(1); 1.851-6].

¶ 3431 Figuring the tax. Regulated investment companies are taxed on investment company taxable income at the same rates as corporations in general. Investment company taxable income is taxable income [¶ 3102] with the following adjustments: (1) Excess of net long-term capital gain over net short-term capital loss is excluded; (2) No net operating loss deduction is allowed; (3) Special deductions listed in ¶ 3113 are not allowed (except organizational expenditures); (4) Dividends paid (other than capital gain and exempt-interest dividends) can be deducted. When shareholders can choose cash or stock [¶ 1709], the dividends paid deduction is the cash amount [Sec. 1.305-2(b)].

In addition, a tax of 30% is imposed on the excess of net long-term capital gain over (a) net short-term capital loss, and (b) capital gain dividends paid during the tax year [Sec. 852; 1.852-2, 1.852-3]. See (a) below for treatment of undistributed long-term capital gain under certain conditions.

(a) **Capital gain dividends.** A capital gain dividend is any dividend (or part of it) so designated by the investment company in a written notice mailed to its shareholders within 45 days (or 55 days in the case of a nominee acting as a custodian of a unit investment trust) after the end of the mutual fund's tax year. The capital gain dividend cannot be more than the excess of the net long-term capital gain over the short-term capital loss. Capital gain dividends received by the shareholders are treated by them as long-term capital gains[1] [Sec. 852(b)(3); 1.852-2(b); 1.852-4(c)]. Distributions, after 1963 by a unit investment trust, from the sale of securities, to redeem a holder's interest will qualify [Sec. 852(d); 1.852-10].

NOTE: A capital loss carryover does not reduce the earnings and profits of a taxable year available for the payment of dividends, but does reduce the amount of a dividend that may be designated as a capital gain dividend.

Undistributed long-term capital gain. Regulated investment companies may treat undistributed long-term capital gain as if: (a) it had been distributed to the shareholders; (b) the capital gains tax had been paid by the shareholder (rather than the company); and (c) the amount constructively distributed (less the capital gains tax) had been reinvested by the shareholder in the company. The shareholder (1) includes this amount in figuring his long-term capital gain; (2) gets a credit against his tax equal to the capital gains tax paid by the company on the amount; and (3) adds the amount (less the tax) to the basis of his shares. Within 30 days after the close of the tax year, the company must file Form 2438 and pay the tax on the undistributed gain. A notice of the amount constructively distributed must be given to each shareholder on Form 2439 within 45 days (or 55 days in the case of a nominee acting as a unit investment trust's custodian) after the end of the fund's tax year. The shareholder should attach Form 2439 to his return to substantiate the credit claimed [Sec. 852(b)(3)(D); 1.852-4, 1.852-9(b)].

Shares held for less than 31 days. If a shareholder held shares for less than 31 days, and received, or was deemed to have received, a capital gain dividend in that period, any loss on the sale of the shares is treated as a long-term capital loss to the extent of the capital gain dividend. Special rules apply in determining the holding period [Sec. 852(b)(4); 1.852-4(d)].

(b) **Exempt-interest dividend** is any dividend (or part of it) so designated by the investment company in a written notice mailed to its shareholders within 45 days after the close of its tax year. Exempt-interest dividends are allowed for tax years starting after 1975 only if, at the close of each quarter of its tax year, at least 50% of the value of the investment company's total assets is tax-exempt obligations. The amount of the dividend cannot be more than the excess of the exempt interest over the disallowed exempt-interest deductions. Shareholders treat exempt-interest dividends as interest excludable from gross income [Sec. 852(b)(5)].

(c) **Foreign tax credit allowed to shareholders.** Instead of taking a credit or deduction for foreign taxes on its own return, a regulated investment company may elect to have its shareholders take the credit or deduction on their returns. Although the investment company loses the credit or deduction for the foreign taxes, it may add the amount of such taxes to its dividends paid deduction.[1] The shareholder's proportionate share of the foreign taxes must be included in his gross income and treated as paid by him. To qualify for the election, the investment company must have more than 50% of the value of its total assets at the close of the tax year invested in foreign securities, and must distribute at least 90% of its investment company taxable income. A notice of the election must be sent to shareholders within 45 days (or 55 days in the case of a nominee acting as a unit investment trust's custodian) after the end of the fund's tax year [Sec. 853; 1.853-1—1.853-4]. For explanation of the foreign tax credit, see ¶ 3701 et seq.

(d) Shareholders' dividends received exclusion or deduction. Capital gain dividends do not qualify for the individual's exclusion or the corporate deduction for dividends received [Sec. 854(a); 1.854-1].

If a regulated investment company gets less than 75% of its gross income (excluding gain from sale of securities) from dividends, only a portion of the dividends received by the company's stockholders qualifies for the individual exclusion or the corporate deduction. That portion is figured as follows [Sec. 854(b)(1), (3); 1.854-1—1.854-3]:

$$\text{Dividend from regulated investment company} \times \frac{\text{Dividends received by the company}}{\text{Company's gross income}}$$

The amount applied to the individual exclusion or corporate deduction cannot be more than the amount stated in the notice sent to shareholders within 45 days (or 55 days in the case of a nominee acting as a unit investment trust's custodian) after the end of the fund's tax year [Sec. 854(b)(2); 1.854-2].

(e) Dividends declared after close of tax year, but before the filing date of the return, may, if the company elects, be treated as having been paid in the tax year covered by the return. However, they must actually be paid to the shareholders not later than the date of the next regular dividend payment after the declaration and within 12 months after the close of the tax year. These dividends are treated by the shareholders as income of the tax year in which the dividends are actually distributed. The necessary notice to shareholders must be given not later than 45 days after the close of the tax year in which the distribution is made [Sec. 855; 1.855-1].

(f) Tax preference items for minimum tax. Regulated investment companies are not subject to the minimum tax to the extent they pass through tax preferences to their shareholders. The shareholders are subject to the minimum tax on capital gains tax preferences passed through to them to the extent these preferences are attributable to capital gain dividends (¶ 2403; 3201(b)) [Sec. 58(f); Prop. Reg. 1.58-6].

¶ 3432 Real estate investment trusts. A real estate investment trust may elect to be taxed in a manner substantially similar to a regulated investment company [¶ 3431]. However, unlike a regulated investment company, dividends from a real estate investment trust do not qualify for the exclusion, there is no pass-through of the foreign tax credit, and no special provision for undistributed capital gains.

Election. The trust makes the election by computing its taxable income as a real estate investment trust in its return for the first tax year for which it wants the election to apply. The election is irrevocable [Sec. 856(c); 1.856-2(b)].

Footnotes appear at end of this Chapter.

(a) General requirements. In addition to the income (b), and investment (c) requirements explained below, the corporation, trust or association must [Sec. 856(a); 1.856-1]:

- Be managed by one or more trustees or directors.
- Have beneficial interests represented by transferable shares or certificates.
- Be taxable as a domestic corporation (but for the provisions for these trusts).
- Be beneficially owned by at least 100 persons (for at least 335 days of a tax year); and 5 or less persons may not own, either actually or constructively, more than 50% of the stock. Qualified employees' pension or profit-sharing trusts [¶ 3024] qualify as "persons." [1]

For tax years starting after 10-4-76, a real estate investment trust will not be disqualified for holding property held primarily for sale to customers in the ordinary course of business, but will be subject to a 100% tax on net income from such sales ("prohibited transactions"), excluding foreclosures [Sec. 857(b)(6)].

NOTE: A real estate investment trust may acquire foreclosure property if it elects to pay a special tax on the income from such property, and disposes of the property normally within 2 years [Sec. 856(e); Temp. Reg. 10.3].

(b) Gross income requirement [Sec. 856(c); 1.856-2—1.856-4]:

- 90% (95% after 1979) or more of the trust's gross income must come from dividends; interest; real property rents; gains from the sale of stock, securities, and real property; and abatements and refunds of real property taxes.
- 75% or more of the trust's income must be from real property. This includes rents; interest on obligations secured by mortgages on real property; gain from the sale of real property and stock in, and distributions from, other qualified real estate trusts.
- Gains from short-term security sales, and sales of real property held less than 4 years must be less than 30% of the trust's gross income. This does not include property involuntarily converted.

NOTE: For tax years starting after 10-4-76, failure to meet the 75% and 90% tests will not result in disqualification if: (1) the trust sets forth the source and nature of gross income on its tax return; (2) incorrect information is not included on the return with the intent to evade tax; and (3) failure to meet the tests is due to reasonable cause—not willful neglect. A 100% tax is imposed on the greater of the amounts by which the trust exceeded either the 75% or 90% tests. [Sec. 856(c)(7), 857(b)(5)].

(c) Diversification of income. At the close of each quarter of the tax year [Sec. 856(c)(5)]:

- 75% or more of the value of the trust's total assets must be in real estate assets, cash and cash items (including receivables), and Government securities; and
- The other 25% of the trust's total assets may be in securities of other corporations, but securities of any one corporation are limited to 5% of the trust's total assets, and 10% of the issuer's voting securities.

(d) Distribution of income. The trust must distribute as dividends (not counting capital gains dividends) at least 90% (95% after 1979) of its real estate investment trust taxable income. The dividends may be declared and paid during the tax year, or after the close of the tax year,[2] generally under the same conditions as regulated investment companies (¶ 3431(d)) [Sec. 857, 858; 1.857-1—1.857-8,

1.858-1]. "Real estate investment trust taxable income" is similar to investment company taxable income [¶ 3431] and includes any increase in income resulting from a change in accounting method.³ For tax years ending after 10-4-76, real estate investment trust taxable income is taxable income with the following adjustments: (1) special deductions listed in ¶ 3113 are not allowed (except for organizational expenses); (2) dividends paid (computed without net income from foreclosure property) can be deducted; (3) any increase in income from a change in accounting method is included; and (4) net income from foreclosure property is excluded [Sec. 857(b)(2)(A)-(D)].

Deduction for deficiency dividends. If on audit an adjustment to real estate investment trust income or deductions means that distributions to shareholders for the year being audited were insufficient to meet the 90% requirement (95% after 1979), the real estate investment trust can make current distributions to its shareholders up to the net amount of the adjustment. Such deficiency dividend distributions are deducted in the year under audit, not the year paid. However, shareholders are taxable in the year paid, whether or not they were shareholders in the year under audit. If failure to pay out sufficient dividends is due to fraud or if the real estate investment trust willfully failed to file a return, the deficiency dividend procedure is not available and the real estate investment trust will lose its status [Sec. 859]. These rules apply to deficiency determinations made after 10-4-76.

Capital gains tax. If a real estate investment trust has a net capital gain in a tax year ending after 10-4-76, a tax is imposed equal to the sum of: (1) the tax (as computed on corporations in general) on real estate investment trust taxable income (figured without net capital gain and with the deduction for dividends paid), plus (2) 30% of the excess of net capital gain over the deduction for dividends paid [Sec. 857(b)(3)(A)].

(e) Net operating loss carryover. For tax years ending after 10-4-76, a real estate investment trust cannot carry back a net operating loss. Instead, an eight-year carryover is allowed [Sec. 172(b)(1)(E)].

(f) Records and information required. The trust must keep records of all its investments. It also must keep records of the actual stock ownership in the Revenue District where it files its return. For this, the trust must ask some record shareholders to supply the names of the actual stock owners each year. These are record holders of 5% or more of stock when there are 2,000 or more shareholders; holders of 1% or more when shareholders are between 200 and 2,000; holders of ½% or more for 200 or less shareholders. Shareholders who do not give the information to the trust must attach it to their income tax return. A trust that does not keep this ownership record is taxed as an ordinary corporation [Sec. 857; 1.857-6, 1.857-7].

(g) Tax preference items for minimum tax. Like any trust, the real estate investment trust treats the same items as tax preferences as individual taxpayers do [¶ 2403(d); 3020(d)]. However, the real estate investment trust pays the tax and passes through the preferences in the same way as regulated investment companies (¶ 3431(e)) [Sec. 58(f)]. The only exception is that the investment trust does not pass through excess real property depreciation (¶ 2403(a)) [Sec. 58(f)(2); Prop. Reg. 1.58-6].

Footnotes appear at end of this Chapter.

¶ 3432

BANKS AND TRUST COMPANIES

¶ 3433 **The tax on banks and trust companies.** Banks and trust companies generally have the same income and deductions, and are subject to the same taxes, as ordinary business corporations. But there are special rules.

(a) **Special rules for all banks and trust companies.**

Sale of securities of banks. In tax years starting after 7-11-69, gains and losses from the sale or exchange of securities by a bank are treated as ordinary gains and losses [Sec. 1.582-1(d)]. A transition rule applies capital gains treatment to gains on the sale or exchange of securities held on 7-11-69 [Sec. 1.582-1(e)]. "Securities" include bonds, debentures, notes, or certificates or other evidence of indebtedness [Sec. 582(c)]. In tax years starting before 7-12-69, net gains were treated as capital gains and losses were treated as ordinary [Sec. 1.582-1(c)]. Worthless bonds are discussed in ¶ 2312(b).

Worthless stock in affiliated bank. If a bank owns directly at least 80% of each class of stock of another bank, stock in the other bank is not treated as a capital asset [Sec. 582(b); 1.582-1]. If the stock becomes worthless, the loss is not restricted to the capital loss provisions. See also ¶ 2208.

Reserve for bad debts. Special rules apply to U.S. banks and trust companies and foreign banks whose interest on loans is effectively connected with a banking business in the U.S. In tax years starting before 7-12-69, banks were allowed additions to bad debt reserves of 0.8% of eligible loans outstanding at year's end until the total reserve built up to 2.4%.[1] In tax years starting after 7-11-69, banks are limited to the following percentages at year's end: 1.8% for tax years starting after 7-11-69 and before 1976; 1.2% for tax years starting after 1975 and before 1982; and 0.6% for tax years starting after 1981. If the reserve at the start of any of these periods is less than the ceiling, no more than one-fifth of the difference may be added in any one year. If the reserve equals or exceeds the ceiling at the start of the period, the reserve need not be decreased but the addition in any tax year is limited to the amount necessary to restore the reserve to its level at the beginning of the period or to the ceiling for the period, whichever is greater. For years before 1988 a bank may, and for 1988 and later the bank must, compute reserves on the basis of its own average experience for the taxable and five preceding years [Sec. 585; Prop. Reg. 1.585-2].

The excess of the deduction allowed for a reasonable addition to a reserve for bad debts over the deduction based on the institution's actual experience is a tax preference item for the minimum tax (¶ 2403) [Sec. 57(a)(7); Prop. Regs. 1.57-0, 1.57-1(g)]. A bank changing to the bad debt reserve method needs Revenue Service consent [¶ 2708].

Bank depositors' guaranty fund. Transfers to a "Depositors' guaranty fund" required by state law, can be deducted if the fund is not an asset of the bank. When such amount is set up as a reserve that is an asset of the bank, only amounts actually paid out can be deducted [Sec. 1.162-13].

Net operating loss carryback-carryover. Banks are allowed a 10-year carryback (as well as the 5-year carryover) for net operating losses sustained in any tax year after 1975. The same rule applies to Banks for Cooperatives for losses in years after 1969 [Sec. 172(b)(1)(F), (G)].

(b) **Special rules for mutual banks and loan associations.** Mutual savings banks, cooperative banks, domestic building and loan associations,[2] and certain other saving institutions also are subject to the same income taxes as ordinary business corporations. There are some special provisions:

Deduction for dividends paid to depositors or holders of accounts is allowed for amounts paid (or credited to the accounts) as dividends or interest on deposits or withdrawable accounts, if the amounts are withdrawable on demand subject only to customary notice of intention to withdraw [Sec. 591; 1.591-1]. Except for a liquidation year, the deduction for any year is limited to amounts paid or credited for a 12-month period with an allowance for grace interest or dividends. The excess may be deducted in later years (within the deduction allowed for 12 months or equally over 10 years) [Sec. 461(e); 1.461-1].

Reserve for bad debts. These so-called "thrift institutions" qualify for a special way of figuring deductions for the addition to the reserve for bad debts [Sec. 593(a); 1.593-5]. The addition is the sum of (a) the addition to the reserve for non-real property loans computed under the 5-year experience method used by commercial banks, plus (b) the amount added by the bank to the reserve for losses on qualifying real property loans. The addition to the reserve for real property loans is limited to the largest of 3 figures: (1) an amount based on the 5-year experience method used by commercial banks; (2) an amount based on a percentage of taxable income (this percentage is revised downward from 60% over a 10-year period until it is fixed at 40% for 1979 and later) with special rules dependent on the percentage of qualifying investment assets held by the taxpayer; (3) an amount based on the percentage method allowed banks less the amount of non-real property [Sec. 593(b); Prop. Reg. 1.593-6A].

Except when the experience method is used, the addition cannot exceed the amount by which 12% of the total deposits at year's end exceed the sum of surplus, undivided profits and reserves at the start of the year [Sec. 593; 1.593-6(e); Prop. Reg. 1.593-6A(e)].

The excess of the deduction allowed for a reasonable addition to a reserve for bad debts over the deduction based on the institution's actual experience is a tax preference item subject to minimum tax (¶ 2403) [Sec. 57(a)(7); Prop. Reg. 1.57-0, 1.57-1(g)].

Depreciation. Adjustment to basis must be made for depreciation for all prior years (including pre-tax period) [Sec. 1016(a)(3); 1.1016-9].

Amortization of bond premium. Basis of exempt or partially exempt bonds must be adjusted to reflect amortization from date of acquisition (including pre-tax period). Basis of taxable bond is only adjusted from date of election to amortize [Sec. 1016(a)(5); 1.1016-9].

Life insurance department. The income of the life insurance department of mutual savings banks is taxed as life insurance company income, if the bank keeps separate records for that department [Sec. 594; 1.594-1].

Foreclosures. When these mutual savings associations take over property securing a debt by foreclosure or other arrangement, they have no gain or loss at that time; nor can they take a worthless debt deduction then. The property is the equivalent of the debt. Its basis is the adjusted basis of the unpaid debt plus costs of acquisition. Later receipts reduce the "debt" and a loss is a bad debt [Sec. 595; 1.595-1].

Insurance premiums paid by savings and loan associations. Prepayment of "additional premiums" to Federal Savings and Loan Insurance Corporation is treated as a capital payment and is not deductible by a state-chartered savings and loan association.[3]

Footnotes appear at end of this Chapter.

¶ 3433

INSURANCE COMPANIES

¶ **3434 The tax on insurance companies.** Insurance companies may be classified as (a) life insurance companies; (b) insurance companies other than life or mutual; (c) mutual insurance companies other than life, marine or fire; or (d) foreign insurance companies. They must file returns on a calendar year basis. Insurance companies filing a consolidated return may adopt the common parent's tax year even if it is not the calendar year [Sec. 843; 1.6012-2].

(a) **Life insurance companies** are taxed under Sections 801-820. A 3-phase tax base is provided: the first tax is on a portion of investment income; the second is on 50% of the underwriting income; the third is on the remaining 50% when it is distributed to shareholders or certain other conditions exist. A normal tax and surtax are imposed at the same rates as for ordinary corporations [Sec. 802(a)(1); 1.802-3]. The tax is imposed on life insurance taxable income as defined in Sec. 802(b). Life insurance companies are taxed on both investment and underwriting income [Sec. 802; 1.802-4]. The excess of long-term capital gain over net short-term capital loss is taxed as it is in an ordinary corporation (¶ 3202) [Sec. 802(a)(2); 1.802-3(f)]. An operations loss deduction is allowed in place of the net operating loss deduction of corporations in general [Sec. 812; 1.812-2(a)]. Special relief is given to certain small and new life insurance companies and to insurance company branches in Canada or Mexico. The return is made on Form 1120L.

(b) **Insurance companies other than life or mutual** are taxed under Sec. 831. Mutual marine and certain mutual fire or flood insurance companies and factory mutuals are also taxed under this section. These insurance companies are taxed at the same rates as corporations generally, and in the same manner, except for the computation of gross income and net income [Sec. 831, 832; 1.831-3, 1.832-4, 1.832-5]. The return is made on Form 1120. Any mutual insurance companies engaged in writing marine, fire and casualty insurance may elect to be taxed under Sec. 831 on total income [Sec. 831(c); 1.831-4].

(c) **Mutual insurance companies other than life, marine or fire.** All mutual insurance companies are taxed under Sec. 821, except the following: (1) life insurance companies taxable under Sec. 802 and 811 [(a) above]; (2) mutual marine and mutual fire or flood insurance companies taxable under Sec. 831 [(b) above]; and (3) mutual insurance companies exempt from tax under Sec. 501(c)(15) [¶ 3436]. Mutual insurance companies, taxable under Sec. 821, are subject to a tax on a specially defined "mutual insurance company taxable income" [Sec. 821(b); 1.821-4, 1.822-5]. The tax is as follows: (1) the lesser of (a) 20% of taxable income up to $25,000 plus 22% of taxable income over $25,000, or (b) 44% of the taxable income over $6,000; plus (2) 26% of taxable income over $50,000. For tax years ending after 12-31-78, the rate is the lesser of (a) 22% of taxable income or (b) 44% of taxable income in excess of $6,000, plus the surtax of 26% on taxable income over $50,000 [Sec. 821(a)]. There are special provisions for companies with concentrated risks, for small companies, for mutual insurance companies filing consolidated returns after 1980, and for reciprocals or inter-insurers [Sec. 821, 822, 823, 826, 831; 1.821-4, 1.822-8, 1.823-6, 1.823-8, 1.826-1, 1.826-7]. The return is made on Form 1120M.

(d) **Foreign insurance companies** are taxed on their effectively connected U.S. business income [¶ 3711] at the same rates as similar domestic insurance companies; their remaining U.S. income is taxed at a 30% or lower treaty rate [Sec. 842]. A special rule applies to foreign life insurance companies when their surplus held in the U.S. is less than a specified minimum figure [Sec. 819; 1.819-2].

EXEMPT ORGANIZATIONS

¶ **3435 Exempt organizations in general.** The Internal Revenue Code allows an exemption from income tax to those organizations that may generally be described as nonprofit organizations [Sec. 501(a)]. These organizations may be in the form of a trust or a corporation. They are exempt only if they apply for an exemption as one of those organizations described in Sec. 501(c), (d), (e) or (f) [¶ 3436] or as an employee pension, profit-sharing or stock bonus plan qualified under Sec. 401(a) [¶ 3024]. Despite the exemption, an organization is subject to tax on unrelated business income [¶ 3445 et seq.].

The Tax Reform Act of 1969 includes a statutory definition of private foundations. In general, they are religious, charitable or educational exempt organizations that are essentially private in nature [¶ 3437]. The Act applies strict requirements and severe penalties to private foundations for specified acts (or failures to act) [¶ 3438 et seq.].

¶ **3436 Types of exempt organizations.** The following types of organizations, with exceptions, qualify for exemption:

Corporations organized under an Act of Congress, which are instrumentalities of the U.S. exempt from federal income taxes under such act [Sec. 501(c)(1)].

Corporations paying all income to exempt corporations. [Sec. 501(c)(2); 1.501(c)(2)-1].

Religious, charitable, educational, etc., organizations. [Sec. 501(c)(3); 1.501(c)(3)-1].

Churches, conventions or associations of churches [Sec. 501(c)(3); 1.501(c)(3)-1].

Civic leagues or organizations operated exclusively for the promotion of social welfare. [Sec. 501(c)(4); 1.501(c)(4)-1].

Labor, agricultural, or horticultural organizations[2] (including certain fishermen's organizations) [Sec. 501(c)(5), (g); 1.501(c)(5)-1].

Business leagues, chambers of commerce, real estate boards, boards of trade or professional football leagues, not organized for profit whose earnings do not benefit any private shareholder or individual[3] [Sec. 501(c)(6); 1.501(c)(6)-1].

Clubs organized and operated substantially for pleasure, recreation, and other nonprofitable purposes, whose net earnings do not benefit any private shareholder[4] (but not if charter, bylaws or other written policies provide for discrimination in tax years starting after 10-20-76) [Sec. 501(c)(7), (i); 1.501(c)(7)-1].

Fraternal beneficiary societies, orders, or associations operating under the lodge system and providing insurance benefits to its members or their dependents[5] [Sec. 501(c)(8); 1.501(c)(8)-1].

Voluntary employees' beneficiary associations [Sec. 501(c)(9)].

Fraternal orders operating under the lodge system and not providing insurance benefits for members [Sec. 501(c)(10); 1.501(c)(10)-1].

Teachers' retirement fund associations [Sec. 501(c)(11)].

Benevolent life insurance associations, mutual ditch or irrigation companies, mutual or cooperative telephone companies, or like organizations [Sec. 501(c)(12); 1.501(c)(12)-1].

Cemetery companies [Sec. 501(c)(13); 1.501(c)(13)-1].

Credit unions [Sec. 501(c)(14)(A)].

Banks providing reserves and deposit insurance[6] [Sec. 501(c)(14)(B), (C)].

Mutual insurance companies or associations other than life or marine [Sec. 501(c)(15); 1.501(c)(15)-1]. See also ¶ 3434(c).

Corporations organized by farmers' cooperatives [Sec. 501(c)(16); 1.501(c)(16)-1].

Qualified supplemental unemployment benefit trust [Sec. 501(c)(17); 1.501(c)(17)-1].

Trusts forming part of pension plans, [Sec. 1.501(c)(18)-1].

Veterans' organizations [Sec. 501(c)(19); 1.501(c)(19)-1].

Trusts forming part of qualified group legal services plan for tax years starting after 1976 and ending before 1982 [Sec. 501(c)(20)].

Footnotes appear at end of this Chapter.

¶ **3436**

Athletic organizations promoting amateur sports competition [Sec. 501(c)(3)].

Religious or apostolic associations or corporations [Sec. 501(d); 1.501(d)-1].

Hospital service organizations [Sec. 501(e)].

Cooperative service organizations of operating educational organizations (school investment funds) [Sec. 501(f)].

Farmers' cooperative marketing and purchasing associations [Sec. 521; 1.521-1].

Political organizations operated primarily to influence selection, appointment, nomination or election of public office seekers. A fund maintained by an elected official to receive contributions for his newsletters can also qualify as a political organization [Sec. 527; Prop. Reg. 1.527-1—7].

Qualified homeowners' associations (e.g., condominium management associations and residential real estate management associations) [Sec. 528].

EXAMPLES OF EXEMPT ORGANIZATIONS

Clubs: College fraternities,[7] country clubs[8] (even though club got its principal income from a bar or restaurant, if only members or guests were served);[9] riding clubs (as long as admission charged to outsiders for annual rodeo is merely to defray expenses).[10]

Farmers' cooperatives: Cooperative organization operating a farmers' market.[11] A farmers' cooperative will not lose its exempt status for doing business with or for the United States or its agencies[12] [Sec. 521; 1.521-1].

Religious, charitable, educational etc., organizations: Daughters of American Revolution; Salvation Army; Red Cross; Navy Relief Society; U.S. Lawn Tennis Association;[13] Woodrow Wilson Foundation; the U.S.O.; U.S. Olympic Assoc.[14]

Business leagues, etc.: Fruit growers association organized to promote sale of apples grown in state;[15] organization to promote sale and use of processed agricultural product.[16]

EXAMPLES OF NONEXEMPT ORGANIZATIONS

Clubs: Automobile clubs.[17]

Farmers' cooperatives: Cooperative advertising association;[18] scavenger service;[19] corporation marketing building materials on cooperative basis.[20]

Cemeteries: Corporation operating cemetery used only by organizer and his descendants.[21]

Religious, charitable, educational, etc., organizations: Journal of Accountancy Inc.,[22] Jockey Club of New York;[23] private hospital operated for benefit of physicians in charge.[24]

Business leagues, etc.: Stock exchange; commodity exchange; nurses' association operated primarily as an employment agency for its members;[25] business league operated primarily to publish yearbook comprised largely of members' paid advertisements.[26]

(a) Feeder organizations. An organization operated primarily for the purpose of carrying on a trade or business for profit cannot claim tax exemption on the ground that all its profits are payable to one or more exempt organizations [Sec. 502(a)]. Accordingly, an organization turning over income to another exempt organization is not exempt unless it proves that it is not primarily a business for profit; it must rely on its own activities of an exempt nature to gain tax exemption. A feeder organization is taxable on its entire income, not just the portion it designates as its unrelated business income. "Trade or business," for this rule, does not include rental by an organization of its realty or of personal property rented out with such realty unless it is more than incidental in amount. "Rents," for this purpose, are similar to those excluded for unrelated business taxable income [see ¶ 3448(b)]. It also does not include business in which substantially all the work is performed voluntarily, nor one that sells merchandise substantially all of which is donated (for example, a thrift shop) [Sec. 502(b); 1.502-1(d)].

(b) Application for exemption. Every organization claiming exemption must file an application for exemption with the Revenue Service. Special forms are provided for the various types of organizations: for organizations claiming exemption under Sec. 501(c)(3), Form 1023; under Sec. 501(c)(2), (4)—(10), (12), (13), (15), (17) and (19), Form 1024; under Sec. 521 (farmers' cooperative associations),

Form 1028; and under Sec. 528 (homeowners' associations), Form 1120-H. Organizations for which no special form is provided must file an application showing the character of the organization, its purposes, activities, sources and disposition of income, whether any income is credited to surplus or may benefit a private shareholder or individual, and all facts affecting its exemption. A copy of the articles of incorporation and the latest financial statement must be attached to the application [Sec. 1.501(a)-1]. A determination letter also can be obtained before operations.[27] Subordinate organizations under the control of a central organization can apply for exemptions on a group basis.[28]

The application and supporting papers are open to public inspection. The Revenue Service can withhold information that may adversely affect the organization or the national defense. Upon request the Revenue Service must supply the basis upon which an exemption is granted [Sec. 6104(a); 301.6104-1].

In addition to the proof of exemption, exempt corporations, with certain exceptions, must file annual information returns; see ¶ 3537.

> **NOTE:** Religious, charitable and educational organizations organized after 10-9-69 and claiming an exception under Sec. 501(c)(3) must notify the Revenue Service, unless exempted (¶ 3437(a)) [Sec. 508; 1.508-1].

(c) Disallowed losses. No deduction is allowed for the loss on a sale between an exempt organization and a taxpayer that controls it. Control by an individual taxpayer's family is the same as control by the individual [Sec. 267(b)(9); 1.267(b)-1]. See also ¶ 2223.

(d) Loss of exemption. Supplemental unemployment benefit plans, qualified employee pension, profit-sharing or stock bonus plans and certain specific other employee pension plans lose their exempt status if they engage in the prohibited acts defined in the Code [Sec. 503; 1.503(a)-1]. Examples of prohibited acts are the payment of unreasonable compensation or lending of money at low interest rates to persons connected with the organization [Sec. 503(b); 1.503(b)-1]. An organization that loses its exempt status under Sec. 501(c)(3) because of excessive lobbying occurring after 10-4-76 can never become exempt under Sec. 501(c)(4) as a social welfare organization [Sec. 504]. Those religious, charitable and educational organizations that are private foundations are subject to a number of penalty taxes for engaging in prohibited acts [¶ 3438 et seq.] but lose their exemption only for "willful repeated acts" or a "willful and flagrant act" (¶ 3437(b)) [Sec. 507(a)].

Lobbying expenditures. To avoid losing their exempt status due to excessive lobbying, public charities (except for churches and affiliated group members) can elect to be subject to a tax equal to 25% of their excess lobbying expenditures for the tax year. "Excess lobbying expenditures" are defined as the greater of (1) the excess of lobbying expenditures over the lobbying nontaxable amount, or (2) the excess of grass roots expenditures over 25% of the lobbying nontaxable amount. Grass roots and lobbying expenditures are both attempts to influence legislation, but grass roots doesn't include communication with a government official or employee. The "lobbying nontaxable amount" is a certain percentage of the lobbying expenditures [Sec. 501(h); 504; 4911].

¶ 3437 Private foundations defined. In general, private foundations are exempt organizations organized exclusively for religious, charitable and educational purposes [¶ 3436] except those that are churches, hospitals, schools, public charities and other broadly publicly supported organizations. For example, symphony societies, garden clubs, alumni associations, the Boy Scouts of America and parent-teacher associations are usually not private foundations. The Code defines private foundations as those exempt religious, charitable and educational organizations [Sec. 501(c)(3)] that do *not* meet any of the following four descriptions [Sec. 509]:

(1) A church, a school or educational organization that supports state schools, a hospital or medical research association, a governmental unit, or a charitable organization that is supported by the government or the general public [Sec. 170(b)(1)(A), 509(a)(1; 1.170A-9]. To qualify, a medical research organization must conduct medical research continuously in conjunction with a qualified tax-exempt hospital. It is not disqualified merely because the organization does not commit itself to spend every contribution for medical research within 5 years of receipt [Sec. 1.509(a)-2(b)].

NOTE: The public support tests used for public charities described above differ in many important respects from those used for the publicly supported organizations described in (2) below. For detailed descriptions of the above public charities that qualify under Sec. 170(b)(1)(A), see ¶ 1943(a).

(2) An organization that normally receives (a) from the general public (persons who are not disqualified [¶ 3440(a)]) and from governmental units, more than 1/3 of its annual support in any combination of (1) gifts, grants, contributions or membership fees and (2) gross receipts from admissions, sales or services performed in a related trade or business, and (b) no more than 1/3 of its annual support from the sum of (1) gross investment income and (2) the excess of unrelated business taxable income from businesses acquired after 6-30-75 [¶ 3448] over the unrelated business income tax (¶ 3445) [Sec. 509(a)(2); 1.509(a)-3]. Contributions and payment for services are both counted as support (for example, a $10 gift plus $5 ticket payment would make up $15 public support). But payments by any person or government bureau for services rendered cannot exceed $5,000 or 1% of the total support, whichever is greater [Sec. 1.509(a)-3]. Gross investment income includes interest, dividends, rents and royalties, but not net capital gains [Sec. 509(e)]. In addition to gifts and contributions, gross investment income and gross receipts, the total support of an organization also includes net income from unrelated business activities [¶ 3446] but not net capital gains [Sec. 509(d)].

Example: Y receives total support of $600,000 for 1977: $10,000 each from Bureau O and Bureau P for services rendered; $240,000 gifts of substantial contributors [¶ 3440(b)]; $150,000 of gross investment income; and $150,000 for services rendered and $40,000 of gifts, from the general public. Y's public support is $202,000—$190,000 from the general public and $6,000 each from Bureaus O and P. Its total support is $600,000. The payments from O and P are taken into account only to the extent of 1% of that amount. For 1977, therefore, Y would pass both the one-third support test ($202,000 is more than 1/3 of $600,000 total support), and the one-third gross investment income test ($150,000 is less than 1/3 of total support).

Failing the above support test is not necessarily fatal, since the Revenue Service may look at the experience of an organization over a 4-year period to determine its "normal" sources of support [Sec. 1.509(a)-3(c)]. Special rules are provided for new organizations [Sec. 1.509(a)-3(d), (e)].

(3) An organization exclusively for the benefit of one or more organizations described in (1) or (2) above [Sec. 509(a)(3); 1.509(a)-4].

(4) An organization operated exclusively to test for public safety [Sec. 509(a)(4)]. The broad public support test mentioned in (2) above, does not apply to such an organization [Sec. 1.509(a)-1].

(a) Notification of status. Because the activities of private foundations are severely restricted [¶ 3439], the Revenue Service must know of a foundation's existence and status. Both new *and* old charitable organizations are presumed to be private foundations unless they claim public charity status [Sec. 1.508-1(b)]. Therefore, any organization formed after 10-9-69 that claims to be a charitable exempt organization must notify the Revenue Service on Form 1023 [Sec. 1.508-1(a)]. The organization should provide information that it is not a private foundation, plus any further information necessary to establish that it qualifies as a public charity [Sec. 1.508-1(b)(2)]. An organization that fails to give notice by 15 months from the end of the month in which it was organized, will not be exempt [Sec. 508(a); 1.508-1(a)]. If the organization's tax-exempt status was recognized before 7-14-70, the notice is filed on Form 4653; otherwise it is filed on Form 1023 [Sec. 508(b); 1.508-1(b)(2)]. No deductions are allowed for charitable contributions received after the loss of exemption [Sec. 508(d)(2); 1.508-2].

The following organizations are not required to give notice: churches (including church organizations, religious schools, mission societies and youth groups); public charities whose annual gross income normally is $5,000 or less: subordinate organizations (except private foundations) covered by a group exemption letter: and certain non-exempt charitable trusts (see ¶ 3453) [Sec. 508(c); 1.508-1(a)(3), (b)(7)].

(b) Tax on termination of private foundation status. A private foundation may want to give up that status to avoid the restrictions on its conduct [¶ 3439]. Or the Revenue Service may give notice of the forfeiture of exempt status for willful and flagrant violations of the prohibitions on foundations [Sec. 507(a); 1.507-1]. In either case, tax assessments recapture the aggregate tax benefits (with interest) flowing from the foundation's prior exempt status [Sec. 507(c); 1.507-5, 1.507-8]. The recaptured tax benefits—from 1913 on—are (1) the taxes saved by all substantial contributors [¶ 3440] through deductions of contributions for income, estate and gift taxes, and (2) all taxes the foundation would have paid on its income if it had not been exempt [Sec. 507(d)]. The recapture tax cannot exceed the value of the foundation's net assets [Sec. 507(e); 1.507-4, 1.507-7]. The Revenue Service may abate the tax if the foundation itself goes public and so operates for at least 5 years after 1969, or if it distributes its assets to one or more public charities that have existed continuously for at least 5 years [Sec. 507(b); 1.507-9]. The foundation can avoid the tax by terminating its status and operating as a public charity within the 12 months starting with the first tax year beginning after 1969, or during the 60 months starting with the first day of any tax year beginning after 1969 [Sec. 1.507-2(b)]. The foundation must notify the Revenue Service of its termination before the start of either of these periods [Sec. 1.507-2(b)]. If this tax is imposed on the foundation, deductions for gifts and bequests to the foundation are not allowed [Sec. 508(d)(1); 1.508-2]. Special rules apply in the case of transfers of assets by one private foundation to another [Sec. 1.507-3, 1.507-8].

¶ 3438 Tax on investment income. Private foundations must pay a 4% tax on their net investment income for the tax year [Sec. 4940; 53.4940-1]. Investment income includes interest, dividends, rents and royalties, to the extent they are not taxed as unrelated business income [¶ 3445]. Net capital gains are also subject to the investment tax. Capital losses are taken into account only as an offset to gains. The deductions from gross investment income are the ordinary and necessary expenses paid or incurred in producing the income [Sec. 4940(c); 53.4940-1(e)]. This tax is reported on Form 990. Foreign private foundations pay a 4% tax on *gross* investment income from U.S. sources [Sec. 4948(a); 53.4948-1(a)]. This tax also applies to nonexempt private foundations, to the extent that it plus the unrelated business income tax [¶ 3445] that would have been imposed exceeds the foundation's regular tax [Sec. 53.4940-1(b)].

¶ 3439 Prohibited acts of private foundations. Severe sanctions in the form of heavy excise taxes are imposed on private foundations for certain prohibited acts (or failures to act). These taxes apply as well to the foundation manager and in certain cases to substantial contributors to the foundation [¶ 3440(b)]. Also, government officials may be penalized for dealings with the foundation. There is

Footnotes appear at end of this Chapter.

also a tax on the termination of the exempt status of the foundation [¶ 3437(b)]. And if a violation is willful and flagrant, or if the foundation, its manager, a disqualified person [¶ 3440] or government official is liable for excise tax for a prior violation, a penalty equal to the amount of the tax is also imposed on the violator [Sec. 6684; 301.6684-1]. Since the taxes are excises, they are not deductible as taxes by the payor [¶ 1911].

Briefly, penalized acts are: (1) self-dealing [¶ 3440]; (2) failure to distribute income [¶ 3441]; (3) excessive holdings in a business [¶ 3442]; (4) investments which jeopardize the charitable purpose [¶ 3443]; and (5) improper expenditures (for example, propaganda to influence legislation) [¶ 3444].

Prohibitions included in governing instrument. Governing instruments of private foundations must include provisions prohibiting income accumulations and the other prohibited acts [Sec. 508(e)(1); 1.508-3].[1] Gifts and bequests to foundations not complying with this requirement are not deductible [Sec. 508(d)(2)(A)]. Private foundations must also file information returns and annual reports [¶ 3537(c)].

¶ 3440 Tax on self-dealing. Disqualified persons and the foundation manager are penalized by an excise tax for specific acts of self-dealing [Sec. 4941; 53.4941(a)-1]. A self-dealing act may be a direct or indirect transaction, whether or not it results in a benefit or detriment to the foundation. Punishable acts of self-dealing are specifically set forth in the Code [Sec. 4941(d); 53.4941(d)-1—3].

(a) Disqualified persons. A disqualified person is: (1) a substantial contributor (see (b) below); or (2) the foundation manager; or (3) the owner of over 20% of (i) the voting power in a corporation, or (ii) profits interest of a partnership, or (iii) beneficial interest in a trust or unincorporated business, if the corporation, partnership, trust or business itself is a substantial contributor; or (4) a member of the family of any of the above; or (5) a corporation, partnership, trust or estate in which any of the foregoing persons owns more than a 35% interest; or (6) related foundations (for the tax on excess business holdings only) [¶ 3442] and government officials (for the tax on self-dealing only) [Sec. 4946; 53.4946-1].

Attribution rules apply in determining stock ownership and beneficial interest (¶ 2223(d)) [Sec. 4946(a)(3); 53.4946-1(d), (e)].

(b) Substantial contributor is any person (including a corporation) who alone or with his spouse has contributed or bequeathed a total of more than $5,000 to a private foundation, but only if such gifts and bequests exceed 2% of all gifts and bequests received from all donors by the end of the foundation's tax year. If a person is a substantial contributor in any year, he remains such for all later years [Sec. 507(d)(2); 1.507-6].

(c) Initial taxes. A tax is imposed on the disqualified person at 5% of the amount involved in the self-dealing. The foundation manager who knowingly participated is subject to a 2½% tax ($10,000 maximum) [Sec. 4941(a); 53.4941(a)-1]. A government official is liable only if he knowingly participated in the self-dealing. The tax is reported on Form 4720 by private foundations with Form 990 (or Form 1041-A by non-exempt trusts).

(d) Additional taxes. The disqualified person is liable for an additional tax of 200% of the amount involved if the self-dealing act is not corrected within 90 days after the deficiency notice is mailed. The foundation manager is liable for 50% of the amount involved if he refuses to agree to a correction. If several persons are liable for the tax, they are jointly and severally liable, but the limit on management liability is $10,000 for each act of self-dealing [Sec. 4941(b), (c)(2); 53.4941(b)-1, 53.4941(c)-1, 53.4941(e)-1(d)].

¶ **3441 Tax on undistributed income.** Sanctions are imposed on private foundations that do not distribute income currently. Instead of the foundation losing its exemption for unreasonable accumulations as under former law, the foundation is subject to tax on its accumulations. To avoid the tax, the foundation must distribute its income in the year received or in the next year (or a minimum percentage of its assets, if that is higher). The tax is 15% of the foundation's undistributed income less qualifying distributions. An additional tax of 100% of the undistributed income is imposed if the foundation fails to make the necessary distributions within 90 days after the deficiency notice [Sec. 4942; 53.4942(a)-1].

Subject to transition rules, the mandatory payout provisions apply to tax years starting after 1969. However, in general, the tax does not apply if the organization was created before 5-27-69 and is mandatorily required to accumulate.[1] Nor does it apply to private operating foundations [Sec. 4942(a)(1)].

Private operating foundation. An operating foundation is one that spends at least 85% of its adjusted net income directly for the active conduct of its exempt activities [Sec. 53.4942(b)-1]. In addition to satisfying the income test above, the foundation must also be one either (1) at least 65% of whose assets are directly devoted to such purposes, or (2) whose charitable distributions are at least ⅔ of the minimum investment return for the year (see below), or (3) at least 85% of whose support (other than investment income) comes from the general public and from 5 or more independent organizations with not more than 25% being derived from any one such organization, and not over half of whose support is from gross investment income [Sec. 53.4942(b)-2]. Examples of private operating foundations are public museums, Colonial Williamsburg and Jackson Hole in Wyoming.[2] Form 1023 or Form 4653 is used [Sec. 508(b); 1.508-1(b)(2)].

(a) **Undistributed income** is the adjusted net income less qualifying distributions. To prevent avoidance of income distribution by investing in growth stock or nonproductive land, the minimum investment return, if higher, is substituted for adjusted net income [Sec. 4942(c), (d), (f); 53.4942(a)-2].

Minimum investment return (less any unrelated business tax or investment tax) if it exceeds the foundation's adjusted net income, is the basis for figuring the minimum payout. For tax years starting after 1975, the minimum investment return is 5% (6% for years starting in 1975) of the excess of the aggregate fair market value of the foundation's assets not used to carry out its exempt functions over the indebtedness incurred to acquire the assets [Sec. 4942(e)].[3] To the extent the failure to make required payouts results from incorrect asset valuation in good faith, the foundation can avoid the tax by promptly making deficiency distributions [Sec. 4942(a), (e); 53.4942(a)-1(b); 53.4942(a)-2(c)].

(b) **Qualifying payouts.** Qualifying payouts (reductions of tax base) are direct expenditures for charitable purposes or for assets to be used for such purposes. They also include payouts to public charities and operating foundations and payouts to other private foundations if the recipient pays it out for charitable purposes by the end of the following tax year. Although the payouts must be made in the year the income is received or the year after, the foundation may set aside funds up to 5 years for major projects. Any set-asides must have advance approval of the Revenue Service.

Payouts generally first reduce undistributed income of the prior year, then of the current year, then corpus. The foundation can elect to apply payout in excess of the undistributed income of the immediately preceding year to the undistributed income of a designated earlier year [Sec. 4942(h); 53.4942(a)-3(d)].

Footnotes appear at end of this Chapter.

¶ **3442 Tax on excess business holdings.** An excise tax is imposed on a private foundation if it has excess business holdings. The rate is 5% of the value of the excess holdings [Sec. 4943(a); Prop. Reg. 53.4943-2(a)(1)]. It is imposed on the last day of the foundation's tax year but is determined on that day during the year when excess holdings were the largest [Prop. Reg. Sec. 53.4943-2(a)(2)]. An additional tax of 200% of value is imposed if the excess holdings are not disposed of within a specified period. Permitted holdings vary according to the time of acquisition. Excess business holdings may consist of stock in a corporation or a partnership interest, if not related to the foundation's charitable purpose. The foundation may not hold any interest in a sole proprietorship [Sec. 4943; Prop. Reg. 53.4943-2(b), 53.4943-3].

(a) Holdings acquired after 5-26-69. For acquisitions after 5-26-69, the foundation and all disqualified persons [¶ 3440(a)] may not hold more than 20% of the voting stock of a corporation or a 20% interest in a partnership or trust. The foundation may hold any percent of nonvoting stock if all disqualified persons do not own more than 20% of the voting stock. The permitted holdings are 35% instead, if the corporation's voting stock is under nondisqualified persons' effective control. A *de minimis* rule permits a foundation to own up to 2% of voting stock and all other outstanding stock, regardless of the 20% (or 35%) rules. As to excess holdings resulting from future gifts or bequests, 5 years are allowed to dispose of the excess holdings [Sec. 4943(c); Prop. Reg. 53.4943-3(b), 53.4943-4(b)].

(b) Holdings on 5-26-69. Notwithstanding the 20% (or 35%) rules, the foundation with excess holdings on 5-26-69, together with all disqualified persons, may continue to hold up to 50% of the existing holdings. If the percent of holdings decreases after that date, no additional interest may be acquired except to the extent permitted under the 20% (or 35%) rules. The foundation must reduce the existing excess holdings to 50% within 10 years if the holdings are not more than 75%; or within 15 years if between 75%—95%; or within 20 years if over 95% [Sec. 4943(c)(4); Temp. Reg. Sec. 143.6; Prop. Reg. 53.4943-4(b)(1)].

¶ **3443 Tax on speculative investments.** If a private foundation invests in a manner that jeopardizes the carrying out of its charitable purpose, it and the foundation manager are penalized by an excise tax [Sec. 4944; 53.4944-1—6]. The initial tax on the foundation is 5% of the investment, imposed each year until the earlier of sale or the mailing of a deficiency notice; the additional tax is 25% of the investment if not sold within 90 days after deficiency notice. The foundation manager who knowingly participated without use of reasonable care, is subject to initial and additional taxes of 5% each ($5,000 maximum for initial tax and $10,000 for additional tax) [Sec. 4944(a), (b), (d); 53.4944-1—2; 53.4944-4—5]. The tax is reported on Form 4720 with Form 990, or Form 1041-A.

¶ **3444 Tax on improper expenditures.** If a private foundation makes "taxable expenditures," it and the foundation manager are penalized by an excise tax. The initial tax on the foundation is 10% of the expenditure; an additional tax of 100% is imposed if the foundation does not recover, to the extent possible, within 90 days after deficiency notice. The initial tax on the foundation manager who knowingly participated is 2½% (maximum $5,000) and the additional tax is 50% (maximum $10,000). No tax is imposed if the manager was not willful and used reasonable care [Sec. 4945; 53.4945-1—6]. The tax is reported on Form 4720 with Form 990, or Form 1041-A.

Generally, "taxable expenditures" are outlays: (1) to influence legislation through lobbying or propaganda; (2) to influence election outcomes or to carry on voter registration drives; (3) for certain discriminatory study or travel grants to individuals; (4) to other private nonoperating foundations unless the grantor exercises expenditure responsibility; and (5) for any purpose that would not support a charitable deduction if the foundation were taxable [Sec. 4945(d); 53.4945-2—6].

¶ 3445 **Unrelated business income tax in general.** Otherwise tax-exempt organizations are taxed on income unrelated to the purposes that entitle them to exemption [¶ 3436]. The income subject to tax is from unrelated businesses or is unrelated debt-financed income (¶ 3449) [Sec. 511-515]. The tax rates and the time to pay tax and file returns depend on whether the organization would be taxable as a corporation or as a trust. (These are explained at ¶ 3454 and in Chapter 25.) The unrelated business tax figured either way can be offset by the foreign tax credit (¶ 3701) [Sec. 515]. A charitable deduction is allowed in figuring the unrelated business taxable income [¶ 3448(c)].

Exempt organizations must pay the minimum tax on any tax preferences that enter into the computation of unrelated business taxable income (¶ 2403) [Sec. 511(d); Proposed Reg. 1.511-4].

Background and purpose. The primary objective of the tax is to eliminate unfair competition to taxpaying businesses by taxing exempt organizations on the same basis [Sec. 1.513-1(b)]. Before 1970, many exempt organizations such as churches, social clubs and fraternal beneficiary societies were not subject to the tax, and they engaged in substantial commercial activities.[1] The 1969 Tax Reform Act extended the tax to all exempt organizations except U.S. agencies. Private foundations are subject to this tax as well as the excise taxes discussed at ¶ 3439 et seq.

¶ 3446 **Exempt organizations subject to tax on unrelated business income.-**
All exempt organizations (except U.S. instrumentalities) are subject to the unrelated business tax [Sec. 511; 1.511-2(a)]. However, churches are not subject to tax on income from unrelated businesses operated by them before 5-27-69 until their tax year starting after 1975 [Sec. 512(b)(16); 1.512(b)-1(i)]. Religious orders (and schools run by them) are also exempt from tax on income from a trade or business carried on before 5-27-69 under a license issued by a federal regulatory agency if less than 10% of the income is used annually for unrelated purposes [Sec. 512(b)(17); 1.512(b)-1(j)].

> NOTE: Church books may be examined only to the extent necessary to determine any unrelated business income tax liability and then only if the Regional Commissioner believes it has unrelated business taxable income and gives advance notice. However, this restriction does not interfere with Revenue Service's examination of an organization's religious activities for determining its initial or continuing exempt qualification [Sec. 301.7605-1(c)].

¶ 3447 **What is an unrelated trade or business.** In determining whether a trade or business from which the exempt organization gets income is "unrelated," the need of the organization for the income, or the use it makes of the profits, has no relation to the question. Except as noted below, if the trade or business is not substantially relatd to the exercise or performance by the organization of the charitable, educational, or other purpose constituting the basis for its exemption under Sec. 501, it is an unrelated trade or business [Sec. 513; 1.513-1]. For an exempt employees' trust (a trust forming part of a qualified stock bonus, pension, or profit-sharing plan [¶ 3024]), or an exempt supplemental unemployment benefit trust, "unrelated trade or business" means any trade or business regularly carried on by the trust or by a partnership of which it is a member [Sec. 513(b); 1.513-1]. The income from the business is taxable [Sec. 512; 1.512(a)-1]. Generally, "unrelated trade or business" does not include: (1) qualified public entertainment activities (e.g., fairs and expositions) conducted by exempt charitable, social welfare or agri-

Footnotes appear at end of this Chapter.

¶ **3447**

cultural organizations, or (2), in tax years starting after 10-4-76, qualified conventions or trade shows conducted by exempt unions or trade associations [Sec. 513(d)]. Also, specified services provided by one hospital to others are not unrelated if the services could have been provided tax free by a cooperative organization of exempt hospitals and the services (1) are furnished to hospitals with facilities for 100 patients or less, (2) are consistent with the recipient hospital's exempt purpose, and (3) do not cost more than the actual cost of providing the service [Sec. 513(e)].

In determining whether income of an exempt organization from a trade or business is subject to unrelated business income tax, it is necessary to determine (1) whether it is income from a trade or business *regularly carried on,* or from a sporadic activity, and (2) whether the business is unrelated. The business is substantially related only if the activity (not the proceeds from it) *contributes importantly* to the accomplishment of the exempt purposes of the organization [Sec. 1.513-1].

Example 1: If an exempt organization operates a sandwich stand during the week of an annual county fair, it is not regularly carrying on a business.

Example 2: If an exempt organization operates a public parking lot one day each week, it is regularly carrying on a trade or business.

Example 3: If an exempt organization owns and operates a race track, it would *not* be an occasional activity even though the track ran only a few weeks every year, since such a trade or business usually operates only in a particular season.

Example 4: Milk and cream production from an experimental dairy herd maintained by a research organization is a related business, but the manufacture of ice cream and pastries would be unrelated.

Example 5: A school trains children in singing and dancing for professional careers. Performances before audiences by the students contribute importantly to the school's exempt purpose of training. Thus, the income from admissions to the performances is related and therefore exempt.

Example 6: To improve the trade skills of its members, a trade union conducts refresher training courses and supplies handbooks and training manuals. The payments by the members for these services and materials are for an activity that contributes importantly to one of the union's exempt purposes—to develop and improve the skills of its members—and are related and therefore exempt.

Trade or business activities. A trade or business includes any activity carried on to produce income. It makes no difference if the activity is not profitable; the trade or business could still be unrelated. An activity remains a trade or business even when it is carried on within a larger aggregate of similar activities which may or may not be related to the organization's exempt purpose [Sec. 513(c)]. Advertising income from publications of exempt organizations in excess of expenses or any loss is unrelated (and therefore taxable) whether or not the publications are related to the exempt purpose of the organization[1] [Sec. 1.512(a)-1(f)].

Income exempt from tax. Income from a trade or business is not subject to tax if [Sec. 513(a); 1.513-1(e)]:

- Substantially all the work in carrying it on is performed for the organization without pay. For example, an orphanage runs a second-hand clothing store, all the work being performed by volunteers.
- As to religious, charitable or educational organizations, and state universities, it is carried on primarily for the convenience of its members, students, patients, officers, or employees. For example, a college operates a laundry for laundering dormitory linen and students' clothing.
- A local association of employees organized before 5-27-69 under Sec.

501(c)(4) has income from the sale of work clothes and equipment and items sold through vending machines or by snack bar for the convenience of its members at their usual work place. Income from such association organized after 5-26-69 is taxable [Sec. 1.513-1]. Otherwise exempt sales at places other than the usual work site are unrelated and therefore taxable.

• The trade or business is the selling of merchandise, substantially all of which has been received by the organizations as gifts or contributions: for example, activities commonly known as thrift shops.

NOTE: A separate organization that pays its profits to an exempt organization is not a feeder organization subject to tax if its workers perform without pay or the merchandise that it sells is received as a gift or contribution (¶ 3436(a)) [Sec. 502(b)(2), (3)].

¶ **3448 Income from unrelated business.** (a) **Gross income** from an unrelated trade or business includes both the gross income of an unrelated trade or business regularly carried on by the exempt organization and a percentage of unrelated debt-financed income (¶ 3449) [Sec. 512(a)(1), 514(a)(1)].

NOTE: Depreciation deduction for real or personal property used in the unrelated business may be recaptured as ordinary gain when the property is sold [Sec. 1.1245-2(a); 1.1250-2(d)(6)].

Foreign corporations. Unrelated business income of a foreign organization includes income from U.S. sources that is not effectively connected with a U.S. trade or business as well as all unrelated business income that is effectively connected (¶ 3711) [Sec. 512(a)(2); 1.512(a)-1(g)].

Unrelated business conducted as a partnership. If the unrelated business is conducted as a partnership, with the exempt organization as a partner, the organization must include in its income its distributive share of the gross income of the partnership, less directly connected deductions. It must make the necessary adjustments for the exclusions and deductions in (b) and (c) below. [Sec. 512; 1.512(c)-1].

(b) **Exclusions from gross income.** The following income is excluded in arriving at the taxable income from an unrelated trade or business [Sec. 512(b); 1.512(b)-1]:

• Dividends, interest, and annuities.
• Royalties (including overriding royalties), whether measured by production or by gross or net income from the property.
• Rents from real as well as personal property are generally excluded. However, rents from personal property leased with real property are taxed if they exceed 10% of the total rents from all property leased. In addition, all rents—from real as well as personal property—are taxed if (a) over 50% of the total rents determined when the lessee first places personal property in service, are attributable to personal property, or (b) the total rents are contingent on profits rather than gross receipts. Also, rents from debt-financed property are taxable [¶ 3449].
• Capital gains and losses, except for the cutting of timber treated as a sale or exchange.
• Income taxed as debt-financed income (including otherwise excluded rents, dividends, interest, capital gains, annuities and royalties) [¶ 3449].
• Income derived from research for state and local governments, or the U.S., its agencies or instrumentalities.
• Income from research by a college, university or hospital and by an organi-

zation operating primarily for fundamental research, the results of which are freely available to the general public.

• Income from limited-partnership interest of certain testamentary charitable trusts.

NOTE: The investment income of a private foundation is subject to a 4% tax [¶ 3438].

(c) Deductions from gross income. To arrive at unrelated business taxable income, the exempt organization may deduct from gross income the deductions directly connected with the carrying on of the trade or business. [Sec. 1.512(a)-1]. The following exceptions or limitations, however, apply:

• Any deductions directly connected with items excluded from income are not deducted. See (b) for items of excluded income.
• The deduction for charitable contributions is allowed (whether or not directly connected with the carrying on of the trade or business), but cannot exceed 5% of the unrelated business taxable income of an organization taxed as a corporation figured without the charitable contribution deduction. For an exempt trust's charitable deduction, see ¶ 3451.
• The net operating loss deduction is allowed except that:

(a) Any amount of income or deduction excluded in figuring the unrelated business taxable income is not taken into account in determining the net operating loss for any tax year, the amount of the net operating loss carryback or carryover to any tax year, and the net operating loss deduction for any tax year.

(b) The terms "preceding tax year" and "preceding tax years" do not include any tax year for which the organization was not subject to unrelated business income tax [Sec. 512(b); 1.512(b)-1].

The organization also gets a specific deduction of $1,000. In the case of a diocese, religious order, or association of churches, each parish, individual church or other local unit can claim a specific deduction of the lower of $1,000 or the gross income from the unrelated trade or business carried on by the local unit [Sec. 512(b)(12); 1.512(b)-1(h)].

NOTE: In the case of a trust that is taxed on unrelated business taxable income, there is no deduction for personal exemption [¶ 3012], but the $1,000 specific deduction is allowed.

(d) Special rules. In addition to the postponement of the tax in relation to churches [¶ 3446], special rules also apply to social clubs, voluntary employee benefit associations, veterans' organizations and controlled organizations.

Social clubs generally exclude only exempt function income. Thus, clubs must pay tax on investment income but do not pay tax on dues, fees and similar charges paid by members for club services and facilities rendered to them, their dependents or their guests. In addition, they do not pay tax on investment income that is set aside for religious, charitable or educational purposes. However, income from a club's unrelated business cannot be set aside and exempted from tax. If property used by the social club (for example, a golfing area or fraternity house) is sold and replaced within one year before and 3 years after the sale, gain is recognized only to the extent the amount realized exceeds the cost of replacement. In addition to these special exclusion rules, a social club can deduct directly connected expenses, charitable contributions within a 5% of taxable income limitation, the net operating loss deduction and the $1,000 specific deduction [Sec. 512(a)(3); Prop. Reg. 1.512(a)-3]. In a case involving tax years before 1971, the Tax Court held expenses of social club's nonprofit activities not deductible from income from profit activities.[1]

NOTE: In tax years starting after 10-20-76, the corporate dividends received deduction is not considered directly connected with the production of gross income for social clubs, and is not allowed as a deduction by nonexempt membership organizations.

Nonexempt membership organizations. A special rule applies to social clubs and other membership organizations to prevent those that are exempt from giving up their exempt status and escaping the tax on their business and investment income by using this income to serve the members at less than cost and then deducting the book "loss."[2] Nonexempt membership organizations can deduct the expenses incurred in supplying services, facilities and goods to their members only to the extent of the income received from their members (including income from institutes and trade shows for the education of their members) [Sec. 277; Prop. Reg. 1.277-1]. Any excess can be carried over and deducted from membership income in succeeding years. This rule does not apply to banking institutions, insurance companies, stock and commodity exchanges, or organizations that have elected before 10-9-69 to spread prepaid membership dues over 36 months (¶ 2726(b)) [Sec. 277(b); Prop. Reg. 1.277-2].

Voluntary employee benefit associations are treated under the same special rules as exempt social clubs [Sec. 512(a)(3); Prop. Reg. 1.512(a)-(3)]. In addition, associations can also exclude investment income set aside to provide for the payment of life, sickness, accident or other benefits [Sec. 512(a)(3)(B)(ii)].

Veterans' organizations pay no tax on income from insurance to the extent that the income is used or set aside for insurance or charitable purposes [Sec. 512(a)(4); 1.512(a)-4].

Controlled organizations. Interest, rents, royalties and annuities (but not dividends) received from a corporation over which an exempt organization has 80% control are subject to tax. This rule does not apply to income that is related to the recipient's exempt status, nor to the income of a controlled corporation that is itself exempt except to the extent the income is unrelated to the controlled organization's exempt purposes [Sec. 512(b)(15); 1.512(b)-1]. This special rule prevents an exempt organization from transferring a business to a corporation for "rent" that is 80% or 90% of the business net profits and that is deductible by the controlled corporation. Under this setup, the exempt organization avoided the tax on the business income, and the controlled organization escaped nearly all its tax because of the large "rent" deductions.[3]

¶ **3449 Unrelated debt-financed income.** Unrelated debt-financed income is subject to the unrelated business income tax.

Background and purpose. Before the Tax Reform Act of 1969, certain tax-exempt organizations were subject to the unrelated business tax on rental income from long-term leases of real property to the extent the property was acquired with borrowed money. The Tax Reform Act retained this tax on debt-financed business lease income and broadened it to apply to all exempt organizations and to include other income from properties acquired with borrowed funds. The income from all of these sources is termed unrelated debt-financed income. The main reason for the broadening of the tax is to prevent the use of the tax exemption to reduce taxes for owners of a business by allowing them to convert ordinary income into capital gain and eventually to acquire the business for a tax-exempt organization entirely out of the earnings of that business.¹ This device was used under prior law and upheld by the Supreme Court.²

(a) General rule. The income of an exempt organization from debt-financed property unrelated to the exempt function is included in the computation of unrelated business taxable income in the same proportion that average acquisition indebtedness bears to the property's adjusted basis [Sec. 514(a)(1); 1.514(a)-1(a)]. Unrelated debt-financed gross income does not include income already subject to tax as unrelated business income, but capital gains on the sale of debt-financed property are included [Sec. 514(b)(1)(B); 1.514(b)-1(a), (b)(2)]. The same percentage of gross income is used to determine the allowable deductions [Sec. 514(a)(2); 1.514(a)-1(b)]. Only the percentage of deductions directly connected with the debt-financed property is allowed [Sec. 514(a)(3); 1.514(a)-1(b)].

Example: Business or investment property is acquired by a tax-exempt organization subject to an 80% mortgage. Thus, 80% of the income and 80% of the deductions are taken into account. As the mortgage is paid off, the percentage taken into account diminishes.

(b) Debt-financed property. This is defined as any property (for example, rental real estate, tangible personal property and corporate stock) held to produce income and that has an acquisition indebtedness at any time during the tax year (or during the 12 months preceding its disposal).

Property is not included in this definition: (1) if at least 85% of all its use is substantially related to the organization's exempt purpose (if less than 85% of its use, to the extent of its related use); (2) to the extent its income is already subject to tax as income from the conduct of a trade or business [¶ 3445-3448]; (3) to the extent its income is derived from research activities; and (4) to the extent its use is exempt from the unrelated business tax on income from the conduct of an unrelated trade or business [¶ 3447]. Special rules apply to related exempt organizations and to medical clinics [Sec. 514(b); 1.514(b)-1].

Land acquired for exempt use within 10 years. The tax on unrelated debt-financed income does not apply to income from newly acquired land in the neighborhood of other land owned by the organization and used for an exempt purpose if the organization plans to use the new land for the same exempt purpose within 10 years of acquisition. This exemption also applies if the property is actually used for the exempt purpose within the 10-year period even though it is not neighborhood land or even though the organization is unable to show 5 years after acquisition that it is reasonably certain that the land is to be used for the exempt purpose within the 10-year period. Churches are treated under a more liberal rule: their land income is exempt if they intend to devote the land to an exempt purpose within 15 years after acquisition rather than 10 years, and even though the land is not in the neighborhood of other church property. Special rules apply to structures on the land and to refund procedures if the land is actually used for an exempt purpose within the 10 or 15 years. There is no exemption if the property is subject to a business lease ((d) below) [Sec. 514(b)(3); 1.514(b)-1(d)].

(c) Acquisition indebtedness. Income-producing property is treated as debt-financed property (making income from it taxable) only if there is an acquisition indebtedness attributable to the property. This term is defined as indebtedness incurred in acquiring or improving the property, or indebtedness that would not have been incurred but for the acquisition or improving of the property. If property is acquired subject to a mortgage, the mortgage is acquisition indebtedness even if the organization did not assume the mortgage or agree to pay the debt. However, mortgage indebtedness on property received by devise or bequest or, under certain conditions, by gift may not be acquisition indebtedness. This exception permits an organization receiving such property a 10-year period within which to dispose of it free of tax or to retain it and reduce or discharge the indebtedness.

The extension, renewal or refinancing of an existing indebtedness is not treated as the creation of new indebtedness. Nor is an FHA-insured obligation to finance low- and middle-income housing acquisition indebtedness. A lien, arising from a State or local tax, or special assessment, is not acquisition indebtedness until the underlying tax or assessment becomes due and payable and the organization has had an opportunity to pay it [Sec. 514(c); 1.514(c)-1].

Acquisition indebtedness is the average amount of acquisition indebtedness for the period the property is held during the tax year [Sec. 514(c)(7)].

Special rules apply to determine the basis of debt-financed property acquired in a corporate liquidation [Sec. 514(d); 1.514(d)-1].

¶ **3450 Exempt trusts.** The exemption from tax granted to religious, etc., organizations by Sec. 501(c)(3) applies to an ordinary trust that meets the tests laid down for exemption [¶ 3436]. Like other exempt organizations, they are taxed on unrelated business taxable income [¶ 3451]. If an exempt trust is a private foundation, it is subject to the same taxes and reporting requirements as other private foundations [¶ 3438 et seq.; 3537]. The denial of tax exemption to feeder organizations also applies to trusts [¶ 3436(a)].

> **NOTE:** Charitable remainder annuity trusts and unitrusts, the only types of trusts to which a donor can contribute a remainder interest and get a deduction [¶ 1942(e); 3927; 4022], are exempt from tax [Sec. 664(c); 1.664-1]. However, if a charitable remainder trust has any unrelated business taxable income, the trust is subject to all the income taxes [Sec. 1.664-1(c)].

¶ **3451 Business income tax of exempt trusts.** Exempt trusts are subject to the unrelated business income tax [Sec. 511(b); 1.511-2]. The explanation of this tax at ¶ 3447-3449 applies to exempt trusts, with the following exception: The trust is allowed a charitable deduction from the gross income of the unrelated business [¶ 3448(c)] equivalent to the limited deduction allowed individuals [¶ 1943], but computed on its unrelated business taxable income before the charitable deduction [Sec. 512(b)(11); 1.512(b)-1]. When an exempt trust figures its unrelated business taxable income, the term "unrelated trade or business" means any trade or business regularly carried on by the trust or by a partnership of which it is a member [Sec. 513(b); 1.513-1].

¶ **3452 Trusts claiming charitable deduction.** No charitable contribution deduction is allowable to a trust under Sec. 642(c) for any tax year for amounts allocable to the trust's unrelated business income. As with an exempt trust [¶ 3451], a limited deduction is allowed for contributions allocable to the trust's unrelated business income. The unrelated business income of a non-exempt trust for this purpose means the amount which, if the trust were exempt under Sec. 501(c)(3) would be its unrelated business income [Sec. 681(a); 1.681(a)-2].

¶ **3453 Nonexempt trusts with charitable interests treated as private foundations.** Both charitable and split-interest trusts that are not exempt from tax may be subject to some of the same requirements and restrictions that are imposed on exempt private foundations (¶ 3437 et seq.) [Sec. 4947; Prop. Reg. 53.4947-1]. For tax years ending on or after 12-31-75, both nonexempt charitable trusts and split-interest trusts that are treated as private foundations must file an annual return on Form 5227 [Sec. 53.6011-1(d)].

Charitable trusts. Nonexempt charitable trusts are treated as charitable organizations under Sec. 501(c)(3) (with the exception of the notification requirements [¶ 3436-3437]). Furthermore, if the trust is private in nature and meets the definition of a private foundation [¶ 3437], it is also subject to all of the requirements and restrictions (including the income and excise taxes) that are imposed on private foundations [¶ 3438-3444]. These rules apply to any nonexempt trust that devotes all of its "unexpired interests" (income interests, life or term, and corpus or remainder interests) to charitable purposes and for which a charitable deduction was allowed [Sec. 4947(a)(1); Prop. Reg. 53.4947-1(b)].

Split-interest trusts. A split-interest trust is one that has a noncharitable income beneficiary and a charitable remainder, or vice versa. The split-interest trust is, except as shown below, subject to taxes on private foundations imposed on (1) self-dealing [¶ 3440], (2) excess business holdings [¶ 3442], (3) investments that jeopardize charitable purposes [¶ 3443], and (4) taxable expenditures [¶ 3444]. These taxes apply to amounts transferred in trust on or after 5-27-69 for which a charitable deduction was allowed. (But amounts payable under the terms of the trust to income beneficiaries are taxed only if a charitable deduction was allowed for the income interest.) Other amounts in trust may also be taxed if amounts for which a charitable deduction was allowed are not properly segregated from the other amounts [Sec. 4947(a)(2); Prop. Reg. 53.4947-1(c)]. However, taxes described in (2) and (3) do not apply if the charity is only an income beneficiary and the beneficial interest of the charity in the trust is less than 60% of the value of the trust property, and also where the only interest of charity in the trust is as a remainderman [Sec. 4947(b)(3); Prop. Reg. 53.4947-2].

Revision of trust instrument. No income, estate or gift tax charitable deduction is allowed for a charitable interest in a nonexempt trust unless the trust instrument expressly prohibits the trust from violating the restrictions and requirements to which it is subject [Sec. 508(e), 4947(a)].

¶ 3454 **Unrelated business income tax rates, returns and payments. (a) Rates.** Organizations taxable as corporations are taxed at regular corporate rates explained at ¶ 3102. Trusts are taxed at individual income tax rates explained at ¶ 3020(c) [Sec. 511(a); 1.511-1]. The alternative tax rates apply to exempt organizations subject to the unrelated business income tax only in one isolated instance. That is where the taxpayer elects to treat the cutting of timber, for sale or use in his business, as an actual sale or exchange [Sec. 1201(b); 1.1201-1(c)]. Other capital gains and losses are not included in figuring unrelated business income [¶ 3448(b)] and are disregarded for the alternative tax.

(b) Returns and payments. The unrelated business income tax return (Form 990-T) must be filed by taxpayers having gross income of $1,000 or more included in figuring unrelated business taxable income for the tax year [Sec. 6033; 1.6072-2(c)]. Taxpayers with gross income not exceeding $5,000 need complete only part of the return. Time for filing an unrelated business tax return is covered at ¶ 3517(d). Time for paying unrelated business income tax is at ¶ 3525.

COOPERATIVE ORGANIZATIONS

¶ 3455 **Taxing cooperatives.** Some cooperative corporations and farmers' organizations pay a tax on taxable income at the rates for corporations [Sec. 1381(b); 1.1381-1, 1.1381-2]. Taxable income can be reduced or eliminated by distributions of cooperative earnings to members or patrons [Sec. 1382(a); 1.1382-1]. This section discusses what distributions can be deducted from gross income and the amount included in the patron's income.

(a) Taxable organizations. The cooperative tax rules apply to any cooperative corporation unless it is tax exempt, or supplies electricity or telephone service in rural areas, or is taxed as a mutual savings bank [¶ 3433] or insurance company (¶ 3434) [Sec. 1381(a); 1.1381-1]. The rules also apply to the specially defined Section 521 farmers' cooperative organizations that are otherwise exempt from tax [Sec. 1.1381-2].

(b) Returns. Tax-exempt farmers' cooperatives file income tax returns on Form 990-C by the 15th day of the 9th month after the end of the tax year. This is September 15 for calendar year taxpayers. Other qualified cooperative corporations have until the same time to file if they pay or are obligated to pay 50% or more of patronage earnings as patronage dividends for the latest year they had patronage income [Sec. 6072(d); 1.6072-2(f), 1.6072-2(d)]. Cooperatives must file information returns [¶ 3436(b); 3533].

¶ 3456 Cooperative distributions. Cooperative distributions from earnings may be made in cash, other property, or by written notice of allocation that states the dollar amount allocated and the part that is a patronage dividend. This is commonly called scrip. A patronage dividend is a distribution out of earnings from business done with the payee-patrons. Each payment is based on the amount of business the patron did with the cooperative.

Distributions also may be made by per-unit retain certificates under allocation agreements.[1] A per-unit retain allocation is a patron's share of the proceeds from products marketed for him during the tax year that the cooperative retains at a specified amount per unit sold. The patron receives a per-unit retain certificate (any written notice) showing the amount retained. It differs from scrip in that it represents sales proceeds rather than a share of coopative net earnings.

In addition to patronage distributions and retain certificates, farmers' cooperatives can also distribute earnings on a patronage basis from business done with the U.S. or its agencies or from other sources. These are called nonpatronage payments. Farmers' cooperatives also can pay dividends on capital stock. All cooperatives must keep permanent records to show business done with members and that done with nonmembers[2] [Sec. 1.521-1(a)(1)].

For tax purposes, scrip and per-unit retain certificates are qualified or unqualified. Scrip is qualified when at least 20% of a patronage dividend or nonpatronage payment is paid in cash or qualified check, and the patron is notified in writing that the scrip can be redeemed for cash for at least 90 days after date [Sec. 1388(c)(1)(A); 1.1388-1(c)]. A qualified check is one with notice to the payee that cashing it is a consent to include the amount in income [Sec. 1388(c)(4); 1.1388-1(c)(3)]. Scrip also is qualified if the receiver consents to include the amount in income [Sec. 1388(c)(1)(B); 1.1388-1(c)(3)]. This can be an irrevocable consent shown by being a member of the cooperative after notice that membership means consent, or it can be a continuing revocable written consent [Sec. 1388(b)(2); 1.1388-1(c)(3)]. Cashing a qualified check within 90 days after the end of the cooperative payment period [¶ 3457] is a consent to include that amount in income. Assignment of future qualified scrip to the cooperative to pay for patron's purchase on conditional sale does not disqualify the scrip.[3]

Per-unit retain certificates are qualified only when the patron has consented to include the amount retained in his income. Consent is indicated the same way as for patronage dividends [Sec. 1388(h)].

¶ 3457 Deduction for distributions. Any cooperative organization the tax rules apply to [¶ 3455] can deduct patronage dividends [¶ 3456] paid from patronage income of the tax year and per-unit retain allocations if:

- Patronage dividends are paid under an enforceable written obligation made before the cooperative received the amounts distributed. This obligation may be stated in state law, corporate charter or by-laws, or other documents or agreements [Sec. 1388(a)(2); 1.1388-1(a)(1)].

Footnotes appear at end of this Chapter.

- Patronage dividends are paid in cash, qualified scrip, or other property (not unqualified scrip). Amounts paid to redeem unqualified scrip are deducted; but scrip used to redeem scrip cannot be deducted. A qualified check cashed within 90 days after the end of the payment period is counted as cash [Sec. 1382(c), (d); 1.1382-1, 1.1382-2].
- Per-unit retain allocations for the current year are paid in cash, qualified certificates, or other property (except nonqualified per-unit certificates) [Sec. 1382(b)]. Payments to redeem unqualified certificates are deductible, unless redeemed by other certificates [Sec. 1383].
- The patronage dividend or per-unit retain allocation is paid during the tax year or within 8 months and 15 days after the year ends [Sec. 1382(d); 1.1382-4].

NOTE: Patronage dividends are included in gross income and deducted, but per-unit retain allocations are treated as exclusions from gross income [Sec. 1382].

Distributions from earnings of prior years are deductible in the year the earnings are included in income [Sec. 1.1382-6]. Patronage from pooling arrangements is income for the year the pool closes, but the marketing of products can be treated as occurring during any of the tax years the pool is open [Sec. 1382(e); 1.1382-5].

(a) **Farmers' cooperatives.** In addition to patronage dividends (above), exempt farmers' cooperatives can also deduct: (a) dividends paid on capital stock during the tax year, and (b) distributions on a patronage basis from non-patronage business earnings during its tax year when paid in money, property, or qualified scrip within its tax year or within 8½ months thereafter [Sec. 1382(c), (d); 1.1382-3; 1.1382-4]. There is no deduction for payments made by a borrowing cooperative to the Federal Bank for Cooperatives to buy Class C stock in the bank.[1]

(b) **Tax reduction for redemption of unqualified scrip or certificates.** The tax for the year unqualified scrip or retain certificates are redeemed may be reduced by treating the redemption payment as a deductible amount. The tax for the redemption year is the lesser of (1) the tax computed with the redemption deduction or (2) the tax computed without the deduction, less the tax that would have been saved in the prior years, if the amount could have been deducted then. If the prior years' tax savings is more than the current year's tax without the redemption deduction, the excess is refunded or credited to the cooperative. If the second tax above is paid, the redemption deduction is used to adjust earnings and profits, but does not enter into other tax computations, such as taxable income or loss or net operating loss carryback or carryover [Sec. 1383; 1.1383-1].

The deduction allowed for redemption of scrip cannot exceed the dollar amount of the scrip. Deduction of any excess depends on the nature of the payment. For example, it may be deductible as interest. When the redemption is made within the payment period under the 8½-months rule explained in (a) above that could apply to more than one tax year, the deduction must be taken for the earliest year [Sec. 1.1382-3(d)].

¶ **3458 Patrons' income from cooperative.** Generally, a member of a cooperative reports patronage dividends, nonpatronage payments [¶ 3456] and per-unit retains as ordinary income when received. This does not apply to unqualified scrip or nonqualified retain certificates. All or part of some patronage dividends may be excluded or reported as capital gain [Sec. 1385; 1.1385-1(a)].

(a) **Ordinary income.** A member includes in income the amount of cash, the stated dollar amount of qualified scrip, and a fair market value of other property received as a nonpatronage payment or a patronage dividend that cannot be excluded ((b) below) [Sec. 1.1385-1(c), (d)]. The stated dollar amount of qualified retain certificates received is also included [Sec. 1385(a)].

Unqualified scrip or nonqualified certificates received are not included in income until they are redeemed or otherwise disposed of. The member's basis for the scrip or certificate is zero. Its basis to anyone acquiring it from a decedent is always the decedent's basis—never fair market value. Any gain is reported when the scrip or certificate is redeemed, sold or otherwise disposed of by the holder. If its basis is less than its stated dollar amount, the difference is ordinary income to the extent of the gain [Sec. 1.1385-1(b)].

(b) Excluded patronage dividends. Certain patronage dividends, including unqualified scrip, can be excluded. The exclusion depends on the kind of property that is the source of the dividend, or whether the patron owns it during the tax year he receives the dividend.

The amount of a dividend based on the purchase of personal items or services for business is excluded [sec. 1.1385-1(c)(1)].

The amount based on the purchase of a capital asset or depreciable business property is excluded up to the adjusted basis of property the member still owns during the tax year he receives the dividend. If the dividend amount for the purchase is more than the adjusted basis, the excess is ordinary income. The property basis is reduced by the amount of the exclusion, effective on the first day of the tax year the dividend is received [Sec. 1.1385-1(c)(2)].

When a patron does not own a capital asset or depreciable business property during the year he receives the dividend, the amount based on the purchase or sale of a capital asset is excluded if a loss related to the property could not be deducted [¶ 2200]. If a loss could be deducted, and the asset was held for more than 6 months, the amount is treated as long-term capital gain [Sec. 1.1385-1(c)(2)(ii)].

A dividend amount based on the sale of a capital asset or depreciable business property is added to the price received for the property when the dividend is received the same year the property is sold [Sec. 1.1385-1(c)(2)(iii)].

NOTE: The full amount of a patronage dividend must be reported as ordinary income if a part cannot be excluded [Sec. 1.1385-1(c)(2)(iv)].

SMALL BUSINESS INVESTMENT COMPANIES

¶ 3459 Small Business Investment Companies receive the following special tax treatment:

(1) Stockholders can treat a loss on the sale (except a short sale[1] [¶ 1608]), exchange or worthlessness of the stock as an ordinary loss. The loss does not have to be offset against gains from sales of stock,[2] and it qualifies as a business loss for net operating loss deduction purposes [Sec. 1242; 1.1242-1].

(2) The company can treat a loss from the sale, exchange or worthlessness of stock received under the conversion privilege of debentures bought from small businesses as an ordinary loss [Sec. 1243; 1.1243-1]. Ordinary loss treatment also applies to sales or exchanges of the convertible debentures in tax years starting before 7-11-74 unless the company elects to have capital loss treatment apply to tax years starting after 7-11-69 [Sec. 1.582-1(f)].[3]

(3) The company gets a 100% dividends received deduction [Sec. 243; 1.243-1].

A taxpayer claiming any of these deductions must file a statement with the return showing it is entitled to the special treatment [Sec. 1.1242-1(c); 1.1243-1(b)].

NOTE: These benefits are not available to a taxpayer while its license to operate under the Act is suspended by the Small Business Administration.[4]

(a) Personal holding company tax. A small business investment company is exempt from the personal holding company tax, unless any of its shareholders owns 5% or more of a small business concern receiving funds from the investment company [Sec. 542(c)(8)]. See ¶ 3403.

(b) Accumulated earnings tax. A small business investment company is not subject to the accumulated earnings tax as a "mere holding or investment company" if: (1) it complies with the 1958 Act and the regulations of the Small Business Administration, *and* (2) it is actively in the business of providing equity capital for small incorporated businesses [Sec. 1.533-1(d)].

DOMESTIC INTERNATIONAL SALES CORPORATIONS (DISC)

¶ 3460 Tax deferral for export sales profits. DISCs are mostly selling subsidiaries of a domestic parent corporation that have elected the tax beneficial status [(a) below]. A DISC itself is exempt from income taxes [Sec. 991; 1.991-1]. But the income of a DISC is at some point fully taxed to its shareholders [(b) below]. The shareholder's tax, however, if partly postponed because it is normally applied only to 50% of the DISC's income for year, or if income is distributed or the DISC status ends or shareholder sells his stock.

Background and purpose. The 1971 Revenue Act provided a system of tax deferral for Domestic International Sales Corporations and their shareholders. It is designed to increase exports and to remove discrimination against those who export through U.S. corporations.

(a) What corporations may elect. To qualify as a DISC, a corporation must meet the following requirements: (1) It must be a domestic corporation; (2) It can have only one class of stock whose par or stated value is at least $2,500 on each day of its tax year; (3) It must elect the DISC status[1] (see below); (4) It must have its own bank account on each day of the year; (5) It must maintain separate books and records; (6) At least 95% of the corporation's gross receipts must be qualified export receipts; (7) At least 95% of the adjusted basis of its assets at the end of its tax year must be qualified export assets.[2] Natural resources, energy products and products whose export is restricted under the 1969 Export Administration Act, are not qualified export assets [Sec. 992, 993; 1.992-1]. Proposed regulations define export receipts, export assets, producer's loans and such; qualified export receipts do not include, for example, receipts from agricultural products exported under certain government subsidized programs [Prop. Regs. Sec. 1.993-1—1.993-7]. However, a corporation that fails to meet the gross receipts or assets tests may still qualify, if it makes a qualifying distribution to its stockholders [Sec. 992(c); 1.992-3].

A DISC can make loans of its tax-deferred profits to its parent or other producer for export. The loan interest is an export receipt, and the obligation is an export asset. Dividends from a related foreign export corporation are also export receipts and securities of such corporation are export assets [Sec. 993; Prop. Regs. 1.993-1—7].

Generally, a DISC can choose any hybrid accounting method [¶ 2701(a)]. But if it is a member of a controlled group, it cannot choose a method that will result in distortion of income when applied to transactions between the DISC and other members of the group [Sec. 1.991-1(b)(2)].

How to elect. A corporation electing DISC status must file Form 4876 with the service center with which the corporation would file its income tax return if it were not a DISC [Sec. 1.992-2]. The form be signed by a person authorized to sign the corporation return. A corporation electing DISC status in its first taxable year must do so within the first 90 days of such year. Election for a taxable year which is not the corporation's first taxable year must be made within 90 days *before* the start of that year. Every shareholder as of the beginning of the first taxable year for which DISC status is elected must consent to the election. A shareholder's consent is binding even on transferees, and cannot be withdrawn after a valid DISC election has been made. Furthermore, after the election is made, new shareholders need not consent since they are bound by the prior election. The election is binding for the first taxable year, but may be revoked for any later year. DISC status is automatically terminated for continued failure to qualify for each of five consecutive years. However, revocation or nonqualification does not bar a later reelection.

Corporations not eligible for DISC status are: Corporations exempt under Sec. 501 [¶ 3436]; personal holding companies [¶ 3400]; banks and savings institutions [¶ 3433]; insurance companies [¶ 3434]; regulated investment companies [¶ 3428]; China Trade Act corporations [¶ 3117(b)]; and Subchapter S corporations (¶ 3140) [Sec. 992(d); 1.992-1(f)].

(b) Tax on DISC's shareholders. Actual or deemed distributions of a DISC's income to the shareholders would end tax deferral, making the nondeferred income currently taxable to the shareholders [Sec. 995, 996; 1.995-1—5; 1.996-1—8].

Deemed distributions. Each shareholder of a DISC is considered to have received a proportionate share of the following amounts as taxable dividends [Sec. 995; 1.995-1—5]: (a) gross interest on producer's loans; (b) gain on certain sales of property which is not an export asset in a tax-free transfer; (c) gain on depreciable property in a tax-free transaction; (d) 50% of DISC taxable income attributable to military property; (e) DISC taxable income attributable to base period export gross receipts; (f) the sum of (i) one-half of the excess of DISC income over the sum of amounts (a) to (e) above, (ii) the amount in (i) above multiplied by the international boycott factor, and (iii) any illegal bribe or kickback made by the DISC; and (g) foreign investments related to producer's loans. In addition, each shareholder is considered to have received distributions of the DISC's accumulated income if it fails to qualify or revokes its election, or when the shareholder disposes of DISC stock at a gain. For tax years beginning after 1975, if a shareholder disposes of DISC stock by distribution, sale or exchange in certain tax-free transactions, the accumulated DISC income is recaptured and deemed distributed as a dividend. The deemed distributions may be distributed later to the shareholders tax free. DISC's with $100,000 or less adjusted taxable income receive special treatment.

Actual distributions charged to the previously taxed income account (PTI) are tax free. But if they exceed stock basis, the shareholder realizes a gain (normally capital gain). Other distributions are fully taxable to the shareholders [Sec. 996; 1.996-1—8].

(c) Special rules are provided for distributions to transferee stockholders, a corporate stockholder of a DISC or former DISC, and transfer of DISC's stock at death (¶ 1507) [Sec. 997, 1014(d); 1.997-1, 1.1014-1(b)]. Liberal inter-company pricing is permitted, regardless of the profit under arm's length rules [Sec. 994; 1.994-1, 1.994-2]. No dividends-received deduction is allowed either for deemed distributions or actual distributions paid out of accumulated DISC income or previously taxed income [Sec. 246(d); 1.246-4].

NOTE: For decedents dying after 12-31-76, the rule on the transfer of DISC stock is repealed.

Chapter 24—Footnotes

Footnotes to Chapter 24

(P-H "FEDERAL TAXES" related references are cited in brackets [ ] at the end of each footnote below.)

Footnote ¶ 3400 [¶ 21,345 et seq.].

Footnote ¶ 3401 [¶ 21,366-21,389].
(1) Rev. Rul. 75-67, 1975-1 CB 169 [¶ 21,384(5)].

Footnote ¶ 3402 [¶ 21,368; 21,393-21,404].

Footnote ¶ 3403 [¶ 21,364].

Footnote ¶ 3404 [¶ 21,411-21,453; 21,580 et seq.].
(1) Wetter Mfg. Co. v. U.S., 29 AFTR 2d 72-917; 458 F.2d 1033 [¶ 21,613(5)].

Footnote ¶ 3405 [¶ 21,411].

Footnote ¶ 3406 [¶ 21,345 et seq.].

Footnote ¶ 3407 [¶ 21,441 et seq.].

Footnote ¶ 3408 [¶ 16,825].

Footnote ¶ 3409 [¶ 21,367].

Footnote ¶ 3411-3412 [¶ 21,471 et seq.].

Footnote ¶ 3413 [¶ 21,471; 21,517].

Footnote ¶ 3414 [¶ 21,471; 21,472; 31,553].

Footnote ¶ 3415 [¶ 21,482].

Footnote ¶ 3416 [¶ 35,271 et seq.].

Footnote ¶ 3428 [¶ 29,750 et seq.].

Footnote ¶ 3429 [¶ 29,751; 29,760].

Footnote ¶ 3430 [¶ 29,751].

Footnote ¶ 3431 [¶ 29,803].
(1) The P-H Capital Adjustments Service lists the dividends paid by regulated investment companies and shows to what extent each is a capital gain dividend.

Footnote ¶ 3432 [¶ 29,820 et seq.].
(1) Rev. Rul. 65-3, 1965-1 CB 267 [¶ 29,830].
(2) Rev. Rul. 64-30, 1964-1 (Pt. 1) CB 232 [¶ 29,850(5)].
(3) Rev. Rul. 64-330, 1964-2 CB 183; as modified by Rev. Rul. 74-192, 1974-1 CB 171 [¶ 29,846(10)].

Footnote ¶ 3433 [¶ 21,750 et seq.].
(1) Rev. Rul. 65-92, 1965-1 CB 112, as modified by Rev. Rul. 74-593, 1974-2 CB 62; Rev. Rul. 66-26, 1966-1 CB 41; Rev. Rul. 68-630, 1968-2 CB 84, as amplified by Rev. Rul. 75-372, 1975-2 CB 73; Rev. Rul. 70-124, 1970-1 CB 38; Rev. Rul. 70-180, 1970-1 CB 40; Rev. Rul. 70-495, 1970-2 CB 53 [¶ 21,835(5)].
(2) Domestic building and loan association includes a domestic savings and loan association and a Federal savings and loan association, substantially all the business of which is confined to making loans to members [Sec. 7701(a)(19)].
(3) Comm. v. Lincoln Savings & Loan Association, 403 US 345, 27 AFTR 2d 71-1542 [¶ 11,112(10)].

Footnote ¶ 3434 [¶ 29,000 et seq.].

Footnote ¶ 3435 [¶ 21,003 et seq.].

Footnote ¶ 3436 [¶ 21,003 et seq.].
(1) TIR-359 [¶ 21,021(25)].
(2) Rev. Rul. 62-17, 1962-1 CB 87 [¶ 21,029.5(5)].

Footnote ¶ 3436 continued
(3) Rev. Rul. 61-177, 1961-2 CB 117 [¶ 21,035(25)].
(4) Rev. Rul. 68-74, 1968-1 CB 267; Rev. Proc. 71-17 (TIR-1083), 1971-1 CB 683 [¶ 21,041(15)].
(5) Grange Ins. Assn. of Calif. v. Comm., 11 AFTR 2d 1423, 317 F.2d 222 [¶ 21,066(12)].
(6) U.S. v. Maryland Savings-Share Ins. Corp., 26 AFTR 2d 70-5679, 400 US 4 [¶ 21,087(15)].
(7) Rev. Rul. 69-573, 1969-2 CB 125 [¶ 21,041(90)].
(8) Coeur d'Alene Country Club v. Viley, 157 F.2d 330, 35 AFTR 120 [¶ 21,041(10)].
(9) Rev. Rul. 44, 1953-1 CB 109 [¶ 21,041(10)].
(10) Clements Buckaroos, ¶ 62,018 P-H Memo TC [¶ 21,041(20)].
(11) Rev. Rul. 67-430, 1967-2 CB 220 [¶ 21,266(25)].
(12) Rev. Rul. 65-5, 1965-1 CB 244 [¶ 21,266(15)].
(13) U.S. Lawn Tennis Assn., ¶ 42,457 P-H Memo BTA [¶ 21,023(90)].
(14) Letter Ruling, 4-15-52, in full at ¶ 76,314 P-H Fed. 1952 [¶ 21,023(90)].
(15) Washington State Apples, Inc., 46 BTA 64 [¶ 21,035(25), (30)].
(16) Rev. Rul. 67-252, 1967-2 CB 195 [¶ 21,035(30)].
(17) Smyth v. Calif. State Auto. Ass'n, 175 F.2d 752, 38 AFTR 120 [¶ 21,041(30)].
(18) National Outdoor Advertising Bureau, 89 F.2d 878, 19 AFTR 619 [¶ 21,261(10)].
(19) Sunset Scavenger Co., Inc., 84 F.2d 453, 17 AFTR 1319 [¶ 21,261(10)].
(20) Rev. Rul. 73-308, 1973-2 CB 193 [¶ 21,261(10)].
(21) Rev. Rul. 65-6, 1965-1 CB 229 [¶ 21,082(30)].
(22) Journal of Accountancy, Inc., 16 BTA 1260 [¶ 21,026.5(5)].
(23) The Jockey Club, 76 F.2d 597, 15 AFTR 1196 [¶ 21,023(70)].
(24) Sonora Community Hospital, 46 TC 519, aff'd. 22 AFTR 2d 5442, 397 F.2d 814 [¶ 21,025(10)].
(25) Rev. Rul. 61-170, 1961-2 CB 112 [¶ 21,023(35)].
(26) Rev. Rul. 65-14, 1965-1 CB 236 [¶ 21,035(15)].
(27) Rev. Proc. 73-7, 1973-1 CB 753; superseded by Rev. Proc. 76-34, IRB 1976-39, [¶ 39,779(5); 54,829].
(28) Rev. Proc. 72-41, 1972-2 CB 820 [¶ 39,779(5)].

Footnote ¶ 3437 [¶ 21,175 et seq.].

Footnote ¶ 3438 [¶ 34,963 et seq.].

Footnote ¶ 3439 [¶ 34,963 et seq.].
(1) Rev. Rul. 70-270, 1970-1 CB 135 [¶ 21,186(25)].

Footnote ¶ 3440 [¶ 34,963 et seq.].

Footnote ¶ 3441 [¶ 34,963 et seq.].
(1) P.L. 91-172, Sec. 101(1)(3).
(2) Senate Report No. 91-552, p. 61, 91st Cong., 1st Sess.
(3) Rev. Rul. 76-193 (IR-1601), 1976-1 CB 357 [¶ 34,969.75(30)].

Footnote ¶ 3442 [¶ 34,963 et seq.].

Footnote ¶ 3443 [¶ 34,963 et seq.].

Footnote ¶ 3444 [¶ 34,963 et seq.].

Chapter 24—Footnotes

Footnote ¶ 3445 [¶ 21,201 et seq.].
(1) Senate Report No. 91-552, p. 67, 91st Cong., 1st Sess.

Footnote ¶ 3446 [¶ 21,202].

Footnote ¶ 3447 [¶ 21,215].
(1) House Report No. 91-413 (Pt. 1), p. 50, 91st Cong., 1st Sess.

Footnote ¶ 3448 [¶ 21,215 et seq.].
(1) Adirondack Legue Club, 55 TC 796; aff'd. 29 AFTR 2d. 72-1083; 458 F.2d 506 [¶ 11,018(10)].
(2) Senate Report No. 91-552, p. 74, 91st Cong., 1st Sess.
(3) Senate Report No. 91-552, p. 73, 91st Cong., 1st Sess.

Footnote ¶ 3449 [¶ 21,236 et seq.].
(1) House Report No. 91-413 (Pt. 1), p. 45, 91st Cong., 1st Sess.
(2) Comm. v. Clay B. Brown, 380 US 563, 15 AFTR 2d 790 [¶ 32,142].

Footnote ¶ 3450 [¶ 28,064 et seq.; 28,473].

Footnote ¶ 3451 [¶ 21,201 et seq.].

Footnote ¶ 3452 [¶ 28,064 et seq.; 28,473].

Footnote ¶ 3453 [¶ 28,064; 28,473].

Footnote ¶ 3454 [¶ 21,201].

Footnote ¶ 3455 [¶ 33,475 et seq.].

Footnote ¶ 3456 [¶ 33,477 et seq.].
(1) Rev. Rul. 68-236, 1968-1 CB 382 [¶ 35,261(5), (30)].
(2) Rev. Rul. 63-58, 1963-1 CB 109 [¶ 33,521(5)].
(3) Rev. Rul. 65-128, 1965-1 CB 432 [¶ 33,557(70)].

Footnote ¶ 3457 33,477 et seq.].
(1) U.S. v. Mississippi Chemical Corp., 29 AFTR 2d 72-671, 92 SCt. 908 [¶ 13,015].

Footnote ¶ 3458 33,531 et seq.].

Footnote ¶ 3459 32,655 et seq.].
(1) Rev. Rul. 63-65, 1963-1 CB 142 [¶ 32,349(5)].
(2) Rev. Rul. 65-291, 1965-2 CB 290 [¶ 32,662(5)].
(3) P.L. 91-172, Sec. 433(d)(2).
(4) Rev. Rul. 62-58, 1962-1 CB 158 [¶ 32,669].

Footnote ¶ 3460 [¶ 30,925].
(1) Rev. Proc. 72-12, 1972-1 CB 733 [¶ 30,967(5)].
(2) Rev. Rul. 72-166, 1972-1 CB 220 [¶ 30,967(10)].

Highlights of Chapter 24
Corporations—Personal Holding Companies, Etc.—
Exempt Organizations

I. **Personal Holding Companies**
  A. **What is personal holding company [¶ 3400-3402]:**
    1. At least 60% of adjusted ordinary gross income (gross income less capital and Sec. 1231 gains) for tax year comes from dividends, interest, royalties, annuities, rents, payments for shareholder's use of corporate property, and payments under personal service contracts ("personal holding company income") [¶ 3401].
    2. Five or less individuals directly or indirectly own over 50% of outstanding stock during last ½ of tax year [¶ 3402].
  B. **Corporations not taxed.** Corporations exempt from income tax, banks, domestic building and loan associations, life insurance and surety companies, certain finance, foreign, and small business investment companies [¶ 3403].
  C. **Taxes imposed [¶ 3400; 3405]:**
    1. 70% of undistributed personal holding company income (D, below) due with income tax [¶ 3405].
    2. 10% minimum tax. Tax preference includes accelerated depreciation on personal property subject to net lease; otherwise same as ordinary corporations [¶ 3400].
  D. **What is undistributed personal holding company income [¶ 3404; 3406].** It is taxable income adjusted as follows:
    1. Increase taxable income by: contributions allowed, interest on U.S. bonds, dividends-received deduction, net operating loss deduction, and certain disallowed depreciation and expenses.
    2. Reduce taxable income by: federal and foreign income taxes, charitable contributions (figured without this deduction), net operating loss for preceding year, excess net long-term capital gain, pre-1934 debt retirement, and U.S. lien.
    3. Subtract following from adjusted taxable income: dividends paid during tax year and within 15th of 3d month after tax year ends, consent dividends, and dividend carryover.

II. **Foreign Personal Holding Companies**
  A. **Tax on U.S. shareholders.** Each includes pro rata share of undistributed foreign personal holding income in income [¶ 3411; 3414].
  B. **Undistributed foreign personal holding company income.** Basically same as in I-D, above [¶ 3413].

III. **Regulated Investment Companies [¶ 3428-3432]**
  A. **Minimum requirements.** At least [¶ 3429; 3430]—
    1. 90% of gross income must be from dividends, interest and stock gains.
    2. 50% of total assets at end of each quarter must be in cash and government or other mutual fund securities (not over 25% may be invested in one company).
    3. 90% of taxable income must be distributed (except venture capital companies).
  B. **Tax on investment company taxable income.** Figured basically same as tax on ordinary corporations except [¶ 3431]:
    1. Excess long-term capital gain over short-term capital loss and capital gain dividends paid during tax year taxed at 30%.
    2. Net capital loss and special deductions disallowed.
    3. Dividends paid (except capital gain dividends) deductible.
    4. Company can let shareholders get foreign tax credit.
    5. Shareholders get no or only part of deduction for capital dividends received.

C. **Real estate investment trusts.** Qualified corporations, trusts, or associations taxed substantially same as regulated investment companies [¶ 3432].

IV. **Banks and Trust Companies.** Basically their income, deductions and taxes are same as those of ordinary corporations except special rules apply to certain investments, bad debt reserve, net operating loss carryback-carryover and such [¶ 3433].

V. **Insurance Companies** [¶ 3434]
   A. Life insurance companies.
   B. Insurance companies other than life or mutual.
   C. Mutual insurance companies other than life, marine or fire.
   D. Foreign insurance companies.

VI. **Exempt organizations**
   A. **How to be exempt.** Organization must fall within description of Code §501(c), (d), (e) or (f).—Status must be applied for [¶ 3435; 3436].
   B. **Feeder organizations not exempt** [¶ 3436(a)].
   C. **Private foundations.** Must pay 4% tax on investment income [¶ 3438] in addition to the following:

Table of Penalty Taxes on Private Foundations [¶ 3439-3444]

Nature of tax	Initial Taxes Foundation	Foundation Manager	Additional Taxes Foundation	Foundation Manager
Self-dealing [¶ 3440]	5% of amount involved*	2½% ($10,000 maximum)	200% of amount involved*	50% ($10,000 maximum)
Undistributed income [¶ 3441]	15% of undistributed income	—	100% of undistributed income	—
Excess business holdings [¶ 3442]	5% of value of excess holdings	—	200% of value of excess holdings	—
Speculative investments [¶ 3443]	5% of amount of jeopardy investments	5% ($5,000 maximum)	25% of amount of jeopardy investments	5% ($10,000 maximum)
Improper expenditures [¶ 3444]	10% of amount of improper expenditures	2½% ($5,000 maximum)	100% of amount of improper expenditures	50% ($10,000 maximum)

* Imposed on "self-dealer," not foundation.

D. **Unrelated business income tax** [¶ 3445-3454]
   1. All exempts (except U.S. agencies) must pay tax on income from unrelated business. Corporations taxed at regular corporate rates; trusts at individual income tax rates [¶ 3445-3447; 3450-3453].
   2. Gross income from unrelated business includes percentage of unrelated debt-financed income [¶ 3448; 3449].
   3. Taxable income from unrelated business excludes dividends, interest, annuities, royalties, rents, capital gains and losses, and such [¶ 3448(b)].
   4. Deductions directly connected with carrying on of trade allowed [¶ 3448(c)].
   5. Special rules for social clubs [¶ 3448(d)].

VII. **Cooperative**
   A. **Cooperative's deduction.** Patronage dividends and per-unit retain allocations generally deductible [¶ 3455-3457].
   B. **Patron's income.** Members report patronage dividends, nonpatronage payments and per-unit retains as ordinary income [¶ 3458].
VIII. **Small Business Investment Companies**
   A. **Stockholders' loss on sale of small business investment company stock is ordinary** [¶ 3459].
   B. **Company exempt from personal holding and accumulated earnings taxes generally** [¶ 3459(a), (b)].
IX. **Domestic International Sales Corporations (DISC)** [¶ 3460]
   A. DISC itself exempt from tax.
   B. Shareholders normally taxed on only 50% of DISC's income for tax year.

FILING THE NEW RETURNS—PAYING TAXES—GETTING REFUNDS

Chapter 25—RETURNS AND PAYMENT OF TAX
(Detailed Table of Contents below)

Chapter 26—ASSESSMENT—COLLECTION—REFUNDS
(Detailed Table of Contents at page 3601)

Chapter 27—FOREIGN INCOME—FOREIGN TAXPAYERS
(Detailed Table of Contents at page 3701)

Chapter 25

RETURNS AND PAYMENT OF TAX
TABLE OF CONTENTS

INDIVIDUAL TAX RETURNS

	¶
Taxpayer's identifying numbers	3500
Who signs the return	3503
Who may file joint returns	3505
How the return is signed	
Forms constituting joint returns	
Joint return after filing separate return	3506
When "late" joint return can be filed	
"Late" separate returns not allowed	
Joint return on death of spouse	3507
Who makes the return	
How the return is signed	
When survivor remarries	
Should you file a joint or separate return	3508
Returns of minors	3509
Return by agent	3510
Return by fiduciary	3511
Who are fiduciaries	
What return form to use	
Fiduciaries not required to file	

CORPORATION TAX RETURNS

	¶
Corporation income tax returns	3512
Determining corporate existence	
Return by receiver or trustee	
What tax return form to use	3513
Exempt organizations	
How return is signed	
Return for short tax year	3514
Consolidated income tax return	3515

TIME AND PLACE FOR FILING TAX RETURNS AND DECLARATIONS

	¶
When returns must be filed	3517
Individual returns	
Corporation returns	
Tax returns for estates and trusts	
Exempt organizations—return of unrelated business income	
DISC returns	
Extension of time to file returns	3518
Businesses with foreign operations and U.S. citizens abroad	
2-month extension for individuals	
90-day extension for corporations	
Declaration of estimated tax	
Where to file returns	3519
Individuals, estates and trusts	
Corporations	
Private foundations	
Returns specially treated	
Use of amended returns	3520

Footnotes appear at end of this Chapter.

SUPPORTING INFORMATION

Additional information that must be filed with return 3521

PAYMENT OF TAX

When individual tax must be paid 3522
When corporation tax must be paid .. 3523
   Payment of estimated tax
   Penalty for underpayment of estimated tax
When estates and trusts pay tax 3524
Exempt organizations 3525
   Unrelated business income
   Private foundations
Extension of time to pay tax 3526
Reporting and payment procedures 3527
   Even dollar reporting
   Paying the tax

INFORMATION RETURNS

Information returns in general 3530
Return for business payments 3531
   Payments to employees
   Payments of fees
   Payments of fixed or determinable income
   Payments of $600 or more not reported
Returns for interest paid 3532
   Returns for $10
   Ownership certificates for bond interest
Returns for dividends paid 3533
   Payments not reported
   Patronage dividends
Returns for stock transfers under employee options 3534
Returns for group-term life insurance premiums 3535
Returns for certain liquidations or terminations 3536
   Report on plan
   Return for distributions
   Exempt organizations
Information returns related to tax-exempt organizations and trusts 3537
   Who must file a return
   Return for transfers to exempt organizations
   Annual reports by private foundations
   Employee benefit plans
Returns for nonexempt trusts claiming charitable deduction 3538
Partnership, fiduciary and Subchapter S corporation returns 3539
Returns for foreign items and foreign organizations 3540
Returns and recordkeeping for minimum tax 3541
Returns, disclosure and recordkeeping for income tax return preparers 3542

POINTERS ON FIGURING THE TAX

Identifying gross income 3545
When the tax rate changes 3546
When there are two related unknown amounts 3547

• Highlights of Chapter 25 .... Page 3561

INDIVIDUAL TAX RETURNS

¶ **3500 Taxpayers' identifying numbers.** The Revenue Service automatic data processing system (ADP) analyzes returns and correlates information reported about every U.S. taxpayer. The key factor in this process is the taxpayer identifying number that must be shown on returns, statements and other documents filed with the Revenue Service [Sec. 6109]. The importance of entering the correct number required cannot be over-emphasized. The omission of, or inaccuracy in, this item will seriously impede processing of the return or other documents.

The identifying number for individuals and estates of decedents is the social security number. They may also have an "employer identification" (EI) number if they are engaged in trade or business or must withhold income tax or social security tax from wages. Corporations, partnerships, investment clubs,[1] trusts and estates, and exempt organizations[2] use the employer identification number [Sec. 6109; 301.6109-1; 301.7701-11, 301.7701-12]. The terms "account number" and "social security number" are no longer used interchangeably. [Sec. 1.6109-1].

Preparers of tax returns who employ others to prepare returns or refund claims must include their employer identification numbers on the documents. Preparers who do the work themselves must include their social security numbers [Sec.

6109(a)(4); Temp. Reg. Sec. 404.6109-1]. There is a penalty for failure to furnish the number. See ¶ 3542.

A return for an individual should include his social security number and, if he is engaged in business, the EI number as well.

Example 1: Johnson operates a retail business. He employes three clerks. His income tax return includes his social security or account number on the return and the self employment income Schedule, SE. Johnson uses his EI number on Schedule C which shows profit and loss from the business.

A fiduciary filing for an individual includes the individual's social security number and when necessary the EI number; for an estate or trust its EI number is used. The fiduciary's own number is not used in either case.

A husband and wife filing a joint return or declaration of estimated tax may use only the husband's number unless she receives income that would require her to file a return or that the payor reports on an information return [Sec. 301.6109-1(b)]. A widow who does not have her own number may use her benefit number (deceased husband's number) if she drew social security benefits before 1-1-63.[3]

Returns filed about payments made to others (generally information returns [¶ 3530] and employer returns on withholding [¶ 2509]) must include the social security number or EI number of the payees. Payees must give their number to the person filing the return when requested. Generally, he need ask for it only once, but the Revenue Service may require new requests[4] [Sec. 301.6109-1(b)]. The request should state that it is made by authority of law. Form 3435 can be used. If the number is not obtained, the payor must file an affidavit with his return stating that the payee refused to give him his number [Sec. 301.6109-1(c)].

Example 2: Alpha Company pays Johnson a $25 dividend. Since the dividend is more than $10, Alpha must file an information return. This means Alpha must ask Johnson for his social security number. Johnson must furnish his number, and Alpha must then include its own and Johnson's number on the form.

Only one number is necessary when a single payment is made to more than one payee. Payments made to fiduciaries or agents should show the number of the principal entitled to the payment. Returns for estates and trusts should show the beneficiaries' numbers [Sec. 301.6109-1(a)].

Nonresident aliens and foreign corporation not doing business in the U.S. generally do not need identification numbers [Sec. 301.6109-1(g)].

Those who do not have a number must apply for one from any Revenue Service or Social Security office. This should be done far enough in advance to permit timely filing of any returns, statements or documents. An employee who is subject to social security or wage withholding must file an application on Form SS-5 within 7 days after he begins work. Employers who withhold taxes must apply for an (EI) number on Form SS-4 within 7 days after wages are first paid. This form can be filed in accordance with its instructions [Sec. 31.6011(b)-1, 31.6011(b)-2, 301.6109-1(2)]. A fiduciary, or authorized person, acting for ten or more estates or trusts that do not report employment or excise taxes may file one application for EI numbers instead of using Form SS-4 for each one.[5]

Taxpayers with (EI) numbers should use them on their own tax and information returns. Employers (other than household) must show their numbers on Form W-2, depositary forms and returns required for wage withholding [Sec. 301.6109-1(a)]. The Revenue Service may assign numbers to those who employ household help. They do not have to apply for a number. Other employers should apply in time to include the numbers when required on returns and other documents they file [Sec. 1.6109-1, 31.6109-1].

Footnotes appear at end of this Chapter.

¶ **3500**

Penalties. There is a $5 penalty for each failure to include any identifying number required in a filed document. The same penalty is imposed on a person who fails to furnish his number to another when required to do so. A failure may be excused if it is shown to be due to reasonable cause [Sec. 6676; 301.6676-1].

¶ **3503 Who signs the return.** An income tax return must be signed by the taxpayer or his authorized agent (¶ 3510) [Sec. 6061; 1.6061-1].

The person who makes a return as a fiduciary, parent or guardian, or executor or administrator must sign it. The husband and wife, or a fiduciary acting for one or both of them,[1] must sign a joint return. A return not signed or incompletely signed may be considered *no return* and subject taxpayer to penalties.[2]

Verification. Individual income tax returns need not be sworn to [Sec. 6065]. But an individual who wilfully makes and signs a return he does not believe is true is subject to the penalty for perjury [¶ 3620]. Persons who are paid to prepare a return for another must verify the return, unless it is part of their work as an employee of the taxpayer [Sec. 1.6065-1]. The Revenue Service may require verified returns of a private foundation (¶ 3437 et seq.) [Sec. 53.6065-1].

¶ **3505 Who may file joint returns.** Two individuals who are husband and wife at the close of the tax year, or on the date one of them dies, can file a joint return instead of separate returns [Sec. 6013(d)(1)]. A guardian appointed for one spouse may file a joint return with the other spouse.[1]

Use of different accounting methods. A husband and wife who use different accounting methods, can file a joint return, if the methods used (cash or accrual basis) accurately reflect the income of each spouse.[2]

When declaration of estimated tax is filed. The filing of a separate or joint declaration of estimated tax does not affect the right to file separate or joint returns. Payments of estimated tax can be allocated between them when a joint declaration is made, but separate returns are filed [¶ 2516].

Liability for tax. If a joint return is filed, the tax is figured on the combined income and deductions of both spouses. A wife may be liable for the full tax on a joint return even if all the income was earned by her husband.[2] Generally, each is liable for the entire tax and any penalties imposed [Sec. 6013(d)(3); 1.6013-4(b)]. However, the innocent spouse is relieved of liability for tax on unreported income if: (1) the amount omitted is attributable to the other spouse and is more than 25% of the gross income stated in the return; (2) the innocent spouse did not and could not know of the omission; and (3) the innocent spouse did not benefit significantly from the omission and, under the circumstances, it would be inequitable to hold the innocent spouse liable for the omissions [Sec. 6013(e); 1.6013-5].

NOTE: During calendar year 1977 only, innocent spouse taxpayers who could not obtain relief because their joint filing tax matters were decided before the relief provisions became law in 1971, may apply for a redetermination of tax liability for any tax years starting in 1962 or later and ending before 1-31-71.[3]

A wife in a community property state is personally liable as to her separate property for half the tax on the community income even if she has no control over it.[4]

(a) How the return is signed. The Revenue Service requires that the return be signed by both spouses or it will not be considered a joint return [Sec. 1.6013-1]. An agent or guardian may sign for either or both spouses [¶ 3510; 3511], and one spouse may sign for the other if authorized under a valid power of attorney attached to the return.[2] However, the non-signing spouse can orally authorize the other spouse to act as his agent if physically unable to sign the joint return, declaration or formal authorization. A statement attached to the return is required [Sec. 1.6012-1(a)(5), 1.6013-1(a)(2), 1.6015(a)-1(f), 1.6015(b)-1(d)].

Some courts hold that a joint return may be filed even though only one spouse signed it.[5] The determination generally turns upon whether they intended to file a joint return, considering all the circumstances.

(b) Forms constituting joint returns. Form 870, Waiver of Restrictions on Assessment and Collection of Deficiency in Tax and Acceptance of Overassessment, Form 1902E, Report of Individual Income Tax Audit Changes, or Form 4549, Income Tax Audit Changes, when executed and signed by husband and wife will constitute a joint return.[6]

¶ **3506 Joint return after filing separate return.** If a separate return is filed for a tax year for which a joint return could have been filed [Sec. 6013(a)], a "late" joint return may be filed, even if the time for filing the return has expired [Sec. 6013(b); 1.6013-2(a)].

Background and purpose. The provision allowing taxpayers to change their election and file joint return rather than separate returns was enacted to lessen the probability of excessive taxes resulting from an improper election.

Tax must be paid. A married couple can file a joint return to replace separate returns only if the tax shown on the joint return is paid in full when the joint return is filed [Sec. 6013(b)(2)(A); 1.6013-2(b)].

All credits, payments, refunds, etc. with respect to the separate return of either spouse will be considered in determining if the tax based on the joint return has been paid [Sec. 6013(b)(1); 1.6013-2(a)].

Elections made in separate returns. Any election by either spouse in his separate return as to the treatment of any income, deduction, or credit cannot be changed in the joint return, if the election would have been irrevocable had the joint return not been made [Sec. 6013(b)(1); 1.6013-2(a)(2)].

(a) When "late" joint return can be filed. A joint return replacing a separate return, must be filed within 3 years from the due date for filing the return for the year (extensions of due date for either spouse do not count) [Sec. 6013(b)]. But it cannot be filed after either spouse:

• is mailed a deficiency notice for the tax year, if the spouse files a timely Tax Court petition as to the notice; or

• starts any court action to recover any part of the tax for the year; or

• concludes a closing agreement for the year, or compromises a civil or criminal case against either for the year [Sec. 6013(b)(2); 1.6013-2(b)].

(b) "Late" separate returns not allowed. If a joint return has been filed, the spouses may not, after the due date of the return of either one, elect to file separate returns [Sec. 1.6013-1(a)]. However, a joint return filed by a surviving husband or wife may be replaced with a separate return by the decedent's administrator or executor [¶ 3507].

¶ **3507 Joint return on death of spouse.** A joint return may be filed even if one spouse dies during the tax year, unless the survivor remarries before the close of the year [Sec. 6013(a)(2); 1.6013-1(d)]. Spouses who have different tax years ordinarily may not file a joint return. An exception is made, however, in the case of

Footnotes appear at end of this Chapter.

¶ **3507**

spouses whose tax years begin on the same day, but end on different days due to the death of either or both of them.

If a husband and wife have different tax years because one of them dies, the joint return is treated as if the tax years of both ended on the date the survivor's tax year closes [Sec. 6013(c); 1.6013-3]. The due date of the joint return is the same as if the death had not occurred [¶ 3517].

(a) Who makes the return. Generally, when a spouse dies, the joint return may be made in his behalf only by the executor or administrator.

Return by survivor. The surviving husband or wife may file a joint return if *all* the following conditions are met:

• no return has been made by the deceased spouse for the tax year for which the joint return is to be made;

• no executor or administrator has been appointed by the time the joint return is made; and

• no executor or administrator is appointed before the due date for filing the return of the survivor [Sec. 6013(a)(3); 1.6013-1(d)(3)].

All three conditions must be present for each tax year of the deceased spouse for which a joint return may be made, if more than one tax year is involved.

Example: Husband and wife are both on the calendar year basis. If the wife dies in January 1978, the husband may, if the conditions are satisfied, file a joint return for himself and deceased wife for the calendar year 1977. If on a separate determination, the conditions are again satisfied, he may also file a joint return for himself and deceased wife for the calendar year 1978.

An executor or administrator who is later appointed can disaffirm a joint return previously made by the surviving husband or wife [Sec. 6013(a)(3); 1.6013-1(d)(5)]. This relieves the decedent's estate from the joint and several tax liability attaching to the filing of a joint return. The disaffirmance must be made by filing a separate return for the deceased spouse within one year after the last day prescribed for filing the survivor's return.

If this right is exercised by the executor or administrator, the joint return previously filed by the survivor is treated as his or her separate return, and the tax liability is recomputed [Sec. 6013(a)(3); 1.6013-1(d)(5)].

➢OBSERVATION➔ An executor has been compelled to enter into a joint return for a decedent when failure to file a joint return would have resulted in loss of the benefits of income splitting.[1]

"Late" joint return. A surviving spouse cannot file a late joint return [¶ 3506]. This must be done by the decedent's administrator or executor [Sec. 6013(b)(1); 1.6013-2(a)(3)].

(b) How the return is signed. If an executor or administrator has been appointed, both he and the surviving husband or wife must sign the joint return. If no executor or administrator has been appointed, the joint return may be signed in either of the following ways:[2]

John Jones
John Jones (Surviving Spouse)
or
John Jones (Taxpayer and Surviving Spouse)

If a refund is due, Form 1310, Statement of Claimant to Refund Due on Behalf of Deceased Taxpayer, must be filed by the person claiming the refund. The form may be obtained from the Revenue Service.[2] Copy of the death certificate must accompany Form 1310.

(c) When survivor remarries. A joint return cannot be filed for a decedent spouse, if the surviving husband or wife remarries before the close of the tax year in which the spouse dies [Sec. 6013(a)(2); 1.6013-1(d)(2)]. The income splitting benefit allowed to a surviving spouse when there are dependent children. [¶ 1107; 3504] also is lost when the survivor remarries.

¶ 3508 Should you file a joint or separate return. The gross income requirement for a married couple filing jointly in tax years ending in 1977 is $4,700. For married persons filing separately, the gross income requirement is $750. When a husband and wife file a joint return, the income and deductions of both are combined in figuring the adjusted gross income and the aggregate taxable income.[1] In most cases, aside from the effect of income averaging [¶ 2401], a joint return will be better than separate returns, because the income splitting benefits result in the income being taxed in effect at lower rates. On separate returns, the husband and wife are each limited to a $1,000 for 1977 ($500 before 1977; $1,500 after 1977) capital loss deduction [¶ 1613(b)].

Community property states. Generally, a husband and wife residing in a community property state [¶ 1300(e)] can save taxes by filing a joint return and splitting all their income. If they file separate returns they can divide only the income from community property. Any separate income must be reported on the separate return of the taxpayer who has the separate income.

A joint return, however, will not always result in less tax in community property states. Separate returns may result in less tax if both spouses have separate income and one has big medical expenses. But note that when community property is taxed one-half to each spouse, the deductions must be divided the same way.[2]

¶ 3509 Returns of minors. A minor must file a return, if he meets the gross income requirements for single or married taxpayers (¶ 1100) [Sec. 6012(a)(1)]. His parent or guardian must make, sign, and file the return for him, if he is unable to do so [Sec. 1.6012-1(a)(4); 1.6012-3(b)(3)].

   NOTE: "Parent" means an individual who under state law is entitled to the services of a child because he has parental rights and duties to the child.

(a) Deductions. For federal income tax purposes, the minor is a separate taxpayer. He is entitled to a separate exemption deduction, and entitled to take as deductions the anounts paid out by him or on his behalf if the amounts are due to his earnings and are otherwise deductible [¶ 1100(a); 1312].

(b) Vacation earnings. If a child is paid for services during school vacation periods or at other times, his pay need not be subject to withholding and he will not be liable for any tax unless the amount received exceeds $2,950. There will be no withholding if he files a certificate of nontaxability with his employer [¶ 2506(c)].

¶ 3510 Return by agent. The tax return may be made by an agent, if the taxpayer is unable to make it because of disease or injury or because he is absent from the United States for a period of at least 60 days before the return is due. An agent also may make the return if the taxpayer's District Director, upon receipt of the taxpayer's application showing good cause, gives his permission. Form 2848 should be filed with the return. An agent may submit a photographic copy of a

Footnotes appear at end of this Chapter.

¶ 3510

valid power of attorney in place of the official form. If another reproduction is used, the copy must be certified. These rules also apply to declarations of estimated tax [Sec. 6012(b), 6015; 1.6012-1, 1.6015(a)-1; 601.-504(e)]. See ¶ 2516; 2517.

¶ 3511 **Return by fiduciary.** In general, if an individual would be required to make a return [¶ 1100], a fiduciary acting for him is required to file one [Sec. 6012(b)].

(a) Who are fiduciaries. The term "fiduciary" means a guardian, trustee, executor, administrator, receiver, conservator, or any person acting in any fiduciary capacity for any person [Sec. 7701(a)(6); 301.7701-6].
Fiduciaries required to file returns include the following [Sec. 6012(b)]:

- Guardian or a committee of an insane person [Sec. 1.6012-3(b)(3)].
- Guardian of a minor unless the minor himself makes the return or causes it to be made [Sec. 1.6012-3(b)(3)]. See also ¶ 3509.
- Guardian of a taxpayer who has disappeared. If his spouse is appointed guardian, she may file a joint return for herself and as guardian of her missing husband, if the other requirements are met[1] [¶ 3505].
- Executor or administrator for decedent [Sec. 1.6012-3(b)(1)]. See ¶ 3020; 3507; 3517.
- Trustee of a trust [¶ 3020].

Example: The guardian of an insane person must file a return for the estate, if the gross income from the ward's estate is $600 or more [¶ 3020(c)].

(b) What return form to use. The guardian, executor or administrator must make the return for an individual on Form 1040 or 1040A [Sec. 6012(b); 1.6012-3(b)]. The return for an estate or trust is made on Form 1041.

How the return is signed. The person making the return must sign and indicate the capacity in which he is acting. If there are two or more joint fiduciaries, one can execute the return [Sec. 6012(b)(5); 1.6012-3(c)].

(c) Fiduciaries not required to file. A receiver who is in charge of only a portion of the taxpayer's property need not make a return. A receiver who stands in place of an individual has a duty to file a return if the individual does not file it [Sec. 6012(b); 1.6012-3(b)].
A trustee in bankruptcy may not file a return, in his capacity as trustee, for a bankrupt individual. The bankrupt files his own return.[2]

NOTE: The trustee in bankruptcy files Form 1041 for the income of a bankrupt partnership.[3]

CORPORATION TAX RETURNS

¶ 3512 **Corporation income tax returns.** Every corporation not expressly exempt must file an *income tax* return, even if it has no taxable income. Returns must be filed by the corporation for as long as it remains in existence [Sec. 6012(a); 1.6012-2(a)]. Returns must include identifying numbers (¶ 3500) [Sec. 301.6109-1(d)].
Corporations, that received a charter, but have never perfected their organization, transacted business or received any income from any source may be relieved of the duty of filing a return upon application to the District Director [Sec. 6012(a)(2); 1.6012-2(a)(2)].

(a) Determining corporate existence. Generally, a corporation is not in existence after it ceases business and dissolves, retaining no assets, even if it is still treated as a continuing corporation under state law to wind up its affairs. If the corporation has valuable claims for which it will bring suit, it has retained assets, and it continues in existence. A corporation that is turned over to receivers who continue to operate it does not go out of existence [Sec. 1.6012-2(a)(2)].

RETURNS NOT REQUIRED

When a charter was granted, but never exercised there was no de facto corporation, and no liability for corporation tax.[1]

A corporation ceases to exist after its charter is revoked and the income from continued operation is taxed to the sole proprietor.[2]

RETURNS REQUIRED

Corporation returns must be filed in the following cases: when a partnership is incorporated, but business is conducted the same as before its incorporation;[3] when a corporation, which has ceased business, retains a small sum of cash to pay state taxes to preserve its corporate charter,[4] or has valuable claims for which it will bring suit [Sec. 1.6012-1(a)(2)]; when a corporation has dissolved before the date its return was due[5] or before passage of a retroactive tax law or law changing the rates of tax.[6] (The corporation is not relieved from tax liability for the period it was in existence.)

(b) Return by receiver or trustee. A receiver having possession or title to all or substantially all of the business or property of a corporation must file the corporation returns, whether he is liquidating the corporation or operating its business. Trustees in dissolution and trustees in bankruptcy have the same status as receivers [Sec. 6012(b)(3); 1.6012-3(b)(4)].

¶ **3513 What tax return form to use.** Form 1120 is used by all ordinary business corporations. Corporations electing to be treated as a partnership [¶ 3140-3146] file Form 1120S.

(a) Exempt organizations. Unrelated business income of exempt corporations is reported on Form 990-T [¶ 3454]. Exempt farm cooperatives use Form 990-C to report income [¶ 3455].

(b) How return is signed. Corporation income tax returns must be signed by hand[1] and verified by the president, vice-president, treasurer, assistant treasurer, chief accounting officer or any other officer authorized to act [Sec. 6062, 6065; 1.6062-1, 1.6065-1].

¶ **3514 Return for short tax year.** A corporation in existence during any part of the tax year must file a tax return [Sec. 1.6012-2(a)(2)]. The closing date of the first return of the newly organized corporation depends on whether it uses the calendar year or a fiscal year as its accounting period. A fiscal year may be adopted without permission of the Revenue Service.[1]

> **Example:** If a corporation received its charter and began business on November 15, 1977, and wished to adopt the calendar year, its first return would be for the period November 15, to December 31, 1977, and subsequent returns would be for the calendar years following. If the corporation wished to adopt a fiscal year ending January 31, its first return would be for the period November 15, 1977, to January 31, 1978, and subsequent returns for the fiscal years following.

A return for a corporation from the date of incorporation to the end of its first accounting period is considered to be for a period of 12 months. It is not a fractional year return, and the income need not be put on an annual basis [Sec. 443].

Footnotes appear at end of this Chapter.

Returns for periods of less than twelve months due to change of accounting periods must be put on an annual basis [¶ 2717].

¶ 3515 Consolidated income tax return. An affiliated group of corporations, under certain conditions [¶ 3222], may file a consolidated return [Sec. 1501]. The common parent makes the return for the group on Form 1120, to which it attaches Form 851. Once a consolidated return in filed, the practice must be continued while the group remains in existence, unless the Commissioner grants permission to discontinue the consolidated return [Sec. 1.1502-75].

TIME AND PLACE FOR FILING TAX RETURNS AND DECLARATIONS

¶ 3517 When returns must be filed. Returns must be filed by the prescribed due date, unless the time to file has been extended [¶ 3518]. Income tax returns are filed for a calendar year or for a fiscal year. Information returns [¶ 3530 et seq.] generally are filed on a calendar year basis. There is a penalty for failure to file returns on time [¶ 3618].

The time for filing returns for taxes withheld by the payer are discussed at the following paragraphs: wage payments, ¶ 2509; payments to nonresident aliens and interest on tax-free covenant bonds, ¶ 2535.

Due date on Saturday, Sunday, or legal holiday. When the due date for filing a return or performing any other prescribed act falls on Saturday, Sunday or a legal holiday, the act is timely if done on the next day that is not a Saturday, Sunday or legal holiday [Sec. 7503; 301.7503-1].

Filing by mail. Returns (and other claims, documents or statements required to be filed) may be filed by mail if properly addressed to the officer, office or agency where they must be filed and postage paid. If the envelope or wrapper bears a U.S. postmark made by the post office dated on or before the due date of the return (or within the required filing period for other claims or statements), it will be considered filed on time, even if it is received after the due date. A postmark from a private postage meter is acceptable but it must be dated on or before the due date. In addition, the return or other document must be received the same time as one bearing a U.S. postmark. If not so received, the taxpayer must prove that it was timely mailed and give the reason for the delay. Incorrect private postage meter dates must be corrected by the post office. However, the Tax Court has accepted a private postage meter date not so corrected.[1] See also ¶ 3639(a). An extension of time to file extends the due date. A registered mail date is treated as the postmark date, and registration is proof of delivery [Sec. 7502; 301.7502-1]. For timely mailing of tax deposits, see ¶ 3523.

Short tax year. Generally, returns for a period of less than 12 months [¶ 2717] must be filed within the same period after the close of the short period as if the short period were a fiscal year.[2]

(a) Individual returns. Individuals on a calendar year basis must file income tax returns by April 15. Taxpayers using a fiscal year must file by the 15th of the fourth month following the close of the fiscal year [Sec. 6072(a); 1.6072-1(a)]. For declaration of estimated tax, see ¶ 2517.

> **Example 1:** Brown is on a fiscal year ending April 30. He must file his return by August 15.

Joint return by surviving husband or wife. If a surviving husband (or wife) elects to file a joint return with his deceased spouse for the year the spouse dies, the time for filing the joint return is the same as if the death had not occurred.

Example 2: John Jones and his wife Mary are both calendar year taxpayers. If Mary dies during 1977, the joint return must be filed by April 17, 1978.

Example 3: James Grey and his wife Joan both file returns on a fiscal year basis ending June 30th. If James dies on December 1, 1977, the joint return must be filed by October 16, 1978.

A "late" joint return replacing separate returns of the husband and wife may be filed after the due date of the return for the tax year [¶ 3506].

Final return for decedent. The executor or administrator of a decdent must file the decedent's last return. It is due the same date a return would have been due had decedent lived the entire tax year [Sec. 1.6072-1].

Nonresident aliens who do not have wages subject to withholding, and partnerships of all nonresident aliens, file returns by the 15th day of the sixth month following the close of the tax year [Sec. 1.6031-1(e); 1.6072-1(c)].

(b) Corporation returns. Income tax returns of corporations on the calendar year basis must be filed by March 15. Fiscal year returns must be filed by the 15th of the third month following the close of the fiscal year [Sec. 6072(b); 1.6072-2]. Corporations are not required to file declarations of estimated tax. For payment due dates, see ¶ 3523.

A corporation that goes out of existence during its annual accounting period must file its income tax return by the 15th day of the third month after it ceased business and dissolved, unless the District Director grants an extension (¶ 3518) [Sec. 1.6071-1(b); 1.6072-2(a)]. It may, however, file its return immediately upon completion of liquidation, and may elect to pay the tax in installments [¶ 3523].[2]

Foreign corporations not having an office or place of business in the U.S. file their income tax returns by the 15th day of the sixth month following the close of the tax year [Sec. 1.6072-2(b)].

(c) Tax returns for estates and trusts. The fiduciary for an estate or trust [¶ 3001] must file a return [¶ 3020] by the 15th day of the fourth month after the close of the tax year. Returns made on a calendar year basis must be filed by April 15th [Sec. 6072(a); 1.6072-1(b)].

Final return. The last return of an estate or a trust must be filed by the 15th day of the fourth month following the closing of the estate or termination of the trust [Sec. 1.6072-1].

(d) Exempt organizations—return of unrelated business income. Return of unrelated business income on Form 990-T required of certain exempt organizations [¶ 3446; 3454] must be filed by the 15th of the third month following the close of the tax year, if the organization is taxable as a corporation [Sec. 1.6072-2(c)]. Domestic trusts, and foreign trusts having an office or place of business in the U.S., must file the return by the 15th day of the fourth month following the close of the trust's tax year. [Sec. 1.6072-1(a)].

Exempt foreign organization taxable as a corporation and foreign trusts without an office or place of business in the U.S., must file the return by the 15th day of the sixth month following the close of the tax year [Sec. 1.6072-1(c), 1.6072-2(c)].

Footnotes appear at end of this Chapter.

¶ **3517**

(e) **DISC returns.** A Domestic International Sales Corporation [¶ 3460] must file its return by the 15th day of the ninth month after the close of its tax year [Sec. 6072(b)].

¶ 3518 Extension of time to file returns. The Revenue Service can grant a reasonable extension of time to file tax returns, except the return of tax withheld from wages (¶ 2509) [Sec. 6081; 1.6081-1]. Some taxpayers (including private foundations [Sec. 53.6081-1]) have a right to an automatic extension of time to file (see below).

The usual extension of time to file income tax returns granted to corporations is 90 days. Individuals, partnerships, estates and trusts usually get 60 days. (See (b) below.) The extension cannot exceed six months, except in the case of taxpayers who are abroad [Sec. 6081(a)].

Return for short period. The time to file an income tax return for a short period may be extended by the Revenue Service, if the taxpayer shows unusual circumstances [Sec. 1.6071-1(b)].

Application must be filed. An application signed by the taxpayer or his authorized agent must be filed by the return due date with the Internal Revenue office where the return is required to be filed [Sec. 1.6081-1(b)]. The factors beyond taxpayer's control that make the extension necessary must be explained in detail.

Applications (by letter or on Form 2688) for an extension of time to file Form 1040 also must state (i) whether a return was filed on time (including extensions) for each of the three preceding tax years, and (ii) whether a declaration of estimated tax was required and the payments made on time (including extensions), for the year of the request [Sec. 1.6081-1]. U.S. citizens abroad who expect to have exempt foreign earned income [¶ 3725] should use Form 2350, not Form 2688.[1]

>   NOTE: Except in undue hardship cases, no extension of time for filing an individual return will be granted until the automatic 2-month filing extension (see (b) below) has been used [Sec. 1.6081-4(a)(5)].

Partnerships, estates and trusts may use application Form 2758. It must be signed by a partner, or the fiduciary or an officer of an organization having control of the estate or trust.[2]

Approved applications should be attached to the return when it is filed. A return must be filed within 10 days after an application is denied. Any election made on such a return is considered made in time.[3]

Application by agent. If for any reason the taxpayer is unable to sign the application for extension, it may be signed by any person standing in close personal or business relationship to him, if the reasons and relationship are stated [Sec. 1.6081-1(b)(4)]. Corporations also may request extensions through an agent [Sec. 1.6081-1(b)(1)]. Applications filed under a power of attorney must show that fact, but a copy of the power need not be attached.[4]

Time to pay tax. Generally, when an individual, corporation or private foundation gets an extension of time to file, the time to pay the tax is not extended, unless the extension specifies otherwise [Sec. 1.6081-1(a), 1.6081-3(c), 1.6081-4(b); 53.6081-1]. However, taxpayers in (a) below automatically get an extension of time to pay unless the extension states otherwise. Interest will be charged on any tax not paid by due date [¶ 3618].

(a) **Businesses with foreign operations and U.S. citizens abroad.** An automatic extension is granted to the 15th of the sixth month after the end of the tax year to the following [Sec. 1.6081-2]:

- Domestic corporations that transact their business and keep their records and books of account outside U.S. and Puerto Rico.

Example 1: Oversea Trading Corp. is a domestic corporation operating on a calendar year basis. Its records and accounts are kept in its office in Switzerland, because it trades exclusively in Europe. The time to file its corporation tax return is extended to June 15.

- Domestic corporations whose principal income is from sources within possessions of the United States.
- Foreign corporations that maintain an office or place of business within the United States, and foreign partnerships.
- Partnerships that keep their books of account outside U.S. and Puerto Rico.
- American citizens residing or traveling outside U.S. and Puerto Rico.

This includes members of the Armed Forces on duty outside the United States. Members serving in a "combat zone" [¶ 1306] (including those in their support) or those hospitalized outside the U.S. for an injury received in the combat zone, have 180 days after such service to file and pay the tax [Sec. 7508]. For the due date of those in a missing or prisoner of war status, see ¶ 1100(d).

NOTE: Citizens who qualify for exclusion of foreign earned income [¶ 3725] may apply for more than 6 months extension.

No extension application is needed, but a statement must be attached to the return, showing that taxpayer falls within one of the above classes.

(b) 2-month extension for individuals. An individual can get an automatic extension of time to file his Form 1040. He gets this extension by filing an application on Form 4868 by the return due date (¶ 3517(a)) [Sec. 1.6081-4(a)]. The application must show the full amount estimated as tax for the year, and must be accompanied by the estimated tax owed [Sec. 1.6081-4(a)(4)]. A duplicate copy of Form 4868 must be attached to the completed Form 1040 as proof of the extension. Interest is payable from the original due date of the return to the date of payment [¶ 3618].

(c) 90-day extension for corporations. Corporations can also get an automatic extension to the 15th day of the third month after the month of the due date of the return by filing Form 7004 by the due date. This form is an application for extension with a statement in place of a tentative return [Sec. 6081(a); 1.6081-3]. The extension may be terminated on 10 days' written notice [Sec. 6081(b); 1.6081-3(d)]. A corporation that has already obtained an automatic 3-month extension by filing Form 7004 may apply for an additional extension by filing Form 7005. This request for an additional extension is not automatic and must be specifically granted by the Director of the Service Center where the return will be filed.[5]

Duplicate copies of Forms 7004 and 7005 must accompany the completed returns as proof of the extensions [Sec. 1.6081-3(a)].

Consolidated return. A parent corporation may request extensions for its subsidiaries when a consolidated return is to be filed. The name and address of each member of the affiliated group for which the extension is desired must be listed on Form 7004. The application is filed with the Internal Revenue office where the parent files its return. If a group member does not file a consolidated return, it must attach a copy of Form 7004 to its separate return [Sec. 1.6081-3(b)].

Tax must be paid. The corporation must remit [¶ 3523] the tax it estimates it will have to pay. If it elects to pay in installments, it must remit 50% of its esti-

¶ 3518

mate [Sec. 1.6081-3(a)]. Payment may not be required if Form 1138 for a net operating loss carryback [¶ 3630(c)] is filed at the same time.[6] Any overpayment based on a tentative return will be refunded without the filing of a refund claim, nevertheless a claim should be made on the final return or refund claim form [¶ 3626] as a protection against not receiving the overpayment [Sec. 301.6402-4].

When Form 7004 is used, interest is payable from the original due date of the corporate return on any tax not shown on the form. When installment payments are elected [¶ 3523], interest on any unpaid tax reported on Form 7004 runs from the installment due dates.[7]

Example 2: The Excel Corporation got a 90-day extension to file its calendar year 1977 return. It filed Form 7004 showing estimated taxes of $24,100, and paid an installment of $15,400, even though only $12,050 (50% × $24,100) was required. The final return showed a tax due of $25,100. The corporation must pay interest at the current rate [¶ 3628] on $1,000 until it is paid, since that is the amount of actual tax not shown on Form 7004.[8]

(d) Declaration of estimated tax. The District or Service Center Director can grant an extension of time to file declarations of estimated tax on written application filed before the due date [Sec. 6081; 1.6073-4]. The maximum extension (except for taxpayers abroad) is 6 months, but the usual extension granted is 15 days [Sec. 601.104(b)]. For corporate estimated tax payments, see ¶ 3523(a).

An extension of time to file an individual's declaration also extends the time to pay the estimated tax *without interest*. However, the penalty for any underpayment of tax [¶ 2519] is figured from the original due date for the declaration [Sec. 1.6153-4].

¶ 3519 Where to file returns. Generally, returns for income tax, self-employment tax and an individual's declaration of estimated tax will be filed in the Revenue District where the taxpayer resides or has a principal place of business, or at the Service Center that serves that district. However, the Revenue Service may designate special filing places for specific returns. Information returns generally are filed at a Service Center [¶ 3530]. Amended returns also must be filed at a Service Center unless they are hand carried [Sec. 1.6091-2]. For return of taxes withheld from wages, see ¶ 2509(c).

(a) Individuals, estates and trusts. Tax returns and declarations of estimated tax may be hand delivered to the District Director for the district where the person making the return has his legal residence or principal place of business. Until regulations or instructions require returns that are not hand delivered to be filed at Service Centers, they may be mailed to the District Director [Sec. 6091; 1.6091-2].

(b) Corporations. Corporation tax returns may be hand delivered to the District Director of the district where the principal place of business or principal office or agency is located [Sec. 6091; 1.6091-2]. That is, where the books are kept.[1] Just as for individuals, returns not hand delivered may be mailed to the District Director until regulations or instructions require that they be sent to a Service Center.

(c) Private foundations. The rules above for returns by individuals and corporations also apply to private foundations. In exceptional cases, the Commissioner may allow returns to be filed in any district [Sec. 53.6091-1, 2].

(d) Returns specially treated. Nonresident aliens, foreign corporations, taxpayers with no residence or place of business in a revenue district, U.S. citizens who live outside the U.S. for the return period, persons who exclude foreign earned income [¶ 3725], taxpayers subject to termination assessments [¶ 3612(b)], or income from U.S. possessions or Puerto Rico [¶ 3727] and corporations claiming the special Western Hemisphere or China Trade Act deduction [¶ 3117] may be required to file their returns at a specially designated Revenue Service office. Currently, individuals and fiduciaries file with the District Director at Baltimore, Maryland if they have no principal residence or place of business in an internal revenue district, but the following taxpayers file returns with the Director of International Operations at Washington, D.C. (or an address designated by the instructions to the return form): U.S. citizens who live outside the U.S. for the return period; citizens of U.S. possessions; nonresident aliens or fiduciaries and foreign corporations with no U.S. place of business [Sec. 6091; 1.6091-2, 1.6091-3].

NOTE: Locations of District Directors' offices and Service Centers are listed in P-H Federal Taxes ¶ 39,920 et seq. and in the instructions to the returns. The locations also can be obtained at your local post office.

¶ 3520 Use of amended returns. A taxpayer can correct an error in a return he has filed by filing an amended return. For this purpose, individuals must use Form 1040X and corporations Form 1120X. Other taxpayers may use a regular return form [Sec. 301.6402-3(a)]. The amended regular return can be filed on a return form for the same year as the return being corrected or another year's return if changed to show the correct year. The words, "Amended Return" should be written or printed at the top of the regular return form. You must explain the error that is being corrected. The Revenue Service is not compelled to accept an amended return.[1]

NOTE: Refund or credit claims filed for individuals and corporations can no longer be made on amended returns (Form 1040 or 1120) [Sec. 301.6402-3(b)].

(a) Payment of tax. If more tax is due because of a correction, it should be paid with the amended return. Interest and penalties are imposed for delinquent returns [¶ 3618].

(b) Credit or refund. If taxpayer is entitled to a credit or refund of income tax as a result of the correction, Forms 1040X, 1120X or the amended return (regular return form for taxpayers other than individuals or corporations) will serve as a claim for refund or credit. The claim must be filed before the limitation period expires [¶ 3623].

NOTE: Taxpayers may no longer use Form 843 to apply for refunds overpayments of income taxes [Sec. 301.6402-3(b)].

(c) Changing elections. Form 1040X, 1120X or an amended regular return may be used to change the election with respect to the standard deduction or the return form. A married couple can file a joint return to replace separate returns under certain conditions [¶ 3506].

SUPPORTING INFORMATION

¶ 3521 Additional information that must be filed with the return. Income tax returns must be executed and filed in accordance with the regulations and the instructions with the return [Sec. 6011(a)]. Preparing and filing returns, therefore, involves more than merely reporting income and deductions, and figuring the tax. It is necessary to include or attach to the return, any required supporting information or statement.

Footnotes appear at end of this Chapter.

Information and statements required. The supporting information, statements, etc., that are called for by the form instructions and regulations is given below.

Bad debts. Statement substantiating the deduction [Sec. 1.166-1]. *Individuals* are required to show (a) nature of the debt; (b) name and family or business relationship, if any, of debtor; (c) when due; (d) efforts made to collect, and (e) how determined to be worthless.[1] As to the reserve method, see also Sec. 1.166-4.

Bingo, keno, slot machine winnings. Starting 3-1-77, Form W-2G must be filed for winnings of $1,000 or more. Between 2-1-77 and 2-28-77, the reportable amount was $600[2] [Temp. Reg. Sec. 7.6041-1].

Blind persons. A taxpayer claiming exemption for partial blindness of himself, his spouse, or both, must attach to his return, a certificate from a qualified physician or a registered optometrist stating that (1) the central visual acuity of the "blind" person does not exceed 20/200 in the better eye with correcting lenses, or (2) the fields of vision are so limited that the widest diameter of the visual field subtends an angle no greater than 20 degrees. If the blindness is total, a statement must be attached to the return setting forth that fact [Sec. 1.151-1(d)(3), (4)]. See also ¶ 1114(a).

Capitalized taxes. An election to capitalize taxes is made by filing a statement with the return indicating the items to be capitalized [Sec. 1.266-1(c)(3)].

Capital loss carryover. Statement showing how the carryover is figured [capital gain and loss schedule].

Charitable contributions. Name and address of each organization to which a contribution was made and the amount. Attach statement showing how the deduction is figured. If a deduction of more than $200 is claimed for contributed property, an appraisal and statement of other details must be submitted [Sec. 1.170A-1(a)(2)].

A special election can be made to reduce all contributions of capital gain property by ½ the appreciation to get the higher limitation for the charitable deduction [¶ 1942(b)].

Corporations deducting contributions paid within 2½ months after the tax year [¶ 3118] must attach the directors' resolution and verify its adoption during the tax year [Sec. 1.170A-11(b)].

Commodity Credit Corp. loans. A taxpayer electing to include such loans in gross income should file a statement showing the details of the loans.

For reference purposes only, a list of the

Common trust funds. A copy of the plan for the fund must accompany the first return filed for the fund. Plan amendments must be filed with the return for the year they are adopted [Sec. 1.6032-1].

Consent dividends. Corporation claiming a credit for consent dividends must file: (1) Forms 972 (shareholder's consent) executed by each consenting shareholder; and (2) Form 973 [Sec. 1.565-1].

Consolidated returns. Form 851, Affiliations Schedule, must be attached to the parent corporation's consolidated return. Form 1122 for each subsidiary must be attached to the first consolidated return and a copy filed with the subsidiary's District Director by the consolidated return due date [Sec. 1.1502-75].

Depletion data. Mineral property [Sec. 1.611-2(g)]. Percentage depletion [Sec. 1.613-5]. Timber [Sec. 1.611-3(h)]. See instructions to Form 1120.

Depreciable property. Depreciation claimed must be supported by detailed schedules showing: description of the property; date of acquisition; cost or other basis of the asset; amount of depreciation allowed or allowable in prior years; method under which the depreciation allowance is claimed; rate of depreciation or expected useful life of the asset; and depreciation allowance claimed for current year. Optional Form 4562 can be attached to the return.

Similar information, including deductions by prior owners, should be filed with the return for the year Sec. 1250 property [¶ 1619] is acquired, except in like-kind exchanges or through involuntary conversions [Sec. 1.1250-2(f)].

A special election applies to changing the method of depreciation on depreciable real property [Sec. 167(e)(3)]. See ¶ 1619(b); 2010(c).

Depreciation. If the Class Life ADR system is elected [¶ 2033], detailed information must be furnished showing: the asset guideline class for each vintage account; the asset depreciation period selected for each vintage account; the first-year convention adopted for the election year; the vintage account's basis and salvage value; the amount of any property improvements; and a description of the property [Sec. 167(m); 1.167(a)-11(f)(2)]. Form 4832 can be used.

In addition, the following special information must be filed as to each asset guideline class for the election year: the total unadjusted basis of all assets retired during the year from each vintage account and the proceeds realized from the retirement; a description of all assets retired during the year; the vintage of the assets retired; reasons for and manner of retirement; and information on expenditures [Sec. 1.167(a)-11(f)(4)].

Development expenditures. Instructions require that election to treat such expenditures as deferred expenses deductible ratably must be made on the return or by filing a statement not later than 6 months after filing the return.

DISC shareholder election. Each shareholder of a corporation electing to be treated as a "DISC" [¶ 3460] must sign either a statement of consent on Form 4876 or a separate statement of consent attached to the Form. The statement must be signed by the shareholder and contain the name and address of the electing corporation and the shareholder as well as the number of shares held by him [Temp. Reg. Sec. 12.7(b)].

Dividend carryover. Attach statement showing computations [Sec. 1.564-1].

Dividends paid. Corporation claiming an allowance for dividends paid must file a copy of the dividend resolution and other information [Sec. 1.561-2(c)].

Employees' trusts. Exemption from tax requires filing with the Revenue Service the detailed information required on certain annual return forms (Form 5500 series). See ¶ 3537(d).

Estates and trusts. First return of an estate or trust, when gross income is $5,000 or over, must be accompanied by a copy of the will or trust instrument, and the fiduciary's statement of the provisions he thinks control the taxability of the income. A copy of later trust amendments, and the fiduciary's statement of their effect on taxability of trust income, must be attached to the affected return [Sec. 1.6012-3(a)(2)].

When a nonresident alien beneficiary appoints a person in the U.S. as his agent to make returns, see Sec. 1.6012-1(b)(6); 1.6012-3(b)(2).

If the estate or trust is engaged in trade or business, a schedule must be attached to the return similar to that required in the "profit (or loss) from business" schedule on Form 1040.

If any part of the income of a trust is taxable to the grantor, the income and the related deductions and credits should be shown in a separate statement attached to Form 1041.

An estate or trust is allowed a special election as to its charitable contributions [Sec. 642(c)]. See ¶ 3013.

Exempt income expenses. Taxpayer receiving exempt income, other than interest, must submit a statement showing the amount of such income and, if an expense item is apportioned between exempt and taxable income, the basis of the apportionment [Sec. 1.265-1(d)].

Exemption for dependent. When several persons support an individual, and one is designated to claim the exemption, each of the others who contributed over 10% support must file a declaration that he will not claim the individual as a dependent. Form 2120 may be used.

Exploration expenditures. Merely deducting expenses on the return elects the deduction. Before 1970, a limited as well as an unlimited deduction could be elected. A taxpayer who elected the pre-1970 limited deduction (not subject to recapture) is considered to have elected the unlimited deduction (subject to recapture) for expenditures made after 12-31-69, unless he notifies the Revenue Service to the contrary. Notification must be made with the return for the first tax year that includes post-1969 expenditures. See ¶ 1843.

Extension of time for filing. U.S. citizens residing or traveling abroad are automatically granted two month extension of time for filing the return. A statement must be attached to the return, showing that taxpayer was outside the U.S. on the due date [Sec. 1.6081-2].

If an individual or corporation gets an automatic extension by filing Form 4868 or Form 7004 [¶ 3518], a copy of the form must accompany the completed return [Sec. 1.6081-3, 1.6081-4(a)(5)].

Farmers. Schedule F of Form 1040 must be attached to return of farmers filing on the cash or accrual method.

A special election applies to the handling of farm gains and losses. See ¶ 2226.

A cash basis farmer can elect to include crop insurance proceeds in income for the tax year after crops were destroyed or damaged if the crop income would have been included in income for that year. The election is made by attaching a statement to the return filed for the recovery year. See ¶ 2614 [Sec. 451(d); 1.451-6].

Farm program payments. Persons receiving cash program payments from the

Footnotes appear at end of this Chapter.

¶ **3521**

Department of Agriculture that belong to others may attach Form 4347 to their returns to identify the real owner of the payment.[3]

Foreign income. File Form 2555 with the return to support exclusion of income earned abroad [¶ 3725].

Foreign tax credit. Individuals file Form 1116, corporations Form 1118. If credit is for taxes paid, receipts must be attached to the form; if credit is for taxes accrued, the return on which each such accrued tax was based, must be attached to the form [Sec. 1.905-2].

Gasoline tax credit. Form 4136 may be filed with the return showing the computation for federal gasoline and oil tax credit [¶ 2417].

Installment sales. When installment method is used, the instructions call for current and prior year data as to: (a) Gross sales; (b) cost of goods sold; (c) gross profits; (d) percentage of profits to gross sales; (e) amount collected; and (f) gross profit on amount collected.

On change to installment method, attach statement to the return showing (1) accounting method used before the change; (2) period over which the adjustments must be made; and (3) schedule showing how adjustments are figured [Sec. 1.453-8].

A taxpayer may revoke an election to report on the installment basis. A revocation notice must be filed within 3 years after the date of filing the tax return for year the installment method was elected [Sec. 453(c)(4)]. See ¶ 2804.

Interest—foreign corporations and nonresident aliens. Any such taxpayer who excludes U.S. source interest from gross income must file a statement of the amount and type of such interest [Sec. 1.861-2].

Inventories. If the inventories reported do not agree with the balance sheet, attach a statement explaining the difference. Taxpayer electing to use LIFO method, must file Form 970 with the return for the first year.

After election to use LIFO method, a separate schedule must be submitted each year with the return showing (1) a summary of all inventories; and (2) with respect to LIFO inventories, the computation of the quantities and cost by acquisition levels.

Inventories by dealers in securities.- Describe method used [Sec. 1.471-5].

Involuntary conversion. Details of an involuntary conversion of property at a gain must be reported on the return for the year the gain is realized. Such details relate to the replacement of the converted property, decision not to replace, or expiration of the period for replacement. If replacement occurs in two years none of the gain on the conversion is realized, details of the replacement should be reported on the return for that year [Sec. 1.1033(a)-2(c)(2)].

The election to treat involuntary conversion of a residence as a sale [¶ 1421] must be attached to the return for the year of disposition, with information as to basis, dates, prices and occupancy of old and new residences [Sec. 1.1034-1].

Liquidating distribution. When a shareholder in exchange for property transfers stock to the corporation that issued the stock, the facts and circumstances should be reported on the shareholder's return, unless the property is part of a distribution made in liquidation of the corporation and the corporation is completely liquidated and dissolved within one year after the distribution [Sec. 1.331-1(d)]. See also ¶ 1715-1717.

Liquidation of subsidiary. In a nontaxable liquidation of a subsidiary under Sec. 332 the parent must file (1) a certified copy of the plan for liquidation and of the resolutions authorizing the liquidation; (2) a list of the property received, showing the basis in the hands of the subsidiary and fair market value at date distributed; (3) a statement of any indebtedness of the liquidating corporation to the recipient corporation on the date the plan of liquidation was adopted and on the date of the first liquidating distribution, and the cost to the recipient corporation of any such indebtedness acquired at less than face value; and (4) statement of its ownership of stock of the subsidiary, and its cost or other basis [Sec. 1.332-6].

Long-term contracts. Attach to the return statement that long-term contract method is being used [Sec. 1.451-3].

Losses by fire, storm, or other casualty, or theft. File statement explaining the deduction, with a description of the property, date acquired, cost, subsequent improvements, depreciation allowable, insurance, salvage value, and deductible loss.

Medical expense deduction. If the expense is deductible for both estate and income tax purposes, and it is deducted on the income tax return, file with the return a statement and waiver of the deduction for estate tax purposes [¶ 1945(b)].

Net operating loss deduction. A concise statement showing how the net operating loss deduction is figured should be filed with taxpayer's return.

Organizational expenditures. Election to amortize the expenditures must be made by filing statement with the return showing

(1) description and amount of the expenditures; (2) date incurred or paid; (3) month the corporation began business; and (4) number of months (not less than 60) of amortization period [Sec. 1.248-1]. See also ¶ 3116.

Partnerships. If the return is filed for a syndicate, pool, joint venture, etc., attach a copy of the operating agreement to the return, unless a copy has been previously filed, together with amendments thereto [Form 1065 instructions].

A partner who transfers any part of his partnership interest must file a statement with his return showing: (1) the adjusted basis of his partnership interest and the portion of it that results from unrealized receivables and substantially appreciated inventory items; and (2) the amount he gets for his interest and the portion that results from unrealized receivables or substantially appreciated inventory items [Sec. 1.751-1(a)(3)].

Pension trust payments. To support a deduction claimed under Sec. 403 for payments to an employees' pension trust, the taxpayer must file the appropriate form in the Form 5500 series. See ¶ 3537(d).

Power of attorney. An agent filing for taxpayer may file power of attorney instead of Form 2848. Form 1342, authorizing attorney in fact to file returns of taxes withheld on wages, must accompany first return filed by agent.

Prepaid subscription income. A statement of election to defer prepaid subscription income [¶ 2726] must be filed with the return for the first year to which it applies, showing accounting method, total prepaid subscriptions, period of liability, income for each period and method of allocation [Sec. 1.455-6].

Regulated investment companies. For information to be filed with the returns of certain stockholders of such companies, see Sec. 1.852-7. For real estate investment trusts, see Sec. 1.857-7.

Reorganizations. Each corporation a party to a reorganization must file as part of its return, (1) a certified copy of the plan of reorganization, with a statement under oath or affirmation showing the purposes thereof and transactions incident to the plan; (2) statement of cost or other basis of all property, including stock or securities, transferred; (3) statement showing the amount of stock or securities, other property, or money, received from the exchange and the distributions or other disposition made thereof; and (4) statement of the amount and nature of liabilities assumed. Every taxpayer, other than a corporation a party to the reorganization, who received stock or securities, other property, or money upon a tax-free exchange in connection with a reorganization, must file a statement including (1) cost or other basis of stock or securities transferred in the exchange; and (2) fair market value of stock, securities or other property and money received [Sec. 1.368-3].

Sale of oil or gas properties. Taxpayer claiming the benefit of Sec. 632 must submit a statement explaining how expenses, losses, and other deductions were apportioned between the gross income from such sale and from other sources [Sec. 1.632-1].

Sale of residence. If you sold your residence and none or only part of the gain was recognized because of your age, or because you purchased or built a new residence, attach a statement to the return showing purchase price, date of purchase, and date of occupancy. Form 2119, for figuring recognized gain, may be obtained from District Directors. If you acquire the new residence after your return is filed, you should advise the District Director, giving full details. See ¶ 1416 et seq.

Sale or exchange of real estate, bonds, or stock. The following information is required by the instructions: (a) For real estate, location and description of land, description of improvements; (b) for bonds or other evidences of indebtedness, name of issuing corporation, description of the particular issue, denomination, and amount; (c) for stocks, name of issuing corporation, class of stock, number of shares, capital changes affecting basis (nontaxable stock dividends, other nontaxable distributions, stock rights, etc.). Such changes can be found in the *Prentice-Hall Capital Adjustments Service*. As to the information required about the acquisition of the property and the purchaser, see the "gain or loss" schedule on return.

Stock owned in foreign or domestic corporations. Statement should be attached to corporation's return setting forth the name and address of each foreign company and the number of shares of each class of stock owned. See instructions. If the taxpayer owns 5% or more in value of the stock of a foreign personal holding company, the information required by Sec. 551(d) must also be furnished [Sec. 1.551-4]. As to stock owned in domestic corporations, see "Questions" on return.

Footnotes appear at end of this Chapter.

¶ 3521

Transfer of property to controlled corporation. Every person who received stock or securities of a controlled corporation for property under Sec. 351 must file a complete statement of all the facts, including (1) description of property, together with cost or other adjusted basis at date of transfer; and (2) fair market value of stock, securities or other property or money received. The corporation must submit a similar statement and also state the amount of its outstanding stock and securities after the transfer and the amount owned by each transferor [Sec. 1.351-3].

Withholding tax on wages. Credit for amount withheld is determined by reference to employee's statement received from employer [Form W-2]. This form must be attached to individual's return.

NOTE: Certain boat operators [¶ 2503(a)] must furnish each crewman and the Revenue Service by January 31 of each succeeding calendar year a written statement showing the crewman's identity, the weight of the catch or proceeds allocated to him in the preceding calendar year [Sec. 6050A].

PAYMENT OF TAX

¶ 3522 When individual tax must be paid. Generally, the income tax must be paid by the due date of the return [¶ 3517]. Any balance of the tax not collected through withholding on wages [¶ 2509] or payments of estimated tax [¶ 2517] must be paid by the 15th of the fourth month following the close of the tax year (April 15 for calendar year taxpayers) [Sec. 6151(a); 1.6151-1(a)].

Example: James Harris reports on the basis of a fiscal year ending on June 30. Payment of tax is due by October 15.

(a) Tax figured by Revenue Service. If a taxpayer elects to have the Revenue Service figure the tax [¶ 1103(b)], the tax must be paid within 30 days after the Revenue Service mails a notice of the amount due [Sec. 6151(b)].

(b) Nonresident aliens. Nonresident aliens who do not have wages subject to withholding pay the tax by the 15th of the 6th month after the end of the tax year [Sec. 6072(c), 6151(a); 1.6072-1(c), 1.6151-1(a)].

¶ 3523 When corporation tax must be paid. Payment of income tax generally is due by the 15th of the third calendar month following the close of the tax year. A corporation on the calendar year basis pays by March 15. If it uses a fiscal year and it ends, for example, on June 30, payment is due by September 15 [Sec. 6151(a); 1.6072-2, 1.6151-1(a)].

Tax must be deposited in authorized banks. Domestic corporations must deposit income and estimated taxes in a Federal Reserve bank or authorized commercial bank[1] by the due date. The tax may be paid by one or more separate deposits, but a preinscribed Federal Tax Deposit Form designating Form 503 must be presented for each deposit [Sec. 1.6302-1]. Checks or money orders should be drawn to the order of the bank where deposited. Depositories other than Federal Reserve banks are not required to accept checks drawn on other banks, but they may do so.[1] Corporations that do not receive the prepunched and preinscribed deposit form from the Revenue Service must apply to their District Director or Service Center Director for the form (giving their name, identification number and the tax year involved) in time to make the deposit [Sec. 1.6302-1]. A penalty of 5% of the amount not deposited on time may be imposed [Sec. 6656; 301.6656-1].

A tax deposit mailed 2 or more days before the due date is considered timely even though the deposit is received after the due date. However the taxpayer must prove that he timely mailed the deposit. Registered mail or other competent evidence can be used to prove the mailing date [Sec. 7502].

Foreign corporations. The tax for a foreign corporation having no office or place of business in the U.S. is due by the 15th of the sixth month following close of the tax year [Sec. 6072(c), 6151(a); 1.6072-2(b), 1.6151-1(a)]. Withholding agents may be required to deposit taxes [¶ 2536].

Installment payment of income tax. A corporation can pay the tax in two equal istallments, the first by the 15th of the third month after the close of the tax year, the second within three months later (15th of 6th month after close of the tax year) [Sec. 6152; 1.6152-1(a)]. This privilege is not lost by underpaying a later installment, unless it is revoked by the Revenue Service.[2]

Example 1: The Zenith Corporation is on the calendar year basis. Its tax for 1977 is $90,000. The tax is payable in 2 equal installments of $45,000 each due March 15 and June 15, 1978.

If any installment is not paid when due, the entire tax must be paid on demand by the District Director [Sec. 6152(d); 1.6152-1(d)].

A nonresident foreign corporation not doing business in the U.S. can pay the tax in equal installments on the 15th day of the 6th and 9th month after the end of the tax year.[3]

(a) Payment of estimated tax. Corporations are not required to file declarations of estimated taxes. Payments of estimated taxes are made by deposit with the preinscribed tax deposit form. Unless a receipt is requested from the bank, a taxpayer must keep its own record of each payment.

Every corporation, including certain foreign corporations [¶ 3710(a)] and insurance companies, may have to pay estimated tax. Estimated tax is the excess of the anticipated tax liability (but not the minimum tax on preference items [¶ 2403 et seq.][4]) less any credits and an estimated tax exemption. In any event, payments are required only if the estimated tax can reasonably be expected to exceed $40 [Sec. 6154].

Estimated tax exemption. For 1977 and later years, the temporary estimated tax exemption is zero. Between years 1973 and 1976, the exemption was phased out on a percentage basis that was applied to the full temporary estimated tax exemption. The full estimated tax exemption was based on 22% of the corporation's surtax exemption. In 1976 and 1975, this was $11,000 [22% of the corporation's $50,000 surtax exemption]; in 1974 and 1973, $5,500 [22% × $25,000 surtax exemption]. The phased out percentages were: in 1976, 20%; 1975, 40%; 1974, 60%; 1973, 80%. Thus, corporations with anticipated liability of over $11,000 for tax years starting in 1976, the temporary estimated tax exemption was $2,200 ($11,000 × 20%); in 1975, it was $4,400 ($11,000 × 40%); in 1974, $3,300 ($5,500 × 60%); in 1973, $4,400 ($5,500 × 80%). For corporations with anticipated tax liability of less than $11,000 (in 1976 and 1975) or $5,500 (in 1974 and 1973), the applicable percentage for the appropriate year was applied to the anticipated liability [Sec. 6154(c)]. Form 1120-W may be used to compute the estimated tax.

Paying installments of estimated tax. Corporations required to pay estimated taxes make the deposits as follows [Sec. 6154(b)]:

After	and before	Percent of estimated taxes payable on 15th of 4th month	6th month	9th month	12th month
	4th month	25%	25%	25%	25%
3rd month	6th month		33⅓%	33⅓%	33⅓%
5th month	9th month			50%	50%
8th month	12th month				100%

Footnotes appear at end of this Chapter.

¶ 3523

Any installment can be deposited before the due date of the payment [Sec. 6154(f)].

(b) Penalty for underpayment of estimated tax. If payments of estimated tax are not made when due, a penalty of 7% (9% between 7-1-75 and 1-31-76; 6% before 7-1-75) of the underpayment may be added to the tax. This rate is adjustable as the prime rate (amount charged by commercial banks to large businesses) changes [¶ 3628]. The penalty is figured on the amount by which any installment payment is less than 80% of the amount due on that installment date. The amount due is the part of the tax on the final return which should have been paid by the installment date (¶ 3619) [Sec. 6655].

Example 2: In 1977 the Able Corporation estimates its tax liability to be $100,000. It avoids the underpayment penalty if it pays at least $80,000 (80% of $100,000) in timely installment payments.

Relief provisions. There is no penalty for underpayment of an installment of estimated tax if the estimated tax paid by the installment date is not less than an amount based on any one of the following [Sec. 6655(d)]:

- the previous year's tax;
- the tax on the previous year's income, but at the current year's rate (since facts shown on the prior year's return apply, except for rates, carryovers for investment credit and net operating loss used in that return would be a factor[5]);
- 80% of the tax due on the basis of annualizing the income received for either (a) the first 3 months, in the case of the installment due in the 4th month, or (b) the first 3 or first 5 months, in the case of the installment due in the 6th month, or (c) the first 6 or first 8 months, in the case of the installment due in the 9th month, or (d) the first 9 or first 11 months in the case of the installment due in the 12th month.

Example 3: A calendar year corporation can base the installment of its estimated tax due September 15 on the annualization of its taxable income through either June or August. It can base the installment due December 15 on the annualization of its taxable income through either September or November.

The income is annualized by multiplying it by the number of months in the tax year, and dividing the result by the number of months the income was received [Sec. 6655(b), (d)]. The full amount of any net operating loss carryover is applied before annualizing.[6]

Example 4: A calendar year corporation bases its estimated tax installment due 9-15-78 on its income from 1-1-78 through 8-31-78 which was $280,000. Its income through June 30 was $270,000. Income is annualized as follows:

$280,000 × 12 ÷ 8 = $420,000
$270,000 × 12 ÷ 6 = $540,000

If the corporation pays at least 80% of the estimated tax due for $420,000 (the lesser amount), it has complied with the minimum requirements, and no penalty will be imposed. If one of the other tests results in a still smaller minimum tax, it can base its payment on the method requiring the smallest payment.

How relief provisions are applied. The tests above are applied after using the estimated tax exemption explained in (a) above. Rules for applying the relief provisions are on Form 2220.

Statement required. A claim that the penalty does not apply should be supported by a statement on Form 2220 filed with the return. Form 2220 can be obtained from the District Director [Sec. 1.6655-1(b)].

¶ 3524 When estates and trusts pay tax. Payment of income tax is due by the 15th of the fourth calendar month after the end of the tax year. For a calendar year taxpayer the date is April 15.

Estates can pay the tax in four equal installments, the first on the payment due date, the second by three months, the third by six months, and the fourth by nine months after that date. Thus for a calendar year, installments are due by the 15th of April, July, October and January. Trusts cannot pay in installments [Sec. 6072, 6151(a), 6152(a)(2); 1.6072-1(a), 1.6151-1(a), 1.6152-1(b)].

¶ 3525 Exempt organizations. (a) Unrelated business income. Tax on unrelated business income of certain exempt organizations [¶ 3446; 3454] must be paid in full with the return [¶ 3517(d)], except that exempt organizations taxable as corporations may pay the tax in two equal installments, the 15th of the third month and sixth month following the close of the tax year.[1]

(b) Private foundations. Any excise tax shown on its annual return (Form 990-PF) and any penalty taxes shown on separate Form 4720 must be paid by the 15th day of the 5th month after the close of the tax year for which the returns are filed[2] (¶ 3437) [Sec. 53.6071-1; 53.6151-1].

¶ 3526 Extension of time to pay tax. The Revenue Service may grant a reasonable extension for payment of the tax or any installment. Such extension is granted only where there is a showing that payment on the due date will result in undue hardship. Generally, an extension may exceed 6 months only for persons abroad. A bond for twice the tax may be required [Sec. 6161, 6164; 1.6161-1, 1.6165-1].

Application must be filed on Form 1127 before the due date of the tax or installment for which the extension is requested. Corporations that expect a net operating loss and carryback can apply on Form 1138 for an extension of time to pay part of the previous year's tax [¶ 3630].

Interest charged. Interest at 7% (9% between 7-1-75 and 1-31-76; 6% before 7-1-75) a year accrues from the date the tax was due, until the tax is paid [Sec. 6601(a), 6621; 301.6601-1]. However, the 7% rate is adjustable depending on the prime interest rate charged by banks (¶ 3628) [Sec. 6621].

Deficiency. When the Revenue Service is satisfied that payment of a deficiency on the prescribed date will result in undue hardship, they may extend the time to pay it for not more than 18 months, and in exceptional cases, for a further period not over 12 months [Sec. 6161(b); 1.6161-1].

Private foundations. Similar provisions as those discussed above apply to private foundations subject to excise taxes [¶ 3438 et seq.]. Form 1127 is also used [Sec. 53.6161-1(a), (c), 53.6165-1].

Estimated tax. An extension of time to file a declaration [¶ 3518(d)] extends the time to pay estimated tax for the same period, without interest; but the penalty for underpayment of estimated tax [¶ 2519] runs from the original due date for payment [Sec. 1.6073-4].

Footnotes appear at end of this Chapter.

Foreign expropriation loss recovery. Under special conditions, a corporation can elect to pay the tax attributable to recovery of a foreign expropriation loss [¶ 2241; 2316] in 10 equal annual installments, or apply for an extension of up to 9 years because of hardship. Interest on the unpaid tax is payable annually in either case at a 7% rate (9% between 7-1-75 and 1-31-76; 4% before 7-1-75) or an adjusted prime interest rate (¶ 3628) [Sec. 6167, 6601, 6621]. This applies to amounts received after 1964 for losses after 1958.

¶ 3527 Reporting and payment procedures. (a) Even dollar reporting.- Tax returns may be filed in whole dollar amounts, instead of showing cents. This is done by eliminating any amount less than 50 cents and increasing any amount between 50 cents and 99 cents to the next higher dollar. This method of reporting applies only to the total amounts to be shown on any line of the return. It cannot be used to figure the various items that have to be totaled to determine the final amount on the line. The choice cannot be changed after the due date of the return [Sec. 6102; 301.6102-1].

(b) Paying the tax. Payment may be made in cash or by check, but if the check is not paid by the bank, the taxpayer remains liable for payment of the tax and the penalties are the same as if the check had not been tendered. There is an extra penalty for bad checks [¶ 3618(e)]. Payment may also be made by money order [Sec. 6311; 301.6311-1]. Checks or money orders should be made payable to the "Internal Revenue Service."

Receipts are given by the Revenue Service upon request. This should always be done for cash payments [Sec. 6314; 301.6314-1].

Payment with U.S. obligations. Treasury bills issued at any time for periods of less than one year may be used to pay income, estate and other taxes.[1] U.S. obligations dated after 3-3-71, are not redeemable at par before maturity for paying any taxes. But certain U.S. bonds issued before 3-4-71 can be used to pay estate taxes.[2]

Payment in foreign currency. A U.S. citizen who receives at least 70% of a grant or pay in nonconvertible foreign currency, from funds made available under the Surplus Property Act of 1944, Agricultural Trade Development and Assistance Act of 1954, or the Mutual Education and Exchange Act of 1961, may pay income tax on the amount received in the same currency [Sec. 6316; 301.6316-1—301.6316-9].

Fractions of a cent are disregarded unless it amounts to ½ cent or more, in which case it is increased to one cent [Sec. 6313; 301.6313-1].

Tax less than $1. If the tax due is less than $1, you are instructed by the form not to pay it.

INFORMATION RETURNS

¶ 3530 Information returns in general. The government uses information returns so that persons receiving certain kinds or amounts of income, report it on their income tax return. The information return may report payments made to others, transactions during the year, the taxable status of the taxpayer or other facts. The procedures for reporting on information returns are handled by several variations of Form 1099. For example, dividends are reported on Form 1099-DIV. Form 1099-MISC is for payments of $600 or more in the course of a trade or business for rents, royalties and other fixed or determinable income paid to an individual, partnership or fiduciary. Payment of interest of $10 or more is reported on Form 1099-INT.[1]

Most information returns are prepared on a calendar year-cash basis, even if the person filing the return is on a fiscal year-accrual basis. They generally must be filed at an Internal Revenue Service Center. The locations are listed on the returns. Taxpayers may apply for permission to file Forms 1099, 1087 and Form W-2 on magnetic tape or other media[2] [Sec. 1.9101-1].

When to file. Information returns usually must be filed annually for a calendar year by February 28th of the following year. A summary of the returns is filed at the same time. This summary is Form 1096. In most cases a copy of the information return will be sent to the person named as payee. If not, a statement of the information reported must be delivered to the payee by the January 31st before the return is filed.

An application for an extension of time to file an information return usually must be made to the internal revenue officer with whom the person files the return, or would be, required to file an income tax return [¶ 3519]. It must state the service center where the information return will be filed [Sec. 1.6081-1].

Exceptions exist to the general rules above. For example, information about liquidating corporations [¶ 3536] must be filed at a different time and place. In addition, partnership and Subchapter S corporation returns are filed as a return of income [¶ 3539]. Employers are also required to provide employees only with information returns regarding the moving expense deduction [¶ 1831]. Also, individual income tax return preparers and employer-preparers must file special information returns [¶ 3542].

Information Returns Required

Trade or business payments ($600 or more) [¶ 3531]
  Interest paid [¶ 3532]
  Dividends paid [¶ 3533]
  Employee benefit plans [¶ 3537(d)]
  Employee stock options [¶ 3534]
  Liquidating organizations [¶ 3536]
  Employee group-term life insurance [¶ 3535]
  Self-employed retirement distributions [¶ 3531(a)]
Tax-exempt organizations [¶ 3537]
Pension plan administrators [¶ 3537(d)]
Private foundations [¶ 3537(c)]
Charitable deduction for trust [¶ 3538]
Partnerships, fiduciaries and Subchapter S corporations [¶ 3539]
Foreign corporations [¶ 3540]
Income tax preparers [¶ 3542]

¶ 3531 Return for business payments. An information return must be filed for certain payments totaling $600 or more made in the course of a trade or business. Except for payments to employees ((a), below), the return is made on the appropriate Form 1099, with summary Form 1096, and filed by February 28th of the following year [Sec. 6041; 1.6041-1]. The return requirement is met if a surviving corporation of a merger files a return with all the required information.[1]

What is trade or business. A "trade or business" is not limited to activities for gain or profit [Sec. 1.6041-1(b)]. Tax-exempt organizations must file information returns if they make payments that qualify.[2]

This applies to exempt as well as nonexempt trusts, to insurance companies making payments under any nontrusteed annuity plan, to trustees paying supplemental unemployment benefits from a trust created with employer contributions[3] to self-employed retirement plans [Sec. 1.6041-2(b)], to those making Medicare or Medicaid payments, and to those making direct payments to doctors or others providing health care services under certain insurance plans.

Footnotes appear at end of this Chapter.

Separate returns required. A separate return must be filed for each payee. The payor should report (1) amounts actually paid and (2) amounts credited or set apart to the taxpayer without any substantial limitation or restriction as to time and manner of payment so that they could have been withdrawn by the taxpayer during the calendar year [Sec. 1.6041-1(f)].

Real owner must be disclosed. When anyone who is not the actual owner receives a payment for which an information return must be filed, he must supply the actual owner's name and address to the payor on demand [Sec. 1.6041-5]. Failure to do so is punishable by a $10,000 fine, 1 year in prison, or both [Sec. 7203].

(a) Payments to employees. An employer must report wages on Form W-2 [¶ 2508(a)]. In addition, he must generally report all payments of compensation (whether or not subject to withholding) on Form W-2 if the total of these payments, such as group-term life insurance [¶ 3535] plus wages, equals at least $600. At his option, the employer may use more than one Form W-2 to report components of reportable amounts paid to each employee. Life insurance companies may report commissions paid to full-time life insurance salesmen and any taxable group-term life insurance premiums on the same or separate Form 1099 with transmittal Form 1096 instead of Form W-2 and W-3 [Sec. 1.6041-2(a); 1.6052-1]. Taxable compensation not subject to withholding payable to nonresident employees and foreign corporations is reported by the withholding agent on Form 1042S (instead of W-2) with transmittal Form 1042 due annually on March 15 [Sec. 1.1461-2(c)]. The time for filing Forms W-2 and W-3 is the same as for the reporting of withheld taxes [¶ 2509(c)]. When Form W-3 does not include any wages subject to withholding, it may be filed by February 28th of the following year [¶ 1.6041-2(a)(4); 1.6052-1(b)]. Returns made on Forms 1096 and 1099 must be filed by the same date with the Revenue Service Center listed in the form instructions. See also ¶ 3519.

Form W-2P must be used to report annuity and pension payments when the payments total $600 or more during the calendar year or when tax has been withheld on these payments. For those payments under $600 or not subject to withholding, use of Form W-2P is optional [Temp. Reg. Sec. 32.1(f)]. Form 1099R must be filed to report lump-sum distributions from profit-sharing and retirement plans.

NOTE: Payments totaling only $10 or more made to an owner-employee [¶ 1839] under a self-employed retirement plan must be reported on Form 1099. The first year contributions to the plan are made for him, the owner-employee must notify the trustee or insurer (for annuity contracts) of that fact not later than February 28th of the following year [Sec. 6047(b); 1.6047-1].

A corporation must report income of $600 or more realized by a former employee from a disqualfying disposition of stock acquired by the exercise of a qualified stock option on Form 1099-MISC if the information is available to the corporation.[4]

(b) Payments of fees. Fees of $600 or more paid in the course of a trade or business to attorneys, public accountants, physicians, and members of other professions generally must be reported on Form 1099-MISC[5] [Sec. 1.6041-1(d)(2)]. Since the regulation refers to payments made to a person and the definition of "persons" includes a partnership, it would appear that information returns should be filed not only for fees paid to individuals but also for fees paid to professional partnerships (lawyers, accountants, etc.), if the other requirements are met. Form 1099-MED is used for filing information returns for payments to health care service suppliers.[6]

(c) Payment of fixed or determinable income. A return must be filed for rent, royalties, annuities, and other fixed or determinable income of $600 or more on Form 1099-MISC. Only payments in the course of a trade or business during the calendar year to an individual citizen or resident, a resident fiduciary, or a resident partnership, any member of which is a citizen or resident, must be reported [Sec. 1.6041-1(a), 1.6041-3]. A resident partnership is one engaged in trade or business in the U.S. [Sec. 301.7701-5]. Literary agents must report the gross amount of royalties received for their authors before deducting commissions, fees and expenses.[7] Gas and oil royalties must be reported on a gross basis.[8] See ¶ 3532 for interest payments; [3533 for dividends.

Example 2: Sloan works on straight salary for Agency Insurance, a partnership. In 1977, he was paid $9,800 commissions direct from insurance companies. He, in turn, paid the $9,800 to Agency. Sloan must file an information return for the payment.[9] If Agency were a corporation, Sloan would not have to file.

Rent payments. Rent paid directly to a landlord (other than a corporation) in the course of a trade or business must be reported, if payments for the year amount to $600 or more. However, the tenant is not required to make a report, if the rent is paid to a real estate agent. The agent must file the information return, if payments by the agent to the landlord (other than a corporation) during the year amount to $600 or more. The agent must report the gross amount collected for the landlord before deducting his commission or expenses.[10] If the landlord is a corporation, no return is required from either the tenant or the agent [Sec. 1.6041-1(a); 1.6041-3].

(d) Payments of $600 or more not reported. Except for returns required for payment of $10 or more for interest [¶ 3532] and dividends [¶ 3533], Forms 1099 need not be filed for the following [Sec. 1.6041-3]:

• Payment to a corporation, but Form 1099-MED must be filed for payments to a corporate health care service supplier.[6]
• Distributions or salaries to partners or distributions to beneficiaries of an estate or trust, that are shown in the partnership return, Schedule K-1 (Form 1065) [¶ 3539] or the fiduciary's return, Form 1041 [¶ 3020].
• Rent paid by a tenant to a real estate agent.[10] See ¶ 3531(c).
• Payments by a broker to his customers [¶ 3532; 3533].
• Bills paid for merchandise, telegrams, telephone, freight, storage, and similar charges.
• Compensation reported on Forms W-2, W-3 and 941 [¶ 2508(a); 2509].
• Income paid for tax-free covenant bonds or to nonresident aliens and reported for tax withholding on Forms 1000, 1001, 1042 and 1042S. See ¶ 2535; 2536; 3532.
• Distributions to shareholders reported on Form 1120S.
• Bank interest paid on and after 9-9-68 on deposits evidenced by negotiable certificates of deposits. See also ¶ 3532(a).
• Payments by banking and lending institutions when acting as collection agents [Sec. 1.6041-3(q)].
• Distributions to DISC shareholders reported on Schedule K, Form 1120-DISC.

¶ 3532 Returns for interest paid. Interest payments totaling $600 or more paid in the course of business generally must be reported [¶ 3531]. The return shows the amount paid and the payee's name and address. The payor can demand the name and address of the actual owner of the payment [Sec. 6041(a), (d) 1.6041-1(a), 1.6041-5]. Some interest must be reported when $10 or more is paid or cred-

Footnotes appear at end of this Chapter.

ited during the calendar year [Sec. 6049]. Foreign interest also must be reported [¶ 3540].

(a) **Returns for $10.** Returns on Forms 1096 and 1099-INT must be filed by the payor for interest totaling $10 or more paid or credited to any person on: bank deposits (except certain deposits evidenced by negotiable certificates of deposits); corporate obligations (evidences of indebtedness) in registered form; deposits or obligations of mutual savings banks or similar organizations (these *may* be called "dividends");[1] funds left with insurance companies at interest; deposits with stockbrokers or securities dealers [Sec. 6049; 1.6049-1(a), 1.6049-2(a)]. A nominee receiving interest for another, reports his payment to the real owner on Form 1087-INT. Some nominees who report the payments on fiduciary return (Form 1041) need not file Forms 1087, if the fiduciary return discloses the actual owner [Sec. 1.6049-1].

Original issue discount on certain corporate indebtedness issued after 5-27-69 is includible in the holder's income [¶ 1629] and must be reported by the corporation on Form 1099-OID [Sec. 1.6049-1(a)(1)(ii)]. Nominees file Form 1087-OID. If several obligations of one issue were held for the same period of time and each obligation had the same amount of total discount for the year, ratable monthly portions of original issue discount, issue prices and stated redemption prices, the corporation may file a single Form 1099-OID with respect to the holder. Similar permission is given to nominees filing Form 1087-OID.[2]

Original issue discount on deferred interest savings accounts, certificates of deposit and other deposit arrangements made or renewed after 12-31-70 and over one year in length is also includible in the holder's income [¶ 2722(a)] and must be reported by financial institutions on Forms 1096 and 1099-OID [Sec. 1.1232-1(d)]. This also applies to face-amount certificates issued after 12-31-74 [Sec. 1.1232-1(c)(3)].

NOTE: Returns may be filed by separate accounts receiving interest of $10 or more [Sec. 1.6049-1(a)(1)].

Tax-exempt interest from a state or local government or a U.S. instrumentality need not be reported. Foreign corporations, nonresident individuals, and partnerships with a nonresident alien partner do not have to report interest paid, when they do no business, and have no business office, in the U.S. [Sec. 6049(b)(2); 1.6049-2(b)].

The return may be filed any time in the last quarter of the year after the final payment for the year is made. It must be filed at a Service Center [¶ 3530] by February 28th of the following year [Sec. 1.6049-1(c)].

Notice to payee. The payor must give the payee a statement that the payments are being reported to the Revenue Service, with the amount and the payor's name and address. A copy of the return (Form 1099-INT or Form 1087-INT) is used. The notice may be sent during the last quarter of the year with the final payment for the year, or after November 30 after the last payment. It must be delivered by January 31st of the following year. Mailing to the payee's last known address is sufficient. A 30-day extension of time may be granted on application to the District Director's office where the payor files income tax returns [Sec. 1.6049-3]. A statement is required for original issue discount of $10 or more includible in the gross income of holders of certain corporate bonds including face-amount certificates issued after 12-31-74 (¶ 1629) and certain financial institution deposit arrangements (¶ 2722) [Sec. 6049(c)(2); 1.6049-1].

For time-savings accounts, banks and other payors must report on Form 1099-INT the entire interest paid or credited a depositor on his premature withdrawal and the amount of loss (forfeiture penalty) deductible by the depositor. They must also indicate on Form 1099-INT their method of reporting the interest and the penalty [¶ 1801(a)].[3]

(b) Ownership certificates for bond interest (Forms 1000 or 1001) may be required. They are filed when presenting interest coupons for payment. They serve as an information return and also as a guide to the debtor corporation or paying agent for determining whether tax is to be withheld and the rate of tax that will apply. Ownership certificates are usually prepared, or at least signed, by the payee. They are necessary for interest payments on registered bonds. If they are not furnished by the owner, the withholding agent must prepare them [Sec. 1.1461-1(g)]. The certificates are filed with the return of withheld tax [¶ 2535].

¶ **3533 Returns for dividends paid.** Corporations paying dividends totaling $10 or more to any person during a calendar year, and stockbrokers paying a substitute for such dividends, must file returns on Forms 1096 and 1099-DIV. A record owner who receives dividends as a nominee files Form 1087-DIV to report his payment to the actual owner [Sec. 1.6042-2]. The dividend payor may demand the name of the actual owner, and failure to supply it subjects the nominee to penalties (see ¶ 3532). Some record owners who file a fiduciary return (Form 1041) that discloses the actual owner of the dividends need not file Form 1087-DIV. Nominees receiving dividends as custodians of mutual fund investment trusts file Forms 1096 and 1099-DIV unless the regulated investment company directly notifies the actual owners [Sec. 1.6042-2(a)].

The return may be filed during the last quarter of the year after the final dividend payment. It must be filed at a Service Center [¶ 3530] by February 28th of the following year [Sec. 1.6042-2]. The payor must give payees the same kind of statement for dividends as is required for interest, and the same dates apply, except for mutual fund unit investment trusts which must deliver notice by February 10, not January 31 (see ¶ 3522(a)) [Sec. 1.6042-4].

If a corporation pays nontaxable dividends to its shareholders, it must file Form 5452 with the Revenue Service by February 28. If the required information is not supplied, the distribution may be considered fully taxable.[1]

(a) Payments not reported. Information returns are not required for:

• Dividends paid to, or by, any domestic or foreign government or subdivision, or an international organization [Sec. 1.6042-2(a)(2)];

• Distributions or payments by nonresident foreign corporations [Sec. 1.6042-3(b)(1)];

• Distributions or payments to nonresident aliens and foreign corporations or their nominees and subject to withholding at the source [¶ 2535; Sec. 1441, 1442; 1.6042-3(b)(2), (3)];

• Undistributed taxable income allocated to shareholders of electing small business corporations [Sec. 1.6042-3(b)(4); ¶ 3142(b)].

(b) Patronage dividends. Exempt farmers' cooperatives and corporations taxed as cooperatives [¶ 3455] must report patronage dividends and per-unit retain allocations [¶ 3456] of $10 or more on Form 1099-PATR and send statements to the payees. The filing times are the same as for ordinary dividends [Sec. 521, 6044; 1.6044-1—1.6044-5].

Consumer cooperatives may apply for exemption from reporting. To qualify, at least 85% of the gross receipts for the preceding tax year, or 85% of the total gross receipts for 3 preceding tax years, must have been received for retail sales of goods or services for personal, living or family use. Returns must be filed until the exemption is granted. The exemption is lost after the first tax year gross receipts from retail sales drop below 70%. The application is filed on Form 3491 with the

District Director's office where the cooperative has its principle place of business [Sec. 1.6044-4].

¶ 3534 Returns for stock transfers under employee options. A corporation must file Form 3921 to report the transfer of stock when a qualified or restricted stock option [¶ 1327] is exercised. It also must file Form 3922 to report each transfer of stock that was acquired for less than 100% of value under a stock purchase plan, or for less than 95% of value under a restricted option plan [Sec. 6039; 1.6039-1, 1.6039-2].

The returns must be filed at a Service Center [¶ 3530] by February 28th of the following year with a covering summary, Form 4067.[1] A statement or copy of the Form 3921 or Form 3922 filed must be sent by January 31st to the person who exercises the option or transfers the stock.

¶ 3535 Returns for group-term life insurance premiums. An employer who pays group-term life insurance premiums taxable to the employee [¶ 1307] reports the taxable amount for each employee on Form W-2 and the summary Form W-3 [Sec. 6052; 1.6052-1]. Insurance companies may report the taxable amount for full-time insurance salesmen on the same or separate Form 1099 and summary Form 1096. It may be entered on the same or separate Form W-2 that reports an employee's tax wthheld from wages. The same filing requirements apply (see ¶ 2509), except that if the Form W-3 does not report any tax withheld from wages, it may be filed by February 28, instead of February 10. The employee's copy of Forms W-2 or 1099 serves as the statement that must be given to the employee by the January 31st preceding the filing date [Sec. 1.6052-1; 1.6052-2].

¶ 3536 Returns for certain liquidations or terminations. A corporation in dissolution or liquidating any part of its capital stock files a report of the plan and the distributions made.

(a) Report on plan. A corporation is required to file an information return (Form 966) with the Internal Revenue office where it must file its income tax return within thirty days after the adoption of a resolution or plan for dissolution of the corporation or for the liquidation of the whole or any part of its capital stock [Sec. 6043; 1.6043-1]. The return must be accompanied by a certified copy of the resolution or plan and all amendments to it [Sec. 1.6043-1(b)].

(b) Return for distributions. Information returns (Form 1099L) must be filed for distributions in liquidation of $600 or more. They must state the names and addresses of the recipients of liquidating dividends, and the amount. These returns, accompanied by Form 1096, must be filed at an Internal Revenue Service Center [¶ 3530] by February 28 of the year after the calendar year the distribution is made [Sec. 6043; 1.6043-2].

(c) Exempt organizations. In general, organizatons exempt from tax [¶ 3435] in any of their last 5 years before their liquidation, termination or contraction in a tax year starting after 1969 are required to file a return. Churches, religious groups and any exempt organization (other than a private foundation [¶ 3437]) whose annual gross receipts normally are not over $5,000 are excused from filing. Private foundations are required to file. However, any organization can be excused from filing by the Revenue Service. Qualified employee plans may be excused if the employer files a return [Sec. 6043(b)]. See also ¶ 3537(a).

NOTE: Proposed regulations would require corporations to file Form 966-E on or before the 30th day after the event that caused the liquidation; trusts would file on or before the 30th day after termination [Prop. Reg. Sec. 1.6043-3].

¶ **3537 Information returns related to tax-exempt organizations and trusts.-**
Organizations exempt from tax file an annual information return, unless they are specifically excused from filing [Sec. 6033(a)]. If the return is not filed, the organization may lose its exemption.[1] They also report unrelated business income [¶ 3454] and payments of income to others [¶ 3531 et seq.]. Organizations claiming exemption from tax [¶ 3436(b)] must file with the District Director as proof of their exemption the application form prescribed in the regulations describing the organization and its functions [Sec. 1.501(a)-1]. An exempt organization maintaining funded pension or annuity plans for their employees must meet special filing requirements in addition to filing the annual information return [see (a) and (d) below]. After 10-3-76, electing exempt organizations subject to lobbying expenditures rules must file information returns. If the organization is a member of an affiliated group, it must also file a return for itself as well as the entire group [Sec. 6033(b)(6)—(8)].

(a) **Who must file a return.** Generally, organizations exempt from tax [¶ 3436] must file annual information returns. Exceptions from filing are in two classes: mandatory and discretionary [Sec. 6033; 1.6033-2].

The mandatory class includes churches, certain religious organizations and six types of organizations (but not private foundations [¶ 3437 et seq.]) if annual gross receipts are normally not over $5,000 [Sec. 6033(a)(2)(A), (C); 1.6033-2(g)(1)]:

• Educational organizations.

• Charitable organizations or organizations for the prevention of cruelty to children or animals supported with government or public funds.

• Religious organizations, and educational or charitable organizations above that are controlled by exempt religious organizations. However, "affiliated church auxiliaries" must file returns. These include affiliated schools (not below the college level), hospitals, orphanages (only those that have separate legal status apart from the affiliated church) and senior citizens' homes [Sec. 1.6033-2(g)(5)].

• Fraternal beneficiary societies, with the lodge system and providing benefits to members.

• Corporations wholly owned by the U.S. or its instrumentalities.

The discretionary class includes those organizations that the Revenue Service relieves from filing a return when it is unnecessary to the efficient administration of the tax laws [Sec. 6033(a)(2)(B); 1.6033-2(g)(2)].

Exempt organizations required to file annual information returns use Form 990 [Sec. 1.6033-2(a)]. Employee trusts for qualified pension and profit-sharing plans file returns in the Form 5500 series [see (d) below]. Group returns can be filed by a parent organization for two or more organizations [Sec. 1.6033-2(d)]. The returns must be filed on or before the 15th day of the fifth month after the close of the organization year. Religious and apostolic organizations with a common treasury file Form 1065 on or before the 15th day of the fourth month after the close of the tax year [Sec. 1.60331-2(e)]. The usual penalties are imposed when there has been a failure to file a return (¶ 3617) [Sec. 1.6033-2(f)].

Form 990 requires exempt organizations to provide information on gross income, disbursements and deductions, net worth at the beginning and end of the tax year, and other information relating to the organization's activities [Sec. 6033(b); 1.6033-2(a)]. Organizations with gross receipts over $10,000 and all private foundations must also include balance sheets at the beginning and end of the tax year. In addition, private foundations must provide the names and addresses of substantial contributors, information on investment income and a list of capital gains and losses. The information (except as to contributors) is open to public inspection on request [Sec. 6104; 301.6104-2].

Form 990 must be filed with the Internal Revenue Service Center, 11601 Roosevelt Blvd., Philadelphia, Pa. 19155.

Footnotes appear at end of this Chapter.

NOTE: Form 990 is used for exempt organizations except private foundations use 990-PF. Organizations with gross receipts of $10,000 or less that are not private foundations will provide less detailed information than private foundations and organizations with gross income over $10,000 [Sec. 1.6033-2(a)(1)].

Form 4720 must also be filed if certain excise taxes are imposed [¶ 3440(c), (d); 3442—3444]. For exempt organizations liquidating, terminating or dissolving, see ¶ 3536(c).

(b) Return for transfers to exempt organizations. Any taxpayer who transfers income-producing property having a fair market value over $50,000 to an exempt organization is required to file Form 4629 on or before the 90th day after the transfer. The return must include the names and addresses of the transferor and transferee, the identifying number of the transferor, decription of the property, date of transfer, whether the property is subject to a lien, and if so, its amount [Sec. 6050; 1.6050-1].

(c) Annual reports by private foundations. In addition to Form 990, a foundation manager of a private foundation [¶ 3437] with at least $5,000 worth of assets must also file an annual report for the foundation at the end of the tax year. The manager can use Form 990-AR or the foundation's own published annual report, if all the required information appears on the form or in the attachments to it [Sec. 6056(a); 1.6056-1 (a)(3)].

The report must provide information on: (1) gross income; (2) expenses; (3) disbursements; (4) a balance sheet; (5) an itemized statement of assets; (6) total contributions received; (7) a detailed list of all grants made or approved; (8) the foundation's address; (9) the names and addresses of the foundation managers; and (10) a list of all substantial contributors [¶ 3449(b)] or others having an interest in the foundation.

The annual report is filed at the same time and place as Form 990 and is open to inspection. For penalties imposed for failure to meet the requirement, see ¶ 3617 [Sec. 6056(d), 6104(d); 1.6056-1].

(d) Employee benefit plans. Any employer or plan administrator (including a self-employed individual) who maintains an employee pension benefit plan [¶ 1838; 3024] must file one or more of the following information returns:[2]

• Form 5500—Annual Return/Report of Employee Benefit Plan (with 100 or more participants). This form requires information relating to the plan entity (single employer, multiemployer, etc.) number of participants, plan amendment, termination, merger or consolidation with another plan, funding methods, fiduciaries' compensation and a detailed statement of plan assets and liabilities as well as a statement of income and expenditures. Other information required relates to bonding, excluded employees, and integration with social security, Railroad retirement, or other plan.

• Form 5500-C—Annual Return/Report of Employee Benefit Plan (with fewer than 100 participants, none of whom is an owner-employee). Form 5500-C is a shortened version of Form 5500 and Schedule B (Form 5500), below if applicable, must be filed with the return.

• Form 5500-K (Annual Return/Report of Employee Benefit Plan for Sole Proprietorships and Partnerships) must be filed by sole proprietors or partnerships for Keogh (H.R. 10) plans which have fewer than 100 participants and at least one owner-employee. Any Keogh plan not having an owner-employee as a participant must file Form 5500 or 5500-C. If applicable, Schedule B (Form 5500), below, must be filed with the return.

• Schedule A (Form 5500), Insurance information, is attached to Forms 5500, 5500-C and 5500-K if the benefits under the plan are provided by an insurance company. This schedule, when applicable, is not filed with the IRS but with the Labor Dept.

• Schedule B (Form 5500), Actuarial Information, is attached to Forms 5500, 5500-C and 5500-K for most defined benefit plans.

In addition, employers or plan administrators may be required to file the following supporting statements with Forms 5500, 5500-C or 5500-K: Form 5501 (Summary of plans of employer); Form 5504 (Deduction for payments made for employees other than self-employed) and Form 5505 (Deduction for payments made on behalf of self-employed individuals).

When to file. The above forms must be filed by the last day of the 7th month after the close of the plan's tax year.

Exempt organizations maintaining custodial accounts for its employees and qualified government and church plans must also file annual returns/reports in addition to Form 990.

Where to file. IRS forms (Form 5500 series above, and supporting schedules) must be filed with the appropriate Service Center designated in the instructions. However, a foreign corporation should file with the Service Center at 11601 Roosevelt Boulevard, Philadelphia, Pa. 19155.

Public inspection of documents. Application papers (including my letter or other document issued by the Revenue Service pertaining to applications filed after 10-31-76) determination letters, annual returns, and other filed documents of certain retirement plans are open to public inspection upon request. Public inspection does not include the right to see a participant's compensation [Sec. 6104(a), (b)].

¶ **3538 Returns for nonexempt trusts claiming charitable deduction.** Nonexempt trusts [¶ 3453] and trusts (not including simple trusts [¶ 3005]) claiming a deduction for amounts paid or permanently set aside [¶ 3013] are required to file an annual information return. Form 1041-A is used for this purpose and filed by the 15th day of the 4th month following the close of the tax year [Sec. 642(c); 6034; Proposed Reg. 1.6034-1(a)(1)]. Charitable nonexempt trusts must also file Form 990; split interest nonexempt trusts file Form 1041-A only. Charitable remainder annuity trusts and charitable remainder unitrusts [Sec. 664(d); 1.664-1—3] must file Form 1041-B in addition to Form 1041-A [Sec. 1.6012-3(a)(6)].

Information on return. The information required includes: the charitable deduction for the year; amounts deducted in prior years, but not paid out by the start of the tax year, and current payments from prior deductions; current and prior payments to charity out of principal; current gross income and expenses; and a balance sheet for the start of the year [Sec. 6034(a)]. This information is open to public inspection except as to contributors [Sec. 6104; 301.6104-2].

¶ **3539 Partnership, fiduciary and Subchapter S corporation returns.** Information returns must be filed by a partnership, fiduciary, and by a corporation electing partnership-type taxation.

(a) Partnership returns. The partnership return, Form 1065, is an information return of the partnerhip income and its distribution to the partners [¶ 2901 et seq.] It must be filed by the 15th day of the 4th month following the close of the partnership tax year [Sec. 6031; 1.6031-1]. If all partners are nonresident aliens the return may be filed by the 15th day of the 6th month after the tax year. A partnership not engaged in U.S. trade or business and having no U.S. source income need not file a return. A return may be filed with the District Director for the district where the principal office or place of business is located or, if none, with the Director, International Operations Division, unless instructions require filing elsewhere [Sec. 1.6031-1].

(b) Fiduciary returns. In addition to filing Form 1041 [¶ 3511], a fiduciary must attach separate Schedule K-1 to the form for each beneficiary of an estate or trust. This indicates each beneficiary's share of income, deductions and credits [¶ 3020(c); 3021]. The fiduciary should give Copy B to the beneficiary by the end of the month following the close of the taxable year of the estate or trust.[1]

Fiduciaries [¶ 3511 (a)] must give written notice of qualification as an executor or receiver, usually within 10 days from the appointment or authorization to act, to the District Director with whom the taxpayer was required to file returns. The notice must generally contain names and addresses of the taxpayer, the fiduciary, the court dealing with the proceedings along with certain dates [Sec. 6036; 301.6036-1]. The notice of qualification can also be provided when the fiduciary files a notice of figuciary relationship, Form 56 [Sec. 6903; 301.6036-1(c), 301.6903-1].

(c) Subchapter S corporation returns. A corporation that elects partnership-type taxation [¶ 3140 et seq.] must file an information return on Form 1120S for each tax year during its election. See ¶ 3141(c).

¶ 3540 Returns for foreign items and foreign organizations. (a) Foreign items. The term "foreign items" means interest on the bonds of a foreign country or interest or dividends on the bonds or stock of a nonresident foreign corporation not having a fiscal or paying agent in the United States [Sec. 1.6041-4(b)]. Form 4683 must be filed for a tax year in which a taxpayer has a financial interest in or authority over a foreign account.[1]

Who files return. Form 1099-INT and Form 1099-DIV must be prepared and filed by the bank or collecting agent for collections totaling $600 or more for a citizen, resident alien, resident fiduciary, or partnership, any member of which is a citizen or resident. Forms 1099 and the summary Form 1096 must be filed by February 28 at an internal Revenue Service Center [¶ 3530]. The payer can demand the name and address of the real owner [Sec. 6041; 1.6041-4—1.6041-6].

License required. The collecting agency must get a license from the Commissioner [Sec. 7001; 301.7001-1].

(b) Foreign corporations. Information returns about foreign corporations must be filed on Form 959 when a U.S. person owns 5% or more of the value of its stock, and on Form 2952 when a U.S. person controls the corporation [Sec. 6038, 6046]. A U.S. person is a U.S. citizen or resident, a domestic corporation or partnership, or an estate or trust that is not a foreign estate or trust [Sec. 7701(a)(30), (31)]. Stock indirectly owned is counted for the 5% ownership requirement. This includes stock owned by an individual's brothers and sisters (whole or half blood), spouse, ancestors and lineal descendants [Sec. 6046(c)].

A U.S. person controls a foreign corporation when he owns stock with more than 50% of the total voting power or more than 50% of the total value of all stock of the corporation, or of another corporation that owns the same percentage of the foreign corporation stock [Sec. 6038(d)(1)]. The rules for constructive ownership of stock [¶ 1727] to determine control apply with these changes: stock owned by a non-U.S. person who is a partner or beneficiary is not attributed to a U.S. partnership, trust or estate; stock owned by a corporation is attributed to a 10% or more shareholder in proportion to his holding; but stock of a 50% or more shareholder who is not a U.S. person is not attributed to a U.S. corporation [Sec. 1.6038-2(c)].

Who must file. *Form 959* must be filed by a U.S. person that acquires, or increases holdings to, 5% or more of the stock value, and whenever 5% or more of the stock value is added to any holding. These owners also must file Form 959 when the corporation is reorganized or the holding drops below 5%. 5% or more owners who later become U.S. persons must file the return. The regulations allow combined returns and omission of some items covered in another shareholder's return [Sec. 1.6046-1(a), (c), (e)]. Officers and directors who are U.S. citizens or residents also must file Form 959 [Sec. 6046(a)].

Form 2952 must be filed by a U.S. person in control of the corporation for 30 consecutive days during the corporation's annual accounting period that ends with or within the U.S. person's tax year [Sec. 1.6038-2(e)].

When to file. *Form 959* must be filed within 90 days after the liability arises. It is filed with the Internal Revenue Service Center, 11601 Roosevelt Blvd., Philadelphia, Pa. The Service Center can extend the time [Sec. 1.6046-1(j)].

Form 2952 is an annual return that must be filed in duplicate with the U.S. person's income tax return by the due date [¶ 3517, 3519]. The Revenue Service can extend the time to file. An application to extend time to file an income tax return includes Form 2952 [Sec. 1.6038-2(i), (j)].

Information required. *Form 959* returns filed by shareholders must give considerable information about the corporation and its organization or reorganization covering dates, names, addresses, assets, income tax returns filed, business activity, accounting statements, previous Forms 959 filed, and other detailed information [Sec. 1.6046-1(c)(3)]. Officers and directors need file only information about 5% or more stockholders [Sec. 1.6046-1(a)].

Form 2952 returns must give detailed information for the accounting, period covered by the return about earnings and profits, distributions, transactions with U.S. persons, sales and purchases of patents and similar property, compensation paid and received and other items [Sec. 1.6038-2(f), (g), (h)].

Penalties. Failure to file a timely or complete Form 959 is subject to a $1,000 civil penalty that can be assessed or collected without a deficiency notice. This is in addition to any criminal penalty [Sec. 1.6046-1(k)].

Failure to file a timely or complete Form 2952 (minor omissions may be excused) reduces by 10% the U.S. person's foreign tax amount used to compute the foreign tax credit, unless it is a credit carryback or carryover or the credit of a corporate stockholder derived from a foreign corporation [¶ 3703 et seq.] already reduced for failure to file Form 2952. If the failure to file continues for 90 days after notice from the Revenue Service, the penalty reduction is increased 5% for each 3-month period after the 90-day period. Failure to file may be excused for reasonable cause. The penalty reduction for each failure can not be more than the greater of the foreign corporation's income for the accounting period or $10,000 [Sec. 1.6038-2].

(c) Foreign trusts. Within 90 days after any U.S. person creates or transfers property to a foreign trust, the grantor, transferor or fiduciary of a testamentary trust must file a return on Form 3520 with the Service Center, Philadelphia, Pa. Contributions to an employees' trust need not be reported. A penalty of 5% of the amount transferred can be collected without deficiency notice for failure to file. The maximum penalty is $1,000. This is in addition to any criminal penalty [Sec. 6048, 6677; 16.3-1].

Footnotes appear at end of this Chapter.

¶ 3540

NOTE: For tax years ending after 1975, each taxpayer taxed under the grantor trust rules because the foreign trusts have one or more U.S. beneficiaries [¶ 3022], must file information returns. This applies to foreign trusts created after 5-21-74, and to property transfers to such trusts after that date. A 5% penalty applies for failure to file [Sec. 6048(c), 6077].

¶ 3541 Returns and recordkeeping for minimum tax. All individuals with tax preference items in excess of $10,000 ($5,000 if married and filing separately) must file Form 4625, even if no minimum tax is due [¶ 2403]. Any minimum tax liability is added to and paid with the income tax liability shown on Form 1040.

Corporations must file Form 4626 if they have tax preference items in excess of $10,000. An estate or trust must file Form 4626 if its tax preference items exceed $10,000 or if these items allocated to the estate or trust exceed its portion of the $10,000 exclusion.[1] Corporations file Form 4626 with Form 1120, estates and trusts with Form 1041. Any minimum tax liability is added to the other income tax liability.

Records to be kept. Proposed regulations would require taxpayers with amounts of preference items to keep permanent records available. The records required would vary with the type of item [Proposed Reg. 1.57-5]:

(a) Accelerated depreciation on real property or leased personal property, depletion, amortization of certified pollution control facilities or railroad rolling stock: when and how the property was acquired and placed in service, taxpayer's basis on the date of acquisition and how the basis was determined; the useful life of the property on the date it was placed in service, and the amount and date of all adjustments made to basis, with explanations.

(b) Stock options: the stock's fair market value at the date the option was exercised, the option price and the manner in which it was determined.

(c) Reserves for losses on bad debts of financial institutions: the amount of debts written off and the amount of loans outstanding for the tax year and the five preceding tax years; record would also have to be kept for the first tax year that a part of a net operating loss was attributable to tax preference items and each succeeding year in which there is a portion of net operating loss or a net operating loss carryover attributable to tax preferences. Also, all the facts necessary to determine the amount of deferred minimum tax liability would have to be included [¶ 2403].

¶ 3542 Disclosure, recordkeeping, and returns for income tax preparers. Generally, a preparer is any person (including a partnership or corporation) who prepares for compensation, all or a substantial portion of another's income tax return or refund claim. A person is not an income tax preparer where he merely furnishes typing, reproducing or mechanical assistance in preparing the return. He is also not a preparer where he is hired by his employer to prepare the employer's or employees' returns. Fiduciaries of trusts or estates are not preparers where they prepare returns or refund claims for the estate or trust. Under certain circumstances, a person who files a refund claim as a result of a Revenue Service audit is not a preparer [Sec. 7701(36); Temp. Reg. Sec. 404.7701-1].

Requirements relating to preparation are described "April 15 requirements" and those relating to annual information returns are "July 31 requirements."

April 15 requirements. A preparer must sign each return (signing includes affixing an appropriate identifying number and address) and furnish a copy to the taxpayer. Also, he must retain copies or lists of returns for three years following the close of the return period. The lists should contain the names and addresses of the taxpayers for whom the returns were prepared and must be available for inspection on request by the district director [Sec. 6107; Temp. Reg. Sec.

404.6107-1]. A $25 penalty is imposed on the preparer for failing to sign the return or refund claim, for failing to furnish a copy of the return or claim to the taxpayer, or for failing to furnish his identifying number on the return or claim. The penalty is $50 for failure to retain copies or list of returns or for failure to make these items available for inspection on request. The maximum penalty under this latter provision is $25,000. However, these penalties do not apply if failure is due to reasonable cause [Sec. 6695; Temp. Reg. Sec. 404.6695-1, 2].

July 31 requirements. Employers of income tax preparers must file Form 5717, an annual information return, on or before July 31 following the close of a return period. The "return period" is the 12-month period starting on July 1 of each year and ending on June 30 of the following year. Preparers who are not employers are considered their own employers and file individually. Partners, however, are considered partnership employees. As a result, a partnership must file on behalf of partner preparers as well as employee preparers [Sec. 6060; Temp. Reg. Sec. 404.6060-1]. A $100 penalty is imposed for each failure to file a return and a $5 penalty is imposed for each failure to include a required item of information in the return. The maximum penalty under these provisions is $20,000 for any return period. However, these penalties do not apply if failure is due to reasonable cause [Sec. 6695(e); Temp. Reg. Sec. 404.6695-2].

NOTE: Negligent, intentional or willful understatement of tax liability by tax preparers is covered by other civil penalties provisions. See ¶ 3617(e).

POINTERS ON FIGURING THE TAX

¶ 3545 Identifying gross income. Your records should enable you to identify the source of gross income included in your return and the amount. If they do not, you may pay more tax than you should, or you may be subject to penalties for underpaying your tax. Here are some of the rules for proper identification of gross income:

- *Capital gains and losses.* When there are capital gains and losses, the proper gross income amount is the capital gain without any deduction for the long-term capital gain deduction [¶ 1612]. There is a special rule for long-term capital gains of an estate or trust set aside or paid out as charitable contributions [¶ 3013].

- *Income from business.* Gross income of a busines is not the same as its gross receipts. It is total receipts less cost of goods sold plus any miscellaneous income [¶ 2601(a)]. See also ¶ 3610.

- *Gross income of partner.* When it is necessary to determine the gross income of a partner, the amount includes his distributive share of the gross income of the partnership [Sec. 702(c); 1.702-1(c)]. See ¶ 2909.

- *Rents.* All rents received must be included in gross income, even if expenses paid out exceed income and produce a loss. The fact that expenses exceed income has no bearing on what is gross income.[1]

ITEMS AFFECTED BY GROSS INCOME

Deductions: charitable contribution deduction of estates and trusts [¶ 3013]; limitation on the deduction for hobby losses [¶ 2225].

Exemptions: exemption for a dependent [¶ 1116]; exemption for a spouse on a separate return [¶ 1112].

Filing returns: requirement for filing an individual return [¶ 1100]; requirement for filing the individual's declaration of estimated tax [¶ 2516].

Limitations on assessments [¶ 3610].

Tax liability: liability for the personal holding company tax [¶ 3401]; the tax on

Footnotes appear at end of this Chapter.

¶ 3545

nonresident aliens and foreign corporations [¶ 3711]; the tax on income from sources in U.S. possessions [¶ 3727].

¶ 3546 When the tax rate changes. If the tax rate is increased or decreased, a special method of figuring the tax is required, unless the change takes place on the first day of the tax year.

To figure the tax in such a situation:
(1) Figure a tentative tax for the entire tax year at the old rate.
(2) Figure a second tentative tax for the entire tax year at the new rate.
(3) Add: (a) the tentative tax in (1) above multiplied by the number of days in the tax year before the rate change and divided by the number of days in the entire tax year; and (b) tentative tax in (2) above multiplied by the number of days in the period on and after the rate change and divided by the number of days in the entire tax year [Sec. 21(a); 1.21-1]. The result is the actual tax for the tax year.

Effective date of change. If the date is changed for tax years "beginning after" or "ending after" a certain date, the following day is the effective date of the change. If the rate is changed for tax years "beginning on or after" a certain date, that date is the effective date of the change [Sec. 21(c)].

¶ 3547 When there are two related unknown amounts. In figuring the federal income tax, cases sometimes arise in which the amounts of two or more unknowns are dependent upon each other. For example, under the federal income tax law, a state income tax is deductible. Under some state income taxes, the federal income tax for the same year is deductible. The federal tax cannot be determined until the state tax is known, and the state tax can not be determined until the federal tax is known. Several methods can be used to solve this type of problem.

(a) Trial and error method. The problem can be solved by the so-called trial and error method. This method, despite its name, is not a matter of guess work, but an accurate mathematical solution.

Example: Before deducting the state income tax the corporation's 1977 taxable income for federal income tax purposes was $100,000.

Before deducting the federal income tax, the corporation's taxable income for state income tax purposes was $104,000 (the difference being due to interest on state obligations, taxable on the state return, but exempt on the federal).

The state rate is 6% of net (taxable) income.

$104,000.00 × 6% = $6,240.00 .... First trial state tax
$100,000.00
    6,240.00

($93,760.00 × 48%) — $13,500† = $31,504.80 .... First trial federal tax

$104,000.00
   31,504.80

$ 72,495.20 × 6% = $4,349.71 .... Second trial state tax
$100,000.00
    4,349.71

($95,650.29 × 48%) — $13,500† = $32,412.14 .... Second trial federal tax

$104,000.00
   32,412.14

$ 71,587.86 × 6% = $4,295.27 .... Third trial state tax
$100,000.00
    4,295.27

($95,704.73 × 48%) — $13,500† = $32,438.27 .... Third trial federal tax

$104,000.00
 32,438.27
─────────
$ 71,561.73 × 6% = $4,293.70 .... Fourth trial state tax

$100,000.00
  4,293.70
─────────
($95,706.30 × 48%) − $13,500† = $32,439.02 .... Fourth trial federal tax

$104,000.00
 32,439.02
─────────
$ 71,560.98 × 6% = $4,293.66 .... Fifth trial state tax

$100,000.00
  4,293.66
─────────
($95,706.34 × 48%) − $13,500† = $32,439.04 .... Fifth trial federal tax

$104,000.00
 32,439.04
─────────
$ 71,560.96 × 6% = $4,293.66 .... Since this is the same as the fifth
trial state tax, it is FINAL

† Subtracting the $13,500 gives effect to the surtax exemption of $50,000 which is multiplied by current tax rates and the $50,000 surtax exemption ($50,000 × 27% = $13,500). See also ¶ 3523(a).

(b) Using a formula. The same problem can be solved with these formulas.

$$S = \frac{r(T + \$13{,}500 - RD)}{1 - rR} \qquad F = \frac{RD - (rRT) - \$13{,}500}{1 - rR}$$

In the formulas:
S = state tax
F = federal tax
D = taxable income (federal)

T = taxable income (state)
R = federal tax rate (48%)
r = state tax rate

When we substitute the values from (a) in the formula we find:

State Tax

$$S = \frac{.06\,(\$104{,}000 + \$13{,}500 - .48 \times \$100{,}000)}{1 - (.06 \times .48)} = \frac{.06\,(\$117{,}500 - \$48{,}000)}{1 - .0288}$$

$$\frac{.06\,(\$69{,}500)}{.9712} = \frac{\$4{,}170}{.9712} = \$4{,}293.66 \text{ (state tax)}$$

Federal Tax

$$F = \frac{.48 \times \$100{,}000 - (.06 \times .48 \times \$104{,}000) - \$13{,}500}{1 - (.06 \times .48)} =$$

$$\frac{\$48{,}000 - \$2{,}995.20 - \$13{,}500}{1 - .0288} = \frac{\$31{,}504.80}{.9712} = \$32{,}439.04 \text{ (federal tax)}$$

Footnotes appear at end of this Chapter.

¶ 3547

When a corporation's income is $50,000 or less, the formulas would drop the $13,500 amount because the surtax exemption is not involved:

$$S = \frac{r(T - RD)}{1 - rR} \qquad F = \frac{R(D - rT)}{1 - rR}$$

Footnotes to Chapter 25

(P-H "Federal Taxes" related references are cited in brackets [ ] at the end of each footnote below.)

Footnote ¶ 3500 [¶ 35,476 et seq.; 37,381].
(1) Rev. Rul. 64-8, 1964-1 CB 480 [¶ 35,484(90)].
(2) Rev. Rul. 63-247, 1963-2 CB 612 [¶ 35,484(115)].
(3) Rev. Prov. 66-29, 1966-1 CB 656 [¶ 35,484(9)].
(4) Rev. Prov. 66-47, 1966-2 CB 1255 [¶ 35,484(10)].
(5) Rev. Proc. 70-22, 1970-2 CB 503 [¶ 35,484(65)].

Footnote ¶ 3503 [¶ 35,306 et seq.].
(1) Rev. Rul. 67-191, 1967-1 CB 318 [¶ 35,069(16)].
(2) Reaves v Comm., 8 AFTR 2d 5619, 295 F.2d 336 [¶ 37,213(15)].

Footnote ¶ 3505 [¶ 35,061; 35,071 et seq.].
(1) Rev. Rul. 67-191, 1967-1 CB 318 [¶ 35,069(16)].
(2) Treas. Dept. booklet "Your Federal Income Tax" (1977 Ed.), p. 13.
(3) P.L. 94-455, Sec. 2114.
(4) U.S. v. Mitchell, 27 AFTR 2d 71-1457, 403 US 190 [¶ 37,227(15)].
(5) Heim v. Comm., 1 AFTR 2d 660, 251 F.2d 44; Kann v. Comm., 45 AFTR 309, 210 F.2d 247; Olsen, W.E., ¶ 48,086 P-H TC Memo. See also McCord v. Granger, 43 AFTR 125, 201 F.2d 103, holding wife's failure to sign made return husband's separate return, even though it included wife's income [¶ 35,070(5)(15)].
(6) Rev. Rul. 74-203, 1974-1 CB 330 [¶ 35,070(10)].

Footnote ¶ 3506 [¶ 35,069].

Footnote ¶ 3507 [¶ 35,061].
(1) Est. of Frank J. Floyd (Orphan's Ct., Pa. 1951), 43 AFTR 1301 [¶ 35,071(20)].
(2) Treas. Dept. booklet, "Your Federal Income Tax" (1977 Ed.), p. 15.

Footnote ¶ 3508 [¶ 35,061; 41.151].
(1) Taft v. Helvering, 311 US 195, 24 AFTR 1076 [¶ 35,073(5)].
(2) Stewart v. Comm., 95 F.2d 821, 21 AFTR 20 [¶ 41,242].

Footnote ¶ 3509 [¶ 35,056].

Footnote ¶ 3510 [¶ 35,056].

Footnote ¶ 3511 [¶ 35,059 et seq.].
(1) Rev. Rul. 55-387, 1955-1 CB 131 [¶ 35,059(60); 35,069(15)].
(2) Rev. Rul. 72-387, 1972-2 CB 632 [¶ 35,059(20)].
(3) Rev. Rul. 68-48, 1968-1 CB 301 [¶ 35,059(45)].

Footnote ¶ 3512 [¶ 35,057 et seq.].
(1) Florida Grocery Co., 1 BTA 412; Central Auto Market, 7 BTA 973 [¶ 35,057(10)].
(2) Wootan, ¶ 55,191 P-H Memo TC [¶ 35,057(60)].
(3) Waldron Co., 2 BTA 715 [¶ 35,057(5)].
(4) Treas. Dept. booklet "Tax Guide for Small Business" (1977 Ed.), p. 4.
(5) U.S. v. General Insp. & Ldg. Co., 192 F. 223, 1 AFTR 182 [¶ 37,024(110)].

Footnote ¶ 3512 continued
(6) Updike v. U.S., 8 F.2d 913, 5 AFTR 5720 [¶ 35,057(55)].

Footnote ¶ 3513 [¶ 35,057].
(1) Treas. Dept. booklet "Tax Guide for Small Business" (1977 Ed.), p. 170.

Footnote ¶ 3514 [¶ 20,045 et seq.; 35,057].
(1) Rev. Rul. 66-68, 1966-1 CB 197 [¶ 20,023(5)].

Footnote ¶ 3515 [¶ 34,345 et seq.].

Footnote ¶ 3517 [¶ 35,336 et seq.; 35,521].
(1) Leventis, Jr., 49 TC 353 [¶ 39,371(30)].
(2) Rev. Rul. 71-129, 1971-1 CB 397 [¶ 35,360(20)].

Footnote ¶ 3518 [¶ 35,366 et seq.; 39,439].
(1) Instructions to Form 2350 [¶ 35,376(29)].
(2) Rev. Rul. 64-214, 1964-2 CB 472 [¶ 35,376(60)].
(3) Instructions to Form 2758 [¶ 35,378(5), (10)].
(4) Instructions to Form 2688 [¶ 35,376(10)].
(5) Instructions to Form 7005.
(6) Rev. Rul. 63-222, 1963-2 CB 605 [¶ 35,375(30)].
(7) Instructions to Form 7004; Rev. Rul. 54-426, 1954-2 CB 39; Rev. Rul 68-258, 1968-1 CB 541 [¶ 37,024(5), (10)].
(8) Lorillard Co., v. U.S. 338 F.2d 499, 14 AFTR 2d 5982 [¶ 35,375(6)].

Footnote ¶ 3519 [¶ 35,386].
(1) Rev. Rul. 73-11, 1973-1 CB 591 [¶ 35,396(20)].

Footnote ¶ 3520 [¶ 35,036].
(1) Bartlett v. Delaney, 173 F.2d 535, 37 AFTR 1157 [¶ 35,042(35)].

Footnote ¶ 3521 [¶ 35,016].
(1) Treas. Dept. booklet "Your Federal Income Tax" (1977 Ed.), p. 118.
(2) IR 1767, 2-28-77 [¶ 55,281].
(3) TIR-956, 1-1-68 [¶ 35,218(60)].

Footnote ¶ 3522 [¶ 35,506].

Footnote ¶ 3523 [¶ 35,521; 35,523].
(1) Treas. Dept. Circ. No. 1079 prescribes how banks are authorized [¶ 35,706].
(2) Rev. Rul. 68-258, 1968-1 CB 541 [¶ 35,518(5)].
(3) Instructions to Form 1120F.
(4) Instructions to Form 1120-W.
(5) Rev. Rul. 69-308, 1969-1 CB 304; Rev. Rul. 72-388, 1972-2 CB 643 [¶ 37,318.35(15)].
(6) Rev. Rul. 67-93, 1967-1 CB 366 [¶ 37,318.35(15)].

Footnote ¶ 3524 [¶ 35,506 et seq.].

Footnote ¶ 3525 [¶ 21,201].
(1) Instructions to Form 990-T.
(2) Instructions to Forms 990-PF and 4720.

Footnote ¶ 3526 [¶ 35,531 et seq.].

Footnote ¶ 3527 [¶ 35,755 et seq.].
(1) 31 USC 754.

Chapter 25—Footnotes

Footnote ¶ 3527 continued
(2) P.L. 92-5, Sec. 4.

Footnote ¶ 3530 [¶ 35,201 et seq.].
(1) Instructions to Form 1096.
(2) Rev. Proc. 74-42, 1974-2 CB 466 [¶ 35,299.50(5)].

Footnote ¶ 3531 [¶ 35,201 et seq.].
(1) Rev. Rul. 69-556, 1969-2 CB 242 [¶ 35,218(35)].
(2) Rev. Rul. 56-176, 1956-1 CB 560 [¶ 35,218(20)].
(3) Rev. Rul. 62-54, 1962-1 CB 285 [¶ 35,218(30)].
(4) Rev. Rul. 71-52, 1971-1 CB 278 [¶ 35,219(16)].
(5) Instructions to Form 1096.
(6) Rev. Rul. 69-595, 1969-2 CB 242; Rev. Rul. 70-608, 1970-2 CB 286 [¶ 35,222(70); 35,223(40)].
(7) Rev. Rul. 65-129, 1965-1 CB 519; Rev. Rul. 67-197, 1971-1 CB 319 [¶ 35,222(15)].
(8) Rev. Rul. 66-198, 1966-2 CB 488 [¶ 35,223(25)].
(9) Rev. Rul. 64-36, 1964-1 CB 446 [¶ 35,222(10)].
(10) Rev. Rul. 54-571, 1954-2 CB 235 [¶ 35,222(15)].

Footnote ¶ 3532 [¶ 35,293 et seq.].
(1) Rev. Rul. 73-221, 1973-1 CB 298 [¶ 35,293].
(2) Rev. Proc. 71-10, 1971-1 CB 677 [¶ 35,299(5)].
(3) Rev. Rul. 73-511, 1973-2 CB 402, clarified by Rev. Rul. 75-21, IRB 1975-3 [¶ 20,137(7)].

Footnote ¶ 3533 [¶ 35,226 et seq.].
(1) Instructions to Form 1096; Rev. Proc. 75-17

Footnote ¶ 3533 continued
1975-1 CB 677 [¶ 35,235(15)].

Footnote ¶ 3534 [¶ 35,191].
(1) Instructions to Forms 3921, 3922; Rev. Rul. 66-117, 1966-1 CB 265 [¶ 35,198(10)].

Footnote ¶ 3535 [¶ 35,300].

Footnote ¶ 3536 [¶ 35,241].

Footnote ¶ 3537 [¶ 21,006; 35,131].
(1) Rev. Rul. 59-95, 1959-1 CB 627 [¶ 35,137(5)].
(2) Instructions to Forms 5500, 5500-C, 5500-K.

Footnote ¶ 3538 [¶ 35,141].

Footnote ¶ 3539 [¶ 35,111; 35,161; 35,171; 38,051].
(1) Instructions to Form 1041 (Sch. K-1).

Footnote ¶ 3540 [¶ 35,181; 35,221].
(1) Instructions to Form 4683.

Footnote ¶ 3541 [¶ 6125].
(1) Instructions to Form 4626.

Footnote ¶ 3545 [¶ 35,055].
(1) T. K. Lewis, ¶ 50,015 P-H Memo TC [¶ 35,055(10)].

Footnote ¶ 3546 [¶ 3427.10].

Footnote ¶ 3547 [¶ 1104].

Highlights of Chapter 25
Returns and Payment of Tax

I. **Individual Tax Returns**
   A. **Taxpayer's identifying numbers.** Give correct number on returns [¶ 3500]:
      1. Individuals use social security number plus employer identification number if in business.
      2. Corporations, partnerships, investment clubs, trusts, estates and exempt organizations use employer identification number.
      3. Fiduciary filing for individual uses individual's number only.
      4. Returns of payments to others must show payees' social security or EI numbers.
      5. Income tax preparers must furnish numbers.
         a. Employers of preparers must use their employer identification numbers.
         b. Other individual preparers use their social security account numbers.
   B. **Who signs return [¶ 3503]:**
      1. Taxpayer or authorized agent such as fiduciary, guardian, or executor.
      2. Joint return must be signed by husband *and* wife (or fiduciary or agent) [¶ 3505].
      3. Returns need not be verified except as to persons paid to prepare returns.
   C. **Who may file joint returns [¶ 3505]:**
      1. Must be husband and wife at close of tax year, or on date one dies.
      2. Joint return allowed, even if:
         a. Different accounting methods used.
         b. Separate estimated tax declarations filed.
         c. One spouse dies [see E below].
      3. Tax on joint return figured on combined income and deductions. Each spouse liable for entire tax, but innocent spouse may be excused.
      4. Filing of certain forms may constitute election to file a joint return.
   D. **Joint return after filing separate return [¶ 3506]:**
      1. Allowed if:
         a. Joint return could have been filed when separate return filed, and
         b. Tax paid in full when "late" joint return filed.
      2. "Late" joint return must be filed within 3 years of due date for filing (extensions not counted), but not after:
         a. Deficiency notice received and Tax Court petition filed, or
         b. Any court action started to recover any part of tax, or
         c. Closing agreement reached or civil or criminal case compromised.
      3. "Late" separate returns not allowed after joint return.
   E. **Joint return on death of spouse [¶ 3507].** Allowed even if one spouse dies during year, unless survivor remarries.
      1. Joint return for deceased generally made by executor or administrator, but survivor may file if:
         a. No return made by decedent for tax year joint return made, *and*
         b. No executor or administrator appointed by time joint return made, *and*
         c. No executor or administrator appointed by filing due date for survivor's return.
      2. Survivor-filed joint return can be disaffirmed by later appointed executor or administrator.
      3. Survivor cannot file "late" joint return (must be done by executor or administrator).

II. **Corporation Tax Returns**
   A. **What corporations must file [¶ 3512]:**

1. Every corporation not specifically exempt must file, even if no taxable income.
2. Must file as long as corporation exists. Corporation not dissolved if:
   a. It has valuable claims for which it will sue, or
   b. Receiver continues operation.
3. Receiver or trustee liquidating or operating business must file, if holding or owning corporate business or property.

B. **Return forms [¶ 3513]:**
1. Ordinary business corporation uses Form 1120.
2. Corporation electing partnership treatment uses Form 1120S.
3. Exempt corporations use Form 990-T for unrelated business income tax.
4. Exempt farm cooperatives use Form 990-C.
5. Return signed by hand and verified by authorized officer.

C. **Returns for short tax year not annualized unless it is due to change of accounting period [¶ 3514].**

D. **Consolidated returns.** Common parent files group return on Form 1120 with Form 851 attached. Filing continued while group exists, unless IRS consents [¶ 3515].

III. **Time and place for Filing Returns and Declarations**
  A. **When returns must be filed [¶ 3517]:**
   1. General rules:
      a. By prescribed due date. But if due date on Saturday, Sunday or legal holiday, due next day.
      b. Filing by mail must be postmarked by due date. Registered mail date is postmark date.
      c. File short tax year returns after period closes as if short period were fiscal year.
   2. Individual returns [¶ 3517(a)]:
      a. File by 15th of 4th month after tax year closes. (April 15 on calendar year basis.)
      b. Joint return by surviving spouse for year spouse died due same as if no death.
      c. Final return for decedent due as if decedent lived throughout year.
      d. Nonresident aliens with no wages file by 15th of 6th month after year-end.
   3. Corporation returns [¶ 3517(b)].
      a. File by 15th of 3d month after year-end (March 15 on calendar year basis).
      b. Dissolving corporations file by 15th of 3d month after dissolving, or on liquidation.
      c. Foreign corporations with no U.S. office file by 15th of 6th month after year-end.
   4. Estate and trust returns [¶ 3517(c)]:
      a. File by 15th of 4th month after year-end. (April 15 on calendar year basis.)
      b. Final returns due by 15th of 4th month after closing.
   5. Exempt organizations' return of unrelated business income[¶ 3517(d)]:
      a. Organizations taxed as corporations file by 15th of 3d month after year-end.
      b. Trusts taxed as individuals file by 15th of 4th month after year-end.
      c. Foreign organizations taxed as corporations without U.S. office file by 15th of 6th month after year-end.
   6. DISC returns due by 15th of 9th month after year-end [¶ 3517(e)].
  B. **Extension of time to file returns [¶ 3518]:**
   1. Extension does not generally extend time to pay, unless specified to contrary. Interest at the current rate on any tax not paid by due date.
   2. Usual extension applied for by return due date:
      a. 90 days for corporations.
      b. 60 days for individuals, partnerships, estates and trusts.
      c. Cannot exceed 6 months (except for taxpayers who are abroad).
      d. Short period return extension granted only under unusual circumstances.
   3. Automatic extensions [¶ 3518(a)]:
      a. Granted to 15th of 6th month after year-end for:

1) Domestic corporations doing business and keeping records abroad.
2) Domestic corporations with principal income from U.S. possessions.
3) Foreign corporations with U.S. Office and foreign partnerships.
4) Partnerships keeping records abroad.
5) American citizens abroad.
  b. 2-month extension for individuals. File Form 4868 by return due date accompanied by full amount estimated tax owed.
  c. 90-day extension for corporations. File Form 7004 by return due date with full or 50% of estimated tax owed.
 C. **Where to file returns.** Usually in Revenue District where taxpayer resides or has principal place of business, or Service Center for that district [¶ 3519].
 D. **Amended returns [¶ 3520]:**
  1. Individuals use Form 1140X.
  2. Corporations use Form 1120X.
  3. Other taxpayers use regular return form but must write "Amended Return" at top and explain error being corrected.
IV. **Supporting Information and Statements Often Required by Regulations and Return Form Instructions [¶ 3521]**
V. **Payment of Tax**
 A. **Individuals.** Pay by 15th of 4th month after tax year ends (April 15 for calendar year taxpayers) except [¶ 3522]:
  1. Tax figured by Revenue Service due within 30 days after notice.
  2. Nonresident aliens with no wages pay by 15th of 6th month after tax year ends.
 B. **Corporations.**
  1. Pay by 15th of 3d month after tax year ends (March 15 for calendar year corporations) [¶ 3523].
  2. Deposit in authorized banks with preinscribed federal deposit form designating Form 503.
  3. Foreign corporations with no U.S. office pay by 15th of 6th month after tax year ends.
  4. Tax payable in 2 equal installments: by 15th of 3d and 6th month after tax year ends, except nonresident foreign corporation not doing business in U.S. by 15th of 6th and 9th month.
  5. Estimated tax [¶ 3523(a)]:
   a. Amount due is excess of anticipated tax less estimated tax exemption ($2,200 for 1976) and credits.
   b. Pay with federal tax deposit form designating Form 503 if over $40.
   c. Penalty is 7% (9% between 7-1-75 and 1-31-76; 6% before 7-1-75) or an adjusted prime interest rate [¶ 3628] of amount by which installment payment is less than 80% of amount due on installment date. No penalty if installment payment not less than amount based on one of following:
    1) Previous year's tax.
    2) Tax on previous year's income, but at current year's rate.
    3) 80% of tax due on basis of annualizing income received.
 C. **Estates and trusts.** Pay by 15th of 4th month after tax year ends (April 15 for calendar year taxpayers) [¶ 3524]:
  1. Estates can pay in 4 equal installments: by 15th of 4th, 7th and 10th after year-end and Jan. of following year.
  2. Trusts cannot pay in installments.
 D. **Exempt organizations.** Pay unrelated business income tax in full with return, except, if taxable as corporation, tax payable by 15th of 3d and 6th month after tax year ends. Private foundations pay excise and penalty taxes by 15th of 5th month after tax year ends [¶ 3525].
 E. **Extensions of time to pay [¶ 3526]:**
  1. Generally granted only in hardship cases.
  2. Apply on Form 1127 before payment due date.

3. 7% (9% between 7-1-75 and 1-31-76; 6% before 7-1-75) or an adjustable rate [¶ 3628] of interest from date due till paid.
4. Deficiency payment extension for 18 months (in exceptional cases 12 month further extension possible).
5. Items 1 to 4 also apply to private foundations.

F. **Even dollar reporting allowed for total amounts shown on return [¶ 3527(a)].**

G. **Tax payable by cash, check or money order [¶ 3527(b)]:**
   1. Accept only Treasury bills issued anytime for periods under 1 year.
   2. Payment in foreign currency allowed to taxpayers receiving at least 70% of pay in nonconvertible foreign currency.

VI. Information Returns

A. **In general [¶ 3530]:**
   1. Various Forms 1099 must be used to report specific type payments.
   2. Generally prepared on calendar year-cash basis, even if filer on fiscal year-accrual basis. File by Feb. 28 of following year.
   3. Summary form (Form 1096) filed at same time as Forms 1099.
   4. Send statement to payee by Jan. 31 before filing date.
   5. Application for extension may be granted.
   6. Exceptions for liquidating corporations, partnerships and Subchapter S corporations.

B. **Return for business payments totaling $600 or more [¶ 3531]:**
   1. Required for certain payments made in course of business.
   2. Payments to employees [¶ 3531(a)]:
      a. Report on specified Forms 1099 compensation not reported on Form W-2, or Form 1042 (nonresident employees).
      b. Report on Form W-2P annuity, pension or retired pay payments.
      c. Report on Form 1099R lump-sum profit-sharing or retirement payments.
      d. Report on Form 1099-MISC income realized by former employee from certain stock dispositions, if information available.
   3. Report fees paid in course of business to attorneys, physicians, or other professionals [¶ 3531(b)].
   4. Report on Form 1099-MISC fixed or determinable income (rents, royalties, annuities) paid in course of business to individual citizens or residents, resident fiduciaries, or resident partnerships with a member who is a resident or citizen [¶ 3531(c)].
   5. Payments of $600 or more not reported if made to corporations or under other exceptions.

C. **Returns for interest paid [¶ 3532]:**
   1. Generally reportable if $600 or more paid in course of business.
   2. File Forms 1096 and 1099-INT for $10 or more interest paid or credited to person on [¶ 3532(a)]:
      a. Banks deposits (even if called "dividends").
      b. Corporate obligations in registered form.
      c. Funds left with insurance companies at interest.
      d. Deposits with stockbrokers or securities dealers.
   3. Nominees report payment to real owner on Form 1087-INT.
   4. Form 1099-OID used to report original issue discount.
   5. File ownership certificates for bond interest on Forms 1000 and 1001 signed by payee [¶ 3532(b)].

D. **Returns for dividends paid [¶ 3533]:**
   1. File Forms 1096 and 1099-DIV if paying $10 or more total dividends to one person.
   2. Record owner reports payment to real owner on Form 1087-DIV.
   3. Returns not required for:
      a. Payments by foreign governments or corporations.
      b. Payments to nonresident aliens and foreign corporations, their nominees, and subject to withholding.

c. Undistributed taxable income allocated to shareholders of electing small business corporations.
4. Exempt farmers' cooperatives report patronage dividends of $10 or more [¶ 3533(b)].

E. **Returns for stock transfers under employee options [¶ 3534]:**
1. Use Form 3921 if qualified or restricted stock option exercised.
2. Use Form 3922 if stock acquired for less than:
    a. 100% of value under stock purchase plan, or
    b. 95% of value under restricted option plan.

F. **Employer's returns for group-term life insurance premiums on Forms W-2 and W-3 [¶ 3535].**

G. **Returns on liquidations or terminations [¶ 3536]:**
1. File Form 966 within 30 days after adoption of plan to liquidate.
2. File Form 1099L for distributions of $600 or more.
3. Exempt organizations generally not excused from filing except:
    a. Churches, religious groups and exempt organizations with gross receipts under $5,000.
    b. Qualified employee plans if employer files.

H. **Information returns related to exempt organizations, trust and pension plans [¶ 3537]:**
1. Generally, exempts file annual information return on Form 990:
    a. Religious and apostolic organizations file Form 1065.
    b. Form 990 gives information on income, disbursements, deductions, net worth at beginning and end of year. If gross receipts over $10,000, balance sheets required.
    c. Private foundations file Form 990-PF providing identification of substantial contributors, investment income information and list of capital gains and losses.
    d. Form 4720 also required if excise taxes imposed.
2. Exception from filing:
    a. Mandatory class includes churches, religious organizations and certain organizations (not private foundations) with annual gross receipts under $5,000.
    b. Discretionary class includes those excused by IRS.
3. Group returns filed by parent.
4. Due by 15th of 4th month after organization's year ends, with Philadelphia Service Center.
5. Return for transfers to exempt organizations filed on Form 4629 by 90th day after transfer.
6. Private foundations, in addition to Form 990-PF, file annual reports on Form 990-AR at same time and place as Form 990.
7. Employer or plan administrator files returns/reports for employee benefit plans on:
    a. Form 5500, 5500-C or 5500-K, whichever is appropriate.
    b. Insurance information must be provided on Schedule A (Form 5500); actuarial information on Schedule B (Form 5500).
    c. Supporting statements may be required:
        1. Form 5501 (Summary of plans of employer).
        2. Form 5504 (Deduction for payments made for employees other than self-employed).
        3. Form 5505 (Deduction for payments made on behalf of self-employed individuals).
8. Returns/reports for employee benefit plans are due by last day of 7th month after end of plan's tax year.

I. **Returns for nonexempt trusts claiming charitable deduction [¶ 3538]:**
1. File annual information return on Form 1041-A.
2. Due by 15th of 4th month after tax year ends.

3. Charitable nonexempt trusts file Form 990 also; charitable remainder annuity trusts and charitable remainder unitrusts file Form 1041-B also; split interest nonexempt trusts file Form 1041-A only.

J. **Partnership, fiduciary and Subchapter S corporation returns [¶ 3539]:**
  1. File on Form 1065 showing income and distribution to partners
     a. By 15th of 4th month after partnership tax year ends (15th day of 6th month if all partners are nonresident aliens).
     b. No return if not engaged in U.S. trade and no U.S. source income.
  2. File fiduciary returns on Form 1041 with Schedule K-1 attached for each estate or trust beneficiary. Written notice required within 10 days from qualification as executor or receiver.
  3. Subchapter S corporation returns on Form 1120S required for each year.

K. **Returns for foreign items and foreign organizations [¶ 3540]:**
  1. Bank or agent for collections of $600 or more of foreign items for a citizen or resident must file Forms 1096 and 1099-INT, 1099-DIV by Feb. 28.
  2. Foreign corporations:
     a. U.S. person owning 5% or more of value of foreign corporation's stock must file Form 959 within 90 days after liability arises, with Director of International Operations (extendable).
     b. U.S. person in control of foreign corporation for 30 consecutive days during corporation's annual accounting period ending with or within U.S. person's tax year files Form 2952 with his income tax return.
  3. Foreign trusts file Form 3520 within 90 days after U.S. Person creates or transfers property to foreign trust.

L. **Returns for minimum tax [¶ 3541].**

M. **Disclosure, recordkeeping and returns, for income tax preparers [¶ 3542]:**
  1. Certain disclosure and recordkeeping requirements must be met: penalties apply for failure to meet requirements.
  2. Annual returns due by July 31; penalty applies for failure to file or disclose required information.

VII. **Pointers on Figuring the Tax**
  A. Records should properly identify source and amount of gross income [¶ 3545].
  B. How to figure tax if tax rate changes [¶ 3546].
  C. When there are 2 related unknown amounts, tax can be figured by trial and error or formula method [¶ 3547].

Chapter 26

ASSESSMENT—COLLECTION—REFUNDS

TABLE OF CONTENTS

	¶
What happens after return is filed	3600

EXAMINATION OF RETURNS

Examination procedure 3601
   Preliminary examination
   Returns audited
   Books and records
Audit procedure 3602
   Taxpayer cooperation
   Examiner's finding

PROCEDURE ON PROPOSED DEFICIENCY ASSESSMENT

The district conference 3603
   Procedure after audit
   Presenting the case
   Taxpayer's action after conference
The 30-day letter 3604
The 90-day letter 3605
   What taxpayer can do
   When deficiency is assessed
Waiver by taxpayer 3606
   Effect of waiver
   Waiver as closing agreement
The Appellate Division hearing 3607
   Protest
   Hearing procedure
   Results of hearing
Agreements settling tax claims 3608
   Compromise
   Closing agreements
Appearance at tax proceedings 3609
   Admission to practice before Internal Revenue Service
   Persons preparing returns
   Power of attorney required
   Tax information authorization

ASSESSMENT AND COLLECTION OF TAX

When tax must be assessed and collected 3610
   Suit to collect tax
   When assessment period begins
   Gross income not reported
   Extension of time
   Private foundations
Special limitation periods 3611
   Gain from sale of residence

   Involuntary conversion
   Transferee liability
   Personal holding company information
   "Late" joint return
   Deficiency on carryback
   Exploration expenses
When assessment period is reduced 3612
   Request for prompt assessment
   Termination assessments
   Jeopardy assessment
   Administrative and court review
   Bankruptcy
When limitation period is suspended .. 3613
Liability for tax of another taxpayer 3614
   Transferred assets
   Parent's liability for child
How tax is collected 3615
   Distraint
   Collection by suit
   Liens
   Set-off or counterclaim
   Payroll deductions
   Suit to prevent collection

PENALTIES

Kinds of penalties 3616
Penalties for failure to file returns 3617
Interest and penalties for failure to pay tax 3618
   Interest charged
   Penalty for failure to make timely payment
   Penalty for failure to pay deficiency
   Negligence and fraud penalty
   Payment with bad check
   Failure to deposit taxes
   Penalty as to excise taxes on private foundations
   Special taxes on retirement plans
   Penalties on income tax preparers
   Special tax on public charities
Penalty for underpayment of corporation estimated tax 3619
Criminal penalties 3620

REFUNDS AND CREDITS

Overpayment of tax 3621

Footnotes appear at end of this Chapter.

¶	¶
Refund claims 3622	Declaratory judgments on transfers of property from U.S.
Overpayment by withholding or estimated tax	**Appearance before Tax Court** 3636
Payment of assessed deficiency	Admission to practice
When taxpayer appeals to Tax Court	Application must be filed
Time for filing refund claims 3623	**Jurisdiction of Tax Court** 3637
Three-year limitation	Items subject to review
Two-year limitation	Deficiencies
Time extended by waiver	Issues raised by pleadings
Special periods for filing refund claims 3624	Matters raised before Revenue Service
Bad debts and worthless securities	Who files petition
Carrybacks	Service of papers
Taxes paid or credited	**Authority of regulations** 3638
Qualified retirement plans	**How proceeding begins** 3639
Amount of refund limited 3625	When to file petition
Form of refund claim 3626	Request for place of hearing
Statement of claim	Filing fee
Amending the claim	**The petition** 3640
Amended tax returns as claims	Form
Filing the refund claim 3627	Contents
Administrative procedure	**The Commissioner's answer** 3641
Decision on claim	Filing
Interest on refunds 3628	Contents
Credit for overpayment	**Petitioner's reply** 3642
No review of interest allowed	Filing
Special provisions	Contents
Suit to recover tax 3629	**Amended or supplemental pleadings** .. 3643
When to file	Amendment
Where to file	Supplemental pleadings
When 90-day letter is issued	Amendment conforming pleadings to proof
Appeal from lower court	Filing
Recovery of refunds paid	**Judgment without trial** 3644
Special rules for excise taxes on private foundations and special taxes on retirement plans	**Time and place for hearing** 3645
	Postponement
Quick refunds for carrybacks 3630	Discovery
Application	Admissions
Procedure on claim	Stipulations
Time to pay corporate tax extended	**How to take depositions** 3646
	The Tax Court hearing 3647
When limitation periods do not apply 3631	Burden of proof
Inconsistent determination required	Argument
	Rehearing
Relief without inconsistent determination	Tax briefs
	The Tax Court Report 3648
	Rule 155
THE UNITED STATES TAX COURT	Procedure after decision
	Review of Tax Court decision 3649
What the Tax Court does 3635	Appeals
Place of trial	Bond to stay assessment and collection
Proving a case	
Small tax case procedure	Effect of Courts of Appeals decisions
Declaratory judgments on qualification of retirement plans	
Declaratory judgments—exempt status and classification	• **Highlights of Chapter 26** .... Page 3661

¶ 3600 What happens after return is filed. A taxpayer's filed return is his assessment of the tax due for the tax year. The Revenue Service first examines it for accuracy, completeness and correct form. The returns are then sorted and classified, and many are selected for audit. The procedure for examination, assessment and collection of deficiencies, refund of tax, and the work of the Tax Court, is explained in this chapter. Collection of tax at the source is explained in Chapter 15.

EXAMINATION OF RETURNS

¶ **3601 Examination procedure.** All business and individual tax returns are now processed by an electronic automatic data system that checks the accuracy of the return, the right to any refund claimed and inclusion of income reported on information returns [¶ 3530]. The key to the system is the taxpayer identification number [¶ 3500]. Finally, all the information about the taxpayer is coordinated on magnetic tape at the computer center in Martinsburg, West Virginia. The system also locates persons who do not file returns as required.

(a) Preliminary examination. If a mathematical error is discovered in the taxpayer's figures—an amount wrongly transferred from one schedule to another, a mistake in addition, subtraction or multiplication—the Revenue Service sends a notice to the taxpayer, with a bill for any additional tax due [Sec. 601.105]. If an overpayment resulted, the excess is applied to future installments of tax [Sec. 6403] or is credited or refunded [Sec. 6402; 301.6402-1].

Procedures for third party summonses. Generally, after 2-28-77, a notice of summons must be given to a taxpayer if the IRS has summoned his books and records from a bank, brokerage house, accountant, attorney or other third-party recordkeeper. Notice by the IRS is due within three days after service of summons but no later than fourteen days of its return date. After notice, the taxpayer can intervene in a summons enforcement proceeding, or stay compliance with the summons by sending written instructions not to comply within 14 days after notice of summons to the third party. If the taxpayer chooses to stay compliance a copy of the notice not to comply must be sent to the IRS. When the taxpayer intervenes or stays compliance the limitation period on assessment or criminal prosecutions is suspended [Sec. 7609].

Witnesses, on application, may be reimbursed for per diem and mileage costs for appearing. Witnesses, other than the taxpayer or his representative, may be reimbursed for direct costs incurred in locating, copying and transporting any summoned records other than those in which the taxpayer has a proprietary interest [Sec. 7610].

Exceptions. Generally, these procedures do not apply to a summons issued solely to discover a bank account number or to aid collection of a judgment or assessment [Sec. 7609(c)(2)]. Moreover, these procedures are not to be made available to a "John Doe" summons (see below), or to a summons issued against a taxpayer's employer, or to a summons used to determine if records exist [Sec. 7609(a)(4)].

Constitutionality of summonses. The Supreme Court has ruled that a taxpayer's privilege against self-incrimination and right of privacy is no bar to a summons directing his accountant-tax preparer or attorney to produce his business and tax records.[1] The Court has also sanctioned using a "John Doe" summons to investigate bank records to identify a depositor involved in an unusual financial deal.[2] Furthermore, neither banks nor depositors have a right of privacy to be protected since records obtained are public business records under federal banking laws.[3]

NOTE: After 2-28-77, generally the IRS is authorized to serve a "John Doe" summons only after court approval [Sec. 7609(f)].

Footnotes appear at end of this Chapter.

¶ **3601**

(b) Returns audited. All income tax returns are subject to audit or review by the Audit Division of the office of the District Director.[4] [Sec. 601.105(b)]. This Division is made up of men thoroughly familiar with all phases of tax law and accounting, and is divided into three groups. They are: (1) agents specializing in taxes other than income taxes, (2) agents specializing in returns of a certain size, and (3) a group of highly specialized internal revenue agents. Depending upon the type of tax or the amount involved, the return is sent to one of these groups for review. Agents from the other groups are on hand, and, if a taxpayer is liable for different kinds of taxes (income, social security, excise, etc.) or penalties, the audit of all his returns is made at one time.

NOTE: "Private letter" rulings and similar determinations made by the Revenue Service for individual taxpayers must be made public but subject to certain restraints [Sec. 6104, 6110].

How returns are selected. Those selected include: returns reporting income aove a designated level; returns showing substantial income not subject to withholding; returns by enterprises shown to be error prone; returns with unusual dependency exemptions, or disproportionately large deductions; business returns that show a lower than normal gross profit ratio. Some returns are selected purely at random. Returns that call for large refunds receive a prerefund audit. Also, failure to answer inventory questions may invite an audit.

The Revenue Service will also select returns at random for its Taxpayer Compliance Measurement Program. (TCMP). The purpose of this program is to furnish the Revenue Service with statistics on the type and number of errors that the taxpayers are making and to provide a starting point for solutions to any problems uncovered. Some of the most common omissions that have turned up for individual returns are Form W-2 missing, incomplete or incorrect address or identifying number, incorrect blocks checked for dependents, entries on the wrong line, and failure to sign the return.[5]

Items subject to audit. Certain items invite tax audits. Particular attention is paid to deductions for charitable contributions, disability exclusion, medical expense deduction, unreimbursed business expenses of salespersons or executives, and blanket expense allowances by employers.

Auditors also examine closely expense deductions for club dues, entertainment, travel, maintenance of automobiles, yachts, airplanes, company supported residences, and other items that may disguise expenses incurred for a personal purpose. A taxpayer who fails to keep adequate records of business expenses may find that his deductions for such expenses are disallowed.

(c) Books and records. The taxpayer is responsible for keeping books and records that are adequate for audit purposes [Sec. 1.6001-1]. If the taxpayer uses an automatic accounting system, it should be set up so that records are available when the Revenue Service requests them. In addition, at regular intervals, the general and subsidiary ledger balances should be written out and income and expense account totals should be printed out and balanced with control accounts.[6]

¶ **3602 Audit procedure.** A return selected for audit may be subjected to an office audit or a field audit. An office audit may require an interview at the District Director's office or only the submission of information by mail [Sec. 601.105].[1] A field audit is made where the taxpayer keeps his books and records. The revenue agent "examiner" will arrange a mutually satisfactory date for an interview or field audit.

(a) Taxpayer cooperation. A taxpayer who receives notice of examination should produce all records required by the examiner, and cooperate with him in every way possible in a routine examination. Nothing is gained by placing obstacles in the way of an examiner. He can compel the production of all books and records he needs [Sec. 7602; 301.7602-1]. Failure to appear or produce books and records when a summons is issued is punishable by fine, imprisonment, or both [Sec. 7210, 7601; 301.7601-1 et seq.].

Fraud investigation. In cases involving possible charges of fraud, the taxpayer should be more cautious. If he learns that the agent investigating the case is from the Intelligence Division, a so-called Special Agent, or if the regular auditing agent does anything or says anything to indicate that this examination is not purely a routine examination, the taxpayer should get professional advice before giving the agent any information. If the taxpayer cooperates in these circumstances without professional advice, he risks the danger that he will help to make a case against himself during the investigation. The Revenue Service can examine the books of a taxpayer without showing probable cause if it suspects fraud, even if the year had been previously audited,[2] or was otherwise closed by the statute of limitations.[3] Evidence obtained by a routine tax investigation is not admissible in a fraud proceeding, unless the taxpayer had been warned of his right to remain silent and his right to have a lawyer[4] or accountant.[5] However, these warnings need not be given for "noncustodial interrogations" during criminal tax investigations.[6]

(b) Examiner's finding. At the close of an audit, the examiner states his findings to the taxpayer orally or by letter, and indicates the amount of any deficiency he finds [Sec. 601.105(c)]. The taxpayer should ask his tax adviser for advice when he receives the statement. If the taxpayer agrees with the result, he may consent to the assessment of the deficiency on Form 870 [¶ 3606]. This generally closes the case. The case will not be reopened to make an adjustment unfavorable to the taxpayer, unless: (1) there is evidence of fraud, malfeasance, collusion, concealment or material misrepresentation; (2) there was substantial error based on an established Service position existing at the time of the previous examination; or (3) failure to reopen would be a serious administrative omission. This does not apply to cases closed beyond the district level or Office of International Operations[7] [Sec. 601.105(j)].

When taxpayer disagrees. If the taxpayer disagrees with the examiner after an office correspondence audit, he may request a district conference [¶ 3606] within the period specified in the form letter sent to the taxpayer that includes the examiner's findings. After an office interview audit, he can ask for a conference then or wait for the form letter with the examiner's findings and a statement of the taxpayer's available appeal procedures [Sec. 601.105]. After a field audit, the case report is sent to the district review staff. The taxpayer then receives a 30-day letter which gives him 30 days in which to arrange for a district conference, or he may take one of several other alternative actions [¶ 3604]. If the issues are complicated the taxpayer may be asked to bypass the district conference.[8] A taxpayer who does not want a district conference after an office audit may apply for an Appellate Division hearing [¶ 3607] within 30 days after he receives the examiner's findings. A taxpayer who does not respond within 30 days after notice of the examiner's findings will receive a 90-day letter [¶ 3605]. In some cases the District Director or taxpayer can ask for technical advice from the National Office [Sec. 601.105].

PROCEDURE ON PROPOSED DEFICIENCY ASSESSMENT

¶ 3603 The district conference. The district conference, held in the district office, gives the taxpayer a chance to discuss the examiner's report. Generally, it is conducted by a conferee selected by the Conference Staff Chief who may settle certain issues that involve $2,500[1] or less. The examining agent usually does not at-

Footnotes appear at end of this Chapter.

tend. The taxpayer may be represented by a person qualified to practice before the Revenue Service [¶ 3609].

> NOTE: Protests, briefs or statements for any conference should be filed at least 5 days before the meeting. But conference date may be postponed by mutual consent, and taxpayer may submit additional evidence within a reasonable time after the meeting [Sec. 601.502].

If a taxpayer who disagrees with the examiner wants a district conference he must ask for it. The procedure depends on whether there was an office or field audit.

(a) Procedure after audit. After an office audit, the taxpayer need only request the conference when he receives the examiner's findings and the amount of the proposed deficiency [¶ 3602]. A formal protest need not be filed [Sec. 601.105].

Field audit. A conference cannot be arranged after a field audit until the taxpayer receives a 30-day letter [¶ 3604]. A formal protest must be filed if the proposed adjustment is more than $2,500, but not if the amount is $2,500 or less. Instructions for preparing protests accompany the 30-day letter [Sec. 601.105]. The taxpayer will be encouraged to bypass the district conference, if it appears there is little possibility of settling the case there.

(b) Presenting the case. Conference decisions are based on the examiner's report, additional facts shown in the taxpayer's statement or brief submitted with the request for a conference, and any other facts disclosed during the conference.

If the facts are disputed, the taxayer must present the correct facts as he sees them. This can be done in writing, by documentary evidence and by affidavit. Legal questions can best be submitted in writing so the authorities may be cited and analyzed. For this reason, it is recommended that a request for a conference be in writing with an attached statement of facts and authorities. A protest must state the facts and the law and authorities relied on.[2]

At the end of the conference, the conferee may concede some or all of the taxpayer's contentions, insist on some or all of the examiner's contentions, or assert an increased deficiency based on admissions by the taxpayer or the attorney made in the course of the conference.

(c) Taxpayer's action after conference. The taxpayer has a choice of actions at the end of the conference.

- He may accept the conferee's proposal and sign a waiver form [¶ 3606].
- He may disagree with the decision. He will then receive a copy of the conference report and a 30-day letter [¶ 3604], if he has not already received one.
- He may ask that a formal deficiency notice (90-day letter) be issued so that he can appeal to the Tax Court, or pay the tax, claim refund, and sue for recovery [¶ 3629].

When agreement is reached. When the taxpayer accepts the proposal made at the end of the conference, the conferee prepares a conference report of the facts and conclusions reached. This is sent to the Regional Commissioner for "post-review." If it is approved, the case is transferred to the District Director's office for collection. The case may be reopened after post-review, especially if there is substantial error,[3] or evidence of fraud or misrepresentation [Sec. 601.105(i), (j)].

¶ 3604 The 30-day letter. A taxpayer who refuses to accept an examiner's deficiency finding after a field audit, or who cannot agree with the determination at a district conference following an office audit, will receive a "30-day letter" [Sec. 601.105]. This is a form letter which states the proposed determination of the Revenue Service, describes the taxpayer's further appeal rights and advises him that he has 30 days to inform the District Director of his course of action. If the audit was an office audit, he may file a written protest and request an Appellate Division hearing [¶ 3607]. If the taxpayer had a field audit, he may request a district conference [¶ 3603]. He may instead file a formal protest and request an Appellate Division hearing rather than a district conference. If he decides to accept the examiner's finding at this point, he may file Form 870, limiting interest on the deficiency, and have the deficiency assessed and collected. If he does nothing, he will receive a 90-day letter [¶ 3605].

NOTE: Where the period for tax assessment is about to expire, a 90-day letter [¶ 3605] can be issued without the necessity of a 30-day letter even though the case may be in the examination or conference stage [Sec. 601.105(f)].

¶ 3605 **The 90-day letter** is a formal notice of the deficiency determined. It is sent by registered or certified mail, and may be received any time after the district conference [¶ 3603], after the period allowed in the 30-day letter if no Form 870 was signed or protest filed, or after the Appellate Division hearing [¶ 3607]. Mailing to the taxpayer's last known address or to his accountant[1] is sufficient [Sec. 6212(b)(1)]. The details are usually given in an attached statement, with notice that within 90 days from the date of mailing (150 days for taxpayers located outside the United States and District of Columbia) the taxpayer may petition the Tax Court for redetermining the deficiency. A copy of Form 870 is sent with the 90-day letter.

The Revenue Service can assess and collect the deficiency after the time for filing a petition with the Tax Court expires, even if the taxpayer does not actually receive a notice mailed to his last known address.[2]

Notice for joint return. When a husband and wife file a joint return, the notice of deficiency may be a single joint notice. However, if either spouse notifies the Commissioner that they have separate residences, the identical joint notice must be sent to each spouse[3] [Sec. 6212(b)(2); 301.6212-1].

When there is a fiduciary. Generally, a fiduciary assumes the powers, rights, duties, and privileges of the taxpayer [Sec. 6903; 301.6903-1]. A fiduciary is required to give the Revenue Service notice that he is acting in a fiduciary capacity [Sec. 6903(b)]. If this notice is not filed, the deficiency notice does not have to be sent to the fiduciary; it can be sent to the last known address of the taxpayer (see above). A fiduciary may be relieved from further liability by filing written notice and proof that his fiduciary capacity has ended [Sec. 301.6903-1].

10-day notice. The following fiduciaries must file a notice within 10 days of the time they qualify [Sec. 6036; 301.6036-1]:

• Receiver or trustee in bankruptcy, or other persons in control of debtor's assets; qualified by appointment or authority to act. (If the Treasury Department is given notice of the proceeding under the Bankruptcy Act a fiduciary notice is not necessary).
• Receiver in receivership proceeding (including foreclosure) in any U.S. or state court; qualified by appointment, authority to act, or by taking possession of debtor's assets.
• Assignee for benefit of creditors; qualified on the date of assignment.

NOTE: The fiduciary notice must be filed with the District Director where the person he acts for is required to file returns.

Excise taxes. The Revenue Service will issue a deficiency notice if it determines that a deficiency exists in excise taxes payable by a private foundation (¶ 3440 et seq.), or payable on certain retirement plans [¶ 3618(h)], or payable by a real estate investment trust [Sec. 6212].

Footnotes appear at end of this Chapter.

(a) **What taxpayer can do.** A taxpayer has four choices when he receives a 90-day letter.

• He may do nothing. Then the deficiency will be assessed at the close of the 90-day (or 150-day) period and referred to the Collection Division.

• He may sign Form 870 (thus limiting interest on the deficiency [¶ 3606]). Then the deficiency will be assessed and referred to the Collection Division.

• He may seek a hearing or a rehearing before the Appellate Division [¶ 3607]. (This hearing or rehearing does not extend his time to petition the Tax Court.)

• He may file a petition with the Tax Court before the 90 (or 150) days have passed.

Time for filing Tax Court petition. The day the notice is mailed is not counted in fixing the 90 or 150-day period, but the day the petition is filed is counted.[4] If the last day is a Saturday, Sunday or legal holiday in the District of Columbia, it is not counted as the 90th or 150th day [Sec. 6213(a); 301.6213-1]. The 150-day period applies even for a temporary absence from the U.S., for any reason.[5] A properly addressed petition mailed to the Tax Court is timely filed with a post office postmark dated before the due date [Sec. 7502]. A postmark from a private postage meter is acceptable but it must be dated on or before the due date. See also ¶ 3517; 3639(a).

(b) **When deficiency is assessed.** The deficiency in tax will not be assessed or collected during the 90 (or 150) day period for filing a Tax Court petition. If a petition is filed during this period, the tax is not assessed until the Tax Court decision becomes final [Sec. 6213(a); 301.6213-1(a)]. There are six exceptions when an immediate assessment can be made.

Immediate assessment. Assessment or collection before the 90 (or 150) day period is allowed in the following situations:

• An insufficient payment due to a mathematical or clerical error on the return may be collected. Notice of an amount due because of the error is not treated as a notice of deficiency. An abatement of the assessment in the notice is allowed if the taxpayer files a request within 60 days after notice is sent [Sec. 6213(b); 301.6213-1(b)].

• Taxpayer signs a waiver on Form 870 [Sec. 6213(d); 301.6213-1(d)].

• A "jeopardy assessment" can be made when delay might prevent the assessment or collection of a deficiency (a jeopardy assessment may be made before the 90-day deficiency notice is sent, but a deficiency notice must be issued within 60 days of the assessment) [Sec. 6861; 301.6861-1].

NOTE: A termination assessment [¶ 3612(b)] does not end the tax year, so a deficiency notice need not be given within 60 days of the assessment [Sec. 6212(c)].

• On the filing or approval of a petition, appointment of receiver, or adjudication in bankruptcy (¶ 3612) [Sec. 6871(a); 301.6871(a)-1].

• When tax is paid. A payment made after a deficiency notice has been mailed will not deprive the Tax Court of jurisdiction over the deficiency determined without regard to the payment [Sec. 6213(b)(3); 301.6213-1(b)].

• When a petition for review of the Tax Court's decision is filed with a Court of Appeals, unless a bond is filed with the Tax Court [¶ 3649(b)].

¶ 3606 Waiver by taxpayer. Taxpayer may be asked to sign a "Waiver of Restrictions on Assessment and Collection of Deficiency in Tax and Acceptance of

Overassessments" [¶ 3602-3605]. Form 870 is used for income tax purposes; Form 890 for estate tax and Form 890a for gift tax.

(a) **Effect of waiver.** Taxpayer by signing the waiver form gives up the right to have an assessment deferred until after the 90-day period provided in the formal notice of deficiency [¶ 3605]. When an overassessment of tax has been made, the taxpayer and the District Director or his representative can sign the waiver form as an agreement of overassessment. If more than one year or different taxes are involved, the taxpayer may waive the restrictions on immediate assessment of a deficiency for one year or type of tax, while agreeing to an overassessment of another year's tax liability or type of tax. By waiving his rights, the taxpayer stops the interest [¶ 3628] on the deficiency during the period from 30 days after filing the waiver to the date of notice and demand for payment [Sec. 6601(c); 301.6601-1(d)].

(b) **Waiver as closing agreement.** Generally, a waiver form does not bar a claim for refund[1] or an assessment.[2] However, provisions barring refund claims are valid when inserted in the form.[3] See also ¶ 3626.

¶ 3607 The Appellate Division hearing. The Appellate Division hearing generally is arranged at the taxpayer's request when he is dissatisfied with the results of the district conference [¶ 3603]. However, the hearing may be granted without a prior district conference [Sec. 601.106].

(a) **Protest.** Generally a formal protest must be filed with the District Director for a case the taxpayer wants reviewed by the Appellate Division. The contents of the protest are described in the Instructions for Unagreed Income, Estate and Gift Tax Cases.[1] The protest must be verified. However, the Appellate Division will consider unagreed cases for amounts of $2,500 or less at the taxpayer's written request after a 30-day letter [¶ 3604] is issued and the taxpayer has had a district conference [¶ 3603].[2] Generally the Appellate Division will not consider a case after a 90-day letter [¶ 3605] is issued until a Tax Court petition [¶ 3639] is filed [Sec. 601.106].

(b) **Hearing procedure.** Hearings before the Appellate Division, like the district conference, are informal. While the district conference deals largely with questions of fact, the Appellate Division's hearing turns upon issues of tax law. The facts established at a district conference are not subject to review except for purposes of settlement. The question to be decided is whether, on the basis of those facts, the courts will in their interpretation of the law decide in favor of the Revenue Service or the taxpayer.

Taxpayer's proof. New facts to be added to the record must be submitted as affidavits. If important evidence bearing on a basic issue is presented for the first time when the case is before the Appellate Division, the information will be turned over to the District Director. The Appellate Division will not consider for the first time, on appeal, evidence not previously available to the District Director [Sec. 601.106].

The taxpayer may be required to submit important evidence by affidavit. A statement of additional facts and points of law on which the taxpayer bases his exceptions may be presented in technical brief form. If the issue is at all complicated, this is generally advisable.

(c) **Results of hearing.** Both the taxpayer and the Revenue Service generally will concede something to avoid the delay, expense, and chance of a court appeal.

Footnotes appear at end of this Chapter.

When the Revenue Service would have a clear-cut case before any court, the Appellate Division will not offer any reduction. But if there is doubt as to the position that the courts might take on the points at issue, the Appellate Division will offer to reduce the proposed deficiency.

When there is agreement. If the conferee and the taxpayer reach an agreement, the taxpayer will sign Form 870-AD. An attorney or accountant representing a taxpayer signs for the taxpayer. The matter then is turned over to the District Director for assessment and collection. Form 870-AD is an offer of waiver and does not stop the running of interest until 30 days after the offer is accepted.[3]

When there is disagreement. If the taxpayer and conferee cannot agree, the Appellate Division may issue a statutory notice of deficiency (the 90-day letter) [¶ 3605]. If the taxpayer files a petition with the Tax Court within 90 days, the case will turned over to the Regional Counsel to prepare for trial. In order to expedite Tax Court cases, the Revenue Service may require a settlement conference when 90-day letters [¶ 3605] have not been issued.[4] If no petition is filed within this period, the case will be transferred to the District Director for appropriate action.

¶ **3608 Agreements settling tax claims.** Tax claims can be settled by compromise or closing agreement.

(a) **Compromise.** The Revenue Service may compromise a tax case before it has been referred to the Department of Justice. After it has been referred to the Department of Justice, the Attorney General or his delegate can compromise the case.[1] Interest and penalties, as well as taxes, may be compromised [Sec. 7122; 301.7122-1]. Offers in compromise are made on Form 656. They are submitted to the District or Service Center Director, with a financial statement on Form 433 [Sec. 601.203].[2] In some cases, the taxpayer can have a district conference [¶ 3603] and an Appellate Division hearing to discuss the offer.[3] A compromise is a final settlement of liability, and amounts paid cannot be recovered;[4] but the agreement may be rescinded for mutual mistake, fraud, or duress [Sec. 301.7122-1]. A refund for a loss carryback is not barred by an earlier compromise.[5] If a taxpayer fails to pay the compromise amount, the Revenue Service can collect the entire original tax liability.[6]

The Revenue Service compromises a case only when there is some doubt the taxpayer is liable or that the tax can be collected. Authority to compromise is delegated to District Directors or higher officers depending on the kind and amount of tax.[3] An agreement with an unauthorized officer is not an effective compromise.[7]

(b) **Closing agreements.** The Commissioner (or any officer or employee authorized by the Commissioner) and the taxpayer may enter into what is known as a closing agreement (Form 866), to settle taxpayer's complete liability.[8] It is final and conclusive on both the government and the taxpayer. The only exception is when fraud, malfeasance or misrepresentation of a material fact is shown [Sec. 301.7121-1]. The agreement generally is used in cases where the taxpayer has made concessions because of others made by the government, and it is necessary to bar further action by either party. It is also used when a fiduciary desires to be discharged by the court and when corporations are winding up their affairs [Sec. 7121; 301.7121-1]. Form 906 is used to settle only one or more separate issues [Sec. 601.202(b))].

¶ **3609 Appearance at tax proceedings.** Attorneys and certified public accountants may represent taxpayers before the Internal Revenue Service by filing a declaration stating they are currently so qualified in a particular state, possession, territory or commonwealth of the U.S. or in the District of Columbia, and are authorized to act for the designated client [Sec. 10.3]. Other persons generally must be enrolled as agents ((a) below) before they can practice. However, appearance without enrollment is possible in some cases. An individual may appear on his own behalf; full time employees may appear for their employer; corporate officers and partners may appear for their corporation or partnership; fiduciaries or their full time employees may appear for the entity they act for; and return preparers may deal with an examining agent ((b) below) [Sec. 10.7]. The Revenue Service can discipline and disbar any person who appears before it [Sec. 10.50].

> NOTE: Labor unions and trade associations can use Revenue Service appeals procedure through the Appellate Division level when members are denied deductions for dues paid because they are used for lobbying or similar purposes.[1]

The Tax Court has its own rules for admission to practice [¶ 3636].

(a) Admission to practice before Internal Revenue Service. Generally, persons other than attorneys or CPAs must pass a written examination and be enrolled before they can practice before the Revenue Service. Practice includes preparation and filing of documents (except tax returns), communication with the Service and representing clients at conferences [¶ 3603], hearings [¶ 3607] or meetings [Sec.10.2]. Attorneys and CPAs cannot enroll as agents [Sec. 10.4]. Application for examination is made on Form 2587. Application for enrollment is made on Form 23. $25 filing fees must accompany the applications. Successful applicants receive a permanent registration card [Sec. 10.6]. The requirements for admission to practice and the disciplinary procedures may be found in Department Circular No. 230.[2]

> NOTE: Current 5-year enrollment cards issued before 9-13-66 may be converted to permanent enrollment cards by filing Form 23 A within 12 months before or after the expiration date [Sec. 10.6].

(b) Persons preparing returns. An unenrolled person who prepares a tax return, if properly authorized (by filing Form 2848-D, or a similar statment), can represent the taxpayer before the revenue agent or examining officer [¶ 3602] in connection with the return he has prepared.[3] He cannot represent the taxpayer at other proceedings [Sec. 10.7].

Injunction against income tax preparers. Suit may be brought in an appropriate U.S. District Court either to enjoin an income tax preparer from engaging in specified acts or engaging in business as an income tax preparer. However, a $50,000 bond may be posted in some cases to stay the injunction [Sec. 7407].

(c) Power of attorney required. A practitioner should obtain a power of attorney from the taxpayer, covering all responsibilities he may be called upon to exercise for the taxpayer before the Revenue Service.[4] Form 2848 can be used for this purpose. One copy of the power of attorney must be filed in each Revenue Service office where the taxpayer is represented, with one additional copy for each tax year under consideration [Sec. 601.503]. Powers given to enrolled agents need not be notarized [Sec. 601.504]. A power is not necessary if the client is present at the proceedings [Sec. 601.502].

(d) Tax information authorization. A taxpayer's representative must file a tax information authorization to receive confidential information, if a power of attorney is not filed. Form 2848-D can be used. The authorization is not a substitute for a required power of attorney; for example, to receive a refund check [Sec. 601.502—601.504].

Footnotes appear at end of this Chapter.

¶ 3609

ASSESSMENT AND COLLECTION OF TAX

¶ 3610 **When tax must be assessed and collected.** The tax generally must be assessed within three years after the return was filled, but if the taxpayer omitted from the return an amount that is over 25% of the gross income stated on the return, the tax can be assessed within six years [Sec. 6501; 301.6501(a)-1, 301.6501(e)-1]. The assessment is made when an assessment officer signs the summary record of assessment [Sec. 6201-6204; 301.6201—301.6204].

In some situations, tax liability may depend on events occurring after the return is filed and the Revenue Service has the opportunity to assess a deficiency resulting from the later event after the usual limitation period has expired [¶ 3611]. Also, assessment or collection may be prevented during the usual period and additional time is added to the period [¶ 3613].

A tax assessed or collected after the statute of limitations has expired is treated as an overpayment. It will be credited or refunded to the taxpayer, if he files a timely refund claim [Sec. 6401; 301.6401-1].

If a false or fraudulent return is filed with intent to evade the tax, or if no return is filed, the tax may be assessed, or a court proceeding begun to collect the tax without assessment at any time [Sec. 6501(c); 301.6501(c)-1]. An unsigned or incompletely signed return may be treated as *no return* at all.[1]

Interest on deficiency. Interest on a deficiency may be assessed and collected during the period the tax itself can be collected [Sec. 6601(g)].

(a) Suit to collect tax. The government may collect the tax by levy [¶ 3615(a)] or by suit within 6 years after a timely assessment has been made. A judgment against the taxpayer does not change the period for collection by levy [Sec. 6502(a); 301.6502-1]. The collection period may be extended by written agreement between the taxpayer and District Director before the period ends. Collection time may be extended after the period ends, if a levy was made during the period, and the extension is agreed upon before the levy is released [Sec. 6502(a); 301.6502-1(a)]. A suit to collect the tax without assessment can be started within the same period the tax can be assessed [Sec. 301.6501(a)-1].

> **Example 1:** An assessment was made in 1971 and a levy was made in 1976. An agreement can be made in 1978 to release the levy and permit the taxpayer to pay the tax in installments by 1980.

(b) When assessment period begins. If a return is filed before the due date, the assessment period generally runs from the due date. But if the return is for income or social security tax withheld from wages or tax withheld at source [¶ 2535] and is filed before April 15 of the next calendar year, the period runs from that date [Sec. 6501; 301.6501(b)-1].

> **Example 2:** On April 6, 1978, Ames, who reports on the calendar years basis filed his return for 1977, correctly showing a gross income of $10,000. The last day on which an additional assessment may be made (or a court proceeding instituted to collect the tax without assessment) is April 15, 1981.

"Late" joint return. A "late" joint return [¶ 3506], replacing separate returns is considered filed:

- on the date the last separate return was filed, if both spouses filed separate returns (but not earlier than the last date for filing the return of either spouse);
- on the date of filing of the separate return, if only one spouse filed a separate return before making of the joint return, and the other spouse had less than $750 ($1,500 if spouse was 65 or over) of gross income for the tax year (but not earlier than the last day for filing the separate return);

• on the date of the filing of the joint return, if only one spouse filed a separate return, and the other spouse had gross income of $750 ($1,500 if spouse was 65 or over) or more [Sec. 6013(b)(3)(A); 1.6013-2(c)].

A special limitation period applies when a late joint return is filed [¶ 3611].

Wrong return form. If a trust or partnership return is filed in good faith by an association that later is held to be a corporation, the return is treated as the return of the corporation, and the limitation period starts to run with the filing of the return [Sec. 6501(g)(1); 301.6501(g)-1(a)]. A return (Form 1120S) filed under an election to be taxed as a partnership [¶ 3140 et seq.] is treated the same way if the corporation is later found not qualified for the election [Sec. 1.6037-1].

If a taxpayer in good faith files a return as an exempt organization, and later it is held to be a taxable organization or to have unrelated business income[2] [¶ 3445], the statute of limitations starts to run when the return is filed [Sec. 6501(g)(2); 301.6501(g)-1(b)]. The taxpayer is still subject to penalties for failure to file a proper return or to pay tax.[3]

(c) Gross income not reported. The tax may be assessed within six years after the return was filed, if taxpayer fails to report an amount that is more than 25% of the gross income reported on the return [Sec. 6501(e)].

> **Example 3:** If Ames in Example 2 actually omitted more than $2,500 of gross income on his return, the last day for assessment would be April 15, 1984.

Business income. Gross income of a business is the total amount received or accrued from the sale of goods or services before subtracting the cost of sales or services. Any amount disclosed on the return is not considered in determining the 25% omission [Sec. 6501(e)(1)(A); 301.6501(e)-1]. Information in a related return may be considered adequate disclosure if the returns are sufficiently correlated.[4]

(d) Extension of time. The period for assessment or collection may be extended by the filing of a waiver (Form 872) by the taxpayer [Sec. 6501(c)(4); 301.6501(c)-1]. For example, a waiver might be used when the issuance of a 90-day letter would result in a petition to the Tax Court that could be avoided if the taxpayer and the government had ample time to consider thoroughly the questions involved. Form 872-A is used instead of Form 872 for cases where Appellate Division consideration has been requested.[5]

Form 872, entitled "Consent Fixing Limitation upon Assessment of Income and Profits Tax," should not be confused with Form 870 previously discussed. Form 870 permits a proposed deficiency to be assessed immediately and waives the right to file a petition with the Tax Court. Form 872 simply extends the time to make an assessment. The consent may be limited to particular unsettled issues.[6]

(e) Private foundations. The assessment and collection of excise taxes imposed on private foundations [¶ 3440-3444] generally must be made within the 3-year period. This period usually starts when the return was filed for the year in which the act or failure to act giving rise to the taxes occurred. For excise taxes imposed on investment income [¶ 3438], the 3-year period starts when the return was filed for the year in which the taxes were imposed [Sec. 6501(n)]. An additional 1-year period may apply for assessing a deficiency arising from contributions made by private foundations to religious, charitable and educational organizations (¶ 3441) [Sec. 6501(n)(2)]. Form 872-C is used with Form 1023 to extend time to assess taxes on investment income if an organization elects non-private foundation treatment.[7] When the private foundation status is ended [¶ 3437(b)],

Footnotes appear at end of this Chapter.

¶ 3610

the termination tax can be assessed (or a collection proceeding without assessment can start) at any time [Sec. 6501(c)(7)].

> **NOTE:** Deficiencies due to set aside distributions [¶ 3441] may be assessed within 2 years after the tax year to which the set aside relates [Sec. 6501(n)(3)]. This applies to any tax year starting after 12-31-74.

¶ 3611 Special limitation periods. Special limitation periods for assessment apply to sale of a residence, involuntary conversion, transferee liability and some other situations. Adjustments of tax may be allowed after the limitation period expires, under certain conditions [¶ 3631].

(a) **Gain from sale of residence.** When a taxpayer sells his residence at a gain, the time for assessing a deficiency on the gain runs for three years from the date the taxpayer notifies the Revenue Service of (1) his cost of buying a new residence, or (2) his intention not to, or failure to, buy a new residence within the required time. Notice should be given when the purchase occurs, or the intention not to purchase is formed, or the period for replacement expires [Sec. 1034(j); 1.1034-1(i)]. See also ¶ 1416 et seq.

(b) **Involuntary conversion.** If a taxpayer elects not to recognize gain on an involuntary conversion of property, the time for assessing a deficiency on the gain runs for three years from the date the taxpayer notifies the Revenue Service of the replacement of the converted property or of his intention not to replace or of his failure to replace within the required time. The notice is filed where the return was filed for the year the gain on the conversion was realized. The notice should be given in the return for the year when the replacement occurs, or the intention not to replace is formed, or the period for replacement expires [Sec. 1033(a)(3)(C); 1.1033(a)-2(c)(5)]. See also ¶ 1411. The period of assessment for any other deficiency due to the election is also extended [Sec. 1033(a)(3)(D)].

(c) **Transferee liability.** Transferees of property may become liable for taxes of the original owner of the property [¶ 3614(a)]. Liability must be assessed against the first transferee within one year after the time for assessment against the owner expires.[1] When the property passes through several hands, the liability must be assessed within one year after the time to assess liability against the preceding holder expires; but not more than 3 years after the time for assessment against the original owner expires. A court proceeding to collect the tax that is started against the original owner or the last preceding transferee before the time ends to assess against the current holder, extends the time for assessment against the holder to one year after the return of execution in the court proceeding. The time for assessment against a fiduciary expires: (1) one year after the liability arises, or (2) when the period for collecting the tax expires, whichever is later [Sec. 6901(c); 301.6901-1(c)].

If an original owner dies, or goes out of existence, the above time limits do not change [Sec. 6901(e); 301.6901-1(e)]. A request for prompt assessment [¶ 3612(a)] does not shorten the length of time of transferee liability.[2] If the transferor filed a fraudulent return, there is no time limit on assessment against the transferee.[3]

(d) **Personal holding company information.** A special 6-year period for assessment applies when a personal holding company fails to furnish required data on the special schedule of the corporation income tax return or a foreign personal holding company shareholder fails to report a constructive dividend [Sec. 6501; 301.6501(e)-(1), 301.6501(f)-1].

(e) **"Late" joint return.** If a *"late" joint return* replacing separate returns is filed [¶ 3506], the limitation period cannot end less than one year after the joint return is actually filed [Sec. 6013(b)(4); 1.6013-2(d)].

(f) Deficiency on carryback. The time to assess a deficiency due to a carryback of a net operating loss, capital loss, investment credit, work incentive program credit, foreign tax credit or certain oil and gas extraction taxes (see below) is measured from the later year.

Net operating loss, capital loss, and investment work incentive program and employee credits. A deficiency for the tax year to which the carryback is made and attributable to the carryback, may be assessed within the period a deficiency can be assessed for the tax year the carryback was created [Sec. 6501(h), (j), (o), (p); 301.6501(h)-1, 301.6501(j)-1]. If the taxpayer files for a quick refund [¶ 3630], *any* deficiency for the prior year may be assessed within the same period, but the amount cannot be more than the refund less any deficiency attributable only to the carryback [Sec. 6501(m); 301.6501(m)-1, 301.6501(o)-1]. A deficiency from a disallowed investment credit carryover can be assessed and collected even though the year the credit was claimed is barred.[4]

Foreign tax credit. A deficiency due to a carryback of a foreign tax credit [¶ 3703(b)] may be assessed within one year after the time to assess a deficiency for the year from which the credit was carried [Sec. 6501(i); 301.6501(i)-1].

Oil and gas. The same limitation provisions that apply to the foreign tax credit (see above) also apply to carryback and carryover of disallowed oil and gas extraction taxes [Sec. 6501(i)].

(g) Exploration expenses. A deficiency due to the election to use the unlimited exploration expense deduction [¶ 1843] (or its revocation) can be assessed up to 2 years after the election (or revocation) [Sec. 617(a)].

¶ 3612 When assessment period is reduced. The period for assessment of tax may be shortened by a request for prompt assessment. A quick assessment also can be made before the 90-day period [¶ 3605(b)] in bankruptcy proceedings or to prevent tax evasion.

(a) Request for prompt assessment. The assessment period may be shortened to 18 months after a request for prompt assessment is filed for a return of a decedent or a decedent's estate or a return for a dissolved or dissolving corporation. If there has been an omission amounting to over 25% of the gross income reported on the return, of if a personal holding company fails to file the required information schedule, the 6-year period for assessment applies, despite the request for prompt assessment [Sec. 6501(d); 301.6501(d)-1]. When a fiduciary distributes estate assets after 18 months and has no knowledge or reasonable belief a tax is due, he is not personally liable for the tax.[1] For transferee liability, see ¶ 3611(c).

(b) Termination assessments. If a taxpayer (including a corporation in liquidation) intends, by immediate departure from the U.S. or some other way, to avoid the payment of the income tax, the Revenue Service may immediately determine the income tax due and payable for the current or preceding taxable year. However, the taxable year is terminated only for tax computation so that the tax year continues until its normal end. The taxpayer may contest the assessment in the Tax Court in the same manner as a jeopardy assessment (see (c) below). In addition, the Revenue Service (after 2-28-77) must issue a deficiency notice within 60 days after the later of the return due date for the full tax year or the return filing date [Sec. 6851]. A penalty of 25% of the tax or deficiency can be imposed if the taxpayer tries to hamper collection proceedings[2] [Sec. 6658].

Footnotes appear at end of this Chapter.

(c) **Jeopardy assessment.** If a tax or deficiency (income, estate, gift or certain excise taxes) is jeopardized by delay, the Revenue Service can immediately assess the tax and serve notice and demand for immediate payment. The taxpayer may contest liability in the Tax Court. To stay collection, however, the taxpayer must also furnish a bond. To enable him to petition to the Tax Court, the Revenue Service must issue a deficiency notice either before assessment or within 60 days after jeopardy assessment[3] [Sec. 6861; 301.6861-1]. In addition, if administrative and judicial review (see (d) below) is sought, restrictions are imposed on sale of property under a jeopardy or termination assessment [Sec. 6863(b)(3)].

(d) **Administrative and court review.** Starting with notices and demands made after 2-28-77, the Revenue Service must furnish a written detailed statement to the taxpayer within 5 days following the jeopardy or termination assessment stating the reasons for the assessment. The taxpayer has 30 days after receipt to request the IRS to review the correctness of the assessment. After the IRS review, suit can be brought in an appropriate District Court either within 30 days after IRS review or within 30 days after the 16th day after request for review, whichever is earlier. The court must issue, within 20 days after start of the suit, a decision on the reasonableness of the assessment and seizure, if any. It may order abatement, redetermination or other appropriate action. In any case, such orders are not appealable. Upon the taxpayer's request the court may grant an extension of the 20 day period up to 60 days [Sec. 7429].

(e) **Bankruptcy.** Any deficiency is assessed immediately upon the filing or approval (when required) of a petition in bankruptcy, the appointment of a receiver for the taxpayer, or an adjudication of bankruptcy in a liquidation proceeding. This is not a jeopardy assessment, and may not be enforced as one. The bankruptcy court determines any question about the amount and validity of taxes of the bankrupt [Sec. 6871; 301.6871(a)-2]. Under the Bankruptcy Act,[4] a trustee's claim is superior to unfiled tax liens.[5] The government has priority over general creditors for tax claims that fell due within 3 years before bankruptcy. Taxes due more than 3 years generally may be discharged, but there are exceptions (tax liens, no return filed, wilful evasion and taxes withheld from others).[6] A bankrupt's income tax refund check passes to the trustee and is not earnings protected against garnishment.[7] The statute of limitations is suspended if the fiduciary fails to file a notice of appointment [¶ 3613].

Interest on tax claims against a bankrupt estate stops running when the bankruptcy petition is filed,[8] or the earlier date a debtor in possession arrangement starts.[9] Interest on claims originating in the arrangement period runs to the filing of the petition.[9] Penalties for failing to file returns for the arrangement period also may be imposed.[9]

If a petition for redetermination of a deficiency is pending before the Tax Court when a bankruptcy petition is filed (or approved) or at the time of the adjudication of bankruptcy, or appointment of a receiver, the Tax Court does not lose its jurisdiction to redetermine the deficiency. However, petition for redetermination of a deficiency may not be filed with the Tax Court after a bankruptcy petition is filed (or approved), or the adjudication of bankruptcy, or appointment of the receiver [Sec. 6871(b); 301.6871(b)-1].

¶ **3613 When limitation period is suspended.** Some periods are not counted in determining whether the three years, or other applicable period, for assessment and collection of tax has passed [Sec. 6503]. In effect, an equivalent period is added after what ordinarily would be the end of the limitation period. Time spent in a combat zone [¶ 1306] postpones the final date an assessment can be made. See ¶ 3518(a).

(a) Deficiency notice issued. The statute of limitations is suspended while the Commissioner is prohibited from making an assessment due to the issuance of a deficiency letter, and for 60 days after; but the final 60 days start to run on the date a waiver on Form 870 [¶ 3606] is filed.[1] If the proceeding is placed on the docket of the Tax Court, the statute of limitations is suspended until 60 days after the decision of the Tax Court becomes final [Sec. 301.6503(a)-1]. However, a deficiency notice from which no appeal was taken does not suspend running of the statute of limitations on assessment of any additional deficiency shown to be due in a later deficiency notice.[2]

(b) Court control of assets. The statute of limitations is suspended while the assets of the taxpayer are in the control or custody of the court in any U.S. or state court proceeding, and for 6 months after [Sec. 6503(b); 301.6503(b)-1].

(c) Taxpayer out of the U.S. The limitation period is suspended while the taxpayer is outside the U.S. for 6 or more consecutive months. If less than 6 months of the collection period remains when he returns, collection is allowed up to 6 months after his return [Sec. 6503(c); 301.6503(c)-1(b)].

(d) Wrongful levy. The limitation period is suspended when money or other property of another person is wrongfully seized or received. The suspension runs from the time the property is taken until 30 days after it is either voluntarily returned or a judgment in a suit to enjoin the levy or recover the property becomes final. However, the suspension only applies to the extent of the value of the returned property [Sec. 6503(g); 301.6503(g)-1].

(e) Failure to file fiduciary notice in bankruptcy. In bankruptcy or receivership cases, when the fiduciary or receiver has to give notice to the Revenue Service of his appointment, the statute of limitations is suspended from the start of the proceeding until 30 days after receipt of the notice by the Service (but not over 2 years) [Sec. 6872; 301.6872-1].

(f) Foreign expropriation losses. The time to collect tax attributable to the recovery of a loss is extended for the period payment of the tax is extended (¶ 3526) [Sec. 6503(f)].

(g) Private foundation—retirement plans. The limitation period on assessing or collecting excise or termination taxes on private foundations is suspended for one year or when the Revenue Service extends the time for corrective action (¶ 3439 et seq.) [Sec. 6503(h)]. Similar provisions apply to excise taxes [¶ 3618(h)] payable by certain retirement plans [¶ 1839].

¶ 3614 Liability for tax of another taxpayer. (a) Transferred assets. If a taxpayer transfers property to others without adequate consideration, the others may become liable for taxpayer's taxes. Thus, the transferee of the assets of an insolvent transferor is ordinarily liable for the accrued and unpaid taxes of the transferor. The same rule applies when assets have been transferred by a taxpayer who later died or by a corporation that later dissolved or terminated its existence without making adequate provision for tax liabilities, or when the transferor is made insolvent by the transfer.[1]

A "transferee" includes a donee, heir, legatee, devisee, and distributee [Sec. 6901(h); 301.6901-1(b)].

Procedure. Transferee liability is assessed and collected the same as a deficiency (¶ 3603 et seq.) [Sec. 6901; 301.6901-1], but a special limitation period for

Footnotes appear at end of this Chapter.

assessment applies [¶ 3611]. Re-transfer of the assets after notice of liability is issued does not relieve the transferee from liability, unless he did not know about the original transfer.[2] Collection of a transferor's full tax from some transferees does not bar collection of another transferee's share, if those who paid file refund claims.[3] A transferee is not bound by a transferor's stipulation of tax liability not based on the merits of the case.[4]

Limit of liability. The amount of the transferee's liability cannot be more than the assets received. A transferee held liable for more than his share of the tax has a right of recoupment against other transferees of assets of the same taxpayer. Acceptance of an offer in compromise [¶ 3608(a)] from one transferee does not compromise the liabilities of the transferor or other transferees; but since the amount paid is credited against the transferor's tax, the liabilities of other transferees may be affected.[5]

(b) Parent's liability for child. An assessment of tax against a child related to compensation he earns, has the effect of an assessment against the parent [Sec. 6201(c); 301.6201-1(c)]. The government's collection remedies can be enforced against both the parent and the child.

¶ **3615 How tax is collected.**[1] **(a) Distraint.** Any tax due can be collected by levy on taxpayer's property, generally after he fails to pay it within 10 days from notice and demand [Sec. 6331; 301.6331-1]. Levy upon an individual's salary or wages is possible only after the individual first receives written notice. Since the levy is continuous from the date served, the IRS must release the employer by notice when the tax is paid or as soon as the levy becomes unenforceable due to lapse of time [Sec. 6331(d)]. Any person in possession of property that has been levied upon must surrender it unless it is already subject to judicial process [Sec. 6332(a); 301.6332-1(a)]. An insurer need not surrender a life insurance or endowment contract, but must pay over amounts that could be advanced to the taxpayer (generally cash loan value) up to 90 days after notice of levy. Automatic advances agreed upon to keep the insurance in force are not counted if the agreement was made before the insurer had actual knowledge of the levy [Sec. 6332(b); 301.6332-2].

Any person (including corporate officers and employees and partnership members and employees) who fails to turn over property levied on is liable for the amount of tax due up to the value of the property, plus costs and interest. He may also be liable for a penalty of 50% of this amount. The penalty is not credited against the tax liability that is the basis for the levy [Sec. 6332(c); 6621; 301.6332-1(b), (d)]. Surrender of the levied property to the Revenue Service relieves the person from liability to the delinquent taxpayer (or insurance beneficiary) with respect to the property [Sec. 6332(d); 301.6332-1(c)].

Property exempt from levy. Unemployment benefits, workmen's compensation, certain pensions and annuities, mail, certain necessary personal and household items, limited amount of business books and tools, and income needed for the support of a taxpayer's minor children under prior judgment, are specifically exempt from levy.

Where the taxpayer receives income weekly, a minimum exemption of $50 per week, plus $15 for each dependent, is allowed for post 2-28-77 levies. A comparable exemption is allowed to those paid other than weekly but it must be determined under the regulations. Dependents include spouses but not minor children with respect to whom amounts are exempt as support payments under a court decree. [Sec. 6334; Temporary Reg. Sec. 404.6334(d)-1; 301.6334-1].

(b) Collection by suit. If any person liable to pay any tax fails to pay it when due, the tax, with interest and additions, may be collected by a suit in the

U.S. District Court. Suit may also be used to collect fines, penalties and forfeitures [Sec. 7401; 301.7401-1].

(c) Liens. The federal tax is a lien on all the taxpayer's property [Sec. 6321; 301.6321-1 et seq.]. Generally, a demand for payment must be made,[2] but the lien is created at the time the tax is assessed [Sec. 6322]. It then becomes one of the many possible claims competing to be first satisfied out of the taxpayer's property. Until notice of the lien has been properly filed, it is not enforceable against a purchaser, mechanics lienor, judgment lien creditor or holder of a security interest [Sec. 6323(a); Prop. Reg. 301.6323(a)-1]. Even after the lien is filed, it may not be enforced against some persons who do not actually know about the lien or who have certain specific claims against the taxpayer's property [Sec. 6323(b); Prop. Reg. 301.6323(b)-1]. The Supreme Court ruled that when the U.S. had complied with the notice requirements, its tax lien was valid against the good faith purchaser who had taken title without actual knowledge.[3]

Subject to varying conditions that must be met in each case, a filed lien cannot be enforced against the following persons who do not have actual knowledge of the lien at the time: purchasers (or security holders) of securities (stocks, bonds, notes, etc.); purchasers of motor vehicles; purchasers in a casual sale of tangible personal property of less than $250 (household goods, personal effects, property exempt from levy); insurers who issued life insurance, endowment or annuity contracts (also protected for automatic advances [(a) above] after actual knowledge of lien); banks and building and loan associations (for passbook loans). Specific claims protected against a filed tax lien, again subject to varying conditions in each case, are: possessory lien for repair or improvement of personal property; real property tax and assessment liens; mechanics liens for repair and improvement of personal residence at contract price of not more than $1,000; attorney's lien enforceable against a judgment or settlement; purchaser of tangible personal property at retail [Sec. 6323(b); Proposed Reg. 301.6323(b)-1, 301.6323(h)-1].

A limited priority against filed tax liens also is granted under specified conditions for advances made under financing agreements entered into before the tax lien is filed, and certain security interests may be protected for disbursements made within 45 days after the filing before the holder has actual knowledge of the lien [Sec. 6323(c)(d); Proposed Regs. 301.6323(c)-1—3, 301.6323(d)-1, 301.6323(h)-1].

Indexing of liens. Starting on 2-1-77, a tax lien is treated as complying with the filing requirements (see below) only if it is entered and recorded in an appropriate public index. Real property liens are filed at the district office where the property is located. Personal property liens are filed at the district office for the area of the taxpayer's residence [Sec. 6323(f)(4), (g)(2)].

NOTE: The indexing requirement is effective on 6-30-77 for notices filed before 10-4-76.

Filing notice of lien. Notices affecting real property must be filed in the office designated by the state where the property is located. Notices affecting personal property must be filed in the office designated by the state where an individual resides or a corporation or partnership has its principal executive office when the lien is filed. If a state fails to specify an office for filing, or designates more than one, the tax lien is filed with the clerk of the U.S. district court for the judicial district where the property is located (for realty) or where the taxpayer resides or has its principal office (for personalty) [Sec. 6323(f); 301.6323(f)-1]. For property and taxpayers located in the District of Columbia, and taxpayers who live out of the U.S., the lien is filed with the Recorder of Deeds in the District of Columbia. The notice generally must be refiled every 6 years to keep the lien in force [Sec. 6323(f),

Footnotes appear at end of this Chapter.

¶ 3615

(g); Proposed Reg. 301.6323(f)-1, 301.6323(g)-1]. A failure to refile does not bar the filing of a new notice [Sec. 400.1-1(a)].

NOTE: If property subject to a filed tax lien is sold to satisfy a competing lien, the sale is subject to the tax lien if adequate written notice[4] of sale is not sent to the Revenue Service [Sec. 7425(b)]. Also, if the U.S. is not made a party to mortgage or lien foreclosure actions and certain other actions, a filed tax lien that affects the property involved will survive the judgment of sale and if *any* judgment in a civil action discharges a tax lien when the U.S. is not a party, the tax lien keeps its same priority against the property or proceeds of a sale [Sec. 7425(a)].

(d) Set-off or counterclaim. The Revenue Service, within the applicable period of limitations, can set off or credit the amount of any overpayment (including interest on it) against liability for any internal revenue tax [Sec. 6402; 301.6402-1]. Set-off may also be used when the taxpayer claims a refund or credit of one tax [¶ 3622], and he is in default to the government on another tax or contract.

(e) Payroll deductions. The Revenue Service allows employees to arrange payroll deductions to satisfy delinquent taxes. Form 2159, "Agreement for Liquidation of Federal Tax Through Payroll Deductions" is used.

(f) Suit to prevent collection. Generally, no suit to restrain the assessment or collection of any tax can be maintained [Sec. 7421]. This includes suits to restrain enforcement of the liability of a transferee or fiduciary or suits to prevent revoking tax-exempt status.[5] Even if the statute of limitations bars collection or the tax is invalid, injunction will be denied.[6] There are exceptions. Collection of the tax can be enjoined (1) when the taxpayer did not receive a 90-day letter and did not file Form 870 [¶ 3606], and (2) when he has filed a petition with the Tax Court [Sec. 6212(a), 6213(a); 301.6213-1], and (3) when he requests judicial review of jeopardy assessment procedures [¶ 3612(d)]. An injunction also may be allowed when it is clear from the facts and law that the Revenue Service could not win a suit to collect the tax and only an injunction can protect the taxpayer.[7]

Persons, other than a person liable for the tax that is the basis for a levy, may sue the U.S. to recover wrongfully levied property or its proceeds or to enjoin a levy or sale that would injure rights superior to those of the U.S. [Sec. 7426].

PENALTIES

¶ 3616 Kinds of penalties. Penalties may be divided into two classes: (1) Ad valorem penalties added to and assessed as part of the tax; and (2) criminal penalties enforceable only by suit or prosecution. Penalties also are imposed under the "pay-as-you-go" collection system [See ¶ 2512; 2519; 3619] and for failure to supply an identifying number [¶ 3500].

¶ 3617 Penalties for failure to file returns. The penalty for failure to file a return is 5% added to the tax if the delay is for not more than one month, with an additional 5% for each additional month or fraction, but not over 25% total [Sec. 6651(a); 301.6651-1]. The penalty is imposed unless it is shown that the failure is due to reasonable cause and not due to willful neglect.

The addition is figured on the net amount due, rather than the gross amount. Thus, if part of the tax has been prepaid through declaration of estimated tax or withholding on wages, the addition will apply only to the amount that still has to be paid [Sec. 6651(b); 301.6651-1(b)]. In addition, this penalty is reduced by the amount of any penalty for failure to pay tax on time [¶ 3618(b)] in months where both penalties are applicable [Sec. 6651(c)(1)(A); 301.6651-1(a)(1)]. A deficiency notice [¶ 3605] is not required to assess and collect the penalty when there is no deficiency in the tax [Sec. 6659]. If a return is not timely filed the fact that the date prescribed for filing the return falls on a Saturday, Sunday, or legal holiday is immaterial in determining the number of months for imposing the penalty [Sec. 301.6651-1(b)(3)].

(a) What is reasonable cause. Reasonable cause for failure to file means such cause as would prompt an ordinary, intelligent man to act under similar circumstances as did the taxpayer in tardily filing his income tax return.[1] The most acceptable reason (though not always accepted) has been taxpayer's reliance upon advice of competent tax counsel. Taxpayer should prove as many of these facts as he can: (1) he sought advice of counsel, expert in federal income tax matters;[2] (2) he gave his counsel all necessary information and withheld nothing;[3] (3) he acted in good faith on his counsel's advice.[4]

(b) Information returns. There is a $1 penalty for each Form 1099 for business payments [¶ 3531] not filed on time and for each W-2 Form that is not filed on time with Form 941 for the last quarter of the year [¶ 2509]. The same penalty applies to returns for foreign items [¶ 3540] and fishing boat operators [¶ 3521]. The total penalty for any one person for a calendar year cannot be more than $1,000 [Sec. 6652(b); 301.6652-1].

A $10 penalty is imposed for each return required for the following items that is not filed on time [Sec. 6652(a); 301.6652-1]: payment of interest, dividends or patronage dividends of $10 or more [¶ 3532; 3533]; stock transferred under stock options [¶ 3534]; employees' group-term life insurance [¶ 3535].

The total penalty for any one person for a calendar year cannot be more than $25,000. The same penalties apply for failure to give the recipients of the items the statements that must be furnished to them [Sec. 6678; 301.6678-1].

Any penalty may be excused, if the District Director is satisfied there was a reasonable cause for the failure to file [Sec. 6652].

Exempt organizations and certain trusts may incur a penalty of $10 a day (up to $5,000) for late filing of certain required information returns [¶ 3537] unless late filing is due to reasonable cause [Sec. 301.6652-2(f)]. Extensions of time to file are taken into account. Continued failure to file, after notice and demand by the Commissioner, results in a $10-a-day penalty (up to $5,000) on any manager, officer, employer or other individual under a duty to file. A similar penalty applies to responsible persons failing to file or publicize annual reports of private foundations and to employers or plan administrators of certain deferred compensation plans [Sec. 6652(d), (f); 301.6652-2].

Group returns. If a central organization agrees to file a group return for its local organizations, then it, not the local organizations, is responsible for any penalty for failure to timely file [Sec. 301.6652-2(g)].

Failure to file or publicize private foundation's annual report. The manager of a private foundation [¶ 3437 et seq.] with at least $5,000 of assets at any time in the tax year must file an annual report and publish notice of its availability for public inspection [¶ 3537(c)]. Willful failure to do so results in a $1,000 penalty as to each report or notice [Sec. 6685; 301.6685-1]. This penalty is in addition to the penalty for fraudulent report [¶ 3620].

(c) Retirement plans, reports and statements. A retirement plan administrator may incur a $1-a-day penalty for each plan member (up to $5,000) for whom there has been a failure to file a registration statement [¶ 3537(d)]. If he fails to notify the Treasury Secretary of any change in the plan's status, the penalty is $1 a day (up to $1,000) [Sec. 6652(e)]. If he issues a false or fraudulent statement, or wilfully fails to furnish employees with their required statement, the penalty is

Footnotes appear at end of this Chapter.

¶ 3617

$50 for each transgression [Sec. 6690]. A penalty of $1,000 may be imposed for failure to file an actuarial report or statement [Sec. 6692]. They may be avoided upon a showing of reasonable cause. Also, a $10 penalty is imposed for each failure to file a report required from the trustee of an individual retirement account or the issuer of an individual retirement annuity. This penalty may be avoided by a showing of reasonable cause [Sec. 6693].

(d) Declaration of estimated tax. There is no penalty for failure to file the declaration of estimated tax required of individuals [Sec. 6651(d)]. There are penalties for individual [¶ 2519] and corporate [¶ 3619] failure to pay estimated tax.

¶ 3618 Interest and penalties for failure to pay tax. (a) Interest charged. If any amount of tax is not paid when due, interest at 7% a year (9% between 7-1-75 and 1-31-76; 6% before 7-1-75) must be paid from the due date until the tax is paid. However, the 7% rate is adjustable (upward and downward) depending on the prime interest rate charged by commercial banks (¶ 3628) [Sec. 6601(a), 6621; 301.6601-1(a)]. If the tax is being paid in installments, interest on any portion of the tax not shown on the return runs from the due date of the first installment. In the case of an unpaid installment of tax shown on the return, interest runs from the installment due date [Sec. 6601(b)(2); 301.6601-1(c)].

When tax is due. Due date for payment is determined without regard to any extension of time (including an automatic extension) [¶ 3518]. Interest will run during the period of the extension and until payment is made. If payment is demanded before the due date because of jeopardy, interest will not run before the prescribed due date [Sec. 6601(b); 301.6601-1(c)].

Offsetting interest. No interest is imposed on a deficiency to the extent that interest would be concurrently payable on a refund of an overpayment of tax credited against the deficiency [Sec. 6601(f); 301.6601-1(b)]. Thus, if an overpayment and deficiency are equal, the interest on each cancels out for the period both are outstanding at the same time[1] [Sec. 6601(f); 6611(b)].

> **Example:** John Green's tax for 1974 was $2,000. He paid $1,500 on 4-15-75. His tax for 1975 was $1,800, but he paid $2,000 on 4-15-76. The underpayment and overpayment were disclosed by an examination of his returns in March 1977 and the overpayment was credited against the underpayment.
>
> Green must pay interest on the underpayment of $500 from 4-15-75 to 4-15-76 when he made the overpayment of $200. Since interest would be payable on a refund of the $200 overpayment, he does not have to pay interest on $200 of the underpayment from 4-15-76. He must pay interest on $300 of the underpayment.

Carrybacks. Interest on a deficiency that is offset by a carryback of a net operating loss, net capital loss, investment credit or work incentive program credit will run from the original due date of the tax to which the deficiency relates to the end of the later tax year in which the loss or credit arises [Sec. 6601(d); 301.6601-1(e)]. If a net operating loss carryback eliminates an investment credit, no interest is payable on the tax originally offset by the credit.[2]

Additions to tax. There is no interest on interest. However, interest is imposed on any assessable penalty, additional amount, or addition to the tax (except interest[1]), if the additional amount is not paid within 10 days from notice and demand for payment. The interest runs from the date of the notice and demand to the date of payment. However, payment within 10 days after notice and demand for payment stops the interest on the date of such notice and demand [Sec. 6601(e); 301.6601-1(f)].

NOTE: When the tax on a "late" joint return replacing separate returns [¶ 3506] is more than the tax on the separate returns, the excess is treated as a deficiency [Sec. 6013(b)(5); 1.6013-2(e)].

(b) Penalty for failure to make timely payment. A penalty is imposed, in addition to the interest [(a) above], if the amount shown as the tax on any return to which the failure-to-file penalty applies [¶ 3617] is not paid on time. The penalty is ½% of the tax if the failure is for 1 month or less, and an additional ½% for each month or part of a month the failure continues until the penalty reaches 25%. This penalty does not apply: (a) if failure to pay is due to reasonable cause, and (b) to failure to pay any estimated tax [Sec. 6651(a), (d); 301.6651-1(a), (c)]. In the case of automatic filing extensions for individuals [¶ 3518(a)], the penalty is imposed in the absence of reasonable cause; reasonable cause is presumed if the balance due does not exceed 10% of the total tax and is remitted with Form 1040 [Sec. 301.6651-1(c)(1), (3)]. The penalty for failure to file [¶ 3617] is reduced by this penalty [Sec. 301.6651-1(a)(1)].

If a corporation is granted an automatic extension of time for filing, reasonable cause for the underpayment for the extension period is presumed if: (a) at least 50% of the tax is paid by the regular due date of the return and the remainder is paid within 3 months later; (b) the tax shown on its application for extension [¶ 3518(a)], or paid by the regular due date, is at least 90% of the tax shown on its return; and (c) any balance due shown on its return is paid by the return due date, including extensions [Sec. 301.6651-1(c)].

The amount of tax on which the penalty is imposed is the net amount due. Thus, the amount of tax shown on the return is reduced by any amount of tax paid on or before the start of the month for which the tax is being computed. Credits against tax which may be claimed on the return are also subtracted from the amount shown to give the net amount. If the amount required to be shown as tax on any return is less than the amount actually shown as tax, the lower amount is used to figure the penalty [Sec. 6651(b), (c); 301.6651-(d)].

(c) Penalty for failure to pay deficiency. The same ½%-25% penalty as in (b) above applies to failure to pay a deficiency without reasonable cause, within 10 days of the date of notice and demand. This penalty can also be applied to assessments relating to mathematical errors [¶ 3605(b)], but not to estimated tax payments [Sec. 6651; 301.6651-1(a)(3)]. The penalty for failure to file [¶ 3617] reduces the amount of this penalty [Sec. 301.6651-1(a)(3)].

(d) Negligence and fraud penalty. A deficiency in tax due to negligence or fraud is subject to penalty.

If any part of a deficiency is due to negligence, or intentional disregard of rules and regulations, without intent to defraud, 5% of the deficiency is added as a penalty [Sec. 6653(a); 301.6653-1(a)].

If any part of a deficiency is due to fraud, 50% of the deficiency is added as a penalty [Sec. 6653(b); 301.6653-1(b)]. This penalty is in place of the negligence penalty. Furthermore, if a fraud penalty is imposed, no penalty for failure to file a return or pay tax will be imposed for the same deficiency [Sec. 6653(d); 301.6651-1(e); 301.6653-1(b)]. In figuring the penalty, no credit will be given for tax withheld[3] or the tax shown on a delinquent return.[4] A taxpayer convicted of criminal fraud cannot contest a civil fraud determination.[5] A spouse filing jointly is not liable for a fraud penalty against the other spouse unless some part of the underpayment was due to his or her fraud [Sec. 6653(b); 301.6653-1(d)].

(e) Payment with bad check. If tax is paid with a bad check, an additional penalty of 1% of the amount of the check is imposed, unless the check was tendered in good faith and with reasonable cause to believe that it would be paid

Footnotes appear at end of this Chapter.

¶ 3618

upon presentment. If the check is less than $500, the penalty is the lesser of $5, or the amount of the check [Sec. 6657; 301.6657-1].

(f) **Failure to deposit taxes.** Failure to make a required timely tax deposit in a government depositary can result in a penalty of 5% of the underpayment. The penalty does not apply if failure is due to reasonable cause. The period of failure to deposit does not continue beyond the earlier of the due date for payment of tax required to be deposited, or the date of its payment [Sec. 6656; 301.6656-1].

(g) **Penalty as to excise taxes on private foundations.** A penalty equal to 100% of the initial and additional excise taxes [¶ 3440-3444] is imposed on a foundation, its manager, a disqualified person or government official, if: (a) the violation for which tax is imposed was willful and flagrant, or (b) the person was liable for any such tax as to a prior violation in connection with the same or another foundation [Sec. 6684]. The penalty is excused if the District Director is satisfied there was reasonable cause for noncompliance [Sec. 301.6684-1].

(h) **Special taxes on retirement plans.** A nondeductible 6% excise tax is imposed on excess contributions to individual retirement accounts or annuities [Sec. 4973]. In addition, a 10% penalty tax is imposed on premature distribution withdrawals from individual retirement plans with certain exceptions [Sec. 408(f)]. An annual 6% excise tax on excess contributions to a self-employed plan is imposed on an employer for contributions made in tax years [Sec. 4972]. Also, a nondeductible 5% excise tax and in certain cases an additional 100% excise tax is imposed on an employer for underfunding his covered retirement plan. [Sec. 4971].

(i) **Penalties on income tax preparers.** Starting in 1977, preparers must pay penalties where they understate the taxpayer's liability. A $100 penalty is imposed where a preparer negligently or intentionally disregards the federal tax rules and regulations. If he wilfully attempts to understate the taxpayer's liability he is subject to a $500 penalty. Where both penalties apply they may not exceed $500. If the preparer pays 15% of the penalty within 30 days of the notice of the assessment and files a refund claim, the IRS may not proceed to collect any remaining part of the penalty. If the IRS denies the refund claim the preparer can bring suit in the appropriate federal district court. The IRS will be prevented from collecting the balance of the penalty during the period the suit is pending. If the IRS does not rule on the refund claim within six months, the preparer can sue within 30 days after the six-month period. If no suit is brought within this time the IRS can proceed with the collection of the remaining 85% of the penalty. The penalty payment must be abated by the IRS and refundable automatically with interest if a taxpayer's determination reveals no understatement of tax [Sec. 6694; Temporary Reg. Sec. 404.6694-1].

NOTE: Although the regular deficiency procedures [¶ 3605; 3615] do not apply to the collection and assessment of preparer penalties, he should receive the revenue agent's report and a thirty-day letter. If he chooses not to pay the 15% penalty, he can pay the full assessment and file a claim for refund within 3 years after payment [Sec. 6694; 6696; Temporary Reg. Sec. 404.6694-1, 404.6696-1]. See also ¶ 3542.

(j) **Special tax on public charities.** A 25% excise tax is imposed on an electing charitable organization [¶ 1941(a)] if it incurs excess lobbying expenditures to influence legislation [Sec. 4911].

¶ **3619 Penalty for underpayment of corporation estimated tax.** If a corporation underpays its estimated tax [¶ 3523(b)], a charge at the current rate [¶ 3618(a)] on the underpayment is added to the tax [Sec. 6655(a); 1.6655-1]. There is an underpayment if the corporation's final tax return for the year shows that the estimated tax actually paid was less than 80% of the amount that should have been paid [¶ 3523], or, if no return was filed, less than 80% of the actual tax for the year. See also ¶ 3622(a).

The penalty charge runs until the underpayment is paid or until the filing date of the tax return [¶ 3517(b)], whichever is earlier [Sec. 6655(c); 1.6655-1]. This penalty may be assessed and collected without a deficiency notice except when no income tax return has been filed [Sec. 6659(b)].

How to figure the penalty. The penalty is figured for each installment date on the difference between the amount paid and 80% of the amount that should have been paid [Sec. 6655(b); 1.6655-1].

Example: A calendar-year corporation estimated its tax for 1978 at $149,800 and made timely quarterly payments of $37,450 each for the $149,800 estimated tax. The corporate tax return filed on March 15, 1979, showed a tax liability of $195,400. Accordingly, the estimated tax payments should have been $48,850 each ($195,400 ÷ 4). There is an underpayment of $1,630 for each quarterly payment [$48,850 (amount that should have been paid) × 80% = $39,080 − $37,450 (amount paid) = $1,630 (underpayment)]. The total penalty is computed at 7% of $1,630 as follows:

4-17-78 to 3-15-79 (332 days)	$103.78
6-15-78 to 3-15-79 (273 days)	85.34
9-15-78 to 3-15-79 (181 days)	56.58
12-15-78 to 3-15-79 (90 days)	28.13
Total penalty	$273.83

¶ 3620 Criminal penalties. Criminal penalties can be imposed as follows:

• Willful failure to pay the tax or estimated tax, make a return (except an individual declaration of estimated tax), or keep the records and supply the information required by the law and regulations—misdemeanor punishable by fine of $10,000, imprisonment for not over one year, or both [Sec. 7203].

• Willful failure to collect, account for, and pay over any tax by any person required to do so—felony, punishable by fine of $10,000, imprisonment for not more than five years, or both [Sec. 7202].

• Willful attempt to evade or defeat the tax—felony, punishable by fine of $10,000, imprisonment for not more than five years, or both [Sec. 7201].

• Willful making and subscribing of a return in which not every material matter is believed to be true and correct—felony, punishable by fine of $5,000, imprisonment for not more than three years, or both [Sec. 7206]. The penalty applies to separate returns even though they are replaced by a "late" joint return (¶ 3506) [Sec. 6013(b)(5)(B); 1.6013-2(e)(2)].

• Willful filing of any known false or fraudulent document, including an income tax return[1]—misdemeanor, punishable by fine of $1,000, imprisonment of not more than one year, or both. This also applies to filing annual reports by private foundations and not publishing notice of their availability for public inspection (¶ 3537) [Sec. 7207, 301.7207-1].

• Disclosure or use (subject to certain qualifications) or any information furnished a person engaged in the business of preparing returns and declarations, or who does so for compensation, for purposes other than the preparation of the return or declaration—misdemeanor, punishable by fine of $1,000, imprisonment up to one year, or both [Sec. 7216; Proposed Regs. 301.7216-1—3].

Limitation period. The statute of limitations on these offenses is three years in some cases and six years in others, the latter applying mostly to attempts to defraud the Government and willful attempts to evade or defeat the tax [Sec. 6531]. The 6-year limitation period begins to run from the date a return is filed, or its due date, whichever is later.[2]

Footnotes appear at end of this Chapter.

REFUNDS AND CREDITS

¶ 3621 Overpayment of tax. The Revenue Service can refund or credit any overpayment of the tax [Sec. 6402; 301.6402-1].

Overpayments by corporations generally are refunded on the basis of tentative returns without a refund claim and without examining the completed return.[1] However, in most other cases, a claim for refund must be filed. There are special refund procedures for overpayments of corporate estimated tax [¶ 3622(a)] or due to carrybacks of net operating or net capital losses [¶ 3630].

Review of tax return. Before filing a refund claim, the taxpayer should review the entry for each item on the tax return for the year in question and recompute the tax to determine if there is an actual overpayment of the *entire* tax. If this is not done, and the Revenue Service finds errors from which the taxpayer received an advantage, the amount of the overpayment may be reduced or entirely eliminated. An additional tax might even be assessed, if the statute of limitations has not run.[2]

¶ 3622 Refund claims. Claims for refund fall into three classes: claims for taxes paid on the original return, for overpayments through withholding on wages or estimated tax paid, and for payments made on a deficiency notice. It is not necessary to pay the tax under protest to get a refund.

(a) Overpayment by withholding or estimated tax. The excess of the tax withheld on wages and the estimated tax paid over the tax shown as due on the return will be refunded to taxpayer, or, at his election, will be credited against his next year's estimated tax, if any. However, the Revenue Service may credit any overpayment of individual, fiduciary, or corporate income tax against any outstanding tax, interest or penalty owed by the taxpayer [Sec. 301.6402-3]. No refund of estimated tax is allowed before the close of the tax year even though an amended declaration filed after the payment shows no estimated tax liability.[1]

Adjustment for corporate estimated tax overpayment. A corporation overpaying its estimated tax can apply for an adjustment on Form 4466 within 2½ months after the close of its tax year. Actual payments of estimated tax must exceed the current revised estimate of tax liability by at least 10% and by at least $500. The application must be filed and verified [¶ 3513(b)] showing the estimated tax paid, the revised estimated tax liability and the adjustment requested [Sec. 6425]. An addition to tax at the current rate [¶ 3618] is imposed on any excessive adjustment and is computed from the time of the adjustment to the return's due date. If the application is denied, the corporation cannot sue on the application [¶ 3529], but it can claim credit or refund (¶ 3626) [Sec. 6655(g); 1.6425-1—3, 1.6655-5].

(b) Payment of assessed deficiency. A taxpayer may prefer to pay the deficiency and avoid the interest charge. Then he can file a claim for refund, and if the claim is rejected, sue to recover. Or the taxpayer, when the deficiency notice is received, may decide that an appeal to the Tax Court is useless. Later events, for example, a court decision, may change the situation. In that case, a claim for refund still can be made, if it is filed in time.

(c) When taxpayer appeals to Tax Court. If a deficiency notice has been issued, and taxpayer appeals to the Tax Court, generally no refund or credit will be allowed and no suit for recovery of any part of the tax can be maintained in any court. There are three exceptions: (1) overpayment determined by a Tax Court decision that has become final; (2) an amount collected above the amount determined by the Tax Court decision; and (3) any amount collected after the period for levy or suit for collection has expired—the decision of the Tax Court is conclusive as to whether the period of limitation expired before the notice of deficiency was mailed [Sec. 6512(a)].

¶ 3623 **Time for filing refund claims.** Claims must be filed within the time set by law, or no refund will be allowed [Sec. 6511(b); 301.6511(b)-1]. Even mental incompetency does not excuse a failure to file on time.[1] A claim is considered to be filed on the date postmarked [Sec. 301.7502:1]. If the due date falls on a Saturday, Sunday, or legal holiday, the next business day is the due date [¶ 3517]. There are special refund periods [¶ 3624]. Claims can be postponed for Armed Forces personnel in a combat zone [¶ 3518(a)].

(a) **Three-year limitation.** A claim for refund for any tax year ordinarily must be filed within three years of the time the return is filed [Sec. 6511(a)]. If the return was filed before the due date, the 3-year period starts to run from the date the return was due [Sec. 6513(a)].

> **Example 1:** The due date of an individual return for the calendar year 1977 is 4-17-78. If a taxpayer filed his return on 2-16-78, the limitation period starts from 4-17-78. If he filed on 5-19-78, the limitation period starts from 5-19-78.

NOTE: Returns of taxes withheld from wages [¶ 2509; 3827] or withheld at source [¶ 2535] for a year filed before April 15 of the next year are considered filed and the tax paid on that date [Sec. 6513; 301.6513-1].

A claim for refund of excise taxes [¶ 3440-3444] must be made by a private foundation within the 3-year period. Generally, this begins when the return was filed for the year in which the act or failure to act giving rise to these taxes occurred. For excise taxes on investment income [¶ 3438], the period starts when the return was filed for the year the taxes were imposed on the private foundation [Sec. 6511(f)].

(b) **Two-year limitation.** There is an exception to the 3-year period. A claim for refund can be filed within two years from the time the tax is paid, if the 2-year period ends at a later date than the 3-year period [Sec. 6511(a); 301.6511(a)-1]. For this purpose, estimated tax [¶ 2515] and tax withheld at source [¶ 2535] are considered paid on the due date of the return (without extensions), and income tax withheld on wages is considered paid by the wage earner on the 15th day of the 4th month after the tax year it is allowed as a credit [Sec. 6513; 301.6513-1]. In determining the 2-year period, the day the tax was paid is not counted.[2] The 2-year period applies if no return was filed, and also comes into play when taxpayer pays an additional assessment.

> **Example 2:** If a 1977 return was filed and the tax amount paid on 4-15-78, and an additional assessment was paid on 11-15-79, the taxpayer could file a refund claim for the additional assessment up to 11-15-81.

(c) **Time extended by waiver.** The Revenue Service sometimes asks the taxpayer to file a waiver (Form 872) extending the time an assessment can be made against the taxpayer. A waiver filed before the time to file a refund claim expires extends the time to file a claim [Sec. 6511(c); 301.6511(c)-1].

¶ 3624 **Special periods for filing refund claims.** The usual period for filing a refund claim may be extended for particular transactions.

(a) **Bad debts and worthless securities.** A refund claim related to a deduction for a bad debt or a loss from a worthless security, or the effect of these deduc-

Footnotes appear at end of this Chapter.

¶ 3624

tions on the application of a *carryover,* can be filed within 7 years from the date the return *was due,* instead of 3 years from the filing of the return. For a similar claim relating to a *carryback,* the period is 7 years from the due date for filing the return for the year of the net operating loss which results in the carryback, or the period for a net operating loss carryback ((b) below), whichever ends later [Sec. 6511(d); 301.6511(d)-1].

(b) Carrybacks. A refund claim based on an investment credit, work incentive program credit, net operating loss carryback, capital loss carryback or investment credit carryback can be filed up to the end of the 15th day of the 40th month (39th month for a corporation) following the end of the tax year in which the credit was earned or the loss incurred [Sec. 6511(d); 301.6511(d)-7]. A beneficiary of an estate that has a net operating loss carryback, reducing distributable net income of a prior year, can file for refund under this provision.[1]

If a claim for carryback refund is filed under this provision, or if timely application for carryback adjustment [¶ 3630] is made, recovery of an earlier overpayment will be allowed even if the recovery might otherwise be barred [Sec. 301.6511(d)-2, 301.6511(d)-4].

> **Example:** Corey Corporation had a net operating loss for the calendar year 1974. Carryback of the loss to 1973 resulted in overpayment of the 1973 tax. This overpayment can be recovered if a refund claim is filed by March 15, 1978.

A net operating or capital loss after the year a taxpayer has elected to average income [¶ 2401] may increase his averageable income for the election year when the loss is carried back to a base year. A refund claim for the electing year is then treated as a claim based on a net operating or capital loss [Sec. 6511(d)(2)(B)(ii)].

(c) Taxes paid or credited. Foreign taxes paid and overpayments credited to estimated tax, may entitle the taxpayer to a refund.

Foreign taxes. If the claim for credit or refund arises from payment or accrual of taxes to a foreign country or U.S. possession for which credit is allowed against the U.S. tax, the time for filing the claim is 10 years from the due date of the return [Sec. 6511(d)(3); 301.6511(d)-3]. It also applies to credit or refund claims for correcting mathematical errors in figuring the foreign tax, discovering creditable taxes not reported when the tax return was filed, or any other adjustments to the amount of the credit, including those due to the paying of additional foreign taxes.[2] The 10-year limitation period does not extend the time to make an election to credit or deduct foreign tax [¶ 3701], but the Court of Claims disagrees.[3]

Overpayment applied to estimated tax. An overpayment claimed as a credit against estimated tax for the following year [Sec. 6402(b)], is treated as a payment for the year the estimated tax is paid. Ordinarily no claim for credit or refund will be allowed for the year the overpayment was made, and the limitation period on refund or credit starts to run with the second year [Sec. 6513(d); 301.6513-1(d)]. But see ¶ 3622(a) for special refund rule applying to corporations.

(d) Qualified retirement plans. A special period of limitation applies for refund or credit of amounts included in income and subsequently recaptured under qualified plan termination. The 3-year limitation period is extended for one year after the recaptured amount is paid [Sec. 6511(d)(8)].

¶ 3625 Amount of refund limited. If a refund claim is filed during the three-year limitation period the credit or refund cannot exceed the portion of the tax paid within the three years (plus extensions of time granted to file the return) preceding the filing of the claim. If the claim was not filed within the three-year period but was filed on time within the two-year period the credit or refund cannot exceed the portion of the tax paid during the two year period preceding the filing of the claim. If no claim is filed the limit on the amount of credit or refund is determined as if a claim was filed on the date the credit or refund is allowed [Sec. 6511(b); 301.6511(b)-1].

Example 1: ABC Corporation filed its 1977 return and paid the first installment of $1,000 (50%) on March 15, 1978. The other installment of $1,000 was paid on June 15, 1978. Claim for refund of all or any part of the $2,000 tax may be filed by March 15, 1981.

Example 2: Assume the same facts as in Example 1. Assume also that on August 3, 1978, the government assessed an additional tax of $700 for 1977 and the taxpayer paid this amount on August 12, 1979. The taxpayer learned later that it neglected to take sufficient deductions in the 1977 return and for that reason overpaid its tax by $1,000.

If the claim is filed by March 15, 1981 (within 3 years after the return was filed), the entire overpayment of $1,000 may be recovered.

If the claim is filed after March 15, 1981, but by August 13, 1981 (within 2 years after $700 was paid), the refund may not exceed $700.

If the claim is filed after August 13, 1981, the time will have expired and nothing may be recovered.

¶ **3626 Form of refund claim.** Claims for refunds of overpayments of income taxes are made on original tax returns or amended tax returns. See (c), below. Claims for refund of other taxes, interest, penalties, and additions to tax are usually made on Form 843. Before 7-1-76, Form 843 could also be used for refund of income taxes [Sec. 301.6402-2; 301.6402-3].

The Revenue Service may treat an informal refund claim as a valid claim provided such claim is later perfected by a formal refund claim. Form 870 or 890 series on which the taxpayer agrees to an overassessment of income taxes may be considered a valid claim for refund or credit.[1]

(a) Statement of claim. Careful thought should be given to the preparation of the section on reasons advanced for the claim. If the claim is rejected and the taxpayer sues on it, he will generally be precluded from advancing grounds for recovery not stated in the claim.[2] Facts should be fully presented. Legal arguments should be outlined if the claim turns on points of law. An amended return is not necessary in filing a claim for refund based on the original return, but may be a way to establish the amount of the refund.

The statement of the grounds and facts must be verified by a written declaration that it is made under the penalties of perjury [Sec. 301.6402-2(b)].

(b) Amending the claim. Taxpayer can amend or supplement his claim during the time within which he could file a new claim. A claim cannot be amended to change the facts after the statute of limitations has expired;[3] but when the facts are not changed an amendment may be allowed.[4]

(c) Amended tax returns as claims. Individuals who have filed Forms 1040 and 1040A should file their claim for a refund of income taxes on amended return Form 1040X. Also, corporations having filed Form 1120 should use Form 1120X.[5] Other taxpayers file their claims on the appropriate amended income tax return, e.g., trusts use Form 1041 and exempt organizations use Form 990T [Sec. 301.6402-3].

¶ **3627 Filing the refund claim.** The refund claim and supporting evidence, must be filed at the service center for the district in which the tax was paid. Hand-delivered claims are filed in the office of the District Director of Internal Revenue for the district where the tax was paid [Sec. 301.6402-2].

Footnotes appear at end of this Chapter.

¶ **3627**

A separate claim must be made for each tax year or period. It must state in detail each ground upon which a refund is claimed, and facts that will inform the Revenue Service of the exact basis for the claim.

If the claim for refund is made on the return for a decedent, Form 1310 should be attached.[1]

(a) Administrative procedure. If the claim is based on a return, administrative procedure is substantially the same as in cases involving determination of a deficiency. An examiner is assigned when a field investigation is called for. If his report is unacceptable to the taxpayer, he may have a district conference [¶ 3603]. If agreement is not reached at this conference, and there are matters capable of settlement, a hearing may be arranged with the Appellate Division [¶ 3607].

A claim based on payment of a deficiency assessment on which hearings were held, will usually be disallowed on the findings of the hearings.

(b) Decision on claim. When decision on a refund claim is in favor of the taxpayer, a certificate of overassessment is issued by the Revenue Service. If the overassessment exceeds $200,000 ($100,000 before 1977), it must be reported to the Joint Congressional Committee on Internal Revenue Taxation [Sec. 6405; 301.6405-1], except in the case of an overpayment made by a corporation based on a tentative return.[2] The amount involved is credited against any taxes owed by the taxpayer for any year not barred by the statute of limitations [Sec. 6402(a)]. Any balance is refunded.

If the decision is against the taxpayer, he can sue to recover [¶ 3629].

¶ 3628 Interest on refunds. Refunds generally carry interest at the rate of 7% (9% between 7-1-75 and 1-31-76; 6% before 7-1-75) or an adjusted rate (keyed to the prime interest rate to be determined by the Secretary of Treasury for the following year) [Sec. 6611, 6621; 301.6611-1]. The interest runs from the date of the overpayment to a date fixed by the Revenue Service. This date cannot be more than thirty days before the refund check date [Sec. 6611(b)(2); 301.6611-1(g)].

No interest is paid on refunds made within 45 days after the due date of returns filed on or before the due date or on refunds made within 45 days after a late return is filed [Sec. 6611(e)]. For a return filed by registered mail during the extension period, the 45-day period begins on its registration date and not on the date received by the Revenue Service.[1]

> NOTE: Inquiries about refund checks should state the taxpayer's identification number and be addressed to the Revenue Service Center that processed the claim, as indicated on the check.[2]

(a) Credit for overpayment. When an overpayment is credited against a later assessed deficiency instead of being refunded, interest runs from the date of overpayment to the due date of the deficiency[3] [Sec. 6611(b); 301.6611-1(h)]. Penalties are offset against the overpayment before interest is computed.[4] See also ¶ 3618(a).

(b) No review of interest allowed. In the absence of fraud or mathematical mistake, the allowance or failure to allow interest on any credit or refund cannot be reviewed by any administrative or accounting officer, employee, or agent of the U.S. [Sec. 6406].

(c) Special provisions. There are special interest provisions for:

Carrybacks. If the overpayment results from the carryback of a net operating loss, capital loss, investment credit, work incentive program credit, job credit or foreign taxes paid, no interest will be allowed for the period before the close of the tax year the net operating loss, capital loss, work incentive program credit, or investment credit arose, or the foreign tax was paid or accrued [Sec. 6611(f), (g); 301.6611-1(e)].

Deposits. Interest is allowed to taxpayers on refund of deposits made to stop the running of interest against them[5] [Sec. 6401(c); 301.6401-1]. However, the Third Circuit has held that a deposit merely to avoid a jeopardy assessment is not a payment on which interest will accrue.[6]

Excessive withholding or estimated tax.- If the claim is based on excessive withholding from wages or on an excessive estimated tax payment, interest is allowed from the date the final return was due even though the tax was paid earlier [Sec. 6513, 6611(d); 301.6513-1, 301.6611-(d)].

¶ **3629 Suit to recover tax.** Suit to recover tax may be started only if a claim for refund has been filed [Sec. 7422(a)], and only if taxpayer has paid the entire tax, including any deficiency claimed by the government.[1] Interest on the tax need not be paid before suit.[2]

Taxpayer's proof. In a suit to recover, taxpayer has to prove that the tax was overpaid.[3] The suit generally must be based on the same grounds as the refund claim.[4]

(a) When to file. A suit to recover may not be started until after six months from the date the refund claim was filed, unless a decision on the claim is made before then. It must be started before the end of two years from the date of mailing to the taxpayer, by registered or certified mail, of a notice disallowing part or all of the claim [Sec. 6532(a); 301.6532-1]. The period cannot be extended by filing a new refund claim, on the same grounds, after the disallowance.[5]

A 30-day letter disallowing the claim is a decision on the claim.[6]

Extension of time to file. If the last day of the period is a Saturday, Sunday or legal holiday the time is extended to include the next business day [¶ 3517]. The two-year period can be extended for any period agreed upon in writing [Sec. 6532(a)(2); 301.6532-1(b)].

Waiver of notice. If the taxpayer files a written waiver of the requirement that he be mailed a notice of disallowance of his refund claim, the two-year period for filing suit for recovery starts to run on the date the waiver on Form 2297[7] is filed [Sec. 6532(a)(3); 301.6532-1(c)].

(b) Where to file. Suit to recover taxes erroneously or illegally assessed or collected must be brought against the United States [Sec. 7422(f)]. The suit may be instituted either in the Court of Claims at Washington, D.C., or in a Federal District Court.[8] The proper District Court is the court for the judicial district where an individual taxpayer resides or a corporation has its principal place of business or its principal office or agency.[9] Either party has a right to trial by jury.[10] They may agree to move the trial to a district more convenient for the parties and witnesses. There are special rules for corporations that have no principal place of business, office or agency.

(c) When 90-day letter is issued. If taxpayer sues for a refund and a notice of deficiency is issued before the case is heard, taxpayer's appeal of the notice to the Tax Court would result in concurrent jurisdiction in both courts over the same case. To prevent this, the proceedings in taxpayer's suit must be stayed for the 90-day period he can appeal to the Tax Court plus an additional 60 days. Then, if taxpayer appeals to the Tax Court, the other court loses jurisdiction. If taxpayer does not appeal, the other court gets sole jurisdiction [Sec. 7422(e)].[11]

Footnotes appear at end of this Chapter.

(d) Appeal from lower court. Appeal from a District Court decision is to the U.S. Court of Appeals for the circuit in which the District Court is located. Decisions of the various circuits of the U.S. Courts of Appeal may be reviewed in the Supreme Court only on certiorari or certificate.

No appeal lies from a Court of Claims decision except by petition for certiorari or certificate to the U.S. Supreme Court. Petitions for certiorari generally must be made within 90 days after decision is entered. If a good reason is shown, up to an additional sixty days may be granted.

A decision in a refund suit is res judicata as to any subsequent proceedings involving the same claim and the same tax year.[12]

(e) Recovery of refunds paid. The United States can sue to recover an erroneous refund if the suit is begun within 2 years after the refund (within 5 years if the refund was induced by fraud or material misrepresentation) [Sec. 6532(b); 301.6532-2].[13] An alternative is a suit for recovery by the deficiency collection procedure subject to a 6-year period of limitation [¶ 3610].[14]

(f) Special rules for excise taxes on private foundations and special taxes on retirement plans. Payment of the full amount of an excise tax imposed on a private foundation [¶ 3440-3444] or payment of the special taxes imposed on retirement plans [¶ 3618(h)] gives either payor the right to sue for refund, but not if the private foundation or the retirement plan administrator of fiduciary has brought another suit or a Tax Court action for a deficiency as to any other excise or special tax imposed on it. A suit for refund of any excise or special tax will determine all questions as to any of the other taxes imposed for the same act (or failure to act) [Sec. 7422(g)].

¶ 3630 Quick refunds for carrybacks. A net operating loss [¶ 2241 et seq.; 3215 et seq.], corporate net capital loss (sustained in tax years starting after 1969) [¶ 3201], excess investment credit [¶ 2410] or excess work incentive program credit [¶ 2411] for the current year may be carried back to the 3 preceding years to reduce the tax liability reported for those years. Since examination and audit of a refund claim usually takes time, a special procedure allows taxpayers to apply for a speedy refund or credit for an overpayment resulting from a carryback [Sec. 6411; Prop. Reg. 1.6411-1—1.6411-3]. The application is not a refund claim [Sec. 1.6411-1], so a separate claim may be advisable.

Corporations that expect a net operating loss may apply for an extension of time to pay the preceding year's tax (see (c) below).

(a) Application for a tentative carryback adjustment to get a quick refund is filed with the service center for the district where the tax was paid or assessed. It must be filed on or after the due date of the return (including extensions of time to file) for the tax year the loss or credit arises, and before 12 months after the close of the year[1] [Sec. 1.6411-1(c)]. Corporations use Form 1139 and other taxpayers use Form 1045. Corporations that filed Form 1138 for an extension of time to pay tax [(c) below] must file Form 1139 by the last day of the month that includes the due date (including extensions) of the return of tax to be deferred, to get a further extension.

Since Form 1139 is filed after the close of the year the loss is incurred or credit earned, it is based on the exact figures of the tax return. The application must show the tax liability of the previous years affected by a loss carryback and the effect of the recomputation for the carryback.[1] The recomputation is based on the returns of the prior years, if the taxpayer had no additional assessments or refunds for those years [Sec. 1.6411-2]. No other income or deduction adjustments that have not been the subject of a separate refund claim are allowed. For an investment credit carryback, a schedule showing the carryback computation and a recomputation of the credit after the carryback must be attached to the application. The recomputation may be made on Form 3468. Thus, a calendar year taxpayer that has a loss or investment credit in 1977 large enough to reduce the tax liability for the 3 preceding years must file application by 12-31-78 with the required details for the years 1974, 1975 and 1976.

(b) Procedure on claim. The Revenue Service examines the application and credits or refunds any decrease in tax allowed for the carryback within 90 days from the last day of the month in which the tax return due date falls (including extensions of time to file), or within 90 days from the time the application is filed, if that is later [Sec. 6411; 1.6411-3].

The Revenue Service can disallow any application that contains material omissions or mathematical errors that the taxpayer cannot correct within the 90-day period [Sec. 1.6411-3]. In most cases, the Revenue Service allows the amounts shown in the application. If it is later found that the allowances were erroneous, the erroneous part of the allowance may be recovered and an adjustment made against the taxpayer [Sec. 6411(b)]. If the taxpayer is not satisfied, he may file the usual claim for refund [¶ 3626] and sue for recovery [¶ 3629] if the claim is not allowed [Sec. 1.6411-1(b)(2)].

(c) Time to pay corporate tax extended. A corporation that expects operations for the tax year to result in a net operating loss carryback can apply on Form 1138 for an extension of the time for payment of a part of its taxes for the preceding tax year. The extension is based on estimates of the reduction in tax that the carryback will make. Payment will be extended only for the amount of the anticipated refund. If an extension is obtained, the total tax to be paid for the preceding tax year will be determined after the extension ends. The extension ends on the last day of the month in which the return is due for the tax year of the expected net operating loss, or if taxpayer has applied for a speeded-up refund under the special refund procedure noted above, on the date the Commissioner mails notice of his approval or disapproval of the refund application [Sec. 6164; 1.6164-1]. The amount deferred bears interest at 7% (9% between 7-1-75 and 1-31-76; 6% before 7-1-75) or at an adjusted prime interest rate (¶ 3628) [Sec. 6601, 6621; 301.6601-1].

¶ 3631 When limitation periods do not apply. The Code permits correction of improper tax results in certain situations after the time for refund or assessment has passed. An "adjustment" by refund or additional assessment is allowed [Sec. 1311-1315]. Some adjustments can be made only when a determination of tax liability or refund is inconsistent with the treatment of the item in another year or as to another taxpayer. [Sec. 1311(b)].

While the statute often works to the taxpayer's advantage, it should be given the most careful study before filing a claim for refund. A refund claim may open the way for the assessment of a deficiency otherwise barred.

(a) Inconsistent determination required. In these situations, determination of tax liability or refund in the later year must be inconsistent with the treatment in the year barred by the statute of limitations. For instance, in Example 1, the successful assertion that the rent should be included in income for the year received (1973) is inconsistent with the original treatment, which included the item in the year of accrual (1972).

Adjustment will be made in the following circumstances:

Double inclusion of income. A double inclusion of income occurs when there is included in one year income which erroneously has also been included in the income of a previous year now barred by the statute of limitations. Or, an item is included in the income of one taxpayer and erroneously has been included in the income of a related taxpayer [Sec. 1312(1); 1.1312-1].

Example 1: The taxpayer who is on the cash basis erroneously included in his 1972 return an item of $10,000 accrued rent which he actually received in 1973. The taxpayer's 1973 return was filed on April 15, 1974 and the time within which the Commissioner could assess a deficiency did not expire until April 15, 1977. If the Commissioner, on February 3, 1977, asserts a deficiency which is sustained by the Tax Court, the taxpayer would have to pay an additional 1973 tax. He could not, however, file a claim for refund of the 1972 overpayment, since the statute of limitations has expired. Sec. 1312(1) allows an adjustment.

Double deduction. A double deduction occurs when a deduction or credit is allowed in one year (or to one taxpayer) which erroneously has also been allowed in another year (or to a related taxpayer[1] [Sec. 1312(2); 1.1312-2].

Example 2: A taxpayer in his return for 1972 took a casualty loss deduction. After he had filed his return for 1973 and after the statute of limitations for the 1972 return had expired, it was discovered that the loss actually occurred in 1973. The taxpayer, therefore, filed a claim for refund for the year 1973 based upon the allowance of a deduction for the loss in that year, and the claim was allowed by the Commissioner in 1977. Here it is the Commissioner who is barred from opening the 1972 return and who is benefited by Sec. 1312(2).

A double exclusion of gross income occurs when an item of income is included in one year, and then taxpayer gets it excluded because it belonged in a prior year now barred [Sec. 1312(3)(A); 1.1312-3].

Example 3: In 1972 U.S. Motors, Inc. recovers a judgment against General Steel Co. for breach of contract. The judgment is paid, but Steel appeals to a higher court and the judgment is not affirmed until 1973. Motors erroneously includes the recovery in its 1973 return instead of its 1972 return, and in February 1977 filed for refund of the 1973 tax. Since the statute of limitations prevents the Commissioner from assessing a deficiency against the 1972 return, Sec. 1312(3)(A) permits an adjustment.

Affiliated corporations. A deduction or credit of a corporation is treated in a manner inconsistent with the way the item is treated by an affiliated corporation [Sec. 1312(6); 1.1312-6].

Basis of property. Basis of property is determined for any purpose, such as gain or loss, depreciation, depletion, etc., and errors were made with respect to prior transactions in determining inclusions or omissions from gross income, recognition or nonrecognition of gain or loss, deductions of items chargeable to capital account, or charges of items chargeable to capital account that should have been deducted [Sec. 1312(7); 1.1312-7].

Trust items. An item of trust income or deduction is treated in a manner inconsistent with the way the item is treated in the hands of the fiduciary or beneficiary, as the case may be [Sec. 1312(5); 1.1312-5].

(b) Relief without inconsistent determination. There are two situations when relief is possible without the later year being inconsistent with a prior position of the successful party [Sec. 1311(b); 1.1311(b)-1]. When there is no deduction or inclusion made in the prior year, there is no *positive* action as to which the successful party in the dispute over the later year can be said to have taken a position. Compare this with cases where there is, in the prior year, positive inclusion of income or taking of a deduction.

Deduction or credit disallowed. An adjustment can be made to disallow a deduction or credit to which the taxpayer (or related taxpayer) is entitled in a prior year now barred [Sec. 1312(4); 1.1312-4]. However, the deduction or credit in the current year must not have been barred when the taxpayer formally claimed the deduction or credit for the year disallowed [Sec. 1311(b)(2)(B); 1.1311(b)-2]. An adjustment is also allowed when a loss is erroneously treated as an ordinary or capital loss.[2]

Example 4: The taxpayer is on the cash basis. He erroneously fails to deduct a payment made in 1972, and, instead, takes the deduction in 1974. In 1975, a deficiency is assessed on the ground that the deduction in 1974 was erroneous, and the taxpayer replies in writing, claiming the deduction for 1972. In 1977, the Tax Court disallows the deduction for 1974. The statute of limitations bars taking the deduction in 1972. Sec. 1312(4) permits an adjustment.

Unreported income. An adjustment is allowed to exclude income not reported and on which tax was not paid, but which is includible in a prior year of the taxpayer (or of a related taxpayer) [Sec. 1312(3)(B); 1.1312-3(b)]. However, the inclusion in the correct year must not have been barred at the time the Commissioner formally claimed the inclusion for the incorrect year [Sec. 1311(b)(2)(A); 1.1311(b)-2].

Example 5: Assume facts similar to Example 3, except that when the time comes to make out its 1973 return Motors decides that the recovery should not be included in 1973 after all. In 1975 the Commissioner assesses a deficiency in the 1973 return on the ground that the recovery should have been included in the year when the judgment was affirmed. In 1976, the Tax Court rejects the Commissioner's arguments. The statute of limitations prevents the Commissioner from including the recovery in the correct year (1972). Sec. 1312(3)(B) applies. Notice that in Example 3, Motors paid the tax (later suing for refund), but in Example 5 there is no such payment.

THE UNITED STATES TAX COURT

¶ **3635 What the Tax Court does.** The Tax Court is a court of limited jurisdiction [¶ 3637], with powers strictly confined to those conferred by statute. Generally, the court's jurisdiction can be invoked only by a taxpayer after a deficiency or liability notice has been issued [¶ 3605]. But once its jurisdiction is invoked by the filing of the proper petition, the court may try the case de novo, and render a decision on the evidence before it, rather than on the mere review of the evidence before the Revenue Service.

The United States Tax Court is a court of record established under Article I of the U.S. Constitution [Sec. 7441].

(a) Place of trial. The Tax Court or any of its divisions may sit at any place within the United States [Sec. 7445; TC Rule 10(b)]. Consequently a taxpayer may ask that his case be tried at or near the city in which he is located [¶ 3639(b)]. Tax Court proceedings (except a small tax claim proceeding; see (c) below) are governed by the rules of evidence that apply in trials without a jury in the District Court of the District of Columbia [Sec. 7453; TC Rule 143].

(b) Proving a case. The Tax Court can consider only the evidence that the parties produce. Usually, the petitioner has the burden of proof [see ¶ 3641(b)]. He must present sufficient evidence to prove his case as stated in the petition, regardless of what evidence he has already presented to the Revenue Service. However, the Commissioner must prove transferee liability, fraud, and the liability of a foundation manager for knowingly participating in an act of self-dealing, or engaging in certain other wrongful acts (¶ 3439) [Sec. 6902(a); 7454].

(c) Small tax case procedure. The Tax Court has adopted simplified procedures to handle small tax cases. These procedures may be used at the taxpayer's option, concurred in by the Tax Court. The taxpayer files his petition for small tax cases on Form 2 obtainable from th court clerk [TC Rule 175]. A "small tax case" is one in which neither the disputed amount of the deficiency nor the claimed over-

Footnotes appear at end of this Chapter.

¶ **3635**

payment exceeds $1,500, including additions to tax, for a tax year [Sec. 7463; TC Rule 171]. The decision of the court in a small tax case is based on a brief summary opinion and is not reviewable on appeal and will not serve as a precedent for future cases. The court is given discretion in applying the rules of evidence and procedure. If during the trial the court decides that the deficiency or overpayment in dispute should be increased to more than $1,500 the court may transfer the case from the small claims procedure to the regular procedure. But this is done only in unusual cases. The decision in a small tax case proceeding becomes final 90 days after the decision is entered [Sec. 7481(b); TC Rules 170-173].

(d) **Declaratory judgments on qualification of retirement plans.** A petition may be filed with the Tax Court seeking a declaratory judgment on the qualification of a retirement plan or amendments to it. An employer, employee who is an "interested party," or the Pension Benefit Guaranty Corporation may qualify as a petitioner. Before filing, all of the administrative remedies provided by the Revenue Service must be exhausted. Actions for declaratory judgments must be brought within 90 days after the Revenue Service mails its determination notice. If the Revenue Service fails to issue a determination letter within 270 days (plus extensions) after one is requested, an action may be commenced at any time thereafter [Sec. 7476; 1.7476-1—3]. For appeals, see ¶ 3649. The Tax Court is authorized to impose a fee up to $10 for filing the petition [Sec. 7451].

(e) **Declaratory judgments—exempt status and classification.** Where there is a controversy with the IRS over status or classification, an exempt organization or foundation may file a petition for a declaratory judgment to determine its status as a tax-exempt organization, a qualified charitable contribution donee, a private foundation or a private operating foundation. Petition may be filed with the Tax Court, Federal District Court for the District of Columbia and the U.S. Court of Claims. These rules apply to pleadings filed after 4-3-77, where the IRS determination or the organization's request for such determination was made after 1-1-76. Procedural provisions that apply are similar to those covered in (d) above [Sec. 7428].

(f) **Declaratory judgments on transfers of property from U.S.** Petition for a declaratory judgment may be filed with the Tax Court where there is a controversy with IRS over its determination under Sec. 367 (or its failure to make a determination) of the tax avoidance purpose of a corporation in transferring property from the U.S. This rule applies to petitions filed after 10-4-76. The procedural provisions that apply are similar to those covered in (d) above [Sec. 7477].

¶ 3636 **Appearance before Tax Court.** The Tax Court has its own rules of practice. An individual may appear in his own behalf, and a member of a partnership or a corporate officer may appear on behalf of the partnership or corporation. Also, a fiduciary may represent an estate or trust [TC Rule 24]. A tax practitioner must be admitted to practice in the Tax Court before he can represent a client there.

(a) **Admission to practice** is granted on the following basis [TC Rules 24; 200]:
• Attorneys may be admitted without examination if they present a current certificate of admission to practice before the U.S. Supreme Court or the highest court of any state.
• All other new applicants must take a written examination. An oral examination may also be required by the court. After 3 failures an applicant is no longer eligible.
Admission to a state bar, or to practice before the Revenue Service does not automatically carry admission to practice before the Tax Court.

(b) Application must be filed. An attorney, seeking admission to practice before the Tax Court, must file an application for admission with the Admission Clerk. The fee is $10. Applicants other than attorneys seeking admission by examination must pay a $10 fee with their applications and must have three individuals already admitted to practice before the court send letters of sponsorship directly to the court [TC Rule 200].

¶ **3637 Jurisdiction of Tax Court.** The Tax Court may hear appeals from Commissioner's notice of deficiency or liability of income, estate or gift tax, excise taxes on private foundations and employment taxes[1] [Sec. 7442; TC Rule 13].

(a) Items subject to review. The Tax Court has jurisdiction to consider appeals involving constitutional questions,[2] closing agreements,[3] fraud penalties,[4] and the statute of limitations.[5]

(b) Deficiencies. The Tax Court can review only proposed assessments of tax deficiencies. It cannot entertain an appeal based on denial of a refund.[6] But when it assumes jurisdiction on a deficiency issue, it reviews the taxpayer's entire liability for the year at issue, and may find there is an added deficiency or an overpayment [Sec. 6512(b); 301.6512-1]. Generally, the court may not go into years for which no deficiency was asserted;[7] but it may determine the effect of a net operating loss it finds for other years on the taxable income of the deficiency years.[8]

(c) Issues raised by pleadings. The Tax Court is limited to the issues raised in the taxpayer's petition and other pleadings, and the evidence supporting them. When facts material and essential to a decision are omitted from the pleadings the court cannot remedy the defect.[9]

(d) Matters raised before Revenue Service. The jurisdiction of the Tax Court is not limited to the issues raised before the Revenue Service, but it will entertain all issues related to a tax liability raised by the taxpayer's pleadings, including claims of overassessment.[10]

(e) Who files petition. Petition to the Tax Court must be brought by and in the name of the person to whom the deficiency or liability notice was directed, or by and in the full descriptive name of his fiduciary. If there is a variance between the name in the deficiency or liability notice and the correct name, reasons for the variance must be stated in the petition [TC Rule 34(b)].

(f) Service of papers. The petition is served on the Commissioner or his representative by the Clerk of the Tax Court. All other papers required to be served can be done by the parties if the originals together with a certificate of service (Form 13) are filed with the Clerk. Service is complete on mailing whether by registered or certified mail or by hand delivery to a party or his counsel [TC Rule 21(b)].

¶ **3638 Authority of regulations.** The Tax Court will be bound by the regulations of the Internal Revenue Service unless they are found to be unreasonable and inconsistent with the Code.[1]

¶ **3639 How proceeding begins.** A proceeding before the Tax Court is started by filing a petition.

Footnotes appear at end of this Chapter.

(a) **When to file petition.** The petition must be filed within 90 days after mailing of the notice of deficiency or liability to the taxpayer. The period is 150 days for taxpayers not located in the U.S., or for the estate of a decedent dying abroad[1] [Sec. 6213(a); 301.6213-1]. The court cannot extend the time to file.[2] An automatic extension is allowed Armed Forces personnel in a combat zone. See ¶ 3518(a).

The filing period. The day the deficiency notice is mailed is not counted, but the day of filing the petition is counted.[3] The period begins to run from the date the deficiency notice is mailed. A second mailing of a notice generally does not start a new 90-day period, unless the first mailing was abandoned.[4]

NOTE: The filing period for certain excise taxes [¶ 3440-3444] is suspended when the Revenue Service extends the time allowed for making corrections (¶ 3439) [Sec. 6213(e)].

Filing by mail. The petition is considered to be filed on time when it is mailed, postage prepaid, to the proper office within the prescribed time as indicated by the postmark on the envelope. This applies even if it is received after the time has expired. Incorrect private postage meter dates must be corrected by the post office. Since private meters can be predated when mailing machines are used, a postmark not made or corrected by the U.S. Post Office will be considered the delivery date only as provided in the regulations. However, the Tax Court has accepted a private postage meter date not corrected by the post office as a postmark date.[5] If the petition is sent by registered or certified mail the date of registration, or the postmarked date on the certified mail receipt, is the date of mailing [Sec. 7502; 301.7502-1]. When the last day for filing the petition falls on a Saturday, Sunday, or is a legal holiday in the District of Columbia, time for filing is extended to include the next business day of the Court [TC Rule 25].

(b) **Request for place of hearing.** The petition should be accompanied by a request on Form 4 that the hearing on the case be held at or near the city more convenient for the taxpayer [TC Rule 140(a), (b)].

(c) **Filing fee.** A $10 filing fee should be paid at the time of filing the petition [TC Rule 20(b)]. If the fee is not paid when the petition is filed, the court has jurisdiction of the case if the fee is paid within a reasonable time after notice from the court that it must be paid.[6]

¶ **3640 The petition.** An attorney or accountant preparing a petition to the Tax Court should bear in mind that it will consider only the issues that are set out in the petition. The issues and the facts upon which they are based should be covered so completely that when the judge reads the petition, he can tell immediately what the dispute is about and what the facts are. A good rule is to give such a complete presentation that, if the facts alleged can be proved, they can be adopted as findings of fact by the court and be in sufficient detail to justify a decision in favor of the taxpayer.

(a) **Form.** The petition (and all other papers filed with the Tax Court) may be prepared by any process, provided the information is set out in clear and legible type and is substantially in accordance with Form 1. An original and four copies are required [TC Rules 23, 34].

(b) **Contents.** The petition must have a caption showing the name of the petitioner [TC Rule 23].

Body of the petition. The petition has numbered paragraphs stating:

- Petitioner's name and current principal office or residence, and the Revenue Service office where the return for the controversial period was filed.
- The date of mailing of the notice of deficiency or liability on which the petition is based, or other proper allegations showing jurisdiction in the court along with the Revenue Service address issuing the notice.
- The amount of the deficiency or liability, nature of the tax, period for which determined, and the amount in dispute.
- Assignments of every error the petitioner charges has been committed by the Commissioner; each separate assignment must be lettered.
- The facts on which the petitioner relies as sustaining the assignments of error; each subparagraph should be lettered.
- The relief sought by the petitioner.

Signature. The petition must be signed by the petitioner or his counsel (counsel in the individual and not the firm name). The signature of a corporation or unincorporated association must be in the name of the corporation or association by one of its active officers or members; the name, mailing address and telephone number of the petitioner or counsel actually signing must be typed or printed immediately beneath the written signature; mailing address of counsel must include the firm name if it is essential to the mailing address.

Verification. The petition need not be verified after 12-31-73 and only when directed by the court do pleadings need to be verified or accompanied by affidavit [TC Rules 33(a), 34].

Deficiency of liability notice attached. A copy of the notice of deficiency or liability must accompany the petition and each copy of it. If a statement accompanied the notice, the part of it that is material to the issues set out in the assignments of error must also be attached. If the notice referred to earlier notices from the Service that are necessary to explain the determination, the parts material to the issues raised by assignments of error must be attached.

¶ 3641 **The Commissioner's answer.** **(a) Filing.** The Commissioner has 60 days after service of a copy of the petition to file an answer, or 45 days for motions on the petition. If an amended petition is filed, the Commissioner has the same time after service to file an answer or for motions on the petition unless the court fixes a different time [TC Rule 36(a)].

(b) Contents. The Commissioner's answer must fully and completely advise the petitioner and the court of the nature of the defense. It must contain a specific admission or denial of each material allegation contained in the petition or state that the Commissioner lacks knowledge or information to form a belief as to the truth of any allegation. The Commissioner may qualify or deny only part of an allegation. If special matters like res judicata, collateral estoppel, estoppel, waiver, duress, fraud, and statute of limitations are pleaded, a mere denial will not be sufficient to raise this issue. Moreover, the answer must state every ground on which the Commissioner relies and has the burden of proof. In addition, every material allegation in the taxpayer's petition that is not expressly admitted or denied by the Commissioner is deemed admitted. Paragraphs of the answer must be numbered to correspond with those of the petition [TC Rule 36(b), (c); 39].

¶ 3642 **Petitioner's reply.** **(a) Filing.** When the Commissioner's answer alleges material facts, the petitioner has 45 days after service of the answer to file a reply or 30 days for motions on the answer [TC Rule 37(a)]. A reply is not filed in small tax cases [¶ 3635(c)] unless required by the court or the Commissioner [TC Rule 175(c)].

(b) Contents. The reply must contain a specific admission or denial of each material allegation in the answer on which the Commissioner has the burden of proof. Lack of knowledge or information as to the truth of any allegation must be asserted. The reply must state every ground, together with supporting facts, on which the petitioner relies. If special matters like res judicata, collateral estoppel, estoppel, waiver, duress, fraud, and the statute of limitations are raised in the answer, a mere denial in the reply will not be sufficient to raise these issues. In addition, every defense in law or fact must be generally raised in the reply. If the petitioner is not required to serve a reply, he may assert the defense at the trial. Each paragraph in the reply must be numbered to correspond with the paragraphs of the answer [TC Rules 37(b); 39; 40].

Every affirmative allegation in the Commissioner's answer, not expressly admitted or denied by the petitioner in his reply, is considered admitted. If the petitioner does not file a reply, the affirmative allegations in the Commissioner's answer are considered denied unless the Commissioner makes a motion to have specific allegations in the answer admitted [TC Rule 37(c)].

¶ 3643 Amended or supplemental pleadings. (a) Amendment. A pleading may be amended once as a matter of course at any time before a responsive pleading is served. If no responsive pleading is permitted and the case has not been placed on the trial calendar, the pleading may be amended within 30 days after it is served. When the amendment is allowed it relates back to the filing date of the pleading, unless the court on its motion or on the motion of a party orders otherwise [TC Rule 41].

(b) Supplemental pleadings. Supplemental pleadings may be permitted when a party wishes to indicate transactions or occurrences that took place after the pleading. Permission may be granted even though the original pleading is defective [TC Rule 41(c)].

(c) Amendment conforming pleadings to proof. The court can order an amendment of the pleadings to conform them to the evidence presented, on the motion of any party. The evidence will be admitted when the pleadings are amended. No amendment is permitted if the evidence will prejudice the party objecting to its admission [TC Rule 41(b)].

(d) Filing. The amendments that are permitted must be filed with the court at the trial or with the Clerk at Washington, D.C., within the time fixed by the court [TC Rule 41(b)].

¶ 3644 Judgment without trial. A case may be disposed of before trial by a motion for judgment on the pleadings or a motion for a summary judgment. Any party may move for a judgment on the pleadings, but the motion must be made within such time so as not to delay trial. A motion for summary judgment must be made at any time starting 30 days after the pleadings are closed, but it must also be made within such time not to delay trial. Any written response to the motion for summary judgment must be made not later than 10 days before the hearing. A decision on the motion for summary judgment will be rendered only after every genuine issue of material fact has been disposed of [TC Rules 120, 122].

¶ 3645 Time and place for hearing. Upon joinder of issue (generally by filing of an answer or reply, where the answer raises affirmative issues), the court will set a calendar date and a city (generally the one requested by the petitioner

[¶ 3639(b)]) for the hearing. No hearing is necessary if the facts are established by deposition [TC Rule 122(a)].

(a) Postponement. When a case is set for trial and for any reason a postponement is desired, a motion should be made immediately on receipt of the notice setting the hearing. In almost all cases the court is denying motions for continuance made on the day the case is called, or within a few days of that date [TC Rule 134].

(b) Discovery. The parties are urged to obtain the required information through informal consultation or communication. If this can't be done, formal discovery procedures involving interrogatories and the production of documents or things should be followed. Depositions [¶ 3646], may not be used as a discovery device. A party must generally wait 30 days after joinder of issue before he can begin discovery. He must generally complete discovery no later than 75 days prior to the trial date [TC Rules 70-73].

(c) Admissions. Parties may serve written requests for admissions. The requests must be made and completed within the same periods provided for discovery (see (b), above). The matter will be considered admitted if the request is not responded to within a certain period (usually 30 days) [TC Rule 90].

(d) Stipulations. Before the hearing date has been set, taxpayer's counsel may be asked to confer with the Appellate Division and a member of the Regional Counsel's staff to try to settle the case. If the case is settled, a stipulation of settlement will be filed with the court and no trial is required. After the hearing date is set, Regional Counsel will ask for a conference, to agree on facts that are not in dispute, in any case that has not been settled or the facts already agreed upon. Agreements should be entered upon stipulations and filed with the court or presented at the hearing. If either party fails to confer or refuses to stipulate undisputed facts after trial notice is issued, the other can ask for an order to show cause why those facts should not be accepted as established in the case [TC Rule 91].

In addition, the court on its own motion, or at the request of either party, may schedule its own pretrial conference [TC Rule 110].

¶ 3646 How to take depositions. Depositions can be taken by written interrogation, which is unusual, or by oral examination of the witness by both parties [TC Rules 81, 84].

An application on Form 6, to take a deposition must be filed with the court at least 45 days before the trial date. The court supplies the application form. It requires a statement of the witnesses' names and addresses, the subject matter of the testimony, why a deposition is requested, the time and place for taking the testimony and the official who will take the deposition [TC Rule 81].

¶ 3647 The Tax Court hearing. The Tax Court is a trial court, and follows formal trial court precedure, except for small tax cases which are conducted as informally as possible [TC Rule 170]. If the parties have reached a settlement and filed a stipulation to that effect, the court will enter decision accordingly. If, at the calendar date, no settlement has been reached, and both parties answer "ready," the judge or clerk will note the probable date of the hearing.

(a) Burden of proof. As a matter of law, the determination of the Commissioner in the notice of deficiency is prima facie correct. Therefore, any statement of fact in the notice must be accepted by the Tax Court as correct unless the petitioner by competent evidence, can overcome the prima facie correctness of the

Footnotes appear at end of this Chapter.

¶ 3647

determination.[1] The burden of proof in matters covered by the notice of deficiency is on the taxpayer. His counsel should bear in mind that he must not merely establish a case but must *overcome the opposing case.*

(b) **Argument.** At the hearing, petitioner's counsel makes his opening statement, and formally presents his evidence, as would be done in a trial before a United States District Court. Any admissions or stipulations made or depositions taken must be introduced as evidence. He is followed by Commissioner's counsel. If the presentation on behalf of the Commissioner involves affirmative issues, petitioner's counsel has opportunity for rebuttal.

At the end of the hearing, the court may ask the parties to make oral arguments and to file written citations of authorities referred to in the presentations. Unless otherwise directed, each party has 45 days after the conclusion of the hearing within which to file a brief on the issues on which he has the burden of proof. Within 30 days after a brief is filed, the opposing party may file a reply brief [TC Rule 151]. Generally, briefs or oral arguments are not required in small tax cases [TC Rule 177(c)].

(c) **Rehearing.** The court at its discretion may grant a rehearing of a case to permit presentation of newly discovered evidence upon motion made not more than 30 days (except where the court permits) after the Report has been served [TC Rule 161].

(d) **Tax briefs.** A good brief is needed at the end of the hearing. The briefs filed by government counsel in tax cases are uniformly good. If briefs in behalf of the taxpayer are not equally good, the taxpayer's case is jeopardized.

It also is advisable to submit either a quasi-brief or a formal brief at various stages of a tax case. Such a document should accompany a request for a district conference [¶ 3603] or a hearing before the Appellate Division [¶ 3607]. A brief is needed in a suit before the District Court or the Court of Claims, and on appeal from decisions of any of these courts. Briefs are not required in small tax cases [TC Rule 117(c)].

¶ **3648 The Tax Court Report.** After the hearing, the court writes up its findings of fact and opinion in a single discussion called a "Report." Note, that this is not the court's decision. This is important for several reasons. The date of the decision determines the time for filing an appeal from the decision [¶ 3649(a)]. It also controls the period when the statute of limitations on assessment and collection is suspended pending the Tax Court proceedings [¶ 3612]. The decision is a specific order that (1) finds the amount of the deficiency, (2) finds there is no deficiency, or (3) dismisses the case for any reason. The decision is usually entered immediately after publication of the findings of fact and opinion if the court decides the deficiency in the deficiency or liability notice is correct. If it decides the deficiency should be revised, decision is entered after proceedings under Rule 155.

(a) **Rule 155.** Instead of itself determining the tax due, the court may direct the parties to compute the liability under TC Rule 155. Each party submits a computation of tax liability in the light of the court's opinion. If the parties cannot agree, the case is set for argument on the settlement, and the court determines the tax due.

No new issues can be raised under Rule 155,[1] but the court may consent to raising an obvious issue; for instance, that the deficiency was barred by the statute of limitations.[2]

(b) **Procedure after decision.** If the petitioner is satisfied with the Tax Court's decision, his counsel should within 30 days of the serving of the Report, file a determination of the result under Rule 155. If he is dissatisfied with the Tax

Court's decision, counsel has 90 days after the decision is entered within which to file a notice of appeal [Sec. 7483].

¶ 3649 Review of Tax Court decision. The Tax Court has no power to set aside or change its decision once it has become final[1] [Secs. 7481; 301.748-1]. However, the 7th Circuit Court holds that the Tax Court has jurisdiction to re-open such a decision on the grounds that fraud had been committed on the court.[2] Tax Court decisions can be reviewed by the Courts of Appeals to the same extent as decisions of the district courts in civil actions tried without a jury [Sec. 7482(a)]. The U.S. Supreme Court may prescribe rules for review of decisions of the Tax Court [Sec. 7482(c)(2)]. The findings of facts made by a Tax Court judge and the factual inferences the Tax Court draws from the findings are binding, unless they are clearly erroneous. If the reviewing court has a firm conviction that a mistake was made, the Tax Court finding is "clearly erroneous."[3] Decisions in small tax cases are not reviewable (¶ 3635(c)) [Sec. 7481(b)].

(a) Appeals. Appeal from a decision of the Tax Court is made to the U.S. Court of Appeals for the circuit where the petitioner has his legal residence when the notice of appeal is filed. A corporation appeals to the circuit where its principal place of business or principal office or agency is located; if it has none, to the circuit where it filed the return. A petitioner not qualified to appeal to a circuit, appeals to the Court of Appeals for the District of Columbia. However, the parties may agree to have the case reviewed by any U.S. Court of Appeals [Sec. 7482].

The Courts of Appeal are authorized to hear appeals from declaratory decisions of the Tax Court involving the determination of the qualification of retirement plans (or amendments thereto) brought under Sec. 7476. Also, declaratory judgments involving charitable organizations under Sec. 7428 or transfers of property from the U.S. under Sec. 7477 provided the determinations (or requests) were made after 1-1-76 [Sec. 7482].

Time to file. A notice of appeal may be filed by either the Commissioner or the taxpayer within 90 days after the Tax Court's decision is entered. If it is filed by one party, any other party to the proceeding may file a notice of appeal within 120 days after the decision [Sec. 7483]. In certain cases, decisions of Courts of Appeals may be reviewed by the Supreme Court of the United States [¶ 3629(d)].

(b) Bond to stay assessment and collection. Appeal from a Tax Court decision does not act as a stay of assessment or collection of the deficiency determined by the Court. The taxpayer, on or before the date of filing his notice of appeal, must file with the Court a bond not exceeding double the amount of the deficiency, or else a jeopardy bond [Sec. 7485].

(c) Effect of Courts of Appeals decisions. The Tax Court has held that it will follow decisions of the Court of Appeals for the same circuit to which the Tax Court decision can be appealed.[4]

Footnotes to Chapter 26

(P-H "FEDERAL TAXES" related references are cited in brackets [ ] at the end of each footnote below.)

Footnote ¶ 3600 [¶ 35,601 et seq.].

Footnote ¶ 3601 [¶ 35,496; 39,610 et seq.].
(1) Couch v. U.S., 93 US 611, 31 AFTR 2d 73-477; Fisher v. US, 37 AFTR 2d 76-1244, 96 SCt. 1569 [¶ 39,650(30); 56,801].
(2) U.S. v. Bisceglia, 35 AFTR 2d 75-702, 420 US 141 [¶ 39,643(8)].
(3) Miller v. US, 37 AFTR 2d 76-1261, 96 SCt. 1619 [¶ 56,802].
(4) Statement of Organization and Functions, IRB 1970-13 [¶ 41,843(5)].
(5) IRS Document 5632 (1966) [¶ 35,496(5)].
(6) Rev. Proc. 64-12, 1964-1 CB 672 [¶ 35,025(50)].

Footnote ¶ 3602 [¶ 39,610 et seq.].
(1) Statement of Procedural Rules (26 CFR 601) [¶ 39,737].
(2) U.S. v. Powell, 85 SCt 248, 14 AFTR 2d 5942 [¶ 39,652(15)].
(3) Ryan v. U.S., 85 SCt 232, 14 AFTR 2d 5947 [¶ 39,652(15)].
(4) Mathis, Sr. v. U.S., 21 AFTR 2d 1251, 391 US 1 [¶ 38,523(20)].
(5) Tarlowski, 24 AFTR 2d 69-6433 [¶ 38,523(5)].
(6) Beckwith v. US (US Sup. Ct., 4-21-76) 37 AFTR 2d 76-1232 [¶ 76-579].
(7) Rev. Proc. 74-5, 1974-1 CB 416 [¶ 33,186(5)].
(8) Rev. Proc. 74-4, 1974-1 CB 414 [¶ 39,767(5)].

Footnote ¶ 3603 [¶ 39,767].
(1) Rev. Proc. 74-4, 1974-1 CB 414 [¶ 39,767(5)].
(2) IRS Pub. No. 5 (1-69) [¶ 39,768(5)].
(3) Cleveland Tr. Co. v. U.S., 19 AFTR 2d 1770, 266 F. Supp. 824 [¶ 126,562.2(10)].

Footnote ¶ 3604 [¶ 39,737].

Footnote ¶ 3605 [¶ 35,641 et seq.].
(1) Delman, J., ¶ 66,059 P-H Memo TC, affd. 20 AFTR 2d 5543, 384 F.2d 929 [¶ 35,647(50)].
(2) Luhring v. Glotzbach, 9 AFTR 2d 1812 [¶ 35,647(10)].
(3) Du Mais, 40 TC 269 [¶ 35,647(55)].
(4) Chambers v. Lucas, 41 F.2d 299, 8 AFTR 10857 [¶ 35,656(50)].
(5) Mindell v. Comm., 200 F.2d 38, 42 AFTR 907. *Contra:* Hamilton, 13 TC 747 [¶ 35,656(40)].

Footnote ¶ 3606 [¶ 35,658].
(1) Morse v. U.S., 6 AFTR 2d 5353, 183 F. Supp. 847 [¶ 35,658(70)].
(2) Payson v. Comm., 36 AFTR 888, 166 F.2d 1008 [¶ 35,658(10)].
(3) Schaefer v. U.S., 43 AFTR 1297 (DC, Hawaii; 1951) [¶ 35,658(70)].

Footnote ¶ 3607 [¶ 39,738].
(1) IRS Pub. No. 5 (1-69); Rev. Proc. 61-36. 1961-2 CB 575 [¶ 39,768(5)].
(2) Rev. Proc. 68-4, 1968-1 CB 746 [¶ 39,768(5)].
(3) U.S. v. Goldstein, 189 F.2d 752, 40 AFTR 768 [¶ 37,024(50)].
(4) Rev. Proc. 60-18 1960-2 CB 988 [¶ 39,769(15)].

Footnote ¶ 3608 [¶ 38,206 et seq.; 38,251 et seq.].
(1) Op. A.G. 7, XIII-2 CB 445 [¶ 38,260(35)].
(2) The subject is highly technical. In actual cases, the Prentice-Hall Federal Taxes should be consulted [¶ 38,251 et seq.].
(3) Rev. Proc. 64-44, 1964-2 CB 974 as amended by Rev. Proc. 66-53, 1966-2 CB 1266 [¶ 38,257(5); 41,845(135)].
(4) Backus v. U.S., 11 AFTR 422, 59 F.2d 242 [¶ 38,264(10)].
(5) Indianapolis Screw Products Corp. v. U.S., 7 AFTR 2d 833 [¶ 38,268(15)].
(6) U.S. v. Wilson, 182 F. Supp. 567, 5 AFTR 2d 1273; U.S. v. Lane, 303 F. 2d 2011, 9 AFTR 2d 1458 [¶ 38,269].
(7) Parks, E. C., 33 TC 298; U.S. v. Mc Cue, 4 AFTR 2d 5830, 178 F. Supp. 426 [¶ 38,260(5), (40)].
(8) Rev. Proc. 68-16, 1968-1 CB 770 [¶ 38,217(3)].

Footnote ¶ 3609 [¶ 39,747 et seq.; 39,791 et seq.].
(1) P.L. 89-332, 89th Cong., 1st Sess.
(2) Printed in full in 1973 P-H Federal Taxes at ¶ 39,798 et seq.
(3) Rev. Proc. 68-20, 1968-1 CB 812 [¶ 39,876(5)].
(4) Rev. Proc. 66-44, 1966-2 CB 1252 [¶ 39,874(5)].

Footnote ¶ 3610 [¶ 36,401 et seq.].
(1) Reaves v. Comm., 8 AFTR 2d 5619, 295 F. 2d 336 [¶ 37,213(15)].
(2) California Thoroughbred Breeders Assn., 47 TC 335; Rev. Rul. 69-247, 1969-1 CB 303 [¶ 36,447(15)].
(3) Rev. Rul. 60-144, 1960-1 CB 636 [¶ 36,447(5)].
(4) Roschuni, 44 TC 80; Walker, 46 TC 630; Taylor, 24 AFTR 2d 69-5747, 417 F.2d 991 [¶ 36,465(50)].
(5) Rev. Proc. 71-11, 1971-1 CB 678 [¶ 36,475(3)].
(6) Rev. Proc. 68-31, 1968-2 CB 917 [¶ 36,473(23)].
(7) Instructions for Form 1023, Part IV (2).

Footnote ¶ 3611 [¶ 36,401 et seq.; 38,010 et seq.; 38,042 et seq.].
(1) Field v. Comm., 7 AFTR 2d 394, 286 F.2d 960; Negus ¶ 53,075 P-H Memo TC [¶ 38,042(5), (15)].
(2) Rev. Rul. 64-305, 1964-2 CB 503 [¶ 36,466(40)].
(3) Rowen, 18 TC 874 [¶ 38,042(30)].
(4) Rev. Rul. 69-543, 1969-2 CB 1 [¶ 5989(42)].

Footnote ¶ 3612 [¶ 37,611 et seq.; 37,631 et seq.; 37,666 et seq.].
(1) Rev. Rul. 66-43, 1966-1 CB 291 [¶ 37,706(60)].
(2) Rev. Rul. 68-96, 1968-1 CB 566 [¶ 37,331].
(3) Laing v. US, 37 AFTR 2d 76-530, 96 SCt. 473 [¶ 56,667].
(4) 11 USC §1 et seq.
(5) P.L. 89-495; U.S. v. Speers, 16 AFTR 2d 6041, 86 SCt 411 [¶ 37,695(5), (20)].
(6) P.L. 89-496.
(7) Kokoszka v. Belford, 94 SCt. 2431, 34 AFTR 2d 5196 [¶ 36,062(40)].

Footnote ¶ 3612 continued
(8) City of New York v. Saper Tr., 336 US 328, 38 AFTR 491; Marcalus Mfg. Co., Inc., 169 F. Supp. 821, 3 AFTR 2d 427 [¶ 37,697(10), (20)].
(9) Nicholas v. US 17 AFTR 2d 1194, 86 SCt 1674 [¶ 37,697(10)].

Footnote ¶ 3613 [¶ 36,521; 38,051].
(1) Rev. Rul. 66-17, 1966-1 CB 272 [¶ 36,531(40)].
(2) Wilson v. Comm., 60 F.2d 501, 11 AFTR 773 [¶ 36,530(25)].

Footnote ¶ 3614 [¶ 38,010 et seq.].
(1) Keller, 21 BTA 84, affd. 59 F.2d 499, 11 AFTR 521 [¶ 38,022(5)].
(2) Ginsberg v. Comm., 10 AFTR 2d 5134, 305 F.2d 664 [¶ 38,031(35)].
(3) Holmes, 47 TC 622 [¶ 38,031(7)].
(4) Joannes, ¶ 67,138 P-H Memo TC [¶ 38,034(5)].
(5) Rev. Rul. 72-436, 1972-2 CB 643 [¶ 38,272(15)].

Footnote ¶ 3615 [¶ 35,761 et seq.; 35,816 et seq.; 38,741 et seq.; 38,776].
(1) The subject is discussed in detail in P-H Federal Taxes.
(2) Mrizeck v. Long, 4 AFTR 2d 5526 (DC Ill.); U.S. v. Pavenick, 8 AFTR 2d 5565, 197 F. Supp. 257 [¶ 35,773(5)].
(3) U.S. v. Donnelly, 25 AFTR 2d 70-832, 90 SCt 1033 [¶ 35,796(10)].
(4) Rev. Proc. 67-25, 1967-1 CB 626 [¶ 38,831(3)].
(5) Bob Jones University, 94 SCt. 2038, 33 AFTR 2d 74-1279; Alexander v. American United, 94 SCt. 2053, 33 AFTR 2d 74-1289 [¶ 38,782(15)].
(6) Bashara v. Hopkins, 295 Fed. 319, 4 AFTR 3763, cert. denied, 265 US 584 [¶ 38,781(25)].
(7) Enochs v. Williams Packing & Navigation Co., Inc., 82 SCt 1125, 9 AFTR 2d 1594 [¶ 38,780(5)].

Footnote ¶ 3616 [¶ 36,721 et seq.; 37,201 et seq.].

Footnote ¶ 3617 [¶ 37,201 et seq.].
(1) Pearsall & Son, 29 BTA 747 [¶ 37,223(15)].
(2) Safety Tube Corp., 8 TC 757 [¶ 37,225(55)].
(3) Orient Inv. & Fin. Co., Inc., 166 F.2d 601, 36 AFTR 818 [¶ 37,225(10)].
(4) Patino, 13 TC 816, affd. 186 F.2d 962, 40 AFTR 132; Rev. Rul. 172, 1953-2 CB 226; [¶ 37,225(5), (55)].

Footnote ¶ 3618 [¶ 37,010 et seq.; 37,251 et seq.].
(1) For guides on figuring interest when the period that interest is payable is restricted under the law, see Rev. Proc. 60-17, 1960-2 CB 942 [¶ 37,027(30)].
(2) Rev. Rul. 66-317, 1966-2 CB 510 [¶ 37,027(5)].
(3) McGovern, ¶ 55,001 P-H Memo TC [¶ 35,637(20)].
(4) Cirillo v. Comm., 11 AFTR 2d 910, 314 F.2d 478 [¶ 37,283(10)].
(5) Amos v. Comm., 16 AFTR 2d 6061, 360 F.2d 358; Arctic Ice Cream Co., 43 TC 68 [¶ 37,296(5), (10)].

Footnote ¶ 3619 [¶ 37,318 et seq.].

Footnote ¶ 3620 [¶ 38,406 et seq.].
(1) Sansone v. U.S., 15 AFTR 2d 611, 380 US 343 [¶ 38,423(5)].
(2) U.S. v. Habig, 21 AFTR 2d 803, 390 US 222 [¶ 36,726(10)].

Footnote ¶ 3621 [¶ 36,021].
(1) Rev. Rul. 54-425, 1954-2 CB 38 [¶ 36,168(5)].
(2) Lewis v. Reynolds, 284 US 281, 52 SCt 145, 10 AFTR 773 [¶ 36,026(50)].

Footnote ¶ 3622 [¶ 36,041 et seq.].
(1) Rev. Rul. 54-149, 1954-1 CB 159 [¶ 36,083(15)].

Footnote ¶ 3623 [¶ 36,551 et seq.].
(1) Stepka v. U.S., 196 F. Supp. 184, 8 AFTR 2d 5141 [¶ 36,577(20)].
(2) Burnet v. Willingham Loan & Trust Co., 282 US 437, 9 AFTR 957 [¶ 36,442(5)].

Footnote ¶ 3624 [¶ 36,551 et seq.; 36,591 et seq.].
(1) Rev. Rul. 61-20, 1961-1 CB 248 [¶ 36,595(10)].
(2) Rev. Rul. 68-150, 1968-1 CB 564 [¶ 36,596(3)].
(3) Bank of America v. U.S., 19 AFTR 2d 1446, 377 F.2d 575 [¶ 36,596(10)].

Footnote ¶ 3625 [¶ 36,541 et seq.].

Footnote ¶ 3626 [¶ 36,081].
(1) Rev. Rul. 68-65, 1968-1 CB 555 [¶ 36,093(5)].
(2) U.S. v. Felt & Tarrant Mfg. Co., 283 US 269, 9 AFTR 1416 [¶ 36,085(5)].
(3) U.S. v. Andrews, 302 US 517, 58 SCt 315, 19 AFTR 1243; U.S. v. Garbutt Oil Co., 302 US 528, 58 SCt 320, 19 AFTR 1248 [¶ 36,613(5); 36,615(5)].
(4) Caswell v. U.S., 190 F. Supp. 591, 7 AFTR 2d 342 [¶ 36,616(30)].
(5) IRS release (IR-1603, 4-30-76) [¶ 54,678].

Footnote ¶ 3627 [¶ 36,041 et seq.; 36,170; 36,741 et seq.].
(1) Treas. Dept. booklet "Your Federal Income Tax" (1977 Ed.), p. 10.
(2) Rev. Rul. 54-425, 1954-2 CB 38 [¶ 36,170(5)].

Footnote ¶ 3628 [¶ 37,046 et seq.].
(1) Rev. Rul. 74-236, 1974-1 CB 348 [¶ 37,054(3)].
(2) IRS release (3-17-67).
(3) For guides on how to figure interest when the period that interest is payable is restricted under the law, see Rev. Proc. 60-17, 1960-2 CB 942 [¶ 37,027(30)].
(4) McDonald v. U.S., 18 AFTR 2d 5215 (DC Tenn., 6-13-66) [¶ 37,066(8)].
(5) Hanley v. U.S., 105 Ct Cl 638, 63 F. Supp. 73, 34 AFTR 694 [¶ 37,055(10)].
(6) Fortugno v. Comm., 16 AFTR 2d 5938, 353 F.2d 429, cert. denied 11-15-66 [¶ 37,046(10)].

Footnote ¶ 3629 [¶ 36,741 et seq.; 38,801 et seq.].
(1) Flora v. U.S., 78 SCt 1079, 1 AFTR 2d 1925; aff'd 5 AFTR 2d 1046 [¶ 38,804(5)].
(2) Kell-Strom Tool Co., Inc. v. U.S., 205 F. Supp. 190, 10 AFTR 2d 5237 [¶ 38,804(5)].
(3) Roybark v. U.S., 218 F.2d 164, 46 AFTR 1441 [¶ 38,809(5)].
(4) McKeesport Tin Plate Co. v. Heiner, 16 AFTR 169, 77 F.2d 756 [¶ 38,809(20)].
(5) Cullman Motor Co. Inc. v. Patterson, 6 AFTR 2d 5159 [¶ 36,094(10)].
(6) Register Publishing Co. v. U.S., 189 F. Supp. 626, 7 AFTR 2d 772 [¶ 36,747(20)].
(7) Rev. Proc. 57-12, 1957-1 CB 740 [¶ 36,747(20)].
(8) 28 USC Sec. 1346.
(9) 28 USC Sec. 1402.
(10) 28 USC Sec. 2402.

Footnote ¶ 3629 continued
- (11) Jurisdiction is discussed in Prentice-Hall Federal Taxes [¶ 38,840; 38,849].
- (12) U.S. v. C. C. Clark, Inc., 159 F.2d 489, 35 AFTR 801 [¶ 38,872(10)].
- (13) U.S. v. Wurts, 303 US 414, 20 AFTR 803 [¶ 36,749(5)].
- (14) U.S. v. C. & R. Investments, Inc., 28 AFTR 2d 71-5273, affg. 25 AFTR 2d 70-477, 310 F.Supp. 222 [¶ 36,749(15)].

Footnote ¶ 3630 [¶ 36,191 et seq.].
- (1) Instructions for Form 1139.

Footnote ¶ 3631 [¶ 33,141 et seq.].
- (1) Rev. Rul. 72-127, 1972-1 CB 268 [¶ 33,200(20)].
- (2) Rev. Rul. 68-152, 1968-1 CB 369 [¶ 33,191(30)].

Footnote ¶ 3635 [¶ 38,921 et seq.].

Footnote ¶ 3636 [¶ 39,121].

Footnote ¶ 3637 [¶ 36,631 et seq.; 38,936 et seq.].
- (1) Philbin, 26 TC 1159; Clarke, 27 TC 861 [¶ 38,940(10)].
- (2) Independent Life Ins. Co. of America, 17 BTA 757 [¶ 38,940(5)].
- (3) Holmes and Janes, Inc., 30 BTA 74 [¶ 38,940(30)].
- (4) Gutterman & Strauss Co., 1 BTA 243 [¶ 38,940(60)].
- (5) Troy Motor Sales Co., 14 BTA 545 [¶ 38,940(65)].
- (6) Baron, 1 BTA 15 [¶ 38,940(45)].
- (7) Gordon, H.A., Est. 47 TC 462 [¶ 35,665(5)].
- (8) Marcello v. Comm., 19 AFTR 2d 1707, 380 F.2d 494 [¶ 35,665(5)].
- (9) Buffalo Wills Sainte Claire Corp., 2 BTA 364 [¶ 39,147(55)].
- (10) Barry, 1 BTA 156 [¶ 38,940(55)].

Footnote ¶ 3638 [¶ 41,357].
- (1) Topps of Canada, Ltd., 36 TC 326 [¶ 41,357].

Footnote ¶ 3639 [¶ 39,141 et seq.].
- (1) Du Pasquier, 39 TC 854 [¶ 35,656(40)].
- (2) Joannou, 33 TC 868 [¶ 35,656(20)].
- (3) Chambers v. Lucas, 41 F.2d 299, 8 AFTR 10857 [¶ 35,656(50)].
- (4) Boccutto v. Comm., 5 AFTR 2d 1374, 277 F.2d 549; Tenzer v. Comm., 7 AFTR 2d 450, 285 F.2d 956 [¶ 35,656(55)].
- (5) Leventis, Jr., 49 TC 353 [¶ 39,371(30)].
- (6) Weaver v. Blair, 19 F.2d 16, 6 AFTR 6675; Reliance Mfg. Co. v. Blair, 19 F.2d 789, 6 AFTR 6745 [¶ 39,147(20)].

Footnote ¶ 3640 [¶ 39,146 et seq.].

Footnote ¶ 3641 [¶ 39,157].

Footnote ¶ 3642 [¶ 39,158 et seq.].

Footnote ¶ 3643 [¶ 39,168 et seq.].

Footnote ¶ 3644 [¶ 39,193 et seq.].

Footnote ¶ 3645 [¶ 39,197].

Footnote ¶ 3646 [¶ 39,241].

Footnote ¶ 3647 [¶ 39,191 et seq.].
- (1) Tankoos, W. G. Est., ¶ 67,008 P-H Memo TC [¶ 39,252(5)].

Footnote ¶ 3648 [¶ 39,216].
- (1) Bankers Pocahontas Coal Co. v. Burnet, 11 AFTR 1089, 287 U.S. 308 [¶ 39,217(10)].
- (2) Excelsior Motor Mfg. Supply Co. v. Comm. 43 F. 2d 968, 9 AFTR 211, [¶ 39,217(10)].

Footnote ¶ 3649 [¶ 39,271 et. seq.].
- (1) Lasky v. Comm., 352 US 1027, 52 AFTR 337 [¶ 39,202(5)].
- (2) **Kenner v. Comm. 21 AFTR 2d 391, 387 F.2d 689 [¶ 39,202(5)].**
- (3) Comm. v. Duberstein, 5 AFTR 2d 1626, 363 US 278; Imbesi v. Comm. 17 AFTR 2d 1241, 361 F.2d 640 [¶ 39,302(5), (40)].
- (4) Jack E. Golsen, 54 TC 742 [¶ 39,295(5)].

Highlights of Chapter 26
Assessment—Collection—Refunds

I. **Examination of Returns**
   A. **Examination procedure**—processed by electronic automatic data system [¶ 3601]:
      1. Preliminary examination—if mathematical error and [¶ 3601(a)]:
         a. Underpayment results—notice to taxpayer for amount due.
         b. Overpayment results—applied to future tax installments, credited or refunded.
         c. Third-party and "John Doe" summonses can be used for enforcement with certain restrictions.
      2. All returns subject to audit by specialized agents—returns selected both purposefully (income over specified level, unusual exemptions or expenses, etc.) and randomly [¶ 3601(b)].
      3. Taxpayer responsible for keeping adequate records [¶ 3601(c)].
   B. **Audit procedure**—may be either office audit or field audit [¶ 3602]:
      1. Taxpayer cooperation suggested (but if fraud charges possible, professional advice should be sought before releasing information) [¶ 3602(a)].
      2. Examiner's finding—deficiency indicated orally or by letter [¶ 3602(b)]:
         a. Taxpayer agrees—case generally closed with filing of Form 870 (consent to assessment of deficiency).
         b. Taxpayer disagrees—request district conference or apply for Appellate Division hearing.

II. **Procedure on Proposed Deficiency Assessment**
   A. **The district conference**—held in district office to discuss examiner's report [¶ 3603]:
      1. Certain issues involving $2,500 or less may be settled.
      2. Protests, briefs or statements filed 5 days before meeting.
      3. Procedure after audit [¶ 3603(a)]:
         a. Office audit—request conference; no formal protest.
         b. Field audit—cannot be arranged till 30-day letter received; formal protest needed when adjustment over $2,500.
      4. Presenting the case—conference decisions based on examiner's report, taxpayer's statements (or formal brief) and facts disclosed in conference [¶ 3603(b)].
      5. Taxpayer's action after conference [¶ 3603(c)]:
         a. Accept conferee's proposal and sign waiver.
         b. Disagree and receive copy of conference report and 30-day letter (if not already received).
         c. Disagree and request formal deficiency notice (90-day letter) allowing appeal to Tax Court, or pay tax, claim refund, and sue for recovery.
   B. **The 30-day letter**—form letter stating Revenue Service determination, taxpayer's appeal rights and 30-day limit to inform District Director of course of action [¶ 3604].
   C. **The 90-day letter**—formal notice of deficiency determined [¶ 3605]:
      1. Sent by registered or certified mail and received after:
         a. District conference, or
         b. Period allowed in 30-day letter if no Form 870 signed or protest filed, or
         c. Appellate Division hearing.
      2. Taxpayer has 90 days (150 days if outside U.S.) to petition Tax Court for redetermination of deficiency.
      3. Actual receipt not needed for assessment and collection if mailed to taxpayer's last known address.

4. Single joint notice allowed for joint return unless Commissioner notified of separate residences.
5. Fiduciary must give notice of fiduciary capacity (can be sent to taxpayer when no notice)—notice required in 10 days for following:
   a. Receiver or trustee in bankruptcy; qualified by appointment or authority to act (but not if Treasury Dept. notified under Bankruptcy Act),
   b. Receiver in receivership proceeding in any U.S. or state court; qualified by appointment, authority to act, or by taking possession of debtor's assets,
   c. Assignee for benefit of creditors; qualified on date of assignment.
6. What taxpayer can do [¶ 3605(a)]:
   a. Nothing—deficiency assessed at close of 90 (or 150) day period and referred to Collection Division.
   b. Sign Form 870 (thus limiting interest)—deficiency assessed and referred to Collection Division.
   c. Seek Appellate Division hearing or rehearing (does not extend time to petition Tax Court).
   d. File petition with Tax Court before 90 (or 150) days pass.
7. When deficiency assessed—when Tax Court decision final (if petition filed), but immediate assessment allowed when [¶ 3605(b)]:
   a. Insufficient payment due to mathematical or clerical error; abatement is allowed.
   b. Taxpayer signs waiver on Form 870.
   c. Jeopardy or termination assessment needed (if delay might prevent assessment or collection).
   d. Petition, appointment of receiver, or bankruptcy adjudication filed or approved.
   e. Tax is paid after deficiency notice mailed.
   f. Petition for review of Tax Court decision filed with Court of Appeals (unless bond filed with Tax Court).

D. **Waiver by taxpayer**—gives up right to deferral of assessment till after 90-day formal deficiency notice period ends [¶ 3606]:
1. Forms used:
   a. Income tax—Form 870.
   b. Estate tax—Form 890.
   c. Gift tax—Form 890a.
2. Stops the interest on deficiency for period from 30 days after waiver filed to date of notice and demand for payment.
3. Generally, does not bar refund claim or assessment, but provisions barring refund claims valid when inserted [¶ 3606(b)].

E. **The Appellate Division hearing**—generally, formal verified protest required for Appellate Division review [¶ 3607]:
1. Unagreed cases of $2,500 or less considered on written request after 30-day letter.
2. No hearing after 90-day letter issued, until Tax Court petition filed.
3. Hearing procedure—informal [¶ 3607(b)]:
   a. Facts established at district conferences not subject to review (except for settlement purposes).
   b. New facts must be submitted as affidavits.
4. Results of hearing [¶ 3607(c)]:
   a. If possible court appeal clearly favors IRS—no reduction of deficiency offered.
   b. If possible court appeal doubtful—deficiency reduction offered.
   c. When agreement—taxpayer signs Form 870-AD (offer of waiver that stops interest only 30 days after accepted).
   d. When disagreement—90-day letter issued.

F. **Agreements settling tax claims [¶ 3608]:**
1. Compromise—final settlement of liability and amounts paid not recoverable (except for mutual mistake, fraud or duress) [¶ 3608(a)]:

a. Interest and penalties as well as taxes can be compromised.
b. Offers made on Form 656 submitted with financial statement on Form 433.
c. If compromise amount not paid—original amount can be collected.
d. Occurs only when some doubt that taxpayer liable or that tax can be collected.
2. Closing agreements—settles complete liability (except when fraud, malfeasance or misrepresentation) [¶ 3608(b)]:
a. Forms 866 and 906 used.
b. Generally, used when concessions made on both sides, fiduciary desires discharge, or when corporation winding up affairs.

G. Appearance at tax proceedings [¶ 3609]:
1. Unenrolled persons may appear when:
a. Individual appearing on own behalf.
b. Full-time employee appearing for employer.
c. Corporate officer or partner appearing for corporation or partnership.
d. Fiduciaries (or full-time employee) appearing for entity they act for.
e. Properly authorized return preparers appearing for taxpayer they represent (but only before revenue agent or examining officer).
2. Enrolled persons:
a. Attorneys and certified public accountants filing declaration of current qualification appear for authorized clients.
b. Other persons apply for written examination (Form 2587) and, if successful, file for enrollment (Form 23)—receive permanent registration card [¶ 3608(a)].
3. Power of attorney required if client not present at proceeding (Form 2848) [¶ 3608(c)].
4. Tax information authorization to receive confidential information required if power of attorney not filed (Form 2848-D) [¶ 3608(d)].

III. Assessment and Collection of Tax
A. When tax must be assessed and collected—generally, within three years after return filed (but within six if taxpayer omitted amount over 25% of gross income stated on return) [¶ 3610]:
1. Tax assessed or collected after statute of limitations expired treated as overpayment.
2. False or fraudulent return filed with intent to evade tax, or no return filed—no limitation period for collection proceeding.
3. Interest on deficiency assessed and collected during period tax itself collected.
4. Suit to collect tax—within 6 years after timely assessment [¶ 3610(a)]:
a. Judgment against taxpayer does not change period for collection by levy.
b. Collection period extendable by written agreement before period ends.
c. Collection period extendable after period ends if levy made during period and extension agreed to before levy released.
d. Suit to collect without assessment—started within same period tax can be assessed.
5. When assessment period begins [¶ 3610(b)]:
a. Return filed before due date—generally, runs from due date.
b. "Late" joint return replacing separate returns filed:
1) On date last separate return filed, if both filed separate returns (but not before last date for filing of either).
2) On date of filing separate return, if only one filed and other spouse had less than $750 gross income (but not before last date for filing of separate).
3) On date of filing joint return, if only one filed and other spouse had $750 or more gross income.
c. Wrong return filed—limitation period starts with filing of wrong return (penalties for failure to file proper return or to pay tax still apply).
6. Gross income not reported—if more than 25% of gross income reported, assessment within 6 years after return filed [¶ 3610(c)].

7. Period for assessment or collection extendable by filing waiver Form 872 (872-A where Appellate Division consideration requested) [¶ 3610(d)].
8. Private foundations—for excise taxes, generally, within 3 years from date return filed [¶ 3610(e)].

B. **Special limitation periods [¶ 3611]:**
  1. Gain from sale of residence—period runs for three years from date taxpayer notifies IRS of [¶ 3611(a)]:
     a. Cost of buying new residence, or
     b. Intention not to, or failure to, buy new residence within required time.
  2. Involuntary conversion—when elect not to recognize gain, period runs from date taxpayer notifies IRS of [¶ 3611(b)]:
     a. Replacement of converted property,
     b. Intention not to replace, or
     c. Failure to replace within required time.
  3. Transferee liability [¶ 3611(c)]:
     a. Against first transferee—within one year after assessment time against owner expires.
     b. Property passes through several hands—within one year after assessment time against preceding holder expires (but not over 3 years after assessment time against original owner expires).
     c. Court proceeding begun before period ends extends period to one year after return of execution in court proceeding.
     d. Against fiduciary—within later of:
        1) One year after liability arises, or
        2) Period for collecting tax.
     e. Death or end of original owner does not change limits.
     f. Request for prompt assessment does not shorten limits.
     g. Transferor filed fraudulent return—no time limit.
  4. Personal holding company information—within 6 years for specified information [¶ 3611(d)].
  5. "Late" joint return—limitation period cannot end before one year after joint return actually filed [¶ 3611(e)].
  6. Deficiency on carryback of net operating loss, capital loss, disallowed oil and gas extraction taxes, investment credit, work incentive credit or foreign tax credit—time to assess measured from later year [¶ 3611(f)].
  7. Exploration expense—within 2 years after election or revocation [¶ 3611(g)].

C. **When assessment period is reduced [¶ 3612]:**
  1. Request for prompt assessment reduces period to 18 months (for return of decedent or decedent's estate or dissolved or dissolving corporation) [¶ 3612(a)].
  2. Termination assessment against taxpayer intending not to pay by departure from U.S. [¶ 3612(b)].
  3. Jeopardy assessment when taxpayer tries to avoid payment [¶ 3612(c)].
  4. Administrative and court review of termination and jeopardy assessments [¶ 3612(d)].
  5. Upon filing or approval of bankruptcy proceedings [¶ 3612(e)].

D. **When limitation period is suspended [¶ 3613]:**
  1. While taxpayer in combat zone.
  2. While deficiency notice issued and for 60 days after (but only if appealed) [¶ 3613(a)].
  3. While taxpayer's assets in control of court and for 6 months after [¶ 3613(b)].
  4. During period of wrongful levy (from date property taken till 30 days after returned or injunction against levy issued) [¶ 3613(d)].
  5. From start of bankruptcy or receivership proceeding till 30 days after receipt of fiduciary notice (but not over 2 years) [¶ 3613(e)].
  6. While period for payment of tax attributable to recovery of foreign expropriation loss extended [¶ 3613(f)].

7. For assessment or collection or excise or termination taxes on private foundations [¶ 3613(g)].
E. **Liability for tax of another taxpayer [¶ 3614]:**
   1. Transferred assets—generally, same as collection of deficiency [¶ 3614(a)]:
      a. Re-transfer after liability notice does not relieve liability, unless original transfer unknown.
      b. Transferee's liability limited to value of assets received.
   2. Parent liable for assessment against child [¶ 3614(b)].
F. **How tax is collected [¶ 3615]:**
   1. Distraint—levy on taxpayer's property generally after failure to pay within 10 days from notice and demand [¶ 3615(a)]:
      a. Must surrender levied property.
      b. Failure to surrender—liable for amount of tax up to value of property, plus costs, interest and possible 50% penalty.
      c. Surrender relieves person from liability to delinquent taxpayer with respect to property.
      d. Certain property exempt from levy.
   2. Collection by suit in U.S. District Court [¶ 3615(b)].
   3. Liens—federal tax is lien on all taxpayer's property [¶ 3615(c)].
   4. Set-off or counterclaim of overpayment owed taxpayer against liability taxpayer owes [¶ 3615(d)].
   5. Payroll deductions—Form 2159 used [¶ 3615(e)].
   6. Suit to prevent collection not allowed, except when [¶ 3615(f)]:
      a. 90-day letter not received and Form 870 not filed.
      b. Tax Court petition filed.
      c. Timely court appeal of jeopardy assessments.
      d. Clear that IRS could not win suit to collect tax and only injunction can protect taxpayer.

IV. **Penalties**
   A. **Kinds of penalties [¶ 3616]:**
      1. Generally, two classes:
         a. Ad valorem—added to and assessed as part of tax.
         b. Criminal—enforceable only by suit or prosecution.
      2. Also penalties imposed under "pay-as-you-go" collection and for failure to supply identifying number.
   B. **Penalties for failure to file returns [¶ 3617]:**
      1. Generally, 5% of net amount due if delay not more than one month, with additional 5% for each additional month or fraction (but not over 25% total).
      2. Imposed unless reasonable cause (generally, reliance upon advice of competent tax counsel) and no willful neglect shown.
      3. Reduced by penalty for failure to pay tax on time in months where both penalties applicable.
      4. Information returns [¶ 3617(b)]:
         a. $1 penalty ($1,000 maximum per person per calendar year) for late filing:
            1) Form 1099 for business payments.
            2) Form W-2 (with Form 941 for last quarter of year).
            3) Returns for foreign items.
         b. $10 penalty ($25,000 maximum per person per calendar year) for late filing of returns required for:
            1) Payment of interest, dividends or patronage dividends of $10 or more.
            2) Stock transferred under stock options.
            3) Employees' group-term life insurance.
            4) Same penalty for failure to give required statements to recipients of items.
         c. Exempt organizations and trusts:
            1) $10 a day penalty (up to $5,000) for late filing of certain required information returns.

2) Continued failure to file, after notice and demand—$10 a day (up to $5,000) on individual required to file.
   d. Private foundations—$1,000 penalty on manager of private foundation with $5,000 or more assets at any time in tax year for each willful failure to:
      1) File annual report (in addition to penalty for fraudulent report).
      2) Publish notice of availability for public inspection.
   e. Retirement plan administrators:
      1) $1-a-day penalty for failure to:
         (a) file registration statement.
         (b) notify Treasury Secretary of change in plan's status.
      2) $50 penalty for:
         (a) issuing false statements to employees.
         (b) failing to provide employees with required statements.
      3) $1,000 penalty for failure to file actuarial report.
      4) $10 penalty for failure to file required report for individual retirement account or annuity.
5. No penalty for failure to file individual declaration of estimated tax [¶ 3617(d)].

C. **Penalties for failure to pay tax [¶ 3618]:**
1. Interest charged—7% (9% between 7-1-75 and 1-31-76; 6% before 7-1-75) or an adjusted rate a year from due date until tax paid [¶ 3618(a)]:
   a. Payment due date determined without regard to any extension.
   b. Offsetting interest:
      1) No interest on deficiency if concurrent interest on refund due taxpayer.
      2) Offset by carryback of net operating loss, net capital loss, work incentive program credit or investment credit—interest runs from original tax due date to end of later tax year in which loss or credit arises.
   c. No interest on interest, but interest on assessable penalties, additional amounts or additions to tax if not paid within 10 days after notice and demand.
2. Penalty for failure to make timely payment—in addition to interest (above) [¶ 3618(b)]:
   a. Penalty is ½% of net amount due if failure not more than one month, with additional ½% for each additional month or fraction (up to 25%).
   b. Penalty does not apply:
      1) If failure due to reasonable cause.
      2) To failure to pay estimated tax.
3. Penalty for failure to pay deficiency without reasonable cause and within 10 days of notice and demand—same as penalty for failure to make timely payment [¶ 3618(c)]:
   a. Can also be applied to assessments from mathematical errors, but not estimated tax payments.
   b. Penalty for failure to file reduces this penalty.
4. Negligence and fraud penalty [¶ 3618(d)]:
   a. Deficiency due to negligence or intentional disregard of rules and regulations without intent to defraud—penalty is 5% of deficiency.
   b. Deficiency due to fraud—penalty is 50% of deficiency:
      1) Imposed in place of negligence penalty.
      2) If imposed, no penalty for failure to file return or pay tax imposed for same deficiency.
5. Payment with bad check (not tendered in good faith)—penalty is 1% of amount of check (if check less than $500—penalty is lesser of $5 or amount of check) [¶ 3618(e)].
6. Failure to deposit taxes—penalty is 5% of underpayment [¶ 3618(f)].
7. Excise taxes on private foundations—penalty is 100% of initial and additional taxes if:
   a. Violation both willful and flagrant, or

Highlights of Chapter 26

  b. Person was liable for such tax as to prior violation with same or another foundation.
  c. Penalty excused if reasonable cause for noncompliance.
 8. Special taxes on retirement plans—
  a. penalty of 5% stock (100% in some cases) for willful underfunding retirement plan [¶ 3618(h)].
  b. 6% penalty on excess contributions to:
   1) individual retirement accounts;
   2) self-employed plans.
  c. 10% penalty applies to premature withdrawals.
 9. Income tax preparers [¶ 3618(i)]:
  a. Understatement of taxpayer's liability:
   1) Willful, $500 per return.
   2) Negligent, $100 per return.
   3) If both apply, maximum $500 per return.
  b. Abatement applies if no understatement is found.
 10. 25% penalty tax on excess lobbying expenditures by public charities [¶ 3618(j)].

D. Penalty for underpayment of corporation estimated tax [¶ 3619]:
 1. 7% (9% between 7-1-55 and 1-31-76; 6% before 7-1-75) or an adjusted rate [¶ 3628] a year on underpayment until paid or until filing date of tax return (whichever earlier).
 2. Underpayment exists if:
  a. Final tax return for year shows tax actually paid less than 80% of amount should have been paid, or
  b. No return filed, less than 80% of actual tax for year.
 3. Can be assessed and collected without deficiency notice except when no return filed.
 4. Figured for each installment date on difference between amount paid and amount should have been paid.

E. Criminal penalties [¶ 3620].

V. Refund and Credits

A. Overpayment of tax—can be refunded or credited [¶ 3621].

B. Refund claims—generally, three classes [¶ 3622]:
 1. Taxes aid on original returns.
 2. Overpayments through withholding or estimated tax [¶ 3622(a)]:
  a. Individual—elect to refund or credit to next year's tax.
  b. Corporate overpayment of estimated tax—actual payment must exceed estimate by 10% and $500:
   1) Apply for adjustment on Form 4466 within 2½ months after year end.
   2) 7% (9% between 7-1-75 and 1-31-76; 6% before 7-1-75) or an adjusted rate [¶ 3628] a year addition to tax imposed on excessive adjustment computed from time of adjustment to return due date.
   3) If application denied—can claim credit or refund.
 3. Payment of assessed deficiency—file refund claim and, if rejected, sue to recover [¶ 3622(b)].
 4. Appeal of deficiency notice—no refund, credit or suit for recovery allowed, unless [¶ 3622(c)]:
  a. Overpayment determined by finalized Tax Court decision.
  b. Amount collected above amount determined by Tax Court decision.
  c. Amount collected after period for levy or suit for collection expired.

C. Time for filing refund claims—generally, within 3 years of time return filed (if filed before due date—3 years from due date) [¶ 3623]:
 1. Considered filed on postmark date.
 2. Two-year limitation exception—within 2 years from time tax paid, if 2-year period ends later than 3-year period [¶ 3623(b)]:
  a. Estimated tax and tax withheld at source considered paid on return due date (without extensions).

b. Income tax withheld on wages considered paid on 15th of fourth month after tax year.
c. Day tax paid not counted in determining 2-year period.
3. Time extended by waiver Form 872 if filed before refund claim period expires [¶ 3623(c)].

D. **Special periods for filing refund claims [¶ 3624]:**
1. Bad debts and worthless securities deduction—within 7 years from return due date [¶ 3624(a)]:
   a. Effect on carryover—same period as above.
   b. Effect on carryback—within 7 years from return due date for year net operating loss resulted in carryback, *or* within period for net operating loss carryback (whichever ends later).
2. Carrybacks of investment credit, work incentive program credit, net operating loss, or capital loss allow refund claim filing through 15th day of 40th month (39th month for corporation) after tax years in which credit earned or loss incurred [¶ 3624(b)].
3. Taxes paid or credited [¶ 3624(c)]:
   a. Claim arises from payment of foreign taxes—period is 10 years from return due date.
   b. Overpayment claimed as credit against following year estimated tax:
      1) Treated as payment for year estimated tax paid.
      2) Limitation period starts to run with second year.
4. Retirement plans—limitation period begins one year after recaptured amount is paid [¶ 3624(d)].

E. **Amount of refund limited**—cannot exceed portion of tax paid within 3 years (or 2 years, if exception applies) preceding filing of claim [¶ 3625].

F. **Form of refund claim [¶ 3626]:**
1. For overpayment of income taxes:
   (a) Original tax return
   (b) Amended tax returns:
      1) Form 1040X for individuals
      2) Form 1120X for corporations
2. Form 843 used for refund of other taxes, interest, penalties, etc.

G. **Filing the refund claim**—filed at service center for district where tax paid (if hand-delivered—at office of District Director) [¶ 3627]:
1. Administrative procedure—generally, same as cases involving deficiency determination [¶ 3627(a)].
2. Decision on claim [¶ 3627(b)]:
   a. In favor of taxpayer—certificate of overassessment issued and credited against any taxes owed with balance refunded.
   b. Against taxpayer—can sue to recover.

H. **Interest on refunds**—generally, 7% (9% between 7-1-75 and 1-31-76; 6% before 7-1-75) or an adjusted rate set by Treasury Secretary a year from date of overpayment to date fixed by IRS (not more than 30 days before refund check date) [¶ 3628]:
1. No interest if made within 45 days after return due date (if filed on or before due date) or after late return filed.
2. Overpayment credited against later assessed deficiency [¶ 3628(a)]:
   a. Interest from date of overpayment to due date of deficiency.
   b. Penalties offset against overpayment before interest computed.
3. No review of interest allowed, unless fraud or mathematical mistake [¶ 3628(b)].
4. Special interest provisions for carrybacks, deposits and excessive withholding or estimated tax [¶ 3628(c)].

I. **Suit to recover tax**—only if refund claim filed and entire tax (including deficiency, but not interest) paid [¶ 3629]:
1. Taxpayer has burden of proof.

Highlights of Chapter 26

2. When to file—only after 6 months from refund claim filing date (unless decision on claim made before then) and before end of 2 years from mailing date on notice disallowing claim [¶ 3627(a)]:
   a. 2-year limit extendable for any period agreed on in writing.
   b. Written waiver (Form 2297) of disallowance notice mailing requirement starts 2-year limit on date waiver filed.
3. If deficiency notice issued before case heard—taxpayer's suit stayed for 90-day appeal period, plus additional 60 days [¶ 3629(c)].
4. Appeal from District Court to U.S. Court of Appeals [¶ 3629(d)]:
   a. No appeal from Court of Claims decision, except to U.S. Supreme Court.
   b. Refund suit decision is res judicata as to subsequent proceedings involving same claim and same year.
5. Recovery of refunds paid—U.S. can sue to recover erroneous refund by [¶ 3629(e)]:
   a. Suit begun within 2 years after refund (5 years if fraud or material misrepresentation).
   b. Suit for recovery by deficiency collection procedure (subject to 6-year limitation period).
6. Special rule for private foundation excise taxes [¶ 3629(f)].

J. **Quick refunds for carrybacks [¶ 3630]:**
1. Application on Forms 1139 (corporations) and 1045 (other taxpayers) [¶ 3630(a)].
2. Generally amounts in application credited or refunded by later of [¶ 3630(b)]:
   a. 90 days from last day of month when tax return due (including filing extensions), or
   b. 90 days from time application filed.
3. Time to pay corporate tax extended—if net operating loss carryback expected [¶ 3630(c)]:
   a. Apply on Form 1138.
   b. Extension based on estimates of reduction carryback will make payment extended only for amount of anticipated refund.
   c. Extension ends on:
      1) Last day of month when return due for tax year of expected loss, or
      2) Date notice of refund application action mailed (if quick refund procedure followed).
   d. Deferred amount bears interest at 7% (9% between 7-1-75 and 1-31-76; 6% before 7-1-75) or an adjusted rate [¶ 3628].

K. **When limitation periods do not apply**—adjustment by refund or additional assessment allowed after limitation period expired when [¶ 3631]:
1. Inconsistent determination required—determination in later year inconsistent with treatment in year barred by statute of limitations [¶ 3631(a)]:
   a. Double inclusion of income.
   b. Double deduction.
   c. Double exclusion of gross income.
   d. Treatment of deductions or credits of affiliated corporations.
   e. Determination of property basis.
   f. Treatment of item as to trust and fiduciary or beneficiary.
2. Relief without inconsistent determination [¶ 3631(b)]:
   a. Deduction or credit disallowed.
   b. Unreported income.

VI. The United States Tax Court

A. **What the Tax Court does**—court of record with own rules of practice and procedure and own forms [¶ 3635]:
1. Place of trial—anywhere in U.S. [¶ 3635(a)].
2. Proving a case—burden of proof on petitioner [¶ 3635(b)].

3. Small tax case procedure—simplified procedures where neither disputed deficiency nor claimed overpayment exceeds $1,500, including additions, for tax year [¶ 3635(c)].
4. Declaratory judgment petitions for:
   a. qualification of retirement plans or amendments to them [¶ 3635(d)].
   b. determination of exempt status or classification [¶ 3625(e)].
   c. determination of purpose in transferring property from U.S. [¶ 3635(f)].

B. **Appearance before Tax Court [¶ 3636]:**
   1. Individual may appear on own behalf.
   2. Corporate officer, partnership member or fiduciary acting for an estate or trust may appear for that entity.
   3. Tax practitioner must be admitted to practice [¶ 3636(a)].

C. **Jurisdiction of Tax Court**—hears appeals of notice of deficiency or liability of income, estate or gift tax, excise taxes on private foundations and employment taxes. [¶ 3637]:
   1. Considers appeals involving constitutional questions, closing agreements, fraud penalties and statute of limitations [¶ 3637(a)].
   2. Limited to issues raised in petition, pleadings and evidence.
   3. Not limited to issues raised before Revenue Service [¶ 3637(d)].
   4. Petition brought by and in name of person to whom deficiency or liability notice directed (or fiduciary).
   5. Papers other than the petition can be served between the parties if the originals are first filed with the clerk [¶ 3637(f)].

D. **Authority of regulations**—bound by IRS regulations unless found unreasonable and inconsistent with Code [¶ 3638].

E. **How proceeding begins**—by filing petition [¶ 3639]:
   1. Within 90 days (150 days for taxpayers not in U.S. or estate of decedent dying abroad) after deficiency or liability notice mailed [¶ 3639(a)]:
      a. Court cannot extend time.
      b. Day deficiency notice mailed not counted, but day petition filed is counted.
      c. Considered filed on time when mailed and postmark date within prescribed time.
   2. Should request nearby place for hearing [¶ 3639(b)].
   3. $10 filing fee [¶ 3639(c)].

F. **The petition [¶ 3640]:**
   1. Form—may be prepared by any process provided information in clear and legible type, and in accordance with Form "1" [¶ 3640(a)].
   2. Contents—must have caption showing name of petitioner, body of numbered paragraphs, signature and in some cases a verification [¶ 3640(b)].
   3. Copy of deficiency or liability notice must be attached.

G. **Commissioner's answer [¶ 3641]:**
   1. Filing—60 days after service of petition to file answer (or 45 days to file motions in respect to petition) [¶ 3641(a)].
   2. Contents—must fully advise of nature of defense and specifically admit or deny each material statement of fact in petition or indicate lack of knowledge or information about any allegation. [¶ 3641(b)].

H. **Petitioner's reply [¶ 3642]:**
   1. Filing—45 days after service of answer to file reply (or 30 days for motions on answer) when answer alleges material facts [¶ 3642(a)].
   2. Contents—must specifically admit or deny each material allegation and state supporting facts. Lack of knowledge as to the truth of an allegation must be asserted. Mere denial to special matters, such as res judicata, etc., is not sufficient to raise the issue. [¶ 3642(b)].

I. **Amended or supplemental pleadings [¶ 3643]:**
   1. Amendments allowed anytime before responsive pleading served [¶ 3643(a)].

2. Supplemental pleadings are allowed even if original pleading is defective [¶ 3643(b)].
3. Amendments conforming pleadings to proof are allowed but only if the party objecting to their admission would not be prejudiced by their admission [¶ 3643(c)].
4. Filing is with the Court at the trial, or with the Clerk at Washington, D.C. within time fixed by court [¶ 3643(d)].

J. Judgment without trial [¶ 3644]:
1. Motion granted for judgment on pleadings or for summary judgment can dispose of the case before trial.
2. Summary judgment motion can be made anytime starting 30 days after the pleadings are closed.

K. Time and place for hearing—fixed by court upon joinder of issue [¶ 3645]:
1. Postponement possible [¶ 3645(a)].
2. Discovery procedures are used to obtain information from the other party either through informal consultation or communication or through formal procedures as written interrogatories and production of documents or things. In no event may depositions be used as a discovery device. Formal procedures must be completed within 75 days of trial date [¶ 3645(b)].
3. Admission requests are served on the other party under the discovery rules and failure to reply within a reasonable time (usually 30 days) after service will be treated as an admission [¶ 3645(c)].
4. Pre-trial conference—usually to stipulate undisputed facts [¶ 3645(d)].

L. How to take depositions [¶ 3646]:
1. By written interrogation (unusual) or oral examination of witness by both parties.
2. Application to take deposition filed with court by 45 days before trial date.

M. The Tax Court hearing—follows formal trial court procedure [¶ 3647]:
1. Burden of proof in matters covered by deficiency notice is on taxpayer [¶ 3647(a)].
2. After argument and rebuttal—either briefs filed or rehearing granted (rare) [¶ 3647(b), (c)].
3. Briefs, or quasi-briefs advisable at various stages of case [¶ 3647(d)].

N. The Tax Court Report—contains findings of fact and opinion, but is not court *decision* [¶ 3648]:
1. Decision, usually entered immediately after publication of Report (unless Rule 155 followed), is specific order that:
   a. Finds amount of deficiency,
   b. Finds there is no deficiency, or
   c. Dismisses the case for any reason.
2. Rule 155—court directs parties to compute liability in light of court opinion; but if no agreement, judge decides [¶ 3648(a)].
3. Procedure after decision [¶ 3648(b)]:
   a. Petitioner satisfied—file determination of result under Rule 155 within 30 days of serving of Report.
   b. Petitioner dissatisfied—file notice of appeal within 90 days after decision entered.

O. Review of Tax Court decision [¶ 3649]:
1. Tax Court cannot set aside or change decision once final.
2. Decisions reviewable by Courts of Appeal [¶ 3649(a)].
3. Findings of facts binding unless clearly erroneous.
4. Appeal from decision does not stay assessment or collection unless bond filed [¶ 3649(b)].

Chapter 27

FOREIGN INCOME—FOREIGN TAXPAYERS

TABLE OF CONTENTS

¶

CREDIT FOR FOREIGN TAXES

Who can take foreign tax credit	3701
How to get the credit	3702
Limitations on credit	3703
Limits applicable	
Foreign tax carryover and carryback	
Adjustment to credit for foreign tax refund	3705
Credit for corporate shareholders in foreign corporations	3706

FOREIGN TAXPAYERS

How foreign taxpayers are taxed	3707
Resident aliens	3708
Nonresident aliens	3709
Foreign corporations	3710
Income taxed at U.S. rates	3711
Effectively connected U.S. source income	
Effectively connected foreign source income	

¶

What is U.S. source income	3712

TAX TREATIES

Tax treaty provisions	3720

U.S. INCOME FROM FOREIGN SOURCES

Earned income of citizens from sources outside the U.S.	3725
Allowances to U.S. Government officers and employees in foreign service	3726
Income from sources in U.S. possessions	3727
U.S. citizens	
Domestic corporations	
Exclusion for residents of Puerto Rico	
Special rules on foreign investments	3728

• Highlights of Chapter 27 .... Page 3761

CREDIT FOR FOREIGN TAXES

¶ 3701 Who can take foreign tax credit. A U.S. citizen or domestic corporation can elect to take either a credit or a deduction (but not both [Sec. 1.901(c)]) for the amount of income, war profits and excess profits taxes (or any tax in lieu of such taxes) paid or accrued during the tax year to a foreign country or U.S. possession [Sec. 901, 903; 1.901-1(a), 1.903-1(a)]. Resident aliens are allowed the credit but can be barred from taking the credit for taxes paid or accured to their native country by presidential proclamation that the alien's country does not grant a similar credit to U.S. citizens residing there [Sec. 901; 1.901-1]. Nonresident aliens and foreign corporations can take the same credit against the tax on U.S. business income, but not against other income, and only for taxes paid or accrued to a foreign country or U.S. possession on income effectively connected with a U.S. business (¶ 3711) [Sec. 906]. Partnerships apportion the credit for foreign taxes among the individual partners, estates among the beneficiaries [Sec. 901(b); 1.901-1(a)(1)].

Any taxpayer who takes the earned income exclusion on income from sources outside the U.S. cannot also elect a foreign tax credit for foreign taxes paid on amounts excluded from gross income. This rule applies to tax years starting after 1975 (¶ 3725) [Sec. 911(a)].

Participation in international boycott. The foreign tax credit, (as well as the benefits of DISC and deferral of earnings of foreign subsidiaries), generally will be denied any taxpayer agreeing to participate in or cooperate with an international boycott based on race, nationality or religion [Sec. 999]. The denial applies to

Footnotes appear at end of this Chapter.

¶ 3701

those operations which require participation in the boycott. A taxpayer participates in or cooperates with an international boycott if the taxpayer: (1) agrees not to do business in a country which is the object of a boycott, or with a U.S. person engaged in business within that country; (2) agrees not to do business with a company whose ownership or management is made up of individuals of a certain religion, race, or nationality; (3) agrees not to employ individuals of a certain religion, race, or nationality; or (4) agrees not to transport goods on carriers owned or operated by persons not participating in the boycott [Sec. 999(b)(3)]. Under certain limited circumstances, a taxpayer may be allowed to cooperate with an international boycott if sanctioned by U.S. law [Sec. 999(b)(4)].

A taxpayer participating in an international boycott will have the foreign tax credit and other above named benefits reduced by the amount of that benefit which resulted from taxation by countries associated with carrying out a boycott [Sec. 999(c)]. The Revenue Service has issued procedures for determining participation in a boycott.[1]

¶ 3702 **How to get the credit.** An individual must file Form 1116 to get the credit [Sec. 36]. Corporations file Form 1118. A bond (Form 1117) may be required if the foreign tax has not yet been paid [Sec. 1.905-4]. The election made applies to every foreign tax, but the taxpayer can change his election any time before the time to file a claim for credit or refund expires (generally three years [¶ 3623]) for the year the choice is made [Sec. 901(a); 1.901-1(d)]. If a carryback or carryover is involved [¶ 3703(b)], the period is measured from the year from which the excess taxes may be carried.[1]

Ordinarily, a taxpayer on the cash basis takes the credit for foreign taxes in the year they are paid; a taxpayer on the accrual basis for the year accrued. However, a cash basis taxpayer can elect to take the credit for the year the taxes accrue. Double credit for taxes actually paid and taxes accrued can be taken for the year the election is made.[2] The election is binding for all later years [Sec. 905(a); 1.905-1(a)]. If foreign taxes actually paid differ from the amount accrued, the Revenue Service should be notified so the tax can be redetermined [Sec. 905(c); 1.905-3].

> NOTE: A special provision allows a domestic corporation to change prior tax credit elections when it elects to exclude recovery of foreign expropriation losses [¶ 2316(d)] from income [Sec. 1351(d)(3)].

The credit is figured in U.S. dollars.[3] A cash method taxpayer uses the rate of exchange on the date the foreign tax is paid to find the amount of the credit. An accrual basis taxpayer uses the exchange rate in effect on the last day of his tax year.[4] If the credit is for tax paid on dividends received from a foreign corporation, at least 10% of whose stock is owned by the recipient [¶ 3706], the above rules do not apply. The rate of exchange used is the one in effect on the date the foreign subsidiary declares the dividends; not the date the foreign tax is paid.[5]

¶ 3703 **Limitations on credit.** (a) **Limits applicable.** For tax years beginning after 1975, taxpayers generally are required to compute the limitation on the amount of foreign tax that can be used to reduce U.S. tax under the *overall* limitation [Sec. 904(a)]. The taxpayer, in effect, combines taxes paid to foreign countries and U.S. possessions. The credit cannot exceed that proportion of the U.S. tax which U.S. taxable income from sources within that country bears to the entire U.S. taxable income for the same year.

> NOTE: For tax years beginning before 1-1-76, taxpayers were required to compute the limitation on the per-country basis unless they specifically elected the overall limitations. A transitional period has been established for certain mining ventures generating income from foreign sources which still may use the per-country limitation for tax years beginning before 1-1-79 [P.L. 94-455].

The limitation as to interest, as well as to foreign source DISC dividends, must be computed separately from the limitation for all other foreign income [Sec. 904(d)]. These rules do not apply to the following: interest from active conduct of a trade or business (for example, interest on accounts receivable) or from obligations received when the business is disposed of; interest from a banking or financing business; interest received from a corporation if the taxpayer, or one of the members of an affiliated group [¶ 3222] that includes the taxpayer, owns (directly or indirectly) at least 10% of the voting stock; interest from obligations received when the owner of at least 10% of voting stock disposes of the stock or other corporate obligations [Sec. 904(d); 1.904-4]. Special rules apply to the treatment of excess investment interest (¶ 1906) [Prop. Reg. Sec. 1.58-7(b)(2)]. The limit on the amount of foreign tax on "foreign oil and gas extraction income" that may be taken into account for credit is: 52.8% for 1975, 50.4% for 1976, and 48% for 1977 and later years. For tax years ending after 1974, there is no foreign tax credit for payments to a foreign government for oil in place (though payments not allowed as credit are allowed as deductions[1]), if: (1) the taxpayer has no economic interest, and (2) the oil is purchased or sold at a price other than the market price [Sec. 907].

NOTE: Excess foreign tax credits attributable to the percentage depletion allowance [¶ 2104] on foreign mineral income cannot reduce the U.S. tax payable on other foreign income [Sec. 901(e); 1.901-3].

Example: Bellis, Inc., a domestic corporation, had income of $50,000 from the U.S., $50,000 from country X and $50,000 from country Y. Bellis paid a tax of $19,000 to X and $21,000 to Y on the income from those countries. The 1977 tax would be figured as follows:

Taxable income from the U.S.	$50,000	
Taxable income from X	50,000	
Taxable income from Y	50,000	$150,000
U.S. tax before credits:		
Normal tax:		
20% × $25,000	$ 5,000	
plus 22% × $25,000	5,500	
Surtax [48% × ($150,000 − $50,000)]	48,000	
U.S. tax before credits		$ 58,500
Limitation for X and Y combined ($100,000/$150,000 × $58,500)		39,000
Net tax payable		$ 19,500

Special limitations apply for taxes paid or accrued by Western Hemisphere trade corporations that are members of a group of affiliated corporations filing a consolidated return [Sec. 1503(b)].

Other rules. For an individual, estate or trust, taxable income is figured without personal exemption deductions [Sec. 1.904-1(b)]. On a joint return, the credit is applied against the total taxes of the spouses, and the limitation is figured on the total taxable income (without exemption deductions) of both spouses. The taxable income of nonresident aliens and foreign corporations is treated as consisting only of income "effectively connected" with a U.S. business (¶ 3711) [Sec. 906(b)]. The credit cannot be taken against the tax for improper accumulations of earnings [¶ 3130 et seq.], the personal holding company tax [¶ 3400 et seq.], or the minimum tax on tax preference items [¶ 2403].

(b) Foreign tax carryover and carryback. If the tax paid or accrued to foreign countries exceeds the overall limitation [(a) above], the excess may be carried back and taken as a credit in each of the 2 preceding years, and carried forward and taken as a credit in each of the 5 following years. The total credit (that is, the tax for the year plus the carryback or carryover), cannot exceed the limitation for that year. The credit is first carried to the earliest year and then to the next earliest year [Sec. 904(c)]. Nonresident aliens and foreign corporations cannot carry an excess credit to or from a tax year beginning before 1967 [Sec. 906].

> **NOTE:** When the foreign tax credit for interest which must be computed separately exceeds the limitation for interest, the excess is a separate interest carryback or carryover [Sec. 1.904-4(d), (e)].

Carryovers from tax years beginning before 1-1-76, during which the taxpayer was on the per-country limitation, to tax years beginning after 12-31-75, during which the taxpayer is required to be on the overall limitation, are permitted if under the per-country limitation, the taxpayer had excess credits from one or more countries which could be carried forward. The use of these excess credits is limited in that they may be used only to the extent they would have been used had the per-country limitation continued to apply. The amount of credits in the current year computed under the per-country limitation attributable to a specific country from prior years cannot exceed the amount of credits if computed under the overall limitation. If this occurs, the amount of carryovers which may be used as credits are reduced to the amount allowed under the overall limitation [Sec. 904(e)(2)].

Carrybacks from tax years beginning after 12-31-75 to tax years beginning before 1-1-76, when taxpayer was on the per-country limitation, are allowed if, under the rules applicable to overall limitation, any excess credits have arisen in the current year which are available to be carried back. If such a situation exists, the taxpayer must make a computation for the current year to determine if any excess credits would exist under the per-country limitation. If excess credits arise from any country, they can be carried back. The credits are carried back to those years in which excess credits could have been used under the per-country limitation [Sec. 904(e)(3)].

There is no carryback or carryover to a year foreign tax is deducted. A timely election to take a credit for foreign taxes must be made for the year to which the excess is to be carried.[2] For interest on refunds, see ¶ 3628.

(c) Treatment of capital gains from foreign sources. The treatment of income from the sale of capital assets outside the U.S., for purposes of computing the overall limitation, is subject to the following rules [Sec. 904(b)]:

(1) Net U.S. capital losses will offset net foreign capital gains, thus rendering the foreign gain not includable for purposes of computing the overall limitation [Sec. 904(b)(3)].

(2) For corporations, only 30/48ths of the net long-term gain from foreign sources is includable in the computation of the limitation [Sec. 904(b)(2)(A)].

The rules in (1) and (2) apply to tax years beginning after 1975.

(3) Generally, the gain on a sale or exchange of personal property by an individual or corporation outside the U.S. will be considered U.S. source income if the country in which the transaction occurs does not impose a tax equal to at least 10% of the gain [Sec. 904(b)(3)(C)]. This rule does not apply to sales within an individual's country of residence, nor to sales by corporations which meet certain gross income tests. This rule applies to sales or exchanges after 11-12-75.

(d) Recapture of foreign losses. Losses from foreign operations which have served to reduce U.S. tax are subject to recapture when the U.S. company subsequently derives income from abroad. Generally, the recapture is accomplished by treating a portion of foreign income derived in tax years following the loss year, as income from domestic sources. The amount of foreign income so treated is limited to the lesser of the amount of loss or 50% of the foreign taxable income for the year, or such larger percent as the taxpayer may choose [Sec. 904(f)(1)].

Foreign losses include any amounts by which the gross income from sources without the U.S. is exceeded by the sum of expenses, losses, and other deductions allocated to foreign sources and a ratable part of any expenses, losses, or other deductions which cannot definitely be allocated to some item or class of gross income [Sec. 904(f)(2)]. In computing the amount of foreign loss, the net operating loss deduction, capital loss carrybacks and carryovers to that year, foreign expropriation losses, and casualty and theft losses are not taken into account.

There is recapture of a loss on business property used predominantly outside the U.S. which is disposed of prior to the time the loss is recaptured under the general rules. The taxpayer is treated as having a recognized gain in the year he disposes of the property. The gain is the excess of the fair market value of the property disposed over the taxpayer's adjusted basis in the property. In such cases, 100% of the gain (to the extent of losses not previously recaptured) is recaptured [Sec. 904(f)(3)].

¶ 3705 **Adjustment to credit for foreign tax refund.** A taxpayer must inform the Revenue Service when he gets a refund of foreign taxes after he took a credit for them. Any foreign tax on the refund reduces the refund amount. It cannot be deducted or used for a credit. The tax is then redetermined. If the redetermination results in a deficiency, interest on the deficiency before the date of the refund is limited to the interest received with the refund[1] [Sec. 905(c); 1.905-3]. An annual interest is charged from the date of the refund until the deficiency is paid.[2]

¶ 3706 **Credit for corporate shareholders in foreign corporations.** A domestic corporation that owns at least 10% of the voting stock of a foreign corporation can get a tax credit for foreign taxes the foreign corporation paid on its "accumulated profits." The basic requirement is that the domestic corporation receive a dividend paid out of the accumulated profits. The domestic corporation is treated as having paid a portion of the taxes the foreign corporation paid [Sec. 902(a); 1.902-1(a)]. If the foreign corporation in turn owns 10% or more of the voting stock of a second foreign corporation, a part of the second corporation's foreign tax on its accumulated profits is attributed to the domestic corporation when the first foreign corporation receives a dividend from the second foreign corporation (after 1-12-71) [Sec. 902(b)]. The first foreign corporation is then treated as having paid part of the second foreign corporation's foreign tax, and this amount is included in figuring the tax attributed to the domestic corporation. In the same way, if the second foreign corporation owns 10% or more of the voting stock of a third foreign corporation and receives dividends from the third corporation after 1-12-71, part of the third corporation's foreign tax is attributed to the domestic corporation. For a second-tier corporation, the foreign tax credit is not available to a domestic corporation unless its percentage ownership in the first-tier corporation multiplied by the first-tier corporation's percentage of ownership in the second-tier corporation equals 5%. Similarly, a domestic corporation cannot claim the credit resulting from foreign taxation of a third-tier corporation unless its ownership percentage in the first-tier corporation, and the ownership percentage of the first-tier corporation in the second-tier corporation, and the percentage of ownership of the second-tier corporation in the third-tier corporation, when multiplied together, equal or exceed 5 percent [Sec. 902(b)]. These rules generally apply to any distribution received by a domestic corporation after 1977. However, they also apply to distribution received for tax years beginning after 1975 if made out of accumulated profits of a foreign corporation.

> NOTE: The foreign tax credit allowed a corporation receiving dividends from a foreign corporation with less than 20% of its gross income from U.S. sources will not be affected by the special depreciation rule on computing earnings and profits[1] (¶ 2024) [Sec. 312(m)(3)].

Footnotes appear at end of this Chapter.

A domestic corporation that claims the credit must include in its gross income, not only the dividend itself, but also the tax attributable to the dividend from a 10% owned foreign corporation. This is sometimes referred to as a "dividend gross-up."

NOTE: Foreign corporate stockholders are also entitled to this credit for foreign corporation dividends received that are effectively connected with the stockholder's U.S. business [¶ 3711]. The credit applies only to U.S. tax on the foreign corporation's business income [Sec. 906(b)(4)].

(a) **Accumulated profits.** The amount of a foreign corporation's accumulated profits is determined by its gains, profits, and income computed without reduction for foreign taxes on income, war profits, and excess taxes [Sec. 902(c)]. Generally, for tax years beginning after 1975 dividends from less developed country corporations are treated the same as dividends from other foreign countries. The District Director can decide from what year's profits dividends are paid. Dividends are treated as paid from the latest accumulation. But those paid in the first 60 days of any tax year are related to the profits of the preceding year, unless the Director is satisfied they belong to a different year [Sec. 1.902-1(a)(2)].

(b) **How to find the credit.** The amount of foreign tax considered to have been paid by the domestic corporation is determined by the ratio of the dividend received to the "accumulated profits" in excess of foreign taxes [Sec. 902(a)(1)].

The credit derived from its foreign subsidiary is included with any other foreign tax credit the domestic corporation may have, to find its credit limitation for the year [¶ 3703]. The credit is reduced if the domestic corporation fails to file information returns required for controlled foreign corporations [¶ 3540]. The domestic corporation can also get a tax credit related to undistributed earnings of a controlled foreign corporation that it must include in income as dividends [¶ 3728].

NOTE: When a domestic corporation receives a dividend from a foreign corporation, more than half of whose income is effectively connected with a U.S. business [¶ 3711], the foreign tax credit does not apply to dividends eligible for the dividends received deduction (¶ 3114(c)) [Sec. 861(a)(2)(B)].

FOREIGN TAXPAYERS

¶ **3707 How foreign taxpayers are taxed.** Business income of nonresident aliens and foreign corporations is taxed at the same rate as the business income of domestic taxpayers, and their investment income is taxed at a 30% rate. The general rules for taxing these taxpayers are as follows:

1. All income from U.S. sources [¶ 3712] and certain types of income from foreign sources [¶ 3711(b)] are subject to U.S. tax.
2. The U.S. and foreign income that is "effectively connected with the conduct of a U.S. trade or business" [¶ 3711] is taxed basically the same as business income is taxed to domestic taxpayers.
3. The remaining U.S. income—investment income—is taxed at a flat 30% rate (unless the investments are effectively connected with the U.S. business [¶ 3711(a)]). This usually allows investment income to be taxed at a lower rate, and thus encourages investment in the U.S. by foreigners.
4. Expatriates from the U.S. may be subject to U.S. tax on all U.S. source income if they relinquished their citizenship to avoid tax [¶ 3709(c)].

Tax treaties. A foreign taxpayer from a country that has a tax treaty with the U.S. may get special tax treatment for various income items [¶ 3720].

If a foreign country discriminates against U.S. citizens or corporations, the U.S., by proclamation of the President, can double the U.S. tax rate (up to 80% of taxable income) for citizens and corporations of the foreign country or impose the same discriminatory tax on the U.S. income of citizens and corporations of the offending country. The President can also proclaim that the income of certain nonresident aliens and foreign corporations will be taxed according to the law before it was amended by the Foreign Investors Act if the taxes their native country imposes on U.S. citizens are more burdensome than the foreigner's U.S. tax on the same type of income [Sec. 891, 896].

¶ **3708 Resident aliens.** With some exceptions ((b) below), resident aliens are taxed the same as U.S. citizens [Sec. 1.871-1]. Generally, filing and paying taxes are also the same as for U.S. citizens [¶ 3517; 3522; 3827].

(a) Who is a resident alien. An alien actually present in the U.S. who is not a mere transient or sojourner is considered a resident. Whether he is a transient is determined by his intentions regarding the length and nature of his stay in the U.S. [Sec. 1.871-2(b)]. If he lives in the U.S. and has no definite intention as to his stay, he is a resident.

The question of whether an alien is a resident arises primarily with transients who are in the U.S. only for a very brief or fixed period of time.[1] An alien coming to the U.S. for a definite purpose that can be completed promptly is a transient; but if it will take a long time[1] and he makes his home temporarily in the U.S., he becomes a resident. This applies even though he intends to return to his domicile abroad when he finishes what he came for. A "treaty trader" (nonimmigrant alien) who carries on a substantial trade between his country and the U.S. under a commerce treaty is presumed to be a resident if he is in the U.S. for at least a year.[2] When a resident leaving the U.S. has a valid permit to re-enter, he keeps his status as a resident until he takes some definite action that shows he has abandoned the residence.[3]

(b) Special provisions for taxation of resident aliens:

Foreign tax credits. Resident aliens get a foreign tax credit [¶ 3701], but the President may, by proclamation, deny citizens of a particular foreign country the right to take the credit [Sec. 901(c)].

Exempt income. Pay of an alien working in the U.S. as an employee of a foreign government is exempt, if the foreign government grants similar exemption to U.S. citizens. Pay of aliens working in the U.S. for international organizations is also exempt under certain conditions [Sec. 893(a); 1.893-1(a), (b)]. The exemption does not apply to an alien's income from other sources in the U.S., such as writing, speaking tours, radio appearances or other ventures. A resident alien cannot exclude foreign earned income [¶ 3725].

> NOTE: Pay of aliens employed by foreign governments and international organizations is not exempt, if they file waivers under the McCarran Act.[4] However, it still may be exempt under tax treaties or other international agreements.[5]

(c) Dual-status aliens. An alien who has been both a resident alien and a nonresident alien in the same tax year (usually the years of arrival and departure) must file Form 1040 with attached schedules or statements explaining the tax for the portion of the year he was a nonresident alien. Form 1040-NR can be used as an attachment. The dual-status taxpayer cannot take the standard deduction, qualify as a head of household or file a joint return. His total exemptions for his spouse and dependents cannot exceed his taxable income (without regard to exemptions) for the period he was a resident alien. The filing requirements depend on taxpayer's status at the end of the year.[6]

Footnotes appear at end of this Chapter.

¶ 3709 Nonresident aliens. A nonresident alien is taxed on all income from U.S. sources [¶ 3712] and certain business connected income from foreign sources [¶ 3711(b)]. Business connected income from both U.S. and foreign sources is taxed at regular U.S. rates. The gross nonbusiness U.S. source income—investment income—is taxed at a 30% rate [Sec. 871, 872; 1.871-7(a)].

(a) Who is a nonresident alien. A nonresident alien is an individual (including a fiduciary and a citizen of a U.S. possession) who is neither a citizen nor a resident of the U.S. [Sec. 932; 1.871-2(a), 1.932-1(a), 301.7701-5]. See also ¶ 3708. Residents of the Virgin Islands are subject to the U.S. income tax laws, but pay taxes to the Virgin Islands. Special rules apply to residents of Puerto Rico [¶ 3727].

(b) Tax on nonresident aliens. Income effectively connected with a nonresident alien's U.S. business [¶ 3711] is taxed at the same graduated rates that apply to U.S. taxpayers [Sec. 871(b), 873(a); 1.871-8(a)]. Unmarried nonresident aliens use the same rate schedule as single U.S. taxpayers. However, a married nonresident alien must use the one for married individuals filing separately, unless married to a U.S. citizen or resident [¶ 1121].[1] U.S. nonbusiness investment income is taxed at 30% [¶ 3711(a)], or lower treaty rate if applicable [Sec. 871(a), 894(b)]. For an election to treat investment income from realty as business income, see ¶ 3711.

A nonresident alien cannot file a head of household return to get lower rates [Sec. 2(b)(3)(A), 6013(a)(1)(g); 1.2-2(b)(6), 1.6013-1(b)]. However for tax years beginning after 1975, a nonresident alien married to a U.S. citizen or resident can elect to file a joint return. But they must report and pay tax on their worldwide income. For tax years after 1976, unless the taxpayers elect to file a joint return, community income shall be treated as follows: (1) earned income [¶ 3725(a)] other than from a trade or business and a partner's distributive share of partnership income, is the income of the spouse who rendered the personal services; (2) trade or business income and partner's distributive share income are treated as income to the husband or the dominant partner [¶ 3827(b)]; (3) community income derived from the separate property of one spouse is income to that spouse; (4) other community income is treated under applicable community property law [Sec. 879].

NOTE: These adjustments to local community property laws do not apply to joint returns filed for tax years after 1976 and all returns filed for tax years before 1977.

Nonresident aliens cannot compute their tax by averaging income [Sec. 1303(b); 1.1303-1(b)]. They are not subject to self-employment tax [Sec. 1402(b); 1.1402(b)-1(d)].

Capital gains and losses "effectively connected" with nonresident aliens' U.S. trade or business [¶ 3711] are treated the same as for U.S. citizens [¶ 1611 et seq.], and the alternative tax may be used for net long-term gains.

Capital gains from U.S. sources that are *not* business connected are taxed only if the alien spent a total of at least 183 days in the U.S. during the tax year. The tax is 30% of the net capital gain from transactions effected during the year, and the capital loss carryover is not allowed. The calendar year is used if the alien has no established tax year [Sec. 871; 1.871-7(d)(2)]. There is no provision for applying capital losses against other income.

Deductions and credits. A nonresident alien computing taxable income from his U.S. business may take deductions attributable to the effectively connected income, personal casualty or theft losses of property in the U.S., charitable contributions and the personal exemption. Only one personal exemption is allowed except for Canadians and Mexicans; they get the same exemptions as U.S. citizens (¶ 1111 et seq.). The dividend exclusion [¶ 1705] is allowed for effectively connected business dividends, and the foreign tax credit [¶ 3701] is allowed against the tax on business income. No deductions are allowed in computing the tax on nonbusiness U.S. source income [Sec. 873].

Foreign students or exchange visitors under the Mutual Educational and Cultural Exchange Act of 1961 are taxed at domestic rates on the taxable portions of their scholarships and grants (¶ 1303) [Sec. 871(c)]. However, compensation paid by a foreign employer while the student or visitor is in the U.S. under this program is tax-exempt [Sec. 872(b)(3)].

(c) Tax on expatriates. A U.S. citizen who becomes a nonresident alien (after 3-8-65) to avoid income, estate or gift taxes can be taxed at U.S. rates on his U.S. source investment income for ten succeeding years as well as on his effectively connected business income [Sec. 877]. However, this provision applies only if this tax would be greater than his tax as a nonresident alien. Gain from the sale or exchange of stock of a U.S. corporation, of debt obligations of a U.S. person or political subdivision, or of any property located in the U.S. is included as U.S. source income for this purpose regardless of where the sale or exchange occurs or title is transferred. See ¶ 3712. The deductions connected with the expatriate's gross income under this provision are allowed. These include the deductions allowed other nonresident aliens [¶ 3709(b)] and investment losses [¶ 2203], but not capital loss carryovers.

(d) Returns and payment of tax. Deductions and credits are allowed only if a return is filed [Sec. 874(a); 1.874-1(a)]. Nonresident aliens with wages subject to withholding must file returns and pay taxes at the same time and manner as U.S. citizens. Those without wages subject to withholding file a return and pay taxes by the 15th day of the 6th month after the close of the tax year [¶ 3517(a); 3522]. For withholding from nonresident alien, see ¶ 2535.

¶ 3710 Foreign corporations. Any corporation not organized or created in the U.S. is a foreign corporation [Sec. 301.7701-5]. Foreign corporations, like nonresident aliens, pay U.S. tax at different rates for U.S. business connected income and for U.S. nonbusiness income.

(a) Tax on foreign corporations. All income that is effectively connected with a foreign corporation's U.S. business [¶ 3711] is taxed at the regular U.S. corporate rate (¶ 3102) [Sec. 882]. U.S. source nonbusiness investment income [¶ 3711(a)] is taxed at a flat 30% rate unless an applicable treaty rate is lower [Sec. 881, 894(b)]. For an election to treat investment income from real property as business income, see ¶ 3711.

Capital gains and losses. Foreign corporations are taxed only on capital gains effectively connected with U.S. business [Sec. 881, 882(a)]. Other capital gains are not taxed. Foreign corporations may use the alternative tax computation [¶ 3202]. Certain specified rules on nonrecognition of gain [¶ 1405; 3309; 3317; 3334] would not apply to a foreign corporation unless the taxpayer makes an advance showing to the Revenue Service that the transaction was not carried out under a tax avoidance plan[1] [Sec. 367; 1.367-1].

Deductions and credits. Deductions attributable to business connected income and the charitable contribution deduction are allowed in computing taxable income from the U.S. business [Sec. 882(c)]. The corporation may get a foreign tax credit against this tax [¶ 3701]. A return must be filed (except for personal holding companies [¶ 3405]) to get the deductions or credit. Gross nonbusiness income from U.S. sources is subject to the 30% tax.

Footnotes appear at end of this Chapter.

(b) Returns and payment of tax. Foreign corporations generally file Form 1120F. The returns are due (a) by the 15th of the *3rd month* after the end of the tax year if the foreign corporation has an office or place of business in the U.S., or (b) by the 15th of the *6th month* if without an office or place of business in the U.S. [¶ 3517(b)]. Tax in either case is payable in full with the return, or in 2 equal installments [¶ 3523].

¶ 3711 Income taxed at U.S. rates. Only income "effectively connected" with a foreign taxpayer's U.S. business is taxed at U.S. rates. Income is "effectively connected" with the conduct of a trade or business during the tax year only if the taxpayer is engaged in business or has income from real property in the U.S. [see below]. All income from U.S. sources [¶ 3712] is effectively connected business income unless it is investment income that is not derived from activities of the business in the U.S. or from assets used or held by the business in the U.S. [(a) below]. Certain income from foreign sources also may be "effectively connected" business income if the taxpayer has an office or fixed place of business in the U.S. [(b) below].

Real property election. A nonresident alien or foreign corporation can elect to treat all income from U.S. real property held for the production of income as "effectively connected" income [Sec. 871(d), 882(d); 1.871-10]. This allows the taxpayer to deduct taxes, interest and other expenses as if the property was being used in a trade or business. The election includes capital gains from the sale of U.S. real property and certain rents and royalties from mines, wells and other natural deposits and timber, coal and domestic iron ore disposed of with a retained economic interest [¶ 1621(b); 1623].

Trade or business in the U.S. In addition to the usual U.S. trade or business activities, trade or business in the U.S. may include the performance of personal services in the U.S.; also trading in stocks or commodities. When a partnership, estate or trust is engaged in U.S. trade or business, the foreign partners or beneficiaries also are considered to be engaged in trade or business in the U.S. The rules that apply to these situations are spelled out below.

Personal services. If personal services are performed by a nonresident alien for another nonresident alien, a foreign partnership or corporation not engaged in a U.S. business, or a foreign branch of a U.S. citizen or resident, corporation or partnership, the nonresident alien is not considered to be engaged in a U.S. trade or business if: (1) he is temporarily in the U.S. not over 90 days during the tax year, and (2) his pay is not over $3,000 [Sec. 864(b); 1.864-2(b)].

Stock or commodity transactions. Only transactions effected through the taxpayer's office or other fixed place of business in the U.S. are considered as being engaged in a trade or business. Also, a taxpayer trading for his own account is not engaged in a U.S. trade or business, whether he uses a resident broker, custodian or other independent agent, acts for himself or through an employee or a partnership of which he is a member; but this exception does not apply to taxpayers or their partnerships that are dealers or to a corporation (other than one that is a personal holding company or would be if not wholly foreign owned [¶ 3404]) that has its principal office in the U.S. and whose principal business is trading in stocks or securities for its own account [Sec. 864(b)(2); 1.864-2(c), (d)].

(a) Effectively connected U.S. source income. If a nonresident alien or foreign corporation is engaged in business in the U.S., all U.S. source income is effectively connected business income unless it is determined that the income or gain is not derived from assets or activities of the U.S. business. This determination is made only for fixed or determinable periodical income, gain or loss from sale or exchange of capital assets and certain specially treated items [Sec. 864(c)(2), (3); 1.864-3, 1.864-4].

NOTE: U.S. source income found not to be "effectively connected" with a U.S. business is taxed at the flat 30% rate; all other U.S. source income of a foreign taxpayer engaged in business in the U.S. is "effectively connected" business income, taxed at regular rates [¶ 3709(b); 3710(a)].

Fixed or determinable periodical income includes the following: interest, dividends, rents, salaries, wages, premiums, annuities, remuneration, emoluments and other income of this type [Sec. 871(a)(1)(A), 881(a)(1); 1.881-2(b)]. Wages, bonuses, pensions and such, attributable to a nonresident alien's personal services in the U.S. are taxable as "effectively connected" business income only if he is engaged in a trade or business here in the tax year the income is received [Sec. 1.864-4(c)(6)(ii)].

Specially treated items are: lump-sum distributions from exempt employees' trust and annuity plans [¶ 1232(c); 3024(d)], gain from certain disposals of timber, domestic iron ore and coal [¶ 1621(b); 1623], gains from the sale or exchange of certain patents, copyrights, trademarks, and other similar property, that usually are treated as capital gains, and gains attributable to original issue discount as to certain bonds or other evidences of indebtedness (¶ 1629) [Sec. 871(a)(1), 881(a); 1.871-7(c), 1.871-11, 1.881-2(b)].

Factors considered. Two principal factors are considered in determining whether the income, gain or loss is "effectively connected" with the U.S. trade or business. In applying these factors, the accounting treatment of the assets and income will be a material, though not controlling, factor [Sec. 1.864-4(c)]:

(1) Was the income derived from *assets* used, or held for use, in the conduct of the U.S. business? The *asset-use test* ordinarily applies to passive-type income—for example, interest or dividends received from U.S. sources by a foreign taxpayer engaged in manufacturing or selling in the U.S. Generally, income from an asset is "effectively connected" if the asset is (a) held primarily for promoting the present U.S. business, or (b) acquired and held in the ordinary course of the U.S. business, or (c) held in a "direct relationship" to the U.S. business. An asset would be directly related to the business if it is held to meet its present, rather than its anticipated future needs. Generally, investment income of a nonresident alien performing personal services in the U.S. would not be business connected, unless there is a direct economic relationship between the investment and the services. The relationship exists, for example, if an alien buys a U.S. company's stock to secure his job with the company [Sec. 1.864-4(c)].

(2) Were the *activities* of the U.S. business a material factor in the realization of the income? The *business-activities test* ordinarily applies to passive-type income that arises directly from a foreign taxpayer's active conduct of its U.S. business. It is used primarily for dividends, interest and gain or loss from a banking, financial or simlar business, and for royalties from a licensing business [Sec. 1.864-4(c)(3), (5)].

(b) Effectively connected foreign source income. Only 3 types of foreign source income can be effectively connected with a U.S. business: (1) rents and royalties from foreign intangibles; (2) income and gain or loss from stocks and bonds to financial businesses; and (3) income or gain from foreign sales of inventory through a U.S. office. Such income is effectively connected with a U.S. business only if the taxpayer has a U.S. office or fixed place of business. A foreign corporation does not have an office or fixed place of business in the U.S. if its only activities here consist of using an office here to make top management decisions. A taxpayer is considered to have a U.S. place of business if his agent (other than an

Footnotes appear at end of this Chapter.

¶ 3711

independent agent in his own U.S. trade or business) has a fixed place of business in the U.S. and negotiates and makes contracts or regularly fills orders for the taxpayer. Also, a foreign taxpayer has a U.S. office, if his employee regularly uses an office in the U.S. to carry on the employer's U.S. business. However, a U.S. office of a related person (for example, a wholly-owned subsidiary of a foreign taxpayer) is not necessarily treated as taxpayer's office. No foreign income, gain or loss is effectively connected unless the U.S. location is regularly engaged in the activity that produces it and is a material factor in realizing it. Only the amount of income or gain properly allocable to the U.S. place of business is taxable to the foreign taxpayer. In the case of inventory sales abroad, income attributable to the U.S. cannot exceed the amount that would have been realized had the taxpayer sold the goods in the U.S. [Sec. 864(c); 1.864-5—1.864-7].

NOTE: Any foreign tax paid on foreign source income that is effectively connected with taxpayer's U.S. business qualifies for foreign tax credit [¶ 3701].

Some foreign source income is never considered effectively connected with the conduct of a U.S. trade or business. These items are: (1) dividends, interest and royalties paid by a foreign corporation in which the taxpayer actually or constructively owns more than 50% of the voting stock; and (2) Subpart F income [¶ 3728]. However, all foreign source income attributable to the U.S. business of a foreign life insurance company is effectively connected with the conduct of the U.S. business (¶ 3434(d)) [Sec. 864(c)(4); 1.864-5].

¶ 3712 **What is U.S. source income.** Aside from the obvious sources such as U.S. business profits and wages and salaries, U.S. source income includes:

Dividends from U.S. corporations are U.S. source income, unless received from a corporation (a) allowed to exclude income from U.S. possessions [¶ 3727] or (b) deriving more than 80% of its gross income from foreign sources during a 3-year period ending with the tax year preceding the declaration of the dividend or (c) electing the possessions credit (¶ 3727(b)) [Sec. 861(a)(2)(A); 1.861-3(a)(2)].

A portion of the dividends from a foreign corporation at least 50% of whose gross income for the 3-year period preceding the declaration of the dividend was effectively connected with a U.S. business is U.S. source income. The amount is determined by the same ratio that effectively connected business income bears to gross income from all sources [Sec. 861(a)(2)(B); 1.861-3(a)(3)].

Dividends from foreign corporations are U.S. source income to the extent the dividends are treated for dividends received deduction purposes [¶ 3114(a)] as dividends from a domestic corporation, because paid out of earnings and profits accumulated while it was a domestic corporation [Sec. 861(a)(2)(C); 1.861-3(a)(4)].

Dividends from a DISC or former DISC are U.S. source income unless they are qualified export receipts and not considered distributed (¶ 3460(b)) [Sec. 861(a)(2)(D)].

Interest from the U.S., the District of Columbia or any Territory, and interest on obligations of U.S. residents, corporate or otherwise, is U.S. source income [Sec. 861(a)(1)]. However, the following interest income is considered income from foreign sources: (a) interest received by nonresident aliens and foreign corporations on deposits in banks, savings and loan associations and insurance companies that is not effectively connected with a U.S. business [Sec. 861(a)(1)(A), (c); 1.864-4(c)(1)(ii), 1.864-5(d)(3)]; (b) interest received from a resident alien or domestic corporation, if less than 20% of the payor's total gross income during the 3 preceding tax years was received from U.S. sources [Sec. 861(a)(1)(B)]; (c) certain portions of interest received from foreign corporations, less than 50% of whose gross income for the preceding 3-year period was effectively connected with a U.S. business (where it is U.S. source income, the taxable portion is the same proportion of interest that effectively connected income bears to gross income from all sources) [Sec. 861(a)(1)(C), (D)]; and (d) interest on deposits in a foreign branch of a U.S. bank [Sec. 861(a)(1)(F)] or income derived by a foreign central bank of issue from bankers' acceptances [Sec. 861(a)(1)(E)].

Income derived by central banks of issue from U.S. obligations is tax-exempt, unless the obligations are held or used for commercial banking functions or other commercial activities [Sec. 895].

Pay for personal services performed in the U.S. is U.S. source income. However, compensation that meets the 90-day—$3,000 test of ¶ 3711 is not counted as U.S. source income [Sec. 861(a)(3)].

Rents and royalties from property located in U.S. or from any interest in such property, including those from U.S. patents, copyrights, good will, trademarks and like property are U.S. source income [Sec. 861(a)(4); 1.861-5].

Sale of real property. Gains, profits, and income from the sale of real property located in U.S. are U.S. source income [Sec. 861(a)(5); 1.861-6].

Certain aircraft and vessels. Income from the leasing of certain aircraft and vessels to a U.S. person is U.S. source income, if so elected [Sec. 861(e)].

Sale of personal property not produced by taxpayer. Income from the purchase and sale of personal property is treated as derived from the country where the property is sold [Sec. 861(a)(6); 1.861-7]. Income from property bought in a U.S. possession and sold in the U.S. is treated as partly from sources in and partly from sources without the U.S. Income from property bought in the U.S. and sold in a U.S. possession is treated as wholly from within the possession.

Sale of personal property produced by the taxpayer. Gains, profits, and income from property produced by the taxpayer in the U.S. and sold in a foreign country, or vice versa, are treated as income derived from sources partly within and partly without the U.S. Complicated formulas in the regulations give the taxpayer the choice of three ways to figure net income: (1) by separate accounting; (2) by independent factory price; or (3) by allocation [Sec. 863(a), (b); 1.863-3].

Continental shelf areas. Pay received for personal services performed on a mine, oil or gas well, located or being developed on the continental shelf of the U.S. is income from U.S. sources [Sec. 638; 1.638-1, 1.638-2].

Underwriting income from the insurance of U.S. risks is U.S. source income. This is includible for tax years starting after 1976 [Sec. 861(a)(7)].

NOTE: Allocable deductions can be taken from the above-mentioned items of gross income, and only the remainder is includible as U.S. source income. For individuals who do not itemize, the zero bracket amount [¶ 1107] is deductible in full [Sec. 861(b)].

Income from sources outside the U.S. does not have to be included in a foreign taxpayer's gross income unless it is effectively connected with taxpayer's U.S. business [¶ 3711(b)]. This applies to [Sec. 862(a); 1.862-1]: interest and dividends other than that included in U.S. income (above); rents and royalties from property outside the U.S.; pay for personal services performed outside the U.S.; gain from the purchase of personal property within the U.S. and its sale outside the U.S. and, insurance underwriting income (for tax years starting after 1976). The portion of a U.S. civil service annuity or retirement benefit payable to a nonresident alien and attributable to pay for services performed outside the U.S. also is excluded [Sec. 402(a)(4)].

NOTE: Income from continental shelf areas adjacent to a foreign country or U.S. possession is not U.S. source income. This applies only if the foreign country exercises tax jurisdiction over the area [Sec. 638; 1.638-1, 1.638-2].

TAX TREATIES

¶ 3720 Tax treaty provisions. Tax conventions with foreign nations are designed to eliminate double taxation of income and prevent tax evasion. Some income is exempt, while for other income a lower than normal rate of tax (and withholding) is applied [¶¶ 2535; 2537; 3707; 3709(b); 3710(a)]. Similar provisions apply to the taxes of the other party to the convention.

Exchange-of-notes agreements may also relieve earnings from the operation of ships and aircraft from double taxation [Sec. 872(b), 883; 1.883-1]. Such agreements are in effect with several countries.[1]

Footnotes appear at end of this Chapter.

¶ 3720

NOTE: The various treaty provisions are explained in detail in the P-H Federal Taxes and in the P-H Federal Tax Treaties services.

U.S. INCOME FROM FOREIGN SOURCES

¶ 3725 **Earned income of citizens from sources outside the U.S.** U.S. citizens can exclude a limited amount of earned income (except payments by the U.S. or its agencies) from sources outside the U.S. This income is included, however, in determining whether a taxpayer has to file a return [¶ 1100]. Compensation for services abroad under U.S. Government contracts is not excluded if the U.S. or a U.S. agency is the taxpayer's actual employer.[1] Form 2555 must be filed with taxpayer's tax return to support the exclusion.

NOTE: Tax preferences that are stock options or capital gains from foreign sources are taken into account only if they are treated as tax preference items by the foreign country or possession [Prop. Reg. Sec. 1.58-8]. This applies when little or no tax is imposed. Other tax preferences from foreign sources are taken into account to the extent they reduce the taxpayer's income tax (¶ 2403) [Sec. 58(g); Prop. Reg. 1.58-7]. Taxpayers who elect to average income [¶ 2401] must include the net foreign earned income in their computations.

(a) What is earned income. Earned income is wages, salaries, professional fees, commissions from sales of life insurance[2] or other compensation for personal services. If a taxpayer is engaged in a trade or business in which both personal services and capital are material income-producing factors, no more than 30% of his share of the net profits of the business can be excluded[3] [Sec. 911(b); 1.911-1(a)]. The place where services are performed controls in determining whether earned income is from within or without the U.S. [Sec. 1.911-1(a)(6)]. It does not matter where the payment is made.

Deductions. Persons entitled to the exclusion lose any deductions chargeable against the amount excluded [Sec. 911(a)(2); 1.911-1(a)(3)].

Pensions and annuities. No amount received as a pension or annuity can be excluded as foreign earned income; nor can an employee exclude employer contributions to an employee trust or for an annuity contract if they would be taxable to the employee (¶ 1232(d); 3024) [Sec. 72(f), 911(c)(5)].

(b) Who can exclude. A U.S. citizen can exclude foreign earned income when he is a bona fide resident of a foreign country for an uninterrupted period that includes one full tax year; or if he is present there 510 days during a period of 18 consecutive months [Sec. 1.911-2]. An individual who is excused from paying the tax of a foreign country where he earns income, because he claims he is not a resident there, cannot exclude the foreign earned income as a resident of that country [Sec. 911(c)(6)]. Once bona fide foreign residence is established, temporary visits to the U.S. on vacation, sick leave[4] or business trips[5] do not necessarily change the status of a bona fide resident.[6]

(c) Amount allowed. For tax years beginning after 1976, U.S. citizens working abroad who are bona fide residents of foreign countries can exclude a maximum of $15,000 foreign earned income for each complete tax year [Sec. 911(c)(1)]. Employees of U.S. charitable organizations may exclude up to $20,000. Those entitled to exclude under the 510 day- 18-month rule can never exclude more than $15,000 a tax year. If the 18-month period does not include the entire year, the exclusion is a portion of $15,000 prorated on a daily basis [Sec. 911(a)(2)]. The tax is computed by reducing the tax on net taxable income by the sum of the tax on net excluded income plus the zero bracket amount [Sec. 911(d)].

Chapter 27—Foreign Income—Foreign Taxpayers

Example: Dave Johnson, a U.S. resident, worked abroad for 510 days during the period 4-1-76 through 10-1-77. He worked abroad for 250 days in 1977. He gets no exclusion for 1976. His exclusion for 1977 is $10,273.97 [$15,000 × 250/365].

NOTE: The Tax Reform Act of 1976 reduced the exclusion from $20,000 to $15,000 for tax years starting after 1975, but the Tax Reduction and Simplification Act of 1977 changed the effective date to tax years starting after 1976. Therefore, taxpayers who computed their 1976 return based on the $15,000 figure should file an amended return.

Only the amounts received for services performed during a tax year can be excluded within the limit for that year. Payment may be made in the following year; but any amount received after that for those services cannot be excluded at all [Sec. 911(c)(4); 1.911-2].

A husband and wife are each entitled to an exclusion for their own earnings, but only one exclusion is allowed for community income that is earned by only one spouse [Sec. 911(c)(3)].

NOTE: The Tax Court has ruled that if a U.S. citizen receives earned income that qualifies for the exclusion, but his income is partially attributed to his nonresident alien wife in a community property country, the citizen may exclude the entire income. However, the exclusion is not applicable to any income earned by a nonresident alien spouse and attributed to a U.S. citizen by operation of community property law.[7]

Income which is received outside of the foreign country it was earned, in order to avoid tax in that country, is ineligible for exclusion [Sec. 911(c)(8)]. Any additional income received by a taxpayer in excess of the $15,000 maximum exclusion is subject to U.S. tax at the higher rate brackets which would apply if the exclusion were not available [Sec. 911(d)]. These rules apply to tax years beginning after 1975.

Form 2555 should be filed by U.S. citizens earning income abroad and by resident aliens from foreign countries with whom tax treaties are in effect ("nondiscrimination clauses").

(d) Returns due before exclusion established. A taxpayer, whose right to an exclusion has not yet been established when he is required to file his income tax return, must either include all wages earned abroad in his gross income and pay the tax on them or get an extension of time for filing the return. However, when he later establishes a right to the exclusion, he can claim a refund or credit for any taxes overpaid [Sec. 1.911-2(e)(1)].

An extension of time to file the return until the required period for the exclusion is completed may be granted by submitting a Form 2350 to the Revenue Service. (This is in addition to the automatic extension for citizens abroad [¶ 3518].) [Sec. 1.911-2(e)(1)].

¶ 3726 Allowances to U.S. Government officers and employees in foreign service. The following are excluded from gross income: (1) cost-of-living allowances received by government civilian personnel stationed outside the continental U.S.; (2) certain Peace Corps allowances; and (3) certain foreign areas allowances [Sec. 912; 1.912-1, 1.912-2].

¶ 3727 Income from sources in U.S. possessions. (a) **U.S. citizens** are allowed to exclude income received from sources outside the U.S. if within a 3-year period immediately preceding the close of a tax year: (1) at least 80% of gross income is from sources within a U.S. possession, and (2) at least 50% of gross income is derived from the active conduct of a trade or business within a U.S. possession. However, amounts received within the U.S. must be included in gross

Footnotes appear at end of this Chapter.

income whether derived from sources within or without the U.S. [Sec. 931; 1.931-1]. In all other cases, the source of the income is the place where the work is done, not where payment is made.[1]

For this exclusion, U.S. possessions include the Panama Canal Zone, American Samoa, Wake Island, the Midway Islands, but not Puerto Rico, Guam, or the Virgin Islands[2] [Sec. 1.931-1(a)(1)]. The 3-year period is the 36 months immediately before the close of a tax year.[3]

Payments by U.S. Compensation paid by the U.S. to civilian or military personnel for services rendered within a possession of the U.S. may not be excluded [Sec. 931(i); 1.931-1(i)].

Returns. A taxpayer excluding income under the above provisions must file Form 4563 with his individual return. If he receives no income within the U.S., or from sources within the U.S., and is entitled to exclude his income from without the U.S., no return is required [Sec. 1.931-1(b)(4)]. Only one personal exemption is allowed. (No exemption is allowed for spouse, age, blindness or dependents.) No credit is allowed for taxes paid to a foreign country or to a U.S. possession. The taxpayer may not use the standard deduction in computing his tax [Sec. 142(b)].

Citizens of U.S. possessions (except Puerto Rico and Guam) who are not also U.S. citizens or residents are taxed as nonresident aliens (¶ 3709(b)) [Sec. 932; Prop. Reg. 1.932-1].

(b) Domestic corporations. For tax years beginning after 1975, U.S. corporations operating in Puerto Rico and possessions of the U.S. (excluding the Virgin Islands) may elect a separate tax credit. The credit, called the Sec. 936 credit, is granted in lieu of the ordinary foreign tax credit [Sec. 936]. To be eligible, a corporation must have received within a 3-year period immediately preceding the close of the tax year at least 80% of its gross income from sources within a possession, and at least 50% of its gross income from the active conduct of a trade or business within a possession.

The amount of the credit equals that portion of U.S. tax attributable to taxable income from sources outside the U.S., from the active conduct of a trade or business within a U.S. possession and from qualified possession source investment income [Sec. 936(a)(1)]. The latter includes only income from sources within a possession in which the corporation actively conducts business, regardless of whether the business produces any taxable income for the year [Sec. 936(d)(2)]. DISC or former DISC corporations are ineligible for the credit [Sec. 936(f)].

To qualify for the credit, a corporation must make an election as prescribed by the Revenue Service. The election is, generally, effective for a ten-year period and cannot be revoked except by IRS consent [Sec. 936(e)].

(c) Exclusion for residents of Puerto Rico. Puerto Rico has its own tax law, which takes the place of the federal income tax law. Thus, in the case of Puerto Rican residents, the United States income tax is applied to income from sources outside Puerto Rico; for income from sources within Puerto Rico, the Puerto Rican income tax applies.

U.S. citizens who are bona fide residents of Puerto Rico for the entire tax year may exclude income from sources within Puerto Rico, except amounts received as employees of the U.S. Deductions allocable to excluded income are not allowed. A citizen giving up his Puerto Rican residence after 2 or more years may exclude from gross income any income derived from Puerto Rican sources which results from his period of residence there during the tax year [Sec. 933; 1.933-1].

Aliens who are bona fide residents of Puerto Rico during the entire tax year, in general, are taxed the same as aliens who reside in the U.S. [¶ 3708]. However, they can exclude any income from within Puerto Rico, except amounts received as employees of the U.S. Deductions allocable to excluded income are not allowed [Sec. 876; 1.876-1].

¶ **3728 Special rules on foreign investments.** U.S. shareholders of "controlled" foreign corporations are *currently* taxed on certain passive-type income (e.g., dividends, interest and rents), income of sales or service subsidiaries and income from insuring U.S. risks, etc. Also, U.S. shareholders realize *ordinary* income, rather than capital gains, on the sale or redemption of stocks in a controlled foreign corporation or foreign investment company. Ordinary income tax treatment applies also to sales of patents, etc. to a controlled foreign corporation.

Controlled foreign corporations. A U.S. shareholder (corporation, individual, etc.) who owns at least 10% of the stock of a controlled foreign corporation is taxed on its *undistributed* income [Sec. 951]. A controlled foreign corporation is one that is more-than-50% owned by 10% U.S. shareholders [Sec. 957; 1.957-1, 1.957-3]. The rules for constructive ownership of stock [¶ 1727] apply with modifications [¶ 3540(b)]. These rules do not apply to shareholders in a foreign investment company electing current taxation, or a foreign personal holding company (¶ 3411) [Sec. 951(c), (d); 1.951-2, 1.951-3]. Form 3646 must be filed with the shareholder's income tax return.

The U.S. shareholder is taxed on his share of the following kinds of income (Subpart F income) earned by the controlled foreign corporation, unless it is taxed by U.S. as effectively connected U.S. business income (¶ 3711) [Sec. 951 et seq.; 1.954-1—1.954-5]: (1) Income from insuring or reinsuring U.S. risks; (2) personal holding company-type income (dividends, interest, rents, royalties); (3) income from services performed for related persons outside the foreign county; (4) profits from sales of property between related persons for use outside the foreign country; and (5) the income of a corporation resulting from cooperation with an international boycott [¶ 3701].

Exceptions: The U.S. shareholder will not be taxed on income in (2), (3) or (4), if it is: "export trade income" (income from sales, to unrelated persons for use outside the U.S., of property produced, grown or extracted in the U.S.) *and* if this income is reinvested in the export trade business; shipping income, if, for tax years starting after 1975, the profits are reinvested in shipping operations [Sec. 955]; or generally for tax years beginning after 1975, shipping income derived from the use of a vessel or aircraft in foreign commerce *within* the country where the corporation is organized or the ship or vessel registered [Sec. 954]; from a controlled foreign corporation not used to reduce taxes; or totals less than 10% (for tax years starting after 1975, or 30% for earlier years) of the controlled foreign corporation's gross income (but if it totals more than 70% of the gross income, the U.S. shareholder will be taxed on his share of *all* the controlled foreign corporation's income).

NOTE: In addition to the stricter rules noted above, the 1975 Tax Reduction Act also repealed the exception for reinvestment in less developed countries, for tax years starting after 1975.

The U.S. shareholder's basis for his stock is increased by his share of reported Subpart F income and decreased by his share of exempt Subpart F income [Sec. 1.961-1, 1.961-2]. Taxable Subpart F income may not exceed the foreign corporation's earnings and profits for the tax year [Sec. 952].

Footnotes appear at end of this Chapter.

A corporate shareholder or an individual who elects the relief provisions below can get a foreign tax credit for the part of the corporation's tax related to the undistributed income included in the taxpayer's income [Sec. 960; 1.960-1].

Earnings invested in U.S. assets. The U.S. shareholder also will be taxed on his share of the foreign corporation's earnings that are invested in assets in the U.S. that are not needed for the business [Sec. 956; 1.956-1, 1.956-2].

No double tax. To the extent the shareholder pays tax under the above rules, he will not be taxed again when the earnings are distributed [Sec. 959].

Relief provisions. Individual shareholders can elect to have the undistributed income taxed to them *as if* they were U.S. corporations. They are then entitled to the foreign tax credit as though they were a corporation. Amounts actually distributed later will be taxed at ordinary individual rates after deducting amounts previously taxed at corporation rates [Sec. 962; 1.962-1].

Under prior law, corporate shareholders were not taxed on undistributed earnings, if the controlled foreign corporation makes a "minimum distribution." Just how much should be distributed depends on the tax rate in the country where the foreign corporation operates (the higher the tax rate, the smaller the amount that need be distributed). However, for tax years starting after 1975, the "minimum distribution" rule is no longer applicable.

Gain from stock. Gain on redemption, liquidation, or sale of stock in a controlled foreign corporation is ordinary income to 10%-or-more U.S. shareholders, to the extent the gain represents earnings and profits accumulated after 12-31-62 [Sec. 1248(a); 1.1248-1—1.1248-7].

The tax on the individual shareholder cannot exceed the sum of [Sec. 1248(b); 1.1248-4]: (1) The excess of the U.S. income taxes that would have been paid by the foreign corporation if it had been a domestic corporation over the foreign income taxes actually paid by the corporation; and (2) the capital gains tax that would have resulted to the shareholder on the surrender of his stock, if the amount actually received by him on the surrender were diminished by the amount described in (1) above.

NOTE: The exclusion from dividend treatment for sales or exchanges of stock in less-developed country corporations has been repealed for earnings accumulated after 12-31-75 [Sec. 1248(d)(3)].

If a reorganization or liquidation of a foreign corporation occurs which involves transfers of property by a U.S. citizen to a foreign corporation, nonrecognition of gain will be permitted if a request for a ruling that tax avoidance was not involved is filed within 183 days after the beginning of the transfer [Sec. 1248(f)].

Footnotes to Chapter 27

(P-H "FEDERAL TAXES" related references are cited in brackets [ ] at the end of each footnote below.)

Footnote ¶ 3701   [¶ 30,473 et seq.]
(1) Rev. Proc. 77-9, IRB 1977-10 [¶ 55,205].

Footnote ¶ 3702   [¶ 30,473 et seq.; 30,561].
(1) Senate Report No. 1393, p. 16, 86th Cong., 2d Sess.
(2) Jose Ferrer, 35 TC 617 affd., 9 AFTR 2d 1651, 304 F.2d 125 [¶ 30,564(110)].

Footnote ¶ 3702 continued
(3) D.E. Brown, 1 BTA 446; Mead Cycle Co., 10 BTA 887 [¶ 30,509(5)].
(4) Rev. Rul. 73-491, 1973-1 CB 267 [¶ 30,509(5)].
(5) Bon Ami Co., 39 BTA 825 [¶ 30,524(30)].

Footnote ¶ 3703   [¶ 30,509(5); 30,536; 30,536(a)].
(1) Conference Committee Report No. 94-120, p. 69, 94th Cong., 1st Sess.

Chapter 27—Footnotes

Footnote ¶ 3703 continued
(2) Senate Report No. 1393, p. 16, 86th Cong., 2nd Sess.

Footnote ¶ 3705 [¶ 30,575].
(1) The Revenue Service has issued guides on how to figure interest in cases where the period that interest is payable is restricted under the law. Rev. Proc. 60-17, 1960-2 CB 942 modified by Rev. Proc. 62-27, 1962-2 CB 495 [¶ 37,027(30)].
(2) Rev. Rul. 58-244, 1958-1 CB 265 [¶ 30,578(40)].

Footnote ¶ 3706 [¶ 30,515].
(1) Senate Report No. 91-552, p. 178, 91st Cong., 1st Sess.

Footnote ¶ 3707 [¶ 3429; 30,186 et seq.; 30,311 et seq.; 30,371; 30,425].

Footnote ¶ 3708 [¶ 3429; 30,186; 30,191; 30,201].
(1) Rev. Rul. 66-76, 1966-1 CB 238 [¶ 30,210(5)].
(2) Rev. Rul. 64-285, 1964-2 CB 184 [¶ 30,210(10)].
(3) Rev. Rul. 70-461, 1970-2 CB 149 [¶ 30,216(20)].
(4) P.L. 414, 82nd Cong., 66 Stat. 163, §247(b).
(5) Rev. Rul.75-425,1975-2 CB 291 [¶ 30,396(50)].
(6) Rev. Rul. 73-62, 1973-1 CB 56 [¶ 30,270(20)].

Footnote ¶ 3709 [¶ 30,186 et seq.].
(1) Rev. Rul. 72-413, 1972-2 CB 436 [¶ 30,225(15)].

Footnote ¶ 3710 [¶ 30,311 et seq.].
(1) Rev. Proc. 68-23, 1968-1 CB 821; Rev. Proc. 77-5, IRB 1977-5 [¶ 18,316(45); 55,173].

Footnote ¶ 3711 [¶ 30,222].

Footnote ¶ 3712 [¶ 30,058 et seq.]

Footnote ¶ 3720 [¶ 42,001 et seq.]
(1) Dept. of State, Office of the Legal Adviser, Treaty Affairs 4-1-58. For the effect of treaty provisions, see Prentice-Hall, Federal Tax Treaties.

Footnote ¶ 3725 [¶ 30,606 et seq.]
(1) Rev. Rul. 67-87, 1967-1 CB 186; Rev. Rul. 54-483, 1954-2 CB 168; Comm. v. Wolfe, 17 AFTR 2d 875, 361 F.2d 62; U.S. v. Johnson, 20 AFTR 2d 5833, 386 F.2d 824; Comm. v. Mooneyhan, 22 AFTR 2d 5897 [¶ 30,628(10), (20)].
(2) Rev. Rul. 55-497, 1955-2 CB 292 [¶ 30,627(15)].
(3) Rev. Rul. 67-158, 1967-1 CB 188 [¶ 30,627(40)].
(4) Chidester v. U.S., 82 F. Supp. 322, 37 AFTR 1059 [¶ 30,627(10)].
(5) Rose, 16 TC 232 [¶ 30,617(95)].
(6) Meyers v. Comm., 180 F.2d 969, 39 AFTR 186 [¶ 30,617(15)].
(7) Solano, 62 TC 562 [¶ 30,625(60)].

Footnote ¶ 3726 [¶ 30,651 et seq.].

Footnote ¶ 3727 [¶ 30,686 et seq.].
(1) San Carlos Milling Co., Ltd., 24 BTA 1132, affd. 63 F.2d 153, 12 AFTR 152 [¶ 30,706(5)].
(2) Rev. Rul. 70-193, 1970-1 CB 163 [¶ 30,705(20)].
(3) Rev. Rul. 65-260, 1965-2 CB 243 [¶ 30,677(35); 30,706(15)].

Footnote ¶ 3728 [¶ 30,741 et seq.; 30,891(5), (10)].

Highlights of Chapter 27
Foreign Income—Foreign Taxpayers

I. **Credit for Foreign Taxes**
   A. **Who can take foreign tax credit [¶ 3701]:**
      1. U.S. citizens.
      2. Resident aliens, unless the credit is barred by President because alien's country does not grant reciprocal credit.
      3. Nonresident aliens and foreign corporations, on income "effectively connected" with a U.S. business, but only against the tax on U.S. business income.
      4. Partner, or beneficiary of an estate or trust for his proportionate share of foreign taxes.
      5. A domestic corporate stockholder owning at least 10% of a foreign corporation's voting stock and from which it receives dividends, for a share of foreign taxes paid by the foreign corporation and its subsidiaries.
      6. Taxpayers cooperating or participating in international boycott cannot get the credit.
   B. **How to get the credit [¶ 3702]:**
      1. Individual taxpayer must itemize deductions to get credit.
      2. Election to take credit applies to every foreign tax, but can be changed within prescribed periods.
      3. Cash basis taxpayers usually take credit in year foreign taxes are paid; taxpayer on accrual basis in year accrued.
      4. The credit is figured in U.S. dollars.
   C. **Limitations on credit [¶ 3703]:**
      1. Overall limitation applies (total taxes paid to foreign countries and U.S. possessions). Before 1976, overall limitation was elective.
      2. Credit cannot exceed proportion of U.S. tax which taxable income from foreign countries and U.S. possessions bears to entire taxable income for same tax year.
      3. Foreign tax carryover and carryback [¶ 3703(b)]:
         a. Excess of foreign tax over limitation may be carried back as a credit in each of 2 preceding years, and carried forward as credit for each 5 following years.
         b. A timely election to take credit is required for year excess taxes are carried.
   D. **Adjustment to credit for foreign tax refund [¶ 3705]:**
      1. Revenue Service must be notified of refund of foreign taxes after credit was taken for them.
      2. Foreign tax on refund reduces refund—no credit allowed.
   E. **Credit for corporate shareholders in foreign corporations [¶ 3706]:**
      1. Domestic corporation gets a credit for foreign taxes paid by a foreign corporation on its accumulated profits, if:
         a. it owns at least 10% of foreign corporation's voting stock, and
         b. dividends were paid to domestic corporation on accumulated profits.
      2. If foreign corporation in turn owns at least 10% of a second foreign corporation, part of the second corporation's foreign tax paid on accumulated profits is attributed to the domestic corporation, and it will receive a credit, if
         a. it owns at least 5% of the second corporation, and
         b. dividends are paid to the first corporation after 1-12-71.
      3. "Dividend gross-up"—Domestic corporation claiming credit must include in its income the tax attributable to dividend, as well as dividend itself, if the foreign corp. is not a "less developed country corporation."
      4. Accumulated profits defined [¶ 3706(a)]:

5. Computing domestic corporation's credit [¶ 3706(b)].
6. Credit cannot exceed the applicable limitation.

II. **Foreign Taxpayers**
   A. **How foreign taxpayers are taxed [¶ 3707]:**
      1. Tax rate for business income is the same as that for domestic taxpayers.
      2. Investment income is taxed at a 30% rate.
   B. **Resident aliens**—Generally taxed and have the same filing requirements as U.S. citizens [¶ 3708]:
      1. Wages received by alien working in U.S. from foreign government employer are exempt if similar exemption granted U.S. citizens abroad.
      2. Pay of aliens employed by international organizations in U.S. may be exempt.
      3. Dual-status aliens [5 3708(c)]:
         a. Attach tax schedules for part of year they are nonresident aliens.
         b. Filing requirements depend on status at end of year.
   C. **Nonresident aliens** are individuals who are neither citizens nor residents of the U.S. [¶ 3709]:
      1. Income effectively connected with nonresident alien's U.S. business is taxed at the same rate as U.S. taxpayers [¶ 3709(b)].
      2. U.S. nonbusiness investment income is taxed at 30% [¶ 3709(b)].
      3. Capital gains and losses effectively connected with U.S. business are treated the same as for U.S. citizens [¶ 3709(b)].
      4. Nonbusiness connected capital gains are taxed only if alien spent 183 days in U.S. during the year [¶ 3709(b)]:
         a. Tax is 30% of net capital gain.
         b. Capital loss carryover is not allowed.
      5. Nonresident alien may take certain deductions in computing taxable income from U.S. business.
      6. They are not allowed deductions in computing tax on nonbusiness U.S. source income.
      7. Expatriates—U.S. citizen who becomes nonresident alien to avoid taxes can be taxed at U.S. tax rates for ten succeeding years (assuming this tax would be greater than his tax as nonresident alien) [¶ 3709(c)].
      8. Returns and payment of tax [¶ 3709(d)]:
         a. If wages were subject to withholding, filing and payment requirements are same as those for U.S. citizens.
         b. If no withholding, returns must be filed and payment made by 15th day of the 6th month following close of tax year.
   D. **Tax on foreign corporations [¶ 3710]:**
      1. Income effectively connected with corporation's U.S. business is taxed at the regular corporate rate.
      2. U.S. source nonbusiness investment income is generally taxed at a 30% rate.
      3. Capital gains are taxed only if effectively connected with U.S. business.
      4. Business connected income deductions and charitable contributions deductions are allowed [¶ 3710(a)].
      5. Foreign corp. returns are due by the 15th of the 3rd month after end of tax year if corporation has a U.S. business office, or by the 15th of the 6th month if without such office [¶ 3710(b)].
   E. **Income taxed at U.S. rates.** Only income "effectively connected" with a nonresident alien's or foreign corporation's business is taxed at U.S. rates [¶ 3711]:
      1. Foreign taxpayer can elect to treat income from U.S. real property held for production of income as effectively connected income.
      2. Trade or business in the U.S. includes trading in stocks and commodities if transactions are effected through taxpayer's office in U.S.
      3. Generally, personal services performed in the U.S. any time during the year qualify as U.S. trade or business.

4. Membership by a foreign taxpayer in a partnership engaged in a U.S. trade or business, or a beneficiary of an estate or trust similarly engaged qualifies the taxpayer or beneficiary as being in a U.S. trade or business.
5. If foreign taxpayer is engaged in business in U.S., all U.S. source income is effectively connected business income so long as income was from assets or activities of U.S. business. Determination is made only for fixed periodical income, gain or loss from sale of capital assets and specially treated items.
6. Factors considered in determining whether income, gain, or loss was "effectively connected" with U.S. trade or business.
   a. Asset-use test.
   b. Business-activities test.
7. Only 3 types of foreign source income can be effectively connected with a U.S. business [¶ 3711(b)]:
   a. Rents and royalties from foreign intangibles.
   b. Income and gain or loss from stocks and bonds to financial businesses.
   c. Income or gain from foreign sales of inventory through a U.S. office.

F. **U.S. source income includes [¶ 3712]:**
   1. U.S. business profits, wages and salaries.
   2. Other items:
      a. Interest and dividend payments.
      b. Compensation for services in U.S.
      c. Rents and royalties from U.S. property interests.
      d. Gain on sale of U.S. realty.
      e. Gain on sale of personal property sold in U.S. after purchase abroad (except in U.S. possession).

III. Tax Treaties [¶ 3720]
IV. U.S. Income From Foreign Sources
   A. Earned income of citizens from sources outside U.S. [¶ 3725].
      1. Except for payments by the U.S. or its agencies, U.S. citizens can exclude limited amount of earned income from sources outside U.S.
      2. Earned income defined [¶ 3725(a)].
      3. For tax years after 1976, U.S. citizens who are working abroad and are bona fide residents of a foreign country can exclude up to $15,000 for one full tax year.
      4. Taxpayer must either be a bona fide resident for one full tax year or be present in the country for 510 days during an 18 month period. (If 18 month period doesn't include full tax year, $15,000 exclusion is prorated on daily basis.)
      5. Taxpayers working for qualified charitable organizations can exclude up to a maximum of $20,000 per year.
      6. If return due before exclusion established, taxpayer may get an extension of time to file, or pay the tax on the income and later claim a refund or credit.
   B. **Allowances to U.S. Government officers and employees in foreign service excluded [¶ 3726].**
   C. **U.S. citizens or domestic corporations receiving income from within U.S. possessions [¶ 3727].**
      1. Exempt, if:
         a. For the 3 years immediately prior to close of tax year (or, for the "applicable part" of such test period) at least 80% of taxpayer's gross income from sources in a U.S. possession. and
         b. At least 50% as compensation or from active conduct of trade or business in such possession.
      2. U.S. payments to personnel working possessions not excludable.
      3. Residents of Puerto Rico (U.S. citizens or aliens) who are bona fide residents of Puerto Rico for the entire tax year exclude all income from sources in Puerto Rico. Rule does not apply to U.S. employees.
   D. **Special rules on foreign investments [¶ 3728]:**
      1. Shareholder of controlled foreign corporations are currently taxed on:
         a. Certain passive-type income (e.g., dividends, interest, rents, etc.).

b. Income of sales or service subsidiaries.
c. Income from insurance or reinsurance of U.S. risks (life or property).
2. Gain received by a 10% or more U.S. shareholder on sale or redemption of stocks in controlled foreign corporation is, to a limited extent, taxable as ordinary income.
3. Undistributed income is taxable to a shareholder owning at least 10% of stock of controlled foreign corporation. Individuals can elect to have income taxed as if they were corporations, entitling them to corporate foreign tax credit.
4. U.S. shareholders are not currently taxed on certain tax haven types of income of foreign subsidiaries under specified conditions.
5. Gain on sale of foreign investment company stock is taxed as ordinary income to a limited extent.

SOCIAL SECURITY TAXES—ESTATE TAX—GIFT TAX

Chapter 28—SOCIAL SECURITY TAXES
(Detailed Table of Contents below)

Chapter 29—FEDERAL ESTATE TAX
(Detailed Table of Contents at page 3901)

Chapter 30—FEDERAL GIFT TAX
(Detailed Table of Contents at page 4001)

Chapter 28

SOCIAL SECURITY TAXES
TABLE OF CONTENTS

OLD-AGE, SURVIVOR AND DISABILITY INSURANCE, HEALTH INSURANCE FOR THE AGED

¶	
Tax on wages	3800
Covered employment	3803
Exempt employment	3804
Agricultural labor	3805
Domestics	3806
Casual labor	3807
Family employment	3808
Clergymen	3809
Students and trainees	3810
Newsboys and news vendors	3811
Railroad workers	3812
Communist organizations	3813
Non-profit organizations	3814
Government employees	3815
Partially covered employment	3816
Employer-employee relationship	3817
Taxable wages	3818
Payments not taxed as wages	3819

TAXES ON SELF-EMPLOYMENT INCOME

	¶
Tax on self-employed persons	3821
What is self-employment	3822
Self-employment income	3823
Exclusions from self-employment income	3824

RETURNS, PAYMENT AND REFUNDS

	¶
Social security and employer identification numbers	3826
Returns and payment of taxes	3827
Records	3828
Refunds and adjustments	3829
Additions and penalties	3830

UNEMPLOYMENT INSURANCE

	¶
Tax on employers	3834
Wages subject to tax	3837
Return and payment of tax	3838
Credit against federal tax for state payments	3839
Credit allowed under merit rating	3841
Employer's records	3843
Refunds and adjustments	3844
Additions and penalties	3845
Procedure after Revenue service's determination against taxpayer	3846

• Highlights of Chapter 28 .... Page 3861

Footnotes appear at end of this Chapter.

OLD-AGE, SURVIVOR AND DISABILITY INSURANCE, HEALTH INSURANCE FOR THE AGED

¶ **3800 Tax on wages.**[1] All employers of one or more persons, except in excluded classes of employment, are required to pay excise taxes on a limited amount of wages [¶ 3818(a)] paid to employees—an Old-Age, Survivor and Disability Insurance Tax and a Hospitalization Insurance Tax [Sec. 3111]. This combination of taxes is commonly referred to as the social security tax. The tax rates for calendar year 1977 total 5.85% (4.95% OASDI plus 0.90% Hospital Insurance).

NOTE: The rates for calendar years 1978—1980 will total 6.05% (4.95% OASDI plus 1.10% Hospital Insurance).

All employees not engaged in exempt employment [¶ 3804] pay taxes on a limited amount of wages [¶ 3818(a)] at the same rates as the employer. Tips reported to the employer as wages are included in the employee's tax base, but not in the employer's [Sec. 3102(c)]. See also ¶ 2503; 3818.

The amount of the employee tax is withheld by the employer. It is deducted from each salary or wage payment [Sec. 3102; 31.3102-1]. An employer of agricultural workers and domestics may use his own judgment whether to withhold from each payment or wait until the tests for coverage have been met[1] [¶ 3805; 3806]. The tax collected is deposited with an authorized bank or Federal Reserve Bank. If an employer deducts less than the correct amount of tax, he is liable for the full amount [Sec. 31.3102-1(c)], but he is not liable for nonpayment of the tax on tips if he does not have available sufficient employee funds to permit deduction of the employee tax by the 10th day of the month after the tips are considered paid.

The tax is imposed regardless of age. The employee (or self-employed person) must pay the tax on all covered earnings even if he is a minor, or has reached the retirement age, or is getting a social security benefit.

¶ **3803 Covered employment.** Employers and employees are liable for the social security tax only on the wages paid and received in covered employment. So it is important to know what covered employment is.

(a) Employment within U.S. Generally, any service performed in the U.S. by an employee for his employer, regardless of the citizenship or residence of either, is considered covered employment. For this purpose, the U.S. includes the Virgin Islands, Puerto Rico, Guam, and American Samoa. All employment within the U.S. is covered, except for a few occupations specifically exempt [¶ 3804].

(b) Employment outside the U.S. is covered *if* the service is rendered by a U.S. citizen for an American employer [Sec. 3121(b)]. Services that would be exempt if performed in the U.S., remain exempt.

U.S. citizens working outside the U.S. for foreign subsidiaries of U.S. firms that own not less than 20% of the foreign subsidiary's voting stock can be covered at the option of the U.S. firm. It must agree with the Secretary of the Treasury to pay the social security tax for them and cover all the U.S. citizens employed by its subsidiary. The employer must file Form 2032 for such workers to be covered [Sec. 3121(1); 36.3121(1)(1)-(1)].

NOTE: If the foreign subsidiary holds over 50 percent of the voting stock of another foreign company, the U.S. citizens employed by the latter also may be covered.

(c) Maritime and aircraft personnel. *(1) On American craft.* Work outside the U.S. is covered if the contract of hire was made in the U.S., or if while the employee is working on the craft, it touches at a port in the U.S., the Virgin Islands, or Puerto Rico.

(2) On foreign craft. Work on a foreign vessel is covered if performed by U.S. citizens for a U.S. employer. Otherwise work on a foreign vessel within the U.S. is exempt if: (i) performed by an alien or for a foreign employer, and (ii) the individual is employed on *and* in connection with the craft when it is outside the U.S. [Sec. 3121(b)(4); 31.3121(b)(4)-1].

¶ **3804 Exempt employment.** Not all employment within the U.S. is covered. The test for coverage depends on such factors as the amount of pay, the nature of the work performed, the nature of the employer, and whether the employees are covered by some other federal retirement system. Both the Federal Insurance Contributions Act (social security taxes) and the Social Security Act (social security benefits) specifically exempt certain classes of employment: Agricultural labor [¶ 3805]; Domestics [¶ 3806]; Casual labor [¶ 3807]; Family employment [¶ 3808]; Clergymen [¶ 3809]; Students and trainees [¶ 3810]; Newsboys and news vendors [¶ 3811]; Railroad workers [¶ 3812]; Communist organizations [¶ 3813]; Nonprofit organizations [¶ 3814]; Government employees [¶ 3815].

> **NOTE:** Not covered are services on fishing boats with fewer than 10 regular crewmen, if their pay is a share of the fleet's or boat's catch. But this rule does not apply to services for and pay received after 12-31-71 and before 10-4-76 that the employer treated as covered employment [Sec. 3121(b)(20)].

¶ **3805 Agricultural labor.** The test for coverage of farm workers is generally the amount of cash wages they receive from a single employer in a calendar year. Farm workers are covered if they work for any one employer who pays them at least $150 in cash wages in a calendar year or if they work for any one employer 20 or more days in a year for a cash wage on a time basis [Sec. 3121(a)(8)]. Sometimes farm workers are supplied to a farmer by a crew leader. If a crew leader pays his crew members for their work, and the leader himself is not designated as the farmer's employee in writing, the men the leader supplies are considered his employees [Sec. 3121(o)]. The farmer himself is covered as a self-employed person [¶ 3823]. Agricultural workers from any foreign country, admitted on a temporary basis, are not covered [Sec. 3121(b)(1); 31.3121(b)(1)-1].

¶ **3806 Domestics.** A domestic worker in a private nonfarm home is covered only if the individual receives $50 or more cash wages in a calendar quarter regardless of the number of days the person works [Sec. 3121(a)(7)(B); 31.3121(a)(7)-1(a)(2)]. It does not matter whether it is for work done in the quarter of payment or during an earlier quarter [Sec. 31.3121(a)(7)-1(b), (c)]. Although a person performing domestic service is in "employment," he is not "covered" unless he has "wages," since both factors must exist. In figuring both the employer's and the domestic's social security tax, the cash wages may, at the employer's option,[1] be rounded to the nearest dollar [Sec. 3121(i); 31.3121(i)-1].

> ➤**OBSERVATION**➤ The coverage of a domestic worker employed in a farm house depends on the character of the farm. If it is operated for profit, the domestic is considered a farm laborer and is covered only if the worker meets the farm labor test [¶ 3805]. If the farm is operated as a "hobby," that is, used mainly for residential purposes or for the pleasure or recreation of the owner, coverage is governed by the test for nonfarm domestics [Sec. 31.3121(g)-1(f)].

Even "baby sitters" are subject to tax under this provision if they meet the prescribed test. However, licensed practical nurses usually will be considered self-employed rather than domestics [¶ 3817].

Footnotes appear at end of this Chapter.

¶ **3807 Casual labor.** Services not in the course of the employer's trade or business are excluded from covered employment *unless* the employee receives $50 or more in cash for any calendar quarter [Sec. 3121(a)(7)(C); 31.3121(a)(7)-1(b), (c)]. Services for a corporation are not excluded from covered employment under this exception [Sec. 31.3121(a)(7)-1(a)(1)].

¶ **3808 Family employment.** Employment of an individual by a spouse (or, if he is under 21, by his parent) is exempt. A parent employed by his child is covered, except for domestic services in the child's home or other work not in the course of the child's trade or business. However, under special circumstances wages paid to close family members as household help can be wages for social security purposes [Sec. 3121(b)(3); 31.3121(b)(3)-1].

¶ **3809 Clergymen** are not in covered employment when performing duties in the exercise of their ministry. Neither are members of religious organizations when performing duties required by the order [Sec. 3121(b)(8)(A); 31.3121(b)(8)-1]. However, both generally are covered as self-employed persons, unless they oppose coverage on conscientious or religious grounds.

¶ **3810 Students and trainees.** Service performed in the employ of a school, college or university is exempt if performed by a *student* who is enrolled and regularly attending classes at the institution [Sec. 3121(b)(10)(B); 31.3121(b)(10)-2]. However, services performed by a student in a *state* institution are not exempt if the state makes an agreement with the Secretary of Health, Education and Welfare to cover the student (¶ 3815(b)) [Sec. 218(5)(D), S.S.A.].[1] Also, domestic service performed by such a student in a local college club or local chapter of a college fraternity or sorority, is exempt [Sec. 3121(b)(2); 31.3121(b)(2)-1]. Some nonresident alien students are not covered for work in connection with their studies [Sec. 3121(b)(19)].

¶ **3811 Newsboys ad news vendors** under 18 years of age are not covered. Service as a newsboy does not include delivering papers or handbills to any point for further delivery or distribution. News vendors, regardless of age, who sell papers or magazines to the ultimate consumer at a fixed price, their compensation being the excess of such price over what they pay for the papers or magazines, are not in covered employment. This is true, even if the news vendor is guaranteed a minimum amount for such service, or is credited with any unsold papers or magazines that are returned [Sec. 3121(b)(14); 31.3121(b)(14)-1].

¶ **3812 Railroad workers** have their own federal retirement system, so they are excluded from coverage [Sec. 3121(b)((9); 31.3121(b)(9)-1].

¶ **3813 Communist organizations.** Any service in the employ of an organization required to register under the Internal Security Act of 1950 is not covered for any quarter in which the organization is required to be registered [Sec. 3121(b)(17)].

¶ **3814 Nonprofit organizations. (a) Complete exemption.** Religious, charitable, educational, and other organizations exempt from income tax under Sec. 501(c)(3) [¶ 3436] are exempt for social security purposes unless the organization elects to come under the law [Sec. 3121(b)(8)(B); 31.3121(b)(8)-2]. The election is made by filing with the internal revenue officer designated in the filing instructions a certificate of waiver of exemption (SS-15) and a certificate of employees' election (SS-15a) [Sec. 31.3121(k)-1(b)(3)]. If the organization has employees who are covered (or are eligible to be covered) by a state or local government pension or retirement fund or system, and employees who are not so covered or eligible, its employees should be separated into two groups along those lines.

Waivers may be filed for either or both groups. These will be effective for the calendar quarters specified in the certificate. When the certificate is made effective for a quarter earlier than the one in which it is filed, all returns and taxes for the earlier quarters are due on the last day of the month following the quarter in which the certificate is filed [Sec. 3121(k)(1); 31.3121(k)-1(c)(4)].

Employees who do not sign the original certificate continue exempt and are not covered. However, they may later get coverage by filing Supplement Form SS-15(a) within 24 months after the calendar quarter in which the certificate was filed. The supplemental list is effective for service beginning on the first day of the quarter in which the list is filed [Sec. 3121(k)(1)(C)].

All employees hired or rehired after the quarter in which the original certificate is filed are covered on a compulsory basis [Sec. 3121(b)(8)(B)(ii)].

> **NOTE:** Nonprofit organizations that have not filed a waiver but have collected the tax and not sought a refund for paying it will be considered to have filed the required waiver [Sec. 3121(k)(4)].

The organization may terminate its coverage and that of its employees by giving a 2-year notice, but not until after eight years of coverage. Coverage, therefore, must actually run for at least ten years. The organization may withdraw its notice in writing before the end of the quarter when its original notice was to have become effective [Sec. 3121(k)(1)(D); 31.3121(k)-1(d)].

If the organization fails or is no longer able to pay the required taxes, the coverage may be revoked. The Commissioner must give the organization at least 60 days advance written notice that the period covered by the certificate will terminate at the end of the calendar quarter specified in the notice [Sec. 3121(k)(2); 31.3121(k)-1(e)].

(b) Limited exemption. Tax-exempt farmers' cooperatives and organizations exempt from income tax under Code Sec. 501(a) (other than a trust exempt under Sec. 401(a)) are covered for social security tax purposes [¶ 3435]. However, an employee is exempt in any calendar quarter in which he earns less than $50 [Sec. 3121(b)(10)(A); 31.3121(b)(10)-1(a)].

¶ 3815 Government employees. (a) Employees of the U.S. Government and its instrumentalities. These employees are exempt if they are covered by a retirement system established by Congress. Thus, all workers under the civil service retirement system are excluded from coverage. But all members of the U.S. armed services and Peace Corps members are directly covered [Sec. 3121(m), (p)]. Also covered are payments made after 1972 to employees of a Federal Home Loan Bank.

Employees of U.S. instrumentalities also are exempt if (1) there is a provision of law specifically referring to the social security tax which exempts the instrumentality from that tax, or (2) the instrumentality was exempt on December 31, 1950, and its employees are covered by a retirement system set up by the instrumentality itself.

However, exception (2) above does not apply to: (i) employees of corporations wholly owned by the U.S.; (ii) employees of national farm loan associations, a production credit association, a Federal Reserve bank, or a federal credit union; (iii) employees of committees set up under the Commodity Stabilization Service; (iv) certain civilian employees of military post exchanges.

Besides the general exemption for those covered by retirement systems, there are specific exemptions for the President, Vice President, members of Congress, inmates of penal institutions and student nurses in federal hospitals, and for temporary services during disasters [Sec. 3121(b)(5), (6)].

Footnotes appear at end of this Chapter.

(b) Employees of state and local government. Employees of any state, its political subdivisions, or any instrumentality wholly owned by one or more states or political subdivisions (except policemen and firemen in certain states) may be brought into social security coverage through agreements with the Secretary of Health, Education and Welfare [Sec. 218, S.S.A.].[1] Otherwise, they are exempt [Sec. 3121(b)(7); 31.3121(b)(7)-1]. However, assistants engaged by a public official or employee are exempt only if the employment is authorized by a statute.[2] Employees who are presently covered by another retirement system may vote in favor of social security coverage by secret written ballot. If a majority of the members *eligible to vote,* vote in favor of coverage, all will be covered.

Certain states and state-owned instrumentalities can divide their retirement systems into two parts: one part for covered positions and the other part for positions not covered [Sec. 218(d)(6), S.S.A.].

For referendum purposes, any political subdivision or combination of subdivisions may be considered as having a separate retirement system. Each public institution of higher learning also may be considered as having a separate system.

Special rules apply to employees of *publicly owned and operated transportation systems:* Employees are not covered if (a) no part of the system was acquired from private ownership after 1936, or (b) the employees are the beneficiaries of a retirement system that the state constitution protects from impairment. Otherwise, if part of the system was acquired before 1951, all employees are covered. In the case of acquisitions after 1950, only the employees taken over will be covered, if the acquisition is an addition to an existing system, but all employees will be covered if the acquisition is a new system [Sec. 3121(j); 31.3121(j)-1].

(c) Employees of foreign governments are exempt. Services performed for an instrumentality wholly owned by a foreign government may be exempt if the foreign government gives a similar exemption to employees of the U.S. or its instrumentalities. Services performed for an international organization, such as the United Nations, are not covered employment [Sec. 3121(b)(11), (12), (15); 31.3121(b) (11), (12), (15)-1].

> NOTE: U.S. citizens employed by foreign governments or their instrumentalities, or by international organizations, are entitled to coverage as self-employed individuals [¶ 3823(e)].

¶ 3816 Partially covered employment. If an employee performs both exempt and non-exempt service for the same employer, all the employment will be considered non-exempt if one-half or more of the employee's time during any pay period is devoted to non-exempt employment; if less than one-half is devoted to non-exempt employment, all will be exempt. "Pay period" means the period (not more than 31 consecutive days) wages are ordinarily paid to employees by the employer [Sec. 3121(c); 31.3121(c)-1].

This rule does not apply if part of the services rendered by an individual for one person during a pay period is performed as an "employee" and part is performed not as an "employee," for example, as an independent contractor. Services as "employee" are covered, and services not as an "employee" are excluded.[1] But see ¶ 3821-3823 for coverage of self-employed persons.

> NOTE: Domestic service or agricultural labor is employment even if certain pay is not considered "wages." Therefore, the rule does not apply if an employee works part time as a servant in the employer's home (or as a hired hand on his farm) and part time at the employer's place of business. Thus, if the pay for domestic or agricultural services meets the $50 a quarter test [¶ 3807], all of the wages are taxable.[2]

¶ 3817 Employer-employee relationship. The employer and his employees have to pay a tax on the wages paid to the employees who are in covered employment [¶ 3800]. If the wages are paid to an independent contractor, no tax is due from the person paying the compensation. (A tax may be payable by the independent contractor as a self-employed person—see ¶ 3821-3823.) Therefore, it is important to determine if a person who performs work for another is an employee or an independent contractor.

NOTE: A ruling as to whether a person is an employee or self-employed may be obtained from the Revenue Service by submitting Form SS-8.

(a) Who is an employee. Generally, the common law tests for the employer-employee relationship are used [Sec. 3121(d)]. The relationship exists when the person for whom services are performed has the right to control and direct the person who performs the services, not only as to the result to be accomplished by the work, but also as to the details and means to accomplish that result [Sec. 31.3121(d)-1(c)].

(b) Special cases. The following are considered employees (even though they may not be employees under the common law tests) if they perform services for pay in the prescribed circumstances [Sec. 31.3121(d)-1(d)].

A full-time traveling or city salesman (other than an agent-driver or commission-driver mentioned below) is an employee, if he solicits orders for one principal from wholesalers, retailers, contractors, hotels, restaurants and the like, for merchandise and business supplies [Sec. 3121(d)(3)(D). His entire or principal business activity must be devoted to solicitation for one principal. The multiple-line salesman generally is not an "employee" under this provision. If the salesman solicits orders primarily for one principal, he will not be excluded solely because of side line sales activities on behalf of one or more other persons. In this case, the salesman is the employee only of the person for whom he primarily solicits orders and not of the other persons. Note that the common law test is always applied first, and the new tests are only applied if the common law test is not met.

An agent-driver or commission-driver is an "employee" if he distributes meat, vegetable, fruit, bakery, beverage (except milk) products, or handles laundry or dry-cleaning for his principal[1] [Sec. 3121(d)(3)(A)]. This includes a person who operates his own truck or the company's truck, serves customers designated by the company as well as those solicited on his own, and whose pay is a commission on his sales or the difference between the price he charges his customers and the price he pays to the company for the product or service [Sec. 31.3121(d)-1(d)].

Full-time life insurance salesmen are "employees" [Sec. 3121(d)(3)(B)]. In determining the status of a life insurance salesman, the common law test is first applied. If he is an employee under this test, he is an employee regardless of other tests. If he does not meet the common law test, he is covered if his entire or principal business activity is devoted to soliciting life insurance or annuity contracts primarily for one insurance company.[2]

A homeworker is an employee, if he meets the common law tests, or if he meets all the following tests: (a) he does work according to specifications furnished by the person for whom the services are performed on materials furnished by the person, that must be returned to that person or his designee and (b) he is paid at least $50 cash in any calendar quarter [Sec. 3121(a)(10); 3121(d)(3)(C)]. The pay test is based on wages paid in the calendar quarter rather than on pay earned during a calendar quarter [Sec. 31.3121(a)(10)-1]. To be a homeworker substantially all the services as a homeworker must be personally performed by the individual.

The above four exceptions do not apply, and the persons described are not employees, if they have a substantial investment in the facilities used in connection

Footnotes appear at end of this Chapter.

¶ 3817

with their job (other than facilities for transportation), or if the services are in the nature of a single transaction, and not part of a continuing relationship with the employer [Sec. 3121(d)(3)].

(c) **Officers and directors of a corporation.** The law specifically includes "any" officer of a corporation as an employee unless the officer performs no services or only minor ones, and neither receives nor is entitled to any pay [Sec. 3121(d)(1); 31.3121(d)-1(b)].

A director of a corporation is not an employee [Sec. 31.3121(d)-1(b)], and directors' fees are excluded from social security tax. However, he may be an employee if he acts as an officer[3] or if he performs services for the corporation other than taking part in meetings of the board of directors.[4] See ¶ 3823(e) for directors' fees as self-employment income.

Bank directors serving on bank committees are presumed *not* to be employees if the committee (a) consists exclusively of directors or (b) consists primarily of directors and the committee operates like a committee that includes only directors. But the bank must treat committee members who are not directors as employees and pay the tax on their pay unless the bank gets a contrary ruling from the Revenue Service.[5]

(d) **Partners** are not employees of the partnership, so their drawings are not subject to the employer-employee taxes.[6] But they may be subject to the tax on self-employed persons [¶¶ 3821-3823].

¶ 3818 Taxable wages. Wages subject to the social security tax generally include all pay within the limitation explained in (a) below, paid in cash or any other form, to an employee for services for his employer in covered employment [Sec. 3121(a)]. There are a number of exceptions. See ¶ 3819.

Basically, taxable wages are those paid for services in covered employment. Thus, salaries, fees, Christmas gifts and bonuses,[1] bonuses paid in installments to retired employees for past services,[2] employee stock bonus,[3] suggestion awards,[4] sales contest prize awards (cash or cash value paid to salesman directly or to salesman's wife),[5] sales commissions (but not if paid to former customers),[6] are taxable wages. The basis of the wage is immaterial. For example, it is taxable whether paid on an hourly, daily, weekly, monthly or annual basis, or on a piecework or a percentage of the profits basis [Sec. 31.3121(a)-1(c), (d)].

The amount of wages paid in any form other than money is the fair market value of the goods, at the time of payment [Sec. 31.3121(a)-1(e)]. If wages are paid in a foreign currency, the official rate of exchange when the payment is made is used to figure the value of the payment in U.S. currency, both to figure the tax and to determine the limitation on taxable wages.[7]

Tips totaling $20 or more a month received by an employee in the course of his employment by any one employer are counted as taxable wages [Sec. 3121(a)]. The employer only withholds on the reported tips, and only to the extent he can collect the tax out of the employee's wages or other funds [¶ 3827] in the employer's hands; the employee can voluntarily furnish any deficiency [Sec. 3102(c); 31.3402(k)-1(a)(3)]. The social security tax reporting and withholding procedures are the same as those for income tax withholding on tip income [¶¶ 2503(a); 2504(i); 2508(a)]. If the available funds are not enough to cover both liabilities, the social security tax on tips has priority over the withholding tax [Sec. 31.3402(k)-1(c)]. The employee must pay a penalty of 50% of the social security tax due on any tips he willfully fails to report to the employer as required [Sec. 6652(c); 31.6652(c)-1].

Agent-drivers' and commission-drivers' wages. When an agent-driver or commission-driver is an employee [¶ 3817(b)], and he submits a statement of his gross receipts, expenses (other than transportation), and the fair rental value of his truck, to his employer, the difference between his gross receipts and the total of his expenses and the rental value of the truck is his wages. If no statement is furnished, the difference between the price he pays his principal and the suggested selling price is his wages.[8]

(a) Limitation on taxable wages. The first $16,500 in 1977 (with adjustments after 1977 when there is a cost-of-living benefit increase) of wages an employee receives during the calendar year is subject to tax [Sec. 3121(a)]. The employee includes in this amount pay from his employer and any tips of $20 or more a month he receives. The employer counts only the amount he pays the employee.[9]

> **Example 1:** By July 1, 1977, Jones, a waiter, received $9,200 in pay from his employer, and tips of $7,300. If the employee tax was paid on these amounts, Jones' liability is fully satisfied. However, the employer will continue to pay employer tax on the next $7,300 of wages he pays Jones during the year.

If an employee works for more than one employer during a calendar year, each employer withholds employee tax and pays the employer tax as if he were the only employer during the year. (For exception for successor employer, see (b) below.) The employee can apply for a refund or credit for any excess social security tax he paid.

(b) Successor employer. In figuring the wage limitation, a successor employer who takes over a business can count the wages paid by the predecessor to the employees who continue in the employ of the successor employer [Sec. 3121(a)(1); 31.3121(a)(1)-1(b)].

> **Example 2:** If Brown works for Cell Co. for the first four months in 1977 and receives $6,000, and then Byer Co. buys all the assets of Cell (or succeeds to its business by merger), Byer will be subject to the employer tax only on the first $10,500 of wages Byer pays Brown during the remainder of the year.

¶ **3819 Payments not taxed as wages.** The law specifically exempts certain forms of compensation from social security tax.

(a) Payments in kind—board and lodging—meals. Pay in any medium other than cash is not taxable, if paid for (1) domestic service in private home, (2) farm labor, or (3) service not in the course of the employer's trade or business [Sec. 3121(a)(7)(A), 3121(a)(8)(A); 31.3121(a)(7)-1]. If the items are *not* paid for services indicated in (1), (2) and (3) above, they are included in "wages" as follows:

Items furnished employees by employer are taxable wages if their value is an appreciable part of the pay. If the item is of small value compared to total pay and is furnished for employees' health, contentment, good will or efficiency, it is not taxable. Thus, board and lodging furnished employees on vessels or in isolated localities, living quarters furnished apartment house superintendents, and meals furnished restaurant employees are taxable wages [Sec. 31.3121(a)-1(f)]. Lunches voluntarily furnished to promote health and efficiency of employees are not taxable when wage scale is not lowered to reflect their value.[1] Payments made directly to an employee's landlord by the employer are taxable wages.[2]

(b) Traveling and allied expenses. Advances or reimbursements for traveling and similar expenses incurred by an employee in the course of his employer's business are not wages, if the employer identifies the payments. He can do this either by making a separate payment or by specifically indicating the separate amounts if the wages and the expense allowance are combined in a single payment [Sec. 31.3121(a)-1(h)].[3] After 7-1-77, reimbursements for traveling expenses incurred between a taxpayer's residence and work, even though temporary, are tax-

Footnotes appear at end of this Chapter.

able as wages, regardless of the nature of work, distance traveled, mode of transportation or degree of necessity.[4]

(c) **Payments under employee benefit, trust or annuity plans.** Payments made under a *plan* established by the employer on account of retirement, death, sickness or accident disability, or medical or hospital expenses are not taxable wages (under certain conditions) [Sec. 3121(a)(2); 31.3121(a)(2)-1]. This exception applies also to payments made on account of the employee's dependents. See also (d) below. But a payment that would have been made regardless of retirement, death, or disability is not excluded [Sec. 3121(a)(13)]. Payments to an employee or for his benefit under a trust or annuity *plan* qualifying for tax exemption purposes under Sec. 501(a), also are not taxable wages [Sec. 3121(a)(5); 31.3121(a)(5)-1].

(d) **Retirement and insurance payments.** Payments to an employee (or to provide for such payments to him) on account of retirement are not taxable wages [Sec. 3121(a)(3); 31.3121(a)(3)-1], unless the premiums are paid by the employees through a salary reduction agreement.[5] This also applies to premiums paid for employee annuity contracts by organizations exempt under Sec. 501(c)(3)[6] [¶ 3436].

Payments to an employee (or to provide for such payments to him) on account of sickness or accident, disability, or medical or hospitalization expenses are not taxable wages, *if* they are made more than 6 calendar months after the month he leaves [Sec. 3121(a)(4); 31.3121(a)(4)-1].

≫**OBSERVATION**→ The provisions in (c) apply to payments under a formal plan. The provisions in (d) apply even if there is no plan. Note that a payment for sickness or accident disability made within 6 calendar months after the employee leaves is not excluded under (d). If it is made under a formal plan, it would be excluded under (c).

(e) **Other payments.** Employer payments of the employee's social security or state unemployment insurance taxes are not taxable wages. Also excluded are tax deductible moving expenses and payments to an employee (other than sick or vacation pay) after he reaches retirement age if he does not work for the employer during the period for which the payment is made [Sec. 3121(a); 31.3121(a)(6)-1, 31.3121(a)(9)-1, 31.3121(a)(11)-1]. Dismissal payments are taxable wages.[7]

TAXES ON SELF-EMPLOYMENT INCOME

¶ **3821 Tax on self-employed persons.**[1] This tax is levied on the taxable self-employment income of every citizen or resident alien engaged in a non-exempt trade or business [Sec. 1402]. The object of the tax is to provide the self-employed with the same benefits that employees get through the payment of the social security tax on their wages. The rate for tax years starting in 1977 is 7.9% (7.0% OASDI plus 0.9% Hospital Insurance).

NOTE: The rate for tax years starting after 12-31-77 and before 1-1-81 will total 8.10% (7.0% OASDI plus 1.10% Hospital Insurance).

¶ **3822 What is self-employment.** Generally only an individual who carries on a "trade or business" as a proprietor or partner, or who renders services as an independent contractor, is self-employed and has self-employment income. The term "trade or business," however, does not embrace all business endeavors. A person paid for making an occasional speech is not engaged in a trade or business, but may be so considered if he seeks engagements and speaks with reasonable regularity.[1] Illegal activities may be a trade or business.[2]

Clergymen. Clergymen, Christian Science practitioners and members of religious orders (except those who have taken a vow of poverty) are considered self-employed and are subject to self-employment tax, unless they get an exemption on conscientious or religious grounds. Application on Form 4361 must be filed by the due date of the return for the second tax year ending after 1967 or the second tax year their net earnings from these services are at least $400 whichever is later. Individuals already covered cannot apply. Exemption is irrevocable when granted. Coverage generally starts with the first tax year the individual has net earnings of $400 or more (any part of which is from services as a minister, member, or practitioner) and for all succeeding tax years [Sec. 1402(c), 1402(e); 1.1402(c)-3(e)(2), 1.1402(c)-5, 1.1402(e)-2A].

Excluded services. A person will *not* be self-employed if he engages in any of the following:

• Services performed in public office [Sec. 1.1402(c)-2]. However, state and local government officials paid on a fee basis are covered, unless they elected not to be or their state covers them as employees [Sec. 1402(c)(1); 1.1402(c)-3(f)].

• Services performed as a railroad worker [Sec. 1.1402(c)-4]. (These workers have their own retirement system.)

• Services performed by a member of a religious order who has taken a vow of poverty [Sec. 1402(c); 1.1402(c)-5].

• Services by a member of a religious sect can be excluded if the sect provides for dependent members, is opposed to all life, health and accident insurance and has existed since 1950. A member must apply for an exemption on Form 4029. This is filed by his return's due date for the first tax year that includes self-employment income. If none is filed by that date, he has until 3 months after the Revenue Service notifies him that a timely application was not filed [Sec. 1402(h); 1.1402(h)-1].

• Services as a newsboy under the age of 18 [Sec. 1.1402(c)-3(b)].

Obviously pay for services as an "employee" is not pay from "self-employment," except in the case of certain news vendors 18 years of age or over [¶ 3811]. In this connection the term "employee" and "wages" have the meanings explained in ¶ 3817 and 3818.

NOTE: Certain fishing crewmen [¶ 3804] will be treated as self-employed [Sec. 1402(c)(2)(F)].

¶ 3823 Self-employment income. (a) Net earnings. Self-employment income is defined as the net earnings of an individual from self-employment, if he has at least $400 of such earnings in his tax year [Sec. 1402(b)(2); 1.1402(b)-1(c)].

Example 1: Jones had $350 of net earnings from self-employment during his tax year. Even if he earned all of this income in one calendar quarter during that year, he will pay no tax, since he has not earned any self-employment income.

If a self-employed individual has more than one business, his net self-employment income is the total net earnings of all businesses. A loss in one business is deductible from the earnings of the other businesses [Sec. 1.1402(a)-2(c)].

In 1977, self-employment income is limited to $16,500 less net earnings from wages. The taxable base will be adjusted if there is an automatic cost-of-living benefit increase. In those years, the taxable base will be an amount equal to the contribution and benefit base (determined under Sec. 230 of SSA) less net earnings from wages [Sec. 1402(b)(H)(I)].

Example 2: Jones has $17,000 of net earnings from self-employment during 1977, and receives $80 a week in "wages" that year. His taxable self-employment income for the year is $12,340 ($16,500 − $4,160 wages).

Example 3: Williams has $1,000 of net earnings from self-employment during 1977, and receives $16,200 in "wages" that year. His taxable self-employment income for the year is $300

Footnotes appear at end of this Chapter.

($16,500 — $16,200). Since Williams' earnings from self-employment are more than $400, he must pay self-employment tax even though the adjustment for "wages" reduces the taxable amount to below $400.

(b) Optional methods of computing net earnings. A farmer who has net earnings from self-employment of $400 or more in any year and receives less than $16,500 in wages must pay self-employment tax for that year. For any tax year starting in any year after 1974, the taxable base will be adjusted if there is an automatic cost-of-living benefit increase [(a) above]. To determine his net earnings from self-employment, a farmer ordinarily must claim all of his deductions, including depreciation. However, he may use an optional method to figure his net earnings, that does not require listing deductions. This method can be used only to find his self-employment tax, and not to determine his income tax. Under the optional method, if his gross income from farming is not over $2,400, he may consider his net earnings from farming to be two-thirds of his gross income. If his gross income from farming is more than $2,400, and his net earnings from farming are less than $1,600 he may consider his net earnings from farming to be $1,600. Similarly, a self-employed person who is not a farmer may elect an optional method to compute his net earnings if self-employed net earnings are under $1,600 and less than ⅔ of gross nonfarm profits. Use of the nonfarm option is limited to not more than 5 times [Sec. 1402(a); 1.1402(a)-13, 15].

NOTE: A farmer who finds he would get greater benefits under the optional method after he files his benefit claim may file Form 2190 to amend his original return and change to the optional method.[1]

(c) Income earned abroad that qualifies for exclusion from income tax [¶ 3725] is not included as net earnings from self-employment. This rule does not, however, apply to residents of Puerto Rico, the Virgin Islands, Guam or American Samoa. They must treat self-employment income the same as residents of the U.S., except that a Puerto Rican resident must include income from Puerto Rican sources in his gross income [Sec. 1402(a)(6), 7651; 1.1402(a)-2, 1.1402(a)-9, 1.1402(a)-12].

(d) Partners' income. A partner's earnings from self-employment include his distributive share of the partnership net income, whether or not distributed. Guaranteed payments and other items that must be accounted for separately[2] [¶ 2913] also are included in the self-employment income computation. It is the nature of the services of the partnership as such, rather than the services contributed by the individual member, that determines the taxability of the distributive share.

➢**OBSERVATION**➢ Income from a corporation that has elected to be taxed as a partnership [¶ 3140] is not income from self-employment.[3]

If the individual and the partnership are on different tax years, the same rules apply as for income tax [Sec. 1.1402(a)-2(e)]. See ¶ 2920.

If a partner dies before the end of the partnership's tax year, his self-employment net earnings should include his distributive share of the partnership's ordinary income or loss for the partnership tax year, except that attributable to any interest in the partnership after the month he died. For this purpose, the partnership's ordinary income or loss is treated as if it was realized or sustained ratably over the partnership tax year. While the partner's "distributive share" includes the share that goes to his estate or any person succeeding to his rights because of his death, it does not include any share from a partnership interest he did not hold at his death [Sec. 1402(f); 1.1402(f)-1(a)(3)]. Generally, retirement payments received by retired partners are net earnings from self-employment, except for certain periodic payments made by a partnership on account of retirement under a written plan [Sec. 1402(a)(10); 1.1402(a)-17].

(e) Income from other sources. *(1) Directors' fees.* Directors are in a trade or business when not employees. Therefore, their fees and other pay for services as such, including attendance at meetings and serving on standing committees, are earnings from self-employment.[4]

(2) Fiduciaries' fees. Fees received by a fiduciary not in a trade or business are not self-employment income. Usually only a professional fiduciary is considered engaged in a trade or business, and the fees received by him are self-employment income. However, even if an individual is not considered a professional fiduciary, he may be subject to the self-employment tax, if he carries on a business in the administration of the estate.[5]

(3) Research funds. A person who gets funds, under a research grant to do independent research work, which are taxable to him, is an independent contractor. He must include the funds in his self-employment income.[3]

(4) International organizations. A U.S. citizen employed in the U.S. by a foreign government, its instrumentalities or by an international organization is considered a self-employed individual [Sec. 1402(c)(2); 1.1402(c)-3]. If employed by an international organization, he is considered self-employed even though he also is covered by the Civil Service Retirement Act.[6]

(5) Trust income. When beneficiaries have the sole right to operate trust property for their joint profit, their distributive shares of the profits may be self-employment income from a joint venture or partnership.[7]

¶ 3824 **Exclusions from self-employment income.** Not all self-employment income is considered net earnings. The rules are as follows [Sec. 1402(a); 1.1402(a)]:

- *Dividends* are included only by a dealer in stock or securities, and then only if received in the course of his business as a dealer.
- *Interest* on business loans is included, even if the lender is not in the business of making loans. For instance, interest received by a merchant on his accounts or notes receivable is included. Interest on nonbusiness loans is excluded. Interest on corporate and government securities is included only by a dealer in securities.
- *Rentals* from real estate (including rentals in crop shares) less any related deductions are included only by a real estate dealer, and then only if they are received in the course of his business as a dealer. Owners of boarding houses, apartment houses, tourist homes, or motels, where services also are rendered to the occupants, are subject to self-employment taxes. Services are considered rendered if they are primarily for the occupants' convenience. Supplying maid service, for example, constitutes such services, but furnishing heat and light or collecting trash does not.[1] Payments to a supervising beneficiary of trust property and his distributive share of profits from rentals of office space is rental income. He does not render "services" to the occupants.[2] For crop share arrangements, if the owner or tenant has an agreement with another person that the latter will produce commodities on the land with material participation by the owner or tenant in the production income that results is not excluded from self-employment net earnings. The activities of a farm management company agent are disregarded in determining whether the owner or tenant participated materially in farm production. The owner or tenant meets the requirements if he can show he (a) periodically advises or consults with the other party about producing the commodity, (b) periodically inspects the production activities on the land and (c) furnishes a substantial part of the equipment and livestock used in the production activities, or provides funds or assumes financial responsibility.[3]

Footnotes appear at end of this Chapter.

- *Profit or loss from business or profession.* Income and deductions properly reported in Schedule C of Form 1040 are included; but not if related to services not considered as being self-employment [¶ 3822]. No net operating loss is allowable.

➤**OBSERVATION**➔ While the mere receipt of royalties probably is not a trade or business, royalties from a trade or business probably will be considered self-employment income.[4]

- *Gain or loss from disposing of property* is excluded if from (1) the sale or exchange of capital assets; (2) the cutting of timber or disposal of timber, coal or iron ore if the proper election is made [¶ 1621; 1623]; (3) the sale, exchange or involuntary conversion of property other than inventory or property held for sale to customers.
- *Personal exemptions.* No deductions are allowed for personal exemptions.
- *A minister* or member of a religious order, in figuring his self-employment income, must include the rental value of a parsonage, or any rental allowance, as well as meals and lodging furnished him for the church's or order's convenience.[1] If he is a U.S. citizen performing religious services as an employee of an American employer [Sec. 3121(h)] or has a congregation abroad of U.S. citizens, he figures his self-employment income without excluding earned income from sources outside the U.S., and without taking into account the rules in Sec. 931 of income from sources within U.S. possessions [¶ 3727]. "Possessions" do not include the Virgin Islands, Guam or American Samoa.

RETURNS, PAYMENT AND REFUNDS

¶ 3826 Social Security and employer identification numbers. (a) Application by employer. Within 7 days after the first payment of wages, an employer must apply for an identification number by filing Form SS-4. He applies at the local Social Security office, or with the Revenue Service. An employer who hires household domestics may be assigned a number without application [Sec. 31.6011(b)-1].

(b) Application by employee. An employee who does not have a social security number must apply for one on Form SS-5 within 7 days after he is hired. (He must file earlier if he leaves the job before the seventh day. The form is filed with any local Social Security office [Sec. 31.6011(b)-2].

(c) Duties of employer and employee. The employer must include his assigned identification number on all records, correspondence, claims or other returns required under the law and regulations. He is liable for a $5 penalty each time he fails to do so. He should have only one identification number [Sec. 31.6011(b)-1]. If he acquired the business of another employer, he cannot use the number assigned to the other employer.[1]

The names and social security number of each employee must be entered on the records, returns and claims of the employer. If an employee fails to advise the employer as to his social security number, the employer must request the number. The employer is subject to a $5 penalty if he fails to include the number on a return [Sec. 301.6109-1, 301.6676-1]. If an employee has no social security number, the employer must advise him of the requirement. If the employee then fails or refuses to file an application, the employer must state that fact by affidavit when he files his return [¶ 3500]. If the employee does not have a social security number or a receipt when the employer files his return on Form 941, the employer should attach the employee's Form SS-5 or statement. A copy of the Form SS-5 or statement should be kept by the employer [Sec. 31.6011(b)-2; 301.6109-1].

An employee must notify the employer of his social security number and name as soon as he is hired. If he has no social security number, he must show the employer (1) a receipt from the Social Security Administration indicating that an application has been filed, or (2) an application (or statement containing similar information) on Form SS-5, a duplicate of the form the employee has filed or intends to file with the Administration [Sec. 31.6011(b)-2; 301.6109-1]. There is a $5 penalty if he fails to give the employer his number [Sec. 301.6676-1].

(d) Application by self-employed person. A self-employed person engaged in trade or business who does not already have an employer identification number should file Form SS-4 with the Revenue Service [Sec. 301.6109-1(d)(2)].

¶ 3827 Returns and payment of taxes. (a) By employer. Every employer who is subject to social security taxes must make a quarterly return by the last day of the month following the quarter covered by the return. The return is made on Form 941. Separate Schedule A (Form 941) with the wage information for social security use must be attached.[1] Form 942 is used for domestic service and Form 943 for agricultural service [Sec. 31.6011(a)-1]. Combined social security taxes and withheld taxes are paid into an authorized bank. See ¶ 2509 for details.

Tips. The employer must give the employee a statement on Form W-2 of any amount of tax to be paid on tips (cash or charge) that the employer cannot withhold because the employee's wages (without tips) and voluntary payments do not cover it [Sec. 6053; 31.6053-1]. See ¶ 2508. The employee must pay the tax on the deficiency stated on Form W-2, and also compute and pay the tax on tips that he has not reported. Form 4137 must be used to compute the tax on unreported tips. It is attached to the employee's income tax return. Any difference is paid with the return. For penalty on unreported tips, see ¶ 3818.[2]

(b) Reporting self-employment income. Each self-employed individual files an annual return of his self-employment income. The return is due the same date as the regular income tax return [¶ 3517(a)].

If the return covers less than 12 months because of a change in accounting period, self-employment income should not be annualized as taxable income must be [¶ 2717(b)].[3] So the tax must be based on the maximum amount of self-employment income in each of the short periods in a tax year.[4]

The tax is collected through the regular income tax forms. A self-employment tax return must be filed when the net earnings from self-employment are $400 or more, even if no income tax return is due. The tax is computed and the taxable self-employment income is reported on separate Schedule SE, Form 1040. The self-employment schedule picks up the individual's net income from Schedule C, Form 1040, as well as partnership or other joint venture earnings reported on Schedule K-1, Form 1065, farm income reported on Schedule F, Form 1040 and self-employment income of certain ministers and members of religious orders. Adjustments have to be made for items excluded from "net earnings" in self-employment income (¶ 3823) [Sec. 1402(a)] and for "wages" subject to the social security tax [¶ 3818].

➤➤**OBSERVATION**➔ If an individual has received at least $16,500 in wages subject to social security tax in 1977, he does not have any self-employment income nor self-employment income tax for the year, regardless of his actual earnings in self-employment. For any tax year starting in any year after 1974, the taxable wage base will be adjusted if there is an automatic cost-of-living benefit increase [¶ 3823(a)].

Footnotes appear at end of this Chapter.

Husbands and wives cannot split their self-employment income. In joint returns, separate self-employment schedules must be filed for both, if both have net earnings from self-employment of $400 or more. The tax liability, however, is joint and several. Community income is reported in the self-employment schedule by the spouse having the actual control and management of the business, regardless of the community property laws of the state [Sec. 1402(a)(5); 1.1402(a)-1(c)(5)].

Social security taxes on self-employment income must be included in determining an individual's estimated tax [Sec. 6015(c)]. See ¶ 2515(b).

¶ 3828 **Records.** (a) **Employers** must keep accurate records of all wages paid. While no particular form is prescribed the system of accounting must show that the employer's tax liability was correctly figured and taxes paid. The records for *each* employee must show [Sec. 31.6001-5(a)]:

(1) the name, address and account number; (2) the total amount (including any deductions) and date of each wage payment, and the period and character of the services covered by the payment; (3) the amount of pay and reported cash tips[1] subject to the tax; (4) the amount of employees' tax withheld or collected and the date collected, if different from the date of payment.

If the amount in (2) and (3) above are not the same, the reason for the difference should be made a part of the record.

The employer also must keep copies of all returns, schedules, and other statements. The records must be kept for a period of four years after the date the tax became due or was paid, whichever is later [Sec. 31.6001-1(b), (e)].

Statements. Every employer withholding taxes must furnish the employee an annual statement of the withholding by January 31 of the next year (or within 30 days after the last payment of wages is made, if the employee leaves during the year). It must show the total social security or railroad retirement tax withheld, and the separate hospital insurance tax. When social security (or railroad retirement) and income taxes have been withheld, these will be shown on Form W-2, the regular form for showing income tax withheld. (See ¶ 2508 for rules on issuing statements to employees.) If only social security has been withheld (as for farm hands, domestics and the like), the employee should be given a receipt. Form SS-14, or any other form containing the information called for on Form SS-14, may be used [Sec. 6051]. The Commissioner can also require these statements to be furnished at other times, and with additional information. The employer may use a duplicate of the statement as an information return [¶ 3531]. As to tips, see ¶ 2508; 3818; 3827.

(b) **Employees** generally do not have to keep records. It is advisable, however, that they keep permanent records of the name and address of each employer, the period of employment in each case, the taxable wages, the tax withheld and the receipts furnished by the employer. Because they must report monthly tips of $20 or more to their employers, employees also should keep records of tip income. The records of all claimants must be complete and detailed [Sec. 31.6001-1]. See also ¶ 3818.

(c) **Self-employed persons** are not required to keep any specific records. However, like employees, they should keep their own records to establish eligibility for benefits. Also, the self-employment income statement will be included on their income tax return. Since the Revenue Service has 3 years to review the return (longer in some cases), records should be held for at least that long.

¶ 3829 **Refunds and adjustments** are allowed for underpayments and overpayments by both employers and employees. If the employer does not collect enough tax from the employee, or withholds too much, his mistake generally will be reflected on his next return. An error in the employee's tax generally will be matched by an error in the employer's share. For details, see ¶ 2510; 2511.

The limitation period on both assessment and refund is the same as for income taxes. See ¶ 3610; 3623. In general, a refund can be claimed within three years after the filing of the return or within two years from the payment of the tax, whichever is later. Interest on overpayment is 7% [¶ 3628].

Form 941c. If, in a prior return, the employer failed to report, or incorrectly reported, the name, account number or wages of an employee, the employer should file Form 941c, Statement to Correct Information, advising the District Director of the omission or error in his previous return.[1]

Overpayment of self-employment tax. When the taxpayer discovers that he has overpaid his self-employment tax, he can claim a refund before the statute of limitations expires [¶ 3626].[2]

Federal and state employees. Adjustments and refunds of employees working for the U.S. or a wholly owned instrumentality, or employees of any state, its political subdivision, or its wholly owned instrumentality who have come under the law by voluntary agreements [¶ 3815], will be figured as if the head of each agency or instrumentality making a tax return was a separate employer [Sec. 6413(c)].

Government employees entitled to a refund of self-employment taxes because the employer made a voluntary agreement can file the refund claim up to 2 years after the year the agreement is made [Sec. 6511(d)(5)].

¶ 3830 Additions and penalties imposed on the employer for failure to pay the tax, failure to withhold fraudulent returns, and the like, are the same as those for the income tax [¶ 2512]. See also ¶ 3827(a).

UNEMPLOYMENT INSURANCE

¶ 3834 Tax on employers. The tax is imposed on persons who employ one or more individuals for some portion of a day in each of 20 weeks in the current or preceding calendar year, or who pay $1,500 or more of wages in a calendar quarter of a current or preceding calendar year [Sec. 3306(a)]. When the coverage requirement is not met until later in the year, the liability dates back to January 1 of that year. In determining unemployment tax liability, it does not matter whether employees actually perform physical services if an employment relationship exists between the parties. Thus, employees on vacation are counted in determining whether the employer has the required number of employees for the required period of time.[1] On the other hand, pensioners are not counted and the pensions are not taxable [Sec. 31.3306(a)-1].

The tax is 3.4% (3.2% after 1977 if there is no balance of repayable advances made to the extended unemployed compensation account) of the first $4,200 ($6,000 after 1977) of wages paid to each employee [Sec. 3301, 3306(b)(1)].

Mergers. A corporation that results from a statutory merger or consolidation is treated as the same employer as the merged corporation. The continuing corporation is liable for the merged corporation's taxes and entitled to credit for its payments. It continues to file returns and treat the employees as would the merged corporation. The changeover must be explained with the first post-merger return.[2]

¶ 3837 Wages subject to tax. Wages include all pay for "employment" (Payments made in a medium other than cash are measured by their cash value) except:

Footnotes appear at end of this Chapter.

¶ 3837

1. Payments over $4,200 ($6,000 after 1977) by one employer during a calendar year [Sec. 3306(b)(1)]. (Certain successor employers may count wages paid by the prior employer as paid by themselves [Sec. 31.3306(b)(1)-1(b)]. See also ¶ 3818(b).)

2. Payments to or on behalf of employees or their dependents *under a plan or system* providing benefits for (a) retirement, (b) sickness or accident disability, (c) medical or hospitalization expenses in connection with sickness or accident disability, or (d) death [Sec. 3306(b)(2)]. But a payment that would have been made regardless of retirement, death, or disability is not excluded [Sec. 3306(b)(10)].

3. Any payment on account of retirement [Sec. 3306(b)(3)].

4. Any payment for sickness or accident disability or medical and hospital expenses made over six months after the last month the employee was employed [Sec. 3306(b)(4)].

5. Payments, not intended as wages, made from a trust exempt from tax under Sec. 501(a), or payments under or to an annuity plan meeting the requirements of Sec. 401(a)(3), (4), (5), and (6) [Sec. 3306(b)(5)].

6. Payment of the employee's social security tax or any tax imposed under a state unemployment compensation law [Sec. 3306(b)(6)].

7. Pay, other than cash, for services not in the course of the employer's trade or business [Sec. 3306(b)(7)].

8. Any payment, other than vacation or sick pay, made after the month an employee becomes 65, if he does not work for the employer during the period for which the payment is made [Sec. 3306(b)(8)].

9. Any payment of supplemental unemployment benefits (SUB).[1]

10. Tips, unless they are reported by the employee to his employer, and are customarily considered part of his total wages [Sec. 31.3306(b)-1(j)(3)]. For example, tips reported in writing and taken into account under a state's minimum wage law are "Wages." [2] Reporting tips for social security and withholding purposes does not make them subject to the unemployment tax.[3]

In general, rulings as to what constitutes pay for social security tax purposes [¶ 3818] also apply under the Unemployment Tax Act. Reported tips are a major exception.

¶ 3838 Return and payment of tax. Employers must make quarterly deposits of unpaid taxes that exceed $100. These are made for periods ending March 31, June 30 and September 30. Deposits are timely if made by the end of the month following each quarter. Any taxes due in excess of quarterly payments are paid with the annual return. No quarterly deposits are required if the tax for a calendar period, plus any unpaid amount for prior periods in the calendar year, does not exceed $100. Each quarterly deposit must be for the full quarterly tax [Sec. 6157]. The annual return, Form 940, must be based on the calendar year, regardless of the accounting period used by the taxpayer. It must be filed by January 31 of the following year.[1] Employers who make timely quarterly deposits are allowed an additional 10 days to file their returns [Sec. 31.6071(a)-1].

NOTE: The rate of quarterly tax is 0.7% (0.5% after 1977) [Sec. 6157(b)].

The time for filing the return may be extended for not over 6 months on application to the Revenue Service [Sec. 6081(a); 31.6081(a)-1(b)]. The application must include a statement of the reasons for the delay.

If the return instructions call for the return to be filed with a service center, it (together with the remittance) must be so filed, or it may be hand filed at the District Director's office. Otherwise the return, with the remittance attached, is filed with the District Director for the district where the employer's principal place of business is located. If an individual employer has no principal place of business in the U.S., the return is filed at Baltimore, Md. [Sec. 31.6091-1]. If it is shown that undue hardship would result, the time for paying the tax may be extended for not over six months [Sec. 6161(a)(1)].

¶ **3839 Credit against federal tax for state payments. (a) State payments made on or before due date for federal returns.** An employer may credit against his federal tax, contributions under state law he pays *on or before* the due date for filing the federal return (January 31 of the following year). The credit is limited to 90% of the federal tax figured as if the rate were 3%; that is, 2.7% of taxable wages [Sec. 3302(c), (d)]. The standard rate in most states is 2.7%, but if the state tax is over 2.7%, the excess cannot be credited against the federal tax. The employer gets the credit only if the state plan for unemployment compensation is certified by the Secretary of Labor as meeting federal requirements [Sec. 3304(c)]. The employer gets no federal credit for employee contributions required by state law.

(b) State payments made after due date for federal returns. If the employer fails to pay his state taxes by January 31 (or an extended due date of the federal return) he will be limited to a credit of only 90% of the normal 90% tax credit, that is, 2.43% of taxable wages. [Sec. 3302(a)(3)]. However, the state tax must be paid and the credit or refund claim filed within three years after payment of the federal tax [Sec. 6511(a)].

Example 1: In 1977 Employers A and B each have a $100,000 payroll subject to federal and state unemployment taxes. A pays his state contributions *on or before the due date* for filing the federal return. B pays his state contributions *after the due date* for filing the federal return *but* within 3 years after payment of the federal tax. Following is a comparison of the credits allowable and total tax payable for each assuming the state tax rate is 2.7%:

Employer A		**Employer B**	
Federal tax of 3.4%, State tax of 2.7% payable entirely by employer			
State tax	$2,700	State tax	$2,700
Federal tax before credit	$3,400	Federal tax before credit	$3,400
Less: Credit for state tax paid *on or before due date* of fed. return (not to exceed 2.7% rate)	2,700	Less: Credit for state tax paid *after due date* of fed. return *but* within 3 years after payment of federal tax (not to exceed 90% of credit allowable if contributions were paid on time)	2,430
Net federal tax	700	Net federal tax	970
Total state and federal tax. $3,400		Total state and federal tax. $3,670	

Refunds will be granted to employers who pay their federal tax without taking credit for state taxes paid after the due date for filing the federal return but within 3 years after payment of the federal tax. Thus, in the above case, if Employer B pays the $3,400 federal tax on 1-31-78, and later, but on or before 1-31-81, pays his state tax for 1977 and files claim for refund, he can get a refund of the $2,430 (81% of $3,000) credit.

Example 2: For the calendar year 1977, the Rampart Company had a total federal tax of $10,200 (total taxable payroll of $300,000 × 3.4%). The company is liable for total state contributions of $8,100 for the year, but only pays $7,100 by the federal due date. The remaining $1,000 is paid to the state in the middle of February 1978. If the $1,000 had been paid by 1-31-78, it could have been credited against the federal tax, since it would not have exceeded the limitation of $8,100 (2.7% of $300,000). Since the $1,000 was paid after the due date, but within 3 years after payment of the federal tax, the Rampart Company will get a credit of 90% of the $1,000, or $900, plus the credit of $7,100 allowable for the contributions paid on or before 1-31-78. The net liability for the federal tax is $2,200 ($10,200 less $8,000).

Footnotes appear at end of this Chapter.

¶ **3841 Credit allowed under merit rating.** State laws provide for some form of merit rating under which a reduction in the state contribution rate is allowed to employers who, as shown by their benefit and contribution experience, have given steady employment. In order not to penalize an employer who has earned a reduction in the contribution rate under the state law, he will be allowed to credit against the federal tax, not only the amount actually contributed to the state, but also an "additional credit" equal to the difference between his actual contributions and the amount he would have contributed at the higher rate or 2.7%, whichever is lesser [Sec. 3302(b)]. In no case, however, can the total credit for state taxes paid be more than 90% of the federal tax figured at a rate of 3% [Sec. 3302(c), (d)]. The additional credit will not be allowed unless the Secretary of Labor finds that the state law permits the rate reduction under provisions that conform to federal requirements [Sec. 3303].

Example: Both Employer A and Employer B have a taxable payroll of $100,000 for 1977. The federal rate is 3.4% and the state contribution rate is 2.7%. However, the state has reduced Employer B's rate to 1%. In both cases the state payment was made before the due date for filing the federal returns.

Employer A		Employer B		
State tax (2.7% of $100,000)	$2,700	State tax (1% of $100,000)		$1,000
Federal tax before credit	$3,400	Federal tax before credit	$3,400	
Less: Credit for state tax paid (not to exceed 2.7% rate)	2,700	Less: Credit for state tax paid	$1,000	
		Additional credit (difference between $2,700 and $1,000)	1,700	2,700
Net federal tax	700	Net federal tax		700
Total fed. & state tax	$3,400	Total fed. & state tax		$1,700

¶ **3843 Employer's records.** Every employer is required to keep permanent records showing the following information:
1. Total wages paid during calendar year, showing separately taxable pay and nontaxable pay.
2. The amount of contributions paid into each state unemployment fund, with respect to services subject to the state tax, showing separately (a) payments made and not deducted from the employees' pay, and (b) payments made and deducted (or to be deducted) from the employees' pay.
3. The information required to be shown on the return and the extent of the tax liability.

An employer who considers that he is not subject to tax should keep records showing the number of individuals employed on each day [Sec. 31.6001-4(b)].

The records must be accessible for inspection and preserved for four years from the due date of the tax for the year to which they relate [Sec. 31.6001-1].

¶ **3844 Refunds and adjustments.** Taxes, including interest, penalties and additions, that have been erroneously, illegally or wrongfully collected, may be credited or refunded to the taxpayer [Sec. 6402(a)]. The claim for refund should be filed with the Revenue Service [¶ 3626]. They must be filed within three years after filing the return or two years after paying the tax, whichever period expires later [Sec. 6511].

¶ **3845 Additions and penalties** for failure to file required returns, failure to pay taxes when due, false returns, and the like are similar to those shown in ¶ 2512.

¶ 3846 Procedure after Revenue Service's determination against taxpayer.-
Except in the case of the tax on self-employment income, there is no provision of law that gives the Tax Court jurisdiction over social security tax cases. Accordingly, after a determination by the Revenue Service that liability has been incurred, the employer must pay the taxes. His only recourse is to file a claim for refund or credit [¶ 3829; 3844] and if it is disallowed or no action is taken, suit for refund may be started. No suit may be started until after six months from the date of filing the claim, unless the Revenue Service gives a decision within that time, nor after two years from the date of mailing by registered mail by the Revenue Service to the taxpayer of a notice of disallowance of the part of the claim to which the suit or proceeding relates.[1]

Footnotes to Chapter 28

(P-H "FEDERAL TAXES" related references are cited in brackets [ ] at the end of the following footnotes.)

Footnote ¶ 3800
(1) The P-H "Payroll Report" volume contains complete coverage and details on benefit payments.

Footnote ¶ 3806
(1) Instructions (1977 Ed.), Form 942, p. 4.

Footnote ¶ 3810
(1) The P-H "Payroll Report" volume contains complete coverage and details.

Footnote ¶ 3815
(1) The P-H "Payroll Report" volume contains complete coverage and details.
(2) Rev. Rul. 61-21, 1961-1 CB 431.

Footnote ¶ 3816
(1) Treas. Dept. letter ruling, 1-12-43.
(2) Rev. Rul. 55-386, 1955-1 CB 120; Rev. Rul. 55-707, 1955-2 CB 420 [¶ 34,618(d)].

Footnote ¶ 3817
(1) Mim. Coll. 6787, 1952-1 CB 192 [¶ 34,701].
(2) Mim. Coll. 6571, 1951-1 CB 95; see also Rev. Rul. 54-309, 1954-2 CB 261; Rev. Rul. 54-312, 1954-2 CB 327 [¶ 34,701; 34,082(75)].
(3) Rev. Rul. 57-246, 1957-1 CB 338 [¶ 34,182(65); 34,689].
(4) Mim. Coll. 5217, 1941-2 CB 220; SSB v. Warren, 141 F.2d 974.
(5) Rev. Rul. 68-597, 1968-2 CB 463 [¶ 34,689].
(6) Rev. Rul. 69-184, 1969-1 CB 256 [¶ 34,699].

Footnote ¶ 3818
(1) Rev. Rul. 71-53, 1971-1, CB 279 [¶ 34,568].
(2) Rev. Rul. 57-92, 1957-1, CB 306.
(3) Indianapolis Glove Co. v. U.S., 96 F.2d 816, 21 AFTR 268 [¶ 11,760(20)].
(4) Rev. Rul. 70-471, 1970-2 CB 471 [¶ 34,555].
(5) Rev. Rul. 68-216, 1968-1 CB 413 [¶ 34,836].
(6) Rev. Rul. 68-452, 1969-2 CB 181 [¶ 34,538].
(7) Treasury Dept. letter to Prentice-Hall, Inc., 10-17-50.
(8) Rev. Rul. 73-260, 1973-1 CB 412 [¶ 34,586; 34,701].

Footnote ¶ 3818 continued
(9) Rev. Rul. 66-75, 1966-1 CB 231 [¶ 34,572].

Footnote ¶ 3819
(1) SST 302, 1938-1 CB 456.
(2) Rev. Rul. 54-384, 1954-2 CB 336 [¶ 8379].
(3) Patton v. Fed. Sec. Agency, 69 F.Supp. 282.
(4) Rev. Rul. 76-453, IRB 1976-47; Announc. 77-23, IRB 1977-7 [¶ 54,980; 55,214].
(5) Rev. Rul. 65-208, 1965-2 CB 383 [¶ 34,539].
(6) Rev. Rul. 53-181, 1953-2 CB 111 [¶ 34,539].
(7) Rev. Rul. 74-252, 1974-1 CB 287 [¶ 34,537(d)].

Footnote ¶ 3821
(1) The tax on self-employed persons has been upheld. Cain v. U.S., 211 F.2d 375, 45 AFTR 801 [¶ 34,006; 38,047(5)].

Footnote ¶ 3822
(1) Rev. Rul. 55-431, 1955-2 CB 312 [¶ 34,080(20)].
(2) Rev. Rul. 60-77, 1960-1 CB 386 [¶ 34,697; 34,080(65)].

Footnote ¶ 3823
(1) Rev. Proc. 57-14, 1957-1 CB 744 [¶ 34,092(15)].
(2) Rev. Rul. 65-272, 1965-2 CB 217 [¶ 34,089(50)].
(3) Rev. Rul. 59-221, 1959-1 CB 225 [¶ 34,080(50)].
(4) Rev. Rul. 57-246, 1957-1 CB 388; Rev. Rul. 68-595, 1968-2 CB 378 [¶ 34,082(65)].
(5) IRS Pub. 533, "Information on Self-Employment Tax" (1976 Ed.), pp. 2-3.
(6) Rev. Rul. 66-69, 1966-1 CB 72 [¶ 34,082(40)].
(7) Rev. Rul. 64-220, 1964-2 CB 335 [¶ 34,077(20)].

Footnote ¶ 3824
(1) IRS Pub. No. 533, "Information on Self-Employment Tax" (1976 Ed.), p. 3.
(2) Rev. Rul. 64-220, 1964-2 CB 335 [¶ 34,077(20)].
(3) Rev. Rul. 57-58, 1957-1 CB 270 [¶ 34,077(35)].
(4) Letter from J. B. Dunlap, Comm'r, to Prentice-Hall, Inc., 11-29-51; Rev. Rul. 55-385, 1955-1 CB 100 [¶ 34,080(5)].

Footnote ¶ 3826
(1) Treas. Dept. booklet "Employer's Tax Guide" (1976 Ed.), p. 3.

Footnote ¶ 3827
(1) Announcement 59-42, IRB 1959-16; Form 941, Instructions p.2.
(2) Treas. Dept. booklet "Your Federal Income Tax" (1977 Ed.), p. 34.
(3) Rev. Rul. 53-94, 1953-1 CB 84 [¶ 34,008(10)].
(4) Rev. Rul. 69-410, 1969-2 CB 167 [¶ 34,008(10)].

Footnote ¶ 3828
(1) Treas. Dept. booklet "Employer's Tax Guide" (1976 Ed.), p. 12.

Footnote ¶ 3829

Footnote ¶ 3829 continued
(1) Instructions to Form 941c.
(2) Rev. Rul. 56-297, 1956-1 CB 564 [¶ 36,091(15)].

Footnote ¶ 3834
(1) Rev. Rul. 71-87, 1971-1 CB 290.
(2) Rev. Rul. 62-60, 1962-1 CB 186 [¶ 34,877].

Footnote ¶ 3837
(1) Rev. Rul. 56-249, 1956-1 CB 488; Rev. Rul. 60-330, 1960-2 CB 46 [¶ 34,813(b)].
(2) Rev. Rul. 66-369, 1966-2 CB 451 [¶ 34,572].
(3) Rev. Rul. 66-54, 1966-1 CB 241.

Footnote ¶ 3838
(1) Treas. Dept. booklet "Tax Guide for Small Business" (1977 Ed.), p. 74. Treas. Dept. Booklet "Employer's Tax Guide" (1976 Ed.), p. 7.

Footnote ¶ 3846
(1) SST 297, 1938-1 CB 382.

Highlights of Chapter 28
Social Security Taxes

I. **Old-age, Survivor and Disability Insurance and Health Insurance for Aged**
   A. **Tax on wages [¶ 3800]:**
      1. Employer:
         a. Social security taxes must be paid by those employing one or more.
         b. Tips are not included as wages in employer's tax base.
      2. Employee:
         a. Limited amount of wages from covered employment is subject to the tax at the same rates paid by employer.
         b. It is withheld by employer and deposited in authorized bank.
   B. **Covered employment includes [¶ 3803]:**
      1. Employment within U.S. (regardless of citizenship or residence of employer or employee or whether business illegal).
      2. Employment outside U.S. by U.S. citizen involving services for:
         a. American-employer.
         b. Foreign subsidiaries of U.S. firms that own less than 20% of the foreign subsidiary's voting stock (coverage is optional with U.S. firm).
         c. Employers of maritime and aircraft personnel on American or foreign crafts providing certain conditions are present.
   C. **Certain classes of U.S. employment are exempt**—Due to nature of work performed, nature of employer, and whether employees covered by other federal retirement system [¶ 3804].
   D. **Agricultural labor [¶ 3805]:**
      1. Farm workers are covered, if:
         a. They work for any one employer who pays them $150 in cash wages in calendar year, or
         b. They work 20 or more days for an employer and are paid a cash wage on a time basis.
      2. Farmer is covered as self-employed person.
      3. Workers from foreign countries admitted on temporary basis aren't covered.
   E. **Domestics [¶ 3806]:**
      1. Covered if receive $50 or more cash wages in calendar quarter.
      2. Usually, licensed practical nurses are considered self-employed.
   F. **Casual labor [¶ 3807]:** If services not performed in employer's trade or business, person is not covered unless he receives $50 in cash for any calendar quarter.
   G. **Family employment [¶ 3808]:**
      1. Individual employed by spouse, or by parent if under 21, is exempt.
      2. Generally, parent employed by child is covered.
      3. Employment of close family members may be covered.
   H. **Clergymen or members of religious organization [¶ 3809]:**
      1. Not covered as employees when performing religious functions.
      2. Covered as self-employed persons unless they oppose coverage on conscientious or religious grounds.
   I. **Students [¶ 3810]:**
      1. Performing services while attending school is not covered.
      2. At state institutions are covered if state agrees with HEW to cover student.
   J. **Newsboys and news vendors [¶ 3811]:**
      1. Under 18, not covered.

2. News vendors who sell to the ultimate consumer and receive profit as their compensation are not covered.
K. **Railroad workers**—Covered by their own federal retirement system [¶ 3812].
L. **Services of registered Communists**—Not covered [¶ 3813].
M. **Non-profit organizations [¶ 3814]:**
   1. Religious, charitable, educational, etc. organizations, not covered unless organization elects otherwise. Employees must file election certificate to be covered where organization has made such election [¶ 3814(a)].
   2. Organizations exempt from income tax under Sec. 501(a) (other than an exempt trust under Sec. 401(a)) or farmer cooperative exempt under Sec. 521, are covered. Employee is not covered where he earns less than $50 in calendar quarter [¶ 3814(b)].
N. **Government employees [¶ 3815]:**
   1. Federal employees:
      a. Employees under federal retirement system are exempt.
      b. Under certain conditions employees of U.S. instrumentalities are exempt.
   2. State and local employees:
      a. Generally covered if they file agreement with Secretary of HEW.
      b. Special rules apply to employees of public transportation systems.
   3. Employees of foreign or international organizations are exempt.
O. **Partially covered employment [¶ 3816]:**
   1. Employee performing exempt and non-exempt service for employer:
      a. All employment non-exempt if one-half or more of time devoted to non-exempt work.
      b. All employment is exempt if one-half or more of time devoted to exempt work.
   2. Rule in 1, above, does not apply if part of services performed as employee and other part performed in some other capacity.
P. **Employer-employee relationship [¶ 3817]:**
   1. Relationship exists where employer controls the person performing services both as to result of work, and means to accomplish result [¶ 3817(a)].
   2. Following are employees even though they do not meet the control test in 1, above [¶ 3817(b)]:
      a. Full-time traveling or city salesman if he solicits business for one principal.
      b. Agent-driver or commission driver if he delivers food products (except milk), or transports laundry for his principal.
      c. Full-time life insurance salesman.
      d. Homeworker if he meets test in 1, above, or meets following tests:
         1) Works according to specifications and materials furnished by person for whom services rendered (materials must be returned), and
         2) Is paid $50 cash in any calendar quarter.
      e. The exceptions in 2(a)-(d), above, do not apply if person:
         1) Has substantial investment in job facilities, or
         2) If work involves only single transaction with employer.
   3. Corporate officers are employees, but directors are not [¶ 3817(c)].
   4. Partners are not employees [¶ 3817(d)].
Q. **Taxable wages [¶ 3818]:**
   1. They are paid for services in covered employment.
   2. Cash tips totaling $20 or more a month are taxable wages.
   3. Limitation on taxable wages:
      a. First $16,500 of wages received in calendar year 1977 (with adjustments after 1977 when there is a cost-of-living benefit increase).
      b. If employee works for more than one employer, each employer withholds and pays the tax as if he were the only employer during the year.
      c. If employer succeeds another he can include amounts paid by predecessor in determining amount to be withheld.

R. **Payments not subject to social security tax [¶ 3819]:**
  1. Payments other than in cash:
     a. Not taxable where paid for domestics, farm labor or service not in employer's business.
     b. If items are not paid for services in (a), they are taxable if they are an appreciable part of pay.
  2. If items are small in relation to pay and are provided for employee's welfare and efficiency they are not taxable.
  3. Advances or reimbursements for traveling and related expenses aren't taxable if employer identifies payments [¶ 3819(b)].
  4. Payments under employee benefit, trust or annuity plans established by employer are generally not taxable [¶ 3819(c)].
  5. Payments to employee on account of retirement aren't taxable wages, unless premiums paid from employee's salary [¶ 3819(d)].
  6. Payments to employee on account of sickness or accident made more than 6 months after he leaves employment are not taxable [¶ 3819(d)].
  7. Other payments considered in determining their taxability [¶ 3819(e)].

II. **Taxes on Self-employment Income**
  A. **In general [¶ 3821]:**
    1. By paying tax, self-employed are entitled to same benefits as employees who pay tax on wages.
    2. Tax is imposed on citizen or resident alien engaged in business.
  B. **Self-employment defined [¶ 3822]:**
    1. A person is self-employed if he carries on a trade or business as:
       a. A proprietor or partner, or
       b. Independent contractor.
    2. Clergymen, Christian Science Practitioners, and members of religious orders (except those who take vow of poverty).
    3. Following persons are not self-employed:
       a. Public officials.
       b. Railroad workers.
       c. Members of religious orders who have taken poverty oath.
       d. Members of religious sect, if certain requirements are met.
       e. Newsboys under 18.
  C. **Self-employment income [¶ 3823]:**
    1. Net earnings must be at least $400.
    2. Tax base is limited to $16,500 in 1977, less net earnings from wages. For any tax year starting in any year after 1974, the taxable base will be adjusted if there is an automatic cost-of-living benefit increase [¶ 3823(a)].
    3. Income from farming [¶ 3823(b)]:
       a. Farmer must pay self-employment tax where net earnings from self-employment income for the year total $400 or more and less than $16,500 is received in wages in 1977 and with adjustment after 1977 if there is an automatic cost-of-living benefit increase.
       b. Farmers may use an optional method in computing net earnings which does not require listing deductions; other self-employeds can use this method if they meet certain requirements.
    4. Foreign income exempt from income tax is generally not included as net earnings from self-employment [¶ 3823(c)].
    5. Partner's net earnings from self-employment income includes his distributive share of partnership net income whether distributed or not [¶ 3823(d)].
    6. Income from other sources [¶ 3823(e)]:
       a. Director's fees are generally self-employment income.
       b. Fees to fiduciary (not in business) are not self-employment income.
       c. Funds to do independent research work are self-employment income.
       d. Compensation paid to U.S. citizens working in U.S. for foreign government or international organization is self-employment income.

e. Income from trusts, operated by beneficiaries for their joint profit may be self-employment income.

D. **Exclusions from self-employment income [¶ 3824]:**
 1. Self-employment income does not include:
    a. Dividends, except those received by security dealers.
    b. Interest on nonbusiness loans and interest on corporate and government securities (except where received by dealer).
    c. Rental income, except income received by real estate dealer.
    d. Income from business or profession not considered self-employment.
    e. In certain situations, gain or loss from disposing of property, such as sale or exchange of capital assets.
 2. Special rules:
    a. Personal exemptions are not allowable deductions.
    b. Minister's self-employment income includes rental value of parsonage, rental allowances, and meals and lodging furnished for church's convenience.

III. **Returns, Payment and Refunds**
 A. **Social security and employer identification numbers [¶ 3826]:**
  1. Employee who doesn't have social security number must apply for it by filing Form SS-5 within 7 days after being hired.
  2. Employer must apply for identification number by filing Form SS-4 within 7 days after first wage payments.
  3. Self-employed persons must also make application on Form SS-4 for their identification numbers.
 B. **Returns and payment of tax [¶ 3827]:**
  1. Employers liable for the tax must file a quarterly return (Form 941) on the last day of the month following the quarter covered by return.
  2. Payment of combined social security and withheld income taxes are deposited in authorized bank.
  3. Employer must give employee Form W-2 showing amount of tax to be paid on tips which could not be withheld by employer.
  4. Reporting self-employment income:
     a. Annual return required on same due date as income tax return.
     b. The tax is computed and reported on Schedule SE.
     c. Married couples cannot split their self-employment income.
 C. **Records [¶ 3828]:**
  1. Employers must keep accurate records of wages, and supply employees with Form W-2 by January 31 of following year.
  2. Generally employees or self-employed persons do not have to keep records.
 D. **Refunds and adjustments [¶ 3829]:**
  1. Allowed for underpayments and overpayments.
  2. Special rules apply to Government employees.
 E. **Additions to tax and penalties** for fraud, failure to pay tax or withhold etc., are imposed the same as those for income tax [¶ 3830].

IV. **Unemployment Insurance**
 A. **Liability of employers [¶ 3834]:**
  1. Tax is imposed if person employs one or more employees in each of 20 weeks in current or preceding calendar year, or pays $1,500 or more in wages in a calendar quarter of current or preceding calendar year.
  2. The rate is 3.4% of first $4,200 of wages.
 B. **Taxable wages**—All pay for employment with certain exceptions [¶ 3837].
 C. **Return and payment of tax [¶ 3838]:**
  1. Unpaid taxes that exceed $100 must be deposited quarterly.
  2. Annual return Form 940 must be filed by January 31 of following year. 10-day extension granted where timely deposits made.
 D. **Credit against federal tax for state payments [¶ 3839]:**

1. A credit up to 2.7% of taxable wages is allowed against federal tax for state taxes paid on or before due date of federal return.
2. If state taxes not paid by due date of federal return, only up to 2.43% of taxable wages is allowed as a credit.

E. **Employer paying reduced rate** because he provided steady employment is granted an "additional credit" [¶ 3841].

F. **Employer's records**—shows taxable and nontaxable pay and other pertinent tax information [¶ 3843].

G. **Employers may get refund [¶ 3844].**

H. **Additions to tax or penalties** are similar to those for income taxes [¶ 3845].

I. **If employer disputes tax liability**—Must nevertheless pay tax, file claim for refund or credit, bring suit for refund if IRS denies credit or refund [¶ 3846].

Chapter 29

FEDERAL ESTATE TAX

TABLE OF CONTENTS

	¶		¶
The federal estate tax	3900	What deductions are allowed	3926
		Charitable and similar transfers	3927
THE GROSS ESTATE		The specific exemption	3928
Property included in the gross estate	3901	**THE MARITAL DEDUCTION**	
Joint estates and tenancies by the entirety	3904	What the marital deduction is	3929
Community property	3905	**THE TAX AND CREDITS**	
Property subject to dower and curtesy	3906	Table for estate tax	3934
Powers of appointment	3907	Credit for federal gift tax	3935
Property subject to power of appointment	3908	Credit for state inheritance or estate tax	3936
Transfers in contemplation of death	3909	Table for maximum credit for state death taxes	3937
Transfers reserving right to use, enjoyment, or income	3910	Credit for foreign estate tax	3938
Transfers taking effect at death	3911	Credit for tax on prior transfers	3939
Transfers reserving power to alter, amend, revoke or terminate	3912	Unified credit	3940
Transfers for inadequate consideration	3913	How to determine the Federal estate tax	3941
Life insurance	3914	**PROCEDURE**	
Annuity, pension or profit-sharing plans or trusts	3915	Return	3943
Generation-skipping transfers	3916	Payment of tax	3944
VALUATION OF ESTATE PROPERTY		Deficiencies and appeals	3945
How property is valued	3919	Refunds	3946
		Discharge from personal liability	3947
DEDUCTIONS FROM THE GROSS ESTATE		• Highlights of Chapter 29	Page 3961

¶ **3900 The federal estate tax.** The federal estate tax is basically a tax payable when property is transferred at death.[1] It is an excise tax on the right to transfer property at death and is measured by the value of property.

THE GROSS ESTATE

¶ **3901 Property included in the gross estate.** The gross estate of a U.S. citizen or resident is the total value of all property that the decedent had beneficial ownership of at the time of his death. It makes no difference whether the property passes by will or the intestate laws, or where it is located [Sec. 2033; 20.2031-1, 20.2033-1]. Regardless of when any rights were created, the law in effect at the date of decedent's death is controlling as to the property's inclusion in the gross estate [Sec. 2044; 20.2044-1].

¶ **3904 Joint estates and tenancies by the entirety.** Except for the joint interest of spouses described below, the value of the entire property in a joint tenancy is included in the gross estate of the deceased joint tenant unless the survivor

Footnotes appear at end of this Chapter.

¶ **3904**

can prove that he paid part of the property's cost. In that case, the portion representing his contribution is excluded. If the property was acquired by gift, devise or inheritance, only the value of the deceased tenant's fractional interest is included. Property held as tenant by the entirety is subject to the same rules as property held jointly [Sec. 2040; 20.2040-1]. As for a tenant in common, only the fractional interest of the decedent is included [Sec. 2033].

Qualified joint interest created by spouses after 12-31-76. Generally, only one-half of the value of a spouse's joint interest in property is included in the deceased joint tenant's gross estate if it is a "qualified joint interest." An interest is a "qualified joint interest" if (1) it is created by one or both joint tenants, (2) its creation in personal property is a completed gift for gift tax purposes, (3) its creation in real property is a taxable gift on the spouse's timely election, ¶ 4013, and (4) only the decedent and his spouse are the joint tenants [Sec. 2040(b)].

¶ 3905 Community property. Arizona, California, Idaho, Louisiana, Nevada, New Mexico, Texas and Washington have community property laws. Generally, community property is included in a decedent's gross estate only to the extent of the decedent's interest under the state law.[1] Some separate property that was converted from community property by the decedent and the surviving spouse may be treated as community property for the marital deduction [¶ 3929 et seq.].

¶ 3906 Property subject to dower and curtesy. Dower and curtesy interests, or any interest of the surviving spouse created by statute in place of dower and curtesy, are included in the gross estate [Sec. 2034; 20.2034-1]. See ¶ 3929 et seq. for allowance of marital deduction for property passing to a surviving spouse.

¶ 3907 Powers of appointment. Technically, a power of appointment may be either *general* or *limited (special)*. Ordinarily, only property subject to general powers of appointment would be included in the possessor's gross estate [Sec. 2041]. There is an exception for one kind of limited power created after 10-21-42 [¶ 3908]. The date the power was created is of prime importance in considering the question of estate tax liability arising out of powers of appointment.

¶ 3908 Property subject to power of appointment. (a) **Powers created after 10-21-42.** The following rules apply:

General powers. Property is included in the gross estate if it is subject to a general power created after 10-21-42 that is held by a decedent at the time of his death. The property is also included if the decedent exercised or released the power by a transfer (before 1977) in contemplation of death [¶ 3909(a)], or within 3 years of death [¶ 3909(b)], or to take effect at death. A renunciation or disclaimer of the power is not considered a release of the power (but see below). A partial release of the power will not result in the property subject to the modified power escaping estate tax liability if the decedent possesses the modified power at death or if he has exercised this power by a transfer in contemplation of, or taking effect at, his death (¶ 3909; 3911) [Sec. 2041(a)(2); 20.2041-3(d)].

Qualified disclaimers (after 1976). For estates of decedents dying after 1976, the disclaimer rules that apply to the gift tax also apply to the estate tax. See ¶ 4004.

Limited powers. Property subject to a limited power is included in the gross estate only if the power is exercised by creating another power of appointment that can, under state law,[1] in turn be exercised so as to postpone the vesting of the property for a period that can be ascertained without regard to the date of the creation of the first power [Sec. 2041(a)(3); 20.2041-3(e)].

Powers that lapse during the life of the holder of the power have a special rule. It covers annual powers of invasion that lapse when they are not exercised. If the holder does not exercise the power there will be no estate tax liability as to this lapse in years before the year of the holder's death, unless the amount of the authorized invasion exceeds the greater of $5,000, or 5% of the value of the property (either income, principal or both[2]) out of which the power could have been satisfied. If the authorized invasion exceeds this limit, the lapse is treated as a release of the power as to the excess. This amount is included in the gross estate if the release is (before 1977) in contemplation of death [¶ 3909(a)], or (after 1976) within 3 years of death [¶ 3909(b)]. Any undrawn amount the holder could take during the year in which he died also is included [Sec. 2041(b)(2); 20.2041-3(d)].

(b) Powers created before 10-22-42. Property subject to a *general* power created before 10-22-42 is included in the possessor's estate only if the power is exercised by will or by a transfer in contemplation of, or taking effect at, death. An exercise of a power to change the beneficial interests in a trust, when the possessor retains a life interest, also is taxable.[3]

General powers may be completely released at any time without estate tax liability. If the power was partially released before 11-1-51—so that it is no longer a general power—the modified power may be exercised after that without tax liability [Sec. 2041(a)(1)]. If the power is partially released on or after 11-1-51, a later exercise of the reduced power by will or by a transfer in contemplation of, or taking effect at, death will put the property into the gross estate [Sec. 20.2041-2(e)]. Property subject to a *special or limited* power is not included in the possessor's gross estate.

(c) Date power is created. Generally, the date a power of appointment is created is the date when the instrument that provides for it goes into effect; not the later date when the power can be exercised.

A will goes into effect when the testator dies. However, a power of appointment in a will drawn before 10-22-42 by a testator who died before 7-1-49 is treated as a pre-1942 power, unless the will was republished after 10-21-42. A power of appointment created by a trust agreement (or any other document not a will) executed before 10-22-42 is considered a power created before that date even though it cannot be exercised until a later date. If the holder exercises the power by creating a similar power in a new appointee, a new power is created at that time [Sec. 2041(b)(3); 20.2041-1(e)].

¶ 3909 Transfers in contemplation of death. (a) For estates of decedents dying before 1-1-77. A transfer of an interest in property, relinquishment of a power, or exercise or release of a general power of appointment by a decedent *made within three years of death* without adequate and full consideration *is presumed* to have been made in contemplation of death. Unless the executors can prove the contrary, the full value of the property will be subjected to estate tax [Sec. 2035; 20.2035-1(d)]. If the tax authorities contend that any gift was made in contemplation of death, to avoid tax, the executors will usually have to prove that the decedent was prompted to make a gift by a motive essentially associated with life rather than with death. Among the motives that have been held to be associated with life are: (1) to see children enjoying property while the donor lived;[1] (2) to save income taxes[2] (A transfer to a spouse to save income tax may be open to question as a motive associated with life in view of the income-splitting provisions of the Code [¶ 1104]); (3) to save personal property taxes;[3] (4) to make dependents financially independent;[4] (5) to see the family carry on the business;[5] and (6) to induce son to stay in family business.[6] Also, to rebut the presumption that a gift was

Footnotes appear at end of this Chapter.

made "in contemplation of death," the executor should show that the deceased was of sound mind and in good health when the gift was made [Sec. 20.2035-1(c)].

(b) For estates of decedents dying after 12-31-76. The following adjustments must be made for gifts made within 3-years of the decedent's death: (1) the value of a transfer (less $3,000 exclusion) of an interest in property by a decedent within three years of death without adequate and full consideration is taxable and included in the gross estate; (2) under a rule described as the "gross-up" rule, any gift tax paid by the decedent or his estate on gifts made by the decedent or his spouse within three years of death is also includible in gross estate. But the amount of gift tax paid by a spouse on a split gift to a third party, [¶ 4009], is excluded. See ¶ 3935. However, these rules do not apply to transfers made before 1-1-77 [Sec. 2035].

¶ 3910 Transfers reserving right to use, enjoyment, or income. Property transferred by a decedent before his death can be included in the gross estate. It is included if the decedent kept a life interest in the possession or enjoyment of the property or its income. It also is included when the decedent had the right during his life to name the persons to possess or enjoy the property or its income. Property transferred after 6-6-32 is included even if another person had to join with the decedent to name the persons who get the property or income. [Sec. 2036; 20.2036-1]. However, a residence transferred by a husband to his wife without restriction was not included in his gross estate, even though he continued to live there and pay the property tax.[1] In the same way, a district court did not include in a parent's gross estate property transferred from the parent to a child.[2]

If the grantor of an *irrevocable* trust retains no economic interest in, control over, or right to the beneficial enjoyment of either the income or principal of the trust (and such control, interest, or right was not relinquished in contemplation of death), no part of the trust property will be included in the gross estate. The term "irrevocable" implies that the trust is not taxable under the provisions explained in ¶ 3912. When the grantor retains power to accumulate or distribute income, accumulated income and the value of the trust are included in this gross estate.[3] But the Supreme Court held that the value of stock transferred to an irrevocable trust is not included when the grantor retained the power to vote the stock and to prevent the trustee from selling any of the shares [4](does not apply to transfers made after 6-22-76 [Sec. 2036(a)]. If irrevocable *reciprocal* trusts are created (such as those created by a husband and wife for each other as life beneficiaries), the value of the property in each trust will be included in the life beneficiary's estate if the arrangement leaves both grantors in about the same economic position as they would have been had they created trusts naming themselves.[5]

When a donor reserves only part of the income from property, only a corresponding part of the property transferred will be taxable by reason of the reservation. Nontaxable transfers include transfers for a full and adequate consideration in cash or its equivalent[6], and transfers made before 3-4-31 with a retained life estate [Sec. 2036; 20.2036-1].

¶ 3911 Transfers taking effect at death. Property interests transferred by a decedent during his life (except a bona fide sale for adequate consideration) generally must be included in the decedent's gross estate if: (1) the decedent has a reversionary interest in the transferred property which, immediately before his death, was worth more than 5% of the value of the property; and (2) possession or enjoyment of the transferred interest could be obtained only by the transferee surviving the decedent [Sec. 2037; 20.2037-1].

A reversionary interest includes the possibility that the transferred property may return to the decedent or his estate or may be subject to his power of disposition. It does not include reservation of a life estate [¶ 3910] or the possible return of, or power or disposition over, income alone from the property. If the transfer was made before 10-8-49, it is not taxable unless the reversionary interest was retained by the express terms of the instrument of transfer. If the transfer was made after 10-7-49, it is taxable, whether the reversionary interest arises by operation of law or by virtue of an express reservation in the instrument of transfer [Sec. 2037; 20.2037-1].

Survivorship condition. A transfer that takes effect at death is not taxable unless the transferee's possession or enjoyment of the property is dependent upon his surviving the decedent. Thus, if immediately before the transferor's death, the possession or enjoyment by the transferee depends upon his surviving the transferor or some alternative event, such as the expiration of a term of years or the exercise of a power of appointment, the property generally will not be included in the gross estate. However, if the alternative event is "unreal," and the decedent dies before such event, the survivorship condition will be satisfied [Sec. 20.2037-1(a)]. See ¶ 3929 et seq. for allowance of marital deduction for property passing to a surviving spouse in trust.

¶ **3912 Transfers reserving power to alter, amend, revoke or terminate.** The value of any property transferred by the decedent during his life is included in his estate, if at the time of death he had the power to make a substantial change in the beneficial enjoyment of the property transferred, or if he gave up such a power (before 1977) in contemplation of death, (after 1976) within 3 years of death. It does not matter whether the power can be exercised by the grantor alone, or with a beneficiary, even if the beneficiary's interest is substantial and adverse.[1] However, property of a decedent mentally incompetent from 10-1-47 to his death is not included in the gross estate if the power could have been relinquished without gift tax from 1-1-40 to 12-31-47. A trust created before 6-2-24 is not taxable if revocable by the grantor and a beneficiary having a substantial adverse interest. In transfers before 6-23-36, a relinquishment of a power (before 1977) in contemplation of death, (after 1976) within 3 years of death is taxable only if executed by the decedent. In transfers after 6-22-36, the relinquishment by another possessing the power with decedent is taxable in decedent's estate [Sec. 2038; 20.2038-1].

Trust revocable by beneficiary. When a beneficiary (or any person other than the decedent) has exclusive and sole power to revoke or terminate a trust, the trust property is not taxable in the deceased grantor's estate [Sec. 20.2038-1(a)].

Trust revocable by grantor and beneficiaries. In most states, a trust may be revoked by the joint action of the grantor and all the beneficiaries, even though the trust instrument provides that the trust is irrevocable. Thus, when a trust is created and the grantor reserves the power to alter or amend the terms or revoke completely if all the beneficiaries consent, the reservation adds nothing to the rights of the parties. If, in this situation, the decedent's power can be exercised only with the consent of all the beneficiaries, the trust property is not taxable.[2] When, however, the trustee with the consent of all the beneficiaries has the power of revocation or alteration, the value of the property will be included in the grantor's estate, if the grantor reserves the right to remove the trustee at any time and appoint himself as successor-trustee [Sec. 20.2038-1(a)].

Power to change without benefit to grantor. If the grantor of a trust reserves the power to alter or modify it, but not in favor of himself or his estate, the trust corpus will be included in his estate despite the limitation of his power.[3] If a donor of property transfers it to himself as custodian for a minor under the Model Custodian Act [¶ 1225], the property's value is included in the donor's gross estate if he is custodian at his death before the donee reaches 21 years of age.[4] This does not apply when any of the above transfers are made for an adequate consideration in money or money's worth [Sec. 20.2038-1(a)].

¶ **3913 Transfers for an inadequate consideration.** The value of property involved in any of the transfers discussed in ¶ 3907 through ¶ 3912 is included in the gross estate only to the extent the consideration is inadequate. If the transfer is for consideration, but is not a real sale for an adequate and full consideration, the excess of the fair market value of the property transferred over the value of the consideration received is taxed in the decedent's estate. A relinquishment of dower, curtesy or other marital rights of a surviving[1] spouse is not consideration [Sec. 2043; 20.2043-1].

¶ **3914 Life insurance** proceeds payable to the executor or administrator, to the estate, or in fact receivable by or for the benefit of the estate are included in the estate regardless of whether the decedent possessed incidents of ownership in the policies [Sec. 2042; 20.2042-1]. Insurance payable to other beneficiaries is included in the estate if the decedent possessed at death any incidents of ownership, exercisable either alone or with any other person. Proceeds paid to a surviving spouse qualify for the marital deduction [¶ 3929].

Transfer of policies. Proceeds paid to other beneficiaries are not included in the decedent's gross estate if he transferred the incidents of ownership of the policy. For example, the proceeds of group life insurance are not included in the gross estate when the decedent assigns all his rights in the policy including the conversion privilege to his wife.[1] However, the proceeds are included if the policy contained a provision against assignment and an assignment was made before the proceeds were payable.[2]

Proceeds of policies transferred in comtemplation of death are also included in the gross estate [¶ 3909]. However, the proceeds of life insurance policies are not included if the policies are transferred more than three years before death. If the decedent has paid the premiums within three years before his death, only the value of the premiums found to have been paid in comtemplation of death are includible. When a person buys a one-year accidental death policy on his life, naming his children as owners and beneficiaries, and dies within nine months of purchase, the proceeds are includible.[3]

National Service Life Insurance. The proceeds are included in the gross estate for purposes of the estate tax. However, payment of tax can be enforced only from other property and not from the insurance proceeds.[4]

Insurance on another's life. The value of an insurance policy [¶ 3919] owned by the decedent on the life of another is included in the gross estate.[5]

¶ **3915 Annuity, pension or profit-sharing plans or trusts. (a) Annuity plans.** Generally, the value of an annuity or other payment payable under agreement made after March 3, 1931, to any beneficiary by reason of his surviving a decedent is included in the decedent's estate in proportion to the decedent's contribution to the cost of the annuity [Sec. 2039(b); 20.2039-1]. Thus, if a husband bought a joint and survivorship annuity for himself and his wife, and paid the full consideration, the total value of the widow's interest (figured at his death) is included, if each paid half, only half the value is included. See ¶ 3919 for valuation of annuities.

Example: Assume an annuity is valued at $40,000. The decedent's contribution to the total purchase price of $30,000 was $15,000. The amount included in the decedent's estate is $20,000 ($15,000/$30,000 × $40,000).

This proportionate part of the value is included only if before death the decedent was getting or had the right to get payments under the annuity contract or plan, either alone or in conjunction with any other person, for life or for any period not ascertainable without reference to his death, or for a period which did not in fact end before his death [Sec. 2039(a); 20.2039-1(b)].

Life payments. Under a life plan, the employer, insurance company, or trustee is obligated to make payments only for the life of the annuitant (or employee). At his death, all installments stop even though death occurs before a single payment is received. No other person is entitled to receive any payments. No estate tax, therefore, may be imposed.

Refund plan or annuity. A refund plan or annuity usually provides for payments to the annuitant for life, and a refund if death should occur before the contract cost is recovered. If this refund is in cash, the amount actually paid to the beneficiaries upon the annuitant's death is included in the decedent's gross estate. If the plan or annuity provides for continuing the installments after decedent's death, the aggregate amount receivable by the beneficiary, discounted to its present value [¶ 3919], would be included.[1] However, the value of payments made to a widow for life is not included in a decedent employee's gross estate as an annuity when the payments under a contract provides only for his salary and her life payments if he dies while employed.[2] Note that the amounts contributed to a qualified plan by an electing Subchapter S corporation for a shareholder-employee are considered as employee's contributions to the extent they exceed the lesser of $7,500 or 15% of his compensation in each year. The excess must be included in the employee's estate [Prop. Reg. Sec. 20.2039-2(c)].

Survivorship plan or annuity not connected with employment. Under a joint and survivor annuity or a contingent annuity plan, part of the value is included in the decedent's estate [Sec. 2039; 20.2039-1] if: (1) The beneficiary, surviving annuitant, or other recipient is entitled to the payments by reason of surviving the decedent, *and* (2) The decedent up to the time of death was receiving or was entitled to receive payments under the annuity plan.

The value of the annuity going to a beneficiary of a contingent plan or to the surviving annuitant of a joint and survivor annuity plan is included in the decedent's estate in proportion to the decedent's contribution to the cost of the annuity. For the method of determining this value, see ¶ 3919.

(b) Employee benefit plans. The amount included in the decedent's estate depends on the type of plan. Nothing is included for a life plan (see above). When a retirement plan merely provides that the amounts contributed by the employee shall be returned with interest to his named beneficiaries in case of his death before retirement, the sum returned is a part of the decedent's estate.[3]

Annuity and benefit plans. If the decedent was an employee entitled to payments under an employees' annuity or benefit plan, the value of the payments going to his beneficiaries after his death is includible to the extent:

(1) It is based on contributions the decedent employee made to the plan, whether or not the plan qualifies as tax-exempt under Section 401 [¶ 3024];

(2) It is based on the employer's contributions to an unqualified plan made as an inducement to employment or as a substitute for additional pay.

Value of the annuity or other payments is excluded to the extent it is based on contributions made by the employer to a qualified plan [Sec. 2039; 20.2039-1; 20.2039-2] or by the government under the civil service retirement program.[4] The same exclusion applies to annuities paid under the retired serviceman's family pro-

Footnotes appear at end of this Chapter.

¶ 3915

tection plan for deaths after 1965 and to annuities paid under survivor benefit plan for deaths on or after 9-21-72 unless the serviceman elects out of the plan.[5] However, amounts subject to withdrawal when employee died are included in gross estate, even though exact amount cannot be calculated until after his death.[6] Amounts the employee elects to have contributed to a qualified plan rather than paid to him are counted as employer contributions.[7]

Self-employed retirement plans. For estates of decedents dying after 12-31-76, the value of the annuity paid to a self-employed person under an H. R. 10 plan is excluded from gross estate to the extent it is based on income tax deductible contributions made for him. Where the decedent dies before 1977 the annuity based on contributions made for the owner-employee is included in the gross estate [Sec. 2039(c)].

Individual retirement savings plans. For estates of decedents dying after 12-31-76, the value of an annuity based on income tax deductible contributions is excluded from gross estate. Although the exclusion is generally limited to contributions that are deductible for income tax purposes under Sec. 219, it will be allowed for rollover contributions from another qualified plan. When the value of the annuity is attributed to both deductible and nondeductible contributions, a portion of the value that reflects the nondeductible contributions must be included in the gross estate. The amount included in gross estate is determined by multiplying the total value of the annuity by the amount not allowed as an income deduction (excluding rollovers) over total payments. For this purpose, "annuity" means substantially equal periodic payments for life or for at least 36 months after the decedent's death [Sec. 2039(c), (e)].

The above provisions eliminate in most instances any estate tax on payments made to employees under non-contributory qualified plans. The only times such payments will be subject to estate tax are: (1) When the retired worker gets his money in his lifetime *and it is still in his estate when he dies;* (2) When the worker dies before retirement and designates *his estate or his executor* as the beneficiary, or the plan makes such a designation; and (3) For estate of decedents dying after 12-31-76, when the worker receives a *lump-sum payment distribution* [Sec. 2039(c)].

Tax-exempt employers. An exclusion from the gross estate also is provided for an annuity or other payments under a retirement annuity contract purchased by a tax-exempt school or college, publicly supported charity or religious organization for its employee. However, annuity payments by a school or hospital that is an integral part of local government do not qualify for the exclusion.[8] The Tax Court holds that a state-owned university is not an integral part of the state government and therefore qualifies for the exclusion.[9] The amount of the exclusion is the part attributable to the employer's contributions that were excludable from the employee's gross income under the 20% rule in ¶ 1232(e). No part of the annuity payments based on the decedent's contributions is excluded [Sec. 2039(c); 20.2039-2(c)].

Amount of employer's contribution. If the employer contribution cannot be found by a more exact method, the employee contributions can be deducted from the value of the annuity when the employee's (or his survivor's) rights first become fixed under the plan. The result is the amount of the employer's contribution [Sec. 2039; 20.2039-2(c)]. The excludable amount can then be determined as above.

Railroad retirement annuities are not included in an employee's gross estate. However, a lump-sum residual death benefit for which the decedent may designate a beneficiary is included.[10]

(c) Annuity taxed under other provisions. The special provisions of Sec. 2039 do not prevent application of any other provision of law relating to the estate tax. If a contract provides for a refund of a portion of the cost, in the event of the decedent's premature death, payable to the decedent's estate, the refund is treated as any other property of the decedent.

(d) Marital deduction. See ¶ 3929 et seq.

¶ 3916 Generation-skipping transfers. (a) General. Unless the transitional rule applies (see (e) below), these transfers under a trust or similar arrangement are taxable. The tax imposed is substantially equivalent to the estate or gift tax which would have been imposed if the property had been actually transferred outright to each generation. This is achieved by adding the value of the property taxable as a result of the generation-skipping transfer to the other taxable transfers (gift or estate) of the "deemed transferor." The net effect is that the generation-skipping transfer is taxed at the marginal transfer tax rate of the deemed transferor. But the tax is paid out of the proceeds of the trust property and neither the deemed transferor nor his estate is liable for the tax [Sec. 2602-2603; 2612].

(b) Nature of tax. Basically, a generation-skipping transfer is one which splits the benefits between two or more generations that are younger than the generation of the grantor. Generally, the transfer is taxable on the termination of an intervening interest, or on distribution to the beneficiary, and if both events occur at the same time, the transfer is treated as a termination. However, transfers to grandchildren aren't subject to the tax to the extent the total transfers don't exceed $250,000 through each deemed transferor, i.e., the grantor's child who is also the grandchild's parent. Thus, if the grantor has two children each of whom has children, up to $500,000 can be transferred to the grandchildren tax free. The "deemed transferor" is the parent of the transferee who is most closely related to the grantor. When the generation-skipping transfer takes place at the same time or after the death of the deemed transferor, the trust is entitled to the unused portion of his unified credit, the charitable deduction and the credit for tax on prior transfers. If the generation-skipping transfer takes place within nine months after the death of the deemed transferor, the trust is entitled to any reduced rate resulting from an increased marital deduction. In addition, it is entitled to credit for state death taxes and deductions for administration costs and losses. The tax is not imposed on outright transfers, and on distributions of current income from generation-skipping trusts [Sec. 2601-2603; 2611-2614].

(c) How to figure the tax. Finding the generation-skipping tax involves three operations: (1) Figure a tentative tax by applying the graduated rates in the unified estate and gift tax rate schedule, ¶ 3937(b), to sum of: (a) the fair market value of property transferred on the date of transfer (or alternative valuation date); (b) the total fair market value of all prior transfers of the deemed transferor; (c) the total amount of "adjusted taxable" gifts, ¶ 3933(b) of the deemed transferor; (d) the total taxable estate of the deemed transferor. (2) Refigure the tentative tax by applying the graduated rates in the unified estate and gift tax rate schedule, to the sum of the items (b), (c), and (d). (3) Subtract the result in (2) from the tentative tax in (1). The remaining amount is the generation-skipping tax [Sec. 2602].

(d) Reporting procedures. The filing requirements are similar to estate and gift taxes (¶ 3943; 4030). But the minimum filing requirement does not apply to the generation-skipping tax. In addition, a return must be filed even though no tax may be due because of the exclusion for transfers to grandchildren [Sec. 2621].

(e) Transitional rule. The generation-skipping tax does not apply to transfers under a pre-5-1-76 irrevocable trust but only to the extent that the transfers are not made from corpus added to the trust after that date. In addition, the tax does not apply to transfers under any will or revocable trust executed before 5-1-76, if the decedent dies before 1-1-82 without having: (1) amended the will or trust to increase the number of younger generations, or (2) expanded the total value of the interest of all beneficiaries below the grantor. If the grantor or testator is incompetent, the grace period is extended for two years after the disability is removed.[1]

VALUATION OF ESTATE PROPERTY

¶ **3919 How property is valued.** All property is included in the gross estate at its fair market value. The value is determined on date of death or an alternate valuation date [Sec. 20.2031-1(b)]. The price of tangible personal property sold at auction or by newspaper advertising is presumed to be the retail price.[1] A Revenue Service determination of fair market value is accepted as correct until the taxpayer proves it is wrong.[2]

For estates of decedents dying after 12-31-76. The Tax Reform Act of 1976 provides "carryover basis property" rules for purposes of computing income taxes. These rules apply to property acquired from or passing from a decedent dying after 12-31-76. Subject to an important exception and certain adjustments, these "carryover basis property" rules require that the basis of property acquired from a decedent after 12-31-76, be the same in the hands of his executor and heirs as it was in the hands of the decedent immediately before death.

Exception. The basis for determining gain but not loss of all assets is increased to their fair market value on 12-31-76. This is popularly described as the "fresh start" rule. It adds to basis the appreciation in value attributable to the period the decedent held the property before 1-1-77. However, if the appreciation is not reflected in the basis of property held on 12-31-76, then the increase attributed to appreciation is determined by a special rule. See ¶ 1507.

Adjustments. A separate carryover basis property rule allows the aggregate basis of all carryover basis property to be increased to a minimum of $60,000, and apportioned to the separate appreciated assets in an estate on 12-31-76. But this does not apply to nonresident estates. Furthermore, a special exemption of $10,000 applies to household and personal effects for which the executor must make an election. Further additions to basis are allowed for federal and state estate taxes due to the appreciation in the carryover basis and for state death taxes paid by the transferee. Executors must furnish beneficiaries and the Revenue Service information as to the carryover basis of property in the estate. Penalties are imposed for failure to comply. See ¶ 1507.

Statement of valuation furnished by Revenue Service. For estates of decedents dying after 12-31-76, an executor (or legal representative) may request a statement from the Revenue Service explaining its estate tax valuation made for the estate tax return. It must be furnished within 45 days after request or after the Revenue Service determination, whichever is later. But the statement is not binding or final on the Revenue Service as to its methods and computations [Sec. 7515].

Valuation date. The executor may generally elect to value the property either (1) at the date of death, or (2) at an alternate valuation date that ordinarily is 6 months after death. If the property transferred qualifies for the charitable [¶ 3927] or marital deduction [¶ 3929 et seq.], and the executor elects to use the alternate valuation date, the property is valued as of the date of death, with adjustment for any difference in value (not due to lapse of time or to a contingency) as of the date

6 months after death, or the date of distribution, sale, exchange or other disposition [Sec. 20.2032-1(g)]. The election to use the alternate valuation date is made in the estate tax return, filed within 9 months after the decedent's death. The election applies to all the assets.[3] Property (except return of capital) earned or accrued by the estate during the alternate valuation period is not included in the gross estate. The election may be made, even if the value of the gross estate has increased in the year after the decedent died.[4] However, for estates of decedents dying before 1-1-77, the alternate valuation method could not be used, unless the gross estate at date of death was more than the statutory exemption of $60,000 (in effect before 1977) [Sec. 20.2032-1].

(a) Real property. Unless the executor elects the special use valuation for certain qualified real property (see below), the fair market value of real estate is at best a matter of opinion based on expert knowledge of the local and general market. An explanation of the basis of the appraisal must be attached to the estate tax return.[5] Assessed value may not be used [Sec. 20.2031-1(b)].

Farms and closely held realty—special valuation. For estates of decedents dying after 12-31-76, if certain conditions are met, the executor may elect to value real property included in the decedent's estate, which is devoted to farming or closely held business use, on the basis of that property's value as a farm or closely held business, rather than its fair market value determined on the basis of its highest and best use. The special valuation cannot, however, reduce the gross estate by more than $500,000. To qualify for the special valuation these conditions must be met: (1) the decedent was a U.S. citizen or resident; (2) the real and personal property of the farm or closely held business is at least 50% of the gross estate, less expenses; (3) 25% of the gross estate value is qualified farm or closely held business realty (to determine the 50% and 25% full value is used); (4) real property must pass to a qualified heir, for example, spouse, children and close relative and if transfer is in trust, the heir must have a present interest in the trust; (5) the real property was used as a farm or closely held business for 5 of the last 8 years before the decedent's death; and (6) the decedent or a member of his family materially participated in the farm or business operations in 5 out of the 8 years before the decedent's death [Sec. 2032A].

Recapture of estate tax benefits. If within 15 years of the decedent's death, the heir sells or transfers the qualified property to nonfamily members or its use for farming or closely held business purposes is terminated, then the estate tax benefits are recaptured. But if the recapture event occurs after the 10th year and before the end of the 15th year, the amount of recapture is not in full but on a ratable monthly basis. In addition, a special lien applies to all qualified property. It terminates when either the heir dies or 15 years elapse [Sec. 2032A(c)]. See also ¶ 3944.

(b) Stocks and bonds. Generally the fair market value per share or bond is the mean between the highest and lowest selling prices on the valuation date. When there are no sales on the valuation date, the value may be determined by taking a weighted average of the means of prices for the days sales were made (within a reasonable time) last before and next after that date. Lacking actual sales the same process may be applied to bid and asked prices. If both sales and complete bid and asked prices are lacking, the mean of the bid and asked prices for the date either before or after the valuation date may be used [Sec. 20.2031-2]. U.S. savings bonds are includible in the gross estate at their redemption value on the valuation date. Treasury bonds with a market value below par, but redeemable at par to pay estate tax, are included in the gross estate at par.[6] Mutual fund shares are valued at the redemption price[7] [Sec. 20.2031-8(b)]. The carryover basis rules for determining gain on the sale of these stocks and bonds is discussed at ¶ 1507.

(c) Business interests. If a decedent owned an interest in a business as a proprietor or partner, have all the assets of the business (including good will), fairly appraised as of the valuation date. Then fix the net value of the business in an amount that a willing buyer would pay to a willing seller in view of the net value of the assets of the business and its earning capacity [Sec. 20.2031-3]. The value of a business interest may be fixed by a "buy and sell" agreement. To fix the value of the interest for estate tax purposes, the agreement must (1) bind the estate to sell, either by giving the survivors an option or by binding all the parties; (2) set a price which is not so grossly inadequate as to make the agreement a "mere gratuitous promise."[8] Buy and sell agreements are often funded by insurance on the lives of the parties.

NOTE: For estates of decedents dying after 12-31-76, see the special rules above that apply to the valuation of real property held by a closely held business.

(d) Annuities, insurance, life estates, remainders and reversions. The value of annuities (except commercial annuities), life estates, terms for years, remainders and reversions includible in a decedent's estate are determined by separate tables for men and women with interest at 6%, set out in Regulation Sec. 20.2031-10. However, if it is known on the valuation date that the person whose life measures a life or remainder interest will die from an illness in a very short time, the value of interest is based on that fact.[9] In the same way, the value of a reversionary interest is affected by the state of health of the decedent immediately before death,[10] but the Tax Court disagrees.[11] A remainder that cannot be valued by using the actuarial tables in a particular fact situation should be valued under rules in Sec. 20.2031-1.[12] The value of an annuity contract or a life insurance policy on the life of another than the decedent issued by a company engaged in that business is determined by the cost of a comparable contract with that company [Sec. 20.2031-8]. When the decedent-owner and the insured die simultaneously, several Circuits (4th, 5th, 6th and 9th) disagree with the Revenue Service position and hold that the interpolated terminal reserve value plus unearned premiums, and not full maturity value, is the amount includible in the decedent-owner's gross estate.[13]

DEDUCTIONS FROM THE GROSS ESTATE

¶ 3926 What deductions are allowed. Deductions from the value of the gross estate to arrive at the taxable estate include: (1) funeral expenses actually paid[1] by the estate [Sec. 20.2053-2]; (2) administration expenses [Sec. 20.2053-3]; (3) claims enforceable against the estate; (4) taxes accrued but unpaid against the estate; (5) unpaid mortgages upon, or any indebtedness in respect to, property where the value of decedent's interest therein, undiminished by such mortgage or indebtedness is included in the gross estate's value; (6) losses; (7) transfers to exempt charitable, religious, etc., institutions [¶ 3927]; (8) property transferred to a surviving spouse, if it doesn't exceed 50% of the "adjusted gross estate" [¶ 3929 et seq.]; (9) interests passing to orphans for estates of decedents dying after 12-31-76, see (e) below. For estates of decedents dying before 1-1-77, the specific exemption deduction was allowed. See ¶ 3928.

Items 1-5 are deductible only to the extent their payment is authorized by the laws of the jurisdiction under which the estate is administered. They are deductible in full if paid before the date the estate tax return is due. If payment is made on or after that date, the deduction is limited to the value of the property that is included in both the gross estate for federal estate tax purposes and the probate estate under state law [Sec. 2053(a); 2053(c); 20.2053-1]. It should be noted that the only expenses included in this treatment are those incurred in administering property which is included in both the decedent's gross estate and his probate estate [Sec. 2053(b); 2053(c)].

(a) Expenses of administering property included in the decedent's federal gross estate, but not in his state probate estate, can be deducted only if paid before the assessment period expires [Sec. 20.2053-8].

(b) Taxes on income received after death, property taxes accrued after death, and estate, inheritance, and legacy taxes are not deductible. However, a deduction is allowed for the amount of state death tax (for decedents dying after Dec. 31, 1953) or foreign death tax (for decedents dying after June 30, 1955) on a transfer for public, charitable or religious uses [Sec. 2053(d)(1); 20.2053-6, 20.2053-9, 20.2053-10]. (This deduction is not allowed for death taxes paid to a U.S. possession for decedents dying after 9-2-58 [Sec. 2053(d)(1)].) If the deduction is elected, no credit for state death tax [¶ 3936] or foreign death tax [¶ 3938] may be taken for the tax that is deducted [Sec. 2011(e), 2053(d); 20.2011-2].

(c) Claims against the estate. The claim must be based on a personal obligation of the decedent. Interest, if any, to the date of death can be added. The deduction for a claim based on a promise or agreement, such as a debt or unpaid mortgage, is limited to the amount of liability that was incurred in good faith for adequate consideration in money, or money's worth. However, the full amount is allowed on a pledge or agreement for a contribution to charity that would be deductible as a bequest [Sec. 20.2053-4]. Giving up dower or other marital rights is not consideration [Sec. 2043(b); 20.2043-1].

A deduction is allowed for a debt arising out of a property settlement in a divorce decree when the court has power to settle all property rights or change a prior property settlement agreed on. If the court does not have this power, the deduction is limited to the value of the wife's right to support.[2]

Claims against the estate that are waived, or not paid for other reasons, are not deductible; but the claim of a sole beneficiary may be deducted without formal payment.[3]

(d) Losses from fire, storm, shipwreck, or similar casualty, or from theft, can be deducted when not compensated for by insurance, if the losses have not been deducted for income tax purposes [Sec. 2054; 20.2054-1].

(e) Orphan's exclusion. For estates of decedent's dying after 12-31-76, a deduction is allowed for the value of property that passes at death to a decedent's child under the age 21 when there is no surviving spouse of decedent or other known parent. To qualify, the property for which the deduction is claimed must be included in the decedent's gross estate and the child must receive the property or interest. The maximum deduction allowable is $5,000 multiplied by the excess of 21 over the child's age on the date of the decedent's death. But this amount may not exceed the value of the transferred property included in the gross estate. Generally, in most cases, if the child's interest can be treated as a terminable interest under the marital deduction rules, ¶ 3929, it does not qualify for the deduction. The deduction is not allowed to an estate of a divorced parent if the decedent is survived by the other known parent. But the deduction is allowed to an estate of an adoptive parent even though one or both of the natural parents are known and surviving [Sec. 2057].

¶ 3927 Charitable and similar transfers. A deduction from the gross estate is allowed for the value of property transferred for public, charitable, religious, educational, or certain other uses.

Footnotes appear at end of this Chapter.

(a) **Amount of the deduction.** The deduction may not exceed the value of the transferred property included in the gross estate.

Reduced for taxes paid. If under the will or the law where the estate is administered, or the law imposing the tax, any estate, succession, legacy, or inheritance tax is payable in whole or in part out of a deductible charitable transfer, the amount deductible is the balance left after subtracting the tax [Sec. 2055(c); 20.2055-3].

(b) **Transfers that qualify for the deduction.** With some exceptions, the deduction will be allowed if the property was transferred [Sec. 2055; 20.2055-1, 20.2055-4]:

(1) to or for the use of the United States, any State, Territory, any political subdivision thereof, or the District of Columbia, for exclusively public purposes;

(2) to or for the use of any corporation or association organized and operated exclusively for religious, charitable, scientific, literary or educational purposes (including the encouragement of art, the prevention of cruelty to children and animals, and effective 10-5-76, the fostering of national or international amateur sports competition), if no part of its net earnings inures to the benefit of any private stockholder or individual and (for estates of decedents dying before 1977) no substantial part of its activities is carrying on propaganda, or otherwise attempting to influence legislation, and which does not participate in or intervene in (including publishing or distributing statements) any political campaign for a candidate for public office, (for estates of decedents dying after 1976, the organization may not be disqualified under Sec. 501(c)(3) for attempting to influence legislation);

(3) to a trustee or trustees, or a fraternal society, order, or association operating under the lodge system, if the transfers, legacies, bequests, or devises are to be used by the trustee, trustees, fraternal society, order, or association exclusively for religious, charitable, scientific, literary, or educational purposes, or for the prevention of cruelty to children or animals, and (1) no substantial part of the activities of the trustee or trustees, or of the fraternal society, order, or association, is carrying on propaganda, or otherwise attempting to influence legislation, (for estates of decedents dying after 1976 if the trust, fraternal society, order or association is not disqualified as exempt under Sec. 501(c)(3) for attempting to influence legislation), and (2) does not participate in or intervene in (including publishing or distributing statements) any political campaign for a candidate for public office;

(4) to or for the use of any veterans' organization incorporated by Act of Congress, or of its departments or local chapters or posts, if no part of its net earnings inures to the benefit of any private shareholder or individual.

The deduction is not limited, in the estates of citizens or residents, to transfers to domestic corporations or associations, or to trustees for use in the United States [Sec. 20.2055-1].

A deduction is allowed for any portion of the estate that falls into a charitable bequest because of a disclaimer (qualified after 1976) to accept any rights to which the person disclaiming is entitled to under the will [Sec. 2055]. The disclaimer (qualified after 1976) should be filed in the probate court before the estate tax return is filed, ¶ 3943. See also ¶ 4008(b).

Even if there is no express disclaimer, (qualified after 1976) the deduction may be allowed if the holder of a power to consume, invade or appropriate the property dies without exercising it [Sec. 2055(a); 20.2055-1(b); 20.2055-2(c)].

Aged spouse's power of appointment. A deduction may be allowed for property transferred in trust with income payable for life to a spouse who is over 80 when decedent dies and who has a power of appointment over the principal of the trust. The power must be exercisable by will and be broad enough to include religious, charitable, etc. organizations as appointees. An affidavit that the spouse intends to exercise the power in favor of the specified organizations must be made within six months of decedent's death and filed with the decedent's return. There are other conditions that must be fulfilled [Sec. 2055, 6503; 20.2055-1(b)].

Deduction of charitable remainder. No deduction is allowed for the bequest of a charitable remainder unless the remainder interest is in a farm or personal residence or is a trust interest in an annuity trust, unitrust or a pooled income fund [Sec. 642(c)(5), 664; 2055(e)(2); 1.642(c), 1.664-2-4; 20.2055-2(e)(2)].

Donations for conservation purposes. Contributions and transfers for conservation purposes made after 6-13-76 and before 6-14-77 of remainder interests in real property are deductible [Sec. 2055(e)(3)].

≫IMPORTANT→ No transfer of a charitable remainder is deductible for income tax [¶ 1942(e)], gift tax [¶ 4022], or estate tax purposes unless the transfer is in trust and is to an annuity trust, a unitrust or a pooled income fund. Contributed charitable remainders in farms, personal residences and certain conservation property are exceptions to this general rule.

Deduction of charitable income interest. The only charitable income interests that can be deducted are guaranteed annuities or bequests of a fixed percentage distributed yearly of property's fair market value determined annually [Sec. 2055(e)(2)(B); 20.2055-2(e)(1), (2)].

(c) **Transfers that do not qualify.** The estates of decedents dying after 1969 cannot deduct transfers to a private foundation that is subject to tax on loss of exemption or that is not required in the governing instrument to avoid practices that would subject it to penalty taxes (¶ 3437) [Sec. 2055(e)(1); 20.2055-5(a), (b)]. Transfers to foreign private foundations are similarly disallowed [Sec. 20.2055-5(c)]. The transition rules that apply to donations of remainder and income interests to charities also apply to disallowed deductions [Sec. 20.2055-5(b)(2)].

¶ **3928 Specific exemption.** For estates of decedents dying before 1-1-77, a specific exemption of $60,000 is allowed [Sec. 2052]. For estates of decedents dying after 12-31-76, a "unified" credit applies to both estate and gift taxes that is substantially the exemption equivalent. See ¶ 3940.

THE MARITAL DEDUCTION

¶ **3929 What the marital deduction is.** The marital deduction is a deduction that is allowed for the value of property that passes at death to a surviving spouse and it cannot be waived[1] [Sec. 2056; 20.2056(a)-1].

To qualify, the property for which the marital deduction is claimed must be included in decedent's gross estate and the surviving spouse must receive the property or interest. Accordingly, in determining the value of the surviving spouse's interest, there must be taken into account the effect that any estate, inheritance, succession or legacy tax has upon the net value of that interest to the surviving spouse. This means that when the spouse's share of the estate must pay part or all of the death taxes imposed by either federal or state law, the marital deduction is found by subtracting from the value of her interest the amount of those taxes charged against the spouse's share [Sec. 2056(b)(4); 20.2056(b)-4(c)].

Any encumbrance on property or any obligation imposed on the surviving spouse that relates to property passing to a surviving spouse must be taken into account [Sec. 2056(b)(4); 20.2056(b)-4(b)]. No marital deduction is allowed, if the value of the property surrendered is greater than the value of what is received.[2]

A marital deduction is allowed for transfers of property to satisfy pecuniary bequests. The deduction is figured on the value of the transferred property for estate tax purposes. However, no deduction will be allowed (1) unless state law, or the

Footnotes appear at end of this Chapter.

¶ **3929**

terms of the will, clearly limit the executor's discretion so that the spouse will receive property with a date of distribution value at least equal to the pecuniary bequest as used for figuring the estate tax, or (2) the spouse will share in the appreciation or depreciation in value of all of the estate property.[3]

In addition, effective for estates of decedents dying after 12-31-76, the distribution of property with an appreciated "carryover basis," ¶ 3919, by an estate in satisfaction of a pecuniary bequest is a nontaxable transaction but for the appreciation from the date of the decedent's death to the date of distribution. Also, the basis of property to the distributee is the "carryover basis" of the property increased by any gain recognized by the estate or trust on the distribution [Sec. 1014(d), 1023]. See also ¶ 1507.

No marital deduction may be taken with respect to any property passing to the spouse for which a deduction is taken under Sec. 2053 or Sec. 2054 [¶ 3926, items 1-6]. For example, a devise to the wife to satisfy a claim against the estate would not qualify [Sec. 20.2056(a)-2]. Terminable interest [(b) below] and certain disclaimed interests do not qualify.

(a) **Amount of the deduction.** For estates of decedents dying before 1-1-77, the amount of the deduction is limited to 50% of the "adjusted gross estate." For estates of decedents dying after 12-31-76, the marital deduction is limited to the greater of $250,000 or 50% of the "adjusted gross estate." "Adjusted gross estate" is the entire gross estate under Sec. 2031 [¶ 3901—3914] *less* the deductions allowed under Sec. 2053 and Sec. 2054 for funeral, administration and other expenses (¶ 3926, items 1-6) [Sec. 20.2056(c)-1].

When the executor of an estate elects to claim certain expenses of administration as deductions from the gross income of the estate for federal income tax purposes, rather than as deductions from the decedent's gross estate, the deductions so claimed need not be deducted from the gross estate in figuring the adjusted gross estate for arriving at the 50% limitation on the amount of the marital deduction.[4] The marital deduction cannot exceed the value of the surviving spouse's share of the estate. It makes no difference that decedent could have left a greater share.

Adjustment for the gift tax marital deduction. For estates of decedents dying after 12-31-76, and to gifts made after 12-31-76, the maximum estate tax marital deduction must be reduced by the excess of the gift tax marital deduction allowed for gifts made after 1976 (full deduction for first $100,000, none over $100,000 to $200,000, 50% of gifts over $200,000) over 50% of the value of the gifts made after 1976. [Sec. 2056(c)].

Transition rules for bequests passing under formula clauses. Generally, the marital deduction limitation discussed above applies to estates of decedents dying after 12-31-76. However, this does not apply to transfers under wills executed before 1-1-77, or to transfers to trusts before 1-1-77, if the maximum marital deduction clause is not amended after 12-31-76 and before the decedent's death. But the limitations do apply if the state passes legislation to relate formula clauses to the maximum marital deduction. The transitional rules apply to estates of decedents dying after 12-31-76 but before 1-1-79 [Sec. 2056].

When decedent held community property. There is a "special rule" for figuring the adjusted gross estate when decedent held community property. Basically, the method is the same as in estates without community property, except that there is subtracted from the entire gross estate, the value of all community property, but only a part of the allowable deductions under Sec. 2053 and Sec. 2054 (¶ 3926, items 1-6 inclusive).

Marital deduction adjustment in community property states. For estates of decedents dying after 12-31-76, the marital deduction of $250,000 or more, discussed above, must be reduced by either: (1) the decedent's interest in all the community property; or (2) the difference between the value in all of the decedent's community property and the part of the allowable deductions ¶ 3926, items (1)-(6), inclusive that are attributed to the community property [Sec. 2056(c)].

In figuring the marital deduction, if community property is converted into separate property after 12-31-41, and the value of the separate property acquired by the decedent is not more than the value of the separate property acquired by the surviving spouse, all of the separate property is treated as community property. If the value of the separate property acquired by the decedent is more than the value of the separate property acquired by the spouse, only a part of the decedent's portion, proportionate to the value (at the time of the conversion) of the property received by the surviving spouse, is treated as community property [Sec. 2056(c)(2); 20.2056(c)-2].

(b) The terminable interest rule. No deduction will be allowed for property or an interest in property passing to a surviving spouse, if: (1) The interest can terminate or fail; and (2) An interest in the property passes or has passed (for less than adequate consideration) from the decedent to a third person who may possess or enjoy any part of the property after the termination or failure of the surviving spouse's interest [Sec. 2056(b)(1); 20.2056(b)-1].

Exceptions to the terminable interest rule. These are: (1) spouses's survivorship; (2) life estate with power of appointment including certain estate trusts; and (3) proceeds of life insurance, endowment or annuity contracts that pass to surviving spouse in a lump sum [Sec. 2056(b); 20.2056(b)].

Spouse's survivorship. The interest or property passing to the surviving spouse may depend upon the transferee spouse's survival of the decedent for a stated period of time. In such cases the survivorship condition does not affect the marital deduction for the property passing, if the condition can only occur with 6 months, *and* the spouse does in fact meet the condition by surviving the stated period. Also, if a will provides that the spouse's interest will terminate or fail if there is a common disaster involving the spouses, the marital deduction will not be lost if in fact such failure or termination does not occur [Sec. 2056(b)(3); 20.2056(b)-3].

Life estate with power of appointment. When a life estate (whether or not in trust) in property passes from decedent to the surviving spouse, the marital deduction will be allowed for its full value, if (1) the spouse is entitled for life to *all* the income from the entire interest, payable at least annually, and (2) the surviving spouse has a general power of appointment [¶ 3907 et seq.] exercisable (a) during life, or (b) by will.[5] Also when the surviving spouse is to receive only a part of income with a power of appointment over a corresponding part of principal—the deduction is allowed for that part.

The regulations say the part interest must be figured as a fraction or percentage to qualify [Sec. 20.2056(b)-5(c)]. However, the U.S. Supreme Court holds that a part interest in a testamentary trust can be actuarially determined from monthly payments made to the decedent's wife, and that amount qualifies for the deduction.[6]

The spouse must have the power to appoint the entire interest (or a corresponding part of the interest when she receives only part of the income) either to herself or to her estate. It is immaterial if, in addition to this general power, the surviving spouse has one or more lesser powers, such as one to appoint any part of the corpus of the trust for the benefit of another. But the marital deduction is not avail-

¶ 3929

able in this situation if any other person has the power to appoint the surviving spouse's interest to someone other than the spouse [Sec. 2056(b)(5); 20.2056(b)-5].

Estate trusts. For marital deduction purposes, property is deemed to pass to the surviving spouse if it passes to his or her estate. Thus, a marital deduction would be allowed if the trust income is payable to the wife for life and on her death the corpus is payable to her estate, or if the income is to be accumulated for a term of years, or for her life, or in the discretion of the trustee, and the corpus plus accumulated income is to be paid to her estate [Sec. 20.2056(e)-2(b)].

Insurance proceeds. Proceeds of life insurance, endowment, or annuity contracts which pass to the surviving spouse in a lump sum qualify for the marital deduction. In addition, when the proceeds are held by the insurer under an agreement to pay interest or when they are payable in installments, with the balance payable to the estate of the surviving spouse, the deduction applies, since no person other than the surviving spouse has an interest in the proceeds [Sec. 20.2056(e)-2]. If the balance of the proceeds is not payable to the estate of the surviving spouse, the deduction may still be taken under an exception to the terminable interest rule, if the following conditions are met: (1) all payments of installments or interest are to be made to the surviving spouse and to no one else; (2) such amounts are payable annually or more often (the first one, not later than 13 months after the decedent's death); and (3) the surviving spouse has a full power to appoint all (or a specific portion) of the proceeds still held by the insurer at her (or his) death [Sec. 2056; 20.2056(b)-6]. A contract which requires annual or more frequent payments will not be disqualified merely because the surviving spouse must comply with certain formalities (for example, proof of decedent's death)[7] before the first payment is made [Sec. 20.2056(b)-6(d)]. The value of employee annuity qualified for the marital deduction even though payments could be made to employer after surviving spouse died or remarried, because the employer payments did not pass from the decedent under the plan.[8]

THE TAX AND CREDITS

¶ 3934 **Tables for computation of estate tax. (a) Table for computation of estate tax for decedents dying before 1-1-77.** The following table indicates the estate tax where death occurred after August 16, 1954 and before 1-1-77.

Amount of taxable estate	Tax on amount in (A)	Amount of taxable estate in excess of (A) but not in excess of (C) is taxed at rate shown in (D).	
(A)	(B)	(C)	(D)
$0	$0	$5,000	3%
5,000	150	10,000	7%
10,000	500	20,000	11%
20,000	1,600	30,000	14%
30,000	3,000	40,000	18%
40,000	4,800	50,000	22%
50,000	7,000	60,000	25%
60,000	9,500	100,000	28%
100,000	20,700	250,000	30%
250,000	65,700	500,000	32%
500,000	145,700	750,000	35%
750,000	233,200	1,000,000	37%
1,000,000	325,700	1,250,000	39%
1,250,000	423,200	1,500,000	42%
1,500,000	528,200	2,000,000	45%
2,000,000	753,200	2,500,000	49%
2,500,000	998,200	3,000,000	53%
3,000,000	1,263,200	3,500,000	56%
3,500,000	1,543,200	4,000,000	59%
4,000,000	1,838,200	5,000,000	63%
5,000,000	2,468,200	6,000,000	67%
6,000,000	3,138,200	7,000,000	70%
7,000,000	3,838,200	8,000,000	73%
8,000,000	4,568,200	10,000,000	76%
10,000,000	6,088,200	......	77%

Column (A) shows the amount of the taxable estate; that is, the total gross estate less all deductions and an exemption of $60,000.

Column (B) shows the estate tax on the corresponding taxable estate in Column (A).

Column (D) shows the rate applicable to any amount in excess of the taxable estate shown in Column (A) but not in excess of the taxable estate shown in Column (C).

The tax computed by use of this table is the estate tax liability without allowance for any credit for gift tax, for death taxes paid to the states, for foreign death taxes, and for taxes on transfers from prior decedents; it is therefore the maximum federal estate tax payable by any estate.

(b) Table for computation of unified estate and gift tax for decedents dying after 12-31-76 and for gifts made after 12-31-76. The following table indicates the estate and gift tax where the transfers occurred after 12-31-76 [Sec. 2001(c)].

Taxable transfer more than— (A)	But not more than— (B)	Tax on amount in col. (A) (C)	Rate of tax on excess of amount in col. (A) (D)
$ 0	10,000	—	18%
10,000	20,000	1,800	20%
20,000	40,000	3,800	22%
40,000	60,000	8,200	24%
60,000	80,000	13,000	26%
80,000	100,000	18,200	28%
100,000	150,000	23,800	30%
150,000	250,000	38,800	32%
250,000	500,000	70,800	34%
500,000	750,000	155,800	37%
750,000	1,000,000	248,300	39%
1,000,000	1,250,000	345,800	41%
1,250,000	1,500,000	448,300	43%
1,500,000	2,000,000	555,800	45%
2,000,000	2,500,000	780,800	49%
2,500,000	3,000,000	1,025,800	53%
3,000,000	3,500,000	1,290,800	57%
3,500,000	4,000,000	1,575,800	61%
4,000,000	4,500,000	1,880,800	65%
4,500,000	5,000,000	2,205,800	69%
5,000,000	....	2,550,800	70%

Columns (A) and (B) show the amount of taxable transfer. For estate tax, taxable transfer is the total gross estate less all deductions plus the adjusted taxable gifts. For the gift tax, taxable transfer is the gross amount of gifts less deductions and exclusions.

Column (C) shows the tax (estate or gift) on the taxable transfer in Column (A).

Column (D) shows the rate applicable to any amount in excess of the taxable transfer shown in Column (A) but not in excess of the taxable transfer shown in Column (B).

The estate tax computed by use of this table is the tentative estate tax liability without allowance for any credit for gift tax, for death taxes paid to the States, for foreign death taxes, for taxes on transfers from prior decedents, and for the unified credit.

The gift tax computed by the use of this table is the tentative gift tax liability without allowance for the unified credit.

Adjusted taxable gifts. This term includes all lifetime transfers except transfers included in gross estate. Examples of transfers included in gross estate are transfers made within 3 years of death [¶ 3909], and transfers of a decedent

Footnotes appear at end of this Chapter.

¶ 3934

[¶ 3910] in which he has retained certain rights, interests, or powers in the property [Sec. 2001(b)].

¶ 3935 Credit for federal gift tax. **(a) For estates of decedents dying before 1-1-77.** To ease the hardship when a transfer made by a decedent during his life is taxed under both the estate and gift taxes, the gift tax (see Ch. 30) can be credited against the donor's estate tax [Sec. 2012; 20.2012-1]. The credit is allowed, even if the gift tax is paid after the donor's death, and even if the gift tax also is deductible from the gross estate as a debt of the decedent [Sec. 20.2012-1(a)].

Split gifts by husband and wife. When spouses split their gifts [¶ 4012], the credit for the gift tax may be taken in the estate of the spouse who is the actual transferor or donor, and not by the other spouse. The credit is allowed only for the actual gift tax paid on both halves of the gift, not the gift tax payable if the gift had not been split [Sec. 2012(c); 20.2012-1(e)].

How to figure the credit. The credit against the estate tax for the amount of any gift tax paid on property included in the gross estate cannot exceed an amount which bears the same ratio to the estate tax as the value of the gift (for purpose of the gift tax, or the estate tax, whichever is lower[1]) bears to the value of the entire gross estate, reduced by the charitable deduction and the marital deduction [Sec. 2012(a); 20.2012-1(d)]. "Estate tax" as used in this subparagraph is the estate tax reduced by the credit for state death taxes [¶ 3936]. The value of the gift in this ratio must be adjusted to reflect the exclusions and marital or charitable deductions for gift tax purposes, and the marital or charitable deductions for estate tax purposes.

Limitation on credit. The total credit allowed against the estate tax may not exceed the total gift tax paid [Sec. 2012; 20.2012-1(c)].

Gifts made in one quarter. If a donor has made several transfers within a calendar quarter (or calendar year if the gift was made before 1971), and only a part of these transfers is included in his gross estate for purposes of the estate tax, the credit is limited to an amount which bears the same ratio to the total gift tax paid for the calendar quarter as the value of the gift (reduced by any portion excluded or deducted for the annual exclusion, charitable deduction, or the marital deduction) bears to the total taxable gifts (determined without benefit of the gift tax specific exemption) for the quarter [Sec. 2012(d)(1); 20.2012-1(c)].

(b) For estates of decedents dying after 12-31-76. The total gift tax paid on lifetime transfers after 12-31-76 is credited in full against the estate tax. This includes the gift tax paid by a spouse on split gift transfers [Sec. 2001(b), (d)].

> NOTE: Since the gift tax credit is reflected in full for computing the estate tax on lifetime transfers, the treatment of the tax as a deduction in addition to the credit is not necessary under the unified transfer tax approach.

¶ 3936 Credit for state inheritance or estate tax. **(a) For estates of decedents dying before 1-1-77.** If an inheritance, estate, legacy or succession tax has been paid to any state or to the District of Columbia, with respect to property included in the decedent's gross estate, a credit is allowed against the federal estate tax when the taxable estate exceeds $40,000 [Sec. 2011; 20.2011-1]. When a decedent died on or before 9-2-58, the credit is allowed for taxes paid to a U.S. possession.

If a deduction is allowed for state death taxes on a public, religious, or charitable transfer, the tax is excluded from the credit, and adjustment is made to reflect the exclusion [Sec. 2011(e); 20.2011-2]. The maximum credit is a percentage of the taxable estate determined from the table in ¶ 3937 [Sec. 2011; 20.2011-1(b)].

The credit is limited to taxes actually paid and for which credit is claimed within four years after filing the return. The time to claim the credit may be extended when a Tax Court petition is filed, the time to pay the tax is extended, or a timely refund claim for overpayment of tax is filed [Sec. 2011(c); 20.2011-1(c)]. If an executor elects to postpone payment of estate tax on a reversionary or remainder interest [¶ 3944] the credit for state death tax on such interest must be claimed (and the death tax paid) before the extended date for payment of the estate tax [Sec. 2015; 20.2015-1(a)]. If the claim is filed on time, a refund will be allowed based on the claim for credit. The refund will be made without interest[1] [Sec. 2011(c); 20.2011-1(c)]. If taxes for which the credit is claimed are recovered from the state, the person recovering the amount must notify the Revenue Service within 30 days. The Revenue Service can redetermine the Federal estate tax on the basis of the recovery. Any tax due must be paid upon notice and demand [Sec. 2016; 20.2016-1].

(b) For estates of decedents dying after 12-31-76. The maximum allowable credit is a percentage of the Federal "adjusted taxable estate" determined from the state tax credit table in ¶ 3937(b). "Adjusted taxable estate" means the taxable estate less $60,000. But the allowable credit cannot be more than the net estate tax payable [Sec. 2011(b)]. An example of the computation of the credit is included in ¶ 3940(b).

¶ 3937 Tables for computation of maximum credit for State death taxes. (a) Table for computation of the maximum credit for state death tax for decedents dying before 1-1-77. The following table gives the maximum credit allowed against the Federal estate tax for death taxes paid to any state; it is based on the amount of Federal taxable estate when death occurred after 8-16-54 and before 1-1-77 [Sec. 2011]. See also ¶ 3936.

Amount of taxable estate	Maximum credit on taxable estate shown in (A)	Amount of taxable estate in excess of (A) but not more than	Maximum credit on amount in excess of (A) but not in excess of (C)
(A)	(B)	(C)	(D)
$ 40,000	$ 0	$ 90,000	.8%
$ 90,000	$ 400	$ 140,000	1.6%
$ 140,000	$ 1,200	$ 240,000	2.4%
$ 240,000	$ 3,600	$ 440,000	3.2%
$ 440,000	$ 10,000	$ 640,000	4.0%
$ 640,000	$ 18,000	$ 840,000	4.8%
$ 840,000	$ 27,600	$ 1,040,000	5.6%
$ 1,040,000	$ 38,800	$ 1,540,000	6.4%
$ 1,540,000	$ 70,800	$ 2,040,000	7.2%
$ 2,040,000	$ 106,800	$ 2,540,000	8.0%
$ 2,540,000	$ 146,800	$ 3,040,000	8.8%
$ 3,040,000	$ 190,800	$ 3,540,000	9.6%
$ 3,540,000	$ 238,800	$ 4,040,000	10.4%
$ 4,040,000	$ 290,800	$ 5,040,000	11.2%
$ 5,040,000	$ 402,800	$ 6,040,000	12.0%
$ 6,040,000	$ 522,800	$ 7,040,000	12.8%
$ 7,040,000	$ 650,800	$ 8,040,000	13.6%
$ 8,040,000	$ 786,800	$ 9,040,000	14.4%
$ 9,040,000	$ 930,800	$10,040,000	15.2%
$10,040,000	$1,082,800	....	16.0%

Footnotes appear at end of this Chapter.

¶ 3937

(b) Table for computation of the maximum credit for state death taxes for decedents dying after 12-31-76. The following table gives the maximum credit allowed against the Federal estate tax for death taxes paid to any state; it is based on the amount of "adjusted taxable estate" when death occurred after 12-31-76.

Adjusted taxable estate[†] more than—	But not more than—	Maximum Credit on amount in col. (A)	Rate of credit on excess of amount in col. (A)
(A)	(B)	(C)	(D)
$ 40,000	90,000		0.8%
90,000	140,000	400	1.6%
140,000	240,000	1,200	2.4%
240,000	440,000	3,600	3.2%
440,000	640,000	10,000	4.0%
640,000	840,000	18,000	4.8%
840,000	1,040,000	27,600	5.6%
1,040,000	1,540,000	38,800	6.4%
1,540,000	2,040,000	70,800	7.2%
2,040,000	2,540,000	106,800	8.0%
2,540,000	3,040,000	146,800	8.8%
3,040,000	3,540,000	190,800	9.6%
3,540,000	4,040,000	238,800	10.4%
4,040,000	5,040,000	290,800	11.2%
5,040,000	6,040,000	402,800	12.0%
6,040,000	7,040,000	522,800	12.8%
7,040,000	8,040,000	650,800	13.6%
8,040,000	9,040,000	786,800	14.4%
9,040,000	10,040,000	930,800	15.2%
10,040,000		1,082,800	16.0%

[†] Adjusted taxable estate means the taxable estate reduced by $60,000.

¶ **3938 Credit for foreign estate tax.** The estate, with certain limitations, is entitled to a credit against the federal estate tax for an inheritance estate, legacy, or succession tax paid to a foreign country and its political subdivisions, on property, included in the gross estate [Sec. 2014; 20.2014-1]. Possessions of the U.S. are considered foreign countries for this purpose [Sec. 2014(g); 20.2014-1(a)]. No credit is allowed for taxes deducted as a tax on a public, charitable or religious transfer[1] [¶ 3926].

Resident aliens. The President can bar the credit for resident aliens, if a similar credit is not allowed U.S. citizens residing in the resident alien's country [Sec. 2014(h)].

(a) Time to claim the credit. Application for the credit must be made within four years after the filing of the estate tax return. The time to claim the credit may be extended beyond the four-year period (1) to within 60 days after the decision of the Tax Court on a petition for redetermination of a deficiency becomes final or (2) during an extension of time granted for payment of the tax or a deficiency before the expiration date of the extension [Sec. 2014(e); 20.2014-6]. When payment of estate tax on a reversion or remainder interest is postponed [¶ 3944] the credit for foreign death taxes on such interest may be claimed before the time for the postponed payment expires [Sec. 2015; 20.2015-1].

Refunds. If a refund claim is filed on time, refund, without interest, will be allowed based on the claim for credit [Sec. 2014(e); 20.2014-6].

(b) Limitations on credit. The credit is limited to the smaller of:

(1) an amount which bears the same ratio to the foreign death tax (without credit for federal estate tax) as the value of property in the foreign country subjected to foreign death tax and included in the gross estate bears to the value of all property subjected to the foreign death tax [Sec. 20.2014-2]; or

(2) an amount which bears the same ratio to the estate tax (less the gift and state death tax credits and for estates of decedents dying after 1976, the unified tax credit) as the value of property in the foreign country subjected to foreign death tax and included in the gross estate bears to the entire gross estate, reduced by the total amounts allowed as the charitable deduction [¶ 3927], and the marital deduction [¶ 3929 et seq.]. The value of the foreign property in this computation must be reduced by the marital or charitable deduction attributable to that property [Sec. 2014; 20.2014-3].

(c) Recovery of foreign death taxes claimed as credit. When any foreign death tax claimed as a credit is later recovered, the executor or administrator must notify the Revenue Service of the recovery within 30 days. The Revenue Service redetermines the federal estate tax on the basis of the recovery. Any tax due must be paid upon notice and demand. No interest is charged on any tax due as the result of the recovery for any period before the refund is received [Sec. 2016; 20.2016-1].

¶ 3939 Credit for tax on prior transfers. To reduce the burden of successive estate taxes when property passes through more than one taxable estate within a ten-year period, a credit is allowed in figuring the second and subsequent estate taxes for some or all of the previous estate tax.

The credit is available when a decedent's estate includes property that was taxed in the estate of a prior decedent. The credit is based on the value of the property in the estate of the prior decedent. It is applied to all property whose value is included in the estate of the prior decedent.

(a) Transfer of property defined. The term "transfer of property" includes the transmission of property by the prior decedent to the present decedent under any condition or form of ownership that requires the inclusion of the property in the prior decedent's gross estate [Sec. 2013(a); 20.2013-5]. The value of a life estate qualifies even if it is not included in the gross estate of the present decedent.[1]

(b) When the credit is allowed. The credit is permitted for property transferred to the present decedent, if he died within two years before the death of the prior decedent or ten years after [Sec. 2013(a); 20.2013-1]. It is allowed when the prior decedent was married to the present decedent, except for the value allowed as a marital deduction from the prior decedent's estate [Sec. 2013(d); 20.2013-4(b)].

(c) How to figure the credit. The credit is calculated in two ways. The lesser of the two is the one allowed. Each imposes a different limit.

First way. The credit cannot exceed the proportion of the prior decedent's estate tax that the value of the transferred property received by the present decedent bore to the total adjusted taxable estate of the prior decedent. A first trial credit is secured by the following formula:

Footnotes appear at end of this Chapter.

$$\text{Prior decedent's adjusted federal estate tax} \times \frac{\text{Value of transferred property}}{\text{Prior decedent's adjusted taxable estate}} = \text{Maximum credit that will be allowed}$$

The "prior decedent's adjusted estate tax" is the federal estate tax paid on his estate, plus any credits for gift tax or tax on prior transfers allowed the estate. The "prior decedent's adjusted taxable estate" is his taxable estate, plus (for estates of decedents dying after 12-31-76) the specific exemption allowed the estate, but less all death taxes paid [Sec. 2013(b); 20.2013-2].

> NOTE: For estates of decedents dying after 12-31-76, the tax on generation-skipping transfers and the additional estate tax on the disposition of certain farm property or of closely-held property [¶ 3916] are treated as "federal estate taxes" for the credit [Sec. 2013(f), (g)].

Second way. The credit cannot exceed the proportion of the present decedent's estate tax that the value of the property received from the prior decedent bears to the total estate of the present decedent. A second trial credit is secured as follows:

Determine the estate tax on the present decedent's estate, without taking any credit for tax on prior transfers. From this figure, subtract the estate tax that results when the present decedent's estate is reduced by the value of the property transferred. The difference is the second trial credit [Sec. 2013(c); 20.2013-3]. In figuring this trial tax, any charitable deduction must be reduced. The amount is determined by multiplying the full charitable deduction by the proportion that the value of the transferred property bears to the present decedent's gross estate less deductions for expenses and losses (¶ 3926, items 1-6)[2] [Sec. 2013(c)(1)(B); 20.2013-3].

> NOTE: If an estate is entitled to a credit for tax on prior transfers and gift tax credit, the limitation on the gift tax credit [¶ 3935(a)] must be recomputed for purposes of figuring the tax on the gross estate without the transferred property in the second trial credit. The gift tax credit limitation for this computation is affected because (1) the estate tax is smaller and (2) the gift taxed property is a larger part of a gross estate that does not include the property taxed in the prior transfer. An example of this computation is in Rev. Rul. 67-110.[3]

Valuation of transferred property. In computing the two trial credits, the property transferred to the present decedent has the same value as it had in the prior decedent's estate for estate tax purposes. Specific property does not have to be identified; the value of property received from a prior decedent is presumed to be contained in the estate of the present decedent. (For the purpose of valuing the estate of the present decedent, any identifiable property from a prior decedent is, of course, valued according to the general rules at date of death.) But when the property transferred is encumbered in any way, or when the present decedent incurs any obligation imposed by the prior decedent with respect to the property, its value is reduced by an equivalent amount [Sec. 2013(d); 20.2013-4].

The value of the transferred property is also reduced to the extent of death taxes (state or federal) imposed on the property, and the marital deduction allowed in the prior decedent's estate [Sec. 2013(d); 20.2013-4(b)].

If the transferred property could not be valued by recognized principles at prior decedent's death, no credit is allowed.[4]

(d) Amount of credit allowed. The credit is allowed in full if the present decedent dies within two years after the death of the prior decedent. If he dies later than that, the credit is reduced by 20 percent every two years, so that no credit is allowed after the tenth year. The following table shows the percentage of the credit allowed [Sec. 2013(a); 20.2013-1(c)].

Time interval between death of present decedent and prior decedent	Percentage of the full credit allowed against the present decedent's estate tax
0- 2 years	100%
2- 4 years	80%
4- 6 years	60%
6- 8 years	40%
8-10 years	20%
more than 20 years	0%

¶ 3940 **Unified credit.** For estates of resident decedents dying after 12-31-76, a unified credit, instead of exemptions for gift and estate taxes, applies to all transfers, whether made during life or after death. In general, the unified credit used for gift taxes reduces the credit available for estate tax. The gift tax unified credit is reflected as a reduction in subtracting the gift taxes payable for the estate tax computation. Because of this interrelationship between the separate estate tax unified credit and the computation of the estate tax payable, the separate estate tax unified credit does not operate to allow a double credit for both life and death transfers. Thus, the credit is in effect a single "unified" credit for both the estate and gift taxes [Sec. 2010].

➤**OBSERVATION**➤ The unified credit, in part, is substantially equal to the exemptions allowed for gift and estate taxes formerly allowed to estates of decedents dying before 1-1-77. This is reflected in the new filing requirements for estates of decedents dying after 12-31-76. See ¶ 3943.

(a) Unified credit rates. Subject to a transitional rule, in "(b)" below, the credit is phased-in over 5-years as follows: $30,000 in 1977; $34,000 in 1978; $38,000 in 1979; $42,500 in 1980; and $47,000 in 1981 [Sec. 2010(b)]. For the rates that apply to nonresident aliens see (d) below.

(b) Special transition rule. The allowable credit in "(a)" must be reduced by 20% of allowed specific exemption for gifts made by the decedent after 9-8-76 and before 1-1-77 [Sec. 2010(c)].

(c) Limitation on overall credit. The total credit allowed to an estate may not exceed the total estate tax imposed on the estate [Sec. 2010(d)].

(d) Nonresident estates. For an estate of a nonresident alien dying after 12-31-76, a unified credit of $3,600 is allowed. However, if a decedent is a resident of a U.S. possession, the credit is the greater of $3,600, or a proportion of a certain amount which the value of the property situated in U.S. bears to the value of the entire estate wherever situated. The amount to which the ratio is applied is $8,480 in 1977; $10,080 in 1978; $11,680 in 1979; $13,388 in 1980; and $15,075 in 1981 and later [Sec. 2102].

(e) Expatriates. For estates of expatriates dying after 12-31-76, the unified credit of $13,000 is allowed. But the credit allowed may not exceed the tax imposed on the estate [Sec. 2107].

¶ 3941 **How to determine federal estate tax.** (a) **For decedents dying before 1-1-77.** The following example shows how the estate tax is figured. It includes a deduction for property passing to a surviving spouse, a credit for transfers taxed to prior decedents, a credit for gift taxes, and a credit for state inheritance taxes.

Footnotes appear at end of this Chapter.

Chapter 29—Federal Estate Tax

John Allen died on November 3, 1976. At the time of death he had $21,000 in the bank, and owned outright stocks and bonds worth $330,000. On September 23, 1976, he had made a gift of real property worth $99,000 to his wife. The executors made a gift tax return for the third quarter of 1976, listing the taxable gifts of prior years and quarters and paid a gift tax of $15,328.50, and deducted the tax from the gross estate as a debt. However, the executors were unable to prove that this gift had been prompted by a motive associated with life rather than with death. As a result, it was included in the gross estate as a transfer in contemplation of death at the same value ($99,000). Allen also had $50,000 life insurance payable to his estate.

Allen disposed of his estate as follows: securities worth $35,000 to State City for maintenance of public parks; securities worth $90,000 to a daughter; balance of estate in trust to pay the income to his wife for life, corpus at her death to be distributed as the wife shall designate in her will, or if no designation, to children then living. All death taxes were to be paid from the daughter's share of the estate.

Debts of the estate (including the $15,328.50 gift tax paid) and expenses of administration totaled $40,000.

Among the securities owned by the estate were $30,000 in government bonds which Allen had received from the estate of his father, who died three years previously, and whose estate paid a federal estate tax. These same bonds were valued at $33,000 in the father's estate. The estate tax attributable to those bonds in the father's estate was $2,000. See ¶ 3939 for limitations on the credit for tax on transfers from prior decedents.

Allen's executors elected to value the estate as of the date of death. They actually paid a state estate tax of $21,850. The estate tax on Allen's estate is figured as follows:

Step 1—Determining Gross Estate

Item	
(1) Gross estate:	
Transfers by will:	
Cash	$ 21,000.00
Stocks and bonds	330,000.00
Transfers in contemplation of death:	
Real property	99,000.00
Transfer under life insurance policies:	
Proceeds payable to estate	50,000.00
Total value of gross estate	$500,000.00

Step 2—Computing the Marital Deduction

Gross estate	500,000.00
Less: Debts and expenses (item 3)	40,000.00
Adjusted gross estate	$460,000.00
Maximum marital deduction [¶ 3929 et seq.]	$230,000.00
Interests passing to wife for which deduction is allowed—up to 50% of adjusted gross estate:	
Real property	$ 99,000.00
Residue † (after payment of all debts and expenses, taxes, including Federal gift tax, and gift to City)	236,000.00
Total of interests passing to wife and qualifying	$335,000.00

---

† Residue is figured as follows:

Gross estate		$500,000.00
Less:		
Real Property	$99,000.00	
Debts and expenses	40,000.00	
Gift to City	35,000.00	
Bequest to daughter (subject to death taxes)	90,000.00	264,000.00
Residue		$236,000.00

(2) Since the total of the interests passing to the wife is more than 50% of the adjusted gross estate, the marital deduction is allowed in full—$230,000.

Step 3—Deductions

(3)	Debts and expenses	$ 40,000
(4)	Bequest to City	35,000
(5)	Marital deduction	230,000
(6)	Specific exemption	60,000
(7)	Total deductions and exemption	$365,000

Figuring the Estate Tax
Step 4—Taxable Estate

	Gross estate (item 1)	$500,000
	Less: Total deductions and exemptions (item 7)	365,000
(8)	Taxable estate	$135,000

Step 5—Applying the Rates

(9) Estate Tax [¶ 3934] on $135,000 .... $ 31,200

Step 6—Subtraction of Credits

(10)	Credit for State death taxes [¶ 3937]	$ 1,120.00
(11)	Federal gift tax paid	$ 15,328.50
(12)	Maximum credit for gift tax [¶ 3935]:	

$$\frac{30{,}090\dagger\dagger}{235{,}000 \text{ (Gross estate less marital deduction, item 5 and gift to City, item 4)}} \times 30{,}080 \text{ (item 9 less item 10)} \qquad \$ \ 3{,}851.51$$

(13) Credit for taxes on transfers from prior decedents [¶ 3939 et seq.]
Full credit would be $2,000
80% of full credit is allowed .... $ 1,600.00

Net Tax Payable

(14) Estate tax less allowable credits (item 9 less items 10, 12, and 13) .... $ 24,628.49

---

†† This numerator (to the nearest dollar) is the gift-taxed property ($99,000) reduced by the exclusion ($3,000) and an amount having the same ratio to $96,000 as the total allowable marital deduction ($230,000) bears to the total amount deductible for transfers to the survivor without regard to the 50% limitations (net residue plus real property or $236,000 plus $99,000) [Sec. 2012(a), 2012(b)(1)(2)].

(b) For estates of decedents dying after 12-31-76. The following is an example of how the estate tax for the estate of a resident decedent is figured. The computation involves the application of the "gross-up" rule for gifts made within 3-years before death, ¶ 3909(b), "adjusted taxable" gifts, ¶ 3934(b), the marital deduction, ¶ 3929, credit for gift taxes, ¶ 3935, credit for State death taxes, ¶ 3937, and the unified credit, ¶ 3940. Generally, the computation below reflects the major changes made by the Tax Reform Act of 1976.

Assume "A" is the same donor as in the gift tax example at ¶ 4028(b), and that he had assets totaling 5 million. Assume further that he died in 1987, after having made the lifetime gifts to his wife totaling $1,800,000 (computed for gift tax liability at ¶ 4028(b)). Under "A's" will, his remaining estate is bequeathed to his wife. Because "A" paid the gift taxes of $256,290, ¶ 4028(b), in addition to the gifts to his wife ($1,800,000), the remaining estate at death is $2,943,710. The estate administration expenses totaled $292,651. In addition, the executor paid a State estate tax liability of $90,000.

The following is a computation of the estate tax on "A's" estate:

Footnotes appear at end of this Chapter.

¶ 3941

Chapter 29—Federal Estate Tax

Step 1—Ascertainment of Gross Estate

Item
(1) Gross estate:
  Transfers by will:
  Cash $2,943,710.00
(2) Gift within 3-years of death (gift No. 3 less $3,000 annual exclusion, plus the tax paid on the gift—"gross-up") 1,063,530.00
  Total value of gross estate $4,007,240.00

Step 2—Computation of Marital Deduction

Gross estate $4,007,240.00
Less: Administration expenses (item 3) 292,651.00
Adjusted gross estate $3,714,589.00
Maximum marital deduction ¶ 3929 .... 1,857,295.00

Interests passing to wife for which deduction is allowed—greater of $250,000 or 50% of adjusted gross estate: 1,857,295.00

Since the total of the interests passing to the wife is greater than $250,000, 50% of the adjusted gross estate, is allowed as marital deduction ¶ 3929.

Step 3—Deductions

(3) Administration expenses .... $ 292,651.00
(4) Marital deduction 1,857,295.00
(5) Total deductions $2,149,946.00

Computation of Tentative Estate Tax
Step 4—Taxable Estate

Gross (item 1) $4,007,240.00
Less: Total deductions (item 5) 2,149,946.00
(6) Taxable estate $1,857,294.00

Step 5—Tentative tax base

(7) Taxable estate (item 6) $1,857,294.00
(8) Plus: Adjusted taxable gifts (gifts No. 1 and No. 2) 444,000.00
(9) Tentative tax base $2,301,294.00

Step 6—Application of Rates

(10) Estate tax on tentative tax base (Table ¶ 3934(b)) on $2,301,294.00 .. $ 928,434.00

Step 7—Subtraction of Credits

(11) Credit for State death taxes† (Table ¶ 3937(b)) .... $ 89,325.00
(12) Federal gift tax paid ¶ 3935(b) .... $ 256,290.00
(13) Unified credit, ¶ 3940 .... $ 47,000.00

Computation of Net Estate Tax Payable

(14) Estate tax less allowable credits (item 10 less items 11, 12 and 13) .... $ 535,819.00

---

† By fitting the "adjusted taxable estate" of $1,797,294 [$1,857,294, taxable estate less $60,000] into the credit schedule it is found that the maximum allowable credit for State death taxes is $70,800 plus $18,525 [$1,797,294 − $1,540,000] or $89,325.

PROCEDURE

¶ 3943 Return. A return (on Form 706) must be filed within 9 months of death for estates of citizens or residents of the United States if the value of the gross estate exceeds $60,000 for estates of decedents dying before 1-1-77. For returns of estates of decedents dying after 12-31-76, see the discussion below [Sec. 6018, 6075(a); 20.6018-1]. For a deceased resident, the return is filed with the Service Center serving the district where he was domiciled, or with the District Director of the decedent's domicile if the return instructions do not provide filing at a Service Center or if the return is hand carried. If the decedent was a nonresident, it must be filed with the Internal Revenue Service Center, Philadelphia, Pa. 19155[1] [Sec. 6091(b); 20.6091-1]. In exceptional cases, the Commissioner can allow the return to be filed in any district [Sec. 20.6091-2]. The Revenue Service may grant a 6-month extension to file (unless the executor is abroad) if an application filed on Form 4768 is made before return due date to the office where the return will be filed[1] [Sec. 20.6081-1]. Penalties are provided for failure to file returns [¶ 3617; 3619].

Returns for estates of decedents dying after 12-31-76. An estate tax return is not required unless the gross estate exceeds $120,000 in 1977, $134,000 in 1978, $147,000 in 1979, $161,000 in 1980, and $175,000 in 1981 and later. However, to determine the minimum gross estate for filing purposes, certain adjustments must be made for gifts. To compute this amount, subtract from the base filing amount (for example, $120,000 in 1977) the full amount of "adjusted taxable" gifts, ¶ 3934(b) and the specific exemption, if any, for gifts made after 9-8-76 [Sec. 6018].

¶ 3944 Payment of tax. The tax ordinarily is due and payable in full 9 months after the decedent's death, and must be paid with the return by the executor or administrator, or where there is no duly qualified executor or administrator, by the persons in actual or constructive possession [Sec. 2002, 2203; 20.2202-1, 20.2203-1, 20.6151-1]. On application using Form 4768, the District Director or Director of a Service Center may grant a reasonable extension for payment of the tax or any installment. The extension generally may not exceed 12 months from the date fixed for payment. However, for reasonable cause (undue hardships for decedents dying before 1977) the time for paying may be extended up to 10 years [Sec. 6161(a); 20.6161-1].

Liability for tax. The legal representative is personally liable for the tax to the full extent of assets coming into his possession. A transferee may also be liable for payment of the tax, or a deficiency, up to the value of the asset received [Sec. 6324(a), 6901(a); 301.6324-1, 301.6901-1]. For payment with U.S. obligations, see ¶ 3527.

NOTE: Executors for estates of decedents dying after 12-31-76, will be able to elect a special lien procedure instead of his personal liability or bond for payment of the tax.

Remainder interests. The fiduciary may elect to postpone payment of the tax on a reversion or remainder until 6 months after the precedent interest in the property terminates. For estates of decedents dying before 1-1-77, an additional extension of up to 3 years may be granted if payment would result in undue hardship. For estates of decedents dying after 12-31-76, an extension is granted whenever there is reasonable cause [Sec. 6163(a), (b); 20.6163-1]. Notice of the election must be filed with the District Director before the due date for paying the tax [Sec. 20.6163-1]. The executor may be required to furnish security for the amount for which the extension is granted [Sec. 6165; 20.6165-1].

(a) **Installment payments allowed—ten year method.** Except for the 15-year alternative method discussed below, all or part of the tax attributable to a decedent's closely held business interest may be paid in ten or less annual installments at the executor's election [Sec. 6161(a)(2), 6166A; 20.6166-1]. The notice of election must be filed with the District Director on or before the due date of the estate tax return [Sec. 20.6166-1(e)]. The District Director determines whether the interest qualifies for the election.[1] If the executor is not sure that an interest qualifies, he may make a protective election. The notice must state it is a "protective election." If it is found later that the interest does not qualify, the notice (on timely request) will be treated as an application for an extension of time to pay the tax [Sec. 20.6166-1].

Footnotes appear at end of this Chapter.

¶ 3944

A closely held business interest may be a proprietorship, partnership, or stock in a corporation engaged in a trade or business. To qualify for installment payment of tax: (1) the value of the interest included in the gross estate must exceed 35% of the gross estate or 50% of the taxable estate and (2) a partnership or corporation must have 10 or less members, or the value of decedent's interest must be 20% or more of the partnership capital or voting stock of the corporation. Two or more businesses may be treated as one for the 35%—50% rule, if more than 50% of the value of each business is included in the gross estate [Sec. 6166A(c), (d); 20.6166-2].

Payment accelerated. The District Director may require payment of the tax in full if any installment is not paid on time. The tax also must be paid in full when 50% or more of the value of the decedent's interest is withdrawn from the business or 50% or more of the interest is disposed of. The executor must notify the District Director within 30 days from the time he learns of withdrawals or transfers that disqualify the interest for installment payment of tax. He also must file a statement with each installment payment to show the interest still qualifies. After its fourth tax year, undistributed net income of the estate for any tax year must be applied to unpaid installments [Sec. 6166A(h)(3); 20.6166-3].

15-year alternative method. For estates of decedents dying after 12-31-76, for the payment of the estate tax attributable to the decedent's interest in a *farm or other closely-held business*, the executor may elect an alternative method to defer the tax (but not interest on the tax) for up to 5 years and thereafter pay the tax in equal annual installments over the succeeding 10 years. To qualify, the value of the interest in the farm or other closely-held business included in gross estate must exceed 65% of the adjusted gross estate (gross estate less expenses, debts and losses). You may have an interest in a "closely-held business" by being a partner or corporate shareholder having a 20% interest in the partnership or corporation. A notice of election to pay in installments under this method must be filed with the Revenue Service within 60 days after notice and demand is made for payment of the taxes.

The Revenue Service may require payment of the tax in full on failure to pay any installment on time. The tax must be paid in full when $33\frac{1}{3}\%$ or more of the value of decedent's interest is withdrawn from the business or $33\frac{1}{3}\%$ or more of the interest is disposed of. In addition, the executor must inform the Revenue Service as soon as he learns that withdrawals or transfers disqualify the interest. Also, any "undistributed net income" of the estate for any tax year after the due date of the first installment must be applied to unpaid installments [Sec. 6166].

(b) Interest and penalty charged. Interest at 7% (9% between 7-1-75 and 1-31-76; 6% before 7-1-75) or at an adjusted prime interest rate (¶ 3628) is charged on the amount of tax not paid by the due date and on tax not paid during or after an extension period. Interest must be paid annually when installment payments are elected [Sec. 6601, 6621; 20.6166-1(f), 301.6601-1(b)]. Penalties are also provided for failure to pay taxes [¶ 3618(b)]. Unless failure to pay is due to reasonable cause and not willful neglect, this added sanction is $\frac{1}{2}\%$ of the unpaid tax for each month (or part of a month) of delinquency, with a maximum of 25% [Sec. 6651].

15-year alternative method—special interest rate. Rate of 4% applies to the "portion of the estate tax" attributable to farm or closely-held business property under the 15-year alternative method of payment. "Portion of estate tax" means the lesser of $345,800 in tax (equivalent to one million valuation) less the allowable unified credit [¶ 3940], or the amount of tax that is extended. Any excess is paid at the same rates as interest on unpaid tax [Sec. 6601(j)].

¶ **3945 Deficiencies and appeals.** When the return is filed it is examined and checked for accuracy by the Revenue Service. A field examination is usually made before the case is closed.

(a) Time for assessment. The Revenue Service may make an assessment up to 3 years from the date the return is considered to have been filed, or up to 6 years if gross estate items have been omitted amounting to more than 25% of the gross estate returned. If a return is false or fraudulent, or if no return is filed, the tax may be assessed at any time [Sec. 6501; 301.6501(c)-1, 301.6501(e)-1].

(b) Notice of deficiency. If a deficiency is found, the legal representative is informed and unless the matter is settled at once, a notice of deficiency is mailed [Sec. 6211(a), 6212(a); 301.6211-1, 301.6212-1]. A petition for redetermination of a deficiency may be filed with the Tax Court within 90 days after mailing of the deficiency notice, or within 150 days if the addressee is outside the United States [Sec. 6213(a); 301.6213-1].

(c) Installment payments. The portion of a deficiency (not due to fraud, negligence or willful disregard of rules and regulations) attributable to a closely held business interest [¶ 3944] is payable in installments if the executor elected to pay the tax in installments [Sec. 6166(f); 20.6166-1(d)]. Interest at 7% a year (9% between 7-1-75 and 1-31-76; 4% before 7-1-75) or an adjusted prime interest rate (¶ 3628) is payable on the amount deferred [Sec. 6166(g), 6601, 6621]. For estates of decedents dying after 12-31-76, a special 4% interest rule applies to payments elected under the 15-year alternative method. See ¶ 3945(a).

(d) Appeals may be taken the same as in income tax cases. See ¶ 3621(c); ¶ 3629(d) and ¶ 3649(a).

¶ **3946 Refunds. (a) Claims for refund** must be filed within three years after the return was filed or two years after the tax was paid, whichever period expires later [Sec. 6511(a); 301.6511(a)-1]. See ¶ 3623. There is an exception for refund claims resulting from state or foreign death tax credit [¶ 3936; 3938]. The claim should be filed on Form 843 with the Revenue Service [Sec. 301.6402-2].

(b) Suit for refund. Suit to recover tax paid may be instituted only if a claim for refund has been filed [Sec. 7422(a); 301.6402-2]. The suit may not be begun (1) before the expiration of six months from the date of filing unless the Revenue Service renders a decision within that time nor (2) after the expiration of two years from the mailing by registered or certified mail by the Revenue Service to the taxpayer of a notice of disallowance [Sec. 6532(a); 301.6532-1]. Recovery is limited to the amount claimed in the refund claim.[1] Suit may be brought in the Court of Claims at Washington or in the District Court where the claimant resides. See also ¶ 3621 et seq.

NOTE: A request for a deduction for attorney's fees for contesting a deficiency or prosecuting a refund claim need not be set forth in a formal refund claim. The deduction should be claimed when the deficiency is contested or the refund claim is prosecuted [Sec. 20.2053-3(c)].

¶ **3947 Discharge from personal liability.** An executor or administrator (or his authorized attorney[1]) can write to the District Director asking for a determination of the tax and discharge from personal liability. The District Director then

Footnotes appear at end of this Chapter.

must notify him of the amount of the tax within one year (9 months for estates of decedents dying after 1973[2]) after the application is received; or, if the application is made before the return is filed, within one year (9 months for estates of decedents dying after 1973[2]) after the return is filed (but not after the assessment limitation period [¶ 3610 et seq.] expires). Upon paying the amount specified, (or furnishing bond on request for any tax for an estate of a decedent dying after 1970 for which an extension to pay has been granted), the executor or administrator is discharged from personal liability for any deficiency in the tax that may be found later. Trustees of trusts that are part of an estate of a decedent dying after 1970 can also obtain this discharge. However, it is not available to a fiduciary of an estate of a non-resident decedent [Sec. 2204; 20.2204-1, 2].

Lien for personal liability or bond. For estates of decedents dying after 12-31-76, the executor is discharged from personal liability for extended installment tax payments [¶ 3944(a)], if a special lien procedure is elected and the executor with all parties who have an interest in the property subject to the lien, file a signed written consenting agreement. A bond is not required as long as the estate has adequate funds to meet its unpaid tax plus interest [Sec. 6324A].

Footnotes to Chapter 29

(P-H "FEDERAL TAXES" related references are cited in brackets [ ] at the end of each footnote below)

Footnote ¶ 3900 [¶ 120,001 et seq.; 121,001 et seq.].
(1) Treaties ratified and in effect are listed in P-H Federal Taxes ¶ 128,001 et seq. For further details, see P-H Federal Tax Treaties.

Footnote ¶ 3901 [¶ 120,310; 120,330 et seq.].

Footnote ¶ 3904 [¶ 120,400 et seq.].

Footnote ¶ 3905 [¶ 120,405 et seq.].
(1) Sec. 351, Rev. Act of 1948.

Footnote ¶ 3906 [¶ 120,340 et seq.].

Footnote ¶ 3907 [¶ 120,410 et seq.].

Footnote ¶ 3908 [¶ 120,410 et seq.].
(1) Such law exists in Delaware (see P-H Wills, Estates and Trusts Service ¶ 416 and ¶ 1019 Del.).
(2) Rev. Rul. 66-87, 1966-1 CB 217 [¶ 120,418(25)].
(3) Gartland v. Comm., 8 AFTR 2d 6045, 293 F.2d 575 [¶ 120,417(7)].

Footnote ¶ 3909 [¶ 120,350 et seq.].
(1) Greer v. Glenn, 64 F. Supp. 1002, 34 AFTR 1206 [¶ 120,352].
(2) Becker v. St. Louis Union Trust Co., et al., Execs., Est. of Wm. E. Guy, 296 US 48, 56 SCt 78, 16 AFTR 989, overruled on another issue by Helvering v. Hallock, 309 US 122, 23 AFTR 1063 [¶ 120,353.4(5)].
(3) Sharp, 33 BTA 290, affd. 91 F.2d 804, 20 AFTR 191 [¶ 120,353.4].
(4) McGregor, Exec., Est. of David McGregor v. Comm., 82 F.2d 948, 17 AFTR 878 [¶ 120,353.6].
(5) Est. of Wilfred W. Campbell v. Kavanaugh, 114 F. Supp. 780, 44 AFTR 448 [¶ 120,353.7].
(6) Detroit Bk. & Tr. Co. v. U.S., 34 AFTR 2d 74-6257, 369 F. Supp. 672 [¶ 147,922].

Footnote ¶ 3910 [¶ 120,360 et seq.].
(1) Est. of Gutchess, 46 TC 554; Est. of Binkley, 17 AFTR 2d 1392, 358 F.2d 639; Union Planter National Bank (Ladd) v. U.S., 17 AFTR 2d 1453, 361 F.2d 662 [¶ 120,364(57)].
(2) Diehl v. U.S., 21 AFTR 2d 1607; but see Rev. Rul. 70-155, 1970-1 CB 189 [¶ 120,364(57); 120,365(7)].
(3) U.S. v. O'Malley, 383 US 627, 17 AFTR 2d 1393 [¶ 120,384(15)].
(4) U.S. v. Byrum, 408 US 125, 30 AFTR 2d 72-5811 [¶ 120,365(5)].
(5) U.S. v. Grace, 395 US 316, 23 AFTR 2d 69-1954 [¶ 120,364(15)].
(6) Ruby Louise Cain, 37 TC 185 [¶ 120,364(40)].

Footnote ¶ 3911 [¶ 120,370 et seq.].

Footnote ¶ 3912 [¶ 120,380 et seq.].
(1) Helvering v. City Bank Farmers Tr. Co., 296 US 85, 16 AFTR 981 [¶ 120,383.1(5)].
(2) Helvering v. Helmholz, 296 US 93, 56 SCt 68, 16 AFTR 979; White v. Poor, 296 US 101, 56 SCt 66, 16 AFTR 977. Cf. Thorpe's Est. (Fidelity Trust Co.) v. Comm., 164 F.2d 966, 36 AFTR 488 [¶ 120,383.2(5)].
(3) Porter v. Comm., 288 US 436, 53 SCt 451, 12 AFTR 25. See also Comm. v. Est. of Harry Holmes, 326 US 480, 34 AFTR 308 [¶ 120,384(5); 120,384.8].
(4) Rev. Rul. 57-366, 1957-2 CB 618; Rev. Rul. 59-357, 1959-2 CB 212; Rev. Rul. 70-348, 1970-2 CB 193; Stuit, 54 TC 580 [¶ 120,384.2(75); 120,384.8; 125,036(7)].

Footnote ¶ 3913 [¶ 120,430].
(1) Glen, 45 TC 323 [¶ 120,434(15)].

Footnote ¶ 3914 [¶ 120,420 et seq.].
(1) Rev. Rul. 68-334, 1968-1 CB 403; Rev. Rul. 69-54, 1969-1 CB 20; Landorf v. U.S., 23 AFTR 2d 69-1876, 408 F.2d 461; Est. of Gorby, 53 TC 80 [¶ 120,427.5; 120,427.5(10)].
(2) Est. of Bartlett, 54 TC 1590 [¶ 120,355.2(10)].
(3) Rev. Rul. 71-497, 1971-2 CB 329; Bel v. U.S., 29 AFTR 2d 72-1482, 452 F.2d 683 [¶ 120,355.1].
(4) Letter ruling dated 3-14-46 [¶ 120,427.6(25)].
(5) Estate of E. M. Donaldson, 31 TC 729 [¶ 120,335.1(15)].

Footnote ¶ 3915 [¶ 120,390].
(1) P-H Pension and Profit Sharing Service ¶ 5501 et seq.
(2) Fusz, 46 TC 214 [¶ 120,392.1(25)].
(3) Comm. v. Albright, 17 AFTR 2d 1367, 356 F.2d 319 [¶ 120,392.1(30)].
(4) Rev. Rul. 56-1, 1956-1 CB 444 [¶ 120,392.1(5)].
(5) P.L. 89-365; P.L. 92-425.
(6) Rev. Rul. 67-37, 1967-1 CB 271 [¶ 120,392.1(30)].
(7) Rev. Rul. 68-89, 1968-1 CB 402 [¶ 120,392.1(30)].
(8) Rev. Rul. 68-294, 1968-1 CB 46 [¶ 120,392.1(17)].
(9) Est. of Johnson, 56 TC 944 [¶ 143,450].
(10) Rev. Rul. 60-70, 1960-1 CB 372 [¶ 120,336.1(7)].

Footnote ¶ 3916 [¶ 125,501].
(1) Sec. 2006(c), P.L. 94-455.

Footnote ¶ 3919 [¶ 120,310 et seq.].
(1) Rev. Proc. 65-19, 1965-2 CB 1002 [¶ 120,318.4(27)].
(2) Kinney's Est. v. Comm., 80 F.2d 568, 17 AFTR 81 [¶ 120,336.4(5)].
(3) Rosenfield, Adm. v. U.S., 1 AFTR 2d 2169, 254 F.2d 940 [¶ 120,323(5)].
(4) Rev. Rul. 55-333, 1955-1 CB 449 [¶ 120,323(10)].
(5) Instructions for Schedule A, Form 706 [¶ 126,703].
(6) Bankers Trust Co. (Ellis) v. U.S., 7 AFTR 2d 1691, 284 F.2d 537 [¶ 120,318.1(75)].
(7) U.S. v. Cartwright, 31 AFTR 2d 73-1461, 411 US 546; Rev. Proc. 74-3 (TIR 1284) [¶ 142,068; 147,832].
(8) Compare May v. McGowan, 97 F. Supp. 326, aff'd 194 F.2d 396, with Giannini Hoffman, 2 TC 1160 [¶ 120,315, 120,363(30)].
(9) Jenning's Est. v. Comm., 10 TC 323; Miami Beach First National Bank v. U.S., 27 AFTR 2d 71-1785, 443 F.2d 475; Rev. Rul. 66-307, 1966-2 CB 429 [¶ 120,319(15)].
(10) Hall v. U.S., 16 AFTR 2d 6206, 353 F.2d 500 [¶ 120,379(5)].
(11) Estate of Roy, 54 TC 1317 [¶ 120,379(2)].
(12) Rev. Rul. 61-88, 1961-1 CB 417 [¶ 120,319(5)].
(13) Estate of Wien, 27 AFTR 2d 71-1765, 441 F.2d 32; Estate of Meltzer, 27 AFTR 2d 71-1724, 439 F.2d 798; Old Kent Bank and Trust Co., 26

Footnote ¶ 3919 continued
AFTR 2d 70-6025, 430 F.2d 392; Estate of Chown, 26 AFTR 2d 70-6014, 428 F.2d 1395 [¶ 120,335.1(15)].

Footnote ¶ 3926 [¶ 120,530 et seq.; 120,540].
(1) Rev. Rul. 66-234, 1966-2 CB 436 [¶ 120,532(45)].
(2) Rev. Rul. 60-160, 1960-1 CB 374 [¶ 120,535(20)].
(3) Rev. Rul. 60-247, 1960-2 CB 272 [¶ 120,534(40)].

Footnote ¶ 3927 [¶ 120,550 et seq.].

Footnote ¶ 3928 [¶ 120,520 et seq.].

Footnote ¶ 3929 [¶ 120,560 et seq.].
(1) Rev. Rul. 59-123, 1959-1 CB 248 [¶ 120,563(5)].
(2) U.S. v. Stapf, 12 AFTR 2d 6326, 84 S.Ct. 248 [¶ 120,573].
(3) Rev. Proc. 64-19, 1964-1 CB (Pt. 1) 682 [¶ 120,567.1].
(4) Rev. Rul. 55-225, 1955-1 CB 400 [¶ 120,533(45)].
(5) Geyer v. Bookwalter, 7 AFTR 2d 1813, 193 F. Supp. 57 [¶ 120,571(5)].
(6) Northeastern Pa. Nat. Bk. & Tr. Co. v. U.S., 19 AFTR 2d 1874, 386 S.Ct. 1019 [¶ 120,571(56)].
(7) Cornwell, 37 TC 688 [¶ 120,570(15)].
(8) Est. of Wilmar M. Allen, 39 TC 817 [¶ 120,567(45)].

Footnote ¶ 3934 [¶ 120,012].

Footnote ¶ 3935 [¶ 120,120 et seq.].
(1) Rev. Rul. 67-319, 1967-2 CB 319, clarified by Rev. Rul. 74-491, 1974-2 CB 290, [¶ 120,122(35); 142,093].

Footnote ¶ 3936 [¶ 120,110 et seq.].
(1) Rev. Rul. 61-58, 1961-1 CB 414 [¶ 120,113(50)].

Footnote ¶ 3937 [¶ 120,110].

Footnote ¶ 3938 [¶ 120,140 et seq.].
(1) House Report No. 82, 86th Congress, 1st Session.

Footnote ¶ 3939 [¶ 120,130 et seq.].
(1) Rev. Rul. 59-9, 1959-1 CB 232 [¶ 120,132(10)].
(2) Rev. Rul. 60-161, 1960-1 CB 367; Rev. Rul. 61-208, 1961-2 CB 148 [¶ 120,132(20)].
(3) Rev. Rul. 67-110, 1967-1 CB 262 [¶ 120,132(20)].
(4) Rev. Rul. 67-53, 1967-1 CB 265 [¶ 120,132(7)].

Footnote ¶ 3943 [¶ 126,010; 126,703].
(1) Instructions for Form 4768.

Footnote ¶ 3944 [¶ 126,150; 126,400].
(1) Rev. Proc. 60-33, 1960-2 CB 1012 [¶ 126,157(5)].

Footnote ¶ 3945 [¶ 126,200; 126,620].

Footnote ¶ 3946 [¶ 126,300].
(1) Austin Nat'l Bank v. Scofield, 84 F. Supp. 483, 37 AFTR 1604 [¶ 126,361(15)].

Footnote ¶ 3947 [¶ 122,040].
(1) Rev. Rul. 65-186, 1965-2 CB 380 [¶ 122,042(15)].
(2) P.L. 91-614, Sec. 101(f).

Highlights of Chapter 29
Federal Estate Tax

I. **General Description of Estate Tax**
   A. **Estates subject to tax**—Tax covers estates of U.S. citizens or residents whose gross estate includes *all* property wherever located [¶ 3900; 3901].
   B. **Nature of tax**—Excise tax on right to transfer property at death—not property or inheritance tax [¶ 3900].

II. **Gross Estate**
   A. **What's included in estate**—Total value of all property that decedent had beneficial ownership of at death [¶ 3901].
   B. **Joint estates and tenancies by entirety [¶ 3904]:**
      1. Property held in joint tenancy included in deceased tenant's estate unless survivor can prove his contribution.
      2. Only decedent's fractional interest held as tenant in common included in gross estate.
      3. One-half value of joint interest created after 12-31-76 in property held as tenants by entirety included in gross estate if a "qualified joint interest".
   C. **Community property** included only to extent of decedent's interest under state law [¶ 3905]
   D. **Property subject to dower and curtesy** included in estate [¶ 3906]
   E. **Property subject to power of appointment [¶ 3907; 3908]:**
      1. Propety included if subject to general powers created after 10-21-42 that is:
         a. Held by decedent at death, or
         b. Exercised or released by decedent by transfer (before 1977) in contemplation of death (after 1976) within 3-years of death or to take effect at death.
      2. Property subject to special or limited power not included in possessor's estate generally.
      3. Lapse of powers created after 10-21-42 subject to special rule.
      4. Property subject to general power created before 10-22-42 included only if exercised by will or by transfer in contemplation of, or taking effect at death.
   F. **Gifts [¶ 3909]:**
      1. For estates of decedents dying before 1-1-77:
         a. Transfer, power relinquishment, or exercise or release of general power of appointment within 3 years of death without consideration is presumed to have been made in contemplation of death, and included in estate.
         b. Gifts not included in estate if made by motive associated with life, not death [¶ 3909(a)].
      2. For estates of decedents dying after 12-31-76:
         a. One-half of qualified joint interest included in decedent's gross estate.
         b. Certain requirements must be met [¶ 3909(b)].
   G. **Transfers reserving right to use, enjoyment, or income [¶ 3910]:**
      1. Trust property not included in estate if grantor of irrevocable trust retains no control or interest in principal or income.
      2. Property in each irrevocable reciprocal trust includible in life beneficiary's estate.
      3. If only portion of income reserved, corresponding portion of property included in estate.
   H. **Transfers effective at death.** Generally included in estate if:
      1. Decedent's reversionary interest is over 5% of property value, and

2. Transferee's enjoyment of property dependent only on his surviving decedent [¶ 3911].
I. **Transfers reserving power to modify or terminate [¶ 3912]:**
   1. Property transferred during life includible if:
      a. Decedent has power at death to make substantial change in enjoyment, or
      b. He gave up power (before 1977) in contemplation of death (after 1976) within 3-years of death.
   2. Generally includible even if power held jointly by deceased grantor and beneficiary. If trust revocable by grantor and beneficiaries, trust property not includible in his estate.
   3. Not included in grantor's estate if power held by another.
   4. Trust corpus includible in grantor's estate though power cannot benefit him.
   5. Transfers under Model Custodian Act.
J. **Transfers for inadequate consideration includible to extent value exceeds consideration [¶ 3913].**
K. **Life insurance [¶ 3914]:**
   1. Proceeds payable to estate includible, whether or not decedent has incidents or ownership in policy.
   2. Proceeds payable to other beneficiaries includible if decedent possessed incidents of ownership at death. Not included if he transferred incidents before death.
   3. National Service Life Insurance proceeds included.
   4. Value of policy owned by decedent on another's life included.
L. **Annuity, pension or profit-sharing plans or trusts [¶ 3915]:**
   1. Annuity plans:
      a. Value included in proportion to decedent's contribution.
      b. Cash under refund plan or annuity included. If installments continue after death, total amount discounted to present value includible.
      c. Under plans not connected with employment, value of annuity going to contingent plan beneficiary or surviving annuitant includible in proportion to decedent's contributions.
   2. Employee benefit plans:
      a. Return of contributions includible.
      b. Payments to employee's beneficiaries includible to extent based on:
         1) Employee contributions to qualified or unqualified plan;
         2) Employer contributions to unqualified plan as inducement or substitute pay.
      c. Employer contributions to qualified plan generally excluded, but amounts subject to withdrawal when employee died are included.
      d. Rules here apply also to employees under self-employed retirement plans including contributions for owner-employee under annuity plan.
      e. Payments under non-contributory qualified plans generally excluded unless:
         1) Retired worker gets money in his lifetime and it's still in estate at death, or
         2) Worker dies before retirement and estate or executor is beneficiary, or
         3) For estates of decedents dying after 12-31-76, lump-sum distributions.
      f. Special exclusion applies to retirement contracts bought by exempt employers and for estates of decedents dying after 12-31-76, payments under qualified individual retirement savings plans.
      g. Railroad retirement annuities not included except for lump-sum residual death benefits.
   3. Nothing included for life plan.
M. **Generation-skipping transfers [¶ 3916]:**
   1. Special tax applies to transfers to two or more generations that are younger than the generation of the grantor.
   2. Transfer is taxable on termination of intervening interest or on distribution to heir.
   3. Direct transfer to grandchild is excluded up to $250,000 per child.
III. **How to Value Estate Property**

A. Property appraised at "fair market value" [¶ 3919]
B. Executor may elect to value property:
  1. At date of death, or
  2. At alternative valuation date applying these rules:
     a. Property not disposed of in 6 months after death valued as of 6 months after death.
     b. Value at disposition time if disposed of in 6 months.
     c. Property affected by mere lapse of time valued as of death subject to adjustment.
     d. Property transferred to charity or spouse valued as of death, with adjustments.
     e. Election made on estate tax return.
  3. For decedents dying after 12-31-76, special "carryover basis property" rules apply on rule of property by executor.
C. Real property [¶ 3919(a)]:
  1. Best evidence is recent sale of similar property in vicinity.
  2. Assessed value may not be used.
  3. Special valuation applies to farms and closely-held business realty.
D. Stocks and bonds [¶ 3919(b)]:
  1. Averaging highest and lowest sales prices on valuation date.
  2. Finding value without actual sales: use weighted average on recent sales; if none, bid and ask prices used.
  3. U.S. savings bonds valued at redemption value; below-par treasury bonds redeemable at par to pay tax, valued at par.
  4. Mutual funds valued at redemption price.
E. Business interests [¶ 3919(c)]:
  1. Appraise all assets of proprietor's or partner's business to fix net value.
  2. Use "buy and sell" agreements to fix value.
F. Annuities, insurance, life estates, remainders and reversions [¶ 3919(d)]:
  1. Value of annuities (not commercial), etc., found in official tables generally, but value can be affected by state of health.
  2. Special rules for commercial annuities and life insurance policies.

IV. Deduction From Gross Estate
  A. What deductions are allowed [¶ 3926—3928]:
    1. Funeral expenses paid.
    2. Administration expenses, including executor's commissions and attorney's fees.
    3. Claims enforceable against estate.
    4. Taxes accrued but unpaid against estate. Those accrued after death not deductible generally.
    5. Unpaid mortgages if undiminished property value included in estate.
    6. Losses not deducted for income tax.
    7. Charitable transfers.
    8. Marital deduction.
    9. Specific exemption (before 1977) of $60,000 in addition to all other deductions [¶ 3928].
    10. For estates of decedents dying after 12-31-77, orphan exclusion.
  B. Limits on deductions [¶ 3926]:
    1. Items 1—5 above deductible to extent payments authorized by local law.
    2. Items 1—5 fully deductible only if paid before return due date; deduction limited on later payments.
  C. Charitable gifts and the like [¶ 3927]:
    1. Deduction not to exceed value of gift less taxes paid on transfer.
    2. Deductible gifts must go to public, religious, charitable, scientific or educational institutions or veterans' organizations generally.
    3. Property disclaimed by distributee may be deductible.
    4. Transfer to 80-year-old spouse with power of appointment may be deductible.

5. Deduction of charitable remainder allowed for:
    a. Interest 50% of adjusted farm or personal residence.
    b. Charitable remainder annuity trust.
    c. Charitable remainder unitrust.
    d. Pool income fund.
6. Deductible charitable income interest must be guaranteed annuity or bequest of fixed percentage distributed yearly.
7. No deduction for gifts to:
    a. Foreign private foundations.
    b. Private foundations penalized for certain practices.

V. Marital Deduction
A. Value of property passing to surviving spouse deductible (before 1977) up to 50% of adjusted gross estate (after 1976) greater of $250,000 or 50% of adjusted gross estate [¶ 3929].
B. To qualify, property must be:
   a. Included in estate, and
   b. Actually received by surviving spouse. (Tax can reduce deduction.)
C. Marital deduction allowed for transfer to satisfy pecuniary interest.
D. Limits on deduction:
   a. Before 1977, limited to 50% of adjusted gross estate; after 1976, greater of $250,000 or 50% of adjusted gross estate.
   b. Adjusted gross estate is gross estate less certain expenses, applying special computation for community property. Expenses deducted from income not deducted from estate.
   c. If amount passes 50% test, deduction can't exceed spouse's share of estate.
E. Terminable interest rule:
   1. No deduction allowed for property passing to survivor, if:
      a. Interest can terminate or fail, and
      b. Interest in property passes from decedent to 3d person who may enjoy any part of property after termination of survivor's interest.
   2. Exceptions to terminable interest rule, involving:
      a. Spouse's survivorship.
      b. Life estate with power of appointment.
      c. Estate trusts.
      d. Insurance proceeds.

VI. Tax and Credits
A. Credit for federal gift tax (before 1977) [¶ 3935]:
   1. If spouses split gifts, credit taken in actual donor's estate.
   2. Formula for figuring credit given at ¶ 3935(a).
   3. Credit cannot exceed gift tax paid.
   4. For estates of decedents dying after 12-31-77, gift tax paid is reflected in full when computing tax under the unified transfer tax approach.
B. Credit for state inheritance or estate tax [¶ 3936]:
   1. Adjustment for taxes deducted.
   2. Maximum credit figured from tables at ¶ 3937.
   3. Generally credit must be claimed within 4 years after filing return.
   4. Refund of estate tax based on credit allowed.
   5. For estates of decedents dying after 12-31-76, credit determined on specially defined "adjusted taxable estate" [¶ 3936(a)].
C. Credit for foreign estate tax allowed with limitations [¶ 3938]
D. Credit for tax on prior transfers [¶ 3939]:
   1. Formula for figuring credit appears at ¶ 3939(c).
   2. Credit allowed in full if present decedent dies within 2 years of prior decedent's death. If he dies later, credit reduced 20% every 2 years.

Highlights of Chapter 29

VII. Filing, Payment, Assessment and Other Procedures
    A. **Return [¶ 3943]:**
        1. File Form 706 with District Director in whose district decedent lived, in most cases.
        2. Usually due within 9 months of death.
    B. **Payment [¶ 3944]:**
        1. Full payment usually required with return.
        2. Tax attributable to decedent's closely held business interest payable in 10 or less installments (before 1977) in hardship cases (after 1976) reasonable cause only need be shown.
        3. Extension of time to pay may be granted up to 12 months for reasonable cause.
        4. Extension of time to pay may be granted up to 10 years; for decedents of estates dying after 12-31-76, 15-year option payment may be elected.
        5. Penalty for late payment provided.
    C. **Time for assessment generally limited to 3 years from date return properly filed [¶ 3945]**
    D. **Appeal allowed same as in income tax cases [¶ 3945(d)]**
    E. **Refunds [¶ 3946]:**
        1. Claims for refunds filed on Form 843 by later of:
            a. 3 years after return filed, or
            b. 2 years after tax paid.
        2. Suit for refund allowed only after filing refund claim.
    F. **Executor or administrator can request tax determination and discharge from personal liability; for estates of decedents dying after 12-31-76, lien procedure may be substituted [¶ 3947].**

Chapter 30

FEDERAL GIFT TAX

TABLE OF CONTENTS

	¶
The federal gift tax	4000

GROSS AMOUNT OF GIFTS

	¶
What gifts are taxable	4002
Gifts by exercise or release of power of appointment	4003
Taxability of powers	4004
Gifts of community property	4005
Gifts made within three years of death	4006
Transfers for less than an adequate and full consideration	4007
Transfers subject to revocation or change	4008
Gifts by husband or wife to third party	4009

VALUATION OF GIFTS

	¶
How gifts are valued	4010
Annuity contracts, life insurance and employees' trusts	4011
Remainder and reversionary interests	4012
Tenancy by the entirety	4013
United States savings bonds	4014

DEDUCTIONS AND UNIFIED CREDIT

	¶
The individual exclusion	4020
The unified credit	4021
Charitable and similar gifts	4022
Marital deduction	4023

FIGURING THE TAX

	¶
Gifts in prior quarters and years included	4025
How to figure the tax	4026
Rates of tax	4027
Examples of tax computation	4028
Gift tax increases basis of gift	4029

PROCEDURE

	¶
Returns	4030
Payment of the tax	4031
Assessments and deficiencies	4032
Refunds	4033

• Highlights of Chap. 30 .... Page 4061

¶ **4000 The federal gift tax.** The gift tax is an excise tax imposed on the exercise of the donor's right to transfer property as a gift. It is *not* a tax on property as such. The statutory provisions that exempt bonds, notes, bills, and certificates of indebtedness of the Federal Government or its agencies and the interest on them from tax do not apply to the gift tax, since it is a tax on the transfer, and not on the subject matter of the gift [Sec. 25.2511-1]. Although the tax is imposed on the donor, he can make a gift subject to the condition that the donee pay the tax.[1]

GROSS AMOUNT OF GIFTS

¶ **4002 What gifts are taxable.** The term "gift," for gift tax purposes, has a much broader meaning than under the common law or in common usage. Every transfer of money or property, whether made as a sale or otherwise, from one person to another without adequate and full consideration in money or money's worth, is in whole or in part a gift within the meaning of the gift tax law [Sec. 2511, 2512; 25.2511-1]. The donee need not be in existence to make the transfer taxable.[1] However, a sale or other transfer of property made in the ordinary course of business (a transaction which is bona fide, at arm's length, and free from any donative intent) will be considered as made for an adequate consideration. In other words, a bad bargain made in a business context will not be taxed [Sec. 25.2512-8].

The tax applies to all gratuitous transfers of property during taxpayer's life. The transfer may be direct, indirect or a transfer in trust. The property may be real or

Footnotes appear at end of this Chapter.

¶ 4002

personal, tangible or intangible. Thus, whenever property, or property rights or interests, are gratuitously passed to or conferred on another, the gift tax will apply to the transfers, regardless of the means or devices employed or the form of the transaction [Sec. 2501, 2511; 25.2511-1].

Checks or notes. A gift of a donor's check or note is not taxable until it is paid or the check negotiated or the note transferred.[2]

Joint bank accounts. When one person opens a joint bank account with his funds for himself and another, and the other party withdraws funds in the account, the person opening the account has made a taxable gift to the extent of the amount withdrawn, when the withdrawal is made [Sec. 25.2511-1(h)]. But if the person opening the account is married, special provisions of the law may apply [¶ 4005; 4009 and 4023]. The joint bank account rules also apply to joint brokerage accounts opened in a "street name."[3]

Interests in life insurance. A person makes a taxable gift when he buys a life insurance policy payable to a beneficiary other than his estate and names someone else as the owner of the policy. Premiums paid on a policy after ownership is transferred are gifts. It is also a gift when the insured relinquishes the legal incidents of ownership over a policy previously issued, even if the assignee or beneficiary must survive the insured to receive the proceeds [Sec. 25.2511-1(h)].

Transfers that are not gifts. No gift results from the payment, by either husband or wife, of the income tax liability due on a joint return, or from the payment of the gift tax for a calendar quarter (or calendar year if made before 1971) in which husband and wife consent to split their gifts to third parties [¶ 4006; Sec. 25.2511-1(d)]. No gift results when an heir, beneficiary or next of kin may refuse a property transfer from a decedent under state law and does so within a reasonable time [Sec. 25.2511-1(c)].

Gifts entirely exempt. The tax does not apply to gifts made before June 7, 1932. Gifts to charitable organizations,[4] qualified "Sec. 527" political organizations made after 5-7-74 (¶ 3436), and to U.S. and its political subdivisions are also exempt [Sec. 2501(a)]. See also ¶ 4022. The $3,000 annual exclusion is discussed at ¶ 4020, and the unified credit is treated at ¶ 4021.

Generation-skipping trusts are trusts with two or more generations of beneficiaries who belong to generations of beneficiaries that are younger than the generation of the trust's grantor. For example, you have such a trust where there is a transfer in trust by the grantor for his child, then to his grandchild for life, and then to his great grandchild. Under the old rules neither the estate of the child nor the grandchild would have been subject to tax since transfers were taxable only where there was a beneficiary with a general power of appointment or a beneficiary who was the grantor. A gift (or estate) tax is now imposed for terminations of interest or distributions after 4-30-76. See ¶ 3912.

¶ 4003 Gifts by exercise or release of power of appointment. A "power of appointment" is the right to name the persons who are to receive property from the decedent's estate. Technically, the power may be either *general* or *limited (special)*. Ordinarily, only general powers are taxable. There is one exception to the general rule. See ¶ 4004. The person who creates the power is the donor of the power. The person who has the right to exercise it is its possessor. Gift tax liability may arise from exercise or release of the power.

¶ 4004 Taxability of powers. A "general" power of appointment is a power that can be exercised in favor of the possessor, his estate, his creditors or the creditors of his estate [Sec. 2514(c); 25.2514-1(c)(1)]. The following are not "general" powers:

- *Limited powers to consume.* A power to consume principal, limited by an ascertainable standard relating to the health, education, support or maintenance of the possessor of the power [Sec. 25.2514-1(c)(2)].

- *Joint powers.* A pre-1942 power exercisable by the possessor only in conjunction with another person [Sec. 25.2514-2(b)].

However, a post-1942 power exercisable by the possessor only in conjunction with another person is a general power unless the other person is the creator of the power or is a person with a substantial adverse interest, such as a taker in default. When a not-adversely-interested co-holder is a permissible beneficiary, the possessor will be regarded as having a general power of appointment over his share of the property which is determined by dividing the value of the property subject to the power by the number of joint holders, including the possessor, who (or whose estates) are permissible appointees [Sec. 25.2514-3(b)].

(a) Powers created before 10-22-42. Special powers created before 10-22-42 are not taxable. General powers created before 10-22-42 are taxable only if they are exercised.

Release of general power. A pre-1942 general power may be released at any time without gift tax liability. If the power was partially released before November 1, 1951—so that it was no longer a general power—the modified power could be exercised after that without gift tax liability. A partial release of a general power on or after November 1, 1951, will not result in gift tax at that time, but a later exercise of the modified power during life which leaves in the possessor no power to change the disposition of the property, will be a taxable gift [Sec. 2514(a); 25.2514-2].

(b) Powers created after 10-21-42. Special or limited powers created after 10-21-42 are taxable only if exercised by creating another power of appointment that can, under state law,[1] be exercised so as to postpone the vesting of the property for a period that is ascertainable without regard to the date of the creation of the first power [Sec. 25.2514-3(a), (d)]. A general power created after 10-21-42 is taxable when exercised [Sec. 2514(b)].

Release of general power. The complete release of a post-1942 general power after May 31, 1951 is subject to gift tax [Sec. 2514(b)]. When a power was completely released before June 1, 1951 there is no gift tax liability. If a general power was partially released before June 1, 1951, a later exercise during life would not be a taxable gift. A partial release of a general power after May 31, 1951 is not taxable at that time, but a later exercise or release of the modified power during life which leaves the possessor no power to change the disposition of the property is a taxable gift [Sec. 25.2514-3(c)].

Disclaimer. Before 1977, renunciation or disclaimer of the power was not considered a release of the power, if unequivocal and effective under applicable state law. For transfers made after 12-31-76, only a "qualified" disclaimer prevents the person disclaiming from being liable for gift tax. "Qualified" means: (1) in writing; (2) received by the transferor or legal representative within 9 months from the creation of the interest; (3) no benefits were accepted before the making of the disclaimer; and (4) the interest passes to another person and the person disclaiming does not direct the transfer [Sec. 2514; 2518].

Footnotes appear at end of this Chapter.

¶ 4004

When power lapses. A special provision applies to annual powers of invasion that lapse when they are not exercised. If the possessor of the power does not exercise the power there is no gift tax liability with respect to the lapse in any year unless the amount of the authorized invasion exceeds the greater of $5,000 or 5% of the value of the property out of which the power may be satisfied. If the authorized invasion exceeds this limit, the lapse will be treated as a taxable release of the power to the extent of the excess [Sec. 2514(e); 25.2514-3(c)(4)].

¶ **4005 Gifts of community property.** A gift of community property to a third person is regarded as a gift by each spouse of his or her interest in the property. Since each spouse ordinarily is regarded as having a vested interest in one-half of the property, a gift of community property generally would be treated as a gift of one-half the property by each spouse.[1] However, if the wife is regarded as having simply an expectancy of acquiring half of the property on the death of her husband (the theory of pre-1927 California community property), a gift of the property would be treated as a gift of the entire property by the husband.[2] Under present law, the gift of a spouse's separate property can be split with his spouse [¶ 4009]. So even a gift of pre-1927 California community property could be returned as a gift of half the property by each spouse. If the property is divided in a different proportion than the pre-existing community ownership, there will be a gift to the spouse who receives more than his pre-existing share in the property from the other spouse.[3] If separate property of one spouse is converted into community property, there is a gift by the original owner of the interest the other gets in the community property.[4]

¶ **4006 Gifts made within three years of death.** Gifts made after 12-31-76 and within three years of death are subject to the gift tax and are also includible in the decedent's gross estate [¶ 3909]. The gift tax paid is also includible in the estate [¶ 3935]. Before 1-1-77, the gift was includible in the estate only if made in contemplation of death, and the gift tax paid was a credit against the estate tax.

¶ **4007 Transfers for less than an adequate and full consideration.** When property is transferred for less than an adequate and full consideration in money or money's worth, the amount by which the value of the property transferred exceeds the value of the consideration received is deemed a gift. Such amount must be included in determining the amount of gifts made by the donor during the calendar quarter (or calendar year if made before 1971). However, a bona fide transfer in the ordinary course of business, and without donative intent, is considered made for adequate consideration [Sec. 2512(b); 25.2512-8]. A consideration not reducible to a money value, such as love and affection, promise of marriage, etc., is to be wholly disregarded, and the entire value of the property transferred constitutes the amount of the gift [Sec. 25.2512-8]. Also, the release of dower and other marital rights in consideration of marriage is not an adequate and full consideration.[1] A transfer of stock to indemnify a prospective wife for loss of property rights as a result of remarriage is a taxable gift because the donor receives no consideration in money or money's worth.[2]

Divorce settlement. A transfer or release of an interest is made for adequate consideration in a settlement of marital and property rights if: (1) husband and wife have provided in writing for certain transfers or releases of marital and property rights; and (2) a divorce is obtained within two years after the written agreement has been made; and (3) the transfers set forth in the written agreement are (a) in settlement of marital or property rights, or (b) to provide reasonable support allowances for the minor children of the marriage [Sec. 2516; 25.2516-1, 25.2516-2].

¶ **4008 Transfers subject to revocation or change.** If the donor has parted with dominion and control over the property and has no power to change the disposition of it, for his own benefit or for another's, the gift is complete and taxable. However, if on a transfer of property (whether or not in trust), the donor has reserved any power over its disposition, the gift may be wholly incomplete, or partially complete and partially incomplete. Hence, to determine gift tax liability when property has been transferred subject to a reserved power, the terms of the power must be examined [Sec. 25.2511-2].

When gift is incomplete. A transfer from one individual to another (either directly or in trust) is not considered a complete taxable gift when the donor retains a power (1) to revest the beneficial title to the property in himself; or (2) to divest the beneficiaries of their title, even though the donor himself may not get the property back[1] or (3) to name new beneficiaries or change the interests of the beneficiaries [Sec. 25.2511-2(c)]. It is immaterial that the revocable transfer is made without consideration. A donor is considered as himself having the power when he can exercise it with any person not having a substantial adverse interest in the disposition of the transferred property [Sec. 25.2511-2(e)].

Release of retained rights. When a donor after making a transfer subject to revocation, later, before death, parts with all dominion and control over the property transferred, and releases his right to revoke, the once incomplete gift becomes complete and taxable [Sec. 25.2511-2(f)].

Income from revocable trust. If the donor retains the power of revocation over a trust, there is no gift tax liability as to the trust corpus since the gift is incomplete. If the income is paid to a beneficiary other than the donor, the payment is a gift of income and taxable because the grantor (donor) is deemed to receive the income and then turn it over to the beneficiary.[2]

¶ **4009 Gifts by husband or wife to third party.** A husband and wife may elect to treat a gift made by either to a third party as though it were made one half by each. The donor and the spouse are each taxed on one half of the gift [Sec. 2513; 25.2513-1]. This amounts to doubling the annual exclusion and the unified credit [¶ 4020; 4021], and, in effect, makes the annual exclusion $6,000 and the unified credit, $60,000, (for 1977). For gifts of community property, see ¶ 4005.

What gifts may be split. Before a husband and wife can split gifts to a third person, five conditions must exist: (1) the gift must be made after 4-2-48; (2) both must be citizens or residents of the U.S.; (3) the one who makes the gift must not give the other a power of appointment over the property given away; (4) the husband and wife must be married at the time of the gift and must not remarry during the remainder of the calendar quarter (or calendar year if gift was made before 1971); and (5) both must consent to this special treatment as to all gifts made during the calendar quarter (or calendar year if gift was made before 1971) by either while married to the other.

A husband and wife who enter into a prenuptial agreement under which each spouse waives all marital rights in the property of the other will not be denied the gift-splitting privilege if they are otherwise qualified.[1]

Spouse must agree. The consent to this special treatment of gifts must be shown on the returns[2] [Sec. 2513(b); 25.2513-2]. Generally, it may be signified at any time after the close of the calendar quarter (or calendar year if the gift was made before 1971) in which the gift is made, but there are two exceptions:

Footnotes appear at end of this Chapter.

¶ 4009

(1) The consent may not be signified after the 15th day of the second month following the close of the calendar quarter (or April 15th of the following year if the gift was made before 1-1-71) in which the gift is made, if either the husband or the wife file their returns before that date. If neither files a return before that date, the consent may be signified at any time up until the time either one files a return [Sec. 25.2513-2(b)].

(2) The consent may not be signified after a notice of deficiency for the calendar quarter (or calendar year if the gift was made before 1971) in question is mailed to either spouse [Sec. 2513(b); 25.2513-2].

Revocation. A consent signified on or before the due date of the return, can be revoked by filing a revocation in duplicate with the internal revenue officer with whom the return must be filed on or before that date [Sec. 2513(c); 25.2513-3; 25.2513-4].

Consent by representative. If a spouse dies or becomes legally incompetent, the consent may be signified by the executor or administrator of the deceased spouse, by the surviving spouse, if no representative of the deceased spouse is appointed,[3] or by the committee of the incompetent spouse [Sec. 25.2513-2]. If one spouse as agent files a separate return and consent for an absent spouse, the latter must ratify the return and consent within a reasonable time after being able to do so [Sec. 25.6019-1; 25.6019-2].[4]

Liability for tax. When a gift is split the husband becomes liable for the tax of the wife, and the wife for the tax of the husband.

VALUATION OF GIFTS

¶ 4010 How gifts are valued. The valuation of gifts of property is based on the same principles that apply to valuation of property for estate tax purposes [¶ 3919]. However, there is no alternate valuation date for gift tax. The value of property for gift tax purposes is determined at the date of the gift. The value used is fair market value—the price at which the property would change hands between a willing buyer and a willing seller, neither being under any compulsion to buy or sell [Sec. 2512(a); 25.2512-1]. Special valuation rules apply if the donee is required to pay the tax under the terms of the gift.[1] Rules for valuing the following kinds of property appear in the regulations: stocks and bonds (a special alternative valuation method applies to listed bonds); business interests; notes; mutual fund shares; and property subject to an excise tax [Sec. 25.2512-2—25.2512-7]. The Revenue Service has issued a ruling on the factors to be considered in valuing stock of a closely held corporation.[2] Mutual fund shares are valued at their bid (redemption) price[3] [Sec. 25.2512-6(b)]. For gifts made after 12-31-76, the IRS must furnish upon request a written statement explaining the valuation method and any computations. The statement must be furnished within 45 days after the later of the date it is requested or the date of the IRS determination or proposed determination [Sec. 7517].

¶ 4011 Annuity contracts, life insurance and employees' trusts.

Annuities. When a donor transfers an annuity to the donee, the value of the gift depends to a large extent on the annuitant's life expectancy. Therefore, in cases involving gifts of private annuities, the value of such a gift after 12-31-70 is determined on the basis of separate valuation tables for men and women with a 6% interest factor set out in Regulation Sec. 25.2512-9. Value of gifts made on or before 12-31-70 is based on tables set out in Regulation Sec. 25.2512-5.

Life insurance. The value of a gift of a life insurance or a commercial annuity contract is the fair market value of the contract. The fair market value is determined by reference to the charge made by the insurance company for similar policies at the attained age of the insured, and by taking into account prepaid premiums, outstanding debts or liens against the policy, and accrued dividends [Sec. 25.2512-6].

When the gift is a single-premium or fully paid life insurance policy and the purchase and gift are simultaneous, the gift tax value is the actual cost of the policy.[1] If time elapses between the purchase and gift, value is the replacement cost at the date of the gift, not the cash surrender value.[2]

Employees' trusts. When a qualified employees' trust or plan [¶ 3024] gives the employee an option to have an annuity or other payment under the plan payable to a surviving beneficiary, the exercise or nonexercise of the option is not a taxable gift, except to the extent of the employee's contributions to the plan. The taxable gift is the same proportion of the total value of the annuity or payment that the employee's contributions bear to the total contributions. For gifts made after 12-31-76, individual retirement accounts, individual retirement annuities and retirement bonds will be covered by these rules. After 1965, the exercise or nonexercise of an option under the retired servicemen's family protection plan (to provide a survivor annuity instead of a single pension) is not taxed. The excess contributions made by a Subchapter S corporation for a shareholder-employee are counted as employee contributions and are taxable gifts. See also ¶ 3915(b) [Sec. 2517; 25.2517-1].

> NOTE: For transfers after 12-31-76, there will be a gift tax exclusion for a community interest in qualified plans.

Self-employed retirement plans. The same rules apply to employees covered by self-employed retirement plans. For gifts made after 12-31-76, contributions made by a self-employed person to a qualified plan are treated as contributions by an employer to the extent the contributions are deductible for income tax purposes [Sec. 2517(b)].

Tax-exempt organizations. The employee's proportionate contribution to a retirement annuity contract purchased for him by a tax-exempt organization also results in a gift when he has an option to name a beneficiary [Sec. 2517(a); 25.2517-1(b)(1)(iii)]. A tax-exempt organization includes a school, college or publicly supported charity or a religious organization. However, this exclusion does not apply if the public school, college, university or hospital is an integral part of a local government.[3] Payments or contributions made by the employer or former employer toward the purchase of the annuity are considered to have been made by the employee to the extent they are not excludable from gross income under the 20% rule in ¶ 1232(e) [Sec. 2517(b)]. These provisions apply to calendar years after 1957.

Value of annuity as contribution. When an employer's contribution to a pension plan on an employee's account cannot readily be determined by a more exact method, the value of the annuity payable to the employee and his beneficiary can be used as the amount of total contributions to the plan. The amount of the employee's contributions is then deducted from this amount to find the employer's contribution [Sec. 25.2517-1(c)(2)].

¶ 4012 Remainder and reversionary interests. If the donor has a reversionary or remainder interest in property and he transfers it to the donee, the donor's liability for gift tax is determined by means of actuarial tables because the value of

Footnotes appear at end of this Chapter.

¶ 4012

the interest is usually dependent on the life expectancy of the donor [Sec. 25.2512-5(d); 25.2512-9(d)]. All the law requires is transfer of property by gift. There need be no donee is existence in order for gift tax liability to arise. A remainder interest was taxable in full where the grantor had a reversionary interest that couldn't be valued because the grantor had no children and was unmarried at the time of the gift.[1] If the reversionary interest can be valued, it is deductible from the value of the remainder to find the value of the gift of the remainder.[2]

¶ 4013 **Tenancy by the entirety.** A husband and wife frequently take title to real property as tenants by the entirety or as joint tenants with right of survivorship. If the property was purchased with funds of one spouse, or with funds furnished disproportionately by both spouses, the gift tax consequences depend on the year involved. If the transaction occurred before 1955, the spouse who contributed the larger amount is deemed to have made a gift to the other. For years after 1954, however, there is no gift tax liability, regardless of who supplied the consideration, unless they elect to have it taxed as a gift at that time. The rule also applies to additions to the value of the property, such as improvements, or debt reductions [Sec. 25.2515-1]. For joint interests created after 1976, if the election was made to have the transfer treated as a gift, each spouse is treated as having a one-half interest in the property [Sec. 2515(c)(3)]. For interests created before 1977, the amount of the gift was the value of the donor's contribution less the value of his retained interest determined by application of actuarial tables [Sec. 25.2512-9] (See Reg. Sec. 25.2512-5 for gifts made before 1971) to the donor's interest under local law [Sec. 25.2515-2(b)]. The Revenue Service, on request, will furnish a special factor required for the valuation of an actual gift [Sec. 25.2512-5(e); 25.2512-9(e)].

When election is made. The election is considered made when the spouse making the larger contribution files a gift tax return for the calendar quarter (or calendar year if gift was made before 1971) in which the tenancy is created or the value added [Sec. 2515(c); 25.2515-2]. If an election to have the transaction treated as a gift is not made, the termination of the tenancy (other than by the death of a spouse) will result in a gift, unless the proceeds are divided in the ratio in which the consideration was furnished orginially [Sec. 2515(b); 25.2515-3].

Termination of the tenancy may result in a taxable gift to a spouse when a third person furnished the original consideration or even when a spouse made an election of gift on its creation [Sec. 25.2515-4].

¶ 4014 **United States savings bonds.** The value of Series E U.S. savings bonds is the amount at which they are redeemable by the Treasury.[1]

DEDUCTIONS AND UNIFIED CREDIT

¶ 4020 **The individual exclusion.** In determining the amount of gifts for a calendar quarter, the donor may exclude the first $3,000 of gifts made to each donee less the aggregate amount of gifts from the donor to that donee during the preceding calendar quarters of the calendar year [Sec. 2503(b)].

Gifts of future interests. The individual exclusion does not apply to gifts of future interests in property [Sec. 25.2503-3]. Unless the donee has the unqualified right *presently* to use, possess or enjoy the property, the gift is of a future interest, and the donor does not get the individual exclusion. The time when enjoyment begins and not when title vests is controlling.[1] Because each beneficiary of a trust is considered a separate donee, the donor of a gift in trust is allowed an exclusion for each beneficiary with a present interest[2] [Sec. 25.2503-2]. However, an interest in property is not a future interest merely because there is a possibility that it may be diminished by the exercise of a power, if no part of the interest will at any time pass to any person besides the donee [Sec. 2503(b); 25.2503-3(b)].

Gifts to minors. A gift made to or for the benefit of a minor is not a gift of a future interest if (a) the gift property and income from it *may* be spent for the benefit of the donee during his minority *and* (b) the balance not spent will pass outright to the donee at 21, or if he dies before 21, to his estate or as he may appoint under a general power[3] [Sec. 2503(c); 25.2503-4]. The provisions of the "Model Gifts of Securities to Minors Act" and the "Uniform Gifts to Minors Act" as adopted by the individual states generally meet these requirements.[4] A gift in trust under which a minor must act either to end the trust or extend it on terms stated in the trust when he becomes 21, also qualifies for the exclusion.[5] Income from a trust for minors (including a short-term trust), may qualify for the exclusion, even though the principal does not.[6]

Trust income divided. No exclusion is allowed when a trustee has the sole discretion to apportion trust income among stated beneficiaries since the value of each beneficiary's right cannot be determined [Sec. 25.2503-3(c)].[7] However, if a value can be determined for a beneficial share, the exclusion will be allowed to that extent although the exact number of beneficiaries or the exact value of each share is unknown.[8]

The exclusion before 1943. Since the gift tax is imposed on a cumulative basis [¶ 4025] the amount of gifts and the exclusions for preceding years and quarters affect the tax for the current calendar quarter. The individual exclusion before 1939 was $5,000, and did not apply to future interests. For the years 1939 through 1942 the exclusion was $4,000, and did not apply to future interests or gifts in trust [Sec. 25.2504-1].

¶ 4021 The unified credit. In addition to the annual exclusion, the donor is entitled to a unified credit against estate and gift taxes for gifts made after 12-31-76 and for decedents dying after such date. To the extent the credit is used to offset gift taxes the amount actually available to reduce estate taxes will be less. The credit is not renewed annually. It may be used in whole or in part until it is exhausted. The credit replaces the specific exemption and is applied at transitional rates as follows: 1977—$30,000; 1978—$34,000; 1979—$38,000; 1980—$42,500; 1981 and after—$47,000. For gifts made after 9-8-76 and before 1-1-77, the credit is reduced by 20% of the amount allowed as a specific exemption. Only $6,000 of the credit can be applied to gifts made after 12-31-76 and before 7-1-77 [Sec. 2505].

Before 1977—specific exemption. For gifts made before 1977, the donor was allowed a specific exemption of $30,000 against lifetime gifts. This exemption was treated as a deduction against gifts made and was replaced by the unified credit which is a credit against gift tax due.

Before 1943. The specific exemption for the years 1932 through 1935, was $50,000, and for the years 1936-1942, $40,000. If a specific exemption was taken in prior years, for example $40,000 in 1937, the donor is not entitled to any further exemption. In computing the tax for gifts after 1942, only the $30,000 exemption can be deducted from lifetime gifts, that is, you must add back the excess exemption. See ¶ 4028.

Footnotes appear at end of this Chapter.

¶ **4022 Charitable and similar gifts.** The taxpayer may deduct from the gross amount of gifts made during the calendar quarter (calendar year for gifts made before 1971), gifts to or for the use of the following.[1]

(A) the United States, any State, Territory, or political subdivision, or the District of Columbia, for exclusively public purposes;

(B) a corporation, or trust, or community chest, fund, or foundation, organized and operated exclusively for religious, charitable, scientific, literary or educational purposes, or for gifts made after 12-31-76 to foster national or international sports competition (but only if no part of its activities involve the provision of athletic facilities or equipment), including the encouragement of art and the prevention of cruelty to children or animals, no part of the net earnings of which inures to the benefit of any private shareholder or individual, and no substantial part of the activities of which is carrying on propaganda, or otherwise attempting, to influence legislation, or participating in or intervening in (including publishing or distributing statements) any political campaign for a candidate for public office;

NOTE: For gifts made in calendar years starting after 12-31-76, to qualify for the deduction, the exempt organization must not lose its exemption status because of excessive lobbying activities [¶ 3437(d)].

(C) a fraternal society, order, or association, operating under the lodge system, but only if such gifts are to be used exclusively for religious, charitable, scientific, literary, or educational purposes, including the encouragement of art and the prevention of cruelty to children or animals;

(D) posts or organizations of war veterans, or auxiliary units or societies of any such posts or organizations, if such posts, organizations, units, or societies are organized in the United States or any of its possessions, and if no part of their net earnings inures to the benefit of any private shareholder or individual [Sec. 2522(a); 25.2522(a)-1].

Donations of charitable remainder and income interests. A gift of a charitable remainder after 7-31-69 cannot be deducted unless the remainder interest is: (1) in a farm or personal residence; (2) real property (after 6-13-76 and before 6-14-81), if for conservation purposes; or (3) a trust interest in an annuity trust, unitrust or a pooled income fund [Sec. 2522(c)(2)(A); 25.2522(c)-3(c)(2)]. Charitable remainder annuity trusts, unitrusts and pooled income funds are defined and valued the same way for both estate and gift taxes. The only transfers of charitable income interests that can be deducted after 7-31-69 are guaranteed annuities or gifts of a fixed percentage distributed yearly of property's fair market value determined annually [Sec. 2522(c)(2)(B); 25.2522(c)-3(c)(2)].

Disallowance of deduction for donations to private foundations. Transfers to private foundations are not deductible if the foundation is subject to tax on loss of exemptions or is not required in the governing instrument to avoid practices that would subject it to penalty taxes [¶ 3437]. Transfers to foreign private foundations are similarly disallowed [Sec. 2522(c)(1); 25.2522(c)-2]. A contribution to a political party or candidate for public office does not qualify for the charitable deduction.[2] But see ¶ 4002.

Proof required. The Revenue Service may require the donor to submit proof of his right to the deduction [Sec. 25.2522(a)-1(c)].

¶ **4023 Marital deduction.** For gifts made after 12-31-76, there is a lifetime gift tax marital deduction for the first $100,000 in gifts to a spouse. Gifts over $100,000 and up to $200,000 are fully taxed and a 50% deduction is allowed for gifts over $200,000. The deduction is in addition to the $3,000 annual exclusion. Use of the gift tax marital deduction will reduce the estate tax marital deduction (¶ 3929) [Sec. 2523(a)]. Gifts of remainder interests to the spouse or the spouse's estate are valued actuarially before applying the marital deduction [Sec. 25.2523(a)-1(d)].

Pre-1977. Formerly, the gift tax marital deduction was equal to one-half the value of the gift to the spouse. The $3,000 annual exclusion was additionally applicable.

What gifts qualify. These requirements must be met before the deduction will be allowed: (1) the gift must be made after 4-2-48; (2) the donor must be a citizen or resident of U.S.; (3) the donor and donee must be married at the time of the gift; and (4) the gift must be one of an outright interest.

Life estates. *For years after 1954,* the gift of a life estate qualifies as an outright interest if the spouse is entitled for life to all of the income from the entire interest (or a portion of it) with the power to appoint the entire interest (or a portion of it) to herself or her estate. Thus a transfer to a spouse of a legal life estate with an unlimited power to invade corpus would satisfy the requirement. The requirement is not met if the donor gives his or her husband or wife a life estate or other terminable interest in the property and if, in addition, (1) the donor retains or transfers to anyone else (other than his spouse or her estate) for less than full consideration, an interest in the same property, making it possible for him or the other person, their heirs or assigns to possess or enjoy any part of the property after the interest of the donee spouse ends, or if (2) the donor, after the gift, has a power of appointment, the exercise of which makes it possible for anyone else to possess or enjoy any part of the property after the interest of the donee husband or wife ends [Sec. 2523(e); 25.2523(e)-1].

The marital deduction may be allowed for gifts by a husgand or wife to his or her spouse as sole joint tenant or as tenant by the entirety. Such an interest will not be considered a "terminable interest" merely because the donor spouse may survive the donee spouse [Sec. 2523(d); 25.2523(d)-1].

For years before 1955, a gift qualified as an outright interest only if the donor gave the spouse the absolute title, or if the gift was in trust and (a) the donee gets the income for life—payable at least annually—and the power to appoint the principal free of the trust to herself or her estate, or the power to invade the principal, or (b) the income is to be paid to the donee for life or accumulated, and the corpus plus any accumulated income is to be paid to the donee's estate.

When deduction not allowed. A transfer in trust will not qualify for the marital deduction when the principal of the trust consists substantially of property which is not likely to be income-producing during the life of the surviving spouse and the spouse has no power to compel the trustee to make the property productive or convert it to income property within a reasonable time;[1] but a power to retain a residence or other property for the personal use of the spouse will not disqualify the transfer in trust [Sec. 25.2523(e)-1(f)].

The marital deduction is not allowed for gifts of the donor's interest in community property, nor for gifts of the donor's interest in certain separate property which is considered community property for purposes of the marital deduction [Sec. 2523(f); 25.2523(f)-1].

Limitation on amount. The marital deduction is limited to the amount at which the gift is reported in the gift tax return [Sec. 2524; 25.2524-1].

FIGURING THE TAX

¶ 4025 Gifts in prior years and quarters included. The gift tax rates are graduated[¶ 4027]. If a donor could spread his gifts over a period of years and pay a tax on only the gifts for each calendar quarter, he could avoid being taxed at the higher rate. To prevent this, the gift tax is figured on a cumulative basis. In figuring the gift tax liability for a current calendar quarter, gifts made after June 6, 1932 must be included [Sec. 2502(a); 25.2502-1]. Including gifts of prior years before 1971 and quarters after 1970 results in taxing the current gifts at a higher tax rate. The prior years' and quarters' gifts are included at the value reported on the prior gift tax return [Sec. 2504; 25.2504-1].

Footnotes appear at end of this Chapter.

¶ 4025

¶ **4026 How to figure the tax.** Finding the tax payable each year involves the following steps [Sec. 2502; 25.2502-1].

(1) Figure a tentative tax by applying the graduated rates that apply to the year for which the tax is being computed to the total value of all taxable gifts made after June 6, 1932.

(2) Refigure the tax for preceding calendar quarters (starting in 1971) and years (1932-1970) by applying the graduated rates that apply to the quarter for which the tax is being figured to the total value of the taxable gifts made in the preceding calendar quarters and years (but after June 6, 1932).

> NOTE: In making computations in (1) and (2) it should be noted that the specific exemption was replaced by the unified credit for gifts made after 12-31-76. The specific exemption if in effect would enter into the computations in (1) and (2), but the unified credit would not.

(3) Subtract the result in (2) from the tentative tax obtained in (1).
(4) Subtract the unified credit (less unified credit taken previously and 20% of specific exemption allowed after 9-8-76 and before 1-1-77.

> NOTE: The unified credit is not to be subtracted unless the tax liability is being determined for periods after 12-31-76.

¶ **4027 Rates of tax.** The following rates apply to gifts made after December 31, 1941 and before January 1, 1977 [Sec. 2502; 25.2502-1(b)]:

> NOTE: The unified estate and gift tax rate schedule, which is effective for gifts made after 12-31-76, appears at ¶ 3934.

Amount of taxable gifts	Tax on amount in (A)	Amounts of taxable gifts in excess of (A) but not in excess of (C) is taxed at rate shown in (D)	
(A)	(B)	(C)	(D)
0	0	$ 5,000	2¼%
$ 5,000	$ 112.50	10,000	5¼%
10,000	375	20,000	8¼%
20,000	1,200	30,000	10½%
30,000	2,250	40,000	13½%
40,000	3,600	50,000	16½%
50,000	5,250	60,000	18¾%
60,000	7,125	100,000	21 %
100,000	15,525	250,000	22½%
250,000	49,275	500,000	24 %
500,000	109.275	750,000	26¼%
750,000	174,900	1,000,000	27¾%
1,000,000	244,275	1,250,000	29¼%
1,250,000	317,400	1,500,000	31½%
1,500,000	396,150	2,000,000	33¾%
2,000,000	564,900	2,500,000	36¾%
2,500,000	748,650	3,000,000	39¾%
3,000,000	947,400	3,500,000	42 %
3,500,000	1,157,400	4,000,000	44¼%
4,000,000	1,378,650	5,000,000	47¼%
5,000,000	1,851,150	6,000,000	50¼%
6,000,000	2,353,650	7,000,000	52½%
7,000,000	2,878,650	8,000,000	54¾%
8,000,000	3,426,150	10,000,000	57 %
10,000,000	4,566,150	....	57¾%

¶ **4028 Example of a tax computation.** (a) **Pre-1977 gift tax calculation.** The following example shows how the tax is calculated:

John Gresham, a resident citizen of the United States, made the following gifts in 1932, 1934, 1935, 1941 and 1976.

On December 24, 1932, to his wife, $75,000; to his daughter, $40,000; and to his son, $2,000.

On February 12, 1934, a contribution, in trust, of $150,000 to a charitable organization.
On June 22, 1934 to his niece, $2,000.
On August 5, 1934, to his nephew, $6,000.
On December 24, 1934, to his wife, $50,000; to his daughter, $10,000; and to his son, $30,000.
On November 6, 1935, to his son, $50,000.
On January 23, 1941, to his daughter, $99,000.

On January 15, 1976, to his wife $100,000 in cash and the remainder interest in a $100,000 homestead, the donor reserving a life estate in it. At the time of this gift, the donor was 68 years of age.

The gift tax for each of the years is calculated as follows:

Gift Tax for the year 1932

(1)	Gifts made in calendar year 1932:		
	To wife $75,000 (less $5,000 exclusion†)		$ 70,000
	To daughter $40,000 (less $5,000 exclusion)		35,000
	To son $2,000 (less $5,000 exclusion)		0
	Total gifts		$105,000
(2)	Deductions		
	Specific exemption†		50,000

† Under the 1939 Code, the exclusion was $5,000 before 1939, and $4,000 for 1939 through 1942. The exemption was $50,000 from 1932 to 1935, and $40,000 from 1936 to 1942. See ¶ 4020, 4021.

(3)	Taxable gifts in 1932		$ 55,000
	Tax upon gifts of $50,000	$1,125	
	Excess ($5,000 × 5%)	250	
(4)	Gift tax for 1932		$ 1,375

Gift Tax for the year 1934

(5)	Gifts made in calendar year 1934:	
	To a charitable organization, in trust	$150,000
	To niece $2,000 (less $5,000 exclusion)	0
	To nephew $6,000 (less $5,000 exclusion)	1,000
	To wife $50,000 (less $5,000 exclusion)	45,000
	To daughter $10,000 (less $5,000 exclusion)	5,000
	To son $30,000 (less $5,000 exclusion)	25,000
	Total gifts in 1934	$226,000
(6)	Deductions:	
	Charitable gift	$150,000
(7)	Taxable gifts in 1934	$ 76,000

Footnotes appear at end of this Chapter.

(8)	Taxable gifts in 1932 ($50,000 exemption having been taken)		55,000
(9)	Aggregate taxable gifts in 1934 and 1932		$131,000
(10)	Gift tax on aggregate gifts:		
	Tax upon taxable gifts of $100,000	$3,625	
	Excess ($31,000 × 6½%)	2,015	
(11)	Total (tentative) tax on aggregate gifts		$ 5,640
(12)	Less tax on aggregate gifts of preceding year		1,375
(13)	Gift tax for 1934		$ 4,265

Gift Tax for the year 1935

(14)	Gifts made in the calendar year 1935:		
	To son $50,000 (less $5,000 exclusion)		$ 45,000
(15)	Taxable gifts in 1934		76,000
(16)	Taxable gifts in 1932		55,000
(17)	Aggregate taxable gifts in 1935, 1934 and 1932		$176,000
(18)	Gift tax on aggregate gifts:		
	Tax upon taxable gifts of $100,000	$4,200	
	Excess ($76,000 × 9%)	6,840	
(19)	Total (tentative) tax on aggregate gifts		$ 11,040
(20)	Less tax on aggregate gifts ($131,000) of preceding years:		
	Tax upon taxable gifts of $100,000	$4,200	
	Excess ($31,000 × 9%)	2,790	
(21)	Tax on gifts made in preceding years at 1935 rates		6,990
(22)	Gift tax for 1935		$ 4,050

Gift Tax for the year 1941

(23)	Gift made in the calendar year 1941:		
	To daughter, $99,000 (less $4,000 exclusion)		$ 95,000
(24)	Taxable gifts in 1935		45,000
(25)	Taxable gifts in 1934		$ 76,000
(26)	Taxable gifts in 1932 ($50,000 exemption having been taken)	$55,000	
	Add difference between $50,000 exemption previously taken, and that allowed under the 1935 Act	10,000	$ 65,000
(27)	Aggregate taxable gifts for 1941 and prior years		$281,000
(28)	Gift tax on aggregate gifts:		
	Tax upon taxable gifts of $200,000	$19,950	
	Excess ($81,000 × 15%)	12,150	
	Total (tentative) tax on aggregate gifts	$32,100	
	110% thereof (defense-tax)		$ 35,310.00
(29)	Less tax at current rates on gifts made in prior years ($176,000 + $10,000 difference in exemption):		
	Tax upon taxable gifts of $100,000	$ 7,200	
	Excess ($86,000 × 12¾%)	10,965	
	Credit for gifts in prior years	$18,165	
	110% thereof (defense-tax)		$ 19,981.50
(30)	Gift tax for 1941 (including defense-tax)		$ 15,328.50

Gift Tax for quarter after 1970

(31) Gifts made in calendar quarter:

Chapter 30—Federal Gift Tax

	To wife ($100,000 cash less $3,000 exclusion under §2503(b))	$ 97,000.00
	To wife (remainder interest)‡	
	Valuation is based on life expectancy of donor, age 68 at time of gift as shown by Actuarial Table A (1) for Single Life Male [Reg. §25.2512-9(f)], $100,000 × .55923	$ 55,923.00
	Total gifts in the quarter	$152,923.00
(32)	Deductions	
	Marital deduction (one-half of cash gift of $100,000 plus one-half of gift of remainder of $55,923 [¶ 4023])	$ 77,961.50
(33)	Taxable gifts in the quarter	$ 74,961.50
(34)	Total taxable gifts in preceding years	$281,000.00
	Add difference between $40,000 exemption taken in prior years and $30,000 after 1942 [Sec. 2504(a)]	$ 10,000.00
(35)	Aggregate taxable gifts for all quarters after 1970 and for prior years (1932-1970)	$365,961.50
(36)	Gift tax on aggregate gifts:	
	Tax on taxable gifts of $250,000 .... $49,275.00	
	Excess ($115,961.50) × 24%) 27,830.76	$ 77,105.76
(37)	Less tax at current rates on gifts made in prior years ($281,000 plus $10,000 difference in exemption):	
	Tax on taxable gifts of $250,000 .... $49,275.00	
	Excess ($41,000 × 24%) 9,840.00	

‡ Since this is a gift of a future interest the $3,000 exclusion would not be allowed, even if it were not exhausted against the cash gift.

	Credit for gifts in prior years	$ 59,115.00
(38)	Gift tax for the quarter	$ 17,990.76

(b) Post-1976 gift tax calculation. Assume that on January 15, of 1981, 1982, and 1986, "A" a resident of the U.S. made the following gifts to his wife: $450,000 in 1981; $450,000 in 1982 and $900,000 in 1986.

The computation of the gift tax is as follows:

Gift No. 1 (made in 1981)

Gross amount of gift	$450,000.00
Less:	
Annual exclusion	3,000.00
Marital deduction	225,000.00
	228,000.00
Taxable gift	222,000.00
Gift tax on gift No. 1	61,840.00
Less: Unified Credit	47,000.00
Gift tax paid on gift No. 1	14,840.00

Gift No. 2 (made in 1982)

Gross amount of gift	450,000.00
Less:	
Annual exclusion	3,000.00
Marital deduction	225,000.00
	228,000.00
Taxable gift	222,000.00
Gift tax paid on gift No. 2	74,920.00

Footnotes appear at end of this Chapter.

¶ 4028

Gift No. 3 (made in 1986)

Gross amount of gift	$900,000.00
Less:	
Annual exclusion	3,000.00
Marital deduction	450,000.00
	453,000.00
Taxable gift	447,000.00
Gift tax paid on gift No. 3	166,530.00
Tax paid on gift No. 1	14,840.00
Tax paid on gift No. 2	74,920.00
Tax paid on gift No. 3	166,530.00
Total gift taxes paid	$256,290.00

¶ 4029 **Gift tax increases basis of gift.** For gifts made after 12-31-76, the basis of property acquired by gift is increased by the amount of gift tax attributable to the net appreciation on the gift. The increase is limited to the total tax paid [Sec. 1015(d)(6)]. See ¶ 1515.

Gifts made on or after 9-2-58 and before 1-1-77. Gifts made during this period get an increase in basis equal to the gift tax paid and limited only by the fair market value of the gift [Sec. 1015(d)(1)(A)].

Gifts made before 9-2-58. When a gift was made before 9-2-58, and the property was not disposed of before that date, basis of the property is increased by the amount of the gift tax. However, the increase may not be more than the excess of the fair market value of the property at the time of the gift over its basis at that time [Sec. 1015(d)(1)(B); 1.1015-5(a)(1)(i),(ii)].

How to determine increase for several gifts. If gifts are made to more than one person in the same calendar quarter (or year if the gifts were made before 1971), the total gift tax paid by the donor in the quarter is prorated over his gifts for that quarter. In determining the total gifts made, all deductions and the allowable $3,000 exclusions are taken into account, but the unified credit (before 1977, the specific exemption) is not. If more than one gift is made in a calendar quarter to the same person, the $3,000 exclusion is applied against the gifts first in time to determine the gift tax to be used as an adjustment to the basis of each gift [Sec. 1015(d)(2)]. If third-party gifts are split between husband and wife, the gift tax of each is taken into account [Sec. 1015(d)(3)].

PROCEDURE

¶ 4030 **Returns.** For gifts made in 1971 and later years, gift tax liability is figured on the basis of a calendar quarter. For gifts made after 12-31-76, a special rule applies to gifts of $25,000 or less in a quarter. See below. Any individual who makes a gift during a calendar quarter of (1) any future interest in property [¶ 4020] regardless of amount, or (2) a present interest in property in excess of the annual individual exclusion of $3,000, or (3) a present interest in property which together with previous gifts of present interests to the same individual in the calendar year exceeds the annual individual exclusion of $3,000, must file a quarterly return (Form 709). Starting in 1971, a donor reports any qualified charitable transfers [¶ 4022] made during the year on the return for the fourth quarter of the calendar year in which the transfer is made. However, if a return must be filed for a noncharitable gift in an earlier quarter, the qualified charitable transfer is reported at the same time the donor files the return for the noncharitable transfer. A qualified charitable transfer is a gift for which the deduction equals the full amount transferred by gift [¶ 4022]. For example, a transfer of a remainder interest to a charity at the same time the income interest is transferred in trust to a noncharitable donee is not a qualified charitable transfer. Unless an extension is granted, the due date is the 15th day of the second month after the end of the calendar quarter in which the gift is made. The return is required even though no tax is due because of deductions or the specific exemption [Sec. 2503(b), 6019(a), 6075(b), 6091(b)(1); 25.6011-1, 25-6019-1, 25.6075-1, 25.6091-1]. Penalties are provided for failure to file returns and to pay taxes [¶ 3617; 3618(b)].

The return is filed with the Service Center for the District either where the donor resides or has his principal place of business. If the donor has neither in the U.S., he must file with the Service Center at 11601 Roosevelt Blvd., Philadelphia, Pa. 19155. The various regional Service Centers are indicated in the instructions to Form 709. Returns not mailed may be hand carried to the District Director's office either where the donor resides or where his principal place of business is located.

Gifts of $25,000 or less made after 12-31-76. A quarterly gift tax return is not required unless: (1) the taxable gifts during the quarter, plus (2) all other taxable gifts made during the calendar year for which a return has yet to be filed are more than $25,000. This requirement is $12,500 for non-resident aliens. Also, if the total taxable gifts made during the calendar year are $25,000 or less, only one return for the year need be filed. This return is due by the 15th day of the second month following the close of the fourth calendar quarter of the calendar year in which the gifts were made [Sec. 6075(b)(2)].

Split gifts. If a husband and wife elect to split gifts by either to a third party, the spouse who makes the gift is treated as the donor of the entire gift to detemine whether a return must be filed. The other spouse is treated as the donor of half the gift to determine whether he or she also must file a return [Sec. 25.6019-2]. Each must file a return for a gift of a future interest.[1]

Information required. In addition to the information required on the gift tax return, the Revenue Service may ask for appraisal lists of the value of the gifts. If life insurance is the subject of a gift, the donor must obtain a valuation statement on Form 938 from the insurance company, and file it with the Revenue Service [Sec. 25.6001-1]. If the gift was made by means of a trust, a certified or verified copy of the trust instrument must be submitted. In the case of stock of close corporations or inactive stock (which should be valued on the basis of net worth, earning and dividend paying capacity, and other relevant factors), balance sheets, particularly the one nearest the date of the gift, and statements of the net earnings or operating results and dividends paid for each of the 5 preceding years must be submitted. Any other documents, such as appraisal lists, required for an adequate explanation, should be filed with the return [Sec. 25.6019-4].

¶ **4031 Payment of the tax.** Starting in 1971, the full amount of the tax is due and payable by the 15th day of the second month following the close of the calendar quarter in which the gift was made [Sec. 2502(d), 6075(b); 6151(a)]. For gifts made before 1-1-71, the tax was due and payable by the donor by April 15th following the close of the calendar year [Sec. 2502(d), 6151(a); 25.2502-2, 25.6151-1]. If the donor shows that payment by the due date would result in hardship, an extention of time for payment, not to exceed 6 months, may be granted [Sec. 25.6161-1]. Interest at the rate of 7% (9% between 7-1-75 and 1-31-76; 6% before 7-1-75) or an adjusted prime interest rate (¶ 3628) will be charged for the extension period [Sec. 6601(a), 6621; 301.6601-1]. If the tax is not paid by the donor, the donee is liable for the tax up to the value of the gift received [Sec. 6324(b),

Footnotes appear at end of this Chapter.

6901(a); 301.6324-1, 301.6901-1]. An executor or administrator can obtain a release from personal liability from the decedent's gift taxes in much the same way he is released from estate tax liability (¶ 3947) [Sec. 6905; 26.6905-1, 301.6905-1].

¶ 4032 Assessments and deficiencies. The Revenue Service ordinarily has three years from the date the return was filed to make an assessment. If the return omits 25% or more of the taxable gifts made during the year, the Revenue Service has 6 years to make the assessment. However, if no return is filed, or if the donor files a false or fraudulent return, the tax may be assessed at any time [Sec. 6501; 301.6501(a)-1; 301.6501(c)-1].

If the Revenue Service determines a deficiency exists and notifies the taxpayer by registered or certified mail, the taxpayer has 90 days (or 150 days, see ¶ 3639) from the receipt of such notice to file a petition with the Tax Court for a redetermination of the deficiency [Sec. 6213(a); 301.6213-1].

¶ 4033 Refunds. Claims for refund should be made on Form 843 and filed with the Revenue Service [Sec. 301.6402-2]. Generally, the claim must be filed within three years after the return was filed or two years after the tax was paid, whichever is later [Sec. 6511(a); 301.6511(a)-1].

A suit for refund can be filed in the District Court or the Court of Claims; the taxpayer must first file a claim for a refund with the Revenue Service. The suit must be brought at least six months after filing the claim (unless the Revenue Service renders a decision on the claim before then) and within two years from the date of mailing by the Revenue Service of disallowance in part or of all of the refund claim. Payment under protest is not necessary in order to sue for refund [Sec. 6532, 7422; 301.6532-1].

Footnotes to Chapter 30

(P-H "FEDERAL TAXES" related references are cited in brackets [ ] at the end of each footnote below)

Footnote ¶ 4000 [¶ 125,013].
(1) Rev. Rul. 75-72, 1975-1 CB 310 [¶ 142,110].

Footnote ¶ 4002 [¶ 125,001; 125,030; 125,110 et seq.; 125,210; 125,220].
(1) Robinette v. Helvering; Paumgarten v. Helvering, 318 US 184, 63 SCt 540, 30 AFTR 384 [¶ 125,116].
(2) Rev. Rul. 67-396, 1967-2 CB 351 [¶ 125,013(10)].
(3) Rev. Rul. 69-148, 1969-1 CB 226 [¶ 125,112(2)].
(4) The Revenue Service list of qualified receivers of deductible contributions, in book form, may be purchased from the Superintendent of Documents, Government Printing Office, Washington, D.C. 20402.

Footnote ¶ 4003 [¶ 125,140 et seq.].

Footnote ¶ 4004 [¶ 125,140 et seq.].
(1) Such law exists in Delaware (see P-H Wills, Estates and Trusts Service ¶ 416 and ¶ 1019, Del.).

Footnote ¶ 4005 [¶ 125,130].
(1) C.F. Roeser, 2 TC 298 [¶ 125,033(65)].
(2) U.S. v. Robbins, 269 US 315, 46 SCt 148, 5 AFTR 5679 [¶ 41,165].

Footnote ¶ 4005 continued
(3) W. Fleming, 3 TC 974, affd. 155 F.2d 204, 36 AFTR 1569 [¶ 125,117(15)].
(4) Holloway's Est. v. Comm., 175 F.2d 672, 38 AFTR 105 [¶ 125,133(25)].

Footnote ¶ 4006 [¶ 120,352; 125,001].

Footnote ¶ 4007 [¶ 125,126 et seq.; 125,160].
(1) Merrill v. Fahs, 324 US 308, 33 AFTR 587; reh. den. 324 US 888, 33 AFTR 604 [¶ 125,162(5)].
(2) Comm. v. Wemyss, 324 US 303, 65 SCt 652, 33 AFTR 584 [¶ 125,162(5)].

Footnote ¶ 4008 [¶ 125,110 et seq.; 125,116 et seq.].
(1) Sanford v. Comm., 308 US 39, 23 AFTR 756 [¶ 125,115(5)].
(2) Reinecke v. Smith Exs., et al., 289 US 172, 53 SCt 570, 12 AFTR 47.

Footnote ¶ 4009 [¶ 125,130 et seq.].
(1) Rev. Rul. 55-241, 1955-1 CB 470 [¶ 125,132(35)].
(2) Edwin L. Jones, 39 TC 734 [¶ 125,132(5)].
(3) Rev. Rul. 67-55, 1967-1 CB 278 [¶ 125,132(20)].
(4) Rev. Rul. 54-6, 1954-1 CB 205 [¶ 125,132(5)].

Footnote ¶ 4010 [¶ 125,120 et seq.].
(1) Rev. Rul. 75-72, 1975-1 CB 310 [¶ 142,110].

Chapter 30—Footnotes

Footnote ¶ 4010 continued
(2) Rev. Rul. 59-60, 1959-1 CB 237 as modified by Rev. Rul. 65-193, 1965-2 CB 370 [¶ 120,312].
(3) Rev. Proc. 74-3, 1974-1 CB 10; U.S. v. Cartwright, 31 AFTR 2d 73-1461, 411 US 546 [¶ 142,068; 147,832].

Footnote ¶ 4011 [¶ 125,123 et seq.].
(1) Guggenheim v. Rasquin, 312 US 254, 25 AFTR 1166 [¶ 125,123(10)].
(2) U.S. v. Ryerson, 312 US 260, 25 AFTR 1164 [¶ 125,123(15)].
(3) Rev. Rul. 68-294, 1968-1 CB 46 [¶ 125,112(22)].

Footnote ¶ 4012 [¶ 125,120; 125,122].
(1) Robinette v. Helvering; Paumgarten v. Helvering, 318 US 184, 30 AFTR 384 [¶ 125,122].
(2) Smith v. Shaughnessy, 318 US 176, 30 AFTR 388 [¶ 125,122(30)].

Footnote ¶ 4013 [¶ 125,150 et seq.].

Footnote ¶ 4014 [¶ 125,014].
(1) Rev. Rul. 55-278, 1955-1 CB 471 [¶ 125,014(5)].

Footnote ¶ 4020 [¶ 125,030].
(1) Fondren v. Comm., 324 US 18, 33 AFTR 302 [¶ 125,035(5)].
(2) Comm. v. Hutchings, 312 US 393, 25 AFTR 1188 [¶ 125,032(5)].
(3) Bernie C. Clinard, 40 TC 878 [¶ 125,035(25)].
(4) Rev. Rul. 56-86, 1956-1 CB 449; Rev. Rul. 59-357, 1959-2 CB 212 [¶ 125,036(5), (7)].

Footnote ¶ 4020 continued
(5) Rev. Rul. 74-43, 1974-1 CB 285 [¶ 142,059].
(6) Rev. Rul. 68-670, 1968-2 CB 413 [¶ 125,033(74)].
(7) Rev. Rul. 55-303, 1955-1 CB 471 [¶ 125,034(5)].
(8) Rev. Rul. 55-678; 55-679, 1955-2 CB 389-391 [¶ 125,033(5)].

Footnote ¶ 4021 [¶ 125,210 et seq.].

Footnote ¶ 4022 [¶ 125,200 et seq.].
(1) The Revenue Service publishes a list. See ¶ 4004, footnote (1).
(2) Rev. Rul. 59-57, 1959-1 CB 626 [¶ 125,222(40)].

Footnote ¶ 4023 [¶ 125,230 et seq., 125,240].
(1) Estate of Charles C. Smith, 23 TC 367 [¶ 125,232(15)].

Footnote ¶ 4025 [¶ 125,020 et seq.].

Footnote ¶ 4026 [¶ 125,021].

Footnote ¶ 4027 [¶ 125,021 et seq.].

Footnote ¶ 4028 [¶ 125,023].

Footnote ¶ 4029 [¶ 125,001].

Footnote ¶ 4030 [¶ 126,000 et seq.].
(1) True v. U.S., 17 AFTR 2d 1317, 354 F.2d 323 [¶ 125,132(25)].

Footnote ¶ 4031 [¶ 126,150 et seq.].

Footnote ¶ 4032 [¶ 126,200 et seq.].

Footnote ¶ 4033 [¶ 126,300 et seq.].

Highlights of Chapter 30
Federal Gift Tax

I. **Federal Gift Tax is an excise tax** on right to transfer property as gift [¶ 4000].
II. **Gross Amount of Gifts**
   A. **What gifts are taxable [¶ 4002]:**
      1. Includes all gratuitous transfers (direct, indirect or transfer in trust) of property (real or personal, tangible or intangible) during taxpayer's life.
      2. Joint bank accounts:
         a. Generally gift results where person who did not make the deposit makes the withdrawal.
         b. Special rules apply to married persons.
      3. Interest in life insurance:
         a. A gift is made where a policy is purchased naming another as the owner, and making it payable to beneficiary other than purchaser's estate.
         b. Gift is made where insured gives up legal incidents of ownership over policy.
      4. Generation-skipping transfers are taxable upon termination or distribution.
      5. No gift results if:
         a. Husband or wife pays liability on joint income tax return.
         b. One spouse pays gift tax for split gifts to third party.
         c. Heir, next of kin, beneficiary refuse to take inherited property.
   B. **Gifts entirely exempt:**
      1. Gifts made before 6-7-32.
      2. Gifts to exempt religious, charitable, educational, etc., organizations.
      3. Gifts made after 5-7-74 to qualified "Sec. 527" political organizations.
      4. Gifts to U.S. and political subdivisions.
   C. **Gifts by exercise or release of power of appointment [¶ 4003]:**
      1. Tax liability may arise from exercise or release of the power.
      2. Generally, only general power is taxable.
   D. **General power defined [¶ 4004]:**
      1. A power exercisable in favor of possessor, his estate, his creditors, or creditors of his estate.
      2. Post-1942 power exercisable by possessor only in conjunction with another person is a general power unless other person created the power or has substantial adverse interest. Such pre-1942 power is a joint power.
      3. Limited power is one to consume principal with such consumption being limited by possessor's health, education, etc., needs.
   E. **Taxability of powers**—Depends on:
      1. Kind of power.
      2. Date created.
      3. Whether release executed.
      4. Date of release.
      5. Powers created before 10-22-42 [¶ 4004(a)]:
         a. Special pre-10-22-42 powers not taxable.
         b. General pre-10-22-42 powers taxable only if exercised.
         c. Special rules apply to partial releases of general powers.
      6. Powers created after 10-21-42 [¶ 4004(b)]:
         a. Certain special or limited powers are taxed.
         b. General power taxed on exercise.
         c. Release of general power.
            1) Complete release after 5-31-51 is taxed.

2) Partial release after 5-31-51 not taxed at time of release, but a later exercise or release of the modified power may be taxed.
3) A qualified disclaimer is not a release.
7. Lapse of annual power of invasion:
a. Generally no tax results unless amount of authorized invasion exceeds $5,000 or 5% of value of property out of which power may be satisfied, whichever is greater.
b. Where invasion exceeds limit the lapse is treated as a taxable release of power to extent of excess.

F. Gifts of community property [¶ 4005]:
1. Gifts to third persons—Generally each spouse treated as giving gift of one-half of community property.
2. Division of property—Conversion into separate property results in no taxable gift where property divided as to spouses' proportionate interests.
3. Addition of property—Where separate property of spouse converted into community property there is a gift to the other spouse.

G. Gifts made within three years of death [¶ 4006]:
1. Taxable, although property included in deceased donor's estate.
2. Gift tax paid includible in gross estate.

H. Transfer for less than an adequate and full consideration [¶ 4007]:
1. Transaction treated as taxable gift to the extent of the excess in value.
2. Generally entire value of gifts of property transferred constitutes gift if consideration not reducible to money value.
3. Marital rights as consideration:
a. Release of dower or other marital rights is not considered adequate consideration.
b. Divorce settlement: certain conditions must be met before interest treated as adequate consideration.

I. Transfers subject to revocation or change [¶ 4008]:
1. If property transferred subject to donor's reserve power over disposition, gift may be incomplete and not taxable.
2. Retention of certain powers makes gift incomplete.
3. When donor releases power to revoke, gift may become complete and taxable.
4. Income from revocable trust: If paid to beneficiary other than donor, gift of income is deemed made by donor.

J. Gifts by husband or wife to third party [¶ 4009]:
1. Treated as gift of one-half by each.
2. Each spouse taxed on one-half.
3. Treatment doubles annual exclusion and unified credit.
4. Five conditions must be met before gift can be split.
5. Spouse must agree:
a. Consent must be shown on returns.
b. Signified at any time after close of calendar quarter (calendar year if gift made before 1-1-71) except:
1) After 15th day of 2nd month following close of calendar quarter if either files return before that date.
2) After notice of deficiency is mailed to either spouse.
6. Timely revocation of consent may be filed before due date of return.
7. Consent by representative is allowed.
8. Each spouse liable for tax of other.

III. Valuation of Gifts
A. How gifts are valued [¶ 4010]:
1. Value determined at date of gift.
2. Alternative valuation date not used.
3. Value generally is the fair market value.
4. Regulations contain rules for valuing stocks and bonds, business interests, notes, mutual fund shares, property subject to excise tax.

5. Taxpayer can request written valuation method or computations.
B. **Annuity contracts, life insurance and employees' trusts [¶ 4011]:**
   1. Annuities:
      a. Value depends on annuitant's life expectancy.
      b. Tables set out in regulations determine separate valuation for men and women.
   2. Value of life insurance or commercial annuity contract is the fair market value.
   3. Employees' trusts:
      a. Qualified plans: Where there is an option to have annuity or other payment payable to surviving beneficiary, there is a taxable gift to extent of employee's contribution to the plan.
      b. Self-employed retirement plans: Contributions as owner-employee treated the same as employee contributions.
      c. Employee's proportionate contribution to retirement annuity contract purchased by tax-exempt organization is taxable when employee can name beneficiary.
C. **Remainder and reversionary interests**—If these interests are transferred donor's tax liability depends on his life expectancy determined by actuarial tables [¶ 4012].
D. **Tenancy by the entirety [¶ 4013]:**
   If one spouse purchases property to be jointly held with other spouse, or pays a disproportionate amount along with the spouse for its purchase, generally no gift tax liability. However:
   a. If the transaction was made before 1955 a gift is deemed to have been made.
   b. After 1954, spouse making larger contribution may elect to have transaction taxed as gift when he files his gift tax return. If no election made, gift will result when tenancy ends (except by death), and then only if proceeds are not divided in proportion to the consideration furnished.
   c. After 1976, if election in b. is made, each spouse is treated as owning one-half.
E. **Value of unified savings bonds** is their redemption value [¶ 4014].
IV. **Deduction and Unified Credit**
   A. **The individual exclusion [¶ 4020]:**
      1. First $3,000 of gifts to each donee.
      2. Gifts of future interests:
         a. $4,000 exclusion does not apply where donee does not have unqualified right to presently use, possess, or enjoy the property.
         b. Gifts to minors are not gifts of future interests if:
            1) Property and income may be spent for minor's benefit during minority.
            2) Balance if any will pass to him at 21, or if he dies before 21 to his estate or to someone he may appoint under general power.
      3. Where trustee can apportion trust income among beneficiaries, no exclusion allowed since beneficiary's right cannot be determined.
   B. **The unified credit [¶ 4021]:**
      1. Taxpayer gets credit against gift tax due in transitional amounts: 1977—$30,000; 1978—$34,000; 1979—$38,000; 1980—$42,500; 1981 and after—$47,000. This is a lifetime credit and is in addition to $3,000 annual exclusion.
      2. 1943—1976: Specific exemption of $30,000 allowed against total gifts made.
      3. 1936—1942: Specific exemption was $40,000.
      4. 1932—1935: Specific exemption was $50,000.
   C. **Charitable and similar gifts [¶ 4022]:**
      1. Gifts to U.S., states, subdivisions, and certain exempt religious, charitable, etc., organizations may be deducted from gross amount of gifts made during calendar quarter (calendar year for gifts made after 1971).
      2. Gift of charitable remainder made after 7-31-69 can't be deducted unless remainder interest is in:
         a. A farm or personal residence, or
         b. Trust interest in annuity trust, unitrust or pooled income fund, or

c. Real property (after 6-13-76 and before 6-14-77), if for conservation purposes.
3. The only transfers of charitable income interests that can be deducted after 7-31-69 are:
   a. Guaranteed annuities.
   b. Gifts of a fixed percentage distributed yearly of property's fair market value determined annually.
4. Under certain conditions no deduction is allowed for transfers to private foundations.

D. **Marital deduction [¶ 4023]:**
1. After 1976, married donor can deduct 1st $100,000 of gifts to spouse, 2nd $100,000 is taxed in full, and 50% of excess over $200,000 is taxed.
2. Before 1977, married donor deducted one-half of all gifts to spouse.
3. What gifts qualify:
   a. Gift must be made after 4-2-48.
   b. Donor must be U.S. citizen or resident.
   c. Spouses must be married at time of gift.
   d. Only gifts of outright interests qualify
4. Life estates qualifying as outright interest:
   a. For years after 1954: Qualifies as outright interest if spouse entitled to receive income for life, plus power to appoint entire interest (or portion) to herself or her estate.
   b. For years before 1955: Qualifies as outright interest only if donor gave spouse absolute title or if gift was in trust and other conditions were met.
5. When deduction not allowed:
   a. Certain nonincome-producing trust property.
   b. Donor's interest in community property.
   c. Gifts of donor's interest in certain separate property that is considered community property for purposes of the marital deduction.
6. Marital deduction is limited to amount at which the gift is reported on return.

V. **Figuring the Tax**

A. **Gift in prior years and quarter included [¶ 4025]:**
1. Gift tax rates are graduated and tax figured on cumulative basis.
2. In figuring liability for current calendar quarter, gifts made after 6-6-32 must be included.

B. **Figuring the tax**—Involves four basic steps [¶ 4026].
C. **Rates of tax [¶ 4027].**
D. **Examples of computation [¶ 4028].**
E. **Gift tax increases basis of gift [¶ 4029]:**
1. After 1976, increase basis of gift by portion of gift taxes attributable to net appreciation. The increase is limited by gift tax paid.
2. After 9-2-58 and before 1-1-77, increase basis of gift by gift tax paid. Increase not in excess of fair market value of gift.
3. For gifts made before 9-2-58 (and not disposed of by then) increase limited to excess of fair market value of property at time of gift over its basis at that time.
4. Donor must prorate gift tax to gifts made to different persons. In determining total gifts made, deductions and exclusions taken into account, but the lifetime exemption is not.

VI. **Procedure**

A. **Returns [¶ 4030]:**
1. For gifts made after 1970, tax liability computed and returns filed on calendar quarter basis. See "4" for special rule for gifts under $25,000 in a quarter.
2. Return required for gifts of:
   a. Any future interest in property, or
   b. A present interest in excess of $3,000 exclusion per donee, or
   c. A present interest which together with previous gifts of present interests to same donee in the calendar year exceed $3,000.

3. Due date is 15th day of 2nd month after the end of the quarter in which gift made.
4. After 12-31-76, quarterly returns are not required unless: taxable gifts during quarter plus all other gifts during calendar year for which a return has not been filed, are over $25,000.
5. Generally, charitable transfers are reported on return for fourth quarter unless earlier return for noncharitable gift is filed.
6. Generally, return filed with Service Center for District where donor resides or where his principal place of business located.
7. Split gifts—Spouse who makes gift is treated as donor of entire gift to deterime whether return must be filed. Other spouse is treated as donor of half the gift to determine whether he or she must also file.
8. Information required—Appraisal lists and any other valuation data may be asked for by Revenue Service.

B. **Payment of the tax [¶ 4031]:**
1. Payment due in full with quarterly return.
2. Extension of time to pay (up to 6 months) may be granted in hardship cases.
3. Donee can be liable for tax if donor does not pay it; executor or administrator, on timely and proper application, can get personal discharge.

C. **Assessment and deficiences [¶ 4032]:**
1. Generally 3 years from return due date for assessments:
   a. Omission of 25% or more of taxable gifts lets Revenue Service assess within 6 years.
   b. If no return filed, or false or fraudulent return, tax can be assessed at any time.
2. Deficiency—Taxpayer generally has 90 days to petition Tax Court for redetermination.

D. **Refunds [¶ 4033]:**
1. Form 843 is used.
2. Form must be filed within:
   a. 2 years after tax paid, or
   b. 3 years after return filed, whichever is later.
3. Suits for refund filed in District Court or Court of Claims:
   a. Claim must first be filed.
   b. Generally, suit must be brought at least 6 months after filing claim and within 2 years of notice of disallowance.

HOW TAX FUNDAMENTALS ARE APPLIED*

AN INTRODUCTION TO TAX PLANNING
(Detailed Table of Contents below)

AN OVERVIEW OF TAX SHELTERS
(Detailed Table of Contents at page 4601)

TAX CONSIDERATIONS IN ESTATE PLANNING
(Detailed Table of Contents at page 4701)

AN INTRODUCTION TO TAX PLANNING
TABLE OF CONTENTS

¶

TAX PLANNING IN GENERAL

Objectives of tax planning 4501
Guides to tax savings 4502

CHOOSING THE BEST FORM OF DOING BUSINESS

Selection of entity in general 4505
Tax advantages in sole proprietorship 4506
Tax advantages of the partnership form 4507
   Minimizing taxes by the partnership agreement
   Reporting a partner's distributive share
Tax advantages of incorporating the business 4508
Tax advantages of electing Subchapter S tax treatment 4509

TAX PLANNING IN ACCOUNTING METHODS

Accounting methods in general 4510
Using the cash receipts and disbursements method 4511

¶

What are the advantages of the cash method
What are the pitfalls of the cash method
How to handle attributed income
Using the accrual method 4512
What are the advantages of the accrual method
What are the pitfalls of the accrual method
What are other permissible methods of accounting 4513
Using hybrid accounting methods 4514
What are the planning considerations 4515
   Selecting the appropriate method
   Tax planning in inventory
   Using the long-term contract method
   Using installment sales

TAX PLANNING IN ACCOUNTING PERIODS

How to choose the right tax year 4520
What are the choices in selecting an accounting period 4521

---

* Acknowledgment is gratefully given to Allan S. Rosenbaum, Ph.D., CPA and Don L. Ricketts, J.D., LLM, CPA, for the preparation of this Section.

What to consider in adopting a tax year 4522
Selecting a natural business year 4523
   What are advantages of a natural business year
   What are the disadvantages of a natural business year

TAX CONSIDERATIONS IN BUSINESS DECISIONS

Method of financing for a corporation 4530
Tax planning in equipment transactions 4531
   The availability of the investment credit
   The depreciation alternatives
   Leasing or buying equipment
   Buying new or used property
   Selling or trading-in property
Acquiring a new business 4532
   How startup or pre-opening expenses are treated
   How to handle expenses of investigating a new investment

   Buying the corporate assets or the corporate stock

TAX PLANNING IN REALIZATION AND RECOGNITION OF INCOME

What is the character of the income .. 4540
   Exclusions
   Ordinary income versus capital gain
Achieving tax savings by income-splitting 4541
   Tax savings by sharing income with your spouse
   Using gifts to shift income
   Using family partnerships to shift income
   Shifting income through lease arrangements
   What are the pitfalls in shifting income
Tax planning on when income is recognized 4542
   Tax savings through year-end planning
   Tax savings through deferred reporting

TAX PLANNING IN GENERAL

It is of primary importance to carefully interpret and apply the tax laws. Proper planning leads to tax minimization or avoidance, which is acceptable. Tax evasion, which is not acceptable, cannot and should not be tolerated. Many transactions can be arranged or structured to minimize tax burdens. However, the tax planner must always consider possible pitfalls that may exist such as the application of the doctrines or theories relating to substance versus form, "sham" transactions, "step" transactions and anticipatory assignment of income.

This section deals with certain overall objectives of tax planning and some guides that aid in achieving those objectives.

¶ 4501 **Objectives of tax planning.** The objective of tax planning is to minimize the burden of taxation. Tax planning or the minimization of the tax liability is the subject of this section. The condensation of volumes of planning ideas and techniques, as well as the interaction of the tax laws, require the warning that the contents of this section are introductory in nature. They are intended to highlight in general terms certain approaches and alternatives that could lead to minimizing the taxpayer's tax burdens. Expertise in this area may be acquired only by continuous in-depth study and research.

¶ 4502 **Guides to tax savings.** There are certain guideposts that can be used in tax planning. These will assist in achieving the objective of tax planning: tax savings. The road to tax savings has at least 10 main branches. They point the direction tax-saving efforts should take. This section deals with some of these guideposts:

• Keep income stable to avoid top rate brackets.
• Speed up or defer income and expenses to take advantage of anticipated higher or lower tax rates.

- Spread income among several taxpayers.
- Spread income over several years to keep out of higher tax brackets and postpone tax.
- Transform ordinary income into long-term capital gain.
- Take full advantage of all exemptions and deductions.
- Take advantage of elections.
- Use tax-free money to expand business operations.
- Select the best form for your business operations.
- Set up business deals along lines that make overall use of tax rates, earning potential, losses and assets that can be depreciated.

CHOOSING THE BEST FORM OF DOING BUSINESS

The proper selection of the form of doing business is a significant factor in the process to minimize the tax burden. It should be noted that before a decision is made as to what form to give to the business, the comparative tax costs of the different methods of doing business should be considered, as well as the various nontax factors.

For a complete discussion on choosing the best form of doing business, see ¶ 3152 et seq.

¶ **4505 Selection of entity in general.** In the typical case, selecting the type of entity used to conduct a trade or business will depend on both tax and nontax considerations. For example, the corporate form might be selected despite tax reasons if limited liability, continuity and transferability of interests are of major importance. Further, if a large number of investors are to be owners of the business, the corporate form is usually preferred to the partnership form even if use of a limited partnership would result in limiting liability for the limited partners.

¶ **4506 Tax advantages in sole proprietorship.** A sole proprietorship is an unincorporated business conducted by a single individual. The fact that the net profit or loss from the business is figured separately from the owner's income from other sources gives him an important tax advantage. In figuring the net profit or loss, all the business expenses are subtracted. Then when the net profit of nonbusiness income is added, the individual still gets the deductions for contributions, interests, taxes, medical expenses and the like.

¶ **4507 Tax advantages of the partnership form.** For tax purposes, a partnership is an association under which two or more persons join together to carry on a trade or business and share its profits and losses. Unlike a corporation, a partnership is not a taxable entity but rather is a conduit through which tax consequences resulting from its activities flow through to the individual partners. Generally, there are two types of partnerships—a general partnership under which partners are personally liable for partnership debts, and a limited partnership under which the limited partners are liable for partnership debts only to the extent of their capital contributions. See ¶ 2900 et seq.

Since partners reflect their share of various items on their own returns, a partner has no tax advantage over a sole proprietor as to the taxation of current income. However, the partnership form, as compared to the corporate form, does avoid the double tax problem [¶ 4508]. A partnership has some other advantages over the corporation:

- A partner can deduct his share of the partnership losses. This is not the case for a shareholder [¶ 2908(a)].
- Partners pay only one capital gains tax [¶ 2911].

¶ 4507

- A partner can deduct his share of certain deductible items on his return but a shareholder gets no benefit from the deductions except as they are reflected in corporate taxable income and in dividends [¶ 2913].

(a) Minimizing taxes by the partnership agreement. The partner's share of each item is generally fixed by the partnership agreement. The agreement may allocate different items in different proportions. See ¶ 2909.

The agreement includes any change agreed to by all the partners or made under its terms. Changes as to a particular tax year are possible up to the original due date of the partnership return for that year.

≫**OBSERVATION→** It is advisable to try to anticipate the tax problems that may lie ahead when organizing a partnership. The agreement should spell out precisely how various items of the partnership are to be handled.

The following are among the items that should be handled on the partnership agreement:

- How contributed property is to be allocated. See ¶ 2910(a).
- How undivided interests are to be allocated. See ¶ 2910(b).
- How salary and interest payments are to be handled. See ¶ 2923(d).
- How payments to retiring partners are to be handled. See ¶ 2941.

(b) Reporting a partner's distributive share. The partnership must report each partner's share of various items on Form 1065. Items not covered by the partnership agreement are shared in the general profit and loss ratio. See ¶ 2908 regarding special and retroactive allocations of partnership income and loss.

≫**WATCH THIS→** This ratio applies if the principal purpose of the provision covering the item lacks substantial economic effect.

A partner may deduct his share of partnership losses (including capital losses) only up to the extent the partner is "at risk" as to his partnership interest at the end of the partnership year. Generally, a taxpayer is "at risk" to the extent of money or the basis of property which is contributed to the partnership and also for loans for which personal liability is assumed or property is pledged, other than property which secures the loan. See ¶ 2736; 2908.

≫**SUGGESTION→** To the extent that a particular partner's adjusted basis is insufficient to cover losses, a partner who wants a deduction for the loss in the year sustained should pay his distributive share of the partnership loss before the end of the partnership year. This can be done by contributing to the partnership before the close of its tax year sufficient money to cover the partner's distributive share of the partnership's loss.

¶ 4508 Tax advantages of incorporating the business. A corporation, unlike a partnership or proprietorship is generally a separate taxable entity. Thus, federal income tax is imposed at the corporate level and another tax is imposed on the earnings as they are distributed to the stockholders.

≫**OBSERVATION→** This "double tax" is minimized, to some extent, by the dividend exclusion [¶ 1705].

For a discussion of the major characteristics of a corporation, see ¶ 3101(a). For a discussion on comparing tax rates and in determining the tax cost of the corporate form of doing business, see ¶ 3152(b), (c).

Corporations have certain tax advantages over unincorporated businesses. The most important of these advantages relate to splitting income, disposing of business interests and availability of fringe benefits for stockholder-employees. See ¶ 3153.

¶ 4509 Tax advantages of electing Subchapter S tax treatment. Certain closely-held corporations have an additional advantage over incorporated businesses. They can elect special tax treatment. See ¶ 3140 et seq.

In a Subchapter S corporation, the tax consequences generally flow through to the stockholders as if the corporation were a nontaxable conduit.

For a discussion of the advantages in electing Subchapter S tax treatment, see ¶ 3154.

TAX PLANNING IN ACCOUNTING METHODS

The accounting method that is best for the taxpayer depends primarily on the type and size of the business. Generally, the only tax requirement the taxpayer must adhere to is that the method for figuring taxable income must be the same as the one regularly used in keeping the books and clearly reflect income.

¶ 4510 Accounting methods in general. The method selected by the taxpayer must clearly reflect income and be regularly used. If not, the Revenue Service can require the taxpayer to adopt one. See ¶ 2701 et seq.

¶ 4511 Using the cash receipts and disbursements method. The cash receipts and disbursements method of accounting to figure taxable income is generally similar to the accountants' concept of a cash method of accounting. The taxpayer reports income as he gets it and deducts expenses as they are paid. See ¶ 2702.

(a) What are the advantages of the cash method. Although the cash method taxpayer has limited control over when income must be reported, he has nearly complete control over when expenses can be deducted. The taxpayer does not report income until it is received. If he does not want to receive income in a particular year, he can delay billing the customer or client. Once the customer or client is billed, the income must be reported when paid. An expense item does not have to be recorded until actually paid by the taxpayer. A cash method taxpayer can select certain bills to be paid at year-end, deferring the balance to the next year. In addition, at year-end, the taxpayer is often in a position to pay certain bills in advance, thereby bringing more deductions into the current year. See also ¶ 4515(a); 4601.

(b) What are the pitfalls of the cash method. Certain limitations on the strictly cash method should be pointed out. Seldom does the actual cash receipts and disbursements of a particular year truly reflect the income for that year. Often the resulting figure of net income is quite different from that actually earned during the year. Unless it is very carefully watched, the cash method often results in distortions of income from year to year. Sometimes income is taxed at a much higher rate than it should be since it is received in a good year in which it was not earned and added to the normal income of that year.

(c) How to handle attributed income. One of the most effective ways of averaging income is to defer the necessity of reporting until it suits the taxpayer's tax convenience. It would be a comparatively simple task for cash basis taxpayers who would report income as received if it weren't for the constructive receipt doctrine

[¶ 2703]. Two tests must be satisfied to bring the doctrine into play: (1) Income must be credited to taxpayer's account or set apart for him; and (2) Income must be free of limitation or restriction.

In order for the "credited or set apart" tests to be satisfied a definite determinable amount must be involved and earmarked as belonging to the taxpayer. Normally, amounts set apart for the taxpayer, but placed in escrow for some legitimate reason, will not be income to the taxpayer until the funds are released.

One of the main points of contention in the area of constructive receipt involves compensation. Two areas of controversy involve stockholders and deferred compensation plans.

≫OBSERVATION→ If the employer and employee are "related," then transactions between such related taxpayers should be drawn and executed with the utmost care. A deferred compensation plan will probably be successful if it is (1) negotiated in a bona fide manner at arm's length and (2) set and executed before the employee becomes entitled to any of the compensation subject to the plan.

¶ 4512 **Using the accrual method.** Income is included in the tax year when all events have occurred that fix the right to receive it and deductions are allowable for the tax year in which all the events have occurred that establish the fact of the liability giving rise to the deduction [¶ 2706].

The amounts taken into account must be reasonably accurate for both income recognition and allowable deductions.

≫OBSERVATION→ Generally, the accrual method is distinguishable from the cash method. Under the accrual method, for purposes of recognition, the emphasis is on the occurring of an all-events test that either fixes the right to receive the income or establishes the fact of the liability giving rise to the deduction. Under the cash method, the emphasis is on actual or constructive receipt as to income recognition and the actual payment for expenditures.

(a) What are the advantages of the accrual method. The accrual method should be used if the taxpayer's business is made up of many and complex transactions during the year. This method will reflect income more accurately than the cash method. Also, to a large extent, the taxpayer's income and expenses will be "matched" for each year. This is especially true if the taxpayer is using a "natural business year" [¶ 4523]. The following are some items that ought to be considered:

▶**Controlling income.** Amounts due for services are taken into income when billed. Sales are taken into income when shipped. If the taxpayer uses the accrual method, he can control which year the item will be taxed by fixing the date of the billing or shipping.

▶**Work in process account.** Many accrual method taxpayers report as income not only the amount actually billed, but the value of all unbilled work at the end of the year. To effectuate this method of reporting income, the taxpayer sets up an inventory or work in process account. A business that fixes its charges principally on a time basis will find that the use of a work in process account eliminates a great amount of distortion. If approximately the same time is spent each year, at approximately the same rates, each year's total income will be approximately identical. Dates of billing and collection will not enter into how net income is determined for the year.

≫WATCH THIS→ A shift to this method should not be made when there is a large amount of unbilled charges on the books at the start of the year. A new enterprise could well adopt the accrual method, with a work in process account, as a means of equalizing income from year to year.

▶**Effect of business recessions.** During business downturns, collections are slow. Many good accounts go bad. The cash method taxpayer finds that during this period his income is much lower than before. When the business upturn occurs, the taxpayer may find his current work being paid for promptly and that he is collecting bills sent out in prior years. As a result, there is a severe distortion of income. During the bad years, his income has been low and his tax small. After the business upturn, his income becomes abnormally high and what the taxpayer earned during the recession years is now being taxed in the highest brackets. The accrual method taxpayer can minimize fluctuations of this type by a careful handling of bad debts [¶ 2311; 2744].

(b) What are the pitfalls of the accrual method. The taxpayer must report income that has not been received in cash. As a result, the percentage of cash receipts that must be set aside for income tax may be greater than the tax rate. Also, there is no control of expenses through making or withholding payment. The only control of expenses is through controlling the dates that they are actually incurred.

≫**OBSERVATION**→ The taxpayer can control his year-end shipping and buying to achieve the desired income level.

¶ 4513 What are other permissible methods of accounting. Certain other methods are specifically permitted that can be separated into two categories: (1) special methods of accounting for income and expenses in general (for example, the installment method [¶ 2801 et seq.], long-term contract method [¶ 2842], and the crop method [¶ 2614]) and (2) special methods of accounting for particular items of income and expense (for example, research and experimental expenditures [¶ 1842], soil and water conservation expenditures [¶ 1845], and expenditures by farmers for fertilizer, etc. [¶ 1844]).

¶ 4514 Using hybrid accounting methods. Any combination of accounting methods provided for by law is permitted so long as the combination clearly reflects income and is consistently used. When a taxpayer accounts for sales and purchases on an accrual method, the cash method may be used for all other items of income and expense. However, if a taxpayer accounts for gross income from his trade or business using a cash method, the same method must be used in computing the expenses of the trade or business.

≫**WATCH THIS**→ If the taxpayer uses a non-approved method, the Revenue Service may insist that the taxpayer change to an accepted method or it may ignore the incorrect handling of the accounts and perhaps require a change when it will result in increased taxes.

¶ 4515 What are the planning considerations. The previous discussion has touched on, in a general way, certain planning aspects as well as some of the advantages found in the cash and accrual methods. This paragraph deals with further planning considerations: selecting the appropriate method; inventory; long-term contracts; and installment sales.

(a) Selecting the appropriate method. Selecting an overall method of accounting is an extremely important decision for a taxpayer when, because of the character of either his trade or business or investment activities, the option to select either the cash or accrual method is available to him.

The cash method may result in bunching deductible expenses in the earlier years of a newly formed business or investment and in postponing the recognition of gross income until years subsequent to the initial years. See also ¶ 4511; 4532.

¶ **4515**

To the extent that a taxpayer can legally plan postponing his tax liability, these funds are available for plowback into his trade or business or for use in other investment activities.

>>OBSERVATION→ It must be kept in mind, that generally the taxes are only deferred and will eventually become due.

A taxpayer starting a new trade or business may, in the initial years, suffer from a cash shortage. It may be advantageous, therefore, to adopt an accounting method that accelerates or "bunches" the allowable deductions in the initial years. This can reduce the tax liability that might otherwise have been due if the allowable deductions and income were matched, as would generally be the case under the accrual method. Alternatively, if it is anticipated that only marginal amounts of income will be generated in the initial years, perhaps it might be more advantageous to select an accounting method where income and expenses are matched. See ¶ 4512.

>>OBSERVATION→ In selecting an accounting method you should consider many variables, both tax and financial.

The cash method has been most advantageously used in investment activities principally because of the deferral element which results from mismatching. This use of the cash method in investment activities and the advantages derived will be further illustrated in the discussion of various tax shelters [¶ 4601 et seq.].

(b) Tax planning in inventory. Various options are available when it comes to identifying and valuing inventories. In identifying the goods in the closing inventory, generally, either the first-in, first-out method (FIFO) or the last-in first-out method (LIFO) is available. Other methods also are available and may be used by the taxpayer so long as such method conforms as nearly as possible to the best accounting practice in the trade or business and most clearly reflects income [¶ 2600 et seq.].

The LIFO inventory method, although considerably more complex than other inventory methods, has certain advantages and disadvantages which the taxpayer must consider before electing its use. See ¶ 2606(a).

>>WATCH THIS→ Since ending inventory under the LIFO method involves aggregate costs incurred at earlier dates, the taxpayer should maintain a constant vigil to avoid the possibility of liquidating a part of this inventory. In this case, the taxpayer might be forced to match earlier incurred and lower costs against recently transacted sales that are probably greater than what the sales price might have been in terms of dollars received during the year in which the inventory costs were incurred. If this liquidation occurs, these so-called "paper profits" can result in a serious cash shortage for the taxpayer and just may happen during a period when the taxpayer can least afford the cash outflow.

Alternatively, if a taxpayer is using an inventory method other than LIFO and during an inflationary period decides to adopt the LIFO method, depending upon the dollar-size of his inventory and the inflation rate, the change in the inventory method can produce tax savings of a significant amount.

If a taxpayer elects the LIFO method, such method must also be used for financial reporting purposes. This conformity is not required in adopting an inventory method other than LIFO.

(c) Using the long-term contract method. Work under construction contracts often is not finished in the year work is begun. Profits and losses ordinarily cannot be figured before the jobs are finished. Still the builder must file an annual return. To mitigate the accounting problem, either of two long-term contract methods are allowed: the completed contract method (the reporting of all income and related expenses is deferred until the job is completed); or the percentage of completion method (the income from the job is reported in proportion to the percent of work that is finished) [¶ 2842].

➤➤OBSERVATION➤ With the completed contract method, the taxpayer has the use of tax dollars during the intervening period which under the percentage of completion method would have to be paid. The value of this deferral varies with the cost of money and the time element involved for the particular taxpayer.

What are the advantages of the percentage of completion method. The following are the advantages along with the possible pitfalls involved in the percentage of completion method:

• It reflects income from long-term contracts as it is earned up to each stage of completion, perhaps, more accurately than any other method.

➤➤PITFALL➤ A profit may be shown in one year and a loss in another while the contract is still partially completed. This may distort the profit and loss picture for the interim years and completely vary with the overall net profit or loss on final completion.

• It avoids "bunching" of income all in one year, as under the completed contract method.

➤➤PITFALL➤ The percent of completion cannot always be accurately estimated for any interim period especially where subsurface work is involved.

What are the advantages of the completed contract method. The following are the advantages along with the possible pitfalls involved in the completed contract method:

• It avoids the reporting of profit for interim years as under the percentage of completion method. Profit so reported may prove fictitious in the end; the final result may be a net loss.

➤➤PITFALL➤ Completion of many profitable contracts in one year may mean a higher tax. Completion of many unprofitable contracts in one year may pile up a huge loss that will have no real advantage, even with the net operating loss provisions.

• It generally may be more conservative and accurate than the percentage of completion method.
• It defers the tax to future years. This is worthwhile if a lower tax rate is foreseeable.

➤➤PITFALL➤ Since the tax is deferred to future years, taxpayer risks the possibility of a higher tax rate.

➤➤PITFALL➤ If a corporation or partnership ends its business before the contracts are completed, it still must report the profit earned up to the date business ends.

(d) Using installment sales. The installment method of reporting gross income allows a taxpayer the opportunity to recognize a proportionate part of profits from certain sales during the years when cash or a cash equivalent is received. Therefore, a taxpayer could defer any taxes, otherwise due, until the time the

¶ 4515

means are available to pay the taxes. Without this, a taxpayer would be required to pay taxes in the year in which the sale was made. This relief applies to installment sales by dealers in personal property, certain sales of real property and casual sales of personal property [¶ 2801 et seq.].

➤OBSERVATION➤ As with other planning considerations, the value of this relief provision is with the deferral aspect.

In using the installment method, the taxpayer must strictly adhere to the rules to avoid being disqualified. Also special consideration must be given to the imputed interest rule [¶ 2840].

TAX PLANNING IN ACCOUNTING PERIODS

It is possible, by selecting the first closing period and by its change when desirable later on, to accomplish sizable tax savings. In practically every case, these savings are permanent. It is not like the situation where the taxpayer defers or accelerates income or expenses. In that case, the taxpayer may find, when the next year's return is due no net savings has been accomplished whatever.

¶ 4520 **How to choose the right tax year.** Generally, when you open a business, you have a choice of accounting periods. Last minute or a haphazard consideration could mean forfeiting the right choice. You may wind up with a tax year not only ill-suited to your business needs, but one that may cost you more taxes as well. It is true that you can later change your method (and often it will pay to do so), but it is not always easy to accomplish. To begin with, you may need the consent of the Revenue Service, proving to them that you have a valid business reason.

¶ 4521 **What are the choices in selecting an accounting period.** The taxpayer has three choices: (1) calendar year; (2) fiscal year; or (3) 52-53 week fiscal year. Most income tax returns cover an accounting period of 12 months. On two occasions, however, a taxpayer's accounting period is less than 12 months: (1) when a first or final return is filed; or (2) when the accounting period is changed [¶ 2714; 2717].

Special rules apply to partnerships in their choice of accounting periods. See ¶ 2921.

¶ 4522 **What to consider in adopting a tax year.** Before a taxpayer selects an accounting period, the following should be considered:
- Advantages of the "natural business year" [¶ 4523].
- Advantages of dividing the business into 13 months (52-53 week year) [¶ 2714(b)].
- If the business has peak income in some months and heavy expenses in others, the first tax year should embrace the peak periods of income and deductions.
- If income and deductions are pretty evenly matched already, consider ending the first tax year just before more anticipated profits. In the meantime, deferred tax money can be put to work in the business.

➤WATCH THIS➤ The taxpayer should be careful that the deferred income does not put him into a higher tax bracket in the next year.

- Always consider the effect of the choice on future tax years not just the first tax year.

¶ 4523 **Selecting a natural business year.** A "natural business year" is a 12-month period that ends when business activities are at their lowest point.

(a) What are the advantages of a natural business year. The following are the main advantages in using a natural business year:
- Taxpayer's financial statements will be more accurate. Estimates of valuation will apply to the smallest amounts of inventory and receivables taxpayer has during the year.
- Taxpayer is in a better position to "match" his income with related costs and expenses of producing it. This will enable him to present a truer picture of his real net income for the year.
- Inventory can be more easily taken.

(b) What are the disadvantages of a natural business year. The following are some of the disadvantages in adopting a natural business year:
- Taxpayer's first period after the change will leave him without any figures for comparative study.
- When other members of an industry are using a different period, it is hard to compare taxpayer's results against theirs.
- Vacation policies may have to be changed—especially if taxpayer's year ends in the summer and he needs help in taking inventory.

TAX CONSIDERATIONS IN BUSINESS DECISIONS

As discussed earlier, tax considerations are important factors in making the basic decision on selecting the most appropriate form of business entity. See ¶ 4505 et seq. This section covers some additional business decisions when tax considerations may influence a choice between alternative courses of action.

¶ 4530 **Method of financing for a corporation.** When a corporation needs additional financing for a relatively long period of time, the alternatives generally consist of either selling new equity issues (preferred or common stock) or borrowing funds under long-term loans. The principal tax consideration as to this type of business decision relates to the basic difference in deductibility treatment between interest paid and dividend distributions by the corporation [¶ 1905; 3127]. Thus, total tax may be reduced by selecting the debt approach rather than the equity approach. In addition, the sales commissions and other marketing expenses for a new stock issue would generally be considered an offset to the amount realized from issuing the stock with the result that there would be no deduction for these expenses. On the other hand, expenses of selling a debt obligation would be amortizable over the term of the loan as a deductible expense [¶ 3116].

For a closely-held corporation when the stockholders are also holders of the corporate debt, the principal pitfall for disallowing the interest is that the corporation is "thinly" capitalized and, therefore, the debt is in effect treated as another class of stock issued by the corporation. Another concern is that the terms of the debt obligation may be so lacking in substance as true debt that it may be characterized as stock for tax purposes, that is, the obligation described as a debt does not bear a fixed interest rate or has no definite principal repayment provision [¶ 1901].

¶ 4531 **Tax planning in equipment transactions.** In many cases, the business owner or manager must choose between alternatives when considering to acquire additional or replacement equipment. Some of the factors to be considered are:

¶ 4531

- The availability of the investment credit.
- The depreciation alternatives.
- The leasing or buying of equipment.
- The buying of new or used property.
- The selling or trading-in of property.

(a) **The availability of the investment credit.** The taxpayer can use tax money to finance the cost of buying machinery and equipment, if it qualifies for the investment credit [¶ 2410].

≫OBSERVATION→ A greater investment credit on a costlier and more fully automated piece of equipment may result in a more favorable and shorter payback period in comparison to a less expensive piece of equipment assuming the payback period is otherwise equal.

(b) **The depreciation alternatives.** Because of the options as to depreciation methods available to taxpayers, considerable planning is possible and should be undertaken by the taxpayer. The use of accelerated methods will result in an earlier and faster recovery of the cost outlay. However, the taxpayer may want to attempt to forecast cash flow over a period of years and then select a method that will aid in planning for the cash needs of the business. If the cash needs are greater in the earlier years, then accelerated methods will be advantageous. If the cash needs are not that severe in the earlier years, perhaps the straight line method will be sufficient. If the important variable is quick cost recovery, then only the accelerated methods can satisfy this objective. See ¶ 2010 et seq.

(c) **Leasing or buying equipment.** Tax considerations will often play an important part in choosing between buying or leasing new equipment. The basic consideration is that rental payments are generally deductible as paid or incurred [¶ 1826(e)]. The cost of purchased equipment must be capitalized and depreciated over its estimated useful life [¶ 1808; 2000 et seq.]. In comparing the alternative approaches, the factors to be considered include:

- The available depreciation methods.
- The property's useful life and contemplated lease term.
- The overall lease cost and the purchase price.
- Salvage value.
- The availablity of the investment credit for purchased property or the credit passthrough from the lessor [¶ 2410(f)].

≫OBSERVATION→ As when selecting between alternative purchases, there is no generalized preference standard. In a given case, only by actually calculating and evaluating all the facts will the best alternative be indicated on whether to buy or lease.

≫WATCH THIS→ One of the pitfalls in this area involves the situation where the Revenue Service would characterize a lease as a purchase [¶ 1826(e)]. Thus, even if the lease approach appeared to be preferred in a given case, these characterization rules could eliminate any tax advantages under a lease since it would be treated as a purchase in substance.

(d) **Buying new or used property.** In choosing between buying new or used equipment, the best approach might be dictated by tax considerations in a given case. A factor to be considered is what depreciation methods are available. Used equipment does not qualify for all the maximum accelerated methods [¶ 2012(a); 2013]. Another factor is the ceiling on used equipment as qualified investment for investment credit purposes [¶ 2410(a)].

(e) Selling or trading-in property. When a decision concerns disposing of used equipment, tax considerations may play an important part in choosing between selling the old equipment or trading it in on new equipment. Among the tax factors to be considered are:

- The depreciation recapture rules [¶ 1619].
- The investment credit recapture rules [¶ 2410(e)].
- The treatment of like kind exchanges [¶ 1406; 1517].
- The availability of Sec. 1231 gains or losses [¶ 1618].
- The lower cost basis on which the investment credit applies in a trade-in [¶ 2410(a)].

¶ 4532 Acquiring a new business. When acquiring a new business is being considered, many tax considerations come into play. Among these are the following basic factors:

- Treating start-up or pre-opening expenses.
- Handling expenses of investigating a new investment.
- Buying the corporate assets or the corporate stock.

≫**OBSERVATION**→ The above considerations by no means exhaust all the possibilities. No attempt is made to cover the complex corporate reorganization area [¶ 3300 et seq.].

(a) How start-up or pre-opening expenses are treated. Generally, expenses incurred before starting a trade or business must be capitalized [¶ 1808]. These expenses would be amortizable only if estimated useful life could be determined [¶ 2001]. Otherwise, the capitalized expenses could be written off only when the business was terminated.

Tax planning in this area might involve choices as between actually starting or postponing business on a particular date and carefully documenting the date on which business was started. In addition, the tax factors might have a bearing on the initial personnel policies of the new business.

(b) How to handle expenses of investigating a new investment. Generally, the "searching" expenses, such as traveling expenses, are not currently deductible [¶ 1829(a)]. After an investment is made, the expenses thereafter incurred by an investor to protect the investment are generally deductible [¶ 1806]. The so-called "investigation expenses" would be recoverable only when the investment was sold, disposed of or abandoned [¶ 2210].

(c) Buying the corporate assets or the corporate stock. The alternative of either buying the corporate assets or the stock of the corporation which owns the assets is significant for the seller as to the recognized gain or loss.

For the buyer, the best choice will generally depend on a number of factors, including the overall value of the business and the tax basis and nature of the assets used in the business. If there are significant amounts of low basis depreciable assets, the buyer would have an incentive to buy assets rather than stock to achieve a higher basis for depreciation purposes. In addition, the buyer generally has a disincentive to assign a large part of the price to goodwill since it would not generally be amortizable as an intangible asset with an ascertainable useful life. On the other hand, the seller would benefit from capital gains treatment from a sale of stock or assignment of a greater amount of an aggregate price for assets to goodwill and other capital assets rather than depreciable property subject to recapture or a covenant not to compete [¶ 1524; 1601; 4540(b)]. When the seller will only sell the stock, the buyer could first create a new corporation which would then buy the old corporation's stock. The old corporation would then be the subsidiary of the new

¶ 4532

corporation. If the subsidiary is liquidated into the parent corporation within two years of the purchase, the assets received in the liquidation would then get a stepped-up basis equal to the price paid for the subsidiary's stock. Allocating basis to particular assets would be made as to relative fair market values [¶ 3334]. Part of this amount could nevertheless be assigned to goodwill but, in the appropriate circumstances, a step-up in basis for depreciable property could be available. However, in this type of liquidation, there would be potential recapture problems as well as the loss of attributes of the liquidated subsidiary (including eliminating the operating loss, unused investment tax credit, and capital loss carryovers) [¶ 3336; 3337].

The same step-up in basis result could be obtained if the buyer purchases the corporation's stock and then later adopts a plan of liquidation that qualifies as a one-month liquidation. However, part of the liquidation distributions could be treated as dividend income [¶ 3335].

>>**OBSERVATION**> The buyer must evaluate the alternative approaches on the basis of the facts and circumstances of the case to choose the best approach.

>>**WATCH THIS**> The student should be aware that tax planning may include not entering into transactions because of adverse tax consequences. As an illustration, the temporary investment of corporate funds may have a tax impact, for example, the passive income generated might tip the corporation into personal holding company status [¶ 3400] or result in revocation of Subchapter S status [¶ 3141(a)].

TAX PLANNING IN REALIZATION AND RECOGNITION OF INCOME

The principal tax planning considerations involving the recognition of income relate to: (1) the character of income, particularly if it is ordinary income or long-term capital gain eligible for special treatment; (2) the taxpayer who realizes the income or gain; and (3) the tax year in which the income or gain must be reported.

¶ **4540   What is the character of the income.**   A threshold issue is whether an item qualifies as an exclusion. Once it is found that it must be included in income, then the nature of that income must be determined (ordinary or capital gain).

(a)   **Exclusions.**   In many cases, tax planning by an individual is either not available or of limited practical use in qualifying for a particular exclusion. Included within this category would be exclusions for life insurance proceeds [¶ 1213], employee death benefits [¶ 1218], bequests and gifts [¶ 1225], scholarships [¶ 1303], damages for personal injuries [¶ 1226] and certain reimbursed living expenses [¶ 2204(c)]. Here, the tax consequences are usually outside taxpayer's control. This means that the results are generally determined by a standard contract issued by an insurer providing the payments, or a court judgment indicating the type of injury for which damages are awarded.

What can be done.   Some effective tax planning techniques could apply to certain transactions. This might result in items either being excluded entirely from taxable income or their being postponed. Some of these are:

• Selecting an installment option in a life insurance policy in which a beneficiary-spouse could exclude up to $1,000 interest annually [¶ 1213(c)].

>>**OBSERVATION**>   Here is where a limited amount of "after-the-fact" tax planning might be available.

- Earning less income while qualifying for excludable disability or social security payments.

≫**OBSERVATION**➤ Here it might be appropriate to see if the taxpayer would be better off to earn less income to maximize the excludable payments. Naturally, this would arise only in certain cases usually involving elderly taxpayers.

- Investing in tax-exempts.

≫**OBSERVATION**➤ This is the principal exclusion for which there is an opportunity for effective tax planning. Generally, the consideration to invest in these would depend on their yield and the taxpayer's marginal tax rate. For example, a taxpayer in a 60% bracket would be better off economically by investing in a sound tax-exempt obligation if its yield exceeds 40% of the yield offered under a sound taxable obligation.

- Adopting a qualified retirement plan.

≫**OBSERVATION**➤ The deductibility of contributions and the tax-exempt status of the plans can provide tax saving benefits the same way as a limited exclusion until the taxpayer or his beneficiaries actually receive distributions.

- Replacing a residence sold at a gain or property involuntarily converted [¶ 1410; 1416].

≫**OBSERVATION**➤ This deferral can operate almost as a complete or partial exclusion. In addition, the limited exclusion for gain when a taxpayer 65 or over sells his residence can be an important consideration in timing the sale to qualify for the exclusion [¶ 1423].

- Marital settlements.

≫**OBSERVATION**➤ The tax consequences will generally depend on the divorce decree. The decree will have a bearing on the amount of child support and who can claim the dependency exemptions [¶ 1116(a); 1320]. Also, certain tax consequences can depend on the amount of appreciated property transferred in a property settlement [¶ 1505].

(b) Ordinary income versus capital gain. An important question on which the tax impact depends is whether the gain or loss is an ordinary or capital gain or loss. Generally, tax savings are found if a gain is treated as a long-term capital gain eligible for special treatment [¶ 1601 et seq.]. On the other hand, greater tax savings usually are available if losses are treated as being unlimited to offset against ordinary income rather than capital losses to offset capital gains or otherwise limited to $2,000 for 1977 and $3,000 for 1978 and thereafter for a year when in excess of other capital gains [¶ 1613].

The tax savings as to long-term capital gains will also depend on the holding period [¶ 1605 et seq.].

≫**OBSERVATION**➤ The timing of a disposition may be an important aspect of tax planning. For stocks and securities, the timing of replacement investments could be important in avoiding the "wash sale" rule [¶ 2221].

Some factors determining capital gain eligibility. The kind of property in a transaction will determine if it is eligible for long-term capital gain treatment.

¶ 4540

However, this eligibility often depends on the way a transaction is carried out. Some transactions or factors determining eligibility are:

• Transferring ordinary income property to a corporation controlled by the transferor who later sells the stock [¶ 1405].

➤**OBSERVATION**➤ This approach should be used with caution since the tax-free nature of the corporation's organization could be denied on step transaction grounds since the sale was contemplated when the corporation was organized. If this results, the taxpayer may be subject to the recapture rules [¶ 1619; 2410(e)].

• Contract terms.

➤**OBSERVATION**➤ There are significant tax planning considerations for both the buyer and seller for assigning part of a purchase price to a covenant not to compete. A covenant not to compete is not considered a capital asset so the seller would not get capital gain for it. However, the buyer has a tax incentive to assign as much of the price to it since it could be amortized over its term. On the other hand, there would be no deduction for goodwill until the business was disposed of later [¶ 1524; 1601]. Also, assigning the price to capital assets (land and buildings) and ordinary income property (inventory and accounts receivable) will determine current tax consequences to the seller and future ones to the buyer. In addition, contract terms are crucial as to the character of income in a patent sale [¶ 1601(j)], or either in selling mineral rights or receiving royalties for their extraction [¶ 1623; 2101].

• Depreciation allowed before property is sold [¶ 1619].

➤**OBSERVATION**➤ Tax planning in selecting the depreciation method for real property necessarily involves considering when the property will be disposed of. However, there may still be an overall savings from using an accelerated method even if recapture occurs because of the time value of money.

• Who is to receive the property.

➤**OBSERVATION**➤ Proper tax planning often dictates that the buyer's relationship to the seller be examined. Depreciable property sold to a related person will generally produce ordinary income [¶ 1625].

• If property is subdivided or is entirely sold [¶ 1631].

Some alternative considerations to capital gain treatment. Although income may not be eligible for capital gain treatment, considerable savings may be achieved if the ordinary income is treated as earned income for maximum tax purposes [¶ 2402]. Another consideration in distributions from qualified retirement plans is to be sure that lump-sum payments are made within one tax year of the taxpayer so it qualifies for the special averaging rules [¶ 3024(d)]. In addition, the taxpayer may have a choice between receiving periodic payments taxable as an annuity and lump-sum distributions eligible for the special averaging. Here, selecting the best option for tax purposes will depend on factors such as the magnitude of the taxpayer's other income and the state of his health.

¶ **4541 Achieving tax savings by income-splitting.** You have a right to split your income with almost anyone at all. As a practical matter, you will probably want to spread it among members of your immediate family. For one thing, to transfer income you must transfer ownership and control of the property that produces it. Naturally, you are likely to prefer that a relative rather than an outsider have control. In addition, the benefits of income-splitting are basically family benefits. You increase family income by reducing family taxes. You may reduce the eventual tax when your estate passes to your family. See ¶ 4701 et seq.

▶▶OBSERVATION▶ Consider carefully the pitfalls of income-splitting particularly the assignment of income rules. See (e) below.

The tax savings from income-splitting usually results from applying the lower marginal rates under the progressive rate schedule. This is the case since two or more family members report only part of the total income that would be subject to higher marginal rates if reported by one of them.

(a) **Tax savings by sharing income with your spouse.** On a joint return, you get the benefits of splitting your income with your spouse, even if all the income is actually yours. Therefore, you would usually gain no tax advantage by switching actual income to your spouse. One exception to this is the dividend exclusion. Only a person who actually receives dividends is entitled to an exclusion. If your spouse owns no stock, the maximum exclusion on a joint return will be $100, even if your dividend is much greater [¶ 1705(a)].

(b) **Using gifts to shift income.** One of the most frequently used means of shifting income to family members is to give them income-producing property. Future income from the property will be taxable to them at their rates.

▶▶OBSERVATION▶ Consider the unified estate and gift tax when giving property to family members [¶ 3935; 4001 et seq.]. See also ¶ 4703.

(c) **Using family partnerships to shift income.** Income-splitting can be achieved by shifting income through a family partnership arrangement. Your children can be made partners in your business even if they are minors who are not able to take part in the actual management of the business. They can be made partners by merely giving them a capital interest in the business. The transfer can also be made by selling them an interest on credit and have them pay for this out of their partnership income. Using a family partnership is subject to special rules. See ¶ 2904; 2905.

(d) **Shifting income through lease arrangements.** A taxpayer can shift income from one family member to another through the use of a lease arrangement and the payment of rent. As long as the rental terms are consistent with an arm's-length transaction, a lease of property from one family member to another is perfectly valid.

(e) **What are the pitfalls in shifting income.** In shifting income among family members or to low-bracket taxpayers, the following should be carefully considered:
- The grantor trust rules [¶ 3022].
- The special family partnership rules [¶ 2904; 2905].
- The effect of estate and gift taxes [¶ 3900 et seq.; 4000 et seq.].
- The constructive receipt rules [¶ 2703].
- The reasonableness of compensation rules [¶ 1816].
- The assignment of income rules [¶ 2704].

¶ 4542 **Tax planning on when income is recognized.** An initial consideration in tax planning as it relates to the tax year in which income is recognized involves the accounting method used by the taxpayer. This subject has been covered at length in ¶ 4510 et seq. Some other tax planning considerations are covered here as they relate to recognition.

Generally, the cash method will result in recognizing income when cash is in hand with which to pay income taxes. An exception to this would arise when property received is treated as the equivalent of cash.

Although tax deferral opportunities are usually greater with the cash method, this method can cause the bunching of income. The bunching-of-income problem can be reduced somewhat by income averaging [¶ 2401].

(a) Tax savings through year-end planning. In many cases, tax planning as to the timing of gain recognition involves completing or postponing year-end transactions. Factors that would encourage completing transactions before the end of a tax year include loss taking on stocks to offset gains realized during the year or to generate income to use a net operating loss carryover. Factors encouraging postponing transactions until the following tax year include tax deferral opportunities for gains or to offset a gain against an anticipated loss from another transaction to be completed in the next tax year.

(b) Tax savings through deferred reporting. An important consideration in an installment sale is whether it will qualify for the installment method [¶ 2800; 2811]. Here, it might be advantageous to limit the amount to be received in the tax year of sale to ensure qualifying.

A second approach for deferred reporting is by the so-called deferred payment sale. The seller is entitled to receive proceeds tax-free until the basis has been recovered. Excess receipts are then taxable as received [¶ 2816].

≫PITFALL→ The buyer's promise to pay must not be the equivalent of cash, such as a negotiable note or other note secured by the property. Thus, deferred payment reporting will be available only when future payments are due under the bare promise to pay by the buyer. In many cases, this type of transaction is risky and therefore not acceptable for nontax reasons.

AN OVERVIEW OF TAX SHELTERS

TABLE OF CONTENTS

TAX SHELTERS IN GENERAL

What are tax shelters 4601
What are the elements of tax shelters 4602
   What is deferral
   What is leverage
   Converting ordinary income into capital gains
What form of business to use 4603
   Using the partnership
   Choosing other forms of business

COMMON SHELTERING ACTIVITIES

Investing in real estate 4605
   Advantages of real estate investment in general
   What are the benefits available
Investing in farm operations 4606
   What are the special tax rules
   Areas of farm tax shelters
Investing in oil and gas drilling shelters 4607
Investing in movie shelters 4608
   Film purchase tax shelter
   Film production tax shelter

TAX SHELTERS IN GENERAL

Minimizing taxes is clearly an objective of most taxpayers. For some, this objective is more easily achievable. Generally, these are the taxpayers with sufficient capital saved, a current income stream that places them in at least a 50% marginal income tax bracket and who invest in various activities that produce artificial losses. However, in many cases the artificial losses result in real losses particularly when the investment's economic viability is subordinated to the tax benefits derived.

¶ 4601 **What are tax shelters.** Generally, tax shelters are investments through which artificial or noneconomic tax losses flow to individuals while the investment might also yield a positive cash flow. These artificial losses are then claimed by the investors as deductions against their other income, usually salaries, professional income or income from a trade or business and from investment activities. The use of this kind of a deduction to offset other income is referred to as "sheltering" other income. The investment generating the loss is known as a tax shelter.

   Artificial losses. Generally, the artificial losses produced by tax shelters arise principally from the following factors:
- Using cash receipts and disbursements method of accounting.
- Accelerated depreciation.
- Electing a fast writeoff of a capital asset or an immediate expense of an otherwise capitalized expenditure.

     ≫OBSERVATION→ Most tax shelters rely on a mismatching of income and expense, deferring or postponing recognition of the income and accelerating or bunching recognition of the expenses.

   ¶ 4602 **What are the elements of tax shelters.** There are several elements that make up a tax shelter investment (not all shelters contain all these elements):
- Deferral.
- Leverage.
- Conversion of ordinary income to capital gains.

¶ 4602

(a) **What is deferral.** Deferral is accomplished by mismatching income and expenses. Deductions are accelerated to reduce an individual's tax liability in the early years of the transaction instead of matching deductions against the income that is eventually generated from the investment. The results of deferral are: (1) the investment activity produces artificial or non-economic tax losses; (2) these tax losses are used to shelter or reduce the investor's other income; and (3) federal income taxes that would have been owing but for the loss, is postponed or deferred until some future year.

The net effect of deferral is that the taxpayer grants himself an interest-free loan from the federal government during the period of the deferral.

> **Example 1:** If a taxpayer has $100,000 of accelerated deductions and invests the tax savings in 7% tax-exempt bonds (with interest compounded annually) his money will double in less than 11 years. In other words, deferral can be worth as much as total tax forgiveness after a period of time.

Eventually, an investment in a tax shelter may either yield taxable income or the investment may become worthless. In both circumstances, the investor's tax liability may increase in the year or years during which a profit is realized or the investment becomes worthless.

(b) **What is leverage.** Leverage is the use of borrowed funds to make an investment. Generally, an individual will borrow money that will equal or exceed his equity investment. Using borrowed funds has both economic as well as tax benefits. The more that an individual can use borrowed money for an investment the more he can use his own money for other purposes. Also, borrowed funds are treated the same as taxpayer's own funds that he has put up as equity in the investment [¶ 1501].

> **Example 2:** An investment requires $100,000. Baker, a 70% bracket taxpayer, invests $10,000 of his money and borrows the rest for which he is personally liable. In the first year, he has accelerated deductions of $20,000. This reduces his tax liability by $14,000. Here, the deduction in the initial year is greater than his equity and his tax savings is $4,000 more than the amount originally invested.

The use of leverage has increased significance when an investor is not even liable on the borrowed money. This is known as "nonrecourse financing." Nonrecourse loans are related to using a partnership or limited partnership arrangement to make investments. See ¶ 4603(a).

(c) **Converting ordinary income into capital gains.** The process of converting ordinary income into capital gain results principally from the depreciation deduction. In essence, a depreciable asset is recovered by annual depreciation. Depreciation reduces ordinary income and the tax on that ordinary income. When the asset is sold, assuming it is a capital asset, any gain will be taxed at the preferential capital gains rate. However, the conversion benefit has been limited by the recapture rules [¶ 1618; 1619].

¶ **4603 What form of business to use.** Choosing the proper form and method is essential in achieving maximum benefits in a tax shelter investment. Legislation enacted in 1976 has, in many respects, curtailed the options available to taxpayers.

(a) **Using the partnership.** A partner may not deduct partnership losses in excess of the amount which is at risk in the activity at the end of each tax year. A carryover to subsequent tax years for the disallowed loss is provided, subject to the "at risk" limitation in that subsequent tax year. See ¶ 2736 and ¶ 2926 for a discussion of the "at risk" limitation as it applies to certain activities as well as the blanket provisions pertaining to the computation of a partner's adjusted basis. Thus, to the extent that a partnership generates a loss, this loss may be used to shelter other income of the partners.

(b) Choosing other forms of business. The corporate form of doing business does not lend itself to tax shelter investments by individuals since the corporation is a taxpaying entity. Therefore, the tax incidents of its operation remain at the corporate level and do not pass through to its stockholders. The one exception to this treatment is for Subchapter S corporations. Generally, the tax incidents of this business form pass through to its stockholders. However, certain limitations are applied to the Subchapter S corporation which do not exist for the limited partnership. The Subchapter S corporation stockholder is limited in terms of the amounts of losses available [¶ 3143(c)]. There are other limitations that restrict using the Subchapter S corporation as a vehicle through which to make a tax shelter investment: (1) generally, it must not have more than 10 stockholders; however, after the corporation has elected Subchapter S treatment for a period of 5 consecutive tax years, the maximum number of stockholders may increase to not more than 15 stockholders; (2) trusts (other than a "grantor" trust) may not be stockholders; (3) it may not have more than one class of stock; (4) no more than 20% of its gross receipts can come from passive investment (for example, rental income); (5) no provision may be made for special allocation of losses and other items; these items are allocated according to stock ownership [¶ 3141(a); 3142].

Certain tax shelter investments can be organized under an agency relationship. Generally, this is created by a management or service contract in which a promoter or operator serves as an investor's agent. This arrangement has been used most often in cattle tax shelters as well as in oil and gas operations. The main advantage of the agency arrangement is in its flexibility. It can be "custom-tailored" to the investor's needs. One pitfall may be the potential liability to which the investor may be subjected. However, this can be minimized through nonrecourse financing and comprehensive insurance coverage.

COMMON SHELTERING ACTIVITIES

Many object to calling these tax savings plans "tax shelters." A number of these so-called tax shelters represent deliberate tax incentives adopted by Congress to encourage certain types of investment. (Recently, however, the Congress has placed severe restraints on tax shelter activities). Others represent the sophisticated use of speeded-up deductions to vastly increase the ratio of current deductible expenses to actual cash invested. The business situations are as varied as the U.S. economy, covering real estate, farm operations, movie filming financing, oil and gas drilling, equipment leasing and professional sports franchises.

¶ **4605 Investing in real estate.** Generally, a real estate tax shelter is an investment in which a large part of the investor's return comes from realizing tax savings on other income as well as receiving a tax-free cash flow from the investment itself. These shelters take advantage of all the characteristics common to tax shelters: use of limited partnership; cash method of accounting; leverage; converting ordinary income to capital gain; and accelerated depreciation methods.

(a) Advantages of real estate investment in general. A real estate tax shelter investment will not only generate an artificial loss but will also yield a positive cash flow. The mortgage sought is usually of such a magnitude that the equity is at a bare minimum. Thus, leveraging is used quite advantageously. Since the real estate project itself is the security for the mortgage, nonrecourse financing is the result. The partnership "at risk" limitation does not apply to real estate ventures.

If the project appreciates and then is sold, ordinary deductions will have been converted into capital gain, subject to recapture [¶ 1619(b)]. Regardless of this, deferral associated with accelerated depreciation has still been most advantageous because of the time-value of money.

(b) What are the benefits available. During the construction period, a limited amount of interest paid on the construction loan and a limited amount of real estate taxes may be immediately deducted even though there is no income from the property. The amount of the deduction allowed for construction period interest and taxes will vary depending upon the classification of the real property and when construction begins. However, after 1987, a maximum of 10% of the amount of construction period interest and taxes will be allowed as a deduction during the construction period with the remaining 90% being deducted on a straight line basis over the succeeding 9 years after the property is placed in service. For a complete explanation of the provisions dealing with the capitalization and amortization of construction period interest and taxes, see ¶ 2042. Later, after the building is completed, deductions for accelerated depreciation can be taken. The additional first-year allowance for equipment as well as the investment credit may be available to the investors.

¶ 4606 Investing in farm operations. Special tax rules apply to farm operations other than syndicated farm operations and certain corporations and partnerships that can be used to shelter income earned in other economic activities. The major tax advantages are a deferral of tax payments for one or more years, deferral until the taxpayer's taxable income falls to a lower marginal tax bracket, or converting income from ordinary to capital gain. The "at risk" provision has curbed the use of leveraging on a nonrecourse basis [¶ 2736].

(a) What are the special tax rules. The following are some of the special tax rules that help to confer tax benefits on farm operations and on those who engage in farming:

- Use of cash method without inventories [¶ 2614].
- Current deduction for development costs of business assets [¶ 1842; 1844].
- Current deduction of certain land improvement costs [¶ 1845].
- Capital gain treatment on the sale of assets [¶ 1618; 1622].
- Accelerated depreciation [¶ 2000 et seq.].
- Investment credit [¶ 2410].

➤**OBSERVATION**➔ Several rules reduce the deferral and leveraging benefits from farm operations: (1) livestock depreciation recapture [¶ 1619(a)]; (2) holding period rule for noninventory livestock [¶ 1622(a)]; (3) capitalizing citrus and almond grove expenses [¶ 1844(a)]; (4) recapture of land-clearing expenses [¶ 1845(e)]; (5) limitations on deductions related to activities not engaged in for profit [¶ 2225]; (6) at risk provision [¶ 2736]; (7) special farm syndicate rules [¶ 2745]; and (8) accrual accounting rules for certain corporations and partnerships [¶ 2701(d)].

(b) What are the areas of farm tax shelters. Some of the more popular farming tax shelters are in the areas of cattle feeding and breeding, horse breeding, certain tree and field crops, including certain fruits, nuts, vegetables and flowers and shell eggs.

¶ 4607 Investing in oil and gas drilling shelters. The typical situation of investing in oil and gas operations involves most of the features of tax shelters:

- The immediate deduction of intangible drilling and development costs [¶ 2103(c)].
- Leverage subject to the "at risk" provision [¶ 2736].
- Converting ordinary income into capital gains subject to certain recapture rules.

¶ 4608 Investing in movie shelters. Movie shelters rely heavily on deferral and leveraging aspects, although the leveraging aspects have been severely curtailed, see ¶ 2736. Generally, they are classified into two categories: (1) film purchase tax shelter; and (2) film production tax shelter.

(a) Film purchase tax shelter. This category usually uses a limited partnership which buys an already existing film. The film is depreciated by the income forecast method [¶ 2015(c)].

(b) Film production tax shelter. Common to this shelter category is the use of the cash accounting method allowing the partners to deduct the expenses paid on the film's production. Depreciation is not available to the partnership since it does not own the film.

TAX CONSIDERATIONS IN ESTATE PLANNING

TABLE OF CONTENTS

ESTATE PLANNING IN GENERAL

	¶
What are the objectives of estate planning	4701
How objectives are carried out	4702

METHODS OF ESTATE PLANNING

	¶
Incentives for lifetime transfers	4703
Selecting property for gift	
Severance of joint interests in anticipation of death	
Transfers to terminally ill spouse	
Using trusts in estate planning	4704
Using the generation-skipping trust	
Using the charitable remainder trust	
Using the marital deduction in estate planning	4705
Using life insurance in estate planning	4706
Using deferred compensation plans in estate planning	4707
Joint interests	4708
Orphan's exclusion	4709
Stock transfers	4710
How to handle post-mortem planning	4711

ESTATE PLANNING IN GENERAL

The term "estate planning" consists of an arrangement for accumulating, composing and disposing of an individual's property to achieve certain objectives.

¶ 4701 What are the objectives of estate planning. In an estate plan, one of the principal objectives is to carry out the estate owner's desire to provide for his intended beneficiaries after his death. An important aspect of this objective is to maximize the benefits for the beneficiaries through careful analysis and planning to accomplish the estate owner's desires in the most economical way. It is on this aspect, that a given plan's relative success may depend on considering the tax consequences of the alternatives available in achieving the principal objectives of the estate's owner.

¶ 4702 How objectives are carried out. It is often necessary to assemble a team of experts to properly evaluate and structure an estate plan. This depends on the size and composition of an estate as well as the principal objectives of the estate owner. In certain cases, the team of experts would include an accountant, an investment counselor, an insurance underwriter and an attorney. The plan developed for an individual may include a general plan to:

- Change the property's composition or ownership over a period of years.
- Make lifetime transfers on a regular basis.
- Obtain additional life insurance.

»**OBSERVATION**→ A carefully designed estate plan will encompass more than merely preparing a will that provides for disposing of property on the owner's death.

METHODS OF ESTATE PLANNING

This section deals with some of the major considerations to minimize the impact of estate and gift taxes. In general, the facts and circumstances of each case determine if the alternatives are appropriate or available. Specifically, the owner's lifetime needs and obliga-

¶ 4702

tions, the ultimate objectives, and the size and composition of the owner's wealth would have to be considered.

The scope of the material covered is necessarily limited to the simpler forms of estate planning available in the more typical family situation. For example, it does not include coverage of sophisticated techniques involving the so-called net gifts, revocable trusts [¶ 3912; 4008], powers of appointment [¶ 3907; 4003], private annuities or installment sales.

¶ **4703 Incentives for lifetime transfers.** There are several factors encouraging lifetime transfers over those at death:

• An annual $3,000 exclusion for each donee is provided under the gift tax laws [¶ 4020].
• The unified credit can be used against lifetime transfers when the value of property subject to tax may be lower [¶ 3935].
• There will be no gross-up for gift taxes if the transfer is made more than 3 years before the donor's death [¶ 1508; 1515].
• Appreciation occurring after the gift is made will be removed from the donor's transfer tax base unless it is made within 3 years of death or the donor retains strings that cause it to be included in his gross estate [¶ 1515; 4029].

NOTE: There may be income tax advantages for making a gift, e.g., income splitting.

• The unlimited gift tax marital deduction for the first $100,000 in gifts to a spouse may be advantageous [¶ 4023].

NOTE: The donee spouse's estate will be taxed at a much lower rate because he or she owns less property than the donor spouse.

≫OBSERVATION→ It may be desirable to transfer other property so that a closely-held business interest will satisfy the qualification requirements for the special valuation rules [¶ 3919], and the redemption of stock to pay death taxes provisions [¶ 1721].

• The opportunity to treat a gift by a married donor as being made by both the donor and his spouse doubles the amount that can be given tax-free through the unified credit annual exclusion [¶ 4009].

(a) Selecting property for gift. Special consideration must be given to selecting property to be given under a lifetime transfer program. Since property passing by reason of death to a beneficiary, and property transferred by gift generally have a carryover basis from the donor [¶ 1515; 4029], it is often necessary to consider future income tax consequences due to a transfer as well as the estate and gift tax consequences including the gain or loss that will be realized by the donee on a taxable disposition by him.

In a choice between holding property for transfer at death and transferring property during lifetime, the impact of the fresh start adjustment for carryover basis property held on December 31, 1976, must be considered. For highly appreciated property, tax savings may be derived from holding property eligible for the fresh start adjustment for transfer at death since the adjustment will be made upon the owner's death rather than upon the donee's death if a gift is made and the property is held by the donee until his death. For property other than marketable securities when the value has peaked out, this may be extremely important as the holding period formula for apportioning appreciation between pre-1977 years and post-1976 years will include the donee's holding period and result in treating more appreciation as occurring after 1976, and not counted in making the fresh start adjustment to basis [¶ 1507].

>>**OBSERVATION**→ In the case of a choice between property to be sold and property to be given away, the donor may benefit from selling property acquired after 1976 and giving property acquired before 1977 to preserve the right to make the fresh start adjustment in the donee's hands.

In selecting property for a lifetime transfer, the donor must be careful to consider the character of the income that will result from the transfer or from the later disposition by the donee for income taxes.

In addition, the donor must be careful not to select property for a gift if the gift is treated as a disposition triggering the recognition of income [¶ 2831]. Of course, the doctrine of anticipatory assignment of income must be considered in any case where one of the principal objectives is to minimize the donor's income tax liability [¶ 2704]. Assuming that this doctrine would not result in inclusion by donor, consideration of the carryover basis rule for property acquired by gift or inheritance would be diminished if the beneficiary is to be taxed on the income from the property in any event because it will be treated as income in respect of a decedent if retained and transferred at death [¶ 3008].

>>**OBSERVATION**→ In the case of encumbered property, the donor must be aware of the possible application of the part sale-part gift rules under which he would incur an income tax liability in addition to the gift tax. This is particularly a problem in the case where the debt exceeds the basis of the property or in the case of a tax shelter where the losses written off have exceeded the actual basis of the investment.

(b) Severance of joint interests in anticipation of death. In cases where the consideration furnished test for jointly owned property applies [¶ 1509] and would result in including the entire value of the property in the gross estate of an owner who is expected to die within a short time, tax savings could be achieved by transferring the property to a third party. The decedent is considered to have made a transfer of only one-half of the value of the property.[a] The transfer made within 3 years of death would be included in the gross estate only to the extent of one-half the value rather than its full value. Any gift tax paid on the transfer would be taken into account as a credit in computing the estate tax.

(c) Transfers to terminally ill spouse. In the case where a spouse who has relatively little property and is terminally ill, transfer tax savings can be achieved by having the wealthier spouse transfer property (e.g., property not taxed to him because of the gift tax marital deduction) to the ill spouse who will have an estate which is not subject to federal estate tax because of the unified credit [¶ 3935].

¶ 4704 Using trusts in estate planning. The use of inter vivos trusts may be an important vehicle to achieve income tax savings through income splitting. See ¶ 4541. The use of inter vivos or testamentary trusts may also result in estate and gift tax savings [¶ 3002].

(a) Using the generation-skipping trust. If property is passed outright to a decedent's son who later leaves the property to his descendants, the estate tax would be imposed twice. However, if the property is left in trust for the son for his life with the remainder over to his descendants, the estate tax would be imposed only once in this case because the son's life estate would have expired on his death and the remainder over to the son's descendants is not included in the son's estate. The son is not considered to have owned the property passing to his descendants since it passed under the terms of the original transfer.

Footnote ¶ 4703 (a) Estate of A. C. Borner, 25 TC 584 (1955); Estate of D. M. Brockway, 18 TC 488 (1952); and Estate of E. Carvall, 25 TC 654 (1955).

In this case, a generation-skipping tax would be imposed in lieu of the estate tax [¶ 1507; 3912]. However, an exemption of $250,000 is provided for property passing to the grantor's grandchildren [¶ 1507]. An additional exemption of $250,000 would apply if the parents of the son's wife also created a trust for the benefit of the wife during her life with the property then passing to the grandchildren.

>>**OBSERVATION**→ If the son is independently wealthy, the son could be given only a limited power to appoint among lineal descendants without triggering a generation-skipping tax upon his death.

(b) Using the charitable remainder trust. In certain cases, a taxpayer may wish to leave his property to a charity but provide his wife or children with income during their lives. A charitable remainder testamentary trust might be an appropriate vehicle for achieving these objectives and result in estate tax savings. If the trust qualifies, a charitable deduction is allowable for the present value of the remainder interest to the charity [¶ 3927]. In addition, the remainder passing to the charity will not be includible in the life tenant's gross estate.

¶ 4705 Using the marital deduction in estate planning. A deduction for property passing to a surviving spouse is generally allowable up to the greater of 50% of a decedent's adjusted gross estate, or $250,000. A special rule applies for community property [¶ 3929(a)]. Property in which the surviving spouse receives a terminable interest, such as a life estate, does not qualify for the deduction [¶ 3929(b)].

Generally, estate tax savings can be derived from taking maximum advantage of the marital deduction. On the other hand, the overall estate tax burden for the estates of both spouses might be increased by maximum utilization of the marital deduction by the first decedent if the surviving spouse has a substantial estate independent of the property owned by the decedent.

The gift tax marital deduction is unlimited as to the first $100,000 in gifts to a spouse. There is no marital deduction for the second $100,000 in gifts to a spouse and is limited to 50 percent of the value of gifts in excess of $200,000. In the case where the gift tax marital deduction exceeds 50 percent of the gifts, the estate tax marital deduction is reduced by the excess. For small and medium sized estates, up to $475,000 can be passed tax-free to a spouse if the unlimited gift tax marital deduction is used ($100,000 for the gift tax marital deduction, $200,000 for the estate tax marital deduction, and $175,000 in property against which the unified credit can be used). If the unlimited gift tax marital deduction is not used, up to $425,000 can be passed tax-free to a spouse ($250,000 for the estate tax marital deduction and $175,000 in property against which the unified credit can be used).

¶ 4706 Using life insurance in estate planning. For several reasons, insurance coverage is almost always an integral element in a well designed estate plan. An insurance program can be used in the following ways:

- To build an estate.
- Provide cash to ease liquidity problems when the estate contains nonliquid assets (for example, real estate or stock of a closely-held business).
- Enable executors or heirs to satisfy debts, administration expenses and the estate tax liability without disposing of assets at reduced prices that might occur if a liquidation had to be done quickly.
- Provide necessary funds for a buy-sell agreement to dispose of a closely-held business.

NOTE: Insurance proceeds would not be includible in the decedent's gross estate if the incidents of ownership are held by the purchasing partners or stockholders [¶ 3914]. This would also apply if a corporation is the beneficiary and held incidents of ownership. However, the insurance payable to the corporation might be taken into account in determining the value of the stock owned by the decedent.

Insurance is included in a decedent's gross estate if it is paid to his estate or he possessed any of the incidents of ownership on the policy [¶ 3914].

➤**OBSERVATION**➤ An important technique for excluding insurance on an individual's life is to have the contract written so that the beneficiary holds all of the incidents of ownership.

¶ 4707 Using deferred compensation plans in estate planning. Amounts paid under employee retirement plans can be excluded from a decedent's gross estate to the extent due to employer contributions. The Tax Reform Act of 1976 extended the estate tax exclusion to amounts contributed for a self-employed person under a Keogh plan and to amounts contributed under an individual retirement plan. However, the exclusion is available only if lump sum income tax treatment is not chosen or, in the case of an individual retirement account, the benefits are payable to the beneficiary over at least a 3-year period [¶ 3915].

¶ 4708 Joint Interests. The Tax Reform Act of 1976 added a new estate tax fractional interest inclusion rule for property which was jointly owned by spouses with the right of survivorship. This rule applies to joint interests created after December 31, 1976, which were subject to gift tax at the time of creation. In the case of joint interests in real property, the donor spouse must elect to treat the creation of the joint interest as a gift. If the provision applies, one-half of the value of the property is included in the estate of the spouse who dies first. If the fractional interest inclusion rule does not apply, the property is included in the gross estate in proportion to the consideration furnished by each spouse.

➤**OBSERVATION**➤ In a typical case where the working spouse has furnished most of the consideration and is the first to die, tax savings can be achieved under the fractional interest rule. However, if the spouse who did not furnish the consideration is the first to die, a greater estate tax will ordinarily be incurred under the fractional interest rule. [¶ 1509; 3904].

¶ 4709 Orphan's exclusion. The Tax Reform Act of 1976 added a limited deduction for property passing to the minor orphans of the decedent [¶ 3926]. The deduction is available only if the transfer satisfies certain terminable interest rules, e.g., a life estate or other terminable interest will not qualify for the deduction. In appropriate cases, a limited amount of tax savings can be achieved by properly structuring a disposition for the benefit of the decedent's orphaned children.

¶ 4710 Stock transfers. The Tax Reform Act of 1976 contained a provision for the inclusion of stock transferred if the decedent had retained voting rights [¶ 3910]. This provision applies where the decedent had directly retained voting rights or had exercised the voting rights in a fiduciary capacity because he had named himself a trustee of the trust to which the stock transfer was made.

➤**OBSERVATION**➤ To avoid this inclusion rule, the donor of voting stock should be certain that voting rights are not considered to be retained. This might involve having the donor's spouse be the trustee eligible to vote stock transferred to a trust for the benefit of the donor's children.

¶ 4711 How to handle post-mortem planning. Generally, there are a few post-mortem tax planning opportunities available to an executor or a decedent's beneficiary. These would include settlement options for a surviving spouse in a life insurance policy to qualify for annual $1,000 interest exclusion. It would also involve identifying income in respect of a decedent items with a view toward timing the recognition of income by the recipient to avoid income bunching problems to the extent practicable.

Included within this category of planning would be the alternative approaches for raising funds to pay the estate tax. Interest payable to the government for extensions of time to pay the estate tax would qualify as an interest deduction by an estate for income tax purposes but not as an administration expense to figure the taxable estate. On the other hand, interest paid on funds borrowed to pay the estate tax may qualify as an administration expense. Thus, if this approach is taken, the executor may have a choice between deducting the interest for income tax or estate tax purposes. This choice will also arise for other expenditures incurred after the decedent's death if deductible for income tax purposes and also eligible to be treated as an estate administration expense [¶ 3016].

➤**OBSERVATION**➤ The choice of the best alternative generally depends upon the relative marginal estate tax rates compared with the relative marginal income tax rate.

Another planning opportunity may arise when the executor must decide which property must be distributed to particular beneficiaries. This concerns the impact of the carryover basis rule as it affects the income tax consequences to the beneficiaries.

➤**OBSERVATION**➤ Generally, tax savings might be achieved when low basis, highly appreciated property is transferred to a tax-exempt charity to whom a bequest has been made or to a beneficiary in a lower tax bracket. This opportunity would not arise where specific bequests of property are made. Thus, a formula bequest of a portion of the decedent's estate would provide more flexibility for the executor in evaluating the tax savings to be achieved by transferring appreciated property to particular beneficiaries.

The executor and beneficiaries must also consider tax savings available for interests in closely held businesses. The tax benefits for special valuation [¶ 3919], extended payments [¶ 3944], and redemptions of stock to pay death taxes [¶ 1721] must be timely chosen. In the case of the estate tax exclusion for qualified pension, etc., plans, a choice must be made as between favorable income tax treatment for lump sum distributions and the estate tax exclusion. The proper choice will depend upon the relationship between the estate tax potential savings and the income tax savings to the beneficiary. Generally, the election must be made as between periodic payments and a lump sum distribution before the estate tax return is filed.

Using the marital deduction. It is possible to effect tax savings in certain cases by maximizing the marital deduction through actions taken by the beneficiaries after the decedent's death. This is accomplished by having beneficiaries timely execute "disclaimers" so that the amount of property passing to the surviving spouse is increased. In addition, future estate tax savings might be achieved by having the spouse execute a disclaimer [¶ 3929].

➤**OBSERVATION**➤ Typically, this opportunity would arise when the decedent left property to the surviving spouse above the marital deduction limitation. In this case, a disclaimer by the surviving spouse would result in not having the property later pass through the surviving spouse's estate as well as the estate of a succeeding beneficiary. This consideration usually arises when the succeeding beneficiary is the decedent's child and the surviving spouse, and is intended to be the ultimate beneficiary of both.

FEDERAL TAX PROBLEMS
TABLE OF CONTENTS

Assignment	Problems Start at Page
1. Individuals—Returns, Filing Status, Personal Exemptions and Rates	5011
2. Gross Income—Exclusions	5017
3. Gross Income—Inclusions	5023
4. Gain or Loss—Recognition	5032
5. Gain or Loss—Basis	5039
6. Capital Gains and Losses of Individuals	5046
7. Dividends	5058
8. Deductions—Expenses	5065
9. Deductions—Interest, Taxes, Contributions, Medical Expenses	5075
10. Deductions—Depreciation	5083
11. Deductions—Depletion	5089
12. Deductions—Losses	5093
13. Deductions—Bad Debts	5103
14. Alternate Tax Methods—Tax Credits	5108
15. Withholding—Estimated Tax	5113
16. Inventory	5121
17. Accounting	5131
18. Installment and Deferred Payment Sales	5148
19. Partnerships	5153
20. Estates and Trusts	5164
21. Corporations—Normal Tax and Surtax, Income, Deductions	5175
22. Corporations—Capital Gains and Losses, Net Operating Loss, Etc.	5186
23. Corporations—Reorganizations	5197
24. Corporations—Personal Holding Companies, Etc.—Exempt Organizations	5204
25. Returns and Payment of Tax	5209
26. Assessment—Collection—Refunds	5213
27. Foreign Income—Foreign Taxpayers	5217
28. Social Security Taxes	5222
29. Federal Estate Tax	5227
30. Federal Gift Tax	5234

ASSIGNMENT NO. 1

INDIVIDUALS—RETURNS, FILING STATUS, PERSONAL EXEMPTIONS, AND RATES

(*Note: In the following problems, unless otherwise specified, assume that the "tax year" is calendar year 1977, that the taxpayer and his spouse, if any, are resident citizens, under 65 and are not blind, and that the taxpayer is not entitled to any credit against tax other than those shown.*)

Problem 1-1

(a) Harry Heliny, who is a bachelor and became 65 years old on 6-13-77, received $3,600 in salary and rental income from his proprietorship during the year. His net earnings from self-employment income were $395. Must he file a return?

(b) Amy King, who is 20 years old and a student, earned $2,900 during her vacation. Her boss deducted withholding tax from her pay. Should she file a return?

(c) Richard Lee, married and living with his wife Janet, received $4,200 gross income from investments during the year. Janet had dividend and interest income of $450 for the year. They were not dependents of another taxpayer. Must either or both of them file a tax return?

(d) Would your answer to (c) be different if Richard and Janet were living separately?

Problem 1-2

Throughout 1977, Jack Wein and Ann Kowl lived together as husband and wife. Explain briefly whether they can file a joint return for the year in each of the following circumstances:

(a) They made preparations to get married on New Year's Eve by the captain of a cruise. However, due to a storm, the ceremony was not performed until one hour past midnight. Jack and Ann lived in a state where common law marriage is not recognized.

(b) Would your answer to (a) be the same if Jack and Ann lived in a state where common law marriage is recognized?

(c) What would be your answer to (a) if the ceremony took place on December 31, but Ann died of a heart attack that day?

(d) In (c), would it make any difference if Ann had no income of her own but Jack had a large income?

Problem 1-3

Laurette Gemstone became a widow in 1975. She furnishes all the cost of maintaining her home. Would she qualify as a surviving spouse for 1977 if:

(a) Clifford, her dependent grandchild, lives with her?

(b) Clifford, her self-supporting son, lives with her?

(c) Laurette's husband died in 1974 (instead of 1975), and Clifford, her dependent son, lives with her?

(d) Clifford, her dependent son, lives with her but spends his vacation with his aunt during the summer months?

(e) Laurette married W. C. Fielding in December, 1977?

Problem 1-4

Rita Alberto and her sister each contributed half of their mother's support, with Rita claiming the dependency exemption this year through a multiple support agreement. Rita also claims dependency exemptions for her father and brother whom she fully supports. The father, mother and brother live in a farm house rented and maintained by Rita. Rita and her self-supporting sister shared a city apartment. Rita paid ⅔ of the cost of maintaining the apartment until the end of

November. On December 1, Rita married a Singapore diplomat, but she keeps her U.S. citizenship. Can Rita claim head of household status? Explain your answer.

Problem 1-5

(a) In 1977, Roseping who was divorced, had itemized deductions of $2,400. Should he elect to itemize deductions? Explain.

(b) Mew is single in 1977 but plans to get married in 1978. His itemized deductions for taxes and interest total $2,200. In addition, he has pledged a $1,000 contribution to his church payable next year. He expects his and his wife's combined income, interest payments and taxes in 1978 will be about the same as those of his in 1977. He asks you, his tax adviser, to suggest a way he can increase his deductions for maximum tax savings. What do you suggest?

Problem 1-6

Gertrude Renaud's husband left home on April 1, 1976, and never returned. Throughout 1977, she was employed as a dental technician and paid the expenses of an apartment for herself and her unmarried child, age 17, who lived with her during the entire year. Gertrude had itemized deductions of $1,800. On April 15, 1978, she files her 1977 tax return as a married person filing separately. She elected to itemize, and took the excess itemized deductions of $200 ($1,800— $1,600).

(a) What tax advice would you give her as to her 1977 tax return?

(b) Would your advice be different if Gertrude took her child into her home in the spring of 1977?

Problem 1-7

How many personal exemptions are the following taxpayers entitled to claim, assuming the persons involved are U.S. citizens except as indicated? Explain briefly.

(a) Mark Peabody, single, contributes 75% of the support of his father, who lives alone. His father is 82 years old, blind, and has no income of his own.

(b) Arthur Kaye, who is married and earned $5,000, files a joint return with his wife. His wife receives over half her support from her father.

(c) Roy and Cecile are married to each other. Cecile had $40 in interest from a savings account. Roy earned $15,000 during the year and files a separate return.

(d) Ian Howe, 65, files a joint return with his wife, Mary, 56. He supports Mary's widowed mother, 77, who has been a citizen and resident of Turkey all her life.

Problem 1-8

What is the number of personal exemptions in each of the following cases, assuming the persons supported are U.S. residents?

(a) Harry Klein and his wife have 3 children. On December 1, Harry and his wife decided to live apart. He and the oldest child moved to an apartment. The wife and 2 younger children remained in their home. No legal separation proceedings were instituted. Harry continued to be the sole support of his wife and 3 children, who had no independent incomes. Harry files a separate return.

(b) Claude Walker was divorced by his wife, Yvonne, on January 1. They had one child, Barbara, who lived with Yvonne under the terms of the divorce decree which also specified that Claude was entitled to the exemption deduction. Yvonne furnished full support for Barbara for the entire year. Barbara had no income or deductions.

Problem 1-9

State whether or not the taxpayer in each of the following cases is entitled to an exemption for a dependent, assuming the person supported is a U.S. citizen:

(a) Nelson Clemens furnished 51% of the support of his widowed sister. She gets $2,000 a year in social security benefits and earns $700 a year as a baby sitter.

(b) Shelley Ronalds contributes 60% of the support of his mother-in-law, Karen Aprilton. She earns $740 in a part-time job. She and her husband file a joint return to minimize the tax on his income. Can Shelley claim an exemption deduction for his mother-in-law?

(c) Would your answer to (b) be different if Karen and her husband filed separate returns?

(d) What would be your answer to (c) if Karen had earnings of $760?

(e) John Young supports his widowed mother for 5 months of the year at a cost of $4,000. His brother, George, supports her the rest of the year at a cost of $3,900. The mother has no income of her own. Is John, George, or neither one entitled to an exemption for the mother?

(f) Ivan Mikelo furnishes 51% of the actual support of his 24-year-old son, Clifford, an unmarried student at Worcester College. Clifford earns $3,000 during the year as a waiter in a fraternity house.

(g) Frank Cecill supports Tina, age 15, the niece of Frank's wife Bertha. Tina is the daughter of Bertha's deceased brother. She has no income or deductions and lives with her mother. Would Frank be entitled to an exemption for supporting Tina, if he files a joint return?

(h) Assume the same facts as in (g), except that Tina is Frank's cousin. Is Frank entitled to an exemption?

Problem 1-10

(a) Dick, Willie, Charlie and Andrew all help support their sister Lucy who has no income of her own. Dick provides 45% of her support; Willie 31%; Charlie 14% and Andrew 10%. Can any of the brothers claim a dependency exemption for Lucy? Explain.

(b) Would your answer to (a) be different if Dick provides 52% of the support and each of the other 3 brothers provides 16%?

Problem 1-11

During the year Ronald gave $3,000 for the support of his mother Cecile, who lives with him in the home he fully maintains. Cecile subleases her house from which she collects $2,000 in rents, less $1,500 in rental expenses. Ronald, who is single, wants to get an exemption for her. As a tax adviser, can you suggest any way he can do this, assuming his mother wants to maintain control over the property?

Problem 1-12

State whether Ben Howe may take an exemption for each of the following. Assume all live in the U.S. and are not married. Explain briefly.

(a) John Tucker, Ben's 16-year-old nephew. The boy was mentally handicapped and the state paid $1,800 annually for the child's education and training. $600 in trust income, received during the year from a trust set up by the boy's deceased father, was used for John's support. Ben contributed $2,000 during the year for the boy's support. Ben has legally adopted John as his child.

(b) Norma Martin, a neighbor and friend. Two years ago she suffered a stroke and has lived in Ben's house ever since. Norma had no income and was fully supported by Ben. She died in October, 1977.

(c) Cathy, Ben's 20-year-old daughter. She lives with Ben's ex-wife. During the tax year Ben contributed $600 for Cathy's support, while her mother contributed $2,500. Cathy has no income and does not receive support from any other source. Under a written separation agreement, Ben is entitled to a dependency exemption for Cathy.

Problem 1-13

Mary Jane's husband Charlie, died in 1974 and she did not remarry. She lives with her mother-in-law in an apartment completely paid for by Mary Jane, earned $18,000 during the year, and had itemized deductions of $4,000.

(a) Assuming Mary Jane supports her mother-in-law who had no income of her own, what is Mary Jane's (1) marital status? (2) tax table income? (3) tax?

(b) Would your answer to (a) be different if Charlie died in 1975 instead?

(c) Would your answer to (a) be different if Mary Jane's mother-in-law supports herself?

(d) Would your answer to (b) be different if Mary Jane also lives with her dependent foster child for the entire year?

Problem 1-14

Mort Black's wages were $17,000 a year. His interest from savings bank and net rental income totalled $20,000. His allowable deductions for property taxes, mortgage interest and church contributions were $5,250 during the year. Mort is single and has no dependents. (1) What is Mort's taxable income? (2) What is his tax before credits?

Problems 1-15

Dick Bank earned $19,000 during the year. His wife, Helena earned $6,000. Dick's itemized deductions were $2,500, and Helena's were $1,000.

Compute (1) their tax table income (a) on a joint return and (b) on separate returns; (2) their tax (a) on a joint return and (b) on separate returns.

SUPPLEMENTAL PROBLEMS

Problem 1-16

All the individuals in this problem live in the U.S.

(a) Mable Newton, single, supports her cousin, Cynthia, and Cynthia's daughter, Kay. During the year Cynthia had no income, but Kay earned $800 from baby-sitting which she puts away in a savings account. They all lived together until Dec. 30, when Cynthia moved out of Mabel's house to live with her new husband, Leighton. However, Kay continued to stay with Mabel. Leighton filed a separate return for the tax year. How many exemptions can Mabel claim? Explain.

(b) Paul Lund's wife Linda is blind. So is their 16-year-old daughter Tina whom Paul fully supports. Linda's only income was a $5 cash award from a cooking contest. Tina worked full-time as an actress. She earned $7,000 during the year and invested the amount in securities. How many exemptions can Paul claim on a joint return? On a separate return?

(c) Bill and Mary Kant are divorced parents of 2 children, ages 2 and 8. Under a 1976 divorce decree, Mary has custody of the children and is entitled to their exemptions. During the year, Bill paid $1,200 for the support of the younger child and Mary paid $1,199 for his support. In addition, Bill paid $600 for the support of the older child in return for Mary's written agreement signed this year that assigns the dependency exemption of that child to him. Mary provided $500 for the support of that child. How many exemptions can Bill claim?

Problem 1-17

(a) On Feb. 1, Bill Hunter's mother who lived all her life in Italy and was dependent on him for support, came to the U. S. on an immigrant visa to live with him permanently. On March 11, Bill's wife, Norma, legally divorced him, and on Nov. 30, his mother died. The divorce decree specified that Norma was to have custody of their only child for 7 months of each year and be entitled to the dependency exemption for him. The child has no income of his own. The cost of his support was paid by both parents, with Bill contributing $1,100 and Norma $900 of the support. All except Bill's mother were U.S. citizens. How many personal exemptions does Bill get?

(b) What would your answer to (a) be, if Bill gave $1,200 to the child's support and Norma gave $1,100?

(c) Would your answer to (a) be different if the Hunters have 2 children and Bill gave $1,115 each to the support of each child and Norma gave $1,100 each? (Assume the divorce decree gave Norma the right to claim the exemption for both children.)

Assignment 1—Problems

★ Problem 1-18 ★

Phil Hall, 56, is the owner of the Keystone Dairy store in State College, Pennsylvania. He lives at 47 Engle St. His social security number is 123-45-6789.

Hall has been a widower since his wife, Karen died on 11-1-76. His two children John, age 19, and JoAnne, age 16, live with him. John is a full-time college student, and during his vacations earned $2,000 in wages. Hall fully supports both his children.

Fill in the following schedule to give Hall the best possible tax result.

Please print or type	Name (If joint return, give first names and initials of both)	Last name	Your social security number
	Present home address (Number and street, including apartment number, or rural route)		Spouse's social security no.
	City, town or post office, State and ZIP code	Occupation — Yours ▶ Spouse's ▶	

Filing Status		Exemptions	
1 ☐	Single (Check only ONE box)	6a Regular ☐ Yourself ☐ Spouse	Enter number of boxes checked ▶
2 ☐	Married filing joint return (even if only one had income)	b First names of your dependent children who lived with you_____	Enter number ▶
3 ☐	Married filing separately. If spouse is also filing give spouse's social security number in designated space above and enter full name here ▶	c Number of other dependents ▶ d Total (add lines 6a, b, and c) . . . . . . ▶	
4 ☐	Unmarried Head of Household. you qualify ▶	e Age 65 or older . ☐ Yourself ☐ Spouse Blind . . . . ☐ Yourself ☐ Spouse	Enter number of boxes checked ▶
5 ☐	Qualifying widow(er) with dependent child (Year spouse died ▶ 19).	f TOTAL (add lines 6d and e) . . . . ▶	

Cumulative Problem 1-19
(Answer (a) or (b) as directed.)

(a) Patsy and David Lewis were married in 1970. On January 1 of this year their 2 sons were killed in a fire. On December 9, Patsy gave birth to a girl who was born blind. David had gross income of $28,000. During the year he had a $2,800 in unreimbursed travel expenses incurred while away from home in connection with his job. In addition, he paid $2,510 in property taxes, $1,000 in mortgage interest and $900 in charitable contributions. (1) Compute their tax table income on a joint return. (2) How many personal exemptions are they entitled to? (3) Compute their tax.

(b) John Carrington, a widower since 1975, earned $15,000 during the year. His only other income was $500 interest on a bank account. He contributed $450 to his church and $200 to a public library. His mortgage interest and property tax on his residence amounted to $1,520. On June 15, Matty, his 17-year old daughter, married Kenneth McKinzie who moved into the Carringtons' home. Kenneth's only income was $790 that he used to support himself from January 1 until June 15. Kenneth died on December 28, a few days before his eighteenth birthday. After the marriage, John continued to fully support his daughter and his son-in-law at a cost of $5,600. Matty went to work in July and earned $1,200 as a waitress which she saved to furnish an apartment where she intends to live. She did not file a joint return. (1) Figure John's tax table income. (2) How many personal exemptions is John entitled to? (3) Compute his tax liability.

Discussion Problem 1-20

There is general agreement that the present tax structure is a steeply progressive one. Despite the recent simplification of the tax system by the 1977 Tax Reduction and Simplification Act, the highest tax rate remains 70%, with the lowest income taxpayers still paying approximately 14%. Therefore, a number of proposals have been advanced to limit the spread between the bottom and top marginal tax rates to, say, 15 percentage points.

(a) What sound economic arguments can you think of to support this proposal?

(b) In the light of the present state of the economy, what arguments can you think of against the proposal?

Research Problem 1-21

During the tax year, Warren Wolfe paid $4,000 for his daughter Barbara to go to college and travel during her vacation. Besides this amount, Barbara received $5,000 from the estate of her grandfather who died that year. Barbara bought a $4,300 sports car with her money and put the balance in a savings account.

Warren claimed Barbara as a dependent. But a Revenue Service Agent has disallowed the dependency exemption. The agent maintained that since Barbara's total support was $8,300 ($4,000 from her father plus the $4,300 she spent on herself with her own money), Warren has failed to prove he furnished half of Barbara's support.

Warren has asked you, as a tax expert, whether he should appeal from the disallowance. He thinks the price of a car is not a type of expense which may be used to determine the support test of a dependent. How would you advise him?

1. To find the answer, use the Prentice-Hall Complete Federal Tax Equipment in your school or local library. Give your answer fully explained. In it, show authorities, citing law and opinions applicable, and the P-H Federal Tax Equipment paragraphs where they may be found.

2. Enumerate and explain carefully every step you take in reaching your result. These are extremely important—just as important as the conclusion itself.

Tax Reasoning Problem 1-22

After his divorce, Brown paid the expenses of maintaining the family home, which continued to be the principal residence of his ex-wife and their 3 daughters. He owned the house but never lived there. Instead he maintained another home as his principal residence. Can he claim head-of-household-status, assuming that the daughters are his dependents? Explain.

ASSIGNMENT No. 2
GROSS INCOME—EXCLUSIONS

(Note: In the following problems, unless otherwise specified, assume that the "tax year" is the calendar year 1977, that the taxpayer and his spouse, if any, are resident citizens, under 65 and are not blind and that the taxpayer is not entitled to any credits against the tax other than those shown.)

Problem 2-1

In January, John McCreedy purchased a vacant lot for $18,500, and five months later sold it for $20,000.

John is a bartender at the Last Chance Saloon. In 1977, he received $11,000 in wages and $2,000 in tips. In July, he inherited $5,000 worth of Yazoo City Bonds from his aunt Louella. In December, he was paid $650 in interest on the bonds. He also received $90 in interest on a savings account during 1977. John is single with no dependents. He had $4,700 in itemized deductions for the year. What is his gross income? Tax table income?

Problem 2-2

Bertha DeBlues owned a local nightclub before it was condemned by the city to make room for a school. Bertha invested the $65,000 award by depositing half in a mutual savings bank and the other half in the city's arbitrage bonds. The city invested all bond proceeds in higher yield securities until plans for the school could be made final. During the year, Bertha received interest of $1,500 on the condemnation award and $1,200 from the bonds. She also received $2,000 in dividends earned on her deposit with the mutual savings bank. What interest, if any, must Bertha include in her gross income?

Problem 2-3

(a) During the year, Jesse Channel received the following interest payments: $400 on an industrial development bond, the proceeds of which were used to construct a sports complex (total bond issue was for $80 million); $100 on a Jersey City Public Housing Authority bond; and $30 on a U.S. Treasury bond issued last year. What items of interest, if any, may Jesse exclude on his return?

(b) Jesse had overpaid his 1975 federal income tax, and in July 1977 received a check from the government for the amount of the overpayment, plus $26 in interest. May Jesse exclude the interest on his return?

Problem 2-4

Susan Parker, age 37, lost her husband last year in a boating accident in Paraguay. Living with her are her two minor children, Hymie and Floyd, and her maiden aunt, Lavinia. Susan is the sole support of both Lavinia and the children. During the year Susan earned $13,200 as a tour guide at Blimp Baby Buggy Corporation, and $6,000 moonlighting as a dancer at Abdul's Arabian Oasis. She owned the following bonds and received the following interest during the year: (a) $7,300 worth of Blimp Baby Buggy at 8½% which paid interest of $620.50; (b) $2,900 worth of City of Akron at 6% which paid interest of $174; and (c) $1,500 worth of U.S. Treasury 5½% bonds issued in 1968, bought at par and held at the end of the year which paid interest of $82.50. She also had a savings account from which she received $61.97 in interest. Her itemized deductions totaled $7,150 for the year.

(a) What is Susan's tax table income?
(b) How many exemptions can she claim?
(c) What is her tax?

Problem 2-5

(a) Terence Mackson had a $100,000 life insurance policy with his mother as beneficiary. His premiums on the policy were $120 a month. When his mother died in March he sold the policy to his brother Ken for $10,000. Ken became the beneficiary under the transfer. He paid the premiums on the first of each month beginning in April. On October 10 Terence died. In December, Ken received the full amount of the insurance proceeds. Did Ken have to pay any tax on these proceeds? Explain.

(b) Rod Roman died on January 1. His wife Iris was the beneficiary of his $100,000 life insurance policy. Instead of taking the $100,000 Iris agreed to take $6,000 in interest each year for 10 years. After the 10th year she was to receive the $100,000. Iris received her first interest payment in December of this year. Must Iris pay tax on the payment?

Problem 2-6

Rose Allen died on July 1, 1976. Her husband Francis was the sole beneficiary of her $50,000 life insurance policy. Francis elected to receive five annual installments of $10,500 ($500 was guaranteed interest). First payment was received on July 1, 1977. One month later Francis assigned his rights under the policy to his brother Bert for $40,000.

(a) What amount, if any, is includible in Francis's gross income?
(b) Would Bert include in gross income any portion of the payments he receives under the assignment?

Problem 2-7

Carlo Ameretto bought an endowment contract for $33,000 which paid him $250 a month for a 15-year period. Early this year, when 36 months were remaining on the contract, Carlo elected to take $10,000 in lump-sum payment in full discharge of the original obligations under the contract. How much, if any, of the lump-sum payment can Carlo exclude from gross income?

Problem 2-8

Discuss the taxability of the following:

(a) In September, Archer Thomas, single and age 53, was injured while at work in the Sun City Concrete plant. He was hospitalized for six weeks. During his hospitalization he continued to receive his salary of $300 a week. When Archer left the hospital his doctors told him he would not be allowed to take on any gainful employment for at least 18 months. He retired under the company disability plan and for the last nine weeks of the year received $200 a week in disability benefits. Up to the time Archer went on disability he had received $12,900 in salary (43 × $300). He also received $500 in bank interest during the year. He had no other income and no deductions for adjusted gross income.

What amount, if any, of the disability benefits may Archer exclude?

(b) Edgar Trooper, a state policeman, was shot while making an arrest. Edgar was not covered under the state's workmen's compensation laws. Under a special state statute he received full salary for the five weeks he missed work. This was one-third higher than the maximum allowed by the state's workmen's compensation laws.

(c) On April 1, Winnie Nobel received a bequest of $100,000 under her mother's will. On December 31, the bank credited her savings account with $3,000 interest.

Would your answer be different if Winnie's mother's will created a $100,000 trust and the income from the trust was bequeathed to Winnie?

(d) Sidney Mozart, world renowned pianist, injured his hand in an auto accident. He was awarded damages of $300,000.

Sidney's brother Hubert was the owner of a restaurant. During a waiters' strike, many of his customers were turned away by threatening pickets. He recovered $3,000 against the waiters' union for loss of profits.

Problem 2-9

Martha Muldoon, a carpenter employed by Quicky Homes Co., suffered a broken leg when heavy beams fell on her. She was unable to work for 12 weeks. During this time she did not receive her salary but did receive $135 weekly under the company group accident plan. Each year, Quicky Homes paid part of the total premiums for the group insurance. The remaining cost was paid by the employees through payroll deductions. In the last three policy years the premiums were $10,000 each year, and Quicky Homes contributions were $3,500, $4,500 and $4,000. What amount, if any, received by Martha under the accident plan can be excluded?

Problem 2-10

Caroline Grimaldi, an elderly widow, bought an installment annuity contract for $37,500, which would pay her $150 a month for life beginning January 1, 1977. On the annuity starting date, her nearest birthday was 67.

If Mrs. Grimaldi dies before the $37,500 is recovered, the payments are to be made to her sister, age 43. Determine what amount Caroline can exclude each year.

Problem 2-11

(a) Mary Kay bought an annuity contract on 1-2-76, her 64th birthday, for $21,096. Under the terms of the contract, she is to receive $900 annually for 3 years, starting 1-1-77, and after 3 years, $1,500, annually for the rest of her life. Mary received her first payment on June 1, 1977. What amount of annuity income must Mary report as gross income for 1977?

(b) Would your answer be different if she were paid the same amount on the same date in 1978? Explain.

Note: In determining your answers, refer to the actuarial tables at pages 1216-1217.

Problem 2-12

Asco Co. has a qualified contributory pension plan for its employees. Asco contributed a total $50,000, including $4,000 during 1975 on behalf of Maxie Wright, its plant engineer. During the course of his employment, Maxie paid in $8,000 to the plan. In 1975, Maxie was paid his regular salary of $30,000. Maxie retired on 1-1-76, his 60th birthday, and started receiving an annuity of $400 a month. Where applicable, refer to the tables on pages 1216-1217.

(a) What income should Maxie have reported as wages on his return for 1975?

(b) What amount must he include in gross income for 1976 on account of the annuity? For 1977? For 1978?

(c) What would your answer to (b) be if Asco's contribution was $24,000 and Maxie's was $15,000?

SUPPLEMENTAL PROBLEMS

Problem 2-13

Harry Bryce, 66, pays over one-half the support of his stepson, Athos, age 20, who lived 8 months with Harry during the year. Athos was enrolled throughout the year in the Bronx Institute of Accountancy, a correspondence school. Harry's wife, Fanny, died October 1, 1976. During the year, Harry received a salary of $22,500 from the Copperhead Corp. and also received the following amounts of interest payments: $400 on U.S. Treasury 5% bonds issued in 1971, $200 interest on a New York State condemnation award, $380 on City of Topeka bonds, $300 on State of Maine Sports Authority bonds, and $75 on a federal income tax refund for a previous year. All bonds and securities were held at the end of the year and no bonds were bought at a premium. Harry's itemized deductions totaled $6,100. Athos had net income of $750 during the year from the sale of jewelry at flea markets on weekends. (1) Determine Harry's tax table income and his total number of personal exemptions. (2) What is his tax?

★ Problem 2-14 ★

Phil Hall purchased a life insurance policy in 1966 on his wife's life. The policy was worth $80,000 at her death in 1976. Hall, as the sole beneficiary, elected under the policy to take $10,000 a year for 10 years. In 1977 the insurance company paid him $10,000. What amount, if any, can Hall exclude from gross income?

★ **Problem 2-15** ★

Phil Hall purchased from Lion Mutual a single life annuity contract on himself at a cost of $18,900. The contract specified that he would receive $100 per month on reaching age 56 on 9-1-77. What amount, if any, can Hall exclude from his gross income in 1977? Fill in the following schedule.

Part I Pension and Annuity Income.

1 Name of payer_____
2 Did your employer contribute part of the cost? . . . . ☐ Yes ☐ No
  If "Yes," is your contribution recoverable within 3 years of the annuity starting date? . . . . ☐ Yes ☐ No
  If "Yes," show: Your contribution $_____, Contribution recovered in prior years . . . | 2 |
3 Amount received this year . . . . | 3 |
4 Amount excludable this year . . . . | 4 |
5 Taxable portion (subtract line 4 from line 3) . . . . | 5 |

★★ **Problem 2-16** ★★

The Atlas Machinery Corp. received $180 in interest on a refund of a prior year's federal income tax. In addition, it received the following interest payments on government bonds it owned:

State of Ohio bonds $300
U.S. Treasury 2½% bonds, issued in June, 1947 250
City of Tampa bonds 500
Industrial development bonds issued on 7-1-70 by the State of Ohio as part of a $6 million bond issue for trade shows and convention facilities 475

Fill in the following schedule:
Interest on obligations of the United States and U.S. instrumentalities ....
Other interest ....

Cumulative Problem 2-17
(Answer (a) or (b) as directed)

(a) Larry and Molly Walter are both employed as management consultants by Shockley's Short Circuit, an electrical appliance manufacturer. Their respective weekly gross salaries are $300 and $400. They have a dependent child, age 16, living at home.

In March, Larry became ill with pneumonia. He was absent from work for six weeks. During this time, he received $150 a week under the state disability insurance program. His employer Shockley paid him each week the difference between the $150 and his weekly salary of $300.

Some time ago, Larry purchased a joint and survivorship annuity for $25,000. Under the contract Larry is to receive $100 a month for life and, after his death, Molly is to be paid $150 a month for life. Larry received his first payment on January 2, 1977. At the annuity starting date, Molly's nearest birthday (February, 1977) is 66 and Larry's (April, 1977) is 64. (To determine what amount of the $1,200 annual annuity payment Larry can exclude each year, use the tables on pages 1216—1217.)

Larry owned bonds at the end of the year which he had bought at par. These paid him the following interest: $800 on $10,000 Shockley's Short Circuit, Inc., bonds issued in 1965; $1,445 on $17,000 City of Frazier bonds issued in 1967; and $1,650 on $22,000 Dingle Dangle Dairy, Inc., bonds issued in 1971.

Besides their deductions for exemptions, the Walters had other allowable itemized deductions of $7,801.60.

Compute (1) the Walters' tax table income on a joint return and determine the allowable number of personal exemptions; (2) their tax.

(b) During the first three months of the year Wilbur Peacock, age 64, was unemployed and received state unemployment insurance benefits totaling $1,200. His employer, the Columbus Aircraft Company, had suspended operations in December 1976 but continued to pay its employees supplemental unemployment benefits. Wilbur received $300 from Columbus in benefits during his period of unemployment. On April 1, Wilbur returned to work and continued to work for the remainder of the year receiving his monthly salary of $1,000.

In May, Wilbur's wife Penelope, was killed in an airplane accident. Penelope would have been 65 in June.

Wilbur was the sole beneficiary of a $100,000 policy on her life. He elected under the policy to receive the proceeds in ten annual installments of $12,000 ($10,000 principal and $2,000 interest). Wilbur received his first payment on July 1.

During the year, Wilbur inherited money from his late uncle Cosmo. Under Cosmo's will Wilbur was to receive a total sum of $12,000. It was to be paid in 3 equal installments from income from rental property which Cosmo had owned and which was placed in trust under his will. Wilbur invested half of the bequest in corporate bonds issued by the Lost Nickel Vending Machine Co., which by year's end had earned $1,500 interest. He also received additional interest on the following: $625 on $20,000 U.S. Treasury 3¼% bonds issued in 1961; $450 on $5,000 City of Philadelphia bonds issued in 1966; and $225 on an account with the Big Sur Savings and Loan Ass'n.

In December, Wilbur settled a lawsuit which arose from his wife's accident. He received $100,000 ($80,000 for loss of life and $20,000 punitive damages).

Paula, Wilbur's 19-year old daughter lived at home during the year and earned $5,000 driving a taxi. Wilbur had deductions for adjusted gross income of $1,200 and other allowable itemized deductions of $6,100.

Determine (1) Wilbur's tax table income and allowable number of personal exemptions; (2) his tax.

Cumulative Problem 2-18

Calvin Zipp, age 61, is a chief engineer for the Central Mining Company. On December 31 of last year his wife Norma and his son James, age 19, were involved in an auto accident. Norma was killed instantly. She was 66 years old when she died. James was hospitalized for three weeks but later fully recovered. In May, he began working in a local restaurant. He continued work until he entered college in September. His earnings for the year were $3,500, $2,000 of which was used for his support. James paid his first year's tuition with a $2,000 scholarship given to him by his school. Calvin contributed $2,200 towards James' support during the year.

During 1977, Calvin earned $19,000 in salary from the mining company and received a $4,000 retainer fee from an oil company for consulting services. On Jan. 2, 1977, $2,000 was placed in trust for Calvin under the will of his uncle. Under the terms of the trust Calvin was to receive any income from the trust principal. On Nov. 1, Calvin received $200 in accordance with these terms. On Nov. 30, he surrendered his $5,000 life insurance policy for $4,000. Up to the time of surrender he had paid $3,800 in premiums. On Dec. 1, he won a lawsuit against the Centerville News. The News had written articles claiming he was responsible for a mining disaster. He was paid $35,000 in compensatory damages and $5,000 punitive damages.

On July 1 of last year Zipp purchased a joint and survivorship annuity contract for $55,680. The policy provides for payments of $300 a month for life, and after his death, payments of $100 a month for life to his sister Gertrude. The annuity starting date was Jan. 2, 1977. Calvin's nearest birthday on that date was 61, and Gertrude's was 66. Monthly payments actually began on April 1, 1977.

Zipp paid the rent for his widowed mother who was 80 years old. Rental payments totaled $1,500 for the year. His mother's only income for the year was $1,800 in social security benefits. She used $1,400 of the payments for her support. Zipp fully supported his sister's 19-year-old daughter who was a full-time student at an out-of-state college. She worked at the school library earning $700 during the year. She also received during the year $125 in interest on state highway bonds. The niece included all the money in her savings account.

Zipp had deductions for adjusted gross income of $3,000 and itemized deductions of $5,300.

Determine (1) Zipp's tax table income and allowable personal exemptions; (2) his tax.

Discussion Problem 2-19

The exemption of the interest on state and local obligations has come under examination to find alternative approaches to using this device to aid state and local governments. It has been recognized that these governments have come to rely heavily on the exemption to meet their capital needs. On the other hand, the tax-exempt obligations permit high-bracket taxpayers to escape their share of the tax burden.

(a) What arguments can you present in favor of retaining the present exemption for state and local obligations?

(b) What arguments can you present against retaining the present exemption for state and local obligations?

Research Problem 2-20

Sarah Klingel was the sole beneficiary of her husband's $75,000 insurance policy. Her husband died on April 1, 1976. She elected to receive the proceeds of the policy in 240 monthly installments. Each payment included $62 in interest. In reporting her 1976 income, Sarah excluded the interest payments under Sec. 101(d)(1)(B) which permits a surviving spouse to exclude up to $1,000 of such interest each year. In May 1977 Sarah married Ted Bullwinkle. In filing her 1977 return Sarah is uncertain whether she should exclude those interest payments received after she remarried. She consults you for advice.

Use the Prentice-Hall Complete Federal Tax Equipment in your school or local library to find the answer.

1. Give your opinion. In it show authorities citing law, regulations, interpretations and decisions applicable, and the P-H Tax Equipment paragraphs where they may be found.

2. Enumerate and explain carefully each step you take in reaching your result. These are just as important as the result.

Tax Reasoning Problem 2-21

When Masters borrowed $40,000, Thrifty Finance Corp. required him to take out a $20,000 life insurance policy naming it beneficiary. Thrifty would be entitled to the proceeds to the extent of any outstanding loan balance. Any excess would go to Masters' wife. When Masters died, the outstanding balance exceeded the insurance proceeds. Can Thrifty exclude the proceeds from income because they were received by reason of the insurer's death? Explain.

ASSIGNMENT No. 3

GROSS INCOME—INCLUSIONS

(Note: In the following problems, unless otherwise specified, assume that the "tax year" is the calendar year 1977, that the taxpayer and his spouse, if any, are resident citizens, under 65 and are not blind and that the taxpayer is not entitled to any credits against the tax other than those shown.)

Problem 3-1

(a) Upon his retirement in June, Percy Quackenbush, president of Short Fall Oil Corp. received from the board of directors of the company $5,000 in cash. The minutes of the director's meeting read that the $5,000 was given to Percy "in recognition of his long and dedicated service to the company." Percy received $30,000 in salary while president in 1977. Under the company's payroll savings plan $2,000 was deducted from this amount to purchase Series E Government bonds. From July through December Percy received $12,000 from the company's pension plan. Percy never contributed to the plan and none of the company's payments to the plan were taxable to him. Which of these items, if any, would be taxable?

(b) Zelda Xanadu, an exotic dancer at the Acropolis Cafe, earned during 1977 $12,000 in salary and $1,500 in tips. At Christmas time, her boss gave her a turkey valued at $10. Each Sunday Zelda directed the choir at the local church and at the end of the year the minister gave her a $100 bond in appreciation of her efforts. During the year, Zelda served on a jury and she was paid $120 in jury fees. She also received $30 to reimburse her for costs of commuting to and from the courthouse. Which of these items, if any, would be taxable?

Problem 3-2

(a) During the year, the ticket agents of the Rockline Railroad had charged many of the railroad's passengers fares in excess of those approved by the Interstate Commerce Commission. The names of the passengers making the excess payments were not known. The railroad placed each excess payment in a separate fund. Were these excess payments income to the railroad?

(b) Kubler Kable, an unemployed actor living in New York, was asked by a Hollywood film company to appear in its new picture "Volcano." Kubler was flown to Hollywood on the company's jet. If Kubler had taken a commercial airline it would have cost him $300. In Hollywood Kubler signed his movie contract. He immediately had his furniture and clothing moved to his Hollywood apartment. Kubler made a two day trip to New York to close the sale on his home. The film company paid all of his expenses of the trip ($700) and reimbursed him for his moving expenses ($4,000) and for the loss on the sale of his home ($3,000). What amounts, if any, must Kubler include in his income?

(c) In February, Gloworm Lighting Company, under a corporate resolution, gave to its president, Rex Ripplemeier, $12,000. The resolution stated that $10,000 was for Ripplemeier's federal income taxes and $2,000 for counseling fees incurred by Ripplemeier in making private investments. For the past several years the company had paid the president's income taxes. How much, if any, of the $12,000 must Ripplemeier include in his income?

Problem 3-3

Dexter Honeycutt, sole owner of Honeydew Construction Company, contracted with the Garrison Construction Company not to engage in any construction projects in a neighboring city for at least three years. In consideration for the promise, he received $10,000. During the year, he also received a $500 award from the Bay City Home Builder's Association for outstanding civic achievement. After completing the construction of a garage for a neighbor he had the neighbor pay the price of the garage ($3,000) to Bay City's Community Chest.

Which of the items received by Dexter, if any, would be taxable?

Problem 3-4

(a) George "Bonzo" Benedict, star fullback for the Atlantic City Boardwalks, was honored by the Football Writers' Association as "Player of the Year." George was awarded an all-expense paid world cruise, valued at $6,000. Set forth arguments as to whether or not the value of the award is includible in gross income.

(b) Mabel Murcer, a long-time employee of Prescott Publishing, spent over $3,000 during the year for medical treatments which ultimately cured a serious lung condition. In November, the board of directors of Prescott adopted this resolution: "Further resolved that Prescott Publishing, Inc. pay to Mabel Murcer, its employee, because of the high esteem and affection in which she is held, $3,000, the amount she paid for medical treatments. This is a gift from the company and not extra compensation." In December, the shareholders approved the resolution. For the tax year, the corporation did not deduct the $3,000 as an expense. What reasons can you supply to support Mabel's claim that the payment was a gift?

Problem 3-5

(a) Clement Fuller, a bacteriologist, was awarded a fellowship of $24,000 by the Rene Foundation, a tax-exempt organization. The grant was made so that Fuller could continue his cancer research. Under the terms of the grant, Fuller receives $6,000 a year for 4 years. Monthly payments began in January 1977 and will continue until December 1980. How much of the grant, if any, must he include in his gross income?

(b) Hugh Hancock received a post-doctorate fellowship grant of $9,000 from a state university for a 36-month period starting 7-1-77, when it was paid to him in full. Must he include any part of the grant in his gross income?

Problem 3-6

(a) During the year Ann Pie, widow of David Pie, received $20,000 from the profit-sharing plan of David's employer. This was the total accumulation in David's account in the noncontributory plan when he died. Under the terms of the plan, in the case of termination of employment or death each participating employee will have earned a 10% vested interest in the amount accumulated in his account for each year of his plan participation. David had been a participant for 8 years. How much must Ann include in her gross income?

(b) What would your answer to (a) be if David had been in the plan for 5 years?

(c) What would your answer to (a) be if David had been in the plan for 11 years?

(d) How would you answer (a), (b) and (c), above, assuming that the plan qualifies for tax exemption?

Problem 3-7

(a) Gordan Company awarded $5,000 to Kenneth Denese when he recommended its computer machine to his employer. Later, when Gordan got a big contract from Kenneth's employer, it charged the $5,000 payment to contract costs. Is the $5,000 taxable to Kenneth?

(b) Laurette Sohn gets $20 each week from the 2 riders in her car pool. Her gasoline, oil, and maintenance expenses for the trips are $14. How much, if anything, is taxable?

(c) Michael Peters received from his town's lighting company a 3-year tuition-free scholarship toward his Ph.D. He was selected because of his college achievements. Beyond a letter acknowledging and accepting the award, nothing further was required of him. Is the scholarship taxable?

Problem 3-8

Victor Lee, 54 years old, is employed by Maurice Fairfield and Daniel Bethesda. Both employers provide group-term life insurance coverage for their employees. Victor's coverage with Maurice Fairfield is $35,000 and with Daniel Bethesda, $45,000. Victor pays premiums of $50 a year under the group plan provided by Bethesda. What is the taxable amount includible in his income for the current year?

Problem 3-9

Fred Seacord is a financial adviser of the Sweeting Corporation under an agreement that calls for an annual payment of $10,000 for his services. During the year he received $7,000 in cash from the corporation. At the end of the year he received from the corporation 50 shares of the Sweeting common stock with a $50 par value and a fair market value of $60 a share. In July, Sweeting gave Fred tax-exempt municipal bonds with a $1,000 face value and $1,100 fair market value. On July 1, one of Sweeting's customers gave Sweeting a 90-day note for $3,000 to pay his bills. On August 1, Sweeting gave Fred the note, but on September 15 the customer went bankrupt and Fred could collect nothing when the note became due. What is Fred's gross income from these transactions?

Problem 3-10

Dixie Hemmings, age 23, is a junior account executive for the Atlas Advertising Agency. The agency provides group-term life insurance for its employees. Dixie is covered by a $90,000 policy. She pays $2 a month in premiums and the agency pays the rest. Dixie's mother is the beneficiary of the policy. Dixie was paid a monthly salary. Instead of receiving cash for the month of December, she received $1,000 in City of Baltimore bonds and 25 shares of the agency's stock. The shares at the time of their receipt had a par value of $30 a share and a fair market value of $35 a share. Dixie attended night classes in advertising at Crabcake Community College. The agency told Dixie that she must take the course and maintain a "B" average if she were to continue working for the agency. The agency paid $800 for her books and tuition during the year. Which, if any, of the above items must Dixie include in her gross income? Explain your answer.

Problem 3-11

Bill Chester, age 39, works for Sherman Corporation. During the tax year he was insured for $150,000 group-term life insurance. He paid $1.00 of the cost of each $1,000 of coverage, and Sherman paid the balance. What amount, if any, must Bill include in his gross income?

Problem 3-12

On 8-1-76, Albert Reita bought a $2,500 par value 6% debenture of the Great Neck Co., a domestic corporation. He paid $2,400 for the bond. Interest on the bond is due and payable on the first of February and August. On 6-1-77, he sold the bond to Yolande Chain for $2,550 (including accrued interest). On 10-1-77 Yolande sold the bond to Paul Setan for $2,585 (including accrued interest).
 (a) What interest, if any, should Albert report for the year?
 (b) What interest, if any, should Yolande report for the year?
 (c) What gain, if any, should Albert report from the sale of the bond?
 (d) What gain, if any, should Yolande report from the sale of the bond?

Problem 3-13

(a) In 1976, Elmer Grade leased his unimproved lakeshore property to "Codfish" Hunter for use as a trout fishing camp. The lease did not require Hunter to pay any rent. Instead, Hunter was required to erect a cabin on the property before the lease expired. Hunter completed the cabin in 1977 at a cost of $8,100. The building when completed had a fair market value of $10,000. The lease expired December 31, 1977, and was not renewed. How did the improvement affect Elmer's gross income for 1977?

(b) In late 1974, Elmer Grade leased another parcel of lakeshore property to Hunter for use as a private beach. The lease was for 3 years at an annual rental of $3,000 payable in October of each year. The lot cost Elmer $2,500 fifteen years ago. On January 2, 1977, it was agreed that Hunter could erect several cabanas on the property for his customer's use. Hunter's cost of construction of the cabanas totaled $5,000. When completed in March 1977, the cabanas had a fair market value of $7,500. The lease expired on December 31, 1977 and was not renewed. A month later, Elmer sold the property for $22,000. What amount, if any, must Elmer include in income from this property in 1977?

Problem 3-14

James Fagen owns a tract of land in a prosperous business community. On 12-1-76, he entered into a lease agreement with the Friteg Corporation. The lease began on 1-1-77 and was to run for 20 years. The annual rent was $15,000. Friteg could terminate the lease at anytime by paying a penalty equal to $2,000 for each year which remained under the lease.

Friteg also was required under the lease to construct a building. The building, completed on 3-1-77, cost Friteg $75,000 to build. At the end of the lease the building was to revert to Fagen. In October 1977, Friteg gave notice that it would terminate the lease on 12-31-77.

By the end of 1977, Friteg had fulfilled its obligations under the lease, including the payment of the penalty for breaking the lease. On 12-31-77, the building had a fair market value of $80,000.

What gross income must Fagen report from these transactions for 1977?

Problem 3-15

E. Casper Coggins, an attorney, owns 20% of the stock of a fast food chain. In January, upon approval of the company's board of directors, the company loaned Coggins $5,000. The company had a very profitable year and in December it released Coggins of his obligation to pay the debt. Coggins leased his law office from his father-in-law. When he fell behind in the rental payments his father-in-law informed him that he would not have to pay the rent for the months he was in arrears. The rents amounted to $1,200.

What income, if any did Coggins realize from these transactions?

Problem 3-16

On July 31, Duncan Fife, a custom furniture maker, owed the following amounts to his creditors: $10,000 to Alberts Co., $20,000 to Buttle Co., and $30,000 to Cloey Co. His business assets on July 31 totaled $80,000. On August 1, Fife transferred a piece of machinery with an adjusted basis of $5,000 to Alberts in settlement of his $10,000 debt.

In September, Fife's assets totaled $45,000 and he still owed $20,000 and $30,000 to Buttle and Cloey. Buttle Co. accepted $10,000 in complete satisfaction of the debt owed to it.

In December, Fife's assets totaled $20,000 and his only remaining creditor, Cloey was still owed $30,000. Fife was adjudicated bankrupt under Section 14 of the Bankruptcy Act and the proceeds from the sale of his assets were used to satisfy the debt to Cloey.

Does Fife realize any income from these transactions? Explain.

Problem 3-17

Frank Bozza purchased an empty lot in downtown Detroit from Kerry Kristen for $16,500 ($9,500 cash and a $7,000 first mortgage on which Frank was personally liable). He settled the mortgage for $5,500, at which time the value of the property was $13,000.

(a) What income, if any, did Bozza receive and what is the basis of his parcel of realty?

(b) What would be your answer to (a) if the value of the property were $5,000 at the time of the settlement?

(c) What would be your answer to (a) if the $5,500 mortgage was cancelled as the result of an agreement made under the Bankruptcy Act? At the time of confirmation of the agreement the property had a fair market value of $13,000.

Problem 3-18

Last year, Marsha McMahon was granted a divorce under a civil decree from her husband Jim. The agreement incident to the divorce specified that Jim was to pay Marsha $1,000 a month:

$400 for Marsha's support until she should remarry. One-half of the amount was to be paid from a trust fund established for Jim by his father. The other half was to be paid from an annuity contract purchased by Jim.

$200 to go to reduce the mortgage on their jointly owned home. Both were liable on the home mortgage.

$300 for child support ($100 a month for the support of their child Hermione, age 8, and $100 each for the support of Jim's two stepchildren from Marsha's previous marriages). The two stepchildren were Lothario, age 12 and Xavier, age 21. Marsha was legally obligated to support only Lothario.

$100 of each monthly payment was for medical treatment of Marsha's allergies.

In addition to the $1,000 monthly payment, Jim had to pay the monthly $30 premium on a life insurance policy assigned to Marsha and naming her irrevocable beneficiary. Determine what payments are taxable to Marsha, and deductible by Jim.

Problem 3-19

Is the taxpayer required to include the following items in gross income during the tax year? Explain briefly.

(a) During the year, Arthur Mannix Corporation gave Cecile Vaughn, an employee, 100 shares of Mannix stock valued at $20 a share for her services. Under the terms of the transfer, Cecile promises to resell the stock to Mannix at $20 a share if she leaves her job for any reason within the next 10 years.

(b) The shares of the C. T. Corporation, a closely held corporation, are not regularly traded. During the year, C. T. transferred to Ivan Fanboy, an employee, 100 shares of its stock subject to the sole condition that if he or his estate wishes to sell the stock at anytime, it must be offered to C. T. for repurchase at its then existing book value.

Problem 3-20

During the year, H. S. Young Co. transferred to Edward Ladin, an employee, a new $35,000 home in which his interest is nontransferable and is subject to a substantial risk of forfeiture for a 5-year period. However, H. S. allows Edward to live in the house rent free. Five years later, Edward pays H. S. $30,000 for the house which has a then market value of $40,000. Did Edward have any income from these transactions? Explain.

Problem 3-21

On 1-14-77, Jack Doyle, an employee of the Uptown Maintenance Corporation, received an option to buy 100 shares of his company stock at $15 a share, the fair market value of the stock on that date. The option was granted under a qualified stock option plan adopted on 5-14-76 and approved by the stockholders on 6-30-76. The option was nontransferable and was scheduled to expire 7-1-81. When he received the option, Jack owned no other options and no stock of any kind. On 2-3-77, Jack exercised his option and paid $1,500 for 100 shares of Uptown Maintenance stock, which had a fair market value of $19 a share on that date. Jack sold his stock for $20 a share on 10-1-77. He was still an employee of Uptown at the time.

(a) Did Jack receive any income from these transactions? Explain.

(b) Would your answer to (a) be different if the option were granted under a plan adopted on 5-28-76 and had no readily ascertainable market value when received by Jack?

Problem 3-22

On 6-1-74, Huberger Corporation granted to Gertrude Renaud, an employee, an option under a qualified employee stock purchase plan to buy 100 shares of the company stock for $85 a share. The fair market value of the share on that date was $100 a share. On 6-1-75, Gertrude exercised her option. On 1-2-77, she sold the stock for $150 a share.

What is the amount of gross income Gertrude should report?

Problem 3-23

Prentegast Pretzel Co., wishing to divest itself of interests in other companies, sold to its largest shareholder, Mortimer Scaggs, 100 shares of Miami Metal Corporation stock and 200 shares of Heavenly Lace Company stock. Scaggs paid $30 a share for the Miami stock and $40 a share for the Heavenly stock. At the time of the purchase both stocks were selling on the New York Stock Exchange for $60 a share. Prentegast Pretzel Co. always showed good earnings. It had earnings and profits in excess of $100,000 at the time of the sale to Scaggs. Four months after the purchase, Scaggs sold the 300 shares for $80 a share. What tax consequences, if any, resulted from these transactions?

SUPPLEMENTAL PROBLEMS

Problem 3-24

(a) Jack Swanson and his son, Paul, both worked for the Acme Steel Co. One day, both died in a fire that swept through their two-family house. Jack left his wife, Mary, and a daughter, Sue. Paul left his wife, Grace, and a son, Jeff. The company followed its policy of paying a certain percentage of salary to the relatives of an employee who dies. As a result, the following payments were made: (1) $9,000 to Mary ($7,000 for her husband and $2,000 for her son); (2) $3,000 to Sue ($2,000 for her father and $1,000 for her brother); (3) $5,000 to Grace (who receives nothing for her father-in-law's death); and (4) $3,000 to Jeff ($2,000 for his father and $1,000 for his grandfather). What amount, if any, can Mary, Sue, Grace and Jeff exclude from income?

(b) Would the exclusions, if any, differ if the same amounts were received, but Jack and Paul had worked for two separate companies? Explain.

(c) Assuming the facts as in (a), would the amounts differ if Acme Steel (in excess of the normal salary percentage, but still on account of Jack's death) gratuitously paid Mary an extra $10,000?

Problem 3-25

Pattie Crown earned $16,500 (51 weeks wages, plus commissions) during the year as a salesperson for the Atlas Real Estate Agency. Her son, Amos, age 15, and her father William, age 65, lived with her during the entire year. She provided more than one half the support of her father who was blind. He had only $30 income (bank interest) during the year.

Pattie was divorced in 1975. Under the divorce decree she was to receive $2,000 a year for Amos's support and $3,000 a year for her support. Payments for her support were to be made until Amos reached the age of 18, or until Pattie remarried or died. During 1977, she received $4,000 in payments from her former husband. Pattie provided $2,200 towards the child's support during 1977.

Pattie recovered $2,000 in compensatory damages for injuries sustained in an automobile accident. $1,800 of this amount was for pain and suffering, and $200 for loss of wages for one week.

On August 1, Pattie won $1,500 at the local race track. The following night, however, she lost $1,800 at a "Las Vegas Night" at her local church.

Pattie held a $2,000 bond issued by Friends of Lost Parakeets, a tax-exempt organization. The bond paid 7% annual interest. On December 31 she received her annual interest payment.

Pattie's deductions for adjusted gross income totaled $800. In addition to her deductions for exemptions, she had deductible taxes and contributions totalling $1,400.

Determine (1) Pattie's tax table income and allowable number of personal exemptions; (2) her tax.

★ Problem 3-26 ★

On 2-20-77, Phil Hall won the first prize in a chess tournament, and received a cash prize of $1,500.

The Central State University named Hall its outstanding alumnus of the year in recognition of his scholarly article published several years ago in a noted farm journal. The award was worth $100.

On June 11, Hall's uncle Steve gave him, as a gift, a $20,000 corporate bond. On December 1, 1977, the bond paid 7% interest on the par value. At the time of the gift, the bond was worth $19,900.

During the year, Hall had interest income of $200 from Farmer's Bank and $1,150 from Mercantile Bank. Hall also received $600 in interest from his Port of N. Y. Authority bonds.

Which of the above items must be included in Hall's gross income? Explain.

Cumulative Problem 3-27
(Answer (a) or (b) as directed)

Rick Forbes, age 33, was divorced several years ago and has been living with his father in his father's home ever since. He pays all of the expenses of maintaining the household and provides more than half his father's support. His father, age 65, received $700 during the year as a school crossing guard. He also received $30 interest on a savings account, $40 in interest on Florida State highway bonds and $1,800 in social security benefits.

Forbes does not pay alimony to his former wife. However, during the year he paid $1,400 for the support of his 3-year old son Morris who was living with his mother. The divorce decree provided that the mother was entitled to claim the dependency exemption. Morris's mother provided $800 for the child's support during the year.

Forbes earned $30,000 during the year as a pilot for Transcontinental Airways. He received the company's annual suggestion award for recommending a change in engine design. The award was 100 shares of company stock with a par value of $25 a share, and fair market value of $50. On July 1, the company gave to Forbes a qualified stock option to purchase 50 shares of company stock at the July 1 market value of $60 a share. The option was granted under a plan adopted on 5-3-76. Forbes exercised the option on September 1 and purchased 50 shares. The stock's fair market value on September 1 was $70 a share. Forbes was also covered by $100,000 group-term life insurance policy paid for by his employer with Morris as the beneficiary. The company paid $120 in premiums on Forbes' policy during the year.

Forbes owed his brother-in-law $800. On October 1, Forbes gave him gold coins he had purchased in France two months before for $600. The coins, given in complete satisfaction of the debt, had a market price of $860 when delivered to his brother-in-law.

Rick's other income included: $150 interest on a 1½% bond of the Lockhead Corporation purchased at par and $450 in interest on bank deposits.

His allowable itemized deductions for interest, taxes and contributions totaled $5,810. Compute Forbes' lowest tax before credits.

(b) George Guttenburg was recently promoted to the position of assistant internal auditor for the Tenderloin Press Co. George was paid a salary of $40,000 during the year. At Christmas, he received a cash bonus of $500 and a "basket of cheer" valued at $50. The Revenue Service, investigating Tenderloin, disallowed $10,000 of George's salary as a deduction ruling that such amount was unreasonable compensation.

George was insured under a company paid group life insurance policy. Tenderloin was the beneficiary. It paid $1,400 in premiums during the year on coverage of $100,000. The company also paid the premiums on a $60,000 ordinary life insurance policy on George. George's mother was the beneficiary and the company paid $1,600 in premiums on the policy during the year. All of Tenderloin's employees were covered by a group health and hospitalization plan. The plan cost the company $120 a year for each employee.

Tenderloin had a nondiscriminatory stock purchase plan covering all employees. Last January, George received an option to buy 100 shares of Tenderloin stock for $25 a share. At the time the option was granted the stock had a fair market value of $28 a share. In January, 1977 George exercised the option when the value of the stock was $30 per share. Two months later, he sold the stock for $40 per share.

George received the following amounts during the year:

(a) $500 refund on his 1976 federal income tax and $45 in interest on the refund.

(b) $180 in winnings from the state lottery.

(c) $100 in interest on U.S. Treasury notes issued in 1956 and $200 in interest on New York City bonds issued in 1974.

George owed his car mechanic $200. George prepared the mechanic's tax returns for 1976 in exchange for cancellation of the debt.

George is single. He pays the cost of maintaining his mother in a nursing home. The only income the mother received during the year was $800 in dividends on Pennsylvania Tubing Company stock, and $30 interest on a savings account. $100 of the dividends on the mother's stock was excludable. George's itemized deductions amounted to $6,700 for the year. Figure George's lowest tax before credits (rounded-off to the nearest dollar).

Cumulative Problem 3-28

Mary Barnes and her husband Roger were separated in 1976 and divorced in April, 1977. Under the divorce decree, Roger was to pay Mary a total of $72,000 in alimony. The alimony was to be paid in the following manner: $12,000 in July, 1977 and the balance of $60,000 in 15 annual installments of $4,000. Mary had custody of their six year old son Larry. The divorce decree stated that Roger was to get the dependency exemption for Larry. During 1977, Roger made support payments for Larry totaling $1,000. Mary provided $1,300 towards the child's support during the year, including the rental value of her apartment. In July Mary received her alimony payment of $12,000.

Mary is an editor for Homewood Publishing Company. During 1977 she received $12,000 in salary. The state paid her $200 in disability benefits when she was absent from work for two weeks due to illness. Mary is covered by an $80,000 group-term life insurance policy at her job. She is 33 years old. She does not contribute to the insurance plan. Mary's son is beneficiary of the plan. On January 2, 1976, the Homewood Publishing Co. adopted a written qualified stock option plan for its key employees. It granted Mary the option to purchase 100 shares of its stock at $15 a share. On January 2, 1976 the stock had a fair market value of $15 a share. In July of 1977 Mary exercised the option and purchased the 100 shares when they had a fair market value of $20 a share. Mary purchased some books from her employer at a 40% discount. The purchase price was $40 less than it would have been if she purchased them in a bookstore.

Mary's mother Millie, age 66, lived with Mary during the entire year. Mary's support for her mother, including rental value of her room and medical expenses, totaled $1,400 for the year. Millie received $1,800 in social security benefits and $20 in interest from a savings account during the year. Millie used $800 of the social security benefits for her own support.

Mary was very active in her local church, assisting greatly in fund raising activities and teaching religious classes to children. The parishioners of the church presented her with a gold watch, valued at $200, in recognition of her services. She also received $100 in interest on a state industrial development bond. The bond proceeds were used to construct a track for horse racing. Mary was awarded $3,000 in settlement of a court action contesting her father's will.

She had no deductions for adjusted gross income and her itemized deductions amounted to $2,100.

Determine (1) Mary's tax table income and personal exemptions; (2) her tax.

Research Problems 3-29

David Link is executive director of the Institute for Juvenile Drug Abuse, a home for teenage drug addicts. In addition to his routine administrative duties, Link has a number of special responsibilities which demand a great deal of his time. For example, he must be available at all times to provide counsel and guidance to his students. In light of the heavy personal demands upon the executive director, the Institute requires, as a convenience for the employer, that Link reside on the premises of the Institute and be available on a 24-hour-a-day basis. Therefore, Link and his family resided on the premises of the Institute in a house provided by the Institute. In addition to the house, the Institute provided Link and his family with free groceries for their meals, including certain non-food items such as napkins, soap, etc., from the Institute's commissary. Link solicits your advice, as a noted tax expert, on whether the cost of the meals and groceries furnished to him by his employer is excludable from his gross income. What would you tell him?

1. To find the answer use the Prentice-Hall Complete Federal Tax Equipment in your school or local library. Give your answer fully explained. In it show authorities, citing law and opinions applicable, and the P-H Federal Tax Equipment paragraphs where they may be found.

2. Enumerate and explain carefully every step you take in reaching your result. These are extremely important—just as important as the conclusion itself.

Tax Reasoning Problem 3-30

When Mason Smith and his wife were divorced, he was ordered to pay her $350 per month. It seemed clear that $200 of the monthly payment was intended for child support. The agreement provided that the payment would go to $200 if she remarried. In addition, reductions in the payments were to be made as each child reached 21. The decree did not fix any specific amount for child support. Are the payments taxable to the wife? Explain.

ASSIGNMENT No. 4

GAIN OR LOSS—RECOGNITION

(Note: In the following problems, unless otherwise specified, assume that the "tax year" is the calendar year 1977, that the taxpayer and his spouse, if any, are resident citizens, under 65 and are not blind and that the taxpayer is not entitled to any credits against the tax other than those shown.)

Problem 4-1

On July 1, Lena Peru sold land and a residence to Ezra Brazil. Lena received $60,000 in cash, a note for $20,000, and 20 shares of Apex Corporation stock. The Apex stock had a par value of $500 a share and a fair market value of $1,000 a share when received.

The sales contract read that "80% of the amount paid for the property was for the land." As part of the sales agreement Ezra agreed to pay the $1,500 in property taxes which Lena owed on the property ($1,000 on the land and $500 on the residence).

Lena had purchased the land five years ago for $60,000. The following year she constructed a house on the property for $20,000 and up to the date of sale had made improvements on the house costing $7,000. Lena had used a portion of the residence for her business. Using the straight line method of depreciation she was allowed depreciation deductions totalling $2,000.

What, if any, gain or loss is recognized on the sale of the property? Assume any gain or loss to be ordinary.

Problem 4-2

(a) In nontaxable exchanges not involving boot, is any gain or loss ever recognized? Explain your answer.

(b) In the following situations explain whether gain or loss would be recognized.

(1) Thompson, the record owner of 100 shares of nonvoting Crane Corporation preferred stock exchanged his stock for 100 shares of nonvoting Crane Corporation common stock owned by Harris. The exchange was not made under a conversion privilege in the preferred stock certificate.

(2) Would your answer in (1) be different if Harris was the owner of 100 shares of preferred stock with voting rights?

(3) Able is the owner of a motor boat which he and his family use for water skiing. Due to the pollution of the lake where the boat is docked, an ordinance was passed limiting the size of the motors which could be used on the lake. Hearing of this new regulation, Able exchanged his old motor boat for a new one which complied with the limitations contained in the ordinance.

(4) Rhodes owns 15,000 of 20,000 shares of nonvoting preferred stock of the Dome Corporation and 20,000 of 40,000 shares of the voting common stock. In exchange for services he had performed for the corporation, he received 12,000 shares of voting common stock and 3,000 shares of nonvoting preferred stock.

(5) Would your answer to (4) be different if Rhodes had received 10,000 shares of voting common stock and 3,000 shares of nonvoting preferred stock for which he transferred property of an equivalent fair market value to the corporation?

Problem 4-3

(a) Oscar Wells sold his airplane having an adjusted basis of $22,000 for $17,500 and his auto having an adjusted basis of $2,000 for $2,500. He used the airplane and auto solely for pleasure. How much of a gain or loss, if any, will be recognized on these sales? Explain.

(b) Jerry Harpo owned an auto junkyard. In July, he granted the Ace Trucking Company an easement for a road to run through the middle of his property. Ace trucks were to use the road to get to a new parking terminal. After the road was completed, Jerry constructed a series of crossings across the road which he used in towing wrecked autos across his property. Was the grant of the easement a sale of the property? Explain.

Problem 4-4

Mike Hall's real estate business has sales listings for some lucrative building lots which he purchased for $50,000 and which are now worth $80,000. An opportunity arises for him to exchange the lots for ownership of an apartment house with an adjusted basis of $70,000 and a fair market value of $120,000. Does Hall have a recognized gain when he exchanges the building lots for the apartment house and if so, how much?

Problem 4-5

John Plouff owned 150 shares of preferred nonvoting stock in Fighting Irish Distillers, Inc. He had purchased this stock for $37 per share. He also owned 500 shares of common stock in the same corporation. He paid $22 per share for the common.

Fighting Irish issued new common stock and gave its shareholders the option of exchanging three shares of the old common stock for two shares of the newly issued common stock.

In which of the following transactions is gain or loss recognized by Plouff? Explain.

(a) In exercising his option, Plouff exchanged 375 shares of the old common stock for 250 shares of the new common stock. The new common stock has a fair market value of $36 per share.

(b) Plouff exchanged the remaining 125 shares of his old issue of common stock for 50 shares of common stock of the P.U. Boilermaker Corporation. The Boilermaker Corporation stock had a fair market value of $77 per share.

(c) Plouff exchanged all his preferred nonvoting stock for $7,500 worth of Fighting Irish 8% bonds bought at par owned by another Fighting Irish stockholder.

No reorganization was involved in any of the above exchanges.

Problem 4-6

Tim Pass and Phil Card organized the Tutti-Frutti Ice Cream Corporation with 1000 shares of stock with a fair market value of $25 a share. Tim transferred property with a fair market value of $16,400 in exchange for 820 shares of stock, while Phil transferred property with a fair market value of $1,600 for 80 shares of stock. At the same time, the corporation issued to Pete Visco 100 shares of its stock in payment for substantial organizational and promotional services rendered by Pete for the benefit of the corporation. Visco transferred no property to the corporation. Tim and Phil were under no obligation to pay for Pete's services. Does either Tim, Phil, or Pete have a recognized gain or loss? Explain.

Problem 4-7

Indicate whether the following exchanges of stock are nontaxable. Assume no corporate reorganization. Explain your answer.

(a) Exchange of common stock in Alpine Corporation for preferred stock in Brookside Corp.

(b) Exchange of common stock in Alpine Corporation for common stock in Brookside Corp.

(c) Exchange of voting preferred stock in Alpine Corp. for nonvoting preferred stock in Alpine Corp.

(d) Exercising a conversion privilege, and exchanging Alpine's preferred stock for Alpine's common stock.

(e) Exercising a conversion privilege, and exchanging Alpine's bonds for Alpine's common stock.

(f) Exercising a conversion privilege, and exchanging Alpine's bonds for Brookside's stock.

Problem 4-8

Wishing to become a rancher, John Jones exchanged a piece of land in Phoenix, Arizona with a basis of $50,000 for a ranch in Coyote Bluffs, Wyoming, valued at $60,000, and farm machinery valued at $10,000. Jones had purchased the land in Phoenix several years ago as an investment. What, if any, is recognized gain on the exchange? Explain.

Problem 4-9

(a) Harmon Herzog, a building contractor, exchanged a warehouse used in his business for a piece of commercial land on which he hoped to construct a housing development. He also gave a dump truck and $5,000 cash. At the time of the exchange the warehouse had a fair market value of $100,000 and an adjusted basis of $80,000. The dump truck had a fair market value of $2,000 and an adjusted basis of $1,000. The fair market value of the land at the time of the exchange was $120,000. What, if any, was Herzog's recognized gain or loss on the exchange? What is Herzog's basis of the land acquired?

(b) Oscar Owens, a printer, had an old printing machine. It had an adjusted basis of $6,000. He exchanged it for a new one valued at $9,000. The manufacturer allowed Oscar a trade-in allowance of $4,000 on his old machine, and Oscar paid the balance of $5,000 in cash. What, if any, was Owens' recognized gain or loss? What is Owens' basis of the new machine acquired?

Problem 4-10

Louis transferred to Johnson commercial real estate with an adjusted basis of $15,000. In return he received similar real estate with a fair market value of $15,100, $5,000 cash, a $1,000 note, and stock with a basis of $1,000 and a fair market value of $2,000. What, if any, is Louis' realized and recognized gain or loss on the transaction?

Problem 4-11

State whether gain or loss will be recognized on each of the following exchanges, and give reasons:

(a) A parcel of commercially zoned real estate in Philadelphia for a truck farm in New Jersey.

(b) A 99-year commercial leasehold for a warehouse in Florida.

(c) A printing press given by one printer to another for 100 shares of electric company stock.

(d) An exchange of 500 square feet of plywood by a lumber retailer for a fork lift truck to be used in retailer's business.

(e) New York City bonds for a chicken farm in Texas.

Problem 4-12

In each of the following exchanges state whether or not gain or loss will be recognized. Explain.

(a) A whole life policy with a basis of $5,000 is exchanged for a 5-year term policy (no cash surrender value) with a basis of $5,500.

(b) Life, endowment and fixed annuity policies are exchanged prior to maturity for three variable annuity contracts.

(c) An endowment policy with a basis of $19,600 is exchanged for a paid-up life insurance policy with a basis of $16,500 and $3,500 in cash.

Assume all contracts relate to the same individual.

Problem 4-13

Mike Meteor owned the Regis apartment building which was subject to a $5,000 mortgage. The building had been purchased for $50,000. A total of $10,000

had been taken in depreciation on the building. Meteor exchanged the Regis receiving: (1) an apartment building known as the Windsor and (2) $5,000 in cash to satisfy the mortgage on the Regis. The Windsor had been owned by Charlie Muller and was purchased for $55,000. At the date of the exchange, $15,000 in depreciation had been allowed on the Windsor and its fair market value was $42,500.
(a) What is Meteor's realized gain or loss, if any?
(b) What is Meteor's recognized gain or loss, if any?

Problem 4-14

Constance Fairweather, a collector of rare books, exchanged a first edition for another collector's Persian rug with a fair market value of $6,000. The adjusted basis of the book was $3,000.
(a) What, if any, is Constance's recognized gain or loss?
(b) Assume instead that Constance exchanged the book for a rare 15th Century book with a fair market value of $10,000. What, if any, is her recognized gain or loss?
(c) Assume the same facts as in (b) except that Constance also received $1,000 in cash. What, if any, is her recognized gain or loss?
(d) Again assume the same facts as in (b) except that Constance also gave Beaver City municipal bonds with an adjusted basis of $5,000 and a fair market value of $1,000. What, if any, is Constance's recognized gain or loss?

Problem 4-15

Butler, a tool and die maker, purchased a new lathe for $4,000. Discovering that the lathe was too large for its intended purpose, he arranged an exchange of the lathe for a smaller one with a fair market value of $2,500. Instead of returning the price differential in cash, the dealer and Butler agreed that Butler would accept 100 pounds of steel valued at $1,700. What, if any, is Butler's recognized gain or loss on the transaction?

Problem 4-16

Baker owns an apartment house with an adjusted basis of $500,000, but which is subject to a mortgage of $150,000. On April 1, he transferred the apartment house to Carter, receiving in exchange $50,000 in cash and another apartment house with a fair market value on that date of $600,000. The transfer to Carter is made subject to the $150,000 mortgage. What is Baker's realized and recognized gain on the exchange, if any?

Problem 4-17

In November of last year, Selwyn Smythe, owner of "The Jungle," a popular downtown nightclub, was notified by the Gulf City Urban Redevelopment Commission that his establishment was condemned. In January of this year, Selwyn received a condemnation award of $75,000 for the property. The adjusted basis of the property was $50,000. Six months later, he purchased an office building in nearby Port Morley for $70,000.
(a) Assuming that Selwyn made a proper and timely election with his return as to nonrecognition of gain, did he have any recognized gain or loss?
(b) Would your answer to (a) be different if the condemnation award had been for $65,000?
(c) Would your answer to (a) be different if the condemnation award had been for $45,000?
(d) Would your answer to (a) be different if Selwyn purchased a summer home on Long Island with the condemnation award rather than an office building?
(e) Would your answer to (a) be different if Selwyn's nightclub was destroyed by fire and he received $75,000 in insurance proceeds rather than a condemnation award?

Problem 4-18

(a) Moynahan was startled one evening when he saw on the evening news that the state highway authority has decided to run a 6 lane superhighway through his front yard. He confirmed this information the next day with his brother-in-law Willard who was a writer for a local newspaper. Two weeks later he sold his home for $36,000 to the Blackman Realty Co. The adjusted basis of the home was $30,000. Three weeks later he purchased a new home for $32,000. Assuming that he made a proper and timely election with his return as to nonrecognition of gain, did he have any recognized gain or loss?

(b) Roland Rustic owned a two story building. The first floor housed his antique shop, the second his apartment. A fire totally destroyed the building but the antiques were saved. The adjusted basis of the store at the time of the fire was $30,000 and the adjusted basis of his apartment was $20,000. Rustic's insurance company awarded him $49,000 for the building ($31,000 for the shop and $18,000 for the apartment). Rustic purchased another antique shop several months later with $35,000 of the purchase price going for the building. He did not purchase a new home. Assuming that he made a proper and timely election with his return as to nonrecognition of gain, did he have any recognized gain or loss?

(c) Assume the same facts in (b), except that Rustic's building was condemned and he received a condemnation award instead of insurance proceeds. Did he have any recognized gain or loss?

SUPPLEMENTAL PROBLEMS
Problem 4-19

(a) Bob Brand was the owner of a house in which he had resided for a period of twenty years. The adjusted basis of the house was $15,000. Because his home was now too large for him, Brand decided to buy a new home. He was able to sell his home for $38,000 and the new owner agreed to assume the balance of the mortgage on the home which amounted to $4,000. Brand spent $1,000 each for brokers commissions and fixing-up expenses. The cost of the new home was $25,000. Compute the realized and recognized gain or loss, if any, on the transaction.

(b) Would your answer to (a) be different if Brand were 66 years old at the time of the sale? If so, how?

(c) Assume that the adjusted basis of Brand's home was $15,000 and that it was not encumbered by any mortgages. Before he could sell it, his home was seized due to condemnation proceedings and the authorities awarded him $35,000 on March 15, 1977. After much looking, Brand bought a new home for $25,000 from the proceeds of the award on October 31, 1978. Compute the realized and recognized gain or loss, if any, on the transaction. Could Brand have elected to treat the condemnation as a sale?

Cumulative Problem 4-20

Harry Fleetwood, 44, single, operated a combination limousine dealership and rental service in which he both sold and rented limousines.

In February, Harry traded a limousine, which he had been renting, for a station wagon. When exchanged, the old limousine had an adjusted basis of $1,800 and a fair market value of $2,500. The station wagon had a fair market value of $2,600. The wagon was used one-half the time in Harry's business and one-half the time for Harry's personal use.

In March, a fire in Harry's showroom destroyed one of the limousines that was being held for sale. The limousine at the time of the fire had an adjusted basis of $5,000 and a fair market value of $6,000. Harry's insurance company paid him $6,000 for the destroyed vehicle. Harry used the proceeds to purchase another limousine from his supplier. The price was $5,500. Instead of holding the new limousine for sale, he used the limousine in his passenger carrying service.

Harry had purchased a bungalow in the mountains 10 years ago for $40,000. The bungalow had been used up until January of this year solely for family vacations. In February, he began renting it out. In April, he exchanged it for a farm in Rhode Island which had a fair market value of $45,000. At the time of the exchange, the bungalow had an adjusted basis of $50,000 and a fair market value of $53,000.

Harry had owed $200 to the owner of a local service station. The debt was cancelled when Harry, under agreement with the station owner, transported the latter's son from his college in Maine to his home for the holidays.

Harry's net profits from the sale and rental of limousines for the year were $25,000. His itemized deductions totaled $2,000. He received the following amounts of interest during the year: $150 on a local sewer authority bond, $300 on his savings account, and $80 on a Wake Island Redevelopment Agency bond.

Compute Harry's tax before credits. Assume any gain or loss to be ordinary. Assume also that Harry made the proper elections.

Cumulative Problem 4-21
(Answer (a) or (b) as directed)

(a) Elmo Axelrod, a 64 year-old attorney has been married twice. His first wife Adele, died in 1975. They had one child, Arden. Arden is now 6 years old, blind and lives with Elmo. In January 1976, Elmo married Beatrice. In August 1976, they had a child, Sybil. In November 1976, they were divorced. Beatrice was granted custody of Sybil. During 1977 Elmo provided $1,000 for the child's support and Beatrice provided $600. During 1977 Elmo was involved in the following exchanges:

(1) In January, Elmo paid $200 for 100 shares of preferred stock in the Bedlow Corporation. Two months later, he exercised a conversion privilege in the share certificates and exchanged with Bedlow the 100 shares for 125 shares of common stock of Bedlow. The fair market value of the shares received in the exchange was $300.

(2) In March, Elmo purchased a piece of land for $10,000 on which he intended to build a residence. In June, the state condemned the land and in return gave him a similar piece valued at $12,000.

(3) In July, Elmo's father gave him a car. The following month Elmo exchanged the car for his neighbor's car. As part of the deal, Elmo had to also give his neighbor $200. Elmo's basis in the automobile at the time of the exchange was $1,000. The value of the neighbor's car was $2,000. Elmo used the cars solely for pleasure.

(4) Elmo had purchased his residence several years ago for $60,000. The house has nine rooms, three of which (or approximately 1/3 of the house) were always used for his law practice. In September, he sold the house. The amount realized on the sale was $75,000. The following month, he purchased a new one for $72,000, again using one-third of the house for his practice. At the time of the sale, Elmo's adjusted basis in the office portion of the old residence was $17,500 (depreciation of $2,500 was taken on this portion of the residence) and his basis in the residential portion was $40,000.

Elmo's net profit from his law practice for 1977 was $35,000. This did not include any net gain (or deductible loss) from the transactions discussed above. In addition, he received $10,000 in a libel action ($3,000 of this amount was punitive damages). His itemized deductions for the year totaled $8,000.

Compute Axelrod's lowest tax before any credits. Assume any gain (or loss) is treated as ordinary. Assume also in your answer that Elmo made proper elections.

(b) Steven Small is the owner of an automobile rental agency. Last month one of the cars belonging to his fleet was stolen and Small received an insurance payment of $4,800. The adjusted basis of the stolen car was $3,000. Three weeks after the theft, Small used the insurance proceeds to purchase a new car to be used in the business for $4,500. Small elected to apply the provisions for nonrecognition of gain on the involuntary conversion.

At the same time, Small purchased an additional car for his business, whose fair market value was $4,300. Small traded-in an old fleet car and he received an allowance of $2,800. In addition, he paid $1,500 in cash. The old car had an adjusted basis of $2,000.

(1) What is the recognized gain or loss, if any, on the above transactions?

(2) Net income from the auto rental business and any taxable gain or loss from the above transactions totaled $34,000. In addition, he received $150 interest on his Port of N.Y. Authority bonds and $350 interest on the Welco Corporation bonds that he owned. Small rented out a number of garages that he owned to the Crestview Sanitation Company, and he received net rental income after depreciation and taxes of $4,000. Under the will of his late Uncle Jason, Small received a devise of $20,000. He also received $600 in interest from the money he had on deposit in the Crestview National Bank. Small is divorced and is the sole support of his father who lives with him. The father has no income of his own. Small paid $2,400 in alimony to his ex-wife pursuant to the divorce decree, which obligates him to pay $2,400 per year to his ex-wife until she dies or remarries. The decree also gave sole custody of their only child to Small's ex-wife and provided that she was entitled to the personal exemption for the child. Small gave $1,500 which constituted almost the entire yearly support for the child. In addition to the above, Small's other itemized deductions totaled $6,000. Compute the tax liability of Small before any credits to which he may be entitled.

Research Problem 4-22

Michael Bell is the owner of timberland. During the year, a severe hurricane struck the timberland, uprooting a considerable number of the trees. The timber was not insured and Bell realized that if he allowed the fallen trees to remain in that condition, they would soon decay or would be rendered totally worthless by insects. Fortunately, Bell was able to sell the damaged timber, and realize a gain from the sale. Bell used the sale proceeds to purchase other standing timber. He is uncertain about whether or not he must report the gain he realized on the sale. He consults you, a tax expert, for advice concerning the nonrecognition of gain in regard to involuntary conversions. What would you advise? Explain.

Use the Prentice-Hall Complete Federal Tax Equipment in your school or local library to find your answer. Do the following:

1. Give and explain your opinion. In it, show authorities, citing the decisions applicable, and the P-H Federal Tax Equipment paragraphs where they may be found.

2. Enumerate and explain carefully each and every step you take in reaching your result.

Tax Reasoning Problem 4-23

To get zoning approval for his residential subdivision, Harrison had to set aside a school site. When needed, Harrison would transfer the site to the local school district or, if a price could not be agreed on, the school district would condemn the property. The school district condemned the property. Can Harrison get nonrecognition of gain by buying replacement property? Explain.

Tax Reasoning Problem 4-24

Acme Corp. was organized five years ago to build and rent housing. The apartments suffered excessive and recurring acts of vandalism. As a result of the continued vandalism, Acme sold the property and realized a gain on the sale. It then reinvested the proceeds in similar property and elected to postpone the gain under the nonrecognition provisions of Sec. 1033. Was this a valid election? Explain.

ASSIGNMENT No. 5

GAIN OR LOSS—BASIS

(*Note:* In the following problems, unless otherwise specified, assume that the "tax year" is the calendar year 1977, that the taxpayer and his spouse, if any, are resident citizens, under 65 and are not blind and that the taxpayer is not entitled to any credits against the tax other than those shown.)

Problem 5-1

In February, Margo Anthony purchased an apartment building for $200,000. She paid $4,000 for a new roof and $6,000 for new electrical wiring to comply with local safety regulations. She also incurred $1,800 in legal fees and purchase commissions.

In June, she had built attached parking garages for the building at a cost of $30,000. In September, a fire in the building's basement caused $2,500 worth of damage to the walls and ceiling. Nothing was done to repair the damage. Insurance proceeds of $1,200 were received for the damage. Margo took a casualty loss deduction on her return for the remainder of the damage. She also took a depreciation deduction of $6,000 on her return.

What is the building's adjusted basis at the end of the year?

Problem 5-2

Katie Kimble owned a little plant shop in Guruville, Nevada. Katie incurred very large gambling losses and she notified her wealthy nephew Sean that the bank was about to foreclose. In January, Sean agreed to buy the land and building from her. Although the property was worth $25,000, he paid Katie $20,000 cash and assumed payment of the $15,000 mortgage on the building. Sean incurred the following expenses in connection with the purchase: brokerage commissions, $2,000; lawyer's fees to acquire and perfect title, $500; back real estate taxes, $200 (all the parties concerned had agreed to this); and surveying expenses, $50. In March, Sean renovated the building at a cost of $3,000 and opened a restaurant. By the end of the year, the business failed, and Sean sold the property for $35,000. Sean had taken a depreciation deduction of $2,000 on the building for the year. What is his recognized gain or loss, if any, on the sale of the property?

Problem 5-3

In 1910, Mulray Corp. purchased land outside Los Angeles for $5,000. Valuable water rights on the property made its fair market value soar to $70,000 as of 3-1-13. On 1-2-27, Mulray completed a dam on the property for $280,000. It had a useful life of 70 years (depreciation was $4,000 a year).

On 1-2-77, Mulray Corp. sold the property for $200,000. What is its gain or loss, if any, on the transaction?

Problem 5-4

On April 6, 1974, Mary Smith purchased a summer home. The home cost $39,000, including purchase commissions and legal fees. Mary died on 7-19-77 leaving the home to her son Michael. The home had a fair market value of $48,000 on the date Mary died. Michael received title to the home under Mary's will on 12-15-77. Its fair market value when received was $49,000. What is Michael's basis in the property?

Problem 5-5

(a) Esther Spumanti inherited a bond of the Scales Corporation from her aunt. Her aunt purchased the bond in 1970 for $1,500. On December 31, 1976, the bond's market value was $1,600. On the date of her aunt's death, January 21, 1977, the value of the bond was $1,650, and on March 17, 1977, the date Esther received the bond, it was quoted at $1,750. In December, Esther sold the bond for $1,900. How much gain, if any, was recognized by Esther on the sale of the bond?

(b) How would your answer in (a) differ if Esther sold the bond for $1,400. Explain.

(c) Leonard Kramer's uncle purchased stock on January 2, 1976 for $1,000. The uncle died on April 1, 1977 when the stock's fair market value was $2,000. On December 31, 1976 the value of the stock was $1,500. Under the uncle's will, Leonard was granted a cash bequest of $2,500. On September 2, 1977, when the value of the stock was $2,500, Leonard received from his uncle's executor the stock in lieu of the cash bequest. On December 31, 1977, Leonard sold the stock for $2,800. What gain or loss, if any, did Leonard recognize on the sale? Assume in your answer that fair market value on date of death was used for estate tax purposes, and that the gain recognized on the distribution was $500.

Problem 5-6

On 1-1-71, George and Martha Becker, husband and wife, bought an office building for $120,000 and held it as tenants by the entirety. Each paid one-half of the purchase price, and each had a one-half interest in the income from the property. The Beckers filed joint returns during the period they held the property. Each year they took a $3,500 depreciation deduction on the property. George Becker died on 1-1-77, when the building had a fair market value of $150,000. One-half of this value ($75,000), was included in his estate. What was Martha's adjusted basis in the property after George's death?

Problem 5-7

(a) In 1975, Grey purchased a business machine for $10,000. On 1-2-77, he made a gift of the machine to Jones. Grey was not liable for any gift tax. At the time of the gift the machine had a fair market value of $7,000. Jones sold the machine on 4-1-77 for $8,000. What was Jones' gain or loss if any, on the sale?

(b) On 1-1-62, Aunt Katy gave 400 shares of oil stock to her niece Priscilla. The value of the stock on 1-1-62 was $40,000. Katy paid a gift tax of $3,600 on the transfer. Katy's husband had given her the stock in 1931 when it had a value of $20,000. The husband had purchased the stock the year before for $37,000. On 1-2-77, Priscilla sold the stock for $40,500. What was Priscilla's gain or loss, if any, on the sale?

Problem 5-8

On 1-2-71, Wilmer Eakins bought a professional building for $95,000. It had an estimated useful life of 50 years. On 1-2-74, Wilmer gave the building, which then had a fair market value of $110,000, to his nephew, Ewald. Wilmer paid a gift tax of $10,000. On 1-2-77, Ewald sold the building for $115,000. During the period he and his uncle owned the building, depreciation was $2,000 a year.

(a) What, if any, is Ewald's gain or loss from the sale?

(b) Assume Ewald received $90,000 from the sale, what would be his gain or loss, if any?

Problem 5-9

Fred Dixon is in the construction business. He exchanged a cement mixer which he had purchased two years ago for $11,000 for a smaller machine having a fair market value of $9,800. Depreciation of $2,000 had been taken on the old cement mixer. Dixon received $1,000 in cash from the dealer in addition to a note which had a fair market value of $1,200. Compute Dixon's realized and recognized gain or loss, and the basis of the new mixer.

Problem 5-10

(a) On 1-2-74, Wellington Bisque, who operates the Belle Art Cinema, purchased a piece of movie equipment for $5,000. On 1-2-77, he traded this for a new one. The new one listed for $7,500 and he was allowed $3,500 as a trade-in allowance on the old equipment. He paid the balance of $4,000 in cash. Wellington had taken a depreciation deduction of $400 each year on the old equipment. What is his basis in the new one?

(b) Assume Wellington traded the old equipment for a new smaller model with a fair market value of $3,500, and also received $450 in cash. What, if any, recognized gain or loss would Wellington have on the transaction? What is his basis in the new equipment?

(c) Assume the same facts as in (b), except that Wellington received $100 in cash. What is his recognized gain or loss on the transaction, if any? What is the basis of the new machine?

Problem 5-11

Dan Hill owns Tract X, a parcel of land that had been given to him as a gift by Steve Moore on 7-1-73. On that date, the property had a fair market value of $12,000 and Moore's basis was $9,000.

On 4-1-77, he exchanged Tract X for 2 smaller tracts; Tract A with a value of $6,000 and Tract B with a value of $4,000 and also received $3,000 cash on the date of the exchange. Tract X had a fair market value of $15,000 on 4-1-77. What is the basis of each tract received by Hill?

Problem 5-12

Roger Nome owns property with an adjusted basis of $150,000, on which there is an outstanding mortgage of $50,000. Nome organized Key Corporation to which he transferred the property in exchange for all the stock of the corporation. The corporation assumed the outstanding mortgage on the property. The fair market value of the stock transferred to Nome was $225,000.

(a) What gain, if any, is recognized by Nome?
(b) What is the basis of the stock which Nome received?

Problem 5-13

(a) Bob Galik used a delivery truck in his laundry business. The truck had an adjusted basis of $14,500, when it was destroyed by a tornado. Bob received $11,500 on his business insurance policy. He immediately purchased a similar truck for $15,200. Does Bob have a recognized gain or loss? What is the new truck's basis?

(b) Nora Barry owned shore property on Lake Michigan which she purchased in 1972 for $200,000. In early 1977, the property had a fair market value of $250,000. In February 1977, the state of Indiana condemned Nora's property to construct a nuclear-powered sewage treatment plant. In March, 1977, she received a $260,000 award from the state. Within 6 months she purchased 3 nearby parcels of lakeshore property totaling about the same acreage as the condemned land. She paid $126,000 for parcel number 1, $63,000 for parcel number 2, and $21,000 for parcel number 3. Nora elected to apply the rules for nonrecognition of gain on an involuntary conversion. Does Nora have a recognized gain or loss? What is the basis of each of the new parcels?

Problem 5-14

(a) Debbie Chick made the following purchases of Drake Duck Down Corporation stock: 150 shares in 1974 at $20 per share; 200 shares in 1975 at $29 per share; and 300 shares in 1976 at $30 per share. In 1977 she sold 400 shares for $12,400. She was able to identify 360 shares of those sold through stock certificates, but had no other records of her purchases. The stock certificates identified 60 of the shares bought in 1974, 100 of the shares bought in 1975, and 200 of the shares bought in 1976 as part of those sold.

(1) What is her recognized gain on the sale?
(2) Assuming Debbie had kept a complete record of her stock purchases, which blocks of stock should she have sold to get the least amount of recognized gain?
(3) What would her recognized gain then be?

(b) In a tax-free merger of Madison Corp. with Unger Corp., Mr. Smith, a stockholder in Unger, received 1,000 shares of Madison stock in exchange for the 2,000 shares he held in Unger. Smith had purchased the Unger stock in lots of 100 over a five-year period. Shares of Madison (the surviving corporation) were traceable through stock certificate numbers to specific shares of Unger. Explain the method Smith should use in determining the basis of his newly acquired shares of Madison stock.

Problem 5-15

Paul Maganzini, owner of Southside Sportstowne, a large sporting goods store, obtained a patent from the government for a new form of cleated athletic shoe designed to lessen the chance of injury resulting from play on artificially surfaced fields. Paul spent $5,500 for consultation fees and $2,000 for other necessary expenses incurred to obtain the patent. Paul experimented on ways to improve the patented shoe and spent $1,800 in fees for advice from experts and $1,500 for materials used in making experimental models. Paul estimates the value of his time spent in trying to improve the shoe is $5,000. None of these costs were deducted as research and experimental expenditures. Paul sold the patent and the exclusive rights to it to the Kedsdidas Shoe Corporation for $75,000. What is his recognized gain or loss on the sale?

Problem 5-16

Mitchell Perone, age 35, purchased a home on 1-2-67 for $25,000. He incurred brokerage commissions of $350 on the purchase. A year later he added a garage costing $3,500. On 6-1-77, he entered into a contract of sale on his residence. The contract was completed on 7-1-77. The sale price was $42,000. In selling the home he incurred brokerage commissions of $900 and advertising expenses of $100. In preparing the house for sale he had it painted on 1-5-77 and replaced some shingles on 5-30-77. The paint job cost him $500 and the shingles $300. Payment of these amounts were made as soon as the work was completed. Perone did not deduct the sale commissions as a moving expense on his 1977 return. On 6-2-77, Perone completed the purchase of a new home for $38,000. He occupied the home on 7-2-77.

What is the basis of the new residence? What is Perone's recognized gain or loss, if any?

Problem 5-17

On 1-1-73, Alan Lane purchased a plot of land upon which he intended to erect a professional building. The cost of the land was $75,000. Construction on the building began in 1974. A loan was taken out to finance the construction of the building. Interest on the loan had totaled $7,500 by the end of 1977. Realizing that he did not have sufficient funds to complete his project, Lane began advertising for the property's sale on December 1, 1977. On 12-31-77, Lane sold the property for $200,000. Advertisements for the sale had cost Lane $1,400. Materials for the partially completed building had cost him $65,000. From 1973 through 1977 Lane had paid $4,800 in real estate taxes on the property. He never deducted these taxes on his previous returns. If Lane elected to capitalize his expenses, determine his gain or loss on the sale of the property, if any.

SUPPLEMENTAL PROBLEMS
Problem 5-18

Dan Rock, a professional fisherman, was involved in the following transactions during the year:

(a) In January, he traded a fishing boat "Betsy" with an adjusted basis of $54,500 for a fishing boat "Carla" valued at $67,000 and gave stock valued at $12,000. The stock originally cost him $13,500.

(b) In September, he exchanged the fishing boat "Carla" in (a) above which was now valued at $65,000 for another fishing boat "Fifi" valued at $68,000. Assume "Carla's" adjusted basis was the same as calculated in (a) above. He also received $2,000 in cash and a boat trailer worth $900.

(c) In December, a fire totally destroyed the marina at which the fishing boat "Fifi" was moored. The boat was a total loss. Assume that at the time of the fire "Fifi's" adjusted basis was the same as calculated in (b) above. Insurance proceeds were $67,300. He purchased an identical fishing boat "Lulu" for $70,000.

What is the basis of each of the properties acquired? What is the recognized gain or loss on each transaction? Explain.

Problem 5-19

In 1975, Edwin Smith purchased a parcel of land located in Michigan's Upper Peninsula for $500,000. A ski lodge and a chair lift were situated on the land. The fair market value of the land was $200,000; the ski lodge was valued at $250,000; the chair lift was valued at $50,000. In 1977, Smith sold the ski lodge for $300,000, properly allowing $15,000 for depreciation. What is his gain on the sale? How is it calculated? Explain.

Problem 5-20

On 5-1-75, Avery Austin bought an apartment house for $400,000 and put a $170,000 mortgage on it. During the period Austin owned it, depreciation on the building amounted to $5,000 a year. After 2 years, Austin tired of city life, and on 5-1-77 exchanged the building for a cattle ranch worth $400,000 owned by Caleb Cornfield. Cornfield took the apartment house subject to Austin's mortgage, which at the time of the exchange, amounted to $150,000. Determine the amount of Austin's recognized gain and the basis of the ranch.

Problem 5-21

What is the recognized gain, if any, and the basis of the stock received in the following transactions? Explain.

(a) Lee Passaro transferred an apartment building with an adjusted basis of $150,000, to the Sturgis Corporation in exchange for 83% of its stock worth $83,000, $70,000 in cash and a new automobile with a fair market value of $6,500.

(b) Joan Johnson exchanged $6,800 worth of home heating oil for 81% of the stock of the Sea Slick Tuna Corporation.

Cumulative Problem 5-22

Ava O'Reilly, 32 and single, is employed as a financial analyst by the Skidmore Tire Co. and receives a monthly salary of $2,000. In February, Ava bought 500 shares of Fountain Corp. stock for $4,000. In June, when the shares had a fair market value of $4,500 she exchanged them for 600 shares of Jetstream, Inc. stock, worth $5,000. The exchange was not part of a corporate reorganization.

In July, Ava travelled to Switzerland on vacation. She deposited $3,000 in a Zurich bank, for possible emergencies. She requested the bank to open an account for her and to convert her money to francs. She later withdrew the money before returning home without ever using the account. When the funds were converted back into dollars, an increase in the value of the franc resulted in Ava receiving $3,300.

While on her vacation, Ava's car was destroyed by fire. Its adjusted basis was $3,600. The insurance proceeds amounted to $3,900 and were received by Ava in May. Soon afterward she bought a new car for $4,100.

Ava's mother is a widow and lives alone in her own apartment. Ava paid rent, utility charges, and upkeep on her mother's apartment. These amounts totalled $1,800 for the year. Her brothers, Tom and Jerry, each gave their mother $500 during the year for food, clothing and medical expenses. The parties did not enter into a multiple support agreement. The mother received $2,000 in social security payments during the year. She used one-half of these benefits for her own support.

Ava had received $85 interest during the year on a savings account. In December, Ava was asked, by a local college, to review the bond offering of a corporation in which the school was considering investing. The school agreed to donate the

$75 she was to receive to the Headache Research Fund, an exempt organization. Ava had itemized deductions of $2,000.

Compute Ava's lowest tax before credits (rounding off to the nearest dollar). Assume any gain or loss is ordinary, and also assume Ava made the proper elections.

Cumulative Problem 5-23

(Answer (a) or (b) as directed)

(a) Benton Slugwell, an artist, had net earnings of $15,000 during 1977 from the sale of his paintings. Benton is single and lives alone. His 65th birthday is on January 1, 1978.

Benton owns an apartment building and a vacant piece of land which he leases. During the year he received net rentals of $12,000 from the apartment building. The vacant land was purchased in 1961 for $35,000. Benton began leasing the property to the Balzac Corporation that year at an annual rental of $16,000 with Balzac agreeing to pay the property taxes. The lease was for 20 years. In June, Balzac notified Benton that it was going to terminate the lease on July 1. It sent to Benton $8,900 ($8,000 rent and $900 property taxes) due for the first half of the year. In October, the state condemned the land to make way for a public highway and Benton received a condemnation award of $125,000. In December, Benton invested $100,000 of the award in a ranch for raising horses. The remaining $25,000 was used to reduce the mortgage on his apartment building. Benton also received in December, $3,000 in legal damages recovered from the Balzac Corporation for lost rentals during 1977.

Benton exchanged one of his better paintings, "The Sleeping Frog", with a fellow artist for one of his. "The Sleeping Frog" had a fair market value of $1,000 at the time of the exchange. It had cost $100 in painting supplies to make. The painting Benton received had a fair market value of $1,200 at the time of the exchange.

Benton received during the year $3,000 in interest on bonds issued by Saint Katherine Hospital, a tax-exempt organization. He also received $2,000 in interest on bonds issued by New York State.

Benton received in March $1,000 from a trust set up under his mother's will. Under the terms of the will the trust was to pay Benton a total of $3,000 in three annual installments. The installments were to be paid out of the trusts's income.

Benton fully supported his half brother Carl for the past several years. Carl lived in a nursing home during this period. Carl was 66 when he died in February 1977. He had no income in 1977.

Benton had itemized deductions of $9,400 for 1977.

Compute Benton's lowest tax before credits for 1977. Assume any gains and losses are ordinary.

(b) Tom Bailey, a dentist, owned a ten room cooperative apartment which he purchased for $90,000. He used eight of the rooms as his family residence, and the others as his dental office. Depreciation on the portion used as an office totaled $6,000. Bailey sold the apartment this year for the sum of $110,000, incurring selling expenses of $4,000 and fixing-up expenses, for the residential portion of the home, of $5,000. He immediately purchased a new residence for $85,000.

Bailey is married and has two children from his present marriage, Jonas and Nancy, ages 6 and 12. The children live with Bailey and his wife Ann. He also has a child, Richard, from a prior marriage. Richard, age 17, moved away from the family last year and now maintains a $75 a month apartment where he lives. He supports himself by panhandling. During the year Bailey gave Richard a total of $250 towards his support. Bailey earned $38,000 from his dental practice for the year. He entered the "Lucky Sweepstakes" contest and received the second prize of $2,000. He also received a $7,000 settlement as the result of a will contest concerning the estate of his deceased mother. Interest on his savings account amounted to $950. He had itemized deductions of $8,350.

(1) What is the realized and recognized gain or loss, if any, on the sale of the apartment?

(2) What is the tax liability of the Baileys before any credits, assuming that they elect to file a joint return? Assume any recognized gain is treated as ordinary income.

Research Problem 5-24

Midland Corp. and Cook Corp. were both subject to I.C.C. regulation. Midland, in early 1977, sought to sell its assets to Cook in return for 20,000 shares of Cook stock. An agreement for the sale was drawn on March 15, 1977. On April 1, 1977, Cook took full control of Midland with the I.C.C. giving the acquisition its temporary approval. The acquisition required final approval by the I.C.C., but both Midland and Cook were convinced that final approval would follow as a matter of course.

With the I.C.C.'s grant of temporary approval to the acquisition, Cook assumed all management duties of Midland and ran the business. On October 1, 1977, the expected I.C.C. final approval to the acquisition was given.

Midland valued the Cook stock it received as of April 1, the date the I.C.C. gave its temporary approval. They claimed that their amount realized was $100,000, the fair market value of the stock on that date. The government claims that the proper valuation date should be October 1, the date the I.C.C. gave its final approval. Midland consults you and asks if the Cook stock received can be valued as of April 1, or must the date of final approval govern the valuation.

Use the Prentice-Hall Complete Federal Tax Equipment in your school or local library to find your answer. Do the following:

1. Give and explain your opinion. In it, show authorities, citing the decisions applicable, and the P-H Federal Tax Equipment paragraphs where they may be found.

2. Enumerate and explain carefully each and every step you take in reaching your result.

ASSIGNMENT No. 6
CAPITAL GAINS AND LOSSES OF INDIVIDUALS

(Note: In the following problems, unless otherwise specified, assume that the "tax year" is calendar year 1977, that the taxpayer and his spouse, if any, are resident citizens, under 65 and are not blind and that the taxpayer is not entitled to any credit against tax other than those shown.

Problem 6-1

Which of the following items is a capital asset? Explain.

(a) An electronic calculator owned and used by the Dynasty Restaurant.

(b) An electronic calculator owned and used by Frank Lowman to figure his household budget and personal income tax.

(c) An electronic calculator held for sale to customers by the C. K. Business Machines Company.

(d) An office building owned and occupied by the Wellington Co.

(e) The private residence of the vice president of Wellington Co.

(f) $100,000 face amount West Virginia Turnpike revenue bonds owned by a housewife.

(g) The personal notes written and owned by a retired senator who used them to deliver speeches during his tenure of office.

(h) Letters of praise received and owned by a retired senator from the President and colleagues.

(i) A patent on an automatic leaf raker held by the inventor.

Problem 6-2

Daniel Lawrence owned and operated the Kirkdale Milk Company selling processed milk and other dairy products to retail and wholesale customers. In his 8 years of operating the business, Daniel had acquired an excellent reputation. This year, he sold out to the Virginia Milk Company. In the contract, no mention was made of milk routes or customer lists. Virginia, however, obtained the benefit of these by continuing to use the Kirkdale Milk Company name and its route men. To protect itself, Virginia inserted the following clause into the agreement:

" . . . the seller covenants and agrees with the Company . . . that he will not engage . . . in a similar business . . . for a period of 12 years . . . "

"The said Company, in consideration of the agreement of said individual, covenants and agrees to pay him the sum of $100,000 . . . "

(a) Will Daniel get capital gain treatment on the above payment?

(b) Can you suggest another way Daniel could allocate the payment to his advantage?

Problem 6-3

Peter Jacobs is the sole owner of an unincorporated business. On 12-31-77, he sold all the assets of his business to Philip David for their fair market value. The assets of the business were comprised of the following:

		Basis	Fair Market Value
(a)	Ending inventory	$18,000	$37,000
(b)	Stock acquired on 1-1-73 for investment	5,000	8,000
(c)	Accounts receivable	12,000	10,000
(d)	Patent acquired on 1-1-77 for investment	5,000	3,000
(e)	Goodwill created by Jacobs	—0—	17,000
		$40,000	$75,000

What is the nature and amount of any gain or loss to Jacobs on the transaction?

Problem 6-4

Terry Shane, a dog breeder, bought a parcel of land as investment property in January of this year. In each of the following situations, indicate whether or not Shane would have a capital gain or loss, and, if so, whether it would be long-term or short-term:

(a) In August, a neighboring landowner paid him $8,000 for his property.
(b) He rented the property all year for $300 per month.
(c) In September, the state seized his land in condemnation proceedings and awarded him $6,800.
(d) He sold the land for $8,400 in October.
(e) In August, he gave the property to his cousin for her birthday.
(f) He traded the land for stock in November.
(g) Assume that Shane had bought securities (instead of land) for $8,000 and that they were worth $2,500 at the close of his tax year.

Problem 6-5

Michael Halen bought 100 shares of Roslyn Court Corporation convertible preferred stock on Jan. 11 for $5,000. On April 15, he turned in these shares to Roslyn for 100 shares of their common stock. On Oct. 12, Michael sold the stock for $7,500.

(a) Does he have a long- or short-term capital gain? Explain.
(b) What would be your answer to (a) if Michael sold the stock on Oct. 11 instead?

Problem 6-6

Percy Howard died on 9-14-77, leaving 100 shares of Dobbs Ferry Co. stock to his wife Mary. Percy bought the stock on 8-1-77 for $14,000. At his death, it was worth $12,000. On 12-10-77, when the estate was distributed, the stock was worth $13,000. Mary sold the stock on 12-11-77 for $12,900. State whether she has a short-term or long-term capital gain or loss, and the amount.

Problem 6-7

Joseph Peterson bought 100 shares of the Gemstone Imports Co. stock for $6,000 in 1973. On 12-13-76, he gave the stock to his daughter Lynn. The stock's fair market value on that day was $5,300. No gift tax was payable. Lynn sold the stock on 2-1-77. State whether there is a short-term or long-term capital gain or loss, and the amount of the gain or loss if the stock was sold at: (a) $6,150; (b) $4,800; (c) $5,700.

Problem 6-8

On 1-22-77, Amy King instructed her broker to sell short 100 shares of Cornell Co. stock at $25 a share. State the amount of gain or loss in each of the following situations and whether it is a long-term or short-term capital gain or loss:

(a) On 8-1-77, Amy delivered 100 shares of Cornell Co. stock to cover the short sale. She had bought those 100 shares at $20 on 12-11-76.
(b) Amy owned no Cornell Co. stock on 1-22-77. On 12-11-77, she bought 100 shares of Cornell at $21 and on the same day delivered them to cover the short sale.
(c) On 1-22-77, Amy owned 100 shares of Cornell Co. stock that she had bought at $30 a share on 1-11-76. On 2-25-77, she bought another 100 shares of that stock at $31 which she used to cover the short sale. On 2-26-77, she sold the shares she had bought on 1-11-76 for $32 a share.

Problem 6-9

State whether Anna Stone has a long-term or short-term capital gain or loss in the following situations and the amount of her gain or loss.

(a) On 12-11-76, Anna Stone bought 100 shares of Pheebee Fashion Co. Class A preferred stock for $20,000. On 1-11-77, she exchanged that stock for 100 shares of that company's Class B preferred stock which was worth $250 a share on that day. On 6-13-77, she sold all her Pheebee stock for $30,000.

(b) In 1950, Anna Stone bought 200 shares of Wellesley Data Company common stock for $40,000. On 10-10-77, she bought 300 more shares of that stock for $90,000. On 12-12-77, she sold 100 shares of her Wellesley stock for $21,000 through her broker, without identifying the lot sold.

Problem 6-10

Compute the long-term capital gain deduction in each of the following:

(a) Net long-term capital gain or loss .... $5,000 GAIN
    Net short-term capital gain or loss .... $3,000 LOSS
(b) Net long-term capital gain or loss .... $2,000 GAIN
    Net short-term capital gain or loss .... $1,000 GAIN
(c) Net long-term capital gain or loss .... NONE
    Net short-term capital gain or loss .... $5,000 GAIN
(d) Net long-term capital gain or loss .... $4,000 GAIN
    Net short-term capital gain or loss .... NONE

Problem 6-11

George Valentine's record of stock transactions during the year is shown below. Compute his net long-term and short-term capital gains or losses, if any, and the amount of gain or loss to be included in his adjusted gross income.

Stock	Bought	Sold
Bow Wow Corp.	5-1-71 for $1,700	12-12-77 for $1,000
Sheffield Co.	1-11-77 for $ 500	12-11-77 for $2,000
Mass. Fishing Co.	6-13-77 for $3,000	7-3-77 for $1,700
Barker Trust Corp.	2-14-77 for $5,000	9-15-77 for $7,000

Problem 6-12

David King earned $19,250 in wages and had the following capital gains and losses during the year: short-term capital gain, $200; short-term capital loss, $650; long-term capital gain, $2,200; and long-term capital loss, $195. King also had a long-term capital loss carryover of $625 and a short-term capital loss carryover of $250. Compute King's adjusted gross income for the year.

Problem 6-13

(a) Miller's income from salary and taxable interest is $32,000. His capital asset transactions during the year were as follows:

January 23	Bought Leeds, Inc. stock for $8,850.
	Bought Cosmic Corp. stock for $1,520
September 17	Sold Leeds, Inc. stock for $5,650
November 26	Sold Cosmic Corp. stock for $2,160.

What is Miller's adjusted gross income this year and what, if any, is his loss carryover to next year?

(b) Blair's income from salary and taxable interest is $18,400. His capital asset transactions during the year were as follows:

February 15	Bought Argo Corp. stock for $9,000.
August 5	Bought Belon Corp. stock for $6,200.
December 3	Sold Argo Corp. stock for $2,300.
	Sold Belon Corp. stock for $6,700.

What is Blair's adjusted gross income this year and what, if any, is his loss carryover to next year?

Problem 6-14

Mark Doren earned a salary of $46,000 a year. He is single and has no dependents. He had a net short-term capital loss of $4,100. His itemized deductions were $5,000. He incurred no net capital losses in prior years.

(a) What is Mark's taxable income? What is the amount of the loss carryover, if any?
(b) What would be your answer to (a) if Mark's loss was long-term?

Problem 6-15

Walter King, a bachelor, had the following capital asset transactions from 1975 through 1978. For each of those years, he had taxable income of $48,000 without taking into account the capital asset transactions.

	Long-term gains	Long-term losses	Short-term gains	Short-term losses
1975	$14,000	($19,000)	—0—	—0—
1976	$ 3,000	—0—	$2,000	—0—
1977	—0—	($ 800)	—0—	($900)
1978	—0—	($ 7,200)	—0—	—0—

What is the amount of his taxable income each year, taking into account the capital transactions? Explain how his taxable income may be affected by the capital transactions.

Problem 6-16

Lester Pinter is married. During the year, he had a long-term capital gain of $70,000 from investments. His taxable income for the year was $75,000. His wife has no income or deductions. Compute Pinter's lowest tax before credits for the year.

Problem 6-17

Compute the lowest tax before any tax credit in (a) and (b) below.
(a) Claude Walker is single and received $35,000 in salary during the year. He also received taxable interest of $1,000. His excess net long-term capital gain over short-term capital loss was $60,000. His itemized deductions were $5,250.
(b) Robert Sperber is married and has 2 dependent children. His wife has no income or deductions. During the year Robert received a salary of $42,000 and taxable interest of $500. He also had a net long-term capital gain of $36,000 and a net short-term capital loss of $4,000. Robert's itemized deductions were $5,500.

Problem 6-18

(a) On 12-31-67, Russell Hemmert bought an apartment building for rental purposes, the purchase price being $300,000. He sold the building on 12-31-77 for $224,900. An accelerated method of depreciation was used and the deductions for depreciation totaled $120,379, of which $29,250 was deducted prior to 1970 and $19,405 was deducted after 1975. Straight line depreciation would have been $7,500 per year. Hemmert had no other taxable transactions during the year. How much of the gain will be ordinary income and how much will be Sec. 1231 gain (round off figures to nearest dollar)?

(b) On 12-31-77 Donald Monroe sold a business machine for $42,500. He had purchased the machine on 1-2-75 for $40,000. An accelerated method of depreciation was used and the deductions for depreciation totaled $10,840. Straight line depreciation would have been $1,750 per year. Monroe had no other taxable transactions during the year. How much of Monroe's gain, if any, will be ordinary income and how much will be Sec. 1231 gain?

Problem 6-19

(a) During the year, Arthur Mannix received $4,000 from insurance for a painting stolen from his home. He had paid $3,000 for it. A fire damaged his living room furniture. The furniture was not insured and he suffered a $3,500 loss. He had a gain of $5,000 when the government condemned and paid him for a portion of his business property. He sold an apartment building at a gain of $14,000 of which $3,000 was recaptured as ordinary gain. He also sold a delivery truck used entirely for business at $800 loss. All of the above assets were held more than 9 months. Compute his gains and losses and explain how they are treated for income tax purposes.

(b) John Dunlop had the following transactions during the tax year: He sold a factory at a $20,000 loss. He received $100,000 in insurance proceeds for the fire loss of another factory with an adjusted basis of $150,000. He sold a business garage at a $9,000 gain, of which $8,000 was recaptured ordinary income. He received a $60,000 condemnation award for his factory's unimproved parking lot with a $40,000 basis. In addition, his insurance company paid him $2,000 for the loss of his new TV set (cost $200) and antique collections (bought for $1,800) when his house was robbed. The company also paid him $85,000 for his vacation home which was completely destroyed by a flood. The home had cost him $16,000 but was worth $85,000 before the flood. Dunlop also had a $2,000 damage on his uninsured personal automobile caused in an accident. He had owned all of the above assets over 9 months. What were his gains and losses, and how are they treated for income tax purposes? Explain.

Problem 6-20

(a) On 7-1-75, Charles Willer bought a $5,000 20-year bond of the Chatsworth Ave. Corp. for $4,100, the day it was issued. The bond was issued for long-term financing. He sold the bond to Leonard Gordon on 1-3-77 for $4,300. How would Charles' gain be taxed? How much is Leonard's monthly portion of the discount includable in his income?

(b) Gordon Valentine bought a $5,000 15-year bond of the Woodlake Co. for $4,500 on 1-2-69, the day it was issued. Woodlake issued the bonds for long-term financing to build a warehouse. On 2-1-77, the bond was redeemed. Gordon received $4,600 for the bond. How will his gain be taxed?

Problem 6-21

(a) Grant Stume, a stone mason, bought 100 acres of abandoned farmland in 1970 for investment purposes. He made no improvements on the property while he owned it. In 1977, he subdivided the land and began selling lots. He sold one lot for $7,200 (basis, $5,000), one lot for $9,000 (basis, $6,200) and three more lots for $6,900 each (basis, $4,800 each). These transactions were Stume's first venture into the real estate field. How will these transactions be taxed?

(b) Assuming the same facts as in (a), what will be the tax results if Stume sells 3 more lots in 1978 for $10,000 each (basis, $7,000 each)?

(c) Assuming the same facts as in (a), what will be the tax results if Stume does not sell any more lots until 1983, when he sells 2 lots for $12,000 each (basis, $7,100 each)?

Problem 6-22

Franklin Motion Picture Co., a small business corporation, engaged in film production, issued 4,000 shares of its common stock to Ivan Clifford on 10-20-71 at $30 a share. When the company ran into financial troubles in 1972, Ivan who was genuinely optimistic about Franklin's future, made a capital contribution of $35,000. However, the critics consistently gave the Franklin pictures bad reviews and the company stock price went down sharply. On 1-14-77, Ivan sold all his stock for $8 a share.

(a) How would Ivan treat the transaction on his 1977 return, assuming that he is married and files a joint return?

(b) Would your answer to (a) be the same if Ivan is divorced?

SUPPLEMENTAL PROBLEMS

Problem 6-23

Shelley Reynolds is married and has no dependents. His income from net rentals and taxable interest for the year was $50,000. His itemized deductions were $6,000. His wife has no income or deductions. During the year, he made the following sales:

		Date sold	Sales price
(1)	100 shares of K.L. Co., Common, bought 12-20-75	1-2-77	$12,000
(2)	200 shares of K.C. Corp. pfd. bought 7-11-76	4-11-77	10,000
(3)	300 shares of T.Y. Co., Common, received 12-22-76	1-12-77	3,000
(4)	400 C.K. Co. 6% bonds received 12-25-76	1-22-77	5,100
(5)	50 shares of Y. T. Co. Class A common received 12-23-76	1-23-77	15,200

Shelley paid $10,000 for the K.L. stock and $10,400 for the K. C. stock. He received the T. Y. stock under his father's will. This stock was valued at $2,800 on 12-22-76; $2,600 on 11-30-76 (date his father died); and $2,700 on 11-13-76 (date his father bought it). The executor made no alternative valuation.

The C. K. bonds were originally bought by Shelley's mother in 1972 for $6,600. When they were valued at $5,600 on 12-25-76, she gave them to Shelley as a present. She paid a gift tax of $36.

The Class A of Y.T. common stock was received in exchange for Class B common stock of Y.T. Co. which Shelley had bought on 6-26-73 for $5,100. The Class A stock had a fair market value of $14,000 on 12-23-76.

(a) Compute Shelley's capital gain or loss on each transaction and explain whether it is short-term or long-term.

(b) Compute Shelley's lowest tax before credits.

Problem 6-24

(a) Paul Rose owned and rented an apartment building. Construction on it was completed 1-2-77 at a cost of $100,000. He began renting it immediately. If he uses straight line depreciation, the deduction would be $2,500 a year. Assume he decides to use an accelerated method of depreciation to give him a total deduction of $36,975 in 9 years. Assume also that he sells the building for $77,025 on 12-31-85. Compute his gain or loss on the sale (round off all figures to the nearest dollar). How would he report his gain or loss? Explain.

(b) What would your answer to (a) be, if Paul sells his building for $78,025 instead of $77,025?

(c) Jackie Princeton built and began renting an apartment building on 1-2-69. The building cost $50,000. Straight line depreciation would have been $1,000 a year, but he took an accelerated depreciation. On 12-31-77, Jackie sold the building for $40,737, having deducted $15,373 in depreciation (with $2,000 taken before 1970 and $2,946 taken after 1975). What are his gains or losses and how should he report them (round off all figures to the nearest dollar)? Explain.

Problem 6-25

George Simon received the following amounts during the tax year: Net rentals, $65,000; interest on bank deposit, $4,530; taxable pension, $300; cash inheritance from the estate of his deceased father, $125,000; interest on Port of New York Authority bonds, $5,470.

Simon sold the following stock during the year:

On 3-8-77, he sold 1,000 shares of Duton Corp. stock for $45,800 that he had purchased on 5-17-76 for $38,000.

On 6-5-77, he sold 200 shares of Winlux Corp. stock for $2,000. He had purchased 100 shares on 9-20-75 for $1,400 and 300 shares on 12-14-76 for $2,400. Simon could not identify the lots from which the shares were sold.

On 8-20-77, he sold 450 shares of Pemco, Inc. for $22,500. He had received this stock as a legacy from the estate of his father on 5-17-77. His father had bought the stock in January, 1977, for $41 a share. The stock was worth $42 per share when his father died and $44 per share when distributed.

On 11-29-77, he sold 5,000 shares of Valdot, Inc. for $85,000. The stock had been purchased on 5-27-76 for $71,000.

On 12-10-77, he sold 1,640 shares of Navco Corp. stock for $22 per share. The stock had been purchased on 7-9-77 for $54,400.

His itemized deductions amounted to $7,450. Simon is married and filed a joint return with his wife, who had no income or deductions of her own. Compute Simon's lowest tax before any credits, rounding off figures to the nearest dollar.

★ Problem 6-26 ★

Phil Hall whose social security no. is 123-45-6789, had the following transactions during the year:

On 2-28-77, Hall sold 10 shares of the Hub Co. common stock for $500 which he had acquired on 5-31-76 for $976. On the same day, he also sold for $1,200 the R&R stock he received as a gift from his sister in 1974. At the time of the gift the stock had an adjusted basis of $1,500 to his sister and a fair market value of $1,000. Hall's sister paid a gift tax of $50 on the stock.

When Hall's wife Karen died on 11-1-76 her will provided that Phil was to get her 15 Ajax bonds. She had bought the bonds on 2-7-66 for $900. At her death they were valued at $750. The executor did not elect the alternate valuation date. Hall received the bonds on 3-1-77 when they were worth $800. He sold them on 3-21-77 for $926.

On 5-1-77, Hall signed a contract to sell his Bellefonte, Pa. residence which he had acquired on 3-6-57. The sale was completed on 6-1-77. His Bellefonte residence had an adjusted basis of $40,000 and he sold it for $52,000. In selling the home he paid brokerage commissions of $1,000 and advertising expenses of $200. Hall did not deduct these expenses as moving expenses.

In preparing the house for sale he had new wallpaper put in on 1-16-77 at a cost of $200, and a complete paint job undertaken on 4-15-77 at a cost of $800. He paid these amounts as soon as the work was completed.

On 5-10-77, Hall purchased and occupied his new home in State College, Pa. The new residence which was a renovated building, cost him $49,200.

Hall bought a summer cottage in New Jersey on 2-12-70 for $9,000. In 1972 he built a porch for the cottage at a cost of $1,000.

On 5-8-77, the cottage was completely destroyed by flooding. Hall received an insurance award of $12,500. He had no intention of replacing the property.

On 1-2-77, Hall sold two machines (a 1-ton machine and a 2-ton machine) that he used in his business. Hall sold the 1-ton machine for $4,500 and the 2-ton machine for $6,250. They had both been purchased on 1-2-72. The 1-ton machine cost $10,000 and the 2-ton machine cost $7,500. A full year's depreciation under the straight line method was $1,000 for the 1-ton machine, and $750 for the other.

Hall's uninsured gold watch bought 12-24-76 for $600 was stolen on 9-8-77. It was worth $600 when stolen.

Fill in the following schedules and attach any necessary statements.

1978   Assignment 6—Problems   5053

SCHEDULE D (Form 1040)
Department of the Treasury
Internal Revenue Service

Capital Gains and Losses (Examples of property to be reported on this Schedule are gains and losses on stocks, bonds, and similar investments, and gains (but not losses) on personal assets such as a home or jewelry.)
▶ Attach to Form 1040.

Name(s) as shown on Form 1040

Social security number

Part I — Short-term Capital Gains and Losses—Assets Held Not More Than 9 Months

a. Kind of property and description (Example, 100 shares of "Z" Co.)	b. Date acquired (Mo., day, yr.)	c. Date sold (Mo., day, yr.)	d. Gross sales price	e. Cost or other basis, as adjusted and expense of sale	f. Gain or (loss) (d less e)
1					

2 Enter your share of net short-term gain or (loss) from partnerships and fiduciaries
3 Enter net gain or (loss), combine lines 1 and 2
4 Short-term capital loss carryover attributable to years beginning after 1969
5 Net short-term gain or (loss), combine lines 3 and 4

Part II — Long-term Capital Gains and Losses—Assets Held More Than 9 Months

6					

7 Capital gain distributions
8 Enter gain, if applicable, from Form 4797, line 4(a)(1)
9 Enter your share of net long-term gain or (loss) from partnerships and fiduciaries
10 Enter your share of net long-term gain from small business corporations (Subchapter S)
11 Net gain or (loss), combine lines 6 through 10
12 Long-term capital loss carryover attributable to years beginning after 1969
13 Net long-term gain or (loss), combine lines 11 and 12

Part III — Summary of Parts I and II

14 Combine lines 5 and 13, and enter the net gain or (loss) here
15 If line 14 shows a gain—
   a Enter 50% of line 13 or 50% of line 14, whichever is smaller
      Enter zero if there is a loss or no entry on line 13
   b Subtract line 15a from line 14. Enter here and on Form 1040, line 30a

5054

Capital Gains and Losses of Individuals

1978

Form **4797**
Department of the Treasury
Internal Revenue Service

Supplemental Schedule of Gains and Losses
Sales, Exchanges and Involuntary Conversions under
Sections 1231, 1245, 1250, 1251, 1252, and 1254
To be filed with Form 1040, 1041, 1065, 1120, etc.

Name(s) as shown on return | Identifying number as shown on page 1 of your tax return

Part I — Sales or Exchanges of Property Used in Trade or Business, and Involuntary Conversions (Section 1231)

SECTION A.—Involuntary Conversions Due to Casualty and Theft

a. Kind of property (if necessary, attach additional descriptive details not shown below)	b. Date acquired (mo., day, yr.)	c. Date sold (mo., day, yr.)	d. Gross sales price	e. Depreciation allowed (or allowable) since acquisition	f. Cost or other basis, cost of subsequent improvements (if not purchased, attach explanation) and expense of sale	g. Gain or loss (d plus e less f)
1						

2 Combine the amounts on line 1. Enter here, and on the appropriate line as follows . . . .
  (a) For all except partnership returns:
    (1) If line 2 is zero or a gain, enter such amount in column g, line 3.
    (2) If line 2 is a loss, enter the loss on line 5.
  (b) For partnership returns: Enter the amount shown on line 2 above, on Schedule K (Form 1065), line 6.

SECTION B.—Sales or Exchanges of Property Used in Trade or Business and Certain Involuntary Conversions (Not Reportable in Section A)

3						

4 Combine the amounts on line 3. Enter here, and on the appropriate line as follows . . . .
  (a) For all except partnership returns:
    (1) If line 4 is a gain, enter such gain as a long-term capital gain on Schedule D (Form 1040, 1120, etc.) that is being filed.
    (2) If line 4 is zero or a loss, enter such amount on line 6.
  (b) For partnership returns: Enter the amount shown on line 4 above, on Schedule K (Form 1065), line 7.

Part II — Ordinary Gains and Losses

a. Kind of property (if necessary, attach additional descriptive details not shown below)	b. Date acquired (mo., day, yr.)	c. Date sold (mo., day, yr.)	d. Gross sales price	e. Depreciation allowed (or allowable) since acquisition	f. Cost or other basis, cost of subsequent improvements (if not purchased, attach explanation) and expense of sale	g. Gain or loss (d plus e less f)
5 Amount, if any, from line 2(a)(2)						
6 Amount, if any, from line 4(a)(2)						
7 Gain, if any, from page 2, line 22						
8						

9 Combine amounts on lines 5 through 8. Enter here, and on the appropriate line as follows . . . .
  (a) For all except individual returns: Enter the gain or (loss) shown on line 9, on the line provided for on the return (Form 1120, etc.) being filed.
  (b) For individual returns:
    (1) If the gain or (loss) on line 9, includes losses which are to be treated as an itemized deduction on Schedule A (Form 1040) _____ enter the total of such loss(es) here and include on Schedule A (Form 1040), line 29—identify as "loss from Form 4797, line 9(b)(1)" . . . .
    (2) Redetermine the gain or (loss) on line 9, excluding the loss (if any) entered on line 9(b)(1). Enter here and on Form 1040, line 31 . . . .

Assignment 6—Problems

Part III   Gain From Disposition of Property Under Sections 1245, 1250, 1251, 1252, 1254—Assets Held More than Six Months

10 Description of sections 1245, 1250, 1251, 1252, and 1254 property:			Date acquired (mo., day, yr.)	Date sold (mo., day, yr.)
(A)				
(B)				
(C)				
(D)				

Relate lines 10(A) through 10(D) to these columns ▶ ▶ ▶ ▶	Property (A)	Property (B)	Property (C)	Property (D)
11 Gross sales price				
12 Cost or other basis and expense of sale				
13 Depreciation (or depletion) allowed (or allowable)				
14 Adjusted basis, line 12 less line 13				
15 Total gain, line 11 less line 14				
16 If section 1245 property: (a) Depreciation allowed (or allowable) after applicable date				
(b) Enter smaller of line 15 or 16(a)				

Summary of Part III Gains (Complete Property columns (A) through (D) through line 20(b) before going to line 21)

21 Total gains for all properties (add columns (A) through (D), line 15) . . . .
22 Add columns (A) through (D), lines 16(b),   Enter here and on line 7 . . .
23 Subtract line 22 from line 21. Enter here and in appropriate Section in Part I

Cumulative Problem 6-27

David Shapiro, a real estate salesman, earned $31,375 in salary and commissions during the year.

Shapiro had the following stock transactions during the year: On May 1, sold 400 shares of Delos Corp. for $14,000, that he had purchased on January 2 for $7,400; on Oct. 17, sold 600 shares of Amlon Corp. for $800, that he had purchased on January 17 for $2 a share; on Oct. 23, sold 1,200 shares of United Pipeline Corp. for $21,600, that he had purchased on Jan. 13 for $22 per share; on December 13, sold 4,400 shares of Belman Corp. for $15 per share, that he had purchased for $40,000 on March 12.

In addition, he received $340 in interest on his bank account, $215 in dividends on his stock in Drambo Ltd. of Canada, and a $45,000 judgment from a personal injury action, of which $25,000 represented punitive damages.

His itemized deductions amounted to $9,740. He is divorced and pays $2,100 in child support for each of his 2 infant children who live with his ex-wife. His ex-wife contributed $1,000 each to the support of the children. The divorce decree provided that the wife was entitled to the dependency exemptions for the children.

Compute Shapiro's lowest tax payable before any credits.

Cumulative Problem 6-28

(Answer (a) or (b) as directed)

(a) Ted Baer, 48, works for Transamer Steel Corp. and earns $27,850 a year. He has two children: Christopher, 13, and Robin, 19. Chris attends a private school for 8 months of the year and lives with his father the rest of the time. Baer fully supports his son. Robin lived with and was fully supported by her father until November 3 when she got married and moved away. Baer's wife, Ann, died last year on December 30. One week after her death, Baer received a check for $25,000 as sole beneficiary of Ann's only insurance policy. One month later, he received $7,000 in death benefit payments from Pied Piper Publishers, the company where his wife had been employed before her death. Pied Piper paid death benefits only to the spouses of deceased employees, not to their children.

In 1970, Baer bought 25 shares of Crazy Creations, Inc. for $10 a share. Last year, on December 26, Baer acquired 40 more shares for $20 a share. This year, Baer had the following stock transactions:

Feb. 12 .... Bought 100 shares of Keepfit Corp. for $700.
Mar. 19 .... Bought 50 shares of Health Havens, Inc. for $850.
26 .... Bought 30 shares of Nature's Foods, Inc. at $42 a share.
Apr. 9 .... Sold 200 shares of Baby Books, Inc. for $5,400. (Baer had received this stock as a legacy from his wife when her estate was distributed on March 8 of this year. Ann had bought the stock for $1,400 on 1-22-72. The stock was worth $17 a share when she died, $18 on 12-31-76, and $23 a share when distributed. The executor did not elect the alternate valuation date.)
May 14 .... Sold 65 shares of Dreamy Cream Co. for $650. (He had bought them in 1973 at $19 a share.)
June 4 .... Sold 42 shares of Crazy Creations, Inc. at $15 per share. (Baer could not identify the lots from which the shares were sold.)
July 19 .... Bought 80 shares of Exercise Spas, Inc. for $32 a share.
Sold 35 shares of Keepfit Corp. for $1,645.
Nov. 6 .... Sold 60 shares of Exercise Spas, Inc. at $18 a share.
Dec. 24 .... Sold 40 shares of Health Havens, Inc. at $11 a share.
Sold 15 shares of Nature's Foods, Inc. for $900.

During the year, Baer received $845 interest from bank accounts and $95 in dividends (after the dividend exclusion) from domestic corporation stock he owned. He also received $2,800 in net rentals from a small piece of beachfront property that he inherited from his wife. His wife had bought the property several years ago for $10,000. The fair market value of the property on the date of her death was $15,000. Its fair market value dropped to $14,700 on 12-31-76 due to a storm damage.

In September, the beachfront Baer had inherited from his wife on March 8 was seized by the state in a condemnation proceeding and Baer was awarded $18,000. He decided to use the money to buy a cabin cruiser for his personal use and, in October, bought one for $19,000.

In December, Health Havens, Inc. was declared bankrupt and all its outstanding stock became worthless.

Baer's itemized deductions totaled $3,870. Baer's daughter, Robin, filed a joint return for the year to get income-splitting benefits. Last year, Baer filed a joint return.

Compute (1) Baer's tax table income; (2) tax liability.

(b) Robert Keller is a certified public accountant. His earnings for the year were $36,500. He received $475 interest on his bank deposits and $225 in dividends (after dividend exclusion) from stock in Genesco Corp. of California. In addition, a debt of $1,000 which Keller owed to John Phillips was cancelled in consideration of Keller's accounting services performed for Phillips.

Keller had the following stock transactions during the year: *Purchases:* February 7th, 500 shares of Colex Inc., stock for $4,000; June 21st, 85 shares of Lilman Corp. stock for $24 per share; August 13th, 1,150 shares of Rayon Inc., stock for $59,800. *Sales:* November 21st, 400 shares of Colex Inc. stock for $25 per share; September 4th, 85 shares of Lilman Corp. stock for $2,440; December 13th, 1,000 shares of Rayon Inc., stock for $48 per share.

On January 2, Keller sold his car, used exclusively for business, for $3,700. The car, purchased on January 2 of last year, had an adjusted basis of $2,750 and depreciation amounted to $800.

Keller is single, and provides the entire support for his cousin, Alex, who lived with him for the entire year. Keller had other itemized deductions of $7,175.

Compute Keller's lowest tax payable before any credits.

Discussion Problem 6-29

The present tax treatment of capital gains and losses has been criticized on economic grounds. Proponents of more liberal treatment argue that the present system imposes a significant barrier to the mobility of investable funds. They contend that imposition of tax on realized capital gains has the effect of reducing the present value of the future income, i.e., the capital sum realized. Accordingly, the tax tends to weigh the taxpayer's choice in favor of retaining the asset and enjoying its enhanced future returns.

(a) What arguments can you present in favor of more liberal treatment of capital gains and losses?

(b) What arguments can you present against a more liberal treatment of capital gains and losses?

Research Problem 6-30

Aubrey Lee became a vice-president of the South Sea Investment Co. in 1963, and in 1974 received under a contract made in 1963 restricted stock options to buy 300,000 shares of its unissued stock at $10 a share. Recently he became involved in a proxy battle for control of the company. To strengthen his voting position, he exercised his option on 12-19-76 and bought 300,000 shares. Despite the purchase, the result of the fight remained in doubt, and Aubrey decided to sell out. A week after acquiring the shares, he negotiated an agreement with the rival group to sell his interest at $23 a share. The purchasers agreed at that time to accept any reasonable arrangement that would enable Aubrey to get the best tax result possible, so long as they would get the voting rights of the 300,000 shares within 3 weeks from the agreement. Aubrey comes to you for advice on how to transfer his voting rights immediately and still hold on to the stock for the 9-month period required for long-term capital gains treatment. What would you advise?

1. To find the answer, use the Prentice-Hall Complete Federal Tax Equipment in your school or local library. Give your answer fully explained. In it, show authorities, citing law and opinions applicable, and the P-H Federal Tax Equipment paragraphs where they may be found.

2. Enumerate and explain carefully every step you take in reaching your result. These are extremely important—just as important as the conclusion itself.

Tax Reasoning Problem 6-31

Ten years ago, Brown bought a 50-acre tract for $4,000 as an investment. Since then, the surrounding land became developed and the value of Brown's property has increased. One developer offered him $100,000. However, a local real estate broker has told Brown that he could gross at least $150,000 if he subdivides and sells off the lots. The sale to the developer will give Brown a capital gain of $96,000. Brown knows he could subdivide the tract into 100 lots and sell each lot for $1,500. His selling expenses for each lot would total $75. Brown comes to you for advice on the tax consequences of selling to the developer or subdividing. Either transaction could be carried out in about the same length of time. This would be his only transaction during the year. What do you advise? Explain.

ASSIGNMENT No. 7
DIVIDENDS

(Note: In the following problems, unless otherwise specified, assume that the "tax year" is calendar year 1977, that the taxpayer and his spouse, if any, are resident citizens under 65 and are not blind and that the taxpayer is not entitled to any credit against tax other than those shown.)

Problem 7-1

Zeaker Corporation has 2,000 shares of common stock issued and outstanding. Laurie London owns 1,000 shares. Zeaker had no accumulated earnings at the beginning of the current calendar tax year. Earnings and profits for the year amounted to $80,000. Starting on March 15, Zeaker made quarterly distributions of $22,000 in cash and property during the year to its shareholders. What dividends did Laurie receive? Is the full amount included in gross income?

Problem 7-2

The Woodlake Corp. was organized in 1970 with an authorized and issued capital stock of $800,000. It has 1,000 shares of common stock issued and outstanding. Its current earnings and profits for the tax year are $80,000. At the start of the year, its accumulated earnings and profits were $50,000. During the year Woodlake paid 4 quarterly dividends of $50,000 each on the last day of March, June, September and December. Norman Sherman owns 100 shares of Woodlake. He gave Ed Tucci half of his stock on July 30 as a gift. What is the amount of taxable dividends received by Norman and Ed?

Problem 7-3

Alex Friedman is a 51% shareholder and president of Larchmont Corp., which has accumulated earnings and profits of $250,000. He needs $100,000 to complete a personal business transaction, but cannot afford to pay taxes on $100,000 additional gross income for the tax year. Based on these facts alone, make the necessary arrangements for Alex to use the corporate funds to complete his personal transaction.

Problem 7-4

(a) During the year, Tony Shewn who is single, received the following dividends on stock he owns in domestic corporations: March 15, $40; June 15, $50; September 15, $60; December 15, $100. How much can he exclude from gross income?

(b) On December 23, Tony married Evelyn who owns no stock. How much can they exclude if they file a joint return?

(c) Would your answer to (b) be the same if on marrying Evelyn, Tony gave her as a gift half of his stock?

(d) Would your answer to (b) be the same if Tony married Evelyn on December 1 instead, and she owned half of the stock on that date?

(e) How much can Tony and Evelyn each exclude in (d) if they file a separate return?

Problem 7-5

Victor Lee and his wife Virginia, received the following dividends during the year:

$35 from Cambridge Foods, Inc., a New York corporation, on stock owned by Virginia; $55 from Lonborg Fishery, Ltd., a Canadian corporation, on stock owned by the Lees jointly; $60 from Bonang Co., an Indonesian corporation, on stock owned by Virginia; $25 from White Plains Motel, Inc., a Massachusetts corporation, on stock owned by Victor.

Victor also received $200 from H. H. L. Fund, a regulated investment company, on 100 shares owned by him. The fund notified him that 80 cents per share was a dividend from investment income and $1.20 from capital gains.

How much can Victor and Virginia exclude on a joint return? On separate returns? Identify which dividends qualify for the dividend exclusion.

Problem 7-6

In 1972, Ian Dantist bought 200 shares of Ton Shipping Co. common stock for $16,000. On 8-15-77, the company declared a taxable stock dividend and Ian received 50 shares of preferred stock that had a fair market value of $6,000. When he received the dividend, the value of the common stock was $14,000. On 10-15-77, Ian sold 50 shares of the common stock at $82 a share and all the preferred shares at $150 a share.

(a) What income, if any, did Ian realize when he received the stock dividend?
(b) State whether Ian's sale of the stock resulted in a long-term or short-term capital gain or loss and the amount?
(c) What would be your answer to (a) and (b) if the stock dividend was nontaxable (assuming there was no tax avoidance scheme)?

Problem 7-7

Randy Young bought 900 shares of Arthur Hardware common stock on 12-30-75. He paid $36,000. On 1-22-77, Arthur Hardware declared a nontaxable stock dividend of one share of common stock for each 3 shares of common stock owned by the shareholders. Randy received 300 additional shares which had a fair market value of $8,000. On 7-7-77, Randy sold 100 old shares and 200 new shares of Arthur Hardware at $31 a share.

(a) What is the basis of each of Randy's old and new shares after the dividend?
(b) What was the amount of his capital gain or loss on the sale?
(c) Is this a long-term or short-term gain or loss?

Problem 7-8

Last year, Joe Peters bought 100 shares of Gibbons Corp. common stock for $8,000. This year, Gibbons declared a taxable dividend of one share of preferred stock for each share of common stock. When Joe received the preferred stock on October 18, its fair market value was $30 a share and the fair market value of the common stock was $85 a share. On December 15, he sold 50 shares of common stock at $90 a share and 50 shares of preferred stock at $28 a share. Compute Joe Peters' adjusted gross income from these transactions.

Problem 7-9

Tommy Holt owns 100 shares of F. F. Products Co. common bought in 1975 at $90 a share. On 2-6-77, he received 100 nontaxable rights from F. F. to buy 100 additional F. F. common at $100 a share. On the same day, the stock was traded in the open market at $110 ex-rights and the rights at $10 each. Holt sold all his rights on 2-7-77 for $1,000. He made a huge profit from other capital transactions in 1977.

(a) Assuming that he wants to minimize his 1977 tax, how would be report his gain or loss on the above transaction?
(b) Would your answer to (a) be different if in 1977 Holt had a net capital loss of $900 over the $2,000 deduction limit?

Problem 7-10

In 1976, Charles bought 100 shares of stock of the Natura Cosmetics Corporation at $120 a share. On 7-1-77, he received 100 rights entitling him to subscribe to 100 additional shares of stock at $150 a share. At the time the rights were issued, the stock was valued at $180 a share ex-rights and the rights at $28 each.

(a) What is the basis of each right assuming an exercise or sale?
(b) Charles sold 30 rights on 8-1-77 for $20 each. State whether his gain or loss is a short-term or long-term gain or loss and the amount.

(c) He turned in the remaining 70 rights with the necessary cash for 70 new shares on 9-1-77. What is the basis of the new shares?

(d) On 12-1-77, Charles sold 50 of the old shares for $200 each. State whether his gain or loss is short-term or long-term capital gain or loss and the amount.

(e) On 12-1-77, Charles sold 10 of the new shares for $200 each. State whether his gain or loss is short-term or long-term capital gain or loss and the amount.

Problem 7-11

David Jule bought 100 shares of Plastic Surgical Equipment Co. common stock at $100 a share in 1975. On 1-20-77, the corporation issued nontaxable rights to its shareholders (one right for each share) giving them the privilege of buying convertible bonds for $125 a bond in the ratio of one new bond for each 4 rights exercised by the shareholder. The bonds had a principal amount of $125, but for $5 each bond could be converted to one share of common stock. At the time the bond rights were issued, the stock was worth $190 a share and the rights $10 each, due entirely to the conversion privilege. On 2-25-77, David sold 20 rights for $240, exercised the remaining 80 rights, elected to allocate basis, and converted his bonds to common stock. On 10-20-77, David sold the old and new stock for $280 a share. State the amount of gain or loss recognized.

Problem 7-12

In each of the following cases, state the amount of Clifford Miklo's gain or loss. Also, explain whether it is ordinary, or short-term or long-term capital gain or loss. Assume the stock redemptions were not essentially equivalent to a taxable dividend.

(a) In 1971, Clifford bought 200 shares of Newark Daily News Co. common stock for $40,000. In 1977, he received $38,000 for his stock when the company was completely liquidated.

(b) Mamaroneck Hotel, Inc., issued a new Class A common stock in December, 1975, for funds to build a new ballroom, and Clifford bought 100 shares for $9,000. In December, 1976, Mamaroneck adopted a plan to redeem all the Class A stock. In 1977, the company paid Clifford $10,000 for his shares.

(c) In 1930, Clifford bought 300 shares of Edico Corp. preferred stock for $12,000. In 1977, Edico adopted a plan to redeem all of its preferred stock, and Clifford received $3,000.

Problem 7-13

Lee Corporation has 5,000 shares of authorized common stock issued and outstanding. Tibbet owns 3,995 shares, Zevell owns 5 shares, and Taylor, a key employee, owns 1,000 shares. Taylor also has an option to buy up to 30% of the corporate stock. At present he has only enough money to buy 200 shares at book value, the option price. He has insisted he will leave the company unless he becomes a 30% shareholder. To keep him as an employee, Tibbett sold him 200 shares of his stock at the option price and transferred 1,000 shares to the corporation at the same price. The corporation's accumulated earnings and profits were more than sufficient to pay Tibbet.

Can Tibbet report the sale of 1,200 shares as a capital transaction? Explain.

Problem 7-14

Two years ago, Paul Rosaline bought 100 shares of the Yolandy Co.'s outstanding 200 shares of common stock for $30,000. The other 100 shares belong to Anna Stone who is unrelated to Paul. Paul and Anna each also own one-half of the Phebeen Corp.'s outstanding 200 shares of common stock. The cost of Phebeen stock to Paul was $10,000. During the year, Phebeen has accumulated earnings and profits of $60,000, and Paul sold 30 shares of the Yolandy stock to it for $50,000. All of the common stock of Yolandy and Phebeen are voting stock.

(a) Explain whether the stock transfer is, or is not, substantially disproportionate.

(b) How should Paul report the transfer on his income tax return, assuming the stock redemption was not essentially equivalent to a taxable dividend?

(c) What are the bases of the Yolandy stock to Phebeen, and the Phebeen stock to Paul, after the sale?

Problem 7-15

Larry Daniel owns all of the stock of the A. B. Manufacturing Company and the X. Y. Distributing Company. The basis of his stock in each company is $20,000. The accumulated earnings and profits of each company exceeded $70,000 at the beginning of the year and each company operated at a profit during the year. On December 27, Daniel sold half of his stock in the A. B. Manufacturing Company to the X. Y. Distributing Company for $65,000, its fair market value.

How should Daniel treat the sale of the stock for income tax purposes? After the sale, what are Daniel's basis of his distributing company stock and the distributing company's basis of the newly acquired stock?

SUPPLEMENTAL PROBLEMS

Problem 7-16

Justin and Betty Easter received the following dividends during the tax year:

$90 from Perry Nursing Home Inc., a New York business corporation, on stock owned by Betty Easter.

$550 from Christina, Ltd., a Canadian company, on stock owned by the Easters jointly.

$100 from Nimura, a Japanese corporation, on stock owned by Betty.

$250 from Wein & Company, a New Jersey corporation, on stock owned by Justin.

$150 from Aldan Housing Unlimited, a U. S. real estate investment trust, on shares owned by Betty.

$100 from S. L. Bridge Supply Co., a California corporation, on stock owned by Justin. S. L.'s current and accumulated earnings and profits were sufficient to pay only 80% of the dividend.

$400 from Peter Management Fund, a U. S. regulated investment company, on 200 shares owned by Justin. The Fund notified him that $0.75 per share was a dividend from investment income, and $1.25 from capital gains.

Aldar, Inc., a New York corporation, declared a 15% common stock dividend for 1977. Justin received 15 shares on December 15, with a fair market value of $15 a share, on the stock he owned. The company notified him that the dividend was nontaxable.

(a) What is the dividend received exclusion for Mr. and Mrs. Justin Easter on a joint return? State which dividends qualify for the exclusion, and which do not.

(b) What would be your answer to (a), on a separate return?

Problem 7-17

John Vellone is married and has an adopted son, Albert. On 1-1-73, John and his wife each received 100 shares of Millburn Paint Co. stock from John's father as a wedding present.

On 1-1-77, John loaned $500 to the Millburn Paint Co. and received a 30-day promissory note.

On 5-1-77, John gave his son Albert 40 shares of Millburn stock to avoid payment of tax in the event the stock was redeemed. On 6-1-77, Millburn Paint Co. redeemed both John's and Albert's stock.

John was unable to collect the amount of the Millburn loan until 9-1-77.

Assuming the parties filed the necessary agreements with the Revenue Service as to notice of future interest in Millburn, was there a complete redemption of John's and Albert's stock?

★ Problem 7-18 ★

During the year, Phil Hall received the following from taxable domestic corporations:

Dividends

$2,000 cash distribution from the earnings of Rockview Corp., on preferred stock.

50 shares of common stock of the Old Quaker Corp. of Pennsylvania (par value $20 a share and fair market value of $35 a share when received) on a 2-to-1 split of the Old Quaker Corp. common stock. The distribution was proportionate among the stockholders.

$424 from the Beacon Mutual Fund. The Fund notified Hall that $74 of the distribution was nontaxable.

Fill in the following schedule. What is the amount of dividend exclusion, if any, which Hall may be entitled to?

Part I   Dividend Income

Note: *If gross dividends (including capital gain distributions) and other distributions on stock are $400 or less, do not complete this part.*

1 Gross dividends (including capital gain distributions) and other distributions on stock. (List payers and amounts—write (H), (W), (J), for stock held by husband, wife, or jointly)

2 Total of line 1 . . . .
3 Capital gain distributions
4 Nontaxable distributions
5 Total (add lines 3 and 4) . . . . .
6 Dividends before exclusion (subtract line 5 from line 2).

★★ **Problem 7-19** ★★

The Atlas Machinery Corp. received a 10% stock dividend on 300 shares of Samson Steel Corp. common stock. That stock, originally issued at $10 par value on 2-1-75, was worth $50 on the date the dividend was paid. The Samson Steel Corp. issued common stocks only, and did not pay any cash dividend during the year. In addition, Atlas received the following cash dividends paid from profits accumulated since 2-28-13 by the corporations shown below. All the corporations mentioned, except the Hercule Rubber Cie., are incorporated in the United States. The Hercule Rubber Cie. was incorporated in France, has no income from U.S. sources, has never engaged in business in this country, and is not subject to U.S. taxes.

Smith Ironworks Corp.	$1,275
Stevens Steel Co.	825
Hercule Rubber Cie.	650

Fill in the following schedule:

Assignment 7—Problems

Schedule C—DIVIDENDS

1	Domestic corporation subject to 85% deduction	....
2	Certain preferred stock of public utilities	....
3	Foreign corporation subject to 85% deduction	....
4	Dividends from wholly-owned foreign subsidiaries subject to 100% deduction (section 245(b))	....
5	Other dividends from foreign corporations	....
6	Includable income from controlled foreign corporations under subpart F (attach Forms 3646)	....
7	Foreign dividend gross-up (section 78)	....
8	Qualifying dividends from affiliated groups and subject to the 100% deduction (section 243(a)(3))	....
9	Qualifying dividends from affiliated groups and subject to provisions of section 1564(b)	....
10	Taxable dividends from DISC or former DISC not included in line 1 (section 246(d))	....
11	Other dividends	_____
12	Total	

Cumulative Problem 7-20

During the year, in addition to a salary of $30,000, Anthony Delia also received the following income: $95 cash dividends from Eddico Motor Corp., a taxable domestic corporation; $315 interest on bonds issued by the Port of New York Authority; $500 interest on U. S. Treasury bonds issued in 1948; $205 interest from a bank account.

During the year Anthony made a profit of $7,350 from selling an oil painting bought 8 years ago for his home.

On 6-13-75, Anthony bought 100 shares of D'Arco Co. common stock at $11 a share. On 1-11-77, he received 10 additional shares of D'Arco common as a nontaxable dividend. When he received these shares, the stock had a market value of $20 per share. On 1-23-77, he sold all his D'Arco stock at $25 a share.

On 2-3-77, the C. K. Corp., a domestic corporation, paid a taxable dividend in the stock of the T. Z. Company. Anthony owned 100 shares of C. K. common and received 20 shares of T. Z. preferred with a par value of $50 a share and market value of $75 a share. The C. K. Corp.'s earnings and profits during the year were well over its distributions.

Compute Anthony's adjusted gross income.

Cumulative Problem 7-21

(Answer (a) and (b) as directed)

(a) Fred Mayvous works for the Shaw Bros. Theatre at a salary of $20,000 a year.

In 1974, Fred bought 100 shares of C. F. & Co.'s 7% preferred stock for $6,000. In 1975, instead of paying dividends on the preferred, the company issued rights of equal value to buy its common stock at $50 a share when the fair market value of the common was $60 a share. Fred received 100 rights which he exercised on 1-5-77 when the fair market value of the common was $55 a share. In January of 1977, a business competitor won an important law suit against C.F. On 1-22-77, Fred sold 90 shares of the preferred stock for $900 and all of the common stock for $8,000. On June 13, he took 8 shares of new 8½% preferred stock issued by C. F. & Co. in exchange for his remaining 10 shares of 7% preferred. He immediately sold the new preferred stock for $600. During the year, Fred received a $55 dividend on the common stock and a $95 dividend on the preferred, both paid out of the company's accumulated earnings.

Compute Fred Mayvous's adjusted gross income.

(b) On 2-3-27, Ivan Fein bought 100 shares of Josay Corp. common stock for $1,200. In January of 1977, the company declared a nontaxable stock dividend in common stock and on 2-3-77, Ivan received 20 additional shares with a market value of $13 a share. On 6-28-77, he sold the 20 new shares and 40 of the old shares for $14 a share.

On 1-6-77, Ivan received $1,000 in cancellation of a bond of the Cynamite Corp. issued in 1958. The bond, which had a face value of $1,000, was being retired. He had bought it for $750 a year ago when the company was having financial troubles.

On 1-11-77, the Hommocks Co. paid a taxable dividend in preferred stock of the Janyboo Corp. Ivan owned 100 shares of the Hommocks common, and received 12 shares of the Janyboo preferred with a par value of $20 a share and market value of $50 a share. The Hommocks Co. had accumulated earnings and profits well over all its distributions.

Ivan also had the following income during the year: $1,500 social security benefit payments; $560 interest on Doring Fine Corp. bonds; and $6,700 in cash dividends from domestic taxable corporations. Compute Ivan Fein's adjusted gross income.

Research Problem 7-22

Sally Brown and her three brothers are the only children of the late Frank Brown who died in 1976. These five were the only owners of the Metropolitan Baseball Club, Inc. To keep corporate ownership within the family, they agreed any transfer of the stock must be subject to the right of any present owners to buy the stock at a low fixed price. Frank Brown's will left his Club stock in equal shares to four separate trusts for Sally and her brothers. In order to obtain funds to pay her share of the death taxes on her father's estate, Sally exercised her option rights and bought the stock from the trust in her favor. This stock was then redeemed by Club, Inc. at its fair market value, and Sally used part of the proceeds to pay her share of the death taxes.

Sally's lawyer had advised Sally to follow the Internal Revenue Code requirements for capital gain treatment of the stock redemption. However, the lawyer has noticed that an IRC Regulation prohibits capital gain treatment to a stockholder who has purchased the stock from one to whom the stock was passed by the decedent. He is afraid the corporate distribution to Sally might be treated as dividend because she purchased the stock from the trust. How would you, a tax expert, answer the lawyer?

Use the Prentice-Hall Complete Federal Tax Equipment in your school or local library to find your answer. Do the following:

1. Give your opinion, fully explained. In it, show authorities, citing law, regulations, interpretations and opinions applicable, and the P-H Federal Tax Equipment paragraphs where they may be found.

2. Enumerate and explain carefully every step you take in reaching your result. These are extremely important—just as important as the result.

Tax Reasoning Problem 7-23

Mrs. Brown and her children owned all of Family Corp.'s stock held in a voting trust. The company redeemed all of her stock. But she continued to be a voting trustee, although all of her other interest in the corporation was terminated. Can she receive capital gain treatment? Explain.

ASSIGNMENT No. 8
DEDUCTIONS—EXPENSES

(Note: In the following problems, unless otherwise specified, assume that the "tax year" is the calendar year 1977, that the taxpayer and his spouse, if any, are resident citizens, under 65 and are not blind, and that the taxpayer is not entitled to any credits against the tax other than those shown.)

Problem 8-1

Ted Robinson is the president of Zome Ltd., a corporation engaged in the development of weapons for the military. An additional employee was needed to do highly secretive work. James Harris was being considered for the position and a private investigating firm was hired to compile a report on Harris' background. Robinson paid the investigating firm personally, since if Harris were to be hired he would have access to the corporate books and might discover that he had been investigated. Discuss the deductibility of the fee paid by Robinson.

Problem 8-2

Which of the following may be claimed as deductible expenses paid or incurred in carrying on a trade or business? Explain.
   (a)   Cost to antique dealer of heat and electricity for his shop.
   (b)   Expenses of candidate seeking reelection.
   (c)   State net income tax on yearly business profits.
   (d)   Cost of planting wheat which is never harvested.
   (e)   Wages paid to caretaker of vacant former residence now listed for sale.
   (f)   Costs incurred by salesman in using auto to visit customers.
   (g)   Delicatessen owner's cost of advertising Christmas special in newspaper.

Problem 8-3

(a)   Ernie Nevers is employed as an electrical engineer by the Gridiron Corporation. Because of tight construction schedules during the year, Ernie frequently had to bring work home. He had a separate room in his home which was used exclusively as an office where he reviewed blueprints and work schedules. His employer did not require him to maintain an office in his home. Ernie claims a deduction of $1,500 for the cost of maintaining the home office. Will this deduction be denied? Explain.

(b)   Jean Stickley works full-time as a math teacher at a local junior high school. In order to supplement her income she also runs a wholesale jewelry business. She converted a garage on her property into an office and storage area for the jewelry. Jean realized a gross income of $2,500 for the year on sales of jewelry to area merchants. The total cost of maintaining the office for business purposes was $2,800. Jean's deductions for taxes and other nonbusiness costs allocable to the office were $900. How much can she deduct for the use of the office?

Problem 8-4

Edward Murphy is an executive with a local television station. In April of last year, Murphy represented his employer at a broadcaster's convention in Denver. His total traveling expenses for the trip amounted to $800. It was the practice in Murphy's office for the employer to promptly reimburse an employee for business-related expenses upon filing and verification of the employee's claim. Murphy neglected to file such a claim and now asks you, his tax advisor, whether or not he may deduct his $800 in expenses in arriving at adjusted gross income on his return. What would you advise him?

Problem 8-5

John Riggins owned a mountain cottage which he built for personal use and to gain income from seasonal rentals. John rented the cottage to some ski enthusiasts for the first three and last two months of the year, at a monthly rental of $700.

During these periods, John incurred expenses of $800 for utilities and heat and $400 for maintenance. Friends of John rented the cottage for July and August at a total rental of $1,000. John incurred utility costs of $200 and maintenance costs of $175 during this rental period. The total depreciation attributable to the rental periods was $950. Taxes and interest on the property amounted to $2,300 for the year. John and his family used the cottage for the entire month of September.

How much, if any, of the expenses and depreciation will John be able to deduct?

Problem 8-6

Pat McCormick owns a two-family home in which he occupied one of the two apartments. The other apartment was vacant from January 1 through April 30. On May 1, Pat rented the apartment to a Mr. and Mrs. Corry for $200 a month. The Corrys remained tenants of the apartment throughout the remainder of the year. Pat incurred the following expenses on the home: decorating expenses, $300; depreciation, $360; maintenance costs, $432; real estate taxes, $1,410. In addition, Pat spent $1,500 in capreting the Corrys' apartment once they moved in. What is McCormick's deduction, if any, for adjusted gross income on the home?

Problem 8-7

Barton Baton is president of Half-Note Corporation, manufacturers of musical instruments and sheet music. How would you advise Barton on the deductibility of the following expenses incurred by Half-Note during the year?

(a) Cost of converting the heating system of Half-Note's west coast plant to solar heat.

(b) Expense of installing a new accounting and cost system.

(c) $50,000 paid to Downbeat Record Company to cease all further sales of sheet music.

(d) $10,000 in legal fees incurred in suit against competitor to stop use of trademark similar to Half-Note's.

(e) $200 fine for violation of local fire code.

(f) $100 penalty paid for failure to pay state income tax on time.

Problem 8-8

(a) John Puff was Underwood Realty Corporation's top salesman. During the year, he received a base salary of $5,200 and $15,000 in commissions. At the beginning of each month John received an advance commissiion of $500. Only in January and February did he fail to earn at least $500 in commissions. In January, he had earned commissions of $300 and in February, $400. It was company policy, however, not to have unearned advanced commissions returned where the salesman's annual commissions exceeded $10,000.

What payments to John are deductible as business expenses by Underwood?

(b) In January, Marilyn Dutkavich, an architect, purchased as an investment, 10 acres of land in the Rocky Mountain ski area of Montana for $85,000. The land was purchased through a licensed real estate broker. The broker's commission on the purchase was $8,500. In December, Marilyn sold her Montana acreage through the same broker for $100,000. The broker's commission on the sale was $10,000.

(1) How should Marilyn treat the purchase and sales commissions on her return?

(2) Would your answer differ, if Marilyn became a licensed real estate broker after she purchased the land, and sold the land through one of her salesmen, whom she paid a $2,000 commission?

Problem 8-9

John Redding is employed by Mitco Corporation as its sales manager. During the tax year he received $8,000 in salary and $12,000 in sales commissions. As the result of his outstanding sales record this year, he received a bonus of $1,000. Redding also received $2,000 for services he had performed two years ago, payment being authorized by a resolution of the board of directors passed last year. Discuss the deductibility of these items by Mitco Corporation in the current tax year.

Problem 8-10

Tom Boyer was employed as an aeronautical engineer by Jetronics, Inc., a major aerospace corporation. Tom was considered a promising aircraft designer by his employer. After working at Jetronics for a year, Tom joined the U.S. Air Force as a 2nd Lieutenant. Jetronics continued to make payments to Boyer during his military service. These payments were made in return for past services rendered. However, they were primarily motivated by Jetronics' desire to retain the services of experienced and promising personnel after release from the Armed Forces. Are Jetronics' payments to Boyer deductible by the corporation?

Problem 8-11

Dr. Charles Balzak was a brain surgeon practicing in Gulfport. In February, a medical malpractice suit was filed against him by a former patient who claimed Balzak had injected him with a poisonous drug. The county medical board instituted an immediate hearing on the matter and Balzak was suspended from practice pending the outcome of the suit. His attorney billed him $850 for representing him at the hearing.

A month later a newspaper article in the Gulfport Chronicle accused Dr. Balzak of "butchery." Upon meeting him on the street, Balzak struck the reporter who wrote the news article. The reporter brought criminal assault charges against the doctor. Balzak was later found guilty and his attorney's fees amounted to $1,000.

Dr. Balzak brought a libel suit against the Gulfport Chronicle to restore his damaged reputation. The newspaper settled out of court and Balzak's attorney billed him $900.

The malpractice suit finally reached trial and Balzak was found guilty following a jury trial. His defense cost $5,000 in legal fees.

Balzak also incurred $400 in accountant's fees in a successful challenge to a Revenue Service income tax deficiency which had been assessed for a prior year.

Which, if any, of the professional fees are deductible?

Problem 8-12

Miller Richards owned a three-story building. On the first floor he operated a health food store. He used the second floor as his apartment and rented the third floor. In April, a hurricane damaged the building. Miller replaced shingles on the roof at a cost of $300. Ceilings in the rented apartment were repainted at a cost of $200. The wooden floor of the health food store was replaced by a concrete floor with vinyl tile. The cost of the new floor was $1,000. Assuming that the three floors are of equal size, explain which of the expenses, if any, are deductible as ordinary and necessary business expenses.

Problem 8-13

Edward Dugan, a commercial photographer, rented a loft on January 1 of last year. He subdivided the loft into two areas, one to be used as his studio and the other as his living area. The lease provided for an annual rental of $6,000. On July 1, Dugan paid his landlord $1,000 in order to cancel his lease, and he moved into an apartment with an annual rental of $3,240. On August 1, he rented a store for use as a studio. He took a two-year lease and paid an advance rental for the two years of $9,600.

What deductions for rent, if any, is Dugan entitled to in his return? Explain.

Problem 8-14

(a) Woodrow Carstairs and Arthur Rubens are partners in an advertising agency. The agency had financial problems and Carstairs wanted to liquidate the partnership. To keep the agency going, Rubens borrowed from the bank and took out life insurance naming the bank as beneficiary. He took out a second policy and named Carstairs as beneficiary to induce him to stay in the business. Can Rubens deduct the premiums? Explain.

(b) Joe Cataldi is a construction supervisor for Hardcastle Homes Company. The company pays him an annual salary of $12,000 and pays the premiums on a $15,000 insurance policy on his life, of which Joe's wife is beneficiary. The annual premiums amount to $1,000. Can the company deduct the cost of the premiums? Explain.

Problem 8-15

(a) Ann and Bob Lueck live in Miami, Florida, where Ann is a tenured college professor and Bob is a media analyst for an advertising agency. In February, Bob was transferred to Jacksonville. Not wishing to commute between the two cities, Bob rented an apartment in Jacksonville where he lived during the week. Ann was not able to move to Jacksonville until June when her contract expired. Can Bob deduct all his meals and lodging costs for the period from February through June?

(b) Wilmer Eakins lives in Houston, where he works for an oil drilling company. In April, he was assigned to work on a project 75 miles from Houston for a six-month period. Eakins made daily trips in a company car with a co-worker from his residence to his temporary job. He incurred $600 in expenses for meals while at the temporary job site. Are these expenses deductible?

(c) Dennis Meehan, a real estate broker whose home and business are in Ohio, made a seven-day trip to Las Vagas to relax and gamble. While there, he signed a million dollar business-lease contract that took three days of negotiation. His plane fare was $400. His meals and lodging cost $75 a day. To what deduction, if any, is Meehan entitled?

Problem 8-16

In April, Fred Scott accepted a job offer from a corporation in a distant state. Scott and his family made two house-hunting trips in May. They drove 800 miles spending another $500 on motel bills and food during these trips. The Scotts sold their home and in the process had to pay $300 for "points" so the buyer could obtain a mortgage. After moving the 150 miles to the new job location, the Scotts were unable to find suitable housing immediately so they lived in a motel for 3 weeks at a cost of $550 and spent another $475 for meals during that time. The cost of moving their household goods was $700. They also used their two family cars to move household effects with Scott and his wife driving the 150 miles. Cost of meals enroute was $20. In purchasing their new home at the new location, they paid a real estate commission of $1,000. Compute the maximum moving expense deduction that would be allowed on the Scotts' return for the year.

Problem 8-17

Determine if any of the following qualify as educational expenses. Explain.

(a) Steven Brown, personnel manager at Combine Corporation, took evening courses that will result in his receiving a Master's degree in Personnel Administration.

(b) Raymond Ralph, an attorney with a general practice, wanted to become a tax specialist. He enrolled in a part-time program at a nearby law school that leads to a Master's degree in taxation.

(c) Cheryl Webber taught English in a local high school for three years. To obtain greater knowledge of her subject area she decided to take graduate courses. She resigned her position and enrolled in a full-time one-year Master's program. She intended to continue teaching at another school upon completion of the program.

(d) Horace Hinckle, a labor relations specialist, took a special 10-day course in Miami designed to acquaint him with recent trends in the labor field. He incurred costs for course fees, travel, meals and lodging.

Problem 8-18

In 1973, John Pillar, a pharmacist, purchased a drug store. He immediately hired two full-time pharmacists and a part-time stock clerk to assist him in his business.

On January 2, 1976, he set up a self-employed retirement plan for himself, but did not include his employees. His earned income from the pharmacy for 1976 was $30,000. He contributed $5,000 to the plan for that year following his accountant's advice. What must John now do if his plan is to qualify for 1977?

Problem 8-19

Ecks Corp., a manufacturer of explosives, contracts with Yates Corp. to attempt through research and experimentation to create a new process of making certain explosives. Because of the danger involved in such an undertaking, Yates is compelled to acquire an isolated tract of land on which to conduct the work. It is agreed that when the project is completed, Yates will transfer this tract to Ecks. Do the amounts Ecks paid to Yates for the cost of the tract qualify as research and experimental expenditures? Explain.

SUPPLEMENTAL PROBLEMS
Problem 8-20

Florence Martin is an attorney. She earned $20,000 from her law practice during the tax year. She was divorced two years ago and was awarded sole custody of the only child of the marriage, Linda, age 4. The divorce decree provides that Florence is to receive $22,500, to be paid over a period of 15 years at a rate of $1,500 each year, of which $550 per year was specifically made payable for the support of Linda. The decree provides that Florence's ex-husband is entitled to the personal exemption for Linda.

Florence rents a seven-room apartment for $560 per month. Two of the rooms are used exclusively as her office, and she and her daughter live in the others.

Florence owns an automobile and she drove a total of 12,000 miles during the tax year, one-half of which was for business purposes. The total gas, oil, maintenance expense and other fixed costs on the car was $1,500, and automobile insurance premiums amounted to $500.

On numerous occasions, Florence took her clients to lunch for the purpose of business discussions. Her expenses in this regard amounted to $700 for the year. Florence employs one secretary in her law office and pays her a yearly salary of $7,000. In order to keep abreast of recent developments in the law, Florence attended two legal symposiums at a cost of $50 each.

In addition, she incurred legal expenses of $2,200 in the successful defense of a malpractice suit brought against her by a disgruntled client.

Other expenses included $200 to the Internal Revenue Service as a penalty for the late payment of last year's tax, and $100 to an accountant for preparing last year's tax return. Deductible charitable contributions amounted to $400. She also had miscellaneous itemized deductions of $2,000.

Assuming that Florence has no other income or deductions, what is her tax table income?

★ Problem 8-21 ★

During 1977, Phil Hall, who owns the Keystone Dairy store, paid $19,000 in wages to his store personnel. He also paid $5,000 to a domestic servant to take care of his house.

Hall had to do extensive driving to different dairy farms in the county to order products for his dairy. He used an old pick-up truck that had been fully depreciated under the straight line method for this field work. During the year he logged 32,500 miles. He spent $1,500 for gas, $900 for oil and repairs and $800 insurance on the truck during the year.

Hall paid his attorney $1,500 to inquire into a possible merger with the Good Taste Dairy. He also paid the attorney $150 to draw up a will.

Deductions—Expenses

On May 1, he spent $300 to obtain parts for one of his refrigerators to keep it in operating condition.

On 9-1-77, Hall obtained a lease for 1 year for a warehouse for his dairy store. The rental was $600 a month. On 10-1-77, Hall paid the landlord the full year's rental. Hall also paid an annual rental of $10,000 for the store.

Hall spent $1,500 on fire insurance premiums in 1977: $1,000 for the store and $500 for his home. He also paid $200 in theft insurance premiums for the store.

What would be his maximum current deductible expenses?

★★ Problem 8-22 ★★

The Atlas Machinery Corp. had the following expenses for the year:

Salaries (office and sales)	$37,625
Commissions—salespersons	52,165
Freight and cartage outward	2,673
Postage	479
Telephone and telegraph	682
Stationery	326
Legal and accounting fees	2,200
General expenses	3,271
Advertising expenses	874

The corporation paid the following salaries to the officers who devoted their full time to the business:

Adam Baker, President, Soc. Sec. No. 153-36-5299	$48,000
Chet Downs, Vice President, Soc. Sec. No. 143-42-6178	$31,000
Earl Fisher, Sec.-Treas., Soc. Sec. No. 154-41-7565	$26,000

In addition, the corporation paid $30,000 to Mrs. George Hunt, Soc. Sec. No. 120-34-7659, who is listed as a vice-president of the corporation. Mrs. Hunt, whose deceased husband founded the corporation in 1928, is 80 years old and owns 40% of the stock. She lives in Florida and is completely inactive in the corporation's business operations.

Baker, the President, owns 22% of the outstanding common stock; Downs, 10%; and Fisher, 8%. None of the officers owns any preferred stock. The address of the Atlas Machinery Corp. is 118 Commerce St., Cleveland, Ohio 44103.

During the tax year, the corporation charged to repair account an amount totaling $4,237. Included in this amount is an item of $1,975 for alteration to the factory building made under orders of the City Fire Department whose rules were being violated. Also included is an anticipated expense of $800 for repair of a special machine used in the factory.

Fill in the following items and schedules:

Items

A. Compensation of officers .... $ ....
B. Salaries and wages ....
C. Repairs ....
D. Other deductions ....

Schedule E — Compensation of Officers

1. Name of officer	2. Social security number	3. Title	4. Time devoted to business	Percent of corporation stock owned		7. Amount of compensation	8. Expense account allowances
				5. Common	6. Preferred		
Total compensation of officers							

Other Deductions Listed (Item "D" above)

....
....
....
....
....

Cumulative Problem 8-23

John Row and his wife, Margie, lived in Chicago during January 1977. He worked as a photographer for a Chicago syndicated newspaper. Margie was on a leave of absence from North University where she had taught journalism. They have twin girls, age 4.

On January 15, John was informed by his employer that he was being transferred to another syndicate-owned newspaper located in Honolulu. John sold the Chicago residence, which was in his name, for $57,000. In selling the home which had an adjusted basis of $45,000, the Rows incurred $5,000 in broker's fees and $2,500 in painting expenses in sprucing-up their old home to facilitate its sale. The Chicago home had been bought in October of the previous year.

On February 1st, the Rows moved into their new home in Honolulu, which also was in John's name. The new residence cost $46,500. John started work with the Honolulu newspaper during the first week in February and was on its staff for the entire year. Also in February, Margie accepted a position as professor of journalism at Honolulu University.

In relocating to Honolulu the Rows paid $5,400 to move the family and furnishings. In April, John received a $4,700 partial reimbursement from his employer for these expenses.

In October, one of John's photographs was chosen as "best news photograph of the year" by the Illinois Media Guild, and John was awarded a $1,000 cash prize.

In November, Margie inherited an apartment building from her late aunt Francine. She received net rentals from the building of $800 during the last two months of the year.

In December, Margie won $3,450 on a T.V. game show.

John was divorced from his first wife, Rowena, in 1970. Under the terms of the divorce decree, he had to make quarterly payments of $240 to her.

John and Margie earned $24,000, and $28,000 yearly, at their respective jobs.

During the year, Margie received $850 in interest on a savings account, $295 in interest on a City of Port Huron bond, and $500 in dividends from the Louisiana Sugar Corporation.

The Rows' allowable deductions for charitable contributions, interest and local taxes came to $7,440.

Compute the tax liability, before credits, of Mr. & Mrs. Row on a joint return. Assume that John did not elect to deduct the broker's fee on the sale of his home as a moving expense.

Cumulative Problem 8-24

(Answer (a), (b) or (c) as directed)

(a) Dave and Christina Nocjar are married and are the parents of twin boys, age 3. Dave is the sole support of the twins and his widowed mother, who lives in a nursing home. Christina had no income during the year. Dave works at two jobs throughout the year. Monday through Thursday of each week, he is employed as an assistant district attorney in Lorain, Ohio. On Friday and Saturday, he works in Cleveland (a distance of 100-plus miles) as a lecturer on criminal law at the local police academy. Dave drives from Lorain to Cleveland on Friday morning and returns to Lorain on Saturday afternoon. Compute the tax liability (rounded off to the nearest dollar), if any, before any credits on a joint return from the following breakdown of Dave and Christina's personal records as of December 31:

Deductions—Expenses

	Debit	Credit
Salary for full year—Lorain, Ohio		$47,500
Salary for full year—Cleveland, Ohio		3,250
Bank interest received		69
Dividends received by Dave:		
Rancid Restaurants, Inc. $273		
Insipid Industries, Inc. 142		415
Profit on sale of Huebland Corp. stock (cost $3,500 on Feb. 1; sold Nov. 15 for $4,276)		776
Gross rents—from apartment house owned for 10 years		4,900
Fee paid to Superintendent of apartment house	$ 1,200	
Cost of replacing broken roofing shingles—for apartment house	275	
Heat, light, plumbing and misc. expenses—for apartment house	2,525	
Loss on sale of Lover Bros. Corp. stock (cost $1,800 on Aug. 5; sold for $1,000 on Dec. 2)	800	
Meals, lodging and transportation expenses on trips to Cleveland	1,400	
Charitable contributions	2,000	
Property tax—for residence	850	
Interest—paid on mortgaged residence	500	
Household expenses (food, gas, electric, etc.)	22,800	
Other miscellaneous personal expenses	24,560	
	$56,910	$56,910

(Note: Disregard any depreciation deduction for the apartment house.)

(b) Joe Michel, a real estate broker, received commissions of $37,500 during the tax year. In addition, he had the following transactions:

On November 11, he sold 200 shares of Dicon Corp. stock for $22,000 that he had purchased on February 1 for $60 per share.

On November 5, he sold 1,200 shares of Remto Corp. stock for $4,200 that he had purchased on June 14 for $6,200.

On December 21, he sold a parcel of real estate for $85,000 that he had purchased on March 6 for $68,000. Joe paid a finder's fee of $3,200 on the purchase and $4,000 on the sale.

Joe is married. His wife has no income or deductions of her own. He fully supports his son Wayne, age 21, who is a full-time college student. Wayne earned $1,200 during the summer working as a waiter which he deposited in his savings account. Joe's allowable deductions for interest, taxes and charitable contributions total $4,600.

(1) What is the lowest tax payable before any credits of Mr. & Mrs. Michel on their joint return?

(2) How would your answer in (1) differ, if at all, assuming Joe was a used car salesman?

(c) Frank Stanley received $42,000 in commissions as an outside salesman for the Keenform Dress Manufacturing Corporation. Since Frank had to have numerous bulky samples of material with him at all times, he was forced to rent a trailer, at a cost of $550, which he attached to his car. Frank also had expenses of $835 in traveling from his office to various customers, and $300 on lunches for customers in the course of his visits to them during the year.

Frank is being considered by the company for a managerial position, but company policy requires that managers have at least 2 years of formal business management education. During the year, Frank enrolled for management courses in a local university. He paid $450 for tuition and books and spent $50 in traveling to his classes.

On February 15, Frank sold his home for $44,500. In January he had the house papered and painted at a cost of $2,250 to help sell it. He paid the broker's commission of $2,570 and the papering and painting costs on February 25. He had bought the house for $26,000 in 1970. On April 15, Frank bought a new home for $41,500.

Frank owns an office building that he rents to a law firm. During the year he spent $4,500 to install a central air conditioning unit. In addition, he installed new lighting fixtures at a cost of $3,200 and repainted some of the offices at a cost of $2,250. His other expenses during the year included: wages for maintenance man, $8,000; insurance, $1,100; heat, light and other expenses, $4,400. He was entitled to deduct $3,350 for depreciation. The law firm paid a rental of $48,000 for the year.

On August 16, Frank sold 100 shares of Western Enterprises, Inc. for $4,550 that he bought for $3,275 on June 10. On October 4, he sold 75 shares of United Gas Corp. for $7,680 that he bought on July 25, for $9,500. On December 6, he sold 335 shares of Unique Fabric Corp. for $2,640. He had bought the shares on March 4 for $3,560. On December 27, Frank sold 2,500 shares of Abco Corp. for $13,575 that he bought on February 12 for $4,850.

During the year Frank received $2,170 in dividends from stock in taxable domestic corporations.

Frank's allowable deductions for contributions, interest and taxes amounted to $8,850. Frank is married. He is the sole support of his 2 children. His wife and children had no income of their own.

Compute the lowest tax payable by Frank and his wife, before any credits.

Cumulative Problem 8-25

Jean Dejour, age 66, and his wife Heloise, age 65, purchased a home in San Francisco twelve years ago for $60,000. Jean and Heloise never made any improvements on the property.

Jean has been under contract with Piccadilly Publications to write four magazine articles a year. His earnings from his writings totaled $22,000. He had $3,000 in business deductions (including $400 for depreciation on the office in his home) for 1977. Heloise worked as a school librarian and for this she received $7,000 in wages for the first five months of the year. Living with the Dejours for the past several years has been Heloise's 83-year old invalid mother Elvira. She received $2,000 in social security payments during 1977 and $800 in interest from a savings account. Jean contributed $1,600 towards his mother-in-law's support during the year and Elvira contributed $800 for her own support.

In February, Jean accepted a temporary position as a television commentator in New York City. His plane fare to New York was $200. He stayed at a hotel during the two months he worked in New York. His hotel room cost $2,800 and his meals $600. He also paid $300 in cab fares in riding between the hotel and the television studio.

On a weekend in March, Jean returned to San Francisco to visit his wife who became ill. Cost of the plane fare to and from San Francisco was $500.

In early April, Jean finished his assignment and returned to San Francisco. His plane fare back to San Francisco was $250. He received $10,000 in salary for his New York assignment.

In June, Jean was offered a job as a television news commentator in New Orleans. He agreed to accept the job beginning in September. In August, he went to New Orleans to rent an apartment. The trip cost him $1,600.

In early September, the Dejours sold their residence for $75,000 and moved to New Orleans. The Dejours paid a brokerage commission of $3,000 and lawyer's fees of $800 on the sale of the house. Up to the date of sale Jean had taken $2,400 in depreciation deductions on his home (using straight line method on 1/10 of his home) since he used a portion of his home to write the articles for Piccadilly Publications.

It cost the Dejours $3,000 to move the furniture and household items to their new apartment in New Orleans. $300 of this amount was for moving Elvira's furniture. Jean paid the plane fares ($225 for each of the three).

Jean was paid a salary of $4,000 a month from September to December for his job as news commentator. Heloise did not work during this period.

The Dejours itemized deductions for taxes, interest, and charitable contributions for the year totalled $6,500.

Compute the Dejour's lowest tax before credits on a joint return (round figures off to nearest dollar). Assume they did not take the selling expenses on their home as a moving expense deduction.

Research Problem 8-26

John March is the owner-operator of a 60-foot fishing vessel from which he and his crew fish for tuna and shrimp. Since March and his crew are often at sea for extended periods, he makes it a practice of occasionally taking his crew to lunch or inviting them all to a catered picnic when in port. March does this in order to reward them for their performances and to assure that they will continue to work for him. These meals are provided in addition to their wages and are not treated as compensation for purposes of withholding taxes. The costs of these meals are recorded in a diary which March maintains. Entries in this diary also reflect the dates on which he purchases meals for his crew and the places where they are purchased. In addition to these costs, March spends $300 for an annual Christmas party for his crew. March seeks your advice as a tax expert in order to determine whether he may deduct any portion of the cost of the meals or party. What do you advise?

Use the Prentice-Hall Complete Federal Tax Equipment in your school or local library to find your answer. Do the following:

1. Give your opinion. In it show authorities, citing law regulations, interpretations and decisions applicable, and the P-H Federal Tax Equipment paragraphs where they may be found.

2. Enumerate and explain carefully each step you take in reaching your result. These are extremely important—just as important as the result.

Tax Reasoning Problem 8-27

Pratt is a teacher in a school located in a poverty area of the city. To provide his culturally deprived students with a new educational experience, he equipped an experimental classroom and provided special materials at his own expense. Are Pratt's outlays deductible as ordinary and necessary business expenses? Explain.

Tax Reasoning Problem 8-28

When Kane applied for a flight officer job with an airline he was 40 pounds overweight. He had to lose the excess weight while training at the flight school. After that, his personal clothing did not fit. He spent $500 for new clothes. Can he deduct the cost? Explain.

ASSIGNMENT No. 9

DEDUCTIONS—INTERESTS, TAXES, CONTRIBUTIONS, MEDICAL EXPENSES

(*Note: In the following problems, unless otherwise specified, assume that the "tax year" is the calendar year 1977, that the taxpayer and his spouse, if any, are resident citizens under 65 and are not blind and that the taxpayer is not entitled to any credits against the tax other than those shown.*)

Problem 9-1

(a) O. J. Smith borrowed $1,500 from his bank to buy a new delivery truck to be used in his business. Is the interest he pays on the loan deductible?

(b) If O. J. uses the loan proceeds to buy a car for his wife, could he then deduct the interest he pays?

(c) What is the effect on adjusted gross income if a deduction is allowed in (a) or (b)?

Problem 9-2

Cleo Brown works for the Adams Corporation. Her brother is the company's vice-president in charge of sales and she is a large shareholder. In March, Cleo made a cash bank deposit of $10,000. The money was the proceeds from a loan she received from a local bank the day before. On June 15, Cleo's brother authorized the treasurer of the corporation to pay the July 1 interest payment on Cleo's note. The action was approved by the stockholders on June 20 on the ground that the payments of interest were an anniversary gift. On September 30, the corporation bought the note. It paid the interest due on the note on Oct. 1. Is it entitled to a deduction for the interest payments it paid?

Problem 9-3

Mrs. Angel is liable to Cue Savings & Loan Association on a first mortgage and to Mrs. Bitters on a second mortgage on her summer home at the shore. This year Mrs. Angel had financial trouble and could not make the payments on the second mortgage. Mrs. Bitters agreed to cancel the second mortgage in exchange for the property.

On Nov. 15, after the property was exchanged, Mrs. Bitters died and her husband, Al, received the property under her will. On Dec. 1, Mrs. Angel told Al she would not be able to pay interest due on the first mortgage. Al wants to keep control of the property and made the interest payment to prevent foreclosure by the Savings & Loan Association. Can Al take a deduction for this payment on a separate return this year?

Problem 9-4

State whether an interest deduction should be allowed in the following situations:

(a) Harvey Nebish paid the balance of his daughter's charge account, including interest.

(b) Elmer Tooney paid the interest on a loan taken out by his mother to pay his college tuition.

(c) Mr. & Mrs. Beanstock won the state lottery and paid off their home mortgage, but had to pay a prepayment penalty.

(d) Elsie Extra paid $500 in points to the bank from which she obtained a home mortgage. The points were intended to compensate the bank for its appraisal and notary fees.

Problem 9-5

(a) In 1975, P.J. Arnold incurred an interest obligation of $60,000 on money borrowed for the following: Cease Corp. stock bought on 4-6-75 for $480,000 and sold on 8-15-75 for $483,000; Climate Corp. stock bought on 5-1-75 for $150,000 and sold on 12-31-75 for $155,000; and an unimproved tract of land bought on 1-2-74 for $450,000. Additional information related to these transactions was as follows: $5,175 in dividends received from his Climate Corp. stock; $5,000 per month for renting the property to the Wyco Corp. starting the same day Arnold purchased the land.

Wyco erected a small building for $3,000 by February 15. In March, Arnold and Wyco agreed to terminate the lease on May 1. As part of the agreement, Arnold purchased the building for $3,000. On May 1, Wyco vacated the premises. On 12-31-75, Arnold sold the building for $6,000. Taxes on the land amounted to $2,000 and straight line depreciation on the building during the time he owned it totaled $625. Figure Arnold's interest deduction for tax year 1975 on his joint return. Explain.

(b) In 1976, Arnold had net investment income of $30,000. He had $120,000 in investment interest as follows: $60,000 attributable to 1975 (as stated in (a)) and $60,000 attributable to 1976. Figure Arnold's total investment interest deduction for tax year 1976 on his joint return. Explain.

Problem 9-6

Harry Jones, an engineer, has a $100,000 life insurance policy. He has paid annual premiums of $2,000 on the policy since January 1970. In December 1976 he ran into financial difficulties when his 18-year-old son began going to engineering school as Harry had always planned.

In January 1977 he borrowed $6,000 against the cash surrender value of the policy in order to pay the annual premiums for 1977 through 1979. On this he paid $120 interest (6% of $2,000 premium) for the year. May Jones take an interest deduction on his 1977 return? Explain.

Problem 9-7

Linda Hay, a computer programmer, uses the entire floor of her two-floor home (equivalent to ½ of the total floor space) as an office for sales meetings and for dealings with customers in the normal course of her business. The home has a fair market value of $75,000. This year, she paid $5,000 city-assessed real property taxes. Other taxes she paid this year are: $100 city sales tax on the purchase of office supplies; $600 city income tax on her computer-sales income; $300 U.S. excise tax on use of her telephone, one-half of which was attributed to her computer operations. How would you treat these taxes on Linda's return?

Problem 9-8

State whether or not the following taxes are deductible and, if deductible, indicate how they are shown on the return.

(a) State transfer tax paid by buyer of personal residence.

(b) State transfer tax paid by buyer of warehouse to be used in his business.

(c) Assessment by town for cost of constructing new sewer, paid by home owner.

(d) State gasoline tax paid by owner of private automobile that is used 50% of the time in the owner's activities as an outside salesman.

Problem 9-9

During the year, Donald Pace, a dentist, paid the following taxes in the course of his practice:

a. Federal self-employment taxes of $1,303.50.

b. Social security taxes of $1,930.50 withheld on the wages of his two dental hygienists, Jane and Joan ($965.25 each).

c. Social security taxes of $1,930.50 for Jane and Joan (employer required to pay tax on equal amount of wages).

d. State and federal unemployment taxes of $285.60 (the federal tax was $58.80 after credit for payment of state unemployment taxes was taken).

e. State disability tax of $104 for Joan and Jane.

Which of the above payments of taxes are deductible by Jane, Joan and Donald?

Problem 9-10

During the year, Carter Tracey, an independent TV and radio repairman, paid the following federal taxes: excise taxes on telephone calls, $200 (telephone used one-half for business); excise tax on transportation of electronic equipment by air freight, $125; import tax on receipt of transistor radios from Taiwan, $80; estate tax on legacy received from aunt, $2,000; gasoline tax on business truck, $120; and gasoline tax on personal automobile, $40.

What taxes are deductible by Tracey?

Problem 9-11

L. E. Fant is a retail furrier. During the year he paid the following taxes: $300 federal import taxes on the purchase of materials and supplies, $1,303.50 in federal self-employment taxes, $630 in state income taxes, $80 in state gasoline taxes and $40 in federal gasoline taxes on his automobile (auto used $1/2$ of time for business), $30 state auto registration fee based on the weight of the vehicle, $50 local personal property tax on business equipment based on equipment's value, and $250 in sales taxes ($200 for personal items and $50 for business items).

Fant does some hunting, but only for furs sold in his business. He paid $100 for a state hunting license, a $50 state gun registration fee, and $25 fee for permission to hunt in a local game preserve.

What taxes are deductible, and how would Fant treat them on his return?

Problem 9-12

Pat Worthy, a New York resident, is a wholesale ceramics dealer. While on a trip to Nassau in the Grand Bahama Islands, he visited an antique display and came across 50 pieces of rare pottery which he bought. He shipped 40 to his N.J. warehouse and the remaining 10 pieces to his residence to become part of his personal collection. Pat paid an import tax of $40 a piece. How much, if any, of the federal import taxes may Pat deduct on his federal return?

Problem 9-13

On May 1, 1977, C. C. Claw discovered that he failed to report a stock dividend on his 1975 federal return. He immediately filed an amended return and paid an additional tax of $300 along with an interest payment of $30.

On June 1, 1977, Claw was notified by the state tax commission that he had underpaid his state income tax for 1976. In September, he paid the additional tax due ($60), plus $7 in interest.

What amounts, if any, may Claw deduct on his 1977 return?

Problem 9-14

M. C. Tracer stated business as a travel agent last year. To get capital, he incorporated his business and sold 10% of the stock. The corporation leased office property and in consideration of a lower rent, agreed to pay the real estate taxes on the property. This year the corporation was in financial difficulties and Tracer paid $800 of the property taxes on the office. The corporation paid the balance of $300 and also the rent of $3,500. Tracer also paid $150 in real estate taxes on a hunting cottage that he owns.

What amount, if any, can Tracer deduct? What amounts can the corporation deduct?

Problem 9-15

(a) Bee Brown works as a writer. Her salary this year is $29,000. She received $100 interest from a savings account and $300 dividends from U.S. stock. During the year she paid the following taxes and interest: $2,000 real property taxes on her home, $250 New York City and State income taxes, $300 interest on a personal loan and $60 state gasoline taxes. She contributed $5,000 to the University Hospital and $10,000 to Writers of America Association. The Association is a nonprofit private foundation that operates a writing clinic for unemployed writers. It was organized by Bee's wealthy parents and is fully supported by them. On Dec. 1, Bee sold Rich Company common stock worth $10,000 to her church for $6,000. She had bought the stock on January 15 of this year for $5,000. Bee is not married and has no dependents. Compute her lowest tax table income.

(b) Assume the same facts as in (a), except that Bee sold the Rich Company stock to her church on April 1. How would your answer differ? Explain.

Problem 9-16

Jake Bunting and his wife made the following contributions for the year: Community Chest, $100; Boy Scouts, $75; and $300 to their family church. Mr. Bunting, a member of the local Boy Scout committee, devoted about 60 hours of his time to committee projects. He valued his time at $5 an hour. He also incurred car expenses of $25 in his Boy Scout activities. Mrs. Bunting gave a pint of blood to the local blood bank which was paying professional donors $35 a pint. Assuming that the Buntings' adjusted gross income was $30,000 what is their deduction for contributions on a joint return?

Problem 9-17

(a) Betty Smith is 48 years old. Her husband Fred is 67 years old, permanently disabled and has no income. During the year, Betty paid the following expenses: $260 in premiums for hospitalization insurance for herself and Fred; $45 withheld from wages for social security hospitalization tax; $1.50 a month withheld from wages for premiums for an accident and health policy; $80 for voluntary social security medicare program for Fred; $680 for drugs and medicines; $1,040 for doctor fees; $670 for room, board and care in a hospital; contact lenses for Fred, $185.

Most of the expense was due to an accident Betty had on her job, and she received the following payments: $375 for hospital expenses paid under the hospitalization policy, $2,000 for partial loss of a toe under the accident and health policy.

Betty's adjusted gross income is $18,500. What is her medical deduction on a joint return?

(b) Tim Webb, 69 years of age, is married and the sole support of his blind son, Joe. Neither his wife Karen, age 63, nor Joe have income of their own. During the year, Tim received a salary of $23,000. In addition, he received $200 dividends on AC Corp. stock which he owned. Expenses paid during the year were: $600 for traveling on job-connected business trips; $400 real property taxes on residence; $235 interest on mortgage covering his home; $350 contributions to his church; $300 hospital expenses for himself and wife; $3,150 hospital expenses for his "dependent" son, Joe; $145 on drugs for himself and wife; and $275 on drugs for Joe. Tim had no other dependents. (1) Figure the tax table income to be shown on a joint return filed by Tim and Karen. (2) What is their tax?

SUPPLEMENTAL PROBLEMS

Problem 9-18

C. W. Kole's wife died last year. He continues to support his 70-year-old mother-in-law who lives with him and has no income of her own. During the year, he earned a salary of $20,150, received a $650 cash dividend on stock he owns in Phila. Mfg. Corp. a Pennsylvania corporation, and a $500 payment from an endowment policy he bought on January 3, for $13,440. The policy will pay him 27 more yearly installments of the same amount.

On July 5, he sold a valuable painting for $1,200. He had bought it for his home on February 8, for $800. On April 15, he paid a federal gift tax of $210 on gifts he had made last year. He also made the following payments during the year: State general sales tax, $72; real estate taxes on his home, $1,350; State income tax on last year's income, $110; federal income tax on last year's income, $200; interest on personal loan, $1,320; doctor's bill for his mother-in-law's eye examination,

$15; eyeglasses for her, $30; contribution to his church, $350; contribution to his college, $200.

Kole also paid $380 in doctors' bills and a hospital bill of $210, for himself.

Compute (1) Kole's tax table income (round expenses to the nearest dollar); (2) his tax.

★ Problem 9-19 ★

During the year, Phil Hall had adjusted gross income of $30,000. His medical expenses were: $280 in premiums for hospitalization insurance, $360 for drugs and medicines; $900 for doctor's fees; $300 for hospital care. On 8-1-77, he received $100 for hospital expenses paid under his hospitalization policy.

In 1977, Hall made the following contributions for which he has kept the receipts: $1,500 to his church; $13,500 worth of securities to Central State University that cost him $5,000 in 1957. Hall also contributed $190 worth of ice cream to the Double Fault Club, an informal group of tennis friends that give an annual dinner for ball boys.

Hall paid $660 in property tax on his home, $1,130 in realty taxes on his business property, $250 in state gift taxes, $100 in state income tax. He also paid $50 in state gasoline tax on his personal car and a state inheritance tax of $200 on his wife's estate. Hall paid $2,500 in employer's federal and state payroll taxes from operation of his dairy store.

When Hall moved to his new home he had a blanket mortgage drafted to cover both his residence and business property. Of the $3,000 mortgage interest he paid during the year, 70% is attributable to the business property.

Fill in the following schedule to give Hall maximum itemized deductions:

Itemized Deductions
1. 50% of hospital insurance premiums but not more than $150 ....
2. Total cost of medicine and drugs ....
3. Enter 1% of adjusted gross income ....

4. Subtract line 3 from line 2 ....
5. Other medical, dental expenses (include hospital insurance premiums not entered in 1) ....

6. Total (add lines 4 and 5) ....
7. Enter 3% of adjusted gross income ....
8. Subtract line 7 from line 6 ....
   Total medical deduction (line 1 plus line 8) ..

Contributions.—
1. Cash contributions for which you have receipts ....
2. Other than cash ....
3. Carryover from prior years ....

   Total contributions (add lines 1, 2 and 3) ......
Interest: Home mortgage ....
Installment purchases ....
Other (Specify) ....
....
....
   Total interest expense ....
Taxes—Real estate ....
State and local gasoline ....
General sales ....
State and local income ....
Personal property ....
   Total taxes ....

Cumulative Problem 9-20
Answer (a) or (b) as directed

(a) Larry Friend is the sole support of two daughters: Alice, age 8, and Pat, age 14. Both live with Larry and have no income or deductions of their own. Friend's wife died last year. As an accountant for Acme Sales Company, Larry earned $15,000 for the year and received $2,000 in reimbursed travel allowance expenses. His cash dividends from domestic stock for the year totaled $250. Other income consisted of $100 interest on corporate bonds and $500 incentive award from Acme.

On May 1, Larry's 65th birthday, he received 5 shares of Eastland Corp. stock as a taxable dividend on his Ohio Company stock. When he received the Eastland stock it had a fair market value of $100. By the year's end, its value dropped to $75.

On May 12, he sold 100 shares of United Corporation common stock for $1,000. He received this stock on 12-16-76 as a taxable dividend on 500 shares of Bengal Corporation preferred stock that he bought in 1973 for $10,000. The 100 shares of United common had a fair market value of $700 when received in 1976.

During the year, Friend's actual audited expenses on extended business trips for Acme were $1,500. His charitable gifts for the year were: $300 to the Trinity Church, $50 to Century College, $65 to Girl Scouts, and $500 to Institute for Improved Learning, a private nonprofit institute. He also paid $2,200 interest on the mortgage on his residence, reduced the face amount of the mortgage by $600 and paid the final $200 due on his wife's funeral.

Friend's record of taxes paid during the year was as follows: $200 property tax on his residence; $10 federal tax on sporting goods bought for personal use; $20 annual registration fee (based on weight) for pleasure auto; $25 federal gasoline tax; and $15 state gasoline tax for his pleasure auto.

Compute (1) the tax table income of Larry Friend; (2) his tax.

(b) Sam West retired from his real estate firm after 28 years of service at the end of last year. Sam became 65 years of age on August 31, 1977.

During 1977, he received the following: $5,000, the first of 10 annual payments on an endowment purchased ten years ago for $45,000; $400 in social security benefits; $1,900 from his former partnership for consulting services; $6,500 in cash dividends from domestic corporations; $900 interest on Center City Authority bonds; $16,500 interest on Wonder Corp. bonds; $200 interest on a savings account; and $21,400 in rents from a gasoline service station business. The net rent is $19,900 because Sam's deductions for business expenses of the service station totaled $1,500. Mr. West did not perform any personal services at the station.

Sam's father, who had a substantial income of his own, died in April. On June 1, Sam received the following property under his father's will: $100,000 face amount of Zeppo bonds which had been purchased by his father in 1973 for $90,000 and were worth $95,000 when he died; 100 shares of Sim Company stock that cost Sam's father $2,500 in 1971 and had a fair market value of $3,000 at date of his death. On December 31, 1976, the Zeppo bonds had a fair market value of $98,500 and the Sim Company stock had a fair market value of $4,000.

During the year, Sam made these stock and bond transactions: On July 29, Sam sold 40 shares of Sim Corp. stock for $1,200. He received these shares as a taxable stock dividend on May 3, when they had a fair market value of $50 a share. He had bought 960 shares of Sim Corp. stock in 1970 for $4,000. On August 1, he sold his 100 inherited shares for $4,100.

On September 30, Sam sold Zeppo bonds he inherited from his father for $97,000.

On November 10, Sam sold for $6,400, 200 shares of Garden Corp. stock. West received these shares as a nontaxable stock dividend on August 1, of this year. On that date they had a fair market value of $4,000. He had bought 2,000 shares of Garden Corp. stock in 1969 for $22,000.

Sam's wife, age 68, died on August 31, 1977.

Before her death, Sam had paid his wife $6,000 during 1977 as support payments under a written separation agreement they made in 1975.

On September 2, Sam sold his home for $25,000. He had bought it in 1969 for $19,000 but never made any improvements on it. Two weeks before the sale, he spent $1,000 for repairs and painting. At the sale closing, Sam paid his attorney $150 and the real estate salesman $250. The buyer on the closing date paid the property taxes of $365 for the calendar year. These taxes were due and owing since July 1. Sam also had to pay $100 for points to obtain a mortgage for his buyer. It cost him $900 as a penalty for paying off the mortgage he obtained when he bought the home. Sam bought a cooperative apartment for $19,000 after the sale.

Other taxes paid during the year were: $140 state and city general sales-use taxes and $60 federal tax on personal telephone calls. On June 15, Sam made a gift of a painting having a $5,000 retail value, to a local art museum. Sam had paid $2,000 for the painting in 1972. During the year, he contributed $2,000 to his church and spent $300 for raffle tickets during his church's annual Thanksgiving bazaar. Sam's medical bills were all covered by medical insurance during 1977. The medical insurance premiums totaled $150 for the year.

Sam's wife had no other income during 1977 except social security benefits of $1,000 and no deductions. What is the least income tax before credits for West assuming he makes the proper elections?

Cumulative Problem 9-21

Harold Stern is married. His wife, Lynn, earned $350 during the year, doing typing at home. Harold worked as a machinist and received $8,950 in wages during the year. Also during the year, Harold and Lynn received $400 in dividends on stock they owned jointly in domestic corporations. $100 of this was a stock dividend from the Wood Corporation. All of Wood's stockholders had the right to receive cash or stock.

On September 1, Harold sold 100 shares of Spaed Corporation stock for $1,800 that he received as a gift on 1-1-72 from his father. The fair market value on that date was $1,700. His father's basis was $2,000. No gift tax was paid.

On October 6, Lynn sold stock of the Powderdust Corporation for $8,000 that she received under her mother's will. Her mother died on June 1 when the fair market value of the stock was $10,000. The value as of 12-31-76 was $9,000. When distributed to Lynn on October 1, the stock's fair market value was $9,500. Her mother had bought it on 2-10-73 for $10,000.

In his work as a machinist, Harold incurred the following expenses during 1977: $200 in commuting costs, $50 for goggles and special gloves used on his job, $30 for work shoes worn at home and on his job, and $20 for union dues.

On November 1, Harold gave 100 shares of Star Co. stock to Duchess University. The stock was valued at $30 per share on that date. The stock had been received from his mother in 1970 when the shares were valued at $20 each. Harold's mother had bought the stock 3 years earlier for $10 a share. On 12-1-77, Harold gave Duchess University library a painting valued at $75 when the gift was made. Harold had completed the painting in 1976. He had paid $25 for materials to create the work. Harold mailed a charitable contribution check for $50 to the American Red Cross on 12-31-77.

The Sterns incurred the following personal expenses during 1977: $200 interest on the mortgage on their residence, $70 in finance charges on retail credit card, $200 in real estate taxes, $150 in state income taxes, $30 auto registration fee based on weight, $280 for medical insurance, $400 for doctor bills and $100 in prescription drugs for him and his wife.

They contributed $1,100 for the support of their daughter, Kim, age 19, who is away at school. The $1,100 includes $100 of Kim's doctor bills. Kim is attending college on a $1,000 scholarship but during the summer she earned $1,050, which she used for her own support.

Figure the tax table income of Mr. and Mrs. Stern on a joint return.

Discussion Problem 9-22

The basic principle of equity underlying individual taxation is that equal amounts of income should bear equal tax liabilities. This requires a workable concept of income. The Internal Revenue Code, however, does not define income directly, but arrives at the statutory concept of taxable income by specifying how various types of receipts and expenditures are to be treated. The result has been a continuing loss of uniformity in the income tax base as differential treatment has been provided in many situations, either by specific exclusions, deductions, or other qualification, or by failure to specify inclusion of various types of income. These differential tax provisions result from trying to provide special tax adjustments for special tax situations. The basic difficulty is that forsaking uniformity in one case gives rise to demands for similar concessions in others. This has resulted in a highly nonuniform income tax system that places a premium on tax avoidance devices and increases the relative tax burden on those taxpayers who are unable to take advantage of the special provisions.

To restore the universality of the income tax, it is suggested that it is necessary to define income. For many economists, the best definition of income for tax purposes is the algebraic sum of an individual's consumption expenditures and the change in his net worth during a given period of time. Neither the source of the income, the conditions under which it is received, nor the manner in which it is disposed of should be considered in determining how much of it should be taxed. Similarly, this definition would substitute accrual for realization as a determinant of taxability of an income item.

As a practicable approximation of this definition, it has been suggested that taxable individual income be defined as gross receipts (other than those representing return of the original cost of capital) less the expenses necessarily incurred in obtaining these receipts. In addition, deductions would be allowed for liens on the taxpayer's income, such as income taxes of another jurisdiction, and alimony payments.

(a) What arguments can you give to support this suggestion?
(b) What arguments can you give against this proposal?

Research Problem 9-23

Carla Homebrew is a retired school teacher. On her income tax return last year she claimed a $4,000 medical deduction. The Revenue Service, after audit, disallowed the deduction. Carla engages you, a tax expert, to advise her of her chances for success if she appeals the disallowance. She tells you that the $4,000 medical expense deduction represents the value of medical care which she rendered to herself. She did not pay any doctor for medical services, or pay for treatment at any hospital, nor did she pay for medical insurance. She contends that she is entitled to a deduction for insurance premiums for medical care because she can act as a self-insurer. Similarly, she says that she should not be required to get treatment from either a doctor or a hospital and so may deduct the value of self-treatment. Also, she urges that the Revenue Service should have no right to force her to get treatment from medical practitioners as opposed to caring for herself.

1. Give your opinion. In it show authorities, citing law regulations, interpretations and decisions applicable, and the P-H Federal Tax Equipment paragraphs where they may be found.
2. Enumerate and explain carefully each step you take in reaching your result. These are extremely important—just as important as the result.

Tax Reasoning Problem 9-24

On December 15, Jones asks your advice about donating a hundred shares of his blue-chip stock that he purchased in October of this year. He wishes to contribute the stock to his church or to a private foundation, whichever would give rise to a bigger deduction either this or next tax year. Assume that Jones' adjusted gross income tax is sufficient to support the desired deduction, what would you advise Jones to do?

ASSIGNMENT NO. 10
DEDUCTIONS—DEPRECIATION

(Note: In the following problems, unless otherwise specified, assume that the "tax year" is the calendar year 1977, that the taxpayer and his spouse, if any, are resident citizens under 65 and are not blind and that the taxpayer is not entitled to any credits against the tax other than those shown. In figuring your answers, round off all amounts to the nearest whole dollar.)

Problem 10-1

(a) On 1-1-52, Rob Green entered into an agreement with Acme Realty to lease from it a tract of land for 40 years. There was also an option to renew the lease for a 10-year period. On 1-1-77, Green completed the construction of a building on the land at a cost of $51,000 to conduct some of his business operations. The building had an estimated useful life of 30 years. Assume no salvage value. Green and Acme Realty have always employed the straight line method to determine depreciation on their properties. Who can claim the deduction for the year on the building and how much would it be?

(b) Would your answer be different if Green and Acme Realty were "related parties"?

(c) Assume in (a) above that the building had a useful life of 10 years. How would that affect your answer to (a)?

Problem 10-2

John Howard, a real estate salesman, purchased a car on 1-2-75 for $3,000. Its estimated life is 3 years and its salvage value is $500. He uses it 3 days of the week for business and the rest for pleasure. At the close of 1976, it was determined that the car would be used for 2 more years. If Howard uses the straight line method of depreciation what is his deduction for 1977?

Problem 10-3

During the past few years, Andrews has operated a small store in the suburbs, located in a single story building he owns. In October, Andrews sold out his entire stock and listed the property for rent. On November 1, he bought a two-family house and moved into half of it. He had been living in an apartment. He listed the other half of the house for rent. On January 1, 1978, both the store property and the second half of the house were still vacant.

(a) In his income tax return for the year, may Andrews take a deduction for depreciation on (1) the store property and (2) the two-family house?

(b) Would your answer to (a) be different if Andrews used the second half of his house as guest quarters for visiting relatives during November and December and did not list it for rent until January 1, 1978?

Problem 10-4

On 12-31-77, Kevin Gregory died and left an apartment house to his sister, Mary, for her life and then to her son, John. The building, which Gregory had bought new on 1-1-75 at a cost of $49,000 with no salvage value, had a fair market value at date of death of $61,000. When Mary got the building, its adjusted basis was $45,325 (no adjustments, other than depreciation, were necessary) and its remaining useful life was 37 years. Mary's life expectancy at that time was 25 years.

(a) Assuming straight line depreciation will continue to be used, what depreciation may be taken and by whom?

(b) Would your answer to (a) differ if, immediately upon inheritance, Mary sold her life interest to Sara Jones for $40,000?

Problem 10-5

(a) Ace Builders completed construction of an office building on 6-30-77 and entered into an executory contract of sale with Dana Realty, Inc. on 7-1-77. Dana took immmediate possession and began leasing the offices for terms ranging from 3 to 25 years. Settlement of complicated tax liens delayed the transfer of title to Dana until 9-30-77. Dana paid $740,000 for the building which has an estimated useful life of 40 years and no salvage value. Under the lease terms, tenants are required only to maintain the property, with any repairs and improvements to be made by Dana. What amount of depreciation can Dana take for the current year under the straight line method?

(b) Jim Carson purchased a building in 1969 for $38,000. On 4-1-77, he made a gift of the building to his nephew, Kevin Block. On that date, Carson's adjusted basis in the building (assuming no gift tax was paid on the transfer) was $28,000 and the fair market value was $24,000. Also on that date, the building had a remaining useful life of 14 years and no salvage value. Assuming straight line depreciation is used, what is Block's depreciation deduction for the current year?

Problem 10-6

Debbie Hancock's husband died on 1-1-74, leaving her an office building and lot subject to a $30,000 mortgage. The value of the property as of 1-1-74 was $88,000 ($55,000 for the building). This was the value used by the executor for estate tax purposes. Debbie continued to operate the building. On 1-1-77, she settled the mortgage (amounting at that time to $24,000) for $23,000, and sold the property for $81,440 in cash. Assuming a straight line depreciation rate of 4%, and no salvage value, how much is her recognized gain or loss on the sale?

Problem 10-7

On 1-2-74, Matt James bought a machine for $8,000. It had an estimated useful life of 10 years on the date of purchase and no salvage value. James did not elect the additional first-year depreciation. Using the straight line method he deducted and was allowed $800 in 1974 and 1975, nothing in 1976 and $1,600 this year. Of the $1,600 deduction this year, only $1,280 resulted in a tax benefit. What will be the adjusted basis of the machine the first of January of next year, and what depreciation deduction can James take for next year, using the straight line method?

Problem 10-8

(a) Mark Piller started construction of an office building on land he owned on 10-31-76. The building was completed and ready for use on 4-30-77 at a total cost of $152,000. The building has an estimated useful life of 40 years and a salvage value of $12,000. What is the maximum depreciation Piller can take for the current year, and what method of depreciation is used?

(b) On the completion date in (a) above, Piller also acquired a license with 40-year useful life for $228,000. What is the maximum depreciation he can take on the license for the current year, and what method of depreciation is used?

Problem 10-9

On 1-2-77, Ruth's Creations, Inc., bought a new manufacturing machine. It cost $60,000, with an estimated salvage value of $5,500 and useful life of 8 years.

(a) How much is the current year's depreciation deduction on the machine, if the sum of the years-digits method is used?

(b) What would the machine's adjusted basis be at the end of 8 years if the corporation used the declining balance method?

(c) If after using the accelerated methods in (a) or (b) above, Ruth decides that she wants to recover the entire cost, how can she do it?

Problem 10-10

Herb Andrews bought an apartment building for $75,000 on January 2 of the current year. The building has a useful life of 40 years and a salvage value of $3,000.

(a) What is the largest depreciation allowance Andrews is entitled to for the current year, assuming the building was new?

(b) What would your answer be if he purchased a used apartment building?

(c) What would your answer be if he purchased a new office building?

(d) What would your answer be if he purchased a used office building?

Problem 10-11

Assuming that the additional first-year depreciation allowance is elected, figure the total depreciation for the first and second years for an office machine used in business (with no salvage value), under the following circumstances:

(a) Bought for $12,000 on 7-1-77, with a 10-year useful life and depreciated under the straight line method on an individual return.

(b) Bought for $7,000 on 10-1-77, with an 8-year useful life and depreciated under declining balance method on a joint return.

(c) Bought for $24,000 on 1-2-77, with a 6-year useful life and depreciated under the general rule of the sum of the years-digits method on a joint return.

(d) Bought for $3,000 on 4-1-77, with a 4-year useful life and depreciated under declining balance method on an individual return.

(e) Bought for $13,500 on 1-2-77, with a 20-year useful life and depreciated under the straight line method on a joint return.

Problem 10-12

Merlin Mills, Inc., a cement manufacturer, bought and placed in service four similar machines during the year for use in the manufacturing process. Machine A was bought from the Atlas Sand and Gravel Co. on 4-1-77 at a cost of $20,000 with a $1,200 salvage value. Merlin Mills and Atlas Sand and Gravel are component members of the same controlled group of corporations. Machine B was bought on 5-1-77 at a cost of $15,000 with an $1,800 salvage value. Machine C was bought on 7-1-77 at a cost of $25,000 with a salvage value of $2,500. Machine D was bought on 9-1-77 at a cost of $14,000 with no salvage value. Merlin Mills elects the Class Life Asset Depreciation Range system for depreciation of all its assets this year. Using available elections, compute the maximum straight line depreciation deduction Merlin Mills can take for the year.

Problem 10-13

Anson is a processor and distributor of dairy products. Part of Anson's operation is a bottle washing facility consisting of three machines. Each machine cost $1,000 and was placed in item vintage accounts of 1975. Anson also has a 1975 multiple asset vintage account consisting of three machines. Two of these machines, used in processing butter, each cost $10,000. A third, used in capping bottles, cost $1,000. In 1977, Anson began using paper milk cartons and disposed of all the machines used in the bottling process (washing and capping). Will Anson have a recognized loss in 1977 from these machines? Explain.

SUPPLEMENTAL PROBLEMS

Problem 10-14

Kay and Jim Miller, manufacturers of nonwoven fabrics, bought a used machine on 12-1-76 for $18,000. It had $2,025 salvage value. The Millers elected the Class Life ADR treatment and the limited declining balance depreciation method for the machine. For the current year, the Millers switched to the straight line method. Salvage value remained the same, but the remaining estimated useful life was increased to 10 years on 1-1-77.

Assuming they file joint returns, what is the Millers' depreciation deduction for the current year if they have taken all steps since 12-1-76 to maximize their depreciation deductions?

★ Problem 10-15 ★

On 1-2-72, Phil Hall bought furniture for his dairy store at a cost of $29,000, with a useful life of 10 years. Hall used the straight line method to calculate depreciation and took the additional first-year depreciation. Salvage value was $3,900. On 1-2-77, it is determined that the remaining useful life of the furniture is 6 years.

On 9-1-77, Hall purchased and immediately placed in service a new refrigerated truck for the store. The truck cost Hall $9,000 and had a salvage value of $1,800 and a 6-year useful life. He took the maximum depreciation deduction for the truck, but did not elect the ADR system.

On 10-1-77, Hall purchased and immediately placed in service a new ice cream machine for his store for $500. Its salvage value was $150, and it had a useful life of 5 years. Hall chose the straight line method to compute depreciation on the machine.

Hall is a widower. He filed a joint 1972 return.
Fill in the following schedule.

a. Description of property	b. Date acquired	c. Cost or other basis	d. Depreciation allowed or allowable in prior years	e. Method of computing depreciation	f. Life or rate	g. Depreciation for this year
1 Total additional first-year depreciation (do not include in items below)				→		
2 Other depreciation:						
3 Totals						

★ ★ **Problem 10-16** ★ ★

The books of the Atlas Machinery Corp. show the following capital accounts:
 (a) Concrete factory building. Cost to build on 5-1-70, $210,000. Estimated salvage value, $30,000. Estimated life, 50 years.
 (b) Brick office building. Purchased on 1-2-64 for $95,000 (land excluded). Estimated salvage value, $15,000. Estimated life, 40 years.
 (c) Machinery which cost $60,000 on 1-1-76 had an estimated life of 8 years and no salvage value.
 (d) A patent for a computerized pollution control adjuster was acquired on 1-1-74 for $12,000 at which time it had a life of 10 years.
 (e) New furniture and movable fixtures cost $17,000 on 1-1-77. Estimated salvage value, $1,500. Estimated life, 10 years.
 (f) A new truck was bought on 1-1-77 for $5,400. It had an estimated life of 6 years and no salvage value.

The corporation used the straight line method to figure depreciation for all the tangible assets except the truck. The corporation elected to depreciate the truck using the declining balance method. It elected to take additional first-year depreciation on the furniture and fixtures. It did not elect additional first-year depreciation on the machine bought in 1976. Figure the depreciation for 1977 and fill in the schedule below. Enter original cost or other basis in column 3, less salvage value if that is a factor. The corporation did not elect to depreciate its assets under the Class Life ADR System (Form 4832) or the Guideline Class Life System (Form 5006).

1978   **Assignment 10—Problems**   **5087**

Schedule G — Depreciation

Note: If depreciation is computed by using the Class Life (ADR) System or the Guideline Class Life System, you must file Form 4832 (Class Life (ADR) System) or Form 5006 (Guideline Class Life System) with your return. Check box(es) if you made an election this taxable year to use ☐ Class Life (ADR) System and/or ☐ Guideline Class Life System.

1. Group and guideline class or description of property	2. Date acquired	3. Cost or other basis	4. Depreciation allowed or allowable in prior years	5. Method of computing depreciation	6. Life or rate	7. Depreciation for this year
1 Total additional first-year depreciation (do not include in items below)						
2 Depreciation from Form 4832						
3 Depreciation from Form 5006						
4 Other depreciation:						
Buildings						
Furniture and fixtures						
Transportation equipment						
Machinery and other equipment						
Other (specify)						
5 Totals						

Cumulative Problem 10-17

During the year, Joe Wilson worked Monday through Friday for the Acme Braid Co. From January through June he spent his day on the road collecting on Acme's accounts in the area. For the last half of the year he worked in Acme's central office. On 1-2-77, he bought a new car. It had a useful life of 5 years and cost Joe $6,000. Its salvage value was $1,000.

Joe spent $5,675 during the year for gasoline, oil, repairs and insurance. One-half of the expenses were incurred in the first six months when Joe drove his auto 25,000 miles (20,000 for business use and 5,000 for personal use). The remainder of the year he used the car for commuting to work and for personal use.

On Monday, September 12, Joe was in an accident while on his lunch break and because of his injury did not return to work until Monday, November 7. Under Acme's wage continuation plan, Joe received $250 per week while he was absent from work. Joe's salary would have been $300 a week during this period. During the periods before and after this absence Joe earned $13,200 in wages.

Joe was hospitalized the first week of his absence. During his absence, he incurred the following costs which were not reimbursed: hospital costs, $1,000; drugs, $650; doctor bills, $360.

In 1977, Joe received $450 in dividends from Ohio Instruments. One-third of the company's distribution was in excess of earnings and profits. His wife Karen received a $60 dividend from Tulsa Oil, an Oklahoma corporation. Interest income from a joint savings account totaled $2,830.

During the year Joe paid $280 in medical insurance premiums. His real estate taxes totaled $2,000 and interest on his home mortgage was $2,310.

Joe and Karen have 3 children: Mike 19, Phil 16 and Laurie 12. Mike, an apprentice carpenter earned $2,000 during the year. From January through March and September through December he attended night school at a local branch of the state university. Phil earned $800 as a hot dog vendor during the summer. All three children live at home where Joe provided more than ½ of their support.

   (a) Compute Joe's lowest tax table income for the year.
   (b) How many personal exemptions can Joe claim for the year?

Cumulative Problem 10-18

On 7-1-76, P. A. Nobel bought a truck, for use in his hauling business, for $9,000. He determined from his business experience that the truck he used usually lasted approximately 6 years. The truck has a salvage value of $1,800. Nobel used the sum of the years-digits method of depreciation. The truck was sold on 12-31-77 for $6,400.

Nobel sold a garage in which he kept some of his trucks. The land on which it was located was bought by Nobel on 1-1-69 for $7,000 and on 7-1-69 he completed the garage for $45,000. Nobel began using it for his trucks on 7-30-69. Until he sold the entire property on 12-31-77, for $49,750 (land, $8,054; building

$41,696), he used a declining balance method with a 5% rate. Salvage value was $3,000.

On 1-1-77, Nobel traded an old fork lift bought in 1969 for a new one costing $20,000. By the end of 1975, the old lift, with a $2,500 adjusted basis representing only salvage value, had become fully depreciated. He was, however, allowed $4,000 for the old lift in the trade-in and paid the balance in cash. The new lift had a 6-year life, a salvage value of $2,150, and he used the straight line method to depreciate the new lift.

Nobel bought an auto on 1-1-76 for $3,500. At that time, the auto's estimated useful life was 3 years and estimated salvage of $850. During 1976, the auto was driven 12,000 business miles and 4,000 for pleasure. On his 1976 return, Nobel used the straight line depreciation method to compute his business use depreciation deduction. He sold the auto on 1-2-77 for $2,400.

Net income from Nobel's trucking business (before depreciation and the above transactions) was $38,200. His itemized deductions were $4,600 for the year and he elected the first-year allowance whenever possible. Nobel is married, has two dependent children and files a joint return. (1) What is his tax table income for the year? (2) What is his tax?

Discussion Problem 10-19

The use of methods that provide for larger depreciation deductions in the early years of an asset's useful life than the straight line method allows have been supported as more realistic in a modern setting. Critics of the present accelerated methods contend that these are inappropriate for the recovery of capital investment.

(a) What arguments can you present in favor of accelerated methods as they are now handled?

(b) What arguments can you present against the accelerated methods as they are now handled?

Research Problem 10-20

Ben Parker is considering buying several parcels of property that contain various improvements for $150,000. While the property is zoned for industrial development, the improvements, basically buildings used for low-rent housing, have been depreciated for 60 years as rental property and have a 10-15 year useful life remaining. Ben would like to allocate the purchase price as follows: $60,000 to the land and $90,000 to the buildings (based on market values evaluated on the property's current residential use). However, Ben is afraid the government will want him to allocate the purchase price based on a valuation as industrial development property, not rental property. This valuation would make the land worth $100,000 and the buildings $50,000, and thus, greatly reduce Ben's allowable depreciation deductions. Ben comes to you for advice as to which allocation will probably be allowed. What is your opinion?

1. Give your opinion. In it, show authorities, citing law, regulations, interpretations and decisions applicable, and the P-H Federal Tax Equipment paragraphs where they may be found.

2. Enumerate and explain carefully each step you take in reaching your result. They are extremely important—just as important as the result.

Tax Reasoning Problem 10-21

Mike Cole, a horse trainer, bought Bamboozle on December 1, 1977. He entered the horse in races during December. The horse was registered under Jockey Club rules which state that a horse ages one year every January 1. Assuming that Bamboozle constitutes property used in Cole's trade or business, Cole wonders if he can take a full year's depreciation for 1977 on the horse to comport with Jockey Club rules.

ASSIGNMENT No. 11
DEDUCTIONS—DEPLETION

(Note: In the following problems, unless otherwise specified, assume that the "tax year" is the calendar year 1977, that the taxpayer and his spouse, if any, are resident citizens, under 65 and are not blind, and that the taxpayer is not entitled to any credits against the tax other than those shown.)

Problem 11-1

(a) State three basic differences between the depletion allowance and the depreciation allowance.

(b) Distinguish between legal title to mineral deposits and standing timber, and an "economic interest" in mineral deposits and standing timber.

Problem 11-2

(a) Walter Rich is the owner of a parcel of land which is known to contain large deposits of nickel ore. Being unable to mine the ore himself, he sells the property to Afco Mining Corporation for $1,250,000. Is Rich entitled to a deduction for depletion?

(b) Would your answer in (a) be different if Rich decided not to sell the land, but leased the mineral rights to Afco in exchange for a royalty payment of $4 per ton of ore extracted?

(c) Would your answer in (b) be different if at the same time the agreement was made, Afco paid Rich $20,000 so that it may delay the mining until the following year?

Problem 11-3

Royal Mining owns zinc mines. In 1977 it produced 20,000 tons of zinc ore and sold 13,000 tons during the year. The mines had an adjusted basis of 4 million dollars and the recoverable reserves were estimated at 500,000 tons. The gross income from the property in 1977 was $600,000. Royal had deductions of $300,000 directly related to the property. It also had selling expense deductions of $60,000 of which 50% could be allocated to the zinc mines with the remainder allocable to other business holdings. The company also took a charitable contribution deduction of $80,000.

What is the maximum allowable depletion deduction for the tax year?

Problem 11-4

On 1-2-77, Sludge Oil Co. purchased a parcel of land in Texas for $1,000,000 after estimates had been received that the land contained recoverable units of oil amounting to 15,000,000 barrels. Gross income from the property in 1977 was $200,000. Taxable income from the property (exclusive of depletion) totaled $48,000.

Sludge Oil recovered a total of 500,000 barrels in 1977 but was only able to sell 420,000 barrels. During the year Sludge Oil was involved in several other business ventures. Their taxable income (exclusive of depletion on their oil land) during the year was $50,000.

(a) Assuming Sludge Oil had no net operating loss carryback or capital loss carryback to 1977, what is their depletion deduction?

(b) Would your answer be different in (a) above if during the year Sludge operated the Seaview Refinery which during April refined 50,000 barrels of oil?

(c) What if in (a) above Sludge owned and operated a chain of ABC gas stations in Michigan. What would be their depletion deduction then?

Problem 11-5

The Tin Horn Co. bought a copper mine for $3,000,000 on 1-2-76 when recoverable reserves were estimated at 600,000 units. 40,000 units were extracted in

1976. Gross income from the property was $1,500,000, taxable income was $400,000 without allowance for depletion. 30,000 units were sold during 1976.

On 1-2-77, it is discovered that the property actually contained 700,000 units. 50,000 units were produced during 1977 and 40,000 units were sold.

Gross income from the property in 1977 was $1,200,000 and taxable income was $300,000 without allowance for depletion.

What is the depletion deduction of the copper mine for 1977?

Problem 11-6

(a) J. R. Homesey owned a dozen operating oil and gas interests which he operated as a unit. Interests 1 through 10 he combined and treated as one property. Interests 11 and 12 were operated separately. During the year, J. R. acquired a new operating interest in the same property. What is the result?

(b) Assume that the dozen operating interests were zinc mines. Homesey operated interests 1 through 4 as the Indian Head Mine and interests 5 through 8, in a different but contiguous tract, as the Red Dog Mine. The last four interests were treated as separate properties. Homesey elected to aggregate interests 1 through 7. What is the result?

Problem 11-7

(a) In 1969, Martin Van Pelt acquired four operating oil interests and incurred substantial development expenditures in connection with them. All four interests are in the same parcel of land. Van Pelt made a timely election to treat the interests as four separate properties. In 1977, he discovered a fifth operating oil interest on the same parcel of land and incurred development expenses in relation to it. What would be the result if Van Pelt made no election relative to interest number 5 for 1977?

(b) In 1974, Van Pelt acquired two separate nonoperating oil interests in Tract A. In May 1976, he acquired another nonoperating oil interest in adjacent Tract B. In February 1977, he requested the Revenue Service permission to treat all three separate interests as one property for 1977. What would be the result of his request, assuming the purpose of the aggregation was not tax avoidance?

SUPPLEMENTAL PROBLEMS

Problem 11-8

Under a zinc mine lease, Yukon agrees to pay the owner a royalty of 30 cents a ton mined and sold by Yukon. During the year, Yukon mined and sold 100,000 tons for $600,000. Deductions directly related to the zinc mine totaled $330,000. What is Yukon's percentage depletion allowance for the year?

Problem 11-9

Barry Ridolfo leased oil land to the Redcap Oil Corp., on 1-3-76, for as long a period as oil should be produced on the property. Barry received a bonus of $125,000 for 1976 plus royalties of one-fifth of oil produced on the property in any year. The royalty payments were expected to amount to $900,000. On the date of the lease, Barry's basis in the land was $400,000 and the remaining units (recoverable reserves) were estimated at 2,000 barrels. No oil was produced in 1976.

During 1977, Redcap Oil extracted and sold 100,000 barrels, receiving $1,300,000 in gross income (after processing) from the sale. If the oil were sold at the well site, a gross income of $1,000,000 would have resulted. After taking all deductions except depletion, Redcap Oil's taxable income was $750,000.

In 1977, Barry received $250,000 in royalties from Redcap Oil. Barry's basis for depletion for 1977 was $350,000. His taxable income for the year without regard to the depletion deduction was $300,000.

Assuming that Barry and Redcap Oil have no net operating loss carryback or capital loss carryback to the years involved:

(a) Determine Barry's maximum depletion allowance for 1976.

(b) What would Barry's depletion allowance under the percentage method be for 1977?

(c) Determine Redcap Oil's depletion allowance for 1977 using the percentage method.

Cumulative Problem 11-10

Sandy Beech, a marketing specialist, earned $45,000 during the year working for Pine Products, Inc. in New York City. Sandy lived in Philadelphia but spent the work-week in New York. She incurred expenses for the year of $6,000 for meals and lodging at the Hotel Broadway. Each weekend she returned to Philadelphia by train. Her round-trip travel expenses between the two cities amounted to $2,000.

Sandy was divorced from her husband ten years ago, and in 1977 received $6,100 in periodic alimony payments which were paid out of an annuity contract established by her former husband.

She had a number of expenses during the year, including: $1,500 in state income taxes, $200 to an accountant for preparation of her last year's return, $1,200 to her attorney for an unsuccessful attempt at having her alimony payments increased, $1,200 donation to a local church, $750 donation to the ASPCA, $200 in interest payments on a bank loan, $600 in finance charges on credit card payments, $500 for medical insurance, $3,200 in doctor bills, $450 for prescription medicines, and $285 in sales taxes.

On 1-1-73, Sandy purchased an interest in a producing oil well for $40,000. Her share of the well's income each year was $10,000, less cash expenses of $2,500. On 12-31-77, she sold the interest for $33,000. Her depletion deductions through 12-31-76 totalled $11,000. She qualified for the royalty owner's exemption for 1977.

Compute Sandy's taxable income for the year.

Cumulative Problem 11-11

Blaine Carlin is employed as an engineer for the Roadway Construction Co. at a salary of $15,300. Blaine was divorced last year. He has a son, age 6, living with his former spouse. The divorce decree provided that Blaine would receive the dependency exemption for the child.

Blaine was discharged from the Air Force in 1974. Since that time he has received $200 a month in disability compensation from the Veteran's Administration. He also received $60 in dividends during the year from government insurance.

In January, Blaine was injured when struck by some road equipment. He was out of work a few days but received his regular pay. Blaine received $150 in accident insurance under a plan for which he personally paid. On May 1, Blaine received a workman compensation award of $600 for the injury.

On July 1, the state passed a law requiring engineers working on public roads to obtain a license. Blaine immediately took some refresher courses in engineering to prepare him for the state license exam. The courses lasted through December and cost him $400.

Blaine inherited valuable mining property in January and paid a $20,000 state tax on the inheritance. The following month he leased the land to the Atkins Mining Co. Under the lease, he was to receive a $200,000 bonus plus royalties of one-fourth of the ore produced and sold. On the date of the lease the basis of the land to Blaine was $1,000,000 and the recoverable reserves were estimated at 2,000,000 tons. It is expected that royalty payments will amount to $3,000,000. In December, Blaine received his bonus under the lease.

During the year, Blaine made periodic alimony payments totaling $8,000 to his former spouse. He also paid $1,500 in support for his son. His former wife paid $1,700 for the child's support during the year.

Blaine also made the following expenditures during the year: $1,200 interest on his home mortgage, $1,500 property taxes on his home, $500 for doctors' fees, $200 for drugs and medicines, and $1,000 to the building fund of the college he

had attended. He incurred $5,500 in business expenses. Just before Christmas, Blaine received a $75 bonus from his employer.
(a) Compute Blaine's lowest taxable income for 1977.
(b) What is Blaine's filing status for 1977? Explain.

Discussion Problem 11-12

It is generally agreed that mineral resources, because of their wasting nature and their importance in an industrial economy, are an appropriate concern of public policy. However, the special tax treatment accorded the extractive industries has been a subject of wide controversy. It is maintained that there is no theoretical justification for treating mineral producers in a manner different from other taxpayers and that the revenue loss is considerable.

(a) What arguments can you present against the current tax treatment of income from natural resources as they relate to tax equity and revenue issues?

(b) What arguments can you present in support of the current tax treatment of income from natural resources as they relate to tax equity and revenue issues?

Research Problem 11-13

Steve Cole is the owner of land that he leases to various oil companies. In 1977 he entered into a lease with the Meyer Oil Company. One clause of the lease spoke of a selection bonus payment that Meyer Oil was to pay to Cole. The clause said in part:

The selection bonus payment must be paid even if there has been drilling operations or production from the leased premises prior to the selection bonus date. Meyer Oil can avoid paying the selection bonus only by surrendering the leased premises prior to the date on which the selection bonus payment becomes due.

In computing his 1977 tax, Cole claimed a depletion deduction on the selection bonus received under the lease citing Sec. 612 of the Code. The Commissioner disallowed the deduction calling the above payment a non-depletable delay rental.

Cole comes to you for advice on whether he can take the depletion deduction for the selection bonus described in the lease.

Use the Prentice-Hall Complete Federal Tax Equipment in your school or local library to find your answer. Do the following:

1. Give your opinion. In it, show authorities citing law, regulations, interpretations and decisions applicable, and the P-H Federal Tax Equipment paragraphs where they may be found.

2. Enumerate and explain carefully each step you take in reaching your result. These are extremely important—just as important as the result.

ASSIGNMENT No. 12

DEDUCTIONS—LOSSES

(Note: In the following problems, unless otherwise specified, assume that the "tax year" is the calendar year 1977, that the taxpayer and his spouse, if any, are resident citizens, under 65 and are not blind, and that the taxpayer is not entitled to any credits against the tax other than those shown.)

Problem 12-1

John Singer had the following losses during the year. State whether each is deductible or nondeductible and explain.

(a) He sold his sailboat, used exclusively for pleasure, at a loss.

(b) His valuable watch was stolen.

(c) The shock from an explosion at a nearby chemical plant shattered a large plate glass picture window in his home.

(d) A metal detector that he purchased to prevent shoplifting in his store proved worthless, and was sold at a loss.

(e) He purchased a home and used it as his residence. He moved into an apartment, rented the residence and later sold it at a loss.

Problem 12-2

Three years ago, D. C. Smith leased his garage to the Transit Travel Corp. at an annual rental of $5,000. The lease expired this year and the garage was vacated in July. Smith was unable to lease the property again until December. To what deduction, if any, is Smith entitled for the loss in rentals?

Problem 12-3

Penny Bird, a TV news correspondent, sold her pleasure aircraft at a loss, for which she took a deduction on this year's return. Before 1976, she had been interested in flying for recreation. In 1976, she decided to buy and sell pleasure aircraft for profit while continuing her business activities as a TV news correspondent. The Atlantic Aircraft Company refused to issue her a franchise because of her inexperience in selling aircraft. She was however, able to make a sub-dealer arrangement with a franchised dealer, receiving a representative's discount on all her purchases. Penny bought an aircraft to use as a demonstrator for selling other aircraft in the Atlantic line. She placed many ads in local papers and made repeated efforts to sell the aircraft and all other items of the Atlantic line. Early this year, Penny found that she could not profitably operate the business. As a result, she sold the aircraft at a loss. As Penny's tax advisor, what arguments can you give to support the deduction?

Problem 12-4

(a) Harold reimbursed his sister for losses she sustained on stocks that he had recommended to her. He had agreed to reimburse her for losses. On Harold's personal return for the year, he deducted the loss. Was he correct? Explain.

(b) On May 1, John Henderson bought shares of his brother-in-law's movie company for $10 a share. The company had been experiencing financial difficulties and needed the capital to complete various films in progress. Nevertheless, John believed a profit could be made on the investment. John sold the stock for $5 a share five months later. Could he deduct the loss on his 1977 return?

(c) Suppose John in (b) purchased the shares for $10 a share when they were worthless and the company eventually went bankrupt. Could John take a deduction for the worthless stock?

Problem 12-5

Paul Pommino owns a cold-storage business. Every year, Paul's customers must pick up their stored articles before Paul goes on vacation in November. This year, three days before Paul was going to close, a fire totally destroyed the store and its contents, including the storage bins of two customers, Sal T. Lake and Fanny Wood, who had not yet picked up their goods. Sal had uninsured clothing valued at $950 in his bin, which had been purchased for $1,400. Fanny had a mink coat in her bin, purchased three years ago for $3,100, which was worth $2,600 at the time of the fire. The mink coat was insured and she collected $2,000 from the insurance company. Paul, experiencing financial problems, had no insurance. What deductions, if any, are Paul and his customers entitled to, and how are they treated on their returns?

Problem 12-6

(a) When M. O. Smith decided to retire from the City Health Department, he and Mrs. Smith bought a house and an adjoining small cottage on Center Street. When they took title, they moved into the house, and converted the cottage into a bicycle shop where they repaired and sold bikes. One night the bicycle shop caught fire, and both the house and bicycle shop were severely damaged. Before the fire, the house was worth $25,000 and the bicycle shop $15,000; after the fire, the house was worth $10,000 and the bicycle shop $2,000. The house had cost $20,000 and the bicycle shop had an adjusted basis of $14,000 at the time of the fire. What is their deductible loss, if any, on a joint return, if they received $12,000 from the insurance company on the house and $10,000 on the bicycle shop?

(b) Assume the same facts in (a) except that the fire totally destroyed the bicycle shop. How much loss, if any, may Smith deduct for the bicycle shop?

Problem 12-7

P. T. Travell owns two motels (Motel #1 and Motel #2 with a gift shop) and operates them under a well-known trade name. Both motels have 20 rooms. On January 1, after the annual New Year's party, the 20 rooms in Motel #1 were completely destroyed by fire. They were constructed at a cost of $20,000 and had an adjusted basis on January 1 of $5,000. Their value at the time of the fire was $40,000. Travell used the straight line method in depreciating his motel property. Travell's insurance company paid him $20,000 for the loss to the motel.

An auto bus used in Travell's business was damaged in an accident in March. It had cost $3,500 when purchased new two years ago. Depreciation taken until the accident had left an adjusted basis of $2,000. Travell received $2,300 from the insurance company, the auto's value at the time of the accident.

On April 1, Travell discovered that $1,000 worth of merchandise had been stolen from the gift shop. The property, which cost Travell $500, was not insured.

In June, Travell's summer home was destroyed by a hurricane. Its adjusted basis at the time of the loss was $32,000 and its fair market value was $50,000. Travell's home-owner's insurance policy contained a clause that excluded claims for hurricane damage.

In December, Travell sold restaurant property which he purchased in 1961. His gain on the sale was $6,000.

Compute Travell's net gain or loss for the above. Assume all properties were held for more than nine months.

Problem 12-8

In 1971, Tim Holt purchased his wife a mink coat for $1,500. In 1975, the Holts purchased a watchdog named Bazooka for $300. On December 31, 1975, while the Holts were at a New Year's Eve party, a thief broke into their home and stole a mink coat and Bazooka. The Holts discovered the loss when they returned home on the morning of January 1, 1976. The mink coat had a fair market value of $1,000 when stolen. Local pet shops at that time were selling dogs similar to Bazooka for $250. In February 1976, Holts' insurance company paid them $800 for the mink coat but refused to pay them anything for the dog. The Holts sent a letter to the president of the insurance company stating that their insurance policy did not exclude pets from their coverage. The controversy was settled in 1977, when the company paid the Holts $100 for the dog.

(a) In what years may the loss deductions, if any, be taken?

(b) What are the amounts of the deductions, if any, on the Holts' joint returns for the years involved?

Problem 12-9

(a) In 1972, Joseph Bell purchased a home for $30,000. He used it as his personal residence until 1-2-75 when he rented it to the Smith family under a three-year lease. On 1-2-75, the residence had a fair market value of $31,000. During 1975 and 1976, Bell took depreciation deductions on the residence totaling $2,500. In 1976, a tornado struck the residence and he had a casualty loss deduction of $3,000 in that year. On 1-5-77, he sold the residence for $22,000. How much loss, if any, may Bell deduct on his 1977 return?

(b) Assume the same facts as in (a) except that Bell and the Smith family terminated the lease on 1-3-77 and Bell occupied the property as his personal residence before selling it on 2-1-77 for $22,000. How much loss, if any, could Bell deduct on his 1977 return?

Problem 12-10

(a) John Winthrop purchased 1,000 shares of Unified Products stock on January 12 for $9,400. On July 23, the shares became completely worthless. Winthrop keeps his records on a fiscal year basis ending October 31. How should the loss be treated on Winthrop's return?

(b) Stuart Allan purchased shares of the Abco Engineering Corp. five years ago for $32 per share. In December of this year the stock was listed on the stock exchange at $18 per share. Is Allan entitled to a loss deduction? Explain.

(c) Robert Pirog, a calendar year taxpayer, purchased Cantex Corp. stock three years ago for $12 per share. On September 12 of this year it became completely worthless. Pirog does not wish to take the loss deduction this year since he expects to have large gains in 1978 when the deduction would provide greater tax savings. Will the loss be allowed in 1978? Explain.

(d) Flo Terry purchased 100 shares of Lascoff Corp. stock last year by giving a promissory note for $3,000, the market value of the 100 shares of stock at that time. This year, the corporation declared bankruptcy on July 17, at which time the stock became completely worthless. Flo's promissory note remains unpaid. Is she entitled to a loss deduction in the current tax year? Explain.

Problem 12-11

The Brown Chemical Company planned to build a new office building in New City. To obtain a suitable site, it bought a lot with a warehouse building on it in January, 1977, for $750,000. The estimated value of the land was $500,000 and the warehouse $250,000. Immediately after the purchase, Brown had the warehouse building razed at a cost of $50,000. It realized $5,000 from the sale of material that was salvaged. By the end of 1978, the new office building was constructed at a cost of $3,400,000. The new building was occupied in January of 1979.

What deduction and/or income must the Brown Chemical Company report on its return for 1977?

Problem 12-12

Jenny Tox, an artist, bought 100 shares of common stock of the Crystal Klear Corp. on 9-21-76 for $6,000. On 12-21-76, she bought 50 more shares of substantially the same stock for $3,750 and on 12-27-76, she bought 25 additional shares of the stock for $2,125. On 1-3-77, Jenny sold the 100 shares bought on 9-21-76 for $5,000.

(a) What, if any, is Jenny's loss on the above transactions?

(b) What is the basis of the 75 shares bought in December?

Problem 12-13

(a) Wayne sold stock with a basis of $10,000 to his sister at its market value of $7,500. What is his loss deduction, if any, on the transaction?

(b) Wayne sold a building he owned having a basis of $50,000 to Blue Corp. for $10,000. Wayne owns 52% of Blue Corp. stock. Two months after the sale, Blue Corp. sold the building for $48,000. What is the recognized gain or loss, if any, to Wayne and Blue Corp. on the transactions?

Problem 12-14

Ezra Koppett is a salaried employee. Due to a fire in his home his total allowable deductions for 1977 exceeded his gross income. As a result, he had a net operating loss in 1977 of $22,000. From 1972 through 1975, he had filed returns as a single taxpayer. His reported taxable income for these were as follows: $5,000 for 1972, $5,500 for 1973, $6,000 for 1974, and $6,500 for 1975. In 1976, he was married and filed a joint return reporting taxable income of $10,000. $7,000 of this amount was attributable to Ezra.

How would you advise Ezra to deduct the net operating loss? This problem illustrates the years to which the net operating loss may be taken and against whose income it is taken when joint returns are filed. Adjustments to the net operating loss carryovers are ignored.

Problem 12-15

Jack McCarthy owns a stationery store. In 1977, his gross sales amounted to $143,000. His operating expenses were $155,000. The following items appeared on his 1977 return: loss from business operations, $12,000; nonbusiness capital gains, $3,000; nonbusiness capital losses, $4,100; itemized deductions, $6,100; ordinary nonbusiness income, $2,000; personal exemptions, $1,500; no net operating loss deduction; no business capital gains or losses.

In 1974 McCarthy's taxable income was $3,000. There were no capital losses and there was a long-term capital gain deduction of $1,000. The deduction for personal exemptions was $1,500.

(a) What is the net operating loss for 1977?
(b) What amount of the net operating loss deduction for 1977 may be carried back to 1974?
(c) What is the carryover to 1975?

SUPPLEMENTAL PROBLEMS

Problem 12-16

A. M. Bly owns and drives his own school bus. On 1-2-76, he bought a new bus. He paid $18,000 cash and traded in his old bus, having an adjusted basis of $6,000. The estimated useful life of the new bus was four years and straight line depreciation was taken. Salvage value was $2,000.

Bly owns property on which he erected a pre-fab garage on 10-1-70, at a cost of $1,600. He kept his bus in the garage. On 10-1-76, he enlarged the garage at a cost of $300. The garage and the addition had an estimated life of 10 yers. Straight line depreciation was used. Assume no salvage value.

On 1-1-77, the garage and bus were completely destroyed by fire. The bus was insured, but not the garage. Bly received insurance proceeds of $10,000 for the bus.

On 9-15-77, Bly bought a used car from a dealer for $1,750. The next day he was held up, and not only lost his car, but a diamond ring he had bought on 1-5-67 for $300, but which was then worth $350. Neither the car nor the ring was insured against theft, and at the end of the year neither had been recovered.

Fill in the following schedule and explain the entries:

Assignment 12—Problems

Kind of property	Date acquired	Cost or other basis	Subsequent improvements	Deprec. allowed or allowable since acquisition	Insurance or salvage value	Deductible loss
....	....	....	....	....	....	....
....	....	....	....	....	....	....
....	....	....	....	....	....	....
....	....	....	....	....	....	....

Problem 12-17

(a) During 1974, Scott Fleming purchased on three separate occasions, 100 shares of stock in the Monroe Corporation for personal investment purposes. He paid $10 per share for the first block of 100 shares, $8.80 per share for the second block, and $7.90 per share for the third block. On December 22, 1976, Fleming sold the 300 shares of Monroe Corporation for $9.40 per share. On January 8, 1977 he purchased 250 shares of identical Monroe Corporation stock for $9.00 per share.

(1) Is the loss sustained on the block of stock which he purchased for $10 per share deductible from the gains realized on the identical blocks of stock sold that same day?

(2) What is the basis of the 250 shares of stock purchased on January 8, 1977?

(b) Charles Graf owns a home having an adjusted basis of $40,000. In August, the house was struck by lightning which resulted in a fire causing considerable damage. What is the amount of his deductible loss if:

(1) The actual cash value of the home preceding the casualty was $50,000, and after the casualty was $46,000. Assume that Graf received $1,800 from his insurance carrier.

(2) The actual cash value of the home preceding the casualty was $60,000, and after the casualty was $16,000. Assume that Graf received $30,000 from his insurance carrier.

Problem 12-18

(a) Phillip Smith wanted to offset some of the large gains he had from his stock transactions. State whether or not losses would be allowed on bona fide sales made to the following:

(1) Sold 100 shares of Tillion Business Machines to his brother's friend;
(2) Sold 50 shares of Radio Electronics to his daughter-in-law;
(3) Sold 75 shares of Steel Major Corporation to the Smith Foundation, a charitable organization controlled by his family.

(b) Mr. Boomer is a stockholder in the Basil Corporation. The corporation only has one class of stock outstanding and it is owned as follows:

Mr. Boomer	20%
Mrs. Boomer	25%
His son	30%
His foster child	15%
His godchild	10%

What percentage of stock does Boomer own directly or indirectly?

Problem 12-19

(a) G. O. Marks runs his own retail clothing store and also works part-time as a salesman. He had the following income and deductions during the tax year. What, if any, is his net operating loss?

Income

Interest on municipal bond	$ 100
Interest on corporate bond	1,850
Salary as salesman	1,000

Deductions

Net operating loss deduction	$1,200
Net loss from business (gross receipts $71,000, less expenses $73,000)	2,000
Real estate taxes on residence	250
Interest on mortgage	2,050
Personal exemption	750

(b) During 1977, T. E. White earned $15,000 in his typewriter repair business and made a profit of $400 on the sale of W. O. Box, Inc. stock bought in 1975. He also received $400 in dividends on Omaha Oil stock.

During 1977, he had a deductible loss of $20,000 when his uninsured home burned to the ground; he paid $850 in real property taxes on the house, and his personal exemption is $750. What, if any, is his net operating loss?

Problem 12-20

You are called in to prepare the 1977 tax return for Richard Martin, who owns an appliance store. He is married and has no children. His books and records show the following:

Gross profit from business	$90,000
Business operating expenses	96,000
Dividends received from domestic corporations	750
Interest received on savings deposit	940
Long-term capital gain from sale of stocks	3,000
Long-term capital loss from sale of stocks	(3,800)
Interest paid on personal loan	345
State sales taxes	145
Property taxes paid on residence	1,100
Medical and surgical expenses	1,800

On checking Martin's files for prior years, you discover that he had no income and filed no return for 1974. His wife had no income in any of the years. He filed joint returns with his wife in 1975 and 1976 which showed the following:

1975 Return

Profit from business			$4,000
Dividends after $100 exclusion			400
Interest on savings account			700
Net long-term capital gain		$800	
Less: long-term capital gain deduction		400	400
Adjusted gross income			$5,500
Less itemized deductions:			
Interest on personal loan		$200	
Taxes on residence		900	
State sales tax		150	
Contributions to church		200	
Medical expenses paid	$800		
Less: 3% adjusted gross income	165	635	2,085
			$3,415
Personal exemptions			1,500
Taxable income			$1,915
Net tax paid ($277, tax payable less $60 personal exemption credit)			$ 270

1976 Return

Profit from business	$5,000
Dividends after $100 exclusion	500
Interest on savings account	550

Assignment 12—Problems

Net long-term capital gain		$1,100	
Less: long-term capital gain deduction		550	$ 550
Adjusted gross income			$6,600
Less itemized deductions:			
Interest on personal loan		$250	
Taxes on residence		950	
State sales taxes		100	
Contributions to church		200	
Medical expenses paid	$600		
Less: 3% adjusted gross income	198	402	1,902
			$4,698
Personal exemptions			1,500
Taxable income			$3,198
Net tax paid ($480, tax payable less $70 general credit)			$ 410

Compute Martin's tax liability or overpayments refundable for the years involved.

★ Problem 12-21 ★

On 2-1-77, due to rust, a water heater in Phil Hall's home burst with water flooding the den, leaving a stereo system and a painting completely destroyed. Immediately before the damage the heater had a fair market value of $100, the stereo and painting had a fair market value of $700 and $500, respectively. When initially purchased, the heater cost $300, the stereo $750, and the painting, $380. None of the destroyed items were insured.

On December 4, a used car purchased by Hall for pleasure was completely destroyed in an accident, caused when his car was sideswiped by a drunken driver. The auto had been purchased from Hall's brother for $300 and just before the accident had a fair market value of $465. After the wreck Hall sold the car to a junk dealer for $50. He received $130 in insurance proceeds for the car.

Compute Hall's loss deduction for 1977.

★★ Problem 12-22 ★★

During the year, the Atlas machinery Corp. accrued interest as follows:

Bank loan for general business purposes	$ 2,820.42
Bank loan to purchase City of Tampa bonds	200.00
Bonded indebtedness	2,860.00
Mortgage on building	1,955.58
Mortgage on land	782.00

The corporation accrued the following taxes during the year:

Federal and state social security and unemployment insurance taxes	$14,670.00
Real estate taxes—Cleveland	8,230.00
Ohio franchise and other state taxes	462.00

Fill in the following items and schedules:

Deductions

Interest	$ ....
Taxes	....

Taxes

Nature	Amount	Nature	Amount
....	$	....	$ ....
....	....	....	....
....	....	....	....
....	....		
Total			$ ....

Cumulative Problem 12-23
(Answer (a) or (b) as directed)

F. T. Tott is a self-employed commercial artist. His wife Rose, age 57, is a salaried TV news reporter.

In February, she was transferred to Honolulu, Hawaii. F. T. immediately notified his customers that he would not be able to complete their in-process art selections and returned all advance deposits. F. T. and Rose flew to Honolulu at a cost of $1,500. This was in addition to the $500 spent by F. T. in traveling back and forth before this trip to find a place for them to live in Honolulu. Once there, they took a room in a motel while they looked for accomodations. The motel bill, including meals, came to $275. F. T. and Rose rented an apartment selling their home in Chicago for $39,315 on June 11. The house had been purchased on January 2 and had a basis of $33,000. They paid $1,000 to repaint the house one week before its sale, and incurred $2,500 in broker's commissions.

At the end of March, Rose was seriously injured in an auto accident. Her medical bills were completely covered by insurance. The injury made it impossible for her to continue her work. She exercised her option for early retirement under her pension plan and became eligible to receive $400 a month in pension payments starting July 1. Rose had not contributed to the plan. Payments under the plan from July through December were made to Rose.

During the time in Honolulu, F. T. had net earnings of $22,555 from his art studio. In early April, he and Rose went to Los Angeles to set up F. T.'s art studio there. In furtherance of this intention to set up the business at a new job site, they bought office furniture in Hawaii for $500 to be used in their new business in Los Angeles. The furniture had a five-year useful life.

The plane trip to California from Hawaii cost $600. $90 was paid to ship the office furniture. F. T. and Rose stayed at a motel for 30 days at a cost of $1,000 ($622 for room; $378 for meals) until they found an apartment they wanted in the suburbs of Los Angeles.

On July 1, they rented a store located in downtown Los Angeles for $660 a month. The same day, they bought two used photo-equipment machines from F. T.'s parents for $900 each and two used art reproduction machines for $600 each. The machines each had a useful life of 10 years at that time. The photo-equipment machines had a scrap value of $90 each; the art reproduction machines $60 each. The Totts used the straight line method of depreciation. Rose's friend gave them an electric typewriter and adding machine. The business friend paid $275 for the typewriter when she bought it; it depreciated $50 a year. She paid $250 for the adding machine when she bought it; depreciation was also $50 a year. The Totts were entitled to an $800 depreciation deduction for their assets (other than the photo-equipment and art reproduction machines). Rose spent $100 between July and December on cab and bus fares to get to various art dealers to sell their products.

On November 2, a fire broke out upstairs in the building they rented. Although the fire did not spread, the fire department cut a hole in the floor and water from the hoses destroyed a desk and other office furniture with combined adjusted bases of $3,000. One photo-equipment machine was completely destroyed. They received $1,100 from the insurance company, $900 of which was allocated to the photo-equipment machine. On December 30, they bought a new machine for $870. The Totts elected to apply the nonrecognition provisions to the gain on the fire.

On November 4, a thief broke into the store and took the typewriter and adding machine. The typewriter was stolen 3 years and the adding machine 1 year after they were bought, and they were not recovered by the end of the year. The insurance company paid $300 for the typewriter and $275 for the adding machine, their fair market values.

The Totts' income from the Los Angeles art business was $17,000. Before she retired, Rose earned $10,800 from her TV job. The Totts have one daughter, Pat, age 28, who this fall, started her second year of law school. She earned over $1,500 as a law clerk this summer but is fully supported by her parents. During the year, the Totts paid $3,650 in property taxes on their Chicago home and gave $400 to their alma mater college where they both graduated. F. T. paid the property taxes on January 15 for the entire calendar year. He paid $300 in fire and theft insurance on the business property during the year.

Compute the Totts' lowest tax before credits (rounding off all items to the nearest dollar) on a joint return for 1977. Taxpayers elect to take as a moving expense deduction as much of their selling expenses on their Chicago home as they can.

(b) Rose Stencil, an operations manager for the Tri-State Bank, received a salary of $17,000 this year. On January 15, she sold for $3,000, stock of the Allied Cement Corp., that she had bought on March 5, 1974 for $4,400. Also, stock of the Canadian Steel Corp., bought on 1-2-77 for $500, became completely worthless on 4-15-77 when the corporation was declared bankrupt with no assets and heavy liabilities to creditors. On April 1, she received a nontaxable dividend of 100 shares of Pacific Cooper Corp. common stock on 300 shares of the same common that she had bought in 1974 for $1,600. She sold 300 shares of this stock on 12-22-77, for $2,600. Rose received a suggestion award of $500 from her employer for recommending a more efficient billing system. Rose sold for $2,400 on 4-2-77, investment real estate which she had purchased on 2-2-77 for $2,500.

During the year, Rose made the following payment on her private residence: $500 interest on the mortgage; $1,800 real property taxes; $250 repairs to roof; and $275 for plumbing repairs. A handy-man whom she employed in her home slipped on a broken walk in her yard and was injured. To avoid a possible claim for damages she paid his doctor's bills which were $600. She had no insurance to cover the accident. A small building on Rose's property was removed at a cost of $400, and Rose set up a tennis court. The building has an adjusted basis of $1,800 when removed and a fair market value of $2,000.

On 6-1-77, Rose was divorced from her husband. Under the divorce decree she received a lump-sum payment of $15,000. They have no children. In October she contributed $1,000 to a local hospital, a non-profit institution.

Compute (1) Rose's tax table income; (2) her tax.

Cumulative Problem 12-24

(a) P. Q. Brown bought trucking equipment for $80,000 on 10-1-73. The equipment's estimated useful life was 8 years and had a salvage value of $8,000. Depreciation was figured on the straight line method. Brown did not elect the additional first-year depreciation allowance. On 4-1-77, Brown sold the equipment to the Axle Company, whose stock is wholly owned by him. The sales price was $40,000. An appraisal of the equipment at that time showed that Brown's original estimates of useful life and salvage value were still approximately correct. The Axle Company depreciated the property on the straight line method. On 1-2-78, Axle sold the equipment for $55,000.

(1) What gain or loss should Brown's 1977 return show as a result of the sale of the equipment to Axle Company?

(2) Determine the allowable depreciation deduction that the Axle Company should take on its 1977 return.

(3) Compute the gain or loss that the Axle Company will report from the sale of the equipment in 1978.

(b) Assume that Brown sold the equipment to Axle Company on 4-1-77 for $75,000. Compute the amount of Brown's gain and specify the nature of the gain.

Research Problem 12-25

Early this year, Frank Carlson received a phone call from a hotel employee in Las Vegas telling him that while he had been in Las Vegas he had paid his bills with three $1,000 checks that were not honored when presented at the local bank. After the call, his brother William told him that while in Las Vegas he had forged Frank's name to the three $1,000 checks. In addition, William admitted drawing a $100 check on his brother's account which was paid by the bank when it was presented for payment. Frank demanded return of the forged checks from Las Vegas. After their receipt, he paid the Las Vegas hotel $3,000 with his own check. Frank has not taken any legal action to recover the $100 loss from the bank which honored the $100 forged check, nor has he taken any legal action against his brother. Frank consults you, his tax advisor, as to the possibility of taking a $3,100 theft loss deduction on his tax return. What would you advise?

1. To find the answer use the Prentice-Hall Complete Federal Tax Equipment in your school or local library. Give rown'answer fully explained. In it show authorities, citing law and opinions applicable, and the Federal Tax Equipment paragraphs where they may be found.

2. Enumerate and explain carefully every step you take in reaching your result. These are extremely important—just as important as the conclusion itself.

Tax Reasoning Problem 12-26

Martin bought a nonrefundable annuity for $100,000 having an annual return of $15,000. The expected return was $150,000. He received a payment in the first year but then he died forfeiting the balance of the annuity. Is there a deductible loss? Explain.

Tax Reasoning Problem 12-27

For years, Frank contributed to an employee's stock bonus plan. When his employment ended, Frank's entire account was settled by a distribution of stock. However, at the time, Frank's employer was bankrupt and the stock was worthless. What is the tax result to Frank? What if the employee's stock had some value, although much less than Frank had paid in? Explain.

ASSIGNMENT No. 13
DEDUCTIONS—BAD DEBTS

(Note: In the following problems, unless otherwise specified, assume that the "tax year" is the calendar year 1977, that the taxpayer and his spouse, if any, are resident citizens under 65 and are not blind and that the taxpayer is not entitled to any credits against the tax other than those shown.)

Problem 13-1

This year Jeffrey Stone contributed $3,000 to his local theater group. He advanced the money to get the group started, and it was understood that he would be reimbursed from the profits on the sale of tickets. Although the leaders of the group promised reimbursement, none of them assumed any personal liability for repayment of the $3,000. The theater group did not do well, and after just meeting operating expenses, it closed for good at the end of the season. Is Mr. Stone entitled to a bad debt deduction of $3,000 on his return?

Problem 13-2

Jim Wall owed Stan May $600 which was secured by a note. Bob Holmes, a dealer in commercial paper, bought the note on March 1 for $550. On September 1, Wall went bankrupt. Holmes received $400 from Wall's trustee. Characterize and determine Holmes' bad debt deduction.

Problem 13-3

Christopher Prey, a used car dealer, sold a 1973 auto to Andrew Scott for $1,800 on 1-1-75. Scott gave Prey $500 in cash and an unsecured note for $1,300 payable on 1-1-77. On 9-1-76, Scott's bankruptcy trustee notified Prey that only one-half of the debt would be paid. Prey did not take a loss deduction on his 1976 return. On 6-1-77, the bankruptcy referee notified Prey that there had been an accounting error and only one-quarter of the debt would be paid. Prey was paid this amount. What, if any, loss deduction may Prey take on his 1977 return?

Problem 13-4

(a) Gary and Susan Byrnes were in the process of purchasing their first home. After inspecting various building developments, they decided to have their home custom built. They purchased a plot of land and then contacted the Shoddy Construction Company regarding the building of the home. After the company had approved the architectural plans, Mr. and Mrs. Byrnes signed the construction contract and made an initial deposit of $2,000 towards the cost of the construction. Three weeks later, they learned that the company had become insolvent and could not begin construction of their home. They tried to recover their deposit of $2,000, but were unsuccessful. Are they entitled to a bad debt deduction on their tax return?

(b) Would your answer in (a) differ, if it could be shown that the company never intended to construct any homes, and merely intended to defraud prospective purchasers?

Problem 13-5

Felix Cooper, a clothing wholesaler, loaned Sally Saxe, a customer, $25,000 two years ago to enable her to stay in business. She gave him a personal note for $25,000 and as collateral, stocks of the International Fuels Corp. valued at $25,000. This year the debt became worthless and the value of the International Fuels Corp. stock declined to $20,000 as of 12-31-77. Cooper took a business bad debt deduction of $5,000 on his 1977 return without selling the stocks as security. Was he correct in doing so? Explain.

Problem 13-6

(a) Sidney Petrie was employed by the Snappy Food Corporation. On 4-1-77, the president of Snappy Food asked all employees to advance the corporation money. Sidney was advised that unless he did so, the corporation would not be able to pay his salary and he would be fired. He made a loan of $1,500. On 12-20-77, it was learned that the corporation was financially insolvent due to embezzlement losses. Is Sidney entitled to a bad debt deduction? If so, is the deduction a business or nonbusiness bad debt deduction?

(b) Russ Myers wanted to purchase an antique clock he had seen in a neighborhood shop but could raise only $3,000 of the $4,200 purchase price. He arranged to borrow the needed amount from his friend Matt Powers, and gave Matt a note for $1,200, payable on 9-15-77. At the end of the year, the fair market value of the note was $800. What would be Matt's deduction for a bad debt?

(c) On 5-1-76, David Smith gave a $3,000, 2-year note to Everett Mellon, owner of a stereo discount store, for some stereo equipment Smith purchased. By September 1, David had paid off half the note. He then gave Everett a second note having a one-year maturity date for $1,500. On 3-5-77, Everett sold the first note for $1,800 to John Lange, a dealer in stereo amplifiers. In November 1977, Smith declared bankruptcy and the notes became completely worthless. How will Mellon and Lange treat the notes on their returns?

Problem 13-7

(a) Woody Pinehurst, a successful retail furniture dealer, made loans to Dan Smith who made hand crafted furniture for Woody and other retailers. Woody made several loans to Smith during 1976 to keep Smith's business going. Woody died in early 1977 and willed some of his business assets, including notes receivable, to the Friend's Charity. The Friend's Charity had unrelated business income in 1977. In September 1977, the charity attempted to collect the overdue debts from Smith. Smith, however, was bankrupt and the debts completely worthless. How should the Friend's Charity treat these debts on its 1977 return?

(b) Orville Olgaby was made executor for the estate of Pierre Lovely, a leading woman's fashion designer. Orville was required as the executor to see to it that Pierre's outstanding contractual obligations were fulfilled. He was also required to collect all business debts owed Pierre. In collecting from Pierre's creditors, Orville found $10,000 in debts to be completely worthless. How should Orville treat these debts on Pierre's final return?

(c) Herb Wilson was vice-president of the Anders Corporation receiving a salary of $35,000 a year. The Anders company had been in substantial financial difficulty and there was a $100,000 U. S. tax lien upon the corporation's assets. Wilson executed a guaranty with the U. S. for payment of the taxes. He feared that a foreclosure of the lien would cause the termination of the corporation's business and he would lose his job. Wilson fulfilled his obligation under the guaranty when the company defaulted. The Anders company went bankrupt on Sept. 1, 1977, and Wilson was able to collect only $30,000 from the company. How should Wilson treat this uncollectible debt on his 1977 return?

Problem 13-8

Bill Michaels deals in commercial paper. On January 21, 1977, he advanced $4,000 to his brother Steve on the condition that Steve repay the money when his new shoe store showed a profit. Competition was severe and in December 1977 the shoe store went out of business with huge losses. Is Bill entitled to a bad debt deduction and if so how is it characterized?

Problem 13-9

In 1977, Lauren Mutton changed from the specific charge-off to the reserve method of treating the bad debts from her business. Her books showed that at the end of each of the years 1972 through 1976 her accounts receivable were $18,000, $22,000, $15,000, $17,000 and $19,000, respectively. Her bad debt losses for these

years were $700, $515, $825, $407 and $325, respectively. Her accounts receivable at the end of 1977 totaled $24,000 and her bad debts charged off during the year were $820.
(a) What is her initial reserve for 1977 and how does she compute it?
(b) What would her bad debt deduction be for 1977? Explain.

Problem 13-10

(a) Harris has employed the reserve method to calculate his deduction for bad debts. At the end of 1977 the following information was available:

Average bad debt recoveries	50
1977 accounts receivable	12,000
Average accounts receivable	10,000
Reserve balance	270

In 1974 Harris had bad debt losses of $500. In 1975 there were $250 of bad debt losses and in 1976 he totaled $150 of bad debt losses. On 3-1-75, Harris bought a $500 note in the course of his realty business. He paid $300 for it. In 1977 it became worthless.
How much should be added to Harris' reserve account for 1977?
(b) Wilson wants to change from specific charge-off to the reserve method. In the year of his change to the reserve method he seeks to take an addition to a reserve and a separate bad debt deduction. May he do this?
(c) Campbell, in 1977, has encountered his first bad debt claim. He decides to employ the reserve method but doesn't obtain Revenue Service consent. May he do this?

Problem 13-11

(a) On August 4, Mel Hall bought Acme Corp. debentures for $800. On September 4, Acme went bankrupt and the debentures were completely worthless. How would this affect Hall's return for the year?
(b) Would your answer (a) be different if on September 4, Acme announced its assets were in receivership and that bondholders would receive 25 cents on the dollar?
(c) Answer (a) and (b), above, if instead of Mel Hall the Atlanta Fur Company purchased the debentures.
(d) Answer (b), above, if instead of Mel Hall the People's Trust Bank of N. Y. purchased the debentures.

Problem 13-12

Samuel Green owed $700 to the Hotspot Appliance Company for a vibrating bed he had bought. He gave Hotspot his personal note in this amount, which was due 8-10-77. Samuel's uncle, Arthur Brown, guaranteed payment of the note. In July, Samuel suffered a series of financial setbacks and notified his uncle that he was facing bankruptcy. Samuel was hopeful, however, of collecting a substantial sum from one of his business dealings in the near future. After learning of this, Uncle Arthur cancelled the debt.
(a) Is Uncle Arthur entitled to a deduction for this debt? If so, how should he treat it on his return?
(b) What would be the result if Samuel, facing immediate bankruptcy, had no hope of collecting on the business deal and Uncle Arthur then cancelled the debt?

Problem 13-13

Ben Abrams owns and operates a liquor store. He uses the specific charge-off method to deduct bad debts. During 1976 he had a net operating loss of $1,750, computed as follows:

Deductions—Bad Debts

1976 nonbusiness income			$ 8,000
Income (or loss) from business:			
Gross profit from business		$24,000	
Less: Business deductions (other than bad debt deduction)	$14,000		
Bad debt	12,500	26,500	
Net loss from business			(2,500)
Adjusted gross income			$ 5,500
Less: Excess itemized deductions ($10,450 − $3,200)		$ 7,250	
Deduction for exemptions (taxpayer, wife, 2 children)		3,000	10,250
Income tax net loss shown on the return for 1976			$ 4,750
Less: Adjustment for deduction for exemptions			3,000
Net operating loss for 1976			$ 1,750

The net operating loss of $1,750 was carried back to 1973 reducing the 1973 taxable income to the full extent of the $1,750 carryback.

The $12,500 taken as a bad debt in 1976 was repaid in 1977. How should Abrams treat the recovery of this debt on his 1977 return?

SUPPLEMENTAL PROBLEMS
Problem 13-14

(a) In 1976, Cyrus Decker endorsed a $750 note for his aunt Hilda. Hilda needed the money to pay some gambling debts. When the note became due in 1977, Hilda defaulted, and Cyrus had to pay. He immediately saw a lawyer who advised him to sue Hilda, but an investigation showed that she had no assets and owed large sums to several friends. What deduction, if any, is Cyrus entitled to in his 1977 return?

(b) Brandford Bell gave his personal note for $1,200 to Elmer Oaks for an automobile purchased from Oaks' used car lot. The note was due on November 16, 1977. In October, Bell was on the verge of bankruptcy. In order to pay some of his debts, he made an agreement with his creditors to pay half of the face value of all his outstanding notes. In accordance with the agreement, Oaks received $600 on settlement of the debt. Bell then went bankrupt and was completely without funds.

How much, if any, can Oaks deduct and how should he treat the bad debt on his return?

★★ Problem 13-15 ★★

From experience, the Atlas Machinery Corp. has determined that the amount of bad debts sustained each year is about 5% of the accounts and notes receivable outstanding at the end of the year. Business debts which became worthless and were charged off during 1977 were $9,674 and recoveries came to $423. On 12-31-77, the outstanding accounts and notes receivable were $196,340. The records of the corporation for the six years ending with 1977 show the following:

Schedule F — Bad Debts—Reserve Method

1. Year	2. Trade notes and accounts receivable outstanding at end of year	3. Sales on account	Amount added to reserve — 4. Current year's provision	5. Recoveries	6. Amount charged against reserve	7. Reserve for bad debts at end of year
1972	182,400	1,790,450	5,620	400	5,900	9,120
1973	204,040	1,850,912	6,780	620	6,318	10,202
1974	192,060	1,804,624	7,584	359	8,542	9,603
1975	204,620	2,001,183	9,466	582	9,420	10,231
1976	208,320	2,120,234	9,644	741	10,200	10,416
1977		2,350,620				

Figure the corporation's bad debt deduction for 1977. Fill in the blank spaces above.

Cumulative Problem 13-16

Jim McCarthy is a widower, 60 years old, and lives in Pikesville. His wife passed away in 1976. He has one child, Marie, 22 years of age and a full-time student at Atlantic University. During the year, she worked on holidays and vacations earning $3,200. Jim paid for over half the cost of maintaining the household and contributed over half his daughter's support.

Jim is employed as a labor relations consultant by Pinchpenny, Inc. and received a salary of $42,000 for the year. He also received $23,000 in royalties from the Paymorre Publishing Co., resulting from sales of his book "Collective Bargaining for Beginners."

In 1975, Jim loaned $1,800 to a friend, Ray Marshall, to help Ray buy a new sports car. In July 1977, Marshall died without funds after repaying only $1,000 of the loan.

In 1974, Jim endorsed a note for his brother-in-law who needed money for his business. In November 1977, his brother-in-law went bankrupt and Jim had to pay $2,600 on the note. His brother-in-law was completely without funds and there was no chance of receiving any part of the amount paid.

In October, Jim loaned his small pleasure cruiser to a friend for a trip to Florida. A few days later, the boat was caught in a sudden storm off Cape Hatteras and sank. His friend was saved but the boat was lost. Jim had no insurance on the boat and had paid $12,000 for it only three months earlier. This was considered its value just before the loss.

During the year, Jim paid a $250 premium on a life insurance policy with his daughter as beneficiary and $600 in entertainment expenses connected with his job (for which he was not reimbursed). He also gave $300 to his church and paid $1,100 in state income taxes, $575 in doctor bills, and $2,100 in real estate taxes and mortgage interest.

What is Jim's lowest tax before credits?

Research Problem 13-17

During 1977, Tom Donchez made withdrawals for personal use of $700,000 from his wholly owned corporation, Blue and White, Inc. Donchez executed notes for the withdrawals. These notes contained maturity dates and provided for the payment of interest. The books of Blue and White listed these notes on a loan account of Tom Donchez. There was a prior history of loans by Donchez from Blue and White which were repaid. These loans were $10,000 in 1974 and $15,000 in 1975.

When Donchez made the withdrawals he knew that Blue and White was having serious financial difficulties. Donchez had no tangible means of repayment when he made these large withdrawals.

An accountant from Blue and White Inc. comes to you, a noted tax expert, and asks if the company is eligible for a bad debt deduction under Sec. 166. An independent lending company informs you that they would not have made similar advances to Donchez. How would you advise?

Use the Prentice-Hall Complete Federal Tax Equipment in your school or local library to find your answer. Do the following:

1. Give your opinion. In it show authorities, citing law, regulations, interpretations and decisions applicable, and the P-H Federal Tax Equipment paragraphs where they may be found.

2. Enumerate and explain carefully each step you take in reaching your result. These are extremely important—just as important as the result.

Tax Reasoning Problem 13-18

Bolt was an executive of a complex of trucking companies. For years he personally made loans to customers. These loans promoted goodwill and kept the paying customers solvent. One customer finally became insolvent. Bolt sought to deduct the worthless debt as a business expense. Can he deduct the debt as a business expense?

ASSIGNMENT No. 14

ALTERNATE TAX METHODS—TAX CREDITS

(Note: In the following problems, unless otherwise specified, assume that the "tax year" is the calendar year 1977, that the taxpayer and his spouse, if any, are resident citizens under 65 and are not blind, and that the taxpayer is not entitled to any credits against the tax other than those shown.)

Problem 14-1

(a) Kermit Hennings graduated from college in 1977 at age 22. The day after graduation, he signed a contract with the Jersey Sharks of the World Swim League, receiving a $30,000 bonus for signing. Kermit has worked the past four summers and his taxable income for those years averaged $650. Kermit lived at home during his college years and his parents provided over half his support. Can Kermit average the $30,000 bonus? Explain.

(b) Nelson Argyle graduated from college in 1973 at the age of 21. He immediately went to work for an insurance company, where he worked until December 1974 when he was laid off. He did not return to work until December 1976. He was supported by his parents during 1975 and 1976. During 1977, his taxable income amounted to $19,000. Can Nelson average his income? Explain.

Problem 14-2

During the year, Arthur Young, single, has taxable income of $55,000, consisting of dividends and net rentals. His taxable incomes for tax years 1972 through 1976 were $12,000, $7,000, $6,000, $10,000 and $9,000 respectively, and included both long-term capital gains and ordinary income.

(a) What is Arthur's averageable income for 1977?
(b) Does Arthur qualify for income averaging? Explain.
(c) Assuming that Arthur qualifies for income averaging, how much would he save in taxes by electing to average?

Problem 14-3

Which of the following items qualify for maximum tax treatment? Explain.
(a) A lump-sum distribution through a Keogh retirement plan.
(b) A consulting fee received by a heart specialist.
(c) A gain on the sale of stock held for more than six months.
(d) Wages of a nonresident alien.
(e) The cost of group-term life insurance purchased for employees by their employer.
(f) 50% of a taxpayer's share of the net profits in a dry cleaning business.
(g) A professional athlete's bonus payment received over a ten-year period.
(h) Taxable state pension payments made to taxpayer upon retirement.
(i) Taxable annuity payments received under a life insurance contract.

Problem 14-4

Victor Lee, who is married, receives $155,000 in salary and $60,000 in interest and other income in 1977. During the year, he had unreimbursed travel expenses of $5,000. His excess itemized deductions and personal exemptions total $38,000. His wife has no income or deductions of her own. What is Victor's lowest tax liability before any credits, assuming he never has had any tax preferences?

Problem 14-5

Harriet Harding's salary is $45,000 for the year. She also receives $1,000 in interest from municipal bonds. In addition, she owns a commercial building that provides her with rental income of $25,000 annually. The building cost her $50,000 and had a 50-year useful life with a $5,000 salvage value. She uses the limited declining balance method to figure the depreciation deduction each year. During the year, her stock transactions gave her net long-term capital gains of $50,000. This year, Harriet exercised a qualified stock option when its fair market value was $25,000. The stock had cost her $10,000, its value when the option was granted. Determine what amounts, if any, must Harriet include in computing a minimum tax liability. Explain.

Problem 14-6

Bob Marley, single, had a tax liability before credits of $25,000 for 1977. During the year he received a salary of $100,000. He also had a long-term capital gain of $18,000 on the sale of stock. In November, he exercised a stock option granted to him by his employer. The purchase price of the stock was $10,000, and the fair market at the time of the purchase was $20,000. His adjusted gross income for the year was $110,000. In December he donated a valuable painting, valued at $40,000 to an art museum. Bob's itemized deductions for the year totaled $50,000. He did not have any deductions for medical expenses or casualty losses nor did he have any dependents. Assuming Bob was not entitled to any credits except the general tax credit, compute his minimum tax, if any, for the year.

Problem 14-7

Faith Caswell lives in an apartment with her two minor children. She pays the rent on the apartment and supplies over half the children's support. She was divorced from her husband two years ago. During the past year, Faith worked part-time as a bank teller at a salary of $60 a week. In her spare time, she gave music lessons earning $255 by year's end. Faith also received weekly checks of $55 for child support and $40 alimony. The $40 was payable until she remarried. Assuming Faith had no deductions for adjusted gross income, what is her earned income credit for the year? Explain.

Problem 14-8

Sam and Ruth Price, both 67, are married taxpayers who filed a joint return for 1977. During the year, Sam worked part time as a credit analyst and earned $6,600. He also received $2,950 in pension benefits from a former employer, of which $450 was excludable. Ruth worked in her son's jewelry store on weekends and holidays and earned $2,600. Sam also received $150 a month in social security payments for the entire year. Sam received $200 in dividends from stock in the Maryland Asbestos Company.

What amount can be claimed by the Prices as a credit for the elderly?

Problem 14-9

In May 1977, Johnny Graff bought and used the following equipment for his factory: A $41,000 new machine with a 7-year useful life; a $83,000 used machine with a 6-year useful life; $20,000 worth of used office furnishings with a 3-year useful life; and a $2,000 new machine with a useful life of 2½ years. Johnny is single. His tax before any investment credit is $10,000. What is the maximum amount of his investment credit, assuming he has no other tax credits? Explain.

Problem 14-10

(a) Art Craft, Inc. employed 500 workers in its factory. On 4-1-77, it hired 20 new employees undergoing on-the-job training under a Work Incentive Program certified by the Secretary of Labor. Art Craft paid these trainees the standard salary of $6,120 a year (paid semimonthly). Art Craft is a calendar year taxpayer and owes $23,480 income tax (before credits) for 1977 and has an investment credit of $2,800. Assuming no other credits, what amount, if any, may Art Craft deduct as WIN credit on its 1977 return?

(b) In 1978, Art Craft discovers that other employees performing services comparable to those performed by the Work Incentive employees were actually paid $6,600 a year in 1977. What effect, if any, will this have on Art Craft's return for 1978?

Problem 14-11

Jeffrey and Martha Kaplan have two daughters, Hilda, 3 and Olga, 2. Jeffrey was employed as a lab technician and earned $16,000 for the year. Martha was a full-time medical school student. Because Martha had irregular hours at school, the Kaplans hired a housekeeper to care for the children and paid her a total of $5,000 during the year. Martha worked as a lifeguard during the three summer months in which she did not attend school. She earned $900 during this period.

Compute the Kaplan's child care credit for the year.

Problem 14-12

Keith Jurow made the following campaign contributions during the year: $45 to Ralph Mesa, candidate for county prosecutor; $20 to John Bremen, candidate for the state senate; $30 to the Committee for Clean Air, which sponsored environmentally concerned candidates for public office; $25 to a national political party. In addition, Keith attended a $30 a plate dinner, the proceeds being used to finance the campaign of the incumbent president of Local 1101 of the National Association of Electrical Workers. The evening was primarily devoted to speeches.

Keith's taxable income for the year, before any deduction for political contributions, was $14,000. He is single.

How would you treat the political contributions on his return so as to derive the greatest tax benefit?

SUPPLEMENTAL PROBLEMS
Problem 14-13

Townsend Cooper, a corporate executive, received a salary of $85,000 during the year. In addition, his residentially leased apartment gave him $25,000 in rental income. He had the apartment built at a cost of $250,000 which was completed and he began renting on 1-5-77. It had an estimated useful life of 50 years with no salvage. Cooper used the declining balance method. During the year, he incurred $5,000 in expenses related to the property.

During the year, Cooper made the following stock sales: sold 800 shares of Hudson Bay Paper on 10-3-76 for $35,000 bought 4 years ago for $19,000; sold 350 shares of Rosebud Industries on 12-11-77 for $14,500 bought on 2-10-77 for $10,000; sold 250 shares of Thermatape Corp. on 8-17-77 for $3,100 bought on 3-10-77 for $3,900.

In March, Cooper sold his summer home on Long Island for $65,000. Broker's commissions and fees on the sale amounted to $3,500. The house had an adjusted basis of $29,000 and had been owned by Cooper for ten years.

Cooper is now separated from his wife and they are filing separate returns as they have done for the past four years. Cooper took a depletion deduction of $41,000 on a mineral property he leased which had an adjusted basis of $23,000 due to past depletion deductions. His income from the lease during the year was $67,000. His exemptions and excess itemized deductions total $21,000. Compute Cooper's lowest total tax liability before credits (rounded-off to the nearest dollar).

Cumulative Problem 14-14
Answer (a) or (b) as directed

(a) Ralph Crampden is the sole owner of the Chelsea Cab Co. He comes to you to prepare his tax return bringing his records and returns from prior years. The return for 1976 indicated that his only capital asset transaction resulted in a long-term capital loss of $3,500. He took an allowable deduction up to the limit which figured in producing a taxable income of $32,250. Earlier returns showed the following taxable incomes: 1972, $25,000; 1973, $28,700; 1974, $27,000 and 1975, $33,400. His only stock transaction this year produced a long-term capital gain of $500.

He tells you he was widowed in June 1976 when his wife died in an airline crash. Ralph's only child, Mortimer, goes to private school 8 months of the year and lives with Ralph for the balance. Mortimer earned $1,200 during the summer.

Assignment 14—Problems

Ralph operated his cab company out of a recently rented warehouse which he used as a terminal. The lease term began on 1-1-77 and runs to 1-1-82 with an option to renew for five years. Annual rental was $5,500. On April 1, Ralph had automatic sliding doors installed on the warehouse and had a concrete lining added to the floor. The doors cost $10,000, had an estimated useful life of 20 years with no salvage value. The lining cost $2,500, had an estimated useful life of 10 years and had no salvage value.

On May 1, Ralph bought four new automobiles to be used as taxicabs. Each auto cost $4,200, had a 2-year useful life and salvage value of $200. He paid $1,325 in interest during the year on the bank loan used in the purchase of the autos, which were first used as taxis on July 1. All four were used solely for business. His records indicated that expenditures incurred in operating the cabs amounted to $80,000 (gas, oil, insurance, parking fees and tolls) for the year. You decide to use the straight line method in depreciating his business property and do not take additional first-year depreciation.

Gross receipts for year in operating the business totaled $235,500. The following salaries were paid for the year: $80,000 to 7 drivers and $8,000 to the company bookkeeper. An attorney's fee of $1,400 was paid for services in handling Crampden's business affairs for the year.

Crampden tells you that he wants to deduct a $300 loss which he discovered was missing from the company safe. The bookkeeper had admitted taking the money and agreed to return it as soon as he could obtain it from a friend.

When Ralph's wife died, he elected to take the $100,000 in life insurance proceeds over a 10-year period, receiving $10,000 in proceeds and $1,500 in interest each year. In 1977, he received payment in accordance with the agreement.

During the year, Ralph donated $300 to the Heart Fund and gave $100 to a neighborhood drive conducted to buy a kidney machine to be used by residents of Ralph's community. His medical expenses for the year included: $75 for eyeglasses; $350 for medical insurance; $550 for doctor and dental bills; and $250 for drugs.

Property taxes on his home totaled $1,800 for the year and interest on his home mortgage amounted to $1,525. He also paid $180 in state sales taxes.

Compute Ralph Crampden's lowest tax before credits (rounding-off all figures to the nearest dollar).

(b) Abigail Ames is an investment consultant with the Hudson Investment Group. In 1977, she received a salary of $55,000. Her husband Anthony is a sales representative for the Penny Pen Corp. He earned $40,000 during the year. By year's end, they had received $850 interest from their joint bank account.

Mr. and Mrs. Ames own an office building from which they receive $22,000 in rentals. The property was acquired on 6-1-77 for $55,000 (land, $15,000; building, $40,000). The building has an estimated useful life of 50 years and no salvage value. On 11-1-77, an addition was completed at a cost of $12,000. It had an estimated useful life of 25 years and a salvage value of $2,000. Expenses related to the property were: real estate taxes, $1,400; mortgage interest, $1,200; heat and light, $3,600; insurance, $800; maintenance, $2,000.

In her job with Hudson Investment, Mrs. Ames was required to do extensive traveling. During the year, she met with business clients throughout the country. Her air fare, local transportation, meals and lodging totaled $8,500. Hudson reimbursed $7,500 of these expenses although she was not required to report her expenses to her employer.

In his job, Anthony was required to use the family car, driving 43,400 miles. He recorded $2,600 in operating expenses. He also incurred the following expenses: parking fees and tolls, $555; business cards, $35; telephone calls, $235. He received a $2,000 reimbursement from his employer which did not require an itemization of expenses.

During the year, Mr. and Mrs. Ames were involved in the following stock transactions: On 4-7-77, sold 250 shares of American Fruit Co. for $5,200 purchased on 1-17-77 for $4,000; on 5-1-77, sold 300 shares of Conner Medical, Inc., for $4,500 purchased on 2-5-75 for $3,500; on 12-3-77, sold 400 shares of Jersey Bay Oil Co. for $7,000 purchased on 12-17-76 for $8,200. In addition, stock of the Hebride Corp. purchased on 3-31-77 for $7,000 became completely worthless during the year.

In February, Anthony's uncle Arnold died and left Anthony mining property in Wyoming. Anthony paid $20,000 state tax on the inheritance. Two months later, he leased the land to the Cripple Creek Mining Co. Under the terms of the lease, he was to receive a $250,000 bonus plus royalties of one-fourth of the ore produced and sold. When the lease was signed the basis of the land to Anthony was $1,000,000 and the recoverable reserves were estimated at 3,000,000 tons. The expected royalty payments amounted to $3,000,000. Just prior to Christmas, Anthony received his bonus under the lease.

During the year, Mr. and Mrs. Ames paid the following: fees to doctor and dentist,$1,100; state gasoline taxes for personal use of family car, $175; state sales taxes, $225; interest on personal loans, $300; finance charges on credit card purchases, $185; $18,200 to the National Council of Churches; $10,000 to a cancer research organization at a local hospital; $50,000 to Chesapeake State University building fund.

Compute the lowest tax payable before credits by Mr. and Mrs. Ames (round-off all figures to the nearest dollar).

Tax Reasoning Problem 14-15

The Lakewood Shopping Center had air-conditioning units atop each of its 12 stores. In the town of Centerville, the tax assessor treated them as personal property so the shopping center wonders if it can take the investment credit on their cost.

ASSIGNMENT No. 15

WITHHOLDING—ESTIMATED TAX

(Note: In the following problems, unless otherwise specified, assume that the "tax year" is the calendar year 1977, that the taxpayer and his spouse, if any, are resident citizens, under 65 and are not blind and that the taxpayer is not entitled to any credits against the tax other than those shown. Assume that the withholding rates shown in the text apply for the entire year.)

Problem 15-1

State whether withholding is required in the following cases. Explain your answer.

(a) The American Red Cross paid workers $150 a week for cleaning up debris left by an earthquake.

(b) Harvey Glub, who had posted a bond guaranteeing the work of the Alamo Construction Co., paid Alamo's workers their weekly wage when the company went insolvent.

(c) Cal Hamner paid his son Edward, age 16, $30 a week while working in Cal's hardware store.

(d) Would your answer in (c) be different if Cal owned and operated a farm?

(e) The Akley Corporation paid to a retired vice president a $5,000 annual fee for serving on the board of directors.

Problem 15-2

Simons is a clothing salesman. He receives a semimonthly salary of $900. During the first half of July he received the following amounts in addition to his salary: $75 commissions, $25 bonus, and $60 in traveling expenses previously reported to his employer. The commissions and bonus were paid with the semimonthly wage payment. Simons is married and has submitted to his employer a withholding certificate claiming 2 withholding exemptions. Using the wage-bracket withholding tables figure the amount to be withheld on these payments.

Problem 15-3

State whether the following items received from the employer are subject to withholding:

(a) Daniel Talegate, a truck driver, received a $200 cash award for safe driving.

(b) John Parks, a migrant farm worker, received $200 in severance pay.

(c) James Peer, a machinist, served on a jury and his employer paid him the difference between his jury fee and his normal wage.

(d) Norton Michaels, a salesman, celebrated his tenth anniversary with his firm and was given a 10-week membership to Jack Lagoon's Health Spa to help alleviate his chronic asthma condition.

(e) Tom and Bob, ages 19 and 17, supplemented their family income with wages from delivering newspapers.

(f) Ethel Graham received $100 a week as a maid in a private home, while her sister, Lillian, received $150 a week performing nursing services in a private home.

Problem 15-4

Miss Hunter receives a monthly salary plus sales commissions on advertising accounts. On March 14, the paydate for February, she is entitled to receive $500 regular monthly salary, $400 reimbursement in education expenses for an advance advertising management course required by her employer and a $350 special incentive award. Also, she earned $500 in sales commissions and a winter vacation trip to the Caribbean—the sales prize for the most outstanding advertising "account salesperson" in January. This trip is valued at $2,000 and is reported on Form W-2 as "other compensation." Miss Hunter, a single person, claimed herself and the special withholding allowance as exemptions on her withholding certificate.

Using the percentage method, determine the amount to be withheld from these payments.

Problem 15-5

Jim Hogan opened his own lumberyard on January 1, 1977 with one employee. From January 1 through March 31 each month's social security and withholding taxes were $50. On April 1, Hogan hired an additional employee. Each month's withholding in combined taxes for the period April 1 through September 30 amounted to $95. A monthly total of $180 was withheld in combined taxes for the period of October 1 through December 31 as a result of the hiring of yet another employee.

(a) When must Hogan pay the taxes withheld and how much must he pay?
(b) When must Hogan file returns, assuming that he made timely payments?

Problem 15-6

(a) Mike Landgraf deducted withholding and social security taxes from his employees' pay but failed to deposit the money since he needed the funds in order to pay for a new swimming pool. Landgraf received a notice from the IRS requiring him to deposit the taxes within two banking days thereafter. He inexcusably failed to comply. What are the penalties for Landgraf's noncompliance?

(b) John Ramsey intentionally failed to inform his employer that he could no longer claim his 23-year-old son as a dependent. To what penalties would Ramsey be subject?

Problem 15-7

During the year, Hanes, Inc. withheld $550 from the wages of its employees during the first quarter. The correct amount of tax to be withheld was $495. The quarterly return of the employer showed $550 withheld and paid by Hanes, Inc. In the second quarter $525 was withheld when the correct figure for tax to be withheld was $590. The quarterly return showed a tax of $525 withheld and paid. The company has just discovered these errors and the third quarterly return is due in 10 days for a withholding tax amounting to $450, but only $350 has been withheld from wages during the quarter.

When and how may these errors be corrected?

Problem 15-8

State whether a declaration of estimated tax must be filed by the following. Explain briefly.

(a) White is single. His salary is $19,900. He has other income of $300 in bank interest. His estimated tax is $101.

(b) Smith is married. His only income is his $23,000 salary. His wife has no income. His estimated tax is $93.

(c) Wise is married. His only income is his $10,500 salary. His wife's only income is $135 interest each year. His estimated tax is $103.

(d) Johnson is married. His salary is $10,500 a year. He also receives $600 in interest each year. His wife has no income. His estimated tax is $102.

Problem 15-9

Mildred Fox is married. Her husband, Richard, age 65, is disabled and is not expected to have any gross income during the year. Mildred estimates that during the coming year, she will receive $52,000 in salary and $2,900 in dividends on stock. She also has a net operating loss carryover of $4,600 (after adjustments) from last year. She also expects to pay $2,500 for deductible taxes and interest and $6,000 in doctor's fees. She has properly filed an exemption certificate with her employer who withholds the proper amount of tax from her biweekly paycheck using the percentage method. She does not claim additional allowances for tax credits and itemized deductions on her exemption certificate. Must Mildred file a declaration of estimated tax? Explain briefly, disregarding the general tax credit.

Problem 15-10

Barbara Fielding, a widow, age 66, supports her brother's daughter who lives with her. Barbara's husband died last year. Barbara is a fashion editor for Metropolitan Magazine and during the coming year expects to earn a salary of $46,000 from her job and $3,000 from free-lance writing. She also expects to receive dividends of $300 from Texas Oil Development Co. stock, and interest on her savings account of $200. In addition she expects to make the following expenditures: charitable contributions $500, sales taxes $135, property taxes on her home $1,200, interest on home mortgage $1,000, and $100 in state gasoline taxes. Her employer pays her on the last day of every month and uses the percentage method of withholding. Barbara has filed an exemption certificate with her employer claiming two exemptions and the zero bracket allowance. But additional allowances were not claimed for any tax credits or itemized deductions. Will Barbara be required to file a declaration of estimated tax? Explain (disregard the general tax credit).

Problem 15-11

Mary Alice is a management investment counselor receiving semimonthly consultant fees. Her regular tax on her 1976 tax return plus her self-employment tax for 1976 totaled $7,800. Mary estimated that her taxes would be the same for 1977 and decided she would pay four equal installments of $1,950. She paid all the installments on due dates. However, her consultant fees were substantially doubled in 1977. The regular tax on Mary's return for 1977 plus her self-employment tax for 1977 totaled $15,600.

What penalty, if any, must she pay for the underestimate of tax?

Problem 15-12

Mitchel Roy is an industrial psychologist whose income is received under retainers in equal monthly amounts throughout the year. He estimated that his 1977 income tax would be $6,080 and paid four quarterly installments of $1,520 each on the due dates. Roy's final return showed that his actual tax for the year was $8,400. What penalty must be paid for the underestimate of tax, assuming that the estimate was not based on the previous year's tax?

Problem 15-13

(a) Akhmed Fazi, an Egyptian citizen and resident, is a free-lance drilling consultant to a number of petroleum companies. During the year Fazi did advisory work for Power Petrol, an American oil concern, in its Galveston, Texas office. Fazi's assignment lasted 3 days. What amount, if any, will Power withhold for taxes from Fazi's salary?

(b) Minitronics, Ltd., a Japanese corporation, operates a factory in Missouri from which it ships electronic components to both Canada and Mexico. Must Minitronics withhold for taxes on the wages of its factory's employees?

(c) Paolo Matteone, an Italian citizen and resident, is currently doing graduate work at a major American university under a $5,000-a-year university grant, which has been deemed 80% tax-free. An Italian-American tax treaty provides for a 16% rate on withholding. What is the applicable withholding rate, if any, on Paolo's grant?

SUPPLEMENTAL PROBLEMS

Problem 15-14

Eric Snead is a salesman for the Semco Manufacturing Corporation. He is married with one child, and properly claims three withholding exemptions. Snead receives a yearly salary of $24,000, paid semimonthly on the 15th and last day of each month. He also receives commission payments based upon the volume of his sales. Between May 15 and the end of the month he earned $115 in commissions and is paid this amount plus his regular salary on May 31.

(a) Compute the tax withheld on the May 31 salary plus commission payment using the wage-bracket withholding tables.

(b) Assume that the commission payments are made at the end of every four-month period. The commissions for May 1 to August 31 were $900, and payment was made on September 10. Compute the tax withheld on the August 31 salary payment and the September 10 commission payment, if the wage tables are used for the salary, and the percentage method is used for the supplemental payments.

Problem 15-15

Loren Blue and her husband Jack estimate their salaries for 1977 will be $24,000 and $30,000 respectively. In addition, they fully support their daughter, Pat, who is to be a second-year law student this year. During the year, they expect to receive a $5,000 withdrawal from Loren's company profit-sharing plan and $2,000 in dividends in jointly owned stock. They estimate their only deduction for adjusted gross income will be Jack's travel expense of $3,000. Their itemized deductions are estimated to be $8,000. Loren is paid semimonthly and has filed a withholding exemption certificate with her employer claiming married status and one exemption. Jack claimed married status listing himself and his daughter on his withholding exemption certificate. He is paid on a biweekly basis. His first biweekly period begins January 1, 1977. Neither claimed any additional withholding allowances. Loren and Jack's employer use the percentage method to deduct the proper amount of withholding.

(a) Compute the joint estimated tax for the year. Disregard the general tax credit.

(b) When must they file a joint declaration of estimated tax?

(c) When is the estimated tax payable?

★ Problem 15-16 ★

On April 15, 1977, Phil Hall who is a qualifying widower living with his two dependent children filed his declaration of estimated tax for 1977. He estimated that his yearly income from his dairy store would be $18,000 and that he would receive other income of $35,000. He estimated that his itemized deductions would amount to $11,350. In July 1977, he discovered that his estimated tax would be $100 lower than the original estimate, and he preferred to pay a lower estimated tax.

What is the least amount of Hall's 1977 estimated tax? How does Hall meet his estimated tax obligation?

NOTE: In computing the estimated tax of Phil Hall, disregard any self-employment tax, since this is covered in a later chapter.

Cumulative Problem 15-17

(Answer (a) or (b) as indicated)

(a) Ann Florence, single, is an executive vice-president for the Computer Corporation. Ann works from Monday through Friday and earned a salary this year of $52,000 which was paid biweekly starting Tuesday, January 11, 1977.

Ann transferred to her present job site on July 1. Her records for the move to this job site show these qualified expenses: $600 on pre-move apartment hunting trips (cost includes travel as well as meals and lodging); $500 prepayment of rent on her new apartment; $400 for real estate commission on finding new lessee for the old apartment; $1,705 for moving furniture by truck along with other household goods and personal effects; $457 for driving expenses (includes meals and lodging) to new location; $1,050 ($623 for motel rooms; $427 meals) for temporary housing at new job site while new apartment was being readied. Computer made a full reimbursement on these expenses except for the rent prepayment on the new apartment along with her first paycheck in August.

The capital transactions of Ann Florence are as follows:

On March 1, sold 100 shares of the Domestic Corp. stock at $60 a share that she had bought a year ago for $50 a share.

On June 1, sold 500 shares of the Computer Corp. stock for $4 a share. She received these shares on May 27 from Computer as a stock bonus. The stock, with $15 par value, had a market value of $5 a share on May 27.

On September 1, sold 100 shares of Troy Inc. stock for $20 a share. She had received the stock from her mother on April 1 as a birthday gift when the fair market value was $23 a share. No gift tax was paid. Her mother bought these shares in 1973 for $24 a share.

Ann's job required her to have business conferences at the customer's place of business. To get to these conferences, she used her own auto and paid all the operating costs. Although she can prove that she traveled 200 miles on business during the year and has records of actual expenses, she elected to use the standard mileage rate deduction. On her last business trip, Ann spent $150 for a dinner party for several business clients for which she was not reimbursed even though she submitted a claim.

In November, Computer Corporation sent Ann to Aruba to attend a national computer sales convention. She flew there with her mother for six days spending one day for nonbusiness matters. Computer had agreed to reimburse Ann for her mother's expenses. The trip cost $1,400 which she reported to Computer and for which she was fully reimbursed. The reimbursement was included in her paycheck of December 13. It would have cost $1,060 (first class reservations), if Ann's mother had not accompanied her.

In September, Computer Corporation announced that Ann had won top prize of $250 in a job achievement contest. She was paid the $250 in the September 6 paycheck. On September 16, she received her only dividend check of $425 for the year from Acme Corp. stock she bought five years ago.

Ann fully supports her mother, 68, who lives in a nursing home. She also provided meals and lodgings for a foreign exchange student. The student lived with Ann for 6 months while attending senior high school. The exchange program was underwritten by H.E.W. of the federal government. H.E.W. sent to Ann a reimbursement check in the amount of $45 of her $100 monthly cost.

During the year, Ann paid these expenses; cash contribution to the Big Boy Foundation, a private nonoperating foundation, $6,000; state income taxes, $150; and finance charges on credit card purchases, $700. Her doctor and dental fees totaled $3,000 and prescribed drugs $300. The $3,000 did not include the $600 spent for medical care of her mother. Nor did it include the $1,000 it cost Ann to fly her mother to a Cancer Institute Center for a check-up. Ann was absent from work because of illness from Wednesday, March 23 through Tuesday, May 17. The unreimbursed hospital bill totaled $6,800. Computer, under its wage continuation plan, paid her 4 biweekly payments of $800 each. It kept no records on the payments. Ann can prove she drove 500 transportation miles for her own medical treatments though she kept no records of the actual auto operating expenses.

Ann's properly filed withholding exemption certificate shows she is single and has taken all the exemptions allowed her. She does not claim the zero bracket allowance.

(1) Compute the amounts of withholding tax Computer must deduct from Ann's 1977 paychecks using the percentage method.

(2) Compute the net tax payable or overpayment refundable to which Ann is entitled on her return. Disregard general tax and earned income credits, if any.

(b) Bill Bostel is married and is the sole support of his infant daughter. Bill worked as manager of the Notell Motel, Inc. from January 1 to September 30 during 1977. It used the percentage method of withholding and paid him $4,000 monthly. On October 1, Bill changed his job and was employed as assistant manager by the Grosse Arms Hotel, Inc. at $5,000 monthly. His employer paid him on the 15th and last day of each month and used the percentage method of withholding. In November, Bill won a $500 suggestion award which was included in his regular November 30 paycheck. At Thanksgiving, his employer gave him a turkey, while at Christmas he received a $1,000 bonus, which was included in his regular December 31 paycheck. Both his employers withheld the correct amounts of tax according to Bill's properly filed exemption certificates claiming 3 exemptions.

On Bill's birthday, February 15, his father gave him 100 shares of Trans-Oasis Oil Co. common stock having a then current market value of $40 a share. No gift tax was paid. His father had bought it 5 years ago for $1,600. On December 21, Bill sold the stock at $42 a share. On September 30, he received a $300 cash dividend from Trans-Oasis, a domestic corporation, which had declared the dividend a month ago out of its earnings and profits.

Bill paid these amounts during the year: $3,800 in doctor and dental bills; $800 to his church; $350 in state sales tax; $195 in finance charges; and, $1,700 in body repairs to his car which was severely damaged by a hurricane. The car was uninsured.

(1) Compute the total taxes withheld during the year from Bill Bostel's income.

(2) Compute the net tax payable or overpayment refundable to which Bill is entitled. Disregard any credit for excess social security taxes and any earned income or general tax credits.

Cumulative Problem 15-18

Florence Ellen, a widow, is a full-time computer programmer for Worldwide Company and receives a biweekly salary of $725 on every other Tuesday throughout the year. In addition, the company allows her use of one of their two mobile vans to make calls on customers. Under the company's agreement, she has to pay all the operating costs. Although she can prove that she traveled 5,000 miles on business, she has no record of actual auto expenses. Florence properly filed with Worldwide an exemption certificate that shows she is unmarried and has taken all the exemptions allowed her, but not the zero bracket allowance.

On Feb. 1, Florence fell on ice as she was alighting from the company's van which was parked in the employee's parking lot. As a result of her fall, she fractured several ribs that were a major factor in her developing pneumonia which caused her to be hospitalized for two weeks. Due to this illness, Florence was absent from work for six weeks and returned to work on March 16. She received 4 full paychecks during her absence from the workmen's compensation insurance carrier of Worldwide because her fall was on company property.

On March 21, Florence exercised a nonqualified company stock option, receiving $600 in company stock for the purchase price of $300. This was payable in the March 22 paycheck.

On June 1, Florence signed foster-parent papers with the officials of the U.S. State Department. Under the agreement, she is the sole support of a Vietnamese orphan, age 7. The child joined Florence's household on July 1. (Assume for dependency purposes, that the child is automatically a U.S. citizen on arrival in the U.S.).

During August and September, Florence began moonlighting as a hostess at the Busy Bee, a plush hotel-restaurant complex. During August she received $500 and during September, $600 in tips. Florence reported these amounts in writing to her employer on the 10th of September and October. In addition, Florence received 4 semimonthly paychecks of $50 from this employer. In filing the W-4 withholding certificate, she did not claim any exemptions. Busy Bee uses the percentage method of withholding and withholds on tips at flat rate of 20%. For travel, Florence went to this job from her computer job. She can prove her actual miles traveled was 2,000 business miles but did not keep detailed recordkeeping for depreciation, oil, gas, insurance and the like.

Because she was holding down two jobs during August and September, Florence employed a housekeeper to take care of her foster child while she worked. For these child-care services, she paid $1,000 a month for August and September.

On August 31, Florence sold a diamond for $30,000 that she inherited from her mother who died on Jan. 1 of this year. At the time of her mother's death, the value of the diamond was $25,000. The mother owned the diamond for 20 years before her death having purchased it in 1956 for $5,000. For estate tax purposes, adjustments to basis were not necessary for any federal, state estate taxes or any death taxes attributed to the diamond's appreciation.

Early in December, Florence believed that recent changes in the company had limited the employer's future and had caused internal organizational instability. For these reasons Florence decided to secure new employment as a computer programmer, her same trade or business. On December 2, she paid $200 for typing and printing of a resume to a management consulting agency and paid $10 in postage for mailing copies of the printed resume to prospective employers. As a result of responses, Florence incurred $75 in transportation expenses to attend scheduled evening interviews after work with prospective employers. She also paid $200 in traveling expenses away from home to attend scheduled interviews in several faraway cities. On December 31, she was still employed at Worldwide Corporation.

On Dec. 15, Florence sold 100 shares of Chemical Corp. stock for $100 a share. She inherited the stock from her father who died on July 1. He bought the stock on Jan. 3 for $10 a share and the date of death value of the stock was $50. Florence was the sole support of her father whom she maintained in a home for the aged.

During the year, Florence also paid these expenses: cash contribution to a Vietnamese orphanage in Saigon, $500; sales tax, $300; interest on a personal loan, $195; doctor and dental fees, $900; drugs, $200. These medical expenses did not include $200 for doctor and dental fees for the foster child. Nor did it include the $100 it cost Florence to fly to a diagnostic center in Atlanta, Georgia for a physical check-up she had after suffering pneumonia in February.

On Jan. 15, 1978 and for tax year 1977, Florence who is not covered by any employer profit-sharing or pension plan, opened an individual retirement account at her local savings and loan association. Her contribution is the maximum allowable based on her 1977 compensation. On this same date, Florence filed an estimated tax return and paid $600 for 4th quarter of 1977.

(a) Figure the total amount withheld for income tax by Florence's employers during the year. Use the percentage withholding tables.

(b) Figure Florence's lowest tax liability and net tax payable or refund to which she is entitled for this year.

Research Problem 15-19

During 1977 the Nittany Company employed 100 salesmen in its commercial feed business. Nittany reimbursed its salesmen for the cost of meals purchased by them during noontime on the road. The salesmen were allowed the cost of meals purchased by them in sales territory even though the territory being covered on a day in question may not have required overnight lodging.

The reimbursements paid to the salesmen were the actual cost of the meals and nothing more. There was no reimbursement if a meal was not purchased and the reimbursements were not made on the basis of the salary or commission level of the salesmen.

The salesmen performed no services for Nittany while eating. The salesmen were not on call during their lunch break and they got the free lunch whether they made any sales that day or not.

Nittany comes to you, their tax counselor and asks if the reimbursement for the meals are wages subject to withholding under Sec. 3401. How would you advise them?

Use the Prentice-Hall Complete Federal Tax Equipment in your school or local library to find your answer. Do the following:

1. Give your opinion. In it, show authorities, citing law, regulations, interpretations, and decisions applicable, and the P-H Federal Tax Equipment paragraphs where they may be found.

2. Enumerate and explain carefully each step you take in reaching your result. These are extremely important—just as important as the result.

Tax Reasoning Problem 15-20

The United Prune Pickers struck the Tart Prune Company of Oregon. Tart Prune hired 60 non-union replacements for some of the strikers. When the strike ended Tart Prune made an agreement with the union to pay those striking workers, who could not be rehired, a lump sum equal to the wages they would have earned had there been no strike. Were these payments subject to withholding?

ASSIGNMENT No. 16

INVENTORY

(Note: In the following problems, unless otherwise specified, assume that the "tax year" is the calendar year 1977, that the taxpayer and his spouse, if any, are resident citizens under 65 and are not blind and that the taxpayer is not entitled to any credits against the tax other than those shown.)

Problem 16-1

The Hardy Corporation manufactures high powered rifles. The results of operation for the tax year are as follows:

Rifle sales	$200,000
Purchases of steel bought for manufacturing operations	35,000
Other manufacturing supplies and materials	2,000
Notes payable	150,000
Heat, light and power for manufacturing	5,000
Delivery charges for materials received	750
Inventory depreciation	6,000
Salaries and wages	30,000
Inventory on 1/1/77	125,000
Inventory on 12/31/77	25,000

What is the net cost of goods sold?

Problem 16-2

Teller Corp. uses lower of cost or market for its inventory valuation. It has only two items of inventory on hand on December 31, 1977: a computer bought in 1976 for $2,000 and a copier machine bought the same year for $1,000. The market value of the computer was $1,900 on Dec. 31, 1976 and $2,100 on Dec. 31, 1977. The market value of the copier machine was $1,500 on Dec. 31, 1976 and $900 on Dec. 31, 1977. What is the value of the computer and the copier machine in the closing inventory on December 31, 1977?

Problem 16-3

Lakeland Typewriter Inc. uses the cost method for its inventory valuation and consistently credits the cash discount to a discount account. On 12-31-77, it had 100 typewriters which were bought on 7-1-77 from Arco Corporation at an invoice price of $150 each. Lakeland paid $100 for its freight and delivery charges and received a 10% trade discount as well as $50 cash discount from Arco. These typewriters retail at $300 each. What is their inventory price?

Problem 16-4

Pearl Plastics is a division of the Stupe Oil Co. At the start of the tax year Pearl Plastics had no inventory on hand. During the year Stupe bought $250,000 worth of chemicals for manufacturing plastics for the division, paid $310,000 in wages for direct labor and $30,000 for advertising Pearl Plastics products. Stupe's salesmen received $40,000 in commissions on sales of Pearl Plastics products and Stupe company allocated $10,000 of its overhead expenses to the Pearl Plastics division. By the end of the year, Pearl Plastics had used up all materials in manufacturing 100,000 cartons of plastic wrap, and 88,000 cartons were sold. What is the value of the plastic cartons in Stupe inventory at the end of the year?

Problem 16-5

The following items were recorded in the books of Way Company relating to its opening inventory on 1-1-77:

Item	Quantity	Unit Price Opening Inventory Price 1/1/77
Blenders	12	$15
Radios	10	30
Ranges	10	160
Dry cleaning machines	8	380

The above items were valued at "lower of cost or market" in the ending inventory as of 12-31-76.

(a) On hand on 12-31-77, were all the blenders and dry cleaning machines that were included in the opening inventory on 1-1-77. The market value unit prices on 12-31-77 for the blenders and dry cleaning machines were $21 and $300, respectively. What amount should be reported as the value of the closing inventory at 12-31-77?

(b) Assume that Way Company, a calendar-year taxpayer, decides to switch to "LIFO" method of costing in 1978 from "lower of cost or market." By what date and what procedure would it use to adopt the change?

Problem 16-6

Susie Lin, an expert computer programmer, values her inventory on the basis of the lower of cost or market. At year-end, her closing inventory had models A and B computers on hand. Model A computer cost $100,000 and had a market value of $50,000. Model B cost $15,000 and had a market value of $12,000.

On October 1, Lin signed a noncancellable contract obligating her to deliver Model A computer at a fixed price of $105,000. Before December 31, she learned that demand was rapidly falling for Model B computer in the market place, and she might not be able to realize more than $10,000 in a forced sale. What is Lin's closing inventory valuation?

Problem 16-7

T. R. Butcher, a wholesale meat distributor, had 100,000 pounds of beef with an opening inventory price and cost of 15¢ a pound on 1-1-77. On January 2, 1977, the fair market value went to 20¢ a pound. The beef's fair market value at the end of 1976 was 16¢ a pound. On 12-31-77, Butcher had 40,000 pounds on hand with a fair market value of 13¢ a pound. During the year these purchases were made:

Date	Pounds	Price Per Pound
March 1	45,000	13¢
May 4	25,000	14¢
July 5	30,000	11¢
October 21	18,000	12¢
November 7	20,000	15¢

No record was kept of sales from the several invoices so it is not known to what purchases the 40,000 pounds on hand at the close of the year should be assigned.

Figure the correct opening and closing inventory valuations on the basis of (a) cost; and (b) the lower of cost or market. Explain.

Problem 16-8

M. Far, an appliance retailer, adopted LIFO for 1976 and had an opening inventory of 40 units at $25 per unit for that year. In 1976, he had no sales but he bought 40 units as follows:

April	12	@ $40	$ 480
June	8	@ $39	312
September	12	@ $38	456
December	8	@ $37	296
	40		$1,544

During 1977, he sold 5 units but made no purchases. What is Far's closing inventory on 12-31-77?

Problem 16-9

Brown Company uses the first-in, first-out method. Brown's opening inventory for 1977 consists of 10 units purchased on 12-31-76 for $200 each. During 1977 Brown purchased these units:

February 5	15 at $205
May 5	10 at $206
September 8	8 at $210
December 1	6 at $208

Brown's closing inventory on 12-31-77 is 16 units. He values his inventory at cost.
(a) What was the value of the inventory at the end of 1977?
(b) What is your answer to (a) if Brown Company uses the lifo method.

Problem 16-10

Signal Publishing Company discovered one week after taking inventory for 1977 that its textbooks on mathematics in the closing inventory at the end of the year, valued at $200,000, could not be sold at current market prices. This was due to book-binding manufacturing defects and to new modern math procedures not included in Signal's math textbooks. Twenty days after its closing inventory, the Company spent $1,000 in advertising the textbooks for sale at $50,000. The next day the textbooks were consigned to an agent at that price to handle the sale. His commission, if he sold the books, was 10%.

What is Signal's correct closing inventory valuation for the textbooks for 1977?

Problem 16-11

Although Sally Fox, a leading fur retailer, uses the conventional "retail method" for pricing her inventory, she has obtained the Revenue Service permission to compute mark-downs as well as mark-ups in the computation of the cost-to-retail ratio. Her inventory on 1-1-77 is:

	Cost	Retail Selling Price
Beaver	$100,000	$ 400,000
Mink	300,000	900,000
During 1977, she bought the following:		
Beaver	$200,000	$ 800,000
Mink	100,000	300,000
Sales during the year were:		
Beaver		$ 900,000
Mink		1,000,000

Assume the mark-ups for Beaver were $100,000 and mark-downs for Mink were $200,000 of which $100,000 was charged to "Mink unsalable obsolescence" account for the year. What is the value of her closing inventory for Beaver and Mink?

Problem 16-12

Jumbo Paper Corporation uses the "direct cost" method to value goods in its closing inventory. Under this method Jumbo segregates indirect production costs into fixed and variable production cost classifications. Only variable indirect production costs, such as indirect materials, factory janitorial supplies and utilities, are allocated to its inventoriable costs. Fixed indirect productions costs, such as rents and property taxes on building and machinery used for manufacturing operations, are treated as currently deductible period costs and not allocated to inventoriable costs.

Is Jumbo correct in using this method? Explain.

SUPPLEMENTAL PROBLEMS
Problem 16-13

(a) Cleo Andrews is a fur dealer. On 1-1-77, her entire inventory, having been purchased during 1976, consisted of: 200 Puma fur coats bought at $240 each; 180 Rabbit fur coats bought at $210 each and 6,000 imitation fur gloves bought at $4 each. Their market values on 12-31-76 were: Puma coats, $300 each; Rabbit coats, $200 each; fur gloves, $3 each. During the year Cleo bought 600 Puma coats at $250 each; 500 Rabbit coats at $140 each and 15,000 imitation fur gloves at $3 each (10% discount for cash in 30 days). Cleo always pays net invoice price on delivery.

On 12-31-77, Cleo has in stock: 100 Puma coats, market value $290 each; 100 Rabbit coats, market value $150 each; 5,000 imitation fur gloves, $3 each. In each category Cleo always disposes of her old stock before offering goods bought during the year. She values inventory at lower of cost or market. Her sales for the year totaled $499,000 with $10,000 in returns. She sells the coats with a one-year service guarantee and employs a part-time tailor at $7,500 a year. Cleo's seller replaces a defective coat without charge.

Cleo's other business expenses for the year are: sales clerks' wages, $25,000; taxes, $70,000; delivery truck repairs, $175; advertising, $2,500; telephone, postage and other miscellaneous expenses, $3,500. Depreciation on her building is $8,000, and $450 on her truck.

During the year Cleo found that one of her customers had moved to a foreign country owing her $300 she cannot collect. On 12-31-77, she has $15,000 worth of accounts receivable. She maintains a bad debt reserve and the credit balance on 1-1-77 was $500. Over the years she has found the 3% of receivables are ultimately uncollectible.

What is Cleo's opening and closing inventory? What is her net profit or loss? Use the following schedules.

	Quantity	Cost per unit	Market Value per unit	Total Cost	Total Market Value	Inventory
Inventory 1-1-77:						
	....	$	$	$	$	$ ....
	....	....	....	....	....	....
	....	....	....	....	....	....
Total						$ ....
Inventory 12-31-77:						
	....	$	$	$	$	$ ....
	....	....	....	....	....	....
	....	....	....	....	....	....
Total						$ ....

Total Receipts ...., less returns and allowances $ .... $ ....

Cost of Goods sold:
    Inventory at beginning of year .... $ ....
    Merchandise bought for sale ....
    Labor ....
    Materials and supplies ....
    Other costs ....
    Total .... $ ....
Less inventory at end of year ....

Net cost of goods sold .... $ ....

Gross profit .... $ ....
Other Business Deductions:
    Salaries .... $ ....
    Taxes on business and business property ....
    Losses ....

Bad debts ....
Depreciation and obsolescence ....
Repairs ....
Advertising ....
Other expenses ....
   Total ....
Net profit (or loss) .... $...............

(b) Cleo Andrews is married and has 1 child, age 8. Her husband, who is blind, did not have any income or deductions.

During 1977, she received from Louisiana Telo Corp. $5,000 in cash dividends on 10,000 shares of common stock she owns. She also received from Telo, one share of common stock for each share owned. Telo only had common stock outstanding and all other shareholders were given one share for each share owned. The par value of the stock was $20 a share. The market value of the stock was $50 a share before the dividend was declared and $25 a share after the dividend.

She paid $1,200 real property taxes on their home, and she contributed $7,500 to their church and $15,000 to Good Heart Foundation, a private foundation.

On December 31, 1977, she sold these stocks: Ocean Gold Corp. bought on June 30, 1977 and sold at a $1,000 loss; C. P. Corp., bought on October 1, 1977 and sold at $750 gain; Andrus Corp., bought in November 1975 and sold at a $2,500 gain.

What is the tax before credits if Cleo and her husband filed a joint return?

★ Problem 16-14 ★

Phil Hall's Keystone Dairy Store buys milk products from local dairies and sells ice cream, cheese, butter, eggs and the like. The following information was taken from the books of the store.

Gross sales	$86,775
Sales returns and allowances	850
Cash discount on sales	250
Inventory at beginning of year	8,400
Cash discounts on purchases	300
Purchases	10,700
Materials and supplies	6,000
Inventory at end of year	4,000
Cash on hand from sale of inventory	4,200
Depreciation	4,620
Payroll Taxes	2,500
Realty Taxes	1,130
Rent for warehouse	2,400
Rent for store	10,000
Repairs to refrigerator	300
Salaries and wages	19,000
Fire insurance	1,000
Theft insurance	200
Mortgage interest	2,100
Traveling expenses	3,250
Legal fees	1,500

Phil donated ice cream from his store for an annual dinner given by him and his tennis friends to promote good will. The ice cream was worth $190 but cost the shop $125.

Fill in the following schedules.

5126 Inventory 1978

Profit (or loss) from Business or Profession

Income
1. Gross receipts or sales $ .... Less: returns and allowances $ .... Balance ▶ ... 1
2. Less: Cost of goods sold and/or operations (Schedule C-1, line 8) 2
3. Gross profit 3
4. Other income (attach schedule) 4
5. Total income (add lines 3 and 4) 5

Deductions
6. Depreciation (explain in Schedule C-3) 6
7. Taxes on business and business property (explain in Schedule C-2) 7
8. Rent on business property 8
9. Repairs (explain in Schedule C-2) 9
10. Salaries and wages not included on line 3, Schedule C-1 (exclude any paid to yourself) . 10
11. Insurance 11
12. Legal and professional fees 12
13. Commissions 13
14. Amortization (attach statement) 14
15. (a) Pension and profit-sharing plans .... 15(a)
    (b) Employee benefit programs .... (b)
16. Interest on business indebtedness 16
17. Bad debts arising from sales or services 17
18. Depletion 18
19. Other business expenses (specify):
    (a) ....
    (b) ....
    (c) ....
    (d) ....
    (e) ....
    (f) ....
    (g) ....
    (h) ....
    (i) ....
    (j) ....
    (k) Total other business expenses (add lines 19(a) through 19(j)) ...... 19(k)
20. Total deductions (add lines 6 through 19(k)) 20
21. Net profit or (loss) (subtract line 20 from line 5). Enter here and on Form 1040, line 29. **ALSO** enter on Schedule SE, line 5(a) 21

SCHEDULE C-1.—Cost of Goods Sold and/or Operations

1. Inventory at beginning of year (if different from last year's closing inventory, attach explanation) ... 1
2. Purchases $ .... Less: cost of items withdrawn for personal use $ .... Balance ▶ ... 2
3. Cost of labor (do not include salary paid to yourself) 3
4. Materials and supplies 4
5. Other costs (attach schedule) 5
6. Total of lines 1 through 5 6
7. Less: Inventory at end of year 7
8. Cost of goods sold and/or operations. Enter here and on line 2 above 8

SCHEDULE C-2.—Explanation of Lines 7 and 9

Line No.	Explanation	Amount	Line No.	Explanation	Amount
		$			$

★★ Problem 16-15 ★★

The Atlas Machinery Corp., with offices and factory in Cleveland, Ohio, is a manufacturer of industrial machines. Sales during 1977 came to $1,292,738 and returns and allowances were $8,759. The following information was taken from the Profit and Loss account:

Inventory difference (on 1-1-77, $97,635; on 12-31-77, $89,042)	$ 8,593
Purchases	392,407
Labor	341,935
Heat, light and power	14,230
Freight and cartage inward	2,157
Factory supplies	5,106
Miscellaneous factory expense	597

1978   **Assignment 16—Problems**   **5127**

Fill in the following schedules:

Schedule A — Cost of Goods Sold

1. Inventory at beginning of year . . . . .
2. Merchandise bought for manufacture or sale
3. Salaries and wages . . . .
4. Other costs (attach schedule) . . . . .
5. Total . . . .
6. Less: Inventory at end of year . . . . .
7. Cost of goods sold—Enter on line 2, page 1 .

Schedule—Other Costs

_____
_____
_____
_____
_____
_____

Gross receipts or gross sales .... Less: Returns and allowances ....
Less: Cost of goods sold (Schedule A) and/or operations (attach schedule)
Gross profit ....

Problem 16-16

Socko Co. is a major retailer of household appliances. In 1976, using the "fifo" method to value inventory, Socko's closing inventory was as follows:

Item	Quantity	Unit Cost	Total Cost	Total Retail Sales Price
Brand A	200 units	$ 8.00	$1,600	$2,100
	100 units	7.00	700	520
Brand B	100 units	8.00	800	1,200
Brand C	70 units	11.00	770	1,500
	30 units	12.00	360	720

The Revenue Service granted Socko Co. permission to change to the "lifo" method of valuing inventory for 1977. Socko's purchases in 1977 were as follows:

Date	Item	Quantity	Unit Cost	Total Cost	Total Retail Sales Price
1/10	Brand A	400	$7.50	$3,000	$4,800
4/11	Brand B	500	9.00	4,300*	8,000
6/12	Brand C	150	6.00	900	1,440
10/25	Brand C	100	9.00	900	1,440
11/29	Brand B	500	8.00	3,500*	7,000

* After reduction for late delivery allowances.

Closing inventory for 1977 shows Brand A, 300 units, Brand B, 200 units and Brand C, 150 units.

(a) Find the largest closing inventory value under ordinary "lifo."
(b) Find the lowest closing inventory value if dollar-value costing is used.
(c) Find the closing inventory value assuming the price index is 101, sales for the year totaled $20,000 and Socko in 1977 is merely changing to dollar-value costing for the retail "lifo" method it uses.

Closing inventory for 1976 shows Spring and Summer dresses, 150 each and Fall coats, 80.

(a) Find the largest closing inventory value of goods on hand under ordinary "lifo".

(b) Find the lowest closing inventory value of goods on hand if dollar-value costing is used.

(c) Find the closing inventory value of goods on hand assuming the price index is 104, sales for the year totaled $17,500 and Janis in 1976 is merely changing to dollar-value costing for the retail "lifo" method she uses.

Cumulative Problem 16-17

C. D. Fluz and his wife own and operate as sole proprietorship, a small leather manufacturing company and a retail leather store. The book entries for the manufacturing accounts show these balances at the end of the year:

Inventory 1/1/77	$100,000
Leather bought for manufacture	400,000
Labor	200,000
Heat, light and power for manufacturing	58,369
Factory expenses	700
Inventory depreciation	6,000
Freight-in	1,200
Factory supplies and materials	1,600
Inventory 12/31/77	194,567

The depreciation for manufacturing machines is included in the cost of goods produced. On Jan. 1, Fluzs' books showed these entries for production machinery:

Asset	Date Acq.	Cost	Prior Dep.	Meth.	Life
Machine A	7/1/70	$24,000†	$15,900	Sum dig.	15 yrs.
Machine B	1/5/76	16,000*	4,800	DB	10 yrs.
Machine C	1/3/71	26,000**	19,709	DB	10 yrs.

† No salvage value.
* Before $2,000 1st-year allowance taken in '76.
** Before $2,000 1st-year allowance taken in '71.

The Fluzs use the cost method for its retail inventory valuation and consistently credit the cash discount to an income discount account. Although the Fluzs manufacture most of their leather products sold for retail, they purchase specialty items from other dealers. They also consistently sell all their manufactured leather goods each year so that the opening inventory consists of purchases from other dealers. On all purchases, the Fluzs must pay the freight and delivery charges and they receive trade and cash discounts. The following information was taken from the books at the close of the year for the retail part of the business:

Gross sales	$800,000
Returns and allowances	10,000
Opening and closing inventory	20,000
Purchases	13,000
Trade discounts	1,000
Cash discounts	1,000
Salaries	145,000
Taxes	2,000
Freight and delivery charges	3,000
Utilities and other office expenses	5,000

On Jan. 1, the depreciation accounts considered in determining the net profit of the business showed the following:

Assignment 16—Problems

Asset	Date Acq.	Cost	Prior Dep.	Method	Life
Building	1/2/73	$60,000	$12,000	St. Line	20 yrs.
Furn. & Fix.	1/4/70	3,000	2,625	St. Line	8 yrs.
Delivery truck	1/2/73	7,500	5,000	St. Line	6 yrs.

The Fluzs elect the Class Life system and the modified half-year convention for equipment purchases in 1977. For earlier acquired assets, they use the older system.

This year, Fluzs bought and placed into service two new leather machines— Machine D costing $15,000 on Feb. 1 and Machine E costing $28,000 on March 1. They took the allowable additional first-year depreciation based on a $10,000 limit for each machine and elected declining balance depreciation for both machines. Both machines have the same vintage account. Since Fluzs are in the manufacturing business, the Asset Guideline Class for the equipment is "Class 31.0" with an asset depreciation range of from 9 to 13 years. They chose the higher limit of 13 years as the write-off period.

The Fluzs also bought new office furnishings for $2,400 on April 30. The Asset Guideline class for this category of goods is "Class 70.11" and the Asset Guideline period is 10 years. The depreciation range is from 8 to 12 years and they elect the 12 year class life and the declining balance depreciation on these assets.

On May 1 the Fluzs bought a new business van truck for $10,000; Asset Guideline period, 4 years; Class life depreciation range, 3 to 5 years; Class, 00.241. They elect a 5-year class life and declining balance.

In addition, the Fluzs elect additional first-year depreciation on the new "qualifying property" assets.

On 1-5-77, the Fluzs sold a leather machine for $20,400 that they bought on 1-5-74 for $14,000. Its adjusted basis at the time of the sale was $11,000. Total depreciation taken for 1974 through 1976 was $3,000.

The Fluzs bought on 1-2-73 the building in which their retail and manufacturing operations are located for $60,000 with a useful life of 20 years (assume no salvage value). The Fluzs have consistently deducted this depreciation expense in determining the net profit of the business.

On 1-1-77, the Fluzs reserve for bad debts was $3,000. During the year, they charged $1,500 of bad debts against this reserve. Based on past experiences, it was estimated that 2% of the accounts receivable of $40,000 would be uncollectible bad debts.

On 12-1-77 the Fluzs sold 100 shares of Apex Corp. stock for $4,800 purchased on 12-15-76 for $1,000.

Dividends from domestic corporations were paid to Mr. and Mrs. Fluz totaling $250 ($200 to Mrs. Fluz on stock she owned and $50 to Mr. Fluz for stock he owned).

They paid $3,800 in interest and taxes during the year.

Compute their tax before credits (disregard any self-employment taxes). Round-off all figures to the nearest dollar.

Research Problem 16-18

Steer Enterprises Corporation owns and operates a feedlot in Kansas. The company fattens cattle for market. One-half of the cattle is owned by the feedlot. The other half is supplied by cattle raisers. The raisers are charged a fee for the feed consumed and the yard space used. The company custom feeds and cares for the steers and finds buyers for them. Over the years the feedlot has kept its corporate books on the accrual basis. It now wishes to file its federal income tax returns on the cash basis. The company's representative comes to you, a tax expert, to see if they may report inventoriable costs and income on the cash basis even though their corporate books are on an accrual basis. What would you advise?

1. Give your opinion, fully explained. In it show authorities, citing regulations and decisions applicable, and the P-H Federal Tax Equipment paragraphs where they may be found.

2. Enumerate and explain carefully every step you take in reaching your result.

ASSIGNMENT No. 17

ACCOUNTING

(Note: In the following problems, unless otherwise specified, assume that the "tax year" is the calendar year 1977, that the taxpayer and his spouse, if any, are resident citizens under 65 and are not blind and that the taxpayer is not entitled to any credits against the tax other than those shown. In figuring your answers, round off all amounts to the nearest whole dollar, unless otherwise specified.)

Problem 17-1

Under the terms of a written lease, the monthly rents in a 12-unit apartment building became due and payable in cash on the last day of each preceding month. On 12-31-77, the owner collected the rents for January, 1978, from 11 apartments. The 12th apartment did not pay him the January rent until 1-2-78. In what year should the owner report the income from this last apartment if:
- (a) He is on the cash basis?
- (b) He is on the accrual basis?

Problem 17-2

Paul Field started a brokerage account in June, 1977, that earned profits of $2,400 by the end of the year. Instead of withdrawing these profits, Field continued to play the market through February, 1978, when his entire account was wiped out during a slump in trading. Field reports his income on the cash basis. How should Field have treated the $2,400 in profits?

Problem 17-3

(a) Jim Sands is a cash basis taxpayer. In 1978, while preparing his income tax return for 1977, he discovered uncashed interest coupons of corporate bonds, which had matured and should have been collected in 1977. Should the income be included in his return for 1977?

(b) Jim also discovered that his bank, on December 1, 1976, had credited his account with $95 interest, which it had collected as his agent on a mortgage he owned. Should this be included in his income for 1977?

Problem 17-4

Connie Jimmers, a tennis pro, made a contract with Ed-U-Kate Movies, Inc. to film her style of play. Ed-U-Kate agreed to pay her $50,000 for making the picture. Some time later, but before making the picture, Connie sold her rights under the motion picture contract to her father. Her father declared himself trustee of the rights for Connie's minor children.
- (a) Does Connie have to pay tax on the $50,000?
- (b) Would your answer be the same if Connie had transferred her rights after making the picture, but before receiving payment?

Problem 17-5

Harry Ames, a cash basis taxpayer, has several accounts with Argo Corp., a brokerage firm. In December, 1977, Ames is notified that he owes the firm $50 interest on a margin account debt. In January, 1978, the firm collects $175 on several of Ames' accounts and sends Ames $125 (keeping $50 in settlement of the interest owed). Can Ames deduct the $50 retained by the firm as a paid expense on his return for 1977? Explain.

Problem 17-6

(a) Brandon Mills is a fiscal year taxpayer who uses the LIFO method to value inventory. He wants to change to the FIFO method of inventory valuation for his fiscal year ending 9-30-78. What procedure should be followed and what date is important in making this change?

(b) Would your answer to (a) differ if Brandon Mills was a subsidiary corporation of a consolidated group that uses the FIFO method of inventory valuation?

Problem 17-7

Dick Hall changed his accounting period from a fiscal year ending Oct. 31 to one ending July 31. He filed a return for the short tax year (Nov. 1, 1977 to July 31, 1978). Hall's gross income (before exemption deductions) for the short period was $17,250. He is married and the father of 2 dependent children and does not itemize deductions. Disregarding the alternative method, what is Hall's tax for the short period?

Problem 17-8

Kate Jones received the following items of income. When should they be included in income if Jones is (1) an accrual basis taxpayer, and (2) a cash basis taxpayer?

(a) Jones rents an apartment she owns for $120 a month. On 12-31-77, she received $360 in payment for 3 months rent (December, 1977, and January and February, 1978).

(b) Also on 12-31-77, Jones received $480 from the tenant in (a) to cancel its lease, effective 3-1-78. Under the terms of the lease, it did not expire until 12-31-78.

(c) Jones is paid semimonthly on the 15th and the last day of each month. She received her $430 salary check for the last half of December at 5:30 P.M. on 12-31-77. Because the banks were closed, Jones did not cash the check until 1-3-78.

(d) Would your answer to (c) differ if Jones' employer had asked her not to cash the check until 1-3-78, because it was short of funds?

(e) Would your answer to (c) differ if Jones had not been paid until 1-3-78 because the amount of her compensation had not been determined until 1-2-78?

(f) On 1-3-78, Jones cashed an $82 Long Lumber Co. dividend check she had received in the mail on 12-30-77. The check was dated 12-20-77 (the date the dividend was declared).

(g) On 2-1-78, Jones received $45 interest on bonds of Magnus Motors. Interest on these bonds is payable quarterly for the preceding 3-month period on February 1, May 1, August 1 and November 1.

Problem 17-9

Joe Sherman, an accrual basis taxpayer, sold 200 shares of Parcela, Inc. stock for $12,500. The stock had cost $5,200 on 1-16-75. Sherman's broker completed the sale on the stock exchange on 12-29-77, but delivery of the stock and payment was not made until 1-3-78, the contract settlement date.

(a) When should Sherman report as income the gain from this transaction?
(b) Would your answer to (a) differ if Sherman were a cash basis taxpayer?
(c) Would your answers to (a) and (b) differ if the stock was sold for $4,000?
(d) Would your answers to (a) and (b) differ if Sherman had sold land, not stock? Assume the closing was held on 12-29-77 with all incidents of ownership and title being conveyed to the purchaser on that date, and that Sherman was not paid until 1-3-78.

Problem 17-10

In 1974, the Acme Corp., an accrual method taxpayer, entered into a contract for the sale of Type X clock radios (properly includible in Acme's inventory) with a total contract price of $100,000. Acme estimates that its total inventoriable costs and expenditures for the clock radios will be $50,000. The contract calls for Acme to receive the following advance payments:

1974	$35,000
1975	20,000
1976	15,000
1977	10,000
1978	10,000
1979	10,000

The clock radios are to be delivered pursuant to the customer's request in 1980. It is Acme's tax policy to account for its sales when the goods are delivered. Acme's closing inventory for radios in 1975 is as follows:

Transistor Radios	$300,000
Police Band Radios	180,000
Type X Clock Radios	120,000
Car Radios	60,000

Acme's accountants in their December 1975 meeting have noted in their long-range planning that 1980 will be a big year for the corporation. Gross income is expected to reach peak levels. The accountants note that 1977 will be a year where extensive losses can be expected. What should Acme do to avoid accruing $100,000 in 1980? If Acme chooses the best approach to the problem, detail the tax consequences.

Problem 17-11

(a) Acme Corp. sells computers. In December, 1975, Acme entered into a contract with Wilson Electronics agreeing to pay Wilson $10,000 for certain computer parts to be manufactured by Wilson. Payment under the contract was to be made only after the government approved the parts for safety.

On 11-30-76, government officials acknowledged the safety of Wilson's computer parts. Soon afterwards, Acme received the parts, and on 12-24-76 a representative of Acme hand delivered a $10,000 check to Wilson's treasurer. It was postdated 1-5-77.

If Acme is a cash basis taxpayer, when may it take a business deduction for the acquisition of the parts?

(b) Would your answer be different in (a), if Acme were an accrual basis taxpayer?

(c) Ed Cole, an accrual basis taxpayer, borrowed $1,000 on 7-1-76 giving a three-year note at 6% annual interest. He paid $30 interest on the note on 12-31-76 and repaid the loan and $150 interest on 6-20-77. What is his interest deduction for 1977?

(d) Would your answer be different in (c), if Cole was on the cash basis?

Problem 17-12

Mort Gage, an accrual basis taxpayer, purchased a parcel of land in Sept. 1976 and had a house built on it. On Dec. 1, 1976, when the house was completed, the local tax assessor valued the house and property at $30,000. Mort immediately appealed the valuation to the County Board of Tax Assessors. On Dec. 28, 1976, he received his tax bill for the year. The tax due was based on the $30,000 assessed valuation. On Dec. 29, he placed on deposit with his local bank the amount of the taxes due. The money was to be paid to the local tax collector if he lost his appeal to the County Board. On Jan. 21, 1977, the Board affirmed the valuation set by the local tax assessor. On Jan. 22, Mort notified the bank of the Board's decision and the funds were turned over to the local tax collector. In what year may Mort deduct the property taxes?

Problem 17-13

(a) Hal Wilson, an accrual basis taxpayer, was being sued for patent infringement. He was advised by his attorney that the case would not be tried until 1979 and that he would probably have to pay damages of $15,000. Wilson plans to contest the action but to protect himself in case of an adverse verdict, he set up a reserve fund and contributed $5,000 to it in 1977. Can he deduct this amount in 1977?

(b) Would your answer to (a) be different if Wilson were a cash method taxpayer?

(c) Would your answer to (a) be different if Wilson put the $5,000 in escrow?

(d) Assume in (c) Wilson was a cash method taxpayer. Would your answer to (c) be different?

Problem 17-14

Shane Setter, a student of veterinary medicine, has steady income from a trust fund, but needs extra cash to finish his final year of veterinarian school. On 8-1-77, he borrowed $840 from his sister, Nadine, and $360 from his cousin, Tom. Shane agreed to pay interest on the loans at a rate of 5% a year. He paid $42 to Nadine and $18 to Tom on 8-1-78, as interest for one year. Nadine and Tom are cash basis taxpayers, while Shane is on the accrual basis. All are calendar year taxpayers. What interest deduction, if any, can Shane take for 1977 and 1978?

SUPPLEMENTAL PROBLEMS

Problem 17-15

Lucas Butler, a calendar year taxpayer, has used the cash receipts and disbursements method of accounting since starting his business in 1969. The Commissioner requires him to change to the accrual method for 1977. Butler's taxable income for 1977, figured on the accrual basis, is $15,400. A study of Butler's books reveals the following additional facts:

Accounts receivable:	
December 31, 1976	$4,800
December 31, 1977	5,200
Accounts payable:	
December 31, 1976	4,500
December 31, 1977	4,150
Inventory:	
December 31, 1976	3,900
December 31, 1977	5,100

No other accruals are required at the start or end of 1977.

What adjustments, if any, are necessary to Butler's taxable income as a result of the change, and how should they be reported?

Problem 17-16

Adam Baker, a cash basis taxpayer, is the income beneficiary of a spendthrift trust established by his late father. In a written instrument executed last year, Adam directed the trustee to pay one-third of the trust income to his mother for her support. The trustee started court proceedings to have Adam's action invalidated, claiming that it violated the terms of the trust. Pending trial of the suit, the trustee paid one-third of the trust income into an escrow fund, the proceeds to be paid to Adam's mother or to Adam, depending on the outcome of the suit. This year, the trustee paid $12,600 trust income to Adam and paid $6,300 into the escrow fund. Adam believes that he does not have to pay tax on the $6,300 put into escrow by the trustee since it is disputed income, which he has not received, nor may ever receive. What amount of trust income is taxable to Adam this year? Explain.

Cumulative Problem 17-17

(Answer (a) or (b) as directed)

(a) Mr. Camel is president and 80% shareholder of the Deep Spring Water Co. The company uses the accrual method of accounting and reports its income on a fiscal year basis which runs from Oct. 1 to Sept. 30. On Oct. 1, 1975, the company leased a warehouse from Mr. Camel. The lease was for five years and the rent was $5,000 a year to be paid at the end of each year (Sept. 30). The amount of rent was reasonable. Deep Spring did not make payment under the lease until January 2,

1977, when it paid Camel $25,000 to cover both the amount that was due under the lease and that which would become due. Mr. Camel is a cash basis taxpayer and reports his income on a calendar year basis.

(1) What may Deep Spring deduct and in what year?
(2) How should Mr. Camel report the rental payment in income?
(b) John Miles earned a salary of $20,000 from the Apex Corp. during 1977.

On 12-31-76, he bought a new car giving his 3-year note for $2,000. The note bore interest at 8% per year. On 12-31-77, he prepaid the entire note and interest.

On 12-27-77, the Wolfpack Corp. of North Carolina declared a dividend of $800 payable to John on 12-31-77. John received the check on 1-6-78.

John and his wife Cheryl had been divorced in 1976. Under the divorce decree John was to make periodic alimony payments of $200 a month with $120 of each payment for the support of their son Rob, age 19. During 1977, John sent Cheryl $120 a month under the divorce decree. The divorce decree stated that Cheryl was to have custody of Rob and that she could claim the exemption. During the year she provided $650 in support of her son.

In May 1977, Rob was involved in a car accident. He incurred $2,000 in doctor's bills which his father paid in 3 installments; $1,000 on 8-1-77, $600 on 10-1-77 and $400 on 1-11-78.

During the year, Miles paid $280 in medical insurance, $200 in doctor bills for arthritic condition and $260 in drugs for his arthritis. He paid $1,200 in property taxes, $400 in state inheritance taxes and $350 in state income tax.

In 1977, Rob Miles received the following: $1,000 in state unemployment insurance benefits; $700 for summer work as a lifeguard and $200 interest on a refund of federal tax.

(1) Compute John Miles' tax table income for 1977; (2) tax liability.

Cumulative Problem 17-18

Kent Davis, single, is the sole support of his young cousin, aged 12, who lives with him. He pays all her living expenses and she has no income of her own. Davis, divorced 3 years ago under a final court decree, pays his former wife $700 per month as part of the settlement ($500 of this amount is child support payments for their two children in his wife's custody).

This year, Davis has been granted permission to change his annual accounting period and must file a return for the short period of 4 months ending April 30. During this period, he has the following additional income and expenses:

Net business income	$8,200
Dividends from domestic corporations	340
Savings account interest	82
Interest on federally backed housing bonds	367
State lottery winnings	40
Federal tax refund from prior year's tax	293
State tax refund from prior year's tax	178
State income tax for current year	184
Real estate taxes on personal residence	440
Interest on mortgage on personal residence	232
Contributions to qualified charities	125
State sales tax	89

During 1976, Davis invested $10,000 in a tax shelter involved with the production and distribution of video tapes. By the end of 1976, he had incurred a $12,000 loss and had decided not to invest any more money in the venture until 1979. As of April 30 of this year, Davis had incurred additional losses totalling $1,800.

Assuming Davis can not claim his children as dependents for personal exemption purposes, compute his tax liability for the short period return that he is required to file.

Research Problem 17-19

On March 1, 1975, the United States filed a complaint in condemnation on real property owned by Dave Stutts, and deposited $65,000 in the Registry of the Court as estimated compensation. Title to the property vested in the U.S. on that date and Stutts was entitled to the amount deposited without restrictions as to its use.

On March 26, 1975, Stutts received payments on account from the Registry in the amount of $62,500 having agreed to leave $2,500 in the Registry to cover a possible claim on the property.

Stutts questioned the adequacy of the amount estimated as just compensation and employed attorneys to pursue this issue in the condemnation proceedings before the U. S. District Court. On February 1, 1977, the court entered a judgment that $150,000 was the fair, just, and adequate compensation for the taking of Stutts' property.

Stutts, an accrual basis taxpayer, comes to you for advice. He tells you that in late 1977 he replaced the condemned property with similar property. He knows that the gain from the sale of his property must be reported. He thinks that under the accrual method no amount could be accrued as income until 1977 when events occurred for the first time which fixed, with reasonable certainty, the amount to be received by him as compensation for the taking of his property. On this issue of the time for reporting income, Stutts asks if he realized any gain from the condemnation award in 1976. How would you advise?

1. To find the answer use the Prentice-Hall Complete Federal Tax Equipment in your school or local library. Give your answer fully explained. In it show authorities, citing law and opinions applicable, and the P-H Federal Tax Equipment paragraphs where they may be found.

2. Enumerate and explain carefully every step you take in reaching your result. These are extremely important—just as important as the conclusion itself.

Master Review Problem 17-20

Ed and Mary Grant are married and living together in Rutland, Vermont. They engaged you to prepare their 1977 federal income tax on a joint return and advise you that they wish to take advantage of every tax saving method available. Conferences with them and examination of their records reveal the following facts:

(1) Ed Grant became 65 years old on September 5, 1977. Mary is 55 years old. The Grants have two children; John, 24, a disabled veteran, lives with and is completely supported by his parents; Jane, 23, lived with and was supported by her parents until September 15, 1977, when she married Roger Blake and moved to New York. A third child, James, died on February 10, 1977, at age 21. Prior to his death he also lived with and was supported by his parents. Neither John nor James had any income of their own.

(2) On April 30, 1977, Ed Grant sold an apartment building for $157,744.53 (building, $137,744.53; land, $20,000.00) that he had built in Barre, Vermont, and put in service on January 2, 1964, for $185,000 (building, $165,000; land, $20,000). Mr. Grant used the declining balance method to compute total depreciation deductions of $69,240.81 ($35,844.97 taken before 1970); straight line depreciation would have been $3,300 a year (assume no salvage value). The building contained only residential dwelling units and was fully rented. Rents collected during 1977 up until the time of sale were $15,900; 1977 expenses were: painting, $2,100; repairs, $839.45; taxes, $400; miscellaneous, $180.

(3) In May, 1977, Mr. Grant's house was damaged by a falling tree. Furniture, drapes and carpeting in two second-floor bedrooms were completely destroyed and the first floor ceiling was dangerously weakened. Mr. Grant's insurance company estimated the damage at $10,000. While the house was being repaired the Grants were forced to move into a hotel, thereby incurring expenses

of $2,100 (lodging, $980 and meals, $1,120). Their normal living expenses for this period would have been $1,120. In July, Mr. Grant's insurance company completely reimbursed him for his losses, including extraordinary living expenses.

(4) On October 31, 1977, Mr. Grant sold his home for $43,900 as a result of a sale contract dated September 30, 1977, and moved into an apartment with his wife and son. The Grants had lived in this house since they bought it on December 12, 1955 for $22,000. Mr. Grant had incurred purchase commissions, surveying expenses and recording fees totaling $600 when he bought the house. He also had spent $8,200 for improvements while living there. Commissions and expenses incurred in selling the house were $3,100. To fix up the house prior to its sale, Mr. Grant spent $400 for paper-hanging in May and $800 for painting in July and August. 1977 real estate taxes on the house and land were $1,632 and were paid by Mr. Grant on January 2, 1977. At the closing, the buyer reimbursed Mr. Grant for the prepaid November and December taxes.

(5) During 1977, Mr. Grant owned and operated as a sole proprietorship, Perfect Paper Products, a small paper processing company with its office and plant located at 432 Commerce Street, Montpelier, Vermont. Mr. Grant furnishes you with the following information concerning the operation of his business:

(a) Perfect Paper Products uses a hybrid method of accounting. Purchases and sales are accrued, and expenses are reflected on the cash basis. Mr. Grant's non-business affairs are conducted on the cash basis.

(b) Customer billings for the year totaled $343,813.82 for jobs completed and shipped.

(c) All production is according to specifications of the customer. Mr. Grant purchases raw materials only as needed for orders placed.

(d) Production costs:

Cost of raw materials purchased	$ 41,350.00
Direct labor	163,000.00
Overhead allocated to production	47,200.00

(e) Expenditures taken from business records:

Utilities	$ 1,980.00
Truck driver wages	7,200.00
Office salaries	17,654.00
Real estate taxes	1,070.00
Repairs	16,446.48
Union welfare contribution	600.00
National political party contribution	100.00
Employment taxes	1,179.80
Delivery expense	1,476.00
Rent	1,200.00
Insurance (see (g) below)	8,600.00
Payments to Acme Construction Company (see (h) below)	6,800.00
Miscellaneous business expenses	1,247.32
Office furniture (see (j) below)	12,000.00
City of Montpelier, special sewer assessment	1,350.00

(f) Standard Stationery, Inc., a customer of Perfect Paper Products, was declared bankrupt on April 20, 1977. Mr. Grant's claim against the bankrupt for $8,473.00 proved worthless.

(g) Insurance premiums include:

Business liability for one year	$	575
Employees' Group Life Insurance		725
Fire insurance		5,400
Workmen's Compensation Insurance		1,550
Mr. Grant's medical care insurance		350
Total	$	8,600

(h) Payments to the Acme Construction Company represent 12 monthly installment payments at $480 plus interest due the 30th of each month for a warehouse that was completed and put into use on January 3, 1977. The total price for the building was $45,000, payable in installments as indicated above and under the terms of a written contract signed in October, 1976. The building has an estimated useful life of 50 years and a salvage value of $5,000.

(i) On January 1, 1977, a small garage that Mr. Grant used to store completed orders before delivery was completely destroyed by fire. The garage, which was empty when destroyed, was worth $300 before the fire. It was bought on June 30, 1957 for $9,000. Grant had claimed $8,775 in straight line depreciation up to the time of the fire. Insurance proceeds were $325. Mr. Grant did not replace the garage.

(j) Except for a building bought in 1957, Mr. Grant uses declining balances to compute depreciation on all Perfect Paper Products assets. His depreciable assets at the beginning of the current tax year include: (1) the building built by Acme Construction Company; (2) the building bought on 1-2-57 (cost, $63,000; est. useful life, 50 years; salvage value, $8,000; prior straight line depreciation, $22,000); (3) two furnaces with estimated useful lives of 20 years and salvage values of $2,500 (Furnace #1 cost $16,500 on 1-2-70 and had been depreciated $8,608.11 and Furnace #2 cost $13,000 on 1-2-74 and had been depreciated $3,523.00); (4) a light truck bought on 1-3-77 for $8,700 with estimated salvage value of $800; and (5) office furniture bought for $12,000 and placed in service on 5-20-77 ($750 estimated salvage value). Mr. Grant decides to elect the Class Life ADR system of depreciation for the truck and office furniture. He also elects the modified half-year convention. Mr. Grant reminds you that he wants to maximize his 1977 depreciation deduction in every way possible.

Note: The unadjusted basis in Col. b of the ADR form is the asset's cost reduced for any additional first-year depreciation. Any additional first-year depreciation is reflected on this form in Col. c.

(6) In December, Mr. Grant moved his office to Rutland, Vermont, a town located 58 miles south of Montpelier. He made this permanent move because his principal customers had their headquarters in the Rutland area. Mr. Grant rented office space and employed a secretary on November 15. He actually started working in the Rutland office on December 3. However, he could not find an apartment until January 2, 1978. He traveled to Rutland several times in November in attempts to find an apartment. The cost of these trips was $380. Mrs. Grant and John lived in a hotel in Montpelier and Mr. Grant lived at an athletic club in Rutland from December 3 until they moved into their new apartment on January 3. The living costs for the temporary quarters of Mr. Grant and of Mrs. Grant and John were $965 each. On December 3, Mr. Grant paid his former landlord $1,895 to settle his long-term lease on his former apartment. The actual cost of moving the Grants' furniture and household effects was $1,680 and was paid in January, 1978.

(7) Mr. Grant had the following stock transactions during the year: On April 16, he sold 20 shares of Main Mining Company stock for $400. They were pur-

chased on February 28, 1977, for $600. On May 10, he sold 900 shares of Canamont International, Inc. for $161 per share. The Canamont stocks were bought by Mrs. Grant's uncle for $218 per share and were worth $192 per share when Mrs. Grant inherited them on August 12, 1974. On November 28, Mr. Grant sold 25 shares of Brower Business Corporation stock for $15 per share; these were purchased for $10 per share on February 28, 1977.

(8) Other income includes:

(a) Mary Grant, Ed's wife, was Assistant Vice-President of Vermont Business Women, Inc. She earned an annual salary of $16,500. During 1977, $2,591.52 was withheld from her salary. She worked a 5-day week, Monday through Friday, and was paid biweekly. In June, 1972, while she was an executive trainee, she was given an option under a qualified stock plan to purchase 150 shares of stock of the corporation at $25 per share, its fair market value at that time. In March, 1977, she exercised her option and purchased the 150 shares of stock. Its fair market value then was $80 per share.

(b) Dividends on stock (all held jointly) in 10 different domestic corporations, each of which paid less than $50 for the year. Total dividends received amounted to $426.

(9) Mr. Grant had a mild coronary attack while at work and was taken to the Montpelier General Hospital. Mr. Grant paid $669.55 for drugs and medicine and paid doctor's bills amounting to $956. The remaining balance due on his hospital and medical bills was paid by the insurance company under Grant's medical insurance policy.

(10) Ann Mason, a retired teacher, was hired by the Grants to take care of their son, John, while Mrs. Grant was working. Mrs. Grant paid her $160 per month. She worked the entire year except for March and April when she was on vacation. The Grants also paid $533 in doctor bills for therapy treatments for John, as well as $294 for his drugs and medicine.

(11) Mrs. Grant discovered on December 31, 1977, that her ruby brooch had been stolen from her hotel room. She had purchased the brooch a year ago for $1,000 and it was worth $1,100 when stolen. The uninsured brooch has not been recovered.

(12) The Grants bought new furniture in September for $1,467. They charged their purchases on their SuperCharge credit card and received a bill for $1,467 in October, which they did not pay. In November, they received a bill for $1,489 (the $1,467 past due plus $22 in finance charges) which Mr. Grant paid on November 30.

(13) The Grants paid state sales taxes of $135 during the year.

(14) In 1977, the Grants pledged $200 to their church, of which $94 was paid in 1977. Mr. Grant contributed services to the Boy Scouts with a fair market value of $350. He also traveled 200 miles in his auto in connection with church business. Three suits worth a total of $31 were given to the Salvation Army. They cost Mr. Grant $95 each when he purchased them. Mrs. Grant contributed $155 to an indigent local family who needed help.

(15) On June 2, 1977, the Grants received reimbursement of $458 for medical expenses they paid in 1976. Their 1976 adjusted gross income was $11,486.73, and their 1976 itemized medical expense deduction amounted to $219.

(16) Mr. Grant paid $7,000 in 1977 estimated taxes.

(17) The Grants' daughter, Jane, filed a joint return with her husband, Roger Blake, for 1977.

(18) At the time they filed their 1977 return, the Grants lived in a rented apartment at 1370 South Avenue, Rutland, Vermont.

On the basis of the above information, fill in the necessary schedules and compute the least net tax payable or largest overpayment refundable on a joint return (do not round off any figures or amounts).

5140

Accounting

1978

Schedule 1

Profit (or Loss) from Business or Profession

Gross receipts ...., less returns and allowances $ .... $ ....
Cost of goods sold:
    Inventory at beginning of year .... $................
    Merchandise purchased ....
    Labor ....
    Materials and supplies ....
    Other costs (explain below) ....

    Total .... $................
    Less inventory at end of year ....

    Cost of goods sold .... $ ....

Gross profit .... $ ....
Other business deductions:
    Depreciation (Explain in Schedule below) .... $................
    Taxes on business and business property ....
    Rent ....
    Repairs ....
    Salaries (not deducted above) ....
    Insurance ....
    Interest on business indebtedness ....
    Bad debts ....
    Other business expenses (itemize below) ....

    Total .... $ ....

Net profit .... $ ....

Explanation of Deductions

....
....

Explanation of Deduction for Depreciation

1. Group and guideline class or description of property	2. Date acquired	3. Cost or other basis	4. Depreciation allowed or allowable in prior years	5. Method of computing depreciation	6. Life or rate	7. Depreciation for this year
1 Total additional first-year depreciation (do not include in items below)						
2 Depreciation from Form 4832						
3 Depreciation from Form 5006						
4 Other depreciation:						
Buildings						
Furniture and fixtures						
Transportation equipment						
Machinery and other equipment						
Other (specify)						
5 Totals						

Class Life Asset Depreciation Range (Form 4832)

a. Asset guideline class	b. Unadjusted basis		c. Additional first-year depreciation	d. Gross salvage value (before application of section 167(f))	e. Period (years)	f. Method	g. Depreciation for this taxable year
	(1) Amount placed in service first half of this taxable year	(2) Amount placed in service second half of this taxable year					
Totals							

Depreciation (Furnish the following information by individual accounts for assets placed in service this taxable year) — Identifying number

Schedule 2

Part II. Rent and Royalty Income

(a) Kind and location of property If residential, also write "R"	(b) Total amount of rents	(c) Total amount of royalties	(d) Depreciation (explain below) or depletion (attach computation)	(e) Other expenses (Repairs, etc.— explain below)
Totals				

Net income or (loss) from rents and royalties (column (b) plus column (c) less columns (d) and (e)) .

Schedule for Deductions Claimed Above

Explanation of Column (e), Part II

Item	Amount	Item	Amount	Item	Amount

Schedule for Depreciation Claimed in Part II Above

(a) Description of property	(b) Date acquired	(c) Cost or other basis	(d) Depreciation allowed or allowable in prior years	(e) Method of computing depreciation	(f) Life or rate	(g) Depreciation for this year
1 Total additional first-year depreciation (do not include in items below) →						
2 Totals						

Schedule 3
Capital Gains and Losses

Part I Short-term Capital Gains and Losses—Assets Held Not More Than 9 Months

a. Kind of property and description (Example, 100 shares of "Z" Co.)	b. Date acquired (Mo., day, yr.)	c. Date sold (Mo., day, yr.)	d. Gross sales price	e. Cost or other basis, as adjusted and expense of sale	f. Gain or (loss) (d less e)
1					

2 Enter your share of net short-term gain or (loss) from partnerships and fiduciaries ...... | 2 |
3 Enter net gain or (loss), combine lines 1 and 2 .... | 3 |
4 Short-term capital loss carryover attributable to years beginning after 1969 .... | 4 ( )
5 Net short-term gain or (loss), combine lines 3 and 4 .... | 5 |

Part II Long-term Capital Gains and Losses—Assets Held More Than 9 Months

6					

7 Capital gain distributions .... | 7 |
8 Enter gain, if applicable, from Form 4797, line 4(a)(1) .... | 8 |
9 Enter your share of net long-term gain or (loss) from partnerships and fiduciaries ..... | 9 |
10 Enter your share of net long-term gain from small business corporations (Subchapter S) ... | 10 |
11 Net gain or (loss), combine lines 6 through 10 .... | 11 |
12 Long-term capital loss carryover attributable to years beginning after 1969 .... | 12 ( )
13 Net long-term gain or (loss), combine lines 11 and 12 .... | 13 |

Part III Summary of Parts I and II

14 Combine lines 5 and 13, and enter the net gain or (loss) here .... | 14 |
15 If line 14 shows a gain—
  a Enter 50% of line 13 or 50% of line 14, whichever is smaller.
      Enter zero if there is a loss or no entry on line 13 .... | 15a |

  b Subtract line 15a from line 14. Enter here and in Schedule 5 .... | 15b |
16 If line 14 shows a loss—
  a Enter one of the following amounts:
    (i) If line 5 is zero or a net gain, enter 50% of line 14;
    (ii) If line 13 is zero or a net gain, enter line 14; or,
    (iii) If line 5 and line 13 are net losses, enter amount on line 5 added to 50% of amount on line 13 . . . . | 16a |
  b Enter here and   in Schedule 5,   the smallest of:
    (i) The amount on line 16a;
    (ii) $1,000 ($500 if married and filing a separate return); or,
    (iii) Taxable income, as adjusted . . . . | 16b ( )

1978   **Assignment 17—Problems**   5143

Form 4797: Supplemental Schedule of Gains and Losses

Part I   Sales or Exchanges of Property Used in Trade or Business, and Involuntary Conversions (Section 1231)

SECTION A.—Involuntary Conversions Due to Casualty and Theft

a. Kind of property (if necessary, attach additional descriptive details not shown below)	b. Date acquired (mo., day, yr.)	c. Date sold (mo., day, yr.)	d. Gross sales price	e. Depreciation allowed (or allowable) since acquisition	f. Cost or other basis, cost of subsequent improvements (if not purchased, attach explanation) and expense of sale	g. Gain or loss (d plus e less f)
1						

2 Combine the amounts on line 1. Enter here, and on the appropriate line as follows . . . .
    (a) For all except partnership returns:
       (1) If line 2 is zero or a gain, enter such amount in column g, line 3.
       (2) If line 2 is a loss, enter the loss on line 5.
    (b) For partnership returns: Enter the amount shown on line 2 above, on Schedule K (Form 1065), line 6.

SECTION B.—Sales or Exchanges of Property Used in Trade or Business and Certain Involuntary Conversions (Not Reportable in Section A)

3						

4 Combine the amounts on line 3. Enter here, and on the appropriate line as follows . . . .
    (a) For all except partnership returns:
       (1) If line 4 is a gain, enter such gain as a long-term capital gain on Schedule D (Form 1040, 1120, etc.) that is being filed.
       (2) If line 4 is zero or a loss, enter such amount on line 6.
    (b) For partnership returns: Enter the amount shown on line 4 above, on Schedule K (Form 1065), line 7.

Part II   Ordinary Gains and Losses

a. Kind of property (if necessary, attach additional descriptive details not shown below)	b. Date acquired (mo., day, yr.)	c. Date sold (mo., day, yr.)	d. Gross sales price	e. Depreciation allowed (or allowable) since acquisition	f. Cost or other basis, cost of subsequent improvements (if not purchased, attach explanation) and expense of sale	g. Gain or loss (d plus e less f)
5 Amount, if any, from line 2(a)(2)						
6 Amount, if any, from line 4(a)(2)						
7 Gain, if any, from page 2, line 22						
8						

9 Combine amounts on lines 5 through 8. Enter here, and on the appropriate line as follows . . . .
    (a) For all except individual returns: Enter the gain or (loss) shown on line 9, on the line provided for on the return (Form 1120, etc.) being filed.
    (b) For individual returns:
       (1) If the gain or (loss) on line 9, includes losses which are to be treated as an itemized deduction on Schedule 7, enter the total of such loss(es) here and include on Schedule 7. . . . .
       (2) Redetermine the gain or (loss) on line 9, excluding the loss (if any) entered on line 9(b)(1). Enter here and in Schedule 5. . . . .

5144   Accounting   1978

Part III   Gain From Disposition of Property Under Sections 1245, 1250, 1251, 1252, 1254

Disregard lines 18 and 19 if there are no dispositions of farm property or farmland, or if this form is filed by a partnership.

10 Description of sections 1245, 1250, 1251, 1252, and 1254 property: Date acquired (mo., day, yr.)   Date sold (mo., day, yr.)

(A)
(B)
(C)
(D)

Relate lines 10(A) through 10(D) to these columns ▶ ▶ ▶ ▶	Property (A)	Property (B)	Property (C)	Property (D)

11 Gross sales price
12 Cost or other basis and expense of sale
13 Depreciation (or depletion) allowed (or allowable)
14 Adjusted basis, line 12 less line 13
15 Total gain, line 11 less line 14
16 If section 1245 property:
    (a) Depreciation allowed (or allowable) after applicable date
    (b) Enter smaller of line 15 or 16(a)
17 If section 1250 property:
    (a) Additional depreciation after 12/31/75
    (b) Applicable percentage times the smaller of line 15 or 17(a)
    (c) Excess, if any, of line 15 over line 17(a) (If line 15 does not exceed line 17(a), omit lines 17(d) through 17(h), and enter the amount from line 17(b) on line 17(i))
    (d) Additional depreciation after 12/31/69 and before 1/1/76
    (e) Applicable percentage times the smaller of line 17(c) or line 17(d)
    (f) Excess, if any, of line 17(c) over line 17(d) (If line 17(c) does not exceed line 17(d), omit lines 17(g) and 17(h), and combine the amounts on lines 17(b) and 17(e) on line 17(i))
    (g) Additional depreciation after 12/31/63 and before 1/1/70
    (h) Applicable percentage times the smaller of line 17(f) or 17(g)
    (i) Add lines 17(b), 17(e), and 17(h)
18 If section 1251 property:
    (a) If farmland, enter soil, water, and land clearing expenses for current year and the four preceding years
    (b) If farm property other than land, subtract line 16(b) from line 15; if farmland, enter smaller of line 15 or 18(a)
    (c) Excess deductions account
    (d) Enter smaller of line 18(b) or 18(c)
19 If section 1252 property:
    (a) Soil, water, and land clearing expenses made after 12/31/69
    (b) Amount from line 18(d), if none enter a zero
    (c) Excess, if any, of line 19(a) over line 19(b)
    (d) Line 19(c) times applicable percentage
    (e) Line 15 less line 19(b)
    (f) Enter smaller of line 19(d) or 19(e)
20 If section 1254 property:
    (a) Intangible drilling and development costs deducted after December 31, 1975
    (b) Enter smaller of line 15 or 20(a)

Summary of Part III Gains (Complete Property columns (A) through (D) through line 20(b) before going to line 21)

21 Total gains for all properties (add columns (A) through (D), line 15)
22 Add columns (A) through (D), lines 16(b), 17(i), 18(d), 19(f), and 20(b). Enter here and on line 7
23 Subtract line 22 from line 21. Enter here and in appropriate Section in Part I

Schedule 4: Child and Dependent Care Credit

1. Total expenses paid .... $ ....
2. Less: Amount in excess of:
   (a) $2,000, if one dependent ....
   (b) $4,000, if two or more dependents ....
3. Balance ....
4. Allowable credit (20% of line 3)..   ....

Schedule 5: Income From Sources Other Than Wages

Dividends .... $ ....
Exclusion ....
Taxable dividends ....
Interest ....
Pensions and annuities, rents and royalties (Sched. 2) ....
Business income (Sched. 1) ....
Net gain or (loss) from sale or exchange of capital assets (Sched. 3) ....
Net gain or (loss) from Supplemental Schedule of Gains and Losses (Form 4797)..   ....
Farm income ....
Miscellaneous income ....
Total .... $ ....

Schedule 6: Adjustments

Moving expenses .... $ ....
Employee business expenses ....
Payments to Keogh or individual retirement plans ....
Total adjustments .... $ ....

Schedule 7: Itemized Deductions

Medical and Dental Expense

1. One-half (but not over $150) of insurance premiums for medical care .... $ ....
2. Total cost of medicine and drugs ....
3. Enter 1% of adjusted gross income ....
4. Subtract line 3 from line 2 ....
5. Other medical, dental expenses ....
6. Total (add lines 4 and 5) ....
7. Enter 3% of adjusted gross income ....
8. Subtract line 7 from line 6 ....
9. Total (add lines 1 and 8) ....

Contributions

Total cash contributions .... $............
Other than cash ....
Carryover from prior years ....
Total contributions ....

Taxes

Real estate .... $............
State and local gasoline ....
General sales ....
State and local income ....
Personal property ....
Total taxes ....

Interest Expense

Home mortgage .... $ ....
Other (specify) ....
Total interest expense .... $ ....

Casualty or Theft Loss(es)

1. Loss before adjustments .... $ ....
2. Insurance reimbursement ....
3. $100 limitation 100.00
4. Add lines 2 and 3 ....
5. Casualty or theft loss (line 1 less line 4) .... $ ....

Miscellaneous Deductions
Miscellaneous deductions (specify) .... $ ....

Summary of Itemized Deductions
Total medical and dental expenses .... $ ....
Total contributions ....
Total taxes ....
Total interest expense ....
Casualty and theft loss(es) ....
Total miscellaneous deductions ....
    Total itemized deductions .... $ ....

Schedule 8: Tax Computation
1. Wages, salaries, tips .... $ ....
2. Other income (Sched. 5) ....
3. Total .... $ ....
4. Adjustments (Sched. 6) ....
5. Total income (Adjusted gross income) .... $ ....
6. Less: Excess itemized deductions:
    Itemized deductions (Sched. 7) .... $ ....
    Less: Zero bracket amount ....
7. Balance .... $ ....
8. Less: Deductions for exemptions ....
9. Taxable income .... $ ....
10. Tax .... $ ....
11. Less: Credits:
    (a) Investment credit .... $ ....
    (b) Credit for political contributions ....
    (c) Credit for child care expenses (Sched. 4) ....
    (d) General tax credit: Enter larger of 2% of taxable income, but not more than $180; or $35 per exemption deduction .. ..
12. Balance .... $ ....
13. Minimum tax (Sched. 9) ....
14. Total tax .... $ ....
15. Total income tax withheld .... $ ....
16. Estimated tax payments ....
17. Balance due or Overpayment .... $ ....

Schedule 9: Minimum Tax
1. Items of Tax Preference:
    (a) Excess itemized deductions .... $ ....
    (b) Accelerated depreciation on real property:
        (1) Low-income rental housing under Sec. 167(k) ....
        (2) Other real property ....
    (c) Accelerated depreciation on personal property subject to a lease ....
    (d) Amortization of certified pollution control facilities ....
    (e) Amortization of railroad rolling stock ....
    (f) Amortization of on-the-job training facilities ....
    (g) Amortization of child care facilities ....
    (h) Stock options ....
    (i) Reserves for losses on bad debts of financial institutions ....
    (j) Depletion ....
    (k) Capital gains ....
    (l) Intangible drilling costs ....
2. Total items of tax preference .... $ ....
3. Exclusion: Enter greater of $10,000; or ½ regular taxes (Sched. 8, line 12) .. ..
4. Subtract line 3 from line 2 .... $ ....
5. Multiply amount on line 4 by .15 and enter result .... $ ....

Tax Reasoning Problem 17-21
Acme Corp. had a dispute with the state of California over real estate taxes in San Pedro. Because Acme failed to pay the taxes, the San Pedro property was

"sold" to the state. But the sale was rather unusual for under state law Acme had full use of the property, and title would not vest in the state until the end of five years. In the meantime, the taxes could be paid and the slate wiped clean with Acme keeping title. Was this sale a payment so that accrual basis Acme could claim an immediate deduction?

ASSIGNMENT No. 18
INSTALLMENT AND DEFERRED PAYMENT SALES

(Note: In the following problems, unless otherwise specified, assume that the "tax year" is calendar year 1977, that the taxpayer and spouse, if any, are resident citizens under 65 and are not blind and that taxpayer is not entitled to any credits against tax other than those shown.)

Problem 18-1

Bill Hoffman owns a retail musical instruments store. He regularly sells on the installment plan, and has consistently reported his income on the installment method of accounting. His records disclose the following:

Year	Installment sales	Gross profit	1977 Collections
1975	$100,000	$25,000	$50,000
1976	150,000	45,000	47,000
1977	180,000	50,400	60,000

Compute the total gross profit Bill Hoffman must report on his 1977 return.

Problem 18-2

Lester Pinter Co.'s records show the following installment sales transactions:

Year	Installment accounts receivable as of 12-31-76	Percent of gross profit	Collections in 1977	Uncollectible amounts charged off during 1977
1975	.... $50,000	20%	$20,000	$2,500
1976	 70,000	30%	24,000	4,200
1977	....	35%	70,000	6,000

Lester Pinter uses the installment method of reporting and the specific charge-off method of computing bad debts. The gross profit on the company's 1977 sales is $40,000. What is the amount of unrealized gross profit as of 12-31-77?

Problem 18-3

On 1-8-77, Bill Tow, a dealer who reports on the installment basis, sold a fur coat for $3,000. The coat cost him $1,440. He received a down payment of $600. The balance was payable in 8 monthly installments of $300 each, starting 2-1-77. After paying 3 installments, the buyer defaulted. Under the sales contract, Bill repossessed the coat when it was worth $760.

(a) Compute Bill's total gain or loss for the year, if any, on these transactions.

(b) Would your answer to (a) be different if the coat was worth nothing when repossessed?

Problem 18-4

Larry Eichler is a furniture dealer. He is unmarried with no dependents. Assume his 1977-1979 records would reveal the following facts and figures:

In 1977, he realized from installment sales a gross profit of $5,000 payable in periodic payments over 5 years. From these sales he receives each year (1977, 1978 and 1979) $1,000 in profits. Other income in 1977 was $19,500. His excess itemized deductions and exemption for 1977 totaled $4,000.

In 1978, his gross profit from installment sales would be $9,000 payable in periodic payments over 3 years. From these sales he would receive $3,000 each year (1978, 1979) in profits. He would also receive in 1978, $16,000 in other income. His excess itemized deductions and exemption for 1978 total $4,000.

In 1979, Larry would sell $50,000 of furniture which cost him $45,000. He would receive $10,000 from the sales during the year. His other income during 1979 would total $21,000. His excess itemized deductions and exemption for 1979 would be $4,000.

Assuming that on 1-1-79, Larry Eichler changes from the accrual to the installment method of reporting, what would be his tax for 1979? (Note: In figuring tax liabilities in this problem, disregard tax credits, if any.)

Problem 18-5

On 10-20-77, Smith a cash basis taxpayer sold for $20,000 (exclusive of 7% interest), shares of stock that he had bought on 6-13-77 for $15,000. Smith is not a dealer in stocks. He received $3,000 cash, bonds having a fair market value of $2,000 and a 2-year note issued by Jones which had a face value of $15,000 and a fair market value of $10,000. One-half the note was due in 1978 and the rest in 1979.

(a) Detail the method or methods Smith may use to report the profit or loss on the transaction.

(b) Would your answer differ if Smith had bought the stock on 1-15-77? Explain.

Problem 18-6

Ian Howe sold his summer cottage on 8-1-77 for $26,000. He received $4,000 in cash. The buyer assumed an existing mortgage of $6,000 and gave a 9% purchase-money second mortgage payable $190 per month starting September 1 (calculated to be fully paid in 20 years). The installments for the year included total interest of $478.23. Ian had bought the cottage 15 years ago for $13,500. He plans to use the proceeds of the sale to invest in the stock market.

(a) Can Ian Howe report the gain from the sale on the installment basis?
(b) Figure the amount of gain reportable in 1977.

Problem 18-7

(a) Amos Nance is the sole owner of Kingfisher Farms, Inc., which was formed 5 years ago. The yearly net profits of the company in the last 5 years have steadily increased from $17,000 to $26,000. This year, Amos entered a contract to buy a personal residence from its owner, Bernie Allen, a cash basis taxpayer, who had paid $40,000 for the house in 1972. The contract calls for $15,000 down plus 25% of the net profits of Amos' corporation for the next four years. An appropriate rate of interest on the installment payments is provided for in the contract. Bernie did not replace his residence with a new house. Assume that Bernie receives the following payments (exclusive of interest) from Amos over the next four years:

1978	$7,000
1979	8,250
1980	9,000
1981	9,750

How should Bernie treat the payments (exclusive of interest) received under this contract?

(b) Assume that Bernie sold the property to Amos for $65,000 and, instead of the payments in (a) above, received $30,000 cash and Amos' installment notes of $35,000 payable in 4 equal annual payments starting in 1978. The notes had a fair market value of $32,000 when received in 1977. Assume also that Bernie prefers to use a deferred method of reporting, how should he report the payments received under this agreement?

(c) Would your answer to (b) above differ if the notes had no fair market value when received?

Problem 18-8

On 7-8-77, Jason Andrews sold a vacant lot next to his house to Brad Davis for $18,000, payable as follows: $4,000 cash on the date of sale; assumption of an existing mortgage of $4,600; and a second mortgage for $9,400 payable in five equal annual installments (exclusive of interest), starting one year from the date of sale. The fair market value of the second mortgage was 100% of face value. Jason had owned the land for 12 years and it had an adjusted basis to him of $3,000.

(a) Can Jason report the gain from the sale on the installment basis? Explain.

(b) Compute the amount of gain reportable in 1977 and later that results from this sale.

(c) Would Jason be able to use the installment basis if, instead of the above payments, Brad had paid $4,000 cash, assumed an existing mortgage of $4,000, and taken a second mortgage for $10,000? Explain.

Problem 18-9

On 1-26-77, Leonard Gordon sold for $28,000 a warehouse with an adjusted basis of $32,000 in his hands. He received $7,000 in cash on the date of sale. The balance was to be paid in equal installments of $3,500 (exclusive of 8% interest) during the next 6 years. What amount of gain or loss will be reported this year and in later years? Explain.

Problem 18-10

(a) On 12-1-77, George Johnson, who reports on the cash basis, sold to Madge Valentine for $40,000 (exclusive of interest) 200 shares of stock in Apex Corporation. The shares had been bought on 2-1-77 for $30,000. Johnson received $6,000 cash, bonds having a fair market value of $8,000 (adjusted basis $6,000) and the buyer's 2-year note which had a face value of $26,000 and a fair market value of $20,000 when received. One-half the note was due in 1978 and the rest in 1979. How could Johnson report his gain (loss) on the sale?

(b) What would be your answer to (a) if the note, when received, had no fair market value?

Problem 18-11

In 1973, Alec Martin sold to Bill Hunter real estate for $70,000. Terms: $20,000 cash plus $50,000 8.75% purchase-money mortgage payable $10,000 annually (exclusive of interest) starting in 1974. Alec's adjusted basis for the property was $35,000. He elected installment reporting, and Bill paid the 1974, 1975 and 1976 installments on time. At the beginning of 1977, Bill defaulted, and Alec repossessed the property at a cost of $1,500.

(a) What is Alec Martin's realized gain or loss on the repossession, and how much must he report on his 1977 return? Explain.

(b) What is the basis of the repossessed property?

Problem 18-12

On February 1, 1977, Dan Richards sold a tract of land which he had held since 1975, with an adjusted basis of $9,000 for $14,000, payable as follows: $4,000 down, the rest payable in 4 equal installments (due every 12 months) starting on June 1, 1978. On February 5, 1977, Richards paid the following expenses: commissions on the sale $400, abstract of title $75, and recording fees $25.

(a) What is Richards' gain from this sale?

(b) Can Richards use the installment method to report his profit? Explain.

Problem 18-13

Tom Rains, single, is a construction contractor and calendar year taxpayer. On 2-1-77, he signed a contract for the construction of a new building to be completed by 7-1-79. The contract calls for Rains to be paid $220,000 in 1977 and the balance of $270,000 on completion of the building. Rains estimates that his expenditures for construction will be as follows: $145,000 in 1977; $188,000 in 1978; and $70,500 in 1979. He also estimates that the percentage of completion for each year will be as follows: 35% completed by 12-31-77; 80% completed by 12-31-78; and 100% completed by 6-30-79.

Rains' excess itemized deductions and personal exemptions for 1977 total $5,500. Assume they will remain the same for the next 2 years. Assume also that Rains' estimates are correct and that this contract will provide the only income Rains will receive for these 3 years. Which long-term contract method of reporting income will produce the most favorable tax results for Rains?

Problem 18-14

Pierce Construction Company, a calendar year taxpayer, contracted to build an office building for a total sum of $3,000,000. Pierce began construction in March 1975, and completed the building in February 1977. On 12-31-75, 40% of the work was completed. On 12-31-76, 90% of the work was completed.

The following is a schedule of allowable expenditures incurred by Pierce during the construction, and payments received from the company having the building erected:

	Expenditures	Payments Received
1975	$1,000,000	$1,200,000
1976	1,000,000	1,300,000
1977	300,000	500,000
Total	$2,300,000	$3,000,000

Inventories of supplies and materials were properly taken into account in the determination of the yearly expenses.

(a) How much income must Pierce report on the contract for 1976, if it does not elect any special method of reporting income?

(b) How much income must Pierce report on the contract for 1976, if it elects to use the percentage-of-completion method in reporting income from long-term contracts?

(c) How much income must Pierce report on the contract for 1976, if it elects to use the completed contract method in reporting income from long-term contracts?

Problem 18-15

(a) Jim Fagen sold an antique jade vase for $12,000 on 2-1-77. He had bought it from a private collection 3 years ago for $5,000. The contract of sale provided for payment of $2,000 within 2 weeks, and the balance in 4 equal annual payments starting on 2-1-78. What amount of gain on the sale must Jim report in 1977? Explain.

(b) Would your answer to (a) be the same if the contract provides for $3,800 down payment and 6% interest on the remaining 4 equal installment payments?

Cumulative Problem 18-16

Ken Andrews is a self-employed trucker. On 7-2-75, he purchased and put into service a new Acme truck for his business. It cost $22,000 and had a 10-year useful life. Its salvage value was $4,200. On 1-2-77, Andrews sold the truck to Mike Howe for $17,400 (exclusive of 6% interest on installments) payable as follows: cash $2,900 and a 2-year note for $14,500 with first payment for ½ the note due on 1-2-78. On 2-1-77, Andrews bought a Peerless truck to use in his business. It cost him $12,000 and had a 5-year useful life. Its salvage value was $2,400. During the year he drove the truck 55,000 business miles incurring $200 for repairs, $1,300 for gasoline and $200 for insurance on the vehicle. Other expenses that Andrews incurred in his business, such as for telephone, advertising and legal fees, totaled $720.

Andrews' gross income from his business in 1977 was $31,470. In 1974 Andrews' wife died. He presently shares his home with his son John, age 24, who is single. John is a T.V. repairman and earned $8,500 in 1977. For 7 months of the year John attends night school taking a course in electronics. Ken furnished 60% of John's support.

In July 1977, Ken Andrews injured his back. During the summer he incurred $1,000 in doctor's fees and $770 in hospitalization costs. John had a history of allergies and Ken spent $350 for his son's medications. Ken's medical insurance provided him with $900 reimbursement for his doctor's fees related to his back. He paid medical insurance premiums of $280 during the year.

5152 Installment and Deferred Payment Sales

During the year, Ken paid $1,100 in property taxes, $400 in state income taxes and $120 in state inheritance taxes from his wife's estate. Interest on his home mortgage totaled $1,050. John did not contribute anything to home maintenance.

Assuming Andrews sought to maximize all deductions, what is his lowest tax liability before credits for 1977?

Research Problem 18-17

This year, Frank Enstein sold his interest in certain oil and gas leases for $240,000 cash. The contract of sale provides for a contingent additional consideration, in the amount of 48% of the estimated future net revenues. This estimate is to be made and discounted to the then present value only if the total production from the leases reaches 500,000 barrels of oil. Past production records show this figure will probably be reached within 5 years and will amount to at least $700,000, and probably more. The oil and gas leases had an adjusted basis to Frank of $188,000.

Frank would like to report the sale on the installment basis. While uncertain what the total selling price will be, he is sure it will be at least $940,000 ($240,000 cash and at least $700,000 in contingent consideration). Therefore, the $240,000 payment received in the year of sale is below the 30% limit set by the regulations (30% × $940,000 = $282,000). He figures his percentage of profit to be used to report income on the future payments will be 80% [total profit of $752,000 ($940,000 selling price less $188,000 adjusted basis) divided by contract price of $940,000].

Before making the election on his return, he comes to you for tax advice and asks if he can report the gain on the installment plan. What would you advise?

Use the Prentice-Hall Complete Federal Tax Equipment in your school or local library to find your answer. Do the following:

1. Give your opinion. In it, show authorities, citing law, regulations, interpretations and decisions applicable, and the P-H Federal Tax Equipment paragraphs where they may be found.

2. Enumerate and explain carefully each step you take in reaching your result. These are extremely important—just as important as the result.

Tax Reasoning Problem 18-18

Green bought stock 2 years ago and still owed the original owner $6,000. In July, Green sold the stock to Blake. Blake paid Green $2,000 and agreed to pay him $2,000 a year over the next 9 years. In addition, Blake assumed Green's debt on the stock. Green's basis at the time of the sale was $12,000. Can Green report the gain on the installment method? Explain.

Tax Reasoning Problem 18-19

When Kane sold a farm with a basis of $100,000 for $430,000, the buyer paid $85,000 in cash, assumed a $160,000 mortgage and gave a new mortgage for the balance of the price. Kane had selling expenses of $20,000. Can Kane report the gain on the installment method? Explain.

ASSIGNMENT No. 19

PARTNERSHIPS

(Note: In the following problems, unless otherwise specified, assume that the "tax year" is calendar year 1977, that the taxpayer and his spouse, if any, are resident citizens, under 65 and are not blind and that the taxpayer is not entitled to any credit against tax other than those shown.)

Problem 19-1

(a) Barbara, Ginger and Joan agree that they will rent a store and run a laundromat. Barbara will supply $8,000 cash for rent and other expenses. Ginger will pay $18,000 for machinery. Joan will operate the business. Ginger is to receive 50% of the net income and Barbara and Joan 25% each, until Ginger receives $10,000. After that, each is to receive $1/3$ of the net income. If there is any loss, each will pay $1/3$. Is this a valid partnership for federal income tax purposes?

(b) Alec Martin owns a profitable hardware store. It is his only source of income. He supports his 2 sons ages 21 and 14. What opportunity does Alec have to reduce his income tax?

(c) David Jule is a plastic surgeon. His son William is a medical student. David gives William a $1/4$ interest in his medical practice as a reward for being a good student. Is William a partner for federal income tax purposes?

Problem 19-2

During the calendar year, the partnership of Newton & Leighton had the following income and expenses:

Gross income from sales	$400,000
Cost of goods sold	250,000
Dividends from Lincoln Wine Co.	6,255
Interest on Larchmont City bonds	3,475
Distributive share of ordinary income from Kay & June partnership, in which it is a two-fifth partner	61,000
Net long-term gains	56,000
Distributive share of net long-term gains from Kay & June	2,400
Distributive share of net short-term loss from Kay & June	1,310
Contributions to Community Chest	800
Gain on condemnation of land bought 9 years ago	6,000
Office employees' salaries	120,000
State income taxes	85,000
Other business expenses	51,000

What is the partnership's taxable income or loss?

Problem 19-3

Joe, Peter, Mike and Helen are partners in a bridge construction business. During the year, Joe sold his stock for a long-term capital gain of $5,000. Mike and Helen sold their municipal bonds, and each realized $4,000 in long-term capital gains. Peter realized a $120 gain from the insurance proceeds he collected after his 10-month old car was demolished. In April, Mike lost $3,000 when he sold a diamond bracelet which he had bought in January of this year for investment.

During the year, the partnership lost $4,000 on the sale of Roslyn Gold Company stock held for 4 months. On 1-22-77, the partnership sold a business machine for $11,000. The machine was bought 2 years ago for $10,000; depreciation deduction taken on the machine totalled $6,400. The partnership agreement provides for distribution of 40% of the net profit or loss to Joe and Peter each and 10% to Mike and Helen each. The partnership made no distributions during the year.

(a) What is each partner's net gain or loss from capital asset transactions (before long-term capital gain deduction) for the year?

(b) If the adjusted basis of Helen's partnership interest at the end of the current tax year before any adjustment for partnership losses is $300, what is her net gain or loss from capital asset transactions (before long-term capital gain deduction) for the year?

(c) In (b), suppose you are Helen's tax adviser in 1977. Can you suggest a tax strategy to enable her to reduce her gain or increase her loss for the year?

Problem 19-4

Derek Dew and Leland Florence are business partners. According to the partnership agreement Derek is to share 60% of its net profit or loss, Leland 40%. During the tax year, Derek gave $500 to the Red Cross, Leland gave $200 to the Heart Fund, and the partnership gave $300 to the Salvation Army. Derek received a salary of $16,000 from the partnership, Leland $15,000. Derek paid property taxes of $3,320 on his home and Leland $3,000. Both partners are single and have no dependents. The partnership books show a gross profit of $39,000 for the year. The partnership and the partners all report on a calendar year basis.

Assuming that there were no other deductions to the partnership or to the partners:

(a) What is the partnership taxable income?

(b) Compute each partner's tax table income, giving him the best possible tax result.

Problem 19-5

Robert Sperber and Leonard Gordon are both single and have no dependents. In 1973 they formed the Lockwood Avenue Co., a general partnership. Each has a $7,000 basis for his partnership interest. The partnership agreement provides that the partners will make no withdrawals for the first 4 years of operation, but gains from capital asset transactions are to be distributed. Both are general partners and share the profit and loss equally. Lockwood pays each partner an annual salary of $22,000. The partnership profit and loss statement shows that for 1977 its gross profit and miscellaneous income items totaled $30,000. During the year it had a $6,000 short-term capital loss from the sale of stock, and contributed $1,000 to the New Rochelle Hospital, a nonprofit organization. Each partner also donated $1,000 to the hospital. Sperber paid $3,000 property tax on his home in 1977 and Leonard, $3,200. Sperber had a $1,500 net long-term capital gain from the sale of bonds.

Assuming no other deductions or income:

(a) What is the partnership's taxable income or loss?

(b) Compute each partner's tax table income, giving him the best possible tax result.

(c) If Sperber's partnership basis has been $6,500, what could he have done to minimize his 1977 tax liability?

(d) Would your answer to (c) be the same if Sperber obtains insurance to compensate him for any payments which he must personally make on the transactions under which the partnership has incurred a loss?

Problem 19-6

(a) The A-1 partnership uses a fiscal year ending March 31. Martin, a 30% partner, uses a calendar year. For the year ending 3-31-77, the partnership had taxable income of $90,000. The partnership paid Martin regular monthly guaranteed payments of $200 for services and for the use of capital for the fiscal year ending 3-31-77 and $120 monthly payments for fiscal year starting 4-1-77. What is the total amount of Martin's distributive share of partnership income and guaranteed payment that he must include in his taxable income for calendar 1977?

(b) Assume the same facts as in (a), except that Martin sold his entire interest to Foster on 11-30-77. There was no gain or loss on the sale. From April 1 to 11-30-77 the partnership had taxable income of $50,000. What would Martin include in his return for calendar 1977?

Assignment 19—Problems

(c) The Rapid Transit partnership uses the calendar year basis. Alex, a 40% partner, uses a fiscal year ending September 30. For calendar year 1975, the partnership had taxable income of $50,000, for 1976, $60,000, and for 1977, $80,000. Alex received regular monthly guaranteed payments of $200 in 1975, $230 in 1976, and $180 in 1977. What is the total amount of Alex's distributive share of partnership income and guaranteed payments he must include in his taxable income for fiscal year ending 9-30-77?

(d) Assume the same facts as in (c), except that there were no guaranteed payments, and Alex died on 6-30-77. What is the total amount that must be included in his final return?

Problem 19-7

Jackie Cicilea owns an 85% interest in the capital and profits of the WON partnership, real estate dealers. The partnership is offering for sale a piece of land with a $16,000 basis.

(a) If Jackie buys the property for $15,000 to build a summer home, is the partnership loss deductible?

(b) Jackie changes his mind about building on the plot and sells half of it to his brother Paul for $8,700 to use for camping. What, if any, is Jackie's taxable gain?

(c) Paul also changes his mind and resells his land to the partnership for $14,000. What is Paul's recognized gain or loss? How is it treated?

Problem 19-8

Sandy Andrews, who is a member of the partnership of Andrews and Roy, bought a new business machine for $60,000 on 1-2-76. It had a useful life of 4 years and an estimated salvage value of $5,400 and was immediately put to use in his business. Andrews and the partnership use the sum of the years-digits method of depreciation (general rule) and ignore salvage value wherever possible; otherwise, the straight line method is used. Andrews also deducts additional first-year depreciation if the property qualifies. On 1-1-77, when the machine was worth $59,000, he contributed it to his partnership in return for a capital credit in the same amount. On 10-1-77, the partnership sold the machine for $37,500. It had no other asset transactions in 1977.

(a) What is the partnership basis for the machine at the time of the transfer?

(b) How does the partnership report the gain or loss on the sale?

Problem 19-9

On 1-2-75, Joe Ponasa contributed $13,000 cash and unimproved real estate worth $55,000 for a 50% interest in a manufacturing partnership. He bought the property as an investment in 1974, for $39,000. The partnership held the property as an investment and would use it as security if it needed a loan. The partners and partnership are on a calendar year basis. In 1975, the partnership had a $32,000 loss from operations. It reported taxable income of $46,000 for 1976, and $130,000 for 1977. There were no distributions to the partners in 1976. On 11-10-77, the partnership made a distribution of earnings. It distributed $60,000 in cash to the other partner. The unimproved property Ponasa had contributed, now worth $60,000, was not needed by the partnership, and he agreed to take it instead of a cash distribution. He is not a real estate dealer. Ponasa sold the property for $65,000 on 12-15-77.

(a) What is the basis of Ponasa's partnership interest on 12-31-77?

(b) What gains or losses did Ponasa have from these property transfers?

Problem 19-10

Bill Tow and Kay Wig are equal partners in the partnership of Bill & Kay. The partnership uses the straight line method to depreciate its assets. On 1-2-77, Bill sold his partnership interest to Alfred Wilmar for $70,000 cash. Alfred agreed to assume Bill's share of the partnership liabilities. The balance sheet of the partnership as of 1-1-77 is as follows:

	Assets			Liabilities & Capital		
	Basis	Market Value			Basis	Market Value
Cash	$ 30,000	$ 30,000	Notes payable		$ 90,000	$ 90,000
Accounts receivable	0	30,000	Capital:			
Inventory	60,000	78,000	Bill		40,000	70,000
Land and building	80,000	92,000	Kay		40,000	70,000
	$170,000	$230,000			$170,000	$230,000

What is the amount of Bill's gain or loss on the sale? How is it treated? Explain.

Problem 19-11

(a) What, in problem 19-10, would be the basis of Alfred Wilmar's interest in the partnership?

(b) If the partnership had elected to adjust the basis of partnership property on the transfer of an interest, what gain would Alfred realize, if the partnership sold the inventory for $140,000? Explain your answer.

Problem 19-12

The Kirdale partnership is engaged in the hardware business. The partners are Daniel (30% interest), Lawrence (30% interest) and Michael (40% interest). The partnership balance sheet as of June 30 showed the following:

Assets			Capital		
	Basis	Market Value		Per Books	Market Value
Cash	$ 54,000	$ 54,000			
			Michael	$ 43,200	$ 57,600
Accounts receivable	4,500	7,200			
Hardware	4,500	36,000	Lawrence	32,400	43,200
Land & Building	45,000	46,800	Daniel	32,400	43,200
	$108,000	$144,000		$108,000	$144,000

Straight line depreciation is used for the building which Daniel contributed to the partnership 13 months before he liquidated his partnership interest. On July 1, the partnership distributed the hardware and accounts receivable to Daniel, in complete liquidation of his partnership interest.

(a) What is Daniel's gain or loss on the distribution? How is it treated?

(b) What is the partnership's gain or loss on the distribution? How is it treated?

SUPPLEMENTAL PROBLEMS

Problem 19-13

Lee and Forman formed a partnership on 11-1-76. For capital investment, Lee contributed 75 shares of Cramer Corp. stock he bought in 1974 for $40,000. Forman contributed 75 shares of Raleigh Corp. stock he bought 10-30-76 for $50,000. Each partner received a 50% capital interest in the partnership based on equal values of the stock contributed (each worth $50,000 when contributed). Both Raleigh Corp. and Cramer Corp. are domestic corporations. Lee and Forman are active partners in managing the business. Lee's share of profit or loss is 40% and Forman's share, 60%. In addition, Lee is guaranteed a salary of $20,000 a year, and Forman, $10,000 a year. Both receive 6% interest on their capital investment.

Lee-Forman partnership books show the following income and deductions for 1977:

Gross profit from business	$100,000
Income from rents (treated as business income)	7,000
Interest on bonds of the City of Newark	2,600
Gain on sale of 75 shares of Cramer Corp. stock sold 3-31-77	4,500
Loss on sale of 75 shares of Raleigh Corp. stock sold 2-3-77	3,500
Employees' salaries	8,000
Partner's salary	30,000
Interest paid to partners on capital investment	6,000
Contributions to qualified self-employed retirement plan—Lee, $3,000; Forman, $1,500; Employees, $1,200	5,700
Depreciation on building bought on 1-6-77	3,500
Taxes paid	5,600
Bad debts	1,800
Other business expenses	9,800
Contributions to Community Fund	2,100

(a) What is the book profit or loss?
(b) Compute the partnership's taxable income.

Problem 19-14

C. S. Lee, one of the partners in Problem 19-13, is the sole support of his wife who has no income or deduction of her own. In addition to the information given in the preceding Problem, Lee individually received income and paid expenses in 1977 as follows:

Interest received on Forest Hills Corp. Co. bonds	$ 260
Uninsured theft loss of Lee's home TV set bought in 1975	350
Loss on the sale of Solaya Yacht Co. stock bought on 1-22-76 and sold on 10-10-77	500
Gain on the sale of Lee's china collection bought on 1-11-77 and sold on 1-27-77	6,000
Taxes on residence	1,700
Contributions to FF Lodge (a private operating foundation)	17,000
Other deductions for adjusted gross income	1,200

C. S. Lee's 1976 return showed he had a $6,900 long-term capital loss carryover from 1976 stock transactions.

(a) On the basis of the information above, and on that given in Problem 19-13, compute C. S. Lee's tax table income, giving him the best possible tax result.
(b) Will any 1977 transactions affect C. S. Lee's 1978 tax liability? Explain.

★ Problem 19-15 ★

In 1976 Phil Hall and Jerry Martin formed a partnership called Nittany Co. to sell bumperstickers. Hall's basis for his 50% partnership interest was $4,100. In 1976 Nittany Co. distributed to Hall a parcel of land which had a basis to the partnership of $2,000 and a fair market value of $2,500. The partnership made no other transactions in 1976.

During 1977 Nittany Co. had a $5,000 loss. What loss, if any, can Hall claim on his 1977 return?

Cumulative Problems 19-16
(Answer (a) or (b) as directed)

(a) Ronald Kent and his brother Fred Kent each owned 50% of the Cherry Lawn Noodle Mfg. Corp. stock. Charles Yingly was the production manager, and Paul Tinar the sales manager. In 1973 the Kent brothers dissolved the corporation, and with its assets formed the Rochelle Noodle Co., each contributing his half of the distributed assets. Charles and Paul agreed to continue to run the production and sales activities of the Rochelle Noodle Co. The 4 men also agreed that the brothers would continue to manage the business as before, and that each brother would share a 50% interest in capital and losses of the business, and a 30% interest in the profits and the partnership's charitable donations. Charles and Paul each would get 20% of the profits plus $20,000 a year, whether or not there were any profits. The Kents are calendar-year taxpayers.

Due to the joint efforts of the 4 men, the business made huge profits from year to year. In January, 1977, Ronald needed cash and asked for a return of the C. K. Dog Food Co. stock that originally had been contributed to the business. Ronald and Fred each received the 100 shares they had contributed a year ago. The fair market value of the stock when returned was $500 a share; its basis to Rochelle was $200 a share. The company had no other transactions that affected its capital assets in 1977. It donated $10,000 to the Cancer Fund and had a taxable income of $70,000.

During 1977, Ronald received $5,000 interest on corporate bonds. One bond of the Y. T. Corp. that he bought on January 14 for $800 became completely worthless on July 1. He sold his 100 shares of the C. K. stock in April for $50,000. He paid the following expenses during the year: real property taxes, $750; fee to a tax expert for preparing his income tax return, $200; medical bills for a pedestrian he struck with his car, $1,300; and $500 to his church. He is divorced and has no dependents.

(1) Is Rochelle Noodle Co. a partnership, and if so, who are the partners? Explain.

(2) Compute Ronald Kent's tax liability for 1977 before tax credits, giving him the best possible tax result.

(b) Ivan Jamstone and his uncle, Irving Shea, formed the Teevee Mfg. Co. as a partnership in 1974. The partners share profits and losses equally. The company had the following profit and loss statement for 1977:

Gross receipts from sales	$320,429.25	
Cost of goods sold	153,089.25	
Gross profits from operations	$167,340.00	
Dividends from CT & Co.	5,942.25	
Interest on KL Corp. bonds	1,752.00	
Interest on State of Nevada bonds	2,293.00	
Long-term capital gain	14,765.75	
Gain from sale of machine bought in 1974 with $5,000 depreciation allowance taken on partnership returns	30,047.00	
Bad debt recovery (reserve is not used)	750.00	$222,890.00
Salaries (including $15,000 to each partner)	$ 92,000.00	
Taxes	15,666.50	
Repairs	4,500.00	
Other business expenses	18,000.00	
Contributions	9,371.00	
Interest on notes	1,125.00	
Short-term capital loss	5,317.50	
Interest on capital	7,500.00	$153,480.00
Net profit		$ 69,410.00

During 1977, Ivan received no distributions from the partnership except his salary and $2,225 interest on his capital investment. He had a long-term capital gain of $7,473.74 and a short-term capital gain of $2,230 on personal investments. In addition, he and his former wife received $36,523.50 in dividends from American Synamid Co. stock owned jointly by them.

Ivan was divorced in 1975. His former wife, Laurette, has custody of their 2 sons who received more than ½ their support from the parents. According to their written agreement, Laurette is entitled to claim the children's dependency exemptions. Because Laurette and her daughter by a previous marriage were in a serious accident, Ivan provided more than ½ the support of her and her 22-year old married daughter who files a joint return with her attorney-husband. Ivan gave $2,400 (at $1,200 each) for the support of his 2 sons during the year. His former mother-in-law contributed $1,800 to their support, and Laurette provided $400.

Ivan's summer cottage which cost him $17,700 (including $3,600 for the land) on 6-13-66, was completely destroyed by fire on 1-15-77. The property value immediately before the fire was $18,638 ($4,200 for the land and $14,438 for the building). He had no fire insurance.

During the year, Ivan paid the following expenses: $1,281 in property taxes; $1,347 for hospital bills and treatment of his former wife; $2,090 for the medical treatment of her daughter; $280 for medical insurance; $1,000 to his church; $290 to the American Red Cross; and $125 to his accountant for preparing the tax returns.

(1) Compute the partnership's taxable income for 1977.
(2) Compute Ivan Jamstone's tax liability for 1977, giving him the best possible tax result.

Cumulative Problem 19-17

Dick Princetone and Harry Richards formed a partnership in 1971 for the purpose of manufacturing chess sets. Both the partnership and the partners report on the calendar year basis. The partnership had a taxable income of $25,605 for 1977. Dick devoted his full time to the business, and Harry 80%. The partnership agreement provides for an annual salary of $20,000 for each partner. In addition, Dick shares in 60% of partnership profits and losses, while Harry shares in 40%. Dick is single. Harry is married and files a joint return. During 1977, the partnership was involved in the following transactions:

On January 1, the partnership sold a business machine for $400. The machine was bought and put into service on 1-2-76 for $2,400. At that time, it had a useful life of 5 years with no salvage value. The partnership used the sum of the years-digits depreciation method.

On January 2, the partnership bought and put into service new machinery for $40,000, with a useful life of 7 years and estimated salvage value of $4,000. The partnership elected to take the additional first-year depreciation and the declining balance method of depreciating the asset.

In May, the partnership received a dividend of $10 a share on 100 shares of common stock of Diana Company, a taxable domestic corporation. The stock had been contributed by Dick when the partnership was formed. Dick had paid $17,000 for the stock on the same day he made the contribution, and was credited for that amount to his capital account.

In June, the partnership received insurance proceeds of $700 for the theft of a business machine bought in 1971. At the time of the theft, the machine had an adjusted basis of $900 and a market value of $1,200.

In July, the partnership sold 50 shares of the Diana common for $15,000. It paid sales commission of $50.

On August 1, the partnership bought 100 shares of preferred stock of Simcar Co., a taxable domestic corporation for $6,000. The stock was sold on October 20 for $10,000, less $45 commission.

In November, Harry contributed to the partnership a factory (building and land) with a fair market value of $40,000.

In December, the partnership received $100 interest on Larchmont City bonds. In the same month it donated $400 to the Red Cross.

Throughout the year, Dick took numerous overnight business trips that cost him $1,915. Harry, for the most part, stayed in the office. He did, however, spend $645 in taking customers to lunch while completing sales contracts. The partnership reimbursed the partners for these expenses.

During the year, the partnership distributed $13,000 to each of the partners. In addition, Dick withdrew $9,801.

The capital accounts of the partners as of 1-1-77 were: Dick, $309,217; Harry, $261,744.

On the basis of the above information, fill out the following schedules:

Partners' Distributive Shares	Dick	Harry		Partners' Capital Accounts Reconciled	Dick	Harry
1. Ordinary income (or loss)	$........	$..........		1. Capital account at beginning of year	$........	$........
2. Additional first-year depreciation	....	....		2. Capital contributed during year	....	....
3. Payments to partners—salaries and interest	....	....		3. Ordinary income (or loss)	....	....
4. Qualifying dividends	....	....		4. Income not included in item 3 above, plus nontaxable income	....	....
5. Net short-term gain (or loss) from sale or exchange of capital assets	....	....		5. Losses not included in item 3 above, plus unallowable deductions	....	....
6. Net long-term gain (or loss) from sale or exchange of capital assets	....	....		6. Withdrawals and distributions	....	....
7. Net gain (or loss) from sale or exchange of property under Sec. 1231	....	....		7. Capital account at end of year	....	....
8. Net gain (or loss) from involuntary conversion under Sec. 1231	....	....				
9. Expense account allowance	....	....				
10. Charitable contributions	....	....				
11. Investment in property qualifying for tax credit	....	....				

Research Problem 19-18

The Brown and White limited partnership agreement provides that limited partners are to receive 5% of the annual profits, but guarantees a minimum annual payment regardless of profit or loss. The agreement also provides that these minimum amounts are to be treated as an expense of doing business when computing the company's net profits to determine the general partners' shares of profits.

In 1977, for the first time since the partnership was organized, the limited partners' share of partnership profits was less than the guaranteed payment and they received the guaranteed amount.

Brown and White is your client. An accountant employed by the company has asked you to review the company's Form 1065 filled out by him. In particular, he wants your opinion of his treatment of the minimum payments to the limited partners. In his view, they are guaranteed payments and deductible in full under Sec. 707(c). What would you advise?

Use the Prentice-Hall Complete Federal Tax Equipment in your school or local library to find your answer. Do the following:

1. Give your opinion. In it, show authorities, citing decisions applicable, and the P-H Federal Tax Equipment paragraphs where they may be found.

2. Enumerate and explain carefully each and every step you take in reaching your result. These are extremely important—just as important as the result.

Master Review Problem 19-19

Wally Nilson and Irving Shelley are partners in the firm of Nilson & Shelley which manufactures playing cards. The partners agree to divide the firm's profits and losses equally between them. The partnership keeps its books on the accrual basis for the calendar year, and values its inventories at cost. Neither partner received any expense account allowance. Wally is married, and Irving is single.

The books of Nilson & Shelley for 1977 disclose the following:

	Debit	Credit
Gross sales		$800,000
Returns and allowances	$ 18,000	
Inventory at beginning of year	80,000	
Merchandise bought for sale during year	200,000	
Direct Labor in factory	170,000	
Materials and supplies used in manufacturing	20,000	
Freight and cartage inward	4,000	
Factory power cost	3,000	
Inventory at end of year	67,000	
Interest on Golden Gate Diner Co. bonds		2,500
Interest on bank deposits		1,000
Dividends received on stock of taxble domestic industrial corporations		2,200
Salaries of partners ($20,000 to Wally and $19,000 to Irving)	39,000	
Salaries of clerical workers	20,000	
Salesmen's commissions	60,000	
Rent paid for sales offices in Scarsdale City	6,000	
Ordinary repairs to partnership property	2,500	
Interest on mortgage on factory	800	
N. Y. unincorporated business tax	650	
N. Y. property taxes	4,500	
Unemployment insurance and social security taxes	11,000	
Miscellaneous office expenses (telephone, heat, etc.)	8,000	
Legal fees	900	
Accounting fees for preparing tax returns	800	
Insurance premiums on firm property	14,000	

The partnership has determined from past experience that 6% of its accounts and notes receivable ultimately become uncollectible. The balance in the reserve on January 1 was $4,000. Debts charged off during the year amounted to $5,000. Accounts and notes receivable at the end of 1977 were $96,000. Recoveries during the year totaled $800.

The partnership's depreciable assets are shown below (Note: In column 3 of the depreciation schedule, enter the cost or other basis less salvage value, to the extent that salvage value is a factor.)

Brick factory building acquired 10-1-68 at cost of $55,000. Estimated useful life, 50 years; estimated salvage value, $5,000. Straight line method used.

Furniture and fixtures acquired 7-1-74 at cost of $9,000. Estimated useful life, 5 years; estimated salvage value, $800. Straight line depreciation used.

New machinery bought 1-2-77 at cost of $40,000. Estimated useful life, 10 years; estimated salvage value, $5,000. Declining balance depreciation used. Additional first-year depreciation allowance elected.

New pick-up truck bought 1-3-77 at cost of $8,900. Estimated useful life, 4 years; estimated salvage value, $800. Sum of years-digits method used.

When Nilson & Shelley was formed on 1-29-68, Wally contributed 200 shares of Parker Shirt Co. stock that had cost him $4,000 on 2-25-67. He received a capital credit for $3,000 when the stock was paid in. The partnership sold 100 shares of this stock for $5,500 on 1-22-77. Commissions amounted to $80.

On 2-14-77, the partnership sold 100 shares of Nevada Radio Corp. stock for $7,000. It had bought them on 6-13-75 for $9,300. Commissions were $100.

On 1-30-77, a photostat machine the partnership bought in 1975 was destroyed by fire. Its adjusted basis and value before the fire was $930. Insurance and salvage totaling $430 were recovered. (Assume there is no investment credit recapture on this machine.)

No family, fiduciary or business relationship exists between the partnership or the partners and any of the purchasers in the above transactions.

During the year, the partnership donated $400 to the American Heart Association and $400 to the American Cancer Society. The contributions were not related to the partnership business.

The partners' capital accounts, as shown on the partnership balance sheets, are as follows: at the beginning of the year, Wally, $269,320; Irving, $269,320; at the end of the year, Wally, $360,995; Irving, $359,995. During the year, Wally withdrew $2,000 and Irving $3,000 from the partnership; neither made any capital contributions. The partnership did not make any other distributions to the partners in 1977.

On the basis of the above data, fill in the following schedules:

SCHEDULE 1—DEPRECIATION

1. Kind of property	2. Date acquired	3. Cost or other basis	4. Depreciation in prior years	5. Depreciation method	6. Life or rate	7. Depreciation for this year
Total additional first-year depreciation .... $ ....
....	....	....	....	....	.....	....
....	....	....	....	....	.....	....
....	....	....	....	....	.....	....
....	....	....	....	....	.....	....
....	....	....	....	....	.....	....

Total (enter this amount as depreciation deduction in Sched. 3) $ _____

SCHEDULE 2—COST OF GOODS SOLD

Opening inventory ....
Purchases ....
Cost of labor ....
Other costs per books ....
  Total ....
Less closing inventory ....
Cost of goods sold ....

SCHEDULE 3—INCOME

Gross receipts .... Less: returns and allowances ....
Less: cost of goods sold (Schedule 2) ....
  Gross Profit ....
Nonqualifying dividends ....
Interest (fully taxable) ....
Rents ....
Other income ....
  Total income ....

DEDUCTIONS

Salaries and wages (other than to partners)	$ ....
Payments to partners—salaries and interest	....
Rent	....
Interest	....
Taxes	....
Bad debts	....
Repairs	....
Depreciation (from Schedule 1)	....
Other deductions	....
Total deductions	....
Ordinary income (or loss)	....

SCHEDULE 4—PARTNERS' SHARES OF INCOME, CREDITS, DEDUCTIONS, ETC.

1. Salary, interest and ordinary income (loss) .... $
2. Additional first-year depreciation ....
3. Dividends qualifying for exclusion ....
4. Net short-term capital gain (loss) ....
5. Net long-term capital gain (loss) ....
6. Net gain (loss) from involuntary conversions due to casualty and theft under Sec. 1231 ....
7. Net gain (loss) from sale or exchange of property used in trade or business ....
8. Contributions ....
9. Expense account allowance ....
10. Tax preference items:
    (a) Accelerated depreciation ....
    (b) Capital gains (losses)   (1) Short-term ....
                                   (2) Long-term ....
11. Property qualified for investment credit:
    Basis of new/used investment property   *Life years*
    ....
    ....
12. Other (specify) ....

SCHEDULE 5—RECONCILIATION OF PARTNERS' CAPITAL ACCOUNTS

1. Name of partner	2. Capital account at beginning of year	3. Capital contributed during year	4. Ordinary income	5. Income not included in col. 4 plus nontaxable income	6. Losses not included in col. 4 plus unallowable deductions	7. Withdrawals and distributions	8. Capital account at end of year
....	....	....	....	....	....	....	....
....	....	....	....	....	....	....	....

ASSIGNMENT No. 20

ESTATES AND TRUSTS

(Note: In the following problems, unless otherwise specified, assume that the "tax year" is calendar year 1977, that the taxpayer and his spouse, if any, are resident citizens, under 65 and are not blind, and that the taxpayer is not entitled to any credit against tax other than those shown.)

Problem 20-1

(a) Nelson Howe who died on 2-5-77, created the following trusts under his will:

Trust A—"$6,000 income shall be distributed each year to my daughter, Phebe, age 23, with any remaining income accumulated and distributed to my son Gordon, age 15, when he reaches 21."

Trust B—"Income shall be distributed to my married daughter Denise, if, in the trustee's discretion, she is in financial need."

Trust C—"One-half of the income shall be distributed to my youngest grandchild, Kenneth, and the other half to my oldest grandchild, Eileen. If either grandchild does not survive me, his or her share shall go to my sister, Laura."

To whom is the income from the trusts taxable? State whether each trust is a simple or complex trust.

(b) Nelson's will also directs his executor to transfer his apartment house to his wife "for as long as she lives." On 10-10-77, the executor, with the consent of Nelson's wife and the remaindermen, sold the property to buy Treasury bonds. Is Nelson's wife taxed on the $100,000 gain from the sale?

Problem 20-2

Michael is the sole beneficiary of a trust whose fiscal year ends on January 31. He is on a calendar year basis. The trust requires the trustee to distribute all its income currently, but permits distribution of corpus to Michael if he is in financial need. On 12-31-77, the trustee distributes to Michael all of the trust's $20,000 current income to that date, but made no distribution of corpus. The trust's distributable net income at the end of its tax year is $18,000.

(a) Is the trust a simple or complex trust? Explain.
(b) How much of the trust income must Michael include in his 1977 return?
(c) How much must Michael include in his 1978 return?

Problem 20-3

Arthur Young set up a trust 4 years ago for his wife Katherine. The trust instrument provides that the trust income is to be currently distributed to Katherine during her lifetime. But capital gains are to be allocated to, and all expenses charged off to corpus.

The trust corpus consists of:

(1) 2,000 shares of Solaya Hardware Corp. paying an annual dividend of $35.50 a share;
(2) 3,000 Weinstein Corp. 7% indenture bonds with $100 face value of each bond;
(3) 1,000 Big Apple City 4% bonds with $800 face value of each bond; and
(4) A vacant lot bought 2 years ago for $15,000 as an investment.

In 1977, all 3 securities paid the dividend and interest called for. The Trustee sold the lot for $20,000 to get a capital gain. The expenses of the sale were $800. The trustee paid out $310 in miscellaneous disbursements. Using these facts, compute the following for the year:

(a) Income currently distributable to Katherine.
(b) The trust's distributable net income.

Problem 20-4

When Charlie died on 2-6-77, he left his property to his wife, Mary Jane, in trust for her life. Mary Jane was to receive only the income from the trust property, and on her death, the property was to go outright to Charlie's sister, Josephine. The property included 200 acres of unimproved land which Charlie had bought for investment on 2-5-77. On 3-13-77, while Mary Jane was alive, the land was sold, resulting in a loss.
(a) Who may deduct this loss?
(b) Is the loss a short-term or long-term capital loss?

Problem 20-5

Wellington Lenape created a trust for his wife Alice and his mother Cecile that requires an annual distribution of $30,000 to Alice and $2,000 to Cecile. The trustee has power to invade corpus to make any additional payments to Alice and Cecile that the trustee thinks they need. During the tax year, the trust had a gross income of $40,000 and expenses of $3,000. The trustee distributed $42,000 to Alice and $3,000 to Cecile.

How much must Alice and Cecile include in their respective gross incomes? Explain.

Problem 20-6

Wally Leon died on 2-13-77 at age 70. He was single. Until he died, he was the sole support of his sister, Julie, and her 2 children in his home. He gave her an allowance each month to pay the household bills. Wally's will set up 2 trusts. The executor was directed to transfer one-half of Wally's net estate to each trust on the first day of the year after his death. Under Trust A, Julie is to receive all income of the trust each year for life. At her death the principal will be divided among her children. Under Trust B, the trustee is authorized to pay over to Julie from trust income any funds he decides are necessary to supplement her income from Trust A for her children's support and education. The principal and undistributed income will be divided among her children at the end of 12 years. The will also bequeathed to Julie for her support, all the net income from Wally's estate until the trusts were established. What deduction for personal exemptions is allowed on:
(a) Wally Leon's final return, assuming that he is required to compute his taxable income?
(b) The estate's income tax return?
(c) Income tax returns for Trust A?
(d) Income tax returns for Trust B?
Explain your answers.

Problem 20-7

The Hilderbrand Trust is required by its terms to contribute 10% of each year's income to the St. John's Church, a tax-exempt organization. During the year, the trust received $6,000 rent, $9,000 tax-exempt interest from municipal bonds, and $5,000 long-term capital gains allocated to income. It paid the required contribution to the church. How much charitable contribution can the trust deduct?

Problem 20-8

Andrew Tregunter died on 2-11-77. His wife, Sandra and 2 children survive him. His executor determined that during the year, Andrew had received taxable income of $46,350 (before exemption) up to the date of his death. The taxable income of the estate (before exemption) for the balance of the year was $20,000. Sandra had separate income of her own, but the children had no income and the mother furnished more than ½ their support for the year.

Compute the tax liability before credits against tax for the estate and for Andrew on a separate return. Who must file the necessary returns?

Problem 20-9

(a) Lester Tipley, age 75, bought a $100,000 life insurance policy at an annual premium of $11,750 based on his life expectancy of 9½ years. He immediately set up a trust and transferred the policy to it. He also transferred to the trust $200,000 in bonds paying $14,000 interest a year. The income from the bonds is to be used to pay the insurance premiums. The principal and accumulated interest of the trust will be distributed to him after 10 years, or to his estate if he dies before then. What, if any, trust income is taxable to Lester each year, and how much?

(b) Would your answer to (a) be the same, if the trust income not used to pay premiums must be distributed to Lester's married daughter each year for life and, at her death, the trust principal is to be paid over to her son?

Problem 20-10

On 6-13-76 Michael Chain transferred 2,000 shares of Rosline Court Co. stock to a newly created trust which requires the trust income to be currently distributed to his wife Helen. The trust has the discretion to sell the stock, with Helen's consent, and to reinvest in other securities, but any gain must not be currently distributed. Michael had bought the stock 3 years ago at $24 a share. At the time of the transfer it was worth $28 a share. On 2-15-77, the trustee sold the stock at $30 a share with Helen's consent. Both Michael and the trust are on the calendar year basis. Michael and Helen file joint returns. Helen had no income in 1977, but Michael had taxable income of $60,000. They have no tax preferences. Assuming the trust had no other income for the year, compute the trust's tax liability for 1977.

Problem 20-11

On 1-2-71, K. L. Lou set up an irrevocable trust, and transferred 10,000 shares of T. Y. Corp. 5% preferred stock (face value, $10 a share) to Greatneck Trust Co. as trustee. Under the trust terms, the trustee has the power to accumulate income, or pay all or part of it to K. L.'s friend, Mimi Williams, during her life as it sees fit. At her death, any accumulated income is to be paid as she directs by will, and the corpus is to be paid over to K. L.'s mother. The trustee's expenses and commissions are paid directly by K. L., and have not been charged against the trust income.

The trust has received $5,000 in dividends every year except 1973 when T. Y. paid no dividends. The trustee made no distribution in 1971, and in 1972 distributed only ½ the income. In other years, it distributed all the income it received. In 1977, the trustee distributed $16,000 to Mimi. Assuming that the tax rates for 1977 apply to all tax years:

(a) How much of the 1977 distribution is accumulated income?
(b) How much of the distribution should Mimi include in her 1977 income?

Problem 20-12

Johnny Graff retires on 12-31-83. He receives a lump-sum distribution of $150,000 from his company's qualified profit-sharing plan in which he has participated for 20 calendar years. During 1983, he also receives $19,000 in salary and $1,000 of interest on corporate bonds. His itemized deductions for 1983 are $4,000. His average taxable income for the period 1979-1982 is $14,000. Johnny is married. He and his wife are both 65 years old. They have no other income or deductions. Compute Johnny's lowest possible tax for 1983 before credits, assuming the tax rates then are the same as the 1977 rates.

Problem 20-13

The East Empire Bank maintains the Family Trust Fund as part of its services. The bank established this common trust fund for those of its depositors who want to assure income to their close relatives without the worry of choosing their own investments. Thomas Holt bought shares in the fund for his 2 teenage daughters. During the year, the fund has taxable income from capital gains, dividends and rents. How do the East Empire Bank and the Holt children report and pay the tax on the income of the trust fund?

SUPPLEMENTAL PROBLEMS

Problem 20-14

The terms of a trust, set up by the will of Kenneth Leighton, widower, who died in 1976, require that all trust income be distributed currently, ⅔ to his son,

Assignment 20—Problems

Lincoln, and ⅓ to his daughter, Mabel. Capital gains are allocated to corpus, and no special provision is made for depreciation. The trust earns income from an unincorporated business, domestic corporation stock, and municipal bonds. The trust, Lincoln and Mabel all file tax returns on the calendar year basis. The trustee elects to allocate to business income any expenses not directly attributable to a specific item. The trust had the following items of income and expenses of 1977:

Dividends from domestic corporations	$ 12,000
Interest on municipal bonds	7,000
Long-term capital gains	4,000
Income from business	45,000
Taxes and other expenses attributable to business	3,600
Trustee's commissions allocated to income	2,000
Trustee's commissions allocated to corpus	1,900
Depreciation	3,000

(a) Complete the following schedules, using above items:

Income Required to be Distributed Currently

Dividends .... $..........
Interest ....
Income from business ....

    Total .... $..........
Deductions:
    Expenses attributable to business .... $..........
    Trustee's commissions ....

Income required to be distributed currently .... $..........

Trust Distributable Net Income

Dividends .... $..........
Tax-exempt interest .... $..........
    Less: Expenses allocable to tax-exempt interest ....
Income from business ....

    Total .... $..........
Deductions:
    Expenses attributable to business .... $..........
    Trustee's commissions ....

    Distributable net income .... $..........

Deduction Allowable for Distributions

Distributable net income .... $..........
Less: Tax-exempt interest as adjusted for expenses ....

Deduction allowable for distributions .... $..........

Income Tax Payable by Trust

Dividends .... $..........
Interest ....
Income from business ....
Long-term capital gains ....

    Gross income .... $..........
Deductions:
    Business expenses .... $..........
    Trustee's commissions ....
    Capital gains deduction ....
    Distributions to beneficiaries ....
    Personal exemption ....

Taxable income .... $..........

Income tax payable by trust .... $..........

Amounts Allocable to Beneficiaries

	Dividends	Tax-exempt interest	Business income	Total
Income for trust accounting purposes	$	$	$	$
Less: Business expenses				
Trustee's commissions				
Total deductions				
Character of the amounts in the hands of the beneficiaries	$	$	$	$
Amount distributed to Lincoln	$	$	$	$
Amount distributed to Mabel	$	$	$	$

(b) Give a brief explanation of how the dividend exclusion and the deduction for depreciation are handled.

Problem 20-15

Charlie Sohn died in 1976. His will set up a testamentary trust. The trust instrument provides that one-half of the trust income is to be distributed currently to Mary John Sohn, widow of the deceased, for her life. The remaining trust income may, in the trustee's discretion, either be paid to Michael, the son of the deceased, or paid to designated charities, or accumulated. The trust is to terminate at the death of Mary Jane, and the principal will then be payable to Michael. The trust instrument makes no provision as to depreciation. It allocates capital gains to the principal account under state law. The trust and both beneficiaries file returns on the calendar year basis. The records of the trustee show the following items of income and deduction for 1977:

Rents	$50,000
Dividends of domestic corporations	10,000
Interest on Mott City Sewage Construction bonds	6,000
Interest on U.S. Treasury bonds issued after March 1, 1941	5,000
Long-term capital gains	20,000
Depreciation of rental property	8,000
Expenses attributable to rental property	14,000
Trustee's commissions allocable to income account	3,000
Trustee's commissions allocable to principal account	1,500

The trustee, after distributing one-half the income to Mary Jane, contributed one-fourth of the income to the Cancer Fund and distributed the remaining one-fourth to Michael. The trustee has elected to allocate to the rents any part of his commissions not required to be allocated to a specific item. He did not set up any depreciation reserve.

(a) Fill in the following schedules:

Income for Trust Accounting Purposes

Rents		$
Dividends		
Interest		
Total		$
Deductions:		
Rental expenses	$	
Trustee's commissions		$
Income for trust accounting purposes		$

Distributable Net Income

Rents			$
Dividends			
Taxable interest			
Tax-exempt interest		$	
Less: Trustee's commissions allocable thereto	$		
Charitable contributions allocable thereto			
Total			$

1978   **Assignment 20—Problems**   5169

Deductions:
  Rental expenses .... $ ....
  Trustee's commissions as adjusted ....
  Charitable deductions as adjusted ....
Distributable net income .... $ ....

Deduction Allowable for Distributions

Distributable net income .... $ ....
Less: Tax-exempt interest (as adjusted for expenses and contributions
    allocable thereto) ....
Deduction allowable for distributions .... $ ....

Character of Amounts Distributable to Beneficiaries and Contributed to Charity

	Rents	Dividends	Tax exempt Interest	Taxable Interest	Total
Trust income	$	$	$	$	$ ......
Less:					
Charitable contributions	......	......	......	......	......
Rental expenses	......	......	......	......	......
Trustee's commissions ...	......	......	......	......	......
Total deductions	......	......	......	......	......
Amounts distributable to beneficiaries	$	$	$	$	$ ......

Income Tax Payable by Trust

Rents .... $ ....
Dividends ....
Interest ....
Capital gains ....
  Gross income .... $ ....
Deductions:
  Rental expenses .... $ ....
  Trustee's commissions ....
  Fiduciary's portion of depreciation ....
  Charitable contributions ....
  Capital gains deductions ....
  Distributions to beneficiaries ....
  Personal exemption ....
Taxable income .... $ ....
Income tax payable by trust .... $ ....

(b) Mary Jane Sohn, widow of Charlie Sohn, is 54 years old. She has not remarried and lives with her son, Michael, whom she supports. Her only income during 1977 is the distribution from the trust. She paid $2,000 in property taxes, $500 in state and local income taxes and donated $1,500 to churches and public hospitals in 1977. What is her (1) tax table income? (Round off all items to whole dollars); (2) tax liability?

★ Problem 20-16 ★

Phil Hall and his sister are the beneficiaries of a simple trust. This year the trust's distributable net income was $40,000 and its income was $48,000.

The trust provided that Phil is to receive 80% of its income and his sister, 20%. How much, if any, income received from the trust during the year is taxable to Phil?

Problem 20-17

Paul Jacky was the owner of a half interest in a partnership formed in 1973. The partnership agreement provides that it will make no distributions until 1978. For the fiscal year ending 8-31-77, the partnership had $50,000 taxable income from X-ray equipment rentals.

In 1974, Paul transferred Pierre Motel Co. stock to a trust that provided for income payable to his friend, Rose Pearlsun, for 12 years, with the corpus to return to him. On 1-23-77, he transferred Princetone Machine Co. stock to the same trust. During the trust's fiscal year ending on 7-31-77, the trust received $3,000 in dividends from Pierre, and $2,500 from Princetone.

In July of 1977, Paul's home was completely destroyed by fire. He died of severe burns on September 15, his 65th birthday, as a result of the fire. He had bought his home in 1953 for $35,000. It was worth $40,000 at the time of the fire. His hospital and doctor bills were $3,400, and his drug bills were $470. The executor paid these out of the estate the following June. Paul had no insurance of any kind.

Paul was divorced and had no dependents. His only income in 1977 was $20,000 interest on corporate bonds he owned. In 1977, he paid real property taxes of $800. Compute on a return filed for the decedent (1) **tax table income**; (2) **tax liability**.

Cumulative Problem 20-18

When Sam Martin, a childless widower, 73 years old, died on April 30 of this year, he left an estate consisting of a life insurance policy payable to his estate, a rooming house, 300 shares of Domestic Corporation stock and an $8,000 account in the Crestwood Savings Bank. Sam was a cash basis-calendar year taxpayer. He died without a will, and the probate court immediately appointed Marshall Henry as administrator to handle the assets, locate the heirs and distribute the estate.

On inspection of Sam's accounts, Marshall noticed that Sam's income had always come from investments. His wife who died 5 years ago, never worked during their marriage. Marshall also found that Sam had paid $350 for repairs and maintenance, and $650 in realty taxes on the rooming house. He collected $3,600 in rents. He gave his church $300, and paid $4,200 in state income, sales, property and gasoline taxes during the year. He received a net short-term capital gain of $13,540, a month before he died. Interest credited on the Crestwood Savings account was $110.

The administrator deposited the $20,000 check he received from the life insurance company in a special account paying 5% interest. This account earned $750 in interest for the year.

Sam had bought the rooming house on 1-1-67 for $27,000. $17,000 was allocated to the building and $10,000 to the land. The building had an estimated useful life of 20 years and a salvage value of $2,000. Sam was taking depreciation on a straight line basis. The official state appraiser valued the property as of April 30 of this year, giving a fair market value of $18,000 to the house and $10,000 to the land. The appraiser informed Marshall that the building then had a useful life of 10 years with no salvage value. Marshall decided to follow Sam's method of depreciation. From May 1 to October 31, Marshall collected $5,400 in rents and paid $875 real estate taxes. Marshall got a good offer and sold the house on November 1 of this year for $30,000 ($20,000 building, $10,000 land).

Marshall sold the Domestic Corporation stock on July 10 for $36 a share. Sam had paid $20 per share in 1974. On 12-31-76, it was selling on the stock exchange at $34 a share, and on 4-30-77, at $35 a share. Selling expense totaled $30. The first dividend of 50 cents a share was paid in June to Marshall.

The Crestwood Savings account earned $225 from May 1 to the end of the year. In June, Marshall paid a doctor's bill for $56. Sam had incurred this expense during his final illness in April. In December, Marshall paid administration expenses of $1,235.

Marshall continues filing tax returns on a calendar year basis. The estate is exempt from federal estate tax.

(a) What income tax return or returns will the administrator, Marshall Henry file for this year?

(b) Figure for the required return or returns (1) the decedent's tax table income; (2) the estate's tax liability.

Research Problem 20-19

Lou Brother bought 1,000 shares of the C. K. Dog Food Co. stock for $10,000 in 1975. In November 1976, he worked out a deal to sell his stock to Willie Terry for $20,000. The contract required Lou to put the stock in escrow pending the closing, and obligated Willie to pay $1,000 damage in case of his default. Lou died in December, 1976, but his estate completed the deal 5 weeks later.

A member of the Brother family has suggested to the estate to use a stepped-up basis in this deal under Code Section 1014(a). If the estate follows this advice, it would realize no gain since the stock was worth $20,000 at the time Lou died. The executor of the estate, however, has asked you, a tax expert, to check this out. What would you advise?

1. To find the answer, use the Prentice-Hall Complete Federal Tax Equipment in your school or local library. Give your answer fully explained. In it, show authorities, citing law and opinions applicable, and the P-H Federal Tax Equipment paragraphs where they may be found.

2. Enumerate and explain carefully every step you take in reaching your result. These are extremely important—just as important as the conclusion itself.

Master Review Problem 20-20

By his will, Ronald Change who died on 7-1-68, created a trust under which the beneficiaries are his widow, Edith, and his children Nelson and Shelley. Ronald's children share one-quarter each in the income of the trust, and his widow receives one-half of the income.

The trustee has the power to sell or exchange the trust assets but is required to accumulate the gain from such sales (under local law such gains are allocable to trust corpus). All other income is distributable currently to the beneficiaries. The trust is on a calendar year basis and its books are kept on the cash basis. The executor valued the estate as of the date of death of the testator. The trust instrument makes no allocation of the deduction for depreciation. Expenses for the operation of the trust are payable from income.

Following are the pertinent items of property transferred to the trust (assuming no gift tax was paid on any of the transfers and straight-line depreciation was used whenever applicable):

On 7-1-65, Ronald had received a patent on a tide-reading clock. He had immediately assigned the use of the clock covered by the patent to the Schelling Hardware Co. for an annual royalty of $2,150. On 7-1-68, the patent had a fair market value of $15,000 and a remaining useful life of 15 years. The trust continued to receive the royalties after Ronald died.

On 7-1-77, the trust sold for $68,000 (including land) an office building on which it had collected $6,400 rent for the tax year. Selling expenses were $500. On 7-1-68, the land had a market value of $12,000, and the building had a market value of $58,000 with an estimated useful life of 40 years and no salvage value. The expenses connected with the building for 1977 were: repairs to a boiler, $135; Property taxes, $2,300; heating, $900; insurance, $425; electricity, $70; superintendent's salary, $1,250.

Ronald had bought 200 shares of N. C. Diner Co. common stock on 9-16-67 for $14,500. On the day he died the shares had a market value of $12,300. The trustee sold the 200 shares on 4-27-77 for $12,000. Commissions on the sale were $98.

The trustee on 6-27-77 sold for $17,525 an entire lot of 100 shares of L.S.F. Corp. preferred stock which Ronald had bought on 5-2-68 for $13,500. On the day he died, the shares had a market value of $13,700. Commissions on the sale were $150.

Ronald had bought a Seaboard Corp. bond in 1966 for $250. The bond had a market value of $200 on the date of his death but became completely worthless on 2-19-77.

The books of the trust disclose the following for 1977:

	Debit	Credit
Dividends from taxable domestic corporations		$6,000
Interest on bank deposits		145
Interest on $4,000 U.S. Treasury 3¾% bonds issued 1-1-60		2,150
Interest on bonds of the Larchmont Gas Corp.		400
Legal fees	860	
Accounting fees for preparing tax returns	255	
Rent paid for office space	770	
Wages of part-time clerical worker	1,100	
Insurance of office equipment	220	
Miscellaneous office expenses (stationery, telephone, light, etc.)	635	
Safe deposit box fees (for securities)	50	
Trustee's commission (as provided in the instrument)	1,435	
State stamp taxes paid in connection with security transactions	16	

On 2-15-77, the trust sold for $2,200 ten shares of Cedric William Corporation common stock that it had bought on 1-11-77 for $1,900. Sales commission was $24.

On 12-2-77, the trustee bought out of the trust funds 2 new typewriters for $490 to be used in connection with his trust business. They were stolen a week later before he could use them. The property was not recovered and the trustee collected only $300 from insurance.

The trust held a parking lot from which it collected $17,400 rentals in 1977. It paid rent collection expenses of $2,600 and property taxes of $6,860.

On the basis of the above data, fill in the following schedules.

Schedule 1
Part I—Gains and Losses From Sales or Exchange of Capital Assets

Short-term Capital Gains and Losses—Assets held not more than 9 months

1. Kind of property	2. Date acquired	3. Date Sold	4. Gross Sales Price	5. Depreciation since Acquisition	6. Cost or Other basis and Expense of Sale	7. Gain or Loss (4 plus 5 less 6)
1.	....	....	$	$	$	$ ....
....	....	....	....	....	....	....
2. Net short-term gain or loss						$

Long-term Capital Gains and Losses—Assets held more than 9 months

3. Gain from Part II			$	$	$	$ ....
....	....	....	....	....	....	....
....	....	....	....	....	....	....
4. Net long-term gain or loss						$

	1. Beneficiaries	2. Fiduciary	3. Total
5. Enter net short-term gain or loss from line 2	$	$	$ ....
6. Enter net long-term gain or loss from line 4	....	....	....
7. Total net gain or loss	$	$	$

Computation of Fiduciary's Capital Gains Deduction

8. Long-term capital gain shown on line 6, column 3, above .... $..................
9. Short-term capital loss shown on line 5, column 3, above ....
10. Excess of line 8 over line 9, above .... $..................
11. Long-term capital gains taxable to beneficiaries ....
12. Balance line 10 minus line 11 .... $..................
13. Long-term capital gain deduction (50% of line 12) .... $..................

Part II—Gain From Disposition of Depreciable Property

1. Kind of property	2. Date acq.	3. Date sold	4. Gross sales price	5. Cost or other basis and expense of sale
14.	....	....	....	....
....	....	....	....	....
....	....	....	....	....

6. Depreciation since acquisition	7. Adjusted basis	8. Total gain	9. Ordinary gain	10. Other gain
....	....	....	....	....
....	....	....	....	....
....	....	....	....	....

15. Total ordinary gain. Enter here and in column 7, line 17, Part III ....
16. Total other gain. Enter here and in column 7, line 3, Part I; however, if the gains do not exceed the losses when this amount is combined with other gains and losses from section 1231 property, enter the total of column 10 in column 7, line 17, Part III ....

Part III—Property Other Than Capital Assets

	1. Kind of property	2. Date acq.	3. Date sold	4. Gross sales price	5. Depreciation since acq.	6. Cost or other basis, and expense of sale	7. Gain or loss
17.	....	....	....	....	....	....	....
	....	....	....	....	....	....	
18.	Net gain (or loss). Enter here and on line 5, Schedule 3						

Schedule 2
Depreciation Schedule

Kind of Property	Date acq.	Cost or other basis	Dep. allowed (or allowable) prior yrs.	Method	Rate (%) or life (years)	Dep. for this year
....	....	$	$	....	....	$ ....
....	....	....	....	....	....	....

Schedule 3
Computation of Tax Liability of Trust

Income

1. Dividends .... $ ....
2. Interest ....
3. Gross rents and royalties ....
4. Net gain or loss from sale of capital assets ....
5. Net gain or loss from property other than capital assets ....
6. Total income .... $ ....

Deductions

7. Taxes (Itemize below) .... $ ....
8. Other deductions (Itemize below) ....
9. Deduction for distributions to beneficiaries ....
10. Long-term capital gain deduction ....
11. Dividend exclusion ....
12. Exemption ....
13. Total .... $ ....
14. Taxable income of fiduciary ....
15. Tax payable ....

Explanation of Deduction Claimed on Lines 7 and 8

Line No.	Explanation	Amount	Line No.	Explanation	Amount
....	....	....	....	....	....
....	....	....	....	....	....
....	....	....	....	....	....
....	....	....	....	....	....

Tax Reasoning Problem 20-21

Roger Keenon fully supports his 75-year old Aunt Minnie. In 1977, he paid $3,800 for her support. Minnie has no income other than social security. Keenon is in the 50% income tax bracket. He would thus have to earn $7,600 to pay his aunt's support for the year. He is allowed a dependency exemption for her, but this only saves him $410 in 1977 tax ($35 credit for exemption plus 50% of $750). What taxwise moves would you advise Keenon to take in order for him, in effect, to earn $3,800 to give $3,800?

ASSIGNMENT No. 21

CORPORATIONS

NORMAL TAX AND SURTAX, INCOME, DEDUCTIONS

(Note: In the following problems assume that the "tax year" is the calendar year 1977, unless otherwise specified. In figuring all your answers, round off all amounts to the nearest whole dollar.)

Problem 21-1

Seven small hotel owners in Funn City agree to form Hotel Management Association to increase their profits by reducing their vacant room time. Under the agreement, each owner transfers all his assets to the Association, except the land and building, and receives a share in the association in proportion to the number of rooms in his hotel. The association establishes general standards for all the hotels through a committee of 4 elected annually by all the members, but each hotel is operated by its owner, who is responsible for any negligence on his premises and also for any unpaid debts of the association. The proceeds of operation are deposited in an association bank account from which all expenses are paid. Each owner's share of the profits is distributed to him twice a year.

Under the agreement, the association cannot be dissolved except by a vote of 5 members, and no member can transfer his share except to another member. However, state law provides that any person who cannot recover his investment in a solvent business organization may sue for the dissolution of the organization.

Is the Hotel Management Association taxable as a corporation?

Problem 21-2

Kapon Trucking, Inc., a domestic corporation, had gross income of $92,000 this year that included taxable dividends of $3,500 from another domestic corporation. During the year, the company had the following expenses and allowances:

Salaries	$16,000
Rent	5,200
Advertising	350
Taxes	950
Interest	2,300
Depreciation	3,975
Miscellaneous business expenses	650

Figure the corporation's normal tax and surtax liability.

Problem 21-3

The Hewmatt Mattress Corporation had gross income of $42,840 and itemized deductions of $7,280 for the current tax year. Included in gross income were $8,600 of cash dividends from domestic corporations. The corporation also had tax preferences of $35,450. This is the first year it has ever had tax preferences.

(a) Compute the corporation's tax liability for the current year.
(b) Must Hewmatt file Form 4626, Computation of Minimum Tax?

Problem 21-4

Matt and Dan Horn, brothers, are co-owners of Copper Crafts, Inc. Each has a basis of $40,000 for his stock. Two years ago, the corporation needed cash so Matt and Dan assessed themselves $16,000 each. On January 2, 1977, Matt sold his stock for $95,000 and contributed the gain on this sale to Copper Crafts. The corporation bought new machinery in July for $12,000. In August, Matt contributed a computer worth $6,200 to the corporation. On January 1, 1978, Copper Crafts has the following assets in addition to the new machinery and computer:

	Fair Market Value	Basis
Land (bought 3/74)	$22,000	$16,000
Building (bought 3/74)	26,000	14,000
Equipment (bought 3/74)	5,000	2,000
Certified pollution control facility	8,000	5,000

What is the corporation's bases of all its assets on 1-1-78?

Problem 21-5

Kandroth, Inc., a corporation organized by 12 individuals (all equal stockholders), built and operated bowling alleys. Several years ago, Kandroth needed additional operating funds which it raised through a bond issue. To pay the debt, Kandroth created a sinking fund trust. Last year, Kandroth leased all of their buildings to Max Million. Max agreed to pay $1,500 monthly rent to the corporation and $1,500 a month directly to the corporation's stockholders ($125 monthly to each). The corporation set aside $750 of the monthly rent to defray expenses and gave the remaining $750 to the trustee of the sinking fund, who invested it in various securities. This year, the stockholders and the corporation received $18,000 each under the lease terms; in addition, the sinking fund trust earned $2,000 from investments. What amounts do the corporation and the stockholders include in their returns?

Problem 21-6

In 1977, Worldwide Art, a domestic corporation, had gross profits of $625,000 and deductible expenses of $845,000. It also received the following dividends during the year: (1) $32,500 from stock in Paradise Developers, a real estate investment trust; (2) $47,000 paid out of the earnings and profits of African Artwork, a foreign corporation whose income is 100% effectively connected with a U.S. business and whose stock is wholly owned by Worldwide Art; (3) $210,000 from preferred stock of Western Gas and Electric, a U.S. public utility ($150,000 from stock issued in 1940 for which the utility was allowed a dividends paid deduction, and $60,000 from stock issued in 1968); and (4) $119,500 from 200 shares of Indian Art Importers stock, a domestic corporation (Worldwide bought this stock 3-25-77, 6 days before the dividend record date, and sold it on 4-7-77).
(a) What is Worldwide Art's total income tax for 1977?
(b) What would your answer be if Worldwide Art had been able to increase its deductible expenses by $689 in 1977?

Problem 21-7

Sudamer Pottery, Inc., a Western Hemisphere Trade Corporation, had 1976 taxable income of $48,000 before deducting charitable contributions or the WHTC deduction. Sudamer had no capital gains or losses for 1976 and no net operating loss or capital loss carryovers from previous years, but it did contribute $7,650 to the Red Cross.
(a) What, if any, was Sudamer's WHTC deduction and charitable contribution deduction for 1976?
(b) In 1977, Sudamer had taxable income of $62,500 before deducting charitable contributions or the WHTC deduction. It also had no capital gains or losses and made no charitable contributions for the year. What deductions, if any, is Sudamer entitled to for 1977?

Problem 21-8

In 1977, Pollution-Free Products, Inc., had the following transactions:
(a) The company received $115,000 as the subscription price on the original issue of 1,000 shares of its stock. The par value is $110 per share.
(b) The company sold 200 shares of its own treasury stock for $120 per share. The stock had been reacquired from shareholders at a cost of $117 per share.
(c) The company exchanged 300 shares of its own treasury stock which had been reacquired from shareholders at a cost of $35,100 for a building with a fair market value of $37,000.

(d) The company exchanged a building with an adjusted basis of $30,000 for 250 shares of its own stock with a fair market value of $135 per share. The building had been used in its business for 15 years and had been depreciated under the straight line method.

(e) The company transferred to Jayne Georgetown, in lieu of 3 months salary, 50 shares of its own treasury stock with a fair market value of $120 per share which had been repurchased from shareholders at a cost of $110 per share.

What is the gain or loss, if any, recognized to the corporation from these transactions?

Problem 21-9

The Clean-Air Ecology Corp. issued $500,000 of its 50-year bonds for $650,000 on Dec. 31, 1957. On July 1, 1977, the corporation issued new bonds with a face value of $580,000 for which it received $560,000. These were 20-year bonds. Then, on Dec. 31, 1977, the corporation took $515,000 of this money, added $60,000 from cash surplus, and bought up the bonds it had issued in 1957.

(a) What is the taxable income or deductible expense to the corporation on the issuance of the 1957 bonds, and how is it treated? On the issuance of the 1977 bonds?

(b) What is the taxable income or deductible expense to the corporation on the repurchase of the 1957 bonds, and how is it treated?

Problem 21-10

On 10-1-72, the Anide Corp. issued and sold $850,000 of its 8% bonds, due 5 years from the date, receiving in payment $820,000. On 4-1-77, the corporation redeemed one-half of these bonds for $423,000, with interest on the bonds being paid for $1/3$ of the year. What deductions for interest and discount can the corporation take for 1977?

Problem 21-11

Jim Harris owns 10% of Able Corp. stock and 23% of Baker Corp. stock. Able Corp. owns 7% of Baker Corp. stock worth $15,000, with an adjusted basis of $18,000. All other shareholders of the corporations are unrelated individuals and no one person owns more than 25% of the stock of any corporation. Able Corp. has been accumulating earnings for expansion at the rate of $75,000 a year for 2 years. Able sold its Baker Corp. stock to Harris for $4,000. Harris immediately transferred this stock to Baker Corp. in exchange for land worth $19,500. Baker Corp.'s adjusted basis for the land was $16,000.

What is the gain or loss realized by Harris on the exchange with Baker Corp.?

Problem 21-12

At the beginning of 1977, Kiddie Car Industries, Inc. consisted of the following assets: land and buildings with an adjusted basis of $100,000 (land—$20,000; buildings—$80,000); machinery with an adjusted basis of $11,000 (bought on 1-2-73 for $19,000); furniture and fixtures with an adjusted basis of $2,500 (bought in 1974 for $4,000) and $9,500 cash on hand. On 1-2-77, Kiddie Car adopted a plan of complete liquidation. Assuming that it is neither a collapsible corporation nor a controlled subsidiary and that all necessary filing requirements are met, would Kiddie Car have any recognized gain under the following different situations:

(a) On 6-1-77, Kiddie Car sold all its assets (land, buildings, machinery, furniture and fixtures) at their respective adjusted bases to a competitor for $113,500. On 9-1-77, it distributed the sale proceeds plus the $9,500 cash on hand to its stockholders.

(b) On 6-1-77, Kiddie Car sold its machinery to a competitor for $12,500 and gave its furniture and fixtures to a creditor in settlement of a debt. Kiddie Car had owed the creditor $2,500. On 7-1-77, Kiddie Car sold its land and buildings for $100,000. On 9-1-77, it distributed the sale proceeds plus the $9,500 cash on hand to its stockholders.

(c) On 6-1-77, a fire destroyed all of Kiddie Car's buildings, machinery, furniture and fixtures. Insurance proceeds received totaled $275,000. On 8-1-77, the land was sold for $20,000. On 9-1-77, the corporation distributed the insurance and sale proceeds (assume they did not represent any recapture of depreciation) plus the cash on hand to its stockholders.

(d) Assume the facts as in (c) above except that Kiddie Car retained $4,000 in cash to pay a creditor. The creditor finally asked for and received payment in February, 1978.

Problem 21-13

Danah Corp., a cosmetics manufacturer, is a calendar year taxpayer that has always distributed all earnings and profits to its shareholders. This year, for the first time, it has accumulated profits, instead of distributing them as dividends, in order to meet the following objectives:

1. $50,000 accumulated to purchase 100% of the stock of a competing corporation whose products can be merged into Danah's line of products.
2. $20,000 accumulated to loan the president's son, a 3% stockholder, to set up his own business.
3. $15,000 accumulated to redeem enough of the president's stock after he dies to pay the estate taxes.
4. $50,000 accumulated to build up their inventory to have enough items on hand to fill orders without delay.
5. $35,000 accumulated to purchase bonds of the Araby Oil Co. to be held as an investment.
6. $110,000 accumulated to construct a new factory with construction due to start next year. The corporation now rents a building which is inadequate for its needs.

As a result of the accumulating, Danah has an adjusted taxable income for 1977 of $280,000 (it was $30,000 the year before). Danah had no capital gains, either this year or last, and paid no dividends this year. However, it did pay $70,000 in dividends in January 1978.

(a) Which, if any, of the above six objectives constitute reasonable grounds for accumulating surplus? Which, if any, are unreasonable?

(b) How much accumulated earnings tax, if any, does Danah Corp. have to pay?

Problem 21-14

Midway Mills, Inc., a calendar year corporation, had accumulated earnings and profits of $185,000 at the end of 1976. On 2-17-77, it distributed a taxable dividend of $130,000. In 1977, Midway's long-term capital gain, minus the tax attributable to such gain, totalled $15,000. Midway also retained $55,000 of its 1977 earnings and profits for reasonable business needs. What, if any, is Midway's accumulated earnings credit for 1977?

Problem 21-15

Wetmath Corp. is not a personal holding company, but is unreasonably accumulating surplus. The following facts relate to the tax year 1977:
1. Taxable income, $340,800.
2. Dividends received from taxable domestic corporations, $30,000.
3. Dividends paid in 1977, $62,500.
4. Consent dividends, $3,800.
5. Dividends paid on 3-1-78, $4,450.
6. Charitable contributions, $23,116 of which $16,600 was allowed in computing the corporation income tax.
7. Accumulated earnings credit, $7,850.
8. Net capital loss for 1977, $4,100.

(a) Compute the corporation's income tax and accumulated earnings tax.

(b) How could Wetmath Corp. avoid the accumulated earnings tax for 1977?

Problem 21-16

(a) The Matthews Light Corp., a manufacturer of decorator lamps and lighting fixtures, retained earnings totalling $245,000 for 1977 and allocated these earnings among the four following accounts:

(1) $75,000 into an account for the construction of a new warehouse next to its manufacturing plant. (The company now rents a warehouse several miles away that is inadequate for its needs.) Construction is scheduled to begin in the spring of 1978.

(2) $25,000 is accumulated to build up an inventory of products so that enough items will be on hand to fill orders without delay.

(3) $30,000 is set aside to buy out all the stock of Imaginative Lighting, Inc., a competitor which deals in fixtures that can be merged into Matthews' line of products.

(4) $115,000 into an account to buy bonds of Northern Airlines to be held as investment by the corporation.

Would any of the above accumulations subject the Matthews Light Corp. to an accumulated earnings tax for 1977? Explain.

(b) Assuming that any unreasonable accumulations in (a) above are equal to the corporation's accumulated taxable income for 1977, what would be Matthews' accumulated earnings tax for the year?

Problem 21-17

(a) The Circe Corp., a Pennsylvania corporation with 11 stockholders, was incorporated on January 2, 1977. All the stockholders are U. S. citizens. One of them resides in Rome, Italy. Circe Corp. has only one class of stock with 50,000 shares issued and outstanding. Nine of the stockholders own 5,000 shares each. The remaining two stockholders, John and Jane Miller, are married and own 5,000 shares as joint tenants. Assuming all filing requirements are met, may Circe Corp. elect to be treated as a Subchapter S corporation?

(b) Assuming the same facts as in (a) above, and that a valid election was made, may Circe Corp. continue its election under each of the following different circumstances:

(1) During the year, the Millers receive a final decree of divorce and in the property settlement each is awarded 2,500 shares of Circe stock.

(2) In August, one of the stockholders dies and bequeaths all his Circe stock to an educational trust fund (not a grantor or a voting trust) which holds the stock for the rest of the year.

(3) The Millers sell their stock on the open market. Herbert Jones buys all the shares on June 15, and by August 15 has not acted to terminate the election.

(4) Three of Circe's stockholders decide to form a partnership. In September they transfer ownership of all their individual stockholdings to their partnership.

(5) The Millers sell 3,000 of their shares to a neighbor.

(6) On December 15, the Millers sell 3,000 of their shares to one of Circe's other stockholders.

(7) Gross receipts from sales through November, 1977, total $68,000. On December 15, Circe unexpectedly receives $25,000 in dividends from stock it owns. Gross receipts from sales during December, 1977, total $12,000.

Problem 21-18

Ruth Dana, a high income taxpayer, was asked by three friends to help provide investment capital for a new business. While Dana did not necessarily want to profit from the deal, she also did not want to lose her investment. However, her friends assured her of tax benefits for the company's first few years. On 1-2-75, Dana and her three friends each contributed $50,000 to form Energy Savers, Inc., a calendar year-cash basis corporation, and elected Subchapter S tax treatment. The corporation had net operating losses in the first two years: $100,000 in 1975 and $20,000 in 1976. For 1977, Energy Savers anticipated high earnings. Its undistributed taxable income for 1977 was $140,000. Dana, who wants to avoid a higher tax bracket, sells her stock on 6-30-77 for $50,000, her original investment.

(a) Assuming no dividend distributions were made during 1977, what would Dana's tax consequences be for each of her three years as an Energy Savers stockholder?

(b) Would your answer to (a) be different if Dana had sold her stock on 3-31-77? On 12-30-77?

Problem 21-19

(a) The Ronan Co. has been an electing small business corporation since January, 1975. Joshua Ronan has always been its sole shareholder. In 1975, the company had a net operating loss of $10,000. In 1976, the company had taxable income of $40,000, none of which was distributed. In February, 1977, the company made a $27,000 distribution to Joshua. What is Joshua's net share of previously taxed income immediately after the distribution?

(b) The Baker Co., an electing small business corporation since 1968, has four equal shareholders. For 1977, it has $80,000 in taxable income and current earnings and profits. For 1977, Baker had an excess of $100,000 of net long-term capital gain over net short-term capital loss. At the beginning of the year Baker had substantial accumulated earnings and profits. During the year it distributed $25,000 to each of the shareholders. Mr. Blue, one of the shareholders, reports the $25,000 as long-term capital gain on his 1977 return. Was he correct? Explain your answer.

Problem 21-20

Matthew Douglass plans to start his own business manufacturing and selling plastic items. He had been a sales manager in this field for many years, and is sure former customers will give their business to his new company. Consequently, he estimates that the average annual taxable income from the business will amount to about $125,000. However, the income is expected to vary widely in future years. Douglass wants to use most of the profits for business expansion. He can live comfortably on $45,000 a year, using the remainder of the business income (after taxes) for expansion purposes. He has three grown children who are in professional careers and not interested in working in the business. Douglass is 55, and plans to sell the business and retire at age 65. His wife has no income of her own.

Douglass wants to know whether it would be better for him to operate as a corporation or as a sole proprietor. What would you call to his attention to help him reach a decision?

Consider these questions:

(a) Would there be an over-all tax saving or tax loss the first year of operation (1977) if Douglass operates the business as a corporation? How much? In answering this question, assume the following: taxable business income is $125,000; Douglass will pay himself a salary of $45,000 if he operates the business as a corporation ($125,000 taxable income less $45,000 salary, resulting in taxable income of $80,000 for the corporation and $45,000 to Douglass as an individual); the corporation will not pay any dividends; Douglass has no other income, files a joint return, has no dependents, and does not itemize deductions.

(b) Mention the major tax advantages to Douglass if he operates the business as a corporation under the facts discussed above.

(c) Mention the major tax pitfalls or potential dangers of Douglass' operating his business as a corporation.

(d) Mention two tax advantages Douglass would gain by operating as a corporation and electing Subchapter S tax treatment.

Problem 21-21

The books of M & D, Inc., a domestic corporation, show the following for the current year:

Assignment 21—Problems

Income:			
Gross sales			$2,824,250
Cost of goods sold	$2,365,250		
Sales returns and allowances	86,250	2,451,500	
Gross profit from sales			$372,750
Interest income:			
State of New York bonds		$ 700	
Interest on federal tax refund		325	1,025
Dividend income:			
Bandana, Inc. stock		$ 1,900	
Royal China, Ltd. stock		2,150	4,050
Gain from sale of business machine purchased in 1954 (no post-'61 depreciation)			1,525
Total income			$379,350
Expenses and losses:			
Contributions to qualified charities		$ 11,000	
Insurance premium on policy on life of officer with M & D as beneficiary		2,350	
Depreciation		19,623	
Loss on sale of Bandana, Inc. stock purchased in 1970 for investment		3,250	
Other expenses (deductible items such as wages, salaries, repairs, rent, etc.)		249,327	285,550
Net income before federal income taxes			$93,800

During the current tax year, M & D distributed $36,500 in cash dividends from current earnings and profits and had an increase in retained earnings from $13,153 to $38,249. Its 1977 federal income taxes are $36,204, but it had a $4,000 refund of prior year's federal income tax. M & D was allowed $17,098 in depreciation for income tax purposes. M & D's only investments are in Bandana, Inc. stock, a U.S. domestic corporation, and in Royal China, Ltd., a British corporation that does not do business in the U.S. and is not subject to U.S. federal income tax.

  (a) Compute M & D's taxable income for the current tax year.
  (b) On the basis of the information given, fill in the following schedules:

Schedule M–1 Reconciliation of Income Per Books With Income Per Return

1. Net income per books . . . .
2. Federal income tax . . . .
3. Excess of capital losses over capital gains . . . .
4. Income subject to tax not recorded on books this year (itemize)

5. Expenses recorded on books this year not deducted in this return (itemize)
   (a) Depreciation . . . . $
   (b) Depletion . . . . . $

6.   Total of lines 1 through 5 . . . . .

7. Income recorded on books this year not included in this return (itemize)
   (a) Tax-exempt interest $

8. Deductions in this tax return not charged against book income this year (itemize)
   (a) Depreciation . . $
   (b) Depletion . . $

9.   Total of lines 7 and 8 . . . .
10. Income ———————line 6 less 9 .

Schedule M–2 Analysis of Unappropriated Retained Earnings Per Books

1. Balance at beginning of year . . . .
2. Net income per books . . . .
3. Other increases (itemize)

4.   Total of lines 1, 2, and 3 . . . . . .

5. Distributions: (a) Cash . . . . . .
             (b) Stock . . . . . .
             (c) Property . . . . .
6. Other decreases (itemize)

7.   Total of lines 5 and 6 . . . . .
8. Balance at end of year (line 4 less 7) . . .

★★ Problem 21-22 ★★

On 3-1-77, the Atlas Machinery Corp. leased some land it owned. Annual rent was $2,400. It received a full year's rent at that time.

The Atlas Machinery Corp. owns a patent on a computerized pollution control adjuster. During 1977, it leased the patent to another corporation and received $3,200 in royalties.

Atlas keeps a separate account for "Discount on Purchases" and in its federal income tax returns makes a practice of including the item as "Other Income" rather than as an offset to the cost of purchases. For 1977, the amount shown by the books was $2,508.

In 1977, a suit was started against Atlas to recover a $12,000 balance on a contract for goods delivered. Atlas contends that the goods were not up to standard and it is entitled to a reduction in the contract price. When the suit was started, Atlas deposited $12,000 with an escrow holder, agreed upon with the supplier, pending the outcome of the trial. The case will probably not be tried until 1979.

In addition to the interest on various government bonds and income tax refund (see Problem 2-16), the following interest accrued to the benefit of the Atlas Machinery Corp. in 1977:

	Principal	Interest
Bank deposits	$22,000	$1,540
Bonds of the Clark Corp.	40,000	2,600
Mortgages	37,000	1,800

On 7-1-69, the Atlas Machinery Corp. issued for $110,000, twenty-five year bonds having a face value of $100,000. $20,000 of the bonds were redeemed in 1976. $30,000 were redeemed on 1-1-77 for $29,000 (include as other income the gain on the redemption and amortization of the bonds still outstanding).

During the year, Atlas donated $5,000 to a private operating foundation. Atlas' taxable income (without any contribution deduction, special deductions or net operating loss carryback) in 1977 was $273,552.

Fill in the following schedules:

Gross Income
Interest on loans, notes, mortgages, bonds, bank deposits, etc. ....
Rents ....
Royalties ....
Other income (state nature) ....

Deductions
Contributions ....
Other deductions ....

★★ Problem 21-23 ★★

At the close of business on 12-31-76, the Atlas Machinery Corp.'s books showed a surplus of $249,486. The corporation's income statement for 1977 showed that the net income for the year was $124,575. Its taxable income (before special deductions and net operating loss deduction) for 1977 was $268,552.

During the year, the corporation received $180 in interest on a $3,000 refund of a prior year's federal income tax. It also properly accrued the following interest:

U.S. Treasury 2½% bonds, issued in June, 1947	$ 250
Non-taxable industrial development bonds	475
Bonds of the State of Ohio	300
City of Tampa bonds	500

In its income statement for 1977, the corporation showed the following expenses not allowed as deductions on its income tax return:

Reserve for anticipated expenses	$ 800
Capital expenditure (under income tax law)	1,975

Payments labeled compensation to Mrs. George Hunt, a 40% stockholder not active at all in the business	30,000
Interest paid to carry tax-exempt bonds	200

In 1977, the corporation received $400 for January and February 1978 rental on land.

In 1977, the corporation paid cash dividends of $100,000. Its federal income tax expense per books was $111,877.

Fill in the following reconciliation schedules:

Schedule M–1 Reconciliation of Income Per Books With Income Per Return

1 Net income per books		7 Income recorded on books this year not included in this return (itemize)	
2 Federal income tax		(a) Tax-exempt interest $	
3 Excess of capital losses over capital gains			
4 Income subject to tax not recorded on books this year (itemize)			
		8 Deductions in this tax return not charged against book income this year (itemize)	
5 Expenses recorded on books this year not deducted in this return (itemize)		(a) Depreciation $	
(a) Depreciation $		(b) Depletion $	
(b) Depletion $			
		9 Total of lines 7 and 8	
6 Total of lines 1 through 5		10 Income ———— line 6 less 9	

Schedule M–2 Analysis of Unappropriated Retained Earnings Per Books

1 Balance at beginning of year		5 Distributions: (a) Cash	
2 Net income per books		(b) Stock	
3 Other increases (itemize)		(c) Property	
		6 Other decreases (itemize)	
		7 Total of lines 5 and 6	
4 Total of lines 1, 2, and 3		8 Balance at end of year (line 4 less 7)	

Cumulative Problem 21-24
(Answer (a), (b) or (c) as directed)

(a) Thomas Frank, 76, is the owner of 75% of the stock of Electroil Heating Systems, Inc., an electing small business corporation. In 1977, the corporation had a gross profit from sales of $120,500 and received $2,500 in dividends from domestic corporations. Interest received from bonds of the Rocky Mts. Oil Corp. amounted to $650.

On 4-1-76, the corporation issued and sold at par $200,000 of first mortgage bonds. The market price of the bonds declined steadily, and on 10-15-76, the corporation bought the entire issue in the market for $90,000. The corporation elected to exclude the gain from gross income.

The following expenses were incurred in 1977:

Interest paid	$ 4,260
Bad debts charged off	8,000
Rent for warehouse	6,400
Social security and unemployment taxes	6,790
Officers' salaries	38,000
Clerical and sales salaries	37,000
Real property taxes	2,660
Depreciation on equipment	11,000

On 10-15-77, the corporation sold land for $361,000 to Hope-for-the-Handicapped, Inc., a tax-exempt organization, organized and controlled by Electroil Heating Systems. This was the same land against which the mortgage bonds had been issued on 4-1-76. It had an adjusted basis of $470,000 at the time the bonds were purchased.

Frank is in good health. He has never been married and has supported his blind cousin, Joseph Charles, 67, for the past 50 years. Charles has lived with Frank in his apartment since childhood and has no income of his own.

The only income Frank received was his $3,000 proportionate share of the dividends distributed by Electroil and $18,000 in salary, less $3,857 withholding tax. Frank paid $1,800 in estimated tax. He made no contributions to charity and paid no interest, taxes or medical expenses. Compute Frank's 1977 net tax payable or overpayment refundable.

(b) The Schuyler Movies Corp., a commercial motion picture company, recorded the following items on its books for the tax year 1977:

Income
Gross sales	$827,369
Cash dividends from Ace Film Co. stock	4,020
Interest on bank deposits	1,756

Expenses
Labor involved in manufacturing	$131,250
Other salaries	142,000
Salesmen's commissions	36,760
Rent	10,000
Taxes	1,224
Repairs	620
Bad debts	1,076
Political contributions	2,500
Interest on bonds	3,000
Depreciation	6,215

The corporation values its inventory on the basis of cost. It had an opening inventory of $63,400 and a closing inventory of $87,200. During the year its purchases totaled $210,420.

The corporation had outstanding a $60,000 issue of 5% bonds held by bondholders other than Paragon (below). Under the indenture, the corporation was required to pay a sinking fund trustee $3,000 per year until sufficient funds were accumulated to redeem the bonds. The trustee reported earnings of $1,200 for 1977 from the sinking fund investments.

In addition to the cash dividends recorded above, Schuyler Movies received a dividend from Cartoons, Inc. Instead of the usual $10,000 annual cash dividend, it received title to a piece of property with a fair market value of $12,000. The property's adjusted basis to Cartoons had been $8,000 immediately before the distribution and no gain was recognized by Cartoons as a result of the distribution.

During the year, Schuyler Movies leased a building it owned to Science Studies, Inc. Instead of paying rent to Schuyler Movies, Science Studies paid $3,600 per year directly to Paragon Pictures Co. This was in lieu of Schuyler Movies paying this amount as interest on its bonds held by Paragon Pictures.

Compute the taxable income of Schuyler Movies Corp. for the current tax year. Show the cost of goods sold in a supporting schedule.

(c) The books of Great Gadgets, Inc. show the following income and expenses for 1977:

Income
Gross sales	$420,000
Dividends from taxable domestic corporations	6,800
Interest on bonds of Horn, Inc.	400

Expenses
Real estate taxes	$12,000
Mortgage interest (not including interest listed below)	5,200
Labor used in manufacturing	86,300
Clerical salaries	42,700
Managerial salaries	33,200
Social security and unemployment taxes	6,880
Interest on indebtedness (including interest on corporation's 3% bonds—see below)	6,870
Advertising	1,800

Depreciation	12,260
Auditing and legal fees	1,930

The gross sales figure listed on the books does not reflect sales returns and allowances totaling $1,800. Inventory at Great Gadgets is based on the lower of cost or market from the following figures:

Opening inventory (1-1-77)	$37,900
Closing inventory (12-31-77)	29,600
Merchandise purchased during year	118,230

During the year, Great Gadgets paid $28,000 in estimated income tax. It also donated $500 to the Democratic Party's election campaign.

On 1-20-71, the corporation issued $100,000 of its 10-year bonds for $105,000. On 1-2-77, the corporation redeemed one-fifth of the issue at par.

Compute Great Gadgets' net tax payable or overpayment refundable for 1977.

Discussion Problem 21-25

The tax treatment of dividends has been criticized on two counts: (1) that it is inequitable; and (2) that it results in an imbalance in the method of financing corporate ventures.

(a) What arguments can you give to support these criticisms?

(b) What arguments can you give against any change in the present taxation of dividends?

Research Problem 21-26

In May of this year, Cal-Tex Computers, Inc., a struggling, independent domestic corporation composed of 15 stockholders, anticipated that heavy expenses would arise in order to finish a new warehouse by year's end. It appeared that at least $100,000 additional cash was required from the stockholders to meet these expenses. At a meeting of the stockholders on June 11, an attempt was made to induce all 15 stockholders to contribute the needed cash. However, five of the stockholders refused to make any further investment in Cal-Tex and it was decided to have them redeem their stock in exchange for debentures of the corporation. This was done on June 16 and the remaining ten stockholders contributed the needed $100,000.

After June 16, the five "withdrawing" stockholders no longer participated in the affairs of Cal-Tex. They did not attend stockholders' or directors' meetings; they did not vote and they did not in any manner have any proprietary interest in the corporation or its affairs.

In July, Cal-Tex comes to you, a noted corporate tax counselor to see if it could be treated as a small business corporation, but it is concerned about the number of stockholders required by Sec. 1371.

What would you advise?

Use the Prentice-Hall Complete Federal Tax Equipment in your school or local library to find your answer. Do the following:

1. Give your opinion. In it, show authorities, citing law, regulations, interpretations and decisions applicable, and the P-H Federal Tax Equipment paragraphs where they may be found.

2. Enumerate and explain carefully each step you take in reaching your result. These are extremely important—just as important as the conclusion itself.

Tax Reasoning Problem 21-27

Jaxco is an electing small business corporation. This year its only business activity is from the buying and selling of commodity futures. It seeks your advice on whether the amounts received from trading in the commodity futures disqualify it from being a small business corporation and thus terminate the election. What do you advise? Explain.

ASSIGNMENT No. 22

CORPORATIONS—CAPITAL GAINS AND LOSSES,

NET OPERATING LOSS, ETC.

(Note: In the following problems assume that the "tax year" is the calendar year 1977, unless otherwise specified. In figuring all your answers, round off all amounts to the nearest whole dollar.)

Problem 22-1

Hewmatt, Inc., a furniture manufacturer organized in 1965, was offered $235,000 for its business (excluding cash), the sale to close on 1-3-77. Hewmatt's customers have good credit ratings. The following schedule shows the 1-3-77 bases of the assets and prices allocated to them in the contract:

	Basis	Allocated in contract
Notes and accounts receivable	$65,000	$65,000
Furniture, incomplete or undelivered, cost	$95,000	$110,000
Machinery (held over 9 months with $2,500 depreciation taken after 1961)	$24,500	$ 28,000
Lease (non-depreciable)		$ 12,000
Good will		$ 20,000

Before signing the contract, Hewmatt asks you to determine what recognized gain, if any, they will have to report from the transaction. What will you advise them?

Problem 22-2

The Walter Fergursen Corporation, a manufacturer of fishing equipment, had the following transactions during the tax year:

On January 28, the corporation bought 400 shares of Bow-Wow Co. stock at $29 a share.

On February 4, the corporation bought 200 shares of stock in the Hammocks Corporation at $17 a share.

On March 30, the corporation sold all of its accounts receivable for services rendered in 1976 for $11,245. The basis of the accounts receivable was $14,024.

On October 28, the corporation sold 100 shares of Bow-Wow Co. stock for $2,700.

On November 2, it sold 80 shares of Hammocks Corporation stock for $1,280.

On November 3, the corporation sold the remaining shares of the Hammocks stock for $2,160.

On November 10, it sold the remaining shares of the Bow-Wow stock for $9,600.

What is the corporation's long-term or short-term capital gain or loss for the year?

Problem 22-3

(a) On 12-1-76, the Kimberley Corporation, a dealer in household supplies, bought 1,500 shares of Household Helpers, Inc. stock at $80 a share as an investment. On 8-5-77, Kimberley made a contract to sell all the Household Helpers stock to the Kitchen Kraft Corp. for $85 a share and placed them in escrow until it received all the sale price. On 10-18-77, Kitchen Kraft paid $127,500 and the stock was released to it. How should the Kimberley Corporation report the gain?

(b) Assume the same facts as in (a), except that Kimberley Corporation bought the Household Helpers stock, not for investment, but solely to be able to buy curtain rods produced by Household Helpers because there was a shortage of curtain rods around 12-1-76 and Household Helpers sold its products exclusively to its shareholders. On 8-5-77, Household Helpers began to take orders for curtain rods from non-shareholders. Would your answer to (a) be different?

(c) Assume the same facts as in (b), except that Kimberley sold the stock on 5-19-88. Would this affect your answer to (b) above?

Problem 22-4

The Curtis Corporation had the following transactions during the year:

Kind of Property	Selling Price	Date sold	Basis	Date acquired
M Corp. common stock	$ 4,800	1-5-77	$ 8,800	11-5-54
AT Corp. bonds	10,300	1-5-77	14,900	8-9-76
T Corp. debentures	12,700	7-14-77	11,500	12-1-76
Notes receivable (from sales)	5,000	10-3-77	4,800	2-14-77
HE Corp. bonds	7,500	10-14-77	7,600	6-3-77
W Corp. preferred stock	21,800	12-30-77	14,400	3-7-77

(a) Figure the net short-term capital gain or loss.
(b) Figure the net long-term capital gain or loss.
(c) Figure the net capital gain or loss.

Problem 22-5

The Mattlas Mattress Corp. realized taxable income of $73,000 from the operation of its business. In addition to its regular business operations, it realized the following gains and losses from the sale of stock it held in other companies for investment purposes:

Short-term capital loss	$1,430
Long-term capital loss	4,770
Short-term capital gain	10,120
Long-term capital gain	4,610

What is the total taxable income of the corporation?

Problem 22-6

The Sanoro Corporation, formed on 1-2-76, had a taxable operating income of $40,000 in 1976. The corporation also incurred a net capital loss of $10,000 in that year.

Assume that in 1977, the corporation has an operating income of $70,000 and a net capital loss of $2,000.

Assume that in 1978, the corporation has an operating income of $90,000 and a net capital gain of $9,000.

Assume that the corporation has no more transactions involving capital gains or losses until 1982, when it has a capital gain of $3,000 and an operating income of $110,000.

What is the corporation's taxable income in 1976? 1977? 1978? 1982?

Problem 22-7

The Fine Used Furniture Corp. was incorporated in 1967. From 1972 to 1976 only, it did business as a Subchapter S corporation. In 1977, the corporation revoked its Subchapter S election and, without any change in stock ownership, continued business as an ordinary domestic corporation. It had the following transactions during the year:

Jan. 6—sold a pick-up truck for $3,450 that was bought 2 years ago. The truck had an adjusted basis of $2,000, $1,000 depreciation having been taken to date of sale.

Jan. 20—bought a plot of land for $6,200 on which to store junked furniture.

May 24—sold 200 shares of Barnaby Corp. stock for $3,600. It bought this stock as an investment in December, 1976 for $4,400.

June 17—sold some office machinery for $1,800 that it bought five years before for $5,750. Depreciation on the machinery to the date of sale amounted to $2,850.

Oct. 24—sold the land purchased on January 20 for $7,600.

Oct. 26—sold an old building it had used for storing furniture for $3,150. It cost $7,000 ten years ago, and straight line depreciation to the date of sale amounted to $3,500.

Nov. 4—sold 15 shares of Chicken Little, Inc. stock it bought on 11-23-76 for $180. The selling price, less expenses, was $340.

Nov. 15—sold 3,000 pieces of used furniture to another dealer for $26,150. All this furniture had been purchased before the current year for $29,830.

What is the corporation's net capital gain or loss for the current tax year? How will it be treated on the return?

Problem 22-8

During the current tax year, the Sherman Corporation had the following income and expenses:

Gross sales	$149,965
Cost of goods sold	45,000
Deductible expenses	23,000
Dividend from Mark Dorin Co., a U.S. corporation	1,000

The corporation also had the following gains and losses:

Long-term capital gains	$ 4,200
Long-term capital losses	1,100
Short-term capital gains	2,900
Short-term capital losses	3,900
Gain on sale of a business machine (1969 through 1977 depreciation totaling $235)	670
Loss on sale of another business machine (1970 through 1977 depreciation totaling $500)	35

What is the corporation's tax before credits?

Problem 22-9

(a) The Gotham Glass Corporation's income tax return for 1977 shows deductions exceeding gross income by $63,400. In the return are shown the following items: dividends received deductions of $3,400 on dividends from Albany Builders, Inc., and a prior year net operating loss carryover of $16,000.

(1) What is the net operating loss for 1977?

(2) How much, if any, of the net operating loss resulting in 1977 would be used to offset taxable income for 1974?

(b) The Dianamor Corporation's return for 1974 shows taxable income of $32,500. The corporation had a net operating loss deduction of $51,000 which consisted solely of a net operating loss carried back from 1977. Figure the net operating loss carryover from 1974 to 1975.

Problem 22-10

The Cranmoor Corporation has 20,000 shares of stock outstanding and 5 stockholders, each owning 4,000 shares. In 1976, the corporation sustained a net operating loss of $12,000.

In January 1977, two of Cranmoor's stockholders sell all their stock to an outsider, John Berry. At the corporation's annual meeting in February, Berry points out that the tax structure of a nearby state is much more beneficial to the corporation and proposes a move. The move actually takes place in May and proves beneficial not only for tax purposes but for business, also. The Cranmoor Corporation ends the year with a taxable income, before credits or net operating losses, of $16,500. In December, Amos Ball, one of the remaining original stockholders, sells all his stock to Berry.

(a) What, if any, is Cranmoor's taxable income for 1977? Explain.

(b) Would your answer to (a) differ if, instead of selling, Ball had died and Berry had inherited all his stock in December?

Problem 22-11

(a) On January 2, 1977, Jasmine Roberts bought 30% of the stock of a New Jersey corporation, the Exotic Tea Company, from Rose Hippe, its sole stockholder. In June, Jasmine married Pete Lipley, and on June 15, at Pete's suggestion and with money borrowed from him, Jasmine bought the rest of Rose Hippe's stock. She then reorganized the business, putting her husband in charge of the wholesale division of the firm and opening a retail division under her personal management. Under the Lipleys' supervision, Exotic Tea ended the year with taxable income of $16,200, even though it had been operating at a loss for several years and had a net operating loss carryover from 1976 of $8,700.

Will Exotic Tea be allowed to take the net operating loss carryover from its prior year on its 1977 return? Explain.

(b) Would your answer to (a) differ if Rose Hippe was Jasmine's mother and, in reorganizing the business, the Lipleys moved the firm to a new plant in California, involving a complete change in personnel and customers? Explain.

Problem 22-12

Johnson Oil Company of Austin, Texas owns 85% of all classes of stock of the Brian Oil Co. and 80% of all classes of stock of the Ballock Petroleum Company. Both companies are located in Oklahoma. Brian owns 50% of all classes of stock of an oil company in Saudi Arabia. Ballock owns 30% of all the classes of stock of the same company. All of the outstanding stock in these companies is voting stock. May the four companies file a consolidated return?

SUPPLEMENTAL PROBLEMS

Problem 22-13

Cassidy Tours, Inc., was organized in 1974. During the current year its taxable income from sales was $60,000. Its net capital loss during the year was $2,500. Cassidy had elected Subchapter S tax treatment in its first two years of business and had taxable income of $10,000 (including $1,800 in net capital gains) in 1974 and $16,500 (including $2,600 in net capital gains) in 1975. Early in 1976, Cassidy's stockholders voted not to elect Subchapter S treatment for 1976 or any later years. The taxable income for 1976 was $24,000, of which $3,200 was net capital gain. Figure Cassidy's tax liabilities and refund rights, if any, for these years, assuming that all forms and taxes have been properly filed and paid.

Problem 22-14

During the year, the Danaruth Corporation had gross income (other than capital gains) of $285,000. This included $6,500 in dividends from taxable domestic corporations. The corporation also had a net short-term capital loss of $7,200 and a net long-term capital gain of $18,700. Itemized deductions for the year amounted to $150,575. Figure the total tax liability for the current tax year.

★ ★ Problem 22-15 ★ ★

On 1-2-68, the Atlas Machinery Corp. bought land and a used warehouse building for $180,000 (land, $40,000). The building had no salvage value and was depreciated using the limited declining balance method with a 50-year useful life. It was sold on 1-2-77 for $162,447 ($47,447 for the land).

On 1-2-77, the Atlas Machinery Corp. sold for $30,000, machinery that had been bought for $50,000 on 1-2-72. When it was acquired, the machinery was not expected to have any salvage value at the end of its 10-year useful life. It was depreciated on the straight line method. No additional first-year depreciation had been taken.

A van valued at $13,000 was stolen on 1-1-77. It had been bought for $18,000 on 7-1-74, had a 10-year useful life and $4,000 estimated salvage value, and was depreciated under the straight line method. No investment credit had been taken but additional first-year depreciation was elected and salvage value was disregarded whenever possible. The loss was covered by insurance to the extent of

$5,544. At the end of the year, the thieves were not apprehended and the van had not been recovered. The corporation did not have any other theft loss or involuntary conversion during the year.

The Atlas Machinery Corp. had the following stock transactions in 1977:

On June 28, they sold 10 shares of Trovic Corp. common stock for $65 a share. They had received these shares on 6-14-77 as a stock dividend on 100 shares of the common stock of that company that they owned on that date. The 100 shares had been bought on 6-15-70 for $44 a share. On 6-15-77, the stock, which had a $50 par value, was selling for $60 a share.

On 9-2-77, they sold for $9,000, 100 shares of Beden Corp. common stock that they had bought on 7-1-74 for $4,000.

On 10-11-77, they sold for $4,500, 200 shares of Griele Co. common stock bought on 9-3-72 for $9,000.

On 11-1-77, they sold for $7,000, 200 shares of Sicap Co. preferred stock bought on 2-3-77 for $6,000.

On 12-6-77, they sold for $10,000, 75 shares of the Geva Co. common stock bought on 8-9-77 for $12,000.

In 1976, the Atlas Machinery Corp.'s only capital transaction resulted in a long-term capital loss of $900.

Fill in schedules that appear on following pages:

1978 Assignment 22—Problems 5191

SCHEDULE D

Short-term Capital Gains and Losses—Assets Held 9 Months or Less

a. Kind of property and description (Example, 100 shares of "Z" Co.)	b. Date acquired (mo., day, yr.)	c. Date sold (mo., day, yr.)	d. Gross sales price	e. Cost or other basis and expense of sale	f. Gain or (loss) (d less e)
1					

2 Unused capital loss carryover (attach computation) . . . .
3 Net short-term capital gain or (loss) . . . .

Long-term Capital Gains and Losses—Assets Held More Than 9 Months

4 Enter Section 1231 gain from line 4, **Part I** . . . .
5

6 Net long-term capital gain or (loss) . . . .

Summary of Schedule D Gains and Losses

7 Enter excess of net short-term capital gain (line 3) over net long-term capital loss (line 6) . . . . . .
8 Enter excess of net long-term capital gain (line 6) over net short-term capital loss (line 3) . . . . . .
9 Total of lines 7 and 8. Enter here and on Form 1120, page 1, line 9(a) . . . .

Part I Sales or Exchanges of Property Used in Trade or Business and Certain Involuntary Conversions

3

4 Combine the amounts on line 3. Enter here, and on the appropriate line as follows . . . .
   (1) If line 4 is a gain, enter such gain as a long-term capital gain on Schedule D.
   (2) If line 4 is zero or a loss, enter such amount on line 6, **Part II**.

Part II Ordinary Gains and Losses

a. Kind of property (if necessary, attach additional descriptive details not shown below)	b. Date acquired (mo., day, yr.)	c. Date sold (mo., day, yr.)	d. Gross sales price	e. Depreciation allowed (or allowable) since acquisition	f. Cost or other basis, cost of subsequent improvements (if not purchased, attach explanation) and expense of sale	g. Gain or loss (d plus e less f)

6 Amount, if any, from line 4, **Part I (if amount is zero or a loss)**. . . . .
7 Gain, if any, from page 2, line 22, **Part III**
8

9 Combine amounts on lines 6 through 8. Enter here, and on **Form 1120, page 1, line 9(b)** . . .

Part III — Gain From Disposition of Property Under Sections 1245, 1250, 1251, 1252, 1254—Assets Held More than Nine Months.

10 Description of sections 1245, 1250, 1251, 1252, and 1254 property: | Date acquired (mo., day, yr.) | Date sold (mo., day, yr.)

(A)
(B)
(C)
(D)

Relate lines 10(A) through 10(D) to these columns ▶▶▶▶	Property (A)	Property (B)	Property (C)	Property (D)
11 Gross sales price				
12 Cost or other basis and expense of sale				
13 Depreciation (or depletion) allowed (or allowable)				
14 Adjusted basis, line 12 less line 13				
15 Total gain, line 11 less line 14				
16 If section 1245 property: (a) Depreciation allowed (or allowable) after applicable date				
(b) Enter smaller of line 15 or 16(a)				
17 If section 1250 property: (a) Additional depreciation after 12/31/75				
(b) Applicable percentage times the smaller of line 15 or line 17(a)				
(c) Excess, if any, of line 15 over line 17(a) (If line 15 does not exceed line 17(a), omit lines 17(d) through 17(h), and enter the amount from line 17(b) on line 17(i))				
(d) Additional depreciation after 12/31/69 and before 1/1/76				
(e) Applicable percentage times the smaller of line 17(c) or line 17(d)				
(f) Excess, if any, of line 17(c) over line 17(d) (If line 17(c) does not exceed line 17(d), omit lines 17(g) and 17(h), and combine the amounts on lines 17(b) and 17(e) on line 17(i))				
(g) Additional depreciation after 12/31/63 and before 1/1/70				
(h) Applicable percentage times the smaller of line 17(f) or 17(g)				
(i) Add lines 17(b), 17(e), and 17(h)				

Summary of Part III Gains

21 Total gains for all properties (add columns (A) through (D), line 15)
22 Add columns (A) through (D), lines 16(b), 17(i), ——————— Enter here and on line 7, **Part II**
23 Subtract line 22 from line 21. Enter here and **on line 3, Part I**

Cumulative Problem 22-16

(Answer (a) or (b) as directed)

(a) In 1977, Trukenaid Corporation had gross sales of $182,000 from its business and received dividends of $3,200 from Crestwood Corporation, a domestic corporation, and $2,700 in dividends from Swampland Corporation, a domestic real estate investment trust. Trukenaid's inventory, valued at cost or market, was $31,500 on 1-1-77 and $73,400 on 12-31-77. Material bought for production cost $69,800. Wages for labor involved in manufacturing totalled $46,750. During the tax year Trukenaid incurred the following expenses:

Compensation of officers	$32,000
Office salaries	16,200
Commissions to salesmen	8,250
Rent on business property	3,600
Real estate taxes	1,128
Dividends paid	2,400
Depreciation (including depreciation taken on both used and new vans in (2) and (3) below)	9,250
Advertising	921
Reserve for anticipated repairs	3,800
Interest on outstanding bonds	980
Unemployment and social security taxes	5,552
Miscellaneous deductible expenses	689

1978 **Assignment 22—Problems** 5193

In addition Trukenaid Corporation had the following transactions in 1977:

(1) It sold 50 shares of Eco-Labs Corporation common stock on 2-3-77 for $85 per share. On 2-2-76, Trukenaid, as part of a financial arrangement, had bought an option for $1,500 to buy 100 shares of the stock. It exercised the option on 8-4-76 and bought the 100 shares for $55 per share.

(2) On 10-1-77, Trukenaid exchanged a used delivery van with a fair market value of $2,850 and an adjusted basis of $1,800 for a new van with a fair market value of $5,850. The new van has a 4-year useful life and no salvage value. To equalize the exchange, Trukenaid also gave the remaining 50 shares of Eco-Labs Corporation common stock with the old van. The fair market value of the stock was then $55 per share. Trukenaid had bought the old van in 1975 and had depreciation deductions totalling $3,775.

(3) On 12-1-77, Trukenaid sold its new van to one of its customers that needed this type of van immediately. Straight line depreciation taken to date of sale amounted to $190. The buyer paid $6,200.

Compute Trukenaid Corporation's income tax for the current tax year.

(b) As tax preparer for the Sonola Music Corporation you are provided with a profit and loss statement as shown below. You are also informed that $21,000 cash dividends were distributed during the tax year, and that the retained earnings at the start of the tax year amounted to $78,800.

THE SONOLA MUSIC CORPORATION
Statement of Profit and Loss
For the year ended December 31, 1977

Gross profit from sales		$75,135.00
Deduct General Expenses:		
Office salaries	$8,550.00	
Real estate taxes	1,420.00	
Social security and unemployment taxes	1,190.00	
Depreciation	2,340.00	
Total General Expenses		13,500.00
Net Profit on Operations		$61,635.00
Add Other Income:		
Interest on bonds of New York City	$2,800.00	
Interest on U.S. Telephone Corp. bonds	615.00	
Long-term capital gains	4,000.00	
Dividends from taxable domestic corporations	6,250.00	
Total Other Income		13,665.00
Net Profit on Operations and Other Income		$75,300.00
Deduct Other Expenses:		
Long-term capital losses	$8,600.00	
Cost of new factory floors completed 12-31-77 (charged to expense on the books)	5,750.00	
Charitable contributions	4,525.00	
Addition to reserve for anticipated loss on contract to purchase merchandise	2,875.00	
Total Other Expenses		21,750.00
Net income (before Federal income tax)		$53,550.00

On the basis of the above figures you are asked to:
(1) Figure the corporation's income tax.
(2) Figure the surplus at the close of the tax year.
(3) Fill in the schedules shown below.

Suggestion: To figure the surplus at the close of the tax year, take the following steps: From the net income (before taxes) as shown on the statement of profit and loss ($53,550) subtract the federal income tax paid and dividends distributed. Add the resulting figure to the surplus at the close of the preceding tax year.

Reconciliation Schedule (M-1)

1. Net income per books (after taxes) .... $ ....
2. Federal income tax ....
3. Excess of capital losses over capital gains ....
4. Taxable income not recorded on books this year (itemize) ....
5. Expenses recorded on books this year not deducted in this return:
   (a) Depreciation .... $ ....
   (b) Depletion .... $ ....
   ....
   ....
6. Total of lines 1 through 5 ....
7. Income recorded on books this year but not included in return:
   (a) Nontaxable interest .... $ ....
8. Deductions in this return not charged against book income this year
   (a) Depreciation .... $ ....
   (b) Depletion .... $ ....
   ....
   ....
9. Total of lines 7 and 8 .... $ ....
10. Income (line 6 less line 9) .... $ ....

Analysis of Retained Earnings (M-2)

1. Balance at beginning of year ....
2. Net income per books ....
3. Other increases (to earned surplus) ....
4. Total of lines 1, 2, and 3 ....
5. Distributions to stockholders:
   (a) Cash .... $ ....
   (b) Stock ....
   (c) Property ....
6. Other decreases ....
7. Total of lines 5 and 6 ....
8. Balance end of year (line 4 less line 7) ....

Cumulative Problem 22-17

The West Lake Co., a Pennsylvania corporation organized in 1975, is a manufacturer of pollution control equipment. For 1977, the books and records of the corporation show the following:

Net sales	$530,000
Interest received from savings banks	1,500
Interest received on New York City bonds	525
Interest received on loans	250
Proceeds from life insurance policy on death of corporate officer	15,000
Dividends received from U.S. corporations	1,820
Long-term capital loss from the sale of stocks	15,000
Long-term capital gain from the sale of stocks	13,320
Gain on sale of land held for 7 months	2,000
Gain on sale of office building bought in Feb. 1975 (straight line depreciation used)	2,800
Loss on sale of machinery held 11 months	1,900
Interest on loan to buy New York City bonds	120
Interest on other loans	230
Insurance premiums on lives of corporate officers (the corporation is the beneficiary)	3,000
Cost of goods sold	390,000
Compensation of officers	60,000
Salaries and wages	90,000
Repairs	4,250
Property and sales taxes	7,300
Depreciation	15,920
Advertising	8,500

On checking the corporation's returns for prior years, you find that the corporation paid tax on $24,800 in 1975 and $23,400 in 1976, had a $100 long-term capital loss from its only capital asset transactions prior to the current tax year, and made no charitable contributions. The corporation made no tax elections affecting the current tax year.

Assuming the corporation would rather obtain a refund for prior years than reduce its tax liability in future years compute the corporation's tax liability or the refund due for the years 1975, 1976 and 1977.

Research Problem 22-18

The Blakely Corporation, located in the 4th Circuit of the U. S. Court of Appeals, has a net operating loss for 1977 totalling $90,000. For the tax year 1974, Blakely had $67,000 ordinary income and $150,000 in capital gains. Blakely had used the alternative method to figure its 1974 tax liability of $70,660. This was $27,000 less than its tax would have been under the regular method. For 1975, Blakely had $82,000 taxable income (no capital gains) and paid a tax of $39,360.

Blakely's chief accountant comes to you, a tax specialist, to ask how to apply this $90,000 net operating loss as a carryback to Blakely's prior tax years. The accountant wants to know if Blakely can use its $90,000 net operating loss carryback to reduce its 1974 tax and still leave a $23,000 net operating loss ($90,000 net operating loss — $67,000 ordinary income) to be carried over to 1975. What would you advise the Blakely Corporation?

Use the Prentice-Hall Complete Federal Tax Equipment in your school or local library to find your answer. Do the following:

1. Give your opinion. In it, show authorities, citing law, regulations, interpretations and decision applicable, and the P-H Federal Tax Equipment paragraphs where they may be found.

2. Enumerate and explain carefully each step you take in reaching your result. These are extremely important—just as important as the result.

Master Review Problem 22-19

The assistant treasurer of the Bob Clark Corporation has prepared a worksheet for computing the corporation's taxable income on an accrual basis for the tax year. However, he has separately listed the transactions treated differently for book and tax purposes. The net income per books without these transactions is $74,755. The pertinent information about the transactions is given below. The company has consistently used the fastest depreciation method available but it does not elect the Class Life system for depreciation. The company also does not have an employee stock ownership plan.

On January 2, 1977, the corporation transferred title to the Lincoln Building to Stanley White, a 28% stockholder. The building had been bought in 1962 for $53,040 and had been depreciated $21,420 up to the time of the transfer. The transfer was neither a redemption nor a liquidation. A mortgage of $32,000 on the building was also transferred to White.

On January 4, the corporation sold an electric tool to the Salvation Army for $6,400. It had bought the tool in February, 1967 for $10,000. The tool had a fair market value of $8,000 and an adjusted basis of $4,800 at the time of the sale.

On August 30, the corporation bought some new equipment from the Belleau Co. for $9,000. Instead of paying cash, the corporation gave a note due December 31, 1977. The company books deducted a depreciation expense of $1,980 on the equipment. However, the Belleau Co. forgave the debt on December 31 in an arm's-length transaction.

On September 30, the corporation acquired a new machine with a useful life of 6 years and a salvage value of $500. Its sales price was $4,000 and its cost to the vendor was $3,200. The corporation traded in an old machine of the same type bought in 1970 with an adjusted basis of $1,200, for the new machine. The old machine had a fair market value of $2,300 and the corporation also had to pay $1,800 in cash on the purchase.

During the year, the Chamber of Commerce of Harrison gave the corporation a vacant lot with a fair market value of $10,000. The contribution was made solely to induce Bob Clark to locate in the town of Harrison.

The corporation invested in stocks and bonds traded on the major stock exchanges. During the year, it had a net long-term capital gain of $3,010 and a net short-term capital loss of $2,800. In addition, there was an unused capital loss carryover from 1971 of $2,555.

On November 5, the corporation received $1,040 in interest on a municipal bond.

The corporation has a net operating loss carryover of $18,000 from 1976.

On December 20, the board of directors authorized a contribution of $3,000 to the American Red Cross. It was paid by check on March 8, 1978.

On December 30, the corporation received a used truck from Albert Ritta Co., a domestic corporation, representing a distribution of Ritta's earnings. The Bob Clark Corporation is a 25% stockholder of the Albert Ritta Co. The truck's fair market value on December 30 was $6,660, with an adjusted basis of $5,100 and a useful life of 4 years.

During the year, the corporation received a payment of $205 on an account receivable that had been written off in 1970 as bad debt. No tax benefit resulted from the bad debt deduction, The corporation charges off specific accounts when they are deemed to be uncollectible.

On the basis of the above data, figure the corporation's income tax after credits, assuming the corporation paid an estimated tax of $14,000 for 1977.

(NOTE: To figure Bob Clark's net income before contribution and special deductions, start with the $74,755 book income figure. Then, make the necessary adjustments; for example, certain depreciation allowances should be subtracted.)

ASSIGNMENT No. 23

CORPORATIONS—REORGANIZATIONS

(Note: In the following problems assume that the "tax year" is calendar year 1977, unless otherwise specified. In figuring your answers, round off all amounts to the nearest whole dollar.)

Problem 23-1

Parent I. M. Corporation owns, among its many assets, all the stock of Subsidiary Y. T. Corporation.

(a) On 2-26-77, Subsidiary Y. T. transferred 100 shares of Parent I. M. voting stock and $1,000 cash to Eiline Pie Corporation in exchange for substantially all of Eiline's assets in a reorganization. The assets have a fair market value of $10,000 and adjusted basis of $7,000. The fair market value of the Parent stock is $90 a share, and the adjusted basis is $85 a share.

(b) On 3-1-77, Subsidiary Y. T. transferred 150 shares of Parent I. M. voting stock in exchange for all the stock of the Deen Corp. in a reorganization.

(c) On 6-13-77, Parent I. M. transferred all of the stock of Subsidiary Y. T. to Doris Corporation in exchange for Doris's voting stock in a reorganization.

Identify the above reorganizations by Type. Explain why the corporations involved are, or are not, parties to the reorganization.

Problem 23-2

Natura Corporation is insolvent due to poor management. The stockholders and creditors wanted to salvage the business with new management and agreed to set up this written plan:

"Creditors and Shareholders agree to organize Frank Corporation. 50% of the stock will be issued to Creditors in exchange for their claims against Natura Corporation; 50% of the stock will be issued to Shareholders for cash. Frank Corporation will acquire the assets of Natura Corporation."

In pursuance of the plan, Natura transferred all its assets to Frank Corporation for some cash and in discharge of the creditors' claims now assumed by Frank. The cash was distributed to the Natura stockholders in redemption of their Natura stock, and that corporation was dissolved. Does this transaction qualify as a tax-free reorganization? Explain.

Problem 23-3

Are the following transactions tax-free reorganizations? Explain why they are or are not.

(a) The Fountpen Corporation, organized in New Jersey, owns 75% of the stock of India, Inc. For good business reasons, Fountpen wants full control of India's assets. Fountpen proposes to organize Ballpoint Corporation in Delaware and exchange Fountpen Corporation stock for all of Ballpoint Corporation stock. Ballpoint will exchange all of its Fountpen stock for the assets of India, Inc. India, Inc., then will distribute the Fountpen stock to its stockholders and dissolve. All the corporations will adopt this plan.

(b) Body Beautiful, Inc., owns health clubs. Streamline Saunas Corp. operates in the Body Beautiful clubs. For business reasons, Body Beautiful and Streamline Saunas agree to exchange all of the stock of Streamline for a sufficient number of Body Beautiful voting common stock. Sven Johansen, who owns all the voting preferred stock of Streamline, refuses to accept Body Beautiful stock. He insists on cash for his shares. To satisfy Sven, the Streamline board of directors resolves to call the preferred stock for cash in accordance with the certificate of incorporation. After the redemption of the preferred stock, the exchange of common stock takes place and the holders of the voting common stock receive shares of Body Beautiful for their shares of Streamline Saunas.

Problem 23-4

The Futura Fabrics Corp. had outstanding $750,000 of 10-year 7% bonds that matured on 12-15-77. The corporation was not in a position to pay the bondholders off in cash. It, therefore, offered to exchange these bonds for a like face amount of 5-year 8½% bonds.

Karen Ashley had bought a $1,000 bond in 1974 for $1,050. On 12-15-77, she received a $1,000 5-year 8½% bond in exchange for her 10-year 7% bond. On that date, the new bond had a fair market value of $1,095.

What was the amount of her recognized gain, if any, on this transaction?

Problem 23-5

Andrew Sandymire owned 80 shares of the Hawaii Narcissus Co. stock, costing him $70 a share. Under a qualified reorganization plan, Narcissus was merged into the Huston Corporation. Pursuant to the plan, on 2-27-77, Andrew received in exchange for his stock 80 shares of the Huston stock with a market value of $90 a share, plus a bond in the Huston Corp. worth $1,000.

(a) What is Andrew's recognized gain or loss, if any, from these transactions?
(b) What is his basis of the Huston stock?

Problem 23-6

Peter Masters owned 100 shares of stock in a corporation which was a party to a reorganization. He had paid $55 a share for his stock. Pursuant to the reorganization plan, he received in exchange for his stock a like number of shares of stock in the reorganized company worth $75 a share and bonds in the reorganized company worth $1,500. He later sold the stock for $68 a share. What was his recognized gain or loss, if any, from these transactions? Explain.

Problem 23-7

On 3-1-77, Westwood Paint Co. absorbed Home Decorators, Inc. in a statutory merger. Home Decorators had no accumulated earnings or profits. Esther Farrell owned 600 shares of stock in Home Decorators, worth $4,200. Under the plan of reorganization adopted and filed by the corporation, Esther surrendered her stock and received in exchange: 300 shares of stock in Westwood Paint Co. worth $10 a share, $500 cash, and property with a basis of $700 and a fair market value of $1,200.

If Esther had paid $2,000 for her stock in Home Decorators four years earlier, what is her taxable gain, if any, on the exchange? What is the basis in the new stock?

Problem 23-8

(a) Under a plan of reorganization, Barry Hendricks exchanged 200 shares of stock in Beechwood Corporation, a party to the reorganization, for $6,000 cash and 100 shares in Oakwood Inc., another party to the reorganization. Barry's original stock cost $2,400, and the 100 shares received in exchange were worth $3,500. What is his recognized gain, if any? What is the basis of the Oakwood stock?

(b) Suppose, in connection with the reorganization, that Barry exchanged his 200 shares, costing $2,400, for 200 shares with a value of $2,000 and $1,000 in cash. What would be his recognized gain, if any? What is the basis of the new stock?

Problem 23-9

On 2-2-77, the Silverthorne Corporation entered into a tax-free reorganization with Goldbug, Inc. As of 12-31-76, Silverthorne had capital of $90,000 on its balance sheet and an earned surplus of $9,000 since 2-28-13. Boris Klemke owned 300 shares (par $22) of the 900 shares of Silverthorne stock outstanding. The 300 shares cost him $3,500. Under the plan of reorganization, he exchanged his Silverthorne shares for 200 shares of Goldbug, worth $4,000, and $3,000 in cash. The exchange had the effect of a dividend distribution.

(a) What was Boris' recognized gain on the exchange (including dividend portion)?
(b) How much of the recognized gain is taxable as (1) dividend; (2) gain?
(c) What is Boris' basis for the Goldbug stock?

Problem 23-10

Daniel Virgini bought 2,000 shares of Larry Bridge Contracts Corp. common stock for $30,000 in 1972. In 1977, Larry Bridge merged with Washington Co. in a tax-free reorganization. Daniel received 1,500 shares of Washington Co. common stock valued at $45,000, and 500 shares of Washington Co. preferred stock valued at $15,000, in exchange for all his Larry Bridge stock. Compute Daniel's bases for the Washington Co. common and preferred stock. Explain your answer.

Problem 23-11

Lee Corporation owns all the stock of Stone Corporation, which owns 400 shares of 20,000 outstanding shares of Lee Corporation. On 1-2-77, Stone transferred 400 shares of the Lee voting stock and $3,000 to W. W. Corporation in exchange for substantially all the assets of W. W. in a reorganization. W. W. bought the assets in 1972; they had a fair market value of $35,000 on 1-2-77 and an adjusted basis of $30,000. On 1-2-77, the fair market value of the Lee stock was $80 a share, and its adjusted basis was $76 a share.

On 2-25-77, W. W. sold 100 shares of Lee Corporation stock for $73 a share. What is W. W.'s gain or loss on the sale?

Problem 23-12

H. S. Young, Inc., a manufacturer of poker tables, was organized and started doing business in 1971. Billy Kane and Mary Fashion, who each owned 50% of the Young stock, had differences in 1977 and agreed to split up. On 2-27-77, H. S. Young transferred 50% of its assets to a newly formed corporation, Peterson, Inc., in exchange for all of the Peterson stock. On the same day, H. S. Young transferred the Peterson stock (valued at $500,000) to Mary in exchange for all of her stock in H. S. Young for which she had paid $50,000. Both corporations continued to manufacture poker tables after the exchange.
(a) What income, if any, did Mary realize in the transaction? Explain.
(b) Would your answer be different if H. S. Young started business in 1974?

Problem 23-13

David Patsay and Mark Carlo owned all the stock in the Paylo Co., which has engaged in the manufacture of carpets and trophies for 7 years. David's basis for the stock was $15,000, and Mark's was $12,000. In January, 1977, David decided he would like to handle only the carpet business, and Mark wanted to have exclusive control of the trophy business. To carry out their wishes, on 1-30-77, the Paylo Co. transferred all its assets relating to the carpet business to a newly formed Davay Co. in exchange for all of the Davay Co. stock. David immediately exchanged all his stock in the Paylo Co. for all the stock of the Davay Co., and as a result of the exchange, had an actual gain of $48,000.
(a) How much gain, if any, must David report on his 1977 return? Explain.
(b) What is David's basis for the Davay stock?

Problem 23-14

On 1-31-75, the Downtown Travel Corp. bought all of the authorized common stock of the Sherman Corp. for $200,000. Sherman had no other class of stock. In February, 1976, Downtown decided to liquidate Sherman for good business reasons. The Sherman Corp. shares held by Downtown in February had a fair market value of $225,000. Downtown received no distributions from Sherman before February, 1976. Sherman's basis for its assets was $180,000.
(a) If Downtown goes ahead with its liquidation plan, may it avoid tax on the receipt of the subsidiary's assets?
(b) If Downtown can sell the Sherman assets after the absorption at a profit, how can it minimize the gain?

Problem 23-15

The Weinstein Company and the Salaya Company were both organized on 1-2-73, and both keep their books on a calendar year basis. On 10-10-76, Weinstein acquired the assets of Salaya in a statutory merger. The net capital losses and net capital gains (computed without regard to any capital loss carryovers) of the two corporations are as follows:

	Weinstein	Salaya
1973	0	$8,000 loss
1974	0	12,000 loss
1975	$7,000 gain	1,200 loss
1976	10,950 gain	800 loss (up to Oct. 10)
1977	54,000 gain	

What net capital gain will Weinstein Company report in its return for 1976? For 1977?

Problem 23-16

Edico Corp. and Andrew Co. are calendar year taxpayers. On 2-3-76, Andrew acquired the assets of Edico in a statutory merger. The books of the 2 companies reveal the following information:

	Edico Corp.	Andrew Co.
Accumulated earnings at end of 1975	$50,000	$200,000
Deficit in earnings and profits for period ending 2-3-76	$120,000	
Earnings and profits in 1976		$60,000
Distributions in 1976		

On 1-2-77, Andrew made a cash distribution of $210,000 to Sandy Eucliff, its sole shareholder. How should Sandy report the transaction on his 1977 return? Explain.

SUPPLEMENTAL PROBLEMS
Problem 23-17

In 1971, Wally Leon and Julie Persey organized Haywood Printing and Publishing Corporation with 500 shares of $800 par common stock. Wally got 250 shares of the stock in exchange for a building with a fair market value of $200,000. He had bought the building in 1969 for $180,000. In 1970, he borrowed $172,000 for good business reasons and mortgaged this building. Haywood assumed the $172,000 mortgage. Wally took $20,000 depreciation on the building before he transferred it.

Julie got 250 shares of the stock in exchange for printing equipment with a fair market value of $200,000 and adjusted basis of $80,000. She received the equipment from her father in December, 1970, as a gift, but had never used it in any business until her contribution to Haywood. Julie was told that assumption of a liability by a corporation is not treated as money received in a corporate organization. She decided that as long as the corporation assumed the building mortgage she would get ready cash and escape some taxes by mortgaging the equipment. In 1971, the day before the transfer to Haywood, she borrowed $60,000 and mortgaged the equipment. Haywood assumed the mortgage.

From incorporation until 1-3-77, Wally ran the publishing department and Julie ran the printing department. Haywood Corporation lost money because Wally and Julie could not agree on overall policy and management. They decided each would run his or her own department as a separate business. Haywood Corporation organized two new corporations, Leon Publishing Corporation and Persey Printing Corporation. On 1-3-77, Haywood Corporation transferred half of its assets used in publishing to Leon Corporation, and the other half used in printing to Persey Corporation. Haywood Corporation received all of the stock of Leon and Persey corporations in exchange. On the same day, Wally surrendered his Haywood stock to Haywood Corporation and received all of the Leon stock, par value $60,000. The fair market value was $81,000. Julie also surrendered her Haywood stock to Haywood Corporation and received all of the Persey stock, par value $60,000. The fair market value also was $81,000. Haywood Corporation was then dissolved.

What is Wally's and Julie's realized and recognized gain or loss in 1977? Explain how you arrived at your answer.

Problem 23-18

The M. J. Wellsley Corporation was organized in 1969 to take title to and manage a chain of theatres in Boston. In 1970, it bought stocks in various companies that distributed artificial flowers. By late 1971 it had gained enough know-how about flower marketing to go into the business itself. Since 12-1-71, M. J. has been in both the theatre and flower businesses with varying success and has distributed all its profits. In 1977, it had a $100,000 operating loss due to poor management. On the advice of competent management consultants, M. J.'s board of directors took the following steps to separate the theatre business from the flower business. On 12-15-77, pursuant to a reorganization plan, M. J. transferred its artificial flower business to a newly created corporation, Weinstein, Inc., which continued the business. In exchange, M. J. received 2,500 of the 3,000 shares of Weinstein's common stock, the only class of stock authorized. M. J. realized a gain of $34,000 on the deal. M. J. then immediately distributed all of the Weinstein's stock and the stock bought in 1970 to the M. J. shareholders.

Laura Sohn owned 100 shares of M. J. stock that she had bought in 1972 for $250. On 12-15-77, when the stock was worth $700, she received 50 shares of Weinstein (fair market value, $2 a share; $1 par value), 5 shares of Forever Rose Co. stock (fair market value, $4 a share; $1 par value), and one share of Seaboard Evergreen Co. stock (fair market value, $30; $2 par value). On 12-31-77, Laura sold 50 shares of M. J. for $400, her Weinstein stock for $130 and her Seaboard stock for $5.

(a) How much of M. J.'s $34,000 gain is recognized? Explain.

(b) How much of the distribution is taxed to Laura and what are the bases of her stocks after the distribution?

(c) What are Laura's gains or losses from the stock sales and how are they treated?

Cumulative Problem 23-19

Eric Jason, age 67, is retired and lives alone. His wife died in 1973. His children are self-supporting but he does support a foster daughter who lives in Asia. During 1977, he received $2,250 interest from bank accounts, $13,500 cash dividends from taxable domestic corporations, $10,000 in rental income, and income from the following transactions:

On 1-2-77, he sold 60 shares of Data Figures Inc. at $150 a share. In 1971, he had bought 40 shares of Daylight Auditing Inc. at $275 a share. In 1974, the company paid a 50% nontaxable stock dividend and he received 20 more shares. On 8-15-76, Daylight Auditing merged with Data Figures. In furtherance of the plan of reorganization, Jason exchanged 60 shares of Daylight Auditing for 60 shares of Data Figures plus $20 cash for each share exchanged. The Data stock at the time of the exchange had a fair market value of $125 a share.

On 6-1-77, he sold 10 shares of Ravenol Products Inc. for $325 that he had purchased on 2-1-77 for $375. Jason had a long-term capital loss carryover of $800, of which $200 was from 1969 and $600 from 1976.

On 9-23-77, Jason sold 250 shares of Delux Paper Co. common stock at $10 a share. The stock consisted of lots bought at different times and Jason did not identify the stock sold. Jason supplied the following information for his cost basis: On 8-17-72, he bought 20 shares of Delux Paper stock, $100 par value, at $100 a share. On 6-14-73, he received 20 stock rights allowing him to buy 10 additional shares of common stock, $100 par value, at $100 a share. At the time the rights were issued, the value of the stock was $114 a share and the rights $6 each. Jason exercised the rights and elected to allocate basis. On 1-20-76, the company split its entire common stock 10 for 1. Under the split-up, Jason received 10 $10 par value shares for each $100 par value share owned.

During 1977, he contributed 10 shares of TMC common stock to the American Cancer Society. The stock cost $200 when he bought it on 2-4-77 and was worth $340 when he donated it on 11-4-77. He contributed TMC stock valued at $50 to the Red Cross on the same day; he bought this stock on 2-3-77 at $40. He also contributed an antique chair to the Avant Painting Foundation, a nonoperating private foundation, that was worth $600. He had bought the chair in 1975 for $200. He paid $2,150 in state income and sales taxes in 1977. Interest on a mortgage totaled $1,050.

Figure Jason's tax liability before any credits.

Discussion Problem 23-20

A problem that has attracted considerable public attention concerns the transferability of net operating loss carryovers in corporate mergers. A number of cases involving well-known companies have illustrated the tax savings that may accrue when a profitable company merges with a loss corporation.

The loss carryover is intended primarily as a device for equalizing the tax burden of a company realizing fluctuating profits and losses with that of a company with a stable income over a period of years. Presumably, a change in the superficial characteristics of the company which does not affect its basic economic characteristics should not result in loss of the net operating loss carryover. By the same token, however, a basic change in the corporation should be expected to encounter some limitations on the availability of the loss carryover.

(a) What types of changes in the structure of a business enterprise should result in denial of the loss carryover?

(b) What arguments can you give for allowing the loss carryover under the conditions discussed under (a)?

Research Problem 23-21

The Loretta Corporation wants to buy the cosmetics business of the Frank Evon Corporation, an unrelated corporation established in 1970. However, Loretta does not want to get into Frank Evon's other business of noodle manufacturing which represents about 23% of its assets. At a final stage of their negotiations, Frank Evon's president has suggested the following blueprint with the best possible tax results in mind: His company would immediately transfer all its noodle manufacturing assets to a new company for all its stock. The new stock would be distributed to the Frank Evon stockholders in proportion to their stockholdings. Loretta would then acquire all of Frank Evon's outstanding stock in exchange for Loretta's voting common stock. After the reorganization or recapitalization, Frank Evon would remain as a wholly owned subsidiary of the Loretta Corporation.

The Loretta Corporation board of directors likes the idea, but does not know whether the tax scheme will work. The board has asked you, as a tax expert, for advice. What is your opinion?

Use the Prentice-Hall Complete Federal Tax Equipment in your school or local library to find your answer. Do the following:

1. Give your opinion. In it, show authorities, citing law, regulations, interpretations and decisions applicable, and the P-H Federal Tax Equipment paragraphs where they may be found.

2. Enumerate and explain carefully each step you take in reaching your result. These are extremely important—just as important as the result.

Tax Reasoning Problem 23-22

Acme Corp. acquires Eagle Corp. in a stock-for-stock Type B reorganization.

Since Eagle was in need of additional working capital for expansion purposes, Acme made a cash investment in Eagle to acquire additional stock Eagle had authorized but had not issued. No cash was distributed to Eagle's shareholders. Is this a tax-free reorganization? Explain.

Tax Reasoning Problem 23-23

Ace Mills was interested in the Slade Corp.'s timber cutting contracts. It acquired all of Slade's stock in March 1976, and liquidated this corporation one year later in March 1977, in a tax-free liquidation. In June 1977, Ace began cutting and selling timber. In its return for the year, it elected the special capital gain treatment on the cutting of timber. The Revenue Service contends that this treatment does not apply since Ace had to have held the contracts for 9 months before the election year and Ace only received the contracts in March 1977, on the liquidation of Slade. Ace asks you for tax advice on the matter. What do you advise?

ASSIGNMENT No. 24

CORPORATIONS—PERSONAL HOLDING COMPANIES, ETC.—EXEMPT ORGANIZATIONS

(*Note: In the following problems assume that the "tax year" is the calendar year 1977, unless otherwise specified. In figuring all your answers, round off all amounts to the nearest whole dollar.*)

Problem 24-1

Throughout 1977, Alma Jestik, founder and president of the Majestik Corporation, owned 20% of the issued and outstanding shares of Majestik stock. Her husband, Dan, owned 12% and Dan's sister-in-law, Lori Thomas, owned 8%. Majestik has 20 other employees, not related to Alma, Dan, Lori or each other, and each owned 3% of the stock. Alma and Dan were married until June 23, 1977, when a final divorce decree was granted. On July 3, Alma married Frank Jason, the corporation's personnel director. On August 11, Dan married Mary Jones, the corporation's bookkeeper. Majestik's gross income for 1977 is as follows:

Gross profit from sales of inventory	$ 80,000
Dividends	50,000
Interest	30,000
Gain from sale of business machine	10,000
Net rents from office building	50,000
Total	$220,000

(a) Is the Majestik Corporation a personal holding company for 1977? Explain.

(b) Would your answer to (a) be the same if Alma and Dan remained married to each other throughout 1977? Explain.

Problem 24-2

The Laurasi Cola Corp. had adjusted ordinary gross income of $280,000 in 1976 and again in 1977. The corporation received net rents from tangible property leased to nonshareholders totalling $138,000 in 1976 and $182,000 in 1977. In each of the two years the corporation received $30,000 in adjusted oil and gas royalties and $35,000 in copyright royalties. The remainder of the income in both years was from dividends, and interest on loans. Before each year ended, the nonrent income that exceeded 10% of ordinary gross income was paid out in dividends.

During 1976, the 5,000 outstanding shares of stock in the Laurasi Cola Corp. were owned as follows:

Stockholder	Shares
Aaron Brand	100
Carl Drake	450
Eric Fisher (Aaron Brand's step-brother)	350
Grace Hall	450
Ira Jacobs (Grace Hall's uncle)	450
Karen Lodge (Aaron Brand's sister-in-law)	500
Mark Nelson	200
Olga Peterson	450
Quentin Reed	50
Sam Tyler	450
Ursula Vance (Quentin Reed's grandmother)	400
Warren Xavier	450
Yolanda Zaumen (Mark Nelson's sister)	250
Amy Baker	450

These shareholders were not otherwise related.

In January 1977, Ursula Vance died and all her stock was distributed to her grandson, Quentin Reed. In March 1977, Quentin Reed married Grace Hall.

(a) Was the Laurasi Cola Corp. a personal holding company in 1976? In 1977? Explain.

(b) Which shareholder owned the greatest number of shares actually and constructively in 1976? In 1977? Explain.

Problem 24-3

Themtaw, Inc., is a personal holding company. Based on the following facts, figure its income tax and personal holding company tax, if any, for 1977:

(1) Taxable income (after deductions for charitable contributions and dividends received), $492,250.

(2) Dividends received from taxable domestic corporations, $30,000.

(3) Dividends paid in 1977, $8,600.

(4) Consent dividends, $16,000.

(5) Charitable contributions, $280,000 (all to hospitals), $27,250 of which was allowed in figuring the corporation's income tax.

(6) $11,320 set aside during year to apply toward retirement of indebtedness of $250,000 incurred before 1-1-34.

(7) $6,100 dividends paid on February 15, 1978; their deduction in 1977 was elected.

Problem 24-4

How could the corporation in the preceding Problem avoid the personal holding company tax?

Problem 24-5

Healthgrain, Inc., a calendar year personal holding company, was organized in 1972 with 200 shares of authorized and issued capital stock at $1,000 per share, but with no paid-in surplus. Gary Baker paid $50,000 in 1972 for his 50 shares. By 12-31-77, Healthgrain had an earned surplus of $150,000 available for distribution and made a consent distribution of $10 per share ($2,000) on 12-31-77. The corporation paid no other dividend in 1977, but on March 14, 1978, it did pay a dividend of $5 per share.

(a) What is Healthgrain's dividends paid deduction for undistributed personal holding company income for 1977?

(b) Baker sells all his stock on 1-15-78 for $1,100 per share. What, if any, is his gain or loss on this sale?

Problem 24-6

(a) Carmen Veranda, a U.S. citizen, owns all the stock of the Foreign Fruit Company, a domestic corporation. Foreign Fruit is on the calendar year basis. It owns 400 of the 700 outstanding shares of capital stock of Bananas de Brazil, S.A. The remaining shares are divided equally among 30 other stockholders, all U.S. citizens. Bananas de Brazil, a foreign corporation, is also on the calendar year basis and keeps all its asssets, books and records in its offices in Brazil.

In 1977, due to a severe drought, the Brazil corporation had no bananas to sell and its only income for the year was $85,000 from estates and trusts. It incurred deductible expenses of $15,000. None of Bananas' income was distributed to Foreign Fruit in the U.S. during the year.

Does Foreign Fruit's gross income have to include income the Brazil corporation earned? If so, how much? Explain.

(b) Assuming the same facts as in (a), will your answer differ if, on June 15, Foreign Fruit sold 100 shares of its Bananas de Brazil stock to 10 new stockholders (10 shares each)? No two stockholders are related and all are U.S. citizens.

(c) Would your answer for 1978 differ, if you assume the same facts in (a) for 1978, except that (1) Bananas de Brazil received $145,150 gross income ($85,000 from estates and trusts and $60,150 proceeds from the sale of bananas) and (2) its deductible expenses totalled $23,000 for the year?

Problem 24-7

(a) Grandview Estates, an unincorporated association that specializes in real estate investments and real estate mortgages, had $1,000,000 income for 1977: $630,000 from dividends, interest and rents; and $370,000 in capital gains from the sale of real property and stock. Assuming it meets all other qualifications and makes no capital gain dividends, what amount of distributions must Grandview Estates make to its shareholders if it elects to be taxed as a real estate investment trust?

(b) Could Grandview Estates still elect to be taxed as a real estate investment trust if its $630,000 in earnings and profits were made up as follows: $180,000 from rents; $75,000 from interest on obligations secured by mortgages in real property; $260,000 in dividends from stock in Mason-Dixon Manufacturing Co., a corporation that produces automobile parts; and $115,000 in dividends from stock in Blue Grass Associates, a qualified real estate trust?

Problem 24-8

During 1977, the Andrew Lane Foundation, a charitable tax-exempt organization founded in 1970, received all its income from the following sources:
1. $4,200 from Andrew Lane, the foundation manager.
2. $6,900 from Ruth James, an individual contributor.
3. $1,100 each from four individual contributors.
4. $2,500 each from three individual contributors.
5. $6,000 in long-term capital gains.
6. $13,000 in dividend and interest income.

No contributors were related to each other. Experience shows that the above sources of support are those that the organization normally receives. The organization also paid $2,200 in investment expenses during the year.

Is the Andrew Lane Foundation a private foundation? Explain.

Problem 24-9

The Midway Marine Trust Fund, a tax-exempt trust formed in 1961, owns a printing factory which consists of a building housing two printing presses and other equipment necessary for printing. On January 2, 1977, Midway Marine rents the building and the printing equipment to the New City Times, a local newspaper, for $10,000 a year. The lease states that $9,000 of such rent is for the building and $1,000 for the printing equipment. However, it is determined that notwithstanding the terms of the lease $4,000 of the rent is actually attributable to the printing equipment. During 1977, Midway Marine has $3,000 of deductions, all of which are properly allocable to the rented building. In addition, Midway Marine also receives $2,640 in dividends and $570 in interest during 1977.

Assuming it meets all qualifications necessary to maintain its basic tax-exempt status, how much tax, if any, must Midway Marine pay for the current year? Explain.

Problem 24-10

(a) Landlock College, a tax-exempt educational institution specializing in teaching business administration, owns several acres of unused land. During the year, it leases the land to a sheep farmer. Would the income received by the college be subject to the unrelated business income tax?

(b) Would your answer to (a) differ if Landlock entered into a contract with a livestock company to raise and sell sheep and split the profits?

(c) Would your answer to (b) differ if Landlock College specialized in teaching animal husbandry?

Cumulative Problem 24-11

A statement of income for the calendar year 1977 taken from the books of the

Instant Antiques Corporation and compiled for the benefit of its stockholders is as follows:

Sales and other income:

Gross sales	$450,000	
Dividends from GN Corporation stock	120,000	
Interest on American Phone & Wireless bonds	275,000	
Rent from apartment building	225,000	$1,070,000

Deductions:

Cost of goods sold	$345,000	
Salaries not deducted elsewhere	150,000	
Repairs	4,000	
Interest	6,000	
Property taxes	5,000	
Depreciation, taxes and interest on apartment building	25,000	
Contributions to hospitals and charity	175,000	
Depreciation	20,000	
Advertising	3,000	
Accounting and legal fees	8,000	741,000
Income before provision for income taxes		$ 329,000

Instant Antiques Corp. is a manufacturer of "antique" furniture. During the calendar year 1977 it paid $120,000 in taxable dividends to its shareholders. It usually pays dividends only twice a year (June 1 and December 1), and it plans to follow this procedure for 1978.

An examination of the stock transfer records of Instant Antiques shows that during the last half of the tax year the corporation had 9,000 shares of stock outstanding, 2,250 shares of which were held by various individuals not related to each other, and none of whom are partners. The remaining 6,750 shares were held by 50 stockholders, among whom there were the following family relationships:

George Adams owns 550 shares. His family and relatives own the following number of shares: Wife, 50; Wife's father, 50; Wife's brother, 50; Wife's brother's wife, 50; Father, 50; Brother, 50; Brother's wife, 50; Son, 50; Daughter by former marriage (son's half-sister), 50.

John Bond owns 100 shares. His family and relatives own the following number of shares: Wife, 200; Wife's father, 50; Wife's brother, 50; Wife's brother's wife, 50; Father, 50; Brother, 50; Brother's wife, 50; Son, 200; Daughter by former marriage (son's half-sister), 200.

Dave Clark owns 100 shares. His family and relatives own the following number of shares: Wife, 200; Wife's father, 550; Wife's brother, 50; Wife's brother's wife, 50; Father, 50; Brother, 50; Brother's wife, 50; Son, 200; Daughter by former marriage (son's half-sister), 200.

Tom Drew owns 100 shares. His family and relatives own the following number of shares: Wife, 200; Wife's father, 50; Wife's brother, 50; Wife's brother's wife, 50; Father, 50; Brother, 50; Brother's wife, 800; Son, 200; Daughter by former marriage (son's half-sister), 200.

Bill Evers owns 100 shares. His family and relatives own the following number of shares: Wife, 200; Wife's father, 50; Wife's brother, 50; Wife's brother's wife, 550; Father, 50; Brother, 50; Brother's wife, 50; Son, 200; Daughter by former marriage (son's half-sister), 200.

(a) Does the Instant Antiques Corp. meet the requirements to be classified as a personal holding company for 1977? Explain.

(b) Figure Instant Antiques' total federal tax liability, if any, for 1977.

Research Problem 24-12

Midwest Grain and Supply Co. was organized as a farmers' cooperative in 1974. During 1977, 780 out of the 1,000 equal shareholder-producers of Midwest marketed their produce and purchased their supplies through the cooperative. The

I.R.S. after reviewing Midwest's 1977 activity with its shareholder-producers, has informed the cooperative that its tax-exempt status under Sec. 521 is about to be revoked.

A group of the producers who are interested in seeing Midwest maintain its tax-exempt status comes to you, an accountant who has specialized in agricultural tax matters. The producers are aware of Sec. 521(b) which requires that in order for a cooperative to be exempt, "substantially all" of the cooperative's stock be owned by producers who transact business in the cooperative. They are not sure, however, exactly how this requirement is applied. How would you advise the producers?

Use the Prentice-Hall Complete Federal Tax Equipment in your school or local library to find your answer. Do the following:

1. Give your opinion. In it, show authorities, citing law, regulations, interpretation and decisions applicable, and the P-H Federal Tax Equipment paragraphs where they may be found.

2. Enumerate and explain carefully each step you take in reaching your result. These are extremely important—just as important as the result.

Tax Reasoning Problem 24-13

Jasper Loan Corp. knew that a Subchapter S election terminated if more than 20% of a corporation's gross receipts was from interest or other "passive" income sources. However, it argued that this rule did not apply to its election even though most of its income came from interest on loans it made. The corporation reasoned that "passive" income for Subchapter S purposes is similar to personal holding company income. Since Jasper, as a small loan company, was excluded from the personal holding company rules, it should also be excluded from the Subchapter S "passive" income rule. Is this correct? Explain.

ASSIGNMENT No. 25

RETURNS AND PAYMENT OF TAX

(Note: In the following problems, unless otherwise specified, assume that the "tax year" is the calendar year 1977, that the taxpayer and his spouse, if any, are resident citizens under 65 and are not blind and that the taxpayer is not entitled to any credits against the tax other than those shown.)

Problem 25-1

Frank and Nancy Sohler are a married couple living in a community property state. During the year Frank received a $200,000 commission on the sale of property which he failed to report on his tax return. Nancy neither knew about the nonreporting nor benefited from it. The Sohlers file separate returns. Is Nancy liable for taxes due on one-half of Frank's unreported income?

Problem 25-2

Tom and Susan Fealey filed separate returns for 1977. The Fealeys included payment-in-full with their returns. After the time for filing returns had expired the Fealeys determined that their tax liability would have been greatly reduced by the filing of a joint return. The Fealeys are presently involved in litigation designed to recover part of the tax they paid as a result of their jointly filed 1976 return. Can Tom and Susan now file a joint return for 1977?

Problem 25-3

C. O. Brown was widowed on February 1, 1977. On April 1, he remarried. He prepared and filed on April 15, a joint return for himself and deceased wife for calendar year 1976. On April 18, an executor was appointed for his deceased wife's estate. On April 15, 1978, Brown filed for calendar year 1977, a joint return for himself and his deceased first wife. His second wife filed a separate return for 1977. On April 18, 1978, the executor of the first wife's estate filed a separate return for the deceased spouse for calendar year 1976, seeking to disaffirm the joint return made by Brown.

(a) Was Brown entitled to file joint returns for his deceased wife and himself for tax years 1976 and 1977?

(b) What, if anything, was the effect of the executor's disaffirmance?

Problem 25-4

Which of the following minors must file a 1977 income tax return? How should they report their respective taxes?

(a) Sixteen-year-old Rose White earned $2,000 during the summer working in her mother's yarn shop. Rose donated $250 of her salary to her church's building fund.

(b) Richard Miller, age 20, attends college but works as an ice cream vendor during his spare time and earned $2,500 during the year.

(c) Gloria Gonzales, age 18, earned $450 as a part-time employee in her college's bookstore. Additionally, she earned $1,300 at a summer job and received $75 in interest on her savings account. Gloria used all her funds to cover her college tuition.

Problem 25-5

On March 1, 1977, Brian Kelly, age 35, left on a fishing trip and failed to return home. He has been missing ever since. On December 1, Brian's wife, Rita, age 35, was appointed Brian's legal guardian. Brian had earned during January and February of 1977, a total of $3,500. Subsequent to his departure Brian received $200 in interest on his personal savings account. Rita's only income for the year was $250 in dividends from domestic corporations. Brian and Rita are otherwise entitled to file a joint return. How should the Kellys report their taxes?

Problem 25-6

The Johnson partnership operates a manufacturing business on a fiscal year ending October 31 with Revenue Service permission. Partners Fred and Clark are calendar year taxpayers. They decide to form a corporation to operate the same manufacturing business. On July 1, when a certificate of incorporation is filed in the state office for the Easy Corp., all the partnership assets are transferred. Clark became president of the corporation. Fred's only activity is as a director of the corporation. He is a fiscal year taxpayer with a tax year ending June 30. The corporation continues to use the same fiscal year as the partnership.

What returns must be filed to report and tax the profits of the manufacturing business?

Problem 25-7

Bonny Black, a tax executive, has among her clients the Salfe trust; the estate of Twilly Dandy; Merit Corporation, a foreign corporation; and Merit's secretary-treasurer Reno Bendo, a nonresident alien. All except the Salfe trust are on a calendar year basis. Salfe's fiscal year ends June 30. The Dandy estate was settled 8-14-77. Bonny's husband, Aldo, with whom she filed jointly last year died 9-2-77, and she was appointed his administrator.

(a) When must Bonny's clients file their returns?

(b) When must Bonny file her own return, if she wants to file a joint return? A separate return?

Problem 25-8

You are a tax adviser to Nancy Blue, a famous singer. On April 1, 1978, you realize that due to Miss Blue's frequent traveling, you would not be able to get all the information needed for her 1977 return. Assuming you probably can get the necessary information by June 1, 1978, what steps would you take to avoid, or minimize, any possible penalties?

Problem 25-9

The Racer Corporation has offices in Detroit, Buffalo and Chicago but it keeps its books and permanent official records in Philadelphia where all business transactions are reported. Racer expects to have a $60,000 tax liability less credits for the current tax year. Assume corporation's income was earned evenly over the year.

(a) Where does Racer file its income tax return?

(b) When and how may it pay the tax if it files a return for a calendar year? A fiscal year that ends on May 31?

Problem 25-10

Ohio Steel Cable Company had higher earnings than it anticipated during 1977. Its estimated tax payment due April 15 should have been $100,000. Instead it paid $70,000.

(a) What penalty, if any, must Steel Cable pay on the underpayment of estimated tax?

(b) Assuming there is a penalty in (a), is there any way Steel Cable can avoid such penalty?

Problem 25-11

This year, Matt Falon, heavily mortgaged all his property to maintain his chicken farm. He sold his chickens at a profit and when he filed his 1977 income tax return made timely application for an extension of time for payment of tax. Before the application was acted on, Falon received a notice for a deficiency of tax amounting to 12% of the tax reported. The deficiency was due to an understatement of income resulting from state lottery winnings. Falon acknowledged the deficiency and applied for an extension of time to pay it.

(a) Discuss briefly the basis on which the extensions may be granted.

(b) How will eventual payment of the amounts due be assured?

(c) What, if any, payment will be required in addition to those amounts?
(d) What are the maximum extensions that may be granted?

Problem 25-12

In the following examples what information returns and statements, if any, must the parties send out as a result of their transactions with Elmer Grade, an attorney?

(a) Grade received a salary of $15,000 as corporate counsel of Save Our Wildlife, Inc., a tax-exempt environmental organization.

(b) Grade authorized payments of $4,700 on behalf of Save Our Wildlife to a professional partnership of accountants for services rendered during the year.

(c) $2,400 in annual rental fees were passed on to Grade as landlord by Charles, a real estate agent, who collected the sum of $200 monthly from Earl, the tenant of Grade's premises.

(d) $235 in interest credited to Grade's savings account with the Merchant's Trust Bank.

(e) $550 in interest from a City of Appleton, Wisconsin municipal bond.

(f) $1,160 in corporate dividends received from a domestic corporation by Elmer Grade as owner of record. Grade was, in fact, a nominee who merely paid over the dividends to the true owner, his mother.

Problem 25-13

On 1-2-77, Belt Grinding Associates, Inc. agreed to pay Akramatic Inc. a fee of 10% of Belt Grinding's profits after payment of federal income taxes for the exclusive right to manufacture Akramatic's die-stamping machine. Before paying their 1977 federal tax, Belt Grinding had profits of $100,000 in 1977. Compute Akramatic's 1977 fee using the trial and error method.

Problem 25-14

Before deducting the state income tax, the Wellrod Mfg. Corp. had a taxable income of $60,000 for federal income tax this year. Before deducting the federal income tax, Wellrod's taxable income for state income tax purposes was $42,000 (the difference being due to interest on state bonds, taxable on the state return, but exempt on the federal). The state tax rate is 5% of net (taxable) income.

Use the formula method to find the federal tax and the state tax.

SUPPLEMENTAL PROBLEMS
★★ Problem 25-15 ★★

On 3-1-77, Atlas Machinery Corp., a calendar year corporation, estimated that its taxable income for 1977 would be $265,000. This amount included $9,000 of net long-term capital gain in excess of net short-term capital loss. Assuming the corporation made timely equal quarterly estimated tax deposits based on these figures, fill in the following schedule:

Record of Federal Tax Deposits (List deposits in order of date made):

	Date of deposit	Amount
1st installment		
2nd installment		
3rd installment		
4th installment		

Cumulative Problem 25-16

Allen Corporation was incorporated in March 1976 to manufacture and sell custom made dresses. The 1,000 shares of common stock issued by Allen were its only issue and were owned chiefly by three sisters. Alice who is married, owned 545 shares, her daughter Pat, 5 shares; Mary had 300 shares and Jane 150 shares. Mary and Jane are not married.

In 1977, the three sisters served as officers and supervisory employees. Allen employed 16 workers in production. There are also two office employees. At inventory time, which usually lasts about a month, Allen hires 4 extra employees. All employees received salaries. The sisters' salaries totaled $6,000 a month. Allen files its income tax returns on a calendar year basis. Its combined withheld taxes and social security taxes for all employees averages about $600 a month.

For 1977, after figuring gross sales, cost of goods, inventory at end of the year and all allowable deductions, Allen had taxable income of $201,213. This was earned at approximately $53,000 per quarter-year and the same rate as for 1976. Included in the deductions were fees of $650 paid to an accountant and $700 paid to the firm's attorney. In addition to his annual salary, Allen paid its sales manager a flat $300 for actual travel expenses. The company did not require him to keep a record of his expenses. An item of Allen's costs was $900 paid as royalty to Zipp-Wear Machinery for use of its lint removal machine. In 1977, Allen paid a dividend of $1 a share.

During 1977, Allen's tax adviser recommended that the sisters make a Subchapter S election for 1978.

(a) What returns must Allen file in 1977? Give the form numbers, due dates and general statement of the purpose.

(b) Give the due dates and form number for any other forms that Allen should file for transactions in 1977.

(c) How will Allen determine tax withheld from wages and salary in 1977? What forms are involved?

(d) Discuss the procedure, and forms to be filed if Allen decides to adopt the tax adviser's recommendation.

Research Problem 25-17

Mary and Jeffrey Smith, husband and wife, were foreign nationals who entered the U.S. last year. They want to file a joint income tax return for their "taxable year" of entry into the U.S. and want to adopt the calendar year as their accounting period. The Smiths tell you that their arrival date in the U.S. was May 2 of last year and up to that time they considered themselves nonresident aliens. After arrival, and until December 31 of the taxable year, their status was that of resident aliens.

The Smiths consult you about their filing status. They contend that their joint return covers only the period in which they are resident aliens (May 2 to Dec. 31) and the part of the "taxable year" in which they were foreign nationals (Jan. 1 to May 1) should be excluded from their "taxable year" so that as resident aliens they are qualified to file a joint return for the short-tax year (May 2 to Dec. 31). What advice would you give?

Use the Prentice-Hall Complete Federal Tax Equipment in your school or local library to find your answer. Do the following:

1. Give your opinion. In it, show authorities, citing law, regulations, interpretations and decisions applicable, and the P-H Federal Tax Equipment paragraphs where they may be found.

2. Enumerate and explain carefully each step you take in reaching your result. These are extremely important—just as important as the result.

Tax Reasoning Problem 25-18

Mrs. Ross filed a joint return with her husband from whom she is now divorced. The Revenue Service increased their taxable income because of a fraudulent deduction overstatement of the cost of goods sold by Mr. Ross in his business. Mrs. Ross contends she is not liable because she did not know about the overstatement, did not benefit from it and therefore, she should not be liable on the return. What would you advise?

ASSIGNMENT No. 26

ASSESSMENT—COLLECTION—REFUNDS

(Note: In the following problems assume that the "tax year" is the calendar year 1977, unless otherwise specified.)

Problem 26-1

(a) Two weeks before the statute of limitations was about to expire, an Internal Revenue Service agent disallowed an exemption deduction on T. C. Apple's tax return. Apple did not ask for a district conference. A day later, the Revenue Service mailed out a formal deficiency notice (90-day letter). Apple feels that this letter is not valid since he did not previously get a 30-day letter. Is he correct? Give reasons.

(b) M. C. White had some deductions disallowed by an Internal Revenue Service agent at an office audit. A conference failed to resolve the dispute as the disallowed deductions were based in White's interpretation of the law. White, certain that she is correct, is determined to fight the deficiency and will not accept any settlement short of a total IRS concession. She is anxious to reach a final determination on this matter as soon as possible. What action, if any, would you advise her to take at the end of the conference?

Problem 26-2

After an office audit of the partnership return filed for 1976, a proposed deficiency was determined against Sally and Wendy Hall, equal partners in an advertising firm. The examiner determined that the partnership claimed certain expenses as business deductions which were really personal expenses and that the partnership was not entitled to use an accelerated form of depreciation on certain property.

Each one received a "30-day letter" stating that the examiner's deficiency was based on increased taxable income resulting from the disallowed deductions. The notices further advised them of their appeal rights.

Sally immediately filed a formal protest and asked for an Appellant Division hearing. Wendy decided to accept the examiner's finding and consented to the assessment of the deficiency by executing Form 870 (a waiver of restriction on assessment) at the District Conference. Wendy paid the assessment before Sally had her Division hearing. After an Appellate Division hearing, Sally executed a closing agreement (Form 906) in which she agreed to pay a deficiency for 1976 of $2,500 and the Revenue Service agreed to allow the partnership continued use of accelerated depreciation.

In 1977, Sally discovers she failed to claim her nephew as a qualified dependent on her 1976 return, and Wendy learns about the allowed accelerated depreciation for the partnership in Sally's "Form 906" closing agreement. On these facts, both file refund claims in a District Court. Wendy's refund claim is limited to that part of the assessment attributed to the allowed accelerated depreciation while Sally's claim is for her qualified dependent exemption. Would their claims be successful? Explain.

Problem 26-3

On May 1, 1977 B. Richards received a 90-day formal deficiency notice on his return filed March 1, 1974 for calendar year 1973. He disregarded the notice. On August 1, 1977 he was assessed additional tax on the lottery winnings he had collected in 1973.

(a) Assume the lottery winnings were less than 25% of reported income, what grounds, if any, can B. Richards assert as a defense?

(b) Assume the omission was fraudulent, can B. Richards successfully assert the statute of limitations as a defense against collection?

Problem 26-4

Jane Hall is a resident of State A, and after the arrest of her husband in State B on drug-related charges, State A police obtained a warrant and searched Jane's home on 1-31-77. They found illegal drugs. The next day, the IRS District Director in State A, believing the collection of tax on sales income from illegal drugs might be avoided because the drugs were concealed, notified Jane by letter that her first 30 days of tax year 1977 was closed and an income tax of one-hundred thousand dollars for that period was owing. An assessment for that amount was made on February 1.
 (a) Explain why the government can or cannot assess the tax.
 (b) What can Jane do to challenge the assessment or delay its collection?

Problem 26-5

Helen, Barbara and Elizabeth operate an antique and flea market business which they incorporated several years ago to take advantage of the corporate tax rates. Helen and Barbara each own 20% of the stock and Elizabeth owns 60%. At the end of the current year, they wound up the business and immediately shared all the assets equally. Assuming no income taxes were paid by the corporation for the year, what assessment may the Revenue Service make to collect them?

Problem 26-6

Mary Hart resides in Waco, Texas. On July 1, the Revenue Service filed a notice of tax lien in the district for Waco, Texas. On July 15 Mary entered into a contract with the Ace Repair Company for $950 to repair the roof of her residence. Ace Repair Company completed the roof repair on July 19. The next day it filed and indexed a mechanic's lien against the apartment building for $800 repair after Mary refused to pay the bill. On July 25 Mary was struck by an auto. She immediately brought suit against the operator of the vehicle. She was awarded $10,000 in damages under a settlement agreement executed on August 1. When Mary did not pay her attorney's fee of $3,000, the attorney attached a lien against the proceeds. On August 20 Mary borrowed $300 from Middle Bank using her savings account balance of $1,000 as security for the passbook loan. On November 1, when the first installment was due Mary defaulted. On December 1, Mary sold her residence to a Florida buyer. On December 15 all of the foregoing persons received a notice of levy from the government. The notice declared the tax lien valid against the apartment building and all other assets of Mary in the district. None of the persons had actual notice or knowledge of the existence of the federal lien before December 15. Although the notice of lien was filed in the IRS district where the property was located it was not recorded in the federal tax lien index at the Revenue Service district office.
 (a) Assuming all of the property is located in Waco, Texas, to what extent is the federal tax lien enforceable?
 (b) Would your answer to (a) differ if the federal tax lien had been filed in the federal tax lien index at the district office?

Problem 26-7

Roth finds that he does not have enough cash to pay his tax liability by April 15, 1977. He knows that on August 15 he will complete a transaction that will enable him to pay the $4,000 tax balance due. He seeks your tax advice. He asks you what will happen if he files his return and pays his tax liability at the same time on August 15 when he has the cash. What do you advise? Explain.

Problem 26-8

When Holly Wills checked her 1974 tax figures in March 1977, she realized she had mistaken a 4 for a 6 and overpaid her tax by $300. Holly had filed her 1974 return on time, but because of a shortage in ready funds did not pay the tax until May 15, 1976. When is the last day that Holly can file for a refund:
 (a) If the facts are as related above?
 (b) If Holly had filed the return and paid the tax on April 15, 1975?

(c) If it is assumed that Holly filed no return but paid the tax on April 15, 1975?

Problem 26-9

Harriet and Benny Lee always file timely joint tax returns. On September 12, 1977 they ask you to file a refund claim of taxes paid for years 1969 thru 1971. Their claim is based on net operating losses in tax years 1972 thru 1974. After consultation, you examine their returns for the years involved which show a tax of $290 paid on taxable income of $2,000 for each tax year 1969 and 1970 and a tax of $450 paid on taxable income of $3,000 for 1971. Furthermore, the returns reveal net operating losses of $1,000 for each tax year 1972 and 1973, and a net operating loss of $2,500 for 1974. Moreover, because of your tax expertise, you uncover an unclaimed permissible tax deduction of $100 for tax year 1971.

The Lees used the standard deduction in computing their tax and in 1971 Lees used the Tax Rate Schedule in effect for that year which showed no tax due on taxable income of $500 or less regardless of filing status.

What refund, if any, can you obtain for the Lees assuming you file the claim on 9/12/77? How would you proceed?

Problem 26-10

Sam Clayson filed his 1975 tax return on April 15, 1976. The Revenue Service audited his return and sent him a notice of deficiency on Aug. 19, 1976 for $480. Clayson did not pay the deficiency, but later on Nov. 1, 1977 paid the $480 assessment which followed the deficiency notice. Clayson then had his 1975 return reviewed by Tom Brightner, a college student who had just completed a course in federal taxes. Tom informed Clayson that he had included an item in ordinary income which was actually capital gain. This entitled Clayson to a refund of $1,200 ($720 on his 1975 tax return and the $480 he paid later). When is the last day that Clayson can file a refund claim of the entire overpayment of $1,200?

Problem 26-11

Jane Merlin filed a 1040 return for 1976 on April 4, 1977. With it, she enclosed her W-2 form, which indicated that her employer withheld $580 from her wages, and a check for $120 to pay the total tax liability of $700. On July 1, 1978, the Revenue Service notified Jane that she had been assessed an additional $75. She paid this assessment on August 15, 1978. On September 5, 1978, Jane's employer gave her a corrected W-2 for 1976, and this showed that $780 had been withheld. The firm's bookkeeper had made an error in the amount.

(a) What can Jane do to recover the overpayment?
(b) What amount, if any, will Jane recover if she waits until August 1, 1980 to file a refund claim? Explain.

Problem 26-12

On 8-1-75, Sally H. Rowe received a refund based on her claim for a dependency exemption for her mother on her tax return for the year 1972. On 9-5-77, the Revenue Service was informed that Sally's mother had died in 1971. The IRS immediately started a suit for return of the refund. Sally's attorney has made a motion that the court dismiss the suit as not being timely filed, on the grounds that a suit for a return of a refund must be started within 2 years of the time that the refund was made. Will the motion be sustained or overruled? Explain.

Problem 26-13

Mary Hill filed her return and paid her 1977 tax on April 15, 1978. In August 1978 she had occasion to recheck her return and filed a refund claim on 8-17-78 on the ground she had overstated her income. On 11-19-78, the Revenue Service sent her by certified mail a notice disallowing her claim, and in addition, assessing a deficiency. Mary Hill paid the deficiency, but believing she has a good case, decides to sue.

(a) When is the last day Mary can start suit?
(b) Where can Mary bring the suit?

(c) What must Mary prove to win her case?

Problem 26-14

On Oct. 1, 1977, J. C. Patton mailed a properly addressed petition by certified mail to the Tax Court to redetermine a deficiency. In his July 1, 1977 deficiency notice, the commissioner alleges that J. C. has failed to report 25% or more of his gross income in his 1976 return, filed April 15, 1977. The petition included allegations that denied the 25% omission of gross income as well as a claim for refund for tax year 1974.

Counsel for Revenue Service moves to dismiss the petition because: (1) it was filed more than 90 days after July 1, the date the deficiency notice was mailed; (2) it contained an allegation for a refund which was not within the jurisdiction of the court.

Are these sufficient reasons for dismissal of the petition? Explain.

SUPPLEMENTAL PROBLEMS

Problem 26-15

On 7-1-76, Wendell C. Hope filed his tax return for fiscal year ending on 3-31-76. On 1-15-77, he received a notice for $600 in additional tax, plus penalties and interest. He had not signed Form 870 consenting to the assessment of the deficiency. $50 of the $600 was due to Wendell failing to report a profit-sharing income withdrawal made on July 1, 1975. Since the trustee of the profit-sharing plan did not have to report payments under $600 on an information return, Wendell was hoping to avoid the tax. Wendell paid the total assessment by check on 2-15-77. What was the amount of the check?

Problem 26-16

Oliver C. Brady filed his 1973 income tax return on 4-15-74, paying a tax of $350. On 9-16-76, after his return was examined he paid an additional $85 in tax. On 6-21-77, he discovered that he had omitted taking a deduction on his 1973 return, and he filed for a refund of $100. Assuming that the claim is proper, what will the amount of the refund be? Explain.

Research Problem 26-17

Louis and Harriet Brown are the principal owners in business as transferees of Town Corporation. More than two and one-half years have passed since they paid an income tax assessment against Town Corporation as transferees of its assets. Now Louis and Harriet want to file a claim for refund for the collected taxes with an appropriate District Director. In furtherance of their intent, they consult you, a tax expert. Louis and Harriet assert as their main ground for a timely refund claim that they were not the primary taxpayers, so that the time for filing their refund claim as transferees is of equal duration with the time limit within which the government is authorized to make an assessment—that is, three (3) years. Are they correct in their position?

Use the Prentice-Hall Complete Federal Tax Equipment in your school or local library to find your answer. Do the following.

(1) Give your opinion. In it, show authorities, citing law, regulations, interpretations and decisions applicable, and the P-H Federal Tax Equipment paragraphs where they may be found.

(2) Enumerate and explain carefully each step you take in reaching your result. These are extremely important—just as important as the result.

Tax Reasoning Problem 26-18

Alco Corp., operating under a Subchapter S election, made a disqualifying move 5 days before the end of its tax year. Therefore, Alco lost its Subchapter S status for the entire tax year. As a Subchapter S corporation, it had paid no estimated tax installments during the year. (a) Is Alco subject to a penalty for underpayment of corporate estimated taxes? Explain. (b) What if Alco's election terminated at mid-year? Explain.

ASSIGNMENT No. 27

FOREIGN INCOME—FOREIGN TAXPAYERS

(Note: In the following problems, unless otherwise specified, assume that the "tax year" is the calendar year 1977, that the individual taxpayer and his spouse, if any, are resident citizens under 65 and are not blind and that the taxpayer is not entitled to any credits against the tax other than those shown.)

Problem 27-1

Carol Winslow, a cash basis taxpayer, is a recording artist from California. In January 1977 she received a royalty payment from a London theatre company when her song was used in a play. In December 1977 she received notice that a United Kingdom tax was due on the royalty payment. When she filed her 1977 tax return in April 1978 she had not yet paid the tax. She did not elect to itemize on her return. Could she take a credit for the British tax on her 1977 return?

Problem 27-2

Mel Collins and his wife, June, have 2 infant children for whom they claim dependency exemptions. June had no income during 1977. Mel's taxable income in 1977 before exemption deductions was as follows: $22,000 from U.S. sources, $16,000 of business income from Spain, $2,000 interest on a Spanish bank deposit and $5,000 of business income from Portugal. Collins paid $1,000 to Spain in tax on his business income and $400 on his interest income. He paid $1,204 in tax to Portugal on his business income.

Compute Collins' foreign tax credit for 1977.

Problem 27-3

Morgan Pierrepont, a U.S. citizen, paid income taxes to Iran and Kuwait in 1976 and 1977. He filed the returns on the due dates claiming foreign tax credits under the overall limitation. In 1975, Peirrepont paid income taxes to Egypt and Iran, and filed on the due date claiming a foreign tax credit under the per country limitation. In 1974, Pierrepont paid amounts of tax to Egypt which he claimed as a deduction. Explain briefly why the following are, or are not, correct:

(a) Pierrepont can apply a carryover of foreign tax paid to Egypt in 1975 under the per country limitation, to the foreign tax paid to Iran in 1977.

(b) Pierrepont can apply a carryback of foreign tax paid to Kuwait in 1977 to tax paid Egypt in 1975.

(c) Pierrepont can apply a carryback of foreign tax paid to Iran in 1976 to the tax paid Egypt in 1974.

Problem 27-4

(a) Harold Mann is a United States citizen. During the tax year he had a taxable income of $25,000 from sources within the United States, and income of $20,000 from his holdings in Turkey. Mann paid a tax of $2,000 to Turkey on his income there. Mann is married and is the sole support of his two minor children. His wife had no income or deductions of her own. Assuming that Mann decided to file jointly, compute the net tax payable if he elects to take the foreign tax credit.

(b) Flomur Controls, Inc. is a corporation organized and doing business in the United States. It also does business in Bolivia. For the tax year the company had taxable income of $450,000, which included $150,000 from its operations in Bolivia. It paid Bolivian taxes of $70,000 on its income there. Compute the corporation's income tax with credit for the foreign taxes paid.

Problem 27-5

Bridgewater Fabrics, Inc., a New York corporation, owned 220,000 of a total of 1,500,000 voting shares of Bogside Linens, Ltd., an Irish corporation. Bogside Linens paid the Irish government a tax on its 1977 accumulated profits, and was also able to pay Bridgewater Fabrics a dividend out of accumulated profits. Indus

Thread Co., a less developed country corporation of Pakistan, was a wholly owned subsidiary of Bogside Linens. Indus Thread paid accumulated profit taxes to Pakistan in 1977, and paid Bogside dividends during the year. Explain briefly why, the following are, or are not, correct:

(a) Bridgewater Fabrics is treated as having paid a portion of Bogside Linen's taxes, and can claim a foreign tax credit.

(b) A portion of Indus Thread Co.'s taxes paid to Pakistan cannot be attributed to Bridgewater Fabrics because Bridgewater did not own 10% of Indus Thread Co.'s voting stock.

(c) If Bridgewater Fabrics claims a foreign tax credit for taxes paid by Bogside Linens it must include in gross income any dividends received from Bogside but not any tax attributable to dividends.

Problem 27-6

(a) Alfredo Ponti came to the United States with his wife and family as an attache of the Italian Embassy. In 1977 he bought 350 shares of Continental Copper Co. stock. He left the United States permanently on 6-30-77 after being transferred to a diplomatic post in Africa. On 9-10-77, Carlo cabled his broker in New York and told him to sell all the stock. Carlo contends that he should not be taxed on the gain from the sale. Is he correct? Explain.

(b) Chesapeake Shipbuilding Corp., a domestic corporation, owns and operates a drydock and ship repair business in Baltimore. A part of Chesapeake's operating costs results from wages it pays to crew members of ships owned by foreign corporations. During the year, Chesapeake paid eighty crew members (all citizens and residents of foreign nations) of the "Tannenbaum," a tanker owned by a West German company, $2,800 each. The repair work was completed in two months. Will the crewmen of the "Tannenbaum" be taxed at U.S. rates? Explain.

Problem 27-7

Pierre Cardigan, age 67 and his wife Jackie, age 66, are citizens of Canada residing in Toronto. During the year, he received $60,000 in net income from a sporting goods store in Madison, Wisconsin. On Jan. 2, he sold at a $3,000 gain, 100 shares of Iowa Plastics. He had purchased 200 shares of Iowa Plastics in 1975. During the year he received $4,100 in dividends on his remaining 100 shares.

Pierre's wife had no gross income for the year and was fully supported by her husband.

Compute Pierre's federal income tax, if any, for 1977.

Problem 27-8

Joe and Betty Warren went to Switzerland from the U.S. on 1-1-75. They were representing the Colaco Corp., a Swiss corp., and their job was to collect accounts receivable from the company's rural customers. The Warrens stayed in Switzerland until 8-7-77, when they returned permanently to the U.S. During 1976 and early 1977 they made 2 or 3 short trips to the U.S. on business. On 11-2-77, while in California they received $60,000 from Colaco's Los Angeles representative for their 1977 work in Switzerland. How much of their foreign earned income can they exclude from income for their 1977 U.S. tax? Explain.

Problem 27-9

Joseph Turner is a curator in the Museum of Ancient Art. He and his wife have no children, and Mrs. Turner has no income or deductions of her own. Mr. Turner accepted an appointment as a special consultant to an archeological expedition in Cairo, Egypt. The appointment was to begin on 7-1-77 and to last for the remainder of the year. Turner stayed in Egypt for that entire period.

During the tax year, Turner had the following income: salary, $18,400 paid in the U.S. and $23,000 paid to him in Egypt; dividends, $780 from the Allentown Steel Company and $360 from an Egyptian corporation.

The museum withheld $1,357.80 from his salary. Turner paid $1,890 in taxes to the Egyptian government on the salary that he received while in Egypt and paid

$10 in tax to Egyptian government on the dividends received from the Egyptian corporation. He also paid $7,280 in U.S. estimated taxes.

Turner had the following deductions for the tax year: charitable contributions, $1,900.00; property tax on his home, $1,100; interest on his home mortgage, $675; and state sales tax, $325.

Compute Turner's overpayment or lowest U.S. net tax payable.

Problem 27-10

Rick Savage is an attorney employed by a large New York law firm. His wife, Joan, is a translator for the United Nations. Rick's law firm decided to open a branch office in Paris, and he was assigned to be the supervising attorney. Rick and Joan began residing in Paris on 4-1-75. Joan was able to secure employment with the French government.

Rick received a salary of $2,000 per month payable on the last day of each month. Joan received $7,000 from the French government during 1977. Rick paid $693.15 to France in taxes on his salary, while Joan's income was exempt from French tax. Rick was recalled to the New York office, and he left Paris permanently on 3-31-77. Joan completed her assignment with the French government on 4-30-77, and left Paris to rejoin her husband in New York.

The Savages have no children. They had itemized deductions of $6,500 for the tax year. During the year, $3,359.10 was withheld from Rick's salary.

Compute the tax liability and net tax payable, or overpayment refundable on their joint return for the current year.

★ ★ Problem 27-11 ★ ★

In 1977, the Atlas Machinery Corp. had gross income of $552,341. This includes: (1) cash dividends from taxable domestic corporations, $2,100; and (2) excess of net long-term capital gain over net short-term capital loss, $8,850. The itemized deductions came to $283,789.

During 1977, the corporation received $650 in dividends from the Hercule Rubber Cie., a corporation that was incorporated in France (not a less developed country). The 10% tax owed to France by Atlas was withheld from the dividends. The Atlas Machinery Corp. owned 11% of the voting stock of Hercule Rubber, and did not deduct the withheld tax. Hercule had accumulated profits of $15,400 and paid $2,400 in income taxes to France.

On 1-1-77, the corporation bought new furniture and fixtures with a 10-year useful life for $17,000. It also bought a new van with a 6-year useful life for $5,400 on that date. The corporation took the maximum investment credit allowed. Atlas does not have an employee stock ownership plan.

On 1-2-77, the corporation sold machinery it had bought on 1-2-72 for $50,000. Its expected useful life at the time was 10 years. The corporation took advantage of the investment credit, under a binding contract.

Assume Atlas Machinery Corp. deposited $112,080 in estimated taxes during the year, and fill in the following schedules.

Schedule J — Tax Computation

1 Taxable income (line 30, page 1)	....
2 Enter line 1 or $25,000, whichever is lesser.	....
3 Line 1 less line 2	....
4 Enter line 3 or $25,000, whichever is lesser.	....
5 Line 3 less line 4	....
6 20% of line 2	....
7 22% of line 4	....
8 48% of line 5	....
9 Income tax (Sum of lines 6, 7 and 8 or alternative tax from separate Schedule D, whichever is lesser:	....
10 (a) Foreign tax credit (attach Form 1118)	....
(b) Investment credit (attach Form 3468)	....
(c) Work incentive (WIN) credit (attach Form 4874)	....
11 Total of lines 10(a), (b), and (c)	....
12 Line 9 less line 11	....
13 Personal holding company tax (attach Schedule PH (Form 1120))	....
14 Tax from recomputing a prior year investment credit (attach Form 4255)	....
15 Tax from recomputing a prior year WIN credit (attach computation)	....
16 Minimum tax on tax preference items (attach Form 4626)	....
17 Total tax—Add lines 12 through 16.	....

Alternative Tax Computation

10 Taxable income	....
11 Excess of net long-term capital gain over net short-term capital loss	....
12 Line 10 less line 11	....
13 Enter line 12 or $25,000, whichever is lesser.	....
14 Line 12 less line 13	....
15 Enter line 14 or $25,000, whichever is lesser.	....
16 Line 14 less line 15	....
17 20% of line 13	....
18 22% of line 15	....
19 48% of line 16	....
20 30% of line 11	....
21 Alternative tax—total of lines 17 through 20. If applicable, enter here and on line 9, Schedule J, and write "ALT." in the margin to the right of the entry .	....

Problem 27-12

Farbrek International is a foreign corporation that manufactures exotic cloth in Europe. It has a branch office located in New York that acts as importer and distributor for Farbrek in the U.S. The activities and cash requirements of the New York branch fluctuate. As a result, it has large cash balances for extended periods of time. During periods when large amounts of cash are not required, some of it is invested in U.S. Treasury bills that are later sold when the cash is needed again. Excess cash that is not needed for the business is used to buy U.S. stocks. These are held in a New York brokerage office in Farbrek's name. Officers of the New York branch manage the portfolio, and the dividends and gains on sales are remitted to Farbrek in Germany. The New York branch also carries on its books, stock of Dolly Corporation, a U.S. corporation that makes and sells toys in the United States. Farbrek owns all the Dolly Corporation stock, and directs its operations solely through Dolly's officers. Dividends on the Dolly stock held by the New York office are paid to the branch and commingled with its general funds, even though its own activities generate all the cash it needs for its own branch operations. For sales that are made on credit, the New York office transfers the accounts receivable to Farbrek.

Explain why or why not the following items are effectively connected U.S. business income.

(a) Interest received on the U.S. Treasury bills.
(b) Interest received on overdue accounts receivable.
(c) Income received from stocks held in the U.S. broker's office.
(d) Dividends received on the Dolly Corporation stock.

Discussion Problem 27-13

A question that has stimulated extensive public debate is whether the U.S. tax on the foreign income of foreign subsidiaries should be deferred until the income is remitted to U.S. shareholders. The Revenue Act of 1962 requires that certain undistributed earnings made in industrialized countries (so-called Subpart F income [¶ 3728]) be taxed to U.S. investors in the year they are earned. This reversal of prior law is regarded as a necessary step by some to prevent tax avoidance. However the idea of attributing undistributed foreign earnings to U.S. shareholders when earned is criticized as being detrimental to the best interests of the U.S. Thus, the controversy continues. Considering economic as well as tax factors, advance some arguments for and against the provisions of the Revenue Act of 1962.

Research Problem 27-14

Joan Clarkson, a U.S. citizen, was employed as a teacher in 1976 and 1977 by the Government of the Trust Territory of the Pacific. She lived in the Territory continuously during the two year period. The Trust Territory was established after World War II by the United Nations and is comprised of numerous island chains in the South Pacific. The United Nations granted the United States administrative and legislative powers over the Territory, whose affairs are under the general power of the Dept. of the Interior. Joan's salary, $10,000 per year, was paid from a general fund established by the Government of the Trust Territory composed of U.S. grant money and locally generated revenue. The Territorial government controlled the teachers' salaries, and taxed U.S. citizens, like Joan, on income earned within the Territory.

Joan consults you, a tax expert, as to the treatment of her 1977 income earned while teaching in the Trust Territory. She claims the entire amount can be excluded from gross income because she was a U.S. citizen who resided in a foreign country for an uninterrupted period which included the taxable year in question and had earned income from sources within the foreign country, all of which entitles her to the exemption for income earned abroad. How would you advise her? Explain.

1. To find the answer, use the Prentice-Hall Complete Federal Tax Equipment in your school or local library. Give your answer, fully explained. In it, show authorities, citing law and opinions applicable, and the P-H Federal Tax Equipment paragraphs where they may be found.

2. Enumerate and explain carefully every step you take in reaching your result. These are extremely important—just as important as the conclusion itself.

ASSIGNMENT No. 28

SOCIAL SECURITY TAXES

(*Note: In the following problems assume that the "tax year" is the calendar year 1977, unless otherwise specified.*)

Problem 28-1

T. Gary's CPA staff includes a secretary at $250 a week and a junior accountant at $400 a week. During the year, he paid several different accounting students $60 for one day's accounting research. In September, Gary became a candidate for the local school board. He paid 3 committeemen $40 each to distribute campaign literature. Near the end of the campaign, he asked his junior accountant to organize a rally and distribute literature at the rally. Gary gave him a $40 personal check for his services.

Explain why Gary will or will not pay social security tax on the payments.

Problem 28-2

Which of the following persons are subject to the social security tax?
(a) Gladys Winesap works in her husband's liquor store.
(b) Buck Vanderstein works for the Peace Corps.
(c) Pamela Papoose, age 17, works as babysitter for $10 a week.
(d) Karen Wright is a civil service employee employed by the F.C.C.
(e) Hal Smith is a brakeman on the Puff and Toot Railroad.
(f) John Marshall, a college student, waits on tables at the fraternity house.

Problem 28-3

During the summer of 1977, Bee Mable hired 10 workers to harvest her fruit crop. Five worked from July 1 to July 5 at a $50 a day rate. They were fired by Bee for their union activities. Three more worked from July 1 to July 31; they were paid $140 each in cash wages for the month. The other two workers received $100 for a 6-day week before they quit.

What social security taxes must Mable pay for some or all of the workers? Explain.

Problem 28-4

Clyde Parker owned and operated a haberdashery store for many years. In January, February and March 1977, he had net earnings of $4,500. At the end of March 1977, he sold his business to Mod Styles, Inc. Pursuant to the sales agreement, he was employed by Mod Styles, Inc. starting April 1, 1977 at a salary of $2,000 per month. Because of a disagreement over policies, Parker resigned from Mod Styles, Inc. on August 31, 1977. He went to work for Menswear Clothing Co. on October 1, 1977, at a salary of $3,000 per month, and worked for them the rest of 1977.

(a) Figure Parker's social security tax liability (including any self-employment tax) for the tax year 1977.

(b) Figure the social security tax, if any, that each of Parker's employers must pay for 1977.

(c) Assume that Parker did not resign from Mod Styles, Inc., and that Menswear Clothing Co. purchased Mod Styles, Inc. on October 1, 1977 and carried on the business the rest of the year. What is the amount of social security tax, if any, that Mod Styles, Inc. will have to pay for Parker? What social security tax, if any, will Menswear Clothing Co. have to pay for Parker?

Problem 28-5

Steve Meyers, a retired basketball star, and his brother Joe were partners in the Brothers' Two Cafe. During 1977, Steve received a guaranteed salary of $12,000 from the partnership, and $1,000 in guaranteed interest on his capital investment in the partnership. The partnership had net income of $20,000 in 1977. Steve and his brother shared profits and losses equally.

Steve was also the sole proprietor of a laundromat. The business had a net loss of $10,700 in 1977. Steve also received $4,000 in 1977 for speaking at a sportswriter's dinner.

What employment taxes, if any, is Steve subject to for 1977?

Problem 28-6

Anne Platt, graduate nurse, worked and attended classes throughout the year as a full time student at U-P University School of Medicine under an Ord Foundation scholarship. To meet her living expenses and supplement her scholarship, she assisted in the training of nurses at the University Hospital on a part time basis. During the year, U-P University furnished her meals and lodging worth $750 and paid her $2,500 in cash.

Must Anne pay social security taxes on this income?

Problem 28-7

(a) Mr. Wayne is a farmer. During the tax year, the gross income from his farming operations was $2,340, and the net income amounted to $1,800. Compute Mr. Wayne's self-employment tax using both the standard and optional method.

(b) Assume the same facts as in (a) above, except that Mr. Wayne's gross income from farming was $2,800 and that his net earnings from farming were $1,500. What is Mr. Wayne's self-employment tax using both methods?

(c) Harold Stevens is the owner of the Sound System, a store which sells stereo equipment. During the tax year, the net profits from the business amounted to $26,000, but a $6,000 loss occurred when Harold was forced to sell the building in which the store was located. What is his self-employment tax for 1977?

Problem 28-8

State whether the following items are "nontaxable wages" for social security tax purposes and explain:
(1) Living quarters furnished apartment house superintendents.
(2) Stock bonus paid to an employee.
(3) Payments to an employee from an employer exempt annuity plan.
(4) An incentive bonus.
(5) Air flight expense paid by employer for an employee's Florida vacation.
(6) Reimbursed payment for business travel.
(7) Dismissal payments.

Problem 28-9

In 1977, Sister Mary had $1,000 of ministerial income. Ordained last year, she had taken the vow of poverty. Sister Mary as full time theology professor at a college, received a salary of $16,200 this year. Also, she was credited with a $3,000 grant for a Bible research project. What social security taxes, if any, must she pay for the amounts received?

Problem 28-10

On Jan. 2, 1977 Dick Brown was hired as an outside salesman for Allco Company at an annual salary of $16,200. Allco management was so satisfied with his work that it offered Brown an incentive bonus of $400 to be paid on Dec. 31, 1977 or Jan. 1, 1978 at his option.

During 1977 Brown received $800 from his partnership ABC. In 1978 Brown expects his salary from Allco to be $16,100, but he expects no partnership income.

Assuming Brown is a cash basis taxpayer and that there is no cost of living adjustment to the wage base in 1978, when should he take the bonus so as to pay the least amount of social security taxes for 1977 and 1978 (including self-employment taxes)? Explain.

Problem 28-11

(a) Paul Goodhands sells life insurance for Guardian Life Insurance Company. The company rents office space for Goodhands in a professional building, and pays his telephone expenses. The company also supplies Goodhands with forms, rate books, and advertising material without cost. Goodhands is also licensed to sell real estate. He only occasionally sells real estate, but when he does he uses the office facilities. Should the company deduct social security taxes from Mr. Goodhands' compensation?

(b) John Depleten, a tax attorney, agreed with the local law school to teach a course in federal taxation. Depleten was required to teach regularly scheduled classes and had to give written exams at the end of the semester. Although Depleten had to teach within the framework of the course as described in the school's catalogue, he was given complete discretion as to the areas of the tax law he could cover. Should the school deduct social security taxes from Mr. Depleten's salary?

Problem 28-12

(a) In 1977, John Marion served as the director of the Apex Corporation, a manufacturer of sporting goods. During the year, he received $13,000 for his services. His sole duty was to participate in director's meetings. He received one half of this amount on July 1, and the balance on December 31. He also worked as the ticket manager for the Intercontinental Hockey League during 1977. The league paid him $800 a month from January through May.

What amount of social security or self-employment tax must Marion pay for the year?

(b) Would your answer to (a) be different if Marion had represented the company at various business meetings and promoted Apex's products at sporting events?

Problem 28-13

Between December 18, 1976 and January 9, 1977, the Triplex Mills Corporation made the following payments into its state unemployment insurance fund: $3,200 for wages paid during 1976 and $1,500 for wages paid during 1975. Triplex paid $3,674 federal tax for unemployment insurance for 1976. How much of the above amounts paid into the state fund can be credited against this 1976 federal tax?

Problem 28-14

John and Carol Hart filed a joint return for 1977. During the year, John earned $12,000 in salary as an assistant store manager. John was also a partner in the Acme partnership. His distributive share of the net income from the partnership was 25%. During 1977, Acme's net income was $20,000. John received only one-half of his distributive share in 1977.

Carol owned a gift shop. In 1977, her net income from the shop was $17,000. How do the Harts account for employment taxes on their return?

Problem 28-15

Sam Cartright is a prosperous Kansas attorney who represents many of the farmers in his area, and has a farm of his own. Buford Hogsmith, a law student, works three hours a day from Mon. through Fri. in Cartright's law office doing legal research.

Each Saturday Buford works as a farm hand from 8:00 A.M. to 4:00 P.M. on Cartright's farm. Buford began working for Cartright on Monday, August 1. In 1977 he earned $900 doing legal research and $550 working on the farm. He was paid weekly. Buford was given the month of December off to prepare for and take his law school exams. On January 2, 1978, he continued his work for Cartright.

What is Cartright's federal unemployment tax liability, if any, for 1977?

Problem 28-16

The Wilson Coal Corp. operates in States A & B. State A has a state unemployment contribution tax rate of 2.9%, and State B a rate of 2.4%. Wilson's total taxable payroll in 1977 was $600,000; 60% paid in State A, the rest in State B.

1978 **Assignment 28—Problems** 5225

On 1-2-77, Wilson Coal was informed by State A that due to the company's exemplary record in stabilizing employment the company's contribution rate for 1977 was reduced to 1.6%.

On 1-14-78, Wilson Coal made its state payment to A. On 2-14-78, it made its payment to B. What is Wilson's federal and state tax liability in each state for 1977?

SUPPLEMENTAL PROBLEMS
Problem 28-17

Mr. Lewin was employed as a barber for the first 8 months of the year for which he earned $8,000 (including tips of $20 or more a month). On September 2, 1977, he opened his own barber shop, which he operated as a sole proprietorship. The gross revenues from the shop for the remainder of the year were $14,800, while the total expenses for the business amounted to $11,000. There was a recognized gain of $300 on the sale of one of the barber chairs used in the business. He received $150 in interest on a loan made to his brother-in-law's trucking company.

On September 2, 1977, Mr. Lewin employed two barbers in his shop, Tony and John. Each received a salary of $500 a month. During 1977 Tony reported to Lewin tips of $475 and John reported tips of $385. Tony did not report his tips of $15 for the month of September, and John did not report his tips for the month of December of $177 until January 10, 1978.

(a) Compute Tony's social security tax, if any, for 1977, including any tax he is required to pay on unreported tips.
(b) Compute John's social security tax, if any, for 1977, including any tax he is required to pay on unreported tips.
(c) Compute the amount of employer social security tax, if any, that Mr. Lewin is required to pay on Tony and John's earnings for 1977.
(d) Compute Mr. Lewin's social security and self-employment tax, if any, for 1977.

Problem 28-18

During 1977, the Brewster Shirt Company employed the following non-exempt employees:
Five employees at $1,200 per month from January 1 to December 31.
Seven employees at $1,000 per month from January 1 to December 31.
Three employees at $800 per month for the months of November and December.
The state unemployment tax rate was 2.8%. However, a low rate of unemployment claims had been filed by Brewster's employees and the state had assigned Brewster an experience rate of 2.4% for unemployment tax purposes. This rate was in effect throughout the year. State unemployment taxes were timely paid at the rate of 2.4%.
Compute the federal unemployment tax for the year.

Problem 28-19

State Y imposes a 3% state tax for unemployment insurance on employers. It also imposes a 1% state tax on employees for the same purpose.

On 3-1-77, Y informs Gridco Corp. that due to its record in stabilizing employment in Y its employer contribution rate is to be reduced to 2%. Gridco had a total taxable payroll of $200,000 in Y in 1977.

On 1-11-78, Gridco paid State Y its employee withheld tax. On 3-16-78, it paid its employer contribution. What is Gridco's credit allowance for 1977?

★ Problem 28-20 ★

Phil Hall owns and operates a dairy store. His wife died on 11-1-76 and he has dependent children, John and Joanne. During the year, he purchased and placed into service a new refrigerated truck which cost $9,000 and had a useful life of 6 years, and a new ice cream machine which cost $500 and had a 5-year useful life. His net earnings from the business during 1977 were $17,000. From his partnership interest in the Nittany Co. he had a loss of $2,100 for the year. He had no wages during the year. His 1977 taxable income was $44,950. Hall elects itemized deductions and qualifies as a surviving spouse. He paid an estimated tax (including self-employment tax) of $12,867.10. Fill in the following schedule.

16	Tax, check if from: ☐ Tax Table ☐ Schedule G ☐ Tax Rate Schedule X, Y or Z ☐ Form 2555 OR ☐ Schedule D ☐ Form 4726	16	
17a	Multiply $35.00 by the number of exemptions	17a	
b	**Enter 2% of taxable income up to $180**	17b	
	Enter larger of a or b	17c	
18	Balance. Subtract line 17c from line 16 and enter difference (but not less than zero)	18	
19	Credits	19	
20	Balance. Subtract line 19 from line 18 and enter difference (but not less than zero)	20	
21	Other taxes	21	
22	Total (add lines 20 and 21)	22	
23a	Total Federal income tax withheld. (attach Forms W-2, or W-2P to front)	23a	
b	1977 estimated tax payments (include amount allowed as credit from 1976 return)	23b	
c	Earned income credit.	23c	
d	Amount paid with Form 4868	23d	
e	Other payments	23e	
24	**TOTAL** (add lines 23a through e)	24	
25	If line 22 is larger than line 24, enter **BALANCE DUE IRS**	25	
26	If line 24 is larger than line 22, enter amount **OVERPAID**	26	
27	Amount of line 26 to be **REFUNDED TO YOU**	27	
28	Amount of line 26 to be credited on 1978 estimated tax ▶	28	

Pay amount on line 25 in full with this return. Write social security number and check or money order and make payable to Internal Revenue Service.

Cumulative Problem 28-21

Mr. Crown was employed as a grocery clerk for the first six months of 1977 and earned $3,000. During the year, he also earned $500 as a Christian Science practitioner. On July 1, 1977, he established his own grocery store, which he operated as a sole proprietorship. The results of operations for 1977 are reflected below:

Sales	$30,000
Cost of sales	10,000
Other business expenses	19,000
Gain on sale of depreciable property used in business	10,000
Dividends on securities	500

Figure Mr. Crown's self-employment tax liability for 1977. Assume he did not claim exemption for his Christian Science income.

Tax Reasoning Problem 28-22

During 1977, Mike Jackson was employed as a salesman by the Hub Company. His yearly salary was $11,400 and as a limited partner in Atlas Co. a concern engaged in the stock brokerage business, he received $4,000 of Atlas profits. Other partners of Atlas received larger shares of the profits than did Jackson on account of their active participation in the business. In fact, the Atlas partnership agreement prohibited Jackson from doing anything for the business. He never came to the Atlas offices or performed any services for the partnership. What will be Jackson's social security liability for 1977?

1978

5227

ASSIGNMENT No. 29

FEDERAL ESTATE TAX

(Note: In the following problems, unless otherwise specified, assume that the "tax year" is the calendar year 1977, that the decedent was a citizen and resident of the United States who died after August 16, 1954).

Problem 29-1

M. Jay died on 7-4-77, survived by a brother. An inventory taken shortly after his death reveals these assets: $10,000 life insurance policy the proceeds of which were payable to his brother (Jay owned and retained the right to change the beneficiary of the policy at death); $15,000 in securities registered in Jay's name; $15,000 life insurance policy on Jay applied for by the brother who paid the premiums and is the beneficiary (Jay owed his brother $15,000 when the policy was taken out); and an apartment building in Alaska valued at $36,000. Upon further examination of the estate, the administrator found that one year before death, Jay purchased an annuity contract valued at $10,000. Life payments to Jay under the contract were to begin on 8-1-77. What property would be included in his gross estate? Explain.

Problem 29-2

At the time of his death, M. Deal owned as a single person, a condominium apartment in Florida and a winter residence in Vermont. Each property was declared exempt from local property tax assessments. Deal's executor discovered a $30,000 bank deposit Deal had made in joint names of himself and his father. The deposit agreement provided that upon the death of either Deal or his father, the survivor would be entitled to the full deposit. In addition, by his will, Deal exercised a general power of appointment over the corpus of a $100,000 trust fund. Under the appointment, the trust went to Deal's two nephews in equal shares.

Which items will be included in Deal's gross estate?

Problem 29-3

(a) P. Range, age 70, transferred his house and lot to his daughter and son-in-law without restrictions. Range continues to live in the house after the transfer even though no agreement, expressed or implied, had been made before or after the transfer to create for him such a possessory right. In addition, Range paid the property taxes that became due. The property was worth $63,000. Should any amount be in Range's gross estate when he dies? Explain.

(b) Assume the same facts as in (a) except that Range transferred the property with a proviso in the deed that he was entitled to use the property as long as he lived and his daughter and son-in-law would take possession of the property when he dies. Would your answer be the same? Explain.

Problem 29-4

C.B. Inter Company made a lump-sum payment to Clarence's wife, his designated beneficiary, under the company's noncontributory profit-sharing plan. Clarence worked for the company 40 years and he died before his retirement age of 65. Is the payment included in Clarence's estate?

Problem 29-5

(a) P. J. Wilcox bought a condominium apartment for $20,000 and recorded the property interest in his and his wife's name as joint tenants by the entirety. Under the law of the state where the apartment is located, it is presumed that P. J. made a gift of half the property to his wife. If P. J. dies this year, would $20,000 or $10,000 be included in his gross estate?

(b) Assume the same facts as in (a) except that at the time the interest in the property was recorded, Wilcox also filed a timely gift tax return electing to treat the transfer to his wife as a taxable gift. Would your answer be the same if each interest created in the property is a "qualified joint interest".

Problem 29-6

Carol Tree and her brother Clarence acquired a house by an inter-vivos gift from their mother taking title as tenants in common. Carol and her husband, Jack, already owned a house as joint tenants each having paid one-half the purchase price. They all agreed to sell both houses and buy one larger 2-family house. They were paid $25,000 for Carol and Clarence's house and $35,000 for Carol and Jack's house. In turn, they paid the $60,000 for the new house and took title in the 3 names as tenants in common. Clarence lived on the 1st floor and Jack and Carol on the 2nd floor. When Carol died the house was appraised at $75,000. How much, if any, should be included in Carol's gross estate if these values are accepted for estate tax purposes?

Problem 29-7

William Sheehan died in July 1977 leaving a wife and 2 children. Since the provisions of his will did not satisfy his wife, she elected to take against the will. As a result of this action, she received $3,500 in cash outright and a life interest in a trust, the principal of which is ⅓ the estate.
(a) Will the value of her share be includible in Sheehan's gross estate?
(b) What part of her share, if any, will qualify for the marital deduction?

Problem 29-8

In his will dated 4-1-42, Neil Arthur set up a trust. The income from it was to go to his brother, Alfred, for life. His daughter Mary was named trustee with unrestricted power to distribute the trust corpus when Alfred dies. In June 1946, Neil reopened his will and added a codicil. He also added a clause that Mary did not have to comply with, but asked that she distribute the trust corpus to Mary's children. Neil died 7-1-49. Mary died in an airplane accident in February of this year before Alfred died. Mary did not leave a will.

Will the trust corpus be included in Mary's estate?

Problem 29-9

(a) Henry Gordon died in April 1941. In his will he created a trust, the income to be paid to Gordon's daughter, Mary, for life, with a general power of appointment in Mary over the remainder, exercisable by an instrument to be delivered to the trustee during Mary's life. Mary exercised the power in 1970. She died in 1977. Is the trust property includible in Mary's gross estate?

(b) Another provision in Henry Gordon's will left an apartment house to his son, Mark, for life, remainder as he may designate in his will. Mark died intestate in 1977. Is the value of the apartment house includible in his gross estate?

Problem 29-10

In January 1975, Linda and Alice Dixon, elderly sisters, became life beneficiaries of a $340,000 trust fund with remainder to Linda's daughter, Rene. Each sister was to receive ½ of the trust's annual income. In years that trust income was insufficient to give each sister an annual income of $30,000, the trust instrument gave each sister the noncumulative right to draw up to $25,000 from principal to make up any difference. Trust income in 1975 was $52,000, in 1976 it was $14,000 and in 1977 it was $28,000. Linda never took more than her share of trust income because she thought of Rene as the family heir. Alice also felt this way and in 1975 took only income. In 1976, she had unusual medical expenses and, in addition to ½ the income, took her full share of the trust principal, $23,000 ($30,000 less ½ of $14,000). Both sisters had been in ill health and died in December 1977. Each had received her ½ income for 1977, but had not requested any trust principal. Can any of the remaining trust principal be included in Linda's gross estate? In Alice's gross estate?

Problem 29-11

Harry Horlick was quite ill in 1973, and he spent some time in the hospital. However, he made a rapid recovery, and in 1974 his doctor told him that he was in excellent health, and that he need have no fear of a recurrence of his illness. He had made substantial gifts of money and property to his children in previous years. He believed that a man of wealth should give sums of money to his children during his lifetime while he could advise them as to its proper use. He also wanted to see what his children would do with the money so that he would know better how to dispose of the remainder of his wealth. In 1974, 1975 and 1976 he continued his policy of making gifts to his children. He made total gifts during those years of $200,000. In the early part of 1977 he was struck with a sudden and completely unexpected recurrence of his illness and died a short time later. The Revenue Service contends that the gifts totaling $200,000 made from 1974 through 1976 are includible in Horlick's gross estate as transfers made in contemplation of death.

(a) How would the Revenue Service go about proving that the gifts were in contemplation of death?

(b) Do you agree with the Revenue Service's contention? Explain.

Problem 29-12

Ten years ago, P. C. Steed transferred income-producing securities to an irrevocable trust, with the income payable to his wife, Gloria during her lifetime. At her death the trust property was to be transferred to the American Cancer Society. At the same time, Gloria deeded her income-producing real estate to a trust with the income to be shared equally by P.C. and herself during their joint lives. She reserved to herself the right to transfer by will any remaining interests. P.C. died in 1977, and was survived by Gloria.

(a) What part, if any, of the value of the securities will be included in the P.C. estate? Explain.

(b) Will the property deeded by Gloria become part of her gross estate? Explain.

Problem 29-13

(a) On May 1, 1949, M. C. Rye transferred $150,000 worth of securities in trust to accumulate income for his life. At his death the corpus of the trust was to be paid over to his son, John. John died in 1976. Rye made no change in the trust because he intended to will his estate to his grandson. He knew that under state law the corpus of a trust is returned to the grantor or his estate when all other interests in the trust have ended or lapsed. Rye was killed in an accident in 1977 without having made a will. At the time of his death the trust securities were worth $300,000. What amount of the trust corpus, if any, should be included in Rye's gross estate?

(b) On October 10, 1972, Peter Paul transferred $75,000 in cash in trust to accumulate income for his life. On his death the corpus is payable to his daughter, Rose. If Rose dies before him, $50,000 of the principal is to revert to him and the rest to his wife. In June 1977, Peter tried to sell his interest in the trust. The best offer he could get from any source was $2,714. He did not sell. On July 4th Peter accidentally drowned while boating. At the time of the accident his daughter was 18. What amount of the trust corpus, if any, should be included in Peter's gross estate?

Problem 29-14

Taylor Allen created an inter vivos trust with the income to be divided equally between his two children and upon the death of either, ½ the corpus of the trust is payable to his estate, and upon the death of the survivor the remaining corpus is payable to his estate. Allen reserved the right to alter or amend the terms of the trust or to revoke it completely if both beneficiaries granted their consent. State law allowed the grantor-settlor and beneficiaries of a trust to jointly change or revoke a trust. Allen died in 1977 with the trust terms in effect as stated.

(a) Would the trust property be included in Allen's estate?

(b) Would your answer be the same, if in addition to the reservation stated, Allen had the right to remove the trustee at any time and to appoint himself as successor trustee?

Problem 29-15

When Stella Dow died in 1977, there were 5 policies on her life which became vested in interest.

(1) A $25,000 limited payment policy; this policy was purchased by Stella when she was married and had been fully paid-up in 1973. The sole beneficiary was her husband, Peter. By the terms of the policy, Stella could not change the beneficiary and had no other reserved power over the policy.

(2) A $50,000 policy taken out by Woolton Industries when Stella was appointed its chief purchasing agent. Woolton kept custody of the policy at all times. The proceeds were payable half to the corporation and half to Stella's husband, Peter. Woolton had complete control of the policy except that it could not be surrendered without Peter's consent. Stella owned no Woolton stock.

(3) Two policies, each for $15,000, one payable to Stella's married daughter and the other to her married son. Stella had the right to borrow on each policy and also, to change the beneficiaries.

(4) A policy purchased by Peter. He paid the premiums and had named himself beneficiary.

What amount of the insurance will be included in Stella's gross estate? Explain. None of the policies had been transferred or assigned.

Problem 29-16

Tea Top Insurance Company stock is listed on a Midwest Exchange. T.S. Franco who owned 1,000 shares of this stock died on November 20. His executors elected to value his estate on the date of death. On November 20, the quotations on the exchange for Tea Top stock show the following sales figures: Open, $88; High, $92; Low, $87; Close, $88. What value for the Tea Top Company stock should the executors report in the estate return for the decedent?

Problem 29-17

Barbara Kuhn bequeathed her entire estate to her husband, Joseph, on condition that they did not die in a common disaster, or that Joseph survives her by 4 months. On July 1, the Kuhns were in an auto accident. Barbara died instantly and although Joseph was injured in the accident he survived and remarried on Dec. 1.

(a) Is Barbara's estate entitled to a marital deduction?

(b) Assume the same facts as in (a) except that the condition of the bequest was that they did not die in a common disaster and that Joseph was to survive probate. Would your answer be the same if Joseph survived probate which took 4 months?

Problem 29-18

When Vera Brown died on December 10, 1977, she owned the following property: a home in Maryland worth $40,000; a summer home in Canada worth $12,000; stocks worth $70,000 and $25,000 cash in savings bank accounts.

Under Vera's will, the Maryland property goes to her husband, Paul, for life. After his death the property will go to their daughter unless Paul makes some other disposition of the remainder in his will. The Canadian property goes to her daughter. All other remaining property is divided equally between her husband and daughter after paying debts and expenses of the estate.

Among Vera's effects, the executor found an insurance policy on Vera's life for $30,000 naming her husband as the beneficiary. A memorandum attached to the policy showed Vera had changed the beneficiary from her daughter to her husband on September 15, 1977. The executor also found a deed transferring an office building in Chicago from Vera to her daughter. The deed, dated April 10, 1975 was recorded by the daughter on April 15, 1975. A note on the deed recited a gift tax of $10,275 had been paid on a value of $75,000. A qualified real estate appraiser hired by the executor filed an affidavit deposing that the building had a $90,000 value when Vera died. Also, he paid off a $10,000 mortgage on the Maryland property with cash from the savings accounts. The administration expenses, including commissions, amount to $32,000.

What is the marital deduction for the estate if the executor does not elect an alternate valuation date?

Problem 29-19

Peal Vincent who died in 1977, directed in his will that his wife, Elinor, receive all property Vincent owned or had power to appoint, except for $70,000 in cash given to his church. There were no children.

The Vincent property was a home worth $110,000 on the date Peal died jointly owned by Peal and Elinor as tenants by the entirety. Peal had supplied the entire purchase price in 1963. At the time of the creation of the joint interest, Peal did not elect to treat Elinor's interest as a taxable gift. Peal had personal savings accounts totaling $63,000. He also had $74,000 in joint savings accounts with Elinor to which both had contributed equal amounts. Peal had 2 insurance policies: Policy A provided that the proceeds, $100,000, were payable to Elinor, Peal had transferred in 1973 all his rights to Elinor and she paid the premiums; Policy B was for $150,000 and the proceeds were also payable to Elinor, but Peal could change the beneficiary. There were securities worth $45,000 at the date of death and registered in Peal's and Elinor's names as joint owners; Peal had contributed ⅔ of their original cost, Elinor the rest. Peal also had a general power under the will of his father dated in 1964 to appoint $170,000 as he saw fit. The father died in 1968.

Peal had great interest in art and at death owned a collection appraised at $190,000. Just before he died, Peal had mortgaged his home for $30,000. Other debts, and funeral and administrative expenses of the estate totaled $29,000 and a $4,200 state death tax for property in the residuary estate.

Assume the executor elected to value the assets in gross estate at their date of death value. Peal made no other lifetime transfers for which a gift tax return would have been required. What is the estate tax on Peal's estate? Apply the "unified" estate and gift tax rates. Disregard all credits except the "unified" credit.

Problem 29-20

When Joe Alex died on December 1, 1976, his estate consisted of a home worth $25,000, proceeds of a $10,000 life insurance policy payable to his estate, $5,000 cash and a ⅓ capital interest in a 3-man partnership that operates the XYZ Manufacturing Company. His partnership interest was worth $250,000 when Alex died. The partnership agreement provided that the heir of any deceased partner would be accepted as a partner in the firm.

Joe had bequeathed his entire estate to his only relative, a nephew he had not heard from for 20 years. His will stated he wished his nephew to continue in the partnership as a full ⅓ partner and directed the executor to sell the home if necessary and use any cash in the estate to find the nephew. After spending $20,000 in the search, the executor has just located Joe's nephew in Russia on February 1, 1977. He cannot arrive in the United States until April 15th.

The executor asks you to advise him how he can keep the partnership interest intact for the nephew without paying any penalty or interest, considering that the estate tax due is $47,250, he has only $20,000 cash available, and $17,500 of administration expenses and commissions are still unpaid. What would you advise him?

SUPPLEMENTAL PROBLEM
Problem 29-21

C. Raymond, age 55, decided some time ago to dispose of his assets so that his immediate family could enjoy the property while he was alive. He made his intentions known to his family, business associates and legal counsel. His family were his wife, Esther, his married daughters, Pat and Theresa and his twin sons, Peter and Albert, who were unmarried.

In furtherance of his intentions, in May 1974, Raymond transferred all of his computer business stock worth $25,000 to his daughters. In 1975, he created an inter-vivos trust with $100,000 worth of securities. The income was payable jointly to him and Esther for life, then to the survivor during the survivor's life, and, at the survivor's death, the trust property was to be divided equally between the twin boys.

In 1976, Raymond gave to the Suburban Museum, a cultural institution, by deed of gift his treasured gun collection. In the deed of gift, Raymond reserved to himself the right to the use, possession and enjoyment of the collection during his lifetime and after Raymond's death, for a ten-year period, his twin sons have the right to possession and use of the collection. After that ten-year period, title is to be vested in the museum.

In 1976, Raymond transferred a summer cottage valued at $40,000 located near a resort lake to his daughters and sons as joint tenants.

Raymond died on June 15. His will provided that all property not disposed of during his life is to go to his wife, Esther. His remaining property was his surburban home worth $65,000 with a $25,000 mortgage outstanding against it. All taxes have been paid. On Dec. 15 Esther had several offers from developers offering Esther $200,000 for the house and she directed the executor to sell it. He sold it on Dec. 31 for $250,000.

Raymond's life insurance of $150,000 was paid directly to Esther. The policy gave Raymond the right to change the beneficiary. Raymond was receiving monthly payments under a joint and survivor annuity policy beginning last year. He and Esther bought the policy 5 years ago. He paid $25,000 and she paid $75,000 toward the cost. Under the annuity contract, no payments will be made after Esther's death.

A gun expert hired by the executor appraised the collection at a value of $175,000. Suburban Museum agreed to pay 2% state inheritance tax on transfers to cultural institutions.

(a) List the items included in the gross estate; also list any items that are excluded from the gross estate. Give reasons.

(b) Discuss reasons for alternate valuation dates for estate property. What are possible valuation dates for the Raymond estate?

(c) What deductions are allowed to the estate? Explain.

Cumulative Problem 29-22

Robert Gray, a widower and resident of Ohio, died on November 3, 1977. Upon examining his affairs, his executors found:

1. Gray purchased securities which were valued at $25,000 on the date of his death. These were registered in his name and that of his daughter as joint owners.

2. Gray owned a residence in Columbus valued at $45,000; also a winter home in Florida valued at $40,000. These he willed to his son.

3. Gray exercised by his will a general power of appointment granted to him by his late wife's will over a $250,000 trust fund, which was not includible in her gross estate.

4. Gray created in 1943 an irrevocable trust of $80,000 to pay the income and principal to his children; but reserving to himself power to alter or change the beneficiaries or their proportionate interests, except that he could not name himself or his estate as a beneficiary.

5. In 1972, Gray deposited $52,000 in the Provident bank in the names of himself and his mother jointly. The agreement of deposit provided that upon the death of either Mr. Gray or his mother, the survivor is entitled to the full amount on deposit.

6. In 1975, in order to save income taxes and to give his mother an independent income, Gray created an irrevocable trust of $160,000. All of the trust income

was distributed to his mother. None of it was used to discharge Mr. Gray's legal obligation to support his mother.

7. Mr. Gray was insured for $180,000. Under policies aggregating $145,000 in amount, he had reserved the right to change the beneficiary. Under the rest of the policies, he had no right to change the beneficiary, borrow on the policies, assign them, or otherwise use them for his benefit; all of these powers were vested in Mrs. Gray, his mother, who was named as beneficiary. Mr. Gray paid all the premiums on all the policies.

8. Mr. Gray had been receiving the income from another trust valued at $75,000 created by his deceased wife. The trust instrument provided that at Mr. Gray's death, the corpus should be distributed to his children in equal shares. Mr. Gray had no power to invade the corpus during his lifetime or control its distribution.

9. Mr. Gray left the following additional property to be distributed under his will:

Bank accounts	$ 85,000
Stocks	450,000
Furniture, automobiles, personal effects and fixtures	86,000
State exempt securities	90,000
Life insurance payable to his executors	25,000

During administration of the estate, the executors paid out the following amounts:

To creditors (bona fide claims incurred for an adequate and full consideration)	$ 67,000
Administration expenses	72,000

The executors also paid the following specific bequests:

To Siwash U. (for educational purposes)	$ 70,000
To Siwash U. Boosters Club, a non-profit organization (to provide financial assistance to deserving members of the Siwash football team)	20,000
To Unity Church (for religious purposes)	120,000

The executors also paid state death taxes of $48,000. They elected to value the estate property at date of death, and those are the values indicated above. The executors determined that no gift tax had been paid by Gray on any of his lifetime transfers.

Compute the net estate tax payable.

Discussion Problem 29-23

The marital deduction has been the subject of considerable controversy since it was introduced into law by the Revenue Act of 1948. Some tax experts contend that the deduction should be made more liberal. This was done by the Reform Act of 1976 which increased the deduction. Others urge its curtailment or outright elimination.

(a) What arguments can you give to support the deduction?
(b) What arguments can you give for curtailing or eliminating the deduction?

ASSIGNMENT No. 30

FEDERAL GIFT TAX

(Note: In the following problems, unless otherwise specified, assume that the "tax year" is the calendar year 1977, and the donor is a citizen and resident of the United States.)

Problem 30-1

When W. C. Harris died, he willed his entire estate to his widow, Alice. One of the assets was a $5,000 note signed by the Harris' son, Ben, payable on demand. Ben told Alice he had borrowed the money some years ago. His father had never asked him to repay it, but he could pay her any time she wanted him to. Alice told him to forget the loan, and tore up the note. Was there a taxable gift? Explain.

Problem 30-2

Nancy Wilson's son is married and is about to give up a steady job to start his own business. She wants to be sure the son's family has a steady income for the next several years, so she proposes to transfer $100,000 worth of tax-exempt bonds to her son. The words "Exempt from all tax" is printed on the face of the bonds. Advise Nancy as to whether the gift is taxable gift. Explain.

Problem 30-3

Mary Earl lives in a non-community property state. She bought a summer home in July, 1976 with funds she received from her employer's profit-sharing plan. Title to the property was taken in the joint name of Mary and her husband. In July, 1977, they sold the home, and each deposited half the proceeds in their separate bank accounts. When and under what circumstances may gift tax liability arise from these transactions?

Problem 30-4

Harris Gordon died on April 15, 1977. His will provided the $100,000 worth of stock he owned was to be used to create a trust with the income payable to his wife for life. She also had the power to appoint the entire trust property to one or more of her children or their descendants during her life or to appoint the corpus by will in whatever way she wished. Is there any gift tax liability if Mrs. Gordon exercises her power by transferring the corpus to her married son on July 21, 1977?

Problem 30-5

Sidney Clyde and his wife Mary, each have a one-half vested interest in community property under their state law. The Clydes owned 33,000 shares of Tango Inc. stock as community property and Sidney owned, individually, 4,000 shares. John, their son, owned 1,000 shares. There were no other stockholders. To give John control of the corporation and to equalize their own holdings the Clydes transferred 19,000 of the community property shares to John, and Sidney Clyde relinquished his community property interest in 4,000 shares to make them the separate property of his wife, Mary. No consideration was paid for any of the transfers. What gifts, if any, resulted from these transactions?

Problem 30-6

(a) Jimmy Adams heard that his uncle, Harry, had just placed an order for a new car. Jimmy told him that he would like to buy his old car for $500. The uncle sold the car to Jimmy for $500 although several car dealers had offered the uncle $1,000 for it. Was this transaction a gift?

(b) P. Howard put his condominium apartment on the market for $50,000. Its appraised value was $40,000. To make a quick sale, he let the house go to J. D. Snow for $39,000. Did this sale result in a gift?

Is the above transaction subject to gift tax? Explain.

Problem 30-7

In 1975, Albert Beck established a trust with a principal of $500,000 worth of stocks. Income from the trust is paid annually to Albert's daughter during his life. At his death any stock in the trust will be divided equally between his daughter and his grandson. Albert owns the Wright Materials Co. and has to get large bank loans from time to time to pay for materials, so he put a clause in the trust instrument that gives him the right to require the trustee to deposit all or part of the trust as freely transferable collateral for loans he may need for the business. On January 15, 1977, Albert sold the Wright Materials Co.

Does Albert have a liability for gift tax for a taxable quarter in 1975, 1976, or 1977?

Problem 30-8

On March 16, Miles Minter bought a single premium $25,000 ordinary life policy for $13,650, naming his wife the irrevocable beneficiary. On that day, the policy had a cash surrender value of $13,000.

(a) Has there been a taxable gift as a result of this transaction?

(b) If a gift has been made, what valuation should be used in computing the gift tax?

Problem 30-9

Under a retirement plan of Bram College, Frank Joseph, a tax accounting professor, is to receive an annuity for life when he retires. A provision in the plan allows Frank, either before or after retirement, to designate a surviving beneficiary upon his death. On March 1, 1977, Frank made an irrevocable election whereby he is to receive a lesser annuity, and after his death annuity payments will be continued to his wife. Bram College purchased the retirement annuity contract from a life insurance company at a cost of $20,000 of which Frank reported $4,000 as taxable employee contributions under the 20% exclusion rule for an employee of a tax exempt organization. The premium the company would have charged for the reduced retirement annuity payments for Frank's life alone is $15,000. What is the value of Frank's gift for gift tax purposes?

Problem 30-10

This year, James Richards established a trust fund for the benefit of his 5-year old granddaughter, Denise, the net income to be used for her benefit or accumulated each year until she reaches age 30. Any income accumulated before Denise reaches 21 is to be paid to Denise when she reaches 21 or to her estate if she dies before then. When Denise reaches age 30, she is to receive the principal and income accumulated since she was 21, or if she dies before then, it is to be paid to her estate. Can James take advantage of the individual exclusion? Explain.

Problem 30-11

During their married life, Bob Ames celebrated anniversaries by giving his wife, Clara, a number of gifts. In 1977 on their wedding anniversary, Bob gave Clara a life interest valued at $10,000 in income from an apartment house. On his death, the apartment is to go to their daughter Carol. In 1968, while they were temporarily residing in Spain, he gave her a necklace valued at $5,000. On their wedding anniversary in 1954, when Clara was 52 years old, Bob arranged with his bank that it assume custodial care of 500 shares of a blue chip stock and pay the annual income of $1,500 to Clara for life. If Bob dies before Clara, the stock will go to Carol when Clara dies. In 1967, Bob gave Clara an antique gold pin valued at $7,000. In 1963, the Ames were domiciled in a community property state. Bob bought as community property, a ranch valued at $14,000, and later that same year, on their wedding anniversary, transferred his interest in the ranch to Clara as a gift. For their anniversary in 1947 Bob bought Clara a fine ebony carving worth $6,000.

(a) Which of these gifts qualify for the marital deduction? Explain.

(b) What is the taxable amount of the gifts that qualify for the marital deduction?

Problem 30-12

On March 6, 1977, Sally Evans gave her husband $1,800 in cash. On April 6, she gave him stock worth $102,200. On December 10, she gave him jewelry worth $6,000. What would be the amount of Sally's marital deduction if she made no other gifts after (a) March 6; (b) April 6; (c) December 10?

Problem 30-13

B. R. Stone had an extremely good year in 1977, and on December 25 he decided to share his good fortune with his 12 nephews and nieces. To 11 of them he gave immediate gifts of cash: $5,000 each to 5 of them, $4,000 each to 4 of them, and $3,000 each to 2 of them. For the youngest nephew, Philip, age 9, Stone established an irrevocable trust of $19,000, the income to be used for Philip's benefit until he reaches age 21 and then transferred outright to him or his estate, or as he may appoint if he dies before then. Stone has never made any other gifts and claims the unified credit. What is Stone's gift tax for 1977?

Problem 30-14

On December 10, 1976, Bob Dawson gave his nephew, Tom, and Tom's wife, Alice, $23,000 in domestic stocks for a wedding present, and to his niece, Pat, for an engagement gift, an antique tea-set valued at $11,000. Bob contributed $8,000 to the Boy Scouts. Bob gave his intended wife, Joy, a matched pearl necklace, worth $49,000. Bob, who had been supporting his elderly parents, transferred $65,000 to an irrevocable trust. This provided that trust income was to be paid equally to each parent for life and then to the survivor for life. The survivor was given a general power to appoint the trust corpus by will. Joy gave Bob a diamond studded watch worth $2,900. She also gave Bob, who was very fond of water sports, a yacht worth $46,000. Bob and Joy were married on January 2, 1977. Neither Bob nor Joy had made any other gifts than those described above.

(a) What is the least possible gift tax each must pay for the last quarter of 1976?

(b) What would the tax be if Bob and Joy had postponed all their December 1976 gifts to January 1977 after their marriage and then agreed to split their gifts?

Problem 30-15

Winston Brown bought a ranch in 1975 for $250,000. On Nov. 1, 1977, he advertised it for sale. Brown received a firm offer of $280,000 from several prospective buyers. His wife objected to the sale because she wanted their son to have the property. When the contract was prepared, she refused to sign it or to join in the deed or release her dower rights. Her dower rights alone have no value. The buyer withdrew his original offer, but said he would pay $200,000 for the ranch even if Winston's wife did not join in the sale. On Dec. 1, 1977, Winston and his wife sold the ranch to their son for $20,000.

Determine whether the transfer of the ranch is a taxable gift, and if so, find the lowest gift tax payable for the fourth quarter of 1977, assuming the Browns have never before made a gift in excess of their annual exclusions.

Problem 30-16

Jesse Hill works for Webster Brothers, a partnership owned in equal shares by Harold and Jim Webster. The firm has a qualified contributory self-employment retirement plan. The plan provides for retirement at age 60 and allows members to elect irrevocably a survivor annuity for a beneficiary at that time. Both Jesse and Harold who are married, select their wives for this annuity when they retire. In 1977, Jesse reaches age 60 and retires. His retirement pension is based on a principal sum of $25,000 to which the firm contributed $15,000 and Jesse $10,000. Jesse's wife's survivor annuity is computed from actuarial tables to be worth $8,000.

(a) What is the value of the taxable gift, if any, that Jesse has made to his wife?

(b) What would your answer be if Harold retired and the same facts apply to him and his wife, except that the entire $25,000 was contributed and deducted as an income tax deduction by the firm?

SUPPLEMENTAL PROBLEMS

Problem 30-17

On 1-2-77, Morris Cotton created three $250,000 trusts. The annual income of each trust is $10,000. Income of one trust is to be paid to Morris' wife for life, with the power to appoint the principal in her will. Income of the second trust is to be paid to Morris' daughter and son-in-law for their joint lives with the principal to be paid to the survivor. Income of the third trust is to be paid to Morris' son and daughter-in-law for their joint lives, then to the survivor with the principal being paid to their son when the survivor dies.

Cotton has made these other previous gifts: in 1924, a wedding gift of $10,000 to his wife on June 10th; in 1938, a $50,000 diamond ring to his wife on June 10th; in 1948, on January 2, $10,000 worth of stock each to his son and daughter and on June 10th $50,000 worth of stock to his wife. Morris deducted his full specific exemption when he reported the 1938 gift. Mrs. Cotton has made no gifts of her own property.

What is Mr. and Mrs. Morris' least total gift tax liability for 1977 if they have elected to split all possible gifts and they made no other gifts in 1977?

Problem 30-18

Edith Tite, a widow 77 years old, made the following distributions of property: to her son, $3,000 cash; to her daughter, personal jewelry worth $3,000; $6,000 to the Red Cross for disaster relief; $12,000 in trust to Winsocki University for a scholarship in the name of her grandson, Charles, if Charles should predecease her. Edith also agreed to transfer her $8,000 summer cottage to 17-year old Charles for $5,000 when he completed his military service four years later. She told Charles about the scholarship fund, and that under the terms of the trust, Charles' father, as trustee could, if necessary, use the principal or income for Charles, and if Edith died before him, Charles would get the money outright. Edith figured she did not have to pay a gift tax because of deductions and exclusions, so she did not file a return. Why did she receive a notice of deficiency for gift taxes?

Problem 30-19

Gary Inde has made gifts to his children over many years. On Feb. 2, 1965, he gave his son stock worth $100,000 that he paid $78,000 for in 1963. On Jan. 1, 1967, he gave his daughter an apartment house worth $50,000. He had bought the building on Jan. 1, 1947 for $80,000, made no improvements or additions and deducted $40,000 depreciation for the building on his income tax returns. She continued to deduct $2,000 depreciation each year and made no improvements. In 1975, he gave his son an antique gun collection worth $24,000 that had cost $25,000 and he gave his daughter jewelry valued at $40,000 that cost him $38,000. These were the only gifts Gary has made. He took $15,000 of his specific exemption in 1967 and $15,000 in 1975. He paid all gift taxes due.

During all the taxable quarters of 1977, the children still own all the property they received. What were the properties' adjusted bases on January 1, 1977?

Cumulative Problem 30-20

In 1969, John Beech, age 55 and in good health, started a program of making gifts of his property to his family. He wanted to be free to enjoy himself without the problems of supervising his investments and at the same time provide for his family and cut down his federal estate tax. On March 1, he established a trust with $50,000 worth of stocks that pay an annual dividend of $5,000. The trust income is payable to John's wife, Estella for life. At her death, their son, Ray will receive the trust corpus; but if Estella dies before John, she can appoint him by will to receive the annual income and the corpus will go to Ray at John's death. On September 10th, John also transferred in trust an apartment house worth $70,000 that earns a net rental of $7,000 a year. The trust income is payable annually to his unmarried daughter, Alice, for life. At her death the property is to go to his grandson, son of Ray, or, if Alice should marry, to her children in equal shares.

On April 14, 1970, John gave his wife $150,000 worth of stocks. His daughter died in May, 1970. Alice's will provided that her father, John was to receive all the property in her estate except money. The money is to be paid to her mother after paying all debts, expenses and death taxes. The only property she owned at death was $2,000 cash in savings banks and $70,000 worth of Texas state bonds she had inherited from her grandmother in 1964. She had no debts at her death. Administration expenses for her estate were $1,200 and state death taxes were $212. No commissions were paid.

On July 1, 1971, John established a trust with $100,000 worth of 2½% U.S. Treasury bonds. Income from the trust is to be accumulated until his grandson reaches the age of 35. Income and corpus are to be paid to him then. The maximum specific exemption allowed was used in 1971.

On September 8, 1974, John sold a partnership interest worth $30,000 to his son Ray for $5,000. John's basis for the partnership interest had been reduced to zero at the time. He reported the $5,000 gain on his income tax return for the year.

John made no further gifts. He still owned a house worth $40,000, the Texas state bonds inherited from his daughter, $100,000 worth of stocks and $15,000 in savings bank accounts when he died suddenly of a stroke on December 15, 1976. He owed no personal debts. Administration expenses and executor's commission will be $6,000. His will provides $50,000 worth of stocks is to go to his son and the rest of his entire estate is to go to his wife after paying all death taxes. The state inheritance tax is $4,400.

(a) What is the least total gift tax and estate tax payable (disregarding any interest or penalties) as a result of these events? Explain what actions should be taken to arrive at this lowest total tax.

(b) Assume the same facts as in (a) except that John died on December 15, 1977. Would your answer be the same as in (a)? Explain.

Discussion Problem 30-21

Net receipts from federal estate and gift taxes represent only a small percentage of total federal revenues. The relatively small yield of these taxes in relation to other taxes in the federal revenue system has been remarked both by proponents of more extensive reliance on estate and gift taxes and by those favoring their elimination. The former criticize the present taxes as inadequate to achieve the objectives for which they were enacted. They contend that these taxes were regarded originally as important revenue devices. Opponents of the federal estate and gift taxes contend that their small revenue yield is a reflection of the basic deficiency of these taxes as revenue sources.

(a) Give some arguments in favor of tightening the estate and gift taxes so as to increase the net revenues obtained from them.

(b) Give some arguments in favor of eliminating these taxes.

Research Problem 30-22

Mrs. Hayes transferred property valued at $50,000 to the Wire Corporation. Her husband, Alex, is the director of the corporation and owns 46% of its outstanding stock. The remaining 54% of the stock is owned equally by their sons Carl and Jeffery. On her gift tax return, Mrs. Hayes claimed the $3,000 gift tax exclusion for each of the stockholders. The Revenue Service contested the exclusions on the ground that a gift to a corporation is a gift to its stockholders, and since each stockholder's use, possession, or enjoyment of the gift property or proceeds are dependent upon contingencies beyond his individual control, the gifts are gifts of future interests and do not qualify for the annual exclusion under Sec. 2503(b). Mr. Hayes paid the deficiency resulting from the disallowance. She comes to you seeking your advice as a tax expert on whether to sue for a refund. What advice would you give her?

Use the Prentice-Hall Complete Federal Tax Equipment in your school or local library to find your answer. Do the following:

1. Give your opinion. In it show authorities, citing law, regulations, interpretations and decisions applicable, and the P-H Federal Tax Equipment paragraphs where they may be found.

2. Enumerate and explain carefully each step you take in reaching your result. These are extremely important—just as important as the result.

SHORT CUTS TO TAX KNOWLEDGE

TAX CHARTS AND TABLES
(Detailed Table of Contents below)

"ABC" ROUND-UP OF FEDERAL TAX RULES
(Starts at page 5701)

INTERNAL REVENUE CODE FINDING LIST
(Starts at page 5801)

TAX CHARTS AND TABLES CHECK LIST

	¶		¶
Federal Tax Calendar	5501	Taxes on corporations	5507
		Tax on self-employment income	5512
TAX CHARTS		Social security taxes	5513
Joint return of husband and wife	5503	Railroad retirement tax	5514
Preparing and filing return for decedent	5504	Excise tax rates	5515
Income tax on foreign corporations	5505	Tax Rate Schedules	5516
Income tax on estates and trusts	5506	Tax Tables	5517

¶ 5501   **FEDERAL TAX CALENDAR**
September 15, 1977—December 31, 1978

Last Day   **To**

1977
Sept. 15   Pay undeposited income and social security taxes withheld on wages to authorized depositary if between $200 and $2,000 is withheld in August.
*Pay third installment of individual or corporation 1977 estimated tax.
Sept. 20†   Employers with at least $2,000 undeposited accumulated payroll taxes for quarter-month (Sept. 8-15) pay authorized depositary.
Sept. 27†   Employers with at least $2,000 undeposited accumulated payroll taxes for quarter-month (Sept. 16-22) pay authorized depositary.
Oct. 5†   Employers with at least $2,000 undeposited accumulated payroll taxes for quarter-month (Sept. 23-30) pay authorized depositary.
Oct. 13†   Employers with at least $2,000 undeposited accumulated payroll taxes for quarter-month (Oct. 1-7) pay authorized depositary.
Oct. 15   ††Pay third installment of 1976 estate income tax.
Oct. 19†   Employers with at least $2,000 undeposited accumulated payroll taxes for quarter-month (Oct. 8-15) pay authorized depositary.
Oct. 26†   Employers with at least $2,000 undeposited accumulated payroll taxes for quarter-month (Oct. 16-22) pay authorized depositary.
Oct. 31   Pay undeposited income and social security taxes withheld on wages and file third 1977 quarterly return (Form 941) (but see Nov. 10):
(a) If between $200 and $2,000 withheld in prior quarter (July-Sept.) or in September;
(b) If less than $200 withheld for the quarter.
Pay third installment of federal unemployment tax in full to authorized depositary. Pay installment if tax on wages paid for July, August and September is more than $100 or accumulated tax for January through September is more than $100.
Nov. 3†   Employers with at least $2,000 undeposited accumulated payroll taxes for quarter-month (Oct. 23-31) pay authorized depositary.
Nov. 10†   File third quarterly return (Form 941) of income and social security taxes withheld on wages if timely deposits have been made for July, August and September.

For footnotes, see page 5505.   ¶ 5501

5502 Federal Tax Calendar 1978

Last Day	To
	Employers with at least $2,000 undeposited accumulated payroll taxes for quarter-month (Nov. 1-7) pay authorized depositary.
Nov. 15	Pay undeposited income and social security taxes withheld on wages to authorized depositary if between $200 and $2,000 is withheld in October.
	File third 1977 quarterly gift tax return and pay entire tax.
Nov. 18†	Employers with at least $2,000 undeposited accumulated payroll taxes for quarter-month (Nov. 8-15) pay authorized depositary.
Nov. 28†	Employers with at least $2,000 undeposited accumulated payroll taxes for quarter-month (Nov. 16-22) pay authorized depositary.
Dec. 1	Employers should request new Form W-4 from each employee if exemption changes are to be made by 1-1-78.
Dec. 5†	Employers with at least $2,000 undeposited accumulated payroll taxes for quarter-month (Nov. 23-30) pay authorized depositary.
Dec. 12†	Employers with at least $2,000 undeposited accumulated payroll taxes for quarter-month (Dec. 1-7) pay authorized depositary.
Dec. 15	Pay undeposited income and social security taxes withheld on wages to authorized depositary if between $200 and $2,000 is withheld in November.
	*Pay final installment of corporation's 1977 estimated tax.
Dec. 20†	Employers with at least $2,000 undeposited accumulated payroll taxes for quarter-month (Dec. 8-15) pay authorized depositary.
Dec. 27†	Employers with at least $2,000 undeposited accumulated payroll taxes for quarter-month (Dec. 16-22) pay authorized depositary.
1978	
Jan. 4†	Employers with at least $2,000 undeposited accumulated payroll taxes for quarter-month (Dec. 23-31) pay authorized depositary.
Jan. 11†	Employers with at least $2,000 undeposited accumulated payroll taxes for quarter-month (Jan. 1-7) pay authorized depositary.
Jan. 16	*Pay final installment of individual's 1977 estimated tax; file amended declaration for 1977.
	††Pay final installment of 1976 estate income tax.
	*File farmer's or fisherman's declaration and payment estimated tax for 1977.
Jan. 18	Employers with at least $2,000 undeposited accumulated payroll taxes for quarter-month (Jan. 8-15) pay authorized depositary.
Jan. 25†	Employers with at least $2,000 undeposited accumulated payroll taxes for quarter-month (Jan. 16-22) pay authorized depositary.
Jan. 31	File employer's final return of income taxes withheld in 1977 (but see Feb. 10).
	Furnish statement to employee on Form W-2 showing wages paid and amount of tax withheld during the calendar year 1977.
	*File individual tax return and pay tax for 1977 in lieu of declaration of estimated tax.
	Pay undeposited income and social security taxes withheld on wages and file last 1977 quarterly return (Form 941) (but see Feb. 10):
	(a) If between $200 and $2,000 withheld in prior quarter (Oct.-Dec.) or in December;
	(b) If less than $200 withheld for the quarter.
	File 1977 federal unemployment tax return and pay entire tax (remaining tax for those who have made quarterly payments: but see Feb. 10).
	Furnish information returns to recipients of $10 or more in dividends or interest.
Feb. 3†	Employers with at least $2,000 undeposited accumulated payroll taxes for quarter-month (Jan. 23-31) pay authorized depositary.
Feb. 10†	File fourth 1977 quarterly return (Form 941) of income and social security taxes withheld on wages if timely deposits have been made for October, November and December, 1977.
	Employers with at least $2,000 undeposited accumulated payroll taxes for quarter-month (Feb. 1-7) pay authorized depositary.
	File Form 940 unemployment tax return if timely deposits made for year.
Feb. 15	Pay undeposited income and social security taxes withheld on wages to authorized depositary if between $200 and $2,000 withheld in January.
	File fourth 1977 quarterly gift tax return and pay entire tax.
Feb. 20†	Employers with at least $2,000 undeposited accumulated payroll taxes for quarter-month (Feb. 8-15) pay authorized depositary.
Feb. 27†	Employers with at least $2,000 undeposited accumulated payroll taxes for quarter-month (Feb. 16-22) pay authorized depositary.
Feb. 28	File information returns (reports of payments of $600 or more, $10 dividend and interest payments and information on certain tax-favored stock options).
Mar. 1	*File farmer's or fisherman's tax return and pay tax in lieu of declaration of estimated tax.
Mar. 3†	Employers with at least $2,000 undeposited accumulated payroll taxes for quarter-month (Feb. 23-28) pay authorized depositary.
Mar. 10†	Employers with at least $2,000 undeposited accumulated payroll taxes for quarter-month (Mar. 1-7) pay authorized depositary.

For footnotes, see page 5505.

1978   **Federal Tax Calendar**   5503

Last Day	To
Mar. 15	Pay undeposited income and social security tax withheld on wages to authorized depositary if between $200 and $2,000 withheld in February.
	*File 1977 corporation income tax returns (except certain foreign corporations).
	*Pay first (50%) installment of unpaid 1977 corporation income taxes.
	*File Form 1120S (Subchapter S corporation).
	File report and pay tax withheld at source on other than wages.
Mar. 20†	Employers with at least $2,000 undeposited accumulated payroll taxes for quarter-month (Mar. 8-15) pay authorized depositary.
Mar. 27†	Employers with at least $2,000 undeposited accumulated payroll taxes for quarter-month (Mar. 16-22) pay authorized depositary.
Apr. 5†	Employers with at least $2,000 undeposited accumulated payroll taxes for quarter-month (Mar. 23-31) pay authorized depositary.
Apr. 12†	Employers with at least $2,000 undeposited accumulated payroll taxes for quarter-month (Apr. 1-7) pay authorized depositary.
Apr. 17	††File 1977 estate income tax returns and pay first installment of tax.
	††File 1977 trust income tax returns and pay entire tax.
	*File individual income tax returns for calendar year 1977 (except returns in lieu of declaration of estimated tax; see Jan. 31 and Mar. 1).
	(a) Nonresident citizens and nonresident aliens (other than certain residents of Canada or Mexico) may be excepted.
	(b) Any net tax payable on this return must be paid by this date.
	*File individual declaration of estimated tax for calendar year 1978 and pay first installment of tax.
	*Pay first installment of corporation estimated tax.
	*File 1977 partnership information returns.
Apr. 19†	Employers with at least $2,000 undeposited accumulated payroll taxes for quarter-month (Apr. 8-15) pay authorized depositary.
Apr. 26†	Employers with at least $2,000 undeposited accumulated payroll taxes for quarter-month (Apr. 16-22) pay authorized depositary.
May 1	Pay undeposited income and social security taxes withheld on wages and file first 1978 quarterly return (Form 941) (but see May 10):
	(a) If between $200 and $2,000 withheld in prior quarter (Jan.-Mar.) or in March;
	(b) If less than $200 withheld for the quarter.
	Pay first quarterly federal unemployment tax in full to authorized depositary if unpaid and accumulated tax in January, February and March is more than $100.
May 3†	Employers with at least $2,000 undeposited accumulated payroll taxes for quarter-month (Apr. 23-30) pay authorized depositary.
May 10†	File first 1978 quarterly return (Form 941) of income and social security taxes withheld on wages if timely deposits have been made for January, February and March.
	Employers with at least $2,000 undeposited accumulated payroll taxes for quarter-month (May 1-7) pay authorized depositary.
May 15	Pay undeposited income and social security taxes withheld on wages to authorized depositary if between $200 and $2,000 withheld in April.
	**File 1977 annual information return of exempt organizations.
	File first 1978 quarterly gift tax return and pay entire tax.
May 18†	Employers with at least $2,000 undeposited accumulated payroll taxes for quarter-month (May 8-15) pay authorized depositary.
May 25†	Employers with at least $2,000 undeposited accumulated payroll taxes for quarter-month (May 16-22) pay authorized depositary.
June 5	Employers with at least $2,000 undeposited accumulated payroll taxes for quarter-month (May 23-31) pay authorized depositary.
June 12†	Employers with at least $2,000 undeposited accumulated payroll taxes for quarter-month (June 1-7) pay authorized depositary.
June 15	Pay undeposited income and social security taxes withheld on wages to authorized depositary if between $200 and $2,000 withheld in May.
	*Pay final installment of unpaid balance of 1977 corporation income tax.
	*Pay second installment of individual or corporation 1978 estimated tax.
	*File 1977 individual income tax return for citizens residing or traveling abroad or in Armed Forces overseas and pay tax.
June 20†	Employers with at least $2,000 undeposited accumulated payroll taxes for quarter-month (June 8-15) pay authorized depositary.
June 27†	Employers with at least $2,000 undeposited accumulated payroll taxes for quarter-month (June 16-22) pay authorized depositary.
July 6†	Employers with at least $2,000 undeposited accumulated payroll taxes for quarter-month (June 23-30) pay authorized depositary.
July 12†	Employers with at least $2,000 undeposited accumulated payroll taxes for quarter-month (July 1-7) pay authorized depositary.
July 17	††Pay second installment of 1977 estate income tax.

For footnotes, see page 5505.   ¶ 5501

5504 Federal Tax Calendar 1978

Last Day — **To**

July 19† — Employers with at least $2,000 undeposited accumulated payroll taxes for quarter-month (July 8-15) pay authorized depositary.

July 26† — Employers with at least $2,000 undeposited accumulated payroll taxes for quarter-month (July 16-22) pay authorized depositary.

July 31 — Pay undeposited income and social security taxes withheld on wages and file second 1978 quarterly return (Form 941) (but see Aug. 10):
(a) If between $200 and $2,000 withheld in prior quarter (Apr.-June) or in June;
(b) If less than $200 withheld for the quarter.
Pay second quarterly federal unemployment tax in full to authorized depositary if unpaid and accumulated tax in April, May and June is more than $100.

Aug. 3† — Employers with at least $2,000 undeposited accumulated payroll taxes for quarter-month (July 23-31) pay authorized depositary.

Aug. 10† — File second 1978 quarterly return (Form 941) of income and social security taxes withheld on wages if timely deposits have been made for April, May and June.
Employers with at least $2,000 undeposited accumulated payroll taxes for quarter-month (Aug. 1-7) pay authorized depositary.

Aug. 15 — Pay undeposited income and social security taxes withheld on wages to authorized depositary if between $200 and $2,000 withheld in July.
File second 1978 quarterly gift tax return and pay entire tax.

Aug. 18† — Employers with at least $2,000 undeposited accumulated payroll taxes for quarter-month (Aug. 8-15) pay authorized depositary.

Aug. 25† — Employers with at least $2,000 undeposited accumulated payroll taxes for quarter-month (Aug. 16-22) pay authorized depositary.

Sept. 6† — Employers with at least $2,000 undeposited accumulated payroll taxes for quarter-month (Aug. 23-31) pay authorized depositary.

Sept. 12† — Employers with at least $2,000 undeposited accumulated payroll taxes for quarter-month (Sept. 1-7) pay authorized depositary.

Sept. 15 — Pay undeposited income and social security taxes withheld on wages to authorized depositary if between $200 and $2,000 withheld in August.
*Pay third installment of individual or corporation 1978 estimated tax.

Sept. 20† — Employers with at least $2,000 undeposited accumulated payroll taxes for quarter-month (Sept. 8-15) pay authorized depositary.

Sept. 27† — Employers with at least $2,000 undeposited accumulated payroll taxes for quarter-month (Sept. 16-22) pay authorized depositary.

Oct. 4† — Employers with at least $2,000 undeposited accumulated payroll taxes for quarter-month (Sept. 23-30) pay authorized depositary.

Oct. 11† — Employers with at least $2,000 undeposited accumulated payroll taxes for quarter-month (Oct. 1-7) pay authorized depositary.

Oct. 16 — ††Pay third installment of 1977 estate income tax.

Oct. 18† — Employers with at least $2,000 undeposited accumulated payroll taxes for quarter-month (Oct. 8-15) pay authorized depositary.

Oct. 25† — Employers with at least $2,000 undeposited accumulated payroll taxes for quarter-month (Oct. 16-22) pay authorized depositary.

Oct. 31 — Pay undeposited income and social security taxes withheld on wages and file third 1978 quarterly return (Form 941) (but see Nov. 10):
(a) If between $200 and $2,000 withheld in prior quarter (July-Sept.) or in September;
(b) If less than $200 withheld for the quarter.
Pay third quarterly federal unemployment tax in full to authorized depositary if unpaid and accumulated tax in July, August and September is more than $100.

Nov. 3† — Employers with at least $2,000 undeposited accumulated payroll taxes for quarter-month (Oct. 23-31) pay authorized depositary.

Nov. 10† — File third 1978 quarterly return (Form 941) of income and social security taxes withheld on wages if timely deposits have been made for July, August and September.
Employers with at least $2,000 undeposited accumulated payroll taxes for quarter-month (Nov. 1-7) pay authorized depositary.

Nov. 15 — Pay undeposited income and social security taxes withheld on wages to authorized depositary if between $200 and $2,000 withheld in October.
File third 1978 quarterly gift tax return and pay entire tax.

Nov. 20† — Employers with at least $2,000 undeposited accumulated payroll taxes for quarter-month (Nov. 8-15) pay authorized depositary.

Nov. 28† — Employers with at least $2,000 undeposited accumulated payroll taxes for quarter-month (Nov. 16-22) pay authorized depositary.

Dec. 1 — Employers should request new Form W-4 from each employee if exemption changes are to be made by 1-1-79.

Dec. 5† — Employers with at least $2,000 undeposited accumulated payroll taxes for quarter-month (Nov. 23-30) pay authorized depositary.

For footnotes, see page 5505.

5506 Federal Tax Charts 1978

Divorced or Legally Separated	Joint return not permitted if this status exists on the last day of the tax year. ¶ 1104.
Nonresident Aliens	Joint return not permitted if either spouse is nonresident alien for any part of tax year, unless both elect to be taxed on worldwide income. ¶ 1104.
Estimated Tax—Separate Declarations	Do not preclude the filing of a joint return. ¶ 3505.

General Information to be Furnished on Return

Names	Both husband's and wife's at top of return. Give first names and middle initials of each—not "Mr. and Mrs."
Signatures	Both husband and wife must sign unless one is authorized to sign as agent for the other. ¶ 3505.
Social Security Number	Enter social security numbers for both.
Occupation	Give occupation of each if both are employed.
Form W-2	Copy B of all Withholding Statements of both spouses should be attached to the return.

Personal Exemptions

Husband and Wife	Claim 1 exemption for each, plus old-age and blindness exemption for each. ¶ 1112-1113. **Table users.**—Personal exemptions are built into the tax tables.
Deceased Spouse	Surviving spouse may claim 1 exemption for the spouse who died during the year, plus extra exemption for old-age and blindness, if applicable. ¶ 1112.
Dependents	All dependency exemptions to which either husband or wife is entitled can be claimed. ¶ 1117. It is not necessary that the prescribed relationship exist between the person claimed as a dependent and the spouse furnishing the support. e.g.—Deduction can be claimed for wife's niece supported by the husband. ¶ 1117.

Income

General Rule	Report the combined income. However, income from separate businesses must be reported separately.
Business Income	If there is more than one business, give the information called for in Schedule C, Form 1040, for each.
Income from Property	The amounts of dividends, interest, rents, and royalties to be reported are those of husband and wife combined.

1978 Federal Tax Calendar 5505

Last Day	To
Dec. 12†	Employers with at least $2,000 undeposited accumulated payroll taxes for quarter-month (Dec. 1-7) pay authorized depositary.
Dec. 15	Pay undeposited income and social security taxes withheld on wages to authorized depositary if between $200 and $2,000 withheld in November.
	*Pay final installment of corporation's 1978 estimated tax.
Dec. 20†	Employers with at least $2,000 undeposited accumulated payroll taxes for quarter-month (Dec. 8-15) pay authorized depositary.
Dec. 28†	Employers with at least $2,000 undeposited accumulated payroll taxes for quarter-month (Dec. 16-22) pay authorized depositary.

* Applies to calendar year taxpayers. For return and payment of tax of fiscal year taxpayers, see ¶ 3517; 3522. For declaration and payment of estimated tax of individuals on fiscal year basis, see ¶ 2517(d). Corporate income and estimated tax must be paid to a bank, see ¶ 3523.

** For organizations with calendar year accounting period. Others must file on or before 15th day of 5th month following the close of their annual accounting period.

† For deposits required within 3 banking days after end of quarter-monthly period, any local banking holidays, Saturdays, Sundays and legal holidays are excluded. The next business day would be the due date. The within-3-banking-days rule only applies to employers with combined withheld taxes and employer-employee social security taxes of $2,000 or more. See ¶ 2509(a).

†† For fiduciaries with calendar year accounting period. Others must file on or before the 15th day of the 4th month following the end of their annual accounting period.

TAX CHARTS
¶ 5503   **JOINT RETURN OF HUSBAND AND WIFE**

Tax Savings

General Rule	Tax is less than it would be if separate returns were filed, in most cases. **Incomes approximately equal.**—If the tax table incomes or the taxable incomes (before exemptions) of husband and wife are approximately equal, joint or separate returns may produce the same tax.
Exceptions	**Extremely high medical expenses** [¶ 1945] paid by one spouse might give a deduction on his separate return that would more than offset the advantage of a joint return. Reason: the medical expense deduction figured on the combined adjusted gross income might be smaller. **Net business operating loss** [¶ 2241] sustained by one spouse might give a greater advantage if reported on a separate return and used as a carryback or carryover than if applied against the income of the other spouse for the current year on a joint return. Note.—These exceptions are unusual cases, and whether they apply can only be determined by actual computations.

Who May File

General Rules	The right to make a joint return is not affected by: (1) Relative proportions of income of husband and wife; (2) Fact that all income is that of one spouse; (3) Fact that one spouse reports on accrual basis and other on cash basis; (4) Fact that separate returns were filed for a prior year.
Tax Years	Tax years must begin on the same day.
Death of One Spouse	Surviving (and not remarried) husband or wife can file a joint return if the other spouse died during the year. ¶ 3507. Executor can disaffirm. ¶ 3507.

¶ 5503

¶ 5504 PREPARING AND FILING FINAL RETURN FOR DECEDENT

Generally, a decedent's return is subject to the same provisions that control individual income taxes. If the decedent's gross income for his final year meets the gross income requirement, a return must be filed [¶ 3020; 3511]. A return should be filed even when the income was less than that to get a refund of any tax withheld from wages. However, the return of a decedent does require some special consideration. For example, though a joint return is permitted, one may not be filed if the surviving husband or wife remarries before the close of his or her tax year. The following table presents the information most commonly sought in preparing and filing a decedent's return.

RETURN	SEPARATE	JOINT
FILING By whom	Executor or administrator of decedent's estate [¶ 3511]. If no executor or administrator, beneficiaries may act jointly, or appoint one of their number as agent for filing return.	Generally the executor or administrator of decedent's estate [¶ 3507]. Surviving spouse may file if decedent did not file a return for the tax year and if no executor (continued)

Credits and Refunds

Tax Withheld on Wages	Total of taxes withheld from both husband and wife should be entered on appropriate line of the form.
Payments of Estimated Tax	Total paid on a joint declaration or on separate declarations should be entered on appropriate line of the form.
Refund	If there has been an overpayment of tax the refund check will be made out to husband and wife jointly.
Other Credits	Earned income credit [¶ 2405], credit for the elderly [¶ 2406], general tax credit [¶ 1111(e)], foreign tax credit [¶ 3701], etc.

Amended Returns

Before Due Date	If filed before the due date, a joint return can be substituted for separate returns, or separate returns for a joint return.
After Due Date	A joint return can be substituted for separate returns at any time before the limitation statute expires, but no separate return can be substituted for a joint return after the return due date [¶ 3506].

Self-Employment Tax

Split-Income Benefits	Self-employment income cannot be split [¶ 3827].
Returns	In joint returns, separate schedules must be filed for both husband and wife, if both have net earnings from self-employment of $400 or more [¶ 3827].

1978 Federal Tax Charts 5508

Federal Tax Charts

¶ 5503

Tax Table Method	Figure your tax on tax table income using appropriate table [¶ 5517]. Tax table income is adjusted gross income [¶ 1102(c)] reduced by any excess itemized deductions [¶ 1103(a)] and increased in some cases by any unused zero bracket amount [¶ 1102(f)]. If you don't itemize, tax table income is same as adjusted gross income (in most cases).
Rate Schedule Method	(a) Find your taxable income this way: Start with your adjusted gross income. Reduce AGI by any excess itemized deductions (excess of itemized deductions over $3,200) and deductions for personal exemptions. In certain cases, increase AGI by any unused zero bracket amount. ¶ 1102(f), 1121. (b) Figure your tax on taxable income, using the right column in Schedule Y reproduced at ¶ 5516.

Amount of Tax

Tax Shown on Return	Husband or wife may pay all, or each may pay a part.
General Rule	The entire tax and deficiencies or penalties can be collected from either husband or wife. ¶ 3505.

Liability for Tax

Medical Expenses	Payments of husband and wife are combined. Flat deduction allowed (but not more than $150) for ½ of insurance premiums. Balance of premiums, drug and medicine costs in excess of 1% of combined adjusted gross income, and other medical expenses are deductible to the extent their total amount exceeds 3% of the combined adjusted gross income. ¶ 1945.
Charitable Contributions	Combined: Deduction cannot exceed 50% (20% or 30% in certain cases) of combined adjusted gross income. ¶ 1943.
Deductions Relating to Property	Can be claimed without regard to whether the property is owned by the husband or the wife.
Zero Bracket Amount	$3,200 for married taxpayers filing jointly and surviving spouses. ¶ 1102(e). This amount is, in effect, a fixed standard deduction built into the tax tables.
General Rule	Take the combined deductions of both spouses. However, if you report more than one business, you must itemize business deductions separately.

Deductions

Dividends	Exclude 1st $100 of dividends from domestic corporations received by each spouse. Total exclusion of $200 if each gets at least $100 in dividends. ¶ 1705.
Sales of Property	Report the combined gains and losses on Schedule D, regardless of who owns the property or the form in which title was held. The alternative tax on capital gains is at ¶ 1614.

1978

RETURN	SEPARATE	JOINT
FILING By whom (continued)		or administrator is appointed before the due date for filing the survivor's return or before the joint return is filed.
WHEN For year preceding death	Same date as if taxpayer were alive. ¶ 3517. [Thus, if a calendar year taxpayer dies in February, 1978, a return for 1977 must be filed by April 17, 1978.]	
For year of death	Calendar year taxpayer—April 15 of year following death [¶ 3517]. Fiscal year taxpayer—15th day of 4th month following close of decedent's tax year.	
Postponement	An automatic 2-month extension may be obtained by filing Form 4868 by the return due date. Any estimated tax owed must accompany the form [¶ 3518].	
PERIOD COVERED	Fractional part of year in which decedent was living [¶ 3008(b); 3517]. (When death occurred after close of year, but before return filed for preceding year, two returns are required: one for preceding year, one for year of death.)	
WHERE	File where the taxpayer lived or had a principal place of business [¶ 3519].	
UNDER NAME	Name of decedent, followed by word "Deceased," and date of death, with name, address and relationship to decedent of person filing return.	
SIGNED	Person filing signs. Designates status. Furnishes affidavits or other documentary evidence establishing right to act for decedent.	
LIABILITY	Decedent's estate is liable for tax on separate return filed for decedent.	Decedent's estate and surviving spouse are jointly and severally liable for tax on joint return, unless executor or administrator disaffirms joint return survivor filed [¶ 3507].
PREPARATION Form	1040 or 1040A [¶ 3511].	
Income	Cash basis [¶ 2702]. Accrual basis [¶ 2706]. But there is no accrual when income accrues solely by reason of the decedent's death. Such income is taxable to the person receiving it. Distributive share of partnership [¶ 2908; 3008(b)]. Transfer of installment obligations [¶ 2831].	

¶ 5504

Deductions	Election to itemize deductions is available. Cash basis [¶ 2702]. Accrual basis [¶ 2706].
Exemptions	$750 for each exemption [¶ 1111—1115]. Personal exemptions are built into tax tables.
Rates	Same as living taxpayers [¶ 1121; 1122].
REFUNDS	Form 1310 must be filed with return [¶ 3626(c)].
DECLARATION OF ESTIMATED TAX	No need to file after decedent's death [¶ 2516]. Death terminates obligation to pay future installments. Surviving spouse must continue payments on joint declaration or file amended declaration.

¶ 5505 INCOME TAX ON FOREIGN CORPORATIONS (I.R.C. §881)

Basis of tax is taxable income effectively connected with conduct of U.S. business [¶ 3710]. Tax rates are same as domestic corporations. But U.S. nonbusiness income (generally passive or investment income) is taxed at 30%. Capital gain is taxed only if effectively connected with U.S. business.

¶ 5506 INCOME TAX ON ESTATES AND TRUSTS (I.R.C. §1, 641, 642)

	Basis	Rate
Estates	Taxable income, figured as for individual, except for certain special rules as to deductions and credits. Credit for foreign taxes and exclusion for dividends received allowed only to extent that these items are not allocable to beneficiaries. Deduction for personal exemption, $600. Special rules for charitable deduction. Depreciation and depletion deductions allowed only to extent not allowed to beneficiaries. [¶ 3011-3014; 3019].	Use special rate schedule prescribed for estates and trusts [¶ 3020]
Trusts	Taxable income, figured as for individual, except for certain special rules as to deduction and credits. Credit for foreign taxes and exclusion for dividends received allowed only to extent that these items are not allocable to beneficiaries. Deduction for personal exemption, $100 ($300 when required to distribute all income currently). Special rules for deduction of charitable contributions. Depreciation and depletion deductions allowed only to extent not allowed to beneficiaries. No additional first-year depreciation deduction [¶ 2016; 3011-3014; 3019].	Use special rate schedule prescribed for estates and trusts [¶ 3020]

¶ 5507 TAXES ON CORPORATIONS

Type	Basis	Rates
Domestic Corporations [1] **(for 1977 through 1978)** (IRC §11, 21)	Taxable income up to $25,000[2] Taxable income over $25,000 [¶ 3102 et seq.]	20% 22%
	Taxable income over $50,000	Surtax 26%

Life insurance companies (IRC §802). Basis of tax is taxable income [¶ 3434(a)]. Tax rates are the same as domestic corporations.

Exempt organizations (IRC §507-515, 4940-4948). Basis of tax is unrelated business income [¶ 3448].[3] Tax rates are the same as domestic corporations.[3]

Regulated investment companies (IRC §851, 852). Basis of tax is taxable income [¶ 3431]. Tax rates are the same as domestic corporations. But the alternative capital gain rate of 30% applies to net long-term capital gain less total of net short-term capital loss and capital gain dividends paid [¶ 3431].

Personal holding companies (IRC §541-547). Basis of tax is undistributed personal holding company income [¶ 3404]. Tax rate is 70%.

Accumulated earnings (IRC §531-537). Basis of tax is accumulated taxable income [¶ 3132]. Tax rate up to $100,000 is 27½%; over $100,000, $27,500 plus 38½% of excess over $100,000.

Foreign corporations. For tax basis and rates see ¶ 5505.

Footnote ¶ 5507 (1) Does not include some insurance companies [IRC §801 et seq.] and certain mutual savings banks [IRC §594] that are specially taxed.
(2) Subchapter S corporations [¶ 3140 et seq.] pay only a capital gains tax on net long-term capital gains over $25,000, at the lesser of the regular corporation tax rates or the alternative tax rate.
(3) Private foundations are subject to an annual user tax and various excise taxes for certain prohibited acts or failures to act [¶ 3435 et seq.].

¶ 5512 TAX ON SELF-EMPLOYMENT INCOME
(I.R.C. §1401, 1402)

Applies to individuals with self-employment income of $400 or more, and wages of $16,500 or less [¶ 3823]. The basis of tax is net earnings from self-employment or $16,500 less wages received, whichever is less.[1] The tax rates[2] for tax years beginning in 1974-1977 is 7.9%.

Footnote ¶ 5512 (1) Taxable base will be adjusted if there is an automatic cost of living benefit increase.
(2) Rates include health insurance tax.

¶ 5513 SOCIAL SECURITY TAXES
(I.R.C. §3101, 3111, 3121, 3303, 3306)

Old age, survivor and disability insurance, and health insurance. The tax rates apply for a calendar year at the same rate for an employer and employee. For 1975-1977, the tax rate on each employer and employee is 5.85%. The employer's taxable wage base for 1977 is the first $16,500[1] of wages paid to each employee in nonexempt employment during the calendar year. Employee's tips reported to employer are not included in the employer's tax base

[¶ 3800; 3818(a)]. The employee's taxable wage base for 1977 is the first $16,500[1] of wages during the calendar year (including tips reported to an employer). The employer withholds tax [¶ 3800; 3818(a)].

Unemployment insurance. The tax applies to employers of 1 or more in nonexempt employment on each of 20 or more calendar days during a calendar year, each day being in a different calendar week, or who pay $1,500 or more of wages in a calendar quarter of a current or prior calendar year. The tax is on the first $4,200 of wages paid in a calendar year [¶ 3834 et seq.]. The tax rate is 3.4%, effective 1-1-77.

Footnote ¶ 5513 (1) Same as footnote ¶ 5512(1) above.

¶ 5514 RAILROAD RETIREMENT TAX (I.R.C. §3201, 3202, 3211, 3221)

Imposed on employees, employers and employee representatives. It applies to compensation up to $1,375 for each calendar month.[1] The tax rate for 1975-1977 is 5.85% for employees, 15.35% for employers[2] and 21.2% for employee representatives.[2]

Footnote ¶ 5514 (1) This basis is an amount equal to $1/12$ of the current maximum annual taxable "wages" for social security purposes. See also footnote ¶ 5512(1) above.

(2) Employers also pay an excise tax for each man-hour of paid service at a rate fixed by the Railroad Retirement Board. Employee representatives also pay an income tax equal to the rate of excise tax imposed on employers.

¶ 5515 EXCISE TAX RATES

Retailers' excise taxes: Diesel fuel and special motor fuels ... 4¢ per gal.[1]

Manufacturers' excise taxes:
Trucks, buses, trailers with gross weight over 10,000 lbs. ... 10% of mfrs. price.[2]
Truck and bus parts and accessories ... 8%[2] of mfrs. price
Tires, etc.:
  Highway type ... 10¢ per lb.[3]
  Other ... 5¢ per lb.
  Inner tubes ... 10¢ per lb.[4]
  Tread rubber ... 5¢ per lb. till 10-1-79.
  Laminated tires (nonhighway) ... 1¢ per lb.
Gasoline ... 4¢ per gal.[1]
Lubricating oil ... 6¢ per gal.[5]
Fishing equipment ... 10% of mfrs. price
Pistols and revolvers ... 10% of mfrs. price
Other firearms, shells and cartridges ... 11% of mfrs. price

Airport and airway user taxes:
Fuel and gasoline used in general non-commercial aviation ... 7¢ per gal.[6]

Domestic transportation of persons by air ... 8% of amount paid
International transportation of persons by air (flights starting in U.S.) ... $3 added to amount paid till 6-30-80
Domestic transportation of property by air ... 5% of amount paid till 6-30-80
Annual registration tax on civil aircraft:
  Turbine engine powered aircraft ... $25 plus $3^1/_2$¢ per lb. till 6-30-80
  Other aircraft ... $25 plus 2¢ per lb. of total weight if it exceeds 2,500 lbs.

Miscellaneous excise taxes:
Telephone and teletypewriter service ... 5%[7]
Foreign insurance policies ... 4¢ or 1¢ per dollar of premium
Wagering:
  Wagers ... 2% of amount of wager
  Occupation of accepting wagers ... $500 per year
Coin-operated gaming devices ... $250 per device per year[8]
Use tax on certain highway vehicles ... $3 per 1,000 lbs. per year till 7-1-79[9]
Import tax on oleomargarine ... 15¢ per lb.[10]

Regulatory taxes:
White phosphorus matches . . . 2¢ per hundred[10]
Adulterated butter . . . 10¢ or 15¢ per lb.[10]
Process butter . . . 1/4¢ per lb.[10]
Occupational taxes: adulterated or process butter . . . $48 to $600 per year[10]
Cotton futures . . . 2¢ per lb. till 1-2-77
Bank circulation tax (other than national banks) . . . 1/12 of 1%; 1/6 of 1%; 10%[10]

Alcohol taxes:
Distilled spirits . . . $10.50 per proof gal.
Beer . . . $9 per barrel
Still wines . . . various rates
Rectification tax . . . 30¢ per proof gal.
Occupational taxes:
   Rectifiers . . . $110 or $220 per year

Brewers . . . $55 or $110 per year
Manufacturers of stills . . . $55 per year plus $22 per still
Wholesale dealers . . . $123 or $255 per year
Retail dealers . . . $24 or $54 per year
Other . . . $25 to $100 per year

Tobacco taxes:
Cigarettes . . . $4 or $8.40 per 1,000
Cigars . . . 75¢ or 8 1/2% of wholesale price[11] to $20 per 1,000[11]
Cigarette papers or tubes . . . 1/2 or 1¢ per 50.

Machine guns, etc.:
Transfers . . . $5 or $200 per firearm
Occupational . . . $10 to $500 per year
Making . . . $200 per firearm

Footnote ¶ 5515 (1) 1 1/2¢ after 9-30-79.
(2) 5% as of 10-1-79.
(3) 5¢ as of 10-1-79.
(4) 9¢ as of 10-1-79.
(5) Credit for nonhighway use; see ¶ 2413.
(6) Reached by adding a 3% (5 1/2% after 9-30-79) retailers' tax to 4% (1 1/2% after 9-30-79) manufacturers' tax on gasoline.
(7) Reduced by 1% each year until repeal on 1-1-82.
(8) Credit allowed for state tax up to 80% of federal tax.
(9) 75¢ per 1,000 lbs. from 7-1-79 through 9-30-79. No tax after 9-30-79.
(10) Till 2-1-77.
(11) Effective 2-1-77.

¶ 5516   TAX RATE SCHEDULES

[Table appears on page 5514]

¶ 5517   TAX TABLES

➤**NOTE**→ As we went to press, the Revenue Service has not yet issued the new 1977 tax tables. They will be made available as soon as they are officially released.

1977 Tax Rate Schedules

SCHEDULE X—Single Taxpayers Not Qualifying for Rates in Schedule Y or Z

TAXABLE INCOME		TAX	
Not over $2,200		—0—	
Over—	But not over—		of the amount over—
$2,200	$2,700	14%	$2,200
$2,700	$3,200	$70+15%	$2,700
$3,200	$3,700	$145+16%	$3,200
$3,700	$4,200	$225+17%	$3,700
$4,200	$6,200	$310+19%	$4,200
$6,200	$8,200	$690+21%	$6,200
$8,200	$10,200	$1,110+24%	$8,200
$10,200	$12,200	$1,590+25%	$10,200
$12,200	$14,200	$2,090+27%	$12,200
$14,200	$16,200	$2,630+29%	$14,200
$16,200	$18,200	$3,210+31%	$16,200
$18,200	$20,200	$3,830+34%	$18,200
$20,200	$22,200	$4,510+36%	$20,200
$22,200	$24,200	$5,230+38%	$22,200
$24,200	$28,200	$5,990+40%	$24,200
$28,200	$34,200	$7,590+45%	$28,200
$34,200	$40,200	$10,290+50%	$34,200
$40,200	$46,200	$13,290+55%	$40,200
$46,200	$52,200	$16,590+60%	$46,200
$52,200	$62,200	$20,190+62%	$52,200
$62,200	$72,200	$26,390+64%	$62,200
$72,200	$82,200	$32,790+66%	$72,200
$82,200	$92,200	$39,390+68%	$82,200
$92,200	$102,200	$46,190+69%	$92,200
$102,200	....	$53,090+70%	$102,200

SCHEDULE Y—Married Taxpayers and Qualifying Widows and Widowers

Married Filing Joint Returns and Qualifying Widows and Widowers

TAXABLE INCOME		TAX	
Not over $3,200		—0—	
Over—	But not over—		of the amount over—
$3,200	$4,200	14%	$3,200
$4,200	$5,200	$140+15%	$4,200
$5,200	$6,200	$290+16%	$5,200
$6,200	$7,200	$450+17%	$6,200
$7,200	$11,200	$620+19%	$7,200
$11,200	$15,200	$1,380+22%	$11,200
$15,200	$19,200	$2,260+25%	$15,200
$19,200	$23,200	$3,260+28%	$19,200
$23,200	$27,200	$4,380+32%	$23,200
$27,200	$31,200	$5,660+36%	$27,200
$31,200	$35,200	$7,100+39%	$31,200
$35,200	$39,200	$8,660+42%	$35,200
$39,200	$43,200	$10,340+45%	$39,200
$43,200	$47,200	$12,140+48%	$43,200
$47,200	$55,200	$14,060+50%	$47,200
$55,200	$67,200	$18,060+53%	$55,200
$67,200	$79,200	$24,420+55%	$67,200
$79,200	$91,200	$31,020+58%	$79,200
$91,200	$103,200	$37,980+60%	$91,200
$103,200	$123,200	$45,180+62%	$103,200
$123,200	$143,200	$57,580+64%	$123,200
$143,200	$163,200	$70,380+66%	$143,200
$163,200	$183,200	$83,580+68%	$163,200
$183,200	$203,200	$97,180+69%	$183,200
$203,200	....	$110,980+70%	$203,200

Married Filing Separate Returns

TAXABLE INCOME		TAX	
Not over $1,600		—0—	
Over—	But not over—		of the amount over—
$1,600	$2,100	14%	$1,600
$2,100	$2,600	$70+15%	$2,100
$2,600	$3,100	$145+16%	$2,600
$3,100	$3,600	$225+17%	$3,100
$3,600	$5,600	$310+19%	$3,600
$5,600	$7,600	$690+22%	$5,600
$7,600	$9,600	$1,130+25%	$7,600
$9,600	$11,600	$1,630+28%	$9,600
$11,600	$13,600	$2,190+32%	$11,600
$13,600	$15,600	$2,830+36%	$13,600
$15,600	$17,600	$3,550+39%	$15,600
$17,600	$19,600	$4,330+42%	$17,600
$19,600	$21,600	$5,170+45%	$19,600
$21,600	$23,600	$6,070+48%	$21,600
$23,600	$27,600	$7,030+50%	$23,600
$27,600	$33,600	$9,030+53%	$27,600
$33,600	$39,600	$12,210+55%	$33,600
$39,600	$45,600	$15,510+58%	$39,600
$45,600	$51,600	$18,990+60%	$45,600
$51,600	$61,600	$22,590+62%	$51,600
$61,600	$71,600	$28,790+64%	$61,600
$71,600	$81,600	$35,190+66%	$71,600
$81,600	$91,600	$41,790+68%	$81,600
$91,600	$101,600	$48,590+69%	$91,600
$101,600	....	$55,490+70%	$101,600

SCHEDULE Z—Unmarried or legally separated taxpayers Who Qualify as Heads of Household

TAXABLE INCOME		TAX	
Not over $2,200		—0—	
Over—	But not over—		of the amount over—
$2,200	$3,200	14%	$2,200
$3,200	$4,200	$140+16%	$3,200
$4,200	$6,200	$300+18%	$4,200
$6,200	$8,200	$660+19%	$6,200
$8,200	$10,200	$1,040+22%	$8,200
$10,200	$12,200	$1,480+23%	$10,200
$12,200	$14,200	$1,940+25%	$12,200
$14,200	$16,200	$2,440+27%	$14,200
$16,200	$18,200	$2,980+28%	$16,200
$18,200	$20,200	$3,540+31%	$18,200
$20,200	$22,200	$4,160+32%	$20,200
$22,200	$24,200	$4,800+35%	$22,200
$24,200	$26,200	$5,500+36%	$24,200
$26,200	$28,200	$6,220+38%	$26,200
$28,200	$30,200	$6,980+41%	$28,200
$30,200	$34,200	$7,800+42%	$30,200
$34,200	$38,200	$9,480+45%	$34,200
$38,200	$40,200	$11,280+48%	$38,200
$40,200	$42,200	$12,240+51%	$40,200
$42,200	$46,200	$13,260+52%	$42,200
$46,200	$52,200	$15,340+55%	$46,200
$52,200	$54,200	$18,640+56%	$52,200
$54,200	$66,200	$19,760+58%	$54,200
$66,200	$72,200	$26,720+61%	$66,200
$72,200	$78,200	$30,260+61%	$72,200
$78,200	$82,200	$33,920+62%	$78,200
$82,200	$90,200	$36,400+63%	$82,200
$90,200	$102,200	$41,440+64%	$90,200
$102,200	$122,200	$49,120+66%	$102,200
$122,200	$142,200	$62,320+67%	$122,200
$142,200	$162,200	$75,720+68%	$142,200
$162,200	$182,200	$89,320+69%	$162,200
$182,200	....	$103,120+70%	$182,200

"ABC" ROUND-UP OF FEDERAL TAX RULES

¶ **5701** This section presents, in summary form, many of the more important basic rules of federal taxes that are explained and developed in the Federal Tax Explanation [Chapters 1-30]. The subjects treated below are in alphabetical order.

— A —

Abandonment of property. When business property is abandoned because its usefulness is suddenly ended, a deductible loss results [¶ 2036; 2210]. Capital loss limitation [¶ 1613; 3201] does not apply because there is no sale or exchange. The prospect of abandonment before the end of the normal useful life of property furnishes a ground for an annual obsolescence deduction, in addition to normal depreciation [¶ 2034]. Abandonment of real estate because mortgages, taxes, or other liens exceed its value, is also ground for a deduction.

Accidents. A loss resulting from damage to the taxpayer's property due to an accident is deductible if the accident was not caused by the willful act or negligence of the taxpayer [¶ 2204]. The deduction may also include payments to another for damages arising from taxpayer's business [¶ 2202]. Insurance received reduces the amount of the deductible loss [¶ 2204]. Damages or insurance proceeds received for personal injuries resulting from an accident are not income [¶ 1226], but they may reduce the deduction for medical expenses [¶ 1947]. The part of accident insurance premiums allocated to medical care is included in the deduction for medical expenses [¶ 1946]. Premiums paid for insurance against damage to business property by accident are deductible [¶ 1828(b)]. See also "Employee health and accident plans."

Accountants. Certified public accountants may practice before Revenue Service by filing statement of status [¶ 3609]. Accountants, whether or not certified, may be admitted to practice before the Tax Court [¶ 3636]. Fees paid to accountants are deductible if they qualify as business expenses or as "nonbusiness" expenses, and the deduction includes payments for the preparation of income tax returns or related to refunds or deficiencies [¶ 1806; 1823]. The fees paid to an accountant who renders services as an independent contractor are not subject to withholding of taxes on wages [¶ 2502], but the person making the payments must file an information return if they exceed $600 in any tax year and are made in the course of his trade or business [¶ 3531]. Accountants who prepare tax returns for others must sign the returns. The expenses incurred by an accountant in the practice of his profession are deductible in figuring his adjusted gross income [¶ 1804].

Accounting methods. The taxpayer's method is generally accepted for income tax purposes. It need not be accepted, however, if in the opinion of the Revenue Service it does not clearly reflect the income. The methods ordinarily employed are the cash basis or the accrual basis. A combination of these methods is permitted if income is clearly reflected [¶ 2701]. Special methods ae permitted for long term contracts and installment sales [¶ 2801 et seq.]. Permission of the Revenue Service generally must be obtained to change the method of accounting [¶ 2708].

Accounting periods. The calendar year must be used unless the taxpayer has established a fiscal year. Taxpayer can elect to use a fiscal period that always ends on the same day of the week which either (1) falls nearest to the end of the same calendar month, or (2) occurs last in the same calendar month. His fiscal year would thus vary from 52 to 53 weeks. If no books of account are kept, the calendar year must be used [¶ 2714]. Usually a change of accounting period requires the Revenue Service's permission [¶ 2715]. If husband and wife have different tax years, they cannot file a joint return [¶ 3505]. Split income benefits are available when husband and wife file a joint return [¶ 1104]. Returns for less than 12 months must be annualized if due to a change of accounting period [¶ 2717].

Accrual basis of accounting. Takes income into account when earned, even though not received. Expenses are considered as soon as incurred, whether paid or not. Accrual method ordinarily must be used for purchases and sales when it is necessary to use an inventory [¶ 2706].

Accumulation of income. Because corporation income is taxable to the corporation, and again to the shareholders when distributed, avoidance of the tax on the shareholders by not distributing enough of the year's income, may subject certain corporations to special taxes at high rates [¶ 3130]. For guides for accumulation, see ¶ 3131(b). Generally, accumulation by estates, trusts, partnerships and individuals is not taxed specially, since such income is, in any event, taxable only once. For effect of accumulation of income by complex trusts or private foundations, see ¶ 3023; 3441.

Acquisitions to avoid tax. Deductions, credits and other allowances may be disallowed following acquisition of control of corporations or property, when the main purpose of the acquisition was to get tax benefits that would not otherwise have been enjoyed [¶ 3226].

Adjusted gross income. Adjusted gross income is income less the deductions listed in Sec. 62 of the Code [¶ 1801; 1805]. It is an important factor in the return of an individual because it is used as a basis in determining the amounts deductible for charitable contributions and medical expenses [¶ 1801(a)].

Alimony. Lump sum payments are not income to the wife nor deductible by the husband [¶ 1320]. He may have a taxable gain if he uses appreciated property for payment. Periodic payments which meet the requirements of Sec. 71 are taxable to the wife and are deductible under Sec. 215 by the husband. If the divorce decree or a written instrument incident to the decree, a separation agreement, or decree for support or maintenance names a principal sum of alimony, installment payments in discharge of the obligation do not come under Sec. 71 or 215 unless the decree or instrument directs that the principal sum is to be paid over a period of more than 10 years, and then only to the extent that the installment payment does not exceed 10% of the principal sum. The decree or agreement can also affect the right to claim exemption deductions for the children [¶ 1116].

Amortization. Amortization is the exhaustion of an asset resulting from the passage of time. It means that an amount paid or received is not deducted or reported in one tax year; it is divided over the number of years in the term and a prorated part deducted or reported each year. Provision is made for amortizing: bond premium or discount [¶ 1846; 3125], organization expenses [¶ 3116], research and development expenses [¶ 1842], tenant's improvements [¶ 2002], pollution control facilities [¶ 2040], railroad rolling stock [¶ 2041], coal mine safety equipment [¶ 2042] and expenditures for on-the-job training and child care centers [¶ 2043].

Annuities. A person receiving annuity payments can exclude part of each payment as a return of capital. Generally, the amount excluded is based on the ratio that the cost of the annuity to the annuitant bears to the expected return under the contract. The excludable amount usually remains the same each year as long as the payments continue [¶ 1230]. Special rules apply to variable annuities, joint and survivor annuities [¶ 1231] and annuities received by an employee under a contract purchased by his employer [¶ 1232].

Annuity trust. This is a trust with a charitable remainder that pays a specific sum annually to at least one noncharitable income beneficiary. It is one of the three types of trust to which a charitable remainder can be contributed and a deduction claimed [¶ 1942(e); 3927; 4022]. See also "Pooled income fund" and "Unitrust."

Appreciation in value of property. Generally, appreciation is not income until it is realized by a sale or conversion of the property [¶ 1201]. Neither death nor a gift makes appreciation taxable income to the donor or the decedent. But if a donee uses the donor's basis [¶ 1515], appreciation before and after the gift may be taxed to the donee when he disposes of the property.

Assessment of tax. Generally, the Commissioner must assess additional income taxes within three years after the return was filed [¶ 3610 et seq.]. However, there are numerous exceptions. One of the most important is that there is no time limitation if the return was false or fraudulent with intent to evade tax. If the assessment is made too late, the tax cannot be collected. The time for assessment may be shortened by the taxpayer's request, in certain cases involving income of a decedent or his estate, or of a dissolving corporation [¶ 3612]. Additional time may be added after the normal expiration of the assessment period [¶ 3613].

Asset Depreciation Range system. A taxpayer can elect to base an asset's depreciation on any number of years within the designated range of years for that particular guideline class. The election can be made annually and will apply to all eligible assets placed in service by the taxpayer in that tax year. Taxpayers using the Class Life ADR system must account for assets in item or group accounts by the year placed in service (vintage accounts) [¶ 2033].

Attorneys. Qualified attorneys may practice before the Revenue Service by filing a statement of status [¶ 3609]. Application must be filed to practice before the Tax Court [¶ 3636]. Fees paid to attorneys are deductible if they qualify as business expenses or as "nonbusiness" expenses, and the deduction includes payments for preparing income tax returns or related to refunds and deficiencies [¶ 1804; 1806; 1823]. Fees paid to an attorney who renders services as an independent contractor are not subject to withholding of taxes on wages [¶ 2502], but if fees paid in the course of business are $600 or more, the payor must file an information return [¶ 3531]. An attorney's professional expenses are deductions for adjusted gross income [¶ 1804].

Authors. Large amounts of royalties may qualify for income averaging [¶ 2401]. If an author maintains an office, he can deduct his office expenses and depreciation on his furniture and office equipment. If his office is in his home, he can deduct a portion of the rent, or if he owns the home, a portion of the depreciation [¶ 1807; 1832].

Automobiles. Expenses and depreciation are deductible for automobiles when used for business, but not when used for pleasure [¶ 1829]. Damage to an automobile, whether business or pleasure, may result in a deductible casualty loss [¶ 2204]. A loss on the sale of a pleasure automobile would not be deductible [¶ 2202], but a gain would be taxable as a capital gain [¶ 1600; 1601].

Averaging income. Income averaging relieves the tax burden on almost all individual taxpayers who have large amounts of bunched income by allowing the use of an averaging device that taxes the income of a high income year as if it were spread over a 5-year period. It applies generally to all types of income [¶ 2401].

Avoidance of income tax. The courts have said many times that a device to avoid taxes carried out by legal means is not subject to legal censure. The law itself, in many instances, permits optional methods of arranging business transactions, or for reporting income, one of which will show a lower tax liability than the other.

Awards. An award of damages for loss of life is not taxable [¶ 1226]. Suggestion awards to employees are taxable compensation subject to withholding and deductible by the employer [¶ 2503]. Time when retroactive wage increase awards are deducted depends on whether the employer contested the increase [¶ 2735]. Such payments are subject to withholding on wages [¶ 2503].

— B —

Bad debts. Debts owing to the taxpayer, that become worthless within the tax year may be deductible [¶ 2300 et seq.]. To warrant a deduction, the debt must be real and must have a basis represented by either an amount paid out or an amount previously reported as income. Partial worthlessness may give a partial deduction. If the reserve method is adopted, additions to the reserve may be deducted in lieu of specific bad debt items. See also "Reserves for bad debts." When the debt is represented by "securities" or is of a "nonbusiness" nature, certain of the capital loss limitations apply. Character of the debt as a "business" or "nonbusiness" debt can be established when the debt was created (or acquired) or when it became worthless.

Bankruptcy. A person who goes through bankruptcy may remain liable for a limited amount of taxes he owes. During administration of a bankrupt estate, special rules govern assessment and collection of taxes [¶ 3612(c)]. Taxes have certain priorities in the payment of claims.

Banks. Rates of tax are the same as for other corporations [¶ 3433].

Losses sustained by banks on worthless securities are excepted from the limitation on the deduction of such losses by other taxpayers [¶ 2312(b)]. Gains and losses on the sale or exchange of securities by banks are ordinary gains and losses [¶ 3433]. There is a conclusive presumption of complete or partial worthlessness for debts charged off at the direction of bank examiners [¶ 2312(b)].

Banks are allowed to deduct dividends paid on their preferred stock which is owned by the U.S. or any U.S. instrumentality [¶ 3433]. Mutual savings banks, building and loan associations, savings and loan associations, and cooperative banks can deduct dividends paid to depositors [¶ 3433].

Basis. This term is used to describe the figure which is the starting point in figuring gain or loss, depreciation, and (when the percentage method does not apply) depletion. In the ordinary case of property bought for cash, the basis is cost. A "substituted basis" frequently must be used for property that was not bought [¶ 1500; 1514].

The basis described above is the "unadjusted basis." It may have to be increased or decreased to arrive at the figure on which the amount of gain or loss, depreciation, or depletion is figured. The increases and decreases are described in Sec. 1016(a). They relate to the period during which the property was held. The most common are depreciation (a decrease) and capital expenditures (an increase). The result of these adjustments is called the "adjusted basis" [¶ 1500].

Beneficiaries. Income of an estate or trust which is distributed or distributable to beneficiaries is taxable to them. All distributions from the trust, including payments from corpus, are taxable to the beneficiary, but only to the extent of the trust's distributable net income. Distributable net income is determined the same as taxable income (gross income less deductions) with certain modifications. [¶ 3003; 3004].

Bequests. Property acquired by bequest, devise or inheritance is excluded from gross income, but the income or interest from the property is taxable [¶ 1225; 1314]. To determine gain or loss on the disposition of property thus received, basis generally is the "carry-over basis", which is the greater of the decedent's adjusted basis at death or fair market value on 12-31-76, with certain adjustments [¶ 1507].

Bonds of indebtedness. Interest paid on bonds is deductible [¶ 1900] and interest received is income [¶ 1314]. But if an instrument called a "bond" is really a share of stock, the payments are considered dividends rather than deductible interest. Interest on bonds issued by state or local governments is exempt, except interest on certain industrial development bonds and arbitrage bonds [¶ 1204; 1314].

Basis of bonds purchased is cost. If cost is more than face value, the difference (premium) may be subject to amortization [¶ 1846].

Bonuses. A bonus paid for personal services, is income to the person who receives it [¶ 1302] and deductible (to the extent that is not unreasonable) by the person who pays it [¶ 1819]. Bonuses paid to employees are subject to withholding [¶ 2504(e)].

Books and records. Permanent books of account or records, from which the Revenue Service can check the correct amount of income subject to tax, must be kept by all persons except those whose income is solely from wages or from farming. The right of examination continues until the time for assessment of addtional taxes expires. A person who does not keep books or records runs the risk that the Service may determine his income by an arbitrary method [¶ 2711].

Buildings. A building or land used in the taxpayer's trade or business is not a capital asset [¶ 1601]. However, gains from sales or exchanges of the property may be treated as capital gains under certin conditions [¶ 1618]. The personal residence of the taxpayer (land and building) is a capital asset [¶ 1601]. See also "Sale of residence."

Business buildings are depreciable property and the deduction is ordinarily allowable to the owner of the land. However, if 63) tenant erects a building, he is entitled to recover his cost, either over the term of the lease or over the useful life of the building [¶ 1840].

Business. The application to an individual of a section of the Internal Revenue Code often depends on whether he is engaged in business. For tax purposes, "business" includes a profession [¶ 2202]. Taxable wages of nonresident aliens for employment in the U.S. are considered business income [¶ 3711].

Business entities. The effect of the various taxing statutes upon business entities depends upon how they are classified. The general classes are: corporations [¶ 3100 et seq.], estates [¶ 3000 et seq.], individuals [¶ 1100 et seq.], partnerships [¶ 2900 et seq.], and trusts [¶ 3000 et seq.].

"Business purpose" test. This test originated with the decision of Gregory v. Helvering, in which the Supreme Court disregarded a transaction which was in form a statutory reorganization, because the transaction had no business purpose [¶ 3302]. However, the Service has often applied the rule of the Gregory case to any type of transaction motivated by tax avoidance. In most of the cases where the test is applied, the parties involved do not have adverse economic interests and consequently are not dealing at arm's length.

— C —

Call. A call is an option that gives the investor the right to buy stock from the maker of the call at a stated price within a limited time [¶ 1609].

Cancellation of indebtedness. Cancellation of indebtedness, in whole or in part, may result in the realization of income. However, no income results from: (1) certain cancellations by a bankruptcy court; (2) a cancellation that is a gift; (3) a cancellation where the debtor is insolvent both before and after; and (4) a cancellation that is merely a price adjustment [¶ 1318].

The cancellation that results in income does not have to be a forgiveness. It can, for example, be the purchase by a corporation of its bonds or other obligations for less than the issue price [¶ 3125].

If stockholders borrow money from their corporation, and the corporation later cancels the debt, the result may be dividend income to the stockholders [¶ 1318(e)].

Cancellation of lease or distributorship. Payments to a tenant for cancellation of a lease, or to a distributor for cancellation of a distributorship may be treated as capital gains [¶ 1316; 1601].

Capital expenditure. Capital expenditures are not deductible. Capital expenditures for *tangible* property may be either: (1) additions or improvements to old property; or (2) acquisitions of new property that has a useful life of more than one year. Additions and improvements increase the basis of the property. Capital expenditures generally are recoverable through annual depreciation deductions that reduce the basis of the property. The basis as adjusted is used to measure the gain or loss on a sale or exchange of the property [¶ 1501; 1808].

Capital expenditures for *intangible* property can be recovered by depreciation deductions only if the property has a definitely limited useful life (such as a patent). Intangible property which does not have a definitely limited useful life (such as a trade mark) is not depreciable [¶ 2001].

These rules apply only to business or investment property.

Capital gains and losses. Capital gains usually are subject to less tax than ordinary income, and the deduction for capital losses may be limited. Generally, there can be no capital gain or loss unless a "capital asset" is sold or exchanged, but net gains on certain other property may be treated as a capital gain. Except for certain items specifically excluded by the Revenue Code, any property a taxpayer owns is a capital asset [¶ 1601]. Securities held by investors are capital assets; stock in trade and inventory property are not. The disposition of stock in a "collapsible corporation" is not treated as the sale of a capital asset [¶ 1627]. Property used in a trade or business is not a capital asset, but net gains from sales or exchanges may qualify as capital gains [¶ 1601; 1618-1625].

If the property is a capital asset, the next question is whether the property was held for more than nine months (12 months after 12-31-77). If it was, and the seller is not a corporation, he may be entitled to a long-term capital gain deduction [¶ 1605 et seq.].

Some transactions that ordinarily would not be thought of as a sale or exchange are treated as if there was a sale or exchange and the capital gain and loss provisions apply. These include: retirement of bonds [¶ 1602] and losses from worthlessness of certain stocks and securities [¶ 2203; 2208].

Carrybacks and carryovers of net operating losses. Taxpayers who sustain a business operating loss, or a casualty loss, that is not deductible in the year incurred may offset the loss against income of other years after adjustments. The adjusted "net operating loss" is carried back to each of the three preceding years, and if not there absorbed, may be carried forward to the seven following years [¶ 2241; 2243; 3215; 3216].

Carrying charges. Carrying charges may refer to the charges on installment purchases or to costs incident to ownership of property. The interest portion of installment carrying charges is deductible; if it is not specifically stated, the interest may be computed under a special rule [¶ 1904]. Carrying charges for property generally may be deducted, but the taxpayer can elect to capitalize them instead if they may properly be charged to capital account [¶ 1528].

Carryover basis. This is the basis a beneficiary gets from a decedent in carryover basis property. The basis is increased by the excess of fair market value on 12-31-76 over the adjusted basis at death, and is also increased by certain adjustments [¶ 1507].

Cash basis. Cash basis means that net income is determined by including all income actually or constructively received and deducting only amounts actually paid out [¶ 2702; 2703].

The cash basis of making returns is used by taxpayers who keep books on that basis and by those who *do not* keep books. Ordinarily, it cannot be used for purchases and sales when it is necessary to use an inventory [¶ 2706].

Child care expenses. Credit of 20% of household and dependent care expenses needed to keep taxpayer gainfully employed. Allowed to taxpayer maintaining household for dependent under 15, dependent incapable of self-care or spouse incapable of self-care. Credit is limited to $400 for one dependent and $800 for two or more dependents [¶ 2415].

Children. If a child has a gross income of $2,950 or more in 1977, a return must be filed and any tax due must be paid [¶ 1100]. This is the same as the rule for unmarried adults. The child's income is not included in the parent's return.

A parent can claim, on his return, a $750 exemption for a child if: (1) the gross income of the child is less than $750 or the child is under 19 or a full-time student; and (2) the parent furnishes more than one-half of the child's support [¶ 1118]. A divorced parent must meet additional requirements before he or she can claim the child as an exemption [¶ 1116].

A parent can deduct payments to his child for personal services if the payments meet the tests which govern deductibility of payments to a stranger. The child's gross income must include such payments [¶ 1312; 1815]. A foster child is treated the same as a natural child [¶ 1117].

Closed transactions. If property is sold or exchanged, the time for deducting a loss or (if the taxpayer reports on the accrual basis) reporting a gain is the year the sale or exchange becomes a closed transaction [¶ 2725(a)]. If the seller gets his money and the buyer gets the property during the same year, there is clearly a closed transaction in that year. But because contracts of sale vary according to the circumstances and the type of property involved, and may be entered into in one year and performed in another, many questions can arise. For instance, passage of title and delivery of possession may not be simultaneous, or there may be a question as to whether the buyer's promise to pay is the equivalent of cash.

Closely held corporations. Corporations that have only a few stockholders and are so-called "corporate pocket-books" may become subject to the additional personal holding company tax on income not distributed [¶ 3400 et seq.]. Deductions and losses in transactions between a major stockholder and the corporation may be disallowed under certain circumstances [¶ 2223; 2748], and gain on the sale of depreciable property may be taxed as ordinary income instead of being treated as capital gain from business property [¶ 1625].

Salary deductions must be "reasonable" and "in fact payments purely for services" [¶ 1816]. A closely held corporation frequently has difficulty in meeting these tests as to salaries paid to its officers. Reason: The officers, directors, and stockholders are usually the same persons, and they are not dealing at arm's length.

The question of whether the separate entity of a corporation should be ignored comes up frequently where there is evidence of a motive of tax avoidance. Many of the decisions on this question involve closely held corporations.

Closely held corporations that meet certain requirements may elect partnership-type taxation [¶ 3140 et seq.]. Estate taxes on an interest in a closely held business may be paid in 10 annual installments [¶ 3944].

Collection. Normally taxes are collected through payments by the taxpayer with his return [¶ 1100 et seq.], or through withholding at the source [¶ 2501] or prepayments of estimated tax [¶ 2515; 3523]. Domestic corporations pay their tax at a bank [¶ 3523]. The Government has several remedies for the collection of overdue taxes and additional taxes (deficiencies). They are: distraint, set-off, liens and suits [¶ 3615].

Commissions. Compensation paid on a commission basis is income [¶ 1301]. Commissions paid are deductible if they are a business expense or a "nonbusiness" expense. They are not deductible if they are a personal expense or capital expenditure [¶ 1818].

Compensation for services. Compensation received for services generally is income [¶ 1301], and compensation paid for services (if it is a business or "non-business" expense) is deductible [¶ 1815]. Wages are subject to withholding of tax at the source [¶ 2501]. Withholding is also required on pay to nonresident aliens for services within the U.S. [¶ 2535].

Consolidated returns. An affiliated group of corporations is permitted to file a consolidated income tax return. Foreign corporations and certain types of domestic corporations cannot be included. The rates of tax are the same as on a separate return.

In general, the filing of a consolidated return for one year means that a consolidated return must also be filed for each subsequent year. But, when a law change would make less advantageous the continued filing of consolidated returns, corporations will usually be permitted to make a new election to file a consolidated return or separate returns [¶ 3222].

Constructive income and deductions. The term "constructive income" serves to describe situations where the rule of substance v. form is applied. There can be constructive income to a taxpayer from a transaction when, in form, he receives nothing at all, or something that is not income. To describe these situations the term "as if" has also been used: a transaction is treated for tax purposes "as if" something else had been done than what its form indicates.

For instance, the regulations deal with property bought for less than its fair market value by a stockholder from his corporation or by an employee from his employer. Both types of buyers are taxed on the difference between the value of the property and what they paid. The transaction is treated "as if" the corporation or employer had sold the property for its fair market value and had paid the proceeds to the stockholder as a dividend or to the employee as pay [¶ 1310; 1329].

Constructive receipt of income. Income credited or set apart so that the taxpayer can draw it at any time is constructively received. That it was not actually received does not make any difference. This rule applies to cash basis taxpayers [¶ 2703]. A common example is a bond interest coupon. The interest is taxable in the year the coupon matures, even though the owner delays cashing it until a later year [¶ 2703]. (There can be no constructive receipt of income from one who does not have the funds to pay it.)

Contributions—deductions. Deduction is allowed for charitable contributions. The deductible amount is subject to limitations for both individuals and corporations [¶ 1941; 1943; 3118]. Accrued contributions are not deductible. Payment within the taxable year is necessary [¶ 1941]. Contributions by a partnership are not deductible in figuring its taxable income. Each partner treats his proportionate share as if it had been contributed by him individually [¶ 2915].

Corporations. For income tax purposes, "corporation" means not only the artificial entity usually known as a corporation, but also associations (certain trusts and partnerships) [¶ 3101]. Some corporations organized for charitable or other nonprofit purposes are exempt from tax or taxed only on income from commercial operations [¶ 3435 et seq.; 3445]. But if a nonprofit, charitable, etc. organization is considered a private foundation, it may be subject also to a user tax and excise taxes for prohibited acts or failures to act [¶ 3437 et seq.]. Small business corporations may elect to be taxed as partnerships [¶ 3140 et seq.]. A Domestic International Sales Corporation is also exempt from payment of tax. However, the DISC's income is fully taxed at some point to its stockholders [¶ 3460].

Income and deductions are, in general, the same for corporations as for individuals. Exceptions include the following:

"Adjusted gross income" (Sec. 62), the deduction for personal exemptions (Sec. 151), and the zero bracket amount (Sec. 63) do not apply to corporations [¶ 3112].

Corporations get a "special deduction" for dividends received [¶ 3113 et seq.].

Capital gains and losses and the capital loss carryback and carryover are treated differently [¶ 3201 et seq.].

Cost of goods sold. Cost of goods sold is subtracted from gross receipts to determine gross income of a manufacturing or trading business [¶ 2601]. The cost may be the purchase price, or it may include such items as labor, materials, supplies and indirect expenses incident to the production of goods, and freight charges. Inventories, at the beginning and end of the tax year, are an important factor in the computation of cost, and methods of inventory valuation have been devised for various types of business [¶ 2604 et seq.].

Credits. Credits are allowances against the tax itself. During 1977 they include: income taxes withheld on wages; prepaid estimated taxes; credit for the elderly; earned income credit; employment credit; general tax credit; investment credit; jobs credit and credits for: foreign taxes and taxes of U.S. possessions; taxes withheld on tax-free covenant bond interest; work incentive program expenses; and political campaign contributions [¶ 1103].

— D —

Damages. The taxability of damages received and the deductibility of damages paid depend on the nature of the claim they settle [¶ 1226; 2202(b)].

Deadlines. Last day for filing final income tax returns and making final payment is April 15, for calendar-year individuals (15th of fourth month for fiscal-year individuals). Filing date for final corporation returns is March 15 for calendar-year corporations (15th of third month for fiscal-year corporations) [¶ 3517; 3523]. However, automatic filing extensions can be obtained [¶ 3518].

Dealers. Several special rules apply to dealers in property. The principal characteristics of a dealer are that he has an established business and sells to customers. Property that a person sells as a dealer is not a capital asset. A dealer in securities must identify in his records any securities held for investment, otherwise the securities will be considered as held primarily for sale to customers [¶ 1628]. A dealer in securities can deduct selling commissions as business expenses [¶ 1818]. A dealer in real estate is not permitted to inventory real estate. A dealer who sells personal property on the installment plan can use the installment method to report the income [¶ 2801]. The restriction on the deductions of losses from "wash sales" of securities does not apply to dealers [¶ 2221]. A dealer cannot deduct depreciation on his stock in trade [¶ 2001].

Decedents. The executor or administrator must file a 1977 income tax return for an unmarried decedent whose gross income for the period ending with the date of death was at least $2,950 ($3,600 if 65 or over). For a married decedent, a 1977 return must be filed if (a) his gross income was at least $750 and a single return is filed, or (b) the combined gross income of him and his spouse was at least $4,700 ($5,450 if either spouse was 65 or over)and a joint return is filed. The full $750 exemption for the decedent is allowed.

The estate or beneficiaries of a decedent are taxed on any of his income that accrued, but was not reported because he used the cash basis. Even if he used the accrual basis, the same treatment is given to contingent items that were not accrued by him [¶ 3008(b)].

The basis of a decedent's property in the hands of persons who inherit it, is usually the "carryover basis" [¶ 1507].

A joint return can be filed even though one spouse dies during the year [¶ 3507].

Deficiency in tax. If the Revenue Service determines that the correct amount of tax is greater than shown on the return, the difference is called a "deficiency."

A taxpayer can argue the correctness of a deficiency with the Revenue Service [¶ 3603; 3607]. If he is unsuccessful there, he can appeal to the Tax Court without paying the tax [¶ 3635]. If he pays the tax and does not want to go before the Tax Court, he can file a refund claim and sue in the District Court if the claim is disallowed [¶ 3629].

Deficiencies in the tax bear 7% (9% between 7-1-75 and 1-31-76) interest; there are further additions if due to negligence or fraud [¶ 3617-3619].

Dependents. To get the $750 exemption for a dependent, these tests must be met [¶ 1115 et seq.]:

(1) The gross income of the person supported must be less than $750 unless he or she is a child (including a foster child) of the taxpayer, and (a) is a student, or (b) is under 19.

(2) The taxpayer must furnish over half the actual cost of support, except in the case of certain multiple support agreements.

(3) The person supported must be "related" to taxpayer or a member of his household.

(4) The dependent, if married, generally must not file a joint return.

(5) The dependent must be a U.S. citizen or resident, or a resident of Canada, Mexico, the Republic of Panama or the Canal Zone.

Depletion. An annual deduction for depletion is available to an owner of an economic interest in mines, oil and gas wells, other natural deposits, and timber. Its purpose is to make allowance for the fact that what is received from these sources is not all income, but is in part a return of capital [¶ 2100; 2101].

Depreciation. An annual deduction for depreciation is allowed to the owner of property used in his business or held for the production of income. The purpose of the deduction is to make allowance for the fact that property wears out; therefore, it does not apply to land apart from the improvements on it [¶ 2001]. The effect of the deduction is to reduce the taxable income from the property.

Generally, the annual depreciation of qualified tangible personal property and new residential housing construction can be figured under either the straight line, the declining balance or the sum of the year-digits methods, or any other consistent method. Some or all of the accelerated depreciation allowances, however, are not available for intangible property or for used residential housing and new or used commercial and industrial construction acquired after 7-24-69 [¶ 2010 et seq.]. Taxpayers using the straight line or sum of the years-digits method may have to deduct salvage value before figuring the depreciation rate [¶ 2011-2016].

Additional first-year depreciation allowance applies to business machinery and equipment having a useful life of at least 6 years. Additional allowance is 20% of the first $10,000 cost of the property ($20,000 on a joint return) [¶ 2016].

If property is used in part for business, a proportionate depreciation deduction may be claimed [¶ 2001].

Discounts. A seller can deduct, from gross sales, the discounts that he allows to his purchasers. A purchaser to whom a trade discount is allowed treats the net price as his cost. Cash discounts can be applied in reduction of cost or reported separately as income at the taxpayer's option [¶ 2604(a)]. If a borrower gives his note for more than he receives from the lender, this discount is the same as interest [¶ 1903]. A taxpayer who buys the obligations of others at a discount and later collects more than he paid, is taxed on the difference [¶ 2722]. If a corporation issues bonds at a discount, the net amount of the discount is a deduction, prorated over the life of the bonds [¶ 3125].

The profit to a purchaser of bonds issued at a discount may be part capital gain and part interest [¶ 1629]. The owner of an original issue discount bond issued after 5-27-69 must include the discount in his gross income on a ratable basis over the life of the bond [¶ 1629]. A special rule applies to the time for reporting income from short-term government obligations issued on a discount basis and payable without interest [¶ 2723(c)]. Another special rule applies to noninterest-bearing obligations issued at a discount and redeemable for fixed amounts increasing at stated intervals, for example, U.S. Savings Bonds. The rule in effect gives a cash basis bondholder an option to report the increment in value as it accrues instead of reporting the entire amount when the obligation matures [¶ 2723].

Disputed income. If a taxpayer's right to income is disputed, the time when it should be reported on a return may be in doubt. If the taxpayer has not received the income, the problem only affects accrual basis taxpayers. (Cash basis taxpayers do not include the income until it is received.) In most cases the income accrues when he has an absolute right to receive it, as when a final judgment is entered in his favor [¶ 2728]. If the taxpayer claims he has a right to income and he receives it without any restriction on what he may do with it, the income is reported in the year received, even though someone disputes his right to it. If he must repay the amount in a later year, he gets a deduction for it then [¶ 2729].

Distributable net income. This is a yardstick that limits the amount of estate or trust distributions that beneficiaries must include in their income and also limits the deduction allowed for the distributions [¶ 3004]. Generally, distributable net income is the actual or economic income of an estate or trust.

Dividends. Dividends are income if and to the extent that they are paid from earnings and profits [¶ 1702]. A corporation that receives dividends from another corporation gets a special deduction, usually 85% of the dividend [¶ 3114(a)], or 100% of the dividend if from a related corporation [¶ 3114(b)]. Each individual may exclude up to $100 of dividends received [¶ 1705; 1706].

A corporation can deduct payments for interest, but not for dividends. The right to deduct payments as interest has frequently been contested on the ground that they were in fact dividends [¶ 1901].

Divorce. Returns of a husband and wife for the year a final decree of divorce or separation is entered are affected in several ways. A joint return cannot be filed for that year and the estranged couple loses the right to the split-income benefits [¶ 3505]. Neither can claim a personal exemption for the other. In some cases a new withholding exemption certificate [¶ 2506(b)] and an amended declaration of estimated tax are required [¶ 2516]. If the divorced parents together provide more than half the support of their child, and the child is in custody of one or both his parents for more than half the year, the parent with custody of the child for the longer period can usually claim an exemption deduction. A special rule permits the parent without custody to claim the exemption [¶ 1116].

Doctors. Fees and retainers for professional services are ordinary income. Large amounts of fees in one year may qualify for income averaging [¶ 2401].

Deductions allowable to other professionals apply to a doctor. Office expenses and depreciation on furniture and equipment can be deducted if a doctor maintains an office. If he maintains an office in his home, he may deduct part of the rent, or if he owns the home, a portion of the depreciation [¶ 1807; 1832].

Domestic International Sales Corporation (DISC). This is a domestic corporation with only one class of stock (valued at least $2,500 on each day of year) and whose gross receipts and year-end assets are at least 95% export related. DISC status is elective and allows exemption from federal income tax. However, a DISC's income will, at some point, be fully taxed to its stockholders [¶ 3460].

— E —

Election of methods. The law and regulations often give the taxpayer an option of doing something in either of two ways. These options are usually called "elections." Some require the taxpayer's giving notice to or obtaining the permission of the Revenue Service. Most of them are binding for the year they affect; some are also binding for future years.

Employee death benefits. Payments by an employer or employers to beneficiaries of a deceased employee by reason of the employee's death are exempt up to $5,000, whether or not paid under a contract. The exemption applies to payments from a qualified profit-sharing, pension or stock bonus trust if the benefits are paid within one tax year of the beneficiary by reason of the employee's death. If the beneficiary gets an annuity, he may be able to exclude up to $5,000 of the annuity payments. However, this would not apply to a joint and survivor annuity if the employee died after the due date of the first payment [¶ 1304].

Employee health and accident plans. Payments made under qualified accident and health plans are deductible in full if they are reimbursements for medical expenses or are benefits for loss of arm, leg or bodily function. Disability pay is excludable if taxpayer is not 65, is not at mandatory retirement age, is totally disabled at retirement age, and did not make an irrevocable pre-1-1-77 election for the disability exclusion [¶ 1219].

Employer's contributions to accident and health plans, or to buy group or individual accident and health insurance, are not taxable to the employees [¶ 1220].

Employment. Payments that are "wages" require withholding of income tax by the employer, who pays it over to the government [¶ 2501]. Information returns must be filed by employers who pay compensation not subject to withholding, if total pay is at least $600 [¶ 3531(a)].

Payments that are personal expenses (e.g., wages of domestic help) rather than business or nonbusiness expenses, are not deductible by the employer [¶ 1807], but they are income to the employee. See also "Child care expenses."

Employees can deduct expenses of earning their pay, such as fees to secure employment [¶ 1829], traveling expenses [¶ 1805; 1829], entertainment expenses [¶ 1807; 1830] and union dues [¶ 1807]. Federal and state unemployment benefits are not income [¶ 1217].

Employees' trusts that conform to Sec. 401 are exempt from tax if they meet special requirements established by the Code [¶ 3024]. Employers may deduct, within limits, their contributions to such trusts [¶ 1838].

Estimated tax. Declarations and payments of estimated tax liability are required of individual taxpayers if estimated tax is $100 or more. Declarations are required of (1) single persons, heads of household, surviving spouses or married couples entitled to file jointly (if only one spouse works), expecting over $20,000 gross income, (2) a married person entitled to file jointly, expecting his or her own income to exceed $10,000, if both work, (3) a married person not entitled to file jointly expecting over $5,000 gross income, or (4) anyone expecting over $500 not subject to withholding [¶ 2516]. Self-employment social security tax must be included in the estimated tax [¶ 3827(b)].

Corporations must deposit estimated tax payments in an authorized bank. All corporations with an estimated tax of $40 or more will be on a current payment basis [¶ 3523].

Estoppel. In earlier years, the Revenue Service used the principle of estoppel to prevent a taxpayer from taking advantage of his mistake in a prior year after assessment for the year is barred. Now, in many cases, the mistake of a prior year can be adjusted for equitable tax treatment after the period of assessment has ended [¶ 3631].

Evidence. The findings of the Revenue Service are presumed to be correct. Thus, the taxpayer has the burden of proving the contrary. This rule applies when a taxpayer contests a deficiency before the Tax Court [¶ 3635] and also when he sues to recover a tax that he has already paid.

Many of the entries on returns must be supported by evidence in the form of statements to be filed with the returns. Even if these statements are not called for, it is to the interest of a taxpayer to retain the working papers and other data he used to prepare the return. This will save time and trouble when the government makes an audit. Although estimates and approximations of expenses have been allowed, this has often required litigation that could have been avoided if accurate records had been maintained.

Excess investment interest. A portion of excess investment interest is not deductible if it exceeds $25,000 and net long-term capital gains. One-half of any investment interest that exceeds net investment income plus $25,000 plus net long-term capital gains cannot be deducted [¶ 1906].

Excess itemized deductions. This is the excess of itemized deductions over the zero bracket amount, and is deductible in determining tax table or taxable income [¶ 1103].

Exchanges of property. Generally an exchange of property for other property results in taxable gain or deductible loss, but there are numerous important exceptions [¶ 1401]. Capital gain or loss may be realized in an exchange, as well as a sale [¶ 1602].

Property received in a nontaxable exchange generally has the same basis as the property given up. The gain or loss not recognized at the time of the exchange is recognized later when the property received in exchange is sold [¶ 1517].

Exemptions. There are three general types: (1) exemption from doing something that is required of most others (as filing a return); (2) exclusions of certain items from gross income; (3) allowances of fixed amounts before figuring tax (as personal exemptions).

The personal exemptions allowed to individuals are deducted from adjusted gross income along with excess itemized deductions to obtain the amount on which the tax is figured [¶ 1111].

Certain organizations are entirely exempt from income tax and after having established their right to the exemption are not required to file income tax returns although annual information returns are required [¶ 3435; 3537].

Exclusions from gross income generally, are listed in Chapter 2. Among the important exclusions are gifts and bequests and interest on state and local bonds.

Exemptions from withholding on wages may be allowable: (1) because the payments are not "wages" [¶ 2503]; (2) because of statutory exclusions [¶ 2503]; (3) because the person receiving the payment is not an "employee" [¶ 2502]; (4) because the pay does not exceed the personal exemptions allowable to the employee [¶ 2505]; or (5) because the person certifies that he does not expect to pay tax for the current year, and had no tax liability for the prior year [¶ 2506(c)].

In general, an individual is exempt from filing a 1977 income tax return if his gross income for the year is less than $2,950 if single and under 65, or $3,700 if single and 65 or over. During 1977, married persons who live together and file jointly and are both under 65 are exempt if their gross income is less than $4,700. If either spouse is 65 or over, they must file if their gross income is $5,450 or over; if both are 65 or over, the level is $6,200. If either spouse files a separate return, or if another taxpayer is entitled to an exemption for one of the spouses, the filing requirement is $750. Exemption from filing a declaration of estimated tax depends upon the nature and the amount of the individual's income [¶ 1100; 2516].

Expenses. The most common deductions are business expenses and expenses for production of income ("nonbusiness expenses"). But certain payments may also be deductible as losses. Personal and family expenses are not deductible [¶ 1800-1846].

Exploration and development expenses. Expenses for the exploration of a mine or natural deposit (except oil or gas) may be deducted in full currently and recaptured as ordinary income when the mine goes into production. Development expenses in this area are deductible in the year paid or incurred, or at the option of taxpayer, deducted ratably as the ore or mineral produced is sold [¶ 1843].

Certain intangible drilling and development costs of an oil or gas well may be charged to capital or to expense at the operator's option [¶ 2103(c)]. Farmers also have an option to capitalize or deduct development expenses [¶ 1844; 1845].

— F —

Family transactions. The income tax liability arising from transaction between members of a family is the same as for transactions between strangers except for these special rules in the law—

(1) Losses from sales or exchanges of property between members of a family are disallowed [¶ 2223(a)].

(2) Accrued interest and expenses due to a member of taxpayer's family who is on the cash basis are disallowed unless certain conditions are met [¶ 2748].

(3) Gain on sale of depreciable property between spouses is treated as ordinary income, not capital gain under Sec. 1231 [¶ 1625]. Family partnerships that do not meet special tests may be disregarded for tax purposes [¶ 2904]. See also "Closely held corporations," which are often family organizations [¶ 2223].

Farmers. Taxpayers engaged in farming are subject to the same rates of tax as other persons. Several special rules apply to income and deductions peculiar to farming. [¶ 1622; 1844; 2211; 2614].

Expenditures for soil and water conservation can be deducted (instead of capitalized) up to 25% of the farmer's gross income in any year. If he spends more than 25%, he can carry the excess over and treat it as the initial outlay for that purpose the next year—and so on, indefinitely. These expenses may be recaptured when farm land is sold or exchanged [¶ 1845].

Farmers can elect to report receipt of crop insurance proceeds in the year following the year of recovery for the damage or destruction [¶ 2614(a)].

Certain gains from farm operations may be recaptured as ordinary gains; see "Excess deductions account." See also treatment of "Hobby losses" when certain farm operations are not considered as carried on for profit.

Fiduciaries. A fiduciary must make a return for any individual whose income is in his charge if the individual would be required to file a return [¶ 3511]. On a return of this type, the fiduciary pays all of the tax.

A fiduciary for an estate must make a return if its gross income is $600 or over. A trustee must file a fiduciary return if the trust has gross income of $600 or over or any taxable income for the tax year. The fiduciary pays the tax only on income not distributed or distributable to beneficiaries.

Receivers, trustees in dissolution, trustees in bankruptcy, and assignees, operating the business or property of a corporation, must make returns for it [¶ 3512].

A fiduciary who makes distributions without paying taxes due may become personally liable [¶ 3001].

Reasonable fees paid to a fiduciary of an estate or trust are deductible [¶ 3016]. Fees paid to other assignees (such as a receiver operating a business) are generally deductible as business expenses. The persons who receive the fees are, of course, taxed on them as compensation for services. If the fees are large enough, they may qualify for income averaging [¶ 2401].

Filing. Many of the rights and liabilities of taxpayers depend upon filing a document with the proper official at the proper time. The most common examples are returns, refund claims, and Tax Court petitions.

Individual and corporate returns generally may be hand delivered to a District Director's office, but mailed returns may have to be sent to a Service Center [¶ 3519].

Returns, claims and other documents filed by mail and postmarked before the due date are filed on time, even though received after the due date [¶ 3517].

Fiscal year. See "Accounting periods."

Foreign corporations. Foreign corporations are taxed at U.S. rates on their U.S. business income and at 30% on their gross income from other U.S. sources. Certain foreign source income connected with the taxpayer's U.S. business is also taxed at U.S. rates [¶ 3710].

Foreign exchange. If income is received in foreign money, it should be reported in the income tax return in terms of U.S. money. The rate of exchange at the time of receipt governs. Special rules apply to "blocked" foreign currency [¶ 2730(a)].

Foreign taxes. Foreign taxes are deductible from income tax, except for estate, inheritance and gift taxes, and taxes for local benefits [¶ 1914]. However, instead of deducting them, foreign income and excess profits taxes can be claimed as a credit against the U.S. tax. A credit is usually taken instead of a deduction, because it is more advantageous [¶ 3701].

Estate tax credit is given for foreign death taxes paid by U.S. citizens. Resident aliens are permitted a credit if the foreign country to which the tax is paid allows a similar credit to U.S. citizens residing there [¶ 3938].

Fraud. Fraudulent evasion of taxes carries both civil and criminal penalties [¶ 3616-3620].

— G —

Gain or loss. Taxable gain or deductible loss usually results from a sale or other disposition of property. The most common example of "other disposition" is an exchange, but there can be a gain or loss on a transaction that is not actually a sale or an exchange. However, there are certain types of exchanges on which gain or loss is not recognized [¶ 1400 et seq.] or a loss is not deductible, but a gain is taxable [¶ 2221-2223].

Gifts. A person who receives a gift need not report it as income, but he is taxed on the income he receives after that from the gift property [¶ 1225]. So-called gifts received by an employee from his employer are usually taxed as compensation for services [¶ 1302]. If the owner of property makes a gift of only the *income* from it (for example, a gift of income from a trust fund), the person receiving this income is taxed on it [¶ 1225].

The Revenue Service examines gifts of income-producing property very closely. When there is evidence that one who purported to make a gift continues to have the advantages of owning the property, he may still be taxed on the income [¶ 1225].

A person who sells property that he received as a gift is subject to special rules for determining gain or loss. The general effect of these rules is that the gain is the same as it would have been to the former owner; but as to losses there are special restrictions, to prevent tax avoidance. Basis of the property must be adjusted for any gift tax paid on the gift [¶ 1515].

There is a tax on gifts [¶ 4000 et seq.].

Good will. Good will is a nondepreciable capital asset [¶ 1601]. Gain or loss from a sale of good will results only when the business, or part of it to which the good will attaches, is sold [¶ 1524].

Gross income. Gross income means all income received by the taxpayer from any source, unless exempt from tax. It includes gains, salaries, fees, profits, interest, rents, dividends, etc. [¶ 1300 et seq.].

Guaranty. An endorser or guarantor who has to pay the debt of his principal usually is subrogated to the rights of the creditor. If his claim against the principal debtor is worthless, he is entitled to a deduction, not because of the payment itself, but because the payment gives rise to a claim that becomes a bad debt. If the debt is a nonbusiness debt, the loss is a short-term capital loss [¶ 2315(b)].

A noncorporate guarantor, endorser, or indemnitor who has to pay the debt of the principal is entitled to a business bad debt deduction if (1) the debt is noncorporate, (2) the loan proceeds were used in the borrower's trade or business and (3) the right to collect from the principal debtor was worthless at the time of payment [¶ 2315(b)].

Guardians. A guardian of a minor or an incompetent must make a return for him if the ward would be required to file a return. The guardian must also make a declaration of estimated tax for him if the ward would be required to do so [¶ 2516; 3509; 3511].

— H —

Head of household. An unmarried person, except a nonresident alien, who maintains a home in which his children, their descendants, his stepchildren, or certain other relatives for whom he can claim a dependency exemption, reside, and who contributes over half the cost of maintaining the home, is taxed at a lower rate than other unmarried persons [¶ 1106]. A dependent parent will qualify taxpayer as head of household even though the parent does not live with the taxpayer, if taxpayer pays more than one-half the cost of maintaining the parent's home [¶ 1106]. A married parent who has been abandoned by his or her spouse can also qualify as a head of household.

Hobby losses. Losses from activities that are in fact hobbies and not carried on for profit are not deductible. Generally, an activity is presumed to be engaged in for profit if a profit was made in any 2 or more of the 5 consecutive tax years ending with the current year [¶ 2225].

Holding companies. Most holding companies are taxed the same as other corporations. The exceptions are:

(1) A corporation organized to hold title to property and turn over its income, less expenses, to an exempt corporation is also exempt [¶ 3435; 3436].

(2) A personal holding company is subject to regular corporation income taxes and, in addition, to a special personal holding company tax at high rates on the income that it does not distribute to its shareholders [¶ 3400].

(3) A foreign personal holding company is taxed the same as any foreign corporation and, in addition, certain of its undistributed income is taxed to its United States shareholders [¶ 3411].

Husband and wife. A husband and wife will usually elect to file a joint income tax return to get the split-income benefits [¶ 3508]. As a result, it generally is not necessary for a husband to make a gift of income-producing property to his wife or to make his wife a partner in his business solely to reduce his taxes. But he may give her dividend-paying stocks to increase the dividend exclusion of $200 on a joint return [¶ 1705].

If a husband and wife file a joint return, a $750 exemption may be claimed for each. If the husband files a separate return and the wife has no gross income and is not the dependent of another taxpayer, he can also claim a $750 exemption for her [¶ 1112].

Full split-income benefits are allowed a taxpayer for the year of the death of his spouse, and the following 2 years if there is a dependent child or stepchild living with him [¶ 1104].

Husband and wife who are both employed can split their withholding exemptions and allowances between them any way they see fit [¶ 2505].

— I —

Indebtedness. Repayment of a loan results in no income or deduction except for any interest element.

Indebtedness that is a deferment of payment for property or its use, or services, depends (for its deductibility and taxability) upon the treatment that would have been accorded to a cash payment. For instance, a business expense is deductible [¶ 1804], but a capital expenditure is not [¶ 1808]. An amount received for personal services rendered is income [¶ 1301], but an amount received for property sold figures only in arriving at the gain or loss [¶ 1400]. The time when the deduction is claimed or the income is reported depends on the accounting method of the taxpayer. Thus, a tenant on the accrual basis can deduct business rent when it becomes due, although he does not pay it until a later year [¶ 2735]; a landlord on the cash basis does not report rent as income until he receives it, even though it may have been due in a prior year [¶ 2724].

Cancellation of indebtedness may result in income to the person who owed the money [¶ 1318].

Information returns. Many types of payments that are income to the person receiving them must be reported on information returns by the person who makes the payment. The government thus can check whether a person reports all the income he receives [¶ 3530].

A person who receives income is not excused from reporting it because an information return was not filed. The criminal penalty for failure to file a return applies to information returns [¶ 3620].

Installment sales. Dealers are allowed to report gain from installment sales as installment payments are received instead of reporting the entire gain in one tax year. Other taxpayers also have this privilege for real property sales and casual sales of personal property. However, a loss may not be spread over the payment period [¶ 2800 et seq].

The installment method is particularly advantageous when there is a prospect that the rates of tax in future years will be lower.

Insurance premiums. Life insurance premiums paid by the insured are not deductible, even if the insurance is bought to secure a business loan [¶ 1828]. A corporation cannot deduct premiums on policies covering the lives of its officers or employees if it is the beneficiary. But if the beneficiaries are named by the insured, the premiums are considered additional compensation, deductible by the corporation and taxable to the officer or employee. Premiums paid by an employer on a group-term life insurance policy covering his employees are deductible by the employer but are not income to the employees (up to the first $50,000 of coverage per employee) [¶ 1307; 1828].

Premiums on insurance other than life are deductible if they can be shown to be business or "nonbusiness" expenses [¶ 1828]. Individuals can deduct one-half of insurance premiums paid for medical care up to $150; the balance is included with other medical expenses [¶ 1945].

Insurance proceeds. Life insurance proceeds received by reason of the death of the insured generally are wholly exempt from tax. However, if the policy was transferred for value (except in a tax-free transaction), the death proceeds are taxable, unless the transfer was to the insured, his partner or partnership or to a corporation of which he is an officer or shareholder [¶ 1213].

The interest element of life insurance proceeds payable in installments generally is taxable. But if the beneficiary is the surviving spouse of the insured, the interest element up to $1,000 a year is not taxable [¶ 1213].

Proceeds of endowment policies are income to the extent that they exceed the cost of the policy. If received in installments they are taxed as annuitites [¶ 1230]. Proceeds of accident and health insurance ordinarily are not income [¶ 1219] but their receipt may have the effect of reducing the individuals's deduction for medical expenses [¶ 1945].

Proceeds of insurance against loss of or damage to property are offset against the actual loss and only the excess loss is deductible. If the proceeds exceed the loss, the excess is income which may be treated as capital gain. But all or part of the gain will not be recognized if the taxpayer reinvests the proceeds in similar or related property [¶ 1411 et seq.].

Gain from the surrender of a life insurance policy to the insurance company, or from an endowment policy, is ordinary income, not capital gain [¶ 1214].

Interest. Deduction for interest paid or accrued is allowed whether the indebtedness is business or personal [¶ 1900]. Individuals can deduct interest on business obligations in figuring adjusted gross income; interest on personal obligations is an itemized deduction for figuring taxable income [¶ 1900]. Interest that is a carrying charge may be capitalized instead of deducting it [¶ 1528].

Interest received or credited generally is taxable, except interest on state and municipal bonds. Special rules apply to interest on U. S. Savings Bonds [¶ 2723]. The rule of constructive receipt, as applied to bond interest coupons, makes them taxable in the year they mature, even though they are not cashed until later [¶ 2703]. Interest received on a refund of federal taxes is income [¶ 1203(d)].

Part of the proceeds from an installment or other deferred payment sale may be treated as interest [¶ 2840].

Inventories. When the production, purchase, or sale of merchandise of any kind is an income-producing factor, inventories of the merchandise on hand (including finished goods, work in process, raw materials, and supplies) should be taken at the beginning and end of the year and used in figuring the net profit of the year [¶ 2600]. If it is necessary to use inventories, the books of account must be kept and the returns filed on the accrual basis [¶ 2706].

The two most common methods of valuing inventories are (a) cost and (b) cost or market, whichever is lower [¶ 2604]. There are special rules for inventories by: dealers in securities; farmers and live stock raisers; miners and manufacturers; and retail merchants [¶ 2609]. An optional method of identifying goods in inventory—the "last in, first out" method—is available to all taxpayers [¶ 2606].

If inventory property is sold, the basis is its last inventory value and the capital gain and loss rules do not apply [¶ 1601; 2611].

The method of valuing inventories must be the same from year to year unless the Revenue Service grants the taxpayer's application for a change [¶ 2604].

Inventors. An inventor—amateur or professional—is entitled to capital gain treatment on sale of his right to a patent, unless he sells to a related taxpayer (other than a brother or sister). He must not retain any interest in the patent, but the sale price can be based on production (percentage of sales) [¶ 1601].

The sale can be made before the patent is issued or applied for. The inventor's individual backer who got his interest by putting up money before the invention was completed also can get capital gain treatment. But an inventor's employer or a related taxpayer (except a brother or sister) does not get capital gain treatment [¶ 1601].

Inventors can set up self-employed retirement plans based on income from inventions [¶ 1839].

Investment credit. A taxpayer may offset 10% of his qualified investment in depreciable business machinery and equipment acquired and placed in service after 1-21-75 and before 1-1-81 against income tax. The property must have a useful life of at least 3 years. The useful life determines the amount of the qualified investment. The full cost or other basis qualifies, if the life is at least 7 years. The credit is also available for progress payments on qualified property with an estimated useful life of 7 years or more in the taxpayer's hands and a normal construction period of at least 2 years. The offset for any one tax year is limited, but any excess credit may be carried back 3 years and forward 7 years. The credit is also subject to limitations in the carryover years [¶ 2410].

Credit taken on property disposed of before the end of the useful life that was the basis for the credit is added to the tax for the year of disposition [¶ 2410].

Investors. Investors can deduct many types of expenses connected with their investments [¶ 1806]. Investment property generally is a capital asset [¶ 1601]. Investments in real estate furnish a basis for a depreciation deduction [¶ 2001].

— J —

Jobs credit. Employers get a 50% credit on the first $4,200 of wages paid to a new employee, subject to an overall $100,000 ceiling. The credit is only available in 1977 and 1978. A credit of 10% of the increase in Federal Unemployment Insurance paid to handicapped employees is available, limited to 20% of the jobs credit [¶ 2412].

Joint returns. A joint return must be filed if a husband and wife wish to take advantage of the split-income benefits [¶ 3505; 3508].

— L —

Leases. The principal tax effect of a lease of property is that the rent is income to the landlord and (except where it is not a business expense, as rent paid for a personal residence) deductible by the tenant [¶ 1316; 1840].

If a tenant sublets leased property, he must report the profit or can deduct the loss on the transaction if entered into for profit [¶ 2203].

Amounts received by a tenant for cancellation of a lease are usually treated as capital gain. Amounts received by a landlord for cancellation of a lease are taxable as ordinary income [¶ 1316].

Liquidation of corporations. Distribution in kind does not result in gain or loss to the corporation but may result in gain or loss to the shareholders subject to capital gain and loss limitations [¶ 1717]. If the corporation sells property at a gain and distributes the proceeds to its stockholders, the corporation will not be taxed, if it sells the assets within 12 months after adoption of a plan of complete liquidation, and liquidation is completed within the same 12 months. The gain is taxed to the stockholders as part of their capital gain on the liquidation. If inventory is sold, this rule applies only if the inventory is sold in bulk [¶ 3128]. A special rule governs liquidation of subsidiary corporations [¶ 3334]. If a so-called liquidating dividend is in fact an ordinary dividend it will be taxed as an ordinary dividend. Distributees may be held liable for any unpaid tax of the corporation [¶ 3614(a)]. When the liquidation extends over a period of years, deduction for loss through the liquidation generally is allowed in the year final distribution is made [¶ 1717].

Litigation. Payments may be deductible as business expenses or as losses. Attorney's fees may also be deductible [¶ 1823].

Expenses for the determination of *any* tax liability (including federal, state, or local taxes) are deductible by an individual as a "nonbusiness" expense [¶ 1806].

Long-term contracts. Two special methods can be used, at the option of the taxpayer, to report income from such contracts: the percentage-of-completion or completed contract method [¶ 2842]. Use of either method may result in tax saving.

Losses from sales of property [¶ 1400], worthlessness of property [¶ 2208; 2312] and for certain payments of money may be deductible. Special rules apply to capital losses [¶ 1601 et seq.; 3201 et seq.]. Certain losses are nondeductible including those from wash sales of securities [¶ 2221], and from sales to related taxpayers [¶ 2223]. Theft and embezzlement losses are deductible in the year the loss is discovered [¶ 2205].

— M —

Maximum tax on personal service income. There is a maximum tax on wages, professional fees, personal service compensation and other personal service income. The maximum marginal rate is 50%. A special formula is applied to compute the tax [¶ 2402].

Meals and lodging. Meals and lodging furnished to employees for the convenience of the employer are not taxable, if furnished at the employer's place of business, and the employee is required to accept the lodging as a condition of his employment [¶ 1308].

Medical expenses. Individuals are allowed a flat deduction (up to $150) of one-half the cost of medical care insurance. Deduction is allowed for "other medical expenses" in excess of 3% of adjusted gross income. Besides the usual medical expenses, "other medical expenses" include the balance of medical insurance costs and the cost of drugs and medicines in excess of 1% of adjusted gross income [¶ 1945].

Minimum tax on tax preferences. A minimum tax is imposed on certain items that receive preferential tax treatment. This tax is in addition to the regular income tax and is designed to reach formerly untaxed or lightly taxed incomes of taxpayers with large incomes. The tax is a flat 15% of tax preference items reduced by the greater of $10,000 or one-half the regular income tax paid less credits [¶ 2403]. See "Preference items."

Mortgages. Interest on mortgages, whether on business or residential property, is deductible [¶ 1900].

If reduction of a mortgage debt is gratuitous, no income results to the mortgagor. If the settlement is not gratuitous, taxable income may be realized [¶ 1318].

Sales of mortgaged real estate may be reported on the installment or deferred payment method [¶ 2811; 2816].

Foreclosures are considered sales and the nature of the loss to the mortgagor depends on whether the property is or is not a capital asset [¶ 1601]. The mortgagee may have a gain or loss and/or a bad debt deduction [¶ 2821]. Special rules govern the foreclosure of purchase-money mortgages [¶ 2823].

Moving expenses. Moving expenses incurred by an employee or a self-employed person in connection with the beginning of work at a new job location may be deducted. Both direct costs (for example, the cost of moving household goods) and indirect costs (for example, the cost of househunting trips) are deductible, but there are dollar limitations on the deduction for indirect moving expenses. Deductible moving expenses are deductions for adjusted gross income [¶ 1831].

— N —

Net capital gains. Net capital gains are the excess of net long-term capital gains over any net short-term capital losses. Used by individual and corporate taxpayers to compute the tax under the alternative method [¶ 1614; 3202].

Nonresident aliens are taxed at U.S. rates on their U.S. business income and at 30% on their gross income from other U.S. sources. Certain foreign source income effectively connected with the taxpayer's U.S. business is also taxed at U.S. rates. Charitable contributions, casualty and theft losses, business-related expenses, and one personal exemption (except for Canadians and Mexicans) can be deducted from U.S. business income. Canadians and Mexicans get the same personal exemptions as U.S. citizens. Expatriates who become nonresident aliens to avoid U.S. income, estate or gift taxes are subject to special provisions [¶ 3709].

Nonresident citizens—earned income. If a U.S. citizen is in a foreign country for a full tax year at least 510 days during any consecutive 18 months, income earned in the foreign country is exempt up to $15,000 annually. (A ratable part of the $15,000 is exempt if only part of a year is involved.) Foreign income must be included in gross income to determine whether return must be filed [¶ 3725].

— O —

Obsolescence. A deduction for obsolescence of business property and property held for the production of income is allowed. This permits a greater annual deduction than would be allowed for depreciation alone [¶ 2034]. A loss deduction is allowed for obsolescence of nondepreciable property [¶ 2210].

Operating foundation. An operating foundation is a private foundation that spends substantially all its income directly for charitable purposes, and either devotes half its assets to those purposes or whose support is generally not from private substantial contributors [¶ 3441]. See "Private foundations."

Options. Options are agreements, usually entered into for valuable consideration, to buy, sell, lease or exchange property at the election of the optionee (recipient of the option).

Gain or loss from sale or exchange of, or loss on failure to exercise, an option to buy or sell property is treated the same as if the gain or loss came from sale or exchange of the property underlying the option [¶ 1601(h)].

Gain of grantor of the option on failure of grantee to exercise the option is always ordinary income.

Exercise of an employee unrestricted stock option generally is taxable. However, under tax favored stock options, generally, no income is realized until the stock is disposed of [¶ 1327].

— P —

Partnerships. Partnerships are not taxable as such, but individual partners are taxed on their shares of the income whether distributed or not. Family partnerships formed to avoid tax may be disregarded, and the income taxed as if no partnership had been created. The term "partnership" is not limited to the common law meaning of partnership, but may also include groups (for example, joint ventures) not commonly called partnerships [¶ 2901 et seq.].

Payments for the taxpayer by another. Income may result to one whose taxes or other debts are paid by another. But if such payments are without consideration, they may be nontaxable gifts [¶ 1225; 1316; 1919].

Payments of debts with property. Although the value of the property equals the amount of the debt, gain or loss may result if the value is greater or less than the adjusted basis of the property to the debtor [¶ 1318(h)].

Penalties. The term "penalties" often refers not only to criminal penalties but also to additions to the tax [¶ 3616]. Penalties or additions to the tax for fraud, negligence, or delinquency are not deductible [¶ 1804].

Pensions. In general, pensions received as compensation for past services rendered to payor are taxable income; pensions received as gift or as compensation for personal injury are not taxable [¶ 1304]. Deductibility by payor depends on whether they are ordinary and necessary business expenses [¶ 1838].

Personal holding companies. See "Holding companies."

Pooled income fund. This is a trust made up solely of remainder interests contributed to the charity that maintains the fund. It is one of the three types of trust to which a charitable remainder can be contributed and a deduction claimed [¶ 1942(e); 3927; 4022]. See also "Annuity trust" and "Unitrust."

Preference items. Certain income and deduction items receive preferential tax treatment. Examples of these are capital gains, accelerated depreciation and the like. Some of these preferred items are subject to the minimum tax. This tax is in addition to the regular income tax. It taxes those who have large amounts of tax preferences and thus pay a small income tax in relation to their incomes. As a result of the tax on tax preferences, more taxpayers bear a more equitable share of the tax burden [¶ 2403; 3103]. See "Minimum tax."

Private foundation. In general, these are tax-exempt religious, charitable or educational organizations that are privately rather than publicly supported. Private foundations are subject to a tax on investment income and severe sanctions in the form of heavy excise taxes for specific prohibited acts [¶ 3437 et seq.].

Profit-sharing plans. Under a qualified profit-sharing plan, the employer can deduct currently the portion of business profits contributed to a plan for distribution to employees at a future date [¶ 1838]. Installment payments to an employee from a qualified plan are taxed as an annuity at ordinary income rates. A lump-sum distribution of the employee's entire interest in the plan on his separation from service because of death, retirement or discharge, or at the termination of the plan is taxable partly as long-term capital gain and partly as ordinary income [¶ 3024]. The part of the distribution attributable to the employee's plan participation for periods before 1974 is treated as capital gain. The remaining part is treated as ordinary income but can be averaged under a special averaging rule. Plans may also be set up to cover the self-employed [¶ 1839].

Put. A put is an option that gives an investor the right to sell stock to the maker of the put at a stated price within a limited time [¶ 1609].

— R —

Refunds. A taxpayer who paid more taxes than he owed may get a refund of the overpayment if he files a timely claim [¶ 3622]. If the claim is rejected, the taxpayer may sue to recover the tax [¶ 3629].

Reimbursements. The most common type of reimbursement is the repayment of a loan, and the person who receives the repayment need not report it as income [¶ 1201]. A similar rule applies to reimbursements for expenditures in behalf of another, since they are analogous to loans.

A taxpayer who receives reimbursements for his own expenditures must usually report them as income, unless it can be shown that they are a gift [¶ 1805].

Reimbursement for a loss (insurance or otherwise) reduces the amount of the deduction for the loss [¶ 2204].

Related items for different years. Although, in theory, the income tax is based on the income of the tax year, there are many items of income and deductions that depend on what was done in a prior year. Among the principal examples are sales of property acquired otherwise than by purchase. The gain or loss may depend upon: (1) the value as of a certain date; (2) the basis of the property to a previous owner; or (3) the basis of property that the taxpayer gave in exchange for what he is now selling [¶ 1500 et seq.].

A taxpayer may be bound by the way he treated a transaction in a prior year. He cannot benefit from his own omission or mistake.

Recovery of an item that was previously deducted is income unless it is exempt under the tax benefit rule [¶ 2316].

Rents. A landlord can deduct the expenses of collecting rents. If he is an individual, he can deduct these expenses in figuring his adjusted gross income [¶ 1806].

Rents are one of the types of income that may cause a corporation to be classified as a personal holding company; they are not personal holding company income, however, if they are 50% or more of the corporation's adjusted ordinary gross income [¶ 3401].

Reorganization of corporations. If the reorganization of one or more corporations conforms to certain statutory requirements, no gain or loss may be recognized on certain exchanges of property, or stock or securities related to the reorganizations. This is not an exemption. The gain or loss is taken into account when the property received in exchange is later sold or otherwise disposed of [¶ 3300 et seq.].

Repairs. Cost of repairs is deductible if the property is used for business or the production of income. If the repairs appreciably prolong the life of the property, they are treated as capital expenditures and are not deductible. In the latter case they increase the basis for gain or loss and depreciation [¶ 1825].

A specific repair allowance is set up under the Class Life ADR system [¶ 2033(f)]. This allowance is less than one-year's straight line depreciation on assets in a guideline class. The method is also designed to end controversies as to whether an expenditure is deductible in the year incurred or must be capitalized.

Research and experimental expenditures. These expenditures may be expensed or capitalized, at taxpayer's option [¶ 1842]. If capitalized, they must be amortized over at least 60 months, starting with the month the taxpayer first realizes benefits from the expenditures. If the property resulting from the expenditures has a determinable useful life, the expenditures are recoverable by depreciation or depletion. Election is binding, unless the Revenue Service consents to a change. These provisions do not apply to exploration expenditures to find any ore, oil or gas; nor to land or the cost of depreciable property (but depreciation can be treated as a research or experimental expense) [¶ 1842].

Reserves for bad debts. A reserve is an amount set aside out of current income for the purpose of meeting expenditures to be made in a later tax year. Under the cash basis, deduction may be taken only in the year of payment, and consequently there can be no deduction for a reserve [¶ 2744]. If the books are kept on the accrual basis, a deduction may be taken if there is a *present liability* to support the deduction. A reserve for bad debts is deductible under certain conditions [¶ 2311]. A dealer may set up a reserve for customers' paper he transfers and guarantees.

Resident aliens. With minor exceptions, resident aliens are taxed the same as U.S. citizens (on income from within and without the U.S.). The exceptions relate to the credit for foreign taxes and to certain exemptions [¶ 3708].

Restricted property. Special rules apply to stock or other property, subject to restrictions, that is compensation to a taxpayer. In general, the value of the property is included in the taxpayer's income when his rights to the property become transferable or are not subject to a substantial risk of forfeiture. However, the taxpayer can elect to include the restricted property in his income at the time he receives it [¶ 1326].

Royalties. In general, royalties are payments for use of property. They are taxed as ordinary income [¶ 1316]. Some coal and iron ore royalties are treated as capital gains [¶ 1623].

— S —

Sales may result in taxable gain or deductible loss to seller. See also "Gain or loss"; "Capital gains and losses"; "Closed transactions"; "Installment sales"; "Losses."

Sale of mortgaged property. When property, subject to a mortgage for which its owner had assumed personal liability, is transferred to a purchaser who assumes the mortgage obligation, the amount realized by the seller (original owner) is the cash received plus the amount of the mortgage obligation assumed. A similar rule has been applied when the property was encumbered by a mortgage that was not assumed by the seller (when he originally acquired the property) or by the purchaser [¶ 1400].

Sale of partnership interest. Gain or loss to the partner ordinarily would be capital gain or loss. However, it is ordinary gain or loss to the extent it comes from unrealized appreciation of inventory or unrealized receivables. The partnership can elect to adjust the basis of its assets to reflect the increase or decrease of value over the transferring partner's basis for the interest sold [¶ 2935].

Sale of residence. Ordinarily, gain on the sale of a residence is fully recognized. However, if another residence is purchased within 18 months before or after the sale of the old residence, or if construction of the new residence is started within 18 months before or after selling the old residence, and the new property is used as the principal residence within 2 years after sale of the old residence, gain is recognized only to the extent the adjusted sales price of the old residence exceeds the cost of the new residence. Selling price can be reduced by selling commissions and fixing-up expenses. If taxpayer is 65 or over, all or part of gain may never be taxed [¶ 1416-1423]. Loss on the sale of a residence is not deductible [¶ 2207].

Self-employed retirement plans. Partners and sole proprietors may deduct contributions to pension and profit-sharing plans for their own benefit, subject to limitations [¶ 1839]. Inventors, authors and similar creative people may set up a plan with the income from their creations, and deduct contributions to it.

Short sale. Selling what you do not own but expect to buy at a lower price and deliver at a later date is called selling short [¶ 1608].

Standard deduction. See "zero bracket amount."

Stock dividends. In general, stock dividends are not subject to tax. Among the exceptions to this rule are dividends the shareholders can elect to take in stock or cash and stock distributions that result in an increase in the proportionate interests of some shareholders [¶ 1707].

Surviving spouse. Taxpayer may get the benefits of income splitting for 2 years after the year his spouse dies, if (1) he has not remarried, and (2) he maintains as his home a household in which his child or stepchild resides and he can claim a dependency exemption for the child [¶ 1104].

— T —

Tax benefit rule. Recovery of items deducted in a previous year may result in income if the previous deduction resulted in a tax benefit [¶ 2316(c)]. Basis of property is reduced by amount of excess depreciation allowed that resulted in a tax benefit [¶ 2004].

Taxable income. Taxable income is the amount against which the tax rate schedules are applied to figure the tax. It is determined by subtracting allowable deductions from gross income [¶ 1102 et seq.].

Tax table income. Tax table income is adjusted gross income less excess itemized deductions [¶ 1102(h)].

Tax year. Income is figured on the basis of the taxpayer's tax year. This may be either the calendar year or a fiscal year. A fiscal year means (1) an accounting period of twelve months ending on the last day of any month other than December or (2) an annual accounting period varying from 52 to 53 weeks, subject to certain conditions. If the taxpayer does not keep books, the income must be determined on the basis of the calendar year [¶ 2714].

Taxes as deductible items. State and local taxes on real and personal property are deductible. Accrual-basis taxpayers may elect to deduct real estate taxes ratably over the real estate tax year. [¶ 2740]. If property is sold, the deduction is allocated between the buyer and seller in proportion to the length of time in the property-tax year each held the property [¶ 1920].

State or local income taxes are deductible, but federal income taxes are not. Other deductible taxes include state or local retail sales taxes and state gasoline taxes. Nondeductible taxes include federal or state estate, inheritance and gift taxes [¶ 1910-1919].

Time to report income or take deduction. A large percentage of tax litigation involves questions of time for reporting income or claiming deductions. Controversy arises largely because tax rates change from one year to another, and a difference in income may involve much more tax in some years than in others [¶ 2701 et seq.].

Traveling expenses are deductible if they are ordinary and necessary business or "nonbusiness" expenses as distinguished from personal expenses [¶ 1829].

Business traveling expenses are deductible if 3 conditions are satisfied: (1) the expense must be reasonable and necessary as the term is generally understood (this includes transportation fares and expenses for food and lodging while traveling); (2) the expense must be incurred while away from home (except certain *transportation* expenses); (3) the expense must be directly connected with trade, business or profession of the taxpayer or his employer, and it must be necessary or appropriate to the development of the trade, business or profession [¶ 1829]. An individual's expenses are deductible for adjusted gross income [¶ 1805].

"Nonbusiness" traveling expenses are deductible if incurred in connection with the production or collection of income or the management, conservation or maintenance of property held for the production of income [¶ 1829]. An individual's expenses are deductions for adjusted gross income only if related to property held for the production of rents and royalties [¶ 1806].

Trusts. Ordinarily, the income is taxed either to the fiduciary or the beneficiaries, or in part to each. The income of stock bonus, pension, or profit-sharing trusts created by an employer is exempt if certain requirements are met. To prevent tax avoidance, income may be taxed to the grantor of a trust in certain cases [¶ 3000 et seq.].

— U —

Uncollectible income. Uncollectible income generally need not be accrued [¶ 2719]. If the taxpayer is on the cash basis, this question does not arise.

Unitrust. This is a trust with a charitable remainder that pays a fixed percentage of its assets annually to a noncharitable income beneficiary. It is one of the three types of trusts to which a charitable remainder can be contributed and a deduction claimed [¶ 1942(e); 3927; 4022]. See also "Annuity trust" and "Pooled income fund."

Unpaid expenses and interest. To prevent tax avoidance, the deduction is restricted when the payor and payee occupy specified relationships to each other and the former is on the accrual basis and the latter is on the cash basis. In such case an accrual is not deductible unless the amount is paid or includible in the gross income of the payee within 2½ months after the end of the tax year [¶ 2748].

— V —

Valuation of property. Under certain circumstances the law requires that property be valued as of a certain date. For example, carryover basis property must be valued as of 12-31-76 [¶ 1507-1510]. Property received as a dividend must be valued as of the date of its receipt [¶ 1702].

— W —

Withholding of tax. When the law requires tax to be withheld at the source, a person making a payment to another deducts the tax from the payment and turns it over to the government. A person whose tax is being withheld can claim the amount withheld as a credit against his tax [¶ 2511(a)].

Work incentive program expenses. A tax credit is allowed equal to 20% of wages paid to employees in the first 12 months they are employed under the Work Incentive Program. The credit is subject to limitations and recapture rules [¶ 2411].

— Z —

Zero bracket amount. Zero bracket amount replaced the standard deduction. It is a tax-free amount available to all individuals, based on their filing status: joint return, $3,200; single or head of household, $2,200; married filing separately, $1,600. The zero bracket amount is not elected, it is already figured into the tax tables and rate schedules [¶ 1107].

INTERNAL REVENUE CODE
FINDING LIST

¶5801 The following table shows the location in the Federal Tax Course of the sections of the Internal Revenue Code of 1954. These are cited in the paragraphs indicated.

IRC §	Tax Course ¶	IRC §	Tax Course ¶	IRC §	Tax Course ¶
1	.1121	48(c)	2410(a), (b), (g)	58(f)	3432(f)
1(e)	3726(c)	48(c)(2)	2410(a)	58(g)	.3725
1(f)	3726(c)	48(c)(2)(D)	2913(c)	61	1100; 1201; 1305; 1314; 1316(a)
2(a)	.1105	48(d)	2410(f)	61(a)	1300(a); 1301
2(b)	.1106	48(e)	2410(g); 3140	62	1102(c)
2(b)(3)(A)	3709(b)	48(f)	.3019	62(1)	.2804
2(c)	1104(b)	48(k)	2410(c)	62(2)	1805(a); 1829(b)
3	1107(b); 1122; 3020(a)	50A	2411(f)	62(3)	.1612
11	3102; 3103; 3330(a)	50A(a)	2411(a), (b)	62(9)	3146(a)
21	.3102	50A(a)(3)	2411(b)	63	1102(g); 1107
21(a)	.3546	50A(b)	2411(a), (c)	71 et seq.	.1201
21(c)	.3546	50A(c)	2411(a), (d)	71	.1320
22	3726(c)	50A(c)(3)	2411(b)	71(a)	1320(a)
36	1107(d); 3702	50A(d)	2411(d)	71(b)	1320(c)
37	2406; 2407(a)	50A(d)(2)	2411(b)	72(a)	1215(b)
37(a)	2407(a)	50B	2411; 2411(f)	72(b)	1230(b)
37(b)	2406(a)	50B(a)(2)	2411(a)	72(c)	1230(d)
37(c)	2406(c)	50B(b)	2411(a)	72(c)(3)(A)	1230(e); 1231
37(d)	2406(b)	50B(d)	2411(e)	72(c)(3)(B)	1215(b); 1230(e)
37(e)	2406(c)	50B(e)	2411(e); 3019	72(c)(4)	1230(c)
39	.2417	51-53	2412	72(d)	1232(d)
40	.2411	56	2403; 2906; 2908(c)	72(e)(1)	1216; 1230(f), (g)
41	2412; 2412(a)	56(a)	2403; 3020(d); 3103	72(e)(2)	1214; 1215(a); 1230(g)
41(c)	2412(c)	56(b)	2403(b)	72(f)	1232(d); 3725(a)
41(c)(2)(A)	.2412	56(c)	.3103	72(g)	1230(d)
42	1111(e)	56(d)	.3103	72(h)	1215(c)
43	2405; (a), (b)	56(e)	.3103	72(j)	1230(b)
44	1416(d)	57	2403(a); 2906; 2908(c)	72(k)	1230(b)
44A(a)	.2415	57(a)	2403(a); 3103; 3140; 3400	72(m)	1839(g)
44A(c)(1)	2415(a)	57(a)(4)	2040(a); 2040(b); 3103	72(n)	1232(i)
44A(c)(2)	2415(b)	57(a)(5)	2041; 3103	73	.1312
44A(d)	2415(c)	57(a)(6)	1327; 2403(a)	73(b)	1100(a)
44A(e)	2415(c)	57(a)(7)	3103; 3433(a); 3433(b)	74	1302(c)
44A(f)	2415(e)	57(a)(8)	2102(c); 3103	75	1846(a)
44A(f)(1)	2415(a)	57(a)(9)	1327(b); 1612(b); 3009(b); 3103; 3201(b)	77	2722(d)
44A(f)(6)	2415(d)	57(a)(10)	2043; 3103	78	.3706
44B	2412	57(a)(11)	2103(c)	79(a), (b), (c)	1307(a)
46(a)	2410	57(c)	1906(b)	81	2311(d); 2727
46(b)	2410(d)	58(a)	.2403	82	1301(c)
46(c)	2040; 2410; (a), (c)	58(b)	3103; 3223	83	1232(b), (e)
46(d)	2410(a)	58(c)	3020(d)	83(a), (c)	1326(a)
46(e)	2410(g)	58(d)	.3103	83(b)	1326(b)
46(e)(3)	2410(f)	58(d)(1)	3140; 3143(b)	83(d)	1326(c)
46(f)(4)	.2410	58(d)(2)	3143(b)	83(e)	1326(f)
47	2927(b)	58(c)	3025; 3103	83(f)	1326(d)
47(a)	2410(e); 2935(b)			83(g)	1326(e)
47(b)	2925(a)			83(h)	1819(c)
48(a)	2041; 2410(a), (b)				
48(a)(8)	2018; 2042; 2043; 2410(b)				

Internal Revenue Code Finding List

IRC §	Tax Course ¶	IRC §	Tax Course ¶	IRC §	Tax Course ¶
83(i)	1326(e); 1326(g)	151(e)(1)(A)	1118	166(d)	2307
84	2412(d)	151(e)(1)(B)	1118(a)	166(d)(1)	2310
101 et seq.	1201	151(e)(2)	1119	166(d)(2)	2305
101(a)	1213; 1213(a)	151(e)(4)	1116(b)	166(f)	2315(b)
101(b)	1304(a)	152(a)	1116; 1117(a)	166(g)	2311(d)
101(c)	1213(b); 1304(a)	152(a)(9)	1117(a), (b)	167	2000; 2010; 2011
101(d)	1213(c)	152(a)(10)	1117(b)	167(a)	2001(a)
102	1225	152(b)(2)	1117(a); 1118(a)	167(b)(2)	2012
103	1204	152(b)(3)	1120; 1120(a), (b)	167(b)(3)	2013
103(a)	1203(b)	152(b)(4)	1116(a)	167(b)(4)	2015
103(c), (d)	1204	152(b)(5)	1117(b)	167(c)	2012(a); 2013; 2015
104(a)	1218(a); 1218(b)	152(c)	1116(c)	167(d)	2010(c)
104(a)(2)	1947	152(d)	1116(b)	167(e)	2010(b)
104(a)(3)	1221	152(e)	1116(a)	167(e)(3)	3521
104(a)(4)	1218(c), (e)	153(1)	1112	167(f)	2005
104(b)	1218(c)	153(2)	1112	167(g)	2003
105	1219(a)	161–175	3112	167(h)	2002(c); 3014(b)
105(a)	1221	162	1803; 1838; 1911(b); 3016	167(i)	2012(a)
105(b)	1219(a)	162(a)	1804; 1815; 1825; 1825(a); 1828(b); 1829(b); 1832	167(j)	2017(a), (b), (c)
105(d)	1219(c)			167(k)	2018
107	1308(e)			167(l)	2019
108(a)	1318(j); 3125(f)	162(a)(2)	1829(a)	167(m)	3521
108(b)	3125(a)	162(a)(3)	1826	167(m)(1)-(3)	2033
109	1317; 1317(a)	162(b)	1943(d)	167(n)	2017
110	1316(a)	162(c)	1812	167(o)	2017(b)
111	2316(c); 2316(d)	162(f)	1812	169	2040
112	1306	162(g)	1812	169(f)	2040(a)
114	1805	163(a)	1901; 1904(a); 1906	170	3406
116(a)	1705; 1706(a), (b)			170(a)	1941(c)
116(d)	1705	163(b)	1904(b)	170(a)(3)	1942(e)
117	1303	163(b)(1)	1904	170(b)	1943
118	3106	163(c)	1901	170(b)(1)(A)	1943(a); 3437
118(b)	3106	163(d)	1906(a), (b)		
119	1308(b)	163(d)(4)(B)	2913(a)	170(b)(1)(B)	1943(c)
121	1423; 1526; 2823	164	1912(a); 1914; 1917(a), (b)	170(b)(1)(C)	1943(e)
122	1232(i); 1306			170(b)(1)(D)	1943(b)
123	2204(c)	164(a)	1912(c), (d)	170(b)(1)(D)(i)	1943(b)
141(a)	1108	164(b)(5)	1917(b)	170(b)(1)(D)(ii)	1945(a)
141(b)	1107(a)	164(c)	1917(a)	170(b)(1)(D)(iii)	1942(b); 1943(b); 1945(a)
141(c)	1107(a)	164(d)	1920(a)		
141(d)	1108	164(e)	1918	170(b)(1)(E)	1943(a)
141(e)	1107(a)	165	2205; 3203	170(b)(2)	3118(b); 3406
142(a)	1108	165(a)	2200; 2201; 2209	170(c)	1941(a); 3118
142(b)	1107(c); 3727(a)	165(b)	2201; 2204(d)	170(d)(1)	1944
142(b)(4)	1107(c); 3011	165(c)	2200; 2204(b)	170(d)(1)(A)	1944
143	1108	165(c)(2)	2203	170(d)(2)	3118(c)
143(b)	1104(c)	165(c)(3)	2204	170(e)	1619(c); 1942(b)
144	1109(c)	165(d)	2224	170(e)(1)	1942(b); 3118(b)
144(a)(3)	1109(a)	165(e)	2205(b)		
144(b)	1109(b); 1122(b)	165(g)	2208(a); 2312(a)	170(e)(3)	3118
144(d)	1107(b)	165(g)(2)	2312(a)	170(f)(1)	1941(a)
151	1102(f)	165(g)(3)	2208(a); 2312(a)	170(f)(2)	1942(e)
151(b)	1112(a), (b), (c)	165(h)	2204(e)	170(f)(2)(A)	1942(e)
151(c)	1113	166	2300; 2311	170(f)(3)(A)	1942(d), (e)
151(c)(2)	1113	166(a)(2)	2306	170(f)(3)(B), (C)	1942(e)
151(d)	1114	166(b)	2302	170(f)(4)	1942(e)
151(d)(2)	1114(a)				

Internal Revenue Code Finding List

IRC §	Tax Course ¶	IRC §	Tax Course ¶	IRC §	Tax Course ¶
170(f)(5)	1942(g)	211–217	3112	272	1623
170(f)(6)	1941(a)	212	1803; 1806; 1826; 1828(b); 1838; 1911(b); 3016; 3016(b)	274	1830(a), (b); 2202
170(g)	1943(e)			274(a)	1807
170(h)	1942(f)			274(b)	1830(c)
171	1846(a); 1846(b)	212(3)	1823	274(d)	1829(c); 1830(g)
171(b)(1)	1846(d)	213	1945; 1945(c)	274(h)	1829(a)
171(b)(2)	1846(e); 1846(f)	213(b)	1946(b)	275	1910; 1911(a); 1914
		213(d)	1945(b)	276	1811
		213(e)	1946; (c)	277	3448(d)
172	2204(f); 2241	215	1320	278	1844(a)
172(a)	2244; 3218	216	1902; 1919	279	1905(e)
172(b)	2241(a); 3216	216(b)	1417	280	1807
172(b)(1)	2241(a); 3216	216(c)	2002	280A	1804; 1805
172(b)(1)(B), (C)	2226	217	1831; (a)–(d)	280A(d)(2)	1806(a)
172(b)(1)(F)	3433(a)	217(e)	1416(b); 1831(b)	280A(f)(1)	1806(a)
172(b)(1)(G)	3433(a)	217(g)	1831(c)	280B	2209
172(b)(2)	2243	218	2412; (b)	280C	2412
172(b)(3)	2226; 3216	219	1831(a)	301(b)	1702(b)
172(c)	3217	219(a)	2503(a)	301(b)(1), (2)	3107
172(d)	2242(a); 3219	220	2503(a)	301(b)(1)(D)	3107
172(d)(1)	3217	221(d)(3)	1426	301(c)	1702(a)
172(d)(4)	2242(a)	236	1426	301(d)(1)	1702(b); 1709(b)
172(d)(4)(D)	2242(a)	241	3113	301(d)(2), (3)	3107
172(d)(5)	3217	243	3459	302(b)	1718(a), (c)
172(d)(6)	3217	243(a)(3)	3114(b)	302(c)(2)	1719(a), (b)
172(h)	3143(c)	243(b)	3114(b)	303	1721(a)
173	1528; 1528(a); 1808	243(d)	3114(a)	304	1720(c)
174	1842	244	3114(d)	304(a)	1720(a), (b)
174(a)	1842(a)	245(a), (b)	3114(c)	304(b)(2)	1720(a)
174(b)	1842(b)	246(a), (b), (c)	3114(a)	304(c)(2)	1720(d)
174(c), (d)	1842(c)	246(b)(1), (2)	3114(e)	305	1707(b)
175	1845	246(d)	3460(c)	305(b)	1709(a); 1712; 3307(a)
175(c)	1845; 1845(c)	247	3115	305(c)	1707(c)
175(c)(2)	1845	248	3116	305(d)	1710(a); 1712
175(d)	1845(b)	248(b), (c)	3116	306	1718(b); 1722(a), (b), (c); 3311; 3313; 3317(b)
175(f)	1845(c)	249	3125(b)		
177	1808	262	1815; 1828(a), (b)	307(a)	1708(a)
178(a)	1840; 2002(b)	263(a)	1808	307(b)(1)(2)	1711(a)
178(b)(1)	2002(b)	263(c)	2103(c)	311(a)	3127(a)
178(b)(2)	2002(b)	263(d)	1911(b)	311(b)	3127(b)
178(c)	1840; 2002(b)	263(e)	1808; 1825(a)	311(c)	3127(b)
179	2016	264	1905(b); 1905(c)	311(d)(1)	3127(b)
179(b)	2016	264(a)(1)	1828(a)	311(d)(2)	3127(b)
179(d)	2016(a), (c), (d)	265(1)	1809	312	1700; 3129(g); 3404(b)
179(d)(3)	2016	265(2)	1905(a)	312(a)	3129(a)
179(d)(5)	3014(c)	266	1528	312(b)	3129(b)
180	1844(a)	267	2223; 3018	312(c)	3129(c)
182	1845(d)	267(a)(2)	3018	312(d)	3129(d)
183	2225	267(b)	2223(a); 2748; 3018	312(e)	1720(a); 3129(e)
184	2041	267(b)(2)	2223(b)	312(i)	3129(g)
185	2041	267(b)(3)	3408	312(j)	3129(a)
186	1222	267(b)(9)	2223(c); 3436(c)	312(k)	1701(b); 2024; 3129(f)
188	2043	267(c)	2223(a), (d)	312(l)	3129(a)
189	2042	267(d)	2223(e); 2923(a)	312(m)(3)	3706
190	1812	268	1622(b)	316(a)	1700; 1701(a)
191	2044	269	3226	316(b)	1704; 1704(c)
		271	2301	316(b)(2)	3404(b)
				316(b)(3)	1700

Internal Revenue Code Finding List

IRC §	Tax Course ¶	IRC §	Tax Course ¶	IRC §	Tax Course ¶
318	1727	358(d)	1518(a); 3315(a)	401(d)(4)(A)	1839(c)
318(a)	1727(e)	361	3300; 3309(b); 3310	401(d)(9)	1839(a)
318(a)(2)	1727(b), (c), (d)	361(b)(1)(A)	3309(b)	401(d)(10)	1839(a)
318(a)(3)	1727(b), (c), (d)	361(b)(2)	3311	401(e)	1839(b)
318(a)(5)(C), (D)	1727(f)	362(a)	1518(b)	401(e)(3)	1839(f)
331(a)	1717	362(b)	3314	401(f)	1839(e)
331(a)(1)	1717(a)	362(c)	3106(b)	401(g)	1232(a); 1839(e)
332(b)	3332; 3334	367	1405; 3309; 3317; 3334; 3629; 3710(a)	401(h)	1839(d); 3024(a)
332(c)	3334(a)	367(c)(2)	3317	401(i)	3024(a)
333	3335	368	3300	402(a)	1838(l)
333(a)–(d)	3335(a)	368(a)(1)(A)	3302	402(a)(1)	3024(d)
334(b)	3334(b)	368(a)(1)(B)	3302; 3304	402(a)(2)	3024(d)
334(c)	3335; 3335(c)	368(a)(1)(C)	3302; 3305; 3305(a)	402(a)(4)	3712
336	3128	368(a)(1)(D)	3302; 3306(b)	402(a)(5)	3024(d)
337	3141(d); 3153(b)	368(a)(1)(E)	3307(a)	402(b)	3024(f)
337(a), (b)	3128(a)	368(a)(1)(F)	3302; 3307(b)	402(d)	3024(f)
337(c)	3128(a)	368(a)(2)(A)	3305(c)	402(e)(4)(L)	3024(d)
337(d)	3128(a)	368(a)(2)(B)	3305(a)	403	1232(d); 3521
341	1627	368(a)(2)(C)	3301; 3305(c)	403(a)	1232(b), (c), (d); 1838(l)
346	1716	368(a)(2)(D), (E), (F)	3302; 3303	403(b)	1232(e)
351	1405(b); 1720(c); 3306(c); 3521	368(b)(2)	3301	403(c)	1232(b), (d), (e)
351(a)	1405	368(c)	1405; 3304; 3306(a); 3317(a)	404(a)(1)(C), (D)	1838(d)
351(b)	1408(b)	371	3331(a), (b), (c)	404(a)(2)	1232(a); 1838(g)
351(c)	1405	372	3331(c)	404(a)(3)(A), (B)	1838(e)
351(d)	1405(c)	374	3331(a)	404(a)(4)	1838(c); 1838(i)
354	3300; 3309(a); 3310	381	3338(a)	404(a)(5)	1838(i)
354(a)(2)	3309(a)	381(a)	3336(b); 3338	404(a)(7)	1838(h)
354(b)	3306(b)	381(a), (c)	3336	404(a)(8)	1839(c)
354(b)(1)(A)	3309(a)	381(b)	3336(b)	404(a)(9)(B)	1839(c)
354(c)	3332	381(c)(1)–(19), (22)–(25)	3337	404(b)	1838(j)
354(d)	3331(a)	382(a)	3221	404(c)	1838(i)
355	3309(a); 3316(a)	382(b)	3338; 3338(a)	404(e)(4)	1839(c)
355(a)(1)	3317(a)	382(b)(2)	3338(c)	405	1839(e); 3024(h)
355(a)(2)	3317(b)	382(b)(3)	3338(a)	406	1838(e); 3024(a)
355(a)(3)	3317(c)	382(b)(4)	3338(c)	406(c)	3024(d)
355(b)(1)	3318	382(b)(5)	3338(a), (b)	407	3024(a)
355(b)(2)	3318	382(b)(6)	3338(b)	407(c)	3024(d)
356	3319	382(c)	3338(a)	407(d)	1838(e)
356(a)(1)	3309(a); 3311	383	3339	408	1838(l)
356(a)(2)	3312	385	1901	408(d)(3)	1838(l)
356(b)	3317(c)	401	3915(b)	408(f)	3618(h)
356(c)	3311	401(a)	1838(c); 1838(h); 3024(a); 3435	408(f)(1)	1838(l)
356(d)(1)	3319	401(a)(3)(4)(5) & (6)	3837	409	1838(l)
356(d)(2)(B)	3309(a)	401(c)	1839(b)	409(b)(3)	1838(l)
356(d)(2)(C)	3319	401(c)(2)(C)	1839(b)	415	1838(f); 3024(a)
356(e)	3311; 3319	401(c)(3)	1839(a)	421	1327; (d)
357	1409	401(d)	1839(d)	421(c)(2)	3008(b)
357(a)	1405(a); 3315(a)	401(d)(1)	1839(e)	422	1327(a)
357(b)	1405(a); 3309(b)	401(d)(3)	1839(a)	422(a)(2)	1327(a)
357(c)	1405(b); 3315(b)			422(b)	1327(a)
358(a)(1)	1518(a); 3313; 3314			422(c)	1327(a)
358(a)(2)	1518(a); 3313			422(c)(3)(A)	1327(a)
358(b)(1)	3313			422(c)(4)	1327(a)
358(b)(2)	3320(b)				
358(c)	3320(a)				

Internal Revenue Code Finding List

IRC §	Tax Course ¶	IRC §	Tax Course ¶	IRC §	Tax Course ¶
422(c)(6)	1327(a)	483	2840; 2840(a)	508(d)(2)	3437(a)
423(a)(2)	1327(b)	483(d)	2840(d)	508(d)(2)(A)	1941(a); 3439
423(b)	1327(b)	483(e)	2840(c)		
423(c)	1327(b)	483(f)	2840(e)	508(d)(2)(B)	1941(a)
424	1327(c)	501	3415; 3460(a)	508(d)(3)	1941(a)
425(a)	1327(d)	501(a)	3024(a), (c); 3435; 3814(b); 3837	508(e)	3453
425(d)	1327(d)			508(e)(1), (2)	3439
425(h)	1327(d)	501(b)	3024(b)	509	3437
432(b)(1)	2411	501(c)	3435	509(a)(1)	3437
441(b)	2714(a)	501(c)(1)	3436; 3447	509(a)(2)	1943(a); 3437
441(f)(1)	2714(b)	501(c)(2)	3222(a); 3436; 3436(b)		
441(f)(2)(A)	2714(b)			509(a)(3)	1943(a); 3437
441(f)(2)(B)	2715; 2717(b)	501(c)(3)	1232(e); 1941(a); 2503(a); 3436; 3436(b); 3437; 3450; 3452; 3453; 3814(a); 3819(d)		
				509(a)(4)	3437
443	2717(a), (b); 3020(a); 3514			509(d)	3437
				509(e)	3437
443(b)	2717(b), (c)	501(c)(4)	3436; 3436(b); 3447	511–515	3445
443(c)	1111(d); 2717(b)			511	3446
443(d)	2717(b)	501(c)(5)	3436; 3436(b)	511(a)	3454(a)
446(b)	2707; 2711	501(c)(6)	1232(e); 3436; 3436(b)	511(b)	3451
446(c)	2701(a)			511(d)	3445
446(d)	2701(b)	501(c)(7)	3436; 3436(b)	512	3447; 3448(a)
447	2701(c)	501(c)(8)	3436; 3436(b)	512(a)(1)	3448(a)
451	2719(a)	501(c)(9)	3436; 3436(b)	512(a)(2)	3448(a)
451(b)	3008(b)	501(c)(10)	3436	512(a)(3), (4)	3448(d)
451(d)	2614(a); 3521	501(c)(11)	3436	512(b)	3448(b), (c)
451(e)	2614(a)	501(c)(12)	3436; 3436(b)	512(b)(11)	3451
453	2811	501(c)(13)	3436; 3436(b)	512(b)(12)	3448(c)
453(a)	2801; 2802	501(c)(14)(A)	3436	512(b)(15)	3448(d)
453(b)	2812	501(c)(14)(B)	3436	512(b)(16)	3446
453(b)(2)(A)	2811	501(c)(14)(C)	3436	512(b)(17)	3446
453(c)	2804(a)	501(c)(15)	3434(c); 3436; 3436(b)	513(a)	3447
453(c)(1)	2804			513(b)	3447; 3451
453(c)(3)	2804(a)	501(c)(16)	3436	513(c)	3447
453(c)(4)	2804; 3521	501(c)(17)	3436; 3436(b)	514(a)(1)	3448(a); 3449(a)
453(c)(5)	2804	501(c)(18), (19)	3436	514(a)(2)	3449(a)
453(d)	2831	501(d)	3435; 3436	514(a)(3)	3449(a)
453(d)(4)	2831(b)	501(e)	3435; 3436	514(b)	3449(b)
454(a)	2723(a)	501(f)	3435; 3436	514(b)(1)(B)	3449(a)
454(b)	2723(c)	501(h)	3436(d)	514(b)(3)	3449(b)
455(a), (b), (c)	2726(a)	502	3024(b); 3436(a)	514(c)	3449(c), (d)
455(e)	2726(a)	502(b)	3436(a)	514(c)(7)	3449(c)
456	2726(b)	502(b)(2)	3447	514(d)	3449(c)
461	2735(a), (b)	502(b)(3)	3447	514(f)	3449(d)
461(e)	3433(b)	503	3024(b); 3436(d)	514(f)(3)(A)	3449(d)
461(f)	2735(c)			514(g)(1)	3449(d)
461(g)	2739	503(b)	3436(d)	514(g)(2)	3449(d)
464	1844(d); 2745	504	3436(d)	515	3445
465	2436	507(a)	3436(d); 3437(b)	521	3436; 3533(b)
471	2600	507(b)–(d)	3437(b)	527	3436; 4002
472	2606	507(d)(2)	3440(b)	531	3131–3133
481	2709	507(e)	3437(b)	532(a), (b)	3131
481(a)(2)	2709(b)	508	3436(b)	534	3131(a)
481(b)	2709(a)	508(a)	3437(a)	535	3134
481(b)(4)(C)	2709(c)	508(b)	3437(a); 3441	535(a)	3132
481(b)(4)(D)	2709(c)	508(c)	3437(a)	535(b)	3132(a)
481(c)	2709(a); 2709(c)	508(d)(1)	1941(a); 3437(b)		
482	3225				

IRC §	Tax Course ¶	IRC §	Tax Course ¶	IRC §	Tax Course ¶
535(c)	3132(c)	613(a)	2102(b); 2104(a), (b)	663(b)	3023(c)
537	3131			663(b)(1)	3006(e)
541	3405; 3406	613(b)	2104(a), (b)	663(b)(2)	3006(f)
542(a)(1)	3401	613(c)	2104(b)	663(c)	3006(c)
542(a)(2)	3402	613A(b)–(d)	2104(a)	664	3927(b)
542(b)	3409	614	2107	664(b)	3006(g)
542(c)	3403	614(a)	2100	664(c)	3450
542(c)(8)	3459(a)	614(b)	2107	664(d)	3538
542(d)	3403	614(c)(1)	2108(a)	664(d)(1)	3927(b)
543	3401	614(c)(2)	2108(b)	664(e)	3927(b)
544	3402(a)	614(d)	2106	665(a)	3023
545	3406	614(e)	2109	665(a)(2)	3023(a)
545(a)	3404(a), (c)	615	1843(a)	665(b)	3023; 3023(b); 3023(i)
545(b)	3404(a)	616	1843(c)	665(b)(2)	3023(e)
545(b)(8)	3404(a); 3406	616(a)	1843(b)	665(c)	3023(i)
		616(b)	1843(b)	665(d)	3023(a)
545(b)(9)	3404(a)	616(c)	1843(e)	665(e)	3023(c); 3023(i)
545(c)(2), (4)	3404(a)	617	1843(a), (c)	666	3023(i)
546	3404(a)	617(a)	1843(a); 3611(g)	666(a)	3023(c)
547	3407	617(b)–(d), (f), (h)	1843(a)	666(b)	3023(d)
551	3411; 3414	617(e)	1843(e)	666(c)	3023(d)
551(d)	3414; 3416; 3521	617(g)	1843(a); 2945(a)	666(d)	3023(c)
551(f)	3414	631(a)	1621(a)	666(e)	3023(f); 3023(i)
552(a)	3412	631(b)	1621(b)	667	3023(e); 3023(i)
552(b)	3415	631(c)	1623	667(a)	3023(f)
553	3412	632	3521	667(b)	3023(e), (f)
554	3412	636	2101(e)	667(c)	3023(e)
556	3413	638	3712	668	3023(i)
561	3404(b)	641	3002; 3008(a); 3020(b)	668(a)	3023(e)
562	3404(b)			671	3022
563(a)	3404(b)	642	3013(a); 3445	672(a), (b)	3022(b)
563(b)	3404(b); 3406	642(a)	3011; 3019	673(a)	3022(a)
564	3406	642(b)	3012	673(c)	3022(a)
564(b)	3404(b)	642(c)	3013; 3020(c); 3452; 3521; 3538; 3927(b)	674	3022(b)
565	3404(b)			674(b)	3022(b)
581	2312(b)	642(d)	3015	675	3022(c)
582	2312(b)	642(g)	3016(a)	676	3022(d)
582(b)	2208(a); 3433(a)	642(h)	3011(b); 3015	677	3022(e)
		642(i)	3011	678	3022(f)
582(c)	3433(a)	643	3004; 3023(i)	679(a)(1), (2)	3022(h)
583	3433(a)	643(a)(3)	3009(d)	679(c)(2)	3022(h)
584	3025(b)	643(a)(6)	3009(d)	681(a)	3452
584(b)	3025	644	3022(g)	682	3022(e)
584(c)	3025	651	3005; 3017(a)	691	1619(c)
584(d)	3025	652	3004	691(a)	3008(b)
584(e)	3025(a)	652(a)	3005(a)	691(a)(4)	2831(a); 3008(b)
584(g)	3015	652(b)	3007; 3007(a), (b)		
585	3433(a)	652(c)	3003(b)	691(b)	3008(b)
591	3433(b)	661–663	3006	691(c)	3008(b)
592	3433(b)	661(a)–(c)	3017(b)	691(d)	3008(b)
593	3433(b)	662	3004	702	2519(a); 2908
594	3433(b)	662(a)(1)	3006(a)	702(a)(1)	2911(a)
595	3433(b)	662(a)(2)	3006(b)	702(a)(2)	2911(a)
611(a)	2103(d)	662(b)	3007; 3007(a), (b), (c)	702(a)(3)	2911(b)
611(b)	2101(a)			702(a)(4)	2915
612	2103(a)	662(c)	3003(b)	702(a)(5)	2916
613	2102(b)	663(a)	1225; 3006(a), (d)	702(a)(6)	2917

Internal Revenue Code Finding List

IRC §	Tax Course ¶	IRC §	Tax Course ¶	IRC §	Tax Course ¶
702(c)	2908(b); 3545	751(b)(1)	2944(c)	857(b)(5)	3432(b)
703(a)	2906(a), (b)	751(b)(2)(A)	2944(a)	857(b)(6)	3432(a)
703(a)(2)(A)	1107(c)	751(b)(2)(B)	2944(a)	858	3432(d)
703(b)	2906(c)	751(c)	2944(d)	861(a)(1)	3712
704(a)	2909	751(d)	2944(d)	861(a)(2)	3706(b); 3712
704(b)	2909	751(d)(1)	2944(d)	861(a)(3)	3712
704(c)(1)	2910	751(d)(2)	2944(d)	861(a)(4)	3712
704(c)(2)	2910(a)	752	2926(c)	861(a)(5)	3712
704(c)(3)	2910(b)	752(b)	2927(c)	861(a)(6)	3712
704(d)	2908(a); 2911(a)	753	2941(b)	861(a)(7)	3712
704(e)(1)	2904(a)	754	2930(b); 2937	861(b)	3712
704(e)(2)	2905	755	2938(a)	861(e)	3712
704(e)(3)	2905	761(a)	2900	861(e)(4)	3337
705(a)	2926(a)	761(c)	2909	862(a)	3712
705(b)	2926(b)	801-820	3434(a)	863(a)	3712
706(a)	2920	802	3434(a), (c)	863(b)	3712
706(b)	2921(a)	802(a)(1)	3434(a)	864(b)	3711
706(b)(2)	2921(b)	802(a)(2)	3434(a)	864(c)	3711(b)
706(c)	2922	802(b)	3434(a)	864(c)(2)	3711(a)
707(a)	2923	805(d)(1)	1838(l)	864(c)(3)	3711(a)
707(b)(1)	2923(a)	811	3434(c)	864(c)(4)	3711(b)
707(b)(2)	2923(b)	812	3216; 3434(a)	871	3709; 3709(b)
707(b)(3)	2923(c)	819	3434(d)	871(a)(1)	3711(a)
707(c)	2923(d)	821	3434(c)	871(b)	3709(b)
708(b)(1)	2922(b)	822	3434(c)	871(c)	3709(b)
708(b)(2)	2922(c)	823	3434(c)	871(d)	3711
708(b)(2)(B)	2922(d)	826	3434(c)	872	3709
721	2925(a)	831	3434(b), (c)	872(b)	3720
722	2925(c); 2927(c)	831(c)	3434(b)	872(b)(3)	3709(b)
723	2925(b)	832	3434(b)	873	3709(b)
731	2927(a); 2941(a)	842	3434(d)	874(a)	3709(d)
731(a)(2)	2929(c)	843	3434	875(2)	3711
731(c)	2927(c)	844	3215	876	3727(c)
732	2928	851(a)	3429	877	3709(c)
732(b)	2928(b)	851(b)(1)	3429	879	3709(b)
732(c)	2928(c); 2929	851(b)(2), (3)	3429	881	3710(a)
732(c)(2)	2929(b)	851(b)(4)	3429	881(a)	3711(a)
732(d)	2930; 2930(b)	851(e)(1)	3430	882	3710(a)
733	2926(a); 2928(a)	851(f)	3428	882(d)	3711
734(b)(1)	2932(a)	852	3431	883	3720
734(b)(2)	2932(a)	852(a)	3429	891	3707
735(a)(1)	2945(b)	852(b)(3)	3431(a)	893(a)	3708(b)
735(a)(2)	2945(c)	852(b)(3)(D)	3431(a)	894(b)	3709(b); 3710(a)
735(b)	2928(d); 2945	852(b)(4)	3431(a)	895	3712
736	2935(b)	852(d)	3431(a)	896	3707
736(a)(1)	2941(b)	853	3431(b)	901	3701; 3702; 3703, 3708
736(a)(2)	2941(b)	854(a)	3431(c)	902(a)	3706; 3706(b)
736(b)	2941; 2941(a)	854(b)(1)	3431(c)	902(b)	3706
736(b)(1)	2941(a)	854(b)(2)	3431(c)	902(c)	3706(a)
741	2935; 2935(b)	854(b)(3)	3431(c)	902(d)	3706
742	2936	855	3431(d)	903	3703
743(b)	2930; 2937(a), (b), (c)	856(a)	3432(a)	904(a)	3703(a), (b)
751	2930(a); 2944; 2944(b), (c); 2945(a)	856(c)	3432; 3432(b)	904(b)	3703(c)
		856(c)(5)	3432(c)	904(c)	3703(b)
751(a)	2935(b)	856(c)(7)	3432(b)	904(d)	3703
751(b)	2944(b), (c)	856(e)	3432(a)	904(e)(2), (3)	3703(b)
		857	3432(d), (e)	904(f)	3703(d)

Internal Revenue Code Finding List

IRC §	Tax Course ¶	IRC §	Tax Course ¶	IRC §	Tax Course ¶
905(a)	.3702	1015(d)(1)(A)	.4029	1034(d)	.1419
905(c)	3702; 3705	1015(d)(1)(B)	.4029	1034(e)	.1526
906	3701; 3703(b)	1015(d)(2)	.4029	1034(f)	.1417
906(b)	3703(a)	1015(d)(3)	.4029(b)	1034(g)	.1418
906(b)(4)	.3706	1015(d)(6)	1515(b); 4029	1034(h)	.1420
907	3703(a)	1016	.1500(b)	1034(i)	.1421
911(a)	.3701	1016(a)(1)	1528; 1842(d)	1034(j)	1422; 3611(a)
911(a)(2)	3725(a); 3725(c)			1035(a)	.1407
911(b)	2402(a); 2406(a); 3725(a)	1016(a)(3)	2003(b); 3433(b)	1035(b)	.1407
				1036	.1404
911(c)(1)	3725(c)	1016(a)(5)	1846(a), (b); 3433(b)	1037(a)	.1403
911(c)(3)	3725(c)			1038	.2823
911(c)(4)	3725(c)	1016(a)(6)	.1846(a)	1038(d)	.2823
911(c)(5)	3725(a)	1016(a)(7)	.1526	1039	1426; 1526
911(c)(6)	3725(b)	1016(a)(8)	.2722(d)	1053	.1506(b)
911(c)(8)	3725(c)	1016(a)(11)	.1622(b)	1056	.1521(c)
911(d)	3725(c)	1016(a)(12)	.3404(b)	1071	.1410(d)
912	.3726	1016(a)(14)	.1842(d)	1081–1083	3330(a)
921	3117(a)	1016(b)	.1514	1091	.2221
922	3117(a)	1017	1318(j); 3125(f)	1101–1103	3330(b)
931	1107(c); 1122; 3824	1019	1317; 1317(a)	1201 et seq	.1600
		1021	.1527	1201	.3202
931(i)	3727(a)	1023	1507; 2003(a); 3919(b); 3929	1201(a)	.3202
932	3709(a); 3727(a)			1201(b)	.3454(a)
933	3727(c)	1023(b)	.1507(a)	1201(b)(1)	.1614(b)
936	3727(b)	1023(c)–(g)	.1507(b)	1201(b)(2)	.1614(b)
941	3117(b)	1023(h)	.1507(c)	1201(c)(1)	.1614(b)
951 et seq	3728(a)	1031(a)	.1406	1201(d)(1)	1614(b); 2813
951(c)	3728(a)	1031(b), (c)	.1408(b)	1202	1612; 3009(b); 3201
951(d)	3728(a)	1031(d)	1409; 1517; 1517(f)		
952	3728(a)			1211(a)	.3201
954	.3728	1031(e)	.1406	1211(b)	.1613
955	.3728	1032	.3124	1211(b)(2)	.1613(b)
956	3728(a)	1033	.1411	1212(a)(1)	3201(a)
957	3728(a)	1033(a)	.1413	1212(a)(3)	.3143(a); 3201(a)
959	3728(a)	1033(a)(1)	1411(a)		
960	3728(a)	1033(a)(2)(A)	1413(a); 1414	1212(a)(4)	3201(a)
962	3728(a)	1033(a)(2)(B)	.1412	1212(b)	.1613(c)
991	.3460	1033(a)(3)(A)	1411; 1413(a); 1414	1221	1316(a); 1601; 1601(g); 2723(c)
992	3460(a)				
993–997	.3460	1033(a)(3)(B)	.1412(b)	1222	.1600(b)
999	.3701	1033(a)(3)(C)	3611(b)	1222(1), (2), (5), (6)	.1611(b)
1001	1401; 1500	1033(a)(3)(D)	3611(b)	1222(3), (4), (7), (8)	.1611(c)
1001(b)	.1920(b)	1033(b)	1412(b); 1519	1222(11)	1614(b); 3202
1001(e)	.1510	1033(c)	.1410(c)	1223	.2813
1001(f)	.1416(b)	1033(d)	.1410(b)	1223(1)	1606(c)
1002	.1401	1033(e)	.1410(b)	1223(2)	1606(a); 2925(b)
1011	.1500(b)	1033(f)	1412; 1413(c)	1223(4)	2221(a)
1011(b)	.1942(b)	1033(g)(4)	.1412	1223(5)	1708(b); 1711(c)
1012	1500; 1501; 1920(b)	1034	.2823	1223(6)	1711(c); 1712
		1034(a)	.1416	1223(7)	1606(e)
1013	.2611	1034(b)	1416(b), (c)	1223(8)	.1606
1014	2003(a)	1034(c)	.1419	1223(11)	1606; 3009
1014(a)(1)	3010(a), (c)	1034(c)(1)	.1416(g)	1231	1601(g); 1619(b); 1620; 1622(a), (b); 1943(b); 2206(b); 2242(a); 2813; 2816(a);
1014(d)	1507; 3460(c); 3929	1034(c)(2)	.1416(d)		
1015(a)	1515(a); 3010(a)	1034(c)(3)	.1419		
1015(c)	3010(b)	1034(c)(5)	.1416		

IRC §	Tax Course ¶	IRC §	Tax Course ¶	IRC §	Tax Course ¶
	2823; 2840(e); 2906(a); 2911(b);	1245(d)	3127(b); 3204	1251(d)(6)	2226(c)
	2938(a); 2944(c), (d); 3143(a); 3401	1246	3728(c)	1251(e)(5)	2226(a)
		1247	3728(c)	1252	1622(c); 1717(a); 1845(e); 3127(b); 3129(c)
		1248(a)	3728(a)		
1232	1629	1248(b)	3728(a)		
1232(a)	1630	1248(d)(3)	3728	1252(a)	3128
1232(a)(1)	1602	1248(f)	3728	1252(a)(1)	2226(a)
1232(a)(2)(A)	1629(b)	1249	3728(b)	1253	1601(k); 1808
1232(a)(2)(B)	1629(a)	1250	1619(b), (d), (e); 1620; 1717(a); 2043; 2206(b); 2813; 2909; 2925(a); 2927(a); 2928(c); 2935(b); 2944(d); 2945(a), (b); 3107; 3127(b); 3129(c); 3143(a); 3201; 3204; 3521(a)	1254	1717(a); 2103(c); 3107; 3129(c)
1232(a)(2)(D)(i)	1629				
1232(a)(3)(A)	1629(b)			1301	2401(d)
1232(a)(3)(B)	1629(b)			1302(a)(2)	2401(a); (d)
1232(a)(3)(E)	1629(b)			1302(b)(2)	2401(d)
1232(c)	1629(b)			1303	2401(c)
1233	1608(a)			1303(b)	3709(b)
1233(a)	1608; 1608(c)			1303(c)(2)	2401(c)
1233(b)	1608(c)			1304	2401(d)
1233(b)(1)	1608(a)	1250(a)	1619(c); 3127(b); 3204	1304(b)	2401(b)
1233(b)(2)	1608(a)			1304(b)(1)	1122
1233(c)	1609(b), (c)	1250(d)	1619(c); 2945(a)	1304(b)(2)	3024(d)
1233(d)	1608(a)	1250(d)(2)	1619(c)	1304(c)	2401(e)
1233(e)	1608(c)	1250(d)(3)	3204	1311–1315	3631
1233(e)(2)(A)	1608(b)	1250(d)(4)	1619(d), (e)	1311(b)	3631; 3631(b)
1233(e)(2)(C)	1608(a)	1250(d)(4)(D)	1619(e)	1311(b)(2)(A)	3631(b)
1233(e)(4)	1608(a)	1250(d)(4)(E)	1619(d)	1311(b)(2)(B)	3631(b)
1233(f)	1608(a)	1250(d)(6)	2927(b)	1312(1)	3631(a)
1233(g)	1608(c)	1250(d)(7)(B)	1619(c)	1312(2)	3631(a)
1234	1601(h)	1250(d)(8)	1619(c)	1312(3)(A)	3631(a)
1234(b)	1609(c)	1250(d)(10)	1619(b)	1312(3)(B)	3631(b)
1235	1601(j)	1250(e)	1619(b); 2945(a)	1312(4)	3631(b)
1236	1628	1250(e)(4)	1619(b)	1312(5)	3631(a)
1237	1631	1250(f)	1619(b)	1312(6)	3631(a)
1239	1625	1250(f)(2)	1619(b)	1312(7)	3631(a)
1241	1316(a); 1601(g), (i)	1250(h)	3204	1314(a)	2709(a)
1242	3459	1250(i)	3127(b)	1341	2729(a)
1243	3459	1251	1622(c); 1717(a); 2226; 2226(a); 3127(b); 3129(c)	1341(b)(2)	2729(a)
1244	1632			1346	2316(d)
1244(d)(3)	2242(a)			1348	2402
1245	1620; 1717(a); 2206(b); 2226(a); 2813; 2909; 2925(a); 2927(a); 2928(c); 2935(b); 2944(c); (d); 2945(a), (b); 3107; 3127(b); 3129(c); 3143(a); 3201; 3204			1348(b)	2402(a)
		1251(b)	2226(b)	1351	2316(d)
		1251(b)(4)	2226(b); 2614(a)	1351(b)	2305
				1351(d)(3)	3702
		1251(b)(4)(C)	2708(a)	1371	3140; 3141(a)
		1251(b)(5)(A)	2226(c); 3337	1371(a)	3141(a)
				1371(c)	3141(a)
		1251(b)(5)(B)	2226(c)	1371(d)–(f)	3141(a)
		1251(c)	2226(a), (b); 3128	1372	3140; 3142(b)
1245(a)	1619(a); 2040(a); 2043; 2044; 3127(b); 3204			1372(e)	3141(d)
		1251(c)(2)	2226(b)	1372(e)(1)	3141(b)
		1251(c)(2)(C)	2226(a)	1372(e)(4)	3141(a)
1245(a)(2)	1619(a)	1251(d)(1)	2226(a)	1372(e)(5)	3141(a)
1245(a)(4)	1619(g)	1251(d)(2)	2226(a)	1372(f)	3141(d)
1245(b)	1619(c)	1251(d)(3)	2226(d)	1373	3142(b)
1245(b)(3)	3204	1251(d)(4)	2226(d)	1373(b)	3142(b)
1245(b)(4)	1619(d); (e)	1251(d)(5)	2226(d); 2910(a); 2913; 2925(a)	1374	3143(c)
1245(b)(6)	2927(b); 2945(a)			1375	3142(c)

Internal Revenue Code Finding List

IRC §	Tax Course ¶	IRC §	Tax Course ¶	IRC §	Tax Course ¶
1375(a)(3)	3143(a)	1461	.2536	2036	.3910
1375(b)	3142(b)	1465	2535(a)	2037	.3911
1375(c)	.3142	1482	2729(a)	2038	.3912
1375(d)	3142(c)	1501	3222; 3515	2039	3915(a), (b), (c)
1375(f)	3142(c)	1502	.3222	2039(a)	3915(a)
1376	.3144	1503(b)	3703(b)	2039(b)	3915(a)
1377(a)	.3145	1504(a)	3222(a)	2039(c)	3915(b)
1377(b)	.3145	1504(b)	3222(a)	2040	1509; 3904
1377(c)	.3145	1504(c)	.3222	2040(b)	.3904
1377(d)	.3145	1504(e)	3222(a)	2041	.3907
1378	3143(b)	1551(a)	.3224	2041(a)(1)	3908(b)
1378(a)	3143(b)	1551(b)	.3224	2041(a)(2)	3908(a)
1378(b)	3143(b)	1561(a)	3223; (b)	2041(a)(3)	3908(a)
1378(c)(3)	3143(b)	1563(a)	3223(a)	2041(b)(2)	3908(a)
1379(a)	3146(b)	1563(b)(2)	3223(a)	2041(b)(3)	3908(c)
1379(b)	3146(a)	1563(d)	3223(a)	2042	.3914
1379(b)(3)	3146(a)	1563(e)	3223(a)	2043	.3913
1379(c)	3146(c)	1564	.3223	2043(b)	3926(c)
1381(a)	3455(a)	2001	.3944	2044	.3901
1381(b)	.3455	2001(b)	3934; 3935(b)	2052	.3928
1382	.3457	2001(c)	.3934	2053	3016(b); 3929
1382(a)	.3455	2001(d)	3935(b)	2053(a)	.3926
1382(b)	.3457	2002	.3944	2053(b)	.3926
1382(c)	.3457	2010	.3940	2053(c)	.3926
1382(d)	.3457	2010(b)	3940(a)	2053(d)	3926(b)
1382(e)	.3457	2010(c)	3940(b)	2053(d)(1)	3926(b)
1383	3457; 3457(b)	2010(d)	3940(c)	2054	3926(d); 3929
1385	.3458	2011	3936; 3936(a), (b); 3937(a)	2055	3927(b)
1385(a)	2721(b); 3458(a)			2055(c)	3927(a)
1388(a)(2)	.3457	2011(b)	3936(b)	2055(e)(1)	3927(c)
1388(b)(2)	.3456	2011(c)	3936(a); 3936(c); 3936(d)	2055(e)(2)	3927(b)
1388(c)(1)(A)	.3456			2055(e)(2)(B)	3927(b)
1388(c)(1)(B)	.3456	2011(e)	3926(b); 3936(a)	2056	3929(a)
1388(c)(4)	.3456	2012	3935(a), (b)	2056(b)(1)	3929(b)
1388(h)	.3456	2012(a)	3935(a); 3940	2056(b)(4)	.3929
1401	.3821	2012(b)(1)(2)	.3940	2056(c)	3929(a)
1402	.3821	2012(c)	.3935	2056(c)(2)	3929(a)
1402(a)	3823(b); 3824; 3827(b)	2012(d)(1)	3935(a), (b)	2057	3026(e)
1402(a)(5)	3827(b)	2013(a)	3939(a), (b), (d)	2102	3940(d)
1402(a)(6)	3823(c)	2013(b)	3939(c)	2107	3940(e)
1402(a)(10)	3823(d)	2013(c)	3939(c)	2117	.1303
1402(b)	3709(b)	2013(c)(1)(B)	3939(c)	2203	.3944
1402(b)(1)(H), (I)	3823(a)	2013(d)	3939(b), (c)	2204	.3947
1402(b)(2)	3823(a)	2013(f)	3939(c)	2501	.4002
1402(c)	.3822	2013(g)	3939(c)	2501(a)	.4002
1402(c)(1)	.3822	2014	3938; 3938(b)	2502	4026; 4027
1402(c)(2)	3823(e)	2014(e)	3938(a)	2502(a)	.4025
1402(c)(2)(F)	.3822	2014(g)	.3938	2502(d)	.4031
1402(e)	.3822	2014(h)	.3938	2503(b)	4020; 4030
1402(f)	3823(d)	2015	3936(a); 3938(a)	2503(c)	.4020
1402(h)	.3822	2016	3936(a); 3938(c)	2504	.4025
1402(i)	.3823	2031	3929(a)	2504(a)	.4028
1441	2535; 2535(b), (c); 3533(a)	2032A	3919(a)	2505	.4021
		2032A(c)	3919(a)	2511	.4002
1441(c)	2535(b)	2033	3901; 3904	2512	.4002
1441(e)	3727(b)	2034	.3906	2512(a)	.4010
1442	2535; 3533(a)	2035	1508; 3909(b)	2512(b)	.4007

Internal Revenue Code Finding List

IRC §	Tax Course ¶	IRC §	Tax Course ¶	IRC §	Tax Course ¶
2513	.4009	3121(b)(8)(B)	3814(a)	3402(d)	2512(a)
2513(b)	.4009	3121(b)(8)(B)(ii)	3814(a)	3402(e)	2503(c)
2513(c)	.4009	3121(b)(9)	.3812	3402(f)	2505; 2506(a)
2514(a)	4004(a)	3121(b)(10)(A)	3814(b)	3402(f)(1)(G)	2505(a)
2514(b)	4004(b)	3121(b)(10)(B)	.3810	3402(f)(2)(B)	2506(b)
2514(c)	.4004	3121(b)(11)	3815(c)	3402(f)(3)(B)	2506(b)
2514(e)	4004(b)	3121(b)(12)	3815(c)	3402(f)(6)	.2505
2515(b)	.4013	3121(b)(14)	.3811	3402(h)	2504(c)
2515(c)	.4013	3121(b)(15)	3815(c)	3402(h)(1)	2504(i)
2515(c)(3)	.4013	3121(b)(17)	.3813	3402(i)	2504(j)
2516	.4007	3121(b)(19)	.3810	3402(j)	2503(a)
2517	.4011	3121(b)(20)	2503(a); 3804	3402(k)	2503(a); 2512(a)
2517(a)	.4011	3121(c)	.3816	3402(l)	2506; 2506(b)
2517(b)	.4011	3121(d)	3817(a)	3402(m)	2505; 2505(a); 2505(b)
2518	4004(b)	2131(d)(1)	3817(c)		
2521	.4028	3121(d)(3)	3817(b)	3402(n)	2506(c)
2522(a)	.4022	3121(h)	.3824	3402(o)	2503(a); 2504(k)
2522(c)(1)	.4022	3121(i)	.3806	3402(p)-1	2504(j)
2522(c)(2)	.4022	3121(j)	3815(b)	3402(q)	2503(a)
2523(a)	.4023	3121(k)(l)	3814(a)	3403	2512(a)
2523(d)	.4023	3121(k)(2)	3814(a)	3504	2501(b)
2523(e)	.4023	3121(k)(4)	3814(a)	3505	2501(b)
2523(f)	.4023	3121(l)	3803(b)	4911	3436(d); 3618(j)
2524	.4023	3121(m)	3815(a)	4940	.3438
2601–2603	3916(a)	3121(o)	.3805	4940(c)	.3438
2602	3916; 3916(c)	3121(p)	3815(a)	4941	.3440
2603	.3916	3301	.3834	4941(a)	3440(c)
2611–2614	3916(b)	3302(a)(3)	3839(b)	4941(b)	3440(d)
2612	.3916	3302(c)	3839(a); 3841	4941(c)(2)	3440(d)
2614	1507(d)	3302(d)	3839(a); 3841	4941(d)	.3440
2621	3916(d)	3303	.3841	4942	.3441
3102	.3800	3304(c)	3839(a)	4942(a)(1)	.3441
3102(c)	3800; 3818	3306(a)	.3834	4942(c)	3441(a)
3111	.3800	3306(b)(1)	3834; 3837	4942(d)	3441(a)
3121(a)	3818; 3818(a); 3819(e)	3306(b)(2)-(8)	.3837	4942(e)	3441(a)
		3306(b)(10)	.3837	4942(f)	3441(a)
3121(a)(1)	3818(b)	3401	.2503	4942(h)	3441(b)
3121(a)(2)	3819(c)	3401(a)	2503(a); 2503(b)	4942(j)	1943(a)
3121(a)(3)	3819(d)	3401(a)(13)	2503(b)	4943	3442(a)
3121(a)(4)	3819(d)	3401(a)(14)	2503(a)	4943(a)	.3442
3121(a)(5)	3819(c)	3401(a)(15)	2503(a)	4943(b)	.3442
3121(a)(7)(A)	3819(a)	3401(a)(16)	2503(a)	4943(c)	3442(a)
3121(a)(7)(B)	.3806	3401(a)(17)	2503(a)	4943(c)(4)	3442(b)
3121(a)(7)(C)	.3805	3401(d)	2501(a)	4944	.3443
3121(a)(8)	.3805	3401(d)(1)	2501(b)	4944(a)	.3443
3121(a)(8)(A)	3819(a)	3401(d)(2)	2501(b)	4944(b)	.3443
3121(a)(10)	3817(b)	3401(f)	2503(a)	4944(d)	.3443
3121(a)(13)	3819(c)	3402(a)	2504(a)	4945	.3444
3121(b)	3803(b)	3402(b)(2)	2504(d)	4945(d)	.3444
3121(b)(1)	.3805	3402(b)(3)	2504(d)	4946	3440(a)
3121(b)(2)	.3810	3402(b)(4)	2504(d)	4946(a)(3)	3440(a)
3121(b)(3)	.3808	3402(b)(5)	2504(d)	4947	.3453
3121(b)(4)	3803(c)	3402(c)	2504(b)	4947(a)	.3453
3121(b)(5)	3815(a)	3402(c)(2)	2504(d)	4947(a)(1)	.3453
3121(b)(6)	3815(a)	3402(c)(3)	2504(d)	4947(a)(2)	.3453
3121(b)(7)	3815(b)	3402(c)(4)	2504(d)	4947(b)(3)	.3453
3121(b)(8)(A)	.3809	3402(c)(5)	2504(b)	4948(a)	.3438

5812 Internal Revenue Code Finding List 1978

IRC §	Tax Course ¶	IRC §	Tax Course ¶	IRC §	Tax Course ¶
4948(c)(4)	1941(a)	6034(b)	3020(c)	6091(b)(1)	4030
4971	3618(h)	6035(a)(1)	3416	6102	3527(a)
4972	3618(h)	6035(a)(2)	3416	6104	3537(a); 3538; 3601(b)
4973	1838(l); 3618(h)	6035(b)(1)	3416	6104(a)	3436(b); 3537(d)
4974	1838(l)	6036	3539(b); 3605	6104(b)	3537(d)
6011(a)	3521	6037	3141(c)	6107	3542
6012	3020(c)	6038	3540(b)	6109	3500
6012(a)	1100; 3020(b); 3512	6038(d)(1)	3540(b)	6110	3601(b)
6012(a)(1)	1100(a); 3509	6039	3534	6151(a)	3522; 3522(b); 3523; 3524; 4031
6012(a)(2)	3512	6041	3531; 3540(a)	6151(b)	1103(b); 3522(a)
6012(b)	3510; 3511; 3511(a), (b), (c)	6041(a)	3532	6152	3523
6012(b)(2)	2516(b)	6041(d)	3532	6152(a)(2)	3524
6012(b)(3)	3001(a); 3512(b)	6043	3128(b); 3536(a), (b)	6152(d)	3523
6012(b)(5)	3511(b)	6043(b)	3536(c)	6153	2517(a)
6012(c)	1100(a)	6044	3533(b)	6154	3523(a)
6013	1104(a)	6046	3540(b)	6154(b), (c), (f)	3523(a)
6013(a)	1104(a); 3506	6046(c)	3540(b)	6154(h)	3547(a)
6013(a)(1)	3709(b)	6047(b)	3531(a)	6157	3838
6013(a)(2)	3507; 3507(c)	6048	3540(c)	6157(b), (c)	3838
6013(a)(3)	3507(a)	6049	3532; 3532(a)	6161	3526
6013(b)	3506; 3506(a)	6050	3537(b)	6161(a)	3944
6013(b)(1)	3506; 3507(a)	6050A	3509(b)	6161(a)(l)	3838
6013(b)(2)	3506(a)	6051	2508; 2508(a); 3828(a)	6161(a)(2)	3944(a)
6013(b)(2)(A)	3506	6051(a)	2508(a), (b)	6161(b)	3526
6013(b)(3)(A)	3610(b)	6051(b)	2508(a)	6163(a)	3944(b)
6013(b)(4)	3611(e)	6052	3535	6163(b)	3944(b)
6013(b)(5)	3618(a)	6053	3827(a)	6164	3526; 3630(c)
6013(b)(5)(B)	3620	6053(a)	2503(a)	6165	3944(b)
6013(c)	3507	6056(a)	3537(c)	6166	3944(a), (b)
6013(d)	1945(c)	6056(d)	3537(c)	6166(f)	3945(c)
6013(d)(1)	3505	6057	3537(d)	6166(g)	3945(c)
6013(d)(3)	3505	6058(a)	3537(d)	6166A	3944(a)
6013(e)	3505	6059(a)	3537(d)	6166A(c)	3944(a)
6013(f)	1105	6060	3542	6166A(h)(3)	3944(a)
6013(g)	1104(a)	6061	3503	6167	3526
6013(h)	1104(a)	6062	3513(b)	6201–6204	3610
6014	1103(b)	6065	3503; 3513(b)	6201(c)	3614(b)
6014(a)	2406(c)	6072	3524	6205(a)(1)	2510
6015	2516(c); 3510	6072(a)	3517(a), (c)	6211(a)	3945(b)
6015(a)	2516	6072(b)	3517(b), (e)	6212	3605
6015(b)	2516(a)	6072(c)	3522(b); 3523	6212(a)	3615(f); 3945(b)
6015(c)	2518; 3827(b)	6072(d)	3455(b)	6212(b)(1)	3605
6015(c)(1)	2515(a); 2519(a)	6073	1104(a)	6212(b)(2)	3605
6015(e)	2517(b)	6073(a)	2517(a)	6212(c)	3605(b)
6015(f)	2517(a), (b), (c)	6073(b)	2517(c)	6213(a)	3605(a), (b); 3615(f); 3639(a); 3945(b); 4032
6018	3943	6073(e)	2517(d)		
6019(a)	4030	6075(a)	3943		
6031	3539(a)	6075(b)	4030; 4031	6213(b)	3605(b)
6032	3025	6075(b)(2)	4030	6213(d)	3605(b)
6033	3454(b); 3537(a)	6077	3540(c)	6213(e)	3639(a)
6033(a)	3024(b); 3537	6081	3518; 3518(d)	6302(c)	2509(b)
6033(a)(2)	3537(a)	6081(a)	2508(c); 2517(e); 3518; 3518(c); 3838	6311	3527(b)
6033(b)	3537(a)			6313	3527(b)
6034	3538	6081(b)	3518(c)	6314	3527(b)
6034(a)	3020(c); 3538	6091	3519(a); 3519(b), (d)		
		6091(b)	3943	6316	3527(b)

Internal Revenue Code Finding List

IRC §	Tax Course ¶	IRC §	Tax Course ¶	IRC §	Tax Course ¶
6321	3615(c)	6503(f)	3611(f); 3613(f)	6651(d)	2519; 3617(d); 3618(b)
6322	3615(c)	6503(g)	3613(d)	6652	2512(a); 3617(b)
6323(a)	3615(c)	6503(h)	3613(g)	6652(a)	3617(b)
6323(b)	3615(c)	6511	3844	6652(b)	3617(b)
6323(c), (d)	3615(c)	6511(a)	3623(a),(b); 3829(b); 3839(b); 3946(a); 4033	6652(c)	3818
6323(f)	3615(c)			6652(d)	3617(b)
6323(g)	3615(c)			6652(e)	3617(c)
6324(a)	3944	6511(b)	3623; 3625	6653(a)	3618(d)
6324(b)	4031	6511(c)	3623(c)	6653(b)	2512(a); 3618(d)
6324A	3947	6511(d)	3624(a),(b)	6653(d)	3618(d)
6331	3615(a)	6511(d)(2)(B)(ii)	3624(b)	6654(d)	2519(a)
6332(a)	3615(a)	6511(d)(3)	3624(c)	6654(e)(2)	2519(a)
6332(b)	3615(a)	6511(d)(5)	3829	6655	3523(b)
6332(c)	3615(a)	6511(d)(8)	3624(d)	6655(a)	3619
6332(d)	3615(a)	6511(f)	3623(a)	6655(b)	3523(b); 3619
6334	3615(a)	6512(a)	3622(c)	6655(c)	3619
6401	3610	6512(b)	3637(b)	6655(d)	3523(b)
6401(b)	2511(a)	6513	3623(a),(b); 3628(c)	6655(g)	3622(a)
6401(c)	3628(c)	6513(a)	3623(a)	6656	2512(a); 3523; 3618(f)
6402	3601(a); 3615(d); 3621	6513(d)	3624(c)		
		6531	3620	6657	3618(e)
6402(a)	2511; 2511(a); 3627(b); 3844	6532	4033	6658	3612(b)
		6532(a)	3629(a); 3946(b)	6659	3617
6402(b)	3624(c)	6532(a)(2)	3629(a)	6659(b)	2519(b); 3619
6405	3627(b)	6532(a)(3)	3629(a)	6672	2512(a)
6406	3628(b)	6532(b)	3629(e)	6674	2512(a)
6411	3630; 3630(b)	6601	3630(c); 3944(b); 3945(c)	6676	3500
6411(b)	3630(b)			6677	3540(c)
6413(a)(1)	2510	6601(a)	2512(a); 3526; 3618(a); 4031	6678	3617(b)
6413(c)	3829(c),(e)			6682(a)	2512(b)
6413(c)(3)	2511(a)	6601(b)(2)	3618(a)	6683	3405
6414	2511	6601(c)	3606(a)	6684	3439; 3618(g)
6420	2417	6601(d)	3618(a)	6685	3617(b)
6421	2417	6601(e)	3618(a)	6690	3617(c)
6424	2417	6601(e)(4)	2512(a)	6692	3617(c)
6425	3622	6601(f)	2517(e); 3618(a)	6693	3617(c)
6427	2417	6601(g)	3610	6694	3618(i)
6501	3610; 3610(b); 3611(d); 3945(a); 4032	6601(j)	3944(b)	6695	3542
		6611	3628	6695(e)	3542
6501(c)	3610	6611(b)	3618(a); 3628(a)	6696	3618(i)
6501(c)(4)	3610(d)	6611(b)(2)	3628	6851	3612(b)
6501(c)(7)	3610(e)	6611(d)	3628(c)	6861	3605(b); 3612(c)
6501(d)	3612(a)	6611(e)	3628	6863(b)(3)	3612(c)
6501(e)	3610(c)	6611(f)	3628(c)	6871	3612(c)
6501(g)(1)	3610(b)	6611(g)	3628(c)	6871(a)	3605(b)
6501(g)(2)	3610(b)	6621	3615(a); 3618(a); 3628; 3630(c); 3944(b); 3945(c); 4031	6871(b)	3612(c)
6501(h)	3611(f)			6872	3613(e)
6501(i)	3611(f)			6901	3614(a)
6501(j)	3611(f)				
6501(m)	3611(f)	6651	3618(c); 3944(b),(c)	6901(a)	3944; 4031
6501(n)	3610(e)	6651(a)	2512(a); 3617; 3618(b)	6901(c)	3611(c)
6501(n)(2)	3610(e)			6901(e)	3611(c)
6501(o)	3611(f)	6651(b)	2512(a); 3617; 3618(b)	6901(h)	3614(a)
6502(a)	3610(a)			6902(a)	3635(b)
6503	3613; 3927(b)	6651(c)	3618(b)	6903	3001(b); 3539(b); 3605
6503(b)	3613(b)	6651(c)(1)(A)	3617		
6503(c)	3613(c)				

IRC §	Tax Course ¶	IRC §	Tax Course ¶	IRC §	Tax Course ¶
6903(b)	3605	7422(e)	3629(c)	7485	3649(b)
6905	4031	7422(f)	3629(b)	7502	3517; 3523; 3605(a); 3639(a)
6905(a)	3001(b)	7422(g)	3629(f)		
6905(b)	3001(b)	7425(a)	3615(c)	7502(e)	2509(a)
7001	3540(a)	7425(b)	3615(c)	7503	2509(e); 3517
7121	3407; 3608(b)	7426	3615(f)	7508	3518(a)
7122	3608(a)	7428	3635(e)	7512	2509(d)
7201	2512(a); 3620	7429	3612(d)	7515	3919
7202	2512(a); 3620	7441	3635	7517	4010
7203	2512(a); 2519(b); 3128(b); 3531; 3620	7442	3637	7601	3602(a)
		7445	3635(a)	7602	3602(a)
7204	2512(a)	7451	3635(d)	7609	3601(a)
7205	2512(b)	7453	3635(a)	7610	3601(a)
7206	2512(a); 3620	7454	3635(b)	7651	3823(c)
7207	3620	7463	3635(c)		
7210	3602(a)	7476	3635(d)	7701(a)(3)	3026; 3101
7215	2512(a)	7477	3635(f); 3649(h)	7701(a)(4)	3105
7216	3620	7481	3649	7701(a)(6)	3001; 3511(a)
7401	3615(b)	7481(b)	3635(c); 3649	7701(a)(23)	2715
7407	3609(b)	7482	3649	7701(a)(25)	2735(a), (b)
7421	3615(f)	7482(a)	3649	7701(a)(30)	3540(b)
7422	4033	7482(c)(2)	3649	7701(a)(31)	3540(b)
7422(a)	3629; 3946(b)	7483	3648(a)	7701(36)	3542

INDEX TO EXPLANATION

―――― References are to PARAGRAPH (¶) NUMBERS ――――

— A —

Abandoned parent, returns of. .1104(c)
. head of household, filing as. .1104(c)
. child care expenses. .2415
Abandonment losses. .2036; 2210
Abatement claims. .3626
Abatement of taxes, armed forces. .3025
Abortion as medical expense. .1946(a)
Abroad, taxpayers:
. earned income. .3725
. . net earnings from self-employment. .3823(c)
. returns. .3518(a)
. traveling expenses. .1829
Academic courses, deductibility. .1833
Accelerated depreciation. .1619(b); 2012; 2013
Acceptance by taxpayer, constructive receipt . .2703
Accident benefits:
. deductibility. .1819
. employees' trust paying. .3024(d)
. exclusion. .1218—1222
. wage disability plans. .1221
. . withholding tax. .2504(g)
Accident insurance premiums. .1828(b); 1946; 1947
Accident or health insurance, benefits under . .1218(b); 1221
Account number. .3500
. self-employment tax return. .3826(d)
Accountants:
. expenses of. .1832
. fees:
. . deductibility. .1806; 1808; 1823
. . information returns. .3531
. old-age benefit tax. .3817(b)
. practice before I.R.S.. .3609
. practice before Tax Court. .3636
ACCOUNTING. .2701-2749
. employees' expenses. .1805(c)
ACCOUNTING METHODS. .2701-2711
. accrual basis. .2706
. cash basis. .2702
. change in. .2708; 2804
. . adjustments. .2709
. crop basis. .2614(a)
. farm corporations. .2701(d)
. farmers. .2614(a)
. hybrid system. .2701; 2801
. installment sales. .2801
. . election, revocation of. .2804
. long-term contracts. .2842
. reflection of income. .2707
. reorganizations. .3337
. rounding-off amounts. .2707
. successor corporation. .3337
. tax planning. .4510-4515
. two or more businesses. .2701

ACCOUNTING PERIODS. .2714-2717
. change in. .2715-2717
. . corporations. .2715; 2716
. . newlyweds. .2716(c)
. . partnerships. .2921
. 52-53 week accounting period. .2714(b)
. . change in. .2715; 2716
. husband & wife, different tax years. .2716
. less than 12 mos.: *See* Fractional year

ACCOUNTING PERIODS *(continued)*
. short taxable year: *See* Fractional year
. tax planning. .4520-4523
Accounting practice, change in. .2708
Accounting records: *See* Books and records
Accounting system, automated, records required . .3601
Accounts receivable:
. capital assets. .1601
. net operating loss. .2242(a)
. partnership:
. . distributions. .2928-2932; 2944
. . transfers. .2935
. sale of, bad debt deduction. .2311(d)
Accrual basis. .2706
. advances, long-term contract method. .2726(c)
. change to or from. .2708; 2709
. farm loss recapture. .2226(b); 2708
. tax planning. .4512
. time to report income. .2719-2730
. time to take deductions. .2735-2746
Accumulated earnings tax. .3130-3134
. accumulated earnings credit. .3132(c)
. . disallowance in corporate split-up. .3224
. consent dividends. .1702(d)
. dividends paid deduction. .3132
. small business investment cos. .3459
Accumulation distribution, complex trusts. .3023
Acquisitions to avoid tax. .3226
Actors: *See* Professional people
Actuarial tables, annuities. .1230(b)
Additional first-year depreciation. .2016
Additional taxes: *See* Deficiency in tax
Adjusted basis. .1500(b)
. partnership property. .2937-2942
Adjusted gross estate. .3929(a)
Adjusted gross income:
. capital losses. .1613(a)
. deductions for. .1801(a)
. defined. .1102(b); 1801(a)
. importance of. .1102(c); 1801
. long-term capital gain deduction. .1612(a)
. net oper. loss carryover affecting. .2243

Adjusted ordinary gross income, personal holding companies. .3401
Adjusted sales price, residence. .1416; 1423
Adjustments:
. accounting method changed. .2709; 2804
. annuities. .1230(d)
. corporate estimated tax, overpayments. .3622(a)
. credits, foreign tax refunded. .3705
. foreign personal holding companies. .3413
. inventory distributed to shareholders. .3127
. net operating loss. .2242(a); 3217; 3219
. . carryover. .2243
. partnerships, distributions or transfers. .2938
. purchase price. .1318(c)
. tentative carryback. .3630
. uncollected tips. .2510(c)
. unemployment insurance. .3844
. withheld taxes. .2510
Administration expenses, estates and trusts . .3016
Administrators: *See* Executors and administrators
Admission to practice:
. Revenue Service. .3609(a)

ADMISSION—ALTERNATIVE

———————— References are to PARAGRAPH (¶) NUMBERS ————————

Admission to practice (continued)
. Tax Court. .3636(a)
Adopted child as dependent. .1117; 1120
Adoption expenses. .1807
ADR system: See Class Life Asset Depreciation Range system
Ad valorem penalties. .3617
Advance payments: See Prepaid
Advances:
. accrual basis. .2720(b)
. long-term contract method. .2726(c)
. partners to partnerships. .2212(a)
. relatives. .2308
. salesmen. .1818; 2720(a)
. stockholder to corp.. .2212; 2307; 2309
Advertising expenses:
. capitalization. .1528; 1827; 2738
. deductibility. .1827; 2738
. political purposes. .1811; 2416
Affiliated corporations. .3222; See also Corporations, controlled
. allocation of income, etc.. .3225
. consolidated returns. .3222; 3515
. . extension of time for filing. .3518(a)
. . personal holding company tax. .3409
. . surtax rates. .3102; 3223
. profit-sharing plans. .1838(e)
. surtax exemption. .3223
. worthless securities. .2208(a); 2312
. worthless stock. .2208(b)
Age 65 or over:
. credit for the elderly. .2406
. exempt income. .2406
. exemptions. .1113(a)
. medical insurance. .1946
. returns. .1100; 1101
. sale of residence. .1423
Agents:
. constructive receipt through. .1300(c); 2703
. declaration of estimated tax. .2516(b)
. practice before I.R.S.. .3609
. practice before Tax Court. .3636
. returns by. .3510
. withholding by. .2501(b); 2535(a); 2536
Aggregating interests, for depletion. .2106-2109
. nonoperating interests. .2109
. operating interests. .2106—2108
Agreement: See Contracts
Agricultural labor:
. old-age benefit tax. .3805; 3816
. self-employment tax. .3823(b)
. withholding tax on wages. .2503(b)
Air conditioning units, as medical expense. .1946
Airplane expenses. .1829
Aliens:
. nonresident:
. . as dependents. .1120
. . capital gains or losses. .3709(b)
. . citizens of U.S. poss. as. .3709(a); 3727
. . compensation. .3711
. . credits . . 3709(b)
. . . withholding tax. .2511(b)
. . declaration of estimated tax. .2516(c); 2517(f)
. . deductions. .3709(b)
. . defined. .3709(a)
. . dividends received. .3711
. . effectively connected income. .3709(b); 3711(a)
. . exempt interest, info. required. .3521
. . foreign partnership. .3711
. . foreign tax credit. .3703(b)
. . how taxed. .3707-3712
. . identifying numbers. .3500

Aliens (continued)
. nonresident (continued)
. . income. .3709; 3712
. . income averaging. .2401; 3709(b)
. . interest received. .3711
. . joint returns. .3709(b)
. . liability for tax. .1028(f)
. . . payment of tax. .3522
. . rate chart. .5505
. . rents received. .3711
. . returns. .1100; 3517; 3519(c)
. . royalties received. .3711
. . sale of property. .3711
. . standard deduction: See Zero bracket amount
. . status, change during year. .3708(c)
. . tax rate schedule used. .3709(b)
. . tax table method. .1122
. . tax treaties. .3720
. . trade or business in U.S.. .3709; 3711
. . withholding tax. .2503(a); 2511(b); 2535-2537; 3709(d)
. resident:
. . as dependents. .1120
. . credit for foreign taxes. .3701; 3708(b)
. . defined. .3708(a)
. . estate tax credit. .3938
. . exempt income. .3708(b)
. . how taxed. .3708
. . liability for tax. .1028(e); 3708
. . returns. .1100
. . self-employment tax. .3821
. . status, change during year. .3708
. . tax treaties. .3720
. . treaty trader. .3708(a)
. . withholding tax. .2503(a); 2511(b); 2535-2537; 3709(d)
Alimony:
. annuities funding. .1230(b)
. attorney's fees connected with. .1823
. deductibility. .1320
. dependency exemption. .1116(a)
. partnerships. .2913
. taxability. .1320
. trust. .3022(e)
Allocation:
. basis. .1521
. . bargain sales to charity. .1942
. . casualty loss. .2204; 2206
. . condemnation. .1521(b)
. . demolition of buildings. .2209
. . nontaxable stock rights. .1711
. . sales to related taxpayer. .2223(e)
. distributable net income. .3006; 3007
. dividends, taxable and nontaxable. .1701(c)
. earnings and profits in tax-free distributions . .3129(f)
. loan repayment, principal and interest. .1904
. partnerships farm recapture property. .2910(a)
. purchase price:
. . depreciable and nondepreciable. .2003(d)
. . principal and interest. .1904
. securities bought as unit. .1521
Allotments, armed forces. .1306
Almond groves, expenses of. .1844(a)
Alphabetical roundup of federal taxes. .5701
Alterations: See Improvements; Repairs
ALTERNATE TAX METHODS. .2401-2403
Alternative method of withholding. .2504(c)
Alternative taxes:
. income averaging. .2401
. minimum tax on tax preferences. .1612(b); 2403(a)
. net long-term capital gain. .1614; 3202
. net Capital gain. .1614(b); 3202

ALTERNATIVE—ASSESSMENT

References are to PARAGRAPH (¶) NUMBERS

Alternative taxes (continued)
. unrelated business net income. .3445
Amended returns. .3520; 3626

Amortization:
. bond premium or discount. .1846; 3125
. building and loan associations. .3131
. child care centers. .2043
. construction period interest and taxes. .2042
. convertible bonds. .1846
. cooperative banks. .3433(b)
. dealers in securities. .1846
. mutual savings banks. .3433(b)
. on-the-job training and child care centers. .2043
. pollution-control facility. .2040; 2403(a)
. rehabilitation expenses for historic structures .. 2044
. reorganizations. .3337
Annualizing income. .2717
. self-employment income. .3827(b)
Annual payroll period, percentage method withholding table. .2504(a)
Annuities. .1230-1232
. actuarial tables. .1230(b)
. alimony and separate maintenance payments .. 1230(b); 1320
. basis of contract. .1527
. death benefits. .1304(a)
. dividends received on. .1230(f)
. employees'. .1232; *See also* Employees' trusts
. endowment policy proceeds. .1215(b)
. estate tax. .3915; 3919(d)
. . marital deduction. .3929
. exchanges. .1407
. exolusion ratio. .1230(b)
. expected return. .1230(e)
. federal employees. .1232(g)
. fractional part of year payment. .1230(b)
. gift tax. .4011
. individual retirement arrangements. .1838(l); 3024; 3027
. information returns. .3531
. installment payments. .1230(e)
. interest paid to purchase. .1905
. investment in. .1230(d)
. joint. .1230(e)
. joint and survivor. .1231
. . basis to survivor. .1509
. . death benefits. .1304(a)
. . estate tax. .3915
. . exclusion. .3008(b)
. levy on. .3615(a)
. life expectancy rule. .1230
. maturity. .1230(g)
. premiums paid by exempt organization, withholding. .2503(a)
. private, investment in. .1230(j); 1527
. redemption. .1230(g)
. refund. .1230(d)
. restricted stock plans. .1326
. retirement. .1232; 1838(g)
. . credit for the elderly. .2406
. servicemen. .1232(i); 1304(a)
. starting date. .1230(c)
. state and municipal employees. .1232(h)
. surrender of. .1230(g)
. survivor and joint annuitant. .1231
. transferred for consideration. .1230(d)
. two annuities for single consideration. .1230(i)
. . value. .1230(d)
. variable payment. .1230(h)
. voluntary withholding. .2504(k)

Annuity trust:
. charitable deduction for. .1942(e)
. estate tax, charitable deduction. .3927
. gift tax, charitable deduction. .4022
Anti-trust act violations, litigation expenses. .1823
Appeals:
. estate tax. .3945
. gift tax. .4032
. income tax cases. .3605; 3629; 3635 et seq.
. social security taxes. .3846
Appellate Division, hearings before. .3607
Appraisal fees:
. casualty loss. .1806
. charitable contribution. .1942(a)
Appreciation in value:
. as income. .1201
. charitable contribution of property. .1942(b)
"Arbitrage" transactions. .1608
Architects' fees: *See* Professional people
Armed forces: *See also* Veterans
. allotments. .1306
. annuities. .1232(i); 1303(a)
. bonus. .1218(c); 1306
. compensation. .1306
. court martial, legal expenses of. .1823
. death benefits to family. .1218(c)
. deductions by. .1834
. dependency status of members. .1116(a)
. employer payments. .1306; 1819; 1822(b)
. exempt income. .1218(c); 1232(i); 1306
. expenses of. .1834
. extension of time for filing returns. .3518
. family allowances. .1306
. injuries or sickness, pay for. .1218(c); 1306
. military post exchange employees, social security .. 3815(a)
. miscellaneous payments, facilities. .1218(c)
. missing status, return and tax due date. .1100(d)
. monthly family allowances. .1306
. overseas duty. .1834
. partner in, distributive share. .2905
. payment of tax. .3518(a)
. pensions and other benefits. .1218(c)
. . reduction in retirement pay to buy annuity .. 1218(c); 1232(i)
. . withholding tax. .2503(a)
. quarters or allowance for. .1308(d); 1834
. residence, sale of. .1420
. retirement:
. . income credit. .2406
. . pay. .1218(c)
. . . reduction in to buy annuity. .1218(c); 1232(i)
. . . withholding tax. .2503(a)
. returns. .1100; 3518(a)
. Service Academy pay. .1306
. VA death benefits. .1218(c)
. withholding tax. .2503(a)(b)
. . receipts. .2508
Army and Navy Reservists on active duty, compensation paid by employers:
. deductibility. .1819
. withholding tax. .2503(a)
Artists, commercial, old-age benefit tax. .3817(b)
Art works:
. capital asset status. .1601(f)
. depreciation. .2001
ASSESSMENT OF TAXES 3600 et seq.; 3612
. acceptance of overassessment. .3606
. additional: *See* Deficiency in tax
. bankruptcy. .3612(e)
. bond to stay. .3649(b)

ASSESSMENT OF TAXES (continued)
. closing agreements. .3608(b)
. deficiency. .3605
. failure to pay, penalty:
. . old-age benefit tax. .3830
. . unemployment insurance. .3845
. fiduciary. .3605
. gift tax. .4032
. income established by Comm. .3610(c)
. involuntary conversions. .1411
. jeopardy. .3605(b)
. limitation period. .3611-3613
. . suspension. .3605(b)
. private foundations. .3605; .3610(e)
. request for prompt. .3612(a)
. retirement plans. .3605
. summonses. .3601(a)
. suspension. .3605(b)
. termination. .3605(b); 3612(b)
. transferee liability. .3611
. waiver of limitations. .3610(d)
. waiver of restrictions. .3606
Assessments:
. labor organizations. .1807
. local benefits. .1912(b)
. . litigation expenses. .1823
. stock exchange. .1808
. stockholders. .3106
Asset Depreciation Range system. .2033
Assignments:
. life insurance policy. .1213
. part of trust income, effect of. .3008(b)
. property or property rights, taxable to whom . .2704
. right to decedent's income. .3008(b)
Associations:
. as corporations. .3026; 3101
. as partnerships. .2900
. trust distinguished. .3026
Athletic organizations: *See* exempt organizations
Attorneys:
. bar examination expenses. .1832
. disbarment, expense defending suit. .1823
. expenses of. .1832
. fees:
. . deductibility. .1823; 2204(b); 3016
. . . estate tax. .3926
. . . excessive. .1302(a)
. . information returns. .3531
. malpractice suit, expenses of. .1823
. old-age benefit tax. .3817(b)
. practice before I.R.S.. .3609
. practice before Tax Court. .3636
. withholding tax. .2502
Auctioneers, withholding tax. .2502
Audit Division:
. disagreement with findings. .3603
. examination of returns. .3601(b); 3602
Audit, items subject to. .3601(b)
Auditors, old-age benefit tax. .3817(b)
Aunt as dependent. .1117
Author:
. literary works of, capital asset status. .1601(f)
. profit-sharing plans. .1839(b)
Autoette as medical expense. .1946
Automatic Data Processing. .3500
Automobile:
. business and personal use. .2001(a)
. damage to, loss. .2200; 2204(b)
. dealers, property acquired in trade-in. .1503(b)
. depreciation. .2001(a); 2032

Automobile (continued)
. depreciation (continued)
. . contribution deduction. .1942(c)
. destruction of:
. . insurance proceeds reinvested. .1411
. . loss on. .2200
. exchanged. .1406; 1517
. expenses. .1805; 1808; 1832
. . mileage rate. .1829(c); 1942(c); 1946
. gasoline tax. .1917(a)
. inspection fees. .1912(d)
. insurance premiums. .1828(b); 1832
. license tax. .1912(c)
. loss on sale. .1401(b); 1805; 2200; 2202
. professional expenses. .1832
. registration fees. .1912
Average experience method, reserve for bad debts. .3433(a)
Averaging income. .2401; 3024(d)
Averaging methods, depreciation. .2022(b)
Avoidance of taxes, acquisitions to effect. .3226
Awards:
. condemnation. .1410-1415; 1620
. gross income. .1302(c)
. interest on. .1314
. old-age benefit tax. .3818
. withholding tax. .2503(a)

— B —

Baby-sitters, old-age benefit tax. .3806
Back pay. .1301
. withholding tax. .2503(a)
BAD DEBTS. .2300-2317
. accounts receivable, sale of. .2311(d)
. advances to corp.:
. . employees. .2307
. . stockholders. .2307; 2309
. advances to relatives. .2308
. bank deposits. .2310
. bankruptcy as indication of. .2305
. banks. .2306; 2312(b); 3433
. . minimum tax on preference items. .2403(a); 3433(a)
. basis for deduction. .2302
. bonds, worthless. .2312
. business. .2305
. . partially worthless. .2306
. cancellation of debt. .1318; 2315(a)
. capital loss. .2307
. change of method. .2708
. charge-off. .2306; 2311
. collateral securing. .2305; 2306
. compromise of. .2315(a)
. contingent payment. .2301
. deposits in closed banks. .2310
. determination of worthlessness. .2305
. employee's loan to corp. .2307
. endorsers and guarantors. .2315(b)
. forgiveness of debt. .1318; 2315(a)
. income not previously reported. .2300
. information required. .3521
. insolvency as indication of. .2305
. installment sales. .2803
. legal action as prerequisite for deduction. .2305
. life insurance guaranteeing loan. .2305
. loss distinguished. .2315
. officer's loan to corp... .2307
. partial deduction. .2306; 2307; 2312
. pledged property, sale of. .2317
. political contributions, from. .2301
. receivership as indication of. .2305
. recovery. .2316

BAD—BONDS

References are to PARAGRAPH (¶) NUMBERS

BAD DEBTS *(continued)*
. *recovery (continued)*
. . successor in reorganization. .3337
. refund claims, limitation. .3624(a)
. reserve for. .2311(b)
. . accounts receivables sold. .2311(d)
. . average experience method. .3433
. . banks. .3433(b)
. . recoveries. .2316(b)
. specific charge-off method. .2311(a)
. statute of limitations. .2305; 2315
. "tax benefits" rule. .2316(c)
. time to deduct. .2305; 2743(a)
. trust companies. .2312(b)
. worthlessness, determination. .2305
. worthless securities. .2312

Bail-out, preferred stock. .1722
Bank deposit method of computing income. .2711
Bankruptcy:
. assessment and collection of taxes. .3612(e)
. bad debt deduction, effect on. .2305
. discharge of debts. .1318(f)
. reorganization. .3331
. trustees in:
. . returns. .3511; 3512
. . withholding. .2501

Banks:
. bad debt deductions:
. . as tax preference item. .2403(a); 3433(a)
. . reserve method. .3433
. . worthless securities. .2306; 2312(b)
. bonds owned by, gains and losses. .3433
. closed, deposits in, bad debts. .2310
. commissions on loans. .2722(c)
. committee members, old-age tax. .3817(c)
. common trust funds. .3025
. cooperative: *See* Cooperative banks
. credit cards:
. . charitable contributions, when deductible. .2742
. . finance charges, deductibility. .1901
. depositaries:
. . corporate tax payments. .3523
. . withheld taxes. .2509(a); 3827(a)
. deposits:
. . capital asset. .1601(k)
. . interest:
. . . deductibility. .1901
. . . income. .1314; 2703
. . . loss deduction. .2203
. . withheld taxes. .2509(a)
. directors, old-age benefit tax. .3817(c)
. dividends. .1704(a)
. . exclusion. .1706(a)
. . paid to U.S.. .3433
. foreclosure by. .3433
. loans, commissions. .2722(c)
. mutual savings: *See* Mutual savings banks
. net operating loss. .3216
. personal holding company tax. .3403
. taxation of. .3433
. worthless securities. .2312(b)
. worthless stock owned by. .3433(a)

Baptismal offerings:
. income tax. .1301
. self-employment income. .3824
Bar examination expenses. .1832
Bargain purchase by employee. .1310
Baseball:
. contracts, depreciation. .2001(a)
. players, uniforms. .1807
BASIS FOR GAIN OR LOSS. .1500 et seq. *See also* Gain or loss, basis

Beneficiary:
. accumulation distributions, complex trusts. .3023
. assigned income, taxable to whom. .2704
. basis of property. .1507-1510
. complex trusts. .3006; 3023
. credits. .3008(b); 3019
. . excess distributions thrown back. .3023(f)
. . foreign taxes. .3701
. death benefits paid to. .1304(a)
. deductions. .3008(b)
. depletion. .2002(c); 2101(c); 3014
. depreciation. .2002; 3014
. estate previously taxed. .3939
. estates and complex trusts. .3006
. income taxable to. .3008; 3004
. interest:
. . life insurance proceeds. .1213
. . taxes on transferred property. .1902
. investment credit. .2410(g)
. losses of estate or trust. .3009; 3011
. payment to employee's. .1304(a); 1822(a)
. reversionary interests. .3022(a)
. simple trust. .3005
. stock options. .1327(d)
. taxability. .3003
. trust income for support of. .3022(e)
. undistributed net income. .3023
. year different from estate or trust. .3008(b)
Benefit and retirement plans. .1838; 1839; 3024; 3027. *See also* Profit-sharing plans
Bequests: *See* Inheritance
Betting: *See* Gambling
Bingo winnings,
. return for. .3521
Biweekly payroll period, computation of withholding. .2504
Blind individuals:
. defined. .1114(a)
. exemptions. .1114
. information required. .3521
Blocked foreign income. .2730(a)
Blood donations. .1942(c)
Board and lodging:
. armed forces. .1308; 1834
. as compensation. .1308
. child's payment to parent. .1312
. civil service employees. .1308
. clergymen, self-employment income. .3824
. deductibility. .1805; 1829; 1832
. . employer, by. .1815
. farm help. .1844
. medical expenses. .1946
. nurse's board paid by taxpayer, medical expense. .1946
. old-age benefit tax. .3819(a)
. parent furnishing. .1815
. withholding of taxes. .2503(a)
Board of Tax Appeals: *See* Tax Court
Bonding companies, withholding tax on wages. .2501
Bonds:
. amortization election. .1846
. . reorganizations. .3337
. . successor corporation. .3337
. as investment property. .1406(b)
. capital assets, defined. .1601(a)
. Class B interest coupons. .1204
. compensation in form of. .1307(c)
. convertible. .1404
. . amortization of premium. .1846
. . premium on repurchase, deduction. .3125(b)
. . rights to subscribe to. .1714

Bonds (continued)
. defaulted, surrender of. .1403
. discount. .1629; 3125
. . capital gains and losses. .1629
. exchange of. .1403; 1404; 3307
. exempt. .1203 et seq.
. . amortizable premium. .1846
. . compensation in form of. .1307(c)
. sale of. .1629; 1630
. fair market value, estate tax. .3919(b)
. housing authorities, interest. .1204
. installment sales, payment in year of sale. .2811(a)
. interest:
. . arbitrage. .1204
. . accrued before purchase or sale. .1315
. . constructive receipt. .2703
. . coupons. .1204
. . exempt. .1203; 1204
. . "flat" purchase. .1314
. . gross income. .1314
. . industrial development. .1204
. . information returns. .3532
. . tax-free covenant. .2535(b)
. market discount on municipals. .1204
. ownership certificates. .3532
. partial worthlessness. .2312
. posting by taxpayer. .3649(b)
. premium. .1846; 3125
. redemption of: *See* Bonds, retirement
. retirement:
. . before maturity date. .1314
. . capital gain or loss. .1602
. . gain or loss. .3125
. . rights. .1714
. sale and purchase by corporation of its own. .3125
. sale of, handling losses. .1611
. sale or exchange, information required. .3521
. savings: *See* Federal obligations
. tax-free covenant, interest, withholding on . .2535(b)
. U.S.: *See* Federal obligations
. worthless. .3203
. . bad debts. .2312
. . limitations on refunds. .3624(a)
Bonuses. .1302
. armed forces. .1218(c)
. constructive receipt. .3008(b)
. deductibility. .1815; 1819
. depletion. .2105
. gift distinguished. .1302(a)
. incentive compensation plans. .2737(b)
. mines. .2104; 2105
. oil and gas properties. .2104; 2105
. old-age benefit tax. .3818
. retired employees, old-age tax. .3818
. stock plans, contributions under. .1838
. veterans. .1218(c)
. withholding tax. .2504(e)
Book profit, partnerships. .2907
Books and records. .2710; 3601
. depletion deductions. .2112
. depreciation deductions. .2023
. employees, relating to. .2507
. examination. .3602
. failure to keep:
. . accounting period required. .2714
. . penalties. .3620
. farmers. .2614(a)
. medical expenses. .1946
. minimum tax. .3541
. nontaxable exchanges. .1405
. old-age benefit tax. .3828

Books and records (continued)
. real estate investment trusts. .3432(f)
. retirement plans, public inspection of. .3537(d)
. self-employment income. .3828(c)
. unemployment insurance. .3843
. wage plans. .2507
Books and tuition:
. deductibility. .1833
. taxability. .1307(b)
"Boot":
. installment reporting of. .1408
. nontaxable exchanges. .1408; 1517; 3309; 3311; 3319
. reorganizations. .3309; 3311; 3319
Briefs. .3647
Broadcasting companies, sales or exchanges on FCC orders. .1410
Brokerage accounts, constructive receipt of income. .2703
Brokerage fees. .1818
Brother as dependent. .1117
Building and loan associations:
. bad debt deduction, as tax preference item . .2403(a); 3433(b)
. dividends:
. . exclusion. .1706(a)
. . information returns. .3532(a)
. . time to report. .2721(a)
. taxability. .3433(b)
Buildings: *See also* Real estate
. capital gains and losses. .1619(b)
. demolition loss. .2209
. depreciation, allocation of cost of land and building. .2003(d)
. lessee erecting. .1317; 2002
. newly erected, holding period. .1606
. useful life. .2032
Burglary insurance premiums. .1828(b)
Business:
. bad debts. .2305
. capital assets status. .1601(d)
. casualty losses. .2204(d)
. contributions of products. .2601
. damages for injuries to. .1226
. deductions for adjusted gross income. .1801
. defined. .1601; 2202
. donated products. .1810; 1941(a); 2601
. expenses:
. . capital expenditures distinguished. .1808
. . charitable contributions. .3118
. . contributions to pension trust. .1838
. . deductibility. .1803-1805
. . estates and trusts. .3016
. . personal expenses distinguished. .1807
. . political purposes. .2416
. . time to deduct. .2735
. gross profit from. .2601(a)
. illegal:
. . expenses. .1812
. . income from. .1300(g)
. income from. .2601
. . credit for the elderly . .2406
. . exempt organizations. .3445
. . return requirements. .1100
. information returns. .3531
. insurance. .1331
. interest in, capital asset. .1601(d)
. investigation expenses. .1808
. location, expense of seeking. .1829
. losses. .2202; 2204(d)
. net operating loss: *See* Net operating loss
. principal business, defined. .1829

BUSINESS—CAPITAL   Index—6007

———— References are to PARAGRAPH (¶) NUMBERS ————

Business (continued)
. profit. .2601
. property:
. . capital gains and losses. .1618; 1619
. . . partnerships. .2911
. . depreciation. .2001
. . . recapture of. .1619
. sale of. .1524; 1601(d)
. service not in course of, old-age tax. .3807
. special classes, inventory methods. .2609
. unincorporated, retirement plans of. .1839
. unrelated, exempt organizations. .3447
. valuation of interests, estate tax. .3919(c)
Business insurance. .1331; 1828(b)
Business trusts. .3026

— C —

Calendar of due dates. .5501
Calendar year:
. accounting period. .2714
. change to or from. .2715-2717
"Call," short sales. .1609
Campaign contributions and expenses. .2416
Canada, residents:
. as dependents. .1120
. income tax. .3709(b)
Canal Zone residents as dependents. .1120
Cancellation:
. debt: See Indebtedness, forgiveness
. lease. .1316; 1601(g); 1808; 1826(d); 2724
Capital:
. contributions to:
. . advances by stockholders. .2212; 2309
. . assessments against stockholders. .3106
. . cancellation of debt. .1318(d); 2315(a)
. . corporation. .2212(a); 3106
. . interest. .2923(d)
. . partnership. .2212(a)
. . surrender of stock to corp.. .2212(b)
. distributions. .1701
. expenditures:
. . almond groves. .1844(a)
. . business expenses distinguished. .1808
. . citrus groves. .1844(a)
. . deductibility. .1808
. . demolition of building. .2209
. . drilling and development costs. .2103(c)
. . farmers. .1844(b)
. . loss distinguished. .2212
. . medical expense deduction for. .1946
. . repairs distinguished. .1825
. return of. .1201; 2113; 2816
Capital asset, defined. .1601
Capital gain dividends, regulated investment companies. .3431
CAPITAL GAINS AND LOSSES. .1600 et seq.
. accounts receivable. .1601
. alternative tax. .1614; 3202
. arbitrage transactions. .1608(a)
. averaging. .2401
. bad debts. .2307
. banks. .3433
. bonds issued at discount. .1629
. capital asset, defined. .1601
. capital gain dividends of regulated investment companies. .3431
. carryover. .1613(c); 3201
. . accounting method changed, effect on. .2709
. . bad debt recoveries. .2316(c)
. . information required. .3521

CAPITAL GAINS AND LOSSES (continued)
. carryover (continued)
. . long-term capital gain deduction affected . .1613(a)
. . reorganizations. .3337
. . Subchapter S corp.. .3201(a)
. . successor corporation. .3337
. casualty losses. .1619; 1620
. cattle. .1622
. coal, disposal of. .1623
. commercial or industrial property. .1619(b)
. common trust funds. .3025
. computation. .1613(a)
. computing period assets held. .1606
. condemnation awards. .1620
. copyrights. .1601(f)
. corporations. .3201
. . alternative tax. .3202
. . carrybacks and carryovers. .3201(a)
. . electing partnership-type taxation. .3143(b)
. covenant not to compete. .1601(k)
. dealers in securities. .1628
. deductions for adjusted gross income. .1612
. depreciable property sold to spouse or controlled corporation. .1625
. distributable net income. .3009
. distributor's agreement. .1601(i)
. employees' annuities, lump sum proceeds. .1232(c)
. employees' trust distributions. .3024(d)
. estates and trusts. .3008; 3009
. farmers. .1622
. first-in, first-out rule. .1607
. foreign corporations, taxability. .3710(a)
. gains as tax preference income.. .1612(b); 2403(a); 3201(b)
. gifts. .1606(a)
. gross income, effect on. .3545
. holding period: See Capital gains and losses, period assets held
. husband and wife. .1613(b)
. installment and deferred payment sales. .2813; 2816(a)
. installment obligations. .2831
. involuntary conversions. .1619; 1620
. iron ore, disposal of. .1623
. land and buildings. .1619
. lease cancellation. .1316; 1601(g)
. letter or memorandum. .1601
. like kind exchanges. .1619(d)
. liquidating dividends. .1717
. livestock. .1622
. long-term. .1605; 1611; 1614
. . adjusted gross income. .1611; 1612
. . capital gain dividends of regulated investment companies. .3431
. . charitable contributions as. .3013
. . corporations. .3201; 3202
. . deductibility. .1605; 1611; 1612
. . estates and trusts. .3009(b)
. . partnerships. .2911
. . small business corporations. .3143(a)
. lots. .1631
. machinery and equipment. .1619(a)
. minimum tax. .1612(b); 2403(a); 3201(b)
. net capital gain. .1614(b); 3202
. nonresident aliens. .3709(c)
. options. .1601
. partner and partnership. .2923
. partner's interest. .1601(e)
. partnerships. .2906(a); 2911; 2945
. patents. .1601(j); 1606
. period assets held. .1605-1608

CAPITAL GAINS AND LOSSES (continued)
. period assets held (continued)
. . commodity futures. .1606
. . community property. .1606
. . gift after 12-31-20. .1606(a)
. . optioned property. .1606
. . options. .1601(h)
. . partnership interest. .1606(d)
. . patents. .1606
. . stock dividends:
. . . nontaxable. .1708
. . . taxable. .1709
. . stock rights. .1711-1712
. personal-use property. .1601
. preferred stock bail-out. .1722
. property:
. . acquired in nontaxable exchange. .1606(c)
. . transmitted at death. .1606(b)
. . residence, personal. .1606(e)
. . Sec. 1250 property. .1619(b)
. . securities. .1606
. . short sales. .1608(a)
. . . nontaxable. .1708
. . . taxable. .1709
. . stock option. .1327(c)
. . stock rights. .1711-1713
. . wash sales. .2221(a)
. . worthless securities. .2312
. real property. .1601(b); 1618; 1631
. recapture of depreciation. .1619
. repossessions. .2821; 2823
. residential rental property. .1619(b)
. retirement:
. . bonds. .1602
. . credit for the elderly. .2406
. sale or exchange, necessity for. .1602
. Sec. 1231 gains and losses. .1618-1624
. . casualty losses. .2206(b)
. securities dealers. .1628
. self-employment income. .3824
. short sales. .1608
. short-term. .1605; 1611
. . partnerships. .2911
. short-term obligations issued at discount. .2723(c)
. small business investment companies. .3459
. small business stock. .1632
. stock dividends. .1707-1709
. stock rights. .1710-1712
. timber cutting. .1621
. trust companies. .3433
. worthless securities. .2312
. worthless stock. .2208
Capital gains, throwback rule. .3023(h)
Capital stock: *See* Stock
Capital stock tax, deductibility. .1918
Car pools. .1301
Carriers, employment by, rate chart. .5514
Carryback and carryover:
. acquiring corporation, carryovers. .3336; 3337
. bad debt recoveries. .2316(c)
. bond premium or discount, reorganizations. .3125(e)
. capital gain property, charitable deduction. .1944(a)
. capital loss:
. . accumulated earnings tax. .3133
. . corporations. .3201
. . expropriation losses. .3201(a)
. . individuals. .1613(c)
. . information required. .3521
. . personal holding companies. .3404
. . reorganizations. .3337
. . successor corporation. .3337

Carryback and carryover (continued)
. casualty losses. .2204(f)
. charitable contributions. .1944; 3118
. contributions to employees' trust. .1838
. foreign tax credit. .3703(b)
. . deficiency due to. .3624(c)
. investment credit. .2410
. . deficiency due to. .3611(f); 3618(a)
. investment interest. .1906(b)
. net operating loss: *See also* Net operating loss, carryback and carryover
. . corporations. .3215-3221
. . deficiency due to. .3611(f); 3618(a)
. . estates and trusts. .3015
. . individuals. .2241 et seq.
. . partners. .2241; 2914
. . reorganizations. .3337-3339
. . stock ownership rules. .3221
. . successor corporation. .3336(b); 3337-3339
. overpayment of taxes, refund, interest on. .3628(c)
. refunds due to. .3624(b); 3630
. Subchapter S corp.. .3201(a)
. successor corp., carryovers. .3336; 3337
. tentative adjustments. .3630
. work incentive program credit, deficiency due to. .3611(f); 3618(a)
Carrying charges:
. capitalization. .1528
. installment purchases. .1904
Cartage, cost of goods sold. .2604(a)
Cartoon strip, capital asset status. .1601(f)
Cash basis. .2702
. casualty losses. .2204(e)
. change to or from. .2708; 2709
. earnings and profits. .1701(c)
. reserve for bad debts. .2311(b)
. tax planning. .4511
. time to report income. .2719-2730
. time to take deductions. .2735-2746
Cash expenditure method of computing income. .2711
Cash receipts and disbursements, accounting method. .2702
Casual labor:
. old-age benefit tax. .3807
. withholding tax on wages. .2503(b)
Casual sales, installment plan. .2812
Casualty losses. .2204; 2206
. appraisal fees. .1806
. capital gains and losses. .1619; 1620
. estate tax. .3926
. estates and trusts. .3016
. information required. .3521
. insurance recovery. .2204
. inventory. .2601(a)
. involuntary conversion. .1410-1415
. net operating loss. .2204(f); 2242(a)
. refunds for certain years. .2204(e)
. time for deduction. .2204(e)
. uninsured property. .1620
Catalogs, cost of. .1808
Cattle, sale of. .1622
Certiorari, petition for. .3629
Chaplain: *See* Clergymen
Charitable:
. bequests. .3927
. pooled income fund, estate tax. .3927(b)
. remainder, annuity trust or unitrust:
. . distributions. .3006(g)
. . estate tax. .3927(b)
CHARITABLE CONTRIBUTIONS. .1942; 1943.
See also Contributions, charitable.

CHARITABLE—COMMISSIONS   Index—6009

——————— References are to PARAGRAPH (¶) NUMBERS ———————

Charitable organizations: *See* Exempt organizations
Charts and tables. .5501 et seq.
Check:
. bad, payment with, penalty. .3618(e)
. constructive receipt. .2703
. contributions paid by, when deductible. .1941(c); 2735(e)
. income when. .2703; 2719(a)
. payment by, when deductible. .2735(e)
. payment of taxes by. .3527(b)
Child care day centers:
. credit for federal welfare recipients. .2411(f)
Child care expenses. .2415
. medical expenses as. .1946
Children: *See also* Minors
. adopted, exemption for. .1117
. adoption expenses. .1807
. alimony for support of. .1320
. assessment and collection of tax. .3614(b)
. board and lodging payments to parent. .1312
. care of, expenses for. .2415
. compensation paid by parent. .1815
. dependents. .1117
. employment of parent by, old-age tax. .3808
. expenses attributable to earnings of. .1100(a)
. foster, exemption for. .1117(a); 1118(a)
. income of. .1312
. members of household. .1106(b)
. refunds. .3509
. returns. .3509
. trust income for support of. .3022(e)
. vacation earnings. .3509
. withholding tax on wages. .2502
China Trade Act corporations, dividends from . .1708(a)
. deductions. .3117(b)
. exclusion. .1706(a)
Chiropodists' fees. .1946
Christian Science practioners:
. fees. .1946
. self-employment tax. .3822
Christmas gifts and bonuses:
. buyers. .1830
. employees. .1302(a); 1819
. old-age benefit tax. .3818
Cigar and cigarette taxes. .5515
. state, deductibility. .1912(d)
Circulation expenditures:
. capitalization. .1528
. deductibility. .1808
. time to deduct. .2749
Citrus groves, expenses. .1844(a)
Civil service employees:
. annuities. .1232(g), (h)
. . estate tax. .3915(b)
. . service outside U.S.. .3712
. board and lodging. .1308
. compensation. .1305
. retirement fund payments:
. . service outside U.S.. .3712
. . withholding. .2503(a)
. withheld compensation. .1232(g)
Claims:
. refund: *See* Refunds
. time to deduct. .2735(c)
. transferred assets. .3614(a)
Clarinet and lessons, as medical expense. .1946
Classification of taxpayers. .1028
Classified accounts, depreciation. .2022(b)
. retirement from. .2036

Class Life Asset Depreciation Range system . .2033
. election. .2033(a)
. first-year convention. .2033(d)
. property eligible for. .2033(c)
. repair allowances. .1825(a); 2033(f)
. salvage value. .2005; 2033(e)
. useful life. .2033
. vintage accounts. .2033(b), (d)
. . depreciation reserve. .2033(b)
. . retirement from. .2038
Clergymen:
. allowance for parsonage. .1308(e)
. . self-employment tax. .3824
. fees and offerings. .1301
. . self-employment income. .3824
. old-age benefit tax. .3809
. pensions. .1304(b)
. rental value of dwelling:
. . income tax. .1308(e)
. . self-employment income. .3824
. self-employment tax. .3822; 3824
. withholding tax. .2503(b)
"Clifford" trusts. .3022
Close corporations: *See* Corporations, controlled
Closed transactions. .2725
Closing agreements. .3608(b)
. acceptance of overassessment. .3606
. waiver of restrictions on assessment and collection . .3606
Closing of tax year by Comm.. .3612(c)
Club dues. .1807; 1830
Club stock, loss on sale. .2203
Coal mines. .1623
. percentage depletion. .2102
Coast and Geodetic Survey, withholding tax on pensions. .2503(a)
Coast Guard: *See* Armed forces
Code, Internal Revenue:
. finding list. .5801
. organization of. .1013(a)
Collapsible corporations. .1627
COLLECTION OF TAXES. .3600 et seq.; 3612
. at source: *See* Withholding
. bankruptcy. .3612(e)
. bond to stay. .3649(b)
. closing agreements. .3608(b)
. compromise. .3608(a)
. counterclaims. .3615(d)
. distraint. .3615(a)
. extension of period. .3610; 3611; 3613
. government's remedies for. .3610; 3615
. injunction. .3615(f)
. levy. .3610(a)
. . insurance proceeds. .3615
. . wrongful, limitation on. .3613(d)
. liens. .3615(c)
. limitation period. .3610-3613
. payroll deductions. .3615(e)
. private foundations. .3610(e)
. set-off or counterclaim. .3615(d)
. suit. .3610(a); 3615(b)
. waiver of limitations. .3610(d)
College courses, expense of. .1833
Commissions:
. assigned to third parties. .2704
. bank loans. .2722(c)
. deductibility. .1818
. executors, deductibility. .1806; 3016
. . estate tax. .3926
. gross income. .1301

6010—Index COMMISSIONS—COMPENSATION

References are to PARAGRAPH (¶) NUMBERS

Commissions (continued)
. information returns. .3531
. installment realty sales. .2811(a)
. insurance agents. .1301
. loans and mortgages. .1309; 2707
. moving expenses. .1818(b)
. note in payment. .1309
. old-age benefit tax. .3818
. organizational expenses of corporations. .3116
. withholding tax. .2504(e)
Committee for incompetent, returns. .3511(a)
Commodity Credit Corp. loans:
. income. .2722(d)
. information required. .3521
Commodity futures:
. as stock or securities. .2221
. holding period. .1606
. short sales. .1608(c)
. wash sales of. .2221
Commodity Stabilization Service, social security coverage. .3815(a)

Common trust funds. .3025
. information required. .3521
. net operating loss deduction. .3015
. tax preferences, minimum tax. .3025
Communication, taxes on, rate chart. .5515
Communist organizations, social security coverage. .3813
Community income. .1300(f)
. credit for the elderly. .2406
. medical expenses. .1945(c)
. self-employment tax. .3827(b)
. withholding tax on wages. .2503(a)
Community property:
. adjusted gross estate involving. .3929(a)
. dividends from. .1705(b)
. estate tax. .3905
. . adjusted gross estate. .3929(a)
. . marital deduction. .3929(a)
. gift tax. .4005
. . marital deduction. .4023
. hobby losses. .2225
. income from U.S. possession. .3727
. income tax. .1104(a)
. inherited, holding period of. .1606
. joint returns. .3508
. marital deduction:
. . estate tax. .3929(a)
. . gift tax. .4023
Commuting expenses. .1805; 1829(b)
Compensation:
. additional. .1302(a); 1819; 2737
. . withholding on. .2504(e)
. annuity payments. .1232; 1307(a)
. anticipated, losses. .2202(a)
. armed forces. .1306
. assigned to third parties. .2704
. attached by creditors. .2703
. authorization. .1821
. back pay. .1301; 2503(a)
. board and lodging. .1308
. bonds as. .1307(c)
. bonus: *See* Bonuses
. books and tuition. .1307(b)
. children. .1312; 1815
. civil service employees. .1305
. claim of right to. .1301
. commissions: *See* Commissions
. constructive receipt. .2703
. contingent basis. .1815; 1819
. contributions to pension trust. .1838

Compensation (continued)
. decedent's. .1304; 1822(a); 3008(b)
. . withholding tax. .2503(a)
. deductibility. .1815-1823
. deductions from. .1301; 2703
. disability income. .1219(c)
. discount on purchases, employees. .1310
. dividends distinguished. .1817
. employees attending reserve training:
. . deductibility. .1819
. . withholding tax. .2503(a)
. excessive. .1301; 1817
. exempt organizations. .3436(d)
. fed. employees and officers. .1305; 1308
. gifts distinguished. .1302
. gross income. .1301-1312
. guaranteed annual wage payments. .1307(d)
. health insurance premiums. .1307(a)
. hospitalization insurance premiums. .1307(a)
. income taxes paid by employer for employee .1302(a)
. information returns. .3531
. injuries or sickness. .1219; 1819(b); 1947
. . armed forces. .1218(c)
. . withholding tax. .2504(g)
. insurance premiums. .1307(a)
. life insurance premiums. .1307(a)
. liquidated damages under FLSA. .2503(a)
. lump-sum. .2401
. minors. .1815
. municipal employees and officers. .1305
. nonresident aliens. .3712
. . withholding tax. .2503(a); 2535
. nonresident citizens. .3725
. . information required. .3521
. note in payment. .1309
. officers: *See* Corporations, officers
. other than cash. .1307-1310; 1819
. . old-age benefit tax. .3819(a)
. . withholding tax. .2503(a)
. paid after employee's death. .1304; 1822(a)
. . withholding tax. .2503(a)
. partners. .2923(d)
. pay for property distinguished. .1817
. pensions: *See* Pensions
. percentage basis. .1301; 1815; 1819
. prior years' services. .1821; 2503(a)
. proportionate to stockholdings. .1817
. reasonableness. .1301; 1816
. rental value of dwelling furnished clergyman .1308(e)
. resident aliens. .3708
. resort expenses paid for executives. .1819
. restricted property. .1326; 1819(c)
. retroactive. .2503(a)
. returned to employer. .1301
. state officers and employees. .1305
. stock as. .1307(e); 1819
. . gain or loss. .3124
. . withholding tax. .2503(a)
. stock sales or options to employees. .1328
. . deductibility. .1815
. student loans, discharge of. .1303
. tax-free securities as. .1307(c)
. time to deduct. .2737
. time to report. .2720
. unpaid, bad debt deduction. .2300
. unpaid 2½ mos. after close of year. .2748
. vacation pay. .1815
. . time deductible. .2737(a)
. . withholding tax. .2503(a); 2504(f)
. veterans. .1218(c)

COMPENSATION—CONTRIBUTIONS Index—6011

References are to PARAGRAPH (¶) NUMBERS

Compensation (continued)
. voluntary payments. .1302
. wage disability income. .1219(c)
. withholding on: *See* Withholding
Competition, payments to eliminate. .1808
Completed contract method, long-term contracts . .2842; 4515(c)
Complex trusts:
. accumulation, distribution. .3023
. defined. .3006
. distributions. .3006
. . computations. .3021(b)
. . deduction for. .3017(b)
. . excess. .3023
. throwback rule. .3023
. undistributed net income. .3023
Composer, musical compositions, capital asset . .1601(f)
Composite depreciation accounts. .2022(b); 2036
Composition agreement:
. forgiveness of debt under. .1318(f)
. loss through. .2315(a)
Compromise:
. bad debt deduction due to. .2315(a)
. collection of taxes. .3608(a)
. loss due to. .2315(a)
Condemnation:
. awards. .1410-1415; 1619; 1620
. . interest on. .1204
. basis, allocation. .1521(b)
. capital gain or loss. .1619(e); 1620
. involuntary conversion. .1410-1415
. residence, personal. .1421
Condominiums:
. interest. .1902
. sale or exchange of. .1417
. taxes. .1919
Conferences before I.R.S. .3603; 3909
Congressman, social security coverage. .3815(a)
Consent dividends:
. information required. .3521
. personal holding companies. .3404; 3406
Conservation expenditures. .1845
. partnerships. .2913
Consigned goods, inventory. .2602
Consolidated returns. .3222; 3515
. accounting method changed. .2708(a)
. accounting period changed. .2716; 2717
. annualizing income. .2717
. change in accounting period. .2716; 2717
. extension of time for filing. .3518(a)
. information required. .3521
. personal holding company. .3409
Consolidation. .3303
. carryovers. .3336; 3337
. partnerships. .2922(c)
. stock options, effect on. .1327(d)
Construction workers, traveling expenses. .1829
Constructive dividends. .1703
. omitted from return, limitation on assessment and collection. .3611
Constructive ownership of stock: *See* Stock, constructive ownership
Constructive payment. .1942; 2705
Constructive receipt. .1215(c); 1942; 2703; 2721
Containers, depreciation. .2001(a)
Contest awards, income. .1302(c)
Contested items, time for deduction. .2735(c)
Contingent payments. .2725(a); 2816
. imputed interest. .2840(d)
Contract price, installment realty sales. .2811(a)
Contractors, withholding tax. .2502

Contracts:
. depreciation. .2001(a)
. executory depreciation. .2002
. government, renegotiation of. .2729
. installment sales: *See* Installment and deferred payment sales
. long-term. .2842
. . information required. .3521
. loss of anticipated income. .2202(a)
. patent license, assignment of, taxable to whom . .2704
. personal service, personal holding company income. .3401
. promissory note, to execute. .2703
. state and municipal, profits on. .1330
Contributions:
. accident or health plans. .1220
. benefit plans. .1819; 1838
. . information required. .1838(k)
. business expense. .3118
. capital: *See* Capital, contributions to
. charitable. .1941; 1943
. . amateur sports organizations. .1941(a)
. . appraisal fees. .1942(a)
. . bargain sales. .1942(b)
. . benefit shows. .1941(b)
. . capital gain property. .1944(a)
. . capital gains as source. .3013
. . carryover. .1944; 3118(c)
. . children. .1100(a)
. . common trust funds. .3025
. . conditional transfers. .1942(e)
. . corporations. .3118
. . . reorganizations. .3337
. . double deductions, adjustment for. .1942(e), (g)
. . . corporation carryover. .3118(c)
. . estates and trusts. .3007(c); 3013; 3451-3453; 3538
. . farmer's gift of products. .1810; 2614(c)
. . foreign personal holding companies. .3413
. . future interests. .1942(e)
. . gift tax. .4002; 4022
. . income interest. .1942(e)
. . individuals. .1942; 1943
. . information required. .3521
. . interest adjustments. .1942(g)
. . joint returns. .1943(a)
. . limitation. .1943
. . . estates and trusts. .3013
. . manufacturer's gift of products. .1810; 2601
. . net operating loss carryover involved. .2243
. . partnerships. .2906(a); 2915
. . percentage depletion, effect on. .2104(a)
. . personal holding companies. .3404
. . pledges. .1941(c)
. . property donations. .1942
. . remainder interest. .1942(e)
. . reversionary interests. .1942(e)
. . right to use property. .1942(d)
. . Sec. 1245 or Sec. 1250 property. .1619(c)
. . services donated. .1301; 1942(c)
. . time to deduct. .2742
. . uniform costs. .1942(c)
. . unlimited deduction. .1943(e)
. disability benefit funds, deductibility. .1807; 1913(d)
. employees' annuities. .1232
. employees' trusts. .1838; 3024
. employees' welfare plan. .1838
. Fed. U.I., deductibility. .1913(b)
. information required. .3521
. partnerships, recaptured farm property. .2925(a)

6012—Index CONTRIBUTIONS—CORPORATIONS

———————— References are to PARAGRAPH (¶) NUMBERS ————————

Contributions (continued)
. payment by bank credit card, when deductible . .1941(c)
. payment by check, when deductible. .1941(c)
. pension plans. .1232; 1838
. political. .1103(a); 1811; 2416; 4002
. . bad debts from. .2301
. profit-sharing plans. .1838
. retirement annuities. .1838(g)
. rollover to individual retirement arrangements . .1838(l)
. state unemployment insurance deductibility . .1913(c)
. stock bonus plans. .1838
Controlled corporation: *See* Corporations, controlled
Controlled group:
. additional first-year depreciation. .2016(c)
. defined. .3223
. split-up of. .3224
. surtax exemption. .3223
Convention expenses attending. .1829; 1832
. employees. .1805
Conversions, involuntary: *See* Involuntary conversion
Cooperative banks:
. dividends:
. . exclusion. .1706
. . information returns. .3533
. taxability. .3433(b)
Cooperatives:
. apartments and housing:
. . depreciation of. .2002
. . interest. .1902
. . . partnerships. .2913
. . sale or exchange of. .1416(d); 1417
. . taxes. .1919
. . . partnership. .2913
. consumers, information returns. .3533(b)
. earnings of. .3455
. farmers' associations. .3455
. . old age benefit tax. .3814
. . patronage dividends. .3456-3458; 3533(b)
. service organizations. .3436
Copyrights:
. Capital asset status. .1601(f)
. depreciation. .2001(a); 2032
. gain or loss from sale. .1523
. research and experimental expenditures. .1523
. royalties as personal holding company income . .3401
Corn futures, short sales. .1608(c)
CORPORATIONS. .3100-3460
. accounting period change. .2715; 2716
. accumulated earnings tax. .3131; 3133
. acquisition or disposition of own stock. .3124
. advances by stockholders to. .2212; 2309
. advantages. .3152-3154
. affiliated: *See* Affiliated corporations
. allocation of income, deductions, credits and allowances. .3225
. alternative tax. .3202
. as a partner. .2900
. assessments against shareholders. .3106
. associations taxable as. .3026; 3101
. bond premium on repurchase. .3125(b)
. business trusts as. .3026
. capital gains and losses: *See* Capital gains and losses
. changing corporate structure, fees. .1823
. charitable contributions. .3118
. close: *See* Corporations, controlled

CORPORATIONS (continued)
. collapsible. .1627
. compensation: *See* Compensation
. consolidated returns: *See* Affiliated corporations
. constructive ownership of stock. .1727
. controlled:
. . additional first-year depreciation. .2016(c)
. . affiliated. .3222
. . defined. .1720
. . depreciable property sold to. .1625
. . distributions, effect on earnings and profits . .3129(f)
. . foreign, information required. .3540(b)
. . foreign personal holding companies. .3412
. . liquidation of subsidiary, carryovers. .3336; 3337
. . loss on sale to. .2223(b)
. . nontaxable exchanges. .1405; 1409; 1517(f); 1518; 3306; 3318 et seq.
. . . information required. .3521
. . personal holding companies. .3402
. . reorganization distributions. .3316 et seq.
. . sale of stock to as redemption. .1720
. . securities distributed in reorganization. .3316 et seq.
. . split-up to avoid tax. .3224
. . stock distributed in reorganizations. .3316 et seq.
. . surtax exemption. .3223
. . unrelated business income. .3448(d)
. . wash sales. .2221
. dealing in own stock. .3124
. deductions. .3112
. . special. .3113
. deductions for adjusted gross income. .1801; 3112
. defined. .3101
. directors: *See* Directors
. discharge of indebtedness. .1318; 3125
. dissolving:
. . expenses. .1808
. . returns. .3512; 3517(b)
. distributions: *See* Dividends
. dividends: *See* Dividends
. domestic, defined. .3105
. election not to be taxed. .3140-3146
. . advantages. .3154
. estimated tax. .3523(a)
. exempt: *See* Exempt organizations
. farm, accounting methods. .2701(d)
. farming syndicate expenses. .2745
. foreign: *See* Foreign Corporations
. foreign personal holding companies: *See* Foreign personal holding companies
. foreign tax credit. .3701-3706
. forgiveness of debt by stockholders. .1318(d)
. forgiveness of stockholder's debt. .1318(e)
. gain or loss, property distribution to shareholders . .3127
. identification numbers. .3500
. income. .3105
. information returns. .3521; 3533
. insolvent, reorganizations. .3331
. interest paid for. .1902
. investment counseling fees. .1823
. investment credit. .2410(f)
. investment trusts: *See* regulated investment companies
. joint stock companies as. .3101
. liability for taxes. .1028(b)
. limited partnerships as. .3101
. liquidation or termination. .3128; 3334
. . expenses. .1808
. . information returns. .3536
. . one month. .3335

CORPORATIONS—CREDITS

References are to PARAGRAPH (¶) NUMBERS

CORPORATIONS (continued)
. liquidation or termination (continued)
. . preferred stock bail-out. .1722
. . returns. .3512; 3517(b)
. . tax-free. .3335
. . twelve month. .3128
. loans to stockholders. .1703
. minimum tax on tax preferences. .2403; 3103; 3201(b)
. net operating loss. .3215-3221
. net capital gain. . 3202
. newly organized; income tax returns. .3514
. normal tax. .3102
. officers:
. . compensation. .1816-1817
. . . gift distinguished. .1302
. . entertainment expenses. .1830
. . honorarium. .1302(b)
. . income taxes of, paid by corporation. .1302(a)
. . life insurance premiums. .1307(a); 1828(a)
. . loans by. .2307
. . old-age benefit tax. .3817(c)
. . reasonableness of compensation. .1816
. . stock transferred to. .1302(a)
. . withholding tax. .2502; 2512
. organization expenses. .3116
. . information required. .3521
. overpayments, refunds. .3621
. partnership tax treatment. .3140-3146
. . advantages. .3154
. . self-employment tax on shareholders. .3823(d)
. patronage dividends, info. returns. .3533(b)
. payment of tax. .3523(a)
. personal holding companies: *See* Personal holding companies
. preferred stock bail-out. .1722
. purchase and sale of own stock. .3124
. rate. .3102
. . changed during year. .3546
. . tables. .5507
. . . reconciliation of taxable income. .3110
. regulated investment companies: *See* Regulated investment companies
. related: *See* Corporations, controlled
. rents paid to stockholders. .3108
. reorganizations: *See* Reorganizations
. returns. .3512-3515
. . consolidated or separate. .3222
. . dissolving, annualizing income. .2717
. . extension of time for filing. .3518
. . information. .3533
. . new corp., annualizing income. .2717
. . place of filing. .3519
. . . refunds. .3621
. sale and purchase of own bonds. .3125
. sale and purchase of own stock. .3124
. sales between stockholders and. .2223(b)
. sales, international: *See* Domestic International Sales Corporations
. Secs. 1245 and 1250 property, disposition. .3127; 3201; 3204
. sinking fund. .3109
. small business: *See* Small business corporations
. special treatment. .3100
. spin-off: *See* Spin-off reorganizations
. split-off: • *See* Split-off reorganizations
. split-up: *See* Split-up reorganizations
. stock ownership rule. .1727; 2223(d)
. stockholders, loans by. .2307
. successor, carryovers. .3336; 3337
. surtax. .3102
. . mergers. .3223
. . rate tables. .5507

CORPORATIONS (continued)
. tax preferences, minimum tax. .2403; 3103; 3201(b)
. tax savings. .3152-3154
. taxability. .3100
. taxes paid for. .1919
. underpayment of estimated tax, penalty. .3619
. undistributed taxable income. .3142(b)
. unreasonably accumulating surplus. .3131(b)
. worthless stocks and bonds. .3203
Corpus of estate or trust:
. capital gains and losses. .3009
. defined. .3002
. distribution. .3005(b)
. marital deduction. .3929(b)
Cost:
. allocation of, depreciable and nondepreciable property. .2003(d)
. basis of property. .1501
. defined. .1501
. inventories at. .2604(a)
Cost depletion. .2102; 2103
. aggregation:
. . nonoperating interests. .2109
. . operating interests:
. . . minerals other than oil or gas. .2108
. . . oil or gas. .2107
. single interest as more than one property. .2108(b)
Cost of goods sold. .1915; 2601
. adjustment for donated products. .1810; 2601
Cost-of-living allowances. .3726
Cotton futures, short sales. .1608(c)
Counseling fees, withholding tax. .2503(a)
Counterclaims for taxes. .3615(d)
Coupons:
. interest. .2703
. trading. .2747
Court fees, deductibility. .1806
Court martial, legal expenses of. .1823
Courtesy discounts. .1310
Courts:
. collection of taxes. .3610-3613; 3615
. decisions, weight given to. .1016
. recovery of taxes. .3629
. review of decisions by Supreme Court. .3629(d)
. review of TC decisions. .3649
. social security taxes. .3846
. Tax Court: *See* Tax Court
Cousins as dependents. .1106(b)
Covenant not to compete:
. capital asset status. .1601(k)
. payments for. .1301
Credit insurance, premiums. .1828(b)
Credit unions, returns for. . *See* Exempt organizations
Credits:
. allocation, controlled taxpayers. .3225
. annualizing income. .2717
. beneficiary. .3019
. . excess distributions thrown back. .3023(f)
. child care expenses. .2415
. contributions, political. .2416
. counterclaim by government. .3615(d)
. decedent. .3008(b)
. earned income. .2405
. elderly. .2406
. employee stock ownership plan (ESOP). .2410(h)
. estates and trusts. .3019
. . excess distribution throwback. .3023(f)
. estimated tax overpaid. .2517(a)
. federal welfare recipients, employment of. .2411(f)
. foreign corporations. .3710
. foreign taxes: *See* Foreign taxes

6014—Index   **CREDITS—DEDUCTIONS**   1978

———————— References are to PARAGRAPH (¶) NUMBERS ————————

Credits (continued)
. fractional year returns. .2717
. gas tax. .2417; 3521
. gift tax against estate tax. .3935
. handicapped. .2415
. interest on federal obligations: *See* Federal obligations, interest
. investment. .2410: *See also* Investment credit
. jobs. .2412
. lubricating oil. .2417
. nonresident aliens. .3709
. overpayments. .3628
. partnerships. .2913; 2917
. personal exemptions. .1111(e)
. residence, purchase of. .1416(d)
. social security tax overpaid. .2511(a)
. state inheritance or estate tax against federal estate tax. .3936
. unemployment insurance:
. . contributions to states. .3839; 3841
. . merit rating. .3841
. unified credit, estate and gift tax. .3940
. withheld taxes. .2535(b); 3622
. withheld taxes on wages. .2511
. work incentive program expenses. .2411
Criminal action, expense defending. .1823
Criminal penalties. .3620
Crop basis of accounting. .2614(a)
Crop insurance proceeds. .2614(a)
Crop shares. .2614(b)
Curtesy interest, estate tax. .3906; 3926
Custodian fees. .1806(b)
Customs duties, deductibility. .1911(b); 1916

— D —

Daily payroll period, computation of withholding . .2504
Damages:
. antitrust recoveries. .1226
. contract recoveries. .1226
. deductibility. .2202(b); 2204
. disability. .1226
. loss of profit. .1226
. patent infringement recoveries. .1226
. punitive. .1226
. taxability. .1226; 1301
. time to deduct. .2204(e); 2735(c)
. withholding tax. .2503(a)
Date basis: *See* Capital gains and losses, period assets held
Daughter as dependent. .1117
Dealers in personal property, installment sales . .2801-2804
Dealers in securities:
. amortization of bond premium. .1846
. capital assets. .1628
. capital gains and losses. .1628
. commissions. .1818
. defined. .2221(c)
. inventories. .2609(a)
. . information required. .3521
. security, defined. .1628
. self-employment tax. .3824
. short sales. .1608(a)
. wash sales. .2221(c)
Dealers' reserves. .2727
Death: *See also* Decedents
. compensation paid after employee's. .1304; 1822(a)
. . withholding tax. .2503(a)
. employee's stock option. .1327(d)

Death (continued)
. joint returns. .3505; 3517(a)
. . signatures. .3507(b)
. partner. .2941; 2942
. property transmitted at:
. . basis. .1507-1510
. . capital gain or loss. .1606(b)
. . period held. .1606(b)
. spouse's:
. . declaration of estimated tax. .2516(a)
. . exemptions. .1112(c); 1117
. . withholding. .1112(c); 2506
. transfers within 3 years of:
. . estate tax. .3909
. . gift tax. .4006
Death benefits. .1304
. armed forces. .1218(c)
. unemployment insurance tax. .3837
Debt: *See* Indebtedness; Bad debts
Debt-financed: *See also* Unrelated business
. income. .3449
. property. .3449(b)
Decedents:
. carryover basis property, valuation. .1507
. community property, period held. .1606
. compensation. .1304; 1822(a); 3008(b)
. . withholding tax. .2503(a)
. constructive receipt of income. .3008(b)
. credits. .3008(b)
. declaration of estimated tax. .2516(a)
. deductions. .3008(b); 3011; 3016
. estate. . *See* Estates and trusts
. executors and administrators discharge from personal liability. .3001(b)
. exemption deduction. .1112(c); 3010; 3012
. generation-skipping transfers. .1507(d); 3916; 4004
. income in respect of. .3008(b)
. installment obligations owned by. .2831(a)
. joint return. .3505-3507
. medical expenses. .1945(b)
. . information required. .3521
. property acquired from, basis. .1507-1510; 2003
. rates. .3020
. refund claims. .3626
. returns for. .2717; 3008(b); 3020; 3505-3507; 3517(a); 5504
. . as refund claim. .3626
. withholding tax. .2503(a)
Declaration of estimated tax: *See* Estimated tax
Declaratory judgments. .3536(d), (e), (f)
Declining balance depreciation. .2012; 2014
. change of method. .2010
. Class Life ADR system. .2010; 2012; 2033
. limited. .2012(b)
. useful life, change in. .2012

DEDUCTIONS. .1800-2317: *See also* particular items
. adjusted gross income purposes: *See* Deductions for adjusted gross income
. allocation, controlled taxpayers. .3225
. bad debts. .2300-2317
. China Trade Act Corporations. .3117(b)
. classification of deductible items. .1801
. compensation. .1815-1823
. contributions: *See* Contributions
. corporations. .3112; 3113
. . dividends received. .3114
. decedent. .3008(b)
. depletion. .2100-2113
. depreciation. .2000-2038; 2111
. disallowed. .1802

DEDUCTIONS—DEPENDENTS

References are to PARAGRAPH (¶) NUMBERS

DEDUCTIONS (continued)
. dividends:
. . paid:
. . . personal holding companies. .3404
. . . regulated investment companies. .3431
. . . to U.S.. .3433
. . received:
. . . corporations. .3114
. . . regulated investment companies. .3431
. estate tax purposes. .3926-3928
. estates and trusts. .3011
. . allocation. .3007(c)
. . distributions. .3017
. . exemptions. .1111 et seq.:   See also Exemptions
. . blind individuals. .1114
. . decedents. .3012
. . dependents. .1111; 1115-1120
. . estates and trusts. .3012
. . individuals. .1111 et seq.
. . net operating loss. .2242(a)
. . . carryover. .2243
. . old-age exemptions. .1113
. . partnerships. .2906(b)
. expenses. .1800-1846
. farmers. .1844; 1845
. . cooperative associations of. .3457
. farming syndicate expenses. .2745
. foreign corporations. .3710(a)
. foreign personal holding companies. .3413
. foreign taxes. .3701
. . refunded. .3705
. gambling losses. .1321
. gift tax purposes. .4020-4023
. individual retirement arrangements. .1838(l); 3024; 3027
. interest. .1900-1905
. joint and survivor annuities. .3008(b)
. losses. .2200-2244
. medical expenses. .1945-1947
. net operating loss. .2241-2244; 3215-3221
. nonresident aliens. .3709
. nonresident citizens. .3725
. obsolescence. .2034; 2210
. partnerships. .2906; 2913; 2915
. . distributive shares of partners. .2913
. personal holding companies. .3404
. political contributions. .2416
. public utility, for certain dividends paid. .3115
. recovered, tax benefit rule. .2316(d)
. repaid income. .2729
. restricted property. .1819(c)
. segregation of on return. .2601(a)
. standard: See Zero bracket amount
. taxes. .1910-1920
. tax shelter activities, limit on deductions. .2736
. time to report. .2735-2746
. unharvested crop sold with land. .1622
. unrelated business income. .3448(c)
. Western Hemisphere Trade Corporations. .3117(a)
. withheld taxes. .2501
. zero bracket amount. .1107—1109
Deductions for adjusted gross income. .1102(c); 1801
. advertising expenses. .1827
. alimony. .1320; 1801(a)
. allocation of expenses. .1805(c)
. amortizable bond premium. .1846
. bad debts. .2305; 2307
. beneficiaries of trusts. .2002(c); 2101(c); 3014
. board and lodging. .1805
. business expenses. .1804; 1805
. capital losses. .1611; 1613

Deductions for adjusted gross income (continued)
. casualty losses. .2204(g)
. contributions. .1801
. corporations. .1801
. demolition of buildings. .2209
. depletion. .2100 et seq.
. depreciation. .2000 et seq.
. employees' deductions. .1805
. entertainment expenses. .1830
. estates and trusts. .1801
. farm expenses. .1844
. information required, employees. .1805(c)
. insurance premiums. .1828(c)
. interest. .1900
. investors' expenses. .1806(b)
. life tenants. .2002(c); 2101(c); 3014
. long-term capital gain deduction. .1611; 1612
. long-term capital gains. .1612
. losses. .1613; 1620; 1806; 2200; 2307; 2312
. mine expenditures. .1843
. moving expenses. .1831
. nonbusiness bad debts. .2307
. nonbusiness expenses. .1806
. outside salesperson's expenses. .1805(a)
. professional expenses. .1832
. professional fees. .1823
. rentals. .1826
. rents, attributable to. .1806(a)
. reporting, employees. .1805(c)
. royalties, attributable to. .1806(a)
. segregation of items on returns. .2601(c)
. taxes. .1910
. theft or embezzlement. .2205
. trade and business deductions. .1801
. transportation expenses. .1805; 1829
. traveling expenses. .1805; 1829
. trust property. .1801(a); 3014
. worthless securities. .2312
Deferred payment sales: See Installment and deferred payment sales
Deficiency dividends, personal holding companies . .3406; 3407
. successor in reorganization. .3337
Deficiency in tax. .3604; 3605; 3622
. dividends, personal holding companies. .3406; 3407
. estate tax. .3945
. expense of contesting. .1806; 1823; 3016
. extension of time for payment. .3526
. gift tax. .4032
. interest on. .3618
. investment credit. .3611(f)
. litigation expenses. .1823
. net operating loss. .3611(f)
. ninety-day letter. .3605
. notice. .3605
. penalty for failure to pay. .3618(c)
. thirty-day letter. .3604
. work incentive program credit. .3611(f)
Delay rentals. .2101(b)
. capitalization. .1528
Demolition of buildings. .2209
Dentists:
. depreciation. .2001(a)
. expenses of. .1832
. fees of. .1945 et seq.
. withholding tax. .2502
Department stores, inventories. .2606(b)
Dependents: See also Exemptions
. adopted children. .1117(a)
. alimony for support of. .1320
. blind, exemption. .1114
. born during year. .1115

Dependents (continued)
. care of, expenses for. .1946; 2415
. death during year. .1115
. defined. .1115-1120
. employer payments to. .1822(b)
. exemptions. .1103; 1111; 1115-1120
. foster children. .1117(a); 1118(a)
. gross income affecting exemption. .1118
. . rental income received. .1118
. income, support test. .1116(a)
. in-laws, death or divorce of spouse. .1117
. medical expenses. .1945
. member of household. .1106(b); 1117
. monthly family allowances to, armed forces. .1306
. multiple support agreements. .1116(c)
. old-age exemption. .1113
. relationship of. .1117
. returns. .1118(b); 1119
. state aid received. .1118
. stepchildren. .1118(a)
DEPLETION. .2100-2113
. adjusting basis due to. .2102
. aggregation:
. . nonoperating interests. .2109
. . operating interests:
. . . minerals other than oil or gas. .2108
. . . oil and gas. .2107
. as tax preference item. .2102(b); 2403
. basis for. .2102; 2103
. bonus payments. .2104; 2105
. business interruption insurance proceeds. .2104(b)
. capital additions. .2103(c)
. computation methods. .2102
. cost method. .2102; 2103
. deductibility. .2100-2113
. delay rentals. .2101(b)
. development expenses. .2103(c)
. estates and trusts. .3014
. estimates of recoverable units. .2103(d)
. exploration and development expenditures, mines . .1843
. information required. .3521
. intangible drilling expenses. .2103(c)
. . recapture of. .2103(c)
. mineral production payments. .2101(e)
. mines. .2102-2109
. minimum tax. .2102(b); 2403
. oil and gas properties. .2102; 2103(c); 2104
. partnerships, undivided interests. .2910
. percentage. .2102; 2104
. . distribution from reserve. .2113
. . retailers, refiners. .2104(a)
. . successor in reorganization. .3337
. property defined. .2100; 2106
. records. .2112
. reserves, distributions from. .2113
. revaluation. .2103(b)
. royalties. .2101(b); 2104
. shut-in royalties. .2101(b)
. single interest as more than one property. .2108(b)
. small producer's exemption. .2104(a)
. stripping contractor. .2101
. submerged coastal lands. .2101
. timber, deductibility. .2110; 2112
. trust property. .3014
. who may deduct. .2101
Deposits, bank: *See* Banks, deposits
DEPRECIATION. .2000-2038. *See also* particular item
. ADR system. .2033
. abnormal. .2032
. accelerated, as tax preference item. .1619; 2403(a)

DEPRECIATION (continued)
. additional first-year allowance. .2016; 2033
. adjusted rate. .2011
. adjusting basis. .1500(b); 2004
. agreements. .2010(c)
. allocation cost of land and building. .2003(d)
. allowed or allowable. .2004
. averaging conventions. .2022(b)
. basis for. .2003
. book entries. .2023
. building and loan associations. .3433(b)
. buyer and seller. .2002(a)
. change in method. .2010; 2017(d)
. classified accounts. .2022(b)
. . assets retired. .2036
. Class Life Asset Depreciation Range system. .2033
. component method. .2017
. composite accounts. .2022(b)
. . assets retired. .2036
. computation, methods. .2011-2015
. cooperative apt's and housing. .2002
. cooperative banks. .3433(b)
. declining balance method. .2012; 2014; 2033
. . limited. .2012(b)
. deductions. .2000-2038; 2111
. defined. .2000
. earnings and profits, effect on. .2024
. election:
. . additional first-year allowance. .2016; 2033
. . method. .2010
. . tax benefit. .2004
. estates and trusts. .3014
. excessive. .2004
. exempt organization's status changed. .2003
. failure to take. .2004
. farmers. .2001(a)
. first-year allowance. .2016; 2033
. group accounts. .2022(b)
. . assets retired. .2036
. historic property. .2017(b)
. improvements by lessee. .2002
. income forecast method. .2015(c)
. information required. .2023; 3521
. intangible property. .2001(a)
. inventories. .2001(a)
. item accounts. .2022(a)
. . assets retired. .2036
. leased property. .2002
. leaseholds. .1840
. liberalized methods. .2012-2015
. life estate. .2002
. low income housing. .2018
. methods. .2010-2015
. mines, as expenditure. .1843
. multiple asset accounts. .2022
. . assets retired. .2036
. mutual savings banks. .3433(b)
. operating day method. .2015(b)
. partnership:
. . additional first-year. .2016
. . undivided interest. .2910
. pasture land. .2001
. personal holding companies. .3404
. player contracts. .1619(g)
. professional expenses. .1832
. property accounts. .2022
. property subject to. .2001
. . gift of. .1619(c)
. . liberalized methods. .2012(a)
. public utility property. .2019
. rate. .2032; 2033
. recapture of. .1619

DEPRECIATION—DIVIDENDS

References are to PARAGRAPH (¶) NUMBERS

DEPRECIATION (continued)
. records. .2023
. remaining life plan, sum of the years-digits . .2013(b)
. reorganizations. .3337
. replacement and repairs. .1825(a); 2021; 2033(f)
. reserves. .2021
. . Class Life ADR system. .2033(b)
. . defined. .2033(b); 2113
. . distributions from. .2113
. retirement of assets. .2035-2037
. sale of property. .2001(b)
. salvage proceeds, assets retired. .2036(c)
. salvage value. .2000; 2005; 2033(e)
. schedules. .2023
. stepped-up use of property. .2032
. straight line method. .2011; 2014
. successor corporations. .3337
. sum of years-digits method. .2013; 2014; 2033
. trust property. .3014
. unharvested crop sold with land. .1622
. unit-of-production method. .2015(a)
. useful life. .2032; 2033
. vintage accounts. .2033(b); 2038
. when to deduct. .2001(b)
. who may deduct. .2002
Descendant:
. dependent. .1117
. member of household. .1106(b)
Designs, capital asset status. .1601(f)
Determination letter. .1015(c)
Development expenses:
. capitalization. .1528
. farmers. .1844(a)
. information required. .3521
. mines. .1843(b); 2103(c)
. . successor in reorganization. .3337
Devise: *See* Inheritance
Diesel fuel tax. .5515
Directors:
. damages paid by. .2202(b)
. fees. .1301
. . self-employment income. .3823(e)
. legal expenses. .1823
. liability for accumulated earnings tax. .3130
. old-age benefit tax. .3817(c)
. self-employment tax. .3823(e)
. withholding tax. .2502
Disability:
. benefits:
. . armed forces. .1218(c)
. . deductibility. .1819
. . disability plans. .1219(c)
. . . withholding tax. .2504(g)
. . state law. .1218
. child care expenses. .2415
. compensation during. .1218; 1221
. . armed forces. .1218(c)
. . information required. .2508
. . veterans. .1218(c)
. . withholding tax. .2504(g)
. contributions to state fund, deductibility. .1913(d)
. damages received for. .1226
. . employment connected. .1218; 1219
. medical expenses. .1945-1947
. nonoccupational. .1218; 1219
. nonresident citizens. .3725
. occupational. .1218
. overhead expenses during, insurance for. .1828(b)
. return by agent. .3510
. wage plans. .1219(c)
Disaster losses. .2204(e)

Disbarment, expense defending suit. .1823
Disclaimers, qualified. .3908; 4004(b)
Discount:
. bonds. .3125
. . capital gains and losses. .1629
. cost of goods sold. .2604(a)
. employee, purchase by. .1310
. gross income from property, percentage depletion . .2104
. income. .1309; 2722(b)
. interest deduction. .1903; 2739
. inventories, use in. .2604(a)
. loans purchased at. .2722(b)
. mortgage purchased at. .2722(b)
. municipal bonds, market discount. .1204
. original issue discount, savings certificates. .2722(f)
. reserve for. .2744
. short-term obligations. .2723(c)
. U. S. savings bonds. .2723(a)(b)
Dismissal pay:
. deductibility. .1819; 1838(b)
. old-age benefit tax. .3819(e)
. unemployment insurance tax. .3837
. withholding tax. .2503(a)
Disputed income, time to report. .2728
Dissolution, distributions in, gain or loss. .3128
Distraint for taxes. .3615(a)
Distributions: *See also* Dividends
. accumulation, complex trusts. .3023
. charitable estates and trusts. .3007(c)
. complex trusts: *See* Complex trusts, distributions
. computations, estates and trusts. .3021
. cooperatives. .3456
. corpus of estate or trust. .3005(b)
. depletion of depreciation reserves. .2113
. employees' trust. .3024(d)
. . withholding tax. .2503(a)
. estates and trusts. .3006; 3017
. income of estate or trust. .3004-3007
. liquidating: *See* Dividends, liquidating
. partnership. .2908; 2909; 2918; 2927-2932; 2937-2942
. . family. .2905
. property. .1702(a)
. reorganizations, securities in. .3316 et seq.
. schedule, partnerships. .2918
. securities, reorganizations. .3316 et seq.
. simple trusts. .3005
. . deduction for. .3017(a)
. source of. .1701
. tax-free. .1702(e)
Distributor's agreement, capital assets status . .1601(i)
District Conference. .3603
DIVIDENDS. .1700-1727
. annuity policies. .1230(f)
. assigned. .2704
. banks. .1704(a); 3433
. . exclusion. .1706(a)
. bond rights. .1714
. borrowed stock. .1706(b)
. building and loan associations. .3433(b)
. . exclusion. .1706(a)
. capital gain dividends of regulated investment companies. .3431
. carryover:
. . information required. .3521
. . personal holding companies. .3404
. China Trade Act corporations, exclusion. .1706(a)
. compensation distinguished. .1817
. consent:

6018—Index DIVIDENDS—DIVORCE 1978

References are to PARAGRAPH (¶) NUMBERS

DIVIDENDS (continued)
. consent (continued)
. . accumulated earnings tax. .1702(d)
. . information required. .3521
. . personal holding companies. .1702(d); 3404
. constructive. .1703
. . omitted from return, limitation on assessment and collection. .3611
. constructive receipt. .2721
. cooperative banks. .1706(a)
. corp. electing partnership treatment. .3142
. . credit for the elderly. .2406
. declaration. .1703
. deficiency, personal holding companies. .3406; 3407
. . successor in reorganizations. .3337
. defined. .1700
. depletion reserves. .2113
. depreciation reserves. .2113
. disguised. .1703; 1817
. disporportionate distributions. .1318(e); 1703
. earnings available for. .1701(b)
. effect on earnings and profits. .3129
. elderly income credit. .2406
. election as to medium of payment. .1707; 1709
. endowment policies. .1216
. excessive compensation. .1817
. excessive rents and royalties. .1703
. exclusion. .1705
. exempt. .1216; 1704
. exempt organizations. .1706(a)
. farmers' coop., paid by. .3457
. . exclusion. .1706(a)
. federal land banks. .1704(a)
. federal savings and loan assn.. .1704(a); 1706(a)
. . exclusion. .1706(a)
. foreign sources:
. . corporation:
. . . deduction. .3114(c), (e)
. . . foreign tax credit for. .3706
. . individuals. .1706(a)
. forgiveness of debt. .1318(e)
. information returns. .3533
. insurance companies. .1704
. interest distinguished. .1901
. joint ownership. .1705(b)
. life insurance:
. . policies. .1216; 1704
. . premiums. .1704
. life insurance proceeds as. .1213(d); 1703
. liquidating. .1715-1717; 3128
. . defined. .1715
. . exclusion. .1706(a)
. . information returns. .3536
. . loss deductible when. .1717(b)
. . personal holding companies. .3404
. loans distinguished. .1703
. mutual life insurance companies. .1704
. mutual savings bank. .1706(a)
. National farm loan association. .1704(a)
. nontaxable. .1708; 3404
. . exclusion. .1706(a)
. . preferred stock bail-out. .1722
. paid deduction:
. . accumulated earnings tax. .3132(b)
. . banks and trust companies. .3433
. . personal holding companies. .3404
. . . successor in reorganization. .3337
. . public utilities. .3115
. . regulated investment companies. .3431
. paid for another. .1316
. paid to U.S. or instrumentalities. .3433
. patronage. .3457-3458

DIVIDENDS (continued)
. patronage (continued)
. . exclusion. .1706(a)
. personal holding company income. .3401
. preference. .1707
. preferred stock bail-out. .1722
. profits available for. .1701(c)
. property. .1702(b)
. . corporation, gain or loss. .3127
. . information required. .1717(b)
. . received, corp. deduction for. .3107
. . sold at less than market. .1329; 3126
. proportionate to stockholdings. .1703
. real estate investment trusts. .1706(a)
. received:
. . deductions for:
. . . building and loan associations. .3433(b)
. . . cooperative banks. .3433(b)
. . . corporations. .3107; 3114
. . . . foreign. .3114(c), (e)
. . . mutual savings banks. .3433(b)
. . . public utilities. .3114(d)
. . . regulated invest. companies. .3431
. . . small business invest. companies. .3459
. . exclusion. .1705
. . . beneficiaries. .3011(c)
. . . estates and trusts. .3011(c)
. . foreign sources, corporation foreign tax credit. .3706
. . net operating loss, corporations. .3217
. . nonresident aliens. .3711
. . . withholding tax. .2535
. . partnerships. .2906(b); 2916
. . personal holding companies. .3404
. . public utilities. .3114
. regulated investment companies. .1706(a); 3429; 3431
. rent paid stockholders. .1703
. rent paid to lessor corporation's stockholders. .3108
. reorganizations. .3312
. reporting of, when earnings unknown. .1701(d)
. right to receive, sale of. .1601(k)
. royalties as. .1703
. savings and loan associations. .3433(b)
. . exclusion. .1706(a)
. self-employment income. .3824
. small business corp. shareholders. .1706(a)
. source. .1701
. state tax, deductibility. .1918
. stock. .1707-1709
. . assigned. .2704
. . cost of paying. .1808
. . nontaxable. .1708
. optional. .1707(b)
. . preference. .1707(c)
. . . preferred stock bail-out. .1722
. . redemption. .1718-1720
. . . exclusion. .1706(a)
. . taxable. .1709
. stock of another corporation. .1702(b)
. stock rights. .1707; 1710-1713
. taxability. .1702(a); 1708
. . exclusion. .1705
. . small business corp.. .3142
. tenant paying. .1316
. time to report. .2721
. withdrawals by stockholders. .1703
Divisive reorganizations. .3316 et seq.
. basis of property received. .3320
. carryovers. .3336
Divorce:
. alimony payments. .1320

Divorce (continued)
. credit for elderly. .2406
. declaration of estimated tax, effect on. .2516(a)
. exemptions. .1112; 1116; 1117(a)
. expense of suit. .1823
. gift tax on transfers. .4007
. joint return. .3505
. legal fees. .1806
. life ins. premium paid by husband. .1320
. medical expenses paid by husband. .1320(f)
. property acquired in, basis. .1505
. residence expenses paid by husband. .1320(e)
. retirement income credit. .2406
. standard deduction: *See* Zero bracket amount
. status of individuals. .1108; 1112
. support for child. .1116(a)
. withholding, effect on. .2505; 2506

Doctor:
. depreciation. .1832; 2001(a)
. expenses of. .1832
. fees:
. . deductibility. .1823; 1945-1947
. . information returns. .3531
. interns, hospital, stipends received. .1303
. malpractice suit, expense defending. .1823
. plant, old-age benefit tax. .3817(b)
. self-employment tax. .3822
. stipends received while training. .1303
. withholding tax. .2502

Dollar-value costing. .2606(b)

Domestic International Sales Corporations .3460
. election by shareholders. .3521
. returns. .3517(e)

Domestics:
. board and lodging. .1308
. care of dependents. .2415
. compensation paid to. .1815
. old-age tax. .3806; 3816
. pensions. .1822(a)
. professional expense. .1832
. withholding tax on wages. .2503(b)

Donations: *See* Contributions; Gifts

Dower interests:
. estate tax. .3906; 3926
. release of:
. . estate tax. .3926
. . gift tax. .4007

Drilling costs. .2103(e)
. partnerships. .2913

Drought losses. .2204(b)

Drugs, expense of. .1945; 1946

Due date:
. calendar. .5501
. payment of tax. .3522-3527
. returns. .3517

Dues:
. deductibility. .1807; 1808; 1832; 1941
. prepaid, taxability. .2726(b)

Duties, deductibility. .1911(b); 1916

— E —

Earned income:
. credit on. .2405
. elderly income credit. .2406
. maximum tax on: *See* Personal service income
. nonresident citizens. .3725
. . information required. .3521
. . net earnings from self-employment. .3823(c)
. tax preferences, effect on. .2403(d)

Earnings and profits. .1700; 1701
. after reorganization. .1701(b)
. available for dividends. .1701(b), (c)
. depreciation, effect of. .2024
. distributions, effect on. .3129
. reorganizations. .3337
. small business corp.. .3142(c)(d); 3145
. successor corporation. .3337

Easements. .1401(a)

Educational expenses. .1833

Educational loans, interest. .1904

Educational organizations: *See* Exempt organizations

Effectively connected income. .3711

Elderly, credit for. .2406

Election:
. accounting methods. .2701
. accounting periods. .2715; 2716
. aggregating interests for depletion:
. . nonoperating interests. .2109
. . operating interests:
. . . minerals other than oil or gas. .2108
. . . oil or gas. .2107
. amortization:
. . bond premium. .1846
. bad debt deduction method. .2311(c)
. basis, nontaxable stock rights, allocation. .1711
. capitalization:
. . circulation expenditures. .1528; 1808
. . development expenses. .1528
. . taxes and carrying charges. .1528; 3521
. Class Life ADR system. .2033(a), (d)
. commodity credit loans. .2722(d); 3521
. conservation expenditures. .1845
. consolidated returns. .3222
. corp. taxes as partnership. .3140-3146
. credits for:
. . political contributions. .2416
. . foreign taxes. .3701; 3703
. deduction for political contributions. .2416
. defer foreign income. .2730(a)
. depletion:
. . aggregation:
. . . nonoperating interests. .2109
. . . operating interests:
. . . . minerals other than oil or gas. .2108
. . . . oil or gas. .2107
. . methods. .2102
. depreciation:
. . additional first-year allowance. .2016
. . Class Life ADR system. .2033(a), (d)
. . methods. .2010
. . tax benefit. .2004
. development expenses. .1843; 2103(c)
. discharge of indebtedness. .1318(j)
. . corporations. .3125(f)
. dividends, medium of payment. .1707
. Domestic International Sales Corporations. .3460; 3521
. estates and trusts, sixty-five day rule. .3006(f)
. experimental expenditures. .1842
. exploration expenditures, deduction of, mines . .1843; 3521
. fertilizer and lime expenses. .1844
. 52-53 week year. .2714(b)
. husband and wife:
. . gifts to third party. .4009
. . joint or separate returns. .1112(c); 3505-3508
. income from fed. obligations issued at discount . .2723(a)(b)
. income from U.S. possession. .3727
. installment method. .2800

ELECTION—EMPLOYEES

Election (continued)
. installment method *(continued)*
. . revocation of. .3521
. insurance proceeds in installments. .1215(c)
. inventory method. .2604
. . full absorption method, manufacturers. .2609(c)
. involuntary conversion. .1411
. joint return:
. . after filing separate. .3506
. . death of spouse. .3517(a)
. lots sold on installment basis. .2841
. matured savings bonds. .2723(a)(b)
. mining exploration expenses. .1843(a)
. oil and gas properties, expenditures. .2103(c)
. old-age tax, exempt organizations. .3800; 3814
. organization expenditure deduction. .3116
. partial bad debt deduction. .2306
. partners and partnerships. .2906(c)
. . adjustment of basis. .2937-2942
. partnership tax treatment by corporation .3140-3146
. real property tax accrual. .2740(b)
. regulated investment company tax. .3428
. research expenditures. .1842
. returns, affiliated corporations. .3222
. shareholders taxed as partners. .3140-3146
. soil conservation expenditures. .1845
. standard deduction: *See* zero bracket amount
. timber cutting, as sale. .1621
. valuation for estate tax. .3919
. water conservation expenditures. .1845

Elevators:
. as medical expense. .1946
. depreciation recapture. .1619(a)
. investment credit. .2410(a)

Embezzlement:
. loss. .2205
. proceeds of, taxability. .1300(g)

Employees:
. annuities. .1232
. . contributions, taxability. .1232(b)
. . individual retirement arrangements. .1102(c); 1838(l); 3027
. . payments under:
. . . old-age benefit tax. .3819(c)
. . . taxability. .1232(c), (d)
. . special averaging rule. .3024(d)
. bargain purchases. .1310
. benefit plans, payments under, old-age benefit tax . .3819(c)
. bonuses: *See* Bonuses
. books and tuition. .1307(b)
. business expenses. .1805
. carrying tools, travel expense. .1829(b)
. Christmas gifts, bonuses. .1302(a); 1819
. Christmas parties for. .1830
. commuting expenses. .1805; 1829(b)
. compensation while at reserve training:
. . deductibility. .1819
. . withholding tax. .2503(a)
. constructive ownership of stock. .1328
. contributions:
. . disability benefit funds, deductibility. .1807; 1913(d)
. . employees' annuities. .1232
. . social security. .1913
. convention expenses. .1805
. death benefits. .1304
. . unemployment insurance tax. .3837
. deductions for adjusted gross income. .1805
. defined. .2502; 3817(a)

Employees (continued)
. defined *(continued)*
. . withholding tax. .2502
. directors as. .3817(c)
. discount on purchases. .1310
. exempt organizations, right to elect social security coverage. .3814
. expenses. .1805
. federal: *See* Federal employees and officers
. federal obligations purchased by. .3024(h)
. financial counseling fees paid by employer. .1301
. gift to. .1302(b); 1830
. identification number. .3500
. . application for. .3826(b)
. . failure to give. .2512(c); 3826(b)
. . returns. .3826(b)
. . withholding statements. .2508(a)
. income taxes paid by employer for. .1302
. individual retirement arrangements. .1838(1); 3027
. . withholding on. .2503(a)
. insurance payments, old-age tax. .3819(d)
. life insurance on, premiums. .1307(a); 1828(a)
. loans to corp.. .2307
. moving expenses:
. . deductibility. .1831
. . reimbursed. .1302(b)
. . . withholding tax. .2503(a)
. old-age benefit tax. .3800; 3817(a)
. options to buy stock. .1327; 1328; 2743(b)
. property purchased at less than market. .1310
. receipts:
. . old-age benefit tax. .3828(a)
. . withheld taxes: *See* Withholding, statements to employees
. reimbursed expenses. .1805(b)
. . withholding on. .2503(a)
. restricted stock plans. .1326
. retirement pay, old-age tax. .3819(d)
. rollover contributions, individual retirement arrangements. .1838(l)
. special refund old-age and survivor insurance . .2511(a)
. stock options. .1327; 1328
. . withholding tax on. .2503(a)
. . as tax preference income. .1327(c)
. stock ownership plan (ESOP), credit for. .2410(h)
. stock sold to. .1328
. tax on:
. . deductibility. .1913
. . old-age and survivor insurance. .3800
. termination payments. .1304
. tips:
. . reporting requirements. .2503(a)
. . withholding. .2503(a)
. transportation expenses. .1805; 1829(b)
. traveling expenses. .1829
. variable stock options. .1327(c)
. wage disability income. .1219
. withholding exemption certificates. .2506; 2512(b)
. withholding exemptions. .2505
. withholding tax on wages: *See* Withholding, wages

Employees' stock ownership plan (ESOP) .2410(h)

Employees' stock purchase plan. .1327(b)
. information returns. .3534

Employees' trusts. .3024
. annuities. .3024
. beneficiaries, taxability of proceeds. .3024
. contributions to. .1838; 3024
. . successor in reorganization. .3337
. . withholding tax. .2503(a)

Employees' trusts (continued)
. distributions. .3024(d)
. estate tax. .3915(b)
. federal obligations purchased by. .3024(h)
. gift tax. .4011
. information required. .3024(b); 3521; 3537
. payments under, old-age tax. .3819(c)
. prohibited transactions. .3436(d)
. terminated. .3024(e)
. unrelated business income tax. .3447
Employers:
. compensation paid employees attending reserve training:
. . deductibility. .1819
. . withholding tax. .2503(a)
. contributions:
. . disability benefit funds, deductibility. .1913(d)
. . employees' annuities. .1232
. . employees' trusts. .1838; 3024(c), (e)
. . . withholding tax. .2503(a)
. . federal unemployment insurance, deductibility .1913(b)
. . old-age tax, deductibility. .1913(a)
. . state unemployment insurance, deductibility .1913(c)
. death benefits to employees' beneficiaries. .1304
. federal welfare recipients, employment of. .2411(f)
. identification number. .3500
. . application for. .3826(a)
. . failure to give. .2512(c); 3826(c)
. . returns. .3826(a)
. . . withholding statements. .2508(a)
. insurance premiums on employee policies. .1307(a)
. liability insurance premiums. .1828(b)
. payment of tax withheld. .2509
. receipts for employees, old-age tax. .2508; 3828(a)
. records:
. . old-age benefit tax. .3828(a)
. unemployment insurance. .3843
. . withholding of taxes. .2507
. returns of tax withheld. .2509
. stock ownership plan (ESOP), credit for. .2410(h)
. tax on:
. . deductibility. .1913
. . old-age and survivor insurance. .3800
. . unemployment insurance. .3834
. . . credits against federal tax. .3839
. . termination of business, returns. .2508(a)
. withholding statements: *See* Withholding, statements to employees
. withholding tax on wages. .2501-2512
Employment:
. defined, old-age and survivor insurance. .3803
. expense of seeking or securing. .1805
. part-time, withholding tax on wages. .2504(l)
. temporary:
. . traveling expenses. .1805
. . withholding on wages. .2503(a)
Employment agency fee. .1805
. reimbursed, withholding on. .2503(a)
Employment contract:
. canceled, loss. .2202(a)
. capital asset. .1601(k)
. death benefit under. .1304
· Employment taxes:
. Federal Insurance Contributions Act: *See* Social security, old-age and survivor insurance
. Federal Unemployment Tax Act: *See* Social security, unemployment insurance
. pay-as-you-go tax: *See* Estimated tax; Withholding
. rate charts. .5512-5513

Employment taxes (continued)
. social securities taxes: *See* Social security
Endorsers, bad debt deduction. .2315(b)
. account receivables, sale of. .2311(d)
Endowment insurance:
. contracts. .1230(e)
. dividends on policies. .1216
. exchange of policies. .1407
. installment payments. .1215(b), (c)
. interest paid to buy. .1828(a); 1905
. lump-sum payments. .1215(a)
. proceeds. .1215
Entertainment expenses. .1805; 1830
Entertainment Facility:
. deductibility of cost. .1830
. losses on. .2202
Equipment:
. capital gains and losses. .1619(a)
. contributions of. .1942(c)
. investment credit. .2410(a)
. lessee replacing. .2002
ERISA. .1838(f); 3024
Escrow, payments or property in. .2725(c)
Estate planning, tax considerations in. .4701 et seq.
ESTATE TAX. .3900-3947
. adjusted gross estate. .3929(a)
. administration expenses. .3926
. alternate valuation. .3919
. annuities. .3915; 3919(d)
. appeals. .3945
. applicability. .3901
. bonds. .3919(b)
. business interests. .3919(c)
. carryover basis property, valuation. .1507; 3919
. casualty losses. .3926
. charitable bequests. .3927
. claims against estate. .3926
. community property. .3905; 3929(a)
. credits. .3935 et seq.
. deductibility. .1911(a)
. deductions. .3926-3928
. deficiencies. .3945
. defined. .3900
. discharge from personal liability. .3947
. disclaimed legacy to charity. .3927
. disclaimers affecting marital deduction. .3929
. disclaimers, qualified. .3908
. dower and curtesy. .3906; 3926
. employees' trusts. .3915(b)
. exemptions. .3928
. fire losses. .3926
. foreign, credit against federal estate tax. .3938
. funeral expenses. .3926
. gifts. .3909; 3935
. good will. .3919(c)
. gross estate. .3901-3915; *See also* specific item under Estate tax
. imposition. .3900
. installment payment. .3944
. interest on, deductibility. .3016
. joint estates. .3904
. life estates. .3919(d)
. . marital deduction. .3929
. life insurance. .3914
. . marital deduction. .3929(b)
. losses deductible. .3926
. marital deduction. .3929
. mortgages unpaid. .3926
. mutual fund shares. .3919(b)
. National Service Life Insurance. .3914
. nature of. .3900

ESTATE—ESTATES

References are to PARAGRAPH (¶) NUMBERS

ESTATE TAX (continued)
. orphan's exclusion. .3926
. payment. .3944
. penalty for failure to pay. .3944(b)
. power of appointment. .3907; 3908
. . marital deduction. .3929(b)
. procedure. .3943-3947
. profit-sharing plans. .3915
. property previously taxed. .3939
. Railroad Retirement Act annuities. .3915(b)
. rate tables. .3934
. . state tax credit. .3937
. realty. .3901; 3919(a)
. refunds. .3946
. remainders. .3919(d)
. return. .3943
. reversions. .3919(d)
. revocable transfers. .3911
. self-employed retirement plans. .3915
. securities. .3919(b)
. shipwreck losses. .3926
. situs of property. .3901
. specific exemption. .3928
. state, deductibility. .1912(a)
. stocks. .3919(b)
. storm losses. .3926
. taxes deductible. .3926
. tenancies by the entirety. .3904
. tenancy in common. .3904
. terminable interests, martial deduction. .3929(b)
. theft loss. .3926
. transfers:
. . by will and under intestate law. .3901
. . conditioned on survivorship. .3911
. . contemplation of death. .3909
. . inadequate consideration. .3913
. . property included in transferor's estate. .3939
. . reserving life estate. .3911
. . reserving right to use, enjoyment or income . .3910
. . reversions. .3911
. . subject to power to alter, amend, revoke or terminate. .3912
. unified credit. .3940
. valuation of property. .1507; 3919
. . interest passing to surviving spouse. .3929
. . transferred property. .3939
. value for as basis. .1507
ESTATES AND TRUSTS. .3000 et seq.
. accumulation distributions, complex trusts. .3023
. administration expenses. .1806; 3016
. . deduction from gross estate. .3926
. administrative powers. .3022(c)
. alimony and separate maintenance payments . .3022(e)
. annuity trust, gift tax. .4022
. assoc. distinguished from trust. .3026
. basis of property. .3010
. beneficial enjoyment. .3022(b)
. business expenses. .3016
. business income, exempt trusts. .3445; 3450
. . charitable contributions. .3452
. business trusts. .3026
. capital gains and losses. .3008; 3009
. casualty losses. .3016
. charitable nonexempt trusts. .3453
. common trust funds. .3025
. complex trusts: *See* Complex trusts
. contributions. .3013; 3538
. . adjustment. .3007(c)
. . exempt trusts. .3450
. corpus:

ESTATES AND TRUSTS (continued)
. corpus (continued)
. . capital gains and losses. .3009
. . defined. .3002
. . distributions. .3005(b)
. credits. .3019
. . foreign taxes. .3701; 3703
. . investment. .3019
. decedents: *See* Decedents
. declaration of estimated tax. .2516(c)
. deductions. .3008(b); 3011
. . allocation. .3007(c)
. . for adjusted gross income. .1801(a)
. depletion. .3014
. depreciation. .3014
. determination letter. .3024(b)
. discretionary trusts. .4008
. distributable net income. .3003-3007
. . capital gains and losses. .3009
. distributions. .3004-3007; 3017
. . annuity trusts or unitrusts. .3006(g)
. . computations. .3021
. dividends received. .3011(c)
. employees' trusts. .3024
. . contributions to. .1838; 3024
. . information required. .3521
. . unrelated business income. .3447
. estate planning. .4704
. estate tax: *See* Estate tax
. exemption deduction. .3012
. expenses. .1806; 3016; 3018
. fiduciaries:
. . discharge from personal liability. .3947
. . distribution, deductions. .3004-3007
. . identification number. .3500
. fixed investment trusts. .3026
. foreign. .3023
. . information returns. .3540
. foreign tax credit. .3703
. funeral expenses. .3011
. gross income. .3008
. identification numbers. .3500
. income:
. . accumulations. .3008; 3022(e)
. . . marital deduction. .3929(b)
. . assignment of. .2704
. . distributions. .3004-3007
. . elderly income credit. .2406
. . personal holding company income. .3401
. . self-employment tax. .3823
. . taxable to whom. .1225; 2704; 3003
. . trust, taxable to grantor. .3022
. information returns. .3531
. . exempt trusts. .3537
. inter vivos trusts, defined. .3002
. interest, paid for another. .1902
. investment credit. .3019
. liability for tax. .1028(d); 3002
. life insurance trusts. .3022(e)
. liquidating trusts. .3026
. long-term capital gain deduction. .3009
. losses, disallowed. .3018
. losses deductible by whom. .3009; 3011
. medical expenses. .3011
. minimum tax on tax preferences. .2403
. multiple trusts. .3002
. nature. .3002
. net operating loss deduction. .3015
. nonbusiness expenses. .1806; 3016
. payment of tax. .3524
. pooled income fund. .3927(b); 4022
. powers. .3022
. principal defined. .3002

ESTATES—EXCHANGES

References are to PARAGRAPH (¶) NUMBERS

ESTATES AND TRUSTS (continued)
. private foundations, transfers to. .3927(c)
. rate tables:
. . estate tax. .3934; 3937
. . income tax. .5506
. real estate trusts. .3026
. redemption of stock to pay death taxes. .1721
. residence sold by trust. .1419
. returns. .3000; 3020; 3517(c)
. . information required. .3521
. . place of filing. .3519
. reversionary interests. .3022(a)
. revocable trusts. .3022(d)
. . estate tax. .3912
. . gift tax. .4008
. sale of property. .3009
. separate shares. .3006(c)
. separate trusts. .3002
. short-term. .3022
. simple trusts. .3005
. . distribution computations. .3021(a)
. sixty-five day rule. .3006(f)
. split interest nonexempt trusts. .3453
. standard deduction: *See* Zero bracket amount
. stock:
. . ownership rule. .1727; 2223(d)
. . redemption to pay death taxes. .1721
. S.U.B. trusts, taxability. .3436(d); 3447
. taxable entities. .3002
. taxable income. .3008
. termination of trust. .3003(c)
. testamentary trust, defined. .3002
. throwback rule, complex trusts. .3023
. "tier" distributions. .3006(a)(b)
. trust as association. .3026
. undistributed net income, complex trusts. .3023
. unitrust, gift tax on. .4022
. unrelated business income tax, exempt trusts .3451
. . returns and rates. .3454
. work incentive program expenses. .3019

Estimated tax:
. corporations:
. . declaration. .3523(a)
. . payment schedule. .3523(a)
. . penalty for underpayment. .3523(b); 3619
. individuals. .2515-2519
. . declaration. .3523(a)
. . . agent filing. .3510
. . . amended. .2517(b)
. . . extensions. .2517(e)
. . . failure to file. .2519; 3617(c)
. . . farmers. .2517(c)
. . . fiscal year. .2517(d)
. . . fishermen. .2517(c)
. . . identification numbers. .3500
. . . joint. .2516(a)
. . . nonresident aliens. .2517(f)
. . . persons under disability. .2516(b)
. . . preparation. .2518
. . . return as. .2517(a)
. . . self-employment tax. .2515; 3827(b)
. . . underestimate. .2515, 2519
. . extension of time. .2517(e)
. . failure to pay. .2519
. . farmers. .2517(c)
. . fiscal year. .2517(d)
. . fishermen. .2517(c)
. . installment payments. .2517
. . overestimate. .2515; 2517(a)
. . . refund, interest on. .3628(c)
. . payment. .2517

Estimated tax (continued)
. individuals (continued)
. . penalties. .2519
. overpayment credited to refund. .3624(c)
. refunds. .3622
Evasion of taxes, penalties. .3620
Evidences of indebtedness distinguished from stock. .1901
Examination of returns. .3601
Excess deductions account, farm losses. .2226(b)
Excess itemized deductions. .1102(d), (f), (h); 1103(a)
Exchange funds, partnerships. .2925(a)
Exchanges: *See also* Transfers
. amount realized. .1400
. annuities. .1407
. assumption of liabilities. .1405; 1409; 1517(f); 3305; 3309; 3315
. basis:
. . assumed liabilities. .1405
. . gain or loss. .1500 et seq.
. . property received for other property. .1503(a)
. bonds for stock. .1404
. "boot" connected with. .1408; 1517; 3309; 3311; 3319
. capital gains and losses: *See* Capital gains and losses
. controlled corporation. .1405; 1409; 1518; 3306; 3316 et seq.
. defined. .1402
. fair market value. .1400; 1503
. federal agencies, orders of. .3330
. FCC orders. .1410
. federal reclamation laws, orders of. .1410
. foreign currencies. .1406; 2730(a)
. gain or loss. .1400 et seq.
. information required. .3521
. insurance policies. .1407
. investment property. .1406; 1409
. involuntary conversions. .1410-1415; 1519
. liabilities assumed. .3309; 3315
. like kind, defined. .1406
. mortgaged property. .1409
. necessity for, capital gains and losses. .1602
. nontaxable. .1400 et seq.; 3309 et seq.
. . basis for depreciation. .2003
. . basis of property received. .1514; 1517; 1518
. . . corporation. .3314
. . . distributee-stockholder. .3313
. . "boot". .1408; 1517; 3309; 3311; 3319
. . federal agencies, orders of. .1410; 3330
. . information required. .3521
. . investment credit. .2410(a)
. . liquidation of subsidiaries. .3334
. . period property held. .1606(c)
. . property for securities. .3309
. . SEC orders. .3330
. . securities for securities. .1404; 3309
. . transactions to reduce tax liability. .3302
. partnerships. .2944
. personal-use property. .1406
. productive-use property. .1406
. property for other property. .1401
. property of like kind. .1406
. . basis of property received. .1517
. property used partly for business. .1517(g)
. proportionate interests before and after. .1405
. realty for personalty. .1406
. real estate investment trust. .1405(c)
. regulated investment company. .1405(c)
. reorganizations: *See* Reorganizations
. sales distinguished. .1402
. SEC orders. .3330
. stock for bonds. .1404

6024—Index EXCHANGES—EXEMPTIONS

References are to PARAGRAPH (¶) NUMBERS

Exchanges (continued)
. stock for stock of same corporation. .1404
. taxable, property acquired by. .1503
. tax-free: *See* Exchanges, nontaxable
Excise taxes:
. deductibility. .1910; 1911(b); 1916
. gift tax as. .4000
. included in inventory. .1915(d)
. manufacturers' rate chart. .5515
. refunds for. .2417
. retailers' rate chart. .5515
EXCLUSIONS. .1202. *See also* Exempt income
Executors and administrators:
. basis of property to. .1507; 3010
. bequests in lieu of commissions. .1302(b)
. commissions. .1301
. . deductibility. .1806; 3016
. . . estate tax. .3926
. compensation, bequest in lieu of. .1302(b)
. discharge from personal liability. .3001(b); 3947
. joint returns. .3506; 3507; 3517(a)
. liability for tax. .3944
. returns. .3000; 3020; 3506; 3507; 3517(c)
. sale of residence. .1423
EXEMPT INCOME. .1202-1232
. accident insurance benefits. .1218-1222
. age 65 or over. .2406
. annuities. .1230-1232
. armed forces. .1218(c)
. benefits, health, accident, social security and unemployment. .1217-1222
. clergymen. .1308(e)
. combat pay. .1306
. cost of living allowances. .3726
. damages. .1226
. death benefits. .1304
. deductions distinguished. .1201
. dependents, effect on dependency exemption. .1118
. disability income. .1219(c)
. discharge of indebtedness, from. .1318(j)
. distributions from. .1704(b)
. dividends. .1216
. . life insurance. .1216
. elderly income. .2406
. employees' annuities. .1232
. estates and trusts. .3019
. exclusions defined. .1201
. expenses attributable to. .1809; 3007
. foreign government employees. .3708(b)
. gifts and bequests. .1225; 1302(b)
. health insurance benefits. .1218-1222
. income from U.S. possessions. .3727
. information required. .3521
. inheritance. .1225
. interest. .1203; 1204
. . amortizable premium. .1846
. international organizations. .3708(b)
. life insurance. .1213-1216
. medicare benefits. .1222
. nonresident citizens, earned income. .3725
. . information required. .3521
. partners' distributive share. .2913
. pensions. .1304
. Puerto Rican residents. .3727(b)
. resident aliens. .3708(b)
. servicemen's annuities. .1232(i)
. sick pay: *See* Disability income
. social security benefits. .1217
. statutory exclusions. .1202
. stock dividends. .1708
. stock rights. .1711
. treaty obligations. .1228

EXEMPT INCOME (continued)
. unemployment insurance benefits. .1217(b)
. unrelated business. .3448(b)
. wage disability payments. .1219(c); 2504(g)
Exempt organizations. .3435 et seq.
. additional information required. .3537
. annuities purchased for employees:
. . estate tax. .3915(b)
. . gift tax. .4011
. banks providing reserves and deposit insurance . .3436
. business income. .3445
. business lease income. .3449
. depreciation when status changed. .2003
. disallowed losses. .3436(c)
. dividends received from. .1706(a)
. employees' annuities. .1232(f)
. exempt status lost. .3436(d)
. farmers' co-op associations. .3455
. feeder organizations. .3436(a)
. foreign personal holding co.. .3415
. indebtedness, acquisition of. .3449(c)
. information returns. .3436(b); 3537
. . penalty for filing late. .3617(b)
. installment sale to. .2813
. legal services trust. .3436
. lobbying expenditures. .3436(d); 3618(j)
. loss of exemption. .3436(d)
. old-age benefit tax. .3814
. payment of tax. .3525
. personal holding company status. .3403
. political organizations. .3436
. private foundations: *See* Private foundations
. prohibited transactions. .3436(d)
. proof of exemption. .3436(b)
. sales between taxpayer and. .2233(c)
. trusts. .3450-3454
. . information returns. .3537
. . unrelated business income tax. .3451
. . unrelated debt-financed income. .3449
. . unrelated business income. .3447; 3448
. . returns. .3513(a)
. . tax. .3445
. . . organizations subject to. .3446
. . . payment of. .3525
. withholding tax on wages. .2501
Exempt securities: *See also* Exempt income
. estate tax. .3901
. gift tax. .4000
. interest to buy or carry. .1905(a)
. sale of. .1630
EXEMPTIONS. .1111 et seq.
. adopted children. .1117; 1120
. age 65 or over. .1113(a)
. armed forces. .1218(c)
. blind individuals. .1114
. children of divorced or separated parents. .1116(a)
. corporations exempt: *See* Exempt organizations
. credit for. .1111(e)
. decedents. .1112(c)
. dependents. .1103; 1111; 1115-1120
. depletion, small producers. .2104(a)
. employees' trust. .3024
. estate tax purposes. .3928
. estates and trusts. .3012
. foster children. .1117; 1118(a)
. fractional year return. .1111(d)
. gift taxes purposes. .4002; 4021
. gross income: *See* Exempt income
. husband and wife. .1111-1114
. income: *See* Exempt income
. individuals. .1111 et seq.

EXEMPTIONS—FARMERS

References are to PARAGRAPH (¶) NUMBERS

EXEMPTIONS (continued)
. joint returns. .1112-1114
. multiple support tests. .1116(c)
. . information required. .3521
. net operating loss. .2242(a)
. . carryover. .2243
. nonresident aliens. .3707-3712
. old-age. .1113
. partnerships. .2906(b)
. single person. .1111(a)
. social security taxes, old-age and survivor insurance. .3804
. status determination date. .1112
. . blind individuals. .1114
. . withholding purposes. .2506(b)
. students. .1116(b)
. wages subject to old-age tax. .3819
. withholding, employee's. .2505
. . exemption certificate not filed. .2506
Expatriates, tax on. .3709(c)
EXPENSES. .1800 et seq.; *See also* particular item
. adjusted gross income purposes. .1804; 1805
. advances to salespersons. .1818
. advertising. .1528; 1827; 2738
. airplane. .1829
. allocable to exempt income. .1809; 3007
. . information required. .3521
. automobiles. .1808; 1829
. business: *See* Business expenses
. capital expenditures distinguished. .1808
. care of dependents. .2415
. child care. .2415
. child's earnings. .1100(a)
. contributions of property. .1810; 1942(c)
. deductions. .1800-1846
. deductions for adjusted gross income. .1801
. dependents, care of. .2415
. disallowed:
. . estates and trusts. .3018
. . partnership and related person. .2924
. . unpaid 2½ mos. after end of year. .2748
. donated property. .1810
. education. .1833
. employees'. .1805
. entertainment. .1830
. estates and trusts. .1806; 3016; 3018
. family. .1807; 2415
. farmers. .1844; 1845
. . gift of products. .1810; 1844(a); 2601
. gift of products. .1810; 1942; 2601
. guardianship. .1806
. handicapped or elderly. .1808
. illegal business. .1812
. installment and deferred payment sales. .2814
. insurance premiums. .1807; 1828; 1832
. investors. .1806; 1823
. legal. .1806; 1823
. medical. .1945-1947
. . information required. .3521
. nontrade or nonbusiness. .1806
. ordinary and necessary. .1803(a)
. organization. .3116
. personal. .1807
. personal holding companies. .3404
. political campaign. .2416
. production of income. .1806
. . partnerships. .2913
. professional. .1829; 1832
. refund claims, connected with. .1806; 1823; 3016
. reimbursed. .1805
. . withholding statements. .2508(a)
. . withholding tax. .2503(a)

EXPENSES (continued)
. repairs. .1825; 2033(f)
. reserves. .2744
. residence used for business. .1805; 1832(a)
. stock dividend, cost of paying. .1808
. taxes deductible as. .1910
. unharvested crop sold with land. .1622(b)
. uniforms. .1807
. unpaid 2½ mos. after close of year. .2748
. . estates and trusts. .3018
. . partnership and related person. .2924
. withholding of taxes. .2503(a)
Experimental expenditures, deductibility. .1842
Exploration, expenditures, mines. .1843(a)
. aggregated interests, effect on. .2108(b)
. deficiency due to. .3611(g)
. information, required. .3521
. partnerships. .2913
. successor in reorganization. .3337
Exports, Domestic International Sales Corporations. .3460
Expropriation losses. .2241; 3613(f)
. recoveries. .2316(d); 3526
Extension of time:
. collection of taxes. .3610; 3611; 3613
. declaration of estimated tax. .2517(e)
. deficiency payment. .3618
. estimated tax payment. .2517(e)
. filing Form W-3. .2509(e)
. filing returns. .3518
. . information required. .3521
. information returns. .3530
. payment of tax. .3518; 3526; 3630(c)
. . estate tax. .3944
. . gift tax. .4031
. withholding statements. .2508(c)
Extortion income. .1300(g)

— F —

Facilities:
. entertainment:
. . deductibility of costs. .1830
. . losses on. .2202
. withholding of taxes. .2503(a)
Factory work clothes. .1807
Fair Labor Standards Act:
. back pay. .1301
. . withholding tax. .2503(a)
. liquidated damages paid under. .1301; 2503(a)
Fair market value:
. basis of property. .1501-1510
. defined. .1502(a); 3919
. not ascertainable. .1400; 1502(a); 2816
Family:
. compensation to members of. .1816
. employment by members of, old-age benefit tax. .3808
. expenses. .1807; 2415
. gifts. .1225
. losses. .2223(a)
. moving allowances for, armed forces. .1306
. partnerships. .2904; 2905
. traveling expenses on business trip. .1829
Farm buildings, depreciation. .2001(a)
Farmers:
. accounting methods. .2614(a)
. accounting records. .2614(a)
. benefits received from Gov't. .2614(b)
. business expenses. .1844(a)
. capital expenditures. .1844(b)
. capital gains and losses. .1622

6026—Index FARMERS—FILING

References are to PARAGRAPH (¶) NUMBERS

Farmers (continued)
. citrus grove expenses. .1844(a)
. Commodity Credit loan as income. .2722(d)
. conservation expenditures. .1845
. cooperative associations. .3455
. . dividends received from. .1706(a)
. crop basis. .2614(a)
. crop insurance proceeds. .2614(a)
. declaration and payment of estimated tax. .2517(c)
. deductions. .1844; 1845; 2001(a); 2211
. depreciation. .2001(a)
. development expenses. .1844(a)
. estimated tax. .2517(c)
. exchange of farms. .1406
. expenses of. .1844; 1845
. fertilizer expenses. .1844
. gasoline tax refund. .2417
. gift of products. .1810; 1844(a); 2614(c)
. hobby. .1844(c); 2211
. income from farming. .2614
. information required. .3521
. inventory method. .2615
. land clearing expenses. .1845
. lime expenses. .1844
: livestock, sale of. .1622
. losses. .2211
. . recapture of. .2226
. lubricating oil refund. .2417
. old-age benefit tax. .3805; 3816
. patronage dividends. .3456-3458
. . exclusion. .1706(c)
. price method, inventory. .2615(a)
. products used by family. .2614(c)
. program payments, information required. .3521
. rents received in crop shares. .2614(b)
. returns. .2614(a)
. . information required. .3521
. Sec. 1231 transactions. .1622
. self-employment tax. .3805; 3823(b)
. soil conservation expenditures. .1845
. syndicates, expenses for. .2745
. water conservation expenditures. .1845
. withholding tax on wages. .2503(b)
Farming syndicate expenses. .1844(d); 2745
Father as dependent. .1117
Father-in-law as dependent. .1117
Federal agencies, transactions under orders of . .1410; 1619(f); 3330
Federal credit unions: *See* Exempt organizations
. social security taxes. .3815(a)
Federal employees and officers:
. annuities. .1232(g)
. compensation. .1305; 1308(d)
. cost-of-living allowances. .3726
. old-age benefit tax. .3815(a)
. . refund. .3829
. quarters furnished. .1308(d)
. social security coverage. .3815(a)
. withheld compensation. .1232(g)
. withholding tax. .2503(b)
Federal Home Loan banks employees, social security coverage. .3815(a)
Federal instrumentalities:
. dividends from. .1704(a)
. employee's trust. .3024(h)
. interest on obligations of:
. . exclusion. .1203(c)
. old-age benefit tax. .3815(a)
Federal Insurance Contributions Act: *See* Social security, old-age and survivor insurance
Federal land banks, dividends. .1704(a)

Federal obligations:
. advertising. .1827
. amortizable premium. .1846
. capital asset status. .1601
. compensation paid in. .1307(c)
. employee's trust. .3024(h)
. estate tax, valuation. .3919(b)
. exchanges involving. .1403
. gift tax. .4000
. . valuation, Series E bonds. .4014
. interest:
. . fractional year returns. .2717
. . information returns. .3531
. . issues on or after 3-1-41. .1203(a)
. . savings bonds. .2723(a), (b)
. . . co-ownership. .1314
. . short-term issued at discount. .2723(c)
. loss on redemption of Series H savings bonds . .2723(b)
. payment of tax with. .3527(b)
. redemption, as involuntary conversion. .1410
. short-term issed at discount. .2723(c)
Federal reclamation laws, sale or exchange on order of. .1410
Federal Reserve banks, social security coverage . .3815(a)
Federal Reserve Board, transactions under orders of. .3330
Federal savings and loan association, dividends . .1704(c); 1706(a)
Federal taxes:
. deductibility. .1911
. who may deduct. .1916
Federal Unemployment Tax Act: *See* Social security unemployment insurance
Feeder organizations. .3436(a)
Fees: *See also* particular type
. filing petition with Tax Court. .3639(c)
. gross income. .1301
. information returns. .3531
. practice before Tax Court. .3636
Fellowship awards. .1303
. withholding tax. .2503(a)
Fertilizer expense, deductibility. .1844
Fidelity bonds:
. premiums. .1828(b)
. theft loss. .2205
Fiduciaries: *See also* Estates and trusts
. agent distinguished from. .3001
. capital gains and losses of estates and trusts. .3009
. deduction for distributions. .3004-3007; 3017
. defined. .3001; 3511
. discharge from personal liability, estate tax. .3947
. fees of, deductibility. .1806; 3016
. identification number. .3500
. income taxable to. .3003
. information returns. .3539
. liability for taxes. .3001
. notice of relationship. .3605
. receivers distinguished. .3001
. returns. .3000; 3001; 3020; 3511
. self-employment tax. .3823(e)
Fifo method, inventories. .2605; 2606(a)
52—53-Week accounting period. .2714(b)
. change in. .2715; 2716
FILING STATUS. .1104-1106
. head of household. .1106
. married taxpayers. .1104
. . abandoned spouse. .1104(c)
. . joint returns. .1104(a)
. . separate returns. .1104(c); 3506

References are to PARAGRAPH (¶) NUMBERS

FILING STATUS (continued)
. surviving spouse. .1105
Film production, expenses connected with. .1808
Finance charges, deductibility. .1901; 1904(b)
Finance companies, personal holding company tax. .3403
Financial counseling fees paid by corporation . .1301
Fines, deductibility. .1812
Fire:
. damages paid for fraudulent loss. .2202(b)
. estate tax. .3926
. information required. .3521
. insurance companies, tax on. .3434(b)
. insurance premiums. .1828(b)
. insurance proceeds:
. . casualty losses. .2204
. . involuntary conversion. .1410-1415; 1519
. losses. .1410; 1414; 2200; 2204
Firemen:
. disability payments. .1218
. uniforms. .1807
First-in, first-out rule, stocks. .1522
. capital gains and losses affected by. .1607
Fiscal year:
. change to or from. .2715-2717
. computation of tax. .3546
. election. .2714
. estimated tax. .2517(d)
. payment of tax. .3523
. returns. .3517
Fishermen, estimated tax. .2517(c)
Fishing boat operators, information required . .3521
Fishing crewmen, withholding tax. .2503(a)
Fishing licenses. .1912(d)
"Fixing up" expenses, residence. .1416
Fixtures:
. capital asset status. .1601(d)
. investment credit. .2410(a)
. useful life. .2032
Flood insurance companies, tax on. .3434(b)
Flood losses. .2204
Floor, expense of. .1825
Foreclosures:
. losses. .2223(a); 2743(b)
. mutual savings bank. .3433
Foreign accounts, financial interest in, returns . .3540
Foreign areas allowances. .3726
Foreign conventions, deductions for. .1829
Foreign corporations:
. accumulated profits, domestic corporation tax on . .3706
. controlled. .3728
. credit for foreign taxes. .3703; 3710(a)
. deductions. .3710(a)
. defined. .3105; 3710
. dividends:
. . paid to, withholding tax. .2535
. . received from. .1706(a)
. . . corporation foreign tax credit for. .3706
. effectively connected U.S. source income. .3711(a)
. exempt interest, information required. .3521
. extensions. .3518(a)
. foreign taxes:
. . credit for. .3703; 3710(a)
. . paid by domestic subsidiaries. .3706
. gain or loss. .3710(a)
. how taxed. .3707-3712
. identifying numbers. .3500
. income subject to tax. .3404(a)

Foreign corporations (continued)
. less developed country corp.. .3728
. liability for tax. .1028(g)
. nonresident, payment of tax, time due. .3523
. personal holding company tax. .3403
. . failure to file return. .3405
. rate chart. .5505
. reorganizations, advance ruling needed. .3309, 3317
. returns. .3517(b); 3540(b); 3710(b)
. stock owned in, information. .3521
. Subpart F income. .3728
. . tax-free liquidation, advance ruling needed . .3334
. tax treaties. .3720
. trade or business in U.S.. .3711
. transfers to, advance ruling needed. .1405
. unrelated business income tax. .3448
. U.S. controlled, returns. .3540(b)
Foreign currencies and exchange:
. conversion. .1406; 2730(a)
. payment of taxes with. .3527(b)
Foreign governments:
. confiscation by. .2241
. employees' salaries. .3708(b)
. employment by:
. . old-age benefit tax. .3815(c)
. . self-employment tax. .3815(c); 3823(e)
. . withholding tax. .2503(b)
. taxes of: See Foreign taxes
Foreign insurance companies. .3434(d)
Foreign investment company stock. .3728
. partnerships. .2944(d)
Foreign Investors Act of 1966. .3707-3712
Foreign items, information returns. .3540
Foreign partnerships, trade or business in U.S. . .3711
Foreign personal holding companies. .3411-3416
. adjustments of income. .3413
. amount taxable to members of U.S. group, determination. .3414
. charitable contributions. .3413
. corporation income taxed to U.S. Shareholders . .3414
. deductions. .3413
. defined. .3412
. exempt corporations. .3415
. net operating loss. .3413
. personal holding company tax. .3403
. returns. .3416
. undistributed income. .3413; 3414
Foreign Service officers and employees, allowances to. .3726
Foreign taxes:
. contested, when to credit, accrual basis. .2740(b)
. credit for. .3701-3706
. . aliens. .3701; 3708(b)
. . beneficiaries. .3019
. . contested. .2740(b)
. . deficiency due to carryback. .3624(c)
. . estate tax purposes. .3938
. . foreign corporations. .3701; 3710
. . foreign subsidiaries. .3706
. . information required. .3521
. . interest income. .3703
. . partnerships. .2906(c); 2917
. . rate of exchange. .3702
. . real estate investment trusts. .3432
. . refund of tax. .3629(c); 3705
. . reorganization. .3337
. . resident aliens. .3714
. . unrelated business income tax. .3445

6028—Index FOREIGN—FORMS

―――― References are to PARAGRAPH (¶) NUMBERS ――――

Foreign taxes (continued)
. deductibility. .1914; 3404
. . partnerships. .2917
. refund of. .3624(c); 3705
. treaties. .3720

Foreign taxpayers, how taxed. .3707-3712

Forgiveness of debt: *See* Indebtedness, forgiveness

Forms:
. authorization, joint return. .3505(a)
. petition to Tax Court. .3536(c); 3640
. power of attorney. .3510
. refund claim. .3626
. returns:
. . consolidated. .3515
. . corporations. .3513
. . fiduciaries. .3020
. . individuals. .1101; 3517(a)
. . partnerships. .2906
. source of. .1101
. 1(TC). .3640(a)
. 2(TC). .3635(c)
. 4(TC). .3639(b)
. 6(TC). .3646
. 13(TC). .3637(f)
. 23. .3609
. 23A. .3609
. 56. .3539
. 433. .3608(a)
. 501. .2509(a)
. 503. .3523
. 511. .2509(a)
. 512. .2536
. 656. .3608(a)
. 704. .3943
. 706. .3943
. 709. .4030
. 843. .2243(c); 2511(a), (b); 2717; 3520; 3626-3628; 3630(b); 3946; 4033
. 851. .3515; 3521
. 866. .3608(b)
. 870. .3505(b); 3602; 3604-3606; 3610(d); 3613(a); 3615(f); 3626
. 870-AD. .3607
. 872. .3610(d); 3623(c)
. 872-A. .3610(d)
. 872-C. .3610(e)
. 890. .3606; 3626
. 890a. .3606
. 906. .3608(b)
. 938. .4030
. 940. .3838
. 941. .2503(b); 2508-2511; 3531(d); 3617(b); 3826(c); 3827(a)
. 941c. .3829(b)
. 941E. .2509(b)
. 941M. .2509(d)
. 942. .2509(b); 3827(a)
. 943. .2509(b); 3827(a)
. 957. .3416
. 958. .3416
. 959. .3540(b)
. 964. .3335
. 966. .1717(b); 3128; 3335
. 966-E. .3536
. 970. .2606(c); 3521
. 972. .3521
. 973. .3521
. 982. .1318(j); 3125(f)
. 990. .3537
. 990-A. .3537

Forms (continued)
. 990-AR. .3537
. 990-C. .3455; 3513
. 990-P. .3537(d)
. 990-PF. .3525(b); 3537(a)
. 990-T. .3454(b); 3513; 3517
. 1000. .3531(d); 3532(b)
. 1001. .3531(d); 3532(b)
. 1023. .3436(b); 3610(e)
. 1024-1028. .3436(b)
. 1040. .1101; 1103(b); 1109, 2401; 3020; 3024(g); 3027; 3511(b); 3518; 3519(a); 3521; 3527(b); 3626
. 1040 (Sch. A). .1320; 1829(d); 1846; 1910; 2601(c)
. 1040 (Sch. D). .1422; 3024(g)
. 1040 (Sch. F). .2614(a); 3521; 3827(b)
. 1040 (Sch. G). .2401
. 1040 (Sch. SE). .3827(b)
. 1040A. .1101; 1103(b); 1801(a); 1802; 3020
. 1040-ES. .2515; 2517
. 1040-ES (OIO). .2517(f)
. 1040X. .3520; 3626(c)
. 1041. .3000; 3020-3022; 3511; 3521; 3626
. 1041 (Sch. B). .3020(c)
. 1041 (Sch. C). .3020(c)
. 1041 (Sch. D). .3020(c)
. 1041 (Sch. J). .3023(c), (h)
. 1041 (Sch. K-1). .3000(b); 3020(c); 3021(a), (b); 3539(a)
. 1041A. .3020; 3440(c); 3538
. 1041-B. .3538; 3927(b)
. 1042. .2511(b); 2536; 3531(d)
. 1042S. .2536; 3531(d)
. 1045. .2243(c); 3630(a)
. 1065. .2016(d); 2906; 2918; 3025; 3521; 3531(d); 3539
. 1065 (Sch. K). .2918
. 1065 (Sch. K-1). .2918; 3827(b)
. 1087   3530; 3532(a)
. 1087-DIV. .3533
. 1087-INT. .3532(a)
. 1087-OID. .3532
. 1096. .1702(e); 3016; 3128; 3129(d); 3530; 3532; 3536; 3540(a)
. 1099. .3016; 3404(b); 3530-3533; 3535; 3540; 3617
. 1099-DIV. .1701(d); 3530; 3533; 3540
. 1099-INT. .3530-3533; 3540
. 1099L. .3128; 3536
. 1099-MED. .3531
. 1099-MISC. .3530; 3531
. 1099-OID. .3532
. 1099-PATR. .3533(b)
. 1099R. .3531
. 1116. .3521; 3701
. 1117. .3701
. 1118. .3521; 3701
. 1120. .3100; 3434(b); 3513; 3515; 3521; 3626
. 1120 (Sch. D). .3201
. 1120 (Sch. M-1, M-2). .3110
. 1120 (Sch. P-H). .3405
. 1120-DISC (Sch. K). .3531
. 1120F. .3710
. 1120H. .3436(b)
. 1120L. .3434(a)
. 1120M. .3434(c)
. 1120S. .3100; 3141(c); 3201; 3513; 3531(d); 3539(c); 3610(b)
. 1120S (Sch. M). .3110
. 1120W. .3523(a)
. 1120X. .3520; 3626(c)
. 1122. .3222; 3521
. 1127. .3526
. 1128. .2716; 2921

FORMS—FUTURE   Index—6029

References are to PARAGRAPH (¶) NUMBERS

Forms (continued)
- 1138. .3518(a); 3526; 3630(a)(c)
- 1139. .3630(a)
- 1310. .3507; 3626
- 1342. .3521
- 1902E. .3505(b)
- 2032. .3803
- 2106. .1805
- 2119. .1416(f); 1418; 1422; 3521
- 2120. .1116(c); 3521
- 2159. .3615(e)
- 2190. .3823(b)
- 2210. .2519
- 2220. .3523(b)
- 2271. .2010(c)
- 2297. .3629(a)
- 2350. .3518; 3725
- 2438. .3431
- 2439. .3431
- 2440. .3521
- 2553. .3141(b)
- 2555. .3521; 3725(c)
- 2587. .3609(a)
- 2688. .3518
- 2758. .3518
- 2848. .3600(c); 3510; 3521
- 2848-D. .3609(d)
- 2952. .3540
- 3115. .2010(b); 2012(b); 2311(c); 2609(c)
- 3435. .3500
- 3468. .3630(a)
- 3491. .3533(b)
- 3520. .3540
- 3646. .3728
- 3903. .1805; 1831(e)
- 3921. .3534
- 3922. .3534
- 4029. .3822
- 4067. .3534
- 4070. .2503(a)
- 4136. .2417; 3521
- 4137. .3827(a)
- 4219. .2501(b)
- 4224. .2536
- 4361. .3822
- 4461. .3024(b)
- 4462. .3024(b)
- 4466. .3622(a)
- 4549. .3505(b)
- 4562. .2010(a); 3521
- 4563. .3727(a)
- 4573. .3024(b)
- 4574. .1839(d)
- 4575. .3024(b)
- 4576. .3024(e)
- 4577. .3024(b)
- 4578. .3024(h)
- 4625. .2403; 3541
- 4626. .2403; 3020(d); 3103; 3541
- 4629. .3537(b)
- 4653. .3437
- 4683. .3540
- 4684. .1618(b); 2206
- 4720. .3440(b); 3525(b); 3537
- 4768. .3943; 3944
- 4782. .1831(e)
- 4797. .1618; 1620; 2206(b)
- 4798. .1613(c)
- 4832. .2033(a); 3521
- 4874. .2411
- 4876. .3460; 3521

Forms (continued)
- 4952. .1906
- 4970. .3023(e), (h)
- 4972. .3024
- 5227. .3453
- 5301. .3024(b)
- 5310. .3024(e)
- 5329. .1838(1); 3027
- 5405. .1416(d)
- 5452. .1702(e); 3533
- 5498. .1838(l); 3027
- 5500. .3024(c); 3521; 3537(d)
- 5500-C. .3024(c)
- 5500-K. .3024(c); 3537(d)
- 5500 (Sch. A). .3537(d)
- 5500 (Sch. B). .3537(d)
- 5501. .3537(d)
- 5504. .3537(d)
- 5505. .3537(d)
- 5544. .3024(d)
- 5717. .3542
- 7004. .3518(a); 3521
- SS-4. .3500; 3826(a)(d)
- SS-5. .3500; 3826(b)(c)
- SS-14. .3828(a)
- SS-15. .3814
- SS-15a. .3814
- SS-15a Supplement. .3814
- T. .2110
- W-2. .1101; 1831(e); 2507-2509; 3509; 3521; 3530; 3531; 3535; 3617(b); 3827(a); 3828(a)
- W-2G. .3521
- W-2P. .2504(k); 2509(c); 3531
- W-3. .2509; 3531; 3535
- W-3M. .2509(d)
- W-4. .2506
- W-4E. .2506

Foster child, dependency status. .1117(a); 1118(a)
Foundations, private: *See* Private foundations
Fractional part of cent. .3527(b)
Fractional year:
- annualizing income. .2717
- as taxable year. .2714; 2715
- change in accounting period. .2715; 2717
- corporations. .3514
- exemptions. .1111(d)
- minimum tax. .2403; 2717(b)
- partner. .2921(b)
- return for. .2715; 2717(a); 3517

Franchise:
- capital asset. .1601(k)
- depreciation. .2001(a)

Franchise taxes, accrual. .2740(b)
Fraud:
- assessment and collection of tax. .3610
- colorable gifts. .1225
- expenses defending suit involving. .1823
- penalties. .2512; 2519; 3618

Freight charges, cost of goods sold. .2604(a)
Fringe benefits. .1819
Frost losses. .2204(b)
Fruit trees, depreciation. .2001
Full absorption method, inventories. .2609(c)
Funeral Expenses. .1807; 3011
- estate tax. .3926
- medical expense deduction. .1946

Furniture:
- lessee replacing. .1826
- useful life of. .2033

Future interests:
- contribution of. .1942(e)
- gifts. .4020

— G —

GAIN OR LOSS. .1400 et seq.
. amount realized. .1400
. assets retired. .2035-2038
. basis. .1500 et seq.
. . additions to. .1500(b); 1528
. . adjusted. .1500(b)
. . . partnership property. .2937-2942

. . allocation. .1521
. . amortizable bond premium. .1846
. . annuities, private. .1527
. . annuity contract. .1527
. . bankruptcy reorganization. .3331
. . bargain purchases. .1310
. . capital distributions reducing. .1702(a)
. . carrying charges. .1528
. . consent dividends affecting. .3404
. . contributions to capital by nonshareholder. .3106
. . copyrights. .1523
. . cost. .1501

. . dealer's used cars. .1503(b)
. . defined. .1500
. . depletion adjustment. .2102
. . depletion or depreciation reserve distributed . .2113
. . depreciation adjustment. .1500(b); 1514; 2003; 2004
. . discharge of debt affecting. .1318(j); 3125(f)
. . employees' stock options. .1327
. . estates and trusts. .3010

. . fair market value. .1503
. . first-in, first-out rule. .1522
. . forgiveness of mortgage debt. .1318(i)
. . gifts. .1515
. . . gift tax effect on. .1515(b); 4029
. . good will. .1524
. . improvements. .1500(b)
. . . lessee's. .1317
. . inheritance. .1507-1510
. . installment obligations. .2831
. . inventories. .2611
. . . partnerships. .2913
. . involuntary conversion. .1519

. . life estates. .1510
. . liquidating distribution. .1717
. . liquidation of subsidiaries. .3334
. . March 1, 1913, property acquired before. .1506
. . nontaxable distributions. .1702(a)
. . nontaxable exchanges. .1514; 1517; 1518
. . . corporation. .3314
. . . distributee-stockholder. .3313
. . old residence replaced. .1526
. . option to buy stock. .1327

. . partnerships:
. . . contributions to. .2925
. . . distributions. .2928-2932; 2937-2942
. . . interest in. .2925; 2936
. . patents. .1523

. . property:
. . . acquired by exchange. .1503
. . . acquired by purchase. .1501
. . . acquired from decedent. .1507; 2003
. . . acquired in divorce settlement. .1505
. . . acquired in trade-in. .1503(b)
. . . acquired on involuntary conversion. .1514
. . . acquired through exercise of option to purchase. .1501
. . . bought at less than market. .1310; 1329

GAIN OR LOSS (continued)
. basis (continued)
. . property (continued)
. . . received for services. .1504
. . reductions. .1500(b)
. . remainder interests. .1510
. . reorganizations. .3313 et seq.
. . . corporation. .3314
. . . insolvent. .3331(c)
. . . distributee-stockholder. .3313
. . repossessions. .2821; 2823
. . retired assets. .2037
. . sale of residence by taxpayer 65 or over. .1526
. . sales to related taxpayer. .2223(e)
. . securities bought as unit. .1521
. . selling expenses. .1818
. . sports franchises. .1521(c)
. . stock:
. . . bought at less than market. .1328
. . . dividends. .1707-1709
. . . redeemed through controlled corp.. .1720
. . . rights. .1711-1712
. . . small business corp.. .3144
. . substituted. .1514
. . survivor and joint annuities. .1509
. . survivor interest, joint tenancy. .1509
. . taxable exchanges. .1503
. . theft loss. .2205; 2206(b)
. . trade-in allowances. .1517
. . transfers before death. .1508
. . unharvested corp sold with land. .1622
. . wash sales. .2221
. . valuation for estate tax. .1507
. capital: *See* Capital gains and losses
. carryover basis property, estate tax. .1507; 3919
. condemnation awards. .1410-1415
. corporation:
. . dealing in own stock. .3124
. . property distributions. .3127
. . redeeming stock with appreciated property . .3127(b)
. . selling and buying its bonds. .3125
. . determination. .1500 et seq.
. . distributions in liquidation. .3128
. . dividends paid in property. .1702(b)
. . earnings and profits affected by. .1702(a)
. exchanges: *See* Exchanges
. foreign corporations. .3710(a)
. housing, low-income projects. .1426
. improvements by lessee. .1317
. installment obligations. .2831
. involuntary conversions. .1410-1415; 1519; 1619(e); 1620
. life insurance policy surrendered. .1214
. liquidating dividends. .1717; 3128
. liquidation:
. . foreign corporations, advance ruling needed . .3334
. . subsidiaries. .3334
. municipal obligations. .1403
. nonresident aliens. .3709(b)
. . withholding tax. .2535
. partner and partnership. .2923
. partnerships:
. . contributions to. .2925
. . dissolution. .2928-2932
. . distributions. .2927-2932; 2937-2942
. . exchanges. .2944
. . farm recapture property. .2910(a)
. . interest in:
. . . exchanged. .2944
. . . death or retirement of partner. .2941; 2942
. . . transferred. .2937-2942
. . specially treated items. .2913
. postponement. .1400; 1401(b)

GAIN—GIFTS

GAIN OR LOSS (continued)
. realty sales, deferred payments. .2816(a)
. recognition. .1400 et seq.
. redemption of stock. .3124
. repossessions. .2803; 2821; 2823
. residence, personal. .1416-1423; 2207
. . information required. .1422
. . replaced. .1526
. . . holding period. .1606(e)
. . sale by taxpayer 65 or over. .1423
. retirement:
. . assets. .2036-2038
. . bonds. .1602; 3125
. savings bonds, Series H redeemed before maturity ..2723(b)
. Sec. 751 assets partnerships. .2944-2945
. Sec. 1231 gains and losses. .1618-1624
. self-employment income. .3824
. short-term obligations issued at discount. .2723(c)
. stock, collapsible corporations. .1627
. stock dividends. .1707-1709
. stocks and bonds, sale of. .1611
. wash sales. .2221
Gambling:
. income. .1321
. income averaging. .2401
. . partnerships. .2913
. information returns. .3521
. losses. .1321; 2224
. . partnerships. .2913
Gas wells
. capital additions. .2103(c)
. depreciation. .2111
. percentage depletion. .2102
. sale of, information required. .3521
Gasoline:
. contribution deduction for. .1942(c)
. taxes:
. . deductibility:
. . . federal. .2417
. . . state. .1912(c); 1917(a)
. . federal, credit for. .2417
. . refunded, farmers. .2417
Generation-skipping tax. .1507(d); 3916; 4002
. deduction for income tax. .3008(b)
Geodetic Survey, withholding tax on pensions ..2503(a)
G.I. Bill of Rights, allowances under. .1218(c)
G.I. loan, interest. .1902
Gift tax. .4000 et seq.
. annuities. .4011
. appeals. .4032
. applicability. .4002
. assessments. .4032
. assignment of judgment. .4002
. basis of gift increased by. .1515(b); 4029
. charitable, etc. gifts. .4002
. charitable remainder, donations of. .4022
. community property. .4005
. . marital deduction. .4023
. computation. .4025 et seq.
. consideration arising out of marital relationship ..4007
. credit against federal estate tax. .3935
. deductibility. .1911(a)
. deductions. .4020-4023
. deficiencies. .4032
. discretionary trusts. .4008
. employees' trusts. .4011
. exclusions. .4020
. . splitting gifts. .4009
. . exempt securities. .4000

Gift tax (continued)
. exemptions. .4002; 4021
. . splitting gifts. .4009
. federal obligations. .4000
. . valuation, Series E bond. .4014
. forgiveness of debt. .4002
. gift defined. .4002
. husband or wife gift to third party. .4009
. husband-wife:
. . gifts. .4023
. . returns. .4030
. income interests, donations of. .4022
. income tax payment on joint return. .4002
. irrevocable trusts. .4002; 4020
. joint tenancy. .4002
. . marital deduction. .4023
. liability, donee. .4031
. life insurance policy. .4002; 4011; 4030
. marital deduction. .4023
. municipal obligations. .4000
. nature of. .4000; 4002
. payment. .4031
. . effect on basis. .1515(b); 4029
. power of appointment. .4003; 4004
. . marital deduction. .4023
. prenuptial agreement, splitting gift. .4009
. prior gifts. .4025
. prior quarters and years. .4025
. private foundations, transfers to. .4022
. rates. .4027
. refunds. .4033
. remainder and reversionary interests. .4012
. . marital deduction. .4023
. . returns. .4030
. revocable transfers. .4008
. self-employed retirement plans. .4011
. specific exemption. .4021
. splitting gifts. .4009
. state, deductibility. .1912(a)
. state obligations. .4000
. Tax Court jurisdiction. .4032
. tenancy by entirety. .4002; 4013
. . marital deduction. .4023
. transfers:
. . before death. .4006
. . . inadequate consideration. .4002; 4007
. . . subject to revocation or change. .4008
. . taxable. .4000; 4002
. valuation of property. .4010-4014
Gifts: See also Contributions
. acquired after 12-31-20. .1515
. acquired before 1-1-21. .1515
. basis for gain or loss. .1515; 1810
. . gift tax effect on. .1515(b); 4029
. business, deductibility. .1830
. capital gain or loss. .1606(a)
. clergymen, pensions. .1304(b)
. colorable, taxability. .1225
. compensation distinguished. .1225; 1302
. corp. distribution to nonstockholder. .1302(b)
. defined. .1225; 4002
. depreciable property. .1619(c)
. disclaimer, qualified. .4004(b)
. employees, to. .1830
. estate tax. .3909; 3935
. estates and complex trusts. .3006(d)
. forgiveness of indebtedness. .1318(b)
. future interests. .4020
. income averaging. .2401
. income from. .1225
. installment obligations. .2831
. interest in partnership. .2905

6032—Index   GIFTS—HOME

References are to PARAGRAPH (¶) NUMBERS

Gifts (continued)
. legal advice concerning. .1823
. loan distinguished. .2308
. loss on sale. .2203
. minors, to. .1225(b); 4020
. model custodian acts. .1225
. note given as, interest. .1901
. partnership interest. .2904(a); 2905
. pensions as. .1304(b); 1822(a)
. period held. .1606(a)
. prior quarters' and years'. .4025
. rental value of residence occupied rent-free .1308(c); 1942(d)
. tax: *See* Gift Tax
. taxability. .1225
. transfers before death. .4006
. . holding period. .1606
. unified credit. .3940; 4021
. uniforms gifts to minors act. .1225(b)
. withholding tax. .2503(a)
Good will:
. capital asset status. .1601(d)
. damages for injury to. .1226
. depreciation. .2001(a)
. expenditures for. .1827
. loss for. .2210
. partnerships. .2941(a)
. sale of, gain or loss. .1524
. valuation, estate tax. .3919(c)
Government bonds: *See* Federal obligations
Government employees: *See* Federal employees and officers
Grandchildren as dependents. .1117
Grandparents as dependents. .1117
Grantor, income of trust taxable to. .3003; 3022
Grants, disabled veterans. .1218(c)
Gratuities: *See* Contributions; Gifts
Ground rents. .1901
Gross estate, estate tax. .3901; 3904-3915
Gross income:
. adjusted: *See* Adjusted gross income
. adjusted ordinary. .3401
. decedents. .3008(b)
. defined. .1100; 1201; 1300
. . depletion purposes. .2104
. dependent's, effect on exemption. .1118
. estates and trusts. .3008
. exclusions: *See* Exempt income
. foreign corporations. .3707-3712
. gross receipts distinguished. .2601(a); 3545
. identification. .3545
. inclusions. .1300-1331
. . alimony. .1320
. . bad debts, recovery. .2316
. . compensation. .1301-1312
. . forgiveness of debt. .1318
. . illegal business, income from. .1300(g)
. . improvements by lessee. .1317
. . interest. .1314
. . moving expense reimbursements. .1831
. . rents. .1316
. . royalties. .1316
. . state, city contracts, profit on. .1330
. mistake, amounts received by. .1300(b)
. nonresident aliens. .3712
. personal holding companies. .3401
. regulated investment companies. .3429
. time to report. .2719-2730
. unrelated business. .3448
Gross profit. .2601(a)
Gross receipts:
. gross income distinguished. .3545

Gross receipts (continued)
. gross profit distinguished. .2601(a)
Group accounts, depreciation. .2022(b)
. retirement from. .2036
Growth Savings Certificates. .2722(e)
Guam:
. employment in, old age benefit tax. .3803
. residents, self-employment tax. .3823(c)
Guaranteed annual wage payments:
. deductibility. .1819
. taxability. .1307(d)
. withholding tax. .2503(a)
Guarantors, bad debt deduction. .2315(b)
. accounts receivable, sale of. .2311(d)
Guardian:
. expenses of. .1806
. returns. .3000; 1100; 3509; 3511(a)

— H —

Half-blood brother or sister as dependent. .1117
Half-year convention, Class Life ADR depreciation. .2033(d)
Handicapped persons, expenses of. .1808
Head of household:
. abandoned spouse, filing as. .1104(c)
. aliens, nonresident. .3709(b)
. computation of tax. .1102 et seq.
. cousins as dependents. .1106(b)
. declaration of estimated tax. .2516
. defined. .1106
. determination of status as. .1106
. rates of taxes. .1121
. withholding tax on wages. .2504
Health benefits:
. employees trust paying. .3024(d)
. exclusion. .1218(b); 1220
. wage disability income. .1219(c)
. . withholding tax. .2504(g)
Health care services, payments for, information returns. .3521
Health institute fees as medical expense. .1946
Health insurance:
. amounts received under. .1218(b); 1220; 1221
. premiums. .1307(a); 1946(c); 1947
Hearing aids, medical expense. .1946
Hearings:
. Appellate Division. .3607
. proposed assessments. .3603; 3607
. Tax Court. .3635; 3639; 3645-3648
Heating system, cost of changing. .1808
Hedging transactions, short sales. .1608
Hides, futures, short sales. .1608(c)
Highway use tax. .5515
History:
. early laws. .1002
. Revenue Acts. .1005
. Sixteenth Amendment. .1004
Hobby losses. .2225
Holding period: *See* Capital gains and losses, period assets held
Holiday:
. last day:
. . filing:
. . . refund claim. .3623
. . . returns. .3517
. . . suit. .3629(a)
. . . Tax Court petition. .3605(a); 3639(a)
. . payment:
. . . estimated tax. .2517(a)
. . . tax. .3517
Home: *See also* Residence, personal

Home (continued)
. defined for travel expense deduction. .1829
Homeowners associations: *See* Exempt organizations
Homeworkers, old-age benefit tax. .3817(b)
Honorarium to employee. .1302(b)
Hospital:
. fees. .1946
. interns, stipends received. .1303
Hospital Insurance tax. .3800 et seq.
Hospitalization benefit payments, deductibility . .1819; 1838
Hospitalization insurance:
. medical expense. .1946
. premiums. .1828(b)
. . paid by employer. .1307(a)
. social security program. .1946
Houseboat as residence. .1417
Household expenses. .1106(c); 1807
Household effects, moving expenses. .1831
Household workers: *See* Domestics
Housekeeper: *See* Domestics
Housetrailer as residence. .1417
Housing:
. authorities, interest on bonds. .1204
. low income:
. . depreciation on. .1619(c); 2018
. . gain or loss. .1426; 1526; 1619(b)
. new residential rental, depreciation. .2018
. ordinance requirements, selling property to avoid . .1410
Hunting licenses. .1912(d)
Hurricane damage. .2204
Husband and wife:
. abandoned spouse:
. . separate return. .1104(c)
. . standard deduction. .1108
. accounting periods differ, change to same period . .2716
. additional first-year depreciation. .2016
. alimony: *See* Alimony
. assignment of property by one to other. .2704
. blind, exemptions. .1114
. capital gains and losses. .1613(b)
. change in accounting period. .2716
. child care expenses. .2415; 3521
. community income: *See* Community income
. community property: *See* Community property
. computation of tax. .1102 et seq.
. computation of withholding. .2504
. consent connected with gift to third party. .4009
. contributions. .1943(a)
. credit for elderly. .2406(b)
. death of spouse:
. . exemption. .1112(c)
. . joint return. .1106(a); 3507
. declaration of estimated tax. .2516(a)
. depreciable property sold to spouse. .1625
. dividends received. .1705(a)
. divorce:
. . exemptions. .1112; 1116(a)
. . support of child. .1116(a)
. election, joint or separate returns. .1112
. elderly income credit. .2406
. employment of spouse, old-age tax. .3808
. exemptions. .1111-1114
. gain on sale of residence. .1418; 1423
. gifts between, marital deduction. .4023
. gifts to third party. .4009
. gross income requirements. .1101(a)
. income splitting. .1104(a); 1112(c); 1300(c); 3505-3508; 5503

Husband and wife (continued)
. *income splitting (continued)*
. . change to same accounting period. .2716
. interest deductions. .1902
. joint declaration. .2516(a)
. joint qualified interests. .1509; 3908
. joint returns: *See* Husband and wife, returns, joint
. joint tenancy. .1300(e)
. living apart. .1104(c)
. losses on sales or exchanges between. .2223(a), (e)
. low income allowance. .1108
. marital deduction:
. . estate tax purposes. .3929
. . gift tax purposes. .4023
. medical expenses. .1945
. old-age exemptions. .1113
. rate schedule. .1102-1106
. remarriage, joint return. .3507
. residence sold:
. . nonrecognition of gain. .1418
. . tax-free. .1423
. returns. .1100
. . joint. .1112-1114; 3505-3508; 5503
. . . accounting methods differ. .3505
. . . accounting periods differ. .2716; 3505; 3507
. . . additional first-year depreciation. .2016
. . . advantages. .3508
. . . change to same accounting period. .2716
. . . check list. .5503
. . . child care expenses. .2415
. . . community property states. .3508
. . . contributions. .1943(a)
. . . death. .3505-3507; 3517(a)
. . . dividends received. .1705(a)
. . . election after filing separate. .3506
. . . limitation on assessment and collection . .3610(b); 3611
. . . exemptions. .1112-1114
. . . extension of time. .3506
. . . identifying numbers. .3500
. . . medical expenses. .1945(a)
. . . rate of tax. .1121
. . . remarriage. .3507
. . . self-employment schedules. .3827(b)
. . . signatures. .3505(a)
. . . . deceased spouse. .3507(b)
. . . standard deduction: *See* Zero bracket amount
. . . tenants by the entirety. .1300(d)
. . separate. .1112-1114
. . . additional first-year depreciation. .2016
. . . advantages. .3508
. . . child care expenses. .2415
. . . community property states. .3508
. . . dividends received. .1705(a)
. . . exemptions. .1112-1114
. . . extension granted to one. .3506
. . . nonresident alien. .1104
. . . standard deduction: *See* Zero bracket amount
. . . tenants by the entirety. .1300(d)
. . . tax tables. .1122
. self-employment tax schedules. .3827(b)
. separate returns: *See* Husband and wife, returns, separate
. separate v. joint returns. .3508
. separated. .1104(a); 3505(a)
. . support for child. .1116(a)
. short sales. .1608(a)
. splitting gifts. .4009
. splitting income. .1104(a); 3505-3508; 5503
. . change to same accounting period. .2716
. standard deduction: *See* Zero bracket amount
. tax deductions. .1919

6034—Index — HUSBAND—INFORMATION

References are to PARAGRAPH (¶) NUMBERS

Husband and wife (continued)
. tax tables. .1122
. tenants by the entirety. .1300(d)
. trust income for benefit of. .3022(e)
. wash sales. .2221
. withholding exemptions. .2505
. withholding tax on wages. .2504
. zero bracket amount. .1107-1109

— I —

Identification numbers. .3500(c); *See also* Employers, identification number
Identification of stock. .1522
. capital gains and losses. .1607
Illegal business or transaction:
. employees of, old age tax. .3803(a)
. expenses. .1812
. income from. .1300(g)
. . self-employment tax. .3822
. withholding on employees. .2502
Illness: *See* Disability
Import duties, deductibility. .1911(b); 1916
Improvements:
. adjusting basis for. .1500(b); 1528
. capital expenditure. .1528; 1825
. depreciation. .1825; 2033(f)
. lessee. .1317; 2002
. realty subdivided for sale. .1631
. repairs distinguished. .1825; 2033(f)
. Sec. 1250 property. .1619(b)
Imputed interest. .2811(a); 2840
. affiliated corporations. .3226
Incentive compensation plans. .2737(b)
INCLUSIONS IN GROSS INCOME. .1300 et seq.:
See also Gross income, inclusions
Income:
. adjusted gross: *See* Adjusted gross income
. allocation, controlled taxpayers. .3225
. annualizing. .2717
. anticipated, losses. .2202(a)
. averaging. .2401
. bank deposit method of reconstructing. .2711
. cash expenditure method of reconstructing. .2711
. constructive receipt. .2703
. corporations. .3105
. decedents, in respect of. .3008(b)
. deferred foreign. .2730(a)
. defined. .1201
. disputed, when to report. .2728
. exempt: *See* Exempt income
. foreign, deferred. .2730(a)
. gross: *See* Gross income
. investment, tax on private foundations. .3438
. lump-sum. .2401 et seq.
. membership dues, prepaid. .2726(b)
. net worth method of reconstructing. .2711
. percentage method of reconstructing. .2711
. prepaid. .2724; 2726
. reconstructed by commissioner. .2711
. recovered, patent infringement suit. .2728
. repaid. .2729
. source of:
. . foreign country. .3725
. . possessions of U.S.. .3727
. . Puerto Rico. .3727(b)
. splitting of. .1004; 1300(c); 3505-3508; 5503
. . change to same accounting period. .2716
. . community property states. .3508
. subscriptions, prepaid. .2726(a)
. taxable to whom. .1300(c)
. uncollectible. .2719

Income (continued)
. undistributed net, complex trusts. .3023
. undistributed, private foundations. .3441
. unrelated debt-financed, exempt organizations . .3449
Income averaging. .2401
. capital gains, long-term. .2041
. election. .2401
. gifts, income from. .2401
. profit-sharing payouts. .3024(d)
. wagering income. .2401

Income forecast method, depreciation. .2015(c)
Income-producing property:
. capital asset status. .1601(c)
. expenses. .1806; 1808
Income tax: *See* under particular subject
. deductibility. .1911(a)
Income tax preparers. .3542; 3618(i)
. . identification numbers. .3500
. injunctions. .3609(b)
Incorporation fees. .3116
Indebtedness:
. acquisition of, exempt organizations. .3449(c)
. assumption of:
. . exchanges involving. .1405; 1409; 1517(f)
. . reorganizations. .3305
. discharge of, income from. .1318; 3125(f)
. . election to exclude. .1318(j); 3125(f)
. existence, necessity for interest deduction. .1901
. forgiveness. .1318
. . bad debt deduction. .2315(a)
. . dividend, as. .1703
. . gift tax. .4002
. . income from. .1318
. . . election to exclude. .1318(j); 3125(f)
. . loss. .2315(a)
. interest on. .1900-1905
. property in settlement of. .1318(h)
. stock in payment. .1318(h)
Indemnitors, bad debt deduction. .2315(b); 2311(d)
Indemnity bonds, premiums. .1828
Independent contractors distinguished from employees:
. old-age benefit tax. .3817
. teacher. .1832
. withholding tax. .2502
Indexing of liens. .3615(c)
Individuals:
. computation of tax. .1102 et seq.
. . rate changed during year. .3546
. contributions. .1941; 1943
. estimated tax. .2515-2519
. exemptions. .1111 et seq.
. . credit for. .1111(e)
. maximum tax on personal service income. .2402
. minimum tax on tax preferences. .2403
. rates of taxes. .1121; 1122
. . changed during year. .3546
. realty subdivided for sale. .1631
. returns. .1100 et seq.; 3500-3511; 3519
. tax tables. .1122
. withholding. .2501-2512
Individual retirement arrangements. .1101(b); 1838(l); 3027; 3915(b)
Information releases, Internal Revenue Service . .1015(d)
Information required in returns. .3521
. educational expenses. .1833
. employees' deductions. .1805
. installment method, change to. .2804(b)
. installment sales by dealers. .2801

INFORMATION—INSURANCE Index—6035

References are to PARAGRAPH (¶) NUMBERS

Information required in returns (continued)
. partnership interest, sale of. .2935(c)
. real estate investment trusts shareholders. .3432(f)
Information returns. .3530-3540
. actuaries, enrollment and reports of. .3537(d)
. divisive reorganizations. .3316(b)
. exempt organizations. .3436(b); 3537
. . transfers to. .3537
. fiduciaries. .3539
. foreign personal holding companies. .3416
. identifying numbers. .3500
. liquidation of corporation. .3128
. payments for which returns required. .3531
. penalty, failure to file. .3617
. retirement plans:
. . public inspection of. .3537(d)
. . registration statements of. .3537(d)
. wage disability income. .1219(c)
. withholding statements as. .2509
Inheritance:
. basis for gain or loss. .1507-1510
. capital gain or loss. .1606(b)
. depreciation. .2002; 2003
. exclusion. .1225
. income averaging. .2401
. income from. .1225
. interest on. .1314
. loss on sale. .2203
. period held. .1606(b)
. taxes:
. . credit against federal estate tax. .3936
. . deductibility. .1910; 1912(a)
. . . estate tax purposes. .3926
. . foreign, credit against estate tax. .3938
Initiation fees:
. labor unions. .1807
. stock exchange. .1808
Injunction. .3615(f)
Injuries: *See also* Accident benefits; Disability
. compensation for. .1218-1222; 1819(b); 1947
. . armed forces. .1218(c)
. damages paid for. .2204(b)
. damages received for. .1226
. . expenses of suit. .1823
In-laws as dependents. .1117
Insane persons, returns for. .3511(a)
Insect damage, trees. .2204(b)
Insider profits, taxability. .1226; 1328
Insolvency:
. bad debt deduction, effect on. .2305
. forgiveness of debt. .1318(g)
Insolvent corporations, reorganizations. .3331
Installation costs. .1808
INSTALLMENT AND DEFERRED PAYMENT SALES. .2800 et seq.
. accounting methods. .2800; 2801
. . change of. .2804
. bad debts. .2803
. bonds. .2811(a)
. "boot" received. .1408
. capital gain. .2813; 2816(a)
. carrying charges. .1904
. casual sales. .2812
. change to. .2804
. . partnerships. .2913
. commissions. .2811(a)
. computation of profit. .2802
. contingent payments. .2816
. contract price. .2811(a)
. . imputed interest. .2811(a)
. dealers in personal property. .2801-2804
. discounted notes, collection on. .2816

INSTALLMENT AND DEFERRED PAYMENT SALES (continued)
. election to report. .2800
. . revocation of. .2804
. expenses. .2814
. finance charges. .1904(b)
. good faith payments. .2811(a)
. information required. .2811(b); 3521
. initial payments. .2811(a)
. interest deduction. .1904
. interest, imputed. .2811(a); 2840
. losses. .2803; 2814
. obligations:
. . basis. .2831
. . decedents. .3008(b)
. . gain or loss on disposition. .2831
. . gift of. .2831
. option payments. .2811(a)
. payments in year of sale. .2811(a)
. personal property. .2801-2804; 2812
. real property. .2811; 2816; 2823
. reorganizations. .3337
. repossession. .2803; 2821; 2823
. reserve for bad debts. .2311(b)
. residence, personal. .1416(h)
. Section 1245 and 1250 property. .2813
. selling expenses, realty. .2811(a)
. selling price. .2811(a)
. . imputed interest. .2811(a)
. successor corporations. .3337
. tax-free transfer of obligations. .2831(c)
. tax planning. .4515(d)
Installment payments:
. alimony. .1320
. annuities. .1230(e)
. death benefits. .1304(a)
. deficiency interest. .3618
. endowment contracts. .1215(b)
. estate tax. .3944
. . deficiencies. .3945
. insurance proceeds. .1215(b), (c)
. loans purchased at discount. .2722(b)
. mortgage purchased at discount. .2722(b)
. taxes. .3523(a)
. . extension. .3526
Institutional costs, medical expense. .1946
Instrumentalities of U.S.: *See* Federal instrumentalities
Insurance: *See also* Life insurance
. business interruption proceeds. .1331
. . depletion. .2104(b)
. casualty losses. .2204
. commissions. .1301
. . assigned, taxable to whom. .2704
. companies:
. . dividends. .1704
. . employees' annuities. .1232(f)
. . foreign, tax on. .3434(d)
. . net operating loss. .3215
. . tax on. .3434
. exchange of policies. .1407
. losses reduced by. .2201
. premiums. .1807; 1828; 1832; 1946
. . capitalization. .1528
. . compensation. .1307(a)
. . overhead expenses during disability. .1828(b)
. . prepaid. .2707
. proceeds:
. . involuntary conversion. .1410-1415
. . levy on. .3615
. . theft loss. .2205
. . use and occupancy. .1410
. self, reserve for. .2744

6036—Index — INSURANCE—INVENTORIES — 1978

References are to PARAGRAPH (¶) NUMBERS

Insurance (continued)
. use and occupancy. .1331
Intangible drilling costs. .2103(c)
. recapture of. .2103(c)
Intangible property, depreciation. .2001(a)
Interest:
. accrued:
. . bonds sold between interest dates. .1315
. . deduction disallowed for. .2748
. arbitrage bonds. .1204
. awards. .1314
. bank deposits. .1314; 1901; 2703
. bequests. .1314; 3016
. capital contributions by partners. .2923(d)
. capitalization. .1528
. carrying or finance charges. .1901; 1904(c)
. charitable contribution reduced for. .1942(g)
. condemnation awards. .1204
. condominiums. .1902
. constructive payment. .2705
. constructive receipt. .2703
. cooperative apts. and housing. .1902
. . partnerships. .2913
. coupons. .1204; 2703
. deductions. .1900-1905
. . adjusted gross income. .1900
. . corporate mergers. .1905(e)
. deferred payment sales. .1904
. deferred taxes. .3630(c)
. deficiency in tax. .3618
. . carryback, offset by. .3618(d)
. defined. .1314
. deliquent taxes. .3518; 3618
. deductibility. .1901; 3016
. . recovery. .2316(d)
. . . partnerships. .2913
. . withheld taxes. .2512(a)
. discounted notes. .1903; 2739
. dividends:
. . distinguished. .1901
. . left with company. .1216
. . regulated investment companies. .3431(b)
. elderly income credit. .2406
. exempt. .1203; 1204; 1905(a)
. . amortizable premium. .1846
. . net operating loss. .3217; 3219
. exempt organizations, loans to members. .3436(d)
. extensions granted. .3518; 3526; 3618; 3630(c)
. federal instrumentalities' obligations: *See* Federal instrumentalities
. federal obligations: *See* Federal obligations
. foreign tax credit. .3703
. forgiveness of. .1318(b)
. future gift tax. .4020
. G.I. loan. .1902
. gross income. .1201; 1314
. ground rents. .1901
. growth savings certificates. .2722(e)
. imputed. .2811(a); 2840
. . affiliated corporations. .3225
. indebtedness requirements. .1901; 1902
. industrial development bonds. .1204
. information returns. .3521; 3532
. installment and deferred payment sales. .2840
. installment sales. .1904
. investment expense. .1906
. . Subchapter S corp.. .3140
. joint tenants. .1902
. judgments. .1901
. legacies. .1314; 3016
. life insurance loans. .1905; 2739
. life insurance proceeds. .1213, 1314

Interest (continued)
. life policy converted. .1901
. mortgages. .1314; 1528; 1900; 1902
. municipal obligations. .1204
. nonresident aliens, income of. .3712
. . withholding tax. .2503(a); 2535
. notes. .1314
. notes as gift. .1901
. obligations of U.S.. .1203(a)
. on refunds. .1203(d); 3628
. paid for another. .1902
. passing from decedent, defined. .3929
. personal holding company income. .3401
. points paid. .1900
. possessions of U.S., obligations of. .1203(b)
. prepaid. .1314; 2739
. refunds. .1314
. rent paid to lessor corporation's bondholders. .3108
. repaid on H savings bonds. .2723(b)
. savings accounts, forfeiture penalty. .1102(c); 1801(a); 2203; 3532(a)
. savings bonds. .2723
. self-employment income. .3824
. state obligations. .1204
. tax-free covenant bond, withholding on. .2535(b)
. taxpayer's indebtedness. .1902
. tenants by entirety. .1902
. tenant-stockholders. .1902
. time to deduct. .2705; 2739
. time to report. .2722
. unpaid 2½ mos. after close of year. .2748
. . partnership and related person. .2924
. usurious. .1314
. veterans' loans. .1902
Interest equalization tax, deductibility. .1911(b)
Internal Revenue:
. Code:
. . finding list. .5801
. . organization of. .1013(a)
. service, practice before. .3609
International organizations:
. old-age benefit tax. .3815(c)
. self-emloyment tax. .3815(c); 3823(e)
. withholding tax. .2503(b)
Interns, hospitals, stipends received. .1303
Intestate law, transfers under, estate tax. .3901
In-transit goods, inventory. .2602
Invalid care. .2415
Inventions: *See* Patents
INVENTORIES. .2600 et seq.
. accrual basis mandatory. .2706
. appreciated; *See also* Partnerships, substantially appreciated inventory
. . distribution of, corporations. .3129(b)
. basis. .2611
. book and physical. .2608
. capital assets status. .1601(d)
. casualty loss of. .2204(g)
. change of method. .2604; 2708(a)
. consistency of method. .2604
. cost basis. .2604(a)
. cost or market. .2604(b)
. dealers in securities. .2609(a)
. . information required. .3521
. depreciation. .2001(a)
. distribution to shareholders, gain or loss to corporation. .3127
. dollar-value costing. .2606(b)
. election of method. .2604
. farmers. .2615
. farm-price method. .2615(a)
. fifo method. .2605; 2606(a)

INVENTORIES—LABOR

References are to PARAGRAPH (¶) NUMBERS

INVENTORIES (continued)
. full absorption method, manufacturers. .2609(c)
. function. .2600
. goods unsalable at normal prices. .2607
. information required. .3521
. lifo method. .2606; 2609(e)
. livestock. .2615
. manufacturers. .2609(c)
. methods. .2604-2609
. . disapproved. .2610
. miners. .2609(d)
. partnerships:
. . distributions. .2944-2945
. . transfers. .2935
. perpetual. .2608
. physical. .2608
. pools. .2606(b)
. real estate dealers. .2600
. records. .2710
. reorganizations. .3337
. required. .2600
. retail merchants. .2609(e)
. successor corporation. .3337
. theft loss of. .2205(d)
. unidentifiable goods. .2605
. unit-livestock-price method. .2615(b)
. valuation. .2604-2609
. withdrawals for personal use. .2601
Investigation expenses, new business. .1808
Investment credit. .2410
. carryback and carryforward. .2410(d); 3618(a)
. . deficiency in tax. .3611(f); 3618(a)
. employee stock ownership plan (ESOP). .2410(h)
. estates and trusts. .3019
. Form 1040. .1103
. joint ventures. .2913
. movie films. .2410(c)
. partnerships. .2913
. recapture of. .2410(e)
. refunds, carryback affecting. .3624(b); 3630
. reorganizations. .3337
. Subchapter S corp. .2410(f), (g)
Investment interest. .1906
Investment property:
. depreciation. .2001
. exchanges. .1406; 1409
. expenses. .1806
. legal advice concerning. .1823
. private foundations. .3443
Investment trusts:
. foreign, information returns. .3540
. regulated investment companies: *See* Regulated investment companies
Investors:
. expenses. .1806(b)
. limitations on risk. .2736
Involuntary conversion. .1410-1415
. basis. .1519
. benefit assessments. .1415
. capital gain or loss. .1619(e); 1620
. condemnation awards. .1410-1415
. . interest on. .1204
. deductions for adj. gr. inc.. .1801(a)
. gain. .1410-1415; 1519(c); 3611
. information required. .1411; 3521
. investment credit, effect on. .2410(a)
. loss. .1410; 1411; 1414; 1519(b)
. partnership. .2911
. personal use property. .1601
. proceeds, use and occupancy. .1410
. qualified replacement property. .1413

Involuntary conversion (continued)
. recognition of gain or loss. .1410-1415
. reinvestment of proceeds. .1410-1415; 1619(e)
. reorganizations. .3337
. replacements. .1410-1414; 1519
. . substituted basis. .1514
. residence, personal. .1414(b); 1421
. . replaced. .1526
. . . holding period. .1606(e)
. Sec. 1231 gains and losses. .1620
. self-employment income. .3824
. severance damages. .1415
. successor corporations. .3337
. time for replacement. .1412
. what constitutes. .1410
IRA. .1101(b); 1102(c); 1838(l); 3027
Iron lung and equipment. .1946
Iron ore. .1623
Item accounts, depreciation. .2022(a)
. retirement from. .2036

— J —

Jeopardy assessment. .3605(b); 3612(c)
. interest. .3618
Jewelry:
. inherited, loss on sale. .2203
. lost, loss deduction. .2204(b)
Jobs credit. .2412
Job training benefits, taxability. .1301
Job training, veterans. .1218(c)
Joint and survivor annuities: *See* Annuities, joint and survivor
Joint declarations. .2516(a)
Joint returns: *See* Husband and wife, returns
Joint tenancies. .1300(e)
. dividends received. .1705(b)
. estate tax. .3904
. gift tax. .4002
. . marital deduction. .4023
. interest deduction. .1902
. sale of residence. .1423
. Series E bonds. .1314
. stock:
. . converted to tenancy in common. .1404
. . severed by partition action. .1404
. survivor interest, basis. .1509
Joint ventures:
. as partnerships. .2900
. investment credit. .2913
Judgments:
. assigned, gift tax. .4002
. interest on. .1901
. time to deduct. .2735(c)
. time to report. .2728
Jury fees. .1301
. withholding tax. .2503

— K —

Keno winnings, return for. .3521
Keogh plans. .1801(a); 1839; 3537(d)

— L —

Labor, cost of goods sold. .2604(a)
Labor organizations:
. assessments. .1807
. dues. .1102(d); 1807
. fines against members. .1807
. health insurance fund contributions. .1828(b)

LABOR—LIFE

References are to PARAGRAPH (¶) NUMBERS

Labor organizations (continued)
. initiation fees. .1807
. pension plans negotiated by. .3024
. strike benefits: *See* Strike benefits
. unemployment benefits. .1301
Land:
. capital gains and losses. .1601; 1618
. clearing expenses. .1845
. conservation expenditures. .1845
. depreciation. .2001; 2003(d)
. development, expenses. .1528; 1844
. soil conservation expenditures. .1845
. subdivided. .1631
. water conservation expenditures. .1845
. with unharvested crop, sale of. .1622
Land contract: *See* Installment and deferred payment sales
Landlord: *See* Lessee and lessor
Last-in, first-out, inventories. .2606; 2609(e)
. tax planning. .4515(b)
Laundry costs:
. traveling expense. .1829
. uniforms. .1807
Lawyers: *See* Attorneys
Lease-back income. .3449
Lease-purchase agreements, payments under . .1826(e)
Leases: *See also* Lessee and lessor
. assigned. .2704
. bonus payments, oil, gas or mines. .2104; 2105
. building demolished to obtain. .2209
. cancellation. .1316; 1601(g); 1826(d); 2724
. capital asset status. .1601(g)
. deposit forfeited. .1826(d)
. depreciation. .2001
. exchanged for real estate. .1406
. expense of securing. .1823; 1840
. fair market value. .1502(b)
. income from. .3449
. investment credit. .2410(f)
. option to purchase under. .1826(e)
. renewable. .1840
. sales distinguished. .1826(e)
. title transfer. .1826(e)
Legacies: *See* Inheritance
Legacy taxes:
. deductibility:
. . estate tax purposes. .3926
. . income tax purposes. .1912(a)
. foreign, credit against fed. estate tax. .3938
Legal damages, deductibility of. .2202(b)
Legal expenses. .1806; 1823; 3016
Legislation, payments for influencing. .1941(a)
Lenders, withholding tax on wages. .2501(b)
Lessee and lessor:
. advance rentals. .1826(c)
. bond interest paid for lessor. .1316
. coal royalties. .1623
. depletion. .2101(b); 2104; 2105
. depreciation. .2002
. dividends paid for lessor. .1316
. improvements by lessee. .1317; 2002
. investment credit. .2410(f)
. iron ore royalties. .1623
. lease-purchase agreements, payments under . .1826(e)
. payments to obtain possession. .1840
. payments to third parties. .3108
. replacements by lessee. .2002
. taxes paid for lessor. .1316; 1919
Letter or memorandum, capital asset status. .1601
Levies. .3610(a); 3615

Levies (continued)
. insurance contracts. .3615
. wrongful, suspension period. .3613(d)
Liabilities:
. assumption of:
. . partners and partnerships. .2925
. . reorganizations. .3305
. contested. .2735
. corporate distributions. .3129(c)
Liability insurance premiums. .1828(b); 1832
Libel:
. damages received for. .1226
. suit, expense of. .1823
Libraries, depreciation. .2001(a)
Licenses:
. deductibility as tax. .1912(d)
. depreciation. .2001(a)
Liens. .3615(c)
. estate tax, executor. .3947
. personal holding companies. .3404
Life estates:
. basis for gain or loss. .1510
. capital asset. .1601(k)
. depletion. .2101(c)
. depreciation. .2002
. estate tax. .3919(d)
. . marital deduction. .3929(b)
. gift-tax marital deduction. .4023
Life expectancy, annuities. .1230
Life insurance:
. annuities. .1230
. assignments of policy. .1213
. companies, tax on. .3434(a)
. . personal holding company tax. .3403
. . rate tables. .5507
. dividends on policies. .1216; 1704
. endowment contracts. .1215
. estate planning. .4706
. estate tax. .3914; 3919(d)
. . marital deduction. .3929(b)
. exchange of policies. .1407
. family income rider. .1213(c)
. gift tax. .4002; 4011; 4030
. group, premiums. .1307(a); 1828(a)
. . information returns. .3535
. . withholding statements, included on. .2508(a)
. . withholding tax. .2503(a)
. installment payments. .1215(b), (c)
. interest paid to purchaser. .1828; 1905
. loans:
. . interest. .1905; 2739
. . secured by. .1828(a); 2305
. lump-sum payments. .1215(a)
. options in contract. .1213; 1215(c)
. partners. .1828(a)
. premiums:
. . alimony and separate maintenance payments . .1320(d)
. . as dividends. .1704
. . compensation. .1307(a)
. . deductibility. .1807; 1828
. . split-dollar. .1307(a)
. proceeds. .1213-1216
. . alimony and separate maintenance payments . .1320(d)
. . dividends, as. .1703
. . interest on. .1213; 1314
. . partnerships. .2925
. . shareholders receiving. .1213(d)
. salesmen, old-age benefit tax. .3817(b)
. split-dollar. .1307(a)
. surrender of policy. .1214

LIFE—LOSSES

Life insurance (continued)
. term-form. .1307(a)
. trusts. .3022(e)
Life tenants:
. as a fiduciary. .3001
. depletion. .2002(c); 2101(c); 3014
. depreciation. .2002(c); 2101(c); 3014
Lifo method, inventories. .2606; 2609(e)
. distribution to shareholders. .3127(b)
. dollar-value costing. .2606(b)
. information required. .3521
. tax planning. .4515(b)
Like kind, defined. .1406
Lime expenses of farmers. .1844
Limitations: See also Statute of limitations
. accounting method changed. .2709
. bad debt deduction. .2305; 2315
. capital loss. .1613(a)
. estate tax purposes. .3946
. foreign tax credit. .3703
. individual's tax liability. .1121
. net operating loss, carryover:
. . corporation. .3221
. . reorganization. .3338; 3339
. preferred stock bail-out. .1722(c)
. reorganization exchanges. .3307(b)
. . controlled corporations. .3317
. . exchanges of securities. .3309
. social security tax. .3818(a)
. tax-free exchanges, reorganizations. .3309; 3317
. trust held corporation. .3610(b)
Limited partnership, taxability as corporation
. . .3101
Liquidated damages. .1301; 2503(a)
Liquidating dividends. .1715-1717; 3128
. exclusion. .1706(a)
. information returns. .3536
. loss deductible when. .1717(b)
. personal holding companies. .3404
Liquidation:
. carryovers. .3336; 3337
. corporation. .1722(b); 3128; 3334
. . bonds, amortization of premium for discount, successor corp.. .3125(e)
. . expenses. .1808
. . information returns. .3536
. distribution, gain or loss. .3128
. exempt organizations, information returns . .3536(c)
. foreign corporation, advance ruling needed. .3334
. installment obligations distributed in. .2831(b)
. one month. .3335
. . returns. .3512; 3517(b)
. . tax-free. .3335
. partial. .1716; 3129(e)
. partnership interests. .2918; 2927-2932
. stock options, effect on. .1327
. subsidiaries:
. . basis. .3334
. . gain or loss. .3334
. . twelve-month. .3128
Liquor and liquor dealers, taxes, rate chart. .5515
Literary works, capital asset status. .1601(f)
Litigation expenses. .1806; 1823; 3016
Livestock:
. capital gains and losses. .1622
. depreciation. .1619(a); 2001(a)
. diseased:
. . casualty loss. .2204(b)
. . sale or exchange. .1410
. exchange of. .1406
. expenses. .1844(b)

Livestock (continued)
. inventories. .2615
. losses. .2204(b); 2211
. sale of. .1622
. . diseased. .1410
Living expenses. .1807; 2204(c)
Loan and investment corporations, personal holding company tax. .3403
Loans: See also Advances; Bad debts
. building and loan associations, repaid to U.S. . .3433(b)
. commissions. .1309; 2707; 2722(c)
. Commodity Credit Corporation:
. . income. .2722(d)
. . information required. .3521
. cooperative banks, repaid to U.S.. .3433(b)
. dividends distinguished. .1703
. gifts distinguished. .2308
. guaranteed by U.S., distribution of proceeds . .3129(g)
. installment repayments. .1904
. interest on. .1201; 1900-1905
. . capitalization. .1528
. . deductions. .1900; 1903; 1905; 2739
. . income. .1201
. . veterans. .1902
. life insurance. .1828(a); 2305
. life insurance premiums. .1828(a)
. mutual savings bank, repaid to U.S.. .3433(b)
. payment with proceeds from, time for deduction . .2735(a)
. purchased at discount. .2722(b)
. savings and loan associations, repaid to U.S. . .3433(b)
. stockholder receiving. .1703
Lobbying expenses:
. charitable contribution. .1941(a)
. exempt organization. .3436(d)
Lodging: See Board and lodging
Long-term capital gains and losses: See Capital gains and losses, long-term
Long-term contracts. .2842
. advance payments. .2726(c)
. change in method of reporting. .2708(a)
. information required. .2842; 3521
. tax planning. .4515(c)
LOSSES. .2200-2244: See also Capital gains and losses; Gain or loss
. abandoned property. .1808; 2210
. anticipated profits and wages. .2202(a)
. anticipated, reserve for. .2744
. assets retired. .2036
. attorney fees, part of. .2204(b)
. automobiles:
. . damage to. .2200; 2204(b)
. . sale of. .2202
. bad debts distinguished. .2315
. basis. .2201
. . casualty. .2204
. . gifts. .1515
. . involuntary conversions. .1519(b)
. . March 1, 1913, property acquired before. .1506
. buildings, demolition of. .2209
. business, deductibility. .2202; See also Net operating loss
. cancellation of debts. .2315(a)
. capital expenditures distinguished. .2212
. casualty. .2204; 2206
. . estate tax. .3926
. . information required. .3521
. . net operating loss. .2242(a)
. . refunds. .2204

LOSSES (continued)
. casualty (continued)
. . time for deduction. .2204(e)
. compromised accounts. .2315(a)
. court costs, part of. .2204(b)
. damages. .2202(b); 2204
. deductibility. .1801(a); 2200-2244
. . estate tax. .3926
. demolition of buildings. .2209
. disallowed. .2221-2223
. . estates and trusts. .3018
. . partner and partnership. .2908(a); 2923
. . partnership and related person. .2924
. . personal holding companies. .3408
. disaster. .2204(e)
. dividends paid in property. .1702(b)
. embezzlement. .2205
. expropriation. .2241; 3613(f)
. family. .2223(a)(e)
. farmers. .2211; 2226
. fire: See Fire, losses
. five consecutive years. .2225
. flood. .2204
. foreclosures. .2223(a); 2743(b)
. forgiveness of debt. .2315(a)
. frost. .2204(b)
. gambling. .2224
. hobby. .2225
. hurricane. .2204
. installment and deferred payment sales. .2803; 2814
. interest on redemption Series H savings bonds. .2723(b)
. investigation expenses, new business. .1808
. involuntary conversions. .1410; 1411; 1414; 1519(b); 1620
. life insurance policy surrendered. .1214
. liquidating dividend, time to deduct. .1717(b)
. livestock. .2204(b); 2211
. lost articles. .2204
. mine cave-ins. .2204(b)
. mortgage foreclosures and settlements. .2223(a); 2743(b)
. net operating: See Net operating loss
. nontaxable exchange. .1517
. options not exercised. .1601(h)
. partnerships. .2908; 2913
. pledged property. .2317
. railroad reorganizations. .3332
. recovered after deduction. .2316(d)
. reserves. .2744
. residence, personal. .2207
. retirement of assets, . .2036
. sale of property . .2743(b)
. . adjusted gross income. .1801(a); 2200
. . bona fide sale, necessity for. .2222
. . converted to business use. .2207
. . imputed interest. .2840(b)
. . stocks and bonds. .1611
. short-term obligations issued at discount. .2723(c)
. small business investment companies. .3459
. small business stock. .1632
. smog. .2204(b)
. sonic boom. .2204(b)
. storm. .2204(b)
. surrender of stock. .2212(b)
. termites. .2204(b)
. theft. .2205; 2206; 2242(a)
. time for deduction. .2204(e); 2743(b)
. Trade. .2202;   See also Net operating loss
. transactions for profit. .2203
. vandalism. .2204(b)

LOSSES (continued)
. wash sales. .2221
. worthless securities. .3203
. worthless stock. .2203; 2208
Lots:
. capital gains and losses. .1631
. exchanged for other realty. .1406
. sale of. .2841
Lotteries: See Gambling
Lubricating oil, refund. .2417
Lump-sum income, averaging. .2401
Lump-sum payments:
. alimony. .1320
. allocation between land and building. .2003(d)
. endowment insurance. .1215(a)
. life insurance. .1215(a)
. royalties, nonresident aliens. .2535; 3712
. survivor's insurance benefits, taxability. .1304

— M —

Machinery and equipment:
. capital expenditure. .1528; 1825
. capital gains and losses. .1619(a)
. depreciation. .2001; 2016
. exchanged, "boot" involved. .1408; 1517
. . basis of property received. .1517
. farm. .1844(b)
. investment credit. .2410
. lease agreements. .1826(e)
. lessee replacing. .2002
. purchased during year:
. . additional first-year depreciation. .2016
. . credit for. .2410
. . sum of the years-digits. .2013(a)
. repairs. .1825; 2033(f)
. useful life. .2033
Magazine vendors, old-age benefit tax. .3811
Magazines:
. farm. .1844(a)
. professional expense. .1832
Maids: See Domestics
Mails, fraudulent use of, expenses defending suit. .1823
Malicious prosecution, damages for. .2202(b)
Malpractice suit, expense defending. .1823
Management expenses, cost of goods sold. .2604(a)
Manufacturers:
. excise taxes, rate chart. .5515
. gift of products. .1810
. inventory method. .2606(b); 2609(c)
Marine Corps: See Armed forces
Marine Insurance companies. .3434(b)
Marital deduction:
. estate planning. .4705
. estate tax purposes. .3929
. gift tax purposes. .4023
Marital status:
. abandoned spouse. .1104(c); 1106(a)
. computation of withholding. .2504
. standard deduction. .1108
. when determined. .1109
. zero bracket amount. .1109
Maritime employment, old-age benefit tax. .3803(c)
Market, inventories at. .2604(b)
Marriage: See also Husband and wife
. tax advice in settlement. .1823
Marriage fees, income tax. .1301
Married person: See Husband and wife
Masses, fees. .1301
Maternity clothing as medical expense. .1946

Mattress as medical expense. .1946
Maximum tax on personal service income. .2402
McCarran Act, aliens' foreign employment. .3708(b)
Meals: *See* Board and lodging
Medical examination, employees. .1805
MEDICAL EXPENSES. .1945-1947
. benefit plans. .1838
. capital expenditures as. .1946
. child care expenses as. .1946
. community income. .1945(c)
. decedents. .1945(b)
. defined. .1946
. dependent defined. .1945(c)
. divorced wife. .1320(f)
. estate income tax deduction for. .3011
. home improvement costs. .1946
. information required. .3521
. insurance premiums. .1945; 1946(c)
. joint checking accounts. .1945(c)
. joint returns. .1945(a)
. net operating loss carryover involved. .2243
. partners and partnerships. .2913
. reimbursement. .1219; 1221; 1945(a); 1947
. time to deduct. .1945; 2741
. transplant expenses. .1945(c)
. traveling expenses. .1946
. wage disability income. .1219(c)
Medical reimbursement plans. .1819(b); 1946
Medicare. .1116(a)
. benefits, exempt income. .1222
. voluntary premiums, deductibility. .1819(b); 1946
Membership dues, prepaid. .2726(b)
Mergers. .3303
. carryovers. .3336; 3337
. corporate, interest deduction. .1905(e)
. partnerships. .2922(c)
. stock options, effect on. .1327(d)
. surtax exemption. .3102
. survivor corp., information returns. .3531
Merit rating credit, unemployment insurance. .2730(b); 3841
Metal mines, percentage depletion. .2102
Mexican residents:
. as dependents. .1120
. income tax. .3709(b)
Mileage allowance, automobile:
. business use. .1829(c)
. charitable purposes. .1942(c)
. medical purposes. .1946(e)
Military: *See also* Armed forces
. bases, as U.S. possession. .3727(a)
. pay to employees for reserve training:
. . deductibility. .1819
. . withholding tax. .2503(a)
. service: *See* Armed forces
Military post exchanges, social security coverage. .3815(a)
Mineral production payments, depletion. .2101(e)
Mines:
. capital additions. .2103(c)
. cave-ins, loss deduction. .2204(b)
. depletion. .2100-2113
. depreciation. .2111
. development costs. .1843(b)
. . successor in reorganizations. .3337
. drilling cost. .2103(c)
. . partnerships. .2913
. expenditures. .1843
. exploration:

Mines (continued)
. *exploration (continued)*
. . expenditures. .1843(a)
. . . information required. .3521
. . . partnerships. .2913
. . . successor in reorganization. .3337
. inventory method. .2609(d)
. percentage depletion. .2102
Minimum royalties, depletion. .2101(b)
Minimum tax on tax preferences. .2403
. Adjusted itemized deductions. .2403(a)
. amortization:
. . as tax preference. .2403
. . on-the-job training and child care centers. .2043; 2403
. . pollution control facilities. .2040(b); 2403
. bank's bad debt deduction. .3433(a), (b)
. building and loan associations, bad debt deduction. .3433(b)
. capital gains. .1600(d); 1612(b); 2403(a); 3009(b); 3201
. common trust funds. .3025
. corporations. .2403; 3103
. depletion deduction. .2102(b)
. depreciation, accelerated. .2403(a)
. estates and trusts. .3020(d)
. . net capital gain. .3009(b)
. fractional year. .2717. *See also* Fractional year
. intangible drilling costs. .2403(a)
. net capital gains, corporations. .3201(b)
. net operating loss. .2403(b)
. partnerships. .2906
. partners, investment interest. .2913(a)
. personal holding companies. .3400
. real estate investment trusts. .3432(g)
. records. .3541
. regulated investment companies. .3431(f)
. returns. .3541
. stock options. .1327(a), (c); 2403(a)
. Subchapter S Corp.. .3140
. trust companies' bad debt deduction. .3433(a)
Mining, defined. .2104
Ministers: *See* Clergymen
Minors: *See also* Children
. alimony for support of. .1320(c)
. compensation paid by parent. .1815
. dependents. .1118(a)
. . earnings. .1312
. employment of, by parent, old-age benefit tax. .3808
. expenses attributable to earnings of. .1100(a)
. gifts to. .1225(b); 4020(a)
. income of. .1312
. model custodian act gifts. .1225
. returns. .1100; 3509; 3511(a)
. trust income for support of. .3022(e)
. uniform gift to minors act. .1225(b)
. withholding tax on wages. .2502
. . refunds and credits. .3509
Mistake, amounts received by. .1300(b)
Mitigation of statute of limitations. .3631
Model custodian act gifts. .1225(b)
Money:
. as property. .3334
. borrowed, payment with, time for deduction. .2735(a)
. lost, loss deduction. .2204(b)
. order, payment of tax. .3527(b)
Monthly deposits of withheld taxes. .2509(a)
Monthly family allowances, armed forces. .1306
Monthly payroll period, computation of withholding. .2504
Mortality tables, annuities. .1230(b)

6042—Index   MORTGAGE—NONBUSINESS

———— References are to PARAGRAPH (¶) NUMBERS ————

Mortgage:
. alimony payments to reduce. .1320(e)
. "amount realized" as including. .1400
. assumption of, exchanges involving. .1409; 1517(f)
. commission on. .1309; 2707
. deferred payment sale involving. .2816
. estate tax, real estate valuation. .3919(a)
. foreclosures, loss. .2223(a); 2743(b)
. installment sale involving. .2811
. interest on. .1314; 1528; 1900; 1902
. points. .1900
. prepayment. .1901
. purchased at discount. .2722(b)
. settled for less than face value. .1318(i)
. . depreciation of mortgaged property. .2003
. unpaid deduction for estate tax purposes. .3926
Moth damage, loss deduction. .2204(b)
Mother, as dependent. .1117
Mother-in-law:
. alimony for support of. .1320(c)
. dependent. .1117
Motion picture, rights, capital asset. .1601(f)
Moving expenses. .1805; 1831
. reimbursement. .1302(b)
. . withholding tax. .2503
. social security taxes. .3819
. withholding tax on allowance. .2503(a)
Multiple asset accounts, depreciation. .2022(b)
. retirement from. .2036
Multiple support tests, exemptions. .1116(c)
. information required. .3521
Municipalities:
. contracts with, profits. .1330
. employees and officers:
. . annuities. .1232(h); 1305
. . compensation. .1305
. . old-age benefit tax. .3815(b)
. obligations:
. . amortizable premium. .1846
. . capital asset status. .1601
. . gain or loss. .1403
. . gift tax. .4000
. . industrial development bonds. .1204
. . interest. .1204
. . interest to purchase or carry. .1905(a)
. . market discount. .1204
. taxes:
. . deductibility. .1912
. . who may deduct. .1917
Musical composition, capital asset status. .1601(f)
Mutual funds:
. capital gain dividends. .1702(c); 1706(a); 3431(a), (d), (e)
. dividends from. .1702(c); 1706(a); 3431(a), (d), (e)
. valuation, estate tax. .3919(b)
Mutual Educational and Cultural Exchange Act, amounts received under. .1303
Mutual insurance companies. .3434(b), (c)
Mutual life insurance companies, dividends ..1704
Mutual savings banks:
. bad debt reserve. .3433(b)
. dividends, exclusion. .1706(a)
. investment credit. .2410(g)
. taxability. .3433(b)

— N —

National farm loan association:
. dividends. .1704(a)
. social security coverage. .3815(a)

National Guard training, pay to employees attending:
. deductibility. .1819
. withholding tax. .2503(a)
National Labor Relations Board, back pay, withholding. .2503(a)
Naval service: *See* Armed forces
Negligence penalty. .3618
Nephew, as dependent. .1117
Net lease, investment interest. .1906(c)
Net long-term capital gain, alternative tax. .1614; 3202
NET OPERATING LOSS. .2241-2244; 3215-3221
. accounts receivable sold at loss. .2242(a)
. adjustments. .2242(a); 3217; 3219
. . accounting method changed. .2709
. annualizing income, change in accounting period ..2717
. carryback and carryover. .2241; 2243; 2244; 3215-3221: *See also* Carryback and carryover, net operating loss
. . bad debt recoveries. .2316(c)
. . banks and trust companies. .3433(a)
. . building and loan associations. .3433(b)
. . cooperative banks. .3433(b)
. . elimination of carryover. .3221
. . mutual savings banks. .3433(b)
. . refunds due to. .3624(b); 3630
. . reorganizations. .3337-3339
. . stock ownership rules. .3221
. . successor corporation. .3337-3339
. . table. .3220
. common trust funds. .3025
. computation. .2242-2244; 3217
. corporations. .3215-3221
. deduction. .2241-2244; 3215-3221
. . information required. .3521
. . partnerships. .2914
. . percentage depletion, effect on. .2104(a)
. deficiency due to. .3611(f)
. estates and trusts. .3015
. foreign personal holding companies. .3413
. individuals. .2241-2244
. insurance companies. .3215
. minimum tax on tax preferences, effect of. .2403
. moving expenses. .2242(a)
. nonbusiness deductions defined. .2242(a)
. partnerships. .2241; 2914
. personal holding companies. .3404
. regulated investment companies. .3431
. reorganizations. .3337-3339
. self-employed retirement plans. .2242(a)
. small business corporation. .3143(c)
. small business stock. .2242(a)
. state income taxes. .2242(a)
. stock ownership rules. .3221
. successor corporation. .3337-3339
Net capital gain, alternative tax. .1614(b); 3202
Net worth, figuring income from. .2711
Newsboys:
. old-age benefit tax. .3811
. withholding tax. .2503(b)
Newspaper vendors, withholding tax. .2503(b)
Niece, as dependent. .1117
Ninety-day letter. .3605; 3617; 3629(c)
Nonbusiness bad debts. .2307
Nonbusiness expenses. .1803(b); 1806
. attributable to tax-exempt income. .1809; 3007
. estates and trusts. .1806; 3016
. net operating loss purposes. .2242(a)
. partnerships. .2913

Nonbusiness expenses (continued)
. personal expenses distinguished. .1807
Nonexempt trusts:
. information returns. .3538
. treatment of. .3453
Non-patronage income, farmers' cooperative associations. .3455
Non-profit organizations: *See* Exempt organizations: Exemptions
Nonresident aliens: *See* Aliens, nonresident
Nonresident citizen, compensation, income. .3725
Nonresident foreign corporations: *See* Foreign corporations
Nontaxable:
. bond rights. .1714
. exchanges: *See* Exchanges, nontaxable
. income: *See* Exempt income
. stock dividends. .1708; 3404
. . preferred stock bail-out. .1722
. stock rights. .1711; 3404
Nontrade expenses: *See* Nonbusiness expenses
Normal tax, corporations. .3102
Notary fees, as wages. .2503(b)
Notes:
. capital asset status. .1601
. compensation paid in. .1309
. debt paid by, time for deduction. .2735(a)
. deferred payment sales. .2816
. discounted. .1309; 1903; 2739
. fair market valuea. .1502(b)
. gift, given as, interest. .1901
. interest. .1314
. receivable:
. . capital asset status. .1601
. partnership:
. . . distributions. .2928-2932; 2944
. . . transfers. .2935
. state or political subdivision, interest. .1204
Notice of deficiency, payment after. .3605
Nurses:
. cost of. .1945 et seq.
. student, old-age benefit tax, federal hospitals. .3815(a)

— O —

Obligations:
. corporate: *See* Bonds
. distribution of, effect on earnings and profits. .3129
. federal: *See* Federal obligations
. municipalities: *See* Municipalities, obligations
. state: *See* State, obligations
Obsolescence. .2034
Occupational taxes, rate chart. .5515
Office expenses:
. investors. .1806
. professional people. .1832
Oil properties:
. capital additions. .2103(c)
. depletion. .2101(d); 2102
. depreciation. .2111
. drilling costs. .2103(c)
. . as tax preference. .2403(a)
. investing in. .4607
. sale of, information required. .3521
Old-age and survivor insurance: *See* Social security, old-age and survivor insurance
Old-age exemptions. .1113
Operating day method, depreciation. .2015(b)
Operating losses: *See* Net operating loss

Option:
. capital gain or loss. .1601(h); 1609
. forfeiture of, loss. .1601(h)
. life insurance contracts containing. .1213; 1215(c)
. payments, installment and deferred payment sales. .2811
. purchases by employees. .1328
. real estate purchase, holding period. .1606
. short sales. .1609
. stock purchase:
. . compensation v. gift. .1302(b)
. . constructive ownership. .1727(e)
. . ownership rules. .3402
. straddle. .1609
. variable price. .1327(c)
Optional dividends. .1707
Optional tax method: *See* Tax table method
Orchards, depreciation. .2001
Ordinary gross income, personal holding companies. .3401
Ores, percentage depletion. .2104
Organization and syndication fees, partnerships. .2906(b)
Organization expenses. .3116; 3521
. personal holding companies. .3404
Orphan's exclusion, estate tax. .3926
Osteopaths' fees. .1946
Outside salespersons, expenses. .1805(a). *See also* Salespersons
. educational. .1833
. information required. .1805(a)
. reimbursed. .1805(a)
"Over the counter" stock, holding period. .1606
Overassessment, certificate of. .3627(b)
. agreements as to. .3626
Overcollection of tax from employee. .2510
Overhead expenses:
. cost of goods sold. .2604(a)
. disability insurance covering. .1828(b)
Overlapping items. .2735(d)
Overnight, defined. .1829
Overpayment of taxes:
. counterclaims by government. .3615(d)
. refund: *See* Refunds
. Tax Court finding. .3537(b)
Overriding royalties, depletion. .2101(b)
Overtime pay:
. back pay: *See* Back pay
. withholding tax. .2503(a); 2504(e)
Ownership certificates. .3532(b)

— P —

Paid-in surplus, basis of property acquired as. .1518(b)
Painting and redecorating expenses. .1825
Panama Canal Zone: *See* Possessions of U.S.
Panama residents, dependents, as. .1120
Parents:
. as dependents. .1117
. board and lodging of children. .1312
. defined. .3509
. divorced or separated, exemption for children. .1116(a)
. expenses attributable to child's earnings. .1100(a)
. liability for child's tax. .3614(b)
. members of household. .1106(b)
. returns for children. .3509
. services of children. .1312; 1815
Parsonage:
. allowance to cover cost:
. . income tax. .1308(e)

6044—Index — PARSONAGE—PARTNERSHIPS

References are to PARAGRAPH (¶) NUMBERS

Parsonage (continued)
. allowance to cover cost: (continued)
. . self-employment income. .3824
. rental value:
. . income tax. .1308(e)
. . self-employment income. .3824

PARTNERSHIPS. .2900 et seq.
. accounting period changed. .2921
. advantages over corporation. .3152; 4507
. alimony. .2913
. allocation of earnings, family partnership. .2905
. assets:
. . contributed to. .2925
. . distributed. .2927-2932; 2937-2942
. . substantially appreciated. .2944(d)
. bad debts recovered. .2913
. bona fide. .2904
. book profit or loss. .2907
. capital accounts of partners, reconciliation. .2918
. capital contributions. .2910; 2925
. capital gains and losses. .1601(e); 2911; 2945
. . loss carryover. .2906(a)
. charitable contributions. .2915
. child care expenses. .2913
. compensation of partners. .2923(d)
. conservation expenditures. .2913
. consolidations. .2922(c)
. contributions to. .2910; 2925; 2937(b); 2939(a)
. cooperative housing deductions. .2913
. corporation as against. .3152-3154
. corporation as partner. .2900
. corporation taxed as. .3140-3146
. . dividend exclusion. .1706(a)
. credits. .2913; 2917; 3701; 3703
. death of partner. .2941; 2942
. deceased partner:
. . holding period of surviving partner's interest. .1606(d)
. . self-employment income. .3823(d)
. . share income. .2941; 2942
. . tax year of partnership as affected by. .2922(a)(b)
. declaration of estimated tax. .2516(c)
. deductions. .2906; 2913-2917
. defined. .2900
. depletion. .2910; 2913; 2938(b)
. . undivided interests. .2910
. depreciation. .2910; 2913
. . additional first-year allowance. .2016(d)
. . undivided interests. .2910
. dissolution:
. . assets distributed. .2928-2932
. . taxable year as affected by. .2922
. distribution schedule. .2918
. distributions. .2927-2932; 2937-2942
. distributive shares. .2908; 2909; 2918
. . deductions and exclusions. .2913
. . family partnership. .2905
. . self-employment tax. .3823(d)
. dividends received. .2906(b); 2916
. earned income, maximum tax. .2908(d)
. election binding on partners. .2906(c)
. estate as partner. .2900
. evidence of. .2904
. exemptions. .2906(b)
. expenses:
. . disallowed, partnership and related person. .2924
. . production of income. .2913
. exploration expenditures. .2913
. family. .2904; 2905
. farm losses. .2913
. farm recapture property. .2910(a); 2913; 2925
. foreign. .3711
. . withholding tax. .2535

PARTNERSHIPS (continued)
. foreign investment company stock. .2944(d)
. foreign taxes:
. . credit. .2917; 3701; 3703
. . deductibility. .2906(b); 2917
. gambling transactions. .2913
. gift of interest. .2905; 2922(a)(b)
. gross income of partners. .3545
. guaranteed payments, when partner includes. .2920
. identification numbers. .3500
. income, assigned. .2704
. information required. .3521
. installment method, change to. .2913
. intangible drilling and development costs. .2913
. interest in:
. . capital asset status. .1601(e); 1606(d)
. . exchange of. .2920; 2944
. . . death or retirement of partner. .2941; 2942
. . . information required. .2935
. . gift of. .2905; 2922(a)(b)
. . liquidation of. .2920; 2927-2932
. . ownership rules. .2923(c)
. . sale of. .1601(e); 2920; 2935
. . . information required. .2935(c)
. . transfer of. .2935; 2937-2942
. . . basis. .2936
. . undivided. .2910
. . valuation for estate tax. .3919(c)
. interest on capital contributions. .2923(d)
. . when partner includes. .2920
. inventory, substantially appreciated: See Partnerships, substantially appreciated inventory (below)
. investment credit. .2913
. investment purposes. .2900
. involuntary conversions. .2911
. joint ventures. .2900
. liabilities assumed. .2925
. liability for tax. .1028(c); 2906
. life insurance of partners. .1828(a)
. limited. .3101
. liquidated interests. .2927-2932
. long-term capital gain deduction. .2906(b); 2911
. losses. .2908
. . disallowed. .2908(a); 2923; 2924
. . wash sales. .2221(d)
. medical expenses. .2913
. membership changes. .2922(a)
. mergers. .2922(c)
. minimum tax on tax preferences. .2906; 2908(c); 2913(a)
. moving expense. .1831
. net operating loss deduction. .2241; 2914
. nonbusiness expenses. .2913
. old-age tax, account partners. .3817(d)
. organization and syndication fees. .2906(b)
. pools. .2900
. principal partner, defined. .2921
. property contributions. .2910; 2925
. reconciliation schedule. .2918
. retiring partner. .2941; 2942
. returns. .2906; 3539
. . capital gains and losses. .2911
. salaries of partners. .2923(d)
. . when partner includes. .2920
. sale of assets. .2935
. Sec. 751 assets. .2944-2945
. Sec. 1231 gains or loses. .2911
. Sec. 1245 and 1250 property. .1619; 2909; 2925; 2935; 2941; 2945
. . distributions of. .2945(a)

PARTNERSHIPS—PENSIONS

———— References are to PARAGRAPH (¶) NUMBERS ————

PARTNERSHIPS (continued)
. self-employed retirement plans. .2913
. self-employment tax. .3822
. services contributed. .2925
. soil conservation expenditures. .2913
. split-up of. .2922(d)
. stock ownership rule. .1727; 2223(d)
. substantially appreciated inventory item:
. . defined. .2944(d)
. . distributions. .2944-2945
. . . basis. .2928-2932
. . . gain or loss. .2945(c)
. . . transfers. .2935
. successor in interest. .2941; 2942
. syndicate. .2900
. taxable income. .2906
. tax year. .2921; 2922
. taxes recovered. .2913
. tenancy in common. .2903
. termination. .2922
. transactions between partner and. .2904; 2923
. transfers. .2935; 2937-2942
. trust as partner. .2900
. undivided interests. .2910
. unrealized receivables: *See* Unrealized receivables
. unrelated business income. .3448(a)
. validity. .2904
. wash sales. .2221(d)
. water conservation expenditures. .2913
. withholding tax, partners. .2502
. work incentive program expenses:
. . partners, credit for. .2913(d)
. year different from partner. .2921
Party to reorganization. .3301
Patent license contract, depreciation. .2001
Patents:
. capital asset status. .1601(j)
. cost. .1523
. depreciation. .2001(a); 2032
. fair market value. .1502(b)
. infringements. .1226; 2728
. period held. .1606
. research and experimental expenditures. .1523
. royalties: *See* Royalties
. sale of, gain or loss. .1523
Patronage dividends. .3456-3458
. exclusion. .1706(a)
. information returns. .3533(b)
. time to report. .2721(b)
Pay-As-You-Go Tax: *See* Estimated tax; Withholding, wages
Payment of taxes. .3522-3527
. armed forces. .3518(a)
. by check. .3527(b)
. computations by:
. . Revenue Service. .1103(b); 3522(a)
. . taxpayer. .1103(b)
. estate tax. .3944
. estimated tax. .2517. *See also* Estimated tax
. . corporations. .3523(a)
. exempt organizations. .3525
. extension to pay. .3518; 3526; 3630(c)
. failure to make. .3618; 3620
. . withheld taxes. .2512
. foreign corporations. .3523; 3710
. . personal holding company tax. .3405
. foreign currencies. .3527(b)
. fractional cent. .3527(b)
. gift tax. .4031
. installments. .3523(a)

Payment of taxes (continued)
. installments (continued)
. . extensions. .3526
. interest on delinquencies. .2512(a); 3016; 3518; 3618
. . deductibility. .1901; 3016
. less than $1. .3527(b)
. money order. .3527(b)
. nonresident aliens. .3522(b); 3707-3712
. old-age and survivor insurance. .3827
. personal holding companies. .3405
. private foundations. .3525(b)
. receipts. .3527(b)
. social security taxes. .3827
. time of. .3522-3527
. . extension. .3518; 3526; 3630(c)
. unemployment insurance. .3838
. U.S. obligations as medium of. .3527(b)
. withheld taxes. .2509; 2536
Payments in the year of sale, installment realty sales. .2811(a)
Payroll deductions. .1301; 2703
. collection of tax through. .3615(e)
Payroll taxes: *See* Withholding, wages; Social Security
Peace Corps:
. allowances. .2503(b); 3726
. social security coverage. .3815(a)
Pecuniary interests, marital deduction. .3929
Penal institutions, social security coverage. .3815(a)
Penalties. .3616-3620
. ad valorem. .3617
. criminal. .3620
. estate tax, failure to pay. .3944(b)
. estimated income tax. .2519
. . corporations. .3523(b)
. . underpayment. .3619
. failure to:
. . deposit taxes. .3618(f)
. . furnish information, etc.. .3602; 3617; 3620
. . pay taxes. .3618(b)
. foreign corporation information returns, failure to file. .3540
. identification numbers not given. .2512(c); 3500; 3826(c)
. improperly accumulating surplus. .3130-3134
. income tax preparers. .3618(i)
. interest. .3618(a)
. old-age and survivor insurance. .3830
. payment with bad check. .3618(e)
. public charities. .3618(j)
. private foundations. .3618(g)
. refund of, due to carryback. .3618
. surtax, accumulating surplus. .3130-3134
. unemployment insurance. .3845
. withholding violations. .2512
Pension trusts: *See* Employees' trusts
Pensions:
. armed forces. .1218(c)
. constructive receipt. .2703
. contributions to. .1232; 1838; 3027
. . successor in reorganization. .3337
. deductibility. .1822(a)
. elderly income credit. .2406
. employees, annuities. .1232
. employees' trusts. .3024
. exclusion. .1304
. information as to payments. .3521
. levy on. .3615(a)
. nonresident citizens. .3725
. taxability. .1304
. union assessment for. .1807

6046—Index   **PENSIONS—PRIVATE**   1978

———————— References are to PARAGRAPH (¶) NUMBERS ————————

Pensions (continued)
. veterans. .1218(c)
. withholding tax. .2503(a); 2504(k)
Percentage depletion. .2102; 2104
. aggregation:
. . nonoperating interests. .2109
. . operating interests:
. . . minerals other than oil or gas. .2108
. . . oil and gas. .2107
. coal and iron ore royalties. .1623
. distribution from reserve. .2113
. information required. .3521
. single interest as more than one property. .2108(b)
. successor in reorganization. .3337
Percentage method of computing income. .2711
Percentage method of withholding. .2504(a)
Percentage of completion method, long-term contracts. .2842
Percentage standard deduction: *See* zero bracket amount
Per diem allowances. .1805(c)
Period held: *See* gains and losses, period assets held
Person, defined. .1028
Personal exemption: *See* Exemptions
Personal expenses. .1807
Personal finance companies, personal holding company tax. .3403
PERSONAL HOLDING COMPANIES . .3400-3409
. accrued taxes. .3404
. consent dividends. .1702(d); 3404; 3406
. consolidated returns. .3409
. contributions. .3404
. debt retirement fund. .3404
. deficiency dividends. .3406; 3407
. . successor in reorganization. .3337
. dividends paid deduction. .3404
. . successor in reorganization. .3337
. exempt corporations. .3403
. foreign: *See* Foreign personal holding companies
. foreign taxes. .3404
. liens. .3404
. losses, disallowed. .3408
. minimum tax on tax preferences. .3400
. net operating loss. .3404
. organizational expenses. .3404
. request for prompt assessment. .3612(a)
. retirement of indebtedness. .3404
. small business investment cost. .3459
. stock ownership. .3402
. undistributed income. .3404
. . rate of tax. .3405
. . successor in reorganization. .3337
Personal injuries: *See* Injuries
Personal property:
. casualty losses. .2204(c)
. dealers in, installment sales. .2801-2804
. inherited, loss on sale. .2203
. taxes, deductibility. .1912(c)
Personal service contracts, personal holding company income. .3401
Personal service income, maximum tax on. .2402
Per-unit certificates, time to report. .2721(b)
Philippine Islands, residents as dependents. .1120
Physician *See* Doctor
Player contracts:
. basis of. .1521(c)
. depreciation recapture. .1619(g)
Pledges, charitable. .1941(c)
Points paid, sale of residence. .1416(b), (d); 1831(b); 1900; 2739

Policemen:
. disability payments. .1218
. uniforms. .1807
Political:
. campaign expenses and contributions. .2416
. contributions. .2301; 2416; 4002
. gifts. .1225
. organizations, exempt status. .3436
. purposes, expenses for. .2416
. subdivision:
. . defined. .1204
. . obligations, amortizable premium. .1840
Pollution control facility, amortization of. .2403
Pooled income fund:
. charitable deduction for. .1942(e)
. estate tax, charitable deduction. .3927
. gift tax, charitable deduction. .4022
Possessions of U.S.:
. citizens of. .1120
. . liability for tax. .1028; 3727
. income from:
. . armed forces. .3727
. . exemption. .3105; 3727
. . tax table. .1122
. . U.S. citizens. .1028
. list of. .3727(a)
. obligations of, interest. .1203
. services within, withholding tax. .2503(b)
. source of income. .3727
. taxes of:
. . credit for. .3701-3706; 3727
. . deductibility. .1914; 3404
. trade or business within. .3727
Power of appointment:
. estate tax. .3907; 3908
. . marital deduction. .3929
. gift tax. .4003; 4004
. . marital deduction. .4023
Power of attorney:
. declaration of estimated tax. .2516(b)
. practice before I.R.S.. .3609
. returns. .3510; 3521
Preference dividends. .1707
Preference income, minimum tax on. .2403
Preferred stock bail-out. .1722
Premiums:
. bonds. .1846; 3125
. insurance. .1807; 1828; 1832; 1946
. . compensation. .1307(a)
. . prepaid. .2707
Prepaid income. .2724; 2726
. insurance premiums, deductibility. .2707
. interest. .2739
. membership dues. .2726(b)
. rent. .1826(c); 2724
. subscriptions. .2726(a)
. . circulation expenditures. .2749
. . information required. .3521
Priests: *See* Clergymen
Principal and agent relationship. .2703
Principles of federal taxes. .5701
Prisons, social security coverage. .3815(a)
Private foundations:
. accumulated earnings tax, redemption of stock . .3131
. assessment of taxes. .3610(e)
. collection of taxes. .3610(e)
. deficiency in tax. .3607
. disqualified person, tax on. .3440
. excess business holdings, tax on. .3442
. failure to file report, penalty for. .3617(b)

Private foundations (continued)
. foreign investment income. .3438
. improper expenditures, tax on. .3444
. information returns. .3536
. investment income, tax on. .3438
. investments, speculative, tax on. .3443
. nonexempt trusts as. .3453
. payment of taxes. .3525(b)
. penalties. .3618(g)
. prohibited acts of. .3439
. refunds, claims for. .3623
. returns. .3519
. self-dealing, tax on. .3440
. status, notification of. .3437
. statute of limitations. .3613(g)
. substantial contributor, defined. .3440(b)
. suit for refund. .3629(f)
. termination, tax on. .3437
. transfers to, gift tax. .4022
. undistributed income, tax on. .3441
. unrelated business income. .3445 et seq.
Private operating foundation, defined. .3441
Prizes:
. gross income. .1302(c)
. old-age benefit tax. .3818
. withholding tax. .2503(a)
Production credit associations, social security coverage. .3815(a)
Productive-use property, exchanges. .1406
Professional people:
. depreciation 1832; 2001(a)
. elderly income credit. .2406
. expenses of. .1807; 1829; 1832
. fees:
. . deductibility. .1823
. . information returns. .3531
. self-employment tax. .3822
. transportation expenses. .1832
. withholding tax. .2502
Profits:
. accumulated after 2-28-13. .1701(b)
. anticipated, losses. .2202(a)
. available for dividends. .1701(b)
. brokerage accounts, undrawn. .2703
. business. .2601
. compensation based on. .1301; 1815; 1819
. corp., effect of distributions on. .3129
. defined. .2203
. gross income. .1201
. installment and deferred payment sales. .2802; 2804; 2811(a)
. insurance against loss of. .1331
. loss of, damages recovered. .1226
. taxable year, distribution. .1701(c)
. transactions for, loss on. .2203
. wash sales. .2221
Profit-sharing plans. .3024
. affiliated corporations. .1838(e)
. contributions to. .1838
. . successor in reorganizations. .3337
. . Subchapter S Corp.. .3146
. disability payments from. .1221
. distributions. .1102(c); 3024(d)
. . withholding tax on. .2503(a)
. estate tax. .3915
. exclusion. .1304
. joint. .1838(e)
. self-employed. .1839
. taxability to employees. .3024(d)
Prohibited transactions, private foundations .3439
Promissory notes as cash. .2703

Property: *See also* particular kind
. basis: *See* Gain or loss, basis
. business, depreciation. .2001
. carrying charges. .1528
. casualty or theft losses. .2204-2206
. community: *See* Community property
. compensation in form of. .1307-1310; 1819
. condemnation. .1413(c)
. construction period interest and taxes, amortization of. .2042
. contributed to partnership. .2910; 2925
. contributions in. .1942(b)
. converted to business use:
. . basis for depreciation. .2003(c)
. . loss on sale. .2207
. debt settled by transfer of. .1318(h)
. depreciable. .2001; 2017
. . declining balance method. .2012(a)
. . sold to spouse or controlled corporation. .1625
. . sum of the years-digits. .2013
. dividends. .1702(b); 3107
. gift: *See* Gift tax; Gifts
. held for production of income, capital asset status . .1601(c)
. interests, partnerships. .2910
. investment credit. .2410
. involuntary conversion: *See* Involuntary conversion
. money as. .3334
. mortgaged, exchange of. .1409
. nondepreciable, obsolescence deduction. .2210
. payment for, distinguished from compensation for services. .1817
. period asset held: *See* Capital gains and losses
. rehabilitation expenses for historic structures, amortization of. .2044
. repossessed, investment credit. .2410(a)
. sale:
. . bona fide, necessity for loss deduction. .2222
. . closed transaction. .2725(a)
. . contingent payments. .2725(a)
. . depreciation in year of. .2001(b)
. . nonresident aliens. .3712
. . time to deduct loss. .2743(b)
. taxes: *See also* Real estate, taxes
. . accrual. .2740(b)
. . buyer and seller. .1920
. . deductibility. .1912(c); 1920
. . . estate tax. .3926
. . expenses connected with. .1806
. title to, defending or perfecting. .1806; 1823
. undivided interests, partnerships. .2910
. vacation homes. .1806
. valuation: *See* Valuation
Property distributions:
. by corporation with loan:
. . guaranteed by U.S.. .3121(g)
. inclusions in. .3120(b)
Property dividends:
. effect on corporation's earnings and profits. .3121
. gain or loss to corporation. .3119
. liability against, gain or loss. .3119(c)
. received by corporation. .3116(a)
Proprietor, sole:
. advantages over corporation. .3152-3154; 4506
. inventory. .2604
. self-employment tax. .3822
. tax savings. .3152; 4506
Protest, proposed assessment. .3607(b)
Protesting additional income taxes. .3603 et seq.
Psychologist's fees. .1946

6048—Index PUBLIC—REAL

References are to PARAGRAPH (¶) NUMBERS

Public Health Service, withholding tax on pensions. .2503(a)
Public office functions as trade or business, self-employment tax. .3822
Public policy, deductions disallowed as against . .1823
Public School, employee's annuities. .1232(e)
. Public stenographers, withholding tax. .2502
Public utilities:
. dividends paid by, deduction. .3115
. property, depreciation on. .2019
Puerto Rico:
. citizen of:
. . dependent. .1120
. . returns. .1100
. employment in:
. . old-age benefit tax. .3803
. . withholding tax. .2503(b)
. income tax status. .3727(b)
. residents:
. . declaration of estimated tax. .2516(c)
. . exempt income. .3727(b)
. . income tax. .3709(a)
. . returns. .1100
. . self-employment tax. .3823(c)
. source of income. .3727(b)
Punitive damages, taxability. .1226
Purchase price:
. adjustment, forgiveness of debt. .1318(c)
. allocation:
. . land and building. .2003(d)
. . principal and interest. .1904
"Puts," short sales. .1609(b)

— Q —

Qualified joint interests, husband and wife. .3908
Qualified stock options. .1327(a)
. as tax preference income. .1327(a); 2403(a)
. information returns. .3534
Quarterly deposits of withheld taxes. .2509(a)
Quarterly payroll period, percentage method withholding table. .2504(a)

— R —

Racetrack winnings, withholding tax on. .2503(a)
Radio broadcasting companies, sales or exchanges on FCC orders. .1410
Radio program, capital status. .1601(f)
Radium, depreciation. .2001
Raffle tickets, deductibility of purchase price . .1941(b)
Railroad fares: *See* Traveling expenses
Railroad Retirement Act:
. annuities, estate tax. .3915(b)
. employment covered by, old-age benefit tax. .3812
. tax rate chart. .5514
Railroad Unemployment Insurance Act, benefits, exclusion. .1217(b)
Railroad workers:
. refunds, hospital insurance tax. .2511
. self-employment tax. .3822
. work clothes. .1807
Railroads:
. bankruptcy, discharge of debt. .3125
. reorganizations. .3332
. rolling stock. .2041; 2403
Ranchers: *See* Farmers
Rates of taxes:
. accumulated earnings tax. .3133

Rates of taxes (continued)
. changed during year. .3546
. corporations. .3102; 3710
. decedents. .3020
. estates and trusts, income tax. .3020
. foreign taxpayers. .3707; 3710
. gift tax. .4027
. individuals. .1121; 1122
. nonresident aliens. .3707-3712
. old-age and survivor insurance. .3800
. personal holding companies. .3405
. regulated investment companies. .3431
. self-employment income. .3821
. state:
. . gasoline. .1917(a)
. . sales. .1917(b)
. unemployment insurance. .3834
Raw materials, cost of goods sold. .2604(a)
Real estate:
. abandonment loss. .2210
. adjusted basis. .1500(b); 1528
. agents, information returns. .3531
. allocation of sales price between land and building . .2003(d)
. assessments for local benefits. .1912(b)
. . litigation expenses. .1823
. brokers, self-employment tax. .3824
. capital gains and losses. .1601(b); 1619(b); 1631
. carrying charges. .1528
. commissions. .1818
. deferred payment sales. .2816; 2823
. depreciation. .2001; 2003
. . recapture of. .1619(b)
. exchange of. .1406; 1409
. fair market value. .1502(b)
. . estate tax. .3919(a)
. gross estate. .3901
. info. required on sale or exchange. .3521
. installment sales. .2811; 2823
. inventory. .2600
. March 1, 1913, acquired before. .1506
. mortgaged:
. . depreciation. .2003
. . exchange of. .1409
. renting of, as trade or business. .1601(b)
. residence: *See* Residence, personal
. sales:
. . allocation of price between land and building . .2003(d)
. . closed transactions. .2725(a)
. . contingent payments. .2725(a)
. . deferred payment plan. .2816; 2823
. . inherited. .2203
. . installment basis. .2811; 2823
. . lots. .2841
. . . capital gains and losses. .1631
. . nonresident aliens. .3712
. . personal-use property converted to business use . .2207
. . self-employment income. .3824
. . transaction for profit. .2203
. unconditional, holding period. .1606
. subdivided for sale. .1631
. taxes:
. . accrual. .2740(b)
. . acquisition of property. .1920
. . buyer and seller. .1400; 1501; 1920
. . capitalization. .1528
. . deductibility. .1912(c)
. . . estate tax purposes. .3926
. . expenses for. .1806
. . litigation expenses. .1806

REAL—RELIGIOUS Index—6049

───────── References are to PARAGRAPH (¶) NUMBERS ─────────

Real estate (continued)
. taxes *(continued)*
. . tenant paying. .1316; 1919
. tax shelter. .4601 et seq.
. unimproved as similar to improved. .1413(b)
. valuation, estate tax purposes. .3919(a)
Real estate investment trusts. .3432
. capital gain dividends. .1702(c)
. dividend exclusion. .1706(a)
. exchanges of stock, gain or loss. .1405(c)
. minimum tax on tax preferences. .3432(g)
Rebates, farmers co-op. .3456; 3457
Recapitalization, as reorganization. .3307
Recapture:
. depreciation. .1619
. farm property. .1622(c); 2226; 2708; 2925
. investment credit. .2410
. mining exploration expenditures. .1843(a)
Receipts:
. employer to furnish employee. .3828(a)
. payment of taxes. .3527(b)
. withheld taxes: *See* Withholding, statements to employees
Receivables:
. corporation distributions. .3129(b)
. partnership:
. . distributions. .2928-2932; 2944
. . transfers. .2935
. sale of, bad debt deduction. .2311(b)
. unrealized: *See* Unrealized receivables
Receivers, returns by. .3000; 3511
Receivership:
. bad debt deduction, effect on. .2305
. limitation on assessment of tax. .3612(e)
Recognition of gain or loss. .1400 et seq.
Recomputed basis, recapture of depreciation. .1619(a)
Reconciliation schedule:
. corporations. .3110
. partnerships. .2918
Records: *See* Books and records
Recoveries:
. foreign expropriation losses. .2316(d); 3526
. tax benefit rule. .2316(d)
Recreation:
. benefit plan. .1819; 1838
. expense of. .1806
  redecorating expenses. .1825
Redemption:
. annuities. .1230(g)
. bonds: *See* Bonds, retirement
. distributions, effect on earnings and profits. .3129(e)
. stock: *See also* Dividends, liquidating
. . as dividend. .1718-1720
. . . exclusion. .1706(a)
. . constructive ownership. .1727
. . preferred stock bail-out. .1722
. . sale of to controlled corp. as. .1720
. . to pay death taxes. .1721
. . treated as sale. .1718(a)
Refugees, status. .3708
REFUNDS. .3621 et seq.
. acceleration, special procedures. .3630
. amended returns. .3520
. bad debts. .3624(a)
. carrybacks effecting. .2243(c); 3624(b); 3630
. casualty losses. .2204(e)
. claims for. .3621 et seq.
. . administrative procedure. .3627(a)
. . annualized income. .2717
. . as basis for suit. .3626; 3629
. . dependents. .1118(b)

REFUNDS (continued)
. claims for *(continued)*
. . form. .3626
. . gift tax. .4033
. . limitation on. .3625
. . old-age benefit tax. .3829
. . returns of individuals as. .3626
. . time to file. .3623
. . unemployment insurance. .3844
. . waiver of limitations on assessment and collection. .3623(c)
. counterclaim by government. .3615(d)
. estate tax. .3946
. exempt organizations. .2417
. expenses connected with. .1806; 1823; 3016
. farmers' cooperative associations, made by, to patrons. .3456; 3457
. foreign taxes. .3624(c); 3705
. fractional year returns. .2717
. gasoline tax, farmers. .2417
. gift tax. .4033
. interest on. .1203(d); 1314; 3628
. investment credit, carryback affecting. .3624(c); 3630
. limitations. .3623
. losses, casualty. .2204(e)
. lubricating oil, farmers. .2417
. mathematical errors in return. .3601(a); 3621
. net operating loss:
. . carryback affecting. .2243(c); 3624(b); 3630
. . income averaging. .3624(b)
. old-age and survivor insurance. .3829
. overpayment credited to estimated tax. .3624(c)
. private foundations. .3623(a)
. procedure, interim allowance. .3630
. retirement plans. .3618(h); 3624(d); 3629(f)
. set-off against tax liability. .3615(d)
. social security taxes. .2511(a); 3829; 3844
. subchapter S distributions. .3624(c)
. suit to recover. .3629
. Tax Court jurisdiction. .3622
. unemployment insurance. .3844
. withheld taxes. .1100; 2511; 3509; 3622
. work incentive program expense credit, carryback affecting. .3624(b); 3630
. worthless securities. .3624(a)
Regulated investment companies. .3428-3431
. distribution of income. .3429
. diversification of income. .3429
. dividends. .3429; 3431(b)
. . capital gain. .1702(c)
. . limitations on. .3431(d)
. . paid after close of taxable year. .3431(e)
. . received, exclusion. .1706(a)
. exchanges of stock, gain or loss. .1405(c)
. information required. .3521
. minimum tax on tax preferences. .3431(e)
. rate table. .5507
. shareholders, foreign tax credit. .3431
. venture capital companies. .3430
Reimbursed expenses. .1805(b)
. medical. .1945(a); 1947
. withholding statements included on. .2508
. withholding tax. .2503(a)
Relatives:
. advances to. .2308
. alimony for support of. .1320(c)
. loans from. .2223; 2308; 2748
. members of household. .1106(b)
Religious orders, members of:
. old-age benefit tax. .3809
. self-employment tax. .3822; 3824
. withholding tax. .2503(b)

RELIGIOUS—REORGANIZATIONS

References are to PARAGRAPH (¶) NUMBERS

Religious organizations: *See* Exempt organizations
Relocation payments. .1302(b), (c)
Remainders:
. annuity trust and unitrust. .3927(b)
. basis for gain or loss. .1510
. charitable contributions. .1942(e)
. depreciation. .2002
. estate tax. .3919(d)
. gift tax. .4012
Remaining life plan, sum of the years digits depreciation. .2013(b)
Rentals: *See* Rents
Renting of realty, as trade or business. .1601(b)
Rents:
. advance. .1826(c)
. assigned. .2704
. bond interest paid for landlord. .1316
. constructive receipt. .3108
. crop shares. .2614(b)
. deductibility. .1826; 1832
. deductions attributable to. .1806(a)
. dependent receiving. .1118
. devised property. .1225
. dividends distinguished. .1703
. dividends paid for landlord. .1316
. elderly income credit. .2406
. estate tax, real estate value based on. .3919(a)
. forgiveness of. .1318(b)
. free occupancy. .1308(e)
. . donated. .1942(d)
. gross income. .1316
. improvements in lieu of. .1317(b)
. information returns. .3531
. nonresident aliens receiving. .3711
. . withholding tax. .2535
. paid stockholders. .1703
. paid to lessor corporation's stockholders or bondholders. .3108
. personal holding company income. .3401
. prepaid. .1826(c)
. professional people. .1832; 1833
. safe-deposit box. .1806
. self-employment income. .3824
. taxes paid for landlord. .1316; 1919
. time to report. .2724
. unpaid, bad debt deduction. .2300
REORGANIZATIONS. .3300 et seq.
. accounting methods, successor corp. .3337
. acquiring corp., carryovers. .3336; 3337
. acquisition by one corporation of properties of another. .3305
. acquisition by one corporation of stock of another. .3304
. active business requirement. .3318
. annuity plans, succesor corp.. .3337
. assumption of liabilities. .3305; 3309; 3315
. bad debt recoveries, successor corp.. .3337
. bankruptcy. .3331
. basis of property received:
. . corporation. .3314
. . distributee-stockholder. .3313
. bonds, amortization of premium or discount, successor corp.. .3125(e); 3337
. "boot". .3309; 3311; 3319
. business or corporate purpose. .3302
. capital loss carryover, successor corporation. .3337
. carryovers to successor corp.. .3336; 3337
. change in identity, form, or place of organization. .3307

REORGANIZATIONS (continued)
. charitable contributions, successor corporation. .3337
. consolidations. .3303
. . carryovers. .3336; 3337
. . unemployment insurance tax. .3834
. continuity of interest. .3302
. control defined. .3306; 3317
. credits, unused. .3339
. defined. .3303 et seq.
. depletion, mine tailings. .3337
. depreciation, successor corp.. .3337
. development expenses of mines, successor corporation. .3337
. discharge of debts under. .1318(f)
. distributions of stock and securities, controlled corporations. .3316 et seq.
. dividends. .3312
. divisive. .3316 et seq.
. earnings and profits after. .1701(b)
. earnings and profits, successor corporation. .3337
. employees' trusts successor corp.. .3337
. exploration expenses of mines, successor corporation. .3337
. five-year rule. .3318
. foreign corporations, advance ruling needed. .3309; 3317
. foreign taxes, credit for. .3337-3339
. information required. .3521
. insolvent corporations. .3331
. installment and deferred payment sales, successor corporation. .3337
. inventories, successor corp.. .3337
. investment credit, successor corp.. .3337
. involuntary conversions, successor corporation. .3337
. liabilities assumed. .3309; 3315
. mergers. .3303
. . carryovers. .3336; 3337
. . unemployment insurance tax. .3834
. net operating loss, successor corp.. .3337
. . limitation. .3338; 3339
. nontaxable exchanges. .3309 et seq.
. . basis or property received:
. . . corporation. .3314
. . . distributee-stockholder. .3313
. . federal agencies, orders of. .3330
. . liquidation of subsidiaries. .3334
. . property for securities. .3309
. . SEC orders. .3330
. . securities for securities. .3309
. . transactions to reduce tax liability. .3302
. party to. .3301
. pension plans, successor corporation. .3337
. personal holding companies, carryovers. .3337
. plan of. .3302
. profit-sharing plans, successor corporation. .3337
. recapitalization. .3307
. securities, defined. .3301
. small business stock. .1632
. spin-off: *See* Spin-off reorganizations
. split-off: *See* Split-off reorganizations
. split-up: *See* Split-up reorganizaions
. stock options, effect on. .1327(d)
. "substantially all" defined. .3305
. successor corp., carryovers. .3336; 3337
. transfer of assets to another corporation for controlling stock. .3306
. types, chart of. .3308
. unemployment insurance tax. .3834
. what constitutes. .3303 et seq.

REPAID—RETURNS

References are to PARAGRAPH (¶) NUMBERS

Repaid income. .2729
Repairs:
. Class Life Asset Depreciation Range system . .2033(f)
. deductibility. .1825
. depreciation. .2021(a)
. improvements distinguished. .1825
Replacements:
. depreciation. .2021
. involuntary conversions. .1410-1414; 1519
. repairs distinguished. .1825; 2033(f)
Reports: *See* Returns
Repossession of property. .2803; 2823
Research expenditures, deductibility. .1842
Research workers, self-employment tax. .3823(e)
Reserves:
. bad debts. .2311(b). *See also* Bad debts, reserve for
. . banks. .3433
. . recoveries. .2316
. dealers. .2727
. depletion, distribution from. .2113
. depreciation. .2021
. . defined. .2033; 2113
. . distributions from. .2113
. . expenses and losses. .2744
. self-insurer. .2744
Reservists:
. compensation, withholding on. .2503(a)
. expenses. .1834(a), (b)

Residence, personal:
. adjusted sales price. .1416; 1423
. alimony for expenses of. .1320(b)
. business use of. .1805; 1806; 1832
. capital asset status. .1601(b)
. casualty losses. .2204
. condemnation of. .1421
. credit on purchase of. .1416(d)
. defined. .1417
. depreciation. .2001(a)
. expenses connected with. .1805; 1806
. "fixing up" expenses. .1416
. gain on sale or exchange. .1416-1423; 2207
. . limitation on assessment of deficiency due to . .3611
. . old residence replaced. .1526
. . . holding period. .1606(e)
. gift of, sale or exchange. .1526
. hurricane damage. .2204
. inherited, sale or exchange. .1526
. . loss on sale. .2203
. installment sale of. .1416
. insurance premiums. .1807; 1828(b)
. interest on mortgage. .1900
. involuntary conversion. .1414(b); 1421
. . old residence replaced. .1526
. . . holding period. .1606(e)
. loss on sale. .2207
. mortgage:
. . alimony for payment of. .1320(b)
. . interest. .1900
. . points paid. .1416(b), (d); 1900
. moving expenses. .1416(b); 1526; 1831
. office use. .1805; 1806; 1832
. period held. .1606(e)
. professional people. .1832
. purchase of partially constructed new residence . .1419
. reimbursement for loss on sale. .1302(b); 2204(c)
. rent. .1826(b); 1832
. rent-free occupancy. .1308(e); 1941(b)

Residence, personal (continued)
. repairs. .1825
. sale or exchange of. .1416-1423; 1601; 2207
. . armed forces. .1420
. . cooperative apartments. .1417
. . husband and wife. .1418
. . information required. .3521
. . more than one residence. .1417
. . old residence replaced. .1526
. . . holding period. .1606(e)
. . . information required. .1422
. . residence defined. .1417
. . taxpayer 65 or over. .1423
. sales price. .1416
. taxes. .1912(c); 1919; 1920
. termite damage. .2204(b)
Resident aliens: *See* Aliens, resident
Residential rental property:
. depreciation:
. . methods of. .2017
. . recapture of. .1619(b)
. information returns. .3534
Restricted property as compensation. .1326
. basis of. .1504
. taxation of. .1326
Restricted stock plans. .1326; 1327(c)
Retail merchants, inventories . .2606(b); 2609(e)
Retail sales taxes, state and local, deductibility . .1917(b)
Retailers, excise tax, rate chart. .5515
Retired persons, retirement income credit. .2406. *See also* Individual retirement arrangements, Pensions, Profit-sharing plans, Retirement
Retirement:
. assets. .2035-2038
. bonuses after, old-age benefit tax. .3818
. income: *See also* Pensions
. . credit for elderly. .2406
. indebtedness, personal holding companies. .3404
. individual arrangements. .1838(l); 2503(a); 3027
. pay: *See also* Pensions
. . servicemen funding annuities with reductions of . .1232(i)
. . unemployment insurance tax. .3837
. plans:
. . declaratory judgment. .3635(d)
. . failure to file reports, statements. .3617(c)
. . public inspection of records. .3537(d)
. . refunds. .3624(d); 3629(f)
. . special taxes on. .3618(h)
. reports and statements, penalties. .3617(c)
. savings, withholding. .2503(a)
RETURNS. .1100 et seq.; 3500 et seq.
. administrative handling. .3601
. age 65 or over. .1100
. agent. .3510
. amended. .3519; 3520
. . refund claim as necessitating. .3626
. armed forces. .3518(a)
. as declarations of estimated tax. .2517(a)
. as refund claims. .3626
. audit of. .3601
. bankruptcy and receivership. .3511; 3512
. children. .3509
. committee for incompetent. .3511(a)
. common trust funds. .3025
. consolidated. .3222; 3515: *See also* Consolidated returns
. . extension of time for filing. .3518(a)
. . information required. .3521
. . personal holding company. .3409

6052—Index — RETURNS—SALES

References are to PARAGRAPH (¶) NUMBERS

RETURNS (continued)
. corporations. .3512-3515
. . extension of time for filing. .3518(a)
. . small business. .3141(c)
. decedents. .3008(b); 3012; 3020; 3505-3507; 3517(a); 5504
. declarations, estimated tax: *See* Estimated tax
. delinquent, unemployment insurance. .3845
. Domestic International Sales Corporations . .3517(e)
. due date. .3517
. errors in. .3601(a); 3621
. estate tax. .3943
. estates and trusts. .3001; 3020; 3517(c)
. examination by Government. .3601
. executors and administrators. .3001; 3012; 3020; 3506; 3507; 3517(a), (c)
. exempt organizations. .3436
. . unrelated business income. .3513(a)
. expenses connected with. .1823
. extension of time for filing. .3518
. . joint returns. .3506
. failure to file. .3617; 3620
. . limitation on assessment and collection. .3610
. . withheld taxes. .2512(a)
. failure to sign. .3503
. false or fraudulent. .3610; 3618; 3620
. . old-age benefit tax. .3830
. . unemployment insurance. .3845
. farmers. .2614(a)
. . information required. .3521
. farmers' coop. assn.. .3455
. fiduciary. .3001; 3020; 3511
. filing:
. . when. .3517; 3518
. . where. .3519; 3530
. final. .3517
. fiscal year. .3517
. foreign corps. .3540(b); 3710
. foreign personal holding companies. .3416
. forms:
. . consolidated. .3515
. . income tax:
. . . corporations. .3100
. . . individuals. .1101
. fractional year. .2717
. . change in accounting period. .2715
. . corporations. .3514
. fraudulent. .3610; 3618; 3620
. . old-age benefit tax. .3830
. . unemployment insurance. .3845
. gift tax. .4030
. guardian. .1100; 3509; 3511(a)
. husband and wife: *See* Husband and wife, returns
. identifying numbers on. .3500; 3826
. income tax preparers. .3542
. individuals. .1100 et seq.; 3500-3511
. information at source: *See* Information returns
. information required in. .3521
. . employee's expenses. .1805(b)
. insane persons. .3511(a)
. joint: *See* Husband and wife, returns
. mathematics errors. .3601(a); 3621
. military forces. .3518(a)
. minimum tax. .3541
. mining exploration expenses. .1843(a)
. minors. .1100; 3509; 3511(a)
. nonresident aliens. .1100; 3517(a); 3707-3712
. old-age and survivor insurance. .3827
. partnership. .2906; 3539(a)
. personal holding companies. .3405

RETURNS (continued)
. postmarks. .3517; 3605
. power of attorney. .3510; 3521
. preliminary examination. .3601(a)
. private postage meter: *See* Returns, postmarks
. receivers. .3511
. requirements. .1100; 3512
. rounding off amounts. .3527(a)
. segregation of items. .2601(c)
. self-employment income. .1100(c)
. self-employment tax. .3827(b)
. separate v. joint. .3508
. short taxable year: *See* Returns, fractional year
. signatures. .3503
. . corporations. .3513(b)
. . joint return. .3505(a)
. small business corporations. .3141(c)
. social security taxes. .3827; 3838
. source of forms. .1101
. statements required in. .3521
. time for filing. .3517
. . extension. .3518; 3521
. trustees in bankruptcy. .3511
. unemployment insurance. .3838
. verification. .3503; 3513
. wards. .3511(a)
. who must file. .1101
. withheld taxes. .2509; 2536
Revenue agents:
. examination of returns. .3602
. hearings before. .3603
Reversionary interests. .3022(a)
. charitable contributions. .1942(e)
. gift tax valuation. .4012
Reversions, estate tax. .3919(d)
Reviews: *See* Appeals
Revolving credit plans. .2801
. accounting method, change of. .2804
Rewards. .1302(c)
Rights, stock: *See* Stock rights
Rollover contributions, individual retirement arrangements. .1838(l)
Roof, expense of. .1825
Room and board: *See* Board and lodging
Royalties:
. as U.S. source income. .3712
. as constructive dividends. .1703
. coal. .1623
. deductions attributable to. .1806(b)
. depletion. .2101(b); 2104-2106
. dividends. .1703
. elderly income credit. .2406
. gross income. .1316
. information returns. .3531
. iron ore. .1623
. nonresident aliens receiving. .3711
. . withholding tax. .2535
. personal holding company income. .3401
. self-employment income. .3824
Rulings, weight given to. .1015(e)

— S —

S. U. B. trusts:
. information returns. .3531
. taxability. .3436; 3447
Safe-deposit box rental. .1806
Salaries: *See* Compensation
Sales: *See also* particular item
. amount realized. .1400
. basis for gain or loss. .1500 et seq.

SALES—SERVICES Index—6053

───── References are to PARAGRAPH (¶) NUMBERS ─────

Sales (continued)
. casual: *See* Installment and deferred payment sales
. closed transactions. .2725
. commissions. .1818
. contingent payments. .2725(a)
. deferred payment: *See* Installment and deferred payment sales
. exchanges distinguished. .1402
. FCC ordering. .1410
. gain or loss. .1400 et seq.
. installment: *See* Installment and deferred payment sales
. liquidating dividend distinguished. .1715
. necessity for, capital gains and losses. .1602
. partnership interest. .1601(e); 2935
. profits as gross income. .1201
. real estate: *See* Real estate; Residence, personal
. short:
. . capital gains and losses. .1608
. . closed transaction. .1608(b); 2725(b)
. stock redemptions treated as. .1718(a)
. wash. .2221

Sales tax:
. capitalization. .1528
. state, deductibility. .1912(c); 1917(b)

Salespersons:
. advances to. .1818; 2720(a)
. deductions for adjusted gross income. .1805(a)
. old-age benefit tax. .3817(b)
. outside:
. . expenses. .1805(a)
. . . information required. .1805(a)
. . . reimbursed. .1805(a), (b)
. . uniforms. .1807

Salvage value. .2005
. additional first-year depreciation. .2016
. Class Life Asset Depreciation Range system .2033(e)
. declining balance depreciation. .2012
. losses reduced by. .2201; 2204
. rate adjusted for, straight line method. .2011

Samoa:
. employment in, old-age tax. .3803
. residents, self-employment tax. .3823(c)

Saturday, last day:
. filing:
. . refund claim. .3623
. . returns. .3517
. . suit. .3629(a)
. . Tax Court petition. .3605(a); 3639(a)
. payment:
. . estimated tax. .2517(a)
. . tax. .3517

Savings and loan associations:
. dividends:
. . paid, information returns. .3532
. . received from, exclusion. .1706(a)
. taxability. .3433(b)

Savings bonds: *See* Federal obligations

Scholarships. .1303
. as support. .1116(b)
. withholding tax. .2503(a)

School expenses. .1807; 1833
. paid by employer. .1307(b)
. veterans. .1218(c)

Seamen, old-age benefit tax. .3803(c)

Sec. 306 stock. .1722; 3311

Sec. 1231 gains and losses. .1618-1624
. partnerships. .2911

Sec. 1244 stock. .1632

Sec. 1245 and 1250 property:
. contributions. .1619(c)
. corporations. .3201; 3204
. defined. .1619
. distributed: in liquidation. .3128
. . to shareholders. .3127
. gifts of. .1619(c)
. information required. .3521
. installment sale. .2813
. multiple asset accounts. .2022
. partnerships. .2909; 2925; 2935; 2941; 2945
. unrelated business income. .3448

Securities:
. commissions. .1818
. convertible, ownership rules. .3402
. dealers: *See* Dealers in securities
. defined. .1628; 3301
. dividends paid in. .1702(b)
. fair market value, estate tax. .3919(b)
. reorganization distributions. .3316 et seq.
. sale or exchange, personal holding company income. .3401
. short sales. .1608
. tax-exempt: *See* Exempt securities
. wash sales. .2221
. "when issued" basis. .1608(b)
. worthless. .3203
. . limitations on refunds. .3624(a)
. year-end transaction. .2725(b)

Securities and Exchange Commission, Transactions under orders of. .1619(f); 3330

Securities dealer: *See* Dealers in securities

Seeing eye dog, medical expense. .1946

Seizure and Sale. .3610(a); 3615

Self-employed retirement plans. .1839
. accident or health benefits received under. .1221
. annuities, estate tax. .3915
. contributions to. .1801(a); 1839(b)
. gift tax. .4011
. partnerships. .2913
. trustees' fees, deductibility. .1806

Self-employment, defined. .3822

Self-employment income:
. defined. .3823(a)
. income tax return requirement. .1100(c)

Self-employment tax: *See* Social security, self-employment tax

Self-insurance, reserve for. .2744

Selling expenses:
. amount realized. .1400
. cost of goods sold. .2604(a)
. estate tax deduction. .1818; 3016
. installment realty sales. .2811(a)
. moving expenses. .1831(b)
. property bought or sold. .1818
. realty subdivided for sale. .1631

Selling price, installment realty sales. .2811(a)

Semiannual payroll period, percentage method withholding table. .2504(a)

Semimonthly payroll period, computation of withholding. .2504

Separation:
. agreement or decree, alimony. .1320
. suit, expense of. .1823
. support of dependents. .1116

Servants: *See* Domestics

Service charges, tips, withholding tax. .2503(a)

Servicemen: *See also* Armed forces
. annuities. .1232(i); 3915(b)

Services:
. contribution of. .1942(c)
. property received for, basis. .1504

SERVICES—SOCIAL

Services (continued)
. withholding. .2503
Severance damages. .1415
Sewer assessment. .1912(b)
Sham sales. .2222
Shareholders: *See* Stockholders
Shipwreck losses, estate tax. .3926
Short period: *See* Fractional year
Short sales:
. arbitrage transactions. .1608(a)
. "calls". .1609(b)
. capital gains and losses. .1608
. closed transaction. .1608(b); 2725(b)
. commodity futures. .1608(c)
. defined. .1608
. dividends on borrowed stock. .1806
. . exclusion. .1706(b)
. options. .1608(b)
. "puts". .1609(b)
. securities dealers. .1608(a)
. small business investment co. stock. .1608(a)
. "straddle" transactions. .1609(a)
. substantially identical property defined. .1608(a)
Short tax year: *See* Fractional year
Short-term capital gains and losses: *See* Capital gains and losses, short term
Short-term obligations issued at discount .2723(c)
Short-term trusts. .3022
Shrinkage in value. .2208
Shut-in royalties. .2101(b)
Sick pay: *See* Disability
Sickness: *See* Disability
Signatures, joint returns. .3503
Simple trust. .3005
. distribution deductions. .3017(a)
. distribution computations. .3021(a)
. exemption deduction. .3012
Singers: *See* Professional people
Single persons:
. computation of tax. .1102
. exemptions. .1111(a)
. gross income requirements. .1101
. rate schedule. .1103; 1121
. standard deduction: *See* Zero bracket amount
. tax tables. .1122
. withholding tax on wages. .2504
Sinking fund, corporation. .3109
Sister as dependent. .1117
Slander suit:
. damages. .1226
. expenses of. .1823
Slot machine winnings, return for. .3521
Small business corporation. 3140-3146
. defined. .3141(a)
. information required. .3141(c)
. investment credit. .2410(g); 3141(b)
. partnership tax treatment. .3140-3146
. . advantages. .3154
. . dividend exclusion. .1706(a)
Small business investment co.. .3459
. personal holding company tax. .3403
. short sale of stock of. .1608(a)
Small business stock:
. loss. .1632
. net operating loss. .2242(a)
Social clubs, dues to. .1807
Social security benefits, taxability. .1217
Social security numbers, as identification numbers. .3500
SOCIAL SECURITY. .3800 et seq.
. appeals. .3846

SOCIAL SECURITY (continued)
. as wages subject to withholding. .2503(a)
. benefits payable, taxabilty. .1217
. . exemptions, effect on. .1118
. deductibility. .1913
. farm workers. .3805
. hospital insurance tax. .3800 et seq.
. medical expense deduction for. .1946
. number as identification. .3500
. old-age and survivor insurance. .3800 et seq.
. . adjustments. .3829
. . appeals. .3846
. . Communist organizations. .3813
. . covered employment. .3803
. . crew leader, defined. .3805
. . deductibility. .1913(a)
. . employees:
. . . defined. .3817(a)
. . . tax on. .3800
. . employer, tax on. .3800
. . employer-employee relationship. .3817
. . employers subject to. .3800
. . employment. .3803
. . exemptions. .3804
. . overpayments. .2511(a)
. . . withholding statements. .2508
. . payment of tax. .3827
. . penalties. .3830
. . rates. .3800; 5512; 5513
. . records. .3828
. . refunds. .3829
. . returns. .3827
. . successor employer. .3818(b)
. . . withholding statements. .2508
. . wages subject to. .3803; 3818
. . . limitation. .3818(a)
. . withholding tax. .2503(a)
. rate chart. .5512; 5513
. rulings, appeals from. .3846
. self-employment tax. .3821 et seq.
. . American Samoa residents. .3823(c)
. . capital gains and losses. .3824
. . clergymen. .3822
. . community income. .3827(b)
. . corp. shareholders electing partnership, tax . .3823(d)
. . declaration of estimated tax. .2515; 3827
. . deductibility. .1913(a)
. . distributive share of partnership. .3823(d)
. . dividends. .3824
. . excluded income. .3824
. . exemptions. .3822
. . farm income. .3823(b)
. . Guam residents. .3823(c)
. . interest. .3824
. . net earnings from self-employment, defined . .3824
. . net operating loss. .3824
. . nonresident citizens. .3823(c)
. . overpayment. .3829(d)
. . partnership income. .3823(d)
. . professions. .3822
. . public office functions. .3822
. . Puerto Rico residents. .3823(c)
. . railroad workers. .3822
. . rate chart. .5512
. . rates. .3821
. . records. .3828(c)
. . rentals from realty. .3824
. . research grants. .3823(e)
. . royalties. .3824
. . securities dealer. .3824

SOCIAL SECURITY (continued)
. self-employment tax (continued)
. . self-employment income, defined. .3823
. . timber cutting. .3824
. . trade or business income. .3822
. . Virgin Islands residents. .3823(c)
. tips. .2503(a); 2508(a); 3818; 3828(b)
. unemployment insurance. .3834 et seq.
. . adjustments. .3844
. . appeals. .3846
. . benefits, taxability. .1217
. . credits:
. . . contributions to States. .3839; 3841
. . . merit rating. .2730(b); 3841
. . deductibility. .1913(b)(c)
. . employers subject to. .3834
. . payment of tax. .3838
. . penalties. .3845
. . rates. .3834; 5513
. . records. .3843
. . refunds. .3844
. . return. .3838
. . state-federal system. .3839 et seq.
. . wages subject to. .3837
. . withholding tax. .2503(a)
Soil conservation expenditures. .1845
. partnerships. .2913
Sole proprietor: *See* Proprietor, sole
Sonic boom damages. .2204(b)
Son as dependent. .1117
Son-in-law as dependent. .1117
Sources of federal tax law. .1013 et seq.
Special assessments for local benefits. .1912(b)
Specific charge-off method, bad debts. .2311
Speculative investment, expenses. .1806
Spin-off reorganizations. .3316 et seq.
. basis of property received. .3320
. carryovers. .3336
Split-dollar life insurance. .1307(a)
Split-off reorganizations. .3316 et seq.
. basis of property received. .3320
. carryovers. .3336
Split-up reorganizations. .3316 et seq.
. basis of property received. .3320
. carryovers. .3336
. disallowance of surtax exemption and accumulated earnings credit. .3224
Splitting gifts. .4009
Splitting of income. .1104; 3505-3508; 5503
. change to same accounting period. .2716
. community property states. .3508
. tax planning, use in. .4541
Sports franchises, basis, allocation of. .1521(c)
Spouse: *See* Husband and wife
Stamp taxes, capitalization of. .1528; 1912(b)
STANDARD DEDUCTION: *See* Zero bracket amount
State:
. bonus to armed forces. .1218(c)
. contracts, profit on. .1330
. disability benefit contributions, deductibility. .1807
. dividends tax. .1918
. employees and officers:
. . annuities. .1232(h)
. . compensation. .1305
. . meal allowance. .1308(a)
. . old-age benefit tax. .3815(b)
. . . refunds. .3829(e)
. obligations:
. . amortizable premium. .1846
. . capital asset status. .1601
. . estate tax. .3900
. . gift tax. .4000

State (continued)
. obligations (continued)
. . interest on. .1204
. . interest to purchase or carry. .1905(a)
. . sale of, gain or loss. .1630
. taxes:
. . accrual. .2740(b)
. . capitalization. .1528
. . deductibility. .1912; 1913
. . . estate tax purposes. .3926
. . who may deduct. .1917
. unemployment insurance, benefits, exclusion . .1217(b)
. unemployment insurance taxes:
. . credit against Federal tax. .3839; 3841
. . deductibility. .1913(c)
State aid received by dependents. .1118
State highway patrol officers, allowance for meals. .1308(a)
Statements required with returns. .3521
Statute of limitations: *See also* Limitations
. assessment and collection. .3610 et seq.
. foreign tax carrybacks. .3611(f)
. mitigation of effect of. .2709(a); 3631
. penalties. .3620
. petition to Tax Court. .3605(a)
. private foundations. .3613(g)
. refunds and credits. .3623; 3624; 3829; 3844
. retirement plans. .3613(g)
. suit to recover taxes. .3620
. suspension. .3613
Statutory stock options. .1327
Stepchild:
. alimony for support of. .1320(c)
. as dependent. .1117
. member of household. .1106(a), (b)
Steprelatives as dependents. .1117
Stillborn child as dependent. .1115
Stock:
. acquisition by another corporation, as reorganization. .3304
. appreciation in value. .1201
. as investment property. .1406
. bail-out. .1722
. bonds exchanged for. .1404; 3307
. bonus plans:
. . contributions under. .1838
. . . withholding tax. .2503(a)
. book entry sale or exchange. .1522
. broker's fees. .1818
. capital asset, defined. .1601(a)
. certificates, as identification. .1522
. commissions. .1818
. compensation paid in. .1307(e); 1819
. . gain or loss. .3124
. . withholding tax. .2503(a)
. constructive ownership. .1727; 2223(d); 3402
. . net operating loss carryover. .3221
. . stock options. .1327
. contribution of, when deductible. .2742
. controlled foreign corporations, sale of. .3728
. corporation dealing in own. .3124
. debt settled by transfer of. .1318(h)
. dividends: *See* Dividends, stock
. employee purchase. .1328
. employer transfer to employee. .1400
. evidences of indebtedness distinguished. .1901
. exchange of. .1404
. . reorganizations. .3304
. fair market value. .1400; 1502(b)
. . estate tax. .3919(b)
. first-in, first-out rule. .1522ª
. identification of. .1522

6056—Index — STOCK—SUBSTANTIALLY

Stock (continued)
. installment sale. .2812
. joint tenancy:
. . converted to tenancy in common. .1404
. . dividends. .1705(b)
. . severed by partition action. .1404
. losses, transaction for profit. .2203
. option to purchase:
. . at less than market. .1327
. . as tax preference. .1327(b); 2403(a)
. . compensation v. gift. .1302(b)
. . constructive ownership. .1727(e)
. "over the counter" transactions. .1606
. ownership:
. . net operating loss carryover. .3221
. . personal holding companies. .3402
. . sales between corporation and stockholders . .2223(b)(d)
. personal holding company income. .3401
. preferred stock bail-out. .1722
. purchase and sale by corp. of own. .3124
. redemption. .1718; 3127(b). See also Dividends, liquidating
. . as dividends. .1718-1720
. . . exclusion. .1706(a)
. . constructive ownership. .1727
. . preferred stock bail-out. .1722
. . to pay death taxes. .1721
. reorganization distributions. .3306; 3316 et seq.
. rights. .1707; 1710-1712
. . basis. .1710-1712
. . effect on corporation's earnings and profits . .3129(d)
. . election as to medium of payment. .1712
. . holding period. .1712
. . nontaxable. .1711
. . . date basis. .1712
. . . holding period. .1712
. . preferred stock bail-out. .1722
. . sale proceeds. .1712
. . taxable. .1707; 1712
. sale of:
. . closed transaction. .2725(b)
. . losses. .1611
. . small business. .1632
. . to controlled corp. as redemption. .1720
. sale or exchange, info. required. .3521
. short sales:
. . capital gains and losses. .1608
. . closed transaction. .1608(b)
. shrinkage in value. .2208
. small business. .1632
. splits. .1708
. tenancy in common converted from joint tenancy . .1404
. transferred to officer. .1302(a)
. treasury, gain or loss. .3124
. warrants. See Stock, rights
. wash sales. .2221
. "when issued" basis. .1608(b)
. worthless. .3203
. . affiliated bank stock, of. .3433(a)
. . losses. .2203; 2208
. year-end transaction. .2725(b)
Stock exchange:
. assessments, dues and fees. .1808
. quotations, value based on. .1502(b)
. sales on, closed transaction. .2725(b)
. securities sold on, period held. .1606
Stock purchase plan options. .1327(b)
Stockholders:
. advances to corporations by. .2212; 2307; 2309

Stockholders (continued)
. assessments against. .3106
. compensation paid to. .1816; 1817
. cooperative apartments and housing:
. . interest. .1902
. . taxes. .1919
. dissolved corporation, transferee liability. .3614(a)
. dividends: See Dividends
. election:
. . form of dividend payment. .1707(b)
. . to be taxed on corporate earnings. .3140-3146; 3154
. . . self-employment tax. .3823(d)
. forgiveness of corporate debt. .1318(d); 2315(a)
. interest paid for. .1902
. legal advice to protect interests. .1823
. life insurance proceeds as dividends. .1213(d)
. loans from corporation. .1703
. nontaxable exchanges, basis of property received . .3313
. property purchased at less than market. .1329; 3126
. regulated investment companies foreign tax credit . .3431
. rent-free occupancy of corp. building. .1308(c)
. rent paid to. .1703
. rent paid to lessor corporation's. .3108
. sales between corporation and. .2223(b)
. small business corporations, taxability. .1632; 3140-3146
. taxes paid for. .1918; 1919
. transferee liability. .3614(a)
. withdrawals, as dividends. .1703
Storm insurance premiums. .1828(b)
Storm losses. .1410-1414; 2204(b)
. estate tax. .3926
. information required. .3521
"Straddle" transactions, options. .1609
Straight line method, depreciation. .3011
. change to, from declining balance. .2012
. useful life, change in. .2003
Strike benefits:
. income tax. .1301
. withholding tax. .2503(a)
Students:
. charitable deduction for certain. .1942(f)
. exemptions. .1116(b); 1118(a)
. foreign. .3709(b)
. loans, discharged of. .1303
. old-age benefit tax. .3810
. . withholding on. .2503(a); 2535
Subchapter S Corp. .3140 et seq.
. information returns. .3539
. retirement plans, deduction. .1102(c); 3146(a)
Subchapter S distributions, refund claims . .3624(c)
Subcontractors, withholding tax. .2502
Subpart F income. .3728
Subscription income, prepaid. .2726(a)
. information required. .3521
Subscriptions to periodicals. .1832; 1844(a)
Subsidiaries:
. foreign, credit for taxes of. .3706
. liquidation:
. . basis. .3334
. . gain or loss. .3128; 3334
. . information required. .3521
Subsidies. .1225
Subsistence allowances, veterans. .1218(c)
Substantially identical, defined:
. short sales. .1608(a)
. wash sales. .2221(b)

SUBSTITUTE—TAXABLE

References are to PARAGRAPH (¶) NUMBERS

Substitute employees, withholding tax. .2502
Substituted basis. .1514 et seq.
Succession taxes:
. deductibility. .1912(a)
. foreign, credit against federal estate tax. .3938
Successor corporation, carryovers. .3336; 3337
Successor-employer, old-age benefit tax. .3818(b)
. withholding. .2508(a); 2509
Suggestion awards. .1302(c)
. old-age benefit tax. .3818
. withholding tax. .2503(a)
Suit:
. bad debt deduction as necessitating. .2305
. collection of taxes. .3610(a); 3615(b)
. declaratory judgments. .3635(d)
. expenses of. .1806; 1823; 3016
. recovery of taxes. .3629
. . erroneous refund. .3629
. . estate tax. .3946
. . gift tax. .4033
. social security taxes. .3846
Sum of the years-digits method, depreciation . .2013; 2014; 2033
Summonses, tax collection. .3601(a)
Sunday, last day:
. filing:
. . refund claim. .3623
. . returns. .3517
. . suit. .3629(a)
. . Tax Court petition. .3605(a); 3639(a)
. payment:
. . estimated tax. .2517(a)
. . tax. .3517
Supplemental payments:
. contributions, deductibility. .1819
. taxability. .1217(b); 1307(d)
. withholding. .2503(a); 2504(e)
Supplemental unemployment benefit trusts:
. information returns. .3531
. taxability. .1217(b); 1307(d)
Supplies:
. contributions of. .1942(c)
. cost of goods sold. .2604(a)
Support of dependents. .1116
Supreme Court, review of decisions by. .3629(d)
Sureties:
. bad debt deduction. .2315(b)
. personal holding company tax. .3403
. withholding tax on wages. .2501
Surety bond, theft loss. .2205
Surety companies, personal holding company tax . .3403
Surgical insurance premiums. .1828(b)
Surplus:
. analysis of. .3110
. unreasonable accumulation. .3130-3134
Surtax:
. corporations. .3102
. exemption. .3102
. . affiliated corporations. .3114(b); 3223
. . disallowance. .3224
Surviving spouse:
. community property, period held. .1606
. declaration of estimated tax. .2516(a)
. determination of status as . .1105
. income-splitting. .3505
. interest, life insurance proceeds. .1213
. rate of tax. .1121
. splitting income. .1105
. withholding tax on wages. .2504

Survivor insurance: *See* Social Security, old-age and survivor insurance
Sweepstakes: *See* Gambling
Swimming pool as medical expense. .1946
Swindling, income from. .1300(g)
Syndicates as partnerships. .2900

— T —

Tables and charts. .5501, et seq.
Tables, use of in estate tax valuation. .3919(d)
"Tax benefit" rule:
. bad debts. .2316(c), (d)
. depreciation. .2004
Tax briefs. .3647
Tax Court. .3635 et seq.
. admissions. .3645(c)
. appeal from decision of. .3648(b); 3649
. briefs. .3647
. declaratory judgments. .3635(d)
. depositions. .3646
. discovery. .3645(b)
. evidence. .3635
. hearings before. .3635; 3639; 3645-3648
. judgment without trial. .3644
. jurisdiction. .3637
. overpayment found by. .3637(b)
. petition to. .3605; 3635; 3639
. . amendment of. .3643
. . Commissioner's answer. .3641
. . . petitioner's reply. .3642
. . contents. .3640
. . estate tax. .3945
. . gift tax. .4032
. . who may file. .3637(e)
. pleadings. .3643; 3646(b)-(d)
. practice before. .3636
. refunds. .3622
. regulations, Revenue Service, weight given to . .3638
. rehearings. .3647
. reports. .3648
. Rule 155. .3648(a)
. service of papers. .3637(f)
. small tax case procedure. .3635(c)
. social security cases, jurisdiction. .3846
. stipulations. .3645(d)
TAX CREDITS. .2405 et seq, *See also* Credits
Tax information authorization. .3609(d)
Tax planning. .1019; 4501 et seq.
Tax shelters, overview of. .4601 et seq.
Tax tables. .1122
. credit for foreign taxes. .3701
. standard deduction: *See* Zero bracket amount
. tax figured by Revenue Service or taxpayer . .1103(b)
. who may use. .1122
Tax Treaties. .2537; 3720
Taxable income:
. computation of. .1103; 1201
. corporations. .3105
. defined. .1201
. dividends on matured policies. .1216
. estate and trusts. .3003
. 52-53 week year. .2714(b)
. foreign corporations. .3710

Taxable income (continued)
. individuals. .1102
. partnerships. .2906
Tax year:
. change in. .2715-2717
. closing by Commissioner. .3612(c)
. defined. .2714
. . fractional year return. .2715
. different:
. . beneficiary and estate or trust. .3003(b); 3021
. . common trust fund and participants. .3025
. . joint return. .3507
. . partner and partnership. .2921; 2922
. earnings or profits of, distribution. .1701(c)
. less than 12 months: *See* Fractional year
. partnerships. .2921; 2922
TAXES. .1910-1920. *See also* particular type
. accrual. .2740(b)
. amortization during construction period. .2042
. capitalization. .1528
. . information required. .3521
. condominiums. .1919
. contested. .2735(c)
. cooperative apartments and housing. .1919
. . partnerships. .2913
. deductibility. .1910-1920
. . adjusted gross income. .1804; 1910
. . estate tax purposes. .3926
. . period when taken. .2740
. . trial and error method. .3547
. delinquent interest on. .3618
. . deductibility. .1901
. litigation expenses. .1806
. paid for another. .1302(a); 1316; 1919
. private foundations. .3437-3444
. recovery exclusion. .2316(d)
. . partnerships. .2913
. reserved interests. .1919
. state and local, deductibility. .1912
. time to deduct. .2740
TAX-EXEMPT ORGANIZATIONS: *See* Exempt organizations
Taxicab drivers:
. old-age benefit tax. .3817(b)
. tips. .1301
Taxpayers:
. classification of. .1028
. disappearance. .1100(d)
. limitation on deductions. .2736
Teachers:
. expenses of. .1833(a)
Telephone and telegraph taxes. .5515
. deductibility. .1910
Telephone costs, employee's. .1805
Tenancy in common. .1300(e)
. dividends received. .1705(b)
. estate tax. .3904
. partnership. .2903
. sale of residence. .1423
. stock, converted from joint tenancy. .1404
Tenant: *See* Lessee and Lessor
Tenant stockholders:
. interest. .1902
. taxes. .1919
Tenants by entirety. .1300(d)
. dividends received. .1705(b)
. estate tax. .3904
. gift tax. .4002; 4013
. . marital deduction. .4023
. interest deduction. .1902
. survivor interest, basis. .1509
. tax deductions. .1919
Terminable interests:

Terminable interests (continued)
. estate tax, marital deduction. .3929(b)
. holder as a fiduciary. .3001
Termination assessment. .3605(b); 3612(b); 3618
. review of. .3612(d)
Termination payments to employees. .1304
Termites, damage by. .2004(b)
Territories of U.S., obligations of. .1204
Theatre tickets for customers. .1830
Theatrical production, capital asset. .1601(f)
Theft:
. insurance premiums covering. .1828(b)
. involuntary conversions. .1411
. loss deduction. .2205; 2206
. . amount of. .2205; 2206
. . estate tax. .3926
. . information required. .3521
. . net operating loss computation. .2242(a)
. . time for. .2205
. recovery costs. .2205
. Sec. 1231 gains and losses. .1620; 2206
. uninsured property. .1620
Thin incorporation. .1901
Third parties, payments to. .2704; 3108
Thirty-day letter. .3604
Throwback rule, estates and trusts. .3023
Tier distributions, complex trusts. .3006
Timber:
. capital asset. .1621
. cutting or disposal of. .1621
. depletion. .2110
. . records. .2112
. depreciation. .2111
. self-employment income. .3824
. turpentine contained in, depletion. .2110
Tips:
. estimating for withholding purposes. .2504(i)
. gross income. .1301
. reporting requirements, employee. .2503(a); 2507(b); 3828(b)
. social security taxes. .3818; 3837
. supplemental payments, reporting as. .2504(e)
. uncollected withholding, employer adjustment of .2510(c)
. withholding statements. .2508(a)
. withholding tax. .2503(a); 3818; 3827
Title to property:
. expense of defending. .1806; 1808; 1823
. inventories. .2602
Tobacco taxes:
. rate chart. .5515
. state, deductibility. .1912(d)
Tools, cost of. .1102
Tornado relief. .1302(b)
Trade: *See* Business
Trade acceptances, capital asset. .1601(k)
Trade associations, dues to. .1807
Trade brands, depreciation. .2001(a)
Trade-in allowance, basis for gain or loss. .1503(b); 1517
Trade marks:
. depreciation. .2001(a)
. expenses. .1808
Trade names, depreciation. .2001(a)
Traders in Securities:
. commissions. .1818
. wash sales. .2221(c)
Trading stamps and coupons. .2747
Trailer as residence. .1417
Transferees, liability for tax. .3614(a)
. interest deduction. .1902
. limitation on assessment. .3611

Transfers:
. assets to another corp. for controlling stock as reorganization. .3306
. at death. .1508
. before death. .1508
. claims in cases of transferred assets. .3614(a)
. estate tax: See Estate tax
. generation-skipping tax. .3916
. gift tax: See Gift tax
. partnership interest. .2935; 2937-2942
. . basis. .2936
Transportation employees, old-age benefit tax . .3815(b)
Transportation expenses:
. adjusted gross income. .1102(c); 1829(b)
. armed forces. .1834(b)
. carrying tools. .1829(b)
. employees. .1805; 1829
. . information required. .1805
. . reimbursed. .1805
. medical expense. .1946
. old-age benefit tax. .3819(b)
. professional people. .1832
. reimbursed. .1805
. reservists. .1834(b)
. school children. .1330
Transportation taxes. .5515
Traveling expenses. .1829
. adjusted gross income. .1102(c); 1803
. construction workers. .1829
. deductibility. .1805; 1829
. donated services. .1942(c)
. employees. .1805
. . information required. .1805
. . reimbursed. .1805
. family member accompanying taxpayer. .1829
. "home," defined. .1829
. information required, employees. .1805
. medical expenses. .1946
. more than one business. .1829
. moving to new residence. .1831
. nonbusiness expenses. .1803(b); 1806
. old-age benefit tax. .3819(b)
. "overnight," defined. .1829
. professional people. .1832
. reimbursements. .1805(b); 1829
. relative accompanying taxpayer. .1829
. temporary employment. .1829
. vacation combined with business. .1829
. withholding tax. .2503(a)
Treasury stock, gain or loss. .3124
Treaties:
. foreign taxpayers affected by. .3707
. presidential proclamation, rates. .3707
. tax convention with foreign countries. .2537; 3707; 3720
Treaty trader. .3708(a)
Treble damages, taxability. .1226
Trees:
. damage to, loss deduction. .2204(b)
. depreciation. .2001
Trial and error method, two unknowns. .3547
Trust companies:
. bad debt deductions, reserve method. .3433
. bonds owned by, gains and losses. .3433
. dividends paid to U.S.. .3433
. personal holding company tax. .3403
. taxation of. .3433
. worthless securities. .2312(b)
Trustees in bankruptcy:

. returns. .3511; 3512
. withholding. .2501
Trusts: See Estates and trusts
Tuition. .1307(b); 1807; 1833
. medical expense allocation. .1946
. parochial schools, contribution deduction. .1941(b)
. veterans. .1218(c)
TVA employees, social security coverage. .3815(a)

— U —

Uncle as dependent. .1117
Uncollectible income. .2719
Unconstitutional taxes, recovery. .2316(d)
Undercollection of withholding tax. .2510
Underestimate of estimated tax. .2515; 2519; 3523(b)
Undistributed income:
. complex trusts. .3023
. foreign personal holding companies. .3413; 3414
. personal holding companies. .3404
. small business corporations. .3142(b)
Unemployment benefit payments:
. deductibility. .1819; 1913(c)
. levy on. .3615(a)
. taxability. .1217(b); 1307(d)
Unemployment Insurance: See Social security, unemployment insurance
Unharvested crop, sale with land. .1622
. recapture as ordinary income. .2226(a)
Unified credit:
. estate tax. .3940
. gift tax. .4021
Uniforms:
. armed forces. .1834
. expenses of. .1102; 1805(b); 1807
. . charitable deduction. .1942(c)
. reservists. .1834
Uniform gift to minors acts. .1225(b)
Unions: See Labor organizations
United Nations: See International organizations
United States:
. defined. .1028(a)
. guaranteed loan, distribution of proceeds. .3129(g)
. obligations: See Federal obligations
. publications, capital asset status. .1601
. services outside, withholding tax on wages . .2503(b)
. suit against. .3629
Unit-livestock-price method, inventories. .2615(b)
Unit-of-production method, depreciation. .2015(a)
Unitrust:
. charitable deduction for. .1942(e)
. estate tax, charitable deduction. .3927
. gift tax, charitable deduction. .4022
Unrealized receivables:
. defined:
. . corporation. .3129(b)
. . partnership. .2944(d)
. distributions:
. . corporation, effect on earning & profit. .3129(b)
. . partnerships. .2944-2945
. . . basis. .2928-2932
. . . gain or loss. .2945(b)
. transfers, partnership. .2935
Unrelated business. .3445-3454
. income from. .3448
. . tax. .3445
. . . returns. .3454(b); 3517(d)
. . . time of payment. .3525

Urban renewal projects, relocation payments . .1302(b)
Use and occupancy insurance:
. premiums. .1828(b)
. proceeds. .1331
Use tax, state:
. capitalization. .1528
. deductibility. .1912(c)
Useful life:
. depreciation. .2032
. . Class Life Asset Depreciation Range system . .2033
. . change in:
. . . declining balance. .2012; 2033
. . . straight line method. .2003; 2033
. . . sum of the years-digits method. .2013; 2033
. . guidelines. .2033
. . structural life distinguished. .2033
. investment credit. .2410(c)
Usurious interest. .1314

— V —

Vacation earnings of children. .3509
Vacation homes, expenses connected with. .1806
Vacation pay:
. deductibility. .1815; 1819
. nonresident citizens. .3725
. time deductible. .2737(a)
. unemployment insurance tax. .3837
. withholding tax. .2503(a); 2504(f)
Valuation: See also Fair market value
. annuities. .1230(d)
. carryover basis property, estate tax. .3919
. estate tax purposes. .3919
. . transferred property. .3939
. gift tax purposes. .4010-4014
. increase in. .1201
. inventories. .2604; 2609
. shrinkage. .2208
Vandalism damage. .2204(b)
Vasectomy as medical expense. .1946(a)
Venture capital companies. .3430
Verification of returns. .3503; 3513
Veterans: See also Armed forces
. bonuses. .1218(c)
. compensation. .1306
. dependency status. .1116(a)
. disability payments. .1218(c)
. exempt income. .1218(c)
. interest on G. I. loans. .1902
. life insurance:
. . dividends. .1216
. . estate tax. .3914
. on-the-job training. .1218(c)
. pensions and other benefits paid to. .1218(c)
. subsistence allowance. .1218(c)
. tuition and subsistence allowances. .1218(c)
Veterans' Benefit Act, insurance dividends. .1216
Veterinarians, withholding tax. .2502
Virgin Islands:
. employment in, old-age benefit tax. .3803
. residents:
. . income tax. .3709(a)
. . self-employment tax. .3823(c)
Vitamins, medical expense. .1946
Vocational courses, deductibility. .1833(b)
Vocational trainees. .1303
Voting trust certificates exchanged for stock . .1404

— W —

Wage-bracket withholding. .2504(b)
Wage continuation plans: See Disability
Wagering gains and losses: See Gambling
Wagers, tax on. .5515
Wages: See Compensation
. levy on. .3615(a)
. social
. social security taxes: See Social security
. withholding tax: See Withholding, wages
Waiters, tips. .1301; See also Tips
Waivers:
. form. .3606
. limit on assessment and collection. .3610(d)
. refund limitation extended by. .3623(c)
. restrictions on assessment and collection of deficiency. .3606
Walsh-Healey Public Contracts Act. .1301
Wards, returns for. .3511(a)
Warrants:
. payment in . .1330
. stock: See also Stock, rights
Wash sales. .2221
Water:
. conservation expenditures. .1845
. . partnerships. .2913
. test holes dug for. .2210
Weekly deposits of withheld taxes. .2509(a)
Weekly payroll period, computation of withholding. .2504
Western Hemisphere Trade Corporation, deduction. .3117(a)
. net operating loss. .3217; 3219
Wheat futures, short sales. .1608(c)
Wheel chair as medical expense. .1946
"When issued" transactions. .1608(b)
Wholesale merchants, inventories. .2606(b)
Widow:
. child care expenses. .2415
. declaration of estimated tax. .2516(a)
. elderly income credit. .2406
. interest, life insurance proceeds. .1213
. payments to employees. .1304(a)
. splitting income. .1105
Widower:
. child care expenses. .2415
. declaration of estimated tax. .2516(a)
. elderly income credit. .2406
. splitting income. .1105
Will:
. contest:
. . amount received in settlement. .1225
. . attorneys' fees. .1823
. estate or trust:
. . first return. .3020
. . income. .3008(a)
. expense of preparing. .1823
WITHHOLDING. .2501-2512
. additional. .2515
. adjustments. .2507; 2510
. agent. .2535(a); 2536
. allowances, computation of. .2505(b)
. . penalty. .2512(b)
. . table. .2505(b)
. annuity payments. .2504(k)
. at source. .2501 et seq.
. . foreign corporations. .2535-2537; 3710
. . foreign partnerships. .2535

———————References are to PARAGRAPH (¶) NUMBERS ———————

WITHHOLDING (continued)
. at source *(continued)*
. . nonresident aliens. .2535-2537; 3709(d)
. . payment of tax. .2536
. . payments on which tax must be withheld. .2535
. . returns. .2536
. . tax treaties with foreign countries. .2537
. . who must withhold. .2535(a)
. certificate of nontaxability. .2506(c)
. computation of. .2504
. counseling fees. .2503(a)
. divorce, effect of. .2505(c); 2506
. exemption certificates. .2506
. . penalties. .2512
. excluded employment. .2503(b)
. exemptions. .2505
. . change of status. .2506(b)
. . exemption certificate not filed. .2506
. . withholding allowances. .2505(b)
. fishing crewmen. .2503(a)
. illegal business. .2502
. marital status, effect on. .2504
. nonwage payments. .2504(k)
. part-time employment. .2504(l)
. penalties. .2512
. pension payments. .2504(k)
. percentage method. .2504(a)
. receipts: *See* Withholding, statements to employees
. records. .2507
. retirement savings. .2503(a)
. returns and payment of taxes. .2509-2512
. . nonresident aliens. .2536
. standard deduction allowance: *See* Withholding, zero bracket allowance
. statements to employees. .2508
. . as information returns. .2509
. . corrected. .2508
. . failure to furnish. .2512(a)
. . fraudulent. .2512(a)
. . overcollection of social security taxes. .2508
. . penalties. .2512(a)
. . return accompanied by. .2508
. . tips. .2508(a)
. . undercollection of social security taxes. .2508
. . what to include. .2508(a)
. status determination dates. .2506(b)
. tables. .2504
. voluntary. .2504(j)
. wage-bracket method. .2504(b)
. wagering winnings. .2503(a); 3521
. wages. .250-2512
. alternative method. .2504(c)
. . amount to be withheld. .2504
. . annualizing of. .2504(d)
. . annuity premiums paid by exempt organization . .2503(a)
. . average estimated wages. .2504(i)
. . board and lodging. .2503(a)
. . credits and refunds. .2511; 3521; 3622

WITHHOLDING (continued)
. alternative method *(continued)*
. . employer-employee relationship. .2502
. . employers required to withhold. .2502
. . employment agency fee, reimbursed. .2503(a)
. . guaranteed annual wage payments. .2503(a)
. . jury fees. .2503(b)
. . moving expense allowance. .2503(a)
. . nonresident aliens. .2503(a); 2535; 2536
. . overcollection. .2510
. . . refund, interest on. .3628(c)
. . paid for multi-employers. .2504(h)
. . paid without regard to payroll periods. .2504(d)
. . payroll period. .2504
. . Peace Corps allowance. .2503(b)
. . refunds and credits. .2511; 3521; 3622
. . rounding off. .2504(a)
. . services, outside U.S.. .2503(b)
. . substitute employees. .2502
. . supplemental payments. .2504(e)
. . supplemental unemployment benefits. .2503(a)
. . temporary employment. .2503(a)
. . tips. .2504(e)
. . . supplemental payments, reported as. .2504(e)
. . traveling expenses. .2503(a)
. . undercollections. .2510
. . wage disability payments. .2504(g)
. who must withhold. .2502; 2535; 2536
. zero bracket allowance. .2505(a)
Withholding tax, fishing crewmen . .2503(a)
Witnesses:
. examination, Tax Court. .3646
. fees, paid to, withholding. .2503(b)
Work clothes. .1807
Work incentive program expenses, credit for . .2411
. carryback and carryforward, deficiency due to . .3618(a)
. deficiency due to. .3611(f)
. estates and trusts. .3019
. partners, credit for. .2913(d)
. refunds, carryback affecting. .3624(b); 3630
Workmen's compensation insurance. .1218; 1947
. premiums. .1828(b)
Worthless stocks and bonds: *See* Bond, worthless; Stock, worthless

— X —

X-rays, cost of. .1946

— Y —

Year: *See* Specific kind, e.g., Fiscal year; Tax year
Year-end stock transactions. .2725(b)

— Z —

ZERO BRACKET AMOUNT . .1107-1109.